ROTHMANS FOOTBALL YEARBOOK 1979-80

EDITOR: JACK ROLLIN

COMPILED BY
LESLIE VERNON AND JACK ROLLIN

QUEEN ANNE PRESS
MACDONALD AND JANE'S: LONDON & SYDNEY

© Brickfield Publications Ltd. 1979

House Editor: **Ronnie Kerr**

Front Cover: The players are (clockwise): Kevin Keegan; Osvaldo Ardiles; Sandy Jardine; Trevor Francis; Laurie Cunningham.

(Photographs courtesy of Colorsport, as are all other photographs in this book)

All rights reserved. No part of this publication may be reproduced, stored in a retrieval system, or transmitted in any form or by any means electrical, mechanical, photocopied, recorded, or otherwise, without the prior permission of the publisher. This book is sold subject to the condition that it shall not by way of trade or otherwise, be lent, re-sold, hired out, or otherwise circulated without the publisher's prior consent in any form of binding or cover other than that in which it is published and without a similar condition including this condition being imposed on the subsequent purchaser.

ISBN 0354 09083 6

Published by Queen Anne Press
Macdonald and Jane's Publishers Limited
Paulton House, 8 Shepherdess Walk, London N1 7LW

Typeset in Times Roman by
Waterlow, London.

Printed and bound in England by
Hazell Watson & Viney Limited
Aylesbury, Bucks.

CONTENTS

Rothmans Foreword	7
Editorial	8
Introduction and Acknowledgements	9
Rothmans Football Awards 1979	10
Diary: July 1978 – July 1979	11
Footballer of the Year and PFA Awards	43
Manager of the Year	44
European Footballer of the Year	45

THE FOOTBALL LEAGUE: THE CLUBS

Review of the League Season	47
Introduction to the Club Section	48
League Position Progress Charts	49
The Football League Clubs, in alphabetical order	53

THE FOOTBALL LEAGUE: STATISTICS

League Tables 1978-79	
Divisions 1 & 2	423
Divisions 3 & 4	424
Honours List 1888-89 to 1978-79	425
Hat-trick heroes	431
Leading scorers 1978-79	432
Career records of present-day League goalscorers	434
Transfer Trail 1978-79	435
Leading Goalscorers since World War II	439
Football League Attendances	445

THE FA CUP

Review of the FA Cup 1978-79	450
FA Cup results 1978-79	451
FA Cup match details 1978-79	454
FA Cup final results since 1872	464
FA Cup wins, appearances in the final, appearances in the semi-finals	465

THE FOOTBALL LEAGUE CUP

Review of the League Cup 1978-79	466
League Cup results 1978-79	467
League Cup run-down 1961-78	468
League Cup match details 1978-79	486
League Cup final results since 1961	495

SCOTTISH FOOTBALL

Review of the Season	510
Scottish League Referees	511
The Scottish League clubs, in alphabetical order	512
Scottish League tables 1978-79	588
Scottish League Honours List	590
Scottish FA Cup details 1978-79	593
Scottish League Cup details 1978-79	597
Scottish League Cup finals details 1946-79	602
Scottish FA Cup finals 1874-1979	605
Scottish League Cup finals 1946-79	606
Post-War Scottish FA Cup finals	607

IRISH AND WELSH FOOTBALL

Irish Football	610
Welsh Football	613

MISCELLANEOUS

The Managers	616
Major British Records	622
Some International Records	627
Firsts in Football	628
Some Other Records	629
History of Football Part 2: 1939-1955	631
Anglo Scottish Cup 1978-79	651
FA Charity Shield 1908-78	652
England v Young England	652

BRITISH INTERNATIONAL FOOTBALL

Review of the Season	653
British International Championship winners 1883-1979	653
British International Championship 1979	659
Other International and Representative Games 1978-79	668
Other British International Results 1908 to 1979	660
British and Irish International goalscorers from 1946	658
British and Irish International Appearances	671
Under-23 Appearances 1954-76	929
Under-21 Appearances	936
Under-21 Internationals 1978-79	669
'B' and Unofficial Internationals	938
England's Full International Teams 1872-1978	773
Ireland's Full International Teams 1882-1978	808
Scotland's Full International Teams 1872-1978	830
Wales' Full International Teams 1876-1978	858

EUROPEAN FOOTBALL

Review of the Season	715
The European Championship	717
European Championship 1978-80	721
The European Under-21 Championship 1978-80	726
European Club Tournaments 1978-79	727
European Cup Finals 1956-79	733
European Cup History	734
Cup-Winners' Cup History	747
Fairs & UEFA Cup History	757
Full Record of British clubs in Europe 1978-79	881
Progress of British and Irish clubs in Europe	886
Summary of appearances by British and Irish Clubs in Europe	889
European Nations Section	892
Super Cup	654
UEFA Youth Tournament 1978-79	939

WORLD FOOTBALL

The World Cup 1930-78	920
All Time Record of 1978 Finalists	927
World Club Championship	716
South American Championships	928
Copa Libertadores	928
North American Soccer League	41

OTHER LEAGUE, YOUTH AND SCHOOLS FOOTBALL

English Youth International Football	940
FA Youth Challenge Cup	943
England Youth Caps	945
FA County Youth Challenge Cup	957
The Southern League and Northern Premier League	951
Isthmian League 1978-79	958
FA Challenge Trophy	963
Hitachi Cup	965
FA Sunday Cup	966
AFA Football	971
FA Challenge Vase	972
FA Representative Matches 1934-78	975
Schools Football	995
Olympic Football	998

INFORMATION SECTION

Addresses	421
The Laws of the Game	970
Football League Referees	989
FA Staff Coaches	994
The Football League Fixtures 1979-80	990
The Press	997
European, International, and Representative Fixtures	1000

FOREWORD BY ROTHMANS OF PALL MALL

Three successive victories in the European Cup Final must reassure even the most cynical observer that British football still ranks with the best in the world.

And with both Nottingham Forest and Liverpool competing in the competition again this season there is every prospect of that trophy remaining with us even longer.

Liverpool and Nottingham Forest also finished at the head of the Football League, with Forest taking the League Cup Final again to keep the names of Clough and Taylor on everybody's lips. Arsenal played so many games on their way to winning the FA Cup that they too must have felt that they had won a League competition!

Mr Keith Kotch, managing director of Broadstrood Press Ltd and its associate company, GKW Publications Ltd, died in St Mary's Hospital, Harrow Road, on 21 June. He was 59.

A memorial service held in St Bride's, Fleet Street, on 27 June was attended by more than one hundred relatives, friends, colleagues and representatives from New Scotland Yard, industry, the publishing world and the field of sport.

He leaves a widow, Laurie Purden, MBE, the well-known editor of *Woman's Journal*, two daughters and a son and daughter by a previous marriage.

Keith Kotch spent most of his business life in different areas of the publishing world. He became assistant general manager of Hulton Press during the heyday of *Picture Post*. After the closure of that magazine in the late 50s, he helped form Vernon Holding and Partners Ltd, the independent distributors of magazines.

Later he was associated with the Bagenal Harvey Organisation, the specialist sports agency, with particular responsibility for book publishing including the *Rothmans Football Yearbook*, which later he controlled under Brickfield Publications.

EDITORIAL BOARD

Jack Rollin *(Chairman)*, Bobby Charlton, C.B.E., David Coleman, Ted Croker, Jimmy Hill, Brian James, Leslie Vernon.

ADVISORY PANEL

Denis Follows, C.B.E.
Denis Compton, C.B.E.: *Arsenal & England*
Phil Isaacs: *Sportsman Club*
Sir Walter Winterbottom, C.B.E.: *Honorary Vice-President F.A.*
John Morgan: *Daily Star*
John Bromley: *London Weekend Television*
Cliff Lloyd: *Secretary, Professional Footballers' Association*
Bernard Audley: *AGB Research*
George Pullin: *Rothmans of Pall Mall*
Tom Finney, O.B.E.: *Preston North End & England*

Tony Pullein: *Founder, England Football Supporters Association*
Joe Mercer, O.B.E.: *Director, Coventry City*
Sam Leitch: *Thames Television*
Jarvis Astaire: *Anglo-American Sporting Club*
Neville Holtham: *Sports Editor, The Sunday People*
Brian Moore: *London Weekend Television*
R. E. Hadingham, O.B.E. M.C.: *Slazengers Ltd.*
Geoffrey Irvine: *The Bagenal Harvey Organisation Ltd.*
J.N.H. Rice.
Trevor Morris, O.B.E.: *Secretary, Welsh Football Association*

EDITORIAL

Jack Rollin

As the postponement of the World Congress for Clairvoyants due to unforeseen circumstances revealed, not even the most obvious in life is wholly predictable. Thus while Football League attendances for 1978–79 reached a post-war low of 24,540,627 a view of them through the crystal ball is anything but clear.

In the wake of the worst winter for 16 years causing countless postponements and rearranged matches crammed into the last weeks with no promotion or relegation issues at stake for many of the clubs involved, not to mention the attendant problems of that undercurrent of unpleasantness which is either just below the surface on the terraces or about to erupt into something more distasteful, then further examination is needed.

Indeed the figures show a surprisingly healthy attitude from the public to want to go out and watch their football whatever the elements, which becomes more evident when the overall total for last season was seen to be only some 350,000 down on the previous worst in 1975–76.

What did emerge from the statistics was that the gap between the successful and the unsuccessful is continuing to widen. While Manchester United showed their ability to match the candy bar charisma of that TV commercial which said 'very popular is United' in averaging 46,430 and the champions Liverpool played sweetly in attracting 46,406 on average, it was a different taste for the allsorts in the Fourth Division.

Here four clubs had attendances averaging under 2,000: Crewe Alexandra, Darlington, Halifax Town and Rochdale. The first three had to apply for re-election and Rochdale just pulled away from the bottom four in the last few weeks.

Oddly enough the returns from the Fourth Division at 2,308,297 were not the poorest of all time; in the 1974–75 season they were only 1,992,684. What helped last season was Barnsley's being watched by an average of 11,048. Needless to say they were one of the promoted sides.

Both the Third and Second Divisions can also claim to have suffered more severely in the past and in Division One the final tally of 12,704,549 was actually better than the figures produced in 1960–61, 1961–62, 1962–63 (the previous winter of discontent), 1963–64, 1965–66 and 1974–75, and only marginally below 1964–65.

In 1965–66 the *overall* figures were 2½ million up on the 1978–79 attendances.

The early 1960s were seasons prior to the advent of extensive coverage on Television. But who could really say that the money derived from this source is not an essential ingredient of the modern game – except perhaps the clubs lower down the divisions who have suffered more during the last decade and a half in this respect.

And while income from commercial expansion is also benefiting the financial returns, there must be no effort spared to ensure that the turnstiles keep clicking away at least at their present levels.

Almost certainly there will be some general moves towards the introduction of more seated accommodation during the next decade though this will in no way ensure increased attendances.

A team which maintains a winning sequence will invariably attract more spectators than an unsuccessful side in a palatial stadium. Thus arguments about an overall standard of football will inevitably take second place to the bare facts of winning and losing.

However the game will never exist in any form if the gap between the clubs at the top and those at the bottom in any one division is allowed to grow. The plain simple truth is that some people must be prepared to support the teams that lose.

But perhaps out of this basic requirement which must be fostered, might come the reality that if the entertainment value on the field improves it could act as a stimulant to the Football League competition as a whole.

INTRODUCTION

The tenth year of Rothmans Football Yearbook presents a milestone which we have marked by an increased coverage of certain aspects of the game.

Also by popular request we have been able to re-introduce some features which have had to be left out in recent years, including the line-ups of the England, Scotland, Northern Ireland and Wales international teams since they began official matches and the results of all European Cup matches played since the start of these competitions.

Part Two of our historical survey takes us up to 1954–55 a date chosen as a breaking off point for the season by season statistical review of English League and Cup football, because it was the one prior to the beginning of European competition.

Among the more familiar features are line-ups, goalscorers and attendances of matches played in the Football League and Scottish League as well as the League Cup, FA Cup, Scottish League Cup and Scottish Cup. There are the usual separate sections for Welsh, Irish and Continental football and an article on American football.

An asterisk * against a player's name in the club section denotes that a free transfer was granted to the person in question at the end of the 1978–79 season. Transfers since then have been noted up to the end of May as well as references in the Diary and club section for subsequent major moves.

While transfer fees have escalated it has also become almost impossible to reach any accurate figure with the levies which now accompany these amounts, and since such fees are not publicly disclosed, this is one area where it could be said that somebody pays their money and you can take your choice!

Again we would like to thank the various organisations who have helped to make this a complete book and we are especially grateful to Mrs Sandra Whiteside of the Football League, Mike McNamara of the Football Association, Lionel Francis who assisted in the compilation of certain sections and Alan Elliott for his efforts on the Scottish scene.

LESLIE VERNON
JACK ROLLIN

ACKNOWLEDGEMENTS

The compilers wish to thank the many individuals and organisations whose ready co-operation has produced material for this volume and in particular: Jill C. Bradley, Glynis Firth, Mike Foster, Chris J. Whalley (all from the Football League), Adrian Titcombe (The Football Association), The Scottish Football Association, The Welsh Football Association, The Scottish League, The Secretaries of all Football League and Scottish League clubs, Malcolm Brodie, Glyn Evans (The English Schools FA), A. J. Suggate (AFA), Maurice Golesworthy, John Hamon, Ken Goldman, John Pyke, Paul Lamb and Paul Weaver.

ROTHMANS FOOTBALL AWARDS 1979

The following six people are to receive special awards from Rothmans for having made a worthwhile contribution to the wide spectrum of the game in season 1978–79.

LIAM BRADY. The Cup Final fittingly marked this brilliant Irishman's finest game of the season. Still smarting from the previous year's failure on the same pitch when he was not fully fit his superb dribbling skill took him into the penalty area before the second Arsenal goal and his accurate cross found scorer Stapleton. And during those tense last seconds of the game he coldly moved into the opposing half and then released his pass just at the right moment. It resulted in another Arsenal goal which had a 'made by Brady' hallmark on it. A mesmeric playmaker, he is also a regular goalgetter and was elected by his fellow professionals as their 'Player of the Year'.

RAY CLEMENCE. As most great goalkeepers, Clemence regards every goal scored against him as a personal insult. He is a perfectionist. Liverpool – and naturally the ever present Clemence – only conceded 16 League goals in 42 matches: an all time First Division record. It was an incredible feat if one considers that we are not talking about an ultra-defensive outfit, but one which won the championship with a record 68 points and scored 85 goals in the process. And as England's goalkeeper he has maintained his international status effectively.

BRIAN CLOUGH. Clough has achieved the seemingly impossible with Nottingham Forest. In their first season after promotion into Division One, they won the championship and the League Cup. Last season they successfully defended the League Cup, finished second in the League, and to cap it all, won the most coveted prize in club football, the European Cup. Clough, a national figure who is impersonated on TV as often as the Prime Minister, likes to hide behind the facade of an intrepid, dilletante squash player, who gives interviews to the world's press dressed in shorts and swinging a racket. But he is a sensitive man, an outstanding manager immensely proud of his profession and a fighter for good causes.

ROSS JENKINS. Since Graham Taylor took over at Watford, they have progressed from the Fourth Division into the Second in two consecutive promotion seasons. This feat was achieved through some judicious but by no means spectacular buying of players, sound commercial management and last but certainly not least, by motivating the players to give their best. Jenkins a tall, menacing figure to opposing defences whose scoring rate has improved dramatically in recent seasons, topped the Football League list with 29 goals plus four in the FA Cup and four in the League Cup.

DANNY McGRAIN. This Celtic full-back was highly regarded in international circles as a cultured defender with attacking ideas; a player scrupulously fair, but tough and resolute. Sadly, at the peak of his career he suffered a serious injury and was out of the game for over a year. He came back last December and his leadership inspired an astonishing transformation in the club's fortunes. In their last 18 games, they collected 29 points, beat Rangers in the decisive match and took the championship of the Scottish Premier Division.

JOHN TOSHACK. The ex-Liverpool star, who is now player-manager of ambitious Swansea City, deserves his selection on two counts. He has taken the Welsh team from the Fourth to the Second Division in two seasons and in the process, revitalised football in South Wales. At the same time, he earned himself a recall to the Welsh national team and scored a hat-trick against Scotland in the British International Championship match. Toshack who used to star in a double act with Kevin Keegan at Liverpool, has found several talented youngsters at Swansea, who complement him just as effectively. He has also bought shrewdly from his old club and elsewhere, and blended them in splendidly.

LESLIE VERNON

DIARY 1978-79

July

MacLeod stays with the Scots... Foreign invasion begins... Tribunal fixes its first transfer fee

1. Kevin Sheedy, an 18-year-old Hereford midfielder joins Liverpool for an £80,000 fee... Crystal Palace pay £200,000 for Mike Elwiss of Preston... Denis Howell says that it is illogical for sport to refuse sponsorship money from tobacco firms... Chelsea players are offered large bonus pyaments if the club is successful.
2. Hans Krankl, star of Rapid Vienna, signs for Barcelona... Rainer Bonhof joins Valencia... Ron Greenwood calls a meeting of First Division managers at Bisham Abbey to discuss the lessons to be learned from the World Cup – only eight of them take part plus Greenwood's 'B' team manager, Bobby Robson of Ipswich.
3. Leeds sack Jimmy Armfield after four years at Elland Road. It is rumoured that Don Howe and Lawrie McMenemy are the chief contenders for the job.
5. Arsenal pay £70,000 for Plymouth 'keeper Paul Barron... George Best is sent off in an NASL game for 'fighting'... Chelsea are spending around £200,000 to comply with the new Grounds Safety regulations.
6. Ally MacLeod is to stay on as Scotland manager. A motion to remove him was defeated at a meeting of the SFA – said secretary Ernie Walker.
10. Sensational transfer news from Argentina – Tottenham sign World Cup star Osvaldo Ardiles and Ricardo Villa for an estimated combined fee of £700,000. Ardiles costs £325,000 from Huracan and Villa slightly more from Racing Club. Keith Burkinshaw, Tottenham's manager says: 'The Department of Employment told me that there wouldn't be any problem. I never expected to get both players. It proves that Tottenham think big and want to be the best club in the country... Scotland blacklisted Don Masson and Lou Macari. In an ambiguous statement issued by the FA they say: 'Don Masson having admitted giving false information to our medical officer on a most important issue and having expressed publicly that he would prefer not to play for Scotland, could be accommodated in his desire.' On Macari: 'The team manager in selecting players in the future, is recommended to bear in mind the vehement complaints against the association and its arrangements by the player Lou Macari. He should give serious consideration to the advisability of subjecting the player again to these arrangements which he professes to find unsatisfactory'.
11. English football welcomes the introduction of foreign players into our domestic game. Peter Taylor, Tottenham's international winger says: 'The arrival of Ardiles and Villa is magical news. It's bound to affect attendances and create interest everywhere we go. Tommy Docherty: 'Spurs have pulled off a marvellous coup'. Ron Greenwood: 'I congratulate Tottenham on their enterprise. Ardiles was one of the best players in the World Cup'. The voice of dissent came from the PFA's Cliff Lloyd: 'I don't think we would stand for a big influx of Argentinians to this country'... The European Cup draw pairs Liverpool with Nottingham Forest; Ipswich will play the Dutch team AZ Alkmaar in the Cup-Winners Cup.
12. Tottenham Hotspur continue to create football history – they sign John Lacy of Fulham but the transfer fee is not agreed upon by the two clubs. It will be decided by the Football League Tribunal according to the new 'freedom of contract' regulations... Willie Johnston will be allowed to play in West Bromwich Albion's UEFA-Cup matches as the ban imposed on him by FIFA does not apply... Peterborough pay club record £60,000 for West Ham defender Bill Green.
13. The International Board abolishes the 'played on-side' clause from the off-side rule. In future a ball deflected by an opponent will not put a player on-side. The second change in the laws of the game concerns free kicks taken from the goal area. From now on the kick can be taken from any point on the same side of the area where the offence occurred. Thus a defending side will no longer be penalized by having to take the kick from a restricted position near a goal post... Doncaster Rovers collect £25,000 plus a player, Mickey French, from Swindon Town for Ian Miller.
14. George Reader, much respected chairman of Southampton, dies at the age of 81... Luton Town sign Bob Hatton from Blackpool for £50,000.
16. Birmingham pay £50,000 for Neil Freeman, the young Southend goalkeeper...

12 Ron Futcher joins up with his twin brother Paul again – this time at Manchester City for a fee of £75,000 ... Disc-jockey David Hamilton is invited to become a Fulham Director.

18 It is reported that both Manchester clubs are interested in Gerry Francis, but he has to prove his fitness first ... Terry Cooper, the veteran defender, moves to Bristol City for £20,000 ... Bristol Rovers pay the same amount for Walsall striker Miah Dennehy.

19 Alejandro Sabella, a 23-year-old River Plate player signs for Sheffield United. Harry Haslam says: 'I am delighted to have pulled off this £160,000 deal. To get a player of his ability is marvellous for me and the club.'

21 Gordon Taylor, member of executive committee of the PFA says: 'If the trickle of foreign players becomes a flow, it would be detrimental to our members. Whatever way you look at it, there could already be two English players out of a job at Tottenham because of the Argentinians. There is also the wider issue of the possible effect on the future of English football.'

24 Lawrie McMenemy decides to stay with Southampton and refuses the offer to manage Leeds ... Everton sign Newcastle midfielder Geoff Nulty for £40,000.

25 Everton agree to pay £325,000 for Micky Walsh, the Blackpool striker ... Givens, another Eire international, moves from QPR to Birmingham for £150,000 ... Manchester City make an inquiry for Kazimierz Deyna of Legia Warsaw, the the 102-times capped Poland midfielder.

26 The Independent Tribunal decides that Tottenham should pay £200,000 for John Lacy to Fulham – £50,000 less than Fulham's valuation ... Oxford are told that they can sign Garry Briggs of Middlesbrough for £12,500 instead of the £60,000 sought by the selling club ... Derek Hales is back with Charlton for a £70,000 fee paid to West Ham. The striker left Charlton two seasons ago for £300,000 when he joined Derby.

27 The *Daily Express* says: 'The State yesterday pumped £1 million into professional football. In a unique and momentous move, the Government, through the Sports Council, have broken down the barriers that have kept Soccer clubs isolated from their fans. The State grant is to be handed out to 18 League clubs to develop facilities at their grounds that can be used by the local community, integrating the playing staff. The money is to be used to develop outside pitches, floodlighting and general sports halls and to pay staff – called motivators – to organise and co-ordinate activities. The long-term repercussions of the project, simply called 'Football and the Community', were spelled out by the game's top administrator League secretary Alan Hardaker. 'What it means is that the State have at last accepted that the local professional soccer team can be the fulcrum on which a successful community can work. It is the greatest step forward that has taken place in football in the 20 years that I have been associated with the game.' Dickie Jeeps, chairman of the Sports Council, said: 'It could help to reduce hooliganism by giving fans a link with clubs outside match days.' The clubs receiving cash are: Middlesbrough (£50,460), Carlisle (£25,000), Sheffield Wednesday (£55,000), Huddersfield (£41,666), Sheffield United (£41,000), Leicester (£55,000), Notts Co (£32,813), Norwich (£63,150), Arsenal (£52,500), Chelsea (£58,250), QPR (£37,500), Charlton (£58,250), Portsmouth (£66,750), Reading (£33,200), Bristol City (£49,000), Aston Villa (£150,000), Wolves (£5,000), West Bromwich (£5,000).

28 Theresa Bennett is told by a High Court Judge, that the Football Association were correct in banning her from playing for a boys' club team. The 12-year-old girl was beaten at the Appeal Court in a dispute between the FA and the Equal Opportunities Commission. Master of the Rolls, Lord Denning, said in his judgment: 'It is plain as can be that football does not come within the act.'

29 Frank Sibley of QPR the League's youngest manager resigns ... Manchester United supporters are involved once again in a 'pre-season' scandal – this time in Cologne, West Germany. Dave Sexton made an appeal at half time, but there were several arrests. The score of the meaningless friendly: Cologne 1 Manchester U 1.

30 The Football League Management Committee accepts the registration of the three Argentinians imported by Tottenham and Sheffield U ... Southampton sign the Partizan Belgrade defender Ivan Golac for a £50,000 fee – but the money goes to the player ... Alec Stock is taking over QPR – temporarily.

31 Player imports by League clubs from non-Common Market countries are banned temporarily by the Government. No one else will be allowed in until talks take place between the Department of Employment and the PFA.

August

Dave Mackay goes Arabic... Forest show no charity... Jock Stein joins Leeds... Liverpool make early progress... Ron Greenwood praises the foreigners

2   Cardiff City sign Micky Burns of Newcastle for a club record fee of £75,000... Liam Brady will miss an early season match because of the automatic ban for being sent off in Cologne... Roberto Rivelino signs for a Saudi Arabian club.

3   The FA are to clamp down on clubs trying to cheat the 20 points disciplinary totting up system. If a player is suspended, matches in future cannot be rearranged to make him available. Also, after the first suspension, a further 10 penalty points will incur another ban.

5   Bertie Vogts suffers a broken leg injury in his team's opening cup match of the season – he might not be able to play again... Dave Mackay leaves Walsall, and signs a contract worth £40,000 in Kuwait... In the Anglo-Scottish Cup, Bristol City beat local rivals Rovers 6-1.

6   George Petchey decides to stay with Millwall, and turns down an offer to manage QPR.

7   Manchester United celebrate their Centenary Year by defeating Real Madrid 4-0 at Old Trafford in a friendly... Walsall axe assistant manager Des Anderson.

8   Ardiles and Villa make their debuts for Tottenham at Antwerp in Belgium where the Londoners win 3-1. Keith Burkinshaw says: 'No doubt about it, Tottenham will be exciting to watch. These Argentinians will stretch everyone in the team. And considering they have had only one day's training, they fitted in far better than we could have hoped'... Arsenal beat Celtic 3-0 at Glasgow... QPR pay a club record £210,000 for Orient defender Glenn Roeder.

9   Manchester City chairman, Peter Swales, returns from Warsaw with the news that Kazimierz Deyna is willing to sign for his club... Now it is up to the Polish Government and the English Department of Employment to make the move possible... Chairman Sir William Dugdale and two directors resign at Aston Villa over the contract wrangle concerning manager Ron Saunders... Tommy Smith turns down an offer to become Walsall's player/manager.

10 Steve Burtenshaw leaves Everton to become QPR's new manager. He spent four months in 1974 at Loftus Road as coach under Gordon Jago... John Lacy is sent off in Tottenham's friendly against Venlo in Holland... Joe Jordan suffers the same fate in Denmark where Manchester United win 1-0 v Holstebro... Ron Saunders is given a six-year contract by Aston Villa.

11 Geoff Salmons joins Chesterfield from Leicester for a £35,000 fee.

12 Nottingham F thrash Ipswich 5-0 in the Charity Shield game at Wembley (68,000 – receipts £192,000). It was Forest's first win in this traditional pre-season showpiece, and the highest margin recorded since 1968... Both Derek Hales (Charlton) and John Mitchell (Millwall) score for their new clubs in the first round of the League Cup. Richard Finney of Rotherham registers the season's first hat-trick in his team's 5-0 win over Hartlepool.

13 Alan Kennedy, Newcastle's 23-year-old defender signs for Liverpool in a £300,000 deal... Middlesbrough are negotiating to buy the Argentinian World Cup star, Rene Houseman... Malcolm Allison appeals against his life touchline ban. 'I've served more time than Ronnie Biggs did for the Great Train Robbery', said the Plymouth manager.

14 Liverpool beat Celtic at Glasgow 3-2 in a testimonial match for Jock Stein, the 62,000 crowd pay £80,000... Phil Hoadley the Orient defender contacts Norwich in view of 'a job' there. He signs for the 'Canaries' in this first ever 'do-it-yourself' deal. The transfer fee will be settled later – either by the clubs or by the Tribunal.

15 Colin Viljoen cuts short a month's trial with QPR and signs for – Manchester City! The cost – £100,000... Clive Thomas sends off Chris Kamara of Swindon in the League Cup tie against his old club, Portsmouth.

16 John Matthews joins Sheffield United for £90,000 from Arsenal, and Derby winger Terry Curran goes to Southampton for £60,000... Wigan beat Tranmere 2-1 in the second leg of the Football League Cup tie and reach round two. It is the first entry in the club's history as they are 'new boys' in the Football League.

17 John Gorman, out of football for 17 months, starts the season at left full-back for Spurs... Leeds approach Jock Stein to take over as manager... Ipswich beat Ajax for the signature of Arnold Muhren. The Dutchman joins the East Anglian club

from Twente Enschede for £140,000 ... Port Vale pay £40,000 for Wolves midfielder Ken Todd.

19 Ricardo Villa scores the equalizer for Tottenham at Nottingham, thus grabbing the headlines on the opening day of the League season. While the champions drop one point Liverpool squeeze home 2-1 v QPR and Everton register their customary win at Chelsea. Only Norwich win by more than a single goal margin in the First Division – 3-1 v newly promoted Southampton. In Division Two, Luton win 6-1 after a 0-1 deficit at half-time v Oldham and West Ham beat Notts Co 5-2. Two hat-tricksters – David Cross (West Ham) and Brian Joicey (Barnsley). The aggregate attendance is 50,000 more than on the opening day of last season.

21 Jock Stein is the new manager of Leeds United. The ex-Celtic boss signs a three-year contract said to be worth £85,000. Stein says 'I did not want to stay with Celtic as a director. I feel I have too much to offer to football and I wanted closer involvement' ... Peter Withe moves to Newcastle from Forest for £225,000. Brian Clough says: 'This means we now need two new players instead of one' ... Preston NE sign Eric Potts from Brighton for £40,000.

22 Nottingham F drop another point at Coventry, while top-form Liverpool win 3-0 at Ipswich – Kenny Dalglish scoring twice. Crowd trouble at Wolverhampton where Chelsea win 1-0 through a Tommy Langley goal ... First points in Division One for Southampton and Bolton who draw 2-2 at The Dell. The Yugoslav Ivan Golac makes his debut in this match for the home team having received Home Office clearance to play less than two hours before the kick-off ... Ellis of Portsmouth is sent off at York – the score 5-3 to the home club. Other players dismissed: Roffey (Orient), Entwistle (Sunderland) and Youlden of Aldershot.

23 A ticker-tape welcome for the Argentinian stars by the Tottenham crowd ends in an anti-climax when visiting Aston Villa win 4-1 ... Manchester United beat Leeds at Elland Road 3-2 ... In Division Two, West Ham continue their bid for a quick return to the top flight with a 3-0 away win over Newcastle ... Alan Ashman is the new manager of Walsall.

24 Willie Johnston asks for a transfer at WBA. He was put on the subs bench in their first two league matches ... Norwich are told to pay £110,000 for Phil Hoadley to Orient by the Independent Transfer Tribunal. John Bond complains about the decision, saying that the Tribunal's job was intended to be 'normalising' fees not inflating them' ... Berger Isthmian League club Oxford City will wear the 'Buzby' telephone symbol on their jerseys as part of a sponsorship scheme by the Post Office.

25 Derby County pay £45,000 for young Newcastle defender Aidan McCaffrey, but refuse an Everton transfer bid for Colin Todd ... Birmingham are bidding for Brazilian World Cup star Dirceu. The player is available but his club, Vasco da Gama, want a £425,000 cash payment for him.

26 Liverpool win 4-1 at Manchester City and lead the table with maximum points after three matches. Other 100 per cent teams in the league – Everton, WBA, Stoke, Chester, Barnsley, and Reading. Peterborough and Plymouth collect four points each – they only played two games so far ... Don Masson goes back to Notts Co as player/coach for a £30,000 fee.

28 Liverpool, last season's League Cup finalists, are the first team to be beaten in round two. In the only match played on this Monday, Sheffield U beat them 1-0 ... Cosmos beat Tampa Bay Rowdies 3-1 in the final of the USA Championship play-off in front of a near 75,000 crowd ... Chelsea are bidding for Duncan McKenzie of Everton.

29 A Tommy Smith tackle puts Ardiles out of the League Cup tie at Swansea where a 24,335 all-ticket audience see the teams draw 2-2. Arsenal lose at Rotherham, and Bristol City are beaten by Crystal Palace. Everton inflict an 8-0 thrashing on Wimbledon – their heaviest defeat since they joined the league. Bob Latchford gets five, Dobson a hat-trick.

30 Transfers off – Houseman to Middlesbrough, Dirceu to Birmingham ... First Division clubs out of the League Cup – Ipswich, Wolves, Coventry – all beaten by lower division clubs. ... Manchester United have a narrow escape at home to Stockport. The visitors, who in fact switched the game to Old Trafford, lead 2-1 with five minutes to go, when Gordon McQueen is sent off! But Sammy McIlroy equalizes and Jimmy Greenhoff gets the winner from a penalty.

31 The ninth edition of *Rothmans Football Yearbook* is launched at a reception in the Tower Hotel. Ron Greenwood praised the publication in his speech, saying that it was an invaluable guide for managers, journalists and supporters alike. He also welcomed the introduction of foreign players into English football. 'They have acted as a stimulant on our soccer. They have created a feeling of expectancy, excitement and glamour. To deny clubs work permits for their foreign players is a head-in-the-sand attitude'... Malcolm Macdonald needs another knee operation and will be out of football for two months... The Chelsea-McKenzie deal falls through, but Mike Buckley joins Sunderland for £80,000 from Everton... George Armstrong goes to Stockport for £5,000.

September

League Cup shocks ... England do well in Europe ... but their fans are banned from travelling ... MacLeod joins Ayr

2   On the third Saturday of the League season, Liverpool thrash Tottenham 7-0 at Anfield. Dalglish scores twice, sub Johnston twice, Ray Kennedy, Neal (pen), and McDermott who gets the goal which is later described by manager Bob Paisley as 'one of the best in the club's history'... As both Everton and WBA drop points, Liverpool are now the only 100 per centers in Division One. Stoke lead Division Two with seven points, and newly promoted Swansea are the leaders of the Third Division. Barnsley, with Allan Clarke, the ex-Leeds forward, as their player/manager, top Division Four with maximum points... Five players were sent off including Sam Allardyce of Bolton... A new name on the scoring list – Steve Hunt, back in England from Cosmos, gets the first Coventry goal at Derby, where Gordon Milne's team win 2-0.

4   Peter Osgood, back in England, wishes 'to sell himself' to a club, preferably to Chelsea. 'For £30,000, I am still a bargain', he said, 'Chelsea would get their money back, because people would come and see me play'... The Scottish FA's report on the World Cup puts the blame on the players for the failure. 'No matter what arrangements the committee make or what the manager may do, if the team does not produce form on the day they must fail. The biggest disappointment was the failure of the team to exhibit traditional Scottish spirit and fight'... Orient sign Paul Went of Cardiff for £30,000... John Froggatt goes from Port Vale to Northampton for £8,000.

5   Don Revie, holidaying in England, is willing to face an FA commission to clear his name... John Robson, the Aston Villa full-back, is suffering from Multiple Sclerosis. Due to this serious illness, he has to give up the game, and Villa are arranging a testimonial for him... Trevor Francis is injured in training and might miss six weeks' football... The League Cup provides further surprises – in replays, Darlington beat Fulham, and Peterborough ko Middlesbrough... Southend pay a club record £50,000 to Sheffield W for defender Dave Cusack.
Further shocks in the League Cup – Swansea beat 'expensive' Tottenham at White Hart Lane 3-1, and Peterborough progress at the expense of First Division Middlesbrough... Duncan McKenzie signs for Chelsea for £165,000 – the London club's first substantial expenditure on a player in four years.

8   Leighton James rejoins Burnley for a record £165,000 transfer fee – he was originally sold by Burnley to Derby for £300,000 four years ago... Phil Boersma joins the 'Anfield Old Boys' contingent at Swansea for £35,000 to Luton... Tottenham manager Keith Burkinshaw drops five players for the Bristol City game, including talented youngsters Glenn Hoddle and Neil McNab.

9   Liverpool still remain invincible – their 3-0 at Birmingham gives them full points after five games with a goal difference of 19-2: Closest rivals remain Everton (2-0 v Middlesbrough) and Coventry (3-2 v Chelsea). In this match, Duncan McKenzie makes a goalscoring debut for Chelsea ... Charlie George is sent off in Bolton for retaliation... Stoke City, Swansea, and the only other 100 per centers Barnsley, lead the lower divisions... In Scotland Celtic beat Rangers 3-1 in front of a 55,000 crowd... Tottenham, with Ardiles and Villa, register their first win of the season – 1-0 against Bristol City at White Hart Lane through a Dave Rodgers own goal. Rodgers did the same 'trick' a week ago at Wolves, but previously scored a winning goal for his club.

10 Brian Clough threatens to close a part of the Nottingham F ground if the fans carry on with their obscene chanting and baiting of the opposition. 'They are making me sick', says the manager, 'I would rather have a smaller crowd of decent people watching our home matches.'

11 Six clubs are facing FA fines due to their bad disciplinary record during the past season ... Kenny Burns is not included in the Scotland party for their international against Austria.

12 Celtic fans stage a riot at Burnley. The Anglo-Scottish tie is suspended by the referee for 10 minutes because of a crowd invasion. Finally Billy McNeill, Celtic's manager, brings his team back on the pitch to calm the fans ... Players are sent off at Swindon and at Northampton in league matches.

13 European club football opens with a 2-0 surprise Nottingham F win over Cup holders, Liverpool. Unknown 22-year-old Gary Birtles scores the first goal, and full-back Colin Barrett the second. Brian Clough remains cautious: 'Two goals might not be enough at Anfield' ... Rangers lose only 1-0 to Juventus in Turin in the same competition. In the Cup-Winners Cup, Ipswich fight a creditable goalless draw at AZ Alkmaar, and the English clubs all seem favourites to reach round two in the UEFA Cup – three wins, one away draw ... But Wrexham lose 3-0 at Rijeka, where John Roberts is sent off ... Bobby Gould moves again – this time to Hereford for a £10,000 fee.

14 Ian Callaghan is the latest ex-Liverpool recruit for Swansea ... Chesterfield sign Swindon defender Colin Prophett for £15,000 ... Derby buy the striker they wanted to supplement George – he is John Duncan of Spurs, for £150,000.

15 Tommy Docherty sells Colin Todd for £330,000 to Everton. It is his 30th transfer deal since he took over Derby a year ago. He has sold 16 players for the estimated total of £1 million and signed 14 at the cost of about £250,000 more – but deal Number 31 is already lined up as Gerry Ryan is on offer for £80,000.

16 Liverpool maintain their 100 per cent record in the league by beating Coventry 1-0. Now they are two points ahead of closest challengers Everton ... Duncan McKenzie's home debut at Chelsea ends in a disastrous 4-1 home defeat against Manchester City. Ron Futcher scores a hat-trick for the visitors, and Ray Wilkins is substituted after just over one hour's play. Tottenham score their first away win at Leeds and QPR achieve a similar result at Middlesbrough ... Crystal Palace go on top of Division Two, where the Stoke v Brighton game is postponed due to a 'flu epidemic in the 'Seasiders' camp.

18 Bobby Finch, 28, full-back of Hillingdon Borough, dies of a heart attack 48 hours after playing in an FA Cup match ... The full England side selected to play Denmark shows two changes – Clemence for Shilton in goal and Latchford for the injured Trevor Francis in attack.

19 Birmingham sign Alberto Tarantini, the Argentinian World Cup star defender for a club record £259,000, but the deal has to be ratified by the FA ... England U-21 scrape home 2-1 in Copenhagen against Denmark – Ken Sansom of Crystal Palace is the journalists' choice as the only real success ... Littlewoods raise their maximum Treble Chance dividend to £750,000 to keep up with inflation ... Twelve clubs are fined by the FA for accumulating more than 175 disciplinary 'points' last season. Southampton are hardest hit with a £1,250 fine, QPR must pay £800. The others penalized were Crystal Palace, Fulham, Blackpool, Bristol C, Oldham, Crewe, Sheffield U, Hartlepool Halifax and Hereford.

20 England win a spectacular high-scoring match in Copenhagen in the European Championship. Kevin Keegan scores with two headers in the first half, but the Danes equalise through a Simonsen penalty, and a goal by the Ajax player, Arnesen. Latchford gets a disputed third goal after the break, and Neal makes it 4-2. Minutes before the end, Rontved once again narrows the gap – 4-3! Ron Greenwood says: 'I'm an advocate of attacking football – but that was carrying it to extremes' ... In the same group, the historic first encounter between the Republic of Ireland and N Ireland ends in a disappointing goalless draw. The afternoon kick-off helps with crowd control, and there is relatively little trouble ... Scotland lose 3-2 in Vienna, after making a gallant come-back with goals by McQueen and Gray to close a 3-0 deficit ... Swindon buy Andy Rowland from Bury for £85,000, and collect £65,000 for Guthrie from Fulham.

22 Steve Harrison of Blackpool signs for Watford for £25,000.

23 The Burnley v Sunderland 'grudge' game makes headlines on this stormy Saturday. Two Sunderland players are sent-off – Mick Docherty and Joe Bolton – and three others are booked. Afterwards Sunderland manager Jimmy Adamson is accused of 'inciting his players because he dislikes Burnley where he was sacked two years ago'. Despite the handicap, the nine-men visitors win 2-1 ... Liverpool drop their first point of the season at West Brom, Everton keep up the chase with a

2-0 victory over bottom-of-the-table Wolves . . . Ross Jenkins scores all four Watford goals in his team's 4-2 home win over Oxford . . . Tragic event outside a football ground – a Chelsea supporter is pushed under a Birmingham bus and dies . . . Kevin Keegan, the latest captive of the BBC makes his first appearance as a 'Match of the Day' guest, and praises the attitude of the current England side . . . Tommy Smith is sent off at Chester for dissent – his club Swansea, lose 2-0.

24 Johan Cruyff offers to play for Cosmos against Chelsea for nothing – in order to help the finances of the struggling London club.

25 Nigel Stevenson, another Swansea player, is sent off at Carlisle where the Welsh team are beaten 2-0 . . . Alan Ball will appear in front of an FA Disciplinary Committee in connection with remarks made in his autobiography concerning an alleged illegal payment from Don Revie, the then Leeds manager – Alan Mullery raids the transfer market and buys Gerry Ryan from Derby.

26 Ally McLeod resigns as Scotland manager, and takes over Ayr United . . . A near 40,000 crowd creates a carnival atmosphere at Stamford Bridge where Cosmos draw with Chelsea 1-1. Both Beckenbauer and Cruyff play for the US club . . . Everton establish a new European competition club record by beating Finn Harps 10-0 on aggregate in the UEFA Cup.

27 European Cup sensations – both last year's finalists, Liverpool and Bruges, are out in the first round. Liverpool can only draw 0-0 with Forest, and the Belgians lose on a 4-3 aggregate to Wisla Krakow. But Rangers defeat Juventus 2-0, and it is generally a very good start for the British clubs in Europe . . . No casualties for England in either the Cup Winners or UEFA Cups and Aberdeen and Hibernian also survive. Wrexham go out to Rijeka of Yugoslavia on a 3-2 aggregate.

28 A compromise plan drawn up by Sports Minister, Denis Howell and John Grant, Minister of Employment, is accepted by the various football organisations. According to this agreement, established foreign players will be given permits to join British clubs. The two earliest contracts ratified will be those of Tarantini to Birmingham and Golac's pro-forms to Southampton . . . The FA puts a complete ban on fans travelling to Dublin for the Republic's match v England. They have taken this stand because of fans' misbehaviour in Luxembourg and Denmark when England were the visitors . . . Micky Droy is out of football for the rest of the year with a kidney ailment . . . Micky Burns joins Middlesbrough for £75,000 from Cardiff.

29 Orient pay a club record £55,000 for Spurs striker Ian Moores.

30 Nottingham Forest win 2-1 at Aston Villa, thus equalling Leeds United's record of 34 consecutive unbeaten league games. But Liverpool are still top of the table following their 3-0 (Case hat-trick) win over Bolton. The only other unbeaten team, Everton, draw 2-2 at Bristol. A last minute Joe Jordan goal clinches the points for United in the Manchester derby . . . Chelsea lose their fourth home game – out of four! After the match, manager Ken Shellito says: 'It was disgusting. My players behave like primadonnas. If necessary I'll sell the lot, because our wonderful supporters cannot be insulted again.' Later it is revealed that Chelsea are bidding for the services of Johan Cruyff. West Brom's Tony Brown equals the club's goalscoring record in the 3-1 win at Stamford Bridge.

October

Stein is new Scottish boss . . . New record for Forest . . . Jimmy Adamson joins Leeds as boss . . . Liverpool's first League defeat . . .

2 The Scottish FA refuse to name their choice for the team manager's job after a seven hour meeting. But he is certain to be Jock Stein, who hasn't signed a contract with Leeds yet . . . Len Cantello is sent off in the second League Cup replay between WBA and Leeds. Leeds win with a Paul Hart goal.

3 QPR end Swansea's League Cup run with a 2-0 win at Loftus Road.

4 League Cup shock at Old Trafford – Watford beat United 2-1 with two second-half goals by Luther Blissett . . . Exeter also triumph over a First Division side – they defeat Bolton at home 2-1. Aston Villa draw with Crystal Palace 1-1, and after youngster Gary Shelton is carried off with a bad leg injury, manager Ron Saunders launches an attack on Palace. 'You keep reading about these supposed football sides, but they come and try to kick you off the pitch' . . . Jock Stein accepts the Scottish FA's offer to become their national team manager; 'Money didn't come into it', he said, 'but my family didn't want to live in the Leeds area.' Stein stayed

only one day longer than Brian Clough four years ago, who was sacked after 44 days ... John Sharpe is transferred to Gillingham for £30,000.

5   Chelsea chairman, Brian Mears, flies to Yugoslavia to try to persuade Miljan Miljanic to join the club as technical director ... Aston Villa ask for a postponement of their Saturday league game due to a spate of injuries, but the League refuses ... Giant killers Exeter and Watford are drawn against each other in the League Cup, but the top clash will be between the holders, Nottingham F, and Everton at Goodison.

6   Ian Moores scores both goals on his debut for Orient at Charlton – 2-0 ... Sheffield Wednesday pay £60,000 for Mike Pickering from Southampton.

7   Liverpool establish a three-point lead on top of Division One with a 4-1 away win at Norwich ... Still unbeaten are Everton and Nottingham F ... Crystal Palace head the Second Division following their 3-1 home win over Brighton ... Bryan Robson scores a hat-trick for West Ham against Millwall at Upton Park, where a large police contingent is needed to keep the rival fans apart – 70 arrests and several injuries ... Midweek giantkillers Watford are beaten at Chester ... Shrewsbury and Wimbledon are the leaders of the lower divisions.

9   Brian Clough and Peter Taylor travel with the England Youth party to Las Palmas for an international tournament: 'I am not interested in the results' says Clough, 'but I wish to provide some players for Ron Greenwood's 1982 World Cup team ... The FA co-opt as honorary members of their council four 'footballing greats' – Sir Walter Winterbottom, Bobby Charlton, Stan Cullis and Tom Finney.

10 The League Cup replay between Palace and Aston Villa goes to extra-time, but a no-goals draw means another clash. Allan Evans was sent off ... There is a move within the FA to censure their Chairman Sir Harold Thomson for remarks made during a Council meeting earlier in the year ... Jeremy Charles is included in the Wales squad v Malta.

11 FIFA ban George Best at the request of the FA – he will not be allowed to play anywhere until the dispute between him and Fulham is settled ... Denmark and Bulgaria draw in their European Championship match ... Millwall pay £65,000 to Brighton for Tony Towner ... Newport buy David Bruton from Swansea for a club record £15,000 ... Middlesbrough also spend – £233,333 on Terry Cochrane of Burnley.

12 Sammy Chapman, former Nottingham Forest skipper, wins a test case in court concerning players' testimonials. In future, the income from such games will be tax-free ... Miljan Miljanic arrives to spend a trial period with Chelsea ... Alberto Tarantini will make his debut for Birmingham at White Hart Lane against Tottenham ... Preston pay £35,000 for Brian Taylor of Plymouth ... Fulham clinch the John Beck deal – £70,000 to Coventry.

13 Unlucky Friday for some – Mike Summerbee is sent off in Stockport's 0-0 draw v Barnsley ... Derek Jeffries, another ex-Manchester City player is sent off against Tranmere and his team Chester are beaten 6-2 ... At Darlington, six players are booked in the game with Crewe, and after an incident the police move onto the pitch to separate the players ... Brian Clough says that Forest's aim is still to win the league, and the club is willing to spend one million pounds to strengthen the squad.

14 Liverpool, Everton and Nottingham F continue their unbeaten runs. Liverpool thrash Derby 5-0, their record now reads: played 10, won 9, drew 1. Goals 33-4! Everton win 1-0 at Ipswich and Forest 3-1 at Bristol, where three penalties are awarded by referee Clive Thomas and are all converted ... Chelsea watched by prospective new technical director, Miljan Miljanic, pull back a 0-3 deficit at home against Bolton, and score four goals in the last 15 minutes for their first home win of the season ... Tarantini's opening game for Birmingham ends in defeat at Tottenham.

16 Aston Villa ko Crystal Palace in the League Cup at the third attempt 3-0 ... Jim Smith, Birmingham manager, reveals that Tarantini's signature only cost £259,000 with £90,000 of it to the player.

17 Phil Thompson is back in the England squad, which includes no uncapped player ... Wales manager Mike Smith is trying to secure the release of Beringen forward Nick Deacy, and Jock Stein leaves out three Scotland-based players from his squad, but drafts in Frank Gray of Leeds.

18 Nottingham F clinch a surprise win in Greece. McGovern scores early on, Birtles adds a second, then Viera of AEK is sent off. The Greeks reduce the gap to 2-1 with a second-half penalty ... Rangers draw 0-0 with PSV at home ... In the Cup

Winners' Cup, Ipswich only manage a narrow 1-0 win over Innsbruck through a John Wark penalty, and Aberdeen are well beaten in Dusseldorf... Mixed fortunes for the British teams in the UEFA Cup – Manchester City registering the most convincing win, 4-0 v Standard Liege... Wrexham treble their club record pay-out as they buy back Joey Jones from Liverpool for £210,000... Brentford also spend – £33,000 on Jim McNichol from Luton, and £25,000 for Dean Smith of Leicester.

19 Alan Hudson joins Seattle Sounders for a £100,000 fee, but he will not play for them until January. Hudson's last match in an Arsenal shirt was the FA Cup final.

21 Liverpool, Everton and Nottingham F remain unbeaten after 11 games in the First Division. But the day's best score is Albion's 7-1 win over Coventry. Both Regis and Cunningham score twice... In Division Two Crystal Palace are undefeated after a goalless draw at Wrexham... Watford take over the lead in Division Three and Wimbledon are still on top of the Fourth Division despite their first setback of the season – 0-3 at Huddersfield.

23 The England team will be unchanged against the Republic of Ireland on Wednesday. This is the first time that Ron Greenwood keeps the same side – despite Emlyn Hughes' absence from Liverpool's team since mid-September... Willie Bell gives up his job as manager of Lincoln in order to join a religious sect in America. He will coach a team, Campus Crusade for Christ, which hope to gain converts to Christianity through sport... Paul Hinshelwood of Crystal Palace will have a cartilage operation, while his brother Martin is advised to retire.

24 Alan Buckley moves to Birmingham from Walsall for £175,000... Steve Kember is back at the Palace – it is a £50,000 move for the Leicester midfielder... Larry Lloyd withdraws his transfer request at Nottingham... Scotland's Under 21 side beat Norway 5-1.

25 An exciting match ends 1-1 at Dublin between England and the Republic of Ireland. Bob Latchford scores early on, but Daly equalises in the middle of the first half... N Ireland beat Denmark in the same European Championship group 2-1 with goals by subs Derek Spence and Trevor Anderson... Scotland have a narrow escape v Norway at Hampden – they squeeze home 3-2 with a late Archie Gemmill penalty... Jimmy Adamson is the new Leeds manager. He signs a three-year contract. Inevitably his old club Sunderland are linked with Brian Clough... Ian Edwards of Chester scores four times for Wales in their 7-0 win over Malta. This scoring feat equals Mel Charles' all-time best, and the margin of victory is a Welsh record for this century.

26 Ken Burton resigns as joint manager of the England Youth team with Brian Clough and Peter Taylor. It is understood that Burton, the only full-time member of Greenwood's managerial set-up, felt that it was wrong that Clough should run the team on a match-days only basis... Shrewsbury pay £30,000 for David Tong of Blackpool.

27 Bill Ashcroft is sent off, but Middlesbrough still manage to beat Aston Villa 2-0 in Birmingham – a fixture brought forward because of the Motor Show... Johnny Cartwright will take over from Ken Burton as England Youth manager.

28 First defeat for Liverpool in the league. They are beaten at Everton 1-0 through an Andy King goal. It is the first Everton success in this local derby since 1971... Nottingham F keep their unbeaten record at Southampton, where they draw 0-0... Leeds, under new boss Adamson, beat Derby 4-0... Stoke take over the lead in Division Two, Watford and Wimbledon lead the lower sections... Dundee U head the table in the Scottish Premier Division.

30 Bolton pay a club record £250,000 for midfielder Neil McNab of Tottenham... In future there's got to be an outright winner in the Home Championship. If countries finish level on points, they won't share the title, but goal difference will decide, or if necessary, goals for... Birmingham put a blanket ban on all their players going to the USA for the summer... Both Ron Atkinson and Terry Venables turn down lucrative offers from abroad.

31 Four Ipswich players are carpeted after they break the curfew in Innsbruck... Leeds goalkeeper David Stewart goes to WBA for £75,000... Cambridge pay £50,000 – a club record – for Northampton striker Derrick Christie... Bradford City manager John Napier resigns, and Halifax sack their boss Jimmy Lawson.

November

Rangers excel ... Managerial axe continues to fall ... PFA's new Chairman ... London Weekend's TV scoop

1 Nottingham F make sure of a place in the European Cup quarter-finals with a 5-1 home win over AEK. But the best result of the night is achieved by Glasgow Rangers: 3-2 in Eindhoven against PSV ... In the Cup-Winners' Cup, Ipswich hang on to their slender lead in Austria, but Aberdeen are out ... Paul Mariner is sent off in Innsbruck ... UEFA Cup progress for Manchester City, WBA and Arsenal, but Everton lose 1-0 in Prague where Dukla go into the third round ... Gary Owen is sent off at Liege, and Liam Brady gets the red card treatment at Highbury, where two Yugoslavs are also dismissed in a bruising match ... Overall, six W German and six British clubs are still involved in the European competitions, while all other countries are reduced to one or two representatives.

2 Brian Clough is staying with Nottingham F, although he would like to refuse the Sunderland offer personally.

4 Three home wins and eight draws in the First Division. Nottingham F and Everton play out a goalless stalemate, both are still unbeaten in the league ... Stoke increase their lead to three points in Division Two with a 1-0 away win at Sheffield ... Shrewsbury take over the lead in Division Three, as both Watford and Swansea are beaten ... Reading are the new leaders of the Fourth Division ... Frank Stapleton scores his first ever hat-trick for Arsenal in their 4-1 victory over Ipswich – a revenge for May's Cup final defeat.

6 Cardiff sack Jimmy Andrews after five years with the Welsh club ... Lincoln give their vacant managerial job to Colin Murphy, former Derby boss ... Swansea pay £70,000 for Leighton Phillips to Aston Villa and Oxford bring Ray Graydon back from Washington Diplomats for £40,000.

7 Nottingham F continue their unbeaten run at the expense of Everton – a 3-2 League Cup win at Goodison! Away wins also in the same competition for Stoke and Charlton and for Leeds at QPR. Brighton beat Peterborough 1-0 at Hove ... Spurs defender Mike Stead signs for Southend for £50,000 ... Ted MacDougall does not wish to play for Southampton any longer and Paul Bradshaw asks for a move at Wolves ... Eric Gates stages a walk out at Ipswich.

8 Three more away wins in the fourth round of the League Cup and one draw, Reading v Southampton. Manchester City win 3-1 at Norwich with two late Channon goals. Watford beat Exeter 2-0, and Luton supply the shock result with a 2-0 victory at Villa Park. Andy Gray is taken to hospital early on with a leg injury, and Aston Villa never recover from the blow .... Brian Clough and Peter Taylor won't go to Monaco next week with the England Youth team. There are injury problems at Nottingham, but Clough says that he won't be rushed into 'panic buying' ... Kazimierz Deyna, 102 times capped for Poland, signs for Manchester City ... Sammy Chung is sacked at Wolves 18 months after guiding the club to promotion.

9 John Barnwell walks out at Peterborough, because the club is not ambitious enough. He also puts in an application for the vacant managerial jobs at Wolves and Sunderland ... Port Vale pay a club record £40,000 for Bury midfielder Peter Farrell.

10 Manchester U are ordered to pay an extra £22,000 to Bournemouth for Ted MacDougall by the Law Courts. It is part of a complicated transfer arrangement related to MacDougall's goalscoring for the Old Trafford club. On the same day, MacDougall goes back to Bournemouth on a free transfer from Southampton.

12 The top teams in Division One go marching on – Liverpool, Everton, Nottingham F, WBA and Arsenal all win ... Stoke are beaten at home by Cambridge U as the field bunches in the Second Division. Five players are sent off, two of them after the final whistle at the Rotherham v Colchester game where Richard Dawson and Mike Packer were involved in an incident as they trooped off the pitch ... Rangers and Celtic draw 1-1 in Scotland, where Dundee U still head the league race.

14 Lawrie McMenemy is officially approached by Sunderland ... Gordon Taylor is the new PFA Chairman – he wishes to start a clean up campaign against illegal tackles ... Bryan Hamilton joins Swindon for a £20,000 transfer fee ... Liam Brady's UEFA suspension is cut from three to two matches ... Tommy Docherty opens his case against Willie Morgan and Granada TV in the Courts by saying that the interview broadcast has damaged his reputation ... Fulham and Wimbledon

would like to build a new stadium in South London which they would share. They are hoping to get Government help for the one million pound project.

15 Tommy Docherty withdraws from the libel case after admitting that he lied under oath concerning Denis Law. He has to pay costs of £30,000. Derby County call an emergency Board meeting to discuss their manager's future with the club... Lawrie McMenemy is staying with Southampton, as he turns down the Sunderland offer... Fulham are fined £15,000 for 'financial irregularities', which include paying players' expenses, hotel bills etc... John Bond signs a nine-year contract with Norwich... Leighton James is back in the Wales squad for their European tie v Turkey... Exeter pay £25,000 to Millwall for Ian Pearson, and sell Tony Kellow for £105,000 to Blackpool.

16 The front pages of the newspapers are occupied with football news for the second day – ITV have sensationally signed a separate agreement with the Football League, giving them the right to screen league and League Cup ties exclusively for three years! The contract is worth five million pounds to the clubs, and is effectively halving the amount of football on TV. The BBC say that they will fight the deal – they do not want to lose their 'Match of the Day' programme... Tommy Docherty is suspended for seven days by Derby. Assistant manager Frank Blunstone takes over while the Board consider the implication of Docherty's court case... Millwall pay £100,000 for Nick Chatterton to Palace. Tony Hazell goes in the other direction for £25,000... Fulham are negotiating with the Brazilian ace Paulo Cesar, who is in London... Manchester U's mammoth bid for Coventry 'keeper Jim Blyth founders on a medical report concerning the player's future in the game.

18 Liverpool beat Manchester C with a disputed penalty... Everton draw at Arsenal and Nottingham F draw with QPR – both are still undefeated in the league, but Everton are now three points behind Liverpool... Burnley beat Fulham 5-3, but Bristol R and Charlton go even better – 5-5 at Eastville... Crystal Palace are the new leaders of Division Two following their draw at West Ham... Watford are two points ahead in Division Three, and Wimbledon are the top club in Division Four... Jimmy Hill asks for a re-think on the TV deal: 'It wasn't an honourable agreement', he says, 'It was railroaded through, the clubs didn't even know whose bid they were accepting'.

20 After a weekend of speculation, John Barnwell is named as the new Wolves manager... Stan Anderson leaves Doncaster and joins Greaves at Bolton... Jimmy Hill is organizing a petition amongst league chairmen to reconsider the new TV deal. The Department of Fair Trading also looks into the implications of the ITV monopoly... Stan Bowles is suspended for three matches.

21 Crystal Palace draw away from the field in Division Two with a 3-1 win over Sheffield U... Barnwell starts with a 1-0 away win at Bristol City with Wolves. He also takes Richie Barker, the Shrewsbury manager, with him to Molyneux.

22 Good start for English clubs in the UEFA Cup Third Round – Arsenal only lose 1-0 at Belgrade, and WBA draw at Valencia 1-1, where Laurie Cunningham scores and stars for them... Tottenham play out a goalless draw with Liverpool at White Hart Lane and Chelsea lose at Leeds... Stoke join Crystal Palace at the top of Division Two by beating Oldham 4-0.

23 John Gordon, Scotland's top referee, and linesmen Rollo Kyle and David McCartney are suspended by the Scottish Football Association after admitting that they accepted gifts from AC Milan before their UEFA Cup tie against Levski Spartak. Milan were fined £8,000 by UEFA for taking these officials on a buying spree which went beyond the accepted limits of hospitality... Docherty is reinstated as Derby County's manager... The BBC are suing London Weekend Television and the Football League in connection with the recent exclusive deal ... Manchester City draw in Milan 2-2. The game ends in an off-field riot with the fans letting off smoke bombs and fireworks... Vancouver sign Trevor Whymark (£150,000) but the player may play for Ipswich until February next year... Fulham abandon their attempt to sign Paulo Cesar – negotiations broke down after financial demands were made by the player.

24 On his second day back in business, Tommy Docherty raids the transfer market and pays £250,000 for Steve Sims of Leicester.

25 Jimmy Greaves of Barnet sent off, Malcolm Allison's Plymouth beaten by Worcester – these are the FA Cup round one headlines... Billy Bremner the new manager of Doncaster, and Kenny Clements breaks a leg against Ipswich – this is

the league news... Liverpool are still two points in front after beating Middlesbrough 2-0... Chelsea are last following their latest home defeat v Manchester U. Micky Thomas – a £300,000 midweek signing – makes an encouraging debut for the visitors.

27 Viv Anderson, the 22-year-old Nottingham F full-back, is going to be the first black player to represent England in a full international. There are five other changes for the game against Czechoslovakia: Shilton, Thompson, Currie, Woodcock and Cherry come in for players who take their places on the subs' bench. Greenwood says: 'The team is in fact a squad of 20, and this time those who have been challenging for a place get an opportunity to play'... Stan Bowles denies the drug-taking allegations he has made against himself in the *Daily Star*. 'I was misquoted', states the QPR forward.

28 Steve Daley scores the only goal of the match between the Czechoslovakia and England 'B' teams in Prague... The Sims to Derby transfer is stopped on medical grounds.

29 On the icy pitch at Wembley, Czechoslovakia lead England a merry dance, but Peter Shilton saves the day by a series of magnificent stops. At the other end, Michalik blunders, and England win 1-0 with a goal officially credited to Steve Coppell... In European Championship matches, N Ireland collect two unexpected points in Bulgaria, Wales beat Turkey 1-0 at Wrexham, but Scotland lose in Portugal... Luton pay £100,000 for Aston Villa reserve 'keeper Jake Findlay.

30 Malcolm Allison's touch-line ban is lifted... The FA, with the sponsorship of the Coca-Cola company, introduces an award scheme for children. It is designed to give every schoolboy a chance to develop the basic skills of the game.

December

Winter shows its hand... Forest lose at last... MacLeod moves to Motherwell... FA ban Don Revie... Stan Seymour dies... Keegan's honour.

1 Peter Osgood is back with Chelsea. After four years he rejoins the club for a £30,000 fee to Philadelphia Furies... Mick Martin goes to Newcastle for £100,000 from West Brom.

2 Thirty-four league games are cancelled due to frost and ice in England and Scotland – the Pools Panel 'decides' the outcome of these fictional matches. But Arsenal do play Liverpool and beat them 1-0 with a scrambled goal credited to David Price... In Division Two Crystal Palace strengthen their position on top of the table by beating Newcastle.

3 QPR chairman Jim Gregory indicates that he is willing to resign. 'The abuse from the crowd begins to affect my family' he says... Charlie George is available for transfer – West Brom and Southampton are bidding for him.

4 Rob Rensenbrink scores in the last minute to secure a 3-1 lead for Anderlecht over Liverpool in the Super Cup... Millwall chairman Herbert Burnige resigns.

5 The three Scottish referees involved in the AC Milan bribery allegations each receive a three years' suspension from the Scottish FA.

6 Convincing victories for Manchester C and WBA in the UEFA Cup, but Arsenal can only draw with Red Star Belgrade at Highbury and are eliminated... Brian Clough joins the hunt for Charlie George.

7 Charlie George is barred from joining Forest by the Derby board, because the two clubs are rivals for the same local support... Another Scottish referee, Billy Reid, admits receiving gifts from AC Milan before a European match.

9 Terry McDermott scores twice in Liverpool's 2-0 victory over Nottingham F. This is Forest's first league defeat since 26 November 1977 – a 42-match unbeaten run of 21 wins and 21 draws; Brian Clough says: 'I congratulated our lads on a magnificent run. This defeat means a slight relief – but we would have felt better if we hadn't lost'... Everton win at Birmingham, and West Brom beat Middlesbrough 2-0. The three bottom clubs lose again... Crystal Palace increase their lead to two points in Division Two. Watford and Swansea are level top in Division Three and Wimbledon still lead Division Four.

11 Miljan Miljanic rejects Chelsea and accepts an offer to manage the Yugoslav national team.

12 Southampton beat Manchester C 2-1 in the League Cup... Ray Wilkins suffers a ligament injury in the Chelsea v Crystal Palace testimonial match for Charlie

Cooke ... Bruce Rioch goes on loan to Birmingham ... After 78 days with Ayr U, Ally MacLeod moves to Motherwell for a reputed salary of £20,000 per year.

13 Ken Shellito resigns at Chelsea. Frank Upton, first team coach takes over temporarily. His first job is to rubber-stamp Ken Swain's £100,000 transfer to Aston Villa ... Billy Elliot is back at Sunderland after a five-year absence when he sued the club for wrongful dismissal. His present contract runs until the end of the season ... In the League Cup, Nottingham F beat Brighton, and Leeds defeat Luton. Stoke and Watford draw 0-0 at the Victoria Ground ... In Scotland, Rangers and Aberdeen reach the final ... Burnley clinch the Anglo-Scottish Cup by beating Oldham in a two-legged final.

14 Danny Blanchflower is appointed Chelsea manager – he will stay in the job until the end of the season and will stay in the Northern Ireland job as well.

15 Southampton clinch the Charlie George transfer at £400,000.

16 Liverpool lose at Bristol 1-0, Everton drop one point at home to Leeds, but West Brom, Nottingham F and Arsenal all win to close up the top of the table race ... Chelsea lose 7-2 at Middlesbrough where Micky Burns scores four times. Wolves and Birmingham are also beaten – the bottom three are now five points adrift of the field ... In Division Two, with the exception of Sunderland, all leading promotion contenders win .. . Maidstone are the giant killers in the FA Cup Second Round. They beat Exeter, while Woking force a replay at Swansea.

17 Former England manager, Don Revie, spends four hours with the FA Committee discussing his departure 17 months ago. Previously Alan Ball faced the same charge of 'bringing the game into disrepute' for admitting that he had accepted money illegally from Revie when the then Leeds manager tried to persuade Ball to leave Blackpool ... Alan Ashman leaves Walsall, and considers court action against the club ... Steve Fox signs for Wrexham in a £90,000 deal ... Aston Villa sign Joe Ward from Clyde for £80,000.

19 The FA imposes a ten-year ban on Don Revie dated from his unscheduled departure in July 1977. The charge is 'bringing the game into disrepute' – Revie broke his contract with the FA, abandoned his England job and went to work in the United Arab Emirates. After he signed a contract with the Arabs in secret, he offered to resign his England post and asked for £50,000 tax-free compensation. Revie says: 'Since learning of the decision I have been talking over my next move with my solicitors. I am leaving everything in their hands'. Although the ban only applies in England, it is the most severe in the history of English football. Alan Ball was also punished for publishing an account of how he received illegal payments from Revie, when he (Ball) was at Blackpool. He is fined £3,000. Revie has denied these allegations ... In a fog-bound Anfield Liverpool beat Anderlecht 2-1 but lose the Super Cup on a 4-3 aggregate ... League clubs Swansea and Colchester progress in the FA Cup at the expense of minnows, Woking and Leatherhead respectively.

20 Watford pay £200,000 to Leicester for Steve Sims. This is not only a club record, but also an all-time high for a Third Division club ... Newport buy Kevin Moore from Swansea for £12,000 ... Manchester U manager Dave Sexton refuses to allow David McCreery to join Derby: 'Too many of our staff and players went to Derby', he says. But Docherty makes his offer firmer by putting it in writing to the United board.

21 The Charlie George to Southampton deal is off ... and then finally on again, after an £18,000 loan is repaid to Derby ... Docherty buys Dave Webb from Leicester for £12,000 ... Malcolm Macdonald is back on the treatment table and won't play again until February.

23 Everton, the last unbeaten club in the league, are beaten 3-2 at Coventry and so fail to take advantage of the cancellation of Liverpool's home fixture. But Arsenal draw nearer to the leaders with a 5-0 win at White Hart Lane v Tottenham. Alan Sunderland scores his first hat-trick for the club. Chelsea break their losing sequence with a 0-0 draw at home to Bristol City ... Malcolm Poskett scores three times in Brighton's 4-1 win at Charlton, both Crystal Palace and Stoke draw ... Mick Docherty of Sunderland is sent-off at Nottingham ... Stan Seymour, known as 'Mr Newcastle', dies at the age of 84 ... Kevin Keegan also gets a hat-trick – his first for Hamburg ... Cesar Luis Menotti resigns his job as Argentina's national team manager.

26 Boxing Day football reinforces the top three's position in Division One. Liverpool win at Old Trafford, West Brom beat Arsenal at Highbury, and injury-stricken Everton narrowly defeat Manchester C ... At the bottom of the table Wolves score

a last minute penalty against Birmingham. Mark Dennis allegedly insults the referee in the tunnel and gets sent off ... Chelsea collect a point from a goalless draw at Southampton ... Several leading clubs lose ground in the promotion race of Division Two. West Ham lose at home to Orient, Crystal P and Stoke drop a point each ... Hat-tricks by Maybank (Brighton) and Guthrie (Fulham) help these teams to substantial victories. Marinello, a £30,000 buy from Motherwell, supplies the chances for Guthrie ... Swindon beat Swansea at Vetch Field, and are now in the thick of the promotion race in Division Three – Watford and Shrewsbury draw in front of an over 20,000 crowd at Vicarage Road.

27 Kevin Keegan is elected 'European Footballer of the Year'. He receives 87 points in the voting, six more than Hans Krankl, Rensenbrink was third ... Glen Hoddle is fined by Tottenham for missing training after he was dropped against QPR. His transfer request is refused ... Brian Harris, 42, is returning to Cardiff as Assistant-Manager.

28 Bristol Rovers collect a club record £180,000 for Paul Randall from Stoke City ... Ray Wilkins will be out of football for several weeks with a ligament injury ... Parsons scores an extra-time winner direct from a corner kick for Wimbledon at Bournemouth in the FA Cup replay.

30 West Bromwich beat Manchester U 5-3 in a see-saw game at Old Trafford, playing arguably the best football of the season. But Everton miss their chance to overtake Liverpool whose game is postponed, when they draw 1-1 with Tottenham ... In Division Two, Crystal Palace and Stoke end the year as joint leaders, while Watford and Wimbledon are still top teams in the lower division.

January

The weather disrupts the programme ... Record transfers in reality and theory ...Bill McCracken dies.

1 Arctic weather hits the New Year's Day programme, and only three games are completed. West Bromwich, using special boots, beat Bristol City, and are now level on top of the table with Liverpool and Everton who have played one game more ... Coventry make a substantial bid for Kevin Beattie of Ipswich.

2 Alex Stepney signs for Dallas Tornados ... Cliff Lloyd's suggestion that managers should have a say in judging whether games should go on or not on frozen pitches, is rejected by Alan Hardaker ... Beattie is not for sale – says Bobby Robson.

4 The big freeze threatens the week-end football programme – there will be early inspections everywhere ... Luton pay £50,000 for Oldham striker Steve Taylor.

5 West Bromwich Albion finalizes the David Mills transfer. They pay an English record of £482,222 for the Middlesbrough striker ... Malcolm Allison is back with Manchester City. He will be 'coaching overlord' working with Tony Book. 'City has a special attraction for me. I would have refused any other job' said Allison. City will pay Plymouth £35,000 compensation. Plymouth quickly replaced the manager with Bobby Saxton, the Exeter boss.

6 Only three ties survive the freeze – an all-time low for the third round, equalling that of 1963. In all three games, the lower division teams do well – Leicester beat Norwich, Shrewsbury defeat Cambridge and Sheffield Wednesday force a draw against Arsenal.

9 ITV's 'Snatch of the Day' deal with the League is banned by the Office of Fair Trading. According to the Restrictive Trade Practices Order 1976, the agreement should have been registered with that office before it came into operation. The ruling creates confusion concerning next years' television coverage of League football, but Alan Hardaker says: 'The League has been advised that the agreement – if it had to be registered – was registered in due time. There is no question of the Football League having to renegotiate the agreement ... The FA Cup gets under way with a few shocks. Charlton only draw at home with non-League Maidstone. Five minutes from the end Charlton forwards Mick Flanagan and Derek Hales exchanged blows, and referee Brian Martin sends them both off! ... Arsenal v Sheffield W 1-1 after extra time at Highbury, Fulham beat QPR and Newport ko West Ham ... In the League Cup quarter-final re-play at Vicarage Road Paul Richardson equalizes a Jenkins goal, but in extra-time Luther Blissett scores twice, putting Watford into the semi-finals for the first time in the club's history.

10   Further suprises in the Cup – Tottenham take the lead through a Peter Taylor penalty against Altrincham, but the visitors equalize five minutes from the end through Geoff Johnson. Sunderland defeat top First Division club, Everton, and Southend force a replay against Liverpool on a snow-covered pitch at Roots Hall ... John Deehan is sent off at Nottingham, where Forest beat Villa 2-0.

11   At last the record transfer deal between Arsenal and Ipswich concerning Brian Talbot goes through – £450,000! ... Norwich put three players including Martin Chivers on the transfer list.

12   Following Tuesday's punch-up, Charlton 'sack' Derek Hales, and fine the other culprit Mick Flanagan £250. Both players will miss the replay with Maidstone ... Walsall buy Ian Turner from Southampton, and Ernie Moss goes back to Chesterfield from Mansfield.

13   Bill Taylor leaves Manchester City – after collecting compensation for his contract ... Doug Collins is the new player-manager of Rochdale ... Only 13 games beat the freeze, the Pools Panel is in operation for the third time this season ... But in the games played, WBA grab a point at Norwich, and they are on top of the table for the first time in 25 years ... Arsenal's new boy Talbot helps the team to come back from a halfway 0-1 deficit, to beat Nottingham F 2-1 at Highbury ... Alan Biley scores a hat-trick for Cambridge against struggling Cardiff.

15   After 330 minutes' football, there is still no decision between Arsenal and Third Division Sheffield W in the FA Cup. Jack Charlton's team hold the Londoners to a 2-2 draw at Leicester ... Other surprises – Aldershot beat Sheffield United, Crystal Palace ko Middlesbrough, and Manchester City can only draw with Rotherham ... Rumours persist that Trevor Francis is for sale for £1 million! Birmingham say that he is not available.

16   Tottenham finish the Altrincham march with a Colin Lee hat-trick – 3-0! Preston beat Derby in another FA Cup tie, and Newcastle defeat Torquay.

17   The Arsenal v Sheffield W Cup marathon continues. The first replay ended 1-1, the second 2-2, the third today at Leicester 3-3! But the record is held by Oxford City and Alvechurch who needed 11 hours' football to settle the issue in 1971 ... Stoke lose at home to Oldham 1-0. The teams played on the original date, but the referee called the game off with Stoke leading 2-0. Unlucky ... In an interesting League Cup semi-final first leg, Nottingham F beat Watford 3-1. Blissett opens the scoring, but two goals from Birtles put the home side ahead. Shortly before the end, Robertson adds an important third goal.

18   Nottingham F and Rangers miss each other in the European Cup quarter-final draw. Forest play Grasshoppers; the Scottish champions meet Cologne ... Ipswich will play Barcelona for the second season running, WBA and Manchester City get Red Star Belgrade and B Moenchengladbach respectively ... Gordon Clark joins QPR as assistant manager.

20   Another weather-hit Saturday ... All leading teams have a rest day, but Leeds close the gap with one more away win – 2-1 at Tottenham ... The promotion candidates collect one point each in Division II except West Ham, 1-0 winners at Bristol R ... Bill McCracken, the Irishman who was responsible for the change in the off-side laws in the twenties, dies nine days before his 96th birthday. As a scout in later years, he discovered Pat Jennings for Watford.

22   The nine hours Cup marathon comes to an end – Arsenal beat Sheffield W in the fourth replay by two goals to nil. Scorers: Steve Gatting and Frank Stapleton.

23   Manchester City put Mike Channon on the transfer list. Tony Book says: 'He is not being made the scapegoat for our problems. But he has found it difficult to adjust to the way we play'. Channon said: 'I like to go forward to get the early ball and City build up slowly'.

24   Phil Boyer is sent off in the first leg of the League Cup semi-final at Leeds. Currie and Hankin put the home team in front, but Southampton equalize – 2-2. Boyer was booked for a foul on Flynn, then in the 81st minute he was shown the red card for dissent ... Derek Hales must be paid by Charlton until 14 February, when his case will again be discussed by the Disciplinary Committee ... Gordon Hill has a cartilage operation – he'll be out for at least six weeks.

25   Danny Blanchflower spends £200,000 on a young Scot, Eammon Bannon, a midfield player from Hearts. The money comes from the Steve Wicks deal – he has gone to Derby for a club record income of £275,000 ... Alec Stock is back in management with Fourth Division Bournemouth ... The England U-21 squad includes Luther Blissett of Watford. The Jamaica-born striker could have played

26 for any of the Home Counties, and was approached by Wales manager, Mike Smith. But he chose England.

26 Birmingham finally decide to put Trevor Francis on the transfer list. The asking price is £1 million! Surprisingly he is not in the England squad for the Northern Ireland match, but Laurie Cunningham is included for the first time.

27 Only five FA Cup ties are played due to weather and pitch conditions. Two of them are drawn, but Nottingham F and Arsenal duly win at home against lower class opposition. Shrewsbury provide the shock by beating Manchester City 2-0 at Gay Meadow. Paul Maguire and Sammy Chapman score the goals. It is the second time this season that a team coached by Malcolm Allison has gone out of the Cup – earlier Plymouth lost to Worcester City.

28 Ipswich are fined £1,200 by UEFA, and Paul Mariner is suspended for two games. Ted Croker says: 'There is no fixture crisis yet, the FA Cup will be played-off as scheduled'.

29 Norman Hunter is sent off for the fourth time in his career at Selhurst Park, where Bristol City crash 3-0 to Palace in the Cup. Tom Ritchie is also dismissed by referee Kevin McNally ... Swindon make a £250,000 bid for Channon, but he has no wish to play in the Third Division ... Willie Maddren of Middlesbrough has to give up the game due to knee injury ... Cardiff sign Colin Sullivan for £60,000 from Norwich.

30 Nottingham Forest are back at Wembley for the second successive year in the League Cup final. They achieve a comfortable 0-0 draw at Watford in the return leg of the semi-final. Their opponents will be Southampton in the final, 3-2 aggregate winners over Leeds – Terry Curran scores the only goal of the match at the Dell ... Ipswich beat Orient in the FA Cup replay in London, and Aldershot go into the fifth round by defeating Swindon.

31 Fulham draw with Manchester United at Craven Cottage in the Cup – record receipts of £44,763 collected ... In the League, Everton fail to take the opportunity of topping the table – they drop a home point against Villa.

February

Trevor Francis becomes the £1 million man ... the Pools Panel are frequently in action ... Foreigners continue to be imported.

1 Wrexham beat Stockport 6-2 in the Cup – a match which was postponed nine times ... Brian Clough and Peter Taylor request a release from the England Youth job. They are too busy with Nottingham Forest, still engaged in four major competitions ... Swindon pay £80,000 for Watford striker Alan Mayes ... Keith Weller goes to the States – New England Teamen fork out £40,000 to Leicester.

2 Don Revie sues the FA over his ten years' ban. His solicitors say: 'Mr Revie and his lawyers feel that the sentence which was passed was savage and out of all proportion'.

3 The Pools Panel is in action again, but ten First Division games are played. Liverpool beat West Brom 2-1 at Anfield and are on top of the table again as Everton lose at Wolves ... Ron Harris comes on as substitute for Chelsea in his 600th League game for the club. Ray Wilkins scores twice for a 2-1 win over Birmingham ... Brighton go on top in Division Two by beating Leicester 3-1.

5 Negotiations between Nottingham F and Birmingham for Trevor Francis are deadlocked, because the selling club demand £1 million plus the player's share and VAT ... Derby put Gerry Daly on the transfer list ... Luther Blissett is in the England U-21 line-up against Wales.

6 A Glenn Hoddle goal gives England U-21 victory over Wales U-21 at Swansea – 1-0 ... Manchester City are willing to pay £100,000 for Barry Silkman of Plymouth ... The Inverness Thistle v Falkirk Scottish Cup tie is postponed for a record 20th time ... Ron Greenwood selects his usual European Championship side for the Northern Ireland match – Clemence in, Shilton out, and there are no new caps.

7 A convincing 4-0 win against Northern Ireland puts England on top of their European Championship qualifying group. In front of a full-house at Wembley, Kevin Keegan puts England ahead in the first half, Latchford scores twice and Watson once in the second. Ron Greenwood says that teamwork and understanding were the key to England's good run, but there are still some problems left to solve. Blanchflower acknowledges that his team were second best, but thought that the

score-line was harsh. He also complained about some refereeing decisions... Barry Silkman fails a medical and will not be joining Manchester City.

8 Gerry Daly is suspended by Derby for two weeks... The Trevor Francis deal is nearing completion at Nottingham. The only snag – Clough's insistence that the player must not go to the USA during the summer... Tottenham sign Gordon Smith from Aston Villa for £150,000.

9 Nottingham F sign Trevor Francis for a staggering fee of £975,000. According to the *Daily Mail*, it is over £1 million, because apart from the fee Forest are paying, the £97,500 levy and the eight per cent VAT of £78,000 make the total cost £1,150,500! Surprisingly Brian Clough also agrees that Francis can go to America in the summer. 'Trevor is under contract to go to Detroit and we had no alternative' he said. Francis says :'I am going to the best side in the First Division. But the American side of things was quite a factor'... John Pickering is the new Blackburn manager and Jimmy Armfield is chief executive... Derek Hales is back with Charlton, a reprieved man after the recent ban.

10 Francis makes his Forest debut – in the third team at Notts Co in front of a crowd of 40... Everton and Stoke take over the lead in the top divisions. An Andy King hat-trick helps Everton to a 4-1 win over Bristol City, while Liverpool and West Bromwich are idle due to postponements... Stoke draw at Palace, Brighton lose at Preston, West Ham and Sunderland share the points at Upton Park.

12 Manchester United are through to the fifth round of the Cup with a 1-0 win over Fulham. Jimmy Greenhoff scores in the replay at Old Trafford... Southampton also reach that stage with a similar win against Preston away. But Tottenham can only draw with Wrexham 3-3... The FA investigate Trevor Francis's appearance in the Nottingham F third team. He wasn't properly registered with the club then. The League also say that they did not receive the player's registration.

13 Liverpool are back on top of the table through a 1-0 home win over Birmingham. Graeme Souness hits the winning goal... Arsenal beat QPR at Loftus Road. 2-1, and are now second... All other games are postponed and there is very little hope of completing the Fourth Round of the Cup in time for Saturday's scheduled fifth Round.

14 Ipswich get their second Dutchman. Bobby Robson pays £200,000 for Frans Thijssen of Twente Enschede... Barry Silkman goes to Luton on loan.

15 Birmingham City and WBA fly to Guernsey to play each other in a friendly – there is little prospect of football in Britain this week... Billy Hails leaves Peterborough. The club is hoping to persuade Geoff Hurst to take over.

16 Garth Crooks of Stoke is the latest coloured player to be included in an England squad. He is drafted into the U-21 party for the friendly against Holland... Bobby Moore might make a come back with Barking, the Berger Isthmian League club... Chelsea sign John Docherty of East Stirling for £50,000... Jimmy Andrews, sacked by Cardiff earlier in the season, is suing the club for £30,000.

17 For the first time in history, an entire FA Cup round is wiped out by the weather. Only five League matches are played, and the sole First Division game, Southampton defeat Everton 3-0. Manager Gordon Lee described the pitch as a 'deathtrap'. Alan Ball answers: 'He frightened his players to such an extent that they didn't play.'

19 Mike Flanagan walks out on Charlton, because his proposed transfer to an American club is not finalised. His wife is quoted: 'Mike would rather not work than be forced into a move he doesn't want'. Andy Nelson says: 'I don't care where he goes. I just hope it's sooner rather than later'... Southampton transfer-list nine players... Trevor Francis plays his first 18 minutes' football in the Forest league team – in a friendly at Exeter.

20 Aldershot and Shrewsbury draw in a dramatic Cup tie at the Recreation Ground, when both sides score in the last minutes – 2-2... Manchester U win at Colchester with a late Jimmy Greenhoff goal.

21 In a hard-fought Cup tie replay, Tottenham beat Wrexham 3-2 after extra time. Chris Jones scores all three goals... In the League. Liverpool thrash Norwich 6-0 and are now three points clear of the field... Chelsea suffer another setback – 1-3 v Coventry. This was their eighth home League defeat of the season... Fulham sign the Orient striker, Peter Kitchen, for £150,000... Middlesbrough bring another Yugoslav player into the country – Bosco Jankovic for £100,000... The *Daily Mail* says: 'Referee Bob Perkins, who claimed on TV that he had quit soccer because

28 he feared for his life after an FA Cup tie, actually resigned because of a rap from the Football League'.
22 Yet another record transfer deal surprises the football world – Phil Parkes goes from QPR to West Ham for a combined expenditure of £527,000. This is a record for a goalkeeper and for a Second Division club. 'If you want quality you have to pay for it' says John Lyall, the West Ham manager. 'It is one way of expressing our gratitude to our fans'. Falkirk beat Inverness Thistle at Inverness at the 30th attempt in the history-making Scottish Cup tie which was postponed since original date 6 January ... Lincoln sell Tommy Tynan to Newport for £25,000 ... The Holland v England U-21 friendly is off because of the state of pitches in Holland ... Geoff Hurst will not be taking over Peterborough ... The transfer season deadline is extended three weeks up to the 29 March ... Gerry Daly's suspension by Derby Co is outlawed by a Football League Committee. He was talking to the newspapers without the club's permission.
23 Cardiff C pay £120,000 for Ronnie Moore of Tranmere. It is a record figure for both clubs.
24 Practically a full programme on a Saturday brings luck to Liverpool. They win 2-0 at Derby, while rivals Arsenal, WBA, and Everton lose. Now Paisley's team are five points clear at the top of the table ... Charlton suspend Mike Flanagan, and lose Derek Hales with a suspected fracture ... Gary Rowell scores a hat-trick in the Tyneside derby, won by Sunderland 4-1 ... New signing Phil Parkes keeps a clean sheet at Upton Park ... West Ham beat Oldham 3-0 ... Alan Mayes, an £80,000 buy from Watford, scores a hat-trick for Swindon on his debut ... Les Bradd also nets three times – in the last 10 minutes at Barnsley, where his Stockport team draw 4-4 ... Ally MacLeod, now Motherwell's manager, transfer lists 12 players ... Peter Morris accepts the manager's job at Peterborough after a spell on the Newcastle staff.
26 First home defeat for Nottingham F since April 1977 – 1-0 v Arsenal in the fifth round of the Cup. Stapleton scores against the run of play ... Wolves also win 1-0 away – at Crystal Palace. Ipswich beat Bristol R 6-1, and Shrewsbury reach the sixth round for the first time in the club's history by beating Aldershot in extra time 3-1 ... Everton pay £80,000 for Sheffield U striker Imre Varadi.
27 Tom Reynolds, FIFA referee, leaves the English League to take up a post in the USA ... Mervyn Day is on the transfer list at West Ham.
28 Tottenham and Liverpool reach the sixth round of the FA Cup by beating Second Division opposition. Spurs won at Oldham 1-0 and Liverpool easily beat Burnley at home 3-0 ... Kevin Hird of Blackburn goes to Leeds for £357,000 – a record not only for Blackburn, but Leeds and for a full-back in England ... Young England win 1-0 in Rome in a UEFA Youth Cup qualifying match ... Fort Lauderdale go to court over George Best. They quarrel with Fulham over the player's registration .... Heavy overnight snow covered Leicester's hot-air balloon. It was impossible to clear in time for the Fulham match, so it was postponed because of 'snow on balloon' said the referee.

March

TV in a turmoil over a new joint offer ... Forest have Cup successes at home and abroad ... George Best makes the headlines again.

1 West Bromwich beat Leeds in the FA Cup replay 2-0 in extra time. It was the seventh meeting between the clubs this season in League and domestic Cups ... Petar Borota of Partizan Belgrade signs for Chelsea in a £70,000 transfer deal.
3 Expensive signings, Trevor Francis and David Mills play their first full League games for their new clubs. Mills scores for WBA in their 3-1 win at Coventry, but Francis has a quiet game as Forest draw 1-1 with Ipswich ... Liverpool drop one point at Stamford Bridge where they draw 0-0 ... Four of the five Second Division serious promotion candidates win – Stoke beat the fifth, West Ham 2-0. Watford and Reading top the table in the lower divisions.
6 Liverpool's second goalless draw – this time at Coventry, keeps them on track for the title, although Everton win at Middlesbrough ... Keith Bertschin breaks a leg in the relegation battle against QPR – Birmingham win 3-1 ... Brighton's win at Oldham puts them on top of Division Two ... Both Ipswich and West Bromwich will be forced to use youngsters in their European ties tomorrow due to injuries,

illness and suspensions... Only a Dieter Muller goal separates the teams at Cologne where Rangers lose 1-0 in the European Cup. Manager John Greig says that he is delighted with the result.

7 Mixed fortunes for the English clubs in the quarter-finals of the European competitions. Nottingham F fall behind against Grasshoppers, but Birtles equalizes before half-time. Robertson adds a second goal early in the second half. A 'grandstand' finish brings two late goals – Gemmill, Lloyd – and Forest win 4-1 in the European Cup. In the Cup Winners' Cup, Eric Gates scores twice for Ipswich, but an Esteban goal makes the overall score 2-1 with the return leg to come in Barcelona. UEFA-Cup – Red Star Belgrade beat WBA 1-0 at home, and Borussia Moenchengladbach finish all square 1-1, at Maine Road against Manchester City... Mike Flanagan re-emerges from hiding and says he no longer wishes to play for Charlton because of his personal differences with Derek Hales... Fulham issue a writ in order to recover the £15,000 fine paid earlier to a joint committee of the League and FA... Tommy Smith of Swansea is suspended for one match by the Welsh FA – this is his third ban in six months.

9 Gordon Borland, Millwall's secretary, dies at the age of 64. He was with the South London club since the middle fifties.

10 Predictably, Liverpool are the only club to reach the semi-finals of the FA Cup. The other two ties, and the fifth round match between West Bromwich and Southampton, all finish level. Kenny Dalglish gets Liverpool's winner at Ipswich, where in the first half Clemence has to make some outstanding saves to keep a clean sheet once again. At Tottenham, an Ardiles header gives the home team a half-time lead but Micky Thomas scores his first goal for Manchester United to equalize in the 63rd minute... Visitors Shrewsbury also level the score after falling behind at Molineux. Rafferty scores for Wolves, Atkins five minutes from the end for Shrewsbury... West Brom break the Southampton defensive record at the Hawthorns, but the game ends 1-1 with Boyer and Ally Brown the scorers... In the League, Chelsea lose their new Yugoslav 'keeper, Borota, with facial injuries after 27 minutes' play at Norwich. Tommy Langley takes over in goal, and Norwich win 2-0... Both Second Division promotion struggles played in London end goalless, West Ham home to Brighton, and Fulham v Crystal Palace. Sunderland are now third, after beating Oldham 3-0... Derby face a top-level probe by the FA following an official complaint by Dundee United. The Scottish club alleges that Derby's assistant manager, Frank Blunstone, approached their player Dave Narey last September concerning a possible transfer. Dundee United's manager, Jim McLean say: 'I am sickened by Derby's tactics. To take one of my players aside in the transit lounge at an airport is disgraceful'.

12 Oldham pay club record £60,000 for Simon Stainrod of Sheffield United... Southampton progress in the Cup: Boyer scores an extra-time winner in a 2-1 win over tiring WBA... Northampton sack Mike Keen – their third manager to go in three seasons.

13 Shrewsbury's Cup run is over – they lose at home to Wolves, 3-1. Richie Barker, assistant manager of Wolverhampton, who up until three months ago was with Shrewsbury, says: 'It would have been embarrassing to have been beaten here. I am still living in the town'... The Merseyside Derby ends all-square. Kenny Dalglish scores for Liverpool but Andy King equalizes in the 74th minute – Liverpool still lead the table with two points and matches in hand over Everton... A new sports complex including an all-seater football stadium might be built at the present Millwall ground. The ten million pounds' sponsorship is offered by a supermarket chain.

14 Manchester United will play Liverpool in one of the FA Cup semi-finals at Maine Road. They beat Tottenham 2-0 in the replay with goals by Jordan and McIlroy... A useful win for Crystal Palace at Sunderland in the League halts the Wearsiders 10 match unbeaten run.

15 Duncan McKenzie joins Blackburn for a £100,000 fee... Hereford pay £20,000 for Winston White of Leicester... But QPR's substantial bid for Preston forward Mick Robinson is turned down.

16 Steve Elliott goes to Preston for a club record £95,000 from Nottingham F.

17 Forest become the first team to win the League Cup in two successive seasons. Following an indifferent first-half, Garry Birtles equalizes an earlier David Peach goal, then scores a second to put Forest ahead. Archie Gemmill supplies the pass for Tony Woodcock to score the third. Southampton hit back through Nick

Holmes, but it is too late – 3-2. An excellent match watched by a well-behaved capacity crowd paying over £430,000 for the privilege... The League programme is again badly hit by the weather, and the Pools Panel is in action again... QPR beat Chelsea 3-1 in a First Division relegation clash at Stamford Bridge... Brighton's Teddy Maybank was sent off against Sheffield United, to be followed into the dressing room by the visitor's Mike Guy in the 24th minute. Brighton win 2-0 and are top of the table again... A ball with a new design is introduced by the League at their Cup final. It is white with red segments and the League's crest. It is manufactured only in Britain and sales will benefit the clubs financially. According to the *Daily Mail*, Southampton complained about the ball at half-time, thinking it too soft, but referee Peter Reeves declined to change it.

18 Liam Brady is elected 'Player of the Year' by his fellow professionals. He receives the trophy at a glittering dinner at the London Hilton Hotel, where Tom Finney is given a Merit award, and Cyrille Regis is chosen as 'Young Player of the Year'.

19 Southampton and Arsenal draw their FA Cup sixth round match at the Dell. Austin Hayes puts the home team ahead, but a goalkeeper's mistake gives David Price the opportunity to equalize... Norwich goalies Kevin Keelan and Clive Baker are out for the rest of the season – the club hopes to borrow Kieron Baker from neighbouring Ipswich.

20 Manchester City are out of the UEFA Cup – beaten 3-1 away by Moenchengladbach... In the League, Liverpool continue their march to the title by beating Wolves 2-0... Peter Ward scores twice for Brighton in their 2-1 win at Bristol Rovers – now they are three points clear of the field... Swansea beat Watford 3-2 at home in a stormy game, in which Steve Sims is sent off... Shrewsbury, who paid a club record £40,000 for Trevor Birch of Liverpool, lose 5-0 at Blackpool... Martin Chivers joins his old clubmate Alan Mullery at Brighton for a £15,000 fee to Norwich... George Best goes to the High Court to be reinstated: he wants to play for Fort Lauderdale Strikers.

21 Nottingham Forest draw with Grasshoppers in the second leg of the European Cup, and reach the semi-finals on a 5-2 aggregate... But all the other English clubs left in Europe fare badly: WBA score first against Red Star Belgrade, only to be foiled by a late Sestic goal. Ipswich lose 1-0 at Barcelona, and are eliminated on the away goals ruling... In the FA Cup, Alan Sunderland scores twice at Highbury to give Arsenal a 2-0 win over Southampton in the sixth round replay. Charlie George makes his first appearance for the visitors – his first game since early December.

22 A peace formula has been worked out between the BBC, ITV and the League concerning the 'Snatch of the Day' affair. For a reputed £10 million joint fee for the next four seasons, the two channels will cover football alternatively on Saturdays or Sundays. Next season the BBC would still have exclusive right to Saturday night football, but the following season ITV would have that right. The deal has to be approved by the club chairmen at their special meeting next week... It is rumoured that Bobby Robson has been approached by Barcelona and has been offered a two years' contract... Rangers only draw at home with Cologne and are out of the European Cup.

23 Nottingham Forest are paired with Cologne in the European Cup. Brian Clough says: 'I am not too worried. They are all difficult matches at this stage. I don't think I will be getting in touch with Kevin Keegan in Hamburg, because his predictions have been a bit adrift'.

24 Kenny Dalglish scores his 50th goal for Liverpool in 101 appearances. David Johnson adds another and Liverpool beat Ipswich 2-0 at Anfield. Now they are five points ahead of the field... Andy Ritchie, a deputy for the injured Joe Jordan, gets a hat-trick in Manchester United's 4-1 win over Leeds... Chelsea lose again at home (to Wolves) and look certain to be relegated – Brighton are the only club to drop a point – the rest of the leading teams all win in Division Two. But Gary Rowell of Sunderland is badly injured, and might be out for the rest of the season... Carlisle are second on goal difference in Division Three, where it now seems that any three of the top six could be promoted – Watford's lead is cut to two points over three clubs... Grimsby take over the lead in Division Four, while Aldershot, Wimbledon and Reading are beaten... Sunderland pay £125,000 for Leicester full-back Steve Whitworth.

26 George Best loses his court case against Fulham – his suspension stays... West Bromwich win against Derby and are still only two points behind Liverpool on

points dropped ... Bristol City pay £95,000 to Ajax Amsterdam for winger Gert Meijer ... Gordon Lee is charged with 'bringing the game into disrepute' in connection with remarks made by him about the Southampton pitch and match referee Colin Downey.

27 Sunderland win 1-0 at Stoke with an early Mick Docherty goal, and Crystal Palace earn one point at Charlton – it is still any three from five in the Second Division promotion race ... Willie Johnston declines to join QPR and goes to Canada instead to play for the Vancouver Whitecaps ... Emlyn Hughes collects over £39,000 in his testimonial match against Moenchengladbach. It is estimated that the Liverpool captain will benefit from all functions to the tune of a record £100,000.

28 The club chairmen turn down the proposed TV deal – they prefer a two-year agreement because of the possibility of a longer deal to be overtaken by inflation ... Despite the High Court judgment in London, FIFA lift the ban on George Best. He is allowed to play for Fort Lauderdale ... Nottingham F beat Chelsea 6-0. Trevor Francis doesn't score but has an outstanding match in midfield – Martin O'Neill registers a hat-trick.

29 On the last day of the transfer market, a score of players change clubs. There is a straight swap between Everton and QPR – Peter Eastoe goes to Goodison and Mickey Walsh becomes a Ranger. Everton also sign Brian Kidd from Manchester City for £150,000. Southampton sell three forwards – Terry Curran (£100,000) to Sheffield Wednesday, Tony Sealy (£50,000) to Crystal Palace, and Tony Funnell (£50,000) to Gillingham. Les Tibbott goes from Ipswich to Sheffield United for £100,000 ... Bristol City sign a Finnish player, Pertti Jantunen ... Barry Silkman finally achieves his ambition and becomes a Manchester City player – Plymouth collect £65,000.

31 Arsenal are back at Wembley for the second year running. They beat Wolves 2-0 in the FA Cup semi-final with second-half goals by Stapleton and Sunderland. In the other semi-final Liverpool and Manchester United draw 2-2. Kenny Dalglish puts Liverpool ahead, but Jordan equalizes. After Terry McDermott misses a penalty, Brian Greenhoff scores a second goal for United. Alan Hansen makes it level six minutes from time ... In the League the main interest centres on the Second Division promotion race – Sunderland and Crystal Palace win, Brighton and West Ham take one point each, but Stoke surprisingly lose at home to Blackburn. Near the end of the Crystal Palace v Cardiff match, three players, Swindlehurst (Palace), Dwyer and Pontin (Cardiff) are sent off ... Newcomers Walsh, Silkman and Meijer score in their respective debuts for QPR, Manchester City and Bristol City ... Rangers win the Scottish League Cup by beating Aberdeen 2-1.

April

Liverpool's grip on the title race strengthens ... Forest reach the European Cup Final the hard way ... Kenny Dalglish is the Football writers' choice as Player of the Year.

1 Ron Challis of Tonbridge in Kent is selected to referee the FA Cup final. He is 46, and has one more season on the League list.

2 Sheffield U beat West Ham 3-0 – a blow to the London's club promotion hopes ... Stan Bowles is dropped from the QPR side for the vital relegation battle against Bristol City.

3 Bristol City beat QPR 2-0 and Wolves collect two points by defeating Tottenham 3-2 – Kenny Hibbitt scores the winner in the last minute – now Rangers are four points behind Wolves and First Division safety ... Crystal Palace grab an important away point in their battle for promotion at Oldham ... Gerd Muller joins the US club Fort Lauderdale ... Sammy Nelson scores for both sides in the 1-1 draw at Highbury against Coventry. After his excellent equalizer, he runs behind the goal and drops his shorts. The gesture is caught by a press photographer, and the Irish international faces disciplinary action.

4 Manchester United reach the FA Cup final for the third time in four years. At Goodison Park, they beat Liverpool in the semi-final replay 1-0 with a 78th minute goal by Jimmy Greenhoff ... Sammy Nelson is banned for two matches and fined two weeks' wages for the 'shorts-dropping' incident. But the player also faces an FA disciplinary tribunal ... Gordon Lee is cleared of any charges of bringing the game into disrepute ... The England team qualify for the UEFA Youth Tournament in Austria. They beat Italy 2-0 (aggregate 3-0) at Villa Park. Les Carter

(Palace) and the Italian, Stolgato, are sent off . . . West Bromwich beat Manchester City 4-0 in the League, and are now only four points behind the leaders, Liverpool, with a game in hand.

5 Arsenal lose the toss, and Manchester United will play in their usual red-and-white outfit at Wembley in the Cup final . . . A debt collector is assigned to recover around £400,000 Fulham owe to a building firm – the deadline is next Tuesday.

7 Liverpool are back at their best, and beat Arsenal 3-0 at Anfield . . . West Bromwich keep up the chase for the title with a 1-0 victory over rivals Everton. Ally Brown scores in the 83rd minute . . . Nottingham Forest's confidence grows for Wednesday's European Cup semi-final by beating Chelsea at Stamford Bridge 3-1. Trevor Francis is amongst the scorers, but his namesake Gerry is in trouble at Bolton where he is sent off after 37 minutes for a foul on Roy Greaves. Francis accuses the Bolton player of 'play-acting' . . . QPR lose and are still four points behind Wolves in the race for First Division safety . . . None of the leading promotion candidates win in Division Two – they all draw except Palace, 1-0 losers at Newcastle.

9 West Ham improve their promotion chances with a narrow home win over Luton . . . sixty league managers meet at Bisham Abbey to discuss the current problems of football . . . Jimmy Adamson criticises Jimmy Hill for spotlighting his player, Ray Hankin's misbehaviour in the televised match against Ipswich.

10 A best of the season crowd at Highbury, of 54,000, see Arsenal beat Tottenham 1-0 with a Stapleton goal . . . Liverpool win by the same score at Wolves, stretching their lead to six points on top of the league.

11 In a fascinating European Cup semi-final, Nottingham F draw with Cologne 3-3 at the City ground. Roger Van Gool and Dieter Muller score in the first 20 minutes for the West Germans, and Birtles makes it 1-2 before the break. Goals by Bowyer and Robertson give Forest the lead, but Japanese substitute Okudera, equalizes within 30 seconds of coming on the pitch. After the game Brian Clough blames goalkeeper Shilton for two of the German goals, but is still optimistic about the outcome of the tie. 'Only a fool would write us off. We go there full of confidence' . . . In the other semi-final, Austria Vienna and Malmo draw 0-0 . . . Ron Futcher is transferred from Manchester City to Minnesota Kicks for £120,000.

13 Good Friday football brings a dull goalless draw to QPR against Norwich, and a thriller to the Dell where WBA equalize in the last minute against Southampton. Both Brighton and Sunderland register away victories in the Division Two promotion race. Shock result of the day – Watford 0 Colchester 3.

14 West Bromwich Albion drop another point – home to Arsenal, while Liverpool revenge their FA Cup defeat against Manchester United by beating them 2-0. Now, it seems that Liverpool are certain to win the title . . . At the other end of the table both QPR and Wolves grab one away point each – Wolves have a three points advantage over the Londoners with two games in hand . . . Four of the five Second Division promotion candidates win their away fixtures, the sole casualties being Brighton, beaten 3-1 at Cardiff . . . The Third Division 'derby' between Shrewsbury and Watford ends 1-1, and Swansea earn two important points at Swindon. Phil Boersma suffers a broken leg injury in this match.

16 Chelsea's fate is sealed on this Easter Monday at Highbury where they lose 5-2 – now they are definitely relegated . . . Liverpool lose at Aston Villa, and Bob Paisley says: 'We were absolute rubbish. The League is still wide open' . . . The Nottingham Forest management is also unhappy with the team's efforts against Leeds in the goalless draw. 'We shall make changes' promises Peter Taylor . . . Sunderland surprisingly lose at home to Blackburn, West Ham and Stoke drop home points – only Brighton win of the teams jostling for a place in the First Division next season.

17 West Bromwich lose at Bristol 1-0, and are six points behind Liverpool. A disappointed Ron Atkinson says: 'We should have taken a maximum six points from our holiday games to have a realistic chance of the title – we collected only two points' . . . Both Crystal Palace and Stoke win their home matches against Charlton and Bristol R respectively . . . Watford break their Southend jinx – not one victory in seven previous games – and beat them 2-0 for much needed points which keep them on top of the table.

18 Sammy Nelson is fined £750 and suspended for two games by the FA for 'bringing the game into disrepute'. The charge refers to the 'shorts-dropping' incident in the Coventry match at Highbury. Nelson will be available for the Cup final, but David O'Leary is doubtful following an ankle injury sustained in a benefit match at Portsmouth for Eoin Hand . . . Nottingham F drop another home point, and

assistant manager Peter Taylor says: 'I can't see us catching Liverpool now. Now we shall concentrate on the European Cup. We shall surprise a few people at Cologne next Wednesday' . . . Alan Hardaker warns that football might be off the TV screens next season, unless the chairmen agree to accept the latest combined BBC-ITV offer. A decision will be made at the League AGM on 1 June . . . Wolves central defender, George Berry, is called up by Wales for their European Championship match v West Germany. He has a Jamaican father and a Welsh mother – Barry is the first black Welsh international since Ted Parrish fifty years ago.

19 Arsenal offer new improved three-year contracts to the Terry Neill-Don Howe manager/coach partnership . . . If Forest reach the European Cup final, their players will not be called up for England duty during the Home Championships says Ron Greenwood.

21 Willie Young is sent off at Derby where Arsenal lose 2-0. Later referee Kevin McNally makes it clear that the nature of Young's offence will not affect the player's chance of playing in the Cup Final . . . Birmingham are certain to be relegated after a 2-0 home defeat against Nottingham F . . . Liverpool win at home, and WBA drop a point against Wolves . . . Both Stoke and Sunderland win away games – they now look favourites for promotion with Brighton or Crystal Palace to join them in Division One next season . . . Swansea take over on top of Division Three – Watford lose at Swindon . . . Alan Ball completes 100 League appearances for Southampton. He is the first player to achieve this with four different clubs – the others were Blackpool, Everton and Arsenal.

23 Peter Barnes and Asa Hartford are dropped by Manchester City for the Middlesbrough match. The two internationals might be leaving the club. Tony Book says: 'I can't afford to call on players who have their minds on something else' . . . John Barnwell, the Wolves manager, is involved in a serious car accident. He is in hospital with skull and facial injuries . . . Tarantini signs for Talleres of Cordoba (Agentina) for £225,000 . . . Frank Worthington is going to Dallas Tornado on a loan transfer.

24 Borussia Moenchengladbach reach the UEFA Cup final by beating Duisburg 4-1 (aggregate 6-3) . . . Both Liverpool and WBA drop one point in away matches . . . Wolves are safe after beating Derby 4-0 . . . Watford and Swindon lose, Shrewsbury win in their Third Division promotion race.

25 Nottingham Forest reach the European Cup final by winning 1-0 at Cologne. Ian Bowyer scores with a header following a corner in the 65th minute. The Clough-Taylor partnership regards this surprise win as their 'finest hour'. Clough says: 'Tonight we practised everything we have ever preached in the game. There was no dissent from the players, no shady tackling. We worked tremendously hard and gave a performance that everyone connected with the club can be proud of ' . . . Forest will play Malmo in the final – 1-0 home winners over Austria Vienna . . . In the Cup Winners' Cup, a Krankl penalty puts Barcelona in the final against Fortuna Dusseldorf – 4-3 aggregate winners over Banik Ostrava . . . Red Star Belgrade ko Hertha Berlin, thus preventing an all-German UEFA Cup final . . . In the League, Arsenal suffer their heaviest defeat of the season at Villa Park where they are beaten 5-1. Leeds beat Bolton by the same score. Sunderland score six goals against Sheffield United (6-2) and go on top of the Second Division.

26 Kenny Dalglish of Liverpool is the 'Footballer of the Year', having received as many votes as the rest of the nominations put together in the Football Writers Association poll . . . Frank Blunstone, Derby County's assistant manager, is fined £500 for making an illegal approach to Dave Narey, Dundee United's international defender.

28 Liverpool draw 0-0 at Nottingham, and keep their seven points lead on top of Division One . . . QPR beat Coventry 5-1, Clive Allen, 17, son of former manager Les Allen, scores a hat-trick. But Derby secure a point at Manchester United, and need only one more to send Rangers down . . . High drama in the Second Division promotion race. Brighton and Crystal Palace both win at home and Stoke drop one point against Newcastle. Sunderland lose 2-1 against Cardiff at Roker Park in front of a 36,526 crowd. A Wilf Rostron penalty is saved . . . At West Ham, Dai Davies, Wrexham's Welsh international goalkeeper, is sent off for manhandling referee Ken Baker, after he allowed a goal to stand despite an obvious handling offence by 'Pop' Robson. Fullback Cegielski goes into goal and is not beaten during the remaining 62 minutes' play, but Bobby Shinton

heads an equalizer near the final whistle, 1-1. John Lyall says: 'I told the boys we had let our supporters down. We still have a slight chance of promotion, but on this display we don't deserve to have it' . . . Gillingham beat Shrewsbury in the Third Division promotion clash, an Alan Waddle hat-trick secures two points for Swansea, but Watford drop another valuable point – at home to Plymouth. Grimsby and Reading are certain to be promoted from Division Four with Barnsley, and Wimbledon odds-on favourites to accompany them . . . In Scotland, table-toppers Dundee United are beaten again – now it looks like the familiar Rangers v Celtic race to settle the championship.

30 Wolves beat Nottingham F 1-0 – their third League defeat of the season. Malmo's manager Bob Houghton sees the match, and says that he is not deceived by Forest's poor form . . . Trevor Brooking tries out his injured ankle in Steve Perryman's testimonial game at White Hart Lane. He collects around £25,000 from a 17,000 gate. Brooking is still not certain whether he is fit to play for West Ham or England later in May . . . John Cartwright was appointed full-time England Youth Manager with a three year contract . . . Brian Flynn will miss the Wales v Germany European Championship tie because of injury. John Mahoney deputises. George Berry of Wolves and John Toshack are both included in the Welsh line-up. But both Northern Ireland and Eire lose League players through injury or club calls – Pat Rice, David O'Leary and Steve Heighway are not available.

May

Liverpool break records and make Bob Paisley's anniversary a memorable one . . . Arsenal win a dramatic Cup Final . . . England are the Home International champions . . . Forest Kings of Europe.

1 Liverpool show true championship form at Bolton, winning 4-1. WBA keep up the chase by getting two points at Goodison, but bar a miracle the race is over.

2 Wales are beaten at home 2-0 by West Germany. Zimmermann scores in the first half following a Kaltz cross, and the same player makes a goal with another cross which is headed in by Klaus Fischer. But Northern Ireland win 2-0 against Bulgaria in a match at Belfast watched by Ron Greenwood, who said: 'I don't think Bulgaria can play as badly as that ever again. I understand their squad is split because of the Olympics and there could be some new players in the side against England'. In the third European Championship match in Dublin, Eire beat Denmark 2-0 – rather luckily. Despite Danish pressure, Daly scores in the first half and Givens in the second . . . Elsewhere Poland beat Holland 2-0, and Austria draw with Belgium 0-0 . . . Emlyn Hughes is retained in the England squad for the Home Championship and the European tour. Also included is Ken Sansom of Crystal Palace . . . Watford recover from a poor spell at last with a 1-0 win at home v Chester.

3 The Managers and Secretaries Association will appoint a paid full-time supremo. 'The Association wishes to have a bigger say in the game in the future' says their secretary Ken Friar of Arsenal . . . Liverpool spend £300,000 on Frank McGarvey of St Mirren.

4 QPR are relegated. They lead three times at Leeds but the home team equalize and Ray Hankin puts paid to the Londoners' hopes with the winner – 4-3.

5 On the last Saturday of the League season, several issues are settled. Brighton and Stoke are definitely promoted, and Crystal Palace need one point from their last game against Burnley at home to join them next season in the First Division. Brighton, after taking a 3-0 half-time lead, win easily at Newcastle 3-1. Stoke also win away – 1-0 at Notts County with a goal by Paul Richardson in the 88th minute. Sunderland and Crystal Palace also win away matches, but West Ham lose at Blackburn and are out of the promotion race. Charlton are practically safe after beating Oldham 2-0. Blackburn are relegated, and only near miracles can save Millwall and Sheffield United. Watford win at Sheffield, Swansea draw at Plymouth and Swindon beat Gillingham in their promotion battle 3-1. Terry Nicholl of Gillingham is sent off, and there is some trouble in the tunnel leading to the dressing rooms after the match. Wilf Tranter, Swindon's coach, is taken to hospital with facial injuries, and the police interview two Gillingham players. Bob Smith, Swindon's manager says: 'I've rarely seen players react like this to a defeat. I was

proud of the way my team conducted themselves'... Frank Sibley resigns at Walsall – the club is relegated... Norwich draw their 23rd League match of the season – a record... Steve Death has kept a clean sheet for Reading in their last eleven matches. That equals the record held by Graeme Crawford of York.

7 Hector Monro, ex-President of the Scottish Rugby Union is the new Minister for Sport. He has been Opposition spokesman for five years on sport, and takes over from Denis Howell, in the new Tory Government... Keith Blunt, manager of Sutton United, will work with Bob Houghton in Malmo from August... Manchester United beat Wolves 3-2, but Brian Greenhoff limps off in the first half and is doubtful for Wembley... After the Wrexham v Luton match (2-0), Denis Mortimer, Luton's chairman, bursts into the officials room and says: 'You are the worst referee I have ever seen'. Referee Colin Seal will report him to the League... Promotion candidates Gillingham and Shrewsbury draw their away matches.

8 Liverpool clinch the championship for a record eleventh time on the 40th anniversary of Bob Paisley's arrival to Anfield. They beat Aston Villa 3-0, and now have 64 points from 40 matches, with the goal difference of 81-16! Paisley says: 'The atmosphere was overpowering, and I was worried that all the publicity about my anniversary might upset the players' concentration'... Swindon win 2-1 at Brentford, where Bill Dodgin decides to stay with the club. He had an offer to link up with Blanchflower at Chelsea... Barnsley move into the Third Division after beating Grimsby in front of a crowd of over 21,000... Peter Nicholas of Crystal Palace is called up by Wales for the Home Internationals.

9 Red Star Belgrade and Borussia Moenchengladbach draw 1-1 in the first leg of the UEFA Cup final... Portugal win 1-0 in Oslo against Norway in the European Championship... Nottingham Forest beat Manchester City 3-1, and complete two League seasons – since promotion – without a home defeat!

10 QPR sack Steve Burtenshaw after 10 months of his three years' contract is completed. Chairman Jim Gregory says: 'My duty is not to managers, not players, but to our supporters. I'm the same as them – I want only success for QPR. If I can't smell success there has to be a change'. Burtenshaw says at the Football Writers' Association dinner: 'I am shocked and disappointed'... At the dinner Kenny Dalglish was presented with the Footballer of the Year award by the very first winner, Sir Stanley Matthews... Both Cup finalists announce a clean bill of health, and will be able to field their first choice sides at Wembley.

11 Crystal Palace clinch the Second Division title in front of a crowd of 51,801. After a nervous first half, Walsh and Swindlehurst score for a 2-0 victory over Burnley. Terry Venables says: 'We got what we deserved. The lads were brilliant. They played with their heads and did all we asked of them... Sensation at the other corner of London as well. Tommy Docherty rejoins QPR as manager. He was once in charge of the London club eleven years ago, but only for 28 days. 'This time I intend to stay longer' says Docherty, who left Derby after 18 months there. The new boss sees his team beaten 4-0 by Ipswich at Loftus Road in their last League match in the First Division... Wimbledon are sure of promotion to Division Three after beating York 2-1. Fittingly, top scorers, Cork and Leslie get their goals in this vital game... Swansea are also sure of stepping up a grade for the second year in succession. Player/manager John Toshack gets the winner against Chesterfield.

12 Arsenal win a dramatic Cup final. Talbot and Stapleton score for them in the first-half, but four minutes from the end McQueen reduces the arrears, and less than two minutes later, McIlroy equalises. Within a minute a Brady-Rix move gives Alan Sunderland the opening to score the winning goal – 3-2! Terry Neill: 'This final may not be remembered for its flowing football, but it will live on in the memory for its explosive finish'. Dave Sexton: 'It was a cruel result. After fighting back to cancel out Arsenal's two-goal lead, we were thinking of extra-time and lost concentration'. A crowd of 100,000 paid £500,000 at Wembley... In the the Scottish Cup final, Rangers and Hibernian draw 0-0 – the attendance figures are also disappointing, just over 50,000.

14 Watford are promoted to Division Two. They beat Hull 4-0 at Vicarage Road in front of a best-of-season 26,397 crowd. 'I've never been so relieved in my life' says chairman Elton John... Peter Bonetti plays his 600th League game for Chelsea before moving to Scotland. It is a 1-1 draw against Arsenal at Stamford Bridge. Malcolm Macdonald, back after injury, scores for the 'Gunners'... Ray Hankin is censured by the FA for bringing the game into disrepute... Garry Collier of Bristol City negotiates his own transfer to Coventry. The fee will be

decided by a tribunal. Alan Dicks, manager of Bristol City is annoyed. 'We are already seeing the system abused' . . . Leeds pay a club record £370,000 for Swansea striker, Alan Curtis.

15 Swindon are out of the promotion race after their 5-2 defeat at Blackpool . . . Manager John Pickering is leaving relegated Blackburn.

16 Barcelona win the European Cup Winners' Cup. The score is 2-2 after 90 minutes' play at Basle against Fortuna Dusseldorf, but Rexach and Krankl score for Barcelona in extra-time before Seel makes the final score 4-3 to the Spanish team . . . Rangers and Hibernian play out yet another goalless stalemate in the Scottish Cup final – three and a half hours' football without a goal . . . Manchester City bid £750,000 for Mike Flanagan of Charlton . . . A Chinese national team will tour England in August.

17 FIFA decide that in the 1982 World Cup finals in Spain there will be 24 participants . . . Only eight players are fit to train when the England squad meet in Manchester to prepare for the Home Championships . . . There is a police investigation in progress into the affairs of Derby County. It is in connection with transfer deals, and the police are working under the Prevention of Corruption Act. Club Secretary, Stuart Webb cuts short his holiday in Majorca to assist the investigation. Former manager, Tommy Docherty says 'I have no idea what it is about' . . . Arsenal are reported to be interested in Mick Flanagan and Johan Neeskens . . . Liverpool win 3-0 at Leeds, and their championship haul of 68 points is a new record. They only conceded 16 goals in the 42 matches, another all-time First Division record! For scoring 85 goals they will receive a special £50,000 prize from *The Sun* newspaper – surely Liverpool's best-ever season in the League!

18 Nottingham Forest clinch the runners-up spot by beating West Bromwich Albion at The Hawthorns. Trevor Francis scores the only goal of the match. West Brom fail to equal or better their all-time 60 points for a season and finish third in the League.

19 John Toshack scores a hat-trick for Wales in their 3-0 win at Cardiff over Scotland. He combines well with his Swansea colleagues, James and Curtis. Jock Stein introduces Burley and Wark from Ipswich, and Hegarty of Dundee United into his senior team, but is not happy with the performance . . . Two early England goals (Watson, Coppell) effectively finish the match as a contest in Belfast, where Northern Ireland have their worst match under Danny Blanchflower – according to the manager himself. At one point, Gerry Armstrong and Terry Cochrane are involved in a scuffle . . . Bulgaria beat Eire in the European Championship in Sofia – Jimmy Holmes of Spurs is taken off with a broken leg . . . Stafford Rangers win the FA Trophy at Wembley. They defeat Kettering in the final in front of a 32,000 crowd.

20 Arsenal manager Terry Neill is having talks with Johan Neeskens. The 27-year old Dutch international is negotiating with several clubs and might decide to sign for the Londoners . . . Mike Flanagan turns down a £750,000 move to Manchester City.

21 Geoff Hurst leaves Southern League Telford to join Chelsea as first team coach . . . Millwall win the FA Youth Cup beating Manchester City 2-0 at The Den . . . Celtic are the champions of Scotland – they beat Rangers 4-2 in a decisive match for the title. Celtic are one goal down when their player John Doyle is sent-off, but the ten-man side equalize and go on to win with two goals in the last five minutes of the match.

22 Scotland beat Northern Ireland 1-0 with a goal by Arthur Graham of Leeds . . . Ron Greenwood makes six changes in the England team for the Wales match at Wembley, giving caps to newcomers, Kenny Sansom of Crystal Palace and Laurie Cunningham of WBA . . . In the match celebrating the 75th anniversary of FIFA in Berne, Argentina and Holland draw 0-0. Argentina win the ensuing penalty contest 8-7 . . . The Republic of Eire are beaten 3-1 by West Germany in a Dublin friendly . . . The very last League match of a long season is played at Millwall where the already doomed home team lose 2-0 to Preston.

23 England draw with defensive Wales 0-0 at Wembley in front of a 70,000 crowd – a record for this fixture. After the match Ron Greenwood praises debutant, Ken Sansom, but also expresses his disappointment with the England front players' finishing. Mike Smith said: 'We played badly in the first 20 minutes, but then we settled down. Now we must go to Belfast to win handsomely' . . . Borussia Moenchengladbach win the UEFA Cup for the second time in the West German club's

history. An Allan Simonsen penalty gives them a 1-0 home win (2-1 aggregate) over Red Star Belgrade.

24 Billy Elliott, who narrowly failed to lead Sunderland to promotion, is sacked by the club ... Crystal Palace pay £465,000 record transfer fee for Gerry Francis of QPR ... The England Youth team open with a 3-0 win over Czechoslovakia in the annual UEFA Tournament in Austria ... Shrewsbury win the Welsh Cup, beating Wrexham 2-1 on aggregate in the final ... Johan Cruyff comes back from retirement and signs for the American club, Los Angeles Aztecs.

25 Northern Ireland find some form against Wales in a better-than-average international match at Belfast. Derek Spence scores for the home team, and Robbie James equalizes in the second half – 1-1. Danny Blanchflower says: 'We were unlucky. I was delighted with the performance'. Mike Smith: 'The early Irish goal was a tremendous blow, it took us too long to recover' ... Ken Shellito, who spent 23 years with Chelsea before resigning as manager in December, is to join QPR as coach ... Bob Paisley is Bell's 'Manager of the Year' for the third time in four seasons. He receives a cheque for £2500 from the Bell's Whisky firm at a Lunch in London. Divisional awards go to Terry Venables, Graham Turner and Maurice Evans. Brian Clough is given a consolation prize of £500 plus an inscribed silver salver.

26 Scotland take a first-half lead against England at Wembley through John Wark, but Peter Barnes equalizes before the break. Goals by Steve Coppell and Kevin Keegan give the home team a 3-1 win and the Home Championship title. Ron Greenwood said that the Scots 'bossed' the first half, England the second, and that a Ray Clemence save was the turning point of the match ... Tom Maule, Secretary of the Scottish Football League is fired – his successor is Jim Farry.

28 England reach the semi-finals of the UEFA-Youth Tournament with a 2-0 win over West Germany ... Rangers win the Scottish Cup. The second replay stood at 2-2 after 90 minutes' play, but in extra time, an Arthur Duncan own-goal decides the issue ... Liverpool sign Avi Cohen from Maccabi Tel Aviv for £200,000 ... Kettering and Altrincham are the nominated clubs to apply for League status at the AGM.

29 Johny Giles plays his last game for the national team of the Republic of Ireland. It is a 0-0 draw against Argentina at Dublin.

30 Nottingham Forest win the European Cup. In the Munich final they defeat the Swedish club Malmo 1-0 with a goal in first-half injury time by Trevor Francis. This is Francis's first ever European competitive club match. The game is spoilt by Malmo's defensive tactics, but Brian Clough is satisfied:'We are worthy successors to Liverpool as European champions. As far as my career is concerned, tonight is a marvellous milestone, but it doesn't mean as much to me as winning the First Division title. The first time we did that at Derby was the highlight of my life and nothing will surpass it' ... WBA pay £450,000 for Gary Owen to Manchester City ... Fulham are served with a winding-up petition by General Securities who took over the club's debt to McAlpines, the builders of their new stand.

31 Both Brian Clough and Peter Taylor are staying with Nottingham Forest. They signed new four-year contracts with the club ... England lose the semi-final of the UEFA-Youth Tournament against Bulgaria 1-0. Clive Allen hits a last minute penalty kick against the post ... In the semi-professional tournament, Holland beat Italy 3-0, and England beat Scotland 5-1 in the semi-finals ... Don McAllister and Terry Naylor are both sent off in Tottenham's tour match in Tokyo against Fiorentina.

June

TV football is saved ... New look for League Cup ... England go down bravely in Vienna ...

1 The Annual Meeting of the Football League votes in favour of the new television deal with the BBC and ITV. For an inflation allowed for £10 million in the next four years, the two channels will alternately cover football on Saturdays and Sunday programmes. Next season the usual arrangement will be in operation, the season after, ITV will have the Saturday slot – the system is nicknamed 'Swap of the Day' by *The Sun*. Jimmy Hill (Coventry City) speaks in favour of the deal, but launches an attack on the League for not pursuing the possibility of 'shirt advertising': 'We could collect £400,000 each' he says, 'and here we are haggling over

£25,000'. Other decisions taken at the meeting: the loaning of players to American clubs during the close season is banned. The first two rounds of the League Cup will be played on the home and away basis next season. The bottom four clubs are re-elected to the League. Sunday football proposed by Fulham is rejected ... New York Cosmos sack Eddie Firmani.

2   With goals by new boy Peter Nicholas of Crystal Palace and Brian Flynn, Wales win 2-0 at Malta in the European Championship ... England beat France 4-3 on penalty kicks, following a 0-0 draw in Vienna in the third place play-off of the UEFA-Youth Tournament: 'We must produce more technically skilful players' says manager John Cartwright ... Argentina finish their European tour with a 3-1 win at Hampden Park. Diego Maradona is the star of an excellent South American side, and scores the third Argentinian goal. Leopoldo Luque gets the other two, and Arthur Graham scores Scotlands consolation goal minutes before the end ... Bobby Shinton negotiates his own transfer from Wrexham to Manchester City, but there is a dispute between the clubs over the size of the fee.

3   England win the Semi-Pro Tournament by beating Holland 1-0 in the final at Stafford.

4   Tottenham beat Dundee U in the final of the Japan Cup in Tokyo with goals by Gordon Smith and Osvaldo Ardiles ... According to a *Daily Mail* report, Fulham will be reimbursed by the FA with the £15,000 'fine' which they had to pay for alleged irregularities ... Coventry pay £250,000 for David Jones of Everton.

5   Young England win 3-1 in Bulgaria in the European U-21 Championship. Kevin Reeves of Norwich scores twice and Cyrille Regis once ... Len Ashurst turns down an offer to manage his old club, Sunderland.

6   England are in a commanding position in Group One of the European Championship after their easy 3-0 win in Sofia. Kevin Keegan scores the first goal in the 33rd minute from a Brooking pass, and within one minute early in the second-half, Watson and Barnes head goals to make the game safe against the plodding Bulgarians ... Northern Ireland's trip is less rewarding – they are beaten 4-0 in Denmark, where 21-year-old Preben Elkjaer scores a hat-trick for the home team and Allan Simonsen gets the other one ... Sheffield Wednesday sign Ian Mellor from Chester for £60,000.

7   Scotland also take a step towards the European Championship finals with a convincing 4-0 win in Oslo against Norway. Joe Jordan, Kenny Dalglish and John Robertson score in the first half, and Gordon McQueen in the second. In the U-21 match, the same two countries draw 2-2 ... Ken Knighton, formerly coach under Billy Elliott, is appointed manager of Sunderland.

9   England's Under-21's win a friendly against Sweden 2-1 with WBA players, Bryan Robson and Cyrille Regis, the scorers.

10 Sweden celebrate the 75th Anniversary of their Football Association by drawing with England 0-0 in Stockholm. Ron Greenwood makes nine changes from the team which played in Sofia – only Kevin Keegan and Dave Watson keep their places. But even the late introduction of substitutes, Trevor Brooking and Ray Wilkins, is unable to change the pattern of the rather tame play – only goalkeepers Peter Shilton and Jan Moller excel with some important saves ... Billy Elliott is the new boss at Darlington.

11 Werder Bremen, the West German club, are making a bid for David Watson ... Johan Neeskens disappoints Arsenal by signing a five year's contract for Cosmos ... John Bailey of Blackburn moves to Everton. The price will be decided by the Tribunal because the clubs cannot agree ... Kevin Beattie goes into hospital for another knee operation ... Terry Cooper goes to Bristol Rovers as player/coach.

12 The 'B' international between England and Austria is abandoned after 60 minutes' play because of a storm. England were leading 1-0 with a Bryan Robson goal.

13 Despite a brave fight-back, England's unbeaten record – last defeat February 1978 – comes to an end in Vienna. Austria take a 2-0 lead through Pezzey and Welzl, but Keegan scores with a header, Another Welzl goal makes it 3-1 before the break. Coppell from close-in, and Wilkins equalize, After 70 minutes Pezzey heads the winner for Austria past Clemence, who came in for Shilton at half-time – 4-3! Greenwood said: 'We certainly proved that we are a team with plenty of character and spirit, and there was enough evidence to suggest that we are progressing on the right lines' ... Aston Villa pay £220,000 for Tony Morley from Burnley.

14 The Football Association begin to negotiate a new deal with the TV companies. The coverage of FA Cup matches and internationals will cost a great deal more in

the future to both the BBC and ITV... Bryan 'Pop' Robson returns to Sunderland from West Ham for £45,000... Norman Hunter joins his ex-Leeds team-mate Allan Clarke at Barnsley as player/coach... Notts Co collect a club record £150,000 for Mick Vinter from Wrexham.

16 Olympiakos Pireaus fail to turn-up for the Greek championship play-off match, and opponents AEK Athens are awarded the title. The two clubs finished level on points after 34 matches.

18 Alan Curbishley goes to Birmingham from West Ham for a £225,000 fee... Jim Montgomery, the veteran Birmingham goalkeeper, joins Nottingham Forest on a one-year contract... Andras Torocsik, selected to play for a World XI in Buenos Aires, is badly injured in a car accident in Hungary.

19 The Football League are set to sell the League Cup final to one of the TV companies for live transmission. All other games are brought forward to the Friday night... An FA commission rubber-stamps Mick Flanagan's two weeks' suspension by Charlton... John Mortimore, back from Portugal, is to join Southampton, as assistant manager.

20 Dave Watson joins Werder Bremen, the West German First Division club... Everton buy goalkeeper Martin Hodge from Plymouth... Servette complete a treble in Switzerland by winning the Cup – previously they had clinched the League Cup and the Championship... Andy Lochhead, Oldham's coach, is sacked... Gianni Rivera announces his retirement.

21 Tommy Docherty puts Rachid Harkouk and Derek Richardson on the transfer list... Terry Neill travels to Argentina to look for players. Arsenal chairman Denis Hill-Wood says: 'We have given Terry permission to start talks if he sees a likely player. The transfer prices in this country are ridiculous. If you see a promising young player, the club ask £400,000 for him – far too much even these days. We will buy anyone, provided he is a good player, a decent type and can speak good English'.

22 John Hart, a 41-year-old car dealer, bids to get control of Birmingham City. He makes an offer for the block of shares owned by club chairman Keith Coombs... Roger Brown of Bournemouth joins Norwich City.

23 Sir Harold Thompson is re-elected as chairman of the Football Association. Sir Denis Follows, former secretary, has been invited to become an honorary FA vice-president.

25 Fulham hand over a cheque for £273,856 to the High Court as payment for the building cost of their Riverside Stand... Leeds United will be allowed to stage FA Cup ties at Elland Road – the ban has been lifted by the FA... Manchester City are paying £765,000 for the young Preston striker Mick Robinson – it is the second highest ever transfer fee in English football... Newcastle buy full-back Ian Davies from Norwich for £175,000... The Rest of the World XI beat Argentina 2-1 in Buenos Aires. Scorers: Galvan (og) and Zico; and Maradona for the World Champions. Tardelli of Italy is sent off in the second half.

26 Brighton pay £130,000 for Portsmouth centre-half Steve Foster... Southend and Huddersfield complete an exchange deal – Micky Laverick joins the Yorkshire club (£35,000) and Terry Gray comes to Southend (£45,000).

27 'It is unlikely that Arsenal will sign an Argentinian player' says Denis Hill-Wood, the club's chairman... Real Madrid open negotiations to sign Laurie Cunningham of WBA... Tommy Docherty's first signing for QPR is Scottish forward Peter Davidson from Berwick Rangers for £40,000... Alan Buckley rejoins Walsall as player/manager for a £175,000 fee.

28 Asa Hartford goes to Nottingham F for £450,000, but reserve goalkeeper Chris Woods leaves the European Cup holders. He goes to QPR for £235,000... Laurie Cunningham travels to Madrid to sign for £900,000. 'The deal will cost Real more than the Francis deal cost Forest' says Albion director, John Gordon.

July

2 John Hollins is wanted by Norwich, Luton and Arsenal... Athletic Bilbao the Spanish First Division club would like to employ Bobby Robson as manager.

3 Ipswich are willing to let Robson go, but Chairman Cobbold says that Bilbao must pay substantial compensation. 'If it had been an English club, we would not have let him go', said Patrick Cobbold, 'but we are good friends and we wouldn't stand in his way this time.' The Bilbao job is reputedly worth £100,000 per year... Colin

Addison, assistant manager of WBA, is wanted by Derby County, where Michael Dunford has taken over as Secretary from Stuart Webb ... Brian Little agrees to a move to Birmingham from Aston Villa. The striker will cost the Second Division club £615,000. In turn the Villa manager is spending £75,000 on 21-year-old Grimsby forward Terry Donovan; a figure which will be doubled when he has played 40 first team games.

4 John Hollins, who was first persuaded by manager Tommy Docherty to stay at QPR will go to Arsenal in a £75,000 deal after all. 'Joining Arsenal means a fresh challenge to me and I know I can still play top class football because I have looked after myself,' says the 33-year-old Hollins ... Watford pay £15,000 for Lincoln forward John Ward ... Manchester City and Wrexham resolve the Bobby Shinton transfer wrangle by agreeing on a £300,000 price tag put on the player ... UEFA announce that England will only be allowed to enter three teams for the 1980-81 UEFA Cup. This decision is in line with the new rules governing the number of teams each country can nominate in future for this competition.

Here are the detailed regulations:

Over the past few years, the Organizing Committee of the UEFA Club Competitions and the Executive Committee of the European Football Union (UEFA) have made a close study of the organization of the UEFA Cup, trying to find a new system which would ensure that the number of clubs entered by each national federation would be based more upon sporting merit than has been the case in the past. The Executive Committee has, however, remained true to the statutory principle whereby every member association of UEFA still has the right to at least one representative in each of the three European Club Competitions. At its latest meeting in Zurich on July 11, the Executive approved the following official new regulations for the UEFA Cup:

1. The 64 places in the UEFA Cup shall be allocated as follows:

   3 Associations with 4 teams each = 12
   5 Associations with 3 teams each = 15
   13 Associations with 2 teams each = 26
   11 Associations with 1 team each = 11
   —
   32   64

Liechtenstein and Wales, neither of which organizes a national league championship of its own, shall not enter teams for the UEFA Cup. Places which are still vacant after the entry for deadline shall be used to increase the number of Associations entitled to three teams.

2. The allocation of places in the competition is to be based on a table drawn up from the performances of teams in the five preceding seasons of the three European Competitions (Champion Clubs' Cup, Cup Winners' Cup and UEFA Cup). This table is to be updated every year, with the results from the earliest of the five seasons being eliminated every year. The table will be based upon the following points system:

   win   = 2 points
   draw   = 1 point
   defeat = 0 points

In addition, teams will be awarded one bonus point for reaching the quarter-finals, another for the semi-finals and another for the final. The points thus attained by the teams of each country will then be added together and divided by the number of teams entered by that country. This will produce a coefficient which will be calculated to the thousandth of a point, a figure which will not then be rounded off. In the event of two coefficients being equal, the Organizing Committee shall have the final decision.

Points shall only be awarded for matches which have actually taken place, and in accordance with the match results officially registered with UEFA. Series of penalty-kicks taken to decide a drawn tie will have no influence on the result of the match proper. The Member Associations shall be informed of the general classification after every season of European Competitions, and this shall be taken as the basis for determining the number of teams representing each of the Member Associations in the following season's UEFA Cup Tournament. Any situation which may arise and which is not covered by these official provisions, will be finally decided upon by the Organizing Committee.

These new regulations can only enter into force as from 1980-81 season, since the Member Associations have to be informed of the number of places they have in the following season's UEFA Cup before the start of their own national league championship, which is decisive for participation in the tournament the following year; furthermore, league seasons differ somewhat from one country to another. For the 1979-80 season, therefore, the current system will remain valid.

The number of teams taking part in the 1980-81 tournament will then be calculated according to the coefficients derived from the 1974-75, 1975-76, 1976-77, 1977-78 and 1978-79 seasons. Thus the number of places allotted to each country for the 1980-81 season will not be known until the end of the 1978-79 season.

Following a proposal from the French Football Association, and upon the recommendation of the Organizing Committee of the Club Competitions, the Executive Committee also decided that:

- should the holder of the UEFA Cup not qualify for the following season's tournament or either of the other two European Club Competitions, the Organizing Committee may – if so requested by the National Association of the club concerned – admit the Cup-holders to the UEFA Cup tournament that year, without this being at the expense of the total contingent of the Association in question.
- In such an event, the Cup-holder will be allotted a place left vacant by a team from another Association, should such a vacancy exist.
- Should there be no such vacant places and the participation of the Cup-holder would increase the total number of teams to 65, a preliminary round shall be played between two teams drawn by lot from among those which have not been seeded for that year's tournament.

This new regulation comes into effect immediately, and will be included next year in the official Regulations of the UEFA Club Competitions.

NORTH AMERICAN SOCCER LEAGUE

The 1979 season was the 13th in the history of the North American Soccer League. Originally it had been the success of televising the 1966 World Cup Final which had sparked off the idea of providing a professional major soccer league on a coast to coast basis.

Such was the interest aroused that two rival leagues were established. The governing bodies in the United States and Canada decided between them that there was not room for two leagues and urged them to combine. But reacting in the same way as Americans invariably do to events like an oil crisis they ignored it.

The outcome of the rivals lobbying for the right to be considered the official organisation was finally won by the United Soccer Association (USA) but the National Professional Soccer League decided to operate sanctioned or not and recruited players from all over the world for the 1967 season.

The USA, cunningly initialled, decided to import whole teams and brought over Wolverhampton Wanderers, Sunderland, Hibernian, Bangu, Cagliari, Stoke City, Glentoran, Shamrock Rovers and Aberdeen to represent various towns and cities.

The NPSL began with ten new clubs but in December 1967 the two rivals agreed to merge and the North American Soccer League was born for 1968.

Between 1968 and 1975 the new League's fortunes swung with the uncontrolled motion of a dinghy in a storm producing 17, 5, 6, 8, 8, 9, 15 and 20 competitors during this period.

Forty-four different teams were involved in the League though several switched franchise to other cities. Only St Louis Stars remained in constant membership while though Dallas Tornado were in the USA in 1967 they stayed in the NASL.

NASL Champions

1967	Los Angeles Wolves (USA)
	Oakland Clippers (NPSL)
1968	Atlanta Chiefs
1969	Kansas City Spurs
1970	Rochester Lancers
1971	Dallas Tornado
1972	New York Cosmos
1973	Philadelphia Atoms
1974	Los Angeles Aztecs
1975	Tampa Bay Rowdies
1976	Toronto Metros-Croatia
1977	New York Cosmos
1978	New York Cosmos

If one player was responsible for putting soccer on a more even keel it was Pele, signed by New York Cosmos in 1975. By the time he had played his last match on 1 October 1977 before a crowd of 75,646 at the Giants Stadium, East Rutherford, New Jersey, the game had caught the imagination of a public hitherto devoted to the Americans' more traditional sports of American Football, Ice-Hockey, Baseball and Basketball.

Cosmos had added Franz Beckenbauer (West Germany), Giorgio Chinaglia (Italy) and Dennis Tueart (England) among a host of other leading international players.

Yet of the 24 teams competing in the 1978 NASL, Cosmos average gate of 47,856 for their 15 home matches in the regular schedule compared with Chicago Sting's pin-prick of 4,187 and the gap between the successful and unsuccessful was patently obvious from this table:

Team	Average
New York Cosmos	47,856
Minnesota Kicks	30,926
Seattle Sounders	22,578
Tampa Bay Rowdies	18,123
Vancouver Whitecaps	15,736
San Jose Earthquakes	14,281
Detroit Express	12,193
Oakland Stompers	11,929
New England Tea Men	11,858
Portland Timbers	11,803
Tulsa Roughnecks	11,270
California Surf	11,171
Washington Diplomats	10,782
Fort Lauderdale Strikers	10,479
Memphis Rogues	9518
Los Angeles Aztecs	9235
Dallas Tornado	8980
Philadelphia Fury	8279
Colorado Caribou	7417
Rochester Lancers	6760
Toronto Metros-Croatia	6233
Houston Hurricane	5805
San Diego Sockers	5323
Chicago Sting	4187

Unsuccessful clubs have not had much chance to dwell on their misery. The transferring of the franchise has been very much a part of the soccer scene in the States and again in the 1979 season though no new teams were produced, two switched addresses with the Oakland Stompers becoming the Edmonton Drillers and the Colorado Caribou changing to Atlanta Chiefs.

In a survey of the players who regularly appeared in the 1978 NASL most were from England (129). The United States of America provided 101 and the rest came as follows: Canada 33, Yugoslavia 32, Scotland 30, West Germany 12, Ireland 11, South Africa 9, Northern Ireland 6, Argentine, Bermuda, Brazil and Holland four each, Spain and Wales three each; Hungary, Italy, Poland, Portugal and Trinidad two each; Angola, Barbados, Costa Rica, Cyprus, Denmark, Finland, Ghana, Greece, Haiti, Iran, Israel, Nigeria, Peru, Turkey, and Uruguay one each.

In 1979 the names of established but ageing stars from Europe like Gerd Muller and Johan Cruyff had been added to the attractiveness of the NASL. But a short-term outlook is all they can expect. On the other hand Trevor Francis the £1 million Forester has continued his association with Detroit Express and Johan Neeskens has signed for Cosmos.

The League plans to reduce the number of foreigners each year by making it compulsory for all teams to field at least one more American born player each season.

Meanwhile with such refinements as a 35 yard offside law, synthetic pitches which are not conducive to tackling, 'shoot-outs' to eliminate drawn games and bonus points, the country which gave the world Disneyland has provided a Mickey Mouse football industry.

JACK ROLLIN

FOOTBALLER OF THE YEAR

The Football Writers Association was founded in 1947, and it was proposed that the members should elect the Footballer of the Year at the end of each season. The first recipient of the Award, a statuette of a footballer on a square plinth, was one of the all-time greats, Stanley Matthews. The Award, presented at a dinner held in London during Cup Final week, is given 'to the Player, who by precept and example on and off the field, shall have been considered to have done most for football during that season'. To this day, this Award has remained the most prestigious for any player, and the dinner in his honour is an important occasion for English football.

When Kevin Keegan left Liverpool, it was felt that it was an impossible task for Bob Paisley to acquire an adequate replacement for him. However, he paid a then record fee for the established Scottish international forward, Kenny Dalglish. Although he had been a star performer for Celtic during their championship-winning years, there was still a question-mark against his ability to adapt to the faster pace of English League football. This he has done brilliantly, his goal-scoring record speaks for itself, and his excellent distribution gives opportunities to others. Dalglish is certainly a worthy recipient of the highest honour English football can offer to any individual.

Leslie Vernon

Award Winners

1947-48 Stanley Matthews (Blackpool), 1948-49 Johnny Carey (Manchester U), 1949-50 Joe Mercer (Arsenal), 1950-51 Harry Johnston (Blackpool), 1951-52 Billy Wright (Wolverhampton W), 1952-53 Nat Lofthouse (Bolton W), 1953-54 Tom Finney (Preston NE), 1954-55 Don Revie (Manchester C), 1955-56 Bert Trautmann (Manchester C), 1956-57 Tom Finney (Preston NE), 1957-58 Danny Blanchflower (Tottenham H), 1958-59 Syd Owen (Luton T), 1959-60 Bill Slater (Wolverhampton W), 1960-61 Danny Blanchflower (Tottenham H), 1961-62 Jimmy Adamson (Burnley), 1962-63 Stanley Matthews (Stoke C), 1963-64 Bobby Moore (West Ham U), 1964-65 Bobby Collins (Leeds U), 1965-66 Bobby Charlton (Manchester U), 1966-67 Jackie Charlton (Leeds U), 1967-68 George Best (Manchester U), 1968-69 Dave Mackay (Derby C) shared with Tony Book (Manchester C), 1969-70 Billy Bremner (Leeds U), 1970-71 Frank McLintock (Arsenal), 1971-72 Gordon Banks (Stoke C), 1972-73 Pat Jennings (Tottenham H), 1973-74 Ian Callaghan (Liverpool), 1974-75 Alan Mullery (Fulham), 1975-76 Kevin Keegan (Liverpool), 1976-77 Emlyn Hughes (Liverpool), 1977-78 Kenny Burns (Nottingham F).

THE P.F.A. AWARDS 1979

Once again, the members of the Professional Footballers' Association were asked to vote for several individual awards and to select four teams representing the divisions of the Football League.

Player of the Year—Liam Brady (Arsenal)
Previous Winners—Andy Gray (Aston V); Pat Jennings (Tottenham H); Colin Todd (Derby Co); Norman Hunter (Leeds U); Peter Shilton (Nottingham F)

Young Player of the Year—Cyrille Regis (WBA)
Previous Winners—Andy Gray (Aston V); Peter Barnes (Manchester C); Mervyn Day (West Ham U); Kevin Beattie (Ipswich T); Tony Woodcock (Nottingham F)

PFA Merit Award—Tom Finney
Previous Winners—Jack Taylor; George Eastham; Dennis Law; Bobby Charlton; Bill Shankly

DIVISION 1: Peter Shilton (Nottingham F); Viv Anderson (Nottingham F), David O'Leary (Arsenal), Dave Watson (Manchester C), Derek Statham (WBA), Liam Brady (Arsenal), Tony Currie (Leeds U), Osvaldo Ardiles (Tottenham H), Cyrille Regis (WBA), Kenny Dalglish (Liverpool), Laurie Cunningham (WBA).

DIVISION 2: Mark Wallington (Leicester C); Kevin Hird (Leeds U), Mark Lawrenson (Brighton & HA), Mike Doyle (Stoke C), Ken Sansom (C Palace), Trevor Brooking (West Ham U), Howard Kendall (Stoke C), Brian Horton (Brighton & HA), Bryan Robson (West Ham U), Mike Flanagan (Charlton Ath), Peter Withe (Newcastle U).

DIVISION 3: Chris Turner (Sheffield W); John Stirk (Watford), Steve Sims (Watford), Ian MacDonald (Carlisle U), Trevor Storton (Chester), John Breckin (Rotherham), Brian Hornsby (Sheffield W), Ray McHale (Swindon T), Ian Callaghan (Swansea C), Luther Blissett (Watford), Ross Jenkins (Watford), Alan Curtis (Swansea C).
'(McDonald and Storton tied with the same votes and are both included in the side)'

DIVISION 4: Steve Death (Reading); Gary Peters (Reading), Steve Foster (Portsmouth), Mike McCarthy (Barnsley), Kevin Moore (Grimsby T), Joe Waters (Grimsby T), Richie Bowman (Reading), Alan Little (Barnsley), Alan Cork (Wimbledon), Les Bradd (Stockport Co), Allan Clarke (Barnsley).

Bell's Football Managers Awards 1978-79

AUGUST: MANAGER OF THE MONTH: **Ron Atkinson** (WBA); Division Two: **Alan Durban** (Stoke C); Division Three: **Alan Oakes** (Chester); Division Four: **Maurice Evans** (Reading). SEPTEMBER: MANAGER OF THE MONTH: **Brian Clough** (Nottingham F); Division Two: **Terry Venables** (Crystal Palace); Division Three: **John Toshack** (Swansea C); Division Four: **Dario Gradi** (Wimbledon). OCTOBER: MANAGER OF THE MONTH: **Gordon Lee** (Everton); Division Two: **Andy Nelson** (Charlton Ath); Division Three: **Graham Taylor** (Watford); Division Four: **Ian McNeill** (Wigan Ath). NOVEMBER: MANAGER OF THE MONTH: **Brian Clough** (Nottingham F); Division Two: **Harry Potts** (Burnley); Division Three: **Bob Smith** (Swindon T); Division Four: **Jimmy Dickinson** (Portsmouth). DECEMBER: MANAGER OF THE MONTH: **Ron Atkinson** (WBA); Division Two: **Alan Mullery** (Brighton & HA); Division Three: **Graham Taylor** (Watford); Division Four: **Allan Clarke** (Barnsley). JANUARY: MANAGER OF THE MONTH: **Graham Turner** (Shrewsbury T); Division One: **Lawrie McMenemy** (Southampton); Division Two: **Terry Venables** (Crystal Palace); Division Four: **Tom McAnearney** (Aldershot). FEBRUARY: MANAGER OF THE MONTH: **Bob Paisley** (Liverpool); Division Two: **John Lyall** (West Ham U); Division Three: **Gerry Summers** (Gillingham); Division Four: **John Newman** (Grimsby T). MARCH: MANAGER OF THE MONTH: **Brian Clough** (Nottingham F); Division Two: **Billy Elliott** (Sunderland); Division Three: **Dave Smith** (Southend U); Division Four: **Len Ashurst** (Newport Co). APRIL: MANAGER OF THE MONTH: **Brian Clough** (Nottingham F); Division Two: **Richie Morgan** (Cardiff C); Division Three: **Bill Dodgin** (Brentford); Division Four: **John Newman** (Grimsby T).

MANAGER OF THE YEAR

Bob Paisley, whose amazing record since he took over as manager of Liverpool five years ago reads: European Cup victors (twice), UEFA Cup and now a third and record-breaking League Division One championship, was named Bell's Scotch Whisky Football Manager of the Year.

Paisley, who earlier in May celebrated 40 years at Anfield, received a cheque for £2,500 at a lunch in London. It was his third Manager of the Year title in four seasons. The award was decided by a panel of 25 leading football writers and commentators.

Brian Clough – last year's Manager of the Year and Paisley's chief rival for the 1979 title – received a special award of a cheque for £500 and an inscribed salver.

DIVISIONAL MANAGER OF THE SEASON AWARDS

The Divisional Manager of the Season awards – each a cheque for £500 and an inscribed salver – went to: **Terry Venables** (Crystal Palace) in Division Two; **Graham Turner** (Shrewsbury Town) in Division Three; and **Maurice Evans** (Reading) Division Four.

The presentations of these awards were made by Lord Westwood, President of The Football League, who nominate the Divisional awards.

European Footballer of the Year 1978

When Kevin Keegan finished runner-up as 1977 European Footballer of the Year, one thought that his best chance to take the title had disappeared. After all, he was the star performer in that season's Champions' Cup final, a game which usually tilts the balance as far as the panel members are concerned.

In any case, '78 was a World Cup year, and it is traditional that the leading European player is chosen from those who took part in the global confrontation. As far back as 1958, Raymond Kopa was elected, to be followed by Jozef Masopust, Bobby Charlton, Gerd Muller and Johan Cruyff in subsequent World Cup years.

But the panel bravely ignored the obvious claims of certain players, and put the brilliant Hamburg-based Englishman on top of the heap. Keegan was an excellent footballer when with Liverpool, but since he has been playing in West Germany, his all-round game has improved a great deal. Now, he is able to outfox close-marking defenders as well as teams which prefer the English-style zonal marking system.

Against N. Ireland, Keegan scored a courageous goal when his quick-thinking put him a step ahead of all those around him. Later in the same game, a classic back-headed pass gave Latchford the easiest of chances to score.

Kevin Keegan, known as the 'Mighty Mouse' in Germany, is a world-class player, he excels in the role of goal-maker and goal-taker alike, and is a worthy recipient of this, one of the highest honours in the game. Hans Krankl, the Austrian scoring machine, finished second, and the mercurial Robby Rensenbrink, third.

Leslie Vernon

Points awarded
87 Kevin Keegan (Hamburg)
81 Hans Krankl (Barcelona)
50 Robby Rensenbrink (Anderlecht)
28 Roberto Bettega (Juventus)
23 Paolo Rossi (Lanerossi Vicenza)
20 Ronnie Hellstrom (Kaiserslautern), Rudi Krol (Ajax)
10 Kenny Dalglish (Liverpool), Allan Simonsen (B Moenchengladbach)
 9 Peter Shilton (Nottingham F)
 7 Arie Haan (Anderlecht)
 6 Rene Van der Kerkhof (PSV Eindhoven)
 5 Willy Van der Kerkhof (PSV Eindhoven), Antonio Cabrini (Juventus)
 4 Zdenek Nehoda (Dukla Prague), Graeme Souness (Liverpool), Johan Cruyff (ex-Barcelona)
 3 Marian Masny (Slovan Bratislava)
 2 Archie Gemmill (Nottingham F), Marius Tresor (Marseille)
 1 Francois Van der Elst (Anderlecht), Michel Platini (Nancy), Zbigniew Boniek (Stal Mielec), Franco Causio (Juventus), Johan Neeskens (Barcelona), Jose Alves (Benfica), Hansi Muller (Stuttgart), Didier Six (Marseille), Karl-Heinz Rummenigge (Bayern Munich), Rainer Bonhof (Valencia).

Past winners
1956 Stanley Matthews (Blackpool); 1957 Alfredo di Stefano (Real Madrid); 1958 Raymond Kopa (Real Madrid); 1959 Alfredo di Stefano (Real Madrid); 1960 Luis Suarez (Barcelona); 1961 Omar Sivori (Juventus); 1962 Josef Masopust (Dukla Prague); 1963 Lev Yashin (Dynamo Moscow); 1964 Denis Law (Manchester U); 1965 Eusebio (Benfica); 1966 Bobby Charlton (Manchester U); 1967 Florian Albert (Ferencvaros); 1968 George Best (Manchester U); 1969 Gianni Rivera (Milan); 1970 Gerd Muller (Bayern Munich); 1971 Johan Cruyff (Ajax); 1972 Franz Beckenbauer (Bayern Munich); 1973 Johan Cruyff (Barcelona); 1974 Johan Cruyff (Barcelona); 1975 Oleg Blokhin (Dynamo Kiev); 1976 Franz Beckenbauer (Bayern Munich); 1977 Allan Simonsen (B Moenchengladbach).

THE FOOTBALL LEAGUE CLUBS

Featuring a review of the 1978-79 League season, and full details of each of the 92 clubs in the Football League.

Officials, statistics, ground information, full 1978-79 League record, career details of the players.

THE FOOTBALL LEAGUE OFFICIALS

President
Lord Westwood (*Newcastle United*)

Vice-Presidents
R. W. Lord (*Burnley*)
R. Wragg (*Sheffield United*)

Management Committee
J. F. Wiseman (*Birmingham City*)
Sir Matt Busby (*Manchester United*)
J. B. Mears (*Chelsea*)
Dr. C. S. Grossmark (*Gillingham*)
G. H. C. Needler (*Hull City*)
R. Daniel (*Plymouth Argyle*)
J. J. Dunnett MA, (Cantab), LLB, MP (*Notts County*)

Life Members
F. A. Would (*Grimsby Town*)
E. M. Gliksten (*Charlton Athletic*)
L. T. Shipman CBE (*Leicester City*)

General Secretary
A. Hardaker OBE, Lytham St Annes, Lancashire

Deputy General Secretary
G. E. Readle

Assistant General Secretary
R. H. G. Kelly FCIS

Assistant Secretary
N. J. Thomas FCA

Review of the Season

Just before the League season ended, a season in which foreign footballers flocked in, transfer fees shot up and snow heaped down, someone worked out that if Liverpool never won another League match and Arsenal never failed to win another League match – it would still be three full seasons before Liverpool's place in history could be usurped.

It may have been a bizarre statistic, but it served well to underline the awe felt about Bob Paisley's team as they took the title to Anfield for a record eleventh year (Arsenal, on eight, are their nearest challengers). The scale of Liverpool's achievement was indeed so massive as to encourage odd perspectives like that.

Not only did they win, they won superbly. They smashed the all-time record of 67 points, they set an all-time record for conceding fewest goals (16 in 42 matches) and just in case there were any out-dated fools still muttering 'Liverpool, boring' they picked up a £50,000 newspaper prize for hitting a target of 84 goals. Good sides, even *very* good sides, were hit for three, four and occasionally six, as Liverpool cut loose in a manner they have never quite equalled before. Kenny Dalglish, the Scot bought the previous season to replace the irreplaceable Kevin Keegan, was a towering influence in this.

After an early falter (at the time they lost in Europe to Nottingham Forest) Liverpool seemed always bound to do it. So the interest was principally in who would chase them hardest. Curiously it wasn't the expected Forest (whose results if not their play had looked a shade cramped). Nor their dour neighbours Everton, but West Bromwich Albion. And most were prepared to applaud them all along the way.

Albion had got a lot of it right: they had a bright young manager, Ron Atkinson, who in turn had given chances and encouragement to a trio of black players, and Albion's 'multi-coloured skill shop' was admired far beyond the Midlands (as far as Peking in fact, for in 1978 Albion had toured to China) and had the weather not unbalanced their rhythm from New Year – when they stood alongside Liverpool on equal points – Albion might have got closer. Liverpool are surely the team of the decade– they can afford to let Albion be known as the team of the season.

At the bottom, Birmingham were in trouble from the start. Their star Trevor Francis came back late from America and was then soon hurt. Birmingham were doomed before he recovered and was sold to Forest as the country's first million pound player. The experimental deal with North America had not served Birmingham well – nor had their initiative with South America. Involved with the import of Argentinians that gave the season so splendid a new flavour, Birmingham's choice – Alberto Tarantini – settled less well than the others; perhaps because he never played in his World Cup role at left back. Down with Birmingham went London strugglers QPR and Chelsea: both took new managers with them. Danny Blanchflower's lyrical optimism gave Chelsea heart but not defensive back; Tommy Docherty's grit was purchased to start rubbing the edges off a new side being built for the Second Division.

The way back has been trail-blazed by London neighbours Crystal Palace who climbed back on the last day of perhaps the most enthralling promotion battle within memory. Up with them went Brighton and Stoke – and few pretend it is coincidence that what these clubs have so much in common is a young manager (respectively Terry Venables, Alan Mullery and Alan Durban) full of drive, deft with words, and marked by a clear missionary zeal. Their impact on a game increasingly gripped by a real managerial revolution may become enormous.

But more than these three were involved in an epic struggle. West Ham lost their England man Trevor Brooking for the 10 final matches and thus their chance – even though they lashed out late with £500,000 to make Phil Parkes the most expensive goalkeeper in history. Sunderland can trace their downfall to that daft day they lost at home to bottom team Blackburn.

And losing at home to Blackburn committed Sheffield United to a first season in Division Three, where they will join their neighbours Wednesday to render a great city with two major grounds without a side among the country's top 42 teams. Irony here is that United's manager Harry Haslam, the moving force behind the importation of foreign stars (he bought the Argentinian Alex Sabella for himself) should gain so little from his initiative.

Up from the Third came Watford, who led by a street and then barely made it in a highly dramatic sort of season perhaps best appreciated by their chairman Elton John;

with them marched the best footballing side Shrewsbury (moulded by a succession of these same young managerial lions, Durban, Richie Barker, Graham Turner) and Swansea. The Swansea success was appreciated widely . . . for the continuation it gave to the splendid careers of the five ex-Liverpool men gathered around player-manager John Toshack: and the effect it had on a revival of 'Welshness' in the city's soccer. Four Swansea men were included in current Wales teams.

Up from the Fourth came the big, strong Reading side and a Grimsby team whose bright football was given edge by Joe Waters' shooting. With them strode Barnsley, carried on a wave of support that included a 21,000 crowd for their promotion night. Next season Barnsley will meet both Sheffield teams and Rotherham in what is already being nick-named 'Third Division – Yorks' and when they rope in Chesterfield and Mansfield, bristling local derbies will be epidemic.

No one, finally was thrown out. Possibly the voting reflected the feeling that only the very rich and powerful had ridden through the worst footballing weather in history untouched: Halifax, for example, could point out that they had not a single home match between mid-December and March. If for them 1978-79 was all about enduring, we luckier lookers-on will surely best remember Anfield and Osvaldo Ardiles, West Bromwich and Viv Anderson, a League year of players and places in which great clubs like Arsenal and the two at Manchester failed to shine . . . and yet were scarcely missed.

BRIAN JAMES

Introduction to Club Section

Because of the disruption of the original fixture list for 1978-79 and subsequent postponement of many matches which elongated the season, we have taken advantage of the lateness thus produced to provide information on the club section which embraces another month.

In the past our final 'copy date' had been roughly 1 June but in this edition there has been an extension to allow for major transfers. Even so, not all the changes which would normally have affected new colours and finalisation of transfers during this period will be found on the following pages, since 'page 4' refers specifically to the retained lists at the end of the 1978-79 season. But details of players subsequently transferred will appear under their former clubs.

But basically the formula is as before with four pages devoted to each of the 92 League clubs. On 'page 1' there is a potted history of the club since it entered the League, as well as a list of the achievements attained during its existence.

As to 'pages 2 and 3' of this section, these appear as they have done so in recent years. On 'page 4' despite the continuing problem of reproducing a vast amount of material in a small space, all contract players who were attached to the club at the end of the 1978-79 season plus those who were signed up to the end of May 1979 are featured with their individual details.

In addition any player who was either on non-contract or associated schoolboy forms and actually played in the League side is also noted separately.

Where clubs have retained the League registration of a player who has not been on the playing strength for various reasons, these have been listed at the foot of the page. Details of their playing records can be found in earlier editions, of course.

Similarly with a few clubs, specific players who did not appear in the League side in 1978-79 might have been included without details of their previous history but again last year's edition will have covered their careers.

As far as height and weight are concerned, as we have stated previously, the players report for training after our press deadline and this information may be missing for certain comparative newcomers to the ranks of the Football League.

We would like to thank the club secretaries who were kind enough to inform us of changes affecting their club and also those who again allowed us to reproduce their badges. These badges add a touch of individuality to the pages and provide a welcome presentation.

JACK ROLLIN

DIVISION ONE LEAGUE POSITION PROGRESS CHART

	Sept 2	9	16	23	30	Oct 7	14	21	28	Nov 4	11	18	25	Dec 2	9	16	23	30	Jan 6	13	20	27	Feb 3	10	17	24	Mar 3	10	17	24	31	April 7	14	21	May 28	5	Final Position
Arsenal	9	13	11	10	9	8	7	7	5	5	5	5	5	4	4	4	4	4	4	4	4	4	4	4	2	2	3	4	4	5	5	6	5	6	6	6	7
Aston Villa	6	5	5	7	12	10	8	10	10	9	7	7	9	10	10	11	11	11	11	11	11	11	11	11	12	12	11	12	11	12	12	10	14	10	8	8	8
Birmingham C	17	21	22	21	22	22	22	22	22	22	22	22	21	21	21	22	22	22	22	22	22	22	22	22	22	22	22	22	22	21	21	21	21	21	21	21	21
Bolton W	20	14	18	16	18	17	15	18	22	19	19	19	19	17	17	17	17	17	18	17	18	18	18	18	18	18	18	17	17	17	16	17	16	17	17	17	17
Bristol C	7	12	8	6	5	9	11	9	11	10	12	13	11	11	10	7	7	7	7	7	7	7	7	10	13	14	9	8	9	11	12	13					13
Chelsea	16	18	20	20	21	21	21	20	20	22	22	22	22	22	22	20	21	21	21	21	21	21	21	21	21	21	21	18	17	17	18	22	22	22	22	22	22
Coventry C	2	2	3	3	4	3	7	10	8	8	6	6	6	6	6	7	6	8	8	8	8	8	8	10	11	13	11	8	8	7	7	8	9	9	9	10	10
Derby Co	18	19	16	13	17	16	18	16	19	16	13	13	11	12	13	14	14	13	14	15	16	16	15	15	16	17	17	18	18	18	18	18	18	19	19	19	19
Everton	4	3	2	2	2	2	2	2	2	2	2	2	2	2	2	2	2	2	3	3	3	2	2	3	1	3	2	2	2	2	2	4	4	4	4	4	4
Ipswich	14	17	15	18	13	14	15	18	15	17	18	15	16	16	16	13	13	15	12	12	14	14	13	14	9	12	12	10	9	7	8	7	7	7	7	7	6
Leeds U	5	9	14	12	11	13	14	14	12	14	14	10	10	9	9	8	6	6	5	5	5	5	5	5	6	6	5	4	5	6	5	6	5	5	5	5	5
Liverpool	1	1	1	1	1	1	1	1	1	1	1	1	1	1	1	1	1	1	1	1	1	1	1	2	2	2	1	1	1	1	1	1	1	1	1	1	1
Manchester C	15	10	7	4	10	7	5	5	6	7	10	12	13	14	15	14	15	15	12	15	15	15	15	16	16	15	15	15	16	15	16	17	16	16	14	14	15
Manchester U	8	8	10	9	7	7	6	6	7	8	6	7	7	9	6	7	9	10	11	10	10	11	9	9	9	10	7	7	7	7	7	8	13	11	10	10	9
Middlesbrough	13	16	19	19	19	19	17	14	14	15	16	15	14	16	17	18	18	18	17	17	18	17	17	17	17	17	16	16	16	15	14	10	13	11	11	12	12
Nottingham F	10	6	9	8	6	4	3	3	4	4	3	3	3	4	4	5	5	5	5	6	6	6	6	6	6	6	5	4	3	6	4	3	2	3	3	3	2
Norwich C	11	11	6	11	8	11	12	12	13	12	11	10	14	14	15	13	15	12	13	14	14	13	12	13	14	15	10	10	9	11	12	15	14	15	16	16	16
QPR	22	22	17	15	16	15	13	13	16	15	17	16	18	19	18	19	18	19	19	19	19	19	19	20	20	20	20	19	20	19	20	20	20	20	20	20	20
Southampton	12	7	12	14	15	18	16	19	18	16	17	18	15	12	11	13	13	16	12	13	13	13	16	12	9	13	13	9	8	9	15	13	11	13	12	13	14
Tottenham H	21	15	13	17	14	12	8	14	11	9	9	11	9	8	8	8	11	10	9	9	9	9	9	9	8	8	12	11	10	10	13	13	15	14	15	16	11
WBA	3	4	4	5	3	6	4	4	3	3	3	3	3	3	3	3	3	3	3	2	1	1	1	3	4	5	3	3	3	3	3	3	3	3	2	2	3
Wolverhampton W	19	20	21	22	20	20	20	20	21	21	21	20	20	20	20	21	20	20	20	20	20	20	20	20	20	18	20	19	19	19	19	19	19	19	18	18	18

1978 / 1979

DIVISION TWO LEAGUE POSITION PROGRESS CHART

	1978																1979															Final Position
		Sept				Oct				Nov				Dec				Jan				Feb				Mar				April	May	
	2	9	16	23	30	7	14	21	28	4	11	18	25	2	9	16	23	30	6	13	20	27	3	10	17	24	3	10	17	24	31	7	14	21	28	5	
Blackburn R	14	20	20	21	21	21	21	20	20	19	19	20	20	20	20	20	21	21	21	20	20	20	22	22	22	22	21	22	22	22	22	22	22	22	22	22	22
Brighton & HA	5	3	5	10	3	9	4	10	12	8	6	11	12	7	7	4	4	3	3	3	3	3	1	2	1	1	1	1	1	1	1	1	2	1	1	1	2
Bristol R	12	6	11	6	7	5	9	6	6	5	7	8	9	10	12	13	14	12	13	13	13	13	11	12	14	13	15	14	13	14	13	13	13	13	13	16	16
Burnley	6	4	8	13	9	7	11	7	7	7	8	5	5	8	11	8	8	7	7	7	8	8	14	15	14	10	9	9	9	7	7	7	9	10	10	13
Cambridge U	10	15	15	15	15	12	15	16	16	14	12	14	15	15	8	13	15	12	12	12	12	12	14	12	12	11	13	11	11	12	11	12	10	11	12	12	12
Cardiff C	22	22	22	20	17	19	19	19	15	17	20	21	21	21	21	22	20	20	21	21	21	21	20	21	18	14	11	11	11	20	13	14	15	12	13	13	9
Charlton Ath	15	16	17	16	12	16	12	9	5	4	5	7	11	12	10	11	11	10	10	11	11	11	8	8	10	8	9	12	13	14	15	17	18	17	18	19
Crystal Palace	2	2	1	1	4	3	1	2	1	3	2	1	1	1	1	1	1	1	1	1	1	1	2	3	3	3	2	3	2	2	3	2	3	4	4	4	1
Fulham	18	9	10	4	4	3	5	5	3	6	3	4	4	5	8	10	5	5	5	6	6	6	6	7	6	7	8	8	8	8	8	8	7	7	7	10
Leicester C	16	19	19	14	11	13	17	18	18	16	15	16	17	14	17	18	18	16	16	16	16	14	14	11	16	15	14	16	12	13	13	16	15	18	14	18
Luton T	8	14	9	9	10	8	8	4	10	12	14	13	13	13	13	16	17	17	14	14	14	12	12	14	13	14	12	8	11	14	16	17	15	18	14	14
Millwall	21	18	21	22	22	22	22	22	22	22	22	22	22	22	22	22	22	22	22	22	22	22	22	22	21	21	21	21	21	22	21	22	22	21	21	21
Newcastle U	20	10	12	12	8	6	6	11	8	11	10	12	10	11	9	6	5	8	8	9	9	10	11	11	12	15	10	15	16	14	11	12	12	11	11	8
Notts Co	19	12	7	7	14	10	7	12	11	13	11	9	7	6	5	7	7	9	9	10	10	8	9	9	7	10	15	7	6	6	6	6	6	6	6	6
Oldham Ath	7	11	6	11	16	16	18	18	19	17	15	16	16	17	14	15	16	17	18	18	18	19	19	20	19	20	18	19	19	20	20	20	20	16	19	14
Orient	11	17	18	19	19	17	16	16	15	18	18	18	18	16	17	14	11	11	11	11	11	7	6	7	7	8	8	9	9	9	7	9	9	8	9	11
Preston NE	9	8	16	17	20	20	20	21	21	21	19	19	19	18	18	17	15	14	15	17	17	17	16	15	16	16	13	12	10	10	10	11	10	10	10	8	7
Sheffield U	17	21	14	18	18	14	14	13	14	15	17	17	18	19	19	19	19	19	19	19	19	19	18	18	18	18	19	19	18	18	18	19	18	19	20	20	20
Stoke C	1	1	2	2	2	2	2	2	2	1	1	2	2	2	2	2	2	2	2	2	2	2	3	3	3	3	3	1	2	4	4	3	4	2	3	3	3
Sunderland	13	13	13	8	5	11	10	8	9	10	9	6	6	4	4	5	6	6	6	5	5	5	5	5	5	5	5	3	4	4	3	4	3	3	3	3	4
West Ham U	4	7	4	3	6	4	3	5	4	2	4	3	3	3	3	3	3	4	4	4	4	4	4	4	4	5	5	5	5	5	5	5	5	5	5	5
Wrexham	3	5	3	5	13	15	13	14	13	9	13	10	8	9	6	9	9	13	14	15	15	17	17	17	17	17	17	17	17	17	17	16	14	17	17	15

DIVISION THREE LEAGUE POSITION PROGRESS CHART

1978 / 1979

	Sept				Oct				Nov				Dec				Jan				Feb				Mar				April			May	Final Position
	2	9	16	23	30	7	14	21	28	4	11	18	25	2	9	16	23	30	6	13	20	27	3	10	17	24	3	10	17	24	31	7	14	21	28	5	
Blackpool	13	18	14	12	10	6	10	8	10	15	15	16	16	16	16	16	13	13	13	13	13	15	15	13	13	13	9	9	13	14	15	15	15	12
Brentford	18	12	18	19	21	22	23	23	23	22	23	23	21	22	22	21	19	19	19	18	17	17	15	15	17	18	17	18	14	15	14	11	10	10
Bury	19	20	22	21	22	21	18	20	20	19	20	20	20	21	21	22	20	21	19	19	20	18	19	18	20	19	18	20	19	18	18	17	19	18
Carlisle U	12	7	6	7	6	7	7	9	7	8	8	7	7	7	7	8	6	7	6	7	7	7	6	6	5	6	5	4	5	5	6	6	9	6
Chester	4	5	11	10	5	4	6	6	5	6	6	5	5	6	6	6	11	10	11	11	10	10	10	10	11	11	12	11	12	12	10	6	5	14	16
Chesterfield	9	13	17	13	12	8	12	11	12	9	11	11	11	13	10	10	10	12	12	12	14	14	14	14	16	15	13	15	18	19	19	19	18	20
Colchester U	15	21	15	15	14	11	9	14	13	10	14	12	12	12	11	15	16	16	16	16	16	16	18	19	14	11	12	11	9	8	8	8	7
Exeter C	20	17	19	18	16	15	19	10	15	12	12	15	13	14	9	9	6	6	4	4	4	2	5	5	8	8	9	8	8	7	7	7
Gillingham	14	16	12	11	9	10	5	4	8	4	4	6	6	4	5	4	4	4	4	6	5	5	5	5	8	9	4	4	3	4	3	3	5	4
Hull C	7	3	3	4	11	12	14	18	16	17	14	14	15	15	18	19	17	15	15	15	15	14	16	16	18	16	14	14	11	10	12	10	9	8
Lincoln C	21	24	23	24	24	24	24	24	24	24	24	24	24	24	24	24	24	24	24	24	24	24	24	22	22	22	22	24	24	24	24	24	24	24
Mansfield T	16	10	16	17	18	21	21	21	21	21	21	21	21	17	17	18	18	18	18	18	18	22	22	22	22	22	22	21	21	21	21	22	23	20	19
Oxford U	24	23	20	22	19	19	20	18	21	19	19	19	17	17	17	17	14	14	14	14	14	14	13	12	14	16	18	17	13	15	13	13	14	12	11
Peterborough U	3	4	4	5	8	9	8	13	17	18	18	18	18	20	20	20	20	22	22	20	19	19	20	21	21	21	21	22	22	22	22	22	21	21
Plymouth Arg	8	15	8	6	4	5	4	7	8	13	13	8	8	9	8	9	9	8	12	8	8	8	8	9	7	7	8	10	10	17	11	11	13	13	15
Rotherham U	10	8	10	9	7	13	15	12	16	14	10	9	9	8	8	9	5	7	7	8	7	7	10	10	13	12	13	15	17	16	16	16	16	17
Sheffield W	17	11	13	16	18	17	16	17	14	11	11	13	13	14	14	15	16	17	18	17	17	18	19	20	20	19	17	15	16	16	16	18	16	17
Shrewsbury T	6	2	5	3	1	2	1	2	1	2	1	2	3	3	3	3	2	2	2	2	2	2	2	2	2	3	2	3	4	3	4	5	4	3	1
Southend U	11	14	7	8	15	14	11	15	6	7	7	10	10	10	8	10	11	9	11	9	11	11	9	10	9	11	9	7	7	8	9	12	11	13
Swansea C	1	1	1	1	3	3	3	3	3	3	2	3	3	3	2	2	3	3	3	3	3	3	4	4	5	5	4	5	2	2	2	2	2	2
Swindon T	5	9	9	14	13	16	13	5	9	5	5	4	4	5	4	5	5	5	5	5	5	5	7	7	6	6	4	5	6	6	5	6	3	6	4	5
Tranmere R	23	22	24	23	22	23	22	22	22	23	22	22	22	23	23	23	23	22	23	23	23	23	23	22	23	23	23	23	23	23	23	23	23	23
Walsall	22	19	21	20	20	20	17	21	11	17	16	17	17	18	15	15	18	21	20	21	22	22	18	17	15	18	20	19	20	21	20	20	21	21	22	22
Watford	2	6	2	1	2	2	2	1	2	1	2	1	2	2	1	1	1	1	1	1	1	1	1	1	1	1	1	1	1	1	1	1	1	1	2	2

DIVISION FOUR LEAGUE POSITION PROGRESS CHART

	1978																1979														Final Position
	Sept 2	9	16	23	30	Oct 7	14	21	28	Nov 4	11	18	25	Dec 2	9	16	23	30	Jan 6	13	20	27	Feb 3	10	17	24	Mar 3	10	17	24	31	Apr 7	14	21	28	May 5	Final
Aldershot	6	5	5	9	14	9	9	7	8	6	6	6	6	5	5	5	5	5	4	4	3	3	2	1	2	3	3	2	3	3	3	3	3	3	5	5	5
Barnsley	1	1	1	1	2	2	2	2	4	3	3	3	3	4	4	4	4	4	5	5	6	6	6	6	7	7	7	6	6	6	6	4	5	4	4	3	4
AFC Bournemouth	15	17	12	10	6	8	8	12	10	7	8	7	7	8	8	8	15	16	16	16	16	14	16	10	10	10	10	10	9	12	15	17	18	18	18	17	18
Bradford C	13	12	14	16	15	18	16	20	20	21	21	18	18	19	18	19	11	13	13	14	13	15	16	16	16	13	13	17	10	12	11	14	11	14	14	13	15
Crewe Alex	24	20	18	21	20	19	21	21	21	21	22	22	22	22	22	22	22	22	22	22	22	22	22	22	22	22	22	22	22	21	22	22	22	23	23	23	24
Darlington	17	19	17	20	19	17	19	22	18	20	19	19	19	20	20	20	20	20	20	20	20	21	20	21	21	21	21	21	21	22	21	21	21	21	21	22	21
Doncaster R	11	14	19	18	22	22	22	19	22	19	20	21	21	21	21	21	21	21	21	21	21	21	20	20	17	15	13	16	14	14	17	19	20	20	19	20	22
Grimsby T	4	4	6	4	4	4	4	3	3	4	5	5	6	6	6	6	4	4	4	4	4	3	3	5	5	5	5	4	3	1	2	1	2	1	2	2	2
Halifax T	19	22	23	23	23	24	24	24	24	24	24	24	24	24	24	24	24	24	24	24	24	24	24	24	24	24	24	24	24	24	24	24	24	24	24	23	23
Hartlepool U	12	8	10	7	12	13	12	10	9	12	9	14	16	13	15	14	15	11	12	13	13	12	13	13	12	14	16	17	16	19	17	18	19	20	19	19	13
Hereford U	16	18	15	14	13	14	14	11	11	13	14	10	10	7	11	10	10	11	11	12	13	12	12	11	13	11	11	11	11	10	11	10	12	9	10	12	14
Huddersfield T	21	16	20	17	17	16	22	18	19	16	15	15	13	15	13	15	16	17	16	17	17	17	17	18	18	20	18	16	18	16	16	12	9	10	10	12	9
Newport Co	18	21	22	22	21	20	17	17	17	17	17	17	15	17	15	12	12	18	8	9	8	8	8	8	8	8	8	7	7	8	7	8	8	8	8	7	8
Northampton T	8	13	7	12	8	6	6	9	12	10	12	13	14	16	17	18	18	18	18	18	18	18	19	19	19	18	22	20	20	20	20	19	15	17	17	18	19
Portsmouth	14	10	9	5	7	5	5	5	5	5	4	4	4	2	3	3	2	2	2	1	1	1	1	4	4	4	5	5	7	8	8	7	7	7	7	8	7
Port Vale	9	9	11	15	16	15	13	14	16	14	11	12	12	10	11	9	17	11	8	9	9	10	12	12	15	15	15	12	13	13	14	16	15	16	16	16	16
Reading	2	2	3	3	3	3	3	2	2	2	2	1	2	3	2	2	3	3	3	3	3	5	5	3	3	3	1	1	2	2	1	1	2	1	1	1	1
Rochdale	20	23	24	24	24	24	23	23	23	23	23	23	20	23	23	23	23	23	23	23	23	23	23	23	23	23	23	23	18	18	18	23	22	22	22	21	20
Scunthorpe U	5	7	13	11	11	12	15	13	15	17	16	20	20	21	13	12	13	13	12	12	14	15	17	17	19	19	19	18	18	10	10	13	16	17	16	14	12
Stockport Co	10	11	4	8	5	7	7	6	7	9	8	11	11	9	9	9	10	9	9	10	10	10	11	14	14	12	9	9	10	10	10	10	13	11	13	15	17
Torquay U	22	15	16	6	9	10	10	8	6	8	7	8	8	12	12	14	13	14	15	11	9	11	9	14	14	14	13	12	9	9	10	13	11	10	9	9	11
Wigan Ath	23	24	21	19	18	21	18	15	13	11	13	9	11	7	7	7	7	7	7	7	7	7	7	6	6	6	7	5	4	5	5	4	6	6	6	6	6
Wimbledon	3	3	3	1	1	1	1	1	1	1	1	2	1	1	1	1	1	1	2	2	2	2	1	2	2	2	2	3	4	4	4	5	4	6	6	4	3
York C	7	6	8	13	10	11	11	16	14	15	18	16	16	14	15	16	19	19	19	19	19	19	19	20	20	19	20	17	16	15	14	14	15	13	12	11	10

ALDERSHOT

DIV. 4

President: S. C. Salter.
Chairman: R. J. Driver.
Vice-Chairman: F. G. Wiltshire, F.S.V.A.
Directors: S. R. Hooker, L. C. Eustace, M. E. J. Hall. R. H. Lemarre.
Team Manager: Tom McAnearney.
Secretary/Commercial Manager: M. A. Cosway.
Year Formed: 1926. *Turned Professional* 1927.
Limited Company: 1927.
Football League Record:
   1932 Elected to Division 3(S).   1973–76 Division 3.
   1958–1973 Division 4.   1976– Division 4.

Honours: Football League: best season: 8th Division 3, 1973–74. *F.A. Cup,* best season: 5th Rd.1932–33, 5th Rd. replay 1978–79, *Football League Cup,* best season: Never past 2nd Rd.

Record Victory: 8-1 v Gateshead, Division 4, Sept. 13th, 1958.

Record Defeat: 0-9 v Bristol C., Division 3(S) ,Dec. 28th, 1946.

Most League Points: 57, Division 4, 1978–79.

Most League Goals: 83, Division 4, 1963–64.

Highest League Scorer in Season: John Dungworth, 26, Division 4, 1978–79.

Most League Goals in Total Aggregate: Jack Howarth, 171, 1965–71; 1972–77.

Most Capped Player: Peter Scott, 1 (10), Northern Ireland.

Most League Appearances: Len Walker, 450, 1964–76.

Record Transfer Fee Received: £30,000 and 2 players from Leicester City for Joe Jopling Sept. 1970.

Record Transfer Fee Paid: £22,000 to Torquay U. for Dave Tomlin, Aug. 1978.

Managers Since the War: Bill McCracken, Gordon Clark, Harry Evans, Dave Smith, Tom McAnearney, Jimmy Melia, Cliff Huxford.

Address of Supporters Club: c/o Recreation Ground, High St., Aldershot.

Recreation ground: High St., Aldershot, **GU11 1TW.** Telephone Aldershot 20211. *Record attendance:* 19,138 v Carlisle U., F.A. Cup 4th Rd. Replay, January 1970. *Record receipts:* £11,850 v Shrewsbury T. F.A. Cup 5th Rd., February 20, 1979. *Ground capacity:* 16,000 (14,000 under cover).

How to get there: Aldershot railway station is on the main line from London's Waterloo; the ground is five minutes walk from the station. Many buses run from the town centre on match days.
Match tickets: Can be booked in advance by telephoning ground. Available 2 weeks prior to match.
Car parking: Car parks within ¾ mile of the ground.
Entertainments/catering facilities: Members' club, Sportsman's club.
Club shop: Run by Supporters' Club; sells all types of souvenirs.
Handbooks/programmes: Programmes only available on sale.
Extra information: Harry Brooks scored five goals for Aldershot in each of two successive F.A. Cup ties in the 1945–46 season.

Club Colours: Red shirts, blue and white edging, white shorts with blue and red trim, red stockings with blue and white turnover.
Change Colours: White shirts, with blue and red edging, blue shorts with white and red trim, white stockings with blue and red turnover.
Club Captain: Joe Jopling.
Trainer: John Anderson.
Coach: Dave Turner.
Club Nickname: 'Shots'.

ALDERSHOT 1978-79 LEAGUE RECORD

Match No.	Date	Venue	Opponents	Result	H/T Score	League Pos'n	Goalscorers	Attendance
1	Aug 19	H	Wimbledon	D 1-1	1-1	—	Wooler	3510
2	22	A	Newport Co	W 2-1	2-1	—	Dungworth, Brodie	3374
3	26	A	Rochdale	D 1-1	0-0	8	Brodie	1026
4	Sept 2	H	Halifax T	W 1-0	0-0	6	Edwards	2884
5	9	A	Port Vale	D 1-1	0-0	5	Dixon	3045
6	12	H	Bradford C	W 6-0	4-0	—	Dungworth 2, Shanahan, Middleton (og), Dixon, Longhorn	3344
7	16	A	Torquay U	L 1-2	0-2	5	Shanahan	2998
8	23	H	Portsmouth	L 0-2	0-1	9		8967
9	26	A	Scunthorpe U	L 0-2	0-1			2566
10	30	H	Darlington	D 1-1	0-1	14	Dungworth	2560
11	Oct 7	A	AFC Bournemouth	W 1-0	1-0	9	Dungworth	4605
12	14	H	Hartlepool U	D 1-1	0-0	9	Shanahan	2968
13	17	H	Barnsley	W 1-0	0-0		Dungworth (pen)	3622
14	21	A	Hereford U	D 1-1	1-1	7	Dungworth	3835
15	27	A	Crewe Alex	D 1-1	1-0	8	Dixon	1937
16	Nov 4	H	Grimsby T	W 2-0	1-0	6	Shanahan, McGregor	3536
17	11	A	Halifax T	D 1-1	1-1	6	Dungworth	1438
18	18	H	Rochdale	W 1-0	1-0	6	Dungworth (pen)	3043
19	Dec 2	A	Huddersfield T	D 0-0	0-0	5		3138
20	9	H	Doncaster R	W 2-1	1-1	5	Dungworth, Howitt	3030
21	23	H	Stockport Co	W 3-2	0-2	5	Dungworth 2 (1 pen), Jopling	3115
22	26	A	Northampton T	W 3-2	2-1	—	Needham 2, Dungworth	3325
23	30	A	Wigan Ath	L 2-3	1-2	5	McGregor, Wooler	7289
24	Jan 13	H	Port Vale	D 1-1	0-0	4	Brodie	3608
25	20	H	Torquay U	W 1-0	0-0	3	Dungworth	3658
26	Feb 3	H	Scunthorpe U	W 2-0	1-0	2	Needham, Dungworth	3669
27	6	H	Reading	D 2-2	2-2	—	Dungworth, Brodie	7732
28	24	A	Hartlepool U	D 2-2	2-1	3	Dungworth, Brodie	2863
29	Mar 3	H	Hereford U	W 2-0	1-0	3	Needham 2	3932
30	7	A	Bradford C	W 2-0	1-0	—	Needham, Dungworth	3866
31	10	H	Crewe Alex	W 3-0	2-0	2	Dungworth, Brodie, Needham	3947
32	17	A	Grimsby T	D 0-0	0-0	2		6121
33	20	H	AFC Bournemouth	W 1-0	0-0	—	Edwards	5490
34	24	H	Newport Co	L 2-3	0-1	3	Tomlin, Dungworth	5243
35	27	A	Wimbledon	L 1-3	0-1	—	Longhorn	5382
36	31	H	York C	D 1-1	0-0	3	Needham	2110
37	Apr 3	A	Darlington	L 1-2	1-0	—	Needham	1267
38	7	H	Huddersfield T	W 1-0	1-0	3	Dungworth	4215
39	9	A	Stockport Co	D 2-2	1-1	—	Dungworth (pen), Henson (og)	2190
40	14	H	Northampton T	W 2-0	1-0	3	Dungworth 2	4438
41	16	A	Reading	L 0-4	0-2	—		13,273
42	21	H	Wigan Ath	W 1-0	0-0	3	Dungworth (pen)	5466
43	24	A	Barnsley	L 0-2	0-2	—		12,718
44	28	A	Doncaster R	D 1-1	1-1	5	Tomlin	1539
45	May 5	H	York C	W 1-0	0-0	5	Crosby	3675
46	15	A	Portsmouth	D 1-1	1-1	—	Dungworth	6238

Final League Position: 5

Goalscorers

League (63): Dungworth 26 (5 pens), Needham 9, Brodie 6, Shanahan 4, Dixon 3, Edwards 2, Longhorn 2, McGregor 2, Tomlin 2, Wooler 2, Crosby 1, Howitt 1, Jopling 1, Own Goals 2.
F.A. Cup (11): Dungworth 8 (1 pen), Shanahan 2, Crosby.

League Cup	First Round	Millwall (h)	0-1
		(a)	0-1
F.A. Cup	First Round	Weymouth (h)	1-1
		(a)	2-0
	Second Round	Barking (a)	2-1
	Third Round	Sheffield U (a)	0-0
		(h)	1-0
	Fourth Round	Swindon T (h)	2-1
	Fifth Round	Shrewsbury T (h)	2-2
		(a)	1-3 (a.e.t.)

Johnson	Edwards	Wooler	Dixon	Youlden	Earls	Longhorn	Brodie	McGregor	Dungworth	Tomlin	Howitt	Jopling	Hooper	Needham	Shanahan	Crosby	Green	Scott	Match No.
1	2*	3	4	5	6	7	8	9	10	11	12								1
1	2	3	4	5		7	8	11*	10		12	6	9						2
1	2	3	4		5	7	8	11	10			6	9						3
1	2	3	4	5		7	8	11	10			6		9					4
1	2	3	4	5		7	8	11	10			6	9						5
1	2	3	4	5		7	8	11	10			6			9				6
1	2	3	4	5		7	8	11	10*12		6				9				7
1	2	3	4	5			8	11	10	12		6	7	9*					8
1	2	3	4	5		7*	8		10	11		6			9	12			9
1	2*	3	4	5			8		10	11		6			9	7	12		10
1	2	3	4	5		7	8	11	10			6			9*12				11
1	2	3	4	5		7	8*11		10	12		6			9				12
1	2	3	4	5		7	8	11	10			6			9				13
1	2	3*	4	5		7	8	11	10			6			9	12			14
1	2	3	4	6		8		11	10		5				9	7			15
1	2	3	4	5		7	8	11	10			6			9*12				16
1	2	3	4	5		7	8	11	10			6		9					17
1	2	3	4	5		7	8	11	10			6		9					18
1	2	3	4	5			8	11	10						9	7			19
1	2*	3	4	5		12	8	11	10		6					9	7		20
1		3	4	5*		12	8	11	10			2	6		9	7			21
1		3	4	5		12	8*11		10			2	6		9	7			22
1		3	4	5		8		11	10			2	6		9	7			23
1		3	4	5			8	11	10			2	6		9	7			24
1		3	4	5			8	11	10			2	6		9	7			25
1		3	4	5			8	11	10			2	6		9	7			26
1		3	4	5		12	8	11*10				2	6		9	7			27
1	5	3				4	8	11	10			2	6		9	7			28
1	3			5		4	8	11	10			2	6		9	7			29
1	2	12		5		4*	8	11	10			3	6		9	7			30
1	3	12		5		4	8*11		10			2	6		9	7			31
1	3	12	4	5			8	11*10				2	6		9	7			32
1	2		4	5			8*11		10			3	6	12	9	7			33
1	2	6*12	5			4		11	10	8		3			9	7			34
1	3*		4	5			8	11	10			2	6	12	9	7			35
1	2	5*	4				8	11	10			3	6	12	9	7			36
1	6		4*	5			8	11	10			3			9	7	12	2	37
1	2*	12	5			4		11	10	8		3	6		9	7			38
1				5		4		11	10	8		2	6		9	7	3		39
1				5		4	8	11	10			3	6		9	7		2	40
1		12	5	6		4	8	11	10			2*			9	7	3		41
1				5		4	8	11	10			3	6		9	7		2	42
1			4	5		12	8	11	10			3*	6		9	7		2	43
1			4	5			8		10	11		3	6		9	7		2	44
1			4	5			8		10	11		3	6			9	7	2	45
1		3	4	5			8		10	11			6			9	7	2	46
46	31	31	36	43	3	30	38	41	46	9	28	39	3	29	14	30		9	
		+1s		+5s		+5s					+3s	+2s		+3s		+4s	+2s		

ALDERSHOT—PLAYERS

Player and position	Ht	Wt	Birthplace	Clubs	League Appearance	Goals
Goalkeepers						
Glen Johnson	6 2	13 6	Barrow	Arsenal	—	—
				Doncaster R	95	—
				Walsall (on loan)	3	—
				Aldershot	249	—
Ken Dodds	5 11	11 5	Portsmouth	Sunderland	—	—
				Mansfield T (on loan)	—	—
				Aldershot	—	—
Defenders						
Will Dixon	5 8	10 6	London	Arsenal	—	—
				Reading	150+3	—
				Colchester U	—	—
				Swindon T	134+6	10
				Aldershot	81+5	5
David Howitt	5 11	12 4	Birmingham	Birmingham C	2	—
				Bury	11+9	4
				Workington	30+5	1
				Aldershot	112+10	1
Tommy Youlden	6 0½	12 9	London	Arsenal	—	—
				Portsmouth	82+8	1
				Reading	161+2	3
				Aldershot	78	1
Joe Jopling	6 0	12 13	South Shields	Aldershot	35	1
				Leicester C	2+1	—
				Torquay U (on loan)	6	—
				Aldershot	159+9	5
*Michael Earls	6 0	11 12	Limerick	Southampton	8	—
				Aldershot	68+5	—
Alan Wooler	5 10	11 0	Poole	Reading	38	—
				West Ham U	3+1	—
				Aldershot	110+2	3
Peter Scott (N. Ireland)	5 9	11 4	Liverpool	Everton	42+2	1
				Southport (on loan)	4	—
				York C	99+1	4
				Aldershot	9	—
Nigel Edwards	5 11	11 10	Wrexham	Chester	280+9	15
				Rotherham U (on loan)	—	—
				Aldershot	31	2
Midfield						
*Wynne Hooper	5 9	10 12	Neath	Newport Co	166+14	21
				Swindon T	4+2	—
				Aldershot	21+19	1
Dennis Longhorn	5 11	11 0	Southampton	Bournemouth	23+8	1
				Mansfield T	93+3	5
				Sunderland	35+5	3
				Sheffield U	34+2	1
				Aldershot	42+5	3
Malcolm Crosby	5 9½	11 0	South Shields	Aldershot	175+20	13
Adie Green	6 0	10 9	Leicester	Leicester C	—	—
				Rochdale (on loan)	7	—
				Aldershot	0+2	—
Forwards						
Murray Brodie	5 11½	12 13	Glasgow	Leicester C	3	2
				Aldershot	326+8	61
Alex McGregor	5 10	10 8	Glasgow	Ayr U	24+5	1
				Hibernian	—	—
				Shrewsbury T	46+3	7
				Aldershot	113+1	10
Andy Needham	5 11	11 6	Oldham	Birmingham C	2+1	1
				Blackburn R	4+1	—
				Aldershot	73+3	21
John Dungworth	6 0	10 7	Rotherham	Huddersfield T	18+5	1
				Barnsley (on loan)	2+1	1
				Oldham Ath	2+2	—
				Rochdale (on loan)	14	3
				Aldershot	91	49
*Paul Findley	5 9	11 0	Farnham	Aldershot	—	—
David Tomlin	5 10	11 9	Nuneaton	Leicester C	20+7	2
				Torquay U	37+1	2
				Aldershot	9+3	2
Terry Shanahan	5 10	11 0	Paddington	Tottenham H	—	—
				Ipswich T	3+1	—
				Blackburn R (on loan)	6	—
				Halifax T	88+8	23
				Chesterfield	56+4	28
				Millwall	13+7	5
				Bournemouth	14+4	1
				Aldershot	14	4
Steve Bambridge	5 11	10 12	London	Aldershot	0+2	—
Brian Lucas	5 7	10 12	Farnborough	Aldershot	—	—
Mickey French	6 0	12 4	Eastbourne	QPR	—	—
				Brentford	56+9	16
				Swindon T	5+5	1
				Doncaster R	36	5

Free Transfers: *Gerry Gurr, *John Sainty

ARSENAL   DIV. 1

Chairman: D. J. C. Hill-Wood, M.C., M.A.
Directors: Sir Robert Bellinger, C.B.E., D.Sc., S. C. McIntyre, M.B.E., F.C.I.S., The Rev. N. F. Bone, T. D., P. D. Hill-Wood, A. Wood, W. R. Wall.
Manager: Terry Neill.   *Secretary:* K. J. Friar.
Assistant Manager/Chief Scout: Wilf Dixon.
Chief Coach: Don Howe.
Year Formed: 1886.   *Turned Pro.* 1891.   *Ltd. Co.* 1893.
Former Names: 1886–91, Royal Arsenal; 1891–1914, Woolwich Arsenal.
Former Grounds: 1886–87, Plumstead Common; 1887–88, Sportsman Ground; 1888–90, Manor Ground; 1890–93, Invicta Ground; 1893–1913, Manor Ground; 1913– Highbury.
Football League Record:
  1893 Elected to Division 2.   1913–19 Division 2.
  1904–13 Division 1.   1919–   Division 1.

Honours: Football League, Division 1, Champions: 1930–31, 1932–33, 1933–34, 1934–35, 1937–38, 1947–48, 1952–53, 1970–71; Runners-up: 1925–26, 1931–32, 1972–73; Division 2, Runners-up: 1903–04. *F.A. Cup,* Winners: 1929–30, 1935–36, 1949–50 1970–71, 1978–79; Runners-up: 1926–27, 1931–32, 1951–52, 1971–72, 1977–78. *Double Performed:* 1970–71. *League Cup* Runners-up: 1967–68, 1968–69. **European Competitions:** *Fairs Cup:* 1963–64, 1969–70 (winners), 1970–71. *European Cup:* 1971–72. *UEFA Cup:* 1978–79

Record Victory: 12-0 v Loughborough T., Division 2, Mar. 12th, 1900.
Record Defeat: 0-8 v Loughborough T., Division 2, Dec. 12th, 1896.
Most League Points: 66, Division 1, 1930–31.
Most League Goals: 127, Division 1, 1930–31.
Highest League Scorer in Season: Ted Drake, 42, 1934–35.
Most League Goals in Total Aggregate: Cliff Bastin, 150, 1930–47.
Most Capped Player: Pat Rice, 48, Northern Ireland.
Most League Appearances: George Armstrong, 500, 1960–77.
Record Transfer Fee Received: £180,000 from Liverpool for Ray Kennedy, July 1974.
Record Transfer Fee Paid: £450,000 to Ipswich T. for Brian Talbot, Jan. 1979.
Managers Since the War: George Allison, Tom Whittaker, Jack Crayston, George Swindin, Billy Wright, Bertie Mee.
Address of Club Shop or Boutique: Gunners Shop, Arsenal Stadium, Highbury, N.5.

Arsenal Stadium, Highbury, London N.5. Telephone 01-226-0304. *Ground capacity:* 60,000. *Record attendance:* 73,295 v Sunderland, Div 1, March 9, 1935. *Record receipts:* £51,477 v Anderlecht, Fairs Cup Final, April 28, 1970. *Telegraphs:* 'Gunneretic London N.5.' *Pitch measurements:* 110 yds × 71 yds.

How to get there: Arsenal Underground Station (Piccadilly Line) is within one minute of the ground. Finsbury Park (Piccadilly and Victoria) and Drayton Park (Northern) are also within walking distance. Buses 4a, 19, 106, 141a, 236.
Match tickets: Postal application one calendar month prior to the match. Prices and availability of tickets can be checked with the club on their Ansafone Service (01)–359-0131.
Car parking: Parking is allowed in the adjacent streets under the control of the Police.
Entertainments/catering facilities: West Stand restaurant is open Mon.–Fri. for the general public and on match days for ticket holders in the West Stand Upper tier. East Stand restaurant is open on match days only for ticket holders in the East Stand Upper tier. Reservations for both restaurants can be made by telephoning (01)–226-4968. There are also extensive refreshment bars around the ground.
Club shop: Shop in Avenell Road, Highbury, is open Mon.–Fri. 9.30 am. - 5 pm. On Saturday first team matches it is open from 1.00 pm. - 5.30 pm. Other shops in the ground are open on match days.
Handbooks/programmes: Handbooks and programmes can be obtained from the club shop. Programmes available on subscription.
Extra information: In 1970–71 Arsenal became the fourth club to achieve the Football League and F.A. Cup double.
Club Colours: Red shirts with white sleeves, white shorts, red and white stockings.
Change Colours: Yellow shirts with blue shorts, yellow stockings.
Club Captain: Pat Rice
Club Nickname: 'Gunners'.

ARSENAL 1978-79 LEAGUE RECORD

Match No.	Date	Venue	Opponents	Result	H/T Score	League Pos'n	Goalscorers	Attendance
1	Aug 19	H	Leeds U	D 2-2	1-1	—	Brady 2 (1 a pen)	42,057
2	22	A	Manchester C	D 1-1	1-0	—	Macdonald	39,506
3	26	A	Everton	L 0-1	0-0	15		41,179
4	Sept 2	H	QPR	W 5-1	4-0	9	Rix 2, Brady, Stapleton 2	33,474
5	9	A	Nottingham F	L 1-2	1-0	13	Brady	28,124
6	16	H	Bolton W	W 1-0	0-0	11	Stapleton	31,024
7	23	H	Manchester U	D 1-1	1-1	10	Price	45,393
8	30	A	Middlesbrough	W 3-2	1-1	9	O'Leary, Price, Walford	14,404
9	Oct 7	H	Aston Villa	D 1-1	1-0	8	Sunderland	34,537
10	14	A	Wolverhampton W	L 0-1	0-0	9		19,664
11	21	H	Southampton	W 1-0	0-0	7	Brady	33,074
12	28	A	Bristol C	W 3-1	2-1	7	Brady 2 (1 a pen), Stapleton	27,016
13	Nov 4	H	Ipswich T	W 4-1	3-1	5	Stapleton 3, Nelson	35,269
14	11	A	Leeds U	W 1-0	1-0	5	Gatting	33,961
15	18	H	Everton	D 2-2	0-1	5	Brady 2 (1 a pen)	39,801
16	25	A	Coventry C	D 1-1	0-0	5	Stapleton	26,786
17	Dec 2	H	Liverpool	W 1-0	1-0	5	Price	51,902
18	9	A	Norwich C	D 0-0	0-0	4		20,165
19	16	H	Derby Co	W 2-0	1-0	4	Price, Stapleton	26,943
20	23	A	Tottenham H	W 5-0	2-0	4	Sunderland 3, Stapleton, Brady	42,073
21	26	H	WBA	L 1-2	0-2	4	Brady (pen)	40,055
22	30	H	Birmingham C	W 3-1	1-1	4	Stapleton, Rice, Sunderland	27,877
23	Jan 13	H	Nottingham F	W 2-1	0-1	4	Price, Stapleton	52,158
24	Feb 3	A	Manchester U	W 2-0	0-0	4	Sunderland 2	45,460
25	10	H	Middlesbrough	D 0-0	0-0	4		28,371
26	13	A	QPR	W 2-1	0-0	—	Price, Brady	21,125
27	24	H	Wolverhampton W	L 0-1	0-1	2		32,215
28	Mar 3	A	Southampton	L 0-2	0-1	4		25,052
29	10	H	Bristol C	W 2-0	2-0	3	Rix, Stapleton	24,408
30	17	A	Ipswich T	L 0-2	0-1	4		26,407
31	24	H	Manchester C	D 1-1	0-1	4	Sunderland	35,014
32	26	A	Bolton W	L 2-4	1-2	—	Price, Heeley	20,704
33	Apr 3	H	Coventry C	D 1-1	0-1	—	Nelson	30,091
34	7	A	Liverpool	L 0-3	0-0	6		47,297
35	10	H	Tottenham H	W 1-0	0-0	—	Stapleton	54,041
36	14	A	WBA	D 1-1	1-0	5	Brady	28,353
37	16	H	Chelsea	W 5-2	2-0	—	O'Leary, Stapleton 2, Sunderland, Price	37,232
38	21	A	Derby C	L 0-2	0-2	6		18,674
39	25	A	Aston Villa	L 1-5	1-0	—	Stapleton	26,168
40	28	H	Norwich C	D 1-1	0-0	6	Walford	28,885
41	May 5	A	Birmingham C	D 0-0	0-0	6		14,015
42	14	A	Chelsea	D 1-1	0-1	—	Macdonald	28,386

Final League Position: 7

Goalscorers

League (61): Stapleton 17, Brady 13 (4 pens), Sunderland 9, Price 8, Rix 3, Macdonald 2, Nelson 2, O'Leary 2, Walford 2, Gatting 1, Rice 1, Heeley 1.
League Cup (1): Stapleton.
F.A. Cup (20): Sunderland 6, Stapleton 6, Talbot 2, Brady 2, Young 2, Price, Gatting.

League Cup	Second Round	Rotherham U (a)	1-3
F.A. Cup	Third Round	Sheffield W (a)	1-1
		(h)	1-1 (a.e.t.)
			2-2 (a.e.t.) (at Leicester)
			3-3 (a.e.t.) (at Leicester)
			2-0 (at Leicester)
	Fourth Round	Notts Co (h)	2-0
	Fifth Round	Nottingham F (a)	1-0
	Sixth Round	Southampton (a)	1-1
		(h)	2-0
	Semi-Final	Wolverhampton W	2-0 (at Villa Park)
	Final	Manchester U	3-2 (at Wembley)

Jennings	Devine	Nelson	Price	O'Leary	Young	Brady	Sunderland	Macdonald	Stapleton	Harvey	Kosmina	Barron	Rice	Walford	Rix	Heeley	Stead	Gatting	Talbot	McDermott	Brignall	Vaessen	Match No.
1	2	3	4*	5	6	7	8	9	10	11	12												1
	7	3	4	5	6		8	9	10			1	2	11									2
	11*	3	4	5	6	7	8	9	10			1	2	12									3
1		3	4	5	6	7	8		10				2	9	11								4
1		3	4	5*	6	7	8		10	12			2	9	11								5
1		3	4		6	7	8	9					2	5	11	10							6
1		3	4	5	6	7	8	9					2	10*	11	12							7
1	10*	3	4	5	6	7	8	9					2	12	11								8
1		3	4	5	6	7	8	9					2	10	11								9
1		3	4	5	6	7	8*	9					2	10	11		12						10
1		3			6	7		9					2	10	11	8	4	5					11
1		3	4	5*	6	7		9					2	12	11	10		8					12
1		3	4	5	6	7	8	9					2		11			10					13
1		3	4	5	6	7	8	9					2		11			10					14
1		3	4	5	6	7	8	9					2		11			10					15
1		3	4*	5	6	7	8	9					2	10	11	12							16
1		3	4	5	6	7	8	9					2		11			10					17
1		3*	4	5	6	7	8	9					2	12	11			10					18
1			4	5	6	7	8	9					2	3	11			10					19
1			4	5	6	7	8	9					2	3	11			10					20
1			4	5	6	7	8	9					2	3	11			10					21
1			4	5	6	7	8	9					2	3	11			10					22
1		3	10	5	6	7	8	9						2	11				4				23
1		3	10	5	6	7	8	9					2		11				4				24
1		3	10	5	6	7	8	9					2		11				4				25
1		3	10	5	6*	7	8	9					2	12	11				4				26
1			10	5		7	8	9					2	6	11			3	4				27
1		3	10	5		7		9					2	6	11	12		8*	4				28
1		3	10	5		7		9					2	6	11	8*			4	12			29
1		3	10*	5		7	8	9					2	6	11			12	4				30
1		3	10	5	6*		8	9					2		11	7			4	12			31
1		3	10	5			8	9					2	6	11	12		7	4*				32
1		3		5	6		8	9					2	12	11	10*		7	4				33
1			10	5	6		8	9*					2	3	11			7	4	12			34
1			10	5	6	7	8	9					2	3	11				4				35
1		3	10	5		7	8	9*					2	6	11			12	4				36
1		3	10	5		7	8	9					2	6	11				4				37
1			10		6	7	8	9					2	5	11			3	4				38
1	6		10			7	8	9					2	3	11			5	4				39
1	2	3	10			7	8	9						6	11			5	4				40
		3	10*	5	6	7	8	9				1	2	12	11				4				41
1	10	3		5	6	7		9					2		11				4		8		42
39	7	33	39	37	33	37	37	4	41	1	—	3	39	26	39	6	1	19	20	—	—	1	
									+ 1s	+ 1s				+ 7s		+ 4s	+ 1s	+ 2s		+ 2s	+ 1s		

ARSENAL—PLAYERS

Player and position	Ht	Wt	Birthplace	Clubs	League Appearances	Goals
Goalkeepers						
Pat Jennings (N. Ireland)	6 0	12 6	Newry, Co. Down	Watford Tottenham H Arsenal	48 472 81	— — —
Bob Wilson (Scotland)	6 0½	12 12	Chesterfield	Arsenal	234	—
(Contract cancelled November 1978)						
Paul Barron	6 2	13 5	London	Plymouth Arg Arsenal	44 3	— —
Nicky Sullivan	5 11½	11 9	London	Arsenal	—	—
Defenders						
Sammy Nelson (N. Ireland)	5 10	11 0	Belfast	Arsenal	210+9	8
Willie Young	6 3	12 10	Edinburgh	Aberdeen Tottenham H Arsenal	132 54 82	10 3 4
Pat Rice (N. Ireland)	5 8	11 7	Belfast	Arsenal	365+4	11
David O'Leary (Eire)	5 11	11 3	London	Arsenal	138	5
John Devine	5 10½	12 1	Dublin	Arsenal	10	—
Steve Gatting	5 11	11 11	Middlesex	Arsenal	19+2	1
Kevin Stead	5 10	11 0	West Ham	Tottenham H Arsenal	— 1+1	— —
Steve Walford	6 1	11 7	Highgate	Tottenham H Arsenal	1+1 28+10	— 2
Steve Brignall	5 7½	10 8	Kent	Arsenal	0+1	—
Keith Flight	5 8½	10 10	Woolwich	Arsenal	—	—
Chris Whyte	6 1	11 10	London	Arsenal	—	—
Midfield						
Graham Rix	5 9	11 0	Doncaster	Arsenal	80+5	6
David Price	5 11	12 2	Caterham	Arsenal Peterborough U (on loan)	86+6 6	14 1
Richie Powling	5 7	11 6	Barking	Arsenal	50+5	3
Liam Brady (Eire)	5 7	10 7	Dublin	Arsenal	193+8	36
Alan Hudson (England)	5 10½	12 1	Chelsea	Chelsea Stoke C Arsenal	144+1 105 36	10 9 —
(Contract cancelled October 1978)						
Jimmy Harvey	5 9½	11 4	Lurgan	Glenavon Arsenal	(not known) 2+1	—
Mark Heeley	5 6	9 0	Peterborough	Peterborough U Arsenal	12+5 9+6	3 1
Cliff Cant	5 11	11 11	London	Arsenal	—	—
Brian Talbot (England)	5 10	12 0	Ipswich	Ipswich T Arsenal	177 20	25 —
Dermot Drummy	5 6¾	10 4	London	Arsenal	—	—
Forwards						
Frank Stapleton (Eire)	5 11	12 7	Dublin	Arsenal	144+2	47
Malcolm Macdonald (England)	5 8	11 3	Fulham	Fulham Luton T Newcastle U Arsenal	10+3 88< br>187 84	5 49 95 42
Alan Sunderland	5 9	11 6¼	Mexborough	Wolverhampton W Arsenal	139+19 60	30 13
John Kosmina	5 11	12 4	Australia	Arsenal	0+1	—
(Contract cancelled March 1979)						
Brian McDermott	5 8	9 12	London	Arsenal	0+2	—
Paul Vaessen 1 app (Apprentice)						

ASTON VILLA DIV. 1

Chairman: Sir William Dugdale.
Vice Chairman: R. F. Bendall.
Directors: A. C. Smith, W. E. Houghton, H. G. Cressman, H. D. Ellis, D. J. Bendall.
Manager: Ron Saunders.   *Secretary:* Steven Stride.
Commercial Manager: Eric Woodward.   *Year Formed:* 1874.
Turned Professional: 1885.   *Limited Company:* 1896.
Previous Grounds: 1874–76, Aston Park; 1876–97, Perry Barr; 1897–, Villa Park.

Football League Record:
1888 Original Member of the League.

1936–38 Division 2.	1967–70 Division 2.
1938–59 Division 1.	1970–72 Division 3.
1959–60 Division 2.	1972–75 Division 2.
1960–67 Division 1.	1975– Division 1.

Honours: *League*, Division 1, Champions: 1893–94, 1895–96, 1896–97, 1898–1899, 1899–1900, 1909–10; Runners-up: 1888–89, 1902–03, 1907–08, 1910–11, 1912–13, 1913–14, 1930–31, 1932–33, Division 2, Champions: 1937–38, 1959–60; Runners-up 1974–75. Division 3, Champions: 1971–72. *F.A. Cup*, Winners: 1887, 1895, 1897, 1905, 1913, 1920, 1957 (seven wins stands as the record); Runners-up: 1892, 1924. *Football League Cup*, Winners: 1961, 1975, 1977; Runners-up: 1963, 1971.
European Competitions: UEFA Cup 1975–76, 1977–78.
Record Victory: 13-0 v Wednesbury Old Athletic, F.A. Cup 1st Rd., 1886.
Record Defeat: 1-8 v Blackburn R., F.A. Cup 3rd Rd., 1888–89.
Most League Points: 70, Division 3, 1971–72.
Most League Goals: 128, Division 1, 1930–31.
Highest League Scorer in Season: 49, 'Pongo' Waring, Division 1, 1930–31.
Most League Goals in Total Aggregate: 213, Harry Hampton, 1904–20 and Billy Walker, 1919–34.
Most League Appearances: 560, Charlie Aitken 1961–76.
Most Capped Player: Peter McParland, 33 (34), N. Ireland.
Record Transfer Fee Received: £200,000 from Derby Co. for Bruce Rioch, March 1974.
Record Transfer Fee Paid: £250,000 to Newcastle U. for Tommy Craig, Jan. 1978.
Managers Since the War: Alex Massie, George Martin, Eric Houghton, Joe Mercer, Dick Taylor, Tommy Cummings, Tommy Docherty, Vic Crowe.
Address of Club Shop or Boutique: c/o Villa ground.

Villa Park, Trinity Rd., Birmingham B6 6HE. Telephone 021-327 6604. 24 hour answering service 021-328 1722. *Telegraphic Address:* 'Villa, Birmingham 6'. *Ground capacity:* 48,000.
Record attendance: 76,588 v Derby County, F.A. Cup, 6th Rd., March 2, 1946. *Record receipts:* £88,000, F.A. Cup semi-final, Ipswich T. v West Ham U., April 5, 1975. *Club record:* £90,000 UEFA Cup quarter-final v Barcelona March 1 1978. *Pitch measurements:* 115 yds × 75 yds.

How to get there: Bus 5 from Corporation Street to Witton Square. Special buses from Priory Ringway and Hall of Memory (city centre). Birmingham New Street railway station is near the centre. The ground is ½ mile from link to the motorway.
Match tickets: Postal applications one month in advance, personal applications two weeks in advance.
Car parking: Serpentine Car Park in Aston Hall Road. Side-street parking also available.
Entertainments/catering facilities: Lions Club (members only) adjacent to the ground. Many refreshment points around the ground.
Club Shop: Adjacent to the ground; sells all types of souvenirs.
Handbooks/programmes: Programmes available on seasonal subscription.
Extra information: Aston Villa are one of only four clubs to achieve the Football League and F.A. Cup double; they did so in 1896–97.
Club Colours: Claret shirts with light blue sleeves, white shorts, blue stockings. *Change Colours:* White shirts with claret and light blue collar and cuffs, blue shorts, white stockings. *Club Nickname:* 'The Villans'

ASTON VILLA 1978-79 LEAGUE RECORD

Match No.	Date	Venue	Opponents	Result	H/T Score	League Pos'n	Goalscorers	Attendance
1	Aug 19	H	Wolverhampton W	W 1-0	0-0	—	Gray	43,922
2	23	A	Tottenham H	W 4-1	1-0	—	Evans A, Gregory, Little, Shelton	47,892
3	26	A	Bristol C	L 0-1	0-0	6		23,493
4	Sept 2	H	Southampton	D 1-1	1-1	6	Gray	34,067
5	9	A	Ipswich T	W 2-0	1-0	5	Gregory, Gray (pen)	22,166
6	16	H	Everton	D 1-1	1-1	5	Craig	38,636
7	23	A	QPR	L 0-1	0-0	7		16,410
8	30	H	Nottingham F	L 1-2	1-0	12	Craig (pen)	36,735
9	Oct 7	A	Arsenal	D 1-1	0-1	10	Gregory	34,537
10	14	H	Manchester U	D 2-2	2-0	10	Gregory 2	36,204
11	21	A	Birmingham C	W 1-0	1-0	8	Gray	36,145
12	27	H	Middlesbrough	L 0-2	0-1	10		32,615
13	Nov 4	H	Manchester C	D 1-1	0-0	10	Deehan	32,724
14	11	A	Wolverhampton W	W 4-0	2-0	9	Shelton, McNaught, Deehan, Mortimer	23,289
15	18	H	Bristol C	W 2-0	0-0	7	Deehan, Cowans	27,621
16	21	A	Southampton	L 0-2	0-2	—		20,880
17	25	H	WBA	D 1-1	0-1	9	Evans A	35,085
18	Dec 9	A	Chelsea	W 1-0	1-0	10	Evans A	19,080
19	16	H	Norwich C	D 1-1	0-0	10	McQuire (og)	26,228
20	23	A	Derby Co	D 0-0	0-0	9		20,109
21	26	H	Leeds U	D 2-2	2-0	10	Gregory 2	40,973
22	Jan 31	A	Everton	D 1-1	0-0	—	Shelton	29,079
23	Feb 24	A	Manchester U	D 1-1	0-0	12	Albiston (og)	44,437
24	Mar 3	H	Birmingham C	W 1-0	0-0	11	Cowans	42,419
25	7	H	Bolton W	W 3-0	3-0	—	Gray, Swain, Jones (og)	28,053
26	10	A	Middlesbrough	L 0-2	0-0	8		16,562
27	20	H	QPR	W 3-1	1-0	—	Evans A, Gidman (pen), Mortimer	24,310
28	24	H	Tottenham H	L 2-3	2-0	11	Gidman (pen), Gray	35,486
29	28	H	Coventry C	D 1-1	0-0	—	Evans A	25,670
30	Apr 4	A	Nottingham F	L 0-4	0-1	—		27,056
31	7	A	Coventry C	D 1-1	0-1	12	Deehan	23,690
32	11	H	Derby Co	D 3-3	1-2	—	Cowans 2, Gidman (pen)	21,884
33	14	A	Leeds U	L 0-1	0-1	14		24,281
34	16	H	Liverpool	W 3-1	2-0	—	Evans, Thompson (og), Deehan	44,029
35	21	A	Norwich C	W 2-1	1-1	10	Shelton, Cropley	15,061
36	25	H	Arsenal	W 5-1	0-1	—	Shelton 3 (1 pen), Deehan 2	26,168
37	28	H	Chelsea	W 2-1	0-1	8	Wilkins G (og), Deehan	29,219
38	May 2	H	Ipswich T	D 2-2	2-1	—	Swain, Deehan	26,636
39	5	A	Bolton W	D 0-0	0-0	8		17,394
40	8	A	Liverpool	L 0-3	0-2	—		50,570
41	11	H	WBA	L 0-1	0-1	—		35,991
42	15	A	Manchester C	W 3-2	0-1	—	Cropley, Mortimer, Deehan	30,028

Final League Position: 8

Goalscorers

League (59): Deehan 10, Gregory 7, Shelton 7 (1 pen), Gray 6 (1 pen), Evans A 6, Cowans 4, Mortimer 3, Gidman 3 (3 pens), Craig 2 (1 pen), Swain 2, Cropley 2, Little 1, McNaught 1, Own Goals 5.

League Cup (5): Gray 2, Shelton, Little, Gregory

League Cup	Second Round	Sheffield W (h)	1-0
	Third Round	C Palace (h)	1-1
		(a)	0-0 (a.e.t.)
			3-0 (at Coventry)
	Fourth Road	Luton T (h)	0-2
FA Cup	Third Round	Nottingham F (a)	0-2

	Rimmer	Gidman	Smith	Evans A	McNaught	Mortimer	Shelton	Little	Gray	Cowans	Carrodus	Gregory	Shaw	Jenkins	Craig	Evans D	Williams	Deehan	Phillips	Young	Gibson	Linton	Cropley	Swain	Ward	Ormsby	Match No.
	1	2	3	4	5	6	7	8	9*	10	11	12															1
	1	2	3	4	5	6	7	8		10	11	9															2
	1	2	3	4	5	6	7*	8		10	11	9	12														3
	1	2	3	4	5	6	7	8	9	10	11																4
	1	2*	3	4	5	6		8	9	10			7		12 11												5
	1			4	5	6	11*	8	9	10			3			7	2	12									6
	1			4	5	6	11	8		10			3			7	2		9*12								7
	1			4	5	6	11	8		10*	2	12	7			3	9										8
	1			4	5	6		8		11	2		7			3	9	10									9
	1	2			5				9	11	6		7			3	8	4	10								10
	1	2		4	5	6		8	9			10			7		3		11								11
	1	2		4	5	6		8	9			10			7		3		12 11*								12
	1	2*		12	5	6		8	9			11			7		3	10	4								13
	1	2		4	5	6	7	8				10	11				3	9									14
	1	2		4*	5	6	7					10	11				3	9		12	8						15
	1	2*12		4	5	6	7					10	11				3	9		8							16
	1	2		4	5	6						10	11	8	7		3	9									17
	1	2	3	4	5	6						10	11	8*	7			9				12					18
	1	2		4	5	6						10	11		7		3	8			9						19
	1	2		4	5	6	11					10			7		3	8			9						20
	1	2		4	5	6						10	11		7		3	9			8						21
	1	2		9	5		6	11*				10	4		7		3				12	8					22
	1	2		5			6	11				10	4		7		3					8	9				23
	1	2		5		6			8	9 10	4				7		3					11					24
	1	2		5					8	9*10	4				7		3	12				6	11				25
	1			5					8	9 10	4				7		3				2	6	11				26
	1	2		5		6		8*	9	10	4				7		3					12	11				27
	1	2		5		6		8	9	10	4				7		3						11				28
	1			5		6		8	9	10	4				7		3				2		11				29
	1	2		4	5	6		8	9		3				7								10	11			30
	1	2		4	5	6		8	7		3							9					10	11			31
	1	2			5	6*		8	7							12	9		3				10	11	4		32
	1	2		4	5	6		8	7		6						9		3				10	11			33
	1	2		4	5	6			7		8						9		3				10	11			34
	1	2			5*	6	7		8		4						9		3 12				10	11			35
	1	2				6	8		7		4						9		3				10	11		5	36
	1	2		5		6	8		7		4						9		3				10	11			37
	1	2		5		6	8		7		4						9		3				10	11			38
	1	2		8	5	6			7		4						9		3				10	11			39
	1	2		8	5	6			7		4						9		3 12				10*11				40
	1	2		4*	5	6	7				8						9		3 12				10 11				41
	1	2			5	6	7	8			4						9		3				10 11				42
	42	36	6	36	32	38	19	24	15	34	6	38	2	—	23	2	21	25	3	3	11	4	15	24	1	2	
		+ 1s	+ 1s										+ 1s	+ 1s	+ 2s		+ 2s	+ 1s	+ 2s				+ 1s	+ 4s	+ 2s		

ASTON VILLA—PLAYERS

Player and position	Ht	Wt	Birthplace	Clubs	League Appearances	Goals
Goalkeepers						
Nigel Spink	6 1	13 10	Chelmsford	Aston Villa	—	—
Jimmy Rimmer (England)	5 11	11 12	Southport	Manchester U	34	—
				Swansea C (on loan)	17	—
				Arsenal	124	—
				Aston Villa	84	—
Defenders						
John Gidman (England)	5 10	11 0	Liverpool	Liverpool	—	—
				Aston Villa	192	9
John Robson (Contract cancelled November 1978)	5 8	10 3	Consett	Derby Co	171+1	3
				Aston V	141+3	1
David Evans	5 10	12 1	West Bromwich	Aston V	2	—
Colin Gibson	5 8	10 10	Bridport	Aston V	11+1	—
Kenneth McNaught	5 11	11 1	Kirkcaldy	Everton	64+2	3
				Aston V	72	3
Allan Evans	6 0	11 12	Dunfermline	Dunfermline Ath	116	15
				Aston V	45+1	7
Gary Williams	5 9	11 7	Wolverhampton	Aston V	21+2	—
Midfield						
Dennis Mortimer	5 10	12 0	Liverpool	Coventry C	179+14	10
				Aston V	135	10
Frank Carrodus	5 9	10 11	Manchester	Manchester C	33+9	1
				Aston V	151	7
Alex Cropley (Scotland)	5 8	10 0	Aldershot	Hibernian	110+4	24
				Arsenal	29+1	5
				Aston V	64+2	7
Gordon Cowans	5 8	9 2	County Durham	Aston V	79+9	14
Tom Craig (Scotland)	5 7½	11 7	Aberdeen	Aberdeen	43+2	8
				Sheffield W	210+4	38
				Newcastle U	122+1	23
				Aston V	27	2
Gary Shelton	5 7	10 0	Nottingham	Walsall	12+12	—
				Aston V	19	7
John Gregory	6 1	11 0	Scunthorpe	Northampton T	178	8
				Aston V	59+6	10
David Cunningham	5 5	9 5	Kirkcaldy	Brechin C	44+5	6
				Southend U	56+4	4
				Hartlepool (on loan)	10+2	1
				Swindon T	18+5	3
				Peterborough (on loan)	4	1
				Aston V	—	—
Brendan Ormsby	5 10½	11 3	Birmingham	Aston V	2	—
Gary Stirland	5 8½	10 2	Middlesbrough	Aston V	—	—
Eamonn Deacy	5 8½	10 10	Galway	Aston V	—	—
Forwards						
Brian Little (England)	5 8	11 2	Durham	Aston V	213+5	55
Andy Gray (Scotland)	5 10	11 5	Glasgow	Dundee U	61+1	36
				Aston V	112+1	54
John Deehan	5 11	11 13	Solihull	Aston V	101+3	42
Ivor Linton	5 10	10 13	West Bromwich	Aston V	4+7	—
Adrian O'Dowd	5 11	11 0	Solihull	Aston V	—	—
Ken Swain	5 11	11 7	Liverpool	Chelsea	114+5	26
				WBA (on loan)	—	—
				Aston V	24	2
Joe Ward	6 0	12 5	Glasgow	Clyde	103+25	39
				Aston V	1	—
Gary Shaw	5 10	11 9	Birmingham	Aston V	2+1	—
Lee Jenkins	5 10	11 11½	West Bromwich	Aston V	0+2	—
William Young	5 7	11 7	Glasgow	Aston V	3	—
Kevin Ready	5 11½	11 11½	Wymondham	Aston V	—	—

Free transfer: *Alan Ollis

BARNSLEY   DIV. 3

Chairman: E. S. Dennis.
Directors: A. Raynor, J.P., R. F. Potter, G. Pallister, G. Buckle, N. W. B. Moody, J.P., C. Williams.
General Manager: Johnny Steele.
Secretary: Michael Spinks.
Team Manager: Allan Clarke
Year Formed: 1887. *Turned Professional:* 1888.
Limited Company: 1899.
Previous Name: Barnsley St. Peter's.
Football League Record:

1898 Elected to Division 2.	1955–59 Division 2.
1932–34 Division 3(N).	1959–65 Division 3.
1934–38 Division 2.	1965–68 Division 4.
1938–39 Division 3(N).	1968–72 Division 3.
1946–53 Division 2.	1972–79 Division 4.
1953–55 Division 3(N).	1979– Division 3.

Honours: *Football League*, best season: 3rd, Division 2, 1914–15, 1921–22. Division 3(N) Champions: 1933–34, 1938–39, 1954–55. Runners-up: 1953–54. Division 4, Runners-up: 1967–68. Promoted: 1978–79. *F.A. Cup*, Winners: 1912; Runners-up: 1910. *Football League Cup*, best season: 3rd Rd., 1962–63.
Record Victory: 9-0 v Loughborough T. Div. 2, Jan. 28th, 1899 and v Accrington Stanley at Accrington, Division 3(N), Feb. 3rd, 1934.
Record Defeat: 0-9 v Notts. Co., Division 2, Nov. 19th, 1927.
Most League Points: 67, Division 3(N), 1938–39.
Most League Goals: 118, Division 3(N), 1933–34.
Highest League Scorer in Season: Cecil McCormack, 33, Division 2, 1950–51.
Most League Goals in Total Aggregate: Ernest Hine, 123, 1921–26, 1934–38.
Most Capped Player: Eddie McMorran, 9 (15), Ireland.
Most League Appearances: Barry Murphy, 514, 1962–78.
Record Transfer Fee Received: £60,000 from West Ham U. for Anton Otulakowski, Oct. 1976.
Record Transfer Fee Paid: £45,000 to Leeds U for Allan Clarke June 1978.
Managers Since the War: Angus Seed, Tim Ward, Johnny Steele, John McSeveney, Jim Iley.

Oakwell Ground, Grove St., Barnsley. Telephone Barnsley 0226 84113. *Ground capacity:* 38,500 (15,000 under cover). *Record attendance:* 40,255 v Stoke C. February 15, 1936 F.A. Cup 5th Round. *Record receipts:* £16,146 v Rotherham U., December 16, 1978 FA Cup 2nd Rd. *Pitch measurements:* 111 yds × 75 yds.

How to get there: Fairly frequent train service from Sheffield and Leeds to Exchange Station Barnsley. No special buses, just the normal services, and no buses from town centre because the ground is so close.
Match tickets: Stand seats bookable two weeks in advance.
Car parking: Official club park adjacent to the ground holds 600 cars; parking fee 10p. The Yorkshire Traction Company Park, also adjacent, holds another 800 at the same fee. There is a free public park in Queens Road, two minutes from the ground. The M1 runs approximately two miles from the ground.
Entertainments/catering facilities: Football club social club is adjacent to the ground. Seven tea bars sited around the ground sell hot drinks and pies; six of them sell alcoholic drinks.
Club shop: Inside the ground; sells all types of souvenirs.
Handbooks/programmes: Programmes available on subscription.
Extra information: For post-match entertainment, there is Rebeccas night club in Queens Road.

Club Colours: Red shirts, white shorts, white stockings.
Change Colours: White shirts, black shorts, black stockings.
Club Captain:
Club Nickname: 'The Tykes'.

BARNSLEY 1978-79 LEAGUE RECORD

Match No.	Date	Venue	Opponents	Result Score	H/T Score	League Pos'n	Goalscorers	Attendance
1	Aug 19	H	Halifax T	W 4-2	1-0	—	Joicey 3, Little	5634
2	23	A	Crewe Alex	W 2-0	1-0	—	Clarke, Peachey	2500
3	26	A	Bradford C	W 2-1	2-1	1	Pugh, Peachey	8341
4	Sept 2	H	York C	W 3-0	2-0	1	Millar, Clarke, Pugh	8599
5	9	A	Scunthorpe U	W 1-0	0-0	1	Little	7612
6	12	H	Torquay U	L 1-2	0-2	—	Clarke	12,844
7	16	H	Huddersfield T	W 1-0	0-0	1	Clarke	11,566
8	23	A	Doncaster R	D 2-2	1-2	2	Millar, Riley	9380
9	26	A	Darlington	D 0-0	0-0	—		3475
10	30	H	Reading	W 3-1	0-0	2	Little, Saunders, Pugh	10,058
11	Oct 7	H	Northampton T	D 1-1	1-0	2	Clarke	10,102
12	13	A	Stockport Co	D 0-0	0-0	2		9054
13	17	A	Aldershot	L 0-1	0-0	—		3622
14	21	H	Wigan Ath	D 0-0	0-0	4		9841
15	28	A	Newport Co	D 1-1	1-0	4	Bell	4570
16	Nov 4	H	Wimbledon	W 3-1	1-0	3	Bell 2, Riley	11,761
17	11	A	York C	W 1-0	0-0	3	Bell	6900
18	18	H	Bradford C	L 0-1	0-1	3		11,695
19	Dec 9	A	Rochdale	W 3-0	3-0	4	Bell, Millar, Clarke	3136
20	23	H	Hartlepool U	D 1-1	0-1	4	Graham	5914
21	26	H	Port Vale	W 6-2	3-1	—	Clarke 3, Little, Graham, Millar	10,532
22	Jan 31	A	Torquay U	L 2-3	2-2	—	Bell, Graham	2714
23	Feb 10	A	Reading	L 0-1	0-1	6		6604
24	24	H	Stockport Co	D 4-4	2-0	7	Graham 2, Bell 2	9153
25	28	A	Hereford U	D 1-1	0-1	—	Collins	3100
26	Mar 3	A	Wigan Ath	D 1-1	0-0	7	Clarke (pen)	9427
27	6	H	AFC Bournemouth	W 1-0	1-0	—	Graham	7599
28	10	H	Newport Co	W 1-0	1-0	6	Clarke	9428
29	13	H	Scunthorpe U	W 4-1	1-0	—	Graham 3, McCarthy	9308
30	24	H	Crewe Alex	W 3-1	2-1	6	Bell (pen), Pugh, Little	8945
31	27	A	Halifax T	W 2-0	0-0	—	Graham, Bell (pen)	5654
32	30	H	Portsmouth	D 1-1	0-0	6	Graham	12,928
33	Apr 3	H	Doncaster R	W 3-0	1-0	—	Clarke, McCarthy, Riley	12,082
34	7	A	AFC Bournemouth	W 2-0	2-0	4	Little, Bell	3265
35	12	A	Hartlepool U	W 1-0	1-0	—	Bell	11,398
36	14	A	Port Vale	L 2-3	1-1	5	Graham, Keenan (og)	5226
37	16	H	Hereford U	W 2-1	1-1	—	Bell 2	12,260
38	21	A	Grimsby T	L 0-2	0-1	4		15,875
39	24	H	Aldershot	W 2-0	2-0	—	Bell (pen), Dungworth (og)	12,718
40	26	A	Northampton T	W 1-0	1-0	—	Bell	3305
41	28	H	Rochdale	L 0-3	0-2	4		12,051
42	30	H	Darlington	D 1-1	1-0	—	Little	10,974
43	May 2	A	Huddersfield T	L 0-1	0-1	—		9382
44	5	A	Portsmouth	W 1-0	1-0	3	Bell	8761
45	8	H	Grimsby T	W 2-1	0-0	—	Saunders, Bell	21,261
46	14	A	Wimbledon	D 1-1	0-1	—	Chambers	5794

Final League Position: 4

Goalscorers

League (73): Bell 18 (3 pens), Clarke 12 (1 pen), Graham 12, Little 7, Millar 4, Pugh 4, Joicey 3, Riley 3, McCarthy 2, Peachey 2, Saunders 2, Chambers 1, Collins 1, Own Goals 2.
League Cup (1): Little.
F.A. Cup (7): Clarke 2, Reed 2, Riley, Bell, Own Goal 1.

League Cup	First Round	Chesterfield (h)	1-2
		(a)	0-0
F.A. Cup	First Round	Worksop (h)	5-1
	Second Round	Rotherham U (h)	1-1
		(a)	1-2

Springett	Collins	Chambers	Pugh	Saunders	McCarthy	Little	Clarke	Joicey	Peachey	Millar	Riley	Prendergast	Speedie	Bell	Reed	Graham	Mallender	Copley	Banks	Match No.
1	2	3	4	5	6	7	8	9	10	11*	12									1
1	2	3	4	5	6	7	8			11	10	9								2
1	2	3	4	5	6	7	8	12	11	10		9*								3
1	2	3	4	5	6	7	8	12	11	10		9*								4
1	2	3*	4	5	6	7	8	12	11			9	10							5
1	2	3*	4	5	6	7	8			11	10	9	12							6
1	2	3	4	5	6	7*	8	10	12	11		9								7
1	2	3	4	5	6	7	8		10	11		9								8
1	2	3	4	5	6	7	8			11	10	9								9
1	2	3	4	5	6	7	8		10	11		9*	12							10
1	2	3	4	5	6	7	8			11	10	9*	12							11
1	2	3	4	5	6	7	8	12	11*	10		9								12
1	2	3	4	5	6	7	8	12	11*	10		9								13
1	2	3	4	5	6		8	11		10		9*	12	7						14
1	2	3	4	5	6	7		10*		11	9		12	8						15
1	2	3	4	5	6		8	10		11	9		12	7*						16
1	2	3	4	5	6		8	9*		10	7		12	11						17
1	2	3	4	5	6		8			10*	9		12	11	7					18
1	2	3	4*	5	6		8			10	9	12		11	7					19
1	2	3	4	5	6	7				10	9			11	8					20
1	2	3	4	5	6	7	8			10	12			11*	9					21
1	3		2*	5	6	7	8			10	4	12		11	9					22
1	2	3		5	6	4	8			10	7*			11	9	12				23
	2	3		5	6	4	8			10	7			11	9	1				24
1	2	3	4	5	6	7	8			10				11	9					25
1	2	3	4	5	6	7	8			10*	9			11			12			26
1	2	3	4	5	6	7	8			10				11	9					27
1	2	3	4	5	6	7	8			10				11	9					28
1	2	3	4	5	6	7	8			10				11	9					29
1	2	3	4	5	6	7	8			10				11	9					30
1	2	3	4	5	6	7				10	8			11	9					31
1	2	3	4	5	6	7	8*			10	12			11	9					32
1	2	3	4	5	6	7	8			10	12			11*	9					33
1	2	3	4	5	6	7				10	8			11	9					34
1	2	3		5	6	7	8			10	4			11	9					35
1	2	3	4	5	6	7				10*	8			11	9		12			36
1	2	3	4	5	6	7	8			10*	12			11	9					37
1	2	3	4	5	6	7	8*			10	12			11	9					38
1	2	3	4	5	6	7			8		10	11		9						39
1	2	3	4	5	6				10	8	12	7	11			9*				40
1	2	3	4	5		6	10			8	12	7	11			9*				41
1	2	3	4	5	6	7	8*			10	12			11	9					42
1	2	3	4	5	6	7				10	8			11	9					43
1	2	3	4	5	6	7				10	8			11	9					44
1	2	3	4*	5	6	7				10	8	12		11	9					45
1	2	3		5	6	7				10	8	4		11	9					46
45	46	45	42	46	46	40	34	6	12	43	34	1	5	32	1	27	1			
								+5s	+1s		+7s	+8s	+5s			+1s	+2s			

BARNSLEY—PLAYERS

Player and position	Ht	Wt	Birthplace	Clubs	League Appearances	Goals
Goalkeeper						
Peter Springett	5 10	11 6	Fulham	QPR	139	—
				Sheffield W	180	—
				Barnsley	182	—
Gary Copley (non-contract)				Barnsley	1	—
Defenders						
Philip Chambers	5 8	11 4	Barnsley	Barnsley	240+1	8
*Barrie Murphy	5 11	11 4	Crookham	Barnsley	509+5	3
Graham Pugh	5 9	11 2	Hoole	Sheffield W	137+4	8
				Huddersfield T	80	1
				Chester	67+2	3
				Barnsley	109+1	8
John Collins	5 9	11 0	Rhymney	Tottenham H	2	—
				Portsmouth	71+3	—
				Halifax T	82	1
				Sheffield W	7	—
				Barnsley	107+1	1
*John Saunders	6 1	12 6	Worksop	Mansfield T	90	2
				Huddersfield T	123	1
				Barnsley	149	7
Mike McCarthy	6 1	13 0	Barnsley	Barnsley	92	3
*Ian Burgin	5 8	11 6	Barnsley	Barnsley	—	—
*David Markham	5 8	11 0	Rotherham	Barnsley	—	—
*Gary Mallender	5 8	10 0	Barnsley	Barnsley	0+2	—
Midfield						
Alistair Millar	5 9	10 7	Glasgow	Barnsley	274+13	16
Alan Little	5 10	12 3	Co. Durham	Aston V	2+1	—
				Southend U	102+1	12
				Barnsley	84	14
David Speedie	5 7	10 4	Glenrothes	Barnsley	5+5	—
Ian Banks	5 9	11 13	Mexborough	Barnsley	0+2	—
Forwards						
*Peter Price	5 10	11 0	Wrexham	Liverpool	—	—
				Peterborough U	114+5	61
				Northampton T (on loan)	—	—
				Portsmouth	13+1	2
				Peterborough U (on loan)	2	—
				Barnsley	72+7	28
Brian Joicey (Retired)	6 0	12 2	Winlaton	Coventry C	31+8	9
				Sheffield W	144+1	48
				Barnsley	77+16	42
Glyn Riley	5 10	11 11	Barnsley	Barnsley	45+12	5
*Mike Prendergast	5 7	12 4	Denaby Main	Sheffield W	171+12	53
				Barnsley	12+8	2
				Halifax T (on loan)	4	1
Derek Bell	5 8	11 5	Wyberton	Derby Co	—	—
				Halifax T	104+8	21
				Sheffield W (on loan)	5	1
				Barnsley	32	18
Allan Clarke (England)	6 0	11 1	Willenhall	Walsall	72	41
				Fulham	85+1	45
				Leicester C	36	12
				Leeds U	270+3	110
				Barnsley	34	12
Tommy Graham	5 9	10 10	Glasgow	Aston V	—	—
				Barnsley	27	12
Graham Reed (apprentice)	5 10½	12 0	Doncaster	Barnsley	1	—

Free transfer: *Sean Cullen

BIRMINGHAM CITY   DIV. 2

President:
Chairman: C. K. Coombs.
Directors: H. Dare, J. F. Wiseman, N. Bosworth, LL.B. D. M. Coombs, R. Burman.
Manager: Jim Smith.   *Limited Company:* 1888.
Secretary: Alan Instone.   *Coach:* Norman Bodell
Physiotherapist: J. E. Williams.
Year Formed: 1875.   *Turned Professional:* 1885.
Previous Grounds: Waste ground near Arthur St., 1875; Muntz St., Small Heath, 1877; St. Andrew's, 1906.
Previous Name: 1875–88, Small Heath Alliance; 1888, dropped 'Alliance'; became Birmingham, 1905; became Birmingham City, 1945.

Football League Record:
Division One: 1894–96; 1901–02; 1903–08; 1921–39; 1948–50; 1955–65; 1972–79.
Division Two: 1892–94; 1896–1901; 1902–03; 1908–21; 1946–48; 1950–55; 1965–72; 1979–

Honours: Football League, best season: 6th, Division 1, 1955–56. Division 2, Champions: 1892–93, 1920–21, 1947–48, 1954–55; Runners-up: 1893–94, 1900–01, 1902–03, 1971–72, *F.A. Cup,* Runners-up: 1931, 1956, *Football League Cup,* Winners: 1963. **European Competitions:** *European Fairs Cup:* 1955–58, 1958–60 (Finalists), 1960–61 (Finalists), 1960–62.

Record Victory: 12-0 v Walsall Town Swifts, Division 2, Dec. 17th, 1892 and v Doncaster R., Division 2, Apr. 11th, 1903.

Record Defeat: 1-9 v Sheffield W., Division 1, Dec. 13th, 1930.

Most League Points: 59, Division 2, 1947–48.

Most League Goals: 103, Division 2, 1893–94 (only 28 games).

Highest League Scorer in Season: Joe Bradford, 29, Division 1, 1927–28.

Most Capped Player: Malcolm Page, 28, Wales.

Most League Appearances: Gil Merrick, 486, 1946–60.

Most League Goals in Total Aggregate: Joe Bradford, 249, 1920–35.

Record Transfer Fee Received: £975,000 from Nottingham Forest for Trevor Francis, Feb. 1979.

Record Transfer Fee Paid: £259,000 to Boca Juniors for Alberto Tarantini, Oct. 1978.

Managers Since the War: Ted Goodier, Harry Storer, Bob Brocklebank, Arthur Turner, Pat Beasley, Gil Merrick, Joe Mallett, Stan Cullis, Fred Goodwin, Willie Bell, Sir Alf Ramsey.

Address of Supporters Club: St. Andrew's Club, St. Andrew's, Birmingham 9.

Address of Club Shop or Boutique: The Beautique, 26 Cattell Road, Birmingham 9.

St. Andrews, Birmingham B9 4NH. Telephone 021-772 0101/2689. *Ground capacity:* 41,000 (9,009 seats). *Record Attendance:* 66,844 v Everton, F.A. Cup, 5th Round, February 11, 1939. *Record Receipts:* £37,794.40 v Leeds Utd., F.A. Cup, 4th Round, January 29, 1977. *Pitch measurements:* 115 yds × 75 yds.

How to get there: Buses 97, 98, 99, from Carr's Lane, City Centre, Specials from Albert Street and Hall of Memory, Broad Street. Nearest railway station, Birmingham New Street. By road; via M1, M45, and A45 to Small Heath area of Birmingham and via Cattell Road (sixth turning on the right past Small Heath Park) to the ground; via M6 (exit 6, Gravelly Hill) and A38M (Aston Expressway), leave Expressway at first exit, left into Dartmouth Street, and then via Lawley Street and Watery Lane onto the Coventry Road. Turn left and then take left fork into Cattell Road.

Match tickets: Bookable three weeks in advance.
Car parking: Public car park in Coventry Road and Cattrell Road.
Entertainments/catering facilities: Catering points inside the ground.
Club shop: Sells all types of souvenirs.
Handbooks/programmes: Programmes on sale on match days in and outside the ground; subscription rates available on request.
Extra information: In their away League programme in 1947–48, Birmingham let in only 11 goals; this is the best away performance in Division 2 since World War II.
Club Colours: Royal blue shirts, three vertical stripes on sleeves, white shorts blue trim, white stockings with blue hoops on turnover.
Change Colours: Yellow shirts, three blue vertical stripes on sleeves, yellow shorts blue trim, yellow stockings with blue hoops on turnover.
Club Nickname: 'Blues'.   *Club Captain:*   *Chief Scout:* Don Dorman.

BIRMINGHAM CITY 1978–79 LEAGUE RECORD

Match No.	Date	Venue	Opponents	Result	H/T Score	League Pos'n	Goalscorers	Attendance
1	Aug 19	A	Manchester U	L 0-1	0-0	—		56,136
2	22	H	Middlesbrough	L 1-3	1-3	—	Bertschin	24,182
3	26	H	Derby Co	D 1-1	1-1	20	Givens	21,963
4	Sept 2	A	Bolton W	D 2-2	0-0	17	Francis 2	20,284
5	9	H	Liverpool	L 0-3	0-1	21		31,740
6	16	A	Norwich C	L 0-4	0-1	22		16,407
7	23	H	Chelsea	D 1-1	0-0	21	Givens	18,458
8	30	A	Leeds U	L 0-3	0-1	22		23,331
9	Oct 7	H	Manchester C	L 1-2	0-2	22	Ainscow	18,378
10	14	A	Tottenham H	L 0-1	0-1	22		41,230
11	21	H	Aston Villa	L 0-1	0-1	22		36,145
12	28	A	Coventry C	L 1-2	0-1	22	Givens	25,446
13	Nov 4	A	WBA	L 0-1	0-1	22		31,988
14	11	H	Manchester U	W 5-1	3-1	22	Dillon, Buckley 2, Givens, Calderwood	23,550
15	18	A	Derby Co	L 1-2	1-0	22	Givens	24,720
16	21	H	Bolton W	W 3-0	1-0	—	Dillon, Buckley, Jones P (og)	21,643
17	25	H	Bristol C	D 1-1	0-1	21	Tarantini	21,552
18	Dec 2	A	Southampton	L 0-1	0-0	21		18,967
19	9	H	Everton	L 1-3	0-1	21	Buckley	23,391
20	16	A	Nottingham F	L 0-1	0-0	21		25,224
21	26	A	Wolverhampton W	L 1-2	0-1	22	Buckley	26,315
22	30	A	Arsenal	L 1-3	1-1	22	Francis (pen)	27,877
23	Feb 3	A	Chelsea	L 1-2	0-1	22	Bertschin	22,129
24	10	H	Leeds U	L 0-1	0-1	22		17,620
25	13	A	Liverpool	L 0-1	0-1	—		35,207
26	24	H	Tottenham H	W 1-0	1-0	22	Towers	20,980
27	Mar 3	A	Aston Villa	L 0-1	0-0	22		42,419
28	6	H	QPR	W 3-1	0-0	—	Buckley, Towers (pen), Broadhurst	12,650
29	10	H	Coventry C	D 0-0	0-0	22		17,311
30	24	A	Middlesbrough	L 1-2	1-2	22	Givens	15,013
31	27	H	Norwich C	W 1-0	1-0	—	Givens	12,168
32	31	A	Bristol C	L 1-2	0-1	21	Gallagher	15,584
33	Apr 3	H	Ipswich T	D 1-1	0-1	—	Gallagher	12,499
34	7	H	Southampton	D 2-2	1-0	21	Barrowclough 2 (1 pen)	12,125
35	14	H	Wolverhampton W	D 1-1	1-1	21	Ainscow	20,556
36	17	A	Ipswich T	L 0-3	0-2	—		17,676
37	21	H	Nottingham F	L 0-2	0-1	21		22,189
38	24	H	WBA	D 1-1	0-0	—	Gallagher	19,897
39	28	A	Everton	L 0-1	0-0	21		22,958
40	May 1	A	Manchester C	L 1-3	1-1	—	Lynex	27,366
41	5	H	Arsenal	D 0-0	0-0	21		14,015
42	7	A	QPR	W 3-1	1-1	—	Buckley 2, Darke	9600

Final League Position: 21

Goalscorers

League (37): Buckley 8, Givens 7, Francis 3 (1 pen), Gallagher 3, Ainscow 2, Barrowclough 2 (1 pen), Bertschin 2, Dillon 2, Towers 2 (1 pen), Calderwood 1, Tarantini 1, Broadhurst 1, Lynex 1, Darke 1, Own Goals 1.

League Cup (2): Gallagher, Francis.

League Cup	Second Round	Southampton (h)	2-5
F.A. Cup	Third Round	Burnley (h)	0-2

71

Montgomery	Calderwood	Emmanuel	Towers	Gallagher	Broadhurst	Barrowclough	Ainscow	Bertschin	Givens	Fox	Francis	Page	Pendrey	Freeman	Rathbone	Howard	Dillon	Dennis	Van den Hauwe	Tarantini	Buckley	Rioch	Dark	Ivey	Lynex	Briggs	Match No.
1	2	3	4	5	6	7	8*	9	10	11	12																1
1	2	3	4	5	6	7	12	9	11	10*	8																2
1		7		5	6	4	11	9	10		8	2	3														3
	2	12	4	5		7	10	9		8			1	3		6	11*										4
	2	10	8	5		7	12	9	11				3	1		6*	4										5
		10	8	5	6	12	7	9	11				1	3		2*	4										6
1		10	6	5	2	11	7	9	8			3				4											7
1		10	6	5	2		8	9	11		7					4	3										8
1		10	6	5		11	8	9	12		7					4	3	2*									9
1		10		5	12	11	8	9			7	6				4*	3	2									10
1	8	10		5	2			9	11		7	6					3	4									11
	2	10	4	5		11		9			7	6	1				3		8								12
	2	10	4	5*		11		9			7		1		12		3		6	8							13
		10	4	5				9	11		6		1				7	3	2	8							14
	10*		4	5		12		9	11		6		1				7	3	2	8							15
	10		4	5				9	11		6		1				7	3	2	8							16
	8		4*	5		12		9	11		6		1				7	3	2	10							17
	7		4	5				9	11		6	12	1				8	3		2*	10						18
	2*		4	5		12		9	11	8	6		1				7	3		10							19
1	2			5		11	12	9		8	6						7	3		10*	4						20
1			4	5		11		9*		8	6						10	3	2	12	7						21
1		7		5				9		8	6						11	3	2	10	4						22
1		12	5	4			7	9		8	6	3					11		2	10*							23
			4	5		7*	8	9			2		1				11	3		6	10	12					24
			4	5			8	9	12		2		1				11	3		6	10		7*				25
			4	5			7	8	9		2		1				10	3		6	12	11*					26
			4	5	11		7	8	9		2		1				10	3		6							27
			4	5	12		7	8*	9		2	3	1				10			6	11						28
	3		4	5		11	7		9		2		1				10			6	8						29
			4	5		11	7		9		2		1		6	10	3			8							30
			4	5	12	10	7		9		2	6	1			11	3			8*							31
	12		4	5	8	11	7		9*		2		1			10	3		6								32
	9		4	5		11	7				2		1			10	3		6	8							33
	8			5	4	11	7		9		2		1			10*	3		6		12						34
			4	5	2	7	8		9				1			11	3	12	6	10*							35
	2		4	5		11	7		9		10		1				6	3	8*		12						36
1	2		4	5		10	8		9		7					11	3*		6	12							37
	2			5		11	7		9		4		1			10	3	6	8								38
	2			5*		11	8		9		4		1			7	3	6	10		12						39
	2			5		10	7						1		3	6		4	8*		9	11	12				40
	2			5		10*	7		9				1		6	11	3	4	12		8						41
	2			5		7			9				1			10	3	6	8		12	11*	4				42
13	24	12	31	41	13	26	27	9	38	13	8	32	9	29	2	5	35	31	7	23	24	3	2	3	2	—	
	+ 1s	+ 1s	+ 1s		+ 3s	+ 3s	+ 4s		+ 1s	+ 1s	+ 1s		+ 1s				+ 1s		+ 1s	+ 4s	+ 3s	+ 2s			+ 1s		

BIRMINGHAM CITY—PLAYERS

Player and position	Ht	Wt	Birthplace	Clubs	League Appearances	Goals
Goalkeepers						
*Jim Montgomery	5 10	11 9	Sunderland	Sunderland	537	—
				Southampton (on loan)	5	—
				Birmingham C	66	—
Tony Coton	6 1	11 8	Tamworth	Birmingham C	—	—
Neil Freeman	6 2	14 4	Northampton	Arsenal	—	—
				Northampton (on loan)	—	—
				Grimsby T	33	—
				Southend U	69	—
				Birmingham C	29	—
Defenders						
Joe Gallagher	6 2	11 3	Liverpool	Birmingham C	199+5	16
Gary Pendrey	5 9	11 0	Birmingham	Birmingham C	287+17	4
Jimmy Calderwood	5 9	11 0	Glasgow	Birmingham C	134+10	4
Malcolm Page (Wales)	5 9	10 11	Knucklas, Rads	Birmingham C	322+11	9
*Pat Howard	5 11	12 0	Dodworth	Barnsley	176+1	6
				Newcastle U	182+2	7
				Arsenal	15+1	—
				Birmingham C	40	—
Alberto Tarantini (Argentina)	5 11	11 6	Buenos Aires	Boca J	—	—
				Birmingham C	23	1
(Contract cancelled April 1979)						
Mark Dennis	5 9	10 8	Streatham	Birmingham C	31	—
Pat Van den Hauwe	5 10	10 6	Dendermonde, Belgium	Birmingham C	7+1	—
Paul Brady	5 10	10 8	Birmingham	Birmingham C	—	—
Kevan Broadhurst	5 9½	11 2	Dewsbury	Birmingham C	25+4	2
Midfield						
Stewart Barrowclough	5 7	9 0	Barnsley	Barnsley	9	—
				Newcastle U	201+18	20
				Birmingham C	26+3	2
Kevin Dillon	5 11	10 13	Sunderland	Birmingham C	51+2	3
Tony Towers (England)	5 8½	11 2½	Manchester	Manchester C	117+5	10
				Sunderland	108	19
				Birmingham C	68+2	4
Alan Ainscow	5 6½	9 3½	Bolton	Blackpool	178+14	28
				Birmingham C	27+4	2
Forwards						
Keith Bertschin	6 1	11 8	Enfield	Ipswich T	19+13	8
				Birmingham C	51	13
Alan Buckley	5 6	10 9	Mansfield	Nottingham F	16+2	1
				Walsall	241	125
				Birmingham C	24+4	8
Don Givens (Eire)	6 0	12 2	Limerick	Manchester U	4+4	1
				Luton T	80+3	19
				QPR	242	76
				Birmingham C	38+1	7
Trevor Dark	5 9	10 9	Surrey	Birmingham C	2+3	1
Paul Ivey	5 11	10 8	Westminster	Birmingham C	3+2	—
Steve Lynex	5 9	11 0		WBA	—	—
				Shamrock R	—	—
				Birmingham C	2	—
Paul Maguire	6 0	12 0	Bootle	Blackburn R	—	—
				Birmingham C	—	—

Malcolm Briggs 0+1 sub. (Apprentice)

BLACKBURN ROVERS DIV. 3

President: W. H. Bancroft.
Chairman: D. T. Keighley.
Vice-Chairman: D. Brown.
Directors: A. L. Fryars, W. I. Hubert, W. Fox, Dr. M. Jeffries, T.D.
Chief Executive: Jimmy Armfield.
Secretary: John W. Howarth, A.A.A.I.
Manager: Howard Kendall. *Year Formed:* 1875.
Limited Company: 1897. *Turned Professional:* 1880.
Previous Grounds: 1875, Brookhouse Ground; 1876, Alexandra Meadows; 1881 Leamington Road; 1890, Ewood Park.
Previous Name: Blackburn Grammar School O.B.
Football League Record:
1888 Original Member of the League.
1936–46 Division 2.
1946–47 Division 1.
1947–57 Division 2.
1957–66 Division 1.
1966–71 Division 2.
1971–75 Division 3.
1975–79 Division 2.
1979– Division 3.

Honours: Football League, Division 1, Champions: 1911–12, 1913–14. Division 2, Champions: 1938–39; Runners-up: 1957–58. Division 3, Champions 1974–75. *F.A. Cup,* Winners: 1884, 1885, 1886, 1890, 1891, 1928; Runners-up: 1882, 1960. *Football League Cup,* Semi-Finalists: 1961–62.
Record Victory: 11-0 v Rossendale U., F.A. Cup, 1884–85.
Record Defeat: 0-8 v Arsenal, Division 1, Feb. 25th, 1933.
Most League Points: 60, Division 3, 1974–75.
Most League Goals: 114, Division 2, 1954–55.
Highest League Scorer in Season: Ted Harper, 43, Division 1, 1925–26.
Most Capped Player: Bob Crompton, 41, England.
Most League Appearances: Ronnie Clayton, 580, 1950–69 (and 57 F.A. Cup games).
Most League Goals in Total Aggregate: Tommy Briggs, 140, 1952–58.
Record Transfer Fee Received: £357,000 from Leeds U for Kevin Hird, Feb. 1979.
Record Transfer Fee Paid: £100,000 to Chelsea for Duncan McKenzie, March 1979.
Managers Since the War: Eddie Hapgood, Will Scott, Jack Bruton, Jackie Bestall, John Carey, Dally Duncan, Jack Marshall, Eddie Quigley, John Carey, Ken Furphy, Gordon Lee, Jim Smith, Jim Iley, John Pickering.

Ewood Park, Blackburn BB2 4JF. Telephone Blackburn 55432/55433. *Telegraphic Address:* 'Rovers, Blackburn'. *Ground capacity:* 47,500. *Record attendance:* 61,783 v Bolton W. F.A. Cup, 6th Rd., March 2, 1929. *Record receipts:* £25,307 v Bolton W, Division 2, April 26, 1978. *Pitch measurements:* 166 yds 2ft × 72 yds 2ft.

How to get there: Blackburn is the nearest railway station and Corporation buses run from there to the ground.
Match tickets: Seats can be booked 14 days in advance.
Car parking: Ample street parking around the ground.
Entertainments/catering facilities: Licensed refreshment bars in all parts of the ground.
Club shop: Open every day selling all types of souvenirs.
Handbook/programmes: No handbook. Programmes available on subscription from the club shop.
Extra information: In 1881–82, Blackburn Rovers were unbeaten for 35 successive matches.

Club Colours: Blue and white halved shirts, white shorts, blue stockings with two white rings.
Change Colours: Red shirts, blue shorts, red stockings with blue and white tops.
Club Nickname: 'Blue and Whites'.

BLACKBURN ROVERS 1978-79 LEAGUE RECORD

Match No.	Date	Venue	Opponents	Result	Score	H/T Score	League Pos'n	Goalscorers	Attendance
1	Aug 19	H	Crystal Palace	D	1-1	0-1	—	Metcalfe	9463
2	22	A	Preston NE	L	1-4	1-2	—	Gregory	15,412
3	26	A	Notts Co	L	1-2	1-2	21	Radford	7774
4	Sept 2	H	Orient	W	3-0	1-0	14	Radford, Gregory, Hird (pen)	6781
5	9	A	Newcastle U	L	1-3	1-0	20	Gregory	24,334
6	16	H	Leicester C	D	1-1	1-0	20	Radford	7908
7	23	A	Cardiff C	L	0-2	0-1	21		6248
8	30	H	Charlton Ath	L	1-2	0-0	21	Radford	8341
9	Oct 7	A	Bristol R	L	1-4	1-3	21	Craig	7111
10	14	H	Luton T	D	0-0	0-0	21		7450
11	21	A	Cambridge U	W	1-0	0-0	20	Hird	5240
12	28	H	Wrexham	D	1-1	1-0	20	Craig	9906
13	Nov 3	A	Fulham	W	2-1	1-1	19	Garner 2	12,500
14	11	A	Crystal Palace	L	0-3	0-2	19		17,006
15	18	H	Notts Co	L	3-4	1-3	20	Hird (pen), Craig, Radford	7893
16	21	A	Orient	L	0-2	0-0			4415
17	25	H	Stoke C	D	2-2	0-0	20	Hird, Garner	10,841
18	Dec 9	H	Brighton & H A	D	1-1	1-1	20	Radford	8046
19	16	A	Millwall	D	1-1	0-0	20	Hird	6093
20	26	A	Burnley	L	1-2	0-2	—	Hird	23,090
21	30	A	West Ham U	L	0-4	0-1	21		21,269
22	Jan 17	H	Sunderland	D	1-1	1-1	—	Garner	8130
23	20	A	Leicester C	D	1-1	0-1	20	Garner	13,234
24	Feb 10	A	Charlton Ath	L	0-2	0-1	20		5480
25	24	A	Luton T	L	1-2	1-0	22	Garner	6247
26	28	H	Cardiff C	L	1-4	1-1	—	Garner	7158
27	Mar 10	A	Wrexham	L	1-2	0-1	22	Brotherston	9407
28	14	H	Oldham Ath	L	0-2	0-2	—		8367
29	24	H	Preston N E	L	0-1	0-1	22		17,790
30	28	H	Cambridge U	W	1-0	0-0	—	Fazackerley (pen)	6448
31	31	A	Stoke C	W	2-1	1-1	21	Craig, Brotherston	17,020
32	Apr 4	A	Bristol R	L	0-2	0-1	—		8554
33	7	H	Sheffield U	W	2-0	0-0	21	Aston, Craig	10,762
34	13	A	Oldham Ath	L	0-5	0-3	—		10,056
35	14	H	Burnley	L	1-2	1-0	22	Garner	14,761
36	16	A	Sunderland	W	1-0	1-0	—	Fazackerley (pen)	35,005
37	21	H	Millwall	D	1-1	0-1	22	Waddington	5819
38	25	H	Newcastle U	L	1-3	1-1	—	McKenzie	4902
39	28	A	Brighton & Hove A	L	1-2	0-1	22	Aston	26,141
40	May 2	A	Sheffield U	W	1-0	0-0	—	Round	16,012
41	5	H	West Ham U	W	1-0	0-0	21	McKenzie	7585
42	9	H	Fulham	W	2-1	1-1	—	Taylor, Fazackerley (pen)	4684

Final League Position: 22

Goalscorers

League (41): Garner 8, Hird 6 (2 pens), Radford 6, Craig 5, Fazackerley 3 (3 pens), Gregory 3, Aston 2, Brotherston 2, McKenzie 2, Metcalfe 1, Round 1, Taylor 1, Waddington 1.
League Cup: (1) Gregory
F.A. Cup (2): Brotherston, Radford

League Cup:	Second Round	Exeter C (a)	1-2
F.A. Cup:	Third Round	Millwall (a)	2-1
	Fourth Round	Liverpool (a)	0-1

Bucher	Hird	Bailey	Fowler	Keeley	Waddington	Brotherston	Gregory	Radford	Parkes	Aston	Metcalfe	Fazackerley	Curtis	Garner	Taylor	Craig	Birchenall	Round	Morris	Ramsbottom	Rathbone	Morley	Wagstaffe	Parkin	McKenzie	Coughlin	Match No.
1	2	3	4	5	6	7*	8	9	10	11	12																1
1	2	3	4	5	6	12	8	9	10	11	7*																2
1	2	3	4	5	6	7	8	9	10	11																	3
1	2	3	7	5	10		8	9		11	4	6															4
1		3	7	5	10		8	9		11*	4	6	2	12													5
1	2	3		5	10			9		11	4	6		7	8												6
1	2	3		5	8	7		9		12	4	6		10	11*												7
1	2*	3	8	5	12	7		10			4	6				9	11										8
1		3	8	5	6	7				11*	4	2				9	10	12									9
1	2	3	8	5*	12	7		10			4	6				9	11										10
1	2	3	10	5		7		9			4	6				8	11										11
1	2	3	8	5		7		10*			4	6		12		9	11										12
1	2	3		5		7					4	6	8			9	11	10									13
1	2	3	10	5		7					4	6	8			9	11										14
1	2	3	8	5		7		10			4	6				9	11										15
1	2	3		5		7		8	10		4	6				9	11										16
1	2	3	4	5		7		8	10			6	11	9													17
1	2	3	11	5		7		8	10			6	4	9													18
1	2	3		5		7		8	10			6				9	11	4									19
1	2	3	12	5		7		8		4*	6					9	11	10									20
1	2		7	5			8			4		3	10			9*	11	6	12								21
1	2	3	11	5		7*	9			4	6		8				10	12									22
	2	3	10*	5			8			4	6		9			12	11	7	1								23
1		3	2			7		10		4	6		8			9	11	5									24
1	7	3	2					10		4	6		8			9	11	5									25
1		3	2	5		7	9			4	6		8			12	11*	10									26
			5			7	9			4	6		12			10	8			1	2	3*	11				27
			5			7	9			4	6		8			12	10			1	2	3	11*				28
		11	12			7		10		4*	6		8							1	2	3		5	9		29
		3	8			7		10			6		9							1	2		5	11	4		30
		3	8			7		10			6		9							1	2		5	11	4		31
		3	8			7					6		12	9		10*				1	2		5	11	4		32
		3	8							12	6		10	9		7*				1	2		5	11	4		33
		3	8							11	6			9*		12				1	2		5	10	4		34
		3	8	6	7								9			10				1	2		5	11	4		35
1		3	8	4	9					6	7					10					2		5	11			36
1		3	8	6	7					10	12		9								2		5*	11	4		37
1		3	10		7					6	8		9								2		5	11	4		38
1		3	10		7			12		6	8*		9								2		5	11	4		39
1		3	10		7					11	6			9	5						2			8	4		40
1		3	8		7					11	6		4	9	5				2				10				41
1		3		7							6		4	10	9		5	11				2		8			42
32	22	39	32	26	11	34	5	23	12	10	24	37	2	20	3	28	17	17	2	10	15	3	2	12	13	11	
			+ 2s		+ 2s	+ 1s				+ 3s	+ 1s			+ 5s						+ 2s	+ 1s	+ 2s	+ 2s				

BLACKBURN ROVERS—PLAYERS

Player and position	Ht	Wt	Birthplace	Clubs	League Appearances	Goals
Goalkeepers						
John Butcher	6 2	12 3	Newcastle	Blackburn R	68	—
*Neil Ramsbottom	6 0	12 0	Blackburn	Bury	174	—
				Blackpool	12	—
				Crewe A (on loan)	3	—
				Coventry C	51	—
				Sheffield W	18	—
				Plymouth Arg	39	—
				Blackburn R	10	—
*Mark Shipley	5 11	11 8	Hemsworth	Blackburn R	—	—
Defenders						
Derek Fazackerley	5 11	11 6	Preston	Blackburn R	311+1	11
Glenn Keeley	5 10	12 0	Barking	Ipswich T	4	—
				Newcastle U	43+1	2
				Blackburn R	85+1	—
John Waddington	5 11	11 7	Darwen	Liverpool	—	—
				Blackburn R	139+9	18
John Bailey	5 8	10 9	Liverpool	Blackburn R	115+5	1
*John Curtis	5 8	10 0	Poulton	Blackpool	96+6	—
				Blackburn R	9+1	—
				Wigan Ath (on loan)	9	—
Mike Rathbone			Birmingham	Birmingham C	17+3	—
				Blackburn R	15	—
Brian Morley	5 7	11 3	Fleetwood	Blackburn R	3	—
Bernard Moran	5 7	11 0	Blackburn	Blackburn R	—	—
Midfield						
Stuart Metcalfe	5 7	9 0	Blackburn	Blackburn R	359+9	21
Tony Parkes	5 10	11 0	Sheffield	Blackburn R	291+2	37
Noel Brotherston	5 8½	10 8	Belfast	Tottenham H	1	—
				Blackburn R	72+3	13
Martin Fowler	5 11	12 10	York	Huddersfield T	62+11	2
				Norwich C (on loan)	—	—
				Blackburn R	32+2	—
Russell Coughlin	5 8	11 6	Swansea	Manchester C	—	—
				Blackburn R	11	—
Forwards						
Simon Garner	5 8	11 3	Boston	Blackburn R	20+5	8
David Wagstaffe	5 8	10 8	Manchester	Manchester C	144	8
				Wolverhampton W	324	24
				Blackburn R	72+3	7
				Blackpool	17+2	1
				Blackburn R	2	—
Timothy Parkin	6 1	12 10	Penrith	Blackburn R	13	—
*Roy Taylor	5 8	10 11	Preston	Preston NE	3	—
				Blackburn R	3	1
Paul Round	6 0	11 0	Blackburn	Blackburn R	28+6	5
David Hargreaves (Contract cancelled)	5 8½	11 4	Accrington	Blackburn R	2	—
*John Radford (England)	5 11	12 12	Pontefract	Arsenal	375+4	111
				West Ham U	20	—
				Blackburn R	36	10
Peter Morris	5 7	9 8	Farnworth	Preston NE	—	—
				Blackburn R	2+2	—
John Aston	5 10	11 12	Manchester	Manchester U	139+17	25
				Luton T	171+3	31
				Mansfield T	24+7	4
				Blackburn R	10+3	2
Joe Craig (Scotland)	5 9	11 2	Alloa	Partick T	105+4	44
				Celtic	53+2	23
				Blackburn R	28+2	5
Duncan McKenzie	5 9	11 0	Luton	Nottingham F	105+6	41
				Mansfield T (on loan)	6	7
				Leeds U	64+2	27
				Anderlecht	30	16
				Everton	48	14
				Chelsea	15	4
				Blackburn R	13	2

BLACKPOOL

DIV. 3

President: L. Moore.
Chairman: W. B. Gregson.
Directors: G. Bloor (*Vice-Chairman*), S. Davies, G. S. Parr, P. J. Lawson.
Manager: Bob Stokoe. *Secretary:* W. Smith, A.C.I.S.
Year Formed: 1887. *Limited Company:* 1896.
Turned Professional: 1887.
Previous Grounds: 1887, Raikes Hall Gardens; 1897, Athletic Grounds; 1899, Raikes Hall Gardens; 1899, Bloomfield Road.
Previous Name: 'South Shore' combined with Blackpool in 1899, twelve years after the latter had been formed on the breaking up of the old 'Blackpool St. Johns' club.

Football League Record:
1896 Elected to Division 2.
1899 Failed Re-election.
1900 Re-elected.
1900–30 Division 2.
1930–33 Division 1.
1933–37 Division 2.
1937–67 Division 1.
1967–70 Division 2.
1970–71 Division 1.
1971–78 Division 2.
1978– Division 3.

Honours: Football League, Division 1, Runners-up: 1955–56. Division 2, Champions: 1929–30; Runners-up: 1936–37, 1969–70. *F.A. Cup*, Winners: 1953; Runners-up: 1948, 1951. *Football League Cup*, best season: semi-final, 1962. *Anglo-Italian Cup*, Winners 1971: Runners-up: 1972.
Record Victory: 10-0 v Lanerossi Vicenza, Anglo-Italian tournament, June 10th, 1972.
Record Defeat: 1-10 v Small Heath, Division 2, March 2nd, 1901 and 1-10 v Huddersfield, Division 1, Dec. 13th, 1930.
Most League Points: 58, Division 2, 1929–30 and 1967–68.
Most League Goals: 98, Division 2, 1929–30.
Highest League Scorer in Season: Jimmy Hampson, 45, Division 2, 1929–30.
Most League Goals in Total Aggregate: Jimmy Hampson, 247, 1927–38.
Most Capped Player: Jimmy Armfield, 43, England.
Most League Appearances: Jimmy Armfield, 568, 1952–71.
Record Transfer Fee Received: £325,000 from Everton for Mickey Walsh, August 1978.
Record Transfer Fee Paid: £105,000 to Exeter City for Tony Kellow, Nov. 1978.
Managers Since the War: Joe Smith, Ron Suart, Stan Mortensen, Les Shannon, Jimmy Meadows, Bob Stokoe, Harry Potts, Allan Brown, Jimmy Meadows.
Address of Supporters Club: Blackpool F.C., Supporters Club, Bloomfield Road, Blackpool, Lancs. (*Shop:* Same address as ground.)

Bloomfield Rd. Ground, Blackpool FY1 6JJ. Telephone Blackpool 46118. *Telegraphic address:* 'Football Blackpool'. Ground capacity: 29,540. Record attendance: 39,118 v Manchester U., Division 1, April 1952. Record receipts: £22,223 v Bolton Wanderers, Division 1, December 27, 1977. Pitch measurements: 111 yds × 73 yds.

How to get there: Coliseum bus station, Lytham Road, 10 minutes' walk. Railway: South station (a few minutes' walk from ground) and North station.
Match tickets: Bookable four weeks in advance of the match.
Car parking: Car park for 1,000 cars. Street parking available.
Entertainments/catering facilities: Refreshment and licensed bars. Entertainment after the game at the Supporters' Club by prior arrangement.
Club shop: In Bloomfield Road sells all types of souvenirs.
Handbooks/programmes: Programmes available from the development shop.
Extra information: When England lost 6-3 to Hungary in November 1953, there were four Blackpool players – Stanley Matthews, Stan Mortensen, Harry Johnston, and Ernie Taylor – in the team.
Club Colours: Tangerine shirts with white stripe on sleeves, collars and cuffs, white shorts, tangerine with white trim stockings.
Change Colours: White shirts, tangerine shorts and tangerine stockings.
Club Captain: Peter Suddaby.
First Team Coach: Stan Ternant.
Club Nickname: 'The Seasiders'.

BLACKPOOL 1978-79 LEAGUE RECORD

Match No.	Date	Venue	Opponents	Result	H/T Score	League Pos'n	Goalscorers	Attendance
1	Aug 19	H	Oxford U	W 1-0	0-0	—	Davidson	6215
2	22	H	Watford	L 1-5	1-3	—	Wilson	11,812
3	26	A	Rotherham U	L 1-2	0-2	19	Davidson	4572
4	Sept 2	H	Carlisle U	W 3-1	0-0	13	Spence 3	7789
5	9	A	Shrewsbury T	L 0-2	0-1	18		4179
6	12	H	Chesterfield	D 0-0	0-0	—		6244
7	16	H	Walsall	W 2-1	0-0	14	Spence, McEwan (pen)	8153
8	23	A	Swindon T	W 1-0	0-0	12	Chandler	6607
9	26	H	Gillingham	W 2-0	1-0	—	Wagstaffe, Davidson	5722
10	30	H	Colchester U	L 1-3	0-0	—	Hockaday	3007
11	Oct 7	H	Lincoln C	W 2-0	0-0	6	Spence, Chandler	7080
12	14	A	Southend U	L 0-4	0-2	10		6374
13	18	A	Exeter C	L 0-3	0-3	—		3921
14	21	H	Mansfield T	W 2-0	0-0	8	Chandler, Weston	6633
15	28	A	Plymouth Arg	D 0-0	0-0	10		8886
16	Nov 4	H	Sheffield W	L 0-1	0-1	15		9403
17	11	A	Carlisle U	D 1-1	0-0	15	Chandler	6505
18	18	H	Rotherham U	L 1-2	1-2	16	Sunddaby	6085
19	Dec 9	H	Peterborough U	D 0-0	0-0	16		4280
20	23	H	Chester	W 3-0	1-0	13	Spence 2, Kellow	4106
21	26	A	Tranmere R	W 2-0	0-0	11	Ronson, Bramhall (og)	3491
22	30	A	Swansea C	L 0-1	0-0	13		12,549
23	Feb 3	A	Gillingham	L 0-2	0-0	15		6146
24	6	A	Walsall	L 1-2	0-1	—	Kellow	3711
25	10	H	Colchester U	W 2-1	1-0	13	Spence 2	3448
26	20	H	Hull C	W 3-1	0-1	—	Kellow, Weston, Spence	3636
27	24	H	Southend U	L 1-2	1-2	13	Spence	4566
28	Mar 3	A	Mansfield T	D 1-1	0-0	13	Spence	4829
29	6	A	Bury	W 3-1	1-0	—	Spence 2, Jones	4575
30	10	H	Plymouth Arg	D 0-0	0-0	12		4879
31	14	A	Chesterfield	W 3-1	1-0	—	Ronson 2, Kellow	4638
32	20	H	Shrewsbury T	W 5-0	1-0	—	McEwan 2, Kellow 2, Suddaby	5330
33	24	H	Watford	D 1-1	1-1	9	McEwan	9253
34	28	A	Oxford U	L 0-1	0-0	—		2924
35	31	A	Brentford	L 2-3	2-0	9	Weston 2	6360
36	Apr 7	H	Bury	L 1-2	1-0	13	Kellow	5451
37	13	A	Chester	L 2-4	0-1	—	Jones, Thompson	4439
38	14	H	Tranmere R	W 2-0	2-0	14	Spence, Jones	4798
39	16	A	Hull C	D 0-0	0-0	—		6000
40	21	H	Swansea C	L 1-3	0-1	15	Kellow	5977
41	24	H	Exeter C	D 1-1	0-0	—	Kellow	3136
42	28	A	Peterborough U	W 2-1	0-0	15	Kellow 2	4004
43	May 5	H	Brentford	L 0-1	0-0	15		3464
44	7	A	Lincoln C	W 2-1	0-0	—	Hockaday 2	1949
45	15	H	Swindon T	W 5-2	2-1	—	Chandler, Malone, McEwan (pen), Spence, Hockaday	4191
46	17	A	Sheffield W	L 0-2	0-2	—		7310

Final League Position: 12

Goalscorers

League (61): Spence 16, Kellow 11, McEwan 5 (2 pens), Chandler 5, Weston 4, Hockaday 4, Jones 3, Davidson 3, Ronson 3, Suddaby 2, Wilson 1, Wagstaffe 1, Thompson 1, Malone 1, Own Goal 1.
League Cup (7): Davidson 3, McEwan 2 (2 pens), Spence 1, Own Goal 1.
F.A. Cup (3): McEwan (pen), Chandler, Kellow.

League Cup	First Round	Carlisle U (a)	2-2
		(h)	2-1
	Second Round	Ipswich T (h)	2-0
	Third Round	Manchester C (h)	1-1
		(a)	0-3
F.A. Cup	First Round	Lincoln C (h)	2-1
	Second Round	Bury (a)	1-3

Ward	Gardner	Thompson	Wilson	Suddaby	McEwan	Spence	Tong	Holden	Wagstaffe	Davidson	Hockaday	Waldron	Chandler	Pashley	Ronson	Hesford	Sermanni	Bissell	Weston	Malone	May	Kellow	Jones	Kerr	Hall	Milligan	Bowey	Match No.
1	2	3	4	5	6	7*	8	9	10	11	12																	1
1	2	3	4	5	6	9	8		11	10		7*12																2
1	2	6	4	5	8	9		12	11	10	7*		3															3
1	2	4		5	6	9			11	7			10	3	8													4
1	2	4		5	6	9	8	11*10					12	3	7													5
1	2	4		5	6	9			11	10	7*		12	3	8													6
1	2	4		5	6	9			11	10	7		12	3	8*													7
	2	4		5	6	9*			11	10	12		7	3		1	8											8
	2	4		5	6	9			11*10	12			7	3	8	1												9
	2	6		5	4	9				11		8	3	7	1	12	10*											10
	2	4		5	6	9			12	10	3		7	3	8*	1												11
	2	4		5	6	9			10	11*			7	3	8	1		12										12
1	2	4	12	5	6	9			11*10					3	8			7										13
1	2	4	10*	5	6	9			11				12	3	8			7										14
1	2	4		5	6	9*			11				10	3	8		12	7										15
1	2*	4		5	6	9			11				10	3	8		12	7										16
1		4		5	6	9			11				7	3	8			10	2									17
1				5	6	9			12	11	10		3					7	2	4*	8							18
	2	4			6				12				10	3		1	11	7*	5		8	9						19
		4		5	6	10			12	11			3	7	1			2			8	9*						20
		4		5	6	9			11	10			3	8	1			2			7							21
		4		5	6	9			11*10				3	8	1			2			7	12						22
		4	8	5	6				11*10				3	7	1		12	2			9							23
		4*		5	6				10				3	8	1	12	11	2			7	9						24
		4		5	6	9			11*10				3	8	1			2			7	12						25
				5	6	9			10				11	3		1	8	4	2		7*12							26
	12			5	6	9			10				11	3		1	4	7	2		8*							27
		4		5	6	9			10				11*12	3		1		7	2		8							28
		4		5	6	9			10					3	8	1		11	2		7							29
		4		5	6	9			10					3		1		11	2		8	7						30
		4		5	6	9							3	10	1			11	2		7	8						31
				5	6	9				4			3	10	1			11	2		7	8						32
				5	4	9				6			3	10	1			11	2		7	8						33
		4		5	6	9			12				3	10*	1			11	2		7	8						34
			10*	5	6	9							3	4	1			11	2		7	12	8					35
		12		5	6	9						10	3		1			11	2		7		8*	4				36
		4		5	6	9				7			10	3*	1			11	2		8	12						37
	2	4		5	6	9				11					1			10	3		7	8						38
		4			6	9								1	7			11	2	5	8				3	10		39
		4			6	9						10	1	7*				11	2	5	8	12		3				40
	3	4		5	6	9							10	1				11	2		8	7						41
	6	4		5	3	9			12				10	1				11	2		7	8*						42
	10	5		3	6	9			7					4	1			11*	2		8	12						43
		4		5	6	9			7	11			10	1				3	2*		8	12						44
	12	4		5*	6	9			7	11			10	1				3	2		8							45
	2	4	12		6				7	11			10	1				3*		5	8	9						46
13	22	38	7	42	46	42	2	2	17	23	13	5	18	35	32	33	6	1	29	29	4	25	11	7	1	2	1	
	+	+	+					+	+	+	+	+			+	+			+				+					
	1s	1s	3s					1s	2s	2s	5s	6s			4s	2s			8s									

BLACKPOOL—PLAYERS

Player and position	Ht	Wt	Birthplace	Clubs	League Appearances	Goals
Goalkeepers						
Iain Hesford	6 1½	12 9	Noola, Kenya	Blackpool	47	—
*Bob Ward	6 1	12 0	W Bromwich	WBA	9	—
				Northampton T (on loan)	8	—
				Blackpool	41	—
Defenders						
Peter Suddaby	5 11	12 2	Stockport	Blackpool	315+1	9
Paul Gardner	5 9	11 8	Southport	Blackpool	75+1	—
*Laurence Milligan	5 7	12 0	Liverpool	Blackpool	19	—
				Portsmouth (on loan)	7	—
Max Thompson	6 1	12 10	Liverpool	Liverpool	1	—
				Blackpool	49+2	1
Terry Pashley	5 8	10 12	Chesterfield	Burnley	16+2	—
				Blackpool	35	—
John May	5 11	11 4	Crosby	Blackpool	4	—
Bobby Fleming	5 9	10 12	Edinburgh	Blackpool	—	—
Dick Malone	6 0	12 2	Motherwell	Ayr U	163	5
				Sunderland	235+1	2
				Hartlepool U	36	2
				Blackpool	29	1
Midfield						
Willie Ronson	5 6	9 9	Fleetwood	Blackpool	124+4	12
*John Cruickshank	5 11	11 1	Oldham	Blackpool	—	—
Alan Waldron	5 7½	9 8	Royton	Bolton W	127+14	6
(Contract cancelled April 1979)				Blackpool	22+1	1
Keith Bowey	5 6	9 8	Newcastle	Blackpool	1	—
Pat Coyle	5 10	10 13	Gweedore	Blackpool	—	—
Bobby Tynan	5 10	11 0	Liverpool	Tranmere R	193+2	25
				Blackpool	—	—
Jimmy Hall	5 9	9 3	Bootle	Blackpool	1	—
Vic Davidson	5 9	10 9½	Glasgow	Celtic	13+1	6
(Transferred to Celtic April 1979)				Motherwell	59+7	11
				Blackpool	23+2	3
Brian Jackson	5 8½	11 2	Liverpool	Southport	—	—
				Blackpool	—	—
Forwards						
Jimmy Weston	5 9	10 7	Skelmersdale	Blackpool	65+5	5
Stanley McEwan	5 11	12 2	Cambusrethan	Blackpool	107+7	6
Brian Wilson	5 9	10 5	Newcastle	Blackpool	14+6	2
Derek Spence	6 0	11 0	Belfast	Oldham Ath	5+1	—
(N Ireland)				Bury	140	44
				Olympiakos	—	—
				Blackpool	66+3	18
David Hockaday	5 10	10 9½	Billingham	Blackpool	16+7	4
Jeff Chandler	5 7	10 2	Hammersmith	Blackpool	31+6	7
Tom Sermanni	5 8	11 2	Glasgow	Albion R	138+13	38
				Blackpool	6+4	—
Mel Holden	6 1	10 4	Dundee	Preston NE	69+3	22
(Contract cancelled September 1978)				Sunderland	66+7	23
				Blackpool	2+1	—
Bobby Kerr	5 4½	9 3	Alexandria	Sunderland	355+13	57
				Blackpool	7	—
Shaun Rowlands	5 10	11 5	Doncaster	Blackpool	—	—
Tony Kellow	5 10	12 0	Falmouth	Falmouth	—	—
				Exeter C	107	40
				Blackpool	25	11
Carl Howarth	5 9	9 10	Manchester	Blackpool	—	—
Garry Jones	5 9	10 2	Manchester	Bolton W	195+8	42
				Sheffield U (on loan)	3	1
				Blackpool	11+8	3
*Steve Bissell	5 8½	11 0	Birmingham	Blackpool	1	—

BOLTON WANDERERS DIV. 1

President: J. Battersby.
Chairman: G. Warburton.
Vice-Chairman: J. W. Woods.
Directors: B. Cowsill, J. Lightbown, H. D. Warburton, S. Jones, G. E. Ashworth.
Manager: Ian Greaves.
Asst. Manager: Stan Anderson.
Secretary: Des McBain.   *Year Formed:* 1874.
Turned Professional: 1880.   *Limited Company:* 1895.
Previous Grounds: Park Recreation Ground and Cockle's Field before moving to Pike's Lane Ground 1881; Burnden Park 1895.
Previous Name: 1874–77, Christ Church F.C.; 1877, became Bolton Wanderers.
Football League Record:
1888 Original Member of the League.

1899–1900 Division 2.	1909–10 Division 1.	1935–64 Division 1.
1900–03 Division 1.	1910–11 Division 2.	1964–71 Division 2.
1903–05 Division 2.	1911–33 Division 1.	1971–73 Division 3.
1905–08 Division 1.	1933–35 Division 2.	1973–78 Division 2.
1908–09 Division 2.		1978– Division 1.

Honours: Football League: best season: 3rd, Div. 1, 1891–92, 1920–21, 1924–25. Division 2, Champions: 1908–09, 1977–78; Runners-up: 1899–1900, 1904–05, 1910–11, 1934–35. Division 3 Champions 1972–73. *F.A. Cup,* Winners: 1923, 1926, 1929, 1958; Runners-up: 1894, 1904, 1953. *Football League Cup,* best season: Semi-final, 1976–77.
Record Victory: 13-0 v Sheffield U., F.A. Cup, 2nd Rd., Feb. 1st, 1890.
Record Defeat: 0-7 v Manchester C., Division 1, Mar. 21st, 1936.
Most League Points: 61, Division 3, 1972–73.
Most League Goals: 96, Division 2, 1934–35.
Highest League Scorer in Season: Joe Smith, 38, Division 1, 1920–21.
Most Capped Player: Nat Lofthouse, 33, England.
Most League Appearances: Eddie Hopkinson, 519, 1956–70.
Most League Goals in Total Aggregate: Nat Lofthouse, 255, 1946–61.
Record Transfer Fee Received: £85,000 from Newcastle U. for Wyn Davies, Oct. 1966.
Record Transfer Fee Paid: £350,000 to WBA for Len Cantello, May 1979.
Managers Since the War: Walter Rowley, Bill Ridding, Nat Lofthouse, Jimmy McIlroy, Jimmy Meadows, Nat Lofthouse, Jimmy Armfield.
Address of Supporters Club: Supporters Club, Burnden Park, Manchester Road, Bolton.
Address of Club Shop or Boutique: 'The Happy Shop', Burnden Park, Bolton.

Burnden Park, Bolton, BL3 2QR. Telephone Bolton 389200. Information Service: Bolton 21101. *Ground capacity:* 43,000. *Record attendance:* 69,912 v Manchester C., F.A. Cup, February 18, 1933. *Record receipts:* £53,931 v Everton L.C. semi-final, 2nd Leg, February 15th, 1977. *Pitch measurements:* 113 yds × 76 yds.
How to get there: Local buses 8, 524, 523, 542, 543. The nearest station is Trinity St. in the town centre.
Match tickets: Bookable two weeks in advance.
Car parking: Private car parking only on Burnden forecourt. Large park only 200 yards from the ground. Limited street parking in the vicinity. Multi-storey parks in the town centre.
Entertainments/catering facilities: Prerecorded programmes of news, interviews, and record requests. Burnden Sporting Club not now available to the general public. Refreshment bars in each section of the ground and in the Sporting Club.
Club shop: On main car park. Open Mon-Sat. Send S.A.E. for mail order list.
Handbooks/programmes: Programmes available on subscription from club shop.
Extra information: History of club written by Dr Percy Young.
Club Colours: White shirts, navy blue shorts, white stockings.
Change Colours: Red shirts, white shorts, red stockings white trim.
Club Captain: Roy Greaves.
Club Coach: W. Joyce.
First Team Trainer: Jim Headrige.
Club Nickname: 'Trotters'.

BOLTON WANDERERS 1978–79 LEAGUE RECORD

Match No.	Date	Venue	Opponents	Result	H/T Score	League Pos'n	Goalscorers	Attendance
1	Aug 19	H	Bristol C	L 1-2	1-0	—	Gowling	21,355
2	22	A	Southampton	D 2-2	1-1	—	Worthington 2	21,059
3	26	A	WBA	L 0-4	0-3	21		23,237
4	Sept 2	H	Birmingham C	D 2-2	0-0	20	Worthington 2 (1 a pen)	20,284
5	9	H	Derby Co	W 2-1	0-1	14	Gowling 2	20,331
6	16	A	Arsenal	L 0-1	0-0	18		31,024
7	23	H	Newcastle U	W 3-2	1-2	16	Worthington 2, Whatmore	19,901
8	30	A	Liverpool	L 0-3	0-2	18		47,099
9	Oct 7	H	Leeds U	W 3-1	0-1	17	Morgan, Smith, Worthington	27,751
10	14	A	Chelsea	L 3-4	3-0	17	Gowling 2, Worthington (pen)	19,879
11	21	H	Manchester C	D 2-2	1-1	15	Gowling, Worthington	32,249
12	28	A	Tottenham H	L 0-2	0-1	18		37,337
13	Nov 4	H	Coventry C	D 0-0	0-0	19		22,379
14	11	A	Bristol C	L 1-4	1-1	19	Walsh	18,168
15	18	H	WBA	L 0-1	0-0	19		22,273
16	21	A	Birmingham C	L 0-3	0-1	—		21,643
17	25	H	Nottingham F	L 0-1	0-0	19		25,692
18	Dec 2	A	QPR	W 3-1	3-0	19	Gowling, Worthington 2	11,635
19	9	H	Wolverhampton W	W 3-1	1-0	17	Greaves, Worthington (pen), Gowling	21,006
20	16	A	Ipswich T	L 0-3	0-1	19		16,593
21	22	H	Manchester U	W 3-0	2-0	17	Worthington 2, Gowling	32,390
22	26	A	Middlesborough	D 1-1	1-0	17	Worthington	20,125
23	Feb 3	A	Norwich C	D 0-0	0-0	17		15,369
24	24	H	Chelsea	W 2-1	1-1	17	Burke, McNab	19,457
25	Mar 3	A	Manchester C	L 1-2	0-1	18	Worthington	41,127
26	7	A	Aston Villa	L 0-3	0-3	—		28,053
27	17	A	Coventry C	D 2-2	2-2	18	Worthington, McNab	15,231
28	21	A	Derby Co	L 0-3	0-2	—		15,227
29	24	H	Southampton	W 2-0	0-0	18	Gowling 2	19,879
30	26	H	Arsenal	W 4-2	2-1	—	Gowling 2, Worthington 2 (pens)	20,704
31	31	H	Nottingham F	D 1-1	1-0	17	Gowling	29,015
32	Apr 3	H	Everton	W 3-1	1-1	—	Morgan, Whatmore, Jones	27,263
33	7	H	Q.P.R.	W 2-1	1-1	17	Worthington, Gowling	21,119
34	11	A	Manchester U	W 2-1	0-1	—	Worthington 2	49,617
35	14	H	Middlesborough	D 0-0	0-0	16		22,621
36	16	A	Everton	L 0-1	0-1	—		31,214
37	21	H	Ipswich T	L 2-3	1-2	17	Worthington, Allardyce	20,073
38	25	A	Leeds U	L 1-5	0-2	—	McNab	20,218
39	28	A	Wolverhampton	D 1-1	0-0	17	Whatmore	18,225
40	May 1	H	Liverpool	L 1-4	0-1	—	Souness (og)	35,200
41	5	H	Aston Villa	D 0-0	0-0	17		17,394
42	8	H	Tottenham	L 1-3	1-1	—	Worthington	17,879

Final League Position: 17

Goalscorers

League (54): Worthington 24 (5 pens), Gowling 15, McNab 3, Whatmore 3, Morgan 2, Allardyce 1, Smith 1, Walsh 1, Burke 1, Jones (P) 1, Greaves 1, Own Goals 1.
League Cup (3): Worthington 2 (1 pen), Gowling.
F.A. Cup (1): Smith.

League Cup	Second Round	Chelsea (h)	2-1
	Third Round	Exeter C (a)	1-2
F.A. Cup	Third Round	Bristol C (a)	1-3

McDonagh	Nicholson	Walsh	Greaves	Jones P	Allardyce	Morgan	Whatmore	Train	Gowling	Worthington	Dunne	Jones G	Graham	Burke	Smith	Reid	McNab	Nowak	Match No
1	2	3	4	5	6*	7	8	9	10	11	12								1
1	2*	5	4	12	6	7	8	11	9	10	3								2
1		5	4	2*	6	7	8	11	10	9	3	12							3
1		5	4		6	7	8	11	10	9		2	3						4
1	2	5	4			7	8	11*	9	10	3			6	12				5
1	2	5	4	6		7	8		9	10				3	11				6
1	2	5*	4	6	12	7	8		9	10				3	11				7
1	2	5	4	6		7	8		9	10				3	11				8
1		5	4	2	6	7		8*	9	12				3	11	10			9
1		5	6	2	4	7	12	9*	10					3	11	8			10
1	2	5	4		6	7			9	10				3	11	8			11
1	2	5	4		6	7			9	10				3	11	8			12
1	2	5	4	6		7			9	10	3				8	11			13
1	2	5	4			7	12		9	10	3*			6	8	11			14
1	2	6	4	5		7			9	10				3	8	11			15
1	2	6	4	5		7	12		9	10				3	8*	11			16
1	2	3	4	5	6	7			9	11					8	10			17
1	2	6	4	5		7			9	10	3				8	11			18
1	2	6	4	5		7			9	10	3				8	11			19
1	2	6	4	5		7			9	10	3				8	11			20
1	2	6	4	5		7			9	10	3				8	11			21
1	2	6	4	5		7			9	10	3				8	11			22
1	2	6	4	5		7	9			10	3			8		11			23
1	2		4	6	5	7			9	10	3			8		11			24
1	2	6	4	5		7	12		9	10	3			8*		11			25
1	2	6	4	5		7	12		9	10	3			8*		11			26
1	2	6	4*	5	8	7			9	10	3			12		11			27
1	2	6		5*	8	7	12		9	10				3		11			28
1	2	6	4	5		7	8		9	10	3					11			29
1	2	6	4	5		7	8		9	10	3					11			30
1	2	6	4	5		7	8		9	10	3					11			31
1	2	6	4	5		7	8		9	10	3					11			32
1	2*	6	4	5		7	8		9	10	3					11	12		33
1		6	4	5		7	8		9	10	3	2				11			34
1		6	4	5	12	7	8		9	10	3*	2				11			35
1		3	4	5	6	7	8		9	10		2				11			36
1	2	3		5*	6	7	8		9	10					11		4	12	37
1		6	4		5	7	8			10		2	3	9		11			38
1	10	5	4		6	7	8		9	3		2				11			39
1	2	6	4		5	7	8		10	3		11				9			40
1	2	6	4		5	7	8		10			11	3			9			41
1	2	6	4		5		8		10			11	3*	12		9	7		42
42	34	42	41	31	18	41	23	5	36	42	24	—	9	19	18	14	22	1	
				+ 1s	+ 2s		+ 6s				+ 2s	+ 1s		+ 1s	+ 2s		+ 1s	+ 1s	

BOLTON WANDERERS—PLAYERS

Player and position	Ht	Wt	Birthplace	Clubs	League Appearances	Goals
Goalkeepers						
Jim McDonagh	5 11½	13 12	Rotherham	Rotherham U	121	—
				Manchester U (on loan)	—	—
				Bolton W	119	—
Terry Poole	6 1	13 0	Chesterfield	Huddersfield T	207	—
				Bolton W	—	—
David Felgate	6 1	13 12	Blaenau Ffestiniog	Bolton W	—	—
				Rochdale (on loan)	35	—
Defenders						
Tony Dunne	5 6½	9 11	Dublin	Manchester U	415	2
(Eire) (Contract cancelled April 1979)				Bolton W	166+4	—
Paul Jones	5 11	10 10	Ellesmere Port	Bolton W	300+4	34
Mike Walsh	5 11	11 7	Manchester	Bolton W	97+8	2
Sam Allardyce	6 1½	13 4	Dudley	Bolton W	164+3	19
Mike Graham	5 10	11 3	Lancaster	Bolton W	9+1	—
Peter Nicholson	5 11½	11 8½	Cleator Moor	Blackpool	3+3	—
				Bolton W	249+12	12
Roy Heaney	5 7½	11 11	Liverpool	Bolton W	—	—
*Craig Wardle	6 0	11 12	Radcliffe	Bolton W	—	—
Midfield						
Peter Reid	5 8	11 3	Huyton	Bolton W	160+3	16
Roy Greaves	5 11	11 12	Farnworth	Bolton W	466+6	64
Willie Morgan	5 8	11 2	Glasgow	Burnley	183	19
(Scotland)				Manchester U	236+2	23
				Burnley	12+1	—
				Bolton W	133+1	7
Brian Smith	5 7	11 5	Bolton	Bolton W	43+6	3
				Bradford C (on loan)	8	—
Mike Carter	5 8	10 1	Warrington	Bolton W	—	—
				Mansfield T (on loan)	18	4
David Burke	5 10	10 1	Liverpool	Bolton W	19+1	1
Neil McNab	5 7	10 10	Greenock	Morton	11+3	—
				Tottenham H	63+9	3
				Bolton W	22+1	3
Phillip Wilson	5 6	10 4	Hemsworth	Bolton W	—	—
Tadeusz Nowak	6 0	11 2	Trzcinsko, Poland	Legia	—	—
(Poland)				Bolton W	1+1	—
Forwards						
Neil Whatmore	5 9	11 3	Ellesmere Port	Bolton W	186+14	72
*Jan Novacki	5 6	9 6	Manchester	Bolton W	—	—
				York C (on loan)	24+1	3
Chris Thompson				Bolton W	—	—
Frank Worthington	5 10½	11 10	Halifax	Huddersfield T	166+5	42
(England)				Leicester C	209+1	72
				Bolton W	76+1	35
Alan Gowling	6 0	11 10	Stockport	Manchester U	64+7	18
				Huddersfield T	128	58
				Newcastle U	91+1	30
				Bolton W	42+2	15
John Keighley	5 7½	10 5	Ribchester	Bolton W	—	—
James Moores	5 7	9 10	Macclesfield	Bolton W	—	—

AFC BOURNEMOUTH

DIV. 4

Chairman: H. G. Walker, LL.B.
Directors: E. G. Keep, P. W. Hayward, W. J. L. Mackeen, H. G. Berwick, S. F. Holttum, G. P. Pound, F. Ward, S. A. Latter
Secretary: G. H. MacKrell, A.C.C.A.
Manager: Alec Stock.
Commercial Manager: D. Dowsett.
P.R.O.: J. D. King.   *Year Formed:* 1899.
Turned Professional: 1912.   *Limited Company:* 1914.
Previous Names: Boscombe St. Johns, 1890–99; Boscombe F.C., 1899–1923; Bournemouth & Boscombe Ath. F.C. 1923–1971.
Previous Grounds: 1899–1910, Castlemain Road, Pokesdown, Dean Court 1910.

Football League Record:
Elected to Division 3(S), 1923. Remained a Third Division Club for record number of years until 1970; 1970–71 Division 4. 1971–75, Division 3. 1975– Division 4.

Honours: *Football League,* best season in Division 3, 3rd 1961–62, 1971–72. Division 3(S), Runners-up: 1947–48. Promotion from Division 4: 1970–71. (2nd). *F.A. Cup,* best season: 6th Rd., 1956–57. *Football League Cup,* best season: 4th Rd., 1962, 1964.

Record Victory: 11-0 v Margate, F.A. Cup 1st Rd., Nov. 20th, 1971.

Record Defeat: 1-8 v Bradford C., Division 3, Jan. 24th, 1970.

Most League Points: 62, Division 3, 1971–72.

Most League Goals: 88, Division 3(S), 1956–57.

Highest League Scorer in Season: Ted MacDougall 42, 1970–71.

Most League Goals in Total Aggregate: Ron Eyre. 202, 1924–33.

Most Capped Player: Tommy Godwin, 4 (13), Eire.

Most League Appearances: Ray Bumstead, 412, 1958–70.

Record Transfer Fee Received: £195,000 from Manchester U. for Ted MacDougall, Sept. 1972.

Record Transfer Fee Paid: £70,000 to Cardiff C. for Brian Clark, Oct. 1972.

Managers Since the War: Harry Kinghorn, Harry Lowe, Jack Bruton, Freddie Cox, Don Welsh, Bill McGarry, Reg Flewin, Freddie Cox, John Bond, Trevor Hartley, John Benson.

Address of Supporters Club Shop: The Cherry Bees Shop, Dean Court, Bournemouth, BH7 7AF.

Dean Court Ground, Bournemouth. Telephone Bournemouth 35381. *Telegraphic address:* 'Football Bourn'th'.   *Ground capacity:* 22,000.   *Record attendance:* 28,799 v Manchester U., F.A. Cup 6th Rd., March 2, 1957.   *Record Receipts:* £9,525 v Portsmouth, Division 4, Sept 29, 1978.   *Pitch measurements:* 117 yds × 75 yds.

How to get there: Nearest station Bournemouth on the main line from London (Waterloo). Corporation bus 25.
Car parking: Adequate parking for 1500 cars.
Entertainments/catering facilities: Refreshment points around the ground.
Club shop: Sells all types of souvenirs.
Handbooks/programmes: No handbook. Programmes available on subscription.
Extra information: The club did not compete in the F.A. Cup in 1923–24, their first League season, because their election came too late for them to be exempt from the preliminary rounds.

Club Colours: Red shirts with white trim, black shorts, black stockings with red and white tops.
Change Colours: Navy blue and white vertical striped shirts, white shorts, white stockings.
Club Captain: Keith Miller.   *Club Coach:* Fred Davies.   *Club Nickname:* 'Cherries'.   *Trainer* John Kirk.

AFC BOURNEMOUTH 1978–79 LEAGUE RECORD

Match No.	Date	Venue	Opponents	Result	H/T Score	League Pos.n	Goalscorers	Attendance
1	Aug 19	H	Newport Co	W 3-1	1-0	—	Massey (pen), Finnigan, Walker (og)	3083
2	22	A	Scunthorpe U	L 0-1	0-0	—		2433
3	26	A	Darlington	D 0-0	0-0	12		1890
4	Sept 2	H	Hartlepool U	L 0-1	0-1	15		2658
5	9	A	Crewe Alex	L 0-1	0-0	17		1693
6	12	H	Huddersfield T	W 2-0	0-0	—	Brown, Showers	2416
7	16	H	Rochdale	W 3-1	2-1	13	Barton, Impey, Butler	2674
8	23	A	Port Vale	W 2-1	2-1	10	Massey, Butler M	3140
9	26	A	Doncaster R	D 1-1	1-0	—	Butler M	2441
10	29	H	Portsmouth	W 3-1	1-1	6	Butler M, Showers, Massey	10,056
11	Oct 7	H	Aldershot	L 0-1	0-1	8		4605
12	14	A	Hereford U	D 0-0	0-0	8		3752
13	16	A	Stockport Co	L 0-1	0-0	—		4092
14	21	H	Grimsby T	D 0-0	0-0	12		3399
15	28	A	Halifax T	W 2-0	1-0	10	Massey 2	1184
16	Nov 4	H	Torquay U	W 1-0	0-0	7	Butler M	3747
17	11	A	Hartlepool U	D 0-0	0-0	8		3227
18	18	H	Darlington	D 2-2	1-0	7	Butler M 2	6005
19	Dec 9	H	York C	L 1-2	1-1	8	Walsh (og)	3323
20	23	H	Wimbledon	L 1-2	1-2	8	Lennard	3922
21	26	A	Reading	L 0-1	0-0	—		6706
22	30	A	Bradford C	L 1-2	1-0	15	Brown R	4026
23	Jan 13	H	Crewe Alex	L 0-1	0-1	16		2855
24	Feb 3	H	Doncaster R	W 7-1	1-0	14	Scott 2, MacDougall 2, Lennard, Johnson, Barton	2986
25	6	H	Port Vale	W 3-1	2-0	—	Scott, Brown R, MacDougall	3416
26	10	A	Portsmouth	D 1-1	0-0	10	Johnson	12,172
27	21	H	Northampton T	D 0-0	0-0	—		3990
28	24	H	Hereford U	D 1-1	1-0	10	Brown K	4292
29	Mar 3	A	Grimsby T	L 0-1	0-0	11		5428
30	6	A	Barnsley	L 0-1	0-1	—		7599
31	10	H	Halifax T	W 1-0	0-0	10	MacDougall	3078
32	13	A	Huddersfield T	L 1-2	0-1	—	Borthwick	2268
33	17	A	Torquay U	W 1-0	0-0	10	MacDougall	2159
34	20	A	Aldershot	L 0-1	0-0	—		5490
35	24	H	Scunthorpe U	D 0-0	0-0	9		3028
36	31	A	Wigan Ath	L 0-1	0-1	12		5527
37	Apr 3	A	Rochdale	L 1-2	0-1	—	Butler M	1136
38	7	H	Barnsley	L 0-2	0-2	15		3265
39	10	A	Wimbledon	L 0-4	0-3	—		3205
40	14	H	Reading	D 0-0	0-0	17		5638
41	16	A	Northampton T	L 2-4	1-3	—	Brown K, MacDougall	2253
42	21	H	Bradford C	W 1-0	0-0	18	MacDougall	2679
43	23	H	Stockport Co	W 3-1	1-0	—	MacDougall, Brown K 2	2285
44	28	A	York C	L 1-2	1-2	18	Scott	2171
45	May 1	A	Newport Co	L 0-2	0-0	—		2235
46	5	H	Wigan Ath	W 2-1	0-0	17	Massey, Johnson	3063

Final League Position: 18

Goalscorers

League (47): Butler M 8, MacDougall 8, Massey 6 (1 pen), Brown K 4, Scott 4, Brown R 3, Johnson 3, Barton 2, Lennard 2, Showers 2, Borthwick 1, Finnigan 1, Impey 1, Own Goals 2.
League Cup (1): Brown.
F.A. Cup (4): MacDougall 2, Massey (pen), Butler M.

League Cup	First Round	Exeter C (h)	0-1
		(a)	1-1
F.A. Cup	First Round	Hitchin (h)	2-1
	Second Round	Wimbledon (a)	1-1
		(h)	1-2 (a.e.t.)

87

Allen	Cunningham	Miller	Impey	Brown R	Butler G	Brown K	Showers	Butler M	Massey	Lennard	Finnigan	Johnson	Borthwick	Benson	Barton	MacDougall	Scott	Ferns	Weeks	Holder	Benjafield	Match No.
1	2	3	4	5	6	7	8	9	10	11*12												1
1	2	3	4	5	6	11	8	9	10			7										2
1	2	3	4	5		11		9	10*		8	7	6	12								3
1	2	3	4	5		11*12		9	10		8	7	6									4
1	2	3	4	5		11	12	9		10	8	7		6*								5
1	2	3	4	5		11	8	9	10	7			6									6
1	2	3	4	5		11	8	9	10				6		7							7
1	2	3	4	5		11	8	9	10	7					6							8
1	2	3	4	5		11	8*	9	10			12	7		6							9
1	2	3	4	5		11	8	9	10			12	7*		6							10
1	2	3	4	5		11	8	9	10			12	7*		6							11
1	2	3	4	5		11	8	9	10				6		7							12
1	2	3	4	5		11	8	9	10		12		7*		6							13
1	2	3	4	5		11	8	9	10*			12	6		7							14
1	2	3	4	5		11		9	10			8	7		6							15
1	2	3	4	5		11		9	10			8	7		6							16
1		3	4	5	2	11		9	12			10*	7		6	8						17
1		3	4	5	2	11		9	10	12			7*		6	8						18
1	2	3	4	5				9	10	11		12	7		6*	8						19
1	2	3	4	5			10	9		11			7		6	8						20
1	2	3	4	5			10	9		11			7		6	8						21
1	2	3	4	5		11			10				7		6	8	9					22
1	2		4	5			9		10*	11	6				7	8	12	3				23
1	2		4	5					10	11	7				6	8	9	3				24
1	2	3	4	5		12			10*	11	7				6	8	9					25
1	2	3	4	5		10*		12		11	7				6	8	9					26
1	2	3	4	5				10		11	7				6	8	9					27
1	2	3	4	5		10*		12		11	7				6	8	9					28
1	2	3	6	5				10	12		7*				8	9	4	11				29
1	2	6	4	5				11*		12	7				8	9	3	10				30
1	2	3	4	5					10	11	6				8	9		7				31
1	2	3	4	5				12	10	11*	7				8	9		6				32
1		2	4	5			9*11	10			7				8	12	3	6				33
1		2	4*	5			9	11	10		6				8	12	3	7				34
1	2		4			5	9	11	10*	12	6				8		3	7				35
1		4		5	2		9	11	10		6				8		3	7				36
1	2	4		5			9	12	10	11*	7				8		3		6			37
1	2	4		5			9	11	12		6					10	3		7	8*		38
1		2	4	5	12		9*11	10			7				8		3	6				39
1	2	4		5	10			11			7				8	9	3	6				40
1		2		5	10			11		12	7				8	9	3	4*	6			41
1	2	3	4	5	10					11	7				8	9		6				42
1	2	3	4	5	10					11	7				8	9		6				43
1	2	3	4	5	10					11*	7				8	9	12	6				44
1	2	10	4	5	11			12			7				8	9*	3	6				45
1	2	3	4	5	10			12		11	7				8	9*		6				46
46	39	46	38	45	6	28	14	28	29	18	3	20	42	1	22	29	18	14	3	15	2	
					+2a	+2s		7s	3s	2s	8s		+1s			3s	+1s					

AFC BOURNEMOUTH—PLAYERS

Player and position	Ht	Wt	Birthplace	Clubs	League Appearances	Goals
Goalkeepers						
Ken Allen	6 4	12 10	Thornaby on Tees	Bournemouth	46	—
Defenders						
John Benson	5 10	11 10	Arbroath	Manchester C	44	—
(Contract cancelled January 1979)				Torquay U	233+8	7
				Bournemouth	85+8	—
				Exeter C (on loan)	4	—
				Norwich C	29+2	—
				Bournemouth	56+1	—
John Impey	6 0	12 7	Exeter	Cardiff C	13+4	—
				Bournemouth	126+4	5
*Ian Cunningham	5 11	10 11	Glasgow	Bournemouth	114+8	3
*Geoff Butler	5 7	11 0	Middlesbrough	Middlesbrough	54+1	1
				Chelsea	8+1	—
				Sunderland	0+2	—
				Norwich C	151+2	1
				Bournemouth	102+1	1
Roger Brown	6 1	11 10	Tamworth	Bournemouth	63	3
Gary Borthwick	5 7	10 4	Slough	Bournemouth	47+2	1
Phil Ferns	5 11	11 4	Liverpool	Bournemouth	14+1	—
Tom Heffernan	5 9		Dublin	Tottenham H	—	—
*Jon Moore	5 10	11 3	Cardiff	Bristol R	—	—
				Millwall	119	5
Midfield						
Keith Miller	5 9½	10 10	Lewisham	West Ham U	1+2	—
				Bournemouth	359+1	19
*Dave Lennard	5 9	11 0	Manchester	Bolton W	114+5	3
				Halifax T	97	16
				Blackpool	42+3	9
				Cambridge U	39+1	6
				Chester	73+2	11
				Stockport Co	39	4
				Bournemouth	56+3	4
Trevor Finnigan	5 11	11 0	Bedlington	Blackpool	13+4	3
(Contract cancelled January 1979)				Bournemouth	23+2	5
*Graham Weeks	5 8	10 6	Exeter	Exeter C	49+4	1
				Bournemouth	3	—
Frank Barton	5 9½	11 11½	Barton on Humber	Scunthorpe U	93	26
(Contract cancelled March 1979)				Carlisle U	161+4	22
				Blackpool	18	1
				Grimsby T	123	15
				Bournemouth	66	13
				Hereford U	22	3
				Bournemouth	22	2
Philip Holder	5 4	11 6	Kilburn	Tottenham H	9+4	1
				C Palace	92+2	5
				Bournemouth	15	—
Kenny Brown	5 8	9 0	Barnsley	Barnsley	267+10	24
				Bournemouth	28+2	4
Brian Benjafield	5 9	10 9	Barton on Sea	Bournemouth	2	—
Forwards						
*Peter Johnson	5 8	10 10	Islington	Orient	1+2	—
				C Palace	5+2	—
				Bournemouth	99+8	11
Ted MacDougall	5 10	11 11	Inverness	Liverpool	—	—
(Scotland)				York C	84	34
(Contract cancelled May 1979)				Bournemouth	146	103
				Manchester U	18	5
				West Ham U	24	5
				Norwich C	112	51
				Southampton	86	42
				Bournemouth	29	8
Mick Butler	5 9	10 0	Barnsley	Barnsley	118+2	58
				Huddersfield T	73+6	21
				Bournemouth	28	8
Joey Scott	5 10	12 2	Plymouth	Bournemouth	18+3	4
Steve Massey	5 11	11 0	Stockport	Stockport Co	87+14	20
				Bournemouth	29+7	6

Trevor Wallbridge (non-contract) 0+1 sub

BRADFORD CITY DIV. 4

Chairman: R. Martin.
Vice-Chairman: J. Dunne.
Directors: J. H. Garside, K. D. Morrison, W. Roper, E. Sutcliffe, R. Stead.
Manager: George Mulhall.
Secretary: T. F. Newman.
Year Formed: 1903.
Turned Professional: 1903.
Limited Company: 1908.
Football League Record:

1903 Elected to Division 2.	1961–69 Division 4.
1908–22 Division 1.	1969–72 Division 3
1922–27 Division 2.	1972–77 Division 4.
1927–29 Division 3. (N)	1977–78 Division 3.
1929–37 Division 2.	1978– Division 4.
1937–61 Division 3.	

Honours: *Football League*, highest League position, 5th Division 1, 1910–11. Division 2, Champions: 1907–08. Division 3(N), Champions: 1928–29. *F.A. Cup*, Winners: 1911 (first holders of the present trophy). *Football League Cup* best season: 5th Rd., 1965.

Record Victory: 11-1 v Rotherham U., Division 3(N), Aug. 25th, 1928.
Record Defeat: 1-9 v Colchester U., Division 4, Dec. 30th, 1961.
Most League Points: 63, Division 3(N), 1928–29.
Most League Goals: 128, Division 3(N), 1928–29.
Highest League Scorer in Season: David Layne, 34, Division 4, 1961–62.
Most League Goals in Total Aggregate: Frank O'Rourke, 88, 1906–13.
Most Capped Player: Harry Hampton, 9, Ireland.
Most League Appearances: Ian Cooper, 443, 1965–77.
Record Transfer Fee Received: £40,000 from Peterborough U. for Joe Cooke, Jan. 1979.
Record Transfer Fee Paid: £25,000 to Leeds U. for David McNiven, Feb. 1978.
Managers Since the War: Jack Barker, John Milburn, David Steele, Ivor Powell, Peter Jackson, Bob Brocklebank, Bill Harris, Willie Watson, Grenville Hair, Jimmy Wheeler, Bryan Edwards, Bobby Kennedy, John Napier.

Valley Parade Ground, Bradford BD8 7DY. Telephone Bradford 306062. *Ground capacity:* 23,469. *Record attendance:* 39,146 v Burnley, F.A. Cup 4th Rd., March 11, 1911. *Record receipts:* £27,000 v Southampton, F.A. Cup 6th Rd., March 6, 1976. *Pitch measurements:* 110 yds × 76 yds.

How to get there: Ground situated approximately ¾ mile from city centre along Manningham Lane. Corporation buses 23–26 from Cheapside plus specials. West Yorkshire buses from Chester St. bus station. The nearest railway station is Bradford Exchange. By road, the ground is approximately ¼ mile from Ring Road towards Bradford.
Car parking: Club car park off Valley Parade holds 100 cars. Street parking in most side-streets. No parking in Valley Parade or South Parade.
Entertainments/catering facilities: Hot drinks, pies, crisps, etc. available at snack bars in the ground.
Club shop: Adjacent to ground entrance; sells all types of souvenirs.
Handbooks/programmes: Programmes will be sent on receipt of remittance and S.A.E. c/o City Shop, Valley Parade.
Extra information: A Bradford firm designed the present F.A. Cup, the third actual trophy, in 1910. The first club to win it was Bradford City in 1911.

Club Colours: White shirts with Amber and claret trimmings, white shorts, with amber and claret stripe, White with Amber and Claret trim stockings.
Change Colours: Amber shirts with maroon shorts, amber stockings.
Club Captain: Paul Reaney.
First Team Trainer: Colin Kaye.
Club Nickname: 'The Paraders'.

BRADFORD CITY 1978-79 LEAGUE RECORD

Match No.	Date	Venue	Opponents	Result	H/T Score	League Pos'n	Goalscorers	Attendance
1	Aug 19	A	Portsmouth	W 1-0	1-0	—	Jackson D	8268
2	23	H	Hereford U	W 2-1	2-0	—	Hutchins, Dolan	5376
3	26	H	Barnsley	L 1-2	1-2	9	McNiven	8341
4	Sept 2	A	Northampton T	L 0-1	0-0	13		3320
5	9	H	Stockport Co	D 1-1	0-0	12	Dolan (pen)	5001
6	12	A	Aldershot	L 0-6	0-4	—		3344
7	16	A	Wigan Ath	W 3-1	0-0	15	Cooke, McNiven, Martinez	7090
8	23	H	Newport Co	L 1-3	1-2	16	Cooke	4470
9	27	H	Halifax T	W 3-0	0-0	—	Baines, Cooke, Jackson D	4115
10	30	A	Wimbledon	L 1-2	1-0	15	Baines	2819
11	Oct 7	A	Reading	L 0-3	0-1	19		5651
12	14	H	York C	W 2-1	1-0	16	Cooke, McNiven	4026
13	18	H	Port Vale	L 2-3	0-0	—	McNiven, Cooke	4136
14	21	A	Scunthorpe U	L 2-3	0-1	20	Baines 2	2778
15	28	H	Huddersfield T	D 1-1	0-0	20	Hutchins	5478
16	Nov 4	A	Doncaster R	L 0-2	0-0	21		2981
17	11	H	Northampton T	W 3-0	1-0	21	Hutchins, McNiven, Dolan	3361
18	18	A	Barnsley	W 1-0	1-0	18	Cooke	11,695
19	Dec 9	A	Crewe Alex	W 2-1	0-1	18	Dolan, Cooke	1956
20	26	H	Rochdale	W 1-0	0-0	—	McNiven	4882
21	30	H	AFC Bournemouth	W 2-1	0-1	11	Dolan, Baines	4026
22	Jan 9	A	Grimsby T	L 1-5	0-2	—	Dolan	4975
23	12	A	Stockport Co	L 0-1	0-1	13		3573
24	Feb 14	A	Torquay U	W 2-1	0-1	—	Wood, Robertson	1912
25	24	A	York C	D 2-2	1-1	16	Wood 2	4022
26	27	A	Newport Co	W 4-2	2-1	—	Robertson, Dolan, McNiven 2	4225
27	Mar 3	A	Scunthorpe U	D 1-1	0-0	10	Robertson	4988
28	7	H	Aldershot	L 0-2	0-1	—		3866
29	10	A	Huddersfield T	D 0-0	0-0	13		6188
30	13	H	Reading	L 2-3	0-1	—	Baines, McNiven	3387
31	24	A	Hereford U	L 1-3	0-1	17	Cook	2925
32	28	H	Portsmouth	W 2-0	0-0	—	Dolan, McNiven	2410
33	31	H	Darlington	D 0-0	0-0	15		2643
34	Apr 4	H	Wimbledon	W 1-0	0-0	—	Dolan (pen)	2701
35	7	A	Hartlepool U	D 2-2	0-1	12	Jackson D, Hutchins	2143
36	11	H	Torquay U	W 3-1	0-1	—	Szabo, Baines, Hutchins	2453
37	14	A	Rochdale	L 0-1	0-1	11		2262
38	16	H	Grimsby T	L 1-3	0-2	—	McNiven	4585
39	21	A	AFC Bournemouth	L 0-1	0-1	14		2679
40	24	A	Port Vale	L 1-2	0-0	—	Baines	2262
41	26	A	Halifax T	L 0-2	0-2	—		2343
42	28	H	Crewe Alex	W 6-0	3-0	14	Baines 2, McNiven 3, Martinez	2109
43	30	H	Doncaster R	W 1-0	0-0	—	Johnson	2189
44	May 2	H	Hartlepool U	L 1-2	1-2	—	McNiven	1950
45	5	A	Darlington	D 1-1	1-1	13	Hutchins	1558
46	7	H	Wigan Ath	D 1-1	1-1	—	Jackson P	3748

Final League Position: 15

Goalscorers
League (62): McNiven 15, Baines 10, Dolan 9 (2 pens), Cooke 7, Hutchins 6, Jackson D 3, Robertson 3, Wood 3, Martinez 2, Cook 1, Johnson 1, Szabo 1, Jackson P 1.
League Cup (6): Cooke 2, Johnson, Hutchins, Dolan (pen), Baines.
F.A. Cup (3): Dolan 2 (1 pen), Cooke.

League Cup	First Round	Lincoln C (h)	2-0
		(a)	1-1
	Second Round	Burnley (a)	1-1
		(h)	2-3
F.A. Cup	First Round	Port Vale (h)	1-0
	Second Round	Stockport Co (a)	2-4

Downsborough	Reaney	Wood	Podd	Baines	Middleton	Bates	Dolan	Jackson, D	McNiven	Hutchins	Martinez	Cooke	Watson	Smith	Johnson	Szabo	Robertson	Jackson, P	Gilliver	Cook	Match No.
1	2	3	4	5	6	7	8	9	10	11											1
1	2	3	7	5	6	4	8	9	10*	11	12										2
1	2	3	7	5	6	4	8	9	10	11											3
1	2	3	8	5	6	4	7	11*	10			9	12								4
	2	3	7	5	6	4	8	12	10		11*	9		1							5
	2	3		5	6	4	8		10		11	9		1	7						6
	2	3		5	6	4	8		10		11	9*		1	7	12					7
	2	3		5	6	4	8*		10		11	9		1	7	12					8
1			2	5	6	4		8			11	9	3		7	10					9
1			2	5	6	4		8*	12		11	9	3		7	10					10
1	2	3	7	5			4	6	10	11		9			8						11
1*	2	3	8	5	6	4			10	11		9			7	12					12
	2	3	7*	5	6	4			10	11		9		1	8	12					13
	2	3	7	5	6	4			10	11		9		1	8						14
1		3	2	5	6	4			10	11		9	7		8						15
1		6	2	5		4	8		10	11		9	3		7						16
1	4	6	2	5			8		10	11	7	9	3								17
1	4	6	2	5			8		10	11	7	9	3								18
1	7	6	2		5	4	8		10	11		9	3								19
1	4	6	2		5	7	8		10	11	12		3			9*					20
1	4	6	2	9	5	7	8		10	11			3								21
1*	4	6	2	9	5	7	8		10	11	12		3								22
	4	6	2	5		7	8		9*	11	12		3	1		10					23
1	4*	6	2	5			8		10	11			3		12	7		9			24
1		6	2	5			4		10	11			3		7	8		9			25
1		6	2	5			8		10	11			3		4	7		9			26
1		6	2	5			8		10	11	12		3		4*	9		7			27
1	2	6	3	5			8		10	11					4	7		9			28
1	2	6	3	5			8		10	11					4	7		9			29
1	2	3		5	6	11	8		10		12				4*	7		9			30
	2	3		5		8	4		10		11*			1	12	7	6	9			31
	2	3		5	6	4	8		10					1	9	7					32
	2	3		5	6	8*	4	12	10	11				1	7	9					33
	4*	6	2	5		9	8	12	10	11			3	1		7					34
		6	2		5	9	8	4	10	11			3	1		7					35
		6	2	5		9	8	7		11			3	1	10		4				36
	4	3	2	5		10*	8	7		11			6	1		9	12				37
	4	7	2	5			8		10	11			3	1		9	6				38
	4	6	2	5	12		8		10	11	7*		3	1				9			39
1	4	6	2	5		9	8		10	11			3			7*	12				40
	6	2	5	4		8		10*	11	12			3	1	7	9					41
1		3*	2	5			8		10	11	7		6		9	12	4				42
	4		2	9		6			10	11	7		3	1	8		5				43
		6	2	9			8		10	11	7		3	1	4		5				44
	4		2	9		6			10	11	7		3	1	8		5				45
		5	2	9			8		10	11	7		3	1		6	4				46
25	33	42	39	43	23	30	40	9	42	37	15	16	28	21	24	8	14	8	1	8	
					+ 1s		+ 3s	+ 1s		+ 7s		+ 1s		+ 2s	+ 5s		+ 1s	+ 1s			

BRADFORD CITY—PLAYERS

Players and position	Ht	Wt	Birthplace	Clubs	League Appearances	Goals
Goalkeepers						
Peter Downsborough	5 10½	13 2	Halifax	Halifax T	148	—
				Swindon T	274	—
				Brighton (on loan)	3	—
				Bradford C	225	—
Steve Smith	6 0	12 5	Lydney	Birmingham C	2	—
				Bradford C	21	—
Defenders						
Cec Podd	5 9	10 0	St Kitts, W. Indies	Bradford C	309+6	—
*John Middleton	5 10	11 7	Rawmarsh	Bradford C	188+4	5
Mick Wood	5 11	10 13	Bury	Blackburn R	140+7	2
				Bradford C	54	3
Stephen Baines	6 0	12 12	Newark	Nottingham F	2	—
				Huddersfield T	113+1	10
				Bradford C	53+1	11
Paul Reaney (England)	5 9	11 7½	Fulham	Leeds U	551+6	6
				Bradford C	33	—
Peter Jackson	6 1		Bradford	Bradford C	8+1	1
Midfield						
Gary Watson	5 8	10 6	Bradford	Bradford C	141+13	21
*Rodney Johnson	5 7½	11 4	Leeds	Leeds U	18+3	4
				Doncaster R	106+1	23
				Rotherham U	108+2	8
				Bradford C	190+2	16
Eugene Martinez			Chelmsford	Bradford C	27+12	2
Mick Bates	5 7	10 7	Doncaster	Leeds U	106+21	4
				Walsall	84+1	4
				Bradford C	30	—
Barry Gallagher			Bradford	Bradford C	—	—
Forwards						
Don Hutchins	5 7	10 2	Leicester	Leicester C	4	—
				Plymouth Arg	94+2	23
				Blackburn R	37+3	6
				Bradford C	207	40
Terry Dolan	6 1	11 3	Bradford	Bradford C	—	—
				Bradford PA	46+2	—
				Huddersfield T	157+5	14
				Bradford C	128+1	29
David McNiven	5 6	11 4	Stonehouse	Leeds U	15+7	6
				Bradford C	60+1	20
*Tibor Szabo	5 11	11 10	Bradford	Bradford C	8+5	1
Lammie Robertson	5 10	11 2	Paisley	Burnley	—	—
				Bury	3+2	—
				Halifax T	142+8	20
				Brighton	42+4	9
				Exeter C	132+1	25
				Leicester C	6+1	—
				Peterborough U	12+3	1
				Bradford C	14	3
*David Jackson	5 7	9 12	Bradford	Manchester U	—	—
				Exeter C (on loan)	—	—
				Bradford C	9+3	3

Allan Gilliver 1+1 sub (Non-contract)

BRENTFORD DIV. 3

Chairman: Dan Tana.
Directors: L. F. Davey, W. Hall, B. J. Poyton, E. J. Radley-Smith, M.S., F.R.C.S., L.R.C.P., C. W. Wheatley, R. J. J. Blindell, LL.B.
Manager: Bill Dodgin (Jnr).
Chief Administrator/Secretary: D. R. Piggott.
Year Formed: 1889. *Limited Company:* 1901.
Turned Professional: 1899.
Previous Grounds: Clifden Road 1889–91; Benns Fields, Little Ealing 1891–95; Shotters Field 1895–98; Cross Road, S. Ealing 1898–1900; Boston Park 1900–04; Griffin Park 1904.
Football League Record:
1920 Original Member of Division 3.

1921–33 Division 3(S).	1963–66 Division 3.
1933–35 Division 2.	1966–72 Division 4.
1935–47 Division 1.	1972–73 Division 3.
1947–54 Division 2.	1973–78 Division 4.
1954–62 Division 3(S).	1978– Division 3.
1962–63 Division 4.	

© Brentford Football and Sports Club Limited, 1975

Honours: Football League, Highest Position in Division 1, 5th, 1935-36. Division 2, Champions: 1934–35. Division 3(S), Champions: 1932–33; Runners-up: 1929–30, 1957–58. Division 4, Champions: 1962–63. *F.A. Cup,* best season: 6th Rd., 1938, 1946, 1949. *Football League Cup,* best season: 3rd Rd., 1961, 1969.
Record Victory: 9-0 v Wrexham., Division 3, Oct. 15th, 1963.
Record Defeat: 0-7 v Swansea T., Division 3(S), Nov. 8th, 1924; 0-7 v Walsall, Division 3(S), Jan. 19th, 1957.
Most League Points: 62, Division 3(S), 1932–33; 62, Division 4, 1962–63.
Most League Goals: 98, Division 4, 1962–63.
Highest League Scorer in Season: Jack Holliday, 37, Division 3(S), 1932–33.
Most League Goals in Total Aggregate: Jim Towers, 153, 1954–61.
Most Capped Player: Idris Hopkins, 12, Wales.
Most League Appearances: Ken Coote, 514, 1949–64.
Record Transfer Fee Received: £40,000 from Manchester U. for Stewart Houston, Dec. 1973.
Record Transfer Fee Paid: £33,000 to Luton Town for Jim McNichol, Oct. 1978.
Managers Since the War: Harry Curtis, Jackie Gibbons, Jimmy Bain, Tom Lawton, Bill Dodgin (Snr.), Malcolm McDonald, Tommy Cavanagh, Billy Gray, Jimmy Sirrel, Frank Blunstone, Mike Everitt, John Docherty.
Address of Supporters Club: Same as Football Club.
Address of the Club Shop or Boutique: c/o the Club.

Griffin Park, Braemar Rd., Brentford, Middlesex TW8 0NT. Telephone 01-560-2021. *Ground capacity:* 37,000 (30,500 under cover). *Record attendance:* 39,626 v Preston N.E., F.A. Cup 6th Rd., March 5, 1938. *Record receipts:* £12,809.05 v Watford, Division 3, February 24, 1979. *Pitch measurements* 114 yds × 75 yds.
How to get there: South Ealing (Underground, Piccadilly line). Southern Region trains from Waterloo to Brentford Central. Buses 91, 65, 116, 117, E1, E2, 267. The ground is within a mile of the M4 and A4 roads.
Match tickets: All admission by cash through turnstiles for league games. F.A. Cup-tie seats may be booked in advance.
Car parking: Confined to streets around the ground.
Entertainments/catering facilities: Catering kiosks in the ground. A members' social club, the 'Centre Circle' in Braemar Road, provides entertainment throughout the year.
Club-shop: The Supporters' Association sells all souvenir items. Applications for price lists, etc should be sent to the Sales Secretary, Brentford Football Supporters Association, c/o Brentford F.C., accompanied by S.A.E.
Handbooks/programmes: Programmes not available on subscription.
Extra information: One of only six clubs to win all their home games in a season; Brentford accomplished this feat in 1929–30.
Club Colours: Red and white striped shirts, black shorts, black stockings with red and white hoop tops.
Change Colours: Royal blue shirts, white shorts, red stockings.
Physiotherapist: A E Lyons.
Coach: Tommy Baldwin.
Club Nickname: 'Bees'.

BRENTFORD 1978–79 LEAGUE RECORD

Match No.	Date	Venue	Opponents	Result	H/T Score	League Pos'n	Goalscorers	Attendance
1	Aug 19	A	Shrewsbury T	L 0-1	0-1	—		2348
2	21	H	Colchester U	W 1-0	1-0	—	Kruse	6800
3	26	H	Chesterfield	L 0-3	0-2	18		6150
4	Sept 2	A	Exeter C	D 2-2	2-1	18	McCulloch 2	3604
5	9	H	Hull C	W 1-0	1-0	12	Phillips	6530
6	12	A	Swindon T	L 0-2	0-0	—		6685
7	16	A	Peterborough U	L 1-3	1-2	18	Kruse	5881
8	23	H	Gillingham	L 0-2	0-0	19		6970
9	25	H	Lincoln C	W 2-1	2-1	—	Graham J, Eames	6111
10	30	A	Swansea C	L 1-2	1-1	21	McCulloch	11,470
11	Oct 7	H	Bury	L 0-1	0-0	22		5850
12	14	A	Watford	L 0-2	0-0	23		15,180
13	17	A	Rotherham U	L 0-1	0-0	—		3881
14	21	H	Tranmere R	W 2-0	1-0	23	McCulloch 2	5880
15	28	A	Chester	L 1-3	1-0	23	Smith	4301
16	Nov 4	H	Oxford U	W 3-0	2-0	22	McCulloch, Smith 2	6860
17	11	H	Exeter C	D 0-0	0-0	23		6390
18	18	A	Chesterfield	D 0-0	0-0	23		4584
19	Dec 2	H	Walsall	W 1-0	1-0	21	McCulloch	5130
20	9	A	Mansfield T	L 1-2	0-2	22	McCulloch	4003
21	23	H	Southend U	D 1-1	0-0	21	Phillips	13,189
22	26	H	Plymouth Arg	W 2-1	0-0	20	Smith 2	7360
23	30	H	Carlisle U	D 0-0	0-0	19		6480
24	Jan 20	H	Peterborough U	D 0-0	0-0	18		5750
25	27	A	Gillingham	D 0-0	0-0	17		6899
26	Feb 10	H	Swansea C	W 1-0	0-0	15	Carlton	7250
27	24	H	Watford	D 3-3	2-2	17	Smith, Phillips 2 (1 a pen)	13,860
28	Mar 3	A	Tranmere R	W 1-0	0-0	17	Phillips	1882
29	6	A	Hull C	L 0-1	0-0	—		3418
30	10	H	Chester	W 6-0	1-0	15	Phillips 3, Glover 2, McCulloch	6420
31	13	A	Sheffield W	L 0-1	0-1	—		10,229
32	21	A	Lincoln C	L 0-1	0-1	—		2070
33	24	A	Colchester U	D 1-1	0-0	18	Shrubb	3528
34	26	H	Shrewsbury T	L 2-3	1-2	—	McCulloch, Smith	7760
35	31	H	Blackpool	W 3-2	0-2	17	McNicholl 2, Phillips	6380
36	Apr 4	A	Oxford U	W 1-0	0-0	—	Shrubb	4943
37	7	A	Walsall	W 3-2	3-0	14	Kruse, Phillips 2	3840
38	13	H	Southend U	W 3-0	1-0	—	McCulloch, Kruse, Salmon	11,500
39	14	A	Plymouth Arg	L 1-2	0-1	15	Carlton	6344
40	17	H	Sheffield W	W 2-1	2-0	—	McNichol 2	9050
41	21	A	Carlisle U	L 0-1	0-0	14		3967
42	23	H	Rotherham U	W 1-0	1-0	—	Smith	6710
43	28	H	Mansfield T	W 1-0	0-0	11	Phillips	6830
44	May 5	A	Blackpool	W 1-0	0-0	10	McCulloch	3464
45	8	H	Swindon T	L 1-2	1-1	—	Smith	13,320
46	15	A	Bury	W 3-2	1-2	—	Phillips 2, McCulloch	2152

Final League Position: 10

Goalscorers

League (53): Phillips 14 (1 a pen), McCulloch 13, Smith 9, Kruse 4, McNichol 4, Carlton 2, Glover 2, Shrubb 2, Eames 1, Graham J 1, Salmon 1.

League Cup (1): Rolph.

League Cup	First Round	Watford (a)	0-4
		(h)	1-3
F.A. Cup	First Round	Exeter C (a)	0-1

Porter	Fraser	Tucker	Shrubb	Kruse	Graham, J	Carlton	Graham, W	Allder	McCulloch	Phillips	Allen	Salman	Walker	Smith, D	Rolph	Eames	Frost	Bond	Booker	McNichol	Glover	Silman	Smith, N	Match No.
1	2*	3	4	5	6	7	8	9	10	11	12													1
1*		2	4	5	8	7	6	9	10	11	3										12			2
1		3	4	5	8	7	6*	9	10	11	12	2												3
1		2		5	8	7	6	9	10*	11	3	4	12											4
1		2		5	8	7	6	9	10	11	3	4*	12											5
1		2		5	8	7	6	9	10*	11	3		12								4			6
1	10	2		5	8	7*	6	9		11	3		12								4			7
1	2	3	4	5	8	7*			10	11		6	12		9									8
1	6	3	4	5	8*		12		10	11		2	7			9								9
1	6	3	4	5		8			10	11		2	7			9								10
1	6*	3	4	5	8	7		12	10	11		2			9									11
	12	3	4	5*	8	7			10	11		2						9	1	6				12
		3	4		8	7		5	10	11		2						9	1	6				13
4			2		8	6			10	11		3		7				9	1		5			14
		3	2	5	8*	7			10	11	12		9				4		1	6				15
		3	7	5	6	8			10	11		2	9*		12				1	4				16
		3	7	5	6*	8		9	10			2						1	12	4				17
		3	7	5	6	8			10	11		2						1		4	9			18
7		3	4	6	8		12		10*	11		2						1		5	9			19
		3	7	5	6				10	11		2	9					1		4	8			20
		3	7	5	6	8			10	11		2						1		4	9			21
12		3		5	6		7*	10		11		2	9					1		4	8			22
		3		5	6	7		10		11		2	9					1		4	8			23
3				5	6	7		12	10	11		2	9					1		4	8*			24
3				5	6	7		10		11		2	9					1		4				25
		3	7	5	6	8			10	11		2	9					1		4				26
		3	8	5	6	7			10	11		2	9					1		4				27
		3	8	5	6	7			10	11		2	9					1		4*	12			28
		3	8	5	6			12	10	11		2	9*					1		4	7			29
		3	8	5	6			12	10*	11		2	9					1		4	7			30
		3	8	5	6	7		12		11		2	9*					1		10	4			31
		3	8*	5	6	7			10	11		2	12					1		4	9			32
		3	8	5	6	7		12		11*		2	10					1		4	9			33
		3	8*	5	6	7		12	10	11		2	9					1		4				34
		3	8	5	6	7		12	10	11		2*	9					1		4				35
	2	3	8	5		7		12	10	11			9*					1		4	6			36
	6	3	8	5			12	9	10*	11		2						1		4	7			37
	6	3	2	5				9	10	11		7						1		4	8			38
	8	3	2*	5	10	7		9		11		4	12					1		6				39
	6	3	2	5				9	10	11		7*	12					1		4	8			40
	6	3	2	5		12		9*	10	11		7						1		4	8			41
	6	3	2	5		7			10	11		8	9					1		4				42
	6	3	2	5		7		12	10	11*		8	9					1		4				43
	8	3	2	5		7		9	10	11		4						1		6				44
	6	3	2	5		7		12	10	11		8	9*					1		4				45
	6	3	2	5		7		12	10	11			9					1		4	8*			46
11	21	43	39	44	35	36	8	18	39	46	5	39	2	22	1	2	5	35	2	32	18	1	2	
+2s				+1s	+3s	+12s			+2s	+1s	+5s	+3s						+1s		+1s	+1s		+1s	

BRENTFORD—PLAYERS

Player and position	Ht	Wt	Birthplace	Clubs	League Appearances	Goals
Goalkeepers						
Graham Cox (Contract cancelled September 1978)	5 9½	10 5	London	Brentford	4	—
Len Bond	6 0	12 7	Ilminster	Bristol C	30	—
				Exeter C (on loan)	30	—
				Cardiff C (on loan)	—	—
				Torquay U (on loan)	3	—
				Scunthorpe U (on loan)	8	—
				Colchester U (on loan)	3	—
				Brentford	80	—
Trevor Porter	5 11	11 10	Guildford	Fulham	—	—
				Slough T	—	—
				Brentford	11	—
Defenders						
Danis Salman	5 9	11 0	Famagusta	Brentford	94+7	2
Barry Tucker	5 6	10 7	Swansea	Northampton T	209+5	3
				Brentford	61	—
John Fraser	5 10	10 7	London	Fulham	54+1	1
				Brentford	79+2	2
Pat Kruse	5 11	12 4	Biggleswade	Leicester C	2	—
				Mansfield T (on loan)	6	1
				Torquay U	79	4
				Brentford	99	7
*Mike Allen	5 11	10 8	S. Shields	Middlesbrough	32+3	1
				Brentford	223+10	11
Jim McNichol	6 0	12 6	Glasgow	Ipswich T	—	—
				Luton T	13+2	—
				Brentford	32	4
Midfield						
Jackie Graham	5 7	10 12	Glasgow	Morton	6	1
				Dundee U	21+2	10
				Guildford C (not known)	—	—
				Brentford	341+2	37
Paul Walker	5 6	10 10	London	Brentford	6+8	—
*Gary Rolph	5 10¾	10 10	London	Brentford	8+4	1
David Carlton	5 10¼	11 2	London	Fulham	5+4	—
				Northampton T	99+5	6
				Brentford	100+2	5
Paul Shrubb	5 7	10 4	Guildford	Fulham	—	—
				Hellenic (S Africa)	(not known)	—
				Brentford	94+3	5
Willie Graham	5 8	10 7	Co. Armagh	Northampton T	—	—
				Brentford	36+6	2
Allan Glover	5 9½	12 3	Staines	QPR	5+1	—
				WBA	84+8	8
				Southend U (on loan)	0+1	—
				Brentford (on loan)	6	—
				Orient	37	5
				Brentford	18+1	2
Forwards						
John Murray (Contract cancelled December 1978)	5 8½	11 0	Newcastle	Burnley	20+2	6
				Blackpool	6+2	1
				Bury	117+9	37
				Reading	123+8	44
				Brentford	2+3	1
*David Silman	6 2	12 7	London	Wolverhampton W	—	—
				Brentford	1	—
Terry Johnson (Contract cancelled September 1978)	5 9	10 13	Newcastle	Newcastle U	—	—
				Darlington (on loan)	4	1
				Southend U	155+2	34
				Brentford	98+3	27
Andy McCulloch	6 2	13 6	Northampton	QPR	30+12	10
				Cardiff C	58	24
				Oxford U	41	9
				Brentford	115+2	48
Steve Phillips	5 6	10 7	Edmonton	Birmingham C	15+5	1
				Torquay U (on loan)	6	—
				Northampton T	50+1	8
				Brentford	111	53
Doug Allder	5 10	10 7	Hammersmith	Millwall	191+11	10
				Orient	34+7	—
				Torquay U	—	—
				Watford	1	—
				Brentford	49+12	2
Bob Booker	6 0	12 0	Watford	Brentford	2+1	—
Billy Eames (Contract cancelled)	5 8	11 0	Malta	Portsmouth	9+3	1
				Brentford	2	1
Dean Smith	5 10	11 9	Leicester	Leicester C	8+2	1
				Brentford	22+3	9

BRIGHTON & HOVE ALBION — DIV. 1

Chairman: M. K. Bamber.
Vice-chairman: H. Bloom.
Directors: N. J. Hyams, W. Smith, D. Sizen, K. Wickenden, T. Appleby.
Manager: Alan Mullery, M.B.E.
Secretary: Kenneth Calver.   *Year Formed:* 1900.
Turned Professional: 1900.   *Limited Company:* 1901.
Previous Name: Brighton & Hove Rangers.
Previous Grounds: 1900, Withdean; 1901, County Ground; 1902, Goldstone Ground.

Football League Record:
1920 Original Member of Division 3.   1965–72 Division 3.
1921–1958 Division 3(S).   1972–73 Division 2.
1958–62 Division 2.   1973–77 Division 3.
1962–63 Division 3.   1977–79 Division 2.
1963–65 Division 4.   1979–   Division 1.

Honours: Football League: best season: 2nd, Div 2, 1978–79. Division 3(S), Champions: 1957–58; Runners-up :1953–54, 1955–56, Division 3 Runners-up: 1971–72, 1976–77; Division 4, Champions: 1964–65. *F.A. Cup,* best season: 5th Rd., 1929–30, 1932–33, 1945–46, 1959–60, old 3rd Rd., 1913–14, 1923–24. *Football League Cup,* best season: 5th Rd., 1978–79.

Record Victory: 10-1 v Wisbech, F.A. Cup, 1st Rd., Nov. 13th, 1965.
Record Defeat: 0-9 v Middlesbrough, Division 2, Aug. 23rd, 1958.
Most League Points: 65, Division 3(S), 1955–56, and Division 3, 1971–72.
Most League Goals: 112, Division 3(S), 1955–56.
Highest League Scorer in Season: Peter Ward, 32, Division 3, 1976–77.
Most League Goals in Total Aggregate: Tommy Cook, 113, 1922–29.
Most Capped Player: Jack Jenkins, 8, Wales.
Most League Appearances: 'Tug' Wilson, 509, 1922–36.
Record Transfer Fee Received: £26,000 from Blackburn R. for Ken Beamish, May 1974.
Record Transfer Fee Paid: £195,000 to Fulham for Teddy Maybank, Nov. 1977.
Managers Since the War: Tommy Cook, Don Welsh, Billy Lane, George Curtis, Archie Macaulay, Freddie Goodwin, Pat Saward, Brian Clough, Peter Taylor.
Address of Supporters Club: Albion Shop, Goldstone Ground, Hove.

Goldstone Ground, Old Shoreham Rd., Hove, Sussex, BN3 7DE. Telephone Brighton 739535. *Ground capacity:* 34,500.   *Record attendance:* 36,747 v Fulham, Division 2, December 27, 1958. *Record receipts:* £25,500 v Derby Co. League Cup 4th Round, October 26, 1976. *Pitch measurements:* 112 yds × 75 yds.

How to get there: Buses 5, B5, 9, 26, 40, 55, 19 from Old Steyne and 11 via Brighton station and Old Shoreham Rd. Hove station is five minutes walk from the ground.
Match tickets: Postal bookings for tickets two weeks in advance.
Car parking: Car parking facilities are available a few minutes away at the Greyhound Stadium, Neville Road, and in Hove Station Goods Yard, Sackville Road. There is limited street parking adjacent to the stadium.
Entertainments/catering facilities: Bars and tea stands around the ground.
Club shop: At the ground; sells all types of souvenirs.
Handbooks/programmes: Programmes available by post from the club shop.
Extra information: In 1933–34 Oliver Brown was Brighton's leading scorer with 12 goals; yet he played in only 8 matches! Missed promotion to Division 1, 1977–78 on goal difference.
Club Colours: Blue and white striped shirts, white sleeves, blue shorts, white socks with 2 blue hoops.
Change Colours: Yellow.
Physiotherapist: M. Yaxley.
First Team Coach: Ken Craggs.
Club Nickname: "The Seagulls"

BRIGHTON & HOVE ALBION 1978-79 LEAGUE RECORD

Match No.	Date	Venue	Opponents	Result	H/T Score	League Pos'n	Goalscorers	Attendance
1	Aug 19	A	Wrexham	D 0-0	0-0	—		14,081
2	22	H	Cambridge U	L 0-2	0-0	—		21,548
3	26	H	Sunderland	W 2-0	1-0	12	Ward 2	19,885
4	Sept 2	A	Millwall	W 4-1	1-1	5	Maybank 2, Horton, Poskett	9238
5	9	H	Oldham Ath	W 1-0	1-0	3	Hurst (og)	19,735
6	23	A	Leicester C	L 1-4	0-2	10	Williams	14,307
7	27	A	Stoke C	D 2-2	0-1	—	Ward, Maybank	22,203
8	30	H	Preston NE	W 5-1	4-0	3	Baxter 2 (2 ogs), Ryan, Ward, Clark	19,217
9	Oct 7	A	Crystal Palace	L 1-3	0-0	9	Horton	33,685
10	14	H	Fulham	W 3-0	1-0	4	Ryan 2, Horton	24,606
11	21	A	Burnley	L 0-3	0-0	10		10,271
12	28	H	West Ham U	L 1-2	1-2	12	Sayer	32,634
13	Nov 4	A	Sheffield United	W 1-0	1-0	8	Poskett	16,683
14	11	H	Wrexham	W 2-1	1-0	6	Ryan, Horton	19,659
15	18	A	Sunderland	L 1-2	1-1	11	Poskett	22,738
16	21	H	Millwall	W 3-0	2-0	—	Poskett 2, Ryan	19,408
17	25	H	Notts Co	L 0-1	0-0	12		8851
18	Dec 2	H	Orient	W 2-0	1-0	7	Horton (pen), Sayer	16,691
19	9	A	Blackburn R	D 1-1	1-1	7	Ryan	8046
20	16	H	Luton T	W 3-1	2-0	4	Horton (pen), Rollings, Sayer	16,252
21	23	A	Charlton Ath	W 3-0	0-0	4	Poskett 3	10,135
22	26	H	Cardiff C	W 5-0	3-0	—	Williams, Maybank 3, Horton (pen)	20,172
23	30	H	Newcastle U	W 2-0	1-0	3	Poskett, O'Sullivan	25,812
24	Jan 20	H	Stoke C	D 1-1	1-1	3	Jones (og)	23,076
25	Feb 3	A	Leicester C	W 3-1	2-1	1	Maybank, Sayer, Ward	19,973
26	10	A	Preston NE	L 0-1	0-0	2		11,649
27	17	H	Crystal Palace	D 0-0	0-0	1		23,795
28	24	A	Fulham	W 1-0	0-0	1	Clark	18,640
29	Mar 3	H	Burnley	W 2-1	0-0	2	Horton (pen), Lawrenson	19,402
30	6	A	Oldham Ath	W 3-1	1-0	—	Ward, Rollings, Ryan	4637
31	10	A	West Ham U	D 0-0	0-0	1		35,802
32	17	H	Sheffield U	W 2-0	0-0	1	Lawrenson, Ryan	20,091
33	20	A	Bristol R	W 2-1	1-0	—	Ward 2	8290
34	24	A	Cambridge U	D 0-0	0-0	1		8455
35	31	H	Notts Co	D 0-0	0-0	1		21,398
36	Apr 7	A	Orient	D 3-3	2-2	1	Sayer, Chivers, Clark	11,567
37	13	H	Charlton Ath	W 2-0	1-0	—	Clark, Shaw (og)	30,859
38	14	A	Cardiff C	L 1-3	1-2	1	Ward	12,613
39	16	H	Bristol R	W 3-0	3-0	—	Horton 2 (1 a pen), Maybank	23,024
40	21	A	Luton T	D 1-1	0-1	2	Maybank	13,132
41	28	H	Blackburn R	W 2-1	1-0	1	Maybank, Rollings	26,141
42	May 5	A	Newcastle U	W 3-1	3-0	1	Horton, Ward, Ryan	28,425

Final League Position: 2

Goalscorers

League (72): Horton 11 (5 pens), Maybank 10, Ward 10, Poskett 9, Ryan 9, Sayer 5, Clark 4, Rollings 3, Lawrenson 2, Williams 2, Chivers 1, O'Sullivan 1, own goals 5.
League Cup (6): Ward 3, O'Sullivan, Maybank, Lawrenson.
F.A. Cup (2): Lawrenson, Ryan.

League Cup	Second Round	Millwall (h)	1-0
	Third Round	Burnley (a)	3-1
	Fourth Round	Peterborough U (h)	1-0
	Fifth Round	Nottingham F (a)	1-3
F.A. Cup	Third Round	Wolverhampton W (h)	2-3

Moseley	Tiler	Williams	Horton	Winstanley	Lawrenson	Sayer	Ward	Maybank	Clark	O'Sullivan	Towner	Steele	Rollings	Poskett	Ryan	Cattlin	Chivers	Match No.
1	2	3	4	5	6	7*	8	9	10	11	12							1
	2	3	4	5*	6	7	8	9	10	11	12	1						2
	2	3	4		6		8	9	10	11	7	1	5					3
	2	3	4		6	12		9	10*	11	7	1	5	8				4
	2	3	4		6		8*		10	11	7	1	5	12				5
	2	3	4		6	12	8	9	10*	11	7	1	5					6
	2	3	4		6	12	8	9	10*	11		1	5		7			7
	2	3	4		6	11	8	9	10			1	5		7			8
	2*	3	4		6	12	8	9	10	11		1	5		7			9
1	2	3	4		6		8	9	10	11			5		7			10
1	2	3	4*		6	12	8	9	10	11			5		7			11
1	2	3	4		6	12	8	9	10	11			5*		7			12
1	2	3	4	5	6	10		9	12	11*				8	7			13
1	2	3	4		6	10		9		11			5	8	7			14
1	2	3	4		6	10*	12	9		11			5	8	7			15
1	2	3	4		6	10		9					5	8	7	11		16
1	2	3	4		6		12	9	10				5	8	7*	11		17
1		3	4		6	10	8	9*		11			5	7	12	2		18
1		3	4		6	10	8	12		11			5	9*	7	2		19
1		3	4		6	10	8		12	11			5	9*	7	2		20
1		3	4		6	10		9		11			5	8	7	2		21
1		3	4		6*	10		9	12	11			5	8	7	2		22
1		3	4		6	10		9		11			5	8	7	2		23
1		3	4		6	10	12	9		11			5	8	7*	2		24
1		3	4		6	10	12	9		11			5	8	7*	2		25
		3	4		6	10		9	12	11	1		5	8	7*	2		26
		3	4		6	10	12	9		11	1		5	8*	7	2		27
		3	4		6	10*	8	9	12	11	1		5		7	2		28
		3	4		6		8	9	10	11	1		5		7	2		29
		3	4		6		8	9	10	11	1		5		7	2		30
		3	4		6		8*	9	10	11	1		5	12	7	2		31
		3	4		6		8	9	10	11*	1		5	12	7	2		32
		3	4		6		8		10	11	1		5	9	7	2		33
		3	4		6		8*	12	10	11	1		5	9	7	2		34
		3			6	4	8*		10	11	1		5	12	7	2	9	35
		3			6	4			10	11	1		5	8	7	2	9	36
		3	12		6	4			10	11	1		5	8	7*	2	9	37
		3	4		6	7	8	9	10*	11	1		5	12		2		38
		3	4		6*	10	8	9	5	11	1			12	7	2		39
		3*	4	5		10	8	9	6	11	1			12	7	2		40
		3	4			10	8	9	6		1		5	11	7	2		41
		3	4			10	8	9	6	11	1		5	12	7*	2		42
17	17	42	39	4	39	26	27	35	28	37	4	25	37	21	34	27	3	
	+1s				+6s	+5s	+2s	+5s		+2s			+8s	+1s				

BRIGHTON & HOVE ALBION—PLAYERS

Players and position	Ht	Wt	Birthplace	Clubs	League Appearances	Goals
Goalkeepers						
Eric Steele	5 11	11 3	Newcastle	Newcastle U	—	—
				Peterborough U	124	—
				Brighton	78	—
Graham Moseley	6 0	11 8	Manchester	Blackburn R	—	—
				Derby Co	32	—
				Aston V (on loan)	3	—
				Walsall (on loan)	3	—
				Brighton	21	—
Defenders						
Ken Tiler	5 11	10 12½	Sheffield	Chesterfield	138+1	1
				Brighton	130	—
Andy Rollings	6 0	11 8	N. Weston	Norwich C	4	—
				Brighton	161	9
Graham Winstanley	5 11	11 3	Croxdale	Newcastle U	5+2	—
				Carlisle U	165+1	8
				Brighton	63+1	4
Chris Cattlin	5 11	12 5½	Milnrow	Huddersfield T	59+2	1
				Coventry C	213+4	—
				Brighton	95	1
Mark Lawrenson (Eire)	5 10	10 10	Preston	Preston NE	73	2
				Brighton	79	3
Gary Williams	5 10	11 0	Liverpool	Preston NE	107+5	2
				Brighton	76	2
Glen Geard	5 7	10 3	Brighton	Brighton	—	—
Michael Kerslake	5 10	11 1	London	Fulham	1+2	—
				Brighton	—	—
Midfield						
Brian Horton	5 10	11 4	Hednesford	Port Vale	232+4	33a
				Brighton	137+1	28
Peter O'Sullivan (Wales)	5 6	10 0	Colwyn Bay	Manchester U	—	—
				Brighton	372	35
*Steven Ward	5 11	11 7	Brighton	Brighton	—	—
Paul Clark	5 10	12 5	S Benfleet	Southend U	29+4	1
Giles Stille	5 9	11 9	London	Brighton	—	—
				Brighton	54+5	7
Peter Sayer (Wales)	5 6	10 2	Cardiff	Cardiff C	70+12	14
				Brighton	32+6	6
Forwards						
Mike Ring	5 10	10 6	Brighton	Brighton	—	—
Peter Ward	5 7	10 3	Derbyshire	Brighton	120+5	62
*Mark Elliott	5 9	11 0	Wales	Brighton	3	—
Teddy Maybank	5 10	10 12	London	Chelsea	28	6
				Fulham	27	14
				Brighton	51+2	14
Malcolm Poskett	6 0	11 2	Middlesbrough	Middlesbrough	0+1	—
				Hartlepool	50+1	20
				Brighton	32+10	15
Gerry Ryan (Eire)	5 10	10 12	Dublin	Bohemians	—	—
				Derby Co	30	4
				Brighton	34+1	9
Martin Chivers (England)	6 1½	12 12½	Southampton	Southampton	173+1	97
				Tottenham H	268+10	118
				Servette	—	—
				Norwich C	11	4
				Brighton	3	1

BRISTOL CITY DIV. 1

Chairman: S. F. Kew.
Vice-Chairman: G. C. Griffiths.
Directors: W. G. Garland, H. Bissex, N. B. Jones, D. Callow, P. D. West.
Manager: Alan Dicks.
Commercial Manager/Secretary: A. E. Rance.
Coach: Ken Wimshurst. *Year Formed:* 1894.
Turned Professional: 1897. *Limited Company:* 1897.
Previous Grounds: 1894, St. John's Lane; 1904, Ashton Gate.
Previous Name: 1894–97, Bristol South End.
Football League Record:

1901 Elected to Division 2.	1927–32 Division 2.
1906–11 Division 1.	1932–55 Division 3(S).
1911–22 Division 2.	1955–60 Division 2.
1922–23 Division 3 (S).	1960–65 Division 3.
1923–24 Division 2.	1965–76 Division 2.
1924–27 Division 3(S).	1976– Division 1.

Honours: Football League, Division 1, Runners-up: 1906–07. Division 2, Champions: 1905–06. Runners-up: 1975–76. Division 3(S), Champions: 1922–23, 1926–27, 1954–55; Runners-up: 1937–38. Division 3, Runners-up: 1964–65. *F.A. Cup,* Runners-up: 1909. *Football League Cup,* Semi-final: 1970–71. Welsh Cup winners 1934. *Anglo-Scottish Cup:* 1978–79.
Record Victory: 11-0 v Chichester, F.A. Cup, 1st Rd., Nov. 5th, 1960.
Record Defeat: 0-9 v Coventry C., Division 3(S), Apr. 28th, 1934.
Most League Points: 70, Division 3(S), 1954–55.
Most League Goals: 104, Division 3(S), 1926–27.
Highest League Scorer in Season: Don Clark, 36, Division 3(S), 1946–47.
Most Capped Player: Billy Wedlock, 26, England.
Most League Appearances: John Atyeo, 597, 1951–1966 (+ 48 cup ties).
Most League Goals in Total Aggregate: John Atyeo, 315, 1951–66.
Record Transfer Fee Received: £110,000 from Chelsea for Chris Garland, Sept. 1971.
Record Transfer Fee Paid: £110,000 to Leicester C. for Chris Garland, Nov. 1976.
Managers Since the War: Bob Hewison, Bob Wright, Pat Beasley, Peter Doherty, Fred Ford.
Address of Supporters Club: Supporters Club, Bristol City F.C., Ashton Gate, Bristol BS3 2EJ.
Address of Club Shop or Boutique: City Shop, Ashton Gate, Bristol BS3 2EJ.

Ashton Gate, Bristol BS3 2EJ. Telephone Bristol 632812 (5 lines). *Telegraphic address:* 'City Bristol'. *Ground capacity:* 30,868. *Record attendance:* 43,335 v Preston N.E., F.A. Cup 5th Rd., February 16, 1935. *Record receipts:* £30,000 v Tottenham H, Division 1, January 13, 1979. *Pitch measurements:* 115 yds × 75 yds.

How to get there: Buses 6, 7, 9, 19, 22. Parsons St station is available within walking distance for special trains. Also certain scheduled trains stop there.

Match tickets: Tickets can be booked any length of time before the match; Postal application must include remittance and S.A.E. Personal application not accepted until 3 weeks before the match. No postal bookings taken.

Car parking: Season-ticket holders can obtain season car park parking tickets. Coach parking at Cannons Marsh. There is limited street parking around the ground.

Entertainments/catering facilities: Social club in the main stands. Tea bars in the ground. Alcoholic beverages only obtainable by members of a bona-fide Supporters' Club. There is a wide variety of pre-match entertainment, and some matches are sponsored, so throw-away gifts to the crowd, and programme prizes, are a regular feature.

Club shop: One of the biggest in the country, sells all types of souvenirs, clothing and many other items.

Handbooks/programmes: Programmes not available on subscription but postal applications are accepted.

Extra information: Indoor bowling area in the main stand. Large room available for functions caters for 200 people.

Club Colours: Red shirts, white shorts, red stockings.
Change Colours: White shirts, black shorts, black stockings.
Club Captain: Geoff Merrick.
Club Nickname: 'Robins'.

BRISTOL CITY 1978-79 LEAGUE RECORD

Match No.	Date	Venue	Opponents	Result	H/T Score	League Pos'n	Goalscorer	Attendance
1	Aug 19	A	Bolton W	W 2-1	0-1	—	Mann, Ritchie	21,355
2	22	H	Norwich C	D 1-1	0-1	—	Cormack (pen)	19,274
3	26	H	Aston Villa	W 1-0	0-0	5	Rodgers	23,493
4	Sept 2	A	Wolverhampton W	L 0-2	0-1	7		16,121
5	9	A	Tottenham H	L 0-1	0-1	12		34,035
6	16	H	Southampton	W 3-1	1-1	8	Rodgers, Ritchie 2	21,420
7	23	A	Ipswich T	W 1-0	0-0	6	Ritchie (pen)	20,168
8	30	H	Everton	D 2-2	2-1	5	Gow, Hunter	23,231
9	Oct 7	A	QPR	L 0-1	0-0	9		15,707
10	14	H	Nottingham F	L 1-3	1-2	11	Ritchie (pen)	26,953
11	21	H	Manchester U	W 3-1	1-0	9	Mabbutt 3	47,211
12	28	H	Arsenal	L 1-3	1-2	11	Rodgers	27,016
13	Nov 4	A	Middlesbrough	D 0-0	0-0	11		20,471
14	11	H	Bolton W	W 4-1	1-1	10	Ritchie, Royle 2, Rodgers	18,168
15	18	A	Aston Villa	L 0-2	0-0	12		27,621
16	21	H	Wolverhampton W	L 0-1	0-0	—		17,421
17	25	A	Birmingham C	D 1-1	1-0	13	Mabbutt	21,552
18	Dec 2	H	Derby Co	W 1-0	0-0	11	Gillies	17,487
19	9	A	Leeds U	D 1-1	1-1	11	Royle	22,529
20	16	H	Liverpool	W 1-0	0-0	11	Royle	28,722
21	23	A	Chelsea	D 0-0	0-0	10		19,093
22	26	H	Coventry C	W 5-0	2-0	7	Royle 3, Ritchie, Cormack	22,324
23	30	H	Manchester C	D 1-1	1-0	7	Ritchie	25,253
24	Jan 1	A	WBA	L 1-3	1-2	—	Cormack (pen)	31,593
25	13	H	Tottenham H	D 0-0	0-0	7		28,781
26	Feb 3	H	Ipswich T	W 3-1	2-0	7	Whitehead, Tainton, Gow	17,025
27	10	A	Everton	L 1-4	1-1	7	Whitehead	29,166
28	20	A	Southampton	L 0-2	0-2	—		19,845
29	24	H	Nottingham F	L 0-2	0-2	7		28,008
30	Mar 3	H	Manchester U	L 1-2	1-0	10	Gow	24,784
31	10	A	Arsenal	L 0-2	0-2	13		24,408
32	17	H	Middlesbrough	D 1-1	0-0	14	Gow	12,319
33	24	A	Norwich C	L 0-3	0-3	14		14,507
34	31	H	Birmingham C	W 2-1	1-0	14	Meijer, Garland	15,584
35	Apr 3	H	QPR	W 2-0	0-0	—	Mabbutt 2	15,687
36	7	A	Derby Co	W 1-0	0-0	9	Ritchie	17,090
37	10	H	Chelsea	W 3-1	0-0	—	Rodgers, Mabbutt, Meijer	18,645
38	14	A	Coventry C	L 2-3	0-3	8	Mabbutt, Gow	17,812
39	17	H	WBA	W 1-0	0-0	—	Mabbutt	29,914
40	21	A	Liverpool	L 0-1	0-1	9		43,191
41	28	H	Leeds U	D 0-0	0-0	11		25,388
42	May 5	A	Manchester C	L 0-2	0-1	12		29,739

Final League Position: 13

Goalscorers

League (47): Ritchie 9 (2 pens), Mabbutt 9, Royle 7, Gow 5, Rodgers 5, Cormack 3 (2 pens), Meijer 2, Whitehead 2, Garland 1, Gillies 1, Mann 1, Tainton 1, Hunter 1.

League Cup (1): Ritchie

F.A.Cup (3): Gow, Rodgers, Ritchie

League Cup	Second Round	C. Palace (h)	1-2
F.A. Cup	Third Round	Bolton W. (h)	3-1
	Fourth Round	C. Palace (a)	0-3

Shaw	Sweeney	Cooper	Tainton	Rodgers	Hunter	Garland	Ritchie	Royle	Cormack	Mann	Whitehead	Gillies	Pritchard	Gow	Mabbutt	Bain	Collier	Cashley	Meijer	Jantunen	Match No.
1	2	3	4	5	6	7	8	9	10	11											1
1	2	3	7	5	6	11*	8	9	10	4	12										2
1	11		7	5	6		8	9		10	3	2	4								3
1	2		7	5	6		8	9*12	10	11	3		4								4
1	2		7	5	6		8	9		4	11	3		10							5
1	2		7	5	6		8	9*10	12		3		4	11							6
1	2		7	5	6		8	9		10	3		4	11							7
1	3		7	5	6		8	9		10		2	4	11							8
1	2		7	5	6		8	9		10	11	3	4								9
1	2		7	5	6		8	9		10	12	3*	4	11							10
1	2		7	5	6		8	9		10		3	4	11							11
1	2		7	5	6		8		10*	9		3	4	11	12						12
1	2		7	5	6		8	9				3	4	11	10						13
1	2		7	5	6		8	9		12		3	4	11	10*						14
1	2		7	5	6		8	9		12		3	4	11	10*						15
1	2		7	5	6		8		12	10*11		3	4	9							16
1	3		7	5	6		8	9		10		2	4	11							17
1	2		7	5	6		8	9		10		3	4	11							18
1	2			5	6		8	9	10	7		3	4	11							19
1	2		7	5	6		8	9	10	11*12		3	4								20
1	2		7	5	6		8	9	10		11	3	4								21
1	2		7	5	6		8	9	10		11	3	4								22
1	2		7	5	6*		8	9	10	12	11	3	4								23
1	2		7	5			8	9*10	12	11		3	4		6						24
1	2		7	5	6		8	9	10		11	3	4								25
1	2	3	7	5				9	10		11		4	8		6					26
1	2	3	7	5	6		8	9	10		11		4								27
1	2	3	7	5	6		8*	9	10		11		4	12							28
	2	3	7	5			8	9	10*12				4	11		6	1				29
	3		7		6	8		9		10	11	2	4			5	1				30
1	2		7		6	8	12	9		10	11	3	4*		5						31
1	2		7	5	6		8	9			11	3	4	10							32
1	2		7	5	6		8	9*	12		11	3	4	10							33
1	2	3		5	6	12	8	9*		7			4	10			11				34
1	2	3	7	5	6		8	9		4				10			11				35
1	2	3		5	6		8	9		7	12		4	10*			11				36
1	2	3		5	6		8	9		7*12			4	10			11				37
1	2	3		5*	6		8	9		7	12		4	10			11				38
1	2		7		6		8	9			3		4	10		5	11				39
1	2		7		6		8	9			3		4*10			5	11	12			40
1	2		7		6		8	9			3		4	10		5	11				41
1	2		7		6		8	9		12	3		4	10*		5	11				42
40	42	11	37	36	39	4	39	40	14	23	22	27	1	38	26	3	9	2	9	—	
						+			+	+	+			+	+				+		
						1s			1s	3s	5s 8s			1s	1s				1s		

BRISTOL CITY—PLAYERS

Players and position	Ht	Wt	Birthplace	Clubs	League Appearance	Goods
Goalkeepers						
Ray Cashley	5 10	11 0	Bristol	Bristol C	193	1
John Shaw	6 1	13 7	Stirling	Leeds U	—	—
				Bristol C	114	—
David Mogg	5 9½	10 5	Bristol	Bristol C	—	—
Defenders						
Geoff Merrick	5 9	11 0	Bristol	Bristol C	302+5	9
Garry Collier	6 1	12 0	Bristol	Bristol C	193	3
David Rodgers	6 1½	13 2	Bristol	Bristol C	130+2	9
Gerry Sweeney	5 10	10 10	Glasgow	Celtic	—	—
				Morton	137+2	16
				Bristol C	310+7	22
Don Gillies	5 10	11 5	Glencoe	Morton	45+2	23
				Bristol C	176+16	26
Norman Hunter (England)	5 11½	12 5	Eighton Banks	Leeds U	543	18
				Bristol C	108	4
Paul Stevens	5 7	9 9½	Bristol	Bristol C	1	—
Steve Jasper	5 10	12 4½	Bristol	Bristol C	—	—
Terry Cooper (England)	5 7½	10 9	Castleford	Leeds U	240+10	7
				Middlesbrough	105	1
				Bristol C	11	—
Allan Hay	5 11	11 3	Scotland	Bolton W	—	—
				Bristol C	—	—
Midfield						
Trevor Tainton	5 8	11 7	Bristol	Bristol C	364+27	21
James Mann	5 6	11 1	Poole	Leeds U	2	—
				Bristol C	133+22	16
John Bain (Contract cancelled February 1979)	5 7	9 3	Glasgow	Bristol C	5+1	—
				Brentford (on loan)	17+1	1
Gerry Gow	5 8	10 8	Glasgow	Bristol C	326+7	44
Peter Cormack (Scotland)	5 9	10 13	Edinburgh	Hibernian	182	75
				Nottingham F	74	15
				Liverpool	119+6	21
				Bristol C	58+5	15
Ricky Chandler	5 10	11 1	Bristol	Bristol C	—	—
Pertti Jantunen (Finland)	5 8½	11 7	Lahti Finland	Eskilstuna Sweden	0+1	—
Forwards						
Tom Ritchie	5 11	12 8	Scotland	Bristol C	246+10	59
Kevin Mabbutt	5 7	10 2	Bristol	Bristol C	42+11	13
Shaun Penny	5 8	10 13	Bristol	Bristol C	—	—
Clive Whitehead	5 9	10 7	Birmingham	Bristol C	132+20	10
Chris Garland	5 9½	11 12	Bristol	Bristol C	141	32
				Chelsea	89+3	22
				Leicester C	52+3	15
				Bristol C	25+3	8
Howard Pritchard	5 10	10 8	Cardiff	Bristol C	1	—
Joe Royle (England)	6 1	13 8	Liverpool	Everton	229+2	102
				Manchester C	98+1	23
				Bristol C	66	15
				Hereford U (on loan)	1+1	—
*Colin O'Brien	5 7	11 2	Dunfermline	Bristol C	—	—
Ian Doyle	5 9½	11 4	Torquay	Barnstaple	—	—
				Bristol C	—	—
Geert Meijer (Holland)	6 2	12 0	Amsterdam	Ajax	—	—
				Bristol C	9	2

BRISTOL ROVERS   DIV. 2

President: Duke of Beaufort.   *Chairman:* G. A. W. Holmes.
Vice Chairman: A. I. Seager.
Directors: H. E. L. Brown, C. A. L. Stevens, E. W. H. Godfrey, I. S. P. Stevens, Dr. W. T. Cussen, D. Mearns Milne.
Manager: Bobby Campbell.
Secretary: Peter Terry.
Year Formed: 1883. *Turned Professional:* 1897.
Limited Company: 1896.
Previous Names: 1883, Black Arabs; 1884, Eastville Rovers; 1897, Bristol Eastville Rovers; 1898, Bristol Rovers.
Previous Grounds: Purdown, Ashley Hill and Ridgeway Ground.
Football League Record:
1920 Original Member of Division 3.   1962–74 Division 3.
1921–1953 Division 3(S).   1974– Division 2.
1953–62 Division 2.

Honours: Football League, highest League position: 6th Division 2, 1955–56, 1958–59. Division 3(S), Champions: 1952–53.   Division 3 Runners-up 1973–74. *F.A. Cup,* best season: 6th Rd. 1950–51 and 1957–58.
Football League Cup, best season: 5th Rd., 1970–71, 1971–72.
Record Victory: 7-0 v Swansea Town, Division 2, Oct. 2, 1954; v Brighton Division 3(S), Nov. 29, 1952 and v Shrewsbury Town, Division 3, Mar. 21, 1964.
Record Defeat: 0-12 v Luton T., Division 3(S), Apr. 13th, 1936.
Most League Points: 64, Division 3(S), 1952–53.
Most League Goals: 92, Division 3(S), 1952–53.
Highest League Scorer in Season: Geoff Bradford, 33, Division 3(S), 1952–53.
Most League Goals in Total Aggregate: Geoff Bradford, 245, 1949–64.
Most Capped Player: Matt O'Mahoney, 6, Eire, 1, Ireland.
Most League Appearances: Stuart Taylor, 524, 1966–79.
Record Transfer Fee Received: £180,000 from Stoke City for Paul Randall, Dec. 1978.
Record Transfer Fee Paid: £50,000 to Birmingham C. for Gary Emmanuel, Jan. 1979.
Managers Since the War: Brough Fletcher, Bert Tann, Fred Ford, Bill Dodgin (Snr.), Don Megson.
Address of Supporters Club: 468 Stapleton Road, Bristol.
Address of Club Shop or Boutique: The Rovers Shop, 468 Stapleton Road, Bristol 5.

Bristol Stadium, Eastville, Bristol BS5 6NN. Telephone Bristol 511050. *Ground capacity:* 32,000 (18,000 covered). *Record attendance:* 38,472 v Preston N.E., F.A. Cup 4th Rd., January 30, 1960.   *Record receipts:* £23,275 v Southampton, F.A. Cup 4th Rd., Jan. 28 1978.
Pitch measurements: 110 yds × 70 yds.
How to get there: Buses 51 from Temple Meads Station to Stapleton Rd., five minutes from ground. By car, leave M4 or M5 at M32 junction; M32 runs direct to the ground.
Match tickets: Stand tickets available two weeks prior to the match.
Car parking: Large car parks at Stapleton Rd. and Muller Rd. entrances.
Entertainments/catering facilities: Bars open to the public in both stands. Tea bars on the terraces.
Club shop: In Stapleton Rd.; sells all types of souvenirs.
Handbooks/programmes: Handbooks and programmes available from club shop; programmes can be ordered on subscription.
Extra information: Bristol Rovers went 27 games without defeat in 1952–53, a Third Division (South) record, and 27 games in Division 3 from the start of the season 1973–74 (a Div. 3 record).
Club Colours: Blue and white quartered shirts, white shorts, white stockings with two blue rings on top.
Change Colours: Yellow shirts with blue trim, blue shorts, yellow stockings with blue tops.
Club Nickname: 'The Pirates'.
Player/Coach: Roy Cooper.

BRISTOL ROVERS 1978-79 LEAGUE RECORD

Match No.	Date	Venue	Opponents	Result	H/T Score	League Pos'n	Goalscorers	Attendance
1	Aug 19	H	Fulham	W 3-1	1-0	—	Randall, Gould, Barry	5950
2	22	A	Oldham Ath	L 1-3	0-1	—	Gould	6005
3	26	A	Charlton Ath	L 0-3	0-1	17		7745
4	Sept 2	H	Cardiff C	W 4-2	2-0	12	Grapes (og), Randall, Staniforth 2	6855
5	9	H	Luton T	W 2-0	0-0	6	Staniforth, Randall	6508
6	16	A	West Ham U	L 0-2	0-0	11		22,189
7	23	H	Wrexham	W 2-1	1-1	6	Randall, Williams	7619
8	30	A	Cambridge U	D 1-1	0-0	7	Aitken	5513
9	Oct 7	H	Blackburn R	W 4-1	3-1	5	Randall 3, Williams	7111
10	14	A	Notts Co	L 1-2	0-0	9	White	8646
11	21	H	Orient	W 2-1	1-0	6	Prince, Staniforth	7234
12	28	A	Leicester C	D 0-0	0-0	6		12,498
13	Nov 4	H	Newcastle U	W 2-0	1-0	5	Randall 2	10,582
14	10	A	Fulham	L 0-3	0-0	7		10,296
15	18	H	Charlton Ath	D 5-5	2-3	8	Randall 3, Williams 2	8107
16	25	H	Sheffield U	W 2-1	1-0	9	Staniforth, Randall	8434
17	Dec 2	A	Sunderland	L 0-5	0-1	10		18,864
18	9	H	Millwall	L 0-3	0-0	12		7112
19	16	A	Burnley	L 0-2	0-1	13		9119
20	23	H	Stoke C	D 0-0	0-0	14		7897
21	26	A	Crystal Palace	W 1-0	0-0	—	White	21,605
22	30	H	Preston NE	D 1-1	0-1	12	Hendrie	12,660
23	Jan 16	A	Luton T	L 2-3	2-0	—	White 2	6002
24	20	H	West Ham U	L 0-1	0-1	13		12,418
25	Feb 10	H	Cambridge U	W 2-0	2-0	12	Prince, White	5904
26	24	H	Notts Co	D 2-2	1-2	12	Williams 2	6887
27	Mar 3	A	Orient	D 1-1	0-0	11	White	5078
28	10	A	Leicester C	D 1-1	1-1	12	Williams	6381
29	20	H	Brighton & HA	L 1-2	0-1	—	Staniforth	8290
30	24	H	Oldham Ath	D 0-0	0-0	13		5405
31	31	H	Sheffield U	L 0-1	0-0	15		14,064
32	Apr 4	A	Blackburn R	W 2-0	1-0	—	White, Williams	8554
33	7	H	Sunderland	D 0-0	0-0	15		8003
34	14	H	Crystal Palace	L 0-1	0-0	14		10,986
35	16	A	Brighton & HA	L 0-3	0-3	—		23,024
36	17	A	Stoke C	L 0-2	0-2	—		18,679
37	21	H	Burnley	W 2-0	1-0	13	Jones (pen), White	5947
38	28	A	Millwall	W 3-0	2-0	13	White 2, Williams	5266
39	May 2	A	Newcastle U	L 0-3	0-2	—		9625
40	5	H	Preston NE	L 0-1	0-1	16		5814
41	7	A	Cardiff C	L 0-2	0-1	—		10,185
42	10	A	Wrexham	W 1-0	0-0	—	Williams	6136

Final League Position: 16

Goalscorers

League (48): Randall 13, White 10, Williams 10, Staniforth 6, Gould 2, Prince 2, Aitken 1, Barry 1, Hendrie 1, Jones 1 (pen), own goal 1.
League Cup (2): Aitken, Staniforth.
F.A. Cup (3): White 3.

League Cup	First Round	Hereford U (h)	2-1
		(a)	0-4
F.A. Cup	Third Round	Swansea C (a)	1-0
	Fourth Round	Charlton Ath (h)	1-0
	Fifth Round	Ipswich T (a)	1-6

Thomas	Jones	Bater	Pulis	Taylor	Prince	Dennehy	Williams	Gould	Randall	Barry	Aitken	Staniforth	Day	Hendrie	Lythgoe	Clarke	White	Petts	Harding	Mabbutt	Emmanuel	Brown	Shaw	Palmer	England	Match No.
1	2	3	4	5	6	7	8	9	10	11																1
1	12	3	4	5	7	8*	6	9	10	11	2															2
1	2	3	4	5		7	8	9	10*11		6	12														3
1		3		5	6	7*	9	12	8	11	2	10	4													4
1		3	2	5	6	7	8		10	11		9	4													5
1		3	2	5	6	7*	8		10	11		9	4	12												6
1		3	2	5	6	7	8	9				10	4		11											7
1		3	2*	5	6	7	8	9		12	10		4		11											8
1		3		5	6	7	8	9		2	10		4			11										9
1		3		5	6	7	8	10*		2		4		11	12	9										10
1		3		5	6	7	8	10		2	9	4		11												11
1		3		5	6	7	8	10		2	9	4		11												12
1		3		5	6	7	8	9		2	10	4	12	11*												13
1	6	3		5		7*	8	10		2	9	4	11			12										14
1		3		5	6*	7	8	10	11	2	9	4	12													15
1	3*			5		7	8	10	11	2	9	4	6			12										16
1	3			5		7*	8	10	11	2	9	4	6			12										17
1		3		5	6		8	10	11	2	9	4					7									18
1			5	6	11		8	10		3*	9	2				7	4	12								19
1	3		5	6			8	10			9	2				12	7*	4	11							20
1	2		5				8	9			10	4	12			7*		3	11	6						21
1	3		5		12	8					9	2	7			10		6	11*	4						22
1	2		5		12	8		11	10	4*	7			9			3	6								23
1	3		5		12	8*			6	10	2	11		9			4		7							24
1		3		5	6	7	8				2	11		9			4		10							25
1	2	3		5	6	7	8			12		10*		9			4		11							26
1		3		5	6	7	8			4	9	2				11			10							27
1		3		5		7*	8			6	10	2		11	9			12	4							28
1	2	3		5		7*	8		6	4	10		11	12	9											29
1	2	3		5			8		11*	4	10		7	12	9			6								30
1	2	3		5	6*	7	8			4	10		12		9			11								31
1	2	3		5		7	8			4	10		11		9			6								32
1	2	3		5		7	8			4	11		10		9			6								33
1	2	3		5		7	8			4	10		11*	12	9			6								34
1	2	3		5	11	7	8			4	10				9*			6	12							35
1	2	3		5	6*	7	8			4	10				9	12		11								36
1	2			5	11		8			3					9	7	4	10	6							37
1	2	3		5	11		8			4					9	7		10	6							38
1	2	3		5			8			6					9	7	4	10	11							39
1	2	3		5	6		8*			4					9	7		10	11		12					40
1	2	3		5	6		8			4					9	7		10*11	12							41
1	3						8			4					9	10		12	7	11	6*	2	5			42
42	21	36	7	41	26	29	42	3	21	12	31	31	24	13	6	2	23	9	10	8	21	1	1	1	1	
					+	+					+	+		+	+	+		+			+	+				
					1s	3s					1s	2s		5s	4s	4s	1s				3s	2s	1s			

BRISTOL ROVERS—PLAYERS

Player and position	Ht	Wt	Birthplace	Clubs	League Appearances	Goals
Goalkeepers						
Glyn Jones	6 0	13 1	Newport	Bristol R.	5	—
Martin Thomas	6 1	12 11	Senghenydd	Bristol R.	80	—
Defenders						
Peter Aitken	5 11	12 1	Penarth	Bristol R.	189+4	2
Stuart Taylor	6 4½	14 6	Bristol	Bristol R.	524	26
Phil Bater	5 10½	11 0	Cardiff	Bristol R.	153+1	1
Graham Day	6 1	12 4	Bristol	Bristol R.	129+1	1
(Contract cancelled March 1979)						
Vaughan Jones	5 8½	11 0	Tonyrefail	Bristol R.	22+1	1
Steve Harding	6 1	14 4	Bristol	Bristol C	2	—
				Southend U (on loan)	2	—
				Grimsby T (on loan)	8	—
				Bristol R.	16+1	1
Mike England	6 0	10 10	Bristol	Bristol R.	1	—
David Palmer	5 9	11 0	Bristol	Bristol R.	1	—
Mike Malpas	6 0	12 2	Bristol	Bristol R.	—	—
Midfield						
Frankie Prince	5 9	11 7	Cardiff	Bristol R.	349+2	23
David Williams	5 9	11 6	Cardiff	Bristol R.	154+1	30
Tony Pulis	5 10	10 8	Newport	Bristol R.	41+2	—
Paul Hendrie	5 6	9 8	Glasgow	Birmingham C	19+4	1
				Bristol R.	17+13	1
Mike Barry	5 10	11 6	Hull	Huddersfield T	21+5	—
(Contract cancelled April 1979)				Carlisle U	73+8	10
				Bristol R.	46+1	3
Ashley Griffiths	5 9	10 6	Barry	Bristol R.	—	—
Martin Shaw	5 7	9 12	Bristol	Bristol R.	1+1	—
Gary Emmanuel	5 9	10 8	Birmingham	Birmingham C	61+10	6
				Bristol R.	21	—
*Alan Hoult	5 8	10 8	Burbage	Leicester C	—	—
				Hull C (on loan)	3	1
				Lincoln C (on loan)	2+2	1
				Bristol R.	—	—
Forwards						
Dave Staniforth	6 0	12 1	Chesterfield	Sheffield U	22+4	3
				Bristol R.	135+18	31
Andrew Evans	5 10	10 6	Swansea	Bristol R.	34+8	2
(Retired)						
Steve White	5 11	11 11	Bristol	Bristol R.	31+4	14
Keith Brown	5 9	11 2	Bristol	Bristol R.	1+2	—
Gary Clarke	5 8	10 10	Boston	Bristol R.	2+4	—
Gary Mabbutt	5 10	10 6	Bristol	Bristol R.	8+3	—
Miah Dennehy	5 9	10 13	Cork	Nottingham F	37+4	4
(Eire)				Walsall	123+5	22
				Bristol R.	29+3	—

Paul Petts
 (Apprentice) 9+1 sub

BURNLEY DIV. 2

Chairman: R. W. Lord.
Directors: Dr. R. D. Iven, M.R.C.S.(Eng.), L.R.C.P. (Lond.), M.R.C.G.P., J. Wilde, M.B.E., J. Elgin, J. E. Jackson.
Team Manager: Harry Potts.
Secretary: A. Maddox.
Commercial Manager: Bill Read.
Year Formed: 1882. *Turned Professional:* 1883.
Limited Company: 1897.
Previous Name: 1881–82, Burnley Rovers.
Previous Grounds: 1881, Calder Vale; 1882, Turf Moor.
Football League Record:
  1888 Original Member of the Football League.
  1897–98 Division 2.
  1898–1900 Division 1.
  1900–13 Division 2.
  1913–30 Division 1.
  1930–47 Division 2.
  1947–71 Division 1.
  1971–73 Division 2.
  1973–76 Division 1.
  1976– Division 2.

Honours: Football League, Division 1, Champions: 1920–21, 1959–60; Runners-up: 1919–20, 1961–62. Division 2, Champions: 1897–98, 1972–73; Runners-up: 1912–13, 1946–47. *F.A. Cup,* Winners: 1913–14; Runners-up: 1946–47, 1961–62. *Football League Cup,* best season: Semi Final, 1960–61, 1968–69. *Anglo-Scottish Cup* Winners: 1978–79.
European Competitions: European Cup, 1960–61; *European Fairs Cup,* 1966–67.
Record Victory: 9-0 v Darwen, Division 1, Jan. 9th, 1892, v C. Palace, F.A. Cup, 2nd Rd. Replay 1908–09 and v New Brighton, F.A. Cup, 4th Rd., Jan. 26th, 1957.
Record Defeat: 0-10 v Aston Villa, Division 1, Aug. 29th, 1925 and v Sheffield U., Division 1, Jan. 19th, 1929.
Record 30 consecutive Division 1 games without defeat 1920–21
Most League Points: 62, Division 2, 1972–73.
Most League Goals: 102, Division 1, 1960–61.
Highest League Scorer in Season: George Beel, 35, Division 1, 1927–28.
Most League Goals in Total Aggregate: George Beel, 178, 1923–32.
Most Capped Player: Jimmy McIlroy, 52 (55) Ireland.
Most League Appearances: Jerry Dawson, 530, 1906–29.
Record Transfer Fee Received: £300,000 from Everton for Martin Dobson, August 1974; and from Derby Co. for Leighton James, Nov. 1975.
Record Transfer Fee Paid: £165,000 to QPR for Leighton James, Sept. 1978.
Managers Since the War: Cliff Britton, Frank Hill, Alan Brown, Billy Dougall, Harry Potts, Jimmy Adamson, Joe Brown, Harry Potts.
Address of Club Shop or Boutique: The Claret and Blue Shop, Brunshaw Road, Burnley, Lancs.

Turf Moor, Burnley BB10 4BX. *Telephones: Office:* Burnley (0282) 27777/38021 *Ticket Office and Shop:* Burnley 27777 and 38021. *Ground capacity:* 38,000. *Record attendance:* 54,775 v Huddersfield T., F.A. Cup 3rd Rd., February 23, 1924. *Pitch measurements:* 115yds × 73 yds.
How to get there: Central bus station and the Central railway station are both within 5 minutes walk of the ground, which is near the town centre.
Match tickets: None. Pay at turnstiles £3.20 & £2.80.
Car parking: parks in Church St. and Fulledge Recreation Ground are both chargeable. Each holds about 500 cars, and both are about 5 minutes' walk from stadium.
Entertainments/catering facilities: 'Centre Spot' Social Club underneath Bob Lord Stand—open every night. Seating for 300. Members and bona-fide guests only on match days. Snack, licensed bars are sited around the ground and under the stands.
Club shop: Attached to the Development Office in Brunshaw Rd., Burnley. Telephone: Burnley 27777 and 38021.
Handbooks/programmes: No handbooks. There is a subscription list for League programmes on a seasonal basis; enquiries c/o Club shop.
Club colours: Claret shirts with light blue sleeves, light blue shorts with claret trimming down side and light blue stockings.
Change Colours: All yellow.
Club Captain: Peter Noble.
First Team Trainer: Brian Miller.
Club Nickname: 'Clarets'.

BURNLEY 1978-79 LEAGUE RECORD

Match No.	Date	Venue	Opponents	Result	H/T Score	League Pos'n	Goalscorers	Attendance
1	Aug 19	H	Leicester C	D 2-2	0-1	—	Fletcher, Noble (pen)	12,026
2	22	A	Charlton Ath	D 1-1	1-1	—	Cochrane	8580
3	26	A	Fulham	D 0-0	0-0	11		5407
4	Sept 2	H	Notts Co	W 2-1	1-1	6	Noble (pen), Brennan	9961
5	9	H	West Ham U	W 3-2	1-2	4	Brennan, Fletcher, Thomson	12,303
6	16	A	Sheffield U	L 0-4	0-3	8		15,355
7	23	A	Sunderland	L 1-2	0-0	13	Morley	12,964
8	30	A	Millwall	W 2-0	1-0	9	Fletcher, Noble	5238
9	Oct 7	H	Oldham Ath	W 1-0	0-0	7	Smith	11,648
10	14	A	Stoke C	L 1-3	1-2	11	Ingham	18,437
11	21	H	Brighton & HA	W 3-0	0-0	7	Ingham 2, Brennan	10,271
12	28	A	Preston NE	D 2-2	1-2	7	Kindon, Noble (pen)	15,014
13	Nov 4	H	Crystal Palace	W 2-1	1-0	7	Brennan, Fletcher	11,067
14	11	A	Leicester C	L 1-2	0-0	8	Ingham	12,842
15	18	H	Fulham	W 5-3	2-2	5	Noble 3 (2 pens), James, Kinden	10,393
16	21	A	Notts Co	D 1-1	0-0	—	Ingham	8520
17	25	H	Cambridge U	D 2-2	1-2	5	Ingham, Fletcher	6502
18	Dec 9	A	Orient	L 1-2	1-0	11	Fletcher	4764
19	16	H	Bristol R	W 2-0	1-0	8	Ingham 2	9119
20	23	A	Newcastle U	L 1-3	0-2	8	Noble	23,630
21	26	H	Blackburn R	W 2-1	2-0	—	Fletcher, Noble	23,090
22	30	A	Cardiff C	D 0-0	0-0	7		9807
23	Feb 3	A	Sunderland	L 1-3	1-0	9	James	23,030
24	24	H	Stoke C	L 0-3	0-0	13		13,756
25	Mar 3	A	Brighton & HA	L 1-2	0-0	15	Ingham	19,402
26	6	H	Sheffield U	D 1-1	1-1	—	Fletcher	9000
27	10	H	Preston NE	D 1-1	0-0	14	Noble	15,175
28	13	H	Luton T	W 2-1	1-0	—	Noble 2 (1 a pen)	8000
29	21	H	Wrexham	W 1-0	1-0	—	Fletcher	5000
30	24	H	Charlton Ath	W 2-1	1-1	7	James, Scott	8521
31	31	H	Cambridge U	D 1-1	1-0	9	Robinson	8162
32	Apr 7	A	Luton T	L 1-4	0-2	9	Noble (pen)	6466
33	10	H	Newcastle U	W 1-0	1-0	—	Hall	7742
34	14	A	Blackburn R	W 2-1	0-1	7	Morley, Hall	14,761
35	16	H	Wrexham	D 0-0	0-0	—		9361
36	21	A	Bristol R	L 0-2	0-1	7		5947
37	24	H	West Ham U	L 1-3	1-2	—	Noble	24,139
38	28	H	Orient	L 0-1	0-0	9		7162
39	May 5	A	Cardiff C	D 1-1	1-0	10	Kindon	10,270
40	8	H	Millwall	L 0-1	0-1	—		5737
41	11	A	Crystal Palace	L 0-2	0-0	—		51,801
42	14	A	Oldham Ath	L 0-2	0-1	—		7791

Final League Position: 13

Goalscorers

League (51): Noble 14 (7 pens), Fletcher 9, Ingham 9, Brennan 4, James 3, Kindon 3, Hall 2, Morley 2, Cochrane 1, Robinson 1, Scott 1, Smith 1, Thomson 1.
League Cup (5): Cochrane 2, Noble, Ingham, Brennan.
F.A. Cup (6): Morley, James, Thomson, Fletcher, Ingham, Kindon.

League Cup	Second Round	Bradford C (h)	1-1
		(a)	3-2
	Third Round	Brighton & HA (h)	1-3
F.A. Cup	Third Round	Birmingham C (a)	2-0
	Fourth Round	Sunderland (h)	1-1
		(a)	3-0
	Fifth Round	Liverpool (a)	0-3

Stevenson	Scott	Brennan	Noble	Thomson	Rodaway	Cochrane	Ingham	Fletcher	Kindon	Smith	Hall	James	Morley	Robinson	Arins	Jakub	Young	Robertson	Match No.
1	2	3	4	5	6	7	8	9	10	11									1
1	2	3	4	5	6	7	8	9	10	11									2
1	2	3	4	5	6	7	8	9	10*11		12								3
1	2	3	4	5	6	7	8	9	10	11									4
1	2	3	4	5	6	7		9	10	11	8								5
1	2	3	4	5	6	7		9	10		8	11							6
1	2		4	5	6		3		10	9	8	11	7						7
1	2	3	4	5	6		8	9	10	7		11							8
1	2	3	4	5	6		8	9	10	7		11							9
1	2	3	4	5	6		8	9	10	7		11							10
1	2	3	4	5	6		8	9	10		7	11							11
1	2	3	4	5	6		8	9	10		7	11							12
1	2	3		5	6		8	9	10		7	11	4						13
1	2	3	4	5	6		8	9	10		7	11							14
1		3	4	5	6		8	9	10*		7	11	12	2					15
1		3	4	5	6		8	9	10		7	11		2					16
1		3	4	5	6		8	9	10		7*11		12	2					17
1		3	4	5	6		8	9	10*		7	11	12	2					18
1		3	4	5	6		8	9	10		7	11		2					19
1	2	3	4	5	6		8	9	10		7	11*	12						20
1	2	3	4	5	6		8	9	10		7	11*12							21
1	2*	3	4	5	6		8	9	10		7	11	12						22
1	2	3	4	5	6		8		10		7	11	9						23
1	2	3	4	5	6		8	9	10			11		7					24
1	2	3	4	5	6		8	9	10		7	11							25
1	2	3	4	5	6		8	9*10				11	12			7			26
1	2	3	4	5	6		8*	9	10			11	12			7			27
1	2	3	4	5	6			9	10		12	11		8*		7			28
1	2	3	4	5	6		8	9	10			11				7			29
1	2	3	4	5	6		8	9				11	10			7			30
1	2	3	4	5			8	9	10*			11	12	6		7			31
1	2	3	4	5			8	9	12			11	10	6		7*			32
1	2		4	5	6		8	9*10			7	11	12			3			33
1			4	5	6		8	9	10*		7	11	12		2	3			34
1			4	5	6			9			7	11	10		2	3	8*	12	35
1	2	3	4	5	6		8	9*			7	11	10	12					36
1	2	3	4	5	6		8				12	11	10	9		7*			37
1	2	3	4		6				10		7	11	9	5		8			38
1	2	3	4	5	6		8		10		7	11	9						39
1	2	3	4	5	6		8	12	10		7*11		9						40
1	2	3	4	5	6		8		10		7	11	9						41
1	2	3	4	5			8		10		11		9	6		7			42
42	35	38	41	41	39	6	37	34	37	9	25	37	12	8	7	13	1		
							+1s	+1s			+3s		+7s	+5s		+1s			

BURNLEY—PLAYERS

Player and position	Ht	Wt	Birthplace	Clubs	League Appearances	Goals
Goalkeepers						
Alan Stevenson	6 1	12 2½	Staveley	Chesterfield	104	—
				Burnley	276	—
Tony Norman	6 1	11 10	Mancot N. Wales	Burnley	—	—
Billy O'Rourke	6 0	12 7	Nottingham	Burnley	—	—
Defenders						
Ian Brennan	5 10	11 4½	Easington	Burnley	166+1	11
Jim Thomson	5 11½	12 0	Glasgow	Chelsea	33+6	1
				Burnley	271+3	3
Bob Higgins	6 2	13 6	Bolsover	Burnley	3	—
Derek Scott	5 8	11 12	Gateshead	Burnley	93+1	4
William Rodaway	5 9	12 12	Liverpool	Burnley	168+1	1
Peter Robinson	6 1	12 6	Ashington	Burnley	45+6	3
Tony Arins	5 11	11 8	Chesterfield	Burnley	7	—
Richard Overson	5 11	12 2	Kettering	Burnley	1	—
David Tait	5 9½	12 6	Burnley	Burnley	—	—
Jim Gardiner			Belfast	Portadown	(not known)	
			Belfast	Burnley	—	—
Kevin Young	5 8	9 11	Burnley	Burnley	1	—
Midfield						
Stuart Robertson	5 4	10 0	Glasgow	Burnley	0+1	—
Peter Noble	5 9	10 6	Newcastle	Newcastle U	22+3	7
				Swindon T	212+4	62
				Burnley	230+2	60
William Ingham	5 5½	9 10	Stakeford	Burnley	174+30	24
Joe Jakub	5 6	9 3	Falkirk	Burnley	19	1
Marshall Burke	5 7	9 1	Glasgow	Burnley	6+1	1
Brian Hall	5 7	10 6	Glasgow	Liverpool	140+4	15
				Plymouth Arg	49+2	16
				Burnley	34+4	3
Neil McGregor	5 6	10 9	Leeds	Burnley	—	—
Paul Dixon	5 10½	10 10	Burnley	Burnley	—	—
Jeff Tate	5 7	10 4	Burnley	Burnley	—	—
Forwards						
Paul Fletcher	5 9½	12 10	Bolton	Bolton W	33+3	5
				Burnley	278+2	71
Steve McAdam			Portadown	Portadown	(not known)	
				Burnley	—	—
Tony Morley	5 7	10 0	Ormskirk	Preston NE	78+6	15
				Burnley	78+13	5
Malcolm Smith	5 8	11 0	Stockton	Middlesbrough	32+24	11
				Bury (on loan)	5	1
				Blackpool (on loan)	8	5
				Burnley	60+3	16
Steve Kindon	6 0	12 12	Warrington	Burnley	102+7	28
				Wolverhampton W	111+27	28
				Burnley	64+1	15
Leighton James (Wales)	5 9	10 3	Llwchwr, Glam.	Burnley	180+1	44
				Derby Co	67+1	15
				QPR	27+1	4
				Burnley	37	3
Stuart Pickerill	5 8½	11 2	Burnley	Burnley	—	—
Philip Cavener	5 8	10 7	S. Shields	Burnley	—	—

BURY   DIV. 3

Chairman: R. A. Clarke B.Sc.Tech., F.I.O.B.
Vice-Chairman: Canon J. R. Smith, M.A.
Directors: G. A. Black, A. Metcalfe, Mrs. A. Allen.
Team Manager: Dave Hatton.
Secretary: John Heap.
Year Formed: 1885. *Turned Professional:* 1885.
Limited Company: 1897.
Football League Record:

1894 Elected to Division 2.	1961–67 Division 2.
1895–1912 Division 1.	1967–68 Division 3.
1912–24 Division 2.	1968–69 Division 2.
1924–29 Division 1.	1969–71 Division 3.
1929–57 Division 2.	1971–74 Division 4.
1957–61 Division 3.	1974– Division 3.

Honours: Football League, Highest League Position: 4th, Division 1, 1925–26. Division 2, Champions: 1894–95; Runners-up: 1923–24, Division 3, Champions: 1960–61; Runners-up: 1967–68. *F.A. Cup:* Winners, 1900, 1903, *Football League Cup,* best season, semi-finalists: 1963.
Record Victory: 12–1 v Stockton, F.A. Cup, 1st Rd. Replay, 1896–97.
Record Defeat: 0–10 v Blackburn R., F.A. Cup, 1887–88.
Most League Points: 68, Division 3, 1960–61.
Most League Goals: 108, Division 3, 1960–61.
Highest League Scorer in Season: Norman Bullock, 31, Division 1, 1925–26.
Most League Goals in Total Aggregate: Norman Bullock, 124, 1920–35.
Most Capped Player: Bill Gorman, 11 (14), Eire and (4), Ireland.
Most League Appearances: 506, Norman Bullock, 1920–35.
Record Transfer Fee Received: £85,000 from Swindon Town for Andy Rowland, Sept. 1978.
Record Transfer Fee Paid: £30,000 to Stoke City for David Gregory and £30,000 to Port Vale for Ken Beamish, September, 1978
Managers Since the War: Norman Bullock, John McNeil, Dave Russell, Bob Stokoe, Bert Head, Les Shannon, Jack Marshall, Les Hart, Colin McDonald, Tom McAnearney, Allan Brown, Bobby Smith, Bob Stokoe.
Address of Club Shop or Boutique: Bury F.C., Souvenir Shop, Gigg Lane.

Gigg Lane, Bury BL9 9HR. Telephone 061-764 4881/2. *Ground capacity:* 35,000. *Record attendance:* 35,000 v Bolton, F.A. Cup 3rd Rd., January 9, 1960. *Record receipts:* £22,200 v Nottingham F., L.Cup quarter final, Jan. 17 1978. *Pitch measurements:* 112 yds × 72 yds.

How to get there: Buses 35, 472, 481, 487, 488, 524 from Kay Gardens to within walking distance. The nearest railway station is Bury. Buses run from the station to the ground.
Match tickets: 500 seats in the Reserved Chair section of the main stand may be booked two weeks before the match.
Car parking: Season-ticket holders only may use the car park on match days. But there is ample parking space in the side-streets around the ground.
Entertainments/catering facilities: Social club open during normal licensing hours.
Club shop: At the ground; sells all types of souvenirs.
Handbooks/programmes: Programmes available from club shop.
Extra information: The social club has large dance hall, lounge, and cocktail bars. These facilities may be hired for private functions; tel. 061-764-6771.

Club Colours: White shirts, royal blue shorts, royal blue stockings with white band.
Change Colours: Yellow shirts, yellow shorts, yellow stockings.
Club Captain:
First Team Trainer: Les Hart.
Club Nickname: 'Shakers'.

BURY 1978-79 LEAGUE RECORD

Match No.	Date	Venue	Opponents	Result	H/T Score	League Pos'n	Goalscorers	Attendance
1	Aug 19	A	Swindon T	L 1-2	0-2	—	Keenan	5382
2	22	H	Southend U	D 3-3	0-1	—	Farrell, Tucker, Rowland	3243
3	26	H	Gillingham	D 2-2	2-2	14	Wilson, Overton (og)	3414
4	Sept 2	A	Swansea C	L 0-2	0-1	19		10,500
5	9	A	Oxford U	D 0-0	0-0	20		3699
6	12	H	Plymouth Arg	L 1-2	1-1	—	Robins	3361
7	16	H	Watford	L 1-2	1-0	22	Tucker	4102
8	22	A	Tranmere R	D 0-0	0-0	21		2458
9	26	A	Sheffield W	D 0-0	0-0	—		9000
10	30	H	Chester	D 1-1	1-1	22	Gregory	4056
11	Oct 7	A	Brentford	W 1-0	0-0	21	Beamish	5850
12	14	H	Chesterfield	W 3-0	2-0	18	Gregory, Beamish, Ritson	4306
13	17	H	Walsall	D 1-1	0-1	—	Beamish (pen)	4443
14	21	A	Exeter C	L 1-2	0-2	20	Gregory	3840
15	28	H	Hull C	D 1-1	1-0	20	Gregory	4088
16	Nov 4	A	Peterborough U	D 2-2	0-2	19	Stanton, Wilson	4780
17	11	H	Swansea C	L 0-1	0-0	20		5186
18	18	A	Gillingham	D 3-3	0-1	20	Beamish 2 (1 a pen), Stanton	6291
19	Dec 9	A	Colchester U	D 0-0	0-0	21		2732
20	26	H	Rotherham U	W 3-2	2-0	21	Beamish 2, Gregory	5852
21	30	H	Mansfield T	D 0-0	0-0	21		4009
22	Jan 20	A	Watford	D 3-3	0-2	20	Gregory, Beamish, Whitehead	12,003
23	Feb 10	H	Chester	D 1-1	0-1	19	Stanton	3160
24	13	A	Carlisle U	W 2-1	1-0	—	Hatton, Wilson	4547
25	24	A	Chesterfield	L 1-2	1-2	19	Gregory	4332
26	27	H	Tranmere R	W 1-0	0-0	—	Kennedy	3434
27	Mar 3	A	Exeter C	W 4-2	3-0	15	Beamish 3, Madden	3425
28	6	H	Blackpool	L 1-3	0-1	—	Beamish (pen)	4575
29	10	A	Hull C	L 1-4	1-2	19	Constantine	3940
30	20	H	Oxford U	D 1-1	1-1	—	Beamish	3168
31	24	A	Southend U	D 0-0	0-0	20		8531
32	27	H	Swindon T	L 0-1	0-0	—		3557
33	31	H	Shrewsbury T	W 3-0	0-0	19	Ritson, Wilson, Taylor	3340
34	Apr 3	A	Plymouth Arg	L 0-3	0-1	—		4728
35	7	A	Blackpool	W 2-1	0-1	18	Whitehead 2	5451
36	13	H	Carlisle U	D 2-2	1-2	—	Beamish 2	4838
37	14	A	Rotherham U	L 1-2	0-1	18	Beamish	2726
38	16	H	Lincoln C	D 2-2	2-1	—	Gregory, Lugg	3455
39	21	A	Mansfield T	L 0-3	0-2	18		3976
40	24	H	Walsall	W 1-0	1-0	—	Stanton	2573
41	28	H	Colchester U	D 2-2	1-1	17	Hilton, Wilson	2905
42	May 1	H	Sheffield W	D 0-0	0-0	—		3424
43	5	A	Shrewsbury T	L 0-1	0-0	19		6604
44	9	A	Lincoln C	W 4-1	3-0	—	Gregory, Johnson, Lugg, Wilson	1517
45	15	H	Brentford	L 2-3	2-1	—	Gregory, Taylor	2152
46	19	H	Peterborough U	W 1-0	0-0	—	Wilson	2298

Final League Position: 19

Goalscorers

League (59): Beamish 16 (3 pens), Gregory 10, Wilson 7, Stanton 4, Whitehead 3, Tucker 2, Ritson 2, Lugg 2, Taylor 2, Farrell 1, Keenan 1, Rowland 1, Robins 1, Kennedy 1, Constantine 1, Hatton 1, Hilton 1, Madden 1, Johnson 1, Own Goal 1.
League Cup (1): Rowland.
F.A. Cup (11): Gregory 6, Kennedy, Wilson (pen), Lugg, Beamish, Own Goal 1.

League Cup	First Round	Wrexham (a)	0-2
		(h)	1-2
F.A. Cup	First Round	Wigan Ath (a)	2-2
		(h)	4-1
	Second Round	Blackpool (h)	3-1
	Third Round	Orient (a)	2-3

Forrest	Keenan	Kennedy	Lugg	Tucker	Hatton	Wilson	Farrell	Rowland	Hilton	Taylor	Madden	Stanton	Robins	Bailey	Hamstead	Beamish	Gregory	Ritson	Johnson	Whitehead	Woolfall	Constantine	Mullen	Latchford	Match No.
1	2	3	4	5	6*	7	8	9	10	11	12														1
1	2	3	4	5		6		8	9	10	11		7												2
1	2	3	4	5		6	8	9	10	11	12	7*													3
1	2		4	3	5	6	8	9	10*	11		12	7												4
1		3	4	5	2	7	8	9		10			11	6											5
1	2*	3	4	5	12	7	8	9		11		10	6												6
1		3	2	5			4	8	9	10	11		7	6											7
1		3	2	5	4*	8			12	11		7			6	9	10								8
1		3	4	5		8				11		7			6	9	10	2							9
1		3	4	5		8	12			11		7*			6	9	10	2							10
1		3	4	5		8				11		7			6	9	10	2							11
1		3	4	5		8				11		7			6	9	10	2							12
1		3	4	5		8	12			11		7*			6	9	10	2							13
1		3	4	5		8	12			11		7*			6	9	10	2							14
1		3	4	5		8	7			11					6*	9	10	2	12						15
1		3	4	5		8				11		7				9	10	2	6						16
1		3	4	5		8				11		7				9	10	2	6						17
1		3	4	6		7				11		8				9	10	2	5						18
1		3	4	5		8				11		7	6			9	10	2							19
1		3	4	5		8*				11		7	6	2		9	10		12						20
1		3	2	5		4				11		7			6	8	9	10*	12						21
1		3	4	6		8				11	12	7*	5			9	10		2						22
1		3	4		5	8				11		7				9	10	2	6						23
1		3	4	5	6	8				11		7				9	10	2							24
1		3	4	5	6	8			12	11		7*				9	10	2							25
1		3	4		2	8			11	12		7		6		9	10*		5						26
1		3	4			8			11	10		7	5*		9			6			2	12			27
1		3	4		5*	8			11	10		7			9		12	6			2				28
1		3	4	5		8			11*	10		7			9		12	6			2				29
1		3		5		8			11			7*			9	10	4	12	6			2			30
1	8		4	5		7			11						9	10			2		6	3			31
1		3	7	5		8			11	12						10	4	9	6	2*					32
1	3*		4	6		10			11	12					9	8	5		7	2					33
1		7	5*			8			11	12	3				9	10	4		6	2					34
1	2		4*			8			11	12	7		6		9	10	3		5						35
1			4		3	8			11		7		5		9	10	2		6						36
1			7		2*	8			11	12	6		5		9	10	4		3						37
1			4			8			11		7		5		9	10	2		6	3					38
1	3*		4			8		9	11	12	7		5		10		2		6						39
1			4	5		8			11		7		6		9	10	2			3					40
1			4	5		8			12	11		7		6*	9	10	2			3					41
1			4	5		8				11		7			9	10	2		6	3					42
1			4	5		8				11		7			9	10	2		6	3					43
1			4	5*		8				12		7				10	2	9	6	3	11				44
			4			8				11	6	7				10	2	9	5	3		1			45
			4	5		8				11					9	10	2		6	3	7	1			46
44	5	33	45	36	12	46	8	7	6	45	4	36	4	16	10	35	36	31	3	24	—	16	2	2	

+1s (Tucker), +3s (Wilson), +3s (Rowland), +9s (Taylor), +3s (Stanton), +5s (Beamish), +1s (Johnson), +1s (Woolfall)

115

BURY—PLAYERS

Player and position	Ht	Wt	Birthplace	Clubs	League Appearances	Goals
Goalkeepers						
John Forrest	5 9	11 6	Bury	Bury	377	—
Dave Latchford	6 2	12 9	Birmingham	Birmingham C	206	—
				Wolverhampton W (on loan)	—	—
				Motherwell	8	—
				Barnsley	—	—
				Bury	2	—
Defenders						
Tony Bailey	5 10	11 2	Burton	Derby Co	1	—
				Oldham Ath	26	1
				Bury	124+7	1
Dave Hatton	5 10	11 10	Farnworth	Bolton W	231	7
(Contract cancelled April 1979)				Blackpool	250+1	6
				Bury	96+1	2
Keith Kennedy	5 7	10 8	Sunderland	Newcastle U	1	—
				Bury	287	4
Billy Tucker	5 11	11 10	Kidderminster	Hereford U	135+2	12
				Bury	96	8
Daniel Wilson	5 7	10 3	Wigan	Bury	55+3	8
Dave Constantine	5 8	10 3	Dukinfield	Hyde U	—	—
				Bury	16	1
Ron Evans	5 11	11 7	Manchester	Manchester C	—	—
				Bury	—	—
Alan Whitehead	6 3	12 0	Bury	Bury	30	4
John Ritson	5 9	10 5	Liverpool	Bolton W	321+3	9
				Bury	31	2
Midfield						
Ray Lugg	5 9	10 10	Jarrow	Middlesbrough	34+3	3
				Watford	51+8	3
				Plymouth Arg	22+2	1
				Crewe A	183+2	10
				Bury	45	2
Gordon Taylor	5 6	11 2	Ashton under Lyne	Bolton W	254+5	41
				Birmingham C	156+10	9
				Blackburn R	62+2	3
				Bury	45	2
Paul Hilton	6 1	11 6	Oldham	Bury	6+3	1
Forwards						
Craig Madden	5 8	10 2	Manchester	Bury	5+12	1
George Hamstead	5 6½	10 13	Rotherham	Rotherham U	—	—
(Contract cancelled April 1979)				York C	32+3	1
				Barnsley	147+2	23
				Bury	189+7	29
				Rochdale (on loan)	3+1	—
*Alan Woolfall	5 6	9 12	Liverpool	Bury	46+11	11
Brian Stanton	5 7	10 7	Liverpool	Bury	72+11	14
Steve Johnson	6 0	12 9	Liverpool	Bury	12+7	2
David Gregory	5 9	11 6	Peterborough	Peterborough U	131+11	32
				Stoke C	22+1	3
				Bury	36	10
Ken Beamish	6 0	12 6	Bebbington	Tranmere R	175+1	49
				Brighton	86+10	27
				Blackburn R	86	19
				Port Vale	84+1	29
				Bury	35	16
Steve Mullen	5 7	10 2	Glasgow	Darwen	—	—
				Bury	2+1	—

CAMBRIDGE UNITED   DIV. 2

Chairman: D. A. Ruston.
Vice-Chairman: A. R. Douglas.
Directors: B. C. Moore, R. H. Smart, A. E. Harris, J. Crook, J. E. Cooke.
Manager: John Docherty.   *Secretary:* L. S. Holloway.
General Manager:
Year Formed: 1919.   *Turned Professional:* 1946.
Limited Company: 1948.
Previous Name: Abbey United until 1949.

Football League Record:
1970 Elected to Division 4.
1973–74 Division 3.
1974–77 Division 4.
1977–78 Division 3.
1978– Division 2.

Honours: Football League, Highest Position: Division 2, 12th, 1978–79. Division 3, Runners-up 1977-78. Division 4, Champions 1976–77. *F.A. Cup,* best season: 3rd Rd., 1973–74, 1974–75, *Football League Cup* never beyond 2nd Rd.
Record Victory: 6-0 v Darlington, Sept. 18, 1971.
Record Defeat: 0-6 v Aldershot, Division 3, April 13 1974, and v Darlington, Division 4, September 28 1974.
Most League Points: 65, Division 4, 1976–77.
Most League Goals: 87, Division 4, 1976–77.
Highest League Scorer in a Season: Alan Biley, 21, 1977–78.
Most League Goals in Total Aggregate: Alan Biley, 63, 1975–79.
Most Capped Player: None.
Most League Appearances: Terry Eades, 248, 1970–77.
Record Transfer Fee Received: £35,000 from AFC Bournemouth for Brian Greenhalgh Feb 8, 1974.
Record Transfer Fee Paid: £50,000 to Northampton T for Derrick Christie Oct. 1978.
Managers Since the War: Bill Whittaker, Gerald Williams, Bert Johnson, Roy Kirk, Alan Moore, Bill Leivers, Ron Atkinson.
Address of Supporters Club: 530, Newmarket Rd., Cambridge.

Abbey Stadium, Newmarket Rd., Cambridge. Telephone Teversham (02205) 2170. *Ground capacity:* 12,000. *Record attendance:* 14,000 v Chelsea, Friendly, May 1, 1970. *Record receipts:* £3392 v Mansfield T., April 23, 1973. *Pitch measurements:* 115 yds × 75 yds.

How to get there: Nearest railway station; Cambridge. Buses 180 and 181 run from the station to the town centre; then buses 182 and 183 to the ground, which is situated on the east side of the city.
Match tickets: Reserved seats bookable 14 days in advance. Postal applications must be accompanied by remittance and S.A.E.
Car parking: Limited parking at main entrance; off-street parking allowed, and at Coldhams Common.
Entertainments/catering facilities: Entertainments each evening organised by Supporters' Club. Three canteens open in the ground on match days.
Club shop: Two shops, one at the main entrance, the other inside the ground.
Handbooks/programmes: Handbooks not available.
Extra information: Cambridge are the third youngest professional club in the Football League; they turned professional in 1946.
Club Colours: Shirts black and amber vertical trim. Shorts amber with black trim. Stockings black with amber trim.
Change Colours: White.

CAMBRIDGE UNITED 1978-79 LEAGUE RECORD

Match No.	Date	Venue	Opponents	Result	H/T Score	League Pos'n	Goalscorers	Attendance
1	Aug 19	H	Stoke C	L 0-1	0-0	—		7485
2	22	A	Brighton & HA	W 2-0	0-0		Streete, Winstanley (og)	21,548
3	26	A	Leicester C	D 1-1	0-1	9	Biley	14,148
4	Sept 2	H	Newcastle U	D 0-0	0-0	10		8404
5	9	A	Cardiff C	L 0-1	0-0	15		6154
6	16	H	Charlton Ath	D 1-1	0-1	15	Biley	6166
7	23	A	Luton T	D 1-1	0-1	15	Biley (pen)	10,801
8	30	H	Bristol R	D 1-1	0-0	15	Biley	5513
9	Oct 7	H	Preston NE	W 1-0	1-0	12	Finney	5398
10	14	A	Wrexham	L 0-2	0-1	15		9807
11	21	H	Blackburn R	L 0-1	0-0	16		5240
12	28	A	Notts Co	D 1-1	1-0	16	Biley	8437
13	Nov 4	H	Orient	W 3-1	2-1	14	Biley 2, Finney	6655
14	11	A	Stoke C	W 3-1	2-0	12	Biley (pen), Leach, Garner	19,027
15	18	H	Leicester C	D 1-1	0-0	14	Finney	8875
16	22	A	Newcastle U	L 0-1	0-1	—		20,004
17	25	H	Burnley	D 2-2	2-1	14	Garner, Biley	6502
18	Dec 2	A	West Ham U	L 0-5	0-1	15		21,379
19	9	H	Oldham Ath	D 3-3	2-1	15	Hicks (og), Finney, Biley (pen)	4663
20	16	A	Sunderland	W 2-0	1-0	12	Christie 2	20,841
21	23	H	Crystal Palace	D 0-0	0-0	13		8081
22	26	A	Fulham	L 1-5	0-2	—	Biley (pen)	7814
23	30	A	Sheffield U	D 3-3	0-1	15	Cozens, Biley 2	14,527
24	Jan 13	H	Cardiff C	W 5-0	0-0	12	Finney, Biley 3, Garner	5344
25	Feb 3	H	Luton T	D 0-0	0-0	12		8125
26	10	A	Bristol R	L 0-2	0-2	14		5904
27	24	H	Wrexham	W 1-0	1-0	11	Cegielski (og)	5297
28	Mar 6	A	Charlton Ath	W 3-2	3-0		Biley, Christie, Cozens	6119
29	10	H	Notts Co	L 0-1	0-0	11		5758
30	17	A	Orient	L 0-3	0-0	13		4577
31	20	H	Millwall	W 2-1	0-1	—	Murray, Biley	5301
32	24	A	Brighton & HA	D 0-0	0-0	11		8455
33	28	A	Blackburn R	L 0-1	0-0	—		6448
34	31	H	Burnley	D 1-1	0-1	11	Biley	8162
35	Apr 7	H	West Ham U	D 0-0	0-0	12		11,406
36	10	A	Crystal Palace	D 1-1	1-1	—	Spriggs	21,795
37	14	H	Fulham	W 1-0	1-0	10	Finney	6573
38	17	A	Millwall	L 0-2	0-1	—		6414
39	21	H	Sunderland	L 0-2	0-0	11		10,100
40	24	A	Preston NE	W 2-0	0-0	—	Finney, Buckley	10,136
41	28	A	Oldham Ath	L 1-4	1-2	12	Finney	6185
42	May 5	H	Sheffield U	W 1-0	1-0	12	Spriggs	7255

Final League Position: 12

Goalscorers

League (44): Biley 20 (4 pens), Finney 8, Christie 3, Garner 3, Spriggs 2, Buckley 1, Cozens 1, Leach 1, Murray 1. Streete 1, Own Goals 3.

League Cup (3): Morgan, Finney, Biley (pen).

F.A. Cup (1): Biley

League Cup:	First Round	Northampton T (h)	2-2
		(a)	1-2
F.A. Cup:	Third Round	Shrewsbury T (a)	1-3

Webster	Howard	Smith L	Streete	Fallon	Graham	Cozens	Buckley	Biley	Finney	Murray	Adams	O'Neill	Spriggs	Leach	Stringer	Watson	Christie	Garner	Corbin	Key	Smith M.P.	Match No.
1	2	3	4	5	6	7	8*	9	10	11	12											1
1	2	3	4	5	6	7		11	10	9		8										2
1	2	3	4	5	6	7	12	11	10	9*		8										3
1	2	3	4*	5	6	7	9	11	10	12		8										4
1	2	3	4*	5	6	7		9	11	10	12	8										5
1	2	3	6*	5	4	7	9	11	10			8	12									6
1	2	3		5		7*	9	11	10			8	6	4	12							7
1	2	3		5	7		9	11	10			8	6	4								8
1	2	3		5	7			11	10	9		8	6	4								9
1	2	3		5	7			11	10	9		8	6	4								10
1	2	3		5	12	7		11	10	9*		8	6	4								11
1	2	3		5		7		11	10	9		8	6	4								12
1	2	3		5				11	10			8	6	4		7	9					13
1	2*	3		5		12		11	10			8	6	4		9	7					14
1	2	3		5		12		11	10			8	6	4		9*	7					15
1		3		5	2	7*		11	10			8	6	4		12	9					16
1		3		5				11	10			8	6	4		9	7	2				17
1		3		5				11	10	12		8	6	4		7	9	2*				18
1		3		5				11	10			8	6	4		9	7	2				19
1		3		5	2	9		11	10			8	6	4		7						20
1		3		5	2	9	6	11	10			8		4		7						21
1		3		5	2	9	6	11	10*			8		4		7	12					22
1		3	6	5		9	2	11	10	7		8		4								23
1		3	12	5		7		11*	10			2	6	4		9	8					24
1		3		5		2		11	10			8	6	4		9	7					25
1		3		5	12	2		11	10			8	6*	4		7	9					26
1		3		5	6	2		11	10	9		8		4		7						27
1		3		5	2	6	12	11	10	9		8		4		7*						28
1				5	2	6	3		10	9		8	11	4		7*	12					29
1		3		5	2	6	12	11	10	9		8		4		7*						30
1		3	12	5	2			6	11	10	7	8		4		9*						31
1		3		5	2	12		6	11	10	9	8		4		7*						32
1		3	12	5	2			6*	11	10	9	8		4		7						33
1		3		5	2			6*	11	10	9	8		4		7	12					34
1		3		5	2			9	11	10	6	8		4		7*	12					35
1		3	12	5	2			6	11	10	9	8		4		7*						36
1		3	9	5	2			6	11	10	7	8		4								37
1		3	7	5		2*		6	11	10	9	8		4		12						38
1		3		5	6*	12	2	11	10	9		8		4		7						39
1		3		5	2			6	11	10	9	8		4		7						40
	3			5	2*			6	11	10	9	8		4		7			1	12		41
1				5	2	6	3	11	10		12	8		4		9*	7					42
41	15	40	9	42	28	23	22	41	42	23	1	40	18	36		20	17	3	1			
		+4s		+2s	+4s	+3s		+3s	+1s	+1s		+1s	+1s	+1s		+5s			+1s			

CAMBRIDGE UNITED—PLAYERS

Player and position	Ht	Wt	Birthplace	Clubs	League Appearances	Goals
Goalkeepers						
Malcolm Webster	5 10½	12 6	Rossington	Arsenal	3	—
				Fulham	95	—
				Southend	96	—
				Cambridge U	122	—
Richard Key	6 0	12 4	Coventry	Coventry C.	—	—
				Exeter C	109	—
				Cambridge U	1	—
Defenders						
David Stringer	5 10	11 9	Gt. Yarmouth	Norwich C	417+2	19
				Cambridge U	120	1
Steve Fallon	6 1	11 2	Whittlesey	Cambridge U	170+5	13
Lindsay Smith	5 11	11 1	London	Colchester U	185+27	16
				Cambridge U	67	1
				Charlton Ath (on loan)	1	—
				Millwall (on loan)	4+1	—
Nigel Smith	5 10	11 7	Banstead	Brentford	81+4	—
				Cambridge U	0+1	—
Floyd Streete	6 1	12 8	West Indies	Cambridge U	27+10	5
Midfield						
Stephen Spriggs	5 2	9 0	Doncaster	Huddersfield T	2+2	—
				Cambridge U	163+1	20
Ian Buckley	5 8	11 0	Oldham	Oldham Ath	—	—
				Stockport Co	55+10	2
				Cambridge U	39+6	1
Trevor Howard	5 7	10 10	Kings Lynn	Norwich C	81+43	13
				Bournemouth	86	11
				Cambridge U	105	5
*Kirk Corbin	5 10	11 0		Cambridge U	3	—
Steve Adams	5 5	10 0	Windsor	QPR	—	—
(Contract cancelled October 1978)				Millwall	1	—
				Cambridge U	1+2	—
Peter Graham	5 10	10 4	Barnsley	Barnsley	16+3	—
				Halifax (on loan)	6	—
				Darlington	118+1	43
				Lincoln C	142+16	47
				Cambridge U	28+2	—
Ian Ladd	6 0	11 1	Peterborough	Notts Co	1	—
(Contract cancelled)				Cambridge U	—	—
Mike Leach	6 0	12 0	London	QPR	291+22	61
				Cambridge U	18+1	1
Forwards						
Alan Biley	5 8	10 9	Leighton Buzzard	Luton T	—	—
				Cambridge U	138+5	63
Jim Murray	5 7	10 8	Scotland	Cambridge U	35+12	2
Tom Finney	5 11	11 8	Belfast	Luton T	13+1	5
(N. Ireland)				Sunderland	8+7	1
				Cambridge U	126+4	37
Tom O'Neil	5 7	10 11	Glasgow	Cambridge U	2+5	1
John Cozens	6 0	12 0	London	Notts Co	41+5	13
				Peterborough U	127+5	41
				Cambridge U	39+9	3
Sammy Morgan	6 1	11 0	Belfast	Port Vale	109+4	24
(N. Ireland)				Aston V	35+5	9
(Transferred to Sparta Rotterdam)				Brighton	19+16	9
				Cambridge U	34+3	4
Peter Silvester	5 11	11 8	Wokingham	Reading	76+2	26
(Contract cancelled October 1978)				Norwich C	99+1	36
				Colchester U (on loan)	4	—
				Southend U	79+2	32
				Reading (on loan)	2	—
				Blackburn R (on loan)	5	1
				Washington Diplomats (not known)		
				Cambridge U	2+2	1
Gordon Sweetzer	6 0	11 8	Toronto	Brentford	68+4	40
				Cambridge U	8	3
Roger Avery	—	—		Cambridge U	0+1	—
Derrick Christie	5 8	10 10	Bletchley	Northampton T	116+22	18
				Cambridge U	20+1	3
Bill Garner	6 0	12 0	Leicester	Notts Co	2	—
				Bedford	—	—
				Southend U	101+1	41
				Chelsea	94+11	31
				Cambridge U	17+5	3

CARDIFF CITY DIV. 2

Chairman: R. Grogan, C.Eng., M.I.E.E., M.I.Gas.E., A.M.B.I.M.
Vice-Chairman: J. A. Clemo, Dip. P.E.
Directors: C. Griffiths, E. Jones, J. P. Leonard,
Executive Directors: J. D. Evans, M.A. (Cantab), Counc. J. Hermer (Cantab)
Team Manager: Richie Morgan.
Asst. Manager: Brian Harris.
Secretary: L. G. Hayward.
Year Formed: 1899. *Turned Professional:* 1910.
Limited Company: 1910.
Previous Grounds: Riverside, Sophia Gardens, Old Park and Fir Gardens. Moved to Ninian Park, 1910.
Previous Name: 1899–1910, Riverside.

Football League Record:
  1920 Elected to Division 2.   1952–57 Division 1.
  1921–29 Division 1.   1957–60 Division 2.
  1929–31 Division 2.   1960–62 Division 1.
  1931–47 Division 3(S).   1962–75 Division 2.
  1947–52 Division 2.   1975–76 Division 3.
                                   1976–   Division 2.

Honours: *Football League*, Division 1, Runners-up: 1923–24. Division 2, Runners-up: 1920–21, 1951–52, 1959–60. Division 3(S), Champions: 1946–47. Division 3, Runners-up 1975–76, *F.A. Cup*, Winners: 1926–27 (Only occasion the Cup has been won by a club outside England). Runners-up: 1925. *Football League Cup*, semi-final: 1965–66. Welsh Cup Winners: 20 times. *Charity Shield:* 1927.
European Competitions: *European Cup Winners Cup:* 1964–65, 1965–66, 1967–68, 1968–69, 1969–70, 1970–71, 1971–72, 1973–74, 1974–75, 1976–77, 1977–78.
Record Victory: 9–2 v Thames, Division 3(S), Feb. 6th, 1932.
Record Defeat: 2–11 v Sheffield U., Division 1, Jan. 1st, 1926.
Most League Points: 66, Division 3(S), 1946–47.
Most League Goals: 93, Division 3(S), 1946–47.
Highest League Scorer in Season: Stan Richards, 31, Division 3(S), 1946–47.
Most Capped Player: Alf Sherwood, 39 (41), Wales.
Most League Appearances: Tom Farquharson, 445, 1922–35.
Most League Goals in Total Aggregate: Len Davies, 127, 1921–29.
Record Transfer Fee Received: £110,000 for John Toshack from Liverpool, Nov. 1970.
Record Transfer Fee Paid: £120,000 to Tranmere Rovers for Ronnie Moore, Feb. 1979.
Managers Since the War: Bill McCandless, Cyril Spiers, Trevor Morris, Bill Jones, George Swindin, Jimmy Scoular, Frank O'Farrell, Jimmy Andrews.
Address of Supporters Club: Bluebirds Club, Bluebirds Office, Ninian Park, Cardiff CF1 8SX.
Address of Club Shop or Boutique: Bluebirds Shop, Ninian Park, Cardiff CF1 8SX.

Ninian Park, Cardiff CF1 8SX. Telephone Cardiff 398636/7/8. *Telegraphic address:* 'Soccer Cardiff'. *Ground capacity:* 26,815. *Record attendance:* 61,566, Wales v England, October 14, 1961. *Club record:* 57,800 v Arsenal, Division 1, April 22, 1953. *Record receipts:* £31,728 v Everton F.A. Cup 5th Rd., February 26, 1977. *Pitch measurements:* 114 yds × 78 yds.
How to get there: Corporation bus 2 runs past the ground; special buses run to Ninian Park from the bus station, returning after the match. Nearest railway station: Cardiff Central.
Match tickets: Bookable 14 days in advance by postal application. Details from Ticket Office (tel: Cardiff 398636/7/8).
Entertainments/catering facilities: Refreshment points around the ground.
Club shop: Open on match days; souvenirs available during the week from the Pools Office.
Handbooks/programmes: No handbook. Back numbers of programmes available from Programme Dept., Ninian Park.
Extra information: In 1928–29 Cardiff conceded the least number of goals in the First Division – but were relegated!
Club Colours: Blue shirts with single yellow and white stripe, blue shorts and stockings with yellow and white trim.
Change Colours: Shirts yellow with blue and white vertical stripe on chest. Shorts, yellow with blue and white stripe down sides. Stockings, yellow with blue and white band on turndown.
Club Captain:
Club Nickname: 'Bluebirds'.

CARDIFF CITY 1978–79 LEAGUE RECORD

Match No.	Date	Venue	Opponents	Result	H/T Score	League Pos'n	Goalscorers	Attendance
1	Aug 19	H	Preston NE	D 2-2	2-1	—	Went, Dwyer	7812
2	23	A	Stoke C	L 0-2	0-0	—		16,005
3	26	H	Oldham Ath	L 1-3	1-1	22	Buchanan	6929
4	Sept 2	A	Bristol R	L 2-4	0-2	22	Roberts, Buchanan (pen)	6855
5	9	H	Cambridge U	W 1-0	0-0	22	Buchanan	6154
6	16	A	Luton T	L 1-7	0-2	22	Bishop	7752
7	23	H	Blackburn R	W 2-0	1-0	20	Stevens, Bishop	6248
8	30	A	Wrexham	W 2-1	1-0	17	Buchanan 2 (1 a pen)	11,766
9	Oct 7	H	Notts Co	L 2-3	0-1	19	Buchanan, Stevens	7974
10	14	A	Orient	D 2-2	1-1	19	Buchanan, Stevens	6064
11	21	H	Leicester C	W 1-0	1-0	15	Stevens	8791
12	28	A	Newcastle U	L 0-3	0-1	17		23,462
13	Nov 4	H	Charlton Ath	L 1-4	1-2	20	Stevens	7842
14	11	A	Preston NE	L 1-2	0-2	20	Evans	9268
15	18	A	Oldham Ath	L 1-2	1-0	21	Bishop	5356
16	25	H	Crystal Palace	D 2-2	2-1	21	Evans, Dwyer	8739
17	Dec 2	A	Millwall	L 0-2	0-1	21		5381
18	9	H	Sunderland	D 1-1	1-1	21	Evans (pen)	7178
19	16	A	Sheffield U	L 1-2	0-2	22	Evans (pen)	11,913
20	23	H	Fulham	W 2-0	1-0	20	Evans, Roberts	5558
21	26	A	Brighton & HA	L 0-5	0-3	—		20,172
22	30	A	Burnley	D 0-0	0-0	20		9807
23	Jan 13	A	Cambridge U	L 0-5	0-0	20		5344
24	Feb 24	H	Orient	W 1-0	1-0	20	Buchanan	8256
25	28	A	Blackburn R	W 4-1	1-1	—	Stevens, Grapes, Buchanan, Evans	7158
26	Mar 3	A	Leicester C	W 2-1	0-1	18	Dwyer, Stevens	12,820
27	10	H	Newcastle U	W 2-1	1-0	18	Bishop, Stevens	11,116
28	17	A	Charlton Ath	D 1-1	0-1	18	Buchanan	5658
29	24	H	Stoke C	L 1-3	0-2	19	Buchanan (pen)	14,869
30	27	A	Notts Co	L 0-1	0-1	—		8211
31	31	A	Crystal Palace	L 0-2	0-2	20		18,672
32	Apr 7	H	Millwall	W 2-1	1-0	19	Stevens, Kitchener (og)	7714
33	11	A	Fulham	D 2-2	2-2	—	Dwyer, Money (og)	6067
34	14	H	Brighton & HA	W 3-1	2-1	19	Stevens, Evans, Moore	12,613
35	16	A	West Ham U	D 1-1	0-1	—	Bishop	29,058
36	21	H	Sheffield U	W 4-0	2-0	18	Stevens, Buchanan 3 (1 a pen)	10,590
37	25	H	Luton T	W 2-1	1-0	—	Moore, Stevens	10,549
38	28	A	Sunderland	W 2-1	1-0	14	Moore, Bishop	36,526
39	May 5	H	Burnley	D 1-1	0-1	13	Sullivan	10,270
40	7	H	Bristol R	W 2-0	1-0	—	Stevens, Buchanan (pen)	10,185
41	11	H	West Ham U	D 0-0	0-0	—		13,140
42	14	H	Wrexham	W 1-0	0-0	—	Buchanan	11,910

Final League Position: 9

Goalscorers

League (56): Buchanan 16 (5 pens), Stevens 13, Evans 7 (2 pens), Bishop 6, Dwyer 4, Moore 3, Roberts 2, Grapes 1, Sullivan 1, Went 1, Own Goals 2.

League Cup (2): Buchanan, Bishop.

League Cup:	First Round	Oxford U	(h)	1-2
			(a)	1-2
F.A. Cup:	Third Round	Swindon T	(a)	0-3

Healey	Thomas	Pethard	Campbell	Went	Roberts	Burns	Giles	Dwyer	Bishop	Buchanan	Davies	Byrne	Grapes	Attley	Pontin	Harris	Barber	Stevens	Larmour	Lewis	Evans	Platt	Micallef	Jones	Sullivan	Moore	Match No.
1	2	3	4	5	6	7	8	9	10	11																	1
	2	3	4	5	6	7	8	9	10		1	11															2
	2	3	4	5	6	10	8*	9		11	1		7	12													3
	2	3	4		6	8		9		11	1		7		5	10											4
	2	3	4		6	8		9	10*	11			7		5		1	12									5
	2	5	7		4	8	11	12	9				6		3*		1	10									6
1		3	4					2	10	11*			7	12	5			9	6	8							7
1	12	3	4*					2	10	8			7		5			9	6	11							8
1		3	4					2	10	8			7		5			9	6	11							9
1	12		4*	3				2		8			7		5			9	6	11	10						10
1	4	12		5				3		8			7*	2				9	6	11	10						11
1	4	12	7	3				2		8	6*				5			9		11	10						12
1	6		4	3				2	12	8			7*		5			9		11	10						13
	3		4				8	2	12	7*					5			9	6	11	10	1					14
	3		4					2	8					7	5			9	6	11	10	1					15
	3		4*					2	11	7				8	5			9	6	12	10	1					16
	3	12	4					2	8	11				7	5			9	6		10*	1					17
1	3	12	4					2	8	7				11*	5			9	6		10						18
1	3	8	4					2		7					5			9	6		10	11					19
1	2	3	4		5			9		8*			7					12	6	11	10						20
1	2	3	4		5			10	12				7					8*	6	11	9						21
1	4	3	7					2	9				8	5					6	11	10						22
1	3			4			11	10	9				7	2	5			6		8							23
1			4				5	12	9				7*		6			8			10			2	3	11	24
1			4				6		11				7		5			8			10			2	3	9	25
1		6		2			5	8	11				7		4			10							3	9	26
1		6					5	8	11				7		4			10						2	3	9	27
1			4	2			6	8*11					7		5			10		12					3	9	28
			4	2			5	8	11	1			7		6				12	10*					3	9	29
1			4	2			6	8	11				7		5					9					3	10	30
1			4	2			6	8					7*		5			11	12	9					3	10	31
1	5		4	6				8										11	7	9		12	2		3	10*	32
1			4				6	7	11						5			10		8				2	3	9	33
1	5		4	6				8	7									11		9				2	3	10	34
1			4	5			6	7	11									10		8				2	3	9	35
1	6		4	5			11	8	7									10		9				2	3		36
1	6		4*	5				7	11		12							10		8				2	3	9	37
1			4	5			6	8	7									11		9				2	3	10	38
1			4	5			6	8*	7		12							11		9				2	3	10	39
1			4	5			6		11		7							10		8				2	3	9	40
1			4	5			6		11		7							10		8				2	3	9	41
1			4	5			6		11		7							10		8				2	3	9	42
32	22	14	40	3	28	6	4	39	26	36	4	2	22	8	27	1	2	32	15	13	30	4	1	14	19	18	
	+ 1s	+ 5s						+ 5s					+ 2s	+ 2s				+ 2s	+ 3s	+ 1s				+ 1s			

CARDIFF CITY—PLAYERS

Player and position	Ht	Wt	Birthplace	Clubs	League Appearances	Goals
Goalkeepers						
Ron Healey (Eire)	5 11	13 0	Manchester	Manchester C Coventry C (on loan) Preston (on loan) Cardiff C	30 3 6 132	— — — —
John Davies	6 3	13 2		Cardiff C	4	—
Defenders						
Colin Sullivan	5 8	11 4	Saltash	Plymouth Arg Norwich C Cardiff C	225+5 154+3 19	7 3 1
Phil Dwyer (Wales)	6 0	13 0	Cardiff	Cardiff C	269	27
Albert Larmour	5 10½	11 10	Belfast	Linfield Cardiff C	— 152+2	— —
*Freddie Pethard	5 8	11 7	Glasgow	Celtic Cardiff C	— 161+10	— —
*Richie Morgan	5 11	12 6	Cardiff	Cardiff C	69	1
Keith Pontin	6 1½	12 7	Pontyclun	Cardiff C	70	1
Rod Thomas (Wales)	6 2½	13 1	Glyncorrwg	Swindon T Derby Co Cardiff C	296 89 36+3	5 2 —
Linden Jones	5 6	10 8	New Tredegar	Cardiff C	14	—
Phil Leach	5 11	11 6	Cardiff	Cardiff C	—	—
Paul Miller	5 11	11 3	Cardiff C	Cardiff C	—	—
Dave Roberts (Wales)	5 11	12 5	Southampton	Fulham Oxford U Hull C Cardiff C	21+1 160+1 86 28	— 8 4 2
*Gerry Byrne	5 8	10 6	Glasgow	Cardiff C	11+4	—
Dean Piper	5 9	11 5	Newport	Manchester C Cardiff C	— —	— —
Gary Harris	5 9½	13 0		Cardiff C	1	—
Midfield						
John Buchanan	5 8	11 0	Dingwall	Northampton T Cardiff C	104+10 153+9	25 42
Alan Campbell	5 8	11 7	Arbroath	Charlton Ath Birmingham C Cardiff C	196+2 39+1 116	28 6 2
Steve Grapes	5 7	10 11	Norwich	Norwich C Bournemouth (on loan) Cardiff C	34+7 7 69+7	3 1 3
Chris Williams	5 11	11 7	Brecon	Cardiff C	3	—
Antone Joseph	5 9	11 0	Manchester	Cardiff C	—	—
John Lewis	5 9	11 3	Tredegar	Cardiff C	13+3	—
Tony Parsons	5 8	9 12	Cardiff	Cardiff C	—	—
Forwards						
Tony Evans	5 8	11 7	Liverpool	Blackpool Cardiff C	4+2 120+4	— 47
Robin Friday	5 10	12 0	London	Reading Cardiff C	121 20+1	46 6
Ray Bishop	5 8	10 4	Hengoed	Cardiff C	48+9	14
Paul Davies	5 11	12 9	Kidderminster	Cardiff C	—	—
Gary Stevens	6 1	12 0	Birmingham	Cardiff C	32+2	13
*Christopher Guy	5 7	9 9	Cardiff	Cardiff C	—	—
Robert Sherman	5 10	9 11	Aberystwyth	Cardiff C	—	—
Ronnie Moore	6 0	12 10	Liverpool	Tranmere R Cardiff C	246+1 18	72 3
Constantinous Micallef	5 5	11 4	Cardiff	Cardiff C	1+1	—
Kevin Lloyd			Wolverhampton	Cardiff C	—	—

CARLISLE UNITED

DIV. 3

Chairman: J. A. Bendall.
Directors: H. Sherrard, J. C. Monkhouse, J. W. Cullen, H. A. Jenkins, T. L. Sibson, J. Johnston, J. R. Sheffield, Dr. T. Gardner, M.B., ChB.
Team Manager: Bob Moncur.
Secretary: J. D. Dent.
Year Formed: 1904. *Limited Company:* 1921.
Previous Grounds: 1903–5, Milholme Bank; 1906–9 Devonshire Park; 1910– Brunton Park.

Football League Record:
1928 Elected to Division 3(N).   1965–74 Division 2.
1958–62 Division 4.   1974–75 Division 1.
1962–63 Division 3.   1975–77 Division 2.
1963–64 Division 4.   1977–   Division 3.
1964–65 Division 3.

Honours: Football League, highest position: 22nd Division 1, 1974–75. Promoted from Division 2 (3rd) 1973–74. Division 3, Champions: 1964–65. Division 4, runners-up: 1963–64. *F.A. Cup,* 6th Rd., 1974–75.

Football League Cup, Semi-Finalists: 1969–70.

Record Victory: 8-0 v Hartlepools U., Division 3(N), Sept. 1st, 1928 and v Scunthorpe U. Division 3(N), Dec. 25th, 1952.

Record Defeat: 1-11 v Hull C., Division 3(N), Jan. 14th, 1939.

Most League Points: 62, Division 3(N), 1950–51.

Most League Goals: 113, Division 4, 1963–64.

Highest League Scorer in Season: Jimmy McConnell, 42, Division 3(N), 1928–29.

Most Capped Player: Eric Welsh, 4, Ireland.

Most League Appearances: Alan Ross, 466, 1963–79.

Most League Goals in Total Aggregate: Jimmy McConnell, 126, 1928–32.

Record Transfer Fee Received: £125,000 from Wolverhampton W for Bill Rafferty, March 1978.

Record Transfer Fee Paid: £75,000 to Portsmouth for David Kemp, March 1978.

Managers Since the War: W. Clark, Ivor Broadis, Bill Shankly, Fred Emery, Ivor Broadis, Andy Beattie, Ivor Powell, Alan Ashman, Tim Ward, Bob Stokoe, Ian MacFarlane, Alan Ashman, Dick Young.

Brunton Park, Carlisle, CA1 1LL. Telephone Carlisle 0228-26237.   *Redord attendance:* 27,500 v Birmingham C., F.A. Cup 3rd Rd., January 5, 1957, and v Middlesbrough, F.A. Cup, 5th Rd., February 7, 1970.   *Record receipts:* £20,506 v Manchester U, F.A. Cup 3rd Rd, January 7, 1978.   *Ground capacity:* 25,000.   *Pitch measurements:* 117 yds × 78 yds.

How to get there: City centre one mile away. Ribble buses from the Town Hall. Nearest railway station, Carlisle. By road—exit 43 from the M6, ground ¾ mile away; this avoids the town centre.
Match tickets: Bookable 1–2 weeks in advance by post or personal application.
Car parking: Car park holding 1500 vehicles adjacent to the ground. Limited street parking available.
Entertainments/catering facilities: Supporters Club with extensive bar facilities. Refreshment points around the ground.
Club shop: Caravan in car park open on match days.
Handbooks/programmes: No handbook. Programmes available on subscription.
Extra information: In 1949, Carlisle's player-manager Ivor Broadis transferred himself to Sunderland for £18,000.

Club Colours: Blue shirts with broad white vertical stripe and red piping, white shorts, red stockings.
Change Colours: Yellow shirts, blue shorts, yellow stockings.
Club Captain: Bobby Parker.
Club Trainer/Coach: Martin Harvey.
Club Nickname: 'Cumbrians'

CARLISLE UNITED 1978–79 LEAGUE RECORD

Match No.	Date	Venue	Opponents	Result	Score	H/T Score	League Pos'n	Goalscorers	Attendance
1	Aug 19	A	Hull C	D	1-1	1-1	—	Tait	5062
2	22	H	Chesterfield	D	1-1	0-0	—	Kemp	5232
3	26	H	Walsall	W	1-0	1-0	7	Lumby	4781
4	Sept 2	A	Blackpool	L	1-3	0-0	13	Kemp	7789
5	8	H	Colchester U	W	4-0	4-0	7	McCartney (pen), Bonnyman, Hamilton, Tait	4430
6	12	H	Peterborough U	D	0-0	0-0	—		6283
7	16	A	Lincoln C	D	1-1	0-0	6	McVitie	2577
8	23	H	Southend U	D	0-0	0-0	7		5263
9	25	H	Swansea C	W	2-0	0-0	—	McCartney (pen), Kemp	8489
10	30	A	Mansfield T	L	0-1	0-1	6		4716
11	Oct 7	H	Plymouth Arg	D	1-1	0-0	7	Bonnyman	5731
12	14	A	Sheffield W	D	0-0	0-0	7		10,980
13	17	A	Watford	L	1-2	0-2	—	Joslyn (og)	12,444
14	21	H	Rotherham U	D	1-1	0-0	9	Kemp	5085
15	28	H	Swindon T	W	2-0	1-0	7	Kemp, McCartney (pen)	5141
16	Nov 4	A	Shrewsbury T	D	0-0	0-0	8		4656
17	11	H	Blackpool	D	1-1	0-0	8	Parker	6505
18	18	A	Walsall	W	2-1	1-0	7	Serella (og), Kemp	4441
19	Dec 2	A	Gillingham	D	0-0	0-0	7		4322
20	9	H	Exeter C	D	1-1	1-0	7	Kemp	4568
21	26	H	Chester	W	2-1	1-1	6	Kemp, McVitie	4690
22	30	A	Brentford	D	0-0	0-0	6		6480
23	Jan 20	H	Lincoln C	W	2-0	1-0	7	Ludham, Kemp	3892
24	Feb 2	A	Swansea C	D	0-0	0-0	7		10,821
25	10	A	Mansfield T	W	1-0	1-0	6	Bonnyman	4934
26	13	H	Bury	L	1-2	0-1	—	Bonnyman (pen)	4547
27	17	A	Plymouth Arg	L	0-2	0-2	7		6294
28	24	H	Sheffield W	D	0-0	0-0	7		5675
29	Mar 3	A	Rotherham U	W	3-1	0-1	6	Kemp 2, Tait	3908
30	6	H	Tranmere R	W	2-0	1-0	—	McCartney (pen), Bonnyman	4330
31	10	A	Swindon T	D	0-0	0-0	6		8386
32	12	A	Southend U	D	1-1	0-1	—	Tait	5457
33	17	H	Shrewsbury T	D	1-1	0-0	5	Ludham	5057
34	20	H	Peterborough U	W	4-1	1-1	—	Lumby 2, Kemp 2	4571
35	24	H	Chesterfield	W	3-2	0-0	2	Kemp, Lumby, Tait	4152
36	27	H	Hull C	D	2-2	0-0	—	Kemp, McCartney (pen)	6254
37	31	A	Oxford U	L	1-5	0-2	5	Kemp	3439
38	Apr 2	A	Colchester U	L	1-2	1-0	—	Lumby	2608
39	7	H	Gillingham	W	1-0	0-0	4	Kemp	5130
40	13	A	Bury	D	2-2	2-1	—	Tait, Kemp	4838
41	14	H	Chester	D	1-1	1-0	5	MacDonald	5309
42	16	A	Tranmere R	D	1-1	0-1	—	Lumby	1504
43	21	H	Brentford	W	1-0	0-0	6	Ludham	3967
44	24	H	Watford	W	1-0	1-0	—	Bonnyman	7141
45	28	A	Exeter C	L	2-3	1-2	5	Bonnyman, Tait	4299
46	May 5	H	Oxford U	L	0-1	0-0	6		3811

Final League Position: 6

Goalscorers

League (53): Kemp 18, Tait 7, Bonnyman 7 (1 a pen), Lumby 6, McCartney 5 (5 pens), Ludlam 3, McVitie 2, Parker 1, McDonald 1, Hamilton 1, Own Goals 2.
League Cup (3): Kemp, Bonnyman, Lumby.
F.A. Cup (6): Lumby 2, Kemp 2, McCartney (pen), Tait.

League Cup	First Round	Blackpool (h)	2-2
		(a)	1-2
F.A. Cup	First Round	Halifax T (h)	1-0
	Second Round	Hull C (h)	3-0
	Third Round	Ipswich T (a)	2-3

Swinburne	Hoolickin	McCartney	MacDonald	Tait	Parker	McVitie	Bonnyman	Kemp	Ludham	Hamilton	Lumby	Ross	Sawyers	Collins	Clarke, D	Bannon	McLean	Match No.
1	2	3	4	5	6	7	8	9	10	11								1
1	2	3		5	6	7	8	9	4	11	10							2
1	2	3	4	5*	6	7	8	9	12	11	10							3
1	2	3	4	5	6	7	8	9		11	10							4
1	2	3	4	5	6	7	8	9		11	10							5
1	2	3	4	5	6	7	8	9		11	10							6
1	2	3	4	5	6	7	8	9		11	10							7
1	2	3	4	5	6	7	8	9		11	10							8
1	2	3	4	5	6	7	8	9		11	10							9
1	2	3	4	5	6	7	8	9		11	10							10
1	2	3	4	10	6	7	8	9	5	11								11
1	2	3	4	5	6	7	8	9	10	11								12
1	2	3	4	5	6	7	8	9	10	11								13
1	2	3	4	5	6	7	8	9	10	11								14
	2	3	4	5	6	7	8	9	10	11		1						15
1	2	3	4*	5	6	7	8	9	10	11			12					16
1	2	3		5	6	7	8*	9	10	11				4	12			17
1	2	3		5	6	7	8	9	4	11	10							18
1	2	3		5	6	7	8	9	4	11	10							19
1	2	3	4	10	6	7	8	9	5	11*	12							20
1	2	3		5	6	7	8	10	4	11	9							21
1	2	3*	4	5	6	7	8	10	9	11	12							22
1	2	3	4	5	6	7	8	10	9	11								23
1	2	3	4	5	6	7	8	10	9	11								24
1	2	3	4	5	6	7	8	10	9	11								25
1	2		4	5	6	7	8	10	9	11				3	10			26
1	2		4	5	6	7		10	9	11				3				27
1	2	3	4	5	6	7	8		9	11					10			28
1	2	3	4	5	6	7	8	9	10						11			29
1	2	3	4	5	6	7	8	10	9						11			30
1	2	3	4	5	6	7	8	10	9	12					11*			31
1	2	3	4	5	6	7	8	10	9						11			32
1	2	3	4	5	6	7	8	10	9		12				11*			33
1	2	3	4	5	6	7	8	10	11		9							34
1	2	3	4	5	6	7*	8	9	11		10				12			35
1	2	3	4	5	6	7	8	10	9		11							36
1	2	3	4	5	6	7	8	11	9		10*				12			37
1	2	3	4	5	6	7	8	10	11		9							38
1	2	3	4	5	6	7	8	9	11		10							39
1	2	3	4	5	6	7	8	10	11		9							40
1	2	3	4	5	6	7	8	9	11		10							41
1	2	3	4	12	6	7	8	10	11		9				5*			42
1	2	3	4	5	6	7	8	9	11		10*				12			43
1	2	3	4	5	6	7	8	10	11	9								44
1	2	3	4	5	6	7	8	9	10	11								45
1	2	3	4	5	6	7	8	9	10	11								46
45	46	44	41	45	46	46	45	45	38	31	22	1	—	3	—	2	6	
				+1s					+1s	+1s	+3s			+1s		+1s	+3s	

CARLISLE UNITED—PLAYERS

Player and position	Ht	Wt	Birthplace	Clubs	League Appearances	Goals
Goalkeepers						
*Alan Ross	5 10¾	10 7½	Glasgow	Luton T	—	—
				Carlisle U	465+1	—
Trevor Swinburne	6 0	12 12	East Rainton	Sunderland	10	—
				Sheffield U (on loan)	—	—
				Carlisle U	76	—
Tony Harrison	6 1	13 0	Gateshead	Southport	48	—
				Carlisle U	—	—
Defenders						
Bob Parker	5 9	10 12	Coventry	Coventry C	78+3	—
				Carlisle U	185	5
Bobby Moncur (Scotland) (Non-Contract)	5 9¾	10 9	Perth	Newcastle U	293+3	3
				Sunderland	86	2
				Carlisle U	11	—
Ian MacDonald	6 1	12 4	Rinteln, W Germany	St Johnstone	107+1	2
				Carlisle U	117	5
Steve Hoolickin	5 11	11 2	Manchester	Oldham Ath	8	—
				Bury	140	5
				Carlisle U	82	1
Andy Collins	5 10	10 9	Carlisle	Carlisle U	30	—
Midfield						
Philip Bonnyman	6 0	12 2	Glasgow	Rangers	—	—
				Hamilton A	65+6	7
				Carlisle U	121+3	16
Mike McCartney	5 7	10 12	Edinburgh	WBA	—	—
				Carlisle U	122+8	15
Keith Sawyers	5 8	10 5	Branbury	Carlisle U	5+3	—
Steve Ludlam	5 6	9 11	Chesterfield	Sheffield U	26+1	1
				Carlisle U	54+1	3
Jimmy Hamilton	5 11½	11 4	Uddingtson	Sunderland	9+8	2
				Plymouth Arg	6+2	—
				Bristol R	16+4	1
				Carlisle U	65+2	5
David McLean (Contract cancelled May 1979)	5 8	11 5	Newcastle	Newcastle U	7+2	—
				Carlisle U	9+6	—
Forwards						
Paul Bannon	6 2	11 2	Dublin	Carlisle U	2	—
Jim Lumby	5 9	11 7	Grimsby	Grimsby T	28+3	12
				Scunthorpe U	55	28
				Carlisle U	24+3	7
George McVitie	5 9¾	11 1	Carlisle	Carlisle U	124+4	21
				WBA	42	5
				Oldham Ath	108+5	19
				Carlisle U	141+3	16
Mick Tait	5 11	11 8	North Shields	Oxford U	61+3	23
				Carlisle U	97+5	20
Geoff Fell	5 9	10 9	Carlisle	Carlisle U	0+2	—
David Kemp	5 9	11 0	Harrow	C Palace	32+3	10
				Portsmouth	63+1	30
				Carlisle U	58	22

CHARLTON ATHLETIC DIV. 2

Chairman: E. M. Gliksten.
Directors: W. J. Jenner, C. W. Wheeler, F. W. Boswell, G. E. Neighbour, W. F. Whitehead, N. E. Madsen.
General Manager/Secretary: Benny Fenton.
Manager: Andy Nelson *Ass. Secretary:* Mrs J. P. Doble.
Asst. Manager: Harry Cripps.
Year Formed: 1905. *Turned Professional:* 1920.
Limited Company: 1919.
Previous Grounds: 1906, Siemen's Meadow; 1907, Woolwich Common; 1909, Pound Park; 1913, Horn Lane; 1920, The Valley; 1922, Catford; 1922, The Valley.
Football League Record:
  1921 Elected to Division 3(S).   1936-57 Division 1.
  1929-33 Division 2.   1957-72 Division 2.
  1933-35 Division 3(S).   1972-75 Division 3.
  1935-36 Division 2.   1975-   Division 2.

Honours: *Football League*, Division 1, Runners-up: 1936-37. Division 2, Runners-up: 1935-36. Division 3(S), Champions, 1928-29, 1934-35. Promoted from Division 3 (3rd) 1974-75. *F.A. Cup*, Winners: 1947; Runners-up: 1946. *Football League Cup*, best season: 4th Rd., 1962-63, 1964-65, 1978-79.
Record Victory: 8-1 v Middlesbrough, Division 1, Sept. 12th, 1953.
Record Defeat: 1-11 v Aston Villa, Division 2, Nov. 14th, 1959.
Most League Points: 61, Div 3(S) 1934-5.
Most League Goals: 107, Div. 2, 1957-8.
Highest League Scorer in Season: Ralph Allen, 32, Division 3(S), 1934-35.
Most Capped Player: John Hewie, 19, Scotland.
Most League Appearances: Sam Bartram, 583, 1934-56.
Most Goals in Total Aggregate: Stuart Leary, 153, 1953-62.
Record Transfer Fee Received: £280,000 from Derby Co. for Derek Hales, Dec. 1976.
Record Transfer Fee Paid: £65,000 to Gillingham for Dick Tydeman, Dec. 1976.
Managers Since the War: James Seed, Jimmy Trotter, Frank Hill, Bob Stokoe, Eddie Firmani, Theo Foley.
Address of Supporters Club: Same address as Club.
Address of Club Shop or Boutique: 'The Valley Shop', The Valley, Floyd Road, London SE7 8AW.

The Valley, Floyd Rd., Charlton, London SE7 8AW. Telephone 01-858 6006. *Ground capacity:* under review following extensive redevelopment. *Record attendance:* 75,031 v Aston Villa, F.A. Cup 5th Rd., February 12, 1938. *Record receipts:* £26,014 v West Ham U, League Cup 3rd Round, Sept. 21, 1976. *Pitch measurements:* 114 yds. × 78 yds.
How to get there: Buses 53, 54, 75, 177, 180. Nearest railway station, Charlton, is on the line from London from Charing Cross and Waterloo East. The ground is 3 minutes walk from the station.
Match tickets: Available 2-3 weeks in advance.
Car parking: In ground for season-ticket holders only. Ample off-street parking available.
Entertainments/catering facilities: The Valley Club, Harvey Gardens, and Beer and Snack Bars in the ground.
Club shop: The Valley Shop in ground is open on match days.
Handbooks/programmes: Both available in shops, and programmes on subscription.
Extra information: Charlton are the only club to go from the third to the first division in successive seasons (1934-36) and then finish runners-up.
Club Colours: Red shirts, white shorts, red stockings.
Change Colours: Yellow and black.
Club Captain:
Club Coach: Peter Shearing.
First Team Trainer/Physiotherapist: Charlie Hall.
Club Nickname: 'Haddicks', 'Robins', or 'Valiants'.

CHARLTON ATHLETIC 1978–79 LEAGUE RECORD

Match No.	Date	Venue	Opponents	Result	Score	H/T Score	League Pos'n	Goalscorers	Attendance
1	Aug 19	A	Sunderland	L	0-1	0-1	—		20,486
2	22	H	Burnley	D	1-1	1-1	—	Hales	8580
3	26	H	Bristol R	W	3-0	1-0	8	Campbell, Hales 2 (1 a pen)	7745
4	Sept 2	A	Luton T	L	0-3	0-1	15		8509
5	9	H	Wrexham	D	1-1	1-0	16	Flanagan	8356
6	16	A	Cambridge U	D	1-1	1-0	17	Flanagan	6166
7	22	H	Notts Co	D	1-1	1-1	16	Tydeman	8643
8	30	A	Blackburn R	W	2-1	0-0	12	Robinson 2	8341
9	Oct 6	H	Orient	L	0-2	0-2	16		11,024
10	14	A	Leicester C	W	3-0	2-0	12	Flanagan 2, Brisley	14,278
11	21	H	Newcastle U	W	4-1	1-1	9	Flanagan (pen), Robinson 2, Gritt	11,616
12	28	A	Millwall	W	2-0	1-0	5	Shaw, Shipperley	9546
13	Nov 4	A	Cardiff C	W	4-1	2-1	4	Madden, Robinson, Brisley 2	7842
14	11	H	Sunderland	L	1-2	0-0	5	Madden	11,412
15	18	A	Bristol R	D	5-5	3-2	7	Tydeman, Robinson 2, Flanagan 2	8107
16	21	H	Luton T	L	1-2	1-0	—	Robinson	10,000
17	25	H	Fulham	D	0-0	0-0	11		11,440
18	Dec 9	H	Sheffield U	W	3-1	1-0	10	Shipperley, Flanagan 2	7048
19	12	A	Preston N E	L	1-6	0-3	—	Robinson	8500
20	16	A	West Ham U	L	0-2	0-1	11		23,833
21	23	H	Brighton & HA	L	0-3	0-0	11		10,135
22	26	A	Stoke C	D	2-2	0-1	—	Flanagan 2	20,846
23	30	A	Oldham Ath	W	3-0	2-0	10	Flanagan 2, Hales	4191
24	Feb 3	A	Notts Co	D	1-1	0-0	11	Robinson	7958
25	10	H	Blackburn R	W	2-0	1-0	8	Robinson, Warman	5480
26	24	H	Leicester C	W	1-0	0-0	7	Peacock (pen)	7936
27	Mar 3	A	Newcastle U	L	3-5	2-3	8	Gritt, Shipperley, Robinson	15,006
28	6	A	Cambridge U	L	2-3	2-3	—	Peacock, Gritt	6119
29	10	H	Millwall	L	2-4	2-3	10	Warman, Hales	9908
30	17	H	Cardiff C	D	1-1	1-0	9	Campbell	5658
31	20	A	Orient	L	1-2	0-2	—	Robinson	6457
32	24	A	Burnley	L	1-2	1-1	12	Rodaway (og)	8521
33	27	H	Crystal Palace	D	1-1	1-1	—	Powell	15,065
34	31	A	Fulham	L	1-3	0-1	13	Hales	6955
35	Apr 2	A	Wrexham	D	1-1	1-1	—	Berry	7518
36	7	H	Preston NE	D	1-1	1-0	14	Madden	5836
37	13	A	Brighton & HA	L	0-2	0-1	—		30,859
38	14	H	Stoke C	L	1-4	1-1	15	Hales (pen)	9084
39	17	A	Crystal Palace	L	0-1	0-0	—		30,000
40	21	H	West Ham U	D	0-0	0-0	17		22,816
41	28	A	Sheffield U	L	1-2	0-1	19	Hales	16,888
42	May 5	H	Oldham Ath	W	2-0	1-0	18	Robinson 2	6891

Final League Position: 19

Goalscorers

League (60): Robinson 15, Flanagan 13 (1 pen), Hales 8 (2 pens), Brisley 3, Gritt 3, Madden 3, Shipperley 3, Campbell 2, Peacock 2 (1 a pen), Tydeman 2, Warman 2, Berry 1, Powell 1, Shaw 1, Own Goal 1.
League Cup (12): Peacock 3, Robinson 3, Flanagan 2, Shipperley 2, Hales, Brisley.
F.A. Cup (3): Flanagan, Campbell, Robinson.

League Cup	First Round	Colchester U (a)	3-2
		(h)	0-0
	Second Round	Walsall (a)	2-1
	Third Round	Chesterfield (a)	5-4
	Fourth Round	Stoke C (h)	2-3
F.A. Cup	Third Round	Maidstone (h)	1-1
		(a)	2-1
	Fourth Round	Bristol R (a)	0-1

Wood	Campbell	Berry	Tydeman	Shaw	Dugdale	Brisley	Hales	Flanagan	Madden	Gritt	Peacock	Shipperley	Powell	Robinson	Penfold	Johns	Warman	Churchouse	Booth	Match No.
1	2	3	4	5	6	7	8	9	10	11										1
1	2	3*	4	5	6	7	8	9	10	11	12									2
1	3	2	4		6	11	8	9		12	10	5	7*							3
1	3	2	4		6	7	8	9		11	10	5								4
1	3	6	4				8	9	2	11	10	5		7						5
1	2	6	4				8	9	3	11	10	5		7						6
1	3	6*	4				8	9	2	11	10	5	12	7						7
1	2		4	6		7		9	3	8	11*	5	12	10						8
1	3		4	6*		7		9	2	11	10	5	12	8						9
1	3	2	4	6		7		9	10	11		5		8						10
1	3	6	4	2		7		9	10	11		5		8						11
1	3	6	4	2		7		9	10	11		5		8						12
1	3	6	4	2		7		9	10	11*12		5		8						13
1	3	6	4	2*		7		9	10	11	12	5		8						14
1	3	6	4*	2		7		9	10	11	12	5		8						15
1	2	6		5		10		9	3	4	11		7	8						16
1	3	6		2		7		9	10	4	11	5		8						17
1	3	6		2*		4		9	10		11	5	7	8	12					18
1		6	4	2*		7		9	10		11	5	12	8	3					19
1	3	6		2		7		9	10	4	11	5	12	8*						20
1	3	6		2		4		9	10	7	11*	5	12	8						21
1	3	6		2		7		9	10	4		5	11	8						22
1	3	6		2		7	8	9	10	4		5	11							23
	3	6		2				9	10	4	11*	5	7	8	12	1				24
	2	6				11		9	10	4		5	7	8		1	3			25
10	6		12			4	9*			11	5		7	8	2	1	3			26
	4	6		2		10				9	11	5	7	8		1	3			27
	4	6				10		12	9	11	5		7	8	2*	1	3			28
		3				4	9	10	6	11	5		8	2	1	7				29
1	2	10	5			7	8		6	4	11		9			3				30
1	2	10		5		7	8		6	4	11*		12	9		3				31
1	3	6		2				8	10	4	11	5	7	9						32
1	2	10		3				9	6	4	12	5	7	8*		11				33
1	3	4		2				8	10	6	9	5	7			11*12				34
1	3	12		6			8*	10	4		5	7	9		2	11				35
1	2		4	6				10	8		5	7	9		3	11				36
1	3*12	8	6			9		10	4		5	7			2	11				37
1		6		2		12	9	10	4	11	5*	7	8		3					38
	3	5		2		10		6	9*11		7	8	1		4	12				39
	3	5	4	2		12		6	9	10		7	8	1	11*					40
	3	5		2		10	9	6	4			7	8	1	11					41
	3	5	4	2		12	8	6	9*			7	10	1	11					42
32	39	36	21	33	4	29	20	25	37	38	25	33	21	35	4	10	11	9		
			+2s	+1s		+3s			+1s	+1s	+5s		+7s		+2s			+2s		

CHARLTON ATHLETIC—PLAYERS

Player and position	Ht	Wt	Birthplace	Clubs	League Appearances	Goals
Goalkeepers						
Jeff Wood	6 1	10 9	London	Charlton Ath	130	—
Steve Chalk	6 1	12 3	Southampton	Bournemouth	11	—
(Contract cancelled February 1979)				Charlton Ath	—	—
Defenders						
*Mark Penfold	5 7	10 1	London	Charlton Ath	65+5	—
				Manchester U (on loan)	—	—
Phil Warman	5 6½	11 0	Bromley	Charlton Ath	260	18
Leslie Berry	6 2	11 13	Plumstead	Charlton Ath	129+4	6
David Campbell	6 1	11 8	Edinburgh	Charlton Ath	53+5	3
Alan Dugdale	5 8	12 6½	Kirkby	Coventry C	139+3	—
				Charlton Ath	34	—
Dave Shipperley	6 3	14 0	Hillingdon	Charlton Ath	92+8	8
				Plymouth Arg (on loan)	1	—
				Gillingham	144	2
				Charlton Ath	49	6
Peter Shaw	6 2	13 10	Northolt	Charlton Ath	39+2	1
Lawrie Madden	6 0	12 6	London	Arsenal	—	—
				Charlton Ath	40+2	3
Mark Newson	5 9½	11 0	London	Charlton Ath	—	—
Midfield						
Keith Peacock	5 6½	10 7	Barnhurst	Charlton Ath	512+21	94
(Contract cancelled May 1978)						
Dick Tydeman	6 1¾	12 8	Gillingham	Gillingham	293+2	12
				Charlton Ath	82	4
Steven Gritt	5 10	10 10	Bournemouth	Bournemouth	4+2	3
				Charlton Ath	66+7	6
Terry Brisley	5 6	10 6½	Stepney	Orient	133+9	10
				Southend U (on loan)	8	—
				Millwall	106+1	15
				Charlton Ath	44+4	5
Gary Churchouse	5 9	11 8	Wembley	Windsor & Eton	—	—
				Charlton Ath	9	—
Forwards						
Mike Flanagan	5 9½	11 8	Ilford	Tottenham H	—	—
				Charlton Ath	241+13	85
Colin Powell	5 10	11 10	Hendon	Charlton Ath	230+14	22
(Contract cancelled April 1979)						
Tony Burman	5 8½	11 0	London	Charlton Ath	16+3	3
(Contract cancelled February 1979)						
Lawrence Abrahams	5 11½	11 4	Barking	Charlton Ath	12+4	2
William O'Sullivan			London	Charlton Ath	1+1	—
(Contract cancelled November 1978)						
Martin Robinson	5 8	11 5½	Ilford	Tottenham H	5+1	2
				Charlton Ath	51	22
Leroy Ambrose	5 7½	10 8	St. Vincent, W Indies	Charlton Ath	—	—
Anthony Booth	5 7½	10 3	Biggin Hill	Charlton Ath	0+2	—
Derek Hales	5 9	12 4	Lower Halston	Luton T	5+2	1
				Charlton Ath	126+3	73
				Derby Co	22+1	4
				West Ham U	23+1	10
				Charlton Ath	20	8

CHELSEA DIV. 2

President: The Right Hon. Earl Cadogan, M.C., D.L.
Chairman: J. B. Mears.
Directors: Viscount Chelsea, G. M. Thomson Sir R. S. Attenborough, C.B.E., D. Mears. B. Sc.
Chief Executive: Martin Spencer, F.C.A.
General Manager: Ron Suart.
Team Manager: Danny Blanchflower.
Secretary: Christine Mathews.
P.R.O.: Albert Sewell.
Year Formed: 1905. *Turned Pro.* 1905.
Limited Company: 1905
Football League Record:

1905 Elected to Division 2.	1962–63 Division 2.
1907–10 Division 1.	1963–75 Division 1.
1910–12 Division 2.	1975–77 Division 2.
1912–24 Division 1.	1977–79 Division 1.
1924–30 Division 2.	1979– Division 2.
1930–62 Division 1.	

Honours: Football League, Division 1, Champions: 1954–55, Division 2, Runners-up: 1906–07, 1911–12, 1929–30, 1962–63, 1976–77. *F.A. Cup,* Winners: 1970; Runners-up: 1914–15, 1966–67. *Football League Cup,* Winners: 1964–65. Runners-up: 1971–72.

European Competitions: European Fairs Cup: 1958–60, 1965–66, 1968–69. *European Cup-Winners' Cup:* 1970–71 (winners), 1971–72.

Record Victory: 13-0 v Jeunesse Hautcharage, European Cup Winners' Cup, 1st Rd., Sept. 29th, 1971.

Record Defeat: 1-8 v Wolverhampton W., Division 1, Sept. 26th, 1953.

Most League Points: 57, Division 2, 1906–07.

Most League Goals: 98, Division 1, 1960–61.

Highest League Scorer in Season: Jimmy Greaves, 41, 1960–61.

Most Goals in Total Aggregate: Bobby Tambling, 164, 1958–70.

Most Capped Player: Eddie McCreadie, 23, Scotland.

Most League Appearances: Ron Harris, 616, 1962–79.

Record Transfer Fee Received: £275,000 from Derby Co for Steve Wicks, January 1979.

Record Transfer Fee Paid: £225,000 to Celtic for David Hay, July 1974.

Managers Since the War: Billy Birrell, Ted Drake, Tommy Docherty, Dave Sexton, Ron Suart, Eddie McCreadie, Ken Shellito.

Address of Supporters Club: Same as Football Club.
Address of Club Shop or Boutique: Stamford Bridge, S.W.6.

Stamford Bridge, London S.W.6. Telephone 01-385-5545/6. *Telegraphic address:* 'Chelstam, London S.W.6.' *Ground capacity:* 60,000 (31,500 covered). *Record attendance:* 82,905 v Arsenal, Division 1, October 12, 1935. *Record receipts:* £147,225, F.A. Cup semi-final, Orient v Arsenal, April 8, 1978. *Pitch measurements:* 114 yds × 71 yds.

How to get there: Nearest station is Fulham Broadway on the Underground (District Line). London Transport regular buses to Fulham Broadway, Kings Road, Fulham Road, or Stamford Bridge.
Match tickets: Advance tickets available by postal or personal application. No telephone bookings.
Car Parking: Street parking only.
Entertainments/catering facilities: Licensed bars at all points of the ground.
Club shop: Run by the Football Club; sells all types of souvenirs.
Handbook/programmes: Programmes available on subscription.

Club Colours: All royal blue with white stripe on shorts. White stockings.
Change Colours: Yellow, green, yellow.
Team Captain: Micky Droy.
First Team Coach: Geoff Hurst.
First Team Trainer: Norman Medhurst.
Physiotherapist: Eddie Franklin, M.C.S.P.
Club Nickname: 'Blues'.

CHELSEA 1978-79 LEAGUE RECORD

Match No.	Date	Venue	Opponents	Result	H/T Score	League Pos'n	Goalscorers	Attendance
1	Aug 19	H	Everton	L 0-1	0-1	—		31,755
2	22	A	Wolverhampton W	W 1-0	1-0	—	Langley	22,041
3	26	A	Tottenham H	D 2-2	1-2	9	Swain 2	40,643
4	Sept 2	H	Leeds U	L 0-3	0-1	16		30,099
5	9	A	Coventry C	L 2-3	2-1	18	Langley, McKenzie	24,920
6	16	H	Manchester C	L 1-4	0-3	20	Stanley	28,980
7	23	A	Birmingham C	D 1-1	0-0	20	McKenzie	18,458
8	30	H	WBA	L 1-3	1-1	21	Wicks	20,186
9	Oct 7	A	Derby Co	L 0-1	0-0	21		20,251
10	14	H	Bolton W	W 4-3	0-3	21	Langley, Swain, Walker, Allardyce (og)	19,879
11	21	A	Liverpool	L 0-2	0-1	21		45,775
12	28	H	Norwich C	W 3-2	1-0	20	Swain, Walker, Stanley (pen)	23,941
13	Nov 4	A	QPR	D 0-0	0-0	20		22,878
14	11	A	Everton	L 2-3	1-1	20	McKenzie, Langley	38,694
15	18	H	Tottenham H	L 1-3	1-0	20	Langley	41,594
16	22	A	Leeds U	L 1-2	1-2	—	Langley	24,088
17	25	H	Manchester U	L 0-1	0-0	22		27,156
18	Dec 9	H	Aston Villa	L 0-1	0-1	22		19,080
19	16	A	Middlesbrough	L 2-7	1-3	22	Osgood, Bumstead	15,107
20	23	H	Bristol C	D 0-0	0-0	20		19,093
21	26	A	Southampton	D 0-0	0-0	21		20,770
22	30	A	Ipswich T	L 1-5	0-3	21	Langley	21,439
23	Jan 20	A	Manchester C	W 3-2	1-2	21	McKenzie, Osgood, Walker	31,876
24	Feb 3	H	Birmingham C	W 2-1	1-0	21	Wilkins (R) 2	22,129
25	21	A	Coventry C	L 1-3	1-3	—	Langley	15,282
26	24	A	Bolton W	L 1-2	1-1	21	Bannon	19,457
27	Mar 3	H	Liverpool	D 0-0	0-0	21		40,594
28	10	A	Norwich C	L 0-2	0-1	21		19,071
29	14	A	WBA	L 0-1	0-0	—		20,425
30	17	H	QPR	L 1-3	1-1	21	Shanks (og)	25,871
31	24	H	Wolverhampton W	L 1-2	0-0	21	Langley	20,502
32	28	A	Nottingham F	L 0-6	0-1	—		24,514
33	Apr 4	H	Derby Co	D 1-1	0-0	—	Langley	10,682
34	7	H	Nottingham F	L 1-3	0-2	22	Wilkins (R)	29,213
35	10	A	Bristol C	L 1-3	0-0	—	Langley (pen)	18,645
36	14	H	Southampton	L 1-2	0-2	22	Stanley	18,243
37	16	A	Arsenal	L 2-5	0-2	—	Walker, Langley	37,232
38	21	H	Middlesbrough	W 2-1	1-0	22	Stanley, Wilkins (G)	12,007
39	28	A	Aston Villa	L 1-2	1-0	22	Langley	29,219
40	May 5	H	Ipswich T	L 2-3	2-3	22	Langley 2	15,462
41	14	H	Arsenal	D 1-1	1-0	—	Stanley	28,386
42	16	A	Manchester U	D 1-1	1-1	—	Johnson	38,119

Final League Position: 22

Goalscorers

League (44): Langley 15 (1 pen), Stanley 5 (1 pen), McKenzie 4, Swain 4, Walker 4, Wilkins (R) 3 Osgood 2, Wicks 1, Bannon 1, Wilkins (G) 1, Bumstead 1, Johnson 1, Own Goals 2.
League Cup (1): Langley

League Cup	Second Round	Bolton W (a)	1-2
F.A. Cup	Third Round	Manchester U (a)	0-3

Bonetti	Locke	Harris	Hay	Droy	Wicks	Swain	Wilkins R	Langley	Stanley	Walker	Britton	Lewington	McKenzie	Stride	Iles	Garner	Phillips	Wilkins G	Bumstead	Aylott	Osgood	Nutton	Bannon	Sitton	Borota	Doherty	Frost	Fillery	Chivers	Johnson	Match No.
1	2	3	4	5	6	7	8	9*	10	11	12																				1
1	2	3	4	5	6	7	8	9	10	11																					2
1	2	3	4	5	6	7	8	9	10	11																					3
1	2	3	4	5	6	7	8	9	10	11																					4
1	2	3	5		6	7	8	9	10*		12	4	11																		5
1	2	3	5		6	7	8*	9	10		12	4	11																		6
1	2	6			5	7	8	9	4			10	11	3																	7
1	2	6			5	7	8	9	4	12		10	11*	3																	8
	6	2			5	7	8	9			4	10		3	1	11															9
	4	2			5	11	10	9	8*	12	7	6		3	1																10
	6				5	10	8*	9	4	11	12		7	3		1	2														11
	6				5	10	8	9	4	11			7	3		1	2														12
	6				5	10	8	9	4	11			7	3		1	2														13
	6				5	10	8	9	4	11			7	3		1	2														14
	6				5	10	8	9	4	11			7	3		1	2														15
	6				5		8	9	4	12		11	7*	3	1		2	10													16
	6				5		8	9	4	11		10	7	3	1		2														17
	6				5		8		4	12	11		7*	3	1		2	10	9												18
	6				5			8	11	12	7			3	1		2	4	10	9*											19
	2				5			10	7		11		8	3	1			6		9	4										20
	2				5			10	7*		11	6	8	3		1		12		9	4										21
	2				5			9	7*12	8	10			3		1		6	11		4										22
1	4		5	6				10	7	11			8	3		2			9												23
1	12		5*					8	10	7	11			3		2		9	6	4											24
1	5*							8	10	7	11			3		2		9	6	4	12										25
1								8	10	7	11			3		2		9	6	4	5										26
	9							8	10	7*11				3		2			6	4	5	1	12								27
	9							8	10*		11			3		2	12	7	6	4	5	1									28
	9							8	10		11			3*		2	12		6	4	5	1	7								29
	9							8	12	10	11			3		2			6	4	5	1	7*								30
	7							8	10	12	11			3*		2	9		6	4	5	1									31
	7							8	10	12		11		3		2*	9		6	4	5	1									32
	7		5					8	10		11*			3		2			6	4		1		9	12						33
	7		5					8	10	12				3		2	9		6	4		1		11*							34
	7		5					8	10					3		2	9		6	4		1			11						35
	6							8	7	12				3		2	10	9*	4	5	1			11							36
			5					8	10	11	12			3		2	9*		4	6	1			7							37
1	12		5					8	10	7	11			3*		2			4					9	6						38
1	3		5					8	10	7	11					2	12		4						9*	6					39
1	3		5					8	10	7				2				9	4						12	11*	6				40
1	3		5						10	7	11							8	9	4	6					2					41
	3								10		11							2	7	8				4	5	1			6	9	42
16	8	38	8	14	23	15	35	40	32	23	9	10	15	32	7	1	7	28	6	13	9	15	19	11	12	2	2	6	5	1	
	+2s						+1s	+4s	+7s	+4s							+2s	+2s				+1s		+1s	+1s	+1s					

CHELSEA—PLAYERS

Player and position	Ht	Wt	Birthplace	Clubs	League Appearances	Goals
Goalkeepers						
Peter Bonetti (England)	5 10	11 8	Putney	Chelsea	600	—
John Phillips (Wales)	6 0	10 8	Shrewsbury	Shrewsbury T	51	—
				Aston Villa	15	—
				Chelsea	125	—
				Swansea C (on loan)	—	—
Petar Borota (Yugoslavia)	6 0	12 7	Yugoslavia	Belgrade SC	—	—
				Partizan	—	—
				Chelsea	12	—
Bob Iles	6 1	12 7	Leicester	Weymouth	—	—
				Chelsea	7	—
Defenders						
Ron Harris	5 8	11 7	Hackney	Chelsea	608+8	11
Gary Locke	5 11	11 5	London	Chelsea	180+1	2
Micky Droy	6 4½	15 5	Highbury	Chelsea	155+2	6
Graham Wilkins	5 6¾	10 2	Hayes	Chelsea	94	1
John Sparrow	5 10	12 0	Bethnal Green	Chelsea	52+6	2
				Millwall (on loan)	7	—
Michael Nutton	5 11	10 12	St. John's Wood	Chelsea	15	—
John Sitton	6 0	12 2	Hackney	Chelsea	11+1	—
Gary Chivers	5 11	11 7	Stockwell	Chelsea	5	—
Kevin Hales	5 7	10 4	Dartford	Chelsea	—	—
Lori Jenkins	5 10	11 7	Neath	Chelsea	—	—
Clive Penny	5 8	10 0	Neath	Chelsea	32	—
David Stride	5 9	11 5	Lymington	Chelsea	32	—
David Hay (Scotland)	5 11	11 7	Paisley	Celtic	111+1	8
				Chelsea	107+1	2
Midfield						
Ray Wilkins (England)	5 7	10 10	Hillingdon	Chelsea	176+3	30
Ray Lewington (Contract cancelled February 1979)	5 6	10 5	London	Chelsea	80+5	4
Gary Stanley	5 9½	10 8	Burton-on-Trent	Chelsea	105+4	15
John Bumstead	5 7	10 0	Rotherhithe	Chelsea	6+2	1
Eamonn Bannon	5 10	11 7	Edinburgh	Hearts	70+1	18
				Chelsea	19	1
Mike Fillery	5 10	11 12	Mitcham	Chelsea	6+1	—
Ian Britton	5 5	9 7	Dundee	Chelsea	168+8	22
Forwards						
Tommy Langley	5 11	11 7	London	Chelsea	94+12	30
Clive Walker	5 8¼	11 4	Oxford	Chelsea	44+10	11
Trevor Aylott	6 1	13 10	London	Chelsea	23+3	2
				QPR (on loan)	—	—
Lee Frost	5 8½	10 7	Woking	Chelsea	3+1	—
				Brentford (on loan)	5+1	—
Jim Docherty	5 10	10 5	Broxburn	E Stirling	46+1	28
				Chelsea	2+1	—
Peter Osgood (England)	6 2	12 9	Windsor	Chelsea	267+3	103
				Southampton	122+4	28
				Norwich C (on loan)	3	—
				Chelsea	9	2
Jimmy Clare	5 8	9 9	Islington	Chelsea	—	—
Gary Johnson	5 11	11 7	Peckham	Chelsea	1	1
Chris Sulley	5 8	10 0	Camberwell	Chelsea	—	—
Richard Wilson	5 8	10 7	Orpington	Chelsea	—	—
				Orient (on loan)	—	—
David Stewart (N. Ireland)	5 8	9 3	Belfast	Hull C	45+5	7
				Chelsea	—	—

CHESTER DIV. 3

President: Duke of Westminster. *Chairman:* R. Rowlands.
Vice-Chairman: A. E. Cheshire.
Directors: C. Thompson, L. Lloyd, R. H. Clark, E. J. Owen, R. S. Tresidder.
Team Manager: Alan Oakes. *Secretary:* S. Gandy
Year Formed: 1884. *Turned Professional:* 1902.
Limited Company: 1909.
Previous Grounds: Faulkner Street; Old Showground; 1904, Whipcord Lane; 1906, Sealand Road.
Football League Record:
 1931 Elected Division 3(N). 1975– Division 3.
 1958–75 Division 4.
Honours: Football League, highest position: 5th, Division 3, 1977–78. Division 3(N), Runners-up: 1935–36. *F.A. Cup,* best season: 5th Rd., 1976–77. *Football League Cup:* best season, semi-final, 1974–75. Welsh Cup winners: 1908, 1933, 1947. Debenhams Cup winners: 1977.
Record Victory: 12-0 v York C., Division 3(N), Feb. 1st, 1936.
Record Defeat: 2-11 v Oldham Ath., Division 3(N), Jan. 19th, 1952.
Most League Points: 56, Division 3(N), 1946–47; Division 4, 1964–65.
Most League Goals: 119, Division 4, 1964–65.
Highest League Scorer in Season: Dick Yates, 36, Division 3(N), 1946–47.
Most League Goals in Total Aggregate: Gary Talbot, 83, 1963–67, 1968–70.
Most Capped Player: Bill Lewis, 9 (30), Wales.
Most League Appearances: Ray Gill, 408, 1951–62.
Record Transfer Fee Received: £100,000 from Luton T. for Paul Futcher, June 1974.
Record Transfer Fee Paid: £24,000 to Brighton & HA for Ian Mellor, Feb. 1978.
Managers Since the War: Frank Brown, Louis Page, John Harris, Stan Pearson, Bill Lambton, Peter Hauser, Ken Roberts.
Address of Club Shop or Boutique: 18 Grosvenor St., Chester.

The Stadium, Sealand Rd, Chester CH1 4LW. Telephone Chester 371376. *Ground capacity:* 20,000. *Record attendance:* 20,500 v Chelsea, F.A. Cup 3rd Rd., Replay, January 16 1952. *Record receipts:* £15,854 v Aston Villa, F.L. Cup semi-final first leg, January 15 1975. *Pitch measurements:* 114 yds × 76 yds.

How to get there: Nearest railway station, Chester. Corporation bus to Town Hall Square, where special buses run from the Odeon Cinema to the ground.
Match tickets: No advance booking.
Car parking: Extensive parking at ground.
Entertainments/catering facilities: Catering facilities on ground.
Club shop: In town centre; stocks all types of souvenirs.
Handbooks/programmes: Programmes not available on subscription.
Extra information: Additional programme shop inside the ground.

Club Colours: Royal blue shirts with white stripes, royal blue shorts with red and white trim, white stockings with red and blue ringed top.
Change Colour: All yellow.
First Team Trainer: Vincent Pritchard.
Youth Team Manager: Cliff Sear.
Club Nickname: 'The Seals'.

CHESTER 1978-79 LEAGUE RECORD

Match No.	Date	Venue	Opponents	Result	H/T Score	League Pos'n	Goalscorers	Attendance
1	Aug 19	A	Southend U	W 1-0	0-0	—	Edwards	4223
2	23	H	Walsall	W 2-1	1-1	—	Phillips, Mellor (pen)	4257
3	26	H	Exeter C	W 3-0	1-0	1	Mellor (pen), Edwards 2	3431
4	Sept 2	A	Hull C	L 0-3	0-2	4		5325
5	8	H	Peterborough U	D 1-1	0-0	5	Edwards	4506
6	12	A	Colchester U	L 1-2	0-0	—	Phillips	2311
7	16	A	Gillingham	L 0-1	0-0	11		4743
8	23	H	Swansea C	W 2-0	1-0	10	Mellor, Edwards	8583
9	27	H	Swindon T	W 2-0	1-0	—	Delgado, Oakes	3311
10	30	A	Bury	D 1-1	1-1	5	Edwards	4056
11	Oct 7	H	Watford	W 2-1	1-1	4	Edwards, Phillips	6468
12	13	A	Tranmere R	L 2-6	1-1	6	Edwards, Mellor	5587
13	18	H	Plymouth Arg	D 0-0	0-0	—		3921
14	21	A	Oxford U	D 0-0	0-0	6		3908
15	28	H	Brentford	W 3-1	0-1	5	Edwards 3	4301
16	Nov 4	A	Chesterfield	L 1-3	0-2	6	Raynor	5015
17	11	H	Hull C	W 2-1	2-1	6	Edwards 2	4249
18	18	A	Exeter C	W 1-0	0-0	5	Mellor	3985
19	Dec 9	A	Sheffield W	D 0-0	0-0	6		8872
20	23	A	Blackpool	L 0-3	0-1	7		4106
21	26	H	Carlisle U	L 1-2	1-1	9	Walker	4690
22	Jan 13	A	Peterborough U	L 1-2	0-2	11	Edwards	4445
23	17	H	Colchester U	D 2-2	1-1	—	Henderson, Phillips	2339
24	30	A	Shrewsbury T	L 0-1	0-0	—		6693
25	Feb 3	A	Swindon T	L 0-2	0-1	11		6036
26	10	H	Bury	D 1-1	1-0	11	Henderson	3160
27	21	H	Gillingham	D 1-1	1-1	—	Jeffries	2421
28	24	H	Tranmere R	D 1-1	1-1	11	Raynor (pen)	4375
29	27	A	Swansea C	D 2-2	1-0	—	Henderson, Rayner (pen)	7983
30	Mar 3	H	Oxford U	W 4-1	2-1	10	Oakes, Jones, Phillips, Edwards	2476
31	7	H	Lincoln C	W 5-1	0-1	—	Henderson 3, Edwards, Phillips	2585
32	10	A	Brentford	L 0-6	0-1	10		6420
33	14	H	Rotherham U	L 0-1	0-1	—		2473
34	21	H	Southend U	L 0-1	0-0	—		2108
35	24	A	Walsall	L 1-2	1-0	12	Oakes	2795
36	28	H	Chesterfield	W 3-0	2-0	—	Jones, Livermore, Phillips	1804
37	31	H	Mansfield T	D 1-1	0-0	11	Edwards	2205
38	Apr 7	A	Lincoln C	D 0-0	0-0	12		3489
39	13	H	Blackpool	W 4-2	1-0	—	Oakes, Phillips (pen), Henderson, Edwards	4439
40	14	A	Carlisle U	D 1-1	0-1	12	Phillips	5309
41	16	H	Shrewsbury T	D 0-0	0-0	—		6249
42	21	A	Rotherham U	W 1-0	1-0	10	Edwards	2893
43	24	A	Plymouth Arg	D 2-2	2-1	—	Rayner (pen), Edwards	4686
44	28	H	Sheffield W	D 2-2	1-1	9	Mellor, Phillips	4200
45	May 2	A	Watford	L 0-1	0-1	—		12,167
46	5	A	Mansfield T	L 0-2	0-0	14		4173

Final League Position: 16

Goalscorers
League (57): Edwards 20, Phillips 10 (1 a pen), Henderson 7, Mellor 6 (2 pens), Oakes 4, Raynor 4 (3 pens), Jones 2, Delgado 1, Walker 1, Jeffries 1, Livermore 1.
League Cup (6): Edwards 3, Phillips, Livermore, Mellor.
F.A. Cup (7): Mellor 3, Phillips 2, Jones, Howatt.

League Cup	First Round	Port Vale (a)	3-0
		(h)	1-1
	Second Round	Coventry C (h)	2-1
	Third Round	Norwich C (h)	0-2
F.A. Cup	First Round	Runcorn (h)	1-1
		(a)	5-0
	Second Round	Darlington (a)	1-2

Lloyd	Raynor	Walker	Storton	Jeffries	Oakes	Livermore	Mellor	Edwards	Delgado	Phillips	Jones	Nickeas	Millington	Howat	Sutcliffe	Burns	Felix	Henderson	Rush	Match No.
1	2	3	4	5	6	7	8	9	10	11										1
1	2	3	4	5	6		8	10	9	7	11									2
1	2	3	4	5	6		8	10	9	7	11									3
1	2	3	4	5	6		8	10	9	7*11	12									4
1	2	3	4	5	6		8	10	9	7	11									5
1	2	3	4	5	6		8	10	9	7	11									6
1	3	11	4	5	6		8	10	9	7		2								7
1	3	11	4	5	6		8	10	9	7		2								8
1	2	3	4	5	6		8	10	9	7	11									9
1	3	11	4	5	6		8	10	9	7		2								10
1	3	11	4	5			8	10	9	7	6	2								11
1	3	11*	4	5			8	10	9	7	6	12	2							12
	3		4		6		8	10	9	5	11	7	2	1						13
	3		4	5	6		8	10	9		11	7	2	1						14
	3		4	5	6		8	10	9		11	7	2	1						15
	3		4	5	6		8	10	9		11	7	2	1						16
	3		4	5			8	10	9	6	11	7	2	1						17
1	3		4	5	6		8	10			11	7	2		9					18
1	3		4	5	6		8	10		7	11		2		9					19
1	3	11	4	5			8			6	10		2	9*	7	12				20
1	3	10	4	5			8			6	11		2	9*	7	12				21
1		3	4	5			8	9		6			2		7		10	11		22
1		3	4	5			8	9		6			2		7		10	11		23
1		3	4	5	6		8	9		10			2				7	11		24
1	3		4	5			8	9		6	7		2				10	11		25
1		3	4	5	6		8	12	9		11		2		7*			10		26
1	2	3	4	5	6				9		10				7		8	11		27
1	2	3	4	5	6				9		11*12				7		8	10		28
1	2	3	4	5	6						10	7		9*12			8	11		29
1	2	3	4*	5	6			9			10	7	12	8				11		30
1	2	3	4	5	6			9			10	8		7				11		31
1	2	3	4	5	6			9			10	8		7				11		32
1	3	10	4	5	6		8	9				7	2					11		33
1	3	10	4	5	6			9					2	7			8	11		34
1		3	4	5	6	8		9			10	7	2					11		35
1		3	4	5	6	8		9			10	7	2					11		36
1	12	3*	4	5	6	8		9			11	7	2					10		37
1			4	5	6	8		9			11	7	2		3			10		38
1			4	5	6	8		9			10	7	2	12	3*			11		39
1	3		4	5	6	8	12	9			11	7	2					10*		40
1	3		4	5	6	8		9			10	7	2	12				11*		41
1	2		4		6	8		9			11	7	3		5			10		42
1	5		4		6	8		9			10	7	2		3			11		43
1	2		5			8	9				10	7	6		3		11	4		44
1	5	12	4		6	8	9			10*	7	2			3			11		45
1	5	11	4		6	8		9			7	2			3			10		46
41	36	31	46	40	37	39	21	39	15	40	26	33	5	5	11	7	8	25	1	
	+ 1s	+ 1s				+ 2s				+ 3s	+ 1s			+ 3s	+ 2s					

CHESTER—PLAYERS

Player and position	Ht	Wt	Birthplace	Clubs	League Appearances	Goals
Goalkeepers						
Gren Millington	5 10	11 6	Queensferry	Chester	1	—
				Brighton	—	—
				Chester	167	—
Brian Lloyd (Wales)	6 2	12 7	Rhyl	Stockport Co	32	—
				Southend	46	—
				Wrexham	265	—
				Chester	307	—
Defenders						
Trevor Storton	6 1	12 4	Keighley	Tranmere R	112+6	8
				Liverpool	5	—
				Chester	216	10
Jim Walker	5 10	10 10	Northwich	Derby Co	35+6	3
				Brighton	24+4	4
				Peterborough U	20+11	1
				Chester	95+1	2
Paul Raynor	5 11	11 0	Chester	Chester	87+1	4
Derek Jeffries	5 10½	11 3	Manchester	Manchester C	64+9	—
				C Palace	108	1
				Peterborough U (on loan)	7	—
				Millwall (on loan)	10+1	—
				Chester	63+2	2
Mark Nickeas (Contract cancelled May 1979)	5 9	10 11	Southport	Plymouth Arg	—	—
				Chester	58+2	1
Alan Oakes	6 0	12 10	Winsford	Manchester C	562+3	26
				Chester	126	10
Ron Phillips	5 6½	10 3	Worsley	Bolton W	135+9	17
				Chesterfield (on loan)	5	—
				Bury	68+4	5
				Chester	82	17
Gary Felix	5 8	9 9	Manchester	Leeds U	—	—
				Chester	8	—
Richard Gendall	5 11	11 6	Wrexham	Chester	—	—
David Prestidge	5 9	10 6	Queensferry	Chester	—	—
Forwards						
Paul Lewis	5 7	11 7	Shotton	Chester	—	—
Ian Edwards (Wales)	6 1	12 5	Wrexham	WBA	13+3	3
				Chester	89	31
Ian Howat	5 8	10 7	Wrexham	Chester	25+7	5
David Burns	5 8	10 6	Ellesmere Pt	Chester	17+3	1
Bryn Jones	5 8	10 0	St. Asaph	Chester	42+8	4
Doug Livermore	5 8½	10 5	Liverpool	Liverpool	13+2	—
				Norwich C	113+1	4
				Bournemouth (on loan)	10	—
				Cardiff C	84+4	5
				Chester	71	6
Ian Mellor	6 1	10 12	Manchester	Manchester C	36+4	7
				Norwich C	28+1	2
				Brighton	116+6	31
				Chester	38+2	11
Peter Sutcliffe	5 6	9 0	Manchester	Manchester U	—	—
				Stockport Co	19+8	2
				Port Vale	44+6	6
				Chester	11+3	—
Peter Henderson	6 0	12 4	Berwick on Tweed	Witton A	—	—
				Chester	25	7
Ian Rush (apprentice) 1 app.						
*John Ruggiero	5 10	11 5	Stoke-on-Trent	Stoke C	9	2
				Workington (on loan)	3	—
				Brighton	4+4	2
				Portsmouth (on loan)	6	1

CHESTERFIELD DIV. 3

President: His Grace the Duke of Devonshire, M.C., D.L., J.P.
Vice-President: G. Kenning, D.F.C., T.D., M.A.
Chairman: P. C. J. T. Kirkman, O.B.E.
Vice-Chairman: A. Bates.
Directors: F. Tuckley, E. Brocklehurst, E. I. Gaunt, J. Leedham.
Team Manager: Arthur Cox.
General Manager/Secretary: A. G. Sutherland.
Year Formed: 1866. *Turned Professional:* 1891.
Limited Company: 1871.
Previous Name: Chesterfield Town, 1904.
Football League Record:

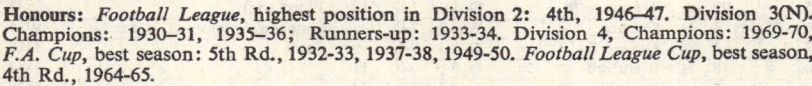

1899 Elected to Division 2.	1936–51 Division 2.
1909 failed re-election.	1951–58 Division 3(N).
1921–31 Division 3(N).	1958–61 Division 3.
1931–33 Division 2.	1961–70 Division 4.
1933–36 Division 3(N).	1970– Division 3.

Honours: *Football League,* highest position in Division 2: 4th, 1946–47. Division 3(N). Champions: 1930–31, 1935–36; Runners-up: 1933–34. Division 4, Champions: 1969–70. *F.A. Cup,* best season: 5th Rd., 1932-33, 1937-38, 1949-50. *Football League Cup,* best season, 4th Rd., 1964-65.

Record Victory: 10-0 v Glossop North End, Division 2, Jan. 17th, 1903.

Record Defeat: 1-9 v Port Vale, Division 2, Sept. 24th, 1932.

Most League Points: 64, Division 4, 1969–70.

Most League Goals: 102, Division 3(N), 1930–31.

Highest League Scorer in Season: Jimmy Cookson, 44, Division 3(N), 1925–26.

Most League Goals in Total Aggregate: Herbert Munday, 112, 1899–1909.

Most Capped Player: Walter McMillen, 4 (7), Ireland.

Most League Appearances: Dave Blakey, 613, 1948–67.

Record Transfer Fee Received: £80,000 for Steve Hardwick from Newcastle U., Feb. 1977.

Record Transfer Fee Paid: £35,000 to Leicester C. for Geoff Salmons, Aug. 1978.

Managers Since the War: Bob Brocklebank, Bob Marshall, Ted Davison, Duggie Livingstone, Tony McShane, Jimmy McGuigan, Joe Shaw.

Address of Club Shop: The Club Shop, Chesterfield F.C.

Recreation Ground, Chesterfield. Telephone Chesterfield 31535. *Ground capacity:* 28,500 (12,000 covered). *Record attendance:* 30,968 v Newcastle U., Division 2, April 7, 1939. *Record receipts:* £4,600 v Aston Villa F.L. Div. 3 August 15, 1970. *Pitch measurements:* 114 yds × 72 yds.

How to get there: Chesterfield railway station is one mile from the ground, via Corporation St., Holywell St., to Saltergate.
Match tickets: Seats in the Centre and Wing Stands may be booked in advance.
Car parking: Street parking permitted around the ground. Also car parks in Saltergate within ¼ mile of the ground.
Entertainments/catering facilities: A social club is sited on the ground at the Saltergate entrance. Entertainment provided at the Aquaries Club, Whittington Moor.
Club shop: At the ground; stocks all types of souvenirs.
Handbooks/programmes: Programmes available on subscription.
Extra information: Arnold Birch, Chesterfield's goalkeeper, scored five goals in 1923–24, all from penalties.

Club Colours: Royal blue shirts, white shorts, royal blue stockings, white tops.
Change Colours: All amber.
Club Trainer/Coach: Harold Roberts.
Club Nickname: 'Blues' or 'Spireites'.

CHESTERFIELD 1978-79 LEAGUE RECORD

Match No.	Date	Venue	Opponents	Result	Score	H/T Score	League Pos'n	Goalscorers	Attendance
1	Aug 19	H	Plymouth Arg	L	1-3	1-0	—	Cottam	3895
2	22	A	Carlisle U	D	1-1	0-0	—	Fern	5232
3	26	A	Brentford	W	3-0	2-0	10	Walker, Fern, Cammack	6150
4	Sept 2	H	Oxford U	D	1-1	1-1	9	Kowalski	4200
5	9	H	Exeter C	L	0-1	0-1	13		3936
6	12	A	Blackpool	D	0-0	0-0	—		6244
7	16	A	Hull C	D	1-1	1-1	17	Tartt	7705
8	23	H	Peterborough U	W	3-1	1-1	13	Kowalski 2, Salmons	3824
9	27	H	Southend U	W	3-2	1-2	—	Salmons, Fern, Cammack	4316
10	30	A	Gillingham	L	1-2	0-2	12	Fern (pen)	4602
11	Oct 7	H	Swansea C	W	2-1	1-1	8	Fern, Cammack	7033
12	14	A	Bury	L	1-3	0-2	12	Flavell	4306
13	18	H	Colchester U	W	2-1	0-0	—	Burton, Walker	4394
14	21	H	Watford	L	0-2	0-1	11		7800
15	27	A	Tranmere R	D	1-1	1-0	12	Flood (og)	2587
16	Nov 4	H	Chester	W	3-1	2-0	9	Simpson, Salmons, Cottam	5015
17	11	A	Oxford U	D	1-1	0-1	9	Fern	3410
18	18	H	Brentford	D	0-0	0-0	11		4584
19	Dec 9	A	Rotherham U	L	0-1	0-0	13		4935
20	16	H	Plymouth Arg	D	1-1	1-0	11	Kowalski	6740
21	23	A	Lincoln C	W	1-0	0-0	10	Fern	2951
22	26	H	Sheffield W	D	3-3	2-2	8	Walker, Fern, Prophett	13,322
23	Jan 13	A	Exeter C	L	1-3	1-2	10	Walker	3671
24	Feb 2	A	Southend U	L	0-2	0-2	12		4322
25	24	H	Bury	W	2-1	2-1	14	Walker 2	4332
26	28	H	Swindon T	D	1-1	0-1	—	Fern	3904
27	Mar 3	A	Watford	L	0-2	0-0	16		12,281
28	7	H	Shrewsbury T	W	2-1	0-0	—	Moss, Fern (pen)	4324
29	10	H	Tranmere R	W	5-2	3-0	11	Salmons 2, Moss, Walker, Fern (pen)	4090
30	14	H	Blackpool	L	1-3	0-1	—	Moss	4638
31	24	H	Carlisle U	L	2-3	0-0	15	McDonald (og), Simpson	4152
32	28	A	Chester	L	0-3	0-2	—		1804
33	31	H	Walsall	D	0-0	0-0	18		3332
34	Apr 4	H	Hull C	L	1-2	1-2	—	Flavell	3003
35	17	A	Swindon T	L	0-1	0-1	19		6176
36	14	A	Sheffield W	L	0-4	0-2	19		12,960
37	16	H	Mansfield T	W	1-0	0-0	—	Walker	4931
38	17	A	Lincoln C	L	1-3	1-1	—	Moss	3364
39	21	A	Shrewsbury T	D	1-1	0-1	19	Simpson (pen)	6360
40	24	A	Colchester U	D	0-0	0-0	—		6273
41	28	H	Rotherham U	W	1-0	1-0	19	Cammack	4160
42	May 5	A	Walsall	W	1-0	1-0	18	Moss	2625
43	8	A	Peterborough U	D	0-0	0-0	—		2338
44	11	A	Swansea C	L	1-2	1-1	—	Walker	25,000
45	19	H	Gillingham	L	0-2	0-1	—		2802
46	21	A	Mansfield T	L	1-2	0-1	—	Kowalski	4159

Final League Position: 20

Goalscorers

League (51): Fern 11 (3 pens), Walker 9, Kowalski 5, Moss 5, Salmons 5, Cammack 4, Simpson 3 (1 a pen), Cottam 2, Flavell 2, Burton 1, Prophett 1, Tartt 1, Own Goals 2.
League Cup (8): Fern 2, Tartt 2, Cottam, Cammack, Flavell, Walker.
F.A. Cup (1): Flavell

League Cup	First Round	Barnsley (a)	2-1
		(h)	0-0
	Second Round	Orient (a)	2-1
	Third Round	Charlton Ath (h)	4-5
F.A. Cup	First Round	Darlington (a)	1-1
		(h)	0-1

Letheran	Tartt	Salmons	O'Neill	Cottam	Hunter	Cammack	Fern	Simpson	Flavell	Kowalski	Dearden	Burton	Walker	Tingay	Prophett	Moss	Chamberlain	Heppolette	Pollard	Higgins	Match No.
1	2	3*	4	5	6	7	8	9	10	11	12										1
1	2	10	6	5	4	7	9		8			3	11								2
1	2	11	6	5	4	7	8			10		3	9								3
1	2	11	6	5	4	7	8*		12	10		3	9								4
1	2	10	6	5	4	8*		9		7	12	3	11								5
1	7	10	6	5	4			12	2	8	11	3	9*								6
	4	11		5	3		8		2	10		7	9	1	6						7
1	4	11		5	6		8		2	10		7	9		3						8
1	7	10		5*	4	12	9		2	8		3	11		6						9
1	7	10		5	4	12	9		2*	8		3	11		6						10
1	7	10		5	4	12	9		2*	8		3	11		6						11
	7	10		5	2	12	9		4*	8		3	11	1	6						12
1	7	10		5	4	12	9		2	8		3*	11		6						13
1	7	10		5*	4	12	9		2	8		3	11		6						14
1	7	10	5		4	12	9	11*	2	8		3			6						15
1	7	10		5	4		9	11	2	8		3			6						16
1	7	10		5	4		9	11	2	8		3*12			6						17
1	7	10*	3	5	4		9	11	2	8			12		6						18
1	7	10		5	4	11		9	2	8	12	3			6*						19
1	7	10		5	2	11	9*		4	8		3	12		6						20
1	7	10		5	4	11	9		2	8		3			6						21
1	2	10		5	4	11	9			8		3	7		6						22
1	4	10		5	2	7	9*		8			3	11		6	12					23
1	2	10		5	4		9			7		3	11		6	8					24
1		10		5	4	12	9		2	7*		3	11		6	8					25
1	7	10		5	4		9		2			3	11		6	8					26
1	2	10	12	5	4		9					3	11		6*	8	7				27
1	2	10		5	4		9		12			3	11		6	8	7*				28
1	2	10		5	4		9		12			3	11		6	8	7*				29
1	2	10*		5	4		9		7			3	11		6	8	12				30
1	4*10			5	3	11	9	12	7			2			6	8					31
1	2*10	6		4		9	12		7			3	11		8		5				32
1		10	4	5			9*12	2	7			11		3	8	6					33
1		10	3	5			9	12	2	7		11*	6		8	4					34
1	6	10	3	5			9		2	7		12	11*		8	4					35
1	6	10*	3	5			9		2	4		12	11		8	7					36
	4		6	5			9		2	7		3	10	1	8	11					37
	4		6	5		12	9		2	7		3	10	1	8	11*					38
			4	5			10		2	7		3	11	1	6	9	8				39
	2		5	4			9			7		3	10	1	6	8	11				40
	2		4		5	10	12			7		3	9	1	6	8	11*				41
	2		5		3	10	9			7		4	11	1	6	8					42
	2		5	4			9			7		3	10	1	6	8	11				43
	2		5	4			9*			7		3	10	1	6	8	11				44
	2		5		10		9*		4	7	12	3	11	1	6	8					45
	2	10	5		4			9	12	7		3*11		1	6			8			46
34	42	37	23	36	40	13	39	10	27	42	1	40	37	12	35	22	1	13	1	1	
	+1s				+9s	+1s	+5s	+2s	+2s	+4s	+2s	+3s			+1s	+1s					

CHESTERFIELD—PLAYERS

Player and position	Ht	Wt	Birthplace	Clubs	League Appearances	Goals
Goalkeepers						
Philip Tingay	5 11	11 12	Chesterfield	Chesterfield	161	—
				Barnsley (on loan)	8	—
Glan Letheran	6 1½	12 4	Llanelli	Leeds U	1	—
				Scunthorpe U (on loan)	27	—
				Chelsea (on loan)	—	—
				Notts Co (on loan)	—	—
				Chesterfield	57	—
Defenders						
Ken Burton	5 7½	11 8	Sheffield	Sheffield W	54+2	2
				Peterborough U (on loan)	3+1	—
				Chesterfield	234+3	6
Sean O'Neill	5 9	12 2	Belfast	Leeds U	—	—
				Chesterfield	184+3	3
Leslie Hunter	6 2	11 10	Middlesborough	Chesterfield	110+8	4
Glyn Chamberlain	5 9	11 4	Chesterfield	Burnley	—	—
				Chesterfield	17+1	—
John Cottam	5 10	11 10	Nottingham	Nottingham F	92+3	4
				Mansfield (on loan)	2	1
				Lincoln C (on loan)	1	—
				Chesterfield	120	7
Andy Higgins	6 3	12 4	Bolsover	Chesterfield	1	—
Bobby Flavell	5 7	9 10	Berwick	Burnley	—	—
				Halifax T	91	7
				Chesterfield	27+2	2
Colin Prophett	5 11	12 2	Crewe	Sheffield W	113+6	7
				Norwich C	34+1	—
				Swindon T	158+2	10
				Chesterfield	35	1
Midfield						
Colin Tartt	5 11	11 8	Liverpool	Port Vale	171+4	7
				Chesterfield	103	4
Ricky Heppolette	5 9	11 5	Bolton	Preston NE	149+5	13
				Orient	113	10
				C Palace	13+2	—
				Chesterfield	46+1	3
Bill Dearden	5 10	10 13	Oldham	Oldham Ath	29+3	2
				Crewe Alex	45+3	7
				Chester	85	22
				Sheffield U	170+5	61
				Chester	35+1	7
				Chesterfield	18+9	2
Geoff Salmons	5 10¾	11 10½	Mexborough	Sheffield U	170+10	8
				Stoke C	115+3	14
				Sheffield U (on loan)	5	—
				Leicester C	25+1	4
				Chesterfield	37	5
Forwards						
Rod Fern	5 11	11 0	Burton-on-Trent	Leicester C	132+17	27
				Luton T	34+5	5
				Chesterfield	150+2	54
Phil Walker	6 0	12 1	Kirby	Chesterfield	47+3	11
Andrew Kowalski	5 10	11 0	Mansfield	Chesterfield	223+8	22
Steve Cammack	5 11	11 1	Sheffield	Sheffield U	21+15	5
				Chesterfield	95+18	21
Gary Simpson	6 0	12 0	Chesterfield	Chesterfield	27+6	7
Stuart Parker	6 1	11 9	Preston	Blackpool	10+6	2
(Contract cancelled September 1978)				Southend U	62+2	23
				Chesterfield	30+4	8
Gary Pollard	6 1	11 10	Staveley	Chesterfield	17+3	—
Ernie Moss	6 1	12 11	Chesterfield	Chesterfield	271	94
				Peterborough U	34+1	9
				Mansfield T	56+1	21
				Chesterfield	22+1	5

COLCHESTER UNITED   DIV. 3

Patron: A. Buck, Q.C., M.P.
President: R. G. R. Chapman, F.R.I.C.S.
Chairman: J. W. Rippingale.
Directors: M. J. Cadman, T. C. M. Dodwell, S. G. Firth, N. F. Fitch, H. R. Piper.
Manager: Bobby Roberts. *Secretary:* Mrs. E. Scott.
Year Formed: 1937. *Turned Professional:* 1937.
Limited Company: 1937.

Football League Record:
 1950 Elected to Division 3(S).   1966–68 Division 3.
 1958–61 Division 3.   1968–74 Division 4.
 1961–62 Division 4.   1974–76 Division 3.
 1962–65 Division 3.   1976–77 Division 4.
 1965–66 Division 4.   1977–   Division 3.

Honours: Football League, Highest position in Division 3(S) 3rd, 1956–57. Division 4, Runners up; 1961–62. *F.A. Cup,* best season: 1970–71, 6th Rd. (Record for a Fourth Division club shared with Oxford United and Bradford City.) *Football League Cup,* best season: 5th Rd. 1974–75.

Record Victory: 9–1 v Bradford C., Division 4, Dec. 30th, 1961.
Record Defeat: 0–7 v Leyton Orient, Division 3(S), Jan. 5th, 1952; 0–7 v Reading, Division 3(S), Sept. 18th, 1957.
Most League Points: 60, Division 4, 1973–74.
Most League Goals: 104, Division 4, 1961–62.
Most League Goals in a Season: Bobby Hunt, 37, Division 4, 1961–62.
Most League Goals in Total Aggregate: Martyn King, 131, 1959–65.
Most Capped Player: None.
Most League Appearances: Peter Wright, 421, 1952–64.
Record Transfer Fee Received: £25,000 from Portsmouth for Colin Garwood, March 1978.
Record Transfer Fee Paid: £15,500 to Darlington for Eddie Rowles, Dec. 1977.
Managers Since the War: Ted Fenton, Jimmy Allen, Jack Butler, Benny Fenton, Neil Franklin, Dick Graham, Jim Smith.

Layer Rd. Ground, Colchester. Telephone (0206) 74042. *Telegraphic address:* 'United Colchester'. *Ground capacity:* 16,150. *Record attendance:* 19,072 v Reading F.A. Cup 1st Rd., November 27, 1948. *Record receipts:* £20,265 v Manchester U., F.A. Cup 5th Rd., February 20, 1979. *Pitch measurements:* 110yds × 71yds.

How to get there: Buses from Osborne Street in Colchester, which is about 2 miles from the railway station.
Match tickets: Stand seats can be booked two weeks in advance (Ticket Office tel: Colchester 72202 or 74042.)
Car parking: Parking facilities in Butt Road and Layer Road, approximately 150 yards past the ground on the south side of Colchester. Free parking in Army Barracks (150 yards).
Entertainments/catering facilities: Refreshment points on the ground.
Club shop: Sells all types of souvenirs; mailing list on request.
Handbooks/programmes: Back numbers of programmes can be ordered from the club shop.
Extra information: In 1947–48, Colchester, then a non-League side, reached the 5th round of the F.A. Cup

Club Colours: Blue and white vertical stripes, blue shorts, white stockings.
Change Colours: Red shirts, black shorts, black stockings.
Club Trainer/Coach: Ray Harford.
Club Nickname: 'The U's.

COLCHESTER UNITED 1978–79 LEAGUE RECORD

Match No.	Date	Venue	Opponents	Result	H/T Score	League Pos'n	Goalscorers	Attendance
1	Aug 19	H	Swansea C	D 2-2	1-0	—	Foley, Rowles	2918
2	21	A	Brentford	L 0-1	0-1	—		6800
3	26	A	Sheffield W	D 0-0	0-0	16		10,685
4	Sept 2	H	Rotherham U	D 0-0	0-0	15		2448
5	8	A	Carlisle U	L 0-4	0-4	21		4430
6	12	H	Chester	W 2-1	0-0	—	Gough, Cook	2311
7	15	H	Shrewsbury T	W 1-0	0-0	15	Foley	2788
8	23	A	Walsall	D 2-2	0-2	15	Gough, Foley	4052
9	27	A	Exeter C	L 1-2	1-1	—	Gough	3421
10	30	H	Blackpool	W 3-1	0-0	14	Gough 2, Rowles	3007
11	Oct 6	A	Swindon T	W 3-2	0-2	11	Rowles, Evans, Gough	3324
12	13	A	Lincoln C	D 0-0	0-0	9		3541
13	18	A	Chesterfield	L 1-2	0-0	—	Dyer	4394
14	20	H	Southend U	D 1-1	0-1	14	Evans	5831
15	28	A	Mansfield T	D 1-1	0-0	13	Wignall	4515
16	Nov 3	H	Plymouth Arg	W 2-1	0-1	10	Bunkell, Gough	4564
17	11	A	Rotherham U	L 0-1	0-1	14		3777
18	18	H	Sheffield W	W 1-0	0-0	12	Wignall	4346
19	Dec 9	A	Bury	D 0-0	0-0	11		2732
20	23	H	Watford	L 0-1	0-1	12		5424
21	26	A	Oxford U	L 0-2	0-0	14		4892
22	Jan 17	A	Chester	D 2-2	1-1	—	Foley 2	2339
23	19	A	Shrewsbury T	L 0-2	0-1	16		2119
24	Feb 2	H	Exeter C	D 2-2	1-0	16	Roberts (og), Allinson (pen)	2767
25	10	A	Blackpool	L 1-2	0-1	18	Allinson	3446
26	23	H	Lincoln C	W 2-0	0-0	16	Lee, Hodge	2861
27	27	H	Walsall	W 2-0	1-0	—	Hodge, Wignall	3135
28	Mar 2	A	Southend U	D 1-1	0-0	12	Lee	6957
29	9	H	Mansfield T	W 1-0	1-0	14	Gough	2866
30	13	A	Hull C	L 0-1	0-0	—		4201
31	17	A	Plymouth Arg	D 1-1	0-0	14	Dyer	5342
32	20	A	Swindon T	W 2-1	0-0	—	Lee 2	6678
33	24	H	Brentford	D 1-1	0-0	11	Hodge (pen)	3528
34	27	A	Swansea C	L 1-4	0-1	—	Lee	11,645
35	31	A	Peterborough U	W 2-1	1-0	12	Gough, Allinson	3559
36	Apr 2	H	Carlisle U	W 2-1	0-1	—	Lee, Wignall	2608
37	6	H	Tranmere R	W 1-0	1-0	9	Lee	2578
38	13	A	Watford	W 3-0	1-0	—	Lee 2, Gough	17,903
39	14	H	Oxford U	D 1-1	1-0	9	Gough	3897
40	16	A	Gillingham	L 0-3	0-1	—		12,030
41	21	H	Hull C	W 2-1	0-0	8	Rowles, Gough	2762
42	24	H	Chesterfield	D 0-0	0-0	8		6273
43	28	A	Bury	D 2-2	1-1	8	Gough, Wright	2905
44	May 4	H	Peterborough U	W 4-2	1-2	8	Foley, Allinson, Dowman 2	2692
45	7	H	Gillingham	D 2-2	0-1	—	Allinson, Gough	6317
46	9	A	Tranmere R	W 5-1	1-0	—	Gough 2, Lee 2, Packer	1016

Final League Position: 7

Goalscorers

League (60): Gough 16, Lee 11, Foley 6, Allinson 5 (1 a pen), Wignall 4, Rowles 4, Hodge 3 (1 a pen) Dyer 2, Dowman 2, Evans 2, Cook 1, Packer 1, Wright 1, Bunkell 1, Own Goal 1.
League Cup (2): Rowles, Dowman.
F.A. Cup (11): Gough 6, Dowman 2, Foley, Lee, Hodge.

League Cup	First Round	Charlton Ath (h)	2-3
		(a)	0-0
F.A. Cup	First Round	Oxford U (h)	4-2
	Second Round	Leatherhead (a)	1-1
		(h)	4-0
	Third Round	Darlington (a)	1-0
	Fourth Round	Newport Co (a)	0-0
		(h)	1-0
	Fifth Round	Manchester U (h)	0-1

Walker	Cook	Packer	Leslie	Wignall	Dowman	Sharkey	Gough	Foley	Rowles	Allinson	Dyer	Wright	Evans	Hodge	Bunkell	Lee	Cotton	Match No.
1	2	3	4	5	6	7	8	9	10	11								1
1	2	3	4	5	6	9*	8	7	10	11	12							2
1	2	3	4*	5	6		8	7	10	11	9	12						3
1	2	4		5	6		8	7	10	11	9	3						4
1	2	3		5	6		8	7	10	11		4	9					5
1	2	3		5	6	12	8	7	10	11	9	4*						6
1	2	3		5	6	4	8	7	10	11	9							7
1	2	3		5	6	4	8	7	10	11	9							8
1	2	3		5	6	4	8	7*12		11	9		10					9
1	2	3		5	6		8		10	11	9		7	4				10
1	2	3		5			8		10	11	9		7	4	6			11
1	2	3		5	6		8			11	9	10	7	4				12
1	2	3		5			8			11	9	6	7	4	10			13
1	2	3		5				6	11		9*10		7	4	12			14
1	2	6		5	7		8			11	3		9	4	10			15
1	2	3*		5	6		8	7		11	12			4	9	10		16
1	2	3		5	6		8	7		11	9*12			4		10		17
1	2	3		5	6		8	7		11				4	10	9		18
1	2	3		5	6		8	7		11	12		10	4	9*			19
1	2	3			6		8		7	11	9	5		4		10		20
1	2	3		5	6		8	7	11	12	9*10			4				21
1	2			5	6		8	7		11	9	3		4	10			22
1	2	10*		5	6		8	7		11	9	3		4	12			23
1	2	12		5	6		8	7		11	9	3		4		10*		24
1	2	9		5	6					10	11	3		4	7	8		25
1	2	7		5	6			8		11	9	3		4		10		26
1	2	7		5	6			8		11	9	3		4		10		27
1	2	7		5	6			8		11	9	3		4		10		28
1	2	7		5			6	8		11	9	3		4		10		29
1	2	7		5	12		6	8		11	9	3		4		10*		30
1	2	6		5			8	7		11	9	3		4		10		31
1	2	7			5		6	8		11	9	3		4		10		32
1	2	7			5		6	8		11	9	3		4		10		33
1	2	3.			5		9	6		8	7	4		11		10		34
1	2	6		5			8	7		10	9	3		4		11		35
1	2	7		5			6	8		11	9	3		4		10		36
1	2	6		5			8*	7	12	11	9	3		4		10		37
1	2	6		5	9		8	7		11		3		4		10		38
1	2	6		5	7		8			11	9	3	12	4*		10		39
1	2	6		5	4		8			11	9	3				10	7	40
1	2			5	6		8		9	10	7	3		4	11			41
1	2			5	4		8		7	11	9	3			6	10		42
1	2			5	6		8	4	9	10	7	3			11			43
1	2	12		5	4		8	6	7	11	9*	3			10			44
1	2	9		5	4		8	6	7	11		3			10			45
1	2	9		5	4		8	6	7	11		3			10			46
46	46	40	3	42	37	5	42	34	19	45	37	33	8	31	10	27	1	
		+2s		+1s	+1s				+2s	1s	+3s	+2s	1s		+2s			

COLCHESTER UNITED—PLAYERS

Player and position	Ht	Wt	Birthplace	Clubs	League Appearances	Goals
Goalkeepers						
Mike Walker	6 1	13 2	Colwyn Bay	Shrewsbury T	7	—
				York C	60	—
				Watford	137	—
				Charlton Ath (on loan)	1	—
				Colchester U	271	—
Bobby Hamilton	5 10	12 7	Irvine	Colchester U	—	—
Defenders						
Michael Cook	5 7	10 11	Enfield	Colchester U	397+4	14
Mike Packer	5 10	11 0	London	Watford	57+11	2
				Crewe Alex (on loan)	12	—
				Colchester U	225+7	10
Steve Wignall	5 11	11 12	Liverpool	Doncaster R	127+3	1
				Nottingham F (on loan)	—	—
				Colchester U	74+2	6
Steve Dowman	5 11	12 4	Manor Park	Colchester U	113+4	19
Steve Wright	6 0	10 11	Clacton	Colchester U	34+2	1
Midfield						
Ray Bunkell	5 9	11 3	Tottenham	Tottenham H	—	—
				Swindon T	52+4	3
				Colchester U	116+12	9
Steve Leslie	5 10	11 0	Brentwood	Colchester U	242+13	35
Paul Dyer	5 9	12 0	Leicester	Notts Co	1+6	—
				Colchester U	121+19	4
Russell Cotton	5 10	11 8	Wellington	Colchester U	2+1	—
Bobby Hodge	5 9½	11 0	Exeter	Exeter C	120+8	1
				Colchester U	31	3
Forwards						
Stephen Foley	6 0	11 4	Clacton	Colchester U	200+8	41
Bobby Gough	5 7	11 0	Birmingham	Walsall	1	—
				Port Vale	189+21	33
				Stockport Co (on loan)	6	—
				Southport	61	6
				Colchester U	149	51
Ian Allinson	5 10	11 0	Hitchin	Colchester U	124+12	18
Eddie Rowles	5 9	11 2	Gosport	Bournemouth	58+8	12
				York C	61+6	14
				Torquay U	54+5	13
				Darlington	96+7	21
				Colchester U	28+2	7
Tony Evans	5 8	10 8	Colchester	Colchester U	13+3	2
Trevor Lee	5 11	11 7	London	Millwall	99+9	23
				Colchester U	27	11

COVENTRY CITY DIV. 1

President: D. H. Robins.
Chairman: J. R. Mead, J.P.
Managing Director: J. W. T. Hill.
Directors: M. F. French, F.C.A., J. W. Jamieson, J. Mercer, O.B.E., P. D. H. Robins, T. Sergeant, F.R.C.S.
Team Manager: Gordon Milne.
Asst. Managers: Bob Dennison and Ron Wylie.
General Secretary: J. D. Dent
Commercial Manager: George Curtis.
Year Formed: 1883. *Turned Professional:* 1908.
Limited Company: 1907. *Former Names:* 1883–98 Singers F.C.; 1898 Coventry City F.C.

Football League Record:
1919 Elected to Division 2.	1958–59 Division 4.
1925–26 Division 3(N).	1959–64 Division 3.
1926–36 Division 3(S).	1964–67 Division 2.
1936–52 Division 2.	1967– Division 1.
1952–58 Division 3(S).	

Honours: *Football League*, highest League position: Division 1, 6th, 1969–70. Division 2, Champions: 1966–67. Division 3, Champions: 1963–64. Division 3(S), Champions: 1935–36; Runners-up: 1933–34. Division 4, Runners-up: 1958–9. *F.A. Cup*, best season: 6th Round, 1962–63, 1966–67, 1972–73; old 4th Rd., 1909–10. *Football League Cup*, best season: 5th Rd., 1964–65, 1970–71, 1973–74. *European Competition: European Fairs Cup:* 1970–71.
Record Victory: 9-0 v Bristol C., Division 3(S), Apr. 28th, 1934.
Record Defeat: 2-10 v Norwich C., Division 3(S), Mar. 15th, 1930.
Most League Points: 60, Division 4, 1958–59; and Division 3, 1963–64.
Most League Goals: 108, Division 3(S), 1931–32.
Highest League Scorer in Season: Clarrie Bourton, 49, Division 3(S), 1931–32.
Most Goals in Total Aggregate: 171, Clarrie Bourton, 1931–37.
Most Capped Player: Dave Clements, 21 (48), N. Ireland.
Most League Appearances: George Curtis, 486, 1956–70.
Record Transfer Fee Received: £200,000 from Arsenal for Jeff Blockley, Oct. 1972.
Record Transfer Fee Paid: £250,000 to Everton for David Jones, June 1979.
Managers Since the War: Dick Bayliss, Billy Frith, Harry Storer, Jack Fairbrother, Jesse Carver, Harry Warren, Billy Frith, Jimmy Hill, Noel Cantwell, Bob Dennison.
Address of Supporters Club: Thackhall Street, Coventry.
Address of Club Shop: 'Sky Blue Shop', Highfield Road, Coventry.

Highfield Rd., Coventry. Telephone Coventry 57171. *Telegraphic address:* 'City Football Coventry'. *Ground capacity:* 48,000 (16,000 covered). *Record attendance:* 51,457 v Wolverhampton W., Division 2, April 29, 1967. *Record receipts:* £45,061 v Liverpool. F.L. Cup 4th Rd., Replay, Dec 20 1977. *Pitch measurements:* 110 yds × 75 yds.
How to get there: Buses from Coventry railway station to town centre (Pool Meadow bus station). Then buses 1, 4, 7, 8, 8A to ground. Also taxi service from station.
Match tickets: Stand seat tickets can be booked 28 days in advance of any home League fixture. Postal applications accepted if sent with correct remittance to the Ticket Office Manager, Coventry City F.C. Highfield Rd. Stadium, Coventry.
Car parking: Street parking permitted all around the ground. Special coach/car park situated at Gosford Green (200 yards from stadium) on Walsgrave Road. (A46.)
Entertainments/catering facilities: Pre-match entertainment at all League and Cup games by Radio Sky Blue; live entertainment from groups and bands at special matches. The Sky Blue Buttery is open for hot and cold snacks before matches for main stand patrons. There are 16 licensed refreshment rooms and lounges, and 11 unlicensed refreshment rooms and lounges around the ground; all are open before the game, at half-time, and after the match. The Grandstand restaurant, recommended by Egon Ronay, is open for lunch Mon. to Fri. and is available in the evening for private dinner parties. On match days it is used as the Vice-Presidents' Club. An executive suite, with accommodation for 60 and full buffet facilities, can also be hired on match days, during the afternoon. Mr. T. Caluori, catering man, Grandstand Restaurant, Highfield Road, Coventry.
Club shop: Sited in the main stand; sells all types of souvenirs. There is a similar shop at the Thackhall St. side of the stadium, attached to the Sky Blue Pools Office.
Handbooks/programmes: Programmes available through a postal service. Special Halliday Yearbook available price 25p on receipt of remittance and large S.A.E.
Extra information: Coventry City Supporters' Club under the Sky Blue stand, Thackhall St. welcome visiting supporters on production of the membership card of their own club. They can attend the evening entertainment if they give 48-hours' notice by post to the secretary, Frank Fountaine, Coventry City S.C., Thackhall St., Coventry.
Club Colours: Sky blue shirts and shorts with navy and white trim, sky blue stockings.
Change Colours: Red shirts and shorts with navy and white trim, red stockings.
Club Captain: Terry Yorath. *Club Nickname:* 'Sky Blues'.

COVENTRY CITY 1978-79 LEAGUE RECORD

Match No.	Date	Venue	Opponents	Result	H/T Score	League Pos'n	Goalscorers	Attendance
1	Aug 19	A	Middlesbrough	W 2-1	0-1	—	Powell, Ferguson	17,956
2	22	H	Nottingham F	D 0-0	0-0	—		28,622
3	26	H	Norwich C	W 4-1	2-0	4	Beck, Powell, Wallace, Ferguson	20,452
4	Sept 2	A	Derby Co	W 2-0	0-0	2	Hunt, Wallace	21,435
5	9	H	Chelsea	W 3-2	1-2	2	Wallace, McDonald, Ferguson	24,920
6	16	A	Liverpool	L 0-1	0-1	3		51,130
7	23	H	Leeds U	D 0-0	0-0	3		27,365
8	30	A	Tottenham H	D 1-1	0-0	4	Ferguson	35,006
9	Oct 7	H	Ipswich T	D 2-2	0-2	3	Green, Thompson	21,859
10	14	A	Manchester C	L 0-2	0-0	7		36,723
11	21	A	WBA	L 1-7	1-3	10	Ferguson	27,381
12	28	H	Birmingham C	W 2-1	1-0	8	Hutchison 2	25,446
13	Nov 4	A	Bolton W	D 0-0	0-0	8		22,379
14	11	H	Middlesbrough	W 2-1	1-0	6	Wallace, Thompson	18,603
15	18	A	Norwich C	L 0-1	0-0	8		17,696
16	21	H	Derby Co	W 4-2	1-2	—	Wallace 2, McDonald, Powell	20,654
17	25	H	Arsenal	D 1-1	0-0	6	Hunt	26,786
18	Dec 9	H	QPR	W 1-0	0-0	6	Thompson	18,717
19	16	A	Southampton	L 0-4	0-2	7		19,102
20	23	H	Everton	W 3-2	0-0	6	Wallace, Thompson, Hunt	22,834
21	26	A	Bristol C	L 0-5	0-2	9		22,324
22	30	A	Wolverhampton W	D 1-1	0-1	8	Hutchison	21,514
23	Feb 3	A	Leeds U	L 0-1	0-1	8		22,928
24	10	H	Tottenham H	L 1-3	1-2	10	McDonald	25,133
25	21	A	Chelsea	W 3-1	3-1	—	Ferguson, Wallace, Powell	15,282
26	24	H	Manchester C	L 0-3	0-1	11		20,116
27	Mar 3	H	WBA	L 1-3	0-1	13	Thompson	25,795
28	6	H	Liverpool	D 0-0	0-0	—		26,629
29	10	A	Birmingham C	D 0-0	0-0	11		17,311
30	13	A	Ipswich T	D 1-1	0-1	—	Thompson	16,095
31	17	H	Bolton W	D 2-2	2-2	8	Wallace, Powell (pen)	15,231
32	20	H	Manchester U	W 4-3	3-1	—	Powell, Thompson, Hutchison, McDonald	26,308
33	24	A	Nottingham F	L 0-3	0-1	8		29,708
34	28	A	Aston Villa	D 1-1	0-0	—	Thompson	25,670
35	Apr 3	A	Arsenal	D 1-1	1-0	—	Nelson (og)	30,091
36	7	H	Aston Villa	D 1-1	1-0	7	Hutchison	23,690
37	10	A	Everton	D 3-3	3-1	—	Wallace 2, Hunt	25,302
38	14	H	Bristol C	W 3-2	3-0	7	Powell (pen), Hutchison, Hunt	17,812
39	16	A	Manchester U	D 0-0	0-0	—		43,075
40	21	H	Southampton	W 4-0	1-0	8	Wallace 3, Blair	17,750
41	28	A	QPR	L 1-5	1-1	9	Wallace	10,950
42	May 5	H	Wolverhampton W	W 3-0	2-0	9	Bannister, Powell 2 (1 a pen)	21,825

Final League Position: 10

Goalscorers

League (58): Wallace 15, Powell 9 (3 pens), Thompson 8, Ferguson 6, Hutchison 6, Hunt 5, McDonald 4, Beck 1, Green 1, Bannister 1, Blair 1, Own Goal 1.
League Cup (1): Thompson
F.A. Cup (2): Blair, Green

League Cup	Second Round	Chester (a)	1-2
F.A. Cup	Third Round	W.B.A. (h)	2-2
		(a)	0-4

Sealey	Osgood	McDonald	Gillespie	Holton	Yorath	Nardiello	Powell	Ferguson	Wallace	Hutchison	Green	Beck	Bannister	Roberts	Hunt	Coop	Hagan	Thompson	Blair	Gooding	Dyson	Blyth	Hateley	Match No.
1	2	3	4	5	6*	7	8	9	10	11	12													1
1	2	3	6*	5		7	10	9	8	11	12	4												2
1	2	3	6	5		7*	10	9	8	11		4	12											3
1		3	6	5			10	9	8	11		4		2	7									4
1		3	6	5			10	9	8	7		4		2	11									5
1		3	6	5			10	9	8	7		4		2	11									6
1		3	6	5	4		10	9	8	7				11	2									7
1		3	6	5	4		10*	9	8	11	12			7	2									8
1		3		5	4		8*		10	7	12			11	2	6	9							9
1		3	6	5	4		10		8	7				11	2		9							10
1		3	6	5*	4		10	9	8	7	12			11	2									11
1	5	3						9	8	11	7		2		6				4	10				12
1	5	3	6				10	9	8	11	7				2				4					13
1	5	3	6				10		8	11	7				2	9	4							14
1	5	3	6				10		8	11		7			2	9	4							15
1	5	3					10		8	11		7*	2	12	6	9	4							16
1	5	3					8		10	11			2	7	6	9	4							17
1		3	6*	5			10	12	8	11				7	2	9	4							18
1		3	12	5			10	6	8*	11				7	2	9	4							19
1		3		5			10		8	11				7	2	9	4		6					20
1	6	3		5			10		8	11				7	2	9	4							21
	2	3		5		7	10	12	8	11				6		9*	4				1			22
		3		5	7		10*	9	8	11				12	2	4		6			1			23
		3		5*	7		10	9	8	11				12	2	6		4			1			24
		3		5	7		10	9	8	11					2	6		4			1			25
		3		5	7		10	9	8	11					2	6*	12	4			1			26
1		3		5			10		8	11	7				2	6	9	4						27
1		3		5	4		10		8	11	7				2	6	9							28
1		3		5	4				8	11	7				2	6	9	10						29
1	3*		5	4					8	11	12		7		2	6	9	10						30
1		3		5	4	7	10		8	11					2	6	?							31
1		3		5	4	7	10		8	11					2	6	9							32
1		3			4	7	10			11*				5	12	2	6	9	8					33
1		3		5	4	7	10		8	11					2	6	9							34
1		3		5	4	7	10			11					2	9	6		8					35
1		3		5	4	7	10		8	11					2	9	6							36
1		3		5	4	7*	10		8	11					2	9	6		12					37
1		3		5	4*	7	10			11					2	9	6	12	8					38
1		3		5		7	10		8	11					2	9	6		4					39
1		3		5		7			10	11					2	9	6		8	4				40
1		3		5		7*	10		8	11					2	9	6		4	12				41
		3				7*	8			11			10	2		6			4	12	5	1	9	42
36	11	42	14	34	21	16	38	16	38	42	6	5	3	17	20	36	12	19	25	2	2	6	1	
			+ 1s				+ 2s					+ 5s	+ 1s	+ 1s		+ 4s		+ 1s	+ 1s	+ 1s	+ 2s			

COVENTRY CITY—PLAYERS

Player and position	Ht	Wt	Birthplace	Clubs	League Appearances	Goals
Goalkeepers						
Jim Blyth (Scotland)	6 1½	13 3	Perth	Preston NE	1	—
				Coventry C	96	—
				Hereford U (on loan)	7	—
Les Sealey	6 1	11 6½	Bethnal Green	Coventry C	49	—
Steve Murcott	6 0	12 0	Birmingham	Coventry C	—	—
Defenders						
Mick Coop	5 11	11 5½	Leamington	Coventry C	354+12	17
				York C (on loan)	4	—
Graham Oakey	5 7	9 10	Worcester	Coventry C	87+1	—
Brian Roberts	5 8½	11 3½	Manchester	Coventry C	57	—
Bobby McDonald	5 9	11 5½	Aberdeen	Aston V	33+6	3
				Coventry C	123	10
Jim Holton (Scotland)	6 1½	13 7	Lesmahagow	WBA	—	—
				Shrewsbury T	67	4
				Manchester U	63	5
				Sunderland	15	—
				Coventry C	67	—
Paul Dyson	6 2	13 7	Birmingham	Coventry C	2	—
Jim Hagan	6 0	11 10	Monkstown	Larne	(not known)	
				Coventry C	12+1	—
Keith Osgood	5 11	11 2	Ealing	Tottenham H	112+1	13
				Coventry C	24+1	1
Kevin Cooper	6 0	12 7	London	Coventry C	—	—
Steve Jacobs	5 8	11 0	London	Coventry C	—	—
Midfield						
Andy Blair	5 8½	10 10	Bedworth	Coventry C	25+1	1
Barry Powell	5 7½	10 0	Kenilworth	Wolverhampton W	58+6	7
				Coventry C	152+2	24
Tommy Hutchison (Scotland)	5 11½	11 2	Cardenden	Alloa Ath	68	4
				Blackpool	164+2	10
				Coventry C	268+2	22
Ray Gooding	5 8	11 4½	Hartlepool	Coventry C	12+2	1
Terry Yorath (Wales)	5 10½	12 3	Cardiff	Leeds U	110+23	10
				Coventry C	99	3
Gary Gillespie	6 2	12 1	Scotland	Falkirk	22	—
				Coventry C	14+1	—
Nick Phillips	5 10	11 2	London	Coventry C	—	—
Dan Thomas	5 7	11 0	Worksop	Coventry C	—	—
Steve Whitton	6 0	12 7	London	Coventry C	—	—
Forwards						
*Tom O'Brien	5 5	10 3	Cork	Coventry C	—	—
Mick Ferguson	6 1¾	12 8½	Newcastle	Coventry C	101+6	41
Alan Green (Contract cancelled March 1979)	5 5½	10 6	Worcester	Coventry C	98+19	30
Donato Nardiello	5 10	10 11	Cardiganshire	Coventry C	28+1	1
Ian Wallace (Scotland)	5 7½	10 9	Glasgow	Dumbarton	32+2	11
				Coventry C	103+2	44
Garry Thompson	6 0	12 9	Birmingham	Coventry C	24+2	10
Gary Bannister	5 7½	10 1	Warrington	Coventry C	3+1	1
Steve Hunt	5 7	10 11	Birmingham	Aston V	4+3	1
				New York C	—	—
				Coventry C	20+4	5
Mark Hateley	6 1	11 7	Liverpool	Coventry C	1	—
Clive Harwood	5 9	11 7	Kent	Coventry C	—	—

Also retained: David Barnes, Peter Bodak.

CREWE ALEXANDRA

DIV. 4

President: D. Plastow.

Chairman: N. Rowlinson.

Directors: J. McHugh, K. Potts, E. Tagg, C. Humphrey, J. Middleton, F. Saville, N. Hassall, R. Clayton.

Manager: Tony Waddington.

Secretary: Ken Dove.

Year Formed: 1877.

Turned Professional: 1893.

Limited Company: 1892.

Football League Record:
1892 Original Member of Division 2.
1896 Failed re-election.
1921 Re-entered Division 3(N).
1958–63 Division 4.
1963–64 Division 3.
1964–68 Division 4.
1968–69 Division 3.
1969– Division 4.

Honours: Football League: Best season Division 2, 10th, 1892–93. *F.A. Cup,* best season: semi-finalists: 1888. *Football League Cup:* 1974–75, 1975–76, 1978–79 3rd Rd.

Record Victory: 8-0 v Rotherham U., Division 3(N), Oct. 1st, 1932.

Record Defeat: 2-13 v Tottenham H., F.A. Cup, 4th Rd. Replay, Feb. 3rd, 1960.

Most League Points: 59, Division 4, 1962–63.

Most League Goals: 95, Division 3(N), 1931–32.

Highest League Scorer in Season: Terry Harkin, 34, Division 4, 1964–65.

Most League Goals in Total Aggregate: Bert Swindells, 126, 1928–37.

Most Capped Player: Bill Lewis, 12 (30), Wales.

Most League Appearances: Tommy Lowry, 436, 1966–78.

Record Transfer Fee Received: £30,000 from Arsenal for Brian Parker, August, 1975.

Record Transfer Fee Paid: £5,000 for Gordon Wallace to Liverpool, Oct. 1967.

Managers Since the War: George Lillycrop, Frank Hill, Arthur Turner, Harry Catterick, Ralph Ward, Maurice Lindley, Harry Ware, Jimmy McGuigan, Ernie Tagg, Dennis Viollet, Jimmy Melia, Ernie Tagg, Harry Gregg, Warwick Rimmer.

Address of Supporters' Club: Registered Office, Crewe Alexandra, Supporters' Association, 131 Edleston Road, Crewe, Cheshire.

Address of Club Shop or Boutique: Gresty Road, Crewe.

Football Ground, Gresty Rd., Crewe. Telephone Crewe 213014. *Telegraphic address:* 'Alex Football Crewe'. *Ground capacity:* 17,000. *Record attendance:* 20,000 v Tottenham H. F.A. Cup 4th Rd., January 30, 1960. *Record receipts:* £4,278 v Preston N.E., F.A. Cup 3rd Rd., Nov. 20, 1976. *Pitch measurements:* 112 yds × 74 yds.

How to get there: Local bus services from outlying districts. The ground is situated just five minutes' walk from Crewe railway station.
Match tickets: Advance booking for important cup ties only.
Car parking: Parking at the ground for 120 cars.
Entertainments/catering facilities: The Alexandra Club adjoining the ground is owned by the club. Refreshment points inside the ground.
Club shop: Situated at the ground; sells all types of souvenirs.
Handbooks/programmes: Handbooks on sale at matches.
Extra information: In 1956–57 the club set an unenviable League record of playing 30 successive games without a win.

Club Colours: Red shirts, white shorts, red and white stockings.
Change Colours: Sky blue shirts and stockings, black shorts.
Club Nickname: 'The Railwaymen'.

CREWE ALEXANDRA 1978-79 LEAGUE RECORD

Match No.	Date	Venue	Opponents	Result	H/T Score	League Pos'n	Goalscorers	Attendance
1	Aug 19	A	Huddersfield T	D 0-0	0-0	—		2838
2	23	H	Barnsley	L 0-2	0-1	—		2500
3	25	H	Port Vale	L 1-5	1-2	23	Bowles	4413
4	Sept 2	A	Portsmouth	L 0-3	0-1	24		7429
5	9	H	AFC Bournemouth	W 1-0	0-0	20	Davies	1693
6	12	A	Newport Co	W 2-1	2-0	—	Coyne 2	3176
7	16	A	Hereford U	L 1-6	1-1	18	Purdie	3493
8	23	H	Grimsby T	L 0-3	0-2	21		2000
9	27	H	Stockport Co	D 2-2	0-1	—	Davies, Coyne	2777
10	30	A	Halifax T	D 0-0	0-0	20		985
11	Oct 7	H	Torquay U	W 6-2	2-1	19	Bowles (pen), Coyne 2, Wilshaw, Davies, Purdie	1854
12	13	A	Darlington	D 1-1	1-1	21	Davies	1919
13	17	A	Wimbledon	D 1-1	0-0	—	Coyne	3555
14	21	H	Hartlepool U	L 0-1	0-1	21		2023
15	27	H	Aldershot	D 1-1	0-1	21	Bowles	1937
16	Nov 4	A	Rochdale	L 1-2	1-0	22	Coyne	1325
17	11	H	Portsmouth	D 0-0	0-0	22		2294
18	18	A	Port Vale	D 2-2	1-1	22	Bowles, Coyne	4607
19	Dec 6	A	Reading	L 0-3	0-2	—		4643
20	9	H	Bradford C	L 1-2	1-0	22	Nelson	1956
21	26	A	Wigan Ath	L 0-1	0-0	—		7586
22	Jan 13	A	AFC Bournemouth	W 1-0	1-0	22	Bowles	2855
23	Feb 6	H	Hereford U	D 0-0	0-0	—		1485
24	10	H	Halifax T	W 1-0	1-0	22	Warnock	1594
25	13	H	Doncaster R	L 2-4	1-2	—	Davies, Bowles	1532
26	20	A	Torquay U	L 0-3	0-1	—		2020
27	23	H	Darlington	D 1-1	0-0	22	Coyne	1474
28	27	A	Grimsby T	D 2-2	2-1	—	Davies 2	6854
29	Mar 3	A	Hartlepool U	D 2-2	1-1	21	Nelson, Coyne	2427
30	5	A	Stockport Co	L 3-4	1-3	—	Davies, Coyne, Bevan	3102
31	10	A	Aldershot	L 0-3	0-2	21		3947
32	13	H	Newport Co	L 0-1	0-0	—		1459
33	24	A	Barnsley	L 1-3	1-2	22	Coyne	8945
34	28	H	Huddersfield T	D 3-3	1-1	—	Bowles 2 (1 pen), Nelson	1382
35	31	A	Scunthorpe U	W 1-0	1-0	21	Nelson	1868
36	Apr 7	H	Reading	L 0-2	0-2	22		1856
37	10	H	Northampton T	L 2-4	2-1	—	Coyne 2	1291
38	14	H	Wigan Ath	D 1-1	0-1	22	Coyne	4604
39	16	A	Doncaster R	L 0-2	0-1	—		1658
40	17	A	Northampton T	L 1-3	0-1	—	Geidmintis (og)	2570
41	21	H	York C	L 0-1	0-1	23		1428
42	25	H	Wimbledon	L 1-2	0-2	—	Coyne	1254
43	28	A	Bradford C	L 0-6	0-3	23		2109
44	May 1	A	York C	L 0-1	0-0	—		2009
45	5	H	Scunthorpe U	L 0-2	0-2	23		1121
46	18	H	Rochdale	L 1-2	0-1	—	Nelson (pen)	2036

Final League Position: 24

Goalscorers
League (43): Coyne 16, Bowles 8 (2 pens), Davies 8, Nelson 5 (1 a pen), Purdie 2, Bevan 1, Warnock 1, Wilshaw 1, Own Goal 1.
League Cup (8): Nelson 3, Bowles 2 (1 a pen), Coyne, Wilshaw, Davies.
F.A. Cup (2): Coyne, Bowles.

League Cup	First Round	Rochdale (h)	1-0
		(a)	4-2
	Second Round	Notts Co (h)	2-0
	Third Round	Luton T (a)	1-2
F.A. Cup	First Round	Nuneaton (a)	2-0
	Second Round	Hartlepool (h)	0-1

Brand	Bevan	Purdie	Wilshaw	Bowles	Rimmer	Davies	Roberts	Nelson	Coyne	Tully	Caswell	Hughes	Cheetham	Robertson	Rafferty	Wilkinson	Dulson	Nicholls	Warnock	Rogan	Spence	White	Match No.
1	2	3	4	5	6	7	8	9	10	11													1
	2	8	6	5	4	7	3	9	10*11		1	12											2
	2	4	6	5		7	8	9	10	11	1		3										3
	6	10	11	5	4	7	8	9*12			1	2	3										4
	4	10	11	5	6	7	8	9			1	2	3										5
	6	10	11	5	4	7	8		9		1	2	3										6
	4	11	10	5	6	7	8		9		1	2	3*12										7
	4	10	8	5	6	7	3	12	9			2*		11	1								8
	2	8	6	5	4	7	3	9	12	10	1		11*										9
	4	6	9	5	3	7	2	8		10	1		11										10
	2	9	6	5	4	7	3		8	10	1		11										11
	2	8	11	5	4	7		10	9		1	3		6									12
	2	8	4	5	12	7		10	9		1		3	11		6*							13
	2	8	4	5		7		10	9		1		3	11		6							14
	2	8	4	5		7	3	10	9		1		11			6							15
	2	10	4	5		7	3	8	9				11	1		6							16
	2	8		5	4	7	10	12	9*				11	1	6	3							17
	6	8	10	5	4	7	3		9				11*	1	2		12						18
	6	8	10	5	4	7	3	9*					11	1	2	12							19
	6	8	10	5	12	7	3*	9			2		11	1		4							20
		8*		5	6	7	4	9					11	1	2	3	12	10					21
6				5	2	7	10	9			1		11			3	4	8					22
6	2			5		7	8	9			1		11			3	4	10					23
6	2			5		7	10	9			1		11		12	3	4	8*					24
6	10			5		7	8*	9	12		1		11		2	3	4						25
6	10			5		7	8	9			1		11		2	3	4						26
6*10				5		7	8	9	12		1				2	3	4	11					27
6	4			5		7	8	9	11					1	2	3		10					28
6	4			5		7	8	9	10					1	2*	3	12	11					29
6				5		7	8		9		2		11	1		3	4	10					30
6	4			5		7	8	12				9	11	1	2	3		10					31
6	4			5		7	8		9				11	1	2*	3		10					32
6	4			5		7			9		2	8	11	1		3		10					33
6	4			5		7		12	9		2	8	11*	1		3		10					34
6	4			5		7		10	9		2	8				3		11	1				35
6	4	12		5		7*		11	9		2	8				3		10	1				36
6	4			5				11	10			8	7		2	3		9	1				37
6	4*			5			12	11	9			8	7	1	2	3		10					38
6	4			5	12		7*11	10				8		1	2	3		9					39
	4*			5	6		12	11	10			8	7	1	2	3		9					40
6				5			12	9*10				8	7	1	2	3	4	11					41
6				5			11		10			8	7	1	2	3	4		9				42
	9		5		11			10			2	8	7	1		3	4						43
6			5	4	9	11		10		1		8	7		2	3							44
6			5	4		11*		10		1		8	7		2	3		12		9			45
	7	3	12		4		6*10	9		1		8		2	5		11						46
1	44	39	20	45	20	38	34	31	32	6	22	12	22	32	20	25	28	10	20	3	1	1	
			+ 2s			+ 3s	+ 3s	+ 4s	+ 4s		+ 1s		+ 1s		+ 1s	+ 1s	+ 3s	+ 1s					

CREWE ALEXANDRA—PLAYERS

Player and position	Ht	Wt	Birthplace	Clubs	League Appearances	Goals
Goalkeepers						
*Peter Caswell	6 0	12 3	Leatherhead	C Palace Crewe A	3 22	— —
Kevin Rafferty	6 1	12 0		Crewe A	20	—
Defenders						
Kevin Lewis	5 9	11 13	Hull	Manchester U Stoke C Crewe A	— 15 —	— — —
Richard Wainwright	5 11	10 7	Crewe	Crewe A	—	—
Paul Bevan	5 11	10 9	Shrewsbury	Shrewsbury T Swansea C Crewe A	67+5 77+2 156+1	1 5 7
*Warwick Rimmer	5 8¼	10 13	Birkenhead	Bolton W Crewe A	426+6 114+14	17 —
Neil Wilkinson	5 7	10 4	Blackburn	Blackburn R Port Vale Crewe A	27+3 7 25+1	— — —
Gary Dulson	5 10	11 8	Nottingham	Nottingham F Port Vale Crewe A	— 108+2 28+1	— 3 —
*Phillip Nicholls	5 11	11 6	Bilston	Wolverhampton Crewe A Bradford C Crewe A	— 155+8 19+2 10+3	— 3 2 —
Paul Bowles	6 2	11 7	Manchester	Manchester U Crewe A	— 168+5	— 20
Danny Bowers	5 8¼	10 2	Stoke	Stoke C Shrewsbury T (on loan) Crewe A	35+4 6 —	2 — —
Midfield						
Paul Mayman	5 8	10 0	Crewe	Crewe A	42+1	3
Hughie Cheetham	5 10	10 5	Manchester	Crewe A	90+3	—
David Davies	6 0	13 5	Rhondda Valley	Swansea C Crewe A	0+1 141+1	— 20
David Hughes (Non-contract)	5 10	11 4	Blackburn	Crewe A	12+1	—
*Steven Wilshaw	5 9	10 0	Stoke	Stoke C Crewe A	— 20+2	— 1
Forwards						
Bernard Purdie	5 9	11 0	Wrexham	Wrexham Chester Crewe A	7+3 54+9 184+9	3 14 44
*Ian Roberts	5 10	10 8	Glasgow	Shrewsbury T Crewe A	93+3 89+4	— —
Colin Spence (Non-contract)	6 0	12 2	Glasgow	Crewe A	10+8	1
Peter Coyne	5 8¼	10 7	Hartlepool	Manchester U Crewe A	1+1 71+6	1 32
*Jimmy Robertson (Scotland)	5 8	9 7	Glasgow	Cowdenbeath St Mirren Tottenham H Arsenal Ipswich T Stoke C Walsall Crewe A	25 52 153+4 45+1 87 99+15 16 32+1	7 14 26 7 10 12 — —
Ted White (Non-contract)	5 10	11 0	Crewe	Crewe A	1	—
Dennis Nelson	5 8	10 4	Edinburgh	Dunfermline Crewe A Reading Crewe A	38+10 65+6 53+6 31+4	17 18 6 5
Neil Warnock	5 9	10 10	Sheffield	Chesterfield Rotherham U Hartlepool U Scunthorpe U Aldershot Barnsley York C Crewe A	19+3 46+8 58+2 63+9 35+2 53+4 1+3 20+1	2 5 5 7 6 10 — 1

CRYSTAL PALACE   DIV. 1

Chairman: R. E. Bloye.
Directors: E. J. Swann, R. S. Briggs, R. R. Varey, S. Stephenson, F. C. Buckley, C. D. Richards, J. C. Williams, A. G. Broughton, N. H. Hunt, O.B.E.
Manager: Terry Venables.
Secretary: Alan Leather.
Commercial Manager: Tony Shaw.
Year Formed: 1905.   *Limited Company:* 1905.
Turned Professional: 1905.
Previous Grounds: 1905, Crystal Palace; 1915, Herne Hill; 1919, The Nest; 1924, Selhurst Park.
Football League Record:

© Crystal Palace F.C. Ltd. Copyright reserved.

1920 Original Members of Division 3.	1964–69 Division 2.
1921–25 Division 2.	1969–73 Division 1.
1925–58 Division 3(S).	1973–74 Division 2.
1958–61 Division 4.	1974–77 Division 3.
1961–64 Division 3.	1977–79 Division 2.
	1979– Division 1.

Honours: *Football League*, best season in Division 1: 18th 1970–71. Division 2: Champions 1978–79. Runners-up: 1968–69. Division 3, Runners-up: 1963–64. Division 3(S), Champions: 1920–21; Runners-up: Division 3(S), 1928–29, 1930–31, 1938–39. Division 4, Runners-up: 1960–61.
F.A. Cup, best season: semi-final 1975–76. *Football League Cup:* 5th Rd., 1968–69, 1970–71.
Record Victory: 9-0 v Barrow, Division 4, Oct. 10th, 1959.
Record Defeat: 4-11 v Manchester C., F.A. Cup, 5th Rd., Feb. 20th, 1926.
Most League Points: 64, Division 4, 1960–61.
Most League Goals: 110, Division 4, 1960–61.
Highest League Scorer in Season: Peter Simpson, 46, Division 3(S), 1930–31.
Most Goals in Total Aggregate: Peter Simpson, 154, 1930–36.
Most Capped Player: Ian Evans, 13, Wales.
Most League Appearances: Terry Long, 432, 1956–69.
Record Transfer Fee Received: £200,000 from Tottenham H for Peter Taylor, September 1976.
Record Transfer Fee Paid: £465,000 to QPR for Gerry Francis, May 1979.
Managers Since the War: George Irwin, Jack Butler, Ronnie Rooke, Fred Dawes, Charlie Slade, Laurie Scott, Cyril Spiers, George Smith, Arthur Rowe, Dick Graham, Bert Head, Malcolm Allison.
Address of Social Section: Social Hall, Selhurst Park, S.E.25, 6PU.
Address of Club Shop or Boutique: Palace Shop; Programme Shop in Old Stand.

Selhurst Park, London, SE25 6PU. Telephone 01-653 3338. *Ground capacity:* 51,000 (21,000 covered). *Record attendance:* 51,801 v Burnley Division 2, May 11, 1979. *Record receipts:* £51,650 v Burnley, Division 2, May 11, 1979.
Pitch measurements: 110 yds × 75 yds.
How to get there: Ground served by three stations—Selhurst (5 minutes walk), Norwood Junction (7 minutes) and Thornton Heath (10 minutes). Buses 68, 75, 154, 157, 12 (to Norwood Junction).
Information service: 01-653 2223.
Match tickets: Seats bookable in advance, postal applications accepted one month in advance and personal application two weeks in advance. Postal applications must be accompanied by S.A.E. and the correct remittance. Cheques must be made payable to Crystal Palace F.C. and name and address must be written on the back. Separate application must be made for each match.
Car parking: Large car park at the ground.
Entertainments/catering facilities: A social hall and catering facilities within the ground.
Club shops: Two shops sell all types of souvenirs.
Handbooks/programmes: Programmes available on subscription.
Extra information: Vic Rouse, the Crystal Palace goalkeeper, was the first Fourth Division player to be capped when he played for Wales v Ireland in 1959.
Club Colours: White shirts with 4 inch diagonal band red over blue, white shorts, white stockings.
Change Colours: Royal blue and red vertical striped shirts, royal blue shorts, royal blue stockings with red and white band.
First Team Coach: Alan Harris.   *Club Captain:* Ian Evans.   *Club Nickname:* 'The Eagles'.

CRYSTAL PALACE 1978–79 LEAGUE RECORD

Match No.	Date	Venue	Opponents	Result	H/T Score	League Pos'n	Goalscorers	Attendance
1	Aug 19	A	Blackburn R	D 1-1	1-0	—	Swindlehurst	9463
2	22	H	Luton T	W 3-1	1-1	—	Swindlehurst, Hilaire, Murphy	17,639
3	26	H	West Ham U	D 1-1	1-1	6	Gilbert	32,611
4	Sept 2	A	Sheffield U	W 2-0	2-0	2	Hilaire, Elwiss	17,388
5	9	H	Sunderland	D 1-1	0-0	2	Chatterton (pen)	21,112
6	16	A	Millwall	W 3-0	1-0	1	Murphy, Chatterton, Nicholas	11,693
7	23	H	Oldham Ath	W 1-0	0-0	1	Swindlehurst	18,318
8	30	A	Stoke C	D 1-1	0-1	2	Murphy	19,070
9	Oct 7	H	Brighton & H A	W 3-1	0-0	1	Hilaire 2, Swindlehurst	33,685
10	14	A	Preston N E	W 3-2	0-1	1	Walsh 2, Elwiss	10,795
11	21	A	Wrexham	D 0-0	0-0	1		15,132
12	28	H	Fulham	L 0-1	0-0	2		28,733
13	Nov 4	A	Burnley	L 1-2	0-1	3	Chatterton (pen)	11,067
14	11	H	Blackburn R	W 3-0	2-0	2	Walsh, Swindlehurst 2 (1 a pen)	17,006
15	18	A	West Ham U	D 1-1	0-1	1	Elwiss	31,245
16	21	H	Sheffield U	W 3-1	2-0	—	Elwiss, Nicholas, Swindlehurst	19,504
17	25	A	Cardiff C	D 2-2	1-2	1	Elwiss, Swindlehurst	8739
18	Dec 2	H	Newcastle U	W 1-0	1-0	1	Elwiss	19,287
19	9	A	Notts Co	D 0-0	0-0	1		11,011
20	16	H	Leicester C	W 3-1	2-0	1	Cannon, Swindlehurst, Elwiss	17,330
21	23	A	Cambridge U	D 0-0	0-0	1		8081
22	26	H	Bristol R	L 0-1	0-0	—		21,605
23	30	H	Orient	D 1-1	1-0	1	Hilaire	20,100
24	Jan 20	H	Millwall	D 0-0	0-0	1		21,142
25	Feb 10	H	Stoke C	D 1-1	0-0	3	Walsh	23,313
26	17	A	Brighton & HA	D 0-0	0-0	2		23,795
27	24	H	Preston NE	D 0-0	0-0	3		17,592
28	Mar 3	H	Wrexham	W 1-0	0-0	3	Walsh	15,154
29	10	A	Fulham	D 0-0	0-0	4		16,654
30	14	A	Sunderland	W 2-1	2-1	—	Hilaire, Cannon	34,986
31	24	A	Luton T	W 1-0	1-0	3	Nicholas	11,008
32	27	A	Crystal Palace	D 1-1	1-1	—	Swindlehurst	15,065
33	31	H	Cardiff C	W 2-0	2-0	2	Smillie, Walsh	18,672
34	Apr 3	A	Oldham Ath	D 0-0	0-0	—		5620
35	7	A	Newcastle U	L 0-1	0-0	3		18,860
36	10	H	Cambridge U	D 1-1	1-1	—	Swindlehurst	21,795
37	14	H	Bristol R	W 1-0	0-0	4	Walsh	10,986
38	17	H	Charlton Ath	W 1-0	0-0	—	Murphy	30,000
39	20	A	Leicester C	D 1-1	0-1	4	Hinshelwood	16,767
40	28	H	Notts Co	W 2-0	1-0	4	Swindlehurst, Murphy	23,880
41	May 5	A	Orient	W 1-0	0-0	4	Swindlehurst	19,945
42	11	H	Burnley	W 2-0	0-0	—	Walsh, Swindlehurst	51,801

Final League Position: 1

Goalscorers

League (51): Swindlehurst 14 (1 a pen), Walsh 8, Elwiss 7, Hilaire 6, Murphy 5, Chatterton 3 (2 pens), Nicholas 3, Cannon 2, Gilbert 1, Hinshelwood 1, Smillie 1.
League Cup (3): Murphy, Swindlehurst, Chatterton (pen).
F.A. Cup (5): Walsh, Sansom, Nicholas, Fenwick, Kember.

League Cup	Second Round	Bristol C (a)	2-1
	Third Round	Aston Villa (a)	1-1
		(h)	0-0 (a.e.t.)
			0-3 (at Coventry)
F.A. Cup	Third Round	Middlesbrough (a)	1-1
		(h)	1-0
	Fourth Round	Bristol C (h)	3-0
	Fifth Round	Wolverhampton W (h)	0-1

Burridge	Hinshelwood	Sansom	Nicholas	Cannon	Gilbert	Chatterton	Murphy	Swindlehurst	Elwiss	Hilaire	Fenwick	Walsh	Kember	Silkman	Smillie	Hazell	Sealy	Match No.
1	2	3	4	5	6	7	8*	9	10	11	12							1
1	2	3	7	5	6	4	8	9	10	11								2
1	2	3	7	5	6	4	8	9	10	11								3
1	2	3	7	5	6	4	8	9	10	11								4
1	2	3	7	5	6	4	8*	9	10	11	12							5
1	2	3	7	5	6	4	8	9	10	11								6
1	2	3	7	5	6	4	8	9	10	11								7
1	2	3	7	5	6	4	8	9	10	11								8
1	2	3	7	5	6	4	8	9*10	11		12							9
1	2	3	7	5	6	4	8		10	11		9						10
1	2*	3	7		6	4	8	9	10	11	5	12						11
1		3	7	5*	6	4	8	9	10	11	2	12						12
1		3	7	5	6	4	12	9	10*11		2		8					13
1		3	7	5	6		8	9		11	2	10	4					14
1		3	7	5	6		8	9	12	11*	2	10	4					15
1		3	7	5	6		8	9	10*		2	11	4	12				16
1		3		5	6		8	9	11	12	4	10	7*		2			17
1		3		5	6		8	9	10		7	11	4		2			18
1		3		5	6		8	9	10		2	11	7		4			19
1		3	7	5	6		8	9	10		2	11	4					20
1	2	3	7	5	6				9	10*12	8	11	4					21
1		3	7	5	6		8	9		12	2	11	4*10					22
1		3	7	5	6		8*	9		10		11	4	12	2			23
1	2	3	7	5	6		8*	9		12	10	11	4					24
1	2	3	7	5	6		8	9			10	11	4					25
1	2	3	7	5	6		10	9			8	11	4					26
1	2	3	7	5	6		8	9		10*		11	4	12				27
1	2	3	7	5	6		8*	9	11			10	4	12				28
1	2	3	7	5	6		8	9	11			10	4					29
1	2*	3	7	5			8	9	10	12		11	4		6			30
1	2	3	7	5	6		8	9	11			10	4					31
1	2	3	7	5	6		8	9	10			11	4					32
1	2	3	7	5	6		8	9				11*	4	10		12		33
1	2	3	7	5	6		8			12		10	4	11*		9		34
1	2	3	7	5	6		8	9	12	10*		11	4					35
1	2	3	7*	5	6		8	9	10			11	4	12				36
1	2	3	7	5	6		8	9*		12		11	4			10		37
1	2	3		5	6		8	9		7		11	4			10		38
1	2	3		5	6		8	9	12	7		11	4*			10		39
1	2	3	7	5	6		8	9	11			10	4					40
1	2	3	7	5	6		8	9	11	4		10						41
1	2	3	7	5	6		8	9	11			10	4					42
42	31	42	37	41	41	13	40	40	19	25	20	30	29	3	5	4		
							+1s		+1s	+6s	+4s	+1s	+3s		+5s	+1s		

CRYSTAL PALACE—PLAYERS

Player and position	Ht	Wt	Birthplace	Clubs	League Appearance	Goals
Goalkeepers						
David Fry	6 0	12 6	Bournemouth	C Palace	1	—
John Burridge	5 10	12 2	Workington	Workington	27	—
				Blackpool	134	—
				Aston V	65	—
				Southend U (on loan)	6	—
				C Palace	52	—
Robert Horn	6 0	13 0	Westminster	C Palace	—	—
Defenders						
Kenny Sansom (England)	5 6	11 6	Camberwell	C Palace	136	2
Ian Evans (Wales)	6 2½	12 7	Egham	QPR	39	2
				C Palace	137	14
Jimmy Cannon	6 0	13 6	Glasgow	C Palace	216+3	13
Peter Nicholas (Wales)	5 8½	11 2	Newport SW's	C Palace	60	4
Kevin Dare	5 9	11 8	Finchley	C Palace	—	—
Billy Gilbert	5 11	11 9	Lewisham	C Palace	59	1
Terry Boyle	5 10	12 3	Ammerford	Tottenham H	—	—
				C Palace	1	—
Chris Sparks	5 10	10 8	Islington	C Palace	—	—
Paul Hinshelwood	5 11	12 1	Bristol	C Palace	129+5	11
Tony Hazell	5 10	11 6	High Wycombe	QPR	361+7	4
				Millwall	153	6
				C Palace	5	—
Midfield						
George Graham (Scotland)	5 11	12 6	Bargeddie	Aston V	8	2
				Chelsea	72	35
				Arsenal	219+8	60
				Manchester U	41+2	2
				Portsmouth	61	5
				C Palace	43+1	2
Gary Lowe	5 11	11 10	Manchester	C Palace	—	—
Jerry Murphy	5 9	11 3	Stepney	C Palace	44+6	5
Neil Smillie	5 6	10 8	Barnsley	C Palace	4+6	1
				Brentford (on loan)	3	—
Terry Fenwick	5 9½	10 6	Camden, Co D	C Palace	30+4	—
Les Carter	5 9	10 8	Farnborough	C Palace	—	—
Steve Lovell	6 0	11 12	Swansea	C Palace	—	—
Tony Paul	5 9	11 0	Islington	C Palace	—	—
Steve Kember	5 9	10 12	Croydon	C Palace	216+2	34
				Chelsea	125+5	13
				Leicester C	115+2	6
				C Palace	29	—
Forwards						
David Swindlehurst	6 2	13 3	Edgware	C Palace	200+12	66
Steve Leahy	5 7	10 6	Battersea	C Palace	—	—
Vince Hilaire	5 6	10 2	Forest Hill	C Palace	51+13	8
Ian Walsh	5 9½	11 2	St. Davids, Pem.	C Palace	44+6	10
Mike Elwiss	6 0	12 6	Doncaster	Doncaster R	106+1	30
				Preston NE	191+1	60
				C Palace	19+1	7
Tony Sealy	5 7	11 2	London	Southampton	2+5	—
				C Palace	4+1	—

DARLINGTON DIV. 4

Chairman: J. L. T. Moore.
Directors: D. Mason, A. Brown, J. B. Hadley, B. J. H. Richardson, E. W. A. McMahon, Dr. M. C. Robson, J. Hunter, C. Parias
Manager: Billy Elliott.
Secretary: Andrew W. Rowell.
Year Formed: 1883. *Turned Professional:* 1908.
Limited Company: 1891.
Football League Record:
  1921 Original Member   1958–66 Division 4.
  Division 3(N).   1966–67 Division 3.
  1925–27 Division 2.   1967–   Division 4.
  1927–58 Division 3(N).

Honours: *Football League*, highest position: 15th, Division 2, 1925–26. Division 3(N), Champions: 1924–25; Runners-up: 1921–22. Division 4, Runners-up: 1965–66. *F.A. Cup*, best season: 3rd Rd., 1910–11; 5th Rd., 1957–58. *Football League Cup*, best season: 5th Rd., 1967–68.

Record Victory: 9-2 v Lincoln C., Division 3 (N), Jan. 7, 1928.

Record Defeat: 0-10 v Doncaster R., Division 4, Jan. 25th, 1964.
Most League Points: 59, Division 4, 1965–66.
Most League Goals: 108, Division 3(N), 1929–30.
Highest League Scorer in Season: David Brown, 39, Division 3(N), 1924–25.
Most League Goals in Total Aggregate: David Brown, 74, 1923–26.
Most Capped Player: None.
Most League Appearances: Ron Greener, 442, 1955–68.
Record Transfer Fee Received: £15,555 from Lincoln C. for Alan Harding, March 1973.
Record Transfer Fee Paid: £17,000 to Notts Co. for Eric Probert, Oct. 1978.
Managers Since the War: Bill Forrest, George Irwin, Bob Gurney, Dick Duckworth, Eddie Carr, Lol Morgan, Jimmy Greenhalgh, Ray Yeoman, Len Richley, Frank Brennan, Allan Jones, Ralph Brand, Dick Conner, Billy Horner, Peter Madden, Len Walker.
Address of Supporters Club: Same as Football Club.

Feethams Ground, Darlington. Telephone Darlington (0325) 65097/67712. *Ground capacity:* 20,000. *Record attendance:* 21,023 v Bolton W., League Cup 3rd Rd., November 14, 1960. *Record receipts:* £4,685.60 v Fulham, League Cup 2nd Rd., replay, September 5, 1978. *Pitch measurements:* 110 yds × 74 yds.

How to get there: Darlington railway station, five minutes walk.
Match tickets: Postal and telephone bookings accepted in advance of the match.
Car parking: Ample parking in surrounding side-streets.
Entertainments/catering facilities: Four nearby cafés. Three snack bars in the ground.
Club shop: Shop inside the ground sells all types of souvenirs.
Handbooks/programmes: No handbook. Programmes available on subscription.
Extra information: The club will make every effort to cater for the disabled, the blind, or any person who has some difficulty seeking entrance because of illness.

Club Colours: White shirts with red trim, black shorts, black stockings.
Change Colours: All royal blue.
First Team Trainer/Coach: Barry Lyons.
Club Nickname: 'The Quakers'.

DARLINGTON 1978-79 LEAGUE RECORD

Match No.	Date	Venue	Opponents	Result	Score	H/T Score	League Pos'n	Goalscorers	Attendance
1	Aug 19	A	Stockport Co	L	0-3	0-3	—		3626
2	22	H	Huddersfield T	W	1-0	0-0	—	Lyons	2549
3	26	H	AFC Bournemouth	D	0-0	0-0	14		1890
4	Sept 2	A	Hereford U	L	0-1	0-1	17		3622
5	9	H	Grimsby T	L	0-1	0-1	19		2220
6	12	A	Northampton T	L	1-4	0-2	—	Ferguson	3442
7	16	A	Halifax T	W	2-0	0-0	17	Stone, Seal	1203
8	23	H	Torquay U	L	1-2	0-1	20	Seal	1613
9	26	H	Barnsley	D	0-0	0-0	—		3475
10	30	A	Aldershot	D	1-1	1-0	19	Paterson	2560
11	Oct 7	A	Hartlepool U	W	2-0	1-0	17	Maitland, Stone	4853
12	13	H	Crewe Alex	D	1-1	1-1	19	Paterson	1919
13	17	H	Reading	L	1-2	1-1	—	Stone	1821
14	21	A	Rochdale	L	1-2	1-1	22	Ferguson	1272
15	28	H	Port Vale	W	4-0	1-0	18	Walsh, Seal 2, Ferguson	1793
16	Nov 4	A	Portsmouth	L	0-3	0-1	20		11,394
17	11	H	Hereford U	W	2-1	1-1	18	Lyons, Walsh	1622
18	18	A	AFC Bournemouth	D	2-2	0-1	19	Seal, Walsh	6005
19	Dec 2	A	Newport Co	L	1-2	1-1	21	Stone	2450
20	9	H	Wigan Ath	D	1-1	1-1	20	Stone	1967
21	23	H	Scunthorpe U	D	2-2	0-0	20	Hague, Walsh	1512
22	26	A	Doncaster R	W	3-2	2-1	—	Wann, Stone, Seal	2889
23	Jan 16	A	Grimsby T	L	2-7	0-6	—	Cochrane, Stone	5378
24	27	A	Torquay U	L	0-1	0-1	20		2321
25	Feb 23	A	Crewe Alex	D	1-1	0-0	21	Stone	1474
26	27	H	Halifax T	W	2-1	1-0	—	Seal, Nattress	1403
27	Mar 3	A	Rochdale	L	0-2	0-1	19		1495
28	6	H	York C	L	0-1	0-1	—		1173
29	10	A	Port Vale	L	1-2	0-0	20	Ferguson	2566
30	24	A	Huddersfield T	D	2-2	1-1	21	Walsh, Peachey	2862
31	27	H	Stockport Co	L	0-1	0-0	—		1086
32	31	A	Bradford C	D	0-0	0-0	22		2643
33	Apr 3	H	Aldershot	W	2-1	0-1	—	Peachey 2	1267
34	7	H	Newport Co	W	1-0	0-0	21	Peachey	1518
35	10	A	Scunthorpe U	L	0-1	0-1	—		1372
36	14	H	Doncaster R	W	3-2	3-1	21	Stone, Walsh, Hedley	1967
37	16	A	York C	L	2-5	2-3	—	Wann, Walsh	2973
38	21	H	Wimbledon	D	1-1	0-0	21	Ferguson	1674
39	25	A	Reading	L	0-1	0-1	—		7117
40	28	A	Wigan Ath	D	2-2	1-2	21	Seal, Walsh	6153
41	30	A	Barnsley	D	1-1	0-1	—	Ferguson	10,974
42	May 5	H	Bradford C	D	1-1	1-1	22	Walsh	1558
43	7	H	Hartlepool U	L	0-1	0-0	—		3513
44	11	H	Portsmouth	W	2-0	0-0	—	Peachey 2	1140
45	14	H	Northampton T	D	0-0	0-0	—		1333
46	17	A	Wimbledon	L	0-2	0-1	—		3638

Final League Position: 21

Goalscorers

League (49): Stone 9, Walsh 9, Seal 8, Ferguson 6, Peachey 6, Lyons 2, Paterson 2, Wann 2, Cochrane 1, Hague 1, Hedley 1, Maitland 1, Nattress 1.
League Cup (6): Craig 2, Lyons 2 (1 pen), Stone, Wann.
F.A. Cup (4): Ferguson 3, Craig.

League Cup	First Round	Mansfield T	(a)	1-0
			(h)	2-2
	Second Round	Fulham	(a)	2-2
			(h)	1-0
	Third Round	Everton	(a)	0-1
F.A. Cup	First Round	Chesterfield	(h)	1-1
			(a)	1-0
	Second Round	Chester	(h)	2-1
	Third Round	Colchester U	(h)	0-1

Burleigh	Nattress	Crosson	Hague	Craig	Stone	Maitland	Lyons	Seal	Probert	Wann	Cochrane	Ferguson	Paterson	Taylor	Walsh	Owers	Peachey	Hedley	Match No.
1	2	3	4	5	6	7	8	9	10	11									1
1	2		4	5	6	7	8	9	10	11	3								2
1	2		4	5	6	7	8*	9	10	11	3	12							3
1	2	12	4	5	6*	7	8	10		11	3	9							4
1	2		4	5	6	7	8*	9	10	11	3	12							5
1	2	3	4	5	6	7*		10	8	11		9	12						6
1	2		4	5	6	7		9	10	11	3	8							7
1	2		4	5	6	7		10	8	11	3	9							8
1	5		4		2	7	8	9	6	11	3		10						9
1	2	12	4		6	7*	5	9	10	11	3	8							10
1	2		4	5	6	7	8	9	10	11	3								11
1	2	12	4	5	6	7		9	10*11		3	8							12
1	2	10	4	5	6	7		9		11	3		8*12						13
1	2		4	5	6	7*		9		11	3	8	12 10						14
1	2	12	4	5	6*	7		10		11	3	9	8						15
1	2	12	4	5	6	7*		10		11	3	9	8						16
1	2	12	4	5		7	6	10*		11	3	9	8						17
	2	4		5	6		7	10		11	3	9	8	1					18
	2		4	5	6		7*10	12	11		3	9	8	1					19
1	2		4	5		6	12	10	8	11	3	9*	7						20
1	2		4	5		6	12	10	8*11		3	7	9						21
1	2		4	5		6	12	9	7	11	3	8*	10						22
1	2		4	5		6	12	9*	7	11	3	8	10						23
1			5	6		4	10	7	11		3	9	8						24
1	4	2		5	6			10	7	8	3	9	11						25
1	4	2		5	6	12		11	7*	8	3	10	9						26
1	4	2		5*	6	7		10		8	3	9	12	11					27
1	4	2		5	6		9	12	10	3		8	7	11*					28
1	4		2	5	6		10	12	8*	3	9		7	11					29
1	2		4	5	6		7		8	3	9		11	10					30
1	2		6	5	4*		7	12	8	3	9		11	10					31
1	2		6	5			7		8	3	9		11	10	4				32
1	2	6		5			7		8	3	11		9	10	4				33
1	2	12		5	6		7		8	3	10		9*	11	4				34
1	6	3		5	2		7		8		10		9	11	4				35
1	3		6	5	2	12	7		8		9*		11	10	4				36
1	2		6	5*	4		7	12	8	3	10		9	11					37
1	2			5	6		7	12	8	3	9		11	10*	4				38
1	2		6	5			7	11	8	3	10		9		4				39
1	2		6	5	7			10	8	3	9		11		4				40
1	2		9	5	3		7	6	8		10		11		4				41
1	2		6	5			7*10		8	3	9		11	12	4				42
1	2			5	7			6*10	8	3	12		11	9	4				43
1	2	3	10	5	7			6	8				11	9	4				44
	2	3		5	10	7		6	8				11	1	9	4			45
	4	2	9*	5	6			11	8	3			12	1	10	7			46
42	45	14	34	44	41	19	26	35	19	46	39	31	6	2	32	4	13	14	
		+ 7s				+ 6s	+ 5s	+ 1s			+ 3s	+ 1s	+ 3s	+ 1s		+ 1s			

DARLINGTON—PLAYERS

Player and position	Ht	Wt	Birthplace	Clubs	League Appearance	Goals
Goalkeepers						
Phil Owers	5 11	10 9	Shildon	Darlington	45	—
				Gillingham	2	—
				Darlington	33	—
Martin Burleigh	5 10	13 1	Durham	Newcastle U	11	—
				Darlington	30	—
				Carlisle U	26	—
				Darlington	71	—
Defenders						
Clive Nattress	6 0	12 4½	Durham	Blackpool	—	—
				Darlington	255+4	11
Len Walker (Non-contract)	5 11	12 4	Darlington	Newcastle U	1	—
				Aldershot	440+10	23
				Darlington	10	—
John Stone	6 0	12 2	Carlinstow	Middlesbrough	2	—
				York C	86	5
				Darlington	120	14
Derek Craig	6 0	11 9	Durham	Newcastle U	13+2	—
				Darlington	160+1	10
Jimmy Cochrane	5 9	11 0	Glasgow	Middlesbrough	3	—
				Darlington	180+1	5
Midfield						
David Crosson	5 9	11 11	Durham	Newcastle U	6	—
				Darlington	108+7	2
Neil Hague	6 0½	12 7	Rotherham	Rotherham U	134+11	23
				Plymouth Arg	98	15
				Bournemouth	89	7
				Huddersfield T	25	2
				Darlington	80	4
Barry Lyons	5 7	10 8	Nottingham	Rotherham U	132	24
				Nottingham F	201+2	28
				York C	80+5	11
				Darlington	97	10
Eric Probert	5 7½	10 9½	South Kirby	Burnley	63+5	11
				Notts Co	122	14
				Huddersfield T (on loan)	—	—
				Darlington	19+1	—
Forwards						
Eric Young (Contract cancelled February 1979)	5 6½	10 3	Stockton on Tees	Manchester U	—	—
				Peterborough U (on loan)	24+1	2
				Walsall (on loan)	8	—
				Stockport Co (on loan)	16	—
				Darlington	123+7	15
Ronnie Ferguson	6 0	12 5	Accrington	Sheffield W	15+1	1
				Scunthorpe U (on loan)	3	—
				Darlington	93+13	18
Dennis Wann	5 8	10 11	Blackpool	Blackpool	10+6	—
				York C	65+1	1
				Chesterfield (on loan)	3	—
				Hartlepool U (on loan)	2	—
				Darlington	119+2	13
Jimmy Seal	5 10	11 8	Pontefract	Wolverhampton W	1	—
				Walsall (on loan)	40	14
				Barnsley	43	12
				York C	152+8	43
				Darlington	109+6	17
Lloyd Maitland	5 7	11 2	Birmingham	Huddersfield T	31+8	2
				Darlington	58+13	6
Tom Paterson (Contract cancelled May 1979)	5 10	11 0	Newcastle	Leicester C	—	—
				Middlesbrough	—	—
				Bournemouth	45+12	10
				Darlington	6+1	2
Alan Walsh	6 0	11 0	Hartlepool	Middlesbrough	0+3	—
				Darlington	32+1	9
John Peachey	6 0	12 1	Cambridge	York C	6+2	3
				Barnsley	116+11	31
				Darlington	18+2	9
Phil Taylor	5 9	10 12	Sheffield	York C	14+7	1
				Darlington	2+3	—

DERBY COUNTY DIV. 1

President: Sam Longson, O.B.E.
Chairman: G. Hardy.
Vice-Chairman: F. W. Innes.
Directors: R. J. Moore, A. B. Atkins, W. Stevenson, R. J. Mulholland.
Manager: Colin Addison.
General Secretary:
Year Formed: 1884.   *Turned Professional:* 1884.
Limited Company: 1896.
Former Grounds: 1884–95, Racecourse Ground; 1895, Baseball Ground.
Football League Record:
  1888 Founder Member of the Football League.
  1907–12 Division 2.
  1912–14 Division 1.
  1914–15 Division 2.
  1915–21 Division 1.
  1921–26 Division 2.
  1926–53 Division 1.
  1953–55 Division 2.
  1955–57 Division 3(N).
  1957–69 Division 2.
  1969– Division 1.

Honours: *Football League:* Division 1, Champions: 1971–72; 1974–75; runners-up: 1895–96, 1929–30, 1935–36. Division 2, Champions: 1911–12, 1914–15, 1968–69; runners-up: 1925–26. Division 3(N), Champions: 1956–57; runners-up: 1955–56. *F. A. Cup*, Winners: 1945–46; runners-up: 1897–98, 1898–99, 1902–03. *Football League Cup*, best season: semi-final, 1967–68.
European Competitions: European Cup 1972–73, 1975–76; UEFA Cup 1974–57, 1976–77.
Record Victory: 12-0 v Finn Harps, UEFA Cup 3rd Rd., 1st leg, September 15, 1976.
Record Defeat: 2-11 v Everton, 1st Rd., F.A. Cup, 1889–90.
Most League Points: 63, Division 2, 1968–69 and 63, Division 3(N), 1955–56, 1956–57.
Most League Goals: 111, Division 3(N), 1956–57.
Highest League Scorer in Season: Jack Bowers, 37, Division 1, 1930–31 and Ray Straw, 37, Division 3(N), 1956–57.
Most Goals in Total Aggregate: Steve Bloomer, 291, 1892–1906 and 1910–14.
Most League Appearances: Jack Parry, 478, 1949–66.
Most Capped Player: Roy McFarland, 28, England.
Record Transfer Fee Received: £400,000 from Southampton for Charlie George, Dec. 1978.
Record Transfer Fee Paid: £300,000 to Burnley for Leighton James, Nov. 1975.
Managers Since the War: Stuart McMillan, Jack Barker, Harry Storer, Tim Ward, Brian Clough, Dave Mackay, Colin Murphy, Tommy Docherty.
Address of Supporters Club: Baseball Ground, Derby.
Address of Club Shop or Boutique: The Ramtique, 55 Osmaston Road, Derby DE1 2JH.

Baseball Ground, Shaftesbury Crescent, Derby DE3 8NB. Telephone Derby 40105. *Telegraphic address:* 'Football Derby'. *Ground capacity:* 37,000 (30,000 covered, 16,000 seats.) *Record attendance:* 41,826 v Tottenham H. Division 1, September 20, 1969. *Record receipts:* £65,000 v Juventus. European Cup semi-final April 25, 1973. *Pitch measurements:* 110 yds × 71 yds.
How to get there: Buses from town centre 60, 88 and 89.   Nearest railway station Derby.
Match tickets: Available 14 days prior to game (£2.50, £2.00, £1.80).
Car parking: Eight car parks within half a mile of the ground run by the club in connection with the local corporation. Street parking half a mile from the ground.
Entertainments/catering facilities: Sportsman Club (members only). Licensed and refreshment bars in all parts of the ground.
Club shop: The Ramtique in Osmaston Road open every week day. Shop on the ground open on match days.
Handbooks/programmes: Yearbook published annually. "The Ram", the club newspaper and official programme, available on subscription c/o The Programme Editor, Derby County F.C. or from local newsagents.
Club Colours: White shirts, blue shorts, blue stockings.
Change Colours: Orange, black, orange.
Club Captain: Roy McFarland.
Club Nickname: 'The Rams'.

DERBY COUNTY 1978-79 LEAGUE RECORD

Match No.	Date	Venue	Opponents	Result	H/T Score	League Pos'n	Goalscorers	Attendance
1	Aug 19	H	Manchester C	D 1-1	0-0	—	George	26,480
2	22	A	Everton	L 1-2	1-0	—	Nish	39,848
3	26	A	Birmingham C	D 1-1	1-1	16	Daly	21,963
4	Sept 2	H	Coventry C	L 0-2	0-0	18		21,435
5	9	A	Bolton W	L 1-2	1-0	19	Daly	20,331
6	16	H	WBA	W 3-2	3-0	16	Duncan, Powell, Daly	23,697
7	23	H	Southampton	W 2-1	0-0	13	George, Nicholl (og)	21,623
8	30	A	Norwich C	L 0-3	0-2	17		16,585
9	Oct 7	H	Chelsea	W 1-0	0-0	16	Harris (og)	20,251
10	14	A	Liverpool	L 0-5	0-1	18		47,475
11	21	H	Tottenham H	D 2-2	1-0	16	Buckley, Duncan	26,181
12	28	A	Leeds U	L 0-4	0-3	19		25,449
13	Nov 4	H	Wolverhampton W	W 4-1	2-0	16	Daly, Hill, Caskey, Duncan	20,658
14	11	A	Manchester C	W 2-1	2-0	13	Duncan, Daly (pen)	37,376
15	18	H	Birmingham C	W 2-1	0-1	13	Daly, Buckley	24,720
16	21	A	Coventry C	L 2-4	2-1	—	Daly (pen) Caskey	20,654
17	25	H	QPR	W 2-1	1-0	11	Daniel Caskey	19,702
18	Dec 2	A	Bristol C	L 0-1	0-0	12		17,487
19	9	H	Manchester U	L 1-3	1-1	13	Daly	25,100
20	16	A	Arsenal	L 0-2	0-1	14		26,943
21	23	H	Aston Villa	D 0-0	0-0	13		20,109
22	26	A	Nottingham F	D 1-1	1-0	13	Daly (pen)	34,256
23	Feb 3	A	Southampton	W 2-1	1-1	15	Duncan, Powell	21,109
24	10	H	Norwich C	D 1-1	0-0	14	Buckley	20,837
25	24	H	Liverpool	L 0-2	0-1	16		27,859
26	28	H	Ipswich T	L 0-1	0-0	—		15,935
27	Mar 3	A	Tottenham H	L 0-2	0-1	16		28,089
28	10	H	Leeds U	L 0-1	0-0	17		22,800
29	13	A	Middlesbrough	L 1-3	0-1	—	Daly (pen)	16,286
30	21	H	Bolton W	W 3-0	2-0	—	McFarland 2, Daly	15,227
31	24	H	Everton	D 0-0	0-0	17		20,814
32	26	A	WBA	L 1-2	1-0	—	Crawford	20,010
33	31	A	QPR	D 2-2	1-2	18	Crawford, Daly	13,988
34	Apr 4	A	Chelsea	D 1-1	0-0	—	McFarland	10,682
35	7	H	Bristol C	L 0-1	0-0	18		17,090
36	11	A	Aston Villa	D 3-3	2-1	—	Greenwood, Powell, Gibson (og)	21,884
37	14	H	Nottingham F	L 1-2	1-2	18	Webb	30,256
38	16	A	Ipswich T	L 1-2	1-2	—	Crawford	19,899
39	21	H	Arsenal	W 2-0	2-0	18	Daly, Buckley	18,674
40	24	H	Wolverhampton W	L 0-4	0-2	—		19,036
41	28	A	Manchester U	D 0-0	0-0	19		42,474
42	May 5	H	Middlesbrough	L 0-3	0-2	19		18,151

Final League Position: 19

Goalscorers

League (44): Daly 13 (4 pens), Duncan 5, Buckley 4, Caskey 3, McFarland 3, Powell 3, Crawford 3 George 2, Nish 1, Hill 1, Daniel 1, Webb 1, Greenwood 1, Own Goals 3.
League Cup (1): Hill

League Cup:	Second Round	Leicester C (a)	1-0
	Third Round	Southampton (a)	0-1
F.A. Cup:	Third Round	Preston N E (a)	0-3

167

Middleton	Langan	Buckley	Nish	McFarland	Todd	Ryan	Powell	George	Daly	Hill	Daniel	Chesters	Carter	Rioch	McCaffery	Duncan	Moreland	Caskey	Clarke	Bartlett	Clayton	McKeller	Webb	Wicks	Greenwood	Spooner	Crawford	Emson	Match No.
1	2	3	4	5	6	7	8	9	10	11																			1
1	2	3	8	5	6	9	7	10	4	11																			2
1	2	3	8	5		9	7*10		4	11		6	12																3
1	2	3	8*	5	6	9	7	10	4		12		11																4
1	2	3	8	5	6	11	9	10	4				7																5
1	2	3	12	5		11*10		8					7	4	6	9													6
1	2	3				6	10		4				7	8	5	9*12	11												7
1	2	3	11	5		7			4					8	6			9	10										8
1	2	3				8	10		4				7	12	5	6*	9	11											9
1	2	3	12			8	10*		4				7		5	6	9	11											10
1	2	3	12			8			4				7		5	9	6		10*11										11
1	2	3				8			4	11		5	7			9	6		10										12
1	2	3		5		8			4	11			7			9	6	10											13
1	2	3		5		8			4	11			7			9	6	10											14
1	2	3				8			4	11		5	7				6	10	9										15
1	2	3	12			8			4	11		5	7				6	9*10											16
1	2	3				8			4			5	7			9	6	10	11										17
1	2	3		5*		8			4	12			7			9	6	10	11										18
1	2	3				5			4	11			7			9	6	10	8										19
		3				8			4	11		5	7			9	6	10	2		1								20
	2	3		5		8			4	11			7				12	9	10		1	6*							21
	2	3		5		8			4	11			7*				12	9	10		1	6							22
	2	3		5		8								4		10*12	9	7			1		6	11					23
	2	3		5		8							7	4		9			10		1		6	11					24
	2	3		5		8			4				7	10		6	9				1			11					25
	2	3		5		8			4				7	10		12	9*				1		6	11					26
	2	3		5		8			4							10	9				1		6	11	7				27
	2	3				8			4							10*	9	7		1	5	6		11		12			28
	2	3				8			4							11	9			1	5	6	7		10				29
1	2	3		5		8			4				7			10						6	9	11					30
1	2	3		5		8			4				7			10						6	9	11					31
1	2	3		5		8			4*				7			11					12	6	9	10					32
1	2	3		5		8			4	12			7*			10						6	9	11					33
1	2	3		5		8			4				7*			10	12					6	9	11					34
1	2	3				8			4*				7			10	12			5		6	9	11					35
1	2	3		5		8										10	4					6	9	11		7			36
	2	3				8			4				7				4			1	5	6	9		11	10			37
	2	3				8			4				7				4			1	5	6	9		11	10			38
	2	3				8			4							7				1	5	6	9		11	10			39
		3				8			4							10		2		1	5	6	9		11	7			40
	2	3		5		8			4							9	10		7	1		6	11						41
	2	3							4							10	6	11*	8	9	1		5	12			7		42
26	40	42	6	24	4	6	41	8	37	12	6		29	7	6	16	27	22	17	3	1	16	9	19	19	1	12	0	
+			+						+	+	+		+			+	+	+				+			+		+		
4s			4s						2s	1s	1s		1s			1s	4s	2s				1s			1s		1s		

DERBY COUNTY—PLAYERS

Player and position	Ht	Wt	Birthplace	Clubs	League Appearances	Goals
Goalkeepers						
John Middleton	6 2	13 7	Lincoln	Nottingham F	90	—
				Derby Co	60	—
David McKellar	6 0	11 8	Ardrossan	Derby Co	16	—
Steve Cherry	5 10	10 12	Nottingham	Derby Co	—	—
Defenders						
Peter Daniel	5 10	11 2	Stanley	Derby Co	187+7	7
(Contract cancelled April 1979)						
David Nish	5 11	11 3	Burton-on-Trent	Leicester C	228	25
(England)				Derby Co	184+4	10
(Contract cancelled April 1979)						
Roy McFarland	5 11½	11 2	Liverpool	Tranmere R	35	—
(England)				Derby Co	391	41
David Langan	5 10	11 2	Dublin	Derby Co	103	—
(Eire)						
Ray Storey	5 7	10 7	Sheffield	Manchester U	—	—
(Contract cancelled April 1979)				Derby Co	—	—
Steve Buckley	5 11	12 4	Brinsley	Luton T	123	4
				Derby Co	60	5
Kevin Murray	5 9		Dundee	Derby Co	—	—
Steve Wicks	6 2	13 0	Reading	Chelsea	117+1	5
				Derby Co	19	—
Vic Moreland	6 1	12 0	Belfast	Glentoran	—	—
(N. Ireland)				Derby Co	27+4	—
Frank Sheridan	6 0	11 0	London	Derby Co	—	—
Steve Blades	5 8	10 7	Peterborough	Derby Co	—	—
Steve Spooner	5 7	11 4	London	Derby Co	1	—
Aidan McCaffery	5 11	11 2	Newcastle	Newcastle U	57+2	4
				Derby Co	6	—
Midfield						
Bruce Rioch	5 11	12 5	Aldershot	Luton T	147+1	47
(Scotland)				Aston V	149+6	34
				Derby Co	106	34
				Everton	30	3
				Birmingham (on loan)	3	1
				Sheffield U (on loan)	8	4
				Derby Co	27+1	—
Steve Powell	5 8	11 0	Derby	Derby Co	187+8	17
Gerry Daly	5 9	10 0	Dublin	Bohemians	(not known)	
(Eire)				Manchester U	107+4	23
				Derby Co	91	30
David Webb	5 10½	12 11	London	Orient	62	3
				Southampton	75	2
				Chelsea	230	21
				QPR	116	7
				Leicester C	32+1	—
				Derby Co	9+1	1
Robert Bowers	5 7	10 0	Dublin	Cliftonville	—	—
				Derby Co	—	—
Jonathan Clark	5 9	10 11	Swansea	Manchester U	0+1	—
				Derby Co	17	—
Forwards						
Colin Chesters	5 11	11 0	Crewe	Derby Co	6+3	1
Paul Bartlett	5 6	10 1	Grimsby	Derby Co	6+6	—
Andy Crawford	5 7	10 4	Filey	Derby Co	15+1	4
Keith Falconer	5 10	11 0	Newcastle	Derby Co	—	—
Gordon Hill	5 7	10 12	Sunbury	Millwall	79+7	20
(England)				Manchester U	100+1	39
				Derby Co	13+2	2
Roy Greenwood	5 10	11 0	Leeds	Hull C	118+8	24
				Sunderland	45+11	9
				Derby Co	19+1	1
John Duncan	5 11	11 4	Lochee	Dundee	121+3	62
				Tottenham H	101+2	53
				Derby Co	16+1	5
Steve Carter	5 8	10 10	Gt Yarmouth	Manchester C	4+2	2
				Notts Co	172+16	21
				Derby Co	29	—
Billy Caskey	5 10	12 4	Belfast	Glentoran	—	—
(N. Ireland)				Derby Co	22+2	3
John Clayton	5 11	11 7	Elgin	Derby Co	1	—
Paul Emson	5 11	11 3	Lincoln	Brigg T	—	—
				Derby Co	6	—

(Free Transfer: *Peter Falconer)

DONCASTER ROVERS   DIV. 4

President: J. C. Morris.
Chairman: A. Phillips.
Directors: H. Bates, K. Jackson, B. Bailey, T. R. Jones, I. M. Jones, D. Harrison.
Team Manager: Billy Bremner.
General Manager/Secretary: J. E. Bennison.
Promotions Manager: A. Chapman (tel. 59679).
Year Formed: 1879.   *Turned Professional:* 1885.
Limited Company: 1905 and 1920.
Previous Grounds: 1880–1916, Intake Ground; 1920–22, Benetthorpe Ground; 1922, Low Pasture, Belle Vue.

Doncaster Rovers Football Club Ltd.
(Founded 1879)

Football League Record:

1901 Elected to Division 2.	1948–50 Division 3(N).
1903 Failed re-election.	1950–58 Division 2.
1904—Re-elected.	1958–59 Division 3.
1905 Failed re-election.	1959–66 Division 4.
1923–35 Re-elected to Division 3(N)	1966–67 Division 3.
1935–37 Division 2.	1967–69 Division 4.
1937–47 Division 3(N).	1969–71 Division 3.
1947–48 Division 2.	1971– Division 4.

Honours: Football League, highest position: Division 2, 7th, 1901–02. Division 3(N), Champions: 1934–35, 1946–47, 1949–50; Runners-up: 1937–38, 1938–39. Division 4, Champions: 1965–66, 1968–69. *F.A. Cup,* best season: 5th Rd., 1951–52, 1953–54, 1954–55, 1955–56. *Football League Cup,* best season: 5th Rd., 1975–76.
Record Victory: 10-0 v Darlington, Division 4, Jan. 25th, 1964.
Record Defeat: 0-12 v Small Heath, Division 2, Apr. 11th, 1903.
Most League Points: 72, Division 3(N), 1946–47.
Most League Goals: 123, Division 3(N), 1946–47.
Highest League Scorer in Season: Clarrie Jordan, 42, Division 3(N), 1946–47.
Most League Goals in Total Aggregate: Tom Keetley, 180, 1923–29.
Most Capped Player: Len Graham, 14, Ireland.
Most League Appearances: Fred Emery, 406, 1925–36.
Record Transfer Fee Received: £70,000 from Preston N.E. for Mike Elwiss, Feb. 1974.
Record Transfer Fee Paid: £10,000 to Stoke C. for John Flowers, Aug. 1966.
Managers Since the War: Bill Marsden, Jackie Bestall, Peter Doherty, Jack Hodgson, Syd Bycroft, Jack Crayston, Jack Bestall, Norman Curtis, Danny Malloy, Oscar Hold, Bill Leivers, Keith Kettleborough, George Raynor, Lawrie McMenemy, Maurice Setters, Stan Anderson.
Address of Supporters Club: Secretary, K. J. Avis, 64 Harrowden Road, Doncaster.
Address of Club Shop or Boutique: On ground.

Belle Vue Ground, Doncaster. Telephone Doncaster 55281. *Telegraphic address:* 'Rovers Doncaster'. *Ground capacity:* 30,000. *Record attendance:* 37,149 v Hull C., Division 3(N), October 2, 1948. *Record receipts:* £8936 v Liverpool, F.A. Cup 3rd Rd., Jan. 8, 1974.
Pitch measurements: 118 yds × 79 yds.
How to get there: Buses from town centre (Duke St.)—Race Course, Hyde Park, and Cantley Estate services. Doncaster railway station is near the town centre.
Match tickets: No advance booking except for Cup ties.
Car parking: Very large car and coach park adjoining the ground. Entrance direct from Great North Road.
Entertainments/catering facilities: Refreshment bars in Main Stand and around the ground, including licensed bars. Social club adjoining ground.
Club shop: In Main Stand, stocks all types of souvenirs.
Handbooks/programmes: Annual handbook on sale at 20p post free or at shop or Supporters Club office. Programmes on sale at shop but not on subscription.
Extra information: Development Association office on ground. Supporters' Club office on ground—minimum subscription 15p (Children and OAPs 10p). Handbook free to members. Phone 59679.
Club Colours: White shirts with red trim on sleeves, white shorts with red stripes on side, red with white turnover stockings.
Change Colours: Yellow shirts with chocolate collar and cuffs, brown shorts, yellow stockings.
First Team Trainer: C. Knowles.
Physiotherapist: J. Cunningham.
Club Nickname: 'Rovers'.

DONCASTER ROVERS 1978-79 LEAGUE RECORD

Match No.	Date	Venue	Opponents	Result	H/T Score	League Pos'n	Goalscorers	Attendance
1	Aug 19	A	Hartlepool U	W 4-3	1-3	—	Snodin, French, Habbin, Lewis	2364
2	26	A	York C	D 1-1	0-1	11	Laidlaw	3609
3	Sept 1	H	Scunthorpe U	D 0-0	0-0	11		4667
4	9	A	Huddersfield T	L 1-2	1-0	14	Owen	4038
5	11	H	Port Vale	L 1-3	0-1	—	Owen	3405
6	16	A	Reading	L 0-3	0-1	19		4867
7	23	H	Barnsley	D 2-2	2-1	18	French, Habbin	9380
8	26	H	AFC Bournemouth	D 1-1	0-1	—	Taylor	2441
9	30	A	Northampton T	L 0-3	0-1	22		3011
10	Oct 7	H	Stockport Co	W 2-0	1-0	22	Owen, Edwards (og)	2742
11	10	H	Torquay U	W 1-0	0-0	—	Owen	2507
12	14	A	Wigan Ath	L 0-1	0-0	20		5788
13	17	H	Portsmouth	L 2-3	1-2	—	Laidlaw, Bentley	2480
14	21	H	Newport Co	D 0-0	0-0	19		2008
15	28	A	Wimbledon	L 2-3	1-3	22	Jones 2	3252
16	Nov 4	H	Bradford C	W 2-0	0-0	19	Bradley, Owen	2981
17	11	A	Scunthorpe U	D 0-0	0-0	20		3250
18	18	H	York C	L 1-2	1-1	21	Bradley	2479
19	Dec 2	H	Rochdale	W 1-0	1-0	19	Owen	1750
20	9	A	Aldershot	L 1-2	1-1	21	Reed	3030
21	26	H	Darlington	L 2-3	1-2	—	Bentley, Owen	2889
22	Jan 16	A	Port Vale	W 3-1	3-1	—	Olney, Laidlaw, Cork	3381
23	30	H	Hereford U	W 1-0	0-0	—	Laidlaw	1719
24	Feb 3	A	AFC Bournemouth	L 1-7	0-1	20	Laidlaw	2986
25	10	H	Northampton T	W 2-0	0-0	17	Bradley, Snodin	1922
26	13	A	Crewe Alex	W 4-2	2-1	—	Laidlaw, Owen 2, Pugh	1532
27	21	A	Stockport Co	W 1-0	0-0	—	Owen	3007
28	24	H	Wigan Ath	L 0-1	0-0	13		4612
29	27	H	Huddersfield T	L 0-2	0-0	—		3419
30	Mar 3	A	Newport Co	L 0-3	0-1	16		2550
31	6	A	Halifax T	D 0-0	0-0	—		1658
32	9	H	Wimbledon	W 1-0	1-0	14	Cox	1927
33	20	H	Reading	D 2-2	0-1	—	Lewis, French	2487
34	23	H	Hartlepool U	D 0-0	0-0	14		2552
35	28	A	Torquay U	L 1-2	1-2	—	French (pen)	1781
36	31	H	Grimsby T	L 0-1	0-0	17		4707
37	Apr 3	A	Barnsley	L 0-3	0-1	—		12,082
38	7	A	Rochdale	L 0-2	0-0	19		1606
39	14	A	Darlington	L 2-3	1-3	21	Snodin, Packer	1967
40	16	H	Crewe Alex	W 2-0	1-0	—	Packer, Cox	1658
41	17	H	Halifax T	D 1-1	1-1	—	Cox	2227
42	21	A	Hereford U	L 0-2	0-1	20		3209
43	24	A	Portsmouth	L 0-4	0-2	—		5869
44	28	H	Aldershot	D 1-1	1-1	19	French	1539
45	30	A	Bradford C	L 0-1	0-0	—		2189
46	May 5	A	Grimsby T	W 4-3	2-2	20	Lewis 3, Laidlaw	10,157

Final League Position: 22

Goalscorers
League (50): Owen 10, Laidlaw 7, French 5 (1 pen), Lewis 5, Bradley 3, Cox 3, Snodin 3, Bentley 2, Habbin 2, Jones 2, Packer 2, Cork 1, Olney 1, Pugh 1, Reed 1. Taylor 1, Own Goal 1.
League Cup (1): French.
F.A. Cup (2): Lewis, Laidlaw.

League Cup	First Round	Sheffield W. (h)	0-1
		(a)	1-0
		(h)	0-1
F.A. Cup	First Round	Huddersfield T. (h)	2-1
	Second Round	Shrewsbury T. (h)	0-3

Peacock	Owen	Robinson	Olney	Bradley	Taylor	Habbin	French	Snodin	Lewis	Laidlaw	Meagen	Bentley	Lally	Cox	Reed	Gilligan	Packer	Hemsley	Cork	Jones	Bowden	Pugh	Cannell	Flanagan	Lister	Austin	Match No.
1	2*	3	4	5	6	7	8	9	10	11	12																1
1	2*		4	5	6	7	10	9	8	11	12	3															2
1	2		4*	5	6	7	10	9	8	11	12	3															3
1	2			5	6	7	10	9*	8	11	12	3	4														4
1	2			5	6	7	10	12	8*11		9	3	4														5
1	9	2		5	6	7	10*		12	11		3	4	8													6
1	9	3		5	6	7	10*		8	11		12	4		2												7
1	9	3		5	6	7			8	11			4		2	10											8
1		3		5		8		10*12	11		7	6	4		2		9										9
1	9			5	6	7	10		8	11			4		2		3										10
1	9			5	6	7*10			8	11			4 12		2		3										11
1	9			5	6	7	10		8*11				4 12		2		3										12
1	9			5	6*	7	10	12		8		11	4		2		3										13
1	9		6	5		7	10	8*		11		3	4 12		2												14
1	2		6	5		7	10		8	11		3							4	9							15
1	12		6	5			8*	7	11			10	2				3	4	9								16
1	10		6	5		12		11	7	8			2*				3	4	9								17
1	12		6	5	3		10	8	7	11			2					4	9*								18
1	9		6	5			10		12	7		8	11*		2		3		4								19
1	9*		6	5			10		12	11	7				2		3	8	4								20
1	8		6	5				12	9	7	10	3			2			4	11*								21
1	8		2	5			9	3		7	10	11	6				4*		12								22
1	11	3	2	5			9			7	4	10	6						8*12								23
1	8*		2	5			9	3		10	7	11	6						4 12								24
1	11		2	5			9	3		7	8	10	6						4								25
1	8		2	5		12	9*	3		7	4	10	6						11								26
1	8		2	5			9*	3	12	7	4	10	6						11								27
1	10		2	5			9*	3	12	8	7	11	6						4								28
1	8		2	5			9*	3	12	7	4	10	6						11								29
1	9*		2	5		12		3	10	7	8		6						11	4							30
1	8		6	5			9	3		7		10*12			2				11		4						31
1			2	5			8	3		7	4		9						11	10	6						32
1				5			8		9	7	4	10							11	6	3	2					33
1			6	5			8		9*	7	4	10		12					11		3	2					34
1			6	5			8	12		4	10		9						11*		3	2	7				35
1			6*	5			9	12		4	10		8						7		3	2	11				36
1	11		6	5		9*		3		4	10	8							7	12		2					37
1			3	5			9	4		7	8	10	6						11			2					38
1			6				8			7	11	4	10		9						5	2	3				39
1			6					3	12	4*10	7	9		8							5	11	2				40
1			6*					3	10	4		2	7	9					12		5	11		8			41
1			6				9	3	8*	4	11	2	10						12		5	7					42
1			6	4			8	3	10		7	2	9*						12		5	11					43
1			6				10	12	9	4		11	2*	8					7		5	3					44
1			5				9	11	8	4	7	10	2								6	3					45
1			5				10	3	9	4	8							12			7	6	11*	2			46
46	29	6	32	42	13	16	36	28	24	38	27	32	33	10	11	1	4	9	7	4	5	16	11	14	9	3	
	+					+		+		+		+			+						+	+	+				
	2s					3s		6s		8s		4s	1s		5s				1s		1s	5s	1s				

DONCASTER ROVERS—PLAYERS

Player and position	Ht	Wt	Birthplace	Clubs	League Appearances	Goals
Goalkeepers						
Dennis Peacock	6 3	14 0	Lincoln	Nottingham F	22	—
				Walsall (on loan)	10	—
				Doncaster R	169	—
Defenders						
*Kevin Olney	6 0	11 0	Doncaster	Doncaster R	65+1	1
Stephen Reed (Retired)	5 9	10 9	Doncaster	Doncaster R	137+2	2
*Fred Robinson	5 10	11 4	Rotherham	Doncaster R	111+8	3
*Ted Hemsley	5 8	11 5	Stoke	Shrewsbury T	234+1	21
				Sheffield U	247	8
				Doncaster R	32	1
*Peter Bowden	5 5	10 7	Liverpool	Doncaster R	22+6	1
David Bradley	6 0	13 0	Manchester	Manchester U	—	—
				Wimbledon (on loan)	7	—
				Doncaster R	42	3
Shaun Flanagan	5 3	9 7	Doncaster	Doncaster R	14	—
Steve Lister			Doncaster	Doncaster R	9	—
Midfield						
David Bentley	5 8½	10 0	Worksop	Rotherham U	243+7	13
				Mansfield T (on loan)	1+3	1
				Chesterfield	53+2	1
				Doncaster R	60+2	2
Tom Meagan	5 9	10 5	Liverpool	Doncaster R	32+5	1
David Cork	5 6	9 5	Doncaster	Manchester U	—	—
				Doncaster R	7	1
Pat Lally	5 10	10 9	Paddington	Millwall	1	—
				York C	68+8	5
				Swansea C	152+8	10
				Aldershot (on loan)	3	—
				Doncaster R	33	—
*Mark Cox				Doncaster R	10+5	—
Forwards						
Ian McConville (Contract cancelled August 1978)	5 8	12 1	Doncaster	Doncaster R	9+2	1
Joe Laidlaw	5 8½	11 12	Wallsend	Middlesbrough	104+7	20
				Carlisle U	146+5	44
				Doncaster R	127+1	27
Glynn Snodin	5 6	9 5	Rotherham	Doncaster R	42+18	5
*Bobby Owen	5 10	10 7	Farnworth	Bury	81+2	38
				Manchester C	18+4	3
				Swansea C (on loan)	5+1	1
				Carlisle U	185+9	51
				Northampton T (on loan)	5	—
				Bury (on loan)	4	1
				Workington (on loan)	8	2
				Doncaster R	74+3	22
*Richard Habbin	5 7	10 6	Cambridge	Reading	204+14	42
				Rotherham U	79+5	19
				Doncaster R	57+3	12
*Stuart Cannell				Doncaster R	22+4	—
Jack Lewis	5 10	11 4	Long Eaton	Lincoln C	47+15	9
				Grimsby T	231+27	74
				Blackburn R	24+4	6
				Doncaster R	24+8	5
Les Packer				Doncaster R	4+1	2
Daral Pugh	5 7	9 1	Sunderland	Doncaster R	16+5	1
*Roy Austin				Doncaster R	3	—

EVERTON DIV. 1

Chairman: P. D. Carter.
Vice-Chairman: T. H. W. Scott.
Directors: J. C. Sharp, A. W. Waterworth, G. A. Watts, K. M. Tamlin, J. Search, D. A. B. Newton.
Manager: Gordon Lee.
Secretary: Jim Greenwood
Year Formed. 1878. *Limited Company:* 1892.
Turned Professional: 1885.
Former Grounds: 1878, Stanley Park, 1882; Priory Road; 1884, Anfield Road; 1892, Goodison Park.
Football League Record:

1888 Founder Member of the Football League.	1931–51 Division 1.
	1951–54 Division 2.
1930–31 Division 2.	1954– Division 1.

Honours: *Football League,* Division 1, Champions: 1890–91, 1914–15, 1927–28, 1931–32, 1938–39, 1962–63, 1969–70; Runners-up: 1889–90, 1894–95, 1901–02, 1904–05, 1908–09, 1911–12. Division 2, Champions: 1930–31; Runners-up: 1953–54. *F.A. Cup,* Winners: 1906, 1933, 1966; Runners-up: 1893, 1897, 1907, 1968. *Football League Cup,* best season: Runners-up 1976–77.

European Competitions: *European Cup:* 1963–64, 1970–71; *European Cup Winners Cup.* 1966–67. *European Fairs Cup:* 1962–63, 1964–65, 1965–66. *UEFA Cup:* 1975–76, 1978–79.

Record Victory: 11-2 v Derby Co., F.A. Cup, 1st Rd., 1889–90.

Record Defeat: 4-10 v Tottenham H., Division 1, Oct. 11th, 1958.

Most League Points: 66, Division 1, 1969–70.

Most League Goals: 121, Division 2, 1930–31.

Highest League Scorer in Season: Dixie Dean, 60, 1927–28.

Most Goals in Total Aggregate: Dixie Dean, 349, 1925–37.

Most League Appearances: Ted Sagar, 465, 1929–53.

Most Capped Player: Alan Ball, 39 (72), England.

Record Transfer Fee Received: £250,000 from QPR for Mickey Walsh, March 1979 and £250,000 from Coventry C for David Jones, June 1979.

Record Transfer Fee Paid: £350,000 to Birmingham C. for Bob Latchford, Feb. 1974.

Managers Since the War: Theo Kelly, Cliff Britton, Ian Buchan, John Carey, Harry Catterick, Billy Bingham.

Address of Supporters Club: 38 City Rd., Liverpool 4.

Goodison Park, Liverpool L4 4EL. Telephone 051-521 2020. *Match ticket information:* 051-523 6642 (24 hr. service). *Ground Capacity:* 58,000. (25,000 seats). *Record attendance:* 78,299 v Liverpool, Division 1, September, 18 1948. *Record receipts:* £174,945 Liverpool v Manchester U F.A. Cup Semi-final Replay, April 4, 1979. *Pitch measurements:* 112 yds × 78 yds.

How to get there: Corporation buses 19 and 44 from Pierhead, 68 from Old Swan 3, 22, 25, 500 from South End of the City and 30, 92, 92a, 92b, 93 from City centre. Nearest railway station, Liverpool Lime Street.

Match tickets: Reserved stand seats are available for all home fixtures (except the match v Liverpool) at anytime during the season, either by post or by personal application to the Box Office at the Goodison Rd. side of the ground. The Box Office is open each weekday from 9 a.m. to 5 p.m. Postal applications should be addressed to the Box Office manager and contain the correct remittance and S.A.E.

Car parking: Extensive parking facilities on site at the corner of Priory Rd. and Utting Ave.

Entertainments/catering facilities: Royal Blue Social Club offers cabaret entertainment each Saturday, visiting parties by arrangement. Royal Blue Restaurant open to the public for lunch on Mondays to Fridays but restricted to members on match days.

Club shop: All souvenirs available from The Toffee Shop in Goodison Rd.; send S.A.E. for mail order list.

Handbooks/programmes: Match-day magazine available on seasonal subscription.

Club Colours: Royal blue shirts with white trim, white shorts, blue trim, white stockings.

Change Colours: Amber shirts, blue trim, amber shorts, blue trim, amber stockings.

Club Coach: Eric Harrison.
Team Captain: Mick Lyons.
Club Nickname: 'Toffeemen' or 'Blues'.

EVERTON 1978–79 LEAGUE RECORD

Match No.	Date	Venue	Opponents	Result	H/T Score	League Pos'n	Goalscorers	Attendance
1	Aug 19	A	Chelsea	W 1-0	1-0	—	King	31,755
2	22	H	Derby Co	W 2-1	0-1	—	King, Nulty	39,848
3	26	H	Arsenal	W 1-0	0-0	3	Thomas	41,179
4	Sept 2	A	Manchester U	D 1-1	1-0	4	King	53,982
5	9	H	Middlesbrough	W 2-0	0-0	3	Lyons, Dobson	36,201
6	16	A	Aston Villa	D 1-1	1-1	2	Walsh	38,636
7	23	H	Wolverhampton W	W 2-0	2-0	2	Latchford, King (pen)	30,895
8	30	A	Bristol C	D 2-2	1-2	2	Latchford 2	23,231
9	Oct 7	H	Southampton	D 0-0	0-0	2		38,769
10	14	A	Ipswich T	W 1-0	1-0	2	Latchford	22,676
11	21	A	QPR	D 1-1	1-0	2	Latchford	21,171
12	28	H	Liverpool	W 1-0	0-0	2	King	53,131
13	Nov 4	A	Nottingham F	D 0-0	0-0	2		35,415
14	11	H	Chelsea	W 3-2	1-1	2	King, Dobson 2	38,694
15	18	A	Arsenal	D 2-2	1-0	2	Ross, Dobson	39,801
16	21	H	Manchester U	W 3-0	2-0	—	Ross, King, Latchford	41,926
17	25	A	Norwich C	W 1-0	0-0	2	Lyons	19,383
18	Dec 9	A	Birmingham C	W 3-1	1-0	2	Ross (pen), Todd, Latchford	23,391
19	16	H	Leeds U	D 1-1	0-1	2	Ross	37,997
20	23	A	Coventry C	L 2-3	0-2	2	Lyons, Latchford	22,834
21	26	H	Manchester C	W 1-0	0-0	2	Wright	46,997
22	30	H	Tottenham H	D 1-1	1-1	2	Lyons	44,363
23	Jan 31	H	Aston Villa	D 1-1	0-0	—	Thomas	29,079
24	Feb 3	A	Wolverhampton W	L 0-1	0-1	3		21,892
25	10	H	Bristol C	W 4-1	1-1	1	King 3, Wright	29,186
26	17	A	Southampton	L 0-3	0-1	3		20,673
27	24	H	Ipswich T	L 0-1	0-1	3		29,031
28	Mar 3	H	QPR	W 2-1	2-0	2	Latchford, Telfer	24,809
29	6	A	Middlesbrough	W 2-1	1-0	—	Jack, Latchford	15,990
30	10	H	Nottingham F	D 1-1	1-1	2	Telfer	37,435
31	13	A	Liverpool	D 1-1	0-1	—	King	52,352
32	24	H	Derby Co	D 0-0	0-0	2		20,814
33	30	H	Norwich C	D 2-2	0-1	2	Lyons 2	28,825
34	Apr 3	A	Bolton W	L 1-3	1-1	—	Ross (pen)	27,263
35	7	A	WBA	L 0-1	0-0	4		29,560
36	10	H	Coventry C	D 3-3	1-3	—	Ross, Latchford, Kidd	25,302
37	14	A	Manchester C	D 0-0	0-0	4		39,711
38	16	H	Bolton W	W 1-0	1-0	—	Higgins	31,214
39	21	A	Leeds U	L 0-1	0-0	4		29,125
40	28	H	Birmingham C	W 1-0	0-0	4	King	22,958
41	May 1	H	WBA	L 0-2	0-1	—		30,038
42	5	A	Tottenham H	D 1-1	1-1	4	Kidd	26,077

Final League Position: 4

Goalscorers

League (52): King 12 (1 pen), Latchford 11, Lyons 6, Ross 6 (2 pens), Dobson 4, Thomas 2, Wright 2, Telfer 2, Kidd 2, Nulty 1, Walsh 1, Todd 1, Jack 1, Higgins 1.

League Cup (11): Latchford 6 (1 pen), Dobson 4, Own Goal 1

F.A. Cup (1): Dobson

League Cup:	Second Round	Wimbledon (h)	8-0
	Third Round	Darlington (h)	1-0
	Fourth Round	Nottingham F (h)	2-3
F.A. Cup	Third Round	Sunderland (a)	1-2

Wood	Darracott	Pejic	Lyons	Higgins	Nulty	King	Dobson	Latchford	Walsh	Thomas	Wright	Todd	Ross	Robinson	Kenyon	Jones	Telfer	Heard	Jack	Barton	Kidd	Eastoe	Match No.
1	2	3	4	5	6	7	8	9	10	11													1
1	2	3	4		6	7	8	9	10	11	5												2
1	2	3	4		6	7	8	9	10	11	5												3
1	2	3	4		6	7	8	9	10	11	5												4
1	2	3	4		6	7	8	9	10	11	5												5
1	2	3	4		6	7	8	9	10	11	5												6
1		3	4			7	8	9	10	11	5	2	6										7
1		3	4			7	8	9	10	11	5	2	6										8
1		3	4			7	8	9	10	11	5	2	6										9
1		3	4	12		7	8	9	10	11*	5	2	6										10
1		3	4*		6	7	8	9	10	11	5	2		12									11
1		3			6	7	8	9	10	11	5	2		4									12
1	2	3				7	8	9	10	11	5	4	6										13
1		3	4			7	8	9	10*11		5	2	6	12									14
1		3	4	12		7	8	9	10	11	5*	2	6										15
1		3	4	12		7	8	9	10*11		5	2	6										16
1		3	4			7	8	9		11	5	2	6		10								17
1		3	10	5		7	8	9		11	2	4	6										18
1		3	4	10	12	7	8*	9		11	5	2	6										19
1			4	10	6	7	8	9		11	5	2			3								20
1			4	10	6	7	8	9			5	2		12	3*11								21
1			4		6	7	8	9			5	3	12	2	10*	11							22
1			4	3		7	8	9	10	11	5	2	6										23
1			4	3		7	8	9	10*11		2	5	6				12						24
1			4	3		10	8	9		11	5	7	6	2									25
1			4	3		10	8	9		11	5	6		2			7						26
1			4	3		7	8	9	12	11*	5	2				10	6						27
1			4	12		7	8*	9		11	5		6	2		10	3						28
1			4	3			8	9		11	5		6			10	2	7					29
1			4	2		7	8	9	12	11	5		6			10*	3						30
1			4			7	8	9		11	5	2	6			10	3						31
1			4	9		7	8			11	5	2	6			10	3						32
1			4	7*		9	8			11	5	2	6			10	3		12				33
1			4			8	7			11		5	6			3	9		2	10			34
1			4			7	8	9		11*		5	6			3			2	10	12		35
1			4			7	8	9*			5		6			3	12		2	10	11		36
1				4	8	9					5	7	6			3*12			2	10	11		37
1			4	5	7		8				9		6			3		8	2	10	11		38
1			4	5		7					9		6			3	8		2	10	11		39
1				4	12	7	8	9			5	6				3			2	10	11*		40
1			4	5		7	8	9				6				3			2	10	11		41
1				5		7	8	9			6	4				3			2	10	11		42
42	7	19	37	20	13	40	40	36	18	33	39	29	26	4	3	11	10	9	1	9	9	7	
			+1s	+5s				+2s				+1s	+3s			+2s	+1s		+1s		+1s		

EVERTON—PLAYERS

Player and position	Ht	Wt	Birthplace	Clubs	League Appearances	Goals
Goalkeepers						
Drew Brand	6 1	11 1	Edinburgh	Everton	2	—
				Crewe A (on loan)	15	—
George Wood	6 3	14 0	Douglas	East Stirling	22	—
(Scotland)				Blackpool	117	—
				Everton	84	—
Defenders						
Roger Kenyon	6 0	11 8	Blackpool	Everton	253+14	6
(Contract cancelled February 1979)						
Billy Wright	5 9	11 6	Liverpool	Everton	42+1	3
Terry Darracott	5 9	11 6	Liverpool	Everton	138+10	—
(Contract cancelled February 1979)						
Mike Pejic	5 6	10 5	Chesterton	Stoke C	274	6
(England)				Everton	76	2
Neil Robinson	5 7	9 11	Liverpool	Everton	13+3	1
David Jones	5 10	12 7	Liverpool	Everton	79+7	1
Michael Lyons	6 0	12 2	Liverpool	Everton	233+18	43
Mark Higgins	6 1	13 3	Buxton	Everton	47+2	2
Ray Deakin	5 8	11 1	Liverpool	Everton	—	—
Tim Heard	5 10	11 0	Hull	Everton	9+1	—
*Steve Adams	5 8	10 7	Preston	Everton	—	—
*Mark Tansey	5 10	10 10	Liverpool	Everton	—	—
Colin Todd	5 9	11 5	Chester le Street	Sunderland	170+3	3
(England)				Derby Co	293	6
				Everton	29	1
John Barton	5 10	11 0	Birmingham	Everton	9+1	—
Kevin Ratcliffe	5 11	11 0	Deeside	Everton	—	—
Midfield						
Martin Dobson	5 11¾	11 8	Blackburn	Bolton W	—	—
(England)				Burnley	220+3	42
				Everton	190	29
Andy King	5 9	10 13	Luton	Luton T	30+3	9
				Everton	121+1	29
Trevor Ross	5 8	10 12	Ashton-U-Lyne	Arsenal	57+1	5
				Everton	44+3	10
Geoff Nulty	5 10	10 9	Prestcott	Burnley	123+7	20
				Newcastle U	101	11
				Everton	13+5	1
Paul Lodge	5 8	10 7	Liverpool	Everton	—	—
Forwards						
Bob Latchford	6 0	12 1	Birmingham	Birmingham C	158+2	68
(England)				Everton	191	94
John Anderson	5 9	10 3	Manchester	Everton	—	—
*David Smallman	5 8	10 4	Connah's Quay	Wrexham	100+1	38
(Wales)				Everton	19+2	5
George Telfer	5 10	11 5	Liverpool	Everton	80+17	20
Martin Murray	5 10	11 11	Dublin	Home Farm	—	—
				Everton	—	—
Ross Jack	5 10	11 2	Inverness	Everton	1	1
Dave Thomas	5 8	11 4	Kirkby in Ashfield	Burnley	152+4	19
(England)				QPR	181+1	29
				Everton	71	4
John Thomas	5 9	11 0	Birmingham	Everton	—	—
				Tranmere R (on loan)	10+1	2
Joe McBride	5 8	10 0	Glasgow	Everton	—	—
Imre Varadi			Paddington	Letchworth	—	—
				Sheffield U	6+4	4
				Everton	—	—
Brian Kidd	6 0	12 12	Manchester	Manchester U	196+8	52
(England)				Arsenal	77	30
				Manchester C	97+1	44
				Everton	9	2
Peter Eastoe	5 10	11 3	Tamworth	Wolverhampton W	4+2	—
				Swindon T	117	46
				QPR	43+3	12
				Everton	7+1	—

EXETER CITY   DIV. 3

President: F. E. J. Dart.
Chairman: L. G. Vallance.
Vice-Chairman: W. O. Rice, M.A. (Cantab)., A.I.B., F.R.G.S.
Directors: F. E. J. Dart, J. R. Cowley, C. Hill, I. Webb, A.C.M.A.
Manager: Brian Godfrey.
Secretary: P. R. Wakeham.
Commercial Manager: E. R. Ellis.
Year Formed: 1904.   *Turned Professional:* 1908.
Limited Company: 1908.

Football League Record:
  1920 Elected Division 3.   1964-66 Division 3.
  1921-1958 Division 3(S)   1966-77 Division 4.
  1958-64 Division 4.   1977-   Division 3.

Honours: *Football League*, highest position in Division 3: 9th, 1978–79. Division 3(S), Runners-up: 1932-33. Division 4 Runners-up 1976-77. *F.A. Cup*, best season: 6th Rd. Replay, 1931. *Football League Cup*, best year: Never beyond 4th Rd. Division 3(S) Cup Winners: 1934.

Record Victory: 8-1 v Coventry C., Division 3(S), Dec. 4th, 1926 and v Aldershot, Division 3(S), May 4th, 1935.

Record Defeat: 0-9 v Notts Co., Division 3(S), Oct. 16th, 1948, 0-9 v Northampton, Division 3(S) Apr. 12, 1958.

Most League Points: 62, Division 4, 1976-77.
Most League Goals: 88, Division 3(S), 1932-33.
Highest League Scorer in Season: Fred Whitlow, 34, Division 3(S), 1932-33.
Most Goals in Total Aggregate: Alan Banks, 105, 1963-66, 1967-73.
Most Capped Player: Dermot Curtis, 1 (17), Eire.
Most League Appearances: Arnold Mitchell, 495, 1952-66.
Record Transfer Fee Received: £105,000 from Blackpool for Tony Kellow, Nov. 1978.
Record Transfer Fee Paid: £25,000 to Millwall for Ian Pearson, Nov. 1978.

Managers Since the War: George Roughton, Norman Kirkman, Norman Dodgin, Bill Thompson, Frank Broome, Glen Wilson, Cyril Spiers, Jack Edwards, Ellis Stuttard, Jock Basford, Frank Broome, John Newman, Bobby Saxton.

Address of Supporters Club: Same as Football Club.
Address of Club Shop or Boutique: The 'Near Post', 2 Blackbury Rd. Exeter.

St James Park, Exeter, EX4 6PX. Telephone Exeter 54073. *Ground capacity:* 16,500. *Record attendance:* 20,984 v Sunderland F.A. Cup 6th Rd. replay, March, 4 1931. *Record receipts:* £18,150 v Wolverhampton Wanderers, F.A. Cup 3rd Rd., January 11, 1978. *Pitch measurements:* 114 yds × 73 yds.

How to get there: City buses A, D, J, K, S from city centre to The Fountain (one-minute walk to the ground). Routes G and J pass both railway stations—Exeter St David's and Exeter Central.
Match tickets: Tickets may be booked in advance usually two weeks before home matches.
Car parking: No car park at the ground. Limited street parking permitted.
Entertainments/catering facilities: Members social club. Subscription £1.00; joint membership £1.50. The club is situated at the ground.
Club shop: Sells all types of souvenirs.
Handbooks/programmes: Handbooks available at 20p; programmes can be ordered on subscription.
Extra information: Membership of the Supporters Association at 25p per year.
Club Colours: White shirts with three red stripes on sleeves, white shorts, red trim, white stockings, red trim.
Change Colours: Green shirts, green shorts, green stockings.
Club Nickname: 'The Grecians'.

EXETER CITY 1978-79 LEAGUE RECORD

Match No.	Date	Venue	Opponents	Result	H/T Score	League Pos'n	Goalscorers	Attendance
1	Aug 19	H	Mansfield T	D 0-0	0-0	—		3704
2	26	A	Chester	L 0-3	0-1	22		3431
3	Sept 2	H	Brentford	D 2-2	1-2	20	Bowker 2	3604
4	9	A	Chesterfield	W 1-0	1-0	17	Kellow	3936
5	13	H	Shrewsbury T	L 0-1	0-0	—		3732
6	16	A	Oxford U	L 2-3	1-0	19	Bowker, Templeman	5441
7	23	H	Hull C	W 3-1	3-1	18	Kellow, Delve, Bowker	3733
8	27	H	Colchester U	W 2-1	1-1	—	Kellow, Bowker	3421
9	30	A	Peterborough	D 1-1	1-0	16	Holman	6714
10	Oct 7	H	Gillingham	D 0-0	0-0	15		4241
11	14	A	Swansea C	L 0-1	0-1	19		10,957
12	18	H	Blackpool	W 3-0	3-0	—	Kellow 2, Bowker	3993
13	21	H	Bury	W 2-1	2-0	10	Kellow, Bowker	3840
14	24	A	Sheffield W	L 1-2	0-0	—	Kellow	11,139
15	28	A	Watford	L 0-1	0-1	15		14,797
16	Nov 4	H	Tranmere R	W 3-0	1-0	12	Bowker 2, Hatch	3526
17	11	A	Brentford	D 0-0	0-0	12		6390
18	18	H	Chester	L 0-1	0-0	15		3985
19	Dec 2	H	Southend U	D 0-0	0-0	13		3195
20	9	A	Carlisle U	D 1-1	0-1	12	Roberts	4568
21	26	H	Walsall	W 3-1	2-0	13	Sims, Randell, Pearson	4159
22	30	H	Lincoln C	W 3-2	2-0	9	Sims 2, Pearson	3810
23	Jan 13	H	Chesterfield	W 3-1	2-1	6	Neville (pen), Delve, Roberts	3671
24	20	H	Oxford U	W 2-0	0-0	6	Neville, Randell	4532
25	Feb 2	A	Colchester U	D 2-2	0-1	6	Neville 2	2767
26	10	H	Peterborough U	W 1-0	0-0	5	Pearson	3844
27	24	H	Swansea C	W 2-1	1-0	5	Delve, Sims	7697
28	27	A	Plymouth Arg	L 2-4	1-3	—	Delve, Sims	12,637
29	Mar 3	A	Bury	L 2-4	0-3	8	Hatch, Giles	3425
30	10	H	Watford	D 0-0	0-0	8		7082
31	16	A	Tranmere R	D 2-2	1-0	9	Sims, Roberts	984
32	24	H	Sheffield W	D 2-2	1-1	8	Neville, Sims	4521
33	26	A	Mansfield T	D 1-1	0-1	—	Bowker	4562
34	31	H	Rotherham U	W 2-0	0-0	8	Randell, Sims	3349
35	Apr 3	A	Swindon T	D 1-1	0-0	—	Sims	7923
36	6	A	Southend U	W 1-0	0-0	8	Neville (pen)	6733
37	11	H	Swindon T	L 1-2	0-2	—	Sims	5548
38	14	A	Walsall	D 2-2	1-2	7	Rogers, Delve	3118
39	17	H	Plymouth Arg	W 1-0	0-0	—	Rogers	8022
40	21	A	Lincoln C	W 1-0	0-0	7	Neville (pen)	2675
41	24	A	Blackpool	D 1-1	0-0	—	Sims	3136
42	28	H	Carlisle U	W 3-2	2-1	7	Neville 2 (1 a pen), Rogers	4229
43	May 5	A	Rotherham U	L 1-2	0-1	7	Bowker	2217
44	7	A	Hull C	L 0-1	0-0	—		4079
45	14	A	Gillingham	L 0-2	0-2	—		8788
46	17	A	Shrewsbury T	L 1-4	1-3	—	Delve	14,441

Final League Position: 9

Goalscorers

League (61): Bowker 11, Sims 11, Neville 9 (4 pens), Kellow 7, Delve 6, Roberts 3, Randell 3, Rogers 3, Pearson 3, Hatch 2, Templeman 1, Holman 1, Giles 1
League Cup (6): Delve 3, Kellow 2, Bowker.
F.A. Cup (1): Forbes.

League Cup	First Round	AFC Bournemouth (a)	1-0
		(h)	1-1
	Second Round	Blackburn R (h)	2-1
	Third Round	Bolton W (h)	2-1
	Fourth Round	Watford (h)	0-2
F.A. Cup	First Round	Brentford (h)	1-0
	Second Round	Maidstone (a)	0-1

O'Keefe	Templeman	Hore	Randell	Giles	Roberts, L	Hodge	Kellow	Bowker	Delve	Hatch	Ingham	Williams	Holman	Mitchell	Neville	Forbes	Pearson	Sims	Main	Rogers	Ireland	Roberts, P	Match No.
1	2	3	4	5	6	7	8	9	10	11													1
1	2	3	4	5	6	7*	8	9	10	11	12												2
1	2	3	4	5	6	7*	8	9	10	11		12											3
1	2	3	4	5	6	7	8	9	10	11													4
1	2	3	4	5	6		8	9	10	11	7												5
1	2	3	4	5	6		8	9	10	11	7*12												6
1	2	3	4	5	6		8	9	7	11		10											7
1	2	3	4	5	6		8	9	10	11	7												8
1	2	3	4	5	6		8	9	10	11	7												9
1	2	3	4	5	6		8	9	10				7	11									10
1	2	3*	4	5	6		8	9	10	11	12			7									11
1	2	3	4	5	6		8	9	10	11				7									12
1	2	3	4	5	6		8	9	10	11				7									13
1	2	3	4	5	6		8	9		11			12	10*	7								14
1	2	3	4	5	6		8	9	10*	11			12		7								15
1	2		4	5	6		8	9	10	11			3		7								16
1	2	3			6		8	9	10	11				5	7	4							17
1	2	3			6			9	10	11				5	7	4	8						18
1	2			5	6			9	10	11				3	7	4	8						19
1		3		5	6			9	10	11				2	7	4	8						20
1	2	3	10	5	6				4	11					7		8	9					21
1	2	6	4	5	3				10	11					7		8	9					22
1	2	3	4	5	6				10	11					7		8	9					23
1	4	3	6	5	2*				10	11					7	12	9	8					24
1	2	3	4	5	6				10	11					7		8	9					25
1	2	3	4	5	6				10	11					7		8	9					26
1	2	3	4		5				11	6					7	8	9	10					27
1	2	3	4	5	6				10	11					7		8	9					28
1	2	3	4	5	6				10	11					7		9	8					29
1	2	3	4	5	6				10	11					7		8	9					30
1	2	3	4	5	6				10*11	12					7		8	9					31
1	2	3		5	6			9		11					7	4	8	10					32
1	2	3	4	5	6			10		11					7		8	9					33
	2	3	4	5	6			10		11					7		8*	9	1	12			34
	2	3	4	5	6				10	11					7			9	1	8			35
	2	3	4	5	6				10	11					7			9	1	8			36
	2	3		5	6				4	10	11				7			9	1	8			37
	2	3		5	6				4	10	11				7			9	1	8			38
	2	3	4	5	6					10	11				7			9	1	8			39
	3	2		5	6					10	11				7	4		9	1	8			40
	2	3	4	5	6					10	11				7			9	1	8			41
	2	3	4	5					12	10	11				6	7		8	1	9*			42
	3	2	4	5					12	10	11*				6	7		9	1	8			43
	2	3	4	5					12	10	11*				6	7		9	1	8			44
	2	3	4	5					8	10	11					7		9*	1		12	6	45
	23		4	5						10	11					7	9		1	8		6	46
33	45	44	38	43	41	4	17	26	42	45	—	2	4	10	36	7	18	25	13	11	—	2	
								+3s				+2s	+1s	+4s			+1s			+1s	+1s		

EXETER CITY—PLAYERS

Player and position	Ht	Wt	Birthplace	Clubs	League Appearances	Goals
Goalkeepers						
John Baugh	6 0	11 9		Exeter C	20	—
Vince O'Keefe	6 2	12 6	Birmingham	Birmingham C	—	—
				Walsall	—	—
				AP Leamington	—	—
				Exeter C	33	—
Ian Main (non-contract)				Exeter C	13	—
Defenders						
Peter Hatch	5 10	11 7	Reading	Oxford U	15+4	2
				Exeter C	234+1	7
Bob Saxton	5 10	11 7	Doncaster	Derby Co	94+2	1
(Contract cancelled August 1978)				Plymouth Arg	224+7	7
				Exeter C	92	3
John Hore	5 8	10 11	St. Austell	Plymouth Arg	393+4	17
				Exeter C	147	—
John Templeman	5 11	11 7	Yapton	Brighton	229+7	16
				Exeter C	195+1	7
Jimmy Giles	6 0	13 3	Kidlington	Swindon T	12+1	—
				Aldershot	81+1	3
				Exeter C	183	6
				Charlton Ath	92+1	6
				Exeter C	66	1
Phil Roberts	5 10	11 0	Cardiff	Bristol R	175+1	6
(Wales)				Portsmouth	152+1	1
(Contract cancelled)				Hereford U	3	—
				Exeter C	2	—
Brian Clarke	6 0	12 0	Dawley	WBA	—	—
(Contract cancelled)				Exeter C	—	—
Richard Forbes (non-contract)				Exeter C	9+1	—
Midfield						
Colin Randell	5 8½	10 8	Skewen	Coventry C	—	—
				Plymouth Arg	137+2	9
				Exeter C	78	4
Keith Bowker	5 9	10 7	W Bromwich	Birmingham C	19+2	5
				Exeter C	110	38
				Cambridge U	12+5	1
				Northampton T (on loan)	4	—
				Exeter C	72+3	20
John Delve	5 8	10 12	Hanworth	QPR	9+6	—
				Plymouth Arg	127+5	6
				Exeter C	53	7
Lee Roberts	6 0	11 6	Wolverhampton	Shrewsbury T	9+6	1
				Exeter C	70+4	5
Anthony Mitchell (non-contract)				Exeter C	10	—
Forwards						
Alan Beer	5 7	10 0	Swansea	Swansea C	9+5	3
(Contract cancelled September 1978)				Exeter C	114	52
*Fred Ingham	5 7	9 10	Manchester	Stockport Co	—	—
				Exeter C	4+4	1
Peter Rogers				Exeter C	11+1	3
				Barnsley		
Ian Pearson	5 9	11 3	Leeds	Millwall	41+3	9
				Plymouth Arg	6+6	—
				Exeter C	18	3
Steve Neville	5 8	10 10	Walthamstow	Southampton	5	1
				Exeter C	36	9
Roy Ireland				Exeter C	0+1	—
John Sims	6 0	12 10	Belper	Derby Co	2+1	—
				Luton T (on loan)	3	1
				Oxford U (on loan)	6+1	1
				Colchester U (on loan)	2	—
				Notts Co	48+13	13
				Exeter C	25	11

FULHAM   DIV. 2

Life-President: Tommy Trinder.
Chairman: E. Clay.
Directors: G. Clay, B. Dalton, D. Peters, E. Burston, D. Hamilton, A. Smith.
Manager: Bobby Campbell.
Assistant Manager: Mike Kelly.
Club Secretary: George Noyce.   *Year Formed:* 1879.
Turned Professional: 1898.   *Limited Company:* 1903.
Previous Name: 1879–98, Fulham St. Andrew's.
Previous Grounds: Lillie Road, Fulham Cross; Barn Elms, Barnes; Ranelagh House; Stansfield's Field, Fulham Road; Half-moon Cricket Ground, Putney; 1896, Craven Cottage.

Football League Record:
1907 Elected to Division 2.	1959-68 Division 1.
1928-32 Division 3(S).	1968-69 Division 2.
1932-49 Division 2.	1969-71 Division 3.
1949-52 Division 1.	1971- Division 2.
1952-59 Division 2.	

Honours: Football League, highest position in Division 1: 10th, 1959-60. Division 2, Champions 1948-49; Runners-up: 1958-59. Division 3(S), Champions: 1931-32. Division 3, Runners-up 1970-71. *F.A. Cup*, best season: Runners-up 1974-5.
Football League Cup, best season: 5th Rd., 1967-68, 1970-71.
Record Victory: 10-1 v Ipswich T., Division 1, Dec. 26th, 1963.
Record Defeat: 0-9 v Wolverhampton W., Division 1, Sept. 16th, 1959.
Most League Points: 60, Division 2, 1958-59, and Division 3, 1970-71.
Most League Goals: 111, Division 3(S), 1931-32.
Highest League Scorer in Season: Frank Newton, 41, Division 3(S), 1931-32.
Most League Goals in Total Aggregate: Bedford Jezzard, 154, 1948-1956.
Most Capped Player: Johnny Haynes, 56, England.
Most League Appearances: Johnny Haynes, 598, 1952-70.
Record Transfer Fee Received: £200,000 from Tottenham H. for John Lacy, July, 1978.
Record Transfer Fee Paid: £150,000 to Orient for Peter Kitchen, Feb. 1979.
Managers Since the War: Jack Peart, Frank Osborne, Doug Livingstone, Bill Dodgin (Snr.), Bedford Jezzard, Vic Buckingham, Bobby Robson, Johnny Haynes, Bill Dodgin (Jnr.), Alec Stock.
Address of Supporters Club: Fulham Travel Club, Craven Cottage, Stevenage Road, S.W.6.

Craven Cottage, Stevenage Rd., Fulham, London, S.W.6. Telephone 01-736 6561/2/3. Pools Office: 736 4634.   *Telegraphic address:* 'Fulhamish, London S.W.6.'   *Ground capacity:* 42,000.   *Record attendance:* 49,335 v Millwall, Division 2, October 8 1938.   *Record receipts:* £44,763 v Manchester U., F.A. Cup, 4th Rd., Jan. 27, 1979.   *Pitch measurements:* 110 yds × 75 yds.
How to get there: Underground stations, Putney Bridge (District Line) and Hammersmith (District, Metropolitan, Piccadilly). Then by bus—30, 74, 85, 93, 220.
Match tickets: The Box Office is now computerised, and seats are bookable at any time during the season.
Car parking: Plentiful parking in streets around the ground.
Entertainments/catering facilities: Social amenities available. Snack bars and licensed bars around the ground.   The Riverside Suite is available for conferences, weddings, parties, etc.
Club shop: Sells all types of souvenirs.
Handbooks/programmes: Both handbooks and programmes available.
Extra information: Fulham Travel Club runs trips to away matches. The Box Office computer is also geared to obtain tickets for the theatre and other London entertainments.
Club Colours: White shirts with black collar, black shorts, white stockings with three black hoops on turnover.
Change Colours: Red with three black stripes. Red shorts with three black stripes. Black stockings with three red hoops on turnover.
Club Captain: Ray Evans.
First Team Trainer: Ron Woolnough.
Club Nickname: 'Cottagers'.

R.F. 79/80—10

FULHAM 1978–79 LEAGUE RECORD

Match No.	Date	Venue	Opponents	Result	H/T Score	League Pos'n	Goalscorers	Attendance
1	Aug 19	A	Bristol R	L 1-3	0-1	—	Margerrison	5950
2	22	H	Wrexham	L 0-1	0-0	—		6135
3	26	H	Burnley	D 0-0	0-0	20		5407
4	Sept 2	A	West Ham U	W 1-0	1-0	18	Margerrison	25,778
5	9	H	Sheffield U	W 2-0	0-0	9	Mahoney, Margerrison	6672
6	16	A	Sunderland	D 1-1	0-0	10	Margerrison (pen)	17,976
7	23	H	Millwall	W 1-0	0-0	4	Greenaway	8941
8	30	A	Oldham Ath	W 2-0	0-0	4	Guthrie, Davies	6972
9	Oct 7	H	Stoke C	W 2-0	1-0	3	Greenaway, Gale	12,531
10	14	A	Brighton & HA	L 0-3	0-1	5		24,606
11	21	H	Preston NE	W 5-3	2-2	3	Davies, Baxter (og), Money, Lock, Guthrie	8719
12	28	A	Crystal Palace	W 1-0	0-0	3	Greenaway	28,733
13	Nov 3	H	Blackburn R	L 1-2	1-1	6	Evans	12,500
14	10	H	Bristol R	W 3-0	0-0	3	Guthrie 2, Beck	10,296
15	18	A	Burnley	L 3-5	2-2	4	Evanson, Guthrie, Gale	10,393
16	21	H	West Ham U	D 0-0	0-0	—		26,556
17	25	A	Charlton Ath	D 0-0	0-0	4		11,440
18	Dec 2	H	Notts Co	D 1-1	1-0	5	Guthrie	7591
19	16	H	Newcastle U	L 1-3	1-2	10	Guthrie	8575
20	23	A	Cardiff C	L 0-2	0-1	10		5558
21	26	H	Cambridge U	W 5-1	2-0	—	Davies, Margerrison, Guthrie 3	7814
22	30	H	Luton T	W 1-0	1-0	5	Aizlewood (og)	8914
23	Jan 20	H	Sunderland	D 2-2	0-1	6	Davies, Guthrie	11,260
24	Feb 6	A	Sheffield U	D 1-1	0-1	6	Margerrison (pen)	12,457
25	10	A	Oldham Ath	W 1-0	1-0	6	Davies	6942
26	24	H	Brighton & HA	L 0-1	0-0	6		18,640
27	Mar 3	A	Preston NE	D 2-2	1-2	6	Kitchen, Guthrie	10,890
28	10	H	Crystal Palace	D 0-0	0-0	6		16,654
29	21	A	Leicester C	L 0-1	0-0	—		10,363
30	24	A	Wrexham	D 1-1	1-0	8	Kitchen	9046
31	27	A	Orient	L 0-1	0-1	—		6645
32	31	H	Charlton Ath	W 3-1	1-0	8	Kitchen, Davies, Evans	6955
33	Apr 4	A	Stoke C	L 0-2	0-0	—		15,243
34	7	A	Notts Co	D 1-1	0-1	8	Guthrie	9465
35	11	H	Cardiff C	D 2-2	2-2	—	Kitchen, Lock (pen)	6067
36	14	H	Cambridge U	L 0-1	0-1	8		6573
37	16	H	Orient	D 2-2	1-1	—	Davies, Lock (pen)	6956
38	21	A	Newcastle U	D 0-0	0-0	8		11,916
39	24	A	Millwall	D 0-0	0-0	—		7397
40	28	H	Leicester C	W 3-0	2-0	7	Strong, Davies 2	7002
41	May 5	A	Luton T	L 0-2	0-1	7		9112
42	9	A	Blackburn R	L 1-2	1-1	—	Kitchen	4684

Final League Position: 10

Goalscorers

League (50): Guthrie 13, Davies 9, Margerrison 6 (2 pens), Kitchen 5, Greenaway 3, Lock 3 (2 pens) Evans 2, Gale 2, Beck 1, Evanson 1, Mahoney 1, Money 1, Strong 1, Own Goals 2.
League Cup (2): Mahoney, Davies.
F.A. Cup (3): Margerrison 2, Davies.

League Cup	Second Round	Darlington (h)	2-2
		(a)	0-1
F.A. Cup	Third Round	QPR (h)	2-0
	Fourth Round	Manchester U (h)	1-1
		(a)	0-1

Peyton	Evans	Strong	Money	Banton	Lock	Bullivant	Gale	Margerrison	Evanson	Davies	Mahoney	Boyd	Guthrie	Greenaway	Beck	Lovell	Marinello	Kitchen	Mason	Hatter	Digweed	Match No.
1	2	3	4	5	6	7	8	9	10	11												1
1	2	3	10	5	4	7	6		11*	8	9	12										2
1	2	3	10	5	4	7	6		11	8	9											3
1	2		4	5	3	7	6	10	11	8	9											4
1	2	3	4	5*10		7	6	12	11	8	9											5
1	2	3	5		4	7	6	10	11	8	9											6
1	2	3	5		4	7	6	10	11*	8			9	12								7
1	2	3	5		4	7	6	10		8			9	11								8
1	2	3	5		4	7	6*10	12		8			9	11								9
1	2	3	5		4	7	6			8			9	11	10							10
1	2	3	5		4	7*	6		12	8			9	11	10							11
1	2	3	5		4	7	6		12	8*			9	11	10							12
1	2	3	5*		4	7	6	12	8				9	11	10							13
1	2	3	5		4	7*	6	12	8				9	11	10							14
1	2	3	5		4		6		8				9	11	10	7						15
1	2	3	5		4		6	7	8				9	11	10							16
1	2	3	5		4		6		11	8			9	7	10							17
1	2	3	5		4	8	6		7				9	11	10							18
1	2	3	5		4	8		12	10*	7			9	11	6							19
1	2	3	5		4	8	6		7				9	11	10							20
1	2	3	5		4	8		6	12	7			9		10*		11					21
1	2	3	5		4*	8		10	6	7			9	12			11					22
1		2*	5	3		4	6	10	12	7			9		8		11					23
1		2	5	6	3	4		10		7			9		8		11					24
1	2	3	5			6	4		10			7	9		8		11					25
1	2	3	5			4	6	7					9		8		11	10				26
1	2	3	5	4	11	6							9		8		7	10				27
1		2	5		3	4	6		11				9		8		7	10				28
1	2	3	5	11	4	6	7	12		9*					8			10				29
1	2	3	5	7	4	6	12	8		9*					11			10				30
1	2	3	5	7	4	6							9	11	8			10				31
1	2	3	5		4		6	8	7				9		11			10				32
1	2	3	5		4		6	11	7				9		8			10				33
1	2	3	5		4		6	11*	7		12		9		8			10				34
1	2		5		4		6	12	7		11*	9			8			10	3			35
1	2	3	5		4		6	11	12	7			9		8			10*				36
1	2	3	5		4		6	11	7				9		8			10				37
1		2	5		4		6		7				9		8		10		3	11		38
1		2	5				6		7				9		8	4	10		3	11		39
1		2	5		4		6		7				9		8		10		3	11		40
	2	3	5		4		6		7				9		8		10			11	1	41
	2	3	5		7		6		4				9		8		12	10*		11	1	42
40	35	41	42	7	39	28	36	20	16	32	7	1	34	14	32	2	8	17	4	5	2	

                             +   +   +   +   +
                             6s 7s   2s   2s   1s

FULHAM—PLAYERS

Player and position	Ht	Wt	Birthplace	Clubs	League Appearances	Goals
Goalkeepers						
Gerry Peyton (Eire)	6 2	13 11	Birmingham	Burnley	30	—
				Fulham	105	—
Perry Digweed	6 0½	11 4	London	Fulham	3	—
Defenders						
Leslie Strong	5 9	10 7	London	C Palace	—	—
				Fulham	234+3	4
Steve Hatter	6 2	13 0	London	Fulham	10	—
Ray Evans	5 10½	12 4	Edmonton	Tottenham H	132+4	2
				Millwall	74	3
				Fulham	86	6
Tony Gale	6 1½	12 4	London	Fulham	74	10
Richard Money	5 11½	11 5	Lowestoft	Scunthorpe U	165+8	4
				Fulham	65	3
Kevin Lock	6 0	11 6	London	West Ham U	122+10	2
				Fulham	39	3
Geoff Banton	5 11	11 7	Ashton-U-Lyne	Bolton W	—	—
				Plymouth Arg	6+1	—
				Fulham	7	—
James Richardson	5 11	11 6	Glasgow	Fulham	—	—
Brian Corner	5 7	9 3	Scotland	Fulham	—	—
Midfield						
John Margerrison	5 10	12 2	Bushey	Tottenham H	—	—
				Fulham	63+8	8
John Evanson	5 9½	10 12	Newcastle-under-Lyme	Oxford U	145+13	10
				Blackpool	63+4	1
				Fulham	84+11	5
John Beck	5 10½	11 9	Edmonton	QPR	32+8	1
				Coventry C	60+9	6
				Fulham	32	1
Brian Gibson	5 9	10 0	Scotland	Fulham	—	—
Clive Day	6 0	11 0	Essex	Fulham	—	—
Peter O'Doherty				Fulham	—	—
Forwards						
Steven Scrivens	5 8	8 12	London	Fulham	3+1	1
				Brentford (on loan)	5	—
Terry Bullivant	5 9	8 9	London	Fulham	79+7	2
George Best (N Ireland)	5 8¼	11 3	Belfast	Manchester U	361	137
				Stockport Co	3	2
				Cork Celtic	not Known	
				Los Angeles Aztecs	not Known	
				Fulham	42	8
John Gummer	5 10	10 12	Essex	Fulham	—	—
Brian Greenaway	5 9	10 1	London	Fulham	41+5	5
Tony Mahoney	6 0	11 12	Barking	Fulham	21+5	4
Tom Mason	5 8	10 6	London	Fulham	5	—
Gordon Davies	5 7	10 6	S Wales	Fulham	36+1	10
Gordon Boyd	5 7	10 4	Glasgow	Fulham	1+2	—
Peter Kitchen	5 8	11 1	Mexborough	Doncaster R	221+7	89
				Ipswich T (on loan)	—	—
				Orient	64+1	28
				Fulham	17	5
Chris Guthrie	6 1	13 2	Dilston-on-Tyne	Newcastle U	3	—
				Southend U	107+1	35
				Sheffield U	58+2	15
				Swindon T	44+1	12
				Fulham	34	13
Peter Marinello	5 8	10 8¾	Edinburgh	Hibernian	42+3	5
				Arsenal	32+6	3
				Portsmouth	92+3	7
				Motherwell	77+12	12
				Fulham	8+1	—
Mark Lovell	5 9	11 5	London	Fulham	4+1	—

GILLINGHAM   DIV. 3

Chairman: Dr. C. S. Grossmark.
Vice-Chairman: C. A. L. Cox.
Directors: J. W. Leech, B. B. Moore.
Manager: Gerry Summers.   *Club Secretary:* R. J. Dennison.
Assistant Manager: Alan Hodgkinson.
Year Formed: 1893.   *Turned Professional:* 1894.
Limited Company: 1893.
Previous Name: New Brompton, 1893–1913.
Football League Record:
  1920 Original Member
     of Division 3.   1958–64 Division 4.
  1921 Division 3(S).   1964–71 Division 3.
  1938 Failed re-election.   1971–74 Division 4.
  1950 Re-elected to Division 3(S).   1974–   Division 3.

Honours: *Football League*, highest position in Division 3: 4th, 1978–79. Division 4, Champions: 1963–64. Runners-up 1973–74. *F.A. Cup*, best season: 5th Rd., 1969–70. *Football League Cup*, best season: 4th Rd., 1964.
Record Victory: 10-1 v Gorleston, F.A. Cup, 1st Rd., Nov. 16th, 1957.
Record Defeat: 2-9 v Nottingham F., Division 3(S), Nov. 18th, 1950.
Most League Points: 62, Division 4, 1973–74.
Most League Goals: 90, Division 4, 1973–74.
Highest League Scorer in Season: Ernie Morgan, 31, Division 3(S), 1954–55.   Brian Yeo, 31, Division 4, 1973–74.
Most League Goals in Total Aggregate: Brian Yeo, 135, 1963–75.
Most Capped Player: Fred Fox, 1, England; Damien Richardson, 1(2), Eire.
Most League Appearances: John Simpson, 571, 1957–72.
Record Transfer Fee Received: £60,000 from Charlton Ath. for Dick Tydeman, Dec. 1976.
Record Transfer Fee Paid: £50,000 to Southampton for Tony Funnell, March 1979.
Managers Since the War: Archie Clark, Harry Barratt, Freddie Cox, Basil Hayward, Andy Nelson, Len Ashurst.
Address of Supporters Club: Gillingham F.C. Supporters' Association, Gordon Road, Gillingham.

Priestfield Stadium, Gillingham. Telephone 0634 51854. *Telegraphic address:* 'Football Gillingham, Kent'. *Ground capacity:* 22,000. *Record attendance:* 23,002 v Q.P.R., F.A. Cup 3rd Rd., January 10, 1948. *Record receipts:* £10,076. *Pitch measurements:* 114yds × 75 yds.

How to get there: Gillingham railway station (six or seven minutes' walk). Bus services are 10 minutes from ground.
Match tickets: Can be reserved by postal application enclosing correct remittance and S.A.E.
Car parking: Park for 500 cars adjoining the ground, entrance in Toronto Rd.
Entertainments/catering facilities: A club house, and several bars around the ground.
Club shop: Sells all types of souvenirs.
Handbooks/programmes: Programmes available on subscription. Handbooks also available.
Extra information: Enquiries about supporters association to Gillingham F.C. Supporters Association, Gordon Rd., Gillingham.

Club Colours: Blue shirts, white shorts, blue stockings, white and blue trim.
Change Colours: White shirts with blue collar and cuffs, blue shorts, white socks.
Club Captain:
Club Nickname: 'The Gills'.

GILLINGHAM 1978–79 LEAGUE RECORD

Match No.	Date	Venue	Opponents	Result	H/T Score	League Pos'n	Goalscorers	Attendance
1	Aug 19	H	Rotherham U	D 0-0	0-0	—		4157
2	21	A	Mansfield T	D 1-1	0-0	—	Price	5745
3	26	A	Bury	D 2-2	2-2	14	Weatherly, Nicholl	3414
4	Sept 2	H	Watford	L 2-3	2-2	14	Overton, Westwood	8248
5	9	A	Tranmere R	D 1-1	0-0	16	Price	1589
6	12	H	Sheffield W	D 0-0	0-0	—		5835
7	16	H	Chester	W 1-0	0-0	12	Richardson	4743
8	23	A	Brentford	W 2-0	0-0	11	Price, Hughes	6970
9	26	A	Blackpool	L 0-2	0-1	—		5772
10	30	H	Chesterfield	W 2-1	2-0	9	Westwood, Richardson	4602
11	Oct 7	A	Exeter C	D 0-0	0-0	10		4241
12	14	H	Hull C	W 2-0	1-0	5	Crabbe (pen), Jolley	5460
13	17	H	Lincoln C	W 4-2	3-1	—	Westwood 2, Jolley, Hughes	5763
14	21	A	Peterborough U	D 1-1	1-0	4	Nicholl	5001
15	28	A	Oxford U	D 1-1	1-1	4	Price	4366
16	Nov 4	H	Swansea C	W 2-0	0-0	4	Price, Crabbe (pen)	11,329
17	11	A	Watford	L 0-1	0-1	4		13,941
18	18	H	Bury	D 3-3	1-0	6	Jolley 2, Richardson	6291
19	Dec 2	H	Carlisle U	D 0-0	0-0	4		4322
20	9	A	Shrewsbury T	D 1-1	0-0	5	Westwood	3924
21	26	A	Southend U	W 1-0	0-0	5	Jolley	6644
22	30	H	Plymouth Arg	W 2-0	1-0	4	Nicholl, Westwood	5961
23	Jan 13	H	Tranmere R	W 3-2	0-2	4	Price, Westwood (pen), Nicholl	5480
24	27	H	Brentford	D 0-0	0-0	4		6899
25	Feb 3	H	Blackpool	W 2-0	0-0	3	Westwood 2 (1 pen)	6146
26	21	A	Chester	D 1-1	1-1	—	Barker	2421
27	24	A	Hull C	W 1-0	1-0	3	Price	4349
28	Mar 3	H	Peterborough U	W 1-0	0-0	3	Richardson	6890
29	6	A	Sheffield Wed	L 1-2	1-1	—	Westwood	8205
30	10	H	Oxford U	W 2-1	0-1	3	Overton, Weatherley	6063
31	16	A	Swansea C	L 1-3	0-2	4	White (pen)	10,832
32	20	H	Walsall	W 1-0	0-0	—	Westwood	3084
33	24	H	Mansfield T	D 0-0	0-0	4		6935
34	27	A	Rotherham U	D 1-1	1-0	—	Westwood	3239
35	31	H	Swindon T	D 2-2	2-2	3	White, Westwood	9460
36	Apr 7	A	Carlisle U	L 0-1	0-0	6		5130
37	10	H	Walsall	W 3-1	1-0	—	White (pen), Price 2	7342
38	14	A	Southend U	W 1-0	0-0	3	Westwood	7291
39	16	H	Colchester U	W 3-0	1-0	—	Price, Westwood, Funnell	12,030
40	21	A	Plymouth Arg	L 1-2	1-1	4	Funnell	5868
41	25	A	Lincoln C	W 4-2	2-1	—	Funnell 2, Westwood, Price	1863
42	28	H	Shrewsbury T	W 2-0	0-0	3	Price 2	14,902
43	May 5	A	Swindon T	L 1-3	0-0	5	Funnell	15,117
44	7	A	Colchester U	D 2-2	0-0	—	Armstrong, Westwood	6317
45	14	H	Exeter C	W 2-0	2-0	—	Price, Funnell	8788
46	19	A	Chesterfield	W 2-0	1-0	—	Westwood, Funnell	2802

Final League Position: 4

Goalscorers
League (65): Westwood 18 (2 pens), Price 14, Funnell 7, Jolley 5, Nicholl 14, Richardson 4, White 3 (2 pens), Crabbe 2 (2 pens), Hughes 2, Overton 2, Weatherley 2, Armstrong 1, Barker 1.
League Cup (2): Price, Young.
F.A. Cup (1): Westwood.

League Cup	First Round	Reading (a)	1-3
		(h)	1-2
F.A. Cup	First Round	Reading (a)	0-0
		(h)	1-2 (a.e.t.)

Hillyard	Knight	Armstrong	Overton	Young	Crabbe	Nicholl	Weatherley	Price	Westwood	Richardson	Walker	White	Hughes	Williams	Sharpe	Buttress	Jolley	Barker	Funnell	Match No.
1	2	3	4	5*	6	7	8	9	10	11	12									1
1	2*	3	4		6	7	8	9	12	10	11	5								2
1		3	4		6	7	8	9	12	10	11	5	2*							3
1		3	4		6	7*	8	9	10	11	12	5		2						4
1	3		4		6		8	9	10	11		7	5			2				5
1	3*	4			6		8	9	10	11	12	5	7			2				6
1					6	7	4	9	10	11		8*	5	3		2	12			7
1	3				6	7	4	9	10	11			5	8		2				8
1	3				6	7	4	9	10	11	12	5*	8			2				9
1		3	4		6	7	5	9	10	11			8			2				10
1		3	4		6	7	5	9	10	11			8			2				11
1	3*		4		6	7	5	9	10	11			8			2	12			12
1			4		3	7	5	9	10	11			8			2	6			13
1		3	4		6	7	5	9	10	11			8			2				14
1		3	4		6	7	5	9	10	11			8			2				15
1		3	4		6	7	5	9	10	11			8			2				16
1		3*	4		6	7	5	9	10	11			8			2	12			17
1			4		3	7	5	9	10	11			8			2	6			18
1		3	4		6	7	5	9*	10	11	12		8			2				19
1		3	4		6	7	5		10	11		9	8			2				20
1		3	4		6	7	5		10	11			8			2	9			21
1		3	4		6	7	5		10	11			8			2	9			22
1		3*	4		6	7	5	12	10	11			8			2	9			23
1			4		6*	7	5	9	10		12		8			2	11	3		24
1			4		6	7	5	9	10				8			2	11	3		25
1			4		6	7	5	9	10	11			8			2		3		26
1			4		6	7	5	9	10	11		8				2		3		27
1			4		6	7	5	9	10	11		8				2		3		28
1			4		6	7	5	9	10	11*			8	12		2		3		29
1			4		6	7	5	9	10				8			2	11	3		30
1			4		6	7*	5	9	10			11	8			2	12	3		31
1			4		6	7	5	9	10			11	8			2		3		32
1			4		6	7	5	9	10				8	12		2	11*	3		33
1	12		4		6*	7	5	9	10			11	8			2		3		34
1			4	2		7	5	9	10				8	6				3	11	35
1	11*		4			7	5	9				10	6			2	12	3	8	36
1	3		4			7	5	9	10			8	6			2			11	37
1			4			7	5	9	10			8	6			2		3	11	38
1			4			7	5	9	10			8	6			2		3	11	39
1			4			7	5	9	10			8	6			2		3	11	40
1			4			7	5	9	10			8	6			2		3	11	41
1			4	2		7	5	9	10			8	6					3	11	42
1	12		4			7	5	9	10*			8	6			2		3	11	43
1	7		4	2			5	9	10			8	6					3	11	44
1	8		4	2		7*	5	9	10			12	6					3	11	45
1	8		4	2		7	5		10	9			6					3	11	46
46	3	24	43	6	34	43	46	41	43	28	4	26	38	1	37	—	9	22	12	
		+2s				+1s	+2s		+6s	+1s	+2s				+1s	+4s				

GILLINGHAM—PLAYERS

Player and position	Ht	Wt	Birthplace	Clubs	League Appearances	Goals
Goalkeepers						
Ron Hillyard	5 10½	11 0	Rotherham	York C	61	—
				Hartlepool (on loan)	23	—
				Bury (on loan)	—	—
				Brighton (on loan)	—	—
				Gillingham	205	—
Steve Wheatley	5 10½	11 0	Durham	Gillingham	4	—
Defenders						
Graham Knight	5 11	11 9½	Gillingham	Gillingham	230+17	9
Gary Armstrong	5 8	10 7	London	Gillingham	81+4	2
Charles Young	6 1	11 6	Nicosia	Aston V	9+1	—
				Gillingham	17	1
Mickey Barker	5 11½	12 11	Durham	Newcastle U	21+2	—
				Gillingham	22	1
John Sharpe	5 11	11 5	Portsmouth	Southampton	21	—
				Gillingham	37	—
Midfield						
Mark Weatherley	5 11	11 8	Ramsgate	Gillingham	88+22	12
Billy Hughes	5 10	10 8	Folkestone	Gillingham	76+10	5
Terry Nicholl	5 9½	10 12	Wilmslow	Crewe Alex	46	7
				Sheffield U	12+10	1
				Southend U	50	3
				Gillingham	123	8
John Overton	5 11	10 10	Rotherham	Aston V	2+1	—
				Halifax T (on loan)	14	2
				Gillingham	111+1	7
Nigel Williams	5 11	11 2	Canterbury	Wolverhampton W	11	—
(Contract cancelled October 1978)				Gillingham	51+2	1
John Crabbe	5 8	10 6	Weymouth	Southampton	8+4	—
				Gillingham	99	9
Mike Buttress	6 0	11 11	Peterborough	Aston V	1+2	—
(Contract cancelled March 1979)				Gillingham	5+2	—
Peter Hobday				Gillingham	—	—
Colin Ford	5 7	10 10		Gillingham	—	—
Steve Bruce	6 0	11 2		Gillingham	—	—
Forwards						
Damien Richardson (Eire)	5 11½	12 0	Dublin	Gillingham	268	89
Danny Westwood	5 10	11 5	Dagenham	QPR	0+1	1
				Gillingham	153+3	57
Terry Jolley	5 11	10 4	London	Gillingham	10+4	5
Ken Price	5 10½	11 3	Wolverhampton	Southend U	1	—
				Gillingham	112+2	42
Pat Walker	5 8	10 10	Dublin	Gillingham	9+11	1
Tony Funnell	5 6½	10 10	Eastbourne	Southampton	13+4	8
				Gillingham	12	7
Dean White				Gillingham	26+1	3

GRIMSBY TOWN   DIV. 3

Chairman: H. C. Hamilton.
Vice-Chairman: R. K. Middleton.
Directors: J. Evans, M.B.E., T. Wilkinson, T. L. Lindley, M. McGarry, T. W. Bygott, A. W. Edwards, P. Sheffield.
Manager: John Newman,   *Secretary:* D. J. Dowse.
Year Formed: 1878.   *Turned Professional:* 1890.
Limited Company: 1890.   *Previous Name:* Grimsby Pelham.
Previous Grounds: Clee Park; Abbey Park.
Football League Record: 1892 Original Member Division 2. 1901–03 Division 1. 1903 Division 2. 1910 Failed Re-election. 1911 Re-elected Division 2. 1920–21 Division 3. 1921–26 Division 3(N). 1926–29 Division 2. 1929–32 Division 1. 1932–34 Division 2. 1934–48 Division 1. 1948–51 Division 2. 1951–56 Division 3(N). 1956–59 Division 2. 1959–62 Division 3. 1962–64 Division 2. 1964–68 Division 3. 1968–72 Division 4. 1972–77 Division 3. 1977–79 Division 4. 1979– Division 3.
Honours: Football League, highest position: Division 1, 5th, 1934–35. Division 2, Champions: 1900–01, 1933–34; Runners-up: 1928–29. Division 3(N), Champions: 1925–26, 1955–56; Runners-up: 1951–52. Division 3, Runners-up: 1961–62. Division 4, Champions: 1971–72; Runners-up 1978–79.
F.A. Cup, best season: Semi-finalists, 1936. 1939. *Football League Cup,* best season: 5th Rd. Replay, 1966.
Record Victory: 9-2 v Darwen, Division 2, Apr. 15th, 1899.
Record Defeat: 1-9 v Arsenal, Division 1, Jan. 28th, 1931.
Most League Points: 68, Division 3(N), 1955–56.
Most League Goals: 103, Division 2, 1933–34.
Most Capped Player: Pat Glover, 7, Wales.
Highest League Scorer in Season: Pat Glover, 42, Division 2, 1933–34.
Most League Goals in Total Aggregate: Pat Glover, 182, 1930–39.
Most League Appearances: Keith Jobling, 448, 1953–69.
Record Transfer Fee Received: £75,000 from Aston V. for Terry Donovan, July 1979.
Record Transfer Fee Paid: £20,000 Rotherham U. for Ron Wigg, January 1975.
Managers Since the War: Charlie Spencer, Bill Shankly, Billy Walsh, Allenby Chilton, Tim Ward, Tom Johnston, Jimmy McGuigan, Don McEvoy, Bill Harvey, Bobby Kennedy, Lawrie McMenemy, Ron Ashman, Tommy Casey.
Address of Club Shop: Junior Club Souvenir Shop, Blundell Park, Cleethorpes.

Blundell Park, Cleethorpes, South Humberside DN35 7PY. Telephone Cleethorpes 61420 and 61803. *Telegraphic address:* 'Football Grimsby'. *Ground capacity:* 24,000. *Record attendance:* 31,657 v Wolverhampton W., F.A. Cup, February 20, 1937. *Record Receipts:* £13,490 v Southampton, F.A. Cup, 3rd Rd., January 7, 1978. *Pitch measurements:* 111yds × 74 yds.
How to get there: Buses 3A, 3F, 9 run to the ground; also football specials from the town centre Nearest railway stations are Cleethorpes and Grimsby Town.
Match tickets: Seating can be booked one month in advance.
Car parking: Parking permitted in all side streets around the ground.
Entertainments/catering facilities: A licensed bar and several snack bars.
Club shop: There are 3 club shops, run by the Grimsby Town Junior Club, selling all types of souvenirs.
Handbooks/programmes: Programmes on sale at matches.
Extra information: Grimsby have played in all six divisions of the Football League—First, Second, Third, Third South, Third North and Fourth.
Club Colours: Black and white striped shirts, black shorts, red stockings.
Change Colour: Red shirts, red shorts and white stockings.
Club Captain: Joe Waters.
Coach: George Kerr.
Club Nickname: 'The Mariners'.

GRIMSBY TOWN 1978-79 LEAGUE RECORD

Match No.	Date	Venue	Opponents	Result	H/T Score	League Pos'n	Goalscorers	Attendance
1	Aug 19	H	Reading	L 1-2	0-2	—	Lester	3918
2	23	A	Wigan Ath	W 3-0	2-0	—	Donovan 2, Moore K	9227
3	26	A	Halifax T	W 2-1	1-1	6	Donovan, Ford	2055
4	Sept 2	H	Torquay U	W 3-0	1-0	4	Darke (og), Brolly, Mawer	3934
5	9	A	Darlington	W 1-0	1-0	4	Brolly	2220
6	12	H	Wimbledon	D 2-2	0-0	—	Waters (pen), Bryant (og)	6794
7	16	H	Hartlepool U	L 0-1	0-0	6		4729
8	23	A	Crewe Alex	W 3-0	2-0	4	Moore K, Liddell 2	2000
9	26	A	Huddersfield T	L 0-2	0-0	—		4238
10	30	H	Rochdale	W 4-0	2-0	4	Brolly 2, Liddell 2	3681
11	Oct 7	A	Port Vale	D 1-1	1-1	4	Liddell	3433
12	14	H	Portsmouth	W 1-0	0-0	4	Moore K	5141
13	17	H	Northampton T	W 4-3	2-2	—	Drinkell 2, Brolly, Young	5529
14	21	A	AFC Bournemouth	D 0-0	0-0	3		3399
15	28	H	Hereford U	D 1-1	0-1	3	Drinkell	5349
16	Nov 4	A	Aldershot	L 0-2	0-1	4		3536
17	11	A	Torquay U	L 1-3	0-1	5	Drinkell	3189
18	18	H	Halifax T	W 2-1	0-1	5	Cumming, Moore K	4128
19	Dec 4	A	Stockport Co	L 1-2	1-1	—	Moore K	3300
20	9	H	Newport Co	W 1-0	1-0	6	Barker	3667
21	23	H	York C	W 3-0	1-0	6	Cumming 3 (1 pen)	4339
22	26	A	Scunthorpe U	L 1-2	1-1	—	Kavanagh (og)	8008
23	Jan 9	A	Bradford C	W 5-1	2-0	—	Ford 3, Cumming, Mitchell	4975
24	16	H	Darlington	W 7-2	6-0	—	Lester 4, Ford, Waters, Moore K	5378
25	20	A	Hartlepool U	L 0-1	0-1	4		2212
26	Feb 3	H	Huddersfield T	W 2-1	1-1	3	Waters, Ford	4919
27	24	A	Portsmouth	W 3-1	2-0	5	Ford 2, Brolly	12,782
28	27	H	Crewe Alex	D 2-2	1-2	—	Ford, Cumming	6854
29	Mar 3	H	AFC Bournemouth	W 1-0	1-0	4	Waters	5428
30	10	A	Hereford U	W 1-0	1-0	4	Price (og)	2939
31	13	A	Rochdale	W 5-2	2-2	—	Ford, Brolly, Liddell, Waters (pen), Mitchell	2345
32	17	H	Aldershot	D 0-0	0-0	3		6121
33	20	H	Wimbledon	W 1-0	1-0	—	Waters	2392
34	24	H	Wigan Ath	W 3-1	2-0	1	Waters, Brolly, Ford	8252
35	28	A	Reading	L 0-4	0-2	—		8394
36	31	A	Doncaster R	W 1-0	0-0	2	Ford	4707
37	Apr 3	H	Port Vale	W 1-0	0-0	—	Brolly	7815
38	7	H	Stockport Co	W 2-1	2-1	1	Cumming, Ford	7495
39	13	A	York C	D 0-0	0-0	—		5401
40	14	H	Scunthorpe U	D 1-1	1-1	2	Drinkell	10,197
41	16	A	Bradford C	W 3-1	2-0	—	Waters, Ford, Drinkell	4585
42	21	H	Barnsley	W 2-0	1-0	1	Crombie, Lester	15,875
43	24	H	Northampton T	W 2-1	0-0	—	Cumming, Waters	3019
44	28	A	Newport Co	D 1-1	1-0	2	Waters	3049
45	May 5	H	Doncaster R	L 3-4	2-2	2	Drinkell, Ford, Cumming	10,157
46	8	A	Barnsley	L 1-2	0-0	—	Lester	21,261

Final League Position: 2

Goalscorers
League (82): Ford 15, Waters 10 (2 pens), Brolly 9, Cumming 9 (1 a pen), Drinkell 7, Lester 7, Liddle 6 Moore K 6, Donovan 3, Mitchell 2, Barker 1, Crombie 1, Mawer 1, Young 1, own goals 4.
League Cup (5): Waters (pen), Lester, Cumming, Mitchell, Donovan.

League Cup	First Round	York C (h)	2-0
		(a)	3-0
	Second Round	Manchester C (a)	0-2
F.A. Cup	First Round	Hartlepool (a)	0-1

Batch	Mawer	Moore, K	Waters	Barker	Crombie	Ford	Donovan	Lester	Mitchell	Cumming	Liddell	Brolly	Young	Partridge	Drinkell	Moore, D	Wiggington	Match No.
1	2	3	4	5	6	7	8	9	10*	11	12							1
1	2	3	4	5	6	7	8	9	10	11*	12							2
1	2	3	4	5	6	7	8	9	10		11							3
1	2	3	4	5	6	7	8	9		10*	12	11						4
1	2	3	4	5	6	7		9			8	11	10					5
1	2	3	4	5	6	7*		9			8	11	10	12				6
1		3	2	5	6	7		9*10			8	11	4	12				7
1	2	3	4	5	6	7					8	11		10	9			8
1	2	3	4	5	6	7					8	11		10	9			9
1	2	3	4	5	6	7					9	11	12	8*10				10
1	2	3	4	5	6	7					9	11		8	10			11
1	2	3	4	5	6	7					9	11	12	8*10				12
1	2	3	4	5	6	7					8	11	10	9				13
1	2	3	4	5	6	7			12		8	11	9*	10				14
1	2	3	4	5	6*	7			12		8	11	9	10				15
1	2	3	4	5	6	7			12		8*11	10		9				16
1		3	4	5	6			11	10		7		8	9	2			17
1		3	4	5	6	12		9	10		11		7*	8	2			18
1		3	4	5	6	12	8	10	11		7		9*	2				19
1		3	4	5	6	7	9	8	10		11				2			20
1		3	4	5	6	7	8	9	10		11				2			21
1		3	4	5	6	7	8	9	10		11*		12		2			22
1		3	4	5	6	7	8	9	10		11				2			23
1		3	4	5	6	7	8	9	10		11				2			24
1		3	4	5	6	7	8	9	10*		11		12		2			25
1		3	4	5	6	7	8	9	10		11				2			26
1		3	4	5	6	7	8	9	10		11				2			27
1		3	4	5	6	7	9*10	11			8		12		2			28
1		3	4		6	7	9	8	10		11*		12		2	5		29
1		3	4		6	7		9	10		11		8		2	5		30
1		3	4		6	8			10	11	9	7			2	5		31
1		3	4		6	7			10	8	9	11			2	5		32
1		3	4		6	7			10	9	8	11			2	5		33
1		3	4		6	8	9	10		11	7				2	5		34
1		3	4		6	8	11	10*		9	7		12		2	5		35
1		3	4		6	8	10		11	9*	7		12		2	5		36
1		3	4		6	8	10		11	9	7				2	5		37
1		3	4		6	8	9		11	10*	7		12		2	5		38
1		3	4		6	8	10		11	9	7				2	5		39
1		3*	4		6	8	12	10	11		7		9		2	5		40
1		3	4		6	8	10*		11	12	7		9		2	5		41
1		3	4		6	8	9		11		7		10		2	5		42
1		3	4		6	8	10		11		7		9		2	5		43
1		3	4		6	8	10		11		7		9		2	5		44
1		3	4		6	8	10		11		7		9		2	5		45
1		3	4		6	8	10		11	12	7		9*		2	5		46
46	15	46	46	28	46	43	4	30	24	31	21	44	7	7	20	30	18	
							+2s	+1s		+3s	+5s		+2s	+1s	+8s			

GRIMSBY TOWN—PLAYERS

Player and position	Ht	Wt	Birthplace	Clubs	League Appearances	Goals
Goalkeepers						
Harry Wainman	6 0	13 6	Hull	Grimsby T	420	—
				Rochdale (on loan)	9	—
Nigel Batch	5 10	12 5	Huddersfield	Grimsby T	64	—
Defenders						
*David Booth	5 10	12 0	Darton	Barnsley	162+3	8
				Grimsby T	199+1	7
Kevin Moore	5 11	11 7	Grimsby	Grimsby T	114+2	6
Martin Young	5 11½	12 10	Grimsby	Grimsby T	87+6	4
David Moore	5 10	12 13	Grimsby	Grimsby T	30	—
*Geoffrey Barker	6 1	13 1	Hull	Hull C	29+1	2
				Southend U (on loan)	25	—
				Darlington	151	6
				Reading	51+1	2
				Grimsby T	66	1
Shaun Mawer	5 7	10 8	Ulceby	Grimsby T	57	1
Clive Wigginton	6 0	12 1	Sheffield	Grimsby T	163+8	6
				Scunthorpe U	88	7
				Lincoln C	60	6
				Grimsby T	18	—
Dean Crombie	5 11	11 7	Lincoln	Lincoln C	33	—
				Grimsby T	46	1
*Steven Graves	5 8	10 10	Grimsby	Grimsby T	—	—
Midfield						
Robert Cumming	5 8	11 4	Airdrie	Grimsby T	127+12	14
Joe Waters (Eire)	5 5	10 5	Limerick	Leicester C	11+2	1
				Grimsby T	156	26
Mike Lester	5 10	11 5	Manchester	Oldham Ath	26+1	1
				Manchester C	1+1	—
				Stockport Co (on loan)	8+1	1
				Washington D	(not known)	
				Grimsby T	45+1	10
Bob Mitchell	5 10	11 0	S Shields	Sunderland	1+2	—
				Blackburn R	17+12	6
				Grimsby T	24	2
Forwards						
Tony Ford	5 9	12 2	Grimsby	Grimsby T	87+12	17
*Malcolm Partridge	6 0½	12 3	Calow	Mansfield T	66+3	20
				Leicester C	24+11	4
				Charlton Ath (on loan)	1+1	—
				Grimsby T	134+4	24
Terry Donovan	5 10	10 6	Liverpool	Grimsby T	52+12	23
Mike Brolly	5 9	10 4	Kilmarnock	Chelsea	7+1	1
				Bristol C	27+3	2
				Grimsby T	130+1	16
Gary Liddell	5 9¼	11 2	Bannockburn	Leeds U	2+1	—
				Grimsby T	72+6	22
Kevin Drinkell	5 10	11 10	Grimsby	Grimsby T	43+15	14
Peter Wainwright	6 0	12 0	Brigg, Lincs	Grimsby T	—	—

HALIFAX TOWN DIV. 4

Chairman: A. Delaney.
Directors: A. W. Mitchell, J. Turner, J. S. Crowther, R. L. Manson.
Manager: George Kirby.
Secretary/Gen. Manager: D. Holland.
Year Formed: 1911.   *Turned Professional:* 1911.
Limited Company: 1911.
Previous Grounds: Sandhall and Exley.
Football League Record:
   1921 Original Member   1963–69 Division 4.
   Division 3(N).   1969–76 Division 3.
   1958–63 Division 3.   1976—   Division 4.

Honours: *Football League*, highest position in Division 3: 3rd 1970–71. Division 3(N), Runners-up: 1934–35. Division 4, Runners-up: 1968–69. *F.A. Cup*, best season: 5th Rd., 1932-33, 1952–53. *Football League Cup*, best season: 4th Rd., 1964.
Record Victory: 7-0 v Bishop Auckland, F.A. Cup 2nd Rd. Replay, Jan. 10th, 1967.
Record Defeat: 0-13 v Stockport Co., Division 3(N), Jan. 6th, 1934.
Most League Points: 57, Division 4, 1968–69.
Most League Goals: 83, Division 3(N), 1957–58.
Most Capped Player: None.
Most League Appearances: John Pickering, 367, 1965–74.
Highest League Scorer in Season: Albert Valentine, 34 Division 3(N), 1934–35.
Most League Goals in Total Aggregate: Ernest Dixon, 129, 1922–30.
Record Transfer Fee Received: £40,000 from Liverpool for Alan Waddle, June, 1973.
Record Transfer Fee Paid: £13,500 to Blackpool for Fred Kemp, Dec. 1971.
Managers Since the War: Jack Breedon, W. Wootton, Jimmy Thomson, Gerald Henry, Bobby Browne, Willie Watson, Billy Burnicle, Harry Hooper, Willie Watson, Vic Metcalfe, Alan Ball, George Kirby, Ray Henderson, George Mulhall, John Quinn, Alan Ball, Jimmy Lawson.
Address of Supporters Club: Same as Football Club.
Address of Club Shop or Boutique: Club Shop, 11 Horton Street, Halifax, Yorks.

Shay Ground, Halifax HX1 2YS. Telephone Halifax 53423. *Ground capacity:* 23,000. *Record attendance:* 36,885 v Tottenham H., F.A. Cup 5th Rd., February 14, 1953. *Record receipts:* £4,898 v Tottenham H., F.A. Cup 5th Rd., February 14, 1953. *Pitch measurements:* 110 yds × 70 yds.

How to get there: Near the town centre within a few minutes walking distance of the bus station and railway station.
Match tickets: Advance booking on application to the secretary.
Car parking: Car park is available; entrance in Shaw Hill.
Entertainments/catering facilities: Social club adjacent to the club office. Catering facilities at points inside the ground.
Club shop: Sells all types of souvenirs.
Handbooks/programmes: Handbooks and programmes available from Supporters Club, c/o Halifax Town A.F.C.
Extra information: In 1929, Halifax played a goalkeeper, Bob Suter, who was 47 years old!

Club Colours: Royal blue shirts with white trim, collar and cuffs, white shorts, blue trim, blue stockings with white tops.
Change Colours: Emerald green and yellow vertical striped shirts, emerald green shorts, yellow stockings.
Team Captain:
Coach: Mick Bullock.
Club Nickname: 'Town'.

HALIFAX TOWN 1978–79 LEAGUE RECORD

Match No.	Date	Venue	Opponents	Result	H/T Score	League Pos'n	Goalscorers	Attendance
1	Aug 19	A	Barnsley	L 2-4	0-1	—	Burke, Bell	5634
2	22	H	Stockport Co	W 2-1	0-1	—	Bell, Bullock	2253
3	26	H	Grimsby T	L 1-2	1-1	17	Bullock	2055
4	Sept 2	A	Aldershot	L 0-1	0-0	19		2884
5	9	A	Torquay U	L 0-2	0-1	22		2048
6	12	H	York C	L 0-1	0-1	—		1701
7	16	H	Darlington	L 0-2	0-0	23		1203
8	23	A	Hartlepool U	L 1-3	0-0	23	Lawson	3947
9	27	A	Bradford C	L 0-3	0-0	—		4115
10	30	H	Crewe Alex	D 0-0	0-0	23		985
11	Oct 7	A	Rochdale	D 1-1	1-0	23	Bell	1579
12	14	H	Port Vale	L 0-3	0-1	24		1591
13	18	A	Wigan Ath	L 0-1	0-1	—		5216
14	21	A	Portsmouth	L 1-3	0-1	24	Firth	12,365
15	28	H	AFC Bournemouth	L 0-2	0-1	24		1184
16	Nov 4	A	Hereford U	D 2-2	2-1	24	Mountford, Dunleavy	3616
17	11	H	Aldershot	D 1-1	1-1	24	Mountford	1438
18	18	A	Grimsby T	L 1-2	1-0	24	Prendergast	4128
19	Dec 2	A	Wimbledon	L 1-2	0-1	24	Campbell	2374
20	9	H	Reading	D 0-0	0-0	24		1401
21	16	H	Wigan Ath	L 1-2	0-2	24	Carroll	2437
22	26	A	Huddersfield T	L 0-2	0-1	—		5341
23	30	A	Northampton T	L 1-2	1-1	24	Nixon	2208
24	Feb 10	A	Crewe Alex	L 0-1	0-1	24		1594
25	24	A	Port Vale	W 1-0	1-0	24	Bentley (og)	3117
26	27	A	Darlington	L 1-2	0-1	—	Mountford	1403
27	Mar 3	H	Portsmouth	W 2-0	2-0	24	Ellis (og), Johnson	1741
28	6	H	Doncaster R	D 0-0	0-0	—		1658
29	10	A	AFC Bournemouth	L 0-1	0-0	24		3078
30	13	A	York C	L 0-2	0-1	—		2196
31	23	A	Stockport Co	W 2-1	0-1	24	Johnson, Campbell	3033
32	27	H	Barnsley	L 0-2	0-0	—		5654
33	31	A	Newport Co	L 0-2	0-1	24		3927
34	Apr 3	H	Torquay U	W 1-0	0-0	—	Trainer	1112
35	7	H	Wimbledon	W 2-1	2-1	24	Trainer, Johnson	1576
36	14	H	Huddersfield T	L 2-3	2-1	24	Mountford, Sidebottom	4027
37	16	A	Scunthorpe U	L 0-1	0-0	—		1624
38	17	A	Doncaster R	D 1-1	1-1	—	Sidebottom	2227
39	21	H	Northampton T	D 2-2	1-2	24	Geidmintis (og), Johnson	1172
40	26	H	Bradford C	W 2-0	2-0	—	Campbell, Dunleavy	2343
41	28	A	Reading	L 0-1	0-1	24		7408
42	May 5	H	Newport Co	L 1-2	0-1	24	Burke	1007
43	7	H	Rochdale	W 2-1	2-0	—	Johnson (pen), Bradley	2150
44	9	H	Hereford U	W 1-0	0-0	—	Johnson	1036
45	14	H	Hartlepool U	L 2-4	1-3	—	Firth, Johnson (pen)	1012
46	18	H	Scunthorpe U	L 2-3	0-1	—	Bradley 2	1037

Final League Position: 23

Goalscorers

League (39): Johnson 7 (2 pens), Mountford 4, Bell 3, Bradley 3, Campbell 3, Bullock 2, Burke 2, Dunleavy 2, Firth 2, Sidebottom 2, Trainer 2, Carroll 1, Lawson 1, Nixon 1, Prendergast 1, Own Goals 3.
League Cup (1): Bullock.

League Cup	First Round	Walsall (a)	1-2
		(h)	0-2
F.A. Cup	First Round	Carlisle U (a)	0-1

Leonard	Trainer	Loska	Smith	Burke	Dunleavy	Nixon	Johnston	Bullock	Lawson	Bell	Hutt	Firth	Mountford	Bradley	Johnson	Carroll	Kennedy	Prendergast	Campbell	Sidebottom	Stafford	Kilner	Match No.
1	2	3	4	5	6	7	8	9	10	11													1
1	2	3	4	5	6	7	8	9	10	11													2
1	2		4	5	6	7	8	9	10	11	3												3
1	2		4	5	6	7		9	10	11	3			8									4
1	2		4	5	6			9	8	11	3	7		10									5
1	2		4	5	6		12	10	11*	3	7	9		8									6
1		3		5	6	11	4	9*			7	10	2	8	12								7
1	5	3			6			9	10	11		4	2	8	7								8
1	4	3			6		11*	9	10			7	2	5	8	12							9
1	4	3		5				10	11			7	9	2	6	8							10
1		3	12	5	6			10	11			7	9*	2	4	8							11
1		3	4	5	6				11*			7	9	2	8	12	10						12
1		3	4	5	6		9	10		2	7			11	8								13
1	2	3	4	5	6		9	10*11		12				8	7								14
1	5	3	4		6	12				2	7		8*			9	10	11					15
1		3	4*	5	6					2	12	7	8			10	9	11					16
1		3	4	5	6	12				2		8	11		7	9	10*						17
1		6	4	5	2	12				3		7	8		10	9	11*						18
1		3	4	5*	6	7				2		8	11		12	9	10						19
1		3	4		6	7				2		8	11		10	9	5						20
1		3	4		6	7				2		8	11	12	10	9*	5						21
1	11		4		6	7				3		9*	2		8	10	12	5					22
1	11		4		6	7				3		12	2			10	9	5	8*				23
1	10		4	5	3						7	9	2	12	8			6	11*				24
1	11		4	6	3						7	9*	2	10	8		12	5					25
			10	4	6	3					7	9	2	11	8		12	5*		1			26
	3	10	4	5	6						7	9	2	11	8					1			27
	5	10	4	6	3						7	9	2	11	8					1			28
	5	10*	4	6	3					12	7	9	2	11	8					1			29
	5	12	4	6	3	9				2	7		11*10		8					1			30
	5	11	4		3	12				2	7		10*		8		9	6		1			31
	5	11*	4		3	12				2	7		10		8		9	6		1			32
	5	11	4		3					2	7		10		8		9	6		1			33
	5	11	4		3					2	7	12	10		8		9*	6		1			34
	5	11	4		3	12				2	7	9	10*		8			6		1			35
	5	11	4		3	12				2	7	9	10*		8			6		1			36
		11	4	5	3	10				2	7	9*		12	8			6		1			37
	6		4	5	2					3	7		11		8		9	10		1			38
	6		4	5	2	12				3	7		10		8		9	11*		1			39
	6	11	4	5	3					2	7			10	8		9			1			40
	6	10*	4	5	3					2	7			11	8		9	12		1			41
	6		4*	5	2					3	7	12	11		8		9	10		1			42
	6			5	3					2	7		4	10	8		9	11		1			43
	6*			5	3					2	7	12	4	10	8		9	11		1			44
	6	12	5*	2						3	7	9	4	10	8			11		1			45
	5		4		3	12				2	7	9	6	10	8			11*		1			46
25	30	34	38	31	46	12	5	10	12	11	31	33	23	19	37	9	28	4	19	21	7	21	
	+ 1s	+ 2s				+ 7s	+ 2s	+ 1s			+ 1s	+ 2s	+ 3s	+ 1s	+ 2s	+ 3s	+ 2s		+ 3s	+ 1s			

HALIFAX TOWN—PLAYERS

Player and position	Ht	Wt	Birthplace	Clubs	League Appearances	Goals
Goalkeeper						
Mick Leonard	5 11	11 0	Carshalton	Halifax T	64	—
Defenders						
Chris Dunleavy	5 10	11 6	Liverpool	Everton	—	—
				Southport	145+2	9
				Chester	74+2	—
				Halifax T	118	8
*Tony Loska	5 8	11 0	Stoke	Shrewsbury T	12	—
				Port Vale	74+6	5
				Chester	103+7	5
				Halifax T	101+1	—
Peter Burke	6 0	11 10	Rotherham	Barnsley	36	1
				Halifax T	44	3
Geoff Hutt	5 8	12 0	Hazelwood	Huddersfield T	245	4
				Blackburn R (on loan)	10	1
				Haarlem (Holland)	(not known)	
				York C	63	1
				Halifax T	31+1	—
*Jack Trainer	6 2½	12 5	Glasgow	Cork Hibs	—	—
				Halifax T	101+4	5
Midfield						
*John Johnson	5 8	10 4	Belfast	Blackpool	19+5	2
				Halifax T (loan)	3+1	1
				Bradford C	55+4	4
				Southport	82	6
				Halifax T	67+6	7
*Jimmy Lawson	5 8	10 10	Middlesbrough	Middlesbrough	20+6	3
				Huddersfield	236+10	42
				Halifax T	93	9
Steve Smith	5 9	10 3	Huddersfield	Huddersfield T	330+9	34
				Bolton W (on loan)	3	—
				Sheffield W	—	—
				Halifax T	78+3	4
Franny Firth	5 10	11 0	Dewsbury	Huddersfield T	26+1	4
				Halifax T	50+2	3
Mick Kennedy	5 10	10 5	Salford	Halifax T	28+2	—
Kevin Johnson	5 6	9 9½	Doncaster	Sheffield W	0+1	—
				Southend U	13+4	1
				Gillingham (on loan)	1	—
				Workington	15	1
				Hartlepool U	60+1	9
				Huddersfield T	80+1	23
				Halifax T	37+2	7
Arnie Sidebottom	6 1	12 1	Barnsley	Manchester U	16	—
(Contract cancelled May 1979)				Huddersfield T	56+5	5
				Halifax T	21	2
Forwards						
*Lee Bradley	5 11	11 5	Manchester	Stockport Co	39+1	4
				Halifax T	62+10	4
Micky Bullock	5 10¾	12 0	Stoke	Birmingham C	27	10
				Oxford U	58+1	15
				Orient	267+10	64
				Halifax T	98+8	19
Bob Mountford	5 11	10 10	Stoke	Port Vale	64+13	9
				Scunthorpe U (on loan)	1+2	—
				Crewe A (on loan)	5	—
				Rochdale	97+1	37
				Huddersfield T	12+2	4
				Halifax T	33+3	7
*Joe Carroll	5 9	10 7	Radcliffe	Oldham Ath	3+1	—
				Halifax T	76+6	14
*Jon Nixon	5 6	10 0	Preston	Notts Co	167+12	32
				Peterborough U	104+6	16
				Shrewsbury T	21+2	3
				Barnsley	6+4	—
				Halifax T	12+7	1
Bobby Campbell	5 11	12 7	Belfast	Aston V	7+3	1
(Contract cancelled May 1979)				Halifax T (on loan)	14+1	—
				Huddersfield T	30+1	9
				Sheffield U	35+2	11
				Huddersfield T	7	3
				Halifax T	19+3	3
Andy Stafford		11 12	Littleborough	Halifax T	7+1	—

HARTLEPOOL UNITED   DIV. 4

President: S. Spaldin.
Chairman: J. V. Barker.
Vice-Chairman: B. H. Crosby.
Directors: N. S. Armstrong, J. O. Curry, S. I. Levinson, C. Thomas.
Manager: Billy Horner.   *Secretary:* W. P. Hillan.
Year Formed: 1908.   *Turned Professional:* 1908.
Limited Company: 1908.
Previous Name: Hartlepools United until 1968. Revived 1977.

Football League Record:
    1921 Original Member of Division 3(N).   1968–69 Division 3.
    1958–68 Division 4.   1969– Division 4.
    Hartlepool until 1977.

Honours: Football League, highest position in Division 3: 22nd, 1968–69. Division 3(N) Runners-up: 1956–57.

F.A. Cup, best seasons 4th Rd. 1954–55, 1977–78. *F.L. Cup,* best season: 4th Rd. 1974–75.
Record Victory: 10-1 v Barrow, Division 4, Apr. 4th, 1959.
Record Defeat: 1-10 v Wrexham, Division 4, Mar. 3rd, 1962.
Most League Points: 60, Division 4, 1967–68.
Most League Goals: 90, Division 3(N), 1956–57.
Highest League Scorer in Season: William Robinson, 28, Division 3(N), 1927–28.
Most League Goals in Total Aggregate: Ken Johnson, 98, 1949–64.
Most Capped Player: Ambrose Fogarty, 1 (11), Eire.
Most League Appearances: Wattie Moore, 448, 1948–64.
Record Transfer Fee Received: £60,000 from Brighton for Malcolm Poskett, Feb. 1978.
Record Transfer Fee Paid: £10,000 to Sunderland for Ambrose Fogarty, Nov. 1963.
Managers Since the War: Fred Westgarth, Ray Middleton, Bill Robinson, Allenby Chilton, Bob Gurney, Alvan Williams, Geoff Twentyman, Brian Clough, Angus McLean, John Simpson, Len Ashurst, Ken Hale.
Club Shop: On ground.

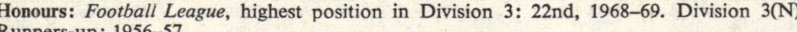

The Victoria Ground. Telephone Hartlepool 72584. 18 Scarborough Street, Hartlepool. Telephone 73492 (Office).   *Ground capacity:* 16,000.   *Record attendance:* 17,426 v Manchester U., F.A. Cup 3rd Rd., January 5, 1957.   *Record receipts:* £17,000 v Leeds U., F.A. Cup January 18, 1979.   *Pitch measurements:* 113 yds × 77 yds.

How to get there: Hartlepool railway station is only a few hundred yards from the ground. Local bus services run scheduled services to Hartlepool.
Match tickets: No pre-booking of tickets.
Car parking: Ample side-street parking.
Entertainments/catering facilities: Two refreshment kiosks inside the ground.
Club shop: Open on match days; stocks all types of souvenirs.
Handbooks/programmes: No handbooks. Programmes available on subscription.
Extra information: Just three years after finishing second in Division III(N) in 1956–57, the club conceded a Fourth Division record 109 goals.

Club Colours: Blue shirts, white shorts, blue stockings.
Change Colours: All red with white stripe on shirt and emblem, red shorts and stockings.
Club Nickname: 'The Pool'.

HARTLEPOOL UNITED 1978-79 LEAGUE RECORD

Match No.	Date	Venue	Opponents	Result	H/T Score	League Pos'n	Goalscorers	Attendance
1	Aug 19	H	Doncaster R	L 3-4	3-1	—	Linacre, Newton, Crumplin	2364
2	23	A	Northampton T	D 1-1	1-1	—	Newton	4288
3	25	H	Portsmouth	D 1-1	1-0	16	Crumplin	3074
4	Sept 2	A	AFC Bournemouth	W 1-0	1-0	12	Newton (pen)	2658
5	9	H	Hereford U	W 2-1	1-0	8	Linacre, Hogan	2995
6	11	A	Stockport Co	L 0-4	0-2	—		4249
7	16	A	Grimsby T	W 1-0	0-0	11	Goldthorpe	4729
8	23	H	Halifax T	W 3-1	0-0	7	Houchen, Newton (pen), Goldthorpe	3947
9	25	H	Newport Co	D 0-0	0-0	—		5491
10	30	A	Torquay U	L 1-4	0-2	12	Houchen	3033
11	Oct 7	H	Darlington	L 0-2	0-1	13		4853
12	14	A	Aldershot	D 1-1	0-0	12	Brooks	2968
13	17	H	Scunthorpe U	D 1-1	1-1	—	Lawrence	2980
14	21	A	Crewe Alex	W 1-0	0-0	10	Smith T	2023
15	28	H	Rochdale	W 5-1	2-0	9	Ayre, Goldthorpe 2, Lawrence, Houchen	3074
16	Nov 4	A	Port Vale	L 0-2	0-1	12		3195
17	11	H	AFC Bournemouth	D 0-0	0-0	9		3227
18	18	A	Portsmouth	L 0-3	0-0	14		10,717
19	Dec 9	H	Wimbledon	D 1-1	0-1	13	Ayre	3098
20	23	A	Barnsley	D 1-1	1-0	15	Goldthorpe	5914
21	26	A	York C	D 1-1	0-0	—	Crumplin	3825
22	Jan 20	H	Grimsby T	W 1-0	1-0	11	Newton (pen)	2212
23	Feb 2	A	Newport Co	L 2-3	1-2	13	Newton (pen), Linacre	3659
24	10	H	Torquay U	W 3-2	1-2	13	Newton 2, Houchen	2376
25	24	H	Aldershot	D 2-2	1-2	12	Ayre, Houchen	2863
26	26	A	Reading	L 1-3	0-2	—	Houchen	6812
27	Mar 3	H	Crewe Alex	D 2-2	1-1	14	Houchen, Crumplin	2427
28	7	A	Hereford U	L 0-1	0-0	—		2119
29	10	A	Rochdale	D 1-1	1-0	16	Crumplin	1931
30	13	H	Stockport Co	L 1-3	0-0	—	Linacre	2403
31	23	A	Doncaster R	D 0-0	0-0	16		2552
32	31	A	Huddersfield T	L 0-2	0-1	19		2420
33	Apr 3	H	Wigan Ath	D 1-1	0-1	—	Smart (og)	2081
34	7	H	Bradford C	D 2-2	1-0	17	Lawrence, Houchen	2143
35	12	A	Barnsley	L 0-1	0-1	—		11,398
36	14	H	York C	D 1-1	1-0	18	Houchen	2343
37	16	A	Wigan Ath	D 2-2	1-0	—	Goldthorpe (pen), Linacre	8217
38	21	H	Reading	D 0-0	0-0	19		2499
39	24	A	Scunthorpe U	L 1-3	0-1	—	Houchen	1226
40	28	A	Wimbledon	L 1-3	0-0	20	Houchen	3546
41	May 2	A	Bradford C	W 2-1	2-1	—	Ayre, Harding	1950
42	5	H	Huddersfield T	W 2-0	1-0	19	Robins (og), Norton	2207
43	7	A	Darlington	W 1-0	0-0	—	Lawrence	3513
44	10	H	Port Vale	L 1-2	0-1	—	Houchen	1996
45	14	A	Halifax T	W 4-2	3-1	—	Lawrence 4	1012
46	17	H	Northampton T	W 2-0	0-0	—	Lawrence, Ayre	1753

Final League Position: 13

Goalscorers

League (57): Houchen 12, Lawrence 9, Newton 8 (4 pens), Goldthorpe 6 (1 pen), Ayre 5, Crumplin 5, Linacre 5, Brooks 1, Harding 1, Hogan 1, Norton 1, Smith T 1, Own Goals 2.
League Cup (1): Newton.
F.A. Cup (4): Newton 2 (2 pens), Goldthorpe, Crumplin.

League Cup	First Round	Rotherham U (a)	0-5
		(h)	1-1
F.A. Cup	First Round	Grimsby T (h)	1-0
	Second Round	Crewe Alex (a)	1-0
	Third Round	Leeds U (h)	2-6

Richardson	Malone	Gorry	Smith, G	Brooks	Ayre	Linacre	Houchen	Newton	Crumplin	Guy	Larkin	Platt	Smith, T	Lawrence	Goldthorpe	Hogan	Loadwick	Edgar	Norton	Harding	Watson	Evans	Match No.
1	2*	3	4	5	6	7	8	9	10	11	12												1
		3	4	5	6	7		9	10*	11		1	2	8	12								2
		3	4*	5	6	7	8	9	10	11		1	2		12								3
		3		5	6	7		9	8	11*		1	2	10	12	4							4
	2		3	5	6	7		9	10	11		1		8	4								5
	2	3	4	5	6	7		9	10	11*		1			12	8							6
		3	2	5	6	7	9	10		12		1		8	11	4*							7
		3	2	5	6	7	10*	9	12			1		8	11	4							8
		3	2	5	6	7	10*	9	12			1		11	8	4							9
		3	2	5	6	7	10	9		12		1		11	8	4*							10
		3	2	5	6	7	9		10	11		1		4	8								11
		3	2	5	6	7	9		10			1		4	11	8							12
			2	5	6	7	11	9	10	12		1	3	4	8*								13
			2	5	6	7	10*	9	12			1	3	4	8		11						14
			2	5	6	7	11	9					3	4	10	8		1					15
			2	5	6	7	10	9					3	4	8		11	1					16
1		3	2	5	6	7	10	9						4	8		11						17
1		3	2	5	6	7*	10	9						4	8		11	12					18
1		3	2	5	6	7	10		9					4	8		11						19
1		3	2	5	6	7		10	9					4	8		11						20
1		3	2	5	6	7		10	9					4	8		11						21
1		3	2			7	12	10	9			5		8*	4	11		6					22
1		3	2	5			7		10	9		6		8	4*	11	12						23
1		3	2	5			7	8	10	9		6			4	11							24
1		3	2	5	6	7	8	10	9						4	11							25
1		3	2	5	6	7	8	10	9*				12		4	11							26
		3		5	6	7	8		9			2	4	10		11	1						27
1		3	2	5	6	7	10		9					4	8		11						28
1		3	2	5*	6	7	8		9			12	4	10		11							29
1		3	2		6	7	10		9			5	4	8*12	11								30
1		3	2		6	7	8		9			5	4		11			10					31
1		3	2			7	10		9				4	5	8		6	11					32
1		3	2		6	7	8		9	10*			12	5		11		4					33
1		3	2*		6	7	8		9			12	10	5		11		4					34
		3	2		6	7	8						9	5	4	12		11*10	1				35
		3	2		6	7	8		12				9	5		11		4*10	1				36
		3	2		6	7	8						9*	5	11			4	10	1	12		37
		3	2		6	7*	8						9	5	11			4	10	1	12		38
		3	2		6		8			12			7	5	11			4*10	1	9			39
		3	4*		6	7	9					2	12	5	8	11			10	1			40
		3	8	5	6	7	9					2	12	4		11			10*	1			41
		3	4*	5	6	7	9						8	2	12	11		10		1			42
		3	4	5	6	7	9						8	2		11		10		1			43
		3	4	5	6	7	9						8	2	12	11*		10		1			44
		3	4	5	6	7	9						8	2		11		10		1			45
		3		5	6	7	9						8	2	4	11		12	10*	1			46
18	3	41	43	34	42	45	38	23	25	7	1	13	15	34	37	20	28	3	8	15	12	1	
						+1s		+4s	+3s	+2s			+2s	+4s	+4s	+3s	+1s		+3s		+2s		

HARTLEPOOL UNITED—PLAYERS

Player and position	Ht	Wt	Birthplace	Clubs	League Appearances	Goals
Goalkeepers						
Graham Richardson	5 10	11 10	Sedgefield	Hartlepool U	53	—
Edward Edgar	5 11	12 4	Bristol	Newcastle U	—	—
(Contract cancelled March 1979)				Hartlepool U	75	—
Gordon Livsey	5 8	12 0	Keighley	Wrexham	79	—
(Contract cancelled July 1978)				Chester	44	—
				Hartlepool U	6	—
John Watson	6 1	13 1	Huddersfield	Huddersfield T	—	—
				Hartlepool U	12	—
Defenders						
Bill Ayre	5 10	12 0	Crookhills	Scarborough	—	—
				Hartlepool U	88	17
George Smith	5 8	10 12	Newcastle	Barrow	91+1	11
				Portsmouth	64	3
				Middlesbrough	74	—
				Birmingham	36+3	—
				Cardiff C	43+2	1
				Swansea C	86+2	8
				Hartlepool U	70	2
*Trevor Smith	6 0	11 3	Middlesbrough	Hartlepool U	27+6	1
Derrick Downing	5 9	10 4	Frickley	Middlesbrough	171+11	39
(Contract cancelled September 1978) Colliery				Orient	100+4	11
				York C	44+3	2
				Hartlepool U	40	4
Steve Brookes	6 0	11 8	Wigan	Southport	65	3
				Hartlepool U	34	1
Martin Gorry	5 10	11 0	Derby	Barnsley	34	3
				Newcastle U	0+1	—
				Hartlepool U	41	—
Graham Normanton	5 9	12 10	Hartlepool	Hartlepool U	—	—
Edward Leighton	6 0		Hartlepool	Hartlepool U	—	—
Midfield						
*Tommy Gibb	5 10½	11 1	West Lothian	Partick T	112	13
				Newcastle U	190+9	12
				Sunderland	7+3	1
				Hartlepool U	40	4
Roy Hogan	5 8	10 6	Hartlepool	Hartlepool U	23+3	1
Derek Loadwick	5 7	12 0	Middlesbrough	Leeds U	—	—
				Stockport Co	84	—
				Hartlepool U	28+1	—
Keith Guy				Newcastle U	—	—
(Contract cancelled January 1979)				Hartlepool U	7+3	—
Phillip Brown	5 8	10 12	Hartlepool	Hartlepool U	—	—
Kenneth Lowe	5 10	11 4	Hartlepool	Hartlepool U	—	—
Gordon Larkin	5 9	11 4	Hartlepool	Hartlepool U	4+2	1
David Norton				Hartlepool U	8+3	1
Forwards						
Keith Houchen	6 2	11 4	Middlesbrough	Hartlepool U	51+1	16
Bob Newton	5 11	12 6	Chesterfield	Huddersfield T	37+5	7
				York C (on loan)	—	—
				Hartlepool U	53	11
Mark Lawrence	6 0	11 2	Middlesbrough	Hartlepool U	36+5	9
Terry Gaffney	5 9	12 0	Hartlepool	Hartlepool U	10+3	1
(Contract cancelled October 1978)						
John Linacre	5 9	11 10	Middlesbrough	Hartlepool U	74+4	5
Chris McMaster	5 8	9 12	Darlington	Hartlepool U	3+1	—
(Contract cancelled October 1978)						
Wayne Goldthorpe	5 10	12 6	Staincross	Huddersfield T	19+7	7
				Bolton W (on loan)	—	—
				Hartlepool U (on loan)	6+1	1
				Arsenal (on loan)	—	—
				Hartlepool U	37+4	6
Alan Harding	5 8	11 6	Sunderland	Darlington	125+4	38
				Lincoln C	203+6	38
				Hartlepool U	15	1
Samuel Hewitt	5 7	11 10	Hartlepool	Hartlepool U	—	—
David Evans	5 10	11 10	Sunderland	Hartlepool U	1+2	—
Ian Crumplin	5 9	11 0	Newcastle	Blue Star	—	—
				Hartlepool U	25+4	5

Also retained: Mike Spelman.

HEREFORD UNITED DIV. 4

Chairman: P. S. Hill, F.R.I.C.S.
Vice-Chairman: J. Jackson.
Directors: D. Vaughan, R. Tidball, J.P., M. Roberts, F. L. Miles, A. J. Phillips.
Player/Manager: Mike Bailey.
Secretary: Bill Stevens.
Football Administrator: Jim Finney.
Year Formed: 1924.   *Turned Professional:* 1924.
Limited Company: 1939.
Ground: Edgar Street Athletic Ground.
Football League Record:
  1972 Elected to Division 4.   1976–77 Division 2.
  1973–76 Division 3.   1977–78 Division 3.
      1978– Division 4.

Honours: Best season *Football League:* Division 3 Champions, 1975–76. Division 4, Runners-up, 1972–73. *F.A. Cup* best season 4th Rd. 1971–72, 1976–77. *F.L.Cup* Best season 3rd Rd. 1974–75.

Record Victory: 11-0 v Thynnes (F.A. Cup), Sept. 1947.

Record Defeat: 0–5 v Wrexham, Dec. 1973, 1–6 v Tranmere R., Jan. 1975, 1–6 v Wolves, Oct. 1976.

Most League Points: 63, Division 3, 1975–76.

Most League Goals: 86, Division 3, 1975–76.

Highest League Scorer in Season: Dixie McNeil, 35, 1975–76.

Most League Appearances: Steve Emery, 198, 1973–79.

Most League Goals in Total Aggregate: Dixie McNeil, 85, 1974–77.

Most Capped Player: Brian Evans, 1(7) Wales.

Record Transfer Fee Recieved: £80,000 for Kevin Sheedy, from Liverpool, July 1978.

Record Transfer Fee Paid: £20,000 to Plymouth Arg for Jim Hinch, Oct. 1973; £20,000 to Lincoln C. for Dixie McNeil, August 1974. £20,000 to Leicester C. for Winston White, March 1979.

Managers Since the War: George Tranter, Alex Massie, Joe Wade, Ray Daniel, Bob Dennison, John Charles, Colin Addison, John Sillett, Tony Ford.

Address of Supporters' Club: Edgar Street, Hereford.
Address of Club Shop: Edgar Street, Hereford.

Edgar Street, Hereford. Telephone Hereford (0432) 4037.
Ground Capacity: 17,500.   *Record Attendance:* 18,114 v Sheffield W., January 1958.   *Record receipts:* £12,666 Bristol C., F.A. Cup 4th Rd., Jan. 26 1974.   *Pitch measurements:* 111 yds x 80 yds.

How to get there: Ground very close to town centre, within five minutes walking distance from Hereford railway station and the bus station.
Match tickets: Tickets can be booked in advance.
Car parking: Parking is available around the ground for approximately 1,000 vehicles.
Entertainments/catering facilities: Canteens on the ground. A social club next to ground.
Club shop: All types of souvenirs sold.
Handbooks/programmes: Programmes available on application to the club shop.
Extra information: As a non-League Club, Hereford reached the first round proper of the F.A. Cup for 21 consecutive seasons.

Club Colours: White shirts with red and black trim, black shorts, white with red and black top stockings.
Change Colours: Red shirts, white and black trim, white shorts, red stockings, white and black trim.

Club Trainer: Peter Isaac.   *Club Nickname:* 'United'.

HEREFORD UNITED 1978-79 LEAGUE RECORD

Match No.	Date	Venue	Opponents	Result	H/T Score	League Pos'n	Goalscorers	Attendance
1	Aug 19	H	Wigan Ath	D 0-0	0-0	—		5674
2	23	A	Bradford C	L 1-2	0-2	—	Holmes K	5376
3	26	A	Torquay U	L 0-1	0-1	18		3074
4	Sept 2	H	Darlington	W 1-0	1-0	16	Barton (pen)	3622
5	9	A	Hartlepool U	L 1-2	0-1	18	Emery (pen)	2995
6	13	H	Reading	D 0-0	0-0	—		3526
7	16	H	Crewe Alex	W 6-1	1-1	16	Gould 2, Jones 2, Bowles (og), Spiring	3493
8	23	A	Rochdale	W 2-0	2-0	14	Gould, Emery (pen)	1068
9	26	A	York C	L 0-1	0-0	—		2358
10	30	H	Port Vale	W 1-0	1-0	13	Holmes K	3963
11	Oct 7	A	Portsmouth	L 0-1	0-0	14		11,949
12	14	H	AFC Bournemouth	D 0-0	0-0	14		3752
13	17	A	Huddersfield T	W 3-2	1-2	—	Gould, Jones 2	2565
14	21	H	Aldershot	D 1-1	1-1	11	Jones	3835
15	28	A	Grimsby T	D 1-1	1-0	11	Spiring	5349
16	Nov 4	H	Halifax T	D 2-2	1-1	13	Jones, Gould	3616
17	11	A	Darlington	L 1-2	1-1	14	Emery (pen)	1622
18	18	H	Torquay U	W 3-1	1-1	10	Crompton, Emery (pen), Gould	3476
19	Dec 9	H	Northampton T	W 4-3	1-2	7	Jones, Holmes W, Burrows, Holmes K	2879
20	16	A	Scunthorpe U	L 2-4	0-1	9	Jones, Bailey	1683
21	22	H	Newport Co	L 0-3	0-2	11		2834
22	26	A	Stockport Co	W 2-0	1-0	—	Holmes W, Stephens	4,630
23	Jan 30	A	Doncaster R	L 0-1	0-0	—		1,719
24	Feb 3	H	York C	W 1-0	1-0	12	Holmes W	3,107
25	6	A	Crewe Alex	D 0-0	0-0	—		1485
26	21	A	Reading	L 0-3	0-2	—		5,639
27	24	A	AFC Bournemouth	D 1-1	0-1	11	Gould	4,292
28	28	H	Barnsley	D 1-1	1-0	—	Gould	3,100
29	Mar 3	A	Aldershot	L 0-2	0-1	13		3,932
30	7	H	Hartlepool U	W 1-0	0-0	—	Emery	2,119
31	10	A	Grimsby T	L 0-1	0-1	11		2,939
32	21	H	Rochdale	D 2-2	1-1	—	White, Gould	2,351
33	24	H	Bradford C	W 3-1	1-0	11	Powell 2, Layton	2,925
34	28	H	Wigan Ath	D 0-0	0-0	—		4,876
35	31	A	Wimbledon	L 0-2	0-1	11		2,636
36	Apr 7	H	Scunthorpe U	W 3-1	2-0	11	McGrellis, Gould 2	2,859
37	11	A	Newport Co	L 1-4	0-2	—	McGrellis	3,771
38	14	H	Stockport Co	W 1-0	1-0	10	McGrellis	3,609
39	16	A	Barnsley	L 1-2	1-1	—	Spiring	12,260
40	21	H	Doncaster R	W 2-0	1-0	12	White 2	3,209
41	25	H	Huddersfield T	W 3-0	0-0	—	Spiring 2, Thomas	2,635
42	28	H	Northampton T	L 1-2	0-1	11	Gould	2,001
43	May 1	A	Port Vale	D 1-1	1-0	—	Gould	2,160
44	5	H	Wimbledon	D 0-0	0-0	11		3,809
45	7	H	Portsmouth	L 0-1	0-1	—		3,707
46	9	A	Halifax T	L 0-1	0-0	—		1,036

Final League Position: 14

Goalscorers

League (53): Gould 13, Jones 8, Emery 5 (4 pens), Spiring 5, Holmes K 3, Holmes W 3, McGrellis 3, White 3, Powell 2, Bailey 1, Barton 1 (pen), Burrows 1, Crompton 1, Layton 1, Stephens 1, Thomas 1, Own Goal 1.

League Cup (5): Jones, Holmes W, Layton, Emery, Barton

League Cup	First Round	Bristol R (a)	1-2
		(h)	4-0
	Second Round	Northampton T (a)	0-0
		(h)	0-1
F.A. Cup	First Round	Newport Co (h)	0-1

Hughes	Roberts	Price	Cornes	Marshall	Barton	Holmes W	Holmes K	Jones	Powell	Spiring	Burrows	O'Hara	Knight	Emery	Phillips	Layton	Stephens	Bailey	Crompton	Gould	Feeley	Hill	Hunt	O'Brien	Hendry	White	Strong	Thomas	McGrellis	Match No.
1	2	3	4	5	6	7	8	9	10	11																				1
1		3	4	5	11	7	8	9		10	2	6																		2
		2	4	5	11	7	8*	9		10	3		1	6	12															3
1		2	4	5	11	7*	8	9		10	3			6			12													4
1		2	4*				8	9		10	3			6		5	7	11	12											5
1		2	4				8	9			3			6		5	7	11		10										6
1		2	4				8	9		12	3			6		5*	7	11		10										7
1		2	4				8	9		10	3			6		5	7	11												8
1		2	4				8	9		11	3			6		5	7			10										9
1	2		4		12		8	9*		10	3			6		5	7	11												10
1		2	4		12		8	9*		10	3			6			5	7		11										11
1		2	4							10	3			6	9	5	7			11	8									12
1		2	4					9		10	3			6		5	7			11	8									13
1		2	4					9		10*	3			6	12	5	7			11	8									14
1			4					9		10	3			2		5	7	6		11	8									15
1	2	4			12			9		10	3			6		5	7*	8		11										16
1	2		4					9		10	3			8		5	7*	6	12	11										17
1	2					7		9		10*	3			6		5		4	8	11		12								18
1			4			11	7	9			3			6		5		2		10	8									19
1			4			7	10	9			3			6		5		2		11	8									20
1			4			11	8	9*			3			6		5	12	2		10	7									21
1	2					11					4			12		5	9	8	6	10*	7		3							22
1	2	4				11	8				3			6				9	10*	7		5	12							23
1	2	5				8					3			6		7		9	11	10		4								24
1	2	4				11	12				3			6			8	9*10		7		5								25
1	2	4				11	9				3			6		7	12		10	8*		5								26
1	2	4					9				3			6	7	5	8		12			11*10								27
1	2	4			12		9*				3			6	11	5	7		10			8								28
1	2	4					9*				3			6	11	5	7	12	10			8								29
1	2	4									3			6	11	5		7	9	10		8								30
1	2	4					7	10			3			6		5			9	11		8								31
1	2	4						9*			3			6		5	12		10	11		8	7							32
1	2							11			3			6*		5	7		10	12		8	9	4						33
1	2							9			3			6		5	11		10			8	7	4						34
1	2*							10			3			6		5	7		11			8	9	4	12					35
1														6		5			9	7	2	8	11	4	3	10				36
1														6		5			10	7	2	8	11	4	3	9				37
1														6	12	5			9	8	2*	10	11	4	3	7				38
1									2					6		5			10	11		8	7	4	3	9				39
1				12					2					6		5			10	11		8*	7	4	3	9				40
1									6					2		5	8		10	7			11	4	3	9				41
1									6					2		5	8		10	7			11	4	3	9				42
1				6										2		5	8		10	7	4		11		3	9				43
1		4		6					7					2		5			10	8			11		3	9				44
1		4		6					7*					2		5	12		10	8			11		3	9				45
		4					12	10	7			1*		2		5				6			8	11	3	9				46
44	3	29	23	14	4	12	19	25	6	24	34	1	2	43	5	38	25	13	6	39	25		9	1	15	15	10	11	11	
						+	+	+		+				+	+	+	+	+	+	+	+		+			+				
						4s	2s	1s		1s				1s	3s	3s	3s	2s	1s	1s	1s		1s			1s				

HEREFORD UNITED—PLAYERS

Player and position	Ht	Wt	Birthplace	Clubs	League Appearances	Goals
Goalkeepers						
Tommy Hughes	6 1	12 4	Dalmuir	Chelsea	11	—
				Aston V	16	—
				Brighton (on loan)	3	—
				Hereford U	176	—
Lyndon Knight	6 1		Lydbrook	Hereford U	2	—
Defenders						
Julian Marshall	6 3	12 0	Swansea	Hereford U	68+1	3
John Layton	6 0	13 2	Hereford	Hereford U	165	13
Steve Emery	5 11	11 10	Hereford	Hereford U	197+1	9
Bryan Bouston	5 6	10 0	Hereford	Hereford U	4+2	—
Phil Burrows	5 8	10 6	Stockton	Manchester C	—	—
				York C	333+2	14
				Plymouth Arg	81	2
				Hereford U	68	1
				Gillingham (on loan)	5	—
Stuart Cornes	6 0	11 1	Usk	Hereford U	36	—
Chris Price	5 7	10 2	Hereford	Hereford U	44	—
David Dixon	6 2		Hereford	Hereford U	—	—
Paul Hunt	5 9		Hereford	Coventry C	—	—
				Hereford U	9	—
Valmore Thomas	5 8	10 6	Worksop	Coventry C	—	—
				Hereford U	11+1	1
Steve Strong (Apprentice)	5 11		Bristol	Hereford U	10	—
Midfield						
Mike Bailey (England)	5 7½	11 2	Wisbech	Charlton Ath	151	20
				Wolverhampton W	360+1	19
				Hereford U	13+3	1
Kyle Holmes	5 7	10 9	Abergavenny	Hereford U	23+2	3
Billy Holmes	5 10	11 2	Balham	Millwall	0+1	—
				Luton T	0+1	—
				Wimbledon	15	5
				Hereford U	21+10	5
Andy Feeley (Apprentice)	5 9		Hereford	Hereford U	25+1	—
Ian Hendry	5 8	10 12	Glasgow	Aston Villa	—	—
				Hereford U	15	—
Henry Hill (non-contract)				Hereford U	0+1	—
Winston White	5 10½		Leicester	Leicester C	10+2	1
				Hereford U	15	3
Gerald O'Hara (non-contract)	5 8	10 11	Wolverhampton	Wolverhampton W	7+2	—
				Hereford U	1	—
Forwards						
Peter Spiring	5 8	11 0	Glastonbury	Bristol C	57+5	16
				Liverpool	—	—
				Luton T	12+3	2
				Hereford U	91+12	16
Steve Crompton	5 10	12 5	Rossety	Hereford U	30+4	6
Ken Stephens	5 7½	10 12	Bristol	WBA	21+1	2
				Walsall	5+2	—
				Bristol R	215+10	13
				Hereford U	51+3	2
Stuart Phillips (apprentice)				Hereford U	6+3	—
David Jones	6 2	14 0	Ruabon	Hereford U	25+1	8
Bobby Gould	5 10	11 5	Coventry	Coventry C	78+3	40
				Arsenal	57+8	16
				Wolverhampton W	39+1	18
				WBA	52	18
				Bristol C	35	15
				West Ham U	46+5	15
				Wolverhampton W	24+10	13
				Bristol R	35+1	12
				Hereford U	39+1	13
Wayne Powell (Contract cancelled May 1979)	5 11	11 0	Newport	Bristol R	25+7	10
				Halifax T (on loan)	4	1
				Hereford U	6	2
Frank McGrellis	5 10	11 6	Falkirk	Coventry C	—	—
				Huddersfield T (on loan)	4+1	—
				Hereford U	11	—

HUDDERSFIELD TOWN DIV. 4

Chairman: K. S. Longbottom.
Directors: S. Kinder, O.B.E., J. Christie, K. C. Padley, C. Senior, M. Ryan, E .A. Lodge.
Manager: Mick Buxton.
Secretary: G. S. Binns.
Year Formed: 1908.
Turned Professional: 1908.   *Limited Company:* 1908.

Football League Record:
1910 Elected to Division 2.	1970–72 Division 1.
1920–52 Division 1.	1972–73 Division 2.
1952–53 Division 2.	1973–75 Division 3.
1953–56 Division 1.	1975– Division 4.
1956–70 Division 2.	

© 1973

Honours: *Football League*, Division 1, Champions: 1923–24, 1924–25, 1925–26; Runners-up: 1926–27, 1927–28, 1933–34. Division 2, Champions: 1969–70; Runners-up; 1919–20, 1952–53. *F.A. Cup*, Winners: 1922; Runners-up: 1920, 1928, 1930, 1938. *Football League Cup*, best season: Semi-finalists, 1967–68. *Record Victory:* 10–1 v Blackpool, Division 1. Dec. 13th, 1930.

Record Defeat: 0–8 v Middlesbrough, Division 1, Sept. 30, 1950.

Most League Points: 64, Division 2, 1919–20.

Most League Goals: 97, Division 2, 1919–20.

Highest Scorer in Season: Sam Taylor, 35, Division 2, 1919–20; George Brown, 35, Division 1, 1925–26.

Most Capped Player: Jimmy Nicholson, 31 (41) N. Ireland.

Most League Appearances: Billy Smith, 520, 1914–34.

Most League Goals in Total Aggregate: George Brown, 142, 1921–29.

Record Transfer Fee Received: £100,000 from Leeds U. for Trevor Cherry, June 1972.

Record Transfer Fee Paid: £65,000 to Manchester U. for Alan Gowling, June 1972.

Managers Since the War: David Steele, George Stephenson, Andy Beattie, Bill Shankly, Eddie Boot, Tom Johnston, Ian Greaves, Bobby Collins, Tom Johnston.

Address of Supporters Club: Supporters Club Offices, 286 Leeds Road, Huddersfield, Yorkshire.

Address of Club Shop or Boutique: The Terriers Souvenir Shop, 286 Leeds Road, Huddersfield.

Leeds Rd., Huddersfield HD1 6PE. Telephone Huddersfield 20335/6.   *Ground capacity:* 48,000.
Record attendance: 67,037 v Arsenal, F.A. Cup 6th Rd., February 27, 1932.   *Record receipts:* £17,577.73p v Bolton W., F.A. Cup 4th Rd., Jan. 24, 1976.   *Pitch measurements:* 115 yds × 75 yds.

How to get there: The ground is one mile from the town centre via Corporation buses 40, 41, 42. On match days special buses run from the centre. By road, the ground can be reached along Leeds Road either from the town centre or from Leeds.
Match tickets: Admission to all parts is by payment at the turnstiles except for special matches. (tel: Huddersfield 36100).
Car parking: Ample parking accommodation on all four sides of the ground; in the region of 6,000 cars can be parked within 200 yards of the turnstiles.
Entertainments/catering facilities: Licensed Presidents Club—members only. 11 unlicensed snack bars around the ground.
Club shop: Close to the ground; sells all types of souvenirs (tel: Huddersfield 31028). Open match days.
Handbooks/programmes: Programmes available on subscription from the club shop.
Extra information: In 1952–53 the club fielded an unchanged defensive line-up throughout the season.
Club Colours: Blue and white striped shirts, white shorts, white stockings.
Change Colours: All yellow.
Club Captain:
Coach: Jim Robson.
Physiotherapist/Coach: John Haselden.
Club Nickname: 'The Terriers'.

HUDDERSFIELD TOWN 1978-79 LEAGUE RECORD

Match No.	Date	Venue	Opponents	Result	Score	H/T Score	League Pos'n	Goalscorers	Attendance
1	Aug 19	H	Crewe Alex	D	0-0	0-0	—		2838
2	22	A	Darlington	L	0-1	0-0	—		2549
3	25	A	Scunthorpe U	L	1-3	0-2	21	Hanvey	3029
4	Sept 2	H	Reading	D	1-1	1-0	21	Bielby (pen)	2951
5	9	H	Doncaster R	W	2-1	0-1	16	Hanvey, Bielby	4038
6	12	A	AFC Bournemouth	L	0-2	0-0	—		2416
7	16	A	Barnsley	L	0-1	0-0	20		11,566
8	23	H	Northampton T	W	1-0	0-0	17	Holmes	3320
9	26	H	Grimsby T	W	2-0	0-0	—	Brolly (og), Campbell	4238
10	29	A	Stockport Co	L	1-3	1-2	17	Bielby (pen)	5554
11	Oct 7	H	Wigan Ath	D	1-1	1-0	16	Bielby (pen)	5150
12	14	A	Newport Co	L	1-2	0-1	22	Robins	3624
13	17	A	Hereford U	L	2-3	2-1	—	Campbell 2	2565
14	21	H	Wimbledon	W	3-0	1-0	18	Robins 2, Bielby	3374
15	28	A	Bradford C	D	1-1	0-0	19	Fletcher	5478
16	Nov 4	H	York C	W	1-0	0-0	16	Sutton	3696
17	11	A	Reading	D	1-1	0-1	15	Robins	6870
18	18	H	Scunthorpe U	W	3-2	0-2	15	Topping, Gray, Fletcher	3375
19	Dec 2	H	Aldershot	D	0-0	0-0	13		3138
20	9	A	Portsmouth	L	0-1	0-1	15		11,615
21	26	H	Halifax T	W	2-0	1-0	—	Fletcher, Robins	5341
22	Jan 1	A	Port Vale	L	0-1	0-0	—		4021
23	Feb 3	A	Grimsby T	L	1-2	1-1	17	Robins	4919
24	17	A	Wigan Ath	L	1-2	1-1	18	Robins	7420
25	24	H	Newport Co	L	0-1	0-1	20		3361
26	27	A	Doncaster R	W	2-0	0-0	—	Holmes, Howey	3419
27	Mar 3	A	Wimbledon	L	1-2	1-0	18	Holmes	3265
28	6	A	Northampton T	W	3-2	0-1	—	Holmes 2, Robins	1623
29	10	H	Bradford C	D	0-0	0-0	18		6188
30	13	H	AFC Bournemouth	W	2-1	1-0	—	Fletcher, Armstrong	2268
31	24	A	Darlington	D	2-2	1-1	18	Robins 2	2862
32	28	A	Crewe Alex	D	3-3	1-1	—	Fletcher 2, Holmes	1382
33	31	H	Hartlepool U	W	2-0	1-0	16	Robins, Holmes	2420
34	Apr 4	A	Stockport Co	D	0-0	0-0	—		2267
35	7	A	Aldershot	L	0-1	0-1	16		4215
36	11	A	Rochdale	W	2-0	1-0	—	Fletcher, Robins	2020
37	14	A	Halifax T	W	3-2	1-0	12	Fletcher 2, Holmes	4027
38	16	H	Port Vale	W	3-2	1-1	—	Robins, Fletcher, Holmes	3236
39	17	H	Rochdale	W	1-0	1-0	—	Fletcher	3346
40	21	A	Torquay U	L	1-2	0-0	9	Holmes	2478
41	25	A	Hereford U	L	0-3	0-0	—		2635
42	28	H	Portsmouth	W	2-0	1-0	10	Robins, Fletcher (pen)	2895
43	30	H	Torquay U	D	1-1	1-0	—	Hart	1624
44	May 2	H	Barnsley	W	1-0	1-0	—	Robins	9328
45	5	A	Hartlepool U	L	0-2	0-1	10		2207
46	19	A	York C	W	3-1	0-0	—	Holmes, Cowling, Robins	2664

Final League Position: 9

Goalscorers

League (57): Robins 16, Fletcher 12, Holmes 11, Bielby 5 (3 pens), Campbell 3, Hanvey 2, Armstrong 1, Cowling 1, Gray 1, Hart 1, Howey 1, Sutton 1, Topping 1, Own Goal 1.
League Cup (2): Holmes (pen), Ripley.
F.A. Cup (1): Fletcher.

League Cup	First Round	Preston N E (a)		0-3
		(h)		2-2
F.A. Cup	First Round	Doncaster R (a)		1-2

Starling	Branagan	Sandercock	Holmes	Sutton	Topping	Howey	Hart	Fletcher	Hanvey	Ripley	McGrellis	Armstrong	Gray	Bielby	Brown	Campbell	Cowling	Gartland	Robins	Lillis	Smith	Brook	Taylor	Match No.
1	2	3	4	5	6	7	8	9	10	11*12														1
1	2	3	4	5	6		8	9	10	12	11*	7												2
1	2	3	4	5	6		8	9*10	12				7	11										3
1	2	3		5	6		8		10		9	4	7	11										4
1		3	4	5	6		8		10		9		7	11	2									5
1		3	4*	5	6		8		10	12	9		7	11	2									6
1		3	4		6		8		5				7	11	2	9	10							7
1			4		6		8		5				7	11	2	9	10	3						8
1			4*		6		8		5				7	11	2	9	10	3	12					9
1			4		6		8*		5				7	11	2	9	12	3	10					10
1		3	4		6		8		5				7	11	2	9			10					11
1		3*			6		8	12	5				7		2	9	11		10	4				12
1					6		8		5				7		2	9	11	3	10	4				13
1		3		5	6		8						7	11	2	9			10	4				14
1		3		5	6		8	12					7	11	2	9			10	4*				15
1		3		5	6		8	12					7*11		2	9			10	4				16
1		3	12	5	6		8	7*						11	2	9			10	4				17
1		3		5	6		8	12					7*11		2	9			10	4				18
1		3		5	6		8	7						11	2	9			10	4				19
1	3			5	6		8	7					12	11	2	9			10	4*				20
1	3			5	6		8	7					4	11	2	9			10					21
1		3		5	6	11	8*		7				4	12	2	9			10					22
1		3		5	6*		4	8					7	11	2	9			10	12				23
1		3	12	6			5	7				8		11	2	9			10	4*				24
1		3	8	5		11	6	7				12			2	9			10	4*				25
1		3	4	5*		11	8	7	6			12			2	9			10					26
1		3	7	6		11	4	9	5						2	8			10					27
1	3		4	6		11	8	7	5						2	9			10					28
1	3		4	6		11	8	9	5					12	2	7*			10					29
1	3		4	6		11	8	7	5				9		2				10					30
1		3	4	6		11	8	7	5				9		2				10					31
1		3	4	5		11	8	7	6				9		2				10					32
1		3	4	6			8	7	5				9	11*	2				10	12				33
1		3	4	6			8	7	5				9	11	2				10					34
1		3	4	6			8	7	5				9	12	11* 2				10					35
1		3	4	6			8	7	5				9	11	2				10					36
1	12	3	4	6			8	7*	5				9	11	2				10					37
1		3	4	6			8	7	5				9	11	2				10					38
	3		4	6			8	7*	5				9	12	11 2				10			1		39
1		3	4	6			8	7	5				9		11 2				10					40
1		3	4	6			8	7	5				9*12	11	2				10					41
1		3	4	6			8	11	5				7		2	9			10					42
1	6	3	4	5			8	7					11		2	9			10					43
1	6	3	4	5			8	7					11		2	9			10					44
1	6	3*12	4				9	7	5				11		2				10		8			45
1	3		4	5			8	7	6				11		2	9			10					46
45	13	36	31	39	23	10	46	31	32	2	4	15	22	29	42	7	25	4	37	11	1	1		

+1s +3s +4s +3s +1s +2s +4s +2s +1s +1s +1s +1s

HUDDERSFIELD TOWN—PLAYERS

Player and position	Ht	Wt	Birthplace	Clubs	League Appearances	Goals
Goalkeepers						
Richard Taylor	6 0½	12 9	Huddersfield	Huddersfield T	92	—
				Wolverhampton W (on loan)	—	—
				Sunderland (on loan)	—	—
Alan Starling	6 1	13 4	Barking	Luton T	7	—
				Torquay U (on loan)	6	—
				Northampton T	238	1
				Huddersfield T	90	—
Defenders						
Peter Hart	5 10	11 12	Mexborough	Huddersfield T	162+2	3
Malcolm Brown	6 2	12 6	Salford	Bury	10	—
				Huddersfield T	72	1
Phil Sandercock	5 10	11 0	Hollymouth	Torquay U	207+6	13
				Huddersfield T	81	1
Chris Topping	6 1	11 12	Selby	York C	410+2	11
				Huddersfield T	23	1
Paul Gartland	5 10½	12 2	Shipley	Huddersfield T	8	—
Jim Branagan	5 10	11 5	Barton	Oldham Ath	24+3	—
				Huddersfield T	37+1	—
David Sutton	5 11	11 0	Tarleton	Plymouth Arg	60+1	—
				Reading (on loan)	9	—
				Huddersfield T	53	1
Brett Mellor	6 0	12 0	Huddersfield	Huddersfield T	1	—
Keith Hanvey	6 0	12 7	Manchester	Manchester C	—	—
				Swansea C	11	—
				Rochdale	121	10
				Grimsby T	54	2
				Huddersfield T	32	2
*David Hepinstall	6 0	12 2	Halifax	Huddersfield T	—	—
Mark Lillis	6 0	12 2	Manchester	Huddersfield T	11+1	—
Midfield						
Terry Gray	5 8	9 2	Bradford	Chelsea	—	—
				Huddersfield T	146+17	36
Terry Armstrong	5 9½	11 11½	Barnsley	Huddersfield T	36+4	2
Ian Holmes	5 7	10 6	Wombwell	Sheffield U	4+2	—
				York C	152+7	30
				Huddersfield T	59+4	18
*Keith Ripley	5 9½	11 0	Normanton	Gainsborough T	—	—
				Huddersfield T	2+3	—
Paul Bielby	5 8	11 10	Darlington	Manchester U	2+2	—
				Hartlepool	74+19	8
				Huddersfield T	29+2	5
Ian Robins	5 9	11 4	Bury	Oldham Ath	202+18	40
				Bury	49	5
				Huddersfield T	37+1	16
Paul Gibson	5 8	10 6	Huddersfield	Huddersfield T	—	—
Daryl Brook	5 9	10 5	Huddersfield	Huddersfield T	1	—
David Cowling	5 7	10 6	Doncaster	Doncaster R	—	—
				Huddersfield T	25+1	1
Forwards						
*Mick Reid	5 7	11 2	Huddersfield	Huddersfield T	—	—
*Peter Howey	5 4	9 8	Kinsley	Huddersfield T	20+2	3
Terry Eccles	6 0½	13 0	Leeds	Blackburn R	33+13	6
(Contract cancelled June 1978)				Mansfield T	115+3	47
				Huddersfield T	41+5	6
Peter Fletcher	6 1	12 0	Manchester	Manchester U	2+5	—
				Hull C	26+10	5
				Stockport Co	43+8	9
				Huddersfield T	31+4	12
Tom Smith				Huddersfield T	0+1	—

HULL CITY DIV. 3

Chairman: R. E. Chapman, B.Sc.
Vice-Chairman: John Needler.
Directors: G. Needler, F.R.I.C.S., J.P., T. G. C. Thomas, M.A., A.C.A., M. J. Kay, Dip. Arch., J.P., G. H. Christopher Needler, B.A., A.C.A., I. J. Blakey, M.C.I.T., F. Inst., T.A.
Team Manager: Ken Houghton.
Assistant Manager:
Gen. Manager/Secretary: M. T. Stone.
Year Formed: 1904.   *Turned Professional:* 1905.
Limited Company: 1905.
Previous Grounds: 1904, Boulevard Ground (Hull R.F.C.); 1905, Anlaby Road (Hull C.C.); 1946, Boothferry Park.
Football League Record:
1905 Elected to Division 2. 1930–33 Division 3(N). 1933–36 Division 2. 1936–49 Division 3(N). 1949–56 Division 2. 1956–58 Division 3(N). 1958–59 Division 3. 1959–60 Division 2. 1960–66 Division 3. 1966–78 Division 2. 1978– Division 3.

Honours: *Football League,* highest position in Div. 2: 3rd, 1909–10. Division 3(N), Champions: 1932–33, 1948–49. Division 3, Champions: 1965–66; Runners-up: 1958–59. *F.A. Cup,* best season: Semi-finalists, 1930.   *Football League Cup,* best season: 4th Rd. 1973–74, 1975–76, 1977–78.

Record Victory: 11-1 v Carlisle U., Division 3(N), Jan. 14th, 1939.

Record Defeat: 0-8 v Wolverhampton W., Division 2, Nov. 4th, 1911.

Most League Points: 69, Division 3, 1965–66.

Most League Goals: 109, Division 3, 1965–66.

Highest League Scorer in Season: Bill McNaughton, 39, Division 3(N), 1932–33.

Most Capped Player: Terry Neill, 15 (59), N. Ireland.

Most League Goals in Total Aggregate: Chris Chilton 195, 1960–71.

Most League Appearances: Andy Davidson, 511, 1947–67.

Record Transfer Fee Received: £200,000 from Manchester U. for Stuart Pearson, May 1974.

Record Transfer Fee Paid: £75,000 to Millwall for Alf Wood, November 1974.

Managers Since the War: Ernest Blackburn, Major Frank Buckley, Raich Carter, Bob Jackson, Bob Brocklebank, Cliff Britton, Terry Neill, John Kaye, Bobby Collins.

Club Shop: Club Shop, Boothferry Park, Hull. In South Stand, also next to Development Association on main car park at front of ground.

Boothferry Park, Hull HU4 6EU. Telephone 0482 52195. *Telegraphic address:* 'Tigers Hull'.   *Ground capacity:* 42,000.   *Record attendance:* 55,019 v Manchester U., F.A. Cup 6th Rd., February 26, 1949.   *Record receipts:* £22,229 v Stoke City F.A. Cup 6th Rd., March 6, 1971.   *Pitch measurements:* 112 yds × 75 yds.

How to get there: Buses 55, 57, 43, 48 from coach station, Ferensway, Hull. Nearest railway stations, Hull and Boothferry Park Halt. Special trains on match days from Hull Paragon to Boothferry Park Halt; admittance to ground through turnstiles on station. Ground situated on A63 to the west of the city.

Match tickets: Tickets for League games may be booked two weeks in advance of the match.

Car parking: Official car park at ground for season passholders only. Public car park, Kempton Road park three minutes walk away; coach parking on Main Car Park.

Entertainments/catering facilities: Catering facilities at points around the ground.

Club shop: In the South Stand, open on League match days, and at ticket office on weekdays.

Handbooks/programmes: Programmes available on subscription.

Extra information: The club's 31 wins in 1965–66 was a Third Division record.

Club Colours: Black and amber stripes, black shorts, amber stockings.

Change Colours: All white.

Club Captain: Stuart Croft.

Club Nickname: 'Tigers'.

HULL CITY 1978-79 LEAGUE RECORD

Match No.	Date	Venue	Opponents	Result	H/T Score	League Pos'n	Goalscorers	Attendance
1	Aug 19	H	Carlisle U	D 1-1	1-1	—	Horswill	5062
2	26	A	Tranmere R	W 3-1	0-0	9	Bannister, Lord, Edwards	1948
3	Sept 2	H	Chester	W 3-0	2-0	7	Edwards 3	5325
4	5	A	Rotherham U	W 2-0	2-0	—	Horswill, Bannister	6389
5	9	A	Brentford	L 0-1	0-1	3		6530
6	12	H	Walsall	W 4-1	1-0	—	Edwards 2, Lord, Bannister	6784
7	16	H	Chesterfield	D 1-1	1-1	3	Bannister	7705
8	23	A	Exeter C	L 1-3	1-3	4	Edwards	3733
9	26	A	Shrewsbury T	L 0-1	0-0	—		3777
10	30	H	Oxford U	L 0-1	0-0	11		5263
11	Oct 7	H	Peterborough U	D 1-1	0-0	12	Lord	4531
12	14	A	Gillingham	L 0-2	0-1	14		5460
13	21	H	Swansea C	D 2-2	0-0	18	Warboys, Haigh	6152
14	23	A	Southend U	L 0-3	0-0	—		6812
15	28	A	Bury	D 1-1	0-1	18	Bannister	4088
16	Nov 4	H	Watford	W 4-0	1-0	16	Edwards, Nisbet, Bannister 2	7739
17	11	A	Chester	L 1-2	1-2	17	Edwards	4249
18	18	H	Tranmere R	W 2-1	1-0	14	Horswill, Edwards	4350
19	Dec 9	A	Swindon T	L 0-2	0-0	18		5697
20	26	H	Mansfield T	W 3-0	2-0	17	Edwards 2, Bannister (pen)	4700
21	Jan 6	A	Walsall	W 2-1	0-1	15	Galvin 2	4061
22	Feb 3	H	Shrewsbury T	D 1-1	1-1	14	Bannister	5129
23	10	A	Oxford U	L 0-1	0-0	16		3420
24	20	A	Blackpool	L 1-3	1-0	—	Warboys	3636
25	24	H	Gillingham	L 0-1	0-1	18		4349
26	Mar 2	A	Swansea C	L 3-5	1-3	20	Horswill, Bannister 2	8849
27	6	H	Brentford	W 1-0	0-0	—	Edwards	3418
28	10	H	Bury	W 4-1	2-1	18	Skipper, Farley, Bannister (pen), Edwards	3940
29	13	H	Colchester U	W 1-0	0-0	—	Stewart	4201
30	24	H	Rotherham U	W 1-0	0-0	14	Hawker	4717
31	27	A	Carlisle U	D 2-2	0-0	—	Roberts, Edwards	6254
32	31	H	Lincoln C	D 0-0	0-0	14		4103
33	Apr 4	A	Chesterfield	W 2-1	2-1	—	Edwards, Galvin	3003
34	7	A	Plymouth Arg	W 4-3	2-1	11	Edwards 2, Skipper, Bannister	5816
35	13	H	Sheffield W	D 1-1	1-0	—	Galvin	10,936
36	14	H	Mansfield T	W 2-0	2-0	10	Bannister, Edwards	5138
37	16	H	Blackpool	D 0-0	0-0	—		6000
38	21	A	Colchester U	L 1-2	0-0	12	Edwards	2762
39	24	H	Southend U	W 2-0	0-0	—	Edwards, McDonald	3960
40	28	A	Swindon T	D 1-1	0-1	10	Bannister	4980
41	May 1	H	Plymouth Arg	W 2-1	0-0	—	Horswill, Edwards	3646
42	5	A	Lincoln C	L 2-4	0-2	9	Roberts, Horswill	2522
43	7	H	Exeter C	W 1-0	0-0	—	Edwards	4079
44	11	A	Peterborough U	L 0-3	0-3	—		1875
45	14	A	Watford	L 0-4	0-1	—		26,397
46	19	A	Sheffield W	W 3-2	2-1	—	McDonald, Roberts, Edwards W	8950

Final League Position: 8

Goalscorers

League (66): Edwards 24, Bannister 15 (2 pens), Horswill 6, Galvin 4, Roberts 3, Lord 3, Skipper 2, McDonald 2, Warboys 2, Nisbet 1, Haigh 1, Farley 1, Stewart 1, Hawker 1.
League Cup (2): Bannister 1, Haigh 1.
F.A. Cup (2): Edwards 1, Own Goal 1.

League Cup	First Round	Peterborough U	(h)	0-1
			(a)	2-1
			(h)	0-1
F.A. Cup	First Round	Stafford	(h)	2-1
	Second Round	Carlisle U	(a)	0-3

Wealands	Nisbet	Devries	Horswill	Croft	Dobson	Haigh	Hood	Edwards	Bannister	Farley	Warboys	Lord	McDonald	Hawker	Galvin	Stewart	Blackburn	Skipper	Roberts	Norrie	Match No.
1	2	3	4	5	6	7	8*	9	10	11	12										1
1	2	3	8*	5	6	4	7	9	10	11		12									2
1	2	3		5	6*	4	7	9	10	11	12	8									3
1	2	3	5	4		6	7	9	10	11		8									4
1	2	3	4			6	7	9	10	11	5	8									5
1	2	3	5			6	7	9	10	11		8	4								6
1	2	3	4	5		6	7	9	10	11			8								7
1	2	3	4	5		6	7*	9	10	11	12	8									8
1	2	3	5	4		6		9	10		7	8		11							9
1	2	3	5	4		6	7	9	10*11	12		8									10
1	2	3	5	4		6	7*	9	10	11		8		12							11
1	2	3	5		4	6		9	10	11		8		7							12
1	2	3	5		4	6		9	10	11	7*	8		12							13
1	2	3	4		5	6		9	10	11		8		7*12							14
1	2	3			5	6	7	9	10	11		8	4								15
1	2	3	4		5	6		9	10	11	7	8									16
1	2	3	4		5	6		9	10	11	7	8									17
	2	3	4		5	6		9	10	11	7	8				1					18
	2	3	4	5	6	7		10	12	11	9	8*				1					19
	2	3	5	4		6		9	10	11		8*		7	12	1					20
	2	3		5	4	6		9	10	11		8		7		1					21
	2	3			5	6		9	10		7	8	4	11		1					22
	2	3			5	6		9	10		7	8	4	11		1					23
	2	3	10*		5	6		9	12	11	7	8	4			1					24
	2	3	10		5	6		9	12	11	7		4	8*		1					25
	2	3	8		5	6		9	10		7		11			1	4				26
	2	3	8		5	6		9	10	11	7					1	4				27
	2	3	4			6		9	10	11	7*		8			1	5	12			28
	2		8	5		6		9	10				4		11	1	3	7			29
	2			5		6		9	10		8		7	12	11*	1	3	4			30
	2		8	5		6		9	10			11*	4	12		1	3	7			31
	2		8*	5		6		9	10				7	11	12	1	3	4			32
	2		8	5		6		9	10				4	11		1	3	7			33
	2		8	5		6	12	9	10				4	11*		1	3	7			34
	2		8	5		6		9*10				12	4	11		1	3	7			35
1	2		8	5		6		9	10				7	11			3	4			36
1	2		8	5		6		9	10				4	11			3	7			37
1	2		8	5		6		9	10	11			7				3	4			38
1	2		8	5*		6		9	10	11		12	4				3	7			39
1	2		8		5	12	9	10	11			4	6				3*	7			40
1.	2		8	12		6	9	10	11			5	4*				3	7			41
1	2		8		3	6		9	10	11		7	5				4				42
1	2		8		5	6	4	9	10	11*		3						7	12		43
1	2		8	3	5	6	4	9	10			11						7			44
1	2		8		12	6		9	10	11		5	7*				4	3			45
1	3	7*	8		6	5	12	9	10	11		2					4				46
28	46	29	40	24	22	45	14	46	43	32	14	23	8	22	15	2	18	17	18	—	
					+ 2s		+ 3s		+ 3s		+ 4s 1s	+ 2s	+	+ 4s 3s	+			+ 1s	+ 1s		

HULL CITY—PLAYERS

Player and position	Ht	Wt	Birthplace	Clubs	League Appearances	Goals
Goalkeepers						
Jeff Wealands	6 0½	12 0	Darlington	Wolverhampton W	—	—
				Northampton (on loan)	—	—
				Darlington	28	—
				Hull C	240	—
Edwin Blackburn	5 9	10 5	Houghton Le Spring	Hull C	39	—
Willie Boyd	5 10½	11 0	Bellshill	Hull C	—	—
				Doncaster R (on loan)	—	—
Defenders						
Gerry Collins (Contract cancelled September 1978)	6 1	12 3	Hamilton	Hull C	—	—
Roger De Vries	5 8½	11 5	Hull	Hull C	280+4	—
Paul Haigh	5 10	11 6	Scarborough	Hull C	133	4
Stuart Croft	5 11	11 5	Ashington	Hull C	141+3	3
Ian Dobson	5 10	11 1	Hull	Hull C	60+6	5
Peter Skipper	5 11	12 6½	Hull	Hull C	17	2
Robert McDonald	6 3	13 5	Hull	Hull C	13+2	2
Midfield						
Malcolm Lord	5 7½	11 10	Driffield	Hull C	271+27	23
Gordon Nisbet	5 10	12 2	Wallsend on Tyne	WBA	136	—
				Hull C	120+3	1
David Hawker	5 7	9 12	Hull	Hull C	26+1	1
Derek Hood	5 10½	11 4	Washington	Hull C	18+3	—
Brian Marwood	5 7	9 13	Easington	Hull C	—	—
Mike Horswill	5 10½	11 0	Annfield Plain	Sunderland	68+1	3
				Manchester C	11+3	—
				Plymouth Arg	98+4	3
				Hull C	40	6
Garreth Roberts	5 4	10 2	Hull	Hull C	18+1	3
Stephen McLaren	5 7½	9 4		Hull C	—	—
Forwards						
Bruce Bannister	5 7½	11 5	Bradford	Bradford C	199+9	61
				Bristol R	202+3	80
				Plymouth Arg	24	7
				Hull C	69+5	19
Alan Warboys	6 0½	13 7	Goldthorpe	Doncaster R	39+2	11
				Sheffield W	66+5	13
				Cardiff C	57+4	27
				Sheffield U	7	—
				Bristol R	141+3	53
				Fulham	19	2
				Hull C	44+5	9
*Chris Hartley	5 7	9 11	Hull	Hull C	—	—
John Farley	5 7	9 12	Stockton	Watford	96+8	8
				Halifax T (on loan)	6	3
				Wolverhampton W	35+5	—
				Blackpool (on loan)	1	—
				Hull C	32	1
Keith Edwards	5 7	10 3	Stockton	Sheffield U	64+6	29
				Hull C	46	24
Craig Norrie	5 10½	10 11½	Hull	Hull C	0+1	—
David Leadbetter	5 7	10 5½		Hull C	—	—

IPSWICH TOWN　　　　　　　　　　　　　　　　　DIV. 1

President: Lady Blanche Cobbold.
Chairman: P. M. Cobbold.
Directors: W. Kerr, H. R. Smith, J. M. Sangster, K. H. Brightwell, J. C. Cobbold.
Manager: Bobby Robson.
Secretary: D. C. Rose.
P. R. O.: Mel Henderson.
Year Formed: 1877.　*Turned Professional:* 1936.
Limited Company: 1936.
Football League Record:
1938 Elected to Division 3(S).　　1961–64 Division 1.
1954–55 Division 2.　　　　　　　1964–68 Division 2.
1955–57 Division 3(S).　　　　　　1968–　　Division 1.
1957–61 Division 2.

Honours: Football League: Division 1, Champions: 1961–62. Division 2, Champions: 1960–61, 1967–68. Division 3(S), Champions: 1953–54, 1956–57. *F.A. Cup,* Winners: 1977–78. *Football League Cup,* best season: 5th Rd., 1966, 1974.
European Competitions: European Cup, 1962–63. *European Cup Winners Cup:* 1978–79. UEFA Cup, 1973–74, 1974–75, 1975–76, 1977–78.
Record Victory: 10-0 v Floriana, Malta, European Cup, 1st Rd., 1962–63.
Record Defeat: 1-10 v Fulham, Division 1, Dec. 26th, 1963.
Most League Points: 64, Division 3(S), 1953–54, 1955–56.
Most League Goals: 106, Division 3(S), 1955–56.
Highest League Scorer in Season: Ted Phillips, 41, Division 3(S), 1956–57.
Most Goals in Total Aggregate: Ray Crawford, 203, 1958–63, 1966–69.
Most Capped Player: Allan Hunter, 45 (51), N. Ireland.
Most League Appearances: Mick Mills, 469, 1966–79.
Record Transfer Fee Received: £450,000 from Arsenal for Brian Talbot, Jan. 1979.
Record Transfer Fee Paid: £220,000 to Plymouth Arg. for Paul Mariner, Oct. 1976.
Managers Since the War: A. Scott Duncan, Alf Ramsey, Jackie Milburn, Bill McGarry.
Address of Supporters Club: Same as Football Club.
Address of Club Shop or Boutique: Same as Football Club.

Portman Rd., Ipswich, Suffolk IP1 2DA. Telephone: Ipswich 219211 (4 lines). *Ground capacity:* 32,000. *Record attendance:* 38,010 v Leeds U., F.A. Cup 6th Rd., March 8, 1975. *Record receipts:* £46,099.50 v Liverpool, F.A. Cup 6th Rd., March 10, 1979. *Pitch measurements:* 112yds × 72yds.

How to get there: The ground is central and only two minutes walk from Ipswich railway station; the town centre is five minutes away. Local buses run past the ground.
Match tickets: All seats sold as season tickets.
Car parking: Large parks in Portman Road, Portman's Walk, and off Princes Street at Greyfriars Park.
Entertainments/catering facilities: 'Centre Spot' bar and restaurant in Portman Road. Bars around the ground.
Club shops: Four on the ground stock all types of souvenirs.
Handbooks/programmes: Programmes available on subscription and an Annual is published.
Extra information: When Ipswich won the First Division title in 1962, five of the side – Bailey, Carberry, Phillips, Elsworthy, and Leadbetter – had been regulars in the Third Division side of the middle fifties.
Club Colours: Blue shirts with three white stripes down each arm, white shorts with three blue stripes, blue stockings with three white stripes.
Change Colours: White shirts with three black stripes down each arm, black shorts with three white stripes, white stockings with three black stripes.
Club Captain: Mick Mills.
First Team Trainer: Cyril Lea.
Club Nickname: 'Town' or 'Blues'.

IPSWICH TOWN 1978–79 LEAGUE RECORD

Match No.	Date	Venue	Opponents	Result	H/T Score	League Pos'n	Goalscorers	Attendance
1	Aug 19	A	WBA	L 1-2	1-1	—	Woods	21,700
2	22	H	Liverpool	L 0-3	0-2	—		28,114
3	26	H	Manchester U	W 3-0	1-0	14	Mariner 2, Talbot	21,894
4	Sept 2	A	Middlesbrough	D 0-0	0-0	14		14,427
5	9	H	Aston Villa	L 0-2	0-1	17		22,166
6	16	A	Wolverhampton W	W 3-1	2-1	15	Mariner, Muhren, Whymark	16,409
7	23	H	Bristol C	L 0-1	0-0	18		20,168
8	30	A	Southampton	W 2-1	2-0	13	Mariner 2	21,264
9	Oct 7	A	Coventry C	D 2-2	2-0	14	Osman, Woods	21,859
10	14	H	Everton	L 0-1	0-1	15		22,676
11	21	A	Nottingham F	L 0-1	0-1	18		28,911
12	28	H	QPR	W 2-1	0-0	15	Gates, Mariner	20,428
13	Nov 4	A	Arsenal	L 1-4	1-3	17	Mariner	35,269
14	11	H	WBA	L 0-1	0-1	18		20,914
15	18	A	Manchester U	L 0-2	0-1	18		42,109
16	21	A	Middlesbrough	W 2-1	1-1	—	Burley, Woods	17,570
17	25	A	Manchester C	W 2-1	0-0	15	Gates, Talbot	38,256
18	Dec 2	H	Leeds U	L 2-3	1-2	16	Beattie, Wark (pen)	22,526
19	9	A	Tottenham H	L 0-1	0-0	16		33,882
20	16	H	Bolton W	W 3-0	1-0	16	Mariner, Gates, Talbot	16,593
21	26	A	Norwich C	D 1-1	0-1	16	Mills	26,336
22	30	H	Chelsea	W 5-1	3-0	13	Osman, Muhren 2, Wark, Mariner	21,439
23	Jan 20	H	Wolverhampton W	W 3-1	2-1	12	Wark 2 (1 a pen), Mariner	17,965
24	Feb 3	A	Bristol C	L 1-3	1-0	14	Mariner	17,025
25	10	A	Southampton	D 0-0	0-0	13		19,520
26	24	A	Everton	W 1-0	1-0	13	Mariner	29,031
27	28	A	Derby Co	W 1-0	0-0	—	Woods	15,935
28	Mar 3	H	Nottingham F	D 1-1	0-1	12	Brazil	27,198
29	13	H	Coventry C	D 1-1	1-0	—	Muhren	16,095
30	17	H	Arsenal	W 2-0	1-0	9	Wark, Rix (og)	26,407
31	24	A	Liverpool	L 0-2	0-1	12		43,243
32	31	H	Manchester C	W 2-1	2-0	12	Geddis, Brazil	20,773
33	Apr 3	A	Birmingham C	D 1-1	1-0	—	Muhren	12,499
34	7	A	Leeds U	D 1-1	0-1	10	Gates	24,153
35	14	A	Norwich C	W 1-0	0-0	9	Thijssen	25,061
36	16	H	Derby Co	W 2-1	2-1	—	Mariner, Mills	19,899
37	17	H	Birmingham C	W 3-0	2-0	—	Gates, Butcher, Brazil	17,676
38	21	A	Bolton W	W 3-2	2-1	7	Brazil 2, Wark	20,073
39	28	H	Tottenham H	W 2-1	2-0	7	Muhren, Brazil	28,179
40	May 2	A	Aston Villa	D 2-2	1-2	—	Muhren 2	26,636
41	5	A	Chelsea	W 3-2	3-2	7	Brazil 2, Woods	15,462
42	11	A	QPR	W 4-0	2-0	—	Gates 2, Brazil, Butcher	9,819

Final League Position: 6

Goalscorers

League (63): Mariner 13, Brazil 9, Muhren 8, Gates 7, Wark 6 (2 pens), Woods 5, Talbot 3, Mills 2, Osman 2, Butcher 2, Burley 1, Beattie 1, Geddis 1, Whymark 1, Thijssen 1, Own goal 1.

F.A. Cup (11): Mariner 3, Muhren 2, Brazil 2, Beattie, Wark, Mills, Geddis.

League Cup	Second Round	Blackpool (a)	0-2
F.A. Cup	Third Round	Carlisle U (h)	3-2
	Fourth Round	Orient (h)	0-0
		(a)	2-0
	Fifth Round	Bristol R (h)	6-1
	Sixth Round	Liverpool (h)	0-1

215

Cooper	Burley	Tibbott	Mills	Osman	Wark	Parkin	Gates	Mariner	Whymark	Woods	Lambert	Talbot	Muhren	Beattie	Brazil	Hunter	Butcher	Geddis	Thijssen	Sivell	Match No.
1	2	3	4	5	6	7	8	9	10*	11	12										1
1	2		3	5	6	7	12	9	10	11		4*	8								2
1	2		3	5	7			9	10	11		4	8	6							3
1	2		3	5	8			9		11	7	4	10	6							4
1	2		3	5	7		8*	9	12	11		4	10	6							5
1	2		3	5	7			9	10	11*		4	8	6	12						6
1	2		3	5	7			9	10*	11		4	8	6	12						7
1	2	3	10	5	7			9		11		4	8	6							8
1	2		3	4	7			9		11		8	10	6		5					9
1	2		3	5	7			9	10	11		4*	8		12	6					10
1	2	3	7*	6	8				12	11		4	10		9	5					11
1	2		3	6	7		11	9	12			4	8			5	10*				12
1		3	2	6	7			9	12	11		4	8			5	10*				13
1		3	2	5	7			9		11*		4	8	6	12		10				14
1	2		3	5	7		10	9		11		4	8*	6			12				15
1	2		3	5	7		10	9		11		4	8	6							16
1	2		3	5	7		10	9		11		4	8	6							17
1	2		3	5	7		10	9		11		4	8	6							18
1	2		3	5	7			9	12	11		4	8		10*	6					19
1	2		3*	6	7	12	8	9		11		4	10			5					20
1	2		3	5	7		10	9		11		4	8			6					21
1	2		3	6	7		10	9		11		4*	8			5	12				22
1	2		4	5	7			9	10	11		8	6								23
1		3	2	5	7	4*		9	10	11		8				6	12				24
1	2	3	4	5	7			9		11		8	6	10*		12					25
1	2	3	4		7			9		11		8	6	10		5					26
1		3	2	5	7			9		11		8		10*		6	12	4			27
1	2		3	5	7			9		11		8		10		6		4			28
1	2		3	5	7		10	9		11		8				6		4			29
1	2		3	5	7		10	9		11		8				6		4			30
1	2	3*	10	5	7			9		11		8		12		6		4			31
1	2		3		7					11	12	8	6	10		5	9*	4			32
1	2		3		7		9			11*		8	6	10		5	12	4			33
1	2		3	5	7		10			11		8	6				9	4			34
	2		3	5	7		8	9		11		10	6*				12	4	1		35
1	2		3	5	7		12	9*	4	11		8				6	10				36
1	2		3	5	7		10			11		8*		9		6	12	4			37
1	2		3	5	7		10*			11		8		9		6	12	4			38
1	2		3	5	7		10			11		8		9		6		4			39
1	2		3	5	7		10			11		8		9		6		4			40
1	2		3	5	7		10*		11	12		8		9		6		4			41
1	2		3	5	7		10		11*			8	12	9		6		4			42
41	38	11	42	39	42	3	20	33	8	41	1	21	41	19	14	4	21	6	16	1	
						+1s	+2s		+5s		+3s			+1s		+5s		+9s			

IPSWICH TOWN—PLAYERS

Player and position	Ht	Wt	Birthplace	Clubs	League Appearances	Goals
Goalkeepers						
Paul Cooper	5 9	10 10	Brierley Hill	Birmingham C	17	—
				Ipswich T	158	—
Laurie Sivell	5 8	11 0	Lowestoft	Ipswich T	113	—
				Lincoln C (on loan)	2	—
*Paul Overton	6 0	11 6	Ely	Ipswich T	1	—
Scott Endersby	5 10	12 4	Lewisham	Ipswich T	—	—
Kieron Baker	6 0½	12	Ryde	Fulham	—	—
				Mansfield T (on loan)	—	—
				Brentford (on loan)	6	—
				Bournemouth	217	—
				Norwich C (on loan)	—	—
Defenders						
George Burley (Scotland)	5 8	10 5	Cumnock	Ipswich T	202	4
Terry Butcher	6 3	11 12	Singapore	Ipswich T	24	2
Allan Hunter (N Ireland)	5 11	12 7	Sion Mills	Oldham Ath	83	1
				Blackburn R	84	2
				Ipswich T	263	6
Mick Mills (England)	5 6	10 8	Godalming	Ipswich T	465+4	18
Dale Roberts	5 8	10 5	Ashington	Ipswich T	17+1	—
Kevin Beattie (England)	5 10	12 2	Carlisle	Ipswich T	208+3	23
Russell Osman	5 9	10 10	Repton	Ipswich T	67	2
Kevin Durrant (Contract cancelled September 1978)				Ipswich T	—	—
Peter Canavan (Deceased)	5 11	11 4	Ash Winning	Ipswich T	—	—
Peter Shields	5 7	10 2	Glasgow	Ipswich T	—	—
Nigel Crouch	5 8	10 7	Ardleigh	Ipswich T	—	—
Don Souter	5 11	11 8	Hammersmith	Ipswich T	—	—
Kevin Steggles	5 11½	12 1	Ditchingham	Ipswich T	—	—
*Stephen Williamson	5 9	11 0	Ashington	Ipswich T	—	—
Midfield						
John Wark (Scotland)	5 8	10 4	Glasgow	Ipswich T	99	21
Roger Osborne	5 9	10 11	Otley	Ipswich T	104+13	9
Eric Gates	5 5	10 4	Ferryhill	Ipswich T	56+27	11
Alec Jamieson (Contract cancelled October 1978)	5 7	10 10	Clydebank	Ipswich T	—	—
Tommy Parkin	5 7	9 6	Gateshead	Ipswich T	3+2	—
				Grimsby T (on loan)	6	—
				Peterborough U (on loan)	3	—
Noel Parkinson	5 8	10 4	Hull	Ipswich T	—	—
Bryan Klug	5 9	10 7	Coventry	Ipswich T	—	—
Stephen McCall	5 11	11 3	Carlisle	Ipswich T	—	—
Arnold Muhren (Holland)	5 10	11 0	Volendam	Twente	(not known)	
				Ipswich T	41	8
Frans Thijssen (Holland)	5 10	11 2	Heumen	Twente	(not known)	
				Ipswich T	16	1
Ron Burns	5 8	10 7	Londonderry	Coleraine	—	—
				Ipswich T	—	—
Forwards						
Clive Woods	5 9	9 10	Norwich	Ipswich T	208+51	22
Mick Lambert	5 8	10 12	Cambridge	Ipswich T	181+30	39
Trevor Whymark (England) (Contract cancelled February 1979)	5 9	10 5	Norfolk	Ipswich T	249+11	74
Robin Turner	5 9	10 8	Carlisle	Ipswich T	12+7	—
David Geddis	5 11	11 2	Carlisle	Ipswich T	26+17	5
				Luton T (on loan)	9+4	4
Paul Mariner (England)	6 0	11 12	Bolton	Plymouth Arg	134+1	56
				Ipswich T	98	34
David Hubbick	5 7½	10 10	S Shields	Ipswich T	—	—
Alan Brazil	5 10	11 3	Glasgow	Ipswich T	14+7	9
Tony Wharton	5 9	10 8	Beverley	Ipswich T	—	—
Mich D'Avray	6 1	12 0	Johannesburg	Ipswich T	—	—

LEEDS UNITED   DIV. 1

President: The Right Hon. The Earl of Harewood, LL.D.
Chairman: M. Cussins.
Vice-Chairman: R. Barker, M.C.I.T, M.B.I.M.
Directors: R. B. Roberts, J.P., F.I.O.B., B. Woodward, J. W. G. Marjason, S. G. Simon, R. R. Roberts.
Manager: Jimmy Adamson.
General Manager/Secretary: K. Archer.
Year Formed: 1919, as Leeds United after disbandment (by F.A. Order) of Leeds City 1904.
Turned Professional: 1920. *Limited Company:* 1920.
Football League Record: 1920 Elected to Division 2. 1924–27 Division 1. 1927–28 Division 2. 1928–31 Division 1. 1931–32 Division 2. 1932–47 Division 1. 1947–56 Division 2. 1956–60 Division 1. 1960–64 Division 2. 1964– Division 1.
Honours: *Football League,* Division 1, Champions: 1968–69, 1973–74; Runners-up: 1964–65, 1965–66, 1969–70, 1970–71, 1971–72. Division 2, Champions: 1923–24, 1963–64; Runners-up: 1927–28, 1931–32, 1955–56. *F.A. Cup,* Winners: 1971-72. Runners-up: 1964–65, 1969–70, 1972–73. *Football League Cup,* Winners: 1967–68.
European Competitions: *European Cup:* 1969–79, Runners -up 1974–75. *European Cup-Winners' Cup:* Runners-up, 1972–73, *European Fairs Cup:* 1965–66, 1966–67 (Runners-up) 1967–68 (winners), 1968–69, 1970–71 (winners). *UEFA Cup:* 1971–72, 1973–74.
Record Victory: 10-0 v Lyn Oslo, European Cup, 1st Rd., 1st Leg, Sept. 17th, 1969.
Record Defeat: 1-8 v Stoke C., Division 1, Aug. 27th, 1934.
Most League Points: 67, Division 1, 1968–69 (First Division Record).
Most League Goals: 98, Division 2, 1927–28.
Highest League Scorer in Season: John Charles, 42, Division 2, 1953–54.
Most League Goals in Total Aggregate: John Charles, 154, 1948–57 and 1962.
Most Capped Player: Billy Bremner, 54, Scotland.
Most League Appearances: Jack Charlton, 629, 1953–73.
Record Transfer Fee Received: £495,000 from Manchester U. for Gordon McQueen, Feb. 1978.
Record Transfer Fee Paid: £370,000 to Swansea C. for Alan Curtis, May 1979.
Managers Since the War: Billy Hampson, Willis Edwards, Major Frank Buckley, Raich Carter, Bill Lambton, Jack Taylor, Don Revie, O.B.E., Brian Clough, Jimmy Armfield, Jock Stein.
Address of Supporters Club: Leeds United Supporters Club, Fullerton Park, Elland Road, Leeds 11.
Address of Club Shop: Leeds United Club Shop, Elland Road, Leeds 11.

Elland Rd., Leeds LS11 0ES. Telephone Leeds 716037 (3 lines). *Telegraphic Address:* 'Football Leeds'. *Ground Capacity:* 43,900. *Record attendance:* 57,892 v Sunderland, F.A. Cup 5th Rd., Replay, March 15, 1967. *Record receipts:* £90,000 v Barcelona, European Cup semi-final first leg, April 9 1975. *Pitch measurements:* 117 × 76 yds.
How to get there: Nearest railway station, Leeds. The city centre is within walking distance from the station and then by Corporation buses to the ground.
Match tickets: Computer installed for sale of match by match tickets.
Car parking: Within one minute of the ground there is a large park owned by the Leeds Greyhound Association; this holds about 1,000 cars. Large park on the Beeston Ring Road owned and operated by the club.
Entertainments/catering facilities: Supporters' social club adjacent to the ground. Snack bars around the ground.
Club shop: This operates at the ground next to the Pools Office and stocks all types of souvenirs.
Handbooks/programmes: Both handbooks and programmes are available from the club shop; programmes are available on subscription.
Extra information: The club have a Robotphone Answering System – the Leeds United Information Service: Leeds 702621. New Football League record established in 1973–74 with a 29-game run of matches without defeat from beginning of the season.
Club Colours: All white with blue and yellow collar and trim.
Change Colours: All yellow with blue and white trim.
Club Captain: Trevor Cherry.
Deputy Manager: Dave Merrington.

LEEDS UNITED 1978-79 LEAGUE RECORD

Match No.	Date	Venue	Opponents	Result	H/T Score	League Pos'n	Goalscorers	Attendance
1	Aug 19	A	Arsenal	D 2-2	1-1	—	Currie, Cherry	42,057
2	23	H	Manchester U	L 2-3	1-2	—	Hart, Gray F (pen)	36,845
3	26	H	Wolverhampton W	W 3-0	2-0	8	Hankin, Gray F (pen), Currie	26,267
4	Sept 2	A	Chelsea	W 3-0	1-0	5	Graham, Hawley 2	30,099
5	9	A	Manchester C	L 0-3	0-2	9		40,125
6	16	H	Tottenham H	L 1-2	1-1	14	Graham	36,062
7	23	A	Coventry C	D 0-0	0-0	12		27,365
8	30	H	Birmingham C	W 3-0	1-0	11	Flynn, Gray F (pen), Hankin	23,331
9	Oct 7	A	Bolton W	L 1-3	1-0	13	Graham	27,751
10	14	H	WBA	L 1-3	1-1	14	Stevenson	25,931
11	21	A	Norwich C	D 2-2	1-0	14	Gray F, Hawley	19,981
12	28	H	Derby Co	W 4-0	3-0	12	Flynn, Hart, Hankin, Hawley	25,449
13	Nov 4	A	Liverpool	D 1-1	1-0	12	Hawley	51,857
14	11	H	Arsenal	L 0-1	0-1	14		33,961
15	18	A	Wolverhampton W	D 1-1	1-1	14	Currie	18,961
16	22	H	Chelsea	W 2-1	2-1	—	Graham, Hankin	24,088
17	25	H	Southampton	W 4-0	2-0	10	Graham, Currie, Golac (og), Madeley	23,592
18	Dec 2	A	Ipswich T	W 3-2	2-1	9	Hankin, Harris, Cherry	22,526
19	9	A	Bristol C	D 1-1	1-1	9	Flynn	22,529
20	16	A	Everton	D 1-1	1-0	9	Hawley	37,997
21	23	H	Middlesbrough	W 3-1	1-1	8	Hawley, Gray E, Currie	27,146
22	26	A	Aston Villa	D 2-2	0-2	6	Gray E 2	40,973
23	30	A	QPR	W 4-1	1-0	6	Hawley 2, Harris, Gray E	17,435
24	Jan 13	H	Manchester C	D 1-1	1-0	5	Hawley	36,303
25	20	A	Tottenham H	W 2-1	1-0	5	Hart, Hankin	36,828
26	Feb 3	H	Coventry C	W 1-0	1-0	5	Currie	22,928
27	10	A	Birmingham C	W 1-0	1-0	5	Gray F (pen)	17,620
28	24	A	WBA	W 2-1	2-1	4	Graham 2	26,426
29	Mar 3	H	Norwich C	D 2-2	1-0	5	Hawley 2	23,038
30	10	A	Derby Co	W 1-0	0-0	4	Hawley	22,800
31	24	H	Manchester U	L 1-4	0-3	5	Hankin	51,191
32	31	A	Southampton	D 2-2	1-0	6	Hawley 2	21,805
33	Apr 7	H	Ipswich T	D 1-1	1-0	5	Cherry	24,153
34	10	A	Middlesbrough	L 0-1	0-1	—		23,260
35	14	H	Aston Villa	W 1-0	1-0	6	Hart	24,281
36	16	A	Nottingham F	D 0-0	0-0	—		37,397
37	21	H	Everton	W 1-0	0-0	5	Currie	29,125
38	25	H	Bolton W	W 5-1	2-0	—	Cherry, Gray F (pen), Hart, Harris, Hawley	20,218
39	28	A	Bristol C	D 0-0	0-0	5		25,388
40	May 4	H	QPR	W 4-3	1-2	5	Graham, Hankin 2, Cherry	20,121
41	15	H	Nottingham F	L 1-2	0-1	—	Cherry	33,544
42	17	H	Liverpool	L 0-3	0-2	—		41,324

Final League Position: 5

Goalscorers

League (70): Hawley 16, Hankin 9, Graham 8, Currie 7, Cherry 6, Gray F 6 (5 pens), Hart 5, Gray E 4, Flynn 3, Harris 3, Madeley 1, Stevenson 1, Own Goal 1.
League Cup (13): Gray E 3, Currie 3, Gray F 2 (1 pen), Hankin 2, Hart, Cherry, Hawley
F.A. Cup: (9) Graham 2, Harris 2, Gray E 2, Gray F 2 (1 pen), Hart

League Cup:	Second Round	WBA (a)	0-0
		(h)	0-0 (aet)
			1-0 (at Maine Rd.)
	Third Round	Sheffield U (a)	4-1
	Fourth Round	QPR (a)	2-0
	Fifth Round	Luton T (h)	4-1
	Semi-Final	Southampton (h)	2-2
		(a)	0-1
F.A. Cup	Third Round	Hartlepool (a)	6-2
	Fourth Round	WBA (a)	3-3
		(a)	0-2 (aet)

Harvey	Madeley	Gray F	Flynn	Hart	Cherry	Harris	Gray E	Hawley	Currie	Graham	Stevenson	Hankin	Stewart	Hampton	Lorimer	Thomas	Parkinson	Hird	Match No.
1	2	3	4	5	6	7	8	9	10	11									1
1	6	3	4	5		7	9		10	11	2	8							2
	6	3	4	5		7*	8	12	10	11	2	9	1						3
	6	3	4	5				9	10	11	2	8	1	7					4
	6	3*	4	5	7	12		9		11	2	8	1	10					5
1	6	3	4	5	10	7				11	2	8			9				6
1	6	3	4	5	10	7				11	2	8			9				7
1	6	10	4	5	3	7				11	2	8			9*	12			8
1	6	10	4	5	3	7	9			11	2	8							9
1	6	9	4	5	3	7			10	11	2	8							10
1	6	3	4	5	2	7	9		10	11		8							11
1	6	3	4	5	2	7	9		10	11		8							12
1	6	3	4	5	2	7	9		10	11		8							13
1	6	3	4	5	2	7			9	10	11	8							14
1	6	3	4	5	2	7	9		10	11		8							15
1	6	3	4	5	2	7	9		10	11		8							16
1	6	3	4	5	2	7			9	10	11	8							17
1	6	3	4	5	2	11	7	9	10			8							18
1	6		4	5	2	11	7		10		3	8			9				19
1	6	3	4	5	2	11	7	9	10			8							20
1	6	3	4	5	2	7	8	9	10	11									21
1	6	3	4	5	2	8	7	9	10	11									22
1	6	3*	4	5	2	11	7	9	10	8					12				23
1	6	3	4	5	2	11	7	9	10	8									24
1		3	4	5		11		9	10	8	2	7			6				25
1	6	7	4		2	9			10	11	3	8			5				26
1	6	7	4	5	2	8*12		9	10	11	3								27
1	6	11	4	5	2	7*		9	10	8	3				12				28
1	6	3	4		2	7		9	10	11						5	8		29
1	6*	3	4	5	2	7	12	9	10	11						8			30
1		8*	4	5	3	7	6	9	10	11	12					2			31
1		3	4	5	6		7	9	10	11		8				2			32
1	6	3	4	5	2		7	9	10*11			8				12			33
1	10	3	4	5	6		7	9		11	12	8*				2			34
1	6	3	4	5	2	12	7*	9		11		8				10			35
1	10	3	4	5	6	7		9		11			8			2			36
1	9	3	4	5	6	7			10	11		8				2			37
1	6	3	4	5	8	7		12	10	11		9*				2			38
1	6	3		5	4	7	10			11		9	8			2			39
1	6	3	4	5	8	7		12	10	11*		9				2			40
1	6	3	4	5	8	7*12		9	10	11						2			41
1	6	3	4	5	8	7	10	9		11						2			42
39	39	41	41	40	38	29	25	29	32	39	14	29	3	4	3	1	3	13	
						+	+	+			+	+				+	+	+	
						2s	3s	3s			1s	1s				1s	2s	1s	

219

LEEDS UNITED—PLAYERS

Player and position	Ht	Wt	Birthplace	Clubs	League Appearances	Goals
Goalkeepers						
David Harvey (Scotland)	5 11	12 3	Leeds	Leeds U	267	—
Henry Smith	6 1½	11 12	Lanarkshire	Leeds U	—	—
John Lukic	6 0	9 0	Chesterfield	Leeds U	—	—
Defenders						
Paul Madeley (England)	6 0	12 6½	Leeds	Leeds U	495+10	24
Peter Hampton	5 7½	11 0	Oldham	Leeds U	46+5	2
Byron Stevenson (Wales)	6 1	11 0	Llanelli	Leeds U	28+4	1
Frankie Gray (Scotland)	5 9½	11 10	Glasgow	Leeds U	188+5	17
Paul Hart	6 2	12 8	Manchester	Stockport Co	88	5
				Blackpool	143	17
				Leeds U	52	5
Keith Parkinson	6 1½	12 6	Preston	Leeds U	12+5	—
*Nick MacNay	5 10	9 0	Leeds	Leeds U	—	—
Barry Tyerman	5 7	8 7	South Shields	Leeds U	—	—
Kevin Hird	5 7	10 6	Colne	Blackburn R	129+3	20
				Leeds U	13+1	—
Duncan Reynard	5 8	11 0	Gosport	Leeds U	—	—
Neil Parker	5 6	10 3	Blackburn	Leeds U	0+1	—
Neil Firm	6 2½	11 2	Bradford	Leeds U	—	—
Midfield						
Trevor Cherry (England)	5 9	11 6	Huddersfield	Huddersfield T	184+2	10
				Leeds U	260+5	20
Tony Currie (England)	5 10½	12 10	Edgware	Watford	17+1	9
				Sheffield U	313	55
				Leeds U	102	11
David Whyte	5 9	11 5	Dunfermline	Leeds U	1+1	—
Peter Savill	5 9	10 12	Bacup	Leeds U	—	—
Billy McGhie	5 9	11 0	Lanark	Leeds U	2	1
Brian Flynn (Wales)	5 3½	9 0	Port Talbot	Burnley	115+5	8
				Leeds U	69+1	4
Peter Daly	5 7	10 0	Hamilton	Leeds U	—	—
David Bennett	5 8½	9 6	Rotherham	Leeds U	—	—
Eddie Gray (Scotland)	5 11	12 7	Glasgow	Leeds U	319+13	49
Forwards						
Carl Harris (Wales)	5 9	11 1	Neath	Leeds U	62+21	12
Peter Lorimer (Scotland) (Contract cancelled March 1979)	5 10	12 0	Dundee	Leeds U	428+21	151
Gwyn Thomas	5 8	11 0	Swansea	Leeds U	8+5	2
Ray Hankin	6 2	14 0	Wallsend	Burnley	110+2	37
				Leeds U	66+1	29
Arthur Graham (Scotland)	5 7½	11 10	Glasgow	Aberdeen	212+8	34
				Leeds U	79	17
John Hawley	6 1	13 5	Withernsea	Hull C	101+13	22
				Leeds U	29+3	16
*Sean Sturman	5 9	11 0	Pontypool	Leeds U	—	—
Alan Clarke	5 9	9 10	Dublin	Leeds U	—	—
Phil Porthouse	5 9	10 0	Jarrow	Leeds U	—	—
David Reid	5 10	11 5	Glasgow	Leeds U	—	—

Free transfers: *Tony Barrowcliffe, *Darren Feeney, *Robert Skilling, *David Thompson, *John MacPhee

LEICESTER CITY DIV. 2

Chairman: D. E. Sharp.
Vice-Chairman: T. W. Shipman.
Directors: W. S. G. Needham, O.B.E., T. E. Bloor, W. G. Page, A. E. Pallett, L. T. Shipman, C.B.E.,
Manager: Jock Wallace.   *Gen. Secretary:* A. K. Bennett.
Year Formed: 1884.
Previous Grounds: 1884, Victoria Park; 1887, Belgrave Road; 1888, Victoria Park; 1891, Filbert Street.
Previous Name: 1884–1919, Leicester Fosse.
Football League Record: 1894 Elected to Division 2. 1908–09 Division 1. 1909–25 Division 2. 1925–35 Division 1. 1935–37 Division 2. 1937–39 Division 1. 1946–54 Division 2. 1954–55 Division 1. 1955–57 Division 2. 1957–69 Division 1. 1969–71 Division 2. 1971–78 Division 1. 1978–   Division 2.

Honours: *Football League,* Division 1, Runners-up: 1928–29. Division 2, Champions: 1924–25, 1936–37, 1953–54, 1956–57; 1970–71. Runners-up: 1907–08.   *F.A. Cup,* Runners-up: 1949, 1961, 1963, 1969.   *Football League Cup,* Winners: 1964; Runners-up: 1965.

European Competitions: *European Cup Winners Cup:* 1961–62.

Record Victory: 10-0 v Portsmouth, Division 1, Oct. 20th, 1928.
Record Defeat: 0-12 (as Leicester Fosse) v Nottingham F., Division 1, Apr. 21st, 1909.
Most League Points: 61, Division 2, 1956–57.
Most League Goals: 109, Division 2, 1956–57.
Highest League Scorer in Season: Arthur Rowley, 44, Division 2, 1956–57.
Most Capped Player: Gordon Banks, 37 (73), England.
Most League Appearances: Adam Black, 530, 1919–35.
Most Goals in Total Aggregate: Arthur Chandler, 262, 1923–35.
Record Transfer Fee Received: £325,000 from Stoke C. for Peter Shilton, November 1974.
Record Transfer Fee Paid: £250,000 to Bruges, Belgium, for Roger Davies, Dec. 1977.
Managers Since the War: Johnny Duncan, Norman Bullock, David Halliday, Matt Gillies, Frank O'Farrell, Jimmy Bloomfield, Frank McLintock.
Address of Club Shop: Leicester City Promotions, Club Shop, City Stadium, Filbert Street, Leicester. Remittance and S.A.E. for price list.

City Stadium, Filbert St., Leicester. Telephone Leicester 555000 (Match information Leicester 551155).   *Ground Capacity:* 34,000.   *Record attendance:* 47,298 v Tottenham, F.A. Cup 5th Rd., February 18, 1928.   *Record receipts:* £23,000 v Arsenal, F.A. Cup 5th Rd., second replay, Feb. 24, 1975.   *Pitch measurements:* 112 yds × 75 yds.

How to get there: Corporation buses from Humberstone Gate and Waterloo St. (opposite railway station) in city centre. Nearest station Leicester. Midland Red run bus services to the town centre from outlying districts.
Match tickets: Seats can be booked from 14 days prior to date of match & S.A.E.
Car parking: Parking adjacent to the ground is for season-ticket holders only. There is nearby street parking and also a public car park about five minutes walk from the ground.
Entertainments/catering facilities: A private season-ticket members bar in the main stand, and catering bars in all sections of the ground.
Club shop: Situated under the main stand; sells all types of souvenirs.
Handbooks/programmes: Both handbooks and programmes are available from the club shop.
Extra information: A league inquiry after Leicester's record defeat discovered that the players had been celebrating a team-mate's wedding!
Club Colours: Blue shirts with white collar and cuffs, white shorts with L.C.F.C. initials on thigh, white stockings with blue tops.
Club Captain: Dennis Rofe.
Physiotherapist: John McVey.
Club Nickname: 'Filberts' and 'Foxes'.

LEICESTER CITY 1978–79 LEAGUE RECORD

Match No.	Date	Venue	Opponents	Result	H/T Score	League Pos'n	Goalscorers	Attendance
1	Aug 19	A	Burnley	D 2-2	1-0	—	Hughes (pen), Christie	12,026
2	23	H	Sheffield U	L 0-1	0-0	—		19,381
3	26	H	Cambridge U	D 1-1	1-0	16	Christie	14,148
4	Sept 2	A	Wrexham	D 0-0	0-0	16		12,785
5	9	H	Notts Co	L 0-1	0-1	19		14,485
6	16	A	Blackburn R	D 1-1	0-1	19	Weller	7908
7	23	H	Brighton & HA	W 4-1	2-0	14	Christie, Hughes 2 (1 a pen), Weller	14,307
8	30	A	Orient	W 1-0	0-0	11	Christie	5430
9	Oct 7	A	Newcastle U	L 0-1	0-0	13		25,374
10	14	H	Charlton Ath	L 0-3	0-2	17		14,278
11	21	A	Cardiff C	L 0-1	0-1	18		8791
12	28	H	Bristol R	D 0-0	0-0	18		12,498
13	Nov 4	A	Luton T	W 1-0	0-0	16	Christie	10,608
14	11	H	Burnley	W 2-1	0-0	15	Weller, Christie	12,842
15	18	A	Cambridge U	D 1-1	0-0	16	Henderson	8875
16	22	H	Wrexham	D 1-1	0-1	—	Christie	14,734
17	25	H	West Ham U	L 1-2	0-1	17	Christie	16,149
18	Dec 2	A	Stoke C	D 0-0	0-0	14		15,950
19	16	A	Crystal Palace	L 1-3	0-2	18	May	17,330
20	23	H	Preston NE	D 1-1	0-0	18	Davies	10,481
21	26	A	Sunderland	D 1-1	1-0	—	Henderson	24,544
22	Jan 1	H	Oldham Ath	W 2-0	2-0	—	Buchanan, Smith	12,757
23	20	H	Blackburn R	D 1-1	1-0	16	May	13,234
24	Feb 3	A	Brighton & HA	L 1-3	1-2	17	Davies	19,973
25	10	H	Orient	W 5-3	3-2	16	Smith, Buchanan, May, Williams, Goodwin	12,050
26	17	H	Newcastle U	W 2-1	2-0	11	Peake, Buchanan	15,106
27	24	A	Charlton Ath	L 0-1	0-0	14		7936
28	Mar 3	H	Cardiff C	L 1-2	1-0	16	Grewcock	12,820
29	10	A	Bristol R	D 1-1	1-1	16	Smith (pen)	6381
30	21	H	Fulham	W 1-0	0-0	—	Buchanan	10,363
31	28	H	Luton T	W 3-0	2-0	—	May, Smith, Williams	10,465
32	31	A	West Ham U	D 1-1	0-0	12	Henderson	23,992
33	Apr 4	A	Millwall	L 0-2	0-1	—		4758
34	7	H	Stoke C	D 1-1	1-1	13	Buchanan	17,502
35	14	H	Sunderland	L 1-2	0-0	13	Henderson	20,740
36	16	A	Oldham Ath	L 1-2	1-1	—	Smith	7179
37	17	A	Preston NE	L 0-4	0-2	—		10,394
38	20	H	Crystal Palace	D 1-1	1-0	16	Smith	16,767
39	24	A	Notts Co	W 1-0	0-0	—	Lineker	8702
40	28	A	Fulham	L 0-3	0-2	15		7002
41	May 5	H	Millwall	D 0-0	0-0	15		12,828
42	8	A	Sheffield U	D 2-2	1-1	—	Peake, Duffy	15,178

Final League Position: 17

Goalscorers

League (43): Christie 8, Smith 6 (1 pen), Buchanan 5, Henderson 4, May 4, Hughes 3 (2 pens), Weller 3, Davies 2, Peake 2, Williams 2, Duffy 1, Goodwin 1, Grewcock 1, Lineker 1.

F.A. Cup (4): Henderson 2, May, Weller.

League Cup	Second Round	Derby Co (h)	0-1
F.A. Cup	Third Round	Norwich C (h)	3-0
	Fourth Round	Oldham Ath (a)	1-3

Wallington	Whitworth	Rofe	Kelly	O'Neill	Webb	Armstrong	Williams	Davies	Hughes	Christie	Goodwin	Kember	May	Sims	Weller	Duffy	White	Welsh	Henderson	Ridley	Reed	Lineker	Buchanan	Smith	Peake	Grewcock	Carr	Lee	Match No
1	2	3	4	5	6	7	8	9	10	11*	12																		1
1	2	3	4	5	6	11	8	10*	7	9	12																		2
1	2	3	4	5	6	7	8	9	10	11*		12																	3
1	2	3	6				12	10*	9	11	8	7	4	5															4
1	2	3	6				12		9		8	4	5	7	10	11*													5
1	2	3	10				9	11		8	6	5	7	4*	12														6
1	2	3	6*				11	9		8	4	5	7	10		12													7
1	2	3	6				9	10		8	4	5	11		7														8
1	2	3	6			12	9	11		8	4	5	7		10*														9
1	2	3	6			10	11	9		8	4	5	7*		12														10
1	2	3	6			10	9	12		8*	4	5	7		11														11
1	2	3	8			6	11*	9			5		7	12	10	4													12
1	2	3	6			4	11	9			5		7	12	10*	8													13
1	2	3	6			4	11	9			5		7		10	8													14
1	2	3	6			5	11	9		4			7		10	8													15
1	2	3	6			4	11	9*					7	5	10	8	12												16
1	2	3	6			5	11	9	12	4			7		10*	8													17
1	2	3	6			5	11	9		4			7		10	8													18
1	2	3				4	10	9	6	5			7		11	8													19
1	2	3				5	10	9	7	4		6			11	8													20
1	2	3	6			4	10	9*	7	5		12			11	8													21
1	2	3				4		8		5					9	6			7	10	11								22
1	2	3		6				12		5		7			10	4			11*	9	8								23
1	2	3	4			6	10			5					9	8*			12	11	7								24
1	2	3	4			6		12	8	5					10*				11	9	7								25
1	2	3	5			6		12	8	4					10*				11	9	7								26
1	2	3	6			4		11		5					9				10	8	7								27
1		3	6	4				2		5					9	12			11	10	7*	8							28
1	2	3		5		4		11*	7	6					9	12			8	10									29
1	2*	3	8	4		6			7	5					9				10	11	12								30
1		3	6	4		8			2	5					9	12			10*	11	7								31
1		3	8	6		4			2	5					9	12			10*	11	7								32
1		3	6	4		8			2	5					9	12			10	11	7*								33
1		3	8	5		4		12	2	6					9				10*	11	7								34
1		3	8	5		4	12		2	6					9				10*	11	7								35
1		3	6	4		8			2	5					9	12			10*	11	7								36
1		3	6*	5		10	8	9	2						12	4		7		11									37
1		3				2		4	5			12			9	6		7	10	11*	8								38
1		3*	4			2		8	5			12			9	6		7	10	11									39
1			2			3*		8	5			6			9	4		7		10		12	11						40
1			5					2				6*	4	9	12		8	10		7		3	11						41
1			4			6		2	5			10			9			7	12		8*	3	11						42
42	29	39	27	23	3	3	32	8	18	23	23	8	36	8	16	7	1	4	31	17		7	17	17	17	1	2	3	
						+3s		+1s	+3s	+5s	+1s				+4s	+1s	+2s	+2s	+7s	+1s		+2s	+1s	+1s					

LEICESTER CITY—PLAYERS

Player and position	*Ht*	*Wt*	*Birthplace*	*Clubs*	*League Appearance*	*Goals*
Goalkeepers						
Mark Wallington	6 1	14 5¼	Sleaford	Walsall	11	—
				Leicester C	204	—
Sean Rafter	6 1¼	12 12½	Rochford	Southend U	23	—
				Leicester C	—	—
Steve Humphries	5 11	12 10½		Leicester C	—	—
*Paul Eason	6 2¼	13 4		Leicester C	—	—
Defenders						
Dennis Rofe	5 7½	11 6¼	Fulham	Orient	170+1	6
				Leicester C	264	3
Malcolm Munro	6 0	12 0	Leicester	Leicester C	69+1	1
Tommy Williams	5 11	11 0	Leicester	Leicester C	63+4	5
Larry May	6 1	12 4¼	Sutton Coldfield	Leicester C	40+2	4
John O'Neill	5 11¾	12 12½	Derry	Leicester C	23	—
Steve Hamilton	5 8½	10 4		Leicester C	—	—
Mark Ratcliffe	5 10¾	10 13½		Leicester C	—	—
Ian Smith (Apprentice)	5 9¼	10 4		Leicester C	—	—
Paul Geddes	6 1½	12 2		Leicester C	—	—
Rory O'Boyle (Apprentice)	5 9	10 12		Leicester C	—	—
Gregor Stevens	5 11	11 8	Scotland	Motherwell	136+3	19
				Leicester C	—	—
Midfield						
Peter Welsh	6 1½	13 0	Coatbridge	Leicester C	5+2	
Keith Weller	5 10	12 1	Islington	Tottenham H	19+2	1
(England)				Millwall	121	38
(Contract cancelled February 1979)				Chelsea	34+4	14
				Leicester C	260+2	37
Mark Goodwin	5 9¾	10 9	Sheffield	Leicester C	37+5	4
Eddie Kelly	5 9½	12 4	Glasgow	Arsenal	168+7	13
				QPR	28	1
				Leicester C	51	1
Steve Convey	5 10	9 12½	Belfast	Leicester C	—	—
Gerald McGowan	0 0	0 0		Leicester C	—	—
Andy Peake	5 9½	10 7		Leicester C	17+1	2
Colin Bell	5 10	11 6		Leicester C	—	—
Andy Geddes	5 9½	11 10		Leicester C	—	—
Everton Carr	5 7	11 1¼		Leicester C	2+1	—
Bobby Smith	5 7½	11 9		Hibs	131+21	19
				Leicester C	17	6
John Ridley	6 1½	12 5		Port Vale	149+7	3
				Leicester C	17+7	—
Gary Lineker	5 9	10 7½		Leicester C	7	1
Mike Duffy	5 10	11 9½		Leicester C	7+4	1
Ian Wilson	5 7½	10 10½		Leicester C	—	—
Forwards						
Roger Davies	6 2½	13 3½	Wolverhampton	Worcester C	Non-league	
(Contract cancelled				Preston NE (on loan)	2	—
				Derby Co	98+16	31
				Bruges	(not known)	
				Leicester C	22+4	6
Trevor Christie	6 1½	12 5¼	Newcastle	Leicester C	28+3	8
Kevin Farmer			Kent	Leicester C	1	—
Billy Hughes	5 8½	11 11	Coatbridge	Sunderland	264+23	74
(Scotland)				Derby Co	17+2	8
				Leicester C	36+1	5
Pat McShane	6 1	11 11		Leicester C	—	—
Neil Grewcock (Apprentice)	5 6	10 11		Leicester C	1	1
Alan Brotherton				Leicester C	—	—
John Allen	6 0½	13 2½		Leicester C	—	—
*Kevin Reed	5 6¾	9 1½		Leicester C	0+1	—
Alan Lee	5 11	12 5		Leicester C	3	00
				Hibernian (on loan)	4+2	—
Martin Henderson	6 0	12 9½		Rangers	27+6	10
				Leicester C	31+2	4
Paul Edmunds	5 8	10 10	Leicester	Leicester C	—	—
David Buchanan	5 7¼	10 4		Leicester C	17+2	5
Frank Cole	5 5	9 2		Leicester C	—	—
David Kirk	5 5½	9 9¼		Leicester C	—	—

LINCOLN CITY   DIV. 4

Chairman: H. W. Dove.
Vice-Chairman: H. C. Sills.
Directors: D. W. Houlston, G. T. Blades, A. C. Davey, M. J. Green.
Manager: Colin Murphy.
Secretary: J. H. Sorby, F.A.A.I.
Year Formed: 1883.   *Turned Professional:* 1892.
Limited Company: 1892.
Previous Grounds: 1883, John O'Gaunt's; 1894, Sincil Bank.
Football League Record: 1892 Original Member of Division 2. Remained in Division 2 until 1920 when they failed re-election but also missed seasons 1908–09 and 1911–12, when not re-elected. 1921–32 Division 3(N). 1932–34 Division 2. 1934–48 Division 3(N). 1948–49 Division 2. 1949–52 Division 3(N). 1952–61 Division 2. 1961–62 Division 3. 1962–76 Division 4. 1976–79 Division 3. 1979– Division 4.

Honours: Football League, highest position in Division 2: 5th, 1901–02. Division 3(N), Champions: 1931–32, 1947–48, 1951–52; Runners-up: 1927–28, 1930–31, 1936–37. Division 4 Champions 1975/6. *F.A. Cup*, best season: 1st Rd. of Second Series (5th Rd. equivalent), 1886–87, 2nd Rd. (5th Rd. equivalent), 1889–90, 1901–02. *Football League Cup*, best season: 4th Rd., 1967–68.

Record Victory: 11-1 v Crewe Alex., Division 3(N), Sept. 29th, 1951.

Record Defeat: 3-11 v Manchester C., Division 2, Mar. 23rd, 1895.

Most League Points: 74, Division 4, 1975–76. (League record)

Most League Goals: 121, Division 3(N), 1951–52.

Highest League Scorer in Season: Allan Hall, 42, Division 3(N), 1931–32.

Most League Goals in Aggregate: Andy Graver, 144, 1950–55 and 1958–61.

Most Capped Players: David Pugh, 3 (7), Wales; Con Moulson, 3 (6) Eire; George Moulson, 3, Eire.

Most League Appearances: Tony Emery, 402, 1946–59.

Record Transfer Fee Received: £29,500 from Leicester C. for Andy Graver, Dec. 1954.

Record Transfer Fee Paid: £36,666 to Sheffield Wednesday for Tommy Tynan, Oct. 1978.

Managers Since the War: Bill Anderson, Bob Chapman, Ron Gray, Bert Loxley, David Herd, Graham Taylor, George Kerr, Willie Bell.

Address of Club Shop or Boutique: Red Imps Shop on Ground.

Sincil Bank, Lincoln. Telephone Lincoln 22224 and 22225. *Ground capacity:* 25,300. *Record attendance:* 23,196 v Derby Co., League Cup 4th Rd., Nov. 15, 1967. *Record receipts:* £9,667 v Sheffield Wed., Div. 3, Oct. 2nd, 1976. *Pitch Measurements:* 110 yds × 75 yds.

How to get there: There is a regular bus service from Lincoln Central Station to the ground, although there are no special buses. Nearest stations are Lincoln Central and Lincoln St Marks.

Car parking: Limited to 150 cars at the ground.

Entertainments/catering facilities: Social club at the ground with light catering before and after the match.

Club shop: Sited on the ground; sells all types of souvenirs.

Handbooks/programmes: Programmes available at each game or by subscription.

Extra information: Frank Keetley scored six times in 21 minutes for Lincoln against Halifax Town, January 16, 1932. Most points, most wins and fewest defeats in a season in division 4.

Club Colours: Red with white vertical striped shirts, black shorts, red and white stockings.

Change Colours: Green shirts, white shorts, green stockings with white tops.

Club Trainer/Coach: Lennie Lawrence.

Physiotherapist: Bert Loxley.

Club Nickname: The 'Red Imps'.

LINCOLN CITY 1978-79 LEAGUE RECORD

Match No.	Date	Venue	Opponents	Result	H/T Score	League Pos'n	Goalscorers	Attendance
1	Aug 19	H	Tranmere R	W 2-1	1-1	—	Hobson, Sunley	2835
2	22	A	Swansea C	L 0-3	0-2	—		16,704
3	26	A	Plymouth Arg	L 1-2	1-1	17	Harding	7806
4	Sept 2	H	Sheffield W	L 1-2	1-1	21	Cooper	7005
5	9	A	Rotherham U	L 0-2	0-1	24		4427
6	13	H	Watford	L 0-5	0-3	—		5924
7	16	H	Carlisle U	D 1-1	0-0	23	Cockerill	2577
8	23	A	Shrewsbury T	L 0-2	0-1	24		2902
9	25	A	Brentford	L 1-3	1-2	—	Cockerill	6110
10	29	H	Walsall	D 1-1	0-1	24	Ward	3371
11	Oct 7	A	Blackpool	L 0-2	0-0	24		7080
12	13	H	Colchester U	D 0-0	0-0	24		3541
13	17	A	Gillingham	L 2-4	1-3	—	Wigginton, Leigh	5763
14	21	H	Swindon T	L 0-3	0-1	24		2982
15	27	A	Southend U	L 0-2	0-2	24		7356
16	Nov 4	H	Mansfield T	L 0-1	0-0	24		3614
17	11	A	Sheffield W	D 0-0	0-0	24		12,590
18	18	H	Plymouth Arg	D 3-3	2-1	24	Fleming 2 (2 pens), Hobson	3670
19	Dec 9	H	Oxford U	D 2-2	0-0	24	Tynan, Wigginton (pen)	2995
20	23	A	Chesterfield	L 0-1	0-0	24		2951
21	26	A	Peterborough U	W 1-0	0-0	24	Watson	4592
22	30	A	Exeter C	L 2-3	0-2	24	Hobson, Cockerill	3810
23	Jan 6	A	Watford	L 0-2	0-2	24		12,132
24	20	A	Carlisle U	L 0-2	0-1	24		3892
25	23	A	Colchester U	L 0-2	0-2	24		2861
26	Mar 3	A	Swindon T	L 0-6	0-4	24		6649
27	7	A	Chester	L 1-5	1-0	—	Sunley	2585
28	10	H	Southend U	D 1-1	1-0	24	Fleming	2559
29	13	A	Walsall	L 1-4	0-0	—	Harford	2794
30	21	H	Brentford	W 1-0	1-0	—	Ward	2070
31	24	H	Swansea C	W 2-1	1-0	24	Harford, Fleming (pen)	3568
32	26	H	Tranmere R	D 0-0	0-0	—		1222
33	31	A	Hull C	D 0-0	0-0	24		4103
34	Apr 4	H	Rotherham U	W 3-0	0-0	—	Sunley, Cockerill, Ward	3347
35	7	H	Chester	D 0-0	0-0	24		3489
36	14	H	Peterborough U	L 0-1	0-0	24		4610
37	16	A	Bury	D 2-2	1-2	—	Laybourne, Fleming (pen)	3455
38	17	A	Chesterfield	W 3-1	1-1	—	Neale, Cockerill 2	3364
39	21	H	Exeter C	L 0-1	0-0	24		2675
40	25	A	Gillingham	L 2-4	1-2	—	Sunley, Fleming	1863
41	28	A	Oxford U	L 1-2	1-1	24	Harford	3249
42	May 2	H	Shrewsbury T	L 1-2	0-0	—	Harford	1677
43	5	H	Hull C	W 4-2	2-0	24	Watson, Hobson 2, Harford	2522
44	7	H	Blackpool	L 1-2	0-0	—	Harford	1949
45	9	H	Bury	L 1-4	0-3	—	Hobson	1517
46	11	A	Mansfield T	L 0-2	0-0	—		4386

Final League Position: 24

Goalscorers

League (41): Cockerill 6, Fleming 6 (4 pens), Harford 6, Hobson 6, Sunley 4, Ward 3, Watson 2, Wigginton 2 (1 a pen), Cooper 1, Harding 1, Laybourne 1, Leigh 1, Neale 1, Tynan 1.
League Cup (1): Hughes.
F.A. Cup (1): Ward.

League Cup	First Round	Bradford C (a)	0-2
		(h)	1-1
F.A. Cup	**First Round**	Blackpool (a)	1-2

Grotier	Wright	Leigh	Hughes	Smith	Cooper	Hobson	Ward	Harford	Sunley	Hubbard	Fleming	Wigginton	Harding	Guest	McCalliog	Cockerill	Burrows	Watson	Turner C	Tynan	Eden	Jones	Neale	Sivell	Loxley	Cross	Laybourne	Creane	Turner I	Match No.
1	2	3	4	5	6	7	8	9	10	11																				1
1	2	3	10	5	6	7	11	9	8	4*12																				2
1	2	3	10		6	7	8*	9	12		4	5	11																	3
1		3	10		6	7	8*	9	12		4	5	11	2																4
1		3	4		6	7		9	10		12	5	11*	2	8															5
1		3	10	12	6	7		8			4*	5		2		9	11													6
1		3	4		6	11		9*10		12	5		2	8	7															7
1		3	4	12	6	7*		9		10	5		2	8	11															8
1		3			6		7		8		10	5	11		2	4	9													9
1		3			6	7	10		8			5			2	4	9	11												10
		3			6	7			8	10		5			2	4	9	11	1											11
		3			6	12			8			5	11*	2	7	4	10	1	9											12
		3		8	6	12			7			5	11	2*	4	10		1	9											13
		3			6	7		8*12			5			2	4	10	11	1	9											14
		3		5	6	7	9		4				11	2			8	1		10										15
		3		5	6		8			4			11	2			10	9	7										1	16
		3		5	6	7	8			4			11	2			10	9											1	17
		3		5	6	7	8			4			11	2			10	9											1	18
		3			6	7* 8	12						5	11	2			10	9		4								1	19
		4			6	7		8					5	11	2			10	9		3								1	20
		3		6		7		8			4	5		2		12	10	9*		11									1	21
		3		6			12	8	9				4	5		2		7	10*			11							1	22
		3		6			12	8	9				4	5	11	2		7					10*	1						23
		3			6	12	8	9		10			5	7	2*		4						11	1						24
1		3		6		11	8	9		2			5	4	7*	10				12										25
1		3		6		11	8*	9		2				4	7	10				12				5						26
1		3		5			10	9	6	2			8	7	11	4														27
1		3				7	8*12	9	6	4				2	10	11									5					28
1		3*				7	8 12	9	6	4				2	10	11									5					29
1					6		8	10	9	2	4				7	11									5	3				30
1					6		8	9	10	7	2				4	11									5	3				31
1					6*12		8	10	9	2	4				7	11									5	3				32
1			6				8	10	9	2	4				7	11									5	3				33
1					6		8	10	9	2	4				7	11									5	3				34
1					6		8	10	9	2	4					11	7*					12			5	3				35
1					6		8	10	9	2	4					11						7			5	3				36
1					6		8*10		9	2	4			12		11						7			5	3				37
1					6				9	2	4			8		11						7			5	3	10			38
1					6		12		9	2	4			7*		11						8			5	3	10			39
1					6	7	8		9		4			2		11	10								5	3				40
1			5	6			9	10		8				2		11	7								4	3				41
1		2			6	7	8	10	9*					12		4	11								5	3				42
1		2			6	7	8	9							4	11	10								5	3				43
1		2 12		6	7	8	9			4*			10	11										5	3				44
1		4	5		7	8	9			2*			10	11										6	3	12			45
1		2	5		7	8	9						4	11	10										6	3				46
32	3	29	13	17	35	27	32	28	27	21	28	19	17	39	9	34	1	21	5	9	1	1	10	2	1	19	17	2	7	
		+ 3s			+ 6s	+ 1s	+ 3s	+ 2s	+ 1s	+ 3s				+ 2s	+ 1s				+ 2s	+ 1s							+ 1s			

LINCOLN CITY—PLAYERS

Player and position	Ht	Wt	Birthplace	Clubs	League Appearance	Goals
Goalkeepers						
Peter Grotier	5 11	12 10	West Ham	West Ham U	50	—
				Cardiff C (on loan)	2	—
				Lincoln C	212	—
Kevin Fox	5 11	10 3	Sheffield	Lincoln C	—	—
Defenders						
Brendan Guest	5 10½	10 9	Nottingham	Lincoln C	82+3	1
Tony Loxley	6 2½	12 6	Nottingham	Lincoln C	1	—
*Dennis Leigh	5 8½	11 7	Doncaster	Doncaster R	33+2	1
				Rotherham U	154+5	10
				Lincoln C	201+5	3
Phil Neale	5 8	11 0	Scunthorpe	Lincoln C	119+5	9
Terry Cooper	5 9	11 7	Cwmbran	Newport Co	64+4	1
				Notts Co	3+6	—
				Lincoln C	268+2	13
				Scunthorpe U (on loan)	4	—
Mick Smith	6 0½	11 9	Sunderland	Linco.n C	20+5	—
Keith Laybourne	5 10	10 11	Sunderland	Lincoln C	18	1
*Graham Cross	6 0	13 0	Leicester	Leicester C	496+3	29
				Chesterfield (on loan)	12	—
				Brighton	46	3
				Preston NE	45	1
				Endersby	—	—
				Lincoln C	19	—
Billy Wright	5 9	12 4	Birmingham	Birmingham C	—	—
				Lincoln C	3	—
Steven Ward	6 0	11 0	Sheffield	Lincoln C	—	—
Midfield						
John Fleming	5 8	11 0	Nottingham	Oxford U	67+8	2
				Lincoln C	109+12	17
Phil Hubbard	5 11	12 2	Lincoln	Lincoln C	150+1	41
(Contract cancelled April 1979)				Norwich C	6+4	1
				Grimsby T	144+2	37
				Lincoln C	99+9	11
David Hughes	5 9	11 2	Birmingham	Aston V	3+1	1
				Lincoln C	15	—
Graham Watson	5 10	11 6	Doncaster	Doncaster R	152+4	34
				Cambridge U	216+3	24
				Lincoln C	21	2
Jim McCalliog	5 9	10 5	Glasgow	Chelsea	7	2
(Scotland)				Sheffield W	150	19
(Contract cancelled March 1979)				Wolverhampton W	158+5	34
				Manchester U	31	7
				Southampton	70+2	8
				Lincoln C	9	—
Forwards						
John Ward	5 8	10 7	Lincoln	Lincoln C	223+17	91
				Workington (on loan)	9+2	3
Glenn Cockerill	5 10½	11 5	Grimsby	Lincoln C	46+6	7
Mick Harford	6 1	12 4	Sunderland	Lincoln C	53+5	15
Alan Eden	5 9	10 8	Sunderland	Lincoln C	5+2	—
Alan Jones	5 6	10 11	Grimethorpe	Huddersfield T	30+2	—
(Contract cancelled April 1979)				Halifax T	109	6
				Chesterfield	39	6
				Lincoln C	24+2	4
Gordon Hobson	5 8	10 4	Sheffield	Lincoln C	32+6	8
David Sunley	5 8	11 6	Shelton	Sheffield W	122+12	21
				Nottingham F (on loan)	1	—
				Hull C	58+11	11
				Lincoln C	27+2	4
David Burrows	5 6	10 0	Bilsthorpe	Lincoln C	1	—
Gerry Creane sub					2+1	—
(Apprentice)						
Tony Cunningham	6 11	12 0	Kingston Jamaica	Lincoln C	—	—

LIVERPOOL   DIV. 1

Chairman: J. W. Smith, J.P.
Directors: C. J. Hill, Coun. S. J. Moss J.P., S. C. Reakes, J.P., H. Cartwright, J. T. Cross, W. D. Corkish.
Team Manager: Bob Paisley.   *Ass./Manager:* Joe Fagan.
General Secretary: P. B. Robinson.
Year Formed: 1892.   *Turned Professional:* 1892.
Limited Company: 1892.
Football League Record:

1893 Elected to Division 2.	1904–05 Division 2.
1894–95 Division 1.	1905–54 Division 1.
1895–96 Division 2.	1954–62 Division 2.
1896–1904 Division 1.	1962– Division 1.

Honours: *Football League,* Division 1, Champions: 1900–01, 1905–06, 1921–22, 1922–23, 1946–47, 1963–64, 1965–66, 1972–73, 1975–76, 1976–77, 1978–79 (Liverpool have a record number of eleven League Championship wins.) Runners-up: 1898–99, 1909–10, 1968–69 1973–74, 1974–75, 1977–78. Division 2, Champions: 1893–94, 1895–96, 1904–05, 1961–62. *F.A. Cup,* Winners: 1965, 1974. Runners-up: 1914, 1950, 1971, 1977. *Football League Cup,* best season: Runners-up 1977–78.

European Competitions: *European Cup:* 1964–65, 1966–67, 1973–74, 1976–77 (winners), 1977–78 (winners), 1978–79. *European Cup Winners' Cup:* 1965–66 (Runners-up) 1971–72, 1974–75. *European Fairs Cup:* 1967–68, 1968–69, 1969–70, 1970–71. *UEFA Cup:* 1972–73 (winners), 1975–76 (winners). *Super Cup:* 1977 (winners), 1978.

Record Victory: 11-0 v Strömsgodset, European Cup-Winners' Cup, Sept. 17th, 1974.

Record Defeat: 1-9 v Birmingham C., Division 2, Dec. 11th, 1954.

Most League Points: 68, Division 1, 1978–79.

Most League Goals: 106, Division 2, 1895–96.

Highest League Scorer in Season: Roger Hunt, 41, Division 2, 1961–62.

Most League Goals in Total Aggregate: Roger Hunt, 245, 1959–69.

Most Capped Player: Emlyn Hughes, 59, England.

Most League Appearances: Ian Callaghan, 640, 1960–78.

Record Transfer Fee Received: £500,000 from Hamburg SV for Kevin Keegan, June 1977.

Record Transfer Fee Paid: £440,000 to Celtic for Kenny Dalglish, Aug. 1977.

Managers Since the War: George Kay, Don Welsh, Phil Taylor, Bill Shankly.

Address of Supporters Club: 212 Lower Breck Road.

Address of Club Shop or Boutique: Same as ground.

Anfield Road, Liverpool 4. Telephone 051–263 2361.   *Telegraphic address:* 'Goalkeeper Liverpool'.   *Ground capacity:* 52,318.   *Record attendance:* 61,905 v Wolverhampton W., F.A. Cup 4th Rd., February 2, 1952.   *Record receipts:* £154,000 Wales v Scotland, World Cup qualifying tie, October 12, 1977.   *Pitch measurements:* 110 yds × 75 yds.

How to get there: Buses 17d from Pier Head and 26, 27 from Castle Street. Nearest stations, Bankhall and Kirkdale.
Match tickets: Postal applications 19 days before the match.
Car parking: Limited street parking around the ground. Large privately owned car park in Priory Road within five minutes walk of the ground.
Entertainments/catering facilities: Licensed refreshment bars in all parts of the ground.
Club shop: Main shop run by the Development Association open Monday–Saturday. Small kiosks in the ground open on match days only.
Handbooks/programmes: No handbook. Programmes available on subscription from the secretary.
Extra information: Liverpool's defensive record of only 16 goals conceded in 1978–79 is the best in First Division history.

Club Colours: All red with white facings.
Change Colours: White shirts with red collars and cuffs, black shorts, white stockings.
Captain: Emlyn Hughes.
First Team Trainer: Ron Moran.
Club Nickname: 'Reds' or 'Pool'.

LIVERPOOL 1978-79 LEAGUE RECORD

Match No	Date	Venue	Opponents	Result	H/T Score	League Pos'n	Goalscorers	Attendance
1	Aug 19	H	QPR	W 2-1	1-1	—	Dalglish, Heighway	50,793
2	22	A	Ipswich T	W 3-0	2-0	—	Souness, Dalglish 2	28,114
3	26	A	Manchester C	W 4-1	2-1	1	Souness 2, Kennedy R, Dalglish	46,710
4	Sept 2	H	Tottenham H	W 7-0	3-0	1	Dalglish 2, Kennedy R, Johnson 2, Neal (pen), McDermott	50,705
5	9	A	Birmingham C	W 3-0	1-0	1	Souness 2, Kennedy A	31,740
6	16	H	Coventry C	W 1-0	1-0	1	Souness	51,130
7	23	A	WBA	D 1-1	0-0	1	Dalglish	38,000
8	30	H	Bolton W	W 3-0	2-0	1	Case 3	47,099
9	Oct 7	A	Norwich C	W 4-1	3-0	1	Heighway 2, Johnson, Case	25,632
10	14	H	Derby Co	W 5-0	1-0	1	Johnson, Kennedy R 2, Dalglish 2	47,475
11	21	H	Chelsea	W 2-0	1-0	1	Johnson, Dalglish	45,775
12	28	A	Everton	L 0-1	0-0	1		53,131
13	Nov 4	H	Leeds U	D 1-1	0-1	1	McDermott (pen)	51,657
14	11	A	QPR	W 3-1	2-1	1	Heighway, Kennedy R, Johnson	26,626
15	18	H	Manchester C	W 1-0	0-0	1	Neal (pen)	47,765
16	22	A	Tottenham H	D 0-0	0-0	—		50,393
17	25	H	Middlesbrough	W 2-0	1-0	1	McDermott, Souness	39,821
18	Dec 2	A	Arsenal	L 0-1	0-1	1		51,902
19	9	H	Nottingham F	W 2-0	1-0	1	McDermott 2 (1 a pen)	51,469
20	16	A	Bristol C	L 0-1	0-0	1		28,722
21	26	A	Manchester U	W 3-0	2-0	1	Kennedy R, Case, Fairclough	54,940
22	Feb 3	H	WBA	W 2-1	1-0	1	Dalglish, Fairclough	52,211
23	13	H	Birmingham C	W 1-0	1-0	—	Souness	35,207
24	21	H	Norwich C	W 6-0	1-0	—	Dalglish 2, Johnson 2, Kennedy A, Kennedy R	35,754
25	24	A	Derby Co	W 2-0	1-0	1	Dalglish, Kennedy R	27,859
26	Mar 3	A	Chelsea	D 0-0	0-0	1		40,594
27	6	A	Coventry C	D 0-0	0-0	—		26,629
28	13	H	Everton	D 1-1	1-0	—	Dalglish	52,352
29	20	H	Wolverhampton W	W 2-0	1-0	—	McDermott, Johnson	39,695
30	24	H	Ipswich T	W 2-0	1-0	1	Dalglish, Johnson	43,243
31	Apr 7	H	Arsenal	W 3-0	0-0	1	Case, Dalglish, McDermott	47,297
32	10	A	Wolverhampton W	W 1-0	1-0	—	Hansen	30,857
33	14	H	Manchester U	W 2-0	1-0	1	Dalglish, Neal	46,608
34	16	A	Aston Villa	W 1-3	0-2	—	Johnson	44,029
35	21	H	Bristol C	W 1-0	1-0	1	Dalglish	43,191
36	24	A	Southampton	D 1-1	1-0	—	Johnson	23,181
37	28	A	Nottingham F	D 0-0	0-0	1		41,898
38	May 1	A	Bolton W	W 4-1	1-0	—	Johnson, Kennedy R 2, Dalglish	35,200
39	5	H	Southampton	W 2-0	1-0	1	Neal 2	46,687
40	8	H	Aston Villa	W 3-0	2-0	—	Kennedy A, Dalglish, McDermott	50,570
41	11	A	Middlesbrough	W 1-0	0-0	—	Johnson	32,244
42	17	A	Leeds U	W 3-0	2-0	—	Johnson 2, Case	41,324

Final League Position: 1

Goalscorers

League (85): Dalglish 21, Johnson 16, Kennedy R 10, Souness 8, McDermott 8 (2 pens), Case 7, Heighway 4, Neal 5 (2 pens), Kennedy A 3, Fairclough 2, Hansen 1.
F.A. Cup (10): Dalglish 4, Johnson 2, Case, Kennedy, R. Souness, Hansen 1.

League Cup	Second Round	Sheffield U (a)	0-1
F.A. Cup	Third Round	Southend U (a)	0-0
		(h)	3-0
	Fourth Round	Blackburn R (h)	1-0
	Fifth Round	Burnley (h)	3-0
	Sixth Round	Ipswich T (a)	1-0
	Semi-Final	Manchester U	2-2 (at Maine Rd)
			0-1 (at Goodison Pk)

Clemence	Neal	Kennedy A	Thompson	Kennedy R	Hughes	Dalglish	Case	Heighway	McDermott	Souness	Johnson	Hansen	Fairclough	Lee	Match No.
1	2	3	4	5	6	7	8	9	10	11					1
1	2	3	4	5	6	7	8	9	10	11					2
1	2	3	4	5	6	7	8	9	10	11					3
1	2	3	4	5	6*	7	8	9	10	11	12				4
1	2	3	4	5		7	8	9	10	11		6			5
1	2	3	4	5	6	7	8	9	10	11					6
1	2	3	4	5	6	7	8	9*	10	11	12				7
1	2	3	4	5		7	8	9	10	11		6			8
1	2	3	4	5		7	8	9		11	10	6			9
1	2	3	4	5		7	8	9		11	10	6			10
1	2	3	4	5		7	8	9		11	10	6			11
1	2	3	4	5		7	8*	9	12	11	10	6			12
1	2	3	4	5		7	8	9	12	11*	10	6			13
1	2	3	4	5		7	8	9		11	10	6			14
1	2	3	4	5		7	8	9		11	10	6			15
1	2	3	4	6		7	8	9	12	11	10*	5			16
1	2	3	4	5		7	8	9	10	11		6			17
1	2	3	4*	5		7	8	9	10	11	12	6			18
1	2	3	4	5		7	8	9	10	11		6			19
1	2	3	4	5		7	8	9*	10	11	12	6			20
1	2		4	5	3	7	8		10	11		6	9		21
1	2	3		5	6	7	8*	12	10	11		4	9		22
1	2	4		5	3	7		8	10	11		6	9		23
1	2	4		5	3	7		9	10	11	8	6			24
1	2	4	6	5	3	7		9	10	11	8				25
1	2	4	6	5	3	7		9	10	11	8				26
1	2		4	5	3	7	9		10	11	8	6			27
1	2		4	5	3	7	9		10	11	8*	6	12		28
1	2		4	5	3	7	9		10	11	8	6			29
1	2		4	5	3	7	9		10	11	8	6			30
1	2	3	4	5		7	8		10	11	9	6			31
1	2	3	4	5		7	9		10	11	8	6			32
1	2	3	4	5		7	8		10	11	9	6			33
1	2	3	4	5		7		8	10	11	9	6			34
1	2	3	4	5		7	8	12	10	11	9*	6			35
1	2	3	4	5		7	8		10		9	6		11	36
1	2	3	4	5		7	8	9*	10	11		6		12	37
1	2	3	4	5		7	8		10	11	9	6			38
1	2	3	4	5		7	8		10	11	9	6			39
1	2	3	4	5		7	8		10	11	9	6			40
1	2	3	4	5		7	8		10	11	9	6			41
1	2	3	4	5		7	8		10	11	9	6			42
42	42	37	39	42	16	42	37	26	34	41	26	34	3	1	
					+2s		+3s			+4s			+1s	+1s	

LIVERPOOL—PLAYERS

Player and position	Ht	Wt	Birthplace	Clubs	League Appearances	Goals
Goalkeepers						
Ray Clemence (England)	5 11½	12 9	Skegness	Scunthorpe U Liverpool	48 388	— —
Steve Ogrizovic	6 3	14 7	Mansfield	Chesterfield Liverpool	16 2	— —
Defenders						
Brian Kettle	5 9	12 13	Prescot	Liverpool	3	—
Phil Neal (England)	5 11	12 2	Irchester	Northampton T Liverpool	184+4 191	29 22
Phil Thompson (England)	6 0	11 8	Liverpool	Liverpool	212+3	7
Emlyn Hughes (England)	5 10½	12 9	Barrow	Blackpool Liverpool	27+1 474	— 35
Jeff Ainsworth	5 9	11 7	Liverpool	Liverpool	—	—
Colin Irwin	6 0	12 6	Liverpool	Liverpool	—	—
Alan Hansen (Scotland)	6 1	13 0	Alloa	Partick T Liverpool	82+4 52	6 1
Derek Carroll	5 5½	9 11	Dublin	Dundalk Liverpool	(not known) —	— —
Alan Harper	5 8	9 7	Liverpool	Liverpool	—	—
Alan Kennedy	5 9	10 7	Sunderland	Newcastle U Liverpool	155+3 37	9 3
David Watson (Non-Contract)	5 11½	11 12	Liverpool	Liverpool	—	—
Alex Cribley	5 11½	12 9	Liverpool	Liverpool	—	—
Michael Halsall	5 10	11 4	Liverpool	Liverpool	—	—
Midfield						
Terry McDermott (England)	5 9	12 13	Kirkby	Bury Newcastle U Liverpool	83+7 55+1 116+8	8 6 16
Ray Kennedy (England)	5 11	13 4	Seaton Delaval	Arsenal Liverpool	156+2 176+3	53 32
Gary McGartney	5 9	10 2	Belfast	Liverpool	—	—
Howard Gayle	5 10½	10 9	Liverpool	Liverpool	—	—
Bob Savage	5 7	11 1	Liverpool	Liverpool	—	—
Graeme Souness (Scotland)	5 11	12 13	Edinburgh	Tottenham H Middlesbrough Liverpool	— 184+2 56	— 22 10
Synan Braddish (Eire)	5 8	10 10	Dublin	Dundalk Liverpool	(not known) —	— —
Kevin Sheedy	5 7	9 2	Hereford	Hereford U Liverpool	47+4 —	4 —
Craig Le Cornu	5 8	10 10	Birkenhead	Liverpool	—	—
Forwards						
Steve Heighway (Eire)	5 10½	11 2	Dublin	Liverpool	306+10	49
Jimmy Case	5 9	12 7	Liverpool	Liverpool	122+6	19
David Fairclough	5 9	11 0	Liverpool	Liverpool	46+21	22
Sammy Lee	5 7	10 1	Liverpool	Liverpool	1+3	1
David Johnson (England)	5 10	12 4	Liverpool	Everton Ipswich T Liverpool	47+3 134+3 52+16	11 35 24
Kenny Dalglish (Scotland)	5 8	11 13	Glasgow	Celtic Liverpool	202+2 84	112 41
Brian Duff	5 10	11 1	Dublin	Dundalk Liverpool	(not known) —	— —
Colin Russell	5 7	10 7	Liverpool	Liverpool	—	—
Jim Williams	5 6½	9 2	Liverpool	Liverpool	—	—
Owen Brown	5 10½	11 10	Liverpool	Liverpool	—	—
Frank McGarvey (Scotland)	5 10	10 7	Kilsyth	St Mirren Liverpool	121+11 —	52 —

LUTON TOWN

DIV. 2

President: T. Hodgson.
Chairman: D. Mortimer.
Directors: H. Richardson, R. J. Smith, E. S. Pearson, LL.M., B.Sc., R. L. Banks, J. R. Yates.
Club Secretary: J. S. Wilkinson.
Company Secretary/Chief Executive: J. R. Smith.
Team Manager: David Pleat.
Year Formed: 1885. *Turned Professional:* 1890.
Limited Company: 1897.
Previous Grounds: 1885, Excelsior, Dallow Lane; 1897, Dunstable Road; 1905, Kenilworth Road.
Football League Record: 1897 Elected to Division 2. 1900 failed re-election. 1920 Division 3. 1921 Division 3(S). 1937–55 Division 2. 1955–60 Division 1. 1960–63 Division 2. 1963–65 Division 3. 1965–68 Division 4. 1968–70 Division 3. 1970–74 Division 2. 1974–75 Division 1. 1975– Division 2.

© L.T.F.C. 1972

Honours: *Football League*, highest position in Division 1: 8th, 1957–58. Division 2, Runners-up: 1954–55, 1973–74. Division 3, Runners-up: 1969–70. Division 4, Champions: 1967–68. Division 3(S), Champions: 1936–37; Runners-up: 1935–36. *F.A. Cup*, best season: Runners-up: 1959. *Football League Cup*, best season: 5th Rd. 1978–79.

Record Victory: 12-0 v Bristol R., Division 3(S), Apr. 13th, 1936.
Record Defeat: 1-9 v Swindon T., Division 3(S), Aug. 28th, 1920.
Most League Points: 66, Division 4, 1967–68 (equalled Division 4 record).
Most League Goals: 103, Division 3(S), 1936–37.
Highest League Scorer in Season: Joe Payne, 55, Division 3(S), 1936–37.
Most Goals in Total Aggregate: 243, Gordon Turner, 1949–64.
Most Capped Player: George Cummins, 19, Eire.
Most League Appearances: Bob Morton, 494, 1948–64.
Record Transfer Fee Received: £350,000 from Manchester C. for Paul Futcher, June 1978.
Record Transfer Fee Paid: £120,000 to Swindon Town for Dave Moss, June 1978.
Managers Since the War: George Martin, Dally Duncan, Syd Owen, Sam Bartram, Bill Harvey, Allan Brown, Alec Stock, Harry Haslam.
Address of Supporters Club: Bobbers Club, Beech Hill Path, Luton.

70–72 Kenilworth Rd. Luton. Telephone Luton (0582) 411622. 24 hour answering service: 0582-33010 *Telegraphic Address:* 'Football Luton'. *Ground capacity:* 25,000 (17,000 covered). *Record attendance:* 30,069 v Blackpool FA Cup 6th Rd. Replay, March 4, 1959. *Record receipts:* £16,100 v Chelsea Div. 1, Jan. 11 1975. *Pitch measurements:* 112yds × 72 yds.

How to get there: Nearest railway station, Luton (six minutes walk). There is also a frequent bus service to and from the town centre to the ground, but the ground is central.
Match tickets: Seats can be booked two weeks before the game.
Car parking: Ample parking facilities adjacent to the ground entrance in Maple Road.
Entertainments/catering facilities: Licensed bars and refreshment bars on ground.
Club shop: Sells all types of souvenirs.
Programmes: Programmes can be obtained from club shop.
Extra information: Joe Payne scored 10 goals against Bristol Rovers in April 1936, a record individual score in a Football League match.
Club Colours: White shirt with orange collar and cuffs, with one navy blue and two orange vertical stripes on left hand side, navy blue shorts with one orange and white vertical stripe down the side, white with orange and navy blue turnover stockings.
Change Colours: White shirts, white orange or navy shorts, white stockings.
Club Captain: Alan West.
First Team Trainer: Reg Game.
Club Nickname: 'Hatters'.

LUTON TOWN 1978-79 LEAGUE RECORD

Match No.	Date	Venue	Opponents	Result	H/T Score	League Pos'n	Goalscorers	Attendance
1	Aug 19	H	Oldham Ath	W 6-1	0-1	—	Hatton 2, Moss 2, Stein, Fuccillo (pen)	8043
2	22	A	Crystal Palace	L 1-3	1-1	—	Fuccillo (pen)	17,639
3	26	A	Newcastle U	L 0-1	0-1	15		24,112
4	Sept 2	H	Charlton Ath	W 3-0	1-0	8	Hatton, Stein, Hill	8509
5	9	A	Bristol R	L 0-2	0-0	14		6508
6	16	H	Cardiff C	W 7-1	2-0	9	Moss 2, Hatton, Stein 2, Fuccillo (pen), Dwyer (og)	7752
7	23	H	Cambridge U	D 1-1	1-0	9	Stein	10,801
8	30	A	Sheffield U	D 1-1	0-1	10	Hatton	15,295
9	Oct 7	H	Wrexham	W 2-1	2-1	8	Stein, Fuccillo	8682
10	14	A	Blackburn R	D 0-0	0-0	8		7450
11	21	H	Notts Co	W 6-0	2-0	4	Hatton, Stein 2, West, Moss, Fuccillo (pen)	8561
12	28	A	Orient	L 2-3	1-1	10	Fuccillo 2	7035
13	Nov 4	H	Leicester C	L 0-1	0-0	12		10,608
14	11	A	Oldham Ath	L 0-2	0-1	14		6876
15	18	H	Newcastle U	W 2-0	1-0	13	Stein, Turner	10,434
16	21	A	Charlton Ath	W 2-1	0-1	—	Moss, Hatton	10,000
17	25	H	Sunderland	L 0-3	0-2	13		10,249
18	Dec 9	H	Preston NE	L 1-2	1-1	13	Price	7036
19	16	A	Brighton & HA	L 1-3	0-2	16	Moss	16,252
20	26	A	Millwall	W 2-0	2-0	—	Moss 2	6068
21	30	A	Fulham	L 0-1	0-1	16		8914
22	Jan 16	H	Bristol R	W 3-2	0-2	—	Moss, Price, Hill	6002
23	Feb 3	A	Cambridge U	D 0-0	0-0	14		8125
24	6	H	Stoke C	D 0-0	0-0	—		6462
25	10	H	Sheffield U	D 1-1	1-0	13	Turner	7025
26	24	H	Blackburn R	W 2-1	0-1	10	West, Turner	6247
27	26	A	West Ham U	L 1-4	0-0	—	Turner	14,205
28	Mar 3	A	Notts Co	L 1-3	0-0	12	Hatton	7624
29	10	H	Orient	W 2-1	1-1	8	Turner, Hill	6003
30	13	A	Burnley	L 1-2	0-1	—	Hatton	8000
31	24	H	Crystal Palace	L 0-1	0-1	14		11,008
32	28	A	Leicester C	L 0-3	0-2	—		10,465
33	31	A	Sunderland	L 0-1	0-0	16		23,358
34	Apr 7	H	Burnley	W 4-1	2-0	16	Hatton 2, Stein, Taylor	6466
35	9	A	West Ham U	L 0-1	0-0	—		25,498
36	14	H	Millwall	D 2-2	2-2	17	Moss 2 (1 a pen)	8292
37	16	A	Stoke C	D 0-0	0-0	—		19,214
38	21	H	Brighton & HA	D 1-1	1-0	15	Williams (og..)	13,132
39	25	A	Cardiff C	L 1-2	0-1	—	Roberts (o.g.)	10,549
40	28	A	Preston NE	D 2-2	0-1	18	Haslegrove (o.g.), Moss	8927
41	May 5	H	Fulham	W 2-0	1-0	14	Beck (o.g.), West	9122
42	7	A	Wrexham	L 0-2	0-1	—		7842

Final League Position: 18

Goalscorers

League (60): Moss 13 (1 a pen), Hatton 11, Stein 10, Fuccillo 7 (4 pens), Turner 5, Hill 3, West 3, Price 2, Taylor 1, Own Goals 5.

League Cup (7): Stein 4, Hatton 2, Hill.

League Cup	Second Round	Wigan Ath (h)	2-0
	Third Round	Crewe Alex (h)	2-1
	Fourth Round	Aston Villa (a)	2-0
	Fifth Round	Leeds U (a)	1-4
F.A. Cup	Third Round	York C (a)	0-2

235

Aleksic	Stephens	Sherlock	Hill	Turner C	Aizlewood	Stein	Fuccillo	Donaghy	Hatton	Moss	Ingram	McNichol	Price	West	Jones	Boersma	Carr	Lawson	Findlay	Taylor	Silkman	Birchenall	Phillipson-Masters	Turner W L	Match No.
1	2	3	4	5	6	7	8	9	10	11															1
1	2	3	7	5	6	9	8*	4	10	11	12														2
1	2*		7	5	3	9		4	10	11		12	6	8											3
1			4	5*	3	9	8	7	10				6	12	2	11									4
1			4	5	3	9	8	7*		11	10		6	12	2										5
1			6	3	5	9	12	7*10	11				4	8	2										6
1			4	5	3	9	12	7*10	11				6	8	2										7
1			4	5	3	9	11	6	10	7			2	8											8
1			4	5	3*	9		6	10	11			2	8	12										9
1			4	5	3	7	9	2	10	11			6	8											10
1			4	5	3	9	8	6	10*11				2	7	12										11
1			5	6	4	9	8	3	10	11			2	7											12
1			4	5	3	9	8	2	10	11			6*	7		12									13
1	12		4*	5	3	9	7	6	10	11			2	8											14
			6	3	9	8		5	10	11			2	7			4	1							15
				5	3	9	8	6	10	11			2	7			4	1							16
			4		3	9	8	6	10	11			2	7	5			1							17
			4	5	3	9	8	6	10	11			2	7				1							18
				5	3	12	8	6	10	11		9*	2	7		4		1							19
			.8	5	3	9		6	10	11			2	7	12	4*		1							20
			8	5*	3	9		6	10	11			2	7	12	4		1							21
	2		8		3	12		6	10	11			5	7		4*			1	9					22
	2		8	5	3			4	10	7			6	11				1		9					23
	2		8	5				4	10	11			6	7			3	1		9					24
	2		8	5	3	9		4	10	11*			6	7				1	12						25
	2		7	5	3	9*			10				6	8		4		1	12	11					26
	2	11	5	3					10				6	4		8		1	9	7					27
	2			5	3			4	10				6	11		8		1	9	7					28
	2		6	5	3	11		4	10					7		8		1	9						29
	2		6	5	3	11		4	10					7		8		1	9						30
	2		7	5	8	11		4	10				3	12		6*		1	9						31
	2		7	5		11		4	10				3	8				1	9		6				32
	2		7			11		4	10*				3	8		12		1	9		6	5			33
	2		6		3	9		4	10	7				8				1	12		11*	5			34
	2	.	7		3	9		4	10	11*				8		6		1	12			5			35
	2		7		3	9*		4	10	11				8				1	12		6	5			36
	2		7		3			4	10				6	8				1	9		11	5			37
	2		7		3			4	10	11				8				1	9		6	5			38
	2		7		3			4	10				6	8				1	9		11	5			39
	2		7		3			4	10	12			6	8				1	9		11*	5			40
	2		7		3	9		4	10	11			6	8				1				5			41
	2		7		3	12		4	10				6	8				1	9			5	11*		42
14	24	2	38	30	39	31	16	40	41	29	2	—	34	37	6	13	5	23	15	3	8	10	1		
+ 1s				+ 3s	+ 2s			+ 1s	+ 1s	+ 1s			+ 3s	+ 4s		+ 2s			+ 5s						

LUTON TOWN—PLAYERS

Player and position	Ht	Wt	Birthplace	Clubs	League Appearances	Goals
Goalkeepers						
Alan Judge	6 0	11 6	Kingsbury	Luton T	—	—
Jake Findlay	6 1	14 6	Blairgowie	Aston V	14	—
				Luton T	23	—
Defenders						
Paul Price	5 11	11 12	St Albans	Luton T	123+1	6
Graham Jones	6 0	12 7	Worsley	Luton T	30+8	—
Gary Sisman	5 8	11 0	Stevenage	Luton T	—	—
Wayne Turner	5 8	10 8	Luton	Luton T	1	—
Chris Turner	6 1	12 9	St. Neots	Peterborough U	308+7	37
(Contract cancelled March 1979)				Luton T	30	5
Mal Donaghy	5 10	12 7	Belfast	Larne	—	—
				Luton T	40	—
Kirk Stephens	5 8¾	11 8	Coventry	Luton T	24+1	—
Mark Aizlewood	6 0	12 8	Newport	Newport Co	35+3	1
				Luton T	39	—
Midfield						
Pasqualle Fuccillo	5 11	11 4	Bedford	Luton T	114+3	21
Ricky Hill	5 9	11 10	London	Luton T	85+6	13
David Carr	5 10	11 8	Aylesham	Luton T	39+4	—
Alan West	5 8½	10 7½	Hyde	Burnley	41+4	3
				Luton T	217+4	14
Alan Birchenall	6 0	12 8	East Ham	Sheffield U	106+1	31
				Chelsea	74+1	20
				C Palace	41	11
				Leicester C	156+7	12
				Notts Co	33	—
				Blackburn R	17+1	—
				Luton T	8	—
Les Harriott	5 7	11 9	Luton	Luton T	—	—
Clive Goodyear	5 11	11 4	Lincoln	Luton T	—	—
Forwards						
Gary Heale	5 11	11 7	Canvey Island	Luton T	7	1
				Exeter C (on loan)	3+1	—
Godfrey Ingram	5 7	10 3	Luton	Luton T	3+3	1
Brian Stein	5 10½	11 8	South Africa	Luton T	49+9	13
Martin Sperrin	5 10	11 0	Edmonton	Luton T	0+1	—
(Contract cancelled December 1978)						
Dave Moss	5 9	11 7	Witney	Swindon T	217+13	60
				Luton T	29+1	13
Bob Hatton	5 11	12 0	Hull	Wolverhampton W	10	7
				Bolton W	23	2
				Northampton T	29+4	8
				Carlisle U	93	38
				Birmingham C	170+5	58
				Blackpool	75	32
				Luton T	41	11
Steve Taylor	5 10	10 8	Oldham	Bolton W	34+6	16
				Port Vale (on loan)	4	2
				Oldham Ath	45+2	25
				Luton T	15+5	1
Seamus Heath	5 8¼	10 5	Belfast	Luton T	—	—
Andy Pearson	5 5	9 9	Newmarket	Luton T	—	—

Not retained: *Peter Lucas, *Steven Sherlock, 2 apps.

MANCHESTER CITY DIV. 1

Chairman: P. J. Swales.
Executive President: S. H. Cussons.
Directors: S. S. Rose, M.B., F.R.C.S., A. E. Alexander, M.S.I.A., R. Harris, J. B. Muir, I. L. G. Niven, M. T. Horwich.
Secretary: J. B. Halford.
General Manager: Tony Book.
Team manager: Malcolm Allison.
Year Formed: 1887 as Ardwick F.C.; 1895 as Manchester City.
Limited Company: 1894.
Turned Professional: 1887 as Ardwick F.C.
Previous Names: 1887–94, Ardwick F.C. (Formed through the amalgamation of West Gorton and Gorton Athletic, the latter having been formed in 1880.)
Previous Grounds: 1880–81, Clowes Street; 1881–82, Kirkmanshulme Cricket Ground; 1882–84, Queens Road; 1884–87, Pink Bank Lane; 1887–94, Hyde Road; (1894–1923, as City); 1923, Maine Rd.
Football League Record: 1892 Ardwick elected founder member of Division 2. 1894 Newly-formed Manchester C. elected to Division 2. Division 1: 1899–1902; 1903–09; 1910–26; 1928–38; 1947–50; 1951–63; 1966– . Division 2: 1902–03; 1909–10; 1926–28; 1938–47; 1950–51; 1963–66.
Honours: Football League, Division 1, Champions: 1936–37, 1967–68; Runners-up: 1903–04, 1920–21, 1976–77. Division 2, Champions: 1898–99, 1902–03, 1909–10, 1927–28, 1946–47, 1965–66; Runners-up: 1895–96, 1950–51. *F.A. Cup,* Winners: 1904, 1934, 1956, 1969; Runners-up: 1926, 1933, 1955. *Football League Cup,* Winners: 1970, 1976. Runners up: 1973–74.
European Competitions: European Cup: 1968–69. *European Cup-Winners' Cup:* 1969–70 (Winners): 1970–71. *UEFA Cup:* 1972–73, 1976–77, 1977–78, 1978–79.
Record Victory: 11-3 v Lincoln C., Division 2, Mar. 23rd, 1895.
Record Defeat: 1-9 v Everton, Division 1, Sept. 3rd, 1906.
Most League Points: 62, Division 2, 1946–47.
Most League Goals: 108, Division 2, 1926–27.
Highest League Scorer in Season: Tommy Johnson, 38, Division 1, 1928–29.
Most League Goals in Total Aggregate: Tommy Johnson, 158, 1919–30.
Most Capped Player: Colin Bell, 48, England.
Most League Appearances: Alan Oakes, 565, 1959–76.
Record Transfer Fee Received: £450,000 from WBA for Gary Owen, June 1979 and £450,000 from Nottingham F for Asa Hartford, July 1979.
Record Transfer Fee Paid: £765,000 to Preston N E for Mick Robinson, June 1979.
Managers Since the War: Wilf Wild, Sam Cowan, Jock Thomson, Les McDowall, George Poyser, Joe Mercer, Malcolm Allison, John Hart, Ron Saunders.
Address of Club Shop or Boutique: O.K. Souvenir Sports Ltd., Maine Road, Moss Side, Manchester M14 7WN.

Maine Road, Moss Side, Manchester M14 7WN. Telephone 061-226-1191/2. *Telegraphic address:* 'Football, Manchester 14'. *Capacity crowd:* 52,500. *Record attendance:* 84,569 v Stoke C., F.A. Cup 6th Rd., March 3, 1934 (British record for any game outside London or Glasgow). *Record receipts:* £140,000 Everton v Liverpool, FA Cup Semi-Final, April 23, 1977. *Pitch measurements:* 119 yds × 79 yds.
How to get there: Corporation specials from Aytoun Street, Piccadilly, in centre of city. Nearest railway station, Manchester Piccadilly.
Match tickets: Advance booking 14 days prior to the match.
Car parking: Kippax Street car park holds approximately 400 cars. Also street parking.
Entertainments/catering facilities: Social club can be used by visiting supporters (contact Mr Roy Clarke). Licensed refreshment points around the ground.
Club shop: Open all week at the ground.
Handbook/programmes: Handbook available. Programmes can be obtained on a mailing list.
Extra information: Manchester City scored more goals in 1937–38 than any other First Division side – but were relegated!
Club Colours: Sky blue shirts with white collar and cuffs, white stripe down sleeve, sky blue shorts with white trimmings, sky blue stockings with white rings on top.
Change Colours: White shirts with red/black stripe diagonally across chest, black shorts, black stockings.
Club Captain:
Club Nickname: 'Citizens'.

MANCHESTER CITY 1978-79 LEAGUE RECORD

Match No.	Date	Venue	Opponents	Result	H/T Score	League Pos'n	Goalscorers	Attendance
1	Aug 19	A	Derby Co	D 1-1	0-0	—	Kidd	26,480
2	22	H	Arsenal	D 1-1	0-1	—	Kidd	39,506
3	26	H	Liverpool	L 1-4	1-2	18	Kidd	46,710
4	Sept 2	A	Norwich C	D 1-1	0-1	15	Channon	18,607
5	9	H	Leeds U	W 3-0	2-0	10	Watson, Palmer 2	40,125
6	16	A	Chelsea	W 4-1	3-0	7	Channon, Futcher R 3	28,980
7	23	H	Tottenham H	W 2-0	0-0	4	Owen, Futcher R	43,471
8	30	A	Manchester U	L 0-1	0-0	10		55,317
9	Oct 7	A	Birmingham C	W 2-1	2-0	7	Kidd, Futcher R	18,378
10	14	H	Coventry C	W 2-0	0-0	5	Owen (2 pens)	36,723
11	21	A	Bolton W	D 2-2	1-1	5	Palmer, Owen	32,249
12	28	H	WBA	D 2-2	2-2	5	Channon, Hartford	40,521
13	Nov 4	A	Aston Villa	D 1-1	0-0	6	Owen (pen)	32,724
14	11	H	Derby Co	L 1-2	0-2	7	Owen (pen)	37,376
15	18	A	Liverpool	L 0-1	0-0	10		47,765
16	25	H	Ipswich T	L 1-2	0-0	12	Hartford	38,256
17	Dec 9	H	Southampton	L 1-2	0-1	14	Power	33,450
18	16	A	QPR	L 1-2	0-0	15	Channon	12,902
19	23	H	Nottingham F	D 0-0	0-0	14		37,012
20	26	A	Everton	L 0-1	0-0	15		46,997
21	30	A	Bristol C	D 1-1	0-1	15	Futcher R	25,253
22	Jan 13	A	Leeds U	D 1-1	0-1	13	Kidd	36,303
23	20	H	Chelsea	L 2-3	2-1	16	Power, Futcher R	31,876
24	Feb 3	A	Tottenham H	W 3-0	2-0	12	Kidd (pen), Barnes, Channon	32,037
25	10	H	Manchester U	L 0-3	0-2	15		46,151
26	24	A	Coventry C	W 3-0	1-0	15	Channon 2, Kidd	20,116
27	27	H	Norwich C	D 2-2	1-1	—	Owen 2 (1 a pen)	30,012
28	Mar 3	H	Bolton W	W 2-1	1-0	14	Channon, Owen (pen)	41,127
29	24	A	Arsenal	D 1-1	1-0	15	Channon	35,014
30	27	A	Wolverhampton W	D 1-1	0-1	—	Channon	19,998
31	31	A	Ipswich T	L 1-2	0-2	16	Silkman	20,773
32	Apr 4	A	WBA	L 0-4	0-2	—		22,314
33	7	H	Wolverhampton W	W 3-1	1-0	16	Channon, Palmer, Silkman	32,298
34	14	H	Everton	D 0-0	0-0	17		39,711
35	17	A	Middlesbrough	L 0-2	0-1	—		19,676
36	21	H	QPR	W 3-1	1-1	16	Silkman, Owen 2	30,694
37	24	H	Middlesbrough	W 1-0	0-0	—	Deyna	28,264
38	28	A	Southampton	L 0-1	0-0	16		19,744
39	May 1	H	Birmingham C	W 3-1	1-1	—	Power, Deyna 2	27,366
40	5	H	Bristol C	W 2-0	1-0	14	Deyna, Hartford	29,739
41	9	A	Nottingham F	L 1-3	0-1	—	Lloyd (og)	21,104
42	15	A	Aston Villa	L 2-3	1-0	—	Deyna 2	30,028

Final League Position: 15

Goalscorers

League (58): Channon 11, Owen 11 (6 pens), Kidd 7 (1 pen), Futcher R 7, Denya 6, Palmer 4, Hartford 3, Power 3, Silkman 3, Watson 1, Barnes 1, Own Goal 1.
League Cup (10): Channon 3, Owen 2 (1 pen), Palmer 1, Booth 1, Barnes 1, Own Goals 2.
F.A. Cup (4): Kidd 2, Owen 1, Barnes 1.

League Cup	Second Round	Grimsby T (h)	2-0
	Third Round	Blackpool (a)	1-1
		(h)	3-0
	Fourth Round	Norwich C (a)	3-1
	Fifth Round	Southampton (a)	1-2
F.A. Cup	Third Round	Rotherham U (h)	0-0
		(a)	4-2
	Fourth Round	Shrewsbury T (a)	0-2

Corrigan	Clements	Donachie	Keegan	Watson	Futcher P	Channon	Hartford	Kidd	Power	Barnes	Booth	Owen	Futcher R	Palmer	Viljoen	Henry	Bell	Deyna	Ranson	Reid	Silkman	Bennett	Match No.
1	2	3	4	5	6	7	8	9	10	11													1
1	2	3	4	5	6	7	10	9	8	11													2
1	2	3	4		6	7	8	9	11		5	10											3
1	2	3			6	7	8		4	11	5	10	9										4
1	2	3		5	6	7	10		4	11		8	9										5
1	2		5	6	7	10		3	11*		8	9		4	12								6
1	2	3		5	6	7	10			11		8	9	4									7
1	2	3		5	6	7	10	9	4	11		8											8
1	2	3		5		7	10	8		11*	4	6	9		12								9
1	2	3		5			10	6		11	4	8	9	7									10
1	2	3		5		8	10		11	6	7	12	9*	4									11
1	2	3			6	7	10	9			5	8	12	11	4*								12
1	2	3			6	7	10	9			5	8		11	4								13
1	2	3		5		7	10	9		11	4	6				8							14
1	2	3		5		7*10		9		11	4	6	12	8									15
1	2*	3		5			10	9	6	11	4	7		12		8							16
1		3	2	5		7	10	9*	6	11	4	12		8									17
1		3		5	2	7	10		6	11	4	8	12		9*								18
1		3		5	4	7	10		6	11		8	9				2						19
1		3		5	6	7	10*		4	11		8	9	12			2						20
1		3		5	4	7	10		6	11		8	9				2						21
1		3	5*	6	7	10	12	4	11			8	9				2						22
1	2		6		7	10	9	3	11	5*	4	12				8							23
1	2	5*	6		7	10	9	3	11		4					8	12						24
1	2	5	6		7	10	9	3	11		8			4									25
1	2		6		7	10	9	3	11	5	4		8										26
1	2		6		7	10	9	3	11	5	4		8										27
1	2	5			7	10	9	3	11	6	4		8										28
1	2	5			7	10		3		6	4		8	9		11							29
1		5			7	10		3	11		4	9*12	8	6				2					30
1		5			7	10		3	11		8	12		6*				2	4	9			31
1	2*		6	7	10		3		5		11	8	4					12	9				32
1	3		6	7*10					5	8	12	11		4					2	9			33
1			5	2	10		3	11	4*		7	8	6							9	12		34
1		5	6		10		3	11			7*	8	4	12	2					9			35
1	2	5			10		3	11	7			4		6	8					9			36
1	3	5	7			11		8				4	6	10					2	9			37
1	3	5	7			11		8				10	6	4					2	9			38
1	3	5	7			11		8				4	6	10					2	9			39
1	3	5	7	10		11						4	6	8					2	9			40
1	3	5	7	10			11					4	6	8					2	9			41
1	3	5*	7	10								12	8	4	6	11	2			9			42
42	15	38	4	33	24	36	39	19	32	29	20	34	10	10	16	13	10	11	8	7	12	—	
						+1s		+1s	+7s	+4s		+2s		+2s			+1s	+1s					

MANCHESTER CITY—PLAYERS

Player and position	Ht	Wt	Birthplace	Clubs	League Appearances	Goals
Goalkeepers						
Joe Corrigan (England)	6 4½	15 11½	Manchester	Manchester C	333	—
Keith MacRae	6 0	11 9	Glasgow	Motherwell	111	—
				Manchester C	53	—
Defenders						
Tommy Booth	6 1	11 12½	Manchester	Manchester C	323+2	25
Willie Donachie (Scotland)	5 9	11 3	Glasgow	Manchester C	328+4	2
Dave Watson (England)	5 11½	11 7	Nottingham	Notts Co	22+1	1
				Rotherham	121	19
				Sunderland	177	27
				Manchester C	146	4
Kenny Clements	6 1	12 6	Manchester	Manchester C	116+3	—
Noel Bradley	5 11½	11 4	Manchester	Manchester C	—	—
Paul Futcher	6 0	12 3	Chester	Chester	20	—
				Luton T	131	1
				Manchester C	24	—
Ray Ranson	5 10	11 5	St Helens	Manchester C	8	—
Nicky Reid	5 9½	11 10	Urmston Manchester	Manchester C	7+1	—
Midfield						
Asa Hartford (Scotland)	5 7	10 6	Clydebank	WBA	206+8	18
				Manchester C	184+1	22
Colin Bell (England)	5 11½	11 6½	Hesleden	Bury	82	25
				Manchester C	393+1	117
Tony Henry	5 11	11 12	Newcastle	Manchester C	14+4	—
Gary Owen	5 9	9 9	St Helens	Manchester C	111+2	19
Paul Power	5 11	10 13	Manchester	Manchester C	102+7	9
Colin Viljoen (England)	5 9	11 8	Johannesburg	Ipswich T	303+2	46
				QPR (on loan)	—	—
				Manchester C	16	—
Kazimierz Deyna (Poland)	5 10½	12 2	Starograd Gdanski	Legia Warsaw	(not known)	
				Manchester C	11+2	6
*Mike Barnes	5 8½	12 5	Manchester	Manchester C	—	—
Forwards						
Peter Barnes (England)	5 10	11 4	Manchester	Manchester C	108+7	15
Roger Palmer	5 10	10 10	Manchester	Manchester C	14+5	7
Mick Channon (England)	6 0½	11 6	Orcheston	Southampton	388+4	155
				Manchester C	69+1	23
Gary Buckley	5 4	9 6	Manchester	Manchester C	—	—
Ron Futcher (Contract cancelled April 1979)	6 0	12 10	Chester	Chester	4	—
				Luton T	116+4	40
				Manchester C	10+7	7
Barry Silkman	5 8	10 13	London	Hereford U	18+19	2
				Crystal Palace	40+8	7
				Plymouth Arg	14	2
				Luton T (on loan)	3	—
				Manchester C	12	3
Dave Bennett	5 10	10 2	Manchester	Manchester C	0+1	—

*Free transfer Chris Gregory

MANCHESTER UNITED   DIV. 1

Chairman: L. C. Edwards.   *Vice-Chairman:* J. A. Gibson.
Directors: W. A. Young, D. D. Haroun, J.P., C. M. Edwards, Sir Matt Busby, C.B.E., K.C.S.G.
Manager: Dave Sexton.   *Secretary:* R. L. Olive.
Ass. Manager: Tommy Cavanagh.
Year Formed: 1878 as Newton Heath; 1902, Manchester United.
Turned Professional: 1885.   *Limited Company:* 1907.
Previous Name: Newton Heath, 1880–1902.
Previous Grounds: 1880–93, North Road, Monsall Road; 1893, Bank Street; 1910, Old Trafford; (Played at Maine Rd. 1941–49).

Football League Record: 1892 Newton Heath Elected to Division 1. 1894–1906 Division 2. 1906–22 Division 1. 1922–25 Division 2. 1925–31 Division 1. 1931–36 Division 2. 1936–37 Division 1. 1937–38 Division 2. 1938–74 Division 1. 1974–75 Division 2. 1975– Division 1.
Honours: *Football League,* Division 1, Champions: 1907–08, 1910–11, 1951–52, 1955–56, 1956–57, 1964–65, 1966–67; Runners-up: 1946–47, 1947–48, 1948–49, 1950–51, 1958–59, 1963–64, 1967–68. Division 2, Champions: 1935–36; 1974–75; Runners-up; 1896–97, 1905–06, 1924–25, 1937–38. *F.A. Cup,* Winners: 1909, 1948, 1963, 1977; Runners-up: 1957, 1958, 1976, 1979. *Football League Cup,* best season: Semi-Finalists; 1969–70, 1970–71, 1974–75, 1978–79. European Competitions: *European Cup,* Semi-finalists: 1956–57, 1957–58, 1965–66, 1968–69; Winners: 1967–68. *European Cup Winners Cup:* 1963–64, 1977–78. *European Fairs Cup,* Semi-finalists: 1964–65. *UEFA Cup:* 1976–77.
Record Victory: 10-0 v Anderlecht, European Cup, preliminary Rd., 1956–57.
Record Defeat: 0-7 v Aston Villa, Division 1, Dec. 27th, 1930.
Most League Points: 64, Division 1, 1956–57.
Most League Goals: 103, Division 1, 1956–57 and 1958–59.
Highest League Scorer in Season: Dennis Viollet, 32, 1959–60.
Most Goals in Total Aggregate: Bobby Charlton, 198, 1956–73.
Most Capped Player: Bobby Charlton, 106, England.
Most League Appearances: Bobby Charlton, 606, 1956–1973.
Record Transfer Fee Received: £250,000 from Derby Co. for Gordon Hill, April 1978.
Record Transfer Fee Paid: £495,000 to Leeds U. for Gordon McQueen, Feb. 1978.
Managers Since the War: Matt Busby, Wilf McGuinness, Sir Matt Busby, Frank O'Farrell, Tommy Docherty.
Address of Club Shop or Boutique: Red Devils Souvenir Shop, Old Trafford.
Address of Supporters Club: Football Ground, Old Trafford (s.a.e. for details).

Old Trafford, Manchester M16 0RA.   Telephone 061-872-1661/2.   *Telegraphic address:* 'Stadium Manchester'.   *Ground capacity:* 58,504.   *Record attendance:* 76,962 Wolves v Grimsby T., F.A. Cup Semi-final, March 25, 1939   *Club record:* 70,504 v Aston Villa, Division 1, December 27, 1920.   *Record receipts:* £111,000, League Cup Final replay, Liverpool v Nottingham Forest, March 22, 1978, £72,000 v Tottenham H. F.A. Cup 6th Rd., replay, March 14, 1979.   *Pitch measurements:* 116 yds. × 76 yds.
How to get there: Special buses from Aytoun Street, Cannon Street, and various points in Manchester and Salford. Frequent train service from Manchester Oxford Road station direct to the Football Ground station, returning after the match. Schedule services from Oxford Road and Knott Mill, Manchester, or from Altrincham, Timperley, and intermediate stations, run to Warwick Road station, only a few minutes walk from the ground.
Match tickets: Seats can be booked from one calendar month before the match. Any not sold by Monday before a Saturday match can be reserved by personal application. For up-to-date ticket information, tel.: 061-872 7771. (24 hour service).
Car parking. Large car parks within easy reach of the ground at Lancashire County Cricket Ground, Talbot Road and Great Stone Road (1,200). White City Stadium, Chester Road (900), Trafford Council car parks (1,630). Alternatively, cars can be parked in Manchester, Altrincham, or at outside intermediate stations and the rest of the journey made by the above train services.
Entertainments/catering facilities: Licensed bars around the ground. Restaurant (not match days).
Club shop: The souvenir shop alongside the ticket office is open throughout the week. Price lists sent on receipt of S.A.E.
Programmes: Available on subscription and application with remittance can be sent to the ground for individual matches. The supporters' club publishes an annual handbook for members only.
Extra Information: The Manchester United Development Association has monthly draws for special prizes and a weekly draw. New agents are always welcome; tel.: 061-872 4676/5208 for full details. There is a travel club for away matches. The club also run their own lottery.
Club Colours: Red shirts with red and white trim, white shorts, black stockings with red tops and white band. *Change Colours:* White shirts with 3 black stripes, black shorts with red and white stripes, white stockings with red and black top. *Club Nickname:* 'Red Devils'.

MANCHESTER UNITED 1978-79 LEAGUE RECORD

Match No.	Date	Venue	Opponents	Result	H/T Score	League Pos'n	Goalscorers	Attendance
1	Aug 19	H	Birmingham C	W 1-0	0-0	—	Jordan	56,136
2	23	A	Leeds U	W 3-2	2-1	—	McQueen, McIlroy, Macari	36,845
3	26	A	Ipswich T	L 0-3	0-1	7		21,894
4	Sept 2	H	Everton	D 1-1	0-1	8	Buchan	53,982
5	9	A	QPR	D 1-1	0-1	8	Greenhoff J	23,477
6	16	H	Nottingham F	D 1-1	0-1	10	Greenhoff J	55,039
7	23	A	Arsenal	D 1-1	1-1	9	Coppell	45,393
8	30	H	Manchester C	W 1-0	0-0	7	Jordan	55,317
9	Oct 7	A	Middlesbrough	W 3-2	2-1	5	Macari 2, Jordan	45,402
10	14	A	Aston Villa	D 2-2	0-2	6	McIlroy, Macari	36,204
11	21	H	Bristol C	L 1-3	0-1	6	Greenhoff J	47,211
12	28	A	Wolverhampton W	W 4-2	3-1	6	Greenhoff J 2, Greenhoff B, Jordan	23,979
13	Nov 4	H	Southampton	D 1-1	1-0	7	Greenhoff J	46,259
14	11	A	Birmingham C	L 1-5	1-3	7	Jordan	23,550
15	18	H	Ipswich T	W 2-0	1-0	6	Coppell, Greenhoff J	42,109
16	21	A	Everton	L 0-3	0-2	—		41,926
17	25	A	Chelsea	W 1-0	0-0	7	Greenhoff J	27,156
18	Dec 9	A	Derby Co	W 3-1	1-1	7	Ritchie 2, Greenhoff J	25,100
19	16	H	Tottenham H	W 2-0	1-0	6	Ritchie, McIlroy	52,026
20	22	A	Bolton W	L 0-3	0-2	7		32,390
21	26	H	Liverpool	L 0-3	0-2	8		54,940
22	30	H	WBA	L 3-5	3-3	9	Greenhoff B, McQueen, McIlroy	45,091
23	Feb 3	A	Arsenal	L 0-2	0-0	11		45,460
24	10	A	Manchester C	W 3-0	2-0	9	Coppell 2, Ritchie	46,151
25	24	H	Aston Villa	D 1-1	0-0	10	Greenhoff J (pen)	44,437
26	28	H	QPR	W 2-0	1-0	—	Greenhoff J, Coppell	36,085
27	Mar 3	A	Bristol C	W 2-1	0-1	7	Ritchie, McQueen	24,784
28	20	A	Coventry C	L 3-4	1-3	—	Coppell 2, McIlroy	26,308
29	24	H	Leeds U	W 4-1	3-0	7	Ritchie 3, Thomas	51,191
30	27	A	Middlesbrough	D 2-2	0-2	—	McQueen, Coppell	20,190
31	Apr 7	A	Norwich C	D 2-2	0-0	8	McQueen, Macari	20,077
32	11	H	Bolton W	L 1-2	1-0	—	Buchan	49,617
33	14	A	Liverpool	L 0-2	0-1	13		46,608
34	16	H	Coventry C	D 0-0	0-0	—		43,075
35	18	A	Nottingham F	D 1-1	0-0	—	Jordan	33,074
36	21	A	Tottenham H	D 1-1	1-0	11	McQueen	36,665
37	25	H	Norwich C	W 1-0	0-0	—	Macari	33,678
38	28	H	Derby Co	D 0-0	0-0	10		42,474
39	30	A	Southampton	D 1-1	1-1	—	Ritchie	21,616
40	May 5	A	WBA	L 0-1	0-1	10		27,862
41	7	H	Wolverhampton W	W 3-2	2-1	—	Ritchie, Coppell 2	39,402
42	16	H	Chelsea	D 1-1	1-1	—	Coppell	38,119

Final League Position: 9

Goalscorers

League (60): Coppell 11, Greenhoff J 11 (1 pen), Ritchie 10, Jordan 6, McQueen 6, Macari 6, McIlroy 5, Buchan 2, Greenhoff B 2, Thomas 1.
League Cup (4): Jordan 2, McIlroy, Greenhoff J (pen).
F.A. Cup (14): Greenhoff J 5, McIlroy 2, Jordan 2, Coppell, Grimes, Thomas, McQueen, Greenhoff B 1.

League Cup	Second Round	Stockport Co	3-2 (at Old Trafford)
	Third Round	Watford (h)	1-2
F.A. Cup	Third Round	Chelsea (h)	3-0
	Fourth Round	Fulham (a)	1-1
		(h)	1-0
	Fifth Round	Colchester U (a)	1-0
	Sixth Round	Tottenham H (a)	1-1
		(h)	2-0
	Semi-Final	Liverpool	2-2 (at Maine Rd)
			1-0 (at Goodison Pk)
	Final	Arsenal	2-3 (at Wembley)

Roche	Greenhoff B	Albiston	McIlroy	McQueen	Buchan	Coppell	Greenhoff J	Jordan	Macari	McCreery	McGrath	Nicholl	Grimes	Houston	Bailey	Sloan	Thomas	Ritchie	Paterson	Connell	Moran	Match No.
1	2	3	4	5	6	7	8	9	10	11												1
1	2	3	4	5	6	7	8	9	10	11												2
1	2	3	4	5	6	7	8	9	10	11*12												3
1	5	3	4		6	7	8	9	10	11*		2	12									4
1	2	3	4	5	6	7	8	9	10	11												5
1	2	3	4	5	6	7	8	9	10	11*		12										6
1	4	2	11	5	6	7	8	9	10					3								7
1	4	2	11	5	6	7	8	9	10					3								8
1		2	4	5	6	7	8*	9	10	11		12		3								9
1		2	4	5	6	7	8	9	10			11		3								10
1	12	2	4*	5	6	7	8	9	10			11		3								11
1	4		11	5*	6	7	8	9	10			2	12	3								12
1	5		4		6	7	8	9	10			2	11	3								13
1	5	12	11		6	7	8	9	10	4		2*		3								14
	4	2	11	5	6	7	8	9			12			3	1	10*						15
	4	2	11	5	6	7	8	9	12					3	1	10*						16
	2		4	5	6	7	8	9	10					3	1		11					17
	2		4	5	6	7	8		10					3	1		11	9				18
	2		4	5	6	7	8		10					3*	1		11	9	12			19
	2		4	5	6	7	8*		10		12				1		11	9		3		20
	2		4	5	6	7	8		10						1		11	9		3		21
	2		4	5	6	7	8*		10			3	1	12	11	9						22
	2		10	5	6	7	8*	9		4		3	1		11	12						23
	2	3	4	5	6	7	8		10						1		11	9				24
	2	3	4	5	6	7	8		10*		12				1		11	9				25
	2	3	4	5	6	7	8				10				1		11	9				26
		3	4	5	6	7	8				2	10			1		11	9				27
10		3	4	5	6	7	8	9			2				1		11					28
10		3	4	5	6	7	8*				2				1		11	9	12			29
10		3	4	5	6	7	8	9			2				1		11					30
		2	4	5	6	7	8	9	10					3	1		11					31
		3	4	5	6	7		9	10		2				1		11	8				32
	5	3	4		6	7		9	10		2		12	1		11	8*					33
10		3	4	5	6	7		9	12		2				1		11	8*				34
10		3	4	5	6*	7		9	8		2	12			1		11					35
	6	3	4	5		7		9	10	8	2	12			1		11*					36
		3	4	5	6*	7		9	10	8	2	12			1		11					37
		3	4			7		9	10	2	5	12	6	1		11	8*					38
	2			5		7			10		11	3	1	4		9	8		6			39
	6	2	4	5		7	8	9	10			12	3	1		11*						40
	4*	3			6	7		9	10		2	12	5	1		11	8					41
		2	4	5		7	8	9		10*		6	12	3	1		11					42
14	32	32	40	36	37	42	33	30	31	14	—	19	5	21	28	3	25	16	1	2	1	
	+ 1s	+ 1s							+ 1s	+ 1s	+ 2s	+ 2s	+ 11s	+ 1s		+ 1s		+ 1s	+ 2s			

MANCHESTER UNITED—PLAYERS

Player and position	*Ht*	*Wt*	*Birthplace*	*Clubs*	*League Appearances*	*Goals*
Goalkeepers						
Alex Stepney	6 0	13 3	Mitcham	Millwall	137	—
(England)				Chelsea	1	—
(Contract cancelled February 1979)				Manchester U	433	2
Paddy Roche	6 1	11 5	Dublin	Shelbourne	not known	
(Eire)				Manchester U	41	—
Gary Bailey	6 1	12 0	Ipswich	Manchester U	28	—
Stephen Pears	5 10¾	11 5	Brandon	Manchester U	—	—
Defenders						
Mike Duxbury	5 9¼	10 6	Accrington	Manchester U	—	—
*Alex Forsyth	5 10	12 2	Sinton,	Partick T	52	5
(Scotland)			Scotland	Manchester U	99+2	4
				Rangers (on loan)	16	4
Martin Buchan	5 10¼	12 4	Aberdeen	Aberdeen	129+2	10
(Scotland)				Manchester U	278	4
Martyn Rogers	5 9¼	11 5½	Nottingham	Manchester U	1	—
Arthur Albiston	5 7½	10 10	Scotland	Manchester U	77+6	1
James Nicholl(N.Ire.)	5 9½	11 11½	Canada	Manchester U	110+8	2
Brian Greenhoff	5 10½	12 2	Barnsley	Manchester U	218+3	13
(England)						
Stewart Houston	5 11	12 3	Dunoon	Chelsea	6+3	—
(Scotland)				Brentford	77	9
				Manchester U	190+1	13
Gordon McQueen	6 3½	13 8½	Kilbirnie	St. Mirren	57	5
(Scotland)				Leeds U	140	15
				Manchester U	50	7
Martin Lane	5 11		Timperley	Manchester U	—	—
Alan McFall	5 11	11 0	Belfast	Manchester U	—	—
(Non-contract)						
Tom Connell	5 9¾	11 1	Newry	Coleraine	—	—
				Manchester U	2	—
Alan Davies	5 7½	10 3	Manchester	Manchester U	—	—
Nigel Keen	5 8½	10 13	Barrow	Manchester U	—	—
Chris Roberts	5 7	10 12	Bangor	Manchester U	—	—
*Phil McCandless	5 8½	9 13	Coleraine	Coleraine	—	—
				Manchester U	—	—
Kevin Moran	5 10½	12 6	Dublin	Manchester U	1	—
Barry Knox	5 7½	10 3	Gateshead	Sunderland	—	—
				Manchester U	—	—
Midfield						
Lou Macari	5 5¾	10 10	Edinburgh	Celtic	51+5	27
(Scotland)				Manchester U	223+4	56
*Steve Jones	5 10¾	12 0	Liverpool	Manchester U	—	—
David Haggett	6 0	11 1	Merthyr	Manchester U	—	—
Kel McDermott	5 6	9 10	Belfast	Manchester U	—	—
(apprentice)						
Mickey Thomas	5 6	10 10	Mochdre	Wrexham	217+13	33
(Wales)				Manchester U	25	1
Tom Sloan	5 6	9 9	Ballymena	Ballymena	—	—
(N. Ireland)				Manchester U	3+1	—
Andy Wray	5 7½	9 6	Beverley	Manchester U	—	—
Forwards						
Jimmy Greenhoff	5 9	12 0	Barnsley	Leeds U	89+6	19
				Birmingham C	31	14
				Stoke C	274	76
				Manchester U	82+1	25
Sammy McIlroy	5 9¾	11 8	Belfast	Manchester U	236+21	43
(Northern Ireland)						
Steve Coppell	5 7½	10 12	Liverpool	Tranmere R	35+3	10
(England)				Manchester U	172+1	26
Stuart Pearson	5 9	12 2½	Hull	Hull C	126+3	44
(England)				Manchester U	138+1	55
David McCreery	5 6½	10 6	Belfast	Manchester U	48+29	7
(N. Ireland)						
Chris McGrath	5 9½	10 11	Belfast	Tottenham H	30+8	5
(N. Ireland)				Millwall (on loan)	15	3
				Manchester U	11+15	1
*Ian Ashworth	5 7½	9 0	Accrington	Manchester U	—	—
*John McDermott	5 10¼	11 2	Manchester	Manchester U	—	—
Ashley Grimes	6 0	10 12	Dublin	Manchester U	12+17	2
(Eire)						
Andy Ritchie	5 9½	11 12½	Manchester	Manchester U	20+1	10
Joe Jordan	6 0¾	12 8	Carluke	Morton	7+3	1
(Scotland)				Leeds U	139+31	35
				Manchester U	44	9
Gary Micklewhite	5 6½	9 10½	Southwark	Manchester U	—	—
Gary Worrall	5 9	10 1½	Salford	Manchester U	—	—
Steve Paterson	6 1½	13 2½	Elgin	Manchester U	3+2	—
*Tony Grimshaw	5 6¾	10 0	Manchester	Manchester U	0+1	—
*Geoff Hunter	5 8½	10 4		Manchester U	—	—
Chris Lynam	5 5	9 3	Manchester	Manchester U	—	—
Andy Reynolds	5 3½	9 4	Neath	Manchester U	—	—
(apprentice)						

MANSFIELD TOWN   DIV. 3

Chairman: A. F. Patrick.
Vice-Chairman: J. B. Almond.
Directors: J. A. Brown, J. W. Pratt,
Dr. S. S. Scott, M.B., Ch. B., M.R.C.G.P.
Manager: *Secretary:* J. D. Eaton.
Year Formed: 1905.
Turned Professional: 1905.   *Limited Company:* 1905.
Football League Record: 1931 Elected to Division 3(S). 1932–37 Division 3(N). 1937–47 Division 3(S). 1947–58 Division 3(N). 1958–60 Division 3. 1960–63 Division 4. 1963–72 Division 3. 1972–75 Division 4. 1975–77 Division 3. 1977–78 Division 2. 1978– Division 3.
Honours: Football League, Div. 3 Champions 1976–77. Div. 4 Champions 1974–75. Division 3(N), Runners-up: 1950–51. *F.A. Cup,* best season: 6th Rd., 1968–69. *Football League Cup:* best season: 5th Rd., 1975–76.
Record Victory: 9-2 v Rotherham U., Division 3(N) Dec 27th, 1932 and v Hounslow T., F.A. Cup, 1st Rd. Replay, Nov. 5th, 1962.
Record Defeat: 1-8 v Walsall, Division 3(N), Jan. 19th, 1933.
Most League Points: 68, Division 4, 1974–75.
Most League Goals: 108, Division 4, 1962–63.
Highest League Scorer in Season: Ted Harston, 55, Division 3(N), 1936–37.
Most League Goals in Total Aggregate: Harry Johnson, 104, 1931–36.
Most League Appearances: Don Bradley, 417, 1949–62.
Most Capped Player: None.
Record Transfer Fee Received: £80,000 from Sparta Rotterdam for Ray Clarke, July 1976.
Record Transfer Fee Paid: £30,000 to Newcastle U. for Dennis Martin, March 1978; £30,000 to Walsall for Terry Austin, March 1979
Managers Since the War: Roy Goodall, Freddie Steele, Stan Mercer, Charlie Mitten, Sam Weaver, Raich Carter, Tommy Cummings, Tommy Eggleston, Jock Basford, Danny Williams, David Smith, Peter Morris, Billy Bingham.
Address of Supporters Club: Jackpot Office, c/o the ground.

Field Mill Ground, Quarry Lane, **Mansfield.** Telephone Mansfield 23567. *Telegraphic address:* 'Football, Mansfield'. *Ground capacity:* 23,500. *Record attendance:* 24,467 v Nottingham F., F.A. Cup 3rd Rd., January 10, 1953. *Record receipts:* £13,317 v Carlisle U., F.A. Cup 5th Rd., February 1, 1975. *Pitch measurements:* 115 yds × 72 yds.

How to get there: Buses from town centre to within 300 yards of the ground. Nearest railway station, Alfreton and Mansfield Parkway.
Match tickets: Advance booking 5 days prior to match.
Car parking: Room for 500 cars at the ground and another 3,000 within 500 yards.
Entertainments/catering facilities: No Club room. Licensed tea bars in the ground.
Club shop: Adjacent to the ground; sells all types of souvenirs.
Handbooks/programmes: Both on sale at the club shop.
Extra information: Mansfield became famous giant-killers as a non-League side in 1929. They went to Molineux in the FA Cup 3rd round and beat Wolves 1-0.

Club Colours: Amber shirts, blue shorts, amber stockings.
Change Colours: White shirts with blue and amber trimmings, white shorts, white stockings.
Club Trainer/Coach: Gerry Clarke.
Club Nickname: 'The Stags'.

MANSFIELD TOWN 1978-79 LEAGUE RECORD

Match No.	Date	Venue	Opponents	Result	H/T Score	League Pos'n	Goalscorers	Attendance
1	Aug 19	A	Exeter C	D 0-0	0-0	—		3704
2	21	H	Gillingham	D 1-1	0-0	—	Bird	5745
3	26	H	Southend U	D 1-1	0-1	13	Goodwin	5500
4	Sept 2	A	Swindon T	L 0-1	0-0	16		6195
5	9	A	Plymouth Arg	W 4-1	2-1	10	Syrett, Martin, Saxby M, Miller	6052
6	16	H	Sheffield W	D 1-1	1-0	16	Goodwin	11,366
7	23	A	Rotherham U	L 0-2	0-0	17		5350
8	27	A	Oxford U	L 2-3	1-1	—	Bird, Allen	3998
9	30	H	Carlisle U	W 1-0	1-0	17	Miller	4716
10	Oct 7	A	Shrewsbury T	D 2-2	1-2	18	Moss, Bird	4338
11	14	H	Walsall	L 1-3	0-0	21	Martin	6066
12	17	H	Swansea C	L 2-3	1-3	—	Goodwin, Allen	10,985
13	21	A	Blackpool	L 0-2	0-0	21		6633
14	28	H	Colchester U	D 1-1	0-0	21	Moss	4515
15	Nov 4	A	Lincoln C	W 1-0	0-0	21	Martin	3614
16	11	H	Swindon T	L 0-1	0-1	21		4721
17	13	H	Tranmere R	D 0-0	0-0	—		3929
18	17	A	Southend U	D 1-1	1-1	21	Syrett	7532
19	Dec 2	A	Watford	D 1-1	0-0	19	Goodwin	10,568
20	9	H	Brentford	W 2-1	2-0	19	Curtis (pen), McClelland	4003
21	23	H	Peterborough U	D 1-1	0-0	17	Green (og)	3671
22	26	A	Hull C	L 0-3	0-2	19		4700
23	30	A	Bury	D 0-0	0-0	18		4009
24	Feb 10	A	Carlisle U	L 0-1	0-1	22		4934
25	24	A	Walsall	D 1-1	1-0	22	Bird	4157
26	Mar 3	H	Blackpool	D 1-1	1-0	22	Curtis (pen)	4829
27	9	A	Colchester U	L 0-1	0-1	22		2866
28	12	H	Plymouth Arg	W 5-0	1-0	—	Syrett 2, Carter 2, Hamilton	4325
29	24	A	Gillingham	D 0-0	0-0	22		6935
30	26	H	Exeter C	D 1-1	1-0	—	Allen	4562
31	31	A	Chester	D 1-1	0-0	21	Austin	2205
32	Apr 3	A	Sheffield W	W 2-1	2-0	—	Saxby M, Austin	11,065
33	7	H	Watford	L 0-3	0-1	21		7944
34	14	H	Hull C	L 0-2	0-2	21		5138
35	16	A	Chesterfield	L 0-1	0-0	—		4931
36	17	A	Peterborough U	W 2-1	0-0	—	Austin, Miller	4178
37	21	H	Bury	W 3-0	2-0	20	Forrest (og), Curtis, Carter	3976
38	23	H	Swansea C	D 2-2	1-1	—	Allen, Curtis (pen)	6420
39	28	A	Brentford	L 0-1	0-0	20		6830
40	30	A	Tranmere R	W 2-1	2-1	—	Saxby G, Carter	1121
41	May 5	H	Chester	W 2-0	0-0	20	Austin, Curtis (pen)	4173
42	7	H	Shrewsbury T	D 2-2	1-0	—	Allen, Curtis (pen)	6413
43	11	H	Lincoln C	W 2-0	0-0	—	Saxby M, Austin	4386
44	14	H	Oxford U	D 1-1	0-0	—	Miller	4138
45	19	H	Rotherham U	L 0-1	0-0	—		3913
46	21	H	Chesterfield	W 2-1	1-0	—	Saxby M, Tartt (og)	4159

Final League Position: 18

Goalscorers

League (51): Curtis 6 (5 pens), Allen 5, Austin 5, Bird 4, Goodwin 4, Syrett 4, Saxby M 4, Miller 4, Carter 4, Martin 3, Moss 2, Saxby G 1, McClelland 1, Hamilton 1, Own Goals 3.
League Cup (2): Bird, Miller.

League Cup	First Round	Darlington (h)	0-1
		(a)	2-2
F.A. Cup	First Round	Shrewsbury T (h)	0-2

Arnold	Curtis	Foster B	Bird	Saxby M	McClelland	Miller	Martin	Syrett	Hodgson	Allen	Wood	Coffey	Goodwin	Foster C	Moss	Saxby G	Phillips	Grattan	Dawkins	Hamilton	Carter	New	Austin	Match No.
1	2	3	4	5	6	7	8	9*	10	11	12													1
1		3	2	5	6	7	8	9	10	11	12	4*												2
1		3	2	5	6	7	8	9	10	11			4											3
1		3	2	5	6	7	8	9	10	11*	12		4											4
1	2	3*	11	5	6	7	8	9	10				4	12										5
1	2	3	11	5	6	7*	8	9	10				4		12									6
1	2	3	7	5	6		10	9		11*	12	4	8											7
1	2	3	4	5	6	7	8*			11		10	9			12								8
1		3	2	5	6	7	10*	9		11				8	4	12								9
1		3	2	5	6	7	10*			11			8	9	4	12								10
1		3	2	5	6	4*	11			12		10		8	7	9								11
1	12	3	2*	5	6	7				11		9		8	4	10								12
1	2	3	7	5	6			9		11*		10	12	8	4									13
1		5	3	6	2	7	10*	9		12			4		8		11							14
1		3	6	5	2	7	11	9					10	4	8									15
1	2	3	6	5	10	7	11*	9		12			8		4									16
1	2	3	6*	5	11	7				12			10	8		4								17
1	2	3		5	6	8		9		11	12	10	4					7*						18
1	2	3*	6	5	11		7	9			12		10	4	8									19
1	2*		6	5	11		7	9			12			4	10	8		3						20
1		3	4	5	6		7	9					11	10	8			2						21
1		3	6	5	11		7*	9			12			4	10	8		2						22
1			4	5	6	7*	8	9		12	3		11	10				2						23
1	4		11	5	6		8*	9		10	3		12					2	7					24
1	4	3	10	5	6			9		11	12		8*					2	7					25
1	6	3	4	5			10	9			12		11					2	8*	7				26
	4	3	6	5	9	11*	10			12								2	7	8	1			27
	4	3	6	5		11	10	9*		12								2	7	8	1			28
	5	3	4	10	6	7*	8			12								2	11	9	1			29
	4	3	6	5	9		10			11								2	7	8	1			30
	4	3	6	5			11			9*	12							2	10	7	1	8		31
	4*	3	6	5			10				12	11						2	7	8	1	9		32
	4	3	6	5			11			12		10*						2	8	7	1	9		33
1	4	3	6	5		7	11			12								2	10*	8		9		34
1	4	3	6	5	12	11*	10											2	7	8		9		35
	4		10	5	6	12	11			7	3*							2		8	1	9		36
	4		10	5	6	7*				11	3							2	12	8	1	9		37
	4		10	5	6	7				11*	3							2	12	8	1	9		38
	4		2	5	6	11	10			7	3*			12					8	1	9			39
	4	3	6	5			10			7				11				2		8	1	9		40
	4	3	6	5		12				11		7*		10				2		8	1	9		41
	4	3	6	5		10				7			12	11*				2		8	1	9		42
	4	3	6	5		12				7				10				2	11*	8	1	9		43
		3	6	5	12	11				7			4		8*			2	10		1	9		44
	4	3	6	5	12	7				10					8*			2	11		1	9		45
	4	3		5	6					7			11	12		8		2	10*		1	9		46
28	33	39	44	46	33	28	33	23	6	26	6	2	26	9	12	14	3	1	26	16	18	18	16	
	+ 1s			+ 3s	+ 3s				+ 10s	+ 11s	+ 1s	+ 1s	+ 4s	+ 1s	+ 2s	+ 2s			+ 2s					

MANSFIELD TOWN—PLAYERS

Player and position	Ht	Wt	Birthplace	Clubs	League Appearances	Goals
Goalkeepers						
Rod Arnold	5 10	11 4	Wolverhampton	Wolverhampton W	—	—
				Mansfield T	260	—
Martin New	5 11	12 2	Swindon	Arsenal	—	—
				Mansfield T	18	—
Defenders						
Kevin Bird	5 9	10 12	Doncaster	Doncaster R	—	—
				Mansfield T	239+3	39
Barry Foster	5 9	10 4	Worksop	Mansfield T	226+5	—
Ian Wood	5 10	10 7	Kirkby in Ashfield	Mansfield T	57+12	1
Michael Saxby	6 0	10 0	Mansfield	Mansfield T	76+3	5
Colin Foster	5 9	11 0	Nottingham	Mansfield T	195+10	17
Bob Curtis	5 9½	11 0	Derby	Charlton	334+13	35
				Portadown	—	—
				Cardiff C	—	—
				Bangor	—	—
				Mansfield T	38+1	6
John McClelland	6 1	11 4	Belfast	Mansfield T	33+3	1
Gary Saxby	5 8	10 3	Mansfield	Mansfield T	14+2	1
Derek Dawkins	5 10	11 1	Edmonton	Leicester C	3	—
				Mansfield T	26	—
Leslie McJannet		10 4	Cumnock	Mansfield T	—	—
Adrian Burrows	5 11	11 12	Sutton	Mansfield T	—	—
Midfield						
*Dennis Martin	5 11	10 12	Edinburgh	WBA	14+2	1
				Carlisle U	270+4	48
				Newcastle U	9+2	2
				Mansfield T	46	3
Neville Hamilton	5 8	10 0	Leicester	Leicester C	4	—
				Mansfield T	16+2	1
*Mike Coffey	5 9	9 8	Liverpool	Everton	—	—
				Mansfield T	2+1	—
Nigel Groome (Contract cancelled)	5 7	10 0	Nottingham	Everton	—	—
				Mansfield T	—	—
Forwards						
John Miller	5 8	10 9	Ipswich T	Ipswich T	37+13	3
				Norwich C	22+1	3
				Mansfield T	100+3	14
*Ian Phillips	5 8	11 3	Edinburgh	Mansfield T	18+5	—
David Goodwin	5 11	11 7	Alsager	Stoke C	22+4	3
				Workington (on loan)	7	—
				Mansfield T	38+4	5
Russell Allen	5 9	11 7	Smethwick	Arsenal	—	—
				WBA	—	—
				Cambridge U (on loan)	—	—
				Tranmere R	137+19	44
				Mansfield T	26+10	5
Terry Austin	6 1	12 7	Isleworth	C Palace	—	—
				Ipswich T	10+9	1
				Plymouth Arg	58	18
				Walsall	44+3	19
				Mansfield T	16	5

Also retained: Peter Morris

MIDDLESBROUGH   DIV. 1

Chairman: C. Amer.
Vice-Chairman: G. T. Kitching.
Directors: Dr. U. N. Phillips, E. Varley, J. D. Hatfield, M. McCullagh, K. Amer, E. K. Varley.
Manager: John Neal.
Asst. Manager: Harold Shepherdson, M.B.E.
Secretary: T. H. C. Green, F.A.A.I.
Year Formed: 1876.
Turned Professional: 1889; became amateur 1892, and professional again, 1899.
Limited Company: 1892.
Previous Grounds: 1877, Old Archery Ground, Linthorpe Rd; 1903, Ayresome Park.

Football League Record:
1899 Elected to Division 2.   1928–29 Division 2.   1966–67 Division 3.
1902–24 Division 1.   1929–54 Division 1.   1967–74 Division 2.
1924–27 Division 2.   1954–66 Division 2.   1974–   Division 1.
1927–28 Division 1.

Honours: Football League, highest position in Division 1: 3rd, 1913–14. Division 2, Champions: 1926–27, 1928–29, 1973–74; Runners-up: 1901–02. Division 3, Runners-up: 1966–67. *F.A. Cup*, best season: 6th Rd., 1935–36, 1946–47, 1969–70, 1974–75, 1976–77, 1977–78, old last eight, 1900–01, 1903–04. *Football League Cup*, Semi-final: 1975–76. *Amateur Cup*, Winners: 1895, 1898. Anglo-Scottish Cup Winners: 1975–76.

Record Victory: 9-0 v Brighton & H.A. Division 2, Aug. 23rd, 1958.
Record Defeat: 0-9 v Blackburn R., Division 2, Nov. 6th, 1954.
Most League Points: 65, Division 2, 1973–74.
Most League Goals: 122, Division 2, 1926–27.
Highest League Scorer in Season: George Camsell, 59, Division 2, 1926–27 (record for Division 2).
Most Capped Player: Wilf Mannion, 26, England.
Most League Appearances: Tim Williamson, 563, 1902–23.
Most League Goals in Total Aggregate: George Camsell, 326, 1925–39.
Record Transfer Fee Received: £482,222 from West Bromwich Albion for David Mills, Jan. 1979.
Record Transfer Fee Paid: £233,333 to Burnley for Terry Cochrane, Oct. 1978.
Managers Since the War: David Jack, Walter Rowley, Bob Dennison, Raich Carter, Stan Anderson, Jack Charlton, O.B.E.
Address of Club Shop or Boutique: Warwick Street, Middlesbrough.

Ayresome Park, Middlesbrough, Teesside. Telephone Middlesbrough 89659/85996. *Telegraphic address:* 'Football, Middlesbrough'. *Ground capacity:* 42,000. *Record attendance:* 53,596 v Newcastle U., Division 1, December, 1949. *Record receipts:* £29,982 v Sunderland League Cup 2nd Rd., Sept. 13, 1977. *Pitch measurements:* 115 yds. × 75 yds.
How to get there: Regular buses from the Exchange in Middlesbrough to the ground. Buses also from bus station next to Middlesbrough railway station.
Match tickets: By postal or personal application two weeks prior to the match.
Car parking: Off-street parking near the ground.
Entertainments/catering facilities: Social club (members only); refreshment bars around the ground.
Handbooks/programmes: Programmes available on subscription.
Extra information: When Middlesbrough bought Alf Common from Sunderland in 1905, they paid the first £1,000 transfer fee.
Club Colours: Red shirts with three narrow stripes down sleeve in white; red shorts with same markings and red stockings.
Change Colours: All white.
Club Captain: Stuart Boam.
First Team Trainer: L. Clayton.
Club Coaches: John Coddington, Jimmy Greenhalgh.
Club Nickname: 'The Boro'.

MIDDLESBROUGH 1978-79 LEAGUE RECORD

Match No.	Date	Venue	Opponents	Result	H/T Score	League Pos'n	Goalscorers	Attendance
1	Aug 19	H	Coventry C	L 1-2	1-0	—	Woof	17,956
2	22	H	Birmingham C	W 3-1	3-1	—	Armstrong, Ashcroft, Mills	24,182
3	26	A	Southampton	L 1-2	1-0	13	Armstrong	20,691
4	Sept 2	H	Ipswich T	D 0-0	0-0	13		14,427
5	9	A	Everton	L 0-2	0-0	16		36,201
6	16	H	QPR	L 0-2	0-1	19		12,822
7	23	A	Nottingham F	D 2-2	0-2	19	Mills, Armstrong	26,287
8	30	H	Arsenal	L 2-3	1-1	19	Ashcroft, Mills	14,404
9	Oct 7	A	Manchester U	L 2-3	1-2	19	Mills, Burns	45,402
10	14	H	Norwich C	W 2-0	1-0	19	Peters (og), Mills	18,203
11	21	H	Wolverhampton W	W 2-0	1-0	17	Burns, Armstrong	19,389
12	27	A	Aston Villa	W 2-0	1-0	14	Burns, Cochrane	32,615
13	Nov 4	H	Bristol C	D 0-0	0-0	14		20,471
14	11	A	Coventry C	L 1-2	0-1	15	Burns	18,603
15	18	H	Southampton	W 2-0	1-0	15	Burns, Mills	17,169
16	21	A	Ipswich T	L 1-2	1-1	—	Armstrong	17,570
17	25	A	Liverpool	L 0-2	0-1	16		39,821
18	Dec 9	A	WBA	L 0-2	0-1	18		19,795
19	16	H	Chelsea	W 7-2	3-1	17	Proctor, Burns 4, Armstrong, Cochrane	15,107
20	23	A	Leeds U	L 1-3	1-1	18	Proctor	27,146
21	26	H	Bolton W	D 1-1	0-1	18	Cummins	20,125
22	Jan 20	A	QPR	D 1-1	0-0	17	Hodgson	9899
23	Feb 3	H	Nottingham F	L 1-3	1-1	18	Proctor	31,330
24	10	A	Arsenal	D 0-0	0-0	17		28,371
25	24	A	Norwich C	L 0-1	0-0	19		13,886
26	Mar 3	A	Wolverhampton W	W 3-1	1-1	17	Ashcroft, McAndrew, Shearer	18,782
27	6	H	Everton	L 1-2	0-1	—	Armstrong	15,990
28	10	H	Aston Villa	W 2-0	0-0	16	Proctor, Burns	16,562
29	13	H	Derby Co	W 3-1	1-0	—	Boam, Armstrong, Burns	16,286
30	17	A	Bristol C	D 1-1	0-0	16	Armstrong	12,319
31	24	H	Birmingham C	W 2-1	2-0	16	Burns, Ashcroft	15,013
32	27	H	Manchester U	D 2-2	2-0	—	Armstrong (pen), Proctor	20,190
33	31	H	Tottenham H	W 1-0	1-0	15	Proctor	19,172
34	Apr 7	A	Tottenham H	W 2-1	1-1	14	Proctor, Ashcroft	21,580
35	10	H	Leeds U	W 1-0	1-0	—	Ashcroft	23,260
36	14	A	Bolton W	D 0-0	0-0	10		22,621
37	17	H	Manchester C	W 2-0	1-0	—	Proctor, Burns	19,676
38	21	A	Chelsea	L 1-2	0-1	12	Armstrong	12,007
39	24	A	Manchester C	L 0-1	0-0	—		28,264
40	28	H	WBA	D 1-1	1-0	13	Burns	18,063
41	May 5	A	Derby Co	W 3-0	2-0	11	Cochrane, Proctor, Jankovic	18,151
42	11	H	Liverpool	L 0-1	0-0	—		32,244

Final League Position: 12

Goalscorers
League (57): Burns 14, Armstrong 11 (1 pen), Proctor 9, Ashcroft 6, Mills 6, Cochrane 3, Woof 1, Cummins 1, Hodgson 1, Shearer 1, McAndrew 1, Boam 1, Jankovic 1, Own Goal 1.
F.A. Cup (1): Ashcroft.

League Cup	Second Round	Peterborough U (h)	0-0
		(a)	0-1 (aet)
F.A. Cup	Third Round	C Palace (h)	1-1
		(a)	0-1

Stewart	Craggs	Bailey	Mahoney	Boam	Ramage	McAndrew	Mills	Ashcroft	Woof	Armstrong	Hedley	Procter	Johnston	Johnson	Cummins	Hodgson	Burns	Cochrane	Shearer	Platt	Jankovic	Bell	Match No.
1	2	3	4	5	6	7	8	9	10	11*	12												1
1	2	3	4	5	6		7	9	10	11		8											2
1	2	3	4	5	6		8	9*	10	11		7	12										3
1	2	3	4	5	6		8	9	10	11		7											4
1	2	3	4	5	6	8	10	9		11		7											5
1	2			5	6	10	9	12		11		7*	4	3	8								6
1	2		4	5	6	8*	7	9		11				3	10	12							7
1	2		4	5	6	8	7	9*		11				3	10	12							8
1	2	3	4	5	6	7	8	10		11							9						9
1	2	3	4	5		6	8	9		11								10	7				10
1	2	3	4*	5		6	8	9		11								10	7	12			11
1	2	3	4	5		6	8	9		11								10	7				12
1	2	3	4	5		6	8			11		7				9	10						13
1	2	3	4	5		6	8	9*		11		12						10	7				14
1	2	3	4	5		6	8			11								10	7	9			15
1	2	3	4*	5		6	8	9		11		12						10	7				16
1	2	3	4	5		6*	8	12		11								10	7	9			17
1	2	3	4	5		6		12		11		8*			10			9	7				18
1	2		4	5	6	3				11		8			10			9	7				19
1	2		4*	5	6	3		12		11		8			10			9	7				20
1	2		4	5	6	3				11		8			10			9	7				21
1	2*	3	4	5		6	9			11		8			10	12			7				22
1		4	5		6	2				11		8	3	10	12	9*	7						23
1	2		4	5		6	7*			11		8	3	10	12	9							24
1	2		4	5		6*		9		11		8	3	10	12	7							25
1	2		4	5		6		9*		11		8	3		7	10		12					26
1	2		4	5		6		9		11		8	3		7	10*		12					27
	2		4	5		6		9		11		8	3		7	10				1			28
	2		4	5		6		9		11		8	3		7	10				1			29
	2		4	5		6		9		11		8	3		7	10*				1	12		30
	2		4	5		6		9		11		8	3		10	7*				1	12		31
	2		4	5		6		9*		11		8	3		7	10	12			1			32
	2		4	5		6		9		11		8	3		7	10				1			33
	2		4	5		6		9		11		8	3		7	10				1			34
	2		4	5		6		9*		11		8	3		7	10				1	12		35
	2		4	5		6		9		11		8	3			10				1	7		36
	2	12	4	5		6				11		8	3			10	7			1	9*		37
	2		4	5	6			9		11		8	3	12		10*	7			1			38
	2			5	6		9	12	11			8	3			10*	7			1		4	39
	2		4		5	6		9		11		8	3*			10	7			1	12		40
	2	3	4			6		5		11		8			10		7			1	9		41
	2	3	4	5		6		9		11		8				7				1	10		42
27	41	18	40	40	14	38	17	33	4	42	—	31	1	21	11	13	31	18	2	15	4	1	
	+1s							+4s	+1s			+1s	+2s	+1s		+1s	+6s			+1s	+3s	+4s	

MIDDLESBROUGH—PLAYERS

Player and position	Ht	Wt	Birthplace	Clubs	League Appearances	Goals
Goalkeepers						
Jim Platt (N Ireland)	6 1	12 10	Ballymoney	Middlesbrough	259	—
				Hartlepool U (on loan)	13	—
				Cardiff C (on loan)	4	—
David Brown	6 1	12 10	Hartlepool	Middlesbrough	10	—
Jim Stewart (Scotland)	6 1	13 4	Kilwinning	Kilmarnock	175	—
				Middlesbrough	27	—
Defenders						
John Craggs	5 8½	12 3	Flinthill	Newcastle U	50+2	1
				Middlesbrough	315	11
Bill Maddren (Contract cancelled February 1979)	5 11	12 0	Billingham	Middlesbrough	293+2	19
Stuart Boam	6 1	13 5	Kirkby	Mansfield T	175	2
				Middlesbrough	320	14
Ian Bailey	5 9	11 2	Middlesbrough	Middlesbrough	57+5	—
				Carlisle U (on loan)	7	1
				Doncaster R (on loan)	9	—
Peter Johnson	5 8	10 4	Harrogate	Middlesbrough	25	—
Alan Ramage	6 2	13 3	Guisborough	Middlesbrough	54+1	1
Mike Angus			Middlesbrough	Middlesbrough	—	—
Jeff Peters	5 6	9 12	Wideopen	Middlesbrough	—	—
Ian Stokoe	5 10½	11 9	Prudhoe	Middlesbrough	—	—
Midfield						
Tony McAndrew	5 10	11 4	Lanark	Middlesbrough	131+1	5
Dave Armstrong	5 8	11 4	Durham	Middlesbrough	276+2	42
John Mahoney (Wales)	5 7½	11 4	Cardiff	Crewe Alex	16+2	5
				Stoke C	270+12	25
				Middlesbrough	77	1
Bill Askew	5 6½	10 0	Lumley	Middlesbrough	—	—
Mark Proctor	5 10	11 8	Middlesbrough	Middlesbrough	31+2	9
Graeme Hedley	5 10	10 2	Easington	Middlesbrough	11+4	3
				Sheffield W (on loan)	6	1
				Darlington (on loan)	14	1
Forwards						
Tony Bell			Middlesbrough	Middlesbrough	—	—
William Woof	5 10	11 9	Gateshead	Middlesbrough	10+10	2
				Brighton (on loan)	—	—
				Peterborough (on loan)	2+1	—
Ian Bell	5 9	10 10	Middlesbrough	Middlesbrough	2	—
Stan Cummins	5 4	9 1	Durham	Middlesbrough	35+4	7
Billy Ashcroft	6 1	14 7	Liverpool	Wrexham	196+23	71
				Middlesbrough	69+4	12
David Shearer	5 10	11 13	Inverness	Middlesbrough	6+3	3
				Lake McQuarry	4	—
Craig Johnston	5 9	10 10	Johannesburg	Middlesbrough	5+2	1
Terry Cochrane (N Ireland)	5 7½	10 9	Killyleagh	Coleraine	—	—
				Burnley	62+5	13
				Middlesbrough	18+1	3
Micky Burns	5 7	11 1	Blackpool	Blackpool	173+6	53
				Newcastle U	143+2	39
				Cardiff C	6	—
				Middlesbrough	31	14
David Hodgson	5 10	11 8	Gateshead	Middlesbrough	13+6	1
Bozo Jankovic (Yugoslavia)	6 0	13 4	Sarajevo	Zeljeznicar	(not known)	
				Middlesbrough	4+4	1

MILLWALL   DIV. 3

Chairman: L. C. Eppel.
Directors: W. J. Nelan, J. B. Rickard, R. I. Burr, P. Martinell.
General Secretary: G. I. S. Hortop.
Manager: George Petchey.
Assistant Manager: T. Long.
Year Formed: 1885. *Turned Professional:* 1893.
Limited Company: 1894.
Previous Grounds: 1885, Glengall Road, Millwall; 1886, Back of 'Lord Nelson'; 1890, East Ferry Road; 1901, North Greenwich; 1910, The Den.
Previous Names: 1885, Millwall Rovers; 1889 Millwall Athletic.
Football League Record: 1920 Original Members of Division 3. 1921 Division 3(S). 1928-34 Division 2. 1934-38 Division 3(S). 1938-48 Division 2. 1948-58 Division 3(S). 1958-62 Division 4. 1962-64 Division 3. 1964-65 Division 4. 1965-66 Division 3. 1966-75 Division 2, 1975-76 Division 3. 1976-79 Division 2. 1979– Division 3.
Honours: Football League, Highest position in Division 2: 3rd, 1971-72. Division 3(S)- Champions: 1927-28, 1937-38. Division 3, Runners-up: 1965-66. Division 4, Champions: 1961-62; Runners-up: 1964-65. Longest unbeaten home run: Aug. 24, 1964 to Jan. 14, 1967. *F.A. Cup*, best season: semi-finalists, 1900, 1903, 1937 (First Division 3 side to reach Semi-Final.) *Football League Cup*, best season: 5th Rd., 1973-74, 1976-77.
Record Victory: 9-1 v Torquay U., Division 3(S), Aug. 29th, 1927; v Coventry C., Division 3(S), Nov. 19th, 1927.
Record Defeat: 1-9 v Aston Villa, F.A. Cup, 4th Rd., Jan. 28th, 1946.
Most League Points: 65, Division 3(S), 1927-28; Division 3, 1965-66.
Most League Goals: 127, Division 3(S), 1927-28.
Highest League Scorer in Season: Richard Parker, 37, Division 3(S), 1926-27.
Most Capped Player: Eamonn Dunphy, 22(23), Eire.
Most League Appearances: Barry Kitchener, 489, 1967-1979.
Most League Goals in Total Aggregate: Derek Possee, 79, 1967-73.
Record Transfer Fee Received: £150,000 from Tampa Bay Rowdies, USA, for Nicky Johns, June 1978.
Record Transfer Fee Paid: £100,000 to Fulham for John Mitchell, July 1978; £100,000 to Crystal P. for Nick Chatterton, Nov. 1978.
Managers Since the War: Jack Cock, Charlie Hewitt, Ron Gray, Jimmy Seed, Reg. Smith, Ron Gray, Billy Gray, Benny Fenton, Gordon Jago.
Address of Supporters Club: 470 New Cross Road, Deptford, London SE8.
Address of Club Shop or Boutique: Same.

The Den, Cold Blow Lane, London, SE14 5RH. Telephone 01-639 3143/4./1474 *Ground capacity:* 32,000. *Record attendance:* 48,672 v Derby Co., F.A. Cup 5th Rd., February 20 1937. *Record receipts:* £13,500 v Brighton & H.A., Dicision 3, April 16, 1976 *Pitch measurements:* 112 yds × 74 yds.

How to get there: Buses from Central London and West End: 36, 36A, 36B, 53, 141, 171, 177, 182. From City: 21. Nearest Underground stations, New Cross or New Cross Gate (Metropolitan Line). Also New Cross Gate British Rail station.
Match tickets: Bookable 10-14 days in advance from club office.
Car parking: Car park near the ground. Also ample street parking.
Entertainments/catering facilities: Several licensed refreshment points around the ground. Jubilee Club.
Club shop: Three shops at the ground open on match days.
Programmes: Programmes available on subscription.
Extra information: Millwall went unbeaten for 59 successive League matches at the Den between 1964 and 1967.
Club Colours: Blue shirts, white trim, white shorts, blue stockings.
Change Colours: Red shirts with black and white trim, black shorts, black stockings.
Club Captain: Barry Kitchener.
First Team Physiotherapist: R. Adams.
Club Nickname: 'Lions'.

MILLWALL 1978-79 LEAGUE RECORD

Match No.	Date	Venue	Opponents	Result	H/T Score	League Pos'n	Goalscorers	Attendance
1	Aug 19	H	Newcastle U	W 2-1	0-1	—	Seasman 2	12,105
2	22	A	Notts Co	D 1-1	1-0	—	Lee	6810
3	26	A	Stoke C	L 0-2	0-0	13		15,176
4	Sept 2	H	Brighton & HA	L 1-4	1-1	21	Seasman	9238
5	9	A	Preston NE	D 0-0	0-0	18		8926
6	16	H	Crystal Palace	L 0-3	0-1	21		11,693
7	23	A	Fulham	L 0-1	0-0	22		8941
8	30	H	Burnley	L 0-2	0-1	22		5238
9	Oct 7	A	West Ham U	L 0-3	0-1	22		22,000
10	14	H	Sheffield U	D 1-1	0-0	22	Seasman	6342
11	21	A	Sunderland	L 2-3	1-2	22	Towner, Hamilton B	19,962
12	28	H	Charlton Ath	L 0-2	0-1	22		9546
13	Nov 4	H	Oldham Ath	L 2-3	2-1	22	Wood (og), Hamilton B	5626
14	11	A	Newcastle U	L 0-1	0-0	22		20,561
15	18	H	Stoke C	W 3-0	1-0	22	Mitchell 2, Seasman	6928
16	21	A	Brighton & HA	L 0-3	0-2	—		19,408
17	25	A	Wrexham	L 0-3	0-3	22		7080
18	Dec 2	H	Cardiff C	W 2-0	1-0	22	Mitchell, Dwyer (og)	5381
19	9	A	Bristol R	W 3-0	0-0	22	Chatterton (pen), Mitchell, Chambers (pen)	7112
20	16	H	Blackburn R	D 1-1	0-0	21	Seasman	6093
21	23	A	Orient	L 1-2	1-1	22	Chatterton	6185
22	26	H	Luton T	L 0-2	0-2	—		6068
23	Jan 20	A	Crystal Palace	D 0-0	0-0	22		21,142
24	Feb 24	A	Sheffield U	W 2-0	1-0	21	Walker, Seasman	13,763
25	Mar 3	H	Sunderland	L 0-1	0-0	21		7889
26	10	A	Charlton Ath	W 4-2	3-2	21	Walker 2, Mitchell, Seasman	9908
27	20	A	Cambridge U	L 1-2	1-0	—	Kitchener	5301
28	24	H	Notts Co	L 0-1	0-0	21		5717
29	Apr 4	H	Leicester C	W 2-0	1-0	—	Seasman, Walker	4758
30	7	A	Cardiff C	L 1-2	0-1	22	Chatterton (pen)	7714
31	10	H	Orient	W 2-0	1-0	—	Chambers 2 (1 a pen)	6117
32	14	A	Luton T	D 2-2	2-2	21	Chambers, Seasman	8292
33	17	H	Cambridge U	W 2-0	1-0	—	Cozens (o.g.), Mehmet	6414
34	21	A	Blackburn R	D 1-1	1-0	21	Mehmet	5819
35	24	H	Fulham	D 0-0	0-0	—		7397
36	28	H	Bristol R	L 0-3	0-2	21		5266
37	May 5	A	Leicester C	D 0-0	0-0	22		12,828
38	8	A	Burnley	W 1-0	1-0	—	Walker	5737
39	11	A	Oldham Ath	L 1-4	0-0	—	Tagg	5943
40	14	H	West Ham U	W 2-1	0-1	—	Mehmet, Chatterton	11,917
41	17	H	Wrexham	D 2-2	0-0	—	Kitchener, Mehmet	4865
42	22	H	Preston NE	L 0-2	0-2	—		2833

Final League Position: 21

Goalscorers

League (42): Seasman 10, Mitchell 5, Walker 5, Chambers 4 (2 pens), Chatterton 4 (2 pens), Mehmet 4 Hamilton B 2, Kitchener 2, Lee 1, Tagg 1, Towner 1, Own Goals 3.
League Cup (2): Mitchell, Seasman (pen).
F.A. Cup (1): Walker.

League Cup	First Round	Aldershot (a)	1-0
		(h)	1-0
	Second Round	Brighton & HA (a)	0-1
F.A. Cup	Third Round	Blackburn R (h)	1-2

255

Cuff	Donaldson	Moore	Allen	Tagg	Hazell	Hamilton, B.	Seasman	Mitchell	Pearson	Mehmet	Lee	Kitchener	Walker	Chambers	Hamilton, J.	Cross	Gale	Gregory	Towner	McKenna	Chatterton	Blyth	O'Callaghan	Sparrow	Dibble	Coleman	Roberts	Kinsella	Match No.
1	2	3	4	5	6	7	8*	9	10	11	12																		1
1	2	3	4		6	7		9	10	8	11	5																	2
1	2	3	4	5	6	7		9	10*	12	11		8																3
1	2	3*	4		6	7	8	9		12	11	5	10																4
1	2	3*			6	7	8	9		12		5	10	4	11														5
1	2	3			6	7	8	9	12	4*	11	5	10																6
1	2		3		6	7	8	9		4*		5	10			11	12												7
1	2		4			7	8	10	9*			5	11		12			6	3										8
1	7		4			2*	8	9	10			5	11			12		6	3										9
1	2		6				8	9	10			5	11				4	3	7										10
1	2		6			12	8	9	11			5	10				4*	3	7										11
1	2		6			11	9		8*	4		5	10					3	7	12									12
1	2		6			4	8	9		11		5	10					3	7										13
1	2	3	6			8	9	11		4		5	10					7											14
1	2	3	6			8	9		11			5	10	12				7*	4										15
1	2	3	6			8	9		4			5	10					7	11										16
1	2	3*	6			8	9		4			5	10	12				7	11										17
1	2					8	9					5	10	4			3	7		11	6								18
1	2					8	9					5	10	4			3	7		11	6								19
1	2					8	9	12				5	10	4*			3	7		11	6								20
1	2	3				8	9*	12				5	10	4				7		11	6								21
1	2					8	9	12				5	10	4*			3	7		11	6								22
1	2					8	9	10				5		4			3	7		11	6								23
1	2		12			8	9					5	10	4				3*11		7	6								24
1	2					8	9	12				5	10	4*			3	11		7	6								25
1	2					8	9	11*				5	10	4			3			7	6	12							26
1	2		6			8	9	7				5	10	4						11		3							27
1	2		6			8	9*	12				5	10	4					7	11	3								28
1	2					8	9	12				5	10	4						11	6	7*	3						29
1	2					8		12				5	10*	4					7	6	11	3	9						30
1	2		6			8	9	10				5		4						11		7*	3	12					31
1	2		6			8	9	12				5	10	11						4		7*	3						32
1	2		6			8	9	12				5	10	4				7		11		3*							33
1	2	12	6					8				5	10	4				3	11*	7			9						34
1	2		6					8				5	10	4				3		11	7		9						35
1	2		6					8*				5	10	4				3	11	7		12	9						36
1	2		12				8*					5	10	4				3	11	7	6	9							37
1	2		9					8*				5	10	4				3	7	11	6		12						38
1	2		6					8				5	10	4				3	7	11			9*	12					39
1	2		9			8		12				5	10	4				3*	7	11			6						40
1	2*		9			8		11				5	10	4				3	7				6			12			41
1			6			8	9*					5	10	4				3	7	11	12				2				42
42	41	11	4	26	7	12	35	32	8	20	4	40	38	26	1	1	4	23	25	27	13	7	7	5	2	1			
			+		+		+		+	+		+	+	+				+		+		+		+		+	+		
			1s		2s		1s		1s	13s	1s		2s	1s	1s	1s		1s			3s		2s		1s	1s			

MILLWALL—PLAYERS

Player and position	Ht	Wt	Birthplace	Clubs	League Appearances	Goals
Goalkeeper						
Pat Cuff	6 0	12 4	Middlesbrough	Middlesbrough	31	—
				Grimsby T (on loan)	2	—
				Millwall	42	—
Peter Gleasure	5 11	12 3	Luton	Millwall	—	—
Defenders						
Dave Donaldson	5 10	13 9	London	Arsenal	—	—
				Millwall	192	1
Barry Kitchener	6 1½	14 7½	Dagenham	Millwall	487+2	23
Tony Tagg	6 2¼	13 4	Epsom	QPR	4	—
				Millwall	40+3	1
*Glen Morris	5 11	11 2	Kent	Millwall	—	—
Ian Gale	5 8	10 8	Slough	Millwall	4+1	—
David Gregory	5 7	9 13	Essex	Millwall	23	—
Mel Blyth	6 1	12 2	Norwich	Scunthorpe U	27	3
				C Palace	213+3	9
				Southampton	104+1	7
				C Palace (on loan)	6	—
				Millwall	13	—
Phil Coleman	5 11	11 9	London	Millwall	2	—
Paul Roberts	5 7½	10 2½	London	Millwall	1+1	—
Midfield						
Chris Dibble	5 10	10 4	Surrey	Millwall	7+3	—
Phil Walker	5 9½	12 2½	London	Millwall	143+3	16
Peter Allen	5 9½	11 11½	Hove	Orient	423+7	28
				Millwall	16+2	—
Brian Chambers	5 10	11 4	Newcastle	Sunderland	53+10	5
				Arsenal	1	—
				Luton T	73+3	9
				Millwall	54+5	9
Tony Kinsella	5 8	9 10½	Essex	Millwall	0+1	—
Nicky Chatterton	5 9	11 4	Norwood	C Palace	142+9	31
				Millwall	27	4
Tony Towner	5 6	10 0	Brighton	Brighton	153+9	24
				Millwall	25	1
Andy Massey	5 10	10 3	London	Millwall	—	—
David Mehmet	5 8	10 4	London	Millwall	32+16	8
Forwards						
*David Pearce	6 0	10 11	Middlesex	Millwall	1	—
John Seasman	5 9	10 7	Liverpool	Tranmere R	15+2	2
				Luton T	7+1	—
				Millwall	123+1	34
*Roger Cross	6 0	13 7	London	West Ham U	5+2	1
				Orient (on loan)	4+2	2
				Brentford	62	20
				Fulham	39+1	8
				Brentford	141+4	52
				Millwall	14+4	—
Dean Horrix	5 10	10 5½	Slough	Millwall	—	—
John Hamilton	5 8	10 10		Hibs & Rangers	—	—
(Contract cancelled November 1978)				Millwall	1+1	—
Alan McKenna	5 9½	10 9	Edinburgh	Millwall	0+1	—
John Mitchell	5 11	12 0¼	London	Fulham	158+11	56
				Millwall	32	5
Kevin O'Callaghan	5 8¼	10 9	London	Millwall	7+3	—

NEWCASTLE UNITED　　　　　　　　　　DIV. 2

President and Vice-Chairman: Rt. Hon. Lord Westwood, J.P., F.C.I.S.
Chairman: R. J. Rutherford.
Directors: F. Braithwaite, O.B.E., J. Rush, A.F.C., W. G. McKeag, Dr. D. V. Salkeld, T.D., S. Seymour, R. Mackenzie.
Manager: Bill McGarry.
Secretary: R. Cushing
Assistant Secretary: A. J. Garvie.
Year Formed: 1882. *Turned Professional:* 1889.
Limited Company: 1890.
Previous Name: Newcastle East End until Newcastle U. in 1892.
Previous Grounds: Chillingham Road, Heaton, until 1892.

Football League Record:
1893 Elected to Division 2.
1898–1934 Division 1.
1934–48 Division 2.
1948–61 Division 1.
1961–65 Division 2.
1965–78 Division 1.
1978– Division 2.

Honours: *Football League:* Division 1, Champions: 1904–05, 1906–07, 1908–09, 1926–27. Division 2, Champions: 1964–65; Runners-up: 1897–98, 1947–48. *F.A. Cup,* Winners: 1910, 1924, 1932, 1951, 1952, 1955; Runners-up: 1905, 1906, 1908, 1911, 1974. *Football League Cup:* Runners-up, 1975–76. **European Competitions:** *European Fairs Cup:* 1968–69 (Winners), 1969–70, 1970–71. *UEFA Cup,* 1977–78. *Anglo-Italian Cup,* Winners 1973. *Texaco Cup,* Winners 1973–74, 1974–75.

Record Victory: 13-0 v Newport Co., Division 2, Oct. 5th, 1946.
Record Defeat: 0-9 v Burton Wanderers, Division 2, April, 15, 1895.
Most League Points: 57, Division 2, 1964–65.
Most League Goals: 98, Division 1, 1951–52.
Highest League Scorer in Season: Hughie Gallacher, 36, Division 1, 1926–27.
Most Capped Player: Alf McMichael, 40, Ireland.
Most League Appearances: Jim Lawrence, 432, 1904–22.
Most League Goals in Total Aggregate: Jackie Milburn, 178, 1946–57.
Record Transfer Fee Received: £333,333 from Arsenal for Malcolm Macdonald, Aug. 1976.
Record Transfer Fee Paid: £225,000 to Nottingham Forest for Peter Withe, Aug. 1979.
Managers Since the War: George Martin, Duggie Livingstone, Charlie Mitten, Norman Smith, Joe Harvey, Gordon Lee, Richard Dinnis.
Address of Supporters' Club and Shop: 7 Prudhoe Place, Haymarket, Newcastle-upon-Tyne 1.

St. James' Park, Newcastle-upon-Tyne NE1 4ST Telephone Newcastle 28361/2. Information service 611571. *Telegraphic address:* 'Football, Newcastle-upon-Tyne'. *Ground capacity:* 40,480. *Record attendance:* 68,386 v Chelsea, Division 1, September 3, 1930. *Record receipts:* £42,415 v Ujpest Dozsa, European Fairs Cup Final, May 29, 1969. *Pitch measurements:* 115 yds × 75 yds.
How to get there: The ground is central and within walking distance of the railway station and the town centre.
Match tickets: Personal applications accepted 10 days before a match and postal applications accepted 14 days before a match.
Car parking: Car park on the north side of the ground. Street parking available.
Entertainments/catering facilities: Excellent facilities in the New East Stand. Refreshments available in all parts of the ground.
Club shop: Open daily (except Sundays). Kiosk in St. James' Park open match days 9.30 a.m.—3.00 p.m. Run by supporters' club.
Handbooks/programmes: Handbook, 'Magpie', published by Supporters' Club. Programmes if available can be ordered from the secretary price 15p, old programmes from the Supporters' Club shop/Club Office.
Extra information: United's 13–0 win over Newport County in 1946 was a Second Division record score.
Club Colours: Black and white striped shirts, black shorts, black and white stockings. *Change Colours:* Yellow shirts, green shorts, yellow and green stockings. *First Team Trainer/Coach:*
Club Nickname: 'Magpies'.

NEWCASTLE UNITED 1978–79 LEAGUE RECORD

Match No.	Date	Venue	Opponents	Result	H/T Score	League Pos'n	Goalscorers	Attendance
1	Aug 19	A	Millwall	L 1-2	1-0	—	Barton	12,105
2	23	H	West Ham U	L 0-3	0-1	—		27,233
3	26	H	Luton T	W 1-0	1-0	18	Pearson	24,112
4	Sept 2	A	Cambridge U	D 0-0	0-0	20		8404
5	9	H	Blackburn R	W 3-1	0-1	10	Withe 2, McGhee	24,334
6	16	A	Wrexham	D 0-0	0-0	12		14,091
7	23	H	Orient	D 0-0	0-0	12		26,356
8	30	A	Notts Co	W 2-1	1-0	8	Bird, Connolly	11,813
9	Oct 7	H	Leicester C	W 1-0	0-0	6	Walker	25,374
10	14	A	Sunderland	D 1-1	1-0	6	Withe	35,405
11	21	A	Charlton Ath	L 1-4	1-1	12	Walker	11,616
12	28	H	Cardiff C	W 3-0	1-0	8	Withe, Robinson, Connolly	23,462
13	Nov 4	A	Bristol R	L 0-2	0-1	11		10,582
14	11	H	Millwall	W 1-0	0-0	10	Pearson	20,561
15	18	A	Luton T	L 0-2	0-1	12		10,434
16	22	H	Cambridge U	W 1-0	1-0	—	Bird	20,004
17	25	H	Oldham Ath	D 1-1	0-0	10	McGhee	20,552
18	Dec 2	A	Crystal Palace	L 0-1	0-1	11		19,287
19	9	H	Stoke C	W 2-0	0-0	9	Withe, Connolly	23,447
20	16	A	Fulham	W 3-1	2-1	6	Shoulder, Connolly, Withe	8575
21	23	H	Burnley	W 3-1	2-0	5	Shoulder, Withe, Cassidy	23,630
22	26	A	Sheffield U	L 0-1	0-0	—		23,118
23	30	H	Brighton & HA	L 0-2	0-1	8		25,812
24	Feb 3	A	Orient	L 0-2	0-0	10		7251
25	17	A	Leicester C	L 1-2	0-2	12	Nattrass	15,106
26	24	H	Sunderland	L 1-4	0-2	15	Connolly	35,000
27	Mar 3	H	Charlton Ath	W 5-3	3-2	10	Shoulder 2 (1 a pen), Martin, Mitchell, Connolly	15,006
28	10	A	Cardiff C	L 1-2	0-1	15	Connolly	11,116
29	24	A	West Ham U	L 0-5	0-4	16		24,650
30	31	A	Oldham Ath	W 3-1	1-1	14	Nattrass, Shoulder (pen), Withe	6329
31	Apr 4	H	Preston NE	W 4-3	2-2	—	Withe, Barton, Shoulder, Connolly	12,157
32	7	H	Crystal Palace	W 1-0	0-0	11	Shoulder	18,860
33	10	A	Burnley	L 0-1	0-1	—		7742
34	14	H	Sheffield U	L 1-3	0-2	12	Shoulder	19,121
35	16	A	Preston NE	D 0-0	0-0	—		12,960
36	18	H	Notts Co	L 1-2	0-1	—	Withe	12,000
37	21	H	Fulham	D 0-0	0-0	12		11,916
38	25	A	Blackburn R	W 3-1	1-1	—	Withe 3	4902
39	28	A	Stoke C	D 0-0	0-0	11		23,271
40	May 2	H	Bristol R	W 3-0	2-0	—	Withe, Shoulder, Bird	9625
41	5	H	Brighton & HA	L 1-3	0-3	11	Shoulder	28,425
42	8	H	Wrexham	W 2-0	1-0	—	Shoulder, Pearson	7133

Final League Position: 8

Goalscorers

League (51): Withe 14, Shoulder 11 (2 pens), Connolly 8, Bird 3, Pearson 3, Barton 2, McGhee 2, Nattrass 2, Walker 2, Cassidy 1, Martin 1, Mitchell 1, Robinson 1.

League Cup (1): Pearson.

F.A. Cup (4): Withe 2, Robinson, Nattrass (pen).

League Cup	Second Round	Watford (a)	1-2
F.A. Cup	Third Round	Torquay U (h)	3-1
	Fourth Round	Wolverhampton W (h)	1-1
		(a)	0-1

Mahoney	Kelly	Barker	Cassidy	Bird	Barton	Walker	Pearson	Mitchell	Hibbitt	Connolly	Blackley	Suggett	Withe	Hardwick	Brownlie	McGhee	Nattrass	Scott	Robinson	Nicholson	Martin	Shoulder	Mulgrove	Guy	Parkinson	Wharton	Carr	Manners	Match No.
1	2	3	4	5	6	7	8	9	10	11																			1
1	2	3	4	5		7	9		10	11	6	8																	2
1	2	3	4	5		8			10	11	6	7	9																3
	3		4	5	6		8		10	11		7	9	1	2														4
	3		4*		6		8		10	11	5	7	9	1	2	12													5
	3		4		6			12	10	11	5	7	9	1	2	8*													6
	2		4					12	10	11	6*	7	9	1	3	8	5												7
	2			5				12	10	11	6	4	9	1	3	8*		7											8
	3*			5		7		8	10	11	6	4	9	1	2	12													9
	2			5	6	8		4	10	11		7	9	1	3														10
	2			5	6	8	7*	4	10			12	9	1	3				11										11
	3			5		4			10	11	6	7	9	1	2	12			8*										12
	3			5		4	8		10	11	6	7	9	1	2														13
	3			5		4	8*		10	11	6	7	9	1	2	12													14
	2*				6	4		8	10	11	5	7	9	1	3	12													15
		3		5		8			10		6	7*	9	1	2	12	4		11										16
		3		5		8		12	10		6		9	1	2	7	4*		11										17
				5		8*		3	10	11	6	7	9	1	2				12	4									18
			4	5				3	10	11	6		9	1	2					7	8								19
			4	5	12			3	10	11	6*		9	1	2					8	7								20
	12		4	5*				3	10	11	6		9	1	2					8	7								21
			8	5				3	10	11	6		9	1	2					4	7								22
			8		6			3	10	11		4*	9	1	2					5	7	12							23
				5				3	10		6		9	1	2	8		11*		4	7		12						24
				5	12			3			6		9	1	2		4	10	11*	8	7								25
				5		8		12	10	11	6*		9	1	2		3			4	7								26
				5	8			3	10	11			9	1	2	6				4*	7		12						27
				5	8*			3	10	11	12		9	1	2	6				4	7								28
				5				8*	3	10	11		9	1	2	6				4	7					12			29
			8	5					10	11	6		9	1	2	3				4	7								30
			8	5				6	10	11	3		9	1	2					4	7								31
			8	5					10	11	3		9	1	2	6				4	7								32
			8	5					10	11	3		9	1	2	6				4	7								33
			8					5	10	11	6		9	1	2	3				4	7								34
			8		12			5	10	11	3		9		2	6				4*	7					1			35
			8		4			5	10	11*	3	12	9		2	6					7					1			36
				5	6	8		9			10				2*	3			11	4	7			12		1			37
				3	5			2	10			8	9			6			11	4	7					1			38
				5	6			3	10			8	9			2			11	4	7					1			39
				6	5			3*10	11			8	9			2			12		7					1	4		40
				6	4			3*10	11				9			2			12	8	7					1	5		41
				6	5		8	3	10	11			9			2				4	7					1			42
3	15	5	19	27	21	18		9	26	40	34	28	20	39	31	34	4	21	2	4	5	23	24			8	2		
	+1s		+1s	+2s		+5s					+3s				+6s				+3s					+1s	+1s	+1s	+2s		

NEWCASTLE UNITED—PLAYERS

Player and position	Ht	Wt	Birthplace	Clubs	League Appearances	Goals
Goalkeepers						
Mike Mahoney	5 11	11 10	Bristol	Bristol C	4	—
(Contract cancelled November 1978)				Torquay U	157	—
				Newcastle U	108	—
Steve Hardwick	5 11	13 0	Mansfield	Chesterfield	38	—
				Newcastle U	40	—
Kevin Carr	5 10	10 9	Ashington	Newcastle U	17	—
Kevin Baldwin	6 0	12 8	Gateshead	Newcastle U	—	—
Defenders						
John Bird	6 0	12 0	Doncaster	Doncaster R	48+2	3
				Preston NE	166	9
				Newcastle U	75+3	5
David Barton	6 0	11 7	Bishop Auckland	Newcastle U	35+1	2
Peter Kelly	5 7	10 0	Lothian	Newcastle U	23+2	—
Irving Nattrass	5 10	11 6	Fishburn	Newcastle U	226+12	16
*John Blackley (Scotland)	5 10	11 13	Falkirk	Hibernian	262+1	6
				Newcastle U	46	—
*Steve Burn	5 6	9 12	Newcastle	Newcastle U	—	—
Keith Mulgrove	5 8½	10 12	Haltwhistle	Newcastle U	0+1	—
*Kevin Patterson	5 9½	11 2	Newcastle	Newcastle U	—	—
John Brownlie	5 10	12 0	Calder-Cruix	Hibernian	210+1	14
				Newcastle U	34	—
Stephen Fairless	5 8	11 0	Co Durham	Newcastle U	—	—
Brian Ferguson	5 10	11 0	Irvine	Mansfield T	—	—
				Newcastle U	—	—
Bruce Halliday	5 10	11 6	Sunderland	Newcastle U	—	—
Midfield						
Ralph Callachan	5 10	11 4	Edinburgh	Hearts	75+2	9
(Transferred to Hibernian)				Newcastle U	9	—
*Colin Mullen	5 10	10 0	Gateshead	Newcastle U	—	—
Robin Armstrong	5 10	10 13	Newburn	Newcastle U	—	—
Brian Latty				Newcastle U	—	—
Kevin Pugh	5 0¾	10 5	Corbridge	Newcastle U	0+2	—
Ken Wharton	5 7½	10 0	Newcastle	Newcastle U	—	—
Colin Suggett	5 8	11 8	Washington	Sunderland	83+3	24
				WBA	123+5	20
				Norwich C	200+3	21
				Newcastle U	20+3	—
Mick Martin (Eire)	5 10	11 2	Belfast	Manchester U	33+7	2
				WBA	85+4	11
				Newcastle U	23	1
Forwards						
Tom Cassidy (N Ireland)	5 11¼	13 1	Belfast	Coleraine	(not known)	
				Newcastle U	141+9	16
*Andy Parkinson	6 0	12 12	Johannesburg	Newcastle U	0+3	—
Ken Mitchell	5 11	11 8	Sunderland	Newcastle U	37+5	2
Stuart Robinson	5 7	10 5	Middlesbrough	Newcastle U	11+1	2
Nigel Walker	5 10	10 11	Gateshead	Newcastle U	32+2	2
Mike Larnach (Transferred to Motherwell)	5 9	11 11	Caithness	Clydebank	160	63
				Newcastle U	12+2	—
Mark McGhee (Transferred to Aberdeen)	5 10	12 12	Glasgow	Morton	61+3	37
				Newcastle U	21+7	5
Peter Manners	5 10	10 12	Sunderland	Newcastle U	2	—
Craig McFarlane	6 0	12 12	Dunfermline	Newcastle U	—	—
Jimmy Scott	5 8	11 0	Newcastle	Newcastle U	9+1	—
Terry Hibbitt	5 6	9 10	Bradford	Leeds U	32+13	9
				Newcastle U	138	7
				Birmingham C	110	11
				Newcastle U	40	—
John Connolly (Scotland)	5 9	10 7	Glasgow	St Johnstone	96	41
				Everton	105+3	15
				Birmingham C	49+8	9
				Newcastle U	34	8
Gary Nicholson	5 7½	10 0	Newcastle	Newcastle U	5+3	—
Alan Shoulder	5 5	10 6	Bishop Auckland	Blyth S	—	—
				Newcastle U	24	11
Peter Withe	6 2	12 0	Liverpool	Southport	3	—
				Barrow	1	—
				Arcadia Shepherds	(not known)	
				Wolverhampton W	12+5	3
				Birmingham C	35	9
				Nottingham F	74+1	28
				Newcastle U	39	14
Jim Pearson	5 11½	11 2	Falkirk	St Johnstone	96+9	39
				Everton	76+11	15
				Newcastle U	9	3

NEWPORT COUNTY

DIV. 4

President: S. Jenkins.
Chairman: R. Ford.
Vice-Chairman: G. C. Thorneycroft.
Directors: J. Ford, A. O. Menzies.
Executive Director: F. Carson.
Manager: M. L. Ashurst.
Secretary: Mr. P. Dauncey.
Commercial Manager: Mr. K. James.
Year Formed: 1912.
Turned Professional: 1912.
Limited Company: 1912.
Football League Record: 1920 Original Member of Division 3. 1921 Division 3(S). Dropped out of the Football League in 1931 but re-elected 1932. 1932–39 Division 3(S). 1946–47 Division 2. 1947–58 Division 3(S). 1958–62 Division 3. 1962– Division 4.

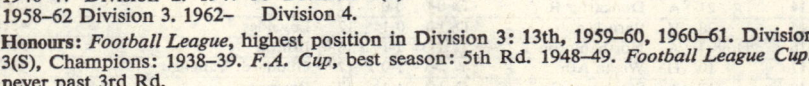

Honours: Football League, highest position in Division 3: 13th, 1959–60, 1960–61. Division 3(S), Champions: 1938–39. *F.A. Cup,* best season: 5th Rd. 1948–49. *Football League Cup:* never past 3rd Rd.

Record Victory: 10-0 v Merthyr Town, Division 3(S), Apr. 10th, 1930.
Record Defeat: 0-13 v Newcastle U., Division 2, Oct. 5th, 1946.
Most League Points: 56, Division 4, 1972–73.
Most League Goals: 85, Division 4, 1964–65.
Highest League Scorer in Season: Tudor Martin, 34, Division 3(S), 1929–30.
Most League Goals in Total Aggregate: Reg Parker, 99, 1948–54.
Most Capped Players: Fred Cook, 2 (8), Jack Nicholls, 2 (4), Alf Sherwood, 2 (41), Bill Thomas 2, Harold Williams 2 (4) (all for Wales).
Most League Appearances: Ray Wilcox, 530, 1946–60.
Record Transfer Fee Received: £50,000 from Luton T. for Mike Aizlewood, March 1978.
Record Transfer Fee Paid: £25,000 to Lincoln C. for Tommy Tynan, Feb, 1979.
Managers Since the War: Billy McCandless, Tom Bromilow, Fred Stansfield, Bill Lucas, Bobby Evans, Bill Lucas, Trevor Morris, Les Graham, Bob Ferguson, Bill Lucas, Brian Harris, Dave Elliot, Jimmy Scoular, Colin Addison.
Address of Supporters Club: Same as Football Club.

Somerton Park, Newport, Mon. Telephone 71543 and 71271. *Ground capacity:* 18,000 (seating 672). *Record attendance:* 24,268 v Cardiff C., Division 3(S), October 16, 1937. *Record receipts:* £14,904 v West Ham U., F.A. Cup 3rd Rd., Jan. 9 1979. *Pitch measurements:* 110 yds × 75 yds.

How to get there: Nearest railway station, Newport. By bus: the Chepstow Road bus to Beechwood and walk down over Somerton Hill; the Corporation Road bus to Cromwell Road and Somerton Park. All buses from bus centre in Dock Street.
Match tickets: Seats can be reserved from the club secretary.
Car parking: Car park at the back of the Social Club Stand in Cromwell Road. Otherwise street parking.
Entertainments/catering facilities: Licensed bar in Supporters' Club. Licensed bar in the Social Club at Cromwell Road; both membership only. Licensed bars on both sides of ground.
Club shop: Sells all types of souvenirs.
Handbooks/programmes: Back issues of programmes available from programme shop. Club history available from Vice-President's club, Somerton Park. Match programmes available on subscription.
Extra information: Newport hold the unenviable record of most defeats in the Third Division—31 in 1961–62.
Club Colours: Amber shirts, black shorts, amber stockings.
Change Colours: All white.
First Team Trainer:
Club Nickname: 'The Ironsides'.

NEWPORT COUNTY 1978-79 LEAGUE RECORD

Match No.	Date	Venue	Opponents	Result	H/T Score	League Pos'n	Goalscorers	Attendance
1	Aug 19	A	AFC Bournemouth	L 1-3	0-1	—	Goddard	3083
2	22	H	Aldershot	L 1-2	1-2	—	Williams	3374
3	26	H	Stockport Co	L 1-2	1-1	24	Goddard (pen)	2659
4	Sept 2	A	Wigan Ath	W 3-2	2-0	18	Sinclair, Goddard, Woods	5319
5	9	A	Reading	L 1-2	1-1	21	Vaughan	5089
6	12	H	Crewe Alex	L 1-2	0-2	—	Woods	3176
7	16	H	Wimbledon	L 1-3	0-0	22	Clark	2903
8	23	A	Bradford C	W 3-1	2-1	22	Sinclair, Lowndes 2	4470
9	25	A	Hartlepool U	D 0-0	0-0	—		5491
10	30	H	York C	D 1-1	1-1	21	Sinclair	3021
11	Oct 7	A	Scunthorpe U	W 3-2	2-1	20	Bailey, Lowndes, Sinclair	2453
12	14	H	Huddersfield T	W 2-1	1-0	17	Goddard 2	3624
13	17	H	Rochdale	D 0-0	0-0	—		3472
14	21	A	Doncaster R	D 0-0	0-0	17		2008
15	28	H	Barnsley	D 1-1	0-1	17	Lowndes	4570
16	Nov 4	A	Northampton T	L 1-3	1-1	18	Bruton	3065
17	10	H	Wigan Ath	W 2-1	1-0	17	Goddard, Vaughan	4142
18	17	A	Stockport Co	D 1-1	1-1	17	Warriner	4009
19	Dec 2	H	Darlington	W 2-1	1-1	15	Goddard, Walden	2450
20	9	A	Grimsby T	L 0-1	0-1	17		3667
21	22	A	Hereford U	W 3-0	2-0	12	Bruton, Goddard, Oakes	2834
22	26	H	Torquay U	D 1-1	1-1	—	Wilson (og)	6930
23	30	H	Port Vale	W 1-0	0-0	8	Goddard (pen)	4104
24	Jan 13	H	Reading	W 3-2	1-2	9	Davies, Goddard 2 (1 pen)	5968
25	Feb 2	H	Hartlepool U	W 3-2	2-1	8	Goddard 2, Lowndes	3659
26	20	A	Portsmouth	L 1-2	1-1	—	Moore	8206
27	24	A	Huddersfield T	W 1-0	1-0	8	Bruton	3361
28	27	H	Bradford C	L 2-4	1-2	—	Oakes, Tynan	4225
29	Mar 3	H	Doncaster R	W 3-0	1-0	8	Moore, Tynan, Lowndes	2550
30	6	A	Wimbledon	D 0-0	0-0	—		2980
31	10	A	Barnsley	L 0-1	0-1	8		9428
32	13	A	Crewe Alex	W 1-0	0-0	—	Tynan	1459
33	16	H	Northampton T	W 2-1	0-0	8	Goddard (pen), Bruton	3018
34	20	A	York C	W 2-1	1-1	—	Tynan, Goddard	2156
35	24	A	Aldershot	W 3-2	1-0	7	Lowndes, Wooler (og), Tynan	5243
36	31	H	Halifax T	W 2-0	1-0	7	Bruton, Vaughan	3927
37	Apr 7	A	Darlington	L 0-1	0-0	8		1518
38	11	H	Hereford U	W 4-1	2-0	—	Goddard, Moore, Oakes, Lowndes	3771
39	14	A	Torquay U	L 0-2	0-0	8		3181
40	16	H	Portsmouth	L 1-2	1-0	—	Goddard (pen)	5421
41	18	H	Scunthorpe U	W 2-0	1-0	—	Thompson, Oakes	2572
42	21	A	Port Vale	D 1-1	0-0	8	Tynan	2444
43	23	A	Rochdale	L 0-1	0-0	—		1200
44	28	H	Grimsby T	D 1-1	0-1	8	Oakes	3049
45	May 1	H	AFC Bournemouth	W 2-0	0-0	—	Tynan, Vaughan	2235
46	5	A	Halifax T	W 2-1	1-0	7	Goddard 2 (1 pen)	1007

Final League Position: 8

Goalscorers

League (66): Goddard 19 (6 pens), Lowndes 8, Tynan 7, Bruton 5, Oakes 5, Sinclair 4, Vaughan 4, Moore 3 Woods 2, Bailey 1, Clark 1, Davies 1, Thompson 1, Walden 1, Warriner 1, Williams 1, Own Goals 2.
League Cup (2): Woods, Williams.
F.A. Cup (5): Goddard 3 (1 pen), Woods, Own Goal 1.

League Cup	First Round	Swansea C (h)	2-1
		(a)	0-5
F.A. Cup	First Round	Hereford U (a)	1-0
	Second Round	Worcester (h)	0-0
		(a)	2-1
	Third Round	West Ham U (h)	2-1
	Fourth Round	Colchester U (h)	0-0
		(a)	0-1

263

Plumley	Byrne	Relish	Thompson	Walker	Davies	Warriner	Goddard	Woods	Armstrong	Williams	Clark	Walden	Vaughan	Sinclair	Lowndes	Oakes	Jones	Bailey	Bruton	Elliott	McGeady	Brown	Lee	Moore	Tynan	Cosslett	Match No.
1	2	3	4	5	6	7	8	9	10	11																	1
1	4	3	10	5	6	2	9	8	7	11*12																	2
1	4*	3	8	5	6		10	9		11		2	7	12													3
1		3	8	5	4	12	10	9*				2	7	11	6												4
1		3	7	4			9	10				2	8	11	6	5											5
1		3	7	4			9	10	12			2	8	11	6*	5											6
1		3*	4				8	10	11		12	2		9	5	6	7										7
1	3*		4	6		9	7			12	2		10	8	5		11										8
1	3		4	6		9	8				2		10	7	5		11										9
1			4	7	3*	9	8		12		2		10	6	5		11										10
1	3			6	4	9	8				2	12	10	7	5		11*										11
1	3		4			9	8*				2	11	10	7	5				6	12							12
1	3		4			8	9				2	11	10	7	5*				6	12							13
1	3		6	4	7	9					2	11	10	8					5								14
1	3		6	4	12	9					2	11	10*	7					5		8						15
1	6*			4	5	9					2	11		7		10	12	3	8								16
1	3			5	4	9	10				2	7		8					6		11						17
1	3	12		5	4	9	10				2	7		8					6		11*						18
1	3	12		5	10	11	9				2	7	8*	4					6								19
1	3		8	5	12	9	10*				2	7	11	4					6								20
1	3		4	5	12	9			10*		2	11		8	7				6								21
	3		4	5		9	10				2	11		8	7				6				1				22
1	3	11	4	5	7	9	10*				2	12		8					6								23
1	3		8	5	4	9	10				2	11		7	6												24
1	3	12	4	5		9					2	11	10	8	7				6*								25
1	3	10			4	9					2	6		8	7				5					11			26
1	3	12		6		9					2			7	5	8	4							11	10*		27
1	3*12			4		9					2			8	5		7	6						11	10		28
1	3		2	4		9								8	5		7	6						11	10		29
1	3*12			4	2	9								8	5	11	6							7	10		30
1	3*12			4	2	9								8	5		7	6						11	10		31
1	3			4		9					2			8	5		7	6						11	10		32
1	3			4	2*	9						12		8	5		7	6						11	10		33
1	3			4		9					2			8	5		7	6						11	10		34
1	3			4		9					2			8	5		7	6						11	10		35
1	3			4		9					2	12		8*	5		7	6						11	10		36
1	3			4		9					2			8	5		7	6						11	10		37
1	3			4		9					2			8	5		7	6						11	10		38
1	3			4		9					2			8	5		7	6						11	10		39
1	3	12		4		9					2			8	5		7*	6						11	10		40
1		4		3	9						2	7		8	5			6						11	10		41
1	12	4		3*	9						2	7		8	5			6						11	10		42
1	3	4			9*						2	7		8	5			6		12				11	10		43
1	3			4	9						2	7		8	5			6						11	10		44
1	3			4	9						2	7		8	5			6						11	10		45
1	3				9						2			8	5		7	6						11	10	4	46
45	26	20	26	6	38	16	46	19	3	3	1	40	23	14	43	34	2	20	34	—	2	2	1	21	20	1	
	+ 7s	+ 2s		+ 4s						+ 1s	+ 1s	+ 3s		+ 4s	+ 1s			+ 1s	+ 2s		+ 1s						

NEWPORT COUNTY—PLAYERS

Player and position	Ht	Wt	Birthplace	Clubs	League Appearances	Goals
Goalkeepers						
Mike Dowler	5 8	11 0	Caldicot	Hereford U	1	—
Gary Plumley	6 0	12 0		Leicester C	—	—
				Newport Co	129	—
Terry Lee	5 11	11 0	Stepney	Tottenham H	1	—
(Contract cancelled March 1979)				Torquay U	106	—
				Newport Co	1	—
Defenders						
Grant Davies	5 10	11 4	Barrow	Preston NE	—	—
				Newport Co	38	1
*Tony Bryne	5 7½	10 6	Rathdowney	Millwall	1	—
(Eire)				Southampton	80+12	3
				Hereford U	54+1	—
				Newport Co	80	1
Ronnie Walker	6 2½	13 8	London	Workington	143+10	3
(Contract cancelled October 1978)				Aldershot (on loan)	—	—
				Newport Co	88+1	5
John Relish	5 8	12 0	Liverpool	Chester	10+1	1
				Bury (on loan)	—	—
				Newport Co	113+11	5
*Greg Steel	6 1	12 4	Clevedon	Newport Co	3	—
*Mike Cosslett	6 4	13 5	Barry	Newport Co	2	—
David Bruton	6 2	14 0	Gloucester	Bristol C	16+1	—
				Swansea C	185+8	19
				Newport Co	40	6
Richard Walden	6 0½	12 10	Hereford	Aldershot	401+4	16
				Sheffield W	100	1
				Newport Co	40	1
Trevor Thompson	5 9	10 12	N Shields	WBA	20	—
				Newport Co	26+2	1
Midfield						
Nigel Vaughan	5 5½	9 10	Newport	Newport Co	33+6	4
Mark Williams	5 4	10 0		Arsenal	—	—
(Contract cancelled November 1978)				Newport Co	59+9	8
John Emanuel	5 8½	12 0	Ferndale	Bristol C	124+4	10
(Wales)				Swindon T (on loan)	6	—
(Contract cancelled November 1978)				Gillingham (on loan)	4	—
				Newport Co	79	4
Ray Guscott	5 9	11 2	Newport	Bristol R	1	—
(Contract cancelled September 1978)				Northampton T	—	—
				Newport Co	12+5	1
Colin Sinclair	5 10	11 2	Edinburgh	Raith R	45+4	14
(Contract cancelled April 1979)				Darlington	201+2	59
				Hereford U	20+2	2
				Newport Co	29+1	5
Keith Oakes	5 10	12 2	Bedworth	Peterborough U	48+14	2
				Newport Co	34	5
Steve Warriner	5 7	10 0	Liverpool	Liverpool	—	—
				Newport Co	16+4	1
John Aldridge				Newport Co	—	—
Forwards						
Mike Hayes	5 11	12 0	Newport	Newport Co	4+1	—
(Non-contract)						
Roderick Jones	5 11	12 0	Rhiwderin	Newport Co	272+18	65
(Contract cancelled November 1978)						
*Eddie Woods	5 11	10 10	Ferndale	Bristol C	1+1	—
				Scunthorpe U (on loan)	4	2
				Newport Co	149+2	54
*Brian Clark	6 1	13 8	Bristol	Bristol C	195	81
				Huddersfield T	28+1	11
				Cardiff C	178+7	78
				Bournemouth	28+2	12
				Millwall	66+5	16
				Cardiff C	19+2	1
				Newport Co	72+8	18
Howard Goddard	5 9	12 0	Shipton Bellinger	Bournemouth	62+2	18
				Swindon T	10+3	—
				Newport Co	83+4	35
Steve Lowndes	5 7	10 7	Cwmbran	Newport Co	44+4	8
John McGeady	5 6	10 0	Glasgow	Sheffield U	13+3	—
(Contract cancelled)				Newport Co	2	—
Neil Bailey	5 9	11 0	Billinge	Burnley	—	—
				Newport Co	20+1	1
Kevin Moore	5 9	11 4	Blackpool	Blackpool	33+5	3
				Bury (on loan)	4	—
				Swansea C	51+4	6
				Newport Co	21	3
Tommy Tynan	5 10	13 0	Liverpool	Liverpool	—	—
				Swansea (on loan)	6	2
				Sheffield W	89+2	31
				Lincoln C	9	1
				Newport Co	20	7

Jeremy Brown 2+1 sub (Non-contract)
Dave Elliott 0+2 sub (Non-contract)

NORTHAMPTON TOWN DIV. 4

Life Vice-President: W. R. Penn.
Chairman: N. S. Ronson.
Vice-Chairman: T. C. Hadland.
Directors: E. P. Northover, G. Taylor, L. Jaffa, F. C. T. Wilson, S. Wilson, W. M. Griggs.
Secretary/General Manager: Dave Bowen.
Team Manager: Clive Walker.
Year Formed: 1897. *Turned Professional:* 1901.
Limited Company: 1901.
Football League Record: 1920 Original Member of Division 3. 1921 Division 3(S). 1958–61 Division 4. 1961–63 Division 3. 1963–65 Division 2. 1965–66 Division 1. 1966–67 Division 2. 1967–68 Division 3. 1968–76 Division 4. 1976–77 Division 3. 1977– Division 4.
Honours: Football League, highest position in Division 1: 21st, 1965–66. Division 2, Runners-up: 1964–65. Division 3, Champions: 1962–63. Division 3(S), Runners-up: 1927–28, 1949–50. Division 4, Promoted: 1960–61 (3rd). Runners-up 1975–76 *F.A. Cup,* best season: 5th Rd., 1933–34, 1949–50, 1969–70. *Football League Cup,* best season: 5th Rd., 1964–65, 1966–67.
Record Victory: 10-0 v Walsall, Division 3(S), Nov. 5th, 1927.
Record Defeat: 0-10 v Bournemouth, Division 3(S), Sept. 2, 1939.
Most League Points: 68, Division 4, 1975–76.
Most League Goals: 109, Division 3, 1962–63; Division 3(S), 1952–53.
Highest League Scorer in Season: Cliff Holton, 36, Division 3, 1961–62.
Most League Goals in Total Aggregate: Jack English, 135, 1947–60.
Most Capped Player: E. Lloyd Davies, 12 (16), Wales.
Most League Appearances: Tommy Fowler, 521, 1946–61 (39 F.A. Cup ties).
Record Transfer Fee Received: £65,000 from Liverpool for Phil Neal, November 1974.
Record Transfer Fee Paid: £20,000 to Coventry C for George Hudson, Mar. 1966.
Managers Since the War: T. Smith, Bob Dennison, David Smith, Dave Bowen, Tony Marchi, Ron Flowers, Bill Baxter, Bill Dodgin (Jnr.), Pat Crerand, John Petts, Mike Keen.
Address of Supporters Club: 195, Abington Avenue, Northampton.

County Ground, Abington Avenue, Northampton NN1 4PS. Telephone Northampton 31553.
Ground capacity: 20,000 (Seating 1,959). *Record attendance.* 24,523 v Fulham, Division 1, April 23, 1966. *Record receipts:* £17,438 v Manchester U. *Pitch measurements:* 120 yds x 75 yds.

How to get there: Nearest railway station, Northampton. Any bus to the town centre, then from Mercer's Row, buses 1, 21, 2 and 14, though only 2 goes right to the ground.
Match tickets: No pre-match booking.
Car parking: No car park, but ample space in nearby side-streets.
Entertainments/catering facilities: Refreshment in hotel and tea bars on ground.
Club shop: 195 Abington Ave—opposite club. Run by the Supporters Club; sells all types of souvenirs.
Handbooks/programmes: Programmes available from the Supporters Club.
Extra information: Ground is shared with Northamptonshire County Cricket Club.

Club Colours: White shirts, claret trim, white shorts, white stockings.
Change Colours: Yellow shirts, claret trim, yellow shorts, yellow stockings. *Club Nickname:* 'Cobblers'.

NORTHAMPTON TOWN 1978-79 LEAGUE RECORD

Match No.	Date	Venue	Opponents	Result	H/T Score	League Pos'n	Goalscorers	Attendance
1	Aug 19	A	Torquay U	W 1-0	0-0	—	Liddle	2966
2	23	H	Hartlepool U	D 1-1	1-1	—	Farrington	4288
3	26	A	Wimbledon	L 1-4	1-3	13	Reilly	2644
4	Sept 2	H	Bradford C	W 1-0	0-0	8	Cordice	3320
5	9	A	York C	L 0-1	0-0	13		2358
6	12	H	Darlington	W 4-1	2-0	—	Froggatt 2, Reilly, Christie	3442
7	15	H	Scunthorpe U	W 1-0	0-0	7	Bryant	3858
8	23	A	Huddersfield T	L 0-1	0-0	12		3320
9	26	A	Port Vale	D 2-2	1-2	—	Farrington, Froggatt	3245
10	30	H	Doncaster R	W 3-0	1-0	8	Mead, Robertson, Christie	3011
11	Oct 7	A	Barnsley	D 1-1	0-1	6	Farrington	10,102
12	14	H	Reading	D 2-2	0-1	6	Farrington, Mead	4694
13	17	A	Grimsby T	L 3-4	2-2	—	Christie, Froggatt, Bryant	5529
14	21	A	Stockport Co	D 2-2	0-2	9	Froggatt, Mead	3867
15	28	A	Wigan Ath	L 0-2	0-0	12		6264
16	Nov 4	H	Newport Co	W 3-1	1-1	10	Froggatt, Farrington, Reilly	3065
17	11	A	Bradford C	L 0-3	0-1	12		3361
18	18	H	Wimbledon	D 1-1	0-1	13	Geidmintis (pen)	3623
19	Dec 2	H	Portsmouth	L 0-2	0-1	14		3592
20	9	A	Hereford U	L 3-4	2-1	16	Hughes (og), Farrington, Reilly	2879
21	26	H	Aldershot	L 2-3	1-2	—	Reilly, McCaffrey	3325
22	30	H	Halifax T	W 2-1	1-1	18	Reilly, McCaffrey	2208
23	Feb 10	A	Doncaster R	L 0-2	0-0	19		1922
24	21	A	AFC Bournemouth	D 0-0	0-0	—		3990
25	24	H	Reading	L 1-5	0-1	18	Reilly	6070
26	Mar 2	A	Stockport Co	L 1-2	0-1	22	Reilly	3009
27	6	H	Huddersfield T	L 2-3	1-0	—	Reilly 2	1623
28	10	H	Wigan Ath	L 2-4	1-3	22	Froggatt, Bryan	2275
29	13	H	Port Vale	W 1-0	0-0	—	Farrington	1572
30	16	A	Newport Co	L 1-2	0-0	20	Froggatt	3018
31	20	A	Scunthorpe U	W 3-0	1-0	—	Reilly 3	1763
32	24	H	Torquay U	L 1-2	1-1	20	Robertson	2194
33	31	H	Rochdale	W 1-0	0-0	20	Robertson	1653
34	Apr 3	H	York C	W 1-0	1-0	—	Froggatt	1628
35	7	A	Portsmouth	L 0-1	0-0	20		8066
36	10	A	Crewe Alex	W 4-2	1-2	—	Robertson, Farrington, Froggatt, Williams	1291
37	14	A	Aldershot	L 0-2	0-1	19		4438
38	16	H	AFC Bournemouth	W 4-2	3-1	—	Reilly 3, Froggatt	2253
39	17	H	Crewe Alex	W 3-1	1-0	—	Reilly 2, Froggatt	2570
40	21	A	Halifax T	D 2-2	2-1	15	McCaffrey, Froggatt	1172
41	24	H	Grimsby T	L 1-2	0-0	—	Williams	3019
42	26	H	Barnsley	L 0-1	0-1	—		3305
43	28	H	Hereford U	W 2-1	1-0	17	Robertson, McCaffrey	2001
44	May 5	A	Rochdale	L 1-4	0-0	18	Reilly	1751
45	14	A	Darlington	D 0-0	0-0	—		1333
46	17	A	Hartlepool U	L 0-2	0-0	—		1753

Final League Position: 19

Goalscorers

League (64): Reilly 19, Froggatt 13, Farrington 8, Robertson 5, McCaffrey 4, Bryant 3, Christie 3, Mead 3, Williams 2, Cordice 1, Geidmintis 1 (pen), Liddle 1, Own Goal 1.
League Cup (6): Reilly 4, Farrington, Christie.

League Cup	First Round	Cambridge U (a)	2-2
		(h)	2-1
	Second Round	Hereford U (h)	0-0
		(a)	1-0
	Third Round	Stoke C (h)	1-3
F.A. Cup	First Round	Portsmouth (a)	0-2

Jayes	Geldmintis	Mead	Woollett	Wassell	Bryant	Farrington	Williams	Reilly	Liddle	Christie	Walker	Robertson	Cordice	Froggatt	Poole	Saunders	Ashenden	Waldock	Bowen	McCaffrey	Matthews	Perkins	Match No.
1	2	3	4	5	6	7	8	9	10	11													1
1	2	3	4	9*	6	7	8	5	10	11	12												2
1		3	4		6	7	8	9	10*	11	2	5					12						3
1	2	3	4		6	7	8	9		11		5	10										4
1	2	3	4		6	7	8	10		11*		5	12	9									5
1	3		4		6	7	8	9		11	2	5*12	10										6
1	2		4		6	7	8	9		11	3	5	10										7
	2	12	4		6	7	8	9		11	3*	5	10	1									8
	2	3	4		6	7	8	9		11		5	10	1									9
	2	3	4		6	7*	8	9		11		5	12	10	1								10
	2	3	4	10	6	7	8*			11		5		9	1	12							11
1	2	3	4	10*	6	7	8	5		11				9		12							12
1	2	3	4		6	7	8	5		11				9		10							13
1	2	3	4*		6	7	8	10		11			12	9		5							14
1	2	3			6	7	8	10		11	12	4		9		5*							15
1	2	3	4	11	6*	7	8	10				5		9			12						16
1	2	3	4	11*	6	7	8	10				5		9		12							17
	2	3	4	11	6	7	8					5	10	9	1								18
1	2	3		11*		7	8	5			12	4	9	10			6						19
1	4	3		11		7	8	9			2	5		10*			6		12				20
1	4	3		12	6	7	8	10			2	5		9					11*				21
1	4	3			6	7	8	10			2*	5		9					12	11			22
1	6	3			4	7	8	10			2	5		9					11				23
1	2	3	4		6	7	8	10				5		9					11				24
1	2	3			6	7	8	4				5	10*	9		12			11				25
	2	3		12	6	7	8*10					5		9	1	4			11				26
	2	3		12	6	7	8*10					5		9	1	4			11				27
1	2	3	4		6	7*		10				5		9		8	12		11				28
	2		4		6	7	8	10				5		9	1	3	12		11*				29
	2		4		3	7	8	10				5		9	1	6*12			11				30
	2	6	4			7	8	10				5		9	1	3			11				31
	2	3	4			7	8	10				5		9	1	6			11				32
1	2	3				7	8	10				5		9				11	4				33
1	2	3				7	8	10				5		9		4		11	6				34
1	2	3				7	8	10				5		9		4	12	11*	6				35
	2	3				7	8	10				5		9	1	4	12	11*	6				36
1	2	3	11			7	8	10				5		9		4			6				37
1	2	3				7	8	9				5		10		4	12		11	6*			38
1	2	3				7	8	10				5		11		4	12		9	6*			39
1	2	3				7	8	10				5		9		6			11	4			40
1	2	3				7	8	10				5		11		4			9	6			41
	2	3				7	8	10*				5		11	1	4	12		9	6			42
	2	3				7	8		12	4	6	10	1	5		9*		11					43
	2					7		10		8			9	1	5	6	3	11	4				44
	3					7	8	2				10	1	4			5	9	11	6			45
	2					7	8	4				9	1	3		5	10	11*	6	12			46
29	45	38	23	10	28	46	44	43	3	15	10	38	4	42	17	24	4	3	2	25	13	—	
			+ 1s		+ 3s					+ 1s		+ 3s		+ 4s			+ 4s	+ 9s		+ 3s	+ 1s		

NORTHAMPTON TOWN—PLAYERS

Player and position	Ht	Wt	Birthplace	Clubs	League Appearances	Goals
Goalkeepers						
Carl Jayes	6 0	12 6	Leicester	Leicester C	5	—
				Northampton T	54	—
Andy Poole	6 0	12 2	Chesterfield	Chesterfield	—	—
				Northampton T	17	—
Defenders						
Keith Williams	5 8	11 3	Burtwood	Aston V	—	—
				Northampton T	86+3	4
*Stuart Robertson	5 11	12 12	Nottingham	Nottingham F	—	—
				Doncaster R	225+3	8
				Northampton T	254	24
Kenneth Parker	6 0	12 10	Northampton T	Northampton T	—	—
(Contract cancelled October 1978)						
*David Liddle				Northampton T	28+3	3
*Peter Mead	5 6	10 1	Luton T	Luton T	—	—
				Northampton T	75+2	4
*Tony Geidmintis	6 0	12 0	London	Workington	323+5	37
				Watford	48+1	—
				Northampton T	63	1
Alan Woollett	5 11	11 3	Leicester	Leicester C	212+15	—
(Contract cancelled May 1979)				Northampton T	23	—
Paul Saunders	5 10	11 10	Watford	Watford	—	—
				Northampton T	24+4	—
Ricky Walker	5 9	11 2	Northampton	Coventry C	—	—
				Northampton T	10+3	—
Midfield						
Jim McNichol	6 3		Greenock	Northampton T	—	—
Andy McGowan	5 8	10 8	Corby	Northampton T	93+12	15
(Contract cancelled April 1979)						
Russell Ashenden				Northampton T	4+9	—
Glen Perkins				Northampton T	0+1	—
Forwards						
George Reilly	6 2	11 10	Bellshill	Northampton T	106+3	43
Peter Hawkins	5 4	9 13	Swansea	Northampton T	49+9	9
(Contract cancelled October 1978)						
John Farrington	5 10	10 6	Lynemouth	Wolverhampton W	31+3	2
				Leicester C	114+3	19
				Cardiff C	23	6
				Northampton T	195+8	26
*Kim Wassell			Wolverhampton	Northampton T	13+7	—
*Neil Cordice	5 10	11 10½	Amersham	Northampton T	4+4	1
John Froggatt	5 11	12 7	Sutton-in-Ashfield	Notts Co	2	—
				Colchester U	155	29
				Port Vale	12+2	3
				Northampton T	42	13
Jim McCaffrey	5 7	9 11	Luton	Nottingham F	2+6	1
				Mansfield T	170+8	21
				Huddersfield T	23+4	—
				Portsmouth	11+1	1
				Northampton T	25	4

Des Waldock 3 apps
 (Apprentice)
Keith Bowen 2+4 subs
 (Non-contract)

NORWICH CITY DIV. 1

President: J. L. Hanly, J.P. *Chairman:* Sir A. South, J.P.
Vice Chairman: G. C. Watling.
Directors: D. S. McCall, E. A. Burrell, I. D. Coutts, F.C.A.
Manager: John Bond.
Asst. Manager: Ken Brown. *Secretary:* A. E. Westwood, J.P.
Commercial Manager: N. S. Mackay.
Ass. Secretary: N. S. Pleasants.
Year Formed: 1905. *Turned Professional:* 1905.
Limited Company: 1905.
Previous Grounds: 1905, Newmarket Road; 1908, The Nest, Rosary Road; 1935, Carrow Road.

Football League Record:
1920 Original Member of Division 3. 1921 Division 3(S). 1934–39 Division 2. 1946–60 Division 3. 1960–72 Division 2. 1972–74 Division 1. 1974–75 Division 2. 1975– Division 1.
Honours: Football League, best season 10th Division 1, 1975–76. Division 2, Champions: 1971–72. Division 3(S), Champions: 1933–34. Division 3, Runners-up: 1959–60. *F.A. Cup*, best season: semi-finalists, 1959 (Division 3 side). *Football League Cup*, best season, Winners: 1962. Runners-up 1973, 1975.
Record Victory: 10–2 v Coventry C., Division 3(S), Mar. 15th, 1930.
Record Defeat: 2–10 v Swindon T., Southern League, Sept. 5th, 1908.
Most League Points: 64, Division 3(S), 1950–51.
Most League Goals: 99, Div. 3(S), 1952–53.
Highest League Scorer in Season: Ralph Hunt, 31, Division 3(S), 1955–56.
Most Capped Player: Ted MacDougall, 7, Scotland.
Most League Appearances: Ron Ashman, 590, 1947–64 (plus 72 Cup games).
Most League Goals in Total Aggregate: Johnny Gavin, 122, 1945–54; 1955–58.
Record Transfer Fee Received: £150,000 from Coventry C. for David Cross, Nov. 1973.
Record Transfer Fee Paid: £145,000 to West Ham U. for Ted MacDougall, Dec. 1973.
Managers Since the War: Cyril Spiers, Dugald Lockhead, Norman Low, Tom Parker, Archie Macauley, Willie Reid, George Swindin, Ron Ashman, Lol Morgan, Ron Saunders.
Address of Supporters Club: 50 King Street, Norwich.
Address of Club Shop or Boutique: 50 King Street, Norwich, also shop on ground.

Carrow Rd., Norwich NR1 1JE. Telephone Norwich 612131. *Match information:* Norwich 612591. *Telegraphic address:* 'Football, Norwich'. *Ground capacity:* 30,000. *Record attendance:* 43,984 v Leicester C., F.A. Cup 6th Rd., March 30, 1963. *Record receipts:* £26,845 v Orient, F.A. Cup 3rd Rd. replay, Jan. 11, 1978. *Pitch measurements:* 114 yds. × 74 yds.
How to get there: Norwich railway station is eight minutes walk from the ground; British Rail run trains from outlying districts on match days. Coach firms also operate special services from surrounding parts Any scheduled bus to the station and then walk.
Match tickets: Personal applications at the previous first-team match to the Advance Ticket Office on the ground, or by post 14 days before the match.
Car parking: Several private car parks within walking distance of the ground. Multi-storey parks in Malt House Road and St Andrews Street. Street parking in Rouen Road, Carrow Hill, Kerrison Road, Cousins Road, and side streets off King Street. Coaches may park at Martineau Lane off the City Ring Road to the south of the city.
Entertainments/catering facilities: Supporters' Club in Rosary Road within walking distance of the ground. Numerous licensed bars in the ground.
Club shop: Sells all types of souvenirs.
Handbooks/programmes: Programmes available on subscription.
Extra information: In 1958–59 Norwich became one of only four clubs (now five) from the Third Division to reach the FA Cup semi-final.
Club Colours: Yellow shirts green trim, green shorts yellow trim, yellow stockings green trim.
Change Colours: White and green.
Club Captain: Duncan Forbes.
Team Captain: Martin Peters.
Club Nickname: 'Canaries'.

NORWICH CITY 1978–79 LEAGUE RECORD

Match No.	Date	Venue	Opponents	Result	H/T Score	League Pos'n	Goalscorers	Attendance
1	Aug 19	H	Southampton	W 3-1	1-0	—	Reeves, Ryan, Chivers	21,133
2	22	A	Bristol C	D 1-1	1-0	—	Ryan (pen)	19,274
3	26	A	Coventry C	L 1-4	0-2	11	Peters	20,452
4	Sept 2	H	Manchester C	D 1-1	1-0	11	Chivers	18,607
5	9	A	WBA	D 2-2	2-1	11	Chivers, Ryan	21,947
6	16	H	Birmingham C	W 4-0	1-0	6	Robson, Ryan (pen), Chivers, Reeves	16,407
7	23	A	Bolton W	L 2-3	2-1	11	Robson, Reeves	19,901
8	30	H	Derby Co	W 3-0	2-0	8	Ryan, Reeves, Robb	16,585
9	Oct 7	H	Liverpool	L 1-4	0-3	11	Ryan (pen)	25,632
10	14	A	Middlesbrough	L 0-2	0-1	12		18,203
11	21	H	Leeds U	D 2-2	0-1	12	Ryan, Peters	19,981
12	28	A	Chelsea	D 3-3	0-1	13	Peters 2, Ryan	23,941
13	Nov 4	H	Tottenham H	D 2-2	1-2	13	Ryan (pen), Peters	25,695
14	11	A	Southampton	D 2-2	1-1	12	Neighbour, Powell	21,183
15	18	H	Coventry C	W 1-0	0-0	11	Bond	17,696
16	25	H	Everton	L 0-1	0-0	14		19,383
17	Dec 9	H	Arsenal	D 0-0	0-0	15		20,165
18	16	A	Aston Villa	D 1-1	0-0	13	Reeves	26,228
19	26	A	Ipswich T	D 1-1	1-0	14	Davies	26,336
20	Jan 13	H	WBA	D 1-1	0-1	14	Peters	20,972
21	31	H	QPR	D 1-1	1-0	—	Davies	14,203
22	Feb 3	H	Bolton W	D 0-0	0-0	13		15,369
23	10	A	Derby Co	D 1-1	0-0	12	Peters	20,837
24	21	A	Liverpool	L 0-6	0-1	—		35,754
25	24	H	Middlesbrough	W 1-0	0-0	14	Peters	13,896
26	27	A	Manchester C	D 2-2	1-1	—	Robson, Peters	30,012
27	Mar 3	A	Leeds U	D 2-2	0-1	15	Bond, Fashanu	23,038
28	7	H	Wolverhampton W	D 0-0	0-0	—		15,427
29	10	H	Chelsea	W 2-0	1-0	10	Fashanu, Peters	19,071
30	14	A	Nottingham F	L 1-2	0-0	—	Fashanu	24,046
31	17	A	Tottenham H	D 0-0	0-0	10		24,982
32	24	H	Bristol C	W 3-0	3-0	9	Neighbour, Evans, Reeves	14,507
33	27	A	Birmingham C	L 0-1	0-1	—		12,168
34	30	A	Everton	D 2-2	1-0	9	Reeves 2	28,825
35	Apr 7	H	Manchester U	D 2-2	0-0	11	Paddon, Robson	20,077
36	13	A	QPR	D 0-0	0-0	—		14,654
37	14	H	Ipswich T	L 0-1	0-0	12		25,061
38	16	A	Wolverhampton W	L 0-1	0-1	—		18,457
39	21	H	Aston Villa	L 1-2	1-1	15	Fashanu	15,061
40	25	A	Manchester U	L 0-1	0-0	—		33,678
41	28	A	Arsenal	D 1-1	0-0	14	Fashanu	28,885
42	May 5	H	Nottingham F	D 1-1	1-0	15	Reeves	17,651

Final League Position: 16

Goalscorers

League (51): Peters 10, Ryan 9 (4 pens), Reeves 9, Fashanu 5, Chivers 4, Robson 4, Neighbour 2, Bond 2, Davies 2, Powell 1, Robb 1, Evans 1, Paddon 1.

League Cup (6): Peters 2, Ryan 2, Reeves 1, Own Goal 1.

League Cup	Second Round	Wrexham (a)	3-1
	Third Round	Chester (a)	2-0
	Fourth Round	Manchester C (h)	1-3
F.A. Cup	Third Round	Leicester C (a)	0-3

Keelan	Bond	Sullivan	Ryan	Hoadley	Powell	Neighbour	Reeves	Chivers	Robson	Peters	McGuire	Baker	Paddon	Robb	Mendham	Davies	Downs	Symonds	Fashanu	Lythgoe	Forbes	Bennett	Hansbury	Evans	Match No.
1	2	3	4	5	6	7	8	9	10	11															1
1	2	3	4	5	6	7	8	9	10	11															2
1	2	3	4	5	6	7	8	9	10	11															3
1	2	3	4	5	6	7	8		9	10	11														4
1	2	3	4	5	6	7	8	9	10*	11	12														5
	2	3	4	5	6	7	8	9	10	11	1														6
	2	3	4	5	6*	7	8	9	10	11	1	12													7
1	2	3	4	5	6	7	8		10*	11			9	12											8
1	2	3	4	5	6	7	8		10	11			9*	12											9
1	2	3	4	5	6	7	8			11	10	9*		12											10
1	2		4	5	6	7	8			11						10	3	9							11
1	2		4	5	6	7	8			11						10	3		9						12
1	2		4	5	6	7	8			11			10*	3	12			9							13
1	2		4	5	6	7	8			11			10	3				9							14
1	2		4	5	6	7	9			8			11	3		10									15
1	2		4	5	6	7	8		12	11			10	3*		9									16
1	2		4	5	6	7	8	9*	12	11				3		10									17
1	2		4	5	6		8	9	10	11	7			3											18
1	2		4	5	6	12	8	9*	10		7			3		11									19
1	2			5	6	7	8			11	4			3		10	9								20
1	2			5	6	7	8			11	4			3		10	9								21
1	2		4	5	6		8			11	10		12	3				9*	7						22
1	2		4		6	7	8*		10	11			9	3						5	12				23
1	2		4	5	6	7		9		11						8		10	3						24
	2		4		6	7*		8	11	12	10			3			9			5		1			25
	2		4	5	6			9	11	7	10			3	8							1			26
	2		4	5	6			9	11	7	10			3	8							1			27
	2			6	7	5		9	11	4	10			3	8							1			28
	2		5	6	7	8		12	11	4	10*			3	9							1			29
	2		5	6	7	8		10	11	4							9					1	3		30
	2		5	6	7	8		9	11*	4				3				12				1	10		31
	2		5	6	7	8		9		4	10			3*	12							1	11		32
	2		5	6	7*	8		9	12	4	10			3								1	11		33
4			5	6	7	8		9		11				3	2							1			34
	2		5	6	7*	8		9	11	4	10			3	12							1			35
	2		5	6		8		9	11	4*	10			3		7	12					1			36
	2*		5	6		8		7	11	4	10			3		9	12					1			37
	2		5	6		8		9	11	4	10			3			12	7*				1			38
	2		5	6		8			11	4	10	7		3		9						1			39
	2		5	6	7	8		9	11	4				3		10						1			40
	2		5	6	7	8			11	4	10			3		9						1			41
	2		5	6	7	8			11	4	10			3		9						1			42
22	42	10	25	39	42	33	38	11	26	38	22	2	16	4	7	26	1	17	13	3	3	—	18	4	
								+	+	+	+		+	+	+	+	+	+	+				+	+	
								1s	3s	1s	2s		1s	1s	1s	1s	2s	2s	3s				1s	1s	

NORWICH CITY—PLAYERS

Player and position	Ht	Wt	Birthplace	Clubs	League Appearances	Goals
Goalkeepers						
Kevin Keelan	5 11	12 0	Calcutta	Aston Villa	5	—
				Wrexham	68	—
				Norwich C	545	—
(Contract cancelled April 1979)						
Roger Hansbury	5 11	12 0	Barnsley	Norwich C	40	—
				Bolton W (on loan)	—	—
				Cambridge U (on loan)	11	—
				Orient (on loan)	—	—
Clive Baker	5 9	11 0	N. Walsham	Norwich C	4	—
Defenders						
David Jones (Wales)	6 1	12 8	Gosport	Bournemouth	128+6	5
				Nottingham F	36	1
				Norwich C	98+2	3
Mel Machin	5 10	11 0	Newcastle under Lyme	Port Vale	29+1	6
				Gillingham	154+1	11
				Bournemouth	110	7
				Norwich C	93+3	4
(Contract cancelled October 1978)						
Mark Halsey	5 6	10 01	Romford	Norwich C	1	—
Tony Powell	5 11	10 3	Bristol	Bournemouth	214+5	10
				Norwich C	197	3
Duncan Forbes	5 11	11 7	Edinburgh	Colchester U	270	2
				Norwich C	284+6	10
				Torquay U (on loan)	7	—
John Ryan	5 11	11 8	Lewisham	Fulham	41+4	1
				Luton T	231+3	10
				Norwich C	103+1	26
(Contract cancelled March 1979)						
Kevin Bond	6 0	12 4	London	Norwich C	69+5	2
Phil Hoadley	5 11	12 2	Battersea	C Palace	62+11	1
				Orient	255	9
				Norwich C	39	—
Robert Carter	5 11	11 7	Kings Lynn	Norwich C	—	—
Kevin Bird	6 3	12 0	Lowestoft	Norwich C	—	—
Midfield						
Billy Steele	5 8	11 0	Kirkmuirhill	Norwich C	56+12	3
				Bournemouth (on loan)	7	2
Mick McGuire	5 7	10 5	Blackpool	Coventry C	60+12	1
				Norwich C	76+5	4
Martin Peters (England)	5 11	12 4	Plaistow	West Ham U	302	79
				Tottenham H	189	46
				Norwich C	166+1	36
Graham Paddon	5 9	11 7	Manchester	Coventry C	3+1	1
				Norwich C	162	19
				West Ham U	115	11
				Norwich C	37+1	1
Mark Nightingale	5 10	10 7	Salisbury	Bournemouth	44+5	4
				C Palace	—	—
				Norwich C	0+1	—
Ian Davies	5 8	10 8	Bristol	Norwich C	29+3	2
Peter Mountford	5 10	10 10	Stoke	Norwich C	—	—
Richard Symonds	6 1	11 5	Longham	Norwich C	17+2	—
David Dunthorne				Norwich C		
(Contract cancelled November 1978)						
Forwards						
Douglas Evans	5 10	11 0	Swansea	Norwich C	13+4	1
Jimmy Neighbour	5 8	11 10	Chingford	Tottenham H	104+15	8
				Norwich C	99+2	5
Kevin Reeves	5 10	11 4	Burley	Bournemouth	60+3	20
				Norwich C	95+1	28
Greg Downs	5 9½	10 7	Carlton	Norwich C	1+2	—
				Torquay U (on loan)	1	1
Phil Lythgoe	5 9	11 0	Norwich	Norwich C	9+2	1
				Bristol R (on loan)	6	—
Keith Robson	5 9½	10 4	Hetton-le-Hole	Newcastle U	14	3
				West Ham U	65+3	13
				Cardiff C	21	5
				Norwich C	36+3	5
Peter Mendham	5 10	11 6	Kings Lynn	Norwich C	7+1	—
David Robb				Norwich C	4+1	1
(Contract cancelled March 1979)						
Dave Bennett	5 11	11 7	Oldham	Manchester C	—	—
				Norwich C	0+1	—
Justin Fashanu	6 1	12 7	London	Norwich C	13+3	5
Steve Goble	5 11	10 6	Wells	Norwich C	—	—
Greg Shepherd	6 1	12 0	Edinburgh	Norwich C	—	—
Alan Cordice	5 11	12 4	West Indies	Norwich C	—	—

NOTTINGHAM FOREST   DIV. 1

President: G. N. Watson, J.P.
Chairman: S. M. Dryden, J.P.
Vice-Chairman: G. E. Macpherson, J.P.
Committee: H. W. Alcock, F.C.A., B. J. Appleby, Q.C., G. T. Thorpe, F. Reacher, F. T. C. Pell, F.C.A., D. C. Pavis, Dr. I. Loch.
Manager: Brian Clough.   *Sec./Treasurer:* K. Smales.
Assistant Manager: Peter Taylor.

Year Formed: 1865.   *Turned Professional:* 1889.
This is a club (200 members) *not* a limited company.
Previous Grounds: 1865, Forest Racecourse; 1879, The Meadows; 1880, Trent Bridge Cricket Ground; 1882, Parkside, Lenton; 1885, Gregory, Lenton; 1890, Town Ground; 1898, City Ground.
Football League Record: 1892 Elected to Division 1. 1906 Division 2. 1907 Division 1. 1911–22 Division 2. 1922–25 Division 1. 1925–49 Division 2. 1949–51 Division 3(S). 1951–57 Division 2. 1957–72 Division 1, 1972–77 Division 2. 1977– Division 1.
Honours: *Football League,* Division 1, Champions: 1977–78; Runners-up: 1966–67, 1978–79. Division 2, Champions: 1906–07, 1921–22; Runners-up: 1956–57. Division 3(S), Champions: 1950–51. *F.A. Cup,* Winners: 1898, 1959. *Anglo-Scottish Cup:* 1976–77 (winners). *Football League Cup:* 1977–78 (winners), 1978–79 (winners).
European Competitions: *Fairs Cup:* 1961–62, 1967–68, *European Cup:* 1978–79 (winners).
Record Victory: 14-0 v Clapton, F.A. Cup, 1st Rd., 1890–91.
Record Defeat: 1-9 v Blackburn R., Division 2, Apr. 10th, 1937.
Most League Points: 70, Div. 3(S), 1950–51.
Most League Goals: 110, Div. 3(S), 1950–51.
Highest League Scorer in Season: Wally Ardron, 36, Division 3(S), 1950–51.
Most Capped Player: Liam O'Kane, 20, N. Ireland.
Most League Appearances: Bob McKinlay, 614, 1951–70.
Most Goals in Total Aggregate: Grenville Morris, 199, 1898–1913.
Record Transfer Fee Received: £240,000 from Leeds U. for Duncan McKenzie, August 1974.
Record Transfer Fee Paid: £975,000 to Birmingham City for Trevor Francis, February 1979.
Managers Since the War: Billy Walker, Andy Beattie, John Carey, Matt Gillies, Dave Mackay, Allan Brown.
Address of Supporters Club: S. Dewar, c/o City Ground, Nottingham.
Address of Club Shop or Boutique: Pools Office, City Ground, Nottingham NG2 5FJ. Forest Sports Shop, Clinton Street West, Nottingham.

City Ground, Nottingham NG2 5FJ. Telephone Nottingham 868236-7-8. Information Desk: 860232. *Telegraphic Address:* 'Forestball, Nottingham'. *Ground capacity:* 41,930 (26,500 covered). *Record attendance:* 49,945 v Manchester U., Division 1, October 28, 1967. *Record receipts:* £120,470 v Cologne, European Cup, semi-final, first-leg, April 11, 1979. *Pitch measurements:* 115 yds × 78 yds.
How to get there: From Nottingham station any bus marked 'Trent Bridge'. Corporation specials from Parliament Street.
Match tickets: Bookable 14 days in advance of the match.
Car parking: Room for 300 cars in the East Stand car park and street parking off the Loughborough and Radcliffe Roads.
Entertainments/catering facilities: Only match-day refreshment bars. Social club situated just outside the ground. Jubilee club on ground (members only).
Club shop: Three shops on the ground sell all types of souvenirs. Also sports shop in city centre.
Handbooks/programmes: Programmes available on subscription from Carrington Publications Ltd., Wilford Crescent East, Trent Bridge, Nottingham.
Extra information: Forest hold the record for the highest away win in the F.A. Cup proper; they beat Clapton 14-0 in 1890-91. They were also the first club to adopt shinguards (1874), the Referee's whistle (1878), three half-backs (1885), the crossbar instead of tape (1891), and oval section goal-posts. Nottingham Forest claim to be the only club to have played against clubs from all four home countries in the F.A. Cup. They are the only club in the Football League which is not a limited company.
Club Colours: Red shirts, white shorts, red stockings.
Change Colours: All yellow.
Club Captain: John McGovern.
First Team Trainer: Jimmy Gordon. *Second Team:* Ron Fenton. *Youth Team:* Liam O'Kane.
Club Nickname: 'Reds'.

NOTTINGHAM FOREST 1978–79 LEAGUE RECORD

Match No.	Date	Venue	Opponents	Result	H/T Score	League Pos'n	Goalscorers	Attendance
1	Aug 19	H	Tottenham H	D 1-1	1-1	—	O'Neill	41,223
2	22	A	Coventry C	D 0-0	0-0	—		28,622
3	26	A	QPR	D 0-0	0-0	10		17,971
4	Sept 2	H	WBA	D 0-0	0-0	10		28,239
5	9	H	Arsenal	W 2-1	0-1	6	Robertson (pen), Bowyer	28,124
6	16	A	Manchester U	D 1-1	1-0	9	Bowyer	55,039
7	23	H	Middlesbrough	D 2-2	2-0	8	Birtles, O'Neill	26,287
8	30	A	Aston Villa	W 2-1	0-1	6	Woodcock, Robertson (pen)	36,735
9	Oct 7	H	Wolverhampton W	W 3-1	1-0	4	Birtles 2, O'Neill	29,313
10	14	A	Bristol C	W 3-1	2-1	3	Birtles, Robertson 2	26,953
11	21	H	Ipswich T	W 1-0	1-0	3	O'Neill	28,911
12	28	A	Southampton	D 0-0	0-0	3		22,530
13	Nov 4	H	Everton	D 0-0	0-0	4		35,415
14	11	A	Tottenham H	W 3-1	0-0	4	Anderson, Robertson, Birtles	50,541
15	18	H	QPR	D 0-0	0-0	4		28,036
16	25	A	Bolton W	W 1-0	0-0	4	Robertson	25,692
17	Dec 9	A	Liverpool	L 0-2	0-1	5		51,469
18	16	H	Birmingham C	W 1-0	0-0	5	Gemmill	25,224
19	23	A	Manchester C	D 0-0	0-0	5		37,012
20	26	H	Derby Co	D 1-1	0-1	5	Woodcock	34,256
21	Jan 13	A	Arsenal	L 1-2	1-0	6	Robertson	52,158
22	Feb 3	A	Middlesbrough	W 3-1	1-1	6	Birtles 2, Robertson (pen)	31,330
23	24	H	Bristol C	W 2-0	2-0	6	Needham, Birtles	28,008
24	Mar 3	A	Ipswich T	D 1-1	1-0	6	Birtles	27,198
25	10	A	Everton	D 1-1	1-1	6	Barrett	37,435
26	14	H	Norwich C	W 2-1	0-0	—	Woodcock 2	24,046
27	24	A	Coventry C	W 3-0	1-0	6	Woodcock, Birtles, Needham	29,706
28	28	H	Chelsea	W 6-0	1-0	—	O'Neill 3, Woodcock 2, Birtles	24,514
29	31	H	Bolton W	D 1-1	0-1	4	Francis	29,015
30	Apr 4	H	Aston Villa	W 4-0	1-0	—	Evans (og), Woodcock, Francis, O'Neill	27,066
31	7	A	Chelsea	W 3-1	2-0	3	Francis, O'Neill, Bowyer	29,213
32	14	A	Derby Co	W 2-1	2-1	3	Birtles, O'Neill	30,256
33	16	H	Leeds U	D 0-0	0-0	—		37,397
34	18	H	Manchester U	D 1-1	0-0	—	Francis	33,074
35	21	A	Birmingham C	W 2-0	1-0	2	Birtles, Robertson	22,189
36	28	H	Liverpool	D 0-0	0-0	3		41,898
37	30	A	Wolverhampton W	L 0-1	0-0	—		23,616
38	May 2	H	Southampton	W 1-0	0-0	—	Francis	20,388
39	5	A	Norwich C	D 1-1	0-1	3	Woodcock	17,651
40	9	H	Manchester C	W 3-1	1-0	—	Birtles, Bowyer, Woodcock	21,104
41	15	A	Leeds U	W 2-1	1-0	—	Mills, Hawley (og)	33,544
42	18	A	WBA	W 1-0	0-0	—	Francis	28,246

Final League Position: 2

Goalscorers

League (61): Birtles 14, O'Neill 10, Woodcock 10, Robertson 9 (3 pens), Francis 6, Bowyer 4, Needham 2, Anderson 1, Gemmill 1, Barrett 1, Mills 1, own goals 2.
League Cup (21): Birtles 6, Robertson 4 (1 pen), Woodcock 3, McGovern 2, Anderson 2, Needham, Burns, Lloyd, O'Neill.
F.A. Cup (5): Needham, Lloyd, McGovern, O'Neill, own goal 1.

League Cup	Second Round	Oldham Ath (a)	0-0
		(h)	4-2
	Third Round	Oxford U (a)	5-0
	Fourth Round	Everton (a)	3-2
	Fifth Round	Brighton & HA (h)	3-1
	Semi-Final	Watford (h)	3-1
		(a)	0-0
	Final	Southampton	3-2 (at Wembley)
F.A. Cup	Third Round	Aston Villa (h)	2-0
	Fourth Round	York C (h)	3-1
	Fifth Round	Arsenal (h)	0-1

Shilton	Anderson	Barrett	McGovern	Needham	Burns	O'Neill	Gemmill	Withe	Woodcock	Robertson	Elliott	Lloyd	Mills	Bowyer	Birtles	O'Hare	Clark	Francis	Gunn	Match No.
1	2	3	4	5	6	7	8	9	10	11										1
1	2	3	4	5	6	7	8		10	11	9									2
1	2	3	4	5	6	7	8		10	11	9									3
1	2	3	4	5	6	7	8		10	11	9									4
1	2	3	4	12	6				10	11		5	7*	8	9					5
1	2	3	4		6		7		10	11		5		8	9					6
1	2	3*	4		6	7			10	11		5		8	9	12				7
1	2		4		6	7	8		10	11		5		3	9					8
1	2		4		6	7	8		10*	11		5		12	9		3			9
1	2		4		6	7	8			11		5			9	10	3			10
1	2		4	5	6	7			10	11				8	9		3			11
1	2		4*12		6		7		10	11		5		3	9	8				12
1	2				6	7	8		10	11		5		3	9	4				13
1	2		4				7		10	11		5	8	3	9	6				14
1	2		4			8			10	11		5	7	3	9	6				15
1	2		4		7	8			10	11		5*		6	9	12	3			16
1	2	8	4			7				11	9	5		6	10		3			17
1	2		4	5			8		10	11		6		7	9		3			18
1	2		4	6	7	8			10	11		5		12	9*		3			19
1	2		4	6	7	8			10	11		5			9		3			20
1	2		4	5	7	8			10	11		6			9		3			21
1	2		4		6	7	8		10	11		5		3	9					22
1	2		4	6		7*	8		10	11		5			9		3	12		23
1	2		4	6		7	8			11		5			9		3	10		24
1		2	4	6					10	11		5		3	9	8		7		25
1		2	4	6			8		10	11		5			9		3	7		26
1	2	3	4	6		7			10	11		5			9			8		27
1	2		4	6		7			10	11		5		3	9			8		28
1	2		4	6		7			10	11		5		3	9			8		29
1	2		4	6		7	8		10	11		5		3				9		30
1	2		4	6		7	8*			11		5	10		12		9	3		31
1	2			5	6	7			10	11		5		4	9		3	8		32
1	2		4		6	7				11		5		8	9		3	10		33
1	2	3	4		6	7			10	11		5		8				9		34
1	2		4		6	7			10	11		5			9		3	8		35
1	2		4		6	7			10	11		5			9		3	8		36
1	2		4		6				10	11		5		3	9	7		8		37
1	2		4		6				10	11		5		8	9		3	7		38
1	2		4		6				10	11		5		8	9		3	7		39
1	2		4		6	7*			10	11		5		12	9		3	8		40
1	2			12	6					11		5	7	10	9	4	3*	8		41
1	2		4		6				10	11		5		3	9	7		8		42
42	40	11	36	23	25	28	24	1	36	42	4	36	4	26	35	9	20	19	1	
		+3s										+3s			+3s		+1s			

275

NOTTINGHAM FOREST—PLAYERS

Player and position	Ht	Wt	Birthplace	Clubs	League Appearances	Goals
Goalkeepers						
Chris Woods	6 0	12 0	Lincs	Nottingham F	—	—
Peter Shilton	6 0	12 10	Leicester	Leicester C	286	1
(England)				Stoke C	110	—
				Nottingham F	79	—
Defenders						
Viv Anderson	5 11	10 4	Nottingham	Nottingham F	147+5	5
(England)						
Bryn Gunn	5 9	10 5	Corley	Nottingham F	4	—
Frank Clark	6 0	12 2	Durham	Newcastle U	388+1	—
				Nottingham F	116+1	1
Colin Barrett	5 11	11 7	Stockport	Manchester C	50+3	—
				Nottingham F	64+5	4
Larry Lloyd	6 2	12 4	Bristol	Bristol R	43	1
(England)				Liverpool	150	4
				Coventry C	50	5
				Nottingham F	88	3
Ken Burns (Scotland)	5 10½	11 0	Glasgow	Birmingham C	163+7	45
				Nottingham F	66	4
David Needham	6 1	12 7	Leicester	Notts Co	428+1	32
				QPR	18	3
				Nottingham F	39+3	6
Midfield						
John McGovern	5 10	10 13	Montrose	Hartlepool	69+3	5
				Derby C	186+4	16
				Leeds U	4	—
				Nottingham F	155	4
John Robertson	5 8	10 9	Uddinston	Nottingham F	225+11	36
(Scotland)						
Ian Bowyer	5 11	11 2½	Ellesmere Port	Manchester C	42+8	13
				Orient	75+3	18
				Nottingham F	191+8	45
Archie Gemmill	5 5	11 2	Paisley	St Mirren	65+2	9
(Scotland)				Preston NE	93+9	13
				Derby Co	261	18
				Nottingham F	56+2	6
Steve Burke	5 9	10 7	Nottingham	Nottingham F	—	—
Forwards						
John O'Hare	5 8½	11 7	Renton	Sunderland	51	14
(Scotland)				Derby C	247+1	65
				Leeds U	6	1
				Nottingham F	87+7	14
Martin O'Neill	5 10	11 3	Kilrea	Nottingham F	208+18	42
(N Ireland)						
Tony Woodcock	5 10	11 0	Nottingham	Nottingham F	109+4	32
(England)				Lincoln C (on loan)	2+2	1
				Doncaster R (on loan)	6	2
Trevor Francis	5 10	11 7	Plymouth	Birmingham C	278+2	118
(England)				Nottingham F	19+1	6
Gary Mills	5 8	11 1		Nottingham F	4	1
Gary Birtles	5 11	10 12	Nottingham	Nottingham F	36	14

NOTTS COUNTY DIV. 2

Chairman: J. J. Dunnett, M.A., LL.B. (Cantab.), M.P.
Directors: L. S. Levin, J.P., R. Sweet.
Manager: Jimmy Sirrel.
Commercial Manager: Stuart J. Burgan, A.Inst.M.
Secretary: Dennis Marshall, F.A.A.I., A.M.B.I.M.
Year Formed: 1862 (the oldest club in the Football League).
Turned Professional: 1885. *Limited Company:* 1888.
Previous Grounds: 1862, The Park; 1863, The Meadows; 1881, Trent Bridge; 1910, Meadow Lane.
Football League Record: 1888 Original Member of the English League. 1893–97 Division 2. 1897–1913 Division 1. 1913–14 Division 2. 1914–20 Division 1. 1920–23 Division 2. 1923–26 Division 1. 1926–30 Division 2. 1930–31 Division 3(S). 1931–35 Division 2. 1935–50 Division 3(S). 1950–58 Division 2. 1958–59 Division 3. 1959–60 Division 4. 1960–64 Division 3. 1964–71 Division 4. 1971–73 Division 3. 1973– Division 2.
Honours: Football League, best season in Division 1: 3rd, 1890–91, 1900–01. Division 2, Champions: 1896–97, 1913–14, 1922–23; Runners-up: 1894–95. Division 3(S), Champions: 1930–31, 1949–50; Runners-up: 1936–37. Division 4, Champions 1970–71; Runners-up: 1959–60. *F.A. Cup,* Winners: 1893–94; Runners-up: 1890–91. *Football League Cup,* best season: 5th Rd., 1963–64, 1972–73, 1975–76.
Record Victory: 15–0 v Thornhill U., F.A. Cup 1st Rd., Oct. 24th, 1885.
Record Defeat: 1-9 v Blackburn R., Division 1, Nov. 16th, 1889; v Aston Villa, Division 1, Sept. 29th, 1888; v Portsmouth, Division 2, Apr. 9th, 1927.
Most League Points: 69, Division 4, 1970–71.
Most League Goals: 107, Division 4, 1959–60.
Highest League Scorer in Season: Tom Keetley, 39, Division 3(S), 1930–31.
Most League Goals in Total Aggregate: Les Bradd, 125, 1967–78.
Most Capped Player: Bill Fallon, 7 (9), Eire.
Most League Appearances: Albert Iremonger, 564, 1904–26.
Record Transfer Fee Received: £150,000 from Wrexham for Mick Vinter, June 1979.
Record Transfer Fee Paid: £80,000 to Kilmarnock for Iain McCulloch, April 1978.
Managers Since the War: Arthur Stollery, Eric Houghton, George Poyser, Tommy Lawton, Frank Hill, Tim Coleman, Eddie Lowe, Jack Burkitt, Andy Beattie, Billy Gray, Jimmy Sirrel, Ron Fenton.
Address of Supporters Club: c/o Club.
Address of Club Shop or Boutique: Souvenir Sales, c/o the Ground.

County Ground, Meadow Lane, Nottingham NG2 3HJ. *Telegraphic address:* 'Notts County F.C. Nottingham'. Telephone General Office: Nottingham 868494; Commercial Manager: Nottingham 868177. Information Service tel: 864152. Sports Hall 865198. *Ground capacity:* 40,000. *Record attendance:* 47,310 v York C., F.A. Cup 6th Rd., March 12, 1955. *Record receipts:* £23,215.62p v Leeds U., F.A. Cup 1st Rd., Jan. 3, 1976. *Pitch measurements:* 117 yds × 76 yds.
How to get there: Nearest railway station Nottingham from there any bus marked 'Trent Bridge'.
Match tickets: Advance bookings can be accepted by post or by personal application 14 days before any home game. S.A.E. must be sent with remittance in postal applications.
Car parking: No street parking around the ground, but ample space in the City of Nottingham Corporation car park on the Cattle Market, Meadow Lane, just 400 yards from the main entrances.
Entertainments/catering facilities: No social club. Tea bars and refreshment points on all sides of the ground.
Club shop: Open daily; situated at the ground.
Programmes: Back copies and subscription rates available from the club.
Extra information: When Notts County won the F.A. Cup in 1893–94, they became the first winners from the Second Division. The club has recently had a Sports Hall built on the Iremonger Road car park. This is available, for hire, to the public at certain times of the day.
Club Colours: Black and white striped shirts, black shorts, white stockings.
Change Colours: Yellow shirts with blue trim, blue shorts, yellow stockings.
Club Captain: Brian Stubbs.
First Team Trainer: Jack Wheeler.
Club Nickname: 'Magpies'.

NOTTS COUNTY 1978–79 LEAGUE RECORD

Match No.	Date	Venue	Opponents	Result	H/T Score	League Pos'n	Goalscorers	Attendance
1	Aug 19	A	West Ham U	L 2-5	0-4	—	McCulloch 2	25,387
2	22	H	Millwall	D 1-1	0-1	—	Vinter	6810
3	26	H	Blackburn R	W 2-1	2-1	14	Blockley, Vinter	7774
4	Sept 2	A	Burnley	L 1-2	1-1	19	McCulloch	9961
5	9	A	Leicester C	W 1-0	1-0	12	Vinter	14,485
6	16	H	Orient	W 1-0	0-0	7	Masson	8094
7	22	A	Charlton Ath	D 1-1	1-1	7	Vinter	8643
8	30	H	Newcastle U	L 1-2	0-1	14	Hooks	11,813
9	Oct 7	A	Cardiff C	W 3-2	1-0	10	Hooks 2, McCulloch	7974
10	14	H	Bristol R	W 2-1	0-0	7	Vinter, O'Brien (pen)	8646
11	21	A	Luton T	L 0-6	0-2	11		8561
12	28	H	Cambridge U	D 1-1	0-1	11	McCulloch	8437
13	Nov 4	A	Wrexham	L 1-3	0-1	13	O'Brien	10,891
14	11	H	West Ham U	W 1-0	0-0	11	O'Brien (pen)	11,002
15	18	A	Blackburn R	W 4-3	3-1	9	Hooks, Vinter, Masson, Hunt	7893
16	21	H	Burnley	D 1-1	0-0	—	Masson	8520
17	25	A	Brighton & HA	W 1-0	0-0	7	Hooks	8851
18	Dec 2	H	Fulham	D 1-1	0-1	6	Hooks	7591
19	9	H	Crystal Palace	D 0-0	0-0	5		11,011
20	16	A	Preston NE	D 1-1	1-0	7	Vinter	10,728
21	23	H	Sunderland	D 1-1	1-1	7	O'Brien (pen)	11,281
22	26	A	Oldham Ath	D 3-3	1-1	—	Hooks, Vinter, Blockley	8161
23	30	A	Stoke C	L 0-2	0-1	9		21,393
24	Jan 20	A	Orient	L 0-3	0-1	10		4803
25	Feb 3	H	Charlton Ath	D 1-1	0-0	8	Mann	7958
26	24	A	Bristol R	D 2-2	2-1	9	Hooks, Vinter	6887
27	Mar 3	H	Luton T	W 3-1	0-0	7	Mann, Hunt, Hooks	7624
28	10	A	Cambridge U	W 1-0	0-0	7	Mann	5758
29	13	H	Sheffield U	W 4-1	1-0	—	Vinter 3, McCulloch	10,372
30	24	A	Millwall	W 1-0	0-0	6	O'Brien	5717
31	27	H	Cardiff C	W 1-0	1-0	—	McCulloch	8211
32	31	A	Brighton & HA	D 0-0	0-0	6		21,398
33	Apr 7	H	Fulham	D 1-1	1-0	6	Blockley	9465
34	10	A	Sheffield U	L 1-5	0-1	—	McCulloch	15,816
35	13	A	Sunderland	L 0-3	0-2	—		34,027
36	14	H	Oldham Ath	D 0-0	0-0	6		7023
37	18	H	Newcastle U	W 2-1	1-0	—	Hooks, O'Brien (pen)	12,000
38	21	H	Preston NE	D 0-0	0-0	6		7009
39	24	H	Leicester C	L 0-1	0-0	—		8702
40	28	A	Crystal Palace	L 0-2	0-1	6		23,880
41	May 1	H	Wrexham	D 1-1	1-1	—	Mair	4374
42	5	H	Stoke C	L 0-1	0-0	6		21,571

Final League Position: 6

Goalscorers

League (48): Vinter 12, Hooks 10, McCulloch 8, O'Brien 6 (4 pens), Blockley 3, Mann 3, Masson 3, Hunt 2, Mair 1.
League Cup (4): Hooks 2, Carter 2.
F.A. Cup (4): Vinter, Hooks, Mann, Masson.

League Cup	First Round	Scunthorpe U (a)	1-0
		(h)	3-0
	Second Round	Crewe Alex (a)	0-2
F.A. Cup	Third Round	Reading (h)	4-2
	Fourth Round	Arsenal (a)	0-2

McManus	Richards	O'Brien	Benjamin	Blockley	Stubbs	Carter	McCulloch	Hooks	Mann	Vinter	McVay	Green	Wood	Hunt	Masson	Mair	Match No.
1	2	3	4	5	6	7	8	9*	10	11	12						1
1	2	3	4	5	6	7	9		10*	11		8	12				2
1	2	3	4	5	6		7	9	8	11			10				3
1	2	3	4	5	6		7	12	10*	11		9	8				4
1	2	3	4	5	6	7				11		9	10	8			5
1	2	3	4	5	6	7				11	-	9	10	8			6
1	2	3	4	5*	6	7		12	11			9	10	8			7
1	2	3	4		5	7	12	6	11			9*	10	8			8
1	2	3	4	5*	6	7	9	10	11			12		8			9
1	2	3	4		5	7	9	6	11				10	8			10
1	2	3	4		5	7	9	6	11	12			10*	8			11
1		3	4		5	7	9	6	11	2	12		10*	8			12
1		3	4		5	7	9	11		2	10		6	8			13
1	2	3	4		5	7	9	6	11				10	8			14
1	2	3	4		5	7	9	6	11	12			10	8*			15
1	2	3	4		5	7	9	6	11				10	8			16
1	2	3	4		5	7	9	6	11				10	8			17
1	2	3	4		5	7	9	6	11				10	8			18
1	2	3	4		5	7	9	6	11				10	8			19
1	2	3	4		5	7	9	6	11				10	8			20
1	2	3	4	6	5	7	9	10	11					8			21
1	2	3	4*12	5		7	9	6	11				10	8			22
1	2	3	4	12	5	7	9	6	11*				10	8			23
1	2	3	4*		5	7	9	6	11	12			10	8			24
1	2	3		4	5	7	9	6	11				10	8			25
1	2	3		4	5	7	9	6	11				10	8			26
1	2	3		4	5	7	9	6	11				10	8			27
1	2	3		4	5	7	9	6*	11	12			10	8			28
1	2	3		4	5	7	9	6	11				10	8			29
1	2	3		4	5	7	9	6	11*	12			10	8			30
1	2	3	12	4	5	7	9	6	11*				10	8			31
1	2	3		4	5	7	9	6	11				10	8			32
1	2	3	12	4	5	7	9	6	11*				10	8			33
1	2	3		4	5	7	9	6	11				10	8			34
1	2	3		4	5	7	9*	6	11		12		10	8			35
1	2	3	12	4	5	7	9*	6	11				10	8			36
1	2	3		4	5	7	9	6	11	12			10	8*			37
1	2	3		4	5	7	9	6	11				10		8		38
1	2	3		4	5	7	9*	12	11				10	8	6		39
1	2	3		4	5*	7	9	6	11	12			10	8			40
1	2			4	5	7	9	12	11			3*10		8	6		41
1	2	3		4	5	7	9	10	11					8	6		42
42	40	41	24	27	42	2	42	36	37	41	3	6	2	36	37	4	
			+3s	+2s				+2s	+3s				+8s	+3s		+1s	

NOTTS COUNTY—PLAYERS

Player and position	Ht	Wt	Birthplace	Clubs	League Appearances	Goals
Goalkeepers						
Eric McManus	6 0	11 2	Limavady, NI	Coventry C	6	—
				Notts Co	229	—
Colin King	6 0	11 8	Edinburgh	Blackpool	—	—
				Clydebank	6	—
				Notts Co	—	—
Defenders						
David McVay	6 1	11 11	Workington	Notts Co	101+12	2
				Torquay U (on loan)	8	—
Pedro Richards	5 8	10 8	London	Notts Co	156	1
Brian Stubbs	6 2	12 0	Keyworth	Notts Co	384+1	20
Tristam Benjamin	6 0	11 1	St Kitts	Notts Co	45+12	2
Ray O'Brien (Eire)	5 9	11 0	Sherbourne	Manchester U	—	—
				Notts Co	198	16
Gary Wood	5 10	11 3	Corby	Notts Co	3	—
Jeff Blockley (England)	6 0½	12 6	Leicester	Coventry C	144+2	6
				Arsenal	52	1
				Leicester C	75+1	2
				Derby Co (on loan)	—	—
				Notts Co	27+2	3
Midfield						
Arthur Mann	5 9	10 10	Burntisland	Hearts	32	—
				Manchester C	32+3	—
				Blackpool (on loan)	3	—
				Notts Co	243+10	21
Gordon Mair	5 9	10 6	Coatbridge	Notts Co	7+2	1
Lloyd Richards	5 8	11 0	Derby	Notts Co	7+2	—
Dave Smith	5 5	10 6	Nottingham	Notts Co	45+5	—
David Hunt	5 11	11 0	Leicester	Derby Co	5	—
				Notts Co	48+1	2
Don Masson (Scotland)	5 8	10 12	Banchory	Middlesborough	51+3	6
				Notts Co	273	81
				QPR	116	18
				Derby Co	23	1
				Notts Co	37	3
Paul Hooks	5 8	10 11	Wallsend	Notts Co	47+11	14
Forwards						
Mick Vinter	5 9	11 0	Boston	Notts Co	135+31	53
Ian McCulloch	5 10	11 0	Kilmarnock	Kilmarnock	104+2	12
				Notts Co	42	8
Rick Green	6 0	10 9	Scunthorpe	Scunthorpe U	66	19
				Chesterfield	45+3	13
				Notts Co	6+3	—

OLDHAM ATHLETIC DIV. 2

Chairman: H. Wilde.
Vice-Chairman: R. Schofield.
Directors: J. Kershaw, F. D. Whitehead, I. H. Stott, G. T. Butterworth, D. A. Brierley, G. Knight.
Manager: Jimmy Frizzell.
Secretary/General Manager: W. Griffiths.
Year Formed: 1894. **Turned Professional:** 1899.
Limited Company: 1906.
Previous Names: 1894, Pine Villa; 1899, Oldham Athletic.
Previous Ground: Sheepfoot Lane; 1905, Boundary Park.
Football League Record: 1907 Elected to Division 2. 1910–23 Division 1. 1923–35 Division 2. 1935–53 Division 3(N). 1953–54 Division 2. 1954–58 Division 3. 1958–63 Division 4. 1963–69 Division 3. 1969–71 Division 4. 1971–74 Division 3. 1974– Division 2.
Honours: *Football League*, Division 1, Runners-up: 1914–15. Division 2, Runners-up: 1909–10. Division 3(N), Champions: 1952–53. Division 3, Champions: 1973–74. Division 4, Runners-up: 1962–63. *F.A. Cup*, best season, semi-finalists: 1913. *Football League Cup*, best season: never past 3rd Rd.
Record Victory: 11-0 v Southport, Division 4, Dec. 26th, 1962.
Record Defeat: 4-13 v Tranmere R., Division 3(N), Dec. 26th, 1935.
Most League Points: 62, Division 3, 1973–74.
Most League Goals: 95, Division 4, 1962–63.
Highest League Scorer in Season: Tom Davis, 33, Division 3(N), 1936–37.
Most League Goals in Total Aggregate: Eric Gemmell, 110, 1947–54.
Most Capped Player: Albert Gray, 9 (23), Wales.
Most League Appearances: Ian Wood, 488, 1966–79.
Record Transfer Fee Received: £85,000 from Vancouver Whitecaps for Carl Valentine, Dec. 1978
Record Transfer Fee paid: £60,000 to Sheffield U., for Simon Stainrod, March 1979.
Managers Since the War: Bob Mellor, Billy Wootton, George Hardwick, Ted Goodier, Peter McKennan, Norman Dodgin, Jack Rowley, Les McDowall, Gordon Hurst, Jimmy McIlroy, Jack Rowley, Gordon Hurst.
Address of Supporters Club:
Address of Club Shop or Boutique: 'Latique', Boundary Park, Oldham.

Boundary Park, Oldham. Telephone 061-624 4972. **Ground capacity:** 30,000 (16,000 covered).
Record attendance: 47,671 v Sheffield W., F.A. Cup 4th Rd., January 25, 1930. **Record receipts:** £18,125 v Tottenham H., F.A. Cup 5th Rd., February 28, 1979. **Pitch measurements:** 110 yds. × 74 yds.
How to get there: Oldham Werneth is the nearest railway station; ordinary bus routes and specials link the station to the ground at Boundary Park.
Match tickets: Tickets can be purchased in advance 12 days before the day of the match: or, if required, they can be sent through the post.
Car parking: Parking for 1,000 cars at the Chadderton End and Ford Stand side of the ground.
Entertainments/catering facilities: A new social club has been built and it holds 350–400 people. It is open after matches and every evening except Mondays, when it is available for private parties. Catering stands around the ground sell hot drinks and pies.
Club shop: A new shop has been opened and sells all the usual souvenirs.
Handbooks/programmes: Programmes on sale at the ground or through the post for 12p plus postage and packing.
Extra information: Oldham's record victory in 1962 is the record for the Fourth Division.
Club Colours: Blue shirts with white trim on sleeves, white shorts with blue stripe down side, white stockings.
Change Colours: Tangerine shirts, blue shorts, tangerine stockings.
Club Captain: Ian Wood. **Team Captain:** John Hurst.
Coach:
Physiotherapist: R. Jay. **Club Nickname:** 'The Latics'.

OLDHAM ATHLETIC 1978–79 LEAGUE RECORD

Match No.	Date	Venue	Opponents	Result	H/T Score	League Pos'n	Goalscorers	Attendance
1	Aug 19	A	Luton T	L 1-6	1-0	—	Wood	8043
2	22	H	Bristol R	W 3-1	1-0	—	Halom, Chapman, Taylor	6005
3	26	A	Cardiff C	W 3-1	1-1	7	Steel 2, Hoolickin	6929
4	Sept 2	H	Stoke C	D 1-1	0-0	7	Steel	11,297
5	9	A	Brighton & HA	L 0-1	0-1	11		19,735
6	16	H	Preston NE	W 2-0	0-0	6	Young 2	9766
7	23	A	Crystal Palace	L 0-1	0-1	11		18,318
8	30	H	Fulham	L 0-2	0-0	16		6972
9	Oct 7	A	Burnley	L 0-1	0-0	18		11,648
10	14	H	West Ham U	D 2-2	0-1	18	Taylor 2	10,143
11	21	A	Sheffield U	L 2-4	1-2	19	Halom, Gardner	14,514
12	28	H	Sunderland	D 0-0	0-0	19		9857
13	Nov 4	A	Millwall	W 3-2	1-2	17	Bell, Hicks 2	5626
14	11	H	Luton T	W 2-0	1-0	16	Halom, Taylor	6876
15	18	H	Cardiff C	W 2-1	0-1	15	Halom, Taylor	5356
16	22	A	Stoke C	L 0-4	0-2	—		17,170
17	25	A	Newcastle U	D 1-1	0-0	15	Valentine	20,522
18	Dec 9	A	Cambridge U	D 3-3	1-2	16	Young, Chapman, Steel	4663
19	16	H	Orient	D 0-0	0-0	15		5169
20	26	H	Notts Co	D 3-3	1-1	—	Hicks, Hurst, Young (pen)	8161
21	30	H	Charlton Ath	L 0-3	0-2	17		4191
22	Jan 1	A	Leicester C	L 0-2	0-2	—		12,757
23	Feb 10	A	Fulham	L 0-1	0-1	19		6942
24	24	A	West Ham U	L 0-3	0-1	19		26,052
25	Mar 3	H	Sheffield U	D 1-1	0-1	20	Bell	6531
26	6	H	Brighton & HA	L 1-3	0-1	—	Young	4637
27	10	A	Sunderland	L 0-3	0-2	20		25,090
28	14	A	Blackburn R	W 2-0	2-0	—	Heaton, Stainrod	8367
29	20	A	Preston NE	D 1-1	0-1	—	Young	12,535
30	24	A	Bristol R	D 0-0	0-0	18		5405
31	31	H	Newcastle U	L 1-3	1-1	19	Heaton	6329
32	Apr 3	H	Crystal Palace	D 0-0	0-0	—		5620
33	7	A	Wrexham	L 0-2	0-1	20		8418
34	13	H	Blackburn R	W 5-0	3-0	—	Young 3, Hilton, Stainrod	10,056
35	14	A	Notts Co	D 0-0	0-0	20		7023
36	16	H	Leicester C	W 2-1	1-1	—	Hicks, Williams (og)	7179
37	21	A	Orient	D 0-0	0-0	20		4340
38	24	A	Wrexham	W 1-0	1-0	—	Hilton	6258
39	28	H	Cambridge U	W 4-1	2-1	16	Stainrod 2, Wood, Young	6185
40	May 5	A	Charlton Ath	L 0-2	0-1	19		6891
41	11	H	Millwall	W 4-1	0-0	—	Heaton 2, Stainrod, Halom	5943
42	14	H	Burnley	W 2-0	1-0	—	Chapman (pen), Heaton	7791

Final League Position: 14

Goalscorers

League (52): Young 10 (1 a pen), Halom 5, Heaton 5, Stainrod 5, Taylor 5, Hicks 4, Steel 4, Chapman 3 (1 a pen), Bell 2, Hilton 2, Wood 2, Gardner 1, Hoolickin 1, Hurst 1, Valentine 1, Own Goal 1.
League Cup (2): Halom, Young.
F.A. Cup (4): Young 3, Wood.

League Cup	Second Round	Nottingham F (h)	0-0
		(a)	2-4
F.A. Cup	Third Round	Stoke C (a)	0-2 (abandoned at half-time)
		(a)	1-0
	Fourth Round	Leicester C (h)	3-1
	Fifth Round	Tottenham H (h)	0-1

McDonnell	Wood	Edwards S	Blair	Holt	Hurst	Gardner	Taylor	Young	Halom	Chapman	Bernard	Heaton	Hoolickin	Hicks	Steel	Hilton	Bell	Valentine	Sinclair	Keegan	Jordan	Stainrod	Match No.
1	2	3	4	5	6	7	8	9	10	11													1
1	2		3	5*	6	12	8	9	10	11	4	7											2
1		4	3		6			9	8	10				2	5	7	11						3
1			3		6	4		9	8	10	2*11				5	7		12					4
1	2		3		6	7		9	8	10					5	11		4					5
1	2		3		6		8	7	9	10	11				5			4					6
1	2		3		6	12	8	9	7	10*		11			5			4					7
1	2		3		6*12		8	9	10	11					5		4	7					8
1	2	6	3			11	12	9	8	10					5*		4	7					9
1	2		3		6	11	8	9		10					5		4	7					10
1	2		3		6	10	8	9	7	11					5		4						11
1	2		3*		6	11	8	9	7	10	12				5		4						12
1	2		3		6	7	8	9	11	10					5		4						13
1	2		3		6	10	8	9	7	11					5		4						14
1	2		3		6	10	8	9	7	11					5		4						15
1	2		3		6	11	8		7	10					5		4-9						16
1	2		3		6		8	9	7	10					5		4	11					17
1	2		3		6	8		9		10					5	11	4	7					18
1	2		3		6	11		9	12	10					5	8*	4	7					19
1	2		3		6	11		9	8	10					5		4	7					20
1		3		5	6	11	12	9	8	10*							4	7	2				21
1	2	3		5	6	11		9*	8	10	4				12			7					22
1	2		11	3*	6			9	8	10					5		4	7	12				23
1	2		3		6	11		9	8	10	12				5*		4		7				24
1	2	5	3		6	9		8		10	11						4		7				25
1	2		3		6	11*		8	9	10	12				5		4		7				26
1	2	3	11		6			9		10					5		4		7	8			27
1	2	3	7		6			9		10	11				5			4		8			28
1	2	3	7		6		9*		10		11				5			4	12	8			29
1	2	3	7		6				10		11				5			4	8	9			30
1	2	3			6	11		8		10	7				5			4		9			31
1	2	3			6			9	7	10	11				5			4		8			32
1	2	3			6			9	7	10	11				5	12		4		8*			33
1		3	5		6			9	7	10	11					4		2		8			34
1	2	4	3*		6	12		9	8	10	11					5		7					35
1	2	3			6			9		10	11				5	4		7		8			36
1		3	2		6				10	11				5	9	7		4		8			37
1	2	3	9		6				10	11				5		7		4		8			38
1	2	3	5		6		8		10		7					11		4		9			39
1	2	3	4		6			9		11					5	8		7		10			40
1		3	2*		6			9	12	10				11	5	7		4		8			41
1		3			6			9*	4	10				11	5	7		2	12	8			42
42	36	21	35	5	41	20	13	37	28	42	2	20		1	34	6	10	22	11	1	19	2	14
			+4s	+2s		+2s				+3s					+1s	+1s	+1s			+1s	+2s		

OLDHAM ATHLETIC—PLAYERS

Player and position	Ht	Wt	Birthplace	Clubs	League Appearances	Goals
Goalkeepers						
John Platt	5 10	11 7	Ashton	Oldham Ath	81	—
Peter McDonnell	6 0½	13 7	Kendal	Bury	1	—
				Liverpool	—	—
				Oldham Ath	42	—
Defenders						
Ian Wood	5 9	11 1	Radcliffe	Oldham Ath	481+7	21
David Holt	5 10	11 0	Padiham	Bury	174+5	9
				Oldham Ath	110+1	—
Keith Hicks	6 0	12 4	Oldham	Oldham Ath	235+2	11
Gary Hoolikin	5 11	11 1	Middleton	Oldham Ath	19	1
John Hurst	5 10	12 7	Blackpool	Everton	336+13	29
				Oldham Ath	110	2
Stephen Edwards	5 9	10 7	Birkenhead	Oldham Ath	26	1
Nick Sinclair	5 11	11 7	Manchester	Oldham Ath	1	—
Midfield						
Ronnie Blair	5 9	11 0	Coleraine	Oldham Ath	74+2	1
(N Ireland)	5 11	11 7	Manchester	Preston NE (on loan)	—	—
				Rochdale	66+5	3
				Oldham Ath	221+7	22
*Les Chapman	5 7	10 4	Oldham	Oldham Ath	75+2	9
				Huddersfield T	120+3	8
				Oldham Ath	186+1	11
Mike Bernard	5 9	12 9	Shrewsbury	Stoke C	124+12	6
(Contract cancelled January 1979)				Everton	139+8	8
				Oldham Ath	6	—
Steve Gardner	5 10	10 5	Hemsworth	Ipswich T	—	—
				Oldham Ath	37+7	2
Mark Hilton	5 9	10 3	Middleton	Oldham Ath	14+2	2
Gerard Keegan	5 6½	10 9	Manchester	Manchester C	32+5	2
				Oldham Ath	19+1	—
*Dave Barnett	5 9½	10 7	Ellesmere Port	Oldham Ath	—	—
Forwards						
Alan Young	6 0	12 0	Kirkcaldy	Oldham Ath	107+15	30
Carl Valentine	5 9	10 7	Manchester	Oldham Ath	55+6	7
(Contract cancelled February 1979)						
Vic Halom	5 10	10 10	Burton	Charlton Ath	8+3	—
				Orient	53	12
				Fulham	66+6	22
				Luton T	57+2	17
				Sunderland	110+3	35
				Oldham Ath	96+2	35
Paul Heaton	5 7	10 0	Hyde	Oldham Ath	21+5	6
Simon Stainrod	6 0½	11 12	Sheffield	Sheffield U	59+8	14
				Oldham Ath	14	5
Jim Steel	6 3	11 0	Dumfries	Oldham Ath	6+1	4
Tim Jordan	5 9	10 4	Littleborough	Oldham Ath	2+2	—

ORIENT

DIV. 2

Chairman: Brian Winston.
Directors: H. S. Zussman, A. J. Harding.
Manager: Jimmy Bloomfield.   *Secretary:* Peter Barnes.
Assistant Manager: Peter Angell.
Year Formed: 1881.   *Turned Professional:* 1901.
Limited Company: 1906.
Previous Names: 1881–46, Clapton Orient; 1946–66, Leyton Orient.
Previous Grounds: Millfields Road, Homerton, Millfields, and Lea Bridge Road.
Football League Record: 1905 Elected to Division 2. 1929–56 Division 3(S). 1956–62 Division 2. 1962–63 Division 1. 1963–66 Division 2. 1966–70 Division 3. 1970– Division 2.
Honours: Football League, best season in Division 1: 22nd, 1962–63. Division 2, Runners-up 1961–62. Division 3, Champions: 1969–70. Division 3(S), Champions: 1955–56; Runners-up 1954–55. *F.A. Cup,* best season: Semi-finalists 1977–78. *Football League Cup,* best season: 5th Rd., 1963.
Record Victory: 9-2 v Aldershot, Division 3(S), Feb. 10th, 1934 and v Chester, League Cup, 3rd Rd., Oct. 15th, 1962.
Record Defeat: 0-8 v Aston Villa, F.A. Cup, 4th Rd., Jan. 30th, 1929.
Most League Points: 66, Division 3(S), 1955–56.
Most League Goals: 106, Division 3(S), 1955–56.
Highest League Scorer in Season: Tom Johnston, 35, Division 2, 1957–58.
Most League Goals in Total Aggregate: Tom Johnston, 121, 1956–58, 59–61.
Most Capped Player: Tony Grealish, 8, Eire.
Most League Appearances: Peter Allen, 430, 1965–78.
Record Transfer Fee Received: £210,000 from Q.P.R. for Glenn Roeder, Aug. 1978.
Record Transfer Fee Paid: £70,000 to West Ham U. for Tommy Taylor May 1979.
Managers Since the War: Charles Hewitt, Neil McBain, Alec Stock, Les Gore, Alec Stock, John Carey, Benny Fenton, Dave Sexton, Dick Graham, Jimmy Bloomfield, George Petchey.
Address of Supporters Section: Same as Ground.
Address of Club Shop: Orient Shop, 369 High Road, Leyton E10.

Leyton Stadium, Brisbane Road, Leyton, London, E10 5NE.   Telephone 01-539 2223/4. *Telegraphic address:* 'The Orient', Leyton E.10.   *Ground capacity:* 25,000 (7,200 seats).   *Record attendance:* 34,345 v West Ham U., F.A. Cup 4th Rd., January 25, 1964.
Record receipts: £37,805.22 v Chelsea, F.A. Cup 5th Rd., February 18, 1978.
Pitch measurements: 110 yds × 75 yds.

How to get there: Buses 69, 58, 278, 241 pass the ground. From the centre of London, journey by underground (Central Line) to Leyton station; the ground is a few minutes walk.   Nearest BR station is Leyton Midland Road (10 minutes' walk).
Match tickets: Can be booked at least two weeks in advance.
Car parking: Street parking around the ground. A National Car Park five minutes from Brisbane Road (off Oliver Road).
Entertainments/catering facilities: Supporters' Section Club and snack bar points around the ground.
Club shop: Sells all types of souvenirs and sportswear.
Handbooks/programmes: Programmes can be obtained on subscription, and back numbers can be ordered from the club shop.
Extra information: The club operates a Pools Section and Travel Service. All enquiries to Mr. B. Blower, commercial manager, club address (tel 01-539 6092).
Club Colours: White shirts two red vertical stripes, white shorts, white stockings.
Change Colours: Red shirts, two white vertical stripes, red shorts, red stockings.
Club Captain: Tony Grealish.
Club Nickname: 'The O's'.

ORIENT 1978-79 LEAGUE RECORD

Match No.	Date	Venue	Opponents	Result	H/T Score	League Pos'n	Goalscorers	Attendance
1	Aug 19	A	Sheffield U	W 2-1	2-1	—	Mayo, Kitchen	19,012
2	22	H	Sunderland	W 3-0	1-0	—	Hughton, Mayo, Grealish	7373
3	26	H	Wrexham	L 0-1	0-0	5		6416
4	Sept 2	A	Blackburn R	L 0-3	0-1	11		6781
5	9	H	Stoke C	L 0-1	0-0	17		6587
6	16	A	Notts Co	L 0-1	0-0	18		8094
7	23	A	Newcastle U	D 0-0	0-0	19		26,356
8	30	H	Leicester C	L 0-1	0-0	19		5430
9	Oct 6	A	Charlton Ath	W 2-0	2-0	17	Moores 2	11,024
10	14	H	Cardiff C	D 2-2	1-1	16	Mayo, Grealish	6064
11	21	A	Bristol R	L 1-2	0-1	17	Moores	7234
12	28	H	Luton T	W 3-2	1-1	15	Coates, Kitchen 2	7035
13	Nov 4	A	Cambridge U	L 1-3	1-2	18	Grealish	6655
14	11	H	Sheffield U	D 1-1	0-0	18	Kitchen (pen)	5540
15	18	A	Wrexham	L 1-3	0-1	18	Moores	9122
16	21	H	Blackburn R	W 2-0	0-0	—	Moores, Mayo	4415
17	25	H	Preston NE	W 2-0	1-0	16	Hughton. Moores	4702
18	Dec 2	A	Brighton & HA	L 0-2	0-1	17		16,691
19	9	H	Burnley	W 2-1	0-1	14	Grealish, Kitchen	4764
20	16	A	Oldham Ath	D 0-0	0-0	14		5169
21	23	H	Millwall	W 2-1	1-1	12	Went, Chiedozie	6185
22	26	A	West Ham U	W 2-0	1-0	—	Mayo, Chiedozie	29,220
23	30	A	Crystal Palace	D 1-1	0-1	11	Mayo	20,100
24	Jan 20	H	Notts Co	W 3-0	1-0	7	Moores 2, Chiedozie	4803
25	Feb 3	A	Newcastle U	W 2-0	0-0	6	Mayo, Kitchen (pen)	7251
26	10	A	Leicester C	L 3-5	2-3	7	Kitchen, Chiedozie 2	12,050
27	24	A	Cardiff C	L 0-1	0-1	8		8256
28	Mar 3	H	Bristol R	D 1-1	0-0	9	Moores (pen)	5078
29	10	A	Luton T	L 1-2	1-1	9	Moores	6003
30	14	A	Stoke C	L 1-3	0-2	—	Mayo	16,183
31	17	H	Cambridge U	W 3-0	0-0	8	Grealish, Mayo, Coates	4577
32	20	H	Charlton Ath	W 2-1	2-0	—	Chiedozie, Whittle	6457
33	24	A	Sunderland	L 0-1	0-0	9		21,189
34	27	H	Fulham	W 1-0	1-0	—	Went (pen)	6645
35	31	A	Preston NE	D 1-1	0-0	7	Moores	9494
36	Apr 7	H	Brighton & HA	D 3-3	2-2	7	Mayo, Coates, Moores	11,567
37	10	A	Millwall	L 0-2	0-1	—		6117
38	14	H	West Ham U	L 0-2	0-1	9		17,517
39	16	A	Fulham	D 2-2	1-1	—	Moores, Banjo	6956
40	21	H	Oldham Ath	D 0-0	0-0	9		4340
41	28	A	Burnley	W 1-0	0-0	8	Mayo	7162
42	May 5	H	Crystal Palace	L 0-1	0-0	9		19,945

Final League Position: 11

Goalscorers

League (51): Moores 13 (1 a pen), Mayo 11, Kitchen 7 (2 pens), Chiedozie 6, Grealish 5, Coates 3, Hughton 2, Went 2 (1 a pen), Banjo 1, Whittle 1.
League Cup (1): Fisher.
F.A. Cup (3): Kitchen 2, Chiedozie.

League Cup	Second Round	Chesterfield (h)	1-2
F.A. Cup	Third Round	Bury (h)	3-2
	Fourth Round	Ipswich T (a)	0-0
		(h)	0-2

Jackson	Fisher	Roffey	Grealish	Gray, N	Hughton	Chiedozie	Banjo	Mayo	Kitchen	Bennett	Godfrey	Smith	Kane	Went	Moores	Coates	Whittle	Clarke	Gray, M	Match No.
1	2	3	4	5	6	7	8	9	10	11										1
1	2	3	4	5	6	7*	8	9	10	11	12									2
1	2		4	5	6	7	8	9	10	11	12	3*								3
1	2	3	4	5	6		8	9	10	11*	7		12							4
1	2	3	4	5	8	7		9	10	11			6							5
1	2	3	4	5	8*	7	12	9	10	11			6							6
1	2	3	4	5		7	8	9	10		11		6							7
1	2	3	4	5		7	8	9	10		11		6							8
1	2	3	4	5	7			9	10				6		8	11				9
1	2	3	4	5	7	12		9	10*				6		8	11				10
1	2	3	4	5	7	11	10	9					6	8						11
1	2	3	4	5	7			9	10				6		8	11				12
1	2	3*	4	5	7	12		9	10				6		8	11				13
1	2	3	4	5	8			9	10				6	11	7					14
1	2	3	4	5	7			9	10				6		8	11				15
1	2	3	4	5	7	12		9	10*				6		8	11				16
1	2	3	4	5	10	7		9					6		8	11				17
1	2	3	4	5	7	10		9					6		8	11				18
1	2*	3	4	5	7	10		9	12				6		8	11				19
1	2	3	4	5	7*	10	12	9	6						8	11				20
1	2	3	4	5		10	7	9	8				6			11				21
1	2	3	4	5		10	12	9	7				6		8	11*				22
1	2	3	4	5	7	10		9	11				6	8						23
1	2	3	4	5		7		9	10				6		8	11				24
1	2	3		5	4	7		9	10				6		8	11				25
1	2	3		5	4	7		9	10				6		8	11				26
1	2	3		5	4	7		9*					6	10	11		8	12		27
1	2	3	4	5		7		9					6	10	11		8			28
1	2	3	4	5	8	7		9					6	10	11					29
1	2	3	4	5	10			9					6	8	11	7				30
1	2	3	4	5		7		9					6	10	11		8			31
1	2	3	4	5		7	11	9					6	8		10				32
1	2	3	4	5		7	11	9		12			6			10*	8			33
1	2	3	4	5	8	7*		9					6		11		10	12		34
1	3		2	5	8	7	4						6	9	11		10			35
1		3	4	5	2	7		9					6		8	11	10			36
1		3	4	5	2	7		9					6		8	11	10			37
1		3	4	5	2	7		9*					6		8	11	10	12		38
1		3	4	5	2	7	9						6		8	11		10		39
1		3	4	5	2	7	9	10					6		8	11				40
1	3	8	4	5	2	7	12	9					6		11			10*		41
1	3		4	5	2	7		9					6		8	11	10			42
42	37	39	39	42	33	33	13	40	22	6	3	1	37	30	30	10	4	1		
		+3s	+4s			+1s			+3s		+1s						+2s	+1s		

ORIENT—PLAYERS

Player and position	Ht	Wt	Birthplace	Clubs	League Appearances	Goals
Goalkeepers						
John Jackson	6 2	13 2	London	C Palace	346	—
				Orient	226	—
*John Smeulders	5 10	12 10	Hackney	Orient	—	—
Mervyn Day	6 2	14 12	Chelmsford	West Ham U	194	—
Defenders						
Michael Bright	5 9	12 2	Chelmsford	Orient	—	—
Peter Bennett	5 10½	11 3	Hillingdon	West Ham U	36+3	3
				Orient	195+4	13
Bill Roffey	5 11	12 6	Stepney	C Palace	24	—
				Orient	154+3	4
Nigel Gray	6 3	12 8	Fulham	Orient	89	1
Bobby Fisher	5 8	11 2	Wembley	Orient	192+6	1
Paul Went	6 0	12 10	Bromley by Bow	Orient	48+2	5
				Charlton Ath	160+2	15
				Fulham	58	3
				Portsmouth	92	5
				Cardiff C	71+1	11
				Orient	37	2
John Kane	5 8½	11 3	Hackney	Orient	0+1	—
Steve Hamberger	6 1	11 8	Hackney	Millwall	—	—
				Walthamstow A	—	—
				Orient	—	—
Tommy Taylor	6 1	14 0	Hornchurch	Orient	112+2	6
				West Ham U	340	8
Midfield						
Tony Grealish (Eire)	5 7	11 7	Paddington	Orient	169+2	10
Chris Henney	5 10	10 8	Forest Gate	Orient	—	—
Tunji Banjo	5 8	11 0	Kensington	Orient	16+7	1
Henry Hughton	5 8½	10 13½	Stratford	Orient	33	2
Ralph Coates (England)	5 7½	11 13	Hetton-le-Hole	Burnley	213+2	26
				Tottenham H	173+15	13
				Orient	30	3
Forwards						
Kevin Godfrey		10 5½	Kennington	Orient	14+3	—
John Chiedozie	5 7	10 2½	Owerri, Nigeria	Orient	60+12	8
Billy Hurley	5 9½	12 6	Leytonstone	Orient	1+1	—
*Derek Clarke	5 8½	11 2	Willenhall	Walsall	6	2
				Wolverhampton W	2+3	—
				Oxford U	172+7	35
				Carlisle U (on loan)	0+1	—
				Orient	30+6	6
Joe Mayo	6 2½	12 11	Tipton	Walsall	2+5	1
				WBA	67+5	16
				Orient	79+1	20
Alan Whittle	5 7	10 4	Liverpool	Everton	72+2	21
				C Palace	103+5	19
				Sheffield U	—	—
				Orient	41+2	6
Mark Gray	5 11	11 3	Tenby	Swansea C	1+1	—
				Fulham	—	—
				Orient	1+1	—
Ian Moores	6 2	13 8	Chesterton	Stoke C	40+10	14
				Tottenham H	25+4	6
				Orient	30	13
Mark Blackhall	6 0	12 2	Upney	Orient	—	—
Mark Smith 1 app (Apprentice)						

OXFORD UNITED

DIV. 3

President: The Duke of Marlborough.
Chairman: W. H. Reeves, B.D.S., L.D.S., R.C.S.
Vice-Chairman: Dr. D. Morris, B.Sc., D.Phil.
Directors: G. Coppock, H. Kimber, P. Marsh.
Manager: Mike Brown.
Secretary: Jim Hunt.
Year Formed: 1896.   *Turned Professional:* 1949.
Limited Company: 1949.
Previous Names: 1896, Headington United; 1960, Oxford United.
Football League Record: 1962 Elected to Division 4. 1965–68 Division 3. 1968–76 Division 2. 1976–   Division 3.
Honours: *Football League*, best season in Division 2: 8th, 1972–73. Division 3. Champions: 1967–68. Division 4, Promoted: 1964–65 (4th). *F.A. Cup*, best season: 6th Rd., 1963–64. (Record for 4th Division Club). *Football League Cup*, best season: 5th Rd., 1969–70.
Record Victory: 7-1 v Barrow, Division 4, Dec. 19th, 1964.
Record Defeat: 0-5 v Cardiff C., Division 2, Feb. 8th, 1969, and v Cardiff C., Division 2, Sept. 12, 1973.
Most League Points: 61, Division 4, 1964–65.
Most League Goals: 87, Division 4, 1964–65.
Highest League Scorer in Season: Colin Booth, 23, Division 4, 1964–65.
Most League Appearances: John Shuker, 480, 1962–77.
Most League Goals in Total Aggregate: Graham Atkinson, 73, 1962–73.
Most Capped Player: David Roberts, 6 (17), Wales.
Record Transfer Fee Received: £70,000 from Hull C. for David Roberts, February 1975.
Record Transfer Fee Paid: £75,000 to Cardiff C. for Andy McCulloch, July 1974.
Managers Since Election to Football League: Arthur Turner, Ron Saunders, Gerry Summers.
Address of the Supporters Club: Supporters Club Offices, Manor Ground, Beech Road, Headington, Oxford.
Address of Club Shop: On ground on match days.

Manor Ground, Beech Road, Headington, Oxford. Telephone Oxford 61503.   *Ground capacity:* 18,000.   *Record attendance:* 22,730 v Preston N.E., F.A. Cup 6th Rd., February 29, 1964. *Record receipts:* £13,825 v Nottingham Forest League Cup 3rd Rd., October 6, 1978.   *Pitch measurements:* 112 yds × 78 yds.

How to get there: Bus 580/1/2 from the city centre. Nearest railway station is Oxford General. From the station take Bus 1 to Queens Lane and then take Bus 581/2/3. By road, take Oxford ring road to the east of the city, following the signs for Headington. Leave the ring road at Green Road roundabout into London Road; the ground is on the right after going straight across at the traffic lights.
Match tickets: Subject to availability tickets may be booked 14 days prior to the match.
Car parking: Parking is available in certain streets around the ground.
Entertainments/catering facilities: Public houses, and cafés, all just minutes from the ground. Refreshments available inside the ground.
Club shop: On ground, offering all types of souvenirs and programmes (open match days only).
Handbook/programmes: Programmes available from the club shop.
Extra information: In five years from joining the Fourth Division, Oxford reached Division Two.

Club Colours: Yellow shirts with blue trim, blue shorts, yellow stockings.
Change Colours: All red.
Club Captain: Les Taylor.
First Team Trainer: Ken Fish.
Club Nickname: The U's.

OXFORD UNITED 1978-79 LEAGUE RECORD

Match No.	Date	Venue	Opponents	Result	H/T Score	League Pos'n	Goalscorers	Attendance
1	Aug 19	A	Blackpool	L 0-1	0-0	—		6215
2	23	H	Shrewsbury T	L 0-1	0-0	—		3877
3	26	H	Swansea C	L 0-2	0-1	24		4947
4	Sept 2	A	Chesterfield	D 1-1	1-1	24	Duncan	4200
5	9	H	Bury	D 0-0	0-0	23		3699
6	11	A	Southend U	L 0-2	0-1	—		5222
7	16	H	Exeter C	W 3-2	0-1	20	Duncan, Foley 2	5441
8	23	A	Watford	L 2-4	1-2	22	McGrogan, Bodel	12,949
9	27	H	Mansfield T	W 3-2	1-1	—	Seacole, Fogg (pen), Foley	3998
10	30	A	Hull C	W 1-0	0-0	19	Foley	5263
11	Oct 7	H	Tranmere R	D 0-0	0-0	19		3853
12	14	A	Peterborough U	D 1-1	1-1	20	Seacole	5472
13	17	A	Sheffield W	D 1-1	1-1	—	Seacole	9431
14	21	H	Chester	D 0-0	0-0	19		3908
15	28	H	Gillingham	D 1-1	1-1	19	McGrogan	4366
16	Nov 4	A	Brentford	L 0-3	0-2	20		6860
17	11	H	Chesterfield	D 1-1	1-0	19	Bodel	3410
18	18	A	Swansea C	D 1-1	1-0	19	Seacole	11,491
19	Dec 2	A	Rotherham U	W 1-0	1-0	17	Foley	3311
20	9	A	Lincoln C	D 2-2	0-0	17	Foley, Hodgson	2995
21	26	H	Colchester U	W 2-0	0-0	15	Foley, Graydon	4892
22	30	H	Walsall	W 2-1	1-0	14	Seacole, Fogg	4231
23	Jan 20	A	Exeter C	L 0-2	0-0	14		4532
24	27	H	Watford	D 1-1	0-1	13	Foley	10,310
25	Feb 10	H	Hull C	W 1-0	0-0	12	Dobson (og)	3420
26	16	A	Tranmere R	L 0-1	0-0	12		1381
27	20	A	Plymouth Arg	W 1-0	0-0	—	Berry	7098
28	24	H	Peterborough U	L 0-2	0-0	12		3842
29	Mar 3	A	Chester	L 1-4	1-2	14	Seacole	2476
30	7	H	Southend U	D 0-0	0-0	—		2913
31	10	A	Gillingham	L 1-2	1-0	16	McGrogan	6063
32	20	A	Bury	D 1-1	1-1	—	Duncan	3168
33	24	A	Shrewsbury T	D 0-0	0-0	17		6791
34	28	H	Blackpool	W 1-0	0-0	—		2924
35	31	H	Carlisle U	W 5-1	2-0	13	Berry 2, McGrogan, Tait (og), Sweetzer	3439
36	Apr 4	H	Brentford	L 0-1	0-0	—		4943
37	7	A	Rotherham U	D 0-0	0-0	15		2734
38	11	H	Plymouth Arg	W 3-2	1-1	—	Graydon 2 (1 a pen), Berry	3299
39	14	A	Colchester U	D 1-1	0-1	13	Taylor	3897
40	16	H	Swindon T	L 0-1	0-0	—		9176
41	21	A	Walsall	W 1-0	1-0	13	Seacole	3396
42	25	H	Sheffield W	D 1-1	0-0	—	White	3243
43	28	H	Lincoln C	W 2-1	1-1	14	Smith (og), Jeffrey	3249
44	May 2	A	Swindon T	L 0-2	0-1	—		8849
45	5	A	Carlisle U	W 1-0	0-0	12	Graydon	3811
46	14	A	Mansfield T	D 1-1	0-0	—	Graydon	4138

Final League Position: 11

Goalscorers

League (44): Foley 8, Seacole 8, Graydon 5 (1 a pen), Berry 4, McGrogan 4, Duncan 3, Fogg 2 (1 a pen), Bodel 2, Hodgson 1, Jeffrey 1, Sweetzer 1, Taylor 1, White 1, Own Goals 3.
League Cup (7): Seacole 2, Taylor, Foley, Fogg (pen), Duncan, Sweetzer.
F.A. Cup (2): Foley, Seacole.

League Cup	First Round	Cardiff C (a)	2-1
		(h)	2-1
	Second Round	Plymouth Arg (h)	1-1
		(a)	2-1 (a.e.t.)
	Third Round	Nottingham F (h)	0-5
F.A. Cup	First Round	Colchester U (a)	2-4

Burton	Doyle	Fogg	Briggs	McIntosh	Jeffrey	McGrogan	Taylor	Foley	Curran	Duncan	Seacole	Kingston	Sweetzer	Stott	Bodel	White	Hodgson	Watson	Graydon	Berry	Milkins	Match No.
1	2	3	4	5	6	7*	8	9	10	11	12											1
1		3	4	5	6	7	8	9		11	10	2										2
1		3	4	5	6	7*	8	9		11	10	2	12									3
1		3	4		6	7	8	9	12	11	10	2		5*								4
1		3	4		6	7	2	9		11	10				5	8						5
1		3	4		6	7	2	9		11	10				5	8						6
1	2	3	4		6	7	8	9		11	10		5									7
1	2	3	4		6	7	8	9*		11	10	12		5								8
1	2	3	4		6	7	8	9		11*	10	12		5								9
1	2*	3	4		6	7	8	9			10				5	12	11					10
1		2		5	6	7*	8	9			11			4	12	10	3					11
1		2		5	6		8	9		7	10			4		11	3					12
1		2		5	6		8	9		7	10			4		11	3					13
1		2		5	6*12		8	9		7	10			4		11	3					14
1		2		5		6	8	9		7	10			4		11	3					15
1	2*	4		5	12	6	8	9		7	10					11	3					16
1			4		6	7	2	9		8	10			5		11	3					17
1		3	4		6		2	9		8	11			5		10		7				18
1		3	4		6		2	9		11	10			5		8		7				19
1		3	4		6		2	9		8	10			5		11		7				20
1		3	4		6		2	9		8	10			5		11		7				21
1		3	4		6		2	9		8	10			5		11*		7	12			22
1		3	4	2			6	9		8	10			5		11		7				23
1		3	4	2			6	9		8	10*			5		11		7	12			24
1		3	4	2			6	9		8	10*			5		11		7	12			25
1		3	5	2	7*		6			8	10	12		4		11		9				26
1		3	4	2	7		8			6	10			5		11		9				27
		3	4	2*12			6	9		11	7			5		10		8	1			28
1		3	4	2*	6	12	8			7	10			5		11		9				29
1		3	4	2	6	7	8			11	10			5				9				30
1		3	4		8	7	2			6	10*	12		5		11		9				31
1		3	4		8	7	2			6	10	12		5		11		9*				32
1		3	4		6	7	2			8	10			5		11		9				33
1		3	4		8	7	2			6	10			5		11		9				34
1		3	4		8	7	2			11	10	12		5		6*		9				35
1		3	4		8	7	2			6	10	12		5		11		9*				36
1		3	4		6		2			8	10			5		11		7	9			37
1		3	4		8		2			6	10			5		11		7	9			38
1		3	4		8	12	2			6	10			5		11		7	9*			39
		3	4		8		2	9		6	10			5	12	11*		7		1		40
		3	4	2	6		8	9		11	10			5				7		1		41
		3	4	2	6		8			11	10			5	12			7	9*	1		42
		3	4*	2	6		8	12			10			5	11			7	9	1		43
		3		4	8		2	9		6	10			5		11		7		1		44
		2		4	8		11	9		6	10			5	12		3	7*		1		45
1			4	2	6		8	9		11	10			5			3	7				46
39	5	44	39	23	40	21	46	31	1	43	45	3	—	2	40	3	31	9	18	16	7	
					+2s	+3s		+1s	+1s		+1s		+8s		+5s				+3s			

OXFORD UNITED—PLAYERS

Player and position	Ht	Wt	Birthplace	Clubs	League Appearances	Goals
Goalkeepers						
Roy Burton	5 10	12 2	Wantage	Oxford U	268	—
John Milkins	6 0½	13 7½	Dagenham	Portsmouth	344	—
				Oxford U	53	—
Steve Foyster	6 3	12 0	Carlton, Collivell	Oxford U	—	—
Defenders						
Andy Bodel	5 11	11 13	Clydebank	Oxford U	126	11
David Fogg	5 10½	11 0	Liverpool	Wrexham	158+2	5
				Oxford U	127+2	
Andy Kingston	5 11	11 2	Oxford	Oxford U	29+1	—
John Doyle	5 9	10 7	Oxford	Oxford U	8	—
Gary Briggs	6 3	12 7	Leeds	Middlesbrough	—	—
				Oxford U	59	2
Ian Stott (non-contract)				Oxford U	8	2
Gary Watson	6 2	11 7	Easington	Oxford U	9	—
Malcolm McIntosh	5 8	11 0	Oxford	Oxford U	23	—
Midfield						
Les Taylor	5 9	10 9	North Shields	Oxford U	164	9
Max Briggs	5 8½	11 4	Barmerton	Norwich C	127+8	—
(Contract cancelled October 1978)				Oxford U	94+3	1
Billy Jeffrey	5 10	11 6	Clydebank	Oxford U	187+3	16
Colin Duncan	5 10	10 13	Plymouth	Oxford U	161+1	6
Phil Emsden	6 0	11 7	Oxford	Oxford U	—	—
Gordon Hodgson	6 0	12 3	Newcastle U	Newcastle U	8+1	—
				Mansfield T	184	23
				Oxford U	31	1
Forwards						
Peter Foley	5 11	10 7	Bicester	Oxford U	149+7	43
Hughie McGrogan	5 9	11 0	Dumbarton	Oxford U	85+22	10
Archie White	5 7	10 8	Dumbarton	Oxford U	7+12	1
Jimmy Sweetzer	5 9¼	11 0	Woking	Oxford U	0+8	1
Jason Seacole	5 9½	11 0	Oxford	Oxford U	97+11	20
Paul Berry	6 0	12 7	Oxford	Oxford U	28+9	5
*Hugh Curran (Scotland)	5 9	11 8	Glasgow	Third Lanark	9	4
				Millwall	57	27
				Norwich C	112	46
				Wolverhampton W	77+5	40
				Oxford U	69+1	26
				Bolton W	40+7	13
				Oxford U	30+5	11
Ray Graydon	5 8	11 0	Bristol	Bristol R	132+2	33
				Aston V	189+4	67
				Coventry C	17+3	5
				Washington D	—	—
				Oxford U	18	5
Nick Merry	5 6	10 7	Chipping Norton	Oxford U	—	—

PETERBOROUGH UNITED   DIV. 4

Chairman: G. H. Woodcock, A.C.I.I.
Vice-Chairman: H. W. Wright.
Directors: S. E. Nicholas, W. O'Neill Wilde, C. Duddington.
Manager: Peter Morris.
Secretary: A. V. Blades.
Commercial Manager: E. Stafford.
Year Formed: 1923.
Turned Professional: 1934.
Limited Company: 1934.
Previous Name: Peterborough and Fletton United until 1934.
Football League Record: 1960 Elected to Division 4. 1961–68 Division 3, when they were demoted for financial irregularities. 1968–74 Division 4. 1974–79 Division 3. 1979– Division 4

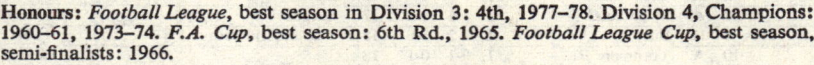

Honours: Football League, best season in Division 3: 4th, 1977–78. Division 4, Champions: 1960–61, 1973–74. *F.A. Cup,* best season: 6th Rd., 1965. *Football League Cup,* best season, semi-finalists: 1966.

Record Victory: 8-1 v Oldham Ath., Division 4, Nov. 26th, 1969.

Record Defeat: 1-8 v Northampton T., F.A. Cup, 2nd Rd. (2nd Replay), 1946–47.

Most League Points: 66, Division 4, 1960–61.

Most League Goals: 134, Division 4, 1960–61.

Highest League Scorer in Season: Terry Bly, 52, Division 4, 1960–61.

Most League Goals in Total Aggregate: Jim Hall, 120, 1967–75.

Most Capped Player: Ollie Conmy, 5, Eire.

Most League Appearances: Tommy Robson, 421, 1968–79.

Record Transfer Fee Received: £100,000 from Luton T. for Chris Turner, June, 1978.

Record Transfer Fee Paid: £60,000 to West Ham U., for Bill Green, July, 1978.

Managers Since Joining Football League: Jimmy Hagan, Jack Fairbrother, Gordon Clark, Norman Rigby, Jim Iley, Noel Cantwell, John Barnwell, Billy Hails.

Address of Supporters Club: Same as Football Club.

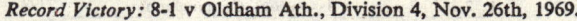

London Road Ground, Peterborough PE2 8AL. Telephone Peterborough (0733) 63947.
Ground capacity: 30,000. *Record attendance:* 30,096 v Swansea T., F.A. Cup 5th Rd., February 20, 1965. *Record receipts:* £17,215 v Leeds U., F.A. Cup 4th Rd., Jan 26 1974.
Pitch measurements: 112 yds × 76 yds.

How to get there: Peterborough Station (20 minutes' walking distance). Bus terminal 400 yards.
Match tickets: Bookable 14 days in advance.
Car parking: Ample parking available at the ground.
Entertainments/catering facilities: Supporters' Club provides entertainments. Licensed refreshment kiosks in the ground.
Club shop: Sells all types of souvenirs (postal requests to Commercial Manager).
Handbooks/programmes: Handbooks available and programmes can be ordered on subscription.
Extra information: Upon joining the Football League in 1960, Peterborough United set up a record in Division Four of scoring 134 goals in their first season.

Club Colours: Blue shirts, white shorts, navy blue stockings with white top.
Change Colours: White shirts, blue shorts, white stockings.
Club Captain:
First Team Trainer/Coach: J. Barron.
Club Nickname: 'The Posh'.

PETERBOROUGH UNITED 1978–79 LEAGUE RECORD

Match No.	Date	Venue	Opponents	Result	H/T Score	League Pos'n	Goalscorers	Attendance
1	Aug 19	H	Sheffield W	W 2-0	0-0	—	Slough, Robson	7468
2	26	A	Watford	W 2-1	0-0	6	Slough 2	12,291
3	Sept 2	H	Tranmere R	W 1-0	0-0	3	Butlin	5229
4	8	A	Chester	D 1-1	0-0	4	Slough (pen)	4506
5	12	H	Carlisle U	D 0-0	0-0	—		6283
6	16	H	Brentford	W 3-1	2-1	4	Butlin, McEwan, Doyle	5881
7	23	A	Chesterfield	L 1-3	1-1	5	Butlin	3824
8	26	A	Walsall	L 1-4	1-2	—	Robertson (pen)	4835
9	30	H	Exeter C	D 1-1	0-1	8	Doyle	6714
10	Oct 7	A	Hull C	D 1-1	0-0	9	Styles	4531
11	14	H	Oxford U	D 1-1	1-1	8	Robson	5472
12	17	A	Swindon T	L 1-3	1-1	—	McEwan	4352
13	21	H	Gillingham	D 1-1	0-1	13	Butlin	5001
14	28	A	Swansea C	L 1-4	1-2	17	Sargent	11,302
15	Nov 4	H	Bury	D 2-2	2-0	18	Doyle, Anderson	4780
16	10	A	Tranmere R	L 0-1	0-1	18		2241
17	14	A	Plymouth Arg	L 2-3	0-2	—	Bason (og), Cunningham	7398
18	H	Watford		L 0-1	0-0	18		8048
19	Dec 6	H	Shrewsbury T	L 0-2	0-2	—		3087
20	9	A	Blackpool	D 0-0	0-0	20		4280
21	23	A	Mansfield T	D 1-1	0-0	20	Holman	3671
22	26	H	Lincoln C	L 0-1	0-0	22		4592
23	30	H	Southend U	L 0-1	0-0	22		3731
24	Jan 13	H	Chester	W 2-1	2-0	20	Robson, Butlin	4445
25	20	A	Brentford	D 0-0	0-0	19		5750
26	Feb 3	H	Walsall	L 0-3	0-1	20		4466
27	10	A	Exeter C	L 0-1	0-0	21		3844
28	24	A	Oxford U	W 2-0	0-0	21	McIntosh (og), Cooke	3842
29	Mar 3	A	Gillingham	L 0-1	0-0	21		6890
30	10	H	Swansea C	W 2-0	0-0	21	Guy 2	5550
31	20	A	Carlisle U	L 1-4	1-1	—	Cooke	4571
32	24	H	Plymouth Arg	W 2-1	1-1	21	Cooke, Smith	4039
33	27	A	Sheffield W	L 0-3	0-1	—		9868
34	31	H	Colchester U	L 1-2	0-1	22	Robson	3559
35	Apr 7	A	Shrewsbury T	L 0-2	0-0	22		5600
36	14	A	Lincoln C	W 1-0	0-0	22	Sargent	4610
37	16	H	Rotherham U	D 1-1	0-1	—	Cuss	3807
38	17	H	Mansfield T	L 1-2	0-0	—	Smith	4178
39	21	A	Southend U	D 0-0	0-0	22		3461
40	24	H	Swindon T	W 2-1	1-0	—	Ross (pen), Cooke	4121
41	28	H	Blackpool	L 1-2	0-0	22	Gynn	4004
42	May 1	A	Rotherham U	D 1-1	0-0	—	Guy	2162
43	4	A	Colchester U	L 2-4	2-1	21	Guy, Cooke	2692
44	8	H	Chesterfield	D 0-0	0-0	—		2338
45	11	H	Hull C	W 3-0	3-0	—	Chard, Cliss, Gynn	1875
46	19	A	Bury	L 0-1	0-0	—		2298

Final League Position: 21

Goalscorers

League (44): Butlin 5, Cooke 5, Slough 4 (1 a pen), Robson 4, Guy 4, Doyle 3, McEwan 2, Sargent 2, Smith 2, Cliss 2, Gynn 2, Robertson 1 (pen), Anderson 1, Styles 1, Cunningham 1, Holman 1, Ross 1 (pen), Chard 1, Own Goals 2.
League Cup (7): Slough 2 (1 a pen), Styles 2, Butlin, Robson, Doyle.
F.A. Cup (2): Butlin, Anderson.

League Cup	First Round	Hull C (a)	1-0
		(h)	1-2
		(a)	1-0
	Second Round	Middlesbrough (a)	0-0
		(h)	1-0 (a.e.t.)
	Third Round	Swindon T (h)	1-1
		(a)	2-0 (a.e.t.)
	Fourth Round	Brighton & HA (a)	0-1
F.A. Cup	First Round	Southend U (a)	2-3

Waugh	Carmichael	Styles	Doyle	Green	Ross	Slough	McEwan	Butlin	Anderson	Quow	Robson	Robertson	Cliss	Hindley	Byatt	Sargent	Cunningham	Holman	Cooke	Smith	Guy	Sharkey	Gynn	Collins	Chard	Match No.
1	2	3	4	5	6	7	8	9	10	11*	12															1
1	2	3	4	5	6	7	8	9	10		11															2
1	2	3	4	5	6	7	8	9	10		11															3
1	2	3	4	5	6	7	8	9	10		11															4
1	2	3	4	5	6	7*	8	9	10	12	11															5
1	2	3	4	5	6		8	9	10		11	7														6
1	2	3	4	5	6		8	9	10*12		11	7														7
1	2	3	4	5	6		8	9	10		11	7														8
1	2	3	4	5	6		8	9	10*		11	7	12													9
1		7	3	4	5	6		8	9	10*		11	12		2											10
1	7*	3		4	5	6	12	8	9	10		11			2											11
1		3	4	5	6*	7	8	9	10		11			2	12											12
1		3	4	5	6	7	8	9			11			2		10										13
1		3	4*	5	6	7	8	9			11	12		2		10										14
1		3	4		6		5	8		10	7		9	2			11									15
1		3	4	5	6		7*	8	9	10			12	2			11									16
1		3	4	5	6		8	9			12	7		2			10*11									17
1		3	4	5	6		8	9			12	7	10	2			11*									18
1		3	4	5	6			9	10*		11	7		2	12	8										19
1		3	4	5	6			9	10		11	7		2*	12	8										20
1		3	4	5	6			9	10		11	7		2		8										21
1		3	4	5	6			9	10		11	7		2		8										22
1		3	4	5	6		9				11	7		2		10	8									23
1	12	3	4	5	6			9	7		11			2			8*10									24
1		3	4	5	6			9	7		11			2			8 10									25
1		3	4	5	6	12	9	7*			11			2			8 10									26
1	7	3	4	5	6		8	9			12			2			11*10									27
1	7	3	4	5	6		8	9	11*		12			2			10									28
1	7	3	4	5	6		8	9			12			2			10*									29
1	7*		4		6		8		11	3		12	2					9	5	10						30
1			4	5			8			3		11	2					10	6	9	7					31
1		3	4		6		10				12		11	2				9	5	7	8*					32
1			4		6		8				11			2				10	5	9	7					33
1	2	3	4		6				10*		11	12						9	5	8	7					34
1	3		4		6		10			12		11	2					9	5	8*	7					35
1	3		4		6				7		10	2	11					5*	9	8	12					36
1	3		4		6			8			11	2		10					5	9*	7	12				37
1	3		4		6			8*			11	2						10	5	12	7	9				38
1	3		4		6	10	8				11	2							5	9	7					39
1	3		4		6	8	7				11	2						10	5		9*		12			40
1	3		4		6	11					10		8					9	5		7	2				41
1	2				6					10	11							9	5*12	8	7	3	4			42
1	5		6	8						10								9	11	7	2	3	4			43
1			5	6	8						12	11						9*	10	7	2	3	4			44
1	12		6	8							11		7			3	9		5	10		2		4*		45
1			6	8							11			2	9				5	10		7	3	4		46
46	25	32	41	30	45	10	33	30	23	5	29	12	15	30	2	9	4	9	18	15	13	11	9	5	5	
	+2s					+1s	+1s		+3s	+7s	+3s	+4s		+1s	+2s				+2s		+2s		+1s			

PETERBOROUGH UNITED—PLAYERS

Player and position	Ht	Wt	Birthplace	Clubs	League Appearances	Goals
Goalkeepers						
Keith Waugh	6 1	12 0	Sunderland	Sunderland	—	—
				Peterborough U	104	—
*Jim Barron	5 11½	11 7	Co. Durham	Wolverhampton W	8	—
				Chelsea	1	—
				Oxford U	152	—
				Nottingham F	155	—
				Swindon T	79	—
				Peterborough U	20	—
Paul Overton	6 1	12 11	Soham	Ipswich T	1	—
				Peterborough U	—	—
John Winters	5 8	11 8	Wisbech	Peterborough U	—	—
Defenders						
Jack Carmichael	5 10	12 11½	Newcastle	Arsenal	—	—
				Peterborough U	294+21	4
*Peter Hindley	5 11	12 0	Worksop	Nottingham F	366	10
				Coventry C	33	—
				Peterborough U	112	1
*Ian Ross	5 9½	11 9	Glasgow	Liverpool	42+5	2
				Aston Villa	175	3
				Peterborough U (on loan)	21	—
				Northampton T (on loan)	2	—
				Notts Co (on loan)	4	1
				Peterborough U	91	—
Denis Byatt	5 11	12 0	Hillingdon	Fulham	—	—
				Peterborough U	2+1	—
Bill Green	6 3	12 8	Newcastle	Hartlepool	128+3	9
				Carlisle U	119	4
				West Ham U	35	1
				Peterborough U	30	—
Archie Styles	5 9	11 0	Liverpool	Everton	22+1	—
				Birmingham C	71+3	3
				Peterborough U	32	1
Michael Gynn	5 5	10 6	Peterborough	Peterborough U	9+2	2
Midfield						
Lyndon Hughes	5 11	11 5	Smethwick	WBA	89+9	3
(Contract cancelled June 1978)				Peterborough U	75+2	5
Tommy Robson	5 8	10 0	Gateshead	Northampton T	73+1	20
				Chelsea	6+1	—
				Newcastle U	46+1	11
				Peterborough U	393+28	104
Bobby Doyle	5 11	10 7	Dunbarton	Barnsley	148+1	16
				Peterborough U	130	10
Alan Slough	5 10	12 5	Luton	Luton T	265+10	28
				Fulham	154	13
				Peterborough U	55+1	10
Phillip Chard	5 8	11 3	Corby	Peterborough U	5+1	1
Tony Smith	5 10	11 13	Sunderland	Newcastle U	1+1	—
				Peterborough U	15	2
Pat Sharkey (N. Ireland)	5 10	11 12	Omagh	Portadown	(not known)	
				Ipswich T	17+1	1
				Millwall (on loan)	7	—
				Mansfield T	31+1	5
				Colchester U	5+1	—
				Peterborough U	11	—
Forwards						
Tony Cliss	5 9	10 0	March	Peterborough U	18+4	3
Gary Sargen	5 9	11 0	Bedford	Norwich C	0+1	—
				Scunthorpe	14+1	1
				Bedford T	(not known)	
				Peterborough U	27+7	5
Billy McEwan	5 10	11 2	Cleveland	Hibernian	59+2	2
				Blackpool	4	—
				Brighton	27	3
				Chesterfield	79+1	7
				Mansfield T	32	3
				Peterborough U	62+1	3
Trevor Anderson (N. Ireland)	5 8½	9 11	Belfast	Portadown	(not known)	
				Manchester U	13+6	2
				Swindon T	128+3	34
				Peterborough U	49	6
Barry Butlin	5 11½	10 4	Roslington	Notts Co	30+1	13
				Derby Co	4	—
				Luton T	56+1	24
				Nottingham F	71+3	17
				Brighton (on loan)	5	2
				Reading (on loan)	5	1
				Peterborough U	64	12
Harry Holman	5 11½	11 8	Exeter	Exeter C	47+5	9
				Peterborough U	9	1
Trevor Quow				Peterborough U	5+3	—
Joe Cooke	5 11	12 0	Dominica	Bradford C	184+20	62
				Peterborough U	18	5
Alan Guy	5 9	11 10	Jarrow	Newcastle U	3+1	—
				Peterborough U	13+2	4
*Rodney Leadbetter						
Steve Collins (apprentice)	5 8	11 3	Corby	Peterborough U	5	—

PLYMOUTH ARGYLE DIV. 3

President: G. H. Gillin, Esq.   *Chairman:* R. Daniel.
Vice-Chairman: P. W. Skinnard, LL.B.
Directors: B. S. Williams, S. J. Williams, B. Ford, L. C. Lovick, P. L. Riley, F.C.A.
Team Manager: Bobby Saxton.
Secretary: Graham Little.
Year Formed: 1886.   *Turned Professional:* 1903.
Limited Company: 1903.
Previous Name: 1886–1903, Argyle Athletic Club.
Football League Record: 1920 Original Member of Division 3. 1921–30 Division 3(S). 1930–50 Division 2. 1950–52 Division 3(S). 1952–56 Division 2. 1956–58. Division 3(S). 1958–59 Division 3. 1959–68 Division 2. 1968–75 Division 3. 1975–77 Division 2. 1977– Division 3.

Honours: Football League, best season in Division 2: 4th, 1931–32, 1952–53. Division 3(S), Champions: 1929–30, 1951–52; Runners-up: 1921–22, 1922–23, 1923–24, 1924–25, 1925–26, 1926–27. (Record of six consecutive years.) Division 3, Champions: 1958–59; Runners-up 1974–75. *F.A. Cup,* best season: 5th Rd., 1952–53. *Football League Cup,* best season: semi-finalists, 1965, 1974.
Record Victory: 8-1 v Millwall, Division 2, Jan. 16th, 1932.
Record Defeat: 0-9 v Stoke C., Division 2, Dec. 17th, 1960.
Most League Points: 68, Division 3(S), 1929–30.
Most League Goals: 107, Division 3(S), 1925–26 and 1951–52.
Highest League Scorer in Season: Jack Cock, 32, Division 3(S), 1925–26.
Most League Goals in Total Aggregate: Sammy Black, 180, 1924–38.
Most Capped Player: Moses Russell, 20 (23) Wales.
Most League Appearances: Sammy Black, 470, 1924–38.
Record Transfer Fee Received: £220,000 from Ipswich Town for Paul Mariner, Oct. 1976.
Record Transfer Fee Paid: £50,000 to Ipswich Town for John Peddelty, Oct. 1976.
Managers Since the War: Jack Tresadern, Jimmy Rae, Jack Rowley, Neil Dougall, Ellis Stuttard, Andy Beattie, Malcolm Allison, Derek Ufton, Billy Bingham, Ellis Stuttard, Tony Waiters, Mike Kelly, Malcolm Allison.
Address of Supporters Association: Same as Football Club.
Address of Club Shop or Boutique: The Pilgrim Shop, Home Park, Plymouth, Devon.

Home Park, Plymouth, Devon. Telephone Plymouth (0752) 52561/2/3. *Ground capacity:* 40,000 (30,000 covered). *Record attendance:* 43,596 v Aston Villa, Division 2, October 10, 1936. *Record receipts:* over £10,000 (official figure not disclosed by club) v Manchester C., League Cup semi-final, Jan. 23, 1974. *Pitch measurements:* 112 yds × 75 yds.

How to get there: Special City buses from the Plymouth bus station at Bretonside. Nearest railway station Plymouth.
Match tickets: Grand Stand and Mayflower Stand tickets are available 2–3 weeks before each first-team game.
Car parking: Car park adjoining the ground holds 2,000 cars.
Entertainments/catering facilities: Eight refreshment bars around the ground.
Club shop: Situated on the ground; sells all types of souvenirs.
Handbooks/programmes: Handbook published annually and sold by the Supporters Association. Programmes sent to all parts of the world.
Extra information: In 1920–21, Plymouth Argyle established a Third Division record by drawing 21 matches.
Club Colours: Green shirts, white shorts, green stockings with white tops.
Change Colours: Green shirts, green shorts, black stockings.
Club Nickname: 'The Pilgrims'.

PLYMOUTH ARGYLE 1978–79 LEAGUE RECORD

Match No.	Date	Venue	Opponents	Result	H/T Score	League Pos'n	Goalscorers	Attendance
1	Aug 19	A	Chesterfield	W 3-1	0-1	—	Fear, Binney, Megson	3895
2	26	H	Lincoln C	W 2-1	1-1	5	Megson, Perrin	7806
3	Sept 1	A	Southend U	L 1-2	1-1	8	Megson	5936
4	9	H	Mansfield T	L 1-4	1-2	15	Binney	6052
5	12	A	Bury	W 2-1	1-1	—	Perrin, Binney	3361
6	16	H	Swindon T	W 2-0	1-0	8	Bason, Binney	6099
7	23	A	Sheffield W	W 3-2	0-1	6	Binney 3	12,088
8	25	A	Tranmere R	L 1-2	0-0	—	Johnson	1907
9	30	H	Rotherham U	W 2-0	2-0	4	Binney 2	6705
10	Oct 7	A	Carlisle U	D 1-1	0-0	5	Perrin	5731
11	14	H	Shrewsbury T	D 1-1	0-1	4	Bason	9901
12	18	A	Chester	D 0-0	0-0	—		3921
13	21	A	Walsall	L 1-2	1-1	7	Binney	5552
14	28	H	Blackpool	D 0-0	0-0	8		8886
15	Nov 3	A	Colchester U	L 1-2	1-0	13	Binney	4564
16	11	H	Southend U	D 1-1	1-1	13	Silkman	6890
17	14	H	Peterborough U	W 3-2	2-0	—	Binney, Rogers, Green (og)	7398
18	18	A	Lincoln C	D 3-3	1-2	8	Fear, Binney (pen), Clarke	3670
19	Dec 9	H	Watford	D 1-1	0-1	9	Silkman	11,907
20	16	H	Chesterfield	D 1-1	0-1	8	Megson	6740
21	26	A	Brentford	L 1-2	0-0	10	Binney	7360
22	30	A	Gillingham	L 0-2	0-1	12		5951
23	Jan 20	A	Swindon T	W 3-1	0-1	8	Trusson, Binney 2	7780
24	27	H	Sheffield W	W 2-0	1-0	8	Binney 2 (1 a pen)	8596
25	Feb 3	H	Tranmere R	D 2-2	2-1	8	Trusson 2	7418
26	10	A	Rotherham U	L 0-1	0-0	9		5237
27	17	H	Carlisle U	W 2-0	2-0	8	Binney 2	6294
28	20	H	Oxford U	L 0-1	0-0	—		7098
29	24	A	Shrewsbury T	L 0-2	0-1	9		6087
30	27	H	Exeter C	W 4-1	3-1	—	Binney (pen), Bason, Johnson, Fear	12,637
31	Mar 3	H	Walsall	W 1-0	0-0	7	Megson	6487
32	10	A	Blackpool	D 0-0	0-0	7		4879
33	12	A	Mansfield T	L 0-5	0-1	—		4325
34	17	H	Colchester U	D 1-1	0-1	8	Binney	5342
35	24	A	Peterborough U	L 1-2	1-1	10	Johnson	4039
36	31	A	Swansea C	L 1-2	0-0	10	Megson	11,412
37	Apr 3	H	Bury	W 3-0	1-0	—	Tucker (og), Harrison, Clarke	4728
38	7	H	Hull C	L 3-4	1-2	10	Trusson, Binney (pen), Clarke	5816
39	11	A	Oxford U	L 2-3	1-1	—	Johnson 2	3299
40	14	H	Brentford	W 2-1	1-0	11	Binney (pen), Johnson	6344
41	17	A	Exeter C	L 0-1	0-0	—		8022
42	21	H	Gillingham	W 2-1	1-1	11	Johnson 2	5868
43	24	H	Chester	D 2-2	1-2	—	Johnson, Megson	4686
44	28	A	Watford	D 2-2	0-1	13	Trusson, Megson	14,816
45	May 1	A	Hull C	L 1-2	0-0	—	Binney	3646
46	5	H	Swansea C	D 2-2	1-0	13	Binney, Bason	13,406

Final League Position: 15

Goalscorers

League (67): Binney 26 (5 pens), Johnson 9, Megson 8, Trusson 5, Bason 4, Fear 3, Clarke 3, Perrin 3, Silkman 1, Harrison 1, Rogers 1, Own Goals 2.
League Cup (5): Fear 2 (1 a pen), Binney 2, Own Goal 1.

League Cup	First Round	Torquay U (h)	1-1
		(a)	2-1
	Second Round	Oxford U (a)	1-1
		(h)	1-2 (a.e.t.)
F.A. Cup	First Round	Worcester (a)	0-2

Burns	Bason	Rogers	Trusson	Foster	Perrin	Fear	Megson	Binney	Taylor	Johnson	Levy	Graves	Harrison	Brennan	Hodge	Hodges	Uzzell	Clarke	Silkman	Upton	McNeill	Chapman	Forde	James	Match No.
1	2	3	4	5	6	7	8	9	10	11															1
1	2	3	4	5	6	10	8	9	7*11	12															2
1	2	3	4	5	6	7	10			11		8*12	9												3
1	2	3	10	5	6	8	7	9		11		12		4*											4
		3	10	5	6		7	9	8	11				4	1	2									5
	2	3	6	5	10	12	7	9	8	11				4*	1										6
	2	3		5	10	8	7	9		4*11					1		12	6							7
	2	3		5	10	8	7	9		4	11				1		6								8
	2*	3	12	5	10	8	7	9		4	11				1		6								9
	2	3*		5	10	8	7	9		4	11	12			1		6								10
	2	3		5	10	8	4	9			11				1		6	7							11
		3	2	5	10	8		9			11		7		1		6	4							12
	2	3		4	10	8		9			11		6		1		5	7							13
		3	5	2	10	8	4*	9			11	12			1		6	7							14
		3	12	5	10	7*	8	9			11				1	2	6	4							15
	2	3		5	10*	8	4	9			11	12			1		6	7							16
	2	3		5		8	7	9				10			1		6	4	11						17
1	2	3		5	10	8*	7	9			11						6	4	12						18
	2			5	10	11	7								1		6	4		3	8	9			19
1	2			5	10*	8	7	9									6	4		3	11	12			20
1	2			5		7	8	9									6	4		3	10	11			21
1	2*			5		7	8	9				10				4	6	11		3	12				22
	4	11	10	5			8	9						1		2	6	7		3					23
	4	11	10	5			8	9						1		2	6	7		3					24
	4	11	8	5		10	7	9						1		2	6			3					25
	4	11	10	5			7	9					8	1		2	6			3					26
	6	11	10*	5			8	9				12	7	1		2	4			3					27
	6	11		5*10		7	9					12	8	1		2	4			3					28
	8	11			9				10			7*	4	1	12	2	5			3		6			29
	7	11			12	8	9*		10				4	1		2	6			3		5			30
	4	11			7	8	9		10			2		1			6			3		5			31
	7	11	10			8	9	6				4		1			2			3		5			32
	6	11	10			8	9	7				2		1			4			3		5			33
		11	10		12	7	9	6				8*		1		3	5			2		4			34
	6	11				8	9	7				10		1		2	5			3		4			35
		11	12		8	10	9	7				3		1		4*	6			2		5			36
		11	10			8	9	7				6		1		3	4			2		5			37
		11	10		12	7	9	8				4		1		3*	6			2		5			38
		11	10			8	9	7				6		1	3		4			2		5			39
	4	11	10			7	9	8				6		1	3	5				2					40
	4		10		11	12	9	7				6		1	3	2		8*				5			41
	4	11				7	9	10				8		1	3	6	5			2					42
	6	11				8	9	7				10		1	3	5	4			2					43
	6		9			8	12					7*11		1	4	5				2		10	3		44
		6				8	9	7				10		1	3	5				2		11	4		45
	6		10			7	9	11				8		1	3	5				2			4		46
8	36	38	24	28	23	22	42	42	8	33	—	5	22	6	38	11	20	35	14	2	27	3	4	15	
		+			+			+			+	+			+	+			+		+	+			
		3s			5s			1s			1s	5s	2s		1s	1s			1s		1s	1s			

299

PLYMOUTH ARGYLE—PLAYERS

Player and position	Ht	Wt	Birthplace	Clubs	League Appearances	Goals
Goalkeepers						
Martin Hodge	5 11	11 0	Southport	Plymouth Arg	43	—
Tony Burns	6 0	13 8	Edenbridge	Arsenal	31	—
(Contract cancelled January 1979)				Brighton	39	—
				Charlton Ath	10	—
				Durban U	—	—
				C Palace	90	—
				Brentford (on loan)	6	—
				Plymouth Arg	8	—
Defenders						
John Uzzell	5 10	11 0	Plymouth	Plymouth Arg	64+1	1
Kevin Hodges	5 7	10 0	Bridport	Plymouth Arg	11+1	—
Tyrone James	6 3	11 0	Paddington	Fulham	18+2	—
				Plymouth Arg	27+1	—
*Geoffrey Battams	5 5	10 1	Plymouth	Plymouth Arg	—	—
*Kevin Pearn	5 10	11 2	Plymouth	Plymouth Arg	—	—
Colin Clarke	6 1½	13 0	Glasgow	Arsenal	—	—
				Oxford U	443+1	23
				Plymouth Arg	35	3
Brian McNeil	5 9	10 12	Newcastle	Bristol C	0+3	—
				Plymouth Arg	27	—
George Foster	5 10	11 2	Plymouth	Plymouth Arg	99+11	6
				Torquay U (on loan)	6	3
Midfield						
Chris Harrison	5 8	10 6	Launceston	Plymouth Arg	73+4	3
Gary Megson	5 11	10 0	Manchester	Plymouth Arg	66	10
Brian Bason	5 9	11 1	Epsom	Chelsea	18+1	1
				Plymouth Arg	58+1	4
Steve Brennan	5 8½	11 0	Mile End	C Palace	2+1	1
				Plymouth Arg	6	—
Steven McCormick	5 7	9 7	Manchester	Manchester C	—	—
				Plymouth Arg	—	—
Leigh Cooper	5 8	10 9	Reading	Plymouth Arg	—	—
Forwards						
Brian Johnson	5 10	11 6	London	Plymouth Arg	146+7	37
				Torquay U (on loan)	5	2
Alan Rogers	5 10	11 4	Plymouth	Plymouth Arg	107+10	5
Mike Trusson	5 10	11 0	Northolt	Plymouth Arg	40+6	7
				Stoke C (on loan)	—	—
Fred Binney	5 10	11 7	Plymouth	Torquay U	5+4	1
				Exeter C	17	11
				Torquay U	19+3	9
				Exeter C	161	79
				Brighton	68+2	35
				Plymouth Arg	60+1	35
Gary Ball	5 7	9 6	St Austell	Plymouth Arg	—	—
Keith Fear	5 7	10 8	Bristol	Bristol C	126+25	33
				Blackburn R (on loan)	5	2
				Hereford U (on loan)	6	—
				Plymouth Arg	39+5	9
Steven Perrin	6 1	12 3	London	C Palace	45+3	11
				Plymouth Arg	34	6
Mark Graves	5 9	10 11	Middlesex	Plymouth Arg	6+5	—
Clevere Forde	5 7	12 0	London	Hounslow	—	—
				Plymouth Arg	4+1	—
Tony Levy	5 10	10 0	Edmonton	Plymouth Arg	0+1	—
Colin Upton	5 7	10 9	Reading	Plymouth Arg	2+1	—
Bill Elliott	5 10	11 6	Poole	Plymouth Arg	—	—

PORTSMOUTH DIV. 4

Vice-Presidents: R. Vernon Stokes, Sir A. L. Blake, M.C., LL.B., K.C.V.O.

Chairman: B. J. Deacon.

Vice-Chairman: J. R. Parkhouse.

Directors: D. K. Deacon, S. W. J. Sloan, G. Gauntlett.

Manager: Frank Burrows.

Company Secretary: W. J. B. Davis.

Chief Executive: J. W. Dickinson M.B.E.

Year Formed: 1898.

Turned Professional: 1898. *Limited Company:* 1898.

Football League Record: 1920 Original Member of Division 3. 1921 Division 3(S). 1924–27 Division 2. 1927–59 Division 1. 1959–61 Division 2. 1961–62 Division 3. 1962–76 Division 2. 1976–78 Division 3. 1978– Division 4.
Honours: *Football League,* Division 1, Champions: 1948–49, 1949–50. Division 2, Runners-up: 1926–27. Division 3(S), Champions: 1923–24. Division 3, Champions: 1961–62. *F.A. Cup,* Winners: 1939; Runners-up: 1929, 1934. *Football League Cup,* best season: 5th Rd., 1961.
Record Victory: 9-1 v Notts Co., Division 2, Apr, 9th, 1927.
Record Defeat: 0-10 v Leicester C., Division 1, Oct. 20th, 1928.
Most League Points: 65, Division 3, 1961–62.
Most League Goals: 87, Division 3(S), 1923–24, Division 2, 1926–27 and **Division 3, 1961–62.**
Highest League Scorer in Season: Billy Haines, 40, Division 2, 1926–27.
Most League Appearances: 764, Jimmy Dickinson, 1946–65.
Most Capped Player: Jimmy Dickinson, 48, England.
Most League Goals in Total Aggregate: Peter Harris, 194, 1946–60.
Record Transfer Fee Received: £130,000 from Brighton for Steve Foster, June 1979.
Record Transfer Fee Paid: £155,000 to Fulham for Paul Went, Dec. 1973.
Managers Since the War: Jack Tinn, Bob Jackson, Eddie Lever, Freddie Cox, George Smith, John Mortimore, Ron Tindall, Ian St. John, Jimmy Dickinson, M.B.E.
Address of Supporters Club: Frogmore Road, Portsmouth.
Address of Club Shop or Boutique: The Club Shop, Portsmouth, 42 Frogmore Road, Portsmouth.

Fratton Park, Frogmore Rd., Portsmouth PO4 8RA. Telephone Portsmouth 31204/5. *Telegraphic address:* 'Pompey Portsm'th'. *Ground capacity:* 46,000 (14,200 covered). *Record attendance:* 51,385 v Derby Co., F.A. Cup 6th Rd., February 26, 1949. *Record receipts:* £18,002 v Arsenal, F.A. Cup 4th Rd. January 23, 1971. *Pitch measurements:* 116 yds × 73 yds.

How to get there: Fratton station on main line from London Waterloo is just four minutes walk from the ground. Buses 17 and 18 from Portsmouth Harbour station and Gosport Ferry Terminal to the ground. Buses also from Portsmouth station.
Match tickets: South Stand centre section (the best seats bookable 10 days in advance.
Car parking: Only side-street parking.
Entertainments/catering facilities: The Pompey public house and reception rooms adjoin the ground and are owned by the club. The Supporters' Club is open to members of the visiting Supporters' Club before and after the match. There are also several bars around the ground.
Club shop: 42 Frogmore Road.
Handbooks/programmes: No handbook. The match-day magazine available on subscription.
Extra information: Portsmouth were the first club to come out of the Third Division to win the League Championship.

Club Colours: Blue shirts with white collars and cuffs, white shorts, red socks.
Change Colours: Red shirts white collar and cuffs, red shorts, white stockings.
Club Captain: John Lathan. *Club Coach:*
Club Nickname: 'Pompey'.

PORTSMOUTH 1978–79 LEAGUE RECORD

Match No.	Date	Venue	Opponents	Result	Score	H/T Score	League Pos'n	Goalscorers	Attendance
1	Aug 19	H	Bradford C	L	0-1	0-1	—		8268
2	22	A	York C	L	3-5	1-1	—	Hemmerman 2, Viney (pen)	2513
3	25	A	Hartlepool U	D	1-1	0-1	19	Davey	3074
4	Sept 2	H	Crewe Alex	W	3-0	1-0	14	Hemmerman 3	7429
5	9	A	Rochdale	W	2-0	2-0	10	Davey, Lathan	1479
6	12	H	Scunthorpe U	D	0-0	0-0	—		10,965
7	16	H	Port Vale	W	2-0	1-0	9	Barnard, Garwood	9937
8	23	A	Aldershot	W	2-0	1-0	5	Hemmerman, Lathan	8967
9	26	H	Wigan Ath	W	1-0	0-0	—	Davey	13,902
10	29	A	AFC Bournemouth	L	1-3	1-1	7	Viney	10,056
11	Oct 7	H	Hereford U	W	1-0	0-0	5	Denyer	11,949
12	14	A	Grimsby T	L	0-1	0-0	5		5141
13	17	A	Doncaster R	W	3-2	2-1	—	Hemmerman 2, Denyer	2480
14	21	H	Halifax T	W	3-1	1-0	5	Garwood 2 (1 a pen), Denyer	12,365
15	28	A	Torquay U	L	1-2	0-1	5	Denyer	4769
16	Nov 4	H	Darlington	W	3-0	1-0	5	Denyer, Garwood, Hemmerman	11,394
17	11	A	Crewe Alex	D	0-0	0-0	4		2294
18	18	H	Hartlepool U	W	3-0	0-0	4	Garwood (pen), Foster, Lathan	10,717
19	Dec 2	A	Northampton T	W	2-0	1-0	2	Garwood, Hemmerman	3592
20	9	H	Huddersfield T	W	1-0	1-0	3	Hemmerman	11,615
21	23	H	Reading	W	4-0	2-0	2	Denyer, Barnard, Hemmerman, Davey	12,541
22	26	A	Wimbledon	W	4-2	1-2	—	Barnard, Wilson, Davey, Hemmerman	7862
23	29	A	Stockport Co	L	2-4	0-1	2	Pullar, Garwood	3795
24	Jan 13	A	Rochdale	D	1-1	0-0	1	Barnard	11,595
25	Feb 3	A	Wigan Ath	L	0-2	0-1	4		8289
26	10	H	AFC Bournemouth	D	1-1	0-0	4	Foster	12,172
27	20	H	Newport Co	W	2-1	1-1	—	Barnard, Davey	8206
28	24	H	Grimsby T	L	1-3	0-2	4	Hemmerman	12,782
29	Mar 3	A	Halifax T	L	0-2	0-2	5		1741
30	10	H	Torquay U	W	1-0	0-0	5	Showers	8689
31	21	A	Port Vale	D	0-0	0-0	—		2738
32	24	H	York C	D	1-1	0-0	8	Showers	9353
33	28	A	Bradford C	L	0-2	0-0	—		2410
34	30	A	Barnsley	D	1-1	0-0	8	Davey	12,928
35	Apr 3	A	Scunthorpe U	D	2-2	1-0	—	Garwood 2	1535
36	7	H	Northampton T	W	1-0	0-0	7	Garwood	8066
37	13	A	Reading	L	0-2	0-1	—		15,054
38	14	H	Wimbledon	D	0-0	0-0	7		11,453
39	16	A	Newport Co	W	2-1	0-1	—	Garwood (pen), Barnard	5421
40	21	H	Stockport Co	D	1-1	1-1	7	Hand	8177
41	24	H	Doncaster R	W	4-0	2-0	—	Garwood 3, Lathan	5869
42	28	A	Huddersfield T	L	0-2	0-1	7		2895
43	May 5	H	Barnsley	L	0-1	0-1	8		8761
44	7	A	Hereford U	W	1-0	1-0	—	Barnard	3707
45	11	A	Darlington	L	0-2	0-0	—		1140
46	15	H	Aldershot	D	1-1	1-1	—	Garwood	6238

Final League Position: 7

Goalscorers

League (62): Garwood 15 (3 pens), Hemmerman 14, Barnard 7, Davey 7, Denyer 6, Lathan 4, Foster 2, Showers 2, Viney 2 (1 pen), Hand 1, Pullar 1, Wilson 1.
League Cup (2): Gilchrist, Pullar.
F.A. Cup (2): Hemmerman 2

League Cup	First Round	Swindon T (h)	0-0
		(a)	2-4
F.A. Cup	First Round	Northampton T (h)	2-0
	Second Round	Reading (h)	0-1

Mellor	Ellis	Viney	Denyer	Foster	Hand	Hemmerman	Lathan	Davey	McIlwraith	Pullar	Garwood	Wilson	Piper	Barnard	McCaffrey	Showers	Milligan	Bryant	James	Roberts	Match No.
1	2	3	4	5	6	7*	8	9	10	11	12										1
1	2	3	4	5	6*	7	8	9	10	11		12									2
1		3	4	5		7	8	9	10	12	11*	2	6								3
1	2	3	4			7	8	9		11			5	6	10						4
1	2	3	4	12		7	8	9		11		6*	5	10							5
1	2	3	4	5		7	8*	9		11	12			6	10						6
1	2	3	4	5		7	8	9*		11	12			6	10						7
1	2	3	4	5		7	8	9		11	12			6	10*						8
1	2	3	4	5		7*	8	9		11	12			6	10						9
1	2	3*	4	5		7	8	9	10	11		12	6								10
1	2	3	4	5		7*	8	9		11	10			6		12					11
1	2	3	4	5		7	8	9	10	11				6							12
1	2	3	4	5		7	8	12	10*11		9			6							13
1	2	3	4	5		7*	8	12	10	11	9			6							14
1	2	3	4	5		7	8	12	10	11	9*		6								15
1	2	3	4	5		7	8	12		11	9			6*10							16
1	2	3	4	5		7	8	6		11	9			10							17
1	2	3	4	5	12	7	8	6		11*	9			10							18
1	2	3	4	5		7	8	6	12	11	9			10*							19
1	2	3	4	5		7	8	6		11	9			10							20
1	2	3	4	5		7	8*	9	12	11		6		10							21
1	2	3	4	5		7	8	6		11		9		10							22
1	2*	3	4	5		7	8	6		11	12	9		10							23
1	2	3	12	5		7	8*	9	4	11		6		10							24
1	2	3	4	5		7*10		6	8	11	9					12					25
1	2	3	12	5		7	8	6	10*11			4		9							26
1	2	3	4	5		7	8	6		11		9		10							27
1	2	3*	4	5		7	8	9		11	12	6		10							28
1	2		4	5		7	8	6		11	12	3		10	9*						29
1	2	3	4	5		7	9	6			8		11	10							30
1	2	12	4			7	8	6				9	5			10	3	11*			31
1	2		4	5		7	8*	6		9			12			10	3	11			32
1	2		4	5		7	8	6				9				10	3	11			33
1	2		4	5		7		6				9	8			10	3	11			34
1	2		4	5			12	6		7		9	8			10	3	11*			35
1	2*		4	5			12	6		7		9	8			10	3	11			36
1			4*	5		7	8	6		12		9	2			10	3	11			37
1	2	3		5*		7	8	6		12	9			4		10		11			38
1	5	3	2				8	6		7	9			4		10		11			39
1	2	3	12		5		8	6		7	9*			4		10		11			40
1	5	3	2				8	6	12	7	9			4*		10		11			41
1	5	3*	2		12	7	8	6	4		9					10		11			42
1	5	3	2				9	6	8	11	7			4		10*		12			43
1	5	3					8	6	4		9			7		10		11	2		44
1	5	3					8	6	4		9			7		10		11	2*12		45
1	5	3					8	6	4		9			7		10		11	2		46
46	44	38	39	35	3	37	43	42	16	35	27	15	14	28	—	19	7	15	3	—	
	+ 1s	+ 3s	+ 1s	+ 2s			+ 2s	+ 4s	+ 3s	+ 3s	+ 8s	+ 3s		+ 1s	+ 1s			+ 1s	+ 1s		

PORTSMOUTH—PLAYERS

Player and position	Ht	Wt	Birthplace	Clubs	League Appearances	Goals
Goalkeepers						
Steve Middleton	6 0	12 7	Portsmouth	Southampton	24	—
(Contract cancelled December 1978)				Torquay U (on loan)	10	—
				Portsmouth	26	—
Peter Mellor	6 2	14 0	Prestbury	Manchester C	—	—
				Burnley	69	—
				Chesterfield (on loan)	4	—
				Fulham	189	—
				Hereford U	32	—
				Portsmouth	46	—
Alan Knight	6 1	13 1½	Balham	Portsmouth	1	—
Defenders						
Peter Ellis	5 11	11 2	Portsmouth	Portsmouth	117+5	—
*Billy Wilson	5 9	11 1	Seaton Delaval	Blackburn R	246+1	—
				Portsmouth	188+6	5
Peter Denyer	5 11	11 9	Hazelmere	Portsmouth	123+8	15
Keith Viney	5 11	11 12	Portsmouth	Portsmouth	79+6	3
*Eoin Hand (Eire)	6 0	12 0	Dublin	Portsmouth	259+1	12
				South Africa	(not known)	
				Portsmouth	15+2	2
Tony Taylor	5 7	11 2	Glasgow	Kilmarnock	20+2	7
(Contract cancelled December 1978)				Celtic	—	—
				Morton	20+2	7
				C Palace	192+3	8
				Southend U	56	1
				Swindon T	20+6	—
				Bristol R	12	—
				Portsmouth	17	—
Keith James (apprentice)				Portsmouth	3+1	—
Midfield						
Stephen Foster	6 0	12 8	Portsmouth	Portsmouth	101+8	6
David Pullar	5 10	10 11	Durham	Portsmouth	84+9	4
Leigh Barnard	5 7½	9 10	Worsley	Portsmouth	36+3	7
Steve Piper	5 10	11 10	Brighton	Brighton	160	9
				Portsmouth	27+2	2
John Lathan	5 7	11 0	Sunderland	Sunderland	43+11	14
				Mansfield T	72+2	14
				Carlisle U	55+6	8
				Barnsley (on loan)	6+1	—
				Portsmouth	55+2	4
Steve Bryant	5 8	10 6	Islington	Birmingham C	34+2	2
				Sheffield W (on loan)	2+1	—
				Northampton T	95+2	5
				Portsmouth	15	—
Jimmy McIlwraith	5 8	10 4	Troon	Motherwell	21+7	2
				Bury	80+9	21
				Portsmouth	16+3	—
Forwards						
Colin Garwood	5 9	10 13	Heacham	Peterborough U	58+8	31
				Oldham Ath	83+9	36
				Huddersfield T	22+6	8
				Colchester U	83+4	25
				Portsmouth	39+8	17
Jeff Hemmerman	5 11	11 0	Hull	Hull C	45+14	10
				Scunthorpe U (on loan)	4+1	1
				Port Vale	13+2	5
				Portsmouth	37	14
Steve Davey	5 7	10 3	Plymouth	Plymouth Arg	214+12	48
				Hereford U	104+3	32
				Portsmouth	42+4	7
Derek Showers (Wales)	5 11	11 4	Merthyr Tydfil	Cardiff C	76+7	10
				Bournemouth	58+2	19
				Portsmouth	19+1	2
Trevor Roberts	6 4	13 8		Portsmouth	0+1	—

PORT VALE DIV. 4

Chairman: A. McPherson.
Vice Chairman: J. Burgess.
Directors: L. W. Cliff, D. Ratcliffe, J.P., D. Leese, J. Lloyd.
Manager: Dennis Butler. *Secretary:* Andrew Waterhouse.
Year Formed: 1876. *Turned Professional:* 1885.
Limited Company: 1911
Previous Name: Burslem Port Vale; became Port Vale, 1913.
Previous Grounds: 1876, Limekin Lane, Longport; 1881, Westport; 1884, Moorland Road, Burslem; 1886, Athletic Ground, Cobridge; 1913, Recreation Ground, Hanley; 1950, Vale Park.
Football League Record: Original Member Division 2, 1892-96. Failed re-election in 1896. Re-elected 1898. Resigned 1907. Returned in Oct., 1919, when they took over the fixtures of Leeds City. 1929-30 Division 3(N). 1930-36 Division 2. 1936-38 Division 3(N). 1938-52 Division 3(S). 1952-54 Division 3(N). 1954-57 Division 2. 1957-58 Division 3(S). 1958-59 Division 4. 1959-65 Division 3. 1965-70 Division 4. 1970-78 Division 3. 1978- Division 4.
Honours: Football League, best season in Division 2: 5th, 1930-31. Division 3(N), Champions: 1929-30, 1953-54; Runners-up: 1952-53. Division 4, Champions: 1958-59; Promoted 1969-70 (4th). *F.A. Cup,* best season, semi-finalists: 1954, when in Division 3. *Football League Cup,* best season: never past 2nd Rd.
Record Victory: 9-1 v Chesterfield, Division 2, Sept. 24th, 1932.
Record Defeat: 0-10 v Sheffield U., Division 2, Dec. 10th, 1892 and v Notts Co., Division 2, Feb. 26th, 1895.
Most League Points: 69, Div. 3(N), 1953-54.
Most League Goals: 110, Division 4, 1958-59.
Highest League Scorer in Season: Wilf Kirkham, 38, Division 2, 1926-27.
Most League Goals in Total Aggregate: Wilf Kirkham, 154, 1923-29, 1931-33.
Most Capped Player: Sammy Morgan, 7 (18) N. Ireland.
Most League Appearances: Roy Sproson, 761, 1950-72.
Record Transfer Fee Received: £30,000 from Brighton for Brian Horton, March 1976.
Record Transfer Fee Paid: £40,000 to Bury for Peter Farrell, Nov. 1978; £40,000 to Wolverhampton W. for Ken Todd, Aug. 1978.
Managers Since the War: Billy Frith, Gordon Hodgson, Ivor Powell, Freddie Steele, Norman Low, Freddie Steele, Jackie Mudie, Sir Stanley Matthews, Gordon Lee, Roy Sproson, Colin Harper, Bob Smith.
Address of Supporters Club: Hamil Rd., Burslem, Stoke on Trent, ST6 1AW.

Vale Park, Burslem, Stoke-on-Trent. Telephone Stoke-on-Trent 814134. *Ground capacity:* 35,000. *Record attendance:* 50,000 v Aston Villa, F.A. Cup 5th Rd., February 20, 1960. *Record receipts:* £11,991 v Burnley, F.A. Cup 4th Rd., Jan. 29 1977. *Pitch measurements:* 116 yds × 76 yds.
How to get there: Nearest railway station, Stoke-on-Trent; there are frequent bus services from the town centre to Burslem.
Match tickets: Not bookable in advance.
Car parking: Parking is available behind the Railway Stand on Hamil Road, and on the Lorne Street side of the ground.
Entertainments/catering facilities: Light refreshments served on the ground. Social club on the Hamil Road side of the ground provides entertainment on certain evenings; membership by subscription.
Club shop: Sells all types of souvenirs.
Handbooks/programmes: Programmes are available on application to the club office or to the club shop.
Extra information: Port Vale are one of only four clubs to reach the F.A. Cup semi-final while in the Third Division; they did so in the 1953-54 season.
Club Colours: White shirts with black trim, black shorts, black stockings.
Change Colours: Yellow shirts, green shorts, yellow stockings.
Trainer: Lol Hamlett.
Club Nickname: 'Valiants'.

PORT VALE 1978-79 LEAGUE RECORD

Match No.	Date	Venue	Opponents	Result	H/T Score	League Pos'n	Goalscorers	Attendance
1	Aug 19	H	Scunthorpe U	D 2-2	1-0	—	Wright, Bromage	3025
2	22	A	Wimbledon	L 0-1	0-1	—		2638
3	25	A	Crewe Alex	W 5-1	2-1	10	Wright 3, Bloor, Beamish	4413
4	Sept 2	H	Rochdale	D 1-1	0-0	9	Beamish	3220
5	9	H	Aldershot	D 1-1	0-0	9	Beamish	3045
6	12	A	Doncaster R	W 3-1	1-0	—	Bromage, Todd, Beamish	3405
7	16	A	Portsmouth	L 0-2	0-1	12		9937
8	23	H	AFC Bournemouth	L 1-2	1-2	15	Griffiths (pen)	3140
9	26	H	Northampton T	D 2-2	2-1	—	Chamberlain 2	3245
10	30	A	Hereford U	L 0-1	0-1	16		3963
11	Oct 7	H	Grimsby T	D 1-1	1-1	15	Chamberlain	3433
12	14	A	Halifax T	W 3-0	1-0	13	Wright 2, Tully	1591
13	18	A	Bradford C	W 3-2	0-0	—	Sutcliffe, Wright, Healy	4136
14	21	H	Torquay U	L 1-2	1-2	14	Todd	4108
15	28	A	Darlington	L 0-4	0-1	16		1793
16	Nov 4	H	Hartlepool U	W 2-0	1-0	14	Chamberlain, Beech	3195
17	11	A	Rochdale	W 1-0	0-0	11	Keenan	1882
18	18	H	Crewe Alex	D 2-2	1-1	12	Farrell (pen), Healy	4607
19	Dec 9	H	Stockport Co	W 2-1	2-1	10	Wright, Farrell (pen)	3689
20	26	A	Barnsley	L 2-6	1-3	—	Todd, Keenan	10,532
21	30	A	Newport Co	L 0-1	0-0	17		4104
22	Jan 1	H	Huddersfield T	W 1-0	0-0	—	Wright	4021
23	9	H	Wigan Ath	W 2-1	1-0	—	Wright, Todd	3744
24	13	A	Aldershot	D 1-1	0-0	8	Sinclair	3608
25	16	H	Doncaster R	L 1-3	1-3	—	Bradley (og)	3381
26	Feb 6	A	AFC Bournemouth	L 1-3	0-2	—	Brown R (og)	3416
27	24	H	Halifax T	L 0-1	0-1	15		3117
28	Mar 3	A	Torquay U	D 2-2	2-0	15	Todd, Wright	1800
29	10	H	Darlington	W 2-1	0-0	15	Hawkins, Beech	2566
30	13	A	Northampton T	L 0-1	0-0	—		1572
31	21	H	Portsmouth	D 0-0	0-0	—		2738
32	24	H	Wimbledon	W 1-0	1-0	12	Beech	2906
33	27	A	Scunthorpe U	L 0-2	0-0	—		1472
34	31	A	Reading	D 0-0	0-0	13		6503
35	Apr 3	A	Grimsby T	L 0-1	0-0	—		7815
36	7	H	York C	D 0-0	0-0	13		2712
37	13	A	Wigan Ath	L 3-5	2-0	—	Wright, Todd 2	8452
38	14	H	Barnsley	W 3-2	1-1	14	Chamberlain N, Wright, Todd	5226
39	16	A	Huddersfield T	L 2-3	1-1	—	Chamberlain N, Beech	3236
40	21	H	Newport Co	D 1-1	0-0	16	Wright	2444
41	24	H	Bradford C	W 2-1	0-0	—	Farrell, Chamberlain N	2262
42	27	A	Stockport Co	D 0-0	0-0	15		3343
43	May 1	H	Hereford U	D 1-1	0-1	—	Hawkins	2160
44	5	H	Reading	L 0-3	0-1	16		3603
45	7	A	York C	L 0-4	0-2	—		2344
46	10	A	Hartlepool U	W 2-1	1-0	—	Sinclair, Farrell	1996

Final League Position: 16

Goalscorers

League (57): Wright 14, Todd 8, Chamberlain N 7, Beamish 4, Beech 4, Farrell 4 (2 pens), Bromage 2, Hawkins 2, Healy 2, Keenan 2, Sinclair 2, Bloor 1, Griffiths 1 (pen), Sutcliffe 1, Tully 1, Own Goals 2.
League Cup (1): Wright.

League Cup	First Round	Chester (h)	0-3
		(a)	1-1
F.A. Cup	First Round	Bradford C (a)	0-1

Connaughton	Wilkinson	Griffiths	Todd	Sproson	Hawkins	Stenson	Bromage	Wright	Beamish	Bentley	Chamberlain N	Froggatt	Bloor	Dance	Sutcliffe	Keenan	Ridley	Sinclair	Healy	Tully	Harris	Beech	Farrell	Delgado	Proudlove	Elsby	Chamberlain M	Match No.
1	2	3	4	5	6	7	8	9	10*	11																	12	1
1	2	3	8*	5	6	11	7	9		4		10	12															2
	2			5*	6	11	8	9	10	3	7	12	4	1														3
	2	3		5	6	11	8	10	9	4	7*		1	12														4
	2	3	8	5	6	11	7*	9	10		12		4	1														5
	2	3	8	5	6*	11	7	9	10		12		4	1														6
	2	3	8	5		11*	7	9	10	6	12		4	1														7
1		3	10	5	6	7	8	9			11		4*			2	12											8
1			10	5	6		8	9		3	11				7	2	4											9
1			10	5	6		8*	9		3	11				7	2	4	12										10
1			10	5	6			9		3	11				7	2	4		8									11
1			8	5	6			9		3	11				7*	2	4		10	12								12
1			8	5	6			9		3	10*				7	2	4		11	12								13
1			8	5	6			9		3	11*				7	2	4		10	12								14
1			8	5	6	4		9		3	11*				7*	2			10		12							15
1				5	6		8	9		3	11					2			10	7	4	12						16
1		12		5	6			9		3*						2			11	7	4	10	8					17
1				5	6			9		3						2			11	7	4	10	8					18
1			4		6			9		3	7*					2			10	11	5	12	8					19
1			4		6			9		3						2	10	11	7			8	5					20
1			7		6			9		3						2	10		5		8	4	11					21
1			10		6	7*		9		3						2			5		8	4	11	12				22
			10		6		8	9		3				1		2	12		5			4	11*	7				23
					6		8	9		3				1		2	10		5			4	11	7				24
			10		6		7	9		3				1		2	12		5		8	4	11*					25
1			7		6			9		3	10					2	12		5		8	4		11*				26
1			10		6		8*	9		3	12					2	11			4	7	5						27
		3	10	5	6			9						1		2		7	11		4	8						28
		3	10	5	6			9						1		2		8	11		4	7						29
		3	10		6			9						1		2		7	11		4	8	5					30
		3	10		6*			9		12				1		2		7	11		4	8	5					31
		3	10					9		6				1		2		7	11		4	8	5					32
		3	10			12		9		6				1		2*		7	11		4	8	5					33
		3	10		2			9		6				1				7	11		4	8	5					34
		3	10		2		11	9		6				1				7			4	8	5					35
		3	8		6			9						1		2		10	11		4	7	5					36
		3	10		6			9		7				1		2			11		4*	8	5			12		37
		3	10		6			9		4	7			1		2						8	5			11		38
		3	10	2	6			9		4*	11			1							12	8	5			7		39
		3	10		6			9		7				1			5		2	8	4					11		40
		3	10		6			9		7				1			4		2	8	5					11		41
		3	10		6			9		7				1			4		2	8	5					11		42
		3	10	12	6			9		7				1			4		2	8	5					11*		43
		3	10		6		11	9		7				1		2					4	8	5					44
		3	10	5	6	12	11	9		7				1		2					4*	8						45
		3	10		6		11*	9						1		2	7				4	8	5			12		46
19	7	26	40	22	43	10	19	46	6	30	22	1	5	27	7	32	6	14	23	5	10	20	27	24	5	3	6	
			+1s	+1s		+1s	+1s			+1s	+4s	+1s	+1s		+1s		+1s	+4s		+3s	+1s	+3s			+2s	+2s		

PORT VALE—PLAYERS

Player and position	Ht	Wt	Birthplace	Clubs	League Appearances	Goals
Goalkeepers						
John Connaughton	5 11	10 12	Wigan	Manchester U	3	—
				Halifax T (on loan)	—	—
				Torquay U (on loan)	—	—
				Sheffield U	—	—
				Port Vale	57	—
*Gregory Lowndes	5 11	10 8	Stoke-on-Trent	Port Vale	—	—
Trevor Dance	5 10	11 13	Durham	Port Vale	43	—
				Stoke C (on loan)	—	—
Defenders						
Mark Nicklin	5 8½	10 4	Stoke	Port Vale	—	—
Gerry Keenan	5 9	11 0	Liverpool	Bury	69+2	3
				Port Vale	32	2
Neil Griffiths	5 10	10 12	Stoke	Chester	89+1	4
				Port Vale	154+3	6
*Dave Harris	6 2	12 4	Stoke	Port Vale	175+1	8
Graham Hawkins	6 0	13 4	Darlaston	Wolverhampton W	28+6	—
				Preston NE	241+4	3
				Blackburn R	108+1	4
				Port Vale	58+1	3
Phil Sproson	6 0	12 0	Trent Vale	Port Vale	22+3	—
Billy Leese	6 1	12 6	Stoke	Port Vale	—	—
Bob Delgado	6 0	12 2	Cardiff	Luton T	—	—
				Carlisle U	25+10	3
				Workington (on loan)	7	—
				Rotherham U	69+1	5
				Chester	125+3	8
				Port Vale	24	—
Alan Bloor	6 0	13 0	Stoke	Stoke C	380+4	17
				Port Vale	5+1	1
Midfield						
Terry Bailey	5 5	11 7	Stafford	Port Vale	161+4	26
(Contract cancelled August 1978)						
Bill Bentley	5 11	13 0	Loughton	Stoke C	44+4	1
				Blackpool	289+7	10
				Port Vale	61+2	—
Paul Bennett	5 9	9 9	Liverpool	Port Vale	—	—
Ken Todd	5 7	9 9	Co Durham	Wolverhampton W	4+1	1
				Port Vale	40+1	8
Brian Sinclair	5 6	10 4	Liverpool	Blackpool	0+2	—
				Port Vale	14+4	2
Peter Farrell	5 7	10 9	Liverpool	Bury	49+5	9
				Port Vale	28	4
Felix Healy	5 11	12 0	Londonderry	Finn Harps	—	—
				Port Vale	23	2
Ian Elsby	5 9	9 0	Stoke	Port Vale	3+2	—
Ged Stenson	5 7	10 2	Bootle	Everton	—	—
				Port Vale	10+1	—
Steven Jones	6 1	10 7	Liverpool	Manchester U	—	—
				Port Vale	—	—
Forwards						
Neville Chamberlain	5 7½	11 5	Stoke	Port Vale	31+5	9
Ken Beech	5 8	10 0	Stoke	Port Vale	81+3	9
Russell Bromage	5 11	11 5	Blurton	Port Vale	25+1	2
Bernie Wright	5 11	13 0	Liverpool	Walsall	15	2
				Everton	10+1	2
				Walsall	145+7	38
				Bradford C	65+1	13
				Port Vale	46	14
Mark Chamberlain	5 8½	9 8	Stoke	Port Vale	6+2	—
*Andy Proudlove	5 9	12 0	Buxton	Sheffield W	10+5	—
				Norwich C	0+1	—
				Hereford U	6+5	—
				Port Vale	5	—
Kevin Tully	5 10	12 4	Manchester	Blackpool	10+1	—
				Cambridge U	40+4	—
				Crewe A	81+5	4
				Port Vale	5+3	1

PRESTON NORTH END DIV. 2

President: Tom Finney O.B.E., J.P.; *Chairman:* Alan R. W. Jones, F.R.I.C.S., J.P.
Vice-Chairman: T. J. Hemmings.
Directors: T. W. S. Croft, K. W. Leeming, T. H. Gore, E. Griffith, M. Johnson, M. H. McCann, A. C. Pilkington.
Team Manager: Nobby Stiles.
Secretary: Ron Severs, F.I.M. Ent.
Year Formed: 1881. *Turned Professional:* 1885.
Limited Company: 1893.
Football League Record: 1888 Original Member of League. 1901–04 Division 2. 1904–12 Division 1. 1912–13 Division 2. 1913–14 Division 1. 1914–15 Division 2. 1919–25 Division 1. 1925–34 Division 2. 1934–49 Division 1. 1949–51 Division 2. 1951–61 Division 1. 1961–70 Division 2. 1970–71 Division 3. 1971–74 Division 2. 1974–78 Division 3. 1978– Division 2.
Honours: Football League, Division 1, Champions: 1888–89 (first champions), 1889–90; Runners-up: 1890–91, 1891–92, 1892–93, 1905–06, 1952–53, 1957–58. Division 2, Champions: 1903–04, 1912–13, 1950–51; Runners-up: 1914–15, 1933–34, Division 3, Champions 1970–71. *F.A. Cup,* Winners: 1889, 1938; Runners-up: 1888, 1922, 1937, 1954, 1964. *Football League Cup,* best season: 4th Rd., 1963, 1966, 1972.
Record Victory: 26-0 v Hyde, F.A. Cup 1st Series, 1st Rd., Oct. 15th, 1887.
Record Defeat: 0-7 v Blackpool, Division 1, May 1st, 1948.
Most League Points: 61, Division 3, 1970-71.
Most League Goals: 100, Division 2, 1927–28 and Division 1, **1957–58**.
Highest League Scorer in Season: Ted Harper, 37, Division 2, **1932–33**.
Most Capped Player: Tom Finney, 76, England.
Most League Appearances: Alan Kelly, 447, 1961–75.
Most League Goals in Total Aggregate: Tom Finney, 187, 1946–60.
Record Transfer Fee Received: £765,000 from Manchester C. for Mick Robinson, June 1979.
Record Transfer Fee Paid: £95,000 to Nottingham F. for Steve Elliott, March 1979.
Managers Since the War: W. Scott, Scot Symon, Frank Hill, Cliff Britton, Jimmy Milne, Bobby Seith, Alan Ball snr, Bobby Charlton C.B.E., Harry Catterick.
Address of Supporters Association: c/o Preston North End F.C., Deepdale, Preston.
Address of Club Shop or Boutique: Lilywhite Shop, Deepdale, Preston.

Deepdale, Preston PR1 6RU. Telephone Preston 795919. *Telegraphic address:* 'Football Preston'. *Ground capacity:* 38,000. *Record attendance:* 42,684 v Arsenal, Division 1, April 23, 1938. *Record receipts:* £24,345.13 Football League Cup 4th Rd., v Southampton February 12, 1979. *Pitch measurements:* 112 yds × 78 yds.

How to get there: Special buses to Deepdale from outlying areas and town centre bus station. Nearest railway station: Preston.
Match tickets: Postal applications, including remittance and S.A.E., may be made 14 days before the match.
Car parking: Club car park on the Deepdale Road (West Stand) side of the ground, holds 1,000 vehicles. Only limited off-street parking.
Entertainments/catering facilities: The ground is well-equipped for normal match-day refreshments.
Club shop: Open on match days. All postal enquiries to: The Commercial Manager, Preston North End Development Association, Deepdale Road, Preston (Tel: Preston 795465).
Handbooks/programmes: No handbook. Programmes available on subscription from the Commercial Manager.
Extra information: The first club to do the League and F.A. Cup double; Preston accomplished this feat in 1888–89.
Club Colours: White shirts, with blue collars and cuffs, white shorts with blue stripes, white stockings.
Change Colours: Yellow shirts, yellow shorts, yellow stockings.
Team Captain: Stephen Doyle.
First Team Trainer: Harry Hubbick.
Club Nickname: 'The Lilywhites' or 'North End'. *Club Captain:* Francis Burns.

PRESTON NORTH END 1978-79 LEAGUE RECORD

Match No.	Date	Venue	Opponents	Result	H/T Score	League Pos'n	Goalscorers	Attendance
1	Aug 19	A	Cardiff C	D 2-2	1-2	—	Bruce 2	7812
2	22	H	Blackburn R	W 4-1	2-1	—	Robinson, Doyle, Bruce 2	15,412
3	26	H	Sheffield U	D 2-2	1-1	4	Robinson 2	13,208
4	Sept 2	A	Sunderland	L 1-3	0-1	9	Robinson	16,819
5	9	H	Millwall	D 0-0	0-0	8		8926
6	16	A	Oldham Ath	L 0-2	0-0	16		9766
7	23	H	Stoke C	L 0-1	0-1	17		14,057
8	30	A	Brighton & HA	L 1-5	0-4	20	Cochrane	19,217
9	Oct 7	A	Cambridge U	L 0-1	0-1	20		5398
10	14	H	Crystal Palace	L 2-3	1-0	20	Haslegrave Thomson	10,795
11	21	A	Fulham	L 3-5	2-2	21	Bruce, Baxter, Coleman	8719
12	28	H	Burnley	D 2-2	2-1	21	Thomson, Bruce	15,014
13	Nov 4	A	West Ham U	L 1-3	1-1	21	Thomson	23,579
14	11	H	Cardiff C	W 2-1	2-0	21	Robinson 2	9268
15	18	A	Sheffield U	W 1-0	0-0	19	Bruce	14,807
16	21	H	Sunderland	W 3-1	1-1	—	Thomson, Robinson, Bruce	13,204
17	25	A	Orient	L 0-2	0-1	19		4702
18	Dec 9	A	Luton T	W 2-1	1-1	18	Robinson (pen), Baxter	7036
19	12	H	Charlton Ath	W 6-1	3-0	—	Coleman, Potts 2, Bruce 2, Robinson	8500
20	16	H	Notts Co	D 1-1	0-1	17	Baxter	10,728
21	23	A	Leicester C	D 1-1	0-0	15	Bruce	10,481
22	26	A	Wrexham	W 2-1	2-0	—	Bruce, Jones (og)	17,820
23	30	H	Bristol R	D 1-1	1-0	14	Bruce	12,660
24	Feb 10	H	Brighton & HA	W 1-0	0-0	15	Bruce	11,649
25	24	A	Crystal Palace	D 0-0	0-0	16		17,592
26	28	H	Stoke C	D 1-1	1-0	—	Bruce	18,177
27	Mar 3	H	Fulham	D 2-2	2-1	13	Bruce, Potts	10,890
28	10	A	Burnley	D 1-1	0-0	13	Bruce	15,175
29	17	H	West Ham U	D 0-0	0-0	12		15,376
30	20	H	Oldham Ath	D 1-1	1-0	—	Coleman	12,535
31	24	A	Blackburn R	W 1-0	1-0	10	Bruce	17,790
32	31	H	Orient	D 1-1	0-0	10	Coleman	9494
33	Apr 4	A	Newcastle U	L 3-4	2-2	—	Robinson 2, Bruce	12,157
34	7	A	Charlton Ath	D 1-1	0-1	10	Coleman	5836
35	14	A	Wrexham	L 1-2	1-2	11	Robinson	13,419
36	16	H	Newcastle U	D 0-0	0-0	—		12,960
37	17	H	Leicester C	W 4-0	2-0	—	Robinson, Bruce 2, Coleman	10,394
38	21	A	Notts Co	D 0-0	0-0	10		7009
39	24	H	Cambridge U	L 0-2	0-0	—		10,136
40	28	H	Luton T	D 2-2	1-0	10	Doyle, Coleman	8927
41	May 5	A	Bristol R	W 1-0	1-0	8	Baxter	5814
42	22	A	Millwall	W 2-0	2-0	—	Bell, Potts	2833

Final League Position: 7

Goalscorers

League (59): Bruce 21, Robinson 13 (1 a pen), Coleman 7, Baxter 4, Potts 4, Thomson 4, Doyle 2, Bell 1, Cochrane 1, Haslegrave 1, Own Goal 1.
League Cup (6): Bruce 3, Baxter, Thomson, Fisher.
F.A. Cup (3): Bruce 2, Burns.

League Cup	First Round	Huddersfield T (h)	3-0
		(a)	2-2
	Second Round	QPR (h)	1-3
F.A. Cup	Third Round	Derby Co (h)	3-0
	Fourth Round	Southampton (h)	0-1

311

Tunks	McMahon	Cameron	Doyle	Baxter	Cross	Burns	Haslegrave	Thomson	Robinson	Bruce	Wilson	Smith	Spavin	Potts	Coleman	Cochrane	Uzelac	O'Riordan	Taylor	Elliott	Bell	Match No.
1	2	3	4	5	6	7	8	9	10	11												1
1		2*	4	5	6	7	8	9	10	11	3	12										2
1			4	5	6	7	2	9*	10	11	3			8	12							3
1			4	5	6	7	2	9	10	11	3			8*	12							4
1	2		6	5		4	8	10*	9	11	3	12		7								5
1	2		4	5		7	8	9	10*	11	3	12			6							6
1	2*		4	5		6	8			11	3	10		7		9	12					7
1	2*			5	6	4	8		9	11	3			10		7	12					8
1			4	5		10*	8	12		11	3			7	2	9	6					9
1	2	3	4	5			8	10	9	11					7			6				10
1	2	3	4	5			8	10	9	11					7			6*	12			11
1	2	3	4	5			8	10	9	11					7			6				12
1	2	3	4	5			8	10	9	11					7			6				13
1		3		5		4	8	10	9	11					7			6	2			14
1		3	12	5		4	8*	10	9	11					7			6	2			15
1		3	12	5		4	8	10*	9	11					7			6	2			16
1		3	4	5		10	8		9	11	12				7			6	2*			17
1		3		5		4	8		9	11				10	7			6	2			18
1		3		5		4	8*		9	11	12			10	7			6	2			19
1		3		5		4	8		9	11				10	7			6	2			20
1		3		5		4	8		9	11				10	7			6	2			21
1		3		5		4	8		9	11				10	7			6	2			22
1		3		5		4	8		9	11				10	7			6	2			23
1		3		5		4	8		9	11				10	7			6	2			24
1		3	12	5		4*	8		9	11				10	7			6	2			25
1		3	4	5			8		9	11				10	7			6	2			26
1		3	4	5			8		9	11				10	7			6	2			27
1		3	4	5			8		9	11				10	7			6	2			28
1		3	4*	5			8			11	12			10	7			6	2	9		29
1		3	4	5			8			11	12			10	7			6	2*	9		30
1		3	8	5						11				10	7			6	2	9	4	31
1		3	4*	5			8	12		11				10	9	7		6	2			32
1		3		5			8	12	9	11				10*	7			6	2	4		33
1		3		5			8		9	11				10	7			6	4	2		34
1		3		5			8		9	11*				10	7			6	2	12	4	35
1		3	12				8		9					10*	7		5	6	2	11	4	36
1		3	4				8		9	11					7		5	6	2	10		37
1		3	4				8		9*	11				12	7		5	6	2	10		38
1		3	4				8*		9	11				12	7		5	6	2	10		39
1		3	10				8		9	11					7		5	6	2	4		40
1		3	4	5			8		9	11				10	7			6	2*	12		41
1		3		5			8	12	9					10*	7		6		2	11	4	42
42	8	36	25	37	5	21	41	13	36	40	8	1	2	25	37	2	7	32	29	5	10	
			+ 4s				+ 4s		+ 4s	+ 3s				+ 4s		+ 2s		+ 1s	+ 2s			

PRESTON NORTH END—PLAYERS

Player and position	Ht	Wt	Birthplace	Clubs	League Appearances	Goals
Goalkeepers						
Roy Tunks	6 0	12 0	Wuppertall	Rotherham J	138	—
				York C (on loan)	4	—
				Ipswich T (on loan)	—	—
				Newcastle U (on loan)	—	—
				Preston NE	196	—
John Kilner	6 0	11 7	Bolton	Preston NE	—	—
				Halifax T (on loan)	21	—
Peter Litchfield	6 2	13 7	Manchester	Droylsden	—	—
				Preston NE	—	—
Defenders						
John McMahon	5 9	11 2	Manchester	Preston NE	256+1	7
				Southend U (on loan)	4	—
Michael Baxter	6 1	11 12	Birmingham	Preston NE	130+1	10
Daniel Cameron	5 7	11 7	Dundee	Sheffield W	31	1
				Colchester U (on loan)	5	—
				Preston NE	90+2	—
Harry Wilson	5 9½	10 12	Hetton-le-Hole	Burnley	12	—
				Brighton	130	4
				Preston NE	26+4	—
Steve Uzelac	5 11	11 4	Doncaster	Doncaster R	182+3	9
				Mansfield T (on loan)	2	—
				Liverpool	—	—
				Preston NE	9	—
				Coventry C	—	—
Brian Taylor	5 10	11 7	Gateshead	Walsall	204+12	25
				Plymouth Arg	34+1	5
				Preston NE	29+1	—
Donald O'Riordan	6 0	11 12	Dublin	Derby Co	2+4	1
				Doncaster R (on loan)	2	—
				Preston NE	32	—
Midfield						
Alex Bruce	5 8	10 3	Dundee	Preston NE	55+7	22
				Newcastle U	16+4	3
				Preston NE	169+2	87
Francis Burns (Scotland)	5 8	10 10	Coatbridge	Manchester U	111+8	6
				Southampton	20+1	—
				Preston NE	215	11
Stephen Doyle	5 9	10 12	Neath	Preston NE	104+16	4
Ricky Thomson	5 9	10 8	Edinburgh	Preston NE	49+10	14
Jimmy Brown	5 10	11 10	Birmingham	Aston V	72+4	2
(Contract cancelled July 1978)				Preston NE	64	3
Gordon Coleman	5 8	10 7	Nottingham	Preston NE	158+12	18
Alan Spavin	5 8	11 4	Lancaster	Preston NE	414+10	26
Sean Haslegrave	5 9	9 2	Stoke	Stoke C	106+7	5
				Nottingham F	5+2	1
				Preston NE	79	1
Graham Bell	5 9	10 6	Middleton	Oldham Ath	166+4	9
				Preston NE	10	1
Andrew McAteer	5 9½	10 12	Preston	Preston NE	—	—
Eric Potts	5 6	10 5	Liverpool	Sheffield W	143+17	21
				Brighton	19+14	5
				Preston NE	25+4	4
Forwards						
Mike Robinson	5 11	12 0	Leicester	Preston NE	45+3	15
John Smith	5 9	10 3	Coatbridge	Preston NE	80+11	4
(Contract cancelled April 1979)						
John Cochrane	5 9	10 5	Bellshill	Preston NE	3+2	2
Jimmy Campbell	5 11	12 0	Warminster	Portadown	(not known)	
(Contract cancelled June 1978)				Preston NE	—	—
Graham Houston	5 8	10 4	Gibraltar	Preston NE	—	—
Stephen Elliott	5 11	11 10	Haltwistle North'land	Nottingham F	4	—
				Preston NE	5+2	—

(Free Transfer: *Alan Byrom)

QUEEN'S PARK RANGERS DIV. 2

Chairman: J. A. Gregory.   *Vice Chairman:* J. C. Gregory.
Directors: R. A. Starnes F.C.I.S., A. D. Farmer M.P.S., B. A. V. Henson F.C.A., S. P. Daverin, L. W. Parris A.C.C.A., A. Williamson.
Manager: Tommy Docherty.
Secretary: R. J. Phillips, F.A.A.I.
Assistant Manager: Gordon Clark.
Year Formed: 1885.   *Turned Professional:* 1898.
Limited Company: 1899.
Previous Name: 1885–87, St. Jude's; 1887, became Queen's Park Rangers.
Previous Grounds: 1885, Welford's Fields; 1888, London Scottish Ground, Brondesbury: Home Farm: Kensal Rise Green: Gun Club, Wormwood Scrubs: Kilburn Cricket Ground; 1899, Kensal Rise Athletic Ground; 1901, Latimer Road, Notting Hill; 1904, Agricultural Society, Park Royal; 1907, Park Royal Ground; 1917, Loftus Road; 1931, White City; 1933, Loftus Road; 1962, White City; 1963, Loftus Road.
Football League Record:
1920 Original Members of Division 3.
1921 Division 3(S).
1948–52 Division 2.
1952–58 Division 3(S).
1958–67 Division 3.
1967–68 Division 2.
1968–69 Division 1.
1969–73 Division 2.
1973–79 Division 1.
1979– Division 2.

Honours: *Football League*, best season in Division 1: 2nd, 1975–76. Division 2, Runners-up: 1967–68, 1972–73. Division 3(S), Champions: 1947–48; Runners-up: 1946–47. Division 3, Champions: 1966–67. *F.A. Cup:* best season: 6th Rd. (or equivalent) 1910, 1914, 1923, 1948, 1970, 1974. *Football League Cup*, Winners: 1966–67. Double: 1966–67, won Division 3 and Football League Cup. **European Competitions:** UEFA Cup 1976-77.
Record Victory: 9-2 v Tranmere R., Division 3, December 3rd, 1960.
Record Defeat: 1-8 v Mansfield T., Division 3, Mar. 15th, 1965, and 1-8 v Manchester U. Division 1, Mar. 19, 1969.
Most League Points: 67, Division 3, 1966–67.
Most League Goals: 111, Division 3, 1961–62.
Highest League Scorer in Season: George Goddard, 37, Division 3(S), 1929–30.
Most League Goals in Total Aggregate: George Goddard, 172, 1926–34.
Most Capped Player: Don Givens, 21 (47), Eire.
Most League Appearances: Tony Ingham, 519, 1950–63.
Record Transfer Fee Received: £527,000 from West Ham U. for Phil Parkes, February 1979
Record Transfer Fee Paid: £250,000 to Everton for Mickey Walsh, March 1979.
Managers Since the War: Dave Mangnall, Jack Taylor, Alec Stock, Tommy Docherty, Les Allen, Gordon Jago, Dave Sexton, Frank Sibley, Steve Burtenshaw.
Address of Supporters Club: c/o Football Club.
Address of Club Shop or Boutique: Supporters Club Shop, Queen's Park Rangers F.C., South Africa Road, London W.12.

South Africa Road, W12 7PA. Telephone 01-743-2618/2670 (01-743-3478/9 Box Office).
Telegraphic address: 'Queu Pear'. *Ground capacity:* 30,000 (23,000 covered).   *Record attendance:* 35,353 v Leeds U., F.L., April 28, 1974. *Record receipts:* £37,931 v Manchester U., Division 1, April 19, 1977. *Pitch measurements:* 112yds × 72yds.
How to get there: Buses 12 and 207. Nos. 11, 49, 72, 88, 105, 220 go near Shepherd's Bush (Metropolitan and Central Lines) and White City (Central Line—five to ten minutes walk).
Match tickets: Seats bookable one month in advance of the match.
Car parking: No club car park, but the White City park, adjacent to the ground, is recommended. Limited parking in side-streets.
Entertainments/catering facilities: Various bars around the ground.
Club shop: Programme shop in South Africa Road and kiosks inside the ground.
Handbooks/programmes: Available from programme shop.
Extra information: Queen's Park Rangers have had more home grounds than any other present Football League club; 12 in all, plus one game at Highbury in 1930.
Club Colours: Blue and white hooped shirts, white shorts, white stockings.
Change Colours: Red and white halved shirts, black shorts, black socks.
Club Captain:
First Team Trainer: Ken Shellito.
Club Nickname: 'Rangers' or 'R's.

QUEENS PARK RANGERS 1978-79 LEAGUE RECORD

Match No.	Date	Venue	Opponents	Result	H/T Score	League Pos'n	Goalscorers	Attendance
1	Aug 19	A	Liverpool	L 1-2	1-1	—	McGee	50,793
2	22	H	WBA	L 0-1	0-0	—		15,481
3	26	H	Nottingham F	D 0-0	0-0	19		17,971
4	Sept 2	A	Arsenal	L 1-5	0-4	22	McGee	33,474
5	9	H	Manchester U	D 1-1	1-0	22	Gillard	23,477
6	16	A	Middlesbrough	W 2-0	1-0	17	Harkouk, Eastoe	12,822
7	23	H	Aston Villa	W 1-0	0-0	15	Harkouk	16,410
8	30	A	Wolverhampton W	L 0-1	0-0	16		14,250
9	Oct 7	H	Bristol C	W 1-0	0-0	15	Busby	15,707
10	14	A	Southampton	D 1-1	0-1	13	Goddard	22,803
11	21	H	Everton	D 1-1	0-1	13	Gillard	21,171
12	28	A	Ipswich T	L 1-2	0-1	16	Francis	20,428
13	Nov 4	H	Chelsea	D 0-0	0-0	15		22,876
14	11	H	Liverpool	L 1-3	1-2	17	Eastoe	26,626
15	18	A	Nottingham F	D 0-0	0-0	16		28,036
16	25	A	Derby Co	L 1-2	0-1	18	Howe	19,702
17	Dec 2	H	Bolton W	L 1-3	0-3	18	Harkouk	11,635
18	9	A	Coventry C	L 0-1	0-0	19		18,717
19	16	H	Manchester C	W 2-1	0-0	18	Hamilton 2	12,902
20	26	A	Tottenham H	D 2-2	1-1	19	Bowles (pen), Shanks	24,845
21	30	H	Leeds U	L 1-4	0-1	19	Eastoe	17,435
22	Jan 20	H	Middlesbrough	D 1-1	0-0	19	Goddard	9899
23	31	A	Norwich C	D 1-1	0-1	—	Francis	14,203
24	Feb 10	A	Wolverhampton W	D 3-3	0-1	19	Roeder, Busby, Gillard	11,814
25	13	H	Arsenal	L 1-2	0-0	—	Shanks	21,125
26	24	H	Southampton	L 0-1	0-1	20		13,636
27	28	A	Manchester U	L 0-2	0-1	—		36,085
28	Mar 3	A	Everton	L 1-2	0-2	20	Goddard	24,809
29	6	A	Birmingham C	L 1-3	0-0	—	Busby	12,650
30	17	H	Chelsea	W 3-1	1-1	19	Goddard, Roeder, Busby	25,871
31	20	H	Aston Villa	L 1-3	0-1	—	Allen	24,310
32	24	A	WBA	L 1-2	0-1	20	McGee	23,678
33	31	H	Derby Co	D 2-2	2-1	20	Goddard, Walsh	13,988
34	Apr 3	A	Bristol C	L 0-2	0-0	—		15,687
35	7	A	Bolton W	L 1-2	1-1	20	Goddard	21,119
36	13	H	Norwich C	D 0-0	0-0	—		14,654
37	14	A	Tottenham H	D 1-1	1-1	20	Clement	28,853
38	21	A	Manchester C	L 1-3	1-1	20	Busby	30,694
39	28	H	Coventry C	W 5-1	1-1	20	Allen 3, Shanks, Walsh (pen)	10,950
40	May 4	A	Leeds U	L 3-4	2-1	—	Walsh, Roeder, Busby	20,121
41	7	H	Birmingham C	L 1-3	1-1	—	Roeder	9600
42	11	H	Ipswich T	L 0-4	0-2	—		9819

Final League Position: 20

Goalscorers

League (45): Busby 6, Goddard 6, Allen 4, Roeder 4, Eastoe 3, McGee 3, Gillard 3, Harkouk 3, Shanks 3, Walsh 3 (1 pen), Francis 2, Hamilton 2, Bowles 1 (pen), Clement 1, Howe 1.

League Cup (5): Eastoe 3, McGee 1, Own Goal 1.

League Cup:	Second Round	Preston N E (a)	3-1
	Third Round	Swansea C (h)	2-0
	Fourth Round	Leeds U (h)	0-2
F.A. Cup:	Third Round	Fulham (a)	0-2

Parkes	Clement	Gillard	Busby	Howe	Hollins	McGee	Francis	Eastoe	Shanks	Bowles	James	Roeder	Harkouk	Goddard	Cunningham	Abbott	Richardson	Allen	Wallace	Hamilton	Elsey	Walsh	Match No.
1	2	3	4	5	6	7	8	9	10	11													1
1	2	3	9*	5	4	12	8	7	6	10	11												2
1		3	9	5	4*11		8	7	6	10		2	12										3
1		3	11	5	6	7	8	9	2	10		4											4
1		3	6	5	4	11	8	7	2	10			9*12										5
1		3	9*	5	4	11		7	2	10			8		6	12							6
1		3	9	5	4	11		7	2	10			8		6								7
		3		5	4	11	8	7	2	10			9		6*12	1							8
1		3	12	5	4	11	8	7	2	10			9*	6									9
1		3*	8	5	4	11		7	2	10			9	12	6								10
1		3	6	5	4	11	8	7	2	10			9										11
1		3	6	5	4	12	8*	7	2	10			9	11									12
1		3	6	5	4	8		7*	2	10			9	11	12								13
1	2	3	8	5	4	9		7	6	10			11										14
1	2	3	9	5	4		8	7	6	10				11									15
1	2	3	9	5	6	12	8	7	4				10		11*								16
1	2	3	10	5	4	11*	8	7	6				9			12							17
1	2	3*10		5	4		7	6				8	11	12		9							18
1	2	3		5	4		8*	9	7	10			6	11		12							19
1	2	3		5	6	12		8	7	10			4	11*		9							20
1	2	3		5*	4		8	7	10			6	11		12	9							21
1	2	3		5	6		8	7	10			4	11			9							22
1	2	3	12	5	4		8	7*10				6	11			9							23
1	2	3	12	5*	4		8	7	10			6	11			9							24
1	2	3	6		4		8	7	10			5	11			9							25
	2	3	6		4		8	7	10			5	11		1	12		9*					26
	2	3	6		4		8	9	7	10			5	11	1								27
	2	3		5	4		8	9*	7	10			6	11	1			12					28
	2*	3	12	5	4		8	9	7	10			6	11	1								29
	2	3	12	5	4		8	9	7	10			6	11*	1								30
	2	3	11	5	4		8	9*	7	10			6			1	12						31
	2	3	9	5	4	10	8	7					6			1			11				32
	2	3*12		5	4		8		7	10			6		11	1						9	33
	2		8	5	6	10		7*					4		11	1	12	3				9	34
	2		10	5	4	7	8						6		11			3				9	35
	2		10	5	4	7		8					6		11	1	12	3*				9	36
	2		7	5	4		8		3	10			6		11	1						9	37
	2	3	4	5		10	8	7					6		11	1						9	38
	2	3	7	5	4			8					6		10	1	11					9	39
		3	7	5	4		8		2				6		10*	1	11		12	9			40
		3		5	4		8		2				6		11	1	10	12		7*	9		41
	2	3	7		4		8		6				5		11	1	10				9		42
24	29	38	29	38	41	18	31	26	41	30	1	27	14	20	9	—	18	4	4	8	2	10	
				+ 6s			+ 4s						+ 1s	+ 3s		+ 2s		+ 6s	+ 1s	+ 3s	+ 1s		

QUEENS PARK RANGERS—PLAYERS

Player and position	Ht	Wt	Birthplace	Clubs	League Appearances	Goals
Goalkeepers						
Derek Richardson	6 1	14 4	London	Chelsea	—	—
				QPR	31	—
Peter Hucker	6 3	14 6	London	QPR		
				Cambridge U	(on loan)	
Defenders						
David Clement (England)	5 10	11 5	London	QPR	403+3	22
Ian Gillard (England)	5 11	12 0	London	QPR	287+3	7
Don Shanks	5 9	10 8	London	Luton T	89+1	2
				QPR	97+4	6
Ron Abbott	6 0	11 0	London	QPR	32+14	4
Ernie Howe	6 1	12 12	London	C Palace	—	—
				Fulham	68+2	10
				QPR	61	2
Glenn Roeder	6 1	12 4½	Woodford	Orient	107+8	4
				QPR	27	4
Midfield						
John Hollins (England)	5 8	11 7	Guildford	Chelsea	436	47
				QPR	148+3	5
Barry Wallace	5 9½	11 4	Plaistow	West Ham U	—	—
				QPR	12+6	—
*Bobby Hale			Hammersmith	QPR	—	—
Karl Elsey	5 10	11 6	Pembroke	QPR	2+1	—
Gerry Francis (England)	5 10	10 8	Hammersmith	QPR	290+5	53
Forwards						
Stan Bowles (England)	5 10	11 4	Manchester	Manchester C	15+2	2
				Bury	5	—
				Crewe A	51	18
				Carlisle U	33	12
				QPR	239	68
Phil Nutt	5 11	11 8	London	QPR	0+4	1
Paul Goddard	5 8½	11 4	Harlington	QPR	23+7	7
Martyn Busby	6 1	12 4	Slough	QPR	71+7	6
				Portsmouth (on loan)	6+1	—
				Notts Co	37	4
				QPR	48+8	9
Paul McGee (Eire)	5 9	11 7	Sligo	Sligo R	—	—
				QPR	31+8	7
Billy Hamilton (N Ireland)	6 1½	12 0	Belfast	Linfield	—	—
				QPR	8+3	2
Rachid Harkouk	6 0	12 4	Chelsea	C Palace	51+3	21
				QPR	14+1	3
Mickey Walsh (Eire)	5 9	11 5	Chorley	Blackpool	172+8	72
				Everton	18+2	1
				QPR	10	3
Clive Allen	5 10	11 0	London	QPR	4+6	4

Free transfer: *Craig Richards

READING

DIV. 3

Chairman: F. V. Waller.
Directors: L. Davies, J. Brooks, K. Parvall, F. J. Briggs, R. Palfreyman.
Manager: Maurice Evans.
Secretary/Manager: R. Bentley.
Year Formed: 1871. **Turned Professional:** 1895.
Limited Company: 1895.
Previous Grounds: 1871, Reading Recreation; Reading Cricket Ground, 1882, Coley Park; 1889, Caversham Cricket Ground; 1896, Elm Park.
Football League Record: 1920 Original Member of Division 3. 1921–26 Division 3(S). 1926–31 Division 2. 1931–58 Division 3(S). 1958–71 Division 3. 1971–76 Division 4. 1976–77 Division 3. 1977–79 Division 4. 1979– Division 3.
Honours: *Football League*, best season in Division 2: 14th, 1926–27. Division 3(S), Champions: 1925–26; Runners-up: 1931–32, 1934–35, 1948–49, 1951–52. Division 4, Champions 1978–79. *F.A. Cup*, best season: semi-finalists, 1927. *Football League Cup*, best season: 4th Rd., 1965, 1966, 1978.

Record Victory: 10-2 v C. Palace, Division 3(S), 1946–47.

Record Defeat: 0-18 v Preston N.E., F.A. Cup, 1st Rd., 1893–94.

Most League Points: 65, Division 4, 1978–79.

Most League Goals: 112, Division 3(S), 1951–52.

Highest League Scorer in Season: Ronnie Blackman, 39, Division 3(S), 1951–52.

Most League Goals in Total Aggregate: Ronnie Blackman, 156, 1947–54.

Most Capped Player: Pat McConnell, 8, Ireland.

Most League Appearances: Dick Spiers, 453, 1955–70.

Record Transfer Fee Received: £60,000 from Southampton for Tommy Jenkins, Dec. 1969.

Record Transfer Fee Paid: £20,000 to West Ham U. for Steve Death, Sept. 1970.

Managers Since the War: Joe Edelston, Ted Drake, Jack Smith, Harry Johnston, Roy Bentley, Jack Mansell, Charlie Hurley.

Address of Supporters Club: Reading Football Supporters Club, Elm Park, Norfolk Road, Reading.

Elm Park, Norfolk Road, Reading. Telephone Reading 57878/9/0. *Ground capacity:* 27,200. *Record attendance:* 33,042 v Brentford, F.A. Cup 5th Rd., February 19, 1927. *Record receipts:* £25,972 v Southampton, League Cup, 4th Rd., November, 8 1978. *Pitch measurements:* 112 yds × 77yds.

How to get there: Corporation specials from St. Mary's Butts (town centre) and from Northumberland Avenue. Usual buses within a few minutes of the ground. Nearest railway station, Reading.
Match tickets: Stand tickets are bookable in advance for all first-team matches 14 days before the match.
Car parking: Space is available for approximately 300 cars adjoining the ground entrance in Norfolk Road and Tilehurst Road.
Entertainments/catering facilities: Catering is available in each of the five stands and also on the terraces
Club shop: Shops in Norfolk Road and on the West Terrace are open on match days selling all types of souvenirs.
Handbooks/programmes: The Supporters' Club produce a handbook and these are available on application to the club. Unsold programmes are available after each match at the programme shop on the West Terrace.
Extra information: Reading first appeared in the F.A. Cup 1st Rd. in 1877; only Notts County of the present League clubs played so long ago.
Club Colours: Blue and white hoops, white shorts, white stockings, two blue rings.
Change Colours: Yellow.
First Team Trainer: Stewart Henderson.
Club Nickname: 'The Royals'.

READING 1978-79 LEAGUE RECORD

Match No.	Date	Venue	Opponents	Result	H/T Score	League Pos'n	Goalscorers	Attendance
1	Aug 19	A	Grimsby T	W 2-1	2-0	—	Earles, Kearns	3918
2	23	H	Rochdale	W 2-0	1-0	—	Earles, Hetzke	4267
3	26	H	Wigan Ath	W 2-0	1-0	2	Kearns (pen), Sanchez	4788
4	Sept 2	A	Huddersfield T	D 1-1	0-1	2	Sanchez	2951
5	9	H	Newport Co	W 2-1	1-1	2	Kearns 2 (1 a pen)	5089
6	13	A	Hereford U	D 0-0	0-0	—		3526
7	16	H	Doncaster R	W 3-0	1-0	2	Bowman, Kearns 2 (1 a pen)	4867
8	23	A	Wimbledon	L 0-1	0-0	3		5001
9	27	H	Torquay U	W 1-0	1-0	—	Bowman (pen)	5722
10	30	A	Barnsley	L 1-3	0-0	3	Bowman (pen)	10,058
11	Oct 7	H	Bradford C	W 3-0	1-0	3	Hetzke, Kearney, Sanchez	5651
12	14	A	Northampton T	D 2-2	0-0	3	Earles 2	4694
13	17	A	Darlington	W 2-1	1-1	—	Sanchez, Kearney	1821
14	21	H	York C	W 3-0	1-0	2	Lewis, Kearney, Hetzke	12,031
15	28	H	Stockport Co	D 3-3	3-3	2	Bowman (pen), Earles, Hetzke	7054
16	Nov 4	A	Scunthorpe U	W 3-0	1-0	1	Peters, Earles, Czuczman (og)	2424
17	11	H	Huddersfield T	D 1-1	1-0	2	Hetzke	6870
18	18	A	Wigan Ath	L 0-3	0-1	2		5858
19	Dec 6	H	Crewe Alex	W 3-0	2-0	—	Bowman 2 (1 a pen), Kearney	4643
20	9	A	Halifax T	D 0-0	0-0	2		1401
21	23	A	Portsmouth	L 0-4	0-2	3		12,541
22	26	H	AFC Bournemouth	W 1-0	0-0	—	Kearney	6706
23	Jan 13	A	Newport Co	L 2-3	2-1	3	Earles, Kearney	5968
24	Feb 3	A	Torquay U	D 1-1	1-0	5	Earles	3495
25	6	A	Aldershot	D 2-2	2-2	—	Lewis, Bowman (pen)	7732
26	10	H	Barnsley	W 1-0	1-0	3	Bennett	6604
27	21	H	Hereford U	W 3-0	2-0	—	Hetzke, Bowman, Earles	5639
28	24	H	Northampton T	W 5-1	1-0	1	Earles, Hetzke, Kearney, Bowman, Kearns	6070
29	26	H	Hartlepool U	W 3-1	2-0	—	Earles 2, Kearns	6812
30	Mar 3	A	York C	W 1-0	1-0	1	Earles	2654
31	9	A	Stockport Co	D 0-0	0-0	1		3560
32	13	A	Bradford C	W 3-2	1-0	—	Kearns, Kearney, Earles	3387
33	16	H	Scunthorpe U	L 0-1	0-0	1		5144
34	20	A	Doncaster R	D 2-2	1-0	—	Kearney, Lewis	2487
35	24	A	Rochdale	L 0-1	0-1	2		1565
36	28	H	Grimsby T	W 4-0	2-0	—	Alexander 4	8394
37	31	H	Port Vale	D 0-0	0-0	1		6503
38	Apr 7	A	Crewe Alex	W 2-0	2-0	2	Kearney, Alexander	1856
39	13	H	Portsmouth	W 2-0	1-0	—	Lewis, Shipley	15,054
40	14	A	AFC Bournemouth	D 0-0	0-0	1		5638
41	16	H	Aldershot	W 4-0	2-0	—	Kearns 2, Alexander, Hetzke	13,273
42	21	A	Hartlepool U	D 0-0	0-0	2		2499
43	25	H	Darlington	W 1-0	1-0	—	Bowman	7117
44	28	H	Halifax T	W 1-0	1-0	1	Hetzke	7408
45	May 2	H	Wimbledon	W 1-0	1-0	—	Alexander	13,131
46	5	A	Port Vale	W 3-0	1-0	1	Hicks, Earles, Alexander	3603

Final League Position: 1

Goalscorers

League (76): Earles 15, Kearns 11 (3 pens), Bowman 10 (5 pens), Kearney 10, Hetzke 9, Alexander 8, Lewis 4, Sanchez 4, Bennett 1, Hicks 1, Peters 1, Shipley 1, Own Goal 1.
League Cup (9): Earles 4, Hetzke 2, Kearns, Lewis, Own Goal 1.
F.A. Cup (5): Kearney 3, Lewis, Alexander.

League Cup	First Round	Gillingham (h)	3-1
		(a)	2-1
	Second Round	Wolverhampton W (h)	1-0
	Third Round	Rotherham U (a)	2-2
		(h)	1-0
	Fourth Round	Southampton (h)	0-0
		(a)	0-2
F.A. Cup	First Round	Gillingham (h)	0-0
		(a)	2-1 (a.e.t.)
	Second Round	Portsmouth (a)	1-0
	Third Round	Notts Co (a)	2-4

Death	Peters	White	Bowman	Hicks	Hetzke	Earles	Williams	Kearns	Sanchez	Lewis	Bennett	Britten	Kearney	Alexander	Wanklyn	Shipley	Match No.
1	2	3	4	5	6	7	8	9	10	11							1
1	2	3	4	5	8	7		9	10	11	6						2
1	2	3	4	5	8	7		9	10	11	6						3
1	2	3	4	5	8	7		9*	10	11	6	12					4
1	2	3	4	5	8	7		9	10	11	6						5
1	2	3	4	5	8	7		9	10	11	6						6
1	2	3	4	5	8*	7		9	10	11	6	12					7
1	2	3	4	5	8	7		9*	10	11	6	12					8
1	2	3	4	5	8	7			10	11	6	9					9
1	2	3	4	5	8	7			10	11	6	9					10
1	2	3	4	5	8	7			10	11	6	9					11
1	2	3	4*	5	8	7		12	10	11	6	9					12
1	2	3	4	5	8	7			10	11	6	9					13
1	2	3	4	5	8	7			10	11	6	9					14
1	2	3	4	5	8	7		12	10*	11	6	9					15
1	2	3	4	5	8	7		10		11	6	9					16
1	2	3	4	5	8	7			10	11	6	9					17
1	2	3	4	5	8	7		12	10*	11	6	9					18
1	2	3	4	5		12		8*	10	11	6	9	7				19
1	2	3	4	5		8			10	11	6	9	7				20
1	2	3	4	5	8	11		12	10		6	9	7*				21
1	2	3	4	5		8			10		6	9	7	11			22
1	2	3	4	5	8	7			10	11	6	9					23
1	2	3	4	5		7		8		11	6	9		10			24
1	2	3	4	5	8	7			12	11	6	9		10*			25
1	2	3	4	5	8	7			12	11	6	9		10*			26
1	2	3	4	5	8	7				11	6	9		10			27
1	2	3	4	5	8*	7		12		11	6	9		10			28
1	2	3	4*	5	8	7		9		11	6		12	10			29
1	2	3		5	4	7		8*	12	11	6	9		10			30
1		3		5	2	7		8	4	11	6	9		10			31
1	2	3		5	4	7		8	12	11	6	9		10*			32
1	2	3		5	4	7		8	12	11	6	9*		10			33
1	2	3		5	4	7		9		11	6	8		10			34
1	2	3		5	4	7		9*		11	6	8		10	12		35
1	2	3		5	8				4	11	6	9	7	10			36
1	2	3		5	8*			12	4	11	6	9	7	10			37
1	2	3		5	8				4	11	6	9	7	10			38
1	2	3		5	8				4	11	6	9	7	10			39
1	2	3		5	8				4	11	6	9	7	10			40
1	2	3		5	8			9	4	11	6		7	10			41
1	2	3	4	5	8				9	11	6		7	10			42
1	2	3	4	5	8	12		9*	11		6		7	10			43
1	2	3	4	5	8	9		12	11		6		7*	10			44
1	2	3	4	5	9	7			11		6		8	10			45
1	2	3	4	5	9	7			11		6		8	10			46
46	45	46	34	46	42	37	1	20	34	40	45	—	31	15	13	11	
						+2s		+7s	+5s		+1s	+2s	+1s		+1s		

READING—PLAYERS

Player and position	Ht	Wt	Birthplace	Clubs	League Appearances	Goals
Goalkeepers						
Steve Death	5 7½	11 0	Elmswell	West Ham U	1	—
				Reading	382	—
*Paul McCullough	6 0	12 5	Birmingham	Torquay U	—	—
				Reading	—	—
Defenders						
Martin Hicks	6 3	13 6	Stratford-upon-Avon	Charlton Ath	—	—
				Reading	65	2
Dave Moreline	5 9	10 8	Stepney	Fulham	63+7	—
				Reading	121	—
Stewert Henderson	5 6	10 11	Bridge of Allan	Chelsea	—	—
				Brighton	201	1
				Reading	138+5	6
Paul Bennett	6 0	12 6	Southampton	Southampton	116	1
				Reading	105	3
Stephen Hetzke	6 2	11 10	Marlborough	Reading	135+6	14
Gary Peters	5 11	11 12	Carshalton	Reading	150+6	7
Mark White	5 9	11 0	Sheffield	Sheffield W	—	—
				Reading	71	—
Wayne Wanklyn	5 7	10 7	Hull	Reading	15+2	—
Midfield						
Richie Bowman	5 6	10 1	London	Charlton Ath	93+3	7
				Reading	105	16
Alan Lewis	5 8	10 12	Oxford	Derby Co	2	—
				Peterborough U (on loan)	10	—
				Brighton	3	—
				Sheffield W (on loan)	—	—
				Reading	73+1	5
*Martyn Britten	5 7	10 7	Bristol	Bristol R	17+3	2
				Reading	6+2	—
Forwards						
Pat Earles	5 7½	10 10	Titchfield	Southampton	4+8	1
				Reading	103+2	35
Jerry Williams	5 11	11 10	Didcot	Reading	11+8	2
Ollie Kearns	6 0	12 0	Banbury	Reading	51+8	29
Mike Kearney	6 0	12 0	Glasgow	Shrewsbury T	143+6	41
				Chester	37+1	5
				Reading	46+7	12
Lawrie Sanchez	6 1	11 11	Reading	Reading	41+6	5
John Alexander	5 11	11 0	Liverpool	Millwall	10+5	2
				Reading	15+1	8

ROCHDALE DIV. 4

Joint Chairmen: F. S. Ratcliffe, B. A. Hindle.
Directors: T. Butterworth, J. B. Foulkes, E. Lord, S. Marks D. H. Wrigley
General Manager: H. Carter.
Player/Manager: Doug Collins.   *Secretary:* J. Butterfield.
Year Formed: 1907.   *Turned Professional:* 1907.
Limited Company: 1910.
Previous Name: Rochdale Town.

Football League Record:
1921 Elected to Division 3(N).   1969–74 Division 3.
1958–59 Division 3.   1974–   Division 4.
1959–69 Division 4.

Honours: Football League, best season in Division 3: 9th, 1969–70. Division 3(N), Runners-up: 1923–24, 1926–27. *F.A. Cup,* best season: 4th Rd., 1970–71. *Football League Cup:* Runners-up, 1962 (record for 4th Division Club).
Record Victory: 8-1 v Chesterfield, Division 3(N), Dec. 18th, 1926.
Record Defeat: 0-8 v Wrexham, Division 3(N), Dec. 28th, 1929.
Most League Points: 62, Division 3(N), 1923–24.
Most League Goals: 105, Division 3(N), 1926–27.
Highest League Scorer in Season: Albert Whitehurst, 44, Division 3(N), 1926–27.
Most League Goals in Total Aggregate: Albert Whitehurst, 117, 1923–28.
Most Capped Player: None.
Most League Appearances: Graham Smith, 317, 1966–74.
Record Transfer Fee Received: £40,000 plus Malcolm Darling from Norwich C. for David Cross, Oct. 1971.
Record Transfer Fee Paid: £12,000 to Sunderland for Alan Weir, June, 1979.
Managers Since the War: Ted Goodier, Jack Warner, Harry Catterick, Jack Marshall, Tony Collins, Bob Stokoe, Len Richley, Dick Conner, Walter Joyce, Brian Green, Mike Ferguson.
Address of Club Shop: Rochdale A.F.C. Soccer Shop, Spotland, Sandy Lane, Rochdale.

Spotland, Willbutts Lane, Rochdale. Telephone 44648/9. *Ground capacity:* 28,000. *Record attendance:* 24,231 v Notts County, F.A. Cup 2nd Rd., December 10, 1949. *Record receipts:* £3996.83p v Coventry C., F.A. Cup 3rd Rd., January 11, 1971. *Pitch measurements:* 113 yds × 75 yds.

How to get there: Football specials run from The Esplanade in the town centre, which is five minutes' walk from Rochdale railway station. Specials also run from the same place for evening matches.

Match tickets: Seats can be reserved in advance.

Car parking: Car parking at the ground and in the adjacent side-streets.

Entertainments/catering facilities: A social club in the car park.

Club shop: Sells all types of souvenirs.

Handbooks/programmes: Programmes not available on subscription.

Extra information: In 1931–32 the club lost 17 Division Three (North) games in a row.

Club Colours: Royal blue and green shirts with white trimmings, white shorts with blue stripe, blue stockings.

Change Colours: Yellow shirts, green shorts, yellow stockings.

Club Nickname: 'The Dale'.

ROCHDALE 1978–79 LEAGUE RECORD

Match No.	Date	Venue	Opponents	Result	H/T Score	League Pos'n	Goalscorers	Attendance
1	Aug 19	H	York C	L 1-2	0-1	—	Scaife	1241
2	23	A	Reading	L 0-2	0-1	—		4267
3	26	H	Aldershot	D 1-1	0-0	20	Owen	1026
4	Sept 2	A	Port Vale	D 1-1	0-0	20	Owen	3220
5	9	H	Portsmouth	L 0-2	0-2	23		1479
6	13	A	Wigan Ath	L 0-3	0-1	—		5746
7	16	A	AFC Bournemouth	L 1-3	1-2	24	Owen	2674
8	23	H	Hereford U	L 0-2	0-2	24		1068
9	25	H	Wimbledon	D 0-0	0-0	—		1263
10	30	A	Grimsby T	L 0-4	0-2	24		3681
11	Oct 7	H	Halifax T	D 1-1	0-1	24	Hoy	1579
12	14	A	Torquay U	D 1-1	1-0	23	Scaife	2873
13	17	A	Newport Co	D 0-0	0-0	—		3472
14	21	H	Darlington	W 2-1	1-1	23	Owen, Esser	1272
15	28	A	Hartlepool U	L 1-5	0-2	23	Esser	3074
16	Nov 4	H	Crewe Alex	W 2-1	0-1	23	Hoy 2 (1 a pen)	1325
17	11	H	Port Vale	L 0-1	0-0	23		1882
18	18	A	Aldershot	L 0-1	0-1	23		3043
19	Dec 2	A	Doncaster R	L 0-1	0-1	23		1750
20	9	H	Barnsley	L 0-3	0-3	23		3136
21	26	A	Bradford C	L 0-1	0-0	—		4882
22	30	A	Scunthorpe U	W 4-0	2-0	23	Jones, Hoy 2, Owen	2620
23	Jan 13	A	Portsmouth	D 1-1	0-0	23	Owen	11,595
24	Feb 3	A	Wimbledon	L 2-3	2-1	23	Jones, Hoy	3166
25	Mar 3	A	Darlington	W 2-0	1-0	23	Jones, Esser	1495
26	10	H	Hartlepool U	D 1-1	0-1	23	Hoy (pen)	1931
27	13	H	Grimsby T	L 2-5	2-2	—	Jones, Snookes	2345
28	19	H	Wigan Ath	L 0-2	0-1	—		3621
29	21	A	Hereford U	D 2-2	1-1	—	Jones 2	2351
30	24	H	Reading	W 1-0	1-0	23	Hoy	1565
31	27	A	York C	L 1-2	0-2	—	Owen	2295
32	31	A	Northampton T	L 0-1	0-0	23		1653
33	Apr 3	H	AFC Bournemouth	W 2-1	1-0	—	Jones, Scott	1136
34	7	H	Doncaster R	W 2-0	0-0	23	Owen 2	1606
35	11	H	Huddersfield T	L 0-2	0-1	—		2020
36	14	H	Bradford C	W 1-0	1-0	23	Scott	2262
37	16	A	Stockport Co	L 0-3	0-1	—		2863
38	17	A	Huddersfield T	L 0-1	0-1	—		3346
39	21	H	Scunthorpe U	W 1-0	1-0	22	Taylor	1224
40	23	H	Newport Co	W 1-0	0-0	—	Esser	1200
41	28	A	Barnsley	W 3-0	2-0	22	Owen 2, Hoy	12,051
42	May 1	H	Stockport Co	W 2-0	0-0	—	Esser, Hoy	2117
43	5	H	Northampton T	W 4-1	0-0	21	Oliver, Jones 2, O'Loughlin	1751
44	7	A	Halifax T	L 1-2	0-2	—	Hilditch	2150
45	9	H	Torquay U	W 1-0	1-0	—	Hilditch	2359
46	18	A	Crewe Alex	W 2-1	1-0	—	Jones, Hilditch	2036

Final League Position: 20

Goalscorers

League (47): Owen 11, Hoy 10 (2 pens), Jones 10, Esser 5, Hilditch 3, Scaife 2, Scott 2, Oliver 1 O'Loughlin 1, Snookes 1, Taylor 1.
League Cup (2): O'Loughlin, Ashworth.

League Cup	First Round	Crewe Alex (a)	0-1
		(h)	2-4
F.A. Cup	First Round	Droylesden (h)	0-1

Slack	Hallows	Snookes	Hart	Scott	Bannon	Scaife	Mullington	Ashworth	Owen	O'Loughlin	Esser	Shyne	Hoy	Hilditch	Price	Morrin	Felgate	Forster	Creamer	Taylor	Jones	Collins	Milne	Oliver	Match No.
1	2	3	4*	5	6	7	8	9	10	11	12														1
	2	3	4	5		6	10	9	7	11	12	1	8*												2
	2	3	4	5		6	10	9	7	11		1	8												3
	2	3	4	5		6		9	7	11	10	1	8												4
	2	3	4	5		6	12	9	7	11*	10	1	8												5
	2		4	5		6	10	12	7	3		1	8	9*11											6
	2		4		5	6	11		10	3		1	8	9 7											7
	2		4	5		6	7	12	11	3	8	1	10	9*											8
	2		4	5		6	11	9	7	3	10	1	8												9
	2	3	4	5		6		9		7	10	1	11	8											10
	2	3	4	5		6	11*		9	8	10		7	12		1									11
	2	3	4	5		6			7	11	10			9	8	1									12
	2	3	4	5		6			7	11	10	12	9*	8		1									13
	2	3	4	5		6		10	11	8		7	9			1									14
	2	3	4	5		6		7	11	10		9	12	8*		1									15
	2	3	4	5		6		9	11	10		7	12	8*		1									16
		3	4	5		6		9*	7	2	11	8	10	12		1									17
		3*	4	5	12	6		11	2	10		7	9	8		1									18
			4	5	2	6		7	3	10		8	9	11		1									19
			4	5	2	6		11	3	10		8*	9	7	1	12									20
		6*	5	12	4			10	8	11		7			1		2	3	9						21
		6	5	12	4*			10	8	11		7			1		3	2	9						22
	6		5	12	4			10	8	11*		7			1		2	3	9						23
	6		5	12	4			8*	10	11		7			1		2	3	9						24
	6		5		4			11	7	10		8			1		2	3	9*12						25
	6		5		4			11	7	10		8			1		2	3	9						26
	6		5*		4			8	10	11		7			1		2	3	9 12						27
		4		5	6			10	11	1		7	12				2	3	9 8*						28
	3	2			4			11	10			7			1		6	5	9 8						29
	6	2			4			11	7			8	12		1		3	5	9 10*						30
	3	2			4			11	10	8		7			1		6	5	9						31
	5	2		4	6*			10	8	11		7	12		1			3	9						32
	3	2	5		8			11	10	7					1		4	6	9						33
	6	2	3	7*				10	8	11			12		1		5	4	9						34
	3	2	5					11	10	8		12	7*		1		4	6	9						35
	6	2	5					11	8			7	9		1		4	3	10*12						36
		2	5					11	10	12		7	9		1		4*	6		8	3				37
		2		5				11	10	7		8	9		1		4	6			3				38
	2				6			8	4	11		7	9		1		5	3		10					39
	3	2		5				10	8	11		7	9		1		6			4					40
	6	2		4				10	8	11		7			1		5	9		3					41
	3	2		5				11	10	8		7			1		6	9		4					42
	6	2		5				10	11	7		9			1		3	8		4					43
	3	2		5				8	10	11		7	12		1		6	9				4*			44
7	3	2		5				10	8			11			1		12	6	9			4*			45
	2	3		5				10	8			7	11		1		12	6	9			4*			46
1	18	35	39	31	15	34	8	9	41	45	37	10	39	19	9	1	35	—	18	26	21	6	1	8	
				+5s	+1s	+2s			+3s	+2s	+8s	+1s			+1s	+2s				+2s	+1s				

ROCHDALE—PLAYERS

Player and position	Ht	Wt	Birthplace	Clubs	League Appearances	Goals
Goalkeepers						
*Chris Shyne	5 11		Rochdale	Rochdale	20	—
Andy Slack	5 9	11 7	Heywood	Rochdale	15	—
Peter Creamer	5 11	11 4	Hartlepool	Middlesbrough	9	—
(Non-contract)				York C (on loan)	4	—
				Doncaster R	31+1	—
				Hartlepool	170+5	9
				Rochdale	18+2	—
Defenders						
Paul Hallows	5 7	10 9	Chester	Bolton W	44+2	—
				Rochdale	192	2
Brian Hart	6 0	11 7	Farnworth	Rochdale	47	—
*Robert Scott	6 2½	13 4	Liverpool	Wrexham	14+4	—
				Reading (on loan)	5	—
				Hartlepool	37	—
				Rochdale	71	3
Ted Oliver	5 6	9 6	Manchester	Rochdale	17+3	1
Ian Bannon	6 0	12 9	Bury	Rochdale	80+6	—
Eric Snookes	5 7	10 0	Birmingham	Preston NE	20	1
				Crewe A	35+1	—
				Southport	106+4	2
				Rochdale	35	1
Brian Taylor	5 11	11 9	Hodthorpe	Middlesbrough	14+4	1
				Doncaster R	118+1	12
				Rochdale	26	1
Graham Wright				Rochdale	—	—
Midfield						
Nigel O'Loughlin	5 8½	10 10	Denbigh	Shrewsbury T	23+10	7
				Rochdale	130+2	9
*Tony Whelan	6 1	11 8	Salford	Manchester U	—	—
				Manchester C	3+3	—
				Rochdale	124	20
*John Price	5 10	11 0	Middlewich	Rochdale	10+2	—
				Burnley	—	—
*Tony Morrin	5 8	11 3	Swindon	Stockport Co	27+5	2
				Barrow	97+3	6
				Exeter C	180+12	15
				Stockport Co	13	1
				Rochdale	29+1	—
Doug Collins	5 8	9 9	Newton	Grimsby T	95+6	11
				Burnley	173+15	18
				Plymouth Arg	22+1	2
				Sunderland	4+2	—
				Rochdale	6+2	—
Mike Milne	5 9	11 0	Aberdeen	Sunderland	—	—
(Contract cancelled)				Rochdale	1+1	—
Phil Mullington	5 10	11 10	Oldham	Oldham Ath	—	—
(Contract cancelled)				Rochdale	59+7	6
				Crewe A	1	—
				Rochdale	8+1	—
Forwards						
David Esser	5 6	10 2	Bowden	Everton	—	—
				Rochdale	77+4	12
*Terry Owen	5 7	11 1	Liverpool	Everton	2	—
				Bradford C	41+11	6
				Chester	161+15	40
				Cambridge U	1	—
				Rochdale	80+3	21
Robert Scaife	6 0	12 4	Northallerton	Middlesbrough	—	—
				Halifax T (on loan)	5+1	1
				Hartlepool	77+3	10
				Rochdale	68	8
Bobby Hoy	5 7½	10 0	Halifax	Huddersfield T	140+4	20
				Blackburn R	13+6	—
				Halifax T	30	7
				York C	10+4	1
				Rochdale	48+2	11
Mark Hilditch				Rochdale	21+9	4
Phil Ashworth	6 0	12 0	Burnley	Blackburn R	—	—
				Bournemouth	30+1	2
				Workington	38+1	7
				Southport	22+2	9
				Rochdale	9+2	—
Chris Jones	5 10	12 3	Altrincham	Manchester C	6+1	2
				Swindon T	49+19	18
				Oldham Ath	3	1
				Walsall	54+5	14
				York C	94+1	33
				Huddersfield T	9+5	2
				Doncaster R	14+6	4
Geoff Forster				Darlington (on loan)	14+2	3
(Non-contract) 0+1				Rochdale	21	10

ROTHERHAM UNITED

DIV. 3

Chairman: Eric Purshouse.
Vice Chairman: L. D. Purshouse.
Director: C. R. Wright.
Manager: Jimmy McGuigan. *Secretary:* G. A. Somerton.
Year Formed: 1884. *Turned Professional:* 1905.
Limited Company: 1920.
Previous Names: 1884, Thornhill United; 1905, Rotherham County; 1925, amalgamated Rotherham Town under Rotherham United.
Previous Grounds: Red House Ground; 1907, Millmoor.
Football League Record:

1893	Elected to Division 2.	1951–68	Division 2.
1896	Failed re-election.	1968–73	Division 3.
1919	Re-elected to Division 2.	1973–75	Division 4.
1923–51 Division 3(N).		1975–	Division 3.

Honours: Football League, best season in Division 2: 3rd, 1954–55 (equal points with Champions and Runners-up). Division 3(N), Champions: 1950–51; Runners-up: 1946–47, 1947–48, 1948–49. *F.A. Cup,* best season: 5th Rd.. 1953, 1968. *Football League Cup,* best season, Runners-up: 1961.

Record Victory: 8-0 v Oldham Ath., Division 3(N), May 26th, 1947.

Record Defeat: 1-11 v Bradford C., Division 3(N), Aug. 25th, 1928.

Most League Points: 71, Division 3(N), 1950–51.

Most League Goals: 114, Division 3(N), 1946–47.

Highest League Scorer in Season: Wally Ardron, 38, Division 3(N), 1946–47.

Most League Goals in Total Aggregate: Gladstone Guest, 130, 1946–56.

Most Capped Player: Harold Millership, 6, Wales.

Most League Appearances: Danny Williams, 459, 1946–62.

Record Transfer Fee Received: £100,000 from Sunderland for Dave Watson, Dec. 1970.

Record Transfer Fee Paid: £27,000 to Sheffield W. for John Quinn, Nov. 1967.

Managers Since the War: Reg Freeman, Andy Smailes, Tom Johnston, Danny Williams, Jack Mansell, Tommy Docherty, Jimmy McAnearney.

Address of Supporters Club: Red and White Shop, c/o Millmoor, Rotherham.

Millmoor Ground, Rotherham. Telephone Rotherham 2434. *Telegraphic address:* 'Holmes Millmoor, Rotherham'. *Ground capacity:* 22,000. *Record attendance:* 25,000 v Sheffield U., Division 2, December 13, 1952 and v Sheffield W., Division 2, January 26, 1952. *Record receipts:* £16,146 v Barnsley, F.A. Cup 2nd Rd., replay January 9, 1979. *Pitch measurements:* 115 yds × 76 yds.

How to get there: Corporation buses from town centre. Also regular service buses from Sheffield to town centre. Nearest railway station, Rotherham on the line from Sheffield.
Match tickets: Seats can be reserved one month before the match.
Car parking: There are parks in Kimberworth Road and Main St. (the municipal car park); both are within easy reach of the ground.
Entertainments/catering facilities: There are refreshment kiosks on all four sides of the ground and also behind the grandstand, and the 'Windmill' where meals may be obtained if booked in advance, and drinks are served during licensing hours.
Club shop: Sited on the forecourt of the ground; stocks all types of souvenirs.
Handbooks/programmes: No handbook, but programmes may be obtained from the club or the club shop.
Extra information: Rotherham full-back Irvine Rhodes scored twice on his debut for Rotherham against Hartlepools in March 1937.

Club Colours: Red shirts, white collar, white sleeves, white (or black) shorts, red stockings.
Change Colours: Blue shirts and shorts with yellow trim, yellow stockings.
Club Coach: Charlie Bell.
Club Nickname: 'The Merry Millers'.

ROTHERHAM UNITED 1978-79 LEAGUE RECORD

Match No.	Date	Venue	Opponents	Result	H/T Score	League Pos'n	Goalscorers	Attendance
1	Aug 19	A	Gillingham	D 0-0	0-0	—		4157
2	26	H	Blackpool	W 2-1	2-0	11	Finney, Breckin	4572
3	Sept 2	A	Colchester U	D 0-0	0-0	10		2448
4	5	H	Hull C	L 0-2	0-2	—		6389
5	9	H	Lincoln C	W 2-0	1-0	8	Finney (pen), Smith	4427
6	12	A	Swansea C	D 4-4	3-1	—	Gwyther 3, Phillips	17,065
7	15	A	Southend U	L 1-2	0-0	10	Gwyther	6527
8	23	H	Mansfield T	W 2-0	0-0	9	Finney, Dawson	5350
9	26	H	Watford	W 2-1	0-1	—	Gwyther, Crawford	6442
10	30	A	Plymouth Arg	L 0-2	0-2	7		6705
11	Oct 7	H	Sheffield W	L 0-1	0-0	13		13,746
12	14	A	Swindon T	L 0-1	0-0	15		4476
13	17	H	Brentford	W 1-0	0-0	—	Flynn	3881
14	21	A	Carlisle U	D 1-1	0-0	12	Phillips	5085
15	28	H	Shrewsbury T	L 1-2	0-2	16	Phillips	4476
16	Nov 4	A	Walsall	W 1-0	1-0	14	Green	5456
17	11	H	Colchester U	W 1-0	1-0	10	Finney	3777
18	18	A	Blackpool	W 2-1	2-1	9	Phillips, Finney	6085
19	Dec 2	A	Oxford U	L 0-1	0-1	10		3311
20	9	H	Chesterfield	W 1-0	0-0	8	Gwyther	4935
21	23	H	Tranmere R	W 3-2	1-1	5	Crawford, Phillips 2	3829
22	26	A	Bury	L 2-3	0-2	7	Phillips 2	5852
23	Feb 3	A	Watford	D 2-2	2-0	10	Phillips, Gwyther	12,857
24	6	A	Southend U	W 2-1	2-1	—	Phillips, Finney (pen)	4478
25	10	H	Plymouth Arg	W 1-0	0-0	8	Gwyther	5237
26	24	H	Swindon T	L 1-3	0-1	10	Phillips	5128
27	Mar 3	H	Carlisle U	L 1-3	1-0	11	Finney	3908
28	6	H	Swansea C	L 0-1	0-0	—		3864
29	14	A	Chester	W 1-0	1-0	—	Gwyther	2473
30	24	A	Hull C	L 0-1	0-0	13		4717
31	27	H	Gillingham	D 1-1	0-1	—	Phillips	3239
32	31	A	Exeter C	L 0-2	0-0	15		3349
33	Apr 4	A	Lincoln C	L 0-3	0-0	—		3347
34	7	H	Oxford U	D 0-0	0-0	17		2734
35	14	H	Bury	W 2-1	1-0	17	Rhodes, Gwyther	2721
36	16	A	Peterborough U	D 1-1	1-0	—	Gwyther	3807
37	18	A	Tranmere R	D 1-1	0-0	—	Phillips	1256
38	21	H	Chester	L 0-1	0-1	16		2893
39	23	A	Brentford	L 0-1	0-1	—		6710
40	28	A	Chesterfield	L 0-1	0-1	18		4160
41	May 1	H	Peterborough U	D 1-1	0-0	—	Finney	2162
42	5	H	Exeter C	W 2-1	1-0	16	Young, Gwyther	2217
43	7	A	Sheffield W	L 1-2	1-1	—	Carr	12,094
44	10	A	Shrewsbury T	L 1-3	1-1	—	Gwyther	8450
45	14	H	Walsall	W 4-1	2-0	—	Finney, Smith (pen), Phillips, Waddington (og)	1996
46	19	A	Mansfield T	W 1-0	0-0	—	Smith (pen)	3913

Final League Position: 17

Goalscorers

League (49): Phillips 14, Gwyther 13, Finney 9 (2 pens), Smith 3 (2 pens), Crawford 2, Young 1, Carr 1, Dawson 1, Green 1, Rhodes 1, Flynn 1, Breckin 1, Own Goal 1.
League Cup (11): Finney 5 (1 pen), Gwyther 2, Crawford 2, Phillips, Green.
F.A. Cup (8): Gwyther 3, Breckin 2, Crawford, Phillips, Green.

League Cup	First Round	Hartlepool (h)	5-0
		(a)	1-1
	Second Round	Arsenal (h)	3-1
	Third Round	Reading (h)	2-2
		(a)	0-1
F.A. Cup	First Round	Workington (h)	3-0
	Second Round	Barnsley (a)	1-1
		(h)	2-1
	Third Round	Manchester C (a)	0-0
		(h)	2-4

McAlister	Forrest	Breckin	Rhodes	Green	Flynn	Finney	Phillips	Gwyther	Crawford	Smith	Vaughan	Wynn	Dawson	Pugh	Stancliffe	Carr	Young	Mountford	Match No.
1	2	3	4	5	6	7	8	9	10	11									1
1	2	3	4	5	6	7	8	9	10	11									2
1	2	3	4	5	6	7	8	9	10	11									3
1	2	3	4	5	6	7	8	9	10	11									4
1	2	3	4	5	6	7	8	9	10	11									5
1	2	3	4	5	6	7	8	9	10	11									6
1	2	3	4	5	6	7	8	9	10	11									7
1	2	3		5		7	8	4	10	11	6*12	9							8
1	6	3		5		4	8	9*10	11		12	7	2						9
1	6	3		5		4	8	9	10	11		7	2						10
1	6	3		5		4	8	9	10	11		7	2						11
1	2	3*		5	6	7	8	9	10	12		11		4					12
1	2			6	3	10	8	4	11		9	7		5					13
1	2	3		6	10	7	8	4	11		9			5					14
1	2	3		5	10	7	8	4	11		9	12		6*					15
1	2	3		5	6	7	8	4	10	11	9								16
1	2	3		5	6	7	8	4	11	10	9*12								17
1	2	3		5	6	7	8	9	10	11					4				18
1	2	3		5	6	7	8	9	10	11					4				19
1	2	3		5	6	7	8	9	10	11					4				20
1	2	3		5	6	7	8	9	10	11					4				21
1	2	3		5	6	7	8	9	11	10					4				22
1	2	3		5	6	7	8	9	10	11					4				23
1	2	3		5	6	7	8	9	11	10					4				24
1	2	3		5	6		8	9	10	11		7			4				25
1	2	3		5	6	7*	8	9	10	11			12		4				26
1	2	3		5	6	7	8	9	10	11					4				27
1	2	3		5	6	7	8	9	11	10					4				28
1	2	3		5	6	7	8	9	11						4	10			29
1	2	3		5	6	7	8	9	11						4	10			30
1	2	3		5	6	7	8	9	11						4	10			31
1	2	3		5	6	7	8	9	11						4	10			32
1	2	3		5	6	7	8	9	11						4	10			33
1	2	3	6	5		7	8		11		9				4	10			34
1	2	3	4	5		7	8	9	11						6	10			35
1	2	3	4	6		7	8	9	11						5	10			36
1	2	3	4	6		7	8	9	11						5	10			37
1	2	3	4	5		7	8	9	11						6	10			38
1	2	3	4	6			8	9	11						5	10	7		39
1	2	3	4	5			8	9		11					6	10	7		40
1	2	3	4	6		7	8			11					5	10	9		41
1	2	3	4	6	12		8	9*		11					5	10	7		42
1	2	3	4	6		7	8			11					5	10	9		43
1	2	3	4	6			7	9		11					5	10	8		44
1	2	3	4	6		7	8			11					5	10	9		45
	2	3	4	6		7	8			11					5	10	9	1	46
45	46	45	20	46	29	41	46	41	39	31	1	6	7	3	33	18	8	1	
					+1s					+1s		+2s	+3s						

ROTHERHAM UNITED—PLAYERS

Player and position	Ht	Wt	Birthplace	Clubs	League Appearances	Goals
Goalkeepers						
Tom McAlister	6 0	11 1	Clydebank	Sheffield U	63	—
				Rotherham U	159	—
*David Kaye	5 10	10 7	Huddersfield T	Rotherham U	—	—
Ray Mountford	6 3	12 7	Mexborough	Manchester U	—	—
				Notts Co (on loan)	—	—
				Rotherham U	1	—
Defenders						
John Breckin	5 9½	11 9	Rotherham	Rotherham U	278+4	7
				Darlington (on loan)	4	—
*Tommy Spencer	5 11	12 9	Glasgow	Celtic	—	—
				Southampton	3	—
				York C	54+3	20
				Workington	167	10
				Lincoln C	67+7	10
				Rotherham U	137+1	10
Gerald Forrest	5 11	10 7	Stockton	Rotherham U	90	—
John Green	5 10	12 1	Rotherham	Rotherham U	125+1	1
Paul Stancliffe	6 0	11 10	Sheffield	Rotherham U	153	5
Ashley Taylor	5 10	10 4	Conisborough	Rotherham U	—	—
John Flynn	6 0	11 7	Workington	Workington	35+3	—
				Sheffield U	185+5	8
				Rotherham U	29+1	1
Steven Galloway	5 10	10 3	Sheffield	Rotherham U	—	—
Midfield						
Peter Nix	5 8	9 5	Rotherham	Rotherham U	15	1
Mark Rhodes	5 9	10 11	Sheffield	Rotherham U	98+2	7
*Kevin Eades	5 5	8 3	Rawmarsh	Rotherham U	1	—
Tommy Young	5 11	12 7	Glasgow	Falkirk	83+9	33
				Tranmere R	170+2	27
				Rotherham U	11+4	1
*Paul Matthews	5 9	10 3	Leicester	Leicester C	56+5	5
				Southend U (on loan)	1	—
				Mansfield T	121+3	6
				Rotherham U	8	—
				Northampton T (on loan	13	—
Dave Smith	5 8	11 13	Thornaby	Middlesbrough	1	—
				Lincoln C	358+13	52
				Rotherham U	31+1	3
Peter Carr	5 9	9 12½	Rawmarsh	Rotherham U	18	1
Forwards						
Alan Crawford	5 7½	9 10	Rotherham	Rotherham U	233+4	49
				Mansfield (on loan)	1+1	—
Richard Finney	5 7	10 4	Rotherham	Rotherham U	198	54
Trevor Phillips	5 6¾	10 3	Rotherham	Rotherham U	289+33	81
David Gwyther	5 10	13 4	Birmingham	Swansea C	213+4	59
				Halifax T	104	26
				Rotherham U	141	35
Richard Dawson	5 9	11 12	Chesterfield	Rotherham U	14+3	2
Steve Winn	5 10½	11 5	Thornaby	Rotherham U	6+2	—
Richard Moon	5 9	11 3½	Maltby	Rotherham U	—	—
Stewart Evans	6 4	11 10	Rotherham	Rotherham U	—	—
Ian Vaughan (apprentice)	1 app.					
Mike Burgess	5 9½	10 1½		Rotherham U	—	—

SCUNTHORPE UNITED — DIV. 4

President: W. H. Pulling. *Chairman:* J. T. Empson.
Vice-Chairman: T. E. Belton
Directors: W. H. Archer, A. Harvey, G. E. Johnson, B. Collen.
Manager: Ron Ashman.
Secretary: Mrs. S. Louth.
Year Formed: 1904. *Turned Professional:* 1912.
Limited Company: 1912.
Previous Name: Amalgamated with Lindsey United to become Scunthorpe United, 1910.
Football League Record:
1950   Elected to Division 3(N)   1968–72 Division 4.
1958–64 Division 2.   1972–73 Division 3.
1964–68 Division 3.   1973–   Division 4.

Honours: Football League, best season in Division 2: 4th, 1961–62. Division 3(N), Champions: 1957–58. *F.A. Cup,* best season: 5th Rd., 1957–58, 1969–70. *Football League Cup,* best season: never past 3rd Rd.
Record Victory: 9-0 v Boston U., F.A. Cup, 1st Rd., Nov. 21st, 1953.
Record Defeat: 0-8 v Carlisle U., Division 3(N), 1952–53.
Most League Points: 66, Division 3(N), 1957–58.
Most League Goals: 88, Division 3(N), 1957–58.
Highest League Scorer in Season: Barrie Thomas, 31, Division 2, 1961–62.
Most League Goals in Total Aggregate: Barrie Thomas, 92, 1959–62, 1964–66.
Most Capped Player: None.
Most League Appearances: Jack Brownsword, 600, 1950–65.
Record Transfer Fee Received: £50,000 from Fulham for Richard Money, Dec. 1977.
Record Transfer Fee Paid: £20,000 to Newcastle U. for Barrie Thomas, Nov. 1964.
Managers Since the War: Leslie Jones, Bill Corkhill, Ron Suart, Tony McShane, Bill Lambton (3 days, shortest ever term of office), Frank Soo, Dick Duckworth, Freddie Goodwin, Ron Ashman, Ron Bradley, Dickie Rooks.
Address of Supporters Club: Scunthorpe U. Supporters and Social Club at Ground.

Old Show Ground, Scunthorpe, South Humberside. Telephone Scunthorpe 2954. *Ground capacity:* 27,000. *Record attendance:* 23,935 v Portsmouth, F.A. Cup 4th Rd., January 30, 1954. *Record receipts:* £7895 v Newcastle U., F.A. Cup 4th Rd., replay, Jan. 30 1974. *Pitch measurements:* 112 yds × 78 yds.

How to get there: Buses 118, 106, 309, 300, 301, 306 run near the ground. Nearest railway station is Scunthorpe By road along A18 from Doncaster via Berkeley Circle, Doncaster Road Hill, and Henderson Avenue; A18 from Grimsby; A15 from Lincoln via Queensway Circle, Ashby Road, Station Roundabout, Church Lane, Exeter Road, and Doncaster Road; via A1 on A638 to Retford, A620 to Gainsborough, A159 to Scunthorpe.
Match tickets: Tickets are bookable up to the day of the match unless advertised otherwise in the local press. No telephone bookings accepted.
Car parking: Club car park adjoining the ground holds 40–50 cars. Ample street parking around the ground.
Entertainments/catering facilities: Catering sub-let to an outside firm; hot drinks and light refreshments served on first-team match days.
Club shop: Three club shops and Development Office on the ground sell all types of souvenirs.
Handbooks/programmes: Programmes available on match days.
Extra information: The club song, 'Scunthorpe United', is available on record.

Club Colours: All red, with white trims on jersey.
Change Colours: All yellow.
Club Nickname: 'The Irons'.

SCUNTHORPE 1978-79 LEAGUE RECORD

Match No.	Date	Venue	Opponents	Result	H/T Score	League Pos'n	Goalscorers	Attendance
1	Aug 19	A	Port Vale	D 2-2	0-1	—	Wigg, Pilling	3025
2	22	H	AFC Bournemouth	W 1-0	0-0	—	Pilling	2433
3	25	H	Huddersfield T	W 3-1	2-0	5	Pilling, Grimes, Kilmore	3029
4	Sept 1	A	Doncaster R	D 0-0	0-0	5		4667
5	9	H	Barnsley	L 0-1	0-0	7		7612
6	12	A	Portsmouth	D 0-0	0-0	—		10,965
7	15	A	Northampton T	L 0-1	0-0	14		3858
8	23	H	Stockport Co	W 1-0	1-0	11	Wigg	2691
9	26	H	Aldershot	W 2-0	1-0	—	Kilmore 2	2566
10	30	A	Wigan Ath	L 0-1	0-0	11		4459
11	Oct 7	H	Newport Co	L 2-3	1-2	12	Deere, Oates	2453
12	14	A	Wimbledon	L 1-3	0-2	15	Wigg	3808
13	17	A	Hartlepool U	D 1-1	1-1	—	Kilmore	2980
14	21	H	Bradford C	W 3-2	1-0	13	Couch, Kilmore 2 (1 a pen)	2778
15	28	A	York C	L 0-1	0-0	15		1970
16	Nov 4	H	Reading	L 0-3	0-1	17		2424
17	11	H	Doncaster R	D 0-0	0-0	16		3250
18	18	A	Huddersfield T	L 2-3	2-0	20	Oates, Keeley	3375
19	Dec 9	A	Torquay U	W 1-0	1-0	19	Kilmore (pen)	2794
20	16	H	Hereford U	W 4-2	1-0	13	Kilmore 2, Pilling, Earl	1683
21	23	A	Darlington	D 2-2	0-0	13	Kilmore 2	1512
22	26	H	Grimsby T	W 2-1	1-1	—	Kilmore (pen), Grimes	8008
23	30	H	Rochdale	L 0-4	0-2	12		2620
24	Feb 3	A	Aldershot	L 0-2	0-1	15		3669
25	26	A	Stockport Co	W 2-0	1-0	—	Kavanagh, Earl	2676
26	Mar 3	A	Bradford C	D 1-1	1-0	17	Pilling	4988
27	10	H	York C	L 2-3	2-1	19	Kilmore (2 pens)	2261
28	13	A	Barnsley	L 1-4	0-1	—	Grimes	9308
29	16	A	Reading	W 1-0	0-0	19	Keeley	5144
30	20	H	Northampton T	L 0-3	0-1	—		1763
31	24	A	AFC Bournemouth	D 0-0	0-0	19		3028
32	27	H	Port Vale	W 2-0	0-0	—	Grimes, Earl	1472
33	31	H	Crewe Alex	L 0-1	0-1	18		1868
34	Apr 3	A	Portsmouth	D 2-2	0-1	—	Couch, Bloomer	1535
35	7	A	Hereford U	L 1-3	0-2	18	Kilmore (pen)	2859
36	10	H	Darlington	W 1-0	1-0	—	Craig (og)	1372
37	14	A	Grimsby T	D 1-1	1-1	16	Kavanagh	10,197
38	16	H	Halifax T	W 1-0	0-0	—	Earl	1624
39	18	A	Newport Co	L 0-2	0-1	—		2572
40	21	A	Rochdale	L 0-1	0-1	17		1224
41	24	H	Hartlepool U	W 3-1	1-0	—	Earl 2, Oates	1226
42	28	H	Torquay U	D 2-2	1-1	16	Kilmore (pen), Earl	1426
43	May 1	H	Wigan Ath	L 0-1	0-0	—		1582
44	5	A	Crewe Alex	W 2-0	2-0	14	Couch 2	1121
45	8	H	Wimbledon	W 2-0	1-0	—	Kilmore (pen), Earl	1777
46	18	A	Halifax T	W 3-2	1-0	—	Couch, Grimes, Gibson	1037

Final League Position: 12

Goalscorers

League (54): Kilmore 17 (8 pens), Earl 8, Couch 5, Grimes 5, Pilling 5, Oates 3, Wigg 3, Kavanagh 2, Keeley 2, Bloomer 1, Deere 1, Gibson 1, Own Goal 1.

F.A. Cup (1): Pilling.

League Cup	First Round	Notts Co (h)	0-1
		(a)	0-3
F.A. Cup	First Round	Sheffield W (h)	1-1
		(a)	0-1

Crawford	Davy	Peacock	Oates	Deere	Czuczman	Grimes	Kilmore	Wigg	Keeley	Pilling	Bloomer	O'Donnell	Gibson	Kavanagh	Couch	Armstrong	Earl	Hall	Match No
1	2	3	4	5	6	7	8*	9	10	11	12								1
1		3	4*	5	6	7	8	9	10	11	12	2							2
1		3		5	6	7	8	9	10	11		2	4						3
1		3	4	5	6	7	8	9	10*11	12		2							4
1		3	4	5	6	7	10	9		11*12		2	8						5
1		3	4	5	6	7	8*	9		11		2	10	12					6
1		3	4	5	6	7	8*	9		11		2	10	12					7
1		3	4	5	6	7	10	9		12		2	8*11						8
1		3	4	5	6	7	8	9		11		2	10						9
1		3*	4	5	6	7	8	9		11		2	12	10					10
1		3	4	5	6		10	9			7	2	8	11					11
1		3	4	5	6	7	10	9		8		2	11						12
1	2		4	5	6	7	8	9		3			10	11*12					13
1	2		4	5	6	7	10		8	3			11	9					14
1	2		4	5		7	8	6	9	3			10	11					15
1	2		4	5	6	7	8	11	9	3			10*12						16
1	2		4		6	7	8	9	11	3		5		10					17
1	2		4	5	6	7	8	9*10		3		11		12					18
1			4	5	6	7	8		10	3		2		11	9				19
1			4	5	6	7	8		10	3		2		11	9				20
1			4	5	6	7	8		10	3		2		11	9				21
1			4	5	6	7	8		11	3		2		10	9				22
1			4*	5	6	7	8	12	10	3		2		11	9				23
1			4	5	6	7	8		11	3		2*12		10	9				24
1			4	5	6	7	8		11	3		2	12	10	9*				25
1	12		4	5	6	7	8		11	3		2		10	9*				26
1			4	5	6	7	8		11	3		2		10	9				27
1			4	5	6	7	8		11	3		2	9	10					28
1			4	5	6	7	12		11	3		2	8	10	9*				29
1			4	5	6	7	12		11	3		2	8*10		9				30
1		3	4	5	6	7	8		11			2		10	9				31
1		3	4	5	6	7	8		11			2		10	9				32
1		3	4	5		7	8					2		10	11	9	6		33
1	12	3*	4	5		7	8			9		2		10	11		6		34
1	12	3*	4	5	6	7	8				11	2		10		9			35
1	12		4	5	2	7	8		9*			3		10	11		6		36
1		3	4	5	6	7	8					2*12	10	9		11			37
1		3	4	5	2	7	8						11	10	12	9*	6		38
1		3	4	5	2	7	8						11	10		9	6		39
1	2	3	4	5		7	8						11*10	12		9	6		40
1	2		4	5	3	7	8							10	9	11	6		41
1		3	4	5	3	7	8						10	11		9	6		42
1		2	4	5	3	7	8						11*10	9		6	12		43
1	2	3	4	5		7	8	6						10	11	9			44
1	2	3	4	5		7	8	6						10	11	9			45
1	2	3	4	5		7	8						11	10	9		6		46
46	12	26	45	45	39	45	44	17	25	29	3	32	14	37	14	—	23	10	
	+	+				+	+		+	+		+	+	+	+		+		
	2s	2s				2s	1s		1s	4s		4s	2s	4s	1s		15		

SCUNTHORPE UNITED—PLAYERS

Player and position	Ht	Wt	Birthplace	Clubs	League Appearances	Goals
Goalkeepers						
Alan O'Meara	5 11	10 10	Grantham	Scunthorpe U	41	—
(Contract cancelled September 1978)						
Graeme Crawford	6 2	13 0	Falkirk	East Stirling	2	—
				Sheffield U	2	—
				Mansfield T (on loan)	2	—
				York C	235	—
				Scunthorpe U	92	—
Jimmy Gordon	5 11	12 5	Stretford	Luton T	—	—
				Lincoln C	4	—
				Reading	—	—
				Scunthorpe U	—	—
Defenders						
John Peacock	5 8½	10 2	Leeds	Scunthorpe U	145+5	1
Bernard Bridges	5 10½	11 7	Doncaster	Scunthorpe U	22+1	—
(Contract cancelled July 1978)						
John O'Donnell	5 10	12 10	Leeds	Leeds U	—	—
				Cambridge U	79	8
				Colchester U (on loan)	1	—
				Hartlepool	30+1	1
				Scunthorpe U	55	—
Stuart Pilling	5 9	10 2	Sheffield	Hull C	—	—
				Scunthorpe U	168+11	14
Steve Deere	6 1½	12 10	Burnham	Norwich C	—	—
				Scunthorpe U	232+6	21
				Hull C	65+1	2
				Barnsley (on loan)	4	—
				Stockport Co (on loan)	6	—
				Scarborough (not known)	—	—
				Scunthorpe U	62	2
Steve Davy	5 8	10 12	Grantham	Scunthorpe U	33+5	—
*Ian Wilkinson	5 11½	13 0	Hemsworth	Scunthorpe U	—	—
Midfield						
Robert Oates	5 11½	11 7	Leeds	Scunthorpe U	169+5	12
Nolan Keeley	5 10	10 12	Barsham	Scunthorpe U	234+4	36
Eamon Kavanagh	5 9½	11 10	Manchester	Manchester C	—	—
				Rochdale	2+2	—
				Workington	123+3	11
				Scunthorpe U	50+4	2
Vincent Grimes	5 9½	11 10	Scunthorpe	Hull C	84+5	9
				Scunthorpe U	63	7
				Bradford C (on loan)	7	1
Dave Gibson	5 5¼	9 10	Seaham	Hull C	19+5	1
				Scunthorpe U	14+4	1
David Hall	5 8½	11 0	Doncaster	Scunthorpe U	10+1	—
Forwards						
Mick Farrell	5 8	9 13	Ilkley	Scunthorpe U	5+4	1
(Contract cancelled July 1978)						
Kevin Kilmore	5 9	10 2	Scunthorpe	Scunthorpe U	88+9	28
Brian Heron	5 8¼	10 8	Dumbarton	Rangers	—	—
(Contract cancelled July 1978)				Motherwell	75	20
				Dumbarton	33+3	10
				Oxford U	40+3	8
				Scunthorpe U	20+5	1
Ron Wigg	6 0	12 2	Dunmow	Orient	—	—
(Contract cancelled March 1979)				Ipswich T	36+2	8
				Watford	92+6	20
				Rotherham U	65	22
				Grimsby T	51+12	11
				Barnsley	14+4	5
				Scunthorpe U	48+2	26
Geoff Couch	5 10¼	10 6	Crowle	Scunthorpe U	20+4	5
*Brian Bloomer	5 10	11 10		Brigg T	—	—
				Scunthorpe U	3+4	1
Steven Earl	5 9	12 4		Scunthorpe U	30	9

SHEFFIELD UNITED   DIV. 3

Chairman: J. C. Hassall.
Vice-Chairman: A. Jackson, J.P., F.R.I.C.S.
Directos: A. A. Bramall, A. H. Laver, K. Lee, F. J. P. O'Gorman, F.R.I.C.S., A. Jackson, J.P., F.R.I.C.S., R. Wragg, M.Inst. B.M.
A. Jackson, J.P., F.R.I.C.S., R. Wragg, M.Inst. B.M.
Manager: Harry Haslam.
Secretary: Richard Chester, F.A.A.I.
Commercial Manager: Derek Dooley.
Asst. Manager: Danny Bergara.
Chief Scout: Neville Briggs.
Year Formed: 1889.   *Turned Professional:* 1889.
Limited Company: 1899.
Football League Record: 1892 Elected to Division 2. 1893-1934 Division 1. 1934-39 Division 2. 1946-49 Division 1. 1949-53 Division 2. 1953-56 Division 1. 1956-61 Division 2. 1961-68 Division 1. 1968-71 Division 2. 1971-76 Division 1. 1976-79 Division 2. 1979- Division 3.

© S.U.F.C.

Honours: Football League. Division 1, Champions: 1897-98; Runners-up: 1896-97, 1899-1900. Division 2, Champions: 1952-53; Runners-up: 1892-93, 1938-39, 1960-61, 1970-71. *F.A. Cup,* Winners: 1899, 1902, 1915, 1925; Runners-up: 1901, 1936. *Football League Cup,* best season: 5th Rd., 1961-62, 1966-67.
Record Victory: 11-2 v Cardiff C., Division 1, Jan. 1st, 1926.
Record Defeat: 0-13 v Bolton W., F.A. Cup, 2nd Rd., Feb. 1st, 1890.
Most League Points: 60, Division 2, 1952-53.
Most League Goals: 102, Division 1, 1925-26.
Highest League Scorer in Season: Jimmy Dunne, 41, Division 1, 1930-31.
Most League Goals in Total Aggregate: Harry Johnson, 205, 1919-30.
Most Capped Player: Billy Gillespie, 25, Ireland.
Most League Appearances: Joe Shaw, 629, 1948-66.
Record Transfer Fee Received: £250,000 from Leeds U., for Tony Currie, June 1976.
Record Transfer Fee Paid: £160,000 to River Plate for Alex Sabella, July, 1978.
Managers Since the War: Ted Davison, Reg Freeman, Joe Mercer, John Harris, Arthur Rowley, John Harris, Ken Furphy, Jimmy Sirrel.
Address of Supporters Club: Secretary, c/o S.U.F.C., Bramall Lane, Sheffield S2 4SU.
Address of Club Shop or Boutique: Lane Souvenir Shop, John Street, Sheffield S2 4SU.

Bramall Lane Ground, Sheffield, S2 4SU. Telephone Sheffield (0742) 738955/6/7. *Telegraphic address:* 'United, Sheffield'. *Ground capacity:* 49,000 (15,300 seats). *Record attendance:* 68,287 v Leeds U., F.A. Cup 5th Rd., February 15, 1936. *Record receipts:* £37,500 v Arsenal, F.A. Cup, 3rd Rd., January 7, 1978. *Pitch measurements:* 117 yds × 75 yds.

How to get there: Buses 34, 35, 38, 42, 45 from the central bus station. Sheffield railway station is within walking distance of the town centre.
Match tickets: Tickets bookable 14 days prior to the match.
Car parking: The ground is five minutes from car parks in the city centre. Ample parking in side-streets around Bramall Lane.
Entertainments/catering facilities: Numerous bars and buffets in the ground.
Club shop: Sells all types of souvenirs.
Handbook/programmes: Mail order service available through the club shop.
Extra information: Lane Social Club offers lounge bars and bier keller.
Club Colours: Red, white and thin black striped shirts, black shorts, white stockings, two red bands on top.
Change Colours: White shirt, red shortstripe down left hand side edged with thin black stripe, black shorts white stockings, red and black top.
Club Captain: Mick Speight.
Chief Coach: Cecil Coldwell.
Club Nickname: 'Blades'.

SHEFFIELD UNITED 1978–79 LEAGUE RECORD

Match No.	Date	Venue	Opponents	Result	H/T Score	League Pos'n	Goalscorers	Attendance
1	Aug 19	H	Orient	L 1-2	1-2	—	Stainrod	19,012
2	23	A	Leicester C	W 1-0	0-0	—	Matthews	19,381
3	26	A	Preston NE	D 2-2	1-1	10	Stainrod, Sabella	13,208
4	Sept 2	H	Crystal Palace	L 0-2	0-2	17		17,388
5	9	A	Fulham	L 0-2	0-0	21		6672
6	16	H	Burnley	W 4-0	3-0	14	Hamson 2 (1 a pen), Franks, Guy	15,355
7	23	A	West Ham U	L 0-2	0-0	18		24,361
8	30	H	Luton T	D 1-1	1-0	18	Anderson	15,295
9	Oct 7	H	Sunderland	W 3-2	0-1	14	Anderson 2, Finnieston	18,873
10	14	A	Millwall	D 1-1	0-0	14	Calvert	6342
11	21	H	Oldham Ath	W 4-2	2-1	13	Finnieston, Matthews, Hamson, Stainrod	14,514
12	28	A	Stoke C	L 1-2	0-1	14	Anderson	21,282
13	Nov 4	H	Brighton & HA	L 0-1	0-1	15		16,683
14	11	A	Orient	D 1-1	0-0	17	Anderson	5540
15	18	H	Preston NE	L 0-1	0-0	17		14,807
16	21	A	Crystal Palace	L 1-3	0-2	—	Varadi	19,504
17	25	A	Bristol R	L 1-2	0-1	18	Finnieston	8434
18	Dec 9	A	Charlton Ath	L 1-3	0-1	19	Varadi	7048
19	16	H	Cardiff C	W 2-1	2-0	19	Anderson, Matthews	11,913
20	26	H	Newcastle U	W 1-0	0-0	—	Garner	23,118
21	30	H	Cambridge U	D 3-3	1-0	19	Varadi 2, Matthews	14,527
22	Feb 6	A	Fulham	D 1-1	1-0	—	Smith	12,457
23	10	A	Luton T	D 1-1	0-1	18	Hamson (pen)	7025
24	24	H	Millwall	L 0-2	0-1	18		13,763
25	28	A	Wrexham	L 0-4	0-2	—		9764
26	Mar 3	A	Oldham Ath	D 1-1	1-0	19	Matthews	6531
27	6	A	Burnley	D 1-1	1-1	—	Kenworthy	9000
28	10	H	Stoke C	D 0-0	0-0	19		20,512
29	13	A	Notts Co	L 1-4	0-1	—	Brown	10,372
30	17	A	Brighton & HA	L 0-2	0-0	19		20,091
31	31	H	Bristol R	W 1-0	0-0	18	Anderson	14,064
32	Apr 2	H	West Ham U	W 3-0	1-0	—	Finnieston, Anderson 2	17,720
33	7	A	Blackburn R	L 0-2	0-0	18		10,762
34	10	H	Notts Co	W 5-1	1-0	—	McPhail, Speight 2, Sabella, Anderson	15,816
35	14	A	Newcastle U	W 3-1	2-0	18	Brownlie (og), Rioch, Anderson	19,121
36	17	H	Wrexham	D 1-1	1-1	—	Kenworthy	19,846
37	21	A	Cardiff C	L 0-4	0-2	19		10,592
38	25	A	Sunderland	L 2-6	1-2	—	Kenworthy, Sabella	29,822
39	28	H	Charlton Ath	W 2-1	1-0	20	Anderson, Guy	16,888
40	May 2	H	Blackburn R	L 0-1	0-0	—		16,012
41	5	A	Cambridge U	L 0-1	0-1	20		7255
42	8	H	Leicester C	D 2-2	1-1	—	Benjamin 2 (2 pens)	15,178

Final League Position: 20

Goalscorers

League (52): Anderson 12, Matthews 5, Finnieston 4, Hamson 4 (2 pens), Varadi 4, Kenworthy 3, Sabella 3, Stainrod 3, Benjamin 2 (2 pens), Guy 2, Speight 2, Brown 1, Calvert 1, Franks 1, Garner 1, McPhail 1, Rioch 1, Smith 1, Own Goal 1.

League Cup (2): Hamson, Calvert.

League Cup	Second Round	Liverpool (h)	1-0
	Third Round	Leeds U (h)	1-4
F.A. Cup	Third Round	Aldershot (h)	0-0
		(a)	0-1

Conroy	Cutbush	Garner	Kenworthy	Franks	Speight	Woodward	Stainrod	Finnieston	Harnson	Sabella	Matthews	Keeley	Calvert	Varadi	Renwick	Guy	Anderson	Johns	Harwood	McPhail	Smith	Flood	Jones	Brown	Tibbott	Rioch	Benjamin	Match No.
1	2	3	4	5	6	7	8	9	10	11																		1
1	2	3			6	7		9	10	11	5	8																2
1	2	3	4*		6	7	12	9	10	11	5	8																3
1	2		12		6	7	8		10	11	5*	4	3	9														4
1	2			4	6	7	9*		10	11	5	8	3		12													5
1	2		4	9	6		12		10	7	5*	8	3		11													6
1	2		4	9	8				11	10	5	6	3		7*	12												7
1	2		6	9	4		7		11		5	8	3		10													8
	2		6	12	4			9	10	11	5		3		7	1	8*											9
1			4	2	6		12	9	11	10*	5		3		7	8												10
1		6	2	4			12	9	11	10	5*	8	3		7													11
1			4	2	8			9	11	10	5	6	3		7													12
1			4	2	6		7	9	11*	10	5	8	3	12														13
1	2	3	6		8			9*	11	10	5		4	12		7												14
1	2	3			6				11	10	5		8*12	4	9	7												15
1	2	3	4		6*			9	11	10			8	12	5	7												16
1		3	6				12	9	11	10	5		4	8	2*	7												17
1		3	6					9	11	10	5		4	8	2*12	7												18
1		3	6	2				9*11	10	5		4	8		7	12												19
1		3	4	2	8				11	10	5		6	9*	12	7												20
1		3	6	2	8				11	10	5		4	9		7												21
1			4		3	9			11	10	6		2			7			5	8								22
1			4*	8	3	9			11	10	6		2			7			5	12								23
1				5	6	9			11	10	4		3			7			2	8								24
1	2			4	3	9			11	10	6					5			7	8								25
1	2	3	4		7				11	10	6		12			5		8		9*								26
1		3	4	2					11	8	7		6			5		9	10									27
1		3	4	2					11	8	7		6			5		9	10									28
1	2	3	4		5				11	10	6		8	12					7*	9								29
1	2	3*	4		8				11	10			6	7		5		12	9									30
1			4		2			9	11	10	7					8		5						3	6			31
1			4		2			9	11	10	6					7		5						3	8			32
1	2		4		7			9	11	10						8		5						12	3	6*		33
1	2		4*		6			9	11	10						7		5						12	3	8		34
1	2		4		8			9	11	10						7		5							3	6		35
1	2		4		6			9	11	10		5				7									3	8		36
1	2		4		8			9*		10		5				7								11	3	6	12	37
1	2	5	4		6				11	10						9	7								3	8		38
1	2	5	4		6			9	11	10						7	8								3			39
1	2	5	4		6			9	11	10*12						8	7								3			40
1	2		4		8				10	11	6					9	7*		5	12					3			41
1	2		4		6					11	8					9			5			10			3	7		42
41	26	19	37	15	39	5	9	23	41	39	31	10	21	6	6	12	28	1	2	15	2	5	1	7	12	8	1	
			+2s		+5s			+1s					+4s	+1s	+3s	+2s			+1s		+1s	+2s			+2s	+1s		

335

SHEFFIELD UNITED—PLAYERS

Player and position	Ht	Wt	Birthplace	Clubs	League Appearances	Goals
Goalkeepers						
Jim Brown (Scotland)	5 11	12 4	Coatbridge	Albion Rovers	79	—
				Chesterfield	47	—
(Contract cancelled March 1979)				Sheffield U	170	—
Steve Conroy	5 11	12 2	Chesterfield	Sheffield U	44	—
Nicky Johns	6 1	12 3	Bristol	Millwall	50	—
				Tampa Bay R	(not known)	
				Charlton Ath (on loan)	10	—
				Sheffield U (on loan)	1	—
Defenders						
Eddie Colquhoun (Scotland)	6 0	12 2	Prestonpans	Bury	81	2
				WBA	46	1
(Contract cancelled December 1978)				Sheffield U	361+3	21
Brian McGarry	5 9¾	11 6	Birmingham	Bromsgrove	(not known)	
				Sheffield U		
Craig Renwick	5 10½	11 2½	Lanark	East Stirling	7+4	—
				Sheffield U	6+1	—
John Cutbush	5 7½	10 7	Malta	Tottenham H	—	—
				Fulham	132+3	3
				Sheffield U	79+2	1
Paul Garner	5 8¾	10 8	Doncaster	Huddersfield T	96	2
				Sheffield U	87	2
Colin Franks	5 11	12 8	Wembley	Watford	99+14	8
(Contract cancelled April 1979)				Sheffield U	139+11	7
Andy Keeley	5 10	11 5	Basildon	Tottenham H	5+1	—
				Sheffield U	26	—
Cliff Calvert	5 11	10 6	Wombwell	York C	62+5	—
(Contract cancelled March 1979)				Sheffield U	78+3	5
Phil Jones (apprentice)	6 0½	12 4	Mansfield	Sheffield U	1	—
Leslie Tibbott	5 10	11 7	Oswestry	Ipswich T	52+2	—
				Sheffield U	12	—
John McPhail	5 10½	12 6	Dundee	Dundee	64+4	—
				Sheffield U	15	1
John Matthews	5 11½	11 13½	London	Arsenal	38+7	2
				Sheffield U	31+1	5
Midfield						
Mick Speight	5 10½	12 3	Upton	Sheffield U	150+14	8
Tony Kenworthy	5 8	10 8	Leeds	Sheffield U	97+3	5
Gary Hamson	5 9½	10 12	Nottingham	Sheffield U	107+1	8
Ian Benjamin (apprentice)	6 0	11 10½	Nottingham	Sheffield U	1+1	2
Richard Harwood	5 7	10 12	Sheffield	Sheffield U	2+1	—
Alex Sabella	5 8	10 13	Buenos Aires	River Plate	(not known)	
				Sheffield U	39	3
†Tom Smith	5 10	12 9	Wolverhampton	Bromsgrove	(not known)	
(Contract cancelled March 1979)				Sheffield U	2+1	1
Mike Guy	5 9	11 1½	Limavady	Coleraine	(not known)	
				Sheffield U	12+6	2
Graham Clark				Sheffield U	—	—
Forwards						
Alan Woodward	5 8¼	11 8¼	Chapeltown	Sheffield U	436+2	158
(Contract cancelled October 1978)						
*Steve McKee	5 8¾	10 4	Belfast	Linfield	(not known)	
				Sheffield U	4+3	—
David Windridge				Sheffield U		
Steve Finnieston	5 11	11 2	Edinburgh	Chelsea	78+2	34
				Cardiff C (on loan)	9	2
				Sheffield U	23	4
Peter Anderson	5 9	11 9	Hendon	Luton T	178+3	34
(Contract cancelled May 1979)				Antwerp	(not known)	
				Tampa Bay R	(not known)	
				Sheffield U (on loan)	28+2	12
Dougie Brown	5 9	12 4	Airdrie	Clydebank	4+8	—
				Sheffield U	7+2	1
John Flood	5 7	9 8½	Glasgow	Sheffield U	5+2	—
Keith Larner	5 7	10 7	Bushey	Letchworth	(not known)	
				Sheffield U	—	—

*Paul Champken
†(See under Huddersfield T)

SHEFFIELD WEDNESDAY DIV. 3

President: The Rt. Hon. The Lord Netherthorpe, LL.D.
Vice-presidents: Sir Andrew Stephen, M.B., Ch.B., R. R. Gunstone, S. Ashton, A. Broomhead, C. Turner.
Chairman: H. E. McGee.
Vice-Chairman: M. Sheppard, J.P., F.C.A.
Directors: R. Whitehead, S. L. Speight, O.B.E., C. Woodward, K. T. Addy, E. Barron.
Manager: Jack Charlton, O.B.E.
Secretary: Eric England, F.A.A.I.
Year Formed: 1867 (fifth oldest League Club).
Turned Professional: 1887. *Limited Company:* 1899.
Previous Grounds: 1867, Highfield; 1869, Myrtle Road; 1877, Sheaf House; 1887, Olive Grove; 1899, Owlerton (since 1912 known as Hillsborough). Some games were played at Endcliffe in the 1880's. Until 1895 Bramall Lane was used for some games.

Football League Record:
1982 Elected to Division 1.	1937–50 Division 2.	1956–58 Division 1.
1899–1900 Division 2.	1950–51 Division 1.	1958–59 Division 2.
1900–20 Division 1.	1951–52 Division 2.	1959–70 Division 1.
1920–26 Division 2.	1952–55 Division 1.	1970–75 Division 2.
1926–37 Division 1.	1955–56 Division 2.	1975– Division 3.

Honours: Football League, Division 1, Champions: 1902–03, 1903–04, 1928–29, 1929–30, runners-up: 1960–61. Division 2, Champions: 1899–1900, 1925–26, 1951–52, 1955–56, 1958–59; Runners-up: 1949–50. *F.A. Cup,* Winners: 1896, 1907, 1935; Runners-up: 1890, 1966. *Football League Cup,* best season: 4th Rd., 1967–68, 1976–77, 1977–78.
European Competitions: Fairs Cup: 1961–62, 1963–64.
Record Victory: 12-0 v Halliwell, F.A. Cup, 1st Rd., Jan. 17th, 1891.
Record Defeat: 0-10 v Aston Villa, Division 1, Oct. 5th, 1912.
Most League Points: 62, Division 2, 1958–59.
Most League Goals: 106, Division 2, 1958–59.
Highest League Scorer in Season: Derek Dooley, 46, Division 2, 1951–52.
Most Capped Player: Ron Springett, 33, England.
Most League Appearances: Andy Wilson, 502, 1900–20.
Most League Goals in Total Aggregate: Andy Wilson, 200, 1900–20.
Record Transfer Fee Received: £120,000 from Newcastle U. for Tommy Craig, January 1975.
Record Transfer Fee Paid: £100,000 to Aberdeen for Tommy Craig, May 1969 and £100,000 to Southampton for Terry Curran, March 1979.
Managers Since the War: Secretary/Manager Eric Taylor, Harry Catterick, Vic Buckingham, Alan Brown, Jack Marshall, Danny Williams, Derek Dooley, Steve Burtenshaw, Len Ashurst.
Address of Supporters Club: Same as Football Club.
Address of Club Shop or Boutique: Owl Shop, Hillsborough, Sheffield S6 1SW.
Club Restaurant: Adjoining South stand.

Hillsborough, Sheffield, S6 1SW. Telephone Sheffield 343123. (Box Office: Sheffield 343122)
Telegraphic address: 'Wednesday, Sheffield 6'. *Ground capacity:* 55,000. *Record attendance:* 72,841 v Manchester C., F.A. Cup 5th Rd., February 17, 1934. *Record receipts:* £144,000, Leeds U. v Manchester U., F.A. Cup Semi-final, April 23, 1977. (Record for F.A. Cup-tie other than the Final.) *Pitch measurements:* 115 yds × 75 yds.
How to get there: Buses 42, 53, 81, 2 from the city centre. Sheffield railway station is close to the centre.
Match tickets: Seats can be booked in advance in the South and North Stands. Postal applications to the Box Office not more than 21 days before the match. Tickets are offered subject to being unsold when the application is received. Remittance and S.A.E. must be enclosed.
Car parking: Street parking available. Also a park at the training ground in Middlewood Road.
Entertainments/catering facilities: Refreshment bars in all parts of the ground.
Club shop: Two shops in the ground sell all types of souvenirs.
Handbooks/programmes: Handbooks available from the secretary. Programmes available on subscription.
Extra information: When Sheffield Wednesday won the First Division title in 1929–30, they finished 10 points ahead of the runners-up.
Club Colours: Royal blue/white striped shirts, royal blue shorts, white stockings. *Change Colours:* Yellow shirts with blue trim, white shorts, yellow socks with blue band. *Club Nickname* 'Owls'.

SHEFFIELD WEDNESDAY 1978-79 LEAGUE RECORD

Match No.	Date	Venue	Opponents	Result	H/T Score	League Pos'n	Goalscorers	Attendance
1	Aug 19	A	Peterborough U	L 0-2	0-0	—		7468
2	26	H	Colchester U	D 0-0	0-0	20		10,685
3	Sept 2	A	Lincoln C	W 2-1	1-1	17	Tynan, Hornsby	7005
4	9	H	Southend U	W 3-2	2-0	11	Hornsby 2 (1 a pen), Grant	11,309
5	12	A	Gillingham	D 0-0	0-0	—		5835
6	16	A	Mansfield T	D 1-1	0-1	13	Hornsby (pen)	11,366
7	23	H	Plymouth Arg	L 2-3	1-0	16	Wylde, Nimmo	12,088
8	26	A	Bury	D 0-0	0-0	—		9000
9	30	A	Swindon T	L 0-3	0-1	18		5857
10	Oct 7	A	Rotherham U	W 1-0	0-0	17	Wylde	13,746
11	14	H	Carlisle U	D 0-0	0-0	16		10,980
12	17	H	Oxford U	D 1-1	1-1	—	Wylde	9431
13	21	A	Shrewsbury T	D 2-2	0-0	17	Hornsby, Wylde	6294
14	24	H	Exeter C	W 2-1	0-0	—	Hornsby, Lowey	11,139
15	28	H	Walsall	L 0-2	0-1	14		12,019
16	Nov 4	A	Blackpool	W 1-0	1-0	11	Hornsby	9403
17	11	H	Lincoln C	D 0-0	0-0	11		12,590
18	18	A	Colchester U	L 0-1	0-0	13		4346
19	Dec 2	A	Swansea C	L 2-4	2-2	14	Wylde, Hornsby	10,000
20	9	H	Chester	D 0-0	0-0	14		8872
21	26	A	Chesterfield	D 3-3	2-2	16	Wylde, Porterfield, Johnson	13,322
22	Jan 27	A	Plymouth Arg	L 0-2	0-1	18		8596
23	Feb 13	A	Southend U	L 1-2	0-1	—	Wylde	4559
24	19	A	Tranmere R	D 1-1	1-1	—	Wylde	2445
25	24	A	Carlisle U	D 0-0	0-0	20		5675
26	Mar 3	H	Shrewsbury T	D 0-0	0-0	19		11,284
27	6	H	Gillingham	W 2-1	1-1	—	Owen, Wylde	8205
28	10	A	Walsall	W 2-0	1-0	17	Lowey, Hornsby	5120
29	13	H	Brentford	W 1-0	1-0	—	Wylde	10,229
30	24	A	Exeter C	D 2-2	1-1	16	Wylde, Hornsby	4521
31	27	H	Peterborough U	W 3-0	1-0	—	Wylde, Johnson, Hornsby (pen)	9868
32	31	A	Watford	L 0-1	0-0	16		15,394
33	Apr 3	H	Mansfield T	L 1-2	0-2	—	Nimmo	11,065
34	7	H	Swansea C	D 0-0	0-0	16		12,101
35	13	A	Hull C	D 1-1	0-1	—	Curran	10,936
36	14	H	Chesterfield	W 4-0	2-0	16	Rushbury, Wylde 2, Johnson	12,960
37	17	A	Brentford	L 1-2	0-2	—	Nimmo	9050
38	21	H	Tranmere R	L 1-2	1-0	17	Hornsby (pen)	9815
39	25	A	Oxford U	D 1-1	0-0	—	Hornsby	3243
40	28	A	Chester	D 2-2	0-1	16	Owen, Lowey	4200
41	May 1	H	Bury	D 0-0	0-0	—		3424
42	5	H	Watford	L 2-3	2-1	17	Hornsby, Shirtliff	13,746
43	7	H	Rotherham U	W 2-1	1-1	—	Mullen, Fleming	12,094
44	11	H	Swindon T	W 2-1	1-0	—	Hornsby, Nimmo	9057
45	17	H	Blackpool	W 2-0	2-0	—	Porterfield, Owen	7310
46	19	H	Hull C	L 2-3	1-2	—	Sterland, Hornsby	8950

Final League Position: 14

Goalscorers

League (53): Hornsby 16 (4 pens), Wylde 14, Nimmo 4, Lowey 3, Owen 3, Johnson 3, Porterfield 2, Curran 1, Fleming 1, Grant 1, Mullen 1, Rushbury 1, Tynan 1, Shirtliff 1, Sterland 1.
League Cup (2): Hornsby, Own Goal 1.
F.A. Cup (14): Hornsby 4 (3 pens), Wylde 3, Lowey 2, Nimmo 2, Leman, Johnson, Rushbury.

League Cup	First Round	Doncaster R (a)	1-0
		(h)	0-1
		(a)	1-0
	Second Round	Aston Villa (a)	0-1
F.A. Cup	First Round	Scunthorpe U (a)	1-1
		(h)	1-0
	Second Round	Tranmere R (a)	1-1
		(h)	4-0
	Third Round	Arsenal (h)	1-1
		(a)	1-1 (a.e.t.)
			2-2 (at Leicester a.e.t.)
			3-3 (at Leicester a.e.t.)
			0-2 (at Leicester)

Bolder	Shirtliff	Grant	Smith	Dowd	Mullen	Owen	Porterfield	Tynan	Johnson	Hornsby	Blackhall	Rushbury	Leman	Wylde	Nimmo	Pickering	Cox	Lowey	Turner	Taylor	Fleming	Curran	Sterland	Match No.
1	2	3	4	5	6	7	8	9	10	11														1
1		3	6	5	7	11	10*	9	8		2	4	12											2
1	2		6		4	7*10	9	8	11	3	5		12											3
1		3		5	6		8	9	10	11	2	4		7										4
1		3		5	6		8	9*10	11	2	4		7	12										5
1		3	12	5	6		10	9*	8	11	2	4		7										6
1		3	5		6		8	9*10	11	2	4		7	12										7
1		3		5	6		8	9*10	11	2	4		7	12										8
1		3	6	5	7	12	8		10	11	2*	4		9										9
1		3	6				8		9	11	2	4	10	7	5									10
1		3	5			12	8		10	11	2	4*	9	7		6								11
		3	4			6	8			11	2	12	9	7		5	1	10*						12
		3	5			9*	8			11	2	4	10	7		6	1	12						13
			4			10	8		6*11		2	3	9	7		5	1	12						14
			5			12	8*		10	11	2	3	6	7		4	1	9						15
			5				8		10	11	2	3	6	7		4		9	1					16
			5				10		6	11	2	3	9	7		4		8	1					17
			5		6	10*	8			11	2	3	9	7		4		12	1					18
			5				8		6	11	2	3	10	7	9	4			1					19
		7	5			10	8		6*11		2	3		12	9	4		1						20
			4				8		6	11	2	3	9	7		5		10	1					21
		12			4		10*		6	11	2	3		7		5		8	1	9				22
	2	4			5		8		6	11		3		7	12			10	1		9*			23
	2	4			5		8		6	11		3	9	7				10	1					24
	2				4		8		6	11		3	9	7		5		10	1					25
	2				5		8*		6	11		3	9	7		4		10	1	12				26
	2				4	9	12		6	11		3		7		5		10	1	8*				27
	2				4		8		6	11		3	9	7		5		10	1					28
	2				4	12	8		6	11		3	9*	7		5		10	1					29
	2	3	5*		6	12	8		10	11				7		4		9	1					30
	2	3			4	9	8		6	11			7	12	5			10*	1					31
	2	3	5		6		8		10	11			7*		4			9	1		12			32
	2	3			4		8		6	11				12	5			10	1		9*	7		33
	2				5		8		6	11	3			9	4			10	1			7		34
	2				4		8		6	11	3		7		5			10	1			9		35
	2				5	12	8		6	11	3			9	10	4			1			7*		36
	2				4		8		6	11	3*		7	12	5			10	1			9		37
	2	3			5		8		6	11				9	10*	4		12	1			7		38
1	2	3	6		4		8		10*11				7		5			12				9		39
1	2*	3			5	12	8			11	6		9		4			10				7		40
1	2	3			4		8			11	6		7		5			10				9		41
1	2				4	12	8		6*11		3		9		5			10				7		42
1	2				4	6	8*		12	11	3				5			10		9	7			43
1	2	3			4	7	8			11	6		10	5				9						44
1	2	3			4	7	8		11*				10	5				6	9			12		45
1	2	3			4	10*	8		12				11	5				6	9		7			46
19	26	26	20	7	35	14	45	8	37	44	21	36	16	36	8	35	4	24	23	4	6	11	1	
	+ 1s	+ 1s			+ 8s	+ 2s	+ 1s		+ 1s	+ 1s	+ 1s	+ 1s	+ 2s	+ 7s		+ 5s		+ 1s		+ 1s	+ 1s			

SHEFFIELD WEDNESDAY—PLAYERS

Player and position	Ht	Wt	Birthplace	Clubs	League Appearances	Goals
Goalkeepers						
Chris Turner	5 10	11 0	Sheffield	Sheffield W	91	—
				Lincoln C (on loan)	5	—
Bob Bolder	6 2	13 13	Dover	Sheffield W	42	—
Brian Cox	5 11	13 0	Sheffield	Sheffield W	4	—
Defenders						
David Rushbury	5 10	11 4	Wolverhampton	WBA	28	—
				Sheffield W	111+1	7
Jimmy Mullen	5 10	11 6	Jarrow	Sheffield W	209+6	8
Hugh Dowd (N Ireland)	6 1	13 0	Lurgan	Glenavon	not known	
				Sheffield W	110+3	—
David Grant	6 0	12 7	Sheffield	Sheffield W	50+1	2
Mark Smith	6 0½	12 6	Sheffield	Sheffield W	22+1	—
Ray Blackhall	5 9	11 0	Ashington	Newcastle U	26+11	—
				Sheffield W	21	—
Mike Pickering	5 11	12 6	Mirfield	Barnsley	100	1
				Southampton	44	—
				Sheffield W	35	—
Peter Shirtliff	6 1	12 0	Chapeltown	Sheffield W	26	1
Midfield						
Dennis Leman	5 5	10 4	Newcastle	Manchester C	10+7	1
				Sheffield W	65+11	8
Ian Porterfield	5 11	12 8	Dunfermline	Raith R	117	17
				Sunderland	218+13	17
				Reading (on loan)	5	—
				Sheffield W	83+1	2
Jeff Johnson	5 8	11 7	Cardiff	Manchester C	4+2	—
				Swansea C (on loan)	37+2	4
				C Palace	82+5	4
				Sheffield W	110+1	5
John Lowey	5 11	12 7	Manchester	Manchester U	—	—
				California S	—	—
				Sheffield W	24+5	3
Kevin Taylor	5 9	10 10	Wakefield	Sheffield W	4+1	—
Forwards						
Rodger Wylde	6 1½	12 0	Sheffield	Sheffield W	142+12	46
				Burnley (on loan)	—	—
Ian Nimmo	5 11	11 8	Boston	Sheffield W	26+19	10
				Peterborough U (on loan)	4	1
Paul Bradshaw (Contract cancelled)	5 6½	10 4	Sheffield	Burnley	11+2	2
				Sheffield W	62+2	9
*Colin Gregson	5 6	11 0	Newcastle	Sheffield W	1+1	—
Gordon Owen	5 6½	10 0	Barnsley	Sheffield W	17+8	3
*Lindsay McKeown	5 9	11 0	Belfast	Manchester U	—	—
				Sheffield W	6+5	—
Brian Hornsby	5 8	10 11	Shellford	Arsenal	23+3	5
				Shrewsbury T	75	16
				Sheffield W	57+1	19
Terry Curran	5 10	11 3	Kinsley	Doncaster R	67+1	11
				Nottingham F	46+2	12
				Bury (on loan)	2	—
				Derby Co	26	2
				Southampton	25+1	—
				Sheffield W	11+1	1
Ian Fleming	5 8	10 7	Maybole	Kilmarnock	86+9	50
				Aberdeen	48+18	12
				Sheffield W	6	1
Brian Strutt	5 10	10 4	Malta	Sheffield W	—	—
Melvyn Sterland (apprentice)					1+1 sub,	1 gl

SHREWSBURY TOWN DIV. 2

President: Sydney Yates. *Chairman:* H. S. Yates.
Directors: L. Tudor-Owen, A. C. Williams, F. C. G. Fry, K. R. Woodhouse.
Player/Manager: Graham Turner.
Secretary: M. J. Starkey, F.A.A.I.
Year Formed: 1886. *Turned Professional:* 1905 (approx.).
Limited Company: 1936.
Previous Ground: Old Shrewsbury Racecourse.

Football League Record:
1950 Elected to Division 3(N).   1974–75 Division 4.
1951–58 Division 3(S).   1975–79 Division 3.
1958–59 Division 4.   1979–   Division 2.
1959–74 Division 3.

Honours: Football League: best season in Division 3: Champions 1978–79. Runners-up Division 4, 1974–75. *F.A. Cup,* best season: 6th Rd., 1978–79 *Football League Cup,* best season, semi-finalists: 1961. Welsh Cup winners: 1891, 1938, 1977, 1979.

Record Victory: 7-0 v Swindon T., Division 3(S), 1954–55.

Record Defeat: 1-8 v Norwich C., Division 3(S), 1952–53 and v Coventry C., Division 3, Oct. 22nd, 1963.

Most League Points: 62, Division 4, 1974–75.

Most League Goals: 101, Division 4, 1958–59.

Highest League Scorer in Season: Arthur Rowley, 38, Division 4, 1958–59.

Most League Goals in Total Aggregate: Arthur Rowley, 152, 1958–65. (While with **Shrewsbury T.**, Arthur Rowley completed his League scoring record of 434 goals.)

Most Capped Player: Jimmy McLaughlin, 5 (12) Ireland.

Most League Appearances: Joe Wallace, 329, 1954–63.

Record Transfer Fee Received: £90,000 from Manchester U. for Jim Holton, Jan. 1973.

Record Transfer Fee Paid: £40,000 to Liverpool for Trevor Birch, March 1979.

Managers Since the War: Sam Crooks, Walter Rowley, Harry Potts, John Spuhler, Arthur Rowley, Harry Gregg, Maurice Evans, Alan Durban, Richie Barker.

Address of Supporters Club and Shop: c/o Football Club.

Gay Meadow, Shrewsbury. Telephone Shrewsbury 56068. *Ground capacity:* 18,000. *Record attendance:* 18,917 v Walsall, Division 3, April 26, 1961. *Record receipts:* £8,328 v Q.P.R., L.C. 2nd Rd., September 9, 1975. *Pitch measurements:* 116 yds × 76 yds.

How to get there: Midland Red schedule bus services from main bus station in Barker Street to the ground. Special coach facilities are arranged by local companies from neighbouring districts. Shrewsbury railway station is 10 minutes walk from the ground.

Car parking: A park adjacent to the ground and a free public car park five minutes walk away.

Entertainments/catering facilities: Buffets are situated on each side of the ground.

Club shop: Sells all types of souvenirs.

Handbooks/programmes: No handbook. Programmes can be obtained through the post at 10p each plus S.A.E.

Extra information: In 1960–61 Shrewsbury met Swindon Town six times in League, F.A. Cup, and League Cup and did not lose once.

Club Colours: Amber shirts with blue stripes, blue shorts, amber stockings.
Change Colours: Red or white.
Club Nickname: 'Town'.

SHREWSBURY TOWN 1978–79 LEAGUE RECORD

Match No.	Date	Venue	Opponents	Result	H/T Score	League Pos'n	Goalscorers	Attendance
1	Aug 19	H	Brentford	W 1-0	1-0	—	Atkins (pen)	2346
2	23	A	Oxford U	W 1-0	0-0	—	Turner	3877
3	26	H	Swindon T	D 0-0	0-0	3		2672
4	Sept 2	A	Walsall	D 1-1	1-1	6	Turner	4269
5	9	H	Blackpool	W 2-0	1-0	2	Biggins, Maguire	4179
6	13	A	Exeter C	W 1-0	0-0	—	Maguire	3732
7	15	A	Colchester U	L 0-1	0-0	5		2788
8	23	H	Lincoln C	W 2-0	1-0	3	Turner, Atkins (pen)	2902
9	26	H	Hull C	W 1-0	0-0	—	Maguire	3777
10	29	A	Southend U	W 1-0	0-0	1	Atkins	6773
11	Oct 7	H	Mansfield T	D 2-2	2-1	1	Maguire 2	4338
12	14	A	Plymouth Arg	D 1-1	1-0	1	Atkins	9901
13	16	A	Tranmere R	D 2-2	0-1	—	Atkins 2 (1 a pen)	3087
14	21	H	Sheffield W	D 2-2	0-0	2	Maguire, Tong	6294
15	28	A	Rotherham U	W 2-1	2-0	2	Turner, Biggins	4476
16	Nov 4	H	Carlisle U	D 0-0	0-0	1		4656
17	10	H	Walsall	D 1-1	1-0	2	Tong	7615
18	18	A	Swindon T	L 1-2	1-0	3	Griffin	7317
19	Dec 6	A	Peterborough U	W 2-0	2-0	—	Atkins, Griffin	3087
20	9	H	Gillingham	D 1-1	0-0	3	Keay	3924
21	23	H	Swansea C	W 3-0	2-0	2	Atkins, Biggins, Maguire	8567
22	26	A	Watford	D 2-2	1-2	2	Chapman, Maguire	20,276
23	Jan 19	A	Colchester U	W 2-0	1-0	2	Biggins, Chapman	2119
24	30	H	Chester	W 1-0	0-0	—	Biggins	6693
25	Feb 3	A	Hull C	D 1-1	1-1	2	Turner	5129
26	9	H	Southend U	W 2-0	2-0	2	Chapman, Atkins (pen)	5749
27	24	H	Plymouth Arg	W 2-0	1-0	2	Maguire, Chapman	6087
28	Mar 3	A	Sheffield W	D 0-0	0-0	2		11,284
29	7	A	Chesterfield	L 1-2	0-0	—	Tong	4324
30	17	A	Carlisle U	D 1-1	0-0	2	Biggins	5057
31	20	A	Blackpool	L 0-5	0-1	—		5330
32	24	H	Oxford U	D 0-0	0-0	3		6791
33	26	A	Brentford	W 3-2	2-1	—	Biggins, Keay, Cross	7760
34	31	A	Bury	L 0-3	0-0	4		3340
35	Apr 7	H	Peterborough U	W 2-0	0-0	3	Cross (pen), King	5600
36	10	A	Swansea C	D 1-1	0-1	—	Atkins	19,566
37	14	H	Watford	D 1-1	1-1	4	Birch	13,320
38	16	A	Chester	D 0-0	0-0	—		6249
39	21	H	Chesterfield	D 1-1	1-0	5	King	6360
40	24	H	Tranmere R	W 2-1	0-0	—	Birch, Maguire	6013
41	28	A	Gillingham	L 0-2	0-0	4		14,902
42	May 2	A	Lincoln C	W 2-1	0-0	—	King, Maguire	1677
43	5	H	Bury	W 1-0	0-0	3	Biggins	6604
44	7	A	Mansfield T	D 2-2	0-1	—	Biggins, Maguire	6413
45	10	H	Rotherham U	W 3-1	1-1	—	King, Tong, Maguire	8450
46	17	H	Exeter C	W 4-1	3-1	—	King 2, Atkins (pen), Tong	14,441

Final League Position: 1

Goalscorers

League (61): Maguire 13, Atkins 11 (5 pens), Biggins 9, King 6, Turner 5, Tong 5, Chapman 4, Griffin 2, Cross 2 (1 pen), Keay 2, Birch 2.
League Cup (2): Cross, Own Goal 1.
F.A. Cup (17): Maguire 5, Chapman 3, Biggins 3, Atkins 2 (1 pen), Turner, Tong, Leonard, Keay.

League Cup	First Round	Stockport Co (h)	1-0
		(a)	1-3
F.A. Cup	First Round	Mansfield T (a)	2-0
	Second Round	Doncaster R (a)	3-0
	Third Round	Cambridge U (h)	3-1
	Fourth Round	Manchester C (h)	2-0
	Fifth Round	Aldershot (a)	2-2
		(h)	3-1 (a.e.t.)
	Sixth Round	Wolverhampton W (a)	1-1
		(h)	1-3

Mulhearn	King	Leonard	Turner	Griffin	Hayes	Cross	Lindsay	Atkins	Biggins	Maguire	Keay	Loughnane	Chapman	Tong	Larkin	Wardle	Birch	Roberts	Match No.
1	2	3	4	5	6	7*	8	9	10	11	12								1
1	2	3	4	5	6		8	9	10	11			7						2
1	2	3	4	5	6		8	9	10	11			7						3
1	2	3	4	5	6		8*	9	10	11			7	12					4
1	2	3	4	5	6		8	9	10	11			7						5
1	2	3	4	5	6		8	9	10	11			7						6
1	2	3*	4	5	6	12	9	8	10	11			7						7
1	2	3	4	5	6		7	9	10	11				8					8
1	2		4	5	6			8	10	11			9	7	3				9
1	2		4	5	6		9	8	10	11			7		3				10
1	2		4	5	6		12	9	10	11			7	8*	3				11
	2	3	4	5	6		8	9	10	11			7			1			12
	2	3	4	5	6		9*	8	10	11			7	12		1			13
1	2	3	4	5	6		8*	9	10	11			7	12					14
1	2*	3	4	5	6	12		9	10	11			7	8					15
1		3	4	5	6			9	10	11			8	7	2				16
	2	3	4	5	6			8	10	11			7	9		1			17
	2	3	4	5	6			9	10	11			7	8		1			18
	2	3	4	5	6			8	10	11			7	9		1			19
	2	3	4	5		8		10	11		6		7	9		1			20
	2		4	5		12	8*	10	11		6		7	9	3	1			21
	2		4	5				8	10	11	6		7	9	3	1			22
	2		4	5				8	10	11	6		7	9	3	1			23
	2		4	5				8	10	11	6		7	9	3	1			24
	2		4	5				8	10	11	6		7	9	3	1			25
	2	3	4	5*		12		8	10	11	6		7	9		1			26
	2	3	4	5				8	10	11	6		7	9		1			27
	2*	3	4	5		12		8	10	11	6		7	9		1			28
		2	4	5				8	10	11	6		7	9	3	1			29
		3	4	5		12	7	8	10	11	6		9*	2		1			30
		3	4	5			7	8	10	11	6		9	2		1			31
		3	4	5	2		12	8	10	11*	6		9			1	7		32
		3		5	2	4	11	8	10		6		9			1	7		33
		3		5		4	11	8	10		6		9*	2		1	7	12	34
1	2			5		4	11	8	10		6		9	3			7		35
1	2			5		4	11	8	10		6		9	3			7		36
1	2			5		4	11	8	10		6		9	3			7		37
1	2			5		4	11	8	10		6		9	3			7		38
1	2			5			8		4	10	11	6	9	3			7		39
1	2			5		4	11	8		10	6		9	3			7		40
1	2			5		4	10	8	12	11*	6		9	3			7		41
1	2			5		4	11		8	10	6		9	3			7		42
1	2			5		4		8	10	11	6		9	3			7		43
1	2			5		4	7	8*	10	11	6		9	3			12		44
1	2			5		4		8	10	11	6		9	3			7		45
1	2			5		4	7	8	10	11	6		9	3					46
26	39	26	32	46	21	14	27	44	44	40	27	3	24	35	25	20	13	—	
						+ 5s	+ 3s				+ 1s		+ 1s	+ 2s		+ 1s	+ 1s		

SHREWSBURY TOWN—PLAYERS

Player and position	Ht	Wt	Birthplace	Clubs	League Appearances	Goals
Goalkeepers						
Ken Mulhearn	6 0	13 11	Liverpool	Everton	—	—
				Stockport Co	100	—
				Manchester C	50	—
				Shrewsbury T	352	—
Bobby Wardle	5 11	11 2	Leeds	Bristol C	—	—
				Shrewsbury T	23	—
Defenders						
Colin Griffin	6 0	11 7	Dudley	Derby Co	—	—
				Shrewsbury T	144+2	5
Jake King	5 10	11 0	Glasgow	Shrewsbury T	224+2	7
Carleton Leonard	5 9	10 3	Oswestry	Shrewsbury T	125+1	1
Jack Keay	6 0	12 6	Glasgow	Celtic	—	—
				Shrewsbury T	47+2	3
Steve Cross	5 10	10 6	Wolverhampton	Shrewsbury T	19+6	2
Anthony Larkin	5 11	11 12	Wrexham	Wrexham	—	—
				Shrewsbury T	25	—
Midfield						
Ian Atkins	5 10	11 0	Birmingham	Shrewsbury T	156+4	32
Graham Turner	5 10	11 13	Ellesmere Port	Wrexham	77	—
				Chester	215+3	5
				Shrewsbury T	250+2	16
Steve Hayes	5 10	11 6	Smethwick	Shrewsbury T	64+3	—
				Torquay U (on loan)	1	—
Jimmy Lindsay	5 7½	12 0	Hamilton	West Ham U	35+3	2
				Watford	64+1	12
				Colchester U	45	6
				Hereford U	79	6
				Shrewsbury T	62+3	—
Bob Chapman	6 0	12 11	Walsall	Nottingham F	347+12	17
(Contract cancelled April 1979)				Notts Co	42	—
				Shrewsbury T	24+1	4
David Tong	5 8	10 1	Blackpool	Blackpool	70+8	7
				Shrewsbury T	35+2	5
Mike Roberts	5 8	10 6	Birmingham	Shrewsbury T	0+1	—
Forwards						
Peter Loughnane	5 9½	11 2	Shrewsbury T	Manchester U	—	—
(Contract cancelled March 1979)				Shrewsbury T	24+7	4
Paul Maguire	5 9	10 12	Glasgow	Shrewsbury T	115+8	26
Steve Biggins	6 0	11 12	Walsall	Shrewsbury T	53+1	16
Trevor Birch	5 11	11 13	Ormskirk	Liverpool	—	—
				Shrewsbury T	13+1	2
Mike Neil	5 9	11 0	Kilmarnock	Shrewsbury T	—	—
Geoff Croft				Shrewsbury T	—	—

SOUTHAMPTON

DIV. 1

President: H. G. Blagrave. *Chairman:* A. A. Woodford
Directors: E. C. Chaplin, J. Corbett, Lt.-Col. Sir George Meyrick (Bart), M.C., T.D., B. G. W. Bowyer, J.P., F. G. Askham, F.C.A., E. T. Bates.
Chief Executive: Ted Bates. *Manager:* Lawrie McMenemy. *Assistant Manager:* John Mortimore.
Secretary: Brian Truscott.
Year Formed: 1885.
Turned Professional: 1894. *Limited Company:* 1897.
Previous Name: Southampton St. Mary's until 1885.
Previous Grounds: 1885, Antelope Ground; 1897, County Cricket Ground; 1898, The Dell.
Football League Record: 1920 Original Members of Division 3. 1921 Division 3(S). 1922–53 Division 2. 1953–58 Division 3(S). 1958–60 Division 3. 1960–66 Division 2. 1966–74 Division 1. 1974–78 Division 2. 1978– Division 1.
Honours: Football League, best season in Division 1; 7th, 1968–69, 1970–71. Division 2, Runners-up: 1965–66, 1977–78. Division 3(S), Champions: 1921–22, Runners-up, 1920–21. Division 3, Champions: 1959–60. *F.A. Cup,* Winners 1975–76; Runners-up: 1900, 1902.
Football League Cup, best season: Runners-up 1978–79.
European Competitions: European Fairs Cup: 1969–70. *UEFA Cup:* 1971–72. *European Cup-Winners' Cup:* 1976–77.
Record Victory: 11-0 v Northampton, Southern League, Dec. 28th, 1901.
Record Defeat: 0-8 v Tottenham H., Division 2, Mar. 28th, 1936, and v Everton, Division 1, Nov. 20 1971.
Most League Points: 61, Division 3(S), 1921–22, and Division 3, 1959–60.
Most League Goals: 112, Div 3(S), 1957–58.
Highest League Scorer in Season: Derek Reeves, 39, Division 3, 1959–60.
Most Capped Player: Mike Channon, 45 (46), England.
Most League Appearances: Terry Paine, 713, 1956–74.
Most League Goals in Total Aggregate: Terry Paine, 160, 1956–74.
Record Transfer Fee Received: £300,000 from Manchester C. for Mike Channon, July 1977.
Record Transfer Fee Paid: £400,000 to Derby Co. for Charlie George, December, 1978.
Managers Since the War: Bill Dodgin (Snr.), Sid Cann, George Roughton, Ted Bates.
Address of Supporters Club: Same as Football Club.

The Dell, Milton Road, Southampton SO9 4XX. Telephone Southampton 39445 and 39633.
Ground capacity: 26,000 *Record attendance:* 31,044 v Manchester U., Division 1, October 8, 1969.
Record receipts: £43,029 v Anderlecht- European Cup-Winners Cup, Quarter-final, Second leg, March 16, 1977. *Pitch measurements:* 110 yds × 72 yds.
How to get there: The ground is 10 minutes walk from Southampton Central station via Hill Lane. Buses 2 and 5 from the city centre pass the ground, which is only 10 minutes walk from the centre.
Match tickets: No seats available, all seats being sold to season-ticket holders. Room on the terraces for 18,500 standing, and admission is through the turnstiles on the day of the match.
Car parking: Only street parking in the vicinity of the ground. Municipal car parks in the city centre.
Entertainments/catering facilities: Licensed bars inside the ground.
Club shop: Situated in Milton Road, and at Hanover Buildings in City Centre.
Handbooks/programmes: Handbooks not published annually. Programmes available on subscription.
Extra information: In 1921–22, Southampton lost only four league games and conceded only 21 goals both Division Three (South) records.
Club Colours: Red and white striped shirts, black shorts, white stockings.
Change Colours: Yellow shirts, blue shorts, yellow stockings.
Club Captain: Alan Ball. *Physiotherapist:* Don Taylor, M.C.S.P., S.R.P.
First Team Trainer: Lew Chatterley *Club Nickname:* 'Saints'.

SOUTHAMPTON 1978-79 LEAGUE RECORD

Match No.	Date	Venue	Opponents	Result Score	H/T Score	League Pos'n	Goalscorers	Attendance
1	Aug 19	A	Norwich C	L 1-3	0-1	—	MacDougall	21,133
2	22	H	Bolton W	D 2-2	1-1	—	MacDougall, Baker	21,059
3	26	H	Middlesbrough	W 2-1	0-1	12	Nicholl, Ball	20,691
4	Sept 2	A	Aston Villa	D 1-1	1-1	12	Nicholl	34,067
5	9	H	Wolverhampton W	W 3-2	1-0	7	Boyer, Waldron, MacDougall	22,060
6	16	A	Bristol C	L 1-3	1-1	12	Holmes	21,420
7	23	A	Derby Co	L 1-2	0-0	14	Peach (pen)	21,623
8	30	H	Ipswich T	L 1-2	0-2	15	MacDougall	21,264
9	Oct 7	A	Everton	D 0-0	0-0	18		38,769
10	14	H	QPR	D 1-1	1-0	16	MacDougall	22,803
11	21	A	Arsenal	L 0-1	0-0	19		33,074
12	28	H	Nottingham F	D 0-0	0-0	17		22,530
13	Nov 4	A	Manchester U	D 1-1	0-1	18	Holmes	46,259
14	11	H	Norwich C	D 2-2	1-1	16	Holmes, Nicholl	21,183
15	18	A	Middlesbrough	L 0-2	0-1	17		17,169
16	21	H	Aston Villa	W 2-0	2-0	—	Baker, Holmes	20,880
17	25	A	Leeds U	L 0-4	0-2	17		23,592
18	Dec 2	H	Birmingham C	W 1-0	0-0	15	Boyer	18,957
19	9	A	Manchester C	W 2-1	1-0	12	Viljoen (og), Boyer	33,450
20	16	H	Coventry C	W 4-0	2-0	12	Waldron, Hebberd, Boyer, Baker	19,102
21	26	H	Chelsea	D 0-0	0-0	12		20,770
22	Jan 17	A	Wolverhampton W	L 0-2	0-2	—		15,104
23	Feb 3	H	Derby Co	L 1-2	1-1	16	Peach (pen)	21,109
24	10	A	Ipswich T	D 0-0	0-0	16		19,520
25	17	A	Everton	W 3-0	1-0	12	Peach (pen), Baker, Boyer	20,673
26	20	H	Bristol C	W 2-0	2-0	—	Hayes, Holmes	19,845
27	24	A	QPR	W 1-0	1-0	9	Holmes	13,636
28	Mar 3	H	Arsenal	W 2-0	1-0	8	Hayes, Waldron	25,052
29	24	A	Bolton W	L 0-2	0-0	18		19,879
30	28	A	Tottenham H	D 0-0	0-0	—		23,570
31	31	H	Leeds U	D 2-2	0-1	13	Waldron 2	21,805
32	Apr 7	A	Birmingham C	D 2-2	0-1	15	Baker, Hayes	12,125
33	13	H	WBA	D 1-1	0-0	—	Waldron	22,063
34	14	A	Chelsea	W 2-1	2-0	11	Peach (pen), Holmes	18,243
35	16	H	Tottenham H	D 3-3	3-0	—	Peach (pen), Ball (pen), Boyer	22,096
36	21	A	Coventry C	L 0-4	0-1	13		17,750
37	24	H	Liverpool	D 1-1	0-1	—	Holmes	23,181
38	28	H	Manchester C	W 1-0	0-0	12	Hebberd	19,744
39	30	H	Manchester U	D 1-1	1-1	—	Boyer	21,616
40	May 2	A	Nottingham F	L 0-1	0-0	—		20,388
41	5	A	Liverpool	L 0-2	0-1	13		46,687
42	8	A	WBA	L 0-1	0-0	—		17,526

Final League Position: 14

Goalscorers

League (47): Holmes 8, Boyer 7, Waldron 6, MacDougall 5, Baker 5, Peach 5 (5 pens), Nicholl 3, Hayes 3, Ball 2 (1 pen), Hebberd 2, Own Goal 1.
League Cup (15): Boyer 4, Hebberd 2, MacDougall 2, Peach 2, Holmes 2, Nicholl, Williams, Curran.
F.A. Cup (7): Boyer 4, Ball, Peach (pen), Hayes.

League Cup	Second Round	Birmingham C (a)	5-2
	Third Round	Derby Co (h)	1-0
	Fourth Round	Reading (a)	0-0
		(h)	2-0
	Fifth Round	Manchester C (h)	2-1
	Semi-Final	Leeds U (a)	2-2
		(h)	1-0
	Final	Nottingham F	2-3 (at Wembley)
F.A. Cup	Third Round	Wimbledon (a)	2-0
	Fourth Round	Preston N E (a)	1-0
	Fifth Round	WBA (a)	1-1
		(h)	2-1 (aet)
	Sixth Round	Arsenal (h)	1-1
		(a)	0-2

Wells	Waldron	Peach	Williams S	Nicholl	Pickering	Ball	Boyer	MacDougall	Baker	Curran	Hebberd	Golac	Andruszewski	Holmes	Hayes	Gennoe	Sealy	Funnell	Williams O	George	Dawtry	Match No.
1	2	3	4	5	6	7	8	9	10*	11	12											1
1	6	3	4	5		7	8	9	10	11*	12	2										2
1	6	3	4	5		7	8	9	10	11		2										3
1	6	3	4	5		7	8	9		11	12	2	10*									4
1	6	3	4	5		7	8	9		11	12	2		10*								5
1	6	3	4	5		7	8	9*		11		2		10	12							6
	6	3	8	5	4	7	9			11	12	2		10*		1						7
	6	3	4		5	7	8	9		11		2		10		1						8
	6		4	5		7	9	10		11	12	3*	2	8		1						9
	6	3	4	5		7	9	8	11*			2		10		1	12					10
	6		4	5		7	8	9	11			2	3	10		1						11
	6	3	4	5		7	8		11*			2		10		1	12	9				12
	6	3	4	5		7	8		11	9	2			10		1						13
	6	3	4	5		7	8		11			2		10		1		9				14
	6		4	5		7	8		11	9*	2	3	10			1	12					15
	6	3	4	5		7	8	11		9	2			10		1						16
	6	3	4	5		7	8	11	12	9*	2			10		1						17
	6	3	4	5		7	8		11	9	2			10		1						18
	6	3	4	5		7	8		11	9	2			10		1						19
	6	3	4*	5		7	8	11		9	2			10		1	12					20
	6	3	4	5		7	8		11	9	2			10		1						21
	6	3	4	5		7	8		11	9	2			10		1						22
	6	3	4	5		7	8		11*	9	2			10		1	12					23
	6	3*	4	5		7	8	12	11	9	2			10		1						24
	6	3		5		7	8	4	11		2			10	9	1						25
	6	3		5		7	8	4	11		2			10	9	1						26
	6	3	4	5		7	8		11		2			10	9	1						27
	6	3	4	5		7	8				2			10	9	1		11				28
1	6		4	5		7	8		11		2	3		10					9			29
1	6	3	4	5		7	8		11		2			10	12				9*			30
1	6	3	4	5		7	8		11		2			10	9							31
	6	3	4			7	8		11		2	5		10	9	1						32
1	6	3	4	5		7	8		11		2			10	9							33
1	6	3	4	5		7	8		11		2			10	9							34
1	6	3	4	5		7	8		11		2			10	9							35
1	6	3	4	5		7	8		11		2			10	9*							36
1	6	3	4	5		7	8		11		2			10	9*		12					37
1	6	3	4	5		7	8	12		9	2*			10			11					38
1	6	3	4			7	8		11	9		5	10				2					39
1	6	3	4			7	8	5		9		2	10						11*	12		40
1	6	3		5		7	8	4		9		2	10	11								41
1	6	3	4	5		7	8		11		10		2	9								42
19	42	38	39	38	3	42	42	10	20	25	16	36	10	38	13	23	—	2	4	2		
									+ 2s	+ 1s	+ 6s			+ 2s	+ 5s	+ 1s		+ 1s				

SOUTHAMPTON—PLAYERS

Player and position	Ht	Wt	Birthplace	Clubs	League Appearances	Goals
Goalkeepers						
Peter Wells	6 1	13 0	Nottingham	Nottingham F	27	—
				Southampton	73	—
Terence Gennoe	6 2½	13 5	Shrewsbury	Bury	3	—
				Blackburn R (on loan)	—	—
				Leeds U (on loan)	—	—
				Halifax T	78	—
				Southampton	23	—
Mark Harrison	6 0¼	12 3½	London	Southampton	—	—
Defenders						
*Paul Arnold	5 9	11 0	Bournemouth	Southampton	—	—
*Timothy Coak	5 4½	10 4	Southampton	Southampton	4	—
David Peach	5 9	11 6	Bedford	Gillingham	186+1	30
				Southampton	200+3	32
Malcolm Waldron	6 0	12 4	Emsworth	Southampton	103+1	6
Manny Andruszewski	5 10	11 9	Eastleigh	Southampton	71	2
Forbes Phillipson-Masters	6 1	12 10	Bournemouth	Southampton	9	—
				Exeter C (on loan)	6	—
				Bournemouth (on loan)	7	2
				Luton T (on loan)	10	—
Chris Nicholl (N Ireland)	6 2	12 9	Wilmslow	Halifax T	42	3
				Luton T	97	6
				Aston V	210	11
				Southampton	77	4
Mark Whitlock	5 1	11 8½	Portsmouth	Southampton	—	—
Ivan Golac (Yugoslavia)	5 10	12 10	Yugoslavia	Partizan	—	—
				Southampton	36	—
Midfield						
Nick Holmes	5 11	11 7	Southampton	Southampton	175+5	35
Graham Baker	5 8½	9 9½	Southampton	Southampton	23+2	6
Alan Ball (England)	5 6	10 5	Farnworth	Blackpool	116	41
				Everton	208	66
				Arsenal	177	45
				Southampton	106	8
Steve Williams	5 10	11 8	London	Southampton	111+1	5
Wayne Pratt	5 8	9 9	Southampton	Southampton	—	—
Martin McGrath	5 10	11 11	London	Southampton	—	—
Forwards						
George Shipley	5 7¼	9 10	Newcastle-on-Tyne	Southampton	—	—
				Reading (on loan)	11+1	1
Kevin Dawtry	5 6	9 13½	Southampton	Southampton	0+1	—
Austin Hayes (Eire)	5 5½	9 10	London	Southampton	15+5	3
Trevor Hebberd	5 11½	11 4	Winchester	Southampton	26+20	5
Phil Boyer (England)	5 8	11 2	Nottingham	Derby C	—	—
				York C	108+1	27
				Bournemouth	140+1	46
				Norwich C	115+1	34
				Southampton	83	24
Oshor Williams	5 10	11 3	Stockton	Manchester U	—	—
				Southampton	4+1	—
				Exeter C (on loan)	2+1	—
Charlie George (England)	5 11	12 0	London	Arsenal	113+20	31
				Derby Co	106	34
				Southampton	2	—
David Puckett	5 7	9 12	Southampton	Southampton	—	—
Mike O'Donoghue	5 9	11 9	London	Southampton	—	—

SOUTHEND UNITED DIV. 3

President: N. L. Mitchell. *Chairman:* Frank Walton.
Directors: J. N. Woodcock, L. H. Lesser, F.C.A., D. A. Smith, G. C. Janes, H. W. Stone, F. Zonfield M. D. Rubin.
Manager: David Smith. *Secretary:* K. Holmes, F.A.A.I.
Year Formed: 1906. *Turned Professional:* 1906.
Limited Company: 1919.
Previous Grounds: 1906, Roots Hall, Prittlewell; 1920, Kursaal; 1934, Southend Stadium; 1955, Roots Hall Football Ground.

Football League Record:
1920 Original Member of Division 3.
1921 Division 3(S).
1958–66 Division 3.
1966–72 Division 4.
1972–76 Division 3.
1976–78 Division 4.
1978– Division 3.

Honours: Football League, best season in Division 3(S): 3rd. 1931–32, 1949–50.   Division 4, Runners up: 1971–72, 1977–78. *F.A. Cup,* best season: old 3rd Rd., 1920–21, 5th Rd., 1925–26, 1951–52, 1975–76.
Football League Cup: best season: never past 3rd Rd.
Record Victory: 10-1 v Golders Green, F.A. Cup, 1st Rd., Nov. 24th, 1934, 10-1 v. Brentwood, F.A. Cup 2nd Rd., Dec. 7th, 1968.
Record Defeat: 1-11 v Northampton, Southern League, Dec. 30th, 1909.
Most League Points: 60, Division 4, 1971–72, 1977–78.
Most League Goals: 92, Division 3(S), 1950–51.
Highest League Scorer in Season: Jim Shankly, 31, 1928–29 and Sammy McCrory, 1957–58, both of Division 3(S).
Most League Goals in Total Aggregate: Roy Hollis, 122, 1953–60.
Most Capped Player: George Mackenzie, 9, Eire.
Most League Appearances: Sandy Anderson, 451, 1950–63.
Record Transfer Fee Received: £120,000 from C. Palace for Peter Taylor, Oct. 1973.
Record Transfer Fee Paid: £50,000 to Sheffield W. for Dave Cusack, Sept., 1978 and £50,000 to Tottenham H. for Mike Stead, Nov., 1978
Managers Since the War: Harry Warren, Eddie Perry, Frank Broome, Ted Fenton, Alvan Williams, Ernie Shepherd, Geoff Hudson, Arthur Rowley.
Address of Supporters Club: 374 Victoria Ave., Southend-on-Sea, Essex.
Address of Club Shop or Boutique: 374 Victoria Avenue, Southend-on-Sea.

Roots Hall Football Ground, Victoria Avenue, Southend-on-Sea. Telephone Southend 40707
Ground capacity: 35,000 (16,000 covered).   *Record attendance:* 31,033 v Liverpool F.A. Cup 3rd Rd., January, 10 1979.   *Record receipts:* £36,599 v Liverpool F.A. Cup 3rd Rd., January 10, 1979.   *Pitch measurements:* 110 yds × 74 yds.

How to get there: Regular buses from Southend Central station in the High Street; the station is on the London line from Fenchurch Street. Southend Victoria, five minutes walk from the ground, is served by trains from Liverpool Street, London.
Match tickets: Seats can be purchased 14 days before the match.
Car parking: Two car parks at the ground hold approximately 700 cars. Ample parking in side-streets.
Entertainments/catering facilities: Tea bars all around the ground. There is a social club for members and *bona fide* visitors.
Club shop: Situated in Victoria Avenue opposite the ground; sells all types of souvenirs.
Handbooks/programmes: Both handbooks and programmes are available from the club shop; programmes are available on subscription.
Extra information: In 1921–22 full-back Jimmy Evans topped Southend's scorers' list with 10 penalties.
Club Colours: Royal blue shirts, red and white trim, white shorts and white stockings with blue and red trim.
Change Colours: Yellow shirts with black trim, yellow shorts and yellow stockings with black trim.
Club Captain: Alan Moody.
Club Trainer/Coach: John Latimer.
Club Nickname: 'The Shrimpers'.

SOUTHEND UNITED 1978-79 LEAGUE RECORD

Match No.	Date	Venue	Opponents	Result	H/T Score	League Pos'n	Goalscorers	Attendance
1	Aug 19	H	Chester	L 0-1	0-0	—		4223
2	22	A	Bury	D 3-3	1-0	—	Morris 2, Laverick	3243
3	26	A	Mansfield T	D 1-1	1-0	15	Parker	5500
4	Sept 1	H	Plymouth Arg	W 2-1	1-1	11	Pountney, Parker	5936
5	9	A	Sheffield W	L 2-3	0-2	14	Morris (pen), Fell	11,309
6	11	H	Oxford U	W 2-0	1-0	—	Fell, Parker	5222
7	15	H	Rotherham U	W 2-1	0-0	7	Fell 2	6527
8	23	A	Carlisle U	D 0-0	0-0	8		5263
9	27	A	Chesterfield	L 2-3	2-1	—	Parker, Abbott	4316
10	29	H	Shrewsbury T	L 0-1	0-0	15		6773
11	Oct 7	A	Walsall	D 1-1	1-1	14	Cusack	4911
12	14	H	Blackpool	W 4-0	2-0	11	Yates, Fell 2, Pountney	6374
13	20	A	Colchester U	D 1-1	1-0	15	Laverick	5831
14	23	H	Hull C	W 3-0	0-0	—	Moody (pen), Dudley, Parker	6812
15	27	H	Lincoln C	W 2-0	2-0	6	Stead, Laverick	7356
16	Nov 4	A	Swindon T	L 0-1	0-0	7		5647
17	11	A	Plymouth Arg	D 1-1	1-1	7	Fell	6890
18	17	H	Mansfield T	D 1-1	1-1	10	Polycarpou	7532
19	Dec 2	A	Exeter C	D 0-0	0-0	8		3195
20	8	H	Swansea C	L 0-2	0-1	10		8935
21	23	H	Brentford	D 1-1	0-0	11	Moody (pen)	13,189
22	26	A	Gillingham	L 0-1	0-0	12		6644
23	30	A	Peterborough U	W 1-0	0-0	8	Laverick	3731
24	Feb 2	H	Chesterfield	W 2-0	2-0	9	Moody (pen), Parker	4322
25	6	A	Rotherham U	L 1-2	1-2	—	Dudley	4478
26	9	A	Shrewsbury T	L 0-2	0-2	10		5749
27	13	H	Sheffield W	W 2-1	1-0	—	Laverick, Dudley	4559
28	24	A	Blackpool	W 2-1	2-1	8	Morris, Pountney	4566
29	Mar 2	H	Colchester U	D 1-1	0-0	9	Parker	6957
30	7	A	Oxford U	D 0-0	0-0	—		2913
31	10	A	Lincoln C	D 1-1	0-1	9	Morris (pen)	2559
32	12	H	Carlisle U	D 1-1	1-0	—	Morris	5457
33	16	H	Swindon T	W 5-3	3-0	7	Stead, Polycarpou 2, Morris (pen), Laverick	4303
34	21	A	Chester	W 1-0	0-0	—	Polycarpou	2108
35	24	H	Bury	D 0-0	0-0	7		8531
36	30	A	Tranmere R	W 2-1	0-0	7	Polycarpou, Pountney	1250
37	Apr 2	H	Watford	W 1-0	0-0	—	Pountney	11,406
38	6	H	Exeter C	L 0-1	0-0	7		6733
39	13	A	Brentford	L 0-3	0-1	—		11,500
40	14	H	Gillingham	L 0-1	0-0	8		7291
41	17	A	Watford	L 0-2	0-1	—		15,835
42	21	H	Peterborough U	D 0-0	0-0	9		3461
43	24	A	Hull C	L 0-2	0-0	—		3960
44	28	A	Swansea C	L 2-3	0-1	12	Parker 2	15,941
45	30	H	Walsall	W 1-0	1-0	—	Parker	2887
46	May 4	H	Tranmere R	L 0-1	0-1	11		3607

Final League Position: 13

Goalscorers

League (51): Parker 10, Fell 7, Morris 7 (3 pens), Laverick 6, Polycarpou 5, Pountney 5, Dudley 3, Moody 3 (3 pens), Stead 2, Abbott 1, Cusack 1, Yates 1.
League Cup (2): Own Goals 2.
F.A. Cup (5): Parker 2, Pountney, Polycarpou, Own Goal 1.

League Cup	First Round	Wimbledon (h)	1-0
		(a)	1-4
F.A. Cup	First Round	Peterborough U (h)	3-2
	Second Round	Watford (a)	1-1
		(h)	1-0
	Third Round	Liverpool (h)	0-0
		(a)	0-3

Cawston	Dudley	Yates	Laverick	Townsend	Moody	Fell	Goodwin	Parker	Pountney	Morris	Hadley	Walker	Polycarpou	Stead	Cusack	Abbott	Franklin	Otulakowski	Horn	Hull	Match No.
1	2	3	4	5	6	7	8	9	10	11											1
1	2	3	4		6	11	10	9	8	7	5										2
1	2	3	4			7		9	10	11	5	6	8								3
1	2	3	4			11		9	8	7	6	5	10								4
1	10	3	4			11		9	8	7	12	6		2*	5						5
1	2	3	4*			11		9	8	7	6		10		5	12					6
1	2	3	4			11		9	8	7	6	12	10		5*						7
1	10	3	4			8		9	7	11	6			2	5						8
1	10	3				11		9	8	7	6	12		2	5	4*					9
1	10	3				11		9	8	7	6	12		2	5	4*					10
1	10	3	4		6	11			8	7	9			2	5						11
1	10	3	4		6	7			8	11	9			2	5						12
1	10	3	4		6	11*			8	7	12		9	2	5						13
1	10	3	4		6			9	8	7			11	2	5						14
1	10	3	4		6			9	8	7			11	2	5						15
1	10	3*	4		6	12		9	11	7			8	2	5						16
1	2		4		6	7		9	8	11			10	3	5						17
1	2		4		6	10*		9	8	7		12	11	3	5						18
1	10	3*	4		6			9	7	11		12	8	2	5						19
1	10*	3	4		6			9	8	7	12		11	2	5						20
1	7		6		4		10	9	8	3	2	11*	5			12					21
1	10		4		6			9	8	7	5	3	11	2							22
1	10	3	4		6	11		9	8	7	5			2							23
1	10	3			2	11		9	8	7	5				4	6					24
1	10	3			6	11		9	8	7	5			2	4						25
1	10	3	12		6	11*		9	8	7	5	2			4						26
1	10	3	11		6			9	8	7	5			2	4						27
1	10	3	11		2			9	8	7	6			4	5						28
1	10	3	11		2			9	8	7	5			4	6						29
1	10	3	11		2			9	8	7	5			4	6						30
1	10	3			2*			9		7	5	12	11	4	6	8					31
1	10	3	12		2	11		9		7	5			4	6	8*					32
1	10	3	11		2			9		7	5*12	8		4	6						33
1	10	3	11		2			9		7	5*12	8		4	6						34
1	10	3	4		6			9	11	7		8	2	5							35
1	10	3*11			2			9	12	7	5		8	4	6						36
1	10	3			6			9	12	7	2*		8	4	5		11				37
1	2	3						9	10	7	6		8	4	5		11				38
1	10	3		5				9	8	7		2		4	6		11				39
	4	3*		5	7			9	8		6	2	12		10		11	1			40
	10	3			6	7		9	8		5	2		4		11		1			41
	10	3			6			9	8*	7		12	2	5		11	1	4			42
	4	3						9	8	7	6		12	2*	5	10	11	1			43
	10	3			5			9	8	7	4			2	6		11	1			44
	4	3						9	8	7	10	6*12		2	5		11	1			45
	4	3						9	8	7	10*	6	12	2	5		11	1			46
39	46	42	29	1	34	22	2	43	40	44	33	11	21	38	37	7	—	9	7	1	
		+2s			+1s			+2s			+3s +8s	+5s			+1s +1s						

SOUTHEND UNITED—PLAYERS

Player and position	Ht	Wt	Birthplace	Clubs	League Appearances	Goals
Goalkeepers						
Graham Horn	6 2	14 1	Westminster	Arsenal	—	—
				Portsmouth (on loan)	22	—
				Luton T	58	—
				Brentford (on loan)	3	—
				Charlton Ath	—	—
				Kettering T	—	—
				Southend U	9	—
				Norwich C	4	—
				Southend U (on loan)	10	—
Mervyn Cawston	6 1	11 6	Norwich	Chicago S	—	—
				Southend U	39	—
Defenders						
Alan Moody	5 11	11 10	Middlesbrough	Middlesbrough	44+2	—
				Southend U	287+1	36
Neil Townsend	6 0	12 7	Long Buckby	Northampton T	65+2	1
(Contract cancelled April 1979)				Southend U	156+1	7
				Norwich C (on loan)	—	—
Tony Hadley	6 0	12 2	Rochford	Southend U	118+11	6
Frank Banks	5 10	11 7	Hull	Southend U	4	—
(Contract cancelled January 1979)				Hull C	284+4	6
				Southend U	75	—
John Walker	5 10	11 9	Rochford	Southend U	11+9	—
Phil Dudley	5 7	9 10	Basildon	Southend U	48+1	3
Steve Yates	6 0	12 13	Burton-on-Trent	Leicester C	12+7	—
				Southend U	69	2
*Paul Kerchell	5 8	11 1	Basildon	Southend U	—	—
Mickey Stead	5 8	11 10	West Ham	Tottenham H	14+1	1
				Swansea C (on loan)	5	2
				Southend U	38	1
David Cusack	6 1½	13 13	Rotherham	Sheffield W	92+3	1
				Southend U	37	1
*Colin Williams	5 8	10 8	Romford	Southend U	—	—
Midfield						
Ron Pountney	5 6	9 13	Bilston	Walsall	1	—
				Port Vale	—	—
				Southend U	104+10	6
Mickey Laverick	5 9	10 9	Trimdon	Mansfield T	73+16	13
				Southend U	108+2	18
Anton Otulakowski	5 7	10 10	Dewsbury	Barnsley	42	2
				West Ham U	10+7	—
				Southend U	9	—
Jeff Hull	5 6	9 1	Rochford	Southend U	1	—
Steve Goodwin	5 8	11 2	Chadderton	Norwich C	2+1	—
				Scunthorpe U (on loan)	2	—
				Southend U	68+7	10
Forwards						
Graham Franklin	5 9	11 3	Bicester	Southend U	1+3	—
Andy Polycarpou	5 7	9 13	Islington	Southend U	40+12	8
Colin Morris	5 7	10 2	Blyth	Burnley	9+1	—
				Southend U	113	21
Derrick Parker	5 10	11 6	Wallsend	Burnley	5+1	2
				Southend U	110	35
Peter Abbott	6 1	12 0	Rotherham	Manchester U	—	—
				Swindon T (on loan)	—	—
				Swansea C	34+7	3
				Crewe A	27+4	8
				Southend U	26+1	4
Gerry Fell	5 11	11 11	Newark	Brighton	65+14	19
				Southend U	42+1	10

STOCKPORT COUNTY   DIV. 4

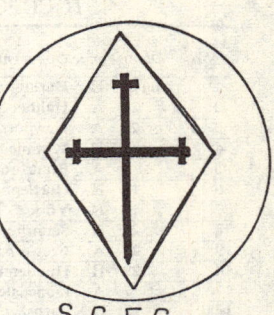

S.C.F.C.

President: A. N. Kirk.
Chairman: F. Pye.
Vice-Chairman: E. Barnes.
Directors: P. Lukic, G. Hopwood, A. M. Barlow, J. Lewis, C. F. Summers.
Chief Executive/Secretary: T. R. McCreery, F.A.A.I.
Manager: Mike Summerbee.
Asst. Manager: Brian Green.
Commercial Manager: John Hill.
Year Formed: 1883.   *Turned Professional:* 1891.
Limited Company: 1908.
Previous Names: Heaton Norris Rovers 1883–88, Heaton Norris 1888–90, Stockport County 1890–
Previous Grounds: 1883 Heaton Norris Recreation Ground, 1884 Heaton Norris Wanderers Cricket Ground, 1885 Chorlton's Farm, Chorlton's Lane, 1886 Heaton Norris Cricket Ground, 1887 Wilkes' Field, Belmont Street, 1889 Nursery Inn, Green Lane, 1902 Edgeley Park.
Football League Record: 1900 Elected to Division 2, 1904 failed re-election, 1905–21 Division 2, 1921–22 Division 3(N), 1922–26 Division 2, 1926–37 Division 3(N), 1937–38 Division 2, 1938–58 Division 3(N), 1958–59 Division 3, 1959–67 Division 4, 1967–70 Division 3, 1970– Division 4.
Honours: Football League, best season in Division 2: 1095–06. Division 3(N) Champions: 1921–22, 1936–37; Runners-up: 1928–29, 1929–30. Division 4, Champions: 1966–67. F.A. Cup, best season: 5th Rd., 1935, 1950. Football League Cup, best season: 4th Rd., 1972–73.
Record Victory: 13–0 v Halifax T., Division 3(N), Jan. 6th, 1934.
Record Defeat: 1–8 v Chesterfield, Division 2, April 19th, 1902.
Most League Points: 64, Division 4, 1966–67.
Most League Goals: 115, Division 3(N), 1933–34.
Highest League Scorer in a Season: Alf Lythgoe, 46, Division 3(N), 1933–34.
Most Goals in Total Aggregate: Jack Connor, 132, 1951–56.
Most Capped Player: Harry Hardy, 1, England.
Most League Appearances: Bob Murray, 465, 1952–63.
Record Transfer Fee Received: £30,000 from Blackpool for Paul Hart, May 1973.
Record Transfer Fee Paid: £16,000 to Luton Town for Dave Lawson, March 1979.
Managers Since the War: Bob Marshall, Andy Beattie, Dick Duckworth, Willie Moir, Reg Flewin, Trevor Porteous, Bert Trautmann, Eddie Quigley, Jimmy Meadows, Walter Galbraith, Matt Woods, Brian Doyle, Jimmy Meadows, Roy Chapman, Eddie Quigley, Alan Thompson.
Address of Programme Editor: H. Jones, 13 Stonepail Close, Gatley, Cheshire.
Address of Supporters Club: Secretary, D. Burfoot, 2 Albion Road, New Mills, Stockport, Cheshire.
Address of Club Shop: Stockport County Promotions Office, Unit 4, The Precinct, Castle Street, Stockport SK3 9AL.

Edgely Park, Hardcastle Road, Stockport, Cheshire SK3 9DD. Telephone: 061-480 8888.
Ground Capacity: 16,500. *Record Attendance:* 27,833 v Liverpool, F.A. Cup 5th Rd., February 11th, 1950. *Record Receipts:* £9,544 F.L. Cup, 3rd Rd., v Everton, September 20th, 1976. *Pitch measurements:* 110 yds × 75 yds.
How to get there: Edgeley Park is situated within a mile of the Mersey Square, the town centre; a few minutes walk via Wellington Road South and Greek Street. The main line railway station lies just off Greek Street and is only five a minute walk to the Ground.
Match tickets: Seats can be reserved in the Main Stand by post or telephone two weeks before the match.
Car parking: Ample street parking around the ground.
Entertainment/catering facilities: Top class caberet club next to the ground; four refreshemnt bars around the ground (not licensed).
Club shop: Small kiosk on ground (due to open August 1979).
Handbook/programmes: The 'Matchday Magazine' is available outside the ground. It is also available on subscription to the Programme Editor and by post.
Extra information: In 1934 Stockport County created a record which is still unsurpassed in a Football League game when they defeated Halifax Town 13-0, eleven goals coming in the second half.
Club Colours: Sky blue shirts with white stripes, dark blue shorts with blue sky trim, white with blue trim stockings.
Change Colours: Yellow shirts, shorts and socks.
Club Captain:
Club Nickname: 'County'.

STOCKPORT COUNTY 1978-79 LEAGUE RECORD

Match No.	Date	Venue	Opponents	Result	H/T Score	League Pos'n	Goalscorers	Attendance
1	Aug 19	H	Darlington	W 3-0	3-0	—	Bradd 2, Craig (og)	3626
2	22	A	Halifax T	L 1-2	1-0	—	Lee	2253
3	26	A	Newport Co	W 2-1	1-1	7	Bradd, Lee	2659
4	Sept 1	H	Wimbledon	L 0-1	0-0	10		5604
5	9	A	Bradford C	D 1-1	0-0	11	Thompson	5001
6	11	H	Hartlepool U	W 4-0	2-0	—	Lee, Edwards, Halford, Thompson	4249
7	15	H	York C	W 2-0	1-0	4	Lee 2	6103
8	23	A	Scunthorpe U	L 0-1	0-1	8		2691
9	27	A	Crewe Alex	D 2-2	1-0	—	Lee, Prudham	2777
10	29	H	Huddersfield T	W 3-1	2-1	5	Bradd 2, Lee	5554
11	Oct 7	A	Doncaster R	L 0-2	0-1	7		2742
12	13	H	Barnsley	D 0-0	0-0	7		9054
13	16	H	AFC Bournemouth	W 1-0	0-0	—	Bradd	4092
14	21	A	Northampton T	D 2-2	2-0	6	Lee, Bradd	3867
15	28	A	Reading	D 3-3	3-3	7	Lee, Thompson 2	7054
16	Nov 3	H	Wigan Ath	L 0-1	0-0	9		8357
17	11	A	Wimbledon	L 0-2	0-1	10		3177
18	17	H	Newport Co	D 1-1	1-1	11	Bradd	4099
19	Dec 4	H	Grimsby T	W 2-1	1-1	—	Lee, Edwards	3300
20	9	A	Port Vale	L 1-2	1-2	9	Bradd	3689
21	23	A	Aldershot	L 2-3	2-0	10	Bradd, Park	3115
22	26	H	Hereford U	L 0-2	0-1	—		4630
23	29	H	Portsmouth	W 4-2	1-0	9	Bradd, Lee 2, Summerbee	3795
24	Jan 12	H	Bradford C	W 1-0	1-0	10	Lee	3573
25	Feb 21	H	Doncaster R	L 0-1	0-0	—		3007
26	24	A	Barnsley	D 4-4	0-2	14	Henson, Bradd 3	9153
27	26	A	Scunthorpe U	L 0-2	0-1	—		2676
28	Mar 2	H	Northampton T	W 2-1	1-0	12	Park 2	3009
29	5	H	Crewe Alex	W 4-3	3-1	—	Bradd 2, Lee, Henson	3102
30	9	H	Reading	D 0-0	0-0	9		3560
31	13	A	Hartlepool U	W 3-1	0-0	—	Henson, Halford, Park	2403
32	17	A	Wigan Ath	L 0-2	0-0	9		7610
33	23	H	Halifax T	L 1-2	0-0	10	Bradd	3033
34	27	A	Darlington	W 1-0	0-0	—	Bradd	1086
35	30	H	Torquay U	L 0-1	0-0	10		2710
36	Apr 4	A	Huddersfield T	D 0-0	0-0	—		2267
37	7	A	Grimsby T	L 1-2	1-2	10	Lee	7495
38	9	H	Aldershot	D 2-2	1-1	—	Lee 2 (1 pen)	2190
39	14	A	Hereford U	L 0-1	0-1	13		3609
40	16	H	Rochdale	W 3-0	1-0	—	Henson 2, Lee	2863
41	21	A	Portsmouth	D 1-1	1-1	11	Lee	8177
42	23	H	AFC Bournemouth	L 1-3	0-1	—	Lee	2285
43	27	H	Port Vale	D 0-0	0-0	13		3343
44	May 1	A	Rochdale	L 0-2	0-0	—		2117
45	5	A	Torquay U	L 0-1	0-1	15		2281
46	14	A	York C	L 0-1	0-0	—		2089

Final League Position: 13

Goalscorers

League (58): Lee 20 (1 a pen), Bradd 18, Henson 5, Park 4, Thompson 4, Edwards 2, Halford 2, Prudham 1 Summerbee 1, Own Goal 1.
League Cup (5): Lee 2, Bradd, Thompson (pen), Park.
F.A. Cup (11): Park 5, Bradd 3, Lee 2, Prudham, Fogarty.

League Cup	First Round	Shrewsbury T (a)	0-1
		(h)	3-1
	Second Round	Manchester U	2-3 (at Old Trafford)
F.A. Cup	First Round	Morecambe (h)	5-1
	Second Round	Bradford C (h)	4-2
	Third Round	Wrexham (a)	2-6

Rogan	Thorpe	Rutter	Thompson	Park	Fogarty	Summerbee	Goodfellow	Bradd	Loadwick	Lee	Halford	Edwards	Prudham	Armstrong	Henson	Smith	Cassidy	Cahill	Lawson	Connor	Seddon	Sumner	Galvin	Match No.
1	2	3	4	5	6	7	8	9*	10	11	12													1
1	2	3	4	5	6	7	8*	9	10	11	12													2
1	2	3	4	6		7		10	8	11		5	9											3
1	2	3	4	5		7*		9	10	11	8	6	12											4
1	2	3	4	5*		7		9	8	10		6	12	11										5
1	2	3	4			7		9	10	11*12		6	5	8										6
1	2	3	4	12		7		9*10		11		6	5	8										7
1	2	3	6	12			4*	9	10	11		5	7	8										8
1	2	3	4	5					10	11		6	9	8	7									9
1	2	3	4	5				9	10	11		6		8	7									10
1	2	3	4	5	12			9	10*11			6		8	7									11
1	2	3		5	4	10		9		11		6		8	7									12
1	2	3		5	4			9		11	12	6*10		8	7									13
1	2	3		5	4	7		9		11		6		8	10									14
1	2	3	12	5	4			10		11		9		8*	7	6								15
1	2	3	10	5	4			9		11		6		8	7									16
1	2	3		5	4	10		9		11	12	6		8*	7									17
1		3		5	4	10		9		11	2	6	8		7									18
1	2	3		5	4	10*		9		11	12	6	8		7									19
1	2	3		5	6	12	10			11	8		9		7*	4								20
1		3	4	5		7		9		11	12	6*		8	10	2								21
1		3	6	5	4	8*		9,		11	12			10	7	2								22
1		3	6	5		10		9		11		4		8	7	2								23
1		3	6	5		8		10		11		4		9	7	2								24
	3		5	4	8*			9		11	12	6		10	7		1	2						25
	4*		10	3				9		11	8	5	12		7	2	1	6						26
			5	6				9		11	8	4	10		7	2	1	3						27
	2	3		6	5	8		9		11		4	7	10			1							28
	2	3		5	6	10*		9		11		4	7	8	12				1					29
	2*	3		5	6	8		9		11		4	7	10	12				1					30
	2	3		5	6			9			11	4	10		7	8			1					31
	2	3		5	4	10*		9		11	8	6			7				1	12				32
	2	3				8		9		11	10	4			7	6			1	5*12				33
	2	3				8		9		11	10	4		6	7	5			1					34
	2	3				8		9		11	10	4	12	6*	7	5			1					35
	2	3				8		9		11	10	4	5	6	7				1					36
	2	3				8*	9			11	5		10	6	7				1		4	12		37
		5	3				9			11	2	4	10	6	7				1		8			38
		5	3				9			11	2	4	10	6	7				1		12	8*		39
		5	3				9			11	2	4	10	6	7				1			8		40
		5	3			10				9	11	2	4		6	7	8		1					41
		5	3				10*	9		11	2	4		6	7	8			1		12			42
		5	3				8	9		11	2	4		6	7	10			1					43
		5	3				8	9		11	2	4	12	6*	7	10			1					44
		5	3				8	9		11	2.	4		6	7	10*			1		12			45
	4	3				8	10			11	2			9	6	5			1				7	46
24	38	45	16	29	20	33	2	45	11	45	21	40	19	34	34	19	4	3	18	1	1	3	1	
			+1s	+2s	+1s				+1s			+9s	+5s		+2s					+1s	+3s	+2s		

STOCKPORT COUNTY—PLAYERS

Player and position	Ht	Wt	Birthplace	Clubs	League Appearances	Goals
Goalkeepers						
Mike Rogan	5 11½	12 4	Fleetwood	Workington	390	—
				Stockport Co	69	—
				Crewe Alex (on loan)	3	—
Dave Lawson	6 0¾	11 0	Newcastle	Bradford PA	13	—
				Huddersfield T	51	—
				Everton	123	—
				Luton T	5	—
				Stockport Co	18	—
*Andy Cassidy	6 1	12 7	Leeds	Sunderland	—	—
				Manchester C	—	—
				Stockport Co	5	—
Defenders						
*Graham Smith	5 10	11 0	Pudsey	Leeds U	—	—
				Rochdale	316+1	2
				Stockport Co	147+4	2
John Rutter	5 9	10 10	Warrington	Wolverhampton W	—	—
				Bournemouth	2+2	—
				Exeter C	31+1	1
				Stockport Co	137	5
Alan Thompson	5 11	12 0	Liverpool	Sheffield W	150+6	3
(Contract cancelled March 1979)				Stockport Co	93+1	17
Paul Edwards	5 10	10 4	Crompton	Manchester U	52+2	—
				Oldham Ath	108+4	7
				Stockport Co	42	2
Paul Cahill	5 9	10 2	Liverpool	Coventry C	—	—
(Contract cancelled)				Portsmouth	95+2	2
				Aldershot (on loan)	2	—
				Tranmere R	5	—
				Stockport Co	3	—
Andy Thorpe	5 11	11 4	Stockport	Stockport Co	42	—
Mike Czuczman	6 1	12 9	Carlisle	Preston NE	—	—
				Grimsby T	108+6	6
				Scunthorpe U	115+1	1
James Connor	5 10	10 8	Stockport	Stockport Co	1+1	—
Midfield						
Ken Fogarty	5 8	11 3	Manchester	Stockport Co	251+4	6
(Contract cancelled April 1979)						
*Carl Halford	5 6	10 10	Oldham	Manchester C	—	—
				Stockport Co	65+9	5
Mike Summerbee	5 10½	11 4	Preston	Swindon T	218	39
(England)				Manchester C	355+2	46
				Burnley	51	—
				Blackpool	3	—
				Stockport Co	75	5
Philip Henson	5 10	9 12	Manchester	Manchester C	12+5	—
				Swansea C (on loan)	1	—
				Sheffield W	65+7	9
				Stockport Co	34+2	5
George Armstrong	5 6	11 2	Hebburn	Arsenal	490+10	53
				Leicester C	14+1	—
				Stockport Co	34	—
Stuart Lee	5 8	10 6	Manchester	Bolton W	77+8	20
				Wrexham	46+8	12
				Stockport Co	45	20
Chris Galvin	5 10	12 3	Huddersfield	Leeds U	7+1	—
				Hull C	132+11	11
				York C (on loan)	22	6
				Stockport Co	1	—
Jimmy Goodfellow	5 8	10 8	Sunderland	Port Vale	77+8	11
(Contract cancelled)				Workington	199	15
				Rotherham	192	8
				Stockport Co	2+1	—
Terry Park	5 11¾	11 6	Liverpool	Wolverhampton W	—	—
(Contract cancelled April 1979)				Stockport Co	74+3	38
Ian Seddon	5 8½	10 0	Prestbury	Bolton W	51+13	4
				Chester	62+11	7
				Stockport Co (on loan)	4	—
				Chesterfield (on loan)	2	—
				Cambridge U	34+3	1
				Rochdale	30+1	3
				Wigan Ath	1	—
				Stockport Co	1+3	—
Forwards						
Eddie Prudham	5 10	11 0	Gateshead	Sheffield W	14+5	2
				Carlisle U	15+2	3
				Hartlepool (on loan)	3	—
				Partick T (on loan)	3+1	3
				Workington (on loan)	15	6
				Stockport Co	56+5	13
Les Bradd	6 1	13 0	Buxton	Rotherham U	3	—
				Notts Co	378+17	125
				Stockport Co	45	18

Alan Sumner 3+2 subs
(Non-contract)

STOKE CITY DIV. 1

Chairman: T. H. Degg.
Vice Chairman: P. Axon.
Directors: J. A. M. Humphreys, A. W. Clubb, A. A. Henshall.
Manager: Alan Durban.
Secretary: M. J. Potts.   *Coach:*
Year Formed: 1863 (second oldest League Club).
Turned Professional: 1885.   *Limited Company:* 1908.
Previous Grounds: 1875, Sweeting's Field; 1878, Victoria Ground (previously known as the Athletic Club Ground).
Football League Record: 1888 Original Members of League. 1890 Not re-elected. 1891 Re-elected. Relegated in 1907, and after one year in Division 2, resigned for financial reasons. Re-elected to Division 2 in 1919. 1922–23 Division 1. 1923–26 Division 2. 1926–27 Division 3(N). 1927–33 Division 2. 1933–53 Division 1. 1953–63 Division 2. 1963–77 Division 1. 1977–79 Division 2. 1979– Division 1.

Honours: Football League, best season in Division 1: 4th, 1935–36, 1946–47. Division 2, Champions: 1932–33, 1962–63; Runners-up: 1921–22. Promoted 1978–79 Division 3(N). Champions: 1926–27. *F.A. Cup,* best season: Semi-finalists, 1899, 1971, 1972. *Football League Cup,* best season; Winners: 1971–72.

European Competitions: *UEFA Cup:* 1972–73, 1974–75.
Record Victory: 10–3 v W.B.A., Division 1, Feb. 4th, 1937.
Record Defeat: 0–10 v Preston N.E., Division 1, Sept 14th, 1889.
Most League Points: 63, Division 3(N), 1926–27.
Most League Goals: 92, Division 3(N), 1926–27.
Highest League Scorer in Season: Freddie Steele, 33, Division 1, 1936–37.
Most League Appearances: Eric Skeels, 506, 1958–76.
Most Capped Player: Gordon Banks 36 (73), England.
Most League Goals in Total Aggregate: Freddie Steele, 142, 1934–49.
Record Transfer Fee Received: £250,000 from Nottingham F. for Peter Shilton, Sept. 1977.
Record Transfer Fee Paid: £325,000 to Leicester C. for Peter Shilton, November 1974.
Managers Since the War: Bob McGrory, Frank Taylor, Tony Waddington, George Eastham, Alan A'Court.
Address of Social Club: c/o Football Club.

Victoria Ground, Stoke-on-Trent. Telephone Stoke-on-Trent 413511. *Telegraphic address:* 'Football, Stoke-on-Trent'. *Ground capacity:* 40,000. *Record attendance:* 51,380 v Arsenal, Division 1, March 29, 1937. *Record receipts:* £31,673 v Sunderland, F.A. Cup, 5th Rd. February 14th, 1976. *Pitch measurements:* 116 yds × 75 yds.

How to get there: Stoke-on-Trent railway station, on the main line from London, is five minutes walk from the ground. No special buses from the town centre because the ground is central. By road, Stoke is well served by the M6 which passes just two miles from the city.
Match tickets: Bookable two weeks before the match. Ticket office No. is Stoke-on-Trent 413961.
Car parking: The official car park in Wheildon Road holds 2,000 cars. Street parking permitted.
Entertainments/catering facilities: Social club. Refreshments obtainable on the ground.
Handbooks/programmes: Programmes available on subscription.
Extra information: Neville Coleman scored seven goals for Stoke against Lincoln City in 1957, a record for a winger in English senior football.

Club Colours: Red and white striped shirts, white shorts and stockings. *Change Colours:* White shirts, black shorts, red stockings.   *Club Captain:* Denis Smith.   *Club Nickname:* 'Potters'

STOKE CITY 1978-79 LEAGUE RECORD

Match No.	Date	Venue	Opponents	Result	H/T Score	League Pos'n	Goalscorers	Attendance
1	Aug 19	A	Cambridge U	W 1-0	0-0	—	Richardson	7485
2	23	H	Cardiff C	W 2-0	0-0	—	Busby, Smith	16,005
3	26	H	Millwall	W 2-0	0-0	1	Busby, Crooks (pen)	15,176
4	Sept 2	A	Oldham Ath	D 1-1	0-0	1	Richardson	11,297
5	9	A	Orient	W 1-0	0-0	1	O'Callaghan	6587
6	23	H	Preston NE	W 1-0	1-0	2	Kendall	14,057
7	27	H	Brighton & HA	D 2-2	1-0	—	Crooks, O'Callaghan	22,203
8	30	H	Crystal Palace	D 1-1	1-0	1	Irvine	19,070
9	Oct 7	A	Fulham	L 0-2	0-1	2		12,531
10	14	H	Burnley	W 3-1	2-1	2	Richardson, Kendall, Irvine	18,437
11	21	A	West Ham U	D 1-1	0-0	2	Richardson	27,859
12	28	H	Sheffield U	W 2-1	1-0	1	O'Callaghan, Crooks (pen)	21,282
13	Nov 4	A	Sunderland	W 1-0	1-0	1	O'Callaghan	25,170
14	11	H	Cambridge U	L 1-3	0-2	1	Irvine	19,027
15	18	A	Millwall	L 0-3	0-1	2		6928
16	22	H	Oldham Ath	W 4-0	2-0	—	O'Callaghan, Irvine, Crooks 2	17,170
17	25	A	Blackburn R	D 2-2	0-0	2	O'Callaghan, Crooks (pen)	10,481
18	Dec 2	H	Leicester C	D 0-0	0-0	2		15,950
19	9	A	Newcastle U	L 0-2	0-0	2		23,447
20	16	H	Wrexham	W 3-0	1-0	2	Crooks 2, Roberts (og)	18,358
21	23	A	Bristol R	D 0-0	0-0	2		7897
22	26	H	Charlton Ath	D 2-2	1-0	—	McGroarty, O'Callaghan	20,846
23	30	H	Notts Co	W 2-0	1-0	2	Irvine, O'Callaghan	21,393
24	Jan 20	A	Brighton & HA	D 1-1	1-1	2	O'Callaghan	23,076
25	Feb 6	A	Luton T	D 0-0	0-0	—		6462
26	10	A	Crystal Palace	D 1-1	0-0	1	Irvine	23,313
27	24	A	Burnley	W 3-0	0-0	2	O'Callaghan, Randall, Crooks	13,756
28	28	H	Preston NE	D 1-1	0-1	—	O'Callaghan	18,177
29	Mar 3	H	West Ham U	W 2-0	1-0	1	Doyle, Randall	24,912
30	10	A	Sheffield U	D 0-0	0-0	2		20,512
31	14	H	Orient	W 3-1	2-0	—	Irvine, Crooks 2	16,183
32	24	A	Cardiff C	W 3-1	2-0	2	Randall, O'Callaghan, Crooks	14,869
33	27	H	Sunderland	L 0-1	0-1	—		24,023
34	31	H	Blackburn R	L 1-2	1-1	4	O'Callaghan	17,020
35	Apr 4	H	Fulham	W 2-0	0-0	—	Smith, Randall	15,243
36	7	A	Leicester C	D 1-1	1-1	2	Busby	17,502
37	14	A	Charlton Ath	W 4-1	1-1	3	Richardson, Randall, O'Callaghan, Irvine	9084
38	16	H	Luton T	D 0-0	0-0	—		19,214
39	17	H	Bristol R	W 2-0	2-0	—	Busby 2	18,679
40	21	A	Wrexham	W 1-0	1-0	1	O'Callaghan	20,211
41	28	H	Newcastle U	D 0-0	0-0	2		23,271
42	May 5	A	Notts Co	W 1-0	0-0	2	Richardson	21,571

Final League Position: 3

Goalscorers

League (58): O'Callaghan 16, Crooks 12 (3 pens), Irvine 8, Richardson 6, Busby 5, Randall 5, Kendall 2, Smith 2, Doyle 1, McGroarty 1.

League Cup (9): Irvine 2, Doyle, Dodd, O'Callaghan, Kendall, Busby, Crooks (pen), Richardson.

League Cup	Second Round	Sunderland (a)	2-0
	Third Round	Northampton T (a)	3-1
	Fourth Round	Charlton Ath (a)	3-2
	Fifth Round	Watford (h)	0-0
		(a)	1-3 (a.e.t.)
F.A. Cup	Third Round	Oldham Ath (h)	2-0 (Abandoned at half-time)
		(h)	0-1

Jones	Marsh	Scott	Kendall	Smith	Doyle	Irvine	Richardson	O'Callaghan	Waddington	Crooks	Busby	Dodd	Conroy	Johnson P	Heath	Cook	Fox	McGroarty	Randall	Johnson P.A.	Sheldon	Match No.
1	2	3	4	5	6	7	8	9*10		11	12											1
1	2	3	4	5	6	8	11		7*10		9	12										2
1	2	3	4	5	6	8	11	12		10	9		7*									3
1	2	3	4	5	6	8	11	9		10*12		7										4
1	2	3	4	5	6	8	11	9		10*12		7										5
1	2	3	4	5	6	8		9		10	12	7	11*									6
1	2	3	4	5	6	8	11*	9		10	12	7										7
1	2	3	4	5	6	8*		9		10	11	7		12								8
1	2	3*	4	5	6		11	9		10	12	7			8							9
1	2		4	5	6	8	11	9		10		7		3								10
1	2	3	4	5	6	8	11	9		10		7										11
1	2	3	4*	5	6	8	11	9		10		7	12									12
1		3	4	5	6	8	11	9		10*		7	12	2								13
1		3	4	5	6	8	11	9		12	10	2	7*									14
1	2	3*	4	5	6	8	11	9		10		7				12						15
1	2		4*	5	6	8	11	9		10		7		3				12				16
1	2		4	5	6	8	11	9		10		7		3*		12						17
1	2		4	5	6	8	11	9		10		7		3								18
1	2	12	4	5	6	8	11	9		10		7*		3								19
	2	3	4	5	6*	8	11	9		10		12				1	7					20
1	2	3	4	5	6	8	11	9		10							7					21
1	2	3	4	5*	6	8	11	9		10		12					7					22
1	2	3	4	5	6	8*11		9		10		12						7				23
1		3	4		6	8	11	9		10		2	5					7				24
1		3*	4	5	6	8	11	9		10	12	2						7				25
1		3	4	5	6		11	9*		10	12	2						7				26
1		3	4	5	6	8	11	9		10		2						7				27
1		3	4	5	6	8	11	9		10		2						7				28
1		3	4	5	6	8	11	9		10		2						7				29
1	2	3	4		6	8	11	9		10		5						7				30
1	2	3	4		6	8	11	9		10		5						7				31
1		3	4	5	6	8	11	9		10		2						7				32
1		3	4	5	6	8	11	9		10	12	2*						7				33
1	2	3	4	5	6	8	11*	9		10	12							7				34
1		3	4	5	6	8	11	9		10		2						7				35
1		3	4	5	6	8	11	9			10*	2		12				7				36
1		3	4	5	6	8	11	9		10*		2	12					7				37
1		3	4*	5	6	8	11	9		10		2	12					7				38
1		3			6*	8	2	9			11	5				10		12	7	4		39
1		3		6		8	2	9		10	11	5						7	4			40
1		3	4	5	6	8	11	9		12	10*	2						7				41
1		3	4	5	6	8	11	9		10		2						7				42
41	24	37	40	38	41	41	40	40	2	38	8	34	3	7	1	1	3	20	2	1		
	+ 1s							+ 1s		+ 2s	+ 10s	+ 4s	+ 4s	+ 1s	+ 1s	+ 2s		+ 1s		+ 1s		

STOKE CITY—PLAYERS

Player and position	Ht	Wt	Birthplace	Clubs	League Appearances	Goals
Goalkeepers						
Roger Jones	5 11	12 13	Upton-on-Severn	Bournemouth	160	—
				Blackburn R	242	—
				Newcastle U	5	—
				Stoke C	82	—
Peter Fox	5 11	12 11	Scunthorpe	Sheffield W	49	—
				West Ham U (on loan)	—	—
				Barnsley (on loan)	1	—
				Stoke C	1	—
Defenders						
*John Marsh	5 6½	11 6	Stoke	Stoke C	346+8	2
*Kevin Lewis	5 9	11 13	Hull	Manchester U	—	—
				Stoke C	15	—
Paul Johnson	5 6	11 10	Stoke	Stoke C	7+1	—
Danny Bowers	5 8¾	10 2	Stoke	Stoke C	35+4	2
				Shrewsbury T (on loan)	6	—
Trevor Brissett	5 9	11 7	Stoke	Stoke C	—	—
Denis Smith	5 11½	12 2	Stoke	Stoke C	355+1	27
Alan Dodd	5 10	11 11	Stoke	Stoke C	230+5	1
Geoff Scott	6 0	11 9	Birmingham	Stoke C	60+2	2
Michael Smith	5 10½	12 4	Stoke	Stoke C	—	—
(Contract cancelled November 1978)						
Mel Pejic	5 7½	10 6	Stoke	Stoke C	—	—
Mike Doyle	6 0	11 9	Manchester	Manchester C	441+8	32
(England)				Stoke C	41	1
Gary Elthick	5 11½	12 0	Brighton	Lewes	—	—
				Stoke C	—	—
Andy Morgan	5 8¾	11 7	Stoke	Stoke C	—	—
Midfield						
*Gary Fenton	5 9	11 2	Stoke	Stoke C	—	—
*Kevin Sheldon	5 5½	9 8	Stoke	Stoke C	10+3	—
Paul Richardson	5 10	11 10	Nottingham	Nottingham F	199+23	17
				Chester	28	2
				Stoke C	72+1	8
Dennis Thorley	6 0	10 10	Stoke	Stoke C	1+1	—
Howard Kendall	5 7	10 13	Ryton-on-Tyne	Preston NE	104	13
				Everton	227+3	21
				Birmingham C	115	16
				Stoke C	82	9
Paul A. Johnson	5 6½	12 2	Stoke	Stoke C	13+2	—
*Mark Cooper	5 10½	12 5	Stoke	Stoke C	—	—
Sammy Irvine	5 6	10 7	Glasgow	Shrewsbury T	198+9	18
				Stoke C	41	8
Adrian Heath	5 4½	8 11	Stoke	Stoke C	1+1	—
Gary Simpson	5 5½	9 13	Sheffield	Stoke C	—	—
Forwards						
Jeff Cook	5 9	11 12	Hartlepool	Stoke C	6+5	1
				Bradford C (on loan)	8	1
*Terry Conroy	5 9¾	11 11	Dublin	Stoke C	244+27	49
(Eire)						
Garth Crooks	5 8	11 0	Stoke	Stoke C	101+6	36
Jim McGroarty	5 6	9 9	Londonderry	Finn Harps	(not known)	
				Stoke C	6+1	2
Viv Busby	6 0	11 12	High Wycombe	Luton T	64+13	16
				Newcastle U (on loan)	4	2
				Fulham	114+4	29
				Norwich C	22	11
				Stoke C	29+11	8
Bren O'Callaghan	6 3	13 12	Bradford	Doncaster R	184+3	65
(Eire)				Stoke C	53+3	22
Paul Randall	6 0	12 2	Liverpool	Bristol R	49+3	33
				Stoke C	20	5
Lee Chapman	6 1½	12 10	Lincoln	Stoke C	—	—
				Plymouth Arg (on loan)	3+1	—
*Steve Nelson						

SUNDERLAND DIV. 2

Chairman: K. I. Collings.
Vice-Chairman: J. M. Ditchburn.
Directors: E. M. Evans, A. D. S. Martin, F. Stewart, F. S. Cronin, T. Cowie.
Manager: Ken Knighton.   *Secretary:* R. M. Linney.
Year Formed: 1879.   *Turned Professional:* 1886.
Limited Company: 1906.
Previous Grounds: 1879, Blue House Field, Hendon; 1881, Ashbrooke; 1883, site of Cooper Street; 1884, Abbs Field, Fulwell; 1886, Newcastle Road; 1898, Roker Park.
Previous Name: 1879–81, Sunderland and District Teachers' A.F.C.
Football League Record:
1890 Elected to Division 1. (record run of 57 seasons). 1958–64 Division 2. 1964–70 Division 1. 1970–76 Division 2. 1976–77 Division 1. 1977– Division 2.
Honours: *Football League*, Division 1, Champions: 1891–92, 1892–93, 1894–95, 1901–02, 1912–13, 1935–36. Runners-up: 1893–94, 1897–98, 1900–01, 1922–23, 1934–35. Division 2, Champions: 1975–76; Runners-up: 1963–64. *F.A. Cup*, Winners: 1937, 1973; Runners-up: 1913. *Football League Cup*, best season: semi-finalists: 1963. **European Competitions:** Cup-Winners' Cup 1973–74.
Record Victory: 11-1 v Fairfield, F.A. Cup, 1st Rd., 1894–95.
Record Defeat: 0-8 v West Ham U., Division 1, Oct. 1968.
Most League Points: 61, Division 2, 1963–64.
Most League Goals: 109, Division 1, 1935–36.
Highest League Scorer in Season: Dave Halliday, 43, Division 1, 1928–29.
Most League Appearances: Jim Montgomery, 537, 1962–77.
Most Capped Player: Billy Bingham, 33 (56), N. Ireland, Martin Harvey, 33, N. Ireland.
Most League Goals in Total Aggregate: Charlie Buchan, 209, 1911–25.
Record Transfer Fee Received: £275,000 from Manchester C. for Dennis Tueart, March 1974.
Record Transfer Fee Paid: £200,000 to Leicester C. for Bob Lee, Sept. 1976.
Managers Since the War: Bill Murray, Alan Brown, George Hardwick, Ian McColl, Alan Brown, Bob Stokoe, Jimmy Adamson, Billy Elliott.
Address of the Supporters Club: c/o Football Club.

Roker Park Ground, Sunderland. Telephone Sunderland 72077 and 58638. *Telegraphic address:* 'Football, Sunderland'. *Ground capacity:* 53,500. *Record attendance:* 75,118 v Derby Co., F.A. Cup 6th Rd. Replay, March 8, 1933. *Record receipts:* £46,767 v Burnley F.A. Cup 4th Rd. Replay, 26 February 1979. *Pitch measurements:* 112 yds. × 72 yds.

How to get there: From Sunderland railway station and Seaburn railway station take buses 123 and 124 to Redby Community Centre: the ground is five minutes walk away. Special buses from the town centre. By road via M1, A690 to Sunderland, and then route to Roker Park is signed.
Match tickets: Seats may be booked 10 days prior to the match.
Car parking: Parking for 1,500 cars, 200 yards from ground.
Entertainments/catering facilities: Hot and cold drinks, pies, sandwiches, etc. available in the ground.
Club shop: Open daily; sells all types of souvenirs.
Handbooks/programmes: Programmes are obtainable on subscription; details from the Club Shop.
Extra information: Sunderland share the highest First Division away win, beating Newcastle United 9-1 in 1908; Newcastle went on to win the League that season!
Club Colours: Red and white striped shirts, black shorts, red stockings with white tops.
Change Colours: Blue shirts with red trim, red shorts with white trim, blue stockings with red tops.
Club Coach:
Club Nickname: 'Rokerites'.

SUNDERLAND 1978-79 LEAGUE RECORD

Match No.	Date	Venue	Opponents	Result	Score	H/T Score	League Pos'n	Goalscorers	Attendance
1	Aug 19	H	Charlton Ath	W	1-0	1-0	—	Rowell	20,486
2	22	A	Orient	L	0-3	0-1	—		7373
3	26	A	Brighton & HA	L	0-2	0-1	19		19,885
4	Sept 2	H	Preston NE	W	3-1	1-0	13	Entwistle, Docherty, Greenwood	16,819
5	9	A	Crystal Palace	D	1-1	0-0	13	Entwistle	21,112
6	16	H	Fulham	D	1-1	0-0	13	Brown	17,976
7	23	A	Burnley	W	2-1	0-0	8	Rowell 2 (1 a pen)	12,964
8	30	H	West Ham U	W	2-1	1-0	5	Rowell 2 (1 a pen)	23,676
9	Oct 7	A	Sheffield U	L	2-3	1-0	11	Rowell, Lee	18,873
10	14	H	Newcastle U	D	1-1	0-1	10	Greenwood	35,405
11	21	H	Millwall	W	3-2	2-1	8	Rowell 2, Brown	19,962
12	28	A	Oldham Ath	D	0-0	0-0	9		9857
13	Nov 4	H	Stoke C	L	0-1	0-0	10		25,170
14	11	A	Charlton Ath	W	2-1	0-0	9	Entwistle, Rowell	11,412
15	18	H	Brighton & HA	W	2-1	1-1	6	Rowell, Clarke	22,738
16	21	A	Preston NE	L	1-3	1-1		Elliott	13,204
17	25	A	Luton T	W	3-0	2-0	6	Rowell 2, Entwistle	10,249
18	Dec 2	H	Bristol R	W	5-0	1-0	4	Entwistle 3, Lee, Rowell	18,864
19	9	A	Cardiff C	D	1-1	1-1	4	Rostron	7178
20	16	H	Cambridge U	L	0-2	0-1	5		20,841
21	23	A	Notts Co	D	1-1	1-1	6	Entwistle	11,281
22	26	H	Leicester C	D	1-1	0-1	—	Clarke	24,544
23	Jan 17	A	Blackburn R	D	1-1	1-1	—	Rowell	8130
24	20	A	Fulham	D	2-2	1-0	—	Bolton, Rowell (pen)	11,260
25	Feb 3	H	Burnley	W	3-1	0-1	5	Rowell (pen), Rostron, Entwistle	23,030
26	10	A	West Ham U	D	3-3	2-1	5	Lee, Rostron 2	24,998
27	24	H	Newcastle U	W	4-1	2-0	5	Rowell 3 (1 a pen), Entwistle	35,000
28	Mar 3	A	Millwall	W	1-0	0-0	5	Entwistle	7889
29	7	H	Wrexham	W	1-0	1-0	—	Bolton	25,017
30	10	H	Oldham Ath	W	3-0	2-0	3	Rowell (pen), Bolton, Rostron	25,090
31	14	H	Crystal Palace	L	1-2	1-2	—	Rostron	34,986
32	24	H	Orient	W	1-0	0-0	4	Rowell	21,189
33	27	A	Stoke C	W	1-0	1-0	—	Docherty	24,023
34	31	H	Luton T	W	1-0	0-0	3	Rostron	23,358
35	Apr 7	A	Bristol R	D	0-0	0-0	4		8003
36	13	H	Notts Co	W	3-0	2-0	—	Lee, Brown, Chisholm	34,027
37	14	A	Leicester C	W	2-1	0-0	2	Docherty, Brown	20,740
38	16	H	Blackburn R	L	0-1	0-1	—		35,005
39	21	A	Cambridge U	W	2-0	0-0	3	Lee, Docherty	10,100
40	25	H	Sheffield U	W	6-2	2-1	—	Rostron 3 (2 pens), Lee, Brown, Gilbert	29,822
41	28	H	Cardiff C	L	1-2	0-1	3	Ashurst	36,526
42	May 5	A	Wrexham	W	2-1	0-0	3	Rostron, Brown	19,133

Final League Position: 4

Goalscorers

League (70): Rowell 21 (6 pens), Entwistle 11, Rostron 11 (2 pens), Brown 6, Lee 6, Docherty 4, Bolton 3, Clarke 2, Greenwood 2, Ashurst 1, Chisholm 1, Elliott 1, Gilbert 1.

F.A. Cup (3): Rowell (pen), Lee, Entwistle.

League Cup	Second Round	Stoke C (h)	0-2
F.A. Cup	Third Round	Everton (h)	2-1
	Fourth Round	Burnley (a)	1-1
		(h)	0-3

Siddall	Henderson	Bolton	Chisholm	Clarke	Ashurst	Kerr	Rostron	Entwistle	Docherty	Rowell	Lee	Elliott	Gilbert	Brown	Greenwood	Buckley	Coady	Arnott	Watson	Gregoire	Whitworth	Match No.
1	2	3	4	5	6	7	8*	9	10	11	12											1
1	2	3	4*		6	7	10	9	8	11	12	5										2
1	2*		5	6	7	10		8	11	9	4	3	12									3
1	2	3	4			9	8	11			5	6		7	10							4
1	2	3	5	12		9	4	11			6	10		8*	7							5
1	2	3	5			9	4	11			6	10	12	8	7*							6
1	2	3	7			10	9	4	11		6		8*12		5							7
1		7	5			3	9	4	11	8	6		10		2							8
1		3	4	5		7*	9	10	11	12	6		8		2							9
1	2	3	7*	5			9	4	11	10	6		8	12								10
1	2	3	7*	5			9	4	11	10	6		8	12								11
1	2	3		5			9	4	11	10	6		8		7							12
1	2	3		5			9	4	11	10	6		8*12		7							13
1	2	3		5		8	9	4	11	10	6				7							14
1	2*	3	4	5		8	9		11	10	6		12		7							15
1	2	3	4*	5		8	9		11	10	6		12		7							16
1	2	3	4	5		8	9		11	10	6				7							17
1	2	3	4	5		8	9		11	10	6				7							18
1	2	3	4	5		8	9		11	10	6				7							19
1	2	3	4*	5		8	9		11	10	6			12	7							20
1	2	3		5		8	9	4	11	10	6				7							21
1	2	3	4*	5		8	9		11	10	6			12	7							22
1	2	3		5		8	9		11	10	6				7	4						23
1	2	3		5		8	9		11	10	6				7	4						24
1	2			5		8	9		11	10	6	3			7	4						25
1	2		7	5		8	9		11	10	6	3				4						26
1	2	3	7	5		8	9	12	11	10	6					4*						27
	2	3	4	5		8	9		11		6				7	10	1					28
1	2	3	7	5		8*	9		11		6				10	4		12				29
1	2	3	7	5		8	9		11		6				10	4						30
1	2	3	7	5		8*	9		11		6		12		10	4						31
1	2	3		5		8	9	4	11	10	6				7							32
1		3	7	5		8	9	4		11	6				10				2			33
1		3*	7	5		11	9	4		10	6		12		8				2			34
1			7	5		11	9*	4		10	6	3	12		8				2			35
1			7		5	8	12	4		11	6	3	9*		10				2			36
1			7		5			4		11	6	3	9		10	8			2			37
1			7		5	8		4			6	3	9		10		10	11	2			38
1				5		9		4		11	6	3	7		10	8			2			39
1				5		8		4		11	6	3	9		10	7			2			40
1		3	7*12	5		10		4		11	6		9			8			2			41
1		3		5		10	12	4		11*	6		9		8	7			2			42
41	30	32	27	33	10	3	34	34	26	32	30	41	12	14	3	30	3	15	1	1	10	
			+1s	+1s			+2s	+1s	+3s	+1s					+8s	+5s			+1s			

SUNDERLAND—PLAYERS

Player and position	Ht	Wt	Birthplace	Clubs	League Appearances	Goals
Goalkeepers						
Barry Siddall	6 0	13 2	Ellesmere Port	Bolton W	137	—
				Sunderland	117	—
Ian Watson	5 11	10 11	North Shields	Sunderland	1	—
Defenders						
Joe Bolton	5 11	11 12	Birley	Sunderland	203+9	11
Jack Ashurst	6 0	11 0	Coatbridge	Sunderland	127+10	4
Jeffrey Clarke	5 11	12 1	Pontefract	Manchester C	13	
				Sunderland	114+2	5
Alan Weir	5 9	10 0	South Shields	Sunderland	1	—
Mick Docherty	5 6	9 8	Preston	Burnley	149+4	—
				Manchester C	8	—
				Sunderland	72+1	6
Mike Coady	5 11	10 3	Dipton	Sunderland	4+1	—
Steve Whitworth (England)	5 9	11 1	Coalville	Leicester C	352+1	—
				Sunderland	10	—
Mike Henderson	5 9	10 8	Gosforth	Sunderland	81+3	2
Midfield						
Tim Gilbert	5 9	11 2½	South Shields	Sunderland	26+2	2
Kevin Arnott	5 9	11 4	Bensham	Sunderland	55+1	6
John Duncan	5 10	11 0	South Shields	Sunderland	—	—
Wilf Rostron	5 6	11 2	Sunderland	Arsenal	55+1	2
				Sunderland	67+1	17
Mike Buckley	5 5	9 6	Manchester	Everton	128+7	10
				Sunderland	30	—
Forwards						
Gary Rowell	5 8	10 9	Seaham	Sunderland	100+7	45
Shaun Elliott	5 11	10 6	Haydin Bridge	Sunderland	85+4	5
Bob Lee	6 1	12 5	Leicester	Leicester C	55+8	17
				Doncaster R (on loan)	14	4
				Sunderland	94+8	31
Alan Brown	6 0	11 11	Easington	Sunderland	25+14	6
*Jimmy Grattan	5 9	10 10	N Ireland	Sunderland	—	—
				Mansfield T (on loan)	1	—
Keith Armstrong	5 8	11 5	Corbridge	Sunderland	7+4	—
(Contract cancelled December 1978)				Newport Co (on loan)	3+1	—
Vince Hutton	5 7½	10 9½	Newcastle	Sunderland	—	—
Roland Gregoire	5 9	10 7	Liverpool	Halifax T	5	—
				Sunderland	6+3	1
Wayne Entwistle	5 11	11 8	Bury	Bury	25+6	7
				Scunthorpe U (on loan)	0+1	—
				Sunderland	41+2	12
Robert Hindmarch	6 2½	13 0	Stannington	Sunderland	—	—
Gordon Chisholm	6 0¾	11 2½	Glasgow	Sunderland	27	1
Colin Crawford	5 7½	10 11	Doagh, Co Antrim	Bangor	—	—
				Sunderland	—	—
David Hamilton	5 7	8 13	South Shields	Sunderland	—	—
John Main	5 7	9 5	Glasgow	Sunderland	—	—
Joe Roddy	5 9	11 4	Stockton	Sunderland	—	—

SWANSEA CITY

DIV. 2

President: P. E. Holden. Chairman: M. Struel.
Vice-Chairman: T. J. Phillips.
Directors: E. P. Walters, I. C. Pursey, P. L. W. Owen, R. G. Jones, W. C. Floyd, D. W. A. Rees.
Team Manager: John Toshack.
Assistant Manager: Terry Medwin
Secretary: G. J. Daniels, F.A.A.I.
Year Formed: About 1900. Turned Professional: 1911.
Limited Company: 1912.
Previous Name: Swansea Town until Feb. 1970.

Football League Record:
1920 Original Member of Division 3.
1921–25 Division 3(S).
1925–47 Division 2.
1947–49 Division 3(S).
1949–65 Division 2.
1965–67 Division 3.
1967–70 Division 4.
1970–73 Division 3.
1973–78 Division 4.
1978–79 Division 3.
1979– Division 2.

Honours: Football League, best season in Division 2: 5th, 1925–26. Division 3(S), Champions: 1924–25, 1948–49, Division 3. Promoted 1978–79. Division 4, Promoted: 1969–70 (3rd), 1977–78 (3rd). F.A. Cup, best season, semi-finalists, 1926, 1964. Football League Cup, best season, 4th Rd., 1964–65, 1976–77. Welsh Cup: Winners 4 times. European Competitions: European Cup Winners Cup, 1961–62, 1966–67.

Record Victory: 8-0 v Hartlepool U., Division 4, April 1st, 1978.

Record Defeat: 1-8 v Fulham, Division 2, Jan. 22nd, 1938.

Most League Points: 62, Division 3(S), 1948–49.

Most League Goals: 90, Division 2, 1956–57.

Highest League Scorer in Season: Cyril Pearce, 35, Division 2, 1931–32.

Most League Goals in Total Aggregate: Ivor Allchurch, 166, 1949–58, 1965–68.

Most Capped Player: Ivor Allchurch, 42 (68), Wales.

Most League Appearances: Wilfred Milne, 585, 1919–37.

Record Transfer Fee Received: £370,000 from Leeds U. for Alan Curtis, May 1979.

Record Transfer Fee Paid: £70,000 to Aston Villa for Leighton Phillips, Nov. 1978.

Managers Since the War: Bill McCandless, Ron Burgess, Trevor Morris, Glyn Davies, Bill Lucas, Roy Bentley, Harry Gregg, Harry Griffiths.

Address of Supporters Club: Vetch Field, Swansea.

Vetch Field, Swansea. Telephone Swansea 42855. Ground capacity: 35,000. Record attendance: 32,796 v Arsenal, F.A. Cup 4th Rd., February 17, 1968. Record receipts: £28,570 v Tottenham H., League Cup, 2nd Rd., August 29, 1978. Pitch measurement: 110 yds. × 70 yds.

How to get there: 5 minutes' walk from bus depot. South Wales Transport Co. Ltd. services from High Street General station to Lower Oxford Street. Parking facilities available at the Quadrant.
Match tickets: Tickets can be reserved in advance.
Car parking: Car park 200 yards from the ground in The Kingsway. Side-street parking available.
Entertainments/catering facilities: Disc jockey programme prior to the match. Licensed bar and refreshment kiosk inside the ground.
Club shop: Situated in William Street; sells all types of souvenirs.
Handbooks/programmes: No handbook. Programmes can be obtained from the Secretary by sending remittance and S.A.E.

Club Colours: All white with black trim.
Change Colours: Yellow shirts with blue and red band, royal blue shorts, royal blue and red stockings.
Player/Coach: Les Chappell.
Club Nickname: 'Swans'.

SWANSEA CITY 1978-79 LEAGUE RECORD

Match No.	Date	Venue	Opponents	Result	H/T Score	League Pos'n	Goalscorers	Attendance
1	Aug 19	A	Colchester U	D 2-2	0-1	—	James R 2	2918
2	22	H	Lincoln C	W 3-0	2-0	—	Charles, Curtis, Waddle	16,704
3	26	A	Oxford U	W 2-0	1-0	2	James R 2	4947
4	Sept 2	H	Bury	W 2-0	1-0	1	James R, Charles	10,500
5	9	A	Watford	W 2-0	2-0	1	Waddle, Moore	17,435
6	12	H	Rotherham U	D 4-4	1-3	—	Charles 2, Curtis 2	17,065
7	16	H	Tranmere R	W 4-3	2-3	1	Charles, Waddle, Bartley, Curtis	16,132
8	23	A	Chester	L 0-2	0-1	2		8583
9	25	A	Carlisle U	L 0-2	0-0	—		8489
10	30	H	Brentford	W 2-1	1-1	3	Charles, James R	11,470
11	Oct 7	A	Chesterfield	L 1-2	0-1	3	Charles	7033
12	14	H	Exeter C	W 1-0	1-0	3	Toshack	10,957
13	17	H	Mansfield T	W 3-2	3-1	—	James R, Baker 2	10,985
14	21	A	Hull C	D 2-2	0-0	3	Toshack, Waddle	6152
15	28	H	Peterborough U	W 4-1	2-1	3	Waddle 2, Toshack, Charles	11,302
16	Nov 4	A	Gillingham	L 0-2	0-0	3		11,329
17	11	A	Bury	W 1-0	0-0	3	James R	5186
18	18	H	Oxford U	D 1-1	0-1	2	Waddle	11,491
19	Dec 2	H	Sheffield W	W 4-2	2-2	2	Boersma, Toshack 2, Charles	10,000
20	8	A	Southend U	W 2-0	1-0	2	Curtis 2	8935
21	23	A	Shrewsbury T	L 0-3	0-2	3		8557
22	26	H	Swindon T	L 1-2	0-1	3	Toshack	16,770
23	30	H	Blackpool	W 1-0	0-0	3	Charles	12,549
24	Feb 2	H	Carlisle U	D 0-0	0-0	4		10,821
25	10	A	Brentford	L 0-1	0-0	4		7250
26	20	A	Walsall	D 1-1	0-0	—	Bartley	6335
27	24	A	Exeter C	L 1-2	0-1	4	Curtis	7697
28	27	H	Chester	D 2-2	0-1	—	Toshack, Stevenson	7983
29	Mar 2	H	Hull C	W 5-3	3-1	5	Smith 2, Toshack 2, Charles	8849
30	6	A	Rotherham U	W 1-0	0-0	—	Waddle	3864
31	10	H	Peterborough U	L 0-2	0-0	4		5550
32	16	H	Gillingham	W 3-1	2-0	3	Curtis, Waddle, Sharpe (og)	10,832
33	20	H	Watford	W 3-2	2-0	—	Curtis 2, James R	19,850
34	24	A	Lincoln C	L 1-2	0-1	5	James R	3568
35	27	H	Colchester U	W 4-1	1-0	—	Waddle 2, James R, Attley	11,645
36	31	H	Plymouth Arg	W 2-1	0-0	2	Stevenson, Waddle	11,412
37	Apr 3	A	Tranmere R	W 2-1	2-0	—	James R, Waddle	3499
38	7	A	Sheffield W	D 0-0	0-0	2		12,101
39	10	H	Shrewsbury T	D 1-1	1-0	—	James R	19,566
40	14	A	Swindon T	W 1-0	1-0	2	James R	16,971
41	17	H	Walsall	D 2-2	0-0	—	Toshack, Waddle	18,096
42	21	A	Blackpool	W 3-1	1-0	1	Curtis, Waddle, Charles	5977
43	23	H	Mansfield T	D 2-2	1-1	—	James R (pen), Waddle	6420
44	28	H	Southend U	W 3-2	1-0	1	Waddle 3	15,941
45	May 5	A	Plymouth Arg	D 2-2	0-1	2	Curtis, Toshack	13,406
46	11	H	Chesterfield	W 2-1	1-1	—	Waddle, Toshack	25,000

Final League Position: 3

Goalscorers

League (83): Waddle 19, James R 14 (1 pen), Curtis 13, Toshack 13, Charles 12, Baker 2, Bartley 2, Stevenson 2, Smith 2, Boersma 1, Attley 1, Moore 1, Own Goal 1.
League Cup (11): James R 4 (1 pen), Curtis 3, Charles 2, Waddle, Toshack.
F.A. Cup (11): Curtis 5, James R 2, Charles 2, Waddle, Toshack.

League Cup	First Round	Newport Co (a)	1-2
		(h)	5-0
	Second Round	Tottenham H (h)	2-2
		(a)	3-1
	Third Round	QPR (a)	0-2
F.A. Cup	First Round	Hillingdon (h)	4-1
	Second Round	Woking (h)	2-2
		(a)	5-3 (a.e.t.)
	Third Round	Bristol R (h)	0-1

Crudgington	Evans	Bartley	Toshack	Bruton	Reeves	Lally	James R	Curtis	Waddle	Moore	Smith	Charles	James A	Stevenson	Morris	Boersma	Marustik	Callaghan	Baker	Phillips	Attley	Match No.
1	2	3	4	5	6	7	8	9	10	11												1
1	2	3	7	5			8	9	10	11	4	6*12										2
1	2	3	5*				8		9	11	6	10	7	4	12							3
1	2	3		12			8	9*10	11		4	7		5	6							4
1	2	3	7*	5			8	9	10	11	4	6	12									5
1	2	3		5			8*	9	10	11	4	6				7	12					6
1	2	3	6	5				9	10	12	4	7*			8		11					7
1	2	3					8	9*10			4	6		5		11	12	7				8
1	2	3							10	8		6		5	4	7	9	11				9
1	2	3		5			8		9	7	4	6*		12	10		11					10
1	2	3		5			8		9	7*	4	6			10		11	12				11
1	2	3	6				8		10	7	4	9		5			11					12
1	2		10				8		9	7	4	6		5		12	11	3*				13
1	2	12	5				8		9	7*	4	6		3		10	11					14
1	2	3	10		12		8		11		4	6		5			7	9*				15
1	2	3	10				8		9		4	6		5		11	7					16
1	2			6			8		9		4			5	3	11		7	10			17
1	2	11	10				8		9		4	6			3		7	5				18
1	2	3	5				8		9	11*		6	12		10		7	4				19
1		3					8	9	10		2	6		5		7	11	4				20
1		3					8	9	10		2	6		5	7*		11	12	4			21
1	2	12	7				8	9	10*		3	6		5			11	4				22
1	2		7				8	9			3	6		5		10*	11	12	4			23
1	2						8	9	10	7	4	6		5			11	3				24
1	2	3	5				8	9	10		4	7*	12				11	6				25
1	2	3	10				8	9			4	6		5			11	7				26
1	2	3	10				8*	9			4	6		5			11		7	12		27
1	2	3	8					9	10		4	12		5			11*		6	7		28
1		3	10				8	9			4	6		5			11		2	7		29
1		3	10*				8	9	12		4	6		5	2		11			7		30
1	2	3			12		8	9	10					5	4		6*11			7		31
1	2	3	10*				8	9	12			6		5			11		4	7		32
1	2	3					8	9	10		12	6		5			11		4	7*		33
1	2*	3					8	9	10		12	6		5			11		4	7		34
1		3					8	9	10		4	6*		5		12	11		2	7		35
1		3					8	9	10		2	6*		5		12	11		4	7		36
1		3					8	9	10		4			5		6	11		2	7		37
1		3					8	9	10		2			5		6	11		4	7		38
1		3	12				8	9	10		4	6*		5			11		2	7		39
1		3					8	9	10		4	12		5		6*	11		2	7		40
1		3	12				8	9*10			4	6		5			11		2	7		41
1	2	3	6*				8	9	10			12		5			11		4	7		42
1	4	3	6				8	9	10					5			11		2	7		43
1	2	3	12				8	9	10			6		5			11		4	7*		44
1	2	3	6				8	9	10			12		5			11		4	7*		45
1	2	3	12				8	9	10			6		5			11		4	7*		46
46	35	40	24	7	2	1	43	34	40	14	34	36	1	36	7	15	2	40	2	28	19	
	+	+	+	+			+	+	+	+	+	+	+		+	+	+		+	+		
	2s	4s	1s	2s			2s	1s	2s	4s	1s	3s	2s		3s	2s			3s	1s		

SWANSEA CITY—PLAYERS

Player and position	Ht	Wt	Birthplace	Clubs	League Appearances	Goals
Goalkeepers						
Keith Barber	5 11	11 6	London	Luton T	142	—
(Contract cancelled November 1978)				Swansea C	42	—
				Cardiff C (on loan)	2	—
Geoff Crudgington	5 11½	12 12½	Wolverhampton	Aston V	4	—
				Bradford C (on loan)	1	—
				Preston NE (on loan)	—	—
				Crewe A	250	—
				Swansea C	46	—
Defenders						
Wyndham Evans	5 9½	12 11½	Llanelli	Swansea C	313+5	19
Danny Bartley	5 8½	11 4½	Paulton	Bristol C	93+6	7
				Swansea C	191+4	8
Steven Morris	6 0	11 0	Swansea	Swansea C	33+6	1
Nigel Stevenson	6 2	11 0	Swansea	Swansea C	38+3	2
Eddie May	6 1½	13 3½	Epping	Southend U	107+4	3
(Contract cancelled October 1978)				Wrexham	329+4	34
				Swansea C	90	8
Brian Attley	5 9	9 12	Cardiff	Cardiff C	73+6	1
				Swansea C	19+1	1
Leighton Phillips	5 10	10 11	Briton Ferry	Cardiff C	169+9	10
(Wales)				Aston V	134+6	4
				Swansea C	28	—
Tommy Smith	5 10½	13 5	Liverpool	Liverpool	467	37
(England)				Swansea C	34+2	2
Midfield						
Leslie Chappell	5 8	10 5	Nottingham	Rotherham U	106+2	37
				Blackburn R	7	—
				Reading	193+8	78
				Doncaster R	57+1	10
				Swansea C	65+2	5
Tony James	5 8	10 0	Swansea	Swansea C	6+4	1
Peter Reeves	5 8	10 7	Swansea	Coventry C	—	—
				Swansea C	2+2	—
Phil Boersma	5 10	11 7	Liverpool	Liverpool	73+10	18
				Wrexham (on loan)	3+2	—
				Middlesbrough	41+6	3
				Luton T	35+1	8
				Swansea C	15+3	1
Chris Marustik	5 8	11 11½	Swansea	Swansea C	2+2	—
Ian Callaghan	5 7	11 11	Liverpool	Liverpool	636+4	49
(England)				Swansea C	40	—
Forwards						
Robbie James	5 10	12 1½	Swansea	Swansea C	245+3	62
(Wales)						
Jeremy Charles	6 1	12 0	Swansea	Swansea C	99+15	39
Ian McCarthy				Swansea C	0+1	—
(Contract cancelled November 1978)						
John Toshack	6 1	12 0	Cardiff	Cardiff C	159+2	74
(Wales)				Liverpool	169+3	74
				Swansea C	37+4	19
Alan Waddle	6 3	13 0	Wallsend	Halifax T	33+6	4
				Liverpool	11+5	1
				Leicester C	11	1
				Swansea C	40+2	19
Mark Baker	5 9	11 4½	Swansea	Swansea C	2+3	2
Alan Curtis	5 11	12 3	Rhondda	Swansea C	244+4	72
(Wales)						

Carl Slee (Contract cancelled April 1979)

SWINDON TOWN   DIV. 3

President: W. H. Castle. *Chairman:* C. J. Green.

Directors: C. Day, A. W. Done, C. Cowley, T. J. R. Kearsley, R. Stephenson, M. W. Earle, W. H. Dore, L. Smart, G. Whittock.

Team Manager: Bob Smith.

Admin. Manager/Secretary: R. Jefferies.

Finance Manager: R. A. Morse.

Year Formed: 1881. *Turned Professional:* 1894.

Limited Company: 1894. *Previous Ground:* 1881–96, The Croft.

Football League Record:

1920 Original Member of Division 3.	1963–65 Division 2.
1921–58 Division 3(S).	1965–69 Division 3.
1958–63 Division 3.	1969–74 Division 2.
	1974– Division 3.

Honours: Football League, best season in Division 2: 5th, 1969–70. Division 3, Runners-up: 1962–63, 1968–69. *F.A. Cup,* best season, semi-finalists: 1910, 1912. *Football League Cup,* best season, Winners: 1968–69. Anglo-Italian Cup, Winners: 1970.

Record Victory: 10-1 v Farnham United Breweries, F.A. Cup, 1st Rd., Nov. 28th, 1925.

Record Defeat: 1-10 v Manchester C., F.A. Cup, 4th Rd. Replay, Jan. 25th, 1930.

Most League Points: 64, Division 3, 1968–69.

Most League Goals: 100, Division 3(S), 1926–27.

Highest League Scorer in Season: Harry Morris, 47, Division 3(S), 1926–27.

Most League Goals in Total Aggregate: Harry Morris, 216, 1926–33.

Most Capped Player: Rod Thomas, 30 (50), Wales.

Most League Appearances: John Trollope, 756, 1960–79.

Record Transfer Fee Received: £150,000 from C. Palace for Don Rogers, Oct. 1972.

Record Transfer Fee Paid: £88,000 to Wolverhampton W. for Peter Eastoe, March 1974.

Managers Since the War: Louis Page, Maurice Lindley, Bert Head, Danny Williams, Fred Ford, Dave Mackay, Les Allen, Danny Williams.

Address of Supporters Club: Swindon Town Supporters Club, County Ground, Swindon, Wilts.

Address of Club Shop: Souvenir and Sports Shop, Swindon Town F.C., County Ground, Swindon.

County Ground, Swindon, Wiltshire. Telephone Ground Swindon 22118. *Ground capacity:* 28,000 (6500 seats). *Record attendance:* 32,000 v Arsenal F.A. Cup 3rd Rd., January 15, 1972. *Record receipts:* £24,494 v Everton, F.A. Cup, 4th Rd., January 29, 1977. *Pitch measurements:* 114 yds × 72 yds.

How to get there: Both Swindon bus and railway stations are half a mile from the ground.

Match tickets: Available 3 weeks in advance.

Car parking: Corporation car park adjacent to the west end of the ground, off County Road.

Club shop: Postal enquiries welcome. All types of souvenirs are stocked.

Handbooks/programmes: Programmes available by postal application, or subscription.

Entaertainment/catering facilities: The Supporters' Club Rendezvous Club and Squash Club in the North Stand. Refreshment kiosks in all parts of the ground. No licensed bars on terraces or stands.

Extra information: Harold Fleming of Swindon Town played 11 times for England before World War 1 when the club were still a non-League side. Separate terrace enclosure available for adults and accompanied children only.

Club Colours: Red shirts with white trimmings, white shorts, red stockings.

Change Colours: All white.

Club Nickname: 'Robins'.

SWINDON TOWN 1978–79 LEAGUE RECORD

Match No.	Date	Venue	Opponents	Result	H/T Score	League Pos'n	Goalscorers	Attendance
1	Aug 19	H	Bury	W 2-1	2-0	—	Bates, Miller	5382
2	21	A	Tranmere R	D 1-1	0-1	—	Carter	2150
3	26	A	Shrewsbury T	D 0-0	0-0	8		2672
4	Sept 2	H	Mansfield T	W 1-0	0-0	5	Bates	6195
5	9	A	Walsall	L 1-4	0-2	9	Williams	5024
6	12	H	Brentford	W 2-0	0-0	—	McHale, Bates	6685
7	16	A	Plymouth Arg	L 0-2	0-1	9		6099
8	23	H	Blackpool	L 0-1	0-0	14		6607
9	27	A	Chester	L 0-2	0-1	—		3311
10	30	H	Sheffield W	W 3-0	1-0	13	Bates, Rowland, Gilchrist	5857
11	Oct 6	A	Colchester U	L 2-3	2-0	16	Gilchrist, Bates	3324
12	14	H	Rotherham U	W 1-0	0-0	13	Bates	4476
13	17	H	Peterborough U	W 3-1	1-1	—	Bates 2, Carter	4352
14	21	A	Lincoln C	W 3-0	1-0	5	McLaughlin, Williams, McHale	2983
15	28	A	Carlisle U	L 0-2	0-1	9		5141
16	Nov 4	H	Southend U	W 1-0	0-0	5	Gilchrist	5647
17	11	A	Mansfield T	W 1-0	1-0	5	Bates	4721
18	18	H	Shrewsbury T	W 2-1	1-0	4	Gilchrist, Aizlewood	7317
19	Dec 9	H	Hull C	W 2-0	0-0	4	Miller, Carter	5697
20	26	A	Swansea C	W 2-1	1-0	4	Bates, Gilchrist	16,770
21	30	A	Watford	L 0-2	0-0	5		15,486
22	Jan 16	H	Walsall	W 4-1	1-0	—	Kamara, Serella (og), Bates, Gilchrist	7282
23	20	A	Plymouth Arg	L 1-3	1-0	5	Carter	7780
24	Feb 3	H	Chester	W 2-0	1-0	5	McHale, Carter	6036
25	24	A	Rotherham U	W 3-1	1-0	6	Mayes 3	5128
26	28	A	Chesterfield	D 1-1	1-0	—	Kamara	3904
27	Mar 3	H	Lincoln C	W 6-0	4-0	4	Rowland 2, Mayes, McHale, Hubbard (og), Bates	6649
28	10	H	Carlisle U	D 0-0	0-0	5		8386
29	16	A	Southend U	L 3-5	0-3	6	Rowland, Mayes, Cawston (og)	4303
30	20	H	Colchester U	L 1-2	0-0	—	Rowland	6678
31	24	H	Tranmere R	W 4-1	2-1	6	Rowland 2, Mayes, McHale	5678
32	27	A	Bury	W 1-0	0-0	—	Rowland	3557
33	31	H	Gillingham	D 2-2	2-2	6	Mayes, Carter	9460
34	Apr 3	H	Exeter C	D 1-1	0-0	—	Rowland	7923
35	7	H	Chesterfield	W 1-0	0-0	5	Carter	6176
36	11	A	Exeter C	W 2-1	2-0	—	Bates, Rowland	5548
37	14	H	Swansea C	L 0-1	0-1	6		16,971
38	16	A	Oxford U	W 1-0	0-0	—	Carter (pen)	9176
39	21	H	Watford	W 2-0	1-0	3	Jenkins (og), Rowland	16,397
40	24	A	Peterborough U	L 1-2	0-1	—	Hamilton	4121
41	28	A	Hull City	D 1-1	1-0	6	Rowland	4980
42	May 2	H	Oxford U	W 2-0	1-0	—	Bates, Carter	8849
43	5	H	Gillingham	W 3-1	0-0	4	Rowland, Mayes 2	15,117
44	8	A	Brentford	W 2-1	1-1	—	Miller, Mayes	13,320
45	11	A	Sheffield W	L 1-2	0-1	—	Mayes	9057
46	15	A	Blackpool	L 2-5	1-2	—	Aizlewood, Carter	4191

Final League Position: 5

Goalscorers

League (74): Bates 14, Rowland 13, Mayes 11, Carter 10 (1 pen), Gilchrist 6, McHale 5, Miller 3, Kamara 2, Aizlewood 2, Williams 2, Hamilton 1, McLoughlin 1, Own Goals 4.
League Cup (7): Aizlewood 2, Guthrie 2, Miller 2, Williams.
F.A. Cup (9): Gilchrist 2, Bates 2, Kamara 2, McHale, Rowland, Carter.

League Cup	First Round	Portsmouth (a)	0-0
		(h)	4-2
	Second Round	West Ham U (a)	2-1
	Third Round	Peterborough U (a)	1-1
		(h)	0-2 (a.e.t.)
F.A. Cup	First Round	March (h)	2-0
	Second Round	Enfield (h)	3-0
	Third Round	Cardiff C (h)	3-0
	Fourth Round	Aldershot (a)	1-2

Ogden	McLaughlin	Ford	McHale	Aizlewood	Stroud	Carter	Williams	Guthric	Bates	Miller	Lewis	Kamara	Gilchrist	Rowland	Trollope	Cunningham	Allan	Hamilton	Mayes	Dornan	Match No.
1	2	3	4	5	6	7*	8	9	10	11	12										1
1	2	3	4	5	6	8	11		10	7*12	9										2
1	2	3	4	5	6	8	10	9*11	7		12										3
1	2	3	4	5	6	8	11	9*10	7		12										4
1	2	3	4	5*	6	8	11	9	10	7	12										5
1	2	3	4	5*	6	8	11	9	10	7	12										6
1	2	3	4	5	6	8		9	11	7*		10	12								7
1	2	3	4	5	6	8	11		10	7				9							8
1		3	4	5	6	8	11		10*	7		12		9	2						9
1		3	4		6	8			10*		5	11	7	9	2	12					10
1		3	4	12	6	8			10		5	11	7	9*	2						11
1	2	3	4	5	6	8			10	7		11	12	9*							12
1	2	3	4	5	6	8	9*		10	7		11	12								13
1	2	3	4	5	6	8*10		9	7			11	12								14
	2	3	4	5	6	8		9	7			10*12			11	1					15
1	2	3	4	5	6	8			10	7		11	9								16
1	2	3	4*	5	6	8			10	7	12	11	9								17
1	2	3	4	5	6	8	12		10	7		11	9*								18
1	2	3	4	5	6	8	12		10	7		11*	9								19
1	2	3	4	5	6	8	12		10	7		11*	9								20
1	2	3	4	5	6	8	12		10	7		11	9*								21
1		3	4	5		8	12		10	7*	6	11	9					2			22
1		3	4	5		8	12		10	7	6*11	9						2			23
		3	4	5	6	8	11		10	7			9				1	2			24
		3	4	5	6	8	11*		12	7				10			1	2	9		25
		3	4	5	6	8			12	7*		11	9				1	2	10		26
		3	4	5	6	8			12	7		11*	9				1	2	10		27
		3	4	5	6	8			12	7*		11	9				1	2	10		28
		3	4	5	6	8	12			7*		11	9				1	2	10		29
		3	4	5	6	8	11		12	7*			9				1	2	10		30
		3	4	5	6	8	11*		12	7			9				1	2	10		31
		3	4	5	6	8	11			7			9	12			1	2	10*		32
		3	4	5	6	8				7		11		10	12		1	2*	9		33
		3	4	5	6	8				7		11	9	2			1		10		34
		3	4	5	6	8	11		12	7				10	2		1		9*		35
		3	4	5	6	8			10*	7		12	9	2			1	11			36
	3*	4	5		6	8			12	7			9	2			1	11	10		37
		3	4	5*	6	8			11	7			9	2			1	12	10		38
		3	4		6	5			10	7			9	2			1	11	8		39
		3	4		6	5			11	7			9	2			1	8	10*12		40
		3	6		5	4			8	7	12		10	2			1	9	11*		41
		3	4	5	6	8*12			11	7			9	2			1		10		42
		3	4	5*	6	8			10	7			9	2			1	12	11		43
		3	4		6	8			11	7	5*		9	2			1	12	10		44
		3	4		6	5			11	7*		12	9	2			1	8	10		45
		3	4	5	6	8	12		11	7*			9	2			1		10		46
22	18	46	46	39	44	46	16	6	34	44	5	22	10	28	16	1	24	18	21	—	
				+ 1s		+ 9s		+ 8s			+ 4s	+ 6s	+ 6s		+ 2s	+ 1s		+ 3s	+ 1s		

SWINDON TOWN—PLAYERS

Player and position	Ht	Wt	Birthplace	Clubs	League Appearances	Goals
Goalkeepers						
Jimmy Allan	6 0	12 3	Inverness	Swindon T	183	—
Kevin Roberts	6 0	13 0	Bristol	Swindon T	1	—
				Grimsby T (on loan)	—	—
Chris Ogden	5 10½	12 6	Oldham	Oldham Ath	128	—
				Swindon T	22	—
Defenders						
John McLaughlin	5 8	10 10	Edmonton	Colchester U	66	2
				Swindon T	199+3	8
Russell Lewis	5 10½	12 13	Neath	Swindon T	10+5	—
John Trollope	6 0½	12 3	Wroughton	Swindon T	753+3	22
Steve Aizlewood	5 11	13 7	Newport	Newport Co	191+6	17
				Swindon T	111+1	10
Andrew Ford	5 11	12 0	Minehead	Bournemouth	—	—
				Southend U	135+2	3
				Swindon T	74+6	1
Kenneth Stroud	5 11	12 0	London	Swindon T	200+9	14
Midfield						
Roy Carter	6 0½	10 12	Torpoint	Hereford U	64+7	9
				Swindon T	66+4	12
Ray McHale	5 9	12 6	Sheffield	Chesterfield	123+1	27
				Halifax T	86	21
				Swindon T	130+2	25
Chris Kamara	6 1	12 0	Middlesbrough	Portsmouth	56+7	7
				Swindon T	59+9	12
Peter Dornan	6 0½	12 0	Belfast	Linfield	—	—
				Sheffield U	1+2	—
				Swindon T	0+1	—
Bryan Hamilton (N Ireland)	5 9	11 4	Belfast	Ipswich T	142+11	43
				Everton	38+3	5
				Millwall	48+1	6
				Swindon T	18+3	1
Brian Williams	5 9	12 1	Manchester	Bury	148+11	19
				QPR	9+10	—
				Swindon T	16+9	2
Forwards						
Augustine Gilligan (Contract cancelled February 1979)	5 8	11 2	Abingdon	Swindon T	3+1	—
				Doncaster R (on loan)	1	—
Chic Bates	6 0	11 12	West Bromwich	Shrewsbury T	160	45
				Swindon T	46+10	15
Andy Rowland	5 11	12 0	Derby	Derby	—	—
				Bury	169+5	58
				Swindon T	28	13
Allan Mayes	5 7	10 10	London	QPR	—	—
				Watford	110+23	31
				Northampton T (on loan)	10	4
				Swindon T	21	11
Ian Miller	5 9	11 7	Perth	Bury	9+6	—
				Nottingham F	—	—
				Doncaster R	124	14
				Swindon T	44	3
Paul Gilchrist	5 11	11 6	Dartford	Charlton Ath	5+2	—
				Fulham (on loan)	—	—
				Doncaster R	22	8
				Southampton	96+11	17
				Portsmouth	38+1	3
				Swindon T	10+6	6
Ken Norman				Swindon T	—	—

TORQUAY UNITED

DIV. 4

Chairman: A. J. Boyce.
Vice-Chairman: M. C. Spedding.
Directors: D. C. Hair, M.R.C.V.S., J. H. Perry, Lt.-Col. W. J. Elliot, M.B.E., F.C.I.S., J. Hudson, L. W. Pope, W. G. Standley, W. W. Rogers.
Player Manager: Mike Green.   *Secretary:* D. J. Easton.
Consultant: Frank O'Farrell.
Year Formed: 1898.   *Turned Professional:* 1921.
Limited Company: 1921.
Previous Name: 1910, Torquay Town; 1921, Torquay United
Previous Grounds: 1898, Teignmouth Road; 1901, Torquay Recreation Ground; 1905, Cricket Field Road; 1907, Torquay Cricket Ground; 1910, Plainmoor.
Football League Record: 1927 Elected to Division 3(S). 1958–60 Division 4. 1960–62 Division 3. 1962–66 Division 3. 1966–72 Division 3. 1972– Division 4.
Honours: *Football League*, best season in Division 3: 4th, 1967–68. Division 3(S), Runners-up: 1956–57. Division 4, Promoted: 1959–60, 1965–66. *F.A. Cup*, best season: 4th Rd. 1949 1955, 1971. *Football League Cup*, never past 3rd Rd.
Record Victory: 9-0 v Swindon T., Division 3(S), March 8th, 1952.
Record Defeat: 2-10 v Fulham, Division 3(S), Sept. 7th, 1931 and v Luton T., Division 3(S), Sept. 2nd, 1933.
Most League Points: 60, Division 4, 1959–60.
Most League Goals: 89, Div. 3(S), 1956–57.
Highest League Scorer in Season: Sammy Collins, 40, Division 3(S), 1955–56.
Most League Goals in Total Aggregate: Sammy Collins, 204, 1948–58.
Most Capped Player: None.
Most League Appearances: Dennis Lewis, 443, 1947–59.
Record Transfer Fee Received: £80,000 from Tottenham H. for Colin Lee, Oct. 1977.
Record Transfer Fee Paid: £15,000 to Leicester C. for David Tearse, Nov. 1971.
Managers Since the War: Jack Butler, John McNeil, Bob John, Alex Massie, Eric Webber, Frank O'Farrell, Allan Brown, Jack Edwards, Malcolm Musgrove, Frank O'Farrell.
Address of Supporters Association: Plainmoor, Torquay, Devon.
Address of Club Shop: The Gull Shop, Torquay United Supporters Association, Plainmoor, Torquay, Devon.

Plainmoor Ground, Torquay, Devon, TQ1 3PS. Telephone Torquay (0803) 38666–7. *Ground capacity:* 22,000. *Record attendance:* 21,908 v Huddersfield T., F.A. Cup 4th Rd., January 29, 1955. *Record receipts:* £10,326 v Tottenham H., F.L. Cup, 3rd Rd., October 6, 1971. *Pitch measurements:* 112 yds × 74 yds.

How to get there: Train to Torquay railway station. Bus 30 runs every 12 minutes from the station to the ground.
Match tickets: Stand seats available a fortnight before the match. Postal applications accepted provided correct remittance and S.A.E. are enclosed.
Car parking: Some street parking. Coaches park at Lymington Road coach station.
Entertainments/catering facilities: 200 Club—a match day venue luxury club—membership £6 (48 hours notice required for membership). Supporters' Social Club—open all week—now completely up-dated with luxury furnishings—membership £1, O.A.Ps. 50p. (48 hours notice required)
Club shop: Sells all types of souvenirs.
Handbooks/programmes: For programmes contact the club shop.
Extra information: Running commentaries of home matches to local hospitals. Twelve free seats supplied to members of the local Rehabilitation Centre of the Royal National Institute for the Blind who can listen to the hospital commentary while experiencing the match atmosphere.
Club Colours: White shirts with blue and yellow vertical stripes on sleeve, blue shorts with yellow and white stripes on side, white stockings with blue and yellow ring on turnover.
Change Colours: Yellow shirts with blue and white vertical stripes on sleeve, yellow shorts with blue and white stripes on side, yellow stockings with blue turnover and yellow ring on turnover.
Club Captain: Clint Boulton. *Club Nickname:* 'The Gulls'. *Team Captain:*

TORQUAY UNITED 1978-79 LEAGUE RECORD

Match No.	Date	Venue	Opponents	Result	H/T Score	League Pos'n	Goalscorers	Attendance
1	Aug 19	H	Northampton T	L 0-1	0-0	—		2966
2	26	H	Hereford U	W 1-0	1-0	15	Davies	3074
3	Sept 2	A	Grimsby T	L 0-3	0-1	22		3934
4	9	H	Halifax T	W 2-0	1-0	15	Lawrence 2	2048
5	12	A	Barnsley	W 2-1	2-0	—	Lawrence, Coffill	12,844
6	16	H	Aldershot	W 2-1	2-0	10	Lawrence, Raper	2998
7	23	A	Darlington	W 2-1	1-0	6	Coffill, Murphy	1613
8	27	A	Reading	L 0-1	0-1	—		5722
9	30	H	Hartlepool U	W 4-1	2-0	9	Cooper 2, Murphy 2 (1 a pen)	3033
10	Oct 7	A	Crewe Alex	L 2-6	1-2	10	Cooper 2	1854
11	10	A	Doncaster R	L 0-1	0-0	—		2507
12	14	H	Rochdale	D 1-1	0-1	10	Green	2873
13	17	A	York C	D 0-0	0-0	—		2084
14	21	H	Port Vale	W 2-1	2-1	8	Murphy, Green	4108
15	28	H	Portsmouth	W 2-1	1-0	6	Lawrence, Murphy	4769
16	Nov 4	A	AFC Bournemouth	L 0-1	0-0	8		3747
17	11	H	Grimsby T	W 3-1	1-0	7	Murphy, Cooper, Lawrence	3189
18	18	A	Hereford U	L 1-3	1-0	8	Cooper	3476
19	Dec 9	H	Scunthorpe U	L 0-1	0-1	12		2794
20	26	A	Newport Co	D 1-1	1-1	—	Murphy	6930
21	Jan 20	A	Aldershot	L 0-1	0-0	15		3658
22	27	H	Darlington	W 1-0	1-0	11	Murphy	2321
23	31	H	Barnsley	W 3-2	2-2	—	Lawrence 3	2714
24	Feb 3	H	Reading	D 1-1	0-1	9	Johnson	3495
25	10	A	Hartlepool U	L 2-3	2-1	9	Coffill, Johnson	2376
26	14	H	Bradford C	L 1-2	1-0	—	Cooper	1912
27	20	H	Crewe Alex	W 3-0	1-0	—	Wilson, Cooper, Murphy	2020
28	28	H	Wimbledon	L 1-6	0-2	—	Murphy	2739
29	Mar 3	H	Port Vale	D 2-2	0-2	9	Lawrence 2	1800
30	10	A	Portsmouth	L 0-1	0-0	12		8689
31	14	A	Wigan Ath	L 1-3	1-2	—	Lawrence	5722
32	17	H	AFC Bournemouth	L 0-1	0-0	13		2159
33	24	A	Northampton T	W 2-1	1-1	13	Green, Lawrence	2194
34	28	H	Doncaster R	W 2-1	2-1	—	Lawrence, Wilson	1781
35	30	A	Stockport Co	W 1-0	1-0	9	Davies	2710
36	Apr 3	A	Halifax T	L 0-1	0-0	—		1112
37	7	H	Wigan Ath	D 1-1	0-1	9	Payne	2969
38	11	A	Bradford C	L 1-3	1-0	—	Cooper	2453
39	14	H	Newport Co	W 2-0	1-0	9	Lawrence 2	3181
40	16	A	Wimbledon	L 0-5	0-4	—		4171
41	21	H	Huddersfield T	W 2-1	0-0	10	Lawrence, Cooper	2478
42	25	A	York C	W 3-0	1-0	—	Cooper 3	1724
43	28	A	Scunthorpe U	D 2-2	1-1	9	Davies, Cox	1426
44	30	A	Huddersfield T	D 1-1	0-1	—	Cooper	1624
45	May 5	H	Stockport Co	W 1-0	1-0	9	Cox	2281
46	9	A	Rochdale	L 0-1	0-1	—		2359

Final League Position: 11

Goalscorers
League (58): Lawrence 17, Cooper 14, Murphy 10 (1 pen), Coffill 3, Davies 3, Green 3, Cox 2, Johnson 2, Wilson 2, Payne 1, Raper 1.
League Cup (2): Lawrence, Murphy.
F.A. Cup (4): Cooper, Wilson, Twitchin, Lawrence.

League Cup	First Round	Plymouth Arg (a)	1-1
		(h)	1-2
F.A. Cup	First Round	Walsall (a)	2-0
	Second Round	AP Leamington (a)	1-0
	Third Round	Newcastle U (a)	1-3

Turner	Twitchin	Parsons	Wilson	Green	Vassallo	Cofill	Darke	Lawrence	Murphy	Raper	Davies	Dunne	Cooper	Payne	Bicknell	Boulton	Johnson	Ritchie	Clarke	Cox	Match No.
1	2	3	4	5	6	7	8	9	10	11											1
1	2	3	12	5		7*	8	9	10	11	4	6									2
1	2	3	12	5		7	6*		10	11	8	4	9								3
1	2		7	5			6	8	10	11	4	3	9								4
1	2		7	5		9	3	8	10	11	4	6									5
1	2		7	4		9	3	10	11*	6	8	5	12								6
1	2		8	5*		9	3	10	11	7	4	6	12								7
1	2		7			9*	3	8	10	11	4	6		5	12						8
1	2		7				3	8	10	11	4*	6	9	5	12						9
1	2		7	5			3	8	10	11*	4	6	9		12						10
1	2		7	5			3	8	10	11	4	6	9								11
1	2		7	5		12	3	8	10	11	4	6	9*								12
1	2	11	7	5		9	3	8	10		4	6									13
1	8	2	7	5		11	3	9	10		4	6									14
1	2	11	7	5		9	3	8	10		4	6									15
1	2	11*	7	5	12	9	3	8	10		4	6									16
1	2		7	5			3	8	10	11	4	6	9								17
1			7	5		12		8	10	11	4*	6	9	3		2					18
1	6		7	5		12		8	10	11	4*	3	9			2					19
1	3	11	7	5		9	2	8	10		4	6									20
1	4	11	7			9	2	8	10*			3	12	6		5					21
1	4	3	7			9	2	8*10				6	12			5	11				22
1	4	3	7			9	2	8				6	10			5	11				23
1	4	3	7			9*	2	8			12	6	10			5	11				24
1	4	3	7			9*	2	8			12	6	10			5	11				25
1	4		7	5			2	8*12		9		6	10	3			11				26
1	3		7				2	8	10	4	11	6	9			5					27
1	2		7	6		12	3	8	10	4*11		9				5					28
1	2		8				3	9	11	4	7	6	10	5							29
1	4		8			12	2*	9	10	7	11	6		5			3				30
1	4		7*			12	2	8	10	9	11	6		5			3				31
1	4		7			11	2	8*10	9		6	12	5				3				32
1	7		12	4		11	2*	9		8	6	10	5				3				33
1	2		10	4		11		8*12		7	6	9	5				3				34
1	2		10	4		11	5	8		7	6	9					3				35
1	2		10	4		11	5*	8	12	7	6	9					3				36
1	2		8*	4		11		9	12	7	6	10	5				3				37
1	2			4		11		8	10	7		9	5	6*			3	12			38
1	2			4		11	12	8		7	6	9	5				3	10*			39
1	2			4		11	12	8		7	6	9	5				3	10*			40
1	2		8	4		12	11	10		7	6	9	5				3*				41
1	2		11	4			10	8		7	6	9	5				3				42
1	2		7	4			12	8	11	6	9	5					3	10*			43
1	2		11	4			10	8		7	6	9	5				3				44
1	2			4	12		10	8		7	6		5				3	11*	9		45
1	2		12			11		8	10	7	6		5			4	3	9*			46
46	45	13	38	33	1	27	33	42	37	21	39	43	28	21	—	11	5	17	4	2	

+4s +1s 8s +3s 4s +2s +5s +3s +1s

TORQUAY UNITED—PLAYERS

Player and position	Ht	Wt	Birthplace	Clubs	League Appearances	Goals
Goalkeepers						
*Geoff Wake	5 10	11 0	Devon	Torquay U	9	—
John Turner	5 11	12 0	Peterlee	Derby Co	—	—
				Doncaster R (on loan)	4	—
				Brighton (on loan)	—	—
				Peterborough U (on loan)	—	—
				Huddersfield T (on loan)	—	—
				Reading	31	—
				Torquay U	46	—
Defenders						
Clinton Boulton	5 10	11 3	Stoke	Port Vale	244	11
				Torquay U	260+2	34
Ian Twitchin	5 6	10 0	Teignmouth	Torquay U	305+25	10
Jimmy Dunne (Eire)	5 9	10 11	Dublin	Millwall	—	—
				Torquay U	125	13
				Fulham	142+1	1
				Torquay U	119+3	4
Mike Green	6 1	12 4	Carlisle	Carlisle U	2	—
				Gillingham	131+1	24
				Bristol R	74+3	2
				Plymouth Arg	108	8
				Torquay U	88	7
*Peter Darke	5 10½	11 0	Exeter	Plymouth Arg	94+6	2
				Exeter C (on loan)	5	—
				Torquay U	58+1	—
*Lindsay Parsons	5 9	11 7	Bristol	Bristol R	354+6	—
				Torquay U	56	—
Jess Payne	6 0	11 0	Leicester	Leicester C	—	—
				Torquay U	25	1
Steve Ritchie	5 11	13 3	Glasgow	Bristol C	1	—
				Morton	54	2
				Hereford U	102	3
				Aberdeen	10	—
				Torquay U	17	—
Midfield						
Barrie Vassallo (Contract cancelled February 1979)	5 8	10 7	Newport, Mon.	Arsenal	—	—
				Plymouth Arg	6+7	2
				Norwich C (on loan)	—	—
				Torquay U	44+2	4
Stuart Clarke	5 10½	11 0	Torquay	Torquay U	4+1	—
*Ken Raper	5 9	10 7	Consett	Stoke C	—	—
				Torquay U	51+1	8
Roy Davies	5 8	11 7	London	Reading	37	2
				Torquay U	39+2	3
*Alan Wilson	5 9		Liverpool	Everton	2	—
				Southport	134	13
				Torquay U	38+4	2
Forwards						
Billy Brown (Contract cnacelled September 1978)	5 9	11 4	Falkirk	Burnley	0+1	—
				Carlisle U	16+3	8
				Newport Co	166+2	49
				Hereford U (on loan)	9	6
				Brentford	16	9
				Torquay U	137+2	47
Peter Coffill	5 8	10 7	Romford	Watford	56+7	6
				Torquay U	54+10	8
Les Lawrence	6 3	11 0	Wolverhampton	Shrewsbury T	10+4	2
				Torquay U	70+9	22
Steve Cooper	5 10	11 0	Stourbridge	Torquay U	38+7	17
Donal Murphy	5 11	11 0	Dublin	Coventry C	33+10	10
				Millwall (on loan)	3	—
				Torquay U	37+4	10
Steve Bicknell (Contract cancelled)			Rugby	Leicester C	6+1	—
				Torquay U	0+3	—
Maurice Cox, 2 apps, 2 gls. (Non-contract)						

TOTTENHAM HOTSPUR DIV. 1

Chairman: S. A. Wale.
Directors: C. F. Cox (*Vice-Chairman*), A. Richardson, G. A. Richardson, D. W. Kennard.
Manager: Keith Burkinshaw. *Secretary:* G. W. Jones.
Asst. Manager: Pat Welton.
Year Formed: 1882. *Turned Professional:* 1895.
Limited Company: 1898.
Previous Grounds: 1882, Tottenham Marshes; 1885, Northumberland Park; 1898, White Hart Lane.
Previous Name: 1882–85, Hotspur Football Club.

Football League Record:
1908 Elected to Division 2.
1909–15 Division 1.
1919–20 Division 2.
1920–28 Division 1.
1928–33 Division 2.
1933–35 Division 1.
1935–50 Division 2.
1950–77 Division 1.
1977–78 Division 2.
1978– Division 1.

Honours: *Football League,* Division 1, Champions: 1950–51, 1960–61; Runners-up: 1921–22, 1951–52, 1956–57, 1962–63. Division 2, Champions: 1919–20, 1949–50; Runners-up: 1908–09, 1932–33. Promoted from Div. 2 1977–78 *F.A. Cup,* Winners: 1901 (as non-league club), 1921, 1961, 1962, 1967. *Football League Cup,* Winners: 1970–71, 1972–73.
European Competitions: European Cup: 1961–62. *European Cup Winners Cup:* 1962–63 (winners), 1963–64, 1967–68. *UEFA Cup:* 1971–72 (winners), 1972–73, 1973–74. (Runners-up).
Record Victory: 13-2 v Crewe Alex, F.A. Cup, 4th Rd. Replay, Feb. 3rd, 1960.
Record Defeat: 0-7 v Liverpool, Division 1, Sept. 2, 1978.
Most League Points: 70, Division 2, 1919–20.
Most League Goals: 115, Division 1, 1960–61.
Highest League Scorer in Season: Jimmy Greaves, 37, Division 1, 1962–63.
Most League Appearances: Pat Jennings 472, 1964–1977.
Most Capped Player: Pat Jennings, 66 (80), N. Ireland.
Most League Goals in Total Aggregate: Jimmy Greaves, 220, 1961–70.
Record Transfer Fee Received: £250,000 for Neil McNab from Bolton W. Nov. 1978.
Record Transfer Fee Paid: £750,000 aggregate fee to Huracan and Racing respectively for Osvaldo Ardiles and Ricardo Villa, July 1978.
Managers Since the War: Joe Hulme, Arthur Rowe, Jimmy Anderson, Bill Nicholson, Terry Neill.
Address of Supporters Club: 744 High Road, N.17.

748 High Rd., Tottenham, N.17. Telephone 01-808 2046. *Ground capacity:* 52,000. *Record attendance:* 75,038 v Sunderland, F.A. Cup 6th Rd., March 5, 1938. *Record receipts:* £49,920 v Feyenoord, UEFA Cup Final 1st leg, May 21, 1974. *Pitch measurements:* 110 yds × 73 yds.

How to get there: Underground to Manor House (Piccadilly line) or Seven Sisters (Victoria line). From Manor House, buses 279, 259; from Seven Sisters 67, 149, 171, 243, 259, 123, 279. White Hart Lane station is three minutes walk from the ground and is served by trains from Liverpool St.
Match tickets: For League matches, seats can be booked not earlier than 21 days before the match. At the Park Lane and Paxton Road ends, there are seats available at the turnstiles.
Car parking: No street parking within a ¼ mile radius of the ground.
Entertainments/catering facilities: Hot food available at snack and chicken bars in the ground.
Club Shop: There is a shop on corner of Park Lane and High Road, and 2 kiosks on the ground which stock over 400 items.
Handbooks/programmes: Programmes available on subscription to shop.
Extra information: Supporters' Club with a present membership of over 7,000 is open to new members; information from the Secretary, Mrs. M. Ellam. (Tel: 808-7430).
Club Colours: White shirts, blue shorts, white stockings.
Change Colours: All yellow with blue trims.
Club Captain: Steve Perryman.
Club Nickname: 'Spurs'.

TOTTENHAM HOTSPUR 1978-79 LEAGUE RECORD

Match No.	Date	Venue	Opponents	Result	H/T Score	League Pos'n	Goalscorers	Attendance
1	Aug 19	A	Nottingham F	D 1-1	1-1	—	Villa	41,223
2	23	H	Aston Villa	L 1-4	0-1	—	Hoddle (pen)	47,892
3	26	H	Chelsea	D 2-2	2-1	17	Duncan, Armstrong	40,632
4	Sept 2	A	Liverpool	L 0-7	0-3	21		50,705
5	9	H	Bristol C	W 1-0	1-0	15	Rodgers (og)	34,035
6	16	A	Leeds U	W 2-1	1-0	13	Taylor, Lee	36,062
7	23	H	Manchester C	L 0-2	0-0	17		43,471
8	30	H	Coventry C	D 1-1	0-0	14	Hoddle	35,006
9	Oct 7	A	WBA	W 1-0	1-0	12	Taylor	33,211
10	14	H	Birmingham C	W 1-0	1-0	8	Ainscow (og)	41,230
11	21	A	Derby Co	D 2-2	0-1	11	Taylor, McAllister	26,181
12	28	H	Bolton W	W 2-0	1-0	9	Lee, Pratt	37,337
13	Nov 4	A	Norwich C	D 2-2	2-1	9	Lee, Taylor	25,695
14	11	H	Nottingham F.	L 1-3	0-0	11	Pratt	50,541
15	18	A	Chelsea	W 3-1	0-1	9	Lee 2, Hoddle	41,594
16	22	H	Liverpool	D 0-0	0-0	—		50,393
17	25	H	Wolverhampton W	W 1-0	1-0	8	Taylor	35,450
18	Dec 9	H	Ipswich T	W 1-0	0-0	8	Pratt	33,882
19	16	A	Manchester U	L 0-2	0-1	8		52,026
20	23	H	Arsenal	L 0-5	0-2	11		42,273
21	26	A	QPR	D 2-2	1-1		Lee, Taylor (pen)	24,845
22	30	A	Everton	D 1-1	1-1	10	Lee	44,363
23	Jan 13	A	Bristol C	D 0-0	0-0	9		28,781
24	20	H	Leeds U	L 1-2	0-1	9	Hoddle	36,828
25	Feb 3	H	Manchester C	L 0-3	0-2	9		32,037
26	10	A	Coventry C	W 3-1	2-1	8	Taylor 2, Lee	25,133
27	24	A	Birmingham C	L 0-1	0-1	8		20,980
28	Mar 3	H	Derby Co	W 2-0	1-0	9	Ardiles 2	28,089
29	17	H	Norwich C	D 0-0	0-0	11		24,982
30	24	A	Aston Villa	W 3-2	0-2	10	Hoddle 2, Jones	35,486
31	28	H	Southampton	D 0-0	0-0	—		23,570
32	31	A	Middlesbrough	L 0-1	0-1	10		19,172
33	Apr 3	A	Wolverhampton W	L 2-3	1-1	—	Jones 2	19,819
34	7	H	Middlesbrough	L 1-2	1-1	13	Taylor (pen)	21,580
35	10	A	Arsenal	L 0-1	0-0	—		54,041
36	14	H	QPR	D 1-1	1-1	15	Perryman	28,853
37	16	A	Southampton	D 3-3	0-3	—	Taylor, Jones, Pratt	22,096
38	21	H	Manchester U	D 1-1	0-1	14	Jones	36,665
39	28	A	Ipswich T	L 1-2	0-2	15	Hoddle (pen)	28,179
40	May 5	H	Everton	D 1-1	1-1	16	Ardiles	26,077
41	8	A	Bolton W	W 3-1	1-1	—	Falco, Allardyce (og), Holmes	17,879
42	14	H	WBA	W 1-0	1-0	—	Villa	24,789

Final League Position: 11

Goalscorers

League (48): Taylor 10 (2 pens), Lee 8, Hoddle 7 (2 pens), Jones 5, Pratt 4, Ardiles 3, Villa 2, Duncan 1, Armstrong 1, McAllister 1, Perryman 1, Falco 1, Holmes 1, Own Goals 3.
League Cup (3): Hoddle, Armstrong, Villa.
F.A. Cup (12): Jones 4, Lee 3, Taylor (pen), Hoddle, Perryman, Ardiles, Own Goal 1.

League Cup	Second Round	Swansea C (a)	2-2
		(h)	1-3
F.A. Cup	Third Round	Altrincham (h)	1-1
			3-0 (at Maine Rd)
	Fourth Round	Wrexham (h)	3-3
		(a)	3-2 (aet)
	Fifth Round	Oldham Ath (a)	1-0
	Sixth Round	Manchester U (h)	1-1
		(a)	0-2

Daines	McAllister	Gorman	Hoddle	Lacy	Perryman	Villa	Ardiles	Armstrong	Moores	Taylor	Pratt	Duncan	McNab	Naylor	Holmes	Lee	Kendall	Jones	Aleksic	Galvin	Beavon	Miller	Smith	Falco	Match No.
1	2	3	4	5	6	7	8	9	10	11*	12														1
1	2	3	4	5	6	7	8	9	10	11															2
1	2	3	4	5	6	7	8	9				10	11												3
1	2		4	5	6	7	8		9			10	11	3											4
1	2	3		5	6	7	8			11	10				4	9									5
1	2	3		5	6	7*	8	12		11	10				4	9									6
1	2	3		5	6*	7	8	12		11	10				4	9									7
1	2	3	12	5	6		8	7*		11	10				4	9									8
1	3		7		6		8	5		11	10	2			4	9									9
1	3		10	5	6		8			11	7	2			4	9									10
1	3		10	5	6		8			11	7	2			4	9									11
1	3		10*	5	6	12	8			11	7	2			4	9									12
	3		10	5	6	12	8*			11	7	2			4	9	1								13
	3		10	5	6	12	8*			11	7	2			4	9	1								14
	2		10	5	6		8			11	7				4	9	1								15
	3	2	10*	5	6	12	8			11	7				4	9	1								16
	2	3	10*	5	6	12	8			11	7				4	9	1								17
	2	3	10	5	6		8			11	7				4	9	1								18
	2	3	10	5	6	12	8			11	7				4*	9	1								19
		3	10	5	6		8			11	7*	2			4	9	1	12							20
	3		5		6	4	8			11	7	2				9	1	10							21
	3		5		6	4	8			11	7	2				9	1	10							22
	3		5		6	4	8			11	7			2		9	1	10							23
	2		4	5	6		8			11	7				3	9		10	1						24
	2		4	5	6		8	9		11					3		1			7	10				25
	10		4	5	6		8*	12		11	7			2	3	9	1								26
			4	5	6	9		8		11	7			2	3		1	10							27
9			4	5	6	11	8				7			2	3		1	10							28
	3		10	5	6	11	8*			12	7			2	4	9	1								29
	3		10	5	6	11	8				7			2	4		1	9							30
	3		10	5	6	11	8				7			2	4		1	9							31
	3		10	5	6	11	8*				7			2	4	12	1	9							32
	3		10	5	6	11				8	7			2	4		1	9							33
	3		10		6	11	7			8	5			2	4		1	9							34
1	3		10		6	11				8	7			2	4			9			5				35
1	4		10		6	11				8	7			2	3			9			5				36
	3				6	8	10			11	7			2	4		1	9			5				37
	3		8	5	6	7	10			11	2						1	9			4				38
	3		10	5	6	11	8				7				2			9	1		4				39
	3		10		6	11	8				7		5	2			1	9	1		4				40
	3*		10		6	11	8				7		5	2			1			4	12	9			41
	5		10	4	6	11	8				7			2			1	9				3			42
14	38	15	34	35	42	26	38	7	2	32	37	2	2	22	33	26	23	18	5	1	7	1	1		43
			+1s			+6s		+3s		+1s	+1s				+1s	+1s					+1s				

TOTTENHAM HOTSPUR—PLAYERS

Player and position	Ht	Wt	Birthplace	Clubs	League Appearances	Goals
Goalkeepers						
Barry Daines	5 11½	11 8	Whitham	Tottenham H	86	—
Mark Kendall	5 11	13 0	Blackwood	Tottenham H	23	—
Milija Aleksic	6 0	13 11	Stafford	Plymouth Arg	32	—
				Ipswich T (on loan)	—	—
				Oxford U (on loan)	—	—
				Luton T	77	—
				Tottenham H	5	—
				Sheffield U (on loan)	—	—
Defenders						
Don McAllister	5 10	11 2	Radcliffe	Bolton W	155+1	2
				Tottenham H	115+3	8
John Gorman	5 8	11 10	Winchburon	Celtic	—	—
(Contract cancelled March 1979)				Carlisle U	228+1	5
				Tottenham H	30	—
James Holmes	5 9	11 7	Dublin	Coventry C	122+6	7
(Eire)				Tottenham H	81	2
Terry Naylor	5 10	11 10	Islington	Tottenham H	231+5	—
Chris Hughton	5 7¾	11 5	West Ham	Tottenham H	—	—
John Lacy	6 1	12 4	Liverpool	Fulham	146+4	7
				Tottenham H	35	—
Gordon Smith	5 9	12 1	Glasgow	St Johnstone	118	11
				Aston V	76+3	—
				Tottenham H	1+1	—
Midfield						
Paul Miller	6 1	12 2	London	Tottenham H	7	—
Steve Perryman	5 8	10 10	Ealing	Tottenham H	392	23
John Pratt	5 8½	10 3	London	Tottenham H	290+18	37
Glen Hoddle	6 0	11 6	Hayes	Tottenham H	120+2	24
Stuart Beavon	5 7¾	9 12½	Wolverhampton	Tottenham H	1	—
Mike Hazard	5 7	10 5	Sunderland	Tottenham H	—	—
Osvaldo Ardiles	5 6	9 10	Cordoba	Huracan	(not known)	
				Tottenham H	38	3
Ricardo Villa	6 0	12 5	Buenos Aires	Racing	(not known)	
				Tottenham H	26+6	2
Giorgio Mazzon	5 10	11 5	London	Tottenham H	—	—
Forwards						
Tony Galvin	5 9	11 5	Huddersfield	Tottenham H	1	—
Chris Jones	5 11	10 7	Jersey	Tottenham H	110+10	25
Gerry Armstrong	5 11	13 2	Belfast	Tottenham H	37+13	6
(N. Ireland)						
Peter Taylor	5 9	11 7	Southend	Southend U	57+18	12
(England)				C Palace	122	33
				Tottenham H	104+2	29
Colin Lee	6 1	11 9	Plymouth	Bristol C	—	—
				Hereford U (on loan)	7+2	—
				Torquay U	35	14
				Tottenham H	49+3	19
Mark Falco	6 0	12 0	Hackney	Tottenham H	1	1
Garry Brooke	5 6	10 5	Bethnal Green	Tottenham H	—	—

TRANMERE ROVERS   DIV. 4

Chairman: W. A. Bothwell.
Vice-Chairman: H. B. Thomas.
Directors: H. A. Bainbridge, F.C.A., G. A. Gould, J.P., F.C.A., R. Moffat, J.P., A. W. Drew.
Secretary: D. Johnson.
Team Manager: John King.
Year Formed: 1883.   *Turned Professional:* 1912.
Limited Company: 1920.
Football League Record: 1921 Original Member of Division 3(N). 1938–39 Division 2. 1939–58 Division 3(N). 1958–61 Division 3. 1961–67 Division 4. 1967–75 Division 3. 1975–76 Division 4. 1976–79 Division 3. 1979–   Division 4.
Honours: *Football League,* best season in Division 2: 22nd, 1938–39. Division 3(N), Champions: 1937–38. *F.A. Cup,* best season: 5th Rd., 1967–68. *Football League Cup,* best season: 4th Rd., 1961. Welsh Cup winners 1935. Promotion to 3rd Division 1966–67, 1975–76.
Record Victory: 13-4 v Oldham Ath., Division 3(N), Dec. 26th, 1935.
Record Defeat: 1-9 v Tottenham H., F.A. Cup, 3rd Rd. Replay, Jan. 14th, 1953.
Most League Points: 60, Division 4, 1964–65.
Most League Goals: 111, Division 3(N), 1930–31.
Highest League Scorer in Season: Bunny Bell, 35, Division 3(N), 1933–34.
Most League Goals in Total Aggregate: Bunny Bell, 104, 1931–36.
Most Capped Player: Albert Gray, 3 (23), Wales.
Most League Appearances: Harold Bell, 595, 1946–64 (including League record of 401 consecutive appearances).
Record Transfer Fee Received: £120,000 from Cardiff C. for Ronnie Moore, Feb. 1979.
Record Transfer Fee Paid: £20,000 to Charlton Ath., for Hugh McAuley, Aug. 1978.
Managers Since the War: Ernie Blackburn, Noel Kelly, Peter Farrell, Walter Galbraith, Dave Russell, Jackie Wright, Ron Yeats.
Address of Supporters Club: Supporters Assn., Prenton Park, Prenton Road West, Birkenhead.

Prenton Park, Prenton Road West, Birkenhead. Telephone 051-608 3677/4194. *Ground capacity:* 25,000. *Record attendance:* 24,424 v Stoke C., F.A. Cup 4th Rd., February 5, 1972. *Record receipts:* £8,982 v Stoke City F.A. Cup 4th Rd., February 5, 1972. *Pitch measurements:* 112 yds × 74 yds.

How to get there: Special buses from railway stations, Hamilton Square and Rock Ferry. Mersey Railway Liverpool, to Hamilton Square, then buses 80 to 90 or 64.
Match tickets: Seats can be booked in advance.
Car parking: Large car park at the back of the stand.
Entertainments/catering facilities: Snack bars in ground. Social club with bar facilities.
Club shop: Run by Supporters' Association.
Handbooks/programmes: Programmes available on subscription.
Extra information: Tranmere's record victory equals the highest score in a League game; in the 13-4 win over Oldham, centre-forward Bunny Bell scored nine goals and missed a penalty!
Club Colours: White shirts with four diagonal royal blue bands from left shoulder, white shorts, royal blue stockings.
Change Colours: Red shirts, white shorts, red stockings.
First Team Trainer/Coach: Eddie Robertson.
Club Nickname: 'Rovers'.

TRANMERE ROVERS 1978-79 LEAGUE RECORD

Match No.	Date	Venue	Opponents	Result	H/T Score	League Pos'n	Goalscorers	Attendance
1	Aug 19	A	Lincoln C	L 1-2	1-1	—	Peplow	2835
2	21	H	Swindon T	D 1-1	1-0	—	Peplow	2150
3	26	H	Hull C	L 1-3	0-0	21	Cliff	1948
4	Sept 2	A	Peterborough U	L 0-1	0-0	23		5229
5	9	H	Gillingham	D 1-1	0-0	22	Peplow	1589
6	16	A	Swansea C	L 3-4	3-2	24	Evans, Moore 2	16,132
7	22	H	Bury	D 0-0	0-0	23		2458
8	25	H	Plymouth Arg	W 2-1	0-0	—	Evans, Moore	1907
9	30	A	Watford	L 0-4	0-1	23		10,753
10	Oct 7	A	Oxford U	D 0-0	0-0	23		3853
11	13	H	Chester	W 6-2	1-1	22	Moore 3, Bramhall, O'Neil (pen) Peplow	5587
12	16	H	Shrewsbury T	D 2-2	1-0	—	Evans, Bramhall	3087
13	21	A	Brentford	L 0-2	0-1	22		5880
14	27	H	Chesterfield	D 1-1	0-1	22	Moore	2587
15	Nov 4	A	Exeter C	L 0-3	0-1	23		3526
16	10	H	Peterborough U	W 1-0	1-0	22	O'Neill	2241
17	13	A	Mansfield T	D 0-0	0-0	—		3929
18	18	A	Hull C	L 1-2	0-1	22	Peplow	4350
19	Dec 9	A	Walsall	L 0-2	0-0	23		2954
20	23	A	Rotherham U	L 2-3	0-1	23	Peplow, Craven	3829
21	26	H	Blackpool	L 0-2	0-0	23		3491
22	Jan 13	A	Gillingham	L 2-3	2-0	23	Evans, Peplow	5480
23	Feb 3	H	Plymouth Arg	D 2-2	1-2	23	Moore (pen), Parry	7418
24	10	H	Watford	D 1-1	1-1	23	Evans	4219
25	16	H	Oxford U	W 1-0	0-0	23	Kerr	1381
26	19	H	Sheffield W	D 1-1	1-1	—	Kerr	2445
27	24	A	Chester	D 1-1	1-1	23	Postlewhite	4375
28	27	A	Bury	L 0-1	0-0	—		3434
29	Mar 3	H	Brentford	L 0-1	0-0	23		1882
30	6	A	Carlisle U	L 0-2	0-1	—		4330
31	10	A	Chesterfield	L 2-5	0-3	23	Evans 2	4090
32	16	H	Exeter C	D 2-2	0-1	23	Kerr, Palios	984
33	24	A	Swindon T	L 1-4	1-2	23	Kerr	5678
34	26	H	Lincoln C	D 0-0	0-0	—		1222
35	30	H	Southend U	L 1-2	0-0	23	Evans	1250
36	Apr 3	A	Swansea C	L 1-2	0-2	—	Evans	3499
37	6	A	Colchester U	L 0-1	0-1	23		2578
38	14	A	Blackpool	L 0-2	0-2	23		4798
39	16	H	Carlisle U	D 1-1	1-0	—	Craven	1504
40	18	H	Rotherham U	D 1-1	0-0	—	Evans	1254
41	21	A	Sheffield W	W 2-1	1-1	23	Evans, Kerr	9815
42	24	A	Shrewsbury T	L 1-2	0-0	—	Thomas	6013
43	27	H	Walsall	D 0-0	0-0	23		1453
44	30	H	Mansfield T	L 1-2	1-2	—	Kerr	1121
45	May 4	A	Southend U	W 1-0	1-0	23	Thomas	3607
46	9	H	Colchester U	L 1-5	0-1	—	Peplow	1016

Final League Position: 23

Goalscorers

League (45): Evans 11, Moore 8 (1 pen), Peplow 8, Kerr 6, Bramhall 2, O'Neill 2 (1 pen), Craven 2, Thomas 2, Cliff 1, Parry 1, Postlewhite 1, Palios 1.
League Cup (2): McAuley, O'Neil.
F.A. Cup (3): Moore 2, McAuley.

League Cup	First Round	Wigan Ath (h)	1-1
		(a)	1-2
F.A. Cup	First Round	Boston (h)	2-1
	Second Round	Sheffield W (h)	1-1
		(a)	0-4

Johnson	Mathias	Flood	Parry	Bramhall	Evans	Peplow	Palios	Moore	O'Neil	McAuley	Kerr	Craven	Cliff	Postlewhite	West	Cahill	Williams	Thomas	Eaton	Griffiths	Whittingham	Match No.
1	2	3	4	5	6	7	8*	9	10	11	12											1
1	2	3	4	5	6	10	7	9	8*11	12												2
1	2	3	4	5	6		7	9	11	10	8*12											3
1	2	3	4	5	6	10	8	9	11		7											4
1	2	3	4	5	6	10	8	9	11		7											5
1	3	2	4	5	6	10	7	9	11		8											6
1	2	3	4	5	10	7	6	9	8	11												7
1	2*	3	4	5	10		6	9	8	11		7	12									8
1	2	3	4	5	6	12	7	9	8	11		10*										9
1	2	3	4	5	10	7		9	8	11			6									10
1	2	3	4	8		6	10	9	7	11			5									11
1	2	3*	4	8		6	10	12	9	7	11		5									12
1	2	3	4	8		6	10		9	7	11		5									13
	2	3	4	8		6	10		9	7	11		5	1								14
	2		4	8		6	10		9	7	11		5	1	3							15
	2	3	4	8*	6	10	12	9	7	11				1	5							16
	2	3	4			6	10		9	7	11		8	1	5							17
	4	11*	2	5	6	10		9	7	12			8	1	3							18
1	2	3	6	4	8	10		9	7	11*		12			5							19
1	2	3	4	5	6	10	8	9	11		7											20
1	2	3	4	5	6	10	8	9	11		7											21
1	2	3	4	8	6	11	7	9			10	5										22
1	2	3	6	4	10	7*11	9	12			8	5										23
1	2	3	4	8*	6		7	9	11	12	10	5										24
1	2	3	4		6		7	9	11	8	10	5										25
1	2	3	4		6		7	9	11	8	10	5										26
1	3	4	2		6		7		8	11	9	10	5									27
1	2	3	4		6		7		8	11	9	10	5									28
1	2	3	4			6	12	10	7	11*	9	8	5									29
1	2		4	8	6		3		7	11	9	10	5									30
1	3		6	4	8		2		7	11	9	10	5									31
1	3		4	5	6	10*12		8	11	9	7	2										32
1	3		4	8	6			7	11	9	10	2			5							33
1	3	2	4	5	6	12		8	11	9	7*		10									34
1	3	2	4	5	6			8	11	9	7*		10			12						35
1	3	2	4*	5	6			7	11	9	12		8			10						36
1	3	2	4	8	6			7	11	9			5			10						37
1		3	4	5*	7			8	11	9	12	2	6			10						38
1	3	2	4		6			8	11	9	7		5			10						39
1	3	2	4		6	12		8*11	9	7			5			10						40
1	3	2	4		6			7	11	9	8		5			10						41
1	3	2	4		6			8	11	9	7		5			10						42
1	3	2	4		6	12		8	11	9	7*		5			10						43
1	3		4	8	6				11	9	12		5			10*	2	7				44
1	2	3	4	6	10	7			8	8			5				9		11*12			45
1	2	3	4	6	10	7			9	8			5					11				46
41	45	40	46	35	46	23	21	26	32	41	22	26	6	31	5	5	1	10	1	3		

+5s +3s +2s +3s +4s +1s +1s +1s +1s

TRANMERE ROVERS—PLAYERS

Player and position	Ht	Wt	Birthplace	Clubs	League Appearances	Goals
Goalkeepers						
Dickie Johnson	6 1	12 10	Liverpool	Tranmere R	260	—
Gordon West (England)	6 1	14 0	Darfield	Blackpool	31	—
				Everton	335	—
				Tranmere R	17	—
Defenders						
Ray Stubbs (Contract cancelled September 1978)	5 10	11 10	Wallasey	Tranmere R	—	—
Ray Mathias	5 9	11 4	Liverpool	Tranmere R	457+5	5
John Bramhall	6 2	13 6	Warrington	Tranmere R	49+4	2
Eddie Flood	5 7	10 0	Liverpool	Liverpool	—	—
				Tranmere R	245+1	5
Dennis Postlewhite	6 0½	12 1	Birkenhead	Tranmere R	31+2	1
Leslie Parry	5 11	11 0	Wallasey	Tranmere R	148+3	2
*David Philpotts	5 11½	11 7	Bramborough	Coventry C	3	—
				Southport (on loan)	8	—
				Tranmere R	174+1	5
Steve Eaton	6 0	11 13	Liverpoo l	Tranmere R	1	—
Midfield						
Steve Peplow	5 8	10 4	Liverpool	Liverpool	2	—
				Swindon T	37+3	11
				Nottingham F	3	—
				Mansfield T (on loan)	4	3
				Tranmere R	171+12	34
Mark Palios	5 8	10 13	Birkenhead	Tranmere R	175+13	25
Clive Evans	5 10	10 9	Birkenhead	Tranmere R	95	13
Eddie Cliff	5 10	11 5	Liverpool	Burnley	20	—
				Notts Co	5	—
				Lincoln C (on loan)	3	—
				Tranmere R	44+6	4
Steve Craven	5 10	11 0	Birkenhead	Tranmere R	29+4	2
Tom O'Neil	5 6½	10 4	St Helens	Manchester U	53	—
				Blackpool (on loan)	7	—
				Southport	192+6	17
				Tranmere R	32	2
Ian Griffiths	5 6	10 2	Birkenhead	Tranmere R	3	—
Forwards						
Hugh McAuley	5 7	9 7	Bootle	Liverpool	—	—
				Tranmere R (on loan)	13	1
				Plymouth Arg	76+1	7
				Charlton Ath	55	9
				Tranmere R	41	2
John Kerr	6 1	12 5	Birkenhead	Tranmere R	22+3	6
John Williams (Non-contract)	6 2	13 6	Liverpool	Tranmere R	1	—
Steve Whittingham (Apprentice)	5 10	11 8	Birkenhead	Tranmere R	0+1	—

WALSALL DIV. 4

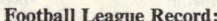

Chairman: K. E. Wheldon.
Directors: J. A. Harris, S. E. Boler, R. Homden, B. E. Bradnack.
Player-Manager: Alan Buckley.
Secretary: H. J. Westmancoat, F.A.A.I.
Year Formed: 1888.
Turned Professional: 1888.
Limited Company: 1921.
Previous Names: Walsall Swifts (Founded 1877) and Walsall Town (Founded 1879) amalgamated in 1888 and were known as Walsall Town Swifts until 1895.

Football League Record:

1982 Elected to Division 2.	1927–31 Division 3(S).	1961–63 Division 2.
1895 failed re-election.	1941–36 Division 3(N).	1963–79 Division 3.
1896–1901 Division 2.	1936–58 Division 3(S).	1979– Division 4.
1901 failed re-election.	1958–60 Division 4.	
1921 Original Member of Division 3(N).	1960–61 Division 3.	

Honours: Football League, best season in Division 2: 6th, 1898–99. Division 4, Champions: 1959–60. Division 3, Runners-up: 1960–61. *F.A. Cup,* best season: 5th Rd., 1939, 1975, 1978, and last 16 1888–89. *Football League Cup,* best season: 4th Rd., 1966–67.
Record Victory: 10-0 v Darwen, Division 2, Mar. 4th, 1899.
Record Defeat: 0-12 v Small Heath, Dec. 17th, 1892 and v Darwen, Dec. 26th, 1896, both Division 2.
Most League Points: 65, Division 4, 1959–60.
Most League Goals: 102, Division 4, 1959–60.
Highest League Scorer in Season: Gilbert Alsop, 40, Division 3(N), 1933–34 and 1934–35.
Most League Goals in Total Aggregate: Tony Richards, 184, 1954–63, and Colin Taylor, 184, 1958–73.
Most Capped Player: Mick Kearns, 15 (16), Eire.
Most League Appearances: Colin Taylor, 459, 1958–63, 1964–68, 1969–73.
Record Transfer Fee Received: £175,000 from Birmingham C. for Alan Buckley, Oct. 1978.
Record Transfer Fee Paid: £175,000 to Birmingham C. for Alan Buckley, June 1979.
Managers Since the War: Harry Hibbs, Tony McPhee, Brough Fletcher, Major Buckley, John Love, Billy Moore, Alf Wood, Ray Shaw, Ron Lewin, Dick Graham, Billy Moore, John Smith, Ronnie Allen, Doug Fraser, Dave Mackay, Alan Ashman, Frank Sibley.
Address of Supporters Club: Saddlers Club, Wallows Lane, Walsall, Staffs.

Fellows Park, Walsall. Telephone 0922 22791. *Telegraphic address:* 'Walsall F.C.. Walsall'.
Ground capacity: 24,100. *Record attendance:* 25,453 v Newcastle U., Division 2, August 29 1961. *Record receipts:* £12,775.35p v Newcastle U., F.A. Cup 4th Rd., January 25 1975. *Pitch measurements:* 113 yds × 73 yds.
How to get there: Corporation specials from Bradford Place. Buses 237 and 238 within walking distance of the ground. Nearest railway stations, Bescot (10 minutes' walk from ground) and Walsall.
Match tickets: Seats can be booked at any time by postal, personal, or telephone application to the ticket office; Hillary Street, Walsall. Tel: 30696.
Car parking: Car park in Hillary Street for 100 cars. Side-street parking available.
Entertainments/catering facilities: Supporters' club adjacent to ground. Tea bars and licensed bars inside the ground.
Club shop: The Boutique, is open on match days.
Programmes: Programmes available on subscription.
Extra information: In 1947, Walsall set a Division 3(S) record by winning 8-0 away at Northampton.
Club Colours: Red shirts, white shorts, green stockings, red top/white band.
Change Colours: Sky blue and white vertical striped shirts, black trim, black shorts, black stockings, sky blue tops.
Club Captain: Colin Harrison.
Club Nickname: 'Saddlers'.

WALSALL 1978-79 LEAGUE RECORD

Match No.	Date	Venue	Opponents	Result	H/T Score	League Pos'n	Goalscorers	Attendance
1	Aug 19	H	Watford	L 2-4	2-2	—	Austin 2	6423
2	23	A	Chester	L 1-2	1-1	—	Kelly	4257
3	26	A	Carlisle U	L 0-1	0-1	23		4781
4	Sept 2	H	Shrewsbury T	D 1-1	1-1	22	Austin	4269
5	9	H	Swindon T	W 4-1	2-0	19	Birch 2 (1 a pen), Austin, King	5024
6	12	A	Hull C	L 1-4	0-1	—	McDonough	6784
7	16	A	Blackpool	L 1-2	0-1	21	Kelly	8153
8	23	H	Colchester U	D 2-2	2-0	20	Buckley, King	4052
9	26	H	Peterborough U	W 4-1	2-1	—	McDonough 2, Austin 2	4835
10	29	A	Lincoln C	D 1-1	1-0	20	Waddington	3371
11	Oct 7	H	Southend U	D 1-1	1-1	20	Buckley (pen)	4911
12	14	A	Mansfield T	W 3-1	0-0	17	Buckley 2, Austin	6066
13	17	A	Bury	D 1-1	1-0	—	McDonough	4443
14	21	H	Plymouth Arg	W 2-1	1-1	16	Buckley, Sbragia	5552
15	28	A	Sheffield W	W 2-0	1-0	11	King, Blackhall (og)	12,019
16	Nov 4	H	Rotherham U	L 0-1	0-1	16		5456
17	10	A	Shrewsbury T	D 1-1	0-1	16	McDonough	7615
18	18	H	Carlisle U	L 1-2	0-1	17	Birch	4441
19	Dec 2	A	Brentford	L 0-1	0-1	18		5130
20	9	H	Tranmere R	W 2-0	1-0	15	Penn, Birch (pen)	2954
21	26	A	Exeter C	L 1-3	0-2	18	Austin	4159
22	30	A	Oxford U	L 1-2	0-1	20	Serella	4231
23	Jan 6	H	Hull C	L 1-2	1-0	20	Caswell	4061
24	16	A	Swindon T	L 1-4	0-1	—	Austin	7282
25	Feb 3	A	Peterborough U	W 3-0	1-0	18	Austin 2, McDonough	4466
26	6	H	Blackpool	W 2-1	1-0	—	Austin, McDonough	3711
27	20	H	Swansea C	D 1-1	0-0	—	Birch (pen)	4335
28	24	H	Mansfield T	D 1-1	0-1	15	Birch	4157
29	27	A	Colchester U	L 0-2	0-1	—		3135
30	Mar 3	A	Plymouth Arg	L 0-1	0-0	18		6487
31	10	H	Sheffield W	L 0-2	0-1	20		5120
32	13	H	Lincoln C	W 4-1	0-0	—	Penn, Austin, Birch, Sbragia	2794
33	20	H	Gillingham	L 0-1	0-0	—		3084
34	24	H	Chester	W 2-1	0-1	19	Birch (pen), Penn	2795
35	27	A	Watford	L 1-3	1-2	—	Serella	11,891
36	31	A	Chesterfield	D 0-0	0-0	20		3322
37	Apr 7	H	Brentford	L 2-3	0-3	20	Williams, Kruse (og)	3840
38	10	A	Gillingham	L 1-3	0-1	—	Syrett	7342
39	14	A	Exeter C	D 2-2	2-1	20	Sbragia, Birch	3118
40	17	A	Swansea C	D 2-2	0-0	—	Syrett 2	18,096
41	21	H	Oxford U	L 0-1	0-1	21		3396
42	24	H	Bury	L 0-1	0-1	—		2573
43	27	A	Tranmere R	D 0-0	0-0	21		1453
44	30	A	Southend U	L 0-1	0-1	—		2887
45	May 5	H	Chesterfield	L 0-1	0-1	22		2625
46	14	A	Rotherham U	L 1-4	0-2	—	Waddington	1996

Final League Position: 22

Goalscorers

League (56): Austin 13, Birch 9 (4 pens), McDonough 7, Buckley 5 (1 a pen), King 3, Penn 3, Sbragia 3, Syrett 3, Waddington 2, Kelly 2, Serella 2, Caswell 1, Williams 1, Own Goals 2.
League Cup (5): Buckley 3 (1 a pen), Birch, Paul.

League Cup	First Round	Halifax T (h)	2-1
		(a)	2-0
	Second Round	Charlton Ath (h)	1-2
F.A. Cup	First Round	Torquay U (h)	0-2

Kearns	Paul	Caswell	Harrison	Serella	King	Birch	Macken	Austin	Buckley	Kelly	Clarke	Waddington S	McDonough	Sbragia	Penn	Waddington P	Turner	Jones	Rees	Williams	Syrett	Green	Mower	Match No.
1	2	3	4	5	6	7	8	9	10	11														1
1	2	3	4	5	6	7	8	9	10	11														2
1	2*	3	4	5	6	7	8	9	10	11	12													3
1		3	4	5	6	7	2	9	10	11	8													4
1		3	4	5	6	7	2	9		11		8	10											5
1		3	4	5	6	7	2	9	10			8	11											6
1		3	4	5	6	7	2	9	10	12		8	11*											7
1		3	4	5	6	7	2	9	10	11		8												8
1		3	4	5	6	7	2	9	10			8	11											9
1		3	4	5	6	7	2	9	10			8	11											10
1	3*		5	6	7	2	9	10	12		8	11	4											11
1		3		5	6	7	2	9	10			8	11	4										12
1		3		5	6	7	2	9	10			8	11	4										13
1		3		5	6	7	2	9	10			8	11	4										14
1	12	3		5	6	7	2*	9		11		10		4	8									15
1	10	3		5	6	7	2	9		11				4	8									16
1		8	3	5	6	7	2	9		11*			10	4	12									17
1		8	3	5	6	7	2	9		11*			10	4	12									18
1	2	3	6		7	4		11		8	10	5*	9	12										19
1	2	3	6			11	4	9				8	5		10									20
1	2	3		4	5		7	6	9	11		8	10											21
1	2	3		4	5	6	7	11		9		8	10											22
1	2	3	6	5		7	4	9		11		8	10											23
	2*	3	4	5		7	11	9			12	8	10	6		1								24
		3	2	5		7		4	9			8	11	6		1	10							25
		3	2	5		7	11	9				8	10	6		1	4							26
		2	3	5		7	11	9				8	10	6		1	4							27
		3	2*	5		7	11	9			12	8	10	6		1	4							28
		3	2	5	12	7	11	9*				8	10	6		1	4							29
		3	2	5	7		11	9				8	10	6		1	4							30
		3	2	5	10	7	11*	9				8	12	6		1	4							31
				5	4	7	2	9		12		8	10*	6	11	1	3							32
1		3		5	8	7	2	9		12			10*	6	11		4							33
	2	3		5	8	7		9		11*			6	10		1	4	12						34
		3		5	7	8	2			11*		10	6	9		1	4	12						35
		3		5		7	2					8*10	6	11		1	4		12	9				36
		3		5		7	2			11	8	6	10		1	4*		12	9					37
		3		5		7	2			10		6			1	4	11	8	9					38
		3		5	4	7				8		6			1	2	11	10	9					39
		3		5	4	7	2			10	12	6			1		11*	8	9					40
		3			4	6	7	2*		10	12	5			1		11	8	9					41
	2	3			4	7		8			5	6	12		1		11*10	9						42
	12	3		5	4	7	2			8	10	6			1		11*		9					43
	8	3		5	4*	7	2			12		10	6		1		11		9					44
	10	2		5	4	7	3*			11			6		1		12	8	9					45
		3		5	4	7				11	8		6		12			10*	91	2				46
24	13	41	30	43	34	45	42	33	13	18	1	33	31	32	10	—	21	15	7	7	11	1	1	
	+ 1s	+ 1s		+ 1s						+ 7s	+ 1s		+ 3s		+ 3s	+ 2s			+ 3s	+ 2s				

WALSALL—PLAYERS

Player and position	Ht	Wt	Birthplace	Clubs	League Appearances	Goals
Goalkeepers						
Mick Kearns (Eire)	6 3	13 12	Banbury	Oxford U	67	—
				Plymouth A (on loan)	1	—
				Charlton Ath (on loan)	4	—
				Walsall	302	—
Ronald Green	6 0	13 3	Birmingham	Walsall	2	—
Ian Turner	6 0	12 5	Middlesbrough	Huddersfield T	—	—
				Grimsby T	26	—
				Walsall (on loan)	3	—
				Southampton	77	—
				Newport Co (on loan)	7	—
				Lincoln C (on loan)	7	—
				Walsall	21	—
Defenders						
Tony Macken (Eire)	5 8	12 6	Waterford	Derby Co	20+3	1
				Portsmouth	10	1
				Walsall	72	—
Colin Harrison	5 10	11 8	Pelsall	Walsall	438+15	33
David Serella	5 9	10 10	King's Lynn	Nottingham F	65+3	2
				Walsall	140+2	7
*Kelvin Clarke	5 11	11 4	Walsall	Walsall	4+5	—
Brian Caswell	5 10	10 7	Wednesbury	Walsall	163+11	7
Steve Jones	6 1	12 1	Eastbourne	QPR	—	—
				Walsall	15	—
Ricky Sbragia	6 0	11 0	Lennoxtown	Birmingham C	14+1	1
				Walsall	32	3
Ian Paul	5 9	11 0	Wolverhampton	Walsall	17+1	—
Ken Mower	6 0½	11 11	Walsall	Walsall	1	—
Midfield						
Alan Birch	5 5	10 2	West Bromwich	Walsall	158+13	23
Jeff King	5 9	11 0	Fauld House	Albion R	40+2	7
				Derby Co	12+2	—
				Notts Co (on loan)	3	—
				Portsmouth (on loan)	4	—
				Walsall	50+1	4
James Kelly	5 6	10 2	Aldergrove	Wolverhampton W	20+2	—
				Wrexham (on loan)	4	—
				Walsall	18+7	2
Steven Waddington	5 4	9 3	Crewe	Stoke C	47+3	5
				Walsall	33	2
Forwards						
Alun Evans (Contract cancelled July 1978)	5 9	11 0	Kidderminster	Wolverhampton W	20+1	4
				Liverpool	77+2	21
				Aston V	53+9	11
				Walsall	78+9	7
Donald Penn	5 10	12 0	Smethwick	Walsall	10+4	3
Dave Syrett	5 11	11 13	Salisbury	Swindon T	110+12	30
				Wolverhampton W (on loan)	—	—
				Mansfield T	65	20
				Walsall	11	3
Roy McDonough	6 1	11 11	Solihull	Birmingham C	2	1
				Walsall	31+3	7
Paul Waddington	5 8	9 12	Oldbury	Walsall	0+2	—
Jimmy Williams	5 9	11 2	Wolverhampton	Walsall	7+2	1

Mark Rees 7+3 subs (Apprentice)

WATFORD   DIV. 2

Life President: J. Bonser.
Chairman: E. John.
Directors: J. Harrowell, H. M. Stratford, G. A. Smith, J. Reid.
Chief Executive & Company Secretary: Eddie Plumley.
General Manager: Graham Taylor.
Assistant Manager: Bertie Mee.
General Secretary: R. E. Rollitt.
Year Formed: 1891.   *Turned Professional:* 1897.
Limited Company: 1909.
Previous Grounds: 1899, Cassio Road; 1919, Vicarage Road.
Football League Record:
1920 Original Member of Division 3.	1972–75 Division 3.
1921–58 Division 3(S).	1975–78 Division 4.
1958–60 Division 4.	1978–79 Division 3.
1960–69 Division 3.	1979– Division 2.
1969–72 Division 2.	

Honours: *Football League*, best season in Division 2: 18th, 1970–71. Division 3, Champions: 1968–69. Runners-up 1978–79. Promoted from Division 4 1959–60, Champions 1977–78 *F.A. Cup*, best season, semi-finalists: 1970.

Football League Cup: best season: semi-finalists, 1978–79.

Record Victory: 10-1 v Lowestoft Town, F.A. Cup, 1st Rd., Nov. 27th, 1926.

Record Defeat: 0-10 v Wolverhampton W., F.A. Cup, 1st Rd. Replay, Jan. 13th, 1912.

Most League Points: 71, Division 4, 1977–78.

Most League Goals: 92, Division 4, 1959–60.

Highest League Scorer in Season: Cliff Holton, 42, Division 4, 1959–60.

Most League Goals in Total Aggregate: Tom Barnett, 144, 1928–39.

Most Capped Player: Frank Hoddinott, 2, Wales; Pat Jennings, 2 (80), N. Ireland.

Most League Appearances: Duncan Welbourne, 411, 1963–74.

Record Transfer Fee Received: £110,000 from West Ham U. for Billy Jennings, September 1974.

Record Transfer Fee Paid: £200,000 to Leicester City for Steve Sims, Dec. 1978.

Managers Since the War: Jack Bray, Eddie Hapgood, Haydn Green, Ron Gray, Len Goulden, Neil McBain, Ron Burgess, Bill McGarry, Ken Furphy, George Kirby, Mike Keen.

Address of Supporters Club: Watford F.C. Supporters Club, Vicarage Road, Watford.

Address of Club Shop or Boutique: Same as Football Club.

Vicarage Road Stadium, Watford WD1 8ER. Telephone Watford 49747–9. *Ground capacity:* 36,500. *Record attendance:* 34,099 v Manchester United, F.A. Cup 4th Rd, February 3 1969. *Record receipts:* £30,497 v Nottingham Forest, F.L. Cup Semi-Final (2nd Leg) January 30, 1979. *Pitch measurements:* 113 yds × 73 yds.

How to get there: Bus 385 from Watford Junction. This and Watford High Street Station are both within walking distance from the ground. Trains from London leave Euston Station.

Match tickets: Stand seats bookable 10 days before each League match. Visiting terrace supporters will be guided by Police to special visitors enclosure.

Car parking: Parking for season ticket holders only at the ground, but several multi-storey car parks a few minutes away.

Entertainments/catering facilities: Pre match entertainment at all League and Cup games by Radio Hornet. Tea kiosks and hot dog stands inside the ground.

Club shops: Shops on the ground sell all type of souvenirs and programmes.

Handbook/programmes: Programmes are available on subscription. Price 20p, plus postage. Handbook will be available for season 1979–80.

Extra information In 1968–69 Watford conceded only 34 goals, a record for the Third Division.

Club colours: Yellow shirts with black/red facings, black shorts, black stockings with red and yellow tops.
Change colours: Red shirts with black/yellow facings, red shorts, red stockings with black and yellow tops.
Club nickname: 'Hornets'.

WATFORD 1978-79 LEAGUE RECORD

Match No.	Date	Venue	Opponents	Result	H/T Score	League Pos'n	Goalscorers	Attendance
1	Aug 19	A	Walsall	W 4-2	2-2	—	Pollard, Joslyn, Garner, Jenkins	6423
2	22	H	Blackpool	W 5-1	3-1	—	Mercer, Jenkins 3, Joslyn	11,812
3	26	H	Peterborough U	L 1-2	0-0	4	Pritchett (pen)	12,291
4	Sept 2	A	Gillingham	W 3-2	2-2	2	Joslyn 2, Blissett	8248
5	9	H	Swansea C	L 0-2	0-2	6		17,435
6	13	A	Lincoln C	W 5-0	3-0	—	Blissett 2, Garner, Pollard, Jenkins	5924
7	16	A	Bury	W 2-1	0-1	2	Bolton, Jenkins	4102
8	23	H	Oxford U	W 4-2	2-1	1	Jenkins 4	12,949
9	26	A	Rotherham U	L 1-2	1-0	—	Blissett	6442
10	30	H	Tranmere R	W 4-0	1-0	2	Jenkins 2, Bolton (pen) Downes	10,753
11	Oct 7	A	Chester	L 1-2	1-1	2	Blissett	6468
12	14	H	Brentford	W 2-0	0-0	2	Jenkins, Blissett	15,180
13	17	H	Carlisle U	W 2-1	2-0	—	Bolton, Pollard	12,444
14	21	A	Chesterfield	W 2-0	1-0	1	Jenkins, Blissett	7800
15	28	H	Exeter C	W 1-0	1-0	1	Blissett	14,797
16	Nov 4	A	Hull C	L 0-4	0-1	2		7739
17	11	H	Gillingham	W 1-0	1-0	1	Jenkins	13,941
18	18	A	Peterborough U	W 1-0	1-0	1	Blissett	8048
19	Dec 2	H	Mansfield T	D 1-1	0-1	1	Train	10,568
20	9	A	Plymouth Arg	D 1-1	1-0	1	Jenkins	11,907
21	23	A	Colchester U	W 1-0	1-0	1	Jenkins	5424
22	26	H	Shrewsbury T	D 2-2	2-1	1	Jenkins 2	20,276
23	30	H	Swindon T	W 2-0	0-0	1	Blissett 2	15,486
24	Jan 6	H	Lincoln C	W 2-0	2-0	1	Blissett 2	12,132
25	20	H	Bury	D 3-3	2-0	1	Blissett 2, Jenkins	12,003
26	27	A	Oxford U	D 1-1	1-0	1	Sims	10,310
27	Feb 3	H	Rotherham U	D 2-2	0-2	1	Jenkins 2	12,857
28	10	A	Tranmere R	D 1-1	1-1	1	Blissett (pen)	4219
29	24	A	Brentford	D 3-3	2-2	1	Pritchett (pen), Blissett, Jenkins	13,880
30	Mar 3	H	Chesterfield	W 2-0	0-0	1	Bolton, Jenkins	12,281
31	10	A	Exeter C	D 0-0	0-0	1		7082
32	20	H	Swansea C	L 2-3	0-2	—	Jenkins, Bolton	19,950
33	24	A	Blackpool	D 1-1	1-1	1	Garner	9253
34	27	H	Walsall	W 3-1	2-1	—	Garner, Blissett 2	11,891
35	31	H	Sheffield W	W 1-0	0-0	1	Pollard	15,394
36	Apr 2	A	Southend U	L 0-1	0-0	—		11,406
37	7	A	Mansfield T	W 3-0	1-0	1	Jenkins 2, Joslyn	7944
38	13	H	Colchester U	L 0-3	0-1	—		17,903
39	14	A	Shrewsbury T	D 1-1	1-1	1	Bolton	13,320
40	17	H	Southend U	W 2-0	1-0	—	Joslyn, Bolton (pen)	15,835
41	21	A	Swindon T	L 0-2	0-1	2		16,397
42	24	A	Carlisle U	L 0-1	0-1	—		7141
43	28	H	Plymouth Arg	D 2-2	1-0	2	Joslyn, Mercer	14,816
44	May 2	H	Chester	W 1-0	1-0	—	Downes	12,167
45	5	A	Sheffield W	W 3-2	1-2	1	Blissett, Jenkins, Bolton (pen)	13,746
46	14	H	Hull C	W 4-0	1-0	—	Joslyn, Jenkins, Bolton (pen), Blissett	26,397

Final League Position: 2

Goalscorers

League (83): Jenkins 29, Blissett 21 (1 pen), Bolton 9 (4 pens), Joslyn 8, Garner 4, Pollard 4, Downes 2, Mercer 2, Pritchett 2 (2 pens), Sims 1, Train 1.
League Cup (17): Blissett 7, Jenkins 4, Downes 2, Joslyn, Bolton, Mayes, Pritchett (pen).
F.A. Cup (4): Jenkins 4.

League Cup	First Round	Brentford (h)	4-0
		(a)	3-1
	Second Round	Newcastle U (h)	2-1
	Third Round	Manchester U (a)	2-1
	Fourth Round	Exeter C (a)	2-0
	Fifth Round	Stoke C (a)	0-0
		(h)	3-1 (a.e.t.)
	Semi-Final	Nottingham F (a)	1-3
		(h)	0-0
F.A. Cup	First Round	Dagenham (h)	3-0
	Second Round	Southend U (h)	1-1
		(a)	0-1

Rankin	Stirl:	Pritchet	Booth	Bolton	Garner	Pollard	Mercer	Jenkins	Joslyn	Downes	Mayes	Blissett	Ellis	Harrison	Sherwood	Cassells	Train	Sims	Match No.
1	2	3	4*	5	6	7	8	9	10	11	12								1
1	2	3	4	5	6	11*	8	9	10	7	12								2
1	2	3	4	5	6	7		9	10	11	8*	12							3
1	2	3	4	5	6	7		9	10	11		8							4
1	2*	3	4	5	6	7		9	10	11	12	8							5
1	2	3	4	5*	6	7		9	10	11		8	12						6
1	2	3*	4	5	6	7		9	10	11		8	12						7
1	2		4	5	6	7		9	10*	11		8	12	3					8
1	2		4	11	6	7*		9	10	12		8	5	3					9
1	2		4	5	6	7		9	10	11	12	8		3*					10
1	2		4	5	6	7		9	10	11		8		3					11
1	2		4	5	6	7		9	10	11		8		3					12
1	2		4	5		7		9	10	11		8	6	3					13
1	2		4	5	6	7		9	10	11*	12	8		3					14
1	2		4	5	6	7*		9	10	11	12	8		3					15
1	2		4	3	6	7		9*	10	11	12	8	5						16
1	2	3	4	5	6			9	10	11		8	7						17
	2	3	4	5	6			9	10	11	8	7		1					18
	2		4	5	6*		9		7	10	8		3	1	12	11			19
	2			5	6	11	9	10	7		8		3	1		4			20
	2		4		6		8	9	7	11			3	1		10	5		21
	2			4	6		8*	9	7	11	12		3	1		10	5		22
	2			4	6	12		9	7		11*	8	3	1		10	5		23
	2	3		11	6	7		9	4			8		1		10	5		24
	2			11	6	7		9	4			8	3	1		10	5		25
	2			11	6	7*		9	4			8	3	1	12	10	5		26
	2		4		6		12	9	10*	7		8	3	1		11	5		27
	2				6	7		9	4	11		8	3	1		10	5		28
	2	3	4	11	6	7		9	12			8		1		10*	5		29
1	2	3	4	6		7	12	9	10	11		8*					5		30
1	2	3	4	6			7	8	9	10	11						5		31
1	2	3	4	6		7	12	9	10	11*		8					5		32
1	2	3	4	5	6	7		9	10	11*		8				12			33
1	2	3	4	5	6	7		9	10			8				11			34
1	2	3	4*	5	6	7	12	9	10			8				11			35
1	2	3	4	5	6		7*	9	10	12		8				11			36
1	2	3	4	5	6	7		9	10			8*			12	11			37
1	2	3	4*	5	6	7		9	10	12		8				11			38
1	2		4	5	6	7		9	10	11		8	3						39
1	2	3	4	5	6	7		9	10	11		8							40
1	2	3	4	5	6	7*		9	10	11		8				12			41
1	2*	3	4	5	6	7	12	9	10			8	3			11			42
	2		5	6		10	9	4	7			8	3	1		11			43
	2		4	5	6		8	9	10	11		7	3	1					44
	2			4	6			9	10	7		8	3	1		11	5		45
	2		4	5	6			9	10	11		7	3	1		8			46
30	46	22	37	43	42	33	9	46	44	34	5	40	23	16	—	20	13		
						+ 1s	+ 5s		+ 1s	+ 3s	+ 8s	+ 1s	+ 3s		+ 3s	+ 1s	+ 1s		

WATFORD—PLAYERS

Player and position	Ht	Wt	Birthplace	Clubs	League Appearances	Goals
Goalkeepers						
Andy Rankin	6 0	12 0	Liverpool	Everton	85	—
				Watford	289	—
Steve Sherwood	6 3	15 0	Selby	Chelsea	16	—
				Brighton (on loan)	—	—
				Millwall (on loan)	1	—
				Brentford (on loan)	62	—
				Watford	40	—
Defenders						
Albert McClenaghan	6 0	13 5	Hamilton	Larne	(not known)	
(Contract cancelled April 1979)				Watford	2	—
Alan Garner	6 0	12 4	Lambeth	Millwall	2	—
				Luton T	88	3
				Watford	190	15
Keith Pritchett	5 9	11 2	Glasgow	Wolverhampton W	—	—
				Doncaster R	6	—
				QPR	3	—
				Brentford	11	1
				Watford	99	6
Trevor How	5 10	12 2	Amersham	Watford	77+1	2
*Sam Ellis	6 0	13 5	Ashton under Lyme	Sheffield W	155+2	1
				Mansfield T	64	7
				Lincoln C	173	33
				Watford	30+4	4
Keith Cassells	5 10	11 2	London	Watford	0+3	—
John Stirk	5 6	9 11	Consett	Ipswich T	6	—
				Watford	46	—
Steve Sims	6 0	13 6	Lincoln	Leicester C	78+1	3
				Watford	13+1	1
Ian Bolton	6 0	11 9	Leicester	Notts Co	61+9	4
				Lincoln C (on loan)	1	—
				Watford	87	15
Paul Kerlin				Watford	—	—
(Contract cancelled September 1978)						
Steve Harrison	5 7	11 1½	Blackpool	Blackpool	141+7	—
				Vancouver W	—	—
				Watford	23	—
Midfield						
Dennis Booth	5 7½	10 5	Stenley Common	Charlton Ath	66+10	5
				Blackpool	12	—
				Southend U	77+1	1
				Lincoln C	162	9
				Watford	68	—
Roger Joslyn	5 10	11 2	Colchester	Colchester U	91+5	4
				Aldershot	186	17
				Watford	167+4	17
Bobby Downes	5 10	11 5	Bloxwich	WBA	—	—
				Peterborough U	24+2	3
				Rochdale	164+10	10
				Watford	184+7	19
Ray Train	5 4	9 7	Nuneaton	Walsall	67+7	11
				Carlisle U	154+1	8
				Sunderland	31+1	1
				Bolton W	49+2	—
				Watford	20+1	1
Forwards						
Ross Jenkins	6 2	12 2	Kensington	C Palace	15	2
				Watford	220+21	91
Keith Mercer	5 10	11 7	Lewisham	Watford	95+23	44
Luther Blissett	5 11	12 0	Jamaica	Watford	59+22	28
Brian Pollard	5 5	9 6	York	York C	151+12	34
				Watford	57+3	7

WEST BROMWICH ALBION   DIV. 1

President: J. W. Gaunt.
Chairman: F. A. Millichip.
Vice-Chairman: T. H. Silk.
Directors: J. Gordon, C. I. Edwards, D. B. Boundy, J. S. Lucas.
Manager: Ron Atkinson.   *Secretary:* A. Everiss, J.P.
Assistant Manager:
Assistant Secretary: Ray Fairfax.
Commercial Manager: Gordon Dimbleby, A.I.E.D.
Assistant Manager: David Jones.
Statistician: Tony Matthews.
Year Formed: 1879.   *Turned Professional:* 1885.
Limited Company: 1891.
Previous Grounds: 1879, Coopers Hill; 1879, Dartmouth Park; 1881, Bunn's Field, Walsall Street; 1882, Four Acres (Dartmouth Cricket Club); 1885, Stoney Lane; 1900, The Hawthorns.   *Previous Name:* 1879–80, West Bromwich Strollers.

Football League Record:
1888 Original Member of the League.   1911–27 Division 1.   1949–73 Division 1.
1901–02 Division 2.   1927–31 Division 2.   1973–76 Division 2.
1902–04 Division 1.   1931–38 Division 1.   1976– Division 1.
1904–11 Division 2.   1938–49 Division 2.

Honours: Football League, Division 1, Champions: 1919–20; Runners-up: 1924–25, 1953–54. Division 2. Champions: 1901–02, 1910–11; Runners-up: 1930–31, 1948–49. Promoted to Division 1 1975–76. *F.A. Cup,* Winners: 1888, 1892, 1931, 1954, 1968; Runners-up: 1886, 1887, 1895, 1912, 1935. *Football League Cup,* Winners: 1965–66; Runners-up 1966–67, 1969–70.
European Competitions: European Cup Winners Cup: 1968–69.   *European Fairs Cup:* 1966–67.
UEFA Cup: 1978–79.
Record Victory: 12-0 v Darwen, Division 1, April 4th, 1892.
Record Defeat: 3-10 v Stoke C., Division 1, Feb. 4th, 1937.
Most League Points: 60, Division 1, 1919–20.
Most League Goals: 105, Division 2, 1929–30.
Highest League Scorer in Season: William 'Ginger' Richardson, 39, Division 1, 1935–36.
Most Capped Player: Stuart Williams, 33 (43), Wales.
Most League Appearances: Tony Brown, 558, 1963–79.
Most League Goals in Total Aggregate: Tony Brown, 215, 1963–79.
Record Transfer Fee Received: £900,000 from Real Madrid for Laurie Cunningham, June 1979.
Record Transfer Fee Paid: £482,222 to Middlesbrough for David Mills, Jan. 1979.
Managers Since the War: Jack Smith, Vic Buckingham, Gordon Clark, Archie Macaulay, Jimmy Hagan, Alan Ashman, Don Howe, John Giles, Ronnie Allen.
Address of Supporters Club: Throstle Club, Birmingham Road, West Bromwich, Staffs.
Address of Club Shop or Boutique: Albion Club Shop, same address as club.

The Hawthorns, West Bromwich B71 4LF. Telephone 021-553 0095. Box Office 021 553 5472. *Ground capacity:* 38,600 (seats 12,500). *Record attendance:* 64,815 v Arsenal, F.A. Cup 6th Rd., March 6, 1937. *Record receipts:* £70,000 v Red Star Belgrade, UEFA Cup, March 21, 1979.
Pitch measurements: 115½ yds × 75½ yds.
How to get there: Buses 72, 74, 75, and 79 from outside Birmingham New Street station run directly to the ground. A special bus service from the centre of West Bromwich to the ground runs every three minutes on match days.
Match tickets: Advance bookings for Centre and Wing Stands accepted six weeks in advance by post including remittance and S.A.E. Telephone bookings are accepted but not before two days prior to the match; tickets reserved by telephone must be collected at least 30 minutes before kick-off. A limited number of unreserved seats in the Paddock are available at Door E1 on the day of the match.
Car parking: Street parking permitted in certain areas, all within 10 minutes walk of the ground.
Entertainments/catering facilities: Post-match entertainment in the Supporters' Club adjoining the ground. Excellent facilities at The Hawthorns Throstle Club alongside the ground includes a full-course lunch, several restaurants within walking distance of the ground. Snack bars in the ground.
Club shop: Situated in the Pools Office in Halfords Lane, and open from 9–5 Mon.–Sat. Stocks over 200 different articles. Excellent mailing service. Price list available on request.
Handbooks/programmes: Handbook & programmes available on subscription.
Extra information: There are 4 Throstle Clubs in the surrounding areas, and the club runs a Junior Throstle Club for the under-15s.
Club Colour: Navy blue and white striped shirts, white shorts and white stockings.
Change Colours: Yellow and green striped shirts, green shorts, yellow stockings.
Club Captain: John Wile.
Coaches: Albert McPherson and Brian Whitehouse.
Club Nicknames: 'Baggies', 'Throstles', 'Albion'.

WEST BROMWICH ALBION 1978–79 LEAGUE RECORD

Match No.	Date	Venue	Opponents	Result	H/T Score	League Pos'n	Goalscorers	Attendance
1	Aug 19	H	Ipswich T	W 2-1	1-1	—	Brown A, Regis	21,700
2	22	A	QPR	W 1-0	0-0	—	Howe (og)	15,481
3	26	H	Bolton W	W 4-0	3-0	2	Brown A, 2, Cunningham, Regis	23,237
4	Sept 2	A	Nottingham F	D 0-0	0-0	3		28,239
5	9	H	Norwich C	D 2-2	1-2	4	Cunningham, Robson	21,947
6	16	A	Derby Co	L 2-3	0-3	4	Cunningham, Regis	23,697
7	23	H	Liverpool	D 1-1	0-0	5	Cunningham	38,000
8	30	A	Chelsea	W 3-1	1-1	3	Regis, Wile, Brown T	20,186
9	Oct 7	H	Tottenham H	L 0-1	0-1	6		33,211
10	14	A	Leeds U	W 3-1	1-1	4	Brown T, Regis 2	25,931
11	21	H	Coventry C	W 7-1	3-0	4	Cantello, Cunningham 2, Regis 2, Brown T, Statham	27,381
12	28	A	Manchester C	D 2-2	2-2	4	Regis, Robson	40,521
13	Nov 4	H	Birmingham C	W 1-0	1-0	3	Trewick	31,988
14	11	A	Ipswich T	W 1-0	1-0	3	Brown A	20,914
15	18	A	Bolton W	W 1-0	0-0	3	Brown A	22,273
16	25	H	Aston Villa	D 1-1	1-0	3	Brown T (pen)	35,085
17	Dec 9	H	Middlesbrough	W 2-0	1-0	3	Regis, Cantello	19,795
18	16	A	Wolverhampton W	W 3-0	1-0	3	Brown A 2, Brown T	29,117
19	26	H	Arsenal	W 2-1	2-0	3	Robson, Brown A	40,055
20	30	A	Manchester U	W 5-3	3-3	3	Brown T 2, Cantello, Cunningham, Regis	45,091
21	Jan 1	H	Bristol C	W 3-1	2-1	—	Brown A 2, Wile	31,593
22	13	A	Norwich C	D 1-1	1-0	1	Regis	20,972
23	Feb 3	A	Liverpool	L 1-2	0-1	2	Brown A	52,211
24	24	H	Leeds U	L 1-2	1-2	5	Brown T	26,426
25	Mar 3	A	Coventry C	W 3-1	1-0	3	Robson, Brown A, Mills	25,795
26	14	H	Chelsea	W 1-0	0-0	—	Brown A	20,425
27	24	H	QPR	W 2-1	1-0	3	Brown A, Cunningham	23,678
28	26	H	Derby Co	W 2-1	0-1	—	Cunningham, Brown A	20,010
29	Apr 4	H	Manchester C	W 4-0	2-0	—	Trewick, Regis, Mills, Summerfield	22,314
30	7	H	Everton	W 1-0	0-0	2	Brown A	29,580
31	13	A	Southampton	D 1-1	0-0	—	Regis	22,063
32	14	H	Arsenal	D 1-1	0-1	2	Brown T	28,353
33	17	A	Bristol C	L 0-1	0-0	—		29,914
34	21	H	Wolverhampton W	D 1-1	0-0	3	Robson	32,385
35	24	A	Birmingham C	D 1-1	0-0	—	Robson	19,897
36	28	A	Middlesbrough	D 1-1	0-1	2	Brown A	18,063
37	May 1	A	Everton	W 2-0	1-0	—	Mills, Robson	30,038
38	5	H	Manchester U	W 1-0	1-0	2	Regis	27,862
39	8	H	Southampton	W 1-0	0-0	—	Brown A	17,526
40	11	A	Aston Villa	W 1-0	1-0	—	Trewick	35,991
41	14	H	Tottenham H	L 0-1	0-1	—		24,789
42	18	H	Nottingham F	L 0-1	0-0	—		28,246

Final League Position: 3

Goalscorers

League (72): Brown A 18, Regis 15, Brown T 9, Cunningham 9, Robson 7, Cantello 3, Trewick 3, Mills 3, Wile 2, Statham 1, Summerfield 1, Own Goal 1.
F.A. Cup (13): Brown A 5, Cunningham 3, Brown T 2, Batson, Regis, Wile.

League Cup	Second Round	Leeds U (h)	0-0
		(a)	0-0 (aet)
			0-1 (at Maine Rd)
F.A. Cup	Third Round	Coventry C (a)	2-2
		(h)	4-0
	Fourth Round	Leeds U (h)	3-3
		(a)	2-0 (aet)
	Fifth Round	Southampton (h)	1-1
		(a)	1-2 (aet)

Godden	Batson	Statham	Brown, T.	Wile	Robertson	Robson	Brown, A.	Regis	Cantello	Cunningham	Johnston	Trewick	Martin	Mills	Summerfield	Bennett	Match No.
1	2	3	4	5	6	7	8	9	10	11							1
1	2	3	4	5	6	7	8	9	10	11							2
1	2	3	4	5	6	8	10	9	7	11*	12						3
1	2	3		5	6	7	8	9	4	10	11						4
1	2	3		5	6	7	8	9	4	10	11						5
1	2	3		5	6	7	8	9		10	11	4					6
1	2	3		5	6	7	8	9	10	4		11					7
1	2	3	11*	5	6	7	8	9	10	4		12					8
1	2	3	11	5	6	7	8	9		4		10					9
1	2	3*	11	5	6	8	10	9	7	4	12						10
1	2	3	11	5	6	7	8	9	10*	4	12						11
1	2	3	11	5	6	7	8	9	10	4							12
1	2		4	5	6	7	8	9	10	11	3						13
1	2		4	5	6	3	8	9	10	11	7						14
1	2		4	5	6	7	8		10	11	3	9					15
1	2	3	4	5	6	7	8	9	10	11							16
1	2	3	4	5	6	7	8	9	10	11							17
1	2	3	4	5	6	7	8	9	10	11							18
1	2	3	4	5	6	7	8	9	10	11							19
1	2	3	4	5	6	7	8	9	10	11							20
1	2	3	4	5	6	7	8	9	10	11							21
1	2	3	4	5	6	7	8	9		11	10						22
1	2	3	4	5	6	7	8	9	10*	11			12				23
1	2	3	4	5	6	7	8*	9	10	11			12				24
1	2	3		5	6	7	8	9		11	4		10				25
1	2	3	4	5	6		8	9*		11	12	7	10				26
1	2	3	4*	5	6	7	8		10	11		12	9				27
1	2	3		5	6	7	8*		10	11	4		9	12			28
1	2*	3		5	6	7		9	10	11	4		8	12			29
1		3		5	6	7	8	9		11	4		10		2		30
1	2	3	12	5	6	7	8	9		11	4		10*				31
1	2	3	4	5	6	7	8	9		11	10						32
1	2	3		5	6	7	8	9	10	11		4					33
1	2	3	4	5	6	7	8	9	10	11							34
1	2	3	4	5	6	7	8*	9	10	11			12				35
1	2	3	4	5	6	7	8	12	10	11*			9				36
1	2	3	4	5	6	7	8	9	10				11				37
1	2	3	4*	5	6	7	8	9		12	10		11				38
1	2	3	12	5	6	7	8	9		4	10*		11				39
1	2	3		5		7	8	9	6	4	10		11				40
1	2	3		5		7	8	9	10	11	4		6				41
1	2	3	4	5		7	8	9	10				11	6			42
42	41	39	29	42	39	41	41	38	32	39	3	19	1	15	—	1	
			+2s						+1s		+1s	+4s	+2s		+3s	+2s	

WEST BROMWICH ALBION—PLAYERS

Player and position	Ht	Wt	Birthplace	Clubs	League Appearances	Goals
Goalkeepers						
Tony Godden	6 1	12 2	Gillingham	Gillingham	—	—
				Preston NE (on loan)	—	—
				WBA	90	—
Mark Grew	5 10	11 2	Bilston	WBA	—	—
				Notts Co (on loan)	—	—
				Wigan Ath (on loan)	4	—
David Stewart (Scotland)	6 1½	13 0	Glasgow	Ayr U	157	—
				Leeds U	55	—
				WBA	—	—
Defenders						
*Paddy Mulligan (Eire)	5 9	11 0	Dublin	Chelsea	55+3	2
				C Palace	57	2
				WBA	109	1
Alistair Robertson	5 9	10 3	Philipstown	WBA	305+2	4
David Arthur	5 8	11 0	Bushbury	WBA	—	—
John Wile	6 1	11 12	Sherburn	Sunderland	—	—
				Peterborough	116+2	7
				WBA	342+1	22
Tony Cooper	5 9	11 0	Crewe	WBA	—	—
(Contract cancelled January 1979)						
Derek Statham	5 5	11 0	Wolverhampton	WBA	95	2
Brendon Batson	5 10	11 7	Grenada	Arsenal	6+4	—
				Cambridge U	162+1	6
				WBA	46	—
Martyn Bennett	6 0	12 11	Birmingham	WBA	1	—
John Anderson	5 10	11 4	Dublin	WBA	—	—
Midfield						
Len Cantello	5 9½	10 8½	Manchester	WBA	297+4	13
Bryan Robson	5 9	11 1	Chester-le-Street	WBA	114+4	21
John Trewick	5 9	10 10	Bedlington	WBA	54+7	8
Wayne Hughes	6 0	12 5	Port Talbot	WBA	3+3	2
(Contract cancelled January 1979)						
John Loveridge	5 7	11 0	Wolverhampton	WBA	—	—
Vernon Hodgson				Birmingham C	—	—
				WBA	—	—
David Mills	5 8	10 0	Whitby	Middlesbrough	278+17	75
				WBA	15+3	3
Remi Moses	5 7	10 10	Birmingham	WBA	—	—
Forwards						
Alistair Brown	6 0	11 0	Musselburgh	Leicester C	93+8	31
				WBA	158+14	48
Tony Brown (England)	5 6½	11 6	Oldham	WBA	549+9	214
Willie Johnston	5 7	11 0	Glasgow	Rangers	210+2	90
(Scotland) (Contract cancelled March 1979)				WBA	203+4	17
Kevin Summerfield	5 11	10 7	Walsall	WBA	0+2	1
Laurie Cunningham	5 8	10 13	Archway	Orient	72+3	15
(England) (Contract cancelled June 1979)				WBA	81+5	20
Derek Monaghan	5 9	11 2	Bromsgrove	WBA	—	—
Cyrille Regis	6 0	13 0	French Guyana	WBA	71+2	25
Barry Cowdrill	5 11	11 5	Birmingham	WBA	—	—
*David Lawrence						
Nicky Cross	5 9	11 0	Birmingham	WBA	—	—

Also retained: Nick Lewis, Robert Page, Phillip Danks, Paul Evans.

WEST HAM UNITED

DIV. 2

President: R. H. Pratt.
Vice-Chairman: B. R. Cearns, F.I.C.S.
Directors: L. C. Cearns, W. F. Cearns, J. Petchey, M. W. Cearns, A.I.B.
Manager: John Lyall.
Secretary: Eddie Chapman, F.A.A.I.
P.R.O.: Jack Helliar.   *Year Formed:* 1900.
Turned Professional: 1900.   *Limited Company:* 1900.
Previous Grounds: Memorial Recreation Ground, Canning Town; 1904 Boleyn Ground.
Football League Record: 1919 Elected to Division 2. 1923–32 Division 1. 1932–58 Division 2. 1958–78 Division 1. 1978– Division 2.
Honours: Football League, best season in Division 1: 6th, 1926–27, 1958–59, 1972–73. Division 2, Champions: 1957–58; runners-up: 1922–23.   *F.A. Cup,* Winners: 1964, 1975; runners-up: 1922–23.   *Football League Cup,* runners-up: 1966. **European Competitions:** *European Cup-Winners Cup:* 1964–65 (Winners), 1965–66, 1975–76 (Runners-up).
Record Victory: 8-0 v Rotherham U., Division 2, 1957–58 and Sunderland, Division 1, Oct. 19th, 1968.
Record Defeat: 2-8 v Blackburn R., Division 1, Dec. 26th, 1963.
Most League Points: 57, Division 2, 1957–58.
Most League Goals: 101, Division 2, 1957–58.
Highest League Scorer in Season: Vic Watson, 41, Division 1, 1929–30.
Most Capped Player: Bobby Moore, 108, England.
Most League Appearances: Bobby Moore, 544, 1958–1974.
Most League Goals in Total Aggregate: Vic Watson, 306, 1920–35.
Record Transfer Fee Received: £225,000 from Birmingham C. for Alan Curbishley, June 1979.
Record Transfer Fee Paid: £527,000 including levies; £475,000 nett. to QPR for Phil Parkes, Feb. 1979.
Managers Since the War: Charlie Paynter, Ted Fenton, Ron Greenwood.
Address of Supporters Club: Castle St., Upton Park, E.13.
Address of Club Shop or Boutique: Hammers Shop, Boleyn Ground, Green Street, Upton Park, London E.13.

Boleyn Ground, Green Street, Upton Park, London E.13. Telephone 01-472 0704.   *Ground capacity:* 39,500.   *Record attendance:* 42,322 v Tottenham H., Division 1, October 17, 1970.   *Record receipts:* £45,397 v Watford, F.A. Cup 3rd Rd., Jan. 7 1978.
Pitch measurements: 110 yds × 72 yds.

How to get there: Nearest station Upton Park (Underground, District Line)—five minutes' walk. Buses from Barking Road, Romford Road and Green Street.
Match tickets: Advance booking, by personal application only, 12 days prior to League matches.
Car parking: Ample side-street parking available.
Entertainments/catering facilities: Refreshment points around the ground.
Club shop: Situated on the ground; sells all types of souvenirs.
Handbooks/programmes: Programmes and handbook available by post from either Sales Service c/o West Ham United F.C. or from Helliar & Sons, 237, Barking Road, London E13 8EQ.
Extra information: Vic Watson's 306 League goals for West Ham is the fourth highest total scored with one club in the history of the competition.

Club Colours: Claret shirts, blue yoke, white shorts and white stockings.
Change Colours: White shirts, sky blue shorts, sky blue stockings.
Club Captain: Billy Bonds.
Physiotherapist: Rob Jenkins.
Club Nickname: 'Hammers'.

WEST HAM UNITED 1978-79 LEAGUE RECORD

Match No.	Date	Venue	Opponents	Result Score	H/T Score	League Pos'n	Goalscorers	Attendance
1	Aug 19	H	Notts Co	W 5-2	4-0	—	Cross 3, Blockley (og), Devonshire	25,387
2	23	A	Newcastle U	W 3-0	1-0	—	Devonshire, Cross, Robson	27,233
3	26	A	Crystal Palace	D 1-1	1-1	2	Taylor, A	32,611
4	Sept 2	H	Fulham	L 0-1	0-1	4		25,778
5	9	A	Burnley	L 2-3	2-1	7	Cross 2	12,303
6	16	H	Bristol R	W 2-0	0-0	4	Robson, Brooking	22,189
7	23	H	Sheffield U	W 2-0	0-0	3	Robson 2 (2 pens)	24,361
8	30	A	Sunderland	L 1-2	0-1	6	Cross	23,676
9	Oct 7	H	Millwall	W 3-0	1-0	4	Robson 3 (1 a pen)	22,000
10	14	A	Oldham Ath	D 2-2	1-0	3	Robson 2	10,143
11	21	H	Stoke C	D 1-1	0-0	5	Brooking	27,859
12	28	A	Brighton & HA	W 2-1	2-1	4	Robson 2	32,634
13	Nov 4	H	Preston NE	W 3-1	1-1	2	Lampard, Devonshire, Cross	23,579
14	11	A	Notts Co	L 0-1	0-0	4		11,002
15	18	H	Crystal Palace	D 1-1	1-0	3	Bonds	31,245
16	21	A	Fulham	D 0-0	0-0	—		26,556
17	25	A	Leicester C	W 2-1	1-0	3	Cross 2	16,149
18	Dec 2	H	Cambridge U	W 5-0	1-0	3	Taylor, A Robson 2, Bonds, Curbishley	21,379
19	9	A	Wrexham	L 3-4	1-2	3	Cross, Lampard, Robson	15,787
20	16	H	Charlton Ath	W 2-0	1-0	3	Robson, Cross	23,833
21	26	H	Orient	L 0-2	0-1	—		29,220
22	30	H	Blackburn R	W 4-0	1-0	4	Robson, Taylor A, Cross, Curtis (og)	21,269
23	Jan 20	A	Bristol R	W 1-0	1-0	4	Robson	12,418
24	Feb 10	H	Sunderland	D 3-3	1-2	4	Cross 2, Robson	24,998
25	24	H	Oldham Ath	W 3-0	1-0	4	Holland, Martin, Robson	26,052
26	26	A	Luton T	W 4-1	0-0	—	Cross 2, Devonshire, Robson	14,205
27	Mar 3	A	Stoke C	L 0-2	0-1	4		24,912
28	10	H	Brighton & HA	D 0-0	0-0	5		35,802
29	17	A	Preston NE	D 0-0	0-0	5		15,376
30	24	H	Newcastle U	W 5-0	4-0	5	Devonshire, Robson, Lampard, McDowell 2	24,650
31	31	H	Leicester C	D 1-1	0-0	5	Robson	23,992
32	Apr 2	A	Sheffield U	L 0-3	0-1	—		17,720
33	7	A	Cambridge U	D 0-0	0-0	5		11,406
34	9	H	Luton T	W 1-0	0-0	—	Carr (og)	25,498
35	14	A	Orient	W 2-0	1-0	5	Holland, Pike	17,517
36	16	H	Cardiff C	D 1-1	1-0	5	Holland	29,058
37	21	A	Charlton Ath	D 0-0	0-0	5		22,816
38	24	H	Burnley	W 3-1	2-1	—	Bonds, Pike, Robson	24,139
39	28	H	Wrexham	D 1-1	1-0	5	Bonds	28,865
40	May 5	A	Blackburn R	L 0-1	0-0	5		7585
41	11	A	Cardiff C	D 0-0	0-0	—		13,140
42	14	A	Millwall	L 1-2	1-0	—	Robson	11,917

Final League Position: 5

Goalscorers

League (70): Robson 24 (3 pens), Cross 17, Devonshire 5, Bonds 4, Holland 3, Lampard 3, Taylor A 3, Brooking 2, Pike 2, McDowell 2, Curbishley 1, Martin 1, Own Goals 3.
League Cup (1): Robson.
F.A. Cup (1): Robson.

League Cup	Second Round	Swindon T (h)	1-2
F.A. Cup	Third Round	Newport Co (a)	1-2

Ferguson	Lampard	Brush	Holland	Taylor, T.	Bonds	Curbishley	Devonshire	Cross	Brooking	Robson	Taylor, A.	Pike	McDowell	Martin	Jennings	Day	Parkes	Morgan	Lansdowne	Brignull	Match No.
1	2	3	4	5	6	7	8	9	10	11											1
1	2	3	4	5	6	7	8	9	10*11	12											2
1	2	3	4	5	6	7	8	9		11	10										3
1	2	3	4	5	6	7		9		11	10*	8	12								4
1	2	3	4	5	6	7	8	9		11			10								5
1	2	3	4	5	6	7	8	9	10	11											6
1	2*	3	4	5	6	7	8		10	11	12		9								7
1		3	4	5	6	7	8	9	10	11			2								8
1	2	3	4	5	6	7	8	9	10	11											9
1	2	3	4	5	6	7*	8	9	10	11	12										10
1		3	4	5	6	7	8	9	10	11			2								11
		3	4	5	6	7	8	9	10	11			2		1						12
	2	3	4	5	6	7	8	9	10	11					1						13
	2	3	4	5	6	7	8	9	10	11					1						14
	2	3	4*	5	6	7	8	9	10	11	12				1						15
	2	3	4	5	6	7	8	9		11	10				1						16
	2	3	4	5	6		7	9		11	10		8		1						17
	2	3	4	5	6	7	8	9		11	10				1						18
	2	3	4	5		7	8	9		11	10			6	1						19
	2	3	4*	5		7	8	9		11	10	12	6		1						20
	2	3		5		7*	8	9		11	10	4	6	12	1						21
	2	3			4		8	9	10	11	7		6	5	1						22
		3			6	4	8	9	10	11	7		2	5	1						23
		3	7	5	6	4	8	9	10	11*			2	12	1						24
		3	7		6	4	8	9	10	11			2	5		1					25
		3	7		6	4	8	9	10	11			2	5		1					26
		3	7		6	4	8	9	10	11			2	5		1					27
	2	3	7		6	4	8	9		11			10	5		1					28
	2	3	7		6		8	9	10	11			4	5		1					29
	2	3	7		6		8	9	10*11		12		4	5		1					30
	2	3	7		6	12	8	9		11			10	4*	5	1					31
	2	3	7		6		8	9		11			10	4	5	1					32
	2*	3	7	5	10		8	9		11			12	4	6	1					33
		3	7	6	4		8			11			10	2	5	1	9				34
		3	7	6	4		8	9		11			10	2	5	1					35
		3	7	6	4		8	9		11			10	2	5	1					36
	12	3	7	6	4		8	9					10	2	5	11*	1				37
		3	7	6	4		8	9		11			10	2	5		1				38
		3	7	6	4		8	9		11			10*	2	5		1	12			39
	2	3	7	6	4		8	9		11	12		10*		5		1				40
	2	3	7	6	4		8	9					10*		5		1	11	12		41
	2	3	7	6	4		8	9	10	11				5			1				42
11	28	42	39	32	39	26	41	40	21	40	10	10	26	22	2	13	18	2			
	+ 1s				+ 1s				+ 3s	+ 4s	+ 2s		+ 2s				+ 1s	+ 1s			

WEST HAM UNITED—PLAYERS

Player and position	Ht	Wt	Birthplace	Clubs	League Appearances	Goals
Goalkeepers						
Bobby Ferguson (Scotland)	5 10½	12 7	Ardrossan	Kilmarnock	73	—
				West Ham U	238	—
				Sheffield W (on loan)	5	—
				Leicester C (on loan)	—	—
				Cardiff C (on loan)	—	—
Gary Moseley	6 0	12 7	Westerham	West Ham U	—	—
Phil Parkes (England)	6 2	14 5	Sedgeley	Walsall	52	—
				QPR	344	—
				West Ham U	18	—
Defenders						
Frank Lampard (England)	5 11	12 9	West Ham	West Ham U	391+1	15
John McDowell	5 10	12 4	East Ham	West Ham U	243+6	8
Paul Brush	5 11	11 7	London	West Ham U	65+1	—
Alvin Martin	6 1	12 6	Bootle	West Ham U	27+2	2
Phil Brignull	5 11	12 6	Stratford	West Ham U	0+1	—
Midfield						
Alan Curbishley	5 9	11 6	Forest Gate	West Ham U	78+7	4
Billy Bonds	6 0½	12 12	Woolwich	Charlton Ath	95	1
				West Ham U	436+1	40
*Mike McGiven	6 0	11 12	Newcastle	Sunderland	107+6	9
				West Ham U	46+2	—
Trevor Brooking (England)	6 0½	13 8	Barking	West Ham U	360+7	61
Pat Holland	5 10	11 6	Limehouse	West Ham U	181+13	16
				Bournemouth (on loan)	10	—
Geoff Pike	5 6	11 0	Clapton	West Ham U	55+10	10
Georgie Cowie	5 8	10 9	Buckie	West Ham U	—	—
Dale Banton	5 10	10 5	Kensington	West Ham U	—	—
Forwards						
Nick Morgan	5 10	12 0	London	West Ham U	2	—
Alan Devonshire	5 10½	10 8	London	West Ham U	100+3	8
Billy Jennings	5 9	10 2	Hackney	Watford	81+12	33
				West Ham U	89+10	33
Alan Taylor	5 9	10 6	Lancaster	Rochdale	55	7
				West Ham U	88+10	25
Bryan Robson	5 6	11 12	Sunderland	Newcastle U	205+1	81
				West Ham U	120	47
				Sunderland	90	34
				West Ham U	107	47
Brian Thomson	5 7	10 4	Morecambe	West Ham U	—	—
David Cross	6 0½	12 0	Bury	Rochdale	50+9	21
				Norwich C	83+1	21
				Coventry C	90+1	29
				WBA	38	19
				West Ham U	61	27
*Gary Pugh	6 0	13 0	Kent	West Ham U	—	—
Bill Lansdowne	6 0	11 8	Epping	West Ham U	0+1	—

WIGAN ATHLETIC DIV. 4

Chairman: Arthur O. Horrocks.

Vice-Chairman: Alan Muir.

Directors: J. Albert Eckersley, Graham D. Gorner, John H. Farrimond.

Secretary: Derek Welsby, F.A.A.I.

Manager: Ian M. McNeill.

Year Formed: 1932.

Honours: **Northern Premier League Champions 1970–71, 1974–75; Northern Premier Cup Winners 1971–72; Northern Premier Shield Winners 1972–73, 1973–74, 1975–76; Cheshire League Champions 1933–34, 1934–35, 1935–36, 1964–65; Lancashire Combination Champions 1947–48, 1950–51, 1952–53, 1953–54.**

Record Victory: 3-0 v Reading Division 4, Nov. 18th, 1978. and 3-0 v Rochdale, Division 4, Sept. 13th, 1978.

Record Defeat: 0-3 v Grimsby T. Division 4, Aug. 23rd, 1978.

Most League Points: 55, Division 4, 1978–79.

Most League Goals: 63, Division 4, 1978–79.

Highest League Scorer in Season: Peter Houghton, 13, Division 4, 1978–79.

Most Capped Player: None.

Most League Appearances: Tommy Gore, Ian Purdie and Jeff Wright, 46, 1978–79.

Most League Goals in Total Aggregate: Peter Houghton, 13, 1978–79.

Managers of note: Ted Goodier, Allan Brown, Gordon Milne.

Address of Social Club: Springfield Park, Wigan.

Springfield Park, Wigan. Telephone: 0942 44433. Telegraphic Address: Springfield, Wigan. *Ground capacity:* 30,000. *Record attendance:* 27,500 v Hereford United, December 1953. *Record receipts:* £9,508 v Sheffield Wednesday, FA Cup, 2nd Rd., 17 December, 1977. *Pitch measurements:* 117 yds × 73 yds.

How to get there: Wigan Wallgate and Wigan North West Railway Stations. Wigan is served by three Motorways, the M6, the M61 and the M62, with convenient access and exit points. Wigan also enjoys the facilities of the main London to Scotland railway line.
Match tickets: Stand – available 14 days prior to game.
Car Park: On ground and within close proximity to ground.
Entertainments/catering facilities: Licensed bar and tea bar in Main Stand, tea bars on ground, Social Club on ground.
Club colours: Blue and white striped shirts, blue shorts, white stockings.
Change colours: White shirts, blue shorts, red stockings.
First team trainer: Ken Banks.
Club Captain: Ian Gillibrand.
Club Nickname: 'The Latics'.

Extra information
Springfield Park covers approximately nine acres and is owned by Wigan Athletic AFC Ltd. The ground will hold over 30,000 spectators with seating accommodation for 1,400 and additional covered standing accommodation for 10,000.
There are terraces on all four sides of the excellent playing area, surrounded by four 114 feet high pylons with 36 lights on each.
The dressing rooms are equipped with plunge baths, slipper baths, showers and medical and physiotherapy equipment.
There are parking facilities for 200 cars.
A lively Social Club and a productive Development Association office are located on the ground.
Wigan has a population of over 300,000 within a radius of 5 miles from the town centre. The actual town population is 89,000.

WIGAN ATHLETIC 1978-79 LEAGUE RECORD

Match No.	Date	Venue	Opponents	Result	H/T Score	League Pos'n	Goalscorers	Attendance
1	Aug 19	A	Hereford U	D 0-0	0-0	—		5674
2	23	H	Grimsby T	L 0-3	0-2	—		9227
3	26	A	Reading	L 0-2	0-1	22		4788
4	Sept 2	H	Newport Co	L 2-3	0-2	23	Hinnigan, Purdie	5319
5	9	A	Wimbledon	L 1-2	1-0	24	Corrigan	3217
6	13	H	Rochdale	W 3-0	0-0	—	Wright, Corrigan, Hinnigan	5746
7	16	H	Bradford C	L 1-3	0-2	21	Purdie	7090
8	23	A	York C	W 1-0	0-0	19	Gore	3307
9	26	A	Portsmouth	L 0-1	0-0	—		13,902
10	30	H	Scunthorpe U	W 1-0	0-0	18	Brownbill	4459
11	Oct 7	A	Huddersfield T	D 1-1	0-1	21	Brownbill	5150
12	14	H	Doncaster R	W 1-0	0-0	18	Ward	5788
13	18	H	Halifax T	W 1-0	1-0	—	Hinnigan	5216
14	21	A	Barnsley	D 0-0	0-0	15		9841
15	28	H	Northampton T	W 2-0	0-0	13	Purdie 2 (1 a pen)	6264
16	Nov 3	A	Stockport Co	W 1-0	0-0	11	Hinnigan	8357
17	10	A	Newport Co	L 1-2	0-1	13	Houghton	4142
18	18	H	Reading	W 3-0	1-0	9	Houghton 2, Ward	5858
19	Dec 9	A	Darlington	D 1-1	1-1	11	Moore	1967
20	16	A	Halifax T	W 2-1	2-0	7	Moore, Purdie	2437
21	26	H	Crewe Alex	W 1-0	0-0	—	Houghton	7586
22	30	H	Aldershot	W 3-2	2-1	7	Moore, Houghton 2	7289
23	Jan 9	A	Port Vale	L 1-2	0-1	—	Wright	3744
24	Feb 3	H	Portsmouth	W 2-0	1-0	7	Wright, Corrigan	8289
25	14	A	Wimbledon	L 1-2	0-2	—	Purdie (pen)	6704
26	17	H	Huddersfield T	W 2-1	1-1	6	Ward 2	7420
27	24	A	Doncaster R	W 1-0	0-0	6	Wright	4612
28	28	H	York C	D 1-1	1-0	—	Houghton	5896
29	Mar 3	H	Barnsley	D 1-1	0-0	6	Wright	9427
30	10	A	Northampton T	W 4-2	3-1	7	Brownbill 2, Purdie, Corrigan	2275
31	14	H	Torquay U	W 3-1	2-1	—	Moore 2, Hinnigan	5722
32	17	H	Stockport Co	W 2-0	0-0	5	Wright, Smart	7610
33	19	A	Rochdale	W 2-0	1-0	—	Purdie, Moore	3621
34	24	A	Grimsby T	L 1-3	0-2	4	Wigginton (og)	8252
35	28	H	Hereford U	D 0-0	0-0	—		4876
36	31	H	AFC Bournemouth	W 1-0	1-0	5	Houghton	5527
37	Apr 3	A	Hartlepool U	D 1-1	1-0	—	Houghton	2081
38	7	A	Torquay U	D 1-1	1-0	5	Houghton	2969
39	13	H	Port Vale	W 5-3	0-2	—	Houghton 3, Brownbill, Moore	8452
40	14	A	Crewe Alex	D 1-1	1-0	4	Purdie (pen)	4604
41	16	H	Hartlepool U	D 2-2	0-1	—	Wright, Purdie	8217
42	21	A	Aldershot	L 0-1	0-0	6		5466
43	28	H	Darlington	D 2-2	2-1	6	Moore, Brownbill	6153
44	May 1	A	Scunthorpe U	W 1-0	0-0	—	Gore	1582
45	5	A	AFC Bournemouth	L 1-2	0-0	6	Purdie	3063
46	7	A	Bradford C	D 1-1	1-1	—	Moore	3748

Final League Position: 6

Goalscorers

League (63): Houghton 13, Purdie 11 (3 pens), Moore 9, Wright 7, Brownbill 6, Hinnigan 5, Corrigan 4, Ward 4, Gore 2, Smart 1, Own Goal 1.
League Cup (3): Corrigan 2, Gore.
F.A. Cup (3): Gore, Houghton, Moore.

League Cup	First Round		Tranmere R (a)	1-1
			(h)	2-1
	Second Round		Luton T (a)	0-2
F.A. Cup	First Round		Bury (h)	2-2
			(a)	1-4

Brown	Hinnigan	Gore	Gillibrand	Ward	Davids	Corrigan	Purdie	Houghton	Wilkie	Wright	Gay	Smart	Crompton	Seddon	Moore	Worswick	Brownbill	Fretwell	Grew	Curtis	Match No.
1	2	3	4	5	6	7	8	9	10	11											1
1	3	2	6	5	4	7	11	9		8	10*		12								2
1		2	6	5	4*	7	8	9	10	11		3	12								3
1	3*	2	6	5		7	11		10	4				8	9	12					4
1	3	4	6	5		7	11			8		2	10		9						5
1	3	4	6	5		7	11			8		2	10		9*	12					6
1	3	4	6	5		7	11			8		2	10*		9	12					7
1	3	4		5	6	7	11			8		2			9	10					8
1	3	4		5	6	7	11		12	8		2			9*	10					9
1	3	4		5	6	7	11			8		2			10	9					10
1	3	4		5		7*11				8		2	12		9	10	6				11
1	3	4		5		7	11			8		2			9	10	6				12
1	3	4		5		7	11	12		8		2			9*	10	6				13
1	3	4		5		7	11	12		8		2			9	10*	6				14
1	3	4		5		7	11	10		8		2			9		6				15
1	3	4		5		7	11	10		8		2			9		6				16
1	3	4		5		7	11*10			8		2			9	12	6				17
1	3	4		5		7	11	10		8		2			9		6				18
1*	3	4		5		7	11	10		8		2			9	12	6				19
	3	4			5	7	11			8		2			9	10	6	1			20
	3	4	5			7	11	9		8		2			10		6	1			21
	3	4	5			7	11	10		8		2			9		6	1			22
		4	5	3		7	11*	9		8		2			10	12	6	1			23
1	3	4	5			7	11	10		8		2			9		6				24
1		2	5			7	11	9		8		3	10			4	6				25
1	3	4	5			7	11	9		8		2	10				6				26
1	3	4	5			7	11	9		8		2	10*		12		6				27
1	3	2	5			7	11	9*		8			10		4	12	6				28
1	3	4	5			7	11			8		2			10	9	6				29
1	3	4	5			7*11				8		2	12		9	10	6				30
1	3	4	5			7	11			8		2			10	9	6				31
1	3	4	5			7	11			8		2			10	9	6				32
1	3	4	5			7	11			8		2			10	9	6				33
1	3*	4	5			7	11	12		8		2			10	9	6				34
1		4	5			7	11*	9		8		3			10	12	6		2		35
1		4	5			7	11	10		8		3			9		6		2		36
1		4	5			7	11	9		8		3			10		6		2		37
1		4	5			7	11	10		8		3			9		6		2		38
1	3	4	5*			7	11	9		8		2			10	12	6				39
1	3	4	5			7	11	9*		8		2			10	12	6				40
1	6	4	5			7*11		9		8		3			10	12			2		41
1	3	4	5	6			11			8		7*12			10	9			2		42
1	3	4	5			7	11			8*			6	12	10	9			2		43
1	3	4		5		7	11			8					10	9	6		2		44
1	3	4		5	12	7	11			8		2			10*	9	6				45
1	3	4		5	12	7	11			8					10	9	6*		2		46
42	39	46	7	44	10	45	46	23	3	46	1	40	7	1	40	—	20	33	4	9	
					+2s			+3s	+1s				+6s		+1s	+1s	+10s				

WIGAN ATHLETIC—PLAYERS

Player and position	Ht	Wt	Birthplace	Clubs	League Appearances	Goals
Goalkeepers						
John Brown	5 11	13 0	Bradford	Preston NE	67	—
				Stockport Co	41	—
				Wigan Ath	42	—
Colin Darcy	6 3	13 9	Wirral	Everton	—	—
(Contract cancelled March 1979)				Bury	4	—
				Wigan Ath	—	—
Defenders						
Joe Hinnigan	6 0	12 0	Liverpool	Wigan Ath	39	5
Noel Ward	6 2½	12 10	Londonderry	Portadown	—	—
				Aberdeen	6+1	—
				Wigan Ath	44	4
Ian Gillibrand	5 8	11 0	Blackburn	Wigan Ath	7	—
Nigel Hart	6 0	11 7	Manchester	Wigan Ath	—	—
Neil Davids	6 0¾	13 9	Bingley	Leeds U	—	—
				Norwich C	2	—
				Northampton T (on loan)	9	—
				Stockport Co (on loan)	5	1
				Swansea C	9	—
				Wigan Ath	10+2	—
Kevin Smart	5 7	10 8	High Heaton	Plymouth Arg	32	—
				Wigan Ath	40	1
Dave Fretwell	5 9	10 9	Normanton	Bradford C	247+1	5
				Wigan Ath	33	—
Midfield						
Tommy Gore	5 7	11 0	Liverpool	Liverpool	—	—
				Tranmere R	—	—
				Wigan Ath	46	2
Jeff Wright	5 11	11 7	Alston	Wigan Ath	46	7
Frank Corrigan	5 10	11 7	Liverpool	Wigan Ath	45	4
Geoff Gay	5 10	10 9	Romford	Bolton W	—	—
(Contract cancelled September 1978)				Exeter C (on loan)	5+1	—
				Southport	40	5
				Wigan Ath	1	—
Forwards						
John Wilkie	5 7	10 7	Dundee	Ross Co	—	—
				Elgin	—	—
				Halifax	29+8	8
				Morton	—	—
				Wigan Ath	3+1	—
Peter Houghton	5 11	12 7	Liverpool	Wigan Ath	23+3	13
Tony Quinn				Wigan Ath	—	—
Mickey Moore	5 9½	10 11	Chorley	Port Vale	13	—
				Wigan Ath	40+1	9
Derek Brownbill	5 9	10 10	Liverpool	Liverpool	1	—
				Port Vale	84+8	13
				Wigan Ath	20+10	6
Micky Worswick				Wigan Ath	0+1	—
(Contract cancelled November 1978)						
Alan Crompton	5 9	10 8	Manchester	Sunderland	—	—
				Blackburn R	2+2	—
				Wigan Ath	7+6	—
Ian Purdie	5 8½	11 0	Motherwell	Aberdeen	36+3	10
				Dundee	55+4	7
				Motherwell	11+5	3
				Wigan Ath	46	11

WIMBLEDON   DIV. 3

President: Bernie Coleman.
Chairman: Ron Noades.
Vice-Chairman: Jimmy Rose.
Directors: B. W. Down, B. S. Rosser, E. C. Gush, G. Collins, J. J. McElligott, S. Hammam, W. Unwin (plus Chairman and Vice-Chairman).
Manager: Dario Gradi.
Secretary: Adrian Cook.
Year Formed: 1889.   *Turned semi-professional:* 1964.
Limited Company: 1964.
Football League Record: 1977–79 Division 4. 1979– Division 3.
Honours: *Southern League,* Champions 1974–75, 1975–76, 1976–77, Cup Winners: 1969–70, 1975–76, Best season in Division 4: 3rd (promoted) 1978–79.
Record Victory: 6-1 v Torquay U., Division 4, February 28, 1979.
Record Defeat: 0-8 v Everton, F.L. Cup 2nd Rd. August 29, 1978.
Most League Appearances: John Leslie, 86, 1977–79.
Most League Goals: John Leslie, 32, 1977–79.
Most League Goals: 78, Division 4, 1978–79.
Most League Points: 61, Division 4, 1978–79.
Highest League Scorer in a Season: Alan Cork, 22, 1978–79.
Record Transfer Fee Received: £8,000 from Hereford for Billy Holmes, 1977–78 season.
Record Transfer Fee Paid: £45,000 to Q.P.R. for Tommy Cunningham, March 1979.
Managers since 1955: Les Henley, Mike Everitt, Dick Graham, Allen Batsford.
Address of Supporters Club and Club shop: Plough Lane Ground, Durnsford Road.

Plough Lane Ground, Durnsford, Wimbledon, S.W.19 (first used in 1912)
Telephone: 01-946 6311

Ground capacity: 15,000.
Record attendance: 18,000 v HMS Victory in the FA Amateur Cup 1932-33.
Record receipts: £30,600 v Leeds United, FA Cup 4th round replay at Crystal Palace, 1974–75.
How to get there: Nearest station Wimbledon or Haydons Road (SR). South Wimbledon Underground. Buses: 77a from Wimbledon, 189 from Tooting.
Match tickets: Available 14 days prior to game for important matches.
Car parking: On ground and in streets quarter mile from ground.
Entertainments/catering facilities: Three licensed bars and tea bars in main stand, Sportsman Public House adjacent to ground and owned by club.
Handbooks/programmes: Supporters Club Handbook published annually. Club magazine 'Outlook' published monthly plus official programme.
Club colours: Yellow and blue shirts, blue shorts, yellow and blue stockings.
Change colours: All white with blue trim.
Club captain: Les Briley.   *Club nickname:* 'The Dons'.

WIMBLEDON 1978-79 LEAGUE RECORD

Match No.	Date	Venue	Opponents	Result	H/T Score	League Pos'n	Goalscorers	Attendance
1	Aug 19	A	Aldershot	D 1-1	1-1	—	Bryant	3510
2	22	H	Port Vale	W 1-0	1-0	—	Cork	2638
3	26	H	Northampton T	W 4-1	3-1	3	Cork 3, Leslie	2644
4	Sept 1	A	Stockport Co	W 1-0	0-0	3	Cork	5604
5	9	H	Wigan Ath	W 2-1	0-1	3	Denny, Eames (pen)	3217
6	12	A	Grimsby T	D 2-2	0-0	—	Bryant, Cork	6794
7	16	A	Newport Co	W 3-1	0-0	3	Leslie 2, Cork	2903
8	23	H	Reading	W 1-0	0-0	1	Cork	5001
9	25	A	Rochdale	D 0-0	0-0	—		1263
10	30	H	Bradford C	W 2-1	0-1	1	Denny, Parsons	2819
11	Oct 7	A	York C	W 4-1	2-0	1	Parsons, Knowles, Leslie, Cork	3329
12	14	H	Scunthorpe U	W 3-1	2-0	1	Leslie 2, Cork	3808
13	17	H	Crewe Alex	D 1-1	0-0	—	Cork	3555
14	21	A	Huddersfield T	L 0-3	0-1	1		3374
15	28	H	Doncaster R	W 3-2	3-1	1	Leslie 2, Cork	3252
16	Nov 4	A	Barnsley	L 1-3	0-1	2	Galvin	11,761
17	11	H	Stockport Co	W 2-0	1-0	1	Denny 2	3177
18	18	A	Northampton T	D 1-1	1-0	1	Leslie	3623
19	Dec 2	H	Halifax T	W 2-1	1-0	1	Cork 2	2374
20	9	A	Hartlepool U	D 1-1	1-0	1	Denny	3098
21	23	A	AFC Bournemouth	W 2-1	2-1	1	Galliers, Briley	3922
22	26	H	Portsmouth	L 2-4	2-1	—	Knowles 2	7862
23	Feb 3	H	Rochdale	W 3-2	1-2	1	Parsons, Galvin, Denny	3166
24	14	A	Wigan Ath	W 2-1	2-0	—	Leslie 2	6704
25	28	A	Torquay U	W 6-1	2-0	—	Cork 4, Haverson, Leslie	2739
26	Mar 3	H	Huddersfield T	W 2-1	0-1	2	Leslie, Driver	3265
27	6	H	Newport Co	D 0-0	0-0	—		2980
28	9	A	Doncaster R	L 0-1	0-1	3		1927
29	20	H	Grimsby T	L 0-1	0-1	—		2392
30	24	A	Port Vale	L 0-1	0-1	5		2906
31	27	H	Aldershot	W 3-1	1-0	—	Knowles, Parsons, Haverson (pen)	5382
32	31	H	Hereford U	W 2-0	1-0	4	Cork, Leslie	2636
33	Apr 4	A	Bradford C	L 0-1	0-0	—		2701
34	7	A	Halifax T	L 1-2	1-2	6	Ketteridge	1576
35	10	H	AFC Bournemouth	W 4-0	3-0	—	Cork 2, Leslie, Parsons	3205
36	14	A	Portsmouth	D 0-0	0-0	6		11,453
37	16	H	Torquay U	W 5-0	4-0	—	Knowles, Galliers, Leslie, Cunningham, Parsons	4171
38	21	A	Darlington	D 1-1	0-0	5	Leslie	1674
39	25	A	Crewe Alex	W 2-1	2-0	—	Leslie, Parsons	1254
40	28	H	Hartlepool U	W 3-1	0-0	3	Cunningham, Smith T (og), Galliers	3546
41	May 2	A	Reading	L 0-1	0-1	—		13,131
42	5	A	Hereford U	D 0-0	0-0	4		3809
43	8	A	Scunthorpe U	L 0-2	0-1	—		1777
44	11	H	York C	W 2-1	0-1	—	Leslie, Cork	3897
45	14	H	Barnsley	D 1-1	1-0	—	Downes	5794
46	17	H	Darlington	W 2-0	1-0	—	Stone (og), Cunningham	3638

Final League Position: 3

Goalscorers

League (78): Cork 22, Leslie 19, Parsons 7, Denny 6, Knowles 5, Cunningham 3, Galliers 3, Bryant 2, Galvin 2, Haverson 2 (1 a pen), Briley 1, Downes 1, Driver 1, Eames 1 (pen), Ketteridge 1, Own Goals 2.
League Cup (4): Galvin, Galliers, Cork, Own Goal 1.
F.A. Cup (4): Cork 2, Denny, Parsons.

League Cup	First Round		Southend U (a)	0-1
			(h)	4-1
	Second Round		Everton (a)	0-8
F.A. Cup	First Round		Gravesend & Northfleet (a)	0-0
			(h)	1-0
	Second Round		AFC Bournemouth (h)	1-1
			(a)	2-1 (a.e.t.)
	Third Round		Southampton (h)	0-2

Goddard	Bryant	Galvin	Donaldson	Eames	Galliers	Leslie	Briley	Cork	Summerill	Parsons	Connell	Denny	Knowles	Ketteridge	Cowley	Perkins	Haverson	Driver	Priddy	Cunningham	Bowgett	Downes	Harwood	Dziadulewicz	Match No.
1	2	3	4	5	6	7	8	9	10	11															1
1	2	3	6	5	4	7	8	10		11	9														2
1	2	5	6	3	4	8	7	10		11*	9	12													3
1	2	5	6	3	4	7*	8	10		11		9	12												4
1	2	5	6	3	4	7		10*		11		9	12	8											5
1	2	5	6	3	4	7		10	11			9	8												6
1	2	5	6	3	4	7		9	11			8	10												7
1	2	5	6	3	4	7		10	11	12		8	9*												8
1	2	5	6	3	4	7		10	11			8	9												9
1	2	5	4	3	6	7*		10		11		8	9	12											10
1	2	5	6	3	4	7		10		11		8	9												11
1	2	5	6	3	4	7*		10		11		8	9		12										12
1	2	5	6	3	4	7		10		11		8*	9		12										13
1	2	5	6	3	4	7		10	12	11			9*		8										14
1	6		5	3	4	7*		10	12	11			9			2	8								15
1	2	5	6		4	7*		10		11			9		12	3	8								16
1		5	6	3	4	7		10		11		9				2	8								17
1		5	6	3*	4	7		10		11		9	12			2	8								18
1		5	6		4	7	8	10		11		9				2	3								19
1		5	6		3	7	8	10		11		9	12			2*	4								20
1	2	5		6	4	7*	8	10				9	12	11		3									21
1	2	5		6	4	7*	8	10					9	11		3	12								22
1	2	5			9	8			11		10	12	4		6	3	7*								23
1	2	5	3		7			10	11		9		8		6	4									24
	2	5		8*	7			10	11		9		3		6	4	12	1							25
1	2	5		8	7			10	11		9*		4		6	3	12								26
1	2	5		8	7			10	11*		9		4		6	3	12								27
1	2	5		3	8	7*		10	11		9		4		6		12								28
1		5		3	8	7	2	10		12	9		4		6		11*								29
1	6	5		3	8	7	2	10		11	9				12	4*									30
1	2*	5			8	7	4	10		11	12	9			6	3									31
1		5		8	7	4	10			11*	12	9			2	3		6							32
1	5			4	7*	8	10				12	9	11		2	3		6							33
1	5				7		4	10		12	8	9	11		2*	3		6							34
1		3		4	7	8*	10			11		9			2	12		6	5						35
1				4	7	8	10			11		9*			2	3	12	6	5						36
1				4	7	8	10			11		9			2	3		6	5						37
1	12			8	7	4	10			11		9			2	3		6*	5						38
1	12			4	7	8	10			11		9			3*	2		6	5						39
1	12			4	7	8	10			11*		9	3			2		6	5						40
1	2	3		4	7	8	10			11		9*	12					6	5						41
1		3		4	7	8	10						9		2	11		6	5						42
1			3	4	7	8	10						9		2	11*		6	5			12			43
1			3	4	7		10			11		12	8		2			6	5	9*					44
1			3*	4	7	8	10			11		12			2			6	5	9					45
1				4	12	8	10						7		2	3		6		11	5*	9			46
45	27	33	23	26	44	44	26	45	5	34	2	24	23	15	3	26	26	3	1	15	11	3	1	1	
		+ 3s			+ 1s				+ 2s	+ 3s		+ 4s	+ 8s	+ 2s	+ 3s		+ 1s	+ 7s				+ 1s			

WIMBLEDON—PLAYERS

Player and position	Ht	Wt	Birthplace	Clubs	League Appearances	Goals
Goalkeepers						
Dickie Guy	6 2	12 8	Greenwich	Wimbledon	13	—
(Contract cancelled November 1978)						
Ray Goddard	5 10	11 9	Fulham	Orient	279	—
				Morton (on loan)	1	—
				Millwall	80	—
				Wimbledon	63	—
Paul Priddy	6 0	11 8	Isleworth	Brentford	121	—
(non-contract)				Wimbledon	1	—
Defenders						
*Jeffrey Bryant	6 0	11 8	Redhill	Fulham	—	—
				Wimbledon	70+3	9
*Dave Donaldson	6 0	11 4	Hounslow	Wimbledon	61	—
*William Smith				Wimbledon	2	—
*Dave Galvin	6 1	11 11	Denaby Main	Wolverhampton W	5	—
				Gillingham	239+6	17
				Wimbledon	73	7
Brian Bithell	5 7	10 9	Winsford	Stoke C	16+1	—
(Contract cancelled October 1978)				Port Vale (on loan)	2	—
				Wimbledon	6	—
Paul Haverson	5 11		Chigwell	QPR	—	—
				Wimbledon	26+1	2
Steve Perkins	5 11	11 0	London	Chelsea	—	—
				QPR	2	—
				Wimbledon	26	—
Paul Bowgett	6 1		Hitchin	Tottenham H	—	—
				Wimbledon	11	—
Tommy Cunningham	6 0	11 3	London	Chelsea	—	—
				QPR	27+3	2
				Wimbledon	15	3
Lee Harwood	6 0		Southall	Southampton	—	—
				Wimbledon	1	—
Midfield						
*Dave Bassett	5 8	11 2	Watford	Watford	—	—
				Chelsea	—	—
				Wimbledon	35	—
Terry Eames	5 10	11 1	Croydon	C Palace	—	—
				Wimbledon	43+1	1
Paul Denny	5 9	10 8	Croydon	Southend U	8+1	2
				Wimbledon	47+7	7
Les Briley	5 6½	9 11	Lambeth	Chelsea	—	—
				Hereford U	60+1	2
				Wimbledon	39+1	2
Wally Downes	5 10		London	Wimbledon	3	1
Mark Dziadulewicz	5 7	9 12	Wimbledon	Southend U	—	—
				Wimbledon	1+1	—
Francis Cowley	5 8¼	10 1	London	Derby Co	—	—
(Contract cancelled April 1979)				Wimbledon	5+3	—
Steve Ketteridge	5 8¼	10 7	Stevenage	Wimbledon	15+2	1
Forwards						
Alan Cork	6 0		Derby	Derby Co	—	—
				Lincoln C (on loan)	5	—
				Wimbledon	62	26
*Roger Connell	6 1	12 4	Wembley	Wimbledon	30+2	14
John Leslie	5 8	11 2	London	Charlton Ath	—	—
				Wimbledon	84+2	16
Steve Galliers	5 6	9 7	Chorley	Wimbledon	66+5	4
Phil Summerill	5 10¼	11 2	Birmingham	Birmingham C	107+8	46
(Contract cancelled December 1978)				Huddersfield T	48+6	11
				Millwall	83+4	20
				Wimbledon	27+4	4
Steve Parsons	6 0	12 7	London	Wimbledon	58+3	12
Phil Driver	5 10		Huddersfield	Luton T	—	—
				Wimbledon	3+7	1
Ray Knowles	5 11		Southall	Wimbledon	23+8	5

WOLVERHAMPTON WANDERERS DIV. 1

President: J. R. Ireland.
Chairman: Harry J. Marshall.
Vice-Chairman: W. C. Sproson.
Directors: G. S. Clark, M. A. Goody, G. P. Devine.
Manager: John Barnwell.   *Secretary:* P. A. Shaw.
Assistant Manager: Richie Barker
Year Formed: 1877.   *Turned Professional:* 1888.
Limited Company: 1923.
Previous Grounds: 1877, Goldthorn Hill; 1884, Dudley Road; 1889, Molineux.
Previous Name: 1880, St. Luke's, Blakenhall combined with The Wanderers to become Wolverhampton Wanderers.
Football League Record: 1888 Original Members of the League. 1906–23 Division 2. 1923–24 Division 3(N). 1924–32 Division 2. 1932–65 Division 1. 1965–67 Division 2. 1967–76 Division 1. 1976–77 Division 2. 1977–   Division 1.
Honours: *Football League*, Division 1, Champions: 1953–54, 1957–58, 1958–59; Runners-up: 1937–38, 1938–39, 1949–50, 1954–55, 1959–60. Division 2, Champions: 1931–32, 1976–77; Runners-up: 1966–67. Division 3(N), Champions: 1923–24. *F.A. Cup*, Winners: 1893, 1908, 1949, 1960; Runners-up: 1889, 1896, 1921, 1939. *Football League Cup*, Winners, 1973–74.
European Competitions: *European Cup:* 1958–59, 1959–60. *European Cup-Winners Cup:* 1960–61. *UEFA Cup:* 1971–72 (Runners-up), 1973–74, 1974–75.
Record Victory: 14-0 v Crosswell's Brewery, F.A. Cup, 2nd Rd., 1886–87.
Record Defeat: 1-10 v Newton Heath, Division 1, Oct. 15th, 1892.
Most League Points: 64, Division 1, 1957–58.
Most League Goals: 115, Division 2, 1931–32.
Highest League Scorer in Season: Dennis Westcott, 37, Division 1, 1946–47.
Most Capped Player: Billy Wright, 105, England (70 consecutive).
Most League Appearances: Billy Wright, 491, 1946–59.
Most League Goals in Total Aggregate: Bill Hartill, 164, 1928–35.
Record Transfer Fee Received: £240,000 from Arsenal for Alan Sunderland, Nov. 1977.
Record Transfer Fee Paid: £150,000 to Hull C. for Peter Daniel, May 1978.
Managers Since the War: Ted Vizard, Stan Cullis, Andy Beattie, Ron Allen, Bill McGarry, Sammy Chung.
Address of Club Shop or Boutique: 'The Lair', Wolverhampton W. F.C., Molineux Grounds, Wolverhampton, Staffordshire.

Molineux Grounds, Wolverhampton WV1 4QR. Telephone Wolverhampton 24053/4. *Telegraphic address:* 'Wanderers, Wolverhampton'. *Ground capacity:* 53,000. *Record attendance:* 61,315 v Liverpool, F.A. Cup 5th Rd., February 11, 1939. *Record receipts:* £54,714 v. Leeds Utd., F.A. Cup 6th Rd., March 19th, 1977. *Pitch measurements:* 115 yds × 72 yds.

How to get there: The ground is within easy walking distance of both Wolverhampton High Level railway station and the town centre. For this reason the local bus company does not operate special services on match days.
Match tickets: Seats are bookable by post one month before the match.
Car parking: Parking is available around 'The West Park', in various side streets, and at the Molineux Hotel.
Entertainments/catering facilities: Entertainment at the Wolves Sporting Club a few yards from the ground. Bars are provided all around the ground.
Club shop: The club shop is situated on the official car park at the ground.
Handbooks/programmes: No handbook. Programmes available on subscription.
Extra information: Wolves scored over 100 First Division goals in four successive seasons (1957–58 to 1960–61).
Club Colours: Old gold shirts, black collar and cuffs, black shorts, old gold stockings. *Change Colours:* White shirt, white shorts, white stockings. *Club Captain:*   *First Team Trainer/Coach:* Brian Owen. *Club Nickname:* 'Wolves'.

WOLVERHAMPTON WANDERERS 1978–79 LEAGUE RECORD

Match No.	Date	Venue	Opponents	Result	H/T Score	League Pos'n	Goalscorers	Attendance
1	Aug 19	A	Aston Villa	L 0-1	0-0	—		43,922
2	22	H	Chelsea	L 0-1	0-1	—		22,041
3	26	A	Leeds U	L 0-3	0-2	22		26,267
4	Sept 2	H	Bristol C	W 2-0	1-0	19	Rodgers (og), Hibbitt	16,121
5	9	A	Southampton	L 2-3	0-1	20	Bell, Daniel (pen)	22,060
6	16	H	Ipswich T	L 1-3	1-2	21	Beattie (og)	16,409
7	23	A	Everton	L 0-2	0-2	22		30,895
8	30	H	QPR	W 1-0	0-0	20	Daniel (pen)	14,250
9	Oct 7	A	Nottingham F	L 1-3	0-1	20	Eves	29,313
10	14	H	Arsenal	W 1-0	0-0	20	Eves	19,664
11	21	A	Middlesbrough	L 0-2	0-1	20		19,389
12	28	H	Manchester U	L 2-4	1-3	21	Hibbitt, Daley	23,979
13	Nov 4	A	Derby Co	L 1-4	0-2	21	Carr	20,658
14	11	H	Aston Villa	L 0-4	0-2	21		23,289
15	18	A	Leeds U	D 1-1	1-1	21	Daniel	18,961
16	21	A	Bristol C	W 1-0	0-0	—	Daley	17,421
17	25	A	Tottenham H	L 0-1	0-1	20		35,450
18	Dec 9	A	Bolton W	L 1-3	0-1	20	Berry	21,006
19	16	H	WBA	L 0-3	0-1	20		29,117
20	26	H	Birmingham C	W 2-1	1-0	20	Hibbitt, Daniel (pen)	26,315
21	30	H	Coventry C	D 1-1	1-0	20	Daley	21,514
22	Jan 17	A	Southampton	W 2-0	2-0	—	Carr, Bell	15,104
23	20	A	Ipswich T	L 1-3	1-2	20	Berry	17,965
24	Feb 3	H	Everton	W 1-0	1-0	20	Daley	21,892
25	10	A	QPR	D 3-3	1-0	20	Bell, Clarke, Patching	11,814
26	24	A	Arsenal	W 1-0	1-0	18	Richards	32,215
27	Mar 3	H	Middlesbrough	L 1-3	1-1	19	Richards	18,782
28	7	A	Norwich C	D 0-0	0-0	—		15,427
29	20	A	Liverpool	L 0-2	0-1	—		39,695
30	24	A	Chelsea	W 2-1	0-0	19	Richards, Rafferty	20,502
31	27	H	Manchester C	D 1-1	1-0	—	Carr	19,998
32	Apr 3	H	Tottenham H	W 3-2	1-1	—	Richards, Daley, Hibbitt	19,819
33	7	A	Manchester C	L 1-3	0-1	19	Hibbitt	32,298
34	10	A	Liverpool	L 0-1	0-1	—		30,857
35	14	H	Birmingham C	D 1-1	1-1	19	Richards	20,556
36	16	H	Norwich C	W 1-0	1-0	—	Hibbitt	18,457
37	21	A	WBA	D 1-1	0-0	19	Richards	32,385
38	24	H	Derby Co	W 4-0	2-0	—	Rafferty, Berry, Daley, Daniel	19,036
39	28	H	Bolton W	D 1-1	0-0	18	Richards	18,225
40	30	H	Nottingham F	W 1-0	0-0	—	Richards	23,613
41	May 5	A	Coventry C	L 0-3	0-2	18		21,825
42	7	A	Manchester U	L 2-3	1-2	—	Bailey (og), Richards	39,402

Final League Position: 18

Goalscorers

League (44): Richards 9, Daley 6, Daniel 5 (3 pens), Bell 3, Carr 3, Berry 3, Rafferty 2, Eves 2, Patching 1, Clarke 1, Own Goals 3.

F.A. Cup (10): Bell 2, Rafferty 2, Daley, Hibbitt, Patching, Carr, Daniel (pen) Own Goal 1.

League Cup:	Second Round	Reading (a)	0-1
F.A. Cup:	Third Round	Brighton & H A (a)	3-2
	Fourth Round	Newcastle U (a)	1-1
		(h)	1-0
	Fifth Round	C. Palace (a)	1-0
	Sixth Round	Shrewsbury T (h)	1-1
		(a)	3-1
	Semi-Final	Arsenal (h)	0-2

Bradshaw	Daniel	Palmer	Parkin	Hazell	McAlle	Hibbitt	Carr	Rafferty	Eves	Daley	Bell	Berry	Richards	Clarke	Patching	Arkwright	Pierce	Brazier	Moss	Black	Match No.
1	2	3	4	5	6	7	8	9	10*	11	12										1
1	2	3	4	5*	6	7	8	10	9	11	12										2
1	2	3	4		6	7	8	10		11		5	9								3
1	2	3	4		6	7	8			11	10	5	9								4
1	2	3	4		6	7*	8	9		11	10	5		12							5
1	4*	2	3	5	6		8	12		11	10		9	7							6
1	4	2	3	5	6		8		12	11	10		9*	7							7
1	4	2	3	5	6		8	9*	10	11				7	12						8
1	4	2	3	5	6		8*		10	11	12			7	9						9
	4	2	3		6	7		12	10	11			8*		9	1	5				10
	4	2*	3		6	7			10	11	12		9		8	1	5				11
	2		3		6	7	8	9	10	11				4		1	5				12
1		2	3	4	6	7	8	9	10	11							5				13
1	4	2	3		6	7	8*	10		9	5	12					11				14
1	4	2	3	5		7		10	8	9	6						11				15
1	4	2	3	5		7	8		10	11	9	6									16
1	4	2	3	5		7*	8	12	10	11	9	6									17
1	4	2	3	5		7	11	10		8	9	6									18
1	4	2	3	5		7	11	10		8	9	6									19
1	4	2	3		5	7	11		10	8	9	6									20
1	4	2	3		5	7	11		10	8	9	6									21
1	4	2	3		5	7	11		10	8	9	6									22
1	4	2	3		5	7	11		10*	8	9	6		12							23
1	4	2	3		6	7	11		10	8	9	5									24
1	4*	2	3		5	7	11			8	9	6		10	12						25
1	4	2	3		5	7	11	12		9	6	10*		8							26
1	4	2	3		5	7*	11		12			6	10	9	8						27
1	4	2	3		5	7	11	9		8		6	10*	12							28
1	4	2	3		5	7	11	9		8		6	10								29
1	4	2	3		5	7	11	9		8		6	10								30
1	4	2	3		5	7	11	9		8		6	10								31
1	4	2	3		5	7	11	9		8		6	10								32
1	4	2	3		5	7	11	9		8		6	10								33
1	4	2	3		5	7	11	9		8		6	10								34
1	4	2	3		5	7*	11	9		8		6	10	12							35
1	4	2	3		5	7	11*	9		8		6	10	12							36
1	4	2	3		5	7		9		8		6	10	11							37
1	4	2	3		5	7		9		8		6	10	11							38
1	4	2	3		5	7		9		8		6	10	11							39
1	4	2	3		5	7	11	9		8			10				6				40
1	4*	2	3	12	5	7	11	9		8			10				6				41
1		2	3		5		7	9		8		6	10	11*				12	4		42
39	40	41	42	12	37	37	36	24	17	39	17	30	19	6	11	3	3	6	1	2	
				+ 1s				+ 3s	+ 2s	+ 1s	+ 4s			+ 2s	+ 5s	+ 1s		+ 1s			

WOLVERHAMPTON WANDERERS—PLAYERS

Player and position	Ht	Wt	Birthplace	Clubs	League Appearances	Goals
Goalkeepers						
Gary Pierce	6 2½	13 4	Bury	Huddersfield T	23	—
				Wolverhampton W	98	—
Paul Bradshaw	6 2½	12 1	Altrincham	Blackburn R	78	—
				Wolverhampton W	73	—
Defenders						
Derek Parkin	5 8½	11 0	Newcastle	Huddersfield T	60+1	1
				Wolverhampton W	420	6
Geoff Palmer	5 10	10 5	Cannock	Wolverhampton W	207	4
Bob Hazell	6 1	12 3	Jamaica	Wolverhampton W	32+1	1
George Berry (Wales)	5 11	11 10	Morpeth	Ipswich T	—	—
				Wolverhampton W	38	3
John McAlle	5 11¼	11 4	Liverpool	Wolverhampton W	369+13	—
Colin Brazier	6 1	11 0	Birmingham	Wolverhampton W	20+2	—
Paul Moss	5 7	10 2	Birmingham	Wolverhampton W	—	—
Peter Daniel	5 8	10 10	Hull	Hull C	113	9
				Wolverhampton W	40	5
John Humphrey	5 10	10 4	Middlesex	Wolverhampton W	—	—
Midfield						
Willie Carr (Scotland)	5 7¾	10 4	Glasgow	Coventry C	245+5	32
				Wolverhampton W	149+3	19
Maurice Daly	5 8	9 10	Dublin	Wolverhampton W	28+4	—
(Eire) (Contract cancelled August 1978)						
Ken Hibbitt	5 10	11 4	Bradford	Bradford PA	13+3	—
				Wolverhampton W	303+11	70
John Black	5 7	11 0	Glasgow	Wolverhampton W	5+1	—
Steve Daley	5 10¼	12 0	Barnsley	Wolverhampton W	191+21	37
Hugh Atkinson	6 0	11 7	Dublin	Wolverhampton W	—	—
Michael Matthews	5 8	10 9	Hull	Wolverhampton W	—	—
Mike Hollifield				Wolverhampton W	—	—
Forwards						
Norman Bell	5 11	12 10	Sunderland	Wolverhampton W	41+9	11
John Richards (England)	5 9	11 1	Warrington	Wolverhampton W	264+13	124
Martin Patching	5 11	11 4	Rotherham	Wolverhampton W	73+12	10
Melvyn Eves	5 10	10 9	Wednesbury	Wolverhampton W	27+4	5
Ian Arkwright	5 8½	10 8	Shafton	Wolverhampton W	3+1	—
Chris Fleming	5 8	9 10	Bangor	Wolverhampton W	—	—
Wayne Clarke	5 11¼	10 6¼	Wolverhampton	Wolverhampton W	6+3	1
Bill Rafferty	5 10	10 7	Glasgow	Coventry C	27	3
				Blackpool	35+1	9
				Plymouth Arg	89+1	35
				Carlisle U	72	27
				Wolverhampton W	37+3	6
Craig Moss	5 8	10 5	Birmingham	Wolverhampton W	1	—

Also retained: Peter Knowles

WREXHAM  DIV. 2

President: W. B. N. Kington, T.D.
Chairman: F. J. Tomlinson.
Directors: T. H. Dodd, H. G. Phillips, A. W. Gaade, G. Morris, R. E. A. Clark, A. Morris, P. Griffiths.
Manager: Arfon Griffiths, M.B.E.
General Secretary: C. N. Wilson, F.A.A.I.
Year Formed: 1873 (oldest Club in Wales).
Turned Professional: 1912. *Limited Company:* 1912.
Previous Ground: Acton Park.

Football League Record:
1921 Original Members of Division 3(N).
1958–60 Division 3.
1960–62 Division 4.
1962–64 Division 3.
1964–70 Division 4.
1970–78 Division 3.
1978– Division 2.

Honours: *Football League,* best season in Division 2: 15th 1978–79, Division 3, Champions 1977–78. Division 3(N), Runners-up 1932–33. Division 4, Runners-up: 1969–70. *F.A. Cup,* best season: 6th Rd., 1973–74, 1977–78. *Football League Cup,* best season 5th Rd., 1961, 1978. *Welsh Cup,* winners 21 times.

European Competition: *Cup-Winners Cup:* 1972–73, 1975–76, 1978–79.

Record Victory: 10-1 v Hartlepools U., Division 4, Mar. 3rd, 1962.

Record Defeat: 0-9 v Brentford, Division 3, Oct. 15th, 1963.

Most League Points: 61, Division 4, 1969–70, Division 3, 1977–78.

Most League Goals: 106, Division 3(N), 1932–33.

Highest League Scorer in Season: Tom Bamford, 44, Division 3(N), 1933–34.

Most League Goals in Total Aggregate: Tom Bamford, 175, 1928–34.

Most Capped Player: Horace Blew, 22, Wales.

Most League Appearances: Arfon Griffiths, 592, 1959–61; 1962–79.

Record Transfer Fee Received: £300,000 from Manchester U. for Mickey Thomas, Nov. 1978 and £300,000 from Manchester C. for Bobby Shinton, July 1979.

Record Transfer Fee Paid: £210,000 to Liverpool for Joey Jones, Oct. 1978.

Managers Since the War: Tom Williams, Les McDowell, Peter Jackson, Cliff Lloyd, John Love, Bill Morris, Ken Barnes, Bill Morris, Jack Rowley, Alvan Williams, John Neal.
Address of Supporters Club: Secretary, John Roberts, 10, Sandringham Rd.

Racecourse Ground, Mold Road, Wrexham. Telephone Wrexham 0978 262129. *Telegraphic address:* 'Football, Wrexham'. *Ground capacity:* 30,000 (18,000 covered). *Record attendance:* 34,445 v Manchester U., F.A. Cup 4th Rd., January 26, 1957. *Record receipts:* £25,107 v Anderlecht, European Cup-Winners' Cup Quarter-Final, March 17, 1976. *Pitch measurements:* 117 yds × 75 yds.

How to get there: Wrexham General railway station is only 200 yards from the ground. Trains run from Chester and Shrewsbury. Bus services from outlying districts to town.
Match tickets: Stand tickets bookable in advance.
Car parking: Parking grounds at St Marks, Bodhyfryd Square, Eagles Meadows, Old Guild Hall, Hill Street, Holt Street, and Town Hill, Hill Street.
Entertainments/catering facilities: A social club and four catering kiosks at the ground.
Club shop: Situated on the Kopside of the ground; stocks all types of souvenirs.
Handbooks/Programmes: No handbook at present. Programmes available on subscription.
Extra information: Season tickets available for all parts of the ground and all stands except the Crispin Lane Stand.

Club Colours: Red shirts with white facings, white shorts with red stripe, white stockings.
Change Colours: White shirts, red trim, black shorts, black stockings with white/red tops.
Club Captain: Gareth Davis.
Club Nickname: 'The Robins'.

WREXHAM 1978-79 LEAGUE RECORD

Match No.	Date	Venue	Opponents	Result	H/T Score	League Pos'n	Goalscorers	Attendance
1	Aug 19	H	Brighton & HA	D 0-0	0-0	—		14,081
2	22	A	Fulham	W 1-0	0-0	—	Lyons	6135
3	26	A	Orient	W 1-0	0-0	3	Whittle (pen)	6416
4	Sept 2	A	Leicester C	D 0-0	0-0	3		12,785
5	9	A	Charlton Ath	D 1-1	0-1	5	Thomas	8356
6	16	H	Newcastle U	D 0-0	0-0	3		14,091
7	23	A	Bristol R	L 1-2	1-1	5	McNeil	7619
8	30	H	Cardiff C	L 1-2	0-1	13	Lyons	11,766
9	Oct 7	A	Luton T	L 1-2	1-2	15	Thomas	8682
10	14	H	Cambridge U	W 2-0	1-0	13	Thomas, Whittle	9807
11	21	H	Crystal Palace	D 0-0	0-0	14		15,132
12	28	A	Blackburn R	D 1-1	0-1	13	Thomas	9906
13	Nov 4	H	Notts Co	W 3-1	1-0	9	McNeil, Thomas (pen), Whittle	10,891
14	11	A	Brighton & HA	L 1-2	0-1	13	Shinton	19,659
15	18	H	Orient	W 3-1	1-0	10	Lyons, Gray (og), Hill	9122
16	22	A	Leicester C	D 1-1	1-0	—	Thomas	14,734
17	25	H	Millwall	W 3-0	3-0	8	McNeil, Hill (pen), Lyons	7080
18	Dec 9	H	West Ham U	W 4-3	2-1	6	Lyons 3 (2 pens), Hill	15,787
19	16	A	Stoke C	L 0-3	0-1	9		18,358
20	26	A	Preston NE	L 1-2	0-2	—	Lyons (pen)	17,820
21	Feb 24	A	Cambridge U	L 0-1	0-1	17		5297
22	28	H	Sheffield U	W 4-0	2-0	—	Whittle, Shinton 2, Fox	9764
23	Mar 3	A	Crystal Palace	L 0-1	0-0	17		15,154
24	7	A	Sunderland	L 0-1	0-1	—		25,017
25	10	H	Blackburn R	W 2-1	1-0	17	Whittle, Buxton	9407
26	21	H	Burnley	L 0-1	0-1	—		5000
27	24	H	Fulham	D 1-1	0-1	17	Whittle	9046
28	Apr 2	H	Charlton Ath	D 1-1	1-1	—	Jones J	7518
29	7	H	Oldham Ath	W 2-0	1-0	17	Shinton 2	8418
30	14	H	Preston NE	W 2-1	2-1	16	Lyons (pen), McNeil	14,419
31	16	A	Burnley	D 0-0	0-0	—		9361
32	17	A	Sheffield U	D 1-1	1-1	—	Tibbott (og)	19,846
33	21	H	Stoke C	L 0-1	0-1	14		20,211
34	24	A	Oldham Ath	L 0-1	0-1	—		6258
35	28	A	West Ham U	D 1-1	0-1	17	Shinton	28,865
36	May 1	A	Notts Co	D 1-1	1-1	—	Giles	4374
37	5	H	Sunderland	L 1-2	0-1	17	Jones J	19,133
38	7	H	Luton T	W 2-0	1-0	—	Buxton, Williams	7842
39	8	A	Newcastle U	L 0-2	0-1	—		7133
40	10	H	Bristol R	L 0-1	0-0	—		6136
41	14	A	Cardiff C	L 0-1	0-0	—		11,910
42	17	A	Millwall	D 2-2	0-0	—	Lyons, Whittle	4865

Final League Position: 15

Goalscorers

League (45): Lyons 10 (4 pens), Whittle 7 (1 a pen), Shinton 6, Thomas 6 (1 a pen), McNeil 4, Hill 3 (1 a pen), Buxton 2, Jones 2, Fox 1, Giles 1, Williams 1, Own Goals 2.

League Cup (5): Davies, Cartwright, Whittle, Shinton, McNeil (pen).

F.A. Cup (11): Lyons 3 (1 a pen), McNeil 3, Shinton 2, Cegielski, Cartwright, Davis.

League Cup	First Round	Bury (h)	2-0
		(a)	2-1
	Second Round	Norwich C (h)	1-3
F.A. Cup	Third Round	Stockport Co (h)	6-2
	Fourth Round	Tottenham H (a)	3-3
		(h)	2-3 (a.e.t.)

Davies	Evans	Dwyer	Davis	Roberts J	Thomas	Shinton	Sutton	McNeil	Whittle	Cartwright	Lyons	Hill	Kenworthy	Williams	Cegielski	Niedzwiecki	Griffiths	Jones J	Giles	Fox	Buxton	Jones F	Roberts I	Match No.
1	2	3	4	5	6	7*	8	9	10	11	12													1
1	2*	3	4	5	6	7	8	9	10	11	12													2
1		2	4	5	6	7	8	9*	10	11	12	3												3
1			4	5	6	7	8	9	10*	11		2		3	12									4
1			4	5	6	7	8	9	10	11		2		3*	12									5
1			4	5	6	7	8	9		3	11	10*	2		12									6
1			4	5	6	7	8	9		3	11	10*	2		12									7
			4	5	6	7*	8	9		3	11	12	2	10		1								8
			4	5	6	7	8	9		3	11	12	2			1	10*							9
	12		4	5	6	7*	8	9		3	11	10	2			1								10
	3		4	5	6	7	8	9	10		11			1		2								11
1	3	4		6	7	8	9			10	12		5	11*	2									12
1	3	4	5	6	7	8	9	11		10*	12				2									13
1	3	4	5	6	7	8	9			10*	11		12		2									14
1	3	4	5	6	7	8	9			10	11				2									15
1	3	4	5	6*	7	8	9			10	11		12		2									16
1	6	4	5		7	8	9			10	11		2		3									17
1	12	3	4	5		7	8	9*		10	11		6		2									18
1	6	10*	4	5		7	8			9	11		2		12	3								19
1	12		4	5*		7	8			9	11		2			3		6	10					20
1			4	5		7	12	9		8	10		2*			3		6	11					21
1				5		7	2	9	12	8	10*		4			3		6	11					22
1				5		7	2	9	12	8	10		4			3*		6	11					23
1				5		7	2		3	8	10		4					6	11	9				24
1				5		7	2	10	8	9*			3					4	6	11	12			25
1				5		7	12	9	3	8	10*		2					4	6	11				26
1	4		5			7	8		9	10	12		2					3	6	11*				27
1	3		5			7	8	12	10	11			2					4	6	9*				28
1	3		5			7	8	9	10	11*			2					4	6	12				29
1	3	4*	5			7	8	9	10	11	12							2	6					30
1	3		5			8	9	10		7			2					4	6	11				31
1	3		5			8		10		7			2					4	6	11	9			32
1	3		5			7	2	10*	8	9								4	6	11	12			33
1	3		5			7	2		8*	9			12					4	6	11	10			34
1	3		5			7	8	9		10*			2					4	6	11	12			35
	3		5			7*	2	9		8			12	4	1				6	11	10			36
1	3		5				8	9					7	2				4	6	11	10			37
1	3						8*	9					7	2				5	6	11	10	4	12	38
1	3		5				8	9		7				2				4	6	11	10			39
1	9		5				8			7				3				2	6	11	10	4		40
1	3		5			7	8	12		9				2				4	6	11	10*			41
	3		5			7		12		9				2	1	8*	4	6	11	10				42
36	3	28	22	40	16	36	39	30	22	23	28	15	2	3	24	6	3	30	23	21	10	2		
	+ 2s	+ 1s				+ 2s	+ 1s	+ 4s		+ 7s	+ 2s		+ 3s	+ 5s		+ 1s		+ 1s	+ 3s		+ 1s			

WREXHAM—PLAYERS

Player and position	Ht	Wt	Birthplace	Clubs	League Appearances	Goals
Goalkeepers						
Eddie Niedzwiecki	6 0	11 0	Wrexham	Wrexham	21	—
Dai Davies (Wales)	6 1	13 3½	Ammanford	Swansea C	9	—
				Everton	83	—
				Swansea C (on loan)	6	—
				Wrexham	66	—
Defenders						
Gareth Davis (Wales)	5 10½	11 7	Bangor	Wrexham	396+6	8
Mickey Evans	5 9¾	11 2	Gaesws	Wrexham	373+12	19
Alan Hill	5 11	11 4	Chester	Wrexham	74+6	3
Wayne Cegielski	6 0	12 0	Bedwellty	Tottenham H	—	—
				Northampton T (on loan)	11	—
				Wrexham	37+10	—
John Roberts (Wales)	6 0	12 2	Swansea	Swansea C	36+1	16
				Northampton T	62	11
				Arsenal	56+3	4
				Birmingham C	61+5	1
				Wrexham	125	5
Steve Kenworthy	6 1	11 6	Wrexham	Wrexham	3	—
Joey Jones (Wales)	5 10	11 7	Llandudno	Wrexham	98	2
				Liverpool	72	3
				Wrexham	30	2
Midfield						
*Arfon Griffiths (Wales)	5 6	10 4½	Wrexham	Wrexham	42	8
				Arsenal	15	2
				Wrexham	544+6	115
Mel Sutton	5 10	10 10	Birmingham	Cardiff C	135+3	5
				Wrexham	288+3	19
Alan Dwyer	5 7	10 7	Liverpool	Wrexham	135+6	2
Les Cartwright (Wales)	5 9	10 13	Aberdare	Coventry C	50+18	3
				Wrexham	64	4
David Giles	5 5	10 4	Cardiff	Cardiff C	51+8	3
				Wrexham	23	1
*Elfyn Edwards	5 10½	11 4	Aberystwyth	Wrexham	—	—
Forwards						
Graham Whittle	5 9	10 3	Liverpool	Wrexham	372+14	90
John Lyons	5 11	11 12	Buckley	Wrexham	63+23	23
Bobby Shinton	5 10	11 7	West Bromwich	Walsall	78+1	20
				Cambridge U	99	25
				Wrexham	128	37
Dixie McNeil	5 10	11 12	Melton Mowbray	Leicester C	—	—
				Exeter C	31	11
				Northampton T	84+1	33
				Lincoln C	96+1	53
				Hereford U	128+1	85
				Wrexham	53+1	17
Steve Buxton	5 5	9 8	Birmingham	Wrexham	10+4	2
Steve Fox	5 7½	11 2	Tamworth	Birmingham C	26+3	1
				Wrexham	21+1	1
Peter Williams	5 8	10 11	Wrexham	Wrexham	3+3	1

Ian Roberts (non-contract) 1 sub
Frank Jones (non-contract) 2 apps

YORK CITY

DIV. 4

Chairman: M. D. B. Sinclair.
Directors: R. B. Strachan, M.A., LL.B., F.C.I.S, F. H. Magson, D. M. Craig, J.P., B. A. Houghton, C. Webb.
Manager: Charlie Wright. *Secretary:* S. B. Winship.
Medical Officer: Dr. A. I. MacLeod.
Year Formed: 1922. *Turned Professional:* 1922.
Limited Company: 1922.
Previous Grounds: 1922, Fulfordgate; 1932, Bootham Crescent.

Football League Record:
1929 Elected to Division 3(N).

1958–59 Division 4.	1971–74 Division 3.
1959–60 Division 3.	1974–76 Division 2.
1960–65 Division 4.	1976–77 Division 3.
1965–66 Division 3.	1977– Division 4.
1966–71 Division 4.	

Honours: Football League: best season: 15th, Div. 2, 1974–75. Division 4, Promoted 1958–59 (3rd), 1964–65 (3rd), 1970–71 (4th). *F.A. Cup,* best season, semi-finalists: 1955, when in Division 3. *Football League Cup,* best season: 5th Rd., 1962.

Record Victory: 9-1 v Southport, Division 3(N), Feb. 2nd, 1957.
Record Defeat: 0-12 v Chester, Division 3(N), Feb. 1st, 1936.
Most League Points: 62, Division 4, 1964–65.
Most League Goals: 92, Division 3(N), 1954–55.
Highest League Scorer in Season: Bill Fenton, 31, Division 3(N), 1951–52; Arthur Bottom, 31, Division 3(N), 1955–56.
Most League Goals in Total Aggregate: Norman Wilkinson, 125, 1954–66.
Most Capped Player: Peter Scott, 7 (10), N. Ireland.
Most League Appearances: Barry Jackson, 481, 1958–70.
Record Transfer Fee Received: £35,000 from Sheffield U. for Cliff Calvert, Oct. 1975.
Record Transfer Fee Paid: £18,000 to AFC Bournemouth for Micky Cave, August 1974.
Managers Since the War: Tom Mitchell, Dick Duckworth, Charlie Spencer, Jimmy McCormack, Sam Bartram, Tom Lockie, Joe Shaw, Tom Johnston, Wilf McGuinness.
Address of Supporters Club: G. J. Mortimer, Secretary, 2 Plantation Grove, Boroughbridge Road, York.

Bootham Crescent, York. Telephone: York 24447. *Telegraphic address:* 'City Football Club, York'. *Ground capacity:* 16,529. *Record attendance:* 28,123 v Huddersfield T., F.A. Cup, 5th Rd., March 5, 1938. *Record receipts:* £9,856 v Arsenal, F.A. Cup 3rd Rd. replay, January 7, 1975. *Pitch measurements:* 115 yds × 75 yds.

How to get there: Buses 2, 2a, and 8 every 10 minutes from York railway station to the ground.
Match tickets: On sale 14 days prior to match.
Car parking: Ample parking in side-streets.
Entertainments/catering facilities: Licensed Social Club open to members only. Three tea bars on the ground. Drinks available at half-time in front of the Popular Stand and in the officials' car park.
Club shop: Selling all types of souvenirs.
Handbooks/programmes: Programmes available on subscription, details available from the Secretary. Programme shop at the ground stocking a wide variety of English, Scottish and non-League programmes.
Extra information: One of only four (now five) Third Division clubs to reach the semi-finals of the F.A. Cup (in 1954-55).
Club Colours: Red shirts with red and blue collar and cuffs, navy blue shorts with white and red stripe. Stockings white with blue and red hoops on turnover.
Change Colours: Gold shirts, gold shorts, and gold stockings.
Club Captain: Roy Kay.
First Team Trainer/Physiotherapist: John Simpson.
Club Nickname: 'Minster Men'.

YORK CITY 1978-79 LEAGUE RECORD

Match No.	Date	Venue	Opponents	Result	H/T Score	League Pos'n	Goalscorers	Attendance
1	Aug 19	A	Rochdale	W 2-1	1-0	—	Staniforth, Randall	1241
2	22	H	Portsmouth	W 5-3	1-1	—	Staniforth 2, Randall 2, Loggie	2513
3	26	H	Doncaster R	D 1-1	0-0	4	Randall	3609
4	Sept 2	A	Barnsley	L 0-3	0-2	7		8599
5	9	H	Northampton T	W 1-0	0-0	6	Staniforth	2358
6	12	A	Halifax T	W 1-0	0-0	—	Randall	1701
7	15	A	Stockport Co	L 0-2	0-1	8		6103
8	23	H	Wigan Ath	L 0-1	0-1	13		3307
9	26	H	Hereford U	W 1-0	0-0	—	Randall	2358
10	30	A	Newport Co	D 1-1	1-1	10	Loggie	3021
11	Oct 7	H	Wimbledon	L 1-4	0-2	11	Loggie	3329
12	14	A	Bradford C	L 1-2	0-1	11	Randall	4026
13	17	H	Torquay U	D 0-0	0-0	—		2084
14	21	A	Reading	L 0-3	0-1	16		12,031
15	28	H	Scunthorpe U	W 1-0	0-0	14	Staniforth	1970
16	Nov 4	A	Huddersfield T	L 0-1	0-0	15		3696
17	11	H	Barnsley	L 0-1	0-0	18		6900
18	18	A	Doncaster R	W 2-1	1-1	16	Randall, Wellings	2479
19	Dec 9	A	AFC Bournemouth	W 2-1	1-1	14	Clements, Staniforth	3323
20	23	A	Grimsby T	L 0-3	0-1	16		4339
21	26	H	Hartlepool U	D 1-1	0-0	—	Faulkner	3825
22	Feb 3	A	Hereford U	L 0-1	0-1	19		3107
23	24	H	Bradford C	D 2-2	1-1	19	Staniforth, Loggie	4022
24	28	A	Wigan Ath	D 1-1	0-1	—	Loggie	5896
25	Mar 3	H	Reading	L 0-1	0-1	20		2654
26	6	A	Darlington	W 1-0	1-0	—	Staniforth	1173
27	10	A	Scunthorpe U	W 3-2	1-2	17	Randall 2, Clements	2261
28	13	H	Halifax T	W 2-0	1-0	—	Loggie, Staniforth	2196
29	20	H	Newport Co	L 1-2	1-1	—	Staniforth	2156
30	24	A	Portsmouth	D 1-1	0-0	15	Loggie	9353
31	27	H	Rochdale	W 2-1	2-0	—	Taylor (og), McDonald	2295
32	31	H	Aldershot	D 1-1	0-0	14	McDonald	2110
33	Apr 3	A	Northampton T	L 0-1	0-1	—		1628
34	7	A	Port Vale	D 0-0	0-0	14		2712
35	13	H	Grimsby T	D 0-0	0-0	—		5401
36	14	A	Hartlepool U	D 1-1	0-1	15	McDonald	2343
37	16	H	Darlington	W 5-2	3-2	—	Staniforth, Ford, Loggie, Stronach McDonald	2973
38	21	A	Crewe Alex	W 1-0	1-0	13	Stronach	1428
39	25	A	Torquay U	L 0-3	0-1	—		1724
40	28	H	AFC Bournemouth	W 2-1	2-1	12	McDonald, Staniforth (pen)	2171
41	May 1	H	Crewe Alex	W 1-0	0-0	—	Ford	2009
42	5	A	Aldershot	L 0-1	0-0	12		3675
43	7	H	Port Vale	W 4-0	2-0	—	Staniforth 3 (1 a pen), McDonald	2344
44	11	A	Wimbledon	L 1-2	1-0	—	Ford	3897
45	14	H	Stockport Co	W 1-0	0-0	—	Wellings	2089
46	19	H	Huddersfield T	L 1-3	0-0	—	Ford	2664

Final League Position: 10

Goalscorers

League (51): Staniforth 15 (2 pens), Randall 10, Loggie 8, McDonald 6, Ford 4, Clements 2, Stronach 2, Wellings 2, Faulkner 1, Own Goal 1.
F.A. Cup (12): Staniforth 4, Wellings 3, Pugh, Ford, Clements, Faulkner, Randall.

League Cup	First Round	Grimsby T (a)	0-2
		(h)	0-3
F.A. Cup	First Round	Blyth (h)	1-1
		(a)	5-3 (a.e.t.)
	Second Round	Scarborough (h)	3-0
	Third Round	Luton T (h)	2-0
	Fourth Round	Nottingham F (a)	1-3

419

	Neenan	Scott	Kay	Young	Faulkner	Clements	Stronach	Randall	Loggie	McDonald	Staniforth	Warnock	Wellings	Bainbridge	Collier	Walsh	Brown	Ford	Pugh	Match No.
	1	2	3	4	5	6	7	8	9	10	11*	12								1
	1	2	3	7	5	6	4	8	9	10	11									2
	1	2	3	7	5	6	4	8	9	10	11									3
	1	2	3	7	5	6	4*	8	9	10	11	12								4
	1	2	3	7	5	6	4	8	9	10	11									5
	1	2	3	7		6	4	8	9	10	11				5					6
	1	2	3	7		6	4	8	9	10	11				5					7
	1	2*	3	7	5	6	10	8	9		11				4	12				8
	1		2	7	5	6		8	9	10	11				4	3				9
	1		3	7	5	6	12	8	9	10	11*				4	2				10
	1		2	7	5	6	8*	9	10		11	12			4	3				11
	1	4	2		5	6		8	9	10	11				7	3				12
		7	2		5	6	4	8	9	10	11				3	1				13
		10	2		5	6	4	8	9*		11	12			3	1	7			14
		2			5	6	4	8	9	10	11				3	1	7			15
		2			5	6		8	9	10	11	12			3*	1	7	4		16
		2			5	6		8	9	10	11	7*			3	1	12	4		17
		2			5	6		8		10	11	9			3	1	7	4		18
		2			5	6		8		10	11	9			3	1	7	4		19
		2			5	6		8		10	11	9			3	1	7	4		20
		2			5	6		8	12	10	11	9*			3	1	7	4		21
		2			5	6		8		10	11	9			3	1	7	4		22
		2			5	6	12	8		10	11	9*			3	1	7	4		23
	1	2			5	6		8	9	10	11				3		7	4		24
	1	2			5	6		8	9	10	11	12			3		7*	4		25
	1	2			5	6		8	9*	10	11	12			3		7	4		26
	1	2			5	6		8	9	10	11				3		7	4		27
	1	2			5	6		8	9	10	11				3		7	4		28
	1	2			5	6		8	9	10	11				3		7	4		29
	1	2			5	6			9	10	11	8			3		7	4		30
	1	2			5	6	12	8*	9	10	11				3		7	4		31
	1	2			5	6		8	9	10	11				3		7	4		32
	1	2			5	6	12	8	9*	10	11				3		7	4		33
		2			5	6		8	9	10	11				3	1	7	4		34
		2			5	6		8	9	10	11				3	1	7	4		35
		2			5	6	12	8*	9	10	11				3	1	7	4		36
		2			5	6	8		9	10	11				3	1	7	4		37
		2			5	6	8		9	10	11				3	1	7	4		38
		2			5	6	8		9	10	11				3	1	7	4		39
		2			5	6	8	12	9*	10	11				3	1	7	4		40
		2			5	6	8	9*	12	10	11				3	1	7	4		41
		2			5	6	8*	12	9	10	11				3	1	7	4		42
		2			5	6	8	9*		10	11	12			3	1	7	4		43
		2			5	6	8	12		10	11	9*			3	1	7	4		44
		2			5	6	8	11		10		9			3	1	7	4		45
		2			5	6	8*	12		10	11	9			3	1	7	4		46
	22	11	46	11	44	46	22	37	36	43	45	1	10	2	5	38	24	32	31	
					+4s	+5s	+2s					+3s	+5s			+1s		+1s		

YORK CITY—PLAYERS

Player and position	Ht	Wt	Birthplace	Clubs	League Appearances	Goals
Goalkeepers						
Joe Neenan	6 2	11 12	Manchester	York C	41	—
Graham Brown	6 1	12 7	Matlock	Millwall	—	—
				Mansfield	142	—
				Doncaster R	53	—
				Swansea C	4	—
				Southport	—	—
				York C	57	—
Defenders						
Steve Faulkner	6 3	13 5	Sheffield	Sheffield U	14+1	—
				Stockport Co (on loan)	3+1	—
				York C	44	1
Steve James	6 0	12 2	Coseley	Manchester U	129	1
				York C	87	1
Andy Clements	5 11	11 2	Swinton	Bolton W	1	—
				Port Vale (on loan)	2+1	—
				York C	75	2
*Peter Bainbridge	5 11	11 10	York	York C	9	—
Jimmy Walsh	5 9	11 0	London	Watford	60+5	—
				York C	38+1	—
Roy Kay	5 9	11 0	Edinburgh	Hearts	140+3	1
				Celtic	5	—
				York C	46	—
Midfield						
Tony Young	5 10	10 13	Urmston	Manchester U	69+14	1
(Contract cancelled November 1978)				Charlton Ath	20	1
				York C	76+2	2
Ian McDonald	5 7	10 5	Barrow	Barrow	30+5	2
				Workington	42	4
				Liverpool	—	—
				Colchester U (on loan)	5	2
				Mansfield T	47+9	4
				York C	73	8
Graham Collier	6 0	11 4	Nottingham	Nottingham F	13+2	2
(Contract cancelled November 1978)				Scunthorpe U	155+6	19
				Barnsley	22+2	2
				York C	5	—
David Pugh	5 10½	11 7	Markham	Newport	73+4	9
				Chesterfield	212+1	12
				Halifax T	91+5	3
				Rotherham U	57+1	—
				York C	31	—
Peter Stronach	5 6	12 0	Seaham	Sunderland	2+1	—
				York C	22+4	2
Gary Ford	5 9	10 7	York	York C	32+1	4
Forwards						
Gordon Staniforth	5 6	9 12	Hull	Hull C	7+5	2
				York C	119	30
Kevin Randall	5 11	12 9	Ashton under Lyme	Bury	4	—
				Chesterfield	257	97
				Notts Co	119+2	38
				Mansfield T	62+4	20
				York C	66+6	18
David Loggie	6 0	11 8	Newbiggin	Burnley	6+1	—
				York C	36+2	8
Barry Wellings	5 7	11 1	Liverpool	Everton	—	—
				York C	10+5	2
John Byrne	5 11	11 6	Manchester	York C	—	—

IMPORTANT FOOTBALL ADDRESSES

The Football Association: 16, Lancaster Gate, London W2 3LW

Scotland—Ernie Walker, 6, Park Gardens, Glasgow G3 7YE

Northern Ireland (Irish FA)—W. J. Drennan, J.P., 20 Windsor Avenue, Belfast BT9 6EG

Wales—Trevor Morris, O.B.E., 3, Fairy Road, Wrexham LL13 7PS

Republic of Ireland (FA of Ireland)—P. J. O'Driscoll, 80, Merrion Square, Dublin, 2

International Federation (FIFA)—Dr. H. Käser, FIFA House, Hitzigweg 11, CH-8032 Zurich, Switzerland

Union of European Football Associations—Mr. H. Bangerter, PO Box 16, CH-3000 Berne 15 Switzerland

THE LEAGUES

The Football League—A. Hardaker, O.B.E., The Football League, Lytham St Annes, Lancs. FY8 1JG. *0253-729421. Telex 67675*

The Scottish League—J. Farry, 188, West Regent Street, Glasgow G2 4RY. *041-248 3844/5*

The Irish League—J. H. Long, 16 Donegall Square South, Belfast.

Alliance Premier League—G. B. Graham, Fairfield, Lydiate Lane, Cloughton on Brock, nr. Preston. *Brock 40582*

Athenian League—G. G. Dell, 'Ardranech', Monument Lane, Chalfont St Peter, Bucks. *Chalfont St Giles 3819*

Central League—D. J. Grimshaw, 118, St Stephens Road, Deepdale, Preston, Lancs., PR1 6TD. *Preston 55898*

Cheshire County League—C. R. Mahood, Burscough Nurseries, Ring O'Bells Lane,Lathom, Ormskirk, Lancs L40 5US. *Rufford 822688*

Town & Country League—A. W. G. Rudd, 'Heathercliff', Gunton Cliff Lowestoft. *Lowestoft 5996*

Football Combination—T. P. R. Kirkup, 15 Oulton Rise, Spinney Hill, Northampton NN3 1EW. *0604-47831*

Hellenic League—D. A. G. Harrison, 107 Thame Road, Haddenham, Aylesbury, Bucks. *Haddenham 290590*

Kent League—D. Baker, 17 Sterling Road, Sittingbourne, Kent. *Sittingbourne 25105*

Lancashire Amateur League—H. Heap, 'Maraldo', Carlton Road, Hale, Altrincham, Cheshire, WA15 8RH. *061-980 2344*

Lancashire Combination—K. H. Dean, 61, Queens Road, Blackburn, Lancs. BB1 1QF

Lancashire Football League—H. E. Lambert, 3, Cravans Avenue, Ewood, Blackburn BB2 4LB. *Blackburn 58561*

Leicestershire Senior League—P. Henwood, 63, Carisbrooke Rd., Leicester LE2 3PF. *Leicester 705475*

London Spartan—A. J. Stephens, 130 Torrington Park, London N12. *01-368 1959*

Manchester League—T. W. Gilgryst, 7, Bowlee Close, Unsworth, Bury, Lancs. *061-766 3082*

Midland Counties League—A. A. Ridsdale, 11 Eskdale Drive, Worksop Notts. *Worksop 475008*

Midland Combination—L. W. James, 175 Barnet Lane, Kingswinford, Brierley Hill, West Midlands *Kingswinford 3459*

Midland Intermediate—J. B. Holmes, 492, Melton Rd., Leicester LE4 7SP. *Leicester 63968*

Mid-Week Football League—Frank P. White, 11 Tulip Way, Clacton-on-Sea, Essex. *Clacton 32750*

Nemean Amateur League—W. Chivers, 58 Laurel Avenue, Potters Bar, Herts. EN6 2AB. *Potters Bar 54969*

Northern Intermediate League—F. R. Vicary, 12, Holmefield Avenue, Thornes, Wakefield, Yorks WF2 7AF. *Wakefield 75013*

Northern League—G. Nicholson, 99, Watling Road, Bishop Auckland, Co. Durham. *Bishop Auckland 2167*

Northern Premier League—R. D. Bayley, 228 Grove Lane, Hale, Altrincham, Cheshire WA15 8PR. *061-980-7007*

North Midlands League—G. Thompson, 7 Wren Park Close, Ridgway, Sheffield.

Old Boys Football League—B. Aldous, Clemitis Cottage, Ongar Road, White Roding, Dunmow, Essex. *White Roding 278*

Peterborough and District League—A. V. Brown, 27, Gloucester Road, Old Fletton, Peterborough

Isthmian League—A. C. F. Turvey, 'Ladymead', 18 Apple Way, Basing, Basingstoke, Hants. *Basingstoke 61789*

Southern Amateur League—F. J. Banner, 10 Oakwood Road, Orpington, Kent. *Farnborough 58720*

South-East Counties League—R. A. Bailey, 10, Highlands Road, New Barnet, Herts. EN5 5AB. *01-449 5131*

Southern League—W. E. Dellow, FCCS, 1, Carmel Close, Great Tylers, Wray Common, Reigate, Surrey RH2 0LS. *Redhill 62585*

South Midlands League—C. Moyse, 33, Markham Crescent, Dunstable, Beds. LU5 4SS. *Dunstable 64682*

South Western League—G. Gazzard, 6 Coastguard Crescent, Penzance, Cornwall. *Penzance 61397*

United Counties League—E. W. Evans, 97, Littlewood Street, Rothwell, Kettering, Northants. *Kettering 710108*

Wearside—J. R. Walsh, 85 Hartington St., Roker, Sunderland, Tyne & Wear. *Sunderland 75513*

Western League—J. Veale, 5, Everest Road, Bristol BS16 2BX. *0272-652699*

The Welsh League—J. T. Burrows, 16, Meyer Street, Thomastown, Tonyrefail, Glam.

West Midland League—C. Gordon Davis, "Roselawns", 42, Ridgewood Avenue, Wollaston, Stourbridge, West Midlands DY8 4QH. *Stourbridge 73241*

West Yorkshire League—W. Keyworth, 2, Hill Court Grove, Branley, Yorks. L13 2AP. *Pudsey 74465*

Yorkshire League—B. Wood, 5, Restmore Avenue, Guiseley, Nr. Leeds, LS20 9DG. *Guiseley 4558 (home); Bradford 29595 (9 a.m. to 5 p.m.)*

R.F. 79/80—22

COUNTY FOOTBALL ASSOCIATIONS

Bedfordshire—P. Burns, 13, Wendover Way, Luton, Beds. LU2 7LS *Luton 30829*

Berks and Bucks—C. J. Twelftree, 42, Bourtonville, Buckingham, Bucks. *Buckingham 2137*

Birmingham County—W. F. Pennick, County F.A. Offices, Rayhall Lane, Great Barr, Birmingham B43 6JE *021-357-4278*

Cambridgeshire—R. E. Rogers, 20, Aingers Road, Histon Cambridge. *Histon 2803*

Cheshire—F. Foden, 549, Crewe Road, Wistaston, Crewe, CW2 6PU. *Crewe 69429*

Cornwall—W. Parnell, 12, Higher Tremena, St Austell PL25 5QQ. *St. Austell 3236*

Cumberland—E. D. Smith, MBE, 4, High Rigg, Brigham, Cockermouth, Cumberland CA13 0TA *Cockermouth 825242*

Derbyshire—H. L. P. Holmes, 82, Friar Gate, Derby *Derby 25835*

Devon County—C. H. Norsworthy, 8, Belair Road, Peverell, Plymouth PL2 3QH. *Plymouth 73550*

Dorset County—P. Hough, 110 Dorchester Rd, Oakdale, Poole Dorset BH15 3SD *0202 746244*

Durham—R. D. Lyons, 'Codeslaw', Ferens Park, Durham DH1 1JZ. *Durham 3653*

East Riding County—C. Branton, 83, Belvedere Road, Hessel, Hull HU13 9JH *Hull 649294*

Essex County—M. S. Jeffers, 54A Eastwood Road Goodmayes, Ilford, Essex. *01-590 7893*

Gloucestershire—E. J. Marsh, 46 Douglas Road, Horfield, Bristol BS7 0JD. *Bristol 46430*

Guernsey—L. A. De La Mare, 'Rock Pond', Grand Rocques, Castel, Guernsey C.I.

Hampshire—R. G. Barnes, 367, Winchester Road, Southampton *Southampton 766884*

Herefordshire—R. A. Doody, Longwynd, Paradise Green, Marden, Hereford. *Sutton St. Nicholas 674*

Hertfordshire—F. Holloway, 115, Tile Kiln Lane, Leverstock Green, Hemel Hempstead HP3 8NX

Hunts County—M. M. Armstrong, 1 Chapel End, Great Giddings, Huntingdon, Cambs. *Winwick 262*

Isle of Man—Mrs. R. Raley, 129 Bucks Road, Douglas, I.O.M.

Jersey—W. A. Nicole, 1, Les Chalets, Queen's Road, St Helier, Jersey, C.I.

Kent County—K. T. Masters, 69 Maidstone Road, Chatham, Kent ME4 6DT. *Medway 43824*

Lancashire—J. Kenyon, 31A, Wellington St., St John's, Blackburn, Lancs. BB1 8AU *Blackburn 64333*

Leicestershire and Rutland—J. B. Holmes, 492, Melton Road, Leicester LE4 7SP. *Leicester 63968*

Lincolnshire—F. S. Richardson, 9 The Avenue, Lincoln. *Lincoln 24917*

Liverpool County—S. A. Rudd, 23 Greenfield Road, Old Swann, Liverpool 13. *051-526-9515*

London—A. F. Monger, Association House, 88, Lewisham High Street, London SE13 5LL. *01-852 4777*

Manchester County—S. Holliday, 87 Hart Road, Fallowfield, Manchester 14. *061-224-5185*

Middlesex County—A. L. Smith, 68, Squires Lane, London N3 2AP *01-346 7565*

Norfolk County—B. G. Smith, 64, Gunton Lane, Costessey, Norwich NOR 32K *Norwich 742894*

Northamptonshire—N. W. Hillier, 36, Watkin Terrace, Northampton NN1 3ER. *Northampton 37071*

North Riding County—T. H. Harper, 125, Westbury Street, Thornaby-on-Tees, Cleveland TS17 6NF *Middlesbrough 67866*

Northumberland—J. Laidler, 80, Riding Dene, Mickley, Stocksfield-on-Tyne, Northumberland, *Stocksfield 2360*

Nottinghamshire—W. T. Annable, 7 Clarendon Street, Nottingham. *Nottingham 48954*

Oxfordshire—S. W. Jacobs, 9, Burrows Close, Headington, Oxford. *Oxford 61187*

Sheffield and Hallamshire—G. Thompson, Clegg House, 253 Pittsmoor Road, Sheffield 3. *Sheffield 27817*

Shropshire—W. B. Jones, 146, Whitchurch Road, Shrewsbury SY1 4EJ *Shrewsbury 3243*

Somerset County—L. G. Webb, 32, North Road, Midsomer Norton, Bath BA3 2QQ. *Midsomer Norton 3176*

Staffordshire—T. Myatt, County Offices, Miller Street, Newcastle-under-Lyme ST5 1HB. *Newcastle-under-Lyme 622585*

Suffolk County—E. A. Brown, 'Shobdon', 68, Fairfield Road, Saxmundham IP17 1BB *Saxmunden 2165*

Surrey County—L. F. J. Smith, 2, Fairfield Avenue, Horley, Surrey RH6 7PD *Horley 4945*

Sussex County—R.F. Reeve, 56, Hawkins Crescent, Shoreham-by-Sea, Sussex BN4 6TP. *Southwick 3444*

Westmorland—J. R. Plumbe, 24, Crescent Green, Kendal LA9 6DR *Kendal 23227*

West Riding County—R. M. Robin, 77 Great, George Street, Leeds LS1 3DR.

Wiltshire—F. J. Peart, 161, Grange Drive, Stratton St Margaret, Swindon. *Stratton St Margaret 2239*

Worcestershire—P. Rushton, 84 Windermere Drive, Warndon, Worcester WR4 9JB. *Worcester 51166*

OTHER USEFUL ADDRESSES

Amateur Football Alliance—W. P. Goss, Room 33, 3rd Floor, 6 Langley Street, London WC2 *01-240 3837/8*

English Schools FA—The Secretary, 4A Eastgate Street, Stafford ST16 2NN. *0285-51142*

Oxford University—Sir Harold Thompson, C.B.E., F.R.S., St. John's College, Oxford.

Cambridge University—S. C. Aston, St. Catherine's College, Cambridge.

Army—Major A. Dobson, M.B.E., Ministry of Defence (A.S.C.B.), Clayton Barracks, Aldershot, Hants.

Royal Air Force—Sqn/Ldr. M. G. T. Standing, 'Kersey', Milton Lawns, Chesham Bois, Amersham, Bucks HP6 6BL. *Amersham 7914*

Royal Navy—Lt.-Cdr. H. A. Sheppard, R.N. Sports Office, H.M.S. Nelson, Portsmouth, Hants. PO1 3HH

Universities Athletic Union—Alun Evans, U.A.U., 28 Woburn Square, London W.C.1. *01-637 4828*

Central Council of Physical Recreation—General Secretary, 70, Brompton Road, London, SW3 1HE. *01-584 6651*

British Olympic Association—6, John Prince's Street, W1M 0DH *01-408 2029*

National Federation of Football Supporters' Clubs—The Secretary, 44, Buxton Road, Luton, Beds.

National Playing Fields Association—Col. R Satterthwaite, O.B.E., 578, Catherine Place London, S.W.1

Professional Footballers' Association—C. Lloyd, 124, Corn Exchange Buildings, Hanging Ditch, Manchester M4 3BN. *061-834 7554*

Referees' Association—O. J. Venning, Summerhill, Kingswinford, West Midlands.

The Association of Football League Referees and Linesmen—R. Hall, Secretary, 59, Woodcock Hill, Kenton, Harrow, Middlesex HA3 0JH

Football League Managers and Secretaries Association—K. Friar, c/o Arsenal FC, Highbury, London, N5

Women's Football Association—Miss P. Gregory, 7, Mayfield Road, London, N.8

The Association of Provincial Football Supporters' Clubs in London—R. W. Peck, Press Officer, 94, Midmoor Road, London SW12 0ET

The Association of Football League Commercial Managers—G. H. Dimbleby, Secretary WBA FC, The Hawthorns, Halfords Lane, West Bromwich B71 4LF

England Supporters Association, R. Coates, Hill End House, Butlers Cross, Aylesbury, Bucks

National Federation of Supporters Clubs, T. Pullein, 1 Kennet Way, Oakley, Basingstone

FOOTBALL LEAGUE TABLES 1978-79

FIRST DIVISION

		HOME						AWAY					
	P	W	D	L	F	A	W	D	L	F	A	Pts.
Liverpool	42	19	2	0	51	4	11	6	4	34	12	68
Nottingham F	42	11	10	0	34	10	10	8	3	27	16	60
West Bromwich A	42	13	5	3	38	15	11	6	4	34	20	59
Everton	42	12	7	2	32	17	5	10	6	20	23	51
Leeds	42	11	4	6	41	25	7	10	4	29	27	50
Ipswich	42	11	4	6	34	21	9	5	7	29	28	49
Arsenal	42	11	8	2	37	18	6	6	9	24	30	48
Aston Villa	42	8	9	4	37	26	7	7	7	22	23	46
Manchester U	42	9	7	5	29	25	6	8	7	31	38	45
Coventry	42	11	7	3	41	29	3	9	9	17	39	44
Tottenham	42	7	8	6	19	25	6	7	8	29	36	41
Middlesbrough	42	10	5	6	33	21	5	5	11	24	29	40
Bristol C	42	11	6	4	34	19	4	4	13	13	32	40
Southampton	42	9	10	2	35	20	3	6	12	12	33	40
Manchester C	42	9	5	7	34	28	4	8	9	24	28	39
Norwich	42	7	10	4	29	19	0	13	8	22	38	37
Bolton	42	10	5	6	36	28	2	6	13	18	47	35
Wolverhampton W	42	10	4	7	26	26	3	4	14	18	42	34
Derby	42	8	5	8	25	25	2	6	13	19	46	31
Queen's Park R	42	4	9	8	24	33	2	4	15	21	40	25
Birmingham	42	5	9	7	24	25	1	1	19	13	39	22
Chelsea	42	3	5	13	23	42	2	5	14	21	50	20

SECOND DIVISION

		HOME						AWAY					
	P	W	D	L	F	A	W	D	L	F	A	Pts.
Crystal Palace	42	12	7	2	30	11	7	12	2	21	13	57
Brighton	42	16	3	2	44	11	7	7	7	28	28	56
Stoke	42	11	7	3	35	15	9	9	3	23	16	56
Sunderland	42	13	3	5	39	19	9	8	4	31	25	55
West Ham	42	12	7	2	46	15	6	7	8	24	24	50
Notts C	42	8	10	3	23	15	6	6	9	25	45	44
Preston	42	7	11	3	36	23	5	7	9	23	34	42
Newcastle	42	13	3	5	35	24	4	5	12	16	31	42
Cardiff	42	12	5	4	34	23	4	5	12	22	47	42
Fulham	42	10	7	4	35	19	3	8	10	15	28	41
Orient	42	11	5	5	32	18	4	5	12	19	33	40
Cambridge	42	7	10	4	22	15	5	6	10	22	37	40
Burnley	42	11	6	4	31	22	3	6	12	20	40	40
Oldham	42	10	7	4	36	23	3	6	12	16	38	39
Wrexham	42	10	6	5	31	16	2	8	11	14	26	38
Bristol R	42	10	6	5	34	23	4	4	13	14	37	38
Leicester	42	7	8	6	28	23	3	9	9	15	29	37
Luton	42	11	5	5	46	24	2	5	14	14	33	36
Charlton	42	6	8	7	28	28	5	5	11	32	41	35
Sheffield U	42	9	6	6	34	24	2	6	13	18	45	34
Millwall	42	7	4	10	22	29	4	6	11	20	32	32
Blackburn	42	5	8	8	24	29	5	2	14	17	43	30

THIRD DIVISION

		HOME						AWAY					
	P	W	D	L	F	A	W	D	L	F	A	Pts.
Shrewsbury	46	14	9	0	36	11	7	10	6	25	30	61
Watford	46	15	5	3	47	22	9	7	7	36	30	60
Swansea	46	16	6	1	57	32	8	6	9	26	29	60
Gillingham	46	15	7	1	39	15	6	10	7	26	27	59
Swindon	46	17	2	4	44	14	8	5	10	30	38	57
Carlisle	46	11	10	2	31	13	4	12	7	22	29	52
Colchester	46	13	9	1	35	19	4	8	11	25	36	51
Hull	46	12	9	2	36	14	7	2	14	30	47	49
Exeter	46	14	6	3	38	18	3	9	11	23	38	49
Brentford	46	14	4	5	35	19	5	5	13	18	30	47
Oxford	46	10	8	5	27	20	4	10	9	17	30	46
Blackpool	46	12	5	6	38	19	6	4	13	23	40	45
Southend	46	11	6	6	30	17	4	9	10	21	32	45
Sheffield W	46	9	8	6	30	22	4	11	8	23	31	45
Plymouth	46	11	9	3	40	27	4	5	14	27	41	44
Chester	46	11	9	3	42	21	3	7	13	15	40	44
Rotherham	46	13	3	7	30	23	4	7	12	19	32	44
Mansfield	46	7	11	5	30	24	5	8	10	21	28	43
Bury	46	6	11	6	35	32	5	9	9	24	33	42
Chesterfield	46	10	5	8	35	34	3	9	11	16	31	40
Peterborough	46	8	7	8	26	24	3	7	13	18	39	36
Walsall	46	7	6	10	34	32	3	6	14	22	39	32
Tranmere	46	4	12	7	26	31	2	4	17	19	47	28
Lincoln	46	5	7	11	26	38	2	4	17	15	50	25

FOURTH DIVISION

		HOME						AWAY					
	P	W	D	L	F	A	W	D	L	F	A	Pts.
Reading	46	19	3	1	49	8	7	10	6	27	27	65
Grimsby	46	15	5	3	51	23	11	4	8	31	26	61
Wimbledon	46	18	3	2	50	20	7	8	8	28	26	61
Barnsley	46	15	5	3	47	23	9	8	6	26	19	61
Aldershot	46	16	5	2	38	14	4	12	7	25	33	57
Wigan	46	14	5	4	40	24	7	8	8	23	24	55
Portsmouth	46	13	7	3	35	12	7	5	11	27	36	52
Newport	46	12	5	6	39	28	9	5	9	27	27	52
Huddersfield	46	13	8	2	32	15	5	3	15	25	38	47
York	46	11	6	6	33	24	7	5	11	18	31	47
Torquay	46	14	4	5	38	24	5	4	14	20	41	46
Scunthorpe	46	12	3	8	33	30	5	8	10	21	30	45
Hartlepool	46	7	12	4	35	28	6	6	11	22	38	44
Hereford	46	12	8	3	35	18	3	5	15	18	35	43
Bradford	46	11	5	7	38	26	6	4	13	24	42	43
Port Vale	46	8	10	5	29	28	6	4	13	28	42	42
Stockport	46	11	5	7	33	21	3	7	13	25	39	40
Bournemouth	46	11	6	6	34	19	3	5	15	13	29	39
Northampton	46	12	4	7	40	30	3	5	15	24	46	39
Rochdale	46	11	4	8	25	26	4	5	14	22	38	39
Darlington	46	8	8	7	25	21	3	7	13	24	45	37
Doncaster	46	8	8	7	25	22	5	3	15	25	51	37
Halifax	46	7	5	11	24	32	2	3	18	15	40	26
Crewe	46	3	7	13	24	41	3	7	13	19	49	26

LEAGUE HONOURS LIST

FOOTBALL LEAGUE

	First	*Pts.*	*Second*	*Pts.*	*Third*	*Pts.*
1888–89a	Preston N.E.	40	Aston Villa	29	Wolverhampton W.	28
1889–90a	Preston N.E.	33	Everton	31	Blackburn R.	27
1890–91a	Everton	29	Preston N.E.	27	Notts. Co.	26
1891–92b	Sunderland	42	Preston N.E.	37	Bolton W.	36

FIRST DIVISION

	First	*Pts.*	*Second*	*Pts.*	*Third*	*Pts.*
1892–93c	Sunderland	48	Preston N.E.	37	Everton	36
1893–94c	Aston Villa	44	Sunderland	38	Derby Co.	36
1894–95c	Sunderland	47	Everton	42	Aston Villa	39
1895–96c	Aston Villa	45	Derby Co.	41	Everton	39
1896–97c	Aston Villa	47	Sheffield U.	36	Derby Co.	36
1897–98c	Sheffield U.	42	Sunderland	37	Wolverhampton W.	35
1898–99d	Aston Villa	45	Liverpool	43	Burnley	39
1899–1900d	Aston Villa	50	Sheffield U.	48	Sunderland	41
1900–1d	Liverpool	45	Sunderland	43	Notts. Co.	40
1901–2d	Sunderland	44	Everton	41	Newcastle U.	37
1902–3d	The Wednesday	42	Aston Villa	41	Sunderland	41
1903–4d	The Wednesday	47	Manchester C.	44	Everton	43
1904–5d	Newcastle U.	48	Everton	47	Manchester C.	46
1905–6e	Liverpool	51	Preston N.E.	47	The Wednesday	44
1906–7e	Newcastle U.	51	Bristol C.	48	Everton	45
1907–8e	Manchester U.	52	Aston Villa	43	Manchester C.	43
1908–9e	Newcastle U.	53	Everton	46	Sunderland	44
1909–10e	Aston Villa	53	Liverpool	48	Blackburn R.	45
1910–11e	Manchester U.	52	Aston Villa	51	Sunderland	45
1911–12e	Blackburn R.	49	Everton	46	Newcastle U.	44
1912–13e	Sunderland	54	Aston Villa	50	Sheffield W.	49
1913–14e	Blackburn R.	51	Aston Villa	44	Middlesbrough	43
1914–15e	Everton	46	Oldham Ath.	45	Blackburn R.	43
1919–20f	W.B.A.	60	Burnley	51	Chelsea	49
1920–21f	Burnley	59	Manchester C.	54	Bolton W.	52
1921–22f	Liverpool	57	Tottenham H.	51	Burnley	49
1922–23f	Liverpool	60	Sunderland	54	Huddersfield	53
1923–24f	*Huddersfield	57	Cardiff C.	57	Sunderland	53
1924–25f	Huddersfield	58	W.B.A.	56	Bolton W.	55
1925–26f	Huddersfield	57	Arsenal	52	Sunderland	48
1926–27f	Newcastle U.	56	Huddersfield	51	Sunderland	49
1927–28f	Everton	53	Huddersfield	51	Leicester C.	48
1928–29f	Sheffield W.	52	Leicester C.	51	Aston Villa	50
1929–30f	Sheffield W.	60	Derby Co.	50	Manchester C.	47
1930–31f	Arsenal	66	Aston Villa	59	Sheffield W.	52
1931–32f	Everton	56	Arsenal	54	Sheffield W.	50
1932–33f	Arsenal	58	Aston Villa	54	Sheffield W.	51
1933–34f	Arsenal	59	Huddersfield	56	Tottenham H.	49
1934–35f	Arsenal	58	Sunderland	54	Sheffield W.	49
1935–36f	Sunderland	56	Derby Co.	48	Huddersfield	48
1936–37f	Manchester C.	57	Charlton Ath.	54	Arsenal	52
1937–38f	Arsenal	52	Wolverhampton W.	51	Preston N.E.	49
1938–39f	Everton	59	Wolverhampton W.	55	Charlton Ath.	50
1946–47f	Liverpool	57	Manchester U.	56	Wolverhampton W.	56
1947–48f	Arsenal	59	Manchester U.	52	Burnley	52
1948–49f	Portsmouth	58	Manchester U.	53	Derby Co.	53
1949–50f	*Portsmouth	53	Wolverhampton W.	53	Sunderland	52
1950–51f	Tottenham H.	60	Manchester U.	56	Blackpool	50
1951–52f	Manchester U.	57	Tottenham H.	53	Arsenal	53
1952–53f	*Arsenal	54	Preston N.E.	54	Wolverhampton W.	51
1953–54f	Wolverhampton W.	57	W.B.A.	53	Huddersfield	51
1954–55f	Chelsea	52	Wolverhampton W.	48	Portsmouth	48
1955–56f	Manchester U.	60	Blackpool	49	Wolverhampton W.	49
1956–57f	Manchester U.	64	Tottenham H.	56	Preston N.E.	56
1957–58f	Wolverhampton W.	64	Preston N.E.	59	Tottenham H.	51
1958–59f	Wolverhampton W.	61	Manchester U.	55	Arsenal	50
1959–60f	Burnley	55	Wolverhampton W.	54	Tottenham H.	53
1960–61f	Tottenham H.	66	Sheffield W.	58	Wolverhampton W.	57

425

	First	Pts.	Second	Pts.	Third	Pts.
1961–62 f	Ipswich T.	56	Burnley	53	Tottenham H.	52
1962–63 f	Everton	61	Tottenham H.	55	Burnley	54
1963–64 f	Liverpool	57	Manchester U.	53	Everton	52
1964–65 f	*Manchester U.	61	Leeds U.	61	Chelsea	56
1965–66 f	Liverpool	61	Leeds U.	55	Burnley	55
1966–67 f	Manchester U.	60	Nottingham F.	56	Tottenham H.	56
1967–68 f	Manchester C.	58	Manchester U.	56	Liverpool	55
1968–69 f	Leeds U.	67	Liverpool	61	Everton	57
1969–70 f	Everton	66	Leeds U.	57	Chelsea	55
1970–71 f	Arsenal	65	Leeds U.	64	Tottenham H.	52
1971–72 f	Derby Co.	58	Leeds U.	57	Liverpool	57
1972–73 f	Liverpool	60	Arsenal	57	Leeds U.	53
1973–74 f	Leeds U.	62	Liverpool	57	Derby Co.	48
1974–75 f	Derby Co.	53	Liverpool	51	Ipswich T.	57
1975–76 f	Liverpool	60	Q.P.R.	59	Manchester U.	56
1976–77 f	Liverpool	57	Manchester C.	56	Ipswich T.	52
1977–78 f	Nottingham F.	64	Liverpool	57	Everton	55
1978–79 f	Liverpool	68	Nottingham F.	60	W.B.A.	59

Maximum points: a, 44; b, 52; c, 60; d, 68; e, 76; f, 84.
No competition during 1915–19 and 1939–46.

SECOND DIVISION

	First	Pts.	Second	Pts.	Third	Pts.
1892–93 a	Small Heath	36	Sheffield U.	35	Darwen	30
1893–94 b	Liverpool	50	Small Heath	42	Notts. Co.	39
1894–95 c	Bury	48	Notts. Co.	39	Newton Heath	38
1895–96 c	*Liverpool	46	Manchester C.	46	Grimsby T.	42
1896–97 c	Notts. Co.	42	Newton Heath	39	Grimsby T.	38
1897–98 c	Burnley	48	Newcastle U.	45	Manchester C.	39
1898–99 d	Manchester C.	52	Glossop N.E.	46	Leicester Fosse	45
1899–1900 d	The Wednesday	54	Bolton W.	52	Small Heath	46
1900–1 d	Grimsby T.	49	Small Heath	48	Burnley	44
1901–2 d	W.B.A.	55	Middlesbrough	51	Preston N.E.	42
1902–3 d	Manchester C.	54	Small Heath	51	Woolwich A.	48
1903–4 d	Preston N.E.	50	Woolwich A.	49	Manchester U.	48
1904–5 d	Liverpool	58	Bolton W.	56	Manchester U.	53
1905–6 e	Bristol C.	66	Manchester U.	62	Chelsea	53
1906–7 e	Nottingham F.	60	Chelsea	57	Leicester Fosse	48
1907–8 e	Bradford C.	54	Leicester Fosse	52	Oldham Ath.	50
1908–9 e	Bolton W.	52	*Tottenham H.	51	W.B.A.	51
1909–10 e	Manchester C.	54	*Oldham Ath.	53	Hull C.	53
1910–11 e	W.B.A.	53	Bolton W.	51	Chelsea	49
1911–12 e	*Derby Co.	54	Chelsea	54	Burnley	52
1912–13 e	Preston N.E.	53	Burnley	50	Birmingham C.	46
1913–14 e	Notts. Co.	53	Bradford P.A.	49	Woolwich A.	49
1914–15 e	Derby Co.	53	Preston N.E.	50	Barnsley	47
1919–20 f	Tottenham H.	70	Huddersfield	64	Birmingham C.	56
1920–21 f	*Birmingham C.	58	Cardiff C.	58	Bristol C.	51
1921–22 f	Nottingham F.	56	Stoke C.	52	Barnsley	52
1922–23 f	Notts. Co.	53	*West Ham U.	51	Leicester C.	51
1923–24 f	Leeds U.	54	*Bury	51	Derby Co.	51
1924–25 f	Leicester C.	59	Manchester U.	57	Derby Co.	55
1925–26 f	Sheffield W.	60	Derby Co.	57	Chelsea	52
1926–27 f	Middlesbrough	62	*Portsmouth	54	Manchester C.	54
1927–28 f	Manchester C.	59	Leeds U.	57	Chelsea	54
1928–29 f	Middlesbrough	55	Grimsby T.	53	Bradford	48
1929–30 f	Blackpool	58	Chelsea	55	Oldham Ath.	53
1930–31 f	Everton	61	W.B.A.	54	Tottenham H.	51
1931–32 f	Wolverhampton W.	56	Leeds U.	54	Stoke C.	52
1932–33 f	Stoke C.	56	Tottenham H.	55	Fulham	50
1933–34 f	Grimsby T.	59	Preston N.E.	52	Bolton W.	51
1934–35 f	Brentford	61	*Bolton W.	56	West Ham U.	56
1935–36 f	Manchester U.	56	Charlton Ath.	55	Sheffield U.	52
1936–37 f	Leicester C.	56	Blackpool	55	Bury	52
1937–38 f	Aston Villa	57	*Manchester U.	53	Sheffield U.	53
1938–39 f	Blackburn R.	55	Sheffield U.	54	Sheffield W.	53
1939–46	Competition cancelled owing to war.					
1946–47 f	Manchester C.	62	Burnley	58	Birmingham C.	55
1947–48 f	Birmingham C.	59	Newcastle U.	56	Southampton	52
1948–49 f	Fulham	57	W.B.A.	56	Southampton	55
1949–50 f	Tottenham H.	61	*Sheffield W.	52	Sheffield U.	52
1950–51 f	Preston N.E.	57	Manchester C.	52	Cardiff C.	50

* Won on goal average

Season	First	Pts	Second	Pts	Third	Pts
1951–52	Sheffield W.	53	*Cardiff C.	51	Birmingham C.	51
1952–53f	Sheffield U.	60	Huddersfield	58	Luton T.	52
1953–54f	*Leicester C.	56	Everton	56	Blackburn R.	55
1954–55f	*Birmingham C.	54	*Luton T.	54	Rotherham U.	54
1955–56f	Sheffield W.	55	Leeds U.	52	Liverpool	48
1956–57f	Leicester C.	61	Nottingham F.	54	Liverpool	53
1957–58f	West Ham U.	57	Blackburn R.	56	Charlton Ath.	55
1958–59f	Sheffield W	62	Fulham	60	Sheffield U.	53
1959–60	Aston Villa	59	Cardiff C.	58	Liverpool	50
1960–61f	Ipswich T.	59	Sheffield U.	58	Liverpool	52
1961–62f	Liverpool	62	Leyton O.	54	Sunderland	53
1962–63f	Stoke C.	53	*Chelsea	52	Sunderland	52
1963–64	Leeds U.	63	Sunderland	61	Preston N.E.	56
1964–65f	Newcastle U.	57	Northampton	56	Bolton W.	50
1965–66	Manchester C.	59	Southampton	54	Coventry C.	53
1966–67f	Coventry C.	59	Wolverhampton W.	58	Carlisle U.	52
1967–68f	Ipswich T.	59	*Q.P.R.	58	Blackpool	58
1968–69f	Derby Co.	63	C. Palace	56	Charlton Ath.	50
1969–70	Huddersfield	60	Blackpool	53	Leicester C.	51
1970–71f	Leicester C.	59	Sheffield U.	56	Cardiff C.	53
1971–72f	Norwich C.	57	Birmingham C.	56	Millwall	55
1972–73f	Burnley	62	Q.P.R.	61	Aston Villa	50
1973–74f	Middlesbrough	65	Luton T.	50	Carlisle U.	49
1974–75f	Manchester U.	61	Aston Villa	58	Norwich C.	53
1975–76f	Sunderland	56	Bristol C.	53	W.B.A.	53
1976–77f	Wolverhampton W.	57	Chelsea	55	Nottingham F.	52
1977–78f	Bolton W.	58	Southampton	57	Tottenham H.	56
1978–79f	Crystal Palace	57	Brighton	56	Stoke C.	56

Maximum points: a, 44; b, 56; c, 60; d, 68; e, 76; f, 84.

THIRD DIVISION

Season	First	Pts	Second	Pts	Third	Pts
1958–59	Plymouth Arg.	62	Hull C.	61	Brentford	57
1959–60	Southampton	61	Norwich C.	59	Shrewsbury T.	52
1960–61	Bury	68	Walsall	62	Q.P.R.	60
1961–62	Portsmouth	65	Grimsby T.	62	Bournemouth	59
1962–63	Northampton	62	Swindon T.	58	Port Vale	54
1963–64	*Coventry C.	60	Crystal Palace	60	Watford	58
1964–65	Carlisle U.	60	*Bristol C.	59	Mansfield T.	59
1965–66	Hull C.	69	Millwall	65	Q.P.R.	57
1966–67	Q.P.R.	67	Middlesbrough	55	Watford	54
1967–68	Oxford U.	57	Bury	56	Shrewsbury T.	55
1968–69	*Watford	64	Swindon T.	64	Luton T.	61
1969–70	Orient	62	Luton T.	60	Bristol R.	56
1970–71	Preston N.E.	61	Fulham	60	Halifax T.	56
1971–72	Aston Villa	70	Brighton	65	Bournemouth	62
1972–73	Bolton W.	61	Nott Co.	57	Blackburn R.	55
1973–74	Oldham Ath.	62	Bristol R.	61	York C.	61
1974–75	Blackburn R.	60	Plymouth Arg.	59	Charlton Ath.	55
1975–76	Hereford U.	63	Cardiff C.	57	Millwall	56
1976–77	Mansfield T.	64	Brighton & H. A.	61	Crystal Palace	59
1977–78	Wrexham	61	Cambridge U.	58	Preston N.E.	56
1978–79	Shrewsbury T.	61	Watford	60	Swansea C.	60

Maximum points: 92.

FOURTH DIVISION

Season	First	Pts	Second	Pts	Third	Pts	Fourth	Pts
1958–59	Port Vale	64	Coventry C.	60	York C.	60	Shrewsbury T.	58
1959–60	Walsall	65	Notts. Co.	60	Torquay U.	60	Watford	57
1960–61	Peterborough U.	66	C. Palace	64	Northampton	60	Bradford P.A.	60
1961–62	†Millwall	56	Colchester U.	55	Wrexham	53	Carlisle U.	52
1962–63	Brentford	62	Oldham Ath.	59	Crewe Alex.	59	Mansfield T.	57
1963–64	*Gillingham	60	Carlisle U.	60	Workington T.	59	Exeter C.	58
1964–65	Brighton	63	Millwall	62	York C.	62	Oxford U.	61
1965–66	*Doncaster R.	59	Darlington	59	Torquay U.	58	Colchester U.	56
1966–67	Stockport Co.	64	Southport	59	Barrow	59	Tranmere R.	58
1967–68	Luton T.	66	Barnsley	61	Hartlepools U.	60	Crewe Alex.	58
1968–69	Doncaster R.	59	Halifax T.	57	Rochdale	56	Bradford C.	56
1969–70	Chesterfield	64	Wrexham	61	Swansea C.	60	Port Vale	59
1970–71	Notts Co.	69	Bournemouth	60	Oldham Ath.	59	York C.	56
1971–72	Grimsby T.	63	Southend U.	60	Brentford	59	Scunthorpe U.	57
1972–73	Southport	62	Hereford U.	58	Cambridge U.	57	*Aldershot	56
1973–74	Peterborough U.	65	Gillingham	62	Colchester U.	60	Bury	59
1974–75	Mansfield T.	68	Shrewsbury T.	62	Rotherham U.	59	Chester	57
1975–76	Lincoln C.	74	Northampton T.	68	Reading	60	Tranmere R.	58
1976–77	Cambridge U.	65	Exeter C.	62	Colchester U.	59	Bradford C.	59
1977–78	Watford	71	Southend U.	60	Swansea C.	56	Brentford	56
1978–79	Reading	65	Grimsby T.	61	Wimbledon	61	Barnsley	61

Maximum points: 92. †Maximum points: 88 due to Accrington Stanley's resignation.
* Won on goal average.

THIRD DIVISION—SOUTH (1921-1958)

	First	Pts.	Second	Pts.	Third	Pts.
1920-21a	C. Palace	59	Southampton	54	Q.P.R.	53
1921-22a	*Southampton	61	Plymouth Arg.	61	Portsmouth	53
1922-23a	Bristol C.	59	Plymouth Arg.	53	Swansea T.	53
1923-24a	Portsmouth	59	Plymouth Arg.	55	Millwall	54
1924-25a	Swansea T.	57	Plymouth Arg.	56	Bristol C.	53
1925-26a	Reading	57	Plymouth Arg.	56	Millwall	53
1926-27a	Bristol C.	62	Plymouth Arg.	60	Millwall	56
1927-28a	Millwall	65	Northampton	55	Plymouth Arg.	53
1928-29a	*Charlton Ath.	54	C. Palace	54	Northampton	52
1929-30a	Plymouth Arg.	68	Brentford	61	Q.P.R.	51
1930-31a	Notts. Co.	59	C. Palace	51	Brentford	50
1931-32a	Fulham	57	Reading	55	Southend U.	53
1932-33a	Brentford	62	Exeter C.	58	Norwich C.	57
1933-34a	Norwich C.	61	Coventry C.	54	Reading	54
1934-35a	Charlton Ath.	61	Reading	53	Coventry C.	51
1935-36a	Coventry C.	57	Luton T.	56	Reading	54
1936-37a	Luton T.	58	Notts. Co.	56	Brighton	53
1937-38a	Millwall	56	Bristol C.	55	Q.P.R.	53
1938-39a	Newport Co.	55	C. Palace	52	Brighton	49
1939-46	Competition cancelled owing to war.					
1946-47a	Cardiff C.	66	Q.P.R.	57	Bristol C.	51
1947-48a	Q.P.R.	61	Bournemouth	57	Walsall	51
1948-49a	Swansea T.	62	Reading	55	Bournemouth	52
1949-50a	Notts. Co.	58	Northampton	51	Southend U.	51
1950-51d	Nottingham F.	70	Norwich C.	64	Reading	57
1951-52d	Plymouth Arg.	66	Reading	61	Norwich C.	61
1952-53d	Bristol R.	64	Millwall	62	Northampton	62
1953-54d	Ipswich T.	64	Brighton	61	Bristol C.	56
1954-55d	Bristol C.	70	Leyton O.	61	Southampton	59
1955-56d	Leyton O.	66	Brighton	65	Ipswich T.	64
1956-57d	*Ipswich T.	59	Torquay U.	59	Colchester U.	58
1957-58d	Brighton	60	Brentford	58	Plymouth Arg.	58

THIRD DIVISION—NORTH (1921-1958)

	First	Pts.	Second	Pts.	Third	Pts.
1921-22b	Stockport Co.	56	Darlington	50	Grimsby T.	50
1922-23b	Nelson	51	Bradford P.A.	47	Walsall	46
1923-24a	Wolverhampton W.	63	Rochdale	62	Chesterfield	54
1924-25a	Darlington	58	Nelson	53	New Brighton	53
1925-26a	Grimsby T.	61	Bradford P.A.	60	Rochdale	59
1926-27a	Stoke C.	63	Rochdale	58	Bradford P.A.	55
1927-28a	Bradford P.A.	63	Lincoln C.	55	Stockport Co.	54
1928-29a	Bradford C.	63	Stockport Co.	62	Wrexham	52
1929-30a	Port Vale	67	Stockport Co.	63	Darlington	50
1930-31a	Chesterfield	58	Lincoln C.	57	Wrexham	54
1931-32c	*Lincoln C.	57	Gateshead	57	Chester	50
1932-33a	Hull C.	59	Wrexham	57	Stockport Co.	54
1933-34a	Barnsley	62	Chesterfield	61	Stockport Co.	59
1934-35a	Doncaster R.	57	Halifax T.	55	Chester	54
1935-36a	Chesterfield	60	Chester	55	Tranmere R.	55
1936-37a	Stockport Co.	60	Lincoln C.	57	Chester	53
1937-38a	Tranmere R.	56	Doncaster R.	54	Hull C.	53
1938-39a	Barnsley	67	Doncaster R.	56	Bradford C.	52
1939-46	Competition cancelled owing to war.					
1946-47a	Doncaster R.	72	Rotherham U.	64	Chester	56
1947-48a	Lincoln C.	60	Rotherham U.	59	Wrexham	50
1948-49a	Hull C.	65	Rotherham U.	62	Doncaster R.	50
1949-50a	Doncaster R.	55	Gateshead	53	Rochdale	51
1950-51d	Rotherham U.	71	Mansfield T.	64	Carlisle U.	62
1951-52d	Lincoln C.	69	Grimsby T.	66	Stockport Co.	59
1952-53d	Oldham Ath.	59	Port Vale	58	Wrexham	56
1953-54d	Port Vale	69	Barnsley	58	Scunthorpe U.	57
1954-55d	Barnsley	65	Accrington S.	61	Scunthorpe U.	58
1955-56d	Grimsby T.	68	Derby Co.	63	Accrington S.	59
1956-57d	Derby Co.	63	Hartlepools U.	59	Accrington S.	58
1957-58d	Scunthorpe U.	66	Accrington S.	59	Bradford C.	57

Maximum points: a, 84; b, 76; c, 80; d, 92.   * Won on goal average.

LEAGUE TITLE WINS

LEAGUE DIVISION 1—Liverpool 11, Arsenal 8, Manchester U 7, Everton 7, Aston Villa 6, Sunderland 6, Newcastle U 4, Sheffield W 4, Huddersfield 3, Wolverhampton W 3, Blackburn R 2, Portsmouth 2, Preston NE 2, Burnley 2, Manchester C 2, Tottenham H 2, Leeds U 2, Derby Co 2, Chelsea 1, Sheffield U 1, WBA 1, Ipswich T 1, Nottingham F 1.

LEAGUE DIVISION 2—Manchester C 6, Leicester C 5, Sheffield W 5, Birmingham C (One as Small Heath) 4, Liverpool 4, Notts Co 3, Preston NE 3, Derby Co 3, Middlesbrough 3, Grimsby T 2, Nottingham F 2, Tottenham H 2, WBA 2, Aston Villa 2, Stoke C 2, Leeds U 2, Ipswich T 2, Burnley 2, Manchester U 2, Wolverhampton W 2, Bolton W 2, Huddersfield 1, Bristo. C 1, Brentford 1, Bury 1, Bradford C 1, Everton 1, Fulham 1, Sheffield U 1, West Ham U 1, Newcastle U 1, Coventry C 1, Blackpool 1, Blackburn R 1, Norwich C 1, Sunderland 1, Crystal Palace 1.

LEAGUE DIVISION 3—Plymouth Arg., Southampton, Bury, Portsmouth, Northampton, Coventry C. Carlisle U., Hull C., Q.P.R., Oxford U., Watford, Leyton O., Preston N.E., Aston Villa, Bolton W., Oldham Ath., Blackburn R., Hereford U., Mansfield T., Wrexham, Shrewsbury T.

LEAGUE DIVISION 4—Doncaster R., Peterborough U. (two); Port Vale, Walsall, Millwall, Brentford, Gillingham, Brighton, Stockport Co., Luton T., Chesterfield, Notts Co., Grimsby T., Southport, Mansfield T., Lincoln C., Cambridge U., Watford, Reading.

To 1957-58

DIVISION 3 (South): Bristol C., 3; Charlton Ath., Ipswich T., Millwall, Notts. Co., Plymouth Arg., Swansea T., 2; Brentford, Bristol R., Cardiff C., C. Palace, Coventry C., Fulham, Leyton O., Luton T., Newport Co., Nottingham F., Norwich C., Portsmouth, Q.P.R., Reading, Southampton, Brighton, 1.

DIVISION 3 (North): Barnsley, Doncaster R., Lincoln C., 3; Chesterfield, Grimsby T., Hull C., Port Vale, Stockport Co., 2; Bradford P.A., Bradford C., Darlington, Derby Co., Nelson, Oldham Ath., Rotherham U., Stoke C., Tranmere R., Wolverhampton W. Scunthorpe U., 1.

RELEGATED CLUBS

1891–92 League extended. Newton Heath, Sheffield W. and Nottingham F. admitted. *Second Division formed* including Darwen.
1892–93 In Test matches, Sheffield U. and Darwen won promotion in place of Notts. Co. and Accrington S.
1893–4 In Tests, Liverpool and Small Heath won promotion. Newton Heath and Darwen relegated.
1894–95 After Tests, Bury promoted Liverpool relegated.
1895–96 After Tests, Liverpool promoted, Small Heath relegated.
1896–97 After Tests, Notts. Co. promoted. Burnley relegated.
1897–98 Test system abolished after success of Stoke C. and Burnley. League extended. Blackburn R. and Newcastle U. elected to First Division. *Automatic promotion and relegation introduced.*

DIVISION 1 TO DIVISION 2

1898–99 Bolton W. and Sheffield W.
1899–1900 Burnley and Glossop
1900–1 Preston N.E. and W.B.A.
1901–2 Small Heath and Manchester C.
1902–3 Grimsby T. and Bolton W.
1903–4 Liverpool and W.B.A.
1904–5 League extended. Bury and Notts. Co. two bottom clubs in First Division, re-elected.
1905–6 Nottingham F. and Wolverhampton W.
1906–7 Derby Co. and Stoke C.
1907–8 Bolton W. and Birmingham C.
1908–9 Manchester C. and Leicester Fosse
1909–10 Bolton W. and Chelsea
1910–11 Bristol C. and Nottingham F.
1911–12 Preston N.E. and Bury
1912–13 Notts. Co. and Woolwich Arsenal
1913–14 Preston N.E. and Derby Co.
1914–15 Tottenham H. and *Chelsea
1919–20 Notts. Co. and Sheffield W.
1920–21 Derby Co. and Bradford
1921–22 Bradford C. and Manchester U.
1922–23 Stoke C. and Oldham Ath.
1923–24 Chelsea and Middlesbrough
1924–25 Preston N.E. and Nottingham F.
1925–26 Manchester C. and Notts. Co.
1926–27 Leeds U. and W.B.A.
1927–28 Tottenham H. and Middlesbrough
1928–29 Bury and Cardiff C.
1929–30 Burnley and Everton
1930–31 Leeds U. and Manchester U.
1931–32 Grimsby T. and West Ham U.
1932–33 Bolton W. and Blackpool
1933–34 Newcastle U. and Sheffield U.
1934–35 Leicester C. and Tottenham H.
1935–36 Aston Villa and Blackburn R.
1936–37 Manchester U. and Sheffield W.
1937–38 Manchester C. and W.B.A.
1938–39 Birmingham C. and Leicester C.
1946–47 Brentford and Leeds U.
1947–48 Blackburn R. and Grimsby T.
1948–49 Preston N.E. and Sheffield U.
1949–50 Manchester C. and Birmingham C.
1950–51 Sheffield W. and Everton
1951–52 Huddersfield and Fulham
1952–53 Stoke C. and Derby Co.
1953–54 Middlesbrough and Liverpool
1954–55 Leicester C. and Sheffield W.
1955–56 Huddersfield and Sheffield U.
1956–57 Charlton Ath. and Cardiff C.
1957–58 Sheffield W. and Sunderland
1958–59 Portsmouth and Aston Villa
1959–60 Luton T. and Leeds U.
1960–61 Preston N.E. and Newcastle U.
1961–62 Chelsea and Cardiff C.
1962–63 Manchester C. and Leyton O.
1963–64 Bolton W. and Ipswich T.
1964–65 Wolverhampton W. and Birmingham C.
1965–66 Northampton T. and Blackburn R.
1966–67 Aston Villa and Blackpool
1967–68 Fulham and Sheffield U.
1968–69 Leicester C. and Q.P.R.
1969–70 Sunderland and Sheffield W.
1970–71 Burnley and Blackpool
1971–72 Huddersfield T. and Nottingham F.
1972–73 C. Palace and W.B.A.
1973–74 Southampton, Manchester U., Norwich C.
1974–75 Luton T., Chelsea, Carlisle U.
1975–76 Wolverhampton W., Burnley, Sheffield U
1976–77 Sunderland, Stoke C., Tottenham H.
1977–78 West Ham U., Newcastle U., Leicester C.
1978–79 Q.P.R., Birmingham C., Chelsea

*Subsequently re-elected to Division 1 when League was extended after the War.

DIVISION 2 TO DIVISION 3

1920–21 Stockport Co.	1953–54 Brentford and Oldham Ath.
1921–22 Bradford and Bristol C.	1954–55 Ipswich T. and Derby Co.
1922–23 Rotherham C. and Wolverhampton W.	1955–56 Plymouth Arg. and Hull C.
1923–24 Nelson and Bristol C.	1956–57 Port Vale and Bury
1924–25 C. Palace and Coventry C.	1957–58 Doncaster R. and Notts. Co.
1925–26 Stoke C. and Stockport Co.	1958–59 Barnsley and Grimsby T.
1926–27 Darlington and Bradford C.	1959–60 Bristol C. and Hull C.
1927–28 Fulham and South Shields	1960–61 Lincoln C. and Portsmouth
1928–29 Port Vale and Clapton O.	1961–62 Brighton and Bristol R.
1929–30 Hull C. and Notts. Co.	1962–63 Walsall and Luton T.
1930–31 Reading and Cardiff C.	1963–64 Grimsby T. and Scunthorpe U.
1931–32 Barnsley and Bristol C.	1964–65 Swindon T. and Swansea T.
1932–33 Chesterfield and Charlton Ath.	1965–66 Middlesbrough and Leyton O.
1933–34 Millwall and Lincoln C.	1966–67 Northampton T. and Bury
1934–35 Oldham Ath. and Notts. Co.	1967–68 Plymouth Arg. and Rotherham U.
1935–36 Port Vale and Hull C.	1968–69 Fulham and Bury
1936–37 Doncaster R. and Bradford C.	1969–70 Preston N.E. and Aston Villa
1937–38 Barnsley and Stockport Co.	1970–71 Blackburn R. and Bolton W.
1938–39 Norwich C. and Tranmere R.	1971–72 Charlton Ath. and Watford
1946–47 Swansea T. and Newport Co.	1972–73 Huddersfield T. and Brighton
1947–48 Doncaster R. and Millwall	1973–74 C. Palace, Preston N. E., Swindon T.
1948–49 Nottingham F. and Lincoln C.	1974–75 Millwall, Cardiff C., Sheffield W.
1949–50 Plymouth Arg. and Bradford	1975–76 Oxford U., York C., Portsmouth
1950–51 Grimsby T. and Chesterfield	1976–77 Carlisle U., Plymouth Arg., Hereford U.
1951–52 Coventry C. and Q.P.R.	1977–78 Blackpool, Mansfield T., Hull C.
1952–53 Southampton and Barnsley	1978–79 Sheffield U., Millwall, Blackburn R.

DIVISION 3 TO DIVISION 4

1958–59 Rochdale, Notts. Co., Doncaster R. and Stockport Co.	1968–69 Oldham Ath., Crewe Alex., Hartlepools U. and Northampton.
1959–60 Accrington S., Wrexham, Mansfield T. and York C.	1969–70 Bournemouth, Southport, Barrow, Stockport Co.
1960–61 Chesterfield, Colchester U., Bradford C. and Tranmere R.	1970–71 Reading, Bury, Doncaster R., Gillingham.
1961–62 Newport Co., Brentford, Lincoln C. and Torquay U.	1971–72 Mansfield T., Barnsley, Torquay U., Bradford C.
1962–63 Bradford, Brighton, Carlisle U. and Halifax T.	1972–73 Rotherham U., Brentford, Swansea C., Scunthorpe U.
1963–64 Millwall, Crewe Alex., Wrexham and Notts. Co.	1973–74 Cambridge U., Shrewsbury T., Southport, Rochdale
1964–65 Luton T., Port Vale, Colchester U. and Barnsley	1974–75 AFC Bournemouth, Tranmere R., Watford, Huddersfield T.
1965–66 Southend U., Exeter C., Brentford and York C.	1975–76 Aldershot, Colchester U., Southend U., Halifax T.
1966–67 Doncaster R., Workington T., Darlington and Swansea T.	1976–77 Reading, Northampton T., Grimsby T., York C.
1967–68 Scunthorpe U., Colchester U., Grimsby T. and Peterborough U. (demoted)	1977–78 Port Vale, Bradford C., Hereford U., Portsmouth
	1978–79 Peterborough U., Walsall, Tranmere R., Lincoln C.

APPLICATIONS FOR RE-ELECTION

FOURTH DIVISION

NINE: Hartlepool.
SIX: Barrow (lost League place to Hereford U. 1972) Southport (lost League place to Wigan Ath. 1978)
FIVE: Lincoln C., Workington (lost League place to Wimbledon 1977) York C.
FOUR: Bradford P.A. (lost League place to Cambridge United 1970), Chester, Newport Co., Stockport Co., Darlington, Crewe.
THREE: Rochdale, Doncaster R., Halifax T.
TWO: Bradford C., Northampton T., Oldham Ath.
ONE: Aldershot, Colchester U., Exeter C., Gateshead (lost League place to Peterborough U. 1960), Grimsby T., Scunthorpe U., Swansea C., Wrexham.
Accrington S. resigned and Oxford U. were elected 1962.
Port Vale were forced to re-apply following expulsion in 1968.

THIRD DIVISIONS NORTH & SOUTH

SEVEN: Walsall.
SIX: Exeter C., Halifax T., Newport Co.
FIVE: Accrington S., Barrow, Gillingham, New Brighton, Southport.
FOUR: Rochdale, Norwich C.
THREE: C. Palace, Crewe Alex., Darlington, Hartlepool, Merthyr T., Swindon T.
TWO: Aberdare Ath., Aldershot, Ashington, Bournemouth, Brentford, Chester, Colchester U., Durham C., Millwall, Nelson, Q.P.R., Rotherham U. ,Southend U., Tranmere R., Watford, Workington T.
ONE: Bradford C., Bradford PA, Brighton, Bristol R., Cardiff C., Carlisle U., Charlton Ath., Gateshead, Grimsby T., Mansfield T., Shrewsbury T., Torquay U., York C.

HAT TRICK HEROES 1978-79

Football League

August
- 19 David Cross 3, West Ham U v Notts Co, Div 2
-     Brian Joicey 3, Barnsley v Halifax T, Div 4
- 22 Ross Jenkins 3, Watford v Blackpool, Div 3
- 25 Bernie Wright 3, Port Vale v Crewe Alex, Div 4
- 26 Alan Cork 3, Wimbledon v Northampton T, Div 4

September
- 2   Derek Spence 3, Blackpool v Carlisle U, Div 3
-     Keith Edwards 3, Hull C v Chester, Div 3
-     Jeff Hemmerman 3, Portsmouth v Crewe Alex, Div 4
- 16 Ron Futcher 3, Manchester C v Chelsea, Div 1
- 23 Fred Binney 3, Plymouth Arg v Sheffield W, Div 3
-     Ross Jenkins 4, Watford v Oxford U, Div 3
- 30 Jimmy Case 3, Liverpool v Bolton W, Div 1

October
- 7   Paul Randall 3, Bristol R v Blackburn R, Div 2
-     Bryan Robson 3, West Ham U v Millwall, Div 2
- 13 Ronnie Moore 3, Tranmere R v Chester, Div 3
- 21 Kevin Mabbutt 3, Bristol C v Manchester U, Div 1
- 28 Ian Edwards 3, Chester v Brentford, Div 3

November
- 4   Frank Stapleton 3, Arsenal v Ipswich T, Div 1
- 18 Paul Randall 3, Bristol R v Charlton Ath, Div 2
-     Peter Noble 3, Burnley v Fulham, Div 2

December
- 2   Wayne Entwistle 3, Sunderland v Bristol R, Div 2
- 9   John Lyons, 3 Wrexham v West Ham U, Div 2
- 16 Micky Burns 4, Middlesbrough v Chelsea, Div 1
- 23 Alan Sunderland 3, Arsenal v Tottenham H, Div 1
-     Malcolm Poskett 3, Brighton & HA v Charlton Ath, Div 2
-     Bob Cumming 3, Grimsby T v York C, Div 4
- 26 Joe Royle 3, Bristol C v Coventry C, Div 1
-     Teddy Maybank 3, Brighton & HA v Cardiff C, Div 2
-     Chris Guthrie 3, Fulham v Cambridge U, Div 2
-     Allan Clarke 3, Barnsley v Port Vale, Div 4

January
- 9   Tony Ford 3, Grimsby T v Bradford C, Div 4
- 13 Alan Biley 3, Cambridge U v Cardiff C, Div 2
- 16 Michael Lester 4, Grimsby T v Darlington, Div 4
- 31 Les Lawrence 3, Torquay U v Barnsley, Div 4

February
- 10 Andy King 3, Everton v Bristol C, Div 1
- 24 Gary Rowell 3, Sunderland v Newcastle U, Div 2
-     Alan Mayes 3, Swindon T v Rotherham U, Div 3
-     Les Bradd 3, Stockport Co v Barnsley, Div 4
- 28 Alan Cork 4, Wimbledon v Torquay U, Div 4

March
- 3   Ken Beamish 3, Bury v Exeter, Div 3
- 10 Steve Phillips 3, Brentford v Chester, Div 3
- 13 Mick Vinter 3, Notts Co v Sheffield U, Div 2
-     Tommy Graham 3, Barnsley v Scunthorpe U, Div 4
- 20 George Reilly 3, Northampton T v Scunthorpe U, Div 4
- 24 Andy Ritchie 3, Manchester U v Leeds U, Div 1
- 28 Martin O'Neill 3, Nottingham F v Chelsea, Div 1
-     John Alexander 4, Reading v Grimsby T, Div 4

April
- 13 Alan Young 3, Oldham Ath v Blackburn R, Div 2
-     Peter Houghton 3, Wigan Ath v Port Vale, Div 4
- 16 George Reilly 3, Northampton T v Bournemouth, Div 4
- 21 Ian Wallace 3, Coventry C v Southampton, Div 1
-     John Buchanan 3, Cardiff C v Sheffield U, Div 2
- 24 Colin Garwood 3, Portsmouth v Doncaster R, Div 4
- 25 Gary Shelton 3, Aston Villa v Arsenal, Div 1
-     Wilf Rostron 3, Sunderland v Sheffield U, Div 2
-     Steve Cooper 3, Torquay U v York C, Div 4
- 28 Clive Allen 3, QPR v Coventry C, Div 1
-     Alan Waddle 3, Swansea C v Southend U, Div 3
-     David McNiven 3, Bradford C v Crewe Alex, Div 4

May
- 5   Jack Lewis 3, Doncaster R v Grimsby T, Div 4
- 7   Gordon Staniforth 3, York C, v Port Vale, Div 4
- 14 Mark Lawrence 4, Hartlepool U v Halifax T, Div 4

League Cup

August
- 12 Trevor Phillips 3, Rotherham U v Hartlepool, Rd 1
- 15 Robbie James 3, Swansea C v Newport Co, Rd 1
- 29 Bob Latchford 5, Everton v Wimbledon, Rd 2
-     Martin Dobson 3, Everton v Wimbledon, Rd 2

FA Cup

November
- 25 Bobby Gough 3, Colchester U v Oxford U, Rd 1
-     Terry Park 3, Stockport Co v Morecambe, Rd 1
-     Ross Jenkins 3, Watford v Dagenham, Rd 1

December
- 19 Alan Curtis 3, Swansea C v Woking, Rd 2 re-play

January
- 16 Colin Lee 3, Tottenham H v Altrincham, Rd 3 re-play

February
- 26 Alan Young 3, Oldham Ath v Leicester C, Rd 4

LEADING SCORERS 1978-79

(Listed in order of League goals scored)

Division 1

	League	FA Cup	FL Cup	Total
Worthington (Bolton W)	24	—	2	26
Dalglish (Liverpool)	21	4	—	25
A Brown (WBA)	18	5	—	23
Stapleton (Arsenal)	17	6	1	24
Johnson (Liverpool)	16	2	—	18
Hawley (Leeds U)	16	—	1	17
Gowling (Bolton W)	15	—	1	16
Langley (Chelsea)	15	—	1	16
Regis (WBA)	15	1	—	16
Wallace (Coventry C)	15	—	—	15
Birtles (Nottingham F)	14	—	6	20
Burns (Middlesbrough)	14	—	—	14
Buckley (Birmingham C)	13	—	3	16
(inc 5 League, 3 LC for Walsall)				
Mariner (Ipswich T)	13	3	—	16
Brady (Arsenal)	13	2	—	15
Daly (Derby Co)	13	—	—	13
King (Everton)	12	—	—	12
J Greenhoff (Manchester U)	11	5	1	17
Latchford (Everton)	11	—	6	17
Channon (Manchester C)	11	—	3	14
Owen (Manchester C)	11	1	2	14
Coppell (Manchester U)	11	1	—	12
Armstrong (Middlesbrough)	11	—	—	11
Woodcock (Nottingham F)	10	1	3	14
O'Neill (Nottingham F)	10	1	1	12
Peters (Norwich C)	10	—	2	12
R Kennedy (Liverpool)	10	1	—	11
Taylor (Tottenham H)	10	1	—	11
Deehan (Aston V)	10	—	—	10
Ritchie (Manchester U	10	—	—	10

Division 2

	League	FA Cup	FL Cup	Total
Robson (West Ham U)	24	1	1	26
Bruce (Preston NE)	21	2	3	26
Rowell (Sunderland)	21	1	—	22
Biley (Cambridge U)	20	1	1	22
Randall (Stoke C)	18	—	—	18
(inc 13 League for Bristol R)				
Cross (West Ham U)	17	—	—	17
Buchanan (Cardiff C)	16	—	1	17
O'Callaghan (Stoke C)	16	—	1	17
Robinson (Charlton Ath)	15	1	3	19
Withe (Newcastle U)	14	2	—	16
Noble (Burnley)	14	—	1	15
Swindlehurst (C Palace)	14	—	1	15
Flanagan (Charlton Ath)	13	1	2	16
Guthrie (Fulham)	13	—	1	14
(inc 1 LC for Swindon T)				
Robinson (Preston NE)	13	—	1	14
Moores (Orient)	13	—	—	13
Moss (Luton T)	13	—	—	13
Stevens (Cardiff C)	13	—	—	13
Kitchen (Fulham)	12	2	—	14
(inc 7 League, 2 FA Cup for Orient)				
Crooks (Stoke C)	12	—	1	13
Vinter (Notts Co)	12	1	—	13
Anderson (Sheffield U)	12	—	—	12
Hatton (Luton T)	11	—	2	13
Moore (Cardiff C)	11	2	—	13
(inc 8 League, 2 FA Cup for Tranmere R)				
Entwistle (Sunderland)	11	1	—	12
Horton (Brighton & HA)	11	—	—	11
Mayo (Orient)	11	—	—	11
Rostron (Sunderland)	11	—	—	11
Shoulder (Newcastle U)	11	—	—	11
Stein (Luton T)	10	—	4	14
Young (Oldham Ath)	10	3	1	14
Hooks (Notts Co)	10	1	—	13
Lyons (Wrexham)	10	3	—	13
Ward (Brighton & HA)	10	—	3	13
White (Bristol R)	10	3	—	13
Maybank (Brighton & HA)	10	—	1	11
Seasman (Millwall)	10	—	1	11
Williams (Bristol R)	10	—	—	10

Division 3

	League	FA Cup	FL Cup	Total
Jenkins (Watford)	29	4	4	37
Binney (Plymouth Arg)	26	–	2	28
Edwards (Hull C)	24	1	–	25
Blissett (Watford)	21	–	7	28
Edwards (Chester)	20	–	3	23
Beamish (Bury)	20	1	–	21
(inc 4 League for Port Vale)				
Waddle (Swansea C)	19	1	1	21
Kellow (Blackpool)	18	1	2	21
(inc 7 League, 2 LC for Exeter)				
Kemp (Carlisle U)	18	2	1	21
Westwood (Gillingham)	18	1	–	19
Austin (Mansfield T)	18	–	–	18
(inc 13 League for Walsall)				
Gough (Colchester U)	16	6	–	22
Hornsby (Sheffield W)	16	4	1	21
Spence (Blackpool)	16	–	1	17
Bannister (Hull C)	15	–	1	16
James (Swansea C)	14	2	4	20
Bates (Swindon T)	14	2	1	17
Wylde (Sheffield W)	14	3	–	17
Phillips (Rotherham U)	14	1	1	16
Rowland (Swindon T)	14	1	1	16
(inc 1 League, 1 LC for Bury)				
Price (Gillingham)	14	–	1	15
Phillips (Brentford)	14	–	–	14
Gwyther (Rotherham U)	13	3	2	18
Maguire (Shrewsbury T)	13	5	–	18
Curtis (Swansea C)	13	5	3	21
Toshack (Swansea C)	13	1	1	15
McCulloch (Brentford)	13	–	–	13

Division 4

	League	FA Cup	FL Cup	Total
Dungworth (Aldershot)	26	8	–	34
Cork (Wimbledon)	22	2	2	26
Lee (Stockport Co)	20	2	2	24
Bell (Barnsley)	21	1	–	22
(inc 3 League for Halifax T)				
Reilly (Northampton T)	19	–	4	23
Goddard (Newport Co)	19	3	–	22
Leslie (Wimbledon)	19	–	–	19
Bradd (Stockport Co)	18	2	1	21
Lawrence (Torquay U)	17	1	1	19
Kilmore (Scunthorpe U)	17	–	–	17
Coyne (Crewe Alex)	16	1	1	18
Robins (Huddersfield T)	16	–	–	16
Earles (Reading)	15	–	4	19
Staniforth (York C)	15	4	–	19
Ford (Grimsby T)	15	–	–	15
Garwood (Portsmouth)	15	–	–	15
Gould (Hereford U)	15	–	–	15
(inc 2 League for Bristol R)				
McNiven (Bradford C)	15	–	–	15
Hemmerman (Portsmouth)	14	2	–	16
Cooper (Torquay U)	14	1	–	15
Wright (Port Vale)	14	–	1	15
MacDougall (AFC Bournemouth)	13	2	2	17
(inc 5 League, 2 LC for Southampton)				
Houghton (Wigan Ath)	13	1	–	13
Froggatt (Northampton T	13	–	–	14

CAREER RECORD OF LEAGUE GOALSCORERS

This is a list of players at present playing, who during their careers have scored 75 or more goals in Football League matches

248	E. MacDougall (AFC Bournemouth)		G. Graham (Crystal Palace)
220	M. Chivers (Brighton & HA)	103	D. Givens (Birmingham C)
	A. Clarke (Barnsley)	101	W. Dearden (Chesterfield)
217	B. Clark (Newport Co)	100	S. Bowles (QPR)
215	T. Brown (WBA)	99	B. Joicey (Barnsley)
209	B. Robson (West Ham U)		S. Pearson (Manchester U)
199	R. McNeil (Wrexham)	97	M. Elwiss (Crystal Palace)
191	M. Macdonald (Arsenal)	96	D. Hales (Charlton Ath)
178	M. Channon (Manchester C)	95	D. McKenzie (Blackburn R)
173	K. Randall (York C)	94	J. Lewis (Doncaster R)
170	F. Binney (Plymouth Arg)		J. O'Hare (Nottingham F)
167	B. Bannister (Hull C)		K. Peacock (Charlton Ath)
	J. Toshack (Swansea C)		J. Ward (Lincoln)
162	R. Latchford (Everton)	93	R. Jenkins (Watford)
161	M. Peters (Norwich C)	91	J. Laidlaw (Doncaster R)
160	A. Ball (Southampton)		A. McCulloch (Brentford)
	R. Gould (Hereford U)	90	R. Gough (Colchester U)
158	A. Woodward (Sheffield U)		P. Graham (Cambridge U)
156	R. Hatton (Luton T)		P. Hubbard (Lincoln)
151	P. Lorimer (Leeds U)		P. Mariner (Ipswich T)
149	F. Worthington (Bolton W)		M. Summerbee (Stockport Co)
143	L. Bradd (Stockport Co)		K. Weller (Leicester C)
142	C. Bell (Manchester C)		G. Whittle (Wrexham)
140	K. Beamish (Bury)	89	J. Murray (Brentford)
	J. Royle (Bristol C)		D. Richardson (Gillingham)
138	F. Clarke (Carlisle U)		S. Davey (Portsmouth)
135	T. Robson (Peterborough U)	87	M. Butler (AFC Bournemouth)
134	A. Buckley (Birmingham C)		W. Hughes (Leicester C)
	J. Greenhoff (Manchester U)		C. Jones (Rochdale)
133	P. Osgood (Chelsea)		B. O'Callaghan (Stoke C)
131	P. Boyer (Southampton)	86	R. Fern (Chesterfield)
129	E. Moss (Chesterfield)		J. Seal (Darlington)
	P. Noble (Burnley)	85	M. Flanagan (Charlton Ath)
128	B. Kidd (Everton)		R. Kennedy (Liverpool)
125	A. Griffiths (Wrexham)	83	R. Cross (Millwall)
124	T. Francis (Nottingham F)		W. Ashcroft (Middlesbrough)
123	B. Rioch (Derby Co)	82	T. Baldwin (Brentford)
122	P. Kitchen (Fulham)		F. Barton (AFC Bournemouth)
121	A. Gowling (Bolton W)		R. Shinton (Wrexham)
	V. Halom (Oldham Ath)	81	P. Summerill (Wimbledon)
	J. Radford (Blackburn R)	80	T. Phillips (Rotherham U)
120	D. Gwyther (Rotherham U)		W. Rafferty (Wolverhampton W)
118	B. Owen (Doncaster R)	79	A. Brown (WBA)
117	C. Garwood (Portsmouth)	78	D. Mills (WBA)
	D. Cross (West Ham U)	77	C. Garland (Bristol C)
115	J. Richards (Wolverhampton W)		A. Harding (Hartlepool)
	A. Warboys (Hull C)	76	I. Bowyer (Nottingham F)
112	A. Bruce (Preston NE)		P. Fletcher (Burnley)
110	R. Graydon (Oxford U)		M. Walsh (QPR)
109	D. Masson (Notts Co)	75	A. Currie (Leeds U)
	D. Shaw (Oldham Ath)		W. Garner (Cambridge U)
108	M. Bullock (Halifax T)		C. Guthrie (Fulham)
106	M. Burns (Middlesbrough)		R. Moore (Cardiff C)

TRANSFER TRAIL 1978-79

These transfers are those which were officially registered by the Football League and Football Association between 1 June 1978 and 30 May 1979.

June 1978

1	J. Stewart	Kilmarnock to Middlesbrough	20	A. Wilson	Southport to Torquay U
1	B. Wellings	Everton to York C	21	A. Harrison	The Football League Ltd to Carlisle U
2	P. Futcher	Luton T to Manchester C	23	M. Donaghy	Larne to Luton T
5	P. Sharkey	Mansfield T to Colchester U	23	R. Green	Chesterfield to Notts Co
6	A. Clarke	Leeds U to Barnsley	23	J Nixon	Barnsley to Halifax T
6	M. New	Arsenal to Mansfield T	24	J. Mitchell	Fulham to Millwall
7	M. Doyle	Manchester C to Stoke C	26	D. Latchford	Birmingham C to Motherwell
7	C. King	Clydebank to Notts Co	28	M. Bates	Walsall to Bradford C
7	P. Stronach	Sunderland to York C	28	P. Graham	Lincoln C to Cambridge U
8	S Finnieston	Chelsea to Sheffield U	28	R. Harkouk	C.rystal Palace to QPR
12	J. Stirk	Ipswich T to Watford	30	S. Irvine	Shrewsbury T to Stoke C
15	M Kerslake	Fulham to Brighton & HA	30	D. Loggie	Burnley to York C
15	B. Wright	Bradford C to Port Vale	30	B. Williams	QPR to Swindon T
20	S. Davey	Hereford U to Portsmouth			

July 1978

1	N. Edwards	Chester to Aldershot	21	N. Freeman	Southend U to Birmingham C
1	P. Roberts	Portsmouth to Hereford U	21	R. Hatton	Blackpool to Luton T
1	K. Sheedy	Hereford U to Liverpool	21	A. Larkin	Wrexham to Shrewsbury T
1	D. Sunley	Hull C to Lincoln C	21	S. Massey	Stockport Co to AFC Bournemouth
5	J. Flynn	Sheffield U to Rotherham U	22	J. Aston	Mansfield T to Blackburn R
5	M. Fowler	Huddersfield T to Blackburn R	22	J. Dennehy	Walsall to Bristol R
6	D. Smith	Lincoln C to Rotherham U	22	D. Gibson	Hull C to Scunthorpe U
7	R. Evans	Manchester C to Bury	25	J. McIlwraith	Bury to Portsmouth
7	R. Lugg	Crewe Alex to Bury	26	M. Butler	Huddersfield T to AFC Bournemouth
10	P. Barron	Plymouth Arg to Arsenal	26	G. Nulty	Newcastle U to Everton
10	A. Crompton	Blackburn R to Wigan Ath	27	V. Davidson	Motherwell to Blackpool
11	E. Snookes	The Football League Ltd to Rochdale	27	M. Holden	Sunderland to Blackpool
12	M Coffey	Everton to Mansfield T	27	R. Tynan	Tranmere R to Blackpool
13	G. Banton	Plymouth Arg to Fulham	28	M. Gorry	Newcastle U to Hartlepool U
13	M. Elwiss	Preston NE to Crystal Palace	29	R. Allen	Tranmere R to Mansfield T
13	M. French	Swindon T to Doncaster R	29	D. Hales	West Ham U to Charlton Ath
17	I. Miller	Doncaster R to Swindon T	29	M. Horswill	Plymouth Arg to Hull C
19	T. Cooper	Middlesbrough to Bristol C	29	J. Lacy	Fulham to Tottenham H
19	W. Green	West Ham U to Peterborough U	31	P. Ashworth	The Football League Ltd to Rochdale
19	A. Styles	Birmingham C to Peterborough U	31	S. Brooks	The Football League Ltd to Hartlepool
20	K. Hanvey	Grimsby T to Huddersfield T	31	G. Crudgington	Crewe Alex to Swansea C
20	C Turner	Peterborough U to Luton T			
21	A. Ainscow	Blackpool to Birmingham C			

Temporary Transfers – July 1978

19	N. Townsend	Southend U to Norwich C	31	E. Probert	Notts Co to Darlington
21	C. Viljoen	Ipswich T to QPR			

August 1978

1	L. Bradd	Notts Co to Stockport Co	7	D. Tomlin	Torquay U to Aldershot
1	S. Brennan	Crystal Palace to Plymouth Arg	8	K. Edwards	Sheffield U to Hull C
1	P. Cuff	Middlesbrough to Millwall	8	J. Thompson	WBA to Newport Co
1	R. Key	Exeter C to Cambridge U	9	C. Ogden	Oldham Ath to Swindon T
1	H McAuley	Charlton Ath to Tranmere R	10	K. Johnson	Huddersfield T to Halifax T
1	R. Walden	Sheffield W to Newport Co	10	J. Kelly	Wolverhampton W to Walsall
3	D. Bradley	Manchester U to Doncaster R	10	G. Roeder	Orient to QPR
3	G. Briggs	Middlesbrough to Oxford U	10	D. Wagstaffe	Blackburn R to Blackpool
3	D. Givens	QPR to Birmingham C	11	J. Turner	Reading to Torquay U
4	M. Burns	Newcastle U to Cardiff C	14	A. Kennedy	Newcastle U to Liverpool
4	R. Flavell	Halifax T to Chesterfield	15	A. Burns	Crystal Palace to Plymouth Arg
5	F. Lewis	Blackburn R to Doncaster R			
5	M. Walsh	Blackpool to Everton	15	G. Salmons	Leicester C to Chesterfield
7	D. Larnach	Newcastle U to Motherwell	16	P. Hoadley	Orient to Norwich C

435

Date	Player	Transfer
16	T. Sloan	Ballymena to Manchester U
16	C. Viljoen	Ipswich T to Manchester C
17	K. Baker	AFC Bournemouth to Ipswich
17	E. Curran	Derby Co to Southampton
17	D. Roberts	Hull C to Cardiff C
17	K. Todd	Wolverhampton W to Port Vale
18	J. Pearson	Everton to Newcastle U
18	T. Smith	Liverpool to Swansea C
19	R. Blackhall	Newcastle U to Sheffield W
19	J. Matthews	Arsenal to Sheffield U
21	R. Callachan	Newcastle U to Hibernian
21	T. Connell	Coleraine to Manchester U
21	P. McCandless	Coleraine to Manchester U
21	C. Suggett	Norwich C to Newcastle U
22	R. Futcher	Luton T to Manchester C
22	W. Goldthorpe	Huddersfield T to Hartlepool
23	P. Bielby	Hartlepool to Huddersfield T
24	J. Brownlie	Hibernian to Newcastle U
24	E. Potts	Brighton & HA to Preston NE
24	P. Withe	Nottingham F to Newcastle U
25	R. Davies	Reading to Torquay U
25	P. Edwards	Oldham Ath to Stockport Co
26	D. Masson	Derby Co to Notts Co
28	A. McCaffrey	Newcastle U to Derby Co
30	J. Capaldi	Aston Villa to Motherwell
30	S. Carter	Notts Co to Derby Co
31	M. Buckley	Everton to Sunderland
31	R. Chapman	Notts Co to Shrewsbury T
31	M. Moore	Port Vale to Wigan Ath

Temporary Transfers – August 1978

Date	Player	Transfer
2	A. Brand	Everton to Crewe Alex
11	F. McGrellis	Coventry C to Huddersfield T
11	P. McDonell	Liverpool to Oldham Ath
14	N. Townsend	Norwich C to Southend U (Transfer back)
15	C. Viljoen	QPR to Ipswich T (Transfer back)
16	D. Gregory	Stoke C to Blackburn R
18	K. Armstrong	Sunderland to Newport Co
18	P. Birchall	The Football League to Blackpool
22	A. Brand	Crewe Alex to Everton (Transfer back)
22	J. Platt	Middlesbrough to Hartlepool
24	P. Birchall	Blackpool to The Football League (Transfer back)
24	T. Pashley	Burnley to Blackpool
31	O. Williams	Southampton to Exeter C

September 1978

Date	Player	Transfer
6	J. Froggatt	Port Vale to Northampton T
7	D. Cusack	Sheffield W to Southend U
7	P. Lally	Swansea C to Doncaster R
7	R. McDonough	Birmingham C to Walsall
7	D. McKenzie	Everton to Chelsea
7	K. Oakes	Peterborough U to Newport Co
7	S. Waddington	Stoke C to Walsall
7	P. Went	Cardiff C to Orient
9	P. Boersma	Luton T to Swansea C
9	L. James	QPR to Burnley
9	P. McDonnell	Liverpool to Oldham Ath
13	R. Gould	Bristol R to Hereford U
14	F. Barton	Hereford U to AFC Bournemouth
14	I. Callaghan	Liverpool to Swansea C
14	J. Duncan	Tottenham H to Derby Co
15	C. Prophett	Swindon T to Chesterfield
19	D. Gregory	Stoke C to Bury
20	K. Beamish	Port Vale to Bury
20	G. Keenan	Bury to Port Vale
20	C. Todd	Derby Co to Everton
21	W. Caskey	Glentoran to Derby Co
21	C. Guthrie	Swindon T to Fulham
21	R. Hodge	Exeter C to Colchester U
21	V. Moreland	Glentoran to Derby Co
21	A. Rowland	Bury to Swindon T
22	J. Ritson	Bolton W to Bury
23	I. Robins	Bury to Huddersfield T
25	G. Ryan	Derby Co to Brighton & HA
26	C. Crawford	Bangor to Sunderland
26	T. Pashley	Burnley to Blackpool
27	G. Hodgson	Mansfield T to Oxford U
28	J. Clark	Manchester U to Derby Co
28	G. Watson	Cambridge U to Lincoln C
29	J. Craig	Celtic to Blackburn R
29	S. Neville	Southampton to Exeter C

Temporary Transfers – September 1978

Date	Player	Transfer
6	K. Roberts	Swindon T to Grimsby T
7	K. Barber	Swansea C to Cardiff C
7	A. Gilligan	Swindon T to Doncaster R
7	J. Sharpe	Southampton to Gillingham
7	M. Stead	Tottenham H to Southend U
21	D. Tong	Blackpool to Shrewsbury T
22	P. Lythgoe	Norwich C to Bristol R

October 1978

Date	Player	Transfer
3	I. Moores	Tottenham H to Orient
3	E. Probert	Notts Co to Darlington
4	J. Sharpe	Southampton to Gillingham
4	M. Burns	Cardiff C to Middlesbrough
5	R. Sbragia	Birmingham C to Walsall
6	P. Healy	Finn Harps to Port Vale
6	M. Pickering	Southampton to Sheffield W
7	T. Tynan	Sheffield W to Lincoln C
7	D. Lawson	Everton to Luton T
9	J. Alexander	Millwall to Reading
11	K. Tully	Crewe Alex to Port Vale
11	N. Wilkinson	Port Vale to Crewe Alex
12	J. Beck	Coventry C to Fulham
12	G. Cochrane	Burnley to Middlesbrough
12	B. Taylor	Plymouth Arg to Preston NE
12	A. Towner	Brighton & HA to Millwall
13	D. Bruton	Swansea C to Newport Co
13	D. Loadwick	Stockport Co to Hartlepool
19	J. Jones	Liverpool to Wrexham
19	J. McNicholl	Luton T to Brentford
19	D. Smith	Leicester C to Brentford
20	A. Walsh	Middlesbrough to Darlington
25	P. Haverson	QPR to Wimbledon
25	S. Perkins	QPR to Wimbledon
26	D. Bell	Halifax T to Barnsley
26	A. Buckley	Walsall to Birmingham C
26	R. Campbell	Huddersfield T to Halifax T
26	J. Ridley	Port Vale to Leicester C
26	D. Tong	Blackpool to Shrewsbury T
27	S. Kember	Leicester C to Crystal Palace

Temporary Transfers – October 1978

2	B. Vassallo	Torquay U to Norwich C	13	B. Silkman	Crystal Palace to Plymouth Arg
5	K. Armstrong	Sunderland to Scunthorpe U	27	M. Prendergast	Barnsley to Halifax T
5	L. Frost	Chelsea to Brentford	31	C. Turner	Lincoln C to Sheffield W (Transfer back)
6	C. Turner	Sheffield W to Lincoln C			
7	D. Felgate	Bolton W to Rochdale	31	I. Turner	Southampton to Lincoln C
12	D. Clarke	Orient to Carlisle U			

November 1978

1	D. Christie	Northampton T to Cambridge U	11	M. Stead	Tottenham H to Southend U
1	T. Lee	Millwall to Colchester U	15	B. Hamilton	Millwall to Swindon T
1	N. McNab	Tottenham H to Bolton W	15	T. Kellow	Exeter C to Blackpool
1	D. Pugh	Rotherham U to York C	16	N. Chatterton	Crystal Palace to Millwall
2	W. Garner	Chelsea to Cambridge U	16	I. Pearson	Millwall to Exeter C
4	D. Stewart	Leeds U to WBA	17	A. Hazell	Millwall to Crystal Palace
8	E. MacDougall	Southampton to AFC Bournemouth	23	M. Thomas	Wrexham to Manchester U
			25	R. Train	Bolton W to Watford
8	L. Phillips	Aston Villa to Swansea C	30	G. Jones	Bolton W to Blackpool
9	P. Farrell	Bury to Port Vale	30	J. Findlay	Aston Villa to Luton T
10	B. Silkman	Crystal Palace to Plymouth Arg			

Temporary Transfers – November 1978

3	D. Cunningham	Swindon T to Peterbourgh U	10	J. Platt	Middlesbrough to Cardiff C
8	R. Malone	Hartlepool U to Blackpool	17	J. Grattan	Sunderland to Mansfield T
9	G. Dulson	Port Vale to Crewe Alex			

December 1978

1	B. McNeill	Bristol C to Plymouth Arg	21	S. Fox	Birmingham C to Wrexham
1	M. Martin	WBA to Newcastle U	21	D. Giles	Cardiff C to Wrexham
5	H. Holman	Exeter C to Peterborough U	21	S. Simms	Leicester C to Watford
8	D. Dawkins	Leicester C to Mansfield T	21	P. Sutcliffe	Port Vale to Chester
9	T. Graham	Aston Villa to Barnsley	21	J. Ward	Clyde to Aston Villa
12	D. Cunningham	Swindon T to Aston Villa	21	N. Warnock	York C to Crewe Alex
13	R. Bowers	Cliftonville to Derby Co	22	D. Webb	Leicester C to Derby Co
13	R. Malone	Hartlepool to Blackpool	24	P. Marinello	Motherwell to Fulham
14	M. Aleksic	Luton T to Tottenham H	24	B. Taylor	Doncaster R to Rochdale
14	K. Swain	Chelsea to Aston Villa	27	C. George	Derby Co to Southampton
19	J. Sims	Notts Co to Exeter C	28	P. Randall	Bristol R to Stoke C
20	R. Delgado	Chester to Port Vale	29	R. Smith	Hibernian to Leicester C

Temporary Transfers – December 1978

5	L. Chapman	Stoke C to Plymouth Arg	19	J. McCaffrey	Portsmouth to Northampton T
6	M. Trusson	Plymouth Arg to Stoke C	22	J. Emmanuel	Birmingham C to Bristol R
14	M. Grew	WBA to Wigan Ath	22	N. Johns	Sheffield U to Charlton Ath
14	B. Rioch	Derby Co to Birmingham C	29	C. O'Brien	Bristol C to Hereford U
15	R. Hansbury	Norwich C to Orient			

January 1979

8	N. Hamilton	Leicester C to Mansfield T	12	I. Turner	Southampton to Walsall
10	R. Greenwood	Sunderland to Derby Co	18	A. Barker	Newcastle U to Gillingham
10	D. Mills	Middlesbrough to WBA	20	S. Jones	QPR to Walsall
11	A. Robertson	Peterborough U to Bradford C	23	G. Dulson	Port Vale to Crewe Alex
			25	J. McCaffrey	Portsmouth to Northampton T
11	B. Talbot	Ipswich T to Arsenal			
11	S. Taylor	Oldham Ath to Luton T	25	S. Wicks	Chelsea to Derby Co
12	J. Cooke	Bradford C to Peterborough U	26	T. Hayes	Luton T to Linfield
			29	E. Bannon	Heart of Midlothian to Chelsea
12	E. Moss	Mansfield T to Chesterfield			
12	E. Thompson	Coventry C to Larne	29	J. Emmanuel	Birmingham C to Bristol R

Temporary Transfers – January 1979

4	L. Sivell	Ipswich T to Lincoln C	22	W. Boyd	Hull C to Doncaster R
20	L. Harwood	Southampton to Wimbledon	22	B. Johnson	Plymouth Arg to Torquay U

February 1979

1	D. Showers	AFC Bournemouth to Portsmouth	19	P. Dornan	Linfield to Swindon T
1	C. Sullivan	Norwich C to Cardiff C	19	J. McPhail	Dundee to Sheffield U
5	G. Keegan	Manchester C to Oldham Ath	20	B. Attley	Cardiff C to Swansea C
8	A. Mayes	Watford to Swindon T	20	L. Harwood	Southampton to Wimbledon
8	G. Smith	Aston Villa to Tottenham H	20	I. Hendry	Aston Villa to Hereford U
13	J. Fleming	Aberdeen to Sheffield W	22	M. Gray	Fulham to Orient
14	T. Francis	Birmingham C to Nottingham F	22	M. Kitchen	Orient to Fulham
			22	P. Parkes	QPR to West Ham U
16	J. Fleeting	Norwich C to Ayr U	23	R. Moore	Tranmere R to Cardiff C
18	K. Moore	Swansea C to Newport Co	23	T. Tynan	Lincoln C to Newport Co

Temporary Transfers – February 1979

2	J. Cook	Stoke C to Bradford C	25	J. Kilner	Preston NE to Halifax T
15	B. Silkman	Plymouth Arg to Luton T			

March 1979

1	J. Docherty	E Stirlingshire to Chelsea	23	D. Brown	Clydebank to Sheffield U
1	I. Varadi	Sheffield U to Everton	25	S. Whitworth	Leicester C to Sunderland
1	D. Wagstaffe	Blackpool to Blackburn R	26	R. Coughlin	Manchester C to Blackburn R
2	K. Hird	Blackburn R to Leeds U			
2	C. Wigginton	Lincoln C to Grimsby T	26	D. Latchford	Motherwell to Bury
3	D. Lawson	Luton T to Stockport Co	27	F. McGrellis	Coventry C to Hereford U
8	A. Guy	Newcastle U to Peterborough U	27	V. Thomas	Coventry C to Hereford U
			28	T. Austin	Walsall to Mansfield T
8	R. Kerr	Sunderland to Blackpool	28	M. McGhee	Newcastle U to Aberdeen
8	A. Smith	Newcastle U to Peterborough U	28	D. Syrett	Mansfield T to Walsall
			29	P. Bowgett	Tottenham H to Wimbledon
13	D. McKenzie	Chelsea to Blackburn R	29	T. Cunningham	QPR to Wimbledon
13	S. Stainrod	Sheffield U to Oldham Ath	29	E. Curran	Southampton to Sheffield W
15	S. Elliott	Nottingham F to Preston NE	29	P. Eastoe	QPR to Everton
16	A. Harding	Lincoln C to Hartlepool	29	A. Funnell	Southampton to Gillingham
16	J. Peachey	Barnsley to Darlington	29	B. Kidd	Manchester C to Everton
16	E. White	Leicester C to Hereford U	29	A. Otulakowski	West Ham U to Southend U
19	G. Bell	Oldham Ath to Preston NE	29	P. Scott	York C to Aldershot
19	P. Sharkey	Colchester U to Peterborough U	29	A. Sealy	Southampton to Crystal Palace
21	T. Birch	Liverpool to Shrewsbury T	29	B. Silkman	Plymouth Arg to Manchester C
21	S. Bryant	Northampton T to Portsmouth	29	L. Tibbott	Ipswich T to Sheffield U
22	M. Chivers	Norwich C to Brighton & HA	29	M. Walsh	Everton to QPR
			30	J. Watson	Huddersfield T to Hartlepool

Temporary Transfers – March 1979

1	M. Carter	Bolton W to Mansfield T	24	K. Baker	Ipswich T to Norwich C
8	P. Holder	Crystal Palace to AFC Bournemouth	24	J. Curtis	Blackburn R to Wigan Ath
			27	G. Hedley	Middlesbrough to Darlington
8	M. Rathbone	Birmingham C to Blackburn R	28	P. Matthews	Rotherham U to Northampton T
12	J. Sparrow	Chelsea to Millwall	28	F. Phillipston-Masters	Southampton to Luton T
14	R. Wilson	Chelsea to Orient			
16	L. Milligan	Blackpool to Portsmouth	29	M. Grew	WBA to Notts Co
22	T. Phillips	Chelsea to Swansea C	30	B. Rioch	Derby Co to Sheffield U
23	M. Aleksic	Tottenham H to Sheffield U	30	M. Rogan	Stockport Co to Crewe Alex
23	G. Johnson	Chelsea to Crystal Palace	30	J. Thomas	Everton to Tranmere R
23	G. Shipley	Southampton to Reading			

April 1979

2	V. Davidson	Blackpool to Celtic	6	P. Holder	Crystal Palace to AFC Bournemouth
4	M. Rathbone	Birmingham C to Blackburn R			

Temporary Transfers – April 1979

16	W. Boyd	Doncaster R to Hull C (Transfer back)

LEADING GOALSCORERS IN EACH DIVISION OF THE FOOTBALL LEAGUE SINCE WORLD WAR II

1946–47

Division 1		Division 2	
D Westcott (Wolverhampton W)	37	C Wayman (Newcastle U)	30
D Reid (Portsmouth)	29	J D Walsh (WBA)	28
F Steele (Stoke C)	29	G Lowrie (Coventry C)	26
R Lewis (Arsenal)	28	G Robledo (Barnsley)	24
S Mortensen (Blackpool)	28		

Division 3 (South)		Division 3 (North)	
D Clark (Bristol C)	36	C Jordan (Doncaster R)	42
M G McPhee (Reading)	31	W Ardron (Rotherham U)	38
S Richards (Cardiff C)	31	R Yates (Chester)	36
A Garrett (Northampton T)	26	P M Cheetham (Lincoln C)	28
J W Stephens (Swindon T)	25		

1947–48

Division 1		Division 2	
R Rooke (Arsenal)	33	E Quigley (Sheffield W)	23
M Fenton (Middlesbrough)	28	A J Wakefield (Leeds U)	22
A Stubbins (Liverpool)	26	D J Walsh (WBA)	22
J Rowley (Manchester U)	23	J Milburn (Newcastle U)	21
S Mortensen (Blackpool)	21	J Downie (Bradford)	19

Division 3 (South)		Division 3 (North)	
L Townsend (Bristol C)	29	J Hutchinson (Lincoln C)	32
D Milligan (Bournemouth & BA)	26	W Ardron (Rotherham U)	27
D Massart (Walsall)	23	J Lindsay (Carlisle U)	26
C Hatton (QPR)	21	T Wyles (Southport)	26
		W F Tunnicliffe (Wrexham)	20

1948–49

Division 1		Division 2	
W Moir (Bolton W)	25	C Wayman (Southampton)	32
F Bowyer (Stoke C)	21	T Briggs (Grimsby T)	26
R Bentley (Chelsea)	20	D Massart (Bury)	25
J Rowley (Manchester U)	20	R Thomas (Fulham)	23
C Vaughan (Charlton Ath)	20	D J Walsh (WBA)	23

Division 3 (South)		Division 3 (North)	
D McGibbon (Bournemouth & BA)	30	W Ardron (Rotherham U)	29
S Richards (Swansea T)	26	A Patrick (York C)	26
J Sewell (Notts County)	26	A Quinn (Darlington)	23
P E Chapman (Walsall)	25	N W Moore (Hull C)	22
W M Jones (Swindon T)	25	E Gemmell (Oldham A)	19

1949–50

Division 1		Division 2	
D Davis (Sunderland)	25	T Briggs (Grimsby T)	35
S Mortensen (Blackpool)	22	C Wayman (Southampton)	24
J Stamps (Derby Co)	22	W Robinson (West Ham U)	23
H Goring (Arsenal)	21	J Lee (Leicester C)	22
J Rowley (Manchester U)	20	L Medley (Tottenham H)	18

Division 3 (South)		Division 3 (North)	
T Lawton (Notts Co)	31	P Doherty (Doncaster R)	26
W Ardron (Nottingham F)	25	R Phillips (Crewe Alex)	26
A J Wakefield (Southend U)	23	A C Burgess (Chester)	24
R Blackman (Reading)	22	E Dodds (Lincoln C)	21
J Devlin (Walsall)	22	D Travis (Accrington Stanley)	20

1950–51

Division 1		Division 2	
S Mortensen (Blackpool)	30	J McCormack (Barnsley)	33
J Lee (Derby Co)	28	A Rowley (Leicester C)	28
N Lofthouse (Bolton W)	21	C Wayman (Preston NE)	27
A McCrae (Middlesbrough)	21	W Robinson (West Ham U)	26
D Reid (Portsmouth)	21		

Division 3 (South)		Division 3 (North)	
W Ardron (Nottingham F)	36	J Shaw (Rotherham U)	37
R Blackman (Reading)	35	R Crosbie (Bradford)	27
J Constantine (Millwall)	27	L E Wildon (Hartlepools U)	26
M Tadman (Plymouth Arg)	23	A Burgess (Chester)	22
		J Nuttall (Southport)	22

1951–52

Division 1		Division 2	
G Robledo (Newcastle U)	33	D Dooley (Sheffield W)	46
R Allen (WBA)	32	A Rowley (Leicester C)	38
J Rowley (Manchester U)	30	W Ardron (Nottingham F)	29
J Dixon (Aston Villa)	26	W Grant (Cardiff C)	26
C Wayman (Preston NE)	24		

Division 3 (South)

R Blackman (Reading)	39	
V Lambden (Bristol R)	29	
M Tadman (Plymouth Arg)	27	
F Ramscar (Northampton T)	24	

Division 3 (North)

A Graver (Lincoln C)	36	
W Cairns (Grimsby T)	32	
W Fenton (York C)	31	
E Gemmell (Oldham A)	28	
D Frost (Halifax T)	24	

1952-53

Division 1

C Wayman (Preston NE)	24
P Harris (Portsmouth)	23
D Lishman (Arsenal)	23

Division 2

A Rowley (Leicester C)	39
B Jezzard (Fulham)	34
J Glazzard (Huddersfield T)	30
J Charles (Leeds U)	26
J Pye (Luton T)	24

Division 3 (South)

G Bradford (Bristol R)	33
R Collins (Torquay U)	27
J English (Northampton T)	26
J Rodgers (Bristol C)	26
W O'Donnell (Northampton T)	26

Division 3 (North)

J Whitehouse (Carlisle U)	29
J Connor (Stockport Co)	26
W Fenton (York C)	24
E Gemmell (Oldham A)	24
D Travis (Chester)	24

1953-54

Division 1

J Glazzard (Huddersfield T)	29
J Nicholls (WBA)	29
R Allen (WBA)	25
J Hancocks (Wolverhampton W)	25
D Wilshaw (Wolverhampton W)	25

Division 2

J Charles (Leeds U)	42
B Jezzard (Fulham)	38
T Briggs (Blackburn R)	32
R Burke (Rotherham U)	32
J W Parker (Everton)	31

Division 3 (South)

J English (Northampton T)	28
R Blackman (Reading)	27
E Day (Southampton)	26
L Graham (Newport Co)	24
J Atyeo (Bristol C)	23

Division 3 (North)

J Connor (Stockport Co)	31
G Ashman (Carlisle U)	30
C Done (Tranmere R)	25
R Brown (Barnsley)	24
K Murray (Mansfield T)	22

1954-55

Division 1

R Allen (WBA)	27
J Glazzard (Huddersfield T)	26
E Firmani (Charlton A)	25
J Hancocks (Wolverhampton W)	25

Division 2

T Briggs (Blackburn R)	33
G Turner (Luton T)	32
W Liddell (Liverpool)	30
J Evans (Liverpool)	29
G Bradford (Bristol R)	27

Division 3 (South)

E Morgan (Gillingham)	31
J Atyeo (Bristol C)	28
E Day (Southampton)	27
R Hollis (Southend U)	27

Division 3 (North)

A Bottom (York C)	30
J Connor (Stockport Co)	30
D Travis (Oldham A)	30
G Stewart (Accrington S)	28
J Whitehouse (Carlisle U)	25

1955-56

Division 1

N Lofthouse (Bolton W)	33
C Fleming (Sunderland)	28
V Keeble (Newcastle U)	26
T Taylor (Manchester U)	25

Division 2

W Gardiner (Leicester C)	34
R Shiner (Sheffield W)	33
T Briggs (Blackburn R)	31
J Atyeo (Bristol C)	30
J Charles (Leeds U)	30

Division 3 (South)

R Collins (Torquay U)	40
R A R Hunt (Norwich C)	31
T Parker (Ipswich T)	30
K McCurley (Colchester U)	29
A Mundy (Brighton & HA)	27

Division 3 (North)

R Crosbie (Grimsby T)	36
G Stewart (Accrington S)	35
W Sowden (Chesterfield)	32
A Bottom (York C)	31
J Connor (Stockport Co)	30

1956-57

Division 1

J Charles (Leeds U)	38
J Mudie (Blackpool)	32
G Turner (Luton T)	30
N Lofthouse (Bolton W)	28

Division 2

A Rowley (Leicester C)	44
B Clough (Middlesbrough)	38
T Briggs (Blackburn R)	32
J Barrett (Nottingham F)	27
T Johnston (Leyton O)	27

Division 3 (South)

E Phillips (Ipswich T)	42
R Collins (Torquay U)	30
S Newsham (Bournemouth & BA)	30
T Dixon (Reading)	28
B Edwards (Swindon T)	25

Division 3 (North)

R Straw (Derby Co)	37
G Stewart (Accrington S)	33
W Tulip (Darlington)	32
R Smith (Bradford)	28
W Gordon (Barrow)	27

1957-58

Division 1

R Smith (Tottenham H)	36
T Thompson (Preston NE)	34
G Turner (Luton T)	33
J Murray (Wolverhampton W)	29
T Finney (Preston NE)	26

Division 2

B Clough (Middlesbrough)	40
T Johnston (Leyton O)	35
J Summers (Charlton Ath)	28
R Rafferty (Grimsby T)	26
J Atyeo (Bristol C)	23

441

Division 3 (South)		Division 3 (North)	
S McCrory (Southend U)	31	A Ackerman (Carlisle U)	35
D Reeves (Southampton)	31	K Williams (Tranmere R)	28
E Towers (Brentford)	29	G Stewart (Accrington Stanley)	27
W Carter (Plymouth Arg)	26	B Jepson (Chester)	25
T Dixon (Reading)	24	J Parker (Bury)	25

1958–59

Division 1		Division 2	
J Greaves (Chelsea)	33	B Clough (Middlesbrough)	42
R Smith (Tottenham H)	32	R Shiner (Sheffield W)	28
R Charlton (Manchester U)	29	R Froggatt (Sheffield W)	26
N Lofthouse (Bolton W)	29	D Pace (Sheffield U)	26
		D Ward (Bristol R)	26
Division 3		Division 4	
E Towers (Brentford)	32	A Rowley (Shrewsbury T)	37
W Bradbury (Hull C)	30	A Woan (Northampton T)	32
J McCole (Bradford C)	28	A Richards (Walsall)	28
C Smith (Hull C)	26	E Calland (Exeter C)	27
T Rowley (Tranmere R)	25	R Straw (Coventry C)	27

1959–60

Division 1		Division 2	
D Viollet (Manchester U)	32	B Clough (Middlesbrough)	39
J Greaves (Chelsea)	29	E Phillips (Ipswich T)	24
J Murray (Wolverhampton W)	29	T Johnston (Leyton Orient)	24
L White (Newcastle U)	28	W Curry (Brighton & HA)	23
D Kevan (WBA)	26	G Hitchens (Aston Villa)	23
Division 3		Division 4	
D Reeves (Southampton)	39	C Holton (Watford)	42
R Hunt (Grimsby T)	33	E Uphill (Watford)	30
A Rowley (Shrewsbury T)	32	J Allan (Bradford)	27
M King (Colchester U)	30	H Llewellyn (Crewe Alex)	25
D Price (Southend U)	28		

1960–61

Division 1		Division 2	
J Greaves (Chelsea)	41	R Crawford (Ipswich T)	39
D Herd (Arsenal)	29	B Clough (Middlesbrough)	34
G Hitchens (Aston Villa)	29	E Phillips (Ipswich T)	30
J Farmer (Wolverhampton W)	28		
R Smith (Tottenham H)	28		
Division 3		Division 4	
A Richards (Walsall)	36	T Bly (Peterborough U)	52
B Bedford (QPR)	33	G Hudson (Accrington Stanley)	35
C Taylor (Walsall)	33	P Burridge (Millwall)	34
C Holton (Watford)	32	J Byrne (Crystal Palace)	30
J Wheeler (Reading)	31	R Summersby (Crystal Palace)	25

1961–62

Division 1		Divison 2	
R Crawford (Ipswich T)	33	R Hunt (Liverpool)	41
D Kevan (WBA)	33	B Thomas (Scunthorpe U)	31
R Charnley (Blackpool)	30	B Clough (Sunderland)	29
E Phillips (Ipswich T)	28	G O'Brien (Southampton)	28
T R Vernon (Everton)	28	A Peacock (Middlesbrough)	24
Division 3		Division 4	
C Holton (Northampton T 36, plus 1 for Watford)	37	R R Hunt (Colchester U)	37
B Bedford (QPR)	36	D Layne (Bradford C)	34
R Rafferty (Grimsby T)	34	M King (Colchester U)	31
T Bly (Peterborough U)	30	F Lord (Crewe Alex)	30
J. Atyeo (Bristol C)	26	J Weir (York C)	28

1962–63

Division 1		Division 2	
J Greaves (Tottenham H)	37	R Tambling (Chelsea)	35
J Baker (Arsenal)	29	A Peacock (Middlesbrough)	31
D Layne (Sheffield W)	29	T Allcock (Norwich C)	26
R Crawford (Ipswich T)	25	J Storrie (Leeds U)	25
		B Clough (Sunderland)	24
Division 3		Division 4	
G Hudson (Coventry C)	30	K Wagstaff (Mansfield T)	34
D Ward (Watford)	29	C Booth (Doncaster R)	34
M King (Colchester U)	26	R Chapman (Mansfield T)	31
A Ashworth (Northampton T)	25	H Lister (Oldham Ath)	30
		F Lord (Crewe Alex)	30

1963–64

Division 1		Division 2	
J Greaves (Tottenham H)	35	R Saunders (Portsmouth)	33
M McEvoy (Blackburn R)	32	A Dawson (Preston NE)	31
R Hunt (Liverpool)	31	D Kevan (Manchester C)	30
D Law (Manchester U)	30	R T Davies (Norwich C)	26
R Crawford (Wolverhampton W 26, plus 2 for Ipswich T)	28	J Crossan (Sunderland)	22

R.F. 79/80—23

Division 3		Division	
A Biggs (Bristol R)	30	H McIlmoyle (Carlisle U)	39
K Wagstaff (Mansfield T)	29	H Green (Bradford C)	29
D Coughlin (Bournemouth & BA)	28	A Spence (Southport)	27
G Hudson (Coventry C)	25	J Dyson (Tranmere R)	26
		J Bonson (Newport Co)	25

1964–65

Division 1		Division 2	
J Greaves (Tottenham H)	29	G O'Brien (Southampton)	34
A McEvoy (Blackburn R)	29	A Dawson (Preston NE)	26
D Law (Manchester U)	28	B Godfrey (Preston NE)	25
F Pickering (Everton)	27	A Bennett (Rotherham U)	24
		F Lee (Bolton W)	23
Division 3		Division 4	
K Wagstaff (Mansfield T 8, plus 23 for Hull C)	31	A Jeffrey (Doncaster R)	36
		T Harkin (Crewe Alex)	35
C Chilton (Hull C)	27	R Stubbs (Torquay U)	31
J Atyeo (Bristol C)	23	K Hector (Bradford)	29
B Bedford (QPR)	23		
A Clarke (Walsall)	23		

1965–66

Division 1		Division 2	
R Hunt (Liverpool)	30	M Chivers (Southampton)	30
W Irvine (Burnley)	29	G Vowden (Birmingham C)	21
T Hateley (Aston Villa)	27	P Knowles (Wolverhampton W)	20
D Herd (Manchester U)	24	J Atyeo (Bristol C)	19
G Hurst (West Ham U)	23		
Division 3		Division 4	
L Allen (QPR)	30	K Hector (Bradford)	34
M Tees (Grimsby T)	28	J O'Rourke (Luton T)	32
K Wagstaff (Hull C)	27	J Dyson (Tranmere R)	29
B Gibbs (Gillingham)	23	L Sheffield (Doncaster R)	28

1966–67

Division 1		Division 2	
R Davies (Southampton)	37	R Gould (Coventry C)	24
G Hurst (West Ham U)	29	F Lee (Bolton W)	22
A Clarke (Fulham)	24	R Crawford (Ipswich T)	21
J Greaves (Tottenham H)	23	K Wagstaff (Hull C)	21
D Law (Manchester U)	23	E Hunt (Wolverhampton W)	20
Division 3		Division 4	
R Marsh (QPR)	30	E Phythian (Hartlepools U)	23
J O'Rourke (Middlesbrough)	27	E Chapman (Lincoln C)	20
I Towers (Oldham Ath)	27	J Mulvaney (Hartlepools U)	19
D Rogers (Swindon T)	25	R Smith (Southend U)	19

1967–68

Division 1		Division 2	
G Best (Manchester U)	28	J Hickton (Middlesbrough)	24
R Davies (Southampton)	28	B Bridges (Birmingham C)	23
J Astle (WBA)	25	K Hector (Derby Co)	21
R Hunt (Liverpool)	25	G Ingram (Blackpool)	18
J Greaves (Tottenham H)	23	R Woodruff (Crystal Palace)	18
Division 3		Division 4	
D Rogers (Swindon T)	25	R Chapman (Port Vale)	25
R Owen (Bury)	25	L Massie (Halifax T)	25
J Fryatt (Torquay U 2 plus 22 for Stockport County)	24	B Rioch (Luton T)	24
		E Loyden (Chester)	22
K Napier (Brighton & HA)	24	K Randall (Chesterfield)	21
G Yardley (Tranmere R)	23		

1968–69

Division 1		Division 2	
J Greaves (Tottenham H)	27	J Toshack (Cardiff C)	22
G Hurst (West Ham U)	25	K Wagstaff (Hull C)	20
J Royle (Everton)	22	J Hickton (Middlesbrough)	18
J Astle (WBA)	21		
Division 3		Division 4	
B Lewis (Luton T)	22	G Talbot (Chester)	22
D Rogers (Swindon T)	22	W Best (Southend U)	20
G Andrews (Southport)	19	J Howarth (Aldershot)	19
W Atkins (Stockport Co)	18	E MacDougall (York C)	19

1969–70

Division 1		Division 2	
J Astle (WBA)	25	J Hickton (Middlesbrough)	24
P Osgood (Chelsea)	23	B Bridges (QPR)	22
J Royle (Everton)	23	J Byrom (Bolton W)	20
B Robson (Newcastle U)	22		
H Curran (Wolverhampton W)	20		

Division 3		Division 4	
G Jones (Bury)	26	A Kinsey (Wrexham)	27
M Macdonald (Luton T)	25	S Brace (Grimsby T)	25
L Chappell (Reading)	24	J Hall (Peterborough U)	24
S Earle (Fulham)	22		
E MacDougall (Bournemouth & BA)	21		

1970–71

Division 1		Division 2	
A Brown (WBA)	28	J Hickton (Middlesbrough)	25
M Chivers (Tottenham H)	21	M Macdonald (Luton T)	24
A Clarke (Leeds U)	19	C Chilton (Hull C)	21
R Kennedy (Arsenal)	19	R Marsh (QPR)	21
		R Hatton (Carlisle U)	18

Division 3		Division 4	
G Ingram (Preston NE)	22	E MacDougall (Bournemouth & BA)	42
D Roberts (Mansfield T)	22	P Aimson (York C)	26
K Randall (Chesterfield)	19	R Crawford (Colchester U)	25
		J Fryatt (Oldham Ath)	24

1971–72

Division 1		Division 2	
F Lee (Manchester C)	33	R Latchford (Birmingham C)	23
M Chivers (Tottenham H)	25	J Galley (Bristol C)	22
P Lorimer (Leeds U)	23	R Hatton (Carlisle U 7 plus 15 for Birmingham C)	22
M Macdonald (Newcastle U)	23	B Clark (Cardiff C)	21
P Osgood (Chelsea)	19	F Casper (Burnley)	18

Division 3		Division 4	
E MacDougall (Bournemouth & BA)	35	P Price (Peterborough U)	28
A Wood (Shrewsbury T)	35	R McNeil (Lincoln C 13 plus 14 for Northampton T)	27
C Gilbert (Rotherham U)	22	M Tees (Grimsby T)	27
L Bradd (Notts Co)	21	W Garner (Southend U)	25
A Lochhead (Aston Villa)	19	J O'Mara (Brentford)	25

1972–73

Division 1		Division 2	
B Robson (West Ham U)	28	D Givens (QPR)	23
J Richards (Wolverhampton W)	27	G Bolland (Millwall)	19
W Dearden (Sheffield U)	20	S Bowles (QPR)	17
R Latchford (Birmingham C)	19	A Gowling (Huddersfield T)	17
		S Pearson (Hull C)	11

Division 3		Division 4	
B Bannister (Bristol R)	25	F Binney (Exeter C)	28
A Horsfield (Charlton Ath)	25	J Hall (Peterborough U)	21
J Byrom (Bolton W)	20	R McNeil (Lincoln C)	21
E Loyden (Tranmere R)	19	A Provan (Southport)	21
K Randall (Notts Co)	19	J Fairbrother (Mansfield T)	20

1973–74

Division 1		Division 2	
M Channon (Southampton)	21	D McKenzie (Nottingham F)	26
F Worthington (Leicester C)	20	A Wood (Millwall)	21
S Bowles (QPR)	19	T Brown (WBA)	19
K Hector (Derby Co)	18	A Foggon (Middlesbrough)	19

Division 3		Division 4	
W Jennings (Watford)	26	B Yeo (Gillingham)	31
J Howarth (Aldershot)	25	F Binney (Exeter C)	25
A Gowling (Huddersfield T)	24	L Chappell (Reading)	24
A Warboys (Bristol R)	22	R Svarc (Colchester U)	24
A Buckley (Walsall)	21		

1974–75

Division 1		Division 2	
M Macdonald (Newcastle U)	21	B Little (Aston Villa)	20
B Kidd (Arsenal)	19	M Channon (Southampton)	19
F Worthington (Leicester C)	18	R Graydon (Aston Villa)	19
K Hibbitt (Wolverhampton W)	17	B Robson (Sunderland)	19
R Latchford (Everton)	17		

Division 3		Division 4	
R McNeil (Hereford U)	31	R Clarke (Mansfield T)	28
P Eastoe (Swindon T)	26	R Habbin (Rotherham U 10 plus 12 for Reading)	22
R Svarc (Colchester U)	24	R Haywood (Shrewsbury T)	21
W Rafferty (Plymouth Arg)	23	P Kitchen (Doncaster R)	21
		E Woods (Newport County)	21

1975–76

Division 1
T MacDougall (Norwich C)	23
J Duncan (Tottenham H)	20
M Macdonald (Newcastle U)	19
J Richards (Wolverhampton W)	17
T Francis (Birmingham C)	17

Division 2
D Hales (Charlton Ath)	28
M Channon (Southampton)	19
T Ritchie (Bristol C)	18
M Walsh (Blackpool)	17
L Bradd (Notts Co)	16

Division 3
R McNeil (Hereford U)	35
A Buckley (Walsall)	34
R Clarke (Mansfield T)	24
F Binney (Brighton & HA)	23
T Evans (Cardiff C)	21

Division 4
R Moore (Tranmere R)	34
J Ward (Lincoln C)	24
N Freeman (Lincoln C)	23

1976–77

Division 1
A Gray (Aston Villa)	25
M Macdonald (Arsenal)	25
B Kidd (Manchester C)	21
T Francis (Birmingham C)	21

Division 2
M Walsh (Blackpool)	26
N Whatmore (Bolton W)	25
S Finnieston (Chelsea)	24
T MacDougall (Southampton)	23
M Flanagan (Charlton Ath)	23

Division 3
P Ward (Brighton & HA)	32
G Whittle (Wrexham)	28
A Bruce (Preston NE)	24
A Crawford (Rotherham U)	23

Division 4
B Joicey (Barnsley)	25
P Kitchen (Doncaster R)	23
J Charles (Swansea C)	23
G Sweetzer (Brentford)	23

1977-78

Division 1
R Latchford (Everton)	30
T Francis (Birmingham C)	25
K Dalglish (Liverpool)	20
I Wallace (Coventry C)	20
R Hankin (Leeds U)	20

Division 2
B Hatton (Blackpool)	22
P Kitchen (Orient)	21
P Randall (Bristol R)	20
S Taylor (Oldham Ath)	20

Division 3
A Bruce (Preston NE)	27
A Buckley (Walsall)	24
A Biley (Cambridge U)	21
J Lumby (Carlisle U) (inc 20 League for Scunthorpe U)	21

Division 4
S Phillips (Brentford)	32
A Curtis (Swansea C)	32
J Dungworth (Aldershot)	23
A McCulloch (Brentford)	22

ATTENDANCES AT FOOTBALL LEAGUE MATCHES

SEASON	MATCHES	TOTAL	DIV: 1
1946/47	1848	35,604,606	15,005,316
1947/48	1848	40,259,130	16,732,341
1948/49	1848	41,271,414	17,914,667
1949/50	1848	40,517,865	17,278,625
1950/51	2028	39,584,967	16,679,454
1951/52	2028	39,015,866	16,110,322
1952/53	2028	37,149,966	16,050,278
1953/54	2028	36,174,590	16,154,915
1954/55	2028	34,133,103	15,087,221
1955/56	2028	33,150,809	14,108,961
1956/57	2028	32,744,405	13,803,037
1957/58	2028	33,562,208	14,468,652
1958/59	2028	33,610,985	14,727,691
1959/60	2028	32,538,611	14,391,227
1960/61	2028	28,619,754	12,926,948
1961/62	2015	27,979,902	12,061,194
1962/63	2028	28,885,852	12,490,239
1963/64	2028	28,535,022	12,486,626
1964/65	2028	27,641,168	12,708,752
1965/66	2028	27,206,980	12,480,644
1966/67	2028	28,902,596	14,242,957
1967/68	2028	30,107,298	15,289,410
1968/69	2028	29,382,172	14,584,851
1969/70	2028	29,600,972	14,868,754
1970/71	2028	28,194,146	13,954,337
1971/72	2028	28,700,729	14,484,603
1972/73	2028	25,448,642	13,998,154
1973/74	2027	24,982,203	13,070,991
1974/75	2028	25,577,977	12,613,178
1975/76	2028	24,896,053	13,089,861
1976/77	2028	26,182,800	13,647,585
1977/78	2028	25,392,872	13,255,677
1978/79	2028	24,540,627	12,704,549

ATTENDANCES AT FOOTBALL LEAGUE MATCHES

SEASON	MATCHES	DIV: 2	DIV: 3 (S)	DIV: 3 (N)
1946/47	1848	11,071,572	5,664,004	3,863,714
1947/48	1848	12,286,350	6,653,610	4,586,829
1948/49	1848	11,353,237	6,998,429	5,005,081
1949/50	1848	11,694,158	7,104,155	4,440,927
1950/51	2028	10,780,580	7,367,884	4,757,109
1951/52	2028	11,066,189	6,958,927	4,880,428
1952/53	2028	9,686,654	6,704,299	4,708,735
1953/54	2028	9,510,053	6,311,508	4,198,114
1954/55	2028	8,988,794	5,996,017	4,051,071
1955/56	2028	9,080,002	5,692,479	4,269,367
1956/57	2028	8,718,162	5,622,189	4,601,017
1957/58	2028	8,663,712	6,097,183	4,332,661
1958/59	2028	8,641,997	5,946,600	4,276,697
1959/60	2028	8,399,627	5,739,707	4,008,050
1960/61	2028	7,033,936	4,784,256	3,874,614
1961/62	2015	7,453,089	5,199,106	3,266,513
1962/63	2028	7,792,770	5,341,362	3,261,481
1963/64	2028	7,594,158	5,419,157	3,035,081
1964/65	2028	6,984,104	4,436,245	3,512,067
1965/66	2028	6,914,757	4,779,150	3,032,429
1966/67	2028	7,253,819	4,421,172	2,984,648
1967/68	2028	7,450,410	4,013,087	3,354,391
1968/69	2028	7,382,390	4,339,656	3,075,275
1969/70	2028	7,581,728	4,223,761	2,926,729
1970/71	2028	7,098,265	4,377,213	2,764,331
1971/72	2028	6,769,308	4,697,392	2,749,426
1972/73	2028	5,631,730	3,737,252	2,081,506
1973/74	2027	6,326,108	3,421,624	2,163,480
1974/75	2028	6,955,970	4,086,145	1,992,684
1975/76	2028	5,798,405	3,948,449	2,059,338
1976/77	2028	6,250,597	4,152,218	2,132,400
1977/78	2028	6,474,763	3,332,042	2,330,390
1978/79	2028	6,153,223	3,374,558	2,308,297

NOTE: *From Season 1958/59 onwards for Div. 3 (S) read Div. 3 and for Div. 3 (N) read Div. 4.*

FOOTBALL LEAGUE ATTENDANCES 1978-79

First Division

	Home	Home average	Away
Arsenal	763,793	36,371	595,970
Aston Villa	689,589	32,838	576,368
Birmingham City	423,439	20,164	547,188
Bolton Wanderers	520,216	24,772	531,488
Bristol City	468,428	22,306	519,047
Chelsea	520,426	24,782	554,570
Coventry City	475,388	22,637	532,162
Derby County	452,654	21,555	524,867
Everton	744,571	35,456	648,732
Ipswich Town	455,125	21,673	513,462
Leeds United	580,291	27,633	641,741
Liverpool	974,541	46,406	775,895
Manchester City	760,256	36,203	591,612
Manchester United	975,029	46,430	637,829
Middlesbrough	387,649	18,459	496,425
Norwich City	375,364	17,874	486,737
Nottingham Forest	621,330	29,587	673,335
Queens Park Rangers	342,021	16,287	497,233
Southampton	447,921	21,330	516,084
Tottenham Hotspur	732,932	34,902	693,212
West Bromwich Albion	556,864	26,517	592,532
Wolverhampton Wanderers	436,722	20,796	558,060
TOTALS	**12,704,549**		**12,704,549**

Second Division

	Home	Home average	Away
Blackburn Rovers	181,449	8,640	288,484
Brighton & Hove Albion	465,035	22,145	323,859
Bristol Rovers	159,461	7,593	242,350
Burnley	225,714	10,748	296,214
Cambridge United	143,822	6,849	250,211
Cardiff City	194,163	9,246	263,270
Charlton Athletic	200,822	9,563	272,484
Crystal Palace	489,173	23,294	328,865
Fulham	212,844	10,135	251,458
Leicester City	297,933	14,187	261,308
Luton Town	184,640	8,792	255,769
Millwall	147,033	7,002	243,754
Newcastle United	437,525	20,834	302,859
Notts County	194,894	9,281	270,107
Oldham Athletic	147,948	7,045	251,289
Orient	153,787	7,323	260,032
Preston North End	254,460	12,117	242,903
Sheffield United	343,111	16,339	271,896
Stoke City	401,619	19,125	324,614
Sunderland	534,541	25,454	310,812
West Ham United	541,343	25,778	377,813
Wrexham	241,906	11,519	262,872
TOTALS	**6,153,223**		**6,153,223**

Third Division

	Home	Home average	Away
Blackpool	129,887	5,647	130,327
Brentford	171,458	7,455	129,532
Bury	86,991	3,782	119,056
Carlisle United	119,695	5,204	130,597
Chester	93,206	4,052	120,279
Chesterfield	110,916	4,822	139,444
Colchester United	78,630	3,419	132,855
Exeter City	101,385	4,408	143,629
Gillingham	164,299	7,143	132,675
Hull City	120,471	5,238	132,271
Lincoln City	72,868	3,168	131,250
Mansfield Town	118,484	5,151	127,552
Oxford United	106,883	4,647	129,397
Peterborough United	106,711	4,635	120,219
Plymouth Argyle	173,099	7,526	138,532
Rotherham United	102,727	4,466	135,556
Sheffield Wednesday	249,783	10,860	174,112
Shrewsbury Town	140,267	6,098	161,692
Southend United	152,024	6,610	137,950
Swansea City	316,152	13,746	181,194
Swindon Town	183,418	7,975	144,940
Tranmere Rovers	50,122	2,179	126,153
Walsall	93,079	4,047	140,337
Watford	332,003	14,435	215,009
TOTALS	3,374,558		3,374,558

Fourth Division

	Home	Home average	Away
A.F.C. Bournemouth	86,452	3,759	86,805
Aldershot	95,752	4,163	96,715
Barnsley	254,102	11,048	144,491
Bradford City	90,249	3,924	91,473
Crewe Alexandra	45,885	1,995	82,200
Darlington	41,568	1,807	94,334
Doncaster Rovers	68,996	2,999	88,250
Grimsby Town	150,140	6,528	119,092
Halifax Town	41,880	1,821	85,648
Hartlepool United	68,921	2,997	93,192
Hereford United	77,492	3,369	89,214
Huddersfield Town	83,929	3,649	100,168
Newport County	85,816	3,731	84,669
Northampton Town	66,590	2,895	83,974
Portsmouth	232,840	10,123	115,012
Port Vale	75,595	3,287	94,512
Reading	175,172	7,616	99,272
Rochdale	40,650	1,767	87,256
Scunthorpe United	62,585	2,721	91,682
Stockport County	95,271	4,142	90,396
Torquay United	61,397	2,669	88,236
Wigan Athletic	154,125	6,701	109,670
Wimbledon	85,372	3,712	101,426
York City	67,518	2,936	90,610
TOTALS	2,308,297		2,308,297

THE FA CUP

THE FOOTBALL ASSOCIATION OFFICIALS

Patron: HER MAJESTY THE QUEEN

President: HRH THE DUKE OF KENT

Honorary Vice-Presidents
His Grace the Duke of Marlborough; The Rt Hon The Earl of Derby, MC; Air Vice-Marshal D. P. Hall, CBE, AFC; Lt-General Sir James Wilson, KBE, MC; Admiral Sir Anthony Morton, KCB; Right Hon Earl of Harewood, LLD; Sir Stanley Rous, CBE; Sir Cyril Hawker; Lord Netherthorpe; Sir Andrew Stephen, MB, ChB; Sir Walter Winterbottom, CBE; Sir Denis Follows, CBE.

Chairman of the Council
Sir Harold Thompson, CBE, FRS (Oxford University)

Vice-Chairman of the Council
A. D. McMullen, MBE (Bedfordshire FA)

Life Vice-Presidents
I. Robinson (Liverpool County FA);
J. W. Bowers (Essex County FA);
G. N. Watson, JP (Nottingham Forest FC);
R. V. Stokes, OBE (Hampshire FA);
E. D. Smith, MBE, JP (Cumberland FA)

Vice-Presidents
A. D. McMullen, MBE (Bedfordshire FA);
Sir Harold Thompson, CBE, FRS (Oxford University);
Rt Hon Lord Westwood, JP, FCIS (Football League);
S. W. Jacobs (Oxfordshire FA);
N. W. Hillier (Northamptonshire FA);
W. H. Webster, CBE (Cambridge University)
E. Kangley (Sheffield and Hallamshire FA)

Secretary
E. Croker, 16 Lancaster Gate, London W2 3LW

FA CUP REVIEW 1978-79

The much disrupted 1978-79 FA Cup season appeared to be moving peacefully towards its conclusion at Wembley like the lifespan of someone who had experienced drama only in the twilight of their existence; Arsenal were leading Manchester United by two first half goals, scored by Brian Talbot and Frank Stapleton.

Then in a violent convulsion, Gordon McQueen reduced the deficit for United in the 86th minute and two minutes later Sammy McIlroy brought the possibility of extra time into more of a reality with the equaliser.

Yet in that very moment United relaxed, assuming the formality of the extra period would produce a psychological advantage. It quickly proved a costly error for Liam Brady and Graham Rix fashioned an attack down the left and Alan Sunderland finished it off on the right with a minute remaining to put the Cup in Arsenal's care after all.

Thus a largely undistinguished final ended in a manner which ensured that it would forever be recalled for its dramatic death throes.

But the last game is but one of many on the long journey to the Empire Stadium and at least for the ultimate winners Arsenal it meant that they could forget the nightmare of their third round tie with Sheffield Wednesday which was only completed at the fifth attempt.

Wednesday had their share of the glory in this prolonged affair, but others also could claim to have moments of magic along the way. The First Round Proper is the starting point for such excitement of course and the giant-killing act albeit of modest proportions came in the result Rochdale 0 Droyslden 1. The Cheshire County League side went on to be deposed by Altrincham of the Northern Premier League in the second round where Berger Isthmian League side Woking audaciously held Swansea City to a 2-2 draw on their own ground before succumbing 5-3 after extra time in Surrey.

Southern League Maidstone United had been quietly plodding away beating Wycombe Wanderers and then Third Division Exeter City each by the only goal to earn a Third Round draw with Charlton Athletic at The Valley. Here two Charlton players were sent off for fighting each other. In the replay at Maidstone the lights failed before Charlton emerged victorious from the gloom.

Altrincham were the only other non-leaguers to have survived as far and they went to another London ground at White Hart Lane to play Tottenham Hotspur. Alas it was not as simple as that.

The weather had taken a grip on the proceedings reducing the original programme to three matches completed and one abandoned on 6 January. Eventually they were all completed though Wrexham and Stockport did not meet until 1 February.

Still at least both non-leaguers could be satisfied with themselves as Altrincham drew 1-1 at Tottenham before losing the replay by three clear goals at Maine Road, Manchester.

A curiosity was Maine Road in fact. On Monday 15 January, Manchester City drew 0-0 with Rotherham United there and three days later came the replay mentioned previously. Then on the Saturday a First Division game was completed there, when almost every other venue was unplayable! And no balloons or undersoil heating...

Shrewsbury Town created history by reaching the sixth round for the first time. They had disposed of Manchester City in the fourth round but were stretched against Aldershot in the next, going 2-1 down away with a minute remaining – but again it was enough time to equalise and win the replay 3-1 after extra time.

Wolverhampton Wanderers ended Shrewsbury's run but not before they had been held at home in the first game. And it was Arsenal who knocked Wolves out in the semi-final at Villa Park with Stapleton and Sunderland responsible for the scoring.

The other semi-final at Maine Road was the glamour one and Liverpool and Manchester United shared four goals in a pulsating encounter. And while the Merseysiders rarely allow anyone a second chance at them, they must have been indiscreet by indulging themselves, for in the replay at Goodison Park a Jimmy Greenhoff goal was sufficient to eliminate them.

Perhaps the surroundings at the home of Everton were not conducive to producing the best for the Anfield club, but it was merely another illustration of the fascinating contortions into which the competition cavorts every year.

JACK ROLLIN

FA CHALLENGE CUP 1978-79

Preliminary Round

Carlisle C v Annfield Plain	4-2
Consett v Eppleton CW	1-1
Crook T v South Bank	1-2
Billingham Synthonia v Tow Law T	2-1
Farsley Celtic v Bridlington T	0-1
North Ferriby U v Selby T	2-0
Accrington Stanley v Lancaster C	1-2
Formby v Ashton U	3-1
Mossley v Burscough	2-1
Nantwich T v Prescot T	1-2
Leek T v Bangor C	2-2
Macclesfield T v Marine	2-4
Alfreton T v Mexborough T	2-5
Appleby Frodingham Ath v Eastwood T	1-2
Heanor T v Boston U	0-3
Holbeach U v Louth U	0-3
Bourne T v Arnold	1-4
Desborough T v Friar Lane OB	0-3
Halesowen T v Bilston	2-0
Kidderminster Harriers v Moor Green	5-0
Brierley Hill Alliance v Alvechurch	0-2
Burton Albion v Oxford C	0-1
Bromsgrove R v Lye Town	3-1
Banbury U v Thame U	4-2
Bury T v Kings Lynn	1-2
Gorleston v Cambridge C	1-0
Haverhill R v Lowestoft T	0-0
Corby T v Barton R	0-1
Newmarket T v Olney T	1-2
Egham T v Camberley T	2-3
Farnborough T v Maidenhead U	1-0
Grays Ath v Cheshunt	5-1
Harlow T v Hemel Hempstead	1-1
Hampton v Banstead Ath	2-0
Harrow Bor v Hertford T	0-2
Chesham U v Berkhamsted T	3-3
Finchley v Hillingdon Bor	0-1
Didcot T v Aylesbury U	1-1
Feltham v Hayes	2-0
Clapton v Barking	1-6
Felixstowe T v Hoddesdon T	1-0
Gravesend & Northfleet v Aveley	6-2
Haringey Bor v Ilford	1-3
Folkstone & Shepway v Bromley	2-1
Margate v Redhill	2-0
East Grinstead v Canterbury C	1-2
Herne Bay v Horsham YMCA	1-1
Eastbourne U v Ashford T	1-0
Faversham T v Hastings U	1-3
Epsom & Ewell v Addlestone	2-0
Horsham v Littlehampton T	4-0
Burgess Hill T v Alton T	1-0
Cowes v Fareham T	0-0
Forest Green R v Calne T	8-1
Frome T v Gloucester C	0-3
Barry T v Mangotsfield U	2-0
Andover v Newbury T	1-1
Glastonbury v Bath C	0-3
Ilminster T v Poole T	1-0
Liskeard Ath v Barnstaple T	1-0
Newquay v Penzance	2-2
Ashington v Bishop Auckland	0-1
Guisborough T v Consett	2-2
Wingate v South Bank	0-0
Shildon v Whitley Bay	3-1
Gateshead v Horden CW	1-0
Wallsend T v Ferryhill Ath	1-0
Willington v Billingham Synthonia	0-1
Easington CW v West Auckland T	2-1
Boldon CA v Durham C	2-0
Washington v Blue Star	3-2
Yorkshire Amateur v Bridlington T	0-0
Whitby T v Worsborough Bridge MW	3-3
Bridlington Trinity v Emley	1-0
Winterton Rangers v North Ferriby U	0-0
Penrith v Lancaster C	0-4
Fleetwood T v Netherfield	0-0
Chorley v Darwen	3-0
Lytham v Barrow	0-2
South Liverpool v Formby	0-3
Hyde U v Skelmersdale U	1-1
Clitheroe v Curzon Ashton	0-1
Leyland Motors v Horwich RMI	1-2
Witton Albion v Mossley	4-2
Radcliffe Bor v Runcorn	0-6
Buxton v Glossop	3-1
Rhyl v Prescot T	2-0
Stalybridge Celtic v Leek T	3-1
New Brighton v Prestwich Heys	1-3
Congleton v Droylsden	1-2
Porthmadog v Marine	3-1
Winsford U v Mexborough T	3-0
Oswestry T v St Helens T	1-1
Frickley Ath v Hednesford T	0-2
New Mills v Denaby U	2-0
Worksop T v Eastwood T	2-1
Brigg T v Spalding U	1-1
Barton T v Boston	1-3
Grantham v Ashby Institute	5-3
Sutton T v Boston U	0-0
Retford T v Stamford	2-1
Enderby T v Gainsborough Trinity	3-4
Skegness T v Louth U	0-1
Wellingborough T v Arnold	1-1
Hinckley Ath v Long Eaton U	5-0
Atherstone T v Belper T	2-0
Irthlingborough D v Friar Lane OB	3-0
Telford U v Halesowen T	0-1
Racing Club (Warwick) v Tamworth	1-1
Dudley T v Gresley R	3-0
Stratford T v Kidderminster Harriers	2-2
Wolverton & BR v Alvechurch	1-2
Redditch U v Tividale	3-2
Bedworth U v Brereton Social	0-0
Sutton Coldfield T v Oxford C	3-0
Worcester C v Bromsgrove R	1-0
Highgate U v Stourbridge	2-1
Darlaston v Evesham U	1-1
Milton Keynes C v Coventry Sporting	2-0
Witney T v Banbury U	0-2
Oldbury U v Willenhall T	1-1
Gornal Ath v Kempston R	0-2
Valley Sports Rugby v Dunstable	2-0
St Neots T v King's Lynn	1-0
Histon v Parson Drove	3-1
Great Yarmouth T v Harwich & Parkeston	1-1
March Town U v Chatteris T	4-1
Thetford U v Gorleston	1-5
Soham Town Rangers v Sudbury T	2-0
Clacton T v Ely C	0-4
Stowmarket v Lowestoft T	0-1
Wisbech T v Barton R	0-2
Potton U v Rushden	0-1
Bedford T v Bishop's Stortford	2-1
Rothwell T v Olney T	1-1
Walton & Hersham v Camberley T	2-3
Ruislip Manor v Southall & Ealing Bor	0-3
Carshalton Ath v Chertsey T	3-0
Slough T v Farnborough T	2-0
Wembley v Grays Ath	0-0

Replays

Eppleton CW v Consett	0-7
Bangor C v Leek T	1-2
Lowestoft T v Haverhill R	2-0
Hemel Hempstead v Harlow T	0-4
Berkhamstead T v Chesham U	1-0
Aylesbury U v Didcot T	2-1
Horsham YMCA v Herne Bay	1-0
Fareham T v Cowes	2-0
Newbury T v Andover	1-2
Penzance v Newquay	2-1

First Round Qualifying

Spennymoor U v Carlisle C	2-1
Evenwood T v North Shields	2-2

451

Leyton-Wingate v Tilbury	1-0
Corinthian-Casuals v Edgware	0-0
Metropolitan Police v Harlow T	1-0
Windsor & Eton v Hampton	1-0
Staines T v Willesden	2-1
Chalfont St Peter v Epping T	0-0
Sutton U v Hertford T	2-1
Uxbridge v Berkhamsted T	2-1
Kingstonian v Tring T	1-0
Boreham Wood v Burnham	3-2
Molesey v Hillingdon Bor	2-2
Wokingham T v Aylesbury U	2-0
Hounslow v St Albans C	1-1
Barnet v Bracknell T	2-1
Marlow v Feltham	(aet) 1-1
Ware v Barking	0-2
Hornchurch v Leytonstone	1-1
Billericay v Chelmsford C	2-1
Letchworth GC v Felixstowe T	5-1
Welling U v Gravesend & Northfleet	1-2
Rainham T v Walthamstow Ave	0-4
Cray Wanderers v Dulwich Hamlet	1-2
Whitstable T v Folkstone & Shepway	1-1
Snowdon CW v Tonbridge AFC	0-3
Croydon v Erith & Belvedere	1-0
Three Bridges v Margate	0-2
Sheppey U v Canterbury C	1-4
Lewes v Ramsgate	1-1
Dover v Eastbourne T	3-0
Maidstone U v Horsham YMCA	2-0
Sittingbourne v Eastbourne U	1-4
Medway v Sidley U	4-1
Bexhill T v Crawley T (at Crawley)	1-1
Ringmer v Hastings U	0-2
Woking v Epsom & Ewell	3-1
Selsey v Tunbridge Wells	2-3
Chichester C v Dorking T	1-1
Southwick v Horsham	1-2
Worthing v Alton T	4-1
Haywards Heath v Wigmore Ath	4-0
Arundel v Bognor Regis T	2-3
Waterlooville v Fareham T	2-0
Trowbridge T v Forest Green R	1-0
Llanelli v Shepton Mallet T	1-3
Cheltenham T v Clevedon T	6-1
Melksham T v Gloucester C	1-0
Ton Pentre v Barry T	0-1
Larkhall Ath v Paulton R	3-3
Chippenham T v Cinderford T	2-2
Merthyr Tydfil v Bridgend T	4-0
Yeovil T v Andover	4-0
Hungerford T v Swaythling	5-1
Bridport v Dorchester T	0-1
Newport IOW v Basingstoke T	0-1
Weston-super-Mare v Bath C	1-2
Salisbury v Welton R	4-0
Bridgwater T v Chard T	1-0
Tiverton T v Ilminster T	1-0
Wadebridge T v Liskeard Ath	0-2
St Blazey v Taunton T	0-3
Bideford v Falmouth T	2-1
Saltash U v Penzance	8-1

Bye: Ilford FC

First Round Qualifying Replays

North Shields v Evenwood T	1-0
Consett v Guisborough T	3-2
South Bank v Wingate	1-1
Bridlington T v Yorkshire Amateur	2-3
Worsborough Bridge MW v Whitby T	0-1
North Ferriby U v Winterton Rangers	0-1
Netherfield v Fleetwood T	1-1
Skelmersdale U v Hyde U	0-1
St Helens T v Oswestry T	0-0
Spalding U v Brigg T	3-4
Boston U v Sutton T	4-0
Arnold v Wellingborough T	2-1
Tamworth v Racing Club (Warwick)	1-0
Kidderminster Harriers v Stratford T	7-0
Brereton Social v Bedworth U	3-2
Evesham U v Darlaston	2-4
Willenhall T v Oldbury U	2-0
Harwich & Parkeston v Great Yarmouth T	4-1
Lowestoft T v Haverhill R	2-0
Olney T v Rothwell T	0-1
Grays Ath v Wembley	4-1
Edgware v Corinthian-Casuals	4-0
Epping T v Chalfont St Peter	1-1
Hillingdon Boro v Molesey	2-1
St Albans C v Hounslow	4-2
Feltham v Marlow	(aet) 3-0
Leytonstone v Hornchurch	4-1
Folkestone & Shepway v Whitstable T	5-0
Ramsgate v Lewes	3-0
Crawley T v Bexhill T	1-1
Dorking T v Chichester C	3-2
Paulton R v Larkhall Ath	2-1
Cinderford T v Chippenham T	2-1
Penzance v Newquay	2-1

Second Replays

Wingate v South Bank at Billingham Synthonia FC	0-0
Fleetwood T v Netherfield at Fleetwood T FC	2-0
Oswestry T v St Helens T at Winsford U FC	3-2
Chalfont St Peter v Epping T at Hoddesdon T FC	0-0
Bexhill T v Crawley T at Hastings U FC	0-1

Third Replays

South Bank v Wingate at Billingham Synthonia FC	2-1
Epping T v Chalfont St Peter at Hounslow FC	1-2

Second Round Qualifying

North Shields v Spennymoor U	0-3
Bishop Auckland v Consett	0-0
Shildon v South Bank	2-1
Gateshead v Wallsend T	6-0
Easington CW v Billingham Synthonia	1-3
Boldon CA v Washington	3-2
Whitby T v Yorkshire Amateur	1-2
Bridlington Trinity v Winterton Rangers	2-2
Fleetwood T v Lancaster C	1-1
Chorley v Barrow	2-1
Hyde U v Formby	2-2
Curzon Ashton v Horwich RMI	1-2
Runcorn v Witton Albion	3-1
Buxton v Rhyl	2-0
Prestwich Heys v Stalybridge Celtic	1-1
Droylsden v Porthmadog	3-1
Oswestry T v Winsford U	0-1
Hednesford T v New Mills	4-0
Brigg T v Worksop T	1-1
Boston v Grantham	0-1
Retford T v Boston U	1-4
Gainsborough Trinity v Louth U	1-1
Hinckley Ath v Arnold	1-0
Atherstone T v Irthlingborough D	1-3
Tamworth v Halesowen T	0-2
Dudley T v Kidderminster Harriers	2-0
Redditch U v Alvechurch	1-0
Brereton Social v Sutton Coldfield T	3-2
Highgate U v Worcester C	5-0
Darlaston v Milton Keynes C	1-0
Willenhall T v Banbury U	3-1
Kempston R v Valley Sports Rugby	3-1
Histon v St Neots T	0-1
Harwich & Parkeston v March Town U	1-1
Soham Town Rangers v Gorleston	0-3
Ely C v Lowestoft T	1-2
Rushden T v Barton R	1-1
Bedford T v Rothwell T	5-2
Southall & Ealing Bor v Camberley T	2-2
Carshalton Ath v Slough T	1-2
Leyton-Wingate v Grays Ath	2-0
Edgware v Metropolitan Police	1-0
Staines T v Windsor & Eton	0-0
Chalfont St Peter v Sutton U	0-2
Kingstonian v Uxbridge	3-0
Boreham Wood v Hillingdon Bor	0-2
St Albans C v Wokingham T	0-0
Barnet v Feltham	3-2

453

Leytonstone v Barking	1-2
Billericay T v Letchworth GC	5-1
Walthamstow Ave v Gravesend & Northfleet	2-3
Dulwich Hamlet v Ilford	4-0
Tonbridge AFC v Folkstone & Shepway	2-3
Croydon v Margate	0-2
Ramsgate v Canterbury C	1-0
Dover v Maidstone U	0-0
Medway v Eastbourne U	0-0
Crawley T v Hastings U	1-2
Tunbridge Wells v Woking	0-2
Dorking T v Horsham	0-2
Haywards Heath v Worthing	1-2
Bognor Regis T v Waterlooville	0-2
Shepton Mallet T v Tonbridge	1-2
Cheltenham T v Melksham T	6-0
Paulton R v Barry T	1-2
Cinderford T v Merthyr Tydfil	0-1
Hungerford T v Yeovil T	4-4
Dorchester T v Basingstoke T	1-0
Salisbury v Bath C	0-2
Bridgwater T v Tiverton T (aet)	5-1
Taunton T v Liskeard Ath	6-0
Bideford v Saltash U	2-0

Second Round Qualifying Replays

Consett v Bishop Auckland	2-1
Winterton Rangers v Bridlington Trinity	2-1
Lancaster C v Fleetwood T	0-1
Formby v Hyde U	2-1
Stalybridge Celtic v Prestwich Heys	4-1
Worksop T v Brigg T	1-1
Louth U v Gainsborough Trinity	1-2
Worcester C v Highgate U	3-2
March Town U v Harwich & Parkeston	2-1
Barton R v Rushden T	3-1
Camberley T v Southall & Ealing Boro	1-3
Windsor & Eton v Staines T	1-0
Wokingham T v St Albans C	4-1
Maidstone U v Dover	1-0
Eastbourne U v Medway	0-0
Yeovil T v Hungerford T	3-0

Second Replays

Brigg T v Worksop T at Gainsborough Trinity FC	0-2
Medway v Eastbourne U at Maidstone U FC	0-6

Third Round Qualifying

Spennymoor U v Consett	0-0
Shildon v Gateshead	1-8
Billingham Synthonia v Boldon CA	0-0
Yorkshire Amateur v Winterton Rangers	1-0
Fleetwood T v Chorley	0-1
Formby v Horwich RMI	0-0
Runcorn v Buxton	1-1
Stalybridge Celtic v Droylsden	1-1
Winsford U v Hednesford T	1-2
Worksop T v Grantham	0-0
Boston U v Gainsborough Trinity	3-0
Hinckley Ath v Irthlingborough D	1-2
Halesowen T v Dudley T	0-1
Redditch U v Brereton Social	0-0
Worcester C v Darlaston	7-1
Willenhall T v Kempston R	0-2
St Neots T v March Town U	2-3
Gorleston v Lowestoft T	3-1
Barton R v Bedford T	0-2
Southall & Ealing Bor v Slough T	1-0
Leyton-Wingate v Edgware	1-1
Windsor & Eton v Sutton U	0-1

Kingstonian v Hillingdon Bor	0-0
Wokingham T v Barnet	0-4
Barking v Billericay T	2-0
Gravesend & Northfleet v Dulwich Hamlet	1-1
Folkestone & Shepway v Margate	0-2
Ramsgate v Maidstone U	1-3
Eastbourne U v Hastings U	2-1
Woking v Horsham	5-2
Worthing v Waterlooville	1-1
Trowbridge T v Cheltenham T	0-4
Barry T v Merthyr Tydfil	0-2
Yeovil T v Dorchester T	2-1
Bath C v Bridgwater T	7-1
Taunton T v Bideford	3-0

Third Round Qualifying Replays

Consett v Spennymoor U	1-2
Boldon CA v Billingham Synthonia (aet)	2-4
Horwich RMI v Formby	5-1
Buxton v Runcorn	0-4
Droylsden v Stalybridge Celtic	3-1
Grantham v Worksop T	0-3
Brereton Social v Redditch U	0-1
Edgware v Leyton-Wingate	3-1
Hillingdon Bor v Kingstonian	3-2
Dulwich Hamlet v Gravesend & Northfleet	0-1
Waterlooville v Worthing	3-0

Fourth Round Qualifying

Chorley v Yorkshire Amateur	4-2
Droylsden v Goole T	2-0
Morecambe v Horwich RMI	3-1
Northwich Victoria v Southport	0-0
Spennymoor v Runcorn	0-0
Billingham Synthonia v Blyth Spartans	0-1
Gateshead v Workington	1-1
Dudley T v Worksop T	0-1
Nuneaton Bor v Matlock T	2-2
Kettering T v Boston U	1-3
AP Leamington v Hednesford T	0-0
Stafford Rangers v Redditch U	2-1
Barking v Bedford T	3-1
Dagenham v Irthlingborough D	0-0
March Town U v Southall & Ealing	2-1
Wealdstone v Kempston R	1-0
Gorleston v Enfield	2-6
Hendon v Hitchin T	1-3
Edgware v Barnet	0-1
Gravesend & Northfleet v Eastbourne U	3-1
Margate v Woking	1-7
Sutton U v Dartford	0-2
Waterlooville v Maidstone U	1-2
Hillingdon Bor v Tooting & Mitcham	2-1
Bath C v Worcester C	1-1
Taunton T v Weymouth	0-2
Cheltenham T v Yeovil T	1-2
Merthyr Tydfil v Minehead	2-0

Fourth Round Qualifying Replays

Southport v Northwich Victoria	2-0
Runcorn v Spennymoor U	2-1
Workington v Gateshead	3-2
Matlock T v Nuneaton Bor	2-2
Hednesford T v AP Leamington	2-3
Irthlingborough D v Dagenham	1-2
Worcester C v Bath C	2-1

Second Replay

Nuneaton Bor v Matlock T at Stafford Rangers FC	1-2

FA CUP DETAILS 1978-79

FIRST ROUND
25 NOV

Aldershot (0) 1 (*Crosby*)
Weymouth (1) 1 (*Hawkins*) 4213
Aldershot: Johnson; Edwards, Wooler, Dixon, Youlden, Jopling, Longhorn (Crosby), Brodie, Needham, Dungworth, McGregor.
Weymouth: Roberts; Lawrence, Durkin, Dyer, Townsend, Iannone, Lowe, Courtney, Leitch, Dove, Hawkins.

Altrincham (2) 4 (*Johnson 2, Bailey, Rogers*)
Southport (2) 3 (*Nolan, Dewnsip, Whittle*) 2153
Altrincham: Eales, Allan, Brooke, Bailey, Owens, Davison, King, Heathcote, Johnson, Rogers, Howard.
Southport: Dalrymple; Woof, Knowles, Pickering, Higham, Wheeldon, Dewsnip, Kisby, Beesley, Nolan (Ferguson), Whittle.

Barnet (1) 3 (*Oliver, Cleary 2, 1 a pen*)
Woking (2) 3 (*James, Love, Field*) 2023
Barnet: Smith; Oliver, Lees, McCormack, Tapping, Townsend, Greaves, Bookman, Brown, Cleary, Price.
Woking: Parsons; Steer, Barrett, Love, Preston, Cottrell, Alexander, Field, Morton, Cosham, James.

Barnsley (1) 5 (*Clarke, Riley, Bell, Reed 2*)
Worksop (0) 1 (*Woods*) 10,433
Barnsley: Springett; Collins, Chambers, Pugh, Saunders, McCarthy, Reed, Clarke, Riley, Millar, Bell.
Worksop: Evans; Parkin, Harmston, Woods, Tandy, Webb, Smith, Conroy (Shaw), Fisher, Vardy, Conroy.

Blackpool (1) 2 (*McEwan pen, Chandler*)
Lincoln (0) 1 (*Ward*) 4375
Blackpool: Hesford; Gardner, Pashley, Malone, Suddaby, McEwan, Weston, Sermanni, Spence, Chandler, Wagstaff (Hockaday).
Lincoln: Turner; Guest, Neale, Fleming (Hubbard), Wigginton, Cooper, Hobson, Ward, Harford, Watson, Harding.

Bournemouth (1) 2 (*Massey pen, Butler M*)
Hitchin (1) 1 (*Taylor*) 5008
Bournemouth: Allen; Butler G, Lennard, Impey, Brown R, Barton, Borthwick, MacDougall, Butler M, Massey, Brown K.
Hitchin: Bradwell; Gear, Baldry, Brimston (Grafton), Martin, Hammond, Whishaw, Carroll, Giggle, Taylor, Harthill.

Bradford C ( ) 1 (*Dolan pen*)
Port Vale (0) 0 5625
Bradford C: Downsborough; Podd, Watson, Reaney, Baines, Wood, Martinez (Bates), Dolan, Cooke, McNiven, Hutchins.
Port Vale: Connaughton; Keenan, Bentley, Todd, Harris, Hawkins, Tully, Farrell, Wright, Beech (Sproson), Healy.

Carlisle (0) 1 (*Lumby*)
Halifax (0) 0 5060
Carlisle: Swinburne; Hoolickin, McCartney, Bonnyman, Tait, Parker, McVitie, Ludlam, Kemp, Lumby, Hamilton.
Halifax: Leonard; Hutt, Loska, Smith, Burke, Dunleavy, Prendergast, Mountford, Campbell, Sidebottom (Carroll), Johnson.

Chester (0) 1 (*Phillips*)
Runcorn (0) 1 (*Keynon*) 5241
Chester: Lloyd; Nickeas, Raynor, Storton, Jeffries, Oakes, Jones, Livermore (Walker), Howat, Mellor, Phillips.
Runcorn: Lloyd; Rutter, Murphy, Rylands, Duff, King, Wilson, Seddon, Whitbread, Kenyon, Spencer.

Chorley (0) 0
Scarborough (1) 1 (*Dunn H A*) 1612
Chorley: Wood; Huddleston, Birchall, Hope, Cartwright, Doyle, Brown, Worswick, Telfer, Done, Garrett.
Scarborough: McKechnie; Fountain, Smith, Dunn, H, Marshall, Donoghue, Lyall, Ellis, Woodall, Abbey, Dunn H A.

Colchester (1) 4 (*Gough 3, Foley*)
Oxford (1) 2 (*Foley, Seacole*) 4170
Colchester: Walker; Cook, Packer, Hodge, Wignall, Dowman, Foley, Gough, Bunkell, Lee (Wright), Allinson.
Oxford: Burton; Taylor, Fogg, Briggs, Bodel, Jeffrey, Graydon, Duncan, Foley, Seacole, Hodgson.

Darlington (0) 1 (*Ferguson*)
Chesterfield (1) 1 (*Flavell*) 2862
Darlington: Owers; Nattrass, Cochrane, Hague, Craig, Stone, Lyons, Walsh, Ferguson, Seal, Wann.
Chesterfield: Letheran; Flavell, O'Neill, Hunter, Cottam, Prophett, Tartt, Kowalski, Fern, Cammack, Walker.

Dartford (0) 1 (*Jones*)
AP Leamington (1) 2 (*Gardner 2*) 1006
Dartford: Hucker; Williams, Tumbridge, Jones, Harris, Horsfield, O'Sullivan, Bray, Smith, Shovelar, Harrison.
AP Leamington: Dulleston; Capewell, Sutheran Jones, Kilkelly, Boot, Taylor, Gorman, Vincent, Gardner, Keeley.

Doncaster (2) 2 (*Lewis, Laidlaw*)
Huddersfield (0) 1 (*Fletcher*) 4330
Doncaster: Peacock; Reed, Snodin, Cork, Bradley, Olney, Habbin (Owen), Lewis, French, Laidlaw, Bentley.
Huddersfield: Starling; Brown, Sandercock, Lillis (Fletcher), Topping, Sutton, Gray, Hart, Cowling, Robins, Bielby.

Exeter (0) 1 (*Forbes*)
Brentford (0) 0 3782
Exeter: O'Keefe; Templeman, Hore, Forbes, Mitchell, Roberts, Neville, Ingham, Bowker, Delve, Hatch.
Brentford: Bond; Salman, Tucker, Shrubb, Kruse, McNichol, Carlton, Graham J (Smith), Glover, McCulloch, Phillips.

Gravesend (0) 0
Wimbledon 0 3758
Gravesend: Smelt; Idle, Sargent, Glozier, Osborne, Jacks, Brown, Hunt, Woon, Dudman, Woolfe (Stonebridge).
Wimbledon: Goddard; Perkins, Haverson, Galliers, Galvin, Donaldson, Leslie, Denny, Connell, Cork, Parsons.

Hartlepool (0) 1 (*Goldthorpe*)
Grimsby (0) 0 3584
Hartlepool: Richardson; Smith G, Gorry, Lawrence, Brooks Ayre, Linacre (Hogan), Goldthorpe, Houchen, Crumplin, Loadwick.
Grimsby: Batch; Moore D, Moore K, Waters, Barker, Crombie, Ford, Mitchell, Drinkell, Cumming (Lester), Brolly.

Hereford (0) 0
Newport (0) 1 (*Goddard pen*) 6939
Hereford: Hughes; Price, Burrows, Cornes, Layton, Emery, Holmes K, Crompton, Jones, Gould, Spiring.
Newport: Plumley; Walden, Byrne, Warriner, Davies, Bruton, Lowndes, Goddard, Woods, Sinclair, Vaughan.

Hull (0) 2 (*Sargeant og, Edwards*)
Stafford (0) 1 (*Wood*) 5411
Hull: Blackburn; Nisbet, DeVries, Horswill, Hood, Haigh, Warboys Lord (Hawker), Edwards, Bannister, Farley.
Stafford: Arnold; Ritchie, Nixon, Sargeant, Seddon, Thomson, Marsden (Wood), Chapman, Jones, Cullerton, Chadwick.

Leatherhead (1) 2 (*Baker, Camp*)
Merthyr (0) 1 (*Pratt*) 2100
Leatherhead: Swannell; Cooper, Brooks, Davies, Reid, Malley, Cook, Salkeld, Kelly, Baker, Camp (Eaton).
Merthyr: Payne; Carter, Wakeham, Holvey, Mullins, Docherty, Jones (Elliott), Sullivan, Pratt, Caviel, Dicks.

Maidstone (0) 1 (*Aitken*)
Wycombe (0) 0 1904
Maidstone: Guy; Kinnear, Edwares, Hill, Aitken, Merrick, Budden, Gregory, Coupland, Fusco, Silvester.
Wycombe: Spittle; Birdseye, Davies, Mead, Phillips, Hardwick, Evans, Holifield, Long (Atkins), Kennedy, Scott.

Mansfield (0) 0
Shrewsbury (1) 2 (*Aitkins, Biggins*) 4881
Mansfield: Arnold; Curtis, Foster B, McClelland, Saxby M, Bird, Miller, Goodwin, Syrett Wood, Allen.
Shrewsbury: Wardle; King, Leonard, Turner, Griffin, Hayes, Chapman, Tong, Atkins, Biggins, Maguire.

Nuneaton (0) 0
Crewe (2) 2 (*Coyne, Bowles*) 4232
Nuneaton: Knight; Cooper, Tysall, Cross, Peake, Lewis, Dale, Fleet, Campbell, Phillips, Smithers.
Crewe: Rafferty; Wilkinson, Roberts (Nelson), Rimmer, Bowles, Bevan, Davies Purdie, Coyne, Wilshaw, Robertson.

Portsmouth (0) 2 (*Hemmerman* 2)
Northampton (0) 0 13,338
Portsmouth: Mellor; Ellis, Viney, Denyer, Foster, Davey, Hemmerman, Lathan, Garwood (Hand), Barnard, Pullar.
Northampton: Jayes; Geidmintis, Mead, Woollett, Robertson, Saunders, Farrington, Williams, Froggatt, Reilly, Wassell (Cordice).

Reading (0) 6,910
Gillingham 0
Reading: Death; Peters, White, Bowman, Hicks Bennett, Alexander, Kearns, Kearney, Sanchez, Lewis (Hetzke).
Gillingham: Hillyard; Sharpe, Armstrong, Overton, Weatherley, Crabbe, Nicholl, Hughes, Price, Westwood, Richardson.

Rochdale (0) 0
Droylsden (1) 1 (*Taylor*) 3252
Rochdale: Shyne; O'Loughlin, Snookes, Hart, Scott, Scaife, Owen, Hoy, Hilditch, Esser, Price.
Droylsden: Litchfield; Hill, Wilkinson, Jackson, Roberts, Gorman, Cooke, Taylor, Nicklin, Hughes, Haughton.

Rotherham (2) 3 (*Gwyther* 2, *Breckin*)
Workington (0) 0 3927
Rotherham: McAlister; Vaughan, Breckin, Stancliffe, Green (Dawson), Flynn, Finney, Phillips, Gwyther, Crawford, Smith.
Workington: Fisher; Leng, Johnston, Endean, McDonald, Brown, Foley, Gill, Gillott, Irving, Reach.

Scunthorpe (0) 1 (*Pilling*)
Sheffield W (0) 1 (*Nimmo*) 8697
Scunthorpe: Crawford; O'Donnell, Pilling, Oates, Deere, Czuczman, Grimes, Kilmore, Wigg, Keeley, Kavanagh.
Sheffield W: Turner; Blackhall, Rushbury, Pickering, Smith, Johnson, Wylde, Nimmo, Leman, Porterfield, Hornsby.

Southend (1) 3 (*Pountney, Carmichael og, Parker*)
Peterborough (1) 2 (*Butlin, Anderson*) 6531
Southend: Cawston; Stead, Yates, Laverick, Cusack, Moody, Morris, Pountney, Parker, Dudley, Polycarpou.
Peterborough: Waugh; Hindley, Styles, Doyle, Carmichael, Ross, Robertson, McEwan, Butlin, Anderson (Sargent), Robson.

Stockport (2) 5 (*Prudham, Bradd, Park* 3)
Morecambe (0) 1 (*Towers*) 3294
Stockport: Rogan; Thorpe, Rutter, Fogarty, Park, Edwards, Henson, Prudham, Bradd, Summerbee, Armstrong.
Morecambe: Byram; Farrell, Newton, Walsh, Street, Heaton (Clayton), Darling, Eatough, Towers, Parry, McLachlan.

Swansea (2) 4 (*James, Charles* 2, *Waddle*)
Hillingdon (0) 1 (*Williams*) 7824
Swansea: Crudgington; Evans, Toshack, Phillips, Smith, Marustik, Callaghan, James, Waddle, Charles, Moore.
Hillingdon: Toogood; Thomas (Armstrong), Williams, Davies, Ryan, Millett, Adams, Wainwright, Reeve, Melledew, Cotton.

Swindon (2) 2 (*Gilchrist, Bates*)
March (0) 0 5633
Swindon: Ogden; McLaughlin, Ford, McHale, Aizlewood, Stroud, Miller, Carter, Gilligan, Bates, Kamara.
March: Dobrowolski; Simmons, Beaver, Smart, Kent L, Eldred, Roos, Kent S, Thomas (Snell), Rowley, Hutchinson.

Tranmere (2) 2 (*McAuley, Moore*)
Boston (0) 1 (*Moyes*) 2424
Tranmere: Johnson; Cahill, Flood, Bramhall, Mathias, Parry, O'Neil, Evans, Moore, Peplow, McAuley.
Boston: Stewart; Phelan, Towle, Poplar, Adamson, Simmonite, Moyes, Hector, Brown, Kabia, Welch.

Walsall (0) 0
Torquay (2) 2 (*Cooper, Wilson*) 4445
Walsall: Kearns; Paul, Harrison, Sbragia, Serella (Penn), King, Birch, Macken, Austin, McDonough, Kelly.
Torquay: Turner; Boulton, Payne, Davies, Green, Dunne, Wilson, Lawrence, Cooper, Murphy, Raper.

Watford (1) 3 (*Jenkins* 3)
Dagenham (0) 0 11,551
Watford: Sherwood; Stirk, Harrison, Mayes, Bolton, Garner, Pollard (Cassells), Pritchett, Jenkins, Joslyn, Downes.
Dagenham: Huttley, Wellman, Scales, Dunwell, Currie, Moore, Harkins, Borland, Fox, Kidd, Holder.

Wealdstone (0) 0
Enfield (1) 5 (*O'Sullivan, Searle, King* 2, *Wright*) 1250
Wealdstone: Cranstone; McVeigh, Fursdon, Morgan, Parratt (Arnold), Barwick, Brinkman, Wilkinson, Moss, Johnson, Briscoe.
Enfield: Moore; Wright, Tone, Jennings, Elley, Gibson, O'Sullivan, Howell, Searle, Bishop, King.

Wigan (0) 2 (*Gore, Houghton*)
Bury (1) 2 (*Gregory, Brown og*) 10,142
Wigan: Brown; Smart, Hinnigan, Gore, Ward, Fretwell, Corrigan, Wright, Houghton, Moore (Brownbill), Purdie.
Bury: Forrest; Ritson, Kennedy Lugg, Tucker, Bailey, Stanton, Wilson, Beamish, Gregory, Tucker.

Worcester (1) 2 (*Phelps, Williams*)
Plymouth (0) 0 8253
Worcester: Cumbes; Barton, Punsheon, Tudor, Phelps, Deehan, Williams J, Stevens, Williams B, Lawrence, Allner (Martin).
Plymouth: Hodge; Bason, Rogers, Silkman, Foster, Clarke, Megson, Fear, Binney, Perrin, Brennan (Trusson).

Yeovil (0) 0
Barking (1) 1 (*Key*) 3030
Yeovil: Parker; Thompson, Cottle, Jones, Dominey, Harrison, Morrall, Platt, Cotton, Flay, Clancy, (Leigh).
Barking: Markwick; Barrett, Makin, Arber, White, Ironton, Ballard, Anderson, Burton, Key, Ashford.

York (1) 1 (*Pugh*)
Blyth (1) 1 (*Johnson pen*) 5088
York: Brown; Kay, Walsh, Pugh, Faulkner, Clements, Ford, Randall, Wellings, McDonald, Staniforth.
Blyth: Clarke; Waterson, Guthrie, Varty. Dixon S, Dixon T, Davies. (Carney) Houghton, Johnson, Shoulder, Dagless.

FIRST ROUND REPLAYS

28 NOV

Blyth (1) 3 (*Shoulder* 2 *pens, Davies*)
York (2) 5 (*Ford, Clements, Wellings* 2, *Staniforth*) aet 3500
Blyth: Clarke; Waterson, Carney S, Varty (Carney R), Dixon S, Dixon T, Houghton, Mutrie, Shoulder, Dagless, Davies.
York: Brown; Kay, Walsh, Pugh, Faulkner, Clements, Ford, Randall, Wellings, McDonald, Staniforth.

Bury (3) 4 (*Gregory* 2, *Kennedy, Wilson pen*)
Wigan (0) 1 (*Moore*) 9342
Bury: Forrest; Ritson, Kennedy, Lugg, Tucker, Whitehead, Stanton, Wilson, Beamish, Gregory, Taylor.
Wigan: Brown; Smart, Hinnigan, Gore, Ward, Fretwell, Corrigan, Wright, Houghton, Moore, Purdie.

Gillingham (1) 1 (*Westwood*)
Reading (1) 2 (*Lewis, Kearney*) aet 6441
Gillingham: Hillyard; Sharpe, Hughes, Overton, Weatherley, Crabbe, Nicholl, Jolley (White), Price, Westwood, Richardson.
Reading: Death; Peters, White, Bowman, Hicks, Bennett, Alexander, Kearns, Kearney, Sanchez, Lewis.

Runcorn (0) 0
Chester (4) 5 (*Mellor* 2, *Jones, Phillips, Howatt*) 4441
Runcorn: Lloyd; Rutter, Murphy, Rylands, Duff, Phillips (Barnes), Wilson, Seddon, Whitbread, Kenyon, Spencer.
Chester: Lloyd; Nickeas, Raynor, Jeffries, Storton, Delgado, Jones, Livermore, Howat, Mellor, Phillips.

Sheffield Wed (0) 1 (*Nimmo*)
Scunthorpe (0) 0 9760
Sheffield W: Turner; Blackhall, Rushbury, Smith, Pickering, Johnson, Wylde, Porterfield, Leman, Nimmo, Hornsby.
Scunthorpe: Crawford; O'Donnell Pilling, Oates, Deere, Czuczman, Grimes, Kilmore, Wigg, Kavanagh, Keeley.

Wimbledon (0) 1 (*Cork*)
Gravesend (0) 0 3369
Wimbledon: Goddard; Perkins, Haverson, Galliers, Galvin, Donaldson, Leslie. Denny, Connell (Briley), Cork, Parsons.
Gravesend: Smelt; Idle, Sargent, Glozier, Osborne, Jacks, Brown, Hunt, Woon, Dudman, Woolfe (Stonebridge).

Woking (1) 3 (*Cosham, Alexander, Morton*)
Barnet (1) 3 (*Brown, Fairbrother* 2) aet 1732
Woking: Parsons; O'Sullivan, Barrett, Love, Martin, Cottrell, Alexander, Field. Morton, Cosham (Adams), James.
Barnet: Smith; Oliver, Lees, McCormack, Tapping, Townsend, Bookman (Foody), Brown, Fairbrother, Cleary, Price.

29 NOV

Weymouth (0) 0
Aldershot (1) 2 (*Shanahan, Dungworth*) 3468
Weymouth: Roberts; Lawrence, Dyer, Durkin, Townsend, Iannone, Lowe, Courtney, Leitch (Henderson), Dove, Hawkins.
Aldershot: Johnson; Edwards, Wooler, Dixon, Youlden, Jopling, Crosby, Brodie, Shanahan, Dungworth, McGregor.

SECOND REPLAY

5 DEC

Barnet (0) 0
Woking (1) 3 (*Love, James, Morton*) at Brentford 2570
Barnet: Smith; Oliver, Lees, McCormack, Tapping, Townsend, Greaves, Bookman (Foody), Fairbrother, Brown, Cleary.
Woking: Parsons; O'Sullivan, Martin, Love, Barrett, Cottrell (Field), Alexander, Adams, Morton, Cosham, James.

FIRST ROUND REPLAY

6 DEC

Chesterfield (0) 0
Darlington (0) 1 (*Ferguson*) 4270
Chesterfield: Letheran; Flavell, Burton, Hunter, Cottam, Prophett, Cammack, Tartt, Fern, Salmons, Walker.
Darlington: Burleigh; Nattrass, Cochrane, Hague, Craig, Stone, Probert, Ferguson, Walsh, Seal, Wann.

SECOND ROUND

16 DEC

AP Leamington (0) 0
Torquay (1) 1 (*Twitchin*) 2200
AP Leamington: Dulleston; Capewell, Sutheran (Houston), Jones, Kilkelly, Boot, Taylor, Gorman, Vincent, Gardner ,Keeley.
Torquay: Turner; Darke, Dunne, Davies. Green, Parsons, Wilson, Lawrence, Cooper, Murphy, Twitchin.

Barking (0) 1 (*Ashford*)
Aldershot (1) 2 (*Dungworth, Shanahan*) 1897
Barking: Markwick; Barrett, Makin, Arber, Waite, Ironton (Dingwall), Ballard, Anderson, Burton, Key, Ashford.
Aldershot: Johnson; Howitt, Wooler, Dixon, Youlden, Jopling, Crosby, Brodie, Shanahan, Dungworth, McGregor (Longhorn).

Barnsley (1) 1 (*Clarke*)
Rotherham (0) 1 (*Crawford*) 15,491
Barnsley: Springett; Collins, Chambers, Pugh, Saunders, McCarthy, Little, Clarke, Riley, Millar, Bell.
Rotherham: McAlister; Forrest, Breckin, Stancliffe, Green, Flynn Finney, Phillips, Gwyther, Crawford, Smith.

Bury (1) 3 (*Lugg, Gregory 2*)
Blackpool (0) 1 (*Kellow*) 6519
Bury: Forrest; Ritson, Kennedy, Lugg, Tucker Bailey, Stanton, Wilson, Beamish, Gregory, Taylor.
Blackpool: Hesford; Gardner, Pashley, Thompson, Malone, Suddaby, Jones, Kellow, Spence, McEwan, Ronson (Davidson).

Carlisle (0) 3 (*Lumby, McCartney pen, Kemp*)
Hull (0) 0 5335
Carlisle: Swinburne; Hoolickin, McCartney, MacDonald, Tait, Parker, McVitie, Bonnyman, Kemp, Ludlam, Lumby.
Hull: Blackburn; Nisbet, DeVries, Horswill, Croft, Haigh, Galvin, Hood, Edwards, Bannister, Farley.

Crewe (0) 0
Hartlepool (1) 1 (*Crumplin*) 2626
Crewe: Rafferty; Wilkinson Dulson, Bevan, Bowles, Roberts, Davies, Purdie, Coyne, Wilshaw (Nelson), Robertson.
Hartlepool: Richardson, Smith, Gorry, Lawrence, Brooks, Ayre, Linacre, Goldthorpe, Crumplin Newton, Loadwick.

Darlington (0) 2 (*Craig, Ferguson*)
Chester (0) 1 (*Mellor*) 2491
Darlington: Burleigh; Nattrass, Cochrane, Hague, Craig, Stone, Probert, Walsh, Ferguson, Seal, Wann.
Chester: Lloyd; Nickeas, Raynor, Storton, Jeffries, Oakes, Delgado (Walker), Livermore, Howat, Mellor. Phillips.

Doncaster (0) 0
Shrewsbury (0) 3 (*Chapman, Maguire 2*) 3720
Doncaster: Peacock; Reed, Snodin, Cork, Bradley, Olney, Laidlaw, Meagan (Owen), French, Lewis, Bentley.
Shrewsbury: Wardle; King, Larkin, Turner, Griffin, Keay, Chapman, Tong, Lindsay, Biggins, Maguire.

Droylsden (0) 0
Altrincham (1) 2 (*Johnson, Brooke*) 2875
Droylsden: Litchfield; Byrne, Wilkinson, Jackson, Roberts, Gorman, Cooke (McMahon), Taylor, Nicklin, Hughes, Haughton.
Altrincham: Eales; Allan, Crossley, Bailey, Owens, Davison, King, Heathcote, Johnson, Brooke, Howard.

Leatherhead (0) 1 (*Kelly*)
Colchester (1) 1 (*Gough*) 2550
Leatherhead: Swannell; Cooper, Eaton, Davies, Reid, Malley, Cook, Salkeld, Kelly, Baker, Camp (Doyle).
Colchester: Walker; Cook, Packer, Hodge, Wignall, Dowman, Foley, Gough, Dyer, Wright, Allinson.

Maidstone (1) 1 (*Hill*)
Exeter (0) 0 3686
Maidstone: Guy; Kinnear, Edwards, Hill, Aitken, Merrick, Budden, Gregory, Coupland (Wallace), Silvester, Fusco.
Exeter: O'Keefe; Hore (Templeman), Mitchell, Forbes, Giles, Roberts, Neville, Pearson, Bowker, Delve, Hatch.

Newport 0
Worcester 0 7196
Newport: Plumley; Walden, Byrne, Davies, Bruton, Thompson, Warriner, Lowndes, Bailey (Oakes), Goddard, Woods.
Worcester: Cumbes; Pemberton, Punsheon, Tudor, Phelps, Martin, Williams J, Stevens, Williams B, Lawrence, Deehan.

Portsmouth (0) 0
Reading (1) 1 (*Alexander*) 17,195
Portsmouth: Mellor; Ellis, Viney, Denyer, Foster, Davey, Hammerman. Lathan, Garwood (Wilson), Barnard, Pullar.
Reading: Death; Peters, White, Bowman, Hicks, Bennett, Alexander (Hetzke), Earles, Kearney, Sanchez, Lewis.

Stockport (3) 4 (*Fogarty, Lee, Bradd, Park*)
Bradford (1) 2 (*Cooke, Dolan*) 5739
Stockport: Rogan; Smith, Rutter, Thompson, Park, Fogarty, Henson, Armstrong, Bradd, Lee, Summerbee.
Bradford: Downsborough; Podd, Watson, Reaney, Middleton, Wood, Bates, Dolan, Cooke, McNiven, Hutchins.

Swansea (1) 2 (*Curtis 2*)
Woking (0) 2 (*Love, Cottrell*) 7172
Swansea: Crudgington; Evans, Smith, Phillips, Stevenson, Charles, Boersma (Bartley), James, Curtis, Waddle, Callaghan.
Woking: Parsons; O'Sullivan, Martin, Love, Barrett, Cottrell, Alexander, Adams, Morton, Cosham, James.

Swindon (0) 3 (*Bates, Carter, Gilchrist*)
Enfield (0) 0 5681
Swindon: Ogden; McLaughlin, Ford, McHale, Aizlewood, Stroud, Miller, Carter, Gilchrist, Bates, Kamara.
Enfield: Moore; Wright, Tone, Jennings, Elley, Gibson, O'Sullivan, Howell, Searle, Bishop, King.

Tranmere (1) 1 (*Moore*)
Sheffield W (0) 1 (*Leman*) 4250
Tranmere: Johnson; Mathias, Flood, Parry, Cahill, Evans, O'Neil, Bramhall, Moore, Peplow, McAuley.
Sheffield W: Turner; Blackhall, Rushbury, Smith, Pickering, Johnson, Wylde, Lowey, Leman, Porterfield, Hornsby.

Watford (0) 1 (*Jenkins*)
Southend (0) 1 (*Parker*)   13,377
Watford: Sherwood; Stirk, Pritchett, Train, How, Garner, Pollard, Blissett (Mayes), Jenkins, Joslyn, Downes.
Southend: Cawston; Stead, Walker, Laverick, Hadley, Moody, Morris, Pountney, Parker, Dudley Polycarpou.

Wimbledon (0) 1 (*Denny*)
Bournemouth (1) 1 (*MacDougall*)   3308
Wimbledon: Goddard; Bryant, Haverson, Galliers, Galvin, Donaldson Leslie, Briley, Denny, Cork, Parsons.
Bournemouth: Allen; Cunningham, Miller, Impey, Brown R, Barton, Borthwick, MacDougall, Butler, Showers, Lennard.

York (2) 3 (*Faulkner, Staniforth 2*)
Scarborough (0) 0   7876
York: Brown; Kay, Walsh, Pugh, Faulkner, Clements, Ford, Randall, Wellings, McDonald, Staniforth.
Scarborough: McKechnie; Fountain, Smith, Dunn H, Marshall, Donoghue, Lyall, Ellis (Harris), Abbey, Smith, Dunn H A.

SECOND ROUND REPLAYS

18 DEC

Southend (1) 1 (*Polycarpou*)
Watford (0) 0   15,463
Southend: Cawston; Stead, Walker, Laverick, Hadley, Moody, Morris, Pountney, Parker, Dudley, Polycarpou.
Watford: Sherwood; Stirk, Harrison, Booth, How, Garner, Pollard, Mercer, Jenkins, Train, Cassells (Joslyn).

Worcester (1) 1 (*Phelps*)
Newport (0) 2 (*Pemberton og, Goddard*)   10,233
Worcester: Cumbes; Pemberton, Punsheon, Tudor, Phelps (Deehan), Martin, Williams J, Stevens, Williams B, Lawrence, Allner.
Newport: Plumley; Walden, Byrne, Thompson, Davies, Bruton, Oakes, Lowndes (Sinclair), Goddard, Clark, Vaughan.

19 DEC

Colchester (1) 4 (*Lee, Gough, Dowman 2*)
Leatherhead (0) 0   3920
Colchester: Walker; Cook, Packer, Hodge, Wignall, Dowman, Wright, Gough, Dyer, Lee, Allinson.
Leatherhead: Swannell; Cooper, Eaton, Davies, Reid, Malley, Cook, Salkeld, Kelly, Baker, Doyle.

Sheffield W (0) 4 (*Wylde 2, Lowey, Hornsby pen.*)
Tranmere (0) 0   7316
Sheffield W: Turner; Blackhall, Rushbury, Smith, Pickering, Johnson, Wylde, Porterfield, Leman, Lowey, Hornsby.
Tranmere: Johnson; Mathias, Flood, Parry, Cahill, Evans, Craven, Bramhall, Moore, Peplow, McAuley (Postlewhite).

Woking (0) 3 (*Morton, Field, Barrett*)
Swansea (3) 5 (*Curtis 3, Toshack, James R*) aet   4500
Woking: Parsons; O'Sullivan, Martin, Love, Barrett, Cottrell, Alexander, Adams, Morton, Cosham (Field), James.
Swansea: Crudgington; Smith, Bartley, Phillips, Stevenson, Morris, Toshack, James R, Curtis, Waddle, Callaghan.

28 DEC

Bournemouth (0) 1 (*MacDougall*)
Wimbledon (0) 2 (*Cork, Parsons*) aet   7192
Bournemouth: Allen; Cunningham, Miller, Impey, Brown R, Barton, Borthwick, MacDougall, Butler M, Showers (Massey), Lennard.
Wimbledon: Goddard; Perkins, Eames, Ketteridge, Galvin, Donaldson (Denny), Parsons, Briley, Knowles, Cork, Haverson.

THIRD ROUND

6 JAN

Leicester (2) 3 (*May, Weller, Henderson*)
Norwich (0) 0   19,680
Leicester: Wallington; Whitworth, Williams, Ridley, May, O'Neill, Weller, Peake, Henderson, Goodwin, Buchanan.
Norwich: Keelan; Bond, Davies, Ryan, Hoadley, Powell, Neighbour, Reeves, Chivers, McGuire, Peters.

Sheffield W (0) 1 (*Johnson*)
Arsenal (1) 1 (*Sunderland*)   33,635
Sheffield W: Turner; Blackhall, Rushbury, Smith, Mullen, Johnson, Wylde, Porterfield, Leman, Lowey, Hornsby.
Arsenal: Jennings; Rice, Walford, Price, O'Leary, Young, Brady, Sunderland, Stapleton, Gatting, Rix.

Shrewsbury (1) 3 (*Maguire, Turner, Chapman*)
Cambridge (0) 1 (*Biley*)   7415
Shrewsbury: Wardle; King, Larkin, Turner, Griffin, Keay, Chapman, Atkins, Tong, Biggins, Maguire.
Cambridge: Webster; Streete, Smith, Stringer, Fallon, Buckley, Murray, Spriggs, Leach (Garner), Finney, Biley.

Stoke (2) 2 (*Irvine 2*)
Oldham (0) 0 *abandoned at half time*   15,991

8 JAN

Swansea (0) 0
Bristol R (1) 1 (*White*)   16,054
Swansea: Crudgington; Evans, Bartley, Smith, Phillips, Charles, Toshack, James, Curtis, Waddle, Callaghan.
Bristol R: Thomas; Day, Taylor, Harding, Bater, Aitken, Williams, White, Hendrie, Staniforth, Mabbutt (Dennehy).

SECOND ROUND REPLAY

9 JAN

Rotherham (1) 2 (*Gwyther, Phillips*)
Barnsley (1) 1 (*Forrest og*)   15,535
Rotherham: McAlister; Forrest, Breckin, Stancliffe, Green, Flynn, Finney, Phillips, Gwyther, Smith, Crawford.
Barnsley: Springett; Collins, Chambers, Pugh, Saunders, McCarthy, Little, Clarke, Riley, Millar, Bell.

THIRD ROUND

Birmingham (0) 0
Burnley (1) 1   15,535
Birmingham: Montgomery; Broadhurst, Dennis, Towers, Gallagher, Page, Dillon, Francis (Bertschin), Buckley, Tarrantini, Givens.
Burnley: Stevenson; Scott, Brennan, Noble, Thomson, Rodaway, Hall, Ingham, Morley, Kindon, James.

459

Brighton (1) 2 (*Lawrence, Ryan*)
Wolves (1) 3 (*Bell, Daley, Williams og*)   25,217
Brighton: Moseley; Cattlin, Williams, Horton, Rollings, Lawrenson, Ryan, Poskett, Maybank (Clark), Sayer, O'Sullivan.
Wolves: Bradshaw; Palmer, Parkin, Daniel, McAlle, Berry, Hibbitt, Daley, Bell, Eves (Brazier), Carr.

Bristol C (0) 3 (*Gow, Rodgers, Ritchie*)
Bolton (0) 1 (*Smith*)   17,392
Bristol C: Shaw; Sweeney, Gillies, Gow, Rodgers, Hunter, Tainton, Ritchie, Royle, Cormack, Whitehead.
Bolton: McDonagh; Nicholson, Dunne, Greaves, Jones P, Walsh, Morgan, Smith, Gowling, Worthington, McNab.

Charlton (0) 1 (*Flanagan*)
Maidstone (1) 1 (*Coupland*)   13,432
Charlton: Wood; Shaw, Campbell, Gritt (Peacock), Shipperley, Berry, Brisley, Hales, Flanagan, Madden, Powell.
Maidstone: Guy; Kinnear, Edwards, Hill, Aitken, Merrick, Silvester, Gregory, Coupland, Fusco, Budden.

Coventry (1) 2 (*Blair, Green*)
WBA (1) 2 (*Cunningham, Brown A*)   38,046
Coventry: Blyth; Hagen, McDonald, Blair, Holton, Coop, Nardiello (Green), Wallace, Thompson, Powell, Hutchison.
WBA: Godden; Batson, Statham, Brown T, Wile, Robertson, Robson, Brown A, Regis, Trewick, Cunningham.

Darlington (0) 0
Colchester (1) 1 (*Hodge*)   3465
Darlington: Burleigh; Nattrass, Cochrane, Hague, Craig, Stone, Probert, Paterson, Seal (Maitland), Wann, Walsh.
Colchester: Walker; Cook, Wright, Hodge, Wignall, Dowman, Foley, Gough, Dyer, Bunkell, Allinson.

Fulham (1) 2 (*Margerrison, Davies*)
QPR (0) 0   21,119
Fulham: Peyton; Strong, Lock, Bullivant, Money, Gale, Davies, Beck, Guthrie, Margerrison, Marinello.
QPR: Parkes; Clement, Gillard, Cunningham, Howe, Hollins, Shanks, Eastoe, Hamilton, Bowles, Busby (Harkouk).

Middlesbrough (0) 1 (*Ashcroft*)
Crystal Palace (1) 1 (*Walsh*)   21,441
Middlesbrough: Stewart; Craggs, Bailey (Ashcroft), Mahoney, Boam, McAndrew, Cochrane, Proctor, Burns, Cummins, Armstrong.
Crystal Palace: Burridge; Hinshelwood, Sansom, Kember, Cannon, Gilbert, Nicholas, Murphy, Swindlehurst, Fenwick, Walsh.

Newport (1) 2 (*Goddard, Woods*)
West Ham (1) 1 (*Robson*)   14,124
Newport: Plumley; Walden, Byrne, Thompson, Davies, Bruton, Oakes, Lowndes, Goddard, Woods, Vaughan.
West Ham: Day; Lampard, Brush, Bonds, Martin, McDowell, Taylor A, Devonshire, Cross, Brooking, Robson.

Notts Co (3) 4 (*Vinter, Hooks, Mann, Masson*)
Reading (0) 2 (*Kearney 2*)   8265
Notts C: McManus; Richards, O'Brien, Blockley, Stubbs, Mann, McCulloch, Masson, Hooks, Hunt, Vinter.
Reading: Death; Peters, White, Bowman, Hicks, Bennett, Alexander (Hetzke), Earles, Kearney, Sanchez, Lewis.

Orient (2) 3 (*Kitchen 2, Chiedozie*)
Bury (2) 2 (*Gregory, Beamish*)   6192
Orient: Jackson; Fisher, Roffey, Grealish, Gray, Went, Hughton, Moores, Mayo, Chiedozie, Kitchen.
Bury: Forrest; Ritson, Kennedy, Lugg, Tucker, Bailey, Stanton, Wilson, Beamish, Gregory, Taylor.

Sheffield U (0) 0
Aldershot (0) 0   16,000
Sheffield U: Conroy; Franks, Garner, Kenworthy, Matthews, Calvert, Anderson, Speight, Varadi, Sabella, Hamson.
Aldershot: Johnson; Howitt, Wooler, Dixon, Youlden, Jopling, Crosby, Brodie, Needham, Dungworth, McGregor.

Swindon (2) 3 (*McHale, Kamara 2*)
Cardiff (0) 0   9983
Swindon: Ogden; McLaughlin, Ford, McHale, Aizlewood, Lewis, Miller, Carter, Gilchrist, Bates, Kamara.
Cardiff: Healey; Dwyer, Roberts, Campbell, Pontin, Larmour, Attley, Bishop (Buchanan), Evans, Thomas, Lewis.

Wimbledon (0) 0
Southampton (0) 2 (*Boyer 2*)   9254
Wimbledon: Goddard; Perkins, Eames, Ketteridge, Galvin, Denny, Parsons, Briley, Knowles (Leslie), Cork, Haverson.
Southampton: Gennoe; Golac, Peach, Williams, Nicholl, Waldron, Ball, Boyer, Hebberd, Holmes, Curran.

York (1) 2 (*Staniforth, Randall*)
Luton (0) 0   6700
York: Brown; Kay, Walsh, Pugh, Faulkner, Clements, Ford, Randall, Loggie, McDonald, Staniforth.
Luton: Findlay; Jones, Aizlewood, Carr, Price, Donaghy, West, Hill, Stein, Hatton, Sherlock.

THIRD ROUND REPLAY

Arsenal (0) 1 (*Brady*)
Sheffield Wed (1) 1 (*Wylde*) aet   37,987
Arsenal: Jennings; Rice, Nelson, Price, O'Leary, Young, Brady, Sunderland, Stapleton, Gatting, Rix.
Sheffield W: Turner; Blackhall, Rushbury, Smith, Shirtliff, Johnson, Wylde, Porterfield, Leman, Lowey, Hornsby.

THIRD ROUND

10 JAN

Ipswich (2) 3 (*Beattie, Muhren, Wark pen*)
Carlisle (1) 2 (*Tait, Kemp*)   19,036
Ipswich: Cooper; Burley, Tibbott, Mills, Osman, Beattie, Wark, Muhren, Mariner, Whymark, Woods.
Carlisle: Swinburne; Hoolickin, McCartney, MacDonald, Tait, Parker, McVitie, Bonnyman, Ludlam, Kemp, Hamilton.

Millwall (0) 1 (*Walker*)
Blackburn (0) 2 (*Brotherston, Radford*) 8354
Millwall: Cuff; Donaldson, Gregory, Chambers, Kitchener, Mehmet, Towner, Seasman, Mitchell, Walker, Chatterton.
Blackburn: Butcher; Hird, Bailey, Metcalfe, Keeley, Fazackerley, Brotherston, Garner, Radford, Round, Birchenall (Morris).

Nottingham F: (0) 2 (*Needham, Evans og*)
Aston Villa (0) 0 29,550
Nottingham F: Shilton, Anderson, Clark, McGovern, Lloyd, Needham, O'Neill, Gemmill, Birtles, Woodcock, Robertson.
Villa: Rimmer; Gidman, Williams, Evans, McNaught, Mortimer, Craig, Swain, Deehan, Cowans, Gregory.

Southend (0) 0
Liverpool (0) 0 31,033
Southend: Cawston; Stead, Yates, Laverick, Hadley, Moody, Morris, Pountney, Parker, Dudley, Fell.
Liverpool: Clemence; Neal, Hughes, Thompson, Kennedy R, Hansen, Dalglish, Case, Fairclough, McDermott (Heighway), Souness.

Sunderland (1) 2 (*Rowell pen, Lee*)
Everton (0) 1 (*Dobson*) 28,602
Sunderland: Siddall; Henderson, Bolton, Docherty, Clarke, Elliott, Buckley, Rostron, Entwistle, Lee, Rowell.
Everton: Wood; Todd, Darracott, Lyons, Wright, Ross, King, Dobson, Latchford, Walsh, Thomas.

Tottenham (1) 1 (*Taylor pen*)
Altrincham (0) 1 (*Johnson*) 31,081
Tottenham: Kendall; McAllister, Holmes, Villa, Lacy, Perryman, Pratt, Ardiles, Lee (Armstrong), Jones, Taylor.
Altrincham: Eales; Allan, Brooke, Bailey (Crossley), Owens, Davison, King, Heathcote, Johnson, Rogers, Howard.

15 JAN

Manchester C (0) 0
Rotherham (0) 0 26,029
Manchester C: Corrigan; Ranson, Donachie, Power, Bell, Futcher P, Channon, Kidd, Futcher R, Hartford, Barnes.
Rotherham: McAlister; Forrest, Breckin, Stancliffe, Green, Flynn, Finney, Phillips, Gwyther, Smith, Crawford.

Manchester U (1) 3 (*Coppell, Grimes, Greenhoff J*)
Chelsea (0) 0 38,500
Manchester U: Bailey; Greenhoff B, Houston, McIlroy, McQueen, Buchan, Coppell, Greenhoff J, Pearson, Nicholl, Grimes.
Chelsea: Bonetti; Wilkins G, Stride, Osgood, Droy, Harris, Britton, McKenzie (Stanley), Langley, Johnson, Walker.

THIRD ROUND REPLAYS

Aldershot (0) 1 (*Dungworth pen*)
Sheffield U (0) 0 8321
Aldershot: Johnson; Howitt, Wooler, Dixon, Youlden, Jopling, Crosby, Brodie, Needham, Dungworth, McGregor.
Sheffield U: Conroy; Franks, Speight, Kenworthy, Matthews, Calvert, Anderson, Guy, Varadi (Stainrod), Sabella, Hamson.

Crystal Palace (1) 1 (*Samson*)
Middlesbrough (0) 0 23,119
Crystal Palace: Burridge; Hinshelwood, Sansom, Kember, Cannon, Gilbert, Nicholas, Murphy, Fenwick, Hilaire, Walsh.
Middlesbrough: Stewart; Craggs, Bailey, Mahoney, Boam, McAndrew, Cochrane, Proctor, Burns (Ashcroft), Cummins, Armstrong.

Maidstone (0) 1 (*Coupland*)
Charlton (1) 2 (*Campbell, Robinson*) 10,500
Maidstone: Guy; Kinnear, Edwards, Hill, Aitken, Merrick, Gregory (Hutton), Coupland, Fusco, Budden, Silvester.
Charlton: Johns; Shaw, Campbell, Gritt, Shipperley, Berry, Brisley, Peacock, Robinson, Madden, Powell.

WBA (2) 4 (*Brown T 2, Batson, Brown A*)
Coventry (0) 0 36,262
WBA: Godden; Batson, Statham, Brown T, Wile, Robertson, Robson (Johnston), Brown A, Regis, Cantello, Cunningham.
Coventry: Blyth; Hagan, McDonald, Blair, Holton, Coop, Nardiello (Green), Wallace, Thompson, Powell, Hutchison.

SECOND REPLAY

Sheffield W (1) 2 (*Hornsby 2, 1 a pen*) *aet* at Leicester
Arsenal (1) 2 (*Brady, Sunderland*) 25,011
Sheffield W: Turner; Blackhall, Rushbury, Smith, Pickering, Johnson, Wylde, Porterfield, Leman, Lowey, Hornsby.
Arsenal: Jennings; Rice, Nelson, Price, O'Leary, Young, Brady, Sunderland, Stapleton, Gatting, Rix.

THIRD ROUND

16 JAN

Newcastle (1) 3 (*Robinson, Nattrass pen, Withe*)
Torquay (1) 1 (*Lawrence*) 21,366
Newcastle: Hardwick; Brownlie, Mitchell, Martin, Nattrass, Blackley, Nicholson (Barton), Cassidy, Withe, Hibbitt, Robinson.
Torquay: Turner; Darke, Twitchin, Davies, Green, Boulton, Wilson, Lawrence, Coffill, Murphy, Parsons (Cooper).

Preston (1) 3 (*Bruce 2, Burns*)
Derby (0) 0 19,884
Preston: Tunks; Taylor, Cameron, Burns, Baxter, O'Riordan, Coleman, Haslegrave, Robinson, Potts, Bruce.
Derby: McKellar; Langan, Buckley, Daly, McFarland, Webb, Carter, Powell, Caskey, Clark, Hill (Duncan).

REPLAY

Altrincham (0) 0
Tottenham (2) 3 (*Lee 3*) at Maine Road 27,878
Altrincham: Eales; Crossley, Brooke, Allan, Owens, Davison, King, Heathcote, Johnson, Rogers, Howard.
Tottenham: Aleksic; McAllister, Holmes, Villa (Naylor), Lacy, Perryman, Pratt, Ardiles, Lee, Jones, Taylor.

THIRD ROUND

17 JAN
Stoke (0) 0
Oldham (1) 1 (*Wood*) 16,554
Stoke: Jones; Dodd, Scott, Kendall, Smith, Doyle, McGroarty, Irvine, O'Callaghan, Crooks, Richardson.
Oldham: McDonnell; Wood, Holt, Bell, Hicks, Hurst, Valentine, Halom, Young, Chapman, Blair.

REPLAYS

Liverpool (1) 3 (*Case, Dalglish, Kennedy R*)
Southend (0) 0 37,797
Liverpool: Clemence, Neal; Hughes, Thompson, Kennedy R, Hansen, Dalglish, Case, Fairclough, McDermott, Souness.
Southend: Cawston; Stead, Yates, Laverick, Hadley, Moody, Morris, Pountney, Parker, Dudley, Fell (Walker).

Rotherham (0) 2 (*Breckin, Green*)
Manchester C (3) 4 (*Owen, Kidd 2, Barnes*) 13,758
Rotherham: McAlister; Forrest, Breckin, Stancliffe, Green, Flynn, Finney, Phillips, Gwyther, Smith, Crawford.
Manchester C: MacRae; Power, Donachie, Owen, Watson, Futcher P, Channon, Deyna, Kidd, Hartford, Barnes.

THIRD REPLAY

Sheffield W (0) 3 (*Rushbury, Lowey, Hornsby pen*)
aet at Leicester
Arsenal (0) 3 (*Stapleton 2, Young*) 17,008
Sheffield W: Turner; Blackhall, Rushbury, Smith, Pickering, Johnson, Wylde, Porterfield, Leman, Lowey, Hornsby.
Arsenal: Jennings; Rice, Nelson, Price, O'Leary, Young, Brady, Sunderland, Stapleton, Gatting, Rix.

THIRD ROUND

18 JAN
Hartlepool (1) 2 (*Newton 2 pens*)
Leeds (3) 6 (*Hart, Graham, Gray E 2, Harris, Gray F pen*) 16,000
Hartlepool: Richardson; Smith G, Gorry, Lawrence, Smith T, Norton, Linacre, Goldthorpe, Crumplin, Newton, Loadwick.
Leeds: Harvey; Cherry, Gray F, Flynn, Hart, Madeley, Gary E, Graham, Hawley, Currie, Harris.

FOURTH REPLAY

22 JAN
Sheffield W (0) 0
Arsenal (2) 2 (*Gatting, Stapleton*) at Leicester 30,275
Arsenal: Jennings; Rice, Nelson, Price, O'Leary, Young, Brady, Sunderland, Stapleton, Gatting, Rix.
Sheffield W: Turner; Blackhall, Rushbury, Smith (Grant), Pickering, Johnson, Wylde, Porterfield, Owen, Lowey, Hornsby.

FOURTH ROUND

27 JAN
Arsenal (0) 2 (*Young, Talbot*)
Notts Co (0) 0 39,173
Arsenal: Jennings; Rice, Nelson, Talbot, O'Leary, Young, Brady, Sunderland, Stapleton, Price, Rix.
Notts Co: McManus; Richards, O'Brien, Blockley, Stubbs, Mann, McCulloch, Masson, Hooks, Hunt, Vinter.

Ipswich (0) 0
Orient (0) 0 23,357
Ipswich: Cooper; Burley, Tibbott, Mills, Osman, Beattie, Wark, Muhren, Mariner, Whymark, Woods.
Orient: Jackson; Fisher, Roffey, Grealish, Gray, Went, Chiedozie, Moores, Mayo, Kitchen, Coates.

R.F. 79/80—24

Newcastle (0) 1 (*Withe*)
Wolves (0) 1 (*Hibbitt*) 30,000
Newcastle: Hardwick; Brownlie, Mitchell, Nattrass, Blackley, Barton, Guy, Martin, Withe, Hibbitt, Robinson (McGhee).
Wolves: Bradshaw; Palmer, Parkin, Daniel, McAlle, Berry, Hibbitt, Daley, Bell, Eves (Brazier), Carr.

Nottingham F (2) 3 (*Lloyd, McGovern, O'Neill*)
York (0) 1 (*Wellings*) 25,228
Nottingham F: Shilton; Anderson, Bowyer, McGovern, Lloyd, Burns, O'Neill, Gemmill, Birtles, Woodcock, Robertson.
York: Brown; Kay, Walsh, Pugh, Faulkner, Clements, Ford, Randall, Loggie (Wellings), McDonald, Staniforth.

Shrewsbury (1) 2 (*Maguire, Chapman*)
Manchester C (0) 0 14,215
Shrewsbury: Wardle; King, Larkin, Turner, Griffin, Keay, Chapman, Atkins, Tong, Biggins, Maguire.
Manchester C: Corrigan; Donachie, Power, Owen, Watson, Futcher P, Channon, Deyna (Bell), Kidd, Hartford, Barnes.

29 JAN
Crystal Palace (1) 3 (*Nicholas, Fenwick, Kember*)
Bristol C (0) 0 21,463
Crystal Palace: Burridge; Hinshelwood, Sansom, Kember, Cannon, Gilbert, Nicholas, Murphy, Fenwick, Swindlehurst, Walsh.
Bristol C: Shaw; Sweeney, Gillies, Gow, Rodgers, Hunter, Ritchie, Royle, Cormack (Mann), Whitehead, Tainton.

30 JAN
Aldershot (2) 2 (*Dungworth 2*)
Swindon (0) 1 (*Rowland*) 10,913
Aldershot: Johnson; Howitt, Wooler, Dixon, Youlden, Jopling, Crosby, Brodie, Needham, Dungworth, McGregor.
Swindon: Allan; Hamilton, Ford, McHale, Aizlewood, Stroud, Miller, Carter, Gilchrist (Rowland), Bates, Williams.

Liverpool (0) 1 (*Dalglish*)
Blackburn (0) 0 43,432
Liverpool: Clemence; Neal, Hughes, Kennedy A, Kennedy R, Hansen, Dalglish, Case, Fairclough, McDermott (Heighway), Souness.
Blackburn: Butcher; Fowler, Bailey, Metcalfe, Round, Fazackerley, Hird, Garner, Craig, Birchenall, Morris (Brotherston).

Newport (0) 0
Colchester (0) 0 10,329
Newport: Plumley; Walden, Byrne, Thompson, Davies, Bruton, Oakes, Lowndes, Goddard, Woods, Vaughan.
Colchester: Walker; Cook, Wright, Hodge, Wignall, Dowman, Foley, Gough, Dyer, Lee, Allinson.

REPLAY

Orient (0) 0
Ipswich (0) 2 (*Mariner 2*) 18,672
Orient: Jackson; Fisher, Roffey (Banjo), Hughton, Gray, Went, Chiedozie, Moores, Mayo, Kitchen, Coates.
Ipswich: Cooper; Burley, Tibbott, Mills, Roberts, Osman, Wark, Muhren, Mariner, Whymark, Woods.

31 JAN

Fulham (0) 1 (*Margerrison*)
Manchester U (1) 1 (*Greenhoff J*) 25,229
Fulham: Peyton; Evans, Strong, Bullivant, Money, Lock, Davies, Beck, Guthrie, Margerrison, Marinello.
Manchester U: Bailey; Greenhoff B, Houston, McIlroy, McQueen, Buchan, Coppell, Greenhoff J, Pearson (Nicholl), Macari, Thomas.

THIRD ROUND

1 FEB

Wrexham (1) 6 (*Cegielski, McNeil 2, Lyons, Cartwright, Shinton*)
Stockport (1) 2 (*Lee, Park*) 7500
Wrexham: Davies, Hill (Sutton), Cegielski, Davis, Roberts, Giles, Shinton, Cartwright, McNeil, Lyons, Fox.
Stockport: Rogan; Smith, Rutter, Thompson, Park, Edwards, Henson, Summerbee, Bradd, Armstrong, Lee (Prudham).

FOURTH ROUND

5 FEB

Bristol R (1) 1 (*White*)
Charlton (0) 0 9623
Bristol R: Thomas; Day, Bater, Harding, Taylor, Prince, Dennehy, Williams, White, Staniforth (Mabbutt), Hendrie.
Charlton: Johns; Shaw, Campbell, Brisley, Shipperley Berry, Powell (Warman), Robinson, Flanagan Madden, Gritt.

Colchester (1) 1 (*Gough*)
Newport (0) 0 7029
Colchester: Walker; Cook, Wright, Hodge, Wignall, Dowman, Foley, Gough, Packer, Lee, Allinson.
Newport: Plumley; Walden, Byrne, Davies, Oakes, Lowndes, Thompson, Sinclair (Relish), Goddard, Bruton, Vaughan.

12 FEB

Preston (0) 0
Southampton (1) 1 (*Ball*) 20,727
Preston: Tunks; Taylor, Cameron, Burns, Baxter, O'Riordan, Coleman, Haslegrave, Robinson, Potts (Doyle), Bruce.
Southampton: Gennoe, Golac, Peach, Williams, Nicholl, Waldron, Ball, Boyer, Hebberd, Holmes, Curran.

Tottenham (2) 3 (*Roberts og, Hoddle Jones*)
Wrexham (2) 3 (*Shinton, Lyons 2, 1 a pen*) 27,120
Tottenham: Kendall; Naylor, Holmes, Hoddle, Lacy, Perryman, Pratt, Gorman, Armstrong (Jones), Lee, Taylor.
Wrexham: Davies, Sutton, Cegielski, Davis, Roberts, Giles, Shinton, Cartwright, McNeil, Lyons, Fox.

REPLAY

Manchester U (0) 1 (*Greenhoff J*)
Fulham (0) 0 41,020
Manchester U: Bailey; Greenhoff B, Albiston, McIlroy, McQueen, Buchan, Coppell, Greenhoff J, Ritchie, Macari, Thomas.
Fulham: Peyton; Evans, Strong, Bullivant, Money, Lock, Davies (Margerrison), Beck, Guthrie, Gale, Marinello.

FIFTH ROUND

20 FEB

Aldershot (0) 2 (*Dungworth 2*)
Shrewsbury (0) 2 (*Maguire, Tong*) 11,895
Aldershot: Johnson; Howitt, Wooler, Dixon, Youlden, Jopling, Crosby, Brodie, Needham, Dungworth, McGregor.
Shrewsbury: Wardle; King, Larkin, Turner, Hayes, Keay, Chapman, Atkins, Tong, Biggins, Maguire.

Colchester (0) 0
Manchester U (0) 1 (*Greenhoff J*) 13,171
Colchester: Walker; Cook, Wright, Hodge, Wignall, Dowman, Packer, Foley, Dyer, Lee, Allinson.
Manchester U: Bailey; Greenhoff B, Albiston, McIlroy, McQueen, Buchan, Coppell, Greenhoff J, Ritchie, Macari, Thomas.

FOURTH ROUND

21 FEB

Burnley (1) 1 (*Thomson*)
Sunderland (0) 1 (*Entwhistle*) 20,000
Burnley: Stevenson; Scott, Brennan, Noble, Thomson, Rodaway, Hall, Ingham, Morley (Fletcher), Kindon, James.
Sunderland: Siddall; Henderson, Bolton, Arnott, Clarke, Elliott, Chisholm, Rostron, Entwistle, Lee, Rowell.

REPLAYS

Wrexham (0) 2 (*Davis, McNeil*)
Tottenham (1) 3 (*Jones 3*) aet 16,050
Wrexham: Davies; Cegielski, Jones, Davis, Roberts, Giles, Shinton, Cartwright. McNeil, Lyons, Fox (Sutton).
Tottenham: Kendall; Naylor, Holmes, Hoddle, Lacy, Perryman, Pratt, Villa, Lee (Armstrong), Jones, Taylor.

22 FEB

Wolves (1) 1 (*Bell*)
Newcastle (0) 0 19,588
Wolves: Bradshaw; Palmer, Parkin, Daniel, McAlle, Berry, Hibbitt, Daley, Bell, Clarke, Carr.
Newcastle: Hardwick; Brownlie, Mitchell (Pearson), Martin, Bird, Blackley Guy, Nattrass, Withe, Hibbitt, Walker.

FOURTH ROUND

26 FEB

WBA (0) 3 (*Cunningham, Brown A, Regis*)
Leeds (1) 3 (*Gray F, Graham, Harris*) 34,000
WBA: Godden; Batson, Statham, Brown T, Wile, Robertson, Robson, Brown A, Regis, Cantello, Cunningham.
Leeds: Harvey; Cherry, Gray F, Flynn, Hart, Madeley, Harris, Stevenson, Hawley, Currie, Graham.

Oldham (1) 3 (*Young 3*)
Leicester (1) 1 (*Henderson*) 11,972
Oldham: McDonnell; Wood, Edwards, Gardner, Blair, Hurst, Steel, Young, Halom Chapman, Heaton.
Leicester: Wallington; Whitworth, Rofe, O'Neill, May, Ridley, Goodwin, Williams, Henderson, Smith, Buchanan (Kelly).

FOURTH ROUND REPLAY

Sunderland (0) 0
Burnley (2) 3 (*Fletcher, Ingham, Kindon*) 37,507
Sunderland: Watson; Henderson, Bolton, Arnott, Clarke, Elliott, Chisholm, Rostron, (Ashurst) Entwistle, Lee, Rowell.
Burnley: Stevenson; Scott, Brennan, Noble, Thomson, Rodaway, Robinson, Ingham, Fletcher, Kindon, James.

FIFTH ROUND

Crystal Palace (0) 0
Wolves (1) 1 (*Patching*) 26,790
Crystal Palace: Burridge; Hinshelwood (Hilaire), Sansom, Kember, Cannon, Gilbert, Nicholas, Murphy, Swindlehurst, Fenwick, Walsh.
Wolves: Bradshaw; Palmer, Parkin, Daniel, McAlle Berry, Hibbitt, Patching, Bell (Daley), Richards, Carr.

Ipswich (4) 6 (*Brazil 2, Mills, Muhren, Geddis, Mariner*)
Bristol R (0) 1 (*White*) 23,231
Ipswich: Cooper, Burley (Geddis), Tibbott, Mills, Osman, Beattie, Wark, Muhren. Mariner, Brazil, Woods.
Bristol R: Thomas; Jones, Bater, Harding, Taylor, Prince, Dennehy, Williams, White, Emmanuel, Hendrie (Staniforth).

Nottingham F (0) 0
Arsenal (0) 1 (*Stapleton*) 35,906
Nottingham F: Shilton; Anderson, Clark, McGovern, Lloyd, Needham, O'Neill, Gemmill, Birtles, Woodcock, Robertson.
Arsenal: Jennings; Rice, Nelson, Talbot, O'Leary, Walford, Brady, Sunderland, Stapleton, Price, Rix.

FIFTH ROUND REPLAY

Shrewsbury (1) 3 (*Biggins 2, Leonard*)
Aldershot (0) 1 (*Dungworth*) aet 13,720
Shrewsbury: Wardle; King, Leonard, Turner, Griffin, Keay, Chapman, Atkins, Tong, Biggins, Maguire.
Aldershot: Johnson; Howitt, Wooler (Edwards), Longhorn, Youlden, Jopling, Crosby, Brodie, Needham, Dungworth, McGregor.

FIFTH ROUND

28 FEB

Liverpool (1) 3 (*Johnson 2, Souness*)
Burnley (0) 0 47,461
Liverpool: Clemence; Neal, Hughes, Kennedy A, Kennedy R, Thompson, Dalglish, Johnson, Heighway, McDermott, Souness.
Burnley: Stevenson; Scott, Brennan, Noble, Thomson, Rodaway, Ingham, Hall, Fletcher, Kindon, James.

Oldham (0) 0
Tottenham (1) 1 (*Perryman*) 16,097
Oldham: McDonnell; Wood, Keegan, Gardner, Blair, Hurst, Steel (Bell), Young, Halom, Chapman, Heaton.
Tottenham: Kendall; Naylor, Holmes, Hoddle, Lacy, Perryman, Pratt, Ardiles, (Lee) McAllister, Jones, Taylor.

FOURTH ROUND REPLAY

1 MARCH

WBA (0) 2 (*Wile, Brown A*)
Leeds (0) 0 aet 31,101
WBA: Godden; Batson, Statham, Brown T, Wile, Robertson, Robson, Brown A, Regis, Cantello, Cunningham.
Leeds: Harvey; Cherry, Gray F, Flynn, Parkinson, Madeley, Harris, Stevenson, Hawley, Currie, Graham.

FIFTH ROUND

10 MARCH

WBA (1) 1 (*Brown A*)
Southampton (1) 1 (*Boyer*) 30,712
WBA: Godden; Batson, Statham, Brown T, Wile, Robertson, Robson, Brown A, Regis, Mills, Cunningham.
Southampton: Gennoe; Golac, Peach, Williams, Nicholl, Waldron, Ball, Boyer, Hayes (Andruszewski), Holmes, Curran.

SIXTH ROUND

Ipswich (0) 0
Liverpool (0) 1 (*Dalglish*) 31,322
Ipswich: Cooper; Burley, Mills, Thijssen, Osman, Butcher, Wark, Muhren, Mariner, Gates (Brazil), Woods.
Liverpool: Clemence; Neal, Hughes, Thompson, Kennedy R, Hansen, Dalglish, Johnson, Case, McDermott, Souness.

Tottenham (1) 1 (*Ardiles*)
Manchester U (0) 1 (*Thomas*) 51,800
Tottenham: Kendall; Naylor, McAllister, Holmes, Lacy, Perryman, Pratt, Ardiles, Jones, Hoddle, Villa (Taylor).
Manchester U: Bailey; Nicholl, Albiston, McIlroy, McQueen, Buchan, Coppell, Greenhoff J, Ritchie (Jordan), Grimes, Thomas.

Wolves (0) 1 (*Rafferty*)
Shrewsbury (0) 1 (*Atkins pen*) 40,946
Wolves: Bradshaw; Palmer, Parkin, Daniel, McAlle, Berry, Hibbitt, Daley, Rafferty, Richards (Patching), Carr.
Shrewsbury: Wardle; Hayes, Leonard, Turner, Griffin, Keay, Chapman, Atkins, Tong, Biggins, Maguire.

FIFTH ROUND REPLAY

12 MARCH

Southampton (0) 2 (*Peach pen, Boyer*)
WBA (0) 1 (*Cunningham*) aet 25,000
Southampton: Gennoe; Golac, Peach, Williams, Nicholl, Waldron, Ball, Boyer, Hayes, Holmes, Curran.
WBA: Godden; Batson, Statham, Brown T, Wile, Robertson, Trewick, Brown A, Regis (Johnston), Mills, Cunningham.

SIXTH ROUND REPLAYS

13 MARCH

Shrewsbury (0) 1 (*Keay*)
Wolves (1) 3 (*Carr, Rafferty, Daniel pen*) 15,279
Shrewsbury: Wardle; Hayes, Leonard, Turner, Griffin, Keay, Chapman, Atkins, Tong, Biggins, Maguire.
Wolves: Bradshaw; Palmer, Parkin, Daniel, McAlle, Berry, Hibbitt, Daley, Rafferty, Richards, Carr.

14 MARCH

Manchester U (1) 2 (*Jordan, McIlroy*)
Tottenham (0) 0 54,510
Manchester U: Bailey; Nicholl, Albiston, McIlroy, McQueen, Buchan, Coppell, Greenhoff J, Jordan, Grimes, Thomas.
Tottenham: Kendall; Naylor, McAllister, Holmes, Lacy, Perryman, Pratt, Ardiles, Jones, Hoddle, Villa.

SIXTH ROUND

19 MARCH

Southampton (0) 1 (*Hayes*)
Arsenal (0) 1 (*Price*) 24,536
Southampton: Gennoe; Golac, Peach, Williams, Nicholl, Waldron, Ball, Boyer, Hayes, Holmes, Curran.
Arsenal: Jennings; Rice, Nelson, Talbot, O'Leary, Young, Brady, Sunderland, Stapleton, Price, Rix.

REPLAY

21 MARCH

Arsenal (1) 2 (*Sunderland 2*)
Southampton (0) 0 44,820
Arsenal: Jennings; Rice, Nelson, Talbot, O'Leary, Young, Brady (Walford), Sunderland, Stapleton, Price, Rix.
Southampton: Wells; Golac, Andruszewski (Baker), Williams, Nicholl, Waldron, Ball, Boyer, Hayes, Holmes, George.

SEMI-FINALS

31 MARCH

Arsenal (0) 2 *(Stapleton, Sunderland)*
Wolves (0) 0 *(at Villa Park)* 46,244
Arsenal: Jennings; Rice, Nelson, Talbot, O'Leary, Young, Gatting, Sunderland, Stapleton, Price, Rix.
Wolves: Bradshaw; Palmer (Patching), Parkin, Daniel, McAlle, Berry, Hibbitt, Daley, Rafferty, Richards, Carr.

Liverpool (1) 2 *(Dalglish, Hansen)* (at Maine Road)
Manchester U (1) 2 *(Jordan, Greenhoff B)* 52,584
Liverpool: Clemence; Neal, Hughes, Thompson, Kennedy R, Hansen, Dalglish, Johnson, Case (Heighway), McDermott, Souness.
Manchester U: Bailey; Nicholl, Albiston, McIlroy, McQueen, Buchan, Coppell, Greenhoff J, Jordan, Greenhoff B, Thomas.

REPLAY

4 APRIL

Manchester U (0) 1 *(Greenhoff J)*
Liverpool (0) 0 *(at Goodison Park)* 53,069
Manchester U: Bailey; Nicholl, Albiston, McIlroy, McQueen, Buchan, Coppell, Greenhoff J, Jordan, Macari (Ritchie), Thomas.
Liverpool: Clemence; Neal, Hughes, Thompson, Kennedy R, Hansen, Dalglish, Johnson (Case), Heighway, McDermott, Souness.

FINAL

12 MAY

Arsenal (2) 3 *(Talbot, Stapleton, Sunderland)*
Manchester U (0) 2 *(McQueen, McIlroy)* 100,000
At Wembley
Arsenal: Jennings; Rice, Nelson, Talbot, O'Leary, Young, Brady, Sunderland, Stapleton, Price (Walford), Rix.
Manchester U: Bailey; Nicholl, Albiston, McIlroy, McQueen, Buchan, Coppell, Greenhoff J, Jordan, Macari, Thomas.

FA CUP FINALS 1872-1979

1872 and 1874-92	Kennington Oval
1873	Lillie Bridge
1893	Fallowfield, Manchester
1894	Everton
1895-1914	Crystal Palace
1901	Replay at Bolton
1910	Replay at Everton
1911	Replay at Old Trafford
1912	Replay at Bramall Lane
1915	Old Trafford, Manchester
1920-22	Stamford Bridge
1923 to date	Wembley
1970	Replay at Old Trafford

Year	Winners	Runners-up	Score
1872	Wanderers	Royal Engineers	1-0
1873	Wanderers	Oxford University	2-0
1874	Oxford University	Royal Engineers	2-0
1875	Royal Engineers	Old Etonians	2-0 after 1-1 draw
1876	Wanderers	Old Etonians	3-0 after 0-0 draw
1877	Wanderers	Oxford University	2-0 after extra time
1878	*Wanderers	Royal Engineers	3-1
1879	Old Etonians	Clapham R	1-0
1880	Clapham R	Oxford University	1-0
1881	Old Carthusians	Old Etonians	3-0
1882	Old Etonians	Blackburn R	1-0
1883	Blackburn Olympic	Old Etonians	2-1 after extra time
1884	Blackburn R	Queen's Park, Glasgow	2-1
1885	Blackburn R	Queen's Park, Glasgow	2-0
1886	†Blackburn R	WBA	2-0 after 0-0 draw
1887	Aston Villa	WBA	2-0
1888	WBA	Preston NE	2-1
1889	Preston NE	Wolverhampton W	3-0
1890	Blackburn R	Sheffield W	6-1
1891	Blackburn R	Notts Co	3-1
1892	WBA	Aston Villa	3-0
1893	Wolverhampton W	Everton	1-0
1894	Notts Co	Bolton W	4-1
1895	Aston Villa	WBA	1-0
1896	Sheffield W	Wolverhampton W	2-1
1897	Aston Villa	Everton	3-2
1898	Nottingham F	Derby Co	3-1
1899	Sheffield U	Derby Co	4-1
1900	Bury	Southampton	4-0
1901	Tottenham H	Sheffield U	3-1 after 2-2 draw
1902	Sheffield U	Southampton	2-1 after 1-1 draw
1903	Bury	Derby Co	6-0
1904	Manchester C	Bolton W	1-0
1905	Aston Villa	Newcastle U	2-0
1906	Everton	Newcastle U	1-0
1907	Sheffield W	Everton	2-1
1908	Wolverhampton W	Newcastle U	3-1
1909	Manchester U	Bristol C	1-0
1910	Newcastle U	Barnsley	2-0 after 1-1 draw
1911	Bradford C	Newcastle U	1-0 after 0-0 draw
1912	Barnsley	WBA	1-0 after extra time
1913	Aston Villa	Sunderland	1-0 after 0-0 draw
1914	Burnley	Liverpool	1-0
1915	Sheffield U	Chelsea	3-0
1920	Aston Villa	Huddersfield	1-0 after extra time
1921	Tottenham H	Wolverhampton W	1-0
1922	Huddersfield	Preston NE	1-0
1923	Bolton W	West Ham U	2-0
1924	Newcastle U	Aston Villa	2-0

Year	Winners	Runners-up	Score
1925	Sheffield U	Cardiff C	1-0
1926	Bolton W	Manchester C	1-0
1927	Cardiff C	Arsenal	1-0
1928	Blackburn R	Huddersfield T	3-1
1929	Bolton W	Portsmouth	2-0
1930	Arsenal	Huddersfield T	2-0
1931	WBA	Birmingham C	2-1
1932	Newcastle U	Arsenal	2-1
1933	Everton	Manchester C	3-0
1934	Manchester C	Portsmouth	2-1
1935	Sheffield W	WBA	4-2
1936	Arsenal	Sheffield U	1-0
1937	Sunderland	Preston NE	3-1
1938	Preston NE	Huddersfield T	1-0 after extra time
1939	Portsmouth	Wolverhampton W	4-1
1946	Derby Co	Charlton Ath	4-1 after extra time
1947	Charlton Ath	Burnley	1-0 after extra time
1948	Manchester U	Blackpool	4-2
1949	Wolverhampton W	Leicester C	3-1
1950	Arsenal	Liverpool	2-0
1951	Newcastle U	Blackpool	2-0
1952	Newcastle U	Arsenal	1-0
1953	Blackpool	Bolton W	4-3
1954	WBA	Preston NE	3-2
1955	Newcastle U	Manchester C	3-1
1956	Manchester C	Birmingham C	3-1
1957	Aston Villa	Manchester U	2-1
1958	Bolton W	Manchester U	2-0
1959	Nottingham F	Luton T	2-1
1960	Wolverhampton W	Blackburn R	3-0
1961	Tottenham H	Leicester C	2-0
1962	Tottenham H	Burnley	3-1
1963	Manchester U	Leicester C	3-1
1964	West Ham U	Preston NE	3-2
1965	Liverpool	Leeds U	2-1 after extra time
1966	Everton	Sheffield W	3-2
1967	Tottenham H	Chelsea	2-1
1968	WBA	Everton	1-0 after extra time
1969	Manchester C	Leicester C	1-0
1970	Chelsea	Leeds U	2-1 after extra time
	(after 2-2 draw, after extra time, at Wembley)		
1971	Arsenal	Liverpool	2-1 after extra time
1972	Leeds U	Arsenal	1-0
1973	Sunderland	Leeds U	1-0
1974	Liverpool	Newcastle U	3-0
1975	West Ham U	Fulham	2-0
1976	Southampton	Manchester U	1-0
1977	Manchester U	Liverpool	2-1
1978	Ipswich T	Arsenal	1-0
1979	Arsenal	Manchester U	3-2

*Won outright, but restored to the Association.

†A special trophy was awarded for third consecutive win.

FA CUP WINS

Aston Villa 7, Blackburn R 6, Newcastle U 6, Arsenal 5, The Wanderers 5, Tottenham H 5, WBA 5, Sheffield U 4, Bolton W 4, Wolverhampton W 4, Manchester C 4, Manchester U 4, Sheffield W 3, Everton 3, Bury 2, Old Etonians 2, Preston NE 2, Nottingham F 2, Sunderland 2, West Ham U 2, Liverpool 2, Barnsley 1, Blackburn Olympic 1, Blackpool 1, Bradford C 1, Burnley 1, Cardiff C 1, Charlton Ath 1, Chelsea 1, Clapham R 1, Derby Co 1, Huddersfield T 1, Notts Co 1, Old Carthusians 1, Oxford University 1, Portsmouth 1, Royal Engineers 1, Leeds U. 1, Southampton 1, Ipswich T 1.

APPEARANCES IN FINALS

Newcastle U 11, WBA 10, Arsenal 10, Aston Villa 9, Blackburn R 8, Manchester U 8, Wolverhampton W 8, Bolton W 7, Preston NE 7, Everton 7, Manchester C 7, Liverpool 6, Old Etonians 6, Sheffield U 6, Huddersfield T 5, *The Wanderers 5, Sheffield W 5, *Tottenham H 5, Derby Co 4, Oxford University 4, Royal Engineers 4, Leeds U 4, Leicester C 4, Blackpool 3, Burnley 3, Chelsea 3, Portsmouth 3, Sunderland 3, West Ham U 3, Southampton 3, Barnsley 2, Birmingham C 2, *Bury 2, Cardiff C 2, Charlton Ath 2, Clapham R 2, Notts Co 2, Queen's Park (Glas) 2, *Nottingham F 2, *Blackburn Olympic 1, *Bradford C 1, Bristol C 1, *Old Carthusians 1, Luton T 1, Fulham 1, Ipswich T 1.

*Denotes undefeated.

APPEARANCES IN SEMI-FINALS

WBA 18, Aston Villa 17, Everton 17, Blackburn R 16, Manchester U 15, Arsenal 14, Sheffield W 13, Derby Co 13, Newcastle U 13, Bolton W 12, Liverpool 12, Wolverhampton W 12, Sunderland 10, Preston NE 10, Sheffield U 10, Chelsea 10, Nottingham F 9, Tottenham H 9, Manchester C 9, Birmingham C 9, Burnley 8, Southampton 8, Huddersfield T, Leeds U 7, Old Etonians 6, Oxford University 6, Leicester C 6, The Wanderers 5, Notts Co 5, Fulham 5, Portsmouth 4, Queen's Park (Glasgow) 4, Royal Engineers 4, West Ham U 4, Blackpool 3, Cardiff C 3, Clapham R 3, Millwall 3, Old Carthusians 3, The Swifts 3, Stoke C 3, Barnsley 2, Blackburn Olympic 2, Bristol C 2, Bury 2, Charlton Ath 2, Grimsby T 2, Ipswich T 2, Swansea T 2, Swindon T 2, Crystal Palace 2, Bradford C 1, Cambridge University 1, Crewe Alex 1, Darwen 1, Derby Junction 1, Glasgow R 1, Hull C 1, Marlow 1, Old Harrovians 1, Oldham Ath 1, Port Vale 1, Reading 1, Shropshire W 1, York C 1, Luton T 1, Norwich C 1, Watford 1, Orient 1.

FOOTBALL LEAGUE CUP 1978-79

The demise of leading First Division clubs in the early stages of the competition has been the most puzzling feature of the League Cup for many years. The casualty rate seems much higher than in the FA Cup, and it is very hard to find a single satisfactory explanation for this phenomenon.

It can be argued that some clubs do not take this tournament seriously, because it interferes with their other more pressing commitments. But when one considers not only the prestige of this well-established cup, but also the vast financial rewards that a Wembley final provides, not to mention a guaranteed place in the UEFA Cup for the winners, this outdated excuse for wholesale failure falls flat on its face.

And the year under review was no exception – no fewer than six First Division teams were k.o'd by lower class opponents in round two, in which the 'creme-de-le-creme' is included in the draw for the first time.

Perhaps these 'giants' weren't quite ready for sudden death combat as early as August? Perhaps the minnows are fitter and full of running at that stage of the season? Perhaps the hard grounds suit the 'fighters' more than the touch-players? Perhaps it is difficult to motivate a 'star' footballer for a midweek fixture in Rotherham?

Whatever the answer, Arsenal were beaten at Rotherham, and the then all-conquering Liverpool lost 1-0 at Sheffield United. Tottenham managed a controversial draw at Swansea, where the Tommy Smith – Osvaldo Ardiles confrontation made the headlines, only to lose 3-1 at home against John Toshack's collection of ancient ex-Liverpool heroes and promising young Welshmen.

The most dramatic encounter of round three was played at Old Trafford, where Manchester United's slender 1-0 lead was first equalized, then destroyed by a rampant Watford side. Luther Blissett headed both goals, thus gaining national recognition for himself.

Holders Nottingham Forest came into the picture at the next stage with a convincing 3-2 win at Goodison, where Everton do not often lose, especially when the prize is a place in the quarter-finals of a cup. Luton's 2-0 win at Villa Park also deserves a mention as yet another giant-killing act. Watford, everybody's favourite underdogs, accounted for Stoke after a replay in the fifth round, and the semi-final pairings were Forest v Watford, Leeds v Southampton.

'This is a very important competition for us,' said Jimmy Adamson, 'because it is now the easiest route into Europe'. However their 2-0 (Currie, Hankin) lead was wiped-out by Holmes and Steve Williams, and in the second-leg at the Dell, a Terry Curran goal was enough to put Lawrie McMenemy's team in the final. Watford opened brightly at Forest, but two goals by Garry Birtles and one by the mercurial John Robertson (a corny adjective, but how true!) gave the holders a 3-1 win to take to Vicarage Road, where they duly drew 0-0. So, Forest were back at Wembley defending the cup, intent on establishing a record by becoming the first club to win this trophy two years in succession.

Terry Gennoe had to make the first save of the final when a Robertson cross was headed straight at him by Birtles. Southampton had a fair share of the play, and their loose but effective man-to-man marking system kept the dangerous Forest forwards quiet. The Yugoslav Golac was shadowing Robertson, Waldron was marking Woodcock, and the tall Chris Nicholl was 'in charge' of young Birtles. In the 17th minute, a marvellous Alan Ball through pass caught the Forest defence flat-footed, Peach ran intelligently into the area, calmly dribbled past Shilton, and slotted the ball into the net for an excellent goal. 'Total football' at its most thrilling – a full-back scoring from an advanced forward position.

Later, an Alan Ball cross went to Boyer, whose attempt was smothered by Shilton. This was an important save, because Southampton's first-half ascendency, which resulted in a single goal lead, wasn't enough. Forest were a different side in the second period, and their excellent spearhead eventually destroyed the faltering Waldron-Nicholl partnership. Birtles equalized with a hooked shot from close-in, then the nervous Gennoe let a ball slip under his body, but there wasn't a Forest player near enough to capitalize on this uncharacteristic error. With Forest well on top, goals had to come, and the two which nailed Southampton were both out of the top drawer.

First, the irresistible Garry Birtles brushed aside the Southampton central defenders and hammered the ball home, then an exquisite Archie Gemmill pass was converted by Tony Woodcock. As a last act of defiance, Nick Holmes scored with a crisp volley, which beat Shilton conclusively. 3-2 to Forest in one of the best finals for years – a deserved victory over a team which 'went' when Alan Ball stopped being effective, and when their defenders were run ragged by talented midfield players and strikers. It has been another good year for the League Cup – a competition which is now an integral part of the English football season.

Leslie Vernon

THE FOOTBALL LEAGUE CUP 1978-79

First Round
Aldershot v Millwall	0-1, 0-1
Barnsley v Chesterfield	1-2, 0-0
Bournemouth v Exeter C	0-1, 1-1
Bradford C v Lincoln C	2-0, 1-1
Bristol R v Hereford U	2-1, 0-4
Cambridge U v Northampton T	2-2, 1-2
Cardiff C v Oxford U	1-2, 1-2
Carlisle U v Blackpool	2-2, 1-2
Colchester U v Charlton Ath	2-3, 0-0
Crewe Alex v Rochdale	1-0, 4-2
Doncaster R v Sheffield W	0-1, 1-0, 0-1
Grimsby T v York C	2-0, 3-0
Hull C v Peterborough U	0-1, 2-1, 0-1
Mansfield T v Darlington	0-1, 2-2
Newport Co v Swansea C	2-1, 0-5
Plymouth Arg v Torquay U	1-1, 2-1
Portsmouth v Swindon T	0-0, 2-4
Port Vale v Chester	0-3, 1-1
Preston NE v Huddersfield T	3-0, 2-2
Reading v Gillingham	3-1, 2-1
Rotherham U v Hartlepool U	5-0, 1-1
Scunthorpe U v Notts Co	0-1, 0-3
Southend U v Wimbledon	1-0, 1-4
Tranmere R v Wigan Ath	1-1, 1-2
Walsall v Halifax T	2-1, 2-0
Watford v Brentford	4-0, 3-1
Wrexham v Bury	2-0, 2-1
Shrewsbury T v Stockport Co	1-0, 1-3

Second Round
Birmingham C v Southampton	2-5
Bolton W v Chelsea	2-1
Brighton v Millwall	1-0
Bristol C v Crystal Palace	1-2
Burnley v Bradford C	1-1, 3-2
Everton v Wimbledon	8-0
Exeter C v Blackburn R	2-1
Fulham v Darlington	2-2, 0-1
Luton T v Wigan Ath	2-0
Manchester C v Grimsby T	2-0
Middlesbrough v Peterborough U	0-0, 0-1
Northampton T v Hereford U	0-0, 1-0
Oldham Ath v Nottingham F	0-0, 2-4
Orient v Chesterfield	1-2
Preston NE v QPR	1-3
Rotherham U v Arsenal	3-1
Sheffield U v Liverpool	1-0
Swansea C v Tottenham H	2-2, 3-1
Walsall v Charlton Ath	1-2
Watford v Newcastle U	2-1
WBA v Leeds U	0-0, 0-0, 0-1
Wrexham v Norwich C	1-3
Aston Villa v Sheffield W	1-0
Blackpool v Ipswich T	2-0
Chester v Coventry C	2-1
Crewe Alex v Notts Co	2-0
Leicester C v Derby Co	0-1
Oxford U v Plymouth Arg	1-1, 2-1
Reading v Wolverhampton W	1-0
Stockport Co v Manchester U	2-3
Sunderland v Stoke C	0-2
West Ham U v Swindon T	1-2

Third Round
Burnley v Brighton	1-3
Everton v Darlington	1-0
Luton T v Crewe Alex	2-1
Northampton T v Stoke C	1-3
Peterborough U v Swindon T	1-1, 2-0
QPR v Swansea C	2-0
Rotherham U v Reading	2-2, 0-1
Southampton v Derby Co	1-0
Blackpool v Manchester C	1-1, 0-3
Chester v Norwich C	0-2
Chesterfield v Charlton Ath	4-5
Exeter C v Bolton W	2-1
Manchester U v Watford	1-2
Oxford U v Nottingham F	0-5
Aston Villa v Crystal Palace	1-1, 0-0, 3-0
Sheffield U v Leeds U	1-4

Fourth Round
Brighton v Peterborough U	1-0
Charlton Ath v Stoke C	2-3
Everton v Nottingham F	2-3
QPR v Leeds U	0-2
Aston Villa v Luton T	0-2
Exeter C v Watford	0-2
Norwich C v Manchester C	1-3
Reading v Southampton	0-0, 0-2

Fifth Round
Southampton v Manchester C	2-1
Leeds U v Luton T	4-1
Nottingham F v Brighton	3-1
Stoke C v Watford	0-0, 1-3

Semi-finals
Nottingham F v Watford	3-1, 0-0
Leeds U v Southampton	2-2, 0-1

Final
Nottingham F v Southampton	3-2

FOOTBALL LEAGUE CUP 1960-61

First Round

Middlesbrough v Cardiff C	3-4
Colchester U v Newcastle U	4-1
*Newport Co v Southampton	2-2, 2-2, 3-5
*Chester v Leyton O	2-2, 0-1
Preston NE v Peterborough U	4-1
*Lincoln C v Bradford	2-2, 0-1
Plymouth Arg v Southport	2-0
York C v Blackburn R	1-3
*Rochdale v Scunthorpe U	1-1, 1-0
*Exeter C v Manchester U	1-1, 1-4
Watford v Derby Co	2-5
Ipswich T v Barnsley	0-2
Oldham Ath v Hartlepool	2-1
*QPR v Port Vale	2-2, 1-3
Everton v Accrington S	3-1
Darlington v C Palace	2-0
West Ham U v Charlton Ath	3-1
*Hull C v Bolton W	0-0, 1-5
Leicester C v Mansfield T	4-0
Bristol R v Fulham	2-1
Coventry C v Barrow	4-2
Stockport Co v Carlisle U	2-0
Millwall v Chelsea	1-7
Doncaster R v Stoke C	3-1
Chelsea v Workington T	4-2
*Swindon T v Shrewsbury T	1-1, 2-2, 0-2
Bradford C v Manchester U	2-1
Derby Co v Barnsley	3-0
Norwich C v Oldham Ath	6-2
Port Vale v Tranmere R	0-2
*Bournemouth v Crewe Alex	1-1, 0-2
Everton v Walsall	3-1
Bury v Sheffield U	3-1

(All the rest byes, except, Arsenal, Tottenham H, Sheffield W, WBA, and Wolverhampton W, who did not compete).

Second Round

*Liverpool v Luton T	1-1, 5-2
Colchester U v Southampton	0-2
Leyton O v Chesterfield	0-1
*Leeds U v Blackpool	0-0, 3-1
Brentford v Sunderland	4-3
Cardiff C v Burnley	0-4
Nottingham F v Halifax T	2-0
*Aldershot v Bristol C	1-1, 0-3
*Gillingham v Preston NE	1-1, 0-3
Aston Villa v Huddersfield	4-1
Bradford v Birmingham C	0-1
*Plymouth Arg v Torquay U	1-1, 2-1
Swansea T v Blackburn R	1-2
Rochdale v Southend U	5-2
Notts Co v Brighton	1-3
*Northampton T v Wrexham	1-1, 0-2
Darlington v West Ham U	3-2
Bolton W v Grimsby T	6-2
Leicester C v Rotherham U	1-2
Reading v Bristol R	3-5
Portsmouth v Coventry C	2-0
Manchester C v Stockport Co	3-0

Third Round

Liverpool v Southampton	1-2
Chesterfield v Leeds U	0-4
*Brentford v Burnley	1-1, 1-2
Nottingham F v Bristol C	2-3
*Preston NE v Aston Villa	3-3, 1-3
*Birmingham C v Plymouth Arg	0-0, 1-1
Blackburn R v Rochdale	2-1
Brighton v Wrexham	0-2
Darlington v Bolton W	1-2
Rotherham U v Bristol R	2-0
Portsmouth v Manchester C	2-0
Doncaster R v Chelsea	0-7
Shrewsbury T v Bradford C	2-1
Derby Co v Norwich C	1-4
Tranmere R v Crewe Alex	2-0
Everton v Bury	3-1

Fourth Round

Southampton v Leeds U	5-4
Burnley v Nottingham F	2-1
*Aston Villa v Plymouth Arg	3-3, 0-0, 5-3
*Blackburn R v Wrexham	1-1, 1-3
Bolton W v Rotherham U	0-2
Portsmouth v Chelsea	1-0
Shrewsbury T v Norwich C	1-0
Tranmere R v Everton	0-4

Fifth Round

Southampton v Burnley	2-4
Aston Villa v Wrexham	3-0
Rotherham U v Portsmouth	3-0
Shrewsbury T v Everton	2-1

Semi-Final

*Burnley v Aston Villa	1-1, 2-2, 1-2
(Replay, Manchester U)	
Aston Villa won 5-4 on aggregate	
*Rotherham U v Shrewsbury T	3-2, 1-1
Rotherham U won 4-3 on aggregate	

* Home Team in first match.

Final 1960-61

Rotherham U 2 Aston Villa 0

(First leg, Rotherham, 12,226, August 22, 1961)

Rotherham U: Ironside; Perry, Morgan; Lambert, Madden, Waterhouse; Webster, Weston, Houghton, Kirkman, Bambridge.

Aston Villa: Sims; Lynn, Lee; Crowe, Dugdale, Deakin; McEwan, Thomson, Brown, Wylie, McParland.

Scorers: Webster, Kirkman.

Aston Villa 3 Rotherham U 0 (after extra time)

(Second leg, Villa Park, 27,000, September 5, 1961)

Aston Villa: Sidebottom; Neal, Lee; Crowe, Dugdale, Deakin; McEwan, O'Neill, McParland, Thomson, Burrows.

Rotherham U: Ironside; Perry, Morgan; Lambert, Madden, Waterhouse; Webster, Weston, Houghton, Kirkman, Bambridge.

Scorers: O'Neill, Burrows, McParland.

Aston Villa won Cup on aggregate 3-2

FOOTBALL LEAGUE CUP 1961–62

First Round
Barnsley v Southport 3-2
Barrow v Portsmouth 0-2
*Birmingham C v Swindon T 1-1, 0-2
Blackpool v Port Vale 2-1
*Bolton W v Sunderland 1-1, 0-1
*Bournemouth v Torquay U 2-2, 1-0
Bradford C v Aston Villa 3-4
Bristol R v Hartlepool 2-1
Bury v Brighton 5-1
Cardiff C v Wrexham 2-0
*Carlisle U v Huddersfield 1-1, 0-3
Chesterfield v Norwich C 2-3
Colchester U v Crewe Alex 1-2
Darlington v Rotherham U 0-1
Doncaster R v Grimsby T 3-2
*Fulham v Sheffield U 1-1, 0-4
Hull C v Bradford P A 4-2
Ipswich T v Manchester C 4-2
Leeds U v Brentford 4-1
Lincoln C v Accrington S 1-0
Luton T v Northampton 2-1
Millwall v Walsall 1-2
Mansfield T v Exeter C 5-2
Newcastle U v Scunthorpe U 2-0
*Newport Co v Shrewsbury T 0-0, 1-3
*Notts Co v Derby Co 2-2, 2-3
Nottingham F v Gillingham 4-1
Oldham Ath v Charlton Ath 1-4
Peterborough U v Blackburn R 1-3
Preston NE v Aldershot 3-1
QPR v Crystal Palace 5-2
Reading v Chester 4-2
*Southampton v Rochdale 0-0, 1-2
Southend U v Stoke C 0-1
Stockport Co v Leyton O 0-1
Tranmere R v Middlesbrough 3-6
Watford v Halifax T 3-0
West Ham U v Plymouth Arg 3-2
Workington T v Coventry C 3-0
York C v Bristol C 3-0
Byes:
Leicester C
Swansea T

Second Round
Barnsley v Workington T 1-3
*Bristol R v Blackburn R 1-1, 0-4
Bury v Hull C 3-4
Charlton Ath v Stoke C 4-1
Leeds U v Huddersfield 3-2
*Leyton O v Blackpool 1-1, 1-5

*Luton T v Rotherham U 0-0, 0-2
*Mansfield T v Cardiff C 1-1, 1-2
Middlesbrough v Crewe Alex 3-2
Norwich C v Lincoln C 3-2
*Portsmouth v Derby Co 1-1, 4-2
QPR v Nottingham F 1-2
Preston NE v Swindon T 3-1
Rochdale v Doncaster R 4-0
*Sheffield U v Newcastle U 2-2, 2-0
Shrewsbury T v Bournemouth 1-3
*Swansea T v Ipswich T 3-3, 2-3
Sunderland v Walsall 5-2
Watford v Reading 3-1
West Ham U v Aston Villa 1-3
York C v Leicester C 2-1

Third Round
Norwich C v Middlesbrough 3-2
Workington T v Blackpool 0-1
Aston Villa v Ipswich T 2-3
Bournemouth v Cardiff C 3-0
*Preston NE v Rotherham U 0-0, 0-3
Sheffield U v Portsmouth 1-0
Sunderland v Hull C 2-1
*York C v Watford 1-1, 2-2, 3-2
Nottingham F v Blackburn R 1-2
Rochdale v Charlton Ath 1-0
Bye:
Leeds U

Fourth Round
Blackburn R v Ipswich T 4-1
*Rotherham U v Leeds U 1-1, 2-1
York C v Bournemouth 1-0
Byes:
Sunderland
Blackpool
Norwich C
Sheffield U
Rochdale

Fifth Round
Sunderland v Norwich C 1-4
*Blackpool v Sheffield U 0-0, 2-0
Rotherham U v Blackburn R 0-1
Rochdale v York C 2-1

Semi-Final
*Norwich C v Blackpool 4-1, 0-2
    Norwich C won 4-3 on aggregate
*Rochdale v Blackburn R 3-1, 1-2
    Rochdale won 4-3 on aggregate

*Home Team in first match.

Final 1961–62

Rochdale 0 Norwich C 3
(First leg, Rochdale, 11,123, April 26, 1962)

Rochdale: Burgin; Milburn, Winton; Bodell, Aspden, Thompson; Wragg, Hepton, Bimpson, Cairns, Whitaker.
Norwich C: Kennon; McCrohan, Ashman; Burton, Butler, Mullett; Mannion, Lythgoe, Scott, Hill, Punton.
Scorers: Lythgoe 2, Punton.

Norwich C 1 Rochdale 0
(Second leg, Norwich, 19,708, May 1, 1962)

Norwich C: Kennon; McCrohan, Ashman; Burton, Butler, Mullett; Mannion, Lythgoe, Scott, Hill, Punton.
Rochdale: Burgin; Milburn, Winton; Bodell, Aspden, Thompson; Whyke, Richardson, Bimpson, Cairns, Whitaker.
Scorer: Hill.

Norwich C won Cup on aggregate 4-0

FOOTBALL LEAGUE CUP 1962–63

First Round
Aldershot v Exeter C	2-0
Barrow v Workington T	3-2
Bradford C v Doncaster R	2-2, 0-2
Brentford v Wrexham	3-0
Chester v Stockport Co	2-0
Crewe Alex v Oldham Ath	2-3
Darlington v Chesterfield	1-0
Halifax T v Mansfield T	2-3
*Hartlepool v Barnsley	1-1, 1-2
Newport Co v Gillingham	2-1
Shrewsbury T v Millwall	3-1
*Southport v Rochdale	0-0, 2-1
Torquay U v Oxford U	2-0
Tranmere R v Carlisle U	2-3
Watford v Colchester U	1-2
*York C v Lincoln C	2-2, 0-2

Second Round
Aldershot v Newport Co	0-3
Aston Villa v Peterborough U	6-1
Barnsley v Grimsby T	3-2
Barrow v Shrewsbury T	3-1
Birmingham C v Doncaster R	5-0
Bradford P A v Huddersfield	3-1
Brentford v Sheffield U	1-4
Brighton v Portsmouth	1-5
Bristol C v Rotherham U	1-2
*Bristol R v Port Vale	2-0
Bury v Lincoln C	2-2, 3-2
Cardiff C v Reading	5-1
Chester v Mansfield T	2-2, 1-0
Coventry C v Swansea T	3-2
*Derby Co v Blackburn R	1-1, 1-3
*Fulham v Bournemouth	4-0
Hull C v Middlesbrough	2-2, 1-1, 3-0
*Leeds U v Crystal Palace	2-1
*Leicester C v Charlton Ath	4-4, 1-2
*Newcastle U v Leyton O	1-1, 2-4
Northampton v Colchester U	2-0
Norwich C v Bolton W	4-0
*Manchester C v Blackpool	0-0, 3-3, 4-2
QPR v Preston NE	1-2
Southampton v Scunthorpe U	1-1, 2-2, 0-3
Southend U v Notts Co	2-3
Southport v Luton T	1-3
Sunderland v Oldham Ath	7-1
Swindon T v Darlington	4-0
Torquay U v Carlisle U	1-2
Walsall v Stoke C	1-2
West Ham U v Plymouth Arg	6-0

Third Round
*Barrow v Birmingham C	1-1, 1-5
Notts Co v Swindon T	5-0
Newport Co v Manchester C	1-2
Barnsley v Luton T	1-2
Leyton O v Chester	9-2
*Bradford P A v Charlton Ath	2-2, 0-1
Bury v Sheffield U	3-1
Bristol R v Cardiff C	2-0
Portsmouth v Coventry C	5-1
Sunderland v Scunthorpe U	2-0
Blackburn R v Leeds U	4-0
Rotherham U v West Ham U	3-1
*Carlisle U v Norwich C	1-1, 0-5
Hull C v Fulham	1-2
Aston Villa v Stoke C	3-1
*Northampton v Preston NE	1-1, 1-2

Fourth Round
Birmingham C v Notts Co	3-2
Manchester C v Luton T	1-0
Leyton O v Charlton Ath	3-2
Bury v Bristol R	3-1
*Portsmouth v Sunderland	0-0, 1-2
Blackburn R v Rotherham U	4-1
Norwich C v Fulham	1-0
Aston Villa v Preston NE	6-2

Fifth Round
Birmingham C v Manchester C	6-0
Leyton O v Bury	0-2
Sunderland v Blackburn R	3-2
Aston Villa v Norwich C	4-1

Semi-Final
*Birmingham C v Bury	3-2, 1-1
Birmingham C won 4-3 on aggregate	
*Sunderland v Aston Villa	1-3, 0-0
Aston Villa won 3-1 on aggregate	

Final 1962–63

Birmingham C 3 Aston Villa 1
(First leg, St. Andrews, 31,850, May 23, 1963)

Birmingham C: Schofield; Lynn, Green; Hennessey, Smith, Beard; Hellawell, Bloomfield, Harris, Leek, Auld.
Aston Villa: Sims; Fraser, Aitken; Crowe, Sleeuwenhoek, Lee; Baker, Graham, Thomson, Wylie, Burrows.
Scorers—Birmingham C: Leek 2, Bloomfield. Aston Villa: Thomson.

Aston Villa 0 Birmingham C 0
(Second leg, Villa Park, 37,921, May 27, 1963)

No change in teams.

Birmingham C won Cup on aggregate 3-1

FOOTBALL LEAGUE CUP 1963–64

First Round
Aldershot v QPR	3-1
Bradford PA v Bradford C	7-3
Carlisle U v Crewe Alex	3-2
Chesterfield v Halifax T	0-1
*Darlington v Barnsley	2-2, 2-6
*Doncaster R v York C	0-0, 0-3
Gillingham v Bristol C	4-2
Lincoln C v Hartlepool	3-2
Mansfield T v Watford	2-1
Newport Co v Millwall	3-4
Oldham Ath v Workington	3-5
Oxford U v Exeter C	0-1
*Reading v Brentford	1-1, 0-2
*Rochdale v Chester	1-1, 5-2
*Shrewsbury T v Bristol R	1-1, 2-6
Southport v Barrow	2-1
Torquay U v Brighton	1-2
Tranmere R v Stockport Co	2-0

Second Round
Aston Villa v Barnsley	3-1
Blackpool v Charlton Ath	7-1
*Bradford PA v Middlesbrough	2-2, 3-2
*Brentford v Bournemouth	0-0, 0-2
*Brighton v Northampton	1-1, 2-3
Bristol R v Crystal Palace	2-0
*Cardiff C v Wrexham	2-2, 1-1 0-3
Colchester U v Fulham	5-3
Gillingham v Bury	3-0
Grimsby T v Rotherham U	1-3
Halifax T v Rochdale	4-2
Hull C v Exeter C	1-0
*Ipswich T v Walsall	0-0, 0-1
Leeds U v Mansfield T	5-1
Leicester C v Aldershot	2-0
Luton T v Coventry C	3-4
Manchester C v Carlisle U	2-0
Millwall v Peterborough U	3-2
Newcastle U v Preston NE	3-0
Norwich C v Birmingham C	2-0
Notts Co v Blackburn R	2-1
*Plymouth Arg v Huddersfield	2-2, 3-3, 1-2
Portsmouth v Derby Co	3-2
*Scunthorpe U v Stoke C	2-2, 3-3, 0-1
Sheffield U v Bolton W	1-2
Southend U v Port Vale	2-1
Swansea T v Sunderland	3-1
Swindon T v Chelsea	3-0
Tranmere R v Southampton	2-0
West Ham U v Leyton O	2-1
Workington v Southport	3-0
*York C v Lincoln C	1-1, 0-2

Third Round
Stoke C v Bolton W	3-0
Bournemouth v Newcastle U	2-1
Rotherham U v Coventry C	4-2
*Millwall v Lincoln C	1-1, 2-1
Notts Co v Bradford PA	3-2
Wrexham v Portsmouth	3-5
Hull C v Manchester C	0-3
Leeds U v Swansea T	2-0
Swindon T v Southend U	3-0
Aston Villa v West Ham U	0-2
Workington v Huddersfield	1-0
Colchester U v Northampton	4-1
Halifax T v Walsall	2-0
Norwich C v Blackpool	1-0
Tranmere R v Leicester C	1-2
*Bristol R v Gillingham	1-1, 1-3

Fourth Round
Stoke C v Bournemouth	2-1
Rotherham U v Millwall	5-2
Notts Co v Portsmouth	3-2
Manchester C v Leeds U	3-1
*Swindon T v West Ham U	3-3, 1-4
Workington v Colchester U	2-1
Halifax T v Norwich C	1-7
Leicester C v Gillingham	4-1

Fifth Round
Stoke C v Rotherham U	3-2
Notts Co v Manchester C	0-1
West Ham U v Workington	6-0
*Norwich C v Leicester C	1-1, 1-2

Semi-Final
*Stoke C v Manchester C	2-0, 0-1
Stoke C won 2-1 on aggregate	
*Leicester C v West Ham U	4-3, 2-0
Leicester C won 6-3 on aggregate	

* Home Team in first match.

Final 1963–64

Stoke C 1 Leicester C 1
(First leg Stoke, 22,309, April 15, 1964)

Stoke C: Leslie, Asprey, Allen, Palmer, Kinnell, Skeels; Dobing, Viollet, Ritchie, McIlroy, Bebbington.

Leicester C: Banks, Sjoberg, Appleton, Dougan, King, Cross; Riley Heath, Keyworth, Gibson, Stringfellow.

Scorers—Stoke C: Bebbington. Leicester C: Gibson.

Leicester C 3 Stoke C 2
(Second leg, Leicester, 25,372, April 22, 1964)

Scorers—Leicester C: Stringfellow, Gibson, Riley. Stoke C: Viollet, Kinnell.

No change in teams.

Leicester C won Cup on aggregate 4-3

FOOTBALL LEAGUE CUP 1964-65

First Round

Barnsley v Lincoln C	2-1
Bradford C v York C	2-0
Brentford v Southend U	0-2
*Brighton v Millwall	2-2, 0-1
Chester v Wrexham	3-0
Chesterfield v Hartlepool	3-0
*Colchester U v Torquay U	1-1, 0-3
Doncaster R v Bradford PA	1-0
Exeter C v Gillingham	2-0
Halifax T v Darlington	1-3
Notts Co v Newport Co	3-2
Port Vale v Luton T	0-1
QPR v Aldershot	5-2
*Southport v Carlisle U	0-0, 0-1
Stockport C v Rochdale	1-3
Tranmere R v Crewe Alex	2-0
Walsall v Oxford U	1-1, 1-6
Workington v Barrow	9-1

Second Round

Birmingham C v Chelsea	0-3
Blackpool v Newcastle U	3-0
Bolton W v Blackburn R	1-5
Bristol R v Chesterfield	0-2
Bournemouth v Northampton	0-2
Bury v Darlington	1-0
Carlisle U v Bristol C	4-1
Charlton Ath v Middlesbrough	2-1
Chester v Derby C	5-4
Coventry C v Ipswich T	4-1
Doncaster R Preston NE	1-0
Exeter C v Bradford C	3-5
Fulham v Oxford U	2-0
Grimsby T v Oldham Ath	3-1
*Hull C v Southend U	0-0, 1-3
Leeds U v Huddersfield	3-2
*Leicester C v Peterborough U	0-0, 2-0
Leyton O v Barnsley	3-0
Luton T v Aston Villa	0-1
Manchester C v Mansfield T	3-5
Millwall v Norwich C	1-2
Plymouth Arg v Sheffield U	2-1
Reading v QPR	4-0
Rotherham U v Rochdale	2-0
Scunthorpe U v Workington	0-1
Southampton v Cardiff C	3-2
*Stoke C v Shrewsbury T	1-1, 1-0
Sunderland v West Ham U	4-1
Swansea T v Swindon T	3-1
Torquay U v Notts Co	1-2
Tranmere R v Crystal Palace	0-2
*Watford v Portsmouth	2-2, 1-2

Third Round

Leeds U v Aston Villa	2-3
*Reading v Fulham	1-1, 3-1
Charlton Ath v Leyton O	2-1
Doncaster R v Bradford C	2-3
*Workington v Blackburn R	0-0, 5-1
Norwich C v Chester	5-3
Chelsea v Notts Co	4-0
*Rotherham U v Swansea T	2-2, 0-2
Stoke C v Southend U	3-1
Bury v Plymouth Arg	0-1
Northampton v Portsmouth	2-1
Chesterfield v Carlisle U	3-1
Coventry v Mansfield T	3-2
Sunderland v Blackpool	4-1
Grimsby T v Leicester C	0-5
Crystal Palace v Southampton	2-0

Fourth Round

Aston Villa v Reading	3-1
Charlton Ath v Bradford C	0-1
Workington v Norwich C	3-0
Chelsea v Swansea T	3-2
*Stoke C v Plymouth Arg	1-1, 1-3
Northampton v Chesterfield	4-1
Coventry C v Sunderland	4-2
*Leicester C v Crystal Palace	0-0, 2-1

Fifth Round

Aston Villa v Bradford C	7-1
*Workington v Chelsea	2-2, 0-2
Plymouth Arg v Northampton	1-0
Coventry C v Leicester C	1-8

Semi-Final

*Aston Villa v Chelsea	2-3, 1-1
Chelsea won 4-3 on aggregate	
*Leicester C v Plymouth Arg	3-2, 1-0
Leicester C won 4-2 on aggregate	

* Home Team in first match.

Final 1964-65

Chelsea 3 Leicester C 2

(First leg, Stamford Bridge, 20,690, March 15, 1965)

Chelsea: Bonetti; Hinton, Harris; Hollins, Young, Boyle; Murray, Graham, McCreadie, Venables, Tambling.

Leicester C: Banks; Sjoberg, Norman; Chalmers, King, Appleton; Hodgson, Cross, Goodfellow, Gibson, Sweenie.

Scorers—Chelsea: Tambling, Venables (penalty), McCreadie. Leicester C: Appleton, Goodfellow.

Leicester C 0 Chelsea 0

(Second leg, Leicester, 26,957, April 5, 1965)

No changes in teams.

Chelsea won Cup on aggregate 3-2

FOOTBALL LEAGUE CUP 1965–66

First Round
*Barrow v Rochdale	1-1, 1-3
*Bournemouth v Aldershot	0-0, 1-2
Bradford P A v Halifax T	1-0
Colchester U v Exeter C	2-1
Crewe Alex v Southport	2-0
*Doncaster R v Barnsley	2-2, 2-1
Hartlepool v Bradford C	1-0
*Luton T v Brighton	1-1, 0-2
*Lincoln C v York C	2-2, 2-4
*Newport Co v Southend U	2-2, 1-3
*Notts Co v Chesterfield	0-0, 1-2
Oldham Ath v Tranmere R	3-2
Oxford U v Millwall	0-1
*Port Vale v Reading	2-2, 0-1
*QPR v Walsall	1-1, 2-3
Scunthorpe U v Darlington	0-2
Shrewsbury T v Torquay U	3-0
Stockport Co v Workington	2-3
Wrexham v Chester	5-2

Second Round
Blackburn R v Northampton	0-1
Brighton v Ipswich T	1-2
*Bristol R v West Ham U	3-3, 2-3
Bury v Huddersfield	0-2
Charlton Ath v Carlisle U	4-1
Swansea v Aston Villa	2-3
Blackpool v Gillingham	5-2
Bolton W v Aldershot	3-0
Chesterfield v Bradford P A	3-0
Colchester U v Middlesbrough	2-4
*Crewe Alex v Cardiff C	1-1, 0-3
Crystal Palace v Grimsby T	0-1
Darlington v Swindon T	2-1
Doncaster R v Burnley	0-4
*Hull C v Derby Co	2-2, 3-4
Leeds U v Hartlepool	4-2
Leyton O v Coventry C	0-3
Manchester C v Leicester C	3-1
Mansfield T v Birmingham C	2-1
Millwall v York C	4-1
Newcastle U v Peterborough U	3-4
Oldham Ath v Portsmouth	1-2
Preston NE v Plymouth Arg	1-0
Reading v Southend U	5-1
Rotherham U v Watford	2-0
Shrewsbury T v Bristol C	1-0
Southampton v Rochdale	3-0
Stoke C v Norwich C	2-1
Sunderland v Sheffield U	2-1
WBA v Walsall	3-1
*Workington v Brentford	0-0, 2-1
Wrexham v Fulham	1-2

Third Round
Leeds U v WBA	2-4
Manchester C v Coventry C	2-3
Fulham v Northampton	5-0
Sunderland v Aston Villa	1-2
*Middlesbrough v Millwall	0-0, 1-3
Peterborough U v Charlton Ath	4-3
*Chesterfield v Stoke C	2-2, 1-2
Burnley v Southampton	3-2
Cardiff C v Portsmouth	2-0
*Derby Co v Reading	1-1, 0-2
*Workington v Ipswich T	1-1, 1-3
Blackpool v Darlington	1-2
Grimsby T v Bolton W	4-2
Huddersfield v Preston NE	0-1
Shrewsbury T v Rotherham U	2-5
West Ham U v Mansfield T	4-0

Fourth Round
*Coventry C v WBA	1-1, 1-6
*Fulham v Aston Villa	1-1, 0-2
Millwall v Peterborough U	1-4
*Stoke C v Burnley	0-0, 1-2
Cardiff C v Reading	5-1
Ipswich T v Darlington	2-0
Grimsby T v Preston NE	4-0
Rotherham U v West Ham U	1-2

Fifth Round
WBA v Aston Villa	3-1
Peterborough U v Burnley	4-0
Cardiff C v Ipswich T	2-1
*Grimsby T v West Ham U	2-2, 0-1

Semi-Final
*WBA v Peterborough U	2-1, 4-2
	WBA won 6-3 on aggregate
*West Ham U v Cardiff C	5-2, 5-1
	West Ham U won on aggregate

*Home Team in first match.

Final 1965–66

West Ham U 2 WBA 1

(First leg, Upton Park, 28,341, March 9, 1966)

West Ham U: Standen, Burnett, Burkett, Peters, Brown, Moore, Brabrook, Boyce, Byrne, Hurst, Dear.
WBA: Potter; Cram, Fairfax, Fraser, Campbell, Williams, Brown, Astle, Kaye, Lovett, Clark.
Scorers—West Ham U: Moore, Byrne. WBA: Astle.

WBA 4 West Ham U 1

(Second leg, WBA, 31,925, March 23, 1966)

WBA: Potter; Cram, Fairfax, Fraser, Campbell, Williams, Brown, Astle, Kaye, Hope, Clark.
West Ham U: Standen; Burnett, Peters, Bovington, Brown, Moore, Brabrook, Boyce, Byrne, Hurst, Sissions.
Scorers—WBA: Kaye, Brown, Clark, Williams. West Ham U: Peters.

WBA won Cup on aggregate 5-3

FOOTBALL LEAGUE CUP 1966-67

First Round
*Aldershot v Luton T	2-2, 2-1
Barnsley v Grimsby T	1-2
Barrow v Oldham Ath	2-1
*Bradford P A v Hartlepools U	2-2, 2-1
*Brentford v Millwall	0-0, 1-0
Brighton v Leyton O	1-0
Bury v Rochdale	2-0
*Bradford C v Doncaster R	1-1, 2-5
Cardiff C v Bristol R	1-0
Chester v Tranmere R	2-5
Chesterfield v Scunthorpe U	2-1
Crewe Alex v Stockport Co	1-2
*Exeter C v Torquay U	2-2, 2-1
*Halifax T v Darlington	0-0, 0-4
Lincoln C v Hull C	1-0
*Middlesbrough v York C	0-0, 1-2
Newport Co v Swansea T	1-2
*Notts Co v Mansfield T	1-1, 0-3
Peterborough U v Oxford U	2-1
*Southend U v Gillingham	0-0, 0-2
Southport v Workington	0-1
Shrewsbury T v Wrexham	6-1
Swindon T v Bournemouth	2-1
Port Vale v Walsall	1-3
QPR v Colchester U	5-0
*Watford v Reading	1-1, 0-1

Second Round
*Aldershot v QPR	1-1, 0-2
*Arsenal v Gillingham	1-1, 1-1, 5-0
Blackburn R v Barrow	4-1
Blackpool v Manchester U	5-1
*Bradford P A v Grimsby T	1-3
Brentford v Ipswich T	2-4
*Bristol C v Swansea T	1-1, 1-2
Bury v Workington	2-3
Cardiff C v Exeter C	0-1
*Carlisle U v Tranmere R	1-1, 2-0
Chelsea v Charlton Ath	5-2
Coventry C v Derby Co	2-1
Darlington v Doncaster R	1-1, 0-2
Fulham v Crystal Palace	2-0
Leeds U v Newcastle U	1-0
*Leicester C v Reading	5-0
Lincoln C v Huddersfield	2-1
Manchester C v Bolton W	3-1
*Northampton v Peterborough U	2-2, 2-0
Norwich C v Brighton	0-1
*Nottingham F v Birmingham C	1-1, 1-2
Preston NE v Crewe Alex	2-0
Southampton v Plymouth Arg	4-3
Sheffield W v Rotherham U	0-1
*Shrewsbury T v Burnley	1-1, 1-5
*Sunderland v Sheffield U	1-1, 0-1
Swindon T v Portsmouth	4-1
WBA v Aston Villa	6-1
West Ham U v Tottenham H	1-0
Wolverhampton W v Mansfield T	2-2
Walsall v Stoke C	2-1
York C v Chesterfield	3-1

Third Round
Swansea T v QPR	1-2
Leicester C v Lincoln C	5-0
*Southampton v Carlisle U	3-3, 1-2
York C v Blackburn R	0-2
Sheffield U v Burnley	2-0
Exeter C v Walsall	1-2
Grimsby T v Workington	3-0
Birmingham C v Ipswich T	2-1
*Brighton v Coventry C	1-1, 3-1
Northampton v Rotherham U	2-1
*Doncaster R v Swindon T	1-1, 2-4
WBA v Manchester C	4-2
*Blackpool v Chelsea	1-1, 3-1
Fulham v Wolverhampton W	5-0
Arsenal v West Ham U	1-3
*Preston NE v Leeds U	1-1, 0-3

Fourth Round
QPR v Leicester C	4-2
Carlisle U v Blackburn R	4-0
Sheffield U v Walsall	2-1
Grimsby T v Birmingham C	2-4
*Brighton v Northampton	1-1, 0-8
Swindon T v WBA	0-2
Blackpool v Fulham	4-2
West Ham U v Leeds U	7-0

Fifth Round
QPR v Carlisle U	2-1
Sheffield U v Birmingham C	2-3
Northampton v WBA	1-3
Blackpool v West Ham U	1-3

Semi-Final
*Birmingham C v QPR	1-4, 1-3
QPR won 7-2 on aggregate	
*WBA v West Ham U	4-0, 2-2
WBA won 6-2 on aggregate	

*Home Team in first match

Final 1966-67: QPR 3 WBA 2

(At Wembley, 97,952, receipts £57,000, March 4, 1967)

QPR: Springett; Hazell, Langley, Sibley, Hunt, Keen, Lazarus, Sanderson, Allen, Marsh, Morgan R (Sub. Morgan (I.).).

WBA: Sheppard; Cram, Williams, Collard, Clarke D., Fraser, Brown, Astle, Kaye, Hope, Clark C., Sub. Foggo).

Scorers—QPR: Morgan R., Marsh, Lazarus. WBA: Clark C. 2.

FOOTBALL LEAGUE CUP 1967–68

First Round
Aldershot v Cardiff C	2-3
Barrow v Southport	1-0
*Bournemouth v Watford	1-1, 0-0, 1-2
Brighton v Colchester U	4-0
*Crewe Alex v Stockport Co	1-1, 0-3
Darlington v York C	1-0
Doncaster R v Scunthorpe U	1-2
Grimsby T v Chesterfield	1-0
Halifax T v Bradford PA	5-0
Hartlepool v Bradford C	2-0
*Luton T v Charlton Ath	1-1, 2-1
Mansfield T v Lincoln C	2-3
Middlesbrough v Barnsley	4-1
Northampton v Peterborough U	3-2
Notts Co v Rotherham U	0-1
Orient v Gillingham	1-3
Oxford U v Swansea T	3-1
Port Vale v Chester	3-0
Reading v Bristol R	3-0
Rochdale v Bury	0-1
Southend U v Brentford	1-0
*Swindon T v Newport Co	1-1, 0-2
*Torquay U v Exeter C	0-0, 3-0
Tranmere R v Wrexham	2-1
Walsall v Shrewsbury T	4-2
*Workington v Oldham Ath	1-1, 1-1, 2-1
Portsmouth v Port Vale	3-1
Plymouth Arg v Birmingham C	0-2
QPR v Hull C	2-1
Scunthorpe U v Nottingham F	0-1
Reading v WBA	3-1
Southend U v Darlington	1-2
Stockport Co v Sheffield W	3-5
Stoke C v Watford	2-0
Sunderland v Halifax T	3-2
Walsall v West Ham U	1-5

Second Round
Barrow v Crystal Palace	1-0
Blackburn R v Brighton	3-1
Bristol C v Everton	0-5
Burnley v Cardiff C	2-1
Carlisle U v Workington	0-2
Coventry v Arsenal	1-2
Derby Co v Hartlepool	4-0
Fulham v Tranmere R	1-0
*Gillingham v Torquay U	2-2, 0-2
*Grimsby T v Bury	2-2, 0-2
Huddersfield v Wolverhampton W	1-0
Ipswich T v Southampton	5-2
Leeds U v Luton T	3-1
Lincoln C v Newcastle U	2-1
*Liverpool v Bolton W	1-1, 2-3
Manchester C v Leicester C	4-0
Middlesbrough v Chelsea	2-1
Millwall v Sheffield U	3-2
Newport Co v Blackpool	0-1
Northampton v Aston Villa	3-1
*Norwich C v Rotherham U	1-1, 2-0
Oxford U v Preston NE	2-1

Third Round
Arsenal v Reading	1-0
Blackburn R v Middlesbrough	3-2
QPR v Oxford U	5-1
Burnley v Nottingham F	3-0
*Workington v Fulham	2-2, 2-6
*Manchester C v Blackpool	1-1, 2-0
Norwich C v Huddersfield	0-1
West Ham U v Bolton W	4-1
Derby Co v Birmingham C	3-1
Lincoln C v Torquay U	4-2
Darlington v Portsmouth	4-1
*Northampton v Millwall	0-0, 1-5
Everton v Sunderland	2-3
Leeds U v Bury	3-0
Sheffield W v Barrow	3-1
Stoke C v Ipswich T	2-1

Fourth Round
Arsenal v Blackburn R	2-1
QPR v Burnley	1-2
Fulham v Manchester C	3-2
Huddersfield v West Ham U	2-0
*Derby Co v Lincoln C	1-1, 3-0
Darlington v Millwall	2-0
Sunderland v Leeds U	0-2
*Sheffield W. v Stoke C	0-0, 1-2

Fifth Round
*Burnley v Arsenal	3-3, 1-2
*Fulham v Huddersfield	1-1, 1-2
Derby Co v Darlington	5-4
Leeds U v Stoke C	2-0

Semi-Final
*Arsenal v Huddersfield	3-2, 3-1
Arsenal won 6-3 on aggregate	
*Derby Co v Leeds U	0-1, 2-3
Leeds U won 4-2 on aggregate	

*Home Team in first match.

Final 1967–68:   Leeds U 1   Arsenal 0
(At Wembley, 97,887, receipts £95,000, March 2, 1968)

Leeds U: Sprake; Reaney, Cooper; Bremner, Charlton, Hunter; Greenhoff, Lorimer, Madeley, Giles, Gray. (Sub. Belfitt).

Arsenal: Furnell; Storey, McNab; McLintock, Simpson, Ure; Radford, Jenkins, Graham, Sammels, Armstrong. (Sub. Neill).

Scorer: Cooper.

FOOTBALL LEAGUE CUP 1968-69

First Round
Aldershot v Brentford	2-4
Bournemouth v Southend U	1-6
Bradford PA v Darlington	0-3
Bradford C v Hartlepool	3-2
Brighton v Oxford U	2-0
Bristol C v Newport Co	2-0
Bristol R v Swansea T	0-2
*Bury v Stockport Co	1-1, 0-1
*Chester v Tranmere R	0-0, 2-2, 1-1, 1-2
Colchester U v Reading	2-0
Derby Co v Chesterfield	3-0
*Doncaster R v Peterborough U	0-0, 0-1
*Gillingham v Orient	2-2, 0-3
*Grimsby T v Notts Co	0-0, 1-0
Halifax T v Hull C	0-3
Lincoln C v Mansfield T	2-1
Luton T v Watford	3-0
*Northampton v Crewe Alex	1-0, 0-1
*Plymouth Arg v Exeter C	0-0, 0-0, 0-1
*Preston NE v Oldham Ath	1-1, 1-0
Scunthorpe U v Rotherham U	2-1
*Southport v Barrow	2-2, 3-1
Swindon T v Torquay U	2-1
Walsall v Shrewsbury T	2-0
Workington v Rochdale	2-1
Wrexham v Port Vale	2-0
York C v Barnsley	3-4

Second Round
Arsenal v Sunderland	1-0
Aston Villa v Tottenham H	1-4
*Barnsley v Millwall	1-1, 1-3
Birmingham C v Chelsea	0-1
*Blackburn R v Stoke C	1-1, 1-0
*Bradford C v Swindon T	1-1, 3-4
Brentford v Hull C	3-0
*Brighton v Luton T	1-1, 2-4
Bristol C v Middlesbrough	1-0
Carlisle U v Cardiff C	2-0
Colchester U v Workington	0-1
Coventry C v Portsmouth	2-0
Crystal Palace v Preston NE	3-1
Darlington v Leicester C	1-2
Derby Co v Stockport Co	5-1
Everton v Tranmere R	4-0
Exeter C v Sheffield W	3-1
*Grimsby T v Burnley	1-1, 0-6
*Huddersfield v Manchester C	0-0, 0-4
Ipswich T v Norwich C	2-4
Leeds U v Charlton Ath	1-0
Liverpool v Sheffield U	4-0
Peterborough U v QPR	4-2
Nottingham F v WBA	2-3
Orient v Fulham	1-0
Scunthorpe U v Lincoln C	2-1
Southampton v Crewe Alex	3-1
Southport v Newcastle U	0-2
West Ham U v Bolton W	7-2
Wolverhampton W v Southend U	1-0
*Wrexham v Blackpool	1-1, 0-3
*Walsall v Swansea T	1-1, 2-3

Third Round
Scunthorpe U v Arsenal	1-6
Liverpool v Swansea T	2-0
Blackpool v Manchester C	1-0
Wolverhampton W v Millwall	5-1
Tottenham H v Exeter C	6-3
Peterborough U v WBA	2-1
Brentford v Norwich C	0-2
Southampton v Newcastle U	4-1
Workington v Burnley	0-1
Carlisle U v Leicester C	0-3
Leyton O v Crystal Palace	0-1
Leeds U v Bristol C	2-1
Everton v Luton T	5-1
*Chelsea v Derby Co	0-0, 1-3
*West Ham U v Coventry C	0-0, 2-3
Swindon T v Blackburn R	1-0

Fourth Round
Arsenal v Liverpool	2-1
Blackpool v Wolverhampton W	2-1
Tottenham H v Peterborough U	1-0
Norwich C v Southampton	0-4
Burnley v Leicester C	4-0
Crystal Palace v Leeds U	2-1
*Everton v Derby Co	0-0, 0-1
*Coventry C v Swindon T	2-2, 0-3

Fifth Round
Arsenal v Blackpool	5-1
Tottenham H v Southampton	1-0
Burnley v Crystal Palace	2-0
*Derby Co v Swindon T	0-0, 0-1

Semi-Final
*Arsenal v Tottenham H	1-0, 1-1
Arsenal won 2-1 on aggregate	
*Burnley v Swindon T	1-2, 2-1, 2-3
(Third match at the Hawthorns)	
Swindon T won 6-5 on aggregate	

* Home Team in first match.

Cup Final 1968-69: Arsenal 1 Swindon T 3
(At Wembley, 98,189, receipts £104,000, March 15, 1969)

Arsenal: Wilson; Storey, McNab, McLintock, Ure, Simpson; Radford, Sammels, Court, Gould, Armstrong. (Sub. Graham).

Swindon T: Downsborough; Thomas, Trollope; Butler, Burrows, Harland; Heath, Smart, Smith, Noble, Rogers. (Sub. Penman).

Scorers—Arsenal: Gould. Swindon T: Smart, Rogers 2.

FOOTBALL LEAGUE CUP 1969–70

First Round
Aldershot v Gillingham	0-1
Barnsley v Halifax T	0-1
Bolton W v Rochdale	6-3
Bournemouth v Bristol R	3-0
Bradford P A v Rotherham U	0-2
Bradford C v Chesterfield	1-1, 1-0
Brighton v Portsmouth	1-0
Chester v Aston Villa	1-2
*Colchester U v Reading	1-1, 3-0
*Crewe Alex v Wrexham	0-0, 0-1
Darlington v York C	3-0
*Exeter C v Bristol C	1-1, 2-3
Grimsby T v Doncaster R	0-2
Mansfield T v Notts Co	3-1
Newport Co v Swansea T	2-3
*Orient v Fulham	0-0, 1-3
Oxford U v Northampton	2-0
*Peterborough U v Luton T	1-1, 2-5
*Plymouth Arg v Torquay U	2-2, 0-1
Preston NE v Bury	0-1
Port Vale v Tranmere R	0-1
Scunthorpe U v Hartlepool	0-2
Shrewsbury T v Walsall	1-0
*Southend U v Brentford	2-2, 0-0, 3-2
Southport v Oldham Ath	5-1
Stockport Co v Blackburn R	0-2
Watford v Lincoln C	2-1
*Workington v Barrow	0-0, 1-3
Sheffield U v Newcastle U	2-0
*Sheffield W v Bournemouth	1-1, 0-1
*Shrewsbury T v Southend U	2-2, 0-2
*Southampton v Arsenal	1-1, 0-2
Southport v Manchester C	0-3
Stoke C v Burnley	0-2
Sunderland v Bradford C	1-2
Swansea T v Swindon T	1-3
Tranmere R v Torquay U	2-1
Watford v Liverpool	1-2
West Ham U v Halifax T	4-2
Wolverhampton W v Tottenham H	1-0

Second Round
Aston Villa v WBA	1-2
Barrow v Nottingham F	1-2
Blackburn R v Doncaster R	4-2
Blackpool v Gillingham	3-1
*Bolton W v Rotherham U	0-0, 3-3, 0-1
Brighton v Birmingham C	2-0
*Bristol C v Leicester C	0-0, 0-0, 1-3
Carlisle U v Huddersfield	2-0
Charlton Ath v Wrexham	0-2
Coventry C v Chelsea	0-1
Crystal Palace v Cardiff C	3-1
Darlington v Everton	0-1
Fulham v Leeds U	0-1
Hartlepool v Derby Co	1-3
Hull C v Norwich C	1-0
Ipswich T v Colchester U	4-0
*Luton T v Millwall	2-2, 1-0
Manchester U v Middlesbrough	1-0
*Mansfield T v QPR	2-2, 0-4
Oxford U v Bury	4-1

Third Round
*Arsenal v Everton	0-0, 0-1
Manchester C v Liverpool	3-2
QPR v Tranmere R	6-0
Brighton v Wolverhampton W	2-3
*Rotherham U v Burnley	1-1, 0-2
Manchester U v Wrexham	2-0
*Crystal Palace v Blackpool	2-2, 1-0
Derby Co v Hull C	3-1
Nottingham F v West Ham U	1-0
Oxford U v Swindon T	1-0
Carlisle U v Blackburn R	2-1
*Leeds U v Chelsea	1-1, 0-2
Bournemouth v Leicester C	0-2
Sheffield U Luton T	3-0
Bradford C v Southend U	2-1
*Ipswich T v WBA	1-1, 0-2

Fourth Round
Manchester C v Everton	2-0
QPR v Wolverhampton W	3-1
*Burnley v Manchester U	0-0, 0-1
*C Palace v Derby Co	1-1, 0-3
Nottingham F v Oxford U	0-1
Carlisle U v Chelsea	1-0
Leicester C v Sheffield U	2-0
WBA v Bradford C	4-0

Fifth Round
Manchester C v QPR	3-0
*Manchester U v Derby Co	0-0, 1-0
*Oxford U v Carlisle U	0-0, 0-1
*Leicester C v WBA	0-0, 1-2

Semi-Final
*Manchester C v Manchester U	2-1, 2-2
Manchester C won 4-3 on aggregate	
*Carlisle U v WBA	1-0, 1-4
WBA won 4-2 on aggregate	

*Home Team in first match.

Final 1969 70: Manchester C 2 WBA 1
(At Wembley, 97,963, receipts, £123,000, March 7, 1970)

Manchester C: Corrigan; Book, Mann; Doyle, Booth, Oakes; Heslop, Bell, Summerbee, Lee, Pardoe. (Sub Bowyer).

WBA: Osborne; Fraser, Wilson; Brown, Talbut, Kaye; Cantello, Suggett, Astle, Hartford, Hope. (Sub Krzywicki).

Scorers: Manchester C: Doyle, Pardoe. WBA: Astle.

FOOTBALL LEAGUE CUP 1970–71

First Round
Aldershot v Brentford	1-0
Aston Villa v Notts Co	4-0
Barnsley v Rotherham U	0-1
Chester v Shrewsbury T	2-1
Colchester U v Cambridge U	5-0
Doncaster R v Darlington	1-1, 1-3
Fulham v Orient	1-0
Gillingham v Luton T	0-1
Halifax T v Bradford C	3-2
Hartlepools U v York C	2-3
Lincoln C v Grimsby T	2-1
Mansfield T v Chesterfield	6-2
Newport Co v Reading	2-1
Portsmouth v Plymouth Arg	2-0
Rochdale v Southport	1-0
Rotherham U v Barnsley	1-0
Scunthorpe U v Northampton T	2-3
Stockport Co v Preston NE	0-1
Torquay U v Bournemouth	1-1, 2-1
Watford v Peterborough U	2-0
Workington T v Barrow	2-0
Birmingham C v Wrexham	3-3, 3-2
Bristol R v Brighton	1-0
Bury v Oldham Ath	1-3
Charlton Ath v Southend U	3-0
Crewe Alex v Tranmere R	2-2, 0-4
Exeter C v Swansea C	0-0, 2-4
Port Vale v Walsall	0-1

Second Round
Carlisle U v Manchester C	2-1
QPR v Cardiff C	4-0
Crystal Palace v Rochdale	3-3, 3-1
Lincoln C v Sunderland	2-1
Torquay U v Preston NE	1-3
Norwich C v Chester	0-0, 2-1
Sheffield W v Chelsea	1-1, 1-2
WBA v Charlton Ath	3-1
Stoke C v Millwall	0-0, 1-2
Oldham Ath v Middlesbrough	2-4
Tranmere R v Coventry C	1-1, 1-2
Derby Co v Halifax T	3-1
Luton T v Workington T	3-0
Bristol R v Newcastle U	2-1
Darlington v Fulham	0-4
Bolton W v Blackburn R	1-0
Mansfield T v Liverpool	0-0, 2-3
Colchester U v Birmingham C	1-1, 1-2
York C v Northampton T	0-0, 1-1, 1-2
Swindon T v Watford	4-2
Sheffield U v Leeds U	1-0
Leicester C v Southampton	3-2
Ipswich T v Arsenal	0-0, 0-4
Portsmouth v Walsall	1-0
Aldershot v Manchester U	1-3
West Ham U v Hull C	1-0
Aston Villa v Burnley	2-0
Oxford U v Wolverhampton W	1-0
Rotherham U v Bristol C	0-0, 0-4
Tottenham H v Swansea C	3-0
Blackpool v Newport Co	4-1
Huddersfield T v Nottingham F	0-0, 0-2

Third Round
Bolton W v Leicester C	1-1, 0-1
Derby Co v Millwall	4-2
Preston NE v WBA	0-1
Crystal Palace v Lincoln C	4-0
Tottenham H v Sheffield U	2-1
Northampton T v Aston Villa	1-1, 0-3
Coventry C v West Ham U	3-1
Birmingham C v Nottingham F	2-1
Luton T v Arsenal	0-1
Norwich C v Bristol R	1-1, 1-3
Carlisle U v Oxford U	3-1
Blackpool v Bristol C	0-1
Manchester U v Portsmouth	1-0
Fulham v QPR	2-0
Swindon T v Liverpool	2-0
Chelsea v Middlesbrough	3-2

Fourth Round
Bristol R v Birmingham C	3-0
Leicester C v Bristol C	2-2, 1-2
Manchester U v Chelsea	2-1
Crystal Palace v Arsenal	0-0, 2-0
Aston Villa v Carlisle U	1-0
Coventry C v Derby Co	1-0
Tottenham H v WBA	5-0
Fulham v Swindon T	1-0

Fifth Round
Bristol R v Aston Villa	1-1, 0-1
Fulham v Bristol C	0-0, 0-1
Tottenham H v Coventry C	4-1
Manchester U v Crystal Palace	4-2

Semi-Final
Bristol C v Tottenham H	1-1, 0-2
Tottenham H won 3-1 on aggregate	
Manchester U v Aston Villa	1-1, 1-2
Aston Villa won 3-2 on aggregate	

Final
Aston Villa v Tottenham H	0-2

Final 1970–71: Aston Villa 0 Tottenham H 2
(At Wembly, 100,000, receipts £132,000 (a record), February 27, 1971)

Aston Villa: Dunn; Bradley, Atken; Godfry, Turnbull, Tiler; McMahon, Rioch, Lochhead, Hamilton, Anderson (Sub. Gibson).

Tottenham H: Jennings; Kinnear, Knowles; Mullery, Collins, Beal; Gilzean, Perryman, Chivers, Peters, Neighbour (Sub Pearce).

Scorer—Tottenham H: Chivers 2.

FOOTBALL LEAGUE CUP 1971–72

First Round
*Aldershot v Southend U	1-1, 2-1
*Aston Villa v Wrexham	2-2, 1-1, 4-3
*Barnsley v Hartlepools	0-0, 1-0
Barrow v Preston NE	0-2
Blackburn R v Workington	2-0
Bournemouth v Portsmouth	2-1
*Bradford C v Bolton W	1-1, 1-2
Charlton Ath v Peterborough	5-1
*Chesterfield v Mansfield T	0-0, 5-0
Colchester U v Brentford	3-1
Crewe Alex v Southport	0-1
Darlington v York C	0-1
Exeter v Bristol R	0-3
Fulham v Cambridge U	4-0
Gillingham v Reading	4-0
Grimsby T v Doncaster R	4-3
*Halifax v Rochdale	1-1, 2-2, 2-0
Newport Co v Torquay U	1-2
Oldham v Bury	1-0
*Orient v Notts Co	1-1, 1-3
Plymouth Arg v Bristol C	1-0
Port Vale v Shrewsbury	0-2
Rotherham U v Sheffield W	0-2
Scunthorpe U v Lincoln C	0-1
Stockport Co v Walsall	1-0
Swansea C v Brighton	0-1
*Tranmere R v Chester	1-1, 3-1
Watford v Northampton T	2-0
Oxford U v Millwall	1-0
QPR v Birmingham C	2-0
Sheffield U v Fulham	3-0
Southampton v Everton	2-1
Southport v Stoke C	1-2
Stockport Co v Watford	0-1
Torquay U v Oldham	2-1
Tranmere R v Preston NE	0-1
WBA v Tottenham H	0-1
*West Ham U v Cardiff C	1-1, 2-1
*York C v Middlesbrough	2-2, 2-1

Second Round
Arsenal v Barnsley	1-0
*Blackburn R v Lincoln C	0-0, 1-4
Bournemouth v Blackpool	0-2
Bristol R v Sunderland	3-1
Carlisle v Sheffield W	5-0
Charlton Ath v Leicester C	3-1
Chelsea v Plymouth Arg	2-0
Chesterfield v Aston Villa	2-3
Colchester U v Swindon T	4-1
Coventry C v Burnley	0-1
Crystal Palace v Luton T	2-0
*Derby Co v Leeds U	0-0, 0-2
Grimsby T v Shrewsbury	2-1
Huddersfield T v Bolton W	0-2
Ipswich T v Manchester U	1-3
Liverpool v Hull C	3-0
Manchester C v Wolverhampton W	4-3
Newcastle U v Halifax T	2-1
Norwich C v Brighton	2-0
Nottingham F v Aldershot	5-1
Notts Co v Gillingham	1-2

Third Round
Arsenal v Newcastle U	4-0
Blackpool v Colchester U	4-0
Bolton W v Manchester C	3-0
Bristol R v Charlton Ath	2-1
*Crystal Palace v Aston Villa	2-2, 0-2
*Gillingham v Grimsby T	1-1, 0-1
Liverpool v Southampton	1-0
*Manchester U v Burnley	1-1, 1-0
Norwich v Carlisle	4-1
*Nottingham F v Chelsea	1-1, 1-2
*Oxford U v Stoke C	1-1, 0-2
QPR v Lincoln C	4-2
Sheffield U v York C	3-2
Torquay U v Tottenham H	1-4
*Watford v Preston NE	1-1, 1-2
*West Ham U v Leeds U	0-0, 1-0

Fourth Round
*Arsenal v Sheffield U	0-0, 0-2
Blackpool v Aston Villa	4-1
*Chelsea v Bolton W	1-1, 6-0
*Grimsby T v Norwich C	1-1, 1-3
*Manchester U v Stoke C	1-1, 0-0, 1-2
*QPR v Bristol R	1-1, 0-1
*Tottenham H v Preston NE	1-1, 2-1
West Ham U v Liverpool	2-1

Fifth Round
Bristol R v Stoke C	2-4
Norwich C v Chelsea	0-1
Tottenham H v Blackpool	2-0
West Ham U v Sheffield U	5-0

Semi-Final
*Chelsea v Tottenham H	3-2, 2-2
Chelsea won 5-4 on aggregate	
*Stoke C v West Ham U	1-2, 1-0, 0-0, 3-2
Stoke C won 5-4 on aggregate	

*Home team in first match.

Final 1971–72: Chelsea 1 Stoke C 2
(At Wembley, 100,000, receipts £132,000 (new record) March 4, 1972)

Chelsea: Bonetti; Mulligan (Baldwin), Harris, Hollins, Dempsey, Webb, Cooke, Garland, Osgood, Hudson, Houseman.

Stoke C: Banks; Marsh, Pejic, Bernard, Smith, Bloor, Conroy, Greenhoff (Maloney), Ritchie, Dobing, Eastham.

Scorers—Chelsea: Osgood, Stoke; Conroy, Eastham.

FOOTBALL LEAGUE CUP 1972–73

First Round
Aston Villa v Hereford U	4-1
*Barnsley v Grimsby T	0-0, 0-2
Blackburn R v Rochdale	0-1
Bolton W v Oldham Ath	3-0
*Bradford C v Stockport Co	1-1, 1-1, 0-2
Brentford v Cambridge U	1-0
Brighton v Exeter C	2-1
*Cardiff C v Bristol R	2-2, 1-3
Chester v Shrewsbury T	4-3
Darlington v Rotherham U	0-1
Gillingham v Colchester U	1-0
Halifax T v Bury	1-2
Hartlepool v Doncaster R	1-0
Mansfield T v Lincoln C	3-1
Northampton T v Charlton Ath	0-3
Notts Co v York C	3-1
Orient v Watford	2-0
Oxford U v Peterborough U	4-0
Plymouth Arg v Bournemouth	0-2
*Reading v Fulham	1-1, 1-1, 0-1
*Scunthorpe U v Chesterfield	0-0, 0-5
Southend U v Aldershot	2-1
Southport v Walsall	4-1
*Swansea C v Newport Co	1-1, 0-3
Torquay U v Portsmouth	1-2
Tranmere R v Port Vale	0-1
Workington v Preston NE	1-0
Wrexham v Crewe Alex	4-0

Second Round
Arsenal v Everton	1-0
*Birmingham C v Luton T	1-1, 1-1, 1-0
*Bournemouth v Blackpool	0-0, 1-1, 1-2
Bristol R v Brighton	4-0
Bury v Grimsby T	1-0
*Carlisle U v Liverpool	1-1, 1-5
Charlton Ath v Mansfield T	4-3
Coventry C v Hartlepool	1-0
Crystal Palace v Stockport Co	0-1
Gillingham v Millwall	0-2
Hull C v Fulham	1-0
Leeds U v Burnley	4-0
Manchester C v Rochdale	4-0
Middlesbrough v Wrexham	2-0
Newport Co v Ipswich T	0-3
Norwich C v Leicester C	2-1
Notts Co v Southport	3-2
Nottingham F v Aston Villa	0-1
*Oxford U v Manchester U	2-2, 1-3
Portsmouth v Chesterfield	0-1
Port Vale v Newcastle U	1-3
Rotherham U v Brentford	2-0
Sheffield W v Bolton W	2-0
*Southampton v Chester	0-0, 2-2, 2-0
Southend U v Chelsea	0-1
Stoke C v Sunderland	3-0
Swindon T v Derby Co	0-1
Tottenham H v Huddersfield T	2-1
WBA v QPR	2-1
West Ham U v Bristol C	2-1
Wolverhampton W v Orient	2-1
Workington v Sheffield U	0-1

Third Round
Arsenal v Rotherham U	5-0
*Aston Villa v Leeds U	1-1, 0-2
Birmingham C v Coventry C	2-1
*Bristol R v Manchester U	1-1, 2-1
Bury v Manchester C	2-0
*Derby Co v Chelsea	0-0, 2-3
Hull C v Norwich C	1-2
Ipswich T v Stoke C	1-2
*Middlesbrough v Tottenham H	1-1, 0-0, 1-2
Millwall v Chesterfield	2-0
Newcastle U v Blackpool	0-3
*Sheffield U v Charlton Ath	0-0, 2-2, 1-0
Southampton v Notts Co	1-3
Stockport Co v West Ham U	2-1
*WBA v Liverpool	1-1, 1-2
Wolverhampton W v Sheffield W	3-1

Fourth Round
Blackpool v Birmingham C	2-0
Bury v Chelsea	0-1
*Liverpool v Leeds U	2-2, 1-0
Notts Co v Stoke C	3-1
Sheffield U v Arsenal	1-2
Stockport Co v Norwich C	1-5
Tottenham H v Millwall	2-0
Wolverhampton W v Bristol R	4-0

Fifth Round
Arsenal v Norwich C	0-3
Chelsea v Notts Co	3-1
*Wolverhampton W v Blackpool	1-1, 1-0
*Liverpool v Tottenham H	1-1, 1-3

Semi-Final
*Chelsea v Norwich C	0-2, 0-1
Norwich C won 3-0 on aggregate	
*Wolverhampton W v Tottenham H	1-2, 2-2
Tottenham H won 4-3 on aggregate	

*Home team in first match.

Final 1972–73: Tottenham H 1 Norwich C 0
(At Wembley, 100,000, receipts £132,000, March 3, 1973)

Tottenham H: Jennings; Kinnear, Knowles, Pratt (Coates), England, Beal, Gilzean, Perryman, Chivers, Peters, Pearce.

Norwich C: Keelan; Payne, Butler, Stringer, Forbes, Briggs, Livermore, Blair (Howard), Cross, Paddon, Anderson.

Scorer: Tottenham H—Coates.

FOOTBALL LEAGUE CUP 1973-74

First Round
*Aldershot v Cambridge U	1-1, 0-3
*Bolton W v Preston NE	1-1, 2-0
AFC Bournemouth v Bristol R	1-0
Brentford v Orient	1-2
Brighton v Charlton Ath	1-2
*Bury v Oldham Ath	0-0, 3-2
Cardiff C v Hereford U	2-0
*Carlisle U v Workington	2-2, 1-0
Chester v Wrexham	0-2
*Chesterfield v Mansfield T	1-1, 2-0
Darlington v Bradford C	2-1
Gillingham v Colchester U	4-2
Grimsby T v Northampton T	2-1
Halifax T v Barnsley	1-1, 1-0
Notts Co v Doncaster R	3-4
*Peterborough U v Scunthorpe U	2-2, 1-2
Portsmouth v Southend U	2-1
*Reading v Watford	2-2, 1-2
Rochdale v Hartlepool	5-3
Rotherham U v Lincoln C	2-1
*Southport v Blackburn R	1-1, 1-3
Stockport Co v Port Vale	2-0
*Swansea C v Exeter C	1-1, 1-2
*Swindon T v Newport Co	3-3, 2-1
Torquay U v Plymouth Arg	0-2
*Tranmere R v Crewe Alex	3-3, 1-0
Walsall v Shrewsbury T	6-1
York City v Huddersfield T	1-0

Second Round
Arsenal v Tranmere R	0-1
*Blackpool v Birmingham C	1-1, 2-4
*A.F.C. Bournemouth v Sheffield W	0-0, 2-2, 1-2
Bury v Cambridge U	2-0
*Cardiff C v Burnley	2-2, 2-3
Chesterfield v Swindon T	1-0
Coventry C v Darlington	5-1
*Derby Co v Sunderland	2-2, 1-1, 0-3
Everton v Reading	1-0
Gillingham v Carlisle U	1-2
Halifax T v Wolverhampton W	0-3
Ipswich T v Leeds U	2-0
*Leicester C v Hull C	3-3, 2-3
*Luton T v Grimsby T	1-1, 0-0, 2-0
Manchester U v Middlesbrough	0-1
*Millwall v Nottingham F	0-0, 3-1
Newcastle U v Doncaster R	6-0
Norwich C v Wrexham	6-2
Orient v Blackburn R	2-0
Oxford U v Fulham	1-1, 0-3
Plymouth Arg v Portsmouth	4-0
QPR v Tottenham H	1-0
Rochdale v Bolton W	0-4
Rotherham U v Exeter C	1-4
*Scunthorpe U v Bristol C	0-0, 1-2
Southampton v Charlton Ath	3-0
Stockport Co v Crystal Palace	1-0
Stoke C v Chelsea	1-0
WBA v Sheffield U	2-1
*West Ham U v Liverpool	2-2, 0-1
*Walsall v Manchester C	0-0, 0-0, 0-4
York City v Aston Villa	1-0

Third Round
*Birmingham C v Newcastle U	2-2, 1-0
*Bristol C v Coventry C	2-2, 1-2
Burnley v Plymouth Arg	1-2
Carlisle U v Manchester C	0-1
Everton v Norwich C	0-1
*Fulham v Ipswich T	2-2, 1-2
Hull C v Stockport Co	4-1
*Luton T v Bury	0-0, 3-2
*Millwall v Bolton W	1-1, 2-1
*Orient v York City	1-1, 1-2
QPR v Sheffield W	8-2
Southampton v Chesterfield	3-0
*Stoke C v Middlesbrough	1-1, 2-1
Sunderland v Liverpool	0-2
*Tranmere R v Wolverhampton W	1-1, 1-2
WBA v Exeter C	1-3

Fourth Round
Coventry C v Stoke C	2-1
*Hull C v Liverpool	0-0, 1-3
Ipswich T v Birmingham C	1-3
Millwall v Luton T	3-1
QPR v Plymouth Arg	0-3
Southampton v Norwich C	0-2
Wolverhampton W v Exeter C	5-1
*York City v Manchester C	0-0, 1-4

Fifth Round
Birmingham C v Plymouth Arg	1-2
*Coventry C v Manchester C	2-2, 2-4
*Millwall v Norwich C	1-1, 1-2
Wolverhampton W v Liverpool	1-0

Semi-Final
*Norwich C v Wolverhampton W	1-1, 0-1
Wolverhampton W won 2-1 on aggregate	
*Plymouth Arg v Manchester C	1-1, 0-2
Manchester C won 3-1 on aggregate	

*Home team in first match.

Final 1973-74: Wolverhampton W 2 Manchester C 1
(At Wembley, 100,000 receipts £165,500, March 2, 1974)

Wolverhampton W: Pierce, Palmer, Parkin, Bailey, Munro, McAlle, Sunderland, Hibbitt, Richards, Dougan, Wagstaffe (Powell).

Manchester C: MacRae; Pardoe, Donachie, Doyle, Booth, Towers, Summerbee, Bell, Lee, Law, Marsh.

Scorers: Wolverhampton W—Hibbitt, Richards; Manchester C—Bell.

FOOTBALL LEAGUE CUP 1974–75

First Round
Barnsley v Halifax T	0-1
Bradford C v Darlington	2-1
Brentford v Aldershot	3-0
Bristol C v Cardiff C	2-1
*Bristol R v Plymouth Arg	0-0, 1-0
Bury v Oldham Ath	2-0
Charlton Ath v Peterborough U	4-0
Chester v Walsall	2-1
Chesterfield v Grimsby T	3-0
Colchester U v Oxford U	1-0
Doncaster R v Mansfield T	2-1
Exeter C v Swansea C	3-1
*Gillingham v AFC Bournemouth	1-1, 1-1, 1-2
*Hereford U v Shrewsbury T	1-1, 1-0
Newport Co v Torquay U	1-0
Northampton T v Port Vale	1-0
Preston NE v Rochdale	1-0
*Reading v Brighton & HA	0-0, 2-2, 0-0, 3-2
*Rotherham U v Lincoln C	1-1, 1-1, 2-1
Scunthorpe U v Sheffield W	1-0
Southend U v Cambridge U	2-0
Southport v Tranmere R	0-2
Stockport Co v Blackburn R	0-2
Swindon T v Portsmouth	0-1
*Watford v Crystal Palace	1-1, 1-5
Workington v Hartlepool	1-2
Wrexham v Crewe Alex	1-2
York C v Huddersfield T	0-2

Second Round
*Arsenal v Leicester C	1-1, 1-2
*Aston Villa v Everton	1-1, 3-0
*Bolton W v Norwich C	0-0, 1-3
*AFC Bournemouth v Hartlepool	1-1, 2-2, 1-1, 0-1
Bradford C v Carlisle U	0-1
Bury v Doncaster R	2-0
Chelsea v Newport Co	4-2
Chester v Blackpool	3-1
Crystal Palace v Bristol C	1-4
Coventry C v Ipswich T	1-2
Crewe Alex v Birmingham C	2-1
Exeter C v Hereford U	0-1
*Huddersfield T v Leeds U	1-1, 1-1, 1-2
Hull C v Burnley	1-2
Liverpool v Brentford	2-1
Luton T v Bristol R	1-0
Manchester C v Scunthorpe U	6-0
Manchester U v Charlton Ath	5-1
*Northampton T v Blackburn R	2-2, 0-1
*Nottingham F v Newcastle U	1-1, 0-3
Portsmouth v Derby Co	1-5

Preston NE v Sunderland	2-0
*QPR v Orient	1-1, 3-0
Reading v Rotherham U	4-2
Sheffield U v Chesterfield	3-1
Southampton v Notts Co	1-0
Southend U v Colchester U	0-2
Stoke C v Halifax T	3-0
Tottenham H v Middlesbrough	0-4
*Tranmere R v West Ham U	0-0, 0-6
WBA v Millwall	1-0
Wolverhampton W v Fulham	1-3

Third Round
*Bristol C v Liverpool	0-0, 0-4
Bury v Leeds U	1-2
*Chelsea v Stoke C	2-2, 1-1, 2-6
Chester v Preston NE	1-0
Colchester U v Carlisle U	2-0
*Crewe Alex v Aston Villa	2-2, 0-1
Fulham v West Ham U	2-1
*Hartlepool v Blackburn R	1-1, 2-1
Ipswich T v Hereford U	4-1
Manchester U v Manchester C	1-0
Middlesbrough v Leicester C	1-0
QPR v Newcastle U	0-4
Reading v Burnley	1-2
Sheffield U v Luton T	2-0
Southampton v Derby Co	5-0
*WBA v Norwich C	1-1, 0-2

Fourth Round
Chester v Leeds U	3-0
*Colchester U v Southampton	0-0, 1-0
*Hartlepool v Aston Villa	1-1, 1-6
Ipswich T v Stoke C	2-1
Liverpool v Middlesbrough	0-1
Manchester U v Burnley	3-2
Newcastle U v Fulham	3-0
*Sheffield U v Norwich C	2-2, 1-2

Fifth Round
Colchester U v Aston Villa	1-2
*Middlesbrough v Manchester U	0-0, 0-3
*Norwich C v Ipswich T	1-1, 2-1
*Newcastle U v Chester	0-0, 0-1

Semi-Final
*Chester v Aston Villa	2-2, 2-3
Aston Villa won 5-4 on aggregate.	
*Manchester U v Newcastle U	2-2, 0-1
Norwich C won 3-2 on aggregate.	

*Home team in first match

Final 1974–75: Aston Villa 1 Norwich C 0
(At Wembley, 100,000, receipts £196,000, March 1, 1975)

Aston Villa: Cumbes; Robson, Aitken, Ross, Nicholl, McDonald, Graydon, Little, Leonard, Hamilton, Carrodus.

Norwich C: Keelan; Machin, Sullivan, Morris, Forbes, Stringer, Miller, MacDougall, Boyer, Suggett, Powell.

FOOTBALL LEAGUE CUP 1975-76

First Round

Aldershot v Portsmouth	1-1, 1-2
Bradford C v York C	2-0, 0-3
Brentford v Brighton & HA	2-1, 1-1
Bury v Rochdale	2-0, 2-0
Cambridge U v Charlton Ath	1-1, 0-3
Cardiff C v Bristol R	1-2, 1-1
Crystal Palace v Colchester U	3-0, 1-3
Crewe Alex v Tranmere R	2-1, 1-2
Darlington v Sheffield W	0-2, 2-0, 5-3
Doncaster R v Grimsby T	3-1, 0-0
Halifax T v Hartlepool	4-1, 1-2
Huddersfield T v Barnsley	2-1, 1-1
Lincoln C v Chesterfield	4-2, 2-3
Mansfield T v Scunthorpe U	4-0, 2-0
Newport Co v Exeter C	1-1, 0-2
Oldham Ath v Workington	3-0, 3-1
Plymouth Arg v AFC Bournemouth	2-0, 2-1
Port Vale v Hereford U	4-2, 0-2, 0-1
Preston NE v Blackburn R	0-0, 0-0
Reading v Gillingham	2-0, 1-1
Rotherham U v Nottingham F	1-2, 1-5
Southend U v Peterborough U	2-0, 0-3
Southport v Stockport Co	3-1, 2-1
Swansea C v Torquay U	1-2, 3-5
Swindon T v Millwall	2-1, 1-0
Walsall v Shrewsbury T	0-0, 1-2
Watford v Northampton T	2-0, 1-1
Wrexham v Chester	3-0, 0-0

Second Round

Aston Villa v Oldham Ath	2-0
Birmingham C v Orient	4-0
Bolton W v Coventry C	1-3
Bury v Middlesbrough	1-2
Carlisle U v Gillingham	2-0
*Charlton Ath v Oxford U	3-3, 1-1, 3-2
Crewe Alex v Chelsea	1-0
Darlington v Luton T	2-1
Derby Co v Huddersfield T	2-1
Doncaster R v Crystal Palace	2-1
*Everton v Arsenal	2-2, 1-0
Halifax T v Sheffield U	2-4
Hereford U v Burnley	1-4
Hull C v Preston NE	4-2
Leeds U v Ipswich T	3-2
Lincoln C v Stoke C	2-1
Manchester U v Brentford	2-1
*Norwich C v Manchester C	1-1, 2-2, 1-6
Notts Co v Sunderland	2-1
Nottingham F v Plymouth Arg	1-0
Peterborough U v Blackpool	2-0
*Portsmouth v Leicester C	1-1, 0-1
Shrewsbury T v QPR	1-4
Southampton v Bristol R	0-1
Southport v Newcastle U	0-6
*Swindon T v Wolverhampton W	2-2, 2-3
*Torquay U v Exeter C	1-1, 2-1
Watford v Tottenham H	0-1
*WBA v Fulham	1-1, 0-1
*West Ham U v Bristol C	0-0, 3-1
Wrexham v Mansfield T	1-2
York C v Liverpool	0-1

Third Round

Aston Villa v Manchester U	1-2
Birmingham C v Wolverhampton W	0-2
*Bristol R v Newcastle U	1-1, 0-2
Crewe Alex v Tottenham H	0-2
Everton v Carlisle U	2-0
Fulham v Peterborough U	0-1
Hull C v Sheffield U	2-0
Leeds U v Notts Co	0-1
Leicester C v Lincoln C	2-1
*Liverpool v Burnley	1-1, 0-1
Manchester C v Nottingham F	2-1
Mansfield T v Coventry C	2-0
Middlesbrough v Derby Co	1-0
*QPR v Charlton Ath	1-1, 3-0
*Torquay U v Doncaster R	1-1, 0-3
West Ham U v Darlington	3-0

Fourth Round

Burnley v Leicester C	2-0
Doncaster R v Hull C	2-1
*Everton v Notts Co	2-2, 0-2
Manchester C v Manchester U	4-0
Mansfield T v Wolverhampton W	1-0
Middlesbrough v Peterborough U	3-0
QPR v Newcastle U	1-3
*Tottenham H v West Ham U	0-0, 2-0

Fifth Round

Burnley v Middlesbrough	0-2
Manchester C v Mansfield T	4-2
Newcastle U v Notts Co	1-0
Tottenham H v Doncaster R	7-2

Semi-Final

Middlesbrough v Manchester C	1-0, 0-4
Manchester C won 4-1 on aggregate.	
Tottenham H v Newcastle U	1-0, 1-3
Newcastle U won 3-2 on aggregate.	

*Home team in first match

Final 1975–76: Manchester C 2 Newcastle U 1

(At Wembley, 100,000, receipts £299,601.16p (a record), February 28, 1976)

Manchester C: Corrigan; Keegan, Donachie, Doyle, Watson, Oakes, Barnes, Booth, Royle, Hartford, Tueart.

Newcastle U: Mahoney; Nattrass, Kennedy, Barrowclough, Keeley, Howard, Burns, Cassidy, Macdonald, Gowling, Craig.

Scorers: Manchester C—Barnes, Tueart; Newcastle U—Gowling.

FOOTBALL LEAGUE CUP 1976-77

First Round
Aldershot v Gillingham	1-1, 0-2
AFC Bournemouth v Torquay U	0-0, 0-1
Bradford C v Oldham Ath	1-1, 3-1
Bury v Preston NE	2-1, 1-1
Cardiff C v Bristol R	2-1, 4-4
Chester v Hereford U	2-0, 3-4
Chesterfield v Rotherham U	3-1, 0-3
Crewe Alex v Tranmere R	2-1, 1-3
Crystal Palace v Portsmouth	2-2, 1-0
Doncaster R v Lincoln C	1-1, 1-1, 2-2
(Doncaster R win on penalties)	
Grimsby T v Sheffield W	0-3, 0-0
Halifax T v Darlington	0-0, 1-1, 1-2
Huddersfield T v Hartlepool	2-0, 2-1
Mansfield T v Scunthorpe U	2-0, 0-2, 1-2
Millwall v Colchester U	2-1, 1-2, 4-4
(Millwall win on penalties)	
Oxford U v Cambridge U	1-0, 0-2
Plymouth Arg v Exeter C	0-1, 0-1
Port Vale v Wrexham	1-1, 0-1
Reading v Peterborough U	2-3, 1-0, 1-3
Rochdale v Blackburn R	0-1, 1-4
Shrewsbury T v Walsall	0-1, 0-1
Southend U v Brighton & HA	1-1, 1-2
Southport v Carlisle U	1-2, 1-0, 2-3
Swansea C v Newport Co	4-1, 0-1
Swindon T v Northampton T	3-2, 0-2
Watford v Brentford	1-1, 2-0
Workington v Stockport Co	0-0, 0-0, 0-2
York C v Barnsley	0-0, 0-0, 1-2

Second Round
Arsenal v Carlisle U	3-2
Aston Villa v Manchester C	3-0
Blackburn R v Stockport Co	1-3
Blackpool v Birmingham C	2-1
Bradford C v Bolton W	1-2
Bristol C v Coventry C	0-1
Bury v Darlington	2-1
Cardiff C v QPR	1-3
Chelsea v Sheffield U	3-1
Chester v Swansea C	2-3
Crystal Palace v Watford	1-3
Doncaster R v Derby Co	1-2
Everton v Cambridge U	3-0
Exeter C v Norwich C	1-3
*Fulham v Peterborough U	1-1, 2-1
Gillingham v Newcastle U	1-2
*Ipswich T v Brighton & HA	0-0, 1-2
*Liverpool v WBA	1-1, 0-1
Manchester U v Tranmere R	5-0

Middlesbrough v Tottenham H	1-2
Northampton T v Huddersfield T	0-1
Orient v Hull C	1-0
Rotherham U v Millwall	1-2
Scunthorpe U v Notts Co	0-2
*Southampton v Charlton Ath	1-1, 1-2
Stoke C v Leeds U	2-1
Sunderland v Luton T	3-1
Torquay U v Burnley	1-0
Walsall v Nottingham F	2-4
West Ham U v Barnsley	3-0
Wolverhampton W v Sheffield W	1-2
Wrexham v Leicester C	1-0

Third Round
Aston Villa v Norwich C	2-1
*Blackpool v Arsenal	1-1, 0-0, 0-2
Charlton Ath v West Ham U	0-1
Chelsea v Huddersfield T	2-0
*Derby Co v Notts Co	1-1, 2-1
*Fulham v Bolton W	2-2, 2-2, 1-2
*Manchester U v Sunderland	2-2, 2-2, 1-0
*Millwall v Orient	0-0, 0-0, 3-0
Newcastle U v Stoke C	3-0
Nottingham F v Coventry C	0-3
QPR v Bury	2-1
Sheffield W v Watford	3-1
Stockport Co v Everton	0-1
Tottenham H v Wrexham	2-3
Torquay U v Swansea C	1-2
WBA v Brighton & HA	0-2

Fourth Round
Arsenal v Chelsea	2-1
Aston Villa v Wrexham	5-1
*Brighton & HA v Derby Co	1-1, 1-2
Everton v Coventry C	3-0
Manchester U v Newcastle U	7-2
Millwall v Sheffield W	3-0
*Swansea C v Bolton W	1-1, 1-5
West Ham U v QPR	0-2

Fifth Round
Aston Villa v Millwall	2-0
Derby Co v Bolton W	1-2
Manchester U v Everton	0-3
QPR v Arsenal	2-1

Semi-Finals
Everton v Bolton W	1-1, 1-0
QPR v Aston Villa	0-0, 2-2, 0-3

*Home team in first match

Final 1976-77: Aston Villa 0 Everton 0
(At Wembley, 100,000, receipts £301,000, March 12, 1977)

Aston Villa: Burridge; Gidman, Robson, Phillips, Nicholl, Mortimer, Deehan, Little, Gray, Cropley, Carrodus.

Everton: Lawson; Jones, Darracott, Lyons, McNaught, King, Hamilton, Dobson, Latchford, McKenzie, Goodlass.

Final, Replay 1975-76: Aston Villa 1 Everton 1 (*aet*)
(At Hillsborough, 55,000, March 16, 1977)

Aston Villa: Burridge; Gidman, Robson, Phillips, Nicholl, Mortimer, Deehan, Little, Gray, Cowans, Carrodus.

Everton: Lawson; Bernard, Darracott, Lyons, McNaught, King, Hamilton (Pearson), Kenyon, Latchford, McKenzie, Goodlass.

Scorers: Aston Villa—Kenyon (og); Everton—Latchford

Final, Second Replay 1975-76: Everton 2 Aston Villa 3 (*aet*)
(At Old Trafford, 54,749, April 13, 1977)

Aston Villa: Burridge; Gidman (Smith), Robson, Phillips, Nicholl, Mortimer, Graydon, Little, Deehan, Cropley, Cowans.

Everton: Lawson; Robinson, Darracott, Lyons, McNaught, King, Hamilton, Dobson, Latchford, Pearson (Seargeant), Goodlass.

Scorers: Everton—Latchford, Lyons; Aston Villa—Little 2, Nicholl.

FOOTBALL LEAGUE CUP 1977-78

First Round

Aldershot v Colchester U	1-1, 1-4
Brentford v Crystal Palace	2-1, 1-5
Bristol R v Walsall	1-2, 0-1
Burnley v Chester	2-0, 0-1
Bury v Crewe Alex	3-0, 1-1
*Cambridge U v Brighton & HA	0-0, 0-0, 0-3
*Chesterfield v Barnsley	4-1, 0-3, 2-0
Darlington v Scunthorpe U	0-0, 1-3
*Exeter C v Plymouth Arg	2-2, 0-0, 1-0
Gillingham v Wimbledon	1-1, 1-3
Grimsby T v Hartlepool	3-0, 2-1
*Hereford U v AFC Bournemouth	2-0, 2-4, 1-2
*Huddersfield T v Carlisle U	1-1, 2-2, 2-1
Mansfield T v Lincoln C	0-1, 0-0
Orient v Fulham	2-0, 1-2
Oxford U v Shrewsbury T	3-0, 2-2
Peterborough U v Bradford C	4-1, 1-1
Portsmouth v Newport Co	3-1, 2-3
*Port Vale v Preston N E	2-1, 1-2, 1-2
Rochdale v Halifax T	1-1, 2-1
*Rotherham U v York C	3-0, 0-3, 1-1
(Rotherham U win on penalties)	
Sheffield W v Doncaster R	5-2, 3-0
Southend U v Northampton T	2-3, 1-2
Swansea C v Swindon T	1-3, 1-2
*Torquay U v Cardiff C	1-0, 2-3, 1-2
Tranmere R v Southport	0-1, 2-2
*Watford v Reading	2-1, 0-1, 5-0
Wrexham v Stockport Co	1-0, 1-1

Second Round

Arsenal v Manchester U	3-2
Birmingham C v Notts Co	0-2
*Blackburn R v Colchester U	1-1, 0-4
*Blackpool v Sheffield W	2-2, 1-3
Bolton W v Lincoln C	1-0
*Brighton & HA v Oldham Ath	0-0, 2-2, 1-2
Bristol C v Stoke C	1-0
Burnley v Norwich C	3-1
Charlton Ath v Wrexham	1-2
Chesterfield v Manchester C	0-1
*Crystal Palace v Southampton	0-0, 1-2
Derby Co v Orient	3-1
Exeter C v Aston Villa	1-3
Grimsby T v Watford	1-2
Huddersfield T v Coventry C	0-2
Ipswich T v Northampton T	5-0
Liverpool v Chelsea	2-0
Newcastle U v Millwall	0-2
Nottingham F v West Ham U	5-0
*Oxford U v Bury	1-1, 0-1
*Peterborough U v Scunthorpe U	1-1, 1-0
Portsmouth v Leicester C	2-0
QPR v AFC Bournemouth	2-0
Rochdale v Leeds U	0-3
Sheffield U v Everton	0-3
*Southport v Hull C	2-2, 0-1
*Sunderland v Middlesbrough	2-2, 0-1
Swindon T v Cardiff C	5-1
Tottenham H v Wimbeldon	4-0
*Walsall v Preston NE	0-0, 1-0
WBA v Rotherham U	4-0
Wolverhampton W v Luton T	1-3

Third Round

Arsenal v Southampton	2-0
Aston Villa v QPR	1-0
Bolton W v Peterborough U	3-1
Burnley v Ipswich T	1-2
*Everton v Middlesbrough	2-2, 2-1
Hull C v Oldham Ath	2-0
Leeds U v Colchester U	4-0
Liverpool v Derby Co	2-0
*Luton T v Manchester C	1-1, 0-0, 2-3
*Millwall v Bury	1-1, 0-2
Nottingham F v Notts Co	4-0
*Portsmouth v Swindon T	1-1, 3-4
Sheffield W v Walsall	2-1
Tottenham H v Coventry C	2-3
WBA v Watford	1-0
Wrexham v Bristol C	1-0

Fourth Round

Arsenal v Hull C	5-1
Bolton W v Leeds U	1-3
Bury v WBA	1-0
Ipswich T v Manchester C	1-2
*Liverpool v Coventry C	2-2, 2-0
Nottingham F v Aston Villa	4-2
Sheffield W v Everton	1-3
Wrexham v Swindon T	2-0

Fifth Round

Bury v Nottingham F	0-3
Leeds U v Everton	4-1
*Manchester C v Arsenal	0-0, 0-1
Wrexham v Liverpool	1-3

SEMI-FINALS

Leeds U v Nottingham F	1-3, 2-4
Liverpool v Arsenal	2-1, 0-0

*Home team in first match

Final 1977-78: Nottingham F 0 Liverpool 0 (*aet*)
(At Wembley, 100,000, March 18, 1978)

Nottingham F: Woods; Anderson, Clark, McGovern (O'Hare), Lloyd, Burns, O'Neill, Bowyer, Withe, Woodcock, Robertson.

Liverpool: Clemence; Neal, Smith, Thompson, Kennedy (Fairclough), Hughes, Dalglish, Case, Heighway, McDermott, Callaghan.

Final, Replay 1977-78: Nottingham F 1 Liverpool 0
(At Old Trafford, 54,375, March 22, 1978)

Nottingham F: Woods; Anderson, Clark, O'Hare, Lloyd, Burns, O'Neill, Bowyer, Withe, Woodcock, Robertson.

Liverpool: Clemence; Neal, Smith, Thompson, Kennedy, Hughes, Dalglish, Case (Fairclough); Heighway, McDermott, Callaghan.

Scorer: Nottingham F—Robertson (pen).

FOOTBALL LEAGUE CUP DETAILS 1978-79

FIRST ROUND, FIRST LEG
12 AUG

Aldershot (0) 0
Millwall (1) 1 (*Mitchell*) 4973
Aldershot: Johnson; Howitt, Wooler, Dixon, Youlden, Jopling, Longhorn, Brodie, Needham, Dungworth, Tomlin (McGregor).
Millwall: Cuff; Donaldson, Moore, Allen, Kitchener, Hazell, Hamilton B, Seasman, Mitchell, Pearson, Walker (Lee).

Barnsley (0) 1 (*Little*)
Chesterfield (1) 2 (*Cottam, Fern*) 8606
Barnsley: Springett; Markham, Collins, Pugh, Joicey, McCarthy, Riley Clarke, Price (Millar), Prendergast, Little.
Chesterfield: Letheran; Tartt, Burton, O'Neill, Cottam, Hunter, Cammack, Fern, Simpson, Kowalski, Flavell.

AFC Bournemouth (0) 0
Exeter C (1) 1 (*Kellow*) 3180
AFC Bournemouth: Baker; Cunningham, Miller, Impey, Brown R, Butler G, Weeks (Johnson), Showers, Butler M, Massey, Brown K.
Exeter C: O'Keefe; Templeman, Hore, Randell, Giles, Roberts, Hodge, Kellow, Bowker Delve, Forbes.

Bradford C (1) 2 (*Cooke, Johnson*)
Lincoln C (0) 0 4980
Bradford C: Downsborough; Podd, Wood, Johnson, Baines, Middleton, Bates, Dolan, Cooke, McNiven, Hutchins.
Lincoln C: Grotier; Wright, Laybourne, Fleming, Wigginton, Cooper, Hobson, Hughes, Harford (Guest), Sunley, Hubbard.

Bristol R (2) 2 (*Aitken, Staniforth*)
Hereford U (0) 1 (*Jones*) 5001
Bristol R: Thomas; Aitken, Bater, Pulis, Taylor, Prince, Dennehy, Williams, Randall (Clarke), Staniforth, Barry.
Hereford U: Hughes; Roberts, Price, Cornes, Layton, Barton (Bailey), Emery, Holmes W, Powell, Jones, Holmes K.

Cambridge U (1) 2 (*Morgan, Finney*)
Northampton T (1) 2 (*Farrington, Reilly*) 4043
Cambridge U: Webster; Howard, Buckley, Smith, Fallon, Cozens, Watson, Spriggs, Morgan, Finney, Biley.
Northampton T: Jayes; Geidmintis, Mead, Woollett, Robertson, Bryant, Farrington, Williams, Reilly, Liddle, Christie.

Cardiff C (0) 1 (*Buchanan*)
Oxford U (2) 2 (*Taylor, Foley*) 4500
Cardiff C: Healey; Thomas, Pethard, Campbell, Dwyer, Larmour (Grapes), Burns, Giles, Went, Bishop, Buchanan.
Oxford U: Burton; Doyle, Fogg, Briggs, McIntosh, Jeffrey, McGrogan (Seacole), Taylor, Foley, Curran, Duncan.

Carlisle U (1) 2 (*Kemp, Bonnyman*)
Blackpool (1) 2 (*McEwan 2 pens*) 5100
Carlisle U: Swinburne; Hoolickin, McCartney, MacDonald, Tait, Parker, McVitie, Bonnyman, Kemp, Lumby, Hamilton.
Blackpool: Ward; Gardner, Milligan, Wilson, Suddaby, McEwan, Hockaday, Tong, Spence, Davidson, Wagstaffe.

Colchester U (1) 2 (*Rowles, Dowman*)
Charlton A (1) 3 (*Hales, Brisley, Robinson*) 3016
Colchester U: Walker; Cook (Sharkey), Packer, Bunkell, Wignall, Dowman, Foley, Gough, Dyer, Rowles, Allinson.
Charlton A: Wood; Berry, Warman, Tydeman Shipperley, Dugdale, Brisley, Peacock (Madden), Hales, Robinson, Gritt.

Crewe Alex (1) 1 (*Nelson*)
Rochdale (0) 0 1914
Crewe Alex: Brand; Bevan, Cheetham, Purdie, Bowles, Wilshaw, Davies, Roberts, Nelson, Coyne (Rimmer), Tully.
Rochdale: Slack; Hallows, Snookes, Hart, Scott, Bannon, Scaife, O'Loughlin Owen, Ashworth, Mullington (Esser).

Doncaster R (0) 0
Sheffield W (1) 1 (*Robinson og*) 7232
Doncaster R: Peacock; Robinson, Bentley, Olney, Bradley, Taylor, Lewis Owen (Snodin), Habbin, French, Laidlaw.
Sheffield W: Bolder; Shirtiff, Grant, Mullen, Dowd, Cusack (Owen), Wylde, Johnson, Tynan, Porterfield, Hornsby.

Grimsby T (1) 2 (*Waters pen, Lester*)
York C (0) 0 3051
Grimsby T: Batch; Mawer, Moore, Waters, Barker, Crombie, Ford, Donovan, Lester, Cumming, Mitchell.
York C: Brown; Scott, Kay, Walsh, Faulkner, Clements, Warnock, Stronach, Loggie, Young, Staniforth.

Hull C (0) 0
Peterborough U (1) 1 (*Slough pen*) 4165
Hull C: Wealands; Nisbet, DeVries, Haigh, Croft, Dobson, Horswill, Hood (Hawker), Edwards, Bannister, Farley.
Peterborough U: Waugh; Carmichael, Styles, Doyle, Green, Ross, Slough, McEwan, Butlin, Anderson, Robson.

Mansfield T (0) 0
Darlington (1) 1 (*Craig*) 4903
Mansfield T: Arnold; Bird, Foster B, Foster C, Saxby, McClelland, Miller, Martin, Syrett, Hodgson, Coffey (Allen).
Darlington: Burleigh; Nattrass, Cochrane, Stone, Craig, Hague, Maitland, Lyons, Seal, Probert, Wann.

Newport Co (2) 2 (*Woods, Williams*)
Swansea C (0) 1 (*Waddle*) 6200
Newport Co: Plumley; Walden, Relish, Byrne, Walker, Davies, Warriner, Thompson (Sinclair), Woods, Goddard, Williams.
Swansea C: Crudgington; Evans, Bartley, Lally Toshack, Bruton, Moore, James R, Curtis, Waddle, Charles (Morris).

Plymouth Arg (0) 1 (*Parsons og*)
Torquay U (0) 1 (*Lawrence*) 7725
Plymouth Arg: Hodge; Bason, Rogers, Trusson, Foster, Megson, Johnson, Taylor, Binney, Perrin, Fear.
Torquay U: Turner; Parsons, Payne, Darke, Green, Dunne, Coffill, Cooper (Lawrence), Murphy, Wilson, Raper.

Portsmouth (0) 0
Swindon T (0) 0 9261
Portsmouth: Mellor; Ellis, Viney, Denyer, Foster, Hand, Hemmerman, Lathan, Davey, Piper, Pullar.
Swindon T: Roberts; McLaughlin, Ford, McHale, Aizlewood, Stroud, Miller (Carter), Kamara, Guthrie, Bates, Williams.

Port Vale (0) 0
Chester (2) 3 *(Edwards 2, Phillips)* 2805
Port Vale: Connaughton; Wilkinson, Bentley, Stenson, Harris, Hawkins, Chamberlain, Moore, Froggatt, Beamish, Bailey.
Chester: Lloyd; Raynor, Walker, Storton, Jeffries, Oakes, Livermore, Delgado, Edwards, Mellor, Phillips.

Preston NE (0) 3 *(Baxter, Bruce 2)*
Huddersfield T (0) 0 6841
Preston NE: Tunks; McMahon, Cameron, Doyle, Baxter, Cross, Cochrane (Bruce), Haslegrave, Robinson, Thomson, Smith.
Huddersfield T: Starling; Brown, Sandercock, Holmes, Sutton, Topping, Howey, Hart, Fletcher, Hanvey, McGrellis.

Reading (0) 3 *(Hetzke, Overton og, Kearns)*
Gillingham (0) 1 *(Price)* 3246
Reading: Death; Peters, White, Bowman, Hicks, Bennett, Earles, Hetzke, Kearns, Sanchez, Lewis.
Gillingham: Hillyard; Knight, Armstrong, Overton, Young, Crabbe, Hunt (Hughes), Weatherley, Price, Westwood, Richardson.

Rotherham U (2) 5 *(Phillips, Finney 3, Gwyther)*
Hartlepool U (0) 0 2431
Rotherham U: McAlister; Forrest, Breckin, Rhodes, Green, Flynn, Finney, Phillips, Gwyther, Smith, Crawford.
Hartlepool U: Richardson; Malone, Gorry, Smith, Brooks, Ayre, Linacre, Guy, Houchen (Larkin), Newton, Crumplin.

Scunthorpe U (0) 0
Notts Co (1) 1 *(Hooks)* 2389
Scunthorpe U: Crawford; O'Donnell, Peacock, Oates, Deere, Czuczman, Grimes, Gibson (Kilmore), Wigg, Keeley, Pilling.
Notts Co: McManus; Richards, O'Brien, Benjamin, Blockley, Stubbs, Carter, Hooks, Vinter, Mann, Wood.

Southend (0) 1 *(Donaldson og)*
Wimbledon (0) 0 4845
Southend U: Horn; Goodwin, Yates, Laverick, Hadley, Moody, Fell, Parker, Abbott, Pountney, Morris.
Wimbledon: Goddard; Bryant, Eames, Denny, Galvin, Donaldson, Leslie, Briley, Connell, Cork, Summerill.

Tranmere R (0) 1 *(McAuley)*
Wigan Ath (0) 1 *(Gore)* 4402
Tranmere R: Johnson; Mathias, Flood, O'Neil, Postlewhite, Palios, Peplow (Kerr), Craven, Moore, Evans, McAuley.
Wigan Ath: Brown; Gore, Hinnigan, Wright, Ward (Davies), Gillibrand, Corrigan, Purdie, Crompton, Wilkie, Houghton.

Walsall (1) 2 *(Buckley, Birch)*
Halifax T (1) 1 *(Bullock)* 4589
Walsall: Kearns; Paul, Caswell (Clarke), Macken, Serella, Harrison, Birch, Kelly, Austin, Buckley, King.
Halifax T: Leonard; Trainer, Loska, Smith, Burke, Dunleavy, Nixon, Lawson, Bullock, Johnson (Bradley), Carroll.

Watford (1) 4 *(Joslyn, Jenkins 2, Downes)*
Brentford (0) 0 9292
Watford: Rankin; Stirk, Pritchett, Booth, Bolton, Garner, Pollard, Mercer (Mayes), Jenkins, Joslyn, Downes.
Brentford: Porter; Salman, Tucker, Shrubb, Kruse, Graham J (Fraser), Graham W, Carlton, Allder, Baldwin, Phillips.

Wrexham (0) 2 *(Davis, Cartwright)*
Bury (0) 0 8004
Wrexham: Davies; Evans, Dwyer, Davis, Cegielski, Thomas, Shinton, Sutton, Lyons (Williams), Whittle, Cartwright.
Bury: Forrest; Keenan (Hilton), Kennedy, Lugg, Tucker, Whitehead, Wilson, Taylor, Rowland, Robins, Farrell.

14 AUG

Shrewsbury T (1) 1 *(Rogan og)*
Stockport C (0) 0 2435
Shrewsbury T: Mulhearn; King, Leonard, Turner, Griffin, Hayes, Cross, Lindsay, Atkins, Biggins, Maguire.
Stockport C: Rogan; Thorpe, Rutter, Thompson, Park, Fogarty, Summerbee, Goodfellow, Bradd, Loadwick, Lee.

FIRST ROUND, SECOND LEG

Rochdale (1) 2 *(O'Loughlin, Ashworth)*
Crewe Alex (1) 4 *(Coyne, Nelson 2, Bowles)* 1344
Rochdale: Slack; Hallows, Snookes, Hart, Scott, Bannon, Owen, Scaife, Ashworth, Mullington (Esser), O'Loughlin.
Crewe Alex: Brand; Bevan, Cheetham, Purdie, Bowles, Wilshaw, Davies, Roberts, Nelson, Coyne, Tully.

15 AUG

Brentford (0) 1 *(Rolph)*
Watford (1) 3 *(Downes, Bolton, Mayes)* 7400
Brentford: Porter; Salman (Wilkins), Tucker, Shrubb, Kruse, Graham, J, Graham W, Carlton, Allder, Rolph, Phillips.
Watford: Rankin; Stirk, Pritchett, Booth, Bolton, Garner, Pollard, Mayes, Jenkins, Joslyn, Downes.

Bury (0) 1 *(Rowland)*
Wrexham (1) 2 *(Whittle, Shinton)* 4568
Bury: Forrest; Keenan, Kennedy, Lugg, Tucker, Hatton, Wilson, Farrell, Rowland, Hilton, Taylor.
Wrexham: Davies; Evans, Dwyer, Davis, Roberts, Thomas, Shinton, Sutton, Lyons (Williams P), Whittle, Cartwright.

Charlton Ath (0) 0
Colchester (0) 0 7205
Charlton Ath: Wood; Campbell, Warman, Tydeman, Shipperley, Dugdale, Brisley, Hales, Robinson, Flanagan, Gritt.
Colchester U: Walker; Sharkey, Packer, Leslie, Wignall, Dowman, Foley, Gough, Dyer, Rowles, Allinson.

Darlington (0) 2 *(Stone, Lyons)*
Mansfield T (0) 2 *(Bird, Miller)* 5000
Darlington: Burleigh; Nattrass, Cochrane, Hague, Craig, Stone, Maitland, Lyons, Seal, Probert, Wann.
Mansfield T: Arnold; Bird, Foster B, Foster C (Coffey), Saxby, McClelland, Miller, Martin, Syrett, Hodgson, Allen.

Exeter C (0) 1 (*Delve*)
AFC Bournemouth (1) 1 (*Brown*) 3865
Exeter C: O'Keefe; Templeman, Hore, Randell, Giles, Roberts, Hodge, Kellow, Bowker, Delve, Hatch.
AFC Bournemouth: Baker; Cunningham, Miller, Impey, Brown R, Butler G, Johnson, Showers, Butler M, Massey, Brown K.

Gillingham (0) 1 (*Young*)
Reading (0) 2 (*Lewis, Earles*) 5914
Gillingham: Hillyard; Knight (Hughes), Armstrong, Overton, Young, Crabbe, Nicholl, Weatherley, Price, Westwood, Richardson.
Reading: Death; Peters, White, Bowman, Hicks, Bennett, Earles, Hetzke, Kearns, Sanchez, Lewis.

Halifax T (0) 0
Walsall (0) 2 (*Paul, Buckley*) 2276
Halifax T: Leonard; Trainer, Loska, Smith, Burke (Bradley), Dunleavy, Nixon, Johnston, Bullock, Lawson, Bell.
Walsall: Kearns; Paul, Caswell, Harrison, Serella, King, Birch, Macken, Austin, Buckley, Kelly.

Hartlepool U (0) 1 (*Newton*)
Rotherham U (0) 1 (*Crawford*) 1746
Hartlepool U: Richardson; Malone, Gorry, Smith, Brooks, Ayre, Linacre, Houchen, Newton, Crumplin, Guy.
Rotherham U: McAlister; Forrest, Breckin, Rhodes, Green, Flynn, Finney, Phillips, Gwyther, Crawford, Smith.

Huddersfield T (1) 2 (*Holmes pen, Ripley*)
Preston NE (0) 2 (*Bruce, Thomson*) 3435
Huddersfield T: Starling; Brown, Sandercock, Holmes, Sutton, Topping, Howey, Hart, Fletcher, Hanvey, McGrellis (Ripley).
Preston NE: Kilner; McMahon, Cameron, Doyle, Baxter, Cross, Coleman, Haslegrave, Robinson, Thomson, Bruce.

Notts Co (2) 3 (*Carter 2, Hooks*)
Scunthorpe U (0) 0 5064
Notts Co: McManus; Richards, O'Brien, Benjamin, Blockley, Stubbs, Carter, McCulloch (Wood) Hooks, Mann, Vinter.
Scunthorpe U: Crawford; O'Donnell, Peacock, Oates, Deere, Czuczman, Grimes, Gibson, Wigg (Kilmore), Keeley, Pilling.

Peterborough U (0) 1 (*Slough*)
Hull C (1) 2 (*Bannister, Haigh*) 4387
Peterborough U: Waugh; Carmichael, Styles, Doyle, Green, Ross, Slough, McEwan, Butlin, Anderson, Robson (Quow).
Hull C: Wealands; Nisbet, DeVries, Cross, Dobson, Haigh, Hood, Horswill, Edwards, Bannister, Farley.

Sheffield W (0) 0
Doncaster R (1) 1 (*French*) 8055
Sheffield W: Bolder; Shirtliff (Owen), Grant, Rushbury, Dowd, Mullen, Wylde, Porterfield, Tynan, Johnson, Hornsby.
Doncaster R: Peacock; Owen, Robinson, Olney, Bradley, Taylor, Habbin, Lewis, Snodin (Meagan), French, Laidlaw.

Swansea C (4) 5 (*James R 3, 1 a pen, Curtis 2*)
Newport Co (0) 0 8734
Swansea C: Crudgington; Evans, Bartley, Toshack, Bruton, Reeves, Lally, James R, Curtis, Waddle, Moore.
Newport Co: Plumley; Walden, Relish, Byrne (Guscott), Walker, Davies, Warriner, Goddard, Woods, Thompson, Williams.

Swindon T (0) 4 (*Aizlewood, Williams, Miller, Guthrie*)
Portsmouth (0) 2 (*Gilchrist, Pullar*) 7343
Swindon T: Ogden; McLaughlin, Ford, McHale, Aizlewood, Stroud, Miller, Kamara, Guthrie, Bates, Williams.
Portsmouth: Mellor; Ellis, Viney, Denyer, Foster, Hand, Hemmerman, Lathan, Gilchrist, McIlwraith, Pullar.

Wimbledon (3) 4 (*Galvin, Galliers, Cork, Townsend og*)
Southend U (1) 1 (*Donaldson og*) 2687
Wimbledon: Goddard; Bryant, Eames, Galliers, Galvin, Donaldson, Leslie (Ketteridge), Briley, Denny, Cork, Summerill.
Southend U: Horn; Hadley, Yates, Laverick, Townsend, Moody, Morris, Pountney, Parker, Abbott (Dudley), Fell.

York (0) 0
Grimsby T (1) 3 (*Cumming, Mitchell, Donovan*) 2668
York C: Brown; Scott, Kay, Young, Faulkner, Clements, Stronach, Walsh (Wellings), Loggie, McDonald, Staniforth.
Grimsby T: Batch; Mawer, Moore, Waters, Barker, Crombie, Ford, Donovan, Lester (Liddell), Mitchell, Cumming.

16 AUG

Blackpool (1) 2 (*Davidson, McCartney og*)
Carlisle U (1) 1 (*Lumby*) 6617
Blackpool: Ward; Gardner, Milligan, Wilson, Suddaby, McEwan, Spence, Tong, Holden (Hockaday), Wagstaffe, Davidson.
Carlisle U: Swinburne; Hoolickin, McCartney, MacDonald, Tait, Parker, McVitie, Bonnyman, Kemp, Lumby, Hamilton.

Chester (1) 1 (*Livermore*)
Port Vale (1) 1 (*Wright*) 3741
Chester: Lloyd; Raynor, Walker, Storton, Jeffries, Oakes, Delgado (Jones), Livermore, Edwards, Mellor, Phillips.
Port Vale: Connaughton; Wilkinson, Griffiths, Bentley, Sproson, Hawkins, Chamberlain, Bromage, Wright, Beamish, Stenson.

Chesterfield 0
Barnsley 0 6278
Chesterfield: Letheran; Tartt, Burton (Salmons), Hunter, Cottam, O'Neill, Cammack, Fern, Simpson, Flavell, Kowalski.
Barnsley: Springett; Collins, Chambers, Pugh, Saunders, McCarthy, Little, Clarke, Joicey, Millar, Peachey.

Hereford U (1) 4 (*Holmes W, Layton, Emery, Barton*)
Bristol R (0) 0 5130
Hereford U: Hughes; Roberts, Price, Cornes, Layton, Emery, Holmes W, Holmes K, Jones, Powell (Spiring), Barton.
Bristol R: Thomas: Aitken, Bater, Pulis, Taylor, Prince, Dennehy, Williams, Hoult (Gould), Randall, Barry.

Lincoln C (0) 1 (*Hughes*)
Bradford C (0) 1 (*Cooke*) 3806
Lincoln C: Grotier; Wright, Laybourne, Fleming, Wigginton, Cooper, Hobson, Sunley (Ward), Harford, Hughes, Hubbard.
Bradford C: Downsborough; Reaney, Wood, Bates, Baines, Middleton, Johnson (Podd), Dolan, Cooke, McNiven, Hutchins.

Millwall (1) 1 (*Seasman pen*)
Aldershot (0) 0   7060
Millwall: Cuff; Donaldson, Moore, Allen, Kitchener, Hazell, Hamilton J, Hamilton B, Mitchell, Seasman, Pearson (Mehmet).
Aldershot: Johnson; Edwards (Howitt), Wooler, Dixon, Youlden, Earls, Longhorn, Brodie, McGregor, Dungworth, Tomlin.

Northampton T (1) 2 (*Christie, Reilly*)
Cambridge U (1) 1 (*Bailey pen*)   4721
Northampton T: Jayes; Geidmintis, Mead, Woollett, Robertson, Bryant, Farrington, Williams, Reilly, Liddle, Christie (Wassell).
Cambridge U: Webster; Howard, Buckley, Smith, Fallon, Graham, Cozens (Streete), Spriggs, Morgan, Finney, Biley.

Oxford U (2) 2 (*Fogg pen, Duncan*)
Cardiff C (0) 1 (*Bishop*)   4760
Oxford U: Burton; Doyle, Fogg, Briggs, McIntosh, Jeffrey, McGrogan, Taylor, Foley, Curran, Duncan.
Cardiff: Healey; Attley, Pethard, Campbell, Dwyer (Bishop), Thomas, Grapes, Giles, Burns, Went, Buchanan.

Stockport Co (2) 3 (*Lee 2, Bradd*)
Shrewsbury T (0) 1 (*Cross*)   4035
Stockport Co: Rogan; Thorpe, Rutter, Thompson, Park, Fogarty, Summerbee, Goodfellow, Bradd, Loadwick, Lee.
Shrewsbury T: Mulhearn; King, Leonard, Turner, Griffin, Hayes, Cross, Lindsay, Atkins, Biggins, Maguire.

Torquay U (0) 1 (*Murphy*)
Plymouth Arg (0) 2 (*Binney 2*)   6999
Torquay U: Turner; Parsons, Payne, Wilson, Green, Dunne, (Lawrence), Coffill, Darke, Cooper, Murphy, Raper.
Plymouth Arg: Burns; Bason, Rogers, Trusson, Foster, Perrin, Fear, Megson, Binney, Taylor, Johnson.

Wigan Ath (1) 2 (*Corrigan 2*)
Tranmere R (1) 1 (*O'Neil*)   8512
Wigan Ath: Brown; Gore, Hinnigan, Wright, Davids, Gillibrand, Corrigan, Crompton, Haughton, Wilkie, Purdie.
Tranmere R: Johnson; Mathias, Flood, Palios (Kerr), Postlewhite, Evans, Craven, O'Neil, Moore, Peplow, McAuley.

FIRST ROUND REPLAYS

22 AUG

Doncaster R (0) 0
Sheffield W (1) 1 (*Hornsby*)   8472
Doncaster R: Peacock; Owen, Robinson, Olney, Bradley, Taylor, Habbin, Lewis, Snodin, French, Laidlaw.
Sheffield W: Bolder; Blackhall (Owan), Grant, Rushbury, Dowd, Smith, Mullen, Porterfield, Tynan, Johnson, Hornsby.

Hull C (0) 0
Peterborough U (0) 1 (*Butlin*)   4996
Hull C: Wealands; Nisbet, DeVries, Croft, Dobson, Haigh, Hood, Horswill, Edwards, Bannister, Farley.
Peterborough U: Waugh; Carmichael, Styles, Doyle, Green, Ross, Slough, McEwan, Butlin, Anderson, Robson.

SECOND ROUND

28 AUG

Sheffield U (0) 1 (*Hamson*)
Liverpool (0) 0   35,753
Sheffield U: Conroy; Cutbush, Garner, Keeley, Matthews, Speight, Woodward, Stainrod, Finnieston (Franks), Hamson, Sabella.
Liverpool: Clemence; Neal, Kennedy A, Thompson, Kennedy R, Hughes, Dalglish, Case (Fairclough), Heighway, McDermott, Souness.

29 AUG

Birmingham C (1) 2 (*Gallagher, Francis*)
Southampton (2) 5 (*Boyer 2, MacDougall 2, Peach*)   18,464
Birmingham C: Montgomery; Page (Towers), Pendrey, Emmanuel, Gallagher, Broadhurst, Barrowclough, Francis, Bertschin, Ainscow, Givens.
Southampton: Wells; Golac, Peach, Williams, Nicholl, Waldron, Ball, Boyer, MacDougall, Andruszewski, Curran.

Bolton W (1) 2 (*Worthington 2, 1 a pen*)
Chelsea (0) 1 (*Langley*)   10,499
Bolton W: McDonagh; Graham, Burke, Greaves, Walsh, Allardyce, Morgan, Whatmore, Gowling, Worthington, Train.
Chelsea: Bonetti; Locke, Harris, Hay, Droy, Wicks, Swain, Wilkins R, Langley, Stanley, Walker.

Brighton & HA (1) 1 (*O'Sullivan*)
Millwall (0) 0   16,748
Brighton & HA: Steele; Tiler, Williams, Horton, Rollings, Lawrenson, Towner (Poskett), Ward, Maybank, Clark, O'Sullivan.
Millwall: Cuff; Donaldson, Moore (Lee), Allen, Kitchener, Hazell, Hamilton B, Seasman, Mitchell, Walker, Mehmet.

Bristol C (0) 1 (*Ritchie*)
Crystal Palace (1) 2 (*Murphy, Swindlehurst*) 10,433
Bristol C: Shaw; Sweeney, Gillies, Mann, Rodgers, Hunter, Tainton, Ritchie, Royle (Garland), Pritchard, Whitehead.
Crystal Palace: Burridge; Hinshelwood, Sansom, Chatterton, Cannon, Gilbert, Murphy, Nicholas, Swindlehurst, Elwiss, Hilaire.

Burnley (0) 1 (*Cochrane*)
Bradford C (0) 1 (*Hutchins*)   9167
Burnley: Stevenson; Scott, Brennan, Noble, Thomson, Rodaway, Cochrane, Ingham, Fletcher, Morley, Smith.
Bradford C: Downsborough; Reaney, Wood, Bates, Baines, Middleton, Podd, Dolan, Jackson (Watson), McNiven, Hutchins.

Everton (3) 8 (*Latchford 5, 1 a pen, Dobson 3*)
Wimbledon (0) 0   23,137
Everton: Wood; Robinson, Pejic, Lyons, Wright, Nulty, King, Dobson, Latchford, Walsh (Ross), Thomas.
Wimbledon: Goddard; Bryant, Eames, Galliers, Galvin, Donaldson, Leslie, Denny, Connell, Cork, Parsons.

Exeter C (0) 2 (*Bowker, Delve*)
Blackburn R (0) 1 (*Gregory*)   4005
Exeter C: O'Keefe; Templeman, Hore, Randell, Giles, Roberts, Hodge, Kellow, Bowker, Delve, Hatch.
Blackburn R: Butcher; Hird, Bailey, Fowler, Keeley, Waddington, Garner, Gregson, Radford, Fazackerley, Aston.

Fulham (2) 2 (*Mahoney, Davies*)
Darlington (2) 2 (*Craig, Wann*) 3894
Fulham: Peyton; Strong, Lock. Money, Banton, Gale, Bullivant, Davies, Mahoney, Margerrison, (Boyd), Evanson
Darlington: Burleigh; Nattrass, Cochrane, Hague, Craig, Stone, Maitland, Lyons, Seal, Probert, Wann.

Luton T (0) 2 (*Stein* 2)
Wigan Ath (0) 0 6618
Luton T: Aleksic; Stephens, Aizlewood, Donaghy. Turner, Price, West, Fuccillo, Stein, Hatton, Moss.
Wigan Ath: Brown; Gore, Smart, Seddon, Ward, Gillibrand, Corrigan, Wright, Houghton, Wilkie (Davids), Purdie.

Manchester C (0) 2 (*Moore og, Palmer*)
Grimsby T (0) 0 21,481
Manchester C: Corrigan; Clements, Power, Keegan, Booth, Futcher P, Channon, Owen, Futcher R (Viljoen), Hartford, Palmer.
Grimsby T: Batch; Mawer, Moore, Waters, Barker, Crombie, Ford, Donovan, Lester. Mitchell, Cumming (Liddell).

Middlesbrough (0) 0
Peterborough U (0) 0 12,803
Middlesbrough: Stewart; Craggs, Bailey, Mahoney, Boam, Ramage, Proctor, Mills, Ashcroft, Woof (Johnston), Armstrong.
Peterborough U: Waugh; Carmichael, Styles, Doyle, Green, Ross, Slough, McEwan, Butlin, Anderson, Robson.

Northampton T (0) 0
Hereford U (0) 0 3991
Northampton T: Jayes; Geidmintis, Mead, Woollett, Robertson, Saunders (Walker), Farrington, Williams, Reilly, Bryant, Christie.
Hereford U: Hughes; Burrows, Price, Cornes, Marshall, Emery, Holmes W, Holmes K, Jones, Spiring, Barton.

Oldham Ath (0) 0
Nottingham F (0) 0 13,793
Oldham Ath: McDonnell; Hoolickin (Edwards), Blair, Gardner, Hicks, Hurst, Steel, Halom, Young, Chapman, Heaton.
Nottingham F: Shilton; Anderson, Barrett, McGovern, Needham, Burns, O'Neill, Gemmill, Elliott, Woodcock, Robertson.

Orient (0) 1 (*Fisher*)
Chesterfield (1) 2 (*Fern, Cammack*) 4667
Orient: Jackson; Fisher, Roffey, Grealish Gray, Hughton, Chiedozie (Godfrey), Banjo, Mayo, Kitchen, Bennett.
Chesterfield: Letheran; Tartt, Burton, Hunter, Cottam, O'Neill, Cammack, Kowalski, Fern, Salmons, Walker.

Preston NE (1) 1 (*Fisher*)
QPR (2) 3 (*Baxter og, Eastoe* 2) 14,913
Preston NE: Tunks; Haslegrave, Williams, Doyle, Baxter, Cross, Burns (Potts), Spavin. Robinson, Thomson, Bruce.
QPR: Parkes; Shanks, Gillard, Hollins, Howe, Roeder, Eastoe, Francis, Busby, Bowles, McGee.

Rotherham U (2) 3 (*Gwyther, Green, Finney*)
Arsenal (1) 1 (*Stapleton*) 10,481
Rotherham U: McAlister; Forrest, Breckin, Rhodes, Green, Flynn, Finney, Phillips, Gwyther, Crawford, Smith.
Arsenal: Jennings; Rice, Nelson, Price, O'Leary, Young, Brady, Sunderland, Macdonald, Stapleton, Rix.

Swansea C (2) 2 (*James R, Charles*)
Tottenham H (1) 2 (*Hoddle, Armstrong*) 24,335
Swansea C: Crudgington; Evans, Bartley, Smith, Stevenson, Charles, Morris, James R, Curtis, Waddle, Moore (Murustik).
Tottenham H: Daines; McAllister, Naylor, Perryman, Lacy, Hoddle, Ardiles (Armstrong), Villa, Duncan, McNab, Taylor.

Walsall (0) 1 (*Buckley pen*)
Charlton Ath (1) 2 (*Peacock, Flanagan*) 4519
Walsall: Kearns; Macken, Caswell, Harrison, Serella, King, Birch, Clarke, Austin, Buckley, Kelly.
Charlton Ath: Wood; Campbell, Berry, Tydeman, Shipperley, Dugdale, Brisley, Hales, Flanagan, Peacock, Gritt.

Watford T (0) 2 (*Blissett* 2)
Newcastle U (1) 1 (*Pearson*) 15,532
Watford T: Rankin; Stirk, Pritchett, Booth, Bolton, Garner, Pollard, Mercer Jenkins, Joslyn (Blissett), Downes.
Newcastle U: Mahoney; Kelly, Barker, Cassidy, Bird, Blackley, Suggett, Pearson (McGhee), Withe, Hibbitt, Connolly.

WBA (0) 0
Leeds U (0) 0 25,064
WBA: Godden; Batson, Statham, Trewick, Wile, Robertson, Robson, Brown A (Martin), Regis, Cunningham, Johnston.
Leeds U: Stewart; Madeley, Gray F, Flynn, Hart, Stevenson, Hampton, Hankin, Hawley, Currie, Graham.

Wrexham (1) 1 (*McNeill pen*)
Norwich C (2) 3 (*Roberts og, Ryan* 2) 12,428
Wrexham: Davies; Hill, Dwyer (Williams), Davis, Roberts, Thomas, Shinton, Sutton, McNeill, Whittle, Cartwright.
Norwich C: Keelan; Bond, Sullivan, Ryan, Hoadley, Powell, Neighbour, Reeves, Chivers, Robson, Peters.

30 AUG

Aston Villa (1) 1 (*Shelton*)
Sheffield W (0) 0 31,152
Aston Villa: Rimmer; Gidman, Smith, Evans, McNaught, Mortimer, Shelton, Little, Gray, Cowans, Carrodus.
Sheffield W: Bolder; Blackhall, Grant, Rushbury, Dowd, Smith, Mullen, Porterfield (Owen), Tynan, Johnson, Hornsby.

Blackpool (1) 2 (*Davidson* 2)
Ipswich T (0) 0 10,029
Blackpool: Ward; Gardner. Pashley, Thompson, Suddaby, McEwan, Hockaday, Ronson, Spence, Davidson, Wilson.
Ipswich T: Cooper, Burley; Mills, Talbot, Osman, Beattie, Parkin (Lambert), Wark, Mariner, Whymark, Woods.

Chester (1) 2 (*Edwards, Mellor*)
Coventry C (0) 1 (*Thompson*) 8598
Chester: Lloyd; Raynor, Walker, Storton, Jeffries, Oakes, Delgado, Livermore, Edwards, Mellor, Phillips.
Coventry C: Sealey; Osgood, McDonald, Beck (Thompson), Holton, Gillespie, Bannister, Wallace, Ferguson, Powell, Hutchison.

Crewe Alex (0) 2 (*Wilshaw, Davies*)
Notts Co (0) 0   3178
Crewe Alex: Caswell; Hughes, Cheetham, Bevan, Bowles, Rimmer, Davies, Roberts, Nelson, Purdie, Wilshaw.
Notts Co: McManus; Richards, O'Brien, Benjamin, Blockley, Stubbs, McCulloch, Masson, Hooks (Hunt), Mann, Vinter.

Leicester C (0) 0
Derby Co (0) 1 (*Hill*)   18,827
Leicester C: Wallington; Whitworth, Rofe, May, Sims, Kelly, Hughes, Goodwin, Christie (Davies), Williams, Armstrong.
Derby Co: Middleton; Langan, Buckley, Daly, McFarland, McCaffrey, Daniel, Nish, Ryan, George, Hill (Chesters).

Oxford U (1) 1 (*Seacole*)
Plymouth Arg (0) 1 (*Fear*)   4255
Oxford U: Burton; Kingston, Fogg, Briggs, Stott, Jeffrey, McGrogan, Taylor, Foley, Seacole, Duncan.
Plymouth Arg: Burns; Bason, Rogers, Brennan, Foster, Perrin, Megson, Fear, Harrison, Trusson, Johnson.

Reading (0) 1 (*Earles*)
Wolverhampton W (0) 0   13,107
Reading: Death; Peters, White, Bowman, Hicks, Bennett, Earles, Hetzke, Kearns, Sanchez, Lewis.
Wolverhampton W: Bradshaw; Daniel, Palmer, Parkin, Berry, McAlle, Hibbitt, Carr, Rafferty, Eves (Bell), Daley.

Stockport Co (0) 2 (*Thompson pen, Park*) at Old Trafford
Manchester U (1) 3 (*Jordan, McIlroy, Greenhoff J pen*)   42,384
Stockport Co: Rogan; Thorpe, Rutter, Thompson, Park, Edwards, Summerbee, Halford, Bradd, Loadwick, Lee.
Manchester U: Roche; Greenhoff B, Albiston, McIlroy, McQueen, Buchan, Coppell, Greenhoff J, Jordan, Macari, Grimes.

Sunderland (0) 0
Stoke C (2) 2 (*Doyle, Irvine*)   12,368
Sunderland: Siddall; Henderson, Bolton, Docherty, Elliott, Ashurst, Kerr, Greenwood, Entwistle, Gilbert, Rowell.
Stoke C: Jones; Marsh, Scott, Kendall, Smith, Doyle, Dodd, Irvine, O'Callaghan, Crooks (Busby), Richardson.

West Ham U (0) 1 (*Robson*)
Swindon T (0) 2 (*Miller, Guthrie*)   19,672
West Ham U: Ferguson; Lampard, Brush, Holland, Taylor T, Bonds, Curbishley, Devonshire, Cross, Taylor A (Pike), Robson.
Swindon T: Ogden; McLaughlin, Ford, McHale, Aizlewood, Stroud, Miller, Carter, Guthrie (Kamara), Bates, Williams.

SECOND ROUND REPLAYS
5 SEPT

Bradford C (2) 2 (*Dolan pen, Baines*)
Burnley (0) 3 (*Noble, Cochrane, Ingham*)   9192
Bradford C: Downsborough; Reaney, Wood, Bates, Baines, Middleton, Podd, Dolan, Cooke, McNiven, Martinez.
Burnley: Stevenson; Scott, Brennan, Noble, Thomson, Rodaway, Cochrane, Ingham, Fletcher, Kindon, Smith.

Darlington (0) 1 (*Lyons pen*)
Fulham (0) 0   5061
Darlington: Burleigh; Nattrass, Cochrane, Hague, Craig, Stone, Maitland, Lyons, Seal, Probert, Wann.
Fulham: Peyton; Strong, Lock, Money, Banton, Gale, Bullivant, Davies, Mahoney, Margerrison, Evanson.

Peterborough U (0) 1 (*Robson*)
Middlesbrough (0) 0   aet 8093
Peterborough U: Waugh; Carmichael, Styles, Doyle, Green, Ross, Slough, McEwan, Butlin, Anderson, Robson.
Middlesbrough: Stewart; Craggs, Bailey, Mahoney (Johnston), Boam, Ramage, Proctor, McAndrew, Ashcroft, Mills, Armstrong.

Plymouth Arg (1) 1 (*Fear pen*)
Oxford U (0) 2 (*Sweetzer, Seacole*)   aet 8424
Plymouth Arg: Burns; Bason, Rogers, Graves, Foster, Perrrin, Megson, Fear, Binney, Trusson, Johnson.
Oxford U: Burton; Taylor, Fogg, Briggs, Bodel, Jeffrey, McGrogan, Sweetzer, Foley (White), Seacole, Duncan.

6 SEPT

Hereford U (0) 0
Northampton T (1) 1 (*Reilly*)   4205
Hereford U: Hughes; Price, Burrows, Cornes (Crompton), Marshall, Emery, Stephens, Holmes K, Jones, Spiring, Bailey.
Northampton T: Jayes; Geidmintis, Mead, Walker, Robertson, Bryant, Farrington, Williams, Reilly, Cordice (Bowen), Christie.

Leeds U 0
WBA 0   aet 29,316
Leeds U: Stewart; Stevenson, Gray F, Flynn, Hart, Madeley, Cherry, Hankin, Hawley, Currie (Gray E), Graham.
WBA: Godden; Batson, Statham, Cunningham, Wile, Robertson, Robson, Brown A, Regis, Cantello, Johnston.

Nottingham F (0) 4 (*Needham, Burns, Woodcock, Robertson pen*)
Oldham Ath (0) 2 (*Halom, Young*)   18,669
Nottingham F: Shilton; Anderson, Barrett, McGovern, Needham, Burns, O'Neill, Gemmill, Elliott, Woodcock, Robertson.
Oldham Ath: McDonnell; Blair, Edwards, Bell, Hicks, Hurst, Valentine (Steel), Halom, Young, Chapman, Gardner.

Tottenham H (0) 1 (*Villa*)
Swansea C (2) 3 (*Toshack, Charles, Curtis*)   33,672
Tottenham H: Daines; Naylor, McAllister, Hoddle, Armstrong, Perryman, Villa, Ardiles, Duncan, Taylor, McNab.
Swansea C: Crudgington; Evans, Bartley, Smith, Bruton, Stevenson, Charles, James R, Curtis, Toshack, Waddle.

SECOND REPLAY
2 OCT

WBA (0) 0
Leeds U (0) 1 (*Hart*)   8164 at Maine Road
WBA: Godden; Batson, Statham, Cunningham, Wile, Robertson, Robson, Brown A, Regis, Cantello, Brown T.
Leeds U: Harvey; Stevenson, Cherry, Flynn, Hart, Madeley, Thomas (Lorimer), Hankin, Gray E, Gray F, Graham.

THIRD ROUND

3 OCT

Burnley (0) 1 (*Brennan*)
Brighton & HA (1) 3 (*Maybank, Ward* 2) 9056
Burnley: Stevenson; Scott, Brennan, Noble, Thomson, Rodaway, Cochrane, Ingham, Fletcher, Kindon, James.
Brighton & HA: Steele; Cattlin, Williams, Horton, Rollings, Lawrenson, Sayer, Ward, Maybank, Clark, O'Sullivan.

Everton (0) 1 (*Dobson*)
Darlington (0) 0 23,682
Everton: Wood; Todd, Pejic, Lyons, Wright, Ross, King, Dobson, Latchford, Walsh, Nulty.
Darlington: Burleigh; Nattrass, Cochrane, Hague, Craig, Stone, Maitland, Lyons, Seal, Probert, Wann.

Luton T (0) 2 (*Hill, Hatton*)
Crewe Alex (0) 1 (*Bowles pen*) 6602
Luton T: Aleksic; Price, Aizlewood, Hill, Turner, Donaghy, West, Fuccillo, Stein, Hatton, Moss.
Crewe Alex: Caswell; Bevan, Roberts, Rimmer, Bowles, Wilshaw, Davies, Purdie, Nelson, Tully (Coyne), Robertson.

Northampton T (1) 1 (*Reilly*)
Stoke C (1) 3 (*Dodd, O'Callaghan, Kendall*) 11,235
Northampton T: Poole; Geidmintis, Mead, Woollett, Robertson, Bryant, Farrington, Williams, Cordice, (Wassell), Reilly, Christie.
Stoke C: Jones; Marsh, Scott, Kendall, Smith, Doyle, Dodd, Heath, O'Callaghan, Crooks, Richardson (Busby).

Peterborough U (0) 1 (*Styles*)
Swindon T (0) 1 (*Aizlewood*) 6132
Peterborough U: Waugh; Hindley, Styles, Doyle, Green, Ross, Carmichael, McEwan, Butlin, Anderson (Robertson), Robson.
Swindon T: Ogden; Trollope, Ford, McHale, Lewis, Stroud, Kamara, Carter, Aizlewood, Bates, Cunningham.

QPR (2) 2 (*McGee, Eastoe*)
Swansea T (0) 0 18,513
QPR: Richardson; Shanks, Gillard, Hollins, Howe, Cunningham, Eastoe, Francis, Harkouk, Bowles (Abbott), McGee.
Swansea C: Crudgington; Evans, Bartley, Smith, Bruton, Stevenson, Boersma (Morris), James R, Waddle, Toshack, Callaghan.

Rotherham U (0) 2 (*Finney pen, Crawford*)
Reading (0) 2 (*Earles* 2) 6847
Rotherham U: McAlister; Forrest, Breckin, Finney, Green, Flynn, Dawson, Phillips, Gwyther, Crawford, Smith.
Reading: Death; Peters, White, Bowman, Hicks, Bennett, Earles, Hetzke, Kearney Sanchez, Lewis.

Southampton (0) 1 (*Boyer*)
Derby Co (0) 0 19,109
Southampton: Gennoe; Golac, Peach (Hebberd), Williams, Nicholl, Waldron, Ball, Boyer, MacDougall, Holmes, Curran.
Derby Co: Middleton; Langan, Buckley, Daly, McFarland (Moreland), McCaffrey, Powell, Clark, Caskey, George, Daniel.

4 OCT

Blackpool (1) 1 (*Spence*)
Manchester C (1) 1 (*Channon*) 18,868
Blackpool: Hesford; Gardner, Pashley, Thompson, Suddaby, McEwan, Chandler, Ronson, Spence (Wagstaffe), Davidson, Hockaday.
Manchester C: Corrigan; Clements, Donachie, Booth, Watson, Power, Channon, Owen, Kidd, Hartford, Barnes (Palmer).

Chester (0) 0
Norwich C (0) 2 (*Reeves, Peters*) 8749
Chester: Lloyd; Nickeas, Raynor, Storton, Jeffries, Oakes, Delgado (Phillips), Livermore, Edwards, Mellor, Walker.
Norwich C: Keelan; Bond, Sullivan, Ryan, Hoadley, Powell, Neighbour, Reeves, Robb, Robson, Peters.

Chesterfield (2) 4 (*Tartt* 2, *Flavell, Walker*)
Charlton Ath (2) 5 (*Robinson* 2, *Peacock* 2, *Flanagan*) 6459
Chesterfield: Letheran; Flavell, Burton, Hunter, O'Neill, Prophett, Tartt, Kowalski, Fern, Salmons, Walker.
Charlton Ath: Wood; Madden, Campbell, Tydeman, Shipperley, Shaw, Robinson, Brisley, Flanagan, Peacock, Gritt.

Exeter C (1) 2 (*Delve, Kellow*)
Bolton W (0) 1 (*Gowling*) 9151
Exeter C: O'Keefe; Templeman, Hore, Randell, Giles, Roberts, Holman, Kellow, Bowker, Delve, Hatch.
Bolton W: Poole; Graham (Reid), Burke, Greaves, Walsh, Allardyce, Morgan, Whatmore, Gowling, Worthington, Smith.

Manchester U (1) 1 (*Jordan*)
Watford (0) 2 (*Blissett* 2) 40,534
Manchester U: Roche; Albiston, Houston, Greenhoff B (McCreery), McQueen, Buchan, Coppell, Greenhoff J, Jordan, McIlroy, Grimes.
Watford: Rankin; Stirk, Harrison, Booth, Bolton, Garner, Pollard, Blissett, Jenkins, Joslyn, Downes.

Oxford (0) 0
Nottingham F (3) 5 (*Birtles, McGovern, O'Neill, Robertson, Anderson*) 14,287
Oxford: Burton; Fogg, Watson, Bodel, McIntosh, Jeffrey, McGrogan, Taylor, Foley, Curran (White), Seacole.
Nottingham F: Shilton; Anderson, Bowyer, McGovern, Lloyd, Burns, O'Neill, Gemmill, Birtles, Woodcock (O'Hare) Robertson.

Aston Villa (1) 1 (*Little*)
Crystal Palace (0) 1 (*Chatterton pen*) 30,690
Aston Villa: Rimmer; Gregory, Williams, Evans, McNaught, Mortimer, Craig, Little, Deehan, Shelton (Phillips), Carrodus.
Crystal Palace: Burridge; Hinshelwood, Sansom, Chatterton, Cannon, Gilbert, Nicholas, Murphy, Swindlehurst, Elwiss, Hilaire.

10 OCT

Sheffield U (0) 1 (*Calvert*)
Leeds U (2) 4 (*Currie, Gray F, Gray E* 2) 40,899
Sheffield U: Johns; Cutbush, Calvert, Kenworthy, Matthews, Speight, Anderson, Harwood, Finnieston, Sabella, Hamson.
Leeds U: Harvey; Stevenson, Cherry, Flynn, Hart, Hampton, Gray E, Hankin, Gray F, Currie, Graham.

THIRD ROUND REPLAYS

Crystal Palace 0
Aston Villa 0 aet 33,155
Crystal Palace: Burridge; Hinshelwood, Sansom, Chatterton, Cannon, Gilbert, Nicholas, Murphy, Swindlehurst (Walsh), Elwiss, Hilaire.
Aston Villa: Rimmer; Gregory, Williams, Evans, McNaught (Ormsby), Mortimer, Craig, Deehan, Gray, Phillips, Carrodus.

Manchester C (0) 3 (*Owen 2, 1 a pen, Booth*)
Blackpool (0) 0 26,213
Manchester C: Corrigan; Clements, Donachie, Booth, Watson, Kidd, Palmer, Owen, Futcher R, Hartford, Barnes.
Blackpool: Hesford; Gardner, Pashley, Thompson, Suddaby, McEwan, Chandler, Ronson, Spence, Davidson, Hockaday.

Swindon T (0) 0
Peterborough U (0) 2 (*Styles, Doyle*) aet 7764
Swindon T: Ogden; Trollope, Ford, McHale, Lewis (Miller), Stroud, Kamara, Carter, Aizlewood, Bates, Cunningham.
Peterborough U: Waugh; Hindley, Styles, Doyle, Green, Ross, Carmichael, McEwan, Butlin, Anderson, Robson.

Reading (1) 1 (*Hetzke*)
Rotherham U (0) 0 12,221
Reading: Death; Peters, White, Bowman, Hicks, Bennett, Earles, Hetzke, Kearney, Sanchez, Lewis.
Rotherham U: McAlister, Pugh, Breckin, Finney, Green, Forrest, Dawson, Phillips, Gwyther, Crawford, Smith.

SECOND REPLAY

16 OCT

Aston Villa (2) 3 (*Gray 2, Gregory*)
Crystal Palace (0) 0 at Coventry 25,445
Aston Villa: Rimmer; Gidman, Williams, Phillips, McNaught, Mortimer, Craig, Little, Gray, Gregory, Carrodus.
Crystal Palace: Burridge; Hinshelwood, Sansom, Chatterton, Cannon (Fenwick), Gilbert, Nicholas, Murphy, Walsh, Elwiss, Hilaire.

FOURTH ROUND

7 NOV

Brighton & HA (0) 1 (*Lawrence*)
Peterborough U (0) 0 21,421
Brighton & HA: Moseley; Tiler, Williams, Horton, Winstanley, Lawrenson, Sayer, Poskett, Maybank (Ward), Clark, O'Sullivan.
Peterborough U: Waugh; Hindley, Styles, Doyle, Green, Ross, Slough, McEwan, Robertson, Anderson, Robson.

Charlton Ath (1) 2 (*Shipperley 2*)
Stoke C (2) 3 (*Irvine, Busby, Crooks pen*) 18,467
Charlton Ath: Wood; Shaw, Campbell (Peacock), Tydeman, Shipperley, Berry, Brisley, Robinson, Flanagan, Madden, Gritt.
Stoke C: Jones; Marsh, Scott, Kendall, Smith, Dodd, Conroy, Irvine, O'Callaghan, Busby (Crooks), Richardson.

493

Everton (1) 2 (*Burns og, Latchford*)
Nottingham F (0) 3 (*Lloyd, Anderson, Woodcock*) 48,503
Everton: Wood; Darracott, Pejic, Todd, Wright, Ross, King, Dobson, Latchford, Walsh, Thomas.
Nottingham F: Shilton; Anderson, Bowyer, O'Hare, Lloyd, Burns (Mills), Gemmill, Needham, Birtles, Woodcock, Robertson.

QPR (0) 0
Leeds U (0) 2 (*Hawley, Hankin*) 22,769
QPR: Parkes; Clement, Gillard, Hollins, Howe, Shanks, Eastoe, Busby, Harkouk (Cunningham), Bowles, McGee.
Leeds U: Harvey; Cherry, Gray F, Flynn, Hart, Madeley, Gray E, Hankin, Hawley, Currie, Graham.

8 NOV

Aston Villa (0) 0
Luton T (0) 2 (*Hatton, Stein*) 32,737
Aston Villa: Rimmer; Gidman, Williams, Evans, McNaught, Mortimer, Craig, Little, Gray (Cowans), Deehan, Gregory.
Luton T: Aleksic; Price, Aizlewood, Hill, Turner, Donaghy, West, Fuccillo, Stein, Hatton, Moss.

Exeter C (0) 0
Watford (1) 2 (*Pritchett pen, Jenkins*) 14,740
Exeter C: O'Keefe; Templeman, Hore, Randell (Holman), Giles, Roberts, Neville, Kellow, Bowker, Delve, Hatch.
Watford: Rankin; Stirk, Pritchett, Booth, Bolton, Garner, Blissett, Mercer (Joslyn), Jenkins, Downes, Mayes.

Norwich C (1) 1 (*Peters*)
Manchester C (0) 3 (*Barnes, Channon 2*) 19,413
Norwich C: Keelan; Bond, Davies, Ryan, Hoadley, Powell, Neighbour, Reeves, Symonds, Mendham, Peters.
Manchester C: Corrigan; Clements, Donachie, Booth, Watson, Viljoen (Futcher P), Channon, Owen, Kidd, Hartford, Barnes.

Reading (0) 0
Southampton (0) 0 24,046
Reading: Death; Peters, White, Bowman, Hicks, Bennett, Earles, Kearns (Sanchez), Kearney, Hetzke, Lewis.
Southampton: Gennoe; Golac, Peach, Williams, Nicholl, Waldron, Ball, Boyer, Hebberd, Holmes, Curran.

FOURTH ROUND REPLAY

14 NOV

Southampton (2) 2 (*Hebberd, Nicholl*)
Reading (0) 0 22,892
Southampton: Gennoe; Golac, Andruszewski, Williams, Nicholl, Waldron, Ball, Boyer, Hebberd, Holmes, Curran (Hayes).
Reading: Death; Peters, White, Bowman, Hicks, Bennett, Earles, Hetzke (Kearns), Kearney, Sanchez, Lewis.

FIFTH ROUND

12 DEC

Southampton (1) 2 (*Boyer, Hebberd*)
Manchester C (0) 1 (*Nicholl og*) 21,500
Southampton: Gennoe; Golac, Peach, Williams, Nicholl, Waldron, Ball, Boyer, Hebberd, Holmes, Curran.
Manchester C: Corrigan; Donachie (Barnes), Power, Booth, Watson, Owen, Channon, Bell, Kidd, Hartford, Deyna.

13 DEC

Leeds U (1) 4 (*Cherry, Currie, Gray E, Gray F pen*)
Luton T (0) 1 (*Stein*)   28,177
Leeds U: Harvey; Cherry, Gray F, Flynn, Hart, Madeley, Gray E, Hankin, Hawley, Currie, Harris.
Luton T: Findlay; Price, Aizlewood, Hill, Turner, Donaghy, West, Fuccillo, Stein, Hatton, Moss.

Nottingham F (1) 3 (*McGovern, Robertson, Birtles*)
Brighton & HA (0) 1 (*Ward*)   30,672
Nottingham F: Shilton; Anderson, Clark, McGovern, Needham, Lloyd, Bowyer, Gemmill, Birtles, Woodcock, Robertson.
Brighton & HA: Moseley; Cattlin, Williams, Horton, Rollings, Lawrenson, Poskett, Ward, Maybank (Clark), Sayer, O'Sullivan.

Stoke C 0
Watford 0   26,070
Stoke C: Jones; Dodd, Scott, Kendall, Smith, Doyle, Heath, Irvine, O'Callaghan, Crooks, Richardson.
Watford: Sherwood; Stirk, Pritchett, Booth, Bolton, Garner, Pollard, Blissett, Jenkins, Joslyn, Downes.

FIFTH ROUND REPLAY

9 JAN

Watford (1) 3 (*Jenkins, Blissett* 2)
Stoke (0) 1 (*Richardson*) aet   21,419
Watford: Sherwood; Stirk, Pritchett, Booth, Bolton, Garner, Pollard, Blissett, Jenkins, Joslyn, Mayes.
Stoke: Jones; Dodd, Bowers, Kendall, Smith, Doyle, McGroarty, Irvine, O'Callaghan, Crooks, Richardson.

SEMI-FINAL FIRST LEG

17 JAN

Nottingham F (1) 3 (*Birtles* 2, *Robertson*)
Watford (1) 1 (*Blissett*)   32,538
Nottingham F: Shilton; Anderson, Clark, McGovern, Lloyd, Needham, O'Neill, Bowyer, Birtles, Woodcock, Robertson.
Watford: Sherwood; Stirk, Pritchett, Booth, Bolton Garner, Pollard, Blissett, Jenkins, Joslyn, Cassells (Mayes).

24 JAN

Leeds U (1) 2 (*Currie, Hankin*)
Southampton (0) 2 (*Holmes, Williams*)   33,415
Leeds: Harvey; Cherry, Gray F, Flynn, Hart, Madeley, Gray E, Hankin, Hawley, Currie, Graham (Harris).
Southampton: Gennoe; Golac, Peach, Williams, Nicholl, Waldron, Ball, Boyer, Hebberd, Holmes, Curran.

SEMI-FINALS SECOND LEG

30 JAN

Southampton (1) 1 (*Curran*)
Leeds U (0) 0   23,645
Southampton: Gennoe; Golac, Peach, Williams, Nicholl, Waldron, Ball, Andruszewski (Baker), Hebberd, Holmes, Curran.
Leeds U: Harvey; Cherry, Gray F, Flynn, Hart, Madeley, Gray E, Hankin, Hawley (Harris), Currie, Graham.

Watford 0
Nottingham F 0   27,656
Watford: Sherwood; Stirk, Harrison, Booth, Bolton, Garner, Pollard (Mercer), Blissett, Jenkins, Joslyn, Downes.
Nottingham F: Shilton; Anderson, Bowyer, McGovern, Lloyd, Burns, O'Neill, Gemmill, Birtles, Woodcock, Robertson.

FINAL

17 MARCH

Nottingham F (0) 3 (*Birtles* 2, *Woodcock*)
Southampton (1) 2 (*Peach, Holmes*)
    100,000 at Wembley
Nottingham F: Shilton; Barrett, Clark, McGovern, Lloyd, Needham, O'Neill, Gemmill, Birtles, Woodcock, Robertson.
Southampton: Gennoe; Golac, Peach, Williams, Nicholl, Waldron, Ball, Boyer, Hayes (Sealy), Holmes, Curran.

FOOTBALL LEAGUE CUP FINALS 1961-1978

Final 1960-61: Rotherham U 2 Aston Villa 0 (First leg, Rotherham, 12,226, 22 August, 1961)
Scorers—Webster, Kirkman.
Aston Villa 3 Rotherham U 0 (after extra time) (Second leg, Villa Park, 27,000, 5 September, 1961)
Scorers—O'Neill, Burrows, McParland. *Aston Villa won on aggregate 3-2.*

Final 1961-62: Rochdale 0 Norwich C 3 (First leg, Rochdale, 11,123, 26 April, 1962)
Scorers—Lythgoe 2, Punton.
Norwich C 1 Rochdale 0 (Second leg, Norwich, 19,708, 1 May 1962)
Scorer—Hill. *Norwich C won on aggregate 4-0*

Final 1962-63: Birmingham C 3 Aston Villa 1 (First leg, St Andrews, 31,850, 23 May, 1963)
Scorers—Birmingham C: Leek 2, Bloomfield. Aston Villa: Thomson.
Aston Villa 0 Birmingham C 0 (Second leg, Villa Park, 37,921, 27 May, 1963)
Birmingham C won on aggregate 3-1

Final 1963-64: Stoke C 1 Leicester C 1 (First leg, Stoke, 22,309, 15 April, 1964)
Scorers—Stoke C: Bebbington. Leicester C: Gibson.
Leicester C 3 Stoke C 2 (Second leg, Leicester, 25,372, 22 April, 1964)
Scorers—Leicester C: Stringfellow, Gibson, Riley. Stoke C: Viollet, Kinnell.
Leicester C won on aggregate 4-3

Final 1964-65: Chelsea 3 Leicester C 2 (First leg, Stamford Bridge, 20,690, 15 March, 1965)
Scorers—Chelsea: Tambling, Venables (penalty), McCreadie. Leicester C: Appleton, Goodfellow.
Leicester C 0 Chelsea 0 (Second leg, Leicester, 26,957, 5 April, 1965)
Chelsea won on aggregate 3-2

Final 1965-66: West Ham U 2 WBA 1 (First leg, Upton Park, 28,341, 9 March, 1966)
Scorers—West Ham U: Moore, Byrne. West Bromwich Albion: Astle.
WBA 4 West Ham U 1 (Second leg, WBA, 31,925, 23 March, 1966)
Scorers—WBA: Kaye, Brown, Clark, Williams. West Ham U: Peters. *WBA won on aggregate 5-3*

Final 1966-67: QPR 3 WBA 2 (At Wembley, 97,952, receipts £57,000, 4 March, 1967)
Scorers—QPR: Morgan (R.), Marsh, Lazarus. WBA: Clark (C) 2.

Final 1967-68: Leeds U 1 Arsenal 0 (At Wembley, 97,887, receipts £95,000, 2 March, 1968)
Scorer: Cooper.

Final 1968-69: Arsenal 1 Swindon T 3 (At Wembley, 98,189, receipts £104,000, 15 March, 1969)
Scorers—Arsenal: Gould. Swindon T: Smart, Rogers 2.

Final 1969-70: Manchester C 2 WBA 1 (At Wembley, 97,963, receipts £123,000, 7 March, 1970)
Scorers—Manchester City: Doyle, Pardoe. WBA: Astle.

Final 1970-71: Aston Villa 0 Tottenham H 2 (At Wembley, 100,000, receipts £132,000, 27 February, 1971)
Scorer—Chivers 2.

Final 1971-72: Chelsea 1 Stoke City 2 (At Wembley, 100,000, receipts £132,000, 4 March, 1972)
Scorers—Chelsea: Osgood. Stoke: Conroy, Eastham.

Final 1972-73: Tottenham H 1 Norwich C 0 (At Wembley, 100,000, receipts £132,000, 3 March, 1973)
Scorer—Coates.

Final 1973-74: Wolverhampton W 2 Manchester C 1 (At Wembley, 100,000, receipts £165,500, 2 March, 1974).
Scorers—Wolverhampton W: Hibbitt, Richards. Manchester C: Bell.

Final 1974-75: Aston Villa 1 Norwich C 0 (At Wembley, 100,000, receipts £196,000, 1 March 1975)
Scorer—Graydon.

Final 1975-76: Manchester C 2 Newcastle U 1 (At Wembley, 100,000, receipts £299,601·16 28 February 1976).
Scorers—Manchester City: Barnes, Tueart. Newcastle U: Gowling.

Final 1976-77: Aston Villa 0 Everton 0 (at Wembley, 100,000, receipts £301,000, 12 March, 1977)
Replay: Aston Villa 1 Everton 1 (at Hillsborough, 16 March 1978).
Scorers—Aston Villa: Kenyon og. Everton: Latchford.
Second replay: Aston Villa 3 Everton 2 (at Old Trafford 54,749, 13 April, 1978)
Scorers—Aston Villa: Little 2, Nicholl. Everton: Latchford, Lyons.

Final 1977-78: Nottingham F 0 Liverpool 0 (at Wembley, 100,000, receipts £425,000, 18 March, 1978).
Replay: Nottingham F 1 Liverpool 0 (at Old Trafford, 54,375, 22 March 1978).
Scorer—Robertson pen.

Alliance Premier League

The 1979-80 season sees the start of the Alliance Premier League, a competition for the most ambitious clubs from the Northern Premier League and Southern League.

Seven Northern Premier sides – Altrincham, Bangor City, Barrow, Boston United, Northwich Victoria, Scarborough and Stafford Rangers and thirteen from the Southern League – Barnet, Bath City, Gravesend and Northfleet, Kettering Town, AP Leamington, Maidstone United, Nuneaton Borough, Redditch United, Telford United, Wealdstone, Weymouth, Worcester City and Yeovil Town will form the new league.

The champions of the Alliance (if their ground meets the requirements of the Football League) will go forward for election into the Football League with the bottom four clubs seeking re-election to the Fourth Division of the Football League.

INTERNATIONAL SEMI-PROFESSIONAL TOURNAMENT 1979

England, Holland, Italy and Scotland competed in a semi-professional tournament, the matches being played at Northwich Victoria FC's ground and that of Stafford Rangers FC between May 31 and June 3 1979.

May 31 1979, Northwich (first semi-final)
Holland 3 Italy 0

May 31 1979, Stafford (second semi-final)
England 5 (*Adamson 3, 2 pens, Mutrie, Whitbread*)
Scotland 1   1,350
England: Arnold; Thompson (Simonite), Davison, Adamson, Peake, Jennings, O'Keefe, Phillips, Mutrie, Houghton (Watson), Whitbread

June 2 1979, Northwick (*match for third place*)
Italy 2 Scotland 1

June 3 1979, Stafford (Final)

England 1 (*O'Keefe*)
Holland 0   2,138
England: Arnold; Thompson (Simonite), Davison, Adamson, Peake, Jennings, O'Keefe, Phillips, Mutrie, Watson, Whitbread

England squad: J. Arnold (Stafford R.), B. Thompson (Yeovil T.), J. Davison (Altrincham), D. Adamson (Boston U.), T. Peake (Nuneaton B), A. Jennings (Enfield) (capt.), E. O'Keefe (Mossley), B. Phillips (Nuneaton B), L. Mutrie (Blyth Spartans), J. Watson (Wealdstone), B. Whitbread (Runcorn), G. Simonite (Boston U.), B. Parker (Yeovil T.), K. Houghton (Blyth Spartans), R. Clayton (Kettering), S. Chapman (Stafford R.).

PLAYFAIR FOOTBALL ANNUAL 1979-80

Edited by Peter Dunk and Lionel Francis

The hugely successful pocket-sized guide to the football season containing all the most important facts and figures of British and international football.

80p paperback   **256 pp**

F.A. NON-LEAGUE FOOTBALL ANNUAL 1979-80

Edited by Tony Williams

The only annual of its kind, this popular title in the *Playfair* series contains information on more than 300 leading non-league clubs.

85p paperback   **304pp**
4pp black and white photos

Available from bookshops or in case of difficulty send cheque/PO payable to Macdonald & Jane's to: QAP Direct Sales, 9 Partridge Drive, Orpington, Kent, England, including 10% postage and packing (UK only). Please allow up to 28 days for delivery, subject to availability.

Football League Representative Teams 1891-1976

1891 Alliance	1892 Scot. Lge.	1893 Scot. Lge.	1894 Irish Lge.	1894 Scot. Lge.
1 Trainer	1 Reader	1 Rowley	1 Reader	1 Sutcliffe
2 Brandon	2 Holmes	2 Clare	2 Howarth	2 Crabtree
3 Ross	3 Gow	3 Howarth	3 Thickett	3 Holmes
4 Calderhead	4 Reynolds	4 Needham	4 Perry	4 Reynolds
5 Dewar	5 Gardiner	5 Perry	5 Holt	5 Holt
6 Wilson	6 Groves	6 Reynolds	6 Crabtree	6 Needham
7 Athersmith	7 Bassett	7 Bassett	7 Wykes	7 Athersmith
8 McInnes	8 McInnes	8 Geary	8 Hammond	8 Goodall
9 Goodall	9 Goodall	9 Southworth	9 Geary	9 Devey
10 Chadwick	10 Chadwick	10 Wood	10 Wheldon	10 Wheldon
11 Daft	11 Daft	11 Schofield	11 Wood	11 Spikesley
Millwall April 20: 1-1 *Chadwick*	Bolton April 11: 2-2 *Bassett, McInnes*	Glasgow April 8: 4-3 *Begbie (og), Wood, Geary, Bassett*	Belfast Feb. 10: 4-2 *Wheldon, Geary, Wykes, A.N.Other*	Liverpool April 21: 1-1 *Goodall*

1895 Scot. Lge.	1895 Irish Lge.	1896 Scot. Lge.	1896 Irish Lge.	1897 Scot. Lge.
1 Storer	1 Baddeley	1 Sutcliffe	1 Reader	1 Sutcliffe
2 Holmes	2 Eccles G	2 Spencer	2 Spencer	2 Spencer
3 Crabtree	3 Swift J	3 Williams	3 Williams	3 Williams
4 Reynolds	4 Turner	4 Perry	4 Higgins W	4 Crabtree
5 Crawshaw	5 Chatt	5 Higgins J	5 Higgins J	5 Crawshaw
6 Needham	6 Chapman	6 Crabtree	6 Malpas	6 Needham
7 Athersmith	7 Williams	7 Athersmith	7 Bassett	7 Athersmith
8 Becton	8 Finnerhan	8 Bloomer	8 Bloomer	8 Bloomer
9 Devey	9 McCairns	9 Goodall	9 Beats	9 Devey
10 Hodgetts	10 Flewitt	10 Becton	10 Wood	10 Chadwick
11 Smith S	11 Dorrell	11 Devey	11 Bradshaw	11 Bradshaw
Glasgow April 13: 4-1 *Devey, Becton 3*	Stoke Nov. 9: 2-2 *Williams, Finnerhan*	Liverpool April 11: 5-1 *Devey, Athersmith, Becton 2, Goodall*	Belfast Nov. 7: 2-0 *Beats, Bloomer*	Glasgow April 24: 0-3

1897 Irish Lge.	1898 Scot. Lge.	1898 Irish Lge.	1899 Scot. Lge.	1899 Irish Lge.
1 Williams	1 Foulke	1 Sutcliffe	1 Hillman	1 Hillman
2 Earp	2 Thickett	2 Crabtree	2 Prescott	2 Spencer
3 Pumfrey	3 Langley	3 Williams	3 Crabtree	3 Williams
4 Booth	4 Perry	4 Booth	4 Frank Forman	4 Fitchett
5 Morren	5 Morren	5 Crawshaw	5 Crawshaw	5 Leeming
6 Holmes	6 Needham	6 Needham	6 Settle	6 Needham
7 Bryant	7 Athersmith	7 Forman	7 Athersmith	7 Johnson
8 Bloomer	8 Wood	8 Bloomer	8 Bloomer	8 Bloomer
9 Beats	9 Beats	9 Farrall	9 Toman	9 Beats
10 Wheldon	10 Wheldon	10 Fletcher	10 Eccles	10 Settle
11 Schofield	11 Smith S	11 Turner J	11 Turner J	11 Hurst
Manchester Nov. 6: 8-1 *Bloomer 2, Beats 2, Wheldon 2, Schofield 2*	Birmingham April 8: 1-2 *Beats*	Belfast Nov. 5: 5-1 *Bloomer, Farrall 2, Fletcher, Needham*	Glasgow April 1: 4-1 *Athersmith 2, Bloomer, Settle*	Bolton Nov. 11: 3-1 *Bloomer 2, Settle*

1900 Scot. Lge.	1900 Irish Lge.	1901 Scot. Lge.	1901 Irish Lge.	1902 Scot. Lge.
1 Foulke	1 Kingsley	1 Kingsley	1 George	1 Kingsley
2 Spencer	2 Layton	2 Balmer	2 Glover	2 Crompton
3 Crabtree	3 Evans	3 Crabtree	3 Iremonger J	3 Iremonger J
4 Griffiths	4 Needham	4 Bull	4 Fitchett	4 Wolstenholme
5 Wigmore	5 Forman	5 Bannister	5 Crawshaw	5 Bannister
6 Norris	6 Fitchett	6 Needham	6 Abbot	6 Houlker
7 Athersmith	7 Sharp	7 Whittaker	7 Goddard	7 Hogg
8 Bloomer	8 Bloomer	8 Athersmith	8 Bloomer	8 Bloomer
9 Hedley	9 Hogg	9 Raybould	9 Wood	9 Beats
10 Settle	10 Sagar	10 Sagar	10 Wooldridge	10 Settle
11 Miller	11 Cox	11 Blackburn	11 Wharton	11 Cox
Crystal Palace March 31: 2-2 *Bloomer, Hedley*	Belfast Nov. 10: 4-2 *Hogg 3, Bloomer*	Glasgow March 16: 2-6 *Athersmith, Raybould*	Plumstead, London Nov. 9: 9-0 *Bloomer 4, Wooldridge 3, Wood 2*	Newcastle March 8: 6-3 *Bloomer 2, Cox, Hogg 3*

1902 Irish Lge.	1903 Scot. Lge.	1903 Irish Lge.	1904 Scot. Lge.	1904 Irish Lge.
1 Baddeley	1 Baddeley	1 Sutcliffe	1 Baddeley	1 Ashcroft
2 Glover	2 Spencer	2 Spencer	2 Crompton	2 Jones J
3 Iremonger J	3 Crompton	3 Iremonger J	3 Burgess	3 Burgess
4 Nurse	4 Johnson	4 Frost	4 Frost	4 Ashworth
5 Booth	5 Booth	5 Crawshaw	5 Greenhalgh	5 Crawshaw
6 McDonald	6 Abbott	6 Needham	6 Abbot	6 Bradshaw
7 Hogg	7 Davies	7 Sharp	7 Rutherford	7 Stokes
8 Bloomer	8 Bloomer	8 Bloomer	8 Bloomer	8 Shearman
9 Calvey	9 Raybould	9 Hogg	9 Raybould	9 Jones W H
10 Sagar	10 Capes	10 Sagar	10 Shearman	10 Munday
11 Lipsham	11 Spiksley	11 Lockett	11 Cox	11 Bridgett
Belfast Oct. 11: 3-2 *Bloomer 2, Calvey*	Glasgow March 14: 3-0 *Spiksley, Raybould, Davies*	Bradford Oct. 10: 2-1 *Bloomer, Sagar*	Manchester April 4: 2-1 *Bloomer, Raybould*	Belfast Oct. 15: 2-0 *Stokes, Jones*

1905 Scot. Lge.	1905 Irish Lge.	1906 Scot. Lge.	1906 Irish Lge.	1907 Scot. Lge.
1 Linacre	1 Maskrey	1 Ashcroft	1 Robinson	1 Robinson
2 Spencer	2 Glover	2 Glover	2 Spencer	2 Crompton
3 Burgess	3 Burgess	3 Burgess	3 Carr	3 Pennington
4 Wolstenholme	4 Makepeace	4 Warren	4 Warren	4 Warren
5 Roberts	5 Sands	5 Veitch	5 Roberts	5 Roberts
6 Leake	6 Bradshaw	6 Bradley	6 Craythorne	6 Abbott
7 Stokes	7 Dorsett	7 Bond	7 Sharp	7 Stokes
8 Bloomer	8 Rouse	8 Common	8 Coleman	8 Coleman
9 Parkinson	9 Hampton	9 Shepherd	9 Hilsdon	9 Thornley
10 Bache	10 Veitch	10 Bache	10 Rouse	10 Bache
11 Hardman	11 Lipsham	11 Conlin	11 Bridgett	11 Hall
Glasgow March 11: 3-2 *Roberts, Bloomer, Parkinson*	Manchester Oct. 14: 4-0 *Hampton 2, Veitch 2*	Chelsea March 24: 6-2 *Shepherd 4 Common, Bache*	Belfast Oct. 13: 6-0 *Sharp, Coleman, Hilsdon 3, Rouse*	Glasgow March 2: 0-0

1907 Irish Lge.	1908 Scot. Lge.	1908 Irish Lge.	1909 Scot. Lge.	1909 Irish Lge.
1 Williamson	1 Hardy	1 Hardy	1 Hardy	1 Matthews
2 Crompton	2 Crompton	2 Crompton	2 Crompton	2 Benson
3 Burgess	3 Burgess	3 Maltby	3 Whitson	3 Cowell
4 Greenhalgh	4 Warren	4 Warren	4 Hunt	4 Greenhalgh
5 Crawshaw	5 Wedlock	5 Wedlock	5 Roberts	5 Wedlock
6 Makepeace	6 Greenhalgh	6 Makepeace	6 Makepeace	6 Lintott
7 Raine	7 Tickle	7 Wallace	7 Stokes	7 Goddard
8 Hibbert	8 Smith J	8 Woodward	8 Latheron	8 Holley
9 Thornley	9 Hilsdon	9 Halse	9 Woodward	9 Freeman
10 Bache	10 West	10 Bradshaw	10 Bradshaw	10 Stewart
11 Hilton	11 Hall	11 Mordue	11 Smith A	11 Wall
Sunderland Oct. 12: 6-3 *Hibbert, Crawshaw 2, Thornley, Bache, Hilton*	Villa Park, Birmingham Feb. 29: 2-0 *Greenhalgh, Hilsdon*	Belfast Oct. 10: 5-0 *Woodward 2, Mordue, Warren, Halse*	Glasgow Feb. 27: 1-3 *Woodward*	Oldham Oct. 9: 8-1 *Freeman 4, Benson, Lintott, Holley, Stewart*

1910 Scot. Lge.	1910 Southern Lge.	1910 Irish Lge.	1910 Southern Lge.	1911 Scot. Lge.
1 Dawson	1 Lievesley	1 Williamson	1 Lunn	1 Dawson
2 Crompton	2 Downs	2 Balmer	2 Johnston	2 Crompton
3 Hayes	3 Rodway	3 Maltby	3 Maltby	3 Pennington
4 Brittleton	4 Taylor	4 Duckworth	4 Duckworth	4 Veitch
5 Harrop	5 Harrop	5 Buckley	5 Buckley	5 Roberts
6 Makepeace	6 Moffat	6 Veitch	6 Bradshaw	6 Bradshaw
7 Garbutt	7 Goddard	7 Broad	7 Mordue	7 Simpson
8 Holley	8 Stewart	8 Holley	8 Coleman	8 Bloomer
9 Parkinson	9 Parkinson	9 Hibbert	9 Hibbert	9 Shepherd
10 Bache	10 Bache	10 Stewart	10 Stewart	10 Bache
11 Wall	11 Middlemiss	11 Conlin	11 Wall	11 Henshall
Blackburn Feb. 26: 2-3 *Brittleton, Parkinson*	Chelsea April 11: 2-2 *Stewart, Parkinson*	Belfast Oct. 8: 6-2 *Holley, Hibbert, Stewart 2, Conlin 2*	Tottenham Nov. 14: 2-3 *Bradshaw, Hibbert*	Ibrox Park March 4: 1-1 *Henshall*

1911 Southern Lge.	1911 Irish Lge.	1912 Scot. Lge.	1912 Southern Lge.	1912 Irish Lge.
1 Iremonger A	1 Iremonger A	1 Williamson	1 Williamson	1 Williamson
2 Hofton	2 Hofton	2 Crompton	2 Longworth	2 Crompton
3 Pennington	3 Pennington	3 Pennington	3 Fletcher	3 Pennington
4 Duckworth	4 Duckworth	4 Duckworth	4 Moffat	4 Brittleton
5 Roberts	5 Roberts	5 Boyle	5 Fay	5 Roberts
6 Hunter	6 Hunter	6 Fay	6 McNeal	6 McNeal
7 Simpson	7 Simpson	7 Wallace	7 Goddard	7 Simpson
8 Halse	8 Halse	8 Buchan	8 Buchan	8 Buchan
9 Hampton	9 Hampton	9 Freeman	9 West	9 Freeman
10 Buck	10 Buck	10 Holley	10 Bradshaw	10 Bradshaw
11 Shearman	11 Shearman	11 Mordue	11 Wall	11 Wall
Stoke Oct. 9: 2-1 *Roberts, Hampton*	Anfield Oct. 16: 4-0 *Hampton 4*	Middlesbrough Feb. 17: 2-0 *Freeman, Mordue*	Old Trafford Sept. 30: 2-1 *Buchan, Bradshaw*	Belfast Oct. 23: 0-0

The European Cup remained in England when Nottingham Forest defeated Malmo 1–0 in the final. The picture shows the winning goal, brilliantly headed by Trevor Francis.

It was Liverpool's year in the League, and also Kenny Dalglish's: he was the overwhelming choice for Footballer of the Year.

Frank Stapleton scores Arsenal's second goal in the FA Cup final. At that point the Gunners looked home and dry, but an astonishing finish saw Manchester United draw level, only to lose to a last-minute goal.

Some dazzling performances for Hamburg and for England gained Kevin Keegan the honour of becoming the fifth British winner of the European Footballer of the Year award.

The 1978–79 season saw the first influx of foreign players into the English League. None proved more successful than Osvaldo Ardiles, who joined Spurs after his brilliant performances in the Argentinian World Cup-winning team.

Viv Anderson booked his place in the record books when he became the first black player to play for England. He is seen here in the match against Hungary.

In Scotland Celtic took the Championship and Rangers the Cup. The picture comes from one of their tussles last year, at Hampden.

When the World Champions toured Europe in 1979 they unveiled a new star who was hailed as 'the new Pele' – Diego Maradona. He is pictured here in Argentina's 3–1 defeat of Scotland.

1913 Scot. Lge.	1913 Irish Lge.	1914 Southern Lge.	1914 Scot. Lge.	1914 Irish Lge.
1 Beale	1 Hardy	1 Hardy	1 Hardy	1 Pearson
2 Downs	2 Crompton	2 Crompton	2 Crompton	2 Crompton
3 Fletcher	3 Pennington	3 Pennington	3 Boocock	3 Boocock
4 Cuggy	4 Cuggy	4 Cuggy	4 Barber	4 Fleetwood
5 Boyle	5 Whalley	5 Harrop	5 Boyle	5 Harrop
6 Uttley	6 Watson	6 McNeal	6 McNeal	6 Watson
7 Wallace	7 Wallace	7 Wallace	7 Jephcott	7 Simpson
8 Buchan	8 Shea	8 Shea	8 Stephenson	8 Buchan
9 Halse	9 Freeman	9 Elliott	9 Peart	9 Bache
10 Woodward	10 Holley	10 Latheron	10 Hodgson	10 Latheron
11 Hodkinson	11 Martin	11 Martin	11 Mosscrop	11 Brooks
Hampden Park March 1: 1-4 *Logan* og	Belfast Oct. 1: 2-0 *Watson, Holley*	Millwall Feb. 9: 3-1 *Shea 3*	Burnley March 21: 2-3 *Boyle, Nellies* og	West Bromwich Oct. 7: 2-1 *Latheron 2*

1914 Southern Lge.	1915 Scot. Lge.	1919 Irish Lge.	1920 Scot. Lge.	1921 Scot. Lge.
1 Reynolds	1 Smith W E	1 Hardy	1 Hardy	1 Mew
2 Crompton	2 Longworth	2 Longworth	2 Longworth	2 Cresswell
3 Boocock	3 English	3 Cook	3 Pennington	3 Silcock
4 Harrow	4 Fleetwood	4 Curry	4 Bambery	4 Bamber
5 Fleetwood	5 Roberts	5 McCall	5 McCall	5 Wilson
6 Watson	6 McNeal	6 Watson	6 Grimsdell	6 Bromilow
7 Walden	7 Chedgzoy	7 Jephcott	7 Chedgzoy	7 Chedgzoy
8 Stephenson	8 Buchan	8 Stephenson	8 Kelly	8 Kelly
9 Halse	9 Elliott	9 Browell	9 Cock	9 Buchan
10 Latheron	10 Latheron	10 Clennell	10 Morris	10 Chambers
11 Hodkinson	11 Martin	11 Crisp	11 Smith W H	11 Paterson
Highbury Oct. 26: 2-1 *Stephenson 2*	Celtic Park March 20: 4-1 *Chedgzoy, Latheron, Elliott, Martin*	Anfield Nov. 19: 2-2 *Stephenson, Clennell*	Hampden Park March 20: 4-0 *Kelly, Cock, Morris 2*	Highbury March 12: 1-0 *Buchan*

1921 Irish Lge.	1922 Scot. Lge.	1922 Irish Lge.	1923 Scot. Lge.	1923 Irish Lge.
1 Dawson	1 Dawson	1 Pearson	1 Taylor	1 Pym
2 Lucas	2 Lucas	2 Clay	2 Cresswell	2 Ashurst
3 Silcock	3 Wadsworth	3 Maitland	3 Wadsworth	3 Jones H
4 Richardson	4 Smith B	4 Kean	4 Moss	4 Healless
5 McClure	5 Wilson	5 Wadsworth	5 Wilson	5 Wilson
6 Watson	6 Bromilow	6 Meehan	6 Bromilow	6 Meehan
7 Chedgzoy	7 Grimshaw	7 Carr	7 Carr	7 Chedgzoy
8 Buchan	8 Kelly	8 Jack	8 Buchan	8 Kelly
9 Walker	9 Chambers	9 Roberts	9 Bullock	9 Bradford
10 Barnes	10 Barnes	10 Cross	10 Chambers	10 Chambers
11 Tunstall	11 Smith W H	11 Dorrell	11 Tunstall	11 Tunstall
Belfast Oct. 1: 1-0 *Chedgzoy*	Ibrox Park March 18: 3-0 *Chambers 2, Smith W. H.*	Bolton Oct. 4: 5-1 *Roberts 2, Jack 2, Cross*	Newcastle Feb. 17: 2-1 *Bullock, Chambers*	Belfast Sept. 29: 6-2 *Bradford 4, Chambers, Chedgzoy*

1924 Scot. Lge.	1924 Irish Lge.	1925 Scot. Lge.	1925 Irish Lge.	1926 Scot. Lge.
1 Taylor	1 Hardy	1 Pym	1 Howard Baker	1 Hardy
2 Cresswell	2 Baker	2 Lucas	2 Lucas	2 Goodall
3 Wadsworth	3 Wadsworth	3 Jones J W	3 Wadsworth	3 Silcock
4 Moss	4 Kean	4 Hill	4 Baker A	4 Edwards
5 Hill	5 Wilson	5 Wilson	5 Spencer	5 Hill
6 Bromilow	6 Bromilow	6 Graham	6 Bromilow	6 Green
7 Mercer	7 Spencer	7 Kelly	7 York	7 York
8 Kelly	8 Kelly	8 Roberts	8 Puddefoot	8 Brown
9 Bradford	9 Bedford	9 Puddefoot	9 Kirkham	9 Bedford
10 Chambers	10 Elkes	10 Elkes	10 Walker	10 Walker
11 Tunstall	11 Ellis	11 Seymour	11 Dorrell	11 Ruffell
Ibrox Park March 15: 1-1 *Chambers*	Cliftonville Oct. 11: 5-0 *Kelly, Bradford* 4	Goodison Park March 14: 4-3 *Roberts* 2, *Puddefoot, Elkes*	Anfield Oct. 7: 5-1 *Kirkham* 2, *Walker* 2 *Dorrell*	Celtic Park March 13: 2-0 *Bedford, Ruffell*

1926 Irish Lge.	1926 The Army	1927 Scot. Lge.	1927 Irish Lge.	1928 Scot. Lge.
1 Tremelling	1 Callendar	1 Brown	1 Tremelling	1 Hacking
2 Cooper	2 Forster	2 Goodall	2 Goodall	2 Goodall
3 Wadsworth	3 McConnell	3 Jones H	3 Finney	3 Jones H
4 Edwards	4 Oliver	4 Edwards	4 Edwards	4 Edwards
5 Kean	5 Townrow	5 Elkes	5 Spencer	5 Kean
6 Green	6 Graham	6 Green	6 Hardy	6 Bishop
7 Spence	7 Hulme	7 Urwin	7 Hulme	7 Hulme
8 Hine	8 Buchan	8 Cross	8 Johnson	8 Jack
9 Roberts	9 Parker	9 Chandler	9 Dean	9 Dean
10 Walker	10 Miller	10 Walker	10 Carr	10 Bradford
11 Amos	11 Penn	11 Ruffell	11 Seymour	11 Smith W H
Belfast Oct. 9: 6-1 *Spence, Roberts* 3 *Walker, Amos*	Millwall Oct. 28: 4-1	Leicester March 19: 2-2 *Elkes, Walker*	Newcastle Sept. 21: 9-1 *Dean* 4, *Hulme, Johnson* 3, *Seymour*	Glasgow March 10: 6-2 *Hulme* 2, *Dean* 2, *Smith, McStay* (og)

1928 Irish Lge.	1928 Scot. Lge.	1929 Irish Lge.	1929 Scot. Lge.	1930 Irish Lge.
1 Tremelling	1 Hacking	1 Davies	1 Hibbs	1 Brown
2 Cooper	2 Smart	2 Cresswell	2 Cresswell	2 Goodall
3 Blenkinsop	3 Blenkinsop	3 Jones H	3 Blenkinsop	3 Hapgood
4 Edwards	4 Edwards	4 Edwards	4 Edwards	4 Strange
5 Wilson	5 Hart	5 Hart	5 Hart	5 Webster
6 Campbell	6 Campbell	6 Campbell	6 Marsden	6 Cadwell
7 Bruton	7 Hulme	7 Toseland	7 Adcock	7 Crooks
8 Jack	8 Hine	8 Hine	8 Hine	8 Jack
9 Dean	9 Dean	9 Hampson	9 Jack	9 Hampson
10 Johnson	10 Bradford	10 Bradford	10 Johnson	10 Walker
11 Ruffell	11 Rigby	11 Page	11 Brook	11 Houghton
Belfast Sept. 22: 5-0 *Dean* 2, *Johnson* 2, *Jack*	Villa Park, Birmingham Nov. 7: 2-1 *Hine, Dean*	Liverpool Sept. 25: 7-2 *Hampson, Bradford* 5, *Hine*	Ibrox Park Nov. 2: 1-2 *Jack*	Belfast Sept. 24: 2-2 *Hampson* 2

1930 Scot. Lge.	1931 Irish Lge.	1931 Scot. Lge.	1932 Irish Lge.	1932 Scot. Lge.
1 Spiers	1 Turner	1 Hibbs	1 Moss	1 Hibbs
2 Goodall	2 Jackson	2 Goodall	2 Cooper	2 Goodall
3 Blenkinsop	3 Keeping	3 Blenkinsop	3 Blenkinsop	3 Blenkinsop
4 Strange	4 Edwards	4 Edwards W	4 Stoker	4 Strange
5 Leach	5 Graham	5 Graham	5 O'Dowd	5 Talbot
6 Campbell	6 Tate	6 Edwards J	6 Weaver	6 Campbell
7 Crooks	7 Hulme	7 Crooks	7 Worrall	7 Hulme
8 Hodgson	8 Beresford	8 Smith J W	8 Hine	8 Smith J W
9 Hampson	9 Hampson	9 Dean	9 Brown G	9 Brown G
10 Carter	10 Bestall	10 Bestall	10 Pickering	10 Johnson
11 Houghton	11 Houghton	11 Bastin	11 Wood	11 Houghton
Tottenham Nov. 5: 7-3 *Campbell, Hodgson, Hampson 3, Crooks 2*	Blackpool Sept. 23: 4-0 *Hampson 3, Houghton*	Celtic Park Nov. 7: 3-4 *Bastin 2, Smith*	Belfast Oct. 1: 5-2 *Brown 3, Wood, Worrall*	Maine Road, Manchester Nov. 9: 0-3

1933 Irish Lge.	1934 Scot. Lge.	1934 Irish Lge.	1934 Scot. Lge.	1935 Irish Lge.
1 Sagar	1 Sagar	1 Sagar	1 Moss	1 Swift
2 Beeson	2 Shaw	2 Cooper	2 Cooper	2 Beeson
3 Trentham	3 Blenkinsop	3 Roughton	3 Hapgood	3 Barkas
4 Britton	4 Willingham	4 Britton	4 Britton	4 Crayston
5 Allen	5 Allen	5 Cowan	5 Barker	5 Barker
6 Copping	6 Copping	6 Robinson	6 Bray	6 Robinson
7 Crooks	7 Bruton	7 Matthews	7 Matthews	7 Worrall
8 Grosvenor	8 Beresford	8 Carter	8 Bowden	8 Carter
9 Bowers	9 Bowers	9 Tilson	9 Tilson	9 Lythgoe
10 Bastin	10 Weaver	10 Westwood	10 Hall	10 Westwood
11 Brook	11 Bastin	11 Brook	11 Brook	11 Boyes
Preston Oct. 4: 4-0 *Bowers 2, Crooks Bastin*	Ibrox Park Feb. 10: 2-2 *Beresford, Bowers*	Belfast Sept. 19: 6-1 *Tilson 2, Matthews, Brook 2, Westwood*	Chelsea Oct. 31: 2-1 *Brook 2*	Blackpool Sept. 25: 1-2 *Boyes*

1935 Scot. Lge.	1936 Irish Lge.	1936 Scot. Lge.	1937 Scot. Lge.	1937 Irish Lge.
1 Sagar	1 Sagar	1 Holdcroft	1 Woodley	1 Woodley
2 Male	2 Rochford	2 Male	2 Sproston	2 Sproston
3 Hapgood	3 Shaw	3 Catlin	3 Barkas	3 Barkas
4 Smith S C	4 Willingham	4 Britton	4 Willingham	4 Willingham
5 Young	5 Barker	5 Gee	5 Cullis	5 Young
6 Bray	6 Bray	6 Keen	6 Bray	6 Bray
7 Birkett	7 Birkett	7 Crooks	7 Matthews	7 Geldard
8 Bowden	8 Bestall	8 Richardson	8 Galley	8 Hall
9 Camsell	9 Steele	9 Dean	9 Steele	9 Mills
10 Tilson	10 Westwood	10 Westwood	10 Westwood	10 Goulden
11 Brook	11 Brook	11 Bastin	11 Ashall	11 Brook
Ibrox Park Oct. 30: 2-2 *Bowden, Camsell*	Belfast Sept. 23: 2-3 *Steele, Westwood*	Goodison Park Oct. 21: 2-0 *Westwood, Bastin*	Glasgow Sept. 22: 0-1	Blackpool Oct. 6: 3-0 *Goulden, Mills, Hall*

1938 Irish Lge.	1938 Scot. Lge.	1947 Irish Lge.	1947 Scot. Lge.	1947 Lge. of Ireland
1 Woodley	1 Woodley	1 Swift	1 Ditchburn	1 Ditchburn
2 Sproston	2 Sproston	2 Scott	2 Scott	2 Woodruff
3 Hapgood	3 Greenhalgh	3 Hardwick	3 Hardwick	3 Robinson
4 Willingham	4 Willingham	4 Wright	4 Taylor	4 Taylor
5 Cullis	5 Cullis	5 Franklin	5 Franklin	5 Pryde
6 Welsh	6 Gardiner	6 Johnston	6 Burgess	6 Mercer
7 Matthews	8 Matthews	7 Matthews	7 Matthews	7 Matthews
8 Robinson	8 Hall	8 Mannion	8 Carter	8 Mortensen
9 Lawton	9 Lawton	9 Lawton	9 Westcott	9 Stubbins
10 Goulden	10 Dix	10 Hagan	10 Mannion	10 Hagan
11 Morton	11 Boyes	11 Kippax	11 Kippax	11 Ormston
Belfast Sept. 21: 8-2 *Lawton 4, Morton Welsh, Goulden, Robinson*	Wolverhampton Nov. 2: 3-1 *Dix 2, Boyes*	Goodison Park Feb. 19: 4-2 *Kippax 2, Lawton 2*	Hampden Park March 12: 3-1 *Mannion 2, Westcott*	Dublin April 30: 3-1 *Mortensen 2, Stubbins*

1947 Irish Lge.	1948 Scot. Lge	1948 Lge. of Ireland	1948 Irish Lge.	1949 Scot. Lge.
1 Merrick	1 Ditchburn	1 Ditchburn	1 Ditchburn	1 Swift
2 Woodruff	2 Mozley	2 Scott	2 Ramsey	2 Scott
3 Robinson	3 Hardwick	3 Walton	3 Robinson	3 Westwood
4 Taylor	4 Harvey	4 Taylor	4 Blenkinsop	4 Attwell
5 Brown	5 Leuty	5 Compton L	5 Jones W H	5 Franklin
6 Emptage	6 Taylor	6 Blenkinsop	6 Wright	6 Harris
7 Matthews	7 Matthews	7 Finney	7 Matthews	7 Finney
8 Pye	8 Morris	8 Carter	8 Morris	8 Mortensen
9 Stubbins	9 Mortensen	9 Stubbins	9 Milburn	9 Milburn
10 Hagan	10 Mannion	10 Rowley	10 Shackleton	10 Mannion
11 Langton	11 Langton	11 Ormston	11 Langton	11 Langton
Belfast Oct. 22: 4-3 *McMillan (og), Stubbins, Pye, Hagan*	Newcastle March 17: 1-1 *Mortensen*	Preston April 14: 4-0 *Stubbins 2, Rowley 2*	Anfield Sept. 20: 5-1 *Shackleton, Milburn 3, Morris*	Ibrox Park March 23: 3-0 *Milburn, Finney Mortensen*

1949 Lge. of Ireland	1950 Lge. of Ireland	1950 Scot Lge.	1950 Irish Lge.	1950 Irish Lge.
1 Merrick	1 Merrick	1 Williams	1 Merrick	1 Allen
2 Ellerington	2 Scott	2 Ramsey	2 Milburn S	2 Milburn S
3 Westwood	3 Eckersley	3 Aston	3 Eckersley	3 Pallister
4 Johnston	4 Nicholson	4 Wright	4 Harvey	4 Johnston
5 Leuty	5 Franklin	5 Franklin	5 Whittaker	5 Cummings
6 Wright A	6 Bell	6 Dickinson	6 Musson	6 Bell
7 Harris	7 Finney	7 Hancocks	7 Harris	7 Finney
8 Gibson	8 Mannion	8 Mannion	8 Morris	8 Morris
9 Bentley	9 Lofthouse	9 Mortensen	9 Milburn J	9 Stubbins
10 Shackleton	10 Baily	10 Baily	10 Wainwright	10 Baily
11 Ormston	11 Langton	11 Langton	11 Metcalfe	11 Langton
Dublin May 4: 5-0 *Shackleton 2, Bentley 2, Harris*	Wolverhampton Feb 15: 7-0 *Mannion 3, Lofthouse 2, Finney Baily*	Middlesbrough March 22: 3-1 *Mortensen 2, Baily*	Belfast April 26: 3-1 *Milburn, J. 3*	Blackpool Oct. 18: 6-3 *Stubbins 5, Morris*

1950 Scot. Lge.	1951 Lge. of Ireland	1951 Lge. of Ireland	1951 Scot. Lge.	1952 Irish Lge.
1 Ditchburn	1 Williams	1 Allen	1 Merrick	1 Merrick
2 Ramsey	2 Ramsey	2 Robinson	2 Ramsey	2 Ball
3 Aston	3 Eckersley	3 Smith L	3 Smith L	3 Garrett
4 Wright	4 Wright	4 Harvey	4 Wright	4 Wright
5 Taylor	5 Taylor	5 Barnes	5 Barrass	5 Froggatt
6 Cockburn	6 Dickinson	6 Dickinson	6 Dickinson	6 Dickinson
7 Hancocks	7 Hurst	7 Finney	7 Finney	7 Finney
8 Mortensen	8 Mannion	8 Thompson	8 Sewell	8 Broadis
9 Lofthouse	9 Lofthouse	9 Lofthouse	9 Lofthouse	9 Lofthouse
10 Morris	10 Baily	10 Hassall	10 Phillips	10 Pearson
11 Finney	11 Langton	11 Langton	11 Medley	11 Rowley
Ibrox Park Nov. 29: 0-1	Dublin April 4: 1-0 *Lofthouse*	Goodison Park Oct. 10: 9-1 *Thompson 4, Lofthouse 2, Finney, Langton, Coffey (og)*	Hillsborough, Sheffield Oct. 31: 2-1 *Lofthouse, Finney*	Belfast March 26: 9-0 *Lofthouse 3, Pearson 3, Finney 2, Broadis*

1952 Irish Lge.	1953 Lge. of Ireland	1953 Scot. Lge.	1953 Danish Comb'tn.	1953 Irish Lge.
1 Merrick	1 Williams	1 Merrick	1 Williams	1 Merrick
2 Ramsey	2 Wade	2 Green	2 Ramsey	2 Green
3 Garrett	3 Eckersley	3 Smith L	3 Eckersley	3 Eckersley
4 Wright	4 Wright	4 Wright	4 Wright	4 Wright
5 Froggatt	5 Froggatt	5 Froggatt J	5 Owen	5 Johnston
6 Dickinson	6 Dickinson	6 Dickinson	6 Barlow	6 Dickinson
7 Finney	7 Finney	7 Finney	7 Harris	7 Finney
8 Sewell	8 Bentley	8 Broadis	8 Sewell	8 Quixall
9 Lofthouse	9 Jezzard	9 Lofthouse	9 Jezzard	9 Lofthouse
10 Baily	10 Broadis	10 Froggatt R	10 Lishman	10 Hassall
11 Elliott	11 Elliott	11 Elliott	11 Roper	11 Robb
Wolverhampton Sept. 24: 7-1 *Lofthouse 6, Ramsey*	Dublin March 17: 2-0 *Bentley 2*	Ibrox Park March 25: 0-1	Copenhagen May 5: 4-0 *Lishman 2, Jezzard, Wright*	Belfast Sept. 23: 5-0 *Lofthouse 3, Hassall 2*

1954 Lge. of Ireland	1954 Scot. Lge.	1954 Lge. of Ireland	1954 Irish Lge.	1955 Scot. Lge.
1 Merrick	1 Merrick	1 Wood	1 Wood	1 Matthews
2 Rickaby	2 Ball	2 Foulkes	2 Meadows	2 Foulkes
3 Byrne	3 Willemse	3 Mansell J	3 Byrne	3 Mansell
4 Wright	4 Wright	4 Wheeler	4 Phillips	4 Armstrong
5 Dugdale	5 Owen	5 Wright	5 Wright	5 Marston
6 Barlow	6 Bell	6 Barlow	6 Edwards	6 Edwards
7 Berry	7 Harris	7 Matthews	7 Hooper	7 Hooper
8 Revie	8 Sewell	8 Revie	8 Baily	8 Atyeo
9 Lofthouse	9 Jezzard	9 Lofthouse	9 Lofthouse	9 Bentley
10 Sewell	10 Haynes	10 Haynes	10 Hassall	10 Evans
11 Metcalfe	11 Mullen	11 Finney	11 Elliott	11 Blunstone
Maine Road, Manchester Feb. 10: 9-1 *Revie 3, Sewell 3, Berry 2, Lofthouse*	Chelsea April 28: 4-0 *Jezzard 2, Sewell, Haynes*	Dublin Sept. 22: 6-0 *Revie 3, Matthews, Lofthouse, Haynes*	Anfield Oct. 20: 4-2 *Hassall, Hooper, Lofthouse, Elliott*	Hampden Park March 16: 2-3 *Evans, Bentley*

1955 Scots. Lge.	1955 Lge. of Ireland	1956 Irish Lge.	1956 Lge. of Ireland	1956 Irish Lge.
1 Williams	1 Baynham	1 Baynham	1 Matthews	1 Wood
2 Hall	2 Hall	2 Armfield	2 Hall	2 Hall
3 Byrne	3 Byrne	3 Byrne	3 Byrne	3 Langley
4 McGarry	4 Clayton R.	4 Clayton R	4 Clayton	4 Clayton R
5 Wright	5 Wright	5 Wicks	5 Wright	5 Wright
6 Dickinson	6 Dickinson	6 Iley	6 Edwards	6 Flowers
7 Finney	7 Finney	7 Harris	7 Astall	7 Matthews
8 Turner	8 Atyeo	8 Quixall	8 Quixall	8 Haynes
9 Lofthouse	9 Lofthouse	9 Taylor	9 Taylor	9 Lofthouse
10 Haynes	10 Haynes	10 Haynes	10 Viollet	10 Rowley A
11 Hogg	11 Perry	11 Grainger	11 Grainger	11 Grainger
Hillsborough Sheffield Oct. 26: 4-2 *Turner, Lofthouse 2, Finney*	Goodison Park Dec. 7: 5-1 *Perry, Atyeo, Byrne, Clayton, Mackey og*	Belfast April 25: 2-5 *Davis og, Taylor*	Dublin Sept. 19: 3-3 *Astall, Taylor, Viollet*	Newcastle Oct. 31: 3-2 *Lofthouse, Grainger, Haynes*

1957 Scot. Lge.	1957 Lge. of Ireland	1957 Irish Lge.	1958 Scot. Lge.	1958 Scot. Lge.
1 Hodgkinson	1 Sims	1 Hopkinson	1 McDonald	1 Hopkinson
2 Howe	2 Armfield	2 Bond	2 Howe	2 Bond
3 Sillett P	3 Moran	3 Garrett	3 Banks	3 Shaw G
4 Clayton	4 Barlow	4 Clayton	4 Clamp	4 Malcolm
5 Wright	5 Charlton J	5 Smith T	5 Wright	5 Shaw J
6 Edwards	6 Pearce	6 Flowers	6 Pearce	6 Hey
7 Hooper	7 Kaye	7 Brabrook	7 Douglas	7 Wilkinson
8 Thompson	8 Broadbent	8 Stevens	8 Robson	8 Quixall
9 Finney	9 Tindall	9 Murray	9 Allen	9 Clough
10 Stokes	10 Parry	10 Haynes	10 Kevan	10 Greaves
11 Pilkington	11 Hooper	11 A'Court	11 Finney	11 Pilkington
Ibrox Park March 13: 2-3 *Pilkington, Thompson*	Leeds Oct. 9: 3-1 *Broadbent, Parry 2*	Belfast Oct. 30: 4-2 *Haynes, Murray, Brabrook, A'Court*	Newcastle March 26: 4-1 *Kevan, 3 Allen*	Ibrox Park Oct. 8: 1-1 *Clough*

1958 Irish Lge.	1959 Lge of Ireland	1959 Irish Lge.	1959 Lge. of Ireland	1960 Scot. Lge.
1 McDonald	1 Springett	1 Springett	1 Springett	1 Kelsey
2 Hartle	2 Howe	2 Howe	2 Armfield	2 Armfield
3 Shaw G	3 Shaw G	3 Wilson	3 Allen	3 Moran
4 Wheeler	4 Clayton	4 Clayton	4 Clayton	4 Robson
5 Shaw J	5 Gratrix	5 Smith T	5 Swan	5 Knapp
6 McGuinness	6 Flowers	6 Flowers	6 Kay	6 Mackay
7 Clapton	7 Wilkinson	7 Connelly	7 Connelly	7 Hooper
8 Harris J	8 Broadbent	8 Dobing	8 Dobing	8 Bloomfield
9 White	9 Viollet	9 Clough	9 Viollet	9 White
10 Haynes	10 Haynes	10 Eastham	10 Parry	10 Greaves
110 A'Court	11 Holden	11 Scanlon	11 Holliday	11 Jones C
Anfield Nov. 12: 5-2 *Haynes, A'Court, White 3*	Dublin March 17: 0-0	Belfast Sept. 23: 5-0 *Clough 5*	Blackburn Nov. 4: 2-0 *Viollet, Connelly*	Highbury March 23: 1-0 *Hooper*

1960 Lge. of Ireland	1960 Irish Lge.	1960 Italian Lge.	1961 Scot. Lge.	1961 Lge. of Ireland
1 Sims	1 Trautmann	1 Springett (Trautmann)	1 Springett	1 Springett
2 Sillet J	2 Angus	2 Armfield	2 Howe	2 Armfield
3 Allen	3 Armfield	3 Megson	3 McNeil	3 Wilson
4 Clayton R	4 Blanchflower	4 Robson	4 Robson	4 Robson
5 Woods	5 Adamson	5 Swan	5 Swan	5 Swan
6 McGrath	6 Mackay	6 Flowers	6 Flowers	6 Flowers
7 Brabrook	7 Jones C	7 Jones (Woosnam)	7 Brabrook	7 Connelly
8 Dobing	8 White	8 McIlroy	8 Greaves	8 Douglas
9 Moore	9 Law	9 Law	9 Hitchens	9 Pointer
10 Greaves	10 McIlroy	10 Haynes	10 Fantham	10 Haynes
11 Blunstone	11 Connelly	11 McParland	11 Charlton R	11 Charlton R
Dublin Sept. 14: 4-0 *Dobing 3, Greaves*	Blackpool Oct. 12: 5-2 *Blanchflower, Connelly, Law 2, McIlroy*	Milan Nov. 1: 2-4 *Law, McParland*	Ibrox Park March 22: 2-3 *Hitchens, Swan*	Eastville, Bristol Oct. 11: 5-2 *Douglas 2, Haynes, Connelly, Nolan og*

1961 Irish Lge.	1961 Italian Lge.	1962 Scot. Lge.	1962 Irish Lge.	1962 Italian Lge.
1 Banks	1 Springett	1 Springett	1 Banks	1 Springett
2 Howe	2 Armfield	2 Armfield	2 Armfield	2 Armfield
3 Shaw G	3 Wilson	3 Wilson	3 Wilson	3 Wilson
4 Miller	4 Kay	4 Miller	4 Moore	4 Moore
5 Labone	5 Swan	5 Swan	5 Sleeuwenhoek	5 Labone
6 Kay	6 Flowers	6 Flowers	6 Appleton	6 Flowers
7 Connelly	7 Connelly	7 Jackson	7 Douglas	7 Connelly
8 Hill	8 Fantham	8 Hunt	8 Hill	8 Greaves
9 Crawford	9 Pointer	9 Crawford	9 Crawford	9 Allen
10 Fantham	10 Haynes	10 Haynes	10 Byrne	10 Douglas
11 Harris	11 Charlton R	11 Charlton R	11 O'Grady	11 O'Grady
Belfast Nov. 1: 6-1 *Crawford 2, Harris, Kay, Fantham, Miller*	Old Trafford, Manchester Nov. 8: 0-2	Villa Park, Birmingham March 21: 3-4 *Hunt 2, Haynes*	Norwich Oct. 31: 3-1 *Crawford 3*	Highbury Nov. 29: 3-2 *O'Grady, Allen, Greaves*

1963 Lge. of Ireland	1964 Scot. Lge.	1964 Italian Lge.	1964 Irish Lge.	1965 Scot. Lge.
1 Waiters	1 Waiters	1 Waiters (Banks)	1 Waiters	1 Waiters
2 Armfield	2 Cohen	2 Cohen	2 Badger	2 Thomson
3 Wilson	3 Thomson	3 Thomson	3 Newton	3 Wilson
4 Milne	4 Milne	4 Mullery	4 Mullery	4 Stiles
5 Moore	5 Flowers	5 Norman	5 Flowers	5 Charlton J
6 Peters	6 Moore	6 Flowers	6 Hunter	6 Hunter
7 Callaghan	7 Paine	7 Paine	7 Paine	7 Paine
8 Hunt	8 Greaves	8 Hunt	8 Hunt	8 Greaves
9 Byrne	9 Byrne	9 Pickering	9 Wignall	9 Bridges
10 Melia	10 Kay	10 Charlton R	10 Venables	10 Ball
11 O'Grady	11 Thompson	11 Thompson	11 Temple	11 Charlton R
Dublin Oct. 2: 1-2 *Byrne*	Sunderland March 18: 2-2 *Byrne, Greaves*	Milan May 9: 0-1	Belfast Oct. 28: 4-0 *Paine, Wignall 3*	Hampden Park March 17: 2-2 *Charlton J, Bridges*

1965 Lge. of Ireland	1966 Scot. Lge.	1966 Irish Lge.	1967 Scot. Lge.	1967 Belgian Lge.	1967 Lge. of Ireland
1 Banks	1 Springett	1 Bonetti	1 Bonetti	1 Banks	1 Grummitt
2 Cohen	2 Reaney	2 Cohen	2 Badger	2 Badger	2 Smith W
3 Newton	3 Newton	3 Wilson	3 Newton	3 Charlton J	3 Wilson
4 O'Neill	4 Stiles	4 Peters	4 Hollins	4 Moore	4 Bailey
5 Charlton J	5 Charlton J	5 Charlton J	5 Labone	5 Hunter	5 Mobley
6 Hunter	6 Hunter	6 Moore	6 Moore	6 Peters	6 Moore
7 Thompson	7 Ball	7 Paine	7 Callaghan	7 Ball	7 Sammels
8 Ball	8 Greaves	8 Byrne	8 Greaves	8 Hollins	8 Greaves
9 Kaye	9 Kaye	9 Hurst	9 Clarke	9 Wignall	9 Ritchie
10 Harris	10 Eastham	10 Eastham	10 Hurst	10 Clarke	10 Chivers
11 Temple	11 Charlton R	11 Connelly	11 Thompson	11 Hurst	11 Bell
Hull Oct. 27: 5-0 Ball 2, Kaye 2, Charlton	Newcastle March 16: 1-3 Greaves	Plymouth Sept. 21: 12-0 Byrne 4, Eastham 2, Connelly 2, Hurst 2, Paine 2	Hampden Park March 15: 3-0 Clarke 2, Hurst	Brussels Sept. 27: 2-2 Peters, Clarke	Dublin Nov. 8: 7-2 Greaves, Chivers 3, Ritchie 2, Sammels

1968 Scot. Lge.	1968 Irish Lge.	1969 Scot. Lge.	1969 Lge. of Ireland	1970 Scot. Lge.	1970 Irish Lge.
1 Stepney	1 West	1 Bonetti	1 Bonetti	1 Stepney (Glazier)	1 Shilton
2 Newton	2 Thomson	2 Smith W	2 Reaney	2 Smith W	2 Edwards
3 Knowles	3 McNab	3 Hughes	3 Clark	3 Hughes	3 Robson
4 Stiles	4 Bailey	4 Osgood	4 Harvey (Woodward)	4 Newton	4 Nish
5 Labone	5 Labone	5 McGrath	5 Madeley	5 McFarland	5 Sadler
6 Moore	6 Smith T	6 Oakes	6 Hunter	6 Todd	6 Harvey
7 Ball	7 Radford	7 Coates	7 Robson	7 Coates	7 Coates
8 Hunt	8 Bell	8 Casper	8 Bailey	8 Kidd (Peters)	8 Hector
9 Hurst	9 Osgood	9 Royle	9 Summerbee	9 Astle	9 Astle
10 Charlton, R.	10 Hurst	10 Ball	10 Lee	10 Harvey	10 Peters
11 Peters	11 Thompson	11 Tambling	11 Morrissey	11 Rogers	11 Storey-Moore
Middlesbrough March 20: 2-0 Hunt, Newton	Belfast Nov. 27: 1-0 Hurst	Hampden Park March 26: 3-1 Casper, Ball, Tambling	Barnsley Sept. 10: 3-0 Robson, Bailey Summerbee	Coventry March 18: 3-2 Astle 2, Rogers	Norwich Sept 23: 5-0 Peters, Astle 2, Brown, Hector

1971 Scot. Lge.	1971 Lge. of Ireland	1972 Scot. Lge.	1973 Scot. Lge.	1974 Scot. Lge.	1976 Scot. Lge.
1 Jackson	1 Banks	1 Clemence	1 Shilton	1 Clemence	1 Shilton
2 Reaney	2 Lawler	2 Lawler	2 Mills	2 Storey	2 Cherry
3 Parkin	3 Nish	3 Nish	3 Nish	3 Nish	3 Mills
4 Hollins	4 Storey	4 Doyle	4 McFarland	4 Dobson	4 Doyle
5 McFarland	5 McFarland	5 Blockley	5 Kendall	5 McFarland	5 McFarland
6 Moore	6 Sadler	6 Moore	6 Moore	6 Todd	6 Todd
7 Coates	7 Woodward	7 Hughes	7 Weller	7 Bowles	7 Wilkins
8 Brown	8 Hector	8 MacDonald	8 Channon	8 Bell	8 Channon
9 Hurst	9 Radford	9 Hurst	9 Worthington	9 Latchford (Hector)	9 Greenhoff
10 O'Neill	10 Osgood	10 Currie	10 Richards	10 Brooking	10 Currie
11 Storey-Moore	11 Hughes	11 Wagstaffe	11 Bell	11 Tueart	11 Tueart
Hampden Park March 17: 1-0 Coates	Dublin Sept. 22: 2-1 Osgood, Radford	Middlesbrough March 15: 3-2 Currie 2, Doyle	Hampden Park March 27: 2-2 Channon 2	Maine Road March 29: 5-0 Bell, Brown (og) Tueart, Brooking, Bowles	Hampden Park March 17: 1-0 Cherry

SCOTTISH LEAGUE REPRESENTATIVE TEAMS

v IRISH LEAGUE
Played 60. Scotland won 55, Ireland 5

Year	Venue	Goals S.L.	Goals I.L.	Year	Venue	Goals S.L.	Goals I.L.	Year	Venue	Goals S.L.	Goals I.L.
1893	Belfast	2	3	1920	Belfast	2	0	1940–46	Not played		
1894	Glasgow	6	2	1921	Glasgow	3	0	1947	Belfast	7	4
1895	Belfast	4	1	1922	Glasgow	3	0	1948	Glasgow	3	0
1896	Glasgow	3	2	1923	Glasgow	3	0	1949	Belfast	1	0
1897	Belfast	2	0	1924	Belfast	1	0	1950	Glasgow	8	1
1898	Dundee	5	0	1925	Edinburgh	3	0	1951	Belfast	4	0
1899	Belfast	1	3	1926	Belfast	7	3	1952	Glasgow	3	0
1900	Edinburgh	6	0	1927	Edinburgh	5	2	1953	Belfast	5	1
1901	Belfast	2	1	1928	Belfast	2	1	1954	Glasgow	4	0
1902	Dundee	3	0	1929	Glasgow	8	2	1955	Belfast	5	1
1903	Belfast	0	1	1930	Belfast	4	1	1956	Glasgow	3	0
1904	Paisley	3	1	1931	Glasgow	5	0	1957	Belfast	7	1
1905–8	Not played			1932	Belfast	2	3	1958	Glasgow	7	0
1909	Glasgow	2	1	1933	Glasgow	4	1	1959	Belfast	5	0
1910	Glasgow	2	0	1934	Belfast	0	3	1960	Glasgow	7	1
1911	Belfast	3	1	1935	Belfast	3	2	1961	Belfast	2	1
1912	Glasgow	3	0	1936	Belfast	3	2	1962	Glasgow	7	0
1913	Belfast	3	1	1937	Glasgow	5	2	1964	Belfast	4	1
1914	Belfast	2	1	1938	Belfast	3	2	1966	Glasgow	6	2
1915	Belfast	2	1	1939	Glasgow	6	1	1968	Belfast	2	0
1916–19	Not played			1939†	Belfast	3	2	1970	Glasgow	5	2
								1978	Motherwell	1	1

†Played in season 1939–40 prior to the outbreak of war.

v LEAGUE OF IRELAND

Year	Venue	Goals S.L.	Goals L.o.I.	Year	Venue	Goals S.L.	Goals L.o.I.	Year	Venue	Goals S.L.	Goals L.o.I.
1938	Dublin	1	2	1955	Glasgow	5	0	1962	Dublin	1	1
1948	Dublin	2	0	1956	Dublin	4	2	1963	Glasgow	11	0
1949	Glasgow	5	1	1957	Glasgow	3	1	1965	Dublin	2	2
1950	Dublin	1	0	1958	Dublin	5	1	1967	Glasgow	6	0
1951	Glasgow	7	0	1959	Glasgow	1	0	1969	Dublin	0	0
1952	Dublin	2	0	1960	Dublin	4	1	1970	Glasgow	1	0
1953	Glasgow	5	1	1961	Glasgow	5	1	1971	Glasgow	1	0
1954	Dublin	3	1								

JUBILEE APPEAL

Glasgow Select 2 Football League 1 (h-t 0-1)
Hampden Park, May 17 1977.

Glasgow; Rough; McGrain, Whittaker, Jardine, McDonald, Forsyth, McLean (McNaughton), Dalglish, Craig, MacDonald, Johnstone (Somner).

League; Corrigan; Clements, Peach, Stanley, Watson, Wilkins R, Francis T, Channon, Royle (Barnes), Owen, Tueart

Scorers: Jardine pen., Dalglish; Tueart.

Review of the Scottish Season

One of the beauties of any game is the vast opportunity it gives for comment – and it is not unknown for the loudest comments to come from the least expert and least knowledgeable. This season has produced ample talking points, but the game has gone on, and has been none the worse for them.

The enforced break in mid-season because of the weather was an unmitigated nuisance to most clubs, to say the least. It was disastrous financially, and an appalling wrecker of training programmes. When matches were played, the crowds consisted of the hardy – perhaps foolhardy – few, who froze while the players slid and slipped. Loud was the cry for a proper break, and football through the summer.

One effect of this enforced break was a rip-roaring finish to the season. Each league held its interest to the end. Last season Dundee United looked to be slightly flattered by their position, but this year they were for the most part business-like and assured. It was in many ways a tragedy that, in the final days, they lost to both Rangers and Celtic, and in doing so seemed overawed in finding themselves so near to the promised land. Congratulations to them, and to manager Jim McLean, for so long acting as convincing leaders; they are a young team with much potential, and their turn must come if they stay together. It was good to see several of their players receiving international recognition at different levels.

For a long while the top clubs were within easy reach of each other; even well into February, only five points separated the first eight teams, and it looked to be almost anyone's championship. Such is the league, however, that one suspects that, at the end of the day, Rangers and Celtic will be at the sharp end: so indeed it was. Celtic looked anything but good early on, and as far on as April, when they were convincingly beaten by Dundee United at Tannadice, they seemed oddly uncertain of themselves. What was it that gave them the urge to reach the summit? Can there be any doubt that the return of Danny McGrain inspired them, and gave them the confidence in themselves so badly missing before.

Rangers puddled away as usual: a poor start, a strong middle period, and then, in the end, they lost the vital game to Celtic, and that was that. Injuries upset their plans more than others – Tom Forsyth's, in particular. But they seemed to lose their way when the atmosphere was lacking: contrast their magnificent displays in Europe with some of the lack-lustre episodes in front of meagre crowds on the lesser grounds.

Hearts had a long spell down the table. Although once or twice they almost broke free, they never did, and they finished the season in some disarray with ten consecutive losses. Hibs, whom they overhauled for a brief moment, finished strongly. Of the rest, St Mirren might have achieved more with greater consistency; Partick always looked safe, but had a thin finish, whilst Morton were inevitably entertaining – Andy Ritchie was never long out of the picture, and frequent moments of magic earned him a well-deserved Player of the Year award.

Motherwell lost touch and, apparently, heart early in the season. A period of rebuilding, with youth in evidence, suggests that there may be a realistic challenge in the First Division next season. It was an unsettled term for them, both on and off the field: as early as mid-September they were at the foot of the table, and they never left it.

Dundee emerged quickly as solid front-runners in the First Division. When they fell behind in number of games played, Clydebank, never far from the top, and Kilmarnock, working their way up from the nether regions, disputed the lead, with assistance from Ayr United and – thanks to the devoted pitch preparation of many enthusiasts – Hamilton Academicals. In the end Kilmarnock pipped Clydebank by the narrowest of margins for the honour of joining Dundee in the move upwards. At the other end, Arbroath looked to have lost their way in the first half of the season, but they had a good run and emerged well up the table, leaving Queen of the South and Montrose stranded, though St Johnstone only pulled away during the final fixtures.

So to Division Two, where there was an extraordinary conclusion to the competition: for some time Falkirk moved confidently forward in command of a large lead, and Dunfermline, with games in hand, looked a snip. Then things started to go wrong: East Fife, lacking any consistency, none the less took Falkirk to the cleaners three times; Dunfermline huffed and puffed; and all the while Berwick Rangers calmly garnered the points and, all of a sudden, were clear at the top and uncatchable. Well done! Falkirk and Dunfermline were left to fight it out for the other promotion place, and the latter managed the draw they needed in the battle of the giants, in mid-May, by which time winter was nearly over.

The League Cup again proved successful in its present form, though the final was not contested until late March. For once Celtic failed to reach it, having lost to Rangers in an exciting semi-final. There were few early surprises, though Montrose, Arbroath and Ayr did well in reaching the quarter-finals. Rangers took the trophy in the final against Aberdeen, and thoroughly deserved to do so.

The Cup started in the thick of winter, and there were heavy delays. Falkirk eventually played their second round match in Inverness at the end of February, and just about achieved a record in the number of 29 postponed dates. There was little giant-killing, and events moved smoothly to a final between Rangers and Hibernian, who had managed to reverse a League Cup semi-final result against Aberdeen. The first final was a pretty boring do, and the second achieved little more except an extra half-hour. The third game, before a sparse crowd, was a good and exciting contest with Rangers deserving their success, but Hibs gaining very much from a stout effort. Victory in the Cup has eluded them for a very long time: they cannot be denied if they continue to show this sort of dedication.

Internationally Jock Stein obviously has a bit to do to reorganise, but he refuses to be hurried, and there are many ready to trust him and his experience, and to wait. The vociferous vandals who wreck our national image and Wembley Stadium do not give us much encouragement, but there is no doubt that the players are there. There have been distinct signs of revival, but, as the game against the Argentinians showed, there is a long way to go. This is the time to get behind the manager we have all wanted and to give him the support and understanding he needs.

Alan Elliott

Scottish League Referees 1978-79

H Alexander (Irvine)
W Anderson (East Kilbride)
R R Cuthill (Edinburgh)
M Delaney (Cleland)
D S Downie (Edinburgh)
A Ferguson (Giffnock)
I M D Foote (Glasgow)
A C Harris (Liff)
K J Hope (Clarkston)
T Kellock (East Kilbride)
W P Knowles (Inverurie)
A G M McFaull (Glasgow)
B R McGinlay (Glasgow)
A McGunnigle (Glasgow)
T Muirhead (Stenhousemuir)
D A Murdoch (Bothwell)
E H Pringle (Edinburgh)
D Ramsey (Edinburgh)
J R S Renton (Cowdenbeath)
B Robertson (East Kilbride)
G B Smith (Edinburgh)
K Stewart (Glasgow)
D F T Syme (Rutherglen)
R B Valentine (Dundee)
A W Waddell (Edinburgh)
J A R Wales (Cumbernauld)
C J White (Clarkston)

ABERDEEN   PREM. DIV.

Year Formed: 1903.
Ground: Pittodrie Stadium. *Size:* 110×71 yds. *Capacity:* 24,000 (all seated).
Telephone: Aberdeen 21428, 53497.
Manager: Alec Ferguson *Assistant-Manager:* Pat Stanton
Secretary: *Trainer:* Teddy Scott.
Club Colours: Scarlet shirts, white collars and cuffs, scarlet shorts with single white stripe, red stockings and white tops.
Club Nickname: 'The Dons'.
Record Attendance: 45,061, v Hearts, Scottish Cup, 4th Rd, March 13th, 1954.
(Present Aberdeen F.C. have had no other home but Pittodrie.)
European Competitions Entered: Fairs Cup, 1968–69; Cup Winners Cup, 1967–68, 1970–71, 1978–79, UEFA Cup 1971–72, 1972–73, 1973–74, 1977–78.
Record Transfer Fee Received: £180,000 from Everton for Joe Harper, December 1972.

1978–79 LEAGUE RECORD

Match No.	Date	Venue	Opponents	Result	H/T Score	League Pos'n	Goalscorers	Attendance
1	Aug 12	A	Hearts	W 4-1	2-1	—	Harper, Davidson, Archibald 2	11,500
2	19	H	Morton	W 3-1	1-1	1	Harper 3	14,500
3	26	A	Dundee U	D 1-1	1-0	2	Harper	10,000
4	Sept 9	H	Motherwell	W 4-0	1-0	2	Harper 2 (1 a pen), Archibald 2	13,200
5	16	A	Rangers	D 1-1	0-1	2	Sullivan	25,000
6	23	A	Hibernian	L 1-2	1-2	3	Jarvie	12,086
7	30	H	Partick T	D 1-1	0-1	3	Archibald	11,100
8	Oct 7	H	Celtic	W 4-1	3-1	3	Harper (pen), Archibald 2, Jarvie	25,000
9	14	A	St Mirren	L 1-2	0-0	4	Harper	10,973
10	21	H	Hearts	L 1-2	0-1	4	Harper (pen)	12,750
11	28	A	Morton	L 1-2	1-2	5	Jarvie	7000
12	Nov 4	H	Dundee U	W 1-0	1-0	2	Harper (pen)	14,850
13	11	A	Motherwell	D 1-1	0-0	3	Scanlon	5448
14	18	H	Rangers	D 0-0	0-0	3		26,000
15	25	H	Hibernian	W 4-1	2-0	2	Harper 2, Fleming, Sullivan	14,250
16	Dec 9	A	Celtic	D 0-0	0-0	3		24,000
17	16	H	St Mirren	D 1-1	0-1	3	McMaster	12,700
18	23	A	Hearts	D 0-0	0-0	3		9500
19	30	H	Morton	L 1-2	0-0	3	Harper	8000
20	Jan 20	A	Hibernian	D 1-1	1-0	3	Harper	6000
21	Feb 24	A	St Mirren	D 2-2	1-0	4	Strachan, Archibald	11,500
22	28	H	Partick T	W 2-1	0-0	—	McMaster, Archibald	12,500
23	Mar 3	A	Celtic	L 0-1	0-0	2		26,000
24	17	H	Dundee U	L 0-2	0-0	4		10,000
25	26	H	Motherwell	W 8-0	3-0	—	Harper 3, Archibald 2, Strachan, McMaster, Davidson	7000
26	Apr 4	A	Morton	W 1-0	1-0	—	Cooper	7000
27	7	H	Hibernian	D 0-0	0-0	5		10,000
28	14	A	Partick T	W 1-0	1-0	3	McGhee	6000
29	18	A	Motherwell	D 1-1	0-0	—	McLeish	2672
30	21	A	Celtic	D 1-1	1-1	4	Strachan	19,400
31	25	H	Rangers	W 2-1	1-0	—	McGhee, Archibald	17,000
32	28	H	St Mirren	L 1-2	1-0	4	Archibald	13,000
33	May 2	H	Hearts	W 5-0	2-0	—	McGhee 2, Strachan, Scanlon, Sullivan	6000
34	5	A	Dundee U	D 2-2	0-1	4	Jarvie, Strachan (pen)	7822
35	7	A	Rangers	L 0-2	0-0	—		28,000
36	11	A	Partick T	W 2-1	1-0	—	Harper, Sullivan	4000

Final League Position: 4

Goalscorers

League (59): Harper 19 (4 pens), Archibald 13, Strachan 5 (1 a pen), Jarvie 4, McGhee 4, Sullivan 4, McMaster 3, Davidson 2, Scanlon 2, Cooper 1, Fleming 1, McLeish 1.
League Cup (25): Harper 9 (2 pens), Archibald 3, Kennedy 3, Sullivan 3, Scanlon 2, Davidson 1, Fleming 1, Jarvie 1, McLelland 1, Rougvie 1.
Cup (12): Archibald 4, Harper 3, Scanlon 2, Davidson 1, McMaster 1, Miller 1.

Honours

Scottish League: Division 1, Champions: 1954–55, Runners-up: 1910–11, 1936–37, 1955–56, 1970–71, 1971–72. Premier Division, Runners-up: 1977–78.
Scottish Cup: Winners: 1947, 1970, Runners-up: 1937, 1953, 1954, 1959, 1967, 1978.
Scottish League Cup: Winners: 1945–46, 1955–56, 1976–77. Runners-up: 1946–47, 1978–79.
Drybrough Cup: Winners: 1971.

Record Victory: 13-0 v Peterhead, Feb. 9th, 1923 (Scottish Cup).
Record Defeat: 2-9 v Dundee, Apr. 17th, 1909.
Most League Points: 61, 1935–36.
Most Individual League Goals in Season: 38, Benny Yorston, Division 1, 1929–30.
Most Capped Player: Bobby Clark 17, Scotland.

Clark R	Leighton J	Gardiner J	Kennedy RS	McLelland C	McLeish A	McMaster J	Garner W	Miller W	Strachan G	Sullivan D	Archibald S	Jarvie A	Rougvie D	Harper J	Fleming I	Davidson D	Scanlon I	Smith J	Ritchie S	Cooper N	Considine D	Hamilton D	McGhee M	Watson A	Match No.
1	2	3		4	5	6		7	8	10		9		11*12											1
1	2	3		4	5	6		7	8	10		9		11*		12									2
1	2	3		4	5	6		7	8*10			9	12	11†13											3
1	2	3		4	5	6	12	7*	8	10		9		11											4
1	2	3	5	4		6	12	7	8*10	13		9		11†											4
1	2	3	5	4		6		7*	8	10	12	9		13	11†										6
1	2	3	5	4		6	7		8	10		9	12	11*											7
1	2	3	5	4		6	7	11	8	10		9													8
1	2	3*	5	4		6	7†11		8	10	12	9		13											9
1	2*	3	5	4†		6	13	7	8	10		9	12	11											10
1			5	4		6		7	8	10	2	9	12	11†13		3*									11
1		3	5			6	7	11	8	10†	2	9	4*		12	13									12
1	2	3		4*		6	7	11		10	5	9	8†	13			12								13
1	2	3		4		6	7	10	8		5	9	12	11*											14
1	2	3		4*		6	7	10		12	5	9	8	11†			13								15
1	2	3		4*		6	7	11	12	10	5	9	8												16
1	2	3		4		6	7	10	8		5	9	12	11*											17
1	2	3		4			7	10†	8*		5	9	12	11			6	13							18
1	2	3		4		6	7*10		8		5	9	13	11†		12									19
1	2	3				6	4*	7	12	10	5	9		11†	8		13								20
1	2			4		6	11	7	8	10*	5			12	9			3							21
1	2		6	4			11	7	8	10*	5	12		9				3							22
1	2	3		4		6	11†	7	8	10*	5	12		9			13								23
1	2	3	13	4*			6	12	7	8	10	5	9†	11											24
1	2	3		4			6	12	7*	8	10	5	9	11											25
	1	2	3	5			6	11		10		9							4			7	8		26
	1	2	3	5†			6	11		10	13	9							4*	12		7	8		27
1		2		4	12		6	10	9*	8		5		11						3		7			28
1		2		4			5	6	10	9*	8	12		11						3		7			29
1		2		4			5	6	10	9	8			11						3		7			30
1			3	4	12		5	6	10	9*	8			11						2		7			31
1		2		4	11*	5	6	10	9	8		12								3		7			32
1	2					5	6	4	9	8	10			11						3		7			33
1		2		4			5	6	9		8	10		11						3		7			34
1		2		4			5	6	10	9	8			11						3		7			35
1							5	6	10	4	8			9			11		12	3	2	7*			36
23	11	2	32	25	18	24	12	34	26	32	30	24	16	25	4	7	22	0	1	3	3	9	11	2	
				+ 1s	+ 2s				+ 5s			+ 2s	+ 2s	+ 4s	+ 3s	+ 8s	+ 2s		+ 6s	+ 2s		+ 4s	+ 3s	+ 1s	

AIRDRIEONIANS   DIV. 1

Year Formed: 1878.
Ground: Broomfield Park.   *Size:* 112 × 68 yds.   *Capacity:* 26,000 (2,000 seats).
Telephone: Airdrie 62067.
Manager: Bobby Watson.   *Coach: First Team:* W. Humphries.   *Second Team:* R. Morrison
Secretary: George W. Peat C.A.
Club Colours: White shirt with red diamond, white shorts, black stockings with red and white tops.
Club Nickname: 'Diamonds' or 'Waysiders'.
Record Attendance: 24,000 v Hearts, Scottish Cup, March 8th, 1952.

1978–79 LEAGUE RECORD

Match No.	Date	Venue	Opponents	Result	H/T Score	League Pos'n	Goalscorers	Attendance
1	Aug 12	H	Queen of the S	W 4-1	2-0	—	Clark 2, Goldthorp, Lapsley	2500
2	19	A	Kilmarnock	L 0-2	0-0	5		2700
3	26	H	Hamilton A	W 4-1	1-0	3	Clark, McCann, McGuire, Lapsley (pen)	2000
4	Sept 6	H	Ayr U	L 2-4	1-1	—	Clark, Lapsley (pen)	3000
5	9	A	Dumbarton	D 1-1	0-0	6	McCann	2000
6	13	A	Montrose	D 2-2	1-1	—	McGuire, Walker	900
7	16	H	Raith R	W 3-0	1-0	4	Goldthorp 2, Houston (og)	2000
8	23	A	St Johnstone	W 2-0	1-0	3	Clark, Goldthorp	1548
9	27	H	Clydebank	D 1-1	0-0	—	Jonquin	3500
10	30	H	Stirling Albion	W 2-1	1-0	3	Clark, Lapsley (pen)	2000
11	Oct 7	A	Clyde	L 1-2	0-2	4	Clark	2127
12	14	H	Arbroath	D 1-1	0-0	6	Short	2000
13	21	A	Dundee	L 0-1	0-0	7		5600
14	28	H	Kilmarnock	W 4-1	3-0	6	Clark 2 (1 a pen), McCormack, Smith	3000
15	Nov 4	A	Hamilton A	L 0-2	0-2	6		1800
16	11	H	Dumbarton	L 3-6	1-3	7	Clark 2 (1 a pen), Goldthorp	1500
17	18	A	Raith R	L 0-2	0-1	8		1800
18	25	H	St Johnstone	L 0-1	0-0	8		1500
19	Dec 9	H	Clyde	D 2-2	1-1	10	March 2	2500
20	16	A	Arbroath	D 3-3	0-1	8	Clark, McCulloch, Goldthorp	807
21	26	H	Dundee	L 0-2	0-0	9		2700
22	Feb 28	H	Arbroath	W 2-0	1-0	—	Lapsley 2 (2 pens)	2000
23	Mar 3	A	Queen of the S	W 3-1	0-0	8	McGuire, Goldthorp 2	900
24	7	A	Clyde	W 3-2	1-0	—	Clark, McGuire, Goldthorp	600
25	10	A	Ayr U	D 0-0	0-0	7		3525
26	14	H	Hamilton A	W 2-1	2-1	—	Clark, Kirkland	900
27	24	A	Clydebank	L 1-4	0-2	7	Clark	1500
28	27	A	St Johnstone	W 3-1	1-0	—	McGuire, Goldthorp 2	1646
29	31	H	Queen of the S	W 5-1	2-1	7	Clark, Goldthorp 4 (1 a pen)	600
30	Apr 4	H	Raith R	L 0-1	0-0	—		2000
31	7	H	Clydebank	L 1-3	0-0	8	March (pen)	1200
32	11	A	Kilmarnock	L 0-1	0-1	—		3000
33	14	A	Stirling Albion	L 1-2	1-1	8	Goldthorp	1000
34	18	H	Montrose	D 1-1	0-0	—	McVeigh	2000
35	21	H	Dundee	L 2-4	1-2	8	McVeigh, March (pen)	3500
36	25	A	Stirling Albion	W 2-1	1-0	—	Clark 2	1000
37	28	H	Ayr U	W 2-0	1-0	6	Clark, McVeigh	1500
38	May 2	A	Dumbarton	W 1-0	0-0	—	McKeown	500
39	5	H	Montrose	W 8-2	2-2	6	Clark 4, McGuire 3 (1 a pen) McVeigh	1000

Final League Position: 6.

Goalscorers
League (72): Clark 23 (2 pens), Goldthorp 16 (1 a pen), McGuire 8 (1 a pen), Lapsley 6 (5 pens), McVeigh 4, March 4 (2 pens), McCann 2, Jonquin 1, Kirkland 1, McCormack 1, McCulloch 1, McKeown 1, Short 1, Smith 1, Walker 1, own goal 1.
League Cup (10): Clark 2, Goldthorp 2, Lapsley 2 (2 pens), Walker 2, Jonquin 1, McCann 1.
Cup (1): Clark 1.

Honours
Scottish League: Division 1, Runners-up: 1922–23, 1923–24, 1924–25, 1925–26.
Division 2, Champions: 1902–03, 1954–55, 1973–74, Runners-up: 1900–01, 1946–47, 1949–50, 1965–66.
Scottish Cup: Winners: 1924, Runners-up 1975.
Scottish League Cup: None.
Spring Cup: Winners: 1975–76.
Record Victory: 11-1 v Falkirk, Division, 1950–51.
Record Defeat: 1-11 v Hibernian, Division 1, 1959–60.
Most League Points: 60, Division 2, 1973–74.
Most Individual League Goals in Season: 45, H. G. Yarnall, Division 1, 1916–17.
Most Capped Player: Jimmy Crapnell, 9, Scotland.
Highest goalscorers in British league football 1973–74 with 102 goals.

Poulton M	McGarr E	Jonquin P	Cowan M	Lapsley J	Black J	Short M	March J	Walker T	Veitch T	Henderson W	Clark A	McKeown B	Anderson N	McCann K	Goldthorp J	Smith H	McPhee R	Wilson W	McGuire W	McCormack R	McCulloch W	Docherty A	Ross J	McVeigh J	Gordon I	Kirkland B	Rodgers J	McClymont J	Erwin H	Match No.
1	2		3	5				4			8		6	7	9	10			11											1
1	2	12	3	5				4			8		6	7	9	10			11*											2
1	2		3	5				4			8		6	7	9	10			11											3
1	2		3	5				4			8		6	7	9	10			11											4
1	2		3	5				4			8		6	7	9	10	12		11*											5
	1	2	3	5				4			8		6	7	9	10			12					11*						6
1	2	12	3	5				4			8		6	7	9	10*			11											7
1	2		3	6	4					10	8		5	7	9			12	11*											8
1	2		3	5				4			8		6	7	9		10*12	11												9
1	2		3	5				4			8		6	7	9	10	12	11*												10
1	2		3	5				4			8	10	6	7	9			11												11
1		3	10	5	2	13	4			7*	8†	6		9				12	11											12
1		3	10	4	2	5	6				8			9	7			11												13
1		3	10	4*	2	5	6				8	12		7				13	11	9†										14
1		3	10	4	2	5					8	13	6			7*			11	9†12										15
1		3	10	4	2	5					6	12	13	7*	8				11	9†										16
	1	2		3	5						9	8	4	7*10	11†12	13		6												17
	1	2		3	5		12				9		4	7*10	8			11	6											18
	1	2		10	5	6					11		4		9			7		8	3									19
1		2*		10	5		6	12			11		4	13	9			7†		8	3									20
	1	2		10	5		6	13		12			4		9			7*		8†	3	11								21
	1	2		6			5	8	4		9							11		10	3	7								22
	1	2		6			5	7	4		8				9	12		11		10	3*									23
	1	2	3	6			5	7	4		8				9	10		11												24
	1	2	3	6			5	7	4		8				9	10		11*						12						25
	1	2	3	6			5	7	4		8				9	10								11						26
	1	2	3	6*			5	7	4		8				9†10			12						11	13					27
	1		2	3			5	7	4		8	12	6		9			11*					10							28
	1		2	3			5	7	4		8	12	6		9			11					10*							29
	1		2	3			5	7	4		8		6		9								10	11						30
	1	2	3	6			5		4		8	7	10		9*			11						12						31
	1		3†	6			5	7	4		8	12			9			11			2*		10	13						32
	1		3	6*			5	7	4		8	12			9			11			2		10†13							33
	1		3			2	5	6	4		8			9				7					10	11						34
	1		3	6		2	5	7	4		8	10						11					9							35
	1		3	6*		2	5	7	4		8	10						11					9							36
	1	2		3	12		5	6			8	7	4					11*					9	10						37
	1	2		3			5	6			8	7	4		9			11					10			3	12	2		38
	1			4			5	6*			8	7						11					9†10	13	3	12	2			39
6	33	25	18	38	22	8	25	31	15	1	38	6	26	14	31	18	1	33	3	7	7	2	11	3	4	1	0	1		
		+		+			+	+		+		+	+		+	+		+	+				+				+			
		2s		1s			2s	2s		1s		6s	2s	1s		1s	4s	3s	3s				1s				3s	2s	2s	

ALBION ROVERS   DIV. 2

Year Formed: 1882. *Ground:* Cliftonhill Park. *Capacity:* 10,000 (580 seats). *Telephone:* Coatbridge 32350
Manager: Sam Goodwin *Secretary:* David Lyttle. *Club Colours:* Primrose shirts, with red trim and number, red shorts, primrose stockings.
Record Attendance: 27,381 v Rangers, Scottish Cup, 2nd Rd, Feb 8th, 1936.
Previous Grounds: Meadow Park, Whifflet, 1881-1919.
Club Nickname: "The Wee Rovers".

1978-79 LEAGUE RECORD

Match No.	Date	Venue	Opponents	Result	H/T Score	League Pos'n	Goalscorers	Attendance
1	Aug 12	A	East Fife	W 2-0	1-0	—	Cleland 2	642
2	19	H	Falkirk	D 1-1	0-1	3	Cleland	1500
3	26	A	Stranraer	L 1-3	0-1	5	Hart	1200
4	Sept 6	A	Dunfermline Ath	L 1-2	1-2	—	Hart	1800
5	9	H	Meadowbank T	L 1-2	1-1	12	Cleland	300
6	13	H	Forfar Ath	W 3-0	1-0	—	Allan, Cleland 2 (1 a pen)	300
7	16	A	Berwick R	L 0-2	0-2	12		882
8	23	H	Alloa	L 1-2	0-1	12	Cleland (pen)	500
9	26	A	East Stirling	D 3-3	0-3	—	Hart, Shields, McGillivray	400
10	30	A	Queen's Park	L 0-2	0-1	13		873
11	Oct 7	H	Brechin C	W 3-2	2-1	10	Leishman 2, Franchetti	400
12	14	A	Cowdenbeath	L 1-4	1-1	12	Hill	500
13	21	H	Stenhousemuir	L 0-1	0-1	14		300
14	28	A	Falkirk	L 1-2	0-2	14	Shields	2000
15	Nov 4	H	Stranraer	W 2-1	0-0	13	Hart 2	300
16	11	A	Meadowbank T	L 0-2	0-2	13		200
17	25	A	Alloa	W 6-2	2-1	13	Main, Cleland 2, Shields, Loughran 2	750
18	Dec 9	A	Brechin C	D 1-1	0-1	13	Cleland (pen)	300
19	23	A	Stenhousemuir	L 2-3	0-2	14	Hart, Coyle	430
20	Feb 17	H	Stranraer	W 1-0	0-0	14	Hill	600
21	24	A	Cowdenbeath	L 1-3	1-2	14	Cleland	400
22	Mar 3	A	East Fife	W 2-1	0-1	14	Main, Cleland	747
23	10	H	Dunfermline Ath	D 1-1	1-0	14	Cleland	800
24	13	H	Cowdenbeath	D 1-1	1-0	—	Cleland	500
25	28	A	Berwick R	L 1-5	0-2	—	Cleland	1000
26	31	H	East Fife	W 2-0	0-0	14	Cleland 2	300
27	Apr 3	H	Meadowbank T	W 2-0	2-0	—	Franchetti, Cleland	300
28	7	A	East Stirling	W 1-0	1-0	11	Hill	200
29	14	H	Queen's Park	W 1-0	1-0	10	Franchetti	500
30	16	A	Forfar Ath	D 1-1	1-0	—	Cleland	700
31	18	H	Queen's Park	W 4-0	1-0	—	Cleland 2, Hill, Leishman	400
32	21	A	Stenhousemuir	W 3-2	2-1	8	Franchetti, Hill, Cleland	300
33	25	H	Berwick R	L 0-2	0-0	—		600
34	28	H	Dunfermline Ath	W 1-0	0-0	9	Gillespie	1000
35	May 1	H	Falkirk	D 0-0	0-0	—		700
36	3	H	Brechin C	D 2-2	1-1	—	Cleland (pen), Leishman	300
37	6	A	Forfar Ath	D 1-1	0-1	—	Hart	600
38	8	H	East Stirling	D 1-1	1-1	—	Cleland	300
39	10	H	Alloa	W 2-1	1-1	—	Leishman, Robertson J	250

Final League Position: 7

Goalscorers

League (57): Cleland 24 (4 pens), Hart 7, Hill 5, Leishman 5, Franchetti 4, Shields 3, Loughran 2, Main 2, Allan 1, Coyle 1, Gillespie 1, McGillivray 1, Robertson J 1.
League Cup (0).
Cup (4): Loughran 2, Cleland 1, Main 1.

Honours
Scottish League: Division 2 Champions 1933-34; Runners-up: 1913-14, 1937-38, 1947-48.
Scottish Cup: Finalists 1920.

Record Victory: 10-0 v Brechin C, Division 2, 1937-38.
Record Defeat: 1-9 v Motherwell Division 1, 1936-37.
Most League Points: 54, Division 2, 1929-30.
Most Individual League Goals in Season: Jim Renwick, 41, 1932-33.
Most Capped Player: Jock White, 1(2), Scotland.

Orr J	Balavage J	Livingstone B	McLeod D	McGregor J	Main D	Doran M	Franchetti R	Shields D	Loughran G	Taylor A	Leishman W	Cleland B	Muldoon W	Allan P	Coyle A	Hill H	Hart I	McGillivray J	Gillespie I	McKee W	McLean D	Flavell G	McLeod J	Boyce K	Bonnar J	Reilly J	Robertson I	Robertson J	Match No.
1			3		4	5					6	9	2	7		8	11*			12	10								1
1			3		4	5					6	9	2	7	13	8*	10†	11		12									2
1			3	6		9	5				4	10	2	7*	12	8†	13	11											3
1			3	6		4	5				2	9	8		7		10	11											4
1		2*	3	6		13					5	10	7	4	8	12		11	9†										5
1			3	6			5				4	9	2	8		7	10	11											6
1		12	3	6			5				4	9	2	7	13	8*	10†	11											7
1		2*	3	6		13		12				9†	4		7	8	10	11				5							8
	1		3	6		4*	5				2	9	8	7†		10	12	11	13										9
	1	2	3	6		13			7*		5		4	8†	12	10	9	11											10
1			3	6		10	5				4		2	7*	13	8	9†	11	12										11
1			3	6*	2	9	5				4		8	13	7†	10	12	11											12
1			3	6		9	5	7			2		10	8*	12	4†		11			13								13
1			3	6		13	9	7			5		4	8*	11		10†	12		2									14
1			3	6*			9	7			5		4		8	10	11	12		2									15
1			3	6		4	5	7				10		13	8	9*	11†	12		2									16
1			3	11		4	5	8			6	9	10	7*		12				2									17
1			3	11		4	5	8			6	9	10		12	7†	13			2*									18
	1		3	6*		4	5	11				9†	10	7	12	8	13			2									19
	1		3	6		4	5	11				9	10	7		8				2									20
	1		3	6			5			4	9	2	13	7		8	10*		11†	12									21
	1		3	4		6					5	9	11	2	7	8	10*		12										22
	1		3	4		6		12	11*	5	9			2		8	10		7										23
	1		3	4		6		12	11	5	9			2		8	10		7*										24
	1		3	4		6		7	11	5	9			2		8	10												25
	1		3	6		13		12		5	9			2	7	4	10		8*	11†									26
	1		3	6		11		8		5	9			2	7	4	10												27
	1		3	6		8		10*		5	9			2	7	4			11	12									28
	1		3	6		8		12		5	9			2	7	4	10*		11										29
			3	6		10				5	9			2	7	4			11					1	8				30
	1		3	6		8				5	9			2	7	4	10		11										31
	1		3	6		10		9*	8	5				2	7	4	12		11										32
	1		3	6		10				5	9	8		2	7	4			11										33
	1		3	6		10		8*		5	9	12		2	7	4			11										34
	1		3	6		10		8		5				2	7	4	9		11										35
	1		3			10		8*		5	9	12		2	7	4			11							6			36
	1		3	6		10		8*		5	9	13		2	7	4	12		11†										37
	1		3	6		10		11		5	9			2	7	4	8												38
	1		3	6		10				5	9			2	7	4											8		39
9	27	2	3	37	38	1	30	18	17	3	35	31	24	31	22	34	23	14	15	2	1	7	1	0	1	1	1		
				+1s				+5s			+5s			+3s	+2s	+8s	+2s	+7s	+2s	+1s	+8s				+1s				

ALLOA   DIV. 2

Year Formed: 1883. *Ground:* Recreation Ground. *Size:* 110 × 75 yds. *Capacity:* 9,000.
Telephone: Alloa 722695. *Manager:* Hugh Wilson.
Secretary: George Ormiston.
Club Colours: Gold with black trim, black shorts, gold socks with black tops.
Club Nickname: 'The Wasps'.
Record attendance: 13,000 v Dunfermline Ath., Scottish Cup 3rd. Rd., replay, Feb. 26th, 1939.

1978–79 LEAGUE RECORD

Match No.	Date	Venue	Opponents	Result	H/T Score	League Pos'n	Goalscorers	Attendance
1	Aug 12	A	Stranraer	L 0-4	0-3	—		1100
2	19	H	Brechin C	D 1-1	0-1	12	Cochrane	800
3	26	A	Stenhousemuir	W 2-0	2-0	9	Irvine, Hamilton	500
4	Sept 6	A	Falkirk	L 0-1	0-1	—		2500
5	9	H	Dunfermline Ath	D 1-1	0-1	11	Miller (pen)	1275
6	13	H	Berwick R	W 2-1	0-1	—	Irvine, Wallace	500
7	16	H	Cowdenbeath	L 2-4	1-3	11	Hamilton, Miller (pen)	789
8	23	A	Albion R	W 2-1	1-0	9	Irvine 2	500
9	27	H	Queen's Park	W 1-0	0-0	—	Irvine	500
10	30	H	Meadowbank T	D 1-1	1-0	7	Carberry	800
11	Oct 7	A	East Stirling	L 2-3	0-2	7	Irvine, Henderson	800
12	14	A	Forfar Ath	L 1-2	0-2	7	Cochrane	1066
13	21	H	East Fife	D 0-0	0-0	7		800
14	28	A	Brechin C	L 2-4	0-1	11	Steele, Morrison	300
15	Nov 4	H	Stenhousemuir	W 2-1	1-1	8	Irvine 2	500
16	11	A	Dunfermline Ath	D 2-2	1-2	8	Cochrane, Miller (pen)	3000
17	18	H	Cowdenbeath	W 4-0	3-0	6	Irvine 2, Morrison, McLeod	800
18	25	H	Albion R	L 2-6	1-2	8	Irvine, Miller	750
19	Dec 2	A	Meadowbank T	W 1-0	1-0	6	Miller (pen)	250
20	9	H	East Stirling	D 2-2	1-1	6	Carberry, Morrison	450
21	23	A	East Fife	L 0-3	0-2	8		1136
22	Feb 3	A	Berwick R	W 1-0	0-0	7	Morrison	865
23	10	A	East Stirling	L 1-3	1-3	7	Morrison	600
24	24	H	Forfar Ath	W 2-0	1-0	7	Cochrane, McLeod	639
25	Mar 3	H	Stranraer	W 3-1	2-0	6	Kelly 2, Irvine	550
26	6	A	Stenhousemuir	W 1-0	1-0	—	Irvine	500
27	10	H	Falkirk	D 3-3	0-1	5	Carberry, Holt, Donald	1800
28	17	A	Berwick R	L 2-3	1-1	6	Cochrane 2	740
29	24	H	Queen's Park	D 1-1	1-0	5	Kelly (pen)	715
30	28	A	Forfar Ath	L 0-2	0-1	—		869
31	31	H	Stranraer	L 0-1	0-0	6		450
32	Apr 4	A	Cowdenbeath	L 1-5	1-0	—	Muir	300
33	7	A	Queen's Park	W 1-0	0-0	5	Kelly	7000
34	14	A	Meadowbank T	D 1-1	0-1	6	Muir	200
35	18	H	Brechin C	W 1-0	0-0	—	Kelly	450
36	21	H	East Fife	W 4-3	4-0	5	Hamilton 2, Miller, Kelly	600
37	28	H	Falkirk	W 2-0	1-0	5	Kelly, McIntosh	1250
38	May 5	H	Dunfermline Ath	W 2-0	1-0	5	Hamilton, McIntosh	2000
39	10	A	Albion R	L 1-2	1-1	—	Morrison	250

Final League Position 6

Goalscorers

League (57): Irvine 13, Kelly 7 (1 a pen), Cochrane 6, Miller 6 (4 pens), Morrison 6, Hamilton 5, Carberry 3, McIntosh 2, McLeod 2, Muir 2, Donald 1, Henderson 1, Holt 1, Steele 1, Wallace 1.
League Cup (6): Miller 2 (1 a pen), Morrison 2, Cochrane 1, Steele 1.
Cup (2): Holt 1, Morrison 1.

Honours

Scottish League: Division 2 Champions 1921–22; Runners-up 1938–39, 1976–77.
Record Victory: 9-2 v Forfar, Division 2, March 18th, 1933.
Record Defeat: 0-10 v Dundee, Division 2, March 8th, 1947.
Most League Points: 60, 1921–22.
Most Individual League Goals in Season: 49, Wee Crilley, Division 2, 1931–22.
Most Capped Player: Jock Hepburn 1, Scotland.

McNab D	Wallace J	McCann H	Nolt A	Henderson I	Carberry R	Miller D	Cochrane J	Hamilton L	Morrison W	Donald J	Kelly W	McGarry B	Ivine W	Lawson S	Connor J	Steele T	McLeod D	Dunn P	McIntosh C	Muir J	Inglis T	Ferguson J	Hargreaves D	Letham P		Match No.
1	2	3		4	6	7	5		11	9		10				8										1
1	2	3	8	6	7	5	10*11†	9		13	4	12														2
1	3	2	12	8*	6	13	5	11		9	4	10†		7												3
1	3	2	7	8	6		5	11		9	4	10														4
1	3	2		8	6	12	5	11		13	4*	9				7†10										5
1	11	2		3*	4	8	7	5	9	13		10					12	6†								6
1	11	2		3*	4	8	7	5	9	13		10					12	6†								7
1	3	2	5		12	6	7	8	13	11	9†	10	4*													8
1	3	2	5		12	6	7	8*13	11†	9		10	4													9
1	3	2	5		8	6	7*		11	12	9	10	4													10
1	3	2	5	12	8		7	6*11		9†		10	4			13										11
1		2		3	8	6	7	5	9			10	4			11										12
1		2	5*	3	11	6			10	12	8†		9	4		13	7									13
1		2		3	4	6	8	5	10	11		9				7										14
1	3		5	2	10	6	7		12		9*	11	4			8										15
1	3	4	5	2	9	6	7		11			10	12			8*										16
1	3	4	5	2	11	6*	7†		9		12	10	13			8										17
1	3	4	5		11†	6	7		9		13	10	2*			12	8									18
1	3	4		2	11	6	7		9†13			10	12				8*	5								19
1	3	4	5	2	11	6	7*		9			10				12	8									20
1	3			2	11†	6	7*	5	9		12	10	4			13	8									21
1		2	5	5	3	11		7	6	9		10	4			12	8*									22
1		2*	5	3	8	6	7	11†	9			10	4			13	12									23
1	3		5	2	11†	6	7*		9	12	13	4	10			8										24
1	3		5	2		6	7		10*		9	4	11			12	8									25
1	3		5	2		6	7†13	11	12	9		4	10				8*									26
1	3		5	2	8	6	7*13	11	12	9†		4	10													27
1	3		5	2	8	6	7	12	11*		9	4	10													28
1	3		5*		6		9	12	8	11	10	4	7	2												29
1			5	3	8	6	7	13	9	11	12	4†10*	2													30
1	13		6	3		12	8†	5	10	11	9		4		2	7*										31
1	3	5*		. 2		6		12	9	10	13	4		7					11†	8						32
1	12	2*	5	3			6†		4	9	11	13				10	8			7						33
1	13	2	5	3			6		4	9	11	12				10†	8*			7						34
1		2	5	3			10		4	6	11	13					8*			7		12	9†			35
1	12	2	5	3			6	8	4	10	11	9				7*										36
1		2	5	3			6	8†	4	11	12	9	13						10	7*						37
1		2	5	3			6		4	8	11	9							10	7						38
1		2	5	3			6		4	11		9							7		8	10				39
39	23	29	29	29	26	34	30	23	35	14	20	12	29	15	1	7	20	1	2	7	1	1	1	1		
	+			+	+	+	+	+	+		+	+	+	+		+	+			+						
	4s			1s	1s	2s	1s	2s	6s	3s	7s	12s	1s	1s		3s			10s	2s				1s		

ARBROATH DIV. 1.

Year Formed: 1878. *Ground:* Gayfield Park. *Capacity:* 15,000. *Telephone:* Arbroath 72157.
Manager: Albert Henderson.
Trainer: Dave Easson. *Club Colours:* Maroon shirts, white shorts, maroon stockings.
Club Nickname: 'Red Lichties'.
Record Attendance: 13,510 v Rangers, Scottish Cup 3rd Rd, Feb. 23rd, 1952.
Record Transfer Fee received: £35,000 from Aberdeen for Billy Pirie, March 1974 and £35,000 from St Mirren for Jim Bone, Jan 1978.

1977–78 LEAGUE RECORD

Match No.	Date	Venue	Opponents	Result	H/T Score	League Pos'n	Goalscorers	Attendance
1	Aug 12	H	Dumbarton	D 1-1	0-1	—	Mylles	1156
2	19	A	Dundee	L 0-2	0-2	13		6826
3	26	H	Montrose	L 1-3	1-2	14	Cargill	1472
4	Sept 2	A	Clydebank	L 2-5	1-2	—	Kidd, Mylles	400
5	9	A	Hamilton A	L 1-3	0-3	14	Kidd	1500
6	13	H	Queen of the S	D 1-1	1-0	—	Kidd	804
7	16	H	St Johnstone	W 3-0	2-0	13	Kidd, Gavine 2	1056
8	23	A	Stirling Albion	L 1-2	0-1	13	Gavine	850
9	27	A	Ayr U	L 0-3	0-1	—		2500
10	30	H	Raith R	L 0-5	0-3	14		1238
11	Oct 7	A	Kilmarnock	L 1-3	1-2	14	Fletcher (pen)	2000
12	14	A	Airdrieonians	D 1-1	0-0	14	Mitchell	2000
13	21	H	Clyde	L 0-2	0-1	14		1098
14	28	H	Dundee	L 0-1	0-0	14		3852
15	Nov 4	A	Montrose	L 0-3	0-0	14		1200
16	11	H	Hamilton A	W 3-0	0-0	14	Yule, Fletcher 2	1000
17	18	A	St Johnstone	D 1-1	0-0	14	Kidd	1516
18	25	H	Stirling Albion	W 1-0	1-0	14	Kidd	859
19	Dec 9	A	Kilmarnock	W 3-2	2-0	14	Yule 2, Wilson	880
20	16	H	Airdrieonians	D 3-3	1-0	14	Yule, Wilson 2	807
21	23	A	Clyde	L 0-1	0-0	14		1000
22	Jan 20	H	Stirling Albion	D 0-0	0-0	14		777
23	Feb 10	H	Kilmarnock	L 0-1	0-0	14		1284
24	21	H	Montrose	W 4-0	1-0	—	Wilson, Fletcher, Kydd 2	988
25	24	A	Queen of the S	D 1-1	0-0	12	Yule	1100
26	28	A	Airdrieonians	L 0-2	0-1	—		2000
27	Mar 3	H	Dumbarton	D 1-1	0-0	12	Yule	863
28	7	A	Hamilton A	L 0-2	0-0	—		1200
29	10	A	Clydebank	D 2-2	0-0	12	Carson, Gavine	1500
30	17	A	Queen of the S	D 2-2	2-2	11	Yule, Mylles	900
31	24	H	Ayr U	W 4-1	1-0	11	McKenzie, Mylles 3	992
32	31	A	Dumbarton	W 1-0	1-0	11	Mylles	450
33	Apr 4	H	St Johnstone	W 3-1	3-1	—	Gavine 2, Mylles	1348
34	7	H	Ayr U	L 2-3	0-1	11	Kidd (pen), Mylles	1012
35	14	A	Raith R	W 2-1	1-0	10	Yule, Fletcher	1200
36	18	A	Raith R	L 0-1	0-0	—		1000
37	21	H	Clyde	W 2-0	2-0	10	Gavine, Carson	1043
38	28	H	Clydebank	D 1-1	0-1	11	Yule	1238
39	May 6	A	Dundee	W 2-0	1-0	—	Kidd, McLaren (og)	8385

Final League Position 10.

Goalscorers

League (50): Mylles 9, Yule 9, Kidd 8 (1 a pen), Gavine 7, Fletcher 5 (1 a pen), Wilson 4, Carson 2, Kydd 2, Cargill 1, McKenzie 1, Mitchell 1, own goal 1.
League Cup (6): McKenzie 2, Cargill 1, Fletcher 1, Gavine 1, Yule 1.
Cup (0).

Honours

Scottish League: Division 2 Runners-up 1934-35, 1958-59, 1967-68, 1971-72.
Record Victory: 36-0 v Bon Accord, Scottish Cup 1st Rd, Sep. 12th, 1885.
Record Defeat: 0-8 v Kilmarnock, Division 2, 1948-49.
Most League Points: 57, Division 2, 1966-67.
Most Individual League Goals in Season: 45, Dave Easson, Division 2, 1958-59.
Most Capped Player: Ned Doig, 2(6), Scotland.

Lister J	Rylance D	Cargill T	Follon N	Carson J	Fettes A	Mitchell J	Kydd L	Smith J	Wells W	Fletcher J	Kidd A	Gavine W	McKenzie A	Yule T	Grant I	Mylles S	Edwards A	Wilson T	Durno D	Neil M	Match No.
1	3	4			8	6			5	7		9	2	11	10						1
1	3	4		8*	6				5	7	10	9	2	12	13	11†					2
1	3	4			6*		8	5	7	10		9	2	12		11					3
1	3	4		8	6			7	5*		10	9†	2	11	12	13					4
1	3	4		5	6			7	12		10	9	2	13	11†	8*					5
1	3	4		5	6		10		7	8			2	11			9				6
1	3	4		5	6	7	8		12	10*		9	2	11†		13					7
1	3	4		5	6	7*	8			10		9	2	11†12		13					8
1	3	4		5	6	13	8†	12		10		9	2	11*				7			9
1	3*	8		5	6	13	12	4		7	10	9†	2	11							10
1	3	4	2	12	6*				5	7†10		9	8	13			11				11
1	3	4	2	5	6	12				7*10		9	8	11							12
1	3	4	2	5	13	12				7	10	9*	6	11†		8					13
1	3	4	2		6*		13	5	11	10			7	12			8†	9			14
1	3	4	2		6			5	8*11	10		7	12					9			15
1	3	4		13	6*			5	7	10	12	2	11				8†	9			16
1	3	4		10	6			5	8	7		2	11*	12				9			17
1	3	4		10	6			5	8	7	12	2	11					9*			18
1	3	4		10	6	12		5	7*		13	2	11				8†	9			19
1	3	4		10	6	7*	8	5				12	2	11				9			20
1	3	4	2		6			5		7		10	11		12		8*	9			21
1	3	4		8				5	7	10		2	11				6	9			22
1	3	4		5	6	12	8		7*10	13		2	11					9†			23
1	3	4		5	6		8		7	10		2	11					9			24
1	3	4		5	6	13	8*		7	10	12	2	11					9†			25
1	3	4		5	6		8		7	10	9	2	11*	12							26
1	3	4		5	6				7	10	8	2	11		12			9*			27
1	3	4		5	12		6*		7	10	8	2	11		13			9†			28
1	3	4		5		7*	6		12	10	8	2	11		9						29
1	3	5			4		6		7	10	8	2	11		9						30
1	3	4		5			6		7*10	8		2	11		9	12					31
1	3	4		5	12		6*		13	10	8	2	11		9	7†					32
1	3	4		5			6		7	10	8	2	11*		9	12					33
1	3	4		5	12		6*		7	10	8	2	11†		9	13					34
1	3	4		5	12		6*		7†10	8		2	11		9	13					35
1	3	4		5		12	6		7	10	8	2	11*		9						36
1	3	4		5	12		6*		7†10	8		2	11		9	13					37
1	3	4		5	12		6*		7†10	8		2	11		9	13					38
1	3	4		5			6		7	10	8*	2	11					9	12		39
39	39	39	6	32	26	4	20	4	15	30	36	27	33	1	14	6	17	0	2		
			+	+	+	+		+	+	+			+	+	+		+	+			
			2s	7s	8s	2s		3s	2s				6s	6s	3s	8s		6s	1s		

R.F. 79/80—27

AYR UNITED

DIV. 1

Year Formed: 1910.
Ground: Somerset Park.   *Size:* 111×75yds.   *Capacity:* 18,500 (1,500 seats).
Telephone: Ayr 63435.
Manager: Willie McLean.   *Coach:* George Caldwell.
Secretary: John Robertson.
Club Colours: White shirts with black facings, black shorts, white stockings.
Club Nickname: 'The Honest Men'.
Record Attendance: 25,225 v Rangers, Division 1, Sept 13, 1969.

1978–79 LEAGUE RECORD

Match No.	Date		Venue	Opponents	Result	H/T Score	League Pos'n	Goalscorers	Attendance
1	Aug	12	H	Dundee	L 0-1	0-1	—		3875
2		19	A	Queen of the S	L 0-1	0-1	14		2000
3		26	H	Kilmarnock	D 0-0	0-0	13		5000
4	Sept	6	A	Airdrieonians	W 4-2	1-1	—	McCall 2, McLaughlin, Cramond	3000
5		9	A	Raith R	D 0-0	0-0	9		1800
6		13	H	Hamilton A	L 1-2	0-1	—	Cramond	2359
7		16	H	Dumbarton	L 2-5	1-0	12	Phillips, McLelland	2146
8		23	A	Clyde	W 1-0	0-0	11	McCall	1500
9		27	H	Arbroath	W 3-0	1-0	—	McCall, McLaughlin 2	2500
10		30	H	St Johnstone	W 1-0	1-0	8	Masterton	3239
11	Oct	7	A	Stirling Albion	W 2-1	0-0	8	Phillips, McAllister	1600
12		14	A	Montrose	W 6-4	3-1	7	McSherry, Phillips 2, Masterton, McLaughlin 2	1300
13		21	H	Clydebank	W 4-3	2-0	6	Phillips 2, Masterton, Christie	3843
14		28	H	Queen of the S	D 1-1	1-0	5	McLaughlin (pen)	3822
15	Nov	4	A	Kilmarnock	W 2-1	0-0	3	McCall, Christie	6200
16		11	H	Raith R	W 3-0	2-0	3	McCall, Cramond, Reilly	3663
17		18	A	Dumbarton	L 0-2	0-0	5		2500
18		25	H	Clyde	W 2-0	2-0	3	Phillips, McLaughlin	3841
19	Dec	9	A	Stirling Albion	L 0-1	0-0	3		2711
20		16	H	Montrose	W 5-0	1-0	3	Phillips, McLaughlin 4 (1 a pen)	2505
21		23	A	Clydebank	L 1-3	0-1	4	McSherry	2000
22		30	A	Queen of the S	W 1-0	0-0	3	Christie	1500
23	Feb	3	A	Hamilton A	L 1-3	1-1	5	Christie	3000
24		10	H	Stirling Albion	W 2-0	1-0	3	Wells, McLaughlin (pen)	2751
25		24	H	Montrose	W 5-0	3-0	3	Masterton, Cramond, Phillips, Christie, D'Arcy B (og)	2500
26		28	A	Clyde	W 5-0	1-0	—	Phillips 3, McLaughlin 2 (1 a pen)	1500
27	Mar	7	H	Kilmarnock	W 2-1	0-0	—	Phillips, Wells	5693
28		10	H	Airdrieonians	D 0-0	0-0	2		3525
29		14	A	Raith R	L 0-2	0-0	—		1200
30		17	H	Hamilton A	W 2-1	1-1	3	Phillips, McLaughlin (pen)	2422
31		24	A	Arbroath	L 1-4	0-1	3	McLaughlin	992
32		31	H	Dundee	L 1-2	1-1	5	McLaughlin (pen)	2970
33	Apr	7	A	Arbroath	W 3-2	1-0	5	McSherry 2, McCutcheon	1072
34		14	H	St Johnstone	W 4-2	0-0	4	Christie, Masterton, McCutcheon, McNeill (og)	2432
35		18	H	Dumbarton	W 1-0	0-0	—	McLaughlin (pen)	2000
36		21	A	Clydebank	W 1-0	1-0	4	McCutcheon	1000
37		28	A	Airdrieonians	L 0-2	0-0	4		1500
38	May	5	A	St Johnstone	L 2-4	1-3	4	McCutcheon 2	1458
39		10	A	Dundee	D 2-2	0-1	—	McSherry, McLaughlin	7692

Final League Position: 4

Goalscorers
League (71): McLaughlin 19 (7 pens), Phillips 14, Christie 6, McCall 6, McCutcheon 5, McSherry 5, Masterton 5, Cramond 4, Wells 2, McAllister 1, McLelland 1, Reilly 1, own goals 2.
League Cup: (11): McLaughlin 4 (1 a pen), McLelland 3, Cramond 2, McCall 2.
Cup: (6): McLaughlin 3 (1 a pen), Phillips 2, McLelland 1.

Honours
Scottish League: Division 2, Champions: 1911-12, 1912-13, 1927-28, 1936-37, 1958-59, 1965-66. Runners-up: 1910-11, 1955-56, 1968-69.
Scottish Cup: None.
Scottish League Cup: None.
Record Victory: 11-1 v Dumbarton, League Cup, Aug. 13th, 1952.
Record Defeat: 0-9 v Rangers, Division 1, Nov. 16th, 1929, and Hearts, Division 1, Feb. 28th, 1931.
Most League Points: 60, Division 2, 1958-59.
Most Individual League Goals in Season: Jimmy Smith 66 in 1927-28.
Most Capped Player: Jim Nisbet, 3, Scotland.

Sproat H	Northcote R	Wells D	Connor R	Kelly W	Scott R	McColl W	McAllister I	Fleeting J	Phillips J	Hannah R	McCall C W	McSherry J	McLaughlin B	Masterton D	Reilly R	Cramond G	McCutcheon D	McLelland S	Christie G	Roos G	Hyslop J	McIlwraith J	Brown C	Match No.
1	2	3	6		8	5		7*			4	10			11		9	12						1
1				4	5		13			10	7	6			11	8*	9†		12					2
1	2	3		10	5				4	7			8*13		11		9†12	6						3
1	2	3		6	5				8	10	12	7			11		9*		4					4
1	2	3	6	8	5			4	10*			7			11		9	12						5
1	2	3	6	8	5			4			7				10		9	11						6
	1	2*	3	6		5		7	8		12				10		9	11	4					7
1	2	3	6	4	5				10	11	7	9*		8			12							8
1	2	3			5				7	6	8	9			10		11	4						9
1	2	3		12	5		13		7	6	8	9*			10		11†	4						10
1	2	3		4	5		12		7	6	8	9*			10		11							11
1	2*	3	12	4	5		7†			6	8	9	13	10			11							12
1	2	3		4	5		7			6	8	9			10		11							13
1	2	3		4	5		7*			6	8	9	12	10			11							14
1	2	3		4	5		7*		12	6	8				10		9	11						15
1	2	3		4	5		12		7*		8			6	10		9	11						16
1	2		3	4	5		13		7†	6*	8		12	10			9	11						17
1	2		3	4	5		7			6	8				10		9	11*12						18
1	2		3	4	5		11			7	8			6			10	9*12						19
1	2		3	4	5		7			6	8				10		9	11						20
1	2	3		4	5		7			6	8	12			10		9*11							21
1		3	2	4	5		7			6	8*	9	12	10			11							22
1	2	3	13	4	5		12			6	8	9†			10		7*11							23
1	2	3			5	4	7			6	8	9*			10		12	11						24
1	2	12	3*	6	5	4	7†				8	13			10		9	11						25
1	2		3	6	5	4	7			12	8				10		9*11							26
1	2		3	6	5	4	7				8				10		9	11						27
1	2		3*	6	5	4	7			12	8	13			10		9†11							28
1	2	12	3*	6	5	4	7			13	8				10		9†11							29
1	2	3		6	5	4	9			7	8	12			10		11*							30
1	2	3		6	5	4	9*			8	7	12			10†		11		13					31
1	2	3		12	5	4	7			6*	8	9			10		11†		13					32
1		3		2	5	4				6	8	9			10	7	11							33
1		3		2	5	4	7			6	8	12			10	9*	11							34
1	2			3	5	4				6	8	9			10	7	11							35
1		3		2	5	4				6	8	9			10	7	11							36
1		3		2	5	4				6	8	9			10	7	11*			12				37
1	12	3		2	5	4*				13	8	9			10	7	11			6†				38
1	2	3		9	5	4				6	8				10	7	11							39
38	33	27	16	1	34	39	16	21	5	9	27	38	17	1	39	8	20	33	0	5	0	1		
	+	+	+		+		+			+	+	+	+	+		+	+	+	+	+				
	1s	2s	2s		2s		6s			1s	5s	1s	7s	4s		1s	4s	2s	1s	2s		1s		

BERWICK RANGERS   DIV. 1

Year Formed: 1881. *Ground:* Shielfield Park. *Size:* 112×76 yds. *Capacity:* 10,500.
Telephone: Berwick 7424. *Player-Manager:* Dave Smith.
Secretary: Dennis McCleary.
Club Colours: Gold shirts with black vertical stripes, black shorts with two gold stripes, gold stockings, black tops.
Record Attendance: 13,365 v Rangers, Scottish Cup, 1st Rd, Jan. 28th, 1967.
Club Nickname: 'The Wee Rangers'.

1978–79 LEAGUE RECORD

Match No.	Date	Venue	Opponents	Result	H/T Score	League Pos'n	Goalscorers	Attendance
1	Aug 12	A	Falkirk	L 0-6	0-1	—		1500
2	19	H	Stenhousemuir	W 6-1	2-1	9	Morton 2, Tait, Rutherford, McLeod, Smith D (pen)	1092
3	26	H	Meadowbank T	D 0-0	0-0	8		1110
4	Sept 6	A	Queen's Park	W 1-0	1-0	—	McLeod	500
5	9	H	East Fife	L 1-2	0-2	8	Halley (og)	900
6	13	A	Alloa	L 1-2	1-0	—	Smith I	500
7	16	H	Albion R	W 2-0	2-0	6	McLean, Morton (pen)	882
8	23	A	Brechin C	W 2-1	2-1	5	McLean, Brown	400
9	27	H	Cowdenbeath	W 4-1	1-0	—	McLean, Morton, Moyes, McLeod	750
10	30	H	East Stirling	W 5-2	0-1	4	Tait 2, Morton 3 (1 a pen)	1063
11	Oct 7	A	Forfar Ath	D 2-2	0-2	3	McLean 2	1011
12	14	H	Dunfermline Ath	D 2-2	1-1	4	Smith G, Davidson	1544
13	21	H	Stranraer	D 1-1	1-0	4	Morton	294
14	28	A	Stenhousemuir	W 2-0	2-0	3	Tait 2	500
15	Nov 3	A	Meadowbank T	W 5-0	2-0	—	Morton 2, McLean, Wheatley, Davidson	600
16	11	A	East Fife	W 4-2	1-2	3	McLean, Morton 2 (1 a pen) Wheatley	1170
17	25	H	Brechin C	W 2-0	1-0	3	McDowell, Smith D (pen)	900
18	Dec 9	H	Forfar Ath	L 2-4	1-3	3	Tait, Smith G	1000
19	16	A	East Fife	L 1-2	1-2	3	McLean	868
20	23	A	Stranraer	D 0-0	0-0	2		700
21	Feb 3	H	Alloa	L 0-1	0-0	3		865
22	10	H	Forfar Ath	W 1-0	0-0	2	McLean	816
23	24	H	Dunfermline Ath	D 0-0	0-0	2		1500
24	Mar 3	A	Falkirk	D 1-1	0-1	2	Smith D	2000
25	7	A	Meadowbank T	W 1-0	0-0	—	McLeod	400
26	10	H	Queen's Park	D 1-1	1-1	3	Morton	800
27	17	H	Alloa	W 3-2	1-1	3	Smith G, Davidson 2	740
28	28	H	Albion R	W 5-1	2-0	—	Smith G 3, Morton (pen), Davidson	1000
29	31	H	Falkirk	D 1-1	0-0	2	Smith G	1200
30	Apr 4	H	Brechin C	W 1-0	1-0	—	Smith G	900
31	7	A	Cowdenbeath	W 3-1	2-0	2	Tait 3	400
32	10	H	Stenhousemuir	W 3-2	1-1	—	Tait 2, Wheatley	800
33	14	H	East Stirling	W 5-1	0-1	2	Morton 2, Jobson 3 (1 a pen)	1270
34	19	A	East Stirling	W 4-1	3-0	—	Morton (pen), Georgeson, McLeod, Davidson	500
35	21	A	Stranraer	W 5-1	1-1	1	Morton 2, Georgeson, Moyes, Davidson	1100
36	25	A	Albion R	W 2-0	0-0	—	Morton (pen), Davidson	600
37	28	A	Queen's Park	D 1-1	0-0	1	Georgeson	800
38	May 2	A	Cowdenbeath	W 2-1	2-0	—	Tait, Davidson	800
39	13	A	Dunfermline Ath	L 0-1	0-0	—		4500

Final League Position: 1.

Goalscorers
League (82): Morton 20 (6 pens), Tait 12, Davidson 9, McLean 9, Smith G 8, McLeod 5, Georgeson 3, Jobson 3 (1 a pen), Smith D 3 (2 pens), Wheatley 3, Moyes 2, Brown 1, McDowell 1, Rutherford 1, Smith I 1, own goal 1.
League Cup (4): McLean 3, Rutherford 1.
Cup (3): Smith G 2, Jobson 1.

Honours
Scottish League: Division 2, Champions: 1978–79
Record Victory: 8-1 v Forfar Athletic.
Record Defeat: 0-8 v Morton and 1-9 v Dundee United.
Most League Points: 54, Division 2, 1978–79.
Most Individual League Goals in Season: Ken Bowron, 38, Division 2, 1963-64.
Most League Goals: 83—1961-62 (Division 2).
Most League Appearances: 282 Alistair Campbell 1955-62.
Best Cup Run: 1963 League Cup Semi-Final 1-3 v Rangers (Hampden).
Extra information: Only Scottish League club with home ground in England.

Frame C	Skilling A	McLaren I	Laing G	Walker A	Smith D	Wheatley S	McDowell R W	Jobson J	Tait E J	Smith I R	Marshall B	Morton J	Moyes D	Rutherford K	Brown D	McLeod I A	Penman D	McLean D	Romaines S	Davidson P	Smith G	McAveety P	Georgeson R	Huntington R	Forrester J	Jones D	Match No.
1		2	3	4			5	13	10	7*		6		9	12	11			8†								1
1		2	3	4				13	10†	7		6*		5		11	12	8	9								2
1		2	3	7	4			12	11			6		5*		10		8	9								3
1		2	3	4*10	5				7			6	9	12		11		8									4
1		2	3	5	4	6			8	9*	7	10	12			11											5
1		2	3*	4	6†	5			7			10	8	12		11		9	13								6
1		2		4		5*			7			6	11	12	9	3		8	10								7
1		2		4	12	5			7			6	11	13	9*	3		8	10†								8
	1			4		5		10	12			6	11	2		3		8	9*	7							9
	1	12		4		5		10	13			6	11	2*		3		8	9†	7							10
1				4		5		10	13			6	11	2		3		8	9*	7							11
1		2		4		5		10				6	11			3		8	7	9							12
1				4		5		10	2			6	11			3		8	12	7*	9						13
1				4	11	5		10	12			6	2			3		8	9	7*							14
1				4	11	5		10				6	2			3		8	9	7							15
	1			4	11	5		10				6	2	12		3*		8		7	9						16
1		3		4	11	5		10	9				2					8	6	7							17
1				4	10	5		13	3			6		12				8	9†	7	11		2*				18
	1			4	11	5			12			6		2		3*		8	9	7	10						19
	1			4	11	5			9			6		2		3		8		7*12			10				20
1		2*		11	10			8†		12		5	9	4		3		13		6	7						21
1		2		11	10			7	9	12				4		3*		13	5†	6	8						22
	1			6	11		4	13	10			5*	8	2		3		12	7	9†							23
1				4	11			6	10				2			3		8		7	9	5					24
1				4	11			13	10*			6†	2			3		12		7	9	5			8		25
1				4	11				10*			6	2			3				7	9	5	12		8		26
1				4	11					10*		6	2			3		12†	13	7	9	5	8				27
1				4	11							6	2			3			10	7	9	5	8				28
1				5	11			12				7	2	3*		4†		13		8	10	6	9				29
1					11	9						6	2	5		3				7	10	4	8				30
1				4	11			10				6	2			3				7	9	5	8				31
1				4	11			10				6	2			3				7	9	5	8				32
1				4	11†			12	10*			6	2	13		3				7	9	5	8				33
1				4	12			10				6	11	2		3				7	9	5*	8				34
1				4	11							6	10	2		3				7	9	5	8				35
1				4	11							6	10	2		3				7	9	5	8				36
1				4*11				13	12			6†	10	2		3				7	9	5	8				37
1				4	11			10				6	2			3				7	9	5	8				38
1				4	11			10				6	2			3		9	7		5	8					39
33	3	3	12	6	39	28	20	4	21	13	1	36	31	18	2	37	0	19	16	31	23	16	13	1	1	2	
			+		+			+	+			+	+			+	+		+		+		+				
			1s		2s			6s	4s	7s			8s	1s			1s	6s	3s		1s		1s				

BRECHIN CITY

DIV. 2

Year Formed: 1906. *Ground:* Glebe Park. *Size* 110×67 yds. *Capacity:* 10,000. *Telephone:* Brechin 2856. *Manager:* Ian Stewart. *Secretary:* George Johnston. *Club Colours:* Red shirts, shorts and stockings. *Club Nickname:* 'City'. *Record Attendance:* 8123 v Aberdeen, Scottish Cup, 3rd round, Feb. 3rd, 1973.

1977–78 LEAGUE RECORD

Match No.	Date	Venue	Opponents	Result	H/T Score	League Pos'n	Goalscorers	Attendance
1	Aug 12	H	Cowdenbeath	D 1-1	1-0	—	Laing	400
2	19	A	Alloa	D 1-1	1-0	8	Watt (pen)	800
3	26	H	Forfar Ath	W 3-2	3-1	3	Robb 2, Watt (pen)	700
4	Sept 6	H	Meadowbank T	D 2-2	0-1	—	Campbell R, Campbell I	400
5	9	A	Stranraer	L 0-1	0-0	6		900
6	13	A	Dunfermline Ath	D 1-1	1-0	—	Elvin	1000
7	16	H	East Stirling	D 1-1	0-0	7	Gillespie	500
8	23	H	Berwick R	L 1-2	1-2	10	Kyles	400
9	27	A	East Fife	D 0-0	0-0	—		821
10	30	H	Falkirk	L 1-4	1-1	10	Gillespie	500
11	Oct 7	A	Albion R	L 2-3	1-2	12	Cairns, Campbell I	400
12	14	A	Stenhousemuir	L 2-4	1-3	13	Campbell I 2	500
13	21	H	Queen's Park	W 2-1	1-1	12	Gillespie, Wylie (og)	300
14	28	H	Alloa	W 4-2	1-0	9	Gillespie 2, Campbell I, Robb	300
15	Nov 4	A	Forfar Ath	D 2-2	0-1	10	Grant, Glover	1255
16	11	H	Stranraer	L 2-4	0-1	10	Cairns, Campbell I	750
17	25	A	Berwick R	L 0-2	0-1	12		900
18	Dec 6	H	East Stirling	W 3-1	2-0	—	Glover, Campbell I 2	300
19	9	H	Albion R	D 1-1	1-0	10	Campbell I	300
20	23	A	Queen's Park	D 1-1	0-1	10	Campbell I	700
21	Feb 28	A	East Stirling	L 2-3	2-2	—	Cairns, Gillespie	150
22	Mar 3	A	Cowdenbeath	D 0-0	0-0	13		300
23	7	H	Dunfermline Ath	L 1-6	1-2	—	Campbell I	400
24	10	A	Meadowbank T	W 3-0	2-0	13	Robb, Reid, Conroy (og)	400
25	24	A	East Fife	L 0-1	0-0	13		989
26	28	H	Stenhousemuir	L 1-3	1-1	—	Gillespie	400
27	31	H	Cowdenbeath	W 2-1	1-0	13	Watt (pen), Gillespie	400
28	Apr 4	A	Berwick R	L 0-1	0-1	—		900
29	7	H	East Fife	D 1-1	0-1	13	Gillespie	320
30	11	H	Stranraer	L 1-2	1-1	—	Cairns	300
31	14	A	Falkirk	L 0-3	0-1	14		2000
32	16	H	Dunfermline Ath	D 0-0	0-0	—		650
33	18	A	Alloa	L 0-1	0-0	—		450
34	21	H	Queen's Park	D 1-1	0-0	13	Campbell I	600
35	23	H	Forfar Ath	W 1-0	0-0	—	Campbell I	800
36	25	A	Falkirk	L 0-2	0-0	—		1200
37	28	H	Meadowbank T	W 2-1	1-1	11	Johnston, Campbell I	300
38	30	H	Stenhousemuir	W 2-1	2-0	—	Johnston, Gillespie	400
39	May 3	A	Albion R	D 2-2	1-1	—	Campbell I 2	300

Final League Position: 11

Goalscorers

League (49): Campbell I 16, Gillespie 10, Cairns 4, Robb 4, Watt 3 (3 pens), Glover 2, Johnston 2, Campbell R 1, Elvin 1, Grant 1, Kyles 1, Laing 1, Reid 1, own goals 2.
League Cup (1): Campbell R 1.
Cup (1): own goal 1.

Honours
Record Victory: 12-1 v Thornhill, Scottish Cup, 1st Rd. Jan 28th, 1926.
Record Defeat: 1-10 v Dunfermline Ath, Division 2, 1929-30.
Most League Points: 42, Division 2, 1955-56, 1958-59.
Most Individual Goals: Davie Paris, 51 (all games), 1948-49.

Ritchie J B	Reilly G	Watt D C	Cairns D	Campbell R	McLeod D	Reid B	Sime J	Sutherland W	Elvin C	Laing W	Gillespie R J	Campbell I	Simpson D	Glover S E	Robb R	Kyles J	Gardner G	Brown T F R	Stewart I	Mellis A	Grant I H	Johnston H G F	Markie P	McNicoll B	Bailkie D	Paterson I	Match No.
1	2			6	4		10†			8	11	3	7		5	12		13	9*								1
1	2	3		6*	4		10			8	7	12	13		5	11			9†								2
1		2	6	10	4	3	5			8		12	11			7			9*								3
	1	2	6	10	4	3	5			8		11*		12	7							9					4
	1	2	6	10	4	3*	5			8	13	9		12	7†11												5
	1	2	6	10	4	3				8		7	11	5	9												6
	1	2	6		4	11	3*			8	12	9	7	5		10†		13									7
	1	2	3	10	4	12				8		9*	7	5	11	6											8
	1	2	6		4	3		12	8		9	7		5	11	10*											9
	1	2			4	3	6*12	8			9	11		5	7†10			13									10
1	2	6			4	3				8		9	11	5	7	10*	12										11
1	2				4	3	13	10	6			9		5	8	7*			12	11†							12
1		2	3	10	4		5			8	11	9		6*12					7								13
1		2		10	4	3	5			8	11†	9		6	12			13	7*								14
1		2		10	4	3	5			8	11	9*		6				12	7								15
1		2	3	10*	4		5			8	11†	9		6		12		13	7								16
1		2		10	4	3	5	12	8		11†	9		6*				13	7								17
1		2	12	4*	3	5				8	13	10		6	11			9†	7								18
1		2		4		3	5*			8	12	10		6	11	13		9	7†								19
1		2		4		3	5	7*	8		12	9		6	11			10†		13							20
1		2	3	4	13				8†		7	9		5	11	10			12		6*						21
1		2	3	4			5		8		9	7			12	10			11		6*						22
1		2	3*	4			5		8†		9	7			12	10			11	6	13						23
1		2		4		3	5		8		9	11	12		7*					6	10						24
1			3	4		2	5	11*	8		9	7		12						6	10						25
1			3	4		2	5	11*	8		9†	7		13					12	6	10						26
1	4	3	12			2*	5	13	8		9	7							11	6	10†						27
1	4	3*12				2	5	11	8		9†	7							13	6	10						28
1	2		4			3	5	12	8		7	9							11	6	10*						29
1			3	4		2	5	10*	8		7	9		12					11	6							30
1		2		4		3		11	8		12	9		5	7					6	10*						31
1		2	3	4			10	8			9	7*		5	11				12	6							32
1		2	3	4	12		10	8			7*	9		5	11					6							33
1		2	3	4*		12		10†	8		13	7		5	11			9		6							34
1		2	3*10		4		12	8			7†	9		5	11				13	6							35
1			10		4	3		8				9	2	5	7			12	11*	6							36
1	2		10		4	3		8		7*	9			5	11					6	12						37
1	2				4	3		8			13	7		5	11*				12	6	10			9†			38
1	2		10		4	3		8				7		5	11					6					9		39
30	9	35	23	30	18	28	28	10	39	2	26	38	1	27	22	12	0	6	0	2	13	17	10	1	1	1	
			+ 3s		+ 4s	+ 1s	+ 6s				+ 2s	+ 8s	+ 1s		+ 4s	+ 7s		+ 2s	+ 1s	+ 5s	+ 2s	+ 2s	+ 7s		+ 2s		

CELTIC PREM. DIV.

Year Formed: 1888. *Ground:* Celtic Park. *Size:* 115×75 yds. *Capacity:* 67,500 (9,000 seats). *Telephone* 041-554 2710. *Manager:* Billy McNeill. *Secretary:* Desmond White C.A. *Ass. Manager:* John Clark. *Club Colours:* Green and white hooped shirts, white shorts. *Club nickname:* 'The Bhoys'. *Record Attendance:* 92,000 v Rangers, Division I, Jan 1st, 1938. *European Competitions Entered:* European Cup, 1966-67 (Winners); 1967-68, 1969-70 (Finalists), 1970-71, 1971-72, 1972-73, 1973-74, 1974-75, 1976-77. Cup Winners Cup, 1963-64, 1965-66, 1975-76; Fairs Cup, 1962-63, 1964-65; UEFA Cup; 1976-77. *Coronation Cup:* 1953. *Empire Exhibition Cup:* 1938.

1978-79 LEAGUE RECORD

Match No.	Date	Venue	Opponents	Result	H/T Score	League Pos'n	Goalscorers	Attendance
1	Aug 12	A	Morton	W 2-1	1-0	—	Glavin, McDonald	16,000
2	19	H	Hearts	W 4-0	2-0	2	Conn 2, Burns, McAdam	24,000
3	26	H	Motherwell	W 5-1	1-1	1	Conn 2, Aitken 2, McAdam	19,710
4	Sept 9	H	Rangers	W 3-1	2-0	1	McAdam 2, McCluskey	60,000
5	16	H	Hibernian	L 0-1	0-1	1		27,000
6	23	A	Partick T	W 3-2	1-2	1	Lynch (pen), Aitken, McDonald	23,000
7	30	H	St Mirren	W 2-1	1-0	1	Lynch (pen), Conn	26,000
8	Oct 7	A	Aberdeen	L 1-4	1-3	1	McAdam	25,000
9	14	A	Dundee U	L 0-1	0-1	1		17,726
10	21	H	Morton	D 0-0	0-0	1		24,000
11	28	H	Hearts	L 0-2	0-0	2		18,500
12	Nov 4	H	Motherwell	L 1-2	1-1	3	McAdam	21,000
13	11	A	Rangers	D 1-1	0-0	4	Lynch	53,000
14	18	A	Hibernian	D 2-2	1-1	4	Provan, MacLeod	22,000
15	25	H	Partick T	W 1-0	0-0	3	McAdam	26,000
16	Dec 9	H	Aberdeen	D 0-0	0-0	4		24,000
17	16	H	Dundee U	D 1-1	1-0	4	Lynch (pen)	21,000
18	23	A	Morton	L 0-1	0-0	5		13,000
19	Mar 3	A	Aberdeen	W 1-0	0-0	8	Conn	26,000
20	17	H	Motherwell	W 2-1	1-0	6	Lennox 2	16,000
21	28	H	Morton	W 3-0	2-0	—	Provan, Burns, Glavin	16,000
22	31	A	Hibernian	L 1-2	0-2	7	Glavin (pen)	18,000
23	Apr 4	A	Motherwell	W 4-3	3-1	—	McGrain 2, Doyle, Lennox	8744
24	7	H	Partick T	W 2-0	1-0	6	Conroy, Lynch	19,000
25	11	A	Dundee U	L 1-2	1-1	—	Davidson	14,424
26	14	A	St Mirren	W 1-0	1-0	4	McCluskey	19,721
27	18	A	Hearts	W 3-0	1-0	—	Conroy, Burns, MacLeod	21,000
28	21	H	Aberdeen	D 1-1	1-1	3	Lynch (pen)	19,400
29	25	H	St Mirren	W 2-1	0-1	—	Aitken, Edvaldsson	18,000
30	28	H	Dundee U	W 2-1	1-0	2	Doyle, Lynch (pen)	37,000
31	May 2	H	Hibernian	W 3-1	1-0	—	McGrain, Provan, Conroy	23,000
32	5	A	Rangers	L 0-1	0-0	3		52,841
33	7	A	Partick T	W 2-1	1-1	—	Provan, McCluskey	18,000
34	11	A*	St Mirren	W 2-0	0-0	—	Lennox, McCluskey	22,000
35	14	H	Hearts	W 1-0	0-0	—	Conroy	18,000
36	21	H	Rangers	W 4-2	0-1	—	Aitken, McCluskey, MacLeod, Jackson (og)	52,000

*At Ibrox

Final League Position 1

Goalscorers

League (61): Lynch 7 (5 pens), McAdam 7, Conn 6, Aitken 5, McCluskey 5, Conroy, 4, Lennox 4, Provan 4, Burns 3, Glavin 3 (1 a pen), McGrain 3, MacLeod 3, Doyle 2, McDonald 2, Davidson 1, Edvaldsson 1, own goal 1.
League Cup (20): McAdam 6, Doyle 3, Lynch 3 (2 pens), Glavin 2 (1 a pen), Aitken 1, Conn 1, Conroy 1, Edvaldsson 1, Lennox 1, McDonald 1.
Cup (9): McCluskey 3, Lynch 2 (2 pens), Burns 1, Doyle 1, Lennox 1, own goal 1.

Honours
Scottish League: Division 1 Champions: 1892–93, 1893–94, 1895–96, 1897–98, 1904–5, 1905–6, 1906–7, 1907–8, 1908–9, 1909–10, 1913–14, 1914–15, 1915–16, 1916–17, 1918–19, 1921–22, 1925–26, 1935–36, 1937–38, 1953–54, 1965–66, 1966–67, 1967–68, 1968–69, 1969–70, 1970–71, 1971–72, 1972–73, 1973–74. Runners-up: 16 times. Premier Division, 1977, 1979. Runners-up 1976. *Scottish Cup:* Winners: 1892, 1899, 1900, 1904, 1907, 1908, 1911, 1912, 1914, 1923, 1925, 1927, 1931, 1933, 1937, 1951 1954, 1965, 1967, 1969, 1971, 1972, 1974, 1975, 1977. Runners-up: 14 times. *Scottish League Cup:* Winners: 1956–57, 1957–58, 1965–66, 1966–67, 1967–68, 1968–69, 1969–70, 1974–75. Runners-up: 7 times. *Record Victory:* 11-0 v Dundee, Division 1, Oct 26th, 1895. *Record Defeat:* 0-8 Motherwell, Division 1, 1936–37. *Most League Points:* 67, 1915–16, 1921–22. *Most Individual League Goals in Season:* 50, James McGrory, 1935–36. *Most Goals in Total Aggregate:* 397, James McGrory 1922–39. *Most Capped Player:* Bobby Evans, 48, Scotland.

Latchford P	Baines R	Bonnar P	McGrain D	Lynch A	Sneddon A	Filippi J	McDonald R	Aitken R	Casey J	Galvin R	Doyle J	Edvaldsson J	Wilson P	Provan D	Burns T	Conn A	McAdam T	Conroy M	McCluskey G	Lennox R	Mackie P	Craig J	MacLeod M	Davidson V	Match No.
1			3	2	5		4	12	8	7*	6				10	11	9								1
1		3		2	5		4	13	8	7*	6	12			10†11		9								2
1		3		2	5		4		8	7	6				10	11	9								3
1			3	2			4	12	6	7	5				10*		9	8	11†		13				4
1			3	2			4		6*12		5				10	7	9	8	11						5
1			3	2	5		4				6				7	10	8	9	12	11*					6
1			3	2			4		6		5				7	10	11	9	8						7
1			3	2	5		4		12		6*				7	10†		9	8	11	13				8
1				2	5		4				6*			7	3	10†	9	8	13	11	12				9
1			3	2	5		4				6				7	10*		9	8	12	11				10
1			3	2	5		4				6				7	10*	8	9		11		12			11
	1		3	2		5	4				6				7	10	11	9				8			12
	1		3	2	5		4			11	6				7	10		9				8			13
	1		3		2*	5	4	12		11	6				7			9		10†13		8			14
	1		3	2	5		4	10		11	6				7			9				8			15
	1		3	2	5		4			11	6				7	10	12	9*				8			16
	1		3	2	5		4	10		11	6					7		9*		12		8			17
	1		3	2	5		4				6				7	10*11		9		12		8			18
1			2	3			12	5	4			11			6	7	10*	9				8			19
		1	2	3				5	4			11			6	7	10		12			8*			20
1			2			3	5*4			8	11				7	10			12	9					21
1			2				3		4	8	11	5			7†10			6*13	12						22
	1	2							4		11	5				7	10		6	8		3	9		23
1		2	3						4		11	5			7	10		8				6	9		24
1		2	3						4			5			7	10	13	8*12	11†			6	9		25
1		2	3						4			5			7		9	8	11			6	10		26
1		2	3						4			5			7*12		9	8	11			6	10		27
1		2	3						4		13	5			7	10	12	8	11†			6	9*		28
1		2	3						4		11	5			7	10		8				6	9		29
1		2	3						4		11	5			7	10		8	9			6			30
1		2							4		11	5			7	10		6	9			3	8		31
1		2	13						4		11	5			7	10†	12	6	9			3	8*		32
1		2	3						4		11				7			5	8	9		6	10		33
1		2	3						4		11				7	10		5		9	12	6	8*		34
1		2	3*						4		11	6			7			5	8	9	12		10		35
1		2	3						4		11	6			7			5	8*	9	12		10		36
27	7	2	18	27	4	19	18	36	1	9	23	34	0	30	28	12	24	20	16	6	0	23	12		
					+			+	+	+		+			+	+	+	+	+	+	+	+	+		
					1s			1s		4s	1s	2s		1s			1s	1s	4s	1s	5s	8s	2s	1s	

CLYDE

DIV. 1

Year Formed: 1878.
Ground: Shawfield Stadium, Glasgow C.5. *Size:* 110 × 70 yds. *Capacity:* 25,000 (2,000 seats).
Telephone: 041-647 6329.
Manager: Craig Brown
Secretary: John McBeth.
Club Colours: White shirts with red facings, black shorts, red stockings.
Club Nickname: 'The Bully Wee'.
Record Attendance: 52,000 v Rangers, Division 1, Nov. 21st, 1908.

1978–79 LEAGUE RECORD

Match No.	Date	Venue	Opponents	Result	H/T Score	League Pos'd	Goalscorers	Attendance
1	Aug 12	H	Raith R	W 3-1	3-0	—	Ward, O'Neill, Myles (og)	951
2	19	A	Montrose	D 2-2	1-1	2	Marshall 2	1100
3	26	H	Queen of the S	W 3-0	0-0	2	Ahern 2, O'Neill	1160
4	Sept 6	A	Stirling Albion	W 4-1	0-0	—	Ward 2, Marshall, Hood	1150
5	9	A	St Johnstone	D 1-1	0-0	1	Ward	1414
6	13	H	Dumbarton	W 1-0	1-0	—	Ahern (pen)	1200
7	16	A	Dundee	L 0-2	0-1	3		6899
8	23	H	Ayr U	L 0-1	0-0	4		1500
9	26	H	Kilmarnock	D 1-1	0-0	—	Grant	1301
10	30	A	Clydebank	W 4-1	2-0	2	Hood 2, Grant 2	2500
11	Oct 7	H	Airdrieonians	W 2-1	2-0	2	McCabe, Brogan	2127
12	14	H	Hamilton A	L 2-3	0-1	3	Ward, Grant	1838
13	21	A	Arbroath	W 2-0	1-0	2	O'Neill, Anderson	1098
14	28	H	Montrose	L 2-4	1-0	4	Grant, Ferris	900
15	Nov 4	A	Queen of the S	L 0-3	0-1	5		1000
16	11	H	St Johnstone	W 6-4	1-1	5	Ward 4, Grant, Hood	1000
17	18	H	Dundee	W 2-1	2-0	4	Hood, Ahern	2368
18	25	A	Ayr U	L 0-2	0-2	6		3841
19	Dec 2	H	Clydebank	L 1-2	1-0	6	Hood	2052
20	9	A	Airdrieonians	D 2-2	1-1	6	Ward, Marshall	2500
21	16	A	Hamilton A	D 3-3	2-1	6	Hood, Ahern (pen), Grant	2500
22	23	H	Arbroath	W 1-0	0-0	5	McCabe	1000
23	Feb 21	H	Queen of the S	W 3-0	2-0	—	Grant, O'Neill, Marshall	800
24	24	A	Hamilton A	L 0-2	0-2	6		2500
25	28	H	Ayr U	L 0-5	0-1	—		1500
26	Mar 3	A	Raith R	W 2-1	0-1	6	McCabe, Houston (og)	1500
27	7	H	Airdrieonians	L 2-3	0-1	—	Ahern, Kean	600
28	10	H	Stirling Albion	D 0-0	0-0	6		1000
29	14	A	St Johnstone	W 1-0	0-0	—	Marshall	1757
30	17	A	Dumbarton	L 0-3	0-2	6		1000
31	24	A	Kilmarnock	L 1-2	0-2	6	Ahern (pen)	2500
32	31	H	Raith R	D 1-1	0-1	6	Marshall	1000
33	Apr 4	A	Dumbarton	D 0-0	0-0	—		700
34	7	H	Kilmarnock	L 0-1	0-1	6		1500
35	11	A	Montrose	L 0-4	0-2	—		600
36	14	H	Clydebank	L 0-1	0-0	6		1050
37	18	A	Dundee	L 0-2	0-1	—		5222
38	21	A	Arbroath	L 0-2	0-2	7		1043
39	28	A	Stirling Albion	L 2-3	1-1	8	Ahern, Kean	750

Final League Position 9.

Goalscorers

League (54): Ward 10, Ahern 8 (3 pens), Grant 8, Hood 7, Marshall 7, O'Neill 4, McCabe 3, Kean 2, Anderson 1, Brogan 1, Ferris 1, own goals 2.
League Cup (3): Ahern 1 (1 a pen), O'Neill 1, Ward 1.
Cup (1): Ahern 1 (1 a pen).

Honours
Scottish League: Division 2, Champions: 1904–5, 1951–52, 1956–57, 1961–62, 1972–73, 1977–78. Runners-up 1903–4, 1905–6, 1925–26, 1963–64.
Scottish FA Cup: Winners: 1939, 1955, 1958. Runners-up: 1910, 1912, 1949.
Scottish League Cup: None.
Record Victory: 11-1 v Cowdenbeath, Division 2, Oct. 6th, 1951.
Record Defeat: 0-11 v Rangers, Scottish Cup, 4th Rd., 1880–81.
Most League Points: 64, Division 2, 1956–57.
Most Individual League Goals in Season: 32, Bill Boyd, 1932–33.
Most capped player: Tommy Ring, 12, Clyde.

Arrol J	Young G	Anderson E	Martin J	Clougherty M	Kinnear B	Ferris R	McNaughton S	Brogan J	Grant A	Kean J	O'Neill T	Ahern B	Hood N	Marshall G	Ward J	McCabe G	Henderson I	Thorburn R	McGettrick J	Nelson J	Mitchell B	Match No.
1	3	2	4	5				8*12		7	6			9	11	10						1
1	3	2	4	5					7		8	6		9	11	10						2
1	3	12	4	2				5*	7†		8	6	13	9	11	10						3
1	3	2	4	5	12				13		8†	6	9	7*11	10							4
1	3	2	4	5							8	6	9	7	11	10						5
1	3	2	4	5	12						8	6	9	7*11	10							6
1	3	2	4	5*				12	13		8	6	9	7	11†10							7
1	3	2	4	5	13	12	11†				8	6	9	7*		10						8
1		2	7	4	5				3	8		6	9	11		10						9
1	2	7	4	5		12		3*	8	10	6	9			11							10
1	3	2	4	5				7*	8		11	6	9	12		10						11
1	3	2	4					5	8		9	6	7	12	11*10							12
1	3		4	5	2*13	11		8		7	6		9†12									13
1	3		4	5	2			11	8		7*	6	9		12	10						14
1	2		4	5*	3			11	8		7	6	13	12	9	10†						15
1	3	12	4					2	8		5	6	9	11	7*10							16
1	3		4	5				2	8	10	6	9		7	11							17
1	3	2	4	5					8			6	9	7*11	10	12						18
1	3		4	5				2	8		7	6	9		11	10						19
1	3		4	5				2	11	12	8	6		7*	9	10						20
1	2	12		5				4	8	11†	7	6	9	13		10	3*					21
1	2			5				4	8	12	7*	6	9	11		10	3					22
1	2		4		13			5	7	12	8	6	9	11*		10†	3					23
1	2		4		12			5	8	13	7	6	9	11†		10	3*					24
1	2		4					5	8*11		7	6	9			10	3	12				25
1	2		4	5				7	8*12			6	9	11†		10	3	13				26
1	2		4	5				7	12		6	9	8			10	11	3*				27
1	3	13	4	5				8	7*10		6	9†		12	11	2						28
1	3		4	5				8		11	7	6		9		10	2					29
1	3		4	5				8	12	11	7	6				10	9*	2				30
1	3		4	5	12			8*		11	7	6	9	13		10†	2					31
1	2		4	5	3*				12		7	10	6	9	11†		13	8				32
1	2		4	5	3					7	10	6	9			11		8				33
1	3		4		2			5*12	7	10†	6	9	11			13		8				34
	1		4	5	3			6	8†	9		12	13	11		10		2	7*			35
1	3		4	5				2	12	7*10	6	9	11			8						36
1	3		4	5	13			2		7	10	6	9	11†		12		8*				37
	1	3	4	5	12				8	11	10	6	13	9†		7		2*				38
1	3		4	5	12				8	13	10	6	9			11†		2*	7			39
37	2	38	12	37	33	7	0	29	23	13	34	38	30	25	14	33	3	6	13	1	1	
				+	+	+	+	+	+				+	+	+	+	+	+	+			
				4s		7s	6s	1s	6s	7s			1s	4s	6s	1s	4s	1s	2s			

CLYDEBANK　　　　　　　　　　　　　　　　　　　　　　　DIV. 1

Year Formed: 1965.　*Ground:* Kilbowie Park.　*Size:* 110 × 68 yds.　*Capacity:* 13,500.
Telephone: 041 952 2887.　*Secretary:* Mrs. M. Baxter.　*Team Manager:* W. Munro.
Club Colours: White shirts with red and black vertical stripes on the left breast and red stripe on sleeves, white shorts with red and black vertical stripe and white stockings with red and black tops.
Club Nicknames: The 'Bankies'.
Record Attendance: 14,900 v Hibs., Scottish Cup, 1st Rd., Feb. 10th, 1965.

1978–79 LEAGUE RECORD

Match No.	Date	Venue	Opponents	Result	H/T Score	League Pos'n	Goalscorers	Attendance
1	Aug 12	H	Kilmarnock	W 2-1	0-0	—	Miller, McDougall	2000
2	19	A	Raith R	L 2-4	1-4	9	Miller 2	1982
3	26	H	Dumbarton	D 1-1	0-1	8	Miller	2000
4	Sept 6	H	Arbroath	W 5-2	2-1	—	Miller, McDougall 2, Colgan, McCormack	400
5	9	A	Montrose	W 3-1	2-0	3	Miller 2, McCormack	1000
6	13	H	Stirling Albion	W 5-2	3-1	—	Miller 2, McDougall, Fallon, Hall	800
7	16	H	Hamilton A	W 4-1	1-1	2	Miller, Hall, McCormack, McDougall	1000
8	23	A	Dundee	L 0-2	0-0	2		7272
9	27	A	Airdrieonians	D 1-1	0-0	—	Given	3500
10	30	H	Clyde	L 1-4	0-2	4	McCormack (pen)	2500
11	Oct 7	A	St Johnstone	W 3-2	3-0	3	Miller, McDougall, Houston	1390
12	14	H	Queen of the S	W 2-0	1-0	2	Miller, McDougall	600
13	21	A	Ayr U	L 3-4	0-2	5	McDougall, Fanning, McCormack (pen)	3843
14	28	H	Raith R	W 2-1	1-0	2	McDougall, McCormack (pen)	1000
15	Nov 4	A	Dumbarton	W 2-1	2-0	2	Miller, Given	3000
16	11	H	Montrose	W 1-0	1-0	2	McDougall	892
17	18	A	Hamilton A	L 0-1	0-0	2		1500
18	25	H	Dundee	W 2-1	1-0	2	Miller, McDougall	3500
19	Dec 2	A	Clyde	W 2-1	0-1	2	Miller 2	2052
20	16	A	Queen of the S	L 1-2	0-1	2	Given	1100
21	23	H	Ayr U	W 3-1	1-0	2	Miller, Colgan, Brown	2000
22	Feb 17	H	Hamilton A	W 3-1	1-0	2	Miller, McDougall, Houston	1500
23	21	A	Dundee	L 1-2	1-1	—	McCormack	5901
24	28	H	Queen of the S	W 3-1	2-1	—	Miller 2, McDougall	1500
25	Mar 3	A	Kilmarnock	D 0-0	0-0	3		3500
26	7	H	St Johnstone	W 3-0	1-0	—	Miller, McDougall 2	2500
27	10	H	Arbroath	D 2-2	0-0	3	Miller 2	1500
28	13	A	Stirling Albion	W 3-2	1-2	—	Miller, McCormack, Hall	1000
29	17	A	Stirling Albion	D 0-0	0-0	2		900
30	24	H	Airdrieonians	W 4-1	2-0	2	Miller 2, McDougall 2	1500
31	28	A	Montrose	W 2-1	1-1	—	McDougall 2	600
32	31	H	Kilmarnock	L 1-2	0-2	2	McDougall	2500
33	Apr 7	A	Airdrieonians	W 3-1	0-0	2	Miller 2, McLaughlin	1200
34	14	A	Clyde	W 1-0	0-0	2	McCormack	1050
35	18	H	St Johnstone	W 1-0	1-0	—	McDougall	700
36	21	H	Ayr U	L 0-1	0-1	3		1000
37	25	H	Dumbarton	W 3-1	1-0	—	McDougall 2, McCormack (pen)	2000
38	28	A	Arbroath	D 1-1	1-0	3	McDougall	1238
39	May 2	A	Raith R	W 2-1	1-1	—	McIntyre, McDougall	1000

Final League Position: 3

Goalscorers

League (78): Miller 28, McDougall 25, McCormack 10 (2 pens), Given 3, Hall 3, Colgan 2, Houston 2, Brown 1, Fallon 1, Fanning 1, McIntyre 1, McLaughlin 1.
League Cup (5): McCormack 2 (1 a pen), Miller 2, McDougall 1.
Cup (5): McDougall 2, Miller 2, McCormack 1.

Honours

Scottish League: Division 1 Runners-up 1976-77. Division 2 Champions 1975-76.
Spring Cup: Runners-up 1975-76.
Record Victory: 7-1 v Hamilton, Division 2, Nov. 20th, 1971.
Record Defeat: 0-7 v Falkirk, Scottish League, Division 2, Sept. 20th 1969.
Most League Points: 44, Division 2, 1974-75.
Most Individual League Goals in Season: Tony Moy 24, Division 2, 1967-68.

Gallacher J	Bryan J	Hall N	Abel G	Gourlay I	Fallon J	Gervaise A	McCormack J	Fanning J	O'Rourke H	Given J	Miller B	Houston D	Brown D	McCulloch D	McLaughlin G	McDougall F	McIntyre J	Colgan G	Ross J			Match No.
1	2	3	4		5	12		6*	9	8	7	10		13				11†				1
1	2	3	4		5	12		6*	9	8	7	10		11								2
1	2	3	4		5	6		11*	9	8	7	10		12								3
1	2	3*	4		5	6		10	9	8		12				7		11				4
1	2	3	4		5	6		10	9	8						7		11				5
1	2	3	4		5	6		10	9	8						7		11				6
1	2	3	4*		5	6		10	9	8		12				7		11				7
1	2	3	4		5	6		10	9	8*13	12					7		11†				8
1	2	3	4		5	6		10	9	8						7		11				9
1*	2	3	4		5	6		10	9	8	12					7		11				10
	1	2	3	4*12	5	6		10	9	8						7		11				11
	1	4	3	2	5	6		10	9	8						7		11*12				12
	1	2	3	8*	4	5	6	10	9			12				7		11†13				13
1	2	3	4		5	6		10	9*	8						7		11	12			14
1	6	3	2	4	5			10	9	8	12				7*			11				15
1	2	3	4		5	6		10	9*	8	12					7		11				16
1	2	3	4		5	6		10	9	8	12					7		11*				17
1	2	3	4		5	6		10*	9	8	12					7		11				18
1	2	3	4		5	6		10	9	8						7		11				19
1	6	3	2	4	5			10	9	8						7		11				20
1		3		4	2	5			6	9	8	10*				7		11	12			21
1	2	3	4		5	6		10	9	8	12					7		11*				22
1	2	3	4		5	6		10*	9	8	13			12	7			11†				23
1	2	3	4		5	6		10	9	8						7		11				24
1	2	3	4		5	6		10	9	8				12				11	7*			25
1	2	3	4		5			10	9	8			6		7			11				26
1	2	3	4		5			10	9	8			6		7	12		11*				27
	1	2	3	4		5			10	9	8		6		7			11				28
1	2	3	4		5			10		8			6		7	9		11				29
1	2	3	4		5			10	9	8			6		7			11				30
1	2	3	4		5	12		10	9	8*			6		7			11				31
1	2	3	4		5			10	8	9			6		7			11				32
1	2	3	4		5	6			9	8			10		7			11				33
1	2	3	12	4	5	6		9		8				10*	7			11				34
1	2	3	4		5	6		10	9	8					7			11				35
1	2	3	4		5	6*		10	9	8						7	12	11				36
1	2	3	4		5	6		10	9	8					7			11				37
1	2			4	13	5	3*	10	9†	8			6		7	12		11				38
1	2			4	12	5		6	9*	8			3		7	10		11				39
35	4	38	37	4	38	1	39	26	0	38	37	38	4	3	11	36	2	37	1			
				+1s		+3s		+2s	+1s					+8s	+4s	+2s	+2s	+3s		+4s		

COWDENBEATH   DIV. 2

Year Formed: 1881. *Ground:* Central Park. *Size:* 110×70 yds. *Telephone:* Cowdenbeath 511205.
Manager: Patrick Wilson.
Secretary: J. Purdie. *Club Colours:* Royal blue shirt with new style emblem, white shorts, white stockings with blue and white tops. *Club Nickname:* 'Cowden'.
Record Attendance: 25,586 v Rangers, League Cup Quarter Final, Sept. 21st, 1949.
Previous Grounds: North End Park, 1881–1917.

1978–79 LEAGUE RECORD

Match No.	Date	Venue	Opponents	Result	Score	H/T Score	League Pos'n	Goalscorers	Attendance
1	Aug 12	A	Brechin C	D	1-1	0-1	—	Steele	400
2	19	H	Meadowbank T	W	2-1	1-0	6	Steele 2	400
3	26	A	Dunfermline Ath	L	0-3	0-2	10		2000
4	Sept 6	H	Stranraer	W	2-0	1-0	—	Caithness, Steele	400
5	9	H	Stenhousemuir	L	1-2	1-2	9	Caithness	400
6	13	A	East Stirling	L	1-4	1-3	—	Caithness	300
7	16	A	Alloa	W	4-2	3-1	9	Caithness, Marshall 2, Hunter	789
8	23	H	East Fife	W	1-0	1-0	6	Steele	1027
9	27	A	Berwick R	L	1-4	0-1	—	Harley	750
10	30	H	Forfar Ath	W	2-1	0-0	8	Liddle, Steele	600
11	Oct 7	A	Queen's Park	D	1-1	0-0	6	Liddle	854
12	14	H	Albion R	W	4-1	1-1	6	Caithness, Harley 2, Steele	500
13	21	A	Falkirk	L	1-2	0-1	6	Purdie	2000
14	28	A	Meadowbank T	W	2-0	1-0	5	Harley, Markey (pen)	500
15	Nov 4	H	Dunfermline Ath	D	1-1	0-1	4	Harley	2792
16	11	A	Stenhousemuir	D	1-1	0-0	5	Caithness	500
17	18	A	Alloa	L	0-4	0-3	5		800
18	25	H	East Fife	D	1-1	0-1	4	Harley	600
19	Dec 2	A	Forfar Ath	L	2-4	1-3	7	Steele, Milne	1882
20	9	H	Queen's Park	D	2-2	1-2	7	Purdie, Markey (pen)	300
21	Jan 20	A	East Fife	W	1-0	1-0	6	Steele	888
22	Feb 24	H	Albion R	W	3-1	2-1	6	Steele, Liddle, Markey (pen)	400
23	28	A	Stenhousemuir	D	0-0	0-0	—		400
24	Mar 3	H	Brechin C	D	0-0	0-0	5		300
25	10	A	Stranraer	W	4-2	2-2	6	Harley, Liddle, Milne, Hunter	600
26	13	A	Albion R	D	1-1	0-1	—	Steele	500
27	31	A	Brechin C	L	1-2	0-1	7	Steele	400
28	Apr 4	H	Alloa	W	5-1	0-1	—	Ferrier 3, Steele, Purdie	300
29	7	H	Berwick R	L	1-3	0-2	7	Davies	400
30	14	A	Forfar Ath	L	0-2	0-1	8		950
31	18	A	Dunfermline Ath	L	0-2	0-1	—		3000
32	21	H	Falkirk	D	1-1	0-1	9	Purdie	725
33	25	H	Meadowbank T	W	4-1	2-1	—	Steele 2, Paterson, Russell	300
34	28	H	Stranraer	W	3-1	1-1	8	Steele 2, Hunter	400
35	30	A	Queen's Park	W	2-1	1-0	—	Steele 2	731
36	May 2	A	Berwick R	L	1-2	0-2	—	Steele	800
37	5	H	East Stirling	L	1-2	0-1	6	Fair	400
38	8	A	Falkirk	W	3-0	2-0	—	Marshall, Liddle, Milne	1000
39	10	H	East Stirling	W	2-1	0-0	—	Marshall, Harley	300

Final League Position: 5

Goalscorers

League (63): Steele 20, Harley 8, Caithness 6, Liddle 5, Marshall 4, Purdie 4, Ferrier 3, Hunter 3, Markey 3 (3 pens), Milne 3, Davies 1, Fair 1, Paterson 1, Russell 1.
League Cup (3): Harley 2, Steele 1 (pen).
Cup (3): Hunter 1, Liddle 1, Markey 1.

Honours

Scottish League: Division 2 Champions 1913–14, 1914–15, 1938–39; Runners-up 1921–22, 1923–24, 1969–70.
Record Victory: 12-0 v St. Johnstone, Scottish Cup 1st Rd., Jan 21st., 1928.
Record Defeat: 1-11 v Clyde, Division 2, Oct. 6th 1951.
Most League Points: 60, Division 2, 1938–39.
Most Individual League Goals in Season: Willie Devlin, 40, Division 1, 1925–26.
Most Capped Player: Alec Venters 1 (3).

McGarr E	Meikle J	Putka A	Cooper J	Thomson J	Markey J	Ferguson K	Purdie B	Aitken R	Ward M	Fair D	Carpenter A	Paterson D	Hunter G	Marshall J	Liddle J	Caithness M	Harlty J	Graham R	Steele N	Davies J	Milne J	Dyce A	McCallum J	McAndrew J	Ferrier B	Adair G	Kane G	Russell R	Allan R	Anderson J	Match No.
1			2	6		12				13	3		10†	9			7		4*11	5	8										1
1			2	6		12					3	13	8	9†			7		4*11	5	10										2
1			2	6							3*		8†	9		13	7	4	11	5	10	12									3
1					2					4	3			10		7	9		11	5	8	6									4
1					2	12				4	3		13	10†		7*	9		11	5	8	6									5
	1		12	3	2					4			10*13	7	9†			11	8	6		5									6
		1	8	3	2	4				12			13	7	9*11†			10	5	6											7
		1	8*	3		4	2			12				7		11	9		10	5	6										8
		1	8†	3		4*	2						13	7		11	9		10	5	6		12								9
			1	8†	3	4*	2						10	7	12	11	13		9	5	6										10
			1	12	3	13	2						4	10†	9	7*	8		11	5	6										11
			1	3			2						4	10	9	7	8		11	5	6										12
			1	3		12	2						4	10	9	7	8*		11	5	6										13
			1	3		10	2						4	12	9*	7	8		11	5	6										14
			1	3		12	2						4*	8	9	11†	7		10		6	13	5								15
			1	3		12	2						4	8	9*11†		7		10		6	13	5								16
			1	6	3		2						4	12	9*11		7		10	8			5								17
			1	3		10	2						4	11†	9*13		7		12	5	8	6									18
			1	3		10*	2						4	9	12	7			11	5	8	6									19
			1	3		8	2		12				4	11	9	7				5	10*	6									20
			1	3		11	2						4	9		7*	8		10	5	12	6									21
			1	3	2	10							4*12	9		7			11	5	8	6									22
			1	3	2	10							4		9	7			11	5	8	6									23
			1	3	2	10†							4	13	9		12		11	5	8	6		7*							24
			1	3		8	2						4		9	7			11	5	10	6									25
	1			3		10	2						4	7	9				11	5	8	6									26
			1	3		10	2						4*12	9	13				11	5	8	6		7†							27
			1	3		10	2							9					11	5	8	6		4		7					28
			1	3		10†	2						13	9			7		11	5	8	6		4*12							29
			1	3		10	2*		12				4		9	7			11	5	8	6									30
			1	3						12				9	7	11	13		10†	5	8*	6		2			4				31
			1	3		4	2			13	10		9	7*12					11		6			8†			5				32
			1	3		4	2		7	10	9								11	8	6						5				33
			1	3	2	4				12	10		9*		7				11	8	6						5				34
			1*	3	2	4					7	10			12	9			11	8	6						5				35
				3	2	4					7	10				9			11	8	6						5	1			36
				3	2			4			7	10				9			11	8	6						5	1			37
				3		10		2			4		9	11			12			8	6					7*	5	1			38
				3		10		2			4		9	11			12	13		8†	6					7*	5	1			39
5	1	3	26	8	37	11	25	10	12	6	5	1	27	29	25	19	26	3	35	27	27	35	0	4	6	0	3	9	3	1	
						+ 2s				+ 7s			+ 4s	+ 2s	+ 1s	+ 6s	+ 5s	+ 3s	+ 4s		+ 6s		+ 2s		+ 1s	+ 1s	+ 2s	+ 1s		+ 1s	

535

DUMBARTON DIV. 1

Year Formed: 1872. *Ground:* Boghead Park. *Capacity:* 18,000. *Telephone:* Dumbarton 62569.
Manager: Davy Wilson.
Secretary: John Hosie.
Club Colours: White with gold horizontal band between two black bands, white shorts and stockings.
Club Nickname: 'Sons'.
Record Attendance: 18,000 v Raith Rovers, Scottish Cup 7th Rd, Mar 2nd, 1957.
Previous Name: Dumbarton Athletic.

1978–79 LEAGUE RECORD

#	Date		Opponent	Res	HT	Pos	Scorers	Att
1	Aug 12	A	Arbroath	D 1-1	1-0	—	Blair	1156
2	19	H	Stirling Albion	L 0-1	0-0	12		1500
3	26	A	Clydebank	D 1-1	1-0	10	Brown	2000
4	Sept 6	A	Kilmarnock	D 0-0	0-0	—		2500
5	9	H	Airdrieonians	D 1-1	0-0	11	McNeil	2000
6	13	A	Clyde	L 0-1	0-1	—		1200
7	16	A	Ayr U	W 5-2	0-1	8	Muir, Whiteford D 3, MacLeod M	2146
8	23	H	Hamilton A	W 2-0	1-0	6	Fyfe, Whiteford D	1000
9	27	H	Dundee	D 0-0	0-0	—		1700
10	30	H	Montrose	W 4-1	4-1	5	Fyfe, McCluskey (pen), Gallagher B, McNeil	2000
11	Oct 7	A	Raith R	D 0-0	0-0	5		2720
12	14	H	St Johnstone	W 2-0	0-0	5	McLean, Whiteford D	1500
13	21	A	Queen of the S	W 2-0	1-0	3	Blair, McCluskey (pen)	1000
14	28	A	Stirling Albion	D 1-1	1-0	3	Fyfe	1400
15	Nov 4	H	Clydebank	L 1-2	0-2	4	McLean	3000
16	11	A	Airdrieonians	W 6-3	3-1	4	Blair 3, McCluskey (pen), Muir, Coyle J	1500
17	18	H	Ayr U	W 2-0	0-0	3	Blair, Fyfe	2500
18	25	A	Hamilton A	L 0-5	0-2	5		1500
19	Dec 9	H	Raith R	L 1-3	0-2	7	Houston (og)	800
20	16	A	St Johnstone	D 2-2	1-0	7	Blair, Sharp	1537
21	Mar 3	A	Arbroath	D 1-1	0-0	7	Blair	863
22	13	H	Kilmarnock	L 0-3	0-1	—		2000
23	17	H	Clyde	W 3-0	2-0	8	Blair, McNeil, MacLeod A	1000
24	20	A	St Johnstone	D 2-2	0-1	—	Sinclair, Whiteford J	1360
25	24	A	Dundee	L 0-2	0-1	8		5547
26	28	H	Raith R	W 3-1	1-0	—	Whiteford J 3	500
27	31	H	Arbroath	L 0-1	0-1	8		450
28	Apr 4	H	Clyde	D 0-0	0-0	—		700
29	7	H	Dundee	W 3-2	2-1	7	Brown, Gallagher B 2	1500
30	14	A	Montrose	L 1-2	1-0	7	Gallagher B	800
31	16	H	Hamilton A	W 3-0	2-0	—	Fyfe 2, Brown	1700
32	18	A	Ayr U	L 0-1	0-0	—		2000
33	21	A	Queen of the S	W 3-1	2-0	6	Whiteford D, Gallagher B, Fyfe	400
34	25	A	Clydebank	L 1-3	0-1	—	Sinclair	2000
35	28	H	Kilmarnock	L 1-3	0-1	7	Findlay	3000
36	May 2	H	Airdrieonians	L 0-1	0-0	—		500
37	5	H	Queen of the S	W 4-1	2-0	7	Coyle J, Brown, Gallagher B 2	300
38	7	H	Stirling Albion	L 0-2	0-2	—		400
39	9	A	Montrose	W 2-0	1-0	—	Gallagher B, Whiteford D	400

Final League Position: 7

Goalscorers

League (58): Blair 9, Gallagher B 8, Fyfe 7, Whiteford D 7, Brown 4, Whiteford J 4, McCluskey 3 (3 pens), McNeil 3, Coyle J 2, McLean 2, Muir 2, Sinclair 2, Findlay 1, MacLeod A 1, MacLeod M 1, Sharp 1, own goal 1.
League Cup (0).
Cup (4): Sharp 2, Blair 1, Gallagher B 1.

Honours
Original members of Scottish League 1890.
Scottish League: Division 1 Champions 1890-91 (shared with Rangers), 1891-92; Division 2 Champions 1910-11, 1971-72. Runners-up 1907-08.
Scottish Cup: Winners 1883; Finalists 1881, 1882, 1887, 1891, 1897.
Record Victory: 8-0 v Cowdenbeath, Division 2, March 28th, 1964.
Record Defeat: 1-11 v Ayr United, League Cup, August 13th, 1952.
Most League Points: 52, Division 2, 1971-72.
Most Individual League Goals in Season: Kenny Wilson, 38, Division 2, 1971-72.
Most Capped Player: John Lindsay, 8, Scotland; James McAulay, 8, Scotland.

Williams L	Hunter D	Campbell R	Sinclair G	McCluskey P	McNeil D	Gallagher J	Whiteford D	Muir J	Brown A	Anderson I	Findlay G	MacLeod M	Gallagher B	Whiteford J	Fyfe G	McLean H	MacLeod A	Blair R	Coyle J	Govan D	Sharp G	Coyle T	Russell W	Rowan J	Match No.
1		2	4	3	5	11		7				6	9		8		10								1
1		2*	4	3	5	11†10						6		8		12	9	7	13						2
1			4*	3	5		9	7				6		8	11†	2	10	12	13						3
1		2	4	3	5		9	7				6		8	11		10								4
1			4	3	5	11†10		7				6		9*12	13	2	8								5
1			4	3	5	11†	2	7				6		9†13	8*12		10								6
1			4	3	5	11	2	13				6	9*		7	8	12	10†							7
	1		4*	3	5	11		12				6	9		7	8	2	10							8
	1		4	3	5	11						6	9		7	8	2	10							9
	1		4	3	5	11		13				6	9†		7	8*	2	10	12						10
	1		4	3	5	11	12	9				6			7	8*	2	10							11
	1		4	3	5	11†12		9*				6			7	8	2	10	13						12
	1		4	3	5	11						6	9		7	8	2	10							13
	1	12	4†	3*	5		13					6	9		7	8	2	10	11						14
	1	2	4	3	5		11						9		7	8	6	10*12							15
1		2	4		5		6						9†		7	8*	3	10	11		13	12			16
	1	2	4		5		6						9*		7		3	10	11	12	8				17
	1	2	4		5			6					9		7		3	10	11	12	8*				18
	1	2*	4		5		6						9		7†	8	3	10	11	12					19
	1	2	4	3	5								7		9	8		11	6*		10	12			20
	1	2	4	3	5	11		7					8			12		10	6*	9					21
	1	2	4	3	5	12		7					8†		13			11	10	6	9*				22
1		2	4	3	5	11†		7					8	12	13			10*	9	6					23
1		2	4	3	5	11		7					8	12				10*	9	6					24
1		2	4	3*	5	13		7					8	9	12			10	11†	6					25
1		3	2	4		5	11						8	9	7			10		6					26
1		3	2	4		5	13		11†				8	9	7*			10		6		12			27
1		2	4	3	5	11		7					8	9				10		6					28
1		3*	2	4		5	12	7		10			8	9				11		6					29
1		3	2*	4		5	12	7		10†			8	9	13			11		6					30
1		2	4		5	11		7					8	9	10					6					31
1		3		4		5	11		2	10			8	9	7					6					32
1		2	4		5	11		7			12		8	9*10				3		6					33
1		2	4		5	11		7					8	9	10			3		6					34
1		3	2			5			4	10			8	9*			11		6			7	12		35
1		3	2	4		5		9					8	12	10*		11			6		7			36
1		3	2	4		5			7	12	10		8				11*		6			9			37
1		3	2	4		5			7		10		8				11		6			9			38
1		2	4		5	11			7	10			8				3		6			9			39
24	15	10	27	38	22	39	22	9	25	1	7	14	32	13	25	15	29	26	25	0	3	8	0	0	
			+			+	+	+	+				+	+	+			+	+	+	+	+	+	+	
			1s			5s	2s	4s	1s		1s		3s	6s	2s		3s		5s	2s	3s	3s	1s	1s	

DUNDEE

PREM. DIV.

Year Formed: 1893.
Ground: Dens Park. *Size:* 110 x 75 yds. *Capacity:* 38,500 (4,750 seats).
Telephone: Dundee 86104.
Manager: Tommy Gemmell. *Coaches:* Hugh Robertson, Willie Wallace.
Secretary: Ian Gellatly. *Physiotherapist:* Eric Ferguson.
Club Colours: Dark blue shirts and shorts with red and white stripes, red stockings.
Club Nickname: 'Dark Blues' or 'The Dee'.
Record Attendance: 43,024, v Rangers, Scottish Cup, 1953.
Previous Name: East End and 'Our Boys' amalgamated to become Dundee in 1893.
Previous Ground: Caroline Park 1893-98.
European Competitions Entered: European Cup, 1962-63 (semi-final); Cup Winners Cup, 1964-65; Fairs Cup, 1967-68 (semi-final), UEFA Cup 1971-72, 1974-75.
Record Transfer Fee Received: £140,000 from Tottenham H. for John Duncan, Oct. 1974

1978–79 LEAGUE RECORD

Match No.	Date	Venue	Opponents	Result	H/T Score	League Pos'n	Goalscorers	Attendance
1	Aug 12	A	Ayr U	W 1-0	1-0	—	Redford	3875
2	19	H	Arbroath	W 2-0	2-0	1	Pirie, Sinclair	6826
3	26	A	St Johnstone	W 2-0	0-0	1	Pirie 2	3875
4	Sept 6	H	Montrose	D 1-1	0-1	1	Phillip	4708
5	9	A	Kilmarnock	D 1-1	0-1	2	Lamb	3000
6	13	H	Raith R	W 4-2	2-2	—	Redford 2, McDougall, Barr	4488
7	16	H	Clyde	W 2-0	1-0	1	Redford, Williamson	6899
8	23	H	Clydebank	W 2-0	0-0	1	Pirie 2	7272
9	27	A	Dumbarton	D 0-0	0-0	—		1700
10	30	H	Hamilton A	W 2-1	1-0	1	Shirra, McGhee	3000
11	Oct 7	H	Queen of the S	W 5-0	0-0	1	Redford, McGhee, Sinclair, Williamson 2	5837
12	14	A	Stirling Albion	L 0-1	0-0	1		2850
13	21	H	Airdrieonians	W 1-0	0-0	1	Shirra	5600
14	28	A	Arbroath	W 1-0	0-0	1	Wells (og)	3852
15	Nov 4	H	St Johnstone	D 1-1	0-0	1	Caldwell	5918
16	11	H	Kilmarnock	D 0-0	0-0	1		5620
17	18	A	Clyde	L 1-2	0-2	1	Glennie	2368
18	25	A	Clydebank	L 1-2	0-1	1	Sinclair	3500
19	Dec 2	H	Hamilton A	D 1-1	1-1	1	Pirie	4646
20	9	A	Queen of the S	L 1-3	1-1	1	Williamson	1350
21	16	H	Stirling Albion	W 2-1	0-0	1	Pirie, Burns (og)	4642
22	23	A	Airdrieonians	W 2-0	0-0	1	Pirie, Murphy	2700
23	Feb 21	H	Clydebank	W 2-1	1-1	—	Redford 2	5901
24	Mar 14	A	Montrose	W 2-0	1-0	—	Redford, Lamb	1800
25	24	H	Dumbarton	W 2-0	1-0	5	Pirie (pen), Shirra	5547
26	28	A	Stirling Albion	W 1-0	0-0	—	Pirie	2000
27	31	A	Ayr U	W 2-1	1-1	3	Pirie (pen), Sinclair	2970
28	Apr 4	H	Queen of the S	W 4-0	1-0	—	Pirie 2 (1 a pen), Sinclair 2	4546
29	7	A	Dumbarton	L 2-3	1-2	3	Pirie, Redford	1500
30	11	A	Raith R	W 2-1	0-0	—	McLaren, Redford	2769
31	14	H	Hamilton A	W 4-3	1-2	3	Sinclair 2, McLaren, Shirra	5804
32	18	H	Clyde	W 2-0	1-0	—	Pirie, McLaren	5222
33	21	A	Airdrieonians	W 4-2	2-1	2	Sinclair, Shirra, Redford 2	3500
34	25	A	Kilmarnock	L 1-2	0-0	—	Murphy	5000
35	28	H	Montrose	W 1-0	1-0	2	Pirie (pen)	6000
36	May 2	A	St Johnstone	L 2-3	1-2	—	Sinclair, Schaedler	5840
37	6	H	Arbroath	L 0-2	0-1	—		8385
38	8	H	Raith R	W 2-0	0-0	—	Redford, McLaren	6450
39	10	H	Ayr U	D 2-2	1-0	—	Redford 2	7692

Final League Position: 1

Goalscorers

League (68): Pirie 16 (4 pens), Redford 15, Sinclair 10, Shirra 5, McLaren 4, Williamson 4, Lamb 2, McGhee 2, Murphy 2, Barr 1, Caldwell 1, Glennie 1, McDougall 1, Phillip 1, Schaedler 1, own goals 2.
League Cup (1): Sinclair 1.
Cup (8): McLaren 2, Pirie 2 (2 pens), Sinclair 2, Lamb 1, Shirra 1.

Honours
Scottish League: Division 1, Champions: 1961–62, 1978–79, Runners-up: 1902–03, 1906–07, 1908–09 1948–49, Division 2, Champions: 1946–47.
Scottish Cup: Winners: 1910, Runners-up: 1925, 1952, 1964.
Scottish League Cup: Winners: 1951–52, 1952-53, 1973–74. Runners-up: 1967–68.
Record Victory: 10-0 v Alloa, Division 2, March 8th, 1947 and v Dunfermline, Division 2, March 22nd, 1947.
Record Defeat: 0-11 v Celtic, Division 1, Oct. 26th, 1895.
Most League Points: 54, Division 1, 1961–62.
Most Individual League Goals in Season: 38, Dave Halliday, 1923–24.
Most Capped Player: Alex Hamilton, 24, Scotland.

Donaldson A	Schaelder E	Caldwell A	Barr L	Watson W	Phillip I	McLaren S	Glennie R	McPhail J	Sinclair E	Pirie W	Scott J	McGhee A	McDougall I	Redford I	Williamson W	Lamb A	Shirra J	Bradley J	Murphy J	Millar P	McKinnon D	Brown N	Davidson G	Scrimgeour B	McGeachie G	Match No.
1			2	3	6			5	9			10	4	11		7			8							1
1			2	3	6	5		10*	9	12	7			11			4	8								2
1			2	3	6	5		10	9		7	12	11*			4	8									3
1	3		2	6	4	5		8		12	9			11*		7	10									4
1	3	4	2	6		5		10	9			11		12		7	8*									5
1	3		2	5	6			8†	9			11	12	13	10	7	4*									6
1	3		2	6		5			9			11	4	8	10	7										7
1	3		2	6		5		13	9			11	4*	8	10		7†12									8
1	3	8	2	4		5			12			11	7	9	10*		6									9
1	3		2	6		5			9			11	4	8		7	10									10
1	3		2	6		5		13	9			11	4*	8	12	7	10†									11
1	3*		2	6		5		12	9			11		8	4	7	10†13									12
1	3		2*	6		5	12	13	9†			11		8	4	7	10									13
1	12		3	2	6	5		9				11	13	8	4*	7	10†									14
1	3		6	2	4	5		9				11	10	8		7										15
1	3		6	2	4	10		5	9			11		8	7											16
1	3	11		4	6		2	5*10				9	12			7†	8				13					17
1	3	11	2	6	8	4	5	9				7		10												18
1	3		2	6		4	5	8	9*			11		10	7		12									19
1	3		2	6		4	5			12	11*		8	9	7	10										20
1		3	2*	6		4†	5		9	13		12	8	11	7	10										21
1	3			2		4	5		9	10*		7	8	11		6		12								22
1	3		2	6		4	12		9			11		8	10		7					5*				23
1	3					2	5	10*	9			11		4	6		7	8		12						24
1			3			4	5	8	9			11		10	6		7*	2		12						25
1			3			4	5	10	9			11		8	6			2		7						26
1	3		4			2	5	10	9			11		12	6*		8			7						27
1	3		4			8	5	10†	9*			11		12	6		7	2		13						28
1	3		4			8	5	10	9			11			6		12	2		7*						29
1	3	2		4	5				9			11		10	6		7	8								30
1	3*12		4			8	5	10	9				7		6		11	2								31
1		3	4	8†	5			10	9			13	12		7		6*	2								32
1	3		4	8	5			10	9				12	7			6	11*	2							33
1	3		6	4	5			8	9			11	7*		10		12	2								34
1	3		6	4	5		7	9				8		10			11*	2					12			35
1	3		6*			4	5	7	9				8	13	10		11†	2					12			36
1	3					4	5	7	9			12	8†10		11		13	2*					6			37
1	3					8	5	10*	9			11	7		8		12	2					6	4		38
1	3					5		10*	9†			13	11	7		8	12	2					6	4		39
39	27	14	21	34	8	21	36	2	27	30	1	20	8	33	20	22	30	0	10	16	1	0	3	3	3	
								+	+	+	+	+		+	+	+	+	+	+	+			+	+	+	
	1s	1s						1s	1s	4s	1s	4s		8s	4s	2s	2s	2s	1s	6s			1s	3s	2s	

DUNDEE UNITED PREM. DIV.

Year Formed: 1910 as Dundee Hibernians, became Dundee U. in 1923.
Ground: Tannadice Park. *Size:* 110 × 74 yds. *Capacity:* 28,500 (2,500 seats).
Telephone: Dundee 86289.
Secretary: Mrs Helen Lindsay. *Physiotherapist:* Andy Dickson.
Manager: Jim McLean.
Club Colours: Tangerine shirts/black trim, black shorts/tangerine trim.
Club Nickname: 'Terrors'.
Record Attendance: 28,000 v Barcelona, Fairs Cup, 1966.
European Competitions Entered: Fairs Cup, 1966–67, 1969–70, 1970–71. European Cup Winners' Cup: 1974–75, UEFA Cup: 1975–76, 1977–78, 1978–79.
Record Transfer Fee Received: £100,000 from Aston Villa for Andy Gray.

1978–79 LEAGUE RECORD

Match No.	Date	Venue	Opponents	Result	H/T Score	League Pos'n	Goalscorers	Attendance
1	Aug 12	H	Hibernian	D 0-0	0-0	—		6000
2	19	A	Partick T	D 1-1	1-0	4	Frye	4500
3	26	H	Aberdeen	D 1-1	0-1	5	Hegarty	10,000
4	Sept 9	H	Morton	L 1-2	0-0	6	Hegarty	5531
5	16	A	Motherwell	W 1-0	1-0	6	Dodds	3372
6	23	A	St Mirren	W 3-1	2-1	4	Dodds, Narey, Hegarty	8000
7	30	H	Hearts	W 3-1	3-0	4	Kopel, Kirkwood 2	6312
8	Oct 7	A	Rangers	D 1-1	1-0	4	Kirkwood	27,000
9	14	H	Celtic	W 1-0	1-0	2	Kopel	17,726
10	21	A	Hibernian	D 1-1	0-1	2	Payne	8000
11	28	H	Partick T	W 2-0	0-0	1	Dodds, Narey	6055
12	Nov 4	A	Aberdeen	L 0-1	0-1	1		14,850
13	11	A	Morton	L 1-3	0-1	1	Addison	6500
14	18	H	Motherwell	W 2-1	2-1	1	Stewart, Kirkwood	5876
15	25	H	St Mirren	D 1-1	1-1	1	Kirkwood	6896
16	Dec 9	H	Rangers	W 3-0	2-0	1	Dodds, Fleming, Narey (pen)	15,247
17	16	A	Celtic	D 1-1	0-1	1	Narey	21,000
18	23	H	Hibernian	W 2-1	1-0	1	Payne, McNamara (og)	7194
19	Jan 20	A	St Mirren	L 1-2	0-1	1	Sturrock	5000
20	Feb 10	A	Rangers	L 0-1	0-0	2		22,000
21	Mar 3	A	Hibernian	L 0-1	0-0	4		5000
22	7	A	Motherwell	W 4-0	3-0	—	Narey, Sturrock 2, Stewart (pen)	2653
23	10	H	Morton	W 4-1	3-1	1	Stark, Sturrock 2, Kirkwood	6433
24	14	H	Partick T	W 2-1	1-0	—	Holt, Hegarty	6200
25	17	A	Aberdeen	W 2-0	0-0	1	Fleming, Sturrock	10,000
26	24	A	Morton	L 1-3	1-0	1	Dodds	5500
27	28	A	Partick T	W 2-1	1-1	—	Fleming, Kirkwood	4000
28	31	H	Motherwell	W 2-1	0-0	1	Addison 2	5655
29	Apr 4	A	Hearts	L 0-2	0-1	—		6700
30	7	H	St Mirren	W 2-0	0-0	1	Hegarty, Holt	6608
31	11	H	Celtic	W 2-1	1-1	—	Holt, Dodds	14,424
32	14	H	Hearts	W 3-0	2-0	1	Dodds 2, Kirkwood	7800
33	21	H	Rangers	L 1-2	0-2	1	Stewart (pen)	20,264
34	25	H	Hearts	W 2-1	2-0	—	Dodds, Kirkwood	6005
35	28	A	Celtic	L 1-2	1-0	1	Dodds	37,000
36	May 5	H	Aberdeen	D 2-2	1-0	1	Payne, Stewart	7822

Final League Position: 3

Goalscorers

League (56): Dodds 10, Kirkwood 9, Sturrock 6, Hegarty 5, Narey 5 (1 a pen), Stewart 4 (2 pens), Addison 3, Fleming 3, Holt 3, Payne 3, Kopel 2, Frye 1, Stark 1, own goal 1.
League Cup (2): Fleming 1, Sturrock 1.
Cup (0).

Honours
Scottish League: Division 2, Champions: 1924-25, 1928-29, Runners-up: 1930-31, 1959-60.
Scottish Cup: Runners-up: 1973-74.
Scottish League Cup: None.
Record Victory: 14-0 v Nithsdale Wanderers, Scottish Cup, 1st Rd. Jan. 17th, 1931.
Record Defeat: 1-12 v Motherwell, Division 2 1953-54.
Most League Points: 51, Division 2, 1928-29.
Most Individual League Goals in Season: 41, John Coyle, Division 2, 1955-56.
Most Capped Player: Paul Hegarty, 5

McAlpine H	Kopel F	Stark D	Smith W	Fleming G	Hegarty P	Narey D	Robinson R	Sturrock P	Holt J	Kirkwood W	Stewart R	Addison D	Frye J F	Payne G	Dodds D	Honeyman G	Phillip I	Match No.
1	2		4*	5	6			7	10	9	3	8	12	11				1
1	2			5	6	4	7	10			3	8	9	11				2
1	12	2*		4	5	6		7	10		3	8	9	11				3
1	3			4	5	6	13	12	10	9	2*	8	7†11					4
1	3	13	7	8*	5	6	4		10	2			9†12	11				5
1	3		7		5	6	4		10	2	8		9	11				6
1	3		7*	8	5	6	4	12	10	11	2		9†13					7
1	3		7	4	5	6		8*11	10	2	9†		12	13				8
1	3		7	4	5	6		8	10	2	11		9					9
1	3	7*		4	5	6		8	10	2	11	12	9					10
1	3	7		4	5	6		8	10	2	11		9*12					11
1	3	7		4	5	6	13	8	10	2	11†		9*12					12
1	3*	7		4	5	6		8	10	2	11		9†12	13				13
1		3		4	5	6	9	8	10	2	11		12			7*		14
1		3		4	5	6	9*	8	10	2	11	12				7		15
1		3		4	5	6		8	9	11	2	12	10*	7				16
1		3		4	5	6			9	11	2	8	10	7*		12		17
1		3		4	5	6		8	7	10	2		9*11	12				18
1		3		4	5	6		8	11	10	2		9	12		7*		19
1	12	3		9	5	6		8	11	10	2			7		4*		20
1		3		8	5	6		9	7	10	2		13	11†12		4*		21
1		3		10	5	6		8	7	11	2			9		4		22
1		3		10	5	6		8	7	11†	2	12	13	9		4*		23
1		3		10	5	6		8	7	11	2			9		4		24
1		3		10	5	6		8	7	11	2	12		9		4*		25
1	2	3		10	5	6		8	7	11		4		9				26
1		3		10	5	6	4	8		11	2	12		9		7*		27
1		3		4	5	6	13	8	12	10†	2	7		11	9*			28
1		3		9	5	6	11	8	10	12	2	7				4*		29
1		3		4	5	6		8	10	11	2	7		9				30
1		3		4	5	6		8	10	11	2	7		9				31
1		3		4	5	6		8	10	11	2	7*	12	9				32
1		3		4	5	6		8	10	11	2	7	12	9*				33
1		3			5	6		8	10	11	2	7		4	9			34
1	12	3		4	5	6		8*10	11†	2	7		13	9				35
1		3		4	5	6		8	10	12	2	7*		11	9			36
36	11	30	5	33	36	36	8	31	26	32	34	24	5	19	19	2	9	
	+	+					+	+	+	+		+	+	+	+	+	+	
	3s	1s					3s	2s	1s	2s		4s	4s	7s	8s	1s	1s	

R.F. 79/80—28

DUNFERMLINE ATHLETIC   DIV. 2

Year Formed: 1885.
Ground: East End Park. *Size:* 112×72 yds. *Capacity:* 27,500 (3,000 seats).
Telephone: Dunfermline 24295.
Manager: Harry Melrose. *Physiotherapist:* Jim Stevenson.
Secretary: Jim McColville J.P.
Club Colours: White and black vertical striped shirts, black shorts.
Club Nickname: 'The Pars'.
Record Attendance: 27,816 v Celtic, Division 1, 1968.
European Competitions Entered: Cup Winners Cup, 1961–62, 1968–69; Fairs Cup, 1962–63, 1964–65 1965–66, 1966–67, 1969–70.

1978–79 LEAGUE RECORD

Match No.	Date	Venue	Opponents	Result	H/T Score	League Pos'n	Goalscorers	Attendance
1	Aug 12	H	Queen's Park	L 0-3	0-2	—		2000
2	19	A	East Stirling	D 1-1	0-1	11	Thomson	300
3	26	H	Cowdenbeath	W 3-0	2-0	6	Mullin, Dickson 2	2000
4	Sept 6	H	Albion R	W 2-1	2-1	—	Leonard, Hegarty	1800
5	9	A	Alloa	D 1-1	1-0	5	Dunn	1275
6	13	H	Brechin C	D 1-1	0-1	—	Dickson	1000
7	16	H	Stranraer	W 6-1	0-1	3	Leonard 4, Robertson R, Rolland (pen)	1650
8	23	A	Falkirk	D 1-1	0-1	3	Mullin	3000
9	26	A	Forfar Ath	W 2-1	1-0	—	Mullin 2	1203
10	30	A	Stenhousemuir	W 2-1	1-0	2	Rolland, Dickson	1000
11	Oct 7	H	East Fife	W 5-1	2-1	2	Leonard 4, Hegarty	3000
12	14	A	Berwick R	D 2-2	1-1	1	Mullin, Hegarty	1544
13	21	H	Meadowbank T	W 2-1	1-1	1	Salton, Borthwick	4000
14	28	H	East Stirling	W 2-1	0-0	1	Leonard, Rolland (pen)	2770
15	Nov 4	A	Cowdenbeath	D 1-1	1-0	1	Leonard	2792
16	11	H	Alloa	D 2-2	2-1	2	Salton, Hegarty	3000
17	18	A	Stranraer	W 3-0	2-0	2	Mullin, Hegarty, Donnelly	2500
18	25	H	Falkirk	L 1-4	1-2	2	Leonard	4500
19	Dec 9	A	East Fife	L 1-2	1-1	2	Leonard	2087
20	Feb 24	A	Berwick R	D 0-0	0-0	4		1500
21	28	H	Meadowbank T	W 1-0	1-0	—	Mullin	2000
22	Mar 3	H	Queen's Park	D 2-2	1-0	3	Mullin, McLaren	2000
23	7	A	Brechin C	W 6-1	2-1	—	Leonard 3, Hegarty, Mullin, Borthwick	400
24	10	A	Albion R	D 1-1	0-1	2	Rolland (pen)	800
25	13	H	Stenhousemuir	W 1-0	1-0	—	Mullin	2000
26	28	H	East Fife	D 1-1	1-0	—	Leonard	2500
27	30	H	Queen's Park	W 1-0	1-0	—	Leonard	500
28	Apr 7	H	Forfar Ath	W 2-1	1-1	3	Leonard, Mercer	1500
29	12	A	East Stirling	W 2-0	2-0	—	Sharp, Dickson	800
30	14	H	Stenhousemuir	W 2-1	1-1	3	Leonard, Mullin	2000
31	16	A	Brechin C	D 0-0	0-0	—		650
32	18	H	Cowdenbeath	W 2-0	1-0	—	Sharp, Mullin	3000
33	21	A	Meadowbank T	W 3-1	2-0	2	Sharp 2, McLaren	928
34	24	A	Stranraer	L 0-1	0-0	—		1020
35	28	A	Albion R.	L 0-1	0-0	3		1000
36	May 2	H	Forfar Ath	D 2-2	1-2	—	Hegarty, Rolland (pen)	2000
37	5	A	Alloa	L 0-2	0-1	3		2000
38	13	H	Berwick R	W 1-0	0-0	—	Salton	4500
39	16	A	Falkirk	D 1-1	0-0	—	Rolland (pen)	6000

Final League Position: 2

Goalscorers

League (66): Leonard 20, Mullin 12, Hegarty 7, Rolland 6 (5 pens), Dickson 5, Sharp 4, Salton 3, Borthwick 2, McLaren 2, Donnelly 1, Dunn 1, Mercer 1, Robertson 1, Thomson 1.
League Cup (0).
Cup (8): Leonard 4, McLaren 2, Mullin 1, Rolland 1.

Honours
Scottish League: Division 2, Champions: 1925–26. Runners-up: 1912–13, 1933–34, 1954–55, 1957–58, 1972–73, 1978–79.
Scottish Cup: Winners: 1961, 1968. Finalists: 1965.
Scottish League Cup: Finalists: 1949–50.
Record Victory: 11-2 v Stenhousemuir, Division 2, 1930–31.
Record Defeat: 0-10 v Dundee, Division 2, March 22nd, 1947.
Most League Points: 59, Division 2, 1925–26.
Most Individual Goals in Season: 31, Alec Ferguson, 1965–66 (Div. 1), 55, Bobby Skinner 1925–26 (Div. 2).
Most capped player: Andy Wilson, 6 (12) (Scotland); Geir Karlsen, 26 (Norway).

Whyte H	Gallagher K	Mercer B	Thompson R	Robertson R	Scott J	Salton J	Meakin J	Robertson A	Leonard M	Rolland A	Mullin J	Donnelly P	Georgeson R	Dickson A	Morrison R	Borthwick W	Dunn L	Finlayson G	Ross B	Hegarty K	McLaren D	Sharp R	Hunter D	Dunlop R	Match No
1		4	2	10			5	3	9		12		7*	8	11	6									1
1		3	2*	10		4		9			13		7	8	11†	6	12	5							2
1	3	4			5	12	2	9			7*			8†	11	6	10		13						3
1	3	4		5			6	9	2		7			8		10		11							4
1	3*	4	6					9	2		7†12			8	13	5	10	11							5
	1	3		6	5	13		9†2		8			12	7*	4	10		11							6
1	12	3	8	5				9	2		6		7		4	10*		11							7
1		3	4	8	5*			9	2	13	10		7†		6	12		11							8
1		3	4	8				9	2	7	10				5	6		11							9
1		3	4	8				9*	2	7	10	12			5	6		11							10
1		3	4	8				9	2	7	10				5	6		11							11
1		3	4	8	13			9*	2	7	10†	12			5	6		11							12
1		3	4	8	5*			9	2	7†10		13			6	12		11							13
1		3	4	8	5			9	2	7*10		12			6			11							14
1		3	4	8	5			9	2	7	10*				6	12		11							15
1		3	4	10	8	5*		9	2	7†		13			6	12		11							16
1		3	4	8	5			9	2	7	10				6*	12		11							17
1		3	4	13	8†	5		9	2	7*10		12			6			11							18
1		3	4	12	8	5		9	2	7*10†					6			11	13						19
1		3	4		8			9		7*10					5	2		11	12		6				20
1		3	4		8			9	2	7*10					5			12	11		6				21
1		3	4		8		10	9	2	7			12		5				11*		6				22
1		3	4		8	5		9	2	7					10			11			6				23
1		3	4		8	5		9	2	7					10			11			6				24
1		3	4		8	5		9	2	7	10				12			13			6*11*				25
1		3	4		6	5		9	2	7*10		8			13			11†			12				26
1		3	4	13	6	5		9	2	7*				8†12	10				11						27
1		3	4	12	6	5		9	2	7	10	8*							11						28
1		3	4		6	5		9	2	7	10*	8						12	11						29
1		3	4	12	6	5		9	2*	7†10		8						13	11						30
1		3	4	2	6	5		9				8			10				7	11					31
1		3	4	2	6	5		9		7	10	8							11						32
1		3	4	2	6	5		9		7	10	8						12	11*						33
1		3	4	2	6	5		9		7†10*		8		12				13	11						34
1		3	4		6	5		9	2	7		8		13				12		11†	10*				35
1		3	4	12	6*	5		9	2	7	10					8			11						36
1		3	4	12	6	5		9	2	7	10					8		11*							37
1		3	4		6	5		9	2	7	10	8							11						38
1		3	4	12	6	5*		9	2	7†10		8						13	11						39
38	1	35	39	7	37	29	2	4	39	31	33	27	2	19	4	25	12	1	0	22	5	9	6	2	
	+			+		+				+	+			+				+	+	+				+	
	1s			8s		1s				2s				3s 1s				7s	3s 4s 6s		1s 6s 4s			1s	

EAST FIFE DIV. 2

Year Formed: 1903.
Address: Bayview Park, Methil, Fife KY8 3AG, Scotland. *Capacity:* 20,000.
Telephone: Leven 26323.
Manager: Davie Clarke.
Secretary: Tom Clark.
Colours: Gold jerseys, black shorts, black stockings.
Record Attendance: 22,515, v Raith R, Division 1, January 2nd, 1950.
Club Nickname: 'The Fifers'.

1978–79 LEAGUE RECORD

Match No.	Date	Venue	Opponents	Result	H/T Score	League Pos'n	Goalscorers	Attendance
1	Aug 12	H	Albion R	L 0-2	0-1	—		642
2	19	A	Forfar Ath	L 1-3	0-2	13	Huskie	1351
3	26	H	Queen's Park	W 3-2	3-1	13	Methven, Dickson 2	924
4	Sept 6	H	East Stirling	W 5-0	3-0	—	Mackie 3 (1 a pen), Gillies, Cairns	723
5	9	A	Berwick R	W 2-1	2-0	3	Huskie, McIvor	900
6	13	A	Stenhousemuir	W 2-1	0-1	—	Dickson, Gibson	500
7	16	H	Meadowbank T	D 2-2	2-1	4	Mackie, Gillies	1100
8	23	A	Cowdenbeath	L 0-1	0-1	4		1027
9	27	H	Brechin C	D 0-0	0-0	—		821
10	30	H	Stranraer	W 2-0	0-0	5	Dickson 2	1086
11	Oct 7	A	Dunfemline Ath	L 1-5	1-2	5	Mackie	3000
12	14	H	Falkirk	W 1-0	0-0	5	Methven	1597
13	21	A	Alloa	D 0-0	0-0	5		800
14	28	H	Forfar Ath	L 1-2	0-0	6	Clarke	1259
15	Nov 4	A	Queen's Park	D 1-1	0-1	6	Dickson	876
16	11	H	Berwick R	L 2-4	2-1	6	Mackie (pen), Methven	1170
17	18	H	Meadowbank T	L 2-3	2-2	7	Dickson, Methven	939
18	25	A	Cowdenbeath	D 1-1	1-0	7	Wedderburn	600
19	Dec 2	A	Stranraer	W 4-2	3-0	5	Mackie, Dickson, Gibson, Methven	400
20	9	H	Dumfermline Ath	W 2-1	1-1	5	Cairns, Methven	2087
21	16	H	Berwick	W 2-1	2-1	4	Mackie 2	868
22	23	H	Alloa	W 3-0	2-0	4	Dickson, McIvor, Wedderburn	1136
23	Jan 20	A	Cowdenbeath	L 0-1	0-1	4		888
24	Feb 3	H	Stenhousemuir	W 3-0	0-0	2	George, Methven, Clarke	886
25	28	A	Falkirk	W 1-0	0-0	—	Cairns	2500
26	Mar 3	H	Albion R	L 1-2	1-0	4	Methven	747
27	6	A	Forfar Ath	D 1-1	0-0	—	Mackie (pen)	920
28	10	A	East Stirling	W 1-0	0-0	4	Neilson	300
29	20	A	Meadowbank T	W 3-1	1-1	—	Mackie, Neilson, MacIvor	300
30	24	H	Brechin C	W 1-0	0-0	2	Mackie	989
31	28	A	Dunfermline Ath	D 1-1	0-1	—	Neilson	2500
32	31	A	Albion R	L 0-2	0-0	4		300
33	Apr 7	A	Brechin C	D 1-1	1-0	4	Cairns	320
34	10	H	Queen's Park	W 3-0	2-0	—	MacIvor, Methven, Halley	447
35	14	H	Stranraer	L 0-2	0-1	4		949
36	18	A	Falkirk	W 5-2	3-0	—	Methven, Herd 2, Mackie, Neilson	1500
37	21	A	Alloa	L 3-4	0-4	4	Methven, Mackie 2 (1 a pen)	600
38	24	A	Stenhousemuir	D 2-2	0-0	—	Mackie (pen), Rose (og)	500
39	29	A	East Stirling	L 1-2	0-1	—	Mackie (pen)	350

Final League Position: 4

Goalscorers

Leagu (64): Mackie 17 (pens 6), Methven 11, Dickson 9, Cairns 4, MacIvor 4, Neilson 4, Clarke 2, Gibson 2, Gillies 2, Herd 2, Huskie 2, Wedderburn 2, George 1, Halley 1, own goal 1.
League Cup (0).
Cup (2): Dickson 2.

Honours
Scottish League, Division 2, Champions: 1947-48. Runners-up: 1929-39, 1970-71.
Scottish Cup: Winners: 1938 (only Second Division winners). Runners-up: 1927, 1950.
Scottish League Cup: Winners: 1947-48 (only Second Division winners) 1949-50, 1953-54.
Record Victory: 13-2 v Edinburgh City, Division 2, Dec 11th, 1937.
Record Defeat: 0-9 v Hearts, Division 1, Oct 5th, 1957.
Most League Points: 57, Division 2, 1929-30.
Most Individual League Goals in a Season: Henry Morris, 41, Division 2, 1947-48.
Most Capped player: George Aitken 5 (8) Scotland.

Blair A	Heaney G	Gillies W	MacIvor R	George Berry D	Clarke D	Methven C	Cooper B	Huskie J	Mackie K	Halley K	Dickson J	Markie P	Gibson J	Morris R	Cairns R	Herd W	Hegarty K	Wight J	Wedderburn W	Neilson G	Young Q	Korankye N	Porwol A	Match No.
1				3	6	5	8	11†	9		4	13	7	2*10		12								1
1				3	6	5	8	7*	9	4				2	10	12	11							2
1	3				6	5	8*	7	9		4		12	2	10		11							3
1	3	2			6	5	8	7	9	4			11		10									4
1	3	2			6	5	8	7*	9	12	4		11†		10			13						5
1	3	2			6	5	8		9		4				10	11		7						6
1	3	2			6	5	8	7	9*		4		11		10		12							7
1	3	2			6	5	8		9		4		12		10	11		7*						8
1	3	2			6	5	8	7	9		4				10	11								9
1	3	2			6	5	8	7*	9†13		4		12		10	11								10
1	3	2			6	5	8	7*	9†		4		13	12	10	11								11
1	3	2	10*		6	5	8		9		4		7	12		11								12
1	3	2	10		6	5	8		9*	7	4		12			11								13
1	3	2			6	5	8	7*	9	10	4				11		12							14
1	3	10	6		4	5	8*					9	11	2		7		12						15
1	3	2	10		6	5			9*		4		11		8	7		12						16
	1		2	8*	12	5		7	10†	3	9		11		4			13	6					17
	1*	3	2	8	13	4	5†		12	10	9		11		7			6						18
1	3	2*	8		4	5		13	10		9	12	11†		7			6						19
1	3	2	8		4	5			10		9		11		7			6						20
	3	2	8		4	5			10		9		11		7			6		1				21
1	3	2	8		4	5	12				9		11		7 10*			6						22
1	3	2	8		4	5			10		9		11*		7	12		6						23
1	3	2	8		4	5			10†		9			12	7*			6	13	11				24
1	3	2	7		4	5			11		9				6			12	8	10*				25
1	3	2	7		4	5			11		9		12		6				8*10					26
1	3	2	7		4	5			8		9				6				11	10				27
1	3	2	7		4	5			8		9				6				11	10				28
1	3	2	7		4	5			8*		9				6	12			11	10				29
1	3	2	7		4	5			8		9				6				11	10				30
1	3	2	7†		4	5			8		9				6	12		13	11	10*				31
1	3	2	7†		4	5*	13		8		9		12	6				10	11					32
1	3	2			6	5			12	9					8	7		10	11	4*				33
1	3	2			6	5				4	9				7	8		10	11					34
1	3	2			4	5			13	6*					7	8		10	11	9†12				35
1	3	2*			4	5			10	12	9				7	8		6	11					36
1	3				4	5			13	10	2*	9		12	7	8		6†11						37
	1	2*		3	4	5		6	8				12		7	10		9	11					38
		3	12		2	4	5		8	10			11			9		6*	7					39
34	4	35	34		18	6	38	39	15	13	34	7	35	0	15	4	34	18	2	2	16	15	10	0	1
			+			+ +		+ +		+ +		+ +		+	+ + +			+					
		1s		1s	1s			5s	2s	3s		2s	9s	4s		4s	1s	5s	3s	1s		1s		

EAST STIRLING   DIV. 2

Year Formed: 1881.   *Ground:* Firs Park.   *Size:* 112×72 yds.   *Capacity:* 12,000.
Telephone: Falkirk 23583.   *Secretary:* P. I. McKay.   *Manager:* W. P. Lamont.
Club Colours: Black and white 1 inch hoops, black shorts, red stockings.   *Club Nickname:* 'The Shire'.
Record Attendance: 11,500 v Hibernian, Scottish Cup, Feb 10th, 1969.

1978–79 LEAGUE RECORD

Match No.	Date	Venue	Opponents	Result	H/T Score	League Pos'n	Goalscorers	Attendance
1	Aug 12	A	Stenhousemuir	W 2-0	1-0	—	Ashwood, Docherty	300
2	19	H	Dunfermline Ath	D 1-1	1-0	4	Grant	300
3	26	A	Falkirk	L 0-2	0-0	7		3000
4	Sept 6	A	East Fife	L 0-5	0-3	—		723
5	9	H	Queen's Park	W 4-2	1-2	10	Ashwood, Bennett, Blair, Simpson	600
6	13	H	Cowdenbeath	W 4-1	3-1	—	Tempany, Docherty 3 (1 a pen)	300
7	16	A	Brechin C	D 1-1	0-0	5	Blair	500
8	23	A	Meadowbank T	L 1-3	1-2	8	Ashwood	350
9	26	H	Albion R	D 3-3	3-0	—	Ashwood, Docherty 2	400
10	30	A	Berwick R	L 2-5	1-0	9	Docherty, McCulley	1063
11	Oct 7	H	Alloa	W 3-2	2-0	9	Simpson 2, Tempany	800
12	14	A	Stranraer	L 0-1	0-0	8		1000
13	21	H	Forfar Ath	D 1-1	0-0	8	Ashwood	250
14	28	A	Dunfermline Ath	L 1-2	0-0	10	Docherty	2170
15	Nov 4	H	Falkirk	D 1-1	1-0	11	Docherty	3000
16	10	A	Queen's Park	L 0-4	0-3	—		600
17	25	H	Meadowbank T	W 4-1	2-0	10	Blair, Docherty 2 (1 a pen), Grant	100
18	Dec 6	A	Brechin C	L 1-3	0-2	—	Docherty	300
19	9	A	Alloa	D 2-2	1-1	11	Grant 2	450
20	23	A	Forfar Ath	L 0-4	0-2	11		1039
21	Jan 20	A	Meadowbank T	L 1-3	1-1	13	Docherty	400
22	27	H	Stranraer	W 4-1	3-1	10	Docherty, McCormack, Grant, Lamont	400
23	Feb 10	H	Alloa	W 3-1	3-1	10	McCulley, McCormack 2	600
24	24	A	Stranraer	L 2-6	1-4	10	Bennett, Lamont	600
25	28	H	Brechin C	W 3-2	2-2	—	McCormack, Lamont, Grant	150
26	Mar 3	A	Stenhousemuir	L 0-5	0-3	10		500
27	10	H	East Fife	L 0-1	0-0	10		300
28	28	A	Falkirk	D 1-1	0-0	—	Grant	2000
29	31	H	Stenhousemuir	L 1-3	1-1	—	Blair	200
30	Apr 3	H	Queen's Park	W 4-2	4-0	—	Simpson, McCormack, Robertson, Bennett (pen)	300
31	7	H	Albion R	L 0-1	0-1	12		200
32	12	H	Dunfermline Ath	L 0-2	0-2	—		800
33	14	A	Berwick R	L 1-5	1-0	12	McCormack	1270
34	19	H	Berwick R	L 1-4	0-3	—	McCaig	500
35	21	H	Forfar Ath	W 3-1	2-0	12	Ashwood, McCormack, Bennett (pen)	200
36	29	H	East Fife	W 2-1	1-0	—	Blair, Bennett (pen)	350
37	May 5	A	Cowdenbeath	W 2-1	1-0	12	Ashwood, Grant	400
38	8	A	Albion R	D 1-1	1-1	—	Lamont	300
39	10	A	Cowdenbeath	L 1-2	0-0	—	McCulley (pen)	300

Final League Position: 12

Goalscorers

League (61): Docherty 14 (2 pens), Grant 8, Ashwood 7, McCormack 7, Bennett 5 (3 pens), Blair 5, Lamont 4, Simpson 4, McCulley 3 (1 a pen), Tempany 2, McCaig 1, Robertson 1.
League Cup (1): Docherty 1.
Cup (4): Docherty 1 (pen), Lamont 1, McCormack 1, Simpson 1.

Honours
Scottish League: Division 2 Champions 1931–32; Runners-up 1962–63.
Record Victory: 8-2 v Brechin C., Division 2, March 31st, 1962.
Record Defeat: 0-10 v Dundee U., Division 2, March 25th, 1939.
Most League Points: 55, Division 2, 1931–32.
Most Individual League Goals in a Season: Malcolm Morrison, 36, Division 2, 1938–39.
Most Capped Player: Davie Alexander, 2, Scotland.

Morrison A	Cairney R	Neilson D	Stirling R	McRitchie R	Simpson G	Collins J	Rennie I	Blair J	Whiteford D	Bennett A	McCulley R	Lamont P	Ashwood K	Hotchkiss W I	McCormack R	Gallacher W	Williamson J	Robertson I	Docherty T	Eccles M	Grant A	Fraser A J	Tempany W	Kennan A	Woods B J	Gray W	Murphy J	Kelly C	Pollock M	McCaig D	Russell J	McGuinness M	McDonald M	Kilpatrick I
1			5					3	6	4		10	11						9		7	12	2	8*										
1			5					2	6	8	12	10	11						9	3	7	4*												
1		2	13	5					6	10†	7	4	11						9	3	12		8*											
1		2	3*	5				12	6	10	8	4†	7	11					9			13												
1		2	3	6				5		10	4		11						9		7	8												
	1	2	3	6				5		10*	4	8	11						9		7		12											
	1	2		6				5		10	4	8	11*12						9	3	7													
1		5	2	6				3*12	10	8	4	11							9		7													
1		2	3	5				6	10	8	4	11							9		7													
	1	2	13	5				3	6	11	10	8†12							9		7*	4												
1		2	12	5				3	6		10†	4*11							9	13	7	8												
	1	2	12	5				3	6	10	4	11							9		7*	8												
	1	2		5				3	6	10	7	4*11	12						9			8												
	1	2		5*				3	6	10	4	8	11						9		7	12												
	1	3	2					5		10	6	8	11	12					9		7*	4												
	1	2	3					5		10	4	8	11*12						9		7	6												
	1	2	6					5		8	4	10	3	9		11			7															
1		2						5		12	4	8*10†	3	9		11			7		6		13											
	1	2						5		10	8*	4	12	3	9	11			7		6													
	1	3	2					5		8		4*11	12	10		9			7		6†		13											
	1	2*12	5					3	4		8	11†13	10			9			7		6													
		2		6				5	10	8	4		3	11		12			7						1	9*								
1		2		6				5	10	4		11	3	9					7		8													
1*		9	2	13	6†			5	10	4	8		3	11					7	12														
		9	2	6				5	10		8	12	3	11					7												1	4*		
		2	6	5	12			8	10		7*		3	9		11				4														1
	1	9	2	6				5	10	4		3	11						7		8													
	1	2	6					5	10	4		11	3	9					7		8													
	1	2*12	6					5		4	10	8	11	3	9				7															
	1	2	6					5		10	4	12		3	11		8*	9	7															
		1*12	5	3				2		10	7	8	11†	6	9						4	13												
	1		2	6				5		10		4		3	9		11		7										8					
	1	13	2	6				5		10*		8	11†	3	9				7	12	4													
	1	12		6				5			8	2*11	3	13					7		4	10†							9					
	1	2		6				5		10	4		11	3	9				7		4													
		1		2	13	5	6		4	8	10	11		9*		12			7										3†					
		2	6			5		8		3	11		9						7							4			10					
	1	2	6	5	3			10	12	4	11		8						7										9*					
	1	4	6		2	5		10	8	9		11							7											3				
9	14	12	26	23	29	3	3	36	10	34	28	33	29	19	21	1	1	2	21	3	35	2	20	1	1	0	1	1	4	2	1	1		
	+	+	+	+				+	+	+	+	+	+	+	+				+	+	+	+	+		+									
	3s	6s	2s	1s				1s	1s	1s	2s	1s	3s	6s	1s				1s	1s	1s	1s	5s		2s									

Gallagher K 1 v Cowdenbeath May 5

FALKIRK
DIV. 2

Year Formed: 1876.
Ground: Brockville Park. *Size:* 100 × 70 yds. *Capacity:* 24,000 (2,750 seats).
Telephone: Falkirk 24121.
Manager: Billy Little, *Physiotherapist/Trainer:* Tom Logan.
Secretary: R. Shaw. *P.R.O.:* William McFarlane.
Club Colours: Navy blue shirts with white trimmings and white motif, white shorts, navy blue stockings.
Club Nickname: 'The Bairns'.
Record Attendance: 23,100, v Celtic, Scottish Cup, 3rd Rd. Feb. 21st, 1953.

1978–79 LEAGUE RECORD

Match No.	Date	Venue	Opponents	Result	H/T Score	League Pos'n	Goalscorers	Attendance
1	Aug 12	H	Berwick R	W 6-0	1-0	—	McCallan 2, Hamilton (pen), Perry, McRoberts, Mitchell	1500
2	19	A	Albion R	D 1-1	1-0	2	McCallan	1500
3	26	H	East Stirling	W 2-0	0-0	2	McCallan, Hoggan	3000
4	Sept 6	H	Alloa	W 1-0	1-0	—	Stevenson	2500
5	9	A	Forfar Ath	L 0-1	0-0	2		1278
6	13	A	Queen's Park	W 3-0	0-0	—	McCallan, Mitchell, McRoberts	853
7	16	H	Stenhousemuir	W 1-0	1-0	1	Feeney (og)	2500
8	23	H	Dunfermline Ath	D 1-1	1-0	1	Thomson	3000
9	27	A	Stranraer	L 0-1	0-0	—		1250
10	30	A	Brechin C	W 4-1	1-1	1	Oliver, McRoberts 3	500
11	Oct 7	H	Meadowbank T	W 6-0	3-0	1	McCallan 2, Mitchell, Perry, McRoberts, Brown	2000
12	14	A	East Fife	L 0-1	0-0	2		1597
13	21	H	Cowdenbeath	W 2-1	1-0	2	Graham, McRoberts	2000
14	28	H	Albion R	W 2-1	2-0	2	McCallan, Brown	2000
15	Nov 4	A	East Stirling	D 1-1	0-1	2	Hay (pen)	3000
16	11	H	Forfar Ath	W 1-0	1-0	1	Thomson	2000
17	18	A	Stenhousemuir	W 2-1	1-0	1	Oliver, Thomson	2500
18	Dec 2	H	Dunfermline Ath	W 4-1	2-1	1	Hay (pen), Thomson 2, Stevenson	4500
19	Dec 9	A	Meadowbank T	W 2-1	1-0	1	McCallan, Thomson	600
20	Feb 10	A	Meadowbank T	D 1-1	0-0	1	McRoberts	700
21	28	H	East Fife	L 0-1	0-0	—		2500
22	Mar 3	H	Berwick R	D 1-1	1-0	1	Hay (pen)	2000
23	10	A	Alloa	D 3-3	1-1	1	McRoberts 2, Henderson (og)	1800
24	14	H	Queen's Park	W 1-0	1-0	—	Perry	2000
25	17	A	Queen's Park	W 2-1	1-0	1	Hay, Perry	800
26	20	H	Stenhousemuir	D 1-1	0-1	1	McRoberts	1500
27	24	H	Stranraer	W 2-0	1-0	1	Perry, Paterson	2500
28	28	H	East Stirling	D 1-1	0-0	1	Hay (pen)	2000
29	31	A	Berwick R	D 1-1	0-0	1	Stevenson	1200
30	Apr 4	A	Forfar Ath	W 4-1	2-1	1	McDowall, Hay 3 (2 pens)	1000
31	7	A	Stranraer	L 1-2	1-0	1	Stevenson	800
32	14	H	Brechin C	W 3-0	1-0	1	McDowall, Paterson 2	2000
33	18	H	East Fife	L 2-5	0-3	—	McDowall, Graham	1500
34	21	H	Cowdenbeath	D 1-1	1-0	3	Stevenson	725
35	25	H	Brechin C	W 2-0	0-0	—	Graham, Oliver	1200
36	28	A	Alloa	L 0-2	0-1	2		1250
37	May 1	A	Albion R	D 0-0	0-0	—		700
38	8	H	Cowdenbeath	L 0-3	0-2	—		1000
39	16	A	Dunfermline Ath	D 1-1	0-0	—	Perry	6000

Final League Position: 3.

Goalscorers
League (66): McRoberts 11, McCallan 9, Hay 8 (6 pens), Perry 6, Thomson 6, Stevenson 5, Graham 3, McDowall 3, Mitchell 3, Oliver 3, Paterson 3, Brown 2, Hamilton 1 (pen), Hoggan 1, own goals 2.
League Cup (4): McRoberts 2, Hoggan 1, own goal 1.
Cup (6): Brown 2, McCallan 2, McRoberts 1, Perry 1.

Honours
Scottish League: Division 1, Runners-up: 1907-08, 1909-10.
Division 2, Champions: 1935-36, 1969-70, 1974-75. Runners-up: 1904-5, 1951-52, 1960-61.
Scottish Cup: Winners: 1913, 1957. *Scottish League Cup:* Runners-up: 1947-48.
Record Victory: 10-0 v Breadalbane, Scottish Cup, 1st Rd. Jan. 13th, 1923 and Jan. 23rd, 1926.
Record Defeat: 1-11 v Airdrieonians, Division 1, April 28th, 1950-51.
Most League Points: 59, Division 2, 1935-36.
Most Individual League Goals in Season: 43, Evelyn Morrison, Division 1, 1928-29.
Most Capped Player: Alec Parker 14 (15), Scotland.

McKell R	Soutar G	Burrell A	Meakin J	Brown B	Oliver M	Hamilton G	Johnston G	Hay J	Thomson G	Leetion P	McCallan J	McRoberts A	Stevenson W	Mitchell J	Perry J	Hoggan W	Graham R	McFarlane B	Wilson J	McDowall D	Nellies A	Paterson W	Morrison A	Nicol A	Match No.
1	3			5	2	4			8†10	9		6*11	12	7	13										1
1	3			5	2	4			10	9		11	7	8	6										2
1	3			5	2	4			8	9		6*11	7	10	12										3
1	3			5	2	4			9	10	8	6	11	7											4
1	3			5	2	4	12		9	10	8†13	11	7*	6											5
1	3			5	2	4	12		9†10	13	6	11	7*	8											6
1	3			5	2	4	10		9*	8	12	6	11		7										7
1	3			5	2	4	10		9*	8	12	6	11†13		7										8
1	3*	9†		5	2	4	10		13	8	12	6	11		7										9
1			6	8	5	2		12	7*10	9		3	11		4										10
1			6		5	2	4		10	9		3	11	7		8									11
1			5	6		2	4	13	12	9	8	3	11†	7*		10									12
1		8*	5			2	6	13	10†	9	3	11	7		4	12									13
1		6	5			2	4		10	9	3	11*12	7			8									14
1		12	5	4		2	6	10		7	9	3		11		8*									15
1			5	4*		2	6	10	13	11	9	3	12		7	8†									16
1		3	5	12		2	4	10	13	11†	9	6			7		8*								17
1		3	13	5	8*	2	4	10	11†12	9	6				7										18
1		3	13	5	9	2	4	10*11†12		8	6				7										19
1	13	3		5		2	4	10†12		9	8	6		11	7*										20
1	12			5	8	2	4		10*	9	3	11	6	7											21
1		12	5			2	4		10	9	6		7	8				3*11							22
1	13			5	6*			4	12	9	8	3	11†	7				10	2						23
1		12	5			2	4		9	10	3		11	7				8		6*					24
1		6	5			2	4		9	10	3		11	7				8							25
1		6	5			2	4		9	8	3		11	7				10							26
1		6*	5			3	4		12	8	10		11	2				9	7						27
1	3		5			2	4			8	6		11	7				9	10						28
1	2	6	5			3	4		11	8	10	12		7*				9							29
1		3	6	5		2	4		9		7		11	8*12				10							30
1		3	6	5		2	4		9	8	7		11					10							31
1		3	6*	5		2	4			12			11	10	7			9	8						32
1		3	6†	5*		2	4			12		13	11	10	7			9	8						33
1	3*	4				2	5		13	9	8	7	11	12	6†			10							34
1		6		5		2	4*			9	8	3	11	12	7			10							35
1		6		4		2	5	12		9*	8	3	11	7	13			10†							36
1			5	6		2	4			9	8	3	11	7	12			10*							37
1		3		6	5*		2	10	8	12	9		11	7									4		38
1		3		5		2	4		6*	9	8	10	11	7				12							39
39	0	22	14	27	12	37	38	10	11	32	32	34	15	27	30	11	0	3	11	1	9	1	2		
		+3s	+5s		+1s				+7s	+6s	+5s	+4s	+3s	+2s	+3s	+2s	+5s	+1s		+1s					

FORFAR ATHLETIC DIV. 2

Year Formed: 1884. *Ground:* Station Park. *Capacity:* 10,000 (850 seated). *Telephone:* Forfar 63576 and 62817. *Manager:* Archie Knox. *Secretary:* James Robertson.
Club Colours: Sky blue shirts, sky blue shorts, sky blue stockings with navy tops.
Club Nickname: 'Loons'.
Record Attendance: 10,780 v Rangers, Scottish Cup 2nd Rd, Feb. 2nd, 1970.

1978-79 LEAGUE RECORD

Match No.	Date	Venue	Opponents	Result	H/T Score	League Pos'n	Goalscorers	Attendance
1	Aug 12	A	Meadowbank T	D 0-0	0-0	—		200
2	19	H	East Fife	W 3-1	2-0	5	Bennett, Henderson, Dickson (og)	1351
3	26	A	Brechin C	L 2-3	1-3	4	Kinnear, Elvin (og)	700
4	Sept 6	H	Stenhousemuir	D 1-1	0-1	—	Rae (pen)	900
5	9	H	Falkirk	W 1-0	0-0	4	Kinnear	12786
6	13	A	Albion R	L 0-3	0-1	—		300
7	16	A	Queens Park	D 1-1	0-0	8	Reid	886
8	23	H	Stranraer	L 1-3	1-1	11	Henderson	1058
9	26	A	Dunfermline Ath	L 1-2	0-1	—	Hall	1203
10	30	A	Cowdenbeath	L 1-2	0-0	12	Clark	600
11	Oct 7	H	Berwick R	D 2-2	2-0	13	Reid, Rae (pen)	1011
12	14	H	Alloa	W 2-1	2-0	11	Hall, Rae (pen)	1066
13	21	A	East Stirling	D 1-1	0-0	9	Reid	250
14	28	A	East Fife	W 2-1	0-0	7	Kinnear, Knox	1259
15	Nov 4	H	Brechin C	D 2-2	1-0	7	Kinnear, Brash	1255
16	11	A	Falkirk	L 0-1	0-1	9		2000
17	18	H	Queens Park	W 2-1	1-0	8	Reid, Henderson	1116
18	25	A	Stranraer	W 3-0	1-0	6	Clark 2, Brash	700
19	Dec 2	H	Cowdenbeath	W 4-2	3-1	4	Clark, Gallacher, Rae (2 pens)	1882
20	9	A	Berwick R	W 4-2	3-1	4	Clark 3, Reid	1000
21	23	H	East Stirling	W 4-0	2-0	5	Reid, Rae, Henry (pen), Gallacher	1039
22	Feb 10	A	Berwick R	L 0-1	0-0	5		816
23	24	A	Alloa	L 0-2	0-1	5		639
24	Mar 3	A	Meadowbank T	L 0-1	0-0	7		400
25	6	H	East Fife	D 1-1	0-0	—	Rae (pen)	920
26	10	H	Stenhousemuir	D 0-0	0-0	7		919
27	14	H	Stranraer	W 2-0	1-0	—	Henry, Henderson	850
28	28	H	Alloa	W 2-0	1-0	—	McPhee, Clark	869
29	31	A	Meadowbank T	L 2-3	1-2	5	Rae (pen), Henderson	810
30	Apr 4	H	Falkirk	L 1-4	1-2	—	Henderson	1000
31	7	A	Dunfermline Ath	L 1-2	1-1	8	Rae (pen)	1500
32	14	H	Cowdenbeath	W 2-0	1-0	7	Rae, Brown T	950
33	16	H	Albion R	D 1-1	0-1	—	Knox	650
34	21	A	East Stirling	L 1-3	0-2	7	Brown K	200
35	23	A	Brechin C	L 0-1	0-0	—		800
36	25	A	Queen's Park	W 1-0	0-0	—	Rae	850
37	28	A	Stenhousemuir	D 1-1	0-1	7	Clark	300
38	May 2	A	Dunfermline Ath	D 2-2	2-1	—	Reid, Brown K	2000
39	6	H	Albion R	D 1-1	1-0	—	Clark	600

Final League Position: 8.

Goalscorers

League (55): Rae 11 (8 pens), Clark 10, Reid 7, Henderson 6, Kinnear 4, Brash 2, Brown K 2, Gallacher 2, Hall 2, Henry 2 (1 a pen), Knox 2, Bennett 1, Brown T 1, McPhee 1, own goals 2.
League Cup (1): Rae 1.
Cup (5): Reid 2, Gallacher 1, Hall 1, Knox 1.

Record Victory: 9-1 v Stenhousemuir, Division 2, 1968-69.
Record Defeat: 2-10 v Dundee, Division 2, 1938-39.
Most League Points: 47, Division 2, 1968-69.
Most Individual League Goals in Season: Davie Kilgour, 45, Division 2, 1929-30.
Scottish League Cup: Semi-Finalist 1977-78.

McWilliams D	Boardley I	Smith G	Bennett W	Brown K	Brash A Y	Cameron J	Rae A	Hall H	Knox H	Kinnear H	Henry J	Brown T	Reid J	Graham S	Henderson A	Clark J	Campbell K	Gallacher W	Ross D	McPhee I	Farningham R	Match No.
1	12	2	4	5	3		11		9†	6	10				7*13		8					1
1		2	4	5	3	6	11	13	9*10†			12	7				8					2
1	13	2	5		3	6	12	4	9	10	8*		11		7*							3
1		2	4	5	3	6	11	8		10		9*					12	7				4
1		2	8	4	5	3	6	7		11	10						9					5
1	2†	8	4	5	3	6	7	13	11	10					9*			12				6
1	12	2	5		3	6		4	11	10†		9			8*13		7					7
1	2*10		5		3	6	9	4	11					12	7*13		8					8
1		2	5		3	6	7	4*	9†10	12		13	11			8						9
1	2*	4	5	3	6	8			10	7†	9		13	12		11						10
1		2	5	3	6	7	4		10		9				11		8					11
1		2	5	3	6	7	4		10		9				11		8					12
1	3	2	5		6		4	11	10		9				7*12		8					13
1	3	2	5		6	7*	4	11	10		9	12					8					14
1	3	2	5		6	7*	4	11	10†		9	13			12		8					15
1	3*	2	4	5		6	8†	7	11			9	12	13		10						16
1		2	4	5	3	6		10	11*		9		7	12			8					17
1		2	4	5	3	6		10			9		7	11			8					18
1		2	4	5	3	6		12		10*	9		7	11			8					19
1		2	4	5	3	6		7		10	9			11			8					20
1		2	4	5	3	6*11		7		10	9			12			8					21
1	2	10	4	5	3		7*			6		9	12	11								22
1	12	2	4*	5	3	6	13		8		9					7†11	10					23
1		2	4	5	3*	6		8		12	9†			13		7	11	10				24
	1	2	5	3		6	4				9	7				8	11	10				25
1		2	5	3		6	12	4			7		13	9*		8	11†10					26
1			4	5		6	9	2		10		12	7			8	11*	3				27
1			4	5	3		9	2		10			7			8	11	6				28
1		2	4	5*	3	8	9†			10		12			7	11	13	6				29
1		2	4		3	8	9	5		10					7	11		6				30
1	5	2*	4		3	6		8		10		9	13		11†	7		12				31
1	2			5	3	10	7	4		12		9†			11		8	13	6*			32
1	2		4	5	3	6	7	12		10*		9			11		8		6*			33
1	2		4	5	3	10	11	7			9				12		8		6*			34
1			4	5	3		7†	2		10	12	9	13			8	11	6*				35
1			4	5	3	6	7	2		10		9		11			8					36
1			4	5	3	6*12	2			10		9		8	11		7					37
1			4	5	3					6	7	10			9	2	8	11				38
1			4	5	3	12	9		6*13					10	11	2	8			7†		39
38	1	13	29	30	35	32	33	25	27	13	29	5	25	3	18	17	2	34	8	11	1	
		†				†	†	†		†	†	†	†	†	†		†	†	†			
		4s				1s	4s	4s		1s	4s	1s	9s	4s	11s		2s	1s	1s			

HAMILTON ACADEMICAL   DIV. 1

Year Formed: 1875.
Ground: Douglas Park (since 1888). *Size:* 110×72 yds. *Capacity:* 20,000 (1,600 seated).
Telephone: Hamilton 286103
Manager: David McParland
Secretary: Joseph Friel. *P.R.O.:* Alan Dick. *Physiotherapist:* R. Reid. *Coach:* R. Graham
Club Colours: Red and white hooped shirts, white shorts with white stockings.
Club Nickname: 'The Accies'.
Record Attendance: 28,281 v Hearts, Scottish Cup, 3rd Round, Mar 3rd, 1937.
Previous Grounds: Bent Farm, South Avenue, South Haugh.
Record Transfer Fee Received: £30,000 from Dundee United for Paul Hegarty, November, 1974.
Record Transfer Fee Paid: £15,000 to Motherwell for Bobby Graham, July 1977.

1978–79 LEAGUE RECORD

Match No.	Date	Venue	Opponents	Result	H/T Score	League Pos'n	Goalscorers	Attendance
1	Aug 12	A	Stirling Albion	D 0-0	0-0	—		1050
2	19	H	St Johnstone	W 2-1	0-0	3	Howie 2	1200
3	26	A	Airdrieonians	L 1-4	0-1	9	Howie	2000
4	Sept 6	H	Raith R	D 1-1	1-1	—	Graham	2000
5	9	H	Arbroath	W 3-1	3-0	5	Graham 2, Fairlie (pen)	1500
6	13	A	Ayr U	W 2-1	1-0	—	Graham, Howie	2359
7	16	A	Clydebank	L 1-4	1-1	6	Howie	1000
8	23	H	Dumbarton	L 0-2	0-1	9		1000
9	27	H	Queen of the S	W 3-2	3-2	—	Fairlie 3 (1 a pen)	1600
10	30	A	Dundee	L 1-2	0-1	9	Graham	3000
11	Oct 7	A	Montrose	D 1-1	0-0	9	Glavin	800
12	14	A	Clyde	W 3-2	1-0	8	Graham 2, Fairlie (pen)	1838
13	21	H	Kilmarnock	L 2-3	2-0	9	Graham 2	2500
14	28	A	St Johnstone	D 0-0	0-0	9		1284
15	Nov 4	H	Airdrieonians	W 2-0	2-0	8	Glavin, Howie	1800
16	11	A	Arbroath	L 0-3	0-0	9		1000
17	18	H	Clydebank	W 1-0	0-0	7	Glavin	1500
18	25	H	Dumbarton	W 5-0	2-0	7	Graham, Morrison 2, Wright, Glavin	1500
19	Dec 2	A	Dundee	D 1-1	1-1	7	Dempsey	4646
20	9	H	Montrose	W 3-1	1-0	4	Graham, Morrison, Howie	1000
21	16	A	Clyde	D 3-3	1-2	5	Howie, Fairlie (pen), Glavin	2500
22	23	A	Kilmarnock	L 0-4	0-1	6		2850
23	30	H	St Johnstone	W 2-1	2-0	5	McGrogan, Hamilton (og)	2024
24	Feb 3	H	Ayr U	W 3-1	1-1	4	Howie, McManus, Graham	3000
25	17	A	Clydebank	L 1-3	0-1	5	Graham	1500
26	24	H	Clyde	W 2-0	2-0	5	McManus, Fairlie (pen)	2500
27	28	A	Montrose	W 4-2	1-0	—	Fairlie 2, Graham 2	900
28	Mar 3	H	Stirling Albion	D 1-1	0-1	4	Fairlie (pen)	1500
29	7	H	Arbroath	W 2-0	0-0	—	Howie, Dempsey	1200
30	10	A	Raith R	W 1-0	1-0	1	McCulloch	1000
31	14	A	Airdrieonians	L 1-2	1-2	—	O'Donnell	2000
32	17	A	Ayr U	L 1-2	1-1	4	Graham	2422
33	24	H	Queen of the S	D 0-0	0-0	4		1300
34	31	H	Stirling Albion	W 2-0	1-0	4	Wright, Fairlie	900
35	Apr 7	A	Queen of the S	D 3-3	1-1	4	Wright, Graham 2	500
36	14	A	Dundee	L 3-4	2-1	5	Fairlie, McCulloch, McDowall	5804
37	16	A	Dumbarton	L 0-3	0-2	—		1700
38	21	H	Kilmarnock	W 1-0	0-0	5	Fairlie (pen)	2400
39	28	A	Raith R	L 0-2	0-0	5		1233

Final League Position: 5

Goalscorers
League (62): Graham 18, Fairlie 13 (7 pens), Howie 10, Glavin 5, Morrison 3, Wright 3, Dempsey 2, McCulloch 2, McManus 2, McDowall 1, McGrogan 1, O'Donnell 1, own goal 1.
League Cup (5): Howie 2, Fairlie 1, Wright 1, own goal 1.
Cup (0).

Honours
Scottish League: Division 2 Champions: 1903–04 Runners-up: 1952–53, 1964–65.
Scottish Cup: Runners-up: 1911, 1935.
Record Victory: 10-2 v Cowdenbeath, Division 1, 1932–33.
Record Defeat: 1-11 v Hibernian, Division 1, 1965–66.
Most League Points: 55, Division 2, 1973–74.
Most League Goals: 92, Division 1, 1932–33.
Most Individual League Goals in a Season: 34, David Wilson, 1936–37.
Highest scorer in total aggregate: 246, David Wilson, 1928–39.
Most Capped Players: Jimmy King 2, Bobby Howe 2, Scotland.
Best Season: 4th in Division 1, 1934–35.

Ferguson R	Frew	Kellachan D	Wright B	Fairlie J	Dempsey J	Glavin A	Gormlty J	Young A	O'Donnell J	Alexander E	Grant J	McDoirall G	McManus M	McGrogan J	Howie N	Morrison D	Weir J	Graham R	McQuade A	Reilly J	Canning G	Howe S	Dunsmore G	McCulloch D	McDougall A	Match No.
1	2		3	4	5			7		6			12	11*	9		10	8								1
1	2		3	4	5			7		6			11*	12	9		10	8								2
1	2		3*	4	5			7		6	12		11		9		10	8								3
1		3	7		5					6	10		11*	12	9		4	8	2							4
1	12	3		4	5					6	7			11	9		10	8	2*							5
1	2	3		4	5					6	7			11	9			8								6
1	2	3		4	5				10	6	7	8*		11	9				12	13						7
1	2*	3		12	5	4			10	6	7†	13		11	9			8								8
1		3		4		10				6		5	7	11	9			8	2							9
1	2	3		4	5	10		7		6			11*	12	9			8								10
1		3		4	5	10		7*		6	2		12		9		8		11*		13					11
1		3	2	4	5	10				6			9	13	11†	7*		8			12					12
1		3*		4	5	10				6	2		9	13	11	7†		8			12					13
1	2	3		4	5	10				6	7		11	12				8			9*					14
1	2	3		4	5	10				6	7		11*	12	9			8								15
1	2	3*12		4†	5	10				6	7		11	13	9			8								16
1	2	3	11	7	5	4				6	10				9*	12		8								17
1	2*	3	11	7	5	4				6	10	12			13	9		8†								18
1	2		11	4	5					6	7				9	10		8	3							19
1	2	3	11	4	5					6	10		12		7	9*		8								20
1	2	3		4	5	11				6	10*		12	7	9			8								21
1	2	3		4	5	11				6	10†	13	12	7	9*			8								22
1	2	3		7	5	4				6	10		11		9			8								23
1	2	3		4	5	12				6	7	10*	11		9			8								24
1	2	3*12		4	5				13		7†	10	11		9			8					6			25
1	2	3*		4	5		7			6			11		9			8			12		10			26
1	2			4	5					6	12	7*11			9			8	3				10			27
1	2			4	5					6	7†		11		9	12		8	3*		13		10			28
1	2	3	7	4	5					6		11†13	12	9*				8					10			29
1	2	3	7	4	5					6	11				9			8					10			30
1	2	3	7*	4	5				12	11†	6	13			9			8					10			31
1	2	3			5			7	12	6	4		11		9*			8					10			32
1	2	3		4	5				9†	6	7*		11	13	12			8					10			33
1	2	3	7	4	5					6*		12	11		9†			8					13	10		34
1	2	3	7	4	5	12				6*		13	11		9†			8						10		35
1	2	3*	7	4	5					6		11	13	12				8				9†		10		36
1	2		7	4	5*					6†		11	13		12			8				9		10	3	37
1	2	3*	7	4	5					12	6		9		13			8				11†		10		38
1	2		7	4						12	6	3	5	11†		9*		8					13	10		39
39	33	31	18	36	37	14	1	9	2	38	24	11	19	9	31	7	5	38	6	1	0	4	0	14	2	
		+		+		+			+	+	+	+	+	+	+						+	+	+			
		1s		2s		1s			2s	1s	4s		3s	5s	6s	11s	6s		2s		1s	1s	6s	1s		

HEART OF MIDLOTHIAN   DIV. 1

Year Formed: 1874.
Ground: Tynecastle Park, Gorgie Road, Edinburgh EH11 2NL. *Size:* 110×76 yds. *Capacity:* 49,000 (4,000 seats).
Telephone: 031-337 6132.
Manager: Willie Ormond.
Secretary: James Calder. *Trainer:* Alex Rennie. *Coach:*
Club Colours: Maroon shirts, white collar and cuffs, white shorts, maroon stockings with white tops.
Club Nickname: 'The Maroons'.
Record Attendance: 53,496, v Rangers, Scottish Cup, 3rd Rd. Feb. 13th, 1932.
Previous Grounds: The Meadows, 1873–78; Powderhall, 1878–81; Tynecastle, 1881–86; Tyneside Park, 1886– .
European Competitions Entered: European Cup, 1958–59, 1960–61, Fairs Cup, 1961–62, 1963–64, 1965–66. Cup Winners Cup, 1976–77.
Record Transfer Fee Received: £200,000 from Chelsea for Eamonn Bannon, Jan. 1979.
Record Transfer Fee Paid: £20,000, to Wolverhampton W for George Miller, Nov. 1965.

1978–79 LEAGUE RECORD

Match No.	Date	Venue	Opponents	Result	H/T Score	League Pos'n	Goalscorers	Attendance
1	Aug 12	H	Aberdeen	L 1-4	1-2	—	Bannon	11,500
2	19	A	Celtic	L 0-4	0-2	10		24,000
3	26	H	Hibernian	D 1-1	1-0	9	Park	20,000
4	Sept 9	A	Partick T	L 2-3	0-2	10	Busby, Bannon (pen)	5000
5	16	H	Morton	D 1-1	0-1	9	McQuade	7230
6	23	A	Motherwell	W 1-0	0-0	9	Robertson	5219
7	30	A	Dundee U	L 1-3	0-3	9	Bannon	6312
8	Oct 7	H	St Mirren	D 1-1	1-0	9	Gibson	9475
9	14	H	Rangers	D 0-0	0-0	9		18,159
10	21	A	Aberdeen	W 2-1	1-0	9	McQuade, O'Connor	12,750
11	28	H	Celtic	W 2-0	0-0	9	Busby 2	18,500
12	Nov 4	A	Hibernian	W 2-1	0-0	8	McQuade, O'Connor	21,200
13	11	H	Partick T	L 0-1	0-1	9		12,400
14	18	A	Morton	L 2-3	1-2	9	Bannon (pen), O'Connor	7500
15	25	H	Motherwell	W 3-2	1-1	9	Fraser, O'Connor, Robertson	8984
16	Dec 9	A	St Mirren	L 0-4	0-1	9		6640
17	16	A	Rangers	L 3-5	1-3	9	Busby 2, Bannon	18,000
18	23	H	Aberdeen	D 0-0	0-0	9		9500
19	Jan 20	A	Motherwell	L 2-3	1-1	9	O'Connor Robertson	3881
20	Feb 10	H	St Mirren	L 1-2	1-0	9	Gibson	8000
21	24	H	Rangers	W 3-2	2-2	9	O'Connor 2, Robertson	18,000
22	Mar 17	A	Hibernian	D 1-1	1-1	9	Gibson (pen)	13,297
23	28	H	Hibernian	L 1-2	1-2	—	Gibson	16,000
24	31	A	Morton	D 2-2	1-1	9	Busby, Gibson	6000
25	Apr 4	H	Dundee U	W 2-0	1-0	9	O'Connor, Shaw	6700
26	7	H	Motherwell	W 3-0	1-0	9	Dempsey (og), Fraser 2 (1 a pen)	7000
27	11	A	Partick T	L 0-2	0-1	—		10,000
28	14	H	Dundee U	L 0-3	0-2	9		7800
29	18	H	Celtic	L 0-3	0-1	—		12,000
30	21	A	St Mirren	L 1-2	1-2	9	McQuade	5800
31	25	A	Dundee U	L 1-2	0-2	—	Gibson (pen)	6005
32	28	A	Rangers	L 0-4	0-3	9		21,000
33	May 2	A	Aberdeen	L 0-5	0-2	—		6000
34	5	A	Partick T	L 0-2	0-1	9		4000
35	7	H	Morton	L 0-1	0-1	—		2700
36	14	A	Celtic	L 0-1	0-0	—		18,000

Final League Position: 9

Goalscorers

League (39): O'Connor 8, Busby 6, Gibson 6 (2 pens), Bannon 5 (2 pens), McQuade 4, Robertson 4 Fraser 3 (1 a pen), Park 1, Shaw 1, 1 own goal.
League Cup (2): Bannon 1 (pen), Shaw 1.
Cup (5): Robertson 2, Busby 1, Gibson 1 (pen), O'Connor 1.

Honours

Scottish League: Division 1, Champions: 1894–95, 1896–97, 1957–58, 1959–60. Runners-up: 1893–94, 1898–99, 1903–04, 1905–06, 1914–15, 1937–38, 1953–54, 1956–57, 1958–59, 1964–65, Division 1, Champions: 1977–78.
Scottish Cup: Winners: 1891, 1896, 1901, 1906, 1956, Runners-up: 1903, 1907, 1968, 1976.
Scottish League Cup: Winners: 1954–55, 1958–59, 1959–60, 1962–63. Runners-up 1961–62.
Record Victory: 15-0 v King's Park, Scottish Cup, 2nd Rd, Feb. 13th, 1937.
Record Defeat: 0-7 v Hibernian, Jan 1st, 1973, Division 1.
Most League Points: 62, Division 1, 1957–58.
Most League Goals: 132, Division 1, 1957–58. (Record for Division 1).
Most Individual Goals in Season: 44, Barney Battles, 1930–31.
Highest Scorer in Total Aggregate: 206, Jimmy Wardhaugh, 1946–59.
Most Capped Player: Bobby Walker, 29, Scotland.

Dunlop R	Brough J	Allan T	Kidd W	McNicoll D	Jefferies J	Fraser C	Liddell F	Brown J	Tierney L	Bannon E	Shaw G	Busby A	Smith I	Gibson W	McQuade D	Prentice R	Robertson M	Craig J	Park D	O'Connor D	Black I	Rodger P	Paterson I	Scott D	Stewart R	More C	McLeod K	O'Sullivan D	Match No.
1			2	4	5	3	6		13		8	10		9*		12	11†	7											1
1			2	4	5	3	6		13		8	10†		9		11	7*	12											2
		1		4	3	2	5		10†	8	6		13	9*		11	12	7											3
		1		4	6*	3	5	2	13	8		9		12	7		11†10												4
1			2		4	3	5		12	8	6*10			9	7		11												5
1			2	12	4	3	5		6	8		10*		9	11		7												6
1			2		4*	3	5	13	12	8		10†		9	11		7	6											7
1			2	4		3	5	12	6*	8		10		9	13	11	7†												8
1			2	4	3	6	5			8		10		9*12	11		7												9
1			2*	4	3	6	5	12		8		10		7	12		11*		9										10
1				4	3	6*	5	2	12	8		10		7			11		9										11
1				4	3	6	5	2		8		10		7	11				9										12
1				4	3	6	5	2		8*		10		7	11†		13	12	9										13
1		12		4	3	6	5	2*		8				7†		13	11	10	9										14
1			2	4	3	6	5			8		10		12	11*	7			9										15
1			2	4*		6	5	3		8		10			7†13	11	12		9										16
1			2		4	6	5*	3		8		10		7†13		11	12		9										17
1			2	4	5	3				8		10		7*12		11	6		9										18
1			2	4	5	3		12		8		10		7†13		11	6*		9										19
1			2	4	5	8		3				10		7		11	6		9										20
	1	2		5	8	4	3					10		7	12		11*	6	9										21
	1	2		5	8	4						10		7		12	11*	6	9	3									22
	1	2			4	8	5					10		7		11	6		9	3									23
	1	2		5	8	4	3				6	10		7		11*			9	12									24
	1	2		5	8	4	3				6	10*		7		11			9	12									25
	1	2		5	8	4	3				6	10		7*12		11†			9	13									26
	1	2		5	8		3				6			7		11			9	10	4								27
	1	2		5	8	4	6					10		9	11†13	7	12		3*										28
	1	2			8	5	3	4				10		9*		11	7	6				12							29
	1	2			4		3	8*				10		9	7		11†	6				12	5	13					30
	1	2		4		5	8*10							7	11	12		6	3					9					31
	1	2			4	5	8	6						7*11			10		3					9	12				32
		1		12	4	5	2	8*						7	11		10†		3					13	9	6			33
	1	2			8	5	6							7	11				3					9*10		4	12		34
	1	2				6	5	8						9					3						10	4	11	7	35
	1	2		12	8	5	6							9					3					13	10	4	11†	7*	36
18	2	16	29	26	36	31	22	8	19	8	25	0	33	13	6	27	14	2	18	10	2	0	3	4	4	2	2		
			+ 1s	+ 1s	+ 2s				+ 4s	+ 6s				+ 1s	+ 1s	+ 9s	+ 6s	+ 2s	+ 4s	+ 1s			+ 4s	+ 2s	+ 2s	+ 1s	+ 1s		

HIBERNIAN

PREM. DIV.

Year Formed: 1875. *Ground:* Easter Road Park. *Size:* 112×74 yds. *Capacity:* 50,136 (6636 seats).
Telephone: 031-661-2159.
Manager: Eddie Turnbull. *Secretary:* C. F. Graham. *Trainer:* John Fraser.
Club Colours: Green shirts with white collars and sleeves, white shorts, green and white stockings.
Club Nickname: 'Hi-Bees'.
Record Attendance: 65,840 v Hearts, Division 1, Jan. 2nd, 1950.
Previous Names: Edinburgh Hibernians. *Previous Ground:* Mayfield 1875-80.
European Competitions Entered: European Cup: 1955-56. Cup Winners Cup: 1972-73. Fairs Cup: 1960-61, 1961-62, 1962-63, 1965-66, 1967-68, 1968-69. UEFA Cup: 1973-74, 1974-75, 1975-76, 1976-77, 1978-79.
Record Transfer Fee Received: £150,000 from Arsenal for Alex Cropley, Dec. 1974.
Record Transfer Fee Paid: £120,000 to Everton, February 1974 for Joe Harper.

1978-79 LEAGUE RECORD

Match No.	Date	Venue	Opponents	Result	H/T Score	League Pos'n	Goalscorers	Attendance
1	Aug 12	A	Dundee U	D 0-0	0-0	—		6000
2	19	H	Rangers	D 0-0	0-0	7		23,000
3	26	A	Hearts	D 1-1	0-1	6	MacLeod	20,000
4	Sept 9	H	St Mirren	W 1-0	1-0	4	Higgins	8000
5	16	A	Celtic	W 1-0	1-0	3	Temperley	27,000
6	23	H	Aberdeen	W 2-1	2-1	2	MacLeod (pen), Rae	12,086
7	30	H	Morton	D 1-1	0-1	2	MacLeod	8000
8	Oct 7	A	Motherwell	W 3-2	1-2	2	MacLeod, Hutchinson, Rae	5516
9	14	A	Partick T	L 1-2	1-1	3	Higgins	7000
10	21	H	Dundee U	D 1-1	1-0	3	Rae	8000
11	28	A	Rangers	L 1-2	1-2	3	MacLeod	25,000
12	Nov 4	H	Hearts	L 1-2	0-0	4	Rae	21,200
13	11	A	St Mirren	L 0-1	0-0	7		8000
14	18	H	Celtic	D 2-2	1-1	7	Callachan, Hutchinson	22,000
15	25	A	Aberdeen	L 1-4	0-2	8	Hutchinson	14,250
16	Dec 9	H	Motherwell	D 2-2	1-1	7	Higgins, Hutchinson	6000
17	16	H	Partick T	D 0-0	0-0	7		6000
18	23	A	Dundee U	L 1-2	0-1	8	Bremner	7194
19	Jan 20	H	Aberdeen	D 1-1	0-1	8	Duncan	6000
20	Feb 10	A	Motherwell	W 3-0	1-0	8	Callachan, Bremner, MacLeod	5101
21	24	H	Morton	D 1-1	1-0	7	Bremner	6500
22	Mar 3	H	Dundee U	W 1-0	0-0	6	Bremner	5000
23	14	A	Rangers	L 0-1	0-0	—		15,000
24	17	H	Hearts	D 1-1	1-1	7	Campbell	13,297
25	24	A	St Mirren	W 3-2	1-1	5	MacLeod, Higgins, Campbell	10,000
26	28	A	Hearts	W 2-1	2-1	—	MacLeod, Callachan	16,000
27	31	H	Celtic	W 2-1	2-0	4	Rae, Stewart	18,000
28	Apr 4	H	St Mirren	L 0-2	0-1	—		6000
29	7	A	Aberdeen	D 0-0	0-0	4		10,000
30	14	A	Morton	D 2-2	0-1	6	Callachan 2	7000
31	18	A	Morton	L 0-3	0-1	—		8000
32	21	A	Motherwell	W 4-0	3-0	6	Callachan, Rae, Campbell, Bremner	7000
33	25	A	Partick T	L 1-6	0-4	—	Callachan	5000
34	28	H	Partick T	W 1-0	0-0	6	Callachan	5500
35	May 2	A	Celtic	L 1-3	0-1	—	Callachan	23,000
36	31	H	Rangers	W 2-1	1-0	—	Rae, Watson (og)	4000

Final League Position: 5.

Goalscorers

League (44): Callachan 9, MacLeod 8 (1 a pen), Rae 7, Bremner 5, Higgins 4, Hutchinson 4, Campbell 3, Duncan 1, Stewart 1, Temperley 1, own goal 1.
League Cup (10): MacLeod 3 (1 a pen), Callachan 2, Refvik 2, Rae 1, Smith 1, Stewart 1.
Cup (15): MacLeod 5 (2 pens), Higgins 3, Callachan 2, Rae 2, Brazil 1, Duncan 1, Stewart 1.

Honours

Scottish League: Division 1, Champions: 1902-03, 1947-48, 1950-51, 1951-52; Runners-up: 1896-97, 1946-47, 1949-50, 1952-53, 1973-74, 1974-75 Division 2, Champions: 1893-94; 1894-95; 1932-33.
Scottish Cup Winners: 1887, 1902; Runners-up: 1896, 1914, 1923, 1924, 1947, 1958, 1972, 1979.
Scottish League Cup: Winners: 1972-73; Runners-up: 1950-51, 1968-69, 1974-75.
Drybrough Cup: Winners 1972-73, 1973-74.
Record Victory: 15-1 v Peebles Rovers, Scottish Cup, 2nd Rd. Feb. 11th, 1961.
Record Defeat: 2-9 v Morton, Division 1, 1918-19.
Most League Points: 54, Division 2, 1932-33.
Most Individual League Goals in Season: 42, Joe Baker, Division 1, 1959-60.
Most Capped Player: Lawrie Reilly, 38, Scotland.

McDonald M	McArthur J	Kilgour R	Smith R	Brazil A	Campbell C	McNamara J	Fleming R	Stewart G	Hutchinson R	Bremner D	Murray W	Rae G	Temperley W	Duncan A	Callachan R	MacLeod A	Higgins A	Carroll P	Lambie D	O'Brien S	Mathisen S	Refvik I	Brown S	Farmer J	Match No.
1			3			6	12	5*		2	7	4		9		8	11	10†		13					1
1	2		3			6	5			4	7*13			9	10†	8	11			12					2
1	2		3			6	5			4	7*			9	10	8	11			12					3
1			3			6	5		2		4	7	9	10		8	11								4
1			3			6	4	5			9	7	2	10		8	11								5
1			3			6*	5	12	9†		4	7	2	10		8	11			13					6
1			3			6	5*12	9			4	13	2	10†	8	11		7							7
1			3		12	6	4*	5	9		7		2	10		8	11								8
1		7	6				5	9*			4	12	2	10		8	11								9
1			3			6		5*	9	4		7	12	2	10	8	11								10
1			3			4		5	9	6		7		2	10	8	11								11
1			3			6		5	9	4		7		2	10	8	11								12
1		3 13	10		6	4		5*	9	2		12			8	11			7†						13
1			3			6	5		11	4				2	10	8					7	9			14
1			3			6	5		11	4				2	10	8					7	9			15
1			3			6		5	9*	4	7		12	2	10	8	11								16
1	3	7				6*		5	11	4	13			2	10		8†12				9				17
1	2					6		5	9	4				3	10	8	11					7			18
	1			2		6		5	9	4				3	10	8	12		11		7*				19
	1			2		6		5	9	4	7			3	10	8			11*12						20
	1			2		6				4	7*	5	12	3	10	8	9		11						21
	1			2		6		5	9	4			12	3	10	8	7		11*						22
	1			2	9	6		5		4			7	3	10	8	11								23
	1			2	9	6		5		4			7	3	10	8	11								24
	1			2	9	6		5	7	4				3	10	8*11				12					25
	1			2	9	6		5		4			7	3	10	8	11*				12				26
	1			2	9	6		5		4			7	3	10	8				11					27
	1			2	9	6		5		4			7	3	10	8		12		11*					28
	1			2	9	6		5		4			7	3	10	8				11					29
	1			2	9	6		5	12	4			7	3	10	8*				11					30
	1			2	9	6		5	12	4			7	3	10	8				11*					31
	1			2	9	6		5	12	4*			7	3	10	8				11					32
1	2				9		5		11	4			7	3	10	8				6					33
	1			2	9	6		5		4			7	3	10	8				11					34
	1			2	9	6		5		4			7	3	10	8				11					35
1				2	9	6		5	11	4			7	3		8		12				10	13		36
18	18	5	17	17	16	35	11	27	19	31	6	24	3	35	33	36	21	1	4	2	2	5	10	0	
			+ 1s	+ 1s			+ 1s	+ 2s	+ 3s		+ 1s	+ 3s	+ 5s				+ 2s		+ 2s	+ 5s		+ 2s	+ 1s		

KILMARNOCK PREM. DIV.

Year Founded: 1869.
Ground: Rugby Park. *Size:* 115 × 75 yds. *Capacity:* 34,500 (4,200 seats).
Telephone: Kilmarnock 25184.
Manager: Dave Sneddon. *Hon. Secretary:* David McCulloch.
Trainer/Physiotherapist: Hugh Allan. *Trainer:* Dave Sneddon.
Club Colours: White shirts with blue and white centre panel, white shorts, white stockings.
Club Nickname: 'The Killies'.
Record Attendance: 34,246, v Rangers, League Cup, Aug. 1963.
European Competitions Entered: European Cup: 1965-66; Fairs Cup: 1964-65, 1966-67, 1969-70, 1970-71.
Record Transfer Fee Received: £120,000 from Celtic for David Provan, Sept. 1978

1978-79 LEAGUE RECORD

Match No.	Date	Venue	Opponents	Result Score	H/T Score	League Pos'n	Goalscorers	Attendance
1	Aug 12	A	Clydebank	L 1-2	0-0	—	Cairney	2000
2	19	H	Airdrieonians	W 2-0	0-0	6	Cairney, Maxwell	2700
3	26	A	Ayr U	D 0-0	0-0	6		5000
4	Sept 6	H	Dumbarton	D 0-0	0-0	—		2500
5	9	H	Dundee	D 1-1	1-0	7	Cairney	3000
6	13	A	St Johnstone	D 0-0	0-0	—		1292
7	16	A	Stirling Albion	W 4-1	2-1	5	McDicken, Provan, Doherty, Maxwell	1300
8	23	H	Montrose	D 2-2	1-0	5	Maxwell, Street	3000
9	26	A	Clyde	D 1-1	0-0	—	McDowell	1301
10	30	A	Queen of the S	L 1-2	0-1	7	Street	1200
11	Oct 7	H	Arbroath	W 3-1	2-1	7	McDowell, Maxwell (pen), Jardine	2000
12	14	H	Raith R	W 3-0	2-0	4	Cairney, Hughes, Bourke	3000
13	21	A	Hamilton A	W 3-2	0-2	4	Cairney, Maxwell (pen), Bourke	2500
14	28	A	Airdrieonians	L 1-4	0-3	7	Bourke	3000
15	Nov 4	H	Ayr U	L 1-2	0-0	7	Hughes	6200
16	11	A	Dundee	D 0-0	0-0	6		5620
17	18	H	Stirling Albion	W 5-0	1-0	6	Bourke 2, Gibson, Doherty, Maxwell	3000
18	25	A	Montrose	W 4-0	3-0	4	Maxwell 2, Hughes, Jardine	850
19	Dec 2	H	Queen of the S	D 0-0	0-0	4		2791
20	9	A	Arbroath	L 2-3	0-2	5	Street, Clark J	880
21	16	A	Raith R	W 3-1	1-1	4	Bourke 2, Maxwell	1200
22	23	H	Hamilton A	W 4-0	1-0	3	Bourke 3, Gibson	2850
23	Jan 20	A	Montrose	W 4-1	3-0	2	Bourke, Clarke P, Gibson 2	2000
24	Feb 3	H	St Johnstone	W 3-2	3-0	1	Bourke, Clark J, Hamilton (og)	3200
25	10	A	Arbroath	W 1-0	0-0	1	Gibson	1284
26	24	H	Raith R	W 2-1	0-1	1	Maxwell, Street	3267
27	Mar 3	H	Clydebank	D 0-0	0-0	1		3500
28	7	A	Ayr U	L 1-2	0-0	—	Clark J	5693
29	13	A	Dumbarton	W 3-0	1-0	—	Bourke, Cairney, Maxwell (pen)	2000
30	17	H	St Johnstone	W 3-1	1-1	1	Cairney, Gibson 2	2000
31	24	H	Clyde	W 2-1	2-0	1	Bourke 2	2500
32	31	A	Clydebank	W 2-1	2-0	1	Bourke, Gibson	2500
33	Apr 4	A	Stirling Albion	D 0-0	0-0	1		1800
34	7	A	Clyde	W 1-0	1-0	1	Bourke	1500
35	11	H	Airdrieonians	W 1-0	1-0	—	Bourke	3000
36	14	H	Queen of the S	W 3-1	2-1	1	Bourke, Street, Cairney	2978
37	21	A	Hamilton A	L 0-1	0-0	1		2400
38	25	H	Dundee	W 2-1	0-0	—	Bourke, McDicken	5000
39	28	A	Dumbarton	W 3-1	1-0	1	Bourke, Cairney, Gibson	3000

Final League Position: 2

Goalscorers

League (72): Bourke 21, Maxwell 11 (3 pens), Cairney 9, Gibson 9, Street 5, Clark J 3, Hughes 3, Doherty 2, Jardine 2, McDicken 2, McDowell 2, Clarke P 1, Provan 1, own goal 1.
League Cup (7): Cairney 2, McDicken 1, McDowell 1, Maxwell 1, Street 1, Welsh 1.
Cup (6): Bourke 3, Street 2, Gibson 1.

Honours

Scottish League; Division 1, Champions: 1964–65. Runners-up: 1959–60, 1960–61, 1962–63, 1963–64, 1975–76, 1978–79. Division 2, Champions: 1897–98, 1898–99. Runners-up: 1953–54, 1973–74.
Scottish Cup: Winners: 1920, 1929. Runners-up: 1898, 1932, 1938, 1957, 1960.
Record Victory: 11-1 v Paisley Academicals, Scottish Cup, 1st Rd. Jan. 18th, 1930.
Record Defeat: 0-8 v Hibernian, Division 1, 1925-26, and v Rangers, Division 1, 1936-1937.
Most League Points: 50, Division 1, 1959–60, 1960–61, 1964–65.
Most Individual League Goals in Season: 35, Peerie Cunningham, Division 1, 1927–28.
Most Capped Player: Joe Nibloe 11, Scotland.

McCulloch A	McLean S	Robertson A	Maxwell G	Murdoch W	Clarke P	Welsh F	Jardine I	Provan D	Bourke J	Cairney J	McDicken D	Street R	Clark J	Taylor A	McDowell D	Doherty J	Baird I	Mauchlen A	Hughes J	Gibson I	Armstrong K	Match No.
1	2	3	8		5		4	7		9	6		10		11							1
1	3		8		5	2	4	7		9	6		10		12	11*						2
1	11	3	8		5	2	4			9	6	12	10		7*							3
1	2	3	10		5		4			9*	6		7	11	8			12				4
1	2	3	10		5		4	7		9	6			11	8*12							5
1	2	3*10			5	12	4			9	6		7	11	8†13							6
1	3		10		5	2	4*	7		9	6			11			8	12				7
1	2	3	10		5		4			9	6		7	11	8							8
1	2	3	10		5	12	4*			9†	6		7	11	13	8						9
1	4	12	10		5	2	3*			9	6		7†11		13	8						10
1	2	3	10		5	13	4				6		7*11†		9	8		12				11
1	2	3	8		5		4		9	10	6				12				7	11*		12
1	2	3	8		5		4		9	10	6				12				7	11*		13
1	2	3	8		5		4		9	10	6*				13	12			7	11†		14
1	2	3	11		5	12	4*		9	8†	6			7					10	13		15
1	8	3	12		5	2	4*		9		6								10	11	7	16
1	4	3	8		5†	2*			9	13	6				12				10	11	7	17
1	2	3	8		5		4			9	6		10						11	7		18
1		3	2	12	5		4*		9†13	6			10			8			11	7		19
1	2	3	8	12					9	10†	6	13	11					4	7*	5		20
1	2	3	8		5				9		6		4	11			10		7			21
1	2	3	8		5				9		6		4	11			10		7			22
1	2	3	8		5				9		6	11	4				10		7			23
1	2	3	8		5				9*12		6	11	4				10		7			24
1	2	3	8	10	5				9*12		6	11	4						7			25
1	2	3	8		5*		12		9		6	11	4				10		7			26
1	2	3	8		5		10		9	12	6		4					11*	7			27
1	2	3	8		5		10		9		6	11	4						7			28
1	10	3	8		5	2	4*		9	11		12							7	6		29
1	2	3	8		5		10		9	11			4						7	6		30
1	2	3	8		5				9	11			4			10			7	6		31
1	2	3	8		5				9	11	6		4			10			7			32
1	2	3	8		5				9	11	6		4			10			7			33
1	2	3			5		8		9	11	6	12	4			10			7*			34
1	2	3	8		5		11		9		6	12	4			10			7*			35
1	10	3			5	2	8		9	11	6*12		4						7			36
1	2	3	8*		5		12		9	13	6	11†	4			10			7			37
1	2	3			5		8		9	11	6		4			10			7			38
1	2	3				5	8		9	11	6		4			10			7			39
39	38	36	34	1	37	9	27	4	27	25	36	12	32	2	5	8	0	20	9	24	4	
	+	+	+		+	+	+		+	+		+			+	+	+		+			
	1s	1s	2s		4s	2s			6s	6s					3s	6s	2s		3s			

MEADOWBANK THISTLE

DIV. 2

Year Formed: 1974. (Previously called Ferranti Thistle, founded 1943.) *Ground:* Meadowbank Stadium.
Size: 105 × 75 yards. *Capacity:* 16,000 (at present only main stand, 7,500 seats, is used for football). *Telephone* (Secretary's office): 031-337 2442.
Manager: W. McFarlane. *Secretary:* William L. Mill.
Club Colours: Amber with black trim shirts, black shorts, amber stockings.
Record Attendance: 4000 v Albion Rovers, Scottish League Cup, August 9th, 1974.

1978–79 LEAGUE RECORD

Match No.	Date	Venue	Opponents	Result	H/T Score	League Pos'n	Goalscorers	Attendance
1	Aug 12	H	Forfar Ath	D 0-0	0-0	—		200
2	19	A	Cowdenbeath	L 1-2	0-1	10	Adair	400
3	26	A	Berwick R	D 0-0	0-0	12		1110
4	Sept 6	A	Brechin C	D 2-2	1-0	—	Davidson, Hancock J	400
5	9	A	Albion R	W 2-1	1-1	7	Adair, Downie	300
6	13	H	Stranraer	L 0-1	0-1	—		300
7	16	A	East Fife	D 2-2	1-2	10	Adair, McKenzie	1100
8	23	H	East Stirling	W 3-1	2-1	7	Adair, Davidson, Hancocks	350
9	27	H	Stenhousemuir	W 2-0	1-0	—	Adair, O'Rourke	500
10	30	A	Alloa	D 1-1	0-1	6	Small	800
11	Oct 7	A	Falkirk	L 0-6	0-3	8		2000
12	14	H	Queen's Park	L 0-4	0-0	9		500
13	21	A	Dunfermline	L 1-2	1-1	10	Davidson	4000
14	28	H	Cowdenbeath	L 0-2	0-1	12		500
15	Nov 3	H	Berwick R	L 0-5	0-2	—		600
16	11	H	Albion R	W 2-0	2-0	12	Adair, Leetion	200
17	18	A	East Fife	W 3-2	2-2	10	Small, Hancock, J, Conroy	939
18	25	A	East Stirling	L 1-4	0-2	11	Adair	120
19	Dec 2	H	Alloa	L 0-1	0-1	11		250
20	9	H	Falkirk	L 1-2	0-1	12	Hancock S.	600
21	Jan 20	H	East Stirling	W 3-1	1-1	12	Hancock J, Davidson 2	400
22	Feb 3	A	Stranraer	L 1-3	0-2	13	Strewat	600
23	10	H	Falkirk	D 1-1	0-0	11	McKenzie	700
24	24	A	Queen's Park	D 1-1	1-0	11	Small	850
25	28	A	Dunfermline Ath	L 0-1	0-1	—		2000
26	Mar 3	H	Forfar Ath	W 1-0	0-0	11	Small	400
27	7	H	Berwick R	L 0-1	0-0	—		400
28	10	H	Brechin C	L 0-3	0-2	12		400
29	17	A	Stranraer	L 0-1	0-0	12		400
30	20	H	East Fife	L 1-3	1-1	—	Downie	300
31	24	H	Stenhousemuir	L 1-2	1-2	12	Davidson	300
32	27	A	Queen's Park	L 0-3	0-1	—		400
33	31	A	Forfar Ath	W 3-2	2-1	12	Downie, Wight, Small	810
34	Apr 3	A	Albion R	L 0-2	0-2	—		300
35	7	A	Stenhousemuir	L 0-2	0-0	14		300
36	14	H	Alloa	D 1-1	1-0	13	McKenzie	200
37	21	H	Dunfermline Ath	L 1-3	0-2	14	Hancock J	928
38	25	A	Cowdenbeath	L 1-4	1-2	—	Small	300
39	28	A	Brechin C	L 1-2	1-1	14	Leetion	300

Final League Position: 14

Goalscorers
League (37): Adair 7, Davidson 6, Small 6, Hancock J 4, Downie 3, McKenzie 3, Hancock S 2, Leetion 2, Conroy 1, O'Rourke 1, Stewart 1, Wight 1.
League Cup (0)
Cup (8): Johnston 2, McKenzie 2, Conroy 1, Davidson 1, Hancock J 1 (pen), Small 1.

Honours

Record Victory: 4-1 v Albion Rovers, Division 2, 1975–76.
Record Defeat: 0-8 v Hamilton, Division 2, 1974–75.
Most League Points: 32, Division 2, 1976–77.
Honours: East of Scotland Qualifying Cup Winners 1963–64.
Scottish Qualifying Cup (South) Winners 1973–74.

Sinclair C	Johnston C	Allan T	Porwol A	McKenzie D	Mooney G	Stewart E	Fraser G	Hancock I	Carr S	O'Rourke T	Bough M	Hancock S	McKenna A	Adair G	Wright D	Davidson K	Johnson K	Downie T	Leetion M	Small D	Conroy D	Notman A	McKinnon S	Donaldson G	McGauran H	Match No.
1				5		3	4	6	2		11		9			8	10*	7	12							1
1				5		3	4	6	2		11		9		10	8*	12	7								2
1					4	3	8	6	2		11		9	5	10			7								3
1						3	4	6	2		8		9*	5	11		10	7	12							4
1		12				3	4	6	2		8*		9	5	11		10	7								5
1						3	4	6	2		8		9*	5	11		10	7	12							6
1		12				3	4	6	2		8		9*	5	11†		10	7	13							7
1		12				3	4	6	2		8*		9	5	11		10†	7	13							8
1						3	4	6	2		8		9	5	11		10	7								9
1		7*				3	4	6	2		8		9	5	11		10		12							10
1					11	3	4	6	2		8*		9†	5	13		10	7	12							11
1						3	4	6	2			7	9*	5	11†	12	10	8		13						12
1					6	3	4		2		8	7	10*	5	11†		12	9	13							13
1			5		6	3	4		2		12	7*			11†	9	10	8		13						14
1		12			4	3	13		2		11		9	5			10†	8	7	6*						15
1					6	3	4		2		11†	12	9	5	13			8	7*	10						16
1		12			6	3	4		2		11		9	5			10		7	8*						17
1					6	3	4		2		11		9	5			10	8	7							18
1					6	3	4*		2		12		9†	5	13		10	7	11	8						19
1		8			6	3	4		2		7	13	9*	5	11	12		10†								20
1					6	3	4		2			7		5	11	9		8		10						21
	1	10†			6	3	4		13		12			5	7*	9		2	11	8						22
	1	10			6	3	4					12		5	7*	9	13	2	11	8†						23
	1	8				3	4				7		6	5	11		10	2	9							24
	1	8				3	4		12			7	6*	5	11†		10	2	9	13						25
	1	8				3	4				11	7*		5	12		10	2	9	6						26
	1	8				3	4				11*	7		5	12		10	2	9	6						27
	1	8				3	4		12			7†		5	11	13	10	2	9	6*						28
	1	8				4	3		2			12		5	13	9*	10	7	11†	6						29
	1	8				4	3		2		13			11†	5	9	10	7	12		6*					30
	1	8				4	3		2			7*		5	11	13	10	6	9†	12						31
	1	8					4				3	11†		5	6	13	10	2	9	12		7*				32
	1	8				4	3		2		7			5	11		10	6	9							33
	1	8				4	3		2		11*	7		5			10	6	9	12						34
	1					4	3		2		11		5	8			10	7	9	6						35
	1	9				4	3		8		2		13	12	5	11	10	3	7†				6*			36
	1	12				4	3		8		2		13	11†	5	9	10	7						6*		37
	1	8				6	3		4		2		9		5		10	7	11							38
	1	4				6*	3	10			2		9	13		5	11	2	7	8†	12					39
21	15	2	1	18	3	23	34	38	12	27	1	26	12	21	36	27	7	31	37	21	12	1	1	1	1	
				+		+			+	+		+	+			+	+			+	+					
				6s		1s			4s	5s		6s	6s			5s	3s			9s	7s					

R.F. '79/80—29

MONTROSE   DIV 2.

Year Formed: 1879. *Ground:* Links Park. *Size:* 114 × 66 yards. *Capacity:* 9000. *Telephone:* Montrose 3200.
Manager: Bobby Livingstone.
Secretary: William Coull.
Club Colours: Royal blue shirts, and shorts, white stockings with royal blue tops.
Club Nickname: 'Gable Endies'.
Record Attendance: 8983 v Dundee, 3rd Round Scottish Cup, March 17th, 1973.
Record Transfer Fee received: £30,000 for Kenny Watson from Rangers, August 1975

1978–79 LEAGUE RECORD

Match No.	Date	Venue	Opponents	Result	H/T Score	League Pos'n	Goalscorers	Attendance
1	Aug 12	A	St Johnstone	L 2-3	2-1	—	Murray 2	1234
2	19	H	Clyde	D 2-2	1-1	11	Hair, D'Arcy D	1100
3	26	A	Arbroath	W 3-1	2-1	5	Hair, Murray 2	1472
4	Sept 6	A	Dundee	D 1-1	1-0	—	Robb	4708
5	9	H	Clydebank	L 1-3	0-2	10	Lowe (pen)	1000
6	13	H	Airdrieonians	D 2-2	1-1	—	Murray, Lowe (pen)	900
7	16	A	Queen of the S	W 3-1	2-1	7	Murray 2, McIntosh	1500
8	23	A	Kilmarnock	D 2-2	0-1	7	Hair, Livingstone	3000
9	27	H	Stirling Albion	D 1-1	0-1	—	D'Arcy B	800
10	30	A	Dumbarton	L 1-4	1-4	10	Georgeson	2000
11	Oct 7	H	Hamilton A	D 1-1	0-0	10	Ford	800
12	14	H	Ayr U	L 4-6	1-3	10	Miller, Georgeson 3	1300
13	21	A	Raith R	L 1-3	1-2	11	Livingstone	1500
14	28	A	Clyde	W 4-2	0-1	10	Miller 2, McIntosh 2	900
15	Nov 4	H	Arbroath	W 3-0	0-0	10	Robb, McIntosh, Livingstone	1200
16	11	A	Clydebank	L 0-1	0-1	11		892
17	18	A	Queen of the S	L 1-2	1-2	11	Georgeson	900
18	25	H	Kilmarnock	L 0-4	0-3	11		850
19	Dec 9	A	Hamilton A	L 1-3	0-1	12	Livingstone	1000
20	16	A	Ayr U	L 0-5	0-1	12		2505
21	23	H	Raith R	D 0-0	0-0	13		700
22	Jan 20	A	Kilmarnock	L 1-4	0-3	13	Lowe (pen)	2000
23	Feb 21	A	Arbroath	L 0-4	0-1	—		988
24	24	A	Ayr U	L 0-5	0-3	14		2500
25	28	H	Hamilton A	L 2-4	0-1	—	Miller, Murray	900
26	Mar 3	H	St Johnstone	L 1-3	0-1	14	Lowe (pen)	850
27	7	H	Queen of the S	W 6-1	1-1	—	Robb 3, Miller 2, Clay (og)	550
28	14	H	Dundee	L 0-2	0-1	—		1800
29	24	H	Stirling Albion	L 0-2	0-1	14		900
30	28	H	Clydebank	L 1-2	1-1	—	Livingstone	600
31	31	A	St Johnstone	L 0-4	0-3	14		1325
32	Apr 7	A	Stirling Albion	W 1-0	1-0	14	Robb	800
33	11	H	Clyde	W 4-0	2-0	—	Cormack, Murray 3	600
34	14	H	Dumbarton	W 2-1	0-1	13	Robb 2	800
35	18	A	Airdrionians	D 1-1	0-0	—	Murray	2000
36	21	H	Raith R	D 1-1	1-1	12	Robb	950
37	28	A	Dundee	L 0-1	0-1	13		6000
38	May 5	A	Airdrieonians	L 2-8	2-2	13	Robb, Wright	1000
39	9	H	Dumbarton	L 0-2	0-1	—		400

Final League Position: 13

Goalscorers

League (55): Murray 12, Robb 10, Miller 6, Georgeson 5, Livingstone 5, Lowe 4 (4 pens), McIntosh 4, Hair 3, Cormack 1, D'Arcy B 1, D'Arcy D 1, Ford 1, Wright 1, own goal 1.
League Cup (15): Livingstone 5, Hair 3, Murray 2, Robb 2, Georgeson 1, Lowe 1 (pen), Miller 1.
Cup (2): Miller 1, Murray 1.

Honours
Record Victory: 12-0 v Vale of Leithen, 2nd Round Scot. Cup, January 4th, 1975.
Record Defeat: 0-13 v Aberdeen, Division C, March 17th, 1951.
Most League Points: 53, Division 2, 1974–75.
Most Capped Player: Alexander Keillor, 2 (6) Scotland.

Gorman D	Moffat J	Daun D	D'Arcy B	Johnston D	Taylor K	D'Arcy D	Hair I	Robb D	Miller R	Shiran J	Ford R	Livingstone R	Georgeson R	Lowe M	Walker A	McIntosh J	Murray G	Downie C	Beadie S	Joss K	Cormack B	Mitchell R	Kyles J	Wright A	Match No.
1		3	6*		5	4	13	11			2	9†		10		7	8			12					1
1		3			5	4	13	12			8	9†			2	10	7	11		6*					2
1		3	6		5†	4		7			8	9			2	10*		11		12			13		3
1		3	6		5	4	7	13			8	10	9*	2			11†			12					4
1		3	6		5	4	7	12			8	10	9*	2			11								5
	1	3*	6		5	4	7	13			8	9	10	2		12	11								6
1		2			5	4	7	12			6	10*	9	3		11	8								7
1		3			5	4	11	12			6	13	9*	2		7	10†	8							8
1		8	3		5	4	9*	12			6	10		2		7	11								9
1		3			5	10	8*	12			6	13	11	2		7	9†		4						10
1		3	6		5		11				4	12	9	2	8	7	10*								11
1		3*	6		5	8	12	11			4	7	9	2	10										12
1		3	6*	5		8	13	11†			4	7	9	2	10	12									13
1		3		6	5	4*12	11				8	10	9	2		7									14
1		3		6	5	8*13	11				4	9	10†	2		7	12								15
1		3*		6	5	10	8	11			4	9†	7	2	12		13								16
1		3		5*		6	12	11†			4	8	9	2	10	7	13								17
1		3	6*		5	8	13	11			4	7	9†	2	10					12					18
1		8*	3		5	6	13	12			4	11	9†	2		7			10						19
1		3	6		5	8*10	11				4	12	9	2		7									20
1		3	6		5		9				4	12	8	10		7	11*			2					21
1		3	6		5	8	11	13			4	12	9*10†			7				2					22
1		3	6		5	8*	9	12			2	11†		10		7	13			4					23
	1	2	3	6	5		7				4			10	11		9		8						24
	1	3	6*	4	5	8	10	11						2	7		9		12						25
	1	12	3*	4	5	8	10	11						6	2	7	9								26
	1	2		4	5	8	10	11				9		3	6	7									27
	1	12	2		4		8	9	11	5	6			3	10*	7									28
1		2	6*	4	12	8	10	11			5		9	3	13	7†									29
	1	10	3	6	5		7	11						2		8	9		4						30
1		10	5	3			8	9	11					6	2	12			4*		7				31
	1	8	3		5		11			6				4	2		9	10		7					32
	1	10	3		5		11			6				4	2		9	8		7					33
	1	8	3		5		11			6				4	2		9	10		7					34
	1	8	3		5		11			6				4	2		9	10		7					35
	1	10	3		5	12	11			6				4	2*		9	8		7					36
	1	10			5	2	11			6		13		4	3		9	8†		12			7*		37
	1	8†	3		5	4	11			6				2		9	13	10		12			7*		38
	1	10	3		5	4	11			6				2		9	8						7		39
23	16	9	37	21	12	34	30	28	3	18	10	25	19	18	36	21	21	24	1	9	8	5	1	0	3
		+	+		+	+	+	+		+				+	+	+	+	+	+	+			+		
		1s	1s		1s	1s	9s	11s		7s				2s	3s	4s	1s	1s	4s	2s			1s		

MORTON

PREM. DIV.

Year Formed: 1874. *Limited Company:* 1896.
Ground: Cappielow Park, Greenock PA15 2TY. *Size:* 110 × 71 yds. *Capacity:* 25,000 (2,900 seats).
Telephone: Greenock 23571.
Manager: Benny Rooney.
Secretary: Tom Robertson.
Club Colours: Blue and white hooped shirts, white shorts and stockings.
Club Nickname: 'Ton'.
Record Attendance: 23,500 v Celtic, Division 1, 1922.
European Competitions Entered: Fairs Cup, 1968–69.
Record Transfer Fee Received: £150,000 from Newcastle U. for Mark McGhee, Dec, 1977.

1978–79 LEAGUE RECORD

Match No.	Date	Venue	Opponents	Result	Score	H/T Score	League Pos'n	Goalscorers	Attendance
1	Aug 12	H	Celtic	L	1-2	0-1	—	Ritchie	16,000
2	19	A	Aberdeen	L	1-3	1-1	9	Ritchie	14,500
3	26	H	St Mirren	L	1-3	0-1	10	Ritchie	12,000
4	Sept 9	A	Dundee U	W	2-1	0-0	8	Russell, Rooney (pen)	5531
5	16	A	Hearts	D	1-1	1-0	8	Thomson	7230
6	23	H	Rangers	D	2-2	1-0	8	Ritchie, Scott	16,500
7	30	A	Hibernian	D	1-1	1-0	8	Scott	8000
8	Oct 7	H	Partick T	W	1-0	0-0	8	McNeil	6500
9	14	H	Motherwell	L	1-2	0-0	8	Ritchie	6000
10	21	A	Celtic	D	0-0	0-0	8		24,000
11	28	H	Aberdeen	W	2-1	2-1	8	Ritchie, Russell	7000
12	Nov 4	A	St Mirren	D	0-0	0-0	9		10,000
13	11	H	Dundee U	W	3-1	1-0	8	Ritchie 3 (1 pen)	6500
14	18	H	Hearts	W	3-2	2-1	5	Ritchie, Thomson, Hutchison	7500
15	25	A	Rangers	L	0-3	0-1	7		22,000
16	Dec 9	A	Partick T	L	1-2	0-1	8	Scott	5000
17	16	A	Motherwell	D	1-1	0-0	8	Ritchie (pen)	5347
18	23	H	Celtic	W	1-0	0-0	7	Ritchie (pen)	13,000
19	30	A	Aberdeen	W	2-1	0-0	5	Ritchie, McNeil	8000
20	Jan 20	H	Rangers	L	0-2	0-0	6		18,000
21	Feb 17	H	Partick T	D	2-2	2-1	6	Ritchie, Thomson	7000
22	24	A	Hibernian	D	1-1	0-1	6	Thomson	6500
23	Mar 10	A	Dundee U	L	1-4	1-3	7	Stark (og)	6433
24	14	H	Motherwell	W	6-0	3-0	—	Ritchie, Thomson 2, Tolmie 2, Russell	3000
25	17	A	St Mirren	L	1-3	0-1	5	Ritchie	8500
26	24	H	Dundee U	W	3-1	0-1	4	McNeil, Anderson, Tolmie	5500
27	28	A	Celtic	L	0-3	0-2	—		16,000
28	31	H	Hearts	D	2-2	1-1	5	Ritchie (pen), Thomson	6000
29	Apr 4	H	Aberdeen	L	0-1	0-1	—		7000
30	7	A	Rangers	D	1-1	1-0	7	Russell	18,000
31	11	H	St Mirren	W	1-0	1-0	—	Ritchie	7500
32	14	H	Hibernian	D	2-2	1-0	7	Ritchie (pen), Thomson	7000
33	18	H	Hibernian	W	3-0	1-0	—	Ritchie, Russell, McNeil	8000
34	21	A	Partick T	L	1-2	0-0	7	Ritchie (pen)	6000
35	28	A	Motherwell	D	3-3	2-0	7	Ritchie, Thomson 2	3546
36	May 7	A	Hearts	W	1-0	1-0	—	Thomson	2700

Final League Position: 7

Goalscorers

League (52): Ritchie 22 (6 pens), Thomson 11, Russell 5, McNeil 4, Scott 3, Tolmie 3, Anderson 1, Hutchison 1, Rooney 1 (pen), own goal 1.
League Cup (13): Ritchie 3 (1 pen), Scott 3, Russell 2, Thomson 2, Anderson 1, McNeil 1, Orr 1.
Cup (6): Ritchie 4 (2 pens), Anderson 1, Scott 1.

Honours
Scottish League: Division 1, Champions: 1977–78. Runners-up: 1916–17, Division 2, Champions: 1949–50, 1963–64, 1966–67. Runners-up: 1899–1900, 1928–29, 1936–37.
Scottish Cup: Winners: 1922. Runners-up: 1948.
Scottish League Cup: Runners-up: 1953, 1961, 1963.
Southern League Cup: Runners-up: 1941–42.
Renfrewshire Cup: 36 times winners.
War Shield winners: 1914.
Record Victory: 11-0 Carfin Shamrock, Scot. Cup, 1886.
Record Defeat: 2-8 v Rangers, Division 1, March 15th, 1927.
Most League Points: 69, Division 2, 1966–67.
Most League Goals: 135, Division 2, 1963–64.
Most Individual League Goals in Season: 41, Allan McGraw, Division 2, 1963–64.
Most Capped Player: Jimmy Cowan, 25, Scotland.

Connaghan D	Brcic D	Baines R	Hayes A D M	Holmes J B	Evans B D	Anderson G	Orr N I	McLaren W	Rooney J	Russell R	Tolmie J	Hutchison R	Thomson R	Miller J	Ritchie A	McNeil J	McLean J	Rae D G	Scott A	Match No.
1		2	3	4			5		6	7				8	11			9	10	1
1		2	3		4	5			6	7				8	11		9*12		10	2
1		2	3		4	5			6	7		9		8*11†13			12		10	3
1		2	3	4		5			6	7		9	8		11				10	4
1		2	3			5	4	6	7*			9		8	11	12			10	5
1		2	3			5	4	6	7*			9		8	11	12			10	6
1			3			5	4	6	7			9	2	11	8				10	7
1		2	3			5	4		7			9	6	11	8				10	8
1		2	3	12		5		4		7†		9	6*11	8			13	10		9
1		2	3	4		5		6	7			9		8	11				10	10
1		2	3	4		5		6	7*12			9	8	11					10	11
1		2	3	4		5		6	7			9	8	11					10	12
1		2	3	4		5		6	7			9	8	11					10	13
1		2	3	4		5		6	7*		13	9†	8	11	12				10	14
1		2	3	4		5		6	7*12			9	8	11					10	15
1		2	3	4*		5		6			7	9	8	11	12				10	16
	1	2	3			5	4	6			7	9	8	11					10	17
	1	2	3			5	4	6			8	9		11	7				10	18
	1	2		3	5	4	6				8	9		11	7				10	19
	1	2	3			5	4	6	12			9	8	11	7				10*	20
	1	2	3		4	5	6		9			10	8	11	7*		12			21
	1	2	3		4	5		6			8	9		11	7				10	22
		1	2	3	13		4	5	12	6*			9	8†11	7				10	23
	1	2	3		4	5					12	10*	8	9	6	11	7			24
	1	2	3		4	5	8			12	9*			6	11	7			10	25
	1	2	3		4	5	6*			10	9			8	11	7			12	26
	1	2	3		4	5				10		9	6	8	11	7				27
	1	2	3		4	5			12	10*	9	6	8	11	7					28
	1	2	3		4	5				10	9	6	8	11	7					29
		1	3	4		5	8	6	7	12	9			2	11	10*				30
		1	3	4		5	8	6	7		9			2	11	10				31
		1	3	4		5	8	6	7*		9†10			2	11	12		13		32
		1	3	4			5*	8	12	7†		6	9	2	11	10		13		33
		1	3	4		5	8	12	7			6*	9	2	11	10†		13		34
		1	3	4			5	6	7*10	12		9		2	11	8†		13		35
		1	3			5	4	6	7			8	9	2	11				10	36
16	6	14	35	15	12	35	18	26	23	7	16	30	33	35	21	1	1	24		
			+2s				+1s	+2s	+4s	+3s	+2s				+6s			+3s +6s		

MOTHERWELL
DIV. 1.

Year Formed: 1886.
Ground: Fir Park. *Size:* 110×72 yds. *Capacity:* 31,000 (3,300 seats).
Telephone: Motherwell 61437.
Manager: Ally MacLeod
Secretary: Jack McGraw. *Trainer:* William McKenzie.
Club Colours: Amber with claret and white trim.
Club Nickname: 'Well'.
Record Attendance: 35,632, v Rangers, Scottish Cup, 4th Rd. Replay, Mar. 12th, 1952.
Previous Names: Club formed following the amalgamation of Alpha and Glencairn, Known as Wee Alpha for a year before becoming Motherwell in 1886.
Previous Ground: Roman Park, Dalziel Park.

1978-79 LEAGUE RECORD

Match No.	Date	Venue	Opponents	Result	Score	H/T Score	League Pos'n	Goalscorers	Attendance
1	Aug 12	H	Partick T	L	0-1	0-1	—		3919
2	19	A	St Mirren	W	1-0	1-0	5	Stevens	8000
3	26	H	Celtic	L	1-5	1-1	8	Edvaldsson (og)	19,710
4	Sept 9	A	Aberdeen	L	0-4	0-1	9		13,200
5	16	H	Dundee U	L	0-1	0-1	10		3372
6	23	H	Hearts	L	0-1	0-0	10		5219
7	30	A	Rangers	L	1-4	1-3	10	Clinging	25,000
8	Oct 7	H	Hibernian	L	2-3	2-1	10	Larnach, Clinging	5516
9	14	A	Morton	W	2-1	0-0	10	Pettigrew, Lindsay (pen)	6000
10	21	A	Partick T	L	0-2	0-0	10		6000
11	28	H	St Mirren	L	1-2	1-1	10	Pettigrew	6007
12	Nov 4	A	Celtic	W	2-1	1-1	10	Stevens, McLaren	21,000
13	11	H	Aberdeen	D	1-1	0-0	10	Wilson	5448
14	18	A	Dundee U	L	1-2	1-2	10	Larnach	5876
15	25	A	Hearts	L	2-3	1-1	10	Larnach, Marinello	8984
16	Dec 9	A	Hibernian	D	2-2	1-1	10	Pettigrew 2	6000
17	16	H	Morton	D	1-1	0-0	10	Pettigrew	5347
18	23	H	Partick T	D	1-1	0-1	10	Millar (pen)	5729
19	Jan 20	H	Hearts	W	3-2	1-1	10	Pettigrew, Stevens, Clinging	3881
20	Feb 10	H	Hibernian	L	0-3	0-1	10		5105
21	17	A	St Mirren	L	0-1	0-1	10		7600
22	Mar 3	A	Partick T	D	0-0	0-0	10		5500
23	7	H	Dundee U	L	0-4	0-3	—		2653
24	10	H	St Mirren	L	0-3	0-2	10		4795
25	14	A	Morton	L	0-6	0-3	—		3000
26	17	A	Celtic	L	1-2	0-1	10	Donnelly	16,000
27	26	A	Aberdeen	L	0-8	0-3	—		7000
28	31	A	Dundee U	L	1-2	0-0	10	Irvine	5655
29	Apr 4	H	Celtic	L	3-4	1-3	—	Larnach, Clinging, Stevens	8744
30	7	A	Hearts	L	0-3	0-1	10		7000
31	10	A	Rangers	L	0-3	0-2	—		8000
32	14	H	Rangers	W	2-0	0-0	10	Clinging, Donnelly	14,612
33	18	H	Aberdeen	D	1-1	0-0	—	Stevens	2672
34	21	A	Hibernian	L	0-4	0-3	10		7000
35	28	H	Morton	D	3-3	0-2	10	Irvine 2, Stevens	3546
36	May 2	H	Rangers	L	1-2	1-0	—	Irvine	13,052

Final League Position: 10

Goalscorers

League (33): Pettigrew 6, Stevens 6, Clinging 5, Irvine 4, Larnach 4, Donnelly 2, Lindsay 1 (pen), McLaren 1 Marinello 1, Millar 1 (pen), Wilson 1, own goal 1.
League Cup (6): Marinello 3 (1 a pen), Pettigrew 2, Clinging 1.
Cup (1): Clinging 1.

Honours
Scottish League: Division 1, Champions: 1931–32. Runners-up: 1926–27, 1929–30, 1932–33, 1933–34.
 Division 2, Champions: 1953–54, 1968–69. Runners-up 1894–95, 1902–03.
Scottish Cup: Winners: 1952. Finalists: 1931, 1933, 1939, 1951.
Scottish League Cup: Winners: 1950–51. Finalists: 1954–55.
Record Victory: 12–1 v Dundee U., Division 2, 1953–54.
Record Defeat: 3-8 v Partick T Division 1, Dec. 11th 1971.
Most League Points: 66, Division 1, 1931–32.
Most Individual League Goals in Season: 52, Willie McFadyen, 1931–32.
Highest Scorer in Total Aggregate: Hugh Ferguson, 283, 1916–25.
Most Capped Player: George Stevenson, 12, Scotland.

Latchford D	Rennie S	Smith J	Millar P	Wark J	Boyd J	McLaren S	Kane	McVie W	Hare M	Stevens G	Carr P	Kennedy I	Mackin A	Marinello P	Pettigrew W	Larnach W	Clinging I	Capaldi J	Rafferty S	Wilson P	Meikle	McLeod I	Lindsay J	Shanks M	Mungall S	Sommerville J	Carbery R	Dempsey J	Irvine W	Donnelly J	Leonard P	Match No.
1		2	3	4	10					6			5			8	9	12				7*11										1
1		2	3	4	10					6			5	7			9	11†				13	8*		12							2
1		2	3	4	10					6			5	7	8	9						11										3
1		2	3	4*	10		5			6				7	8	9	11†					12	13									4
1			3	12	10†	5	6							7	8	9*13	4					11		2								5
1			3	12	4*	5	6								8	9	7	10†		11		13	2									6
1			3*		4	5	6					12†	7	8		9	10	13		11			2									7
1				3		5	6	4					7	8		9	10†			11		12	13	2*								8
	1			3			4	5		6			7	8		9	10*			11		12	2									9
	1	8	3			5	6	4					7			9	10			11			2									10
	1		3		10	5	6		4*				7	8	12	9†				11			2	13								11
	1		3		4	5	6	2					7	8		9	10*			11		12										12
	1	10*	3		4	5	6	2					7	8		9	12			11												13
	1	10	3		4	5	6	2*		7	8			9						11†		13	12									14
	1		3			5	6					7		9	10*12			11		4	8	2										15
	1		4	3			5		12				8		9	10†	7		11			6	13	2*								16
	1		4	3	2					6			7	8	9*10	13				11†		5	12									17
1		4	10	3			5		6					8	9					11*		2	7		12							18
1		4	7	3	2*				6					8		9	12			11†		5	10							13		19
1		4	7	3	2			5		6*				8		9	13					12	10†							11		20
1		4	7*	3	2			5		6				8		9	10†			11										13	12	21
1										6		3		8	13	10		4*		7†	2				9		5			11	12	22
1		4*		6								3		8	12	10		7†			2				9		5			11	13	23
1		4*								6		3		8	13	10		7†12			2				9		5			11		24
1			3							6				8	9	12				4	2	7*			5					11	10	25
1			3		4							2			9	10		7*	8	6		12	13		5					11†		26
1	7		3		4*							2			9	10			8	6		12	13			5†				11		27
1	7		3							6					9	12		8*		2							4	5	10	11		28
1	7		3							6				8		9				2							4	5	10	11		29
1	7		3							6				8	12	9				2							4	5	10	11*		30
1	7		3							6				8	12	9		13		2							4*	5	10	11†		31
1	6		3											5	8	7	9			2							4		10	11		32
1			3								2	6		5	8	7	9										4		10	11		33
1			3							6				5	8	7	9		13	12	2						4*		10	11†		34
1	4		3							6				5*	8	7	9				2						11		10	12		35
1	5		3							6					8	7	9				2						4		10	11		36
8	28	14	13	33	9	12	16	2	1	31	6	5	7	14	30	26	29	3	4	18	1	21	7	10	1	3	9	10	9	14	2	
					+ 2s					+ 1s		+ 1s			+ 6s	+ 5s	+ 5s	+ 1s	+ 3s			+ 4s	+ 8s	+ 1s	+ 3s	+ 4s			+ 2s	+ 4s		

PARTICK THISTLE   PREM. DIV.

Year Formed: 1876. *Team Manager:* Robert Auld. *Admin. Manager:* Scot Symon. *Secretary:* J. C. Monachan, C.A. *Address:* Firhill Park, Glasgow, N.W. *Size:* 110×71 yards. *Capacity:* 36,000 (3,500 seated). *Telephone:* 041-946 2673. *Previous Grounds:* Kelvingrove, 1876–81; Jordanvale Park, 1881–83; Muirpark 1883–85; Meadowside Park, 1891–1908; Firhill Park, 1909 (1908–9, Ibrox was used by Partick when they had no ground of their own, but some 'home games' still had to be played away).

Nickname: 'The Jags'. *Colours:* Red and yellow shirts, broad vertical stripes, black shorts, red stockings with black and yellow tops.
Record Attendance: 49,838, v Rangers, Division 1, Feb, 18th, 1922.
European Competitions Entered: Fairs Cup, 1963–64; UEFA Cup, 1973–74.

1978–79 LEAGUE RECORD

Match No.	Date	Venue	Opponents	Result	H/T Score	League Pos'n	Goalscorers	Attendance
1	Aug 12	A	Motherwell	W 1-0	1-0	—	Sheed	3919
2	19	H	Dundee U	D 1-1	0-1	3	Houston	4500
3	26	A	Rangers	D 0-0	0-0	4		28,000
4	Sept 9	H	Hearts	W 3-2	2-0	3	Melrose, Somner 2 (1 a pen)	5000
5	16	A	St Mirren	L 0-1	0-0	5		8000
6	23	H	Celtic	L 2-3	2-1	5	Melrose, Somner (pen)	23,000
7	30	A	Aberdeen	D 1-1	1-0	5	Somner (pen)	11,100
8	Oct 7	A	Morton	L 0-1	0-0	6		6500
9	14	H	Hibernian	W 2-1	1-1	5	O'Hara 2	7000
10	21	H	Motherwell	W 2-0	0-0	5	Somner 2	6000
11	28	A	Dundee U	L 0-2	0-0	6		6055
12	Nov 4	H	Rangers	W 1-0	0-0	5	Houston	21,000
13	11	A	Hearts	W 1-0	1-0	2	O'Hara	12,400
14	18	H	St Mirren	W 2-1	2-1	2	Melrose, Anderson	11,000
15	25	A	Celtic	L 0-1	0-0	4		26,000
16	Dec 9	H	Morton	W 2-1	1-0	2	Houston, Somner	5000
17	16	A	Hibernian	D 0-0	0-0	2		6000
18	23	A	Motherwell	D 1-1	1-0	2	Somner	5729
19	Feb 17	A	Morton	D 2-2	1-2	4	Houston, McAdam	9000
20	28	A	Aberdeen	L 1-2	0-0	—	Melrose	12,500
21	Mar 3	H	Motherwell	D 0-0	0-0	5		5500
22	14	A	Dundee U	L 1-2	0-1	—	McAdam	6200
23	17	H	Rangers	L 0-2	0-1	8		18,665
24	28	H	Dundee U	L 1-2	1-1	—	Melrose	4000
25	31	H	St Mirren	W 3-1	1-0	8	Melrose, McAdam 2	5000
26	Apr 7	A	Celtic	L 0-2	0-1	8		19,000
27	11	A	Hearts	W 2-0	1-0	—	Somner, Park	10,000
28	14	H	Aberdeen	L 0-1	0-1	8		6000
29	21	H	Morton	W 2-1	0-0	8	O'Hara, McLaren (og)	6000
30	25	H	Hibernian	W 6-1	4-0	—	Melrose 3, O'Hara, Somner, Park	5000
31	28	A	Hibernian	L 0-1	0-0	8		5500
32	May 2	A	St Mirren	D 1-1		—	O'Hara	5000
33	5	H	Hearts	W 2-0	1-0	7	Melrose, O'Hara	4000
34	7	H	Celtic	L 1-2	1-1	—	Sonmer	18,000
35	11	H	Aberdeen	L 1-2	0-1	—	O'Hara	4000
36	23	A	Rangers	L 0-1	0-0	—		2000

Final League Position: 8

Goalscorers

League (42): Somner 11 (3 pens), Melrose 10, O'Hara 8, Houston 4, McAdam 4, Park 2, Anderson 1, Sheed 1, own goal 1.
League Cup (3): Craig 1, Gibson 1, own goal 1.
Cup (6): McAdam 2, Somner 2 (2 pens), Anderson 1, Melrose 1.

Honours
Scottish League: Division 1: Champions 1975–76, Division 2: Champions: 1896–97, 1899–1900, 1970–71. Runners-up: 1901–02. *Scottish Cup:* Winners: 1921; Runners-up: 1930. *Scottish League Cup:* Winners: 1971–72. Runners-up: 1953–54, 1956–57, 1958–59. *Most Capped Player*: Alan Rough 26, Scotland. *Most League Points*: 56, Division 2, 1970–71. *Record Victory*: 16-0 v Royal Albert, Scottish Cup, 1st Rd., Jan. 17th, 1931. *Record Defeat*: 1-10 v Dunfermline Ath., Division 1, 1958–59. *Most Individual League Goals in Season*: Alec Hair, 41, Division 1, 1926–27.

Rough A	McLean A	Mackie G	Whittaker B	McGregor G	Campbell J	Marr J	Gibson I	Anderson A	Houston R	Melrose J	McQuade D	O'Hara A	Love A	Somner D	Craig J	Sheed R	Park D	Mackinnon D	Rodman B	McAdam C	McDonald J	Clarke G	Doyle J	Match No.
1			3		4	5	6	2		8	11*		7	9	10				12					1
1			3		4	5	10†	6*	7	8		13		9	12	2		11						2
1			3			6	4	8*		7	12	9		10	11†	2		5	13					3
1			3		5	6			11	8		10	9			7	4	2						4
1			3		5	4	6		7	8*		13	11	9		10†	2	12						5
1			3		4	5	6		7	10		12	11*	9		8	2							6
1			3		4	5	6		7	10†		12	11	9		8*	2	13						7
1			3		4	5	6*		7			8	12	10		11	2	9						8
1			3		4	6		12	7	8		9		10		11	2	5*						9
1			3		4		12		7	8		6	9*10			11	2	5						10
1			3		4			13	7	8*		6	9	10†		11	2	5	12					11
1			3		5	6		4	7	8		9		10		11	2							12
1			3		5	6	12	4	7	8		9		10		11*	2							13
1			3		5	6		4	7	8		9		10		11	2							14
1			3		5*	6		4	7	8		9	12	10		11	2							15
1			3			6	13	4	7	8†		9		10		11	2	12	5*					16
1			3			6	8*	4	7	13		10		9†		11	2	5		12				17
1			3			6		4	7	8		9		10		11	2	5						18
1			3		4		10	6	7			9		8		11	2	5						19
1			3		6	9		4	7	12		10		8		11	2	5*						20
1			3	12	4	5	13	6	7	10*	11†					8	2	9						21
1	2	3			4		11	6				9		10		8	7	5						22
1		3				6	10	4	7	9		12		8*		11	2	5						23
1			3		4	5	6		7	10		12		8*		11	2	9						24
1			3			5		6	4	7	8		12	10		11*	2	9						25
1			3		4*		6		5	12	8†		7	10	13	11	2	9						26
1			3		4		6	5	7	8		9		10		11	2							27
1			3		13	5	6*	4	7	8		12		9†10		11	2							28
1			3		4	5	6*		7	8		9		12	10	11	2							29
1			3		4	5	6		7*	8		9		10		11†	2		12			13		30
1			3		4	6	8		7	12		9	11†10*				2	5				13		31
1			3		4	5			7	8		10	11				2		9			6		32
1			3		4	5			7*	8		9	11†10			12	2	13				6		33
1			3		4	6	8		12	7		9		10		11*	2	5						34
1			3		13	4	7			7		9		10		11†	2*		5	12	6			35
	1		3		5*	4				7†	8	9		12		2		10	13	6				36
35	1	1	36	—	30	29	21	18	31	29	1	26	13	31	1	1	30	35	—	22	1	—	4	
					+ 1s	+ 2s			+ 4s	+ 2s	+ 2s	+ 4s			+ 8s	+ 3s	+ 2s		+ 1s	+ 1s		+ 1s	+ 4s	+ 2s	+ 3s	+ 3s

QUEEN OF THE SOUTH DIV. 2

Year Formed: 1919. *Ground:* Palmerston Park. *Size:* 111 × 73 yds. *Capacity:* 20,000.
Telephone: Dumfries 4853.
Secretary: Lewis Russell.
Colours: Royal blue shirts with white facings, white shorts, royal blue stockings with two white hoops on top.
Club Nickname: 'Queens' or 'The Doonhamers'.
Record Attendance: 24,500 v Hearts, Scottish Cup, 3rd Rd., Feb. 23rd, 1952.

1978–79 LEAGUE RECORD

Match No.	Date	Venue	Opponents	Result	Score	H/T Score	League Pos'n	Goalscorers	Attendance
1	Aug 12	A	Airdrieonians	L	1-4	0-2	—	Bryce	2500
2	19	H	Ayr U	W	1-0	1-0	10	Dickson G	1000
3	26	A	Clyde	L	0-3	0-0	12		1160
4	Sept 6	H	St Johnstone	D	1-1	1-1	—	Bryce	1500
5	9	H	Stirling Albion	L	1-2	0-1	13	Bryce	1000
6	13	A	Arbroath	D	1-1	0-1	—	Bryce	804
7	16	H	Montrose	L	1-3	1-2	14	Mitchell	1500
8	23	A	Raith R	L	0-4	0-1	14		1800
9	27	A	Hamilton A	L	2-3	2-3	—	Coughlin 2	1600
10	30	H	Kilmarnock	W	2-1	1-0	13	Clark, Dickson P	1200
11	Oct 7	A	Dundee	L	0-5	0-0	13		5837
12	14	A	Clydebank	L	0-2	0-1	13		600
13	21	H	Dumbarton	L	0-2	0-1	13		1000
14	28	A	Ayr U	D	1-1	0-1	13	Dempster	3822
15	Nov 4	H	Clyde	W	3-0	1-0	13	Bryce, Coughlin 2	1000
16	11	A	Stirling Albion	L	1-4	0-2	13	Pollock	1000
17	18	H	Montrose	W	2-1	2-1	12	Boyd, McChesney	900
18	25	H	Raith R	W	2-1	0-0	12	Bryce, Coughlin	1000
19	Dec 2	A	Kilmarnock	D	0-0	0-0	12		2791
20	9	H	Dundee	W	3-1	1-1	11	Dempster, Mitchell, Dickson P	1350
21	16	H	Clydebank	W	2-1	1-0	11	Bryce, Dickson P	1100
22	30	H	Ayr U	L	0-1	0-0	11		1500
23	Jan 20	A	Raith R	L	0-3	0-2	11		1200
24	Feb 21	A	Clyde	L	0-3	0-2	—		800
25	24	H	Arbroath	D	1-1	0-0	10	McChesney (pen)	1100
26	28	A	Clydebank	L	1-3	1-2	—	Halley	1500
27	Mar 3	H	Airdrieonians	L	1-3	0-0	11	Bryce	900
28	7	A	Montrose	L	1-6	1-1	—	McChesney (pen)	550
29	10	A	St Johnstone	L	2-5	1-2	13	Bryce, Dickson P	1446
30	17	H	Arbroath	D	2-2	2-2	12	Boyd, Shields	900
31	24	A	Hamilton A	D	0-0	0-0	12		1300
32	31	H	Airdrieonians	L	1-5	1-2	13	Dempster	600
33	Apr 4	A	Dundee	L	0-4	0-1	—		4546
34	7	H	Hamilton A	D	3-3	1-1	13	Bryce 2, Coughlin	500
35	14	A	Kilmarnock	L	1-3	1-2	14	Dempster (pen)	2978
36	21	H	Dumbarton	L	1-3	0-2	14	Coughlin	400
37	28	H	St Johnstone	L	1-2	1-1	14	Dempster	500
38	May 2	H	Stirling Albion	W	3-2	1-1	—	Bryce, McCann, Dempster (pen)	500
39	5	A	Dumbarton	L	1-4	0-2	—	Coughlin	400

Final League Position: 14

Goalscorers
League (43): Bryce 12, Coughlin 8, Dempster 6 (2 pens), Dickson P 4, McChesney 3 (2 pens), Boyd 2, Mitchell 2, Clark 1, Dickson G 1, Halley 1, McCann 1, Pollock 1, Shields 1.
League Cup (0).
Cup (0).

Honours

Scottish League: Division 2: Champions: 1950–51; Runners-up: 1932–33, 1961–62, 1974–75.
Record Victory: 12–1 v Whithorn, 1920.
Record Defeat: 2–10 v Dundee, Division 1, 1962.
Most League Points: 53, Division 2, 1961–62.
Most Individual League Goals in Season: Jimmy Gray, 33, Division 2, 1927-28.
Most Capped Player: Billy Houliston, 3, Scotland.

Ball A	Lyle J	Poulton M	Thorburn R	McChesney I	McMillan W	McLaren W	Boyd C	Clark R	Cloy G	Dempster J	Dickson P	Pollock M	Bryce T	Halley P	Ferrie B	O'Hara T	Hewitson D	Coughlin J	Dickson G	Mitchell I	Shields D	Muldoon W	McCann K	Clark D	Carson R	Alexander R	Robertson G	Match No.
1			3	2	5		12	4			8		9	10		11*			6	7								1
1			3	2			5	4			8	9	10	11					6	7								2
1			3				5	4			8	9	10	11	13			2	12	6*	7†							3
	1		3	2		5		4		9	8		10	11					6	7								4
	1		3	2		5		4		9†	8*13	10	11					6	12	7								5
	1		3	2		12	5	4*		9		8†10	11					13	6	7								6
	1		3	2			5	4			7	12	8	10	11				6	9*								7
	1		3	2			5	4		7		9	10	11				6		8								8
	1			2			5	4	3	7		8*12	11					10	6	9								9
1				2			5	4	3	7	8		11	6				10		9								10
1				2			5	4		7*	8		12	11		3		10	6	9								11
1							5	4	2	7†	8	10	12	11		3		6*13		9								12
1							5*	4	2	12	8		9	11		3		10	6	7								13
1			2				5	4	3	7	8*		9	11		6		10†13	12									14
1			2				5	4	3	7*	8		9	11		6		10	12									15
1			2	13			5	4	3		8*12		9†11	10	6				7									16
1			2				5	4	3		8*12		9	11		6		10		7								17
1			2				5	4	3	7	8*12		9	11		6		10										18
1			2				5	4	3	8			9	11		6		10		7								19
1			2				5	4	3	7	12		9	11		6		10		8*								20
1			2				5*	4	3	7	8	12	9	11		6		10										21
1			2	5				4	3	7	8		9	11		6		10										22
			2				5	4	3	7	8*12		9	11	6			10					1					23
			2	6			5	4	3	7	8	12	9†11*					10					1	13				24
			2				5	4	3	7	8*	6	12	11				10		9			1					25
			2	6			5	4	3	7		8	9	11				10					1					26
			2	6			5	4	3	7	8		9	11				10					1					27
			2	5				4	3	7	8	6	9	11				10					1					28
			2	9			5	4	3	7	8	6	11					10					1					29
	1						10	4	3	7	2	12	8	11*				6			5		9					30
	1		3				8	4		7	2	9			6						5	10	11					31
	1						10	4	3	7	2	9†13				6*		12			5	8	11					32
	1						8*	4	3		2	10	9		6			7		12	5		11					33
	1		2	6			5	4	3		2		9					10		8		11		7				34
	1			6			4	8	3	7	2		9	10*						12	5		11†	13				35
	1		2				5	4	3*	7	9		11	8				10		6				12				36
	1		2				5	4	3*	7	9†		13	6				10		8		11		12				37
	1						5	4		12	2		11	3				10		6			9		7*	8		38
			1	2			5	4		11			3					10					9		7	8	6	39
16	6	10	8	32	8	2	34	39	27	30	30	15	30	33	6	13	1	30	8	22	5	2	9	7	3	2	1	
				+1s	+1s	+1s				+2s	+2s	+8s	+6s			+1s			+3s	+3s	+4s			+4s				

QUEEN'S PARK

DIV. 2

Year Formed: 1867. *Ground:* Hampden Park, Glasgow G42. *Telephone:* 041 632 1275 (ground).
Manager: E. Hunter
Secretary: W. Frank Campbell.
Club Colours: Black and white hooped shirts, white shorts, white stockings with two black hoops on top
Club nickname: 'Spiders'.
(Only amateur club in British senior football)
Record Attendance: 97,000 v Rangers, Scottish Cup 2nd Rd., Feb. 18th, 1933.
(Record for ground—149,547, Scotland v England, 1937)
Previous Grounds: Queens Park Recreation Ground 1867–73; 'First' Hampden (site: approx. Florida Ave. 1873–83; 'Second' Hampden (renamed Cathkin Park and used by Third Lanark F.C. until 1967) 1883–1903)

1978–79 LEAGUE RECORD

Match No.	Date	Venue	Opponents	Result	H/T Score	League Pos.n	Goalscorers	Attendance
1	Aug 12	A	Dunfermline Ath	W 3-0	2-0	—	Horn, Reynolds, McAloon	2000
2	19	H	Stranraer	L 0-1	0-0	7		1060
3	26	A	East Fife	L 2-3	1-3	11	McDonald, Nicholson	924
4	Sept 6	H	Berwick R	L 0-1	0-1	—		500
5	9	A	East Stirling	L 2-4	2-1	14	Nicholson, Ballantyne	800
6	13	H	Falkirk	L 0-3	0-0	—		800
7	16	H	Forfar Ath	D 1-1	0-0	13	McAloon	886
8	23	A	Stenhousemuir	W 2-1	2-0	13	Nicholson, Ballantyne	400
9	27	A	Alloa	L 0-1	0-0	—		500
10	30	H	Albion R	W 2-0	1-0	11	Nicholson, Ballantyne	873
11	Oct 7	H	Cowdenbeath	D 1-1	0-0	11	Ballantyne	854
12	14	A	Meadowbank T	W 4-0	0-0	10	Nicholson, Ballantyne, Wood O'Rourke (og)	500
13	21	A	Brechin C	L 1-2	1-1	11	Sinclair	300
14	28	A	Stranraer	W 2-0	0-0	8	Wood, Ballantyne	1,100
15	Nov 4	H	East Fife	D 1-1	1-0	9	McAloon	816
16	10	H	East Stirling	W 4-0	3-0	—	McAloon 2, Ballantyne, Sinclair	600
17	18	A	Forfar Ath	L 1-2	0-1	9	Ballantyne (pen)	1116
18	25	H	Stenhousemuir	D 0-0	0-0	9		825
19	Dec 9	A	Cowdenbeath	D 2-2	2-1	9	Horn, Ballantyne	300
20	16	H	Stranraer	W 2-1	1-1	8	Wood, McAloon	830
21	23	H	Brechin C	D 1-1	1-0	6	Wilkie	1000
22	Jan 20	A	Stenhousemuir	L 1-5	1-2	7	McAloon	500
23	Feb 24	H	Meadowbank T	D 1-1	0-1	9	Wilkie	850
24	Mar 3	A	Dunfermline	D 2-2	0-1	9	Wood, Reynolds	2000
25	10	A	Berwick R	D 1-1	1-1	9	Ballantyne (pen)	800
26	14	A	Falkirk	L 0-1	0-1	—		2000
27	17	H	Falkirk	L 1-2	0-1	9	Reynolds	800
28	24	A	Alloa	D 1-1	0-1	9	Ballantyne	715
29	27	H	Meadowbank T	W 3-0	1-0	—	Wilkie, Greenfield, McAloon	400
30	30	H	Dunfermline Ath	L 0-1	0-1	—		500
31	Apr 3	A	East Stirling	L 2-4	0-4	—	Ballantyne 2 (2 pens)	300
32	7	H	Alloa	L 0-1	0-0	10		1600
33	10	A	East Fife	L 0-3	0-2	—		447
34	14	A	Albion R	L 0-1	0-1	11		600
35	18	A	Albion R	L 0-4	0-1	—		500
36	21	A	Brechin C	D 1-1	0-0	11	McPherson	600
37	25	H	Forfar Ath	L 0-1	0-0	—		360
38	28	H	Berwick R	D 1-1	0-0	12	Wylie	800
39	30	H	Cowdenbeath	L 1-2	0-1	—	McAloon	731

Final League Position: 13

Goalscorers

League (46): Ballantyne 13 (3 pens), McAloon 9, Nicholson 5, Wood 4, Reynolds 3, Wilkie 3, Horn 2, Sinclair 2, Greenfield 1, McDonald 1, McPherson 1, Wylie 1, own goal 1.
League Cup (6): Ballantyne 3, Horn 1, McDonald 1, Wilkie 1.
Cup (6): Ballantyne 2, Edgar 2, McAloon 1, Wood 1.

Honours
Scottish League: Division 2 Champions 1922–23, 1955–56.
Scottish Cup: Winners 1874, 1875, 1876, 1880, 1881, 1882, 1884, 1886, 1890, 1893; Finalists 1892, 1900.
FA Cup: Finalists 1884, 1885.
Record Victory: 16-0 v St Peters, Scottish Cup, 1st Rd., 1885–86.
Record Defeat: 0-9 v Motherwell, Division 1, April 26, 1930.
Most League Points: 57, Division 2, 1922–23.
Most Individual League Goals in Season: Peter Buchanan, 32, Division 2, 1962–63.
Most Capped Player: Watty Arnold, 14, Scotland.

Wilson G	Atkins D	Preston J	McSkimming R	Dickson R	Aitken J	Cairns M	Reynolds M	Dalziel G	McAloon J	Bowie A	Wood D	Horn A	Edgar R	Nicholson J	Melrose F	Wilkie D	Ballantyne I	McDonald A	Wylie M	Sinclair J	Canning M	McPherson A	Kay M	Irvine A	Greenfield G	Rennie A	Thomson M	Match No.
	1	2	3			5	4	6			7	10		9*	12	11		8										1
	1	2	3			5	4	6			7	9*		10		11		8										2
	1	2	3			5	4*	6			7			10		11	9†	8			13	12						3
	1	2	3				6	5	7			8	10			11	9		4									4
	1	12	3	2		4*		6			7			10		11	9	8†13		5								5
	1	3	10	2		4					7			8		11	9		6		5							6
	1	2	3				6	5	7			8	10			11	9		4									7
	1	2	3	12			6*	5	7			8	10			11	9		4									8
	1	2	3					5	7			8	10			11	9		4									9
	1	2	3	12			6	5	7			8	10			11*	9		4									10
	1	2	3				6	5	7	12		8	10			11	9*		4									11
	1	2*	3		12		6	5	9	13		7	11				10†		4	8								12
	1	2	3				6	5	7	12		8	10†			13	9		4	11								13
	1	2	3				6	5	7			12	10*			11	9		4	8								14
	1	2	3				6	5	7			8*13				11	9†		4	10			12					15
	1		3	2			6	5	7	13	10	12				11*	9†		4	8								16
	1		3	2			6	5	7	12		8				11			4	10								17
	1		3	2†			6	5	7	12		8				11*	9		4	10								18
	1	2	3				6	5	7	9*	8	12				11	10		4									19
	1	2	3				6	5	7	12	8					11	9*		4	10								20
	1	2	3				6	5	7	12	8					11	9*		4	10								21
	1	2	3				6	5	7			8*12				11	9		4	10								22
1		2	3			8		6	5	7						11	9		4	10								23
	1	2	3			8			5	7		6	12			11	9			10					4*			24
	1	2	3			8		6*	5	7			12			11	9			10					4			25
	1		3	2		8		6	5	7						11	9			10					4			26
	1		3	2		8		6*	5	7			12			11	9†		4	10				12				27
	1		3	2*		8		6	5	7			10			11	9		4					12				28
	1	2	3			10*		6	5	7†						11	9		4				13	8		12		29
	1	2	3			8		6	5	7						11	9		4	10								30
	1	2	3				6	5	7							11	9		4				10	8				31
	1	2*	3	13			6	5	10			12				11	9	4					7	8*				32
	1	2	3				6	5	7*				13	12	11†	9		10						8	4			33
	1	2	3			10		6								11	9		4	8		5		7				34
	1	2	3			10		6								11	9		4	8		5		7				35
	1		3	2				6					11	7	9*			4	10		5		12	8				26
1			3	2				6		8			11	7	9			4	10		5							37
1		2	3					6	4				9	12	11*			8	10		5		7					38
	1	2	3					6	4				9		11				10		5		7	8				39
2	15	22	30	39	8	2	15	3	37	30	34	3	17	17	2	37	35	4	31	22	0	8	0	6	5	5		
		+ 1s		+ 3s	+ 1s								+ 8s	+ 1s	+ 9s	+ 3s	+ 1s		+ 1s			+ 1s	+ 1s	+ 1s	+ 2s	+ 2s	1s	

573

RAITH ROVERS   DIV. 1

Year Formed: 1883. *Limited Company:* 1907. *Ground:* Stark's Park. *Capacity:* 28,000. *Telephone:* Kirkcaldy 3514. *Manager:* Gordon Wallace. *Club Secretary:* Mrs M. B. Watters. *Club Colours:* Royal blue, white. *Record Attendance:* 31,306 v Hearts, Scottish Cup 2nd Rd, Feb. 7th 1953. *Previous Grounds:* Robbie's Park 1883–89. *Managers since the war:* Bert Herdman, Hugh Shaw, Doug Cowie, George Farm, Tommy Walker, Jimmy Millar, Bill Baxter, George Farm, Bert Paton, Andy Matthew, Willie McLean.

1978-79 LEAGUE RECORD

Match No.	Date	Venue	Opponents	Result	H/T Score	League Pos'n	Goalscorers	Attendance
1	Aug 12	A	Clyde	L 1-3	0-3	—	Myles	951
2	19	H	Clydebank	W 4-2	4-1	7	Harrow, Wallace 2 (1 a pen), McDonough	1982
3	26	A	Stirling Albion	W 1-0	0-0	4	Forrest	1550
4	Sept 6	A	Hamilton A	D 1-1	1-1	—	Hunter	2000
5	9	H	Ayr U	D 0-0	0-0	4		1800
6	13	H	Dundee	L 2-4	2-2	—	Duncan, Wallace	4488
7	16	A	Airdrieonians	L 0-3	0-1	9		2000
8	23	H	Queen of the S	W 4-0	1-0	8	Wallace, Forrest 3	1897
9	27	A	St Johnstone	D 1-1	1-1	—	Wallace	1412
10	30	A	Arbroath	W 5-0	3-0	6	Wallace 2, Forrest, Urquhart, Thomson D	1238
11	Oct 7	H	Dumbarton	D 0-0	0-0	6		2720
12	14	A	Kilmarnock	L 0-3	0-2	9		3000
13	21	H	Montrose	W 3-1	2-1	8	Harrow, Taylor, Wallace (pen)	1500
14	28	A	Clydebank	L 1-2	0-1	8	Harrow	1000
15	Nov 4	H	Stirling Albion	L 1-2	1-0	9	Candlish	1200
16	11	A	Ayr U	L 0-3	0-2	10		3663
17	18	H	Airdrieonians	W 2-0	1-0	9	Wallace (pen). McFarlane	1800
18	25	A	Queen of the S	L 1-2	0-0	9	Harrow	1000
19	Dec 9	A	Dumbarton	W 3-1	2-0	8	Harrow, Pettie, McDonough	800
20	16	H	Kilmarnock	L 1-3	1-1	9	Wallace	1200
21	23	A	Montrose	D 0-0	0-0	8		700
22	Jan 20	H	Queen of the S	W 3-0	2-0	8	Wallace 2, Harrow	1200
23	Feb 24	A	Kilmarnock	L 1-2	1-0	8	Thomson R	3267
24	Mar 3	H	Clyde	L 1-2	1-0	9	Forrest	1500
25	7	A	Stirling Albion	L 0-3	0-0	—		600
26	10	H	Hamilton A	L 0-1	0-1	10		1000
27	14	H	Ayr U	W 2-0	0-0	—	Duncan, Murray	1200
28	28	A	Dumbarton	L 0-3	0-1	—		500
29	31	A	Clyde	D 1-1	1-0	10	Wallace (pen)	800
30	Apr 4	A	Airdrieonians	W 1-0	0-0	—	Harrow	2000
31	7	A	St Johnstone	L 0-3	0-2	10		1632
32	11	H	Dundee	L 1-2	0-0	—	Harrow	2769
33	14	H	Arbroath	L 1-2	0-1	11	Thomson D	1200
34	18	H	Arbroath	W 1-0	0-0	—	Wallace (pen)	1000
35	21	A	Montrose	D 1-1	1-1	11	McComb	950
36	25	H	St Johnstone	D 0-0	0-0	—		1000
37	28	H	Hamilton A	W 2-0	0-0	10	Harrow, Ford	1333
38	May 2	H	Clydebank	L 1-2	1-1	10	Harrow	1000
39	8	A	Dundee	L 0-2	0-0	—		6450

Final League Position: 11

Goalscorers

League (47): Wallace 14 (5 pens), Harrow 10, Forrest 6, Duncan 2, McDonough 2, Thomson D 2, Candlish 1, Ford 1, Hunter 1, McComb 1, McFarlane 1, Murray 1, Myles 1, Pettie 1, Taylor 1, Thomson R 1, Urquhart 1.
League Cup (10): Wallace 5, Harrow 3, Forrest 2.
Cup (0).

Honours:
Scottish League: Division 2 Champions 1907–08, 1909–10 (shared), 1937–38, 1948–49; Runners-up 1908–09, 1926–27, 1966–67, 1975–76, 1977–78.
Scottish Cup: Finalists 1913.
League Cup: Finalists 1948–49.
Record Victory: 10–1 v Coldstream, Scottish Cup, 2nd Rd., February 13, 1954.
Record Defeat: 2–11 v Morton, Division 2, 1935-36.
Most League Points: 59, Division 2, 1937–38.
Most Individual League Goals in Season: Norman Haywood, 38, Division 2, 1937–38.
Most Capped Player: Dave Morris, 6, Scotland.
Most League Goals: 142, Division 2, 1937–38.
British record goalscorers: (142 goals in 34 Division 2 matches, 1937–38).

McDermott M	Ford R	McDonogh B	Houston T	Candlish C	Hunter D	McComb L	Urquhart D	McFarlane T	Thomson D	Myles J	Harrow A	Taylor J	Forrest G	Duncan R	Pettie G	Wildridge I	Coleman J	Thomson R	Murray T	Wallace G G	Forsyth A	Match No.
1			2	5	3		8†	4		6	10	9		7*	11		13	12				1
1			2	4	3		8		6		9	5		11		12			10*	7		2
1			2	5	3		8		6		9			12	11*				10	7	4	3
1			2	3	10*		8		6		9	5		11					12	7	4	4
1			2	3	10†		8		6		9	5*	13	11					12	7	4	5
1			2	3*	10†		8		6		9	5	13	11					12	7	4	6
1			2		3*		8		6	12	9	5	13	11†					10	7	4	7
1	11		2	3*			8		6		9	5	12		13				10	7	4†	8
1		3	2				8		6		9	5	11		12				10*	7	4	9
1		3	2				8	6*	12		9†	5	11		13				10	7	4	10
1			2	3			8		6	12	9	5*	11		13				10†	7	4	11
1		8	3				11	6†	2		9	5*	13		12				10	7	4	12
1			3				8	2	12		9	5	11		6				10*	7	4	13
1	12		2	3			8	6*	10†		9	5	13		11					7	4	14
1	6		2	3	12		8				5	9	11	7					10*		4	15
1	2		5	3			8		6		9		12	11*	10					7	4	16
1	2		5	3			8*	6			9			11	12				10	7	4	17
1	2		4	3			8*	6			9	5		11	12				10	7		18
1	2		4	3			8	6	5		9			11*	12				10	7		19
1	2		4	3			8†	6*	5		9	13	12		11				10	7		20
1	2		4	3			8*	6	5		9				12			11	10	7		21
1	2		5	3			8	4	6		9			12	11*				10	7		22
1	2			3			8	4	6		9			11					10	7	5	23
1			2	3			8	4	6		9			11	12				10	7*	5	24
1			2	3			8		6		9	4*	11		12				10	7	5	25
1	2			3			4		6		9		13	11	12				10	8† 7	5*	26
1	2			3			4		6		9			11					10	8 7	5	27
1	4	2		3			8		6		9			11					10	7	5	28
1	4	2		3			8		6		9			12	11*				10	7	5	29
1	4	2		3			8		6		9								10	7	5	30
1	4	2*		3			11	8		6				9†		13			10	12 7	5	31
1	2			3			8	4		6				11					10	7	5	32
1	4		5	3			2		6		9			12	11*				10	8 7		33
1	4		2	3			8*	12		6		9		7	11†				10	13	5	34
1	4		2	3			11*	8		6		9		7					10	12	5	35
1	4		2	3			8		6		9			7*	11				10	12	5	36
1	4		2	3			8		6		9			12	11*				10	7	5	37
1	4		2	3			8		6	9				11					10	7	5	38
1	4		2	3			8		6		9			12	11*				10	7	5	39
39	12	21	30	36	4	6	38	22	24	1	38	15	11	25	5	0	0	19	18	34	31	
			†		†		†		†			†	†	†	†	†			†	†		
			1s		1s		1s		4s			1s	16s	12s	2s	1s			4s	3s		

RANGERS   PREM. DIV.

Year Formed: 1873. *Turned Professional:* 1893. *Limited Company:* 1899.
Ground: Ibrox Stadium Glasgow G51 2XD. *Size:* 115×75 yards. *Capacity:* 44,000 (19,500 seated).
Telephone: 041-427 0159. *Manager:* John Greig. *Secretary:* Frank King.
Club Colours: Royal blue shirts with white shorts. Stockings royal blue.
Club Nicknames: 'Blues' or 'Gers'.
Record Attendance: 118,567 v Celtic, Division 1, Jan, 2nd, 1939.
Previous Grounds: Flesher's Haugh on Glasgow Green was shared with Great Eastern F.C.; Kinning Park, Burnbank; Ibrox Park since 1887.
European Competitions Entered: European Cup: 1956–57, 1957–58, 1959–60, 1961–62, 1963–64, 1964–65, 1975–76, 1976–77. European Cup Winners Cup: 1960–61 (finalists), 1962–63, 1966–67 (finalists), 1969–70, 1971–72 (winners), 1973–74, 1977–78; Fairs Cup: 1967–68, 1968–69, 1970–71.
Record Transfer Fee Received: £140,000 from Coventry C. for Colin Stein, Oct. 1972.
Record Transfer Fee Paid: £100,000 to Hibernian for Colin Stein, Oct. 1968.

1978–79 LEAGUE RECORD

Match No.	Date	Venue	Opponents	Result	H/T Score	League Pos'n	Goalscorers	Attendance
1	Aug 12	H	St Mirren	L 0-1	0-0	—		28,000
2	19	A	Hibernian	D 0-0	0-0	8		23,000
3	26	H	Partick T	D 0-0	0-0	7		28,000
4	Sept 9	A	Celtic	L 1-3	0-2	7	Parlane	60,000
5	16	H	Aberdeen	D 1-1	1-0	7	Forsyth A (pen)	25,000
6	23	A	Morton	D 2-2	0-1	7	Parlane, Johnstone	16,500
7	30	H	Motherwell	W 4-1	3-1	6	Smith 2, McLean, Johnstone	25,000
8	Oct 7	H	Dundee U	D 1-1	0-1	5	MacDonald	27,000
9	14	A	Hearts	D 0-0	0-0	7		18,159
10	21	A	St Mirren	W 1-0	1-0	6	Forsyth A (pen)	22,000
11	28	H	Hibernian	W 2-1	2-1	4	Smith, Forsyth A (pen)	25,000
12	Nov 4	A	Partick T	L 0-1	0-0	6		21,000
13	11	H	Celtic	D 1-1	0-0	6	Forsyth A (pen)	53,000
14	18	A	Aberdeen	D 0-0	0-0	6		26,000
15	25	H	Morton	W 3-0	1-0	5	Smith, Johnstone, Cooper	22,000
16	Dec 9	A	Dundee U	L 0-3	0-2	6		15,247
17	16	H	Hearts	W 5-3	3-1	6	Watson, Johnstone 4	18,000
18	23	H	St Mirren	W 1-0	0-0	4	Johnstone	20,000
19	Jan 20	A	Morton	W 2-0	0-0	2	Watson, MacDonald	18,000
20	Feb 10	H	Dundee U	W 1-0	0-0	1	Robertson	22,000
21	24	A	Hearts	L 2-3	2-2	2	Smith, Parlane	18,000
22	Mar 14	H	Hibernian	W 1-0	0-0	—	Smith	15,000
23	17	A	Partick T	W 2-0	1-0	3	Cooper, Urquhart	18,665
24	27	A	St Mirren	W 2-1	1-1	—	Urquhart 2	20,000
25	Apr 7	H	Morton	D 1-1	0-1	2	Cooper	18,000
26	10	A	Motherwell	W 3-0	2-0	—	Smith, Cooper, MacDonald	8000
27	14	A	Motherwell	L 0-2	0-0	2		14,612
28	21	A	Dundee U	W 2-1	2-0	—	Smith, Dawson	20,264
29	25	A	Aberdeen	L 1-2	0-1	—	Smith	17,000
30	28	H	Hearts	W 4-0	3-0	3	Russell 3, Parlane	21,000
31	May 2	A	Motherwell	W 2-1	0-1	—	Smith, Jackson	13,052
32	5	H	Celtic	W 1-0	0-0	2	MacDonald	52,841
33	7	A	Aberdeen	W 2-0	0-0	—	Smith, Cooper	28,000
34	21	A	Celtic	L 2-4	1-0	—	Russell, MacDonald	52,000
35	23	H	Partick T	W 1-0	0-0	—	Johnstone	2000
36	31	A	Hibernian	L 1-2	0-1	—	Urquhart	4000

Final League Position: 2

Goalscorers
League (52): Smith 11, Johnstone 9, Cooper 5, MacDonald 5, Forsyth A 4 (4 pens), Parlane 4, Russell 4, Urquhart 4, Watson 2, Dawson 1, Jackson 1, McLean 1, Robertson 1.
League Cup (22): Smith 5, Cooper 3, Jackson 2, Johnstone 2, Parlane 2, Jardine 1 (pen), MacDonald 1, McLean 1, Miller 1, Russell 1, own goals 3.
Cup (15): Johnstone 4, Cooper 2, MacDonald 2, Forsyth T 1, Jackson 1, Jardine 1 (pen), Russell 1, Smith 1, Urquhart 1, own goal 1.

Honours

Scottish League: Division 1, Champions: 1890–91 (shared with Dumbarton), 1898–99, 1899–1900, 1900–01, 1901–02, 1910–11, 1911–12, 1912–13, 1917–18, 1919–20, 1920–21, 1922–23, 1923–24, 1924–25, 1926–27, 1927–28, 1928–29, 1929–30, 1930–31, 1932–33, 1933–34, 1934–35, 1936–37, 1938–39, 1946–47, 1948–49, 1949–50, 1952–53, 1955–56, 1956–57, 1958–59, 1960–61, 1962–63, 1963–64, 1974–75. Runners-up: 21 times. Premier Division: 1975–76, 1977–78. Runners-up: 1976–77, 1978–79.
Scottish Cup: Winners: 1894, 1897, 1898, 1903, 1928, 1930, 1932, 1934, 1935, 1936, 1948, 1949, 1950, 1953, 1960, 1962, 1963, 1964, 1966, 1973, 1976, 1978, 1979. Runners-up: 11 times.
Scottish League Cup: Winners: 1946–47, 1948–49, 1960–61, 1961–62, 1963–64, 1964–65, 1970–71, 1975–76, 1977–78, 1978. Runners-up: 5 times.
Record Victory: 14-2 v Blairgowrie, Scottish Cup, 1st Rd. Jan 20th, 1934. *Record Defeat:* 2-10 v Airdrie, 1886. *Most League Points:* 76, Division 1, 1920–21. *Most Individual League Goals in Season:* 44, Sam English, Division 1, 1931–32, *Highest Scorer in Total Aggregate:* Bob McPhail, 233, 1927–39. *Most capped Player:* George Young, 53, Scotland. *Most League Appearances:* John Greig, 496.

McCloy P	Miller A	Jardine W	Forsyth A	Watson K	Forsyth T	Jackson C	MacDonald A	Johnstone D	Armour D	Smith G	Russell R	McLean T	Parlane D	Dawson A	Cooper D	Urquhart W	Robertson C	McDonald J	McKay W	Morris E	Strickland D	Match No.
1	2	3	11*	4		5	6	9		10	8	7			12							1
1	12	2	3		4		6	5		10	8	7	9			11*						2
1		2	3	6		4		5		10	8	7	9	11								3
1	12	2	3		4	5	6*	10		11	8	7†	9	13								4
1		2	3		4	5	6	10		11	8	7	9									5
1		2	3		4	5	6	10		11	8	7	9									6
1	12	2	3		4	5*	6	10		11	8	7†	9	13								7
1	5	2	3		4		6	10		11	8	7	9*	12								8
1		2	3		4	5	6	10		11	8	7	9*	12								9
1	12	2	3		4		6	5		10*	8	7	9	11								10
1	12	2	3		4		6	5		10	8	7	9	11*								11
1		2	3	13	4		6	5		10	8	7	9*	11†	12							12
1	11	2	3	10	4		6	5		9	8	7										13
1	2		11			5	6	4		10	8	7	9	3								14
1	4	2	6			5		9		10	8	7		3	11							15
1	4	2	12			5	6	9		10	8*	7	13	3	11†							16
1	2	4		10		5	6	9		12	8	7		3	11*							17
1	2	4		10		5	6	9			8	7		3	11							18
1	2			10	4	5	6	9			8	7		3	11							19
1	2		10*	4		5	6	9		13	8	7		3	11†	12						20
1	2					4	5	6		10	8	7	9	3	11*		12					21
1	2					4	5	6		10	8	7		3	11	9						22
1	2					4	5	6		10	8	7		3	11	9						23
1	2					5	6	4		10	8	7	12	3	11*	9						24
1	2*	4				5	6			10	8	7	12	3	11	9						25
1	2	4				5	6	9		10	8	7		3	11							26
1	2	4				5	6	9	12	10	8†	7*		3	11	13						27
1	2	4				5	10	6		11	8	12	9	3	7*							28
1	2*	4					6	5		10	8	7	9	3	11	12						29
1	2					5	6	4		10	8	7*	9	3	11		12					30
1	2					5	6	4		10	8	7	9	3	11							31
1	2					5	6	4		10	8	7	9	3	11							32
1	2					5	6	4		10	8	7	9	3	11							33
1	12	2				5	6	4		10	8	7*	9	3	11							34
1	12	2	10			5*	6	4			8	7	9†	3	11		13					35
1	4		2	6						12	10	9		3	11†	8	13		5	7*		36
36	10	31	16	11	17	28	33	31	0	31	36	34	21	23	26	6	0	0	1	1		
	+7s		+2s				+2s	+2s			+1s	+3s			+4s	+4s	+2s	+2s		+1s		

ST. JOHNSTONE   DIV. 1

Year Formed: 1884.
Ground: Muirton Park. *Size:* 109 × 74 yds. *Capacity:* 28,000 (2,500 seats).
Telephone: Perth 26961.
Manager: Alec Stuart.
Secretary: George Bell. *Coach:* J. Lambie. *Physiotherapist:* J. Peacock.
Club Colours: Royal blue with white collar and cuffs, white shorts and white stockings with royal blue tops.
Club Nickname: 'Saints'.
Record Attendance: 29,972, v Dundee, Scottish Cup, 2nd Rd. Feb. 10th, 1952.
Previous Ground: Recreation Ground.
European Competition Entered: UEFA Cup 1971-72.

1978-79 LEAGUE RECORD

Match No.	Date	Venue	Opponents	Result	H/T Score	League Pos'd	Goalscorers	Attendance
1	Aug 12	H	Montrose	W 3-2	1-2	—	Brogan 2, Rutherford	1234
2	19	A	Hamilton A	L 1-2	0-0	8	McNeil (pen)	1200
3	26	H	Dundee	L 0-2	0-0	11		3875
4	Sept 6	A	Queen of the S	D 1-1	1-1	—	O'Connor	1500
5	9	H	Clyde	D 1-1	0-0	12	Brogan	1414
6	13	H	Kilmarnock	D 0-0	0-0	—		1292
7	16	A	Arbroath	L 0-3	0-2	10		1056
8	23	H	Airdrieonians	L 0-2	0-1	12		1548
9	27	H	Raith R	D 1-1	1-1	—	McNeil	1412
10	30	A	Ayr U	L 0-1	0-1	12		3239
11	Oct 7	H	Clydebank	L 2-3	0-3	12	Muir 2	1390
12	14	A	Dumbarton	L 0-2	0-0	12		1500
13	21	H	Stirling Albion	D 0-0	0-0	12		1403
14	28	H	Hamilton A	D 0-0	0-0	12		1284
15	Nov 4	A	Dundee	D 1-1	0-0	12	Muir	5918
16	11	A	Clyde	L 4-6	1-1	12	Lawson 2, Rutherford (pen) Hamilton J	1000
17	18	H	Arbroath	D 1-1	0-0	13	Brogan	1516
18	25	A	Airdrieonians	W 1-0	0-0	13	Lawson	1500
19	Dec 16	H	Dumbarton	D 2-2	0-1	13	Thomas, Brannigan	1537
20	23	A	Stirling Albion	W 5-1	2-0	12	Lawson 3, Brannigan, Pelosi	1250
21	30	A	Hamilton A	L 1-2	0-2	12	Brogan	2024
22	Feb 3	A	Kilmarnock	L 2-3	0-3	12	Lawson, McNeil	3200
23	Mar 3	H	Montrose	W 3-1	1-0	13	Lawson, Brannigan, Rutherford	850
24	7	A	Clydebank	L 0-3	0-1	—		2500
25	10	H	Queen of the S	W 5-2	2-1	11	Brogan 3, Rutherford (pen), Lawson	1446
26	14	H	Clyde	L 0-1	0-0	—		1757
27	17	A	Kilmarnock	L 1-3	1-1	13	Lawson	2000
28	20	H	Dumbarton	D 2-2	1-0	—	Lawson, Ward	1360
29	27	A	Airdrieonians	L 1-3	0-1	—	Brannigan	1646
30	31	H	Montrose	W 4-0	3-0	12	Brogan 2, Pelosi, Rutherford	1235
31	Apr 4	A	Arbroath	L 1-3	1-3	—	Brogan	1348
32	7	H	Raith R	W 3-0	2-0	12	Brogan, Pelosi, Ward	1632
33	14	A	Ayr U	L 2-4	0-0	12	Ward, Brannigan	2432
34	18	A	Clydebank	L 0-1	0-1	—		700
35	21	H	Stirling Albion	L 0-2	0-0	13		1400
36	25	H	Raith R	D 0-0	0-0	—		1200
37	28	A	Queen of the S	W 2-1	1-1	12	Ward, Brogan	500
38	May 2	H	Dundee	W 3-2	2-1	—	Pelosi, Rutherford (pen), Brogan	5840
39	5	H	Ayr U	W 4-2	3-1	11	Pelosi, Hamilton J, Rutherford, Redford	1458

Final League Position: 12

Goalscorers

League (57): Brogan 14, Lawson 11, Rutherford 7 (3 pens), Brannigan 5, Pelosi 5, Ward 4, McNeil 3 (1 a pen), Muir 3, Hamilton J 2, O'Connor 1, Redford 1, Thomas 1.
League Cup (0).
Cup (3): Brogan 1, Lawson 1, Thomas 1.

Honours
Scottish League: Division 2, Champions: 1923-24, 1959-60, 1962-63. Runners-up: 1931-32.
Scottish League Cup: Runners-up: 1969-70.
Record Victory: 8-1 v Partick T. Scottish Cup 1969-70.
Record Defeat: 1-10 v Third Lanark, Scottish Cup 1st Round Jan. 24th, 1903.
Most League Points: 56, Division 2, 1923-24.
Most Individual League Goals in Season: Jimmy Benson 36, Division 2, 1931-32.
Most Capped Players: Sandy McLaren 2, Scotland.

Robertson D	Geoghegan A	Fitzpatrick J	O'Brien J	McCall W	Mackay J	Hamilton J	Houston D	Wright J	Brogan J	Hamilton G	Rutherford A	Lawson M	Brannigan A	Montgomery S	McNeil T	O'Connor D	Ross J	Thomas W	Salisbury A	Pelosi J	McLellan L	Weir J	Gray H	Muir J	Redford G	McCoist A	Ward P	Match No.
				2		6		8		5					3	9		7				4	10	11				1
	1			2				8*		6	12				3	9		7	13		5	4	10†11					2
	1			2		6		8		4					3*	9	13	7	11†		5	10	12					3
1				2				8		5					3	9	11*12	7	6			10	4					4
1				2				8		5*					3	9	11	13		7†	6	12	4	10				5
1				2				8		5					3	9	11			7	6		4	10				6
1				2	12			8		5					3	9	11	13		7†	6†		10	4				7
1				2		6		9		5					3		11†	7			10	12	13	8*	4			8
1				2		6		8		5	11				3	9		7*12				4	10					9
1				2		6		8		5	11				3	9		12	7*		4	10						10
1				2		6		10		5	11†				3	9		7*12	13		8		4					11
1						6	11	10		5	4*				3	9†		13	7		8	12	2					12
1								11*10	5	6	12			9	3			7	8		2		4					13
1								11†10	5	6	13	12	9	3				7*	8		2		4					14
1						8		10†	5	6	11	13	9	3				7			2*12		4					15
1						8		10	12	5	6	11	9*	3				7			2	4						16
1						8		10	12	5	6	11		9*	3			7			2		4					17
1			8			10*		9	5	6	11				3			12	7		2		4					18
	1	8†		10				9	5	6	11	13		3*				12	7		2		4					19
1	2			10				8*	5	6	11	9						12	7		3		4					20
1	13			10†				8	5	6	11	9*		3				12	7		2		4					21
1								9	5	8	11	13	10†	3				12	7*		6	2	4					22
1				10				8	5	6	11	9		3				7			2		4					23
1	5							8		6	11	9*		3				12	7		2		4					24
1		9*		10				8	5	6	11	12		3					7		2		4					25
1		9*		10				8	5	6	11	12		3					7		2		4					26
	1	9*						10†	8	5	6	11	12	3				13	7		2		4					27
1	12			6				11	8		5	10	13	3					7		2*		4				9†	28
1				6*				11	8		5	10†	9	3					7		2		4	13		12		29
1	5							12	8		6		9	3				11*	7			10	4	2				30
1	5			10*				8		6		9		3				13	11†	7	12		4	2				31
	1								10	5		11		3					7	6		4	2	8	9			32
	1			13				10	6		11			3				12		7*	5		4	2	8†	9		33
1	2							10	5		11			3							6		4	8	7	9		34
1	2							10	5	11†	6							13	7*		3		4	9	8	12		35
1	2			10				8	5	11				3					7		6		4		9			36
1	2			10				8		5	11†13			3					7		6		4	12		9*		37
1	2			10				8		5	11								7†		6		4	3		9		38
1	2			10†				9		5	11	8	13						7†		6		4	3		12		39
19 20	7	3	5 11	18	7	9	36	15	39	21	14	6	35	11	5	9	4	31	8	31	9	37	8	4	7			
	+ 1s	+ 1s		+ 1s	+ 1s	+ 1s	+ 2s				+ 3s	+ 9s		+ 1s			+ 1s14s	+ 4s	+ 1s	+ 2s	+ 2s	+ 3s		+ 2s		+ 3s		

ST. MIRREN

PREM. DIV.

Year Formed: 1876. *Ground:* St Mirren Park (Also known as Love Street). *Capacity:* 53,000.
Telephone: 041-889-2558
Manager: Jim Clunie, *Secretary:* J. Aitken, *Club Colours:* Black and white stripes, white shorts and white stockings, with two black bands. *Club Nickname:* 'The Buddies'.
Record Attendance: 47,428 v Celtic, Scottish Cup, 4th Rd, Mar 7th, 1925

1978–79 LEAGUE RECORD

Match No.	Date	Venue	Opponents	Result	H/T Score	League Pos'n	Goalscorers	Attendance
1	Aug 12	A	Rangers	W 1-0	0-0	—	Torrance	28,000
2	19	H	Motherwell	L 0-1	0-1	6		8000
3	26	A	Morton	W 3-1	1-0	3	McGarvey, Fitzpatrick, Abercromby	12,000
4	Sept 9	A	Hibernian	L 0-1	0-1	5		8000
5	16	H	Partick T	W 1-0	0-0	4	Stark	8000
6	23	H	Dundee U	L 1-3	1-2	6	Bone	8000
7	30	A	Celtic	L 1-2	0-1	7	Hyslop	26,000
8	Oct 7	A	Hearts	D 1-1	0-1	7	Fitzpatrick	9475
9	14	H	Aberdeen	W 2-1	0-0	6	McGarvey, Bone	10,973
10	21	H	Rangers	L 0-1	0-1	7		22,000
11	28	A	Motherwell	W 2-1	1-1	7	Stark (pen), Richardson	6007
12	Nov 4	H	Morton	D 0-0	0-0	7		10,000
13	11	H	Hibernian	W 1-0	0-0	5	Stark	8000
14	18	A	Partick T	L 1-2	1-2	8	Young	11,000
15	25	A	Dundee U	D 1-1	1-1	6	Torrance	6896
16	Dec 9	H	Hearts	W 4-0	1-0	5	Stark 2, Torrance, Hyslop	6640
17	16	A	Aberdeen	D 1-1	1-0	5	Stark	12,700
18	23	A	Rangers	L 0-1	0-0	6		20,000
19	Jan 20	H	Dundee U	W 2-1	1-0	5	Bone, Torrance	5000
20	Feb 10	A	Hearts	W 2-1	0-1	3	Bone, Fitzpatrick	8000
21	17	H	Motherwell	W 1-0	1-0	2	McGarvey	7600
22	24	H	Aberdeen	D 2-2	0-1	1	McGarvey, Copland	11,500
23	Mar 10	A	Motherwell	W 3-0	2-0	2	McGarvey 3	4795
24	17	H	Morton	W 3-1	1-0	2	McGarvey 2, Bone	8500
25	24	H	Hibernian	L 2-3	1-1	2	McGarvey, Bone	10,000
26	27	H	Rangers	L 1-2	1-1	—	Stark	20,000
27	31	A	Partick T	L 1-3	0-1	3	Bone	5000
28	Apr 4	A	Hibernian	W 2-0	1-0	—	McGarvey, Stark	6000
29	7	A	Dundee U	L 0-2	0-0	3		6608
30	11	A	Morton	L 0-1	0-1	—		7500
31	14	H	Celtic	L 0-1	0-1	5		19,712
32	21	H	Hearts	W 2-1	2-1	5	Torrance, Abercromby	5800
33	25	A	Celtic	L 1-2	1-0	—	McGarvey	18,000
34	28	A	Aberdeen	W 2-1	0-1	5	Torrance, Stark	13,000
35	May 2	H	Partick T	D 1-1	1-1	—	McGarvey	5000
36	11	H*	Celtic	L 0-2	0-0	—		22,000

Final League Postion: 6
*At Ibrox

Goalscorers
League (45): McGarvey 13, Stark 9, Bone 7, Torrance 6, Fitzpatrick 3, Abercromby 2, Hyslop 2, Copland 1, Richardson 1, Young 1.
League Cup (12): Bone 3, McGarvey 3, Fitzpatrick 2, Hyslop 2, Richardson 1, Stark 1.
Cup (3): Fitzpatrick 1, Munro 1, Stark 1.

Honours

Scottish League: Division 1 Champions 1976–77; Division 2 Champions 1967–68; Runners-up 1935–36.
Scottish Cup: Winners 1926, 1959; Finalists 1908, 1934, 1962.
Victory Cup: 1919-20.
Scottish Summer Cup: 1943-44.
League Cup: Finalists 1955–56.
Record Victory: 15-0 v Glasgow University, Scottish Cup 1st Rd, Jan. 30th, 1960.
Record Defeat: 2-9 v Dundee, Division 1, Feb. 29th, 1964.
Most League Points: 62, Division 2, 1967-68.
Most Individual League Goals in Season: 45 Dunky Walker, Division 1, 1921-22.
Most Capped Player: Tommy Jackson, 6, Scotland.

McLean A	Thomson W	Fitzpatrick A	Mowat J	Young J	Copland J	Dunlop A	Abercromby W	Hyslop D	Stark W	McGarvey F	Torrance R	Richardson A	Munro I	Bone J	Sharp R	Docherty B	Beckett A	Weir P	Match No.
1	4			2	6	5	10	7*		11	12		3	9			8		1
1	4			2	6	5	10	7*		11	12	8	3	9					2
	1	4		12	6	5	10		8	11		7	3	9			2		3
	1	4			6	5	10		8	11		7*	3	9	12		2		4
	1	4			6	5	10		8	11			3	9	7		2		5
	1	4			6	5	10		8	11	12		3	9	7*		2		6
	1	4			6	5	10*	7	8	11	12		3	9			2		7
	1	4		2	6	5	10		8*11	12		7	3	9					8
	1	4		2	6	5	10		8	11		7	3	9					9
	1	4		2*	6	5	10		8	11	7		3	9			12		10
	1	4		2	6	5	10		8	11		7	3	9					11
	1	4	3	2	6	5	10*13		8	11†		7		9	12				12
	1	4		2	6	5			8	11	10	7	3	9					13
	1	4	3	2	6	5			8	11	10	7		9					14
	1	4		2	6	5	11	12	8*		10	7	3	9					15
	1	4			6	5	11	12	8		10*	7	3	9			2		16
	1	4			6	5	10	12	8	11*		7	3	9			2		17
	1	4		12	6	5	10†13		8	11		7	3	9			2*		18
	1	4			6	5	12		8*11		10	7	3	9			2		19
	1	4			6	5			8	11	10	7	3	9			2		20
	1	4			6	5			8	11	10	7	3	9			2		21
	1	4		2	6	5			8	11	10	7	3	9					22
	1	4		2	6	5	10		8	11		7	3	9					23
	1	4		2	6	5	10		8	11		7	3	9					24
	1	4		2	6	5	10		8*11	12		7	3	9					25
	1	4		2	6	5	10		8	11		7	3	9					26
	1	4		2	6	5	10		8	11*12		7	3	9					27
	1	4		2	6	5	10		8	11		7	3	9					28
	1	4		2	6	5	10		8	11		7	3	9					29
	1	4		2	6	5	10		8	11		7	3	9					30
	1	4		2	6	5	10†		8*11	13		7	3	9			12		31
	1	4*		2	6	5	10			11	8	12	3	9			7		32
	1	4		2	6	5	10			11	8		3	9			7		33
	1	4		2	6	5	10		7	9	11	13	3*		12		8†		34
	1	4		2	6	5	10		8	9	11	7				3			35
	1	4		2	6	5	10		7	9	8	3				11			36
2	34	36	2	25	36	36	30	3	32	33	14	28	33	33	2	1	12	4	
				+2s			+1s	+5s			+6s	+4s			+2s	+1s	+2s		

R.F. 79/80—30

STENHOUSEMUIR   DIV. 2

Year Formed: 1884:   *Ground:* Ochilview Park.   *Capacity:* 12,000 (500 seated).   *Telephone:* Larbert 2992.
Team Manager: Harry Glasgow.   *Secretary:* Jimmy Weir.   *Trainer:* W. Williamson.
Club Colours: Maroon shirts with white trimmings, white shorts and stockings.
Club Nickname: 'The Warriors'.
Record Attendance: 12,500 v East Fife, Scottish Cup 4th Rd, Mar. 11th, 1950.
Record Receipts: £2,800 v Celtic, Scottish League Cup, quarter final, 1st leg, Sept. 10th, 1975.

1978–79 LEAGUE RECORD

Match No.	Date	Venue	Opponents	Result	Score	H/T Score	League Pos'n	Goalscorers	Attendance
1	Aug 12	H	East Stirling	L	0-2	0-1	—		300
2	19	A	Berwick R	L	1-6	1-2	14	Gordon	1092
3	26	H	Alloa	L	0-2	0-2	14		500
4	Sept 6	A	Forfar Ath	D	1-1	1-0	—	Sweeney	900
5	9	A	Cowdenbeath	W	2-1	2-1	13	Gibb, Sweeney	400
6	13	H	East Fife	L	1-2	1-0	—	Feeney	500
7	16	A	Falkirk	L	0-1	0-1	14		2500
8	23	H	Queen's Park	L	1-2	0-2	14	Feeney	400
9	27	A	Meadowbank T	L	0-2	0-1	—		500
10	30	H	Dunfermline Ath	L	1-2	0-1	14	Wilson F (pen)	1000
11	Oct 7	A	Stranraer	W	1-0	1-0	14	Feeney	1000
12	14	H	Brechin C	W	4-2	3-1	14	Gibb, Sweeney 2, Feeney	500
13	21	A	Albion R	W	1-0	1-0	13	Gibb	300
14	28	H	Berwick R	L	0-2	0-2	13		500
15	Nov 4	A	Alloa	L	1-2	1-1	14	Gibb	500
16	11	H	Cowdenbeath	D	1-1	0-0	14	McNaughton (pen)	500
17	18	H	Falkirk	L	1-2	0-1	14	McNaughton (pen)	2500
18	25	A	Queen's Park	D	0-0	0-0	14		825
19	Dec 9	H	Stranraer	W	4-1	1-1	14	Jenkins, McNaughton 3	200
20	23	H	Albion R	W	3-2	2-0	12	Jenkins, Sweeney, Shields (og)	430
21	Jan 20	H	Queen's Park	W	5-1	2-1	11	Halliday, Feeney, McCullie, McNaughton 2	500
22	Feb 3	A	East Fife	L	0-3	0-0	12		886
23	28	H	Cowdenbeath	D	0-0	0-0	—		400
24	Mar 3	H	East Stirling	W	5-0	3-0	12	Jenkins, Sweeney, McNaughton 3 (1 a pen)	500
25	6	H	Alloa	L	0-1	0-1	—		500
26	10	A	Forfar Ath	D	0-0	0-0	11		919
27	13	H	Dunfermline Ath	L	0-1	0-1	—		2000
28	20	A	Falkirk	D	1-1	1-0	—	Jenkins	1500
29	24	A	Meadowbank T	W	2-1	2-1	10	Feeney, McNaughton	300
30	28	A	Brechin C	W	3-1	1-1	—	Gibb, Rose, Sime (og)	400
31	31	A	East Stirling	W	3-1	1-1	8	Gibb, McNaughton 2 (1 a pen)	200
32	Apr 3	H	Stranraer	L	1-2	1-1	—	Jenkins	300
33	7	H	Meadowbank T	W	2-0	0-0	9	Sweeney 2	300
34	10	A	Berwick R	L	2-3	1-1	—	Jack, Jenkins	800
35	14	A	Dunfermline Ath	L	1-2	1-1	9	McNaughton	2000
36	21	H	Albion R	L	2-3	1-2	10	Sweeney, McNaughton	300
37	24	H	East Fife	D	2-2	0-0	—	Jack, Sweeney	500
38	28	H	Forfar Ath	D	1-1	1-0	10	Sweeney	300
39	30	A	Brechin C	L	1-2	0-2	—	McNaughton	400

Final League Position: 10

Goalscorers

League (54): McNaughton 16 (4 pens), Sweeney 11, Feeney 6, Gibb 6, Jenkins 6, Jack 2, Gordon 1, Halliday 1, McCullie 1, Rose 1, Wilson F 1 (pen), own goals 2.
League Cup (2): Gibb 1, Sweeney 1.
Cup (1): Jenkins 1.

Honours

Record Victory: 9-2 v Dundee U. Division 2, 1936–37.
Record Defeat: 2–11 v Dunfermline Ath. Division 2, 1930–31.
Most League Points: 50, Division 2, 1960–61.
Most League Goals: 99, Division 2, 1960–61.
Most Individual Goals in Season: 29, Evelyn Morrison, Division 2, 1927–28 and R. Murray Division 2, 1936–37.
Record Transfer Fee Received: £10,000 from Rangers for Stewart Kennedy April 1973.
Scottish Cup: 1902–03 (semi-finalists).

Wilson B	Howie B J	Rose A	Rennie A	McCullie R C	Gaines N	Halliday R	Mullen T	Sage J E	McDonald J	Gordon W	Scott J	McNaughton A	Gibb I	Feeney W	Stone D	Sweeney S	Wilson F	Jenkins B	Straczynski M	Jack B	Masterson R	Dunn J	Drummond S	Auchincloss F	Fish A B	Match No.
	1	2		7			8	6	5	4	3		9*12			11†13	10									1
1		2		7			8*	6	5	4	3		13	9			11	10†12								2
1		2		7†			8	6	5*	4	3		13	9			11	10	12							3
1		2	3		10	6	5			4			9	8		11	7*12									4
1		2			10	6	5			4	3		9	8		11	7									5
	1	2			10	6	5			4	3		9	8		11	7									6
1		2		12	10	6	5			4*	3		9	8		11	7†13									7
1		2	3	7		6	5				13		9†	4	12		11	8*								8
1		2	3		10	6	5			4				9		11	7		8							9
1		2	3	8*	10	6	5			4			9	12		11	7									10
1		2			10	6	5			4	3		9	8		11	7									11
1		2			10	6	5			4	3		9	8*12	11	7										12
1		2			10	6	5			4	3		9	8	12	11*	7									13
1		2			10	6	5			4	3		9	8*13	11†	7	12									14
1		2	3	12	10	6	5			4		8	9		11*	7										15
1		2	3			6	5			10		8	9			7		11		4						16
1				13		2	10*	6	5			4	12	8	9		7		11†							17
1		3				2	10	6	5	4			8	9			7		11							18
1		3		12		2	10	6	5	4			8	9			7*		11							19
1			3		2	10	6	5		4		8	9			7		11								20
1		3		7	2	10	6	5		4			8		9			11								21
1		3		7*	2	10	6	5		4			8	12	9†		13	11								22
1		3		10*	2		6	5		4			8	12	9		7	11								23
1		3			2	10	6	5		4			8		9		7	11								24
1		3			2	10	6	5		4			8	12	9*		7	11								25
1		3			2	10	6	5		4			8	9	12		7*	11								26
1		3	2			10	6	5		4			8	7	9			11								27
1		3	2			10	6		5	4			8	7	9			11								28
1		3	2			10	6	12	5	4			8	7	9			11*								29
1		3	2	10*			6	5		4	12	8	7	9			11									30
1		3	2			10	6	5		4			8	7	9			11								31
	1	3	2			10	6	5		4			8	7	9			11								32
1		3	2		12	10†	6	5		4			8	7	9*		13	11								33
1		3	2			10	6	5		4			8				7	11	9							34
1		3	2			10	6	5		4*			8	12				11	9	7						35
1			2		12	10	6*	5		4			8				7	11	9					3		36
		3		12	2			5	6	4			8	9*			7	11	10		1					37
1		3	2					5	6	4			8		12		11	10	9				7*			38
		3			2	10			5	6	4		8				7	11	9		1					39
34	3	32	23	8	13	31	36	37	8	38	10	25	26	24	1	26	13	28	0	7	1	1	2	1	1	
				+			+			+			+	+	+	+	+	+	+							
				5s	2s		1s			3s			6s	4s	4s	2s	1s	3s	2s							

STIRLING ALBION   DIV. 1

Year Formed: 1945. *Ground:* Annfield Park. *Capacity:* 20,000 (900 seated). *Telephone:* Stirling 3584.
Manager: Alex Smith. *Secretary:* Peter Gardiner. *Club Colours:* Red shirts, socks and shorts.
Record Attendance: 26,400 v Celtic, Scottish Cup 4th Rd., March 14th, 1959.

1978-79 LEAGUE RECORD

Match No.	Date	Venue	Opponents	Result	H/T Score	League Pos'n	Goalscorers	Attendance
1	Aug 12	H	Hamilton A	D 0-0	0-0	—		1050
2	19	A	Dumbarton	W 1-0	0-0	4	Armstrong	1500
3	26	H	Raith R	L 0-1	0-0	7		1550
4	Sept 6	H	Clyde	L 1-4	0-0	—	Thomson (pen)	1150
5	9	A	Queen of the S	W 2-1	1-0	8	Nicol, Heggie	1000
6	13	A	Clydebank	L 2-5	1-3	—	Watson, Heggie	800
7	16	H	Kilmarnock	L 1-4	0-2	11	McPhee	1300
8	23	H	Arbroath	W 2-1	1-0	10	Nicol, Kennedy J	850
9	27	A	Montrose	D 1-1	1-0	—	Lowe (og)	800
10	30	A	Airdrionians	L 1-2	0-1	11	Heggie	2000
11	Oct 7	H	Ayr U	L 1-2	0-0	11	Low	1600
12	14	H	Dundee	W 1-0	0-0	11	Heggie	2850
13	21	A	St Johnstone	D 0-0	0-0	10		1403
14	28	H	Dumbarton	D 1-1	0-1	11	Browning (pen)	1400
15	Nov 4	A	Raith R	W 2-1	0-1	11	Steele, Armstrong	1200
16	11	H	Queen of the S	W 4-1	2-0	8	Watson 2, Armstrong (pen), Kennedy A	1000
17	18	A	Kilmarnock	L 0-5	0-1	10		3000
18	25	A	Arbroath	L 0-1	0-1	10		859
19	Dec 9	A	Ayr U	W 1-0	0-0	9	Kelly (og)	2711
20	16	A	Dundee	L 1-2	0-0	10	Steele	4642
21	23	H	St Johnstone	L 1-5	0-2	10	Watson	1250
22	Jan 20	A	Arbroath	D 0-0	0-0	9		777
23	Feb 10	A	Ayr U	L 0-2	0-1	9		2751
24	Mar 3	A	Hamilton A	D 1-1	1-0	10	Brown	1500
25	7	H	Raith R	W 3-0	0-0	—	Steele 2, Gray	600
26	10	A	Clyde	D 0-0	0-0	9		1000
27	13	H	Clydebank	L 2-3	2-1	—	McPhee, Armstrong	1000
28	17	H	Clydebank	D 0-0	0-0	9		900
29	24	A	Montrose	W 2-0	1-0	9	McPhee, McGibbon	900
30	28	H	Dundee	L 0-1	0-0	—		2000
31	31	A	Hamilton A	L 0-2	0-0	9		900
32	Apr 4	H	Kilmarnock	D 0-0	0-0	—		1800
33	7	H	Montrose	L 0-1	0-1	9		800
34	14	H	Airdrieonians	W 2-1	1-1	9	Steele, Kennedy J	1000
35	21	A	St Johnstone	W 2-0	0-0	9	Steele, Rutherford (og)	1400
36	25	H	Airdrieonians	L 1-2	0-1	—	Steele	1000
37	28	H	Clyde	W 3-2	1-1	9	Irving, Kennedy A 2	750
38	May 2	H	Queen of the S	L 2-3	1-1	—	Gray, Boyd (og)	500
39	7	A	Dumbarton	W 2-0	2-0	—	McPhee, Armstrong	400

Final League Position: 8

Goalscorers

League (43): Steele 7, Armstrong 5 (1 pen), Heggie 4, McPhee 4, Watson 4, Kennedy A 3, Gray 2, Kennedy J 2, Nicol 2, Brown 1, Browning 1 (pen), Irving 1, Low 1, McGibbon 1, Thomson 1 (pen), own goals 4.
League Cup (1): McPhee 1.
Cup (0).

Honours

Scottish League: Division 2 Champions 1952–53, 1957–58, 1960–61, 1964–65, 1976–77: Runners-up 1948–49, 1950–51.
Record Victory: 7-0 v Albion R, Division 2, 1947–48; v Montrose, Division 2, 1957–58: v St Mirren, Division 1, 1959–60; v Arbroath, Division 2, 1960–61.
Most League Points: 59, Division 2, 1964–65.
Most Individual League Goals in Season: Michael Lawson, 26, Division 2, 1975–76.

Young G	Arthur G	Burns J	Steedman A	Young R	Nicol G	Moffat G	Brown J	Kennedy J	Watson G	Steele W B	McPhee M	Duffin R	Gray R	Low K	Thomson R	Armstrong G	Browning I	Kennedy A	Dick G	Heggie S	McGibbon R	Beaton R	McLeod T	Skilling A	Irving L	Match No.
1		3		13	6			5	2			7	8	9	10	11†	4*		12							1
1		3		2	6			5	4	12	7				10	11	8		9*							2
1		3		5	6				2	12	7	4			10	11	8*		9							3
1	6	3		5					2		7†		8	12	10	11	4*		9	13						4
1		3		2	6	12	5	4*		7		13			10†11		8		9							5
1		3		2	6			5	4		7				10	11	8		9							6
1		13	4		6			5	3		7	12	2		10†11		8*		9							7
1		3		5	6			4	2					9	10	11	8		7							8
1		3		5	6			4	2	12				9	10	11	8		7*							9
1		3		5	6			4	2				12	9	10	11	8*		7							10
1		3		2	6		5	12			7	4*		8	10	11	13		9†							11
1		3		2	6		5	13	9*	7	4			10†	11	12		8							12
1		3		2	6		5	12	9	7*	4			10	11	13		8†							13
1		3		2	6		5		9†	7		4*13	10		11	12		8							14
1		3			6		5	10	13	12		2	7†		11	9	8		4*							15
1		3		2	6		5	4	12	7				10†		11	9*	8	13							16
1		3		2*	6		5	4	13	7				10†		11	9	8	12							17
1	13	3			6		5	4*		7		2	12		11	9	8†10									18
	1	3		2	6		5	4	9*	7		8			10	11			12							19
	1	3	12	2*	6		5	4	9†	7		8			10	11			13							20
1		3		2		6	5*	4	9	7	12	8			10	11†			13							21
1		3		2	6		5	8*		7	4	9			10	12			11							22
1		3		2	6		5	13	12	11	4	9†			10	8			7*							23
1		3		2	6	8	5	4	11†12			13			10	7*				9						24
1		3		2	6	8	5	4	11	12		13			10	7*				9†						25
1		3		2	6	8	5	4	11†	7	13	12			10					9*						26
1				2	6		5	3	11	7	8	4			10					9						27
1		3		2	6		5	4	11†	7	8	13			10				12	9*						28
1	4	3		2	6		5		11†	7	8*13				10				12	9						29
1		3		2	6	8	5			7		12			10	11				9		4*				30
1		3		2	6	8				7		5			10	13	11†		12	9*		4				31
1		3		2	6	8	5			7		9			10	11						4				32
1				2	6	8	13			7		5			10	11†			12	9*		3	4			33
1		3	12	2	6	8*	5		11	7		4			10				13	9†						34
1		3	13	2	6	8	5		11	7					10				12†	9*				4		35
1		3		2	6	8	5		11	7					10					9				4		36
1	12	3	2		6		5			7†		4*			11	9			13	10				8		37
1		3	2		6		5			7		4			11	9				10				8		38
1		3	2		6		5			7		4			11	9				10				8		39
37	2	5	33	5	31	38	10	35	23	15	33	12	20	7	11	39	22	9	1	16	12	3	1	4	5	
	+ 2s	+ 1s	+ 3s	+ 1s			+ 1s	+ 1s	+ 4s	+ 6s	+ 4s	+ 4s	+ 9s	+ 1s		+ 6s			+ 12s	+ 2s						

STRANRAER   DIV. 2

Year Formed: 1870. *Ground:* Stair Park. *Size:* 110×70 yds. *Capacity:* 5,500.
Telephone: Stranraer 3271. *Manager:*   *Secretary:* James Edmunds.
Club Colours: Royal blue shirts, white shorts, blue stockings with red tops.
Record Attendance: 6,500 v Rangers, Scottish Cup 1st Rd., Jan 24th, 1948.

1978–79 LEAGUE RECORD

Match No.	Date	Venue	Opponents	Result	H/T Score	League Pos'n	Goalscorers	Attendance
1	Aug 12	H	Alloa	W 4-0	3-0	—	Mills, Harvey 3	1100
2	19	A	Queen's Park	W 1-0	0-0	1	Harvey	1060
3	26	H	Albion R	W 3-1	1-0	1	Mills, Harvey, McGuigan (pen)	1200
4	Sept 6	A	Cowdenbeath	L 0-2	0-1	—		400
5	9	H	Brechin C	W 1-0	0-0	1	Hopkins	900
6	13	A	Meadowbank T	W 1-0	1-0	—	Mills	300
7	16	A	Dunfermline Ath	L 1-6	1-0	2	McDonald	1650
8	23	H	Forfar Ath	W 3-1	1-1	2	Steen, Milligan, Hopkins	1058
9	27	H	Falkirk	W 1-0	0-0	—	Steen	1250
10	30	A	East Fife	L 0-2	0-0	3		1086
11	Oct 7	H	Stenhousemuir	L 0-1	0-1	4		1000
12	14	H	East Stirling	W 1-0	0-0	3	McGuigan	1000
13	21	A	Berwick R	D 1-1	0-1	3	Harvey	1294
14	28	H	Queen's Park	L 0-2	0-0	4		1100
15	Nov 4	A	Albion R	L 1-2	0-0	5	Harvey	300
16	11	H	Brechin C	W 4-2	1-0	4	McDonald, McGuigan, Harvey, Robertson (pen)	750
17	18	A	Dunfermline Ath	L 0-3	0-2	4		2500
18	25	H	Forfar Ath	L 0-3	0-1	5		700
19	Dec 2	H	East Fife	L 2-4	0-3	8	McCutcheon, McDonald (pen)	400
20	9	A	Stenhousemuir	L 1-4	1-1	8	McDonald (pen)	200
21	16	A	Queen's Park	L 1-2	1-1	9	Mills	830
22	23	H	Berwick R	D 0-0	0-0	9		700
23	Jan 27	A	East Stirling	L 1-4	1-3	9	McGuigan	400
24	Feb 3	H	Meadowbank T	W 3-1	2-0	8	Hyslop 3 (1 a pen)	600
25	17	A	Albion R	L 0-1	0-0	8		600
26	24	H	East Stirling	W 6-2	4-1	8	Hyslop 2, Tait 2, McDonald, Robertson	600
27	Mar 3	A	Alloa	L 1-3	0-2	8	Hyslop	550
28	10	H	Cowdenbeath	L 2-4	2-2	8	McClymont 2	600
29	14	A	Forfar Ath	L 0-2	0-1	—		850
30	17	H	Meadowbank T	W 1-0	0-0	8	McClymont	400
31	24	H	Falkirk	L 0-2	0-1	8		2500
32	31	A	Alloa	W 1-0	0-0	9	Hay	450
33	Apr 3	A	Stenhousemuir	W 2-1	1-1	—	McGuigan, Mills	300
34	7	H	Falkirk	W 2-1	0-1	6	McCutcheon, Hay (pen)	800
35	11	A	Brechin C	W 2-1	1-1	—	Harvey, McDonald	300
36	14	A	East Fife	W 2-0	1-0	5	Harvey, McCutcheon	949
37	21	H	Berwick R	L 1-5	1-1	6	McGuigan	1100
38	24	H	Dunfermline Ath	W 1-0	0-0	—	Harvey	1020
39	28	A	Cowdenbeath	L 1-3	1-1	6	Hay (pen)	400

Final League Position: 9.

Goalscorers

League (52): Harvey 11, Hyslop 6 (1 a pen), McDonald 6 (2pens), McGuigan 6 (1 a pen), Mills 5, Hay 3 (2 pens), McClymont 3, McCutcheon 3, Hopkins 2, Robertson 2 (1 a pen), Steen 2, Tait 2, Milligan 1.
League Cup (1): Robertson 1.
Cup: McDonald 1 (pen).

Honours
Record Victory: 7-0 v Brechin C, Division 2, 1964–65.
Record Defeat: 1-11 v Queen of the South, Scottish Cup, 1st Rd., 1931–32.
Most League Points: 44, Division 2, 1960–61, 1971–72.
Most Individual Goals in Season: 27, Derek Frye, Division 2, 1977–78.

Taylor J	Greenhorn M	Stewart J	Hopkins J	Hay H	McDonald D	Muir J	Steen J	Calderwood R	Cairney P	Tait R	Mills B	McCutcheon A	Harvey A	Milligan C	McGuigan I	Robertson J	Murdoch H	Hyslop G	McClymont M	Match No.
1			2	4	3	5	7			6	9		8		10	11				1
2			2	4	3		7			6	9*	5	8	12	10	11				2
1			2	4	3	5	7			6	9		8*	12	10	11				3
	1		2	4	7	5	8		3	6	9			10		11				4
1			2	4	3	5	8	7		6	9*	10		12		11				5
1			2	4	3	5	7			6	8	10		9		11				6
1			2*	4	3	5	7	9†12		6		8	13	10		11				7
1			2	4	3	5	7			6	9*	10†13	8	12	11					8
1			2	4	3	5	7			6	9	12	8		10*11					9
1			2	4	3	5	7	12		6	9*13		8		10†11					10
1			2	4	3	5	7			6*	9	13	8	12	10	11†				11
1			2	4	3	5	7	13			8†12	10	6*11	9						12
1			2	4	3	5*	7	12	6		10	8		9	11					13
1			2	4	3	5	7	13	6*	8†12	10			9	11					14
1			2	4	3	5		12	7*		6	8	10	9	11					15
1			2	4	3	5*		12	6	9		8	7	10	11					16
1			2	4	3	5				7	9	12	8	6*10	11					17
1			2	4	3	5	7				9	6	8		10	11				18
1*			7	5	2	4	3	12			8	6	9		10†11	13				19
	1		7	5	2	4	3			8*12	6		9	13	10†11					20
1			2	5	3	4	7				8	6		9	10	11				21
1			2	6	3*	5	7		12	11	4		9	13	10		8†			22
1			2	4	3		7*		5	9	6	8		10	11	12				23
1			2	3		5*	8		6	9	4	13	12	10	11		7†			24
1			2	3		5	8		6	9	4			10	11		7			25
1			2	3	7		12		5	6		4			10	11		9	8*	26
1			2*	3	7				5	6		4	12		10	11		9	8	27
1		13	3	2	5			12	6	11†	4	7*		10				9	8	28
1			2		8	5	7		3		6	4			10	11		9		29
1			2	3	7		6			11*	4	12		10		5	9	8		30
1			2	6	3	5	7			12	4	9		10	11			8*		31
1			2*	6	3	5		12	4	8			9	7	10	11				32
1			2	6	3	5			4	8			9	7	10	11				33
1			2	6	3	5			4	8	12	9	7	10	11*					34
1			2	6	3	5				7	4	9	10	8	11					35
1			2	6	3	5	12				4	9	7*10	11		8				36
1			2	6	3	5	7				4	9	8*10	11		12				37
	1		2	6	3	5			4	7	8	9		10	11					*38
	1		2	6	3	5			4	7*	8	9	12	10	11					39
35	1	3	38	38	37	34	26	2	4	28	30	26	27	15	33	37	1	9	5	
		+1s				+2s		10s	1s	2s	7s	5s	8s	1s			+1s	+1s	+1s	

SCOTTISH LEAGUE 1978-79

Premier Division

	P	W	D	L	F	A	W	D	L	F	A	Pts
			Home						Away			
Celtic	36	13	3	2	32	12	8	3	7	29	25	48
Rangers	36	12	5	1	32	10	6	4	8	20	25	45
Dundee U	36	12	4	2	33	16	6	4	8	23	21	44
Aberdeen	36	9	5	4	39	16	4	9	5	20	20	40
Hibernian	36	7	9	2	23	16	5	4	9	21	32	37
St Mirren	36	8	3	7	23	20	7	3	8	22	21	36
Morton	36	9	4	5	34	23	3	8	7	18	30	36
Partick T	36	10	2	6	31	21	3	6	9	11	18	34
Hearts	36	5	5	8	19	25	3	2	13	20	46	23
Motherwell	36	2	5	11	20	38	3	2	13	13	48	17

First Division

	P	W	D	L	F	A	W	D	L	F	A	Pts
Dundee	39	13	5	1	36	12	11	2	7	32	24	55
Kilmarnock	39	13	5	1	41	14	9	5	6	31	21	54
Clydebank	39	15	2	3	48	23	9	4	6	30	27	54
Ayr U	39	12	3	5	39	19	9	2	8	32	33	47
Hamilton A	39	13	4	2	39	17	4	5	11	23	43	43
Airdrieonians	39	9	4	7	44	33	7	4	8	28	28	40
Dumbarton	39	9	3	8	30	22	5	8	6	28	28	39
Stirling Albion	39	6	4	9	23	29	7	5	8	20	26	35
Clyde	39	8	3	8	30	29	5	5	10	24	36	34
Arbroath	39	8	6	6	33	26	3	5	11	17	35	33
Raith R	39	8	3	8	29	21	4	5	11	19	34	32
St Johnstone	39	6	8	6	32	28	4	3	12	25	38	31
Montrose	39	4	6	9	31	37	4	3	13	24	55	25
Queen of the S	39	8	4	8	31	35	0	4	15	12	58	24

Second Division

	P	W	D	L	F	A	W	D	L	F	A	Pts
Berwick R	39	11	6	3	45	22	11	4	4	37	22	54
Dunfermline Ath	39	13	6	1	41	19	6	8	5	25	21	52
Falkirk	39	13	4	3	39	16	6	8	5	27	21	50
East Fife	39	10	2	7	33	22	7	7	6	31	31	43
Cowdenbeath	39	10	5	4	37	22	6	5	9	26	36	42
Alloa	39	10	7	3	36	26	6	2	11	21	36	41
Albion R	39	9	6	4	28	17	6	4	10	29	39	40
Forfar Ath	39	9	7	4	35	25	4	5	10	20	27	38
Stranraer	39	11	1	7	32	27	7	1	12	20	39	38
Stenhousemuir	39	6	4	10	34	30	6	4	9	20	28	32
Brechin C	39	8	7	5	31	33	1	7	11	18	32	32
East Stirling	39	10	4	5	42	31	2	4	14	19	56	32
Queen's Park	39	4	7	8	19	19	4	5	11	27	38	28
Meadowbank T	39	5	3	11	17	31	3	5	12	20	43	24

Highland League

	P	W	D	L	F	A	Pts
Keith	30	21	6	3	67	25	48
Inverness Caledonian	30	20	5	5	59	26	45
Peterhead	30	19	5	6	62	32	43
Inverness Thistle	30	18	2	10	91	43	38
Ross Co	30	17	4	9	52	33	38
Elgin C	30	14	7	11	64	49	35
Buckie Thistle	30	14	6	10	61	49	34
Deveronvale	30	14	6	10	63	57	34
Rothes	30	9	10	11	47	60	28
Fraserburgh	30	10	7	13	45	50	27
Nairn Co	30	9	6	15	47	56	24
Brora Rangers	30	9	4	17	45	51	22
Clachnacuddin	30	8	3	19	45	75	19
Huntly	30	7	4	19	51	66	18
Forres Mechanics	30	6	3	21	52	94	15
Lossiemouth	30	3	4	23	24	109	10

SCOTTISH LEAGUE HONOURS LIST

*On goal average. †Held jointly after indecisive play-off. ‡Won on deciding match.
††Held jointly. ¶Two points deducted for fielding ineligible player.
Competition suspended 1940–45 during war. ‡‡Two points deducted for registration irregularities.

PREMIER DIVISION
Maximum points 72

	First	Pts.	Second	Pts.	Third	Pts.
1975–76	Rangers	54	Celtic	48	Hibernian	43
1976–77	Celtic	55	Rangers	46	Aberdeen	43
1977–78	Rangers	55	Aberdeen	53	Dundee U.	40
1978–79	Celtic	48	Rangers	45	Dundee U.	44

FIRST DIVISION
Maximum points 52

	First	Pts.	Second	Pts.	Third	Pts.
1975–76	Partick T.	41	Kilmarnock	35	Montrose	30

Maximum points 78

1976–77	St. Mirren	62	Clydebank	58	Dundee	51
1977–78	Morton	58	Hearts	58	Dundee	57
1978–79	Dundee	55	Kilmarnock	54	Clydebank	54

SECOND DIVISION
Maximum points 52

	First	Pts.	Second	Pts.	Third	Pts.
1975–76	Clydebank	40	Raith R.	40	Alloa	35

Maximum points 78

1976–77	Stirling A.	55	Alloa	51	Dunfermline	50
1977–78	Clyde	53	Raith R.	53	Dunfermline	48
1978–79	Berwick R.	54	Dunfermline Ath.	52	Falkirk	50

FIRST DIVISION to 1974–75

	First	Pts.	Second	Pts.	Third	Pts.
1890–1a††	Dumbarton	29	Rangers	29	Celtic	24
1891–2b	Dumbarton	37	Celtic	35	Hearts	30
1892–3a	Celtic	29	Rangers	28	St. Mirren	23
1893–4a	Celtic	29	Hearts	26	St. Bernards	22
1894–5a	Hearts	31	Celtic	26	Rangers	21
1895–6a	Celtic	30	Rangers	26	Hibernian	24
1896–97a	Hearts	28	Hibernian	26	Rangers	25
1897–98a	Celtic	33	Rangers	29	Hibernian	22
1898–99a	Rangers	36	Hearts	26	Celtic	24
1899–1900a	Rangers	32	Celtic	25	Hibernian	24
1900–1c	Rangers	35	Celtic	29	Hibernian	25
1901–2a	Rangers	28	Celtic	26	Hearts	22
1902–3b	Hibernian	37	Dundee	31	Rangers	29
1903–4d	Third Lanark	43	Hearts	39	*Rangers	38
1904–5d‡	Celtic	41	Rangers	41	Third Lanark	35
1905–6e	Celtic	49	Hearts	43	Airdrieonians	38
1906–7f	Celtic	55	Dundee	48	Rangers	45
1907–8f	Celtic	55	Falkirk	51	Rangers	50
1908–9f	Celtic	51	Dundee	50	Clyde	48
1909–10f	Celtic	54	Falkirk	52	Rangers	46
1910–11f	Rangers	52	Aberdeen	48	Falkirk	44
1911–12f	Rangers	51	Celtic	45	Clyde	42
1912–13f	Rangers	53	Celtic	49	*Hearts	41
1913–14g	Celtic	65	Rangers	59	*Hearts	54
1914–15g	Celtic	65	Hearts	61	Rangers	50
1915–16g	Celtic	67	Rangers	56	Morton	51
1916–17g	Celtic	64	Morton	54	Rangers	53
1917–18f	Rangers	56	Celtic	55	Kilmarnock	43
1918–19f	Celtic	58	Rangers	57	Morton	47
1919–20h	Rangers	71	Celtic	68	Motherwell	57
1920–21h	Rangers	76	Celtic	66	Hearts	56
1921–22h	Celtic	67	Rangers	66	Raith R.	56
1922–23g	Rangers	55	Airdrieonians	50	Celtic	46
1923–24g	Rangers	59	Airdrieonians	50	Celtic	41
1924–25g	Rangers	60	Airdrieonians	57	Hibernian	52
1925–26g	Celtic	58	*Airdrieonians	50	Hearts	50
1926–27g	Rangers	56	Motherwell	51	Celtic	49
1927–28g	Rangers	60	*Celtic	55	Motherwell	55
1928–29g	Rangers	67	Celtic	51	Motherwell	50
1929–30g	Rangers	60	Motherwell	55	Aberdeen	53
1930–31g	Rangers	60	Celtic	58	Motherwell	56
1931–32g	Motherwell	66	Rangers	61	Celtic	48
1932–33g	Rangers	62	Motherwell	59	Hearts	50
1933–34g	Rangers	66	Motherwell	62	Celtic	47

	First	Pts	Second	Pts	Third	Pts
1934–35g	Rangers	55	Celtic	52	Hearts	50
1935–36g	Celtic	66	*Rangers	61	Aberdeen	61
1936–37g	Rangers	61	Aberdeen	54	Celtic	52
1937–38g	Celtic	61	Hearts	58	Rangers	49
1938–39g	Rangers	59	Celtic	48	Aberdeen	46
1946–47f	Rangers	46	Hibernian	44	Aberdeen	39
1947–48j	Hibernian	48	Rangers	46	Partick T.	36
1948–49j	Rangers	46	Dundee	45	Hibernian	39
1949–50j	Rangers	50	Hibernian	49	Hearts	43
1950–51j	Hibernian	48	*Rangers	38	Dundee	38
1951–52j	Hibernian	45	Rangers	41	East Fife	37
1952–53j	*Rangers	43	Hibernian	43	East Fife	39
1953–54j	Celtic	43	Hearts	38	Partick T.	35
1954–55j	Aberdeen	49	Celtic	46	Rangers	41
1955–56f	Rangers	52	Aberdeen	46	*Hearts	45
1956–57f	Rangers	55	Hearts	53	Kilmarnock	42
1957–58f	Hearts	62	Rangers	49	Celtic	46
1958–59f	Rangers	50	Hearts	48	Motherwell	44
1959–60f	Hearts	54	Kilmarnock	50	*Rangers	42
1960–61f	Rangers	51	Kilmarnock	50	Third Lanark	42
1961–62f	Dundee	54	Rangers	51	Celtic	46
1962–63f	Rangers	57	Kilmarnock	48	Partick T.	46
1963–64f	Rangers	55	Kilmarnock	49	*Celtic	47
1964–65f	*Kilmarnock	50	Hearts	50	Dunfermline Ath.	49
1965–66f	Celtic	57	Rangers	55	Kilmarnock	45
1966–67f	Celtic	58	Rangers	55	Clyde	46
1967–68f	Celtic	63	Rangers	61	Hibernian	45
1968–69f	Celtic	54	Rangers	49	Dunfermline Ath.	45
1969–70f	Celtic	57	Rangers	45	Hibernian	44
1970–71f	Celtic	56	Aberdeen	54	St. Johnstone	44
1971–72f	Celtic	60	Aberdeen	50	Rangers	44
1972–73f	Celtic	57	Rangers	56	Hibernian	45
1973–74f	Celtic	53	Hibernian	49	Rangers	48
1974–75f	Rangers	56	Hibernian	49	Celtic	45

Maximum points: a, 36; b, 44; c, 40; d, 52; e, 60; f, 68; g, 76; h, 84; j, 60.

SECOND DIVISION to 1974–75

	First	Pts	Second	Pts	Third	Pts
1893–94f	Hibernian	29	Cowlairs	27	Clyde	24
1894–95f	Hibernian	30	Motherwell	22	Port Glasgow	20
1895–96f	Abercorn	27	Leith Ath.	23	Renton	21
1896–97f	Partick T.	31	Leith Ath.	27	Kilmarnock	21
1897–98f	Kilmarnock	29	Port Glasgow	25	Morton	22
1898–99f	Kilmarnock	32	Leith Ath.	27	Port Glasgow	25
1899–1900f	Partick T.	29	Morton	26	Port Glasgow	20
1900–01f	St. Bernard's	26	Airdrieonians	23	Abercorn	21
1901–02f	Port Glasgow	32	Partick T.	31	Motherwell	26
1902–03g	Airdrieonians	35	Motherwell	28	Ayr U.	27
1903–04g	Hamilton A.	37	Clyde	29	Ayr U.	28
1904–05g	Clyde	32	Falkirk	28	Hamilton A.	27
1905–06g	Leith Ath.	34	Clyde	31	Albion R.	27
1906–07g	St. Bernard's	32	Vale of Leven	27	Arthurlie	27
1907–08g	Raith R.	30	Dumbarton	27‡‡	Ayr U.	27
1908–09g	Abercorn	31	Raith R.	28	Vale of Leven	28
1909–10g	Leith Ath.††	33	Raith R.††	33	St. Bernard's	27
1910–11g	Dumbarton	31	Ayr U.	27	Albion R.	25
1911–12g	Ayr U.	35	Abercorn	30	Dumbarton	27
1912–13h	Ayr U.	34	Dunfermline Ath	33	East Stirling	32
1913–14g	Cowdenbeath	31	Albion R.	27	Dunfermline Ath.	26
1914–15h	Cowdenbeath	37	St. Bernard's	37	Leith Ath.	37
1921–22a	†Alloa	60	Cowdenbeath	47	Armadale	48
1922–23a	Queen's Park	57	Clydebank	¶50	St. Johnstone	¶45
1923–24a	St. Johnstone	56	Cowdenbeath	55	Bathgate	44
1924–25a	Dundee U.	50	Clydebank	48	Clyde	47
1925–26a	Dunfermline Ath.	59	Clyde	53	Ayr U.	52
1926–27a	Bo'ness	56	Raith R.	49	Clydebank	45
1927–28a	Ayr U.	54	Third Lanark	45	King's Park	44
1928–29b	Dundee U.	51	Morton	50	Arbroath	47
1929–30a	*Leith Ath.	57	East Fife	57	Albion R.	54
1930–31a	Third Lanark	61	Dundee U.	50	Dunfermline Ath.	47
1931–32a	*East Stirling	55	St. Johnstone	55	*Raith Rovers	46
1932–33c	Hibernian	54	Queen of the S.	49	Dunfermline Ath.	47
1933–34c	Albion R.	45	*Dunfermline Ath.	44	Arbroath	44

	First	Pts.	Second	Pts.	Third	Pts.
1934–35c	Third Lanark	52	Arbroath	50	St. Bernard's	47
1935–36c	Falkirk	59	St. Mirren	52	Morton	48
1936–37c	Ayr U.	54	Morton	51	St. Bernard's	48
1937–38c	Raith R.	59	Albion R.	48	Airdrieonians	47
1938–39c	Cowdenbeath	60	*Alloa	48	East Fife	48
1946–47d	Dundee	45	Airdrieonians	42	East Fife	31
1947–48e	East Fife	53	Albion R.	42	Hamilton A.	40
1948–49e	*Raith R.	42	Stirling Albion	42	*Airdrieonians	41
1949–50e	Morton	47	Airdrieonians	44	*St. Johnstone	36
1950–51e	*Queen of the S.	45	Stirling Albion	45	*Ayr U.	36
1951–52e	Clyde	44	Falkirk	43	Ayr U.	39
1952–53e	Stirling Albion	44	Hamilton A.	43	Queen's Park	37
1953–54e	Motherwell	45	Kilmarnock	42	*Third Lanark	36
1954–55e	Airdrieonians	46	Dunfermline Ath.	42	Hamilton A.	39
1955–56b	Queen's Park	54	Ayr U.	51	St. Johnstone	49
1956–57b	Clyde	64	Third Lanark	51	Cowdenbeath	45
1957–58b	Stirling Albion	55	Dunfermline Ath.	53	Arbroath	47
1958–59b	Ayr U.	60	Arbroath	51	Stenhousemuir	40
1959–60b	St. Johnstone	53	Dundee U.	50	Queen of the S.	49
1960–61b	Stirling Albion	55	Falkirk	54	Stenhousemuir	50
1961–62b	Clyde	54	Queen of the S.	53	Morton	44
1962–63b	St. Johnstone	55	East Stirling	49	Morton	48
1963–64b	Morton	67	Clyde	53	Arbroath	46
1964–65b	Stirling Albion	59	Hamilton A.	50	Queen of the S.	45
1965–66b	Ayr U.	53	Airdrieonians	50	Queen of the S.	49
1966–67b	Morton	69	Raith R.	58	Arbroath	57
1967–68b	St. Mirren	62	Arbroath	53	East Fife	40
1968–69b	Motherwell	64	Ayr U.	53	*East Fife	47
1969–70b	Falkirk	56	Cowdenbeath	55	Queen of the South	58
1970–71b	Partick Thistle	56	East Fife	51	Arbroath	46
1971–72b	Dumbarton	52	Arbroath	52	Stirling Albion	50
1972–73b	Clyde	56	Dunfermline Ath.	52	*Raith R.	47
1973–74b	Airdrieonians	60	Kilmarnock	59	Hamilton A.	55
1974–75a	Falkirk	54	Queen of the S.	53	Montrose	53

Elected to First Division: 1894 Clyde; 1897 Partick T.; 1899 Kilmarnock; 1900 Partick T.; 1902 Partick T. 1903 Airdrieonians.; 1905 Falkirk, Aberdeen and Hamilton A.; 1906 Clyde; 1910 Raith R.; 1913 Ayr U
Maximum points: a, 76; b, 72; c, 68; d, 52; e, 60; f, 36; g, 44; h, 52.

RELEGATED FROM PREMIER DIVISION

1975–76 Dundee, St. Johnstone
1976–77 Hearts, Kilmarnock
1977–78 Ayr U., Clydebank
1978–79 Hearts, Motherwell

RELEGATED FROM DIVISION 1

1975–7o Dunfermline Ath., Clyde
1976–77 Raith R., Falkirk
1977–78 Alloa Ath., East Fife
1978–79 Montrose, Queen of the South

RELEGATED FROM DIVISION 1 TO 1973–74

1921–22*Queen's Park, Dumbarton, Clydebank
1922–23 Albion R., Alloa
1923–24 Clyde, Clydebank
1924–25 Third Lanark. Ayr U.
1925–26 Raith R., Clydebank
1926–27 Morton, Dundee U.
1927–28 Dunfermline Ath., Bo'ness
1928–29 Third Lanark, Raith R.
1929–30 St. Johnstone, Dundee U.
1930–31 Hibernian, East Fife
1931–32 Dundee U., Leith Ath.
1932–33 Morton, East Stirling
1933–34 Third Lanark, Cowdenbeath
1934–35 St. Mirren, Falkirk
1935–36 Airdrieonians, Ayr U.
1936–37 Dunfermline Ath., Albion R.
1937–38 Dundee, Morton
1938–39 Queen's Park, Raith R.
1946–47 Kilmarnock, Hamilton A.
1947–48 Airdrieonians, Queen's Park
1948–49 Morton, Albion R.
1949–50 Queen of the S., Stirling Albion
1950–51 Clyde, Falkirk
1951–52 Morton, Stirling Albion
1952–53 Motherwell, Third Lanark
1953–54 Airdrieonians, Hamilton A.
1954–55 No clubs relegated
1955–56 Stirling Albion, Clyde
1956–57 Dunfermline Ath., Ayr U.
1957–58 East Fife, Queen's Park
1958–59 Queen of the S., Falkirk
1959–60 Arbroath, Stirling Albion
1960–61 Ayr U., Clyde
1961–62 St. Johnstone, Stirling Albion
1962–63 Clyde, Raith R.
1963–64 Queen of the S., East Stirling
1964–65 Airdrieonians Third Lanark
1965–66 Morton. Hamilton A.
1966–67 St. Mirren, Ayr U.
1967–68 Motherwell, Stirling Albion
1968–69 Falkirk, Arbroath
1969–70 Raith R., Partick T.
1970–71 St. Mirren. Cowdenbeath
1971–72 Clyde, Dunfermline Ath.
1972–73 Kilmarnock, Airdrieonians
1973–74 East Fife, Falkirk

* Season 1921–22—only 1 club promoted, 3 clubs relegated.
The Scottish Football League was reconstructed into three divisions at the end of the 1974–75 season, so the usual relegation statistics do not apply.

SCOTTISH CUP 1979

FIRST ROUND

16 DEC

Dunfermline Ath (1) 2 (*Leonard, Rolland pen*) 1981
Albion R (1) 2 (*Main, Loughran*)
Dunfermline Ath: Whyte; Rolland, Mercer, Thomson, Salton, Borthwick, Mullin, Robertson, Leonard, Donnelly, Hegarty.
Albion R: Balavage; Flavell (Coyle), McGregor, Franchetti, Shields, Leishman, Hill, Loughran, Cleland, Muldoon, Main (McGillivray).

Falkirk (0) 2 (*Brown, McCallan*) 2350
Keith (0) 0
Falkirk: McKell; Johnston (Perry), Burrell, Hay, Brown, Stevenson (Thomson), Hoggan, Graham, McRoberts, McCallan, Mitchell.
Keith: Gray; McKay, Martin, Dalgarno, Wilson, Munro, Winton, Duncan, MacDonald (Bruce), O'Hara, Curran (Fraser).

Gala Fairydean (1) 1 (*Chisholm*) 1000
Cowdenbeath (3) 3 (*Markey, Hunter, Liddle*)
Gala Fairydean: McNulty; Mann, Scott, Dick, Sharp, Frizell, Maitland (Noble), Davidson, Johnstone, Miller, Chisholm.
Cowdenbeath: Cooper; Ward, Markey, Hunter, Davies, Dyce, Caithness, Harley, Liddle (Marshall), Purdie (Milne), Steele.

Meadowbank T (1) 1 (*McKenzie*) 1000
Inverness Caledonian (0) 1 (*Penman*)
Meadowbank T: Sinclair; O'Rourke, Fraser, Stewart, Wight, McKenzie, Davidson (Hancock S), Hancock J, Adair (Downie), Leetion, Small.
Inverness Caledonian: McDonald W; Davidson, Corbett, Mackay, Summers, Derby, Penman (Docherty), Dingwall, Kennedy, McIntosh R, Fyfe.

Threave Rovers (0) 0 500
East Stirling (1) 2 (*McCormack, Docherty pen*)
Threave Rovers: Mundell; Gault, Tait, McGinley, Cochrane, Welsh, Davies, Bendall, McElroy (Maxwell), Houston, Semple.
East Stirling: Cairney; Stirling, Hotchkiss, Lamont (McCulley), Blair, McRitchie, Grant, Docherty, McCormack, Bennett, Ashwood.

Vale of Leithen (0) 1 (*Notman pen*) 800
Forfar Ath (2) 4 (*Gallacher, Knox, Hall, Reid*)
Vale of Leithen: McMenemy; Forrest, Crawford, Boyd, Miller, Johnston, Callaghan, O'Donnell, Reid, Hall, Notman.
Forfar Ath: McWilliams; Bennett, Cameron, Brown K, Brash, Rae, Knox, Gallacher, Reid, Henry, Clark (Hall).

FIRST ROUND, REPLAYS

19 DEC

Albion R (1) 2 (*Loughran, Cleland*) 1000
Dunfermline Ath (1) 3 (*Leonard 2, McLaren*)
Albion R: Balavage; Flavell, McGregor, Franchetti, Shields, Leishman, Hill, Muldoon, Cleland, Loughran, Main.
Dunfermline Ath: Whyte; Scott, Mercer, Thomson, Salton, Dunn, McLaren, Robertson, Leonard, Donnelly, Hegarty.

23 DEC

Inverness Caledonian (0) 0 1700
Meadowbank T (1) 3 (*Johnston, Conroy, McKenzie*)
Inverness Caledonian: McDonald W; Davidson, Kennedy, Derby, Summers, Corbett, Docherty (Paul), Mackay, McIntosh R, McIntosh W, Dingwall (Caldwell).
Meadowbank T: Sinclair; Leetion, Fraser, Stewart, Wight, McKenzie, Small, Hancock J (Davidson), Johnston (Adair), Conroy, Hancock S.

SECOND ROUND

13 JAN

Stranraer (0) 1 (*McDonald pen*) 1120
Dunfermline Ath (0) 1 (*McLaren*)
Stranraer: Taylor; Hopkins, McDonald, McCutcheon, Muir, Hay, Steen, Hyslop (Milligan), Harvey (Mills), McGuigan, Robertson.
Dunfermline Ath: Whyte; Scott, Mercer, Thomson, Salton, Dunn, McLaren, Robertson, Leonard, Donnelly, Hegarty (Mullin).

16 JAN

East Fife (2) 2 (*Dickson 2*) 967
Brechin C (0) 1 (*MacIvor (og)*)
East Fife: Blair; MacIvor, Gillies, Clarke, Methven, Wedderburn, Cairns, George, Dickson, Mackie (Herd), Gibson.
Brechin C: Ritchie; Cairns (Grant), Reid, Campbell R, Sime, Glover, Campbell I, Elvin, Gillespie, Sutherland (Kyles), Robb.

Meadowbank T (1) 2 (*Small, Johnston*) 400
Stenhousemuir (1) 1 (*Jenkins*)
Meadowbank T: Sinclair; Leetion, Fraser, Stewart, Wight, Conroy, Small, Hancock J, Johnston, McKenzie, Hancock S.
Stenhousemuir: Wilson B; Gaines, Rose, Gordon, Sage, Mullen, Sweeney, McNaughton, Gibb, Halliday, Jenkins.

17 JAN

Cowdenbeath (0) 0 600
Alloa (0) 0
Cowdenbeath: Cooper; Ward, Markey, Hunter, Davies, Dyce, Caithness, Harley, Liddle, Purdie, Steele.
Alloa: McNab; McCann, Henderson, Lawson, Holt, Miller, Cochrane, Carberry, Morrison, Irvine, McLeod.

Peterhead (0) 2 (*Sievwright, McIntyre*) 1000
Queen's Park (1) 3 (*Edgar 2, Ballantyne*)
Peterhead: McHattie; Lawson, Rennie, Taylor, Sievwright, Masson (Porter), Christie, Duncan, McIntyre, Hamilton, Hunter.
Queen's Park: Preston; McSkimming, Dickson, Wylie, Bowie, McAloon, Sinclair, Wood, Edgar, Ballantyne, Wilkie.

21 JAN

East Stirling (1) 2 (*Lamont, Simpson*) 787
Spartans (3) 3 (*Smith, Bell, McKinnon*)
East Stirling: Cairney; Stirling (Hotchkiss), Blair, Lamont, Simpson, Tempany, Grant, Bennett, Docherty, McCormack, Ashwood.
Spartans: Tevendale; Hepburn, Brough, Beattie, Gardner, Bell, Smith, Whyte (Dunnett), Arnott, Costello (Morrison), McKinnon.

22 JAN

Forfar Ath (1) 1 (*Reid*)   1117
Berwick R (0) 2 (*Smith G, Jobson*)
Forfar Ath: McWilliams; Bennett, Cameron, Brown, Brash, Rae, Gallacher, Knox, Reid, Hall, Clark.
Berwick R: Frame; Laing, McLeod, Smith D, Rutherford, Morton, Davidson, McLean (Marshall), Jobson, Smith G, Moyes.

22 FEB

Inverness Thistle (0) 0   1543
Falkirk (4) 4 (*McRoberts, Brown, Perry, McCallan*)
Inverness Thistle: Rae; Fraser, Black B, Cumming, Milroy, Drews, Black A, Coutts (Macrae), Newlands, Guyan, Inglis (Maclean).
Falkirk: McKell; Johnston, Burrell, Meakin, Brown, Stevenson (Thomson), Hoggan, Oliver, McRoberts, McCallan (Soutar), Perry.

SECOND ROUND, REPLAYS

21 JAN

Alloa (1) 2 (*Holt, Morrison*)   1214
Cowdenbeath (0) 0
Alloa: McNab; McCann, Henderson, (Steele) Lawson, Holt, Miller, Cochrane, Carberry, Morrison, Irvine, McLeod (Hamilton).
Cowdenbeath: Cooper; Ward, Markey, Hunter (Milne), Davies, Dyce, Caithness, Harley, Marshall, Purdie (Liddle), Steele.

22 JAN

Dunfermline Ath (0) 1 (*Mullin*)   3082
Stranraer (0) 0
Dunfermline Ath: Whyte; Scott, Mercer, Thomson, Salton, Dunn, McLaren, Robertson R, Leonard, Donnelly, Hegarty (Mullin).
Stranraer: Taylor; Hopkins, McDonald, McCutcheon, Muir, Hay, Steen, Mills, Harvey, McGuigan, Robertson.

THIRD ROUND

27 JAN

Arbroath (0) 0
Airdrieonians (1) 1 (*Clark*)   1566
Arbroath: Lister; McKenzie, Rylance, Cargill, Wells (Gavine), Fettes, Fletcher (Mylles), Carson, Wilson, Kidd, Yule.
Airdrieonians: McGarr; Jonquin, Docherty, Anderson, Black, Lapsley, McCann, Walker, Clark, Ross, McCulloch.

East Fife (0) 0
Berwick R (0) 1 (*Smith G*)   1666
East Fife: Blair; MacIvor, Gillies, Clarke, Methven, Wedderburn (Young), Cairns, George, Dickson, Mackie (Huskie), Gibson.
Berwick R: Frame; Laing, McLeod, Smith D, Rutherford, Morton, Davidson, Smith G, Jobson, Wheatley, Moyes.

Hamilton A (0) 0
Aberdeen (0) 2 (*Miller Harper*)   10,000
Hamilton A: Ferguson; Frew, Kellachan, Fairlie, Dempsey, Alexander, Grant, Graham, Howie, McDowall, (Morrison), McManus.
Aberdeen: Clark; Kennedy, Considine, Strachan, Rougvie, Miller, Sullivan, Archibald, Harper, Jarvie (McMaster), Scanlon.

Raith R (0) 0
Hearts (1) 2 (*Robertson 2*)   10,000
Raith R: McDermott; McDonough, Candlish, Houston, Forsyth, Thomson D, Wallace, Urquhart (Murray), Harrow, McFarlane, Thomson R (Forrest).
Hearts: Dunlop; Kidd, Brown, McNicoll, Jefferies, Black, Gibson, Busby, O'Connor, Fraser, Robertson.

28 JAN

Dunfermline Ath (0) 1 (*Leonard*)
Hibernian (0) 1 (*Higgins*)   11,801
Dunfermline Ath: Whyte; Scott, Mercer, Thomson, Salton, Hunter, Mullin, Robertson R, Leonard, Donnelly, Hegarty.
Hibernian: McArthur; Brazil, Duncan, Bremner, Stewart, McNamara, MacLeod, Higgins, Hutchinson, Callachan, Lambie (O'Brien).

31 JAN

Clyde (0) 1 (*Ahern pen*)
Kilmarnock (1) 5 (*Bourke 2, Street, 2 Gibson*)   2509
Clyde: Arrol; Anderson, Thorburn, Clougher:y Kinnear (Ferris), Ahern, O'Neill, Brogan, Hood, McCabe (Grant), Marshall.
Kilmarnock: McCulloch; McLean, Robertson, Clark J, Clarke P, McDicken, Gibson, Maxwell, Bourke, Mauchlen, Street.

Clydebank (3) 3 (*Miller 2, McDougall*)   1500
Queen's Park (1) 3 (*Wood, McAloon, Ballantyne*)
Clydebank: Gallacher; Fallon, Abel, Fanning, McCormack, Given, McDougall, Houston, Miller, Brown, Colgan.
Queen's Park: Atkins; McSkimming, Dickson, Wylie, Bowie, McAloon, Wood, Reynolds, Ballantyne, Sinclair, Wilkie.

Meadowbank T (1) 2 (*Hancock J, pen, Davidson*)
Spartans (0) 1 (*Arnott*)   2000
Meadowbank T: Allan; Leetion, Fraser, Stewart (O'Rourke), Wight, Conroy, McKenzie (Hancock S), Hancock J, Small, Davidson, Johnston R.
Spartans: Tevendale; Hepburn, Brough, Beattie, Gardner, Bell (Dunnett), Smith, White (Morrison), Arnott, Costello, McKinnon.

Montrose (1) 2 (*Miller, Murray*)
Celtic (0) 4 (*McCluskey 3, Lynch pen*)   3066
Montrose: Gorman; D'Arcy B, Johnston, Ford, D'Arcy D, Hair, McIntosh, Robb, Livingstone (Murray), Lowe, Miller.
Celtic: Latchford; McGrain, Lynch, Filippi, McDonald, Edvaldsson, Provan, MacLeod, McCluskey, Lennox, Doyle.

12 FEB

Ayr U (0) 4 (*McCLelland, McLaughlin 2, Phillips*)
Queen of the S (0) 0   2750
Ayr U: Sproat; Wells, Kelly (McColl), Fleeting, McAllister, McSherry, Phillips, McLaughlin, McLelland, Cramond, Christie.
Queen of the S: Clark D; McChesney, Cloy, Clark R, Boyd (Mitchell), Ferrie, Dempster, Pollock (Dickson P), Bryce, Coughlin, Halley.

Rangers (1) 3 (*Johnstone, Cooper, Jackson*)
Motherwell (0) 1 (*Clinging*)   12,000
Rangers: McCloy; Jardine, Dawson, Forsyth T, Jackson, MacDonald, McLean, Russell, Johnstone, Watson, Cooper.
Motherwell: Rennie; Boyd, Wark, Smith, McVie, Stevens, Millar, Pettigrew, Larnach, Clinging, Wilson.

19 FEB

Dumbarton (0) 1 (*Gallagher B*)
Alloa (0) 0 1000
Dumbarton: Hunter; Sinclair, McNeil, McCluskey, Gallacher J, MacLeod, Brown, Fyfe, Gallagher B, Blair, Whiteford D.
Alloa: McNab; Henderson, Wallace, McGarry, Holt, Miller, Cochrane, Lawson, Morrison, Irvine, Carberry.

Morton (1) 1 (*Ritchie pen*)
St Johnstone (1) 1 (*Brogan*) 3963
Morton: Brcic; Hayes, Holmes, Anderson, Orr, McLaren, Russell, Miller, Thomson, Scott, Ritchie.
St Johnstone: Geoghegan; Weir, McNeil, Muir, Hamilton G (Montgomery), Rutherford, Pelosi, Brogan, Brannigan, Hamilton J, Lawson.

Stirling Albion (0) 0
Patrick T (0) 2 (*Somner pen, Melrose*) 3000
Stirling Albion: Young; Nicol, Steedman, Duffin, Kennedy, Moffat, McPhee, Watson (Heggie), Steele, McLeod (Browning), Armstrong.
Patrick T: Rough; McKinnon, Whittaker, Anderson, McAdam (Melrose), Campbell, Houston, Somner, Marr, O'Hara, Park.

25 FEB

Dundee (0) 1 (*Pirie pen*)
Falkirk (0) 0 9671
Dundee: Donaldson; Barr, Schaedler, McLaren, Glennie, Watson, Murphy, Lamb (Scrimgeour), Pirie, Shirra, Redford (Davidson).
Falkirk: McKell; Johnston, Burrell (Thomson) (Leetion), Hay, Brown, Stevenson, Hoggan, Oliver, McRoberts, McCallan, Perry.

26 FEB

Dundee U (0) 0
St Mirren (0) 2 (*Fitzpatrick, Stark*) 9279
Dundee U: McAlpine; Stark, Kopel, Phillip, Hegarty, Narey, Addison, Stewart, Sturrock, Kirkwood, Payne.
St Mirren: Thomson; Beckett, Munro, Fitzpatrick, Dunlop, Copland, Richardson, Stark, Bone, Torrance, McGarvey.

THIRD ROUND, REPLAYS

12 FEB

Hibernian (0) 2 (*MacLeod, Callachan*)
Dunfermline Ath (0) 0 5000
Hibernian: McArthur; Brazil, Duncan, Bremner, Stewart, McNamara, Murray, MacLeod, Hutchinson, Callachan, Lambie.
Dunfermline Ath: Whyte; Scott (Borthwick), Mercer, Thomson, Salton, Hunter, Mullin (McLaren), Robertson R, Leonard, Docherty, Hegarty.

Queen's Park (0) 0
Clydebank (0) 1 (*McCormack*) 828
Queen's Park: Atkins; McSkimming, Dickson, Wylie, Bowie, McAloon, Wood, Reynolds, Ballantyne, Sinclair, Wilkie.
Clydebank: Gallacher; Hall, Abel, Fallon, Fanning, Houston, McDougall, McCormack, Miller, Brown, Colgan (Ross).

26 FEB

St Johnstone (1) 2 (*Thomas, Lawson*)
Morton (2) 4 (*Scott, Ritchie* 3, *1 pen*) 3224
St Johnstone: Geoghegan; Weir, McNeil, Muir, Hamilton G, Rutherford, Pelosi (Thomas), Brogan, Brannigan, Hamilton J (Montgomery), Lawson.
Morton: Connaghan; Hayes, Holmes, Anderson, Orr, McLaren, McNeil, Hutchison, Thomson, Scott, Ritchie (Russell).

FOURTH ROUND

21 FEB

Aberdeen (4) 6 (*Archibald* 2, *Scanlon* 2, *McMaster, Harper*)
Ayr U (0) 2 (*Phillips, McLaughlin, pen*) 12,500
Aberdeen: Clark; Kennedy, Considine, McMaster, Rougvie, Miller, Sullivan (Harper), Archibald (Cooper), Scanlon, Jarvie, Strachan.
Ayr U: Sproat; Wells, Kelly, Fleeting, McAllister, McSherry, Phillips, McLaughlin, Connor, Cramond, Christie.

Meadowbank T (0) 0
Hibernian (2) 6 (*MacLeod* 2, *Higgins, Brazil, Duncan, Callachan*) 5029
Meadowbank T: Allan; O'Rourke, Fraser, Stewart, Wight, Conroy (McKenna), Hancock J, McKenzie, Johnston (Davidson), Leetion, Small.
Hibernian: McArthur; Brazil, Duncan, Bremner, Stewart (Rae), McNamara, Murray, McLeod, Hutchinson (Higgins), Callachan, Lambie.

Rangers (1) 1 (*McDonald*)
Kilmarnock (0) 1 (*Bourke*) 17,500
Rangers: McCloy; Jardine, Dawson, Forsyth T (Miller), Jackson, MacDonald, McLean, Russell, Johnstone, Watson (Smith), Cooper.
Kilmarnock: McCulloch; McLean, Robertson, Clark J, Clarke P, McDicken, Gibson, Maxwell (Jardine), Bourke, Mauchlen, Street (Cairney).

24 FEB

Dumbarton (1) 3 (*Sharp* 2, *Blair*)
Clydebank (1) 1 (*McDougall*) 3000
Dumbarton: Hunter; Sinclair, McNeil, McCluskey, Gallacher J, Coyle, Brown, Gallagher B, Sharp, Blair, Whiteford D.
Clydebank: Gallacher; Hall, Abel, Fallon, McCormack, Fanning, McDougal, Houston, Miller, Given, Colgan (Brown).

Partick T (2) 3 (*McAdam* 2, *Somner pen*)
Airdrieonians (0) 0 7000
Partick T: Rough; McKinnon, Whittaker, Anderson, McAdam (Melrose), Campbell, Houston, Somner, Marr, O'Hara (Gibson), Park.
Airdrieonians: McGarr; Jonquin, Docherty (March), Anderson, Black, Lapsley, McCann (McGuire), McCulloch, Ross, Walker, Clark.

26 FEB

Celtic (1) 3 (*Lynch pen, Burns, McDowell (og)*)
Berwick R (0) 0 13,000
Celtic: Latchford; McGrain, Lynch, Aitken, McDonald, Edvaldsson, Provan, MacLeod, McCluskey, (McAdam) Burns, Doyle.
Berwick R: Frame; Rutherford, McLeod, Smith D, McDowell, Jobson, Davidson, Moyes, Smith G, Tait, Wheatley.

3 MAR
Dundee (2) 4 (*Pirie pen, Lamb, Sinclair* 2)
St Mirren (0) 1 (*Munro*) 11,140
Dundee: Donaldson; Barr, Schaedler, McLaren, Glennie, Watson, Murphy, Lamb, Pirie, Sinclair, Shirra.
St Mirren: Thomson; Beckett, Munro, Fitzpatrick, Dunlop, Copland, Richardson, Stark (Torrance), Bone, Abercromby, McGarvey.

Hearts (1) 1 (*Gibson, pen*)
Morton (0) 1 (*Anderson*) 9000
Hearts: Dunlop; Kidd, Brown, Liddell, Jefferies, Craig, Gibson, Fraser, O'Connor, Shaw, Robertson.
Morton: Connaghan; Hayes, Holmes, Anderson, Orr, McLaren, McNeil (Tolmie), Hutchison, Thomson, Scott, Ritchie.

FOURTH ROUND, REPLAYS

26 FEB
Kilmarnock (0) 0
Rangers (1) 1 (*Urquhart*) 16,000
Kilmarnock: McCulloch; McLean, Robertson, Clark J, Clarke P, McDicken, Gibson, Maxwell, Bourke, Mauchlen, Street.
Rangers: McCloy; Jardine, Dawson, Forsyth T, Jackson, MacDonald, Smith, Russell, Johnstone, Urquhart, Cooper.

5 MAR
Morton (0) 0
Hearts (0) 1 (*Busby*) 8000
Morton: Connaghan; Hayes, Holmes, Anderson, Orr, Rooney, McNeil, Miller, Evans, Scott, Ritchie.
Hearts: Brough; Kidd, Brown, Liddell, Jefferies, Craig, Gibson, Fraser, O'Connor, Busby, Robertson.

QUARTER-FINALS

10 MAR
Aberdeen (1) 1 (*Harper*)
Celtic (1) 1 (*Doyle*) 25,000
Aberdeen: Clark; Kennedy, McLelland, McMaster, McLeish, Miller, Sullivan, Archibald, Harper, Scanlon (Davidson), Strachan.
Celtic: Latchford; McGrain, Lynch, Aitken, McDonald, Edvaldsson, Provan, MacLeod, Conn, Burns, Doyle.

Dumbarton (0) 0
Partick T (0) 1 (*Anderson*) 6360
Dumbarton: Hunter; Sinclair, McNeil, McCluskey, Gallacher J, Coyle, Brown, Gallagher B, Sharp, Blair, Whiteford D.
Partick T: Rough; McKinnon, Whittaker, Marr, Campbell, Anderson, Houston, Somner, McAdam, Dickson (O'Hara), Park.

Hibernian (1) 2 (*Stewart, Rae*)
Hearts (0) 1 (*O'Connor*) 22,618
Hibernian: McArthur; Brazil, Duncan, Bremner, Stewart, McNamara, Rae, MacLeod, Hutchison, Callachan, Higgins.
Hearts: Brough; Brown, Black, Liddell, Jefferies, Craig, Gibson (McQuade), Kidd, O'Connor, Busby (Shaw), Robertson.

Rangers (5) 6 (*Jardine pen, Forsyth T, Smith, MacDonald, Russell, Cooper*)
Dundee (2) 3 (*McLaren 2, Shirra*) 25,000
Rangers: McCloy; Jardine, Dawson (Forsyth A), Denny, Forsyth T, MacDonald, McLean, Russell, Urquhart, Smith, Cooper.
Dundee: Donaldson; Barr, Schaedler, McLaren, Glennie, Watson, Lamb, Sinclair, Pirie, Shirra, Murphy (Redford).

QUARTER-FINAL, REPLAY

14 MAR
Celtic (0) 1 (*Lennox*)
Aberdeen (2) 2 (*Davidson, Archibald*) 37,000
Celtic: Latchford; McGrain, Lynch, Aitken, McDonald, Edvaldsson, Provan, MacLeod, Conn (Lennox), Burns, Doyle.
Aberdeen: Clark; Kennedy, McLelland, McMaster, Rougvie, Miller, Sullivan (McLeish), Archibald, Harper (Scanlon), Jarvie, Davidson.

SEMI-FINALS

4 APR
Partick T (0) 0 (*at Hampden Park*)
Rangers (0) 0 26,232
Partick T: Rough; McKinnon, Whittaker, Campbell, Anderson, Gibson, O'Hara (Houston), Melrose, McAdam, Love, Park.
Rangers: McCloy; Jardine, Dawson, Johnstone, Jackson, MacDonald, McLean, Russell, Urquhart, Smith, Cooper.

11 APR
Aberdeen (1) 1 (*Archibald*) (*at Hampden Park*)
Hibernian (2) 2 (*Rae, MacLeod pen*) 9837
Aberdeen: Gardiner; Kennedy, McLelland (Hamilton), Watson (McLeish), Rougvie, Miller, Strachan, Archibald, Harper, Jarvie, Scanlon.
Hibernian: McArthur; Brazil, Duncan, Bremner, Stewart, McNamara, Rae, MacLeod, Campbell, Callachan, Brown.

SEMI-FINAL, REPLAY

16 APR
Partick T (0) 0 (*at Hampden Park*)
Rangers (0) 1 (*Johnstone*) 32,300
Partick T: Rough; McKinnon, Whittaker, Campbell, Anderson (Marr), Gibson (O'Hara), Houston, Melrose, Somner, Love, Park.
Rangers: McCloy; Jardine, Dawson, Johnstone, Jackson, MacDonald, McLean, Russell, Parlane, Smith, Cooper.

FINAL

12 MAY
Hibernian (0) 0 (*at Hampden Park*)
Rangers (0) 0 50,610
Hibernian: McArthur; Brazil, Duncan, Bremner, Stewart, McNamara, Hutchinson (Rae), MacLeod, Campbell, Callachan, Higgins.
Rangers: McCloy; Jardine, Dawson, Johnstone, Jackson, MacDonald (Miller), McLean, Russell, Parlane, Smith, Cooper.
Referee: Mr B R McGinlay (Glasgow).

FINAL, REPLAY

16 MAY
Hibernian (0) 0 (*at Hampden Park*)
Rangers (0) 0 aet 33,504
Hibernian: McArthur; Brazil, Duncan, Bremner, Stewart, McNamara, Rae, MacLeod, Campbell, Callachan, Higgins (Brown).
Rangers: McCloy; Jardine, Dawson, Johnstone, Jackson, MacDonald, McLean (Miller), Russell, Parlane, Smith, Cooper.
Referee: Mr B R McGinlay (Glasgow)

FINAL, 2ND REPLAY

28 MAY
Hibernian (1) 2 (*Higgins,* (*at Hampden Park*)
MacLeod, pen)
Rangers (1) 3 (*Johnstone 2, Duncan (og) aet* 30,602
Hibernian: McArthur; Brazil, Duncan, Bremner, Stewart, McNamara, Rae, MacLeod, Campbell, Callachan (Brown), Higgins (Hutchinson).
Rangers: McCloy; Jardine, Dawson, Johnstone, Jackson, Watson (Miller), McLean (Smith), Russell, Parlane, MacDonald, Cooper.
Referee: Mr I M D Foote (Glasgow).

Scottish League Cup 1978-79

FIRST ROUND

First Leg, 16 AUG
Alloa (1) 4 (*Morrison, Cochrane, Miller 2, 1 pen*)
Stirling Albion (1) 1 (*McPhee*) 1250
Alloa: McNab; McCann, Henderson (Holt), Lawson, Hamilton, Miller, Cochrane, Carberry, Kelly, Morrison, Donald (Wallace).
Stirling Albion: Young G; Watson, Steedman, Young R, Kennedy (Duffin), Moffat, McPhee, Browning, Gray, Thomson, Armstrong.

Berwick R (1) 2 (*McLean 2*)
St Johnstone (0) 0 1473
Berwick R: Frame; Laing, Walker, Smith, Rutherford, Morton, Penman, McLean, Romaines, Tait, McLeod.
St Johnstone: Geoghegan; Mackay, McNeil, Weir, Rutherford, Houston, Thomas, Brogan, O'Connor, Gray, Muir.

Celtic (0) 3 (*McAdam 2, Glavin*)
Dundee (0) 1 (*Sinclair*) 12,000
Celtic: Latchford; Filippi, Sneddon, Aitken, McDonald, Edvaldsson, Doyle, Glavin, McAdam, Burns, Conn.
Dundee: Donaldson; Barr, Watson, Glennie, McDougall, McPhail, Lamb (Shirra), McKinnon, Sinclair, McGhee, Redford.

Dumbarton (0) 0
St Mirren (0) 0 4000
Dumbarton: Williams, Sinclair, McNeil, McCluskey Gallacher J, MacLeod M, Brown, Fyfe, Gallagher B, Blair, Whiteford D.
St Mirren: McLean; Young, Munro, McGettrick, Dunlop, Copland, Torrance, Weir, Bone, Abercromby, McGarvey.

Montrose (2) 4 (*Murray, Hair, Livingstone 2*)
Queen of the S (0) 0 970
Montrose: Gorman; Lowe, D'Arcy B, Hair, D'Arcy D, Johnston, McIntosh, Ford, Livingstone, Walker, Murray.
Queen of the S: Ball; McChesney, Thorburn, Clark, McMillan, Dickson G, Mitchell, Dickson P, Pollock, Bryce, Ferrie.

Rangers (2) 3 (*Parlane, Smith, Johnstone*)
Albion R (0) 0 10,000
Rangers: McCloy; Jardine, Forsyth A, Forsyth T, Johnstone, MacDonald, McLean, Russell (Miller), Parlane, Smith, Cooper (Urquhart).
Albion R: Orr; Muldoon, Main, Franchetti, Shields, Leishman, Allan, Hill, Cleland, Hart (McKee), Loughran (Coyle).

Second Leg, 23 AUG
Albion R (0) 0
Rangers (1) 1 (*Parlane*) 6500
Albion R: Orr; Muldoon, McGregor, Franchetti, Leishman, Allan, Hill, Hart, Coyle, McGillivray, Loughran.
Rangers: McCloy; Jardine, Forsyth A, Forsyth T, (Miller), Johnstone, MacDonald, Strickland, Russell, Parlane, Smith, Urquhart.

Dundee (0) 0
Celtic (2) 3 (*Doyle 2, Conn*) 12,698
Dundee: Donaldson; Barr, Watson, Lamb, Glennie, Phillip, McGhee, McGhee, Shirra, Sinclair, Redford.
Celtic: Latchford; Filippi, Lynch, Aitken, McDonald, Edvaldsson, Doyle (Casey), Glavin, McAdam, Burns, Conn

Queen of the S (0) 0
Montrose (0) 1 (*Murray*) 1500
Queen of the S: Ball; McChesney, Thorburn, Clark, Boyd, Dickson G, Mitchell, Dickson P, Pollock, Bryce, Halley.
Montrose: Gorman; Lowe, D'Arcy B, Hair (Livingstone), D'Arcy D, Ford, McIntosh, Joss, Murray, Walker, Miller.

St Johnstone (0) 0
Berwick R (0) 0 1500
St Johnstone: Geoghegan; Mackay, McNeil, Rutherford, McLellan, Houston, Thomas, Weir (Muir), Brogan, O' Connor, Lawson (Salisbury).
Berwick R: Frame; Laing, Walker, McDowell, Rutherford, Morton, Smith D, McLean, Romaines, Tait, McLeod.

St Mirren (1) 2 (*Bone 2*)
Dumbarton (0) 0 6000
St Mirren: Thomson; Beckett, Munro, Fitzpatrick Dunlop, Young, Hyslop, Abercromby, Bone Richardson, McGarvey.
Dumbarton: Williams; MacLeod A, McNeil, McCluskey, Gallacher J, MacLeod M, Brown, Fyfe, Gallagher B, Blair, Coyle

Stirling Albion (0) 0
Alloa (0) 1 (*Steele*) 1600
Stirling Albion: Young; Brown, Steedman, Watson, Nicol, Moffat, McPhee, Browning (Steele), Heggie, Thomson, Armstrong.
Alloa: McNab; McCann, Henderson (Wallace), McGarry, Hamilton, Miller, Steele, Carberry, Kelly, Irvine, Morrison.

SECOND ROUND

First Leg, 28 AUG
Montrose (1) 1 (*Livingstone*)
East Stirling (0) 1 (*Docherty*) 950
Montrose: Gorman; Lowe, D'Arcy B, Hair, D'Arcy D, Johnston, McIntosh, Ford (Kyles), Livingstone, Walker, Miller.
East Stirling: Morrison; Stirling, Eccles, Bennett, Simpson, Whiteford, McCulley, Tempany, Docherty, Grant, Ashwood.

30 AUG
Airdrieonians (1) 3 (*Lapsley pen, Jonquin, Goldthorp*)
Dunfermline Ath (0) 0 2500
Airdrieonians: Poulton; Jonquin, Lapsley, Walker, Black, Anderson, McCann, Clark, Goldthorp, Smith, McGuire.
Dunfermline Ath: Whyte; Rolland, Mercer, Thomson, Salton, Borthwick, Mullin, Dickson, Leonard, Robertson R, Dunn

Ayr U (0) 1 (*McLaughlin*)
Stranraer (0) 0 2000
Ayr U: Stewart; Wells, Connor, McColl, McAllister, Masterton, McLaughlin, McSherry, McLelland, Christie, Cramond.
Stranraer: Taylor; Hopkins, McDonald, Hay, Muir, Tait, Steen, Harvey, Mills, McGuigan, Robertson.

Berwick R (1) 1 (*McLean*)
St Mirren (1) 3 (*Richardson, Bone, Stark*)   2500
Berwick R: Frame; Rutherford, Walker, Smith D, McDowell, Morton, Moyes, McLean, Romaines, Tait, McLeod.
St Mirren: Thomson; Beckett, Munro, Fitzpatrick, Dunlop, Copland, Richardson, Stark, Bone, Abercromby, McGarvey.

Brechin C (0) 0
Hibernian (1) 3 (*Callachan, Rae, Smith*)   1645
Brechin C: Robertson; Watt, Reid, McLeod, Sime, Cairns, Robb, Elvin, Gillespie, Campbell R, Campbell I.
Hibernian: McDonald; Kilgour, Smith, Bremner, Fleming (Rae), McNamara, O'Brien, MacLeod, Duncan, Callachan, Higgins.

Clyde (2) 3 (*Ahern pen, Ward, O'Neill*)
Motherwell (1) 1 (*Marinello pen*)   4000
Clyde: Arrol; Kinnear, Anderson, Clougherty, Brogan, Ahern, Marshall, O'Neill, Hood, McCabe, Ward.
Motherwell: Latchford; Millar, Wark, Boyd, Mackin, Stevens, Marinello, Pettigrew, Larnach, McLaren, Lindsay.

Cowdenbeath (2) 3 (*Steele pen, Harley 2*)
Hamilton A (1) 2 (*Howie, Davies og*)   600
Cowdenbeath: McGarr; Thomson, Carpenter, Fair, Davies, Dyce, Harley, Milne, Marshall, Purdie, Steele.
Hamilton A: Ferguson; McQuade, Young, Fairlie, Dempsey, Alexander, Grant, Graham, Howie, Weir (Wright), McManus.

Dundee U (1) 2 (*Sturrock, Fleming*)
Celtic (1) 3 (*Conroy, McDonald, Lynch*)   12,648
Dundee U: McAlpine; Stewart, Kopel, Fleming, Hegarty, Narey, Sturrock, Addison, Frye (Kirkwood), Holt, Payne.
Celtic: Latchford; Filippi, Lynch, Aitken, McDonald, Edvaldsson, Doyle, Conroy, McAdam, Burns, Conn (Wilson).

East Fife (0) 0
Arbroath (1) 1 (*McKenzie*)   914
East Fife: Blair; Morris, Gillies, Dickson, Methven, Clarke, Huskie (Gibson), Cooper, Mackie, Cairns, Halley.
Arbroath: Lister; McKenzie, Rylance, Cargill, Wells, Fettes, Fletcher (Mylles), Kydd (Grant) Gavine, Kidd, Yule.

Hearts (0) 1 (*Shaw*)
Morton (0) 3 (*McNeil, Ritchie pen, Scott*)   7000
Hearts: Brough; Brown J, Jefferies, McNicoll, Liddell, Shaw, Robertson, Bannon (Busby), Gibson, Tierney, Prentice (Smith).
Morton: Connaghan; Hayes, Holmes, Anderson, Orr, Rooney (McNeil), Russell (Rae), Miller, Thomson, Scott, Ritchie.

Kilmarnock (2) 2 (*Street, McDowell*)
Alloa (0) 0   2100
Kilmarnock: McCulloch; Welsh, Robertson, Street, Clarke P, McDicken, McDowell, Maxwell, Cairney, Clark J, McLean.
Alloa: McNab; McCann, Wallace, McGarry, Hamilton, Miller, Steele, Carberry, Kelly, Irvine, Morrison (Henderson).

Meadowbank T (0) 0
Aberdeen (3) 5 (*Fleming, Archibald, Sullivan, Kennedy, Jarvie*)   1000
Meadowbank T: Sinclair; O'Rourke, Fraser, Stewart, Wight, Carr, Leetion, Hancock J, Adair (Downie), Davidson, Hancock S.
Aberdeen: Gardiner; Kennedy, McLelland, McMaster, Garner, Miller, Sullivan, Archibald (Fleming), Harper, Jarvie (Strachan), Scanlon.

Patrick T (0) 1 (*McRoberts og*)
Falkirk (0) 1 (*McRoberts*)   3500
Patrick T: Rough; Campbell, Whittaker, Marr, McAdam, O'Hara, Houston, Melrose, McQuade, Somner (Mackie), Craig.
Falkirk: McKell; Johnston, Burrell, Hay, Hamilton, Stevenson, Perry (Thomson), Hoggan, McRoberts, McCallan, Mitchell.

Rangers (2) 3 (*Smith, Cooper, McLean*)
Forfar Ath (0) 0   5000
Rangers: McCloy; Jardine, Forsyth A, Jackson, Johnstone, MacDonald, McLean, Russell, Parlane (Urquhart), Smith, Cooper.
Forfar Ath: McWilliams; Bennett, Cameron, Knox, Brown, Rae, Hall, Gallacher, Reid, Henry (Brash), Kinnear.

Raith R (3) 4 (*Wallace 4*)
Queen's Park (1) 2 (*Ballantyne, McDonald*)   2000
Raith R: McDermott; Urquhart, Candlish, Forsyth, Houston, McFarlane, Wallace, Thomson, Harrow, Murray, Duncan.
Queen's Park: Preston; McSkimming, Dickson, Reynolds, McPherson, McAloon, Wood, McDonald, Horn, Ballantyne, Wilkie.

Stenhousemuir (0) 1 (*Gibb*)
Clydebank (0) 0   500
Stenhousemuir: Wilson B, Rose, Scott, Gordon, Sage, Mullen, Wilson F, Feeney, Gibb, Jenkins, Sweeney.
Clydebank: Gallacher; Hall, Abel, Fallon, McCormack, Fanning, Brown (McDougall), Houston, Miller, Given, McCulloch (Colgan).

Second Leg, 2 SEPT

Aberdeen (2) 4 (*Archibald, Harper 2, Scanlon*)
Meadowbank T (0) 0   6850
Aberdeen: Leighton; Kennedy, McLelland, McMaster, Garner, Miller, Sullivan (Strachan), Archibald Harper, Jarvie, Scanlon.
Meadowbank T: Sinclair; O'Rourke, Fraser, Stewart (Mooney), Wight, Carr, Leetion, Hancock J, Hancock S, Downie, Davidson (Johnston)

Alloa (0) 1 (*Morrison*)
Kilmarnock (1) 1 (*Cairney*)   1300
Alloa: McNab; Henderson (Holt), Wallace, McCann, Hamilton, Miller, Cochrane (Donald), Carberry, Kelly, Irvine, Morrison.
Kilmarnock: McCulloch; McLean, Robertson, Jardine, Clarke P, McDicken, Street, McDowell, Cairney, Maxwell, Clark J.

Arbroath (0) 1 (*Cargill*)
East Fife (0) 0   1006
Arbroath: Lister; McKenzie, Rylance, Cargill, Wells, Fettes, Grant, Carson (Kydd), Gavine, Kidd, Yule (Mylles).
East Fife: Blair; Morris, Gillies, Dickson, Methven, Clarke, Gibson (Huskie), Cooper, Mackie, Cairns, Halley.

Celtic (0) 1 (*Glavin pen*)
Dundee U (0) 0   30,000
Celtic: Latchford; Filippi, Lynch, Aitken, McDonald (Glavin), Edvaldsson, Doyle, Conroy, McAdam, Burns, Wilson (McCluskey).
Dundee U: McAlpine; Stewart, Kopel, Fleming Hegarty, Narey, Sturrock, Addison (Kirkwood), Frye, Holt, Payne.

Cldebank (2) 4 (*McCormack, Miller 2, McDougall*)
Stenhousemuir (1) 1 (*Sweeney*)   1000
Clydebank: Gallacher; Hall, Abel, Fallon, McCormack, Fanning, McDougall, Houston, Miller, Given, Colgan.
Stenhousemuir: Wilson B; Rose, Scott, Gordon, Sage, Mullen, Wilson F, Feeney, Gibb, Jenkins (Halliday), Sweeney.

Dunfermline Ath (0) 0
Airdrieonians (1) 5 (*Goldthorpe, Walker 2, Lapsley pen, Clark*)   2200
Dunfermline Ath: Whyte; Rolland, Mercer, Thomson, Salton, Borthwick, Bowie (Robertson R), Dickson (Ross), Leonard, Dunn, Mullin.
Airdrieonians: Poulton; Jonquin, Lapsley, Walker, Black, Anderson, McCann, Clark, Goldthorp, Smith, McGuire.

East Stirling (0) 0
Montrose (0) 2 (*Livingstone, Robb*) aet   250
East Stirling: Morrison; Stirling Eccles, Tempany (Lamont), Simpson, Whiteford, Grant, McCulley, Docherty, Bennett, Ashwood (Hotchkiss).
Montrose: Gorman; Lowe, D'Arcy B, Walker (Joss), D'Arcy D, Johnston, Miller, Kyles, Murray, Livingstone, Robb.

Falkirk (1) 2 (*Hoggan, Sheed og*) aet
Partick T (1) 2 (*Gibson, Craig*) (*Falkirk won on pens*)   5000
Falkirk: McKell; Johnston, Burrell, Hay, Hamilton, Hoggan, Perry (Thomson), McCallan, Leetion (Stevenson), McRoberts, Mitchell.
Partick T: Rough; Mackie (Sheed), Whittaker, Marr, Campbell, Gibson (Melrose), Houston, O'Hara, McAdam, Somner, Craig.

Forfar Ath (0) 1 (*Rae*)
Rangers (1) 4 (*MacDonald, Cooper, Smith 2*) 5919
Forfar Ath: McWilliams; Bennett, Cameron, Brown K, Brash, Rae, Gallacher, Knox, Reid (Kinnear), Henry, Hall.
Rangers: McCloy; Jardine, Forsyth A, Jackson (Smith), Johnstone, MacDonald, McLean, Russell (Denny), Parlane, Miller, Cooper.

Hamilton A (1) 2 (*Howie, Wright*)
Cowdenbeath (0) 0   1200
Hamilton A: Ferguson; McQuade, Wright, Fairlie, Dempsey, Alexander, Grant (Reilly), Graham, Bowie, Young, McManus.
Cowdenbeath: McGarr; Dyce, Carpenter (Ward), Fair, Davies, Markey (Caithness), Harley, Milne, Marshall, Purdie, Steele.

Hibernian (1) 3 (*MacLeod 2, Callachan*)
Brechin C (1) 1 (*Campbell R*)   5254
Hibernian: McDonald; Bremner, Smith, Rae, Stewart, McNamara, O'Brien, MacLeod, Duncan, Callachan, Higgins.
Brechin C: Robertson; Watt, Reid, McLeod, Sime, Cairns, Robb, Elvin, Gillespie (Brown), Campbell R, Campbell I.

Morton (1) 4 (*Anderson, Ritchie, Russell 2*)
Hearts (1) 1 (*Bannon pen*)   5000
Morton: Connaghan; Hayes, Holmes, Anderson (McNeil), Orr, Rooney, Russell, Miller (Rae), Thomson, Scott, Ritchie.
Hearts: Brough; Brown, Rodger, McNicoll, Jefferies, Liddell, Park, Bannon, Busby, Smith, Robertson.

Motherwell (1) 3 (*Marinello, Pettigrew, Clinging*)
Clyde (0) 0   3803
Motherwell: Latchford; Millar, Wark, Boyd (McLeod), McVie, Stevens, Marinello, Pettigrew, Larnach, McLaren, Clinging.
Clyde: Arrol; Kinnear, Anderson, Clougherty, Brogan, Ahern, Hood, O'Neill, Marshall, McCabe (Martin), Ward.

Queen's Park (1) 4 (*Horn, Wilkie, Ballantyne 2*)
aet (Raith won on pens)
Raith R (1) 2 (*Harrow, Forrest*)   1084
Queen's Park: Preston; McSkimming, Dickson, Reynolds, McPherson, McAloon, Wood, McDonald (Nicholson), Horn, Ballantyne, Wilkie.
Raith R: McDermott; McDonough (Thomson D), Candlish, Forsyth, Houston, McFarlane, Wallace, Urquhart, Harrow, Murray (Duncan), Forrest.

St Mirren (3) 5 (*McGarvey 3, Hyslop 2*)
Berwick R (1) 1 (*Rutherford*)   5200
St Mirren: Thomson; Beckett, Munro, Fitzpatrick, Dunlop, Copland, Hyslop, Stark, Bone, Richardson, McGarvey.
Berwick R: Frame; Laing, Rutherford, McDowell, Tait, Smith D, Morton, McLean, Moyes, McLeod (Romaines), Smith I.

Stranraer (0) 1 (*Robertson*)
Ayr U (0) 3 (*McLelland 2, McLaughlin pen*)   1000
Stranraer: Taylor, Hopkins, McDonald, Hay, Muir Tait, Steen, McCutcheon (Calderwood), Mills, Milligan, Robertson.
Ayr U: Sproat; Wells, Connor, Hyslop, McAllister (McSherry), McColl, McLaughlin, Hannah, McLelland, Masterton (Christie), Cramond.

THIRD ROUND

First Leg, 4 OCT

Arbroath (0) 1 (*Gavine*)
Airdrieonians (0) 1 (*McCann*)   960
Arbroath: Lister; Follon, Rylance, Cargill, Wells, Fettes, Fletcher, McKenzie, Gavine (Mylles), Kidd, Yule.
Airdrieonians: Poulton; Jonquin, Lapsley, Walker, Black, Anderson, McCann, Clark, Goldthorp, Smith (March), Wilson.

Celtic (0) 0
Motherwell (0) 1 (*Pettigrew*)   19,000
Celtic: Latchford; Filippi, Lynch, Aitken, McDonald, Edvaldsson, Provan, Conroy (Glavin), McAdam (McCluskey), Burns, Conn.
Motherwell: Latchford; Shanks, Boyd, Capaldi (Larnach), McVie, Stevens, Marinello, Pettigrew, Clinging (McLeod), McLaren, Lindsay.

Falkirk (0) 0
Ayr U. (1) 2 (*McLaughlin, McCall*)   4500
Falkirk: McKell; Johnston, Stevenson, Oliver, Hamilton, Brown, Hoggan, Hay, McRoberts, McCallan, Mitchell.
Ayr U: Sproat; Wells, Connor, Hyslop (McColl), McAllister, McSherry, McCall, McLaughlin, Masterton, Cramond, Christie.

Hamilton A (0) 0
Aberdeen (1) 1 (*Scanlon*) 4500
Hamilton A: Ferguson; Grant, Kellachan, Fairlie, Dempsey, Alexander, Young (McGrogan), Graham Howie, Glavin, Reilly.
Aberdeen: Leighton; Kennedy, McLelland, McMaster, McLeish, Miller, Davidson, Strachan, Fleming, Jarvie, Scanlon.

Hibernian (1) 1 (*MacLeod pen*)
Clydebank (0) 0 5000
Hibernian: McDonald; Duncan, Smith, Rae, Fleming, McNamara, Murray, MacLeod, Hutchinson, Callachan, Higgins (Temperley).
Clydebank: Hunter; Hall, Abel, Fallon, McCormack, Fanning, McDougall, Houston, Miller, Given, Colgan.

Kilmarnock (2) 2 (*Cairney, Maxwell*)
Morton (0) 0 4000
Kilmarnock: McCulloch; McLean, Robertson, Jardine, Clarke P, McDicken, Doherty, McDowell, Cairney (Street), Maxwell, Clark J.
Morton: Connaghan; Miller, Holmes, McLaren, Orr, Rooney (Rae), Russell, McNeil, Thomson, Scott, Ritchie.

Raith R (2) 3 (*Harrow 2, Forrest*)
Montrose (0) 0 2310
Raith R: McDermott; Houston, Candlish, Forsyth, Taylor, McFarlane, Wallace, Urquhart, Harrow, Murray, Forrest.
Montrose: Gorman; Lowe, Johnston, Ford, D'Arcy D, Joss (Murray), McIntosh, D'Arcy B, Georgeson, Walker, Miller.

Rangers (0) 3 (*Cooper, Miller, Johnstone*)
St Mirren (1) 2 (*Fitzpatrick 2*) 18,000
Rangers: McCloy; Jardine, Forsyth A, Forsyth T, Miller, MacDonald (Cooper), McLean (Watson), Russell, Parlane, Johnstone, Smith.
St Mirren: Thomson; Beckett, Munro, Fitzpatrick, Dunlop, Copland, Hyslop, Stark, Bone, Abercromby, McGarvey.

Second Leg, 10 OCT
Airdrieonians (0) 1 (*Clark*)
Arbroath (2) 2 (*McKenzie, Yule*) 2000
Airdrieonians: Poulton; Jonquin, Lapsley, Clark, Goldthorp, McKeown, McGuire, Walker (Cowan), Black, Anderson, McCann (Henderson).
Arbroath: Lister; Follon, Rylance, Cargill, Wells (Carson), Fettes, Fletcher, McKenzie, Gavine, Kidd Yule.

11 OCT
Aberdeen (5) 7 (*Harper 4, 2 pens, Rougvie, Sullivan, Kennedy*)
Hamilton A (1) 1 (*Fairlie*) 10,000
Aberdeen: Leighton; Kennedy, McLelland, Rougvie (Strachan), McLeish, Miller, Sullivan, Archibald, Harper, Fleming, Scanlon (Simpson).
Hamilton A: Ferguson; Grant (McDowall), Kellachan, Fairlie, Dempsey, Alexander, Young, Graham, Howie, Glavin, Reilly (Wright).

Ayr U (0) 1 (*Cramond*)
Falkirk (0) 1 (*McRoberts*) 3800
Ayr U: Sproat; Wells, Kelly, McColl, McAllister, McSherry, McCall, McLaughlin, Masterton, Cramond, Christie.
Falkirk: McKell; Johnston, Stevenson, Hay, Hamilton, Brown, Perry, Hoggan, McRoberts, McCallan, Mitchell.

Clydebank (0) 1 (*McCormack pen*)
Hibernian (1) 1 (*Stewart*) 2500
Clydebank: Hunter; Gervaise (Brown), Abel, Hall, McCormack, Fanning, McDougall, Houston, Miller, Given, Colgan.
Hibernian: McDonald; Duncan, Smith, Rae, Stewart, McNamara, Campbell, MacLeod, Hutchinson, Callachan, Higgins.

Montrose (2) 5 (*Livingstone, Hair, Miller, Robb, Lowe pen*)
Raith R (1) 1 (*Wallace*) 1400
Montrose: Gorman; Lowe, D'Arcy B, Ford, D'Arcy D, Johnston, Livingstone, Hair, Georgeson (Robb), Walker, Miller.
Raith R: McDermott; Houston, Candlish, Forsyth, Taylor, McFarlane, Wallace, Urquhart, Harrow, Murray, Forrest.

Morton (1) 5 (*Scott 2, Thomson, Orr, Ritchie*)
Kilmarnock (1) 2 (*McDicken, Welsh*) 5000
Morton: Connaghan; Hayes, Holmes, McLaren, Orr, Miller, Russell, McNeil, Thomson, Scott, Ritchie.
Kilmarnock: McCulloch; Welsh, Robertson, Jardine, Clarke P, McDicken, Doherty, McDowell, Bourke, Maxwell, McLean.

Motherwell (0) 1 (*Marinello*)
Celtic (2) 4 (*McAdam 2, Lennox, Aitken*) 17,911
Motherwell: Latchford; Carr (McLeod), Wark, McLaren, McVie, Stevens, Marinello, Pettigrew, Larnach (Kennedy), Clinging, Lindsay.
Celtic: Latchford; Filippi, Burns, Aitken, McDonald, Edvaldsson, Provan, Conroy, McAdam, Glavin, Conn.

St Mirren (0)
Rangers (0) 0 16,000
St Mirren: Thomson; Young (Torrance), Munro, Fitzpatrick, Dunlop, Copland, Richardson, Stark, Bone, Abercromby, McGarvey.
Rangers: McCloy; Jardine, Forsyth A, Forsyth T, Jackson, MacDonald, Miller, Russell, Parlane, Johnstone, Smith.

QUARTER FINALS

First Leg, 8 NOV

Ayr U (1) 3 (*Cramond, McCall, McLelland*)
Aberdeen (2) 3 (*Sullivan, Harper 2*) 6300
Ayr U: Sproat; Wells, Connor, McColl, McAllister, McSherry, McCall, McLaughlin, McLelland, Cramond, Christie.
Aberdeen: Clark; Kennedy, McLelland, McMaster, (Fleming), McLeish, Miller, Strachan, Archibald, Harper, Jarvie, Sullivan.

Montrose (1) 1 (*Hair*)
Celtic (1) 1 (*Lynch, pen*) 3872
Montrose: Gorman; Lowe, D'Arcy B, Ford, D'Arcy D, Taylor, McIntosh (Georgeson), Robb, Livingstone, Hair, Miller.
Celtic: Baines; Filippi, Lynch, Aitken, McDonald, Edvaldsson, Provan (Doyle), Glavin (Casey), McAdam, Burns, McCluskey.

Morton (1) 1 (*Thomson*)
Hibernian (0) 0 8000
Morton: Connaghan; Hayes, Holmes, Evans, Orr, Rooney, Russell, Miller (McLaren), Thomson, Scott, Ritchie.
Hibernian: McDonald; Duncan, Smith, Fleming, Stewart, McNamara, Rae, MacLeod, Hutchinson, Bremner, Higgins (Campbell).

Rangers (0) 1 (*Wells og*)
Arbroath (0) 0   10,000
Rangers: McCloy; Jardine, Forsyth A, Forsyth T, Johnstone, MacDonald, McLean, Russell, Parlane (Armour), Smith, Watson.
Arbroath: Lister; McKenzie, Rylance, Cargill, Wells, Fettes, Fletcher, Edwards (Follon), Wilson, Carson, Yule.

Second Leg, 15 Nov
Aberdeen (2) 3 (*Harper, McLelland, Archibald*)
Ayr U (1) 1 (*McLaughlin*)   14,000
Aberdeen: Gardiner; Kennedy, McLelland, McMaster, Rougvie, Miller, Strachan, Fleming (Scanlon), Harper, Archibald, Sullivan.
Ayr U: Sproat; Wells, Connor, McColl, McAllister, Cramond (Phillips), McSherry, McLaughlin, McLelland, McCall, Christie.

Arbroath (1) 1 (*Flethcer*)
Rangers (1) 2 (*Smith, Russell*)   4000
Arbroath: Lister; McKenzie, Rylance, Cargill, Wells, Fettes (Follon), Kidd, Fletcher, Wilson, Carson (Gavine), Yule.
Rangers: McCloy; Miller, Forsyth A, Jardine, Forsyth T. (Cooper), Watson, McLean, Russell, Johnstone, Urquhart (MacDonald), Smith.

Celtic (3) 3 (*McAdam, Lynch pen, Edvaldsson*)
Montrose (0) 1 (*Georgeson*)   10,000
Celtic: Baines; McGrain, Lynch, Aitken, McDonald, Edvaldsson, Provan, Casey, McAdam (McCluskey), Lennox, Doyle.
Montrose: Gorman; Lowe, D'Arcy B, Ford, D'Arcy D, Hair, McIntosh, Robb, Georgeson, Walker, Livingstone (Murray).

Hibernian (1) 2 (*Refvik* 2)
Morton (0) 0   5000
Hibernian: McDonald, Duncan, Kilgour, Bremner, Fleming, McNamara, Mathison, MacLeod, Refvik, Callachan, Higgins.
Morton: Connaghan; Hayes, Holmes, Evans, Orr, Rooney, Russell, Miller, Thomson, Scott, Ritchie.

SEMI FINALS

13 DEC
(*At Dens Park*)
Aberdeen (0) 1 (*Kennedy*) aet
Hibernian (0) 0   21,048
Aberdeen: Clark; Kennedy, McLelland, Sullivan, Rougvie, Miller, Strachan, Archibald, Harper, Jarvie (McMaster), Scanlon (Cooper).
Hibernian: McDonald; Duncan, Kilgour, Bremner, Stewart, McNamara, Smith, MacLeod, Refvik (Higgins), Callachan, Hutchinson.

(*At Hampden Park*)
Celtic (1) 2 (*Doyle, McAdam*) aet
Rangers (1) 3 (*Jardine pen, Jackson, Casey og*) 49,432
Celtic: Baines; Filippi, Lynch, Aitken, McDonald, Edvaldsson, Provan, Conroy (Casey), McAdam, Burns, Doyle.
Rangers: McCloy; Miller, Dawson, Jardine, Jackson, MacDonald, McLean, Russell, Johnstone, Watson, Cooper (Smith).

FINAL

31 MAR
(*At Hampden Park*)
Aberdeen (0) 1 (*Davidson*)
Rangers (0) 2 (*McMaster og, Jackson*)   54,000
Aberdeen: Clark; Kennedy, McLelland, McMaster, Rougvie, Miller, Strachan, Archibald, Harper, Jarvie (McLeish), Davidson.
Rangers: McCloy; Jardine, Dawson, Johnstone, Jackson, MacDonald, McLean, Russell, Urquhart (Miller), Smith (Parlane), Cooper.
Referee: Mr I M D Foote (Glasgow)

Scottish League Cup Finals

1945–46 ABERDEEN Johnstone; Cooper, McKenna, Cowie, Dunlop, Taylor, Kiddie, Hamilton, Williams, Baird, McCall.
3–2 RANGERS John Shaw; David Gray, Jock Shaw, Watkins, Young, Symon, Waddell, Thornton, Arnison, Duncanson, Caskie. *Scorers:* Aberdeen—Baird, Williamson, Taylor, Rangers—Duncanson, Thornton.

1946–47 RANGERS Brown; Young, Jock Shaw, McColl, Woodburn, Rae, Rutherford, Gillick, Williamson, Thornton, Duncanson.
4–0 ABERDEEN Johnstone; Cooper, McKenna, McLaughlin, Dunlop, Taylor, Harris, Hamilton, Williams, Baird, McCall. *Scorers:* Rangers—Duncanson 2, Williamson, Gillick.

1947–48 EAST FIFE Niven; Laird, Stewart, Philip, Finlay, Aitken, Adams, Davidson (D), Norris, Davidson (J.) Duncan.
0–0 FALKIRK Dawson (J.): Whyte, McPhie, Bolt, Henderson (R.), Whitelaw, Fiddes, Fleck, Aikman, Henderson (J.), Dawson (K.).
EAST FIFE Niven; Laird, Stewart, Phillip, Finlay, Aitken, Adams, Davidson (D.), Norris, Davidson (J.), Duncan.
4–1 FALKIRK Dawson (J.); Whyte, McPhie, Bolt, Henderson (R.), Gallagher, Fiddes, Alison, Aikman, Henderson (J.), Dawson (K.). *Scorers* East Fife—Duncan 3, Adams, Falkirk—Aikman.

1948–49 RANGERS Brown; Young, Jock Shaw, McColl, Woodburn, Cox, Gillick, Paton, Thornton, Duncanson, Rutherford.
2–0 RAITH ROVERS Westland; McLure, McNaught, Young, Colville, Leigh, Hall, Collins, Penman, Brady, Joyner. *Scorers* Rangers—Gillick, Paton.

1949–50 EAST FIFE McGarrity; Laird, Stewart, Philip, Finlay, Aitken, Black, Fleming, Morris, Brown, Duncan.
3–0 DUNFERMLINE ATHLETIC Johnstone; Kirk, McLean, McCall, Clarkson, Whyte, Mayes, Cannon, Henderson, McGairy, Smith. *Scorers* East Fife—Fleming, Duncan, Morris.

1950–51 MOTHERWELL Johnstone; Kilmarnock, Shaw. McLeod, Paton, Redpath, Watters, Forrest, Kelly, Watson, Aitkenhead.
3–0 HIBERNIAN Younger; Govan, Ogilvie, Buchanan, Paterson, Combe, Smith, Johnstone, Reilly Ormond, Bradley. *Scorers:* Motherwell—Kelly, Forrest, Watters.

1951–52 DUNDEE Brown; Fallon, Cowan, Gallacher, Cowie, Boyd, Toner, Pattillo, Flavell, Steel, Christie.
3–2 RANGERS Brown; Young, Little, McColl, Woodburn, Cox, Waddell, Findlay, Thornton, Johnson, Rutherford. *Scorers:* Dundee—Flavell, Pattillo, Boyd. Rangers—Findlay, Thornton.

1952–53 DUNDEE Henderson (R.); Fallon, Frew, Ziesing, Boyd, Cowie, Toner, Henderson (A.), Flavell, Steel, Christie.
2–0 KILMARNOCK Niven; Collins, Hood, Russell, Thyne, Middlemass, Henaughan, Harvey, Mayes, Jack, Murray. *Scorer:* Dundee—Flavell 2.

1953–54 EAST FIFE Curran; Emery, Stewart (S.), Christie, Finlay, McLennan, Stewart (J.), Fleming, Bonthrone, Gardiner, Matthew.
3–2 PARTICK THISTLE Ledgerwood; McGowan, Gibb, Crawford, Davidson, Kerr, McKenzie, Howitt, Sharp, Wright, Walker. *Scorers:* East Fife—Gardiner, Fleming, Christie. Partick—Walker, McKenzie.

1954–55 HEARTS Duff; Parker, McKenzie, Mackay, Glidden, Cumming, Souness, Conn, Bauld, Wardhaugh, Urquhart.
4–2 MOTHERWELL Weir; Kilmarnock, McSeveney, Cox, Paton, Redpath, Hunter, Aitken, Bain, Humphries, Williams. *Scorers:* Hearts—Bauld 3, Wardhaugh. Motherwell—Redpath (pen.), Bain.

1955–56 ABERDEEN Martin; Mitchell, Caldwell, Wilson, Clunie, Glen, Leggat, Yorston, Buckley, Wisher, Hather.
2–1 ST MIRREN Lornie; Lapsley, Mallon, Neilson, Telfer, Holmes, Rodger, Laird, Brown, Gemmell, Callan. *Scorers:* Aberdeen—Mallon (o.g.), Leggat, St Mirren—Holmes.

1956–57 CELTIC Beattie; Haughney, Fallon, Evans, Jack, Peacock, Walsh, Collins, McPhail, Tully, Fernie.
0–0 PARTICK THISTLE Ledgerwood; Kerr, Gibb, Collins, Davidson, Mathers, McKenzie,
a.e.t. Smith (G.), Hogan, Wright, Ewing.
CELTIC Beattie; Haughney, Fallon, Evans, Jack, Peacock, Walsh, Collins, McPhail, Tully, Fernie.
3–0 PARTICK THISTLE Ledgerwood; Kerr, Gibb, Collins, Davidson, Mathers, McKenzie, Smith (G.), Hogan, Wright, Ewing. *Scorers:* Celtic—McPhail 2, Collins.

1957–58	CELTIC	Beattie; Donnelly, Fallon, Fernie, Evans, Peacock, Tully, Collins, McPhail, Wilson, Mochan.
7–1	RANGERS	Niven; Shearer, Caldow, McColl, Valentine, Davis, Scott, Simpson, Murray, Baird, Hubbard. *Scorers:* Celtic—Wilson, Mochan 2, McPhail 3, Fernie. Rangers—Simpson.
1958–59	HEARTS	Marshall; Kirk, Thomson, Mackay, Glidden, Cumming, Hamilton, Murray, Bauld, Wardhaugh, Crawford.
5–1	PARTICK THISTLE	Ledgerwood; Hogan, Donlevy, Mathers, Davidson, Wright, McKenzie, Thomson (L.), Smith, McParland, Ewing. *Scorers:* Hearts—Bauld 2, Murray 2, Hamilton. Partick—Smith.
1959–60	HEARTS	Marshall; Kirk, Thomson, Bowman, Cumming, Higgins, Smith, Crawford, Young, Blackwood, Hamilton.
2–1	THIRD LANARK	Robertson; Lewis, Brown, Reilly, McCallum, Cunningham, McInnes, Craig, Hilley (D.), Gray, Hilley (L.). *Scorers:* Hearts—Hamilton Young. Third Lanark—Gray.
1960–61	RANGERS	Niven; Shearer, Caldow, Davis, Paterson, Baxter, Scott, McMillan, Millar, Brand, Wilson.
2–0	KILMARNOCK	Brown (J.); Richmond, Watson, Beattie, Toner, Kennedy, Brown (H.), McInally, Kerr, Black, Muir. *Scorers:* Rangers—Brand, Scott.
1961–62	RANGERS	Ritchie, Shearer, Caldow, Davis, Paterson, Baxter, Scott, McMillan, Millar, Brand, Wilson.
1–1	HEARTS	Marshall; Kirk, Holt, Cumming, Polland, Higgins, Ferguson, Elliott, Wallace, Gordon, Hamilton. *Scorers:* Rangers—Millar (pen). Hearts—Cumming (pen.)
	RANGERS	Ritchie; Shearer, Caldow, Davis, Baillie, Baxter, Scott, McMillan, Millar, Brand, Wilson.
3–1	HEARTS	Cruickshank; Kirk, Holt, Cumming, Polland, Higgins, Ferguson, Davidson, Bauld, Blackwood, Hamilton. *Scorers:* Rangers—Millar, Brand, McMillan. Hearts—Davidson.
1962–63	HEARTS	Marshall; Polland, Holt, Cumming, Barry, Higgins, Wallace, Paton, Davidson, Hamilton (W.), Hamilton (J.)
1–0	KILMARNOCK	McLaughlan; Richmond, Watson, O'Connor, McGrory, Beattie, Brown, Black, Kerr, McInally, McIlroy. *Scorers:* Hearts—Davidson.
1963–64	RANGERS	Ritchie; Shearer, Provan, Greig, McKinnon, Baxter, Henderson, Willoughby, Forrest, Brand, Watson.
5–0	MORTON	Brown; Boyd, Mallon, Reilly, Kiernan, Strachan, Adamson, Campbell, Stevenson, McGraw, Wilson. *Scorers:* Rangers—Forrest 4, Willoughby.
1964–65	RANGERS	Ritchie; Provan, Caldow, Greig, McKinnon, Wood, Brand, Millar, Forrest, Baxter, Johnston.
2–1	CELTIC	Fallon; Young, Gemmell, Clark, Cushley, Kennedy, Johnstone, Murdoch, Chalmers, Divers, Hughes. *Scorers* Rangers—Forrest 2. Celtic—Johnstone.
1965–66	CELTIC	Simpson; Young, Gemmell, Murdoch, McNeill, Clark, Johnstone, Gallagher, McBride, Lennox, Hughes.
2–1	RANGERS	Ritchie; Johansen, Provan, Wood, McKinnon, Greig, Henderson, Willoughby, Forrest, Wilson, Johnston. *Scorers* Celtic—Hughes (2 pens.). Rangers—Young (o.g.)
1966–67	CELTIC	Simpson; Gemmell, O'Neill, Murdoch, McNeill, Clark, Johnstone, Lennox, McBride, Auld, Hughes. (Chalmers).
1–0	RANGERS	Martin; Johansen, Provan, Greig, McKinnon, Smith (D.), Henderson, Watson, McLean, Smith (A.), Johnston (Wilson). *Scorer* Celtic—Lennox.
1967–68	CELTIC	Simpson; Craig, Gemmell, Murdoch, McNeill, Clark, Chalmers, Lennox, Wallace, Auld (O'Neill), Hughes.
5–3	DUNDEE	Arrol; Wilson (R.), Houston, Murray, Stewart, Stuart, Campbell, McLean (J.), Wilson (S.), McLean (G.), Bryce. *Scorers:* Celtic—Chalmers 2, Wallace, Lennox, Hughes. Dundee—McLean (G.) 2, McLean (J.).
1968–69	CELTIC	Fallon; Craig, Gemmell (Clark), Murdoch, McNeill, Brogan, Johnstone, Wallace, Chalmers Auld, Lennox.
6–2	HIBERNIAN	Allan; Shevlane, Davis, Stanton, Madsen, Blackley, Marinello, Quinn, Cormack, O'Rourke Stevenson. *Scorers:* Celtic—Lennox 3, Wallace, Auld, Craig. Hibernian—O'Rourke, Stevenson.
1969–70	CELTIC	Fallon; Craig, Hay, Murdoch, McNeill, Brogan, Callaghan, Hood, Hughes, Chalmers (Johnstone), Auld.
1–0	ST JOHNSTONE	Donaldson; Lambie, Coburn, Gordon, Rooney, McPhee, Aird, Hall, McCarry (Whitelaw), Connolly, Aitken. *Scorer:* Celtic—Auld.

1970–71 RANGERS McCloy; Jardine, Miller, Conn, McKinnon, Jackson, Henderson, MacDonald A. Johnstone, Stein, Johnston.
1–0 CELTIC Williams; Craig, Quinn, Murdoch, McNeill, Hay, Johnstone, Connelly, Wallace, Hood (Lennox), Macari. *Scorer:* Rangers—Johnstone.

1971–72 PARTICK THISTLE Rough; Hansen, Forsyth, Glavin (Gibson), Campbell, Strachan, McQuade, Coulston, Bone, Rae, Lawrie.
4–1 CELTIC Williams; Hay, Gemmell, Murdoch, Connelly, Brogan, Johnstone (Craig), Dalglish, Hood, Callaghan, Macari. *Scorers:* Partick—Rae, Lawrie, McQuade, Bone. Celtic—Dalglish.

1972–73 HIBERNIAN Herriott; Brownlie, Schaedler, Stanton, Black, Blackley, Edwards, O'Rourke, Gordon, Cropley, Duncan.
2–1 CELTIC Williams; McGrain, Brogan, McCluskey, McNeill, Hay, Johnstone (Callaghan), Connelly, Dalglish, Hood, Macari. *Scorers:* Hibernian—Stanton, O'Rourke. Celtic—Dalglish.

1973–74 DUNDEE Allan; Wilson, Gemmell, Ford, Stewart, Phillip, Duncan, Robinson, Wallace, Scott J, Lambie, (Johnstone), (Scott I).
1–0 CELTIC Hunter; McGrain, Brogan, McCluskey, McNeill, Murray, Hood (Johnstone), Hay (Connelly), Wilson, Lennox, Dalglish. *Scorer:* Dundee—Wallace.

1974–75 CELTIC Hunter; McGrain, Brogan, Murray, McNeill, McCluskey, Johnstone, Dalglish, Deans, Hood, Wilson.
6–3 HIBERNIAN McArthur; Brownlie (Smith), Bremner, Stanton, Spalding, Blackley, Edwards, Cropley, Harper, Munro, Duncan (Murray). *Scorers:* Celtic—Johnstone, Deans 3, Wilson, Murray. Hibernian—Harper 3.

1975–76 RANGERS Kennedy; Jardine, Greig, Forsyth, Jackson, MacDonald, McLean, Stein, Parlane, Johnstone, Young.
1–0 CELTIC Latchford; McGrain, Lynch, McCluskey, McDonald, Edvaldsson, Hood (McNamara), Dalglish, Wilson (Glavin), Callaghan, Lennox. *Scorer:* Rangers—MacDonald.

1976–77 ABERDEEN Clark; Kennedy, Williamson, Smith, Garner, Miller, Sullivan, Scott, Harper, Jarvie (Robb), Graham.
2–1 CELTIC Latchford; McGrain, Lynch, Edvaldsson, McDonald, Aitken, Doyle, Glavin, Dalglish, Burns (Lennox), Wilson. *Scorers:* Aberdeen—Jarvie, Robb. Celtic—Dalglish (pen.)

1977–78 RANGERS Kennedy; Jardine, Greig, Forsyth, Jackson, MacDonald, McLean, Hamilton (Miller), Johnstone, Smith, Cooper (Parlane).
2–1 CELTIC Latchford; Sneddon, Lynch (Wilson), Munro, McDonald, Dowie, Glavin (Doyle),
a.e.t. Edvaldsson, McCluskey, Aitken, Burns. *Scorers:* Rangers—Cooper, Smith. Celtic—Edvaldsson.

SCOTTISH F.A. CUP FINALS 1874-1979

Year	Winners	Runners-up	Score
1874	Queen's Park	Clydesdale	2-0
1875	Queen's Park	Renton	3-0
1876	Queen's Park	Third Lanark	2-0 after 1-1 draw
1877	Vale of Leven	Rangers	3-2 after 0-0 and 1-1 draws
1878	Vale of Leven	Third Lanark	1-0
1879	*Vale of Leven	Rangers	
1880	Queen's Park	Thornlibank	3-0
1881	†Queen's Park	Dumbarton	3-1
1882	Queen's Park	Dumbarton	4-1 after 2-2 draw
1883	Dumbarton	Vale of Leven	2-1 after 2-2 draw
1884	‡Queen's Park	Vale of Leven	
1885	Renton	Vale of Leven	3-1 after 0-0 draw
1886	Queen's Park	Renton	3-1
1887	Hibernian	Dumbarton	2-1
1888	Renton	Cambuslang	6-1
1889	§Third Lanark	Celtic	2-1
1890	Queen's Park	Vale of Leven	2-1 after 1-1 draw
1891	Hearts	Dumbarton	1-0
1892	¶Celtic	Queen's Park	5-1
1893	Queen's Park	Celtic	2-1
1894	Rangers	Celtic	3-1
1895	St. Bernard's	Renton	2-1
1896	Hearts	Hibernian	3-1
1897	Rangers	Dumbarton	5-1
1898	Rangers	Kilmarnock	2-0
1899	Celtic	Rangers	2-0
1900	Celtic	Queen's Park	4-3
1901	Hearts	Celtic	4-3
1902	Hibernian	Celtic	1-0
1903	Rangers	Hearts	2-0 after 1-1 and 0-0 draw
1904	Celtic	Rangers	3-2
1905	Third Lanark	Rangers	3-1 after 0-0 draw
1906	Hearts	Third Lanark	1-0
1907	Celtic	Hearts	3-0
1908	Celtic	St. Mirren	5-1
1909	‖		
1910	Dundee	Clyde	2-1 after 2-2 and 0-0 draws
1911	Celtic	Hamilton A	2-0 after 0-0 draw
1912	Celtic	Clyde	2-0
1913	Falkirk	Raith R.	2-0
1914	Celtic	Hibernian	4-1 after 0-0 draw
1920	Kilmarnock	Albion R.	3-2
1921	Partick T.	Rangers	1-0
1922	Morton	Rangers	1-0
1923	Celtic	Hibernian	1-0
1924	Airdrieonians	Hibernian	2-0
1925	Celtic	Dundee	2-1
1926	St. Mirren	Celtic	2-0
1927	Celtic	East Fife	3-1
1928	Rangers	Celtic	4-0
1929	Kilmarnock	Rangers	2-0
1930	Rangers	Partick T.	2-1 after 0-0 draw
1931	Celtic	Motherwell	4-2 after 2-2 draw
1932	Rangers	Kilmarnock	3-0 after 1-1 draw
1933	Celtic	Motherwell	1-0
1934	Rangers	St. Mirren	5-0
1935	Rangers	Hamilton A	2-1
1936	Rangers	Third Lanark	1-0
1937	Celtic	Aberdeen	2-1
1938	East Fife	Kilmarnock	4-2 after 1-1 draw
1939	Clyde	Motherwell	4-0
1947	Aberdeen	Hibernian	2-1
1948	Rangers	Morton	1-0 after 1-1 draw
1949	Rangers	Clyde	4-1
1950	Rangers	East Fife	3-0
1951	Celtic	Motherwell	1-0
1952	Motherwell	Dundee	4-0

Year	Winners	Runners-up	Score
1953	Rangers	Aberdeen	1-0 after 1-1 draw
1954	Celtic	Aberdeen	2-1
1955	Clyde	Celtic	1-0 after 1-1 draw
1956	Hearts	Celtic	3-1
1957	Falkirk	Kilmarnock	2-1 after 1-1 draw
1958	Clyde	Hibernian	1-0
1959	St. Mirren	Aberdeen	3-1
1960	Rangers	Kilmarnock	2-0
1961	Dunfermline Ath.	Celtic	2-0 after 0-0 draw
1962	Rangers	St. Mirren	2-0
1963	Rangers	Celtic	3-0 after 1-1 draw
1964	Rangers	Dundee	3-1
1965	Celtic	Dunfermline Ath.	3-2
1966	Rangers	Celtic	1-0 after 0-0 draw
1967	Celtic	Aberdeen	2-0
1968	Dunfermline Ath.	Hearts	3-1
1969	Celtic	Rangers	4-0
1970	Aberdeen	Celtic	3-1
1971	Celtic	Rangers	2-1 after 1-1 draw
1972	Celtic	Hibernian	6-1
1973	Rangers	Celtic	3-2
1974	Celtic	Dundee U.	3-0
1975	Celtic	Airdrieonians	3-1
1976	Rangers	Hearts	3-1
1977	Celtic	Rangers	1-0
1978	Rangers	Aberdeen	2-1
1979	Rangers	Hibernian	3-2 after 0-0 and 0-0 draws

‡ Vale of Leven awarded cup, Rangers failed to appear for replay after 1-1 draw.
† After Protest game, Queen's Park 2 Dumbarton 1.
* Queen's Park awarded cup, Vale of Leven failing to appear.
§ Protested replay after Third Lanark had won 3-0.
¶ After mutual protested game which Celtic won 1-0.
‖ Owing to riot, the cup was withheld after two drawn games—Celtic 2-1, Rangers 2-1.

SCOTTISH LEAGUE CUP FINALS 1946-79

Season	Winners	Runners-up	Score
1945–46	Aberdeen	Rangers	3-2
1946–47	Rangers	Aberdeen	4-0
1947–48	East Fife	Falkirk	4-1 after 1-1 draw
1948–49	Rangers	Raith R	2-0
1949–50	East Fife	Dunfermline Ath	3-0
1950–51	Motherwell	Hibernian	3-0
1951–52	Dundee	Rangers	3-2
1952–53	Dundee	Kilmarnock	2-0
1953–54	East Fife	Partick T	3-2
1954–55	Hearts	Motherwell	4-2
1955–56	Aberdeen	St Mirren	2-1
1956–57	Celtic	Partick T	3-0 after 0-0 draw
1957–58	Celtic	Rangers	7-1
1958–59	Hearts	Partick T	5-1
1959–60	Hearts	Third Lanark	2-1
1960–61	Rangers	Kilmarnock	2-0
1961–62	Rangers	Hearts	3-1 after 1-1 draw
1962–63	Hearts	Kilmarnock	1-0
1963–64	Rangers	Morton	5-0
1964–65	Rangers	Celtic	2-1
1965–66	Celtic	Rangers	2-1
1966–67	Celtic	Rangers	1-0
1967–68	Celtic	Dundee	5-3
1968–69	Celtic	Hibernian	6-2
1969–70	Celtic	St Johnstone	1-0
1970–71	Rangers	Celtic	1-0
1971–72	Partick T	Celtic	4-1
1972–73	Hibernian	Celtic	2-1
1973–74	Dundee	Celtic	1-0
1974–75	Celtic	Hibernian	6-3
1975–76	Rangers	Celtic	1-0
1976–77	Aberdeen	Celtic	2-1
1977–78	Rangers	Celtic	2-1
1978–79	Rangers	Aberdeen	2-1

Post-war Scottish FA Cup Finals

1946–47 **ABERDEEN** Johnstone; McKenna, Taylor, McLaughlin, Dunlop, Waddell, Harris, Hamilton, Williams, Baird, McCall.
2–1 **HIBERNIAN** Kerr; Govan, Shaw, Howie, Aird, Kean, Smith, Finnigan, Cuthbertson, Turnbull, Ormond. *Scorers* Aberdeen—Hamilton, Williams. Hibernian—Cuthbertson.

1947–48 **RANGERS** Brown; Young, Shaw, McColl, Woodburn, Cox, Rutherford, Gillick, Thornton, Findlay, Duncanson.
1–1 **MORTON** Cowan; Mitchell, Whigham, Campbell, Miller, Whyte, Hepburn, Murphy, Cupples, Orr, Liddell. *Scorers* Rangers—Gillick. Morton—Whyte.
a.e.t.
RANGERS Brown; Young, Shaw, McColl, Woodburn, Cox, Rutherford, Thornton, Williamson, Duncanson, Gillick.
1–0 **MORTON** Cowan; Mitchell, Whigham, Campbell, Miller, Whyte, Hepburn, Murphy, Cupples, Orr, Liddell. *Scorer* Williamson.

1948–49 **RANGERS** Brown; Young, Shaw, McColl, Woodburn, Cox, Waddell, Duncanson, Thornton, Williamson, Rutherford.
4–1 **CLYDE** Gullan; Gibson, Mennie, Campbell, Milligan, Long, Davies, Wright, Linwood, Galletly, Bootland. *Scorers* Rangers—Young 2 penalties. Clyde—Galletly.

1949–50 **RANGERS** Brown; Young, Shaw, McColl, Woodburn, Cox, Rutherford, Findlay, Thornton, Duncanson, Rae.
3–0 **EAST FIFE** Easson; Laird, Stewart, Philip, Finlay, Aitken, Black, Fleming, Morris, Brown, Duncan. *Scorers* Rangers—Findlay, Thornton 2.

1950–51 **CELTIC** Hunter; Fallon, Rollo, Evans, Boden, Baillie, Weir, Collins, McPhail, Peacock, Tully.
1–0 **MOTHERWELL** Johnstone; Kilmarnock, Shaw, McLeod, Paton, Redpath, Humphries, Forrest, Kelly, Watson, Aitkenhead. *Scorer* Celtic—McPhail.

1951–52 **MOTHERWELL** Johnstone; Kilmarnock, Shaw, Cox, Paton, Redpath, Sloan, Humphries, Kelly, Watson, Aitkenhead.
4–0 **DUNDEE** Henderson; Fallon, Cowan, Gallacher, Cowie, Boyd, Hill, Pattillo, Flavell, Steel, Christie. *Scorers* Motherwell—Watson, Redpath, Humphries, Kelly.

1952–53 **RANGERS** Niven; Young, Little, McColl, Stanners, Pryde, Waddell, Grierson, Paton, Prentice, Hubbard.
1–1 **ABERDEEN** Martin; Mitchell, Shaw, Harris, Young, Allister, Rodger, Yorston, Buckley, Hamilton, Hather. *Scorers* Rangers—Prentice. Aberdeen—Yorston.
RANGERS Niven; Young, Little, McColl, Woodburn, Pryde, Waddell, Grierson, Simpson, Paton, Hubbard.
1–0 **ABERDEEN** Martin; Mitchell, Shaw, Harris, Young, Allister, Rodger, Yorston, Buckley, Hamilton, Hather. *Scorer* Rangers—Simpson.

1953–54 **CELTIC** Bonnar; Haughney, Meechan, Evans, Stein, Peacock, Higgins, Fernie, Fallon, Tully, Mochan.
2–1 **ABERDEEN** Martin; Mitchell, Caldwell, Allister, Young, Glen, Leggat, Hamilton, Buckley, Clunie, Hather *Scorers* Celtic—Young (o.g.), Fallon. Aberdeen—Buckley.

1954–55 **CLYDE** Hewkins; Murphy, Haddock, Granville, Anderson, Laing, Divers, Robertson, Hill, Brown, Ring.
1–1 **CELTIC** Bonnar; Haughney, Meechan, Evans, Stein, Peacock, Collins, Fernie, McPhail, Walsh, Tully. *Scorers* Clyde—Robertson. Celtic—Walsh.
CLYDE Hewkins; Murphy, Haddock, Granville, Anderson, Laing, Divers, Robertson, Hill, Brown, Ring.
1–0 **CELTIC** Bonnar; Haughney, Meechan, Evans, Stein, Peacock, Walsh, Fernie, Fallon, McPhail, Tully. *Scorer:* Clyde—Ring.

1955–56 **HEARTS** Duff; Kirk, McKenzie, McKay, Glidden, Cumming, Young, Conn, Bauld, Wardhaugh, Crawford.
3–1 **CELTIC** Beattie; Meechan, Fallon, Smith, Evans, Peacock, Craig, Haughney, Mochan, Fernie, Tully *Scorers:* Hearts—Crawford 2, Conn. Celtic—Haughney.

1956–57 **FALKIRK** Slater; Parker, Rae, Wright, Irvine, Prentice, Murray, Grierson, Merchant, Moran, O'Hara.
1–1 **KILMARNOCK** Brown; Collins, Stewart (J.), Stewart (R.), Toner, Mackay, Mays, Harvey, Curlett, Black, Burns. *Scorers:* Falkirk—Prentice, (pen.). Kilmarnock—Curlett.
FALKIRK Slater; Parker, Rae, Wright, Irvine, Prentice, Murray, Grierson, Merchant, Moran, O'Hara.
2–1 **KILMARNOCK** Brown; Collins, Stewart (J.), Stewart (R.), Toner, Mackay, Mays, Harvey,
a.e.t. Curlett, Black, Burns. *Scorers:* Falkirk—Merchant, Moran. Kilmarnock—Curlett.

1957–58	**CLYDE**	McCulloch; Murphy, Haddock, Walters, Finlay, Clinton, Herd, Currie, Coyle, Robertson, Ring.
1–0	**HIBERNIAN**	Leslie; Grant, McClelland, Turnbull, Patterson, Baxter, Fraser, Aitken, Baker, Preston, Ormond. *Scorer:* Clyde—Coyle.
1958–59	**ST MIRREN**	Walker; Lapsley, Wilson, Neilson, McGugan, Leishman, Rodger, Bryceland, Baker, Gemmell, Miller.
3–1	**ABERDEEN**	Martin; Caldwell, Hoggs, Brownlee, Clunie, Glen, Ewen, Davidson, Baird, Wishart, Hather. *Scorers:* St. Mirren—Bryceland, Miller, Baker. Aberdeen—Baird.
1959–60	**RANGERS**	Niven; Caldow, Little, McColl, Paterson, Stevenson, Scott, McMillan, Millar, Baird, Wilson.
2–0	**KILMARNOCK**	Brown; Richmond, Watson, Beattie, Toner, Kennedy, Stewart, McInally, Kerr, Black, Muir. *Scorers:* Rangers—Millar 2.
1960–61	**DUNFERMLINE ATHLETIC**	Connaghan; Fraser, Cunningham, Mailer, Williamson, Miller, Peebles, Smith, Dickson, Thomson, Melrose.
0–0	**CELTIC**	Haffey; MacKay, Kennedy, Crerand, McNeill, Clark, Gallagher, Fernie, Hughes, Chalmers, Byrne.
	DUNFERMLINE ATHLETIC	Connaghan; Fraser, Cunningham, Mailer, Miller, Sweeney, Peebles, Smith, Thomson, Dickson, Melrose.
2–0	**CELTIC**	Haffey; MacKay, O'Neil, Crerand, McNeill, Clark, Gallagher, Fernie, Hughes, Chalmers, Byrne. *Scorers:* Dunfermline—Thomson, Dickson.
1961–62	**RANGERS**	Ritchie; Shearer, Caldow, David, McKinnon, Baxter, Henderson, McMillan, Millar, Brand, Wilson.
2–0	**ST MIRREN**	Williamson; Campbell, Wilson, Stewart, Clunie, McLean, Henderson, Bryceland, Kerrigan, Fernie, Beck. *Scorers:* Rangers—Brand, Wilson.
1962–63	**RANGERS**	Ritchie; Shearer, Provan, Greig, McKinnon, Baxter, Henderson, McLean, Millar, Brand, Wilson.
1–1	**CELTIC**	Haffey; MacKay, Kennedy, McNamee, McNeill, Price, Johnstone, Murdoch, Hughes, Divers, Brogan. *Scorers:* Rangers—Brand. Celtic—Murdoch.
	RANGERS	Ritchie; Shearer, Provan, Greig, McKinnon, Baxter, Henderson, McMillan, Millar, Brand, Wilson.
3–0	**CELTIC**	Haffey; MacKay, Kennedy, McNamee, McNeill, Price, Craig, Murdoch, Divers, Chalmers, Hughes. *Scorers:* Rangers—Wilson, Brand 2.
1963–64	**RANGERS**	Ritchie; Shearer, Provan, Greig, McKinnon, Baxter, Henderson, McLean, Millar, Brand, Wilson.
3–1	**DUNDEE**	Slater; Hamilton, Cox, Seith, Ryden, Stuart, Penman, Cousins, Cameron, Gilzean, Robertson. *Scorers:* Rangers—Millar 2, Brand. Dundee—Cameron.
1964–65	**CELTIC**	Fallon; Young, Gemmell, Murdoch, McNeill, Clark, Chalmers, Gallagher, Hughes, Lennox, Auld.
3–2	**DUNFERMLINE ATHLETIC**	Herriot; Callaghan (W.), Lunn, Thomson, McLean, Callaghan (T.), Edwards, Smith, McLaughlin, Melrose, Sinclair. *Scorers:* Celtic—Auld 2, McNeill. Dunfermline—Melrose, McLaughlin.
1965–66	**RANGERS**	Ritchie; Johansen, Provan, Greig, McKinnon, Millar, Wilson, Watson, Forrest, Johnston, Henderson.
0–0	**CELTIC**	Simpson; Young, Gemmell, Murdoch, McNeill, Clark, Johnstone, McBride, Chalmers, Gallagher, Hughes.
	RANGERS	Ritchie; Johansen, Provan, Greig, McKinnon, Millar, Wilson, Watson, McLean, Johnston, Henderson.
1–0	**CELTIC**	Simpson; Craig, Gemmell, Murdoch, McNeill, Clark, Johnstone, McBride, Chalmers, Auld, Hughes. *Scorer:* Rangers—Johansen.
1966–67	**CELTIC**	Simpson; Craig, Gemmell, Murdoch, McNeill, Clark, Johnstone, Wallace, Chalmers, Auld, Lennox.
2–0	**ABERDEEN**	Clark; Whyte, Shewan, Munro, McMillan, Peterson, Wilson, Smith, Storrie, Melrose, Johnston. *Scorers:* Celtic—Wallace 2.
1967–68	**DUNFERMLINE ATHLETIC**	Martin; Callaghan (W.), Lunn, McGarty, Barry, Callaghan (T.), Lister, Paton, Gardner, Robertson, Edwards (Thomson).
3–1	**HEARTS**	Cruickshank; Sneddon, Mann, Anderson, Thomson, (Miller), Jensen, Moller, Townsend, Ford, Irvine, Traynor. *Scorers:* Dunfermline—Gardner 2, Lister pen. Hearts—Lunn (o.g.).
1968–69	**CELTIC**	Fallon; Craig, Gemmell, Murdoch, McNeill, Brogan (Clark), Connelly, Chalmers, Wallace, Lennox, Auld.
4–0	**RANGERS**	Martin; Johansen, Mathieson, Greig, McKinnon, Smith (D.), Henderson, Penman, Ferguson, Johnston, Persson. *Scorers:* Celtic—McNeill, Lennox, Connelly, Chalmers.
1969–70	**ABERDEEN**	Clark; Boel, Murray, Hermiston, McMillan, Buchan, McKay, Robb, Forrest, Harper, Graham.
3–1	**CELTIC**	Williams; Hay, Gemmell, Murdoch, McNeill, Brogan, Johnstone, Wallace, Connelly, Lennox, Hughes (Auld). *Scorers:* Aberdeen—Harper pen., McKay 2. Celtic—Lennox.

1970–71	CELTIC	Williams; Craig, Brogan, Connelly, McNeill, Hay, Johnstone, Lennox, Wallace, Callaghan, Hood (Macari).
1–1	RANGERS	McCloy; Miller, Mathieson, Greig, McKinnon, Jackson, Henderson, Penman, (Johnstone D.), Stein, MacDonald, Johnston (W.). *Scorers:* Celtic—Lennox. Rangers—Johnstone (D.).
	CELTIC	Williams; Craig, Brogan, Connelly, McNeill, Hay, Johnstone, Lennox, Macari, Callaghan, Hood (Wallace).
2–1	RANGERS	McCloy; Denny, Mathieson, Greig, McKinnon, Jackson, Henderson, Penman, (Johnstone D.), Stein, MacDonald, Johnston (W.). *Scorers:* Celtic—Macari, Hood (pen.). Rangers—Craig (o.g.).
1971–72	CELTIC	Williams; Craig, Brogan, Murdoch, McNeill, Connelly, Johnstone, Deans, Macari, Dalglish, Callaghan.
6–1	HIBERNIAN	Herriot; Brownlie, Schaedler, Stanton, Black, Blackley, Edwards, Hazel, Gordon, O'Rourke, Duncan (Auld). *Scorers:* Celtic—Deans 3, McNeill, Macari 2. Hibernian—Gordon.
1972–73	RANGERS	McCloy; Jardine, Mathieson, Greig, Johnstone, MacDonald, McLean, Forsyth, Parlane, Conn, Young.
3–2	CELTIC	Hunter; McGrain, Brogan (Lennox), Murdoch, McNeill, Connelly, Johnstone, Deans, Dalglish, Hay, Callaghan. *Scorers:* Rangers—Parlane, Conn, Forsyth, Celtic—Dalglish, Connelly (pen.).
1973–74	CELTIC	Connachan; McGrain (Callaghan), Brogan, Murray, McNeill, McCluskey, Johnstone, Hood, Deans, Hay, Dalglish.
3–0	DUNDEE UNITED	Davie; Gardner, Kopel, Copland, Smith (D.), (Traynor), Smith (W.), Payne (Rolland), Knox, Gray, Fleming, Houston. *Scorers:* Celtic—Hood, Murray, Deans.
1974–75	CELTIC	Latchford; McGrain, Lynch, Murray, McNeill, McCluskey, Hood, Glavin, Dalglish, Lennox, Wilson.
3–1	AIRDRIE	McWilliams; Jonquin, Cowan, Mnezies, Black, Whiteford, McCann, Walker, McCulloch (March), Lapsley (Reynolds), Wilson. *Scorers:* Celtic—Wilson 2, McCluskey (pen.), Airdrie—McCann.
1975–76	RANGERS	McCloy; Miller, Greig, Forsyth, Jackson, Macdonald, McLean, Hamilton (Jardine), Henderson, McKean, Johnstone.
3–1	HEARTS	Cruickshank; Brown, Burrell (Aird), Jeffries, Gallacher, May, Gibson (Park), Busby, Shaw, Callachan, Prentice. *Scorers:* Rangers—Johnstone 2, Macdonald. Hearts—Shaw.
1976–77	CELTIC	Lathford; McGrain, Lynch, Stanton, McDonald, Aitken, Dalglish, Edvaldsson, Craig, Wilson, Conn.
1–0	RANGERS	Kennedy; Jardine, Greig, Forsyth, Jackson, Watson (Robertson), McLean, Hamilton, Parlane, MacDonald, Johnstone. *Scorer:* Celtic—Lynch pen.
1977–78	RANGERS	McCloy; Jardine, Greig, Forsyth, Jackson, MacDonald, McLean, Russell, Johnstone, Smith, Cooper (Watson).
2–1	ABERDEEN	Clark; Kennedy, Ritchie, McMaster, Garner, Miller, Sullivan, Fleming (Scanlon), Harper, Jarvie, Davidson. *Scorers:* Rangers—MacDonald, Johnstone. Aberdeen—Ritchie.

Irish Football 1978-79

By Malcolm Brodie

Despite the inadequacy of performance in the British Championship – relieved by the improvement against Wales and in particular that undistinguished match against England at Windsor Park, Belfast, it was a comparatively satisfactory international year for Northern Ireland with home and away victories over Bulgaria in the European Championship Group One qualifying series and an away draw with the Republic of Ireland, plus a home win over Denmark.

Manager Danny Blanchflower and his assistant Tommy Cavanagh have, despite limited resources, succeeded in evolving a pattern, giving players a belief in themselves, adopted a positive attacking policy and, perhaps most important of all, ensured there is proper progression from all levels. There is a complete rapport between them – a most effective partnership.

Now they look forward to the visit to Belfast of England and the Republic, two matches which could have a distinct bearing on who tops the Group One table and qualifies for the finals in Italy next summer.

The season, too, saw the resumption of the inter-league series with Scotland – forerunner of a return of the Scots to Belfast for internationals; a junior game with the Scots; and a magnificent show by the Northern Ireland schoolboys side, managed by Ian Russell, who beat the cream of Europe to win the English Schools FA 75th anniversary tournament.

Domestically the standard fell. It was a mediocre season due primarily to postponement of fixtures, upheaval of schedules and the early transfers of some leading players from various clubs.

Linfield, managed by Roy Coyle, retained the Irish League title, a considerable achievement, but the real success story, a rags to riches one, was that of Cliftonville, winners of the Irish Cup and County Antrim Shield. Their resurgence can only be described as phenomenal.

A few years ago Cliftonville, who made it an annual ritual to seek re-election, could call on only about 200 supporters. Now they have almost 5,000 behind them at every match – the Red Army, recruited from various parts of North Belfast. It was appropriate they should win the Cup in their centenary year and also earn the Roy Stewart-Sean Mullan award from the Professional Footballers Association for outstanding services to the game.

Sponsorship, including that of Fiat in the League and Bass in the Irish Cup has again proved of great help and the first benefits are now being seen from the Government £40,000 grants to Irish League clubs with Linfield opening a new £100,000 floodlighting system at Windsor Park, an occasion marked by the visit of Moscow Dynamo.

Generally a season of ups and downs, an amalgam of success and failure. Still, for football to flourish as it does in the Province after 10 traumatic years of civil unrest is something which must be commended.

FINAL LEAGUE TABLES 1978-79

FIAT IRISH LEAGUE

	P	W	D	L	F	A	Pts
Linfield	22	14	6	2	46	21	34
Glenavon	22	11	6	5	42	30	28
Ards	22	11	5	6	47	34	27
Glentoran	22	9	8	5	36	33	26
Portadown	22	10	5	7	35	27	25
Larne	22	10	4	8	42	35	24
Cliftonville	22	7	7	8	31	29	21
Coleraine	22	7	6	9	29	30	20
Crusaders	22	6	8	8	30	33	20
Bangor	22	5	8	9	28	40	18
Ballymena U	22	4	6	12	25	46	14
Distillery	22	2	3	17	19	52	7

FIAT MANAGER OF THE MONTH

December: Joe Kinkead (*Ards*)
January: Victor Hunter (*Coleraine*)
February: Ronnie McFall (*Glentoran*)
March: Billy McClatchey (*Glenavon*)
April: Roy Coyle (*Linfield*)

HENNESSY GOLD CUP

SECTION A

	P	W	D	L	F	A	Pts
Portadown	5	5	0	0	13	3	10
Linfield	5	4	0	1	15	6	8
Glenavon	5	3	0	2	9	11	6
Ards	5	1	1	3	8	14	3
Distillery	5	0	2	3	3	8	2
Bangor	5	0	1	4	6	12	1

SECTION B

	P	W	D	L	F	A	Pts
Cliftonville	5	3	1	1	10	6	7
Glentoran	5	3	1	1	9	7	7
Ballymena U	5	3	0	2	10	8	6
Crusaders	5	2	1	2	7	6	5
Coleraine	5	2	0	3	8	8	4
Larne	5	0	1	4	4	13	1

PLAY-OFF
Portadown 2 (*Gordon, Campbell*) Cliftonville 1 (*Bowers*) (*aet*) (*at Windsor Park, Belfast 22 November 1978*)
Cliftonville: Johnston; McGuicken, Largey, Flanagan, Quinn M, McCurry, McCusker, Milles, Bowers (Hewitt), Platt, O'Connor.
Portadown: McCallum; Smyth, Donegan, Wilson, Kilburn, Cleary, Gordon, Magee, Blackledge (Alexander), Campbell, Quinn A.
Referee: J Haughey (Strabane).
Player of the Tournament: David McCallum (Portadown).
Manager of the Tournament: Bertie Neill (Portadown).

LEAGUE CHAMPIONSHIP ROLL OF HONOUR

1891	Linfield	1911	Linfield	1935	Linfield	1962	Linfield
1892	Linfield	1912	Glentoran	1936	Belfast Celtic	1963	Distillery
1893	Linfield	1913	Glentoran	1937	Belfast Celtic	1964	Glentoran
1894	Glentoran	1914	Linfield	1938	Belfast Celtic	1965	Derry City
1895	Linfield	1915	Belfast Celtic	1939	Belfast Celtic	1966	Linfield
1896	Distillery	1920	Belfast Celtic	1940	Belfast Celtic	1967	Glentoran
1897	Glentoran	1921	Glentoran	1948	Belfast Celtic	1968	Glentoran
1898	Linfield	1922	Linfield	1949	Linfield	1969	Linfield
1899	Distillery	1923	Linfield	1950	Linfield	1970	Glentoran
1900	Belfast Celtic	1924	Queen's Island	1951	Glentoran	1971	Linfield
1901	Distillery	1925	Glentoran	1952	Glenavon	1972	Glentoran
1902	Linfield	1926	Belfast Celtic	1953	Glentoran	1973	Crusaders
1903	Distillery	1927	Belfast Celtic	1954	Linfield	1974	Coleraine
1904	Linfield	1928	Belfast Celtic	1955	Linfield	1975	Linfield
1905	Glentoran	1929	Belfast Celtic	1956	Linfield	1976	Crusaders
1906	Cliftonville/Dist	1930	Linfield	1957	Glentoran	1977	Glentoran
1907	Linfield	1931	Glentoran	1958	Ards	1978	Linfield
1908	Linfield	1932	Linfield	1959	Linfield	1979	Linfield
1909	Linfield	1933	Belfast Celtic	1960	Glenavon		
1910	Cliftonville	1934	Linfield	1961	Linfield		

MORANS ULSTER CUP

	P	W	D	L	F	A	Pts
Linfield	11	8	1	2	28	12	17
Crusaders	11	6	3	2	21	16	15
Ballymena U	11	6	2	3	19	14	14
Cliftonville	11	5	4	2	15	11	14
Glenavon	11	4	5	2	21	20	13
Glentoran	11	4	4	3	15	12	12
Larne	11	3	3	5	16	16	9
Portadown	11	2	5	4	18	19	9
Bangor	11	3	2	6	16	23	8
Coleraine	11	3	2	6	19	26	8
Ards	11	0	7	4	13	18	7
Distillery	11	1	4	6	9	23	6

BASS IRISH CUP 1978–79

Winners £3,000; Runners Up £2,000; defeated semi-finalists £1,000 each; Personality of each round £250 each.

First Round, 3 February
Linfield v Cliftonville	3-4
Ards v Portadown	1-3
Glenavon v Bangor	4-1
Omagh T v RUC	2-6
Distillery v Banbridge T	0-2
Larne v Glentoran	3-2
Coleraine v Downpatrick	5-2
Ballymena U v Crusaders	2-1

RUC v Larne	0-1
Glenavon v Banbridge T	3-2
Ballymena U v Portadown	2-1, 0-0

Semi-finals, 17 March
Portadown v Glenavon (at Windsor Pk)	2-1
Larne v Cliftonville (at The Oval)	0-1, 2-2

Second Round, 24 February
Coleraine v Cliftonville	2-3

Final
Cliftonville v Portadown	3-2
Attendance 15,000	

Cliftonville: Johnston; McGuickan, Largey, Flanagan, Quinn M, McCurry, Bell T, McCusker, Mills (O'Connor), Platt, Adair.
Portadown: McCallum; Smyth, Donegan, Wilson, Kilburn, Cleary, Gordon, Magee (Bell J), Alexander, Campbell, Quinn A.
Referee: Malcolm Wright (Portadown).
Scorers: Cliftonville: Platt (32 mins), Adair (46 mins) Bell (89 mins).
Portadown: Campbell (93 secs), Alexander (77 mins).

BASS PERSONALITY OF ROUNDS
First Round: Drew Trainor, Manager of Banbridge Town.
Second Round: Jackie Hutton (*Cliftonville*).
Semi-finals: Peter McCusker (*Cliftonville*).
Final: Jackie Hutton (*Cliftonville*).

CITY CUP WINNERS

Year	Winner	Year	Winner	Year	Winner	Year	Winner
1895	Linfield	1915	Glentoran	1938	Linfield	1964	Linfield
1896	Glentoran	1920	Linfield	1939	Portadown	1965	Glentoran
1897	Glentoran	1921	Glenavon	1940	Belfast Celtic	1966	Glenavon
1898	Linfield	1922	Linfield	1948	Belfast Celtic	1967	Glentoran
1899	Glentoran	1923	Queen's Island	1949	Belfast Celtic	1968	Linfield
1900	Linfield	1924	Queen's Island	1950	Linfield	1969	Coleraine
1901	Linfield	1925	Queen's Island	1951	Glentoran	1970	Glentoran
1902	Linfield	1926	Belfast Celtic	1952	Linfield	1971	Bangor
1904	Linfield	1927	Linfield	1953	Glentoran	1972	Ballymena U
1905	Distillery	1928	Belfast Celtic	1954	Coleraine	1973	Glentoran
1906	Belfast Celtic	1929	Linfield	1955	Glenavon	1974	Linfield
1907	Belfast Celtic	1930	Belfast Celtic	1956	Glenavon	1975	Glentoran
1908	Linfield	1931	Belfast Celtic	1957	Glentoran	1976	Bangor
1909	Shelbourne	1932	Glentoran	1958	Linfield	1977	Not played
1910	Linfield	1933	Belfast Celtic	1959	Linfield	1978	Not played
1911	Glentoran	1934	Distillery	1960	Distillery	1979	Not played
1912	Glentoran	1935	Derry City	1961	Glenavon		
1913	Distillery	1936	Linfield	1962	Linfield		
1914	Glentoran	1937	Derry City	1963	Distillery		

IRISH CUP FINALS 1880-1979

Year	Result	Year	Result
1880–81	Moyola Park 1, Cliftonville 0	1929–30	Linfield 4, Ballymena 3
1881–82	Queen's Island 2, Cliftonville 1	1930–31	Linfield 3, Ballymena 0
1882–83	Cliftonville 5, Ulster 0	1931–32	Glentoran 2, Linfield 1
1883–84	Distillery 5, Wellington Park 0	1932–33	Glentoran 3, Distillery 1
1884–85	Distillery 2, Limavady 0	1933–34	Linfield 5, Cliftonville 0
1885–86	Distillery 1, Limavady 0	1934–35	Glentoran 1, Larne 0
1886–87	Ulster 3, Cliftonville 0	1935–36	Linfield 2, Derry City 1
1887–88	Cliftonville 2, Distillery 1	1936–37	Belfast Celtic 3, Linfield 0
1888–89	Distillery 5, Y.M.C.A. 4	1937–38	Belfast Celtic 2, Bangor 0
1889–90	Gordon Highlanders 3, Cliftonville 1	1938–39	Linfield 2, Ballymena 0
1890–91	Linfield 4, Ulster 2	1939–40	Ballymena 2, Glenavon 0
1891–92	Linfield 7, The Black Watch 0	1940–41	Belfast Celtic 1, Linfield 0
1892–93	Linfield 5, Cliftonville 1	1941–42	Linfield 3, Glentoran 1
1893–94	Distillery 3, Linfield 2	1942–43	Belfast Celtic 1, Glentoran 0
1894–95	Linfield 10, Bohemians 1	1943–44	Belfast Celtic 2, Linfield 1
1895–96	Distillery 3, Glentoran 1	1944–45	Linfield 4, Glentoran 2
1896–97	Cliftonville 3, Sherwood Foresters 1	1945–46	Linfield 3, Distillery 0
1897–98	Linfield 2, St. Columb's Hall Celtic 0	1946–47	Belfast Celtic 1, Glentoran 0
1898–99	Linfield 2, Glentoran 1	1947–48	Linfield 3, Coleraine 0
1899–1900	Cliftonville 2, Bohemians 1	1948–49	Derry City 3, Glentoran 1
1900–1	Cliftonville 1, Freebooters 0	1949–50	Linfield 2, Distillery 1
1901–2	Linfield 5, Distillery 1	1950–51	Glentoran 3, Ballymena United 1
1902–3	Distillery 3, Bohemians 1	1951–52	Ards 1, Glentoran 0
1903–4	Linfield 5, Derry Celtic 1	1952–53	Linfield 5, Coleraine 0
1904–5	Distillery 3, Shelbourne 0	1953–54	Derry City 1, Glentoran 0
1905–6	Shelbourne 2, Belfast Celtic 0	1954–55	Dundela 3, Glenavon 0
1906–7	Cliftonville 1, Shelbourne 0	1955–56	Distillery 1, Glentoran 0
1907–8	Bohemians 3, Shelbourne 1	1956–57	Glenavon 2, Derry City 0
1908–9	Cliftonville 2, Bohemians 1	1957–58	Ballymena United 2, Linfield 0
1909–10	Distillery 1, Cliftonville 0	1958–59	Glenavon 2, Ballymena United 0
1910–11	Shelbourne 2, Bohemians 1	1959–60	Linfield 5, Ards 1
1911–12	Linfield were awarded Cup. Final not played.	1960–61	Glenavon 5, Linfield 1
1912–13	Linfield 2, Glentoran 0	1961–62	Linfield 4, Portadown 0
1913–14	Glentoran 3, Linfield 1	1962–63	Linfield 2, Distillery 1
1914–15	Linfield 1, Belfast Celtic 0	1963–64	Derry City 2, Glentoran 0
1915–16	Linfield 1, Glentoran 0	1964–65	Coleraine 2, Glenavon 1
1916–17	Glentoran 2, Belfast Celtic 0	1965–66	Glentoran 2, Linfield 0
1917–18	Belfast Celtic 2, Linfield 0	1966–67	Crusaders 3, Glentoran 1
1918–19	Linfield 2, Glentoran 1	1967–68	Crusaders 2, Linfield 0
1919–20	Cup awarded to Shelbourne.	1968–69	Ards 4, Distillery 2
1920–21	Glentoran 2, Glenavon 0	1969–70	Linfield 2, Ballymena United 1
1921–22	Linfield 2, Glenavon 0	1970–71	Distillery 3, Derry City 0
1922–23	Linfield 2, Glentoran 0	1971–72	Coleraine 2, Portadown 1
1923–24	Queen's Island 1, Willowfield 0	1972–73	Glentoran 3, Linfield 2
1924–25	Distillery 2, Glentoran 1	1973–74	Ards 2, Ballymena 1
1925–26	Belfast Celtic 3, Linfield 2	1974–75	Coleraine 1:0:1, Linfield 1:0:0
1926–27	Ards 3, Cliftonville 2	1975–76	Carrick Rangers 2, Linfield 1
1927–28	Willowfield 1, Larne 0	1976–77	Coleraine 4, Linfield 1
1928–29	Ballymena 2, Belfast Celtic 1	1977–78	Linfield 3, Ballymena United 1
		1978–79	Cliftonville 3, Portadown 2

Continued on Page 615

WELSH CUP 1978-79

Qualifying Round
Rhos U v British Steel (Deeside)	1-3
Bangor Ath v Conwy U	0-8
Abergele U v Llandudno Swifts	2-0
Machynlleth v Penrhyncoch	1-0
Llanfair Caereinion v Aber AC	2-3
New Quay v Montgomery T	1-3
Ffostrasol Wanderers v Rhayader T	1-0
Maesteg Park Ath v Brecon C'thians	3-2
Garwv Pontllanfraith	1-4
Cwmbran T v Abercynon Ath	0-3
Pontyclub v Newport YMCA	1-2

First Round
Blaenau Ffestiniog v Pwllheli & Dist	0-5
Colwyn Bay v Caernarvon T	3-0
Conwy U v Porthmadog	2-5
Courtaulds Greenfield v British Steel (Deeside)	4-1
Nantlle Vale v Connah's Quay Nomads	3-1
Flint Town U v Abergele U	4-1
Mold Alexandra v Denbigh T	0-0, 0-1
Brymbo Steelworks v Llay Welfare	2-0
Druids U v Chirk AAA	3-3, 4-0
Gresford Ath v Ruthin	2-0
Caersws v Ffostrasol Wanderers	5-1
Knighton T v Newton	0-1
Berriew v Aberystwyth T	1-1, 0-4
Towyn v Montgomery T	4-0
Llanidloes T v Talgarth	3-1
Aber AC v Presteigne	1-1, 1-6
Machynlleth v Llandrindod Wells	3-0
Welshpool v Oswestry T	2-3
*Bridgnorth T v Worcester C	0-4
†Stourbridge v Brierley Hill All	4-4, 2-3
Maesteg Park Ath v Ebbw Vale	4-1
Ferndale Ath v South Glamorgan Ins	4-1
Cardiff Corinthians v Afan Lido	1-1, 1-2
Caerau Ath v Abercynon Ath	4-2
Caerleon v Newport YMCA	1-1, 1-3
Pontllanfraith v Sully	3-1
Aberaman v Barry T	1-3
Briton Ferry Ath v Ton Pentre	2-2, 0-4
Ammanford T v Milford U	4-0
BP Llandarcy v Llanelli	2-2, 0-2
Morriston T v Pembroke Borough	2-3
Pontardawe Ath v Haverfordwest Co	0-5

*at Worcester
†both games at Stourbridge

Second Round
Colwyn Bay v Kidderminster Harriers	0-2
Pwllheli & District v Nantlle Vale	2-1
Denbigh T v Druids U	3-2
Gresford Ath v Rhyl	1-2
Courtaulds Greenfield v Brymbo S	1-1, 2-0
Porthmadog v Flint Town U	3-2
*Brierley Hill Alliance v Worcester C	2-5
Machynlleth v Newtown	1-2
Presteigne St. Andrews v Oswestry T	1-3
Llanidloes T v Caersws	1-0
Towyn v Aberystwyth T	0-2
Afan Lido v Ton Pentre	2-2, 1-2
Ferndale Ath v Pembroke Borough	1-3
Barry T v Ammanford T	1-2
Merthyr Tydfil v Newport YMCA	3-0
Maesteg Park Ath v Pontllanfraith	0-2
Bridgend T v Caerau Ath	5-2
Llanelli v Haverfordwest Co	0-1

*at Worcester City FC

Third Round
Aberystwyth T v Oswestry T	1-7
Denbigh T v Rhyl	0-2
Courtaulds Greenfield v Llanidloes T	2-1
Pwllheli & District v Kidderminster H	0-2
*Porthmadog v Newtown	0-0, 4-1
Ton Pentre v Pembroke Borough	2-1
†Pontllanfraith v Worcester C	1-5
Merthyr Tydfil v Haverfordwest Co	2-1
Ammanford T. v Bridgend T	1-2

*1st match abandoned after 62 minutes
†played at Worcester City FC

Fourth Round
Chester v Bangor C	0-0, 1-0
Wrexham v Porthmadog	4-1
Courtaulds Greenfield v Oswestry T.	1-6
Shrewsbury T v Rhyl	6-0
Bridgend T v Worcester C	0-3
Swansea C v Kidderminster H	6-1
Newport Co v Ton Pentre	0-2
Cardiff C v Merthyr Tydfil	2-1

Fifth Round
Chester v Oswestry T	4-3
Shrewsbury T v Ton Pentre	3-2
Worcester C v Cardiff C	3-2
Wrexham v Swansea C	3-2

Semi-Finals
Shrewsbury T v Worcester C (at Shrewsbury)	2-0
Chester v Wrexham (at Chester)	0-1

Final

First Leg at Wrexham, 21 May 1979
Wrexham 1
Shrewsbury T 1
Wrexham: Niedzwiecki; Sutton, Dwyer, Cegielski, Roberts, Giles, Shinton, Whittle, Lyons, Buxton, Fox, Williams (sub).
Shrewsbury T: Wardle; King, Larkin, Cross, Hayes, Keay, Birch, Atkins, Tong, Biggins, Lindsay.

Second Leg at Shrewsbury, 24 May 1979
Shrewsbury T 1
Wrexham 0
Shrewsbury T: Wardle; King, Larkin, Cross, Griffin, Keay, Lindsay, Atkins, Tong, Biggins, Maguire.
Wrexham: Niedzwiecki; Sutton, Whittle, Cegielski, Edwards, Giles, Shinton, Williams, McNeil, Lyons, Fox, Buxton (sub).

Referee: G. P. Owen, Menai Bridge (both games).

WELSH INTERMEDIATE CUP 1978-79

First Round
Sunblest U v British Steel (Deeside)	1-0
Penrhyncoch v Newcastle Emlyn	2-0
Aberaeron v Bow Street	1-2
New Quay & District v Bont	3-2
Abercynon Ath v Sully	1-1, 0-3
Liswerry v Abergavenny Thursdays	0-7
Merlins Bridge v Llanelli Steel	1-3
Caldicot T v Brecon Cor	3-3, 5-4

(a.e.t. and Penalties)

Pontardulais T v Alcan	3-8
Girling (Cwmbran) v Cwmbran Celtic	3-1
BSC Whiteheads (Newport) v Risca U	1-7
Pontyclub v Coedffranc	2-0

Second Round
Cemaes Bay v Penmaenmawr Phoenix	4-1
Llandudno Amateur v Sunblest U	1-3
Bangor Ath v Abergele U	0-13
Hawarden R v Burntwood Drury	2-0
St Mary's (Ruabon) v Johnstown RGA	3-0
Lex XI v Gresford Ath	1-1, 2-4
Llanfyllin T v Llanfair Caereinion	2-0
Aber AC v Machynlleth	1-2
Bow Street v Harlech T	4-3
Llanfechain v New Quay & District	1-0
Montgomery T v Penrhycoch	3-1
Dolgellau Ath v Barmouth & Dyffryn	3-0
Girling (Cwmbran) v Caldicot T	0-1
Abergavenny Thursdays v Llanelli Steel	3-2
Alcan v Risca U	1-0
Sully v Pontyclub	2-1

Third Round
Abergele U v Courtaulds Greenfield	2-3
Nantlle Vale v Sunblest U	1-2
Flint Town U v Cemaes Bay	5-1
Rhos U v Caernarvon T	0-3
Caernarvon U v Llanberis Ath	1-3
Conwy U v Blaenau Ffestiniog	1-0
Prestatyn v Denbigh T	1-2
Buckley v Mold Alexandra	2-1
Bala T v Llangollen	3-2
Ruthin v St Mary's (Ruabon)	3-1
Chirk AAA v Hawarden R	1-1, 1-2
Llay Welfare v Brymbo Steelworks	1-2
New Broughton v Gresford Ath	3-1
Rhosddu v Druids U	1-3
Llandrindod W v Aberystwyth T	2-2, 0-6
Llanfyllin T v Bow Street	3-1
UCW Aberystwyth v Presteigne	0-1
Welshpool v Dolgellau Ath	5-1
Llanfechain v Rhayader T	6-1
Llanidloes T v Newtown	2-1
Berriew v Montgomery T	0-1
Machynlleth v Knighton T	1-0
Towyn v Caersws	1-1, 1-4

Fourth Round (continued)
Caldicot T v Treharris Ath	1-1, 1-2
Croesyceiliog v Aberaman	2-0
Pontllanfraith v Afan Lido	3-0
Abergavenny Thursday v Cwmbran T	2-3
Sully v Cardiff Corinthians	0-1
Tynte R v Dafen Welfare	1-4
Alcan v Talgarth	2-1
S Glamorgan Ins v Newport YMCA	0-5
Tonyrefail Welfare v Blaenrhondda	2-6

Fourth Round
New Broughton v Brymbo Steelworks	0-7
†Sunblest U v Caernarvon T	0-0, 1-2
Courtaulds Greenfield v Conwy U	1-1, 2-3
Druids U v Hawarden R	0-0, 5-2
Denbigh T v Bala T	0-1
Ruthin v Llanberis Ath	0-0
Flint Town U v Buckley	1-1, 4-0
Llanfyllin T v Llanfechain	2-0
Caersws v Aberystwyth T	3-1
Machynlleth v Welshpool	0-0, 2-3
Montgomery T v Llanidloes T	1-6
Cardiff Corinthians v Cwmbran T	2-1
Blaenrhondda v Alcan	2-0
Newport YMCA v Treharris Ath	1-1, 0-2
Croesyceiliog v Presteigne St Andrews	2-5
Pontllanfraith v Dafen Welfare	3-1

Fifth Round
Brymbo Steelworks v Flint Town U	3-6
Llanfyllin T v Conwy U	3-0
Ruthin v Caernarvon T	1-0
Druids U v Bala T	1-1, 3-2
Blaenrhondda v Treharris Ath	3-1
Presteigne St Andrews v Llanidloes T	3-1
Caersws v Pontllanfraith	1-3
Welshpool v Cardiff Corinthians	0-4

Sixth Round
Blaenrhondda v Llanfyllin T	4-2
Ruthin v Flint Town U	0-4
Presteigne St Andrews v Cardiff Corinthians	3-3, 0-3
Pontllanfraith v Druids U	2-0

Semi-Finals
Blaenrhondda v Flint Town U	2-3
Cardiff Corinthians v Pontllanfraith	2-5

Final
Flint Town U v Pontllanfraith	0-1

Welsh Intermediate Cup 1975–79
(replacing Welsh Amateur Cup)
1975–76 Cardiff Coll of Ed 2, Shifnal T 1
1976–77 Welshpool 4, Whitchurch Alport 1
1977–78 Caernarvon T 1, Llanidloes T 0

THE WELSH FOOTBALL LEAGUE Final League Tables—1978-79

Premier Division

	P	W	D	L	F	A	Pts
Pontllanfraith	34	23	7	4	73	37	53
Cardiff Corinthians	34	20	4	10	77	45	44
Newport Co	34	14	13	7	55	25	41
Afan Lido	34	17	7	10	43	37	41
Ton Pentre	34	16	8	10	62	42	40
Swansea C	34	15	9	10	61	47	39
Ammanford T	34	14	11	9	47	42	39
Pembroke Boro'	34	16	6	12	63	50	38
Merthyr Tydfil	34	15	7	12	61	58	37
Barry T	34	12	11	11	54	45	35
Caerau Ath	34	13	8	13	45	55	34
Sully	34	13	7	14	42	41	33
Milford U	34	12	8	14	55	45	32
Llanelli	34	11	9	14	41	55	31
Pontlottyn	34	9	10	15	41	57	28
Treharris Ath	34	9	8	17	43	65	26
Ferndale Ath	34	3	6	25	36	90	12
Cardiff College	34	1	7	26	25	88	9

Division 1

	P	W	D	L	F	A	Pts
Maesteg Park Ath	34	23	5	6	64	29	51
Cardiff C	34	17	14	3	75	33	48
Bridgend T	34	20	6	8	66	42	46
Abercynon	34	20	6	8	73	53	46
BP (Llandarcy)	34	16	11	7	44	34	43
Blaenrhondda	34	15	11	8	59	40	41
Briton Ferry Ath	34	15	8	11	62	47	38
Spencer Works	34	16	6	12	57	50	38
Blaenavon Blues	34	15	7	12	59	46	37
Haverfordwest Co.	34	12	8	14	64	48	32
Morriston T	34	11	9	14	40	48	31
Taffs Well	34	12	7	15	54	63	31
Aberaman	34	10	8	16	43	50	28
Caerleon	34	10	5	19	52	60	25
Cwmbran T	34	8	8	18	34	53	24
Garw	34	8	4	22	41	64	20
Port Talbot Ath	34	7	4	23	29	69	18
Pontardawe Ath	34	5	5	24	26	113	15

WELSH FOOTBALL LEAGUE NORTH

Division 1

	P	W	D	L	F	A	Pts
Caernarvon T	20	15	5	0	77	11	35
Pwllheli & Dist	20	14	4	2	47	20	32
Porthmadog	20	13	4	3	85	21	30
Colwyn Bay	20	9	6	5	51	30	24
Nantle Vale	20	10	3	7	58	21	23
Conwy U	20	8	5	7	40	38	21
Bl. Ffestiniog	20	6	6	8	32	40	18
Bangor C	20	5	6	9	34	42	16
Rhos U	20	6	1	13	24	55	13
Rhyl	20	0	3	17	11	78	3
*Llandudno Swifts	20	1	3	16	11	114	3

(* Two points deducted—playing ineligible player)

OTHER IRISH TROPHIES AND COMPETITIONS

Continued from page 612

	Winners	Runners-up
Co Antrim Shield	Cliftonville	Crusaders
Irish League B Division		
Section One	Carrick Rangers	Ballyclare Comrades
Section Two	Linfield Swifts	Glentoran II
George Wilson Cup	Larne Olympic	Bangor
Steel Cup	Cromac Albion	Ballyclare Comrades
Intermediate Cup	RUC	Downpatrick Rec
IFA Youth Cup	Glentoran Oly	Cregagh Swifts
IFA Junior Cup	Conner	Annalong Swifts
IFA Schools Cup	Lisnagarvey	Dundonald

Ulster Footballer of the Year (promoted by Castlereagh Glentoran Supporters Club)	Roy Walsh (Glentoran)
NI Footballer of the Year (FWA)	Ray McGuigan (Glenavon)
Young Footballer of the Year	Jim Smyth (Portadown)
Ulster Personality of the Year	Ian Russell, manager of the NI Schoolboys team.
Manager of the Year (Coaches Association)	Bertie Neill (Portadown)
NI PFA Player of the Year	Roy Walsh (Glentoran)
Most Promising Newcomer	Brian Quinn (Larne)
Mullan-Stewart Award for Meritorious Service	Cliftonville FC

The Managers

A directory of Football League managers with biographical details. In some entries information has been at the discretion of individuals.

ADAMSON, Jimmy. *Manager:* Burnley, Sunderland, Leeds U October 1978–. *Honours:* Division 2 Championship medal 1973. *Coach:* Burnley (six years). *Player:* Burnley 1946–1964. Captain of Division 1 Championship team 1960 and FA Cup team 1962. *Football League representative honours:* Footballer of the Year 1962; Assistant Manager and member of England's 1962 World Cup squad; FA Staff Coach.

ADDISON, Colin. *Manager:* Hereford U (player-manager), Durban C, Notts Co (assistant) Newport Co, West Bromwich Albion (assistant), Derby Co July 1979–. *Honours:* Promotion to Division 3 1973. *Player:* York C, Nottingham Forest, Arsenal, Sheffield U, Hereford U.

ASHURST, Len. *Manager:* Hartlepool, Gillingham, Sheffield W, Newport Co June 1978–. *Player:* Sunderland 1957–1971; Hartlepool 1971–1973. *Honours:* One Under-23 cap for England.

ASHMAN, Ron. *Manager:* Norwich C 1963–1966; Scunthorpe 1967–1973; Grimsby T 1973–1975; Scunthorpe January 1976–. *Honours:* Scunthorpe, Promotion to Division 3 1973. *Player:* Norwich C 1944–1962. *Honours:* League Cup winners medal 1962.

ATKINSON, Ron. *Manager:* Kettering T, Cambridge U, WBA January 1978–. *Honours:* Division 4 Champions 1977. *Player:* Aston Villa, Oxford U, Kettering T. *Honours:* Promotion to Division 3 1965; Division 3 Championship medal 1968.

BAILEY, Mike. *Player-Manager:* Hereford U June 1978–. *Player-Coach:* Minnesota Kicks. *Player:* Charlton Ath, Wolverhampton W. Five Under-23 and two full England caps.

BARNWELL, John. *Manager:* Peterborough U, Wolverhampton W November 1978–. *Player:* Bishop Auckland, Arsenal, Nottingham F, Sheffield U. *Honours:* Youth international, one Under-23 cap for England.

BLANCHFLOWER, Danny. *Manager:* Chelsea December 1978–. (also Northern Ireland) *Player:* Glentoran, Barnsley, Aston Villa, Tottenham H, Northern Ireland. Fifty-six full Northern Ireland caps.

BLOOMFIELD, Jimmy. *Manager:* Orient 1969, Leicester C 1971, Orient September 1977–. *Player:* Brentford, Arsenal, Birmingham C, West Ham U, Plymouth Arg, Orient (player-manager). *Honours:* Two Under-23 caps for England.

BOND, John. *Manager:* AFC Bournemouth; Norwich C November 1973–. *Honours:* AFC Bournemouth, Promotion to Division 3; Norwich C, Promotion to Division 1 1975. *Player:* West Ham U (17 years); Torquay U (3 years). *Honours:* West Ham U Division 2 Championship medal 1958; FA Cup winners medal 1964; Torquay U, Promotion to Division 3 1966.

BOOK, Tony. *Manager:* Manchester C April 1974–. *Honours:* League Cup winners 1976. *Player:* Plymouth Arg 1964–1966; Manchester C 1967–1974. *Honours:* Manchester C. Division 1 Championship medal 1968; European Cup Winners Cup medal 1970; Football League Cup Winners medal 1970; FA Cup Winners medal 1969; 'Footballer of the Year' 1969.

BREMNER, Billy. *Manager:* Doncaster R, November 1978–. *Player:* Leeds U, Hull C. Fifty-four full Scottish caps.

BROWN, Mick. *Manager:* Oxford U October 1975–. *Player:* Hull C (13 years); Lincoln C (1 year); Cambridge U (18 months). *Honours:* Hull C Division 3 Champions medal 1965.

BURKINSHAW, Keith. *Manager:* Tottenham H July 1976–. *Honours:* Promotion to Division 1 1978. *Coach:* Newcastle U 1968–1975; Tottenham H 1975–1976. *Honours:* FA Cup finalists 1974. *Player:* Liverpool 1954–1958; Workington 1958–1965; Scunthorpe U 1965–1968.

BURROWS, Frank. *Manager:* Portsmouth May 1979–. *Assistant Manager:* Swindon T. *Coach:* Portsmouth 1978. *Player:* Raith R, Scunthorpe U, Swindon T, Mansfield T (on loan).

BUTLER, Dennis. *Manager:* Port Vale May 1978–. (formerly assistant manager). *Player:* Bolton W, Rochdale, *Coach:* Bury, Port Vale.

BUXTON, Mick. *Manager:* Huddersfield T October 1978–. *Coach:* Huddersfield T, Southend U. *Player:* Burnley, Halifax T.

CAMPBELL, Bobby. *Manager:* Fulham December 1976–. *Coach:* QPR, Arsenal, Fulham. *Player:* Liverpool, Portsmouth, Aldershot. *Honours:* Division 2 Championship 1977.

CAMPBELL, Bobby. *Manager:* Dumbarton 1961–1962; Bristol R January 1978–. *Coach:* Bristol R (16 years). *Player:* Falkirk 1941–1947; Chelsea 1947–1954; Reading 1954–1961. Five full Scottish caps.

CHARLTON, Jack. OBE. *Manager:* Middlesbrough, Sheffield W October 1977 *Honours:* 'Manager of the Year' 1974. *Player:* Leeds U 1952–1973. *Honours:* Division 2 Championship medal 1964; FA Cup runners-up medal 1965; World Cup winners medal 1966; Fairs Cup runners-up medal 1967; 'Footballer of the Year' 1967; League Cup winners medal 1968; Fairs Cup winners medal 1968; Division 1 championship medal 1969; FA Cup runners-up medal 1970; Fairs Cup winners medal 1971; FA Cup winners medal 1972.

CLARKE, Allan. *Player-manager:* Barnsley May 1978–. *Player:* Walsall, Fulham, Leicester C, Leeds U. *Honours:* Promotion Barnsley 1979; Division 1 championship medal 1974; FA Cup winners medal 1972; runners-up medals 1970, 1973; European Cup runners-up medal 1975; UEFA Cup winners medal 1971. Six Under-23 and nineteen full England caps.

CLOUGH, Brian. *Manager:* Hartlepool, Derby Co, Brighton & HA, Leeds U, Nottingham F January 1975–. *Honours:* Division 2 Championship 1969; Division 1 Championship 1972; Promotion to Division 1 1977; Division 1 Championship 1978; League Cup winners 1978, 1979; European Cup winners 1979; Division 1 runners-up 1979. *Player:* Middlesbrough, Sunderland. *Honours:* Three Under-23 caps and two full caps for England.

COLLINS, Doug. *Player-manager:* Rochdale January 1979–. *Coach:* Derby Co. *Player:* Grimsby T, Burnley, Plymouth Arg, Sunderland, Tulsa Roughnecks.

COX, Arthur. *Manager:* Chesterfield October 1976–. *Coach:* Youth coach Coventry C, chief coach Walsall, Aston Villa, PNE, Halifax T. Assistant Manager Sunderland. *Honours:* Preston NE Division 3 Championship; Sunderland Division 2 Championship; FA Cup winners 1973. *Player:* Coventry C 1955–1958 (broken leg ended career at 18). Joined coaching staff.

DICKS, Alan. *Manager:* Bristol C October 1967–. *Honours:* Promotion to Division 1 1976. *Player:* Chelsea 1951–1958; Southend U 1958–1962; Coventry C 1962–1967.

DOCHERTY, John. *Manager:* Brentford, Cambridge U January 1978–. *Coach:* Cambridge U. *Player:* Brentford 1959–1961; 1965–1968; 1970–1974; Sheffield U 1961–1965; Reading 1968–1970; QPR player/coach 1974–1975.

DOCHERTY, Tommy. *Manager:* Chelsea 1962; Rotherham U 1967; Aston Villa 1969; Porto FC; Scottish Team Manager; Manchester U 1973; Derby Co 1977; QPR May 1979–. *Honours:* Qualified for 1974 World Cup with Scotland; Manchester U, Division 2 Champions 1975; FA Cup winners 1977. *Player:* Celtic 1949; Preston NE 1949–1958; Arsenal 1958–1962. *Honours:* Division 2 Championship medal 1951; 25 full caps for Scotland.

DODGIN, William. *Manager:* QPR, Fulham, Northampton T, Brentford September 1976–. *Honours:* Fulham promotion to Division 2 1971. *Player:* Fulham 1949–1952; Arsenal 1952–1961; Fulham 1961–1965. *Honours:* One Under-23 cap for England.

DURBAN, William Alan. *Manager:* Shrewsbury T, Stoke C February 1978–. *Honours:* Division 4 runners-up 1975. *Player:* Cardiff C 1959–1963; Derby Co 1963–1973; Shrewsbury T 1973–. *Honours:* 27 full caps for Wales; Division 2 Championship medal 1969; Division 1 Championship medal 1972; promotion to Division 3 1975; promotion to Division 1 1979.

ELLIOTT, Billy. *Manager:* Sunderland, Darlington June 1979–. *Coach:* Brann (Norway), Sunderland. *Player:* Bradford Park Avenue, Burnley, Sunderland. Five full England caps.

EVANS, Maurice. *Manager:* Shrewsbury T 1972–1974; Reading May 1977–. *Coach:* Shrewsbury T 1968–1972; Reading 1974–1977. *Honours:* Promotion to Division 3 1968. *Player:* Reading 1953–1967. *Honours:* Football Combination team 1957; Division 3 South team 1957.

FRIZZELL, James. *Manager:* Oldham Ath March 1970–. *Honours:* Winners of Ford Sporting League; Division 3 champions 1974. *Player:* Morton 1957–1960; Oldham Ath 1960–1970. *Honours:* Promotion to Division 3 1963.

GODFREY, Brian. *Manager:* Exeter C January 1979–. *Player:* Everton, Scunthorpe U, Preston NE, Aston Villa, Bristol R, Newport Co. *Honours:* One Under-23 and three full Welsh caps.

GRADI, Dario. *Manager:* Wimbledon January 1978–. Promotion to Division 3 1979 (formerly assistant manager) *Coach:* Chelsea, Derby Co, Wimbledon. *Player:* Sutton U.

GREAVES, Ian. *Manager:* Huddersfield T 1968–1974; Bolton W October 1974–. *Honours:* Huddersfield T Division 2 Champions 1970. *Player:* Manchester U 1952–1960; Lincoln C 1960–1961; Oldham Ath 1961–1963. *Honours:* Manchester U Division 1 Championship medal 1956, FA Cup runners-up medal 1958.

GREEN, Mike. *Player-manager:* Plymouth Arg, Torquay U March 1977–. *Player:* Carlisle U 1965–1968; Gillingham 1968–1971; Bristol R 1971–1974; Plymouth Arg 1974–1977. *Honours:* Promotion to Division 2 Bristol R 1974; Watney Cup winners; Promotion to Division 2 Plymouth Arg 1975; (captained both promotion teams).

GRIFFITHS, Arfon. *Manager:* Wrexham (player-manager) May 1977–. (formerly assistant manager). *Player:* Wrexham, Arsenal, Wrexham (holds club record of League appearances). 17 full caps for Wales.

HASLAM, Harry. *Manager:* Barry T, Luton T, Sheffield U January 1978–. *Honours:* Division 2 runners-up 1974. *Player:* Manchester U, Leyton Orient, Brighton. *Coach:* Gillingham, Luton T.

HATTON, Dave. *Player-Manager:* Bury May 1978–. *Player:* Bury, Blackpool, Bolton W.

HORNER, Billy. *Manager:* Darlington, Hartlepool November 1976–. *Player:* Middlesbrough, Darlington.

HOUGHTON, Ken. *Manager:* Hull C April 1978–. *Player:* Rotherham U, Hull C, Scunthorpe U.

KING, John A. *Manager:* Tranmere R May 1975–. *Player:* Everton; AFC Bournemouth; Tranmere R; Port Vale; Wigan Ath. *Honours:* Promoted to Captain at all clubs excluding Everton.

KIRBY, George. *Manager:* Halifax T, Watford, Halifax T November 1978–. *Player:* Everton, Sheffield W, Plymouth Arg.

KNIGHTON, Ken. *Manager:* Sunderland June 1979–. *Coach:* Sheffield W, Sunderland. *Player:* Wolverhampton W, Oldham Ath, Preston NE, Blackburn R, Hull C, Sheffield W.

LEE, Gordon. *Manager:* Port Vale 1968–1973; Blackburn R 1973–1975; Newcastle U 1975–1977; Everton January 1977–. *Honours:* Port Vale, promotion to Division 3 1971; Blackburn R Division 3 Champions 1975; Newcastle U League Cup runners-up 1976; Division 3 Manager of the Year 1975. *Player:* Aston Villa 1955–1966; Shrewsbury T 1966–1968. *Honours:* Aston Villa, League Cup Winners medal 1961; League Cup runners-up medal 1963.

LYALL, John. *Manager:* West Ham U August 1974–. Previously Assistant Manager 1971. *Honours:* FA Cup Winners 1975. *Player:* West Ham U 1957. *Honours:* Youth International.

McANEARNEY, Thomas. *Manager:* Aldershot 1966–1968; Asst Manager Sheffield W 1968–1970; Crewe Alex 1970; Bury 1970–1972; Aldershot May 1972–. *Honours:* Promotion to Division 3 1973. *Player:* Sheffield W 1951–1965; Peterborough U 1965–1966; Aldershot 1966–1968. *Honours:* Sheffield W, Division 2 Champion medals 1957 and 1959.

McGARRY, William H. *Manager:* Watford; Ipswich T; Wolverhampton W; Saudi Arabia, Newcastle U November 1977–. *Honours:* Ipswich T Division 2 champions 1968; Wolverhampton W League Cup winners 1974. *Player:* Port Vale; Huddersfield T; AFC Bournemouth. *Honours:* Four full England caps.

McGUIGAN, Jimmy. *Manager:* Crewe Alex 1960; Grimsby T 1964; Chesterfield 1967; Rotherham U May 1973. *Honours:* Crewe Alex promotion to Division 3 1963; Chesterfield promotion to Division 3 1970; RotherhamU promotion to Division 3 1975. Division 4 Manager of the Year. *Player:* Hamilton Acad, Sunderland, Stockport Co, Crewe Alex, Rochdale.

McMENEMY, Lawrie. *Manager:* Doncaster R 1968–1971; Grimsby T 1971–1973; Southampton June 1973–. *Honours:* Doncaster R, Division 4 Championship 1969; Grimsby T, Division 4 Championship 1972; Southampton, FA Cup Winners 1976. League Cup runners-up 1979. *Player:* Newcastle U, Gateshead.

McNEILL, Ian. *Manager:* Wigan Ath, May 1968–January 1976 and May 1976–. *Player:* Aberdeen, Brighton, Leicester C, Southend U.

MILNE, Gordon. *Manager:* Coventry C June 1972–. *Player:* Preston NE 1957; Liverpool 1960; Blackpool 1967–1970. *Honours:* 14 full caps for England; Liverpool Division 2 championship medals 1964 and 1966; FA Cup Winners medal 1965.

MONCUR, Bobby. *Manager:* Carlisle U November 1976–. *Player:* Newcastle U, Sunderland. *Honours:* One Under-23 and 16 full Scottish caps (14 years). UEFA Cup 1969; FA Cup runners-up 1974; Division 2 championship medal 1965; Anglo-Italian Cup 1973; Division 2 championship medal 1976.

MORGAN, Richie. *Manager:* Cardiff C, December 1978–. *Player:* Cardiff C (14 years); One Under-23 cap for Wales.

MORRIS, Peter. *Manager:* Mansfield T (player-manager) Peterborough U February 1979–. *Honours:* Division 3 Championship 1977. *Coach:* Norwich C reserve team coach, Newcastle U. *Player:* Mansfield T, Ipswich T, Norwich C, Mansfield T. *Honours:* Mansfield Division 3 and Division 4 promotion; Norwich C and Ipswich T promotion to Division 1.

MULHALL, George. *Manager:* Halifax T 1972–1974, Bradford C November 1978–. *Coach:* Halifax T, Bolton W (assistant-manager).*Player:* Aberdeen, Sunderland, South Africa (player-coach). *Honours:* Three full Scottish caps.

MULLERY, Alan. *Manager:* Brighton July 1976–. *Honours:* Promotion to Division 2 1977, Promotion to Division 1 1979. *Player:* Fulham 1959–1964; Tottenham H 1964 1972; Fulham 1972–1976. *Honours:* 35 England caps; FA Cup winners medal 1967; FA Cup runners-up 1975; League Cup winners medal 1971; UEFA Cup winners medal 1972; Footballer of the Year 1975; Played for Great Britain XI.

MURPHY, Colin. *Manager:* Derby Co, Lincoln C November 1978–. *Coach:* Derby Co (reserve team), Nottingham F (youth team), Notts Co. *Player:* Hastings U, Crystal Palace.

NEAL, John. *Manager:* Wrexham, Middlesbrough May 1977–. *Honours:* Promotion to Division 3 1970; Welsh Cup winners 1972, 1975; Qualified for Cup Winners Cup 1973, 1976 (quarter-finalists). *Player:* Hull C 1949–1955; Swindon T 1956–1958; Aston Villa 1959–1963; Southend U 1964–1967. *Honours:* Aston Villa, Division 2 championship medal 1960; League Cup winners medal 1961.

NEILL, Terry. *Manager:* Hull C, N Ireland, Tottenham H, 1974–1976; Arsenal July 1976–. *Honours:* FA Cup Winners 1979; Runners-up 1978. *Player:* Arsenal 1959–1970; Hull C 1970–1974. *Honours:* Schoolboy, Youth, Under-23, 'B' and 59 full caps for N Ireland.

NELSON, Andrew. *Manager:* Gillingham 1971–1974; Charlton Ath May 1974–. *Honours:* Gillingham, promotion to Division 3 1974; Charlton Ath, promotion to Division 2 1975. *Player:* West Ham U 1953–1958; Ipswich T 1958–1963; Orient 1963–1964; Plymouth Arg 1964–1969. *Honours:* Ipswich T, Division 2 Championship medal 1961; Division 1 Championship medal 1962.

NEWMAN, John H. G. *Manager:* Exeter C, Grimsby T December 1976–. *Honours:* Division 4 runners-up 1979. *Player:* Birmingham C 1951–1958; Leicester C 1958–1960; Plymouth Arg 1960–1968; Exeter C 1968–1970. *Honours:* Birmingham C Division 2 championship medal 1955; FA Cup runners-up 1956; Football League.

OAKES, Alan. *Manager:* Chester September 1976–. *Honours:* Debenhams Cup 1977. *Player:* Manchester C 1959–1976 (565 League appearances–a club record). *Honours:* Division 2 Championship medal 1966; Division 1 Championship 1968; FA Cup winners medal 1969; League Cup winners medal 1970; European Cup Winners Cup medal 1970; Football League representative honours.

PAISLEY, Robert. *Manager:* Liverpool July 1974–. *Honours:* Division 1 Champions 1976, 1977, and 1979 runners-up 1978; UEFA Cup Winners 1976; European Cup Winners 1977, 1978. *Player:* Bishop Auckland 1938–1938; Liverpool 1939–1954. *Honours:* Amateur Cup winners medal 1939; Division 1 Championship medal 1947.

PETCHEY, George. *Manager:* Orient, Millwall January 1978–. *Coach:* Crystal Palace (6 years). *Player:* West Ham U, QPR, Crystal Palace.

PLEAT, David. *Manager:* Nuneaton B, Luton T January 1978–. *Coach:* Luton T *Player:* Nottingham F, Luton T, Shrewsbury T, Exeter C, Peterborough U. *Honours:* England schools and youth international.

POTTS, Harry. *Manager:* Burnley, Blackpool, Burnley February 1977–. *Coach:* Wolverhampton W. *Player:* Burnley, Everton.

ROBERTS, Bobby. *Manager:* Colchester U June 1975–. Promotion to Division 3 1977. *Player:* Motherwell, Leicester C, Mansfield T. *Honours:* One Under-23 cap for Scotland; Scottish League.

ROBSON, Bobby. *Manager:* Fulham 1968; Ipswich T January 1969–. *Honours:* Ipswich T, Texaco Cup winners 1973, FA Cup winners 1978. *Player:* Fulham 1950–1956; WBA 1956–1962; Fulham 1962–1968. *Honours:* Under-23 and 20 full England caps; (World Cups 1958 and 1962); Football League.

SAUNDERS, Ron. *Manager:* Yeovil 1967; Oxford U 1969; Norwich C 1969; Manchester C 1973; Aston Villa June 1974–. *Honours:* Norwich C Champions Division 2 1972; League Cup runners-up 1973; Manchester C League Cup runners-up 1974; Aston Villa League Cup winners 1975 and 1977; Runners-up Division 2 1975; Manager of the Year 1975. *Player:* Everton, Tonbridge, Gillingham, Portsmouth, Watford, Charlton Ath.

SAXTON, Bobby. *Manager:* Exeter C (player-manager) Plymouth Arg January 1979–. *Honours:* Promotion to Division 3 1977. *Player:* Derby Co 1962–1968; Plymouth Arg 1968–1975; Exeter C 1975–. *Honours:* Promotion to Division 2 Plymouth Arg 1975.

SEXTON, David. *Manager:* Orient 1965–1966; Chelsea 1967–1974; QPR 1974–1977; Manchester U July 1977–. *Honours:* FA Cup winners 1970, runners-up 1979; European Cup Winners Cup 1971; League Cup runners-up 1972, 1976. *Player:* Chelmsford 1950–51; Luton T 1951–53; West Ham U 1953–56; Orient 1956–1957; Brighton & HA 1957–1959; Crystal Palace 1959–1961. *Honours:* FA XI v RAF; Third Division South v Third Division North.

SIRREL, Jimmy. *Manager:* Brentford 1965–1969; Notts Co 1969–1975; Sheffield U 1975–1977; Notts Co October 1977–. *Honours:* Notts Co, Division 4 Champions 1971; Division 3 runners-up 1973. *Player:* Glasgow Celtic 1945–1949; Bradford PA 1949–1951; Brighton & HA 1951–1954; Aldershot 1954–1955 (later trainer).

SMITH, Bobby. *Manager:* Bury, Swindon T May 1978–. *Honours:* Promotion to Division 3 1974. *Player:* Manchester U 1959–1964; Scunthorpe U 1964–1966; Grimsby T 1966–1967; Brighton & HA 1967–1970; Chester 1970–1971; Hartlepool 1971–1973; Bury 1973–. *Honours:* England Schoolboy and Youth caps.

SMITH, Dave. *Manager:* Mansfield T 1974–1976; Southend U 1976–. *Honours:* Division 4 Championship 1975, runners-up 1978; Anglo-Scottish Cup semi-finalists 1976; League Cup quarter-finalists 1976. *Coach:* Chief coach Sheffield W 1965–1968; Chief coach Newcastle U 1968–1971; Reserve team manager Arsenal 1971–1974. *Honours:* FA Cup runners-up 1966 Sheffield W; Fairs Cup winners 1969. *Player:* Burnley 1950–1961; Brighton & HA 1961–1962; Bristol C 1962–1963.

SMITH, Jimmy. *Manager:* Boston U 1968–1972; Colchester U 1972–1975; Blackburn R 1975–1978; Birmingham C March 1978–. *Honours:* Boston U Eastern Professional Floodlight Cup winners; Colchester U Promoted from Division 4 1974. *Player:* Sheffield U 1957–1961; Aldershot 1961–1964; Halifax T 1964–1967; Lincoln C 1967–1968; Boston U 1968–1972.

STILES, Nobby. *Manager:* Preston NE July 1977–. *Coach:* Preston NE. *Player:* Manchester U, Middlesbrough, Preston NE. Three Under-23 and 28 full England caps. Member of World Cup winning team 1966.

STOCK, Alec. *Manager:* Yeovil T 1946–1949; Leyton Orient 1949–1958; AS Roma 1958; QPR 1958–1968; Luton T 1969–1972; Fulham 1972–1976; Bournemouth January 1979–. *Honours:* Leyton Orient Division 3 Championship 1956; QPR Division 3 Championship 1967; League Cup winners 1967; Promotion to Division 2 1970; Fulham FA Cup runners up 1975; *Player:* Charlton Ath 1936–1938; QPR 1938–1946.

STOKOE, Bob. *Manager:* Charlton Ath, Rochdale, Carlisle U, Blackpool, Sunderland, Bury, Blackpool May 1978–. *Honours:* Sunderland FA Cup Winners 1973; Division 2 champions 1976. *Player:* Newcastle U (13 years), Bury (Player-manager). *Honours:* FA Cup Winners medal 1955.

SUMMERS, Gerry. *Manager:* Oxford U 1969–1975; Gillingham October 1975–. *Player:* WBA 1951–1957; Sheffield U 1957–1964; Hull C 1964–1966; Walsall 1966–1968; *Honours:* Sheffield U promotion to Division 1 1961; FA Tour 1962, Far East and America.

SUMMERBEE, Mike. *Player-Manager:* Stockport Co March 1978–. *Player:* Swindon T, Manchester C, Burnley, Blackpool, Stockport Co. *Honours:* One Under-23 and eight full England caps.

TAYLOR, Graham. *Manager:* Lincoln C, Watford June 1977–. *Honours:* Division 4 Championship 1976, 1978; Division 3 runners-up 1979. *Player:* Grimsby T 1962–1968; Lincoln C 1968–1972.

TOSHACK, John. *Player-Manager:* Swansea C February 1978–. *Player:* Cardiff C, Liverpool, Swansea C. Promotion 1978, 1979. *Honours:* Three Under-23 and 39 full Welsh caps.

TURNER, Graham. *Player-Manager:* Shrewsbury T December 1978–. *Player:* Wrexham, Chester, Shrewsbury T. *Honours:* Promotion 1979.

VENABLES, Terry. *Manager:* Crystal Palace June 1976–. (formerly coach). *Honours:* Promotion to Division 2 1976, Division 2 Championship 1979. *Player:* Chelsea, Tottenham H, QPR, Crystal Palace. *Honours:* capped at all levels by England schools, youth, Amateur, Under-23 and two full honours; Promotion to Division 1 1963 Chelsea; League Cup winners medal 1965 Chelsea; FA Cup winners medal 1967 Tottenham H.

WADDINGTON, Tony. *Manager:* Stoke C, Crewe Alex June 1979–. Previously Assistant Manager Stoke C 1957, Coach 1952. *Honours:* Division 2 Championship 1963; League Cup winners 1972. *Player:* Manchester U (amateur), Crewe Alex 1946–1951.

WALKER, Clive. *Manager:* Northampton T May 1979–. *Coach:* Northampton T. *Player:* Leicester C, Northampton T, Mansfield T.

WALLACE, Jock. *Manager:* Rangers, Leicester C June 1978–. *Coach:* Hearts, Rangers *Player-Manager:* Berwick R. *Player:* Airdrie, WBA, Workington T, Hereford U. Bedford T.

WRIGHT, Charlie. *Manager:* York C November 1977–. *Coach:* Bolton W. *Player:* Morton, Rangers, Workington, Hong Kong, Grimsby T, Charlton Ath, Bolton W.

Major British Records

No Scottish Premier Division records at present after only four seasons

HIGHEST SCORES

First-Class Match		Arbroath *(Scottish Cup 1st Round)*	36	Bon Accord	0	5.9.1885
International		England	13	Ireland	0	18.2.1882
F.A. Cup Tie		Preston NE *(First Round)*	26	Hyde U	0	15.10.1887
FOOTBALL LEAGUE						
Division 1	(Home)	WBA	12	Darwen	0	4.3.1892
		Nottingham F	12	Leicester Fosse	0	21.4.1909
	(Away)	Newcastle U	1	Sunderland	9	5.12.1908
		Cardiff C	1	Wolverhampton W	9	3.9.1955
Division 2	(Home)	Newcastle U	13	Newport Co	0	5.10.1946
	(Away)	Burslem P V	0	Sheffield U	10	10.12.1892
Division 3	(Home)	Tranmere R	9	Accrington S	0	18.4.1959
		Brentford	9	Wrexham	0	15.10.1963
	(Away)	Halifax T	0	Fulham	8	16.9.1969
		Brighton	2	Bristol R	8	1.12.1973
Division 3(S)	(Home)	Luton T	12	Bristol R	0	13.4.1936
	(Away)	Northampton T	0	Walsall	8	2.2.1947
Division 3(N)	(Home)	Stockport Co	13	Halifax T	0	6.1.1934
	(Away)	Accrington S	0	Barnsley	9	3.2.1934
Division 4	(Home)	Oldham Ath	11	Southport	0	26.12.1962
	(Away)	Crewe Alex	1	Rotherham U	8	8.9.1973
SCOTTISH LEAGUE						
Division 1	(Home)	Celtic	11	Dundee	0	26.10.1895
	(Away)	Airdrieonians	1	Hibernian	11	24.10.1959
Division 2	(Home)	East Fife	13	Edinburgh C	2	11.12.1937
	(Away)	Alloa Ath	0	Dundee	10	8.3.1947

MOST GOALS FOR IN A SEASON

FOOTBALL LEAGUE		Goals	Games	Season
Division 1	Aston V	128	42	1930–31
Division 2	Middlesbrough	122	42	1926–27
Division 3(S)	Millwall	127	42	1927–28
Division 3(N)	Bradford C	128	42	1928–29
Division 3	QPR	111	46	1961–62
Division 4	Peterborough U	134	46	1960–61
SCOTTISH LEAGUE				
Division 1	Hearts	132	34	1957–58
Division 2	Raith R	142	34	1937–38

MOST GOALS AGAINST IN A SEASON

FOOTBALL LEAGUE		Goals	Games	Season
Division 1	Blackpool	125	42	1930–31
Division 2	Darwen	141	34	1898–99
Division 3(S)	Merthyr T	135	42	1929–30
Division 3(N)	Nelson	136	42	1927–28
Division 3	Accrington S	123	46	1959–60
Division 4	Hartlepools U	109	46	1959–60
SCOTTISH LEAGUE				
Division 1	Leith Ath	137	38	1931–32
Division 2	Edinburgh C	146	38	1931–32

FEWEST GOALS AGAINST IN A SEASON

FOOTBALL LEAGUE (min. 42 games)		Goals	Games	Season
Division 1	Liverpool	16	42	1978–79
Division 2	Manchester U	23	42	1924–25
Division 3 (S)	Southampton	21	42	1921–22
Division 3 (N)	Port Vale	21	46	1953–54
Division 3	Peterborough U	33	46	1977–78
Division 4	Gillingham	30	46	1963–64
SCOTTISH LEAGUE (min. 30 games)				
Division 1	Celtic	14	38	1913–14
Division 2	Morton	20	38	1966–67

MOST POINTS IN A SEASON

FOOTBALL LEAGUE		Points	Games	Season
Division 1	Liverpool	68	42	1978–79
Division 2	Tottenham H	70	42	1919–20
Division 3	Aston Villa	70	46	1971–72
Division 3(S)	Nottingham F	70	46	1950–51
	Bristol C	70	46	1954–55
Division 3(N)	Doncaster R	72	42	1946–47
Division 4	Lincoln C	74	46	1975–76
SCOTTISH LEAGUE				
Division 1	Rangers	76	42	1920–21
Division 2	Morton	69	38	1966–67

FEWEST POINTS IN A SEASON

FOOTBALL LEAGUE (min. 34 games)		Points	Games	Season
Division 1	Leeds U	18	42	1946–47
	QPR	18	42	1968–69
	Glossop	18	34	1899–1900
	Notts Co	18	34	1904–05
	Woolwich Arsenal	18	38	1912–13
Division 2	Doncaster R	8	34	1904–05
	Loughborough T	8	34	1899–1900
Division 3	Rochdale	21	46	1973–74
Division 3(S)	Merthyr T	21	42	1924–25 & 1929–30
	QPR	21	42	1925–26
Division 3 (N)	Rochdale	11	40	1931–32
Division 4	Bradford	20	46	1968–69
SCOTTISH LEAGUE (min. 30 games)				
Division 1	Stirling A	6	30	1954–55

MOST WINS IN A SEASON

FOOTBALL LEAGUE		Wins	Games	Season
Division 1	Tottenham H	31	42	1960–61
Division 2	Tottenham H	32	42	1919–20
Division 3 (S)	Millwall	30	42	1927–28
	Plymouth Arg	30	42	1929–30
	Cardiff C	30	42	1946–47
	Nottingham F	30	46	1950–51
	Bristol C	30	46	1954–55
Division 3 (N)	Doncaster R	33	42	1946–47
Division 3	Aston Villa	32	46	1971–72
Division 4	Lincoln C	32	46	1975–76
SCOTTISH LEAGUE				
Division 1	Rangers	35	42	1920–21
Division 2	Morton	33	38	1966–67

RECORD HOME WINS IN A SEASON

Brentford won all 21 games in Division 3 (S), 1929–30

RECORD AWAY WINS IN A SEASON

Doncaster R won 18 of 21 games in Division 3 (N), 1946–47

MOST DEFEATS IN A SEASON

FOOTBALL LEAGUE		Defeats	Games	Season
Division 1	Leeds U	30	42	1946–47
	Blackburn R	30	42	1965–66
Division 2	Tranmere R	31	42	1938–39
Division 3	Newport Co	31	46	1961–62
Division 3 (S)	Merthyr T	29	42	1924–25
Division 3 (N)	Rochdale	33	40	1931–32
Division 4	Workington	32	46	1975–76
SCOTTISH LEAGUE				
Division 1	St Mirren	31	42	1920–21
Division 2	Lochgelly U	30	38	1923–24
	Brechin C	30	36	1962–63
	Forfar Ath	30	38	1974–75

FEWEST DEFEATS IN A SEASON

FOOTBALL LEAGUE		Defeats	Games	Season
Division 1	Preston NE	0	22	1888–89
	Leeds U	2	42	1968–69
Division 2	Liverpool	0	28	1893–94
	Burnley	2	30	1897–98
	Bristol C	2	38	1905–06
	Leeds U	3	42	1963–64
Division 3	QPR	5	46	1966–67
Division 3 (S)	Southampton	4	42	1921–22
	Plymouth Arg	4	42	1929–30
Division 3 (N)	Port Vale	3	46	1953–54
	Doncaster R	3	42	1946–47
	Wolverhampton W	3	42	1923–24
Division 4	Lincoln C	4	46	1975–76
SCOTTISH LEAGUE				
Division 1	Celtic	0	18	1897–98
	Rangers	0	18	1898–99
	Rangers	1	42	1920–21
	Hearts	1	34	1957–58
	Celtic	1	34	1967–68
	Rangers	1	34	1967–68
Division 2	Kilmarnock	0	18	1898–99
	Clyde	1	36	1956–57
	Morton	1	36	1963–64

MOST LEAGUE GOALS IN A SEASON

FOOTBALL LEAGUE		Goals	Actual Games	Season
Division 1	Dixie Dean (Everton)	60	39	1927–28
Division 2	George Camsell (Middlesbrough)	59	37	1926–27
Division 3 (S)	Joe Payne (Luton T)	55	39	1936–37
Division 3 (N)	Ted Harston (Mansfield T)	55	41	1936–37
Division 3	Derek Reeves (Southampton)	39	46	1959–60
Division 4	Terry Bly (Peterborough U)	52	46	1960–61
SCOTTISH LEAGUE				
Division 1	William McFadyen (Motherwell)	52	34	1931–32
Division 2	Jim Smith (Ayr)	66	38	1927–28

FEWEST GOALS FOR IN A SEASON

FOOTBALL LEAGUE (min. 42 games)

		Goals	Games	Season
Division 1	Leicester C.	26	42	1977–78
Division 2	Watford	24	42	1971–72
Division 3 (S)	Crystal Palace	33	42	1950–51
Division 3 (N)	Crewe Alex	32	42	1923–24
Division 3	Stockport Co	27	46	1969–70
Division 4	Bradford	30	46	1967–68
	Workington	30	46	1975–76

SCOTTISH LEAGUE (min. 30 games)

Division 1	Ayr U	20	34	1966–67
Division 2	Lochgelly U	20	38	1923–24

FEWEST WINS IN A SEASON

FOOTBALL LEAGUE

		Wins	Games	Season
Division 1	Stoke	3	22	1889–90
	Woolwich Arsenal	3	38	1912–13
Division 2	Loughborough T	1	34	1899–1900
Division 3 (S)	Merthyr T	6	42	1929–30
Division 3 (N)	Rochdale	4	40	1931–32
Division 3	Rochdale	2	46	1973–74
Division 4	Bradford	4	46	1967–68

SCOTTISH LEAGUE

Division 1	Vale of Leven	0	22	1891–92
Division 2	East Stirlingshire	1	22	1905–06
	Forfar Ath	1	38	1974–75

MOST DRAWN GAMES IN A SEASON

FOOTBALL LEAGUE

		Draws	Games	Season
Division 1	Norwich C.	23	42	1978–79

SCOTTISH LEAGUE

Division 1	Falkirk	17	42	1921–22
Division 1	Falkirk	17	38	1922–23
Division 2	Bo'ness	17	38	1922–23

MOST GOALS IN A GAME

FOOTBALL LEAGUE

Division 1	Ted Drake (Arsenal) 7 goals v Aston Villa	14.12.1935
Division 2	Tommy Briggs (Blackburn R) 7 goals v Bristol R	5.2.1955
	Nevil Coleman (Stoke C) 7 goals v Lincoln C	23.2.1957
Division 3 (S)	Joe Payne (Luton T) 10 goals v Bristol R	13.4.1936
Division 3 (N)	Robert Bell (Tranmere R) 9 goals v Oldham Ath	26.12.1935
Division 3	Steve Earle (Fulham) 5 goals v Halifax T	16.9.1969
	Barrie Thomas (Scunthorpe U) 5 goals v Luton T	24.4.1965
	Keith East (Swindon T) 5 goals v Mansfield T	20.11.1965
	Alf Wood (Shrewsbury T) 5 goals v Blackburn R	2.10.1971
Division 4	Herbert Lister (Oldham Ath) 6 goals v Southport	26.12.1962

SCOTTISH LEAGUE

Division 1	Jimmy McGrory (Celtic) 8 goals v Dunfermline Ath	14.9.1928
Division 2	Owen McNally (Arthurlie) 8 goals v Armadale	1.10.1927
	Jim Dyet (King's Park) 8 goals v Forfar Ath	2.1.1930
	John Calder (Morton) 8 goals v Raith R	18.4.1936
F.A. CUP	Ted MacDougall (Bournemouth) 9 goals v Margate	20.11.1971
SCOTTISH CUP	John Petrie (Arbroath) 13 goals v Bon Accord	5.9.1885

RECORD ATTENDANCES

Football League	83,260	Manchester U v Arsenal, Maine Road	17.1.1948
Scottish League	118,567	Rangers v Celtic, Ibrox Stadium	2.1.1939
F.A. Cup Final	126,047*	Bolton W v West Ham U, Wembley	28.4.1923
European Cup	135,826	Celtic v Leeds U, semi-final at Hampden P	15.4.1970

* It has been estimated that as many as 70,000 more broke in without paying.

MOST CUP WINNERS' MEDALS

F.A. CUP – 5 medals each
James Forrest (Blackburn R) 1884, 1885, 1886, 1890, 1891.
Hon. A. F. Kinnaird (Wanderers) 1873, 1877, 1878, (Old Etonians) 1879, 1882.
C. H. R. Wollaston (Wanderers) 1872, 1873, 1876, 1877, 1878.

SCOTTISH CUP – 7 medals each
Jimmy McMenemy (Celtic) 1904, 1907, 1908, 1911, 1912, 1914, (Partick Thistle) 1921.
Bob McPhail (Airdrieonians) 1924, (Rangers) 1928, 1930, 1932, 1934, 1935, 1936.
Billy McNeill (Celtic) 1965, 1967, 1969, 1971, 1972, 1974, 1975.

MOST LEAGUE GOALS IN A CAREER

		Goals	Games	Season
FOOTBALL LEAGUE				
Arthur Rowley	WBA	4	24	1946–48
	Fulham	27	56	1948–50
	Leicester C	251	303	1950–58
	Shrewsbury T	152	236	1958–65
		434	619	
SCOTTISH LEAGUE				
Jimmy McGrory	Celtic	1	3	1922–23
	Clydebank	13	30	1923–24
	Celtic	396	375	1924–38
		410	408	

MOST GOALS IN AN INTERNATIONAL CAREER

		Goals	Games
England	Bobby Charlton (Manchester U)	49	106
Scotland	Denis Law (Huddersfield T, Manchester C, Torino, Manchester U)	30	55
Ireland	Billy Gillespie (Sheffield U)	13	25
Wales	Trevor Ford (Swansea T, Aston Villa, Sunderland, Cardiff C)	23	38

MOST GOALS IN AN INTERNATIONAL

England	Malcolm Macdonald (Newcastle U) 5 goals v Cyprus, at Wembley	16.4.1975
	Willie Hall (Tottenham H) 5 goals v Ireland, at Old Trafford	16.11.1938
	G O Smith (Corinthians) 5 goals v Ireland, at Sunderland	18.2.1899
	Steve Bloomer (Derby C) 5 goals* v Wales, at Cardiff	16.3.1896
Scotland	Charles Heggie (Rangers) 5 goals v Ireland, at Belfast	20.3.1886
Ireland	Joe Bambrick (Linfield) 6 goals v Wales, at Belfast	1.2.1930
Wales	James Price (Wrexham) 4 goals v Ireland, at Wrexham	25.2.1882
	Mel Charles (Cardiff C) 4 goals v Ireland, at Cardiff	11.4.1962
	Ian Edwards (Chester) 4 goals v Malta, at Wrexham	25.10.78

* There are conflicting reports which make it uncertain whether Bloomer actually scored four or five goals in this game.

Some International Records

HIGHEST SCORES

World Cup match	West Germany	12	Cyprus	0	1969
Olympic Games	Denmark	17	France	1	1908
	Germany	16	USSR	0	1912
International	Germany	13	Finland	0	1940
	Spain	13	Bulgaria	0	1933
European Cup	Feyenoord	12	Reykjavik	2	1969
Cup-Winners' Cup	Sporting Lisbon	16	Apoel Nicosia	1	1963
Fairs & UEFA Cups	1FC Cologne	13	Union Luxembourg	0	1965

GOALSCORING RECORDS

World Cup Final	Geoff Hurst (England) 3 goals v West Germany	1966
World Cup Final tournament	Just Fontaine (France) 13 goals	1958
A major European cup game	Lothar Emmerich (Borussia Dortmund) v Floriana (Cup-Winners' Cup – 6 goals)	1965
Career	Arthur Friedenreich (Brazil) 1329 goals	1910–30
	Pele (Brazil) 1281 goals	1956–78
	Franz 'Bimbo' Binder (Austria, Germany) 1006 goals	1930–1950

MISCELLANEOUS

Brazil set up a record for undefeated matches in the World Cup in the 1958 and 1962 finals playing 13, winning 11, and drawing two. Their run ended when they lost 3-1 to Hungary in the 1966 World Cup.

Hungary went 13 years undefeated at home from after losing 7-2 to Sweden in 1943 until they lost 4-2 to Czechoslovakia in 1956. The Hungarians also had a run of 29 games before losing from their 5-3 defeat against Austria in May 1950 until they lost the World Cup final 3-2 to West Germany in July 1954.

Real Madrid were undefeated in League matches at home from February 1957 when they lost 3-2 to Atletico Madrid until beaten again by Atletico 1-0 in March 1965. Between these defeats they won 114 matches and drew eight.

Ferenc Deak was one of the most prolific goalscorers in League football in the years immediately after the war. In 1945–46 he scored 66 goals for Szentlorinci AC in Hungary, 48 in 1946–47, and 59 in 1948–49 when with Ferencvaros.

Players who have won international caps for three different countries are Ladislav Kubala, capped for Hungary, Czechoslovakia, and Spain in the post-war period, and Alfredo Di Stefano for Argentina, Colombia, and Spain.

The Nordahl brothers Knut, Bertil, and Gunnar won Olympic Gold medals with Sweden in 1948.

In 1955–56 Fiorentina went through 33 Italian League matches without defeat.

Thought to be the longest match on record, Santos (Brazil) and Penarol (Uruguay) played 3½ hours from August 2 to August 3 after kicking off at 9.30 a.m. The match ended 3-3 after interruptions during play, however.

The first international played in Europe other than between British teams was Austria 5 Hungary 0 on October 12 1902. The first match in South America was between Argentina and Uruguay in 1905 and drawn 1-1.

The first transfer fee approaching £1 million was £922,300 for Johan Cruyff from Ajax (Holland) to Barcelona (Spain) in 1973.

FIRSTS IN FOOTBALL

Football League
The first five Football League games were played on September 8 1888. Bolton Wanderers were three goals up in about six minutes against Derby Co, but were eventually beaten 6-3. Cox of Aston Villa scored the first 'own goal', giving Wolverhampton W an early lead, but Villa recovered to draw 1-1.

Huddersfield T became the first team to complete a hat-trick of League Championships—1924–25–26.

F.A. Cup
Tottenham H was the first Southern club to win the Cup when they beat Sheffield U in 1901. Spurs were then members of the Southern League and so were the first and only non-League club to carry off the trophy.

King George V was the first reigning monarch to attend a Cup Final. He saw Burnley beat Liverpool at the Crystal Palace in 1914.

David Jack (Bolton W) scored the first goal in a Wembley Cup Final. This was in 1923 when the crowd broke in to see the Wanderers beat West Ham U 2-0.

Extra time was first played in the Cup Final in 1877. Wanderers and Oxford University were drawing 0-0 at full-time, but Wanderers scored twice in extra time.

Internationals and representative games
The first representative game was played at Battersea Park, March 31 1866, London beating Sheffield by two goals and four touch-downs to nil.

The first official England v Scotland international was played at the West of Scotland Cricket Ground, Partick, November 30 1872, and resulted in a goalless draw.

Wales played their first international in 1876, losing 4-0 to Scotland in Glasgow.

Ireland's first international was against England at Bloomfield, Belfast, in 1882 when the visitors won 13-0.

Caps were first awarded for appearances in internationals in 1886.

The Football League played their first representative game in April 1891. It was against the Football Alliance at Sheffield and resulted in a draw 1-1.

England's first defeat on foreign soil in a full international was against Spain in Madrid in 1929 when the Spaniards won 4-3.

England's first home defeat by a continental country was at Wembley in 1953 when Hungary won 6-3.

Scotland's first home defeat by a foreign team was at Hampden Park in 1950 when Austria won 1-0.

Billy Wright became the first international in Britain to gain 100 caps when he captained England against Scotland at Wembley in April 1959.

Terry Venables was the first player to win international honours for England at five levels – Schoolboy, Youth, Amateur, Under-23 and Full International. He gained his first full cap in October 1964.

Floodlit football
The first-ever game by floodlight was that between two Sheffield Association teams at Bramall Lane, October 14 1878.

The first F.A. Cup tie under floodlights was a replay between Kidderminster Harriers and Brierley Hill Alliance, September 14 1955.

Floolights were first switched on during an international match in England in November 1955 at Wembley —England v Spain.

The first Football League game under floodlights – Portsmouth v Newcastle U, at Fratton Park, February 22 1956.

The first full international played entirely under floodlights in Britain took place at Wembley in 1963 when England beat N Ireland 8-3.

Hat-tricks
The first hat-trick in an F.A. Cup Final was that scored by William Townley for Blackburn R v Sheffield Wednesday in 1890.

Equipment, etc.
Shinguards were first introduced and registered by Sam Widdowson of Nottingham F in 1874. The cross-bar first replaced the tape in 1875, and the whistle was used by the referee for the first time in 1878.

Goalnets were invented and patented by J. A. Brodie of Liverpool in 1890 and were first used in the F.A. Cup Final in 1892.

Substitutes
First substitute in a Football League game – Keith Peacock of Charlton Ath, at Bolton, August 21 1965.

The first instance of a substitute in a home international Championship game was at Wrexham in 1889 when a player named Pugh of Rhostyllen, took over from the injured S. G. Gillam in the Welsh goal against Scotland.

England's first substitute in a full international was Jimmy Mullen (Wolverhampton W) who took over from the injured Jackie Milburn after 10 minutes of the game against Belgium in Brussels, May 18 1950.

The first substitute to score in a Football League game was Bobby Knox (Barrow) v Wrexham, Division 4, August 21 1965.

Transfers
The first four, five, and six-figure transfer fees between British clubs were as follows:
£1,000 – Alf Common, Sunderland to Middlesbrough, 1905.
£10,890 – David Jack, Bolton W to Arsenal, 1928.
£110,000 – Alan Ball Blackpool to Everton, 1966.

Radio and TV
The first match broadcast in England was the First Division game between Arsenal and Sheffield U at Highbury, January 22 1927.
The first Football League game to be televised was Blackpool v Bolton W, September 10 1960.
The first F.A. Cup tie to be televised – other than the Final – was Charlton Ath v Blackburn R, 5th Round, February 8 1947.

Corner-kick
Billy Smith was the first player to score direct from a corner-kick in a Football League game – Huddersfield T v Arsenal, October 11 1924.

Limited Company
The first football club to form itself into a limited liability company was Birmingham City in 1888. At that time they were still known as Small Heath.

Penalty kick
The first player to score from a penalty kick in a Football League match was Heath of Wolverhampton W v Accrington, Division I, September 14 1891.

Professional
The identity of the first professional footballer may never be definitely established, but it was probably J. J. Lang, a Scot who joined Sheffield Wednesday in 1876 after playing for Clydesdale and Glasgow Eastern.

Tour
Oxford University were the first to send a football team on an overseas tour. This was in 1875 when they visited Germany.

Sunday Football
The first Football League game to be played on a Sunday was that between Millwall and Fulham on the morning of January 20 1974. Eleven other Football League games were played later the same day.

SOME OTHER RECORDS

The oldest player ever to appear in the Football League was Neil McBain who played in goal for New Brighton v Hartlepools U, Division 3(N), March 15 1947. He was then aged 52 years 4 months.
The oldest player ever to appear for any of the home countries in a full international was Billy Meredith. He was nearly 46 years of age when he played for Wales v England, March 15 1920.
The record for most appearances in the Football League during one season by a player over 40 years of age was created by Bob McGrory. In his last season as a player with Stoke C (1934–35) he appeared in all 42 First Division games. Bob was then 43 years of age.
The record for most consecutive appearances in the Football League was created by Harold Bell, Tranmere R centre-half. Commencing with the openign game of season 1946–47 Bell did not miss a single game until August 1955 – a run of 401 consecutive Division 3(N) matches, Including FA Cup, Liverpool Senior Cup and Cheshire Bowl games, Bell enjoyed a run of 459 consecutive first team appearances.
Jimmy Dickinson created a club record by making 764 Football League appearances for Portsmouth between 1946 and 1965. In the Scottish League the record for most appearances for a single club was created by Bob Ferrier with a total of 626 for Motherwell between 1918 and 1937.
Billy Wright (Wolverhampton W) set up a world record by playing in 70 consecutive internationals for England, from 1951 to 1959.
Since substitutes were introduced into League football in 1965, Bristol C is the club that has played through the longest spell without calling upon one of these players – a run of 52 League games, 4 FA Cup, and 2 League Cup ties from February 1966 to April 1967.
The shortest player ever to appear in the Football League was outside-right Fred le May who was only 5 ft tall. He played for Thames 1930–31, Watford 1931–32, and Clapton Orient 1932–33. The tallest was Albert Iremonger, Notts Co and Lincoln C goalkeeper 1904–27. He was 6 ft 5 in tall.
The longest FA Cup tie was that in the 4th qualifying round between Alvechurch and Oxford C in 1971. This needed 11 hours (six games) before Alvechurch won 1-0.
The longest single game on record is that between Stockport Co and Doncaster R, March 26 1946. In an effort to reach a decisive result this Third Division (N) cup tie continued for 205 minutes before bad light forced an abandonment.
Rochdale suffered 14 consecutive home defeats in Division 3(N) in 1931–32. This is a Football League record. After beating New Brighton 3-2 on November 7 1931, they did not get another home point until holding Barrow to a goalless draw in their second home game of season 1932–33. During that same period Rochdale suffered one run of 17 consecutive defeats (home and away) – also a Football League record.
In season 1905–06 Bristol C won 14 consecutive Division 2 games. This Football League record was equalled by Preston NE in Division 2 in 1950–51.
The Scottish League record for the longest run of consecutive victories was created by Morton in Division 2 in 1963–64 when they won 23 games in a row.
Nottingham F. were undefeated in a run of 42 First Division games, November 1977 to December 1978. This is a Football League record.
The longest run without defeat in a single season of Football League games is one of 30 matches by Burnley in Division 1 in 1920–21.
In the Scottish League, Celtic created a record by remaining undefeated in a run of 63 games – November 1915 to April 1917.
Blackburn Rovers hold the record for the longest run of consecutive FA Cup ties without defeat. From December 1883 to December 1886 they were unbeaten in 24 Cup ties and won the trophy three times during this period.
Only two players have scored two goals for each side in a Football League game. Sam Wynne did so in a Division 2 game, October 6 1923, scoring twice for Oldham Ath as well as putting two through his own goal for Manchester U. Chris Nicholl (Aston Villa) scored all the goals in a 2-2 draw with Leicester C, Division 1, March 20 1976.

Arthur Chandler scored in each of 16 consecutive Football League games for Leicester C in Division 2 during season 1924–25. This is a League record.

Jimmy Cookson was the player who reached a first century of Football League goals in the shortest time. He made his debut for Chesterfield in 1925 and reached his century in December 1927 with West Bromwich A when figuring in his 87th Football League game.

The record number of goals scored by a player making his Football League debut is five – by George Hilsdon for Chelsea v Glossop, Division 2, September 1 1906.

The record for scoring the fastest goal in a Football League game is claimed by Jim Fryatt. According to Referee Mr. R. J. Simon this player scored for Bradford v Tranmere R only four seconds after the kick-off, April 25 1964. Fastest own goal Pat Kruse (Torquay) for Cambridge U January 3 1977 six seconds.

The fastest goals scored in the FA Cup Final at Wembley were obtained in the first minute. In 1928 John Roscamp put Blackburn R ahead when he charged both the Huddersfield goalkeeper and the ball into the net, and in 1955 Jackie Milburn headed Newcastle U into a first-minute lead over Manchester C.

John McIntyre scored four goals in five minutes for Blackburn R v Everton, Division 1, September 16 1922.

W. G. Richardson also scored four goals in five minutes for WBA, Division 1, November 7 1931, but this was even more remarkable because the feat was achieved in an away game – against West Ham U.

The record number of penalties missed by one side in a Football League Division 1 game is three. Manchester C (Fletcher 2 and Thornley) missed this number against Newcastle U, January 27 1912.

The most penalties scored by a player in a First Division game is three – Billy Walker for Aston Villa v Bradford C, November 12 1921; Charlie Mitten for Manchester U v Aston Villa, March 8 1950, and Ken Barnes for Manchester C v Everton, December 7 1957.

The record number of players from the same club in an England team is seven, Frank Moss, George Male, Eddie Hapgood, Wilf Copping, Raymond Bowden, Ted Drake and Clifford Bastin, all of Arsenal, played against Italy at Highbury, November 14 1934.

The England team twice included all Corinthian players in the 1890s but this cannot be considered a record because the Corinthians were a combined eleven, most of their players also appearing with other clubs.

In season 1925–26 Cardiff C created a Football League record by having as many as 17 internationals on their books. There were 9 Welsh internationals, 4 Scottish, and 4 Irish.

The England team that won the 1966 World Cup created a record for the country by remaining unchanged in six consecutive games – the quarter-final, semi-final and final of the World Cup and their next three games.

England's longest run without defeat is one of 20 games between 1889 and 1896.

The biggest championship winning margin for any division of the Football League is 15 points. Middlesbrough finished that far ahead of the runners-up in Division 2 in 1973–74.

The smallest number of players called upon by a club to complete a season of Football League games is 14 by Liverpool when winning the Championship in 1965–66. Five of their players were ever-present.

In the Scottish League, Dundee called upon only 15 players throughout season 1961–62. They also won the Championship that season and had five players ever-present.

The goalscoring record for a goalkeeper in a single season of Football League games was set up in 1923–24 by Arnold Birch of Chesterfield. In Division 3(N) games that season he scored five goals, all from penalties.

Five men have both played in and managed Football League Championship winning teams: Ted Drake, Arsenal, centre-forward, 1933–34, 1934–35, 1937–38, Chelsea, manager, 1954–55. Bill Nicholson, Tottenham H, right half-back, 1950–51, manager, 1960–61. Alf Ramsey, right-back, Tottenham H, 1950–51, Ipswich T, manager, 1961–62. Joe Mercer, left-half, Everton 1938–39, Arsenal 1947–48, 1952–53, Manchester C, manager, 1967–68. Dave Mackay, left-half, Tottenham H 1960–61, Derby Co, manager, 1974–75. Bob Paisley, Liverpool left half-back, 1946–47, manager 1975–76.

In 1973–74 Leeds U created a Football League record for the longest run without defeat from the start of a season – 29 First Division games before losing 2–3 at Stoke. It could be said that this only equalled Liverpool's run in the Second Division in 1893–94 when they were unbeaten in all 28 games. Their 29th game that season was the extra 'Test Match' to decide promotion and relegation between the First and Second Divisions.

History of Football Part 2: 1939 to 1955

FA Cup results, teams for final; steps in history; Football League tables; England international results.

1939–40 Regional League:	South 'A' – Arsenal
	South 'B' – QPR
	South 'C' – Tottenham H
	South 'D' – Crystal Palace
	Western – Stoke C
	South-Western – Plymouth Arg
	Midland – Wolverhampton W
	East Midland – Chesterfield
	North-West – Bury
	North-East – Huddersfield T
	Scottish West and South – Rangers
	Scottish East and North – Falkirk
	League War Cup – West Ham U
1940–41 Regional League:	North – Preston N E
	South – Crystal Palace
	Scottish Southern – Rangers
	League War Cup – Preston N E
1941–42 Regional League:	North – Blackpool
	South – Leicester C
	London – Arsenal
	Scottish Southern – Rangers
	League War Cup – Wolverhampton W
1942–43 Regional League:	North – Blackpool
	South – Arsenal
	Scottish Southern – Rangers
	League War Cup – Blackpool (North), Arsenal (South)
1943–44 Regional League:	North – Blackpool
	South – Tottenham H
	Scottish Southern – Rangers
	League War Cup – Aston Villa (North), Charlton Ath (South)
1944–45 Regional League:	North – Huddersfield T
	South – Tottenham H
	Scottish Southern – Rangers
	League War Cup – Bolton W (North), Chelsea (South)
1945–46 Regional League:	North – Sheffield U
	South – Birmingham City
	Third South (South) – Crystal Palace
	Third South (North) – QPR
	Third North (West) – Accrington Stanley
	Third North (East) – Darlington
	Third South Cup – Bournemouth
	Third North Cup – Rotherham U
	Scottish 'A' – Rangers
	Scottish 'B' – Dundee

1939–40	11 Nov v Wales (Cardiff)	1-1	Goulden
1939–40	18 Nov v Wales (Wrexham)	3-2	Balmer, Lawton, Martin
1939–40	2 Dec v Scotland (Newcastle)	2-1	Carter, Lawton
1939–40	13 Apr v Wales (Wembley)	0-1	
1939–40	11 May v Scotland (Glasgow)	1-1	Welsh
1940–41	8 Feb v Scotland (Newcastle)	2-3	Lawton, Birkett
1940–41	26 Apr v Wales (Nottingham)	4-1	Welsh 4
1940–41	3 May v Scotland (Glasgow)	3-1	Welsh 2, Goulden
1940–41	7 June v Wales (Cardiff)	3-2	Hagan 2, Welsh
1941–42	4 Oct v Scotland (Wembley)	2-0	Welsh, Hagan
1941–42	25 Oct v Wales (Birmingham)	2-1	Edelston, Hagan
1941–42	17 Jan v Scotland (Wembley)	3-0	Lawton 2, Hagan
1941–42	18 Apr v Scotland (Glasgow)	4-5	Lawton 3, Hagan
1941–42	9 May v Wales (Cardiff)	0-1	
1942–43	10 Oct v Scotland (Wembley)	0-0	
1942–43	24 Oct v Wales (Wolverhampton)	1-2	Lawton
1942–43	27 Feb v Wales (Wembley)	5-3	Westcott 3, Carter 2
1942–43	17 Apr v Scotland (Glasgow)	4-0	Carter 2, Westcott, D Compton
1942–43	8 May v Wales (Cardiff)	1-1	Westcott
1943–44	25 Sep v Wales (Wembley)	8-3	Carter 2, Welsh 3, Hagan 2, D Compton
1943–44	16 Oct v Scotland (Manchester)	8-0	Lawton 4, Matthews, Carter, Hagan 2
1943–44	19 Feb v Scotland (Wembley)	6-2	Mercer, Lawton, Hagan 2, Carter, and an opponent
1943–44	22 Apr v Scotland (Glasgow)	3-2	Carter, Lawton 2
1943–44	6 May v Wales (Cardiff)	2-0	Lawton, Smith
1944–45	16 Sep v Wales (Liverpool)	2-2	Carter, Lawton
1944–45	14 Oct v Scotland (Wembley)	6-2	Carter, Lawton 3, Goulden, Smith
1944–45	3 Feb v Scotland (Birmingham)	3-2	Brown, Mortensen 2
1944–45	14 Apr v Scotland (Glasgow)	6-1	Matthews, Carter, Lawton 2, Brown, Smith
1944–45	5 May v Wales (Cardiff)	3-2	Carter 3
1944–45	26 May v France (Wembley)	2-2	Carter, Lawton
1945–46	15 Sep v Ireland (Belfast)	1-0	Mortensen
1945–46	20 Oct v Wales (West Bromwich)	0-1	
1945–46	19 Jan v Belgium (Wembley)	2-0	Brown, Pye
1945–46	13 Apr v Scotland (Glasgow)	0-1	
1945–46	11 May v Switzerland (Chelsea)	4-1	Carter 2, Lawton, Brown
1945–46	19 May v France (Paris)	1-2	Hagan

England Victory and Wartime Internationals

1946 Victory Internationals. 1940–45 Wartime Internationals. (No caps were awarded for these games.)

Abbreviations, E, England; S, Scotland; W, Wales; I, Ireland; Bel, Belgium; F, France; Sw, Switzerland.

Bacuzzi J D (Fulham), 1940 v W (2); 1941 v S (2), W (2); 1942 v S (3), W; 1943 v S, W; 1946 v F (13)
Balmer J (Everton), 1940 v W (1)
Barrass M W (Bolton W) 1946 v W (1)
Bartram S (Charlton Ath), 1940 v W; 1941 v S, W (3)
Birkett R J E (Newcastle U), 1941 v S (1)
Britton C S (Everton), 1941 v W (2); 1942 v W; 1943 v S (2), v W (3); 1944 v S (2), W (2) (12)
Brook E F (Manchester C), 1940 v W (1)
Broome F H (Aston Villa), 1940 v S (1)
Brown R A J (Charlton Ath), 1945 v W, F, S (2); 1946 v Bel (with Nottingham F) Sw (6)
Buckingham V F (Tottenham H), 1941 v W (2)

Carter H S (Sunderland), 1940 v S; 1943 v S, W (2); 1944 v S (3), W (2); 1945 v W (2), S (2), F; 1946 v I (with Derby Co) F, Sw (17)
Clifton H (Newcastle U), 1940 v S (1)
Compton D C S (Arsenal), 1940 v W; 1941 v S; 1942 v S (2), W; 1943 v S (2), W (2); 1944 v S, W; 1946 v W (12)
Compton L H (Arsenal), 1940 v W; 1943 v S, W; 1944 v S, W (5)
Copping W (Leeds U), 1940 v W (1)
Crayston W J (Arsenal), 1940 v W (1)
Crook W (Blackburn R), 1940 v W (1)
Cullis S (Wolverhampton W), 1940 v S, W (2); 1941 v S (2), W (2); 1942 v S (2), W; 1943 v S (2), W (3); 1944 v S (3), W (2) (20)

Ditchburn, E G (Tottenham H), 1944 v S, W (2)

Edelston M (Reading), 1941 v W; 1942 v S, W (2); 1943 v S (5)
Elliott W B (WBA), 1944 v W; 1946 v S (2)

Fenton E B A (West Ham U), 1940 v W (1)
Fenton M (Middlesbrough), 1946 v W (1)
Finch L C (Barnet), 1941 v W (1)
Fisher F (Millwall) 1941 v W (1)
Flewin R (Portsmouth), 1945 v W (1)
Franklin C F (Stoke C), 1945 v W, S (2), F; 1946 v I, Bel, F, Sw, S, W (10)

Gibbons A H (Tottenham H), 1943 v W (1)
Goslin H A (Bolton W), 1940 v S; 1941 v S; 1942 v S, W (4)
Goulden L A (West Ham U), 1940 v W (2); 1941 v S (2), W; 1945 v S (6)
Greenhalgh N H (Everton), 1940 v S (1)

Hagan J (Sheffield U), 1941 v W (2); 1942 v S (3), W; 1943 v S (2), W (2), 1944 v S (3), W; 1946 v S, F (16)
Hall G W (Tottenham H), 1940 v W (2); 1942 v W (3)
Hanson A J (Chelsea), 1941 v S (1)
Hapgood E A (Arsenal), 1940 v S, W (2); 1941 v S, W; 1942 v S (3), W (2); 1943 v S, W (2) (13)
Harper B (Barnsley), 1940 v S (1)
Hardwick G F M (Middlesbrough), 1941 v W; 1943 v S, W (2); 1944 v S (2), W; 1945 v W (2), F, S (3); 1946 v Bel, F, Sw, S (17)

Johnson W H (Charlton Ath), 1946 v Sw, F (2)
Joy B (Arsenal), 1945 v S (1)

Kinsell T H (WBA), 1946 v I, W (2)
Kirchen A J (Arsenal), 1941 v W; 1942 v S, W (3)

Lawton T (Everton), 1940 v S, W; 1941 v S; 1942 v S (2), W; 1943 v S, W; 1944 v S (3), W; 1945 v W (2), S (3), F; 1946 (with Chelsea) v I, Bel, F, Sw, S (23)
Lewis J W (Walthamstow A), 1940 v W (sub) (1)

Mannion W J (Middlesbrough), 1941 v S (2); 1942 v S (2) (4)
Mapson J D (Sunderland), 1941 v W (1)
Marks G W (Arsenal), 1942 v S (3), W (2); 1943 v S, W (2) (8)
Martin J R (Aston Villa), 1940 v S, W (2)
Mason G W (Coventry C), 1942 v S, W (2)
Matthews S (Stoke C), 1940 v S (2), W (2); 1941 v S; 1942 v S (3), W; 1943 v S (2), W (3); 1944 v S (3), W; 1945 v S (3), W (2), F; 1946 v I, Bel, F, Sw, W (29)
Mercer J (Everton), 1940 v S (2), W; 1941 v S (2); 1942 v S (2), W; 1943 v S (2), W (3); 1944 v S (3), W; 1945 v S (3), W (2), F; 1946 v I, Bel, S, W (27)
Mortensen S H (Blackpool), 1945 v W, S; 1946 v I (3)
Mountford R C (Huddersfield T), 1941 v S (1)
Mullen J (Wolverhampton W), 1943 v W; 1945 v W; 1946 v Bel (3)

Oakes R J (Charlton Ath), 1940 v W (1)

Pearson T U (Newcastle U), 1940 v S (1)
Pye J (Notts Co), 1946 v Bel (1)

Richardson J (Newcastle U), 1940 v S (1)
Rooke R L (Fulham), 1943 v W (1)
Rowley J F (Manchester U), 1944 v W (1)
Roxburgh A W (Blackpool), 1944 v W (1)

Scott L (Arsenal), 1942 v W; 1944 v S (2), W (2); 1945 v W (2), S (3), F; 1946 v I, Bel, Sw, S, W (16)
Shackleton L F (Bradford), 1946 v S (1)
Smith G C (Charlton Ath), 1945 v W (1)
Smith J C R (Millwall), 1940 v S, W; 1941 v W (3)
Smith L G F (Brentford), 1940 v W; 1942 v W; 1944 v S (2), W; 1945 v W, S (3), F; 1946 v I, F, Sw (13)
Soo F (Stoke C), 1942 v W; 1944 v S, W; 1945 v S (3), F; 1946 v I (with Leicester C), W (9)
Sproston B (Manchester C), 1940 v W, S (2)
Stubbins A (Newcastle U), 1946 v W (1)
Swift F V (Manchester C), 1940 v W; 1941 v S; 1943 v S, W; 1944 v S (2); 1945 v W, S (3); 1946 v I, Bel, Sw, S (14)
Swinburne T A (Newcastle U), 1940 v S (1)

Taylor F (Wolverhampton W), 1944 v S (1)

Watson W (Huddersfield T), 1946 v W (1)
Welsh D (Charlton Ath), 1940 v S; 1941 v S, W (2); 1942 v S (2), W; 1944 v W; 1945 v W (9)
Westcott D (Wolverhampton W), 1940 v W; 1943 v S, W (2) (4)
Williams B F (Walsall), 1945 v W, F (with Wolverhampton W); 1946 v F, W (4)
Willingham C K (Huddersfield T), 1940 v W (2), S; 1941 v S; 1942 v S (2) (6)
Woodley V R (Chelsea), 1940 v W, S (2)
Wright W A (Wolverhampton W), 1946 v Bel, F, Sw, S (4)

FA CUP 1945-46

Third Round
Stoke City v Burnley	3-1, 1-2
Huddersfield T v Sheffield U	1-1, 0-2
Mansfield T v Sheffield W	0-0, 0-5
Chesterfield v York C	1-1, 2-3
Bolton W v Blackburn R	1-0, 3-1
Chester v Liverpool	0-2, 1-2
Wrexham v Blackpool	1-4, 1-4
Leeds U v Middlesbrough U	4-4, 2-7
Accrington S v Manchester U	2-2, 1-5
Preston NE v Everton	2-1, 2-2
Charlton Ath v Fulham	3-1, 1-2
Lovell's A v Wolverhampton W	2-4, 1-8
Southampton v Newport C	4-3, 2-1
QPR v Crystal Palace	0-0, 0-0, 1-0
Bristol C v Swansea T	5-1, 2-2
Tottenham H v Brentford	2-2, 0-2
Chelsea v Leicester C	1-1, 2-0
West Ham U v Arsenal	6-0, 0-1
Northampton v Millwall	2-2, 0-3
Coventry C v Aston V	2-1, 0-2
Norwich C v Brighton	1-2, 1-3
Aldershot v Plymouth Arg	2-0, 1-0
Luton T v Derby Co	0-6, 0-3
Cardiff C v WBA	1-1, 0-4
Newcastle U v Barnsley	4-2, 0-3
Rotherham U v Gateshead	2-2, 2-0
Bradford PA v Port Vale	2-1, 1-1
Manchester C v Barrow	6-2, 2-2
Grimsby T v Sunderland	1-3, 1-2
Bury v Rochdale	3-3, 4-2
Birmingham v Portsmouth	1-0, 0-0
Nottm F v Bradford	1-1, 1-1, 0-1
Bolton W v Liverpool	5-0, 0-2
Blackpool v Middlesbrough	3-2, 2-3, 0-1
Manchester U v Preston NE	1-0, 1-3
Charlton Ath v Wolverhampton W	5-2, 1-1
Southampton v QPR	0-1, 3-4
Bristol C v Brentford	2-1, 0-5
Chelsea v West Ham U	2-0, 0-1
Millwall v Aston V	2-4, 1-9
Brighton v Aldershot	3-0, 4-1
Derby Co v WBA	1-0, 3-1
Barnsley v Rotherham U	3-0, 1-2
Bradford PA v Manchester C	1-3, 8-2
Sunderland v Bury	3-1, 4-5
Birmingham v Watford	5-0, 1-1

Fourth Round
Stoke C v Sheffield U	2-0, 2-3
Sheffield W v York C	5-1, 6-1

Fifth Round
Stoke C v Sheffield W	2-0, 0-0
Bolton W v Middlesbrough	1-0, 1-1
Preston NE v Charlton A	1-1, 0-6
QPR v Brentford	1-3, 0-0
Chelsea v Aston V	0-1, 0-1
Brighton v Derby Co	1-4, 0-6
Barnsley v Bradford PA	0-1, 1-1
Sunderland v Birmingham	1-0, 1-3

Sixth Round
Stoke C v Bolton W	0-2, 0-0
Charlton Ath v Brentford	6-3, 3-1
Aston V v Derby Co	3-4, 1-1
Bradford PA v Birmingham	2-2, 0-6

Semi-Final
Bolton W v Charlton Ath	0-2
Derby Co v Birmingham	1-1, 4-0

Final 1945-46: Derby Co ¹4 Charlton Ath ¹1

For this season only, the Competition was played on home and away principle up to Semi-Final round. Ties decided on aggregate of goals. First named team played at home in first tie.

FA CUP 1946-47

Third Round
Charlton Ath v Rochdale	3-1
WBA v Leeds U	2-1
*Blackburn R v Hull C	1-1, 3-0
Millwall v Port Vale	0-3
Northampton T v Preston NE	1-2
Huddersfield T v Barnsley	3-4
Sheffield W v Blackpool	4-1
Everton v Southend U	4-2
Newcastle U v Crystal Palace	6-2
Southampton v Bury	5-1
West Ham U v Leicester C	1-2
Brentford v Cardiff C	1-0
Sheffield U v Carlisle U	3-0
Wolverhampton W v Rotherham U	3-0
*Tottenham H v Stoke C	2-2, 0-1
Chester v Plymouth Arg	2-0
Burnley v Aston Villa	5-1
Coventry C v Newport Co	5-2
Luton T v Notts Co	6-0
Swansea T v Gillingham	4-1
*QPR v Middlesbrough	1-1, 1-3
Chesterfield v Sunderland	2-1
Lincoln C v Nottingham F	0-1
Bradford PA v Manchester U	0-3
Walsall v Liverpool	2-5
*Reading v Grimsby T	2-2, 1-3
Bournemouth v Derby Co	0-2
*Chelsea v Arsenal	1-1, ¹1-1, 2-0
Fulham v Birmingham C	1-2
Doncaster R v Portsmouth	2-3
Manchester C v Gateshead	3-0
Bolton W v Stockport Co	5-1
Preston NE v Barnsley	6-0
Sheffield W v Everton	2-1
Newcastle U v Southampton	3-1
*Brentford v Leicester C	0-0, ¹0-0, 1-4
*Wolverhampton W v Sheffield U	0-0, 0-2
Chester v Stoke C	0-0, 2-3
Burnley v Coventry C	2-0
Luton T v Swansea T	2-0
Middlesbrough v Chesterfield	2-1
Manchester U v Nottingham F	0-2
Liverpool v Grimsby T	2-0
*Chelsea v Derby Co	2-2, ¹0-1
Birmingham C v Portsmouth	1-0
*Bolton W v Manchester C	3-3, 0-1

Fourth Round
WBA v Charlton Ath	1-2
Blackburn R v Port Vale	2-0

Fifth Round
Charlton Ath v Blackburn R	1-0
Sheffield W v Preston NE	0-2
*Newcastle U v Leicester C	1-1, 2-1
Stoke C v Sheffield U	0-1
*Luton T v Burnley	0-0, 0-3
*Nottingham F v Middlesbrough	2-2, 2-6
Liverpool v Derby Co	1-0
Birmingham C v Manchester C	5-0

Sixth Round
Charlton Ath v Preston NE	2-1
Sheffield U v Newcastle U	0-2
*Middlesbrough v Burnley	1-1, 0-1
Liverpool v Birmingham C	¹4-1

Semi-Final
Charlton Ath v Newcastle U	4-0
Burnley v Liverpool	¹0-0, 1-0

Final 1946-47: Charlton Ath ¹1 Burnley 0

*Home club.   ¹After extra time.

1946 England, Northern Ireland, Scotland and Wales rejoined FIFA.
1946 Bolton Disaster. On March 9, 33 people were killed and over 400 injured when crush barriers at Burnden Park, Bolton, gave way during Cup-Tie with Stoke C.
1947 Great Britain beat Rest of Europe 6-1 at Hampden Park, Glasgow.
1947 Doncaster R set up new record in Third Division North with 72 points.

Season	Date	Opponent	Score	Scorers
1946–47	28 Sept	v Ireland (Belfast)	7-2	Carter, Mannion (3), Finney, Lawton, Langton
1946–47	30 Sept	v Rep of Ireland (Dublin)	1-0	Finney
1946–47	13 Nov	v Wales (Manchester)	3-0	Mannion (2), Lawton
1946–47	27 Nov	v Netherlands (Huddersfield)	8-2	Lawton (4), Carter (2), Mannion, Finney
1946–47	12 Apr	v Scotland (Wembley)	1-1	Carter
1944–47	3 May	v France (Highbury)	3-0	Finney, Mannion, Carter
1946–47	18 May	v Switzerland (Zurich)	0-1	
1946–47	25 May	v Portugal (Lisbon)	10-0	Lawton (4), Mortensen (4), Finney, Matthews

1946–47

DIVISION 1

	P	W	D	L	F	A	Pts
Liverpool	42	25	7	10	84	52	57
Manchester U	42	22	12	8	95	54	56
Wolverhampton W	42	25	6	11	98	56	56
Stoke C	42	24	7	11	90	53	55
Blackpool	42	22	6	14	71	70	50
Sheffield U	42	21	7	14	89	75	49
Preston NE	42	18	11	13	76	74	47
Aston Villa	42	18	9	15	67	53	45
Sunderland	42	18	8	16	65	66	44
Everton	42	17	9	16	62	67	43
Middlesbrough	42	17	8	17	73	68	42
Portsmouth	42	16	9	17	66	60	41
Arsenal	42	16	9	17	72	70	41
Derby Co	42	18	5	19	73	79	41
Chelsea	42	16	7	19	69	84	39
Grimsby T	42	13	12	17	61	82	38
Blackburn R	42	14	8	20	45	53	36
Bolton W	42	13	8	21	57	69	34
Charlton Ath	42	11	12	19	57	71	34
Huddersfield	42	13	7	22	53	79	33
Brentford	42	9	7	26	45	88	25
Leeds U	42	6	6	30	45	90	18

DIVISION 2

	P	W	D	L	F	A	Pts
Manchester C	42	26	10	6	78	35	62
Burnley	42	22	14	6	65	29	58
Birmingham C	42	25	5	12	74	33	55
Chesterfield	42	18	14	10	58	44	50
Newcastle U	42	19	10	13	95	62	48
Tottenham H	42	17	14	11	65	53	48
WBA	42	20	8	14	88	75	48
Coventry C	42	16	13	13	66	59	45
Leicester C	42	18	7	17	69	64	43
Barnsley	42	17	8	17	84	86	42
Nottingham F	42	15	10	17	69	74	40
West Ham U	42	16	8	18	70	76	40
Luton T	42	16	7	19	71	73	39
Southampton	42	15	9	18	69	76	39
Fulham	42	15	9	18	63	74	39
Bradford PA	42	14	11	17	65	77	39
Bury	42	12	12	18	80	78	36
Millwall	42	14	8	20	56	79	36
Plymouth Arg	42	14	5	23	79	96	33
Sheffield W	42	12	8	22	67	88	32
Swansea T	42	11	7	24	55	83	29
Newport Co	42	10	3	29	60	133	23

DIVISION 3 (SOUTH)

	P	W	D	L	F	A	Pts
Cardiff C	42	30	6	6	93	30	66
QPR	42	23	11	8	74	40	57
Bristol C	42	20	11	11	94	56	51
Swindon T	42	19	11	12	84	73	49
Walsall	42	17	12	13	74	59	46
Ipswich T	42	16	14	12	61	53	46
Bournemouth	42	18	8	16	72	54	44
Southend U	42	17	10	15	71	60	44
Reading	42	16	11	15	83	74	43
Port Vale	42	17	9	16	68	63	43
Torquay U	42	15	12	15	52	61	42
Notts Co	42	15	10	17	63	63	40
Northampton	42	15	10	17	72	75	40
Bristol R	42	16	8	18	59	69	40
Exeter C	42	15	9	18	60	69	39
Watford	42	17	5	20	61	76	39
Brighton	42	13	12	17	54	72	38
Crystal Palace	42	13	11	18	49	62	37
Leyton O	42	12	8	22	54	75	32
Aldershot	42	10	12	20	48	78	32
Norwich C	42	10	8	24	64	100	28
Mansfield T	42	9	10	23	48	96	28

DIVISION 3 (NORTH)

	P	W	D	L	F	A	Pts
Doncaster R	42	33	6	3	123	40	72
Rotherham U	42	29	6	7	114	53	64
Chester	42	25	6	11	95	51	56
Stockport Co	42	24	2	16	78	53	50
Bradford C	42	20	10	12	62	47	50
Rochdale	42	19	10	13	80	64	48
Wrexham	42	17	12	13	65	51	46
Crewe Alex	42	17	9	16	70	74	43
Barrow	42	17	7	18	54	62	41
Tranmere R	42	17	7	18	66	77	41
Hull C	42	16	8	18	49	53	40
Lincoln C	42	17	5	20	86	87	39
Hartlepools U	42	15	9	18	64	73	39
Gateshead	42	16	6	20	62	72	38
York C	42	14	9	19	67	81	37
Carlisle U	42	14	9	19	70	93	37
Darlington	42	15	6	21	68	80	36
New Brighton	42	14	8	20	57	77	36
Oldham Ath	42	12	8	22	55	80	32
Accrington S	42	14	4	24	56	92	32
Southport	42	7	11	24	53	85	25
Halifax T	42	8	6	28	43	92	22

FA CUP 1947–48

Third Round

*Gillingham v QPR	1-1, 1-3
Mansfield T v Stoke C	2-4
Plymouth Arg v Luton T	2-4
Coventry C v Walsall	2-1
Rotherham U v Brentford	0-3
Hull C v Middlesbrough	1-3
Crewe Alex v Sheffield U	3-1
Derby Co v Chesterfield	2-0
Aston Villa v Manchester U	4-6
Liverpool v Nottingham F	4-1
Charlton Ath v Newcastle U	2-1
Stockport Co v Torquay U	3-0
Manchester C v Barnsley	2-1
Chelsea v Barrow	5-0
Portsmouth v Brighton	4-1
Millwall v Preston NE	1-2
Fulham v Doncaster R	2-0
Bristol R v Swansea T	3-0
Bournemouth v Wolverhampton W	1-2
Grimsby T v Everton	1-4
Blackpool v Leeds U	4-0
Crystal Palace v Chester	0-1
Colchester U v Huddersfield	1-0
Arsenal v Bradford PA	0-1
Southampton v Sunderland	1-0
*Blackburn R v West Ham U	0-0, 4-2
Burnley v Swindon T	0-2
Birmingham C v Notts Co	0-2
Bolton W v Tottenham H	0-2
WBA v Reading	2-0
Leicester C v Bury	1-0
Cardiff C v Sheffield W	1-2
Brentford v Middlesbrough	1-2
Crewe Alex v Derby Co	0-3
Manchester U v Liverpool	³3-0
Charlton Ath v Stockport Co	3-0
Manchester C v Chelsea	2-0
Portsmouth v Preston NE	1-3
Fulham v Bristol R	5-2
*Wolverhampton W v Everton	1-1, 2-3
Blackpool v Chester	4-0
Colchester U v Bradford PA	3-2
Southampton v Blackburn R	3-2
Swindon T v Notts Co	1-0
Tottenham H v WBA	3-1
Leicester C v Sheffield W	2-1

Fourth Round

QPR v Stoke C	3-0
Luton T v Coventry C	3-2

Fifth Round

QPR v Luton T	3-1
Middlesbrough v Derby Co	1-2
Manchester U v Charlton Ath	²2-0
Manchester C v Preston NE	0-1
*Fulham v Everton	1-1, 1-0
Blackpool v Colchester U	5-0
Southampton v Swindon T	3-0
Tottenham H v Leicester C	5-2

Sixth Round

*QPR v Derby Co	1-1, 0-5
Manchester U v Preston NE	4-1
Fulham v Blackpool	0-2
Southampton v Tottenham H	0-1

Semi-Final

Derby Co v Manchester U	³1-3
Blackpool v Tottenham H	³3-1

Final 1947–48: Blackpool 2 Manchester U 4

[1] At Hillsborough. [2] At Villa Park. [3] At Goodison Park. [4] At Huddersfield.

1948 Two players were killed by lightning on the pitch during Army Cup Final at Aldershot, in the presence of the King and Queen.
1948 Record for an English League match, 82,950, Manchester U v Arsenal, January 17, at Maine Road.

1947–48	21 Sept v Belgium (Brussels)	5-2	Lawton 2, Mortensen, Finney 2
1947–48	18 Oct v Wales (Cardiff)	3-0	Finney, Mortensen, Lawton
1947–48	5 Nov v Ireland (Everton)	2-2	Mannion, Lawton
1947–48	19 Nov v Sweden (Highbury)	4-2	Mortensen 3, Lawton
1947–48	10 Apr v Scotland (Glasgow)	2-0	Finney, Mortensen
1947–48	16 May v Italy (Turin)	4-0	Mortensen, Lawton, Finney 2

1947–48

DIVISION 1

	P	W	D	L	F	A	Pts
Arsenal	42	23	13	6	81	32	59
Manchester U	42	19	14	9	81	48	52
Burnley	42	20	12	10	56	43	52
Derby Co	42	19	12	11	77	57	50
Wolverhampton W	42	19	9	14	83	70	47
Aston Villa	42	19	9	14	65	57	47
Preston NE	42	20	7	15	67	68	47
Portsmouth	42	19	7	16	68	50	45
Blackpool	42	17	10	15	57	41	44
Manchester C	42	15	12	15	52	47	42
Liverpool	42	16	10	16	65	61	42
Sheffield U	42	16	10	16	65	70	42
Charlton Ath	42	17	6	19	57	66	40
Everton	42	17	6	19	52	66	40
Stoke C	42	14	10	18	41	55	38
Middlesbrough	42	14	9	19	71	73	37
Bolton W	42	16	5	21	46	58	37
Chelsea	42	14	9	19	53	71	37
Huddersfield	42	12	12	18	51	60	36
Sunderland	42	13	10	19	56	67	36
Blackburn R	42	11	10	21	54	72	32
Grimsby T	42	8	6	28	45	111	22

DIVISION 2

	P	W	D	L	F	A	Pts
Birmingham C	42	22	15	5	55	24	59
Newcastle U	42	24	8	10	72	41	56
Southampton	42	21	10	11	71	53	52
Sheffield W	42	20	11	11	66	53	51
Cardiff C	42	18	11	13	61	58	47
West Ham U	42	16	14	12	55	53	46
WBA	42	18	9	15	63	58	45
Tottenham H	42	15	14	13	56	43	44
Leicester C	42	16	11	15	60	57	43
Coventry C	42	14	13	15	59	52	41
Fulham	42	15	10	17	47	46	40
Barnsley	42	15	10	17	62	64	40
Luton T	42	14	12	16	56	59	40
Bradford PA	42	16	8	18	68	72	40
Brentford	42	13	14	15	44	61	40
Chesterfield	42	16	7	19	54	55	39
Plymouth Arg	42	9	20	13	40	58	38
Leeds U	42	14	8	20	62	72	36
Nottingham F	42	12	11	19	54	60	35
Bury	42	9	16	17	58	68	34
Doncaster R	42	9	11	22	40	66	29
Millwall	42	9	11	22	44	74	29

DIVISION 3 (SOUTH)

	P	W	D	L	F	A	Pts
QPR	42	26	9	7	74	37	61
Bournemouth	42	24	9	9	76	35	57
Walsall	42	21	9	12	70	40	51
Ipswich T	42	23	3	16	67	61	49
Swansea T	42	18	12	12	70	52	48
Notts Co	42	19	8	15	68	59	46
Bristol C	42	18	7	17	77	65	43
Port Vale	42	16	11	15	63	54	43
Southend U	42	15	13	14	51	58	43
Reading	42	15	11	16	56	58	41
Exeter C	42	15	11	16	55	63	41
Newport Co	42	14	13	15	61	73	41
C Palace	42	13	13	16	49	49	39
Northampton	42	14	11	17	58	72	39
Watford	42	14	10	18	57	79	38
Swindon T	42	10	16	16	41	46	36
Leyton O	42	13	10	19	51	73	36
Torquay U	42	11	13	18	63	62	35
Aldershot	42	10	15	17	45	67	35
Bristol R	42	13	8	21	71	75	34
Norwich C	42	13	8	21	61	76	34
Brighton	42	11	12	19	43	73	34

DIVISION 3 (NORTH)

	P	W	D	L	F	A	Pts
Lincoln C	42	26	8	8	81	40	60
Rotherham U	42	25	9	8	95	49	59
Wrexham	42	21	8	13	74	54	50
Gateshead	42	19	11	12	75	57	49
Hull C	42	18	11	13	59	48	47
Accrington S	42	20	6	16	62	59	46
Barrow	42	16	13	13	49	40	45
Mansfield T	42	17	11	14	57	51	45
Carlisle U	42	18	7	17	88	77	43
Crewe Alex	42	18	7	17	61	63	43
Oldham Ath	42	14	13	15	63	64	41
Rochdale	42	15	11	16	48	72	41
York C	42	13	14	15	65	60	40
Bradford C	42	15	10	17	65	66	40
Southport	42	14	11	17	60	63	39
Darlington	42	13	13	16	54	70	39
Stockport Co	42	13	12	17	63	67	38
Tranmere R	42	16	4	22	54	72	36
Hartlepools U	42	14	8	20	51	73	36
Chester	42	13	9	20	64	67	35
Halifax T	42	7	13	22	43	76	27
New Brighton	42	8	9	25	38	81	25

FA CUP 1948–49

Third Round

Manchester U v Bournemouth	6-0
Newcastle U v Bradford PA	0-2
Yeovil T v Bury	3-1
Crewe Alex v Sunderland	0-2
Blackburn R v Hull C	¹1-2
Grimsby T v Exeter C	2-1
Swindon T v Stoke C	1-3
Barnsley v Blackpool	0-1
Wolverhampton W v Chesterfield	6-0
Sheffield U v New Brighton	5-2
*Nottingham F v Liverpool	2-2, 0-4
Plymouth Arg v Notts Co	¹0-1
Lincoln C v WBA	0-1
Gateshead v Aldershot	3-1
Bristol C v Chelsea	1-3
Everton v Manchester C	1-0
*Leicester C v Birmingham C	¹1-1, ¹1-1, 2-1
Preston NE v Mansfield T	2-1
Luton T v West Ham U	3-1
Fulham v Walsall	¹0-1
Brentford v Middlesbrough	3-2
Torquay U v Coventry C	1-0
Burnley v Charlton Ath	¹2-1
Rotherham v Darlington	4-2
*Portsmouth v Stockport Co	7-0
Sheffield W v Southampton	2-1
Leeds U v Newport Co	1 3
QPR v Huddersfield	0-0, 0-5
Derby Co v Southport	4-1
Arsenal v Tottenham H	3-0
Oldham Ath v Cardiff C	2-3
*Aston Villa v Bolton	¹1-1, ¹0-0, ¹2-1
Grimsby T v Hull C	2-3
*Stoke C v Blackpool	¹1-1, 1-0
Sheffield U v Wolverhampton W	0-3
Liverpool v Notts Co	1-0
Gateshead v WBA	¹1-3
Chelsea v Everton	2-0
Leicester C v Preston NE	2-0
Luton T v Walsall	4-0
Brentford v Torquay U	1-0
Rotherham U v Burnley	0-1
Portsmouth v Sheffield W	2-1
*Newport Co v Huddersfield	¹3-3, 3-1
Derby Co v Arsenal	1-0
Aston Villa v Cardiff C	1-2

Fifth Round

Manchester U v Yeovil T	8-0
Stoke C v Hull C	0-2
Wolverhampton W v Liverpool	3-1
WBA v Chelsea	3-0
*Luton T v Leicester C	¹5-5, 3-5
Brentford v Burnley	4-2
Portsmouth v Newport Co	¹3-2
Derby Co v Cardiff C	2-1

Sixth Round

Hull C v Manchester U	0-1
Wolverhampton W v WBA	1-0
Brentford v Leicester C	0-2
Portsmouth v Derby Co	2-1

Semi-Final

Manchester U v Wolverhampton W²	¹1-1, 0-1
Leicester C v Portsmouth³	3-1

Fourth Round

*Manchester U v Bradford PA	¹1-1, ¹1-1, 5-0
Yeovil T v Sunderland	¹2-1

Final 1948–49: Wolverhampton W 3 Leicester C 1

*Home Team in first match. ¹After extra time. ²At Hillsborough. ³At Highbury.

1949 Ex-professional footballers ruled eligible to serve on FA Council, if permission granted.
1949 S F Rous, FA Secretary, knighted.

1948–49	26 Sept v Denmark (Copenhagen)	0-0	
1948–49	9 Oct v Ireland (Belfast)	6-2	Matthews, Milburn, Mortensen 3, Pearson –
1948–49	10 Nov v Wales (Villa Park)	1-0	Finney
1948–49	2 Dec v Switzerland (Highbury)	6-0	Haines 2, Hancocks 2, Rowley, Milburn
1948–49	9 Apr v Scotland (Wembley)	1-3	Milburn
1948–49	13 May v Sweden (Stockholm)	1-3	Finney
1948–49	18 May v Norway (Oslo)	4-1	Mullen, Finney, Spydevoold og, Morris
1948–49	22 May v France (Paris)	3-1	Morris 2, Wright

1948–49

DIVISION 1

	P	W	D	L	F	A	Pts
Portsmouth	42	25	8	9	84	42	58
Manchester U	42	21	11	10	77	44	53
Derby Co	42	22	9	11	74	55	53
Newcastle U	42	20	12	10	70	56	52
Arsenal	42	18	13	11	74	44	49
Wolverhampton W	42	17	12	13	79	66	46
Manchester C	42	15	15	12	47	51	45
Sunderland	42	13	17	12	49	58	43
Charlton Ath	42	15	12	15	63	67	42
Aston Villa	42	16	10	16	60	76	42
Stoke C	42	16	9	17	66	68	41
Liverpool	42	13	14	15	53	43	40
Chelsea	42	12	14	16	69	68	38
Bolton W	42	14	10	18	59	68	38
Burnley	42	12	14	16	43	50	38
Blackpool	42	11	16	15	54	67	38
Birmingham C	42	11	15	16	36	38	37
Everton	42	13	11	18	41	63	37
Middlesbrough	42	11	12	19	46	57	34
Huddersfield	42	12	10	20	40	69	34
Preston NE	42	11	11	20	62	75	33
Sheffield U	42	11	11	20	57	78	33

DIVISION 2

	P	W	D	L	F	A	Pts
Fulham	42	24	9	9	77	37	57
WBA	42	24	8	10	69	39	56
Southampton	42	23	9	10	69	36	55
Cardiff C	42	19	13	10	62	47	51
Tottenham H	42	17	16	9	72	44	50
Chesterfield	42	15	17	10	51	45	47
West Ham U	42	18	10	14	56	58	46
Sheffield W	42	15	13	14	63	56	43
Barnsley	42	14	12	16	62	61	40
Luton T	42	14	12	16	55	57	40
Grimsby T	42	15	10	17	72	76	40
Bury	42	17	6	19	67	76	40
QPR	42	14	11	17	44	62	39
Blackburn R	42	15	8	19	53	63	38
Leeds U	42	12	13	17	55	63	37
Coventry C	42	15	7	20	55	64	37
Bradford PA	42	13	11	18	65	78	37
Brentford	42	11	14	17	42	53	36
Leicester C	42	10	16	16	62	79	36
Plymouth Arg	42	12	12	18	49	64	36
Nottingham F	42	14	7	21	50	54	35
Lincoln C	42	8	12	22	53	91	28

DIVISION 3 (SOUTH)

	P	W	D	L	F	A	Pts
Swansea T	42	27	8	7	87	34	62
Reading	42	25	5	12	77	50	55
Bournemouth	42	22	8	12	69	48	52
Swindon T	42	18	15	9	64	56	51
Bristol R	42	19	10	13	61	51	48
Brighton	42	15	18	9	55	55	48
Ipswich T	42	18	9	15	78	77	45
Millwall	42	17	11	14	63	64	45
Torquay U	42	17	11	14	65	70	45
Norwich C	42	16	12	14	67	49	44
Notts Co	42	19	5	18	102	68	43
Exeter C	42	15	10	17	63	76	40
Port Vale	42	14	11	17	51	54	39
Walsall	42	15	8	19	56	64	38
Newport Co	42	14	9	19	68	92	37
Bristol C	42	11	14	17	44	62	36
Watford	42	10	15	17	41	54	35
Southend U	42	9	16	17	41	46	34
Leyton O	42	11	12	19	58	80	34
Northampton	42	12	9	21	51	62	33
Aldershot	42	11	11	20	48	59	33
C Palace	42	8	11	23	38	76	27

DIVISION 3 (NORTH)

	P	W	D	L	F	A	Pts
Hull C	42	27	11	4	93	28	65
Rotherham U	42	28	6	8	90	46	62
Doncaster R	42	20	10	12	53	40	50
Darlington	42	20	6	16	83	74	46
Gateshead	42	16	13	13	69	58	45
Oldham Ath	42	18	9	15	75	67	45
Rochdale	42	18	9	15	55	53	45
Stockport Co	42	16	11	15	61	56	43
Wrexham	42	17	9	16	56	62	43
Mansfield T	42	14	14	14	52	48	42
Tranmere R	42	13	15	14	46	57	41
Crewe Alex	42	16	9	17	52	74	41
Barrow	42	14	12	16	41	48	40
York C	42	15	9	18	74	74	39
Carlisle U	42	14	11	17	60	77	39
Hartlepools U	42	14	10	18	45	58	38
New Brighton	42	14	8	20	46	58	36
Chester	42	11	13	18	57	56	35
Halifax T	42	12	11	19	45	62	35
Accrington S	42	12	10	20	55	64	34
Southport	42	11	9	22	45	64	31
Bradford C	42	10	9	23	48	77	29

FA CUP 1949–50

Third Round
Arsenal v Sheffield W	1-0
Swansea T v Birmingham C	3-0
Notts Co v Burnley	1-4
Newport Co v Port Vale	1-2
Carlisle U v Leeds U	2-5
Coventry C v Bolton W	1-2
*Cardiff C v WBA	2-2, 1-0
*Charlton Ath v Fulham	2-2, 2-1
Brentford v Chelsea	0-1
Oldham Ath v Newcastle U	2-7
Chesterfield v Yeovil T	3-1
*Aston Villa v Middlesbrough	2-2, 0-0, 2-3
Manchester U v Weymouth	4-0
*Watford v Preston NE	2-2, 1-0
*Portsmouth v Norwich C	1-1, 2-0
Luton T v Grimsby T	3-4
*Blackburn R v Liverpool	0-0, 1-2
Exeter C v Nuneaton B	3-0
Stockport Co v Barnsley	4-2
*Southport v Hull C	0-0, 0-5
Blackpool v Southend U	4-0
Reading v Doncaster R	2-3
*Plymouth Arg v Wolverhampton W	1-1, 0-3
Sheffield U v Leicester C	3-1
QPR v Everton	0-2
West Ham U v Ipswich T	5-1
Stoke C v Tottenham H	0-1
Sunderland v Huddersfield	6-0
Manchester C v Derby Co	3-5
Bury v Rotherham U	5-4
*Northampton v Southampton	1-1, 3-2
Bradford PA v Bournemouth	0-1
*Leeds U v Bolton W	1-1, 3-2
*Charlton Ath v Cardiff C	1-1, 0-2
Chelsea v Newcastle U	3-0
Chesterfield v Middlesbrough	3-2
Watford v Manchester U	0-1
Portsmouth v Grimsby T	5-0
Liverpool v Exeter C	3-1
*Stockport Co v Hull C	0-0, 2-0
Blackpool v Doncaster R	2-1
Wolverhampton W v Sheffield U	0-0, 4-3
West Ham U v Everton	1-2
Tottenham H v Sunderland	5-1
*Bury v Derby Co	2-2, 2-5
*Bournemouth v Northampton	1-1, 1-2

Fourth Round
Arsenal v Swansea T	2-1
Burnley v Port Vale	2-1

Fifth Round
Arsenal v Burnley	2-0
Leeds U v Cardiff C	3-1
*Chesterfield v Chelsea	1-1, 0-3
*Manchester U v Portsmouth	3-3, 3-1
Stockport Co v Liverpool	1-2
*Wolverhampton W v Blackpool	0-0, 0-1
Everton v Tottenham H	1-0
Derby Co v Northampton	4-2

Sixth Round
Arsenal v Leeds U	1-0
Chelsea v Manchester U	2-0
Liverpool v Blackpool	2-1
Derby Co v Everton	1-2

Semi-Final
Arsenal v Chelsea	2-2, 1-0
Liverpool v Everton	2-0

Final 1949–50: Arsenal 2 Liverpool 0

1950 Football League extended from 88 to 92 clubs, only 44 of whom have single vote. The 48 teams in the Third and Fourth Divisions are honorary members and are represented by four votes.

1950 Fourth World Cup. Uruguay defeated Brazil in final game at Rio de Janeiro, watched by 200,000 crowd, paying £125,000. England beat Chile 2-0, but were eliminated after losing to USA 1-0 at Belo Horizonte and 1-0 by Spain in Rio.

1949–50	21 Sept v Rep of Ireland (Everton)	0-2	
1949–50	15 Oct v Wales (Cardiff)	4-1	Mortensen, Milburn 3
1949–50	16 Nov v Ireland (Manchester)	9-2	Rowley 4, Pearson 2, Mortensen 2, Froggatt J
1949–50	30 Nov v Italy (Tottenham)	2-0	Rowley, Wright
1949–50	15 Apr v Scotland (Glasgow)	1-0	Bentley
1949–50	14 May v Portugal (Lisbon)	5-3	Finney 4, Mortensen
1949–50	18 May v Belgium (Brussels)	4-1	Mullen, Mortensen, Mannion, Bentley
1949–50	25 June v Chile (Rio de Janeiro)	2-0	Mortensen, Mannion
1949–50	29 June v USA (Belo Horizonte)	0-1	
1949–50	2 July v Spain (Rio de Janeiro)	0-1	

1949-50

DIVISION 1

	P	W	D	L	F	A	Pts
Portsmouth	42	22	9	11	74	38	53
Wolverhampton W	42	20	13	9	76	49	53
Sunderland	42	21	10	11	83	62	52
Manchester U	42	18	14	10	69	44	50
Newcastle U	42	19	12	11	77	55	50
Arsenal	42	19	11	12	79	55	49
Blackpool	42	17	15	10	46	35	49
Liverpool	42	17	14	11	64	54	48
Middlesbrough	42	20	7	15	59	48	47
Burnley	42	16	13	13	40	40	45
Derby Co	42	17	10	15	69	61	44
Aston Villa	42	15	12	15	61	61	42
Chelsea	42	12	16	14	58	65	40
WBA	42	14	12	16	47	53	40
Huddersfield	42	14	9	19	52	73	37
Bolton W	42	10	14	18	45	59	34
Fulham	42	10	14	18	41	54	34
Everton	42	10	14	18	42	66	34
Stoke C	42	11	12	19	45	75	34
Charlton Ath	42	13	6	23	53	65	32
Manchester C	42	8	13	21	36	68	29
Birmingham C	42	7	14	21	31	67	28

DIVISION 2

	P	W	D	L	F	A	Pts.
Tottenham H	42	27	7	8	81	35	61
Sheffield W	42	18	16	8	67	48	52
Sheffield U	42	19	14	9	68	49	52
Southampton	42	19	14	9	64	48	52
Leeds U	42	17	13	12	54	45	47
Preston NE	42	18	9	15	60	49	45
Hull C	42	17	11	14	64	72	45
Swansea T	42	17	9	16	53	49	43
Brentford	42	15	13	14	44	49	43
Cardiff C	42	16	10	16	41	44	42
Grimsby T	42	16	8	18	74	73	40
Coventry C	42	13	13	16	55	55	39
Barnsley	42	13	13	16	64	67	39
Chesterfield	42	15	9	18	43	47	39
Leicester C	42	12	15	15	55	65	39
Blackburn R	42	14	10	18	55	60	38
Luton T	42	10	18	14	41	51	38
Bury	42	14	9	19	60	65	37
West Ham U	42	12	12	18	53	61	36
QPR	42	11	12	19	40	57	34
Plymouth Arg	42	8	16	18	44	65	32
Bradford PA	42	10	11	21	51	77	31

DIVISION 3 (SOUTH)

	P	W	D	L	F	A	Pts.
Notts Co	42	25	8	9	95	50	58
Northampton	42	20	11	11	72	50	51
Southend U	42	19	13	10	66	48	51
Nottingham F	42	20	9	13	67	39	49
Torquay U	42	19	10	13	66	63	48
Watford	42	16	13	13	45	35	45
C Palace	42	15	14	13	55	54	44
Brighton	42	16	12	14	57	69	44
Bristol R	42	19	5	18	51	51	43
Reading	42	17	8	17	70	64	42
Norwich C	42	16	10	16	65	63	42
Bournemouth	42	16	10	16	57	56	42
Port Vale	42	15	11	16	47	42	41
Swindon T	42	15	11	16	59	62	41
Bristol C	42	15	10	17	60	61	40
Exeter C	42	14	11	17	63	75	39
Ipswich T	42	12	11	19	57	86	35
Leyton O	42	12	11	19	53	85	35
Walsall	42	9	16	17	61	62	34
Aldershot	42	13	8	21	48	60	34
Newport Co	42	13	8	21	67	98	34
Millwall	42	14	4	24	55	63	32

DIVISION 3 (NORTH)

	P	W	D	L	F	A	Pts.
Doncaster R	42	19	17	6	66	38	55
Gateshead	42	23	7	12	87	54	53
Rochdale	42	21	9	12	68	41	51
Lincoln C	42	21	9	12	60	39	51
Tranmere R	42	19	11	12	51	48	49
Rotherham U	42	19	10	13	80	59	48
Crewe Alex	42	17	14	11	68	55	48
Mansfield T	42	18	12	12	66	54	48
Carlisle U	42	16	15	11	68	51	47
Stockport Co	42	19	7	16	55	52	45
Oldham Ath	42	16	11	15	58	63	43
Chester	42	17	6	19	70	79	40
Accrington S	42	16	7	19	57	62	39
New Brighton	42	14	10	18	45	63	38
Barrow	42	14	9	19	47	53	37
Southport	42	12	13	17	51	71	37
Darlington	42	11	13	18	56	69	35
Hartlepools U	42	14	5	23	52	79	33
Bradford C	42	12	8	22	61	76	32
Wrexham	42	10	12	20	39	54	32
Halifax T	42	12	8	22	58	85	32
York C	42	9	13	20	52	70	31

FA CUP 1950–51

Third Round
Newcastle U v Bury	4-1
Bolton W v York C	2-0
*Stoke C v Port Vale	2-2, 1-0
West Ham U v Cardiff C	2-1
Luton T v Portsmouth	2-0
Bristol R v Aldershot	5-1
Hull C v Everton	2-0
Rotherham U v Doncaster R	2-1
Plymouth Arg v Wolverhampton W	1-2
Aston Villa v Burnley	2-0
Leicester C v Preston NE	0-3
Huddersfield v Tottenham H	2-0
Sunderland v Coventry C	2-0
Notts Co v Southampton	3-4
Newport Co v Reading	3-2
Norwich C v Liverpool	3-1
*Charlton Ath v Blackpool	2-2, 0-3
Stockport Co v Brentford	2-1
Mansfield T v Swansea T	2-0
Sheffield U v Gateshead	1-0
*Grimsby T v Exeter C	3-3, 2-4
Rochdale v Chelsea	2-3
QPR v Millwall	3-4
Fulham v Sheffield W	1-0
*Derby Co v WBA	2-2, 1-0
Birmingham C v Manchester C	2-0
Bristol C v Blackburn R	2-1
Brighton v Chesterfield	2-1
Manchester U v Oldham Ath	4-1
Leeds U v Middlesbrough	1-0
*Arsenal v Carlisle U	0-0, 4-1
Northampton T v Barnsley	3-1
Luton T v Bristol R	1-2
Hull C v Rotherham U	2-0
Wolverhampton W v Aston Villa	3-1
Preston NE v Huddersfield	0-2
Sunderland v Southampton	2-0
Newport Co v Norwich C	0-2
Blackpool v Stockport Co	2-1
*Sheffield U v Mansfield T	0-0, 1-2
*Exeter C v Chelsea	1-1, 0-2
Millwall v Fulham	0-1
Derby Co v Birmingham C	1-3
Bristol C v Brighton	1-0
Manchester U v Leeds U	4-0
Arsenal v Northampton	3-2

Fourth Round
Newcastle U v Bolton W	3-2
Stoke C v West Ham U	1-0

Fifth Round
Stoke C v Newcastle U	2-4
Bristol R v Hull C	3-0
Wolverhampton W v Huddersfield	2-0
Sunderland v Norwich C	3-1
Blackpool v Mansfield T	2-0
*Chelsea v Fulham	1-1, 0-3
Birmingham C v Bristol C	2-0
Manchester U v Arsenal	1-0

Sixth Round
*Newcastle U v Bristol R	0-0, 3-1
*Sunderland v Wolverhampton W	1-1, 1-3
Blackpool v Fulham	1-0
Birmingham C v Manchester U	1-0

Semi-Final
Newcastle U v Wolverhampton W	0-0, 2-1
Blackpool v Birmingham C	0-0, 2-1

Final 1950–51: Blackpool 0 Newcastle U 2

1951 Use of white ball legalised.
1951 Sheffield W paid Notts Co the record transfer sum of £34,000 for Jackie Sewell, an inside forward.

1950–51	7 Oct v Ireland (Belfast)	4-1	Baily 2, Lee, Wright
1950–51	15 Nov v Wales (Sunderland)	4-2	Baily 2, Mannion, Milburn
1950–51	22 Nov v Yugoslavia (Highbury)	2-2	Lofthouse 2
1950–51	14 Apr v Scotland (Wembley)	2-3	Hassall, Finney
1950–51	9 May v Argentina (Wembley)	2-1	Milburn, Mortensen
1950–51	19 May v Portugal (Everton)	5-2	Milburn 2, Nicholson, Finney, Hassall

R.F. 79/80—33

1950–51

DIVISION 1

	P	W	D	L	F	A	Pts
Tottenham H	42	25	10	7	82	44	60
Manchester U	42	24	8	10	74	40	56
Blackpool	42	20	10	12	79	53	50
Newcastle U	42	18	13	11	62	53	49
Arsenal	42	19	9	14	73	56	47
Middlesbrough	42	18	11	13	76	65	47
Portsmouth	42	16	15	11	71	68	47
Bolton W	42	19	7	16	64	61	45
Liverpool	42	16	11	15	53	59	43
Burnley	42	14	14	14	48	43	42
Derby Co	42	16	8	18	81	75	40
Sunderland	42	12	16	14	63	73	40
Stoke C	42	13	14	15	50	59	40
Wolverhampton W	42	15	8	19	74	61	38
Aston Villa	42	12	13	17	66	68	37
WBA	42	13	11	18	53	61	37
Charlton Ath	42	14	9	19	63	80	37
Fulham	42	13	11	18	52	68	37
Huddersfield	42	15	6	21	64	92	36
Chelsea	42	12	8	22	53	65	32
Sheffield W	42	12	8	22	64	83	32
Everton	42	12	8	22	48	86	32

DIVISION 2

	P	W	D	L	F	A	Pts
Preston NE	42	26	5	11	91	49	57
Manchester C	42	19	14	9	89	61	52
Cardiff C	42	17	16	9	53	45	50
Birmingham C	42	20	9	13	64	53	49
Leeds U	42	20	8	14	63	55	48
Blackburn R	42	19	8	15	65	66	46
Coventry C	42	19	7	16	75	59	45
Sheffield U	42	16	12	14	72	62	44
Brentford	42	18	8	16	75	74	44
Hull C	42	16	11	15	74	70	43
Doncaster R	42	15	13	14	64	68	43
Southampton	42	15	13	14	66	73	43
West Ham U	42	16	10	16	68	69	42
Leicester C	42	15	11	16	68	58	41
Barnsley	42	15	10	17	74	68	40
QPR	42	15	10	17	71	82	40
Notts Co	42	13	13	16	61	60	39
Swansea T	42	16	4	22	54	77	36
Luton T	42	9	14	19	57	70	32
Bury	42	12	8	22	60	86	32
Chesterfield	42	9	12	21	44	69	30
Grimsby T	42	8	12	22	61	95	28

DIVISION 3 (SOUTH)

	P	W	D	L	F	A	Pts
Nottingham F	46	30	10	6	110	40	70
Norwich C	46	25	14	7	82	45	64
Reading	46	21	15	10	88	53	57
Plymouth Arg	46	24	9	13	85	55	57
Millwall	46	23	10	13	80	57	56
Bristol R	46	20	15	11	64	42	55
Southend U	46	21	10	15	92	69	52
Ipswich T	46	23	6	17	69	58	52
Bournemouth	46	22	7	17	65	57	51
Bristol C	46	20	11	15	64	59	51
Newport Co	46	19	9	18	77	70	47
Port Vale	46	16	13	17	60	65	45
Brighton	46	13	17	16	71	79	43
Exeter C	46	18	6	22	62	85	42
Walsall	46	15	10	21	52	62	40
Colchester U	46	14	12	20	63	76	40
Swindon T	46	18	4	24	55	67	40
Aldershot	46	15	10	21	56	88	40
Leyton O	46	15	8	23	53	75	38
Torquay U	46	14	9	23	64	81	37
Northampton	46	10	16	20	55	67	36
Gillingham	46	13	9	24	69	101	35
Watford	46	9	11	26	54	88	29
C Palace	46	8	11	27	33	84	27

DIVISION 3 (NORTH)

	P	W	D	L	F	A	Pts
Rotherham U	46	31	9	6	103	41	71
Mansfield T	46	26	12	8	78	48	64
Carlisle U	46	25	12	9	79	50	62
Tranmere R	46	24	11	11	83	62	59
Lincoln C	46	25	8	13	89	58	58
Bradford PA	46	23	8	15	90	72	54
Bradford C	46	21	10	15	90	63	52
Gateshead	46	21	8	17	84	62	50
Crewe Alex	46	19	10	17	61	60	48
Stockport Co	46	20	8	18	63	63	48
Rochdale	46	17	11	18	69	62	45
Scunthorpe U	46	13	18	15	58	57	44
Chester	46	17	9	20	62	64	43
Wrexham	46	15	12	19	55	71	42
Oldham Ath	46	16	8	22	73	73	40
Hartlepools U	46	16	7	23	64	66	39
York C	46	12	15	19	66	77	39
Darlington	46	13	13	20	59	77	39
Barrow	46	16	6	24	51	76	38
Shrewsbury T	46	15	7	24	43	74	37
Southport	46	13	10	23	56	72	36
Halifax T	46	11	12	23	50	69	34
Accrington S	46	11	10	25	42	101	32
New Brighton	46	11	8	27	40	90	30

FA CUP 1951–52

Third Round

Newcastle U v Aston Villa	4-2
Scunthorpe U v Tottenham H	0-3
Reading v Swansea T	0-3
Rotherham U v Bury	2-1
Portsmouth v Lincoln C	4-0
Notts Co v Stockton	4-0
Doncaster R v Buxton	2-0
*Middlesbrough v Derby Co	2-2, 2-0
*Nottingham F v Blackburn R	2-2, 0-2
Manchester U v Hull C	0-2
WBA v Bolton W	4-0
*Ipswich T v Gateshead	2-2, 3-3, 1-2
Burnley v Hartlepools U	1-0
*Leicester C v Coventry	1-1, 1-4
Liverpool v Workington T	1-0
*Manchester C v Wolverhampton W	2-2, 1-4
Norwich C v Arsenal	0-5
Barnsley v Colchester U	3-0
*Leyton O v Everton	0-0, 3-1
Fulham v Birmingham C	0-1
Luton T v Charlton Ath	1-0
Brentford v QPR	3-1
*Cardiff C v Swindon T	1-1, 0-1
*Sunderland v Stoke C	0-0, 1-3
*Chelsea v Chester	2-2, 3-2
Huddersfield v Tranmere R	1-2
Rochdale v Leeds U	0-2
Bradford PA v Sheffield W	2-1
Sheffield U v Newport C	2-0
West Ham U v Blackpool	2-1
Southend U v Southampton	3-0
Bristol R v Preston NE	2-0

Fourth Round

Tottenham H v Newcastle U	0-3
Swansea T v Rotherham U	3-0
Notts Co v Portsmouth	1-3
Middlesbrough v Doncaster R	1-4
Blackburn R v Hull C	2-0
Gateshead v WBA	0-2
Burnley v Coventry C	2-0
Liverpool v Wolverhampton W	2-1
Arsenal v Barnsley	4-0
Birmingham C v Leyton O	0-1
*Luton T v Brentford	2-2, 0-0, 3-2
*Swindon T v Stoke C	1-1, 1-0
Chelsea v Tranmere R	4-0
Leeds U v Bradford PA	2-0
*West Ham U v Sheffield U	0-0, 2-4
Southend U v Bristol R	2-1

Fifth Round

Swansea T v Newcastle U	0-1
Portsmouth v Doncaster R	4-0
Blackburn R v WBA	1-0
Burnley v Liverpool	2-0
Leyton O v Arsenal	0-3
Luton T v Swindon T	3-1
*Leeds U v Chelsea	1-1, 1-1, 1-5
Southend U v Sheffield U	1-2

Sixth Round

Portsmouth v Newcastle U	2-4
Blackburn R v Burnley	3-1
Luton T v Arsenal	2-3
Sheffield U v Chelsea	0-1

Semi-Final

Newcastle U v Blackburn R	[1]0-0, 2-1
Arsenal v Chelsea	[2]1-1, 3-0

Final 1951-52: Arsenal 0 Newcastle U 1

[1]At Hillsborough, replay at Leeds. [2]Both games at White Hart Lane.

1952 Nat Lofthouse scored six goals for Football League v League of Ireland, at Wolverhampton, a record.
1952 Billy Wright passed Bob Crompton's record of 42 international caps. He finally retired in 1959 having played 105 times for England (plus 4 victory Internationals).
1952 Newcastle U won the FA Cup for the second successive year, the first club to do so in the twentieth century. The previous team to achieve this feat was Blackburn R in 1890 and 1891.
1952 Hungary defeated Yugoslavia in Final of Olympic Games at Helsinki. This team formed the basis of the side which beat England at Wembley the following year.

1951–52	3 Oct v France (Highbury)	2-2	Firoud (og), Medley
1951–52	20 Oct v Wales (Cardiff)	1-1	Baily
1951–52	14 Nov v Ireland (Villa Park)	2-0	Lofthouse 2
1951–52	28 Nov v Austria (Wembley)	2-2	Ramsey (pen), Lofthouse
1951–52	5 Apr v Scotland (Glasgow)	2-1	Pearson 2
1951–52	18 May v Italy (Florence)	1-1	Broadis
1951–52	25 May v Austria (Vienna)	3-2	Sewell, Lofthouse 2
1951–52	28 May v Switzerland (Zurich)	3-0	Lofthouse 2, Sewell

1951–52

DIVISION 1

	P	W	D	L	F	A	Pts
Manchester U	42	23	11	8	95	52	57
Tottenham H	42	22	9	11	76	51	53
Arsenal	42	21	11	10	80	61	53
Portsmouth	42	20	8	14	68	58	48
Bolton W	42	19	10	13	65	61	48
Aston Villa	42	19	9	14	79	70	47
Preston NE	42	17	12	13	74	54	46
Newcastle U	42	18	9	15	98	73	45
Blackpool	42	18	9	15	64	64	45
Charlton Ath	42	17	10	15	68	63	44
Liverpool	42	12	19	11	57	61	43
Sunderland	42	15	12	15	70	61	42
WBA	42	14	13	15	74	77	41
Burnley	42	15	10	17	56	63	40
Manchester C	42	13	13	16	58	61	39
Wolverhampton W	42	12	14	16	73	73	38
Derby Co	42	15	7	20	63	80	37
Middlesbrough	42	15	6	21	64	88	36
Chelsea	42	14	8	20	52	72	36
Stoke C	42	12	7	23	49	88	31
Huddersfield	42	10	8	24	49	82	28
Fulham	42	8	11	23	58	77	27

DIVISION 2

	P	W	D	L	F	A	Pts
Sheffield W	42	21	11	10	100	66	53
Cardiff C	42	20	11	11	72	54	51
Birmingham C	42	21	9	12	67	56	51
Nottingham F	42	18	13	11	77	62	49
Leicester C	42	19	9	14	78	64	47
Leeds U	42	18	11	13	59	57	47
Everton	42	17	10	15	64	58	44
Luton T	42	16	12	14	77	78	44
Rotherham U	42	17	8	17	73	71	42
Brentford	42	15	12	15	54	55	42
Sheffield U	42	18	5	19	90	76	41
West Ham U	42	15	11	16	67	77	41
Southampton	42	15	11	16	61	73	41
Blackburn R	42	17	6	19	54	63	40
Notts Co	42	16	7	19	71	68	39
Doncaster R	42	13	12	17	55	60	38
Bury	42	15	7	20	67	69	37
Hull C	42	13	11	18	60	70	37
Swansea T	42	12	12	18	72	76	36
Barnsley	42	11	14	17	59	72	36
Coventry C	42	14	6	22	59	82	34
QPR	42	11	12	19	52	81	34

DIVISION 3 (SOUTH)

	P	W	D	L	F	A	Pts
Plymouth Arg	46	29	8	9	107	53	66
Reading	46	29	3	14	112	60	61
Norwich C	46	26	9	11	89	50	61
Millwall	46	23	12	11	74	53	58
Brighton	46	24	10	12	87	63	58
Newport Co	46	21	12	13	77	76	54
Bristol R	46	20	12	14	89	53	52
Northampton	46	22	5	19	93	74	49
Southend U	46	19	10	17	75	66	48
Colchester U	46	17	12	17	56	77	46
Torquay U	46	17	10	19	86	98	44
Aldershot	46	18	8	20	78	89	44
Port Vale	46	14	15	17	50	66	43
Bournemouth	46	16	10	20	69	75	42
Bristol C	46	15	12	19	58	69	42
Swindon T	46	14	14	18	51	68	42
Ipswich T	46	16	9	21	63	74	41
Leyton O	46	16	9	21	55	68	41
C Palace	46	15	9	22	61	80	39
Shrewsbury T	46	13	10	23	62	86	36
Watford	46	13	10	23	57	81	36
Gillingham	46	11	13	22	71	81	35
Exeter C	46	13	9	24	65	86	35
Walsall	46	13	5	28	55	94	31

DIVISION 3 (NORTH)

	P	W	D	L	F	A	Pts
Lincoln C	46	30	9	7	121	52	69
Grimsby T	46	29	8	9	96	45	66
Stockport Co	46	23	13	10	74	40	59
Oldham Ath	46	24	9	13	90	61	57
Gateshead	46	21	11	14	66	49	53
Mansfield T	46	22	8	16	73	60	52
Carlisle U	46	19	13	14	62	57	51
Bradford PA	46	19	12	15	74	64	50
Hartlepools U	46	21	8	17	71	65	50
York C	46	18	13	15	73	52	49
Tranmere R	46	21	6	19	76	71	48
Barrow	46	17	12	17	57	61	46
Chesterfield	46	17	11	18	65	66	45
Scunthorpe U	46	14	16	16	65	74	44
Bradford C	46	16	10	20	61	68	42
Crewe Alex	46	17	8	21	63	82	42
Southport	46	15	11	20	53	71	41
Wrexham	46	15	9	22	63	73	39
Chester	46	15	9	22	72	85	39
Halifax T	46	14	7	25	61	97	35
Rochdale	46	11	13	22	47	79	35
Accrington S.	46	10	12	24	61	92	32
Darlington	46	11	9	26	64	103	31
Workington T	46	11	7	28	50	91	29

FA CUP 1952-53

Third Round
Sheffield W v Blackpool	1-2
Huddersfield v Bristol R	2-0
*Lincoln C v Southampton	1-1, 1-2
Shrewsbury T v Finchley	2-0
Arsenal v Doncaster R	4-0
Grimsby T v Bury	1-3
*Portsmouth v Burnley	1-1, 1-3
*Sunderland v Scunthorpe U	1-1, 2-1
*Tranmere R v Tottenham	1-1, 1-9
Preston NE v Wolverhampton W	5-2
Halifax T v Cardiff C	3-1
Stoke C v Wrexham	2-1
Oldham Ath v Birmingham C	1-3
Newport Co v Sheffield U	1-4
*Derby Co v Chelsea	4-4, 0-1
West Ham U v WBA	1-4
Bolton W v Fulham	3-1
Leicester C v Notts Co	2-4
Luton T v Blackburn R	6-1
Manchester C v Swindon T	7-0
Gateshead v Liverpool	1-0
Hull C v Charlton Ath	3-1
Plymouth Arg v Coventry C	4-1
Barnsley v Brighton	4-3
Everton v Ipswich T	3-2
Mansfield T v Nottingham F	0-1
Millwall v Manchester U	0-1
Walthamstow A v Stockport Co	2-1
Aston Villa v Middlesbrough	3-1
Brentford v Leeds U	2-1
*Rotherham U v Colchester U	2-2, 2-0
Newcastle U v Swansea T	3-0

Fourth Round
Blackpool v Huddersfield	1-0
Shrewsbury T v Southampton	1-4
Arsenal v Bury	6-2
Burnley v Sunderland	2-0
*Preston NE v Tottenham H	2-2, 0-1
Halifax T v Stoke C	1-0
*Sheffield U v Birmingham C	1-1, 1-3
*Chelsea v WBA	1-1, 0-0, 1-1, 4-0
*Bolton W v Notts Co	1-1, 2-2, 1-0
*Manchester C v Luton T	1-1, 1-5
Hull C v Gateshead	1-2
Plymouth Arg v Barnsley	1-0
Everton v Nottingham F	4-1
*Manchester U v Walthamstow A	1-1, 5-2
*Aston Villa v Brentford	0-0, 2-1
Newcastle U v Rotherham U	1-3

Fifth Round
*Blackpool v Southampton	1-1, 2-1
Burnley v Arsenal	0-2
Halifax T v Tottenham H	0-3
Chelsea v Birmingham C	0-4
Luton T v Bolton W	0-1
Plymouth Arg v Gateshead	0-1
Everton v Manchester U	2-1
Rotherham U v Aston Villa	1-3

Sixth Round
Arsenal v Blackpool	1-2
*Birmingham C v Tottenham H	1-1, 2-2[2], 0-1
Gateshead v Bolton W	0-1
Aston Villa v Everton	0-1

Semi-Final
Blackpool v Tottenham H	[1]2-1
Bolton W v Everton	[3]4-3

Final 1952-53: Blackpool 4 Bolton W 3

[1] At Villa Park. [2] At Maine Road. [3] At Wolverhampton.

1953	Derek Dooley, Sheffield W centre forward and top scorer in the Football League with 46 goals the previous season, had a leg amputated after being injured in a League game against Preston NE on February 14.		
1953	The first ever 100,000 crowd watched the Amateur Cup Final between Pegasus and Harwich and Parkeston at Wembley.		
1953	Arsenal won League championship for a record seventh time.		

1952-53	4 Oct v Ireland (Belfast)	2-2	Lofthouse, Elliott
1952-53	12 Nov v Wales (Wembley)	5-2	Lofthouse 2, Finney, Froggatt J, Bentley
1952-53	25 Nov v Belgium (Wembley)	5-0	Elliott 2, Lofthouse 2, Froggatt R
1952-53	18 Apr v Scotland (Wembley)	2-2	Broadis 2
1952-53	17 May v Argentina (Buenos Aires) (Abandoned after 23 minutes)	0-0	
1952-53	24 May v Chile (Santiago)	2-1	Taylor, Lofthouse
1952-53	31 May v Uruguay (Montevideo)	1-2	Taylor
1952-53	8 June v USA (New York)	6-3	Lofthouse 2, Finney 2, Broadis, Froggatt R

1952–53

DIVISION 1

	P	W	D	L	F	A	Pts
Arsenal	42	21	12	9	97	64	54
Preston NE	42	21	12	9	85	60	54
Wolverhampton W	42	19	13	10	86	63	51
WBA	42	21	8	13	66	60	50
Charlton Ath	42	19	11	12	77	63	49
Burnley	42	18	12	12	67	52	48
Blackpool	42	19	9	14	71	70	47
Manchester U	42	18	10	14	69	72	46
Sunderland	42	15	13	14	68	82	43
Tottenham H	42	15	11	16	78	69	41
Aston Villa	42	14	13	15	63	61	41
Cardiff C	42	14	12	16	54	46	40
Middlesbrough	42	14	11	17	70	77	39
Bolton W	42	15	9	18	61	69	39
Portsmouth	42	14	10	18	74	83	38
Newcastle U	42	14	9	19	59	70	37
Liverpool	42	14	8	20	61	82	36
Sheffield W	42	12	11	19	62	72	35
Chelsea	42	12	11	19	56	66	35
Manchester C	42	14	7	21	72	87	35
Stoke C	42	12	10	20	53	66	34
Derby Co	42	11	10	21	59	74	32

DIVISION 2

	P	W	D	L	F	A	Pts
Sheffield U	42	25	10	7	97	55	60
Huddersfield	42	24	10	8	84	33	58
Luton T	42	22	8	12	84	49	52
Plymouth Arg	42	20	9	13	65	60	49
Leicester C	42	18	12	12	89	74	48
Birmingham C	42	19	10	13	71	66	48
Nottingham F	42	18	8	16	77	67	44
Fulham	42	17	10	15	81	71	44
Blackburn R	42	18	8	16	68	65	44
Leeds U	42	14	15	13	71	63	43
Swansea T	42	15	12	15	78	81	42
Rotherham U	42	16	9	17	75	74	41
Doncaster R	42	12	16	14	58	64	40
West Ham U	42	13	13	16	58	60	39
Lincoln C	42	11	17	14	64	71	39
Everton	42	12	14	16	71	75	38
Brentford	42	13	11	18	59	76	37
Hull C	42	14	8	20	57	69	36
Notts Co	42	14	8	20	60	88	36
Bury	42	13	9	20	53	81	35
Southampton	42	10	13	19	68	85	33
Barnsley	42	5	8	29	47	108	18

DIVISION 3 (SOUTH)

	P	W	D	L	F	A	Pts
Bristol R	46	26	12	8	92	46	64
Millwall	46	24	14	8	82	44	62
Northampton	46	26	10	10	109	70	62
Norwich C	46	25	10	11	99	55	60
Bristol C	46	22	15	9	95	61	59
Coventry C	46	19	12	15	77	62	50
Brighton	46	19	12	15	81	75	50
Southend U	46	18	13	15	69	74	49
Bournemouth	46	19	9	18	74	69	47
Watford	46	15	17	14	62	63	47
Reading	46	19	8	19	69	64	46
Torquay U	46	18	9	19	87	88	45
C Palace	46	15	13	18	66	82	43
Leyton O	46	16	10	20	68	73	42
Newport Co	46	16	10	20	70	82	42
Ipswich T	46	13	15	18	60	69	41
Exeter C	46	13	14	19	61	71	40
Swindon T	46	14	12	20	64	79	40
Aldershot	46	12	15	19	61	77	39
Gillingham	46	12	15	19	55	74	39
QPR	46	12	15	19	61	82	39
Colchester U	46	12	14	20	59	76	38
Shrewsbury T	46	12	12	22	68	91	36
Walsall	46	7	10	29	56	118	24

DIVISION 3 (NORTH)

	P	W	D	L	F	A	Pts
Oldham Ath	46	22	15	9	77	45	59
Port Vale	46	20	18	8	67	35	58
Wrexham	46	24	8	14	86	66	56
York C	46	20	13	13	60	45	53
Grimsby T	46	21	10	15	75	59	52
Southport	46	20	11	15	63	60	51
Bradford PA	46	19	12	15	75	61	50
Gateshead	46	17	15	14	76	60	49
Carlisle U	46	18	13	15	82	68	49
Crewe Alex	46	20	8	18	70	68	48
Stockport Co	46	17	13	16	82	69	47
Chesterfield*	46	18	11	17	65	63	47
Tranmere R*	46	21	5	20	65	63	47
Halifax T	46	16	15	15	68	68	47
Scunthorpe U	46	16	14	16	62	56	46
Bradford C	46	14	18	14	75	80	46
Hartlepools U	46	16	14	16	57	61	46
Mansfield T	46	16	14	16	55	62	46
Barrow	46	16	12	18	66	71	44
Chester	46	11	15	20	64	85	37
Darlington	46	14	6	26	58	96	34
Rochdale	46	14	5	27	62	83	33
Workington	46	11	10	25	55	91	32
Accrington S	46	8	11	27	39	89	27

* Equal

FA CUP 1953–54

Third Round
WBA v Chelsea	1-0
Bristol C v Rotherham U	1-3
Burnley v Manchester U	5-3
*Newcastle U v Wigan	2-2, 4-2
Bristol R v Blackburn R	0-1
*Brentford v Hull C	0-0, 2-2, 2-5
Bradford v Manchester C	2-5
*Leeds U v Tottenham H	3-3, 0-1
*Tranmere R v Leyton O	2-2, 1-4
*Grimsby T v Fulham	5-5, 0-0, 1-3
Plymouth Arg v Nottingham F	2-0
Sunderland v Doncaster R	0-2
Cardiff C v Peterborough U	3-1
QPR v Port Vale	0-1
West Ham U v Huddersfield	4-0
Blackpool v Luton T	1-1, 0-0, 1-1, 2-0
*Sheffield W v Sheffield U	1-1, 3-1
Chesterfield v Bury	2-0
Everton v Notts Co	2-1
*Barrow v Swansea T	2-2, 2-4
*Stockport v Headington	0-0, 0-1
Bolton W v Liverpool	1-0
*Wrexham v Scunthorpe U	3-3, 1-3
*Portsmouth v Charlton Ath	3-3, 3-2
Arsenal v Aston Villa	5-1
*Hastings v Norwich C	3-3, 0-3
Stoke C v Hartlepools U	6-2
*Middlesbrough v Leicester C	2-3
*Lincoln C v Walsall	0-0, 1-1, 2-1
Derby Co v Preston NE	0-2
*Ipswich T v Oldham Ath	3-3, 1-0
Wolverhampton W v Birmingham C	1-2

Fourth Round
WBA v Rotherham U	4-0
*Burnley v Newcastle U	1-1, 0-1
*Blackburn R v Hull C	2-2, 1-2
Manchester C v Tottenham H	0-1
Leyton O v Fulham	2-1
Plymouth Arg v Doncaster R	0-2
Cardiff C v Port Vale	0-2
*West Ham U v Blackpool	1-1, 1-3
*Sheffield W v Chesterfield	0-0, 4-2
Everton v Swansea T	3-0
Headington v Bolton W	2-4
*Scunthorpe U v Portsmouth	1-1, 2-2, 0-4
Arsenal v Norwich C	1-2
*Stoke C v Leicester C	0-0, 1-3
Lincoln C v Preston	0-2
Ipswich T v Birmingham C	1-0

Fifth Round
WBA v Newcastle U	3-2
*Hull C v Tottenham H	1-1, 0-1
Leyton O v Doncaster R	3-1
Port Vale v Blackpool	2-0
Sheffield W v Everton	3-1
*Bolton W v Portsmouth	0-0, 2-1
Norwich C v Leicester C	1-2
Preston NE v Ipswich T	6-1

Sixth Round
WBA v Tottenham H	3-0
Leyton O v Port Vale	0-1
*Sheffield W v Bolton W	1-1, 2-0
*Leicester C v Preston NE	1-1, 2-2, 1-3

Semi-Final
WBA v Port Vale	2-1
Sheffield W v Preston NE	0-2

Final 1953–54; Preston NE 2 WBA 3

1953 Football Association celebrated their 90th birthday with a tremendous banquet attended by representatives of almost every country in the world. The match to celebrate this anniversary was England 4, Rest of the World 4. England were saved by a last minute penalty scored by Alf Ramsey.

1953 October, England lost their first ever game at home to a foreign country, 6-3 to Hungary at Wembley.

1953 Stanley Mortensen first player to score hat-trick in FA Cup Final at Wembley. He helped Blackpool defeat Bolton W (who at one time led 3-1).

1954 West Germany defeated Hungary 3-2 in World Cup Final in Berne, Switzerland. England, having survived the qualifying rounds, lost 4-2 in the quarter-finals to Uruguay.

1954 A few weeks earlier, England suffered their heaviest defeat in an international match, losing 7-1 to Hungary in Budapest.

1953–54	10 Oct v Wales (Cardiff)	4-1	Wilshaw 2, Lofthouse 2
1953–54	21 Oct v FIFA (Wembley)	4-4	Mullen 2, Mortensen, Ramsey (pen)
1953–54	11 Nov v Ireland (Everton)	3-1	Hassall 2, Lofthouse
1953–54	25 Nov v Hungary (Wembley)	3-6	Sewell, Mortensen, Ramsey (pen)
1953–54	3 Apr v Scotland (Glasgow)	4-2	Broadis, Nicholls, Allen, Mullen
1953–54	16 May v Yugoslavia (Belgrade)	0-1	
1953–54	23 May v Hungary (Budapest)	1-7	Broadis
1953–54	17 June v Belgium (Basle)	4-4	Broadis 2, Lofthouse 2
1953–54	20 June v Switzerland (Berne)	2-0	Wilshaw, Mullen
1953–54	26 June v Uruguay (Basle)	2-4	Lofthouse, Finney

1953-54

DIVISION 1

	P	W	D	L	F	A	Pts
Wolverhampton W	42	25	7	10	96	56	57
WBA	42	22	9	11	86	63	53
Huddersfield	42	20	11	11	78	61	51
Manchester U	42	18	12	12	73	58	48
Bolton W	42	18	12	12	75	60	48
Blackpool	42	19	10	13	80	69	48
Burnley	42	21	4	17	78	67	46
Chelsea	42	16	12	14	74	68	44
Charlton Ath	42	19	6	17	75	77	44
Cardiff C	42	18	8	16	51	71	44
Preston NE	42	19	5	18	87	58	43
Arsenal	42	15	13	14	75	73	43
Aston Villa	42	16	9	17	70	68	41
Portsmouth	42	14	11	17	81	89	39
Newcastle U	42	14	10	18	72	77	38
Tottenham H	42	16	5	21	65	76	37
Manchester C	42	14	9	19	62	77	37
Sunderland	42	14	8	20	81	89	36
Sheffield W	42	15	6	21	70	91	36
Sheffield U	42	11	11	20	69	90	33
Middlesbrough	42	10	10	22	60	91	30
Liverpool	42	9	10	23	68	97	28

DIVISION 2

	P	W	D	L	F	A	Pts
Leicester C	42	23	10	9	97	60	56
Everton	42	20	16	6	92	58	56
Blackburn R	42	23	9	10	86	50	55
Nottingham F	42	20	12	10	86	59	52
Rotherham U	42	21	7	14	80	67	49
Luton T	42	18	12	12	64	59	48
Birmingham C	42	18	11	13	78	58	47
Fulham	42	17	10	15	98	85	44
Bristol R	42	14	16	12	64	58	44
Leeds U	42	15	13	14	89	81	43
Stoke C	42	12	17	13	71	60	41
Doncaster R	42	16	9	17	59	63	41
West Ham U	42	15	9	18	67	69	39
Notts Co	42	13	13	16	54	74	39
Hull C	42	16	6	20	64	66	38
Lincoln C	42	14	9	19	65	83	37
Bury	42	11	14	17	54	72	36
Derby Co	42	12	11	19	64	82	35
Plymouth Arg	42	9	16	17	65	82	34
Swansea T	42	13	8	21	58	82	34
Brentford	42	10	11	21	40	78	31
Oldham Ath	42	8	9	25	40	89	25

DIVISION 3 (SOUTH)

	P	W	D	L	F	A	Pts
Ipswich T	46	27	10	9	82	51	64
Brighton	46	26	9	11	86	61	61
Bristol C	46	25	6	15	88	66	56
Watford	46	21	10	15	85	69	52
Northampton	46	20	11	15	82	55	51
Southampton	46	22	7	17	76	63	51
Norwich C	46	20	11	15	73	66	51
Reading	46	20	9	17	86	73	49
Exeter C	46	20	8	18	68	58	48
Gillingham	46	19	10	17	61	66	48
Leyton O	46	18	11	17	79	73	47
Millwall	46	19	9	18	74	77	47
Torquay U	46	17	12	17	81	88	46
Coventry C	46	18	9	19	61	56	45
Newport Co	46	19	6	21	61	81	44
Southend U	46	18	7	21	69	71	43
Aldershot	46	17	9	20	74	86	43
QPR	46	16	10	20	60	68	42
Bournemouth*	46	16	8	22	67	70	40
Swindon T*	46	15	10	21	67	70	40
Shrewsbury T	46	14	12	20	65	76	40
C Palace	46	14	12	20	60	86	40
Colchester U	46	10	10	26	50	78	30
Walsall	46	9	8	29	40	87	26

*Equal

DIVISION 3 (NORTH)

	P	W	D	L	F	A	Pts
Port Vale	46	26	17	3	74	21	69
Barnsley	46	24	10	12	77	57	58
Scunthorpe U	46	21	15	10	77	56	57
Gateshead	46	21	13	12	74	55	55
Bradford C	46	22	9	15	60	55	53
Chesterfield	46	19	14	13	76	64	52
Mansfield T	46	20	11	15	88	67	51
Wrexham	46	21	9	16	81	68	51
Bradford PA	46	18	14	14	77	68	50
Stockport Co	46	18	11	17	77	67	47
Southport	46	17	12	17	63	60	46
Barrow	46	16	12	18	72	71	44
Carlisle U	46	14	15	17	83	71	43
Tranmere R	46	18	7	21	59	70	43
Accrington S	46	16	10	20	66	74	42
Crewe Alex	46	14	13	19	49	67	41
Grimsby T	46	16	9	21	51	77	41
Hartlepools U	46	13	14	19	59	65	40
Rochdale	46	15	10	21	59	77	40
Workington T	46	13	14	19	59	80	40
Darlington	46	12	14	20	50	71	38
York C	46	12	13	21	64	86	37
Halifax T	46	12	10	24	44	73	34
Chester	46	11	10	25	48	67	32

FA CUP 1954–55

Third Round
Everton v Southend U	3-1
*Lincoln C v Liverpool	1-1, 0-1
*Leeds U v Torquay U	2-2, 0-4
*Huddersfield v Coventry C	3-3, 2-1
*Hartlepools U v Darlington	1-1, 2-2, 2-0
Sheffield U v Nottingham F	1-
Plymouth Arg v Newcastle U	0-1
*Brentford v Bradford C	1-1, 2-2, 1-0
Sheffield W v Hastings	2-1
Middlesbrough v Notts Co	1-4
Bristol R v Portsmouth	2-1
Chelsea v Walsall	2-0
*Ipswich T v Bishop Auckland	2-2, 1-3
Blackpool v York C	0-2
Gateshead v Tottenham H	0-2
*West Ham U v Port Vale	2-2, 1-3
Blackburn R v Swansea T	0-2
*Bury v Stoke C	1-1, 1-1, 3-3, 2-2, 2-3
Fulham v Preston NE	2-3
Sunderland v Burnley	1-0
Grimsby T v Wolverhampton W	2-5
Arsenal v Cardiff C	1-0
Bournemouth v WBA	0-1
Rochdale v Charlton Ath	1-3
Hull C v Birmingham C	0-2
Bolton W v Millwall	3-1
Watford v Doncaster R	1-2
*Brighton v Aston Villa	2-2, 2-4
Rotherham U v Leicester C	1-0
Luton T v Workington T	5-0
Derby Co v Manchester C	1-3
*Reading v Manchester U	1-1, 1-4

Fourth Round
Everton v Liverpool	0-4
Torquay U v Huddersfield	0-1
Hartlepools U v Nottingham F	1-1, 1-2
Newcastle U v Brentford	3-2
*Sheffield W v Notts Co	1-1, 0-1
Bristol R v Chelsea	1-3
Bishop Auckland v York C	1-3
Tottenham H v Port Vale	4-2
Swansea T v Stoke C	3-1
*Preston NE v Sunderland	3-3, 0-2
Wolverhampton W v Arsenal	1-0
WBA v Charlton Ath	2-4
Birmingham C v Bolton W	2-1
*Doncaster R v Aston Villa	0-0, 2-2, 1-1, 0-0, 3-1
Rotherham U v Luton T	1-5
Manchester C v Manchester U	2-0

Fifth Round
Liverpool v Huddersfield	0-2
*Nottingham F v Newcastle U	1-1, 2-2, 1-2
Notts Co v Chelsea	1-0
York C v Tottenham H	3-1
*Swansea T v Sunderland	2-2, 0-1
Wolverhampton W v Charlton Ath	4-1
Birmingham C v Doncaster R	2-1
Luton T v Manchester C	0-1

Sixth Round
*Huddersfield v Newcastle U	1-1, 0-2
Notts Co v York C	0-1
Sunderland v Wolverhampton W	2-0
Birmingham C v Manchester C	0-1

Semi-Final
Newcastle U v York C	1-1, 2-0
Sunderland v Manchester C	0-1

Final 1954–55: Manchester C 1 Newcastle U 3

1954 Wolverhampton W gained some sort of revenge for England by defeating Moscow Spartak and Honved, including six of the Hungarian team, in memorable matches under the floodlights at Molineux, Wolverhampton.

1954–55	2 Oct v Ireland (Belfast)	2-0	Haynes, Revie
1954–55	10 Nov v Wales (Wembley)	3-2	Bentley 3
1954–55	1 Dec v Germany (Wembley)	3-1	Bentley, Allen, Shackleton
1954–55	2 Apr v Scotland (Wembley)	7-2	Wilshaw 4, Lofthouse 2, Revie
1954–55	15 May v France (Paris)	0-1	
1954–55	18 May v Spain (Madrid)	1-1	Bentley
1954–55	22 May v Portugal (Oporto)	1-3	Bentley

1954-55

DIVISION 1

	P	W	D	L	F	A	Pts
Chelsea	42	20	12	10	81	57	52
Wolverhampton W	42	19	10	13	89	70	48
Portsmouth	42	18	12	12	74	62	48
Sunderland	42	15	18	9	64	54	48
Manchester U	42	20	7	15	84	74	47
Aston Villa	42	20	7	15	72	73	47
Manchester C	42	18	10	14	76	69	46
Newcastle U	42	17	9	16	89	77	43
Arsenal	42	17	9	16	69	63	43
Burnley	42	17	9	16	51	48	43
Everton	42	16	10	16	62	68	42
Huddersfield	42	14	13	15	63	68	41
Sheffield U	42	17	7	18	70	86	41
Preston NE	42	16	8	18	83	64	40
Charlton Ath	42	15	10	17	76	75	40
Tottenham H	42	16	8	18	72	73	40
WBA	42	16	8	18	76	96	40
Bolton W	42	13	13	16	62	69	39
Blackpool	42	14	10	18	60	64	38
Cardiff C	42	13	11	18	62	76	37
Leicester C	42	12	11	19	74	86	35
Sheffield W	42	8	10	24	63	100	26

DIVISION 2

	P	W	D	L	F	A	Pts
Birmingham C	42	22	10	10	92	47	54
Luton T	42	23	8	11	88	53	54
Rotherham U	42	25	4	13	94	64	54
Leeds U	42	23	7	12	70	53	53
Stoke C	42	21	10	11	69	46	52
Blackburn R	42	22	6	14	114	79	50
Notts Co	42	21	6	15	74	71	48
West Ham U	42	18	10	14	74	70	46
Bristol R	42	19	7	16	75	70	45
Swansea T	42	17	9	16	86	83	43
Liverpool	42	16	10	16	92	96	42
Middlesbrough	42	18	6	18	73	82	42
Bury	42	15	11	16	77	72	41
Fulham	42	14	11	17	76	79	39
Nottingham F	42	16	7	19	58	62	39
Lincoln C	42	13	10	19	68	79	36
Port Vale	42	12	11	19	48	71	35
Doncaster R	42	14	7	21	58	95	35
Hull C	42	12	10	20	44	69	34
Plymouth Arg	42	12	7	23	57	82	31
Ipswich T	42	11	6	25	57	92	28
Derby Co	42	7	9	26	53	82	23

DIVISION 3 (SOUTH)

	P	W	D	L	F	A	Pts
Bristol C	46	30	10	6	101	47	70
Leyton O	46	26	9	11	89	47	61
Southampton	46	24	11	11	75	51	59
Gillingham	46	20	15	11	77	66	55
Millwall	46	20	11	15	72	68	51
Brighton	46	20	10	16	76	63	50
Watford	46	18	14	14	71	62	50
Torquay U	46	18	12	16	82	82	48
Coventry C	46	18	11	17	67	59	47
Southend U	46	17	12	17	83	80	46
Brentford*	46	16	14	16	82	82	46
Norwich C*	46	18	10	18	60	60	46
Northampton	46	19	8	19	73	81	46
Aldershot	46	16	13	17	75	71	45
QPR	46	15	14	17	69	75	44
Shrewsbury T	46	16	10	20	70	78	42
Bournemouth	46	12	18	16	57	65	42
Reading	46	13	15	18	65	73	41
Newport Co	46	11	16	19	60	73	38
Crystal Palace	46	11	16	19	52	80	38
Swindon T	46	11	15	20	46	64	37
Exeter C	46	11	15	20	47	73	37
Walsall	46	10	14	22	75	86	34
Colchester U	46	9	13	24	53	91	31

*Equal

DIVISION 3 (NORTH)

	P	W	D	L	F	A	Pts
Barnsley	46	30	5	11	86	46	65
Accrington S	46	25	11	10	96	67	61
Scunthorpe U	46	23	12	11	81	53	58
York C	46	24	10	12	92	63	58
Hartlepools U	46	25	5	16	64	49	55
Chesterfield	46	24	6	16	81	70	54
Gateshead	46	20	12	14	65	69	52
Workington T	46	18	14	14	68	55	50
Stockport Co	46	18	12	16	84	70	48
Oldham Ath	46	19	10	17	74	68	48
Southport	46	16	16	14	47	44	48
Rochdale	46	17	14	15	69	66	48
Mansfield T	46	18	9	19	65	71	45
Halifax T	46	15	13	18	63	67	43
Darlington	46	14	14	18	62	73	42
Bradford PA	46	15	11	20	56	70	41
Barrow	46	17	6	23	70	89	40
Wrexham	46	13	12	21	65	77	38
Tranmere R	46	13	11	22	55	70	37
Carlisle U	46	15	6	25	78	89	36
Bradford C	46	13	10	23	47	55	36
Crewe Alex	46	10	14	22	68	91	34
Grimsby T	46	13	8	25	47	78	34
Chester	46	12	9	25	44	77	33

ANGLO-SCOTTISH CUP 1978-79

Preliminary competition
Group A

	P	W	D	L	F	A (inc. bonus)	Pts.
Burnley	3	2	1	0	7	4	7
Blackburn R	3	2	1	0	3	1	5
Preston NE	3	1	0	2	6	6	3
Blackpool	3	0	0	3	3	8	0

Group B

	P	W	D	L	F	A	Pts.
Oldham Ath	3	2	1	0	3	1	5
Bolton W	3	1	1	1	2	2	3
Sunderland	3	1	0	2	4	4	2
Sheffield U	3	1	0	2	2	3	2

Group C

	P	W	D	L	F	A	Pts.
Bristol C	3	3	0	0	10	1	8
Cardiff C	3	1	0	2	1	2	2
Fulham	3	1	0	2	2	5	2
Bristol R	3	1	0	2	3	8	2

Group D

	P	W	D	L	F	A	Pts.
Mansfield T	3	2	1	0	3	1	5
Notts C	3	2	0	1	5	4	5
Norwich C	3	0	2	1	2	3	2
Orient	3	0	1	2	2	4	1

QUARTER-FINALS, FIRST LEG
12 SEPT
Bristol C (0) 1 (*Ritchie*) 5572
St Mirren (0) 2 (*Sharpe* 2)
Bristol C: Cashley; Sweeney, McNeil, Gow, Rodgers, Hunter, Tainton, Ritchie, Royle, Mabbutt Whitehead (Cormack).
St Mirren: Thomson, Beckett, Munro, Fitzpatrick, Dunlop, Copland, Sharp, Stark, Bone, Abercrombie, McGarvey.

Burnley (0) 1 (*Kindon*) 30,000
Celtic (0) 0
Burnley: Stevenson; Scott, Brennan, Noble, Thomson, Rodaway, Cochrane, Hall, Fletcher, Kindon, James.
Celtic: Latchford; Filippi, Lynch, Aitken, Edvaldsson, Glavin, Doyle, Conroy, McAdam, Burns, McCluskey.

13 SEPT
Morton (0) 3 (*Scott* 2, *Thomson*) 4000
Oldham Ath (0) 0
Morton: Connaghan; Hayes, Holmes, Evans, Orr, Rooney, Russell, Miller, Thomson, Scott, Ritchie (McNeil).
Oldham Ath: McDonnell; Wood, Blair, Bell, Hicks, Hurst, Gardner, Taylor, Young, Chapman, Halom.

Patrick (0) 1 (*Melrose*) 2000
Mansfield T (0) 0
Patrick: Rough; McKee, McKinnon, Anderson, McAdam (Marr), Gibson, Houston, Love, Melrose, Somner, McDonald.
Mansfield T: Arnold; Curtis, Wood, Goodwin, Saxby (M), McClelland, Miller, Martin (Foster C), Syrett, Hodgson, Bird.

QUARTER-FINALS, SECOND LEG
26 SEPT
Oldham Ath (3) 4 (*Valentine, Taylor, Young,* 4415
Hayes og)
Morton (0) 0
Oldham Ath: McDonnell; Wood, Blair, Bell, Hicks, Hurst, Valentine, Taylor, Young, Chapman, Halom.
Morton: Connaghan; Hayes, Holmes, McLaren, Orr, Rooney, Russell, Miller, Thomson, Scott, Ritchie.

St Mirren (1) 2 (*Abercrombie, Hyslop*) 10,000
Bristol C (1) 2 (*Mann, Garland*)
St Mirren: Thomson, Beckett, Munro, Fitzpatrick, Dunlop, Copland, Hyslop, Stark, Bone, Abercrombie, McGarvey.
Bristol C: Shaw, Sweeney, Gillies, Gow, Rodgers, Hunter, Tainton (Bain), Garland, Ritchie, Mabbutt, Mann.

27 SEPT
Celtic (0) 1 (*Lynch pen*) 28,000
Burnley (2) 2 (*Brennan, Kindon*)
Celtic: Latchford; McGrain, Lynch, Aitken, Edvaldsson, Conroy, Provan, Conn, McAdam, Burns Lennox.
Burnley: Stevenson; Scott, Brennan, Noble, Thomson, Rodaway, Ingham, Smith, Fletcher, Kindon, James.

3 OCT
Mansfield T (1) (3) (*Saxby, G, Goodwin* 2) 5,287
Partick (1) (2) (*Somner, Melrose*)
Mansfield T: Arnold (New); Bird, Foster B, Miller, Saxby M, McClelland, Saxby G, Moss, Syrett, Goodwin, (Phillips), Martin.
Partick: Rough; McKinnon, Whittaker, Gibson, McAdam, Campbell (Marr), Houston, Melrose, Love, Somner, O'Hara.
(aet; Mansfield won on penalties 3-1)

SEMI-FINAL, FIRST LEG
17 OCT
Oldham Ath (1) 1 (*Wood pen*) 6.145
St Mirren (0) 1 (*Stark*)
Oldham Ath: McDonnell; Wood, Blair, Bell, Hicks, Hurst, Halom, Taylor, Young, Chapman, Gardner.
St Mirren: Thomson; Young, Munro, Fitzpatrick, Dunlop, Copland, Hyslop, Stark, Bone, Abercrombie, McGarvey.

31 OCT
Mansfield T (1) 1 (*Goodwin*) 5517
Burnley (0) 2 (*Kindon, James*)
Mansfield T: Arnold; McClelland, Foster B, Goodwin, Saxby M, Bird, Miller, (Allen) Moss, Syrett, Phillips, Martin.
Burnley: Stevenson; Scott, Brennan, Noble, Thomson, Rodaway, Hall, Ingham, Fletcher, Kindon, James.

SEMI-FINAL, SECOND LEG
St Mirren (0) 1 (*Stark*) 3000
Oldham Ath (0) 1 (*Young*) (*aet*)
St Mirren: Thomson; Young, Munro, Fitzpatrick, Dunlop, Copland, Richardson, Stark, Bone, Abercrombie, McGarvey.
Oldham Ath: McDonnell; Wood, Edwards, Bell, Hicks, Heaton, Halom, Taylor, Young, Chapman, Gardner.
(*Oldham won 4-2 on penalties*)

7 NOV
Burnley (0) 0 6871
Mansfield T (1) 1 (*Syrett*)
Burnley: Stevenson; Scott, Brennan, Noble, Thomson, Rodaway, Hall, Ingham, Fletcher, Kindon, James.
Mansfield T: Arnold; Curtis, Foster B, Saxby G Coffey), Saxby M, Bird, Miller, McClelland, Syrett, Goodwin, Martin.
(*Burnley won 8-7 on penalties*)

FINAL, FIRST LEG
5 DEC
(Final first-leg)
Oldham (0) 0 (*Young*) 10,456
Burnley (3) 4 (*Kindon* 2, *Noble, Thomson*)
Oldham: McDonnell; Wood, Blair, Bell, Hicks, Hurst, Valentine, Taylor, Young, Chapman, Steel.
Burnley: Stevenson; Arins, Brennan, Noble, Thomson, Rodaway, Hall, Ingham, Fletcher, Kindon, James.

FINAL, SECOND LEG
12 DEC
Burnley (0) 0 10,865
Oldham Ath (1) 1 (*Steel*)
Burnley: Stevenson; Arins, Brennan, Noble, Thomson, Rodaway, Hall, Ingham, Fletcher, Kindon, James.
Oldham Ath: McDonnell; Wood, Blair, Bell, Hicks, Hurst, Valentine, Steel, Young, Chapman, Gardner.

F.A. CHARITY SHIELD WINNERS 1908-78

Year	Winners	Runners-up	Score
1908	Manchester U	QPR	4-0 after 1-1 draw
1909	Newcastle U	Northampton	2-0
1910	Brighton	Aston Villa	1-0
1911	Manchester U	Swindon T	8-4
1912	Blackburn R	QPR	2-1
1913	Professionals	Amateurs	7-2
1919	WBA	Tottenham H	2-0
1920	Tottenham H	Burnley	2-0
1921	Huddersfield	Liverpool	1-0
1923	Professionals	Amateurs	2-0
1924	Professionals	Amateurs	3-1
1925	Amateurs	Professionals	6-1
1926	Amateurs	Professionals	6-3
1927	Cardiff C	Corinthians	2-1
1928	Everton	Blackburn R	2-1
1929	Professionals	Amateurs	3-0
1930	Arsenal	Sheffield W	2-1
1931	Arsenal	WBA	1-0
1932	Everton	Newcastle U	5-3
1933	Arsenal	Everton	3-0
1934	Arsenal	Manchester C	4-0
1935	Sheffield W	Arsenal	1-0
1936	Sunderland	Arsenal	2-1
1937	Manchester C	Sunderland	2-0
1938	Arsenal	Preston NE	2-1
1948	Arsenal	Manchester U	4-3
1949	Portsmouth	Wolverhampton W	1-1
1950	World Cup Team	Canadian Touring Team	4-2
1951	Tottenham H	Newcastle U	2-1
1952	Manchester U	Newcastle U	4-2
1953	Arsenal	Blackpool	3-1
1954	Wolverhampton W	WBA	4-4*
1955	Chelsea	Newcastle U	3-0
1956	Manchester U	Manchester C	1-0
1957	Manchester U	Aston Villa	4-0
1958	Bolton W	Wolverhampton W	4-1
1959	Wolverhampton W	Nottingham F	3-1
1960	Burnley	Wolverhampton W	2-2
1961	Tottenham H	FA XI	3-2
1962	Tottenham H	Ipswich T	5-1
1963	Everton	Manchester U	4-0
1964	Liverpool	West Ham U	2-2*
1965	Manchester U	Liverpool	2-2*
1966	Liverpool	Everton	1-0
1967	Manchester U	Tottenham H	3-3*
1968	Manchester C	WBA	6-1
1969	Leeds U	Manchester C	2-1
1970	Everton	Chelsea	2-1
1971	Leicester	Liverpool	0-0
1972	Manchester C	Aston Villa	1-0
1973	Burnley	Manchester C	1-1
1974	Liverpool†	Leeds	1-1
1975	Derby Co	West Ham U	2-0
1976	Liverpool	Southampton	1-0
1977	Liverpool	Manchester U	0-0*

* Each club retained shield for six months.   † won on penalties

FA Charity Shield 1978

Ipswich (0) 0 Nottingham F (2) 5, 68,000. *Ipswich:* Cooper; Burley, Mills, Talbot, Osman, Wark, Parkin, Gates, Mariner, Whymark (Turner), Woods. *Nottingham F:* Shilton; Anderson, Barrett, McGovern, Lloyd, Burns, O'Neill (Needham), Gemmill, Withe, Woodcock, Robertson.

ENGLAND v YOUNG ENGLAND

Year	Date	Venue	Goals England	YE	Year	Date	Venue	Goals England	YE
1954	April 30	Highbury	2	1	1963	May 24	Highbury	3	2
1955	May 6	Highbury	5	0	1964	May 1	Stamford Bridge	3	0
1957	May 3	Highbury	1	2	1965	April 30	Highbury	2	2
1958	May 2	Stamford Bridge	4	1	1966	May 13	Stamford Bridge	1	1
1959	May 1	Highbury	3	3	1967	May 19	Highbury	0	5
1960	May 6	Highbury	2	1	1968	May 17	Highbury	1	4
1961	May 5	Stamford Bridge	1	1	1969	April 25	Stamford Bridge	0	0
1962	May 4	Highbury	3	2					

British International Review

The re-emergence of an England team as a potent force in world football was perhaps the most positive feature of the 1978-79 season. I do not like to put too much emphasis on results, because a lucky bounce of the ball or a refereeing decision often distorts the overall picture. Nevertheless, 'results' are important, they do go into the history books and stay there long after the actual circumstances of the events are forgotten.

This year, for instance, goalkeeping errors helped England enormously – Michalik, Jennings and Wood all slipped up at Wembley, and Friedl Koncilia gifted Coppell with one of his opportunist goals in Vienna. But, of course, 'they all count', and as a consequence, England did remarkably well in competitive matches.

Ron Greenwood took a calculated gamble when he opted for a positive 4-2-4 attacking formation, and perhaps a lesser one when he sensibly settled on a squad irrespective of club form. Thank goodness, British footballers still regard it as an honour to play for their country (amazingly, this is not necessarily so elsewhere), therefore the players were grateful for the manager's loyalty and performed above their club form in the national jersey.

This is very significant, because apart from a period in the mid-sixties, such a transformation was unthinkable. The Greenwood plan relied on an orthodox four-man zonal defence, with Dave Watson, the king-pin, in the heart of it. Ray Wilkins, in a slightly defensive role, and Trevor Brooking in a more forward position shared the midfield duties with occasional help from 'withdrawn' wingers, Coppell and Barnes.

Kevin Keegan was given free rein to utilize his extraordinary speed and inventiveness, and Bob Latchford was entrusted with the thankless task of acting as a battering ram in the middle of the opponent's defence. The scheme worked with varying degrees of success, and result-wise, one cannot complain when seven points are collected out of a possible eight in the European Championship.

England's defence was slightly wobbly in Copenhagen, but the Danes suffered even more, and a 4-3 win away from home was quite satisfactory. The fixture in Dublin was a more difficult one, because the bulk of the Irish players were drafted from English League clubs and there was no question of an 'inferiority complex' which often overwhelms lesser countries when they face the might of England.

A 1-1 draw against the Republic was followed by an easy win over Northern Ireland at Wembley (4-0), and a surprisingly poor Bulgarian side was also summarily defeated in Sofia – 3-0. Thus Ron Greenwood's troops made it practically certain that England will reach next summer's European Championship Finals in Italy – a pleasant change from the continuous disappointments of the seventies.

England's success automatically means failure for Ireland, while both Wales and Scotland are still in the running for the top place in their respective groups. Indeed, Wales had a marvellous season, but they faltered on the one occasion when it was the most perilous to do so. They lost at home to West Germany 2-0 in this Championship, when Kaltz twice beat the Welsh defence, and his centres were headed home by Zimmermann and Fischer.

Earlier, Wales registered home wins over Malta and Turkey, and a 2-0 win in Valetta means that the decisive game in this group will be played in October, when Mike Smith's team go to West Germany. After the traumatic World Cup fiasco, the Scottish team, perhaps predictably, went to pieces, and following a defeat in Austria, Jock Stein took over at the helm. But the self-destructive streak in Scotland's football was too much for him to eradicate, and after four matches in Europe, they are on four points – three behind leaders Portugal. However, this is a well-balanced group, and a great deal might happen yet.

After the 'first round' of the British Home Championship, the two main talking points were both rather depressing. They concerned the validity and the timing of these series of matches. I questioned both Mike Smith and Jock Stein on the subject, and they said that they'd rather have played at the end of the season, because at that time, it is easier to obtain the release of players from their clubs. A further affirmation of the present system came in the quality of the football itself, which was well above average.

Admittedly, England's lukewarm 2-0 victory in Belfast wouldn't have raised anyone's blood pressure, but on the same day, a glorious John Toshack hat-trick gave Wales a 3-0 win over the Scots. The midweek match at Wembley between England and Wales was an exciting battle, in which the much-changed home side couldn't break down the resolute Welsh defence. – 0-0. Scotland beat Ireland 1-0 with a goal by Arthur Graham, in a game which they should have won much more comfortably.

So, Wales were poised to capture the title in the first year when goal difference was allowed to decide the issue – in the past, countries with the same points total 'shared' the crown of British Champions. But it is never easy to win at Belfast, and an excellent match ended in a 1-1 draw with Ireland perhaps unlucky not to win.

The usual crescendo at Wembley saw a rampant Scotland side overwhelming England in the first-half, with comparative newcomer John Wark of Ipswich putting them ahead. But in the closing minute of this period, the 'Scottish disease' struck again – a half-hit Peter Barnes shot trickled into the net, with goalkeeper George Wood out of position, and too slow to react. Worse to come in the second-half – a Wilkins shot was dropped by the unfortunate Everton 'keeper, and there was busy little Coppell scuttling the ball into the unguarded net.

A gem of a goal put paid to a Scottish revival later, when Keegan picked up the ball in the centre-circle, sprinted past two or three leaden-footed opponents, exchanged a perfect one-two with his partner in telepathy, Brooking, and scored with unerring accuracy; 3-1 – England won the British title for the second year running. This domestic triumph plus the progress in the European Championship made it a highly satisfactory year.

The friendlies were somewhat less successful – a fortuitous narrow win over Czechoslovakia (1-0), a dull, goalless draw in Sweden, and a 4-3 defeat in Vienna, where a remarkable fight-back came to nothing when Pezzey was left unmarked in the 70th minute to head the winning goal. Obviously, there is room for improvement, but England are on the right road – at last!

LESLIE VERNON

SUPER CUP

1972 Ajax beat Rangers 3-1, 3-2
1973 Ajax beat AC Milan 0-1, 6-0
1974 Not contested
1975 Dynamo Kiev beat Bayern Munich 1-0, 2-0
1976 Anderlecht beat Bayern Munich 4-1, 1-2
1977 Liverpool beat Hamburg 1-1, 6-0

1978

First Leg

Anderlecht (2) 3 (*Vercauteren, Van der Elst, Rensenbrink*)
Liverpool (1) 1 (*Case*) 30,000
Anderlecht: De Bree; Van der Elst, Broos, Dusbaba, Thissen, Vercauteren, Nielsen, Geels, Haan, Coeck, Rensenbrink
Liverpool: Clemence; Neal, Kennedy (A), Hughes, Kennedy (R), Hansen, Dalglish, Case, Johnson (Heighway), McDermott, Souness

Second Leg

Liverpool (1) 2 (*Hughes, Fairclough*)
Anderlecht (0) 1 (*Van der Elst*) 23,598
Liverpool: Ogrizovic; Neal, Hughes, Thompson, Kennedy (R), Hansen, Dalglish, Case, Fairclough, McDermott, Souness
Anderlecht: Munaron; Van Binst, Van Toorn, Dusbaba, Thissen, Vercauteren, Van der Elst, Geels (Martens), Haan, Coeck, Rensenbrink

BRITISH HOME INTERNATIONALS

INTERNATIONAL CHAMPIONSHIP WINNERS 1883-1979

Year	Champions	Pts	Year	Champions	Pts	Year	Champions	Pts
1883–84	Scotland	6	1913–14	Ireland	5		England	3
1884–85	Scotland	5	1919–20	Wales	4	1955–56	Scotland	3
1885–86	England	5	1920–21	Scotland	6		Wales	3
	Scotland	5	1921–22	Scotland	4		Ireland	3
1886–87	Scotland	6	1922–23	Scotland	5	1956–57	England	5
1887–88	England	6	1923–24	Wales	6	1957–58	England	4
1888–89	Scotland	6	1924–25	Scotland	6		Ireland	4
1889–90	Scotland	5	1925–26	Scotland	6	1958–59	Ireland	4
	England	5	1926–27	Scotland	4		England	4
1890–91	England	6		England	4		England	4
1891–92	England	6	1927–28	Wales	5	1959–60	Scotland	4
1892–93	England	6	1928–29	Scotland	6		Wales	4
1893–94	Scotland	5	1929–30	England	6	1960–61	England	6
1894–95	England	5	1930–31	Scotland	4	1961–62	Scotland	6
1895–96	Scotland	5		England	4	1962–63	Scotland	6
1896–97	Scotland	5	1931–32	England	6	1963–64	Scotland	4
1897–98	England	5	1932–33	Wales	5		England	4
1898–99	England	6	1933–34	Wales	5		Ireland	4
1899–1900	Scotland	6	1934–35	England	4	1964–65	England	5
1900–01	England	5		Scotland	4	1965–66	England	5
1901–02	Scotland	5	1935–36	Scotland	5	1966–67	Scotland	5
1902–03	England	4	1936–37	Wales	6	1967–68	England	5
	Ireland	4	1937–38	England	4	1968–69	England	6
	Scotland	4	1938–39	England	4		England	4
1903–04	England	4		Scotland	4	1969–70	Scotland	4
1904–05	England	5		Wales	4		Wales	4
1905–06	England	4	1946–47	England	5	1970–71	England	5
	Scotland	4	1947–48	England	5	1971–72	England	4
1906–07	Wales	5	1948–49	Scotland	6		Scotland	4
1907–08	Scotland	5	1949–50	England	6	1972–73	England	6
	England	5	1950–51	Scotland	6	1973–74	England	4
1908–09	England	6	1951–52	Wales	5		Scotland	4
1909–10	Scotland	4		England	5	1974–75	England	4
1910–11	England	5	1952–53	England	4	1975–76	Scotland	6
1911–12	England	5		Scotland	4	1976–77	Scotland	5
	Scotland	5	1953–54	England	6	1977–78	England	6
1912–13	England	4	1954–55	England	6	1978–79	England	5

ENGLAND v SCOTLAND

PLAYED: 97; England won 37, Scotland won 38, Drawn 22. GOALS: England 177, Scotland 164.

Year	Venue	E	S	Year	Venue	E	S	Year	Venue	E	S
1872	Glasgow	0	0	1896	Glasgow	1	2	1925	Glasgow	0	2
1873	Kennington Oval	4	2	1897	Crystal Palace	1	2	1926	Manchester	0	1
1874	Glasgow	1	2	1898	Glasgow	3	1	1927	Glasgow	2	1
1875	Kennington Oval	2	2	1899	Birmingham	2	1	1928	Wembley	1	5
1876	Glasgow	0	3	1900	Glasgow	1	4	1929	Glasgow	0	1
1877	Kennington Oval	1	3	1901	Crystal Palace	2	2	1930	Wembley	5	2
1878	Glasgow	2	7	1902	Birmingham	2	2	1931	Glasgow	0	2
1879	Kennington Oval	5	4	1903	Sheffield	1	2	1932	Wembley	3	0
1880	Glasgow	4	5	1904	Glasgow	1	0	1933	Glasgow	1	2
1881	Kennington Oval	1	6	1905	Crystal Palace	1	0	1934	Wembley	3	0
1882	Glasgow	1	5	1906	Glasgow	1	2	1935	Glasgow	0	2
1883	Sheffield	2	3	1907	Newcastle	1	1	1936	Wembley	1	1
1884	Glasgow	0	1	1908	Glasgow	1	1	1937	Glasgow	1	3
1885	Kennington Oval	1	1	1909	Crystal Palace	2	0	1938	Wembley	0	1
1886	Glasgow	1	1	1910	Glasgow	0	2	1939	Glasgow	2	1
1887	Blackburn	2	3	1911	Everton	1	1	1947	Wembley	1	1
1888	Glasgow	5	0	1912	Glasgow	1	1	1948	Glasgow	2	0
1889	Kennington Oval	2	3	1913	Chelsea	1	0	1949	Wembley	1	3
1890	Glasgow	1	1	1914	Glasgow	1	3	wc1950	Glasgow	1	0
1891	Blackburn	2	1	1920	Sheffield	5	4	1951	Wembley	2	3
1892	Glasgow	4	1	1921	Glasgow	0	3	1952	Wembley	2	1
1893	Richmond	5	2	1922	Aston Villa	0	1	1953	Wembley	2	2
1894	Glasgow	2	2	1923	Glasgow	2	2	wc1954	Glasgow	4	2
1895	Everton	3	0	1924	Wembley	1	1	1955	Wembley	7	2

Year Venue	Goals E S	Year Venue	Goals E S	Year Venue	Goals E S
1956 Glasgow	1 1	1965 Wembley	2 2	1973 Wembley	1 0
1957 Wembley	2 1	1966 Glasgow	4 3	1974 Glasgow	0 2
1958 Glasgow	4 0	EC1967 Wembley	2 3	1975 Wembley	5 1
1959 Wembley	1 0	EC1968 Glasgow	1 1	1976 Glasgow	1 2
1960 Glasgow	1 1	1969 Wembley	4 1	1977 Wembley	1 2
1961 Wembley	9 3	1970 Glasgow	0 0	1978 Glasgow	1 0
1962 Glasgow	0 2	1971 Wembley	3 1	1979 Wembley	3 1
1963 Wembley	1 2	1972 Glasgow	1 0		
1964 Glasgow	0 1	1973 Glasgow	5 0		

WC = World Cup   EC = European Championship

ENGLAND v WALES

PLAYED: 92; England won 60, Wales won 12, Drawn 20, GOALS: England 235, Wales 84.

Year Venue	Goals E W	Year Venue	Goals E W	Year Venue	Goals E W
1879 Kennington Oval	2 1	1909 Nottingham	2 0	1951 Cardiff	1 1
1880 Wrexham	3 2	1910 Cardiff	1 0	1952 Wembley	5 2
1881 Blackburn	0 1	1911 Millwall	3 0	WC1953 Cardiff	4 1
1882 Wrexham	3 5	1912 Wrexham	2 0	1954 Wembley	3 2
1883 Kennington Oval	5 0	1913 Bristol	4 3	1955 Cardiff	1 2
1884 Wrexham	4 0	1914 Cardiff	2 0	1956 Wembley	3 1
1885 Blackburn	1 1	1920 Highbury	1 2	1957 Cardiff	4 0
1886 Wrexham	3 1	1921 Cardiff	0 0	1958 Aston Villa	2 2
1887 Kennington Oval	4 0	1922 Liverpool	1 0	1959 Cardiff	1 1
1888 Crewe	5 1	1923 Cardiff	2 2	1960 Wembley	5 1
1889 Stoke-on-Trent	4 1	1924 Blackburn	1 2	1961 Cardiff	1 1
1890 Wrexham	3 1	1925 Swansea	2 1	1962 Wembley	4 0
1891 Sunderland	4 1	1926 Crystal Palace	1 3	1963 Cardiff	4 0
1892 Wrexham	2 0	1927 Wrexham	3 3	1964 Wembley	2 1
1893 Stoke	6 0	1927 Burnley	1 2	1965 Cardiff	0 0
1894 Wrexham	5 1	1928 Swansea	3 2	EC1966 Wembley	5 1
1894 Queen's Club, Kensington	1 1	1929 Chelsea	6 0	EC1967 Cardiff	3 0
		1930 Wrexham	4 0	1969 Wembley	2 1
1896 Cardiff	9 1	1931 Liverpool	3 1	1970 Cardiff	1 1
1897 Sheffield	4 0	1932 Wrexham	0 0	1971 Wembley	0 0
1898 Wrexham	3 0	1933 Newcastle	1 2	1972 Cardiff	3 0
1899 Bristol	4 0	1934 Cardiff	4 0	WC1972 Cardiff	1 0
1900 Cardiff	1 1	1935 Wolverhampton	1 2	WC1973 Wembley	1 1
1901 Newcastle	6 0	1936 Cardiff	1 2	1973 Wembley	3 0
1902 Wrexham	0 0	1937 Middlesbrough	2 1	1974 Cardiff	2 0
1903 Portsmouth	2 1	1938 Cardiff	2 4	1975 Wembley	2 2
1904 Wrexham	2 2	1946 Manchester	3 0	1976 Wrexham	2 1
1905 Liverpool	3 1	1947 Cardiff	3 0	1976 Cardiff	1 0
1906 Cardiff	1 0	1948 Aston Villa	1 0	1977 Wembley	0 1
1907 Fulham	1 1	WC1949 Cardiff	4 1	1978 Cardiff	3 1
1908 Wrexham	7 1	1950 Sunderland	4 2	1979 Wembley	0 0

ENGLAND v IRELAND

PLAYED: 87; England won 68, Ireland won 6, Drawn 13. GOALS: England 302, Ireland 78.

Year Venue	Goals E I	Year Venue	Goals E I	Year Venue	Goals E I
1882 Belfast	13 0	1905 Middlesbrough	1 1	1932 Blackpool	1 0
1883 Liverpool	7 0	1906 Belfast	5 0	1933 Belfast	3 0
1884 Belfast	8 1	1907 Everton	1 0	1935 Everton	2 1
1885 Manchester	4 0	1908 Belfast	3 1	1935 Belfast	3 1
1886 Belfast	6 1	1909 Bradford	4 0	1936 Stoke	3 1
1887 Sheffield	7 0	1910 Belfast	1 1	1937 Belfast	5 1
1888 Belfast	5 1	1911 Derby	2 1	1938 Manchester	7 0
1889 Everton	6 1	1912 Dublin	6 1	1946 Belfast	7 2
1890 Belfast	9 1	1913 Belfast	1 2	1947 Everton	2 2
1891 Wolverhampton	6 1	1914 Middlesbrough	0 3	1948 Belfast	6 2
1892 Belfast	2 0	1919 Belfast	1 1	WC1949 Manchester	9 2
1893 Birmingham	6 1	1920 Sunderland	2 0	1950 Belfast	4 1
1894 Belfast	2 2	1921 Belfast	1 1	1951 Aston Villa	2 0
1895 Derby	9 0	1922 West Bromwich	2 0	1952 Belfast	2 2
1896 Belfast	2 0	1923 Belfast	1 2	WC1953 Everton	3 1
1897 Nottingham	6 0	1924 Everton	3 1	1954 Belfast	2 0
1898 Belfast	3 2	1925 Belfast	0 0	1955 Wembley	3 0
1899 Sunderland	13 2	1926 Liverpool	3 3	1956 Belfast	1 1
1900 Dublin	2 0	1927 Belfast	0 2	1957 Wembley	2 3
1901 Southampton	3 0	1928 Everton	2 1	1958 Belfast	3 3
1902 Belfast	1 0	1929 Belfast	3 0	1959 Wembley	2 1
1903 Wolverhampton	4 0	1930 Sheffield	5 1	1960 Belfast	5 2
1904 Belfast	3 1	1931 Belfast	6 2	1961 Wembley	1 1

657

Year	Venue	Goals E	I	Year	Venue	Goals E	I	Year	Venue	Goals E	I
1962	Belfast	3	1	1969	Belfast	3	1	1975	Belfast	0	0
1963	Wembley	8	3	1970	Wembley	3	1	1976	Wembley	4	0
1964	Belfast	4	3	1971	Belfast	1	0	1977	Belfast	2	1
1965	Wembley	2	1	1972	Wembley	0	1	1978	Wembley	1	0
EC1966	Belfast	2	0	1973	Everton	2	1	EC1979	Wembley	4	0
EC1967	Wembley	2	0	1974	Wembley	1	0	1979	Belfast	2	0

SCOTLAND v WALES

PLAYED: 94; Scotland won 56, Wales won 16, Drawn 22. GOALS: Scotland 231, Wales 106.

Year	Venue	Goals S	W	Year	Venue	Goals S	W	Year	Venue	Goals S	W
1876	Glasgow	4	0	1908	Dundee	2	1	1951	Glasgow	0	1
1877	Wrexham	2	0	1909	Wrexham	2	3	WC1952	Cardiff	2	1
1878	Glasgow	9	0	1910	Kilmarnock	1	0	1953	Glasgow	3	3
1879	Wrexham	3	0	1911	Cardiff	2	2	1954	Cardiff	1	0
1880	Glasgow	5	1	1912	Tynecastle	1	0	1955	Glasgow	2	0
1881	Wrexham	5	1	1913	Wrexham	0	0	1956	Cardiff	2	2
1882	Glasgow	5	0	1914	Glasgow	0	0	1957	Glasgow	1	1
1883	Wrexham	4	1	1920	Cardiff	1	1	1958	Cardiff	3	0
1884	Glasgow	4	1	1921	Aberdeen	2	1	1959	Glasgow	1	1
1885	Wrexham	8	1	1922	Wrexham	1	2	1960	Cardiff	0	2
1886	Glasgow	4	1	1923	Paisley	2	0	1961	Glasgow	2	0
1887	Wrexham	2	0	1924	Cardiff	0	2	1962	Cardiff	3	2
1888	Edinburgh	5	1	1925	Tynecastle	3	1	1963	Glasgow	2	1
1889	Wrexham	0	0	1926	Cardiff	3	0	1964	Cardiff	2	3
1890	Paisley	5	0	1927	Glasgow	3	0	EC1965	Glasgow	4	1
1891	Wrexham	4	3	1928	Wrexham	2	2	EC1966	Cardiff	1	1
1892	Edinburgh	6	1	1929	Glasgow	4	2	1967	Glasgow	3	2
1893	Wrexham	8	0	1930	Cardiff	4	2	1969	Wrexham	5	3
1894	Kilmarnock	5	2	1931	Glasgow	1	1	1970	Glasgow	0	0
1895	Wrexham	2	2	1932	Wrexham	3	2	1971	Cardiff	0	0
1896	Dundee	4	0	1933	Edinburgh	2	5	1972	Glasgow	1	0
1897	Wrexham	2	2	1934	Cardiff	2	3	1973	Wrexham	2	0
1898	Motherwell	5	2	1935	Aberdeen	3	2	1974	Glasgow	2	0
1899	Wrexham	6	0	1936	Cardiff	1	1	1975	Cardiff	2	2
1900	Aberdeen	5	2	1937	Dundee	1	2	1976	Glasgow	3	1
1901	Wrexham	1	1	1938	Cardiff	1	2	WC1977	Glasgow	1	0
1902	Greenock	5	1	1939	Edinburgh	3	2	1977	Wrexham	0	0
1903	Cardiff	1	0	1946	Wrexham	1	3	WC1977	Liverpool	2	0
1904	Dundee	1	1	1947	Glasgow	1	2	1978	Glasgow	1	1
1905	Wrexham	1	3	WC1948	Cardiff	3	1	1979	Cardiff	0	3
1906	Edinburgh	0	2	1949	Glasgow	2	0				
1907	Wrexham	0	1	1950	Cardiff	3	1				

SCOTLAND v IRELAND

PLAYED: 84; Scotland won 59, Ireland won 13, Drawn 12. GOALS: Scotland 249, Ireland 76.

Year	Venue	Goals S	I	Year	Venue	Goals S	I	Year	Venue	Goals S	I
1884	Belfast	5	0	1912	Belfast	4	1	1951	Belfast	3	0
1885	Glasgow	8	2	1913	Dublin	2	1	1952	Glasgow	1	1
1886	Belfast	7	2	1914	Belfast	1	1	1953	Belfast	3	1
1887	Glasgow	4	1	1920	Glasgow	3	0	1954	Glasgow	2	2
1888	Belfast	10	2	1921	Belfast	2	0	1955	Belfast	1	2
1889	Glasgow	7	0	1922	Glasgow	2	1	1956	Glasgow	1	0
1890	Belfast	4	1	1923	Belfast	1	0	1957	Belfast	1	1
1891	Glasgow	2	1	1924	Glasgow	2	0	1958	Glasgow	2	2
1892	Belfast	3	2	1925	Belfast	3	0	1959	Belfast	4	0
1893	Glasgow	6	1	1926	Glasgow	4	0	1960	Glasgow	5	2
1894	Belfast	2	1	1927	Belfast	2	0	1961	Belfast	6	1
1895	Glasgow	3	1	1928	Glasgow	0	1	1962	Glasgow	5	1
1896	Belfast	3	3	1929	Belfast	7	3	1963	Belfast	1	2
1897	Glasgow	5	1	1930	Glasgow	3	1	1964	Glasgow	3	2
1898	Belfast	3	0	1931	Belfast	0	0	1965	Belfast	2	3
1899	Glasgow	9	1	1932	Glasgow	3	1	1966	Glasgow	2	1
1900	Belfast	3	0	1933	Belfast	4	0	1967	Belfast	0	1
1901	Glasgow	11	0	1934	Glasgow	1	2	1969	Glasgow	1	1
1902	Belfast	5	1	1935	Belfast	1	2	1970	Belfast	1	0
1903	Glasgow	0	2	1936	Edinburgh	2	1	1971	Glasgow	0	1
1904	Dublin	1	1	1937	Belfast	3	1	1972	Glasgow	2	0
1905	Glasgow	4	0	1938	Aberdeen	1	1	1973	Glasgow	1	2
1906	Dublin	1	0	1939	Belfast	2	0	1974	Glasgow	0	1
1907	Glasgow	3	0	1946	Glasgow	0	0	1975	Glasgow	3	0
1908	Dublin	5	0	1947	Belfast	0	2	1976	Glasgow	3	0
1909	Glasgow	5	0	1948	Glasgow	3	2	1977	Glasgow	3	0
1910	Belfast	0	1	1949	Belfast	8	2	1978	Glasgow	1	1
1911	Glasgow	2	0	1950	Glasgow	6	1	1979	Glasgow	1	0

WALES v IRELAND

PLAYED: 86; Wales won 40, Ireland won 26, Drawn 20. GOALS: Wales 176, Ireland 124.

Year	Venue	Goals W.	Goals I.	Year	Venue	Goals W.	Goals I.	Year	Venue	Goals W.	Goals L.
1882	Wrexham	7	1	1911	Belfast	2	1	1952	Swansea	3	0
1883	Belfast	1	1	1912	Cardiff	2	3	1953	Belfast	3	2
1884	Wrexham	6	0	1913	Belfast	1	0	wc1954	Wrexham	1	2
1885	Belfast	8	2	1914	Wrexham	1	2	1955	Belfast	3	2
1886	Wrexham	5	0	1920	Belfast	2	2	1956	Cardiff	1	1
1887	Belfast	1	4	1921	Swansea	2	1	1957	Belfast	0	0
1888	Wrexham	11	0	1922	Belfast	1	1	1958	Cardiff	1	1
1889	Belfast	3	1	1923	Wrexham	0	3	1959	Belfast	1	4
1890	Shrewsbury	5	2	1924	Belfast	1	0	1960	Wrexham	3	2
1891	Belfast	2	7	1925	Wrexham	0	0	1961	Belfast	5	1
1892	Bangor	1	1	1926	Belfast	0	3	1962	Cardiff	4	0
1893	Belfast	3	4	1927	Cardiff	2	2	1963	Belfast	4	1
1894	Swansea	4	1	1928	Belfast	2	1	1964	Cardiff	2	3
1895	Belfast	2	2	1929	Wrexham	2	2	1965	Belfast	5	0
1896	Wrexham	6	1	1930	Belfast	0	7	1966	Cardiff	1	4
1897	Belfast	3	4	1931	Wrexham	3	2	EC1967	Belfast	0	0
1898	Llandudno	0	1	1932	Belfast	0	4	EC1968	Wrexham	2	0
1899	Belfast	0	1	1933	Wrexham	4	1	1969	Belfast	0	0
1900	Llandudno	2	0	1934	Belfast	1	1	1970	Swansea	1	0
1901	Belfast	1	0	1935	Wrexham	3	1	1971	Belfast	0	1
1902	Cardiff	0	3	1936	Belfast	2	3	1972	Wrexham	0	0
1903	Belfast	0	2	1937	Wrexham	4	1	1973	Everton	0	1
1904	Bangor	0	1	1938	Belfast	0	1	1974	Wrexham	1	0
1905	Belfast	2	2	1939	Wrexham	3	1	1975	Belfast	0	1
1906	Wrexham	4	4	1947	Belfast	1	2	1976	Cardiff	1	0
1907	Belfast	3	2	1948	Wrexham	2	0	1977	Belfast	1	1
1908	Aberdare	0	1	1949	Belfast	2	0	1978	Swansea	1	0
1909	Belfast	3	2	wc1950	Wrexham	0	0	1979	Belfast	1	1
1910	Wrexham	4	1	1951	Belfast	2	1				

LEADING INTERNATIONAL SCORERS 1946-79

ENGLAND	N. IRELAND	SCOTLAND	WALES
49 R. Charlton	10 J. Crossan	30 D. Law	23 T. Ford
44 J. Greaves	J. McIlroy	22 L. Reilly	22 I. Allchurch
30 T. Finney	9 G. Best	K. Dalglish	16 C. Jones
N. Lofthouse	W. Bingham	13 W. Steel	15 J. Charles
24 G. Hurst	W. Irvine	12 A. Gilzean	12 J. Toshack
23 S. Mortensen	P. McParland	11 C. Stein	
21 M. Peters	8 D. Dougan	10 R. Collins	
M. Channon		R. Johnstone	
18 Haynes J.			
R. Hunt			
16 T. Lawton			
T. Taylor			
15 K. Keegan			
13 M. Chivers			
R. Smith			
11 B. Douglas			
W. Mannion			

BRITISH INTERNATIONAL CHAMPIONSHIP 1978-79

19 MAY

Northern Ireland (0) 0
England (2) 2 (*Watson, Coppell*) (at Windsor Park) 35,000
Northern Ireland: Jennings; Rice, Nelson, Nicholl J, Nicholl C, Moreland (McGrath), Hamilton, McIlroy, Armstrong, Caskey, Cochrane (Spence).
England: Clemence; Neal, Thompson, Watson, Mills, Wilkins, McDermott, Currie, Coppell, Latchford, Barnes.

Wales (2) 3 (*Toshack* 3)
Scotland (0) 0 (at Ninian Park) 20,371
Wales: Davies; Stevenson, Dwyer, Phillips, Jones, Flynn, Yorath, (Nicholas) Mahoney, Curtis, Toshack, James.
Scotland: Rough; Burley, Hegarty, Hansen, Gray F, Wark, Hartford, Souness, Wallace (Jordan), Dalglish, Graham.

22 MAY

Scotland (0) 1 (*Graham*)
Northern Ireland (0) 0 (at Hampden Park) 28,529
Scotland: Wood; Burley, Gray F, Wark (Narey), McQueen, Souness, Jordan, Hegarty, Dalglish, Hartford, Graham (McGarvey).
Northern Ireland: Jennings; Rice, Nelson, Nicholl J, Hunter, Hamilton, Sloan, McIlroy, Armstrong, Spence, Moreland (Scott).

23 MAY

England (0) 0
Wales (0) 0 (at Wembley) 75,000
England: Corrigan; Cherry, Sansom, Currie (Brooking), Watson, Hughes, Keegan, Wilkins, Latchford (Coppell), McDermott, Cunningham.
Wales: Davies; Stevenson, Jones, Mahoney, Dwyer, Phillips, Yorath, Flynn, James, Toshack (Harris), Curtis.

25 MAY

Northern Ireland (1) 1 (*Spence*)
Wales (0) 1 (*James*) (at Windsor Park) 6,500
Northern Ireland: Jennings; Rice, Nelson, Nicholl C, Hunter, Nicholl J, Hamilton, McIlroy, McCreery (Sloan), Spence, Armstrong.
Wales: Davies; Stevenson, Dwyer, Phillips, Jones, Flynn, Yorath, Mahoney (Nicholas), Toshack, James, Curtis.

26 MAY

England (1) 3 (*Barnes, Coppell, Keegan*)
Scotland (1) 1 (*Wark*) (at Wembley) 100,000
England: Clemence; Neal, Mills, Thompson, Watson, Wilkins, Keegan, Coppell, Latchford, Brooking, Barnes
Scotland: Wood; Burley, Gray F, Wark, McQueen, Hegarty, Dalglish, Souness, Jordan, Hartford, Graham

FINAL TABLE

	P	W	D	L	F	A	Pts.
England	3	2	1	0	5	1	5
Wales	3	1	2	0	4	1	4
Scotland	3	1	0	2	2	6	2
Northern Irelan	3	0	1	2	1	4	1

OTHER BRITISH INTERNATIONAL RESULTS 1908-1979

ENGLAND

v ARGENTINA

Year	Date	Venue	England	Argentina
1951	May 9	Wembley	2	1
1953	May 17	Buenos Aires	0	0 (abandoned 21 mins)
wc1962	June 2	Rancagua	3	1
1964	June 6	Rio de Janeiro	0	1
wc1966	July 23	Wembley	1	0
1974	May 22	Wembley	2	2
1977	June 12	Buenos Aires	1	1

v AUSTRIA

Year	Date	Venue	England	Austria
1908	June 6	Vienna	6	1
1908	June 8	Vienna	11	1
1909	June 1	Vienna	8	1
1930	May 14	Vienna	0	0
1932	Dec. 7	Chelsea	4	3
1936	May 6	Vienna	1	2
1951	Nov. 28	Wembley	2	2
1952	May 25	Vienna	3	2
wc1958	June 15	Boras	2	2
1961	May 27	Vienna	1	3
1962	April 4	Wembley	3	1
1965	Oct. 20	Wembley	2	3
1967	May 27	Vienna	1	0
1973	Sept. 26	Wembley	7	0
1979	June 13	Vienna	3	4

v BELGIUM

Year	Date	Venue	England	Belgium
1921	May 21	Brussels	2	0
1923	Mar. 19	Highbury	6	1
1923	Nov. 1	Antwerp	2	2
1924	Dec. 8	West Bromwich	4	0
1926	May 24	Antwerp	5	3
1927	May 11	Brussels	9	1
1928	May 19	Antwerp	3	1
1929	May 11	Brussels	5	1
1931	May 16	Brussels	4	1
1936	May 9	Brussels	2	3
1947	Sept. 21	Brussels	5	2
1950	May 18	Brussels	4	1
1952	Nov. 26	Wembley	5	0
wc1954	June 17	Basle	4	4*
1964	Oct. 21	Wembley	2	2
1970	Feb. 25	Brussels	3	1

v BOHEMIA

Year	Date	Venue	England	Bohemia
1908	June 13	Prague	4	0

v BRAZIL

Year	Date	Venue	England	Brazil
1956	May 9	Wembley	4	2
wc1958	June 11	Gothenburg	0	0
1959	May 13	Rio de Janeiro	0	2
wc1962	June 10	Vina del Mar	1	3
1963	May 8	Wembley	1	1
1964	May 30	Rio de Janeiro	1	5
1969	June 12	Rio de Janeiro	1	2
wc1970	June 7	Guadalajara	0	1
1976	May 23	Los Angeles	0	1
1977	June 8	Rio	0	0
1978	April 19	Wembley	1	1

v BULGARIA

Year	Date	Venue	England	Bulgaria
wc1962	June 7	Rancagua	0	0
1968	Dec. 11	Wembley	1	1
1974	June 1	Sofia	1	0
EC1979	June 6	Sofia	3	0

v CHILE

Year	Date	Venue	England	Chile
wc1950	June 25	Rio de Janeiro	2	0
1953	May 24	Santiago	2	1

v COLOMBIA

Year	Date	Venue	England	Colombia
1970	May 20	Bogota	4	0

v CYPRUS

Year	Date	Venue	England	Cyprus
EC1975	Apr. 16	Wembley	5	0
EC1975	May 11	Limassol	1	0

v CZECHOSLOVAKIA

Year	Date	Venue	England	Czechoslovakia
1934	May 16	Prague	1	2
1937	Dec. 1	Tottenham	5	4
1963	May 29	Bratislava	4	2
1966	Nov. 2	Wembley	0	0
wc1970	June 11	Guadalajara	1	0
1973	May 27	Prague	1	1
EC1974	Oct. 30	Wembley	3	0
EC1975	Oct. 30	Bratislava	1	2
1978	Nov. 29	Wembley	1	0

v DENMARK

Year	Date	Venue	England	Denmark
1948	Sept. 26	Copenhagen	0	0
1955	Oct. 2	Copenhagen	5	1
wc1956	Dec. 5	Wolverhampton	5	2
wc1957	May 15	Copenhagen	4	1
1966	July 3	Copenhagen	2	0
EC1978	Sept. 20	Copenhagen	4	3

v ECUADOR

Year	Date	Venue	England	Ecuador
1970	May 24	Quito	2	0

v FIFA

Year	Date	Venue	England	FIFA
1938	Oct. 26	Highbury	3	0
1953	Oct. 21	Wembley	4	4
1963	Oct. 23	Wembley	2	1

v FINLAND

Year	Date	Venue	England	Finland
1937	May 20	Helsinki	8	0
1956	May 20	Helsinki	5	1
1966	June 26	Helsinki	3	0
wc1976	June 13	Helsinki	4	1
wc1976	Oct. 13	Wembley	2	1

v FRANCE

Year	Date	Venue	England	France
1923	May 10	Paris	4	1
1924	May 17	Paris	3	1
1925	May 21	Paris	3	2
1927	May 26	Paris	6	0
1928	May 17	Paris	5	1
1929	May 9	Paris	4	1
1931	May 14	Paris	2	5
1933	Dec. 6	Tottenham	4	1
1938	May 26	Paris	4	2

* After extra time.

Year	Date	Venue	England	France
1947	May 3	Highbury	3	0
1949	May 22	Paris	3	1
1951	Oct. 3	Highbury	2	2
1955	May 15	Paris	0	1
1957	Nov. 27	Wembley	4	0
ENC1962	Oct. 3	Sheffield	1	1
ENC1963	Feb. 27	Paris	2	5
WC1966	July 20	Wembley	2	0
1969	Mar. 12	Wembley	5	0

v EAST GERMANY

Year	Date	Venue	England	Germany
1963	June 2	Leipzig	2	1
1970	Nov. 25	Wembley	3	1
1974	May 29	Leipzig	1	1

v WEST GERMANY

Year	Date	Venue	England	Germany
1930	May 10	Berlin	3	3
1935	Dec. 4	Tottenham	3	0
1938	May 14	Berlin	6	3
1954	Dec. 1	Wembley	3	1
1956	May 26	Berlin	3	1
1965	May 12	Nuremberg	1	0
1966	Feb. 23	Wembley	1	0
WC1966	July 30	Wembley	4	2*
1968	June 1	Hanover	0	1
WC1970	June 14	Leon	2	3*
EC1972	April 29	Wembley	1	3
EC1972	May 13	Berlin	0	0
1975	Mar. 12	Wembley	2	0
1978	Feb. 22	Munich	1	2

v GREECE

Year	Date	Venue	England	Greece
EC1971	Apr. 21	Wembley	3	0
EC1971	Dec. 1	Athens	2	0

v HUNGARY

Year	Date	Venue	England	Hungary
1908	June 10	Budapest	7	0
1909	May 29	Budapest	4	2
1909	May 31	Budapest	8	2
1934	May 10	Budapest	1	2
1936	Dec. 2	Highbury	6	2
1953	Nov. 25	Wembley	3	6
1954	May 23	Budapest	1	7
1960	May 22	Budapest	0	2
WC1962	May 31	Rancagua	1	2
1965	May 5	Wembley	1	0
1978	May 24	Wembley	4	1

v REPUBLIC OF IRELAND

Year	Date	Venue	England	Rep. of Ireland
1946	Sept. 30	Dublin	1	0
1949	Sept. 21	Everton	0	2
WC1957	May 8	Wembley	5	1
WC1957	May 19	Dublin	1	1
1964	May 24	Dublin	3	1
1976	Sept. 8	Wembley	1	1
EC1978	Oct. 25	Dublin	1	1

v ITALY

Year	Date	Venue	England	Italy
1933	May 13	Rome	1	1
1934	Nov. 14	Highbury	3	2
1939	May 13	Milan	2	2
1948	May 16	Turin	4	0
1949	Nov. 30	Tottenham	2	0
1952	May 18	Florence	1	1
1959	May 6	Wembley	2	2
1961	May 24	Rome	3	2
1973	June 14	Turin	0	2
1973	Nov. 14	Wembley	0	1
1976	May 28	New York	3	2
WC1976	Nov. 17	Rome	0	2
WC1977	Nov. 16	Wembley	2	0

v LUXEMBOURG

Year	Date	Venue	England	Luxembourg
1927	May 21	Luxembourg	5	2
WC1960	Oct. 19	Luxembourg	9	0
WC1961	Sept. 28	Highbury	4	1
WC1977	Mar. 30	Wembley	5	0
WC1977	Oct. 12	Luxembourg	2	0

v MALTA

Year	Date	Venue	England	Malta
EC1971	Feb. 3	Valletta	1	0
EC1971	May 12	Wembley	5	0

v MEXICO

Year	Date	Venue	England	Mexico
1959	May 24	Mexico City	1	2
1961	May 10	Wembley	8	0
WC1966	July 16	Wembley	2	0
1969	June 1	Mexico City	0	0

v NETHERLANDS

Year	Date	Venue	England	Netherlands
1935	May 18	Amsterdam	1	0
1946	Nov. 27	Huddersfield	8	2
1964	Dec. 9	Amsterdam	1	1
1969	Nov. 5	Amsterdam	1	0
1970	Jan. 14	Wembley	0	0
1977	Feb. 9	Wembley	0	2

v NORWAY

Year	Date	Venue	England	Norway
1937	May 14	Oslo	6	0
1938	Nov. 9	Newcastle	4	0
1949	May 18	Oslo	4	1
1966	June 29	Oslo	6	1

v PERU

Year	Date	Venue	England	Peru
1959	May 17	Lima	1	4
1962	May 20	Lima	4	0

v POLAND

Year	Date	Venue	England	Poland
1966	Jan. 5	Everton	1	1
1966	July 5	Chorzow	1	0
WC1973	June 6	Chorzow	0	2
WC1973	Oct. 17	Wembley	1	1

v PORTUGAL

Year	Date	Venue	England	Portugal
1947	May 25	Lisbon	10	0
1950	May 14	Lisbon	5	3
1951	May 19	Everton	5	2
1955	May 22	Oporto	1	3
1958	May 7	Wembley	2	1
WC1961	May 21	Lisbon	1	1
WC1961	Oct. 25	Wembley	2	0
1964	May 17	Lisbon	4	3
1964	June 4	São Paulo	1	1
WC1966	July 26	Wembley	2	1
1969	Dec. 10	Wembley	1	0
1974	April 3	Lisbon	0	0
EC1974	Nov. 20	Wembley	0	0
EC1975	Nov. 19	Lisbon	1	1

v RUMANIA

Year	Date	Venue	England	Rumania
1939	May 24	Bucharest	2	0
1968	Nov. 6	Bucharest	0	0
1969	Jan. 15	Wembley	1	1
WC1970	June 2	Guadalajara	1	0

v SPAIN

Year	Date	Venue	England	Spain
1929	May 15	Madrid	3	4
1931	Dec. 9	Highbury	7	1
WC1950	July 2	Rio de Janeiro	0	1
1955	May 18	Madrid	1	1
1955	Nov. 30	Wembley	4	1

Year	Date	Venue	Goals	
1960	May 15	Madrid	0	3
1960	Oct. 26	Wembley	4	2
1965	Dec. 8	Madrid	2	0
1967	May 24	Wembley	2	0
EC1968	April 3	Wembley	1	0
EC1968	May 8	Madrid	2	1

v SWEDEN

Year	Date	Venue	England	Sweden
1923	May 21	Stockholm	4	2
1923	May 24	Stockholm	3	1
1937	May 17	Stockholm	4	0
1947	Nov. 19	Highbury	4	2
1949	May 13	Stockholm	1	3
1956	May 16	Stockholm	0	0
1959	Oct. 28	Wembley	2	3
1965	May 16	Gothenburg	2	1
1968	May 22	Wembley	3	1
1979	June 10	Stockholm	0	0

v SWITZERLAND

Year	Date	Venue	England	Switz.
1933	May 20	Berne	4	0
1938	May 21	Zurich	1	2
1947	May 18	Zurich	0	1
1948	Dec. 2	Highbury	6	0
1952	May 28	Zurich	3	0
WC1954	June 20	Berne	2	0
1962	May 9	Wembley	3	1
1963	June 5	Basle	8	1
EC1971	Oct. 13	Basle	3	2
EC1971	Nov. 10	Wembley	1	1
1975	Sept. 3	Basle	2	1
1977	Sept. 7	Wembley	0	0

v USA

Year	Date	Venue	England	USA
WC1950	June 29	Belo Horizonte	0	1
1953	June 8	New York	6	3
1959	May 28	Los Angeles	8	1
1964	May 27	New York	10	0

v USSR

Year	Date	Venue	England	USSR
1958	May 18	Moscow	1	1
WC1958	June 8	Gothenburg	2	2
WC1958	June 17	Gothenburg	0	1
1958	Oct. 22	Wembley	5	0
1967	Dec. 6	Wembley	2	2
ENC1968	June 8	Rome	2	0
1973	June 10	Moscow	2	1

v URUGUAY

Year	Date	Venue	England	Uruguay
1953	May 31	Montevideo	1	2
WC1954	June 26	Basle	2	4
1964	May 6	Wembley	2	1
WC1966	July 11	Wembley	0	0
1969	June 8	Montevideo	2	1
1977	June 15	Montevideo	0	0

v YUGOSLAVIA

Year	Date	Venue	England	Yugo-slavia
1939	May 18	Belgrade	1	2
1950	Nov. 22	Highbury	2	2
1954	May 16	Belgrade	0	1
1956	Nov. 28	Wembley	3	0
1958	May 11	Belgrade	0	5
1960	May 11	Wembley	3	3
1965	May 9	Belgrade	1	1
1966	May 4	Wembley	2	0
EC1968	June 5	Florence	0	1
1972	Oct. 11	Wembley	1	1
1974	June 5	Belgrade	2	2

SCOTLAND

v ARGENTINA

Year	Date	Venue	Scotland	Argentina
1977	June 18	Buenos Aires	1	1
1979	June 2	Glasgow	1	3

v AUSTRIA

Year	Date	Venue	Scotland	Austria
1931	May 16	Vienna	0	5
1933	Nov. 29	Glasgow	2	2
1937	May 9	Vienna	1	1
1950	Dec. 13	Glasgow	0	1
1951	May 27	Vienna	0	4
WC1954	June 16	Zurich	0	1
1955	May 19	Vienna	4	1
1956	May 2	Glasgow	1	1
1960	May 29	Vienna	1	4
1963	May 8	Glasgow	4	1
		(abandoned after 79 mins.)		
WC1968	Nov. 6	Glasgow	2	1
WC1969	Nov. 5	Vienna	0	2
EC1978	Sept. 20	Vienna	2	3

v BELGIUM

Year	Date	Venue	Scotland	Belgium
1947	May 18	Brussels	1	2
1948	April 28	Glasgow	2	0
1951	May 20	Brussels	5	0
EC1971	Feb. 3	Liege	0	3
EC1971	Nov. 10	Aberdeen	1	0
1974	June 2	Brussels	1	2

v BRAZIL

Year	Date	Venue	Scotland	Brazil
1966	June 25	Glasgow	1	1
1972	July 5	Rio	0	1
1973	June 30	Glasgow	0	1
WC1974	June 18	Frankfurt	0	0
1977	June 23	Rio	0	2

v BULGARIA

Year	Date	Venue	Scotland	Bulgaria
1978	Feb. 22	Glasgow	2	1

v CHILE

Year	Date	Venue	Scotland	Chile
1977	June 15	Santiago	4	2

v CYPRUS

Year	Date	Venue	Scotland	Cyprus
WC1968	Dec. 17	Nicosia	5	0
WC1969	May 11	Glasgow	8	0

v CZECHOSLOVAKIA

Year	Date	Venue	Scotland	Czecho-slovakia
1937	May 22	Prague	3	1
1937	Dec. 8	Glasgow	5	0
WC1961	May 14	Bratislava	0	4
WC1961	Sept. 26	Glasgow	3	2
WC1961	Nov. 29	Brussels	2	4*
1972	July 2	Porto Alegre	0	0
WC1973	Sept. 26	Glasgow	2	1
WC1973	Oct. 17	Prague	0	1
WC1976	Oct. 13	Prague	0	2
WC1977	Sept. 21	Glasgow	3	1

v DENMARK

Year	Date	Venue	Scotland	Denmark
1951	May 12	Glasgow	3	1
1952	May 25	Copenhagen	2	1
1968	Oct. 16	Copenhagen	1	0
EC1970	Nov. 11	Glasgow	1	0
EC1971	June 9	Copenhagen	0	1
WC1972	Oct. 18	Copenhagen	4	1
WC1972	Nov. 15	Glasgow	2	0
EC1975	Sept. 3	Copenhagen	1	0
EC1975	Oct. 29	Glasgow	3	1

v FINLAND

Year	Date	Venue	Scotland	Finland
1954	May 25	Helsinki	2	1
WC1964	Oct. 21	Glasgow	3	1
WC1965	May 27	Helsinki	2	1
1976	Sept. 8	Glasgow	6	0

v FRANCE

Year	Date	Venue	Scotland	France
1930	May 18	Paris	2	0
1932	May 8	Paris	3	1
1948	May 23	Paris	0	3
1949	April 27	Glasgow	2	0
1950	May 27	Paris	1	0
1951	May 16	Glasgow	1	0
WC1958	June 15	Orebro	1	2

v EAST GERMANY

Year	Date	Venue	Scotland	E. Germany
1974	Oct. 30	Glasgow	3	0
1977	Sept. 7	East Berlin	0	1

v WEST GERMANY

Year	Date	Venue	Scotland	West Germany
1929	June 1	Berlin	1	1
1936	Oct. 14	Glasgow	2	0
1957	May 22	Stuttgart	3	1
1959	May 6	Glasgow	3	2
1964	May 12	Hanover	2	2
WC1969	April 16	Glasgow	1	1
WC1969	Oct. 22	Hamburg	2	3
1973	Nov. 14	Glasgow	1	1
1974	Mar. 27	Frankfurt	1	2

v HUNGARY

Year	Date	Venue	Scotland	Hungary
1938	Dec. 7	Glasgow	3	1
1954	Dec. 8	Glasgow	2	4
1955	May 29	Budapest	1	3
1958	May 7	Glasgow	1	1
1960	June 5	Budapest	3	3

v IRAN

Year	Date	Venue	Scotland	Iran
WC1978	June 7	Cordoba	1	1

v ITALY

Year	Date	Venue	Scotland	Italy
1931	May 20	Rome	0	3
WC1965	Nov. 9	Glasgow	1	0
WC1965	Dec. 7	Naples	0	3

v LUXEMBOURG

Year	Date	Venue	Scotland	Luxembourg
1947	May 24	Luxembourg	6	0

v NETHERLANDS

Year	Date	Venue	Scotland	Netherlands
1929	June 4	Amsterdam	2	0
1938	May 21	Amsterdam	3	1
1959	May 27	Amsterdam	2	1
1966	May 11	Glasgow	0	3
1968	May 30	Amsterdam	0	0
1971	Dec. 1	Rotterdam	1	2
WC1978	June 11	Mendoza	3	2

v NORWAY

Year	Date	Venue	Scotland	Norway
1929	May 28	Oslo	7	3
1954	May 5	Glasgow	1	0
1954	May 19	Oslo	1	1
1963	June 4	Bergen	3	4
1963	Nov. 7	Glasgow	6	1
1974	June 6	Oslo	2	1
EC1978	Oct. 25	Glasgow	3	2
EC1979	June 7	Oslo	4	0

v PARAGUAY

Year	Date	Venue	Scotland	Paraguay
WC1958	June 11	Norrkoping	2	3

v PERU

Year	Date	Venue	Scotland	Peru
1972	April 26	Glasgow	2	0
WC1978	June 3	Cordoba	1	3

v POLAND

Year	Date	Venue	Scotland	Poland
1958	June 1	Warsaw	2	1
1960	May 4	Glasgow	2	3
WC1965	May 23	Chorzow	1	1
WC1965	Oct. 13	Glasgow	1	2

v PORTUGAL

Year	Date	Venue	Scotland	Portugal
1950	May 21	Lisbon	2	2
1955	May 4	Glasgow	3	0
1959	June 3	Lisbon	0	1
1966	June 18	Glasgow	0	1
EC1971	April 21	Lisbon	0	2
EC1971	Oct. 13	Glasgow	2	1
1975	May 13	Glasgow	1	0
EC1978	Nov. 29	Lisbon	0	1

v RUMANIA

Year	Date	Venue	Scotland	Rumania
EC1975	June 1	Bucharest	1	1
EC1975	Dec. 17	Glasgow	1	1

v SPAIN

Year	Date	Venue	Scotland	Spain
WC1957	May 8	Glasgow	4	2
WC1957	May 26	Madrid	1	4
1963	June 13	Madrid	6	2
1965	May 8	Glasgow	0	0
EC1974	Nov. 20	Glasgow	1	2
EC1975	Feb. 5	Valencia	1	1

v SWEDEN

Year	Date	Venue	Scotland	Sweden
1952	May 30	Stockholm	1	3
1953	May 6	Glasgow	1	2
1975	April 16	Gothenburg	1	1
1977	April 27	Glasgow	3	1

v SWITZERLAND

Year	Date	Venue	Scotland	Switz.
1931	May 24	Geneva	3	2
1948	May 17	Berne	1	2
1950	April 26	Glasgow	3	1
WC1957	May 19	Basle	2	1
WC1957	Nov. 6	Glasgow	3	2
1973	June 22	Berne	0	1
1976	Apr. 7	Glasgow	1	0

v TURKEY

Year	Date	Venue	Scotland	Turkey
1960	June 8	Ankara	2	4

v URUGUAY

Year	Date	Venue	Scotland	Uruguay
wc1954	June 19	Basle	0	7
1962	May 2	Glasgow	2	3

v USA

			Scotland	USA
1952	April 30	Glasgow	6	0

v USSR

			Scotland	USSR
1967	May 10	Glasgow	0	2
1971	June 14	Moscow	0	1

v YUGOSLAVIA

Year	Date	Venue	Scotland	Yugo.
1955	May 15	Belgrade	2	2
1956	Nov. 21	Glasgow	2	0
wc1958	June 8	Vasteras	1	1
1972	June 29	Belo Horizonte	2	2
wc1974	June 22	Frankfurt	1	1

v ZAIRE

			Scotland	Zaire
wc1974	June 14	Dortmund	2	0

WALES

v AUSTRIA

			Wales	Austria
1954	May 9	Vienna	0	2
1955	Nov 23	Wrexham	1	2
EC1974	Sept. 4	Vienna	1	2
EC1975	Nov. 19	Wrexham	1	0

v BELGIUM

			Wales	Belgium
1949	May 22	Liege	1	3
1949	Nov. 23	Cardiff	5	1

v BRAZIL

			Wales	Brazil
wc1958	June 19	Gothenburg	0	1
1962	May 12	Rio de Janeiro	1	3
1962	May 16	São Paulo	1	3
1966	May 14	Rio de Janeiro	1	3
1966	May 18	Belo Horizonte	0	1

v CHILE

			Wales	Chile
1966	May 22	Santiago	0	2

v CZECHOSLOVAKIA

			Wales	Czechoslovakia
wc1957	May 1	Cardiff	1	0
wc1957	May 26	Prague	0	2
EC1971	April 21	Swansea	1	3
EC1971	Oct. 27	Prague	0	1
wc1977	Mar. 30	Wrexham	3	0
wc1977	Nov. 16	Prague	0	1

v DENMARK

			Wales	Denmark
wc1964	Oct. 21	Copenhagen	0	1
wc1965	Dec. 1	Wrexham	4	2

v FINLAND

			Wales	Finland
EC1971	May 26	Helsinki	1	0
EC1971	Oct. 13	Swansea	3	0

v FRANCE

			Wales	France
1933	May 25	Paris	1	1
1939	May 20	Paris	1	2
1953	May 14	Paris	1	6

v EAST GERMANY

			Wales	East Germany
wc1957	May 19	Leipzig	1	2
wc1957	Sept. 25	Cardiff	4	1
wc1969	April 16	Dresden	1	2
wc1969	Oct. 22	Cardiff	1	3

v WEST GERMANY

			Wales	West Germany
1968	May 8	Cardiff	1	1
1969	Mar. 26	Frankfurt	1	1
1976	Oct. 6	Cardiff	0	2
1977	Dec. 14	Dortmund	1	1
EC1979	May 2	Wrexham	0	2

v GREECE

			Wales	Greece
wc1964	Dec. 9	Athens	0	2
wc1965	Mar. 17	Cardiff	4	1

v HUNGARY

			Wales	Hungary
wc1958	June 8	Sanviken	1	1
wc1958	June 17	Stockholm	2	1
1961	May 28	Budapest	2	3
ENC1962	Nov. 7	Budapest	1	3
ENC1963	Mar. 20	Cardiff	1	1
EC1974	Oct. 30	Cardiff	2	0
EC1975	Apr. 16	Budapest	2	1

v IRAN

			Wales	Iran
1978	Apr. 18	Teheran	1	0

v ISRAEL

			Wales	Israel
wc1958	Jan. 15	Tel Aviv	2	0
wc1958	Feb. 5	Cardiff	2	0

v ITALY

			Wales	Italy
1965	May 1	Florence	1	4
wc1968	Oct. 23	Cardiff	0	1
wc1969	Nov. 4	Rome	1	4

v KUWAIT

			Wales	Kuwait
1977	Sept. 6	Wrexham	0	0
1977	Sept. 20	Kuwait	0	0

v LUXEMBOURG

			Wales	Luxembourg
EC1974	Nov. 20	Swansea	5	0
EC1975	May 1	Luxembourg	3	1

v MALTA

			Wales	Malta
EC1978	Oct. 25	Wrexham	7	0
EC1979	June 2	Valletta	2	0

v MEXICO

			Wales	Mexico
wc1958	June 11	Stockholm	1	1
1962	May 22	Mexico City	1	2

v POLAND

			Wales	Poland
wc1973	Mar. 28	Cardiff	2	0
wc1973	Sept. 26	Katowice	0	3

v PORTUGAL

			Wales	Portugal
1949	May 15	Lisbon	2	3
1951	May 12	Cardiff	2	1

v REPUBLIC OF IRELAND

Year	Date	Venue	Wales	Rep. of Ireland
1960	Sept. 28	Dublin	3	2

v RUMANIA

			Wales	Rumania
EC1970	Nov. 11	Cardiff	0	0
EC1971	Nov. 24	Bucharest	0	2

v SPAIN

			Wales	Spain
wc1961	April 19	Cardiff	1	2
wc1961	May 18	Madrid	1	1

v SWEDEN

			Wales	Sweden
wc1958	June 15	Stockholm	0	0

v SWITZERLAND

Year	Date	Venue	Wales	Switz.
1949	May 26	Berne	0	4
1951	May 16	Wrexham	3	2

v TURKEY

			Wales	Turkey
EC1978	Nov. 29	Wrexham	1	0

v REST OF UNITED KINGDOM

			Wales	U.K.
1951	Dec. 5	Cardiff	3	2
1969	July 28	Cardiff	0	1

v USSR

			Wales	USSR
wc1965	May 30	Moscow	1	2
wc1965	Oct. 27	Cardiff	2	1

v YUGOSLAVIA

			Wales	Yugoslavia
1953	May 21	Belgrade	2	5
1954	Nov. 22	Cardiff	1	3
EC1976	April 24	Zagreb	0	2
EC1976	May 22	Cardiff	1	1

NORTHERN IRELAND

v ALBANIA

			North. Ireland	Albania
wc1965	May 7	Belfast	4	1
wc1965	Nov. 24	Tirana	1	1

v ARGENTINA

			North. Ireland	Argentina
wc1958	June 11	Halmstad	1	3

v BELGIUM

			North. Ireland	Belgium
wc1976	Nov. 10	Liege	0	2
wc1977	Nov. 16	Belfast	3	0

v BULGARIA

			North. Ireland	Bulgaria
wc1972	Oct. 18	Sofia	0	3
wc1973	Sept. 26	Sheffield	0	0
EC1978	Nov. 29	Sofia	2	0
EC1979	May 2	Belfast	2	0

v CYPRUS

			North Ireland	Cyprus
EC1971	Feb. 3	Nicosia	3	0
EC1971	April 21	Belfast	5	0
wc1973	Feb. 14	Nicosia	0	1
wc1973	May 8	London	3	0

v CZECHOSLOVAKIA

			North. Ireland	Czechoslovakia
wc1958	June 8	Halmstad	1	0
wc1958	June 17	Malmo	2	1*

v DENMARK

			North. Ireland	Denmark
EC1978	Oct. 25	Belfast	2	1

v FRANCE

			North. Ireland	France
1951	May 12	Belfast	2	2
1952	Nov. 11	Paris	1	3
wc1958	June 19	Norrkoping	0	4

v WEST GERMANY

			North. Ireland	West Germany
wc1958	June 15	Malmo	2	2
wc1960	Oct. 26	Belfast	3	4
wc1961	May 10	Hamburg	1	2
1966	May 7	Belfast	0	2
1977	April 27	Cologne	0	5

v GREECE

			North. Ireland	Greece
wc1961	May 3	Athens	1	2
wc1961	Oct. 17	Belfast	2	0

v ICELAND

			North. Ireland	Iceland
wc1977	June 11	Reykjavik	0	1
wc1977	Sept. 21	Belfast	2	0

v ISRAEL

			North. Ireland	Israel
1968	Sept. 10	Jaffa	3	2
1976	March 3	Tel Aviv	1	1

v ITALY

			North. Ireland	Italy
wc1957	April 25	Rome	0	1
1957	Dec. 4	Belfast	2	2
wc1958	Jan. 15	Belfast	2	1
1961	April 25	Bologna	2	3

v MEXICO

			North. Ireland	Mexico
1966	June 22	Belfast	4	1

v NETHERLANDS

			North. Ireland	Netherlands
1962	May 9	Rotterdam	0	4
wc1965	Mar. 17	Belfast	2	1
wc1965	April 7	Rotterdam	0	0
wc1976	Oct. 13	Rotterdam	2	2
wc1977	Oct. 12	Belfast	0	1

v NORWAY

			North. Ireland	Norway
EC1974	Sept. 4	Oslo	1	2
EC1975	Oct. 29	Belfast	3	0

v POLAND

			North. Ireland	Poland
ENC1962	Oct. 10	Katowice	2	0
ENC1962	Nov. 28	Belfast	2	0

v PORTUGAL

			North. Ireland	Portugal
wc1957	Jan. 16	Lisbon	1	1
wc1957	May 1	Belfast	3	0
wc1973	Mar. 28	Coventry	1	1
wc1973	Nov. 14	Lisbon	1	1

*After extra time

v SPAIN

Year	Date	Venue	North. Ireland	Spain
1958	Oct. 15	Madrid	2	6
1963	May 30	Bilbao	1	1
1963	Oct. 30	Belfast	0	1
EC1970	Nov. 11	Seville	0	3
EC1972	Feb. 16	Hull	1	1

v SWEDEN

Year	Date	Venue	North. Ireland	Sweden
EC1974	Oct. 30	Solna	2	0
EC1975	Sept. 3	Belfast	1	2

v SWITZERLAND

Year	Date	Venue	North. Ireland	Switzerland
WC1964	Oct. 14	Belfast	1	0
WC1964	Nov. 14	Lausanne	1	2

v TURKEY

Year	Date	Venue	N. Ireland	Turkey
WC1968	Oct. 23	Belfast	4	1
WC1968	Dec. 11	Istanbul	3	0

v URUGUAY

Year	Date	Venue	N. Ireland	Uruguay
1964	April 29	Belfast	3	0

v USSR

Year	Date	Venue	N. Ireland	USSR
WC1969	Sept. 10	Belfast	0	0
WC1969	Oct. 22	Moscow	0	2
EC1971	Sept. 22	Moscow	0	1
EC1971	Oct. 13	Belfast	1	1

v YUGOSLAVIA

Year	Date	Venue	North. Ireland	Yugoslavia
EC1975	Mar. 16	Belfast	1	0
EC1975	Nov. 19	Belgrade	0	1

REPUBLIC OF IRELAND

v ARGENTINA

Year	Date	Venue	Rep. of Ireland	Argentina
1951	May 13	Dublin	0	1
1979	May 29	Dublin	0	0

v AUSTRIA

Year	Date	Venue	Rep. of Ireland	Austria
1952	May 7	Vienna	0	6
1953	Mar. 25	Dublin	4	0
1958	Mar. 14	Vienna	1	3
1962	April 8	Dublin	2	3
ENC1963	Sept. 25	Vienna	0	0
ENC1963	Oct. 13	Dublin	3	2
1966	May 22	Vienna	0	1
1968	Nov. 10	Dublin	2	2
EC1971	May 30	Dublin	1	4
EC1971	Oct. 10	Linz	0	6

v BELGIUM

Year	Date	Venue	Rep. of Ireland	Belgium
1928	Feb. 12	Liege	4	2
1929	April 30	Dublin	4	0
1930	May 11	Brussels	3	1
WC1934	Feb. 25	Dublin	4	4
1949	April 24	Dublin	0	2
1950	May 10	Brussels	1	5
1965	Mar. 24	Dublin	0	2
1966	May 25	Liege	3	2

v BRAZIL

Year	Date	Venue	Rep. of Ireland	Brazil
1974	May 5	Rio de Janeiro	1	2

v BULGARIA

Year	Date	Venue	Rep. of Ireland	Bulgaria
WC1977	June 1	Sofia	1	2
WC1977	Oct. 12	Dublin	0	0
EC1979	May 19	Sofia	0	1

v CHILE

Year	Date	Venue	Rep. of Ireland	Chile
1960	Mar. 30	Dublin	2	0
1972	Jun. 21	Recife	1	2
1974	May 12	Santiago	2	1

v CZECHOSLOVAKIA

Year	Date	Venue	Rep. of Ireland	Czech.
1938	May 18	Prague	2	2
ENC1959	April 5	Dublin	2	0
ENC1959	May 10	Bratislava	0	4
WC1961	Oct. 8	Dublin	1	3
WC1961	Oct. 29	Prague	1	7
EC1967	May 21	Dublin	0	2
EC1967	Nov. 22	Prague	2	1
WC1969	May 4	Dublin	1	2
WC1969	Oct. 7	Prague	0	3

v DENMARK

Year	Date	Venue	Rep. of Ireland	Denmark
WC1956	Oct. 3	Dublin	2	1
WC1957	Oct. 2	Copenhagen	2	0
WC1968	Dec. 4	Dublin	1	1
		(abandoned after 51 mins.)		
WC1969	May 27	Copenhagen	0	2
WC1969	Oct. 15	Dublin	1	1
EC1978	May 24	Copenhagen	3	3
EC1979	May 2	Dublin	2	0

v ECUADOR

Year	Date	Venue	Rep. of Ireland	Ecuador
1972	June 19	Natal	3	2

v FINLAND

Year	Date	Venue	Rep. of Ireland	Finland
WC1949	Sept. 8	Dublin	3	0
WC1949	Oct. 9	Helsinki	1	1

v FRANCE

Year	Date	Venue	Rep. of Ireland	France
1937	May 23	Paris	2	0
1952	Nov. 16	Dublin	1	1
WC1953	Oct. 4	Dublin	3	5
WC1953	Nov. 25	Paris	0	1
WC1972	Nov. 15	Dublin	2	1
WC1973	May 19	Paris	1	1
WC1976	Nov. 17	Paris	0	2
WC1977	Mar. 30	Dublin	1	0

v WEST GERMANY

Year	Date	Venue	Rep. of Ireland	West Germany
1935	May 8	Dortmund	1	3
1936	Oct. 17	Dublin	5	2
1939	May 23	Bremen	1	1
1951	Oct. 17	Dublin	3	2
1952	May 4	Cologne	0	3
1955	May 28	Hamburg	1	2
1956	Nov. 25	Dublin	3	0
1960	May 11	Dusseldorf	1	0
1966	May 4	Dublin	0	4
1970	May 9	Berlin	1	2
1979	May 22	Dublin	1	3

v HUNGARY

Year	Date	Venue	Rep. of Ireland	Hungary
1934	Dec. 15	Dublin	2	4
1936	May 3	Budapest	3	3
1936	Dec. 6	Dublin	2	3
1939	Mar. 19	Cork	2	2
1939	May 18	Budapest	2	2
wc1969	June 8	Dublin	1	2
wc1969	Nov. 5	Budapest	0	4

v ICELAND

Year	Date	Venue	Rep. of Ireland	Iceland
ENC1962	Aug. 12	Dublin	4	2
ENC1962	Sept. 2	Reykjavik	1	1

v LUXEMBOURG

Year	Date	Venue	Rep. of Ireland	Luxembourg
1936	May 9	Luxembourg	5	1
wc1953	Oct. 28	Dublin	4	0
wc1954	Mar. 7	Luxembourg	1	0

v IRAN

Year	Date	Venue	Rep. of Ireland	Iran
1972	June 18	Recife	2	1

v N. IRELAND

Year	Date	Venue	Rep. of Ireland	North. Ireland
EC1978	Sept. 20	Dublin	0	0

v ITALY

Year	Date	Venue	Rep. of Ireland	Italy
1926	Mar. 21	Turin	0	3
1927	April 23	Dublin	1	2
EC1970	Dec. 8	Rome	0	3
EC1971	May 10	Dublin	1	2

v NETHERLANDS

Year	Date	Venue	Rep. of Ireland	Netherlands
1932	May 8	Amsterdam	2	0
1934	April 8	Amsterdam	2	5
1935	Dec. 8	Dublin	3	5
1955	May 1	Dublin	1	0
1956	May 10	Rotterdam	4	1

v NORWAY

Year	Date	Venue	Rep. of Ireland	Norway
wc1937	Oct. 10	Oslo	2	3
wc1937	Nov. 7	Dublin	3	3
1950	Nov. 26	Dublin	2	2
1951	May 30	Oslo	3	2
1954	Nov. 8	Dublin	2	1
1955	May 25	Oslo	3	1
1960	Nov. 6	Dublin	3	1
1964	May 13	Oslo	4	1
1973	June 6	Oslo	1	1
1976	Mar. 24	Dublin	3	0
1978	May 21	Oslo	0	0

v POLAND

Year	Date	Venue	Rep. of Ireland	Poland
1938	May 22	Warsaw	0	6
1938	Nov. 13	Dublin	3	2
1958	May 11	Katowice	2	2
1958	Oct. 5	Dublin	2	2
1964	May 10	Cracow	1	3
1964	Oct. 25	Dublin	3	2
1968	May 15	Dublin	2	2
1968	Oct. 30	Katowice	0	1
1970	May 6	Dublin	1	2
1970	Sept. 23	Dublin	0	2
1973	May 16	Wroclaw	0	2
1973	Oct. 21	Dublin	1	0
1976	May 26	Posnan	2	0
1977	April 24	Dublin	0	0
1978	April 12	Lodz	0	3

v PORTUGAL

Year	Date	Venue	Rep. of Ireland	Portugal
1946	June 16	Lisbon	1	3
1947	May 4	Dublin	0	2
1948	May 23	Lisbon	0	2
1949	May 22	Dublin	1	0
1972	June 25	Recife	1	2

v SCOTLAND

Year	Date	Venue	Rep. of Ireland	Scotland
wc1961	May 3	Glasgow	1	4
wc1961	May 7	Dublin	0	3
1963	June 9	Dublin	1	0
1969	Sept. 21	Dublin	1	1

v SPAIN

Year	Date	Venue	Rep. of Ireland	Spain
1931	April 26	Barcelona	1	1
1931	Dec. 13	Dublin	0	5
1946	June 23	Madrid	1	0
1947	Mar. 2	Dublin	3	2
1948	May 30	Barcelona	1	2
1949	June 12	Dublin	1	4
1952	June 1	Madrid	0	6
1955	Nov. 27	Dublin	2	2
ENC1964	Mar. 11	Seville	1	5
ENC1964	April 8	Dublin	0	2
wc1965	May 5	Dublin	1	0
wc1965	Oct. 27	Seville	1	4
wc1965	Nov. 10	Paris	0	1
EC1966	Oct. 23	Dublin	0	0
EC1966	Dec. 7	Valencia	0	2
1977	Feb. 9	Dublin	0	1

v SWEDEN

Year	Date	Venue	Rep. of Ireland	Sweden
wc1949	June 2	Stockholm	1	3
wc1949	Nov. 13	Dublin	1	3
1959	Nov. 1	Dublin	3	2
1960	May 18	Malmo	1	4
EC1970	Oct. 14	Dublin	1	1
EC1970	Oct. 28	Malmo	0	1

v SWITZERLAND

			Rep. of Ireland	Switzerland
1935	May	5 Basle	0	1
1936	Mar.	17 Dublin	1	0
1937	May	17 Berne	1	0
1938	Sept.	18 Dublin	4	0
1948	Dec.	5 Dublin	0	1
EC1975	May	11 Dublin	2	1
EC1975	May	21 Berne	0	1

v TURKEY

			Rep. of Ireland	Turkey
EC1966	Nov.	16 Dublin	2	1
EC1967	Feb.	22 Ankara	1	2
EC1974	Nov.	20 Izmir	1	1
EC1975	Oct.	29 Dublin	4	0
1976	Oct.	13 Ankara	3	3
1978	April	5 Dublin	4	2

v URUGUAY

			Rep. of Ireland	Uruguay
1974	May	8 Montevideo	0	2

v USSR

			Rep. of Ireland	USSR
WC1972	Oct.	18 Dublin	1	2
WC1973	May	13 Moscow	0	1
EC 1974	Oct.	30 Dublin	3	0
EC 1975	May	18 Kiev	1	2

v YUGOSLAVIA

			Rep. of Ireland	Yugoslavia
1955	Sept.	19 Dublin	1	4

WC denotes World Cup Match.
ENC denotes European Nations Championship Match.
EC is European Championship

OTHER BRITISH INTERNATIONAL AND REPRESENTATIVE MATCHES 1978-79

Motherwell, Nov 1 1978
Scottish League 1 (*Pettigrew*)
Irish League 1 (*Armstrong*)   4,427
Scottish League: Rough; Narey, Burns, Stevens, Hegarty, Thomson, Houston, Bannon, Pettigrew, McAdam (Somner), Marinello.
Irish League: Barclay; Kennedy, Cromie, Walsh, Rafferty, Cleary, Sloan, Dornan, Armstrong, Dickson, Murray.

Wembley, Nov 29 1978
England 1 (*Coppell*)
Czechoslovakia 0   92,000
England: Shilton; Anderson, Cherry, Thompson, Watson, Wilkins, Keegan, Coppell, Woodcock (Latchford), Currie, Barnes.
Czechoslovakia: Michalik; Barmos, Vojacek, Jurkemik, Gogh, Stambacher, Kozak, Gajdusek, Jarusek (Panenka), Masny, Nehoda.

Prague, Nov 28 1978
Czechoslovakia B (0) 0
England B (0) 1 (*Daley*)   5,000
Czechoslovakia: Caloun; Mazura, Vaclavicek, Macela, Koubek, Nemec, Novak, Rott, Licka, Briza, Dvorak.
England: Corrigan; Gidman, Sansom, Talbot, Greenhoff B (Hazell), Lyons, Cunningham, Daley, Sunderland, Mortimer (Owen), Flanagan (Regis).

Dublin, May 22 1979
Eire (1) 1 (*Ryan*)
West Germany (1) 3 (*Rummenigge, Kelsch, Hoeness*)   20,000
Eire: Peyton; Gregg, Martin, O'Leary, Mulligan, Grealish, Giles, Brady, Stapleton (Walsh), Givens (O'Callaghan), Ryan.
West Germany: Maier; Kaltz, Cullmann, Forster K H, Forster B, Schuster, Rummenigge, Zimmermann, Hoeness, Allofs, Muller.

Dublin, May 29 1979
Eire (0) 0
Argentina (0) 0   25,000
Eire: Peyton; Gregg, Martin, O'Leary, Mulligan, Grealish, Giles, Brady, Stapleton (O'Callaghan), Walsh, Givens (McGee).
Argentina: Fillol; Villaverde, Tarantini (Gallego), Olguin, Oviedo, Trossero, Houseman, Barbas, Reinaldi (Maradona), Valencia, Perotti (Outes).

Hampden Park, June 2 1979
Scotland (0) 1 (*Graham*)
Argentina (1) 3 (*Luque 2, Maradona*)   61,918
Scotland: Rough (Wood); Burley, Munro, Narey, Hegarty, Hansen, McGarvey, Wark, Dalglish, Hartford (Gray F), Graham.
Argentina: Fillol; Villaverde (Trossero), Tarantini, Olguin, Gallego, Passarella, Houseman (Outes), Barbas, Luque, Maradona, Valencia.

Stockholm, June 10 1979
Sweden (0) 0
England (0) 0   35,691
Sweden: Moller; Borg, Erlandsson (Wernersson), Arvidsson, Aman, Torstensson, Linderoth, Nordgren, Cervin, Gronhagen, Johansson (Nilsson).
England: Shilton; Anderson, Cherry, McDermott (Wilkins), Watson (Thompson), Hughes, Keegan, Francis, Woodcock, Currie (Brooking), Cunningham.

Klagenfurt, June 12 1979
Austria B (0) 0
England B (1) 1 (*Robson*) abandoned after an hour; lightning.   3,500
England: Corrigan; Anderson, Sansom, Williams, Wright, Butcher, Hoddle, Robson, Reeves, Woodcock, Rix.

Vienna, June 13 1979
Austria (3) 4 (*Pezzey 2, Welzl 2*)
England (1) 3 (*Keegan, Coppell, Wilkins*)   60,000
Austria: Koncilia; Robert Sara, Obermeyer, Baumeister, Pezzey, Hattenberger, Welzl (Schachner), Prohaska, Kreuz, Jara, Jurtin.
England: Shilton (Clemence); Neal, Mills, Thompson, Watson, Wilkins, Keegan, Coppell, Latchford, Brooking, Barnes (Cunningham).

UNDER 21 INTERNATIONALS 1978-79

SCOTLAND 3, USA 1
(at Aberdeen, September 17, 1978, 6,000)

Scotland: Thomson; Sneddon, Gillespie, Orr, McLeish, MacLeod (M), Melrose, Jardine, McCluskey, Bannon, Lindsay.
USA: Brcic; Pollihan, Myernick, Droege, Fowles, Davis, Russell, Bandov, Prost, Nanchoff L, Etherington.
Scorers: Scotland: Melrose, Orr, MacLeod (M). USA: Etherington.

DENMARK 1, ENGLAND 2
(at Hvidovre, September 19, 1978, 4,000)

Denmark: Neilsen; Olzyck, Sorensen, Petersen, Madsen, Ziegler, Schafer, Ostergaard, Anderson (Birkedel), Eriksen (Garly), Berggren.
England: Parkes; Wright, Sansom, Williams, Hazell, Futcher P, Owen, Reeves, Regis, Hoddle, Rix.
Scorers: Denmark: Sorensen pen. England: Hoddle, Hazell.

WALES 0, ENGLAND 1
(at Swansea, February 6, 1979, 5,642)

Wales: Thomas M; Jones, Aizlewood, Phillips, Dwyer, Nicholas, Lowndes, Clark, Walsh, Charles, Thomas G (Doyle).
England: Bailey (Woods); Owen, Gilbert (Osman), Wright, Cowans, Sansom, Statham, Blissett, Robson, Reeves, Hoddle.
Scorer: England: Hoddle.

PORTUGAL 0, SCOTLAND 3
(in Lisbon, November 28, 1978, 2,000)

Portugal: Jorge; Lavo, Silva, Alinho, Tobica, Pereirinha, Manuel, Antonio, Jorge, Fontes, Folha.
Scotland: Stewart J; Stewart R, Dawson, Wark, McNichol, Orr, McCluskey, Bannon, MacLeod A, Aitken, Melrose (MacLeod M).
Scorers: Scotland: McCluskey, MacLeod A 2, 1 a pen.

BULGARIA 1, ENGLAND 3
(at Pernik, June 5, 1979, 10,000)

Bulgaria: Laftschis; Balewski, Marinon, Tetschev, Dimitrov, Kotschev, Valkov, Marmkov, Mladenov, Slavkov, Milkov.
England: Bailey; Sansom, Statham, Williams, Gilbert, Wright, Reeves, Hoddle (Robson), Deehan (Blissett), Owen, Regis.
Scorers: Bulgaria: Valcov. England: Reeves 2, Regis.

NORWAY 2, SCOTLAND 2
(at Haugesund, June 10, 1979, 2,000)

Scotland: Thomson; Stewart, Dawson, Aitken, Orr, McNichol, Bannon, MacLeod A, Brazil, MacLeod M, Melrose.
Scorers: Norway: Davidsen, Halversen. Scotland: Bannon, MacLeod A.

SWEDEN 1, ENGLAND 2
(in Vasteraas, June 10, 1979, 4,300)

Sweden: Ravelli T; Magnus Andersson, Mikael Andersson, Holmgren, Jingblad (Sunessen), Mansson, Nilsson (Westergren), Ravelli A, Schiller (Gustavsson), Johansson, Ahlund.
England: Woods; Sansom, Statham, Robson, Osman, Butcher, Reeves, Cowans (Williams), Blissett, Rix (Owen), Regis (Deehan).
Scorers: Sweden: Nilsson. England: Robson, Regis.

International Appearances
(as at 8 June 1979)

This is a list of full international appearances by Englishmen, Irishmen, Scotsmen and Welshmen in matches against the Home Countries and against Foreign Nations. It does not include matches against Commonwealth and Empire countries.

Explanatory code for matches played by all four countries: A, represents Austria; Alb, Albania; Arg, Argentine; B, Bohemia; Bel, Belgium; Br, Brazil; Bul, Bulgaria; Ch, Chile; Co, Columbia; Cy, Cyprus; Cz, Czechoslovakia; D, Denmark; Ec, Ecuador; Ei, Eire; EG, East Germany; F, France; Fi, Finland; G, Germany (pre-war); Gr, Greece; H, Hungary; Ho, Holland; I, Italy; Ic, Iceland; Ir, Iran; Is, Israel; K, Kuwait; L, Luxembourg; M, Mexico; Ma, Malta; N, Norway; Ni, Northern Ireland; P, Portugal; Par, Paraguay; Pe, Peru; Pol, Poland; R, Rumania, R of E, Rest of Europe; R of W, Rest of World; S, Scotland; Se, Sweden; Sp, Spain; Sw, Switzerland; T, Turkey; U, Uruguay; UK, Rest of United Kingdom; US, United States of America; USSR, Russia; W, Wales; WG, West Germany; Y, Yugoslavia. (Note; for purposes of this code, and in order to distinguish from Eire, Northern Ireland is given throughout the series as Ni).

ENGLAND

Abbott, W. (Everton), 1902 v W (1)
A'Court, A. (Liverpool), 1958 v Ni, Br, A, USSR; 1959 v W (5)
Adcock, H. (Leicester C.), 1929 v F, Bel, Sp; 1930 v Ni, W (5)
Alcock, C. W. (Wanderers), 1875 v S (1)
Alderson, J. T. (C. Palace), 1923 v F (1)
Aldridge, A. (W.B.A.), 1888 v Ni, (with Walsall Town Swifts), 1889 v Ni (2)
Allen, A. (Stoke C.), 1960 v Se, W, Ni (3)
Allen, A. (Aston Villa), 1888 v Ni (1)
Allen, H. (Wolverhampton W.), 1888 v S, W, Ni; 1889 v S: 1890 v S (5)
Allen, J. P. (Portsmouth), 1934 v Ni, W (2)
Allen, R. (W.B.A.), 1952 v Sw; 1954 v Y, S; 1955 v WG, W (5)
Alsford, W. J. (Tottenham H.), 1935 v S (1)
Amos, A. (Old Carthusians), 1885 v S; 1886 v W (2)
Anderson, R. D. (Old Etonians), 1879 v W (1)
Anderson, S. (Sunderland), 1962 v A, S (2)
Anderson, V. (Nottingham F.), 1979 v Cz, Se (2)
Angus, J. (Burnley), 1961 v A (1)
Armfield, J. C. (Blackpool), 1959 v Br, Pe, M, US; 1960 v Y, Sp, H, S; 1961 v L, P, Sp, M, I, A, Y, W, Ni, S; 1962, A, Sw, Pe, W, Ni, S, L, P, H, Arg, Bul, Br; 1963 v F (2), Br, EG, Sw, Ni, W, S; 1964 v R of W, W, Ni, S; 1966 v Y, Fi (43)
Armitage, G. H. (Charlton Ath.), 1926 v Ni (1)
Armstrong, K. (Chelsea), 1955 v S (1)
Arnold, J. (Fulham), 1933 v S (1)
Arthur, J. W. H. (Blackburn R.), 1885 v S, Ni; 1886 v W; 1887 v W, Ni (7)
Ashcroft, J. (Woolwich Arsenal), 1906 v Ni, W, S (3)
Ashmore, G. S. (W.B.A.), 1926 v Bel (1)
Ashton, C. T. (Corinthians), 1926 v Ni (1)
Ashurst, W. (Notts. Co.), 1923 v Se (2); 1925 v S, W, Bel (5)
Astall, G. (Birmingham C.), 1956 v Fi, WG (2)
Astle, J. (W.B.A.), 1969 v W; 1970 v S, P, Br (sub), Cz (5)
Aston, J. (Manchester U.), 1949 v S, W, D, Sw, Se, N, F; 1950 v S, W, Ni, Ei, I, P, Bel, Ch. US; 1951 v Ni (17)
Athersmith, W. C. (Aston Villa), 1892 v Ni; 1897 v S, W, Ni; 1898 v S, W, Ni: 1899 v S, W, Ni; 1900 v S, W (12)
Atyeo, P. J. W. (Bristol C.), 1956 v Br, Se, Sp; 1957 v D, Ei (2) (6)
Austin, S. W. (Manchester C.), 1926 v Ni (1)

Bach, P. (Sunderland), 1899 v Ni (1)
Bache, J. W. (Aston Villa), 1903 v W; 1904 v W, Ni; 1905 v S; 1907 v Ni; 1910 v Ni; 1911 v S (7)

Baddeley, T. (Wolverhampton W.), 1903 v S, Ni; 1904 v S, W, Ni (5)
Bagshaw, J. J. (Derby Co.), 1920 v Ni (1)
Bailey, H. P. (Leicester Fosse), 1908 v W, A (2), H, B (5)
Bailey, M. A. (Charlton Ath.), 1964 v US; 1965 v W (2)
Bailey, N. C. (Clapham Rovers), 1878 v S; 1879 v S, W; 1880 v S; 1881 v S; 1882 v S, W; 1883 v S, W; 1884 v S, W, Ni; 1885 v S, W, Ni; 1886 v S, W; 1887 v S, W (19)
Baily, E. F. (Tottenham H.), 1950 v Sp; 1951 v Y, Ni, W; 1952 v A (2), Sw, W; 1953 v Ni (9)
Bain, J. (Oxford University), 1887 v S (1)
Baker, A. (Arsenal), 1928 v W (1)
Baker, B. H. (Everton), 1921 v Bel; (with Chelsea), 1926 v Ni (2)
Baker, J. H. (Hibernian), 1960 v Y, Sp, H, Ni, S; (with Arsenal) 1966 v Sp, Pol. Ni (8)
Ball, A. J. (Blackpool), 1965 v Y, WG, Se; 1966 v S, Sp, Fi, D, U, Arg, P, WG (2), Pol (2); (Everton), 1967 v W, S, Ni, A, Cz, Sp; 1968, W, S, USSR, Sp (2), Y, WG; 1969 v Ni, W, S, R (2), M, Br, U; 1970 v P, Co, Ec, R, Br, Cz (sub), W, S, Bel; 1971 v Ma, EG, Gr, Ma (sub), Ni, S; 1972 v Sw, Gr; (with Arsenal) WG (2), S; 1973 v W (3), Y, S (2) Cz, Ni, Pol; 1974 v P (sub); 1975 v WG, Cy (2), Ni, W, S (72)
Ball, J. (Bury), 1928 v Ni (1)
Balmer, W. (Everton), 1905 v Ni (1)
Bamber, J. (Liverpool), 1921 v W (1)
Bambridge, A. L. (Swifts), 1881 v W; 1883 v W; 1884 v Ni (3)
Bambridge, E. C. (Swifts), 1879 v S; 1880 v S; 1881 v S; 1882 v S, W, Ni; 1883 v W; 1884 v S, W, Ni; 1885 v S, W, Ni; 1886 v S, W; 1887 v S, W, Ni (18)
Bambridge, E. H. (Swifts), 1876 v S (1)
Banks, G. (Leicester C.), 1963 v S, Br, Cz, EG; 1964 v W, Ni, S, R of W, U, P (2), US, Arg; 1965 v Ni, S, H, Y, WG, Se; 1966 v Ni, S, Sp, Pol (2), WG (2), Y, Fi, U, M, F, Arg, P; 1967 v Ni, W, S, Cz; (with Stoke C.), 1968 v W, Ni, S, USSR (2), Sp, WG, Y; 1969 v Ni, S, R (2), F, U, Br; 1970 v W, Ni, S, Ho, Bel, Co, Ec, R, Br, Cz, 1971 v Gr, Ma (2), Ni, S; 1972 v Sw, Gr, WG (2), W, S (73)
Banks, H. E. (Millwall), 1901 v Ni (1)
Banks, T. (Bolton W.), 1958 v USSR (3), Br, A; 1959 v Ni (6)
Bannister, W. (Burnley), 1901 v W; (with Bolton W.), 1902 v Ni (2)
Barclay, R. (Sheffield W.), 1932 v S; 1933 v Ni; 1936 v S (3)

Barkas, S. (Manchester C.), 1936 v Bel; 1937 v S; 1938 v W, Ni, Cz (5)
Barker, J. (Derby Co.), 1935 v I, Ho, S, W, Ni; 1936 v G, A, S, W, Ni; 1937 v W (11)
Barker, R. (Herts Rangers), 1872 v S (1)
Barker, R. R. (Casuals), 1895 v W (1)
Barlow, R. J. (W.B.A.), 1955 v Ni (1)
Barnes, P. S. (Manchester C.) 1978 v I, WG, Br, W, S, H; 1979 v D, Ei, Cz, Ni (2), S, Bul, A (14)
Barnet, H. H. (Royal Engineers), 1882 v Ni (1)
Barrass, M. W. (Bolton W.), 1952 v W, Ni; 1953 v S (3)
Barrett, A. F. (Fulham), 1930 v Ni (1)
Barrett, J. W. (West Ham U.), 1929 v Ni (1)
Barry, L. (Leicester C.), 1928 v F, Bel; 1929 v F, Bel, Sp (5)
Barson, F. (Aston Villa), 1920 v W (1)
Barton, J. (Blackburn R.), 1890 v Ni (1)
Barton P. H. (Birmingham), 1921 v Bel; 1922 v Ni; 1923 v F; 1924 v Bel, S, W; 1925 v Ni (7)
Bassett, W. I. (W.B.A.), 1888 v Ni; 1889 v S, W; 1890 v S, W; 1891 v S, Ni; 1892 v S; 1893 v S, W; 1894 v S; 1895 v S, Ni; 1896 v S, W, Ni (16)
Bastard, S. R. (Upton Park), 1880 v S (1)
Bastin, C. S. (Arsenal), 1932 v W; 1933 v I, Sw; 1934 v S, Ni, W, H, Cz; 1935 v S, Ni, I; 1936 v S, W, G, A; 1937 v W, Ni; 1938 v S, G, Sw, F (21)
Baugh, R. (Stafford Road), 1886 v Ni; (with Wolverhampton W.) 1890 v Ni (2)
Bayliss, A. E. J. M. (W.B.A.), 1891 v Ni (1)
Baynham, R. L. (Luton T.), 1956 v Ni, D, Sp (3)
Beasley, A. (Huddersfield T.), 1939 v S (1)
Beats, W. E. (Wolverhampton W.), 1901 v W; 1902 v S (2)
Beattie, T. K. (Ipswich T.), 1975 v Cy (2), S; 1976 v Sw, P; 1977 v Fi, I (sub), Ho; 1978 v L (sub) (9)
Becton, F. (Preston N.E.), 1895 v Ni; (with Liverpool); 1897 v W (2)
Bedford, H. (Blackpool), 1923 v Se; 1925 v Ni (2)
Bell, C. (Manchester C.), 1968 v Se, WG; 1969 v W, Bul, F, U, Br; 1970 v Ni (sub), Ho (2), P, Br (sub), Cz, WG (sub); 1972 v Gr, WG (2), W, Ni, S; 1973 v W (3), Y, S (2), Ni, Cz, Pol; 1974 v A, Pol, I, W. Ni, S, Arg, EG, Bul, Y; 1975 v Cz, P, WG. Cy (2), Ni, S; 1976 v Sw, C2 (48)
Bennett, W. (Sheffield U.), 1901 v S, W (2)
Benson, R. W. (Sheffield U.), 1913 v Ni (1)
Bentley, R. T. F. (Chelsea), 1949 v Se; 1950 v S, P, Bel, Ch, USA; 1953 v W, Bel; 1955 v W, WG, Sp, P (12)
Beresford, J. (Aston Villa), 1934 v Cz (1)
Berry, A. (Oxford University), 1909 v Ni (1)
Berry, J. J. (Manchester U.), 1953 v Arg, Ch, U; 1956 v Se (4)
Bestall, J. G. (Grimsby T.), 1935 v Ni (1)
Betmead, H. A. (Grimsby T.), 1937 v Fi (1)
Betts, M. P. (Old Harrovians), 1877 v S (1)
Betts, W. (Sheffield W.), 1889 v W. (1)
Beverley, J. (Blackburn R.), 1884 v S, W, Ni (3)
Birkett, R. J. (Clapham Rovers), 1879 v S (1)
Birkett R. J. E. (Middlesbrough), 1936 v Ni (1)
Birley, F. H. (Oxford University), 1874 v S; (with Wanderers), 1875 v S (2)
Bishop, S. M. (Leicester C.), 1927 v S, Bel, L, F (4)
Blackburn, F. (Blackburn R.), 1901 v S; 1902 v Ni; 1904 v S (3)
Blackburn, G. F. (Aston Villa), 1924 v F (1)
Blenkinsop, E. (Sheffield W.), 1928 v F, Bel; 1929 v S, W, Ni, F, Bel, Sp; 1930 v S, W, Ni, G, A; 1931 v S, W, Ni, F, Bel; 1932 v S, W, Ni, Sp; 1933, S W, Ni, A (26)
Bliss, H. (Tottenham H.), 1921 v S (1)

Blockley, J. P. (Arsenal), 1973 v Y (1)
Bloomer, S. (Derby Co.), 1895 v S, Ni; 1896 v W, Ni; 1897 v S, W, Ni; 1898 v S; 1899 v S, W, Ni; 1900 v S; 1901 v S, W; 1902 v S, W, Ni; 1904 v S; 1905 v S, W, Ni; (with Middlesbrough), 1907 v S, W (23)
Blunstone, F. (Chelsea), 1955 v W, S, F, P; 1957 v Y (5)
Bond, R. (Preston N.E.), 1905 v Ni, W; 1906 v S, W, Ni; (with Bradford C.), 1910 v S, W, Ni (8)
Bonetti, P. P. (Chelsea), 1966 v D; 1967 v Sp, A; 1968 v Sp; 1970 v Ho, P, WG (7)
Bonsor, A. G. (Wanderers), 1873 v S; 1875 v S (2).
Booth, F. (Manchester C.), 1905 v Ni (1)
Booth, T. (Blackburn R.), 1898 v W; (with Everton), 1903 v S (2)
Bowden, E. R. (Arsenal), 1935 v W, I; 1936 v W. Ni, A; 1937 v H (6)
Bowser, A. G. (Corinthians), 1924 v Ni, Bel; 1925 v W, Bel; 1927 v W (5)
Bowers, J. W. (Derby Co.), 1934 v S, Ni, W (3)
Bowles, S. (Q.P.R.), 1974 v P, W, Ni; 1977 v I, Ho (5)
Bowser, S. (W.B.A.), 1920 v Ni (1)
Boyer, P. J. (Norwich C.), 1976 v W (1)
Boyes, W. (W.B.A.), 1935 v Ho; (with Everton), 1939 v W, R of E (3)
Boyle, T. W. (Burnley), 1913 v Ni (1)
Brabrook, P. (Chelsea), 1958 v USSR; 1959 v Ni; 1960 v Sp (3)
Bradford, G. R. W. (Bristol R.), 1956 v D (1)
Bradford J. (Birmingham), 1924 v Ni; 1925 v Bel; 1928 v S; 1929 v Ni, W, F, Sp; 1930 v S, Ni, G, A, 1931 v W (12)
Bradley, W. (Manchester U.), 1959 v I, US, M (sub) (3)
Bradshaw, F. (Sheffield W.), 1908 v A (1)
Bradshaw, T. H. (Liverpool), 1897 v Ni (1)
Bradshaw, W. (Blackburn R.), 1910 v W, Ni; 1912 v Ni; 1913 v W (4)
Brann, G. (Swifts), 1886 v S, W; 1891 v W (3)
Brawn, W. F. (Aston Villa), 1904 v W, Ni (2)
Bray, J. (Manchester C.) 1935 v W; 1936 v S, W, Ni, G; 1937 v S (6)
Brayshaw, E. (Sheffield W.), 1887 v Ni (1)
Bridges, B. J. (Chelsea), 1965 v S, H, Y; 1966 v A (4)
Bridgett, A. (Sunderland), 1905 v S; 1908 v S, A (2), H, B; 1909 v Ni, W, H (2), A (11)
Brindle, T. (Darwen), 1880 v S, W (2)
Brittleton, J. T. (Sheffield W.), 1912 v S, W, Ni; 1913 v S; 1914 v W (5)
Britton, C. S. (Everton), 1935 v S, W, Ni, I; 1937 v S, Ni, H, N, Se (9)
Broadbent, P. F. (Wolverhampton W.) 1958 v USSR; 1959 v S, W, Ni, I, Br; 1960 v S (7)
Broadis, I. A. (Manchester C.), 1952 v S, A, I; 1953 v S, Arg, Ch, U, US; (with Newcastle U.), 1954 v S, H, Y, Bel, Sw, U (14)
Brockbank, J. (Cambridge University), 1872 v S (1)
Brodie, J. B. (Wolverhampton W.), 1889 v S, Ni; 1891 v Ni (3)
Bromilow, T. G. (Liverpool), 1921 v W; 1922 v S, W; 1923 v Bel; 1926 v Ni (5)
Bromley-Davenport, W. E. (Oxford University), 1884 v S, W (2)
Brook, E. F. (Manchester C.), 1930 v Ni; 1933 v Sw; 1934 v S, W, Ni, F, H, Cz; 1935 v S, W, Ni, I; 1936 v S, W, Ni; 1937 v H; 1938 v W, Ni (18)
Brooking, T. D. (West Ham U.), 1974 v P, Arg, EG, Bul, Y; 1975 v Cz (sub), P; 1976 v P, W, Br, I, Fi; 1977 v Ei, Fi, I, Ho, Ni, W; 1978 v I, WG, Br, W, S, (sub) H; 1979 v D, Ei, Ni, W (sub), S, Bul, Se (sub), A (32)

W, S, (sub) H; 1979 v D, Ei, Ni, W (sub), S, Bul, Se (sub), A (32)
Brooks, J. (Tottenham H.), 1957 v W, Y, D (3)
Broome, F. H. (Aston Villa), 1938 v G, Sw, F; 1939 v N, I, R, Y (7)
Brown, A. (Aston Villa), 1882 v S, W, N (3)
Brown, A. S. (Sheffield U.), 1904 v W; 1906 v Ni (2)
Brown, A. (W.B.A.), 1971 v W (1)
Brown, G. (Huddersfield T.), 1927 v S, W, Ni, Bel, L, G; 1928 v W; 1929 v S; (with Aston Villa), 1933 v W (9)
Brown, J. (Blackburn R.), 1881 v W; 1882 v Ni; 1885 v S, W, Ni (5)
Brown, J. H. (Sheffield W.), 1927 v S, W, Bel, L F; 1930 v Ni (6)
Brown, K. (West Ham U.), 1960 v Ni (1)
Brown, W. (West Ham U.), 1924 v Bel (1)
Bruton, J. (Burnley), 1928 v F, Bel; 1929 v S (3)
Bryant, W. I. (Clapton), 1925 v F (1)
Buchan, C. M. (Sunderland), 1913 v Ni; 1920 v W; 1921 v W, Bel; 1923 v F; 1924 v S (6)
Buchanan, W. S. (Clapham R.), 1876 v S (1)
Buckley, F. C. (Derby Co.), 1914 v Ni (1)
Bullock, F.E. (Huddersfield T.), 1921 v Ni (1)
Bullock, N. (Bury), 1923 v Bel; 1926 v Ni W;1927 v Ni (3)
Burgess, H. (Manchester C.), 1904 v S, W, Ni; 1906 v S (4)
Burgess, H. (Sheffield W.), 1931 v S, Ni, F, Bel (4)
Burnup, C. J. (Cambridge University), 1896 v S (1)
Burrows, H. (Sheffield W.), 1934 v H, Cz; 1935 v Ho (3)
Burton, F. E. (Nottingham F.), 1889 v Ni (1)
Bury, L. (Cambridge University), 1877 v S; (with Old Etonians), 1879 v W (2)
Butler, J. D. (Arsenal), 1925 v Bel (1)
Butler, W. (Bolton W.), 1924 v S (1)
Byrne, G. (Liverpool), 1963 v S; 1966 v N (2)
Byrne, J. J. (C. Palace), 1962 v Ni; (with West Ham U.), 1963 v Sw; 1964 v S, U, P (2), Ei, Br, Arg; 1965 v W, S (11)
Byrne, R. W. (Manchester U.), 1954 v S, H, Y, Bel, Sw, U; 1955 v S, W Ni, WG, F, Sp, P; 1956 v S, W, Ni, Br, Se, Fi, WG, D, Sp; 1957 v S, W, Ni, Y D (2), Ei (2); 1958 v W, Ni, F (33)

Callaghan, I. R. (Liverpool), 1966 v Fi, F; 1978 v Sw, L (4)
Calvey, J. (Nottingham F.), 1902 v Ni (1)
Campbell, A. F. (Blackburn R.), 1929 v W, Ni;(with Huddersfield T.), 1931 v W, S, Ni; 1932 v W, Ni, Sp (8)
Camsell, G. H. (Middlesbrough), 1929 v F, Bel; 1930 v Ni, W; 1934 v F; 1936 v S, G, A, Bel (9)
Capes, A. J. (Stoke C.), 1903 v S (1)
Carr, J. (Middlesbrough), 1920 v Ni; 1923 v W (2)
Carr, J. (Newcastle U.), 1905 v Ni; 1907 v Ni (2)
Carr, W. H. (Owlerton, Sheffield), 1875 v S (1)
Carter, H. S. (Sunderland), 1934 v S, H; 1936 v G; 1937 v S, Ni, H; (with Derby Co.), 1947 v S, W, Ni, Ei, Ho, F, Sw (13)
Carter, J. H. (W.B.A.), 1926 v Bel; 1929 v Bel, Sp (3)
Catlin, A. E. (Sheffield W.), 1937 v W, Ni, H, N, Se (5)
Chadwick, A. (Southampton), 1900 v S, W (2)
Chadwick, E. (Everton), 1891 v S, W; 1892 v S; 1893 v S; 1894 v S; 1896 v Ni; 1897 v S (7)
Chambers, H. (Liverpool), 1921 v S, W, Bel; 1923 v S, W, Ni, Bel; 1924 v W (8)
Channon, M. R. (Southampton), 1973 v Y, S (2), Ni, W, Cz, USSR, I; 1974 v A, Pol, I, P, W,

673

Ni, S, Arg, EG, Bul, Y; 1975 v Cz, P, WG, Cy (2), Ni (sub), W, S; 1976 v Sw, Cz, P, W, Ni, S, Br, I, Fi; 1977 v Fi, I, L, Ni, W, S, Br (sub, Arg, U; (with Manchester C.), 1978 v Sw (44)
Charlton, J. (Leeds U.) 1965 v S, H, Y, WG, Se; 1966 v W, Ni, S, A, Sp, Pol(2), WG (2), Y, Fi, D, U, M, F, Arg, P; 1967 v W, S, Ni, Cz; 1968 v W. Sp; 1969 v W, R, F; 1970 v Ho (2), P, Cz (35)
Charlton, R. (Manchester U.), 1958 v S, P, Y; 1959 v S, W, Ni, USSR, I, Br, Pe, M, US; 1960 v W, S, Se, Y, Sp, H; 1961 v Ni, W, S, L, P, Sp, M, I, A; 1962 v W, Ni, S, A, Sw, Pe, L, P, H, Arg, Bul, Br; 1963 v S, F, Br, Cz, EG, Sw; 1964 v S, W, Ni, R of W, U, P, Ei, Br, Arg, US (sub); 1965 v Ni, S, Ho; 1966 v W, Ni, S, A, Sp, WG (2), Y, Fi, N, Pol. U, M, F, Arg, P; 1967 v Ni, W, S, Cz; 1968 v W, Ni, S, USSR (2), Sp (2), Se, Y; 1969 v S, W, Ni, R (2), Bul, M, Br; 1970 v W, Ni, Ho (2) P, Co, Ec, Cz, R, Br, WG (106)
Charnley, R. O. (Blackpool), 1963 v F (1)
Charsley, C. C. (Small Heath), 1893 v Ni (1)
Chedgzoy, S. (Everton), 1920 v W; 1921 v W, S, Ni; 1922 v Ni; 1923 v S; 1924 v W; 1925 v Ni (8)
Chenery, C. J. (C. Palace), 1872 v S; 1873 v S; 1874 v S (3)
Cherry, T. J. (Leeds U.), 1976 v W, S (sub), Br, Fi; 1977 v Ei, I, L, Ni, S (sub), Br, Arg, U; 1978 v Sw, L, I, Br, W; 1979 v Cz, W, Se (20)
Chilton, A. (Manchester U.), 1951 v Ni; 1952 v F(2)
Chippendale, H. (Blackburn R.), 1894 v Ni (1)
Chivers, M. (Tottenham H.), 1971 v Ma (2), Gr, Ni, S; 1972 v Sw (1+1 sub), Gr, WG (2), Ni (sub), S; 1973 v W (3), S (2), Ni, Cz, Pol, USSR, I; 1974 v A, Pol (24)
Christian, E. (Old Etonians), 1879 v S (1)
Clamp, E. (Wolverhampton W.), 1958 v USSR (2), Br, A (4)
Clapton, D. R. (Arsenal), 1959 v W (1)
Clare, T. (Stoke C.), 1889 v Ni; 1892 v Ni; 1893 v W; 1894 v S, (4)
Clarke, A. J. (Leeds U.), 1970 v Cz; 1971 v EG, Ma, Ni, W (sub.), S (sub.); 1973 v S (2), W, Cz, Pol, USSR, I; 1974 v A, Pol, I; 1975 v P; 1976 v Cz, P (sub) (19)
Clarke, H. A. (Tottenham H.), 1954 v S (1)
Clay, T. (Tottenham H.), 1920 v W; 1922 v W, S, Ni (4)
Clayton, R. (Blackburn R.), 1956 v Ni, Br, Se, Fi, WG, Sp; 1957 v S, W, Ni, Y, D (2), Ei(2); 1958 v S, W, Ni, F, P, Y, USSR; 1959 v S, W, Ni, USSR, I, Br, Pe, M, US; 1960 v W, Ni, S, Se, Y (35)
Clegg, J. C. (Sheffield W.), 1872 v S (1)
Clegg, W. E. (Sheffield W.), 1873 v S; (with Sheffield Albion), 1879 v W (2)
Clemence, R. N. (Liverpool), 1973 v W (2); 1974 v EG, Bul, Y; 1975 v Cz, P, WG, Cy, Ni, W, S; 1976 v Sw, Cz, P, W (2), Ni, S, Br, Fi; 1977 v Ei, Fi, I, Ho, L, S, Br, Arg, U; 1978 v Sw, L, I, WG, Ni, S; 1979 v D, Ei, Ni (2), S, Bul, A (sub) (43)
Clement, D. T. (Q.P.R.), 1976 v W (sub), W, I; 1977 v I, Ho (5)
Clough, B. H. (Middlesbrough), 1960 v W, Se (2)
Coates, R. (Burnley), 1970 v Ni; 1971 v Gr(sub.), (with Tottenham H.) Ma W (4)
Cobbold, W. N. (Cambridge University), 1883 v S, Ni; 1885 v S, Ni; 1886 v S, W; (with Old Carthusians), 1887 v S, N, W (9)
Cock, J. G. (Huddersfield T.), 1920 v Ni (with Chelsea) v S (2)
Cockburn, H. (Manchester U.), 1947 v W, Ni, Ei; 1948 v S, I; 1949 v S, Ni, D, Sw, Se; 1951 v Arg, P; 1952 v F (13)

Cohen, G. R. (Fulham), 1964 v U, P Ei, US, Br; 1965 v W, S, Ni, Bel, H, Ho, Y, WG, Se; 1966 v W, S, Ni, A, Sp, Pol (2), WG (2), N, D, U, M, F, Arg, P; 1967 v W, S, Ni, Cz, Sp; 1968 v W, Ni (37)
Coleclough, H. (C. Palace), 1914 v W (1)
Coleman, E. H. (Dulwich Hamlet), 1921 v W (1)
Coleman, J. (Woolwich Arsenal), 1907 v Ni (1)
Common, A. (Sheffield U.), 1904 v W, Ni; (with Middlesbrough), 1906 v W (3)
Compton, L. H. (Arsenal), 1951 v W, Y (2)
Conlin, J. (Bradford C.), 1906 v S (1)
Connelly, J. M. (Burnley), 1960 v W, N, S, Se; 1962 v W, A, Sw, P; 1963 v W, F; (with Manchester U.), 1965 v H, Y, Se, 1966 v W, Ni, S, A, N, D, U (20)
Cook, T. E. R. (Brighton), 1925 v W (1)
Cooper, N. C. (Cambridge University), 1893 v Ni (1)
Cooper, T. (Derby Co.), 1928 v Ni, 1929 v W, Ni, S, F, Bel, Sp; 1931 v F; 1932 v W, Sp; 1933 v S; 1934 v S, H, Cz; 1935 v W (15)
Cooper, T. (Leeds U.), 1969 v W, S, F, M; 1970 v Ho, Bel, Co, Ec, R, Cz, Br, WG; 1971 v EG, Ma, Ni, W, S; 1972 v Sw (2); 1975 v P (20)
Coppell, S. J. (Manchester U.), 1978 v I, WG, Br, W, Ni, S, H; 1979 v D, Ei, Cz, Ni (2), W (sub), S, Bul, A (16)
Copping, W. (Leeds U.), 1933 v I, Sw; 1934 v S, Ni, W, F; (with Arsenal), 1935 v Ni, I; 1936 v A, Bel; 1937 v N, Se, Fi; 1938 v S, W, Ni, Cz; 1939 v W, R of E (with Leeds U.), R (20)
Corbett, B. O. (Corinthians), 1901 v W (1)
Corbett, R. (Old Malvernians), 1903 v W (1)
Corbett, W. S. (Birmingham), 1908 v A, H, B (3)
Corrigan, J. T. (Manchester C.), 1976 v I (sub), Br; 1979 v W (3)
Cotterill, G. H. (Cambridge University), 1891 v Ni; (with Old Brightonians), 1892 v W; 1893 v S, Ni (4)
Cottle, J. R. (Bristol C.), 1909 v Ni (1)
Cowan, S. (Manchester C.), 1926 v Bel; 1930 v A; 1931 v Bel (3)
Cowell, A. (Blackburn R.), 1910 v Ni (1)
Cox, J. (Liverpool), 1901 v Ni; 1902 v S; 1903 v S (3)
Cox, J. D. (Derby Co.), 1892 v Ni (1)
Crabtree, J. W. (Burnley), 1894 v Ni; 1895 v Ni, S; (with Aston Villa), 1896 v W, S, Ni; 1899 v S, W, Ni; 1900 v S, W, Ni; 1901 v W; 1902 v W (14)
Crawford, J. F. (Chelsea), 1931 v S (1)
Crawford, R. (Ipswich T.), 1962 v Ni, A (2)
Crawshaw, T. H. (Sheffield W.), 1895 v Ni; 1896 v S, W, Ni; 1897 v S, W, Ni; 1901 v Ni; 1904 v W, Ni (10)
Crayston, W. J. (Arsenal), 1936 v S, W, G, A, Bel; 1938, v W, Ni, Cz (8)
Creek, F. N. S. (Corinthians), 1923 v F (1)
Cresswell, W. (South Shields), 1921 v W, (with Sunderland), 1923 v F; 1924 v Bel; 1925 v Ni; 1926 v W; 1927 v Ni; (with Everton), 1930 v Ni (7)
Crompton, R. (Blackburn R.), 1902 v S, W, Ni; 1903 v S, W; 1904 v S, W, Ni; 1906 v S, W, Ni; 1907 v S, W, Ni; 1908 v S, W, Ni, A (2), H, B; 1909 v S, W, Ni, H (2), A; 1910 v S, W; 1911 v S, W, Ni; 1912 v S, W, Ni; 1913 v S, W, Ni; 1914 v S, W, Ni (41)
Crooks, S. D. (Derby Co.), 1930 v S, G, A; 1931 v S, W, Ni, F, Bel; 1932 v S, W, Ni, Sp; 1933 v Ni, W, A; 1934 v S, Ni, W, F, H, Cz; 1935 v Ni; 1936 v S, W; 1937 v W, H (26)
Crewe, C. (Wolverhampton W.), 1963 v F (1)

Cuggy, F. (Sunderland), 1913 v Ni; 1914 v Ni (2)
Cullis, S. (Wolverhampton W.), 1938 v S, W, Ni, F Cz; 1939 v S, Ni, R of E, N, I, R, Y (12)
Cunliffe, A. (Blackburn R.), 1933 v Ni, W (2)
Cunliffe, D. (Portsmouth), 1900 v Ni (1)
Cunliffe, J. N. (Everton), 1936 v Bel, (1)
Cunningham, L. (W.B.A.), 1979 v W, Se, A (sub) (3)
Currey, E. S. (Oxford University), 1890 v S, W (2)
Currie, A. W. (Sheffield U.), 1972 v Ni; 1973 v USSR, I; 1974 v A, Pol, I; 1976 v Sw; (with Leeds U.) 1977 v Br, W (sub), Ni, S, H (sub); 1979 v Cz, Ni (2), W, Se (17)
Cursham, A. W. (Notts. Co.), 1876 v S; 1877 v S; 1878 v S; 1879 v W; 1883 v S, W (6)
Cursham, H. A. (Notts Co.), 1880 v W; 1882 v S, W Ni; 1883 v S, W, Ni; 1884 v Ni (8)
Daft, H. B. (Notts. Co.), 1889 v Ni; 1890 v S, W 1891 v Ni; 1892 v Ni (5)
Danks, T. (Nottingham F.), 1885 v S (1)
Davenport, J. K. (Bolton W.), 1885 v W; 1890 v Ni (2)
Davis, G. (Derby Co.), 1904 v W, Ni (2)
Davis, H. (Sheffield W.), 1903 v S, W, Ni (3)
Davison, J. E. (Sheffield W.), 1922 v W (1)
Dawson, J. (Burnley), 1922 v S, Ni (2)
Day, S. H. (Old Malvernians), 1906 v Ni, W, S (3)
Dean, W. R. (Everton), 1927 v S. W. F. Bel, L; 1928 v S, W, Ni, F, Bel; 1929 v S, W. Ni; 1931 v S; 1932 v Sp; 1933 v Ni (16)
Deeley, N. V. (Wolverhampton W.), 1959 v Br, Pe (2)
Devey, J. H. G. (Aston Villa), 1892 v Ni; 1894 v Ni (2)
Dewhurst, F. (Preston N.E.), 1886 v W, Ni; 1887 v S, W, Ni; 1888 v S, W, Ni; 1889 v W (9)
Dewhurst, G. P. (Liverpool Ramblers), 1895 v W (1)
Dickinson, J. W. (Portsmouth), 1949 v N, F; 1950 v S, W, Ei, P, Bel, Ch, US, Sp; 1951 v Ni, W, Y; 1952 v W, Ni, S, A (2), I, Sw; 1953 v W, Ni, S, Bel, Arg, Ch, U, US, 1954 v W, Ni, S, R of E, H (2), Y, Bel, Sw, U; 1955 v Sp, P; 1956 v W, Ni. S, D, Sp; 1957 v W, Y, D (48)
Dimmock, J. H. (Tottenham H.), 1921 v S; 1926 v W, Bel (3)
Ditchburn, E. G. (Tottenham H.), 1949 v Sw, Se; 1953 v US; 1957 v W, Y, D (6)
Dix, R. W. (Derby Co.), 1939 v N (1)
Dixon, J. A. (Notts. Co.), 1885 v W (1)
Dobson, A. T. C. (Notts. Co.), 1882 v Ni; 1884 v S, W, Ni (4)
Dobson, C. F. (Notts. Co.), 1886 v Ni (1)
Dobson, J. M. (Burnley), 1974 v P, EG, Bul, Y; 1975 (with Everton) v Cz (5)
Doggart, A. G. (Corinthians), 1924 v Bel (1)
Dorrell, A. R. (Aston Villa), 1925 v W, Bel, F; 1926 v Ni (4)
Douglas, B. (Blackburn R.), 1958 v S, W, Ni, F, P. Y, USSR (2), Br, A; 1959 v S, USSR; 1960 v Y, H; 1961 v Ni, W, S, L, P, Sp, M, I, A; 1962 v W, Ni, S, Pe, L, P H, Arg, Bul, Br; 1963 v S, Br, Sw (36)
Downs, R. W. (Everton), 1921 v Ni (1)
Doyle, M. (Manchester C.), 1976 v W, S (sub), Br, I; 1977 v Ho (5)
Drake, E. J. (Arsenal), 1935 v Ni, I; 1936 v W; 1937 v H; 1938 v F (5)
Ducat, A. (Woolwich Arsenal), 1910 v S, W, Ni; (with Aston Villa), 1920 v S, W; 1921 v Ni (6)
Dunn, A. T. B. (Cambridge University), 1883 v Ni; 1884 v Ni; (with Old Etonians), 1892 v S, W (4)

Earle, S. G. J. (Clapton), 1924 v F; (with West Ham U.) 1928 v Ni (2)
Eastham, G. (Arsenal), 1963 v Br, Cz, EG; 1964 v W, Ni, S, R of W, U, P, Ei, US, Br, Arg; 1965 v H, WG, Se; 1966 v Sp, Pol, D (19)
Eastham, G. R. (Bolton W.), 1935 v Ho (1)
Eckersley, W. (Blackburn R.), 1950 v Sp; 1951 v S, Y, Arg, P; 1952 v A (2), Sw; 1953 v Ni, Arg, Ch, U, US; 1954 v W, Ni, R of E, H (17)
Edwards, D. (Manchester U.), 1955 v S, F, Sp, P; 1956 v S, Br, Se, Fi, WG; 1957 v Ni, Ei (2), D (2); 1958 v W, Ni, F (18)
Edwards, J. H. (Shropshire Wanderers), 1874 v S (1)
Edwards, W. (Leeds U.), 1926 v S, W; 1927 v W, Ni; S, F, Bel, L; 1928 v S, F, Bel; 1929 v S, W, Ni, 1930 v W, Ni (16)
Ellerington, W. (Southampton), 1949 v N, F (2)
Elliott, G. W. (Middlesbrough), 1913 v Ni; 1914 v Ni; 1920 v W (3)
Eliott, W. H. (Burnley), 1952 v I, A; 1953 v Ni, W, Bel (5)
Evans, R. E. (Sheffield U.), 1911 v S, W, Ni; 1912 v W (4)
Ewer, F. H. (Casuals), 1924 v F; 1925 v Bel (2)

Fairclough, P. (Old Foresters), 1878 v S (1)
Fairhurst, D. (Newcastle U.), 1934 v F (1)
Fantham, J. (Sheffield W.), 1962 v L (1)
Felton, W. (Sheffield W.) 1925 v F (1)
Fenton, M. (Middlesbrough), 1938 v S (1)
Field, E. (Clapham Rovers), 1876 v S; 1881 v S (2)
Finney, T. (Preston N.E.), 1947 v W, I, Ei, Ho, F, P; 1948 v S, W, Ni, Bel, Se, I; 1949 v S, W, Ni, Se, N, F; 1950 v S, W, Ni, Ei, I, P, Bel, Ch, US, Sp, 1951 v W, S, Arg, P, 1952 v W, Ni, S, F, I, Sw, A, 1953 v W, Ni, S, Bel, Arg, Ch, U, US; 1954 v W, S, Bel, Sw, U, H, Y; 1955 v WG; 1956 v S, W, Ni, D, Sp; 1957 v S, W, Y, D (2), Ei (2); 1958 v W, S; F, P, Y, USSR (2); 1959 v Ni, USSR (76)
Fleming, H. J. (Swindon T.), 1909 v S, H (2); 1910 v W, Ni; 1911 v W, Ni; 1912 v Ni; 1913 v S, W; 1914 v S (11)
Fletcher, A. (Wolverhampton W.), 1889 v W; 1890 v W (2)
Flowers, R. (Wolverhampton W.), 1955 v F; 1959 v S, W, I, Br, Pe, US, M (sub); 1960 v W, Ni, S, Se, Y, Sp, H; 1961 v Ni, W, S, L, P, Sp, M, I, A; 1962 v Ni, S, A, Sw, Pe, L, P, H, Arg, Bul, Br; 1963 v Ni, W, S, F (2), Sw; 1964 v Ei, US, P; 1965 v W, Ho, WG; 1966 v N (49)
Forman, Frank (Nottingham F.), 1898 v S, Ni; 1899 v S, W, Ni; 1901 v S; 1902 v S, Ni; 1903 v W (9)
Forman, F. R. (Nottingham F.), 1899 v S, W, Ni (3)
Forrest, J. H. (Blackburn R.), 1884 v W; 1885 v S, W, Ni; 1886 v S, W; 1887 v S, W, Ni; 1889 v S; 1890 v Ni (11)
Fort, J. (Millwall), 1921 v Bel (1)
Foster, R. E. (Oxford University), 1900 v W; (with Corinthians), 1901 v W, Ni, S; 1902 v W (5)
Foulke, W. J. (Sheffield U.), 1897 v W (1)
Foulkes, W. A. (Manchester U.), 1955 v Ni (1)
Fox, F. S. (Gillingham), 1925 v F (1)
Francis, G. C. J. (Q.P.R.), 1975 v Cz, P, W, S; 1976 v Sw, Cz, P, W, Ni, S, Br, Fi (12)
Francis, T. (Birmingham C.), 1977 v Ho, L, S, Br; 1978 v Sw, L, I (sub), WG (sub), Br, W, S, H; (Nottingham F.), 1979 v Bul (sub), Se, A (sub) (15)
Franklin, C. F. (Stoke C.), 1947 v S, W, Ni, Ei, Ho, F, Sw, P; 1948 v S, W, Ni, Bel, Se, I; 1949 v S, W, Ni, D, Sw, N, F, Se; 1950 v S, W, Ni, Ei, I (27)

Freeman, B. C. (Everton), 1909 v S, W; (with Burnley), 1912 v S, W, Ni (5)
Froggatt, J. (Portsmouth), 1950 v Ni, I; 1951 v S; 1952 v S, A (2), I, Sw; 1953 v Ni, W, S, Bel, US (13)
Froggatt, R. (Sheffield W.), 1953 v W, S, Bel, US (4)
Fry, C. B. (Corinthians), 1901 v Ni (1)
Furness, W. I. (Leeds U.), 1933 v I (1)

Galley, T. (Wolverhampton W.), 1937 v N, Se (2)
Gardner, T. (Aston Villa), 1934 v Cz; 1935 v Ho (2)
Garfield, B. (W.B.A.), 1898 v Ni (1)
Garratty, W. (Aston Villa), 1903 v W (1)
Garrett, T. (Blackpool), 1952 v S, I; 1954 v W (3)
Gay, L. H. (Cambridge University), 1893 v S; (with Old Brightonians), 1894 v S, W (3)
Geary, F. (Everton), 1890 v Ni; 1891 v S (2)
Geaves, R. L. (Clapham Rovers), 1875 v S (1)
Gee, C. W. (Everton), 1932 v W, Sp; 1937 v Ni (3)
Geldard, A. (Everton), 1933 v I, Sw; 1935 v S; 1938 v Ni (4)
George, C. (Derby Co.), 1977 v Ei (1)
George, W. (Aston Villa), 1902 v S, W, Ni (193)
Gibbins, W. V. T. (Clapton), 1924 v F; 5 v F (22)
Gidman, J. (Aston Villa), 1977 v L (1)
Gillard, I. T. (Q.P.R.), 1975 v WG, W; 1976 v Cz (3)
Gilliat, W. E. (Old Carthusians), 1893 v Ni (1)
Goodall, F. R. (Huddersfield T.), 1926 v S; 1927 v S, F, Bel, L; 1928 v S, W, F, Bel; 1930 v S, G, A; 1931 v S, W, Ni, Bel; 1932 v Ni; 1933 v W, Ni, A, I, Sw; 1934 v W, Ni, F (25)
Goodall, J. (Preston N.E.), 1888 v S, W; 1889 v S, W; (with Derby) 1891 v S, W; 1892 v S; 1893 v W; 1894 v S; 1895 v S, Ni; 1896 v S, W; 1898 v W (14)
Goodhart, H. C. (Old Etonians), 1883 v S, W, Ni (3)
Goodwyn, A. G. (Royal Engineers), 1873 v S (1)
Goodyer, A. C. (Nottingham F.), 1879 v S (1)
Gosling, R. C. (Old Etonians), 1892 v W; 1893 v S; 1894 v W; 1895 v W, S (5)
Gosnell, A. A. (Newcastle U.), 1906 v Ni (1)
Gough, H. C. (Sheffield U.), 1921 v S (1)
Goulden, L. A. (West Ham U.), 1937 v Se, N; 1938 v W, Ni, Cz, G, Sw, F; 1939 v S, W, R of E, I, R, Y (14)
Graham, L. (Millwall), 1925 v S, W (2)
Graham, T. (Nottingham F.), 1931 v F; 1932 v Ni (2)
Grainger, C. (Sheffield U.), 1956 v Br, Se, Fi, WG; 1957 v W, Ni; (with Sunderland), 1957 v S (7)
Greaves, J. (Chelsea), 1959 v Pe, M, US; 1960 v W, Se, Y, Sp; 1961 v Ni, W, S, L, P, Sp, I, A; (with Tottenham H.), 1962 v S, Sw, Pe, H, Arg, Bul, Br; 1963 v Ni, W, S, F (2) Br, Cz, Sw; 1964 v W, Ni, R of W, P (2), Ei, Br, U, Arg; 1965 v Ni, S, Bel, Ho, Y; 1966 v W, A, Y, N, D, Pol, U, M, F; 1967 v S, Sp, A (57)
Green, F. T. (Wanderers), 1876 v S (1)
Green, G. H. (Sheffield U.), 1925 v F; 1926 v S, Bel, W; 1927 v W, Ni; 1928 v F, Bel (8)
Greenhalgh, E. H. (Notts.), 1872 v S; 1873 v S (2)
Greenhoff, B. (Manchester U.), 1976 v W, Ni; 1977 v Ei, Fi, I, Ho, Ni, W, S, Br, Arg, U, Br, W, Ni, S (sub), H (sub) (17)
Greenwood, D. H. (Blackburn R.), 1882 v S, Ni (2)
Grimsdell, A. (Tottenham H.), 1920 v S, W; 1921 v S, Ni; 1923 v W, Ni (6)
Grosvenor, A. T. (Birmingham), 1934 v Ni, W, F (3)
Gunn, W. (Notts. Co.), 1884 v S, W (2)
Gurney, R. (Sunderland), 1935 v S (1)

Hacking, J. (Oldham Ath.), 1929 v S, W, Ni(3)
Hadley, N. (W.B.A.), 1903 v Ni(1)
Hagan, J. (Sheffield U.), 1949 v D (1)
Haines, J. T. W. (W.B.A.), 1949 v Sw (1)
Hall, A. E. (Aston Villa), 1910 v Ni(1)
Hall, G. W. (Tottenham H.), 1934 v F; 1938 v S, W, Ni, Cz; 1939 v S, W, Ni, R of E, I, Y(11)
Hall, J. (Birmingham C.), 1956 v S, W, Ni, Br, Se, Fi, WG, D, Sp; 1957 v S, W, Ni, Y, D (2), Ei(2)(17)
Halse, H. J. (Manchester U.), 1909 v A (1)
Hammond, H. E. D. (Oxford University), 1889 v S (1)
Hampson, J. (Blackpool), 1931 v Ni, W; 1393 v A(3)
Hampton, H. (Aston Villa), 1913 v S, W; 1914 v S, W(4)
Hancocks, J. (Wolverhampton W.), 1949 v Sw; 1950 v W; 1951 v Y (3)
Hapgood, E. (Arsenal), 1933 v I, Sw; 1934 v S, Ni, W, H, Cz; 1935 v S, Ni, W, I, Ho; 1936 v S, Ni, W, G, A, Bel; 1937 v Fi; 1938 v S, G, Sw, F; 1939 v S, W, Ni, R of E, N, I, Y (30)
Hardinge, H. T. W. (Sheffield U.), 1910 v S (1)
Hardman, H. P. (Everton), 1905 v W; 1907 v S, Ni; 1908 v W (4)
Hardwick, G. F. M. (Middlesbrough), 1947 v S, W, Ni, Ei, Ho, F, Sw, P; 1948 v S, W, Ni, Bel, Se (13)
Hardy, H. (Stockport Co.), 1925 v Bel(1)
Hardy, S. (Liverpool), 1907 v S, W, Ni; 1908 v S 1909 v S, W, Ni, H (2), A; 1910 v S, W, Ni; 1912 v Ni (with Aston Villa), 1913 v S; 1914 v Ni, W, S; 1920 v S, W, Ni (21)
Hargreaves, F. W. (Blackburn R.), 1880 v W; 1881 v W; 1882 v Ni (3)
Hargreaves, J. (Blackburn R.), 1881 v S, W(2)
Harper, E. C. (Blackburn R.), 1926 v S(1)
Harris, G. (Burnley), 1966 v Pol(1)
Harris, P. P. (Portsmouth), 1950 v Ei; 1954 v H (2)
Harris, S. S. (Cambridge University), 1904 v S; (with Old Westminsters) 1905 v Ni, W; 1906 v S, W, Ni (6)
Harrison, A. H. (Old Westminsters), 1893 v S, Ni(2)
Harrison, G. (Everton), 1921 v Bel; 1922 v Ni(2)
Harrow, J. H. (Chelsea), 1923 v Ni, Se (2)
Hart, E. (Leeds U.), 1929 v W; 1930 v W, Ni; 1933v S, A; 1934 v S, H, Cz(8)
Hartley, F. (Oxford C.), 1923 v F(1)
Harvey, A. (Wednesbury Strollers), 1881 v W (1)
Harvey, J. C. (Everton), 1971 v Ma (1)
Hassall, H. W. (Huddersfield T.), 1951 v S, Arg, P; 1952 v F; (with Bolton W.), 1954 v Ni(5)
Haworth, G. (Accrington), 1887 v Ni, W, S; 1888 v S; 1890 v S (5)
Hawtrey, J. P. (Old Etonians), 1881 v S, W (2)
Hawkes, R. M. (Luton T.), 1907 v Ni; 1908 v A (2), H, B(5)
Haygarth, E. B. (Swifts), 1875 v S (1)
Haynes, J. N. (Fulham), 1955 v Ni; 1956 v S, Ni, Br, Se, Fi, WG, Sp; 1957 v W, Y, D, Ei (2); 1958 v W, Ni, S, F, P, Y, USSR (3), Br, A; 1959 v S, Ni, USSR, I, Br, Pe, M, US; 1960 v Ni, Y, Sp, H; 1961 v Ni, W, S, L, P, Sp, M, I, A; 1962 v W, Ni, S, A, Sw, Pe, P, H, Arg, Bul, Br(56)
Healless, H. (Blackburn R.), 1925 v Ni; 1928 v S (2)
Hector, K. J. (Derby Co.), 1974 v Pol (sub), I (sub, (2)
Hedley, G. A. (Sheffield U.) 1901 v Ni (1)
Hegan, K. E. (Corinthians), 1923 v Bel, F; 1924 v Ni, Bel(4)
Hellawell, M. S. (Birmingham C.), 1963 v Ni, F (2)
Henfrey, A. G. (Cambridge University), 1891 v Ni;
(with Corinthians), 1892 v W; 1895 v W; 1896 v S, W (5)
Henry, R. P. (Tottenham H.), 1963 v F (1)
Heron, F. (Wanderers), 1876 v S(1)
Heron, G. H. H. (Uxbridge), 1873 v S; 1874 v S; (with Wanderers), 1875 v S; 1876 v S; 1878 v S(5)
Hibbert, W. (Bury), 1910 v S(1)
Hibbs, H. E. (Birmingham), 1930 v S, W, A, G; 1931 v S, W, Ni; 1932 v W, Ni, Sp; 1933 v S, W, Ni, A, I, Sw; 1934 v Ni, W, F; 1935 v S, W, Ni, Ho; 1936 v G, W(25)
Hill, F. (Bolton W.), 1963 v Ni, W(2)
Hill, J. H. (Burnley), 1925 v W; 1926 v S; 1927 v S, Ni, Bel, F; 1928 v Ni, W; 1929 v F, Bel, Sp (11)
Hill, G. A. (Manchester U.), 1976 v I; 1977 v Ei (sub), Fi (sub), L; 1978 v Sw (sub), L (6)
Hill, R. H. (Millwall), 1926 v Bel (1)
Hillman, J. (Burnley), 1899 v Ni(1)
Hills, A. F. (Old Harrovians), 1879 v S (1)
Hilsdon, G. R. (Chelsea), 1907 v Ni; 1908 v S, W, Ni, A, H, B; 1909 v Ni(8)
Hine, E. W. (Leicester C.), 1929 v W, Ni; 1930 v W, Ni; 1932 v W, Ni(6)
Hinton, A. T. (Wolverhampton W.), 1963 v F ; (with Nottingham F.), 1965 v W, Bel(3)
Hitchens, G. A. (Aston Villa), 1961 v M, I, A; (with Inter-Milan), 1962 v Sw, Pe, H, Br(7)
Hobbis, H. H. F. (Charlton Ath.), 1936 v A, Bel(2)
Hodgetts, D. (Aston Villa), 1888 v S, W, Ni; 1892 v S, Ni; 1894 v Ni(6)
Hodgkinson, A. (Sheffield U.), 1957 v S, Ei (2), D; 1961 v W(5)
Hodgson, G. (Liverpool), 1931 v S, Ni, W (3)
Hodkinson, J. (Blackburn R.), 1913 v W, S; 1920 v Ni(3)
Hogg, W. (Sunderland), 1902 v S, W, Ni(3)
Holdcroft, G. H. (Preston N.E.), 1937 v W, Ni (2)
Holden, A. D. (Bolton W.), 1959 v S, I, Br, Pe, M (5)
Holden, G. H. (Wednesday O.A.), 1881 v S; 1884 v S, W, Ni (4)
Holden-White, C. (Corinthians), 1888 v W, S (2)
Holford, T. (Stoke), 1903 v Ni(1)
Holley, G. H. (Sunderland), 1909 v S, W, H (2), A; 1910 v W; 1912 v S, W, Ni; 1913 v S (10)
Holliday, E. (Middlesbrough), 1960 v W, Ni, Se(3)
Hollins, J. W. (Chelsea), 1967 v Sp (1)
Holmes, R. (Preston N.E.), 1888 v Ni; 1891 v S; 1892 v S; 1893 v S, W; 1894 v Ni; 1895 v Ni(7)
Holt, J. (Everton), 1890 v W; 1891 v S, W; 1892 v S, Ni; 1893 v S; 1894 v S, Ni; 1895 v S; (with Reading), 1900 v Ni (10)
Hopkinson, E. (Bolton W.), 1958 v W, Ni, S, F, P, Y; 1959 v S, I, Br, Pe, M, US; 1960 v W, Se(14)
Hossack, A. H. (Corinthians), 1892 v W; 1894 v W (2)
Houghton, W. E. (Aston Villa), 1931 v Ni, W, F, Bel; 1932 v S, Ni; 1933 v A (7)
Houlker, A. E. (Blackburn R.), 1902 v S; (with Portsmouth), 1903 v S, W; (with Southampton), 1906 v W, Ni (5)
Howarth, R. H. (Preston N.E.), 1887 v Ni; 1888 v S, W; 1891 v S; (with Everton), 1894 v Ni (5)
Howe, D. (W.B.A.), 1958 v S, W, Ni, F, P, Y, USSR (3), Br, A; 1959 v S, W, Ni, USSR, I, Br, Pe, M, US; 1960 v W, Ni, Se(23)
Howe, J. R. (Derby Co.), 1948 v I; 1949 v S, Ni(3)
Howell, L. S. (Wanderers), 1873 v S(1)
Howell, R. (Sheffield U.), 1895 v Ni; (with Liverpool) 1899 v S (2)
Hudson, A. A. (Stock C.), 1975 v WG, Cy (2)
Hudson, J. (Sheffield), 1883 v Ni(1)

Hudspeth, F. C. (Newcastle U.), 1926 v Ni (1)
Hufton, A. E. (West Ham U.), 1924 v Bel; 1928 v S, Ni; 1929 v F, Bel, Sp (6)
Hughes, E. W. (Liverpool), 1970 v W, Ni, S, Ho, P, B; 1971 v EG, Ma (2), Gr, W; 1972 v Sw, Gr, WG (2), W, Ni, S; 1973 v W (3), S (2), Pol, USSR, I; 1974 v A, Pol, I, W, Ni, S, Arg, EG, Bul, Y; 1975 v Cz, P, Cy (sub); Ni; 1977v I, L, W, S, Br, Arg, U; 1978 v Sw, L, I, WG, Ni, S, H; 1979 v D, Ei, Ni, W, Se (59)
Hughes, L. (Liverpool), 1950 v Ch, US, Sp (3)
Hulme, J. H. A. (Arsenal), 1927 v S, Bel, F; 1928 v S, Ni, W; 1929 v Ni, W; 1933 v S (9)
Humphreys, P. (Notts Co.), 1903 v S (1)
Hunt, G. S. (Tottenham H.), 1933 v I, Sw, S (3)
Hunt, Rev. K. R. G. (Leyton), 1911 v S, W (2)
Hunt, R. (Liverpool), 1962 v A; 1963 v EG; 1964 v S, US, P; 1965 v W; 1966 v S, Sp, Pol (2), WG (2), Fi, N, U, M, F, Arg, P; 1967 v Ni, W, Cz, Sp, A; 1968 v W, Ni, USSR (2), Sp (2), Se, Y; 1969 v R (2) (34)
Hunter, J. (Sheffield Heeley), 1878 v S; 1880 v S, W; 1881 v S, W; 1882 v S, W (7)
Hunter, N. (Leeds U.), 1966 v WG, Y, Fi, Sp (sub); 1967 v A; 1968 v Sp, Se, Y, WG, USSR; 1969 v R, W; 1970 v Ho, WG (sub); 1971 v Ma; 1972 v WG (2), W, Ni, S; 1973 v W (2), USSR (sub); 1974 v A, Pol, Ni (sub); S; 1975 v Cz (28)
Hurst, G. C. (West Ham U.), 1966 v S, WG (2), Y, Fi, D, Arg, P; 1967 v Ni, W, S, Cz, Sp, A; 1968 v W, Ni, S, Se (sub), WG, USSR (2); 1969 v Ni, S, R (2), Bul, F, M, U, Br; 1970 v W, Ni, S, Ho (1 + 1 sub), Be, Co, Ec, R, Br, WG; 1971 v EG, Gr, W, S; 1972 v Sw (2), Gr, WG (49)

Iremonger, J. (Nottingham F.), 1901 v S; 1902 v Ni (2)

Jack, D. N. B. (Bolton W.), 1924 v S, W; 1928 v F, Bel; (with Arsenal), 1930 v S, G, A; 1993 v W, A (9)
Jackson, E. (Oxford University), 1891 v W (1)
Jarrett, B. G. (Cambridge University), 1876 v S; 1877 v S; 1878 v S (3)
Jefferis, F. (Everton), 1912 v S, W (2)
Jezzard, B. A. G. (Fulham), 1954 v H; 1956 v Ni (2)
Johnson, D. E. (Ipswich T.), 1975 v W, S; 1976 v Sw (3)
Johnson, E. (Saltley College), 1880 v W; (with Stoke), 1884 v Ni (2)
Johnson, J. A. (Stoke C.), 1937 v N, Se, Fi, S, Ni (5)
Johnson, T. C. F. (Manchester C.), 1926 v Bel; 1930 v W; (with Everton), 1932 v S, Sp; 1933 v Ni (5)
Johnson, W. H. (Sheffield U.), 1900 v S, W, Ni; 1903 v S, W, Ni (6)
Johnston, H. (Blackpool), 1947 v S, Ho; 1951 v S; 1953 v Arg, Ch, U, US; 1954 v W, Ni, H (10)
Jones, A. (Walsall Town Swifts), 1882 v S, W; (with Great Lever), 1883 v S (3)
Jones, H. (Blackburn R.), 1927 v S, Bel, L, F; 1928 v S, Ni, (6)
Jones, H. (Nottingham F.), 1923 v F (1)
Jones, M. D. (Sheffield U.), 1965 v WG, Se (with Leeds U.); 1970 v Ho (3)
Jones, W. (Bristol C.), 1901 v Ni (1)
Jones, W. H. (Liverpool), 1950 v P, Bel (2)
Joy, B. (Casuals), 1936 v Bel (1)

Kail, E. I. L. (Dulwich Hamlet), 1929 v F, Bel, Sp (3)
Kay, A. H. (Everton), 1963 v Sw (1)
Kean, F. W. (Sheffield W.), 1923 v S, Bel; 1924 v W; 1925 v Ni; 1926 v Ni, Bel; 1927 v L; (with Bolton W.), 1929 v F, Sp (9)
Keegan, J. K. (Liverpool), 1973 v W (2); 1974 v W, Ni, Arg, EG, Bul, Y; 1975 v Cz, WG, Cy (2), Ni, S; 1976 v Sw, Cy, P, W (2), Ni, S, Br, Fi; 1977 v Ei, Fi, I, Ho, L, (with SV Hamburg) W, Br, Arg, U; 1978 v Sw, I, WG, Br, H; 1979 v D, Ei, Cz, Ni, W, S, Bul, Se, A (46)
Keen, E. R. L. (Derby Co), 1933 v A; 1937 v W, Ni, H (4)
Kelly, R. (Burnley), 1920 v S; 1921 v S, W, Ni; 1922 v S, W; 1923 v S; 1924 v Ni; 1925 v W, Ni, S; (with Sunderland), 1926 v W; (with Huddersfield T.), 1927 v L; 1928 v S (14)
Kennedy, R. (Liverpool), W (2), Ni, S; 1977 v L, W, S, Br (sub), Arg (sub); 1978 v Sw, L (11)
Kenyon-Slaney, W. S. (Wanderers), 1873 v S (1)
Kevan, D. T. (W.B.A.), 1957 v S; 1958 v W, Ni, S, P, Y, USSR (3), Br, A; 1959 v M, US; 1961 v M (14)
Kidd, B. (Manchester U.), 1970 v Ni, Ec (sub) (2)
King, R. S. (Oxford University), 1882 v Ni (1)
Kingsford, R. K. (Wanderers), 1874 v S (1)
Kingsley, M. (Newcastle U.), 1901 v W (1)
Kinsey, G. (Wolverhampton W.), 1892 v W; 1893 v S; (with Derby Co.), 1896 v W, Ni (4)
Kirchen, A. J. (Arsenal), 1937 v N, Se, Fi (3)
Kirton, W. J. (Aston Villa). 1922 v Ni (1)
Knight, A. E. (Portsmouth), 1920 v Ni (1)
Knowles, C. (Tottenham H.), 1968 v USSR, Sp, Se, WG (4)

Labone, B. L. (Everton), 1963 v Ni, W, F; 1967 v Sp, A; 1968 v S, Sp, Se, Y, USSR, WG; 1969 v Ni S, R, Bul, M, U, Br; 1970 v S, W, Bel, Co, Ec, R, Br, WG (26)
Lampard, F, R, G, (West Ham U.), 1973 v Y (1)
Langley, E. J. (Fulham), 1958 v S, P, Y (3)
Langton, R. (Blackburn R.), 1947 v W, Ni, Ei, Ho, F. Sw; 1948 v Se; (with Preston N.E.) 1949 v D, Se; (with Bolton W.), 1950 v S; 1951 v Ni (11)
Latchford, R. D. (Everton), 1978 v I, Br, H; 1979 v D, Ei, Cz (sub), Ni (2), W, S, Bul, A (12)
Latheron, E. G. (Blackburn R.), 1913 v W; 1914 v Ni (2)
Lawler, C. (Liverpool), 1971 v Ma, W, S; 1972 v Sw (4)
Lawton, T. (Everton), 1939 v S, W, Ni, R of E, N I, R, Y; (with Chelsea), 1947 v S, W, Ni, Ei, Ho, F, Sw, P; 1948 v W, Ni, Bel; (with Notts. Co.), 1948 v S, Se, I; 1949 v D (23)
Leach, T. (Sheffield W.), 1931 v W, Ni (2)
Leake, A. (Aston Villa), 1904 v S, Ni; 1905 v S, W, Ni (5)
Lee, E. A. (Southampton), 1904 v W (1)
Lee, F. H. (Manchester C.), 1969 v Ni, W, S, Bul, F, M, U; 1970 v W, Ho (2), P, Bel, Co, Ec, R, Br, WG; 1971 v EG, Gr, Ma, W, S; 1972 v Sw (2), Gr, WG (27)
Lee, J. (Derby Co.), 1951 v Ni (1)
Leighton, J. E. (Nottingham F.), 1886 v Ni (1)
Lilley, H. E. (Sheffield U.), 1892 v W (1)
Linacre, H. J. (Nottingham F.), 1905 v W, S (2)
Lindley, T. (Cambridge University), 1886 v S, W, Ni; 1887 v S, W, Ni; 1888 v S, W, Ni; (with Nottingham F.), 1889 v S; 1890 v S, W; 1891 v Ni (13)
Lindsay, A. (Liverpool) 1974 v Arg, EG, Bul, Y (4)
Lindsay, W. (Wanderers), 1873 v S (1)
Lintott, E. H. (Q.P.R.), 1908 v S, W, Ni; (with Bradford C.), 1909 v S, Ni, H (2) (7)
Lipsham, H. B. (Sheffield U.), 1902 v W (1)
Little, B. (Aston Villa), 1975 v W (sub) (1)
Lloyd, L. V. (Liverpool), 1971 v W; 1972 v Sw, Ni

(3)
Lockett, A. (Stoke), 1903 v Ni (1)
Lodge, L. V. (Cambridge University), 1894 v W, 1895 v S, W; (with Corinthians), 1896 v S, Ni (5)
Lofthouse, J. M. (Blackburn R.), 1885 v S, W, Ni; 1887 v S, W; (with Accrington), 1889 v Ni; (with Blackburn R.) 1890 v Ni (7)
Lofthouse, N. (Bolton W.), 1951 v Y; 1952 v W, Ni, S, A (2), I, Sw; 1953 v W, Ni, S, Bel, Arg, Ch, U, US; 1954 v W, Ni, R of E, Bel, U; 1955 v Ni, S, F, Sp, P; 1956 v W, S, Sp, D, Fi (sub); 1959 v W, USSR (33)
Longworth, E. (Liverpool), 1920 v S; 1921 v Bel; 1923 v S, W, Bel (5)
Lowder, A. (Wolverhampton W.), 1889 v W (1)
Lowe, E. (Aston Villa), 1947 v F, Sw, P (3)
Lucas, T. (Liverpool), 1922 v Ni; 1924 v F; 1926 v Bel (3)
Luntley, E. (Nottingham F.), 1880 v S, W (2)
Lyttelton, Hon. A. (Cambridge University), 1877 v S (1)
Lyttelton, Hon. E. (Cambridge University), 1878 v S (1)

McCall, J. (Preston N.E.), 1913 v S, W; 1914 v S; 1920 v S; 1921 v Ni (5)
McDermott, T. (Liverpool), 1978 v Sw, L (2); 1979 v Ni, W, Se (6)
McDonald, C. A. (Burnley), 1958 v USSR (3), Br, A; 1959 v W, Ni, USSR (8)
McFarland, R. L. (Derby Co.), 1971 v Gr, Ma (2), Ni, S; 1972 v Sw, Gr, WG, W, S; 1973 v W (3), Ni, S, Cz, Pol, USSR, I; 1974 v A, Pol, I, W, Ni; 1976 v Cz, S; 1977 v Ei, I (28)
McGarry, W. H. (Huddersfield T.), 1954 v Sw, U; 1956 v W, D(4)
McGuinness, W. (Manchester U.), 1959 v Ni, M (2)
McInroy, A. (Sunderland), 1927 v Ni (1)
McNab, R. (Arsenal), 1969 v Ni, Bul, R (1+1 sub) (4)
McNeal, R. (W.B.A.), 1914 v S, W (2)
McNeil, M. (Middlesbrough), 1961 v W, Ni, S,L, P, Sp, M, I; 1962 v L (9)
Macaulay, R. H. (Cambridge University), 1881 v S (1)
Macdonald, M. (Newcastle U.), 1972 v W, Ni, S (Sub); 1973 v USSR (sub); 1974 v P, S (sub), Y (sub); 1975 v WG, Cy (2), Ni; 1976 v Sw (sub), Cz, P (14)
Macrae, S. (Notts. Co.), 1883 v S. W, Ni; 1884 v S, W, Ni (6)
Maddison, F. B. (Oxford University), 1872 v S (1)
Madeley, P. E. (Leeds U.), 1971 v Ni; 1972 v Sw (2), Gr, WG (2), W, S, 1973 v S, Cz, Pol, USSR, I; 1974 v A, Pol, 1; 1975 v Cz, P, Cy; 1976 v Cz, P, Fi; 1977 v Ei, Ho (24)
Magee, T. P. (W.B.A.), 1923, v W Se; 1925 v S, Bel, F (5)
Makepeace, H. (Everton), 1906 v S; 1910 v S; 1912 v S, W (4)
Male, C. G. (Arsenal), 1935 v Se, Ni, I, Ho; 1936 v S, W, Ni, G, A, Bel; 1937 v S, Ni, H, N, Se, Fi; 1939 v I, R, Y (19)
Mannion, W. J. (Middlesbrough), 1947 v S, W, Ni, Ei, Ho, F, Sw, P; 1948 v W, Ni, Bel, Se, I; 1949 v N, F; 1950 v S, Ei, P, Bel, Ch, US; 1951 v Ni, W, S, T; 1952 v F (26)
Mariner, P. (Ipswich T.), 1977 v L (sub), Ni; 1978 v L, W (sub), S (5)
Marsden, J. T. (Darwen), 1891 v Ni (1)
Marsden, W. (Sheffield W.), 1930 v W, S, G (3)
Marsh, R. W. (Q.P.R.), 1972 v Sw (sub), (with Manchester C.) WG (sub + 1), W, Ni, S; 1973 v W (2), Y (9)
Marshall, T. (Darwen), 1880 v W; 1881 v W (2)
Martin, H. (Sunderland), 1914 v Ni (1)
Maskrey, H. M. (Derby Co.), 1908 v Ni (1)
Mason, C. (Wolverhampton W.), 1887 v Ni; 1888 v W; 1890 v Ni (3)
Matthews, R. D. (Coventry C.), 1956 v S, Br, Se, WG; 1957 v Ni (5)
Matthews, S. (Stoke C.), 1935 v W, I; 1936 v G, 1937 v S; 1938 v S, W, Cz, G, Sw, F; 1939 v S, W; Ni, R of E, N, I, Y; 1947 v S; (with Blackpool), 1947 v Sw, P; 1948 v S, W, Ni, Bel, I; 1949 v S, W, Ni, D, Sw; 1950 v Sp; 1951 v Ni, S; 1954 v Ni, R of E, H, Bel, U; 1955 v Ni, W, S, F, WG, Sp, P; 1956 v W, Br; 1957 v S, W, Ni, Y, D (2) Ei (54)
Matthews, V. (Sheffield U.), 1928 v F, Bel (2)
Maynard, W. J. (1st Surrey Rifles), 1872 v S; 1876 v S (2)
Meadows, J. (Manchester C.), 1955 v S (1)
Medley, L. D. (Tottenham H.), 1951 v Y, W; 1952 v F, A, W, Ni (6)
Meehan, T. (Chelsea), 1924 v Ni (1)
Melia, J. (Liverpool), 1963 v S, Sw (2)
Mercer, D. W. (Sheffield U.), 1923 v Ni, Bel (2)
Mercer, J. (Everton) 1939 v S, Ni, I, R, Y (5)
Merrick, G. H. (Birmingham C.), 1952 v Ni, S, A (2), I, Sw; 1953 v Ni, W, S, Bel, Arg, Ch, U; 1954 v W, Ni, S, R of E, H (2), Y, Bel, Sw, U (23)
Metcalfe V. (Huddersfield T.), 1951 v Arg. P. (2)
Mew, J. W. (Manchester U.), 1921 v Ni (1)
Middleditch, B. (Corinthians), 1897 v Ni (1)
Milburn, J. E. T. (Newcastle U.), 1949 v S, W, Ni, Sw; 1950 v W, P, Bel, Sp; 1951 v W, Arg, P; 1952 v F; 1956 v D (13)
Miller, B. G. (Burnley), 1961 v A (1)
Miller, H. S. (Charlton Ath.), 1923 v Se (1)
Mills, G. R. (Chelsea), 1938 v W, Ni, Cz (3)
Mills, M. D. (Ipswich T.), 1973 v Y; 1976 v W (2), Ni, S, Br, I (sub), Fi; 1977 v Fi (sub), I, Ni, W, S; 1978 v WG, Br, W, Ni, S, H; 1979 v D, Ei, Ni (2), S, Bul, A (26)
Milne, G. (Liverpool), 1963 v Br, Cz, EG; 1964 v W, Ni, S, R of W, U, P, Ei, Br, Arg; 1965 v Ni, Bel (14)
Milton, C. A. (Arsenal), 1952 v A (1)
Milward, A. (Everton), 1891 v S, W; 1897 v S, W (4)
Mitchell, C. (Upton Park), 1880 v W; 1881 v S 1883 v S, W; 1885 v W (5)
Mitchell, J. F. (Manchester C.), 1925 v Ni (1)
Moffat, H. (Oldham Ath.), 1913 v W (1)
Molyneux, G. (Southampton), 1902 v S; 1903 v S, W, Ni(4)
Moon, W. R. (Old Westminsters), 1888 v S, W; 1889 v S, W; 1890 v S, W; 1891 v S (7)
Moore, H. T. (Notts. Co.), 1883 v Ni; 1885 v W (2)
Moore, J. (Derby Co.), 1923 v Se (1)
Moore, R. F. (West Ham U.), 1962 v Pe, H, Arg, Bul, Br; 1963 v W, Ni, S, F (2), Br, Cz, EG, Sw; 1964 v W, Ni, S, R of W, U, P (2), Ei, Br, Arg; 1965 v Ni, S, Bel, H, Y, WG, Se; 1966 v W, Ni, S, A, Sp, Pol (2), WG (2), N, D, U, M, F, Arg, P; 1967 v W, Ni, S, Cz, Sp, A; 1968 v W, Ni, S, USSR (2), Sp (2), Se, Y, WG; 1969 v Ni, W, S, R, Bul, F, M, U, Br; 1970 v W, Ni, S, Ho, P, Bel, Co, Ec, R, Br, Cz, WG; 1971 v EG, Gr. Ma, Ni, S; 1972 v Sw (2), Gr, WG (2), W, S; 1973 v W (3), Y, S (2), Ni, Cz, Pol, USSR, I; 1974 v I (108)
Moore, W. G. B. (West Ham U.), 1923 v Se (1)
Mordue, J. (Sunderland), 1912 v Ni; 1913 v Ni (2)
Morice, C. J. (Barnes), 1872 v S (1)

Morley, H. (Notts. Co.), 1910 v Ni(1)
Morren, T. (Sheffield U.), 1898 v Ni (1)
Morris, F. (W.B.A.), 1920 v S; 1921 v Ni (2)
Morris, J. (Derby Co.), 1949 v N, F; 1950 v Ei(3)
Morris, W. W. (Wolverhampton W.), 1939 v S, Ni, R (3)
Morse, H. (Notts.), 1879 v S (1)
Mort T. (Aston Villa) 1924 v W, F; 1926 v S (3)
Morten, A. (C. Palace), 1873 v S (1)
Mortensen, S. H. (Blackpool), 1947 v P; 1948 v W, S, Ni, Bel, Se, I; 1949 v S, W, Ni, Se, N; 1950 v S, W, Ni, I, P, Bel, Ch, US, Sp; 1951 v S, Arg; 1954 v R of E, H (25)
Morton, J. R. (West Ham U.), 1938 v Cz(1)
Mosforth, W. (Sheffield W.) 1877 v S; (with Sheffield Albion), 1878 v S; 1879 v S, W; 1880 v S, W; (with Sheffield W.), 1881 v W; 1882 v S, W (9)
Moss, F. (Arsenal), 1934 v S, H, Cz; 1935 v I (4)
Moss, F. (Aston Villa), 1922 v S, Ni; 1923 v Ni; 1924 v S, Bel (5)
Mosscrop, E. (Burnley), 1914 v S, W (2)
Mozley, B. (Derby Co.), 1950 v W, Ni, Ei (3)
Mullen, J. (Wolverhampton W.), 1947 v S; 1949 v N, F; 1950 v Bel (sub), Ch, US; 1954 v W, Ni, S, R of E, Y, Sw (12)
Mullery, A. P. (Tottenham H.), 1965 v Ho; 1967 v Sp, A; 1968 v W, Ni, S, USSR, Sp (2), Se Y; 1969 v Ni, S, R, Bul, F, M, U, Br; 1970 v W, Ni, S (sub), Ho (sub), Bel, P, Co, Ec, R, Cz, WG, Br; 1971 v Ma, EG, Gr; 1972 v Sw(35)

Neal, P. G. (Liverpool), 1976 v W, I; 1977 v W, S, Br, Arg, U; 1978 v Sw, I, WG, Ni, S, H; 1979 v D, Ei, Ni (2), S, Bul, A (20)
Needham, E. (Sheffield U.), 1894 v S; 1895 v S; 1897 v S, W, Ni; 1898 v S, W; 1899 v S, W, Ni; 1900 v S, Ni; 1901 v S, W, Ni; 1902 v W (16)
Newton, K. R. (Blackburn R.), 1966 v S, WG; 1967 v Sp, A; 1968 v W, S, Sp, Se, Y, WG; 1969 v Ni, W, S, R, Bul, M, U, Br, F; (with Everton), 1970 v Ni, S, Ho, Co, Ec, R, Cz, WG (27)
Nicholls, J. (W.B.A.), 1954 v S, Y (2)
Nicholson, W. E. (Tottenham H.), 1951 v P(1)
Nish, D. J. (Derby Co.), 1973 v Ni; 1974 v P, W, Ni, S (5)
Norman, M. (Tottenham H.), 1962 v Pe, H, Arg, Bul, Br; 1963 v S, F, Br, Cz, EG; 1964 v W, Ni, S, R of W, U, P (2), US, Br, Arg; 1965 v Ni, Bel, Ho (23)
Nuttall, H. (Bolton W.), 1928 v W, Ni; 1929 v S (3)

Oakley, W. J. (Oxford University), 1895 v W; 1896 v S, W, Ni; (with Corinthians), 1897 v S, W, Ni; 1898 v S, W, Ni; 1900 v S, W, Ni; 1901 v S, W, Ni (16)
O'Dowd, J. P. (Chelsea), 1932 v S; 1933 v Ni, Sw (3)
O'Grady, M. (Huddersfield T.), 1963 v Ni; (with Leeds U.), 1969 v F (2)
Ogilvie, R. A. M. M. (Clapham R.), 1874 v S (1)
Oliver, L. F. (Fulham), 1929 v Bel (1)
Olney, B. A. (Aston Villa), 1928 v F, Bel (2)
Osborne, F. R. (Fulham), 1923 v Ni, F; (with Tottenham H.), 1925 v Bel; 1926 v Bel (4)
Osborne R. (Leicester C.), 1928 v W (1)
Osgood, P. L. (Chelsea), 1970 v Bel, R, (sub), Cz (sub), 1974 v I (4)
Ottaway, C. J. (Oxford University), 1872 v S; 1874 v S (2)
Owen, J. R. B. (Sheffield), 1874 v S (1)
Owen, S. W. (Luton T.), 1954 v H, Y, Bel (3)

Page, L. A. (Burnley), 1927 v S, W, Bel, L, F; 1928 v W. Ni (7)
Paine, T. L. (Southampton), 1963 v Cz, EG; 1964 v W, Ni, S, R of W, U, US P; 1965 v Ni, H, Y, WG, Se; 1966 v W, A, Y, N, M (19)
Pantling, H. H. (Sheffield U.), 1924 v Ni(1)
Paravacini, P. J. de (Cambridge University), 1883 v S, W, Ni (3)
Parker, T. R. (Southampton), 1925 v F(1)
Parkes, P. B. (Q.P.R.), 1974 v P (1)
Parkinson, J. (Liverpool), 1910 v S, W (2)
Parr, P. C. (Oxford University), 1882 v W(1)
Parry, E. H. (Old Carthusians), 1879 v W; 1882 v W, S (3)
Parry, R. A. (Bolton W.), 1960 v Ni, S (2)
Pawson, F. W. (Cambridge University), 1883 v Ni; (with Swifts), 1885 v Ni (2)
Payne, J. (Luton T.), 1937 v Fi(1)
Peacock, A. (Middlesbrough), 1962 v Arg, Bul; 1963 v Ni, W; (with Leeds U.), 1966 v W, Ni(6)
Peacock. J. (Middlesbrough), 1929 v F, Bel, Sp (3)
Pearson, H. F. (W.B.A.), 1932 v S (1)
Pearson, J. H. (Crewe Alex.), 1892 v Ni (1)
Pearson, J. S. (Manchester U.), 1976 v W, Ni, S, Br, Fi; 1977 v Ei, Ho (sub), W, S, Br, Arg, U; 1978 v I (sub), WG, Ni (15)
Pearson, S. C. (Manchester U.), 1948 v S; 1949 v S, Ni; 1950 v Ni, I, 1951 v P; 1952 v S, I (8)
Pease, W. H. (Middlesbrough), 1927 v W (1)
Pegg, D. (Manchester U.), 1957 v Ei (1)
Pejic, M. (Stoke C.), 1974 v P, W, Ni, S (4)
Pelly, F. R. (Old Foresters), 1893 v Ni; 1894 v S, W (3)
Pennington, J. (W.B.A.), 1907 v S, W; 1908 v S, W, Ni, A; 1909 v S, W, H (2), A; 1910 v S, W; 1911 v S, W, Ni; 1912 v S, W, Ni; 1913 v S, W; 1914 v S, Ni; 1920 v S, W (25)
Pentland, F. B. (Middlesbrough), 1909 v S, W, H (2) A (5)
Perry, C. (W.B.A.), 1890 v Ni; 1891 v Ni; 1893 v W (3)
Perry, T. (W.B.A.), 1898 v W (1)
Perry, W. (Blackpool), 1956 v Ni, S, Sp (3)
Peters, M. (West Ham U.), 1966 v Y, Fi, Pol, M, P, Arg, P, WG; 1967 v Ni, W, S, Cz; 1968 v W, Ni, S, USSR (2), Sp (2), Se, Y; 1969 v Ni, S, R, Bul, F, M, U, Br; 1970 v Ho (2), P (sub), Bel (with Tottenham H.), W, Ni, S, Co, Ec, R, Br, Cz, WG; 1971 v EG, Gr, Ma (2), Ni, W, S; 1972 v Sw, Gr, WG (1+1 sub.) Ni (sub) 1973 v S (2), Ni, W, Cz, Pol, USSR, I; 1974 v A, Pol, I, P, S (67)
Phillips, L. H. (Portsmouth), 1952 v Ni 1955 v W, WG (3)
Pickering, F. (Everton), 1964 v US; 1965 v Ni, Bel (3)
Pickering, J. (Sheffield), 1933 v S (1)
Pike, T. M. (Cambridge University), 1886 v Ni(1)
Pilkington, B. (Burnley), 1955 v Ni (1)
Plant, J. (Bury), 1900 v S (1)
Plum, S. L. (Charlton Ath.), 1923 v F (1)
Pointer, R. (Burnley), 1962 v W, L, P (3)
Porteous, T. S. (Sunderland), 1891 v W (1)
Priest, A. E. (Sheffield U.), 1900 v Ni (1)
Prinsep, J. F. M. (Clapham Rovers), 1879 v S (1)
Puddefoot, S. C. (Blackburn R.), 1926 v S, Ni(2)
Pye, J. (Wolverhampton W.), 1950 v Ei (1)
Pym, R. H. (Bolton W.), 1925 v S, W. 1926 v W(3)

Quantrill, A. (Derby Co.), 1920 v S, W; 1921 v W, Ni (4)

Quixall, A. (Sheffield W.), 1954 v W, Ni, R of E; 1955 v Sp, P (sub) (5)

Radford, J. (Arsenal), 1969 v R; 1972 v Sw (sub) (2)
Raikes, G. B. (Oxford University), 1895 v W; 1896 v W, Ni, S (4)
Ramsey, A. E. (Southampton), 1949 v Sw; (with Tottenham H.), 1950 v S, I, P, Bel, Ch, US, Sp; 1951 v S, Ni, W, Y Arg, P; 1952 v S, W, Ni, F, A (2), I, Sw; 1953 v Ni, W, S, Bel, Arg, Ch, U, US; 1954 v R of E, H (32)
Rawlings, A. (Preston N.E.), 1921 v Bel (1)
Rawlings, W. E. (Southampton), 1922 v S, W (2)
Rawlinson, J. F. P. (Cambridge University), 1882 v Ni (1)
Rawson, H. E. (Royal Engineers), 1875 v S (1)
Rawson, W. S. (Oxford University), 1875 v S; 1877 v S (2)
Read, A. (Tufnell Park), 1921 v Bel (1)
Reader, J. (W.B.A.), 1894 v Ni (1)
Reaney, P. (Leeds U.), 1969 v Bul (sub); 1970 v P; 1971 v Ma (3)
Revie, D. G. (Manchester C.), 1955 v Ni, S, F; 1956 v W, D; 1957 v Ni (6)
Reynolds, J. (W.B.A.), 1892 v S; 1893 v S, W; (with Aston Villa), 1894 v S, Ni; 1895 v S; 1897 v S, W (8)
Richards, C. H. (Nottingham F.), 1898 v Ni (1)
Richards, G. H. (Derby Co.), 1909 v A (1)
Richards, J. P. (Wolverhampton W.), 1973 v Ni (1)
Richardson, J. R. (Newcastle U.), 1933 v I, Sw (2)
Richardson, W. G. (W.B.A.), 1935 v Ho (1)
Rickaby, S. (W.B.A.), 1954 v Ni (1)
Rigby, A. (Blackburn R.), 1927 v S, Bel, L. F; 1928 v W (5)
Rimmer, E. J. (Sheffield W.), 1930 v S, G, A; 1932 v Sp (4)
Rimmer, J. J. (Arsenal), 1976 v I (1)
Robb, G. (Tottenham H.), 1954 v H (1)
Roberts, C. (Manchester U.), 1905 v Ni, W, S (3)
Roberts, F. (Manchester C.), 1925 v S, W, Bel, F (4)
Roberts, H. (Arsenal), 1931 v S (1)
Roberts, H. (Millwall), 1931 v Bel (1)
Roberts, R. (W.B.A.), 1887 v S; 1888 v Ni; 1890 v Ni (3)
Roberts, W. T. (Preston N.E.), 1924 v W, Bel (2)
Robinson, J. (Sheffield W.), 1937 v Fi; 1938 v G, Sw; 1939 v W (4)
Robinson, J. W. (Derby Co.), 1897 v S, Ni; (with New Brighton Tower), 1898 v S, W, Ni; (with Southampton), 1899 v S; 1900 v S, W, Ni; 1901 v Ni (3)
Robson, R. (W.B.A.), 1958 v F, USSR (2), Br, A; 1960 v Sp, H; 1961 v Ni, W, S, L, P, Sp, M, I; 1962 v W, Ni, Sw, L, P (20)
Rose, W. C. (Wolverhampton W.), 1884 v S, W, Ni; (with Preston N.E.) 1886 v Ni; (with Wolverhampton W.), 1891 v Ni (5)
Rostron, T. (Darwen), 1881 v S, W (2)
Rowe, A. (Tottenham H.), 1934 v F (1)
Rowley, J. F. (Manchester U.) 1949 v Sw, Se, F; 1950 v Ni, I; 1952 v S(6)
Rowley, W. (Stoke C.), 1889 v Ni; 1892 v Ni (2)
Royle, J. (Everton), 1971 v Ma; 1973 v Y; (with Manchester C.), 1976 v Ni (sub), I; 1977 v Fi, L (6)
Ruddlesdin, H. (Sheffield W.), 1904 v W, Ni ; 1905 v S (3)
Ruffell, J. W. (West Ham U.), 1926 v S; 1927 v Ni; 1929 v S, W, Ni; 1930 v W (6)

Russell, B. B. (Royal Engineers), 1883 v W (1)
Rutherford, J. (Newcastle U.), 1904 v S; 1907 v S, Ni, W; 1908 v S, Ni, W, A (2), H, B (11)

Sadler, D. (Manchester U.), 1968 v Ni, USSR; 1970 v Ec (sub); 1971 v EG (4)
Sagar C. (Bury), 1900 v Ni; 1902 v W (2)
Sagar, E. (Everton), 1936 v S, Ni, A, Bel (4)
Sandford, E. A. (W.B.A.), 1933 v W (1)
Sandilands, R. R. (Old Westminsters), 1892 v W; 1893 v Ni; 1894 v W; 1895 v W; 1896 v W (5)
Sands, J. (Nottingham F.), 1880 v W (1)
Sansom, K. (C. Palace), 1979 v W (1)
Saunders, F. E. (Swifts), 1888 v W (1)
Savage, A. H. (C. Palace), 1876 v S (1)
Sayer, J. (Stoke), 1887 v Ni (1)
Scattergood, E. (Derby Co.), 1913 v W (1)
Schofield, J. (Stoke), 1892 v W; 1893 v W; 1895 v Ni (3)
Scott, L. (Arsenal), 1947 v S, W, Ni, Ei, Ho, F, Sw, P; 1948 v S, W, Ni, Bel, Se, I; 1949 v W, Ni, D (17)
Scott, W. R. (Brentford), 1937 v W (1)
Seddon, J. (Bolton W.), 1923 v F, Se (2); 1924 v Bel; 1927 v W; 1929 v S (6)
Seed, J. M. (Tottenham H.), 1921 v Bel; 1923 v W, Ni, Bel; 1925 v S (5)
Settle, J. (Bury), 1899, v S, W, Ni; (with Everton), 1902 v S, Ni; 1903 v Ni (6)
Sewell, J. (Sheffield W.), 1952 v Ni, A, Sw; 1953 v Ni; 1954 v H (2) (6)
Sewell, W. R. (Blackburn R.), 1924 v W (1)
Shackleton, L. F. (Sunderland), 1949 v W, D; 1950 v W; 1955 v W, WG (5)
Sharp, J. (Everton), 1903 v Ni; 1905 v S (2)
Shaw, G. E. (W.B.A.), 1932 v S (1)
Shaw, G. L. (Sheffield U.), 1959 v S, W, USSR, I; 1963 v W (5)
Shea, D. (Blackburn R.), 1914 v W, Ni (2)
Shellito, K. J. (Chelsea), 1963 v Cz (1)
Shelton, A. (Notts. Co.), 1889 v Ni; 1890 v S, W; 1891 v S, W; 1892 v S (6)
Shelton, C. (Notts Rangers), 1888 v Ni (1)
Shepherd, A. (Bolton W.), 1906 v S; (with Newcastle U.), 1911 v Ni (2)
Shilton, P. L. (Leicester C.), 1971 v EG, W; 1972 v Sw, Ni; 1973 v Y, S (2), Ni, W, Cz, Pol, USSR, I; 1974 v A, Pol, I, W, Ni, S, Arg; (with Stoke C.) 1975 v Cy; 1977 v Ni, W; (with Nottingham F.) 1978 v W, H; 1979 v Cz, Se, A (28)
Shimwell, E. (Blackpool), 1949 v Se (1)
Shutt, G. (Stoke C.), 1886 v Ni (1)
Silcock, J. (Manchester U.), 1921 v S, W; 1923 v Se (3)
Sillett, R. P. (Chelsea), 1955 v F, Sp, P (3)
Simms, E. (Luton T.), 1922 v Ni (1)
Simpson, J. (Blackburn R.), 1911 v S, W, Ni; 1912 v S, W, Ni; 1913 v S; 1914 v W (8)
Slater, W. J. (Wolverhampton W.) ,1955 v W, WG; 1958 v S, P, Y, USSR (3), Br, A; 1959 v USSR; 1960 v S (12)
Smalley, T. (Wolverhampton W.), 1937 v W (1)
Smart, T. (Aston Villa), 1921 v S; 1924 v S, W; 1926 v Ni; 1930 v W (5)
Smith, A. (Nottingham F.), 1891 v S, W; 1893 v Ni (3)
Smith, A. K. (Oxford University), 1872 v S (1)
Smith, B.(Tottenham H.), 1921 v S; 1922 v W (2)
Smith, C. E. (C. Palace), 1876 v S (1)
Smith, G. D. (Oxford University), 1893 v Ni; 1894 v W, S; 1895 v W; 1896 v Ni, W, S; (with Old Carthusians) 1897 v Ni, W, S; 1898 v Ni, W, S;

(with Corinthians) 1899 v Ni, W, S; 1899 v Ni, W, S; 1901 v S (20)
Smith, H. (Reading), 1905 v W, S; 1906 v W, Ni(4)
Smith, J. (W.B.A.), 1920 v Ni; 1923 v Ni (2)
Smith, Joe (Bolton W.), 1913 v Ni; 1914 v S, W; 1920 v W, Ni (5)
Smith, J. C. R. (Millwall), 1939 v Ni, N (2)
Smith, J. W. (Portsmouth), 1932 v Ni, W, Sp(3)
Smith, Leslie (Brentford), 1939 v R (1)
Smith, Lionel (Arsenal), 1951 v W; 1952 v W, Ni; 1953 v W, S, Bel (6)
Smith, R. A. (Tottenham H.), 1961 v Ni, W, S, L, P, Sp; 1962 v S; 1963 v S, F, Br, Cz, EG; 1964 v W, Ni, R of W (15)
Smith, S. (Aston Villa), 1895 v S (1)
Smith, S. C. (Leicester C.), 1936 v Ni(1)
Smith, T. (Birmingham C.), 1960 v W, Se (2)
Smith, T. (Liverpool), 1971 v W (1)
Smith, W. H. (Huddersfield T.), 1922 v W, S; 1928 v S (3)
Sorby, T. H. (Thursday Wanderers, Sheffield),1879 v W(1)
Southworth, J. (Blackburn R.), 1889 v W; 1891 v W; 1892 v S(3)
Sparks, F. J. (Herts Rangers), 1879 v S; (with Clapham Rovers) 1880 v S, W (3)
Spence, J. W. (Manchester U), 1926 v Bel; 1927 v Ni (2)
Spence, R. (Chelsea), 1936 v A, Bel(2)
Spencer, C. W. (Newcastle U.), 1924 v S; 1925 v W (2)
Spencer, H. (Aston Villa), 1897 v S, W; 1900 v W; 1903 v Ni; 1905 v W, S (6)
Spiksley, F. (Sheffield W.), 1893 v S, W; 1894 v S, Ni; 1896 v Ni; 1898 v S, W (7)
Spilsbury, B. W. (Cambridge University), 1885 v Ni; 1886 v Ni, S(3)
Spouncer, W. A. (Nottingham F.), 1900 v W(1)
Springett, R. D. G. (Sheffield W.), 1960 v Ni, S, Y, Sp, H; 1961 v Ni, S, L, P, Sp, M, I, A; 1962 v W, Ni, S, A, Sw, Pe, L, P, H, Arg, Bul, Br; 1963 v Ni, W, F (2), Sw; 1966 v W, A, N (33)
Sproston, B. (Leeds U.), 1937 v W; 1938 v S, W, Ni, Cz, G, Sw, P; (with Tottenham H.), 1939 v W, R of E; (with Manchester C.), 1939 v N (11)
Squire, R. T. (Cambridge University), 1886 v S, W, Ni(3)
Stanbrough, M. H. (Old Carthusians), 1895 v W(1)
Staniforth, R. (Huddersfield T.), 1954 v S, H, Y, Bel, Sw, U; 1955 v W, WG (8)
Starling, R. W. (Sheffield W.), 1933 v S; (with Aston Villa), 1937 v S (2)
Steele, F. C. (Stoke C.), 1937 v S, W, Ni, N, Se, Fi (6)
Stephenson, C. (Huddersfield T.), 1924 v W (1)
Stephenson, G. T. (Derby Co.), 1928 v F, Bel; (with Sheffield W.), 1931 v F (3)
Stephenson, J. E. (Leeds U.), 1938 v S; 1939 v Ni(2)
Stepney, A. C. (Manchester U.), 1968 v Se(1)
Stewart, J. (Sheffield W.), 1907 v S, W; (with Newcastle U.), 1911 v S (3)
Stiles, N. P. (Manchester U.), 1965 v S, H, Y, Se; 1966 v W, Ni, S, A, Sp, Pol (2), WG (2), N, D, U, M, F, Arg, P, 1967 v Ni, W, S, Cz; 1968 v USSR; 1969 v R; 1970 v Ni, S (28)
Stoker, J. (Birmingham), 1933 v W; 1934 v S, H (3)
Storer, H. (Derby Co.), 1924 v F; 1928 v Ni (2)
Storey P. E. (Arsenal), 1971 v Gr, Ni, S. 1972 v Sw, WG, W, Ni, S; 1973 v W (3), Y, S (2), Ni, Cz, Pol, USSR, I (19)
Storey-Moore, I. (Nottingham F.), 1970 v Ho(1)

R.F. 79/80—35

Strange, A. H. (Sheffield W.), 1930 v S, A, G; 1931 v S, W, Ni, F, Bel; 1932 v S, W, Ni, Sp; 1933 v S, Ni, A, I, Sw; 1934 v Ni, W, F (20)
Stratford, A. H. (Wanderers), 1874 v S(1)
Streten, B. (Luton T.), 1950 v Ni(1)
Sturgess, A. (Sheffield U.), 1911 v Ni; 1914 v S (2)
Summerbee, M. G. (Manchester C.), 1968 v S, Sp, WG; 1972 v Sw, WG (sub), W, Ni; 1973 v USSR (sub)(8)
Sutcliffe, J. W. (Bolton W.), 1893 v W; 1895 v S, Ni; 1901 v S; (with Millwall), 1903 v W (5)
Swan, P. (Sheffield W.), 1960 v Y, Sp, H; 1961 v Ni, W, S, L, P, Sp, M, I, A; 1962 v W. Ni, S, A, Sw, L, P (19)
Swepstone, H. A. (Pilgrims), 1880 v S; 1882 v S, W; 1883 v S, W, Ni (6)
Swift, F. V. (Manchester C.), 1947, v S, W, Ni, El, Hol, F, Sw, P; 1948 v S, W, Ni, Bel, Se, I; 1949v S, W, Ni, D, N (19)

Tait, G. (Birmingham Excelsior), 1881 v W(1)
Talbot, B. (Ipswich T.), 1977 v Ni (sub), S, Br, Arg, U (5)
Tambling, R. V. (Chelsea), 1963 v W, F; 1966 v Y(3)
Tate, J. T. (Aston Villa), 1931 v F, Bel; 1933 v W(3)
Taylor, E. (Blackpool), 1954 v H (1)
Taylor, E. H. (Huddersfield T.), 1923 v S, W, Ni, Bel; 1924 v S, Ni, F; 1926 v S (8)
Taylor, J. G. (Fulham), 1951 v Arg, P (2)
Taylor, P. J. (C. Palace), 1976 v W (sub), W, Ni, S (4)
Taylor, P. H. (Liverpool), 1948 v W, Ni, Se(3)
Taylor, T. (Manchester U.), 1953 v Arg, Ch, U; 1954 v Bel, Sw; 1956 v S, Br, Se, Fi, WG; 1957 v Ni, Y (sub), D (2), Ei (2); 1958 v W, Ni, F(19)
Temple, D. W. (Everton), 1965 v WG(1)
Thickett, H. (Sheffield U.), 1899 v S, W (2)
Thomas, D. (Q.P.R.). 1975 v Cz (sub), P, Cy (sub + 1), W, S (sub); 1976 v Cz (sub), P (sub) (8)
Thompson, P. (Liverpool), 1964 v P (2), Ei, US, Br, Arg; 1965 v Ni, W, S, Bel, Ho; 1966 v Ni; 1968 v Ni, WG; 1970 v S, Ho (sub) (16)
Thompson, P. B. (Liverpool), 1976 v W (2), Ni, S, Br, I Fi; 1977 v Fi; 1979 v Ei (sub), Cz, Ni; S, Bul, Se (sub), A (15)
Thompson, T. (Aston Villa), 1952 v W; (with Preston N.E.), 1957 v S (2)
Thomson, R. A. (Wolverhampton W.), 1964 v Ni, US, P, Arg; 1965 v Bel, Ho, Ni, W (8)
Thornewell, G. (Derby Co.), 1923 v Se (2); 1924 v F; 1925 v F (4)
Thornley, I. (Manchester C.), 1907 v W (1)
Tilson, S. F. (Manchester C.), 1934 v H, Cz; 1935 v W; 1936 v Ni (4)
Titmuss, F. (Southampton), 1922 v W; 1923 v W (2)
Todd, C. (Derby Co.), 1972 v Ni; 1974 v P, W, Ni, S, Arg, EG, Bul, Y; 1975 v P (sub), WG, Cy (2), Ni, W, S; 1976 v Sw, Cz, P, Ni, S, Br, Fi; 1977 v Ei, Fi, Ho (sub), Ni (27)
Toone, G. (Notts. Co.), 1892 v S, W (2)
Topham, A. G. (Casuals), 1894 v W(1)
Topham, R. (Wolverhampton W.), 1893 v Ni; (with Casuals) 1894 v W(2)
Towers, M. A. (Sunderland), 1976 v W, Ni (sub), I (3)
Townley, W. J. (Blackburn R.), 1889 v W; 1890 v Ni (2)
Townrow, J. E. (Clapton Orient), 1925 v S; 1926 v W(2)
Tremelling, D. R. (Birmingham), 1928 v W(1)
Tresadern, J. (West Ham U.), 1923 v S, Se (2)

Tueart, D. (Manchester C.), 1975 v Cy (sub), Ni; 1977 v Fi, Ni, W (sub), S (sub) (6)
Tunstall, F. E. (Sheffield U.), 1923 v S; 1924 v S. W. Ni, F; 1925 v Ni, S (7)
Turnbull, R. J. (Bradford), 1920 v Ni (1)
Turner, A. (Southampton), 1900 v Ni; 1901 v Ni (2)
Turner, H. (Huddersfield T.), 1931 v F, Bel (2)
Turner, J. A. (Bolton W.), 1893 v W; (with Stoke) 1895 v Ni; (with Derby Co.) 1898 v Ni (3)
Tweedy, G. J. (Grimsby T.) 1937 v H (1)

Ufton, D. G. (Charlton Ath.), 1954 v R of E (1)
Underwood, A. (Stoke), 1891-2 v Ni (2)
Urwin, T. (Middlesbrough), 1923 v Se (2); (with Newcastle U.) 1924 v Bel; 1926 v W (4)
Utley, G. (Barnsley), 1913 v Ni (1)

Vaughton, O. H. (Aston Villa), 1882 v S, W, Ni; 1884 v S, W (5)
Veitch, C. C. M. (Newcastle U.), 1906 v S, W, Ni; 1907 v S, W; 1909 v W (6)
Veitch, J. G. (Old Westminsters), 1894 v W (1)
Venables, T. F. (Chelsea), 1965 v Ho, Bel (2)
Vidal, R. W. S. (Oxford University), 1873 v S (1)
Viljoen, C. (Ipswich T.), 1975 v Ni, W (2)
Viollet, D. S. (Manchester U.), 1960 v H; 1962 v L (2)
Von Donop (Royal Engineers), 1873 v S; 1875 v S (2)

Wace, H. (Wanderers), 1878 v S; 1879 v S, W (3)
Wadsworth, S. J. (Huddersfield T.), 1922 v S; 1923 v S, Bel; 1924 v S, Ni; 1925 v S, Ni; 1926 v W; 1927 v Ni (9)
Wainscoat, W. R. (Leeds U.), 1929 v S, (1)
Waiters, A. K. (Blackpool), 1964 v Ei, Br; 1965 v W, Bel, Ho (5)
Walden, F. I. (Tottenham H.), 1914 v S; 1922 v W (2)
Walker, W. H. (Aston Villa), 1921 v Ni; 1922 v Ni, W, S; 1923 v Se (2); 1924 v S; 1925 v Ni, W, S, Bel, F; 1926 v Ni, W, S; 1927 v Ni, W; 1933 v A (18)
Wall, G. (Manchester U.), 1907 v W; 1908 v Ni; 1909 v S; 1910 v W, S; 1912 v S; 1913 v Ni (7)
Wallace, C. W. (Aston Villa), 1913 v W; 1914 v Ni; 1920 v S (3)
Walters, A. M. (Cambridge University), 1885 v S, N, 1886 v S; 1887 v S, W; (Old Carthusians) 1889 v S, W; 1890 v S, W (9)
Walters, P. M. (Oxford University), 1885 v S, Ni; (Old Carthusians), 1886 v S, W, Ni; 1887 v S, W; 1888 v S, Ni; 1889 v S, W; 1890 v S, W (13)
Walton, N. (Blackburn R.), 1890 v Ni (1)
Ward, J. T. (Blackburn Olympic), 1885 v W (1)
Ward, T. V. (Derby Co.), 1948 v Bel; 1949 v W (2)
Waring, T. (Aston Villa), 1931 v F, Bel; 1932 v S, Ni (5)
Warner, C. (Upton Park), 1878 v S (1)
Warren, B. (Derby Co.), 1906 v S, W, Ni; 1907 v S, W, Ni; 1908 v S, W, Ni, A (2), H, B; 1909 v S, Ni, W, H (2) A; 1911 v S, Ni, W (22)
Waterfield, G. S. (Burnley), 1927 v W (1)
Watson, D. V. (Sunderland), 1974 v P, S (sub), Arg, EG, Bul, Y; 1975 v Cz, P, WG, Cy (2), Ni, W, S; (with Manchester C.) 1976 v Sw, Cz (sub), P; 1977 v Ho, L, Ni, W, S, Br, Arg, U; 1978 v Sw, L, I, WG, Br, W, Ni, S, H; 1979 v D, Ei, Cz, Ni (2), W, S, Bul, Se, A (44)
Watson, V. M. (West Ham U.), 1923 v W, S; 1930 v S, G, A (5)
Watson, W. (Burnley), 1913 v S, 1914 v Ni; 1920 v Ni (3)

Watson, W. (Sunderland). 1950 v Ni, I; 1951 v W, Y (4)
Weaver, S. (Newcastle U.), 1932 v S, 1933 v S, Ni (3)
Webb, G. W. (West Ham U.), 1911 v S, W (2)
Webster, M. (Middlesbrough), 1930 v S; A, G (3)
Wedlock, W. J. (Bristol C.), 1907 v S, Ni, W; 1908 v S, Ni, W. A (2),H B; 1909 v S, W, Ni, H (2), A; 1910 v S, W, Ni; 1911 v S, W, Ni; 1912 v S, W Ni; 1914 v W (26)
Weir, D. (Bolton W.), 1889 v S, Ni (2)
Welch, R. de C. (Wanderers), 1872 v S; (with Harrow Chequers), 1874 v S (2)
Weller, K. (Leicester C.) 1974 v W, Ni, S, Arg (4)
Welsh, D. (Charlton Ath.), 1938 v G, Sw; 1939 v R (3)
West, G. (Everton), 1969 v W, Bul, M (3)
Westwood, R. W. (Bolton W.), 1935 v S, W, Ho; 1936 v Ni, G; 1937 v W (6)
Whatley, O. (Aston Villa), 1883 v S, Ni (2)
Wheeler, J. E. (Bolton W.), 1955 v Ni (1)
Wheldon, G. F. (Aston Villa), 1897 v Ni; 1898 v S, W, Ni (4)
White, T. A. (Everton), 1933 v Ni (1)
Whitehead, J. (Accrington), 1893 v W; (with Blackburn R.), 1894 v Ni (2)
Whitfeld, H. (Old Etonians), 1879 v W (1)
Whitham, M. (Sheffield U.), 1892 v Ni (1)
Whitworth, S. (Leicester C.), 1975 v WG, Cy, Ni, W, S; 1976 v Sw, P (7)
Whymark, T. J. (Ipswich T.) 1978 v L (sub) (1)
Widdowson, S. W. (Nottingham F.), 1880 v S (1)
Wignall, F. (Nottingham F.), 1965 v W. Ho (2)
Wilkes, A. (Aston Villa), 1901 v S. W; 1902 v S, W, Ni (5)
Wilkins, R. G. (Chelsea), 1976 v I; 1977 v Ei, Fi, Ni, Br, Arg, U; 1978 v Sw (sub), L, I, WG, W, Ni, S, H; 1979 v D, Ei, Cz, Ni, W, S, Bul, Se (sub), A (24)
Wilkinson, B. (Sheffield U.), 1904 v S (1)
Wilkinson, L. R. (Oxford University), 1891 c W (1)
Williams, B. F. (Wolverhampton W.), 1949 v F; 1950 v S, W, Ei, I, P, Bel, Ch, US, Sp; 1951 v Ni, W, S, Y, Arg, P; 1952 v W, F, 1955 v S, WG, F, Sp, P; 1956 v W (24)
Williams, O. (Clapton Orient), 1923 v W, Ni (2)
Williams, W. (W.B.A.), 1897 v Ni; 1898 v W, Ni, S; 1899 v W, Ni (6)
Williamson, E. C. (Arsenal), 1923 v Se (2) (2)
Williamson, R. G. (Middlesbrough), 1905 v Ni; 1911 v Ni, S, W; 1912 v S, W; 1913 v Ni (7)
Willingham, C. K. (Huddersfield T.), 1937 v Fi; 1938 v S, G, Sw, F; 1938 v S, W, Ni, R of E, N, I, Y (12)
Willis, A. (Tottenham H.), 1952 v F (1)
Wilshaw, D. J. (Wolverhampton W.), 1954 v W, Sw, U; 1955 v S, F, Sp, P; 1956 v W, Ni, Fi, WG; 1957 v Ni (12)
Wilson, C. P. (Hendon), 1884 v S, W (2)
Wilson, C. W. (Oxford University), 1879 v W; 1881 v S (2)
Wilson, G. (Sheffield W.), 1921 v S, W, Bel; 1922 v S, Ni; 1923 v S W, Ni, Bel; 1924 v W, Ni, F (12)
Wilson, G. P. (Corinthians), 1900 v S, W (2)
Wilson, R. (Huddersfield T.), 1960 v S, Y, Sp, H; 1962 v W, Ni, S, A, Sw, Pe, P, H, Arg, Bul, Br; 1963 v Ni F, Br, Cz, EG, Sw; 1964 v W, S, R of W, U, P (2), Ei, Br, Arg; (with Everton) 1965 v S, H, Y, WG, Se; 1966 v WG (sub), W, Ni, A, Sp, Pol (2), Y, Fi, D, U, M, F, Arg, P, WG; 1967 v Ni, W, S, Cz, A; 1968 v Ni, S, USSR (2), Sp (2), Y (63)
Wilson, T. (Huddersfield T.), 1928 v S (1)

Winckworth, W. N. (Old Westminsters), 1892 v W; 1893 v Ni (2)
Windridge, J. E. (Chelsea), 1908 v S, W. Ni A (2), H, B; 1909 v Ni (8)
Wingfield-Stratford, C. V. (Royal Engineers) 1877 v S (1)
Wollaston, C. H. R. (Wanderers), 1874 v S; 1875 v S; 1877 v S; 1880 v S (4)
Wolstenholme, S. (Everton), 1904 v S; (with Blackburn R.) 1905 v W, Ni (3)
Wood, H. (Wolverhampton W.), 1890 v S, W; 1896 v S (3)
Wood R. E. (Manchester U.), 1955 v Ni, W, 1956 v Fi (3)
Woodcock, T. (Nottingham F.), 1978 v Ni; 1979 v Ei (sub), Cz, Bul (sub), Se (5)
Woodger, G. (Oldham Ath.), 1911 v Ni(1)
Woodhall, G. (W.B.A.), 1888 v S, W (2)
Woodley, V. R. (Chelsea), 1937 v S, N, Se, Fi; 1938 v S, W, Ni, Cz, G, Sw, F; 1939 v S, W, Ni, R of E, N, I, R, Y (19)
Woodward, V. J. (Tottenham H.), 1903 v S, W Ni; 1904 v S, Ni; 1905 v S, W, Ni; 1907 v S; 1908 v S, W, Ni; 1908 v A (2), H, B; 1909 v W, Ni, H (2), A; (with Chelsea), 1910 v Ni; 1911 v W (23)
Woosnam, M. (Manchester C.), 1922 v W (1)
Worrall, F. (Portsmouth), 1935 v Ho; 1937 v Ni(2)
Worthington, F. S. (Leicester C.), 1974 v Ni (sub) S, Arg, EG, Bul, Y; 1975 v Cz, P (sub) (8)
Wreford-Brown, C. (Oxford University), 1889 v Ni; (Old Carthusians), 1894 v W; 1895 v W; 1898 v S (4)
Wright, E. G. D. (Cambridge University), 1906 v W (1)
Wright, J. D. (Newcastle U.), 1939 v N (1)
Wright, T. J. (Everton), 1968 v USSR; 1969 v R (2) M (sub), U, Br; 1970 v W, Ho, Bel, R (sub), Br (11)
Wright, W. A. (Wolverhampton W.), 1947 v S, W, Ni, Ei, Ho, F, Sw, P; 1948 v S, W, Ni, Bel, Se, I; 1949 v S, W, Ni, D, Sw, Se, N, F: 1950 v S, W, Ni, Ei, I, P, Bel, Ch, US, Sp; 1951 v Ni, S, Arg; 1952 v W, Ni, S, F, A (2), I, Sw; 1953 v Ni, W, S, Bel, Arg, Ch, U, US; 1954 v W, Ni, S, R of E, H (2), Y, Bel, Sw, U; 1955 v W Ni, S, WG, F, Sp, P; 1956 v Ni, W, S, Br, Se, Fi, WG, D, Sp; 1957 v S, W, Ni, Y, D (2), Ei (2); 1958 v W, Ni, S, P, Y, USSR (3), Br, A, F; 1959 v W, Ni, S, USSR, I, Br, Pe, M, US (105)
Wyllie, J. G. (Wanderers), 1878 v S (1)

Yates, J. (Burnley), 1889 v Ni (1)
York, R. E. (Aston Villa), 1922 v S; 1926 v S (2)
Young, A. (Huddersfield T.), 1933 v W; 1937 v S, H, N, Se; 1938 v G, Sw, F; 1939 v W (9)
Young, G. M. (Sheffield W.), 1965 v W (1)

R. E. Evans also played for Wales against E, Ni, S;
J. Reynolds also played for Ireland against E, W, S.

NORTHERN IRELAND

Addis, D. J. (Cliftonville), 1922 v N (2)(2)
Aherne, T. (Belfast C.), 1947 v E; 1948 v S; 1949 v W; (with Luton T.), 1950 v W (4)
Alexander, A. (Cliftonville), 1895 v S (1)
Allen, C. A. (Cliftonville), 1936 v E (1)
Allen, J. (Limavady), 1887 v E (1)
Anderson, T. (Manchester U.) 1973 v Cy, E, S, W; 1974 v Bul, P (with Swindon T.), 1975 v S (sub); 1976 v Is; 1977 v Ho, Bel, WG, E, S, Ic; 1978 v Ic, Ho, Bel (with Peterborough U), S, E, W; 1979 v D.

Anderson, W. (Linfield), 1898 v W,E, S; 1899 v S (4)
Andrews, W. (Glentoran). 1908 v S; (with Grimsby T.), 1913 v E, S (3)
Armstrong, G. (Tottenham H.), 1977 v WG, E, W (sub), Ic (sub); 1978 v Bel, S, E, W; 1979 v Ei, D, Bul, E, Bul, E, S, W, D (17)

Baird, G. (Distillery), 1896 v S, E, W (3)
Baird, H. (Huddersfield T.), 1939 v E (1)
Balfe, J. (Shelbourne), 1909 v E; 1910 v W (2)
Bambrick, J. (Linfield), 1929 v W, S, E; 1930 v W, S, E; 1932 v W; (with Chelsea), 1935 v W, 1936 v E, S; 1938 v W (11)
Banks, S. J. (Cliftonville), 1937 v W (1)
Barr, H. H. (Linfield), 1962 v E; (with Coventry C.), 1963 v E, Pol (3)
Barron, H. (Cliftonville), 1894 v E, W, S; 1895 v S; 1896 v S; 1897 v E, W (7)
Barry, H. (Bohemians), 1900 v S (1)
Baxter, R. A. (Cliftonville), 1887 v S, W (2)
Bennett, L. V. (Dublin University), 1889 v W (1)
Berry, J. (Cliftonville), 1888 v S, W; 1889 v E (3)
Best, G. (Manchester U.), 1964 v W, U; 1965 v E, Ho (2), S, Sw (2), Alb; 1966 v S, E, Alb; 1967 v E; 1968 v S; 1969 v E, S, W, T; 1970 v E, W, USSR; 1971 v Cy (2), Sp, E, S, W; 1972 v USSR, Sp; 1973 v Bul; 1974 v P; (with Fulham), 1977 v Ho, Bel, WG; 1978 v Ic, Ho (37)
Bingham, W. L. (Sunderland), 1951 v F; 1952 v E,S, W; 1953 v E, S, F, W; 1954 v E, S, W; 1955 v E, S, W; 1956 v E, S, W; 1957 v E, S, W, P (2) I; 1958 v S, E, W, I (2), Arg, Cz (2), WG, F; (with Luton T.), 1959 v E, S, W, Sp; 1960 v S, E, W; (with Everton), 1961 v E, S, WG (2), Gr, I; 1962 v E, Gr; 1963 v E, S, Pol (2), Sp; (with Port Vale), 1964 v S, E, Sp (56)
Black, J. (Glentoran), 1901 v E (1)
Blair, H. (Portadown), 1931 v S; 1932 v S; (with Swansea) 1934 v S (3)
Blair, J. (Cliftonville), 1907 v W E, S; 1908 v E, S (5)
Blair, R. V. (Oldham Ath.), 1975 v Se (sub), S (sub), W; 1976 v Se, Is (5)
Blanchflower, R. D. (Barnsley), 1950 v S, W; 1951 v E, S; (with Aston Villa), F; 1952 v W; 1953 v E, S, W, F; 1954 v E, S, W; (with Tottenham H.), 1955 v E, S, W; 1956 v E, S, W; 1957 v E, S, W, I, P (2); 1958 v E, S, W, I (2), Cz (2), Arg, F, WG; 1959 v E, S, W, Sp; 1960 v E, S, W; 1961 v E, S, W, WG (2); 1962 v E, S, W, Gr, Ho; 1963 v E, S, Pol (2)(56)
Blanchflower, J. (Manchester U.), 1954 v W; 1955 v E, S; 1956 v S, W; 1957 v S, E, P; 1958 v S, E, I(2)(12)
Bookman, L. O. (Bradford C.), 1914 v W; (with Luton T.), 1921 v S, W; 1922 v E (4)
Bothwell, A. W. (Ards), 1926 v S, E, W; 1927 v E, W (5)
Bowler, G. C. (Hull C.), 1950 v E, S, W (3)
Braithwaite, R. S. (Linfield), 1962 v W; 1963 v P, Sp; (with Middlesbrough), 1964 v W, U; 1965 v E, S, Sw (2), Ho (10)
Breen, T. (Belfast C.), 1935 v E, W; 1937 v E, S; (with Manchester U.), 1937 v W; 1938 v E, S; 1939 v W, S (9)
Brennan, B. (Bohemians), 1912 v W (1)
Brennan, R. A. (Luton T.), 1949 v W; (with Birmingham C.), 1950 v E, S, W; (with Fulham), 1951 v E (5)
Briggs, W. R. (Manchester U.), 1962 v W; (with Swansea T.), 1965 v Ho (2)
Brisby, D. (Distillery), 1891 v S (1)

Brolly, T. (Millwall), 1937 v W; 1938 v W; 1939 v E, W (4)
Brookes, E. A. (Shelbourne), 1920 v S (1)
Brown, J. (Glenavon), 1921 v W; (Tranmere R.) 1924 v E, W (3)
Brown, J. (Wolverhampton W.), 1935 v E, W; 1936 v E; (with Coventry C.), 1937 v E. W; 1938 v S, W; (with Birmingham C.), 1939 v E, S, W (10)
Brown, W. G. (Glenavon), 1926 v W (1)
Brown, W. M. (Limavady), 1887 v E (1)
Browne, F. (Cliftonville). 1887 v E, S, W; 1888 v E, S (5)
Browne, R. J. (Leeds U.), 1936 v E, W; 1938 v E, W; 1939 v E, S (6)
Bruce, W. (Glentoran), 1961 v S, 1967 v W (2)
Buckle, H. (Cliftonville), 1882 v E (1)
Buckle, H. R. (Sunderland), 1904 v E; (with Bristol C.), 1908 v W (2)
Burnett, J. (Distillery), 1894 v E, W, S; (with Glentoran), 1895 v E, W (5)
Burnison, J. (Distillery), 1901 v E, W (2)
Burnison, S. (Distillery), 1908 v E; 1910 v E, S; (with Bradford), 1911 v E, S, W; (with Distillery), 1912 v E; 1913 v W (8)
Burns, J. (Glenavon), 1923 v E (1)
Butler, M. P. (Blackpool), 1939 v W (1)
Campbell, A. C. (Crusaders), 1963 v W; 1965 v Sw (2)
Campbell, J. (Cliftonville), 1896 v W; 1897 v E, S, W; (with Distillery), 1898 v E, S, W; (with Cliftonville), 1899 v E, 1900 v S; 1901 v S, W; 1902 v S; 1903 v E; 1904 v S (15)
Campbell, J. P. (Fulham), 1951 v E, S (2)
Campbell, W. G. (Dundee), 1968 v S, E; 1969 v T; 1970 v S, W USSR (6)
Carey, J. J. (Manchester U.), 1947 v E, S, W; 1948 v E; 1949 v E, S, W (7)
Carroll, E. (Glenavon), 1925 v S (1)
Casey, T. (Newcastle U.), 1955 v W; 1956 v W; 1957 v E, S, W I, P (2); 1958 v WG, F; 1959 v Sp (sub); (with Portsmouth), 1959 v E (12)
Cashin, M. (Cliftonville), 1898 v S (1)
Caskey, W. (Derby Co.), 1979 v Bul, E, Bul, E, D (sub) (5)
Cassidy, T. (Newcastle U.), 1971 v E (sub); 1972 v USSR (sub); 1974 v Bul (sub), S, E, W; 1975 v N; 1976 v S, E, W; 1977 v WG (sub) (11)
Chambers, J. (Distillery), 1921 v W; (with Bury) 1928 v E, S, W; 1929 v E, S, W; 1930 v S, W; (with Nottingham F.), 1932 v E, S, W (12)
Chatton H. A. (Partick T.), 1925 v E, S; 1926 v E (3)
Christian, J. (Linfield), 1889 v S (1)
Clarke, R. (Belfast C.), 1901 v E, S (2)
Clements, D. (Coventry C.), 1965 v W, Ho; 1966 v M; 1967 v S, W; 1968 v S, E,; 1969 v T (2), S, W; 1970 v S, E, W, USSR (2); 1971 v Sp, E, S, W, Cz; (with Sheffield W.) 1972 v USSR (2) Sp, E, S, W; 1973 v Bul, Cy (2) P, E, S, W; (with Everton) 1974 v Bul, P, S, E, W; 1975 v N, Y, E S, W; 1976 v Se, Y (with New York Cosmos), E, W (48)
Clugston, J. (Cliftonville), 1888 v W; 1889 v W, S, E; 1890 v E, S; 1891 v E, W; 1892 v E, S, W; 1893 v E, S, W (14)
Cochrane, D. (Leeds), 1939 v E, W; 1947 v E, S, W; 1949 v E, S, W; 1949 v S, W; 1950 v S, E, (12)
Cochrane, M. (Distillery), 1898 v S, W, E; 1899 v E; 1900 v E, S, W; (with Leicester Fosse), 1901 v S (8)
Cochrane, T. (Coleraine), 1976 v N (with Burnley); 1978 v S (sub), E (sub), W (sub); 1979 v Ei (sub), (Middlesbrough), D, Bul, E, Bul, E (10)

Collins, F. (Glasgow C.), 1922 v S (1)
Collins, R. (Cliftonville), 1922 v N (1)
Condy, J. (Distillery), 1882 v W; 1886 v E, S (3)
Connor, J. (Glentoran), 1901 v S, E; (with Belfast C.), 1905 v E, S, W; 1907 v E, S; 1908 v E, S; 1909 v W; 1911 v S, E, W (13)
Connor, M. J. (Brentford), 1903 v S, W; (with Fulham) 1904 v E (3)
Cook, W. (Celtic), 1933 v E, W, S; (with Everton) 1935 v E; 1936 v S, W; 1937 v E, S, W; 1938 v E, S, W; 1939 v E, S, W (15)
Cooke, S. (Belfast YMCA), 1889 v E; (with Cliftonville), 1890 v E, S (3)
Coulter, J. (Belfast C.), 1934 v E, S, W; (with Everton), 1935 v E, S, W; 1937 v S, W; (with Grimsby T.), 1938 v S, W; (with Chelmsford C.), 1939 v S (11)
Cowan, J. (Newcastle U.), 1970 v E (sub) (1)
Cowan, T. S. (Queen's Island), 1925 v W (1)
Coyle, F. (Coleraine), 1956 v E, S; 1957 v P (with Nottingham F.), 1958 v Arg (4)
Coyle R. I. (Sheffield W.), 1973 v P, Cy (sub), W (sub); 1974 v Bul (sub), P (sub) (5)
Craig A. B. (Rangers), 1908 v E, S, W; 1909 v S; (with Morton), 1913 v S, W, 1914 v E, S, W (9)
Craig, D. J. (Newcastle U.), 1967 v W; 1968 v W; 1969 v T (2), E, S, W; 1970 v E, S, W, USSR; 1971 v Cy (2), S, S (sub); 1972 v USSR, S (sub); 1973 v Cy (2), E, S, W; 1974 v Bul, P; 1975 v N (25)
Crawford, S. (Distillery), 1889 v E, W; (with Cliftonville), 1891 v E, S, W; 1893 v E, W (7)
Croft, T. (Queen's Island), 1922 v N (2); 1924 v E (3)
Crone, R. (Distillery), 1889 v S; 1890 v E, S, W (4)
Crone, W. (Distillery), 1882 v W; 1884 v E, S, W; 1886 v E, S, W; 1887 v E; 1888 v E, W; 1889 v S; 1890 v W (12)
Crooks, W. (Manchester U.), 1922 v W (1)
Crossan, E. (Blackburn R.), 1950 v S; 1951 v E; 1955 v W (3)
Crossan, J. A. (Sparta-Rotterdam), 1960 v E; (with Sunderland); 1963 v W, P, Sp; 1964 v E, S, W, U, Sp; 1965 v E, S, Sw (2); (with Manchester C.), v W, Ho (2), Alb; 1966 v S, E, Alb, WG; 1967 v E, S; (with Middlesbrough), 1968 v S (23)
Crothers, C. (Distillery), 1907 v W (1)
Cumming, L. (Huddersfield T.), 1929 v W, S; (with Oldham Ath.), 1930 v E (3)
Cunningham, R. (Ulster), 1892 v S, E, W; 1893 v E (4)
Cunningham, W. E. (St. Mirren), 1951 v W; 1953 v E; 1954 v S; 1955 v S; (with Leicester C.), 1956 v E, S, W; 1957 v E, S, W, I, P (2); 1958 v S, W, I, Cz (2), Arg, WG, F; 1959 v E, S, W; 1960 v E, S, W; (with Dunfermline Ath.), 1971 v W; 1962 v W, Ho (30)
Curran, S. (Belfast C.), 1926 v S, W; 1928 v S (3)
Curran, J. J. (Glenavon), 1922 v W, N (2); (with Pontypridd), 1923 v E, S; (with Glenavon), 1924 v E (6)
Cush, W. W. (Glenavon), 1951 v E, S; 1954 v S, E; 1957 v W, I, P (2); (withLeeds U.), 1958 v I (2), W, Cz (2), Arg, WG, F; 1959 v E, S, W, Sp; 1960 v E, S, W; (with Portadown), 1961 v WG, Gr; 1962 v Gr (26)

Dalrymple, J. P. (Distillery), 1922 v N (2) (2)
Dalton, W. (YMCA), 1888 v S; (with Linfield), 1890 v S, W; 1891 v S, W; 1892 v E, S, W ; 1894 v E, S, W (11)

D'Arcy, S. D. (Chelsea), 1952 v W; 1953 v E; (with Brentford), 1953 v S, W, F (5)
Darling, J. (Linfield), 1897 v E, S; 1900 v S; 1902 v E, S, W; 1903 v E, S, W; 1905 v E, S, W; 1906 v E, S, W; 1908 v W; 1909 v E; 1910 v E, S, W; 1912 v S (21)
Davey, H. H. (Reading), 1926 v E; 1927 v E, S; 1928 v E; (with Portsmouth), 1928 v W (5)
Davis, T. L. (Oldham Ath.), 1937 v E (1)
Davison, J. R. (Cliftonville), 1882 v E, W; 1883 v E, W; 1884 v E, W, S; 1885 v E (8)
Devine, W. (Limavady), 1886 v E, S; 1887 v W; 1888 v W (4)
Dickson, D. (Coleraine), 1970 v S (sub), W; 1973 v Cy, P (4)
Dickson, T. A. (Linfield), 1357 v S (1)
Dickson, W. (Chelsea), 1951 v W. F; 1952 v E, S, W; 1953 v E, S, W, F; (with Arsenal); 1954 v E, W; 1955 v E (12)
Diffin, W. (Belfast C.), 1931 v W (1)
Dill, A. H. (Knock and Down Ath.), 1882 v E, W; (with Cliftonville), 1883 v W; 1884 v E, S, W; 1885 v E, S, W (9)
Doherty, I. (Belfast C.), 1901 v E (1)
Doherty, J. (Cliftonville), 1933 v E, W (2)
Doherty, M. (Derry C.), 1938 v S (1)
Doherty, P. D. (Blackpool), 1935 v E, W; 1936 v E, S; (with Manchester C.), 1937 v E, W; 1938 v E, S; 1939 v E, W; (with Derby Co.), 1947 v E; (with Huddersfield T.), 1947 v W; 1948 v E, W; 1949 v S; (with Doncaster R.), 1951 v S (16)
Donnelly, L. (Distillery), 1913 v W (1)
Doran, J. F. (Brighton), 1921 v E; 1922 v E, W (3)
Dougan, A. D. (Portsmouth), 1958 v Cz; (with Blackburn R.), 1960 v S; 1961 v E, W, I, Gr; (with Aston Villa), 1963 v S, P (2); (with Leicester C.), 1966 v S, E, W, M; Alb, WG; 1967 v E, S; (with Wolverhampton W.), 1967 v W; 1968 v S, W, Is, T (2); 1969 v E, S, W; 1970 v S, E, USSR (2); 1971 v Cy (2), Sp, E, S, W; 1972 v USSR (2), E, S, W; 1973 v Bul, Cy (43)
Douglas, J. P., (Belfast C.), 1947 v E (1)
Dowd, H. O. (Glentoran), 1974 v W; (with Glenavon), 1975 v N (sub), Se (3)
Duggan, H. A. (Leeds U.), 1930 v E; 1931 v E, W; 1933 v E; 1934 v E; 1935 v S, W; 1936 v S (8)
Dunne, J. (Sheffield U.), 1928 v W; 1931 v W, E; 1932 v E, S; 1933 v E, W (7)
Eames, W. L. E. (Dublin U.), 1885 v E, S, W (3)
Eglington, T. J. (Everton), 1947 v S, W; 1948 v E, S, W; 1949 v E (6)
Elder, A. R. (Burnley), 1960 v W; 1961 v S, E, W, WG (2); Gr; 1962 v E, S, Gr; 1963 v E, S, W, P (2), Sp; 1964 v W, U; 1965 v E, S, W, Sw (2), Ho (2), Alb; 1966 v E, S, W, M, Alb; 1967 v E, S, W (with Stoke C.), 1968 v E, W; 1969 v E (sub), S, W; 1970 v USSR (40)
Elleman, A. R. (Cliftonville), 1889 v W; 1890 v E (2)
Elwood, J. H. (Bradford), 1929 v W; 1930 v E (2)
Emerson, W. (Glentoran), 1920 v E, S, W; 1921 v E; 1922 v E, S; (with Burnley), 1922 v W; 1923 v E, S, W; 1924 v E (11)
English, S. (Glasgow R.), 1933 v W, S (2)
Enright, J. (Leeds C.), 1912 v S (1)
Fallon, E. (Aberdeen), 1931 v S; 1933 v S (2)
Farquharson, T. G. (Cardiff C.), 1923 v S, W; 1924 v E, S, W; 1925 v E, S (7)
Farrell, P. (Distillery), 1901 v S W (2)
Farrell, P. (Hibernian), 1938 v W (1)
Farrell, P, D. (Everton), 1947 v S, W; 1948 v E, S, W; 1949 v E, W (7)

Feeney, J. M. (Linsfield), 1947 v S; (with Swansea T.), 1950 v E (2)
Feeney, W. (Glentoran), 1976 v Is (1)
Ferguson, W. (Linfield), 1966 v M; 1967 v E (2)
Ferris, J. (Belfast Celtic), 1920 v E, W; (with Chelsea), 1921 v S, E, (with Belfast C.), 1928 v S (5)
Ferris, R. O. (Birmingham), 1950 v S; 1951 v F; 1952 v S (3)
Finney, T. (Sunderland), 1975 v N, E (sub), S, W; 1976 v N, Y, S (7)
Fitzpatrick, J. C. (Bohemians), 1896 v E, S (2)
Flack, H. (Burnley), 1929 v S (1)
Forbes, G. (Limavady), 1888 v W; (with Distillery), 1891 v E, S (3)
Forde, J. T. (Ards), 1959 v Sp; 1961 v E, S, WG (4)
Foreman, T. A. (Cliftonville), 1899 v S (1)
Forsyth, J. (YMCA), 1888 v E, S (2)
Fox, W. (Ulster), 1887 v E S (2)
Fulton, R, P. (Belfast C.), 1930 v W; 1931 v E, S, W; 1932 v W, E; 1933 v E, S; 1934 v E, W, S; 1935 v E, W, S; 1936 v S, W; 1937 v E, S, W; 1938 v W (20)
Gaffikin, J. (Linfield Ath.), 1890 v S, W; 1891 v S, W; 1892 v E, S, W; 1893 v E, S, W; 1894 v E, S, W; 1895 v E, W (15)
Galbraith, W. (Distillery), 1890 v W (1)
Gallagher, P. (Celtic), 1920 v E, S; 1922 v S; 1923 v S, W; 1924 v S, W; 1925 v S, W, E; (with Falkirk), 1927 v S (11)
Gallogly, C. (Huddersfield T.), 1951 v E, S (2)
Gara, A. (Preston N.E.), 1902 v E, S, W (3)
Gardiner, A. (Cliftonville), 1930 v S. W; 1931 v S; 1932 v E, S (5)
Garrett, J. (Distillery), 1925 v W (1)
Gaston, R. (Oxford U.), 1969 v Is (sub) (1)
Gaukrodger, G. (Linfield), 1895 v W (1)
Gaussen, A. W. (Moyola Park), 1884 v E, S; 1888 v E, W; 1889 v E, W (6)
Geary, J. (Glentoran), 1931 v S; 1932 v S (2)
Gibb, J. T. (Wellington Park), 1884 v S, W; 1885 v S, E, W; 1886 v S; 1887 v S, E, W; 1889 v S (10)
Gibb, T. J. (Cliftonville), 1936 v W (1)
Gibson, W. K. (Cliftonville). 1894 v S, W, E; 1895 v S; 1897 v W; 1898 v S, W, E; 1901 v S, W, E; 1902 v S, W (13)
Gillespie, R. (Hertford), 1886 v E, S, W; 1887 v E, S, W (6)
Gillespie, W. (Sheffield U.), 1913 v E, S; 1914 v E, W; 1920 v S, W; 1921 v E; 1922 v E, S; 1923 v E, S, W; 1924 v E, S, W; 1925 v E, S; 1926 v S, W; 1927 v E, W; 1928 v E; 1929 v E; 1931 v E (25)
Gillespie, W. (West Down), 1889 v W (1)
Goodall, A. L. (Derby Co.), 1899 v S, W; 1900 v E, W; 1901 v E; 1902 v S; 1903 v E, W; (with Glossop), 1904 v E, W (10)
Goodbody, M. F. (Dublin University), 1889 v E; 1891 v W (2)
Gordon, H. (Linfield), 1891 v S; 1892 v E, S, W; 1893 v E, S, W; 1895 v E, W; 1896 v E, S (11)
Gordon, T. (Linfield), 1894 v W; 1895 v E (2)
Gorman, W. C. (Brentford), 1947 v E, S, W; 1948 v W (4)
Gowdy, J. (Glentoran), 1920 v E; (with Queen's Island), 1924 v W; (with Falkirk), 1926 v E, S; 1927 v E, S (6)
Gowdy, W. A. (Hull C.), 1932 v S; (with Sheffield W.), 1933 v S; (with Linfield), 1935 v E, S, W; (with Hibernian), 1936 v W (6)

Graham, W. G. L. (Doncaster R.), 1951 v W, F; 1952 v E, S, W; 1953, v S, F; 1954 v E, W; 1955 v S, W; 1956 v E, E, S; 1959 v E (14)

Greer, W. (Q.P.R.), 1909 v E, S, W (3)

Gregg, H. (Doncaster R.), 1954 v W; 1957 v E, S, W, I, P; 1958 v E, I; (with Manchester U.), 1958 v Cz, Arg, WG, F, W; 1959 v E, W; 1960 v S, E, W; 1961 v E, S; 1962 v S, Gr; 1964 v S, E (24)

Hall, G. (Distillery), 1897 v E (1)

Halligan, W. (Derby Co.), 1911 v W; (with Wolverhampton W.), 1912 v E (2)

Hamil, M. (Manchester U.), 1912 v E; 1914 v E, S; (with Belfast C.), 1920 v E, S, W; (with Manchester C.), 1921 v S (7)

Hamilton, B. (Linfield), 1969 v T; 1971 Cy (2) E, S, W; (with Ipswich T.), 1972 v USSR (1+1 sub), Sp; 1973 v Bul, Cy (2), P, E, S, W; 1974 v Bul, S, E, W; 1975 v N, Se, Y, E; 1976 v Se, N, Y (with Everton), Is, S, E, W; 1977 v Ho, Bel, WG, E, S, W, Ic (with Millwall); 1978 v S, E, W; 1979 v Ei (sub), (Swindon T.), Bul (2), E, S, W, D (48)

Hamilton, J. (Knock), 1882 v E, W (2)

Hamilton, R. (Distillery), 1908 v W (1)

Hamilton, R. (Glasgow R.), 1928 v S; 1929 v E; 1930 v S, E; 1932 v S (5)

Hamilton, W. (Q.P.R.); 1978 v S (sub) (1)

Hamilton, W. D. (Dublin Association), 1885 vW(1)

Hamilton, W. J. (Dublin Association), 1885 v W (1)

Hampton, H. (Bradford C.), 1911 v E, S, W; 1912 v E, W; 1913 v E, S, W; 1914 v E (9)

Hanna, D. R. A. (Portsmouth), 1899 v W (1)

Hanna, J. (Nottingham), 1912 v S, W (2)

Hannon, D. J. (Bohemian), 1908 v E, S; 1911 v E, S; 1912 v W; 1913 v E (6)

Harkin, J. T. (Southport), 1968 v W; 1969 v T, (with Shrewsbury), W (sub); 1970 v USSR; 1971 v Sp (5)

Harland, A. I. (Linfield), 1922 v N (2), 1923 v E (3)

Harris, J. (Cliftonville), 1921 v W (1)

Harris, V. (Shelbourne), 1906 v E; 1907 v E, W; 1908 v E, W, S; (with Everton); 1909 v E, W, S; 1910 v E, S, W; 1911 v E, S, W; 1912 v E; 1913 v E, S; 1914 v S, W (20)

Harvey, M. (Sunderland), 1961 v I; 1962 v Ho; 1963 v W Sp; 1964 v S, E, W, U, Sp; 1965 v E, S, W, Sw (2), Ho (2), Alb; 1966 v S, E, W, M, Alb, WG; 1967 v E, S; 1968 v E, W,; 1969, Is, T (2) v E; 1970 v USSR; 1971 v Cy, W (sub) (33)

Hastings, J. (Knock), 1882 v E, W; (with Ulster), 1883 v W; 1884 v E, S; 1886 v E, S (7)

Hatton, S. (Linfield), 1963 v S, Pol (2)

Hayes, W. E. (Huddersfield T.), 1938 v E, S; 1939 v E, S (4)

Hegan, D. (W.B.A.), 1970 v USSR (with Wolverhampton W.); 1972 v USSR, E, S, W; 1973 v Bul, Cy (7)

Henderson, A. W. (Ulster), 1885 v E, S, W (3)

Hewison, G. (Moyola Park), 1885 v E, S (2)

Hill, M. J. (Norwich C.), 1959 v W; 1960 v W; 1961 v WG; 1962 v S (with Everton), 1964 v S, E, Sp (7)

Hinton, E. (Fulham), 1947 v S, W; 1948 v S, E, W; (Millwall), 1951 v W, F (7)

Hopkins, J. (Brighton), 1926 v E (1)

Houston, J. (Linfield), 1912 v S, W; 1913 v W, (with Everton), 1913 v E, S; 1914 v S (6)

Houston, W. (Linfield), 1933 v W (1)

Houston, W. G. (Moyola Park), 1885 v E, S(2)

Hughes, W. (Bolton W.), 1951 v W (1)

Humphries, W. (Ards), 1962 v W; (with Coventry C.), 1962 v Ho; 1963 v E, S, W, Pol, Sp; 1964 v S, E, Sp; 1965 v S; (with Swansea T.), 1965 v W, Ho, Alb (14)

Hunter, A. (Blackburn R.), 1970 v USSR, 1971 v Cy (2), E, S, W; (with Ipswich T.), 1972 v USSR (2), Sp, E, S, W; 1973 v Bul, Cy (2), P, E, S, W; 1974 v Bul, S, E, W; 1975 v N, Se, Y, E, S, W; 1976 v Se, N, Y, Is, S, E, W; 1977 v Ho, Bel, WG, E, S, W, Ic; 1978 v Ic, Ho, Bel; 1979 v Ei, D, S, W, D (51)

Hunter, A. (Distillery), 1905 v W; 1906 v W, E, S; (with Belfast C.), 1908 v W: 1909 v W, E, S (8)

Hunter, R. J. (Cliftonville), 1884 v E, S, W (3)

Hunter, V. (Coleraine), 1962 v E; 1964 v Sp (2)

Irvine, R. W. (Everton), 1922 v S; 1923 v E, W; 1924 v E, S; 1925 v E; 1926 v E; 1927 v E, W; 1928 v E, S; (with Portsmouth), 1929 v E; 1930 v S; (with Connah's Quay), 1931 v E; (with Derry C.), 1932 v W (15)

Irvine, R. J. (Linfield), 1962 v Ho; 1963 v E, S, W, Pol (2), Sp; (with Stoke C.), 1965 v W (8)

Irvine, W. J. (Burnley), 1963 v W, Sp; 1965 v S, W, Sw, Ho (2), Alb; 1966 v S, E, W, M, Alb; 1967 v E, S, 1968 v E, W; (with Preston N.E.), 1969 v Is, T, E; (with Brighton), 1927 v E, S, W (23)

Irving, S. J. (Dundee), 1923 v S, W; 1924 v S, E, W; 1925 v S, E, W; 1926 v S, W; (with Cardiff C.), 1927 v S, E, W; 1928 v S, E, W; (with Chelsea), 1929 v E; 1931 v W (18)

Jackson, T. (Everton), 1969 v Is, E, S, W; 1970 v USSR (1+1 sub); (with Nottingham F.), 1971 v Sp; 1972 v E, S, W; 1973 v Cy, E, S, W; 1974 v Bul, P, S (sub), E (sub), W (sub); 1975 v N (sub), Se, Y, E, S, W; (with Manchester U.); 1976 v Se, N, Y; 1977 v Ho, Bel, WG, E, S, W Ic (35)

Jamison, J. (Glentoran), 1976 v N(1)

Jennings, P. A. (Watford), 1964 v W, U; (with Tottenham H.), 1965 v E, S, Sw (2), Ho, Alb; 1966 v S, E, W, Alb, WG; 1967 v E, S; 1968 v S, E, W; 1969 v Is, T (2), E, S, W; 1970 v S, E, USSR (2); 1971 v Cy (2), E, S, W; 1972 v USSR, Sp, S, E, W; 1973 v Bul, Cy, P, E, S, W; 1974 v P, S, E, W; 1975 v N, Se, Y, E, S, W; 1976 v Se, N, Y, Is, S, E, W; 1977 v Ho, Bel, WG, E, S, W, Ic; (with Arsenal), 1978 v Ic, Ho, Bel; 1979 v Ei, D, Bul, E, Bul, E, S, W, D (80)

Johnston, H. (Portadown), 1927 v W (1)

Johnston, R. (Old Park), 1885 v S, W (2)

Johnston, S. (Distillery), 1882 v W; 1884 v E; 1886 v E, S (4)

Johnston, S. (Linfield), 1890 v W; 1893 v S, W; 1894 v E (4)

Johnston, S. (Distillery), 1905 v W (1)

Johnston, W. C. (Glenavon), 1962 v W; (with Oldham), 1966 v M (sub) (2)

Jones, J. (Linfield), 1930 v S, W; 1931 v S, W, E; 1932 v S, E; 1933 v S, E, W; 1934 v S, E, W; 1935 v S, E, W; 1936 v E, S; (with Hibernian), 1936 v W; 1937 v E, W, S; (with Glenavon), 1938 v E (23)

Jones, J. (Glenavon), 1956 v W; 1957 v E, W (3)

Jones, S. (Distillery), 1934 v E; (with Blackpool), 1934 v W (2)

Jordan, T. (Linfield), 1895 v E, W (2)

Kavanagh, P. J. (Glasgow C.), 1930 v E (1)

Keane, T. R. (Swansea T.), 1949 v S (1)

Kearns, A. (Distillery), 1900 v E, S, W; 1902 v E, S, W (6)

Keith, R. M. (Newcastle U.), 1958 v E, W, Cz (2), Arg, I, WG, F; 1959 v E, S, W, Sp; 1960 v S, E; 1961 v S, E, W, I, WG (2), Gr; 1962 v W, Ho (23)
Kelly, H. R. (Fulham), 1950 v E, W; (with Southampton), 1951 v E, S (4)
Kelly, J. (Glentoran), 1896 v E (1)
Kelly, J. (Derry C.), 1932 v E, W; 1933 v E, W, S; 1934 v W; 1936 v E, S, W; 1937 v S, E (11)
Kelly, P. (Manchester C.), 1921 v E (1)
Kelly, P. M. (Barnsley), 1950 v S (1)
Kennedy, A. L. (Arsenal), 1923 v W; 1925 v E (2)
Kernaghan, N. (Belfast C.), 1936 v W; 1937 v S; 1938 v E (3)
Kirkwood, H. (Cliftonville), 1904 v W (1)
Kirwan, J. (Tottenham H.), 1900 v W; 1902 v E, W; 1903 v E, S, W; 1904 v E, S, W; 1905 v E, S, W; (with Chelsea), 1906 v E, S, W; 1907 v W; (with Clyde), 1909 v S (17)
Lacey, W. (Everton), 1909 v E, S, W; 1910 v E, S, W; 1911 v E, S, W; 1912 v E; (with Liverpool), 1913 v W; 1914 v E, S, W; 1920 v E, S, W; 1921 v E, S, W; 1922 v E, S; (with New Brighton), 1925 v E (23)
Lawther, W. I. (Sunderland), 1960 v W; 1961 v I; (with Blackburn R.) 1962 v S, Ho (3)
Leatham, J. (Belfast C.), 1939 v W (1)
Ledwidge, J. J. (Shelbourne), 1906 v S, W (2)
Lemon, J. (Glentoran), 1886 v W; 1888 v S; (with Belfast YMCA), 1889 v W (3)
Leslie, W. (YMCA), 1887 v E (1)
Lewis, J. (Glentoran), 1889 v S, E, W; (with Distillery), 1900 v S (4)
Little, J. (Glentoran), 1898 v W (1)
Lockhart, H. (Rossall School), 1884 v W (1)
Lockhart, N. (Linfield), 1947 v E; (with Coventry C.), 1950 v W; 1951 v W; 1952 v W; (with Aston Villa), 1954 v S, E; 1955 v W; 1956 v W (8)
Lowther, R. (Glentoran), 1888 v E, S (2)
Loyal, J. (Clarence), 1891 v S (1)
Lutton, R. J. (Wolverhampton W.), 1970 v S, E 1973 (with West Ham U.), Cy (sub), S (sub), W (sub); 1974 v P (6)
Lyner, D. (Glentoran), 1920 v E, W; 1922 v S, W; (with Manchester U.), 1923 v E; (with Kilmarnock), 1923 v W (6)

McAdams, W. J. (Manchester C.), 1954 v W; 1955 v S; 1957 v E; 1958 v S, I; (with Bolton W.), 1961 v E, S, W, I, WG (2), Gr; 1962 v E, Gr, (with Leeds U.), Ho (15)
M'Alery, J. M. (Cliftonville), 1882 v E, W (2)
M'Alinden, J. (Belfast C.), 1938 v S; 1939 v S; (with Portsmouth), 1947 v E; (with Southend U.), 1949 v E (4)
M'Allen, J. (Linfield), 1898 v E; 1899 v E, S, W; 1900 v E, S, W; 1901 v W; 1902 v S (9)
M'Alpine, W. J. (Cliftonville), 1901 v S (1)
M'Arthur, A. (Distillery), 1884 v W (1)
McAuley, P. (Belfast C.), 1900 v S (1)
M'Cabe, J. J. (Leeds U.), 1949 v S, W; 1950 v E; 1951 v W; 1953 v W; 1954 v S (6)
M'Cabe, W. (Ulster), 1891 v E (1)
M'Cambridge, J. (Ballymena), 1930 v S, W; (with Cardiff C.), 1931 v W; 1932 v E (4)
M'Candless, J. (Bradford), 1912 v W; 1913 v W; 1920 v W, S; 1921 v E (5)
McCandless, W. (Linfield), 1920 v E, W; 1921 v E; (with Rangers), 1921 v W; 1922 v S; 1924 v W, S; 1925 v S; 1929 v W (9)
M'Cann, P. (Belfast C.), 1910 v E, S, W; 1911 v E, (with Glentoran), 1911 v S; 1912 v E; 1913 v W (7)

M'Cashin, J. (Cliftonville), 1896 v W; 1898 v S, W; 1899 v S (4)
M'Cavana, W. T. (Coleraine), 1955 v S; 1956 v E, S (3)
M'Caw, D. (Distillery), 1882 v E (1)
M'Caw, J. H. (Linfield), 1927 v W; 1930 v S; 1931 v E, S, W (5)
M'Clatchey, J. (Distillery), 1886 v E, S, W (3)
M'Clatchey, R. (Distillery), 1895 v S (1)
M'Cleary, J. W. (Cliftonville), 1955 v W (1)
M'Cleery, W. (Cliftonville), 1922 v N; 1930 v E, W; 1931 v E, S, W; 1932 v S, W; 1938 v E, W (10)
McClelland, J. (Arsenal), 1961 v W, I, WG (2), Gr; (with Fulham), 1967 v M (6)
M'Cluggage, A. (Cliftonville), 1922 v N (2) (with Bradford), 1924 v E; (with Burnley), 1927 v S, W; 1928 v S, E, W; 1929 v S, E, W; 1930 v W; 1931 v E, W (14)
M'Clure, G. (Cliftonville), 1907 v S, W; 1908 v E; (with Distillery), 1909 v E (4)
M'Connell, E. (Cliftonville), 1904 v S, W; (with Glentoran), 1905 v S; (with Sunderland), 1906 v E; 1907 v E; 1908 v S, W; (with Sheffield W.), 1909 v S, W; 1910 v S, W, E (12)
M'Connell, W. G. (Bohemians), 1912 v W; 1913 v E, S; 1914 v E, S, W (6)
M'Connell, W. H. (Reading), 1925 v W; 1926 v E, W; 1927 v E, S, W; 1928 v E, W (8)
M'Court, F. J. (Manchester C.), 1952 v E, W; 1953 v E, S, W, F (6)
M'Coy, J. (Distillery), 1896 v W (1)
McCracken, R. (Linfield) 1922 v N (2)
M'Cracken, R. (C. Palace), 1921 v E; 1922 v E, S, W (4)
M'Cracken, W. (Distillery), 1902 v E, W; 1903 v E; 1904 v E, S, W; (with Newcastle U.), 1905 v E, S, W; 1907 v E; 1920 v E; 1922 v E, S, W; (with Hull C.), 1923 v S (15)
McCreery, D. (Manchester U.), 1976 v S (sub), E, W; 1977 v Ho, Bel, WG, E, S, W, Ic; 1978 v Ic, Ho, Bel, S, E, W; 1979 v Ei, D, Bul, E, Bul, W, D (23)
McCrory, S. (Southend U.), 1958 v E (1)
M'Cullough, K. (Belfast C.), 1935 v W; 1936 v E; (with Manchester C.), 1936 v S; 1937 v E, S (5)
McCullough, W. J. (Arsenal), 1961 v I; 1963 v Sp; 1964 v S, E, W, U, Sp; 1965 v E, Sw; (with Millwall), 1967 v E (10)
M'Donald, R. (Glasgow R.), 1930 v S; 1932 v E (2)
M'Donnell, J. (Bohemians), 1911 v E, S; 1912 v W; 1913 v W (4)
M'Faul, W. S. (Linfield), 1967 v E (sub); (with Newcastle U.) 1970 v W; 1971 v Sp; 1972 v USSR; 1973 v Cy; 1974 v Bul (6)
M'Garry, J. K. (Cliftonville), 1951 v W, F, S (3)
M'Gee, G. (Willington Park), 1885 v E, S, W (3)
M'Grath, R. C. (Tottenham H.), 1974 v S, E, W; 1975 v N; 1976 v Is (sub); (with Manchester U.), 1977 v Ho, Bel, WG, E, S, W, Ic; 1978 v Ic, Ho, Bel, S, E, W; 1979 v Bul (sub), E (sub), E (sub) (21)
M'Gregor, S. (Glentoran), 1921 v S (1)
M'Grillen, J. (Clyde), 1924 v S; (with Belfast C.) 1927 v S (2)
M'Ilroy, H. (Cliftonville), 1906 v E (1)
McIlroy, J. (Burnley), 1952 v E, S, W; 1953 v E, S, W; 1954 v E, S, W; 1955 v E, S, W; 1956 v E, S, W; 1957 v E, S, W, I, P (2); 1958 v E, S, W, I (2), Cz (2), Arg, WG, F; 1959 v E, S, W, Sp; 1960 v E, S, W; 1961 v E, W, WG (2) Gr; 1962 v E, S, Gr, Ho; 1963 v E, S, Pol (2); (with Stoke C.), 1963 v W; 1966 v S, E, A (55)

McIlroy, S. B. (Manchester U.), 1972 v Sp, S (sub); 1974 v S, E, W; 1975 v N, Se, Y, E, S, W; 1976 v Se, N, Y, S, E, W; 1977 v Ho, Bel, E, S, W, Ic; 1978 v Ic, Ho, Bel, S, E, W; 1979 v Ei, D, Bul, E, Bul, E, S, W, D (38)
M'Ilvenny, J. (Distillery). 1890 v E; 1891 v E (2)
M'Ilvenny, P. (Distillery), 1924 v W (1)
McKeag, W. (Glentoran), 1968 v S, W (2)
M'Kee, F. W. (Cliftonville), 1906 v S, W; (with Belfast C.), 1914 v E, S, W (5)
M'Kelvie, H. (Glentoran), 1901 v W (1)
McKenna, J. (Huddersfield), 1950 v E, S, W; 1951 v E, S, F; 1952 v E (7)
M'Kenzie, H. (Distillery), 1922 v N (2); 1923 v S (3)
McKenzie, R. (Airdrie), 1967 v W (1)
M'Keown, H. (Linfield), 1892 v E, S, W; 1893 v S, W; 1894 v S, W (7)
M'Kie, H. (Cliftonville), 1895 v E, S, W (3)
M'Kinney, D. (Hull C.), 1921 v S; (with Bradford C.), 1924 v S (2).
McKinney, V. J. (Falkirk), 1966 v WG (1)
M'Knight, J. (Preston N.E.), 1912 v S; (with Glentoran), 1913 v S (2)
McLaughlin, J. C. (Shrewsbury T.), 1962 v E, S, W, Gr; 1963 v W; with (Swansea T.), 1964 v W, U; 1965 v E, W, Sw (2); 1966 v W (12)
M'Lean. T. (Limavady), 1885 v S (1)
M'Mahon, J. (Bohemians), 1934 v S (1)
M'Master, G. (Glentoran), 1897 v E, S, W (3)
McMichael, A. (Newcastle U.), 1950 v E, S; 1951 v E, S, F; 1952 v E, S, W; 1953 v E, S, W, F; 1954 v E, S, W; 1955 v E, W; 1956 v W; 1957 v E, S, W, I, P (2); 1958 v E, S, W, I (2), Cz (2), Arg, WG, F; 1959 v S, W, Sp; 1960 v E, S, W (40)
M'Millan, G. (Distillery), 1903 v E; 1905 v W (2)
McMillan, S. (Manchester U.), 1963 v E, S (2)
M'Millen, W. S. (Manchester U.), 1934 v E; 1935 v S; 1937 v S; (with Chesterfield), 1938 v S, W; 1939 v E, S (7)
McMordie, A. S. (Middlesbrough), 1969 v Is, T (2), E, S, W; 1970 v E, S, W, USSR; 1971 v Cy (2) E, S, W; 1972 v USSR, Sp, E, S, W; 1973; v Bul (21)
McMorran, E. J. (Belfast C.), 1947 v E; (with Barnsley), 1951 v E, S, W; 1952 v E, S, W; 1953 v E, S, F; (with Doncaster R.), 1953 v W; 1954 v E; 1956 v W; 1957 v I, P (15)
M'Mullan, D. (Liverpool), 1926 v E, W; 1927 v S (3)
M'Ninch, J. (Ballymena), 1931 v S; 1932 v S, W (3)
McParland, P. J. (Aston Villa), 1954 v W; 1955 v E, S; 1956 v E, S; 1957 v E, S, W, P; 1958 v E, S, W, I (2), Cz (2), Arg, WG, F; 1959 v E, S, W, Sp; 1960 v E, S, W; 1961 v E, S, W, I, WG (2), Gr; (with Wolverhampton W.), 1962 v Ho (34)
M'Shane, J. (Cliftonville), 1899 v S; 1900 v E, S, W (4)
M'Vickers, J. (Glentoran), 1888 v E; 1889 v S (2)
M'Wha, W. B. R. (Knock), 1882 v E, W; (with Cliftonville) 1883 v E, W; 1884 v E; 1885 v E, W (7)
Macartney, A. (Ulster), 1903 v S, W; (with Linfield) 1904 v S, W; (with Everton) 1905 v E, S; (with Belfast C.), 1907 v E, S, W; 1908 v E, S, W; (with Glentoran) 1909 v E, S, W (15)
Macauley, J. L. (Huddersfield T.) 1911 v E, W; 1912 v E, S; 1913 v E, S (6)
Mackie, J. (Arsenal), 1923 v W; (with Portsmouth), 1935 v S, W (3)
Madden, O. (Norwich C.), 1938 v E (1)
Magill, E. J. (Arsenal), 1962 v E, S, Gr; 1963 v E, S, W, Pol (2), Sp; 1964 v E, S, W, U, Sp; 1965 v E, S, Sw (2), Ho, Alb; 1966 v S, Alb; (with Brighton), 1966 v E, W, WG, M (26)
Maginnis, H. (Linfield), 1900 v E, S, W; 1903 v S, W; 1904 v E, S, W (8)
Maguire, E. (Distillery) 1907 v S (1)
Mahood, J. (Belfast C.), 1926 v S; 1928 v E, S, W; 1929 v E, S, W; 1930 v W; (with Ballymena), 1934 v S (9)
Manderson, R. (Glasgow R.), 1920 v W, S; 1925 v S, E; 1926 v S (5)
Mansfield, J. (Dublin Freebooters), 1901 v E (1)
Martin, C. (Bo'ness), 1925 v S (1)
Martin, C. J. (Glentoran), 1947 v S; (with Leeds U), 1948 v E, S, W; (with Aston Villa), 1949 v E; 1950 v W (6)
Martin, D. (Bo'ness), 1925 v S (1)
Martin, D. C. (Cliftonville), 1882 v E, W; 1883 v E (3)
Martin, D. K. (Belfast C.), 1934 v E, S, W; 1935 v S; (with Wolverhampton W.), 1935 v E; 1936 v W; (with Nottingham F.), 1937 v S; 1938 v E, S; 1939 v S (10)
Mathieson, A. (Luton T.), 1921 v W; 1922 v E (2)
Maxwell, J. (Linfield), 1902 v W; 1903 v W, E; (with Glentoran), 1905 v W, S; (with Belfast C.), 1906 v W; 1907 v S (7)
Meek, H. L. (Glentoran), 1922 v N (2); 1925 v W (3)
Mehaffy, J. A. C. (Queen's Island), 1922 v W (1)
Meldon, J. (Dublin Freebooters), 1899 v S, W (2)
Mercer, H. V. A. (Linfield), 1908 v E (1)
Mercer, J. T. (Distillery), 1898 v E, S, W; 1899 v E; (with Linfield), 1902 v E, W; (with Distillery), 1903 v S, W; (with Derby Co.), 1904 v E, W; 1905 v S (11)
Millar, W. (Barrow), 1932 v W; 1933 v S (2)
Miller, J. (Middlesbrough), 1929 v W S; 1930 v E (3)
Milligan, D. (Chesterfield), 1939 v W (1)
Milne, R. G. (Linfield), 1894 v E, S, W; 1895 v E, W; 1896 v E, S, W; 1897 v E, S; 1898 v E, S, W; 1899 v E, W; 1901 v W; 1902 v E, S, W; 1903 v E, S; 1904 v E, S, W; 1906 v E, S, W (27)
Mitchell, C. (Glentoran), 1934 v W (1)
Mitchell, E. J. (Cliftonville), 1933 v S (1)
Mitchell, W. (Distillery), 1932 v E, W; 1933 v E, W; (with Chelsea), 1934 v W, S; 1935 v S, E; 1936 v S, E; 1937 v E, S, W; 1938 v E, S (15)
Molyneux, T. B. (Ligoniel), 1883 v E, W; (with Cliftonville) 1884 v E, W, S; 1885 v E, W; 1886 v E, W, S; 1888 v S (11)
Montgomery, F. J. (Coleraine), 1955 v E (1)
Moore, C. (Glentoran), 1949 v W (1)
Moore, J. (Linfield Ath.), 1891 v E, S, W (3)
Moore, P. (Aberdeen), 1933 v E (1)
Moore, T. (Ulster), 1887 v S, W (2)
Moorhead, F. W. (Dublin University), 1885 v E (1)
Moorhead, G. (Linfield); 1923 v S; 1928 v S; 1929 v S (3)
Moran, J. (Leeds C.), 1912 v S (1)
Moreland, V. (Derby Co.), 1979 v Bul (sub), Bul (sub), E, S (4)
Morgan, F. G. (Linfield), 1922 v N (2); 1923 v E; (with Nottingham F.), 1924 v S; 1927 v E; 1928 v E, S, W; 1929 v E (9)
Morgan, S. (Port Vale), 1972 v Sp; 1973 v Bul (sub) P, Cy, E, S, W; (with Aston Villa) 1974 v Bul, P, S, E; 1975 v Se; 1976 v Se, N, Y (with Brighton & H.A.), S, W (sub); (Sparta Rotterdam), 1979 v D,
Morrison, J. (Linfield Ath.), 1891 v E, W (2)
Morrison, T. (Glentoran), 1895 v E, S, W; (with Burnley); 1899 v W; 1900 v W; 1902 v E, S (7)

Morrogh, E. (Bohemians), 1896 v S (1)
Morrow, W. J. (Moyola Park), 1883 v E, W; 1884 v S (3)
Muir, R. (Old Park), 1885 v S, W (2)
Mulholland, S. (Celtic), 1906 v S, E (2)
Mulligan, J. (Manchester C.), 1921 v S (1)
Murphy, J. (Bradford C.), 1910 v E, S, W (3)
Murphy, N. (Q.P.R.), 1905 v E, S, W (3)
Murray, J. M. (Motherwell), 1910 v E, S; (with Sheffield W.), 1910 v W (3)

Napier, R. J. (Bolton W.), 1966 v WG (1)
Neill, W. J. T. (Arsenal), 1961 v I, Gr, WG; 1962 v E, S, W, Gr; 1963 v E, W, Pol, Sp; 1964 v S, E, W, U, Sp; 1965 v E, S, W, Sw, Ho (2), Alb; 1966 v S, E, W, Alb, WGM; 1967 v S, W; 1968 v S, E) 1969 v E, S, W, Is, T (2); 1970 v E, W, USSR (2); (with Hull C.), 1971 v Cy, Sp; 1972 v USSR (2), Sp, S, E, W; 1973 v Bul, Cy, (2), P, E, S, W (59)
Nelis P. (Nottingham F.), 1923 v E (1)
Nelson, S. (Arsenal), 1970 v W, E (sub); 1971 v Cy, Sp, E, S, W; 1972 v USSR (2), Sp, E, S, W; 1973 v Bul, Cy, P; 1974 v S, E; 1975 v Se, Y; 1976 v Se, N, Is, E; 1977 v Bel (sub), WG, W, Ic; 1978 v Ic, Ho, Bel, W (sub); 1979 v Ei, D, Bul, E, Bul, E, S, W, D (41)
Nicholl, C. J. (Aston Villa), 1975 v Se, Y, E, S, W; 1976 v Se, N, Y, S, E, W; 1977 v W; (with Southampton), 1978 v Bel (sub), S, E, W; 1979 v Ei, Bul, E, Bul, E, W (22)
Nicholl, J. M. (Manchester U.), 1976 v Is, W (sub); 1977 v Ho, Bel, E, S, W, Ic; 1978 v Ic, Ho, Bel, S, E, W; 1979 v Ei, D, Bul, E, Bul, E, S, W, D (23)
Nicholl, H. (Belfast C.), 1902 v E, W; 1905 v E (3),
Nicholson, J. J. (Manchester U.), 1961 v S, W; 1962 v E, W, Gr, Ho; 1963 v E, S, Pol (2); (with Huddersfield T.), 1965 v W, Ho (2); Alb; 1966 v S, E, W, Alb, M; 1967 v S, W; 1968 v S, E, W; 1969 v S, E, W, T (2); 1970 v E, S, W, USSR (2); 1971 v Cy (2), E, S, W; 1972 v USSR (2)(41)
Nixon, R. (Linfield), 1914 v S (1)
Nolan-Whelan, J. V. (Dublin Freebooters), 1901 E, W; 1902 v S, W (4)

O'Brien, M. T. (Q.P.R.), 1921 v S; (with Leicester C.), 1922 v S, W; 1924 v S, W; (with Hull C.), 1925 v S, E, W; 1926 v W; (with Derby Co.), 1927 v W (10)
O'Connell, P. (Sheffield W.), 1912 v E, S; (with Hull C.), 1914 v E, S, W (5)
O'Doherty, A. (Coleraine), 1970 v E, A, W (sub) (2)
O'Driscoll, J. F. (Swansea T.), 1949 v E, S, W (3)
O'Hagan, C. (Tottenham H.), 1905 v S, W; 1906 v S, W, E; (with Aberdeen), 1907 v E, S, W; 1908 v S, W; 1909 v E (11)
O'Hagan, W. (St. Mirren), 1920 v E, W (2)
O'Hehir, J. C. (Bohemians), 1910 v W (1)
O'Kane, W. J. (Nottingham F.), 1970 v E, W, S (sub); 1971 v Sp, E, S, W; 1972 v USSR (2), 1973 v P, Cy; 1974 v Bul, P, S, E, W; 1975 v N; Se, E, S (20)
O'Mahoney, M. T. (Bristol R.), 1939 v S (1)
O'Neill, J. (Sunderland), 1962 v W (1)
O'Neill, M. H. (Distillery), 1972 v USSR (sub); (with Nottingham F.) Sp (sub), W (sub); 1973 v P, Cy, E, S, W; 1974 v Bul, P, E (sub), W; 1975 v Se, Y, E, S; 1976 v Y; 1977 v E (sub), S; 1978 v Ic, Ho, S, E, W; 1979 v Ei, D, Bul, E, Bul, D (30)
O'Reilly, H. (Dublin Freebooters), 1901 v S, W; 1904 v S (3)

Parke, J. (Linfield), 1964 v S; (with Hibernian), 1964 v E, Sp; (with Sunderland), 1965 v Sw; 1965 v S, W, Ho (2), Alb; 1966 v WG; 1967 v E, S; 1968 v S, E (14)
Peacock, R. (Celtic), 1952 v S; 1953 v F; 1954 v W; 1955 v E, S; 1956 v E, S; 1957 v W, I, P; 1958 v S, E, W, I (2), Arg, Cz (2) WG; 1959 v E, S, W, Sp; 1960 v S, E; 1961 v E, S, I, WG (2), Gr; (with Coleraine), 1962 v S (32)
Peden, J. (Linfield), 1887 v S, W; 1888 v W, E; 1889 v S, E; 1890 v W, S; 1891 v W, E; 1892 v W, E; 1893 v E, S, W; (with Distillery), 1896 v W, E, S; 1897 v W, S; 1898 v W, E, S; (with Linfield), 1899 v W (24)
Percy, J. C. (Belfast YMCA), 1889 v W (1)
Platt, J. A. (Middlesbrough), 1976 v Is (sub); 1978 v S, E, W (4)
Posonby, J. (Distillery), 1895 v S; 1896 v E, S, W; 1897 v E, S, W; 1899 v E (8)
Potts, R. M. C. (Cliftonville), 1833 v E, W (2)
Priestley, T. J. (Coleraine), 1933 v S; (with Chelsea), 1934 v E (2)
Pyper, Jas. (Cliftonville), 1897 v S, W; 1898 S, v E, W; 1899 v S; 1900 v E (7)
Pyper, John (Cliftonville), 1897 v E, S, W; 1899 v E, W; 1900 v E, W, S; 1902 v S (9)
Pyper, M. (Linfield), 1931 v W (1)

Rankine, J. (Alexander), 1883 v E, W (2)
Raper, E. O. (Dublin University), 1886 v W (1)
Rattray, D. (Avoniel), 1882 v E; 1883 v E, W (3)
Rea, B. (Glentoran), 1901 v E (1)
Redmond, J. (Cliftonville), 1884 v W (1)
Reid, G. H. (Cardiff C.), 1923 v S (1)
Reid, J. (Ulster), 1883 v E; 1884 v W; 1887 v S; 1889 v W; 1890 v S, W (6)
Reid, S. E. (Derby Co.), 1934 v E. W; 1936 v E (3)
Reid, W. (Hearts), 1931 v E (1)
Reilly, J. (Portsmouth), 1900 v E; 1902 v E (2)
Renneville, W. T. (Leyton), 1910 v S, E, W; (with Aston Villa), 1911 v W (4)
Reynolds, J. (Distillery), 1890 v E, W; (with Ulster), 1891 v ES, W (5)
Reynolds, R. (Bohemians), 1905 v W (1)
Rice, P. J. (Arsenal), 1969 v Is; 1970 v USSR; 1971 v E, S, W; 1972 v USSR, Sp, E, S, W; 1973 v Bul, Cy, E, S, W; 1974 v Bul, P, S, E, W; 1975 v N, Y, E, S, W; 1976 v Se, N, Y, Is, S, E, W; 1977 v Ho, Bel, WG, E, S, Ic; 1978 v Ic, Ho, Bel; 1979 v Ei, D, E (2), S, W, D (48)
Roberts, F. C. (Glentoran), 1931 v S (1)
Robinson, P. (Distillery), 1920 v S; (with Blackburn R.), 1921 v W (2)
Rollo, D. (Linfield), 1912 v W; 1913 v W; 1914 v W, E; (with Blackburn R.), 1920 v S, W; 1921 v E, S, W; 1922 v E; 1923 v E; 1924 v S, W; 1925 v W; 1926 v E; 1927 v E (16)
Rosbotham, A. (Cliftonville), 1887 v E, S, W; 1888 v E, S, W; 1889 v E (7)
Ross, W. E. (Newcastle U.), 1969 v Is (1)
Rowley, R. W. M. (Southampton), 1929 v S, W; 1930 v W, E; (with Tottenham H.), 1931 v W; 1932 v S (6)
Russell, A. (Linfield), 1947 v E (1)
Russell, S. R. (Bradford C.), 1930 v E, S; (with Derry C.), 1932 v E (3)
Ryan, R. A. (W.B.A.), 1950 v W (1)

Scott, E. (Liverpool), 1920 v S; 1921 v E, S, W; 1922 v E; 1925 v W; 1926 v E, S, W; 1927 v E, S, W; 1928 v E, S, W; 1929 v E, S, W; 1930 v E; 1931 v E; 1932 v S; 1933 v E, S, W; 1934 v E,

S, W; (with Belfast C.), 1935 v S; 1936 v E, S, W (30)
Scott, J. (Grimsby), 1958 v Cz, F (2)
Scott, J. E. (Cliftonville), 1901 v S (1)
Scott, L. J. (Dublin University), 1895 v S, W (2)
Scott, P. W. (Everton), 1975 v W; 1976 v Y (with York C.), Is, S, E (sub), W; 1978 v S, E, W; (Aldershot), 1979 v S (sub) (10)
Scott, T. (Cliftonville), 1894 v E, S; 1895 v S, W; 1896 v S, E, W; 1897 v E, W; 1988 v E, S, W; 1900 v W (13)
Scott, W. (Linfield), 1903 v E, S, W; 1904 v E, S, W; (with Everton) 1905 v E, S; 1907 v E, S; 1908 v E, S, W; 1909 v E, S, W; 1910 v E, S; 1911 v E, W; 1912 v E; (with Leeds City) 1913 v E, S, W (25)
Scraggs, M. J. (Glentoran), 1921 v W; 1922 v E (2)
Seymour, H. C. (Bohemians), 1914 v W (1)
Seymour, J. (Cliftonville), 1907-9 v W (2)
Shanks, T.(Woolwich Arsenal), 1903 v S; 1904 v W; (with Brentford), 1905 v E (3)
Sharkey, P. (Ipswich T.), 1976 v S (1)
Sheehan, Dr. G. (Bohemians), 1899 v S; 1900 v E, W (3)
Sheridan, J. (Everton), 1903 v W, E, S; 1904 v E, S; (with Stoke C.), 1905 v E (6)
Sherrard, J. (Limavady), 1885 v S; 1887 v W 1888; v W (3)
Sherrard, W. (Cliftonville), 1895 v E, W, S (3)
Sherry, J. J. (Bohemians), 1906 v E; 1907 v W (2)
Shields, J. (Southampton), 1957 v S (1)
Silo, M. (Belfast YMCA), 1888 v E (1)
Simpson, W. J. (Glasgow R.), 1951 v W, F; 1954 v E, S; 1955 v E; 1957 v I, P; 1958 v S, E, W, I; 1959 v S (12)
Sinclair, J. (Knock), 1882 v E, W (2)
Slemin, J. C. (Bohemians), 1909 v W (1)
Sloan, A. S. (London Caledonians), 1925 v W (1)
Sloan, D. (Oxford U.), 1969 v Is; 1971 v Sp (2)
Sloan, H. A. de B. (Bohemians), 1903 v E; 1904 v S; 1905 v E; 1906 v S; 1907 v E, W; 1908 v W; 1909 v S (8)
Sloan, J. W. (Arsenal), 1947 v W (1)
Sloan, T. (Cardiff C.), 1926 v S, W. E; 1927 v W, S; 1928 v E, W; 1929 v E; (with Linfield), 1930 v W, S; 1931 v S (11)
Sloan, T (Manchester U.), 1979 v S, W (sub), D (sub) (3)
Small, J. (Clarence), 1887 v E (1)
Small, J. M. (Cliftonville) 1893 v E, S, W (3)
Smith, E. E. (Cardiff C.), 1921 v S; 1923 v W, E; 1924 v E (4)
Smith, J. (Distillery), 1901 v S, W (2)
Smyth, R. H. (Dublin University), 1886 v W (1)
Smyth, S. (Wolverhampton W.), 1948 v E, S, W; 1949 v S, W; 1950 v E, S, W; (with Stoke C.), 1952 v E (9)
Smyth, W. (Distillery), 1949 v E, S; 1954 v S, E (4)
Snape, A. (Airdrie), 1920 v E (1)
Spence, D. W. (Bury), 1975 v Y, E, S, W; 1976 v Se, Is, E, W, S (sub); (with Blackpool); 1977 v Ho (sub), WG (sub), E (sub), S (sub), W (sub), Ic (sub); 1979 v Ei, D (sub), E (sub), Bul (sub), E (sub), S, W, D (23)
Spencer, S. (Distillery), 1890 v E, S; 1892 v E, S, W; 1893 v E (6)
Spiller, E. A. (Cliftonville), 1883 v E, W; 1884 v E, W, S (5)
Stanfield, O. M. (Distillery), 1887 v E, S, W; 1888 v E, S, W; 1889 v E, S, W; 1890 v E, S; 1891 v E, S, W; 1892 v E, S, W; 1893 v E, W; 1894 v E, S, W; 1895 v E, S; 1896 v E, S, W; 1897 v E, S, W (30)
Steele, A. (Charlton Ath.), 1926 v W, S; (with Fulham), 1929 v W, S (4)
Stevenson, A. E. (Rangers), 1934 v E, S, W; (with Everton), 1935 v S; 1936 v S, W; 1937 v E, W; 1938 v E, W; 1939 v E, S, W; 1947 v S, W; 1948 v S (17)
Stewart, A. (Glentoran), 1967 v W; 1968 v S, E; (with Derby Co.), 1968 v W; 1969 v Is, T (1 + 1 sub) (7)
Stewart, D. C., (Hull C.), 1978 v Bel (1)
Stewart, R. H. (St. Columbia Court), 1890 v E, S, W; (with Cliftonville), 1892 v E, S, W; 1893 v E, W; 1894 v E, S, W (11)
Stewart, T, C, (Linfield), 1961 v W (1)
Swan, S. (Linfield). 1899 v S (1)

Taggart, J. (Walsall), 1899 v W (1)
Thompson, F. W. (Cliftonville), 1910 v E, S, W; (with Bradford C.), 1911 v E, (with Linfield), v W; 1912 v E, W; 1913 v E, S, W; (with Clyde), 1914 v v E, S (12)
Thompson, J. (Distillery), 1897 v S (1)
Thompson, J. (Belfast Ath.), 1889 v S (1)
Thunder, P. J. (Bohemians), 1911 v W (1)
Todd, S. J. (Burnley), 1966 v M (sub); 1967 v E; 1968 v W; 1969 v E, S, W; 1970 v S, USSR (Sheffield W.), 1971 v Cy (2) Sp (sub) (11)
Toner, J. (Arsenal), 1922 v W; 1923 v W; 1924 v W, E; 1925 v E, S; (with St. Johnstone), 1927 v E, S (8)
Torrans, R. (Linfield), 1893 v S (1)
Torrans, S. (Linfield), 1889 v S; 1890 v S, W; 1891 v S, W; 1892 v E, S, W; 1893 v E, S; 1894 v E, S, W; 1895 v E; 1896 v E, S, W; 1897 v E, S, W; 1898 v E, S, W; 1899 v E; 1901 v S, W (26)
Trainor, D. (Crusaders), 1967 v W (1)
Tully, C. P. (Glasgow C.), 1949 v E; 1950 v E; 1952 v S; 1953 v E, S, W, F; 1954 v S; 1956 v E; 1959 v Sp (10)
Turner, E. (Cliftonville), 1896 v E, W (2)
Turner, W. (Cliftonville), 1886 v E; 1886 v S; 1888 v S (3)
Twoomey, J. F. (Leeds U.), 1938 v W; 1939 v E (2)

Uprichard, W. N. M. C. (Swindon T.), 1952, v E, S, W; 1953 v E, S; (with Portsmouth), 1953 v W, F; 1955–6 v E, S, W; 1956 v E, S, W; 1958 v S, I, Cz; 1959 v S, Sp (18)

Vernon, J. (Belfast C.), 1947 v E, S; (with W.B.A.), 1947 v W; 1948 v E, S, W; 1949 v E, S, W; 1950 v E, S; 1951 v E, S, W, F; 1952 v S, E (17)

Waddell, T. M. R. (Cliftonville), 1906 v S (1)
Walker, J. (Doncaster R.), 1955 v W (1)
Walker, T. (Bury), 1911 v S (1)
Walsh, D. J. (W.B.A.), 1947 v S, W; 1948 v E, S, W; 1949 v E, S, W; 1950 v W (9)
Walsh, W. (Manchester C.), 1948 v E, S, W; 1949 v E, S (5)
Waring, R. (Distillery), 1899 v E (1)
Warren, P. (Shelbourne), 1913 v E, S (2)
Watson, J. (Ulster), 1883 v E, W; 1886 v E, S, W; 1887 v S, W; 1889 v E, W (9)
Watson, P. (Distillery) v Cy (sub), (1)
Watson, T. (Cardiff C.), 1926 v S (1)
Wattle. J. (Distillery), 1899 v E (1)
Webb, C. G. (Brighton), 1909 v S, W; 1911 v S (3)
Weir, E. (Clyde), 1939 v W (1)
Welsh, E. (Carlisle U.), 1966 v W, WG, M; 1967 v W (4)

Whiteside, T. (Distillery), 1891 v E (1)
Whitfield, E. R. (Dublin University), 1886 v W (1)
Williams, J. R. (Ulster), 1886 v E, W (2)
Williamson, J. (Cliftonville), 1890 v E; 1892 v S, 1893 v S (3)
Willigham, T. (Burnley), 1933 v W; 1934 v S (2)
Willis, G. (Linfield), 1906 v S, W; 1907 v S; 1912 v S (4)
Wilson, H. (Linfield), 1925 v W (1)
Wilson, M. (Distillery), 1884 v E, S, W (3)
Wilson, R. (Cliftonville), 1888 v S (1)
Wilson, S. J. (Glenavon), 1962 v S; 1964 v S; (with Falkirk), 1964 v E, W, U, Sp; 1965 v E, Sw; (with Dundee), 1966 v W, WG; 1967 v S; 1968 v E (12)
Wilton, J. M. (St. Columbia Court), 1888 v E, W; 1889 v S, E; (with Cliftonville), 1890 v E; (with St. Columbia Court), 1892 v W; 1893 v S (7)
Wright, J. (Cliftonville), 1906 v E, S, W; 1907 v E, S, W (6)
Young, S. (Linfield), 1907 v E, S; 1908 v E, S; (with Airdrie), 1909 v E; 1912 v S; (with Linfield), 1914 v E, S, W (9)

SCOTLAND

Adams, J. (Hearts), 1889 v Ni; 1892 v W; 1893 v Ni (3)
Agnew, W. B. (Kilmarnock), 1907 v Ni; 1908 v W Ni (3)
Aird, J. (Burnley), 1954 v N (2), A, U (4)
Aitken, A. (Newcastle U.), 1901 v E; 1902 v E; 1903 v E, W; 1904 v E; 1905 v E, W; 1906 v E; (with Middlesbrough), 1907 v E, W; 1908 v E; (with Leicester Fosse), 1910 v E; 1911 v E, Ni(14)
Aitken, G. G. (East Fife), 1949 v E, F; 1950 v W, Ni, Sw; (with Sunderland), 1953 v W, Ni; 1954 v E (8)
Aitken, R. (Dumbarton), 1886 v E; 1888 v Ni (2)
Aitkenhead, W. A. C. (Blackburn R.), 1912 v Ni (1)
Alexander, D. (East Stirlingshire), 1894 v W, Ni (2)
Allan, D. S. (Queen's Park), 1885 v E, W; 1886 v W (3)
Allan, G. (Liverpool), 1897 v E (1)
Allan, H. (Hearts), 1902 v W (1)
Allan, J. (Queen's Park), 1887 v E, W (2)
Allan, T. (Dundee) 1974 v WG, N (2)
Ancell, R. F. D. (Newcastle U.), 1937 v W, Ni (2)
Anderson, A. (Hearts), 1933 v E; 1934 v A, E, W, Ni; 1935 v E, W, Ni; 1936 v E, W, Ni, 1937 v G, E, W, Ni, A; 1938 v E, W, Ni, Cz, Ho; 1939 v W, H (23)
Anderson, F. (Clydesdale), 1874 v E (1)
Anderson G. (Kilmarnock), 1901 v Ni (1)
Anderson, H. A. (Raith R.), 1914 v W (1)
Anderson, J. (Leicester C.), 1954 v Fi (1)
Anderson, K. (Queen's Park), 1896 v Ni; 1898 v E, Ni (3)
Anderson, W. (Queen's Park), 1882 v E; 1883 v E, W; 1884 v E; 1885 v E, W (6)
Andrews, P. (Eastern), 1875 v E (1)
Archibald, A. (Rangers), 1921 v W; 1922 v W, E; 1923 v Ni; 1924 v E, W; 1931 v E; 1932 v E (8)
Armstrong, M. W. (Aberdeen), 1936 v W, Ni; 1937 v G (3)
Arnott, W. (Queen's Park), 1883 v W; 1884 v E, Ni; 1885 v E, W; 1886 v E; 1887 v E, W; 1888 v E; 1889 v E; 1890 v E; 1891 v E; 1892 v E; 1893 v E (14)
Auld, J. R. (Third Lanark), 1887 v E, W; 1889 v W (3)

Auld, R. (Celtic), 1959 v H, P; 1960 v W (3)

Baird, A. (Queen's Park), 1892 v Ni; 1894 v W (2)
Baird, D. (Hearts), 1890 v Ni; 1891 v E; 1892 v W (3)
Baird, H. (Airdrie), 1956 v A (1)
Baird, J. C. (Vale of Leven), 1876 v E; 1878 v W; 1880 v E (3)
Baird, S. (Rangers), 1957 v Y, Sp (2), Sw, WG; 1958 v F, Ni(7)
Baird, W. U. (St. Bernard), 1897 v Ni(1)
Barbour, A. (Renton), 1885 v Ni (1)
Barker, J. B. (Rangers), 1893 v W; 1894; v W (2)
Barrett, F. (Dundee), 1894 v Ni; 1895 v W (2)
Battles, B. (Celtic), 1901 v E, W, Ni (3)
Battles, B. jun. (Hearts), 1931 v W (1)
Bauld, W. (Hearts), 1950 v E, Sw, P (3)
Baxter, J. C. (Rangers), 1961 v Ni, Ei(2), Cz; 1962 v Ni, W, E, Cz (2), U; 1963 v W, Ni, E, A, N, Ei, Sp; 1964 v W, E, N, WG; 1965 v W, Ni, Fi; (with Sunderland), 1966 v P, Br, Ni, W, E, I; 1967 v W, E, USSR; 1968 v W (34)
Baxter, R. D. (Middlesbrough), 1939 v E, W, H (3)
Beattie, A. (Preston N.E.), 1937 v E, A, Cz; 1938 v E; 1939 v W, Ni, H (7)
Beattie, R. (Preston N.E.), 1939 v W (1)
Begbie, I. (Hearts), 1890 v Ni; 1891 v E; 1982 v W; 1894 v E (4)
Bell, A. (Manchester U.), 1912 v Ni (1)
Bell, J. (Dumbarton), 1890 v Ni; 1892 v E; (with Everton), 1896 v E; 1897 v E; 1898 v E; (with Celtic), 1899 v E, W, Ni; 1900 v E, W (10)
Bell, M. (Hearts), 1901 v W (1)
Bell, W. J. (Leeds U.), 1966 v P, Br (2)
Bennett, A. (Celtic), 1904 v W; 1907 v Ni; 1908 v W; (with Rangers), 1909 v W, Ni, E; (1910 v E, W; 1911 v E, W; 1913 v Ni(11)
Bennie, R. (Airdrieonians), 1925 v W, Ni; 1926 v Ni (3)
Berry, D. (Queen's Park), 1894 v W; 1899 v W, Ni (3)
Berry, W. H. (Queen's Park), 1888 v E; 1889 v E; 1890 v E; 1891 v E (4)
Beveridge, W. W. (Glasgow University), 1879 v E, W; 1880 v W (3)
Black, A. (Hearts), 1938 v Cz, Ho; 1939 v H (3)
Black, D. (Hurlford), 1889 v Ni (1)
Black, I. H. (Southampton), 1948 v E (1)
Blackburn, J. E. (Royal Engineers), 1873 v E (1)
Blacklaw, A. S. (Burnley), 1963 v N, Sp; 1966 v I (3)
Blackley, J. (Hibernian), 1974 v Cz, E, Bel, Z; 1976 v Sw; 1977 v W Se (7)
Blair, D. (Clyde), 1929 v W, Ni; 1931 v E, A, I; 1932 v W, Ni; (with Aston Villa), 1933 v W (8)
Blair, J. (Sheffield W.), 1920 v E, Ni; (with Cardiff C.), 1921 v E; 1922 v E; 1923 v E, W, Ni; 1924 v W (8)
Blair, J. (Motherwell), 1934 v W (1)
Blair, J. A. (Blackpool), 1947 v W (1)
Blair, W. (Third Lanark), 1896 v W (1)
Blessington J. (Celtic), 1894 v E, Ni; 1896 v E, Ni (4)
Blyth, J. A. (Coventry C.), 1978 v Bul, W (2)
Bone, J. (Norwich C.), 1972 v Y (sub); 1973 v D (2)
Bowie, J. (Rangers), 1920 v E, Ni (2)
Bowie, W. (Linthouse), 1891 v Ni (1)
Bowman, G. A. (Montrose), 1892 v Ni (1)
Boyd, J. M. (Newcastle U.), 1934 v Ni (1)
Boyd, R. (Mossend Swifts), 1889 v Ni; 1891 v W (2)
Boyd, W. G. (Clyde), 1931 v I, Sw (2)
Brackenbridge, T. (Hearts), 1888 v Ni (1)

Bradshaw, T. (Bury), 1928 v E (1)
Brand, R. (Rangers), 1961 v Ni, Ei (2); 1962 v Ni, W, Cz, U (8)
Branden, T. (Blackburn R.), 1896 v E (1)
Bremner, D. (Hibernian), 1976 v Sw (1)
Bremner, W. J. (Leeds U.), 1965 v Sp; 1966 v E, Pol, P, Br, I (2); 1967 v W, Ni, E; 1968 v W, E; 1969 v W, E, Ni, D, A, WG, Cy (2); 1970 v Ei, WG, A; 1971 v W, E; 1972 v P, Bel, Ho, Ni, W, E, Y, Cz, Br; 1973 v D (2), E (2), Ni (sub), Sw, Br; 1974 v Cz, WG, Ni, W, E, Bel, N, Z, Br, Y; 1975 v Sp (2); 1976 v D (54)
Brennan, F. (Newcastle U.), 1947 v W, Ni; 1953 v W, Ni, E; 1954 v Ni, E (7)
Breslin, B. (Hibernian), 1897 v W (1)
Brewster, G. (Everton), 1921 v E (1)
Brogan, J. (Celtic), 1971 v W, Ni, P, E (4)
Brown, A. (Middlesbrough), 1904 v E (1)
Brown, A. (St. Mirren), 1890 v W; 1891 v W (2)
Brown, A. D. (East Fife), 1950 v Sw, P, F; (with Blackpool), 1952 v U.S.A., D. Se; 1953 v W; 1954 v W, E, N (2), Fi, A, U (14)
Brown, G. C. P. (Rangers), 1931 v W; 1932 v E, W, Ni; 1933 v E; 1935 v A; E, W; 1936 v E, W; 1937 v G, E, W, Ni, Cz; 1938 v E, W, Cz, Ho (19)
Brown, H. (Partick T.), 1947 v W, Bel, L (3)
Brown, J. (Cambuslang), 1890 v W (1)
Brown, J. B. (Clyde), 1939 v W (1)
Brown, J. G. (Sheffield U.), 1975 v R (1)
Brown, R. (Dumbarton), 1884 v W, Ni (2)
Brown, R. (Rangers), 1947 v Ni; 1949 v Ni; 1952 v E (3)
Brown, R. jun. (Dumbarton), 1885 v W (1)
Brown, W. D. F. (Dundee), 1958 v F; 1959 v E, W, Ni; (with Tottenham H.), 1960 v W, Ni, Pol, A, H, T; 1962 v Ni, W, E, Cz; 1963 v W, Ni, E, A; 1964 v Ni, W, N; 1965 v E, Fi, Pol, Sp; 1966 v Ni, Pol, I (28)
Browning, J. (Celtic), 1914 v W (1)
Brownlie, J. (Hibernian), 1971 v Rus; 1972 v Pe, Ni, E; 1973 v D (2); 1976 v R (7)
Brownlie, J. (Third Lanark), 1909 v E, Ni; 1910 v E, W, Ni; 1911 v W, Ni; 1912 v W, Ni, E; 1913 v W, Ni, E; 1914 v W, Ni, E (16)
Bruce, D. (Vale of Leven), 1890 v W (1)
Bruce, R. F. (Middlesbrough), 1934 v A (1)
Buchan, M. M. (Aberdeen), 1972 v P (sub), Bel; (with Manchester U.), W, Y, Cz, Br; 1973 v D (2), E; 1974 v WG, Ni, W, N, Br, Y; 1975 v EG, Sp, P; 1976 v D, R; 1977 v Fi, Cz, Ch, Arg, Br; 1978 v EG, W (sub), Ni, Pe, Ir, Ho; 1979 v A, N, P (34)
Buchanan, J. (Cambuslang), 1889 v Ni (1)
Buchanan, J. (Rangers), 1929 v E; 1930 v E (2)
Buchanan, P. S. (Chelsea), 1938 v Cz (1)
Buchanan, R. (Abercorn), 1891 v Ni (1)
Buckley, P. (Aberdeen), 1954 v N; 1955 v W, Ni (3)
Buick, A. (Hearts), 1902 v W, Ni (2)
Burley, G. (Ipswich T.), 1979 v W, Ni, E, Arg, N (5)
Burns, F. (Manchester U.), 1970 v A (1)
Burns, K. (Birmingham C.), 1974 v WG; 1975 v EG (sub), Sp (2); 1977 v Cz (sub), W, Se, W (sub); (with Nottingham F.), 1978 v Ni (sub), W, E, Pe, Ir; 1979 v N (14)
Busby, M. W. (Manchester C.), 1934 v W (1)

Cairns, T. (Rangers), 1920 v W; 1922 v E; 1923 v E, W; 1924 v Ni; 1925 v W, E, Ni (8)
Calderhead, D. (Queen of the South W.), 1889 v Ni (1)
Caldow, E. (Rangers), 1957 v Sp (2), Sw, WG; v E, 1958 v Ni, W, Sw, Par, H, Pol, Y, F; 1959 v E, W, Ni, WG, Ho, P; 1960 v E, W, Ni, A, H, T; 1961 v E, W, Ni, Ei (2), Cz; 1962 v Ni, W, E, Cz (2), U; 1963 v W, Ni, E (40)
Callaghan, P. (Hibernian), 1900 v Ni (1)
Callaghan, W. (Dunfermline), 1970 v Ei (sub), W (2)
Cameron, J. (St. Mirren), 1904 v Ni; (with Chelsea), 1909 v E (2)
Cameron, J. (Queen's Park), 1896 v Ni (1)
Cameron, J. (Rangers), 1886 v Ni (1)
Campbell, C. (Queen's Park), 1874 v E; 1877 v E, W; 1878 v E, W; 1879 v E,; 1880 v E; 1881 v E; 1882 v E, W; 1884 v E; 1885 v E; 1886 v E (13)
Campbell, H. (Renton), 1889 v W (1)
Campbell, Jas. (Sheffield W.), 1913 v W (1)
Campbell, J. (South Western), 1880 v W (1)
Campbell, J. (Kilmarnock), 1891 v Ni; 1892 v W (2)
Campbell, John (Celtic), 1893 v E, Ni; 1898 v E, Ni; 1900 v E, Ni; 1901 v E, W, Ni; 1902 v W, Ni; 1903 v W (12)
Campbell, John (Rangers), 1899 v E, W, Ni; 1901 v Ni (4)
Campbell, K. (Liverpool), 1920 v E, W, Ni; (with Partick T.), 1921 v W, Ni; 1922 v W, Ni, E (8)
Campbell, P. (Rangers), 1878 v W; 1879 v W (2)
Campbell, P. (Morton), 1898 v W (1)
Campbell, R. (Chelsea), 1947 v Bel, L; 1950 v Sw, P, F (5)
Campbell, W. (Morton), 1947 v Ni; 1948 v E, Bel, Sw, F (5)
Carabine, J. (Third Lanark), 1938 v Ho; 1939 v E, Ni (3)
Carr, W. M. (Coventry C.), 1970 v Ni, W, E; 1971 v D; 1972 v Pe; 1973 v D (sub) (6)
Cassidy, J. (Celtic), 1921 v W, Ni; 1923 v Ni; 1924 v W (4)
Chalmers, S. (Celtic), 1965 v W, Fi; 1966 v P (sub), Br; 1967 v Ni (5)
Chalmers, W. (Rangers), 1885 v Ni (1)
Chalmers, W. S. (Queen's Park), 1929 v Ni (1)
Chambers, T. (Hearts), 1894 v W (1)
Chaplin, G. D. (Dundee), 1908 v W (1)
Cheyne, A. G. (Aberdeen), 1929 v E, N, G, Ho; 1930 v F (5)
Christie, A. J. (Queen's Park) 1898 v W; 1899 v E, Ni (3)
Christie, R. M. (Queen's Park), 1884 v E (1)
Clark, J. (Celtic), 1966 v Br.; 1967 v W, Ni, USSR (4)
Clark, R. B. (Aberdeen), 1968 v W, Ho; 1970 v Ni; 1971 v W, Ni, E, D, P, USSR; 1972 v Bel, Ni, W, E, Cz, Br; 1973 v D, E (17)
Cleland, J. (Royal Albert), 1891 v Ni (1)
Clements, R. (Leith Ath.), 1891 v Ni (1)
Clunas, W. L. (Sunderland), 1924 v E; 1926 v W (2)
Collier, W. (Raith R.), 1922 v W (1)
Collins, R. Y. (Celtic), 1951 v W, Ni, A; 1955 v Y, A, H; 1956 v Ni, W; 1957 v E, W, Sp (2), Sw, WG; 1958 v Ni, W, Sw, H, Pol, Y, F, Par; (with Everton), 1959, v E, W, Ni, WG, Ho, P; (with Leeds U.); 1965 v E, Pol, Sp (31)
Collins, T. (Hearts), 1909 v W (1)
Colman, D. (Aberdeen), 1911, v E, W, Ni; 1913 v Ni (4)
Colquhoun, E. P. (Sheffield U.), 1972 v P, Ho, Pe, Y, Cz, Br; 1973 v D (2), E (9)
Combe, J. R. (Hibernian), 1948 v E, Bel, Sw (3)
Conn, A. (Hearts), 1956 v A (1)
Conn, A. (Tottenham H.), 1975 v Ni (sub), E (2)

Connachan, E. D. (Dunfermline A.), 1962 v Cz, U (2)
Connelly, G. (Celtic), 1974 v Cz, WG (2)
Connolly, J. (Everton), 1973 v Sw (1)
Connor, J. (Airdrieonians), 1886 v Ni (1)
Connor, J. (Sunderland), 1930 v F; 1932 v Ni; 1934 v E; 1935 v Ni (4)
Cook, W. L. (Bolton W.), 1934 v E; 1935 v W, Ni (3)
Cooke, C. (Dundee), 1966 v W, I; (with Chelsea), P, Br; 1968 v E, Ho; 1969 v W, Ni, A, WG (sub), Cy (2); 1970 v A; 1971 v Bel; 1975 v Sp, P (16)
Cormack, P. B. (Hibernian), 1966 v Br; 1969 v D (sub); 1970 v Ei, WG; (with Nottingham F.), 1971 v D (sub), W, P, E; 1972 v Ho (sub) (9)
Cowan, J. (Aston Villa), 1896 v E; 1897 v E; 1898 v E (3)
Cowan, J. (Morton), 1948 v Bel, Sw, F; 1949 v E, W, F; 1950 v E, W, Ni, Sw, P, F; 1951 v E, W, Ni, A (2), D, F, Bel; 1952 v Ni, W, USA, D, Se (25)
Cowan, W. D. (Newcastle U.), 1924 v E (1)
Cowie, D. (Dundee), 1953 v E, Se; 1954 v Ni, W, Fi, N, A, U; 1955 v W, Ni, A, H; 1956 v W, A; 1957 v Ni, W; 1958 v H, Pol, Y, Par (20)
Cox, C. J. (Hearts), 1948 v F (1)
Cox, S. (Rangers), 1949 v E, F; 1950 v E, F, W, Ni, Sw, P; 1951 v E, D, F, Bel, A; 1952 v Ni, W, USA, D, Se; 1953 v W, Ni, E; 1954 v W, Ni, E (24)
Craig ,A. (Motherwell), 1929 v N, Ho; 1932 v E (3)
Craig, J. (Celtic), 1977 v Se (sub) (1)
Craig, J. P. (Celtic), 1968 v W (1)
Craig, T. (Rangers), 1927 v Ni; 1928 v Ni; 1929 v N, G; 1930 v Ni, E, W (7)
Craig, T. B. (Newcastle U.), 1976 v Sw (1)
Crapnell, J. (Airdrieonians), 1929 v E, N, G; 1930 v F; 1931 v Ni, Sw; 1932 v E, F; 1933 v Ni (9)
Crawford, D. (St. Mirren), 1894 v W, Ni; 1900 v W (3)
Crawford, J. (Queen's Park), 1932 v F, Ni; 1933 v E, W, Ni (5)
Cerand, P. T. (Celtic), 1961 v Ei (2), Cz; 1962 v Ni, W, E, Cz (2), U; 1963 v W, Ni; (with Manchester U.), 1964 v Ni; 1965 v E, Pol, Fi; 1966 v Pol (16)
Cringan, W. (Celtic), 1920 v W; 1922 v E, Ni; 1923 v W, E (5)
Crosbie, J. A. (Ayr U.), 1920 v W; (with Birmingham); 1922 v E (2)
Croal, J. A. (Falkirk) 1913 v Ni; 1914 v E, W (3)
Cropley, A. J. (Hibernian), 1972 v P, Bel (2)
Cross, J. H. (Third Lanark), 1903 v Ni (1)
Cruickshank, J. (Hearts), 1964 v WG; 1970 v W, E; 1971 v D, Bel; 1976 v R (6)
Crum, J. (Celtic), 1936 v E; 1939 v Ni (2)
Cullen, M. J. (Luton T.), 1956 v A (1)
Cumming, D. S. (Middlesbrough), 1938 v E (1)
Cumming, J. (Hearts), 1955 v E, H, P, Y; 1960 v E, Pol, A, H, T (9)
Cummings, G. (Partick T.), 1935 v E; 1936 v W, Ni, (with Aston Villa), G, E; 1938 v W, Ni, Cz; 1939 v E (9)
Cunningham, A. N. (Rangers), 1920 v Ni; 1921 v W, E; 1922 v Ni; 1923 v E, W; 1924 v E, Ni; 1926 v E, Ni; 1927 v E, W (12)
Cunningham, W. C. (Preston N.E.), 1954 v N (2), U, Fi, A; 1955 v W, E, H (8)
Curran, H. P. (Wolverhampton W.), 1970 v A; 1971 v Ni, E, D, USSR (sub) (5)

Dalglish, K. (Celtic), 1972 v Bel (sub), Ho; 1973 v D (1 + 1 sub), E (2), W, Ni, Sw, Br; 1974 v Cz, WG (2), Ni, W, E, Bel, N (sub), Z, Br, Y; 1975 v EG, Sp (sub + 1), Se, P, W, Ni, E, R; 1976 v D (2), R, Sw, Ni, E; 1977 v Fi, Cz, W (2), Se, Ni, E, Ch, Arg, Br; (with Liverpool), 1978 v EG, Cz, W, Bul, Ni (sub), W, E, Pe, Ir, Ho; 1979 v A, N, P, W, Ni, E, Arg, N (65)
Davidson, D. (Queen's Park), 1878 v W; 1879 v W; 1880 v W; 1881 v E, W (5)
Davidson, J. A. (Partick T.), 1954 v N (2), A, U; 1955 v W, Ni, E, H (8)
Davidson, S. (Middlesbrough), 1921 v E (1)
Dawson, J. (Rangers), 1935 v Ni; 1936 v E; 1937 v G, E, W, Ni, A, Cz; 1938 v W, Ho, Ni; 1939 v E, Ni, H (14)
Deans, J. (Celtic), 1975 v EG, Sp (2)
Delaney, J. (Celtic), 1936 v W, Ni; 1937 v G, E, A, Cz; 1938 v Ni; 1939 v W, Ni; (with Manchester U.), 1947 v E; 1948 v E, W, Ni (13)
Devine, A. (Falkirk), 1910 v W (1)
Dewar, G. (Dumbarton), 1888 v Ni; 1889 v E (2)
Dewar, N. (Third Lanark), 1932 v E, F; 1933 v W (3)
Dick, J. (West Ham U.), 1959 v E (1)
Dickie, M. (Rangers), 1897 v Ni; 1899 v Ni; 1900 v W (3)
Dickson, W. (Kilmarnock), 1970 v Ni, W, E; 1971 v D, USSR (5)
Dickson, W. (Dumbarton), 1888 v Ni (1)
Divers, J. (Celtic), 1895 v W (1)
Divers, J. (Celtic), 1939 v Ni (1)
Docherty, T. H. (Preston N.E.), 1952 v W; 1953 v E, Se : 1954 v N (2), A, U; 1955 v W, E, H (2), A; 1957 v E, Y, Sp (2), Sw, WG; 1958 v Ni, W, E, Sw; (with Arsenal), 1959 v W, E, Ni (25)
Dodds, J. (Celtic), 1914 v E, W, Ni (3)
Doig, J. E. (Arbroath), 1887 v Ni; 1889 v Ni; (with Sunderland), 1896 v E; 1899 v E; 1902 v E; 1903 v E (6)
Donachie, W. (Manchester C.), 1972 v Pe, Ni, E, Y, Cz, Br; 1973 v D, E, W, Ni; 1974 v Ni; 1976 v R, Ni, W, E; 1977 v Fi, Cz, W (2), Se, Ni, E, Ch, Arg, Br; 1978 v EG, W, Bul, W, E, Ir, Ho; 1979 v A, N, P (sub), (36)
Donaldson, A. (Bolton W.), 1914 v E, Ni, W; 1920 v E, Ni; 1922 v Ni (6)
Donnachie, J. (Oldham Ath.), 1913 v E; 1914 v B; Ni (3)
Dougall, C. (Birmingham C.), 1947 v W (1)
Dougall, J. (Preston N.E.), 1939 v E (1)
Dougan, R. (Hearts), 1950 v Sw (1)
Douglas, A. (Chelsea), 1911 v Ni (1)
Douglas, J. (Renfrew), 1880 v W (1)
Dowds, P. (Celtic), 1892 v Ni (1)
Downie, R. (Third Lanark), 1892 v W (1)
Doyle, D. (Celtic), 1892 v E; 1893 v W; 1894 v E; 1895 v E, Ni; 1897 v E; 1898 v E, Ni (8)
Doyle, J. (Ayr U.), 1976 v R (1)
Drummond, J. (Falkirk), 1892 v Ni; (with Rangers), 1894 v Ni; 1895 v Ni, E; 1896 v E, Ni; 1897 v Ni; 1898 v E; 1900 v E; 1901 v E; 1920 v E, W, Ni; 1903 v Ni (14)
Dunbar, M. (Cartvale), 1886 v Ni (1)
Duncan, A. (Hibernian), 1975 v P (sub), W, Ni, E, R; 1976 v D (6)
Duncan, D. (Derby Co.), 1933 v E, W; 1934 v A, W; 1935 v E, W; 1936 v E, W, Ni; 1937 v G, E, W, Ni; 1938 v W (14)
Duncan, D. M. (East Fife), 1948 v Bel, Sw, F (3)
Duncan, J. (Alexandra Ath.), 1878 v W; 1882 v W (2)
Duncan, J. (Leicester C.), 1926 v W (1)

Duncanson, J. (Rangers), 1947 v Ni (1)
Dunlop, J. (St. Mirren), 1890 v W (1)
Dunlop, W. (Liverpool), 1906 v E (1)
Dunn, J. (Hibernian), 1925 v W, Ni; 1927 v Ni; 1928 v Ni, E; (with Everton), 1929 v W (6)
Dykes, J. (Hearts), 1938 v Ho; 1939 v Ni (2)

Easson, J. F. (Portsmouth), 1931 v A, Sw; 1934 v W
Ellis, J. (Mossend Swifts), 1892 v Ni (1)
Evans, R. (Celtic), 1949 v E, W, Ni, F; 1950 v W, Ni, Sw, P; 1951 v E, A; 1952 v Ni; 1953 v Se; 1954 v Ni, W, E, N, Fi; 1955 v Ni, P, Y, A, H; 1956 v E, Ni, W, A; 1957 v WG, Sp; 1958 v Ni, W, E, Sw, H, Pol, Y, Par, F; 1959 v E, WG, Ho, P; 1960 v E, Ni, W, Pol; (with Chelsea), 1960 v A, H, T (48)
Ewart, J. (Bradford C.), 1921 v E (1)
Ewing, T. (Partick T.), 1958 v W, E (2)

Farm, G. N. (Blackpool), 1953 v W, Ni, E, Se; 1954 v Ni, W, E; 1959 v WG, Ho, P (10)
Ferguson, J. (Vale of Leven), 1874 v E; 1876 v E, W; 1877 v E, W; 1878 v W (6)
Ferguson, R. (Kilmarnock), 1966 v W, E, Ho, P, Br; 1967 v W, Ni (7)
Fernie, W. (Celtic), 1954 v Fi, A, U; 1955 v W, Ni; 1957 v E, Ni, W, Y; 1958 v W, Sw, Par (12)
Findlay, R. (Kilmarnock), 1898 v W (1)
Fitchie, T. T. (Woolwich Arsenal), 1905 v W; 1906 v W, Ni; (with Queen's Park), 1907 v W (4)
Flavell, R. (Airdrieonians), 1947 v Bel, L (2)
Fleming, C. (East Fife), 1954 v Ni (1)
Fleming, J. W. (Rangers), 1929 v G, Ho; 1930 v E (3)
Fleming, R. (Morton), 1886 v Ni (1)
Forbes, A. R. (Sheffield U.), 1947 v Bel, L, E; 1948 v W, Ni; (with Arsenal), 1950 v E, P, F; 1951 v W, Ni, A; 1952 v W, D, Se (14)
Forbes, J. (Vale of Leven), 1884 v E, W, Ni; 1887 v W, E (5)
Ford, D. (Hearts), 1974 v Cz (sub), WG (sub), W (3)
Forrest, J. (Rangers), 1966 v W, I; (with Aberdeen), 1971 v Bel (sub), D, Rus (5)
Forrest, J. (Motherwell), 1958 v E (1)
Forsyth, A. (Partick T.), 1972 v Y, Cz Br; 1973 v D; (with Manchester U.), E; 1975 v Sp, Ni (sub), R, EG; 1976 v D (10)
Forsyth, C. (Kilmarnock), 1964 v E; 1965 v W Ni, Fi (4)
Forsyth, T. (Motherwell), 1971 v D; (with Rangers) 1974 v Cz; 1976 v Sw, Ni, W, E; 1977 v Fi, Se, W, Ni, E, Ch, Arg, Br; 1978 v Cz, W, Ni, W (sub), E, Pe, Ir (sub), Ho;
Foyers, R. (St. Bernards), 1893 v W; 1894 v W (2)
Fraser, D. M. (W.B.A.), 1968 v Ho; 1969 v Cy (2)
Fraser, J. (Moffat), 1891 v Ni (1)
Fraser, J. M. J. E. (Queen's Park), 1880 v W; 1882 v W, E; 1883 v W, E (5)
Fraser, J. (Dundee), 1907 v Ni (1)
Fraser, W. (Sunderland), 1955 v W, Ni (2)
Fulton, W. (Abercorn), 1884 v Ni (1)
Fyle, J. H. (Third Lanark), 1895 v W (1)

Gabriel, J. (Everton), 1961 v W; 1964 v N (sub) (2)
Gallacher, H. K. (Airdrieonians), 1924 v Ni; 1925 v E, W, Ni; 1926 v W; (with Newcastle U.), 1926 v E, Ni; 1927 v E, W, Ni; 1928 v E, W; 1929 v E, W, Ni; 1930 v W, Ni, F; (with Chelsea), 1934 v E; (with Derby Co.), 1935 v E (20)
Gallacher, P. (Sunderland), 1935 v Ni (1)
Galt, J. H. (Rangers), 1908 v W, Ni (2)
Gardiner, I. (Motherwell), 1958 v W (1)

Gardner, D, R. (Third Lanark), 1897 v W (1)
Gardner, R. (Queen's Park), 1872 v E; 1873 v E; (with Clydesdale), 1874 v E; 1875 v E; 1878 v E (5)
Gemmell, T. (St. Mirren), 1955 v P, Y (2)
Gemmell, T. (Celtic). 1966 v E; 1967 v W, Ni, E, USSR; 1968 v Ni, E; 1969 v W, Ni, E, D, A, WG, Cy; 1970 v E, Ei, WG; 1971 v Bel (18)
Gemmill, A. (Derby Co.), 1971 v Bel; 1972 v P, Ho, Pe, Ni, W, E; 1976 v D, R, Ni, W, E; 1977 v Fi, Cz, W (2), Ni (sub), E (sub), Ch (sub), Arg, Br; 1978 v EG (sub), (with Nottingham F.), Bul, Ni, W, E, (sub), Pe (sub), Ir, Ho; 1979 v A, N, P, N (33)
Gibb, W. (Clydesdale), 1873 v E (1)
Gibson, D. W. (Leicester C.), 1963 v A, N, Ei, Sp; 1964 v Ni; 1965 v W, Fi (7)
Gibson, J. D. (Partick T.), 1926 v E; 1927 v E, W, Ni; (with Aston Villa), 1928 v E, W; 1930 v W, Ni (8)
Gibson, N. (Rangers), 1895 v E, Ni; 1896 v E, Ni; 1897 v E, Ni; 1898 v E; 1899 v E, W, Ni; 1900 v E, Ni; 1901 v W; (with Partick T.), 1905 v Ni (14)
Gilchrist, J. E. (Celtic), 1922 v E (1)
Gilhooly, M. (Hull C.), 1922 v W (1)
Gillespie, G. (Rangers), 1880 v W; 1881 v E, W; 1882 v E; (with Queen's Park), 1886 v W; 1890 v W; 1891 v Ni (7)
Gillespie, Jas. (Third Lanark), 1898 v W (1)
Gillespie, Jno. (Queen's Park), 1896 v W (1)
Gillespie, R. (Queen's Park), 1927 v W; 1931 v W; 1932 v F; 1933 v E (4)
Gillick, T. (Everton), 1937 v A, Cz; 1939 v W, Ni, H (5)
Gilmour, J. (Dundee), 1931 v W (1)
Gilzean, A. J. (Dundee), 1964 v W, E, N, WG; 1965 v Ni; (with Tottenham H.), Sp; 1966 v Ni, W, Pol, I; 1968 v W; 1969 v W, E, WG, Cy (2), A (sub); 1970 v Ni, E (sub) WG, A; 1971 v P (22)
Glavin, R. (Celtic), 1977 v Se (1)
Glen, A. (Aberdeen), 1956 v E, Ni (2)
Glen, R. (Renton), 1895 v W; 1896 v W; (with Hibernian), 1900 v Ni (3)
Gordon, J. E. (Rangers), 1912 v E, Ni; 1913 v E, Ni, W; 1914 v E, Ni; 1920 v W, E, Ni (10)
Gossland, J. (Rangers), 1884 v Ni (1)
Goudle, J. (Abercorn), 1884 v Ni (1)
Gourlay, J. (Cambuslang), 1886 v Ni (1)
Govan, J. (Hibernian), 1948 v E, W, Bel, Sw, F; 1949 v Ni (6)
Gow, D. R. (Rangers), 1888 v E (1)
Gow, J. J. (Queen's Park), 1885 v E (1)
Gow, J. R. (Rangers), 1888 v Ni (1)
Graham, H. (Leeds U.), 1978 v EG (sub); 1979 v A (sub), N, W, Ni, E, Arg, N (8)
Graham, J. A. (Arsenal), 1921 v Ni (1)
Graham, G. (Arsenal), 1972 v P, Ho, Ni, Y, Cz, Br; 1973 v D (2); (with Manchester U.), E, W, Ni, Br (sub) (12)
Graham, J. (Annbank), 1884 v Ni (1)
Grant, J. (Hibernian), 1959 v W, Ni (2)
Gray, A. (Hibernian), 1903 v Ni (1)
Gray, A. M. (Aston Villa), 1976 v R, Sw; 1977 v Fi, Cz; 1979 v A, N,
Gray, D. (Rangers), 1929 v W, Ni, G, Ho; 1930 v W, Ei, Ni; 1931 v W; 1933 v W, Ni (10)
Gray, E. (Leeds U.), 1969 v E, Cy; 1970 v WG, A; 1971 v W, Ni; 1972 v Bel, Ho; 1976 v W, E; 1977 v Fi, W (12)
Gray, F. T. (Leeds U.), 1976 v Sw; 1979 v N, P, W, Ni, E, Arg (sub) (7)
Gray, W. (Pollokshields Ath.), 1886 v E (1)

Green, A. (Blackpool), 1971 v Bel (sub), P (sub), Ni, E; 1972 v W, E, (sub) (6)
Greig, J. (Rangers), 1964 v E, WG; 1965 v W Ni, E, Fi (2), Sp, Pol; 1966 v Ni, W, E, Pol, I (2), P, Ho, Br; 1967 v W, Ni, E; 1968 v Ni, W, E, Ho; 1969 v W, Ni, E, D, A, WG, Cy (2), 1970 v W, E, Ei, WG, A; 1971 v D, Bel, W (sub), Ni, E; 1976 v D (44)
Groves, W. (Hibernian), 1888 v W; (with Celtic), 1889 v Ni; 1890 v E (3)
Guilliland, W. (Queen's Park), 1891 v W; 1892 v Ni; 1894 v E; 1895 v E (4)

Haddock, H. (Clyde), 1955 v E, H (2), P, Y; 1958 v E (6)
Haddow, D. (Rangers), 1894 v E (1)
Haffey, F. (Celtic), 1960 v E; 1961 v E (2)
Hamilton, A. (Queen's Park), 1885 v E, W; 1886 v E; 1888 v E (4)
Hamilton, A. W. (Dundee), 1962 v Cz, U, W, E; 1963 v W, Ni, E, A, N, Ei; 1964 v Ni, W, E, N, WG; 1965 v Ni, W, E, Fi (2), Pol, Sp; 1966 v Pol, Ni (24)
Hamilton, G. (Aberdeen), 1947 v Ni; 1951 v Bel, A; 1954 v N (2) (5)
Hamilton, G. (Port Glasgow Ath.), 1906 v Ni (1)
Hamilton, J. (Queen's Park), 1892 v W; 1893 v E, Ni (3)
Hamilton, J. (St. Mirren), 1924 v Ni (1)
Hamilton, R. C. (Rangers), 1899 v E, W, Ni; 1900 v W; 1901 v E, Ni; 1902 v W, Ni; 1903 v E; 1904 v E; (with Dundee), 1911 v W (11)
Hamilton, T. (Hurlford), 1891 v Ni (1)
Hamilton, T. (Rangers), 1932 v E (1)
Hamilton, W. M. (Hibernian), 1965 v Fi (1)
Hannah, A. B. (Renton), 1888 v W (1)
Hannah, J. (Third Lanark), 1889 v W (1)
Hansen, A. D. (Liverpool), 1979 v W, Arg (2)
Hansen, J. (Patrick T.), 1972 v Bel (sub), Y (sub) (2)
Harkness, J. D. (Queen's Park), 1927 v E, Ni; 1928 v E; (with Hearts), 1929 v W, E, Ni; 1930 v E, W; 1932 v W, F; 1934 v Ni (11)
Harper, J. M. (Aberdeen), 1973 v D (1+1 sub) (with Hibernian); 1976 v D; (with Aberdeen), 1978 v Ir (sub) (4)
Harper, W. (Hibernian), 1923 v E, Ni, W; 1924 v E, Ni, W; 1925 v E, Ni, W; (with Arsenal), 1926 v E, Ni (11)
Harris, J. (Patrick T.), 1921 v W, Ni (2)
Harris, N. (Newcastle U.), 1924 v E (1)
Harrower, W. (Queen's Park), 1882 v E; 1884 v Ni, 1886 v W (3)
Hartford, R. A. (W.B.A.), 1972 v Pe, W (sub), E, Y, Cz, Br; (with Manchester C.), 1976 v D, R, Ni (sub); 1977 v Cz (sub), W (sub), Se, W, Ni, E, Ch, Arg, Br; 1978 v EG (sub), Cz, W, Bul, W, E, Pe, Ir, Ho; 1979 v A, N, P, W, Ni, E, Arg, N (35)
Harvey, D. (Leeds U.), 1973 v D; 1974 v Cz, WG, Ni, W, E, Bel, Z, Br, Y; 1975 v EG, Sp (2); 1976 v D (2); 1977 v Fi (sub) (16)
Hastings, A. C. (Sunderland), 1936 v Ni; 1938 v Ni (2)
Haughney, M. (Celtic), 1954 v E (1)
Hay, D. (Celtic), 1970 v Ni, W, E; 1971 v D, Bel, W, P, Ni; 1972 v P, Bel, Ho; 1973 v W, Ni, E, Sw, Br; 1974 v Cz (2), WG, Ni, W, E, Bel, N, Z, Br, Y (27)
Hay, J. (Celtic), 1905 v Ni; 1909 v Ni; 1910 v W, Ni, E; 1911 v Ni, E; (with Newcastle U.), 1912 v E, W; 1914 v E, Ni (11)
Hegarty, P. (Dundee U.), 1979 v W, Ni, E, Arg, N (sub) (5),

Heggle, C. (Rangers) 1886 v Ni (1)
Henderson, G. H. (Rangers), 1904 v Ni (1)
Henderson, J. G. (Portsmouth), 1953 v Se; 1954 v Ni, E, N; 1956 v W; (with Arsenal), 1959 v W, Ni (7)
Henderson, W. (Rangers), 1963 v W, Ni, E, A, N, Ei, Sp; 1964 v W, Ni, E, N, WG; 1965 v Fi, Pol, E, Sp; 1966 v Ni, W, Pol, I, Ho; 1967 v W, Ni; 1968 v Ho; 1969 v Ni, E, Cy; 1970 v Ei; 1971 v P (29)
Hepburn, J. (Alloa Ath.), 1891 v W (1)
Hepburn, R. (Ayr U.), 1932 v Ni (1)
Herd, A. C. (Hearts), 1915 v Ni (1)
Herd, D. G. (Arsenal), 1959 v E, W, Ni; 1961 v Ei, Cz (5)
Herd, G. (Clyde), 1958 v E; 1960 v H, T; 1961 v W, N (5)
Herriot, J. (Birmingham C.), 1969 v Ni, E, D, Cy (2), W (sub); 1970 v Ei (sub), WG (8)
Hewie, J. D. (Charlton Ath.), 1956 v E, A; 1957 v E, Ni, W, Y, Sp (2), Sw, WG; 1958 v Pol, W, Y, F; 1959 v Ho, P; 1960 v Ni, W, Pol (19)
Higgins, A. (Kilmarnock), 1885 v Ni (1)
Higgins, A. (Newcastle U.), 1910 v E, Ni; 1911 v E, Ni (4)
Highet, T. C. (Queen's Park), 1875 v E; 1876 v E, W; 1878 v E (4)
Hill, D. (Rangers), 1881 v E, W; 1882 v W (3)
Hill, D. A. (Third Lanark), 1906 v Ni (1)
Hill, F. R. (Aberdeen), 1930 v F; 1931 v W, Ni (3)
Hill, J. (Hearts), 1891 v E, 1892 v W (2)
Hogg, G. (Hearts), 1896 v E, Ni (2)
Hogg, J. (Ayr U.), 1922 v Ni (1)
Hogg, R. M. (Celtic), 1937 v Cz (1)
Holm, A. H. (Queen's Park), 1882 v W; 1883 v E, W (3)
Holt, D. D. (Hearts), 1963 v A, N, Ei, Sp; 1964 v WG, (sub) (5)
Holton, J. A. (Manchester U.), 1973 v W, Ni, E, Sw, Br; 1974 v Cz, WG, Ni, W, E, N, Z, Br, Y; 1975 v EG (15)
Hope, R. (W.B.A.), 1968 v Ho; 1969 v D (2)
Houliston, W. (Queen of the South), 1949 v E, Ni, F (3)
Houston, S. M. (Manchester U.), 1976 v D (1)
Howden, W. (Partick T.), 1905 v Ni (1)
Howe, R. (Hamilton A.), 1929 v N, Ho (2)
Howie, J. (Newcastle U.), 1905 v E; 1906 v E; 1908 v E (3)
Howie, H. (Hibernian), 1949 v W (1
Howieson, J. (St. Mirren), 1927 v Ni (1)
Hughes, J. (Celtic), 1965 v Pol, Sp; 1966 v Ni, I (2), 1968 v E; 1969 v A; 1970 v Ei (8)
Hughes, W. (Sunderland), 1975 v Se (sub) (1)
Humphries, W. (Motherwell), 1952 v Se (1)
Hunter, A. (Kilmarnock), 1972 v Pe, Y; (with Celtic), 1973 v E; 1974 v Cz (4)
Hunter, J. (Dundee), 1909 v W (1)
Hunter, J. (Third Lanark), 1874 v E; (with Eastern), 1875 v E; (with Third Lanark), 1876 v E; 1877 v W (4)
Hunter, R. (St. Mirren), 1890 v Ni (1)
Hunter, W. (Motherwell), 1960 v H, T; 1961 v W (3)
Husband, J. (Partick T.), 1947 v W (1)
Hutchison, T. (Coventry C.), 1974 v Cz (2), WG (2), Ni, W, Bel (sub), N, Z (sub), Y (sub); 1975 v EG, Sp (2), P, E (sub), R (sub); 1976 v D (17)
Hutton, J. (Aberdeen), 1923 v E, W, Ni; 1924 v Ni; 1926 v W, E, Ni; (with Blackburn R.), 1927 v Ni; 1928 v W, Ni (10)
Hutton, J. (St. Bernards), 1887 v Ni (1)

Hyslop, T. (Stoke C.), 1896 v E; (with Rangers) 1897 v E (2)
Imlach, J. J. S. (Nottingham F.), 1958 v H, Pol, Y, F (4)
Imrie, W. N. (St. Johnstone), 1929 v N, G, (2)
Inglis, J. (Kilmarnock Ath.), 1884 v Ni(1)
Inglis, J. (Rangers), 1883 v E, W (2)
Irons, J. H. (Queen's Park), 1900 v W (1)

Jackson, A. (Cambuslang), 1886 v W; 1888 v Ni(2)
Jackson, A. (Aberdeen), 1925 v E, W, Ni; (with Huddersfield T.), 1926 v E, W, Ni; 1927 v W, Ni; 1928 v E W; 1929 v E, W, Ni; 1930 v E, W, Ni, F (17)
Jackson, C. (Rangers), 1975 v Se, P (sub), W; 1976 v D, R, Ni, W, E (8)
Jackson, J. (Partick T.), 1931 v A, I, Sw; 1933 v E; (with Chelsea), 1934 v E; 1935 v E; 1936 v W, Ni (8)
Jackson, T. A. (St. Mirren), 1904 v W, E, Ni; 1905 v W; 1907 v W, Ni (6)
James, A. W. (Preston N.E.), 1926 v W; 1928 v E; 1929 v E, Ni; (with Arsenal), 1930 v E, W, Ni; 1933 v W (8)
Jardine, A. (Rangers), 1971 v D (sub); 1972 v P, Bel, Ho; 1973 v E, Sw, Br; 1974 v Cz (2), WG (2), Ni, W, E, Bel, N, Z, Br, Y; 1975 v EG, Sp (2), Se, P, W, Ni, E; 1977 v Se (sub), Ch (sub), Br (sub); 1978 v Cz, W, Ni, Ir (34)
Jarvie, A. (Airdrieonians), 1971 v P (sub), Ni (sub), E (sub) (3)
Jenkinson, T. (Hearts), 1887 v Ni(1)
Johnston, L. H. (Clyde), 1948 v Bel, Sw(2)
Johnston, R. (Sunderland), 1938 v Cz(1)
Johnston, W. (Rangers), 1966 v W, E, Pol, Ho; 1968 v W, E; 1969 v Ni (sub); 1970 v Ni; 1971 v D (with W.B.A.), 1977 v Se, W (sub), Ni, E, Ch, Arg, Br; 1978 v EG, Cz, W, W, E, Pe (22)
Johnstone, D. (Rangers), 1973 v W, Ni, E, Sw, Br; 1975 v EG (sub), Se (sub); 1976 v Sw, Ni (sub), E (sub); 1978 v Bul (sub), Ni, W (13)
Johnstone, J. (Abercorn), 1888 v W (1)
Johnstone, J. (Celtic), 1965 v W, Fi; 1966 v E; 1967 v W, USSR; 1968 v W; 1969 v A, WG; 1970 v E, WG; 1971 v D, E; 1972 v P. Bel, Ho, Ni, E (sub); 1974 v W, E, Bel, N; 1975 v EG, Sp (23)
Johnstone, Jas (Kilmarnock), 1894 v W (1)
Johnstone, J. A. (Hearts), 1930 v W; 1933 v W, Ni (3)
Johnstone, R. (Hibernian), 1951 v E, D, F; 1952 v Ni, E; 1953 v E, Se; 1954 v W, E, N, Fi; 1955 v Ni, H; (with Manchester C.) 1955 v E; 1956 v E, Ni, W (17)
Johnstone, W. (Third Lanark), 1887 v Ni; 1889 v W; 1890 v E (3)
Jordan, J. (Leeds U.), 1973 v E (sub), Sw (sub), Br; 1974 v Cz (sub + 1), WG (sub), Ni (sub), W, E, Bel, N, Z, Br, Y; 1975 v EG, Sp (2); 1976 v Ni, W, E; 1977 v Cz, W, Ni, E; 1978 v EG, Cz, W (with Manchester U.), Bul, Ni, E, Pe, Ir, Ho; 1979 v A, P, W (sub), Ni, E, N (39)

Kay, J. L. (Queen's Park), 1880 v E; 1882 v E, W; 1883 v E, W; 1884 v W (6)
Keillor, A. (Montrose), 1891 v W; 1892 v Ni; (with Dundee), 1894 v Ni; 1895 v W; 1896 v W; 1897 v W (6)
Keir, L. (Dumbarton), 1885 v W; 1886 v Ni; 1887 v E, W; 1888 v E (5)
Kelly, H. T. (Blackpool), 1952 v USA (1)

Kelly, J. (Renton), 1888 v E; (with Celtic), 1889 v E; 1890 v E; 1892 v E; 1893 v E, Ni; 1894 v W; 1896 v Ni(8)
Kelly, J. C. (Barnsley), 1949 v W Ni (2)
Kelso, R. (Renton), 1885 v W, Ni; 1886 v W; 1887 v E, W; 1888 v E; (with Dundee), 1898 v Ni (7)
Kelso, T. (Dundee), 1914 v W (1)
Kennaway, J. (Celtic), 1934 v A, W (2)
Kennedy, A. (Eastern), 1875 v E; 1876 v E, W; (with Third Lanark), 1878 v E; 1882 v W; 1884 v W (6)
Kennedy, J. (Celtic), 1964 v W, E, WG; 1965 v W, Ni, Fi (6)
Kennedy, J. (Hibernian), 1897 v W (1)
Kennedy, S. (Aberdeen), 1978 v Bul, W, E, Pe, Ho; 1979 v A, P,
Kennedy, S. (Partick T.), 1905 v W (1)
Kennedy, S. (Rangers), 1975 v Se, P, W, Ni, E (5)
Ker, G. (Queen's Park), 1880 v W; 1881 v E, W; 1882 v W, E (5)
Ker, W. (Granville), 1872 v E; (with Queen's Park), 1873 v E (2)
Kerr, A. (Partick T.), 1955 v A, H (2)
Kerr, P. (Hibernian), 1924 v Ni(1)
Key, G. (Hearts), 1902 v Ni (1)
Key, W. (Queen's Park), 1907 v Ni(1)
King, A. (Hearts), 1896 v E, W; (with Celtic), 1897 v Ni; 1898 v Ni; 1899 v Ni, W (6)
King, J. (Hamilton A.), 1933 v Ni; 1934 v Ni(2)
King, W. S. (Queen's Park), 1929 v W (1)
Kinloch, J. D. (Partick T.), 1922 v Ni(1)
Kinnaird, A. F. (Wanderers), 1873 v E (1)
Kinnear, D. (Rangers), 1938 v Cz (1)

Lambie, J. A. (Queen's Park), 1886 v Ni; 1887 v Ni; 1888 v E (3)
Lambie, W. A. (Queen's Park), 1892 v Ni; 1893 v W; 1894 v E; 1895 v E, Ni; 1896 v E, Ni; 1897 v E, Ni(9)
Lamont, D. (Pilgrims), 1885 v Ni(1)
Lang, A. (Dumbarton), 1880 v W (1)
Lang, J. J. (Clydesdale), 1876 v W; (with Third Lanark), 1878 v W (2)
Latta, A. (Dumbarton), 1888 v W; 1889 v E (2)
Law, D. (Huddersfield T.), 1959 v W, Ni, Ho, P; 1960 v Ni, W; (with Manchester C.), 1960 v E, Pol, A; 1961 v E, Ni; (with Torino), 1961 v Cz(2); 1962 v E; (with Manchester U.), 1963 v W, Ni, E, A, N, Ei, Sp; 1964 v W, E, N, WG; 1965 v W, Ni, E, Fi (2), Pol, Sp; 1966 v Ni, E, Pol; 1967 v W, E, USSR; 1968 v Ni; 1969 v Ni, A, WG; 1972 v Pe, Ni, W, E, Y, Cz, Br; (with Manchester C.) 1974 v Cz (2) WG (2), Ni, Z (55)
Law, G. (Rangers), 1910 v E, Ni, W (3)
Law, T. (Chelsea), 1928 v E; 1930 v E (2)
Lawrence, J. (Newcastle U.), 1911 v E (1)
Lawrence, T. (Liverpool), 1963 v Ei; 1969 v W, WG (3)
Lawson, D. (St. Mirren), 1923 v E (1)
Leckie, R. (Queen's Park), 1872 v E (1)
Leggat, G. (Aberdeen), 1956 v E; 1957 v W; 1958 v Ni, H, Pol, Y, Par; (with Fulham), 1959 v E, W, Ni, WG, Ho; 1960 v E, Ni, W, Pol, A, H (18)
Lennie, W. (Aberdeen), 1908 v W, Ni (2)
Lennox, R. (Celtic), 1967 v Ni, E, USSR; 1968 v W, E; 1969 v D, A, W G, Cy (sub); 1970 v W (sub)(10)
Leslie, L. G. (Airdrieonians), 1961 v W, Ni, Ei (2), Cz (5)
Liddell, W. (Liverpool), 1947 v W, Ni; 1948 v E, W, Ni; 1950 v E, W, P, F; 1951 v W, Ni, E, A; 1952 v W, Ni, E, USA, D, Se; 1953 v W, Ni, E; 1954 v W; 1955 v P, Y, A, H; 1956 v Ni (28)

Liddle, D. (East Fife),)1931 v A, I, Sw(3)
Lindsay, D. (St. Mirren), 1903 v Ni (1)
Lindsay, J. (Dumbarton), 1880 v W; 1881 v W, E; 1884 v W, E; 1885 v W, E; 1886 v E (8)
Lindsay, J. (Renton), 1888 v E; 1893 v E, Ni (3)
Linwood, A. B. (Clyde), 1950 v W (1)
Little, R. J. (Rangers), 1953 v Se (1)
Livingstone, G.T. (Manchester C.), 1906 v E; (with Rangers), 1907 v W (2)
Lochhead, A. (Third Lanark), 1889 v W (1)
Logan, J. (Ayr U.), 1891 v W (1)
Logan, T. (Falkirk), 1913 v Ni (1)
Logie, J. T. (Arsenal), 1953 v Ni (1)
Loney, W. (Celtic), 1910 v W, Ni (2)
Long, H. (Clyde), 1947 v Ni (1)
Longair, W. (Dundee), 1894 v Ni (1)
Lorimer, P. (Leeds U.), 1970 v A (sub); 1971 v W, Ni, 1972 v Ni (sub), W, E; 1973 v D (2), E (2); 1974 v WG (sub), E, Bel, N, Z, Br, Y; 1975 v Sp (sub); 1976 v D (2), R (21)
Love, A. (Aberdeen), 1931 v A, I, Sw (3)
Low, A. (Falkirk), 1934 v Ni (1)
Low, T. P. (Rangers), 1897 v Ni (1)
Low, W, L. (Newcastle U.), 1911 v E. W; 1912 v Ni; 1920 v E, Ni (5)
Lowe, J. (Cambuslang), 1891 v Ni (1)
Lowe, J. (St. Bernards), 1887 v Ni (1)
Lundie, J. (Hibernian), 1886 v W (1)
Lyall, J. (Sheffield W.), 1905 v E (1)

M'Adam, J. (Third Lanark), 1880 v W (1)
M'Arthur, D. (Celtic), 1895 v E, Ni; 1899 v W (3)
M'Atee, A. (Celtic), 1913 v W (1)
Macari, L. (Celtic), 1972 v W (sub), E, Y, Cz, Br; 1973 v D; (with Manchester U.) E (2), W (sub), Ni (sub); 1975 v Se, P (sub), W, E (sub), R; 1977 v Ni (sub), E (sub), Ch, Arg; 1978 v EG, W, Bul, Pe (sub), Ir;
Macauley, A. R. (Brentford), 1947 v E; (with Arsenal), 1948 v E, W, Ni, Bel, Sw, F (7)
M'Aulay, J. (Dumbarton), 1882 v W; (with Arthurlie), 1884 v Ni (2)
M'Aulay, J. (Dumbarton), 1883 v E, W; 1884 v E; 1885 v E, W; 1886 v E; 1887 v E, W (8)
M'Auley, R. (Rangers), 1932 v Ni, W (2)
M'Bain, E. (St. Mirren), 1894 v W (1)
M'Bain, N. (Manchester U.), 1922 v E; (with Everton), 1923 v Ni; 1924 v W (3)
McBride, J. (Celtic), 1967 v W Ni (2)
M'Bride, P. (Preston N.E.), 1904 v E; 06 v 19E; 1907 v E, W; 1908 v E; 1909 v W (6)
M'Call, J. (Renton), 1886 v W; 1887 v E, W; 1888 v E; 1890 v E (5)
McCalliog, J. (Sheffield W.), 1967 v E, USSR; 1968 v Ni; 1969 v D; (with Wolverhampton W.) 1971 v P (5)
McCallum, N. (Renton), 1888 v Ni (1)
McCann, R. J. (Motherwell), 1959 v WG; 1960 v E, Ni, W; 1961 v E (5)
McCartney, W. (Hibernian), 1902 v Ni (1)
McClory, A. (Motherwell), 1927 v W; 1928 v Ni; 1935 v W (3)
McCloy, P. (Ayr U.), 1924 v E; 1925 v E (2)
McCloy, P. (Rangers), 1973 v W, Ni, Sw, Br (4)
McColl, A. (Renton), 1888 v Ni (1)
McColl, I. M. (Rangers), 1950 v E, F; 1951 v W Ni, Bel; 1957 v E, Ni, W, Y, Sp, Sw, WG; 1958 v Ni, E (14)
McColl, R. S. (Queen's Park), 1896 v W, Ni; 1897 v Ni, 1898 v Ni; 1899 v Ni, E, W; 1900 v E; W; 1901 v E, Ni; (with Newcastle U.), 1902 v E; (with Queen's Park), 1908 v Ni (13)

M'Coll, W. (Renton), 1895 v W (1)
M'Combie, A. (Sunderland), 1903 v E, W; (with Newcastle U.), 1905 v E, W (4)
M'Corkindale, J. (Partick T.), 1891 v W (1)
M'Cormick, R. (Abercorn), 1886 v W (1)
McCrae, D. (St. Mirren), 1929 v N, G (2)
M'Creadie, A. (Rangers), 1893 v W; 1894 v E (2)
McCreadie, E. G. (Chelsea), 1965 v E, Sp, Fi, Pol; 1966 v P, Ni, W, Pol, I; 1967 v E, USSR; 1968 v Ni, W, E, Ho; 1969 v W Ni, E, D, A, WG, Cy (2) (23)
McCulloch, D. (Hearts), 1935 v W; (with Brentford), 1936 v E; 1937 v W, Ni; 1938 v Cz; (with Derby Co.), 1939 v H, W (7)
MacDonald, A. (Rangers), 1976 v Sw (1)
M'Donald, J. (Edinburgh University), 1886 v E (1)
M'Donald, J. (Sunderland), 1956 v W, Ni (2)
MacDougall, E. J. (Norwich C.), 1975 v Se, P, W, Ni, E; 1976 v D, R (7)
McDougall, J. (Liverpool), 1931 v I (2)
McDougall J. (Airdrieonians), 1926 v Ni (1)
M'Dougall, J. (Vale of Leven), 1877 v E, W; 1878 v E; 1879 v E, W (5)
McFayden, W. (Motherwell), 1934 v A, W (2)
Macfarlane, A. (Dundee), 1904 v W; 1906 v W; 1908 v W; 1909 v Ni; 1911 v W (5)
M'Farlane, R. (Greenock Morton), 1896 v W (1)
Macfarlane, W. (Hearts), 1947 v L (1)
McGarr, E. (Aberdeen), 1970 v Ei, A (2)
McGarvey, F. P. (Liverpool), 1979 v Ni (sub), Arg (2)
M'Geoch, A. (Dumbreck), 1876 v E, W; 1877 v E, W (4)
McGhee, J. (Hibernian), 1886 v W (1)
McGonagle, W. (Celtic), 1933 v E; 1934 v A, E, Ni; 1935 v Ni, W (6)
McGrain, D. (Celtic), 1973 v W, Ni, E, Sw, Br; 1974 v Cz (2), WG, W (sub), E, Bel, N, Z, Br, Y; 1975 v Sp, Se, P, W, Ni, E, R; 1976 v D (2), Sw, Ni, W, E; 1977 v Fi, Cz, W (2), Se, Ni, E, Ch, Arg, Br; 1978 v EG, Cz (40)
M'Gregor, J. C. (Vale of Leven), 1877 v E, W; 1878 v E; 1880 v E (4)
McGrory, J. E. (Kilmarnock), 1965 v Ni, Fi; 1966 v P (3)
M'Grory, J. (Celtic), 1928 v Ni; 1931 v E; 1932 v Ni, W; 1933 v E, Ni; 1934 v Ni (7)
M'Guire, W. (Beith), 1881 v E, W (2)
M'Gurk, F. (Birmingham), 1934 v W (1)
M'Hardy, H. (Rangers), 1885 v Ni (1)
M'Inally, T. B. (Celtic), 1926 v Ni; 1927 v W (2)
M'Innes, T. (Cowlairs), 1889 v Ni (1)
M'Intosh, W. (Third Lanark), 1905 v Ni (1)
M'Intyre, A. (Vale of Leven), 1878 v E; 1882 v E (2)
M'Intyre, H. (Rangers), 1880 v W (1)
M'Intyre, J. (Rangers), 1884 v W (1)
McKay, D. (Celtic), 1959 v E, WG, Ho, P; 1960 v E, Pol, A, H, T; 1961 v W, Ni; 1962 v Ni, Cz, U (sub)(4)
Mackay, D. C. (Hearts), 1957 v Sp; 1958 v F; 1959 v W, Ni; (with Tottenham H.), 1959 v WG, E; 1960 v W, Ni, A, Pol, H, T; 1961 v W, Ni, E; 1963 v E, A, N; 1964 v Ni, W, N; 1966 v Ni (22)
M'Kay, J. (Blackburn R.), 1924 v W (1)
M'Kay, R. (Newcastle), 1928 v W (1)
McKean, R. (Rangers), 1976 v Sw (1)
M'Kenzie, D. (Brentford), 1938 v Ni (1)
Mackenzie, J. A. (Partick T.), 1954 v W, E, N, Fi, A, U; 1955 v E, H; 1956 v A (9)
M'Keown, M. (Celtic), 1889 v Ni ;1890 v E (2)
M'Kie, J. (East Stirling), 1898 v W (1)

McKillop, T. R. (Rangers), 1938 v Ho (1)
M'Kinlay, D. (Liverpool), 1922 v W, Ni (2)
McKinnon, A. (Queen's Park), 1874 v E (1)
McKinnon, R. (Rangers), 1966 v W, E, I (2), Ho, Br; 1967 v W, Ni, E; 1968 v Ni, W, E, Ho; 1969 v D, A, WG, Cy; 1970 v Ni, W, E, Ei, WG, A; 1971 v D, Bel, P, Rus, D (28)
M'Kinnon, W. (Dumbarton), 1883 v E, W; 1884 v E, W (4)
M'Kinnon, W. W. (Queen's Park), 1872 v E; 1873 v E; 1874 v E; 1875 v E; 1876 v E, W; 1877 v E; 1878 v E; 1879 v E (9)
McLaren, A. (St. Johnstone), 1929 v N, G, Ho; 1933 v W, Ni (5)
McLaren, A. (Preston N.E.), 1947 v E, Bel, L; 1948 v W (4)
M'Laren, J. (Hibernian), 1888 v W; (with Celtic), 1889 v E; 1890 v E (3)
M'Lean, A. (Celtic), 1926 v W, Ni; 1927 v W, E (4)
M'Lean, D. (St. Bernard,s) 1896 v W; 1897 v Ni (2)
M'Lean, D. (Sheffield W.), 1912 v E (1)
McLean, G. (Dundee) 1968 v Ho (1)
M'Lean, T. (Kilmarnock), 1969 v D, Cy, W; 1970 v Ni, W; 1971 v D (6)
M'Leod, D. (Celtic), 1905 v Ni; 1906 v E, W, Ni(4)
M'Leod, J. (Dumbarton), 1888 v Ni; 1889 v W: 1890 v Ni; 1892 v E; 1893 v W (5)
MacLeod, J. M. (Hibernian), 1961 v E, Ei (2), Cz; 4
M'Leod, W. (Cowlairs), 1886 v Ni (1)
McLintock, A. (Vale of Leven), 1875 v E; 1876 v E; 1880 v E (3)
McLintock, F. (Leicester C.), 1963 v N (sub) Ei, Sp; (with Arsenal), 1965 v Ni; 1967 v USSR; 1970 v Ni; 1971 v W, Ni, E (9)
McLuckie, J. S. (Manchester C.), 1934 v W (1)
M'Mahon, A. (Celtic), 1892 v E; 1893 v E, Ni; 1894 v E; 1901 v Ni; 1902 v W (6)
M'Menemy, J. (Celtic), 1905 v Ni; 1909 v Ni; 1910 v E, W; 1911 v Ni, W, E; 1912 v W; 1914 v W, Ni, E; 1920 v Ni (12)
M'Menemy, J. (Motherwell), 1934 v W (1)
McMillan, J. (St. Bernards), 1897 v W (1)
McMillan, I. L. (Airdrieonians), 1952 v E, USA, D; 1955 v E; 1956 v E; (with Rangers), 1961 v Cz (6)
McMillan, T. (Dumbarton), 1897 v Ni (1)
McMullan, J. (Partick T.), 1920 v W; 1921 v W, Ni, E; 1924 v E Ni; 1925 v E; 1926 v W; (with Manchester C.), 1926 v E; 1927 v E, W; 1928 v E, W; 1929 v W, E, Ni (16)
McNab, A. (Morton), 1921 v E, Ni (2)
McNab, A. (Sunderland), 1937 v A; (with W.B.A.), 1939 v E (2)
McNab, C. D. (Dundee), 1931 v E, W, A, I, Sw; 1932 v E (6)
McNab, J. S. (Liverpool), 1923 v W (1)
M'Nair, A. (Celtic), 1906 v W; 1907 v Ni; 1908 v E, W; 1909 v E; 1910 v W; 1912 v E, W, Ni; 1913 v E; 1914 v E, Ni; 1920 v E, W Ni (15)
McNaught, W. (Raith R.), 1951 v A, W, Ni; 1952 v E; 1955 v Ni (5)
McNeil, H. (Queen's Park), 1874 v E; 1875 v E; 1876 v E, W; 1877 v W; 1878 v E; 1879 v E, W; 1881 v E, W (10)
M'Neil, M. (Rangers), 1876 v W; 1880 v E (2)
McNeill, W. (Celtic), 1961 v E, Ei (2), Cz; 1962 v Ni, E, Cz, U; 1963 v Ei, Sp; 1964 v W, E, WG; 1965 v E, Fi, Pol .Sp; 1966 v Ni, Pol; 1967 v USSR; 1968 v E; 1969 v Cy, W, E, Cy (sub); 1970 v WG; 1972 v Ni, W, E (29)
McPhail, J. (Celtic), 1950 v W; 1951 v W, Ni, A; 1954 v Ni (5)

McPhail, R. (Airdrieonians), 1927 v E; (with Rangers), 1929 v W; 1931 v E, Ni; 1932 v W, Ni, F; 1933 v E, Ni; 1934 v A, Ni; 1935 v E; 1937 v G, E, Cz; 1938 v W, Ni (17)
McPherson, D. (Kilmarnock), 1892 v Ni (1)
McPherson, J. (Kilmarnock), 1888 v W; (with Cowlairs), 1889 v E; 1890 v Ni, E; (with Rangers), 1892 v W; 1894 v E; 1895 v E, Ni; 1897 v Ni (9)
McPherson, J. (Clydesdale), 1875 v E (1)
McPherson, J. (Vale of Leven), 1879 v E, W; 1880 v E; 1881 v W; 1883 v E, W; 1884 v E; 1885 v Ni (8)
McPherson, J. (Hearts), 1891 v E (1)
McPherson, R. (Arthurlie), 1882 v E (1)
McQueen, G. (Leeds U.), 1974 v Bel; 1975 v Sp (2), P, W, Ni, E, R; 1976 v D; 1977 v Cz, W (2), Ni, E; 1978 v EG, Cz, W (with Manchester U.), Bul, Ni, W; 1979 v A, N, P, Ni, E, N (26)
M'Queen, M. (Leith Ath.), 1890 v W; 1891 v W (2)
M'Rorie, D. M. (Morton), 1931 v W (1)
McSpadyen, A. (Partick T.), 1939 v E, H (2)
M'Stay, W. (Celtic), 1921 v W, Ni; 1925 v E, Ni, W; 1926 v E, Ni ,W; 1927 v E, Ni, W; 1928 v W, Ni (13)
M'Tavish, J. (Falkirk), 1910 v Ni (1)
M'Wattie, G. C. (Queen's Park), 1901 v W, Ni (2)
M'William. P. (Newcastle U.), 1905 v E; 1906 v E; 1907 v E, W; 1909 v E, W; 1910 v E; 1911 v W (8)
Madden, J. (Celtic), 1893 v W; 1895 v W (2)
Main, F. R. (Rangers), 1938 v W (1)
Main, J. (Hibernian), 1909 v Ni (1)
Maley, W. (Celtic), 1893 v E, Ni (2)
Marshall, H. (Celtic), 1899 v W; 1900 v Ni (2)
Marshall, J. (Rangers), 1932 v E; 1933 v E; 1934 v E (3)
Marshall, J. (Middlesbrough), 1921 v E, W, Ni; 1922 v E, W, Ni; (with Llanelly), 1924 v W (7)
Marshall, J. (Third Lanark), 1885 v Ni; 1886 v W; 1887 v E, W (4)
Marshall, R. W. (Rangers), 1892 v Ni; 1894 v Ni (2)
Martin, F. (Aberdeen), 1954 v N (2), A, U; 1955 v E, H (6)
Martin, N. (Hibernian), 1965 v Fi, Pol; (with Sunderland), 1966 v I (3)
Martis, J. (Motherwell), 1961 v W (1)
Mason, J. (Third Lanark), 1949 v E, W. Ni; 1950 v Ni; 1951 v Ni, Bel, A (7)
Massie, A. (Hearts), 1932 v Ni, W, F; 1933 v Ni; 1934 v Ni; 1935 v E, Ni, W; 1936 v W, Ni; (with Aston Villa), 1936 v E; 1937 v G, E, W, Ni, A; 1938 v W (18)
Masson, D. S. (Q.P.R.), 1976 v Ni, W, E; 1977 v Fi, Cz, W, Ni, E, Ch, Arg, Br; 1978 v EG, Cz, W, (with Derby Co.), Ni, E, Pe (17)
Mathers, D. (Partick T.), 1954 v Fi (1)
Maxwell, W. S. (Stoke C.), 1898 v E (1)
May, J. (Rangers), 1906 v W, Ni; 1908 v E, Ni; 1909 v W (5)
Meechan, P. (Celtic), 1896 v Ni (1)
Meiklejohn, D. D. (Rangers), 1922 v W; 1924 v W; 1925 v W, Ni, E; 1928 v W, Ni; 1929 v E, Ni; 1930 v E, Ni; 1931 v E; 1932 v W, Ni; 1934 v A (5)
Menzies, A. (Hearts), 1906 v E (1)
Mercer, R. (Hearts), 1912 v W; 1913 v Ni (2)
Middleton, R. (Cowdenbeath), 1930 v Ni (1)
Millar, J. (Rangers), 1897 v E; 1898 v E, W (3)
Millar, J. (Rangers), 1963 v A, Ei (2)
Miller, A. (Hearts), 1939 v W (1)
Miller, J. (St. Mirren), 1931 v E, I Sw; 1932 v F 1934 v E (5)

Miller, P. (Dumbarton), 1882 v E; 1883 v E, W (3)
Miller, T. (Liverpool), 1920 v E; (with Manchester U.), 1921 v E, Ni (3)
Miller, W. (Third Lanark), 1876 v E (1)
Miller, W. (Celtic), 1947 v E, W, Bel, L; 1948 v W, Ni (6)
Miller, W. (Aberdeen), 1975 v R; 1978 v Bul (2)
Mills, W. (Aberdeen), 1936 v W, Ni; 1937 v W (3)
Milne, J. V. (Middlesbrough), 1938 v E; 1939 v E (2)
Mitchell, D. (Rangers), 1890 v Ni; 1892 v E; 1893 v E, Ni; 1894 v E (5)
Mitchell, J. (Kilmarnock), 1908 v Ni; 1910 v Ni, W (3)
Mitchell, R. C. (Newcastle U.), 1951 v D, F (2)
Mochan, N. (Celtic), 1954 v N, A, U (3)
Moir, W. (Bolton W.), 1950 v E (1)
Moncur, R. (Newcastle U.), 1968 v Ho; 1970 v Ni, W, E, Ei; 1971 v D, Bel, W, P, Ni, E, D; 1972 v Pe, Ni, W, E (16)
Morgan, H. (St. Mirren), 1898 v W; (with Liverpool), 1899 v E (2)
Morgan, W. (Burnley), 1968 v Ni; (with Manchester U.) 1972, v Pe, Y, Cz, Br; 1973 v D (2), E (2), W, Ni, Sw, Br; 1974 v Cz (2), WG (2), Ni, Bel (sub), Br, Y (21)
Morris, D. (Raith R.), 1923 v Ni; 1924 v E. Ni; 1925 v E, W, Ni (6)
Morris, H. (East Fife), 1950 v Ni (1)
Morrison, T. (St. Mirren), 1927 v E (1)
Morton, A. L. (Queen's Park), 1920 v W, Ni; (with Rangers), 1921 v E; 1922 v E, W; 1923 v E, W, Ni; 1924 v E, W, Ni; 1925 v E, W, Ni; 1927 v E, Ni; 1928 v E, W, Ni; 1929 v E, W, Ni; 1930 v E, W, Ni; 1931 v E, W, Ni; 1932 v E, W, F (31)
Morton, H. A. (Kilmarnock), 1929 v G, Ho (2)
Mudie, J. K. (Blackpool), 1957 v W, Ni, E, Y, Sw, Sp, (2) WG; 1958 v N, E, W, Sw, H, Pol, Y, Par, F (17)
Muir, W. (Dundee), 1907 v Ni (1)
Muirhead, T. A. (Rangers), 1922 v Ni; 1923 v E; 1924 v W; 1927 v Ni; 1928 v Ni; 1929 v Ni; 1930 v W (8)
Mulhall, G. (Aberdeen). 1960 v Ni; (with Sunderland), 1963 v Ni; 1964 v Ni (3)
Munro, A. D. (Hearts), 1937 v W, Ni; (with Blackpool), 1938 v Ho (3)
Munro, F. M. (Wolverhampton W.), 1971 v Ni (sub), E (sub), D, USSR; 1975 v Se, W (sub), Ni, E, R (9)
Munro, I. (St. Mirren), 1979 v Arg, N (2)
Munro, N. (Abercorn), 1888 v W; 1889 v E (2)
Murdoch, J. (Motherwell), 1931 v Ni (1)
Murdoch, R. (Celtic), 1966 v W, E, I (2); 1967 v Ni; 1968 v Ni; 1969 v W, Ni, E, WG, Cy; 1970 v A (12)
Murphy, F. (Celtic), 1938 v Ho (1)
Murray, J. (Renton), 1895 v W (1)
Murray, J. (Hearts), 1958 v E, H, Pol, Y, F (5)
Murray, J. W. (Vale of Leven), 1890 v W (1)
Murray, P. (Hibernian), 1896 v Ni; 1897 v W (2)
Murray, S. (Aberdeen), 1972 v Bel (1)
Mutch, G. (Preston N.E.) 1938 v E (1)

Napier, C. E. (Celtic), 1932 v E; 1935 v E, W; (with Derby Co.), 1937 v Ni, A (5)
Narey, D. (Dundee U.), 1977 v Se (sub); 1979 v P, Ni (sub), Arg (4)
Neil, R. G. (Hibernian), 1896 v W; (with Rangers), 1900 v W (2)
Neill, R. W. (Queen's Park), 1876 v W; 1877 v E, W; 1878 v W; 1880 v E (5)
Neilles, P. (Hearts), 1914 v W, Ni (2)

Nelson, J. (Cardiff C.), 1922 v W, Ni; 1928 v E; 1930 v F (4)
Niblo, T. D. (Aston Villa), 1904 v E (1)
Nibloe, J. (Kilmarnock), 1929 v E, N, Ho; 1930 v W; 1931 v E, Ni, A, I, Sw; 1932 v E, F (11)
Nisbet, J. (Ayr U.), 1929 v N, G, Ho (3)
Niven, J. B. (Moffatt), 1885 v Ni (1)

O'Donnell, F. (Preston N.E.), 1937 v E, A, Cz; v 1938 E, W (with Blackpool), Ho (6)
Ogilvie, D. H. (Motherwell), 1934 v A (1)
O'Hare, J. (Derby Co.), 1970 v W, Ni, E; 1971 v D, Bel, W, Ni; 1972 v P, Bel, Ho (sub), Pe, Ni, W (13)
Ormond, W. E. (Hibernian), 1954 v E, N, Fi, A, U; 1959 v E (6)
O'Rourke, F. (Airdrieonians), 1907 v Ni (1)
Orr, J. (Kilmarnock), 1892 v W (1)
Orr, R. (Newcastle U.), 1902 v E; 1904 v E (2)
Orr, T. (Morton), 1952 v Ni, W (2)
Orr, W. (Celtic), 1900 v Ni; 1903 v Ni; 1904 v W; (3)
Orrock, R. (Falkirk), 1913 v W (1)
Oswald, J. (Third Lanark), 1889 v E; (with St. Bernards), 1895 v E; (with Rangers); 1897 v W (3)

Parker, A. H. (Falkirk), 1955 v P, Y, A; 1956 v E, Ni, W, A; 1957 v Ni, W, Y; 1958 v Ni, W, E, Sw, (with Everton) Par (15)
Parlane, D. (Rangers), 1973 v W, Sw, Br; 1975 v Sp (sub), Sc, P, W, Ni, E, R; 1976 v D; 1977 v W (12)
Parlane, R. (Vale of Leven), 1878 v W; 1879 v E, W (3)
Paterson, G. D. (Celtic), 1939 v Ni (1)
Paterson, J. (Leicester C.), 1920 v E (1)
Paterson, J. (Cowdenbeath), 1931 v A, I, Sw (3)
Paton, A. (Motherwell), 1952 v D, Se (2)
Paton, D. (St. Bernards), 1896 v W (1)
Paton, M. (Dumbarton), 1883 v E; 1884 v W; 1885 v W, E; 1886 v E (5)
Paton, R. (Vale of Leven), 1879 v E, W (2)
Patrick, J. (St. Mirren), 1897 v E, W (2)
Paul, H. McD. (Queen's Park), 1909 v E, W, Ni (3)
Paul, W. (Partick T.), 1888 v W; 1889 v W; 1890 v W (3)
Paul, W. (Dykebar), 1891 v Ni (1)
Pearson, T. (Newcastle U.), 1947 v E, Bel (2)
Penman, A. (Dundee) 1966 v Ho (1)
Pettigrew, W. (Motherwell), 1976 v Sw, Ni, W; 1977 v W (sub), Se (5)
Phillips, J. (Queen's Park), 1877 v E, W; 1878 v W (3)
Plenderleith, J. B. (Manchester C.), 1961 v Ni (1)
Porteous, W. (Hearts), 1903 v Ni (1)
Pringle, C. (St. Mirren), 1921 v W (1)
Provan, D. (Rangers), 1964 v Ni, N; 1966 v I (2), Ho (5)
Pryce, J. (Hibernians), 1897 v W (1)
Pursell, P. (Queen's Park), 1914 v W (1)

Quinn, J. (Celtic), 1905 v Ni; 1906 v Ni, W; 1908 v Ni, E; 1909 v E, 1910 v E, Ni, W; 1912 v E, W (11)
Quinn, P. (Motherwell), 1961 v E, Ei (2); 1962 v U (4)

Rae, J. (Third Lanark), 1889 v W; 1890 v Ni (2)
Raeside, J. S. (Third Lanark), 1906 v W (1)
Raisbeck, A. G. (Liverpool), 1900 v E; 1901 v E; 1902 v E; 1903 v E, W; 1904 v E; 1906 v E; 1907 v E (8)
Rankin, G. (Vale of Leven), 1890 v Ni; 1891 v E (2);
Rankin, R. (St. Mirren), 1929 v N, G, Ho (3)

Redpath, W. (Motherwell), 1949 v W, Ni; 1951 v E, D, F, Bel, A; 1952 v Ni, E (9)
Reid, J. G. (Airdrieonians), 1914 v W; 1920 v W; 1924 v Ni (3)
Reid, R. (Brentford), 1938 v E, Ni (2)
Reid, W. (Rangers), 1911 v E, W, Ni; 1912 v Ni; 1913 v E, W, Ni; 1914 v E, Ni (9)
Reilly, L. (Hibernian), 1949 v E, W, F; 1950 v W, Ni, Sw, F; 1951 v W, E, D, F, Bel, A; 1952 v Ni, W, E, USA, D, Se; 1953 v Ni, W, E, Se; 1954 v W; 1955 v H (2), P, Y, A, E; 1956 v E, W, Ni, A; 1957 v E, Ni, W, Y (38)
Rennie, H. G. (Hearts), 1900 v E, Ni; (with Hibernian), 1901 v E; 1902 v E, Ni, W; 1903 v Ni, W; 1904 v Ni; 1905 v W; 1906 v Ni; 1908 v Ni, W (13)
Renny-Tailyour, H. W. (Royal Engineers), 1873 v E (1)
Rhind, A. (Queen's Park), 1872 v E (1)
Richmond, A. (Queen's Park), 1906 v W (1)
Richmond, J. T. (Clydesdale), 1877 v E; (with Queen's Park), 1878 v E; 1882 v W (3)
Ring, T. (Clyde), 1953 v Se; 1955 v W, Ni, E, H; 1957 v E, Sp (2), Sw, WG; 1958 v Ni, Sw (12)
Rioch, B. D. (Derby Co.), 1975 v P, W, Ni, E, R; 1976 v D (2), R, Ni, W, E; 1977 v Fi, Cz, W (with Everton), W, Ni, E, Ch, Br; 1978 v Cz, (with Derby Co.), Ni, E, Pe, Ho;
Ritchie, A. (East Stirlingshire), 1891 v W (1)
Ritchie, H. (Hibernian), 1923 v W; 1928 v Ni (2)
Ritchie, J. (Queen's Park), 1897 v W (1)
Ritchie, W. (Rangers) 1962 v U (sub) (1)
Robb, D. T. (Aberdeen), 1971 v W, E, P, D (sub), USSR (5)
Robb, W. (Rangers), 1926 v W; (with Hibernian), 1928 v W (2)
Robertson, A. (Clyde), 1955 v P. A. H; 1958 v Sw, Par (5)
Robertson, G. (Motherwell), 1910 v W; (with Sheffield W.), 1912 v W; 1913 v E, Ni(4)
Robertson, G. (Kilmarnock), 1938 v Cz(1)
Robertson, H. (Dundee), 1962 v Cz(1)
Robertson, J. (Dundee), 1931 v A, I(2)
Robertson, J. (Nottingham F.), 1978 v Ni, Ir; 1979 v P, N (4)
Robertson, J. G. (Tottenham H.), 1965 v W (1)
Robertson, J. T. (Everton), 1898 v E; (with Southampton), 1899 v E; (with Rangers); 1900 v E, W; 1901 v W, Ni, E; 1902 v W, Ni, E; 1903 v E, W; 1904 v E, W, Ni; 1905 v W (16)
Robertson P. (Dundee), 1903 v Ni(1)
Robertson, T. (Queen's Park), 1889 v Ni; 1890 v E; 1891 v W; 1892 v Ni(4)
Robertson, T. (Hearts), 1898 v Ni (1)
Robertson, W. (Dumbarton), 1887 v E, W (2)
Robinson, R. (Dundee); 1974 v WG (sub); 1975 v Se, Ni, R (sub) (4)
Rough, A. (Partick T.), 1976 v Sw, Ni, W, E; 1977 v Fi, Cz, W (2), Se, Ni, E, Ch, Arg, Br; 1978 v Cz, W, Ni, E, Pe, Ir, Ho; 1979 v A, P, W, Arg, N (26)
Rowan, A. (Caledonian), 1880 v E; (with Queen's Park), 1882 v W (2)
Russell, D. (Hearts), 1895 v E, Ni; (with Celtic), 1897 v W; 1898 v Ni: 1901 v W, Ni (6)
Russell, J. (Cambuslang), 1890 v Ni(1)
Russell, W. F. (Airdrieonians), 1924 v W; 1925 v E(2)
Rutherford, E. (Rangers), 1948 v F(1)

St. John, I. (Motherwell), 1959 v WG; 1960 v E, Ni, W, Pol, A; 1961 v E; (with Liverpool), 1962, v Ni, W, E, Cz (2), U; 1963 v W, Ni, E, N, Ei (sub), Sp; 1964 v I; 1965 v E.(21)

Sawers, W. (Dundee), 1895 v W (1)
Scarff, P. (Celtic), 1931 v Ni, E (I)
Schaedler, E. (Hibernian), 1974 v WG (1)
Scott, A. S. (Rangers), 1957 v Ni, Y, WG; 1958 v W, Sw; 1959 v P; 1962 v Ni, W, E, Cz, U; (with Everton), 1964 v W, N; 1965 Fi; 1966 v P, Br(16)
Scott, J. (Hibernian), 1964 v Ho (1)
Scott, J. (Dundee), 1971 v D (sub), USSR(2)
Scott, M. (Airdrieonians), 1898 v W (1)
Scott, R. (Airdrieonians), 1894 v Ni(1)
Scoular, J. (Portsmouth), 1951 v D, F, A; 1952 v E, USA, D, Se; 1953 v W, Ni (9)
Sellar, W. (Battlefield), 1885 v E; 1886 v E; 1887 v E, W; 1888 v E (with Queen's Park), 1891 v E; 1892 v E; 1893 v E, Ni (9)
Semple, W. (Cambuslang), 1886 v W (1)
Shankly, W. (Preston N.E.), 1938 v E; 1939 v E, W, Ni, H (5)
Sharp, J. (Dundee), 1904 v W; (with Woolwich Arsenal), 1907 v W, E; 1908 v E; (with Fulham). 1909 v W (5)
Shaw, D. (Hibernian), 1947 v W, Ni; 1948 v E, Bel, Sw, F; 1949 v W, Ni(8)
Shaw, F. W. (Pollockshields Ath.), 1884 v E, W (2)
Shaw, J. (Rangers), 1947 v E, Bel, Lux; 1948 v Ni(4)
Shearer, R. (Rangers), 1961 v E, Ei (2), Cz (4)
Sillars, D. C. (Queen's Park), 1891 v Ni; 1892 v E; 1893 v W; 1894 v E; 1895 v W (5)
Simpson, J. (Third Lanark), 1895 v E, W, Ni (3)
Simpson, J. (Rangers), 1935 v E, W, Ni; 1936 v E, W, Ni; 1937 v G, E, W, Ni; A, Cz; 1938 v W, Ni, (14)
Simpson, R. C. (Celtic), 1967 v E, USSR; 1968 v Ni, E; 1969 v A (5)
Sinclair, G. L. (Hearts), 1910 v Ni; 1912 v W, Ni(3)
Sinclair, J. W. E. (Leicester C.), 1966 v P (1)
Skene, L. H. (Queen's Park), 1904 v W(1)
Sloan, T. (Third Lanark), 1904 v W (1)
Smellie, R. (Queen's Park), 1887 v Ni; 1888 v W; 1889 v E; 1891 v E; 1893 v E, Ni (6)
Smith, A. (Rangers), 1898 v E; 1900 v E, Ni, W; 1901 v E, Ni, W; 1902 v E, Ni, W; 1903 v E, Ni, W; 1904 v Ni; 1905 v W; 1906 v E, Ni; 1907 v W; 1911 v E, Ni(20)
Smith, D. (Aberdeen), 1966 v Ho; (with Rangers), 1968 v Ho (2)
Smith, G. (Hibernian), 1947 v E, Ni; 1948 v W, Bel, Sw, F; 1952 v E, USA; 1955 v P, Y, A, H; 1956 v E Ni, W; 1957 v Sp (2), Sw (18)
Smith, J. (Rangers), 1935 v W, Ni; 1938 v Ni(2)
Smith, J. (Ayr U.), 1924 v E (1)
Smith, J. (Aberdeen), 1968 v Ho (sub); (with Newcastle U.), 1974 v WG, Ni(sub), W (sub)(4)
Smith, J. E. (Celtic) 1959 v H, P (2)
Smith, Jas. (Queen's Park), 1872 v E; 1873 v E, (2)
Smith, Jno. (Mauchline), 1877 v E, W; 1879 v E, W; (with Edinburgh University), 1880 v E; (with Queen's Park), 1881 v W, E; 1883 v E, W; 1884 v E(10)
Smith, N. (Rangers), 1897 v E; 1898 v W; 1899 v E, W, Ni; 1900 v E, W, Ni; 1901 v Ni, W; 1902 v E, Ni(12)
Smith, R. (Queen's Park), 1872 v E (1)
Smith, T. M. (Kilmarnock), 1934 v E; (with Preston N.E.), 1938 v E (2)
Somers, P. (Celtic), 1905 v E, Ni; 1907 v Ni; 1909 v W (4)
Somers, W. S. (Third Lanark), 1879 v E, W; (with Queen's Park), 1880 v W (3)
Somerville, G. (Queen's Park), 1886 v E (1)
Souness, G. J. (Middlesbrough), 1975 v EG, Sp, Se; (with Liverpool), 1978 v Bul, W, E (sub), Ho; 1979 v A, N, W, Ni, E (12)

Speedie, F. (Rangers), 1903 v E, W, Ni (3)
Speirs, J. H. (Rangers), 1908 v W (1)
Stanton P. (Hibernian), 1966 v Ho; 1969 v Ni; 1970 v E, A; 1971 v D, Bel, P, USSR, D; 1972 v P, Bel, Ho, W; 1973 v W, Ni; 1974 v WG (16)
Stark, J. (Rangers), 1909 v E, Ni (2)
Steel, W. (Morton), 1947 v E, Bel, L; (with Derby Co.), 1948 v F, E, W, Ni; 1949 v E, W, Ni, F; 1950 v E, W, Ni, Sw, P, F; (with Dundee), 1951 v W, Ni, E, A (2), D, F, Bel; 1952 v W; 1953 v W, E, Ni Se (30)
Steele, D. M. (Huddersfield), 1923 v E, W, Ni (3)
Stein, C. (Rangers), 1969 v W, Ni, D, E, Cy (2); 1970 v A (sub), Ni (sub), W, E, Ei, WG; 1971 v D, USSR, Bel, D; 1972 v Cz (sub); (with Coventry C) 1973 v E (2 subs), W (sub) Ni (21)
Stephen, J. F. (Bradford), 1947 v W; 1948 v W (2)
Stevenson, G. (Motherwell), 1928 v W, Ni; 1930 v Ni, E, F; 1931 v E, W; 1932 v W, Ni; 1933 v Ni; 1934 v E; 1935 v Ni (12)
Stewart, A. (Queen's Park), 1888 v Ni; 1889 v W (2)
Stewart, A. (Third Lanark), 1894 v W (1)
Stewart, D. (Dumbarton), 1888 v Ni (1)
Stewart, G. (Queen's Park), 1893 v W; 1894 v Ni; 1897 v Ni (3)
Stewart, D. S., (Leeds U.), 1978 v EG (1)
Stewart, G. (Hibernian), 1906 v W, E; (with Manchester C.), 1907 v E, W (4)
Stewart, J. (Kilmarnock), 1977 v Ch (sub); (Middlesbrough) 1979 v N,
Stewart, W. E. (Queen's Park), 1898 v Ni; 1900 v Ni (2)
Storrier, D. (Celtic), 1899 v E, W, Ni (3)
Summers, W. (St. Mirren), 1926 v E (1)
Symon, J. S. (Rangers), 1939 v H (1)

Tait, T. S. (Sunderland), 1911 v W (1)
Taylor, J. (Queen's Park), 1872 v E; 1873 v E; 1874 v E; 1875 v E; 1876 v E, W (6)
Taylor, J. D. (Dumbarton), 1892 v W; 1893 v W; 1894 v Ni; (with St. Mirren), 1895 v Ni (4)
Taylor, W. (Hearts), 1892 v E (1)
Telfer, W. (Motherwell), 1933 v Ni; 1934 v Ni (2)
Telfer, W. D. (St. Mirren), 1954 v W (1)
Templeton, R. (Aston Villa), 1902 v E; (with Newcastle U.), 1903 v E, W; 1904 v E; (with Woolwich Arsenal), 1905 v W; (with Kilmarnock), 1908 v Ni; 1910 v E, Ni; 1912 v E, Ni; 1913 v W (11)
Thomson, A. (Arthurlie), 1886 v Ni (1)
Thomson, A. (Airdrieonians), 1909 v W; 1909 v Ni (1)
Thomson, A. (Celtic), 1926 v E; 1932 v F; 1933 v W (3)
Thomson, A. (Third Lanark), 1889 v W (1)
Thomson, C. (Hearts), 1904 v Ni; 1905 v E, Ni, W; 1906 v W, Ni; 1907 v E, W, Ni; 1908 v E, W, Ni; (with Sunderland), 1909 v W; 1910 v E; 1911 v Ni; 1912 v E, W; 1913 v E, W; 1914 v E, Ni (21)
Thomson, C. (Sunderland), 1937 v Cz (1)
Thomson, D. (Dundee), 1920 v W (1)
Thomson, J. (Celtic), 1930 v F; 1931 v E, W, Ni (4)
Thomson, J. J. (Queen's Park), 1872 v E; 1873 v E; 1874 v E (3)
Thomson, J. R. (Everton), 1933 v W (1)
Thomson, R. (Celtic), 1932 v W (1)
Thomson, R. W. (Falkirk), 1927 v E (1)
Thomson, S. (Rangers), 1884 v W, Ni (2)
Thomson, W. (Dumbarton), 1892 v W; 1893 v W; 1898 v Ni, W (4)
Thomson, W. (Dundee), 1896 v W (1)
Thornton, W. (Rangers), 1947 v W, Ni; 1948 v E, Ni; 1949 v F; 1952 v D, Se (7)

R.F. 79/80—36

Toner, W. (Kilmarnock), 1959 v W, Ni (2)
Townsley, T. (Falkirk), 1926 v W (1)
Troup, A. (Dundee), 1920 v E; 1921 v W, Ni; 1922 v Ni; (with Everton), 1926 v E (5)
Turnbull, E. (Hibernian), 1948 v Bel, Sw; 1951 v A; 1958 v H, P, Y, Par, F (8)
Turner, T. (Arthurlie), 1884 v W (1)
Turner, W. (Pollockshields), 1885 v Ni; 1886 v Ni (2)

Ure, J. F. (Dundee), 1962 v W, Cz; 1963 v W, Ni, E, A, N, Sp; (with Arsenal), 1964 v Ni, N; 1968 v Ni (11)
Urquhart, D. (Hibernian), 1934 v W (1)

Vallance, T. (Rangers), 1877 v E, W; 1878 v E 1879 v E, W; 1881 v E, W (7)
Venters, A. (Cowdenbeath). 1934 v Ni; (with Rangers), 1936 v E; 1939 v E (3)

Waddell, T. S. (Queen's Park), 1891 v Ni; 1892 v E; 1893 v E, Ni; 1895 v E, Ni (6)
Waddell, W. (Rangers), 1947 v W; 1949 v E, W, Ni, F; 1950 v E, Ni; 1951 v E, D, F, Bel, A; 1952 v Ni, W; 1954 v Ni; 1955 v W, Ni (17)
Wales, H. M. (Motherwell), 1933 v W (1)
Walker, F. (Third Lanark), 1922 v W (1)
Walker, G. (St. Mirren), 1930 v F; 1931 v Ni, A, Sw (4)
Walker, J. (Hearts), 1895 v Ni; 1897 v W; 1898 v Ni; (with Rangers), 1904 v W, Ni (5)
Walker, J. (Swindon T.), 1911, E, W, Ni; 1912 v E, W, Ni; 1913 v E, W, Ni (9)
Walker, R. (Hearts), 1900 v E, W; 1901 v E, W; 1902 v E, W, Ni; 1903 v E, W, Ni; 1904 v E, W, Ni; 1905 v E, W, Ni; 1906 v Ni; 1907 v E, Ni; 1908 v E, W, Ni; 1909 v E, W; 1912 v E, W, Ni; 1913 v E, W (29)
Walker, T. (Hearts), 1935 v E, W; 1936 v E, W, Ni; 1937 v G, E, W, Ni, A, Cz; 1938 v E, W, Ni, Cz, H; 1939 v E, W, Ni, H (20)
Walker, W. (Clyde), 1909 v Ni; 1910 v Ni (2)
Wallace, I. A. (Coventry C.), 1978 v Bul (sub); 1979 v P (sub), W (3)
Wallace, W. S. B. (Hearts), 1965 v Ni; 1966 v E, Ho; (with Celtic), 1967 v E, USSR (sub); 1968 v Ni; 1969 v E (sub) (7)
Wardhaugh, J. (Hearts), 1955 v H; 1957 v Ni (2)
Wark, J. (Ipswich T.), 1979 v W, Ni, E, Arg, N (sub) (5)
Watson, A. (Queen's Park), 1881 v E, W; 1882 v B (3)
Watson, J. (Sunderland), 1903 v E, W; 1904 v E; 1905 v E; (with Middlesbrough), 1909 v E, Ni (5)
Watson, J. (Motherwell), 1948 v Ni; (with Huddersfield T.), 1954 v Ni (2)
Watson, J. A. K. (Rangers), 1878 v W (1)
Watson, P. R. (Blackpool), 1934 v A (1)
Watson, R. (Motherwell), 1971 v USSR (1)
Watson, W. (Falkirk), 1898 v W (1)
Watt, F. (Kilbirnie), 1889 v W, Ni; 1890 v W; 1891 v E (4)
Watt, W. W. (Queen's Park), 1887 v Ni (1)
Waugh, W. (Hearts), 1938 v Cz (1)
Weir, A. (Motherwell), 1959 v WG; 1960 v E, P, A, H, T (5)
Weir, J. (Third Lanark), 1887 v Ni (1)
Weir, J. B. (Queen's Park), 1872 v E; 1874 v E; 1875 v E; 1878 v W (4)
White, John (Albion R.), 1922 v W; (with Hearts), 1923 v Ni (2)

White, J. A. (Falkirk), 1959 v WG, Ho, P; 1960 v Ni; (with Tottenham H.), 1960 v W, Pol, A, T; 1961 v W; 1962 v Ni, W, E, Cz(2); 1963 v W, Ni, E; 1964 v Ni, W, E, N, WG (22)
White, W. (Bolton W.), 1907 v E; 1908 v E (2)
Whitelaw, A. (Vale of Leven), 1887 v Ni; 1890 v W (2)
Wilson, A. (Sheffield W.), 1907 v E; 1908 v E; 1912 v E; 1913 v E, W; 1914 v Ni (6)
Wilson, A. (Portsmouth), 1954 v Fi (1)
Wilson, A. N. (Dunfermline), 1920 v E, W, Ni; 1921 v E, W, Ni; (with Middlesbrough), 1922 v E, W, Ni; 1925 v E, W, Ni (12)
Wilson, D. (Queen's Park), 1900 v W (1)
Wilson, D. (Oldham Ath.), 1913 v E (1)
Wilson, D. (Rangers), 1961 v E, W, Ni, Ei (2), Cz; 1962 v Ni, W, E, Cz, U; 1963 v W, E, A, N, Ei, Sp; 1964 v E, WG; 1965 v Ni, E, Fi (22)
Wilson, G. W. (Hearts), 1904 v W; 1905 v E. Ni; 1906 v W; (with Everton), 1907 v E; (with Newcastle U.) 1909 v E (6)
Wilson, Hugh. (Newmilns), 1890 v W; (with Sunderland), 1897 v E; (with Third Lanark), 1902 v W; 1904 v Ni (4)
Wilson, J. (Vale of Leven), 1888 v W; 1889 v Ni; 1890 v Ni; 1891 v Ni (4)
Wilson, P. (Celtic), 1926 v Ni; 1930 v F; 1931 v Ni; 1933 v E (4)
Wilson, P. (Celtic), 1975 v Sp (sub) (1)
Wilson, R. P. (Arsenal), 1972 v P. Ho (2)
Wiseman, W. (Queen's Park), 1927 v W; 1930 v Ni (2)
Wood, G. (Everton), 1979 v Ni, E, Arg (sub) (3)
Woodburn, W. A. (Rangers), 1947 v E, Bel, L; 1948 v W, Ni; 1949 v E, F; 1950 v E, W, Ni, P, F; 1951 v E, W, Ni, A(2), D, F, Bel; 1952 v E, W, Ni, USA (24)
Wotherspoon, D. N. (Queen's Park), 1872 v E; 1873 v E (2)
Wright, T. (Sunderland), 1953 v W, Ni, E (3)
Wylie, T. G. (Rangers), 1890 v Ni (1)
Yeats, R. (Liverpool), 1965 v W; 1966 v I (2)
Yorston, B. C. (Aberdeen), 1931 v NI (1)
Yorston, H. (Aberdeen), 1955 v W (1)
Young, A. (Hearts), 1960 v E, A (sub), H, T; 1961 v W, Ni; (with Everton), Ei; 1966 v P (8)
Young, A. (Everton), 1905 v E; 1907 v W (2)
Young, G. L. (Rangers), 1947 v E, Ni, Bel, L; 1948 v E, Ni, Bel, Sw, F; 1949 v E, W, Ni, F; 1950 v B, W, Ni, Sw, P, F; 1951 v E, W, Ni, A (2), D, F, Bel; 1952 v E, W, Ni, USA, D, Se; 1953 v W, E, Ni, Se; 1954 v Ni, W; 1955 v W, Ni, P, Y; 1956 v Ni, W, E, A; 1957 v E, Ni, W, Y, Sp, Sw (53)
Young, J. (Celtic), 1906 v Ni (1)
Younger, T. (Hibernian), 1955 v P, Y, A, H; 1956, v E, Ni, W, A; (with Liverpool), 1957 v E, Ni, W, Y, Sp (2), Sw, WG; 1958 v Ni, W, E, Sw, H, Pol, Y, Par (24)

WALES

Adams, H. (Berwyn Rangers), 1882 v Ni, E; (with Druids) 1883 v Ni, E (4)
Allchurch, I. J. (Swansea T.), 1951 v E, Ni, P, Sw; 1952 v E, S, Ni, R of UK; 1953 v S, E, Ni, F, Y; 1954 v S, E, Ni, A; 1955 v S, E, Ni, Y; 1956 v E, S, Ni, A; 1957 v E, S; 1958 v Ni, Is (2), H (2), M, Sw, Br; (with Newcastle U.), 1959 v E, S, Ni; 1960 v E, S; 1961 v Ni, H, Sp (2); 1962 v E, S, Br (2), M; (with Cardiff C.), 1963 v S, E, Ni, H (2); 1964 v E; 1965 v S, E, Ni, Gr, I, Ru; 1966 (with Swansea T.), v USSR, E, S, D, Br (2), Ch (68)
Allchurch, L. (Swansea T.), 1955 v Ni; 1956 v A, 1958 v S, Ni, EG, Is; 1959 v S; (with Sheffield U.), 1962 v S, Ni, Br; 1964 v E (11)
Allen, B. W. (Coventry C.), 1951 v S, E (2)
Arridge, S. (Bootle), 1892 v S, Ni; (with Everton), 1894 v Ni; 1895 v Ni; 1896 v E; (with New Brighton Tower), 1898 v E, Ni; 1899 v E (8)
Astley, D. J. (Charlton Ath.), 1931 v Ni; (with Aston Villa), 1932 v E; 1933 v E, S, Ni; 1934 v E, S; 1935 v S; 1936 v E, Ni; (with Derby Co.), 1939 v E, S; (with Blackpool), F, (13)
Atherton, R. W. (Hibernian), 1899 v E, Ni; 1903 v E, S, Ni; (with Middlesbrough), 1904 v E, S, Ni; 1905 v Ni (9)
Bailiff, W. E. (Llanelly), 1913 v E, S, Ni; 1920 v N (4)
Baker, C. W. (Cardiff C.), 1958 v M; 1960 v S, Ni 1961 v S, E, Ei; 1962 v S (7)
Baker, W. G. (Cardiff C.), 1948 v Ni (1)
Bamford, T. (Wrexham), 1931 v E, S, Ni; 1932 v Ni; 1933 v F (5)
Barnes, W. (Arsenal), 1948 v E, S, Ni; 1949 v E, S, Ni ; 1950 v E, S, Ni, Bel; 1951 v E S, Ni, P; 1952 v E, S. Ni, R of UK; 1954 v E, S; 1955 v S, Y (22)
Bartley, T. (Glossop N.E.), 1898 v E (1)
Beadles, G. H. (Cardiff C.), 1925 v E, S (2)
Bell, W. S. (Shrewsbury Engineers), 1881 v E, S; (with Crewe Alex.), 1886 v E, S, Ni (5)
Bennion, S. R. (Manchester U.), 1926 v S; 1927 v S; 1928 v S, E, Ni; 1929 v S, E, Ni; 1930 v S; 1932 v Ni (10)
Berry, G. F. (Wolverhampton W.), 1979 v WG (1)
Blew, H. (Wrexham), 1899 v E, S, Ni; 1902 v S, Ni; 1903 v E, S; 1904 v E, S, Ni; 1905 v S, Ni; 1906 v E, S, Ni; 1907 v S; 1908 v E, S, Ni; 1909 v E, S; 1910 v E (22)
Boden, T. (Wrexham), 1880 v E (1)
Bostock, A. M. (Shrewsbury), 1892 v Ni (1)
Boulter, L. M. (Brentford), 1939 v Ni (1)
Bowdler, H. E. (Shrewsbury), 1893 v S (1)
Bowdler, J. C. H. (Shrewsbury), 1890 v Ni; (with Wolverhampton W.), 1891 v S; 1892 v Ni; (with Shrewsbury), 1894 v E (4)
Bowen, D. L. (Arsenal), 1955 v S, Y; 1957 v Ni, Cz, EG; 1958 v E, S, Ni, EG. Is(2), H (2), M, Se, Br; 1959 v E, S, Ni (19)
Bowen, E. (Druids), 1880 v S; 1883 v S, (2)
Bowsher, S. J. (Burnley), 1929 v Ni (1)
Britten, T. J. (Parkgrove), 1878 v S; (with Presteigne), 1880 v S (2)
Brookes, S. J. (Llandudno), 1900 v E, Ni (2)
Brown, A. I. (Aberdare Ath.), 1926 v Ni (1)
Bryan, T. (Oswestry), 1886 v E, Ni (2)
Buckland, T. (Bangor), 1899 v E (1)
Burgess, W. A. R. (Tottenham H.), 1947 v E, S, Ni; 1948 v E, S; 1949 v E, S, Ni, P, Bel, Sw; 1950 v E, S, Ni, Bel; 1951 v S, Ni, P, Sw; 1952 v E, S, Ni, R of UK; 1953 v S, E, Ni, F, Y; 1954 v S, E, Ni, A (32)
Burke, T. (Wrexham), 1883 v E; 1884 v S; 1885 v E, S, Ni; (with Newton Heath), 1887 v E, S; 1888 v S (8)
Burnett, T. B. (Ruabon), 1877 v S (1)
Burton, A. D. (Norwich C.), 1963 v Ni, H; (with Newcastle U.), 1964 v E; 1969 v S, E, Ni, I, EG; 1972 v Cz (9)

Butler, A. (Druids), 1900 v S, Ni(2)
Butler, J. (Chirk), 1893 v E, S, Ni(3)

Cartwright, L. (Coventry C.), 1974 v E (sub), S, Ni; 1976 v S (sub); 1977 v WG (sub); (Wrexham) 1978 v Ir (sub); 1979 v Ma
Carty, T. (Wrexham), 1889 v Ni(1)
Challen, J. B. (with Corinthians), 1887 v E, S; 1888 v E; (Wellingborough G. S.), 1890 v E (4)
Chapman, T. (Newtown), 1894 v E, S, Ni; 1895 v S, Ni; (with Manchester C.), 1896 v E; 1897 v E (7)
Charles, M. (Swansea T.), 1955 v Ni; 1956 v E S, A; 1957 v E, Ni, Cz (2), EG; 1958 v E, S, EG, Is (2), H (2), M, Se Br; 1959 v E, S; (with Arsenal), 1961 v Ni, H, Sp (2); 1962 v E, S, (with Cardiff C.), 1962 v Br, Ni; 1963 v S, H (31)
Charles, W. J. (Leeds U.), 1950 v Ni; 1951 v Sw; 1953 v Ni, F, Y; 1954 v E, S, Ni, A; 1955 v S, E, Ni, Y; 1956 v E, S, A, Ni; 1957 v E, S, Ni) 1957 v Cz (2), EG; (with Juventus), 1958 v Is (2), H (2), M, Se) 1960 v S; 1962 v E, Br (2), M; (with Leeds U.), 1963 v S; (with Cardiff C.), 1964 v S; 1965 v S. USSR (38)
Clarke, R. J. (Manchester C.), 1949 v E; 1950 v S, Ni, Bel; 1951 v E, S, Ni, P, Sw; 1952 v S, E, Ni, R of UK; 1953 v S, E; 1954 v E, S, Ni; 1955 v Y, S, E; 1956 v Ni (22)
Collier, D. J. (Grimsby T.), 1921 v S(1)
Collins, W. S. (Llanelly), 1931 v S(1)
Conde, C. (Chirk), 1884 v E, S, Ni (3)
Cook, F. C. (Newport Co.), 1925 v E, S; (with Portsmouth), 1928 v E, S; 1930 v E, S, Ni; 1932 v E, (8)
Crompton, W. (Wrexham), 1931 v E, S, Ni (3)
Cross, E. A. (Wrexham), 1876 v S; 1877 v S(2)
Cross, K. (Druids), 1879 v S; 1881 v E, S (3)
Crowe, V. H. (Aston Villa), 1959 v E, Ni; 1960 v E, Ni; 1961 v S, E, Ni, Ei, H, Sp (2); 1962 v E, S, Br, M; 1963 v H (16)
Cumner, R. H. (Arsenal), 1939 v E, S, Ni (3)
Curtis, A. (Swansea C.), 1976 v E, Y, S, Ni, Y (sub), E; 1977 v WG, S (sub), Ni (sub); 1978 v WG, E, S; 1979 v WG, S (with Leeds U.) E, Ni, Ma (17)
Curtis, E. R. (Cardiff C.), 1928 v S; (with Birmingham), 1932 v S; 1934 v Ni (3)

Daniel, R. W. (Arsenal), 1951 v E, Ni, P; 1952 v E, S, Ni, R of UK; 1953 v S, E, Ni, F, Y; (with Sunderland), 1954 v E, S, Ni; 1955 v E, Ni; 1957 v S, E, Ni, Cz (21)
Darvell, S. (Oxford University), 1897 v S, Ni (2)
Davies, A. (Wrexham), 1876 v S; 1877 v S (2)
Davies, A. (Shrewsbury), 1891 v Ni (1)
Davies, A. (Druids), 1904 v S; (with Middlesbrough), 1905 v S (2)
Davies, A. O. (Barmouth), 1885 v Ni; 1886 v E, S; (with Swifts), 1887 v E, S; 1888 v E, Ni; (with Wrexham), 1889 v S; (with Crewe Alex.), 1890 v E (9)
Davies, C. (Brecon), 1899 v Ni; (with Hereford), 1900 v Ni (2)
Davies, C. (Charlton Ath.), 1972 v R (sub)(1)
Davies, D. (Bolton W.), 1904 v S, Ni; 1908 v E (sub) (3)
Davies, D. W. (Treharris), 1912 v Ni; (with Oldham Ath.), 1913 v Ni (2)
Davies, E. Lloyd (Stoke C.), 1904 v E; 1907 v E, S, Ni; (with Northampton), 1908 v S; 1909 v Ni; 1910 v Ni; 1911 v E, S; 1912 v E, S; 1913 v E, S; 1914 v Ni, E, S (16)

Davies, E. R. (Newcastle U.), 1953 v S, E; 1954 v E, S; 1958 v E, EG (6)
Davies, Rev. H. (Wrexham), 1928 v Ni(1)
Davies, Idwal (Liverpool Marine), 1923 v S(1)
Davies, J. E. (Oswestry), 1885 v E (1)
Davies, Jas. (Wrexham), 1878 v S (1)
Davies, Jno. (Wrexham), 1879 v S (1)
Davies, Jos. (Everton), 1889 v S, Ni; (with Chirk), 1891 v Ni, (with Ardwick), v E, S; (with Sheffield U.), 1895 v E, S, Ni; (with Manchester C.), 1896 v E; (with Millwall). 1897 v E; (with Reading), 1900 v E (11)
Davies, Jos. (Newton Heath), 1888 v E, S, Ni; 1889 v S; 1890 v E; (with Wolverhampton W.), 1892 v E; 1893 v E (7)
Davies, J. P. (Druids), 1883 v E, Ni (2)
Davies, Ll. (Wrexham), 1907 v Ni; 1910 v Ni, S, B; (with Everton), 1911 v S, Ni; 1912 v Ni, S, E; 1913 v Ni, S, E; 1914 v Ni(13)
Davies, L. S. (Cardiff C.), 1922 v E, S, Ni; 1923 v E, S, Ni; 1924 v E, S, Ni; 1925 v S, Ni; 1926 v E; Ni; 1927 v E, Ni; 1928 v S, Ni, E; 1929 v S, Ni, E; 1930 v E, S (23)
Davies, O. (Wrexham), 1890 v S (1)
Davies, R. (Wrexham), 1883 v Ni; 1884 v Ni; 1885 v Ni (3)
Davies, R. (Druids), 1885 v E(1)
Davies, R. L. (Wrexham), 1892 v Ni(1)
Davies, R. O. (Wrexham), 1892 v Ni, E (2)
Davies, R. T. (Norwich C.), 1964 v Ni; 1965 v E; 1966 v Br (2), Ch; (with Southampton), 1967 v S, E, Ni; 1968 v S, Ni, WG; 1969 v S, E, Ni, I, WG, R of UK; 1970 v E, S, Ni; 1971 v Cz, S, E, Ni; 1972 v R, E, S, N; (with Portsmouth) 1974 v E (29)
Davies, R. W. (Bolton W.), 1964 v E; 1965 v E, S, Ni, D, Gr, USSR; 1966 v E, S, Ni, USSR, D, Br (2), Ch (sub); 1967 v S (with Newcastle U.), E; 1968 v S, Ni, WG; 1969 v S, E, Ni, I; 1970 v EG; 1971 v R, Cz; (with Manchester C.) 1972 v E, S, N; (with Manchester U.) 1973 v E, S (sub), Ni; (with Blackpool), 1974 v Pol (34)
Davies, Stanley (Preston N.E.), 1920 v E, S, Ni; (with Everton), 1921 v E, S, Ni; (with W.B.A.), 1922 v E, S, Ni; 1923 v S; 1925 v S, Ni; 1926 v S, E, Ni; 1927 v S; 1928 v S; (with Rotherham U.), 1930 v Ni(18)
Davies, T. (Oswestry), 1886 v E (1)
Davies, T. (Druids), 1903 v E, Ni, S; 1904 v S (4)
Davies, W. (Swansea T.), 1924 v E, S, Ni; (with Cardiff C.), 1925 v E, S, Ni; 1926 v E, S, Ni; 1927 v S; 1928 v Ni; (with Notts. Co.), 1929 v E. S. Ni; 1930 v E. S. Ni (17)
Davies, W. (Wrexham), 1884 v Ni(1)
Davies, William (Wrexham), 1903 v Ni; 1905 v Ni; (with Blackburn R.), 1908 v E, S; 1909 v E, S, Ni; 1911 v E, S, Ni; 1912 v Ni (11)
Davies, W. C. (C. Palace), 1908 v S; (with W.B.A.), 1909 v E; 1910 v S; (with C. Palace), 1914 v E (4)
Davies, W. D. (Everton), 1975 v H, L, S, E, Ni; 1976 v Y (2), E, Ni; 1977 v WG, S (2), Cz, E, Ni; 1978 v K (with Wrexham), S, Cz, WG, Ir, E, S, Ni; 1979 v Ma, T, WG, S, E, Ni, Ma (30)
Davies, W. H. (Oswestry), 1876 v S; 1877 v S; 1879 v E; 1880 v E (4)
Davies, W. O. (Millwall Ath.), 1913 v E, S, Ni; 1914, v S, Ni (5)
Davis, G. (Wrexham), 1978 v Ir, E (sub), Ni
Day, A. (Tottenham H.), 1934 v Ni(1)
Deacy, N. (PSV Eindhoven), 1977 v Cz, S, E, Ni; 1978 v K (sub), S (sub), Cz (sub), WG, Ir, S (sub), Ni; (Beringen) 1979 v T (12)

Dearson, D. J. (Birmingham), 1939 v S, Ni, F (3)
Derrett, S. C. (Cardiff C.), 1969 v S, WG; 1970 v I; 1971 v Fi (4)
Dewey, F. T. (Cardiff Corinthians), 1931 v E, S (20)
Doughty, J. (Druids), 1886 v S; (with Newton Heath), 1887 v S, Ni; 1888 v E, S, Ni; 1889 v S, 1890 v E (8)
Doughty, R. (Newton Heath and Druids), 1888 v S, Ni; (2)
Durban, A. (Derby Co.), 1966 v Br (sub); 1967 v Ni; 1968 v E, S, Ni, WG; 1969 v EG, S, E, Ni, WG; 1970 v E, S, Ni, EG, I; 1971 v R, S, E, Ni, Cz, Fi; 1972 v Fi, Cz, E, S, Ni (27)
Dwyer, P. (Cardiff C.), 1978 v Ir, E, S; 1979 v T, S, E, Ni, Ma (sub) (9)

Edwards, C. (Wrexham), 1878 v S (1)
Edwards, G. (Birmingham), 1947 v E, S, Ni; 1948 v E, S, Ni; (with Cardiff C.), 1949 v Ni, P, Bel, Sw; 1950 v E, S (12)
Edwards, H. (Wrexham Civil Service), 1878 v S; 1880 v E; 1882 v E, S; 1883 v S; 1884 v Ni; 1887 v Ni (7)
Edwards, R. I. (Chester), 1978 v K (sub); 1979 v Ma, WG (3)
Edwards, J. H. (Owestry), 1895 v Ni; 1897 v E, Ni; (with Aberystwyth), 1898 v Ni (4)
Edwards, J. H. (Wanderers), 1876 v S (1)
Edwards, L. T. (Charlton Ath.), 1957 v Ni, EG (2)
Edwards, T. (Linfield), 1932 v S (1)
Egan, W. (Chirk), 1892 v S (1)
Ellis, B. (Motherwell), 1932 v E; 1933 v E, S; 1934 v S; 1936 v E; 1937 v S (6)
Ellis, E. (Nunhead), 1931 v E (with Oswestry), S; 1932 v Ni (3)
Emanuel, W. J. (Bristol C.), 1973 v E (sub), Ni (sub) (2)
England, H. M. (Blackburn R.), 1962 v Ni, Br, M; 1963 v Ni, H; 1964 v E, S, Ni; 1965 v E, S, D, Gr (2), USSR, I; 1966 v S, Ni, USSR, D; (with Tottenham H.), 1967 v S, E; 1968 v E, Ni, WG; 1969 v Ei; 1970 v R of UK, EG E, S, Ni, I; 1971 v R; 1972 v Fi, E, S, Ni; 1973 v E (3), S; 1974 v Pol; 1975 v H, L (44)
Evans, B. C. (Swansea C.), 1972 v Fi, Cz; 1973 v E (2), Pol, S; (with Hereford U.), 1974 v Pol (7)
Evans, D. G. (Reading), 1926 v Ni; 1927 v Ni, E; (with Huddersfield T.), 1929 v S (4)
Evans, H. P. (Cardiff C.), 1922 v E, S, Ni; 1924 v E, S, Ni (6)
Evans, I. (Crystal Palace), 1976 v A, E, Y (2), E, Ni; 1977 v WG, S (2), Cz, E, Ni; 1978 v K (13)
Evans, J. (Cardiff C.), 1912 v Ni; 1913 v Ni; 1914 v S; 1920 v S, Ni; 1922 v Ni; 1923 v E, Ni (8)
Evans, J. (Oswestry), 1893 v Ni; 1894 v E, Ni (3)
Evans, J. H. (Southend U.), 1922 v E, S, Ni; 1923 v S (4)
Evans, Len (Cardiff C.), 1931 v E, S; (with Birmingham), 1934 v Ni (3)
Evans, L. H. (Aberdare Ath.), 1927 v Ni (1)
Evans, M. (Oswestry), 1884 v E (1)
Evans, R. (Clapton), 1902 v Ni (1)
Evans, R. E. (Wrexham), 1906 v E, S; (with Aston Villa), Ni; 1907 v E; 1908 v E, S; (with Sheffield U.), 1909 v S; 1910 v E, S, Ni (10)
Evans, R. O. (Wrexham), 1902 v Ni; 1903 v E, S, Ni; (with Blackburn R.), 1908 v Ni; (with Coventry C.), 1911 v E, Ni; 1912 v E, S, Ni (10)
Evans, R. S. (Swansea T.), 1964 v Ni (1)
Evans, T. J. (Clapton Orient), 1927 v S; 1928 v E, S; (with Newcastle U.), 1928 v Ni (4)

Evans, W. (Tottenham H.), 1933 v Ni; 1934 v E, S; 1935 v E; 1936 v E, Ni (6)
Evans, W. A. W. (Oxford University), 1876 v S; 1877 v S (2)
Evans, W. G. (Bootle), 1890 v E; 1891 v E; (with Aston Villa), 1892 v E (3)
Evelyn, E. C. (Crusaders), 1887 v E (1)
Eyton-Jones, J. A. (Wrexham), 1883 v Ni; 1884 v Ni, E, S (4)
Farmer, G. (Oswestry), 1885 v E, S (2)
Finnigan, R. J. (Wrexham), 1930 v Ni (1)
Flynn, B. (Burnley), 1975 v L (2 subs), H (sub), S, E, Ni; 1976 v A, E, Y (2), E, Ni; 1977 v WG (sub), S (2), Cz, E, Ni; 1978 v K (2), S (with Leeds U.), Cz, WG, Ir (sub), E, S, Ni; 1979 v Ma, T, S, E, Ni, Ma (33)
Ford, T. (Swansea T.), 1947 v S; (with Aston Villa), 1947 v Ni; 1948 v S, Ni; 1949 v E, S, Ni, P, Bel, Sw; 1950 v E, S, Ni, Bel; 1951 v S; (with Sunderland), 1951 v E, Ni, P, Sw; 1952 v E, S, Ni, R of UK; 1953 v S, E, Ni, F, Y; (with Cardiff C.), 1954 v A; 1955 v S, E, Ni, Y; 1956 v S, Ni, E, A; 1957 v S (38)
Foulkes, H. E. (W.B.A.), 1932 v Ni (1)
Foulkes, W. I. (Newcastle), 1952 v E, S, Ni, R of UK; 1953 v E, S, F, Y; 1954 v E, S, Ni (11)
Foulkes, W. T. (Oswestry), 1884 v Ni; 1885 v S (2)
Fowler, J. (Swansea T.), 1925 v E; 1926 v E, Ni; 1927 v S; 1928 v S; 1929 v E (6)

Garner, J. (Aberystwyth), 1896 v S (1)
Gillam, S. G. (Wrexham), 1889 v S, Ni; (with Shrewsbury), 1890 v E, Ni; (with Clapton), 1894 v S (5)
Glascodine, G. (Wrexham), 1879 v E (1)
Glover, E. M. (Grimsby T.), 1932 v S; 1934 v Ni; 1936 v S; 1937 v E, S, Ni; 1939 v Ni (7)
Godding, G. (Wrexham), 1923 v S, Ni (2)
Godfrey, B. C. (Preston N.E.), 1964 v Ni; 1965 v D, I (3)
Goodwin, U. (Ruthin), 1881 v E (1)
Gough, R. T. (Oswestry White Star), 1883 v S, (1)
Gray, A. (Oldham Ath.), 1924 v E, S, Ni; 1925 v E, S, Ni; 1926 v E, S; 1927 v S; (with Manchester C.), 1928 v E, S; 1929 v E, S, Ni; (with Manchester Central), 1930 v S; (with Tranmere R.), 1932 v E, S, Ni; (with Chester), 1937 v E, S, Ni; 1938 v E, S, Ni (24)
Green, A. W. (Aston Villa), 1901 v Ni, (with Notts. Co.), 1903 v E; (with Notts. Co.), 1904 v S, Ni; 1906 v Ni, E, (with Nottingham F.), 1907 v E; 1908 v S (8)
Green C. R. (Birmingham C.), 1965 v USSR, I; 1966 v S, USSR, Br (2); 1967 v E; 1968 v E, S, Ni, WG; 1969 v S, I, Ni (sub) (15)
Green, G. H. (Charlton Ath.), 1938 v Ni; 1939 v B, Ni, F (4)
Grey, Dr. W. (Druids), 1876 v S; 1878 v S (2)
Griffiths, A. T. (Wrexham) 1971 v Cz (sub); 1975 v A, H (2), L (2), E, Ni; 1976 v A, E, S, E (sub), Ni, Y (2); 1977 v WG, S (17)
Griffiths, F. J. (Blackpool), 1900 v E, S (2)
Griffiths, G. (Chirk), 1887 v Ni (1)
Griffiths, J. H. (Swansea T.), 1953 v Ni (1)
Griffiths, M. W. (Leicester C.), 1947 v Ni; 1949 v P, Bel; 1950 v E, S, Bel; 1951 v E, Ni, P, Sw; 1954 v A (11)
Griffiths, P. (Chirk), 1884 v E, Ni; 1888 v E; 1890 v S, Ni; 1891 v Ni (6)
Griffiths, S. (Wrexham), 1902 v S (1)

Griffiths, T. P. (Everton), 1927 v E, Ni; 1929 v B; 1930 v E; 1931 v Ni; 1932 v Ni, S, E; (with Bolton W.), 1933 v F, E, S, Ni; (with Middlesbrough), 1934 v E, S; 1935 v E, Ni; 1936 v S, (with Aston Villa), Ni; 1937 v E, S, Ni (21)

Hallam, J. (Oswestry), 1889 v E (1)
Hanford, H. (Swansea T.), 1934 v Ni; 1935 v S; 1936 v E; (with Sheffield W.), 1936 v Ni; 1938 v E, S; 1939 v F (7)
Harrington, A. C. (Cardiff C.), 1956, v Ni; 1957 v E, S; 1958, v S, Ni, Is(2); 1961 v S, E; 1962 v E, S(11)
Harris, C. S. (Leeds U.), 1976 v E, S; 1978 v WG, Ir, E, S, Ni; 1979 v Ma, T, WG, E (sub), Ma (12)
Harris, W. C. (Middlesbrough), 1954 v A; 1957 v EG, Cz; 1958 v E, S, EG (6)
Harrison, W. C. (Wrexham), 1899 v E; 1900 v B, S, Ni; 1901 v Ni (5)
Hayes, A. (Wrexham), 1890 v Ni; 1894 v Ni(2)
Hennessey, W. T. (Birmingham), 1962 v Ni Br (2) 1963 v S, H (2); 1964 v E, S; 1965 v S, E, D, Gr, R; 1966 v E, USSR; (with Nottingham F.), 1966 v S, Ni, D, Br (2), Ch; 1967 v S, E; 1968 v E, S, Ni; 1969 v WG, EG, R of UK, EG; (with Derby Co.), 1970 v E, S, Ni; 1972 v Fi, Cz, E, S; 1973 v E (39)
Hersee, A. M. (Bangor), 1886 v S, Ni(2)
Hersee, R. (Llandudno), 1886 v Ni (1)
Hewitt, R. (Cardiff C.), 1958 v Ni, Is, Sc, H, Br (5)
Hewitt, T. J. (Wrexham), 1911 v E, S, Ni; (with Chelsea), 1913 v E, S, Ni;(with South Liverpool), 1914 v E, S (8)
Heywood, D. (Druids), 1879 v E (1)
Hibbott, H. (Newtown Excelsior), 1880 v E, S (2)
Hibbott, P. (Newtown), 1885 v S (1)
Higham, G. G. (Oswestry), 1878 v S; 1879 v E (2)
Hill, M. R. (Ipswich T.), 1972 v Cz, R (2)
Hockey, T. (Sheffield U.), 1972, Fi, R; 1973 v E (2); (with Norwich C.) Pol, S, E, Ni; (with Aston Villa), 1974 v Pol (9)
Hoddinott, T. F. (Watford), 1921 v E, S (2)
Hodgkinson, A. V. (Southampton), 1908 v Ni (1)
Hole, B. G. (Cardiff C.), 1963 v Ni; 1964 v Ni; 1964 v S, E, Ni, D, Gr (2), R, I; 1966 v E, S, Ni, R, D, Br (2), Ch; (with Blackburn R.), 1967 v S, E, Ni; 1968 v E, S, Ni, WG; (with Aston Villa), 1969 v I, WG, EG; 1970 v I; (with Swasnea C.), 1971 v R (30)
Hole, W. J. (Swansea T.), 1921 v Ni; 1922 v E; 1923 v E, Ni; 1928 v E, S, Ni; 1929 v E, S (9)
Hollins, D. M. (Newcastle U.), 1962 v Br (sub), M; 1963 v Ni, H; 1964 v E; 1965 v Ni, Gr, I; 1966 v S, D, Br (11)
Hopkins, I. J. (Brentford), 1935 v S, Ni; 1936 v E, Ni; 1937 v E, S, Ni; 1938 v E, Ni; 1939 v E, S, Ni (12)
Hopkins, M. (Tottenham H.), 1956 v Ni; 1957 v Ni, S, E, Cz(2), EG; 1958 v E, S, Ni, EG, Is(2), H(2), M, Se, Br; 1959 v E, S, Ni; 1960 v E, S; 1961 v Ni, H, Sp(2); 1962 v Ni, Br(2), M; 1963 v S, Ni, H(34)
Howell, E. G. (Builth), 1888 v Ni; 1890 v E; 1891 v E (3)
Howells, R. G. (Cardiff C.), 1954 v E, S (2)
Hugh, A. R. (Newport Co.), 1930 v Ni(1)
Hughes, A. (Rhos), 1894 v E, S (2)
Hughes, A. (Chirk), 1907 v Ni (1)
Hughes, A. J. (Aberystwyth), 1879 v S (1)
Hughes, E. (Everton), 1899 v S, Ni; (with Tottenham H.), 1901 v E, S; 1902 v Ni; 1904 v E, Ni, S; 1905 v E, Ni, S; 1906 v E, Ni; 1907 v E (14)

Hughes, E. (Wrexham), 1906 v S; (with Nottingham F.), 1906 v Ni; 1908 v S, E; 1910 v Ni, E, S; 1911 v Ni, E, S; (with Wrexham), 1912 v Ni, E, S; (with Manchester C.), 1913 v E, S; 1914 v Ni (16)
Hughes, F. W. (Northwich Victoria), 1882 v E, Ni; 1883 v E, Ni, S; 1884 v S (6)
Hughes, I. (Luton T.), 1951 v E, Ni, P, Sw (4)
Hughes, J. (Cambridge University), 1877 v S (1)
Hughes, J. (Liverpool), 1905 v E, S, Ni (3)
Hughes, J. I. (Blackburn R.), 1935 v Ni(1)
Hughes, P. W. (Bangor), 1887 v Ni; 1889 v Ni, E(3)
Hughes, W. (Bootle), 1891 v E; 1892 v S, Ni (3)
Hughes, W. A. (Blackburn R.), 1949 v E, Ni, P, Bel, Sw (5)
Hughes, W. M. (Birmingham), 1938 v E, Ni, S, 1939 v E, Ni, S, F; 1947 v E, S, Ni (10)
Humphreys, J. V. (Everton), 1947 v Ni (1)
Humphreys, R. (Druids), 1888 v Ni (1)
Hunter, W. H. (North End, Belfast), 1887 v Ni (1)

Jackson, W. (St. Helens Rec.), 1899 v Ni (1)
James, E. (Chirk), 1893 v E, Ni; 1894 v E, S, Ni; 1898 v E; 1899 v Ni (7)
James, E. G. (Blackpool), 1966 v Br (2), Ch; 1967 v Ni; 1968 v S; 1971 v Cz, S, E, Ni (9)
James, L. (Burnley, 1972 v Cz, R, S (sub); 1973 v E (3), Pol, S, Ni; 1974 v Pol, E, S, Ni; 1975 v A, H (2), L (2), S, E, Ni; 1976 v A; (with Derby Co.), S, E, Y (2), Ni; 1977 v WG, S (2), Cz, E, Ni; 1978 v K (2) (with Q.P.R.), WG; (Burnley) 1979 v T (37)
James, R. (Swansea C.), 1979 v Ma, WG (sub), S, E, Ni, Ma (6)
James, W. (West Ham U.), 1931 v Ni; 1932 v Ni(2)
Jarrett, R. H. (Ruthin), 1889 v Ni; 1890 v S (2)
Jarvis, A. L. (Hull C.), 1967 v S, E, Ni (3)
Jenkins, J. (Brighton), 1924 v Ni, E, S; 1925 v S, Ni; 1926 v E, S; 1927 v S (8)
Jenkins, R. W. (Rhyl), 1902 v Ni (1)
Jenkyns, C. A. L. (Small Heath), 1892 v E, S, Ni; 1895 v E; (with Woolwich Arsenal), 1896 v S; (with Newton Heath), 1897 v Ni; (with Walsall), 1898 v S, E(8)
Jennings, W. (Bolton W.), 1914 v E, S; 1920 v S; 1923 v Ni, E; 1924 v E, S, Ni; 1927 v S, Ni; 1929 v S(11)
John, R. F. (Arsenal), 1923 v S, Ni; 1925 v Ni; 1926 v E; 1927 v E; 1928 v E, Ni; 1930 v E, S; 1932 v E; 1933 v F, Ni; 1935 v Ni; 1936 v S 1937; v E(15)
John, W. R. (Walsall), 1931 v Ni; (with Stoke C.) 1932 v E, S, Ni; 1933 v F; 1934 v E, S; (with Preston N.E.), 1935 v E, S; (with Sheffield U.), 1936 v E, S, Ni; (with Swansea T.), 1939 v E, S (14)
Johnson, M. G. (Swansea T.), 1964 v Ni(1)
Jones, A. F. (Oxford University), 1877 v S (1)
Jones, A. T. (Nottingham F.), 1905 v E; (with Notts Co.), 1906 v E (2)
Jones, Bryn (Wolverhampton W.), 1935 v Ni; 1936 v S, Ni; 1937 v E, S, Ni; 1938 v E, S, Ni; (with Arsenal), 1939 v E, S, Ni; 1947 v S, Ni; 1948 v E; 1949 v S (17)
Jones, B. S. (Swansea T.), 1963 v S, E, Ni, H (2); 1964 v S, Ni; (with Plymouth Arg.), 1965 v D; (with Cardiff C.), 1969 v S, E, Ni, I (sub), WG, EG, R of UK (15).
Jones, Charlie (Nottingham F.), 1926 v E; 1927 v S, Ni; 1928 v E; (with Arsenal), 1930 v E, S; 1932 v E; 1933 v F (7)

Jones, Cliff (Swansea T.), 1954 v A; 1956 v E, Ni, S, A; 1957 v E, S, Ni, Cz (2), EG; 1958 v EG, E, S, Is (2); (with Tottenham H.), 1958 v Ni, H (2), M, Se, Br; 1959 v Ni; 1960 v E, S, Ni; 1961 v S, E, Ni, Sp, H, Ei; 1962 v E, Ni, S, Br (2), M; 1963 v S, Ni, H; 1964 v E, S, Ni; 1965 v E, S, Ni, D, Gr (2), USSR, I; 1967 v S, E; 1968 v E, S, WG; (with Fulham), 1969 v I, R of UK (59)

Jones, C. W. (Birmingham), 1935 v Ni; 1939 v F (2)

Jones, D. (Chirk), 1888 v S, Ni; (with Bolton W.), 1889 v E, S, Ni; 1890 v E, Ni; 1891 v S; 1892 v Ni; 1893 v E; 1894 v E; 1895 v E; 1898 v S; (with Manchester C.), 1900 v E, Ni (15)

Jones, D. E. (Norwich C.), 1976 v S, E (sub); 1978 v S, Cz, WG, Ir, E (6)

Jones, D. O. (Leicester C.), 1934 v E, Ni; 1935 v E, S; 1936 v E, Ni; 1937 v Ni (7)

Jones, Evan (Chelsea), 1910 v S, Ni; (with Oldham Ath.), 1911 v E, S; 1912 v E, S; (with Bolton W.), 1914 v Ni (7)

Jones, F. R. (Bangor), 1885 v E, Ni; 1886 v S (3)

Jones, F. W. (Small Heath), 1893 v S (1)

Jones, G. P. (Wrexham), 1907 v S, Ni (2)

Jones, H. (Aberaman), 1902 v Ni (1)

Jones, Humphrey (Bangor), 1885 v E, Ni, S; 1886 v E, Ni, S; (with Queen's Park), 1887 v E; (with East Stirlingshire), 1889 v E, Ni; 1890 v E, S, Ni; (with Queen's Park), 1891 v E, S (14)

Jones, Ivor (Swansea T.), 1920 v S, Ni; 1921 v Ni, B; 1922 v S, Ni, (with W.B.A.), 1923 v E, Ni; 1924 v S; 1926 v Ni (10)

Jones, J. (Druids), 1876 v S (1)

Jones, J. (Berwyn Rangers), 1883 v S, Ni; 1884 v S (3)

Jones, J. (Wrexham), 1925 v Ni (1)

Jones, Jeffrey (Llandrindod Wells), 1908 v Ni; 1909 v Ni; 1910 v S (3)

Jones, J. L. (Sheffield U.), 1895 v E, S, Ni; 1896 v Ni, S, E; 1897 v Ni, S, E; (with Tottenham H.), 1898 v Ni, E, S; 1899 v E, S, Ni; 1900 v S; 1902 v E,

Jones, J. Love (Stoke C.), 1906 v S; (with Middlesbrough), 1910 v Ni (2)

Jones, J. O. (Bangor), 1901 v S, Ni (2)

Jones, J. P. (Liverpool), 1976 v A, E, S; 1977 v WG, S (2), Cz, E, Ni; 1978 v K (2), S, Cz, WG, Ir, E, S, Ni; (Wrexham), 1979 v Ma, T, WG, S, E, Ni, Ma (25)

Jones, J. T. (Stoke C.), 1912 v E, S, Ni; 1913 v E, N; 1914 v S, Ni; 1920 v E, S, Ni; (with C. Palace), 1921 v E, S; 1922 v E, S, Ni (15)

Jones, K. (Aston Villa), 1950 v S (1)

Jones, Leslie J. (Cardiff C.), 1933 v F; (with Coventry C.), 1935 v Ni; 1936 v S; 1937 v E, S, Ni; (with Arsenal), 1938 v E, S, Ni; 1939 v E, S (11)

Jones, P. W. (Bristol R.), 1971 v Fi (1)

Jones, R. (Bangor), 1887 v S; 1889 v E; (with Crewe Alex.), 1890 v E (3)

Jones, R. (Bangor), 1900 v S, Ni (2)

Jones, R. (Druids), 1899 v S; (with Millwall), 1906 v S, Ni (3)

Jones, R. A. (Druids), 1884 v E, Ni, S; 1885 v S (4)

Jones, R. S. (Everton), 1894 v Ni; (with Leicester Fosse), 1898 v S (2)

Jones, S. (Wrexham), 1887 v Ni; (with Chester), 1890 v S (2)

Jones, S. (Wrexham), 1893 v S, Ni; (with Burton Swifts), 1895 v S; 1896 v E, Ni (5)

Jones, T. (Manchester U.), 1926 v Ni; 1927 v E, Ni; 1930 v Ni (4)

Jones, T. D. (Aberdare), 1908 v Ni (1)

Jones, T. G. (Everton), 1938 v Ni; 1939 v E, S, Ni; 1947 v E, S; 1948 v E, S, Ni; 1949 v E, Ni, P, Bel, Sw; 1950 v E, S, Bel (17)

Jones, T. J. (Sheffield W.), 1932 v Ni; 1933 v F (2)

Jones, W. (Druids), 1899 v E (1)

Jones, W. E. A. (Swansea T.), 1947 v E, S; (with Tottenham H.), 1949 v E, S (4)

Jones, W. J. (Aberdare), 1901 v E, S; (with West Ham U.), 1902 v E, S (4)

Jones, W. Lot (Manchester C.), 1905 v E, Ni; 1906 v E, S, Ni; 1907 v E, S, Ni; 1908 v S; 1909 v E, S, Ni; 1910 v E; 1911 v E; 1913 v E, S; 1914 v S, Ni; (with Southend U.), 1920 v E, Ni (20)

Jones, W. P. (Druids), 1889 v E, Ni; (with Wynstay), 1890 v S, Ni (4)

Jones, W. R. (Aberystwyth), 1897 v S (1)

Keenor, F. C. (Cardiff C.), 1920 v E, Ni; 1921 v E, Ni, S; 1922 v Ni; 1923 v E, Ni, S; 1924 v E, Ni, S; 1925 v E, Ni, S; 1926 v S; 1927 v E, Ni, S; 1928 v E, Ni, S; 1929 v E, Ni, S; 1930 v E, Ni, S; 1931 v E, Ni, S; (with Crewe Alex.), 1933 v S (32)

Kelly, F. C. (Wrexham), 1899 v S, Ni; (with Druids), 1902 v Ni (3)

Kelsey, A. J. (Arsenal), 1954 v E, A; 1955 v S, Ni, Y; 1956 v E, Ni, S, A; 1957 v E, Ni, S, Cz (2), EG; 1958 v E, S, Ni, Is (2), H (2), M, Se, Br; 1959 v E, S; 1960 v E, Ni, S; 1961 v E, Ni, S, H, Sp (2); 1962 v E, S, Ni Br (2) (41)

Kenrick, S. L. (Druids), 1876 v S; 1877 v S; (with Oswestry), 1879 v E, S; (with Shropshire Wanderers), 1881 v E (5)

Ketley, C. F. (Druids), 1882 v Ni (1,

King, J. (Swansea T.), 1955 v E (1)

Kinsey, N. (Norwich C.), 1951 v Ni, P, Sw; 1952 v E; (with Birmingham), 1954 v Ni; 1956 v E, S (7)

Krzywicki, R. L. (Huddersfield T.), 1970 v E, S, (with W.B.A.), Ni, EG, I; 1971 v R, Fi; 1972 v Cz (sub) (8)

Lambert, R. (Liverpool), 1947 v S; 1948 v E; 1949 v P, Bel, Sw (5)

Lathom, G. (Liverpool), 1905 v E, S; 1906 v S; 1907 v E, S, Ni; 1908 v E; 1909 v Ni; (with Southport Central), 1910 v E; (with Cardiff C.), 1913 v Ni (10)

Lawrence, E. (Clapton Orient), 1930 v Ni; (with Notts. Co.), 1932 v S (2)

Lawrence, S. (Swansea T.), 1932 v Ni; 1933 v F; 1934 v S, E, Ni; 1935 v E, S; 1936 v S (8)

Lea, A. (Wrexham), 1889 v E; 1891 v S, Ni; 1893 v Ni (4)

Lea, C. (Ipswich T.), 1965 v Ni, I (2)

Leary, P. (Bangor), 1889 v Ni (1)

Leek, K. (Leicester C.), 1961 v S, E, Ni, H, Sp (2); (with Newcastle U.), 1962 v S; (with Birmingham C.), v Br (sub), M; 1963 v E; 1965 v S, Gr; (with Northampton T.), 1965 v Gr (13)

Lever, A. R. (Leicester C.), 1953 v S (1)

Lewis, B. (Wrexham), 1891 v Ni; 1892 v S, E, Ni; (with Middlesbrough), 1893 v S, E; (with Wrexham), 1894 v S, E, Ni; 1895 v S (10)

Lewis, D. (Arsenal), 1927 v E; 1928 v Ni; 1930 v E (3)

Lewis, D. (Bangor), 1890 v Ni (1)

Lewis, D. J. (Swansea T.), 1933 v E, S (2)

Lewis, J. (Bristol R.), 1906 v E (1)

Lewis, J. (Cardiff C.), 1926 v S (1)

Lewis, T. (Wrexham), 1881 v E, S (2)

Lewis, W. L. (Swansea T.), 1927 v E, Ni; 1929 v S; (with Huddersfield T.), 1930 v E (4)

Lewis, W. (Bangor), 1885 v E; 1886 v E, S; 1887 v E, S; 1888 v E; 1889 v E, Ni, S; (with Crewe Alex.), 1890 v E, S; 1891 v E, S; 1892 v E, S, Ni; (with Chester), 1894 v E, S, Ni; (with Chester), 1895 v S, Ni, E; 1896 v E, S, Ni; (with Manchester C.), 1897 v E, S; (with Chester), 1898 v N, (30)

Lloyd, B. W. (Wrexham), 1976 v A, E, S (3)

Lloyd, J. W. (Wrexham), 1879 v S; (with Newtown), 1885 v S (2)

Lloyd, R. A. (Ruthin), 1891 v Ni; 1895 v S (2)

Lockley, A. (Chirk), 1898 v Ni (1)

Lowrie, G. (Coventry C.), 1948 v E, S, Ni; (with Newcastle U.), 1949 v P (4)

Lucas, P. M. (Leyton Orient), 1962 v Ni, M; 1963 v S, E (4)

Lucas, W. H. (Swansea T.), 1949 v S, Ni, P, Bel, Sw; 1950 v E; 1951 v E (7)

Lumberg, A. (Wrexham), 1929 v Ni; 1930 v E, S; (with Wolverhampton W.), 1932 v S (4)

McMillan, R. (Shrewsbury Engineers), 1881 v E, S (2)

Mahoney, J. F. (Stoke C.), 1968 v E; 1969 v EG; 1971 v Cz; 1973 v E (3), Pol, S, Ni; 1974 v Pol, E, S, Ni; 1975 v A, H (2), L (2), S, E, Ni; 1976 v A, Y (2), E, Ni; 1977 v WG, Cz, S, E, Ni; (with Middlesbrough) 1978 v K (2), S, Cz, Ir, E (sub), S, Ni; 1979 v WG, S, E, Ni, Ma (44)

Martin, T. J. (Newport Co.), 1930 v Ni (1)

Mates, J. (Chirk), 1891 v Ni; 1897 v E, S (3)

Mathews, R. W. (Liverpool), 1921 v Ni; (with Bristol C.),1923 v E; (with Bradford), 1926 v Ni (3)

Matthews, W. (Chester), 1905 v Ni; 1908 v E (2)

Matthias, J. S. (Brymbo), 1896 v S, Ni; (with Shrewsbury), 1897 v E, S; (with Wolverhampton W.), 1899 v S (5)

Matthias, T. J. (Wrexham), 1914 v S, E; 1920 v Ni, S, E; 1921 v S, E, Ni; 1922 v S, E, Ni; 1923 v S, (12)

Mays, A. W. (Wrexham), 1929 v Ni (1)

Medwin, T. C. (Swansea T.), 1953 v Ni, F, Y; (with Tottenham H.), 1957 v E, S, Ni, Cz (2), EG; 1958 v E, S, Ni, Is (2), H (2), M, Br; 1959 v E, S, Ni; 1960 v E, S, Ni; 1961 v S, Ei, Sp; 1963 v E, H (30)

Meredith, C. (Chirk), 1900 v S; 1901 v S, E, Ni; (with Stoke C.), 1902 v E; 1903 v Ni; 1904 v E; (with Leyton), 1970 v E (8)

Meredith, W. H. (Manchester C.), 1895 v E, Ni; 1896 v E, Ni; 1897 v E, Ni, S; 1898 v E, Ni; 1899 v E; 1900 v E, Ni; 1901 v E, Ni; 1902 v E, S; 1903 v E, S, Ni; 1904 v E; 1905 v E, S; (with Manchester U.), 1907 v E, S, Ni; 1908 v E, Ni; 1909 v E, S, Ni; 1910 v E, S, Ni; 1911 v E, S, Ni; 1912 v E, S, Ni; 1913 v E, S, Ni; 1914 v E, S, Ni; 1920 v E, S, Ni. (48)

Mielczarek, R. (Rotherham), 1971 v Fi (1)

Millership, H. (Rotherham Co.), 1920 v E, S, Ni; 1921 v E, S, Ni (6)

Millington, A. H. (W.B.A.), 1963 v S, E, H; (with C. Palace), 1965 v E, USSR; (with Peterborough U.), 1966 v Ch, Br; 1967 v E, Ni; 1968 v Ni, WG; 1969 v I, EG (with Swansea) 1970 v E, S, Ni; 1971 v Cz, Fi; 1972 v Fi (sub), Cz, R (21)

Mills, T. J. (Clapton Orient), 1934 v E, Ni; (with Leicester C.), 1935 v E, S (4)

Mills-Roberts, R. H. (St. Thomas' Hospital), 1885 v E, S, Ni; 1886 v E; 1887 v E; (with Preston N.E.), 1888 v E, Ni; (with Llanberis), 1892 v E (8)

Moore, G. (Cardiff C.), 1960 v E, S, Ni; 1961 v Ei, Sp; (with Chelsea), 1962 v Br; 1963 v Ni, H; (with Manchester U.), 1964 v S, Ni; (with Northampton T.), 1966 v Ni, Ch; (with Charlton Ath.), 1969 v S, E, Ni, R of UK; 1970 v E, S, Ni, I; 1971 v R (21)

Morgan, J. R. (Cambridge U.), 1877 v S; (with Swansea), 1879 v S; (with Derby School Staff); 1880 v E, S; 1881 v E, S; 1882 v E, S, Ni; (with Swansea), 1883 v E (10)

Morgan, J. T. (Wrexham), 1905 v Ni (1)

Morgan-Owen, H. (Oxford University), 1901 v E, S; 1902 v S; 1906 v E, Ni; (with Welshpool), 1907 v S (6)

Morgan-Owen, M. M. (Oxford University), 1897 v S, Ni; 1898 v E, S; 1899 v S; 1900 v E; (with Corinthians), 1903 v S; 1906 v S, E, Ni; 1907 v E (11)

Morley, E. J. (Swansea T.), 1925 v E; (with Clapton Orient), 1929 v E, S, Ni (4)

Morris, A. G. (Aberystwyth), 1986 v E, Ni, S; (with Swindon T.), 1897 v E; 1898 v S; (with Nottingham F.), 1899 v E, S; 1903 v E, S; 1905 v E, S; 1907 v E, S; 1908 v E; 1910 v E, S, Ni; 1911 v E, S, Ni; 1912 v E (21)

Morris, C. (Chirk), 1900 v E, S, Ni; (with Derby Co.), 1901 v E, S, Ni; 1902 v E; 1903 v E, S, Ni; 1904 v Ni; 1905 v E, S, Ni; 1906 v S; 1907 v S; 1908 v E, S; 1909 v E, S, Ni; 1910 v E, S, Ni; (with Huddersfield T.), 1911 v E, S, Ni (27)

Morris, E. (Chirk), 1893 v E, S, Ni (3)

Morris H. (Sheffield U.), 1894 v S; (with Manchester C.), 1896 v E; (with Grimsby T.), 1897 v E (3)

Morris, J. (Oswestry), 1887 v S (1)

Morris, J. (Chirk), 1898 v Ni (1)

Morris, R. (Chirk), 1900 v E, Ni; 1901 v Ni; 1902 v S; (with Shrewsbury T.), 1903 v, E, Ni (6)

Morris, R. (Druids), 1902 v E, S; (with Newtown), 1902 v Ni; (with Liverpool), 1903 v S, Ni; 1904 v E, S, Ni; (with Leeds C.), 1906 v S; (with Grimsby T.), 1907 v Ni; (with Plymouth Arg.), 1908 v Ni (11)

Morris, S. (Birmingham), 1937 v E, S; 1938 v E, S; 1939 v F (5)

Morris, W. (Burnley), 1947 v Ni; 1949 v E; 1952 v S, Ni, R of UK (5)

Moulsdale, J. R. B. (Corinthians), 1925 v Ni (1)

Murphy, J. P. (W.B.A.), 1933 v F, E, Ni; 1934 v E, S; 1935 v E, S, Ni; 1936 v E, S, Ni; 1937 v S, Ni; 1938 v E, S, (15)

Nardiello, D. (Coventry C.), 1978 v Cz, WG (sub)

Neal, J. E. (Colwyn Bay), 1931 v E, S (2)

Newnes, J. (Nelson), 1926 v Ni (1)

Newton, L. F. (Cardiff Corinthians), 1912 v Ni (1)

Nicholas, D. S. (Stoke C.), 1923 v S; (with Swansea T.), 1927 v E, Ni (3)

Nicholas, P. (C. Palace), 1979 v S (sub), Ni (sub), Ma (3)

Nicholls, J. (Newport Co.), 1924 v E, Ni; (with Cardiff C.), 1925 v E, S (4)

Nock, W. (Newtown), 1897 v Ni (1)

Nurse, M. T. G. (Swansea C.), 1960 v E, Ni; 1961 v S, E, H, Ni, Ei, Sp (2); (with Middlesbrough), 1963 v E, H; 1964 v S (12)

O'Callaghan, E. (Tottenham H.), 1929 v Ni; 1930 v S; 1932 v S, E; 1933 v Ni, S, E; 1934 v Ni, S, E; 1935 v E (11)

Oliver, A. (Blackburn R.), 1905 v E (with Bangor), S (2)

O'Sullivan, P. A. (Brighton), 1973 v S (sub); 1976 v S; 1979 v Ma (sub),
Owen, D. (Oswestry), 1879 v E (1)
Owen, E. (Ruthin Grammar School), 1884 v E, Ni, S (3)
Owen, G. (Chirk), 1888 v S; (with Newton Heath), 1889 v S, Ni; 1892 v E; 1893 v Ni (5)
Owen, T. (Oswestry), 1879 v E (1)
Owen, Trevor (Crewe Alex.), 1899 v E, S (2)
Owen, W. (Chirk), 1884 v E; 1885 v Ni; 1887 v E; 1888 v E; 1889 v E, Ni, S; 1890 v S, Ni; 1891 v E, S, Ni; 1892 v E, S; 1893 v S, Ni (16)
Owen, W. P. (Ruthin), 1880 v E, S; 1881 v E. S; 1882 v E, S, Ni; 1883 v E, S; 1884 v E, S, Ni (12)
Owens, J. (Wrexham), 1902 v S (1)

Page, M. E. (Birmingham C.), 1971 v Fi; 1972 v S Ni; 1973 v E (1 + 1 sub), Ni; 1974 v S, Ni; 1975 v H, L, S, E, Ni; 1976 v E, Y (2), E, Ni; 1977 v WG, S; 1978 v K (sub + 1), WG, Ir, E, S; 1979 v Ma, WG (28)
Palmer, D. (Swansea T.), 1957 v Cz; 1958 v E, EG(3)
Parris, J. E. (Bradford), 1932 v Ni (1)
Parry, B. J. (Swansea T.), 1951 v S (1)
Parry, C. (Everton), 1891 v E, S; 1893 v E; 1894 v E; 1895 v E, S; (with Newtown), 1896 v E, S, Ni; 1897 v Ni; 1898 v E, S, Ni (13)
Parry, E. (Liverpool), 1922 v S; 1923 v E, Ni; 1925 v Ni; 1926 v Ni (5)
Parry, H. (Newtown), 1895 v Ni (1)
Parry, M. (Liverpool), 1901 v E, S, Ni; 1902 v E, S, Ni; 1903 v E, S; 1904 v E, Ni; 1906 v E; 1908 v E, S, Ni; 1909 v S (16)
Parry, T. D. (Oswestry), 1900 v E, S, Ni; 1901 v E, S, Ni; 1902 v E (7)
Paul, R. (Swansea T.), 1949 v E, S, Ni, P, Sw; 1950 v E, S, Ni, Bel; (with Manchester C.), 1951 v S, E, Ni, P, Sw; 1952 v E, S, Ni, R of UK; 1953 v S, E, Ni, F, Y; 1954 v E, S, Ni; 1955 v E, Y; 1956 v E, Ni, S, A (33)
Peake, E. (Aberystwyth), 1908 v Ni; (with Liverpool), 1909 v Ni, S, E; 1910 v S, Ni; 1911 v Ni; 1912 v E; 1913 v E, Ni; 1914 v Ni (11)
Peers, E. J. (Wolverhampton W.), 1914 v Ni, S, E; 1920 v E, S; 1921 v S, Ni, E; (with Port Vale), 1922 v E, S, Ni; 1923 v E (12)
Perry, E. (Doncaster R.), 1938 v E, S, Ni (3)
Phennah, E. (Civil Service), 1878 v S (1)
Phillips, C. (Wolverhampton W.), 1931 v Ni; 1932 v E; 1933 v S; 1934 v E, S, Ni; 1935 v E, S, Ni; 1936 v S; (with Aston Villa), 1936 v E, Ni; 1938 v S (13)
Phillips, L. (Cardiff C.), 1971 v Cz, S, E, Ni; 1972 v Cz, R, S, Ni; 1973 v E; 1974 v Pol (sub), Ni; 1975 v A (with Aston Villa), H (2), L (2), S, E, Ni; 1976 v A, E, Y (2), E, Ni; 1977 v WG, S (2), Cz, E; 1978 v K (2), S, Cz, WG, E, S; 1979 v Ma (Swansea C.), T, WG, S, E, Ni, Ma (44)
Phillips, T. J. S. (Chelsea), 1973 v E; 1974 v E; 1975 v H (sub); 1978 v K (4)
Phoenix, H. (Wrexham), 1882 v S (1)
Poland, G. (Wrexham), 1939 v Ni, F(2)
Powell, A. (Leeds U.), 1947 v E, S; 1948 v E, S, Ni; (with Everton), 1949 v E; 1950 v Bel; (with Birmingham), 1951 v S(8)
Powell, D. (Wrexham), 1968 v WG; (with Sheffield U.), 1969 v S, E, Ni, I, WG; 1970 v E, S, Ni, EG; 1971 v R (11)
Powell, I. V. (Q.P.R.), 1947 v E; 1948 v E, S, Ni; (with Aston Villa), 1949 v Bel; 1950 v S, Bel; 1951 v S(8)
Powell, J. (Druids), 1878 v S; 1880 v E, S; 1882 v E, S, Ni; 1883 v E, S, Ni; (with Bolton W.), 1884 v E; (with Newton Heath), 1887 v E, S; 1888 v E, S, Ni (15)
Powell, Seth (W.B.A.), 1885 v S; 1886 v E, Ni; 1891 v E, 5; 1892 v E, S (7)
Price, H. (Aston Villa), 1907 v S; (with Burton U.), 1908 v Ni; (with Wrexham), 1909 v S, E, Ni (5)
Price, J. (Wrexham), 1877 v S; 1878 v S; 1879 v E; 1880 v E, S; 1881 v E, S; (with Druids), 1882 v S, E, Ni; 1883 v S, Ni(12)
Pring, K. D. (Rotherham), 1966 v Ch, D; 1967 v Ni (3)
Pryce-Jones, A. W. (Newtown), 1895 v E (1)
Pryce-Jones, W. E. (Cambridge University), 1887 v S; 1888 v S, E, Ni; 1890 v Ni(5)
Pugh, A. (Rhostyllen), 1889 v S (sub) (1)
Pugh, D. H. (Wrexham), 1896 v S, Ni; 1897 v S, Ni; (with Lincoln C.), 1900 v S; 1901 v S, E (7)
Pugsley, J. (Charlton Ath.), 1930 v Ni(1)
Pullen, W. J. (Plymouth Arg.), 1926 v E(1)

Rankmore, F. E. J. (Peterborough), 1966 v Ch (sub)(1)
Rea, J. C. (Aberystwyth), 1894 v Ni, S, E; 1895 v S; 1896 v S, Ni; 1897 v S, Ni; 1898 v Ni (9)
Reece, G. I. (Sheffield U.), 1966 v E, S, Ni, USSR; 1967 v S; 1969 v R of UK (sub); 1970 v I (sub); 1971 v S, E, Ni, Fi; 1972 v Fi, R, E (sub), S, Ni; (with Cardiff C.), 1973 v E (sub), Ni; 1974 v Pol (sub), E, S, Ni; 1975 v A, H (2), L (2), S, Ni (29)
Reed, W. G. (Ipswich T.), 1955 v S, Y (2)
Rees, R. R. (Coventry C.) 1965 v S, E, Ni, D, Gr (2), I, R; 1966 v E, S, Ni, R, D, Br (2), Ch; 1967 v E, Ni; 1968 v E, S, Ni (with W.B.A.), WG; 1969 v I; (with Nottingham F.), 1969 v WG, EG, S, (sub), R of UK; 1970 v E, S, Ni, EG, I; 1971 v Cz, R, E (sub), Ni (sub), Fi; 1972 v Cz (sub), R (39)
Rees, W. (Cardiff C.), 1949 v Ni, Bel, Sw; (with Tottenham H.), 1950 v Ni (4)
Richards, A. (Barnsley), 1932 v S(1)
Richards, D. (Wolverhampton W.), 1931 v Ni; 1933 v E, S, Ni; 1934 v E, S, Ni; 1935 v E, S, Ni; 1936 v S; (with Brentford), 1936 v E, Ni; 1937 v S, E; (with Birmingham), 1937 v Ni; 1938 v E, S, Ni; 1939 v E, S(21)
Richards, G. (Druids), 1899 v E, S, Ni; (with (Oswestry), 1903 v Ni; (with Shrewsbury), 1904 v S; 1905 v Ni(6)
Richards, R. W. (Wolverhampton W.), 1920 v E, S; 1921 v Ni; 1922 v E, S; (with West Ham U.), 1924 v E, S, Ni; (with Mold), 1926 v S (9)
Richards, S. V. (Cardiff C.), 1947 v E(1)
Richards, W. E. (Fulham), 1933 v Ni(1)
Roach, J. (Oswestry), 1885 v Ni(1)
Robbins, W. W. (Cardiff C.), 1931 v E, S; 1932 v Ni, E, S; (with W.B.A.), 1933 v F, E, S, Ni; 1934 v S; 1936 v S(11)
Roberts, D. F. (Oxford U.), 1973 v Pol, E (sub), Ni; 1974 v E, S; 1975 v A; (with Hull C.), L, Ni; 1976 v S, Ni, Y; 1977 v E (sub), Ni; 1978 v K (1 + sub), S, Ni (18)
Roberts, J. G. (Arsenal), 1971 v S, E, Ni, Fi; 1972 v Fi, E, Ni; (with Birmingham C.), 1973 v E (2), Pol, S, Ni; 1974 v Pol, E, S, Ni; 1975 v A, H, S, F; 1976 v E, S (22)
Roberts, J. H. (Bolton), 1949 v Bel(1)
Roberts, J. (Corwen), 1879 v S; 1880 v E, S; 1882 v E, S, Ni; (with Berwyn R.), 1883 v E(7)
Roberts, J. (Ruthin), 1881 v S; 1882 v S (2)
Roberts, J. (Bradford C.), 1906 v Ni; 1907 v Ni(2)

Roberts, Jas. (Chirk), 1898 v S (1)
Roberts, Jas. (Wrexham), 1913 v S, Ni (2)
Roberts, P. S. (Portsmouth), 1974 v E; 1975 v A, H, L (4)
Roberts, R. (Rhos), 1891 v Ni; (with Crewe Alex.) 1893 v E (2)
Roberts, R. (Druids), 1884 v S; (with Bolton W.); 1837 v S; 1888 v S, E; 1889 v S, E; 1890 v S; 1892 v Ni; (with P.N.E.) v S (9)
Roberts, R. (Wrexham), 1886 v Ni; 1887 v Ni; 1891 v Ni (3)
Roberts, W. (Llangollen), 1879 v E, S; 1880 v E, S; (with Berwyn R.), 1881 v S; 1883 v E, S (7)
Roberts, W. (Wrexham), 1886 v E, S, Ni; 1887 v Ni (4)
Roberts, N. H. (Ruthin), 1882 v E, S; 1883 v E, S, N; (with Rhyl), 1884 v S (6)
Rodrigues, P. J. (Cardiff C.), 1965 v Ni, Gr (2), 1966 v E, R, E, S, D; (with Leicester C.), v Ni, Br (2), Ch; 1967 v S; 1968 v E, S, Ni; 1969 v E, Ni, EG, R of UK; 1970 v E, S, Ni, EG; (with Sheffield W.) 1971 v R, E, S, Cz, Ni; 1972 v Fi, Cz, R, E, Ni (sub); 1973 v E (3), Pol, S, Ni; 1974 v Pol (40)
Rogers, J. P. (Wrexham), 1896 v E, S, Ni (3)
Rogers, W. (Wrexham), 1931 v E, S (2)
Roose, L. R. (Aberystwyth), 1900 v Ni; (with London Welsh), 1901 v E, S, Ni; (with Stoke C.), 1902 v E, S; 1904 v E; (with Everton), 1905 v S, B; (with Stoke C.), 1906 v E, S, Ni; 1907 v E, S, Ni; (with Sunderland), 1908 v E, S; 1909 v E, S, Ni; 1910 v E, S, Ni; 1911 v S (24)
Rouse, R. V. (C. Palace), 1959 v Ni (1)
Rowlands, A. C. (Tranmere R.), 1914 v E (1)
Rowley, T. (Tranmere R.), 1959 v Ni (1)
Russell, M. R. (Merthyr T.), 1912 v S, Ni; 1914 v E; (with Plymouth Arg.), 1920 v E, S, Ni; 1921 v E, S, Ni; 1922 v E, Ni; 1923 v E, S, Ni; 1924 v E, S, Ni; 1925 v E, S; 1926 v E, S; 1928 v S; 1929 v E (23)

Sabine, H. W. (Oswestry), 1887 v Ni (1)
Savin, G. (Oswestry), 1878 v S (1)
Sayer, P. (Cardiff C.), 1977 v Cz, S, E, Ni; 1978 v K (2), S,
Scrine, F. H. (Swansea T.), 1950 v E, Ni (2)
Sear, C. R. (Manchester C.), 1963 v E (1)
Shaw, E. G. (Oswestry), 1882 v Ni; 1884 v S, Ni (3)
Sherwood, A. T. (Cardiff C.), 1947 v E, Ni; 1948 v S, Ni; 1949 v E, S, Ni, P, Sw; 1950 v E, S, Ni, Bel; 1951 v E, S, Ni, P, Sw; 1952 v E, S, Ni, R of UK; 1953 v E, Ni, F, Y; 1954 v E, S, Ni, A; 1955 S, E, Y, Ni; 1956 v E, S, Ni, A; (with Newport Co.), 1957 v E, S (41)
Shone, W. W. (Oswestry), 1879 v E (1)
Shortt, W. W. (Plymouth Arg.), 1947 v Ni; 1950 v Ni, Bel; 1952 v E, S, Ni, R of UK; 1953 v S, E, Ni, F, Y (12)
Showers, D. (Cardiff C.), 1975 v E (sub), Ni (2)
Sidlow, C. (Liverpool), 1947 v E, S; 1948 v E. S, Ni; 1949 v S, 1950 v E (7)
Sisson, H. (Wrexham Olympic), 1885 v Ni; 1886 v S, Ni (3)
Smallman, D. P. (Wrexham), 1974 v E (sub), S (sub), Ni; (with Everton) 1975 v H (sub), E, Ni (sub); 1976 v A (7)
Sprake, G. (Leeds U.), 1964 v S, Ni; 1965 v S, D, Gr; 1966 v E, Ni, USSR; 1967 v S; 1968 v E, S; 1969 v S, E, Ni, WG, R of UK; 1970 v EG, I; 1971 v R, S, E, Ni; 1972 v Fi, E, S, Ni; 1973 v E (2), Pol, S, Ni; 1974 v Pol (with Birmingham C.) S, Ni; 1975 v A, H, L (37)
Stanfield, F. (Cardiff C.), 1949 v S (1)

Stevenson, B. (Leeds U.), 1978 v Ni; 1979 v Ma, T, S, E, Ni, Ma (7)
Stitfall, R. F. (Cardiff C.), 1953 v E; 1957 v Cz (2)
Sullivan, D. (Cardiff C.), 1953 v Ni, F, Y; 1954 v Ni; 1955 v E, Ni; 1957 v E, S; 1958 v Ni, H (2), Se, Br; 1959 v S, Ni; 1960 v E, S (17)

Tapscott, D. R. (Arsenal), 1954 v A; 1955 v S, E, Ni, Y; 1956 v E, Ni, S. A; 1957 v Ni, Cz, EG; (with Cardiff C.), 1959 v E, Ni (14)
Taylor, J. (Wrexham), 1898 v E (1)
Taylor, O. D. S. (Newtown), 1893 v S, Ni; 1894 v S, Ni (4)
Thomas, C. (Druids) 1899 v Ni; 1900 v S (2)
Thomas, D.A.(Swansea T.), 1957 v Cz; 1958 v EG (2).
Thomas, D. S. (Fulham), 1948 v E, S, Ni; 1949 v S (4)
Thomas, E. (Cardiff Corinthians), 1925 v E (1)
Thomas, G. (Wrexham), 1885 v E, S (2)
Thomas, H. (Manchester U.), 1927 v E (1)
Thomas, M. (Wrexham), 1977 v WG, S (1+1 sub), Ni; 1978 v K (sub), S, Cz, Ir, E, Ni (sub); 1979 v Ma (Manchester U.), T, WG, Ma (sub) (14)
Thomas, R. J. (Swindon T.), 1967 v Ni; 1968 v WG; 1969 v E, Ni, I, WG, R of UK; 1970 v E, S, Ni, EG, I; 1971 v S, E, Ni, R, Cz; 1972 v Fi, Cz, R, E, S, Ni; 1973 v E (3), Pol, S, Ni; 1974 v Pol; (with Derby Co.), E, S Ni; 1975 v H (2), L (2), S, E, Ni; 1976 v A. Y. E.; 1977 v Cz, S, E, Ni; 1978 v K, S, (with Cardiff C.) Cz, (50)
Thomas, T. (Bangor), 1898 v S, Ni (2)
Thomas, W. R. (Newport Co.), 1931 v E, S (2)
Thomson, D. (Druids), 1876 v S (1)
Thomson, G. F. (Druids), 1876 v S; 1877 v S (2)
Toshack, J. B. (Cardiff C.), 1969 v S, E, Ni, WG, EG, R of UK; 1970 v EG, I; (with Liverpool), 1971 v S, E, Ni, Fi; 1972 v Fi, E; 1973 v E (3). Pol, S; 1975 v A, H (2), L (2), S, E; 1976 v Y (2), E; 1977 v S; 1978 v R (2) S, Cz; (Swansea C.), 1979 v WG (sub), S, E, Ni, Ma (39)
Townsend, W. (Newtown), 1887 v Ni; 1893 v Ni (2)
Trainer, H. (Wrexham), 1895 v E, S, Ni (3)
Trainer, J. (Bolton W.), 1887 v S; (with Preston N.E.), 1888 v S; 1889 v E; 1890 v S; 1891 v S; 1892 v Ni, S; 1893 v E; 1894 v Ni, E; 1895 v Ni, E; 1896 v S; 1897 v Ni, S, E; 1898 v S, E; 1899 v Ni, S (20)
Turner, H. G. (Charlton Ath.), 1937 v E, S, Ni; 1938 v E, S, Ni; 1939 v Ni, F (8)
Turner, J. (Wrexham), 1892 v E (1)
Turner, R. E. (Wrexham), 1891 v E, Ni (2)
Turner, W. H. (Wrexham) 1887 v E, Ni; 1890 v S; 1891 v S, E (5)

Vaughan, Jas. (Druids), 1893 v E, S, Ni; 1899 v E (4)
Vaughan, John (Oswestry), 1879 v S; 1880 v S; 1881 v E, S; 1882 v E, S, Ni; 1883 v E, S, Ni; (with Bolton W.), 1884 v E (11)
Vaughan, J. O. (Rhyl), 1885 v Ni; 1886 v Ni, E, S (4)
Vaughan, T. (Rhyl), 1885 v E (1)
Vearncombe, G. (Cardiff C.), 1958 v EG; 1961 v Ei (2)
Vernon, T. R. (Blackburn R.), 1957 v Ni, Cz (2), EG; 1958 v E, S, EG, Se; 1959 v S; (with Everton) 1960 v Ni; 1961 v S, E, Ei; 1962 v Ni, Br (2), M; 1963 v S, E, H; 1964 v E, S; (with Stoke C.) 1965 v Ni, Gr, I; 1966 v E, S, Ni, USSR, D; 1967 v Ni; 1968 v E (32)
Villars, A. K. (Cardiff C.), 1974 v E, S, Ni (sub) (3)
Vizard, E. T. (Bolton W.), 1911 v E, S, Ni; 1912 v E, S; 1913 v S; 1914 v E, Ni; 1920 v E; 1921 v E, S, Ni; 1922 v E, S; 1923 v E, Ni; 1924 v E, S, Ni; 1926 v E, S; 1927 v S (22)

Walley, J. T. (Watford), 1971 v Cz(1)
Ward, D. (Bristol R.), 1959 v E; (with Cardiff C.), 1962 v E (2)
Warner, J. (Swansea T.), 1937 v E; (with Manchester U.), 1939 v F (2)
Warren, F. W. (Cardiff C.), 1929 v Ni; (with Middlesbrough), 1931 v Ni; 1933 v F, E; (with Hearts), 1937 v Ni; 1938 v Ni (6)
Watkins, A. E. (Leicester Fosse), 1898 v E, S;(with Aston Villa) 1900 v E, S; (with Millwall), 1904 v Ni (5)
Watkins, W. M. (Stoke), 1902 v E; 1903 v E, S; (with Aston Villa); 1904 v E, S, Ni; (with Sunderland), 1905 v E, S, Ni (with Stoke C.) 1908 v Ni (10)
Webster, C. (Manchester U.), 1957 v Cz; 1958 v H, M, Br (4)
Whatley, W. J. (Tottenham H.), 1939 v E, S (2)
White, P. F. (London Welsh), 1896 v Ni(1)
Wilcocks, A. R. (Oswestry), 1890 v Ni(1)
Wilding, J. (Wrexham O.), 1885 v E, S, Ni; 1886 v E, Ni; (with Bootle), 1887 v E; 1888 v S, Ni;(with Wrexham) 1892 v S (9)
Williams, A. L. (Wrexham) 1931 v E (1)
Williams, B. D. (Swansea T.), 1928 v Ni, E; 1930 v E, S; (with Everton), 1931 v Ni; 1932 v E; 1933 v E, S, Ni; 1935 v Ni(10)
Williams, B. (Bristol C.), 1930 v Ni (1)
Williams, D. R. (Merthyr T.), 1921 v E, S; (with Sheffield W.), 1923 v S; 2926 v S; 1927 v E, Ni; (with Manchester U.), 1929 v E, S (8)
Williams, E. (Crewe Alex.), 1893 v E, S (2)
Williams, E.(Druids) 1901 v E, Ni, S; 1902 v E, Ni(5)
Williams, G. (Chirk), 1893 v S; 1894 v S; 1895 v E, S, Ni; 1898 v Ni (6)
Williams, G. E. (W.B.A.), 1960 v Ni; 1961 v S, E, Ei; 1963 v Ni, H; 1964 v E, S, Ni; 1965 v S, E, Ni, D, Gr (2), R. I. 1966 v Ni, Br (2), Ch; 1967 v S, E, Ni; 1968 v Ni; 1969 v I (26)
Williams, G. G. (Swansea T.), 1961 v Ni, H, Sp (2); 1962 v E(5)
Williams, G. J. J. (Cardiff C.), 1951 v Sw(1)
Williams, G. O. (Wrexham), 1907 v Ni (1)
Williams, H. J. (Swansea), 1965 v Gr (2); 1972 v R (3)
Williams, H. T. (Newport Co), 1949 v Ni, Sw; (with Leeds U.), 1950 v Ni; 1951 v S (4)
Williams, J. T. (Wrexham), 1939 v F (1)
Williams, J. H. (Oswestry), 1884 v E (1)
Williams, J. T. (Middlesbrough), 1925 v Ni (1)
Williams, J. W. (C. Palace), 1912 v S, Ni (2)
Williams, R. (Newcastle U.), 1935 v S E (2),
Williams, R. P. (Caernarvon), 1886 v S(1)
Williams, S. G. (W.B.A.), 1954 v ; 1955 v E, Ni 1956 v E, S, A; 1958 v E, S, Ni, Is (2), H (2), M. Se, Br; 1959 v E, S, Ni; 1960 v E, S, Ni; 1961 v Ni, Ei, H, Sp (2); 1962 v E, S, Ni, Br (2), M; (with Southampton), 1963 v S, E, H (2); 1964 v E, S; 1965 v S, E, D;'1966 v D (43)
Williams, W. (Druids), 1876 v S; 1878 v S; (with Oswestry), 1879 v E, S; (with Druids), 1880 v E, S; 1881 v E, S; 1882 v E, S, Ni; 1883 v Ni(12)
Williams, W. (Northampton), 1925 v S (1)
Witcomb, D. F. (W.B.A.), 1947 v E, S; (with Sheffield W.), 1947 v Ni (3)
Woosnam, A. P. (Leyton Orient), 1959 v S; (with West Ham U.) v E; 1960 v E, S, Ni; 1961 v S, E, Ni, Ei, Sp, H; 1962 v E, S, Ni, Br; (with Aston Villa), 1963 v Ni H (17)
Woosnam, G. (Newton White Star), 1879 v S(1)
Worthington, T. (Newtown), 1894 v S(1)

Wynn, G. A. (Chirk), 1903 v Ni; (with Wrexham) 1909 v E, S, Ni; (with Manchester C.), 1910 v E; 1911 v Ni; 1912 v E, S; 1913 v E, S; 1914 v E, S (12)

Yorath, T. C. (Leeds U.), 1970 v I; 1971 v S, E, Ni; 1972 v Cz, E, S, Ni; 1973 v E, Pol, S; 1974 v Pol, E, S, Ni; 1975 v A, H (2), L (2), S; 1976 v A, E, S, Y (2), E, Ni; (with Coventry C.) 1977 v WG, S (2), Cz, E, Ni; 1978 v K (2), S, Cz, WG, Ir, E, S, Ni; 1979 v T, WG, S, E, Ni (48)

REPUBLIC OF IRELAND

Aherne, T. (Belfast Celtic), 1946 v P, Sp;(Luton T) 1950 v Fi, E, Fi, Se, Bel; 1951 v N, Arg, N; 1952 v WG (2), A, Sp; 1953 v F; 1954 v F (16)
Ambrose, P. (Shamrock R.), 1955 v N, Ho; 1964 v Pol, N, E (5)
Andrews, P. (Bohemians) 1936 v Ho (1)
Arrigan, T. (Waterford), 1938 v N (1)

Bailham, E. (Shamrock R), 1964 v E (1)
Barber, E. (Shelbourne), 1966 v Sp; (Birmingham City) 1966 v Bel (2)
Barry, P. (Fordsons), 1928 v Bel; 1929 v Bel (2)
Bermingham, J. (Bohemians), 1929 v Bel (1)
Bermingham, P. (St James' Gate), 1935 v H (1)
Braddish, S. (Dundalk), 1978 v Pol (1)
Bradshaw, P. (St James' Gate), 1939 v Sw, Pol, H (2), G (5)
Brady, F. (Fordsons), 1926 v I; 1927 v I (2)
Brady, T. R. (Q.P.R.), 1964 v A (2), Sp (2), Pol, N (6)
Brady, W. L. (Arsenal), 1975 v USSR, T, Sw, USSR, Sw; 1976 v T, N, Pol; 1977 v E, T, F (2), Sp, Bul; 1978 v Bul, N; 1979 v Ni, E, D, Bul, WG, Arg (22)
Breen, T. (Manchester U.), 1937 v Sw, F;(Shamrock R.), 1947 v E, Sp, P (5)
Brennan, F. (Drumcondra), 1965 v Bel(1)
Brennan, S. A. (Manchester U.), 1965 v Sp; 1966 v Sp, A, Bel; 1967 v Sp, T, Sp; 1969 v Cz, D, H; 1970 v S, Cz, D, H, Pol(sub), WG; (Waterford), 1971 v Pol, Se, I, (19)
Brown, J. (Coventry C.) 1937 v Sw, F (2)
Browne, W. (Bohemians), 1964 v A, Sp, E (3)
Burke, F. (Cork), 1934 v Bel (1)
Burke, F. (Cork Ath.), 1952 v WG (1)
Burke, J. (Shamrock R.), 1929 v Bel (1)
Byrne, A. B. (Southampton), 1970 v D, Pol, WG, 1971 v Pol, Se (2), I (2), A; 1973 v F, USSR (sub), F, N; 1974 v Pol (14)
Byrne, D. (Shelbourne), 1929 v Bel; (Shamrock R.), 1932 v Sp; (Coleraine), 1934 v Bel (3)
Byrne, J. (Bray Unknowns), 1928 v Bel (1)
Byrne, P. (Shelbourne), 1931 v Sp; 1932 v Ho; (Drumcondra), 1934 v Ho (3)
Byrne, S. (Bohemians), 1931 v Sp (1)

Campbell, N. (St Patrick's Ath.), 1971 v A (sub); (Fortuna, Cologne), 1972 v Iran, Ec, Ch, P; 1973 v USSR, F (sub); 1976 v N; 1977 v Sp, Bul (sub) (10)
Cannon, H. (Bohemians), 1926 v I; 1928 v Bel (2)
Cantwell, N. (West Ham U.), 1954 v L; 1956 v Sp, Ho; 1957 v D, WG, E (2), 1958 v D, Pol, A; 1959 v Pol, Cz (2); 1960 v Se, Ch, Se; 1961 v N (Manchester United), 1961 v S (2); 1962 v Cz (2), A; 1963 v Ic (2), S; 1964 v A, Sp, E; 1965 v Pol, Sp, 1966 v Sp (2); A, Bel; 1967 v Sp, T (36)

Carey, J. J. (Manchester U.) 1938 v N, Cz, Pol; 1939 v Sw, Pol, H (2), G; 1946 v P, Sp; 1947 v E, Sp P; 1948 v P, Sp; 1949 v Sw, Bel, P, Se, Sp; 1950 v Fi, E, Fi, Se; 1951 v N, Arg, N; 1953 v F, A (29)
Carolan, J. (Manchester U.), 1960 v Se, Ch (2)
Carroll, B. (Shelbourne), 1949 v Bel; 1950 v Fi (2)
Carroll, T. R. (Ipswich T.), 1968 v Pol; 1969 v Pol, A, D; 1970 v Cz, Pol, WG; 1971 v Se; (Birmingham C.), 1972 v Iran, Ec, Ch, P; 1973 v USSR (2), Pol, F, N (17)
Chatton, H. A. (Shelbourne), 1931 v Sp; (Dumbarton), 1932 v Sp; (Cork), 1934 v Ho (3)
Clarke, J. (Drogheda U), 1978 v Pol (sub) (1)
Clarke, K. (Drumcondra), 1948 v P, Sp (2)
Clarke, M. (Shamrock R.), 1950 v Bel (1)
Clinton, T. J. (Everton), 1951 v N; 1954 v F, L (3)
Coad, P. (Shamrock R.), 1947 v E, Sp, P; 1948 v P, Sp; 1949 v Sw, Bel, P, Se, 1951 v N (sub); 1952 v Sp (11)
Coffey, T. (Drumcondra), 1950 v Fi (1)
Colfer, M. D. (Shelbourne), 1950 v Bel; 1951 v N (2)
Collins, F. (Jacobs), 1927 v I (1)
Conmy, O. M. (Peterborough U.), 1965 v Bel; 1967 v Cz; 1968 v Cz, Pol; 1970 v Cz (5)
Connolly, J. (Fordsons), 1926 v I (1)
Connolly, N. (Cork), 1937 v G (1)
Conroy, G. A. (Stoke C.), 1970 v Cz, D, H, Pol, WG; 1971 v Pol, Se (2), I; 1973 v USSR, F, USSR, N; 1974 v Pol, Br, U, Ch; 1975 v T, Sw, USSR, Sw; 1976 v T (sub), Pol; 1977 v E, T, Pol (26)
Conway, J. P. (Fulham), 1967 v Sp, T, Sp, 1968 v Cz; 1969 v A (sub), H; 1970 v S, Cz, D, H, Pol, WG; 1971 v I, A; 1974 v U, Ch; 1976 v N, Pol; (with Manchester C.) 1977 v Pol (19)
Corr, P. J. (Everton), 1949 v P, Sp; 1950 v E, Se (4)
Courtney, E. (Cork U.), 1946 v P (1)
Cummins, G. P. (Luton T.), 1954 v L (2); 1955 v N (2), WG; 1956 v Y, Sp; 1958 v D, Pol, A; 1959 v Pol, Cz (2); 1960 v Se, Ch, WG, Se; 1961 v S (2) (19)
Cuneen, T. (Limerick), 1951 v N (1)
Curtis, D. P. (Shelbourne) 1957 v D, WG; (Bristol C.), 1957 v E (2); 1958 v D, Pol, A; (Ipswich T.), 1959 v Pol; 1960 v Se, Ch, WG, Se; 1961 v N, S; 1962 v A; 1963 v Ic (Exeter C.), 1964 v A (17)
Cusack, S. (Limerick), 1953 v F (1)

Daly, G. A. (Manchester U.), 1973 v Pol (sub), N; 1974 v Br (sub), U (sub); 1975 v Sw (sub); 1977 v E, T, F (with Derby Co.), F, Bul; 1978 v Bul, T, D; 1979 v Ni, E, D, Bul (17)
Daly, J. (Shamrock R.), 1932 v Ho; 1935 v Sw (2)
Daly, M. (Wolverhampton W.), 1978 v T, Pol (2)
Daly, P. (Shamrock R.), 1950 v Fi (sub) (1)
Davis, T. L. (Oldham Ath.), 1937 v G, H, (Tranmere R.), 1938 v Cz, Pol (4)
Dempsey, J. T. (Fulham), 1967 v Sp, Cz; 1968 v Cz, Pol; 1969 v Pol, A, D; (Chelsea), 1969 v Cz, D; 1970 v H, WG; 1971 v Pol, Se (2), I; 1972 v Iran, Ec, Ch, P (19)
Dennehy, J. (Cork Hibernians), 1972 v Ec (sub), Ch; (Nottingham F.), 1973 v USSR (sub), Pol, F, N; 1974 v Pol (sub); 1975 v T (sub); (with Walsall) 1976 v Pol (sub); 1977 v Pol (sub) (10)
Desmond, P. (Middlesbrough), 1950 v Fi, E, Fi, Se (4)
Donnelly, J. (Dundalk), 1935 v H, Sw, G; 1936 v Ho, Sw, H, L; 1937 v G, H, 1938 v N (10)

Donnelly, T. (Drumcondra) 1938 v N; (Shamrock R), 1939 v Sw (2)
Donovan, D. C. (Everton), 1955 v N, Ho, N, WG; 1957 v E (5)
Dowdall, C. (Fordsons), 1928 v Bel; (Barnsley), 1929 v Bel; (Cork) 1931 v Sp (3)
Doyle, C. (Shelbourne), 1959 v Cz (1)
Doyle, D. (Shamrock R.), 1926 v I (1)
Doyle, L. (Dolphin), 1932 v Sp (1)
Duffy, B. (Shamrock R.), 1950 v Bel (1)
Duggan, H. A. (Leeds U.), 1927 v I; 1930 v Bel; 1936 v H, L, (Newport Co.), 1938 v N (5)
Dunne, A. P. (Manchester U.), 1962 v A; 1963 v Ic, S; 1964 v A, Sp, Pol, N, E; 1965 v Pol, Sp; 1966 v Sp (2), A, Bel; 1967 v Sp, T, Sp; 1969 v Pol, D, H; 1970 v H; 1971 v Se, I, A; (Bolton W), 1974 v Br (sub), U, Ch; 1975 v T, Sw, USSR, Sw; 1976 v T (32)
Dunne, J. (Sheffield U.), 1930 v Bel; (Arsenal), 1936 v Sw, H, L; (Southampton), 1937 v Sw, F; (Shamrock R.), 1938 v N (2), Cz, Pol; 1939 v Sw, Pol, H (2), G (15)
Dunne, J. C. (Fulham), 1971 v A (1)
Dunne, L. (Manchester C.), 1935 v Sw, G (2)
Dunne, P. A. J. (Manchester U.), 1965 v Sp; 1966 v Sp (2), WG; 1967 v T (5)
Dunne, S. (Luton T.), 1953 v F, A; 1954 v F, L; 1956 v Sp, Ho; 1957 v D, WG, E; 1958 v D, Pol, A; 1959 v Pol; 1960 v WG, Se (15)
Dunne, T. (St Patrick's Ath.), 1956 v Ho; 1957 v D, WG (3)
Dunning, P. (Shelbourne), 1971 v Se, I (2)
Dunphy, E. M. (York C.), 1966 v Sp; (Millwall), 1966 v WG; 1967 v T, Sp, T, Cz; 1968 v Cz, Pol; 1969 v Pol, A, D (2), H; 1970 v D, H, Pol, WG (sub); 1971 v Pol; Se, (2), I (2), A (23)
Dwyer, N. M. (West Ham U.), 1960 v Se, Ch, WG, Se; (Swansea T.), 1961 v W, N, S (2); 1962 v Cz (2); 1964 v Pol (sub), N, E; 1965 v Pol (14)

Egan, R. (Dundalk), 1929 v Bel (1)
Eglington, T. J. (Shamrock R.), 1946 v P, Sp; (Everton), 1947 v E, Sp, P; 1948 v P, 1949 v Sw, P, Se; 1951 v N, Arg; 1952 v WG (2), A, Sp; 1953 v F, A; 1954 v F, L, F; 1955 v N, Ho, WG; 1956 v Sp (24)
Ellis, P. (Bohemians), 1935 v Sw, G; 1936 v Ho, Sw, L; 1937 v G, H (7)

Fagan, E. (Shamrock R.), 1973 v N (sub) (1)
Fagan, F. (Manchester C.), 1955 v N; 1960 v Se; (Derby Co.), 1960 v Ch, WG, Se; 1961 v W, N, S (8)
Fagan, K. (Shamrock R.), 1926 v I (1)
Fallon, S. (Celtic), 1951 v N; 1952 v WG (2), A, Sp; 1953 v F; 1955 v N, WG (8)
Fallon, W. J. (Notts Co.), 1935 v H; 1936 v H; 1937 v H, Sw, F; 1939 v Sw, Pol; (Sheffield W.), 1939 v H, G (9)
Farquharson, T. G. (Cardiff C.), 1929 v Bel; 1930 v Bel; 1931 v Sp; 1932 v Sp (4)
Farrell, P. (Hibernian), 1937 v Sw, F (2)
Farrell, P. D. (Shamrock R.), 1946 v P, Sp; (Everton), 1947 v Sp, P; 1948 v P, Sp; 1949 v Sw, P (sub), Sp; 1950 v E, Fi, Se; 1951 v Arg, N; 1952 v WG (2), A, Sp; 1953 v F, A; 1954 v F (2); 1955 v N, Ho, WG; 1956 v Y, Sp; 1957 v E (28)
Feenan, J. J. (Sunderland), 1937 v Sw, F (2)
Finucane, A. (Limerick), 1967 v T, Cz; 1969 v Cz, D, H; 1970 v S, Cz; 1971 v Se, I, I (sub); 1972 v A (11)

Fitzgerald, F. J. (Waterford), 1955 v Ho; 1956 v Ho (2)
Fitzgerald, P. J. (Leeds U.), 1961 v W, N, S; 1962 v Cz (2) (5)
Fitzpatrick, K. (Limerick), 1970 v Cz (1)
Fitzsimons, A. G. (Middlesbrough), 1950 v Fi, Bel; 1952 v WG (2), A, Sp; 1953 v F, A; 1954 v F, L, F; 1955 v Ho, N, WG; 1956 v Y, Sp, Ho, 1957 v D, WG, E (2); 1958 v D, Pol, A; 1959 v Pol; (Lincoln C.), 1959 v Cz (26)
Flood, J. J. (Shamrock R.), 1926 v I; 1929 v Bel; 1930 v Bel; 1931 v Sp; 1932 v Sp (5)
Fogarty, A. (Sunderland), 1960 v WG, Se; 1961v S; 1962 v Cz (2); 1963 v Ic (2), S (sub); 1964v A (2) (with Hartlepool), Sp (11)
Foley, J. (Cork), 1934 v Bel, Ho; (Celtic), 1935 v H, Sw, G; 1937 v G, H (7)
Foley, M. (Shelbourne), 1926 v I (1)
Foley, T. C. (Northampton T.), 1964 v Sp, Pol, N; 1965 v Pol, Bel; 1966 v Sp (2), WG; 1967 v Cz (9)
Foy, T. (Shamrock R.), 1938 v N; 1939 v H (2)
Fullam, J. (Preston N.E.), 1961 v N; (Shamrock R.), 1964 v Sp, Pol, N; 1966 v A, Bel; 1968 v Pol; 1969 v Pol, A, D; 1970 v Cz (sub) (11)
Fullam, R. (Shamrock R.), 1926 v I; 1927 v I (2)

Gallagher, C. (Celtic), 1967 v T, Cz (2)
Gallagher, M. (Hibernian), 1954 v L (1)
Gallagher, P. (Falkirk), 1932 v Sp (1)
Gannon, E. (Notts Co.) 1949 v Sw; (Sheffield W.), 1949 v Bel, P, Se, Sp; 1950 v Fi; 1951 v N; 1952 v G, A; 1954 v L, F; 1955 v N; (Shelbourne), 1955 v N, WG (14)
Gannon, M. (Shelbourne) 1972 v A (1)
Gaskins, P. (Shamrock R.), 1934 v Bel, Ho; 1935 v H, Sw, G; (St James' Gate), 1938 v Cz, Pol (7)
Gavin, J. T. (Norwich C.), 1950 v Fi (2); 1953 v F; 1954 v L; (Tottenham H.), 1955 v Ho, WG; (Norwich C.), 1957 v D (7)
Geoghegan, M. (St James' Gate), 1937 v G; 1938 v N (2)
Gibbons, A. (St Patrick's Ath.), 1952 v WG; 1954 v L; 1956 v Y, Sp (4)
Gilbert, R. (Shamrock R.), 1966 v WG (1)
Giles, C. (Doncaster R.), 1951 v N (1)
Giles, M. J. (Manchester U.), 1960 v Se, Ch; 1961 v W, N, S (2); 1962 v Cz (2), A; 1963 v Ic, S; (Leeds U.), 1964 v A (2), Sp (2), Pol, N, E; 1965 v Sp; 1966 v Sp (2), A, Bel; 1967 v Sp, T (2); 1969 v A, D, Cz; 1970 v S, Pol, WG; 1971 v I; 1973 v F, USSR; 1974 v Br, U, Ch; 1975 v USSR, T, Sw, USSR, Sw; (with W.B.A.) 1976 v T; 1977 v E, T, F (2), Pol, Bul; (with Shamrock R.), 1978 v Bul T, Pol, N, D; 1979 v Ni, D, Bul, WG, Arg (60)
Givens, D. J. (Manchester U.), 1969 v D, H; 1970 v S, Cz, D, H; (Luton T.), 1970 v Pol, WG; 1971 v Se, I (2), A; 1972 v Iran, Ec, P; 1973 v F, USSR, Pol, F, N; (QPR), 1974 v Pol, Br, U, Ch; 1975 v USSR, T, Sw, USSR, Sw; 1976 v T, N, Pol; 1977 v E, T, F, (2), Sp, Bul; 1978 v Bul N, D; (Birmingham C.), 1979 v Ni (sub), E, D, Bul, WG, Arg (47)
Glen, W. (Shamrock R.), 1927 v I; 1929 v Bel; 1930 v Bel; 1932 v Sp; 1936 v Ho, Sw, H, L (8)
Glynn, D. (Drumcondra), 1952 v WG; 1955 v N (2)
Godwin, T. F. (Shamrock R.), 1949 v P, Se, Sp; 1950 v Fi, E; (Leicester C.), 1950 v Fi, Se, Bel; 1951 v N; (Bournemouth & Boscombe Ath.), 1956 v Ho; 1957 v E; 1958 v D, Pol (13)

Golding, L. (Shamrock R.), 1928 v Bel; 1930 v Bel (2)
Gorman, W. C. (Bury), 1936 v Sw, H, L; 1937 v G, H; 1938 v N, Cz, Pol; 1939 v Sw, Pol, H; (Brentford), 1947 v E, P (13)
Grace, J. (Drumcondra), 1926 v I (1)
Grealish, A. (Orient), 1976 v N, Pol, N, D; 1979 v Ni, E, WG, Arg (8)
Gregg, E. (Bohemians), 1978 v Pol, D (sub); 1979 v E (sub), D, Bul, WG, Arg (7)
Griffith, R (Walsall), 1935 v H (1)
Grimes, A. A. (Manchester U) 1978 v T, Pol, N (sub) (3)

Hale, A. (Aston Villa), 1962 v A; (Doncaster R.) 1963 v Ic; 1964 v Sp (2); (Waterford), 1967 v Sp; 1968 v Pol (sub); 1969 v Pol, A, D; 1970 v S, Cz; 1971 v Pol (sub); 1972 v A (sub) (13)
Hamilton, T. (Shamrock R.), 1959 v Cz (2) (2)
Hand, E. K. (Portsmouth), 1969 v Cz (sub); 1970 v Pol, WG; 1971 v Pol, A; 1973 v USSR, F, USSR, Pol, F; 1974 v Pol, Br, U, Ch; 1975 v T, Sw, USSR, Sw; 1976 v T (19)
Harrington, W. (Cork), 1936 v Ho, Sw, H, L (4)
Hartnett, J. B. (Middlesbrough), 1949 v Sp; 1954 v L (2)
Haverty, J. (Arsenal), 1956 v Ho, 1957 v D, WG, E (2); 1958 v D, Pol, A; 1959 v Pol; 1960 v Se, Ch; 1961 v W, N, S (2); (Blackburn R.), 1962 v Cz (2); (Millwall), 1963 v S; 1964 v A, Sp, Pol, N, E; (Celtic), 1965 v Pol; (Bristol R.), 1965 v Sp; (Shelbourne), 1966 v Sp (2), WG, A, Bel; 1967 v Y, Sp (32)
Hayes, A. W. P. (Southampton), 1979 v D (1)
Hayes, W. E. (Huddersfield T.), 1947 v E, P (2)
Hayes, W. J. (Limerick), 1949 v Bel (1)
Healey, R. (Cardiff C.), 1977 v Pol (1)
Heighway, S. D. (Liverpool), 1971 v Pol, Se (2), I, A; 1973 v USSR; 1975 v USSR, T, USSR : 1976 v T, N; 1977 v E, F (2), Sp, Bul; 1978 v Bul, N, D; 1979 v Ni, Bul (21)
Henderson, B. (Drumcondra), 1948 v P, Sp (2)
Hennessy, J. (Shelbourne), 1956 v Pol, B, Sp; 1966 v WG; (St Patrick's Ath.), 1969 v A (5)
Herrick, J. (Cork Hibernians), 1972 v A, Ch (sub); Shamrock R.), 1973 v F (sub) (3)
Higgins, J. (Birmingham C.), 1951 v Arg (1)
Holmes, J. (Coventry C.), 1971 v A (sub); 1973 v F, USSR, Pol, F, N; 1974 v Pol, Br; 1975 v USSR, Sw; 1976 v T, N, Pol; 1977 v E, T, F, Sp (with Tottenham H), F, Pol, Bul; 1978 v Bul, T, Pol, N, D; 1979 v Ni, E, D, Bul (29)
Horlecher, A. F. (Bohemians), 1930 v Bel; 1932 v Sp, Ho; 1935 v H; 1936 v Ho, Sw (6)
Hoy, M. (Dundalk), 1938 v N; 1939 v Sw, Pol, H (2), G (6)
Hurley, C. J. (Millwall), 1957 v E; 1958 v D, Pol, A; (Sunderland), 1959 v Cz (2); 1960 v Se, Ch, WG, Se; 1961 v W, N, S (2); 1962 v Cz (2), A; 1963 v Ic (2), S; 1964 v A (2), Sp (2), Pol, N; 1965 v Sp; 1966 v WG, A, Bel; 1967 v T, Sp, T, Cz; 1968 v Cz, Pol (2); (Bolton W.), 1969 v D, Cz, H (40)
Hutchinson, F. (Drumcondra), 1935 v Sw, G (2)

Jordan, D. (Wolverhampton W.), 1937 v Sw, F (2)
Jordan, W. (Bohemians), 1934 v Ho; 1938 v N (2)
Kavanagh, P. J. (Celtic), 1931 v Sp; 1932 v Sp (2)
Keane, T. R. (Swansea T.), 1949 v Sw, P, Se, Sp (4)
Kearin, M. (Shamrock R.), 1972 v A (1)
Kearns, F. T. (West Ham U.), 1954 v L (1)

Kearns, M. (Oxford U.), 1970 v Pol (sub), (Walsall), 1974 v Pol (sub), U, Ch; 1976 v N, Pol; 1977 v E, T, F (2), Sp, Bul; 1978 v N, D; 1979 v Ni, E,
Kelly, J. (Derry C.), 1932 v Ho; 1934 v Bel; 1936 v Sw, L(4)
Kelly, J. A. (Drumcondra), 1957 v WG, E; (Preston N. E.), 1962 v A; 1963 v Ic (2), S; 1964 v A (2), Sp (2), Pol; 1965 v Bel; 1966 v A, Bel; 1967 v Sp (2), T, Cz (2), Pol; 1968 v Pol, A, D, Cz, D, H; 1970 v S, D, H, Pol, WG; 1971 v Pol, Se (2), I(2), A; 1972 v Iran, Ec, Ch, P; 1973 v USSR, F, USSR, Pol, F, N, (47)
Kelly, J. P. V. (Wolverhampton W.), 1961 v W, N, S; 1962 v Cz (2)(5)
Kelly, N. (Nottingham F.), 1954 v L (1)
Kendrick, J. (Everton), 1927 v I; 1934 v Bel, Ho; 1936 v Ho(4)
Kennedy, W. (St. James' Gate), 1932 v Ho; 1934 v Bel, Ho(3)
Keogh, J. (Shamrock R.), 1966 v WG (sub)(1)
Keogh, S. (Shamrock R.), 1959 v Pol(1)
Kiernan, F. W. (Shamrock R.), 1951 v Arg, N; (Southampton), 1952 v WG (2), A (5)
Kinnear, J. P. (Tottenham H.), 1967 v T; 1968 v Cz; Pol; 1969 v A; 1970 v Cz, D, H, Pol; 1971 v Se (sub), I; 1972 v Iran, Ec, Ch, P; 1973 v USSR, F; 1974 v Pol, Br, U, Ch; 1975 v USSR, T, Sw, USSR; (with Brighton) 1976 v T (sub) (25)
Kinsella, J. (Shelbourne), 1928 v Bel(1)
Kinsella, P. (Shamrock R.), 1932 v Ho; 1938 v N (2)
Kirkland, A. (Shamrock R.), 1927 v I(1)

Lacey, W. (Shelbourne), 1927 v I; 1928 v Bel; 1930 v Bel (3)
Langan, D. (Derby Co), 1978 v T, N (2)
Lawler, J. F. (Fulham), 1953 v A; 1954 v L, F; 1955 v N, H, N, WG; 1956 v Y (8)
Lawlor, J. C. (Drumcondra), 1949 v Bel; (Doncaster R.), 1951 v N, Arg (3)
Lawlor, M. (Shamrock R.), 1971 v Pol; Se (2), I (sub); 1973 v Pol(5)
Lawrenson, M. (Preston N.E.) 1977 v Pol; (with Brighton), 1978 v Bul, Pol, N (sub); 1979 v Ni, E,
Leech, M. (Shamrock R.), 1969 v Cz, D, H; 1972 v A, Iran, Ec, P; 1973 v USSR (sub)(8)
Lennon, C. (St. James' Gate), 1935 v H, Sw, G (3)
Lennox, G. (Dolphin), 1931 v Sp; 1932 v Sp(2)
Lowry, D. (St. Patrick's Ath.), 1962 v A (sub)(1)
Lunn, R. (Dundalk), 1939 v Sw, Pol(2)
Lynch, J. (Cork Bohemians), 1934 v Bel(1)

McAlinden, J. (Portsmouth), 1946 v P, Sp(2)
McCann, J. (Shamrock R.), 1957 v WG(1)
McCarthy, J. (Bohemians), 1926 v I; 1928 v Bel; 1930 v Bel(3)
McCarthy, M. (Shamrock R.), 1932 v Ho(1)
McConville, T. (Dundalk), 1972 v A; (Waterford), 1973 v USSR, F, USSR, Pol, F(6)
McEvoy, M. A. (Blackburn R.), 1961 v S (2); 1963 v S; 1964 v A, Sp (2), Pol, N, E; 1965 v Pol, Bel, Sp; 1966 v Sp (2); 1967 v Sp, T, Cz(17)
McGee, P. (QPR), 1978 v T, N (sub), D (sub); 1979 v Ni, E, D (sub), Bul (sub), Arg (sub) (8)
McGowan, D. (West Ham U.), 1949 v P, Se, Sp(3)
McGowan, J. (Cork U.), 1947 v Sp(1)
McGrath, M. (Blackburn R.), 1958 v A; 1959 v Pol Cz (2); 1960 v Se, WG, Se; 1961 v W; 1962 v C (2); 1963 v S; 1964 v A (2), E; 1965 v Pol, Bel Sp; 1966 v Sp; (Bradford), 1966 v WG, A, Bel 1967 v T(22)

McGuire, W. (Bohemians) 1936 v Ho(1)
McKenzie, G. (Southend U.), 1938 v N (2), Cz, Pol; 1939 v Sw, Pol, H,(2), G(9)
Mackey, G. (Shamrock R.), 1957 v D, WG, E (3)
McLoughlin, F. (Fordsons), 1930 v Bel; (Cork), 1932 v Sp(2)
McMillan, W. (Belfast Celtic), 1946 v P, Sp(2)
McNally, J. B. (Luton T.), 1959 v Cz; 1961 v Sp; 1963 v Ic(3)
Macken, A. (Derby Co.), 1977 v Sp (1)
Madden, O. (Cork), 1936 v H(1)
Maguire, J. (Shamrock R.), 1929 v Bel(1)
Malone, G. (Shelbourne), 1949 v Bel(1)
Mancini, T. J. (QPR), 1974 v Pol, Br, U, Ch; (Arsenal), 1975 v USSR (5)
Martin, A. (Bo'ness), 1927 v I(1)
Martin, C. J. (Glentoran), 1946 v P (sub), Sp; 1947 v E; (Leeds U.), 1947 v Sp; 1948 v P, Sp; (Aston Villa), 1949 v Sw, Bel, P, Se, Sp; 1950 v Fi, E, Fi, Se, Bel; 1951 v Arg; 1952 v WG, A, Sp; 1954 v F(2), L; 1955 v N, Ho, N, WG; 1956 v Y, Sp, Ho (30)
Martin, M. P. (Bohemians), 1972 v A, Iran, Ec, Ch, P; 1973 v USSR; (Manchester U.), 1973 v USSR, Pol, F, N; 1974 v Pol, Br, U, Ch; 1975 v USSR, T, Sw, USSR, Sw; (with W.B.A.) 1976 v T, N, Pol; 1977 v E, T, F (2), Sp, Pol, Bul; (Newcastle U.) 1979 v D, Bul, WG, Arg (33)
Meagan, M. K. (Everton), 1961 v S; 1962 v A; 1963 v Ic; 1964 v Sp; (Huddersfield T.), 1965 v Bel; 1966 v Sp (2), A, Bel, 1967 v Sp, T, Sp, T, Cz; 1968 v Cz, Pol; (Drogheda), 1970 v S(17)
Meehan, P. (Drumcondra), 1934 v Ho(1)
Monahan, P. (Sligo R.), 1935 v Sw, G(2)
Mooney, J. (Shamrock R.), 1965 v Pol, Bel(2)
Moore, P. (Shamrock R.), 1931 v Sp; 1932 v Ho; (Aberdeen), 1934 v Bel; Ho; 1935 v H, G, (Shamrock R.), 1936 v Ho; 1937 v G, H(9)
Moroney, T. (West Ham U.), 1948 v Sp; 1949 v P, Se, Sp; 1950 v Fi, E, Fi, Bel; 1951 v N (2); 1952 v WG; 1954 v F (12)
Moulson, C. (Lincoln C.), 1936 v H. L.; (Notts Co.), 1937 v H, Sw, F(5)
Moulson, G. B. (Lincoln C.), 1948 v P, Sp; 1949 v Sw(3)
Mucklan, C. (Drogheda U), 1978 v Pol (1)
Muldoon, T. (Aston Villa), 1927 v I(1)
Mulligan, P. M. (Shamrock R.), 1969 v Cz, D, H; 1970 v S, Cz, D; (Chelsea) 1970 v H, Pol, WG; 1971 v Pol, Se, I; 1972 v A, Iran, Ec, Ch, P; 1973 v F, USSR, Pol, F, N; 1974 v Pol, Br, U, Ch; 1975 v USSR, T, Sw, USSR, Sw; (with W.B.A.) 1976 v T, Pol; 1977 v E, T, F (2), Pol, Bul; 1978 v Bul, N, D; 1979 v E, D, Bul (sub), WG, Arg (47)
Munroe, L. (Shamrock R.), 1954 v L(1)
Murphy, A. (Clyde), 1956 v Y(1)
Murray, T. (Dundalk), 1950 v Bel(1)

Newman, W. (Shelbourne), 1969 v D(1)
Nolan, R. (Shamrock R.), 1957 v D, WG, E; 1958 v Pol; 1960 v Ch, WG, Se; 1962 v Cz(2); 1963 v Ic (10)

O'Brien, M. T. (Derby Co.), 1927 v I; (Walsall), 1929 v Bel; (Norwick C.), 1930 v Bel; (Watford), 1932 v Ho (4)
O'Brien, R. (Notts Co.), 1976 v N, Pol; 1977 v Sp, Pol (4)
O'Byrne, L. B. (Shamrock R.), 1949 v Bel (1)
O'Callaghan, B. R. (Stoke C.), 1979 v WG (sub), Arg (sub) (2)

O'Connell, A. (Dundalk), 1967 v Sp; (Bohemians), 1971 v Pol (sub) (2)
O'Connor, T. (Shamrock R.), 1950 v Fi, E, Fi, Se (4)
O'Connor, T. (Fulham), 1968 v Cz; (Dundalk), 1972 v A, Iran (sub), Ec (sub), Ch; (Bohemians), 1973 v F (sub), Pol (sub) (7)
O'Driscoll, J. F. (Swansea T.), 1949 v Sw, Bel, Se (3)
O'Farrell, F. (West Ham U.), 1952 v A; 1953 v A; 1954 v F; 1955 v Ho, N; 1956 v Y, Ho; (Preston N.E.), 1958 v D; 1959 v Cz (9)
O'Flanagan, K. P. (Bohemians), 1938 v N, Cz, Pol; H (2), G; (Arsenal), 1947 v E, Sp, P (10)
O'Flanagan, M. (Bohemians), 1947 v E (1)
O'Kane, P. (Bohemians), 1935 v H, Sw, G (3)
O'Keefe, T. (Cork), 1934 v Bel; (Waterford), 1938 v Cz, Pol (3)
O'Leary, D. (Arsenal), 1977 v E, F (2), Sp, Bul; 1978 v Bul, N, D; 1979 v E, Bul, WG, Arg (12)
O'Mahoney, M. T. (Bristol R.), 1938 v Cz, Pol; 1939 v Sw, Pol, H, G (6)
O'Neill, F. S. (Shamrock R.), 1962 v Cz (2); 1965 v Pol, Bel, Sp; 1966 v Sp (2), WG, A; 1967 v Sp, T, Sp, T; 1969 v Pol, A, D, Cz, D (sub), H (sub); 1972 v A (20)
O'Neill, J. (Everton), 1952 v Sp; 1953 v F, A; 1954 v F, L, F; 1955 v N, Ho, N, WG; 1956 v Y, Sp; 1957 v D; 1958 v M; 1959 v Pol, Cz (2) (17)
O'Neill, J. (Preston N.E.), 1961 v W (1)
O'Neill, W. (Dundalk), 1936 v Ho, Sw, H, L; 1937 v G, H, Sw, F; 1938 v N; 1939 v H, G (11)
O'Reilly, J. (Brideville), 1932 v Ho; (Aberdeen), 1934 v Bel, Ho; (Brideville), 1936 v Ho; Sw, H, L, (St. James' Gate), 1937 v G, H, Sw, F; 1938 v N (2), Cz, Pol; 1939 v Sw, Pol, H (2), G (20)
O'Reilly, J. (Cork U.), 1946 v P, Sp (2)
Peyton, G. (Fulham), 1977 v Sp (sub); 1978 v Bul, T. Pol; 1979 v D, Bul, WG, Arg (8)
Peyton, N. (Shamrock R.), 1957 v WG; (Leeds U.), 1960 v WG, Se (sub); 1961 v W; 1963 v Ic, S (6)
Reid, C. (Brideville)k, 1931 v Sp (1)
Richardson, D. J. (Shamrock R.), 1972 v A (sub); (Gillingham), 1973 v N (sub) (2)
Rigby, A. (St. James' Gate), 1935 v H, Sw, G (3)
Ringstead, A. (Sheffield U.), 1951 v Arg, N; 1952 v WG (2), A, Sp; 1953 v A; 1954 v F; 1955 v N; 1956 v Y, Sp, Ho; 1957 v E (2); 1958 v D, Pol, A; 1959 v Pol, Cz (2) (20)
Robinson, J. (Bohemians), 1928 v Bel; (Dolphin), 1931 v Sp (2)
Roche, P. J. (Shelbourne), 1972 v A; (Manchester U.), 1975 v USSR, T, Sw, USSR, Sw; 1976 v T (7)
Rogers, E. (Blackburn R.), 1968 v Cz, Pol; 1969 v Pol, A, D, Cz, D, H; 1970 v S, D, H; 1971 v I (2), A; (Charlton Ath.), 1972 v Iran, Ec, Ch, P; 1973 v USSR (19)
Ryan, G. (Derby Co.), 1978 v T; (Brighton), 1979 v E, WG (3)
Ryan, R. A. (W.B.A.), 1950 v Se, Bel; 1951 v N, Arg, N; 1952 v WG (2), A, Sp; 1953 v F, A; 1954 v F, L, F; 1955 v N; (Derby Co.), 1956 v Sp (16)

Saward, P. (Millwall), 1954 v L; (Aston Villa), 1957 v E (2); 1958 v D, Pol, A; 1959 v Pol, Cz; 1960 v Se, Ch, WG, Se; 1961 v W, N; (Huddersfield T.), 1961 v S; 1962 v A; 1963 v Ic (2) (18)
Scannell, T. (Southend U.), 1954 v L (1)
Sloan, J. W. (Arsenal), 1946 v P, Sp (2)
Smyth, M. (Shamrock R.), 1969 v Pol (sub) (1)
Squires, J. (Shelbourne), 1934 v Ho (1)
Stapleton, F. (Arsenal), 1977 v T, F, Sp, Bul; 1978 v Bul, N, D; 1979 v Ni, E (sub), D, WG, Arg (12)
Stevenson, A. E. (Dolphin), 1932 v Ho; (Everton), 1947 v E, Sp, P; 1948 v P, Sp; 1949 v Sw (7)
Strahan, F. (Shelbourne), 1964 v Pol, N, E; 1965 v Pol; 1966 v WG (5)
Sullivan, J. (Fordsons), 1928 v Bel (1)
Swan, M. M. G. (Drumcondra), 1960 v Se (sub) (1)
Synnott, N. (Shamrock R), 1978 v T, Pol; 1979 v Ni,

Thomas, P. (Waterford), 1974 v Pol, Br (2)
Traynor, T. J. (Southampton), 1954 v L; 1962 v A; 1963 v Ic (2), S; 1964 v A (2), Sp (8)
Treacy, R. C. P. (W.B.A.), 1966 v WG; 1967 v Sp, Cz; 1968 v Cz; (Charlton Ath.), 1968 v Pol; 1969 v Pol, Cz, D; 1970 v S, D, H (sub), Pol (sub), WG (sub); 1971 v Pol, Se (sub), Se, I, A; (Swindon T.), 1972 v Iran, Ec, Ch, P; 1973 v USSR, F, USSR, Pol, F, N; 1974 v Pol; (Preston N.E.), 1974 v Br; 1975 v USSR, Sw (2); 1976 v T, N (sub), Pol (sub); (with WBA), 1977 v F, Pol; 1978 (with Shamrock R), v T, Pol (2) (41)
Tuohy, L. (Shamrock R.), 1956 v Y; 1959 v Cz (2); (Newcastle U.), 1962 v A; 1963 v Ic (2); (Shamrock R.), 1964 v A; 1965 v Bel (8)
Turner, A. (Celtic), 1963 v S; 1964 v Sp (2)
Turner, C. J. (Southend U.), 1936 v Sw; 1937 v G, H, Sw, F; (West Ham U.), 1938 v N (2), Cz, Pol; 1939 v H (10)

Vernon, J. (Belfast Celtic), 1946 v P, Sp (2)

Walsh, D. J. (W.B.A.), 1946 v P, Sp; 1947 v Sp, P; 1948 v P, Sp; 1949 v Sw, P, Se, Sp; 1950 v E, Fi, Se; 1951 v N; (Aston Villa), v Arg, N; 1952 v Sp; 1953 v A; 1954 v F (2) (20)
Walsh, M. (Blackpool), 1976 v N, Pol; 1977 v F (sub), Pol; (Everton), 1979 v Ni (sub), (Q.P.R.), D (sub), Bul, WG (sub), Arg (9)
Walsh, W. (Manchester C.), 1947 v E, Sp, P; 1948 v P, Sp; 1949 v Bel, 1950 v E; Se, Bel (9)
Waters, J. (Grimsby T.), 1977 v T (1)
Watters, F. (Shelbourne), 1926 v I (1)
Weir, E. (Clyde), 1939 v H (2), G (2)
Whelan, R. (St. Patrick's Ath.), 1964 v A, E (sub) (2)
Whelan, W. (Manchester U.), 1956 v Ho; 1957 v D, E (2) (4)
White, J. J. (Bohemians), 1928 v Bel (1)
Whittaker, R. (Chelsea), 1959 v Cz (1)
Williams, J. (Shamrock R.), 1938 v N (1)

EUROPEAN REVIEW

Participation in European club competitions is becoming vitally important for most leading clubs in Britain and on the Continent. As the insane spending spree on players continues, with transfer fees rocketing sky-high and lucrative contracts being offered to even the most pedestrian performers, the clubs are badly in need of revenue.

Domestic gate receipts are no longer sufficient to cover their extravagant budgeting and consequently they must attain European status to obtain extra cash. But mere qualification is not enough, as first-round elimination is neither financially nor psychologically satisfactory.

Progress must be made, but how can it be achieved? Either by playing extremely well, or ... and here is the rub! European football is becoming increasingly less enjoyable to watch, because teams either use over-defensive tactics on the one hand, or resort to naked brutality on the other. To see such previously distinguished teams as Red Star Belgrade and Barcelona 'cave in' against Arsenal and Ipswich respectively, was a depressing experience.

To observe a player of Johan Neeskens' stature and class deliberately fouling and kicking opponents was an even bigger disappointment. The remedy is in the hands of the referees and the managers. But even the most able official cannot prevent atrocities (he can only punish them), and the managers are guided by the overwhelming need for 'getting a result' – by fair means or foul.

Having said that – to use the most overworked football phrase of the past season – I must exempt Nottingham Forest from the above criticism. Under the visionary guidance of Brian Clough, they are always scrupulously fair, they play attacking, entertaining football, and their victory in the European Cup was fully deserved, although they should send a 'thank you' note to Glasgow Rangers, who earlier in the competition eliminated such dangerous foes as Juventus and PSV Eindhoven.

Thus, perhaps, Forest's passage to the final was made easier, but certainly not too simple. Indeed, it can be said that they played the 'real' final in the very first round when they were paired with holders Liverpool. At that time, in September, Paisley's team were in rampant form, and Forest were struggling to recapture the rhythm of the previous season.

Liverpool were regarded as clear favourites, and that was the trap which possibly cost them the tie. They played an open attacking game at Nottingham, and after Garry Birtles gave the home side the lead, the 'Reds' went forward in search of an equaliser. A brilliant counter-attack resulted in an excellent goal by Colin Barrett, and Forest took a 2-0 lead to Anfield, where a goalless draw was sufficient to give them the tie.

Beating AEK Athens and Grasshoppers didn't pose any great problems to Forest, but the semi-final against Cologne the conquerors of heroic Rangers was a different proposition. The confrontation was written-up by the press as a duel between the Germans' world renowned manager, Hennes Weisweiler, and the brash challenger for the hypothetical 'tactical mastermind' title, Brian Clough.

If we accept this concept, the first-leg was a triumph for the wily German, but his blunders in the home match robbed him of any credit for that. Cologne went two goals up at Nottingham, but Birtles, Ian Bowyer and John Robertson made it 3-2 to the home team. But the Weisweiler master-stroke was still to come – he sent on Yashiko Okudera, and the Japanese substitute sank Forest with an equaliser which crept in under Peter Shilton's slowly descending body.

This was a truly memorable match – one of the few – which illuminated a disagreeable European season. With the home-leg to come, Cologne were destined to reach the Munich final – at least they were convinced that they would do so. But Dieter Muller missed an early chance, and the same player had to go off injured. Weisweiler substituted him with a half-fit mid-fielder, Heinz Flohe, and Forest, playing cagely, scored through the underrated Bowyer.

The final against Malmo was a foregone conclusion – resultwise – although the Swedes beat such illustrious opponents as Dynamo Kiev and Austria WAC on their way to this 'provincial crescendo'. English-born Bob Houghton gave the same orders to his Swedes as, a year earlier, the Austrian-born Ernst Happel gave to his Belgians – 'keep the score down'. A cowardly attitude which produced another dismal 'showpiece'.

The Forest forwards were caught in offside positions time and again, and the only goal of the match was scored by Trevor Francis from a Robertson cross in the injury time of the first half.

If this was a dull game, the Cup Winners' Cup final was a violent one. Barcelona and Fortuna Dusseldorf once more underlined the truism that football is often a substitute for war, and I am sad to record that the main culprits for the mayhem were the the better players, such as Migueli, Neeskens and Gerd Zimmermann. Barcelona won a highly exciting, and, I must confess, entertaining game 4-3 in extra time, with Hans Krankl getting the winner after young Carrasco bamboozled the leg-weary German defence.

Earlier in the competition, Ipswich failed against the eventual winners, and Aberdeen were beaten by the runners-up. Some consolation perhaps for the British entries – not for Wrexham though, early casualties against Rijeka of Yugoslavia.

A good start in the UEFA Cup gave us hope that an English club would regain this trophy last captured by Liverpool, in 1976. West Bromwich Albion were especially effective with consecutive victories against Galatasaray, Braga and the Mario Kempes-Rainer Bonhof outfit, Valencia. But they came a cropper when they faced Red Star Belgrade, whose earlier victims included Arsenal.

Everton went out against Dukla, and Manchester City's dreams died at Moenchengladbach. Eventually, three West German clubs and Red Star reached the semi-finals, where Duisburg and Hertha Berlin failed to make any further progress. Moenchengladbach, led once again by Bertie Vogts, made a draw through an own goal by Jurisic in Belgrade, and the same Yugoslav was ludicrously penalised for an innocuous attempt to take the ball away from Allan Simonsen in the second leg. The diminutive Dane shamelessly converted the penalty . . . who can blame him?

Not a vintage year in Continental club football, but it must be said that European Cup newcomers, Nottingham Forest, ambitious Barcelona and experienced Borussia Moenchengladbach, the three trophy winners, were the best of a mediocre bunch – and they cannot do more than that, can they?

Leslie Vernon

WORLD CLUB CHAMPIONSHIP

Played annually up to 1974 between the winners of the European Cup and the winners of the South American Champions Cup—known as the Copa Libertadores de America.

1960 Real Madrid beat Penarol 0-0, 5-1
1961 Penarol beat Benfica 0-1, 5-0, 2-1
1962 Santos beat Benfica 3-2, 5-2
1963 Santos beat AC Milan 2-4, 4-2, 1-0
1964 Inter-Milan beat Independiente 0-1, 2-0, 1-0
1965 Inter-Milan beat Independiente 3-0, 0-0
1966 Penarol beat Real Madrid 2-0, 2-0
1967 Racing Club beat Celtic 0-1, 2-1, 1-0
1968 Estudiantes beat Manchester United 1-0, 1-1
1969 AC Milan beat Estudiantes 3-0, 1-2
1970 Feyenoord beat Estudiantes 2-2, 1-0
1971 Nacional beat Panathinaikos 1-1, 2-1
1972 Ajax beat Independiente 1-1, 3-0
1973 Independiente beat Juventus 1-0
1974 Atlético Madrid beat Independiente 0-1, 2-0
1975 Independiente and Bayern Munich could not agree dates; no matches.
1976 Bayern Munich beat Cruzeiro 2-0, 0-0
1977 Boca Juniors v Borussia Moenchengladbach 2-2 (second match to be played)

EUROPEAN FOOTBALL CHAMPIONSHIP
(formerly EUROPEAN NATIONS' CUP)

Year	Winners		Runners-up		Venue
1960	USSR	2	Yugoslavia	1	Paris
1964	Spain	2	USSR	1	Madrid
1968	Italy	2	Yugoslavia	0	Rome
			After 1-1 draw		
1972	West Germany	3	USSR	0	Brussels

EUROPEAN NATIONS CUP 1958-60

PRELIMINARY ROUND
Eire 2 Czechoslovakia 0
Czechoslovakia 4, Eire 0

FIRST ROUND
France 7 Greece 1
Greece 1, France 1
USSR 3, Hungary 1
Hungary 0, USSR 1
Rumania 3, Turkey 0
Turkey 2, Rumania 0
Norway 0, Austria 1
Austria 5, Norway 2
Yugoslavia 2, Bulgaria 0
Bulgaria 1, Yugoslavia 1
Portugal 3, East Germany 2
East Germany 0, Portugal 2
Denmark 2, Czechoslovakia 2
Czechoslovakia 5, Denmark 1
Poland 2, Spain 4
Spain 3, Poland 0

QUARTER-FINALS
Portugal 2, Yugoslavia 1
Yugoslavia 5, Portugal 1
France 5, Austria 2
Austria 2, France 4
Rumania 0, Czechoslovakia 2
Czechoslovakia 3, Rumania 0
Russia w.o. Spain withdrew

SEMI-FINALS
Yugoslavia 5, France 4 (in Paris)
USSR 3, Czechoslovakia 0 (in Marseilles)

THIRD PLACE MATCH
Czechoslovakia 2, France 0

FINAL
(Paris, July 10, 1960)
USSR 2, Yugoslavia 1 after extra time
USSR: Yachin; Tchekeli, Kroutikov; Voinov, Maslenkin, Netto; Metreveli, Ivanov, Ponedelnik, Bubukin, Meshki.
Yugoslavia: Vidinic; Durkovic, Jusufi; Zanetic, Miladinovic, Perusic; Sekularac, Jerkovic, Galic, Matus, Kostic.
Scorers: Metreveli, Ponedelnik for USSR, Netto (own goal) for Yugoslavia.

EUROPEAN NATIONS CUP 1962-64

FIRST ROUND
Spain 6, Rumania 0
Rumania 3, Spain 1
Poland 0, Northern Ireland 2
Northern Ireland 2, Poland 0
Denmark 6, Malta 1
Malta 1, Denmark 3
Eire 4, Iceland 2
Iceland 1, Eire 1
Greece withdrew against Albania
East Germany 2, Czechoslovakia 1
Czechoslovakia 1, East Germany 1
Hungary 3, Wales 1
Wales 1, Hungary 1
Italy 6, Turkey 0
Turkey 0, Italy 1
Holland 3, Switzerland 1
Switzerland 1, Holland 1
Norway 0, Sweden 2
Sweden 1, Norway 1
Yugoslavia 3, Belgium 2
Belgium 0, Yugoslavia 1
Bulgaria 3, Portugal 1
Portugal 3, Bulgaria 1
Bulgaria 1, Portugal 0
England 1, France 1
France 5, England 2

SECOND ROUND
Spain 1, Northern Ireland 1
Northern Ireland 0, Spain 1
Denmark 4, Albania 0
Albania 1, Denmark 0
Austria 0, Eire 0
Eire 3, Austria 2
East Germany 1, Hungary 2
Hungary 3, East Germany 3
USSR 2, Italy 0
Italy 1, USSR 1
Holland 1, Luxembourg 1
Luxembourg 2, Holland 1
Yugoslavia 0, Sweden 0
Sweden 3, Yugoslavia 2
Bulgaria 1, France 0
France 3, Bulgaria 1

QUARTER-FINALS
Luxembourg 2, Denmark 2
Denmark 3, Luxembourg 3
Denmark 1, Luxembourg 0
Spain 5, Eire 1
Eire 0, Spain 2
France 1 Hungary 3
Hungary 2, France 1
Sweden 1, USSR 1
USSR 3, Sweden 1

SEMI-FINALS
USSR 3, Denmark 0 (in Barcelona)
Spain 2, Hungary 1 (in Madrid)

THIRD PLACE MATCH
Hungary 3, Denmark 1 after extra time

FINAL
(Madrid, June 21, 1964)
Spain (1) 2, USSR (1) 1
Spain: Iribar; Rivilla, Calleja; Fuste, Olivella, Zoco; Amancio, Pereda, Marcellino, Suarez Lapetra.
USSR: Yachin; Chustikov, Mudrik, Voronin, Shesternjev, Anitchkin; Chislenko, Ivanov, Ponedelnik, Kornaev Khusainov.
Scorers: Pereda, Marcellino for Spain Khusainov for USSR.

EUROPEAN CHAMPIONSHIP 1966–68

GROUP 1
Eire 0, Spain 0
Eire 2, Turkey 1
Spain 2, Eire 0
Turkey 0, Spain 0
Turkey 2, Eire 1
Eire 0, Czechoslovakia 2
Spain 2, Turkey 0
Czechoslovakia 1, Spain 0
Spain 2, Czechoslovakia 1
Czechoslovakia 3, Turkey 0
Turkey 0, Czechoslovakia 0
Czechoslovakia 1, Eire 2

GROUP 2
Norway 0, Bulgaria 0
Portugal 1, Sweden 2
Bulgaria 4, Norway 2
Sweden 1, Portugal 1
Norway 1, Portugal 2
Sweden 0, Bulgaria 2
Norway 3, Sweden 1
Sweden 5, Norway 2
Bulgaria 3, Sweden 0
Portugal 2, Norway 1
Bulgaria 1, Portugal 0
Portugal 0, Bulgaria 0

GROUP 3
Finland 0, Austria 0
Greece 2, Finland 1
Finland 1, Greece 1
USSR 4, Austria 3
USSR 2, Finland 0
Finland 2, USSR 5
Austria 2, Finland 1
Greece 4, Austria 1
Austria 1, USSR 0
Greece 0, USSR 1
Austria 1, Greece 1
USSR 4, Greece 0

GROUP 4
Albania 0, Yugoslavia 2
West Germany 6, Albania 0
Yugoslavia 1, West Germany 0
West Germany 3, Yugoslavia 1
Yugoslavia 4, Albania 0
Albania 0, West Germany 0

GROUP 5
Holland 2, Hungary 2
Hungary 6, Denmark 0
Holland 2, Denmark 0
East Germany 4, Holland 3
Hungary 2, Holland 1
Denmark 0, Hungary 2
Denmark 1, East Germany 1
Holland 1, East Germany 0
Hungary 3, East Germany 1
Denmark 3, Holland 2
East Germany 3, Denmark 2
East Germany 1, Hungary 0

GROUP 6
Cyprus 1, Rumania 5
Rumania 4, Switzerland 2
Italy 3, Rumania 1
Cyprus 0, Italy 2
Rumania 7, Cyprus 0
Switzerland 7, Rumania 1
Italy 5, Cyprus 0
Switzerland 5, Cyprus 0
Switzerland 2, Italy 2
Italy 4, Switzerland 0
Cyprus 2, Switzerland 1
Rumania 0, Italy 1

GROUP 7
Poland 4, Luxembourg 0
France 2, Poland 1
Luxembourg 0, France 3
Luxembourg 0, Belgium 5
Luxembourg 0, Poland 0
Poland 3, Belgium 1
Belgium 2, France 1
Poland 1, France 4
Belgium 2, Poland 4
France 1, Belgium 1
Belgium 3, Luxembourg 0
France 3, Luxembourg 1

GROUP 8
Ireland 0, England 2
Wales 1, Scotland 1
England 5, Wales 1
Scotland 2, Ireland 1
Ireland 0, Wales 0
England 2, Scotland 3
Wales 0, England 3
Ireland 1, Scotland 0
England 2, Ireland 0
Scotland 3, Wales 2
Scotland 1, England 1
Wales 2, Ireland 0

QUARTER-FINALS
England 1, Spain 0
Spain 1, England 2
Bulgaria 3, Italy 2
Italy 2, Bulgaria 0
France 1, Yugoslavia 1
Yugoslavia 5, France 1
Hungary 2, USSR 0
USSR 3, Hungary 0

SEMI-FINALS
Yugoslavia 1, England 0 (in Florence)
Italy 0, USSR 0 (Italy won toss) (in Naples)

THIRD-PLACE MATCH (Rome)
England 2, USSR 0

FINAL (Rome, June 8, 1968)
Italy (0) 1, Yugoslavia (1) 1

Italy: Zoff; Burgnich, Facchetti; Ferrini, Guarneri, Castano; Domenghini, Juliano, Anastasi, Lodetti, Prati.

Yugoslavia: Pantelic; Fazlagic, Damjanovic; Pavlovic, Paunovic, Holcer; Petkovic, Acimovic, Musemic, Trivic, Dzajic.

Scorers: Italy, Domenghini. Yugoslavia, Dzajic.

REPLAYED FINAL (Rome, June 10, 1968)
Italy (2) 2, Yugoslavia (0) 0

Italy: Zoff; Burgnich, Facchetti; Rosato, Guarneri, Salvadore; Domenghini, Mazzola, Anastasi, De Sisti, Riva.

Yugoslavia: Pantelic; Fazlagic, Damjanovic, Pavlovic, Paunovic, Holcer; Hosic, Acimovic, Musemic, Trivic, Dzajic.

Scorers: Riva, Anastasi for Italy.

EUROPEAN CHAMPIONSHIP 1970-72

GROUP 1
Czechoslovakia 1, Finland 1
Rumania 3, Finland 0
Wales 0, Rumania 0
Wales 1, Czechoslovakia 3
Finland 0, Wales 1
Czechoslovakia 1, Rumania 0
Finland 0, Czechoslovakia 4
Finland 0, Rumania 4
Wales 3, Finland 0
Czechoslovakia 1, Wales 0
Rumania 2, Czechoslovakia 1
Rumania 2, Wales 0

GROUP 2
Norway 1, Hungary 3
France 3, Norway 1
Bulgaria 1, Norway 1
Hungary 1, France 1
Bulgaria 3, Hungary 0
Norway 1, Bulgaria 4
Norway 1, France 3
Hungary 2, Bulgaria 0
France 0, Hungary 2
Hungary 4, Norway 0
France 2, Bulgaria 1
Bulgaria 2, France 1

GROUP 3
Greece 0, Switzerland 1
Malta 1, Switzerland 2
Malta 0, England 1
England 3, Greece 0
Switzerland 5, Malta 0
England 5, Malta 0
Malta 1, Greece 1
Switzerland 1, Greece 0
Greece 2, Malta 0
Switzerland 2, England 3
England 1, Switzerland 1
Greece 0, England 3

GROUP 4
Spain 3, Northern Ireland 0
Cyprus 0, Northern Ireland 3
Northern Ireland 5, Cyprus 0
Cyprus 1, USSR 3
Cyprus 0, Spain 2
USSR 2, Spain 1
USSR 6, Cyprus 1
USSR 1, Northern Ireland 0
Northern Ireland 1, USSR 1
Spain 0, USSR 0
Spain 7, Cyprus 0
Northern Ireland 1, Spain 1

GROUP 5
Denmark 0, Portugal 1
Scotland 1, Denmark 0
Belgium 2, Denmark 0
Belgium 3, Scotland 0
Belgium 3, Portugal 0
Portugal 2, Scotland 0
Denmark 1, Scotland 0
Portugal 5, Denmark 0
Denmark 1, Belgium 2
Scotland 2, Portugal 1
Scotland 1, Belgium 0
Portugal 1, Belgium 1

GROUP 6
Eire 1, Sweden 1
Sweden 1, Eire 0
Austria 1, Italy 2
Italy 3, Eire 0
Eire 1, Italy 2
Eire 1, Austria 4
Sweden 1, Austria 0
Sweden 0, Italy 0
Austria 1, Sweden 0
Italy 3, Sweden 0
Austria 6, Eire 0
Italy 2, Austria 2

GROUP 7
Holland 1, Yugoslavia 1
East Germany 1, Holland 0
Luxembourg 0, East Germany 5
Yugoslavia 2, Holland 0
East Germany 2, Luxembourg 1
Luxembourg 0, Yugoslavia 2
Holland 6, Luxembourg 0
East Germany 1, Yugoslavia 2
Holland 3, East Germany 2
Yugoslavia 0, East Germany 0
Yugoslavia 0, Luxembourg 0
Luxembourg 0, Holland 8

GROUP 8
Poland 3, Albania 0
West Germany 1, Turkey 1
Turkey 2, Albania 1
Albania 0, West Germany 1
Turkey 0, West Germany 3
Albania 1, Poland 1
West Germany 2, Albania 0
Poland 5, Turkey 1
Poland 1, West Germany 3
Albania 3, Turkey 0
West Germany 0, Poland 0
Turkey 1, Poland 0

QUARTER-FINALS
England 1, West Germany 3
Italy 0, Belgium 0
Hungary 1, Rumania 1
Yugoslavia 0, USSR 0
West Germany 0, England 0
Belgium 2, Italy 1
USSR 3, Yugoslavia 0
Rumania 2, Hungary 2
Play-off: Hungary 2, Rumania 1

SEMI-FINALS
USSR 1, Hungary 0 (in Brussels)
West Germany 2, Belgium 1 (in Antwerp)

THIRD-PLACE MATCH (Liege)
Belgium 2, Hungary 1

FINAL (Brussels, June 18, 1972)
West Germany (1) 3 (*Muller* 2, *Wimmer*)
USSR (0) 0

West Germany: Maier, Hottges, Schwarzenbeck, Beckenbauer, Breitner, Hoeness, Wimmer, Netzer, Heynkes, Muller, Kremers.

USSR: Rudakov, Dzodzuashvili, Khurtsilava, Kaplichny, Istomin, Troshkin, Kolotov, Baidachni, Konkov (Dolmatov), Banishevski (Kozinkievits), Onishenko.

EUROPEAN CHAMPIONSHIP 1974-76

GROUP 1
England 3, Czechoslovakia 0
England 0, Portugal 0
England 5, Cyprus 0
Czechoslovakia 4, Cyprus 0
Czechoslovakia 5, Portugal 0
Cyprus 0, England 1
Cyprus 0, Portugal 2
Czechoslovakia 2, England 1
Portugal 1, Czechoslovakia 1
Portugal 1, England 1
Cyprus 0, Czechoslovakia 3
Portugal 1, Cyprus 0

GROUP 2
Austria 2, Wales 1
Luxembourg 2, Hungary 4
Wales 2, Hungary 0
Wales 5, Luxembourg 0
Luxembourg 1, Austria 2
Austria 0, Hungary 0
Hungary 1, Wales 2
Luxembourg 1, Wales 3
Hungary 2, Austria 1
Austria 6, Luxembourg 2
Hungary 8, Luxembourg 1
Wales 1, Austria 0

GROUP 3
Norway 2, Northern Ireland 1
Yugoslavia 3, Norway 1
Sweden 0, Northern Ireland 2
Northern Ireland 1, Yugoslavia 0
Sweden 1, Yugoslavia 1
Norway 1, Yugoslavia 3
Sweden 3, Norway 1
Norway 0, Sweden 2
Northern Ireland 1, Sweden 2
Yugoslavia 3, Sweden 0
Northern Ireland 3, Norway 0
Yugoslavia 1, Northern Ireland 0

GROUP 4
Denmark 1, Spain 2
Denmark 0, Rumania 0
Scotland 1, Spain 2
Spain 1, Scotland 1
Spain 1, Rumania 1
Rumania 6, Denmark 1
Rumania 1, Scotland 1
Denmark 0, Scotland 1
Spain 2, Denmark 0
Scotland 3, Denmark 1
Rumania 2, Spain 2
Scotland 1, Rumania 1

GROUP 5
Finland 1, Poland 2
Finland 1, Holland 3
Poland 3, Finland 0
Holland 3, Italy 1
Italy 0, Poland 0
Finland 0, Italy 1
Holland 4, Finland 1
Poland 4, Holland 1
Italy 0, Finland 0
Holland 3, Poland 0
Poland 0, Italy 0
Italy 1, Holland 0

GROUP 6
Eire 3, USSR 0
Turkey 1, Eire 1
Turkey 2, Switzerland 1
USSR 3, Turkey 0
Switzerland 1, Turkey 1
Eire 2, Switzerland 1
USSR 2, Eire 1
Switzerland 1, Eire 0
Switzerland 0, USSR 1
Eire 4, Turkey 0
USSR 4, Switzerland 1
Turkey 1, USSR 0

GROUP 7
Iceland 0, Belgium 2
East Germany 1, Iceland 1
Belgium 2, France 1
France 2, East Germany 2
East Germany 0, Belgium 0
Iceland 0, France 0
Iceland 2, East Germany 1
France 3, Iceland 0
Belgium 1, Iceland 0
Belgium 1, East Germany 2
East Germany 2, France 1
France 0, Belgium 0

GROUP 8
Bulgaria 3, Greece 3
Greece 2, West Germany 2
Greece 2, Bulgaria 1
Malta 0, West Germany 1
Malta 2, Greece 0
Bulgaria 1, West Germany 1
Greece 4, Malta 0
Bulgaria 5, Malta 0
West Germany 1, Greece 1
West Germany 1, Bulgaria 0
Malta 0, Bulgaria 2
West Germany 8, Malta 0

QUARTER-FINALS
Spain 1, West Germany 1
Yugoslavia 2, Wales 0
Czechoslovakia 2, USSR 0
Holland 5, Belgium 0
West Germany 2, Spain 0
USSR 2, Czechoslovakia 2
Wales 1, Yugoslavia 1
Belgium 1, Holland 2

SEMI-FINALS
Czechoslovakia 3, Holland 1 (*after extra time*) (in Zagreb)

West Germany 4, Yugoslavia 2 (*after extra time*) (in Belgrade)

THIRD PLACE MATCH (Zagreb)
Holland 3, Yugoslavia 2 (*after extra time*)

FINAL (Belgrade, 20 June, 1976)
Czechoslovakia (2) 2 (*Svehlik, Dobias*)

West Germany (1) 2 (*Muller, Holzenbein*)
(*after extra time*)
Czechoslovakia won 5-3 *on penalties*

Czechoslovakia: Viktor; Dobias (Vesely. F.), Pivarnik, Ondrus, Capkovic, Gogh, Moder, Panenka, Svehlik (Jurkemik), Masny, Nehoda.

West Germany: Maier; Vogts, Beckenbauer, Schwarzenbeck, Dietz, Bonhof, Wimmer (Flohe), Muller, D., Beer (Bongartz), Hoeness, Holzenbein.

EUROPEAN CHAMPIONSHIP 1978-80
(Henri Delaunay Cup)

GROUP 1

September 20 1978, Copenhagen
Denmark (2) 3 (*Simonsen pen., Arnesen, Rontved*)
England (2) 4 (*Latchford, Keegan 2, Neal*) 47,600
Denmark: Jensen B; Nielsen F, Jensen H M, Rontved, Lerby, Arnesen, Nielsen C, Lund, Simonsen, Nielsen B, (Hansen , A), Kristensen.
England: Clemence; Neal, Mills, Wilkins, Watson, Hughes, Keegan, Coppell, Latchford, Brooking, Barnes.

September 20 1978, Dublin
Eire 0
N Ireland 0 46,000
Eire: Kearns; Grealish, Synott, Daly, Holmes, Lawrenson, Brady, Stapleton (Walsh), Heighway (Givens), Giles, McGee.
N Ireland: Jennings; Rice, Nelson, Nicholl C, Hunter (Hamilton), Nicholl J, O'Neill, McCreery, Armstrong, McIlroy, Spence (Cochrane).

May 24 1978, Copenhagen
Denmark (1) 3 (*Jensen, Nielsen, Lerby*)
Eire (2) 3 (*Stapleton, Grealish, Daly*) 39,000
Denmark: Jensen B; Hansen J, Rontved, Jensen H M, Lerby, Olsen (Hoyland), Nielsen B, Nygaard (Arnesen), Sorensen, Jensen H, Kristensen.
Eire: Kearns (Gregg); Mulligan, O'Leary, Daly, Holmes, Lawrenson, Stapleton, Giles, Grealish, Heighway, Givens (McGee).

October 11 1978, Copenhagen
Denmark (1) 2 (*Nielsen B, Lerby*)
Bulgaria (1) 2 (*Panov, Iliev*) 15,800
Denmark: Kjaer; Nielsen F, Rontved, Larsen, Lerby, Olsen, Hansen H, Arnesen, Lund, Nielsen B, Kristensen.
Bulgaria: Goranov, Nikolov, Stankov P, Bonev, Grantcharov (Iliev), Zdravkov, Gotchev, Slavkov (Ivanov), Mladenov, Panov, Stankov A.

October 25 1978, Dublin
Eire (1) 1 (*Daly*)
England (1) 1 (*Latchford*) 50,000
Eire: Kearns; Mulligan, O'Leary, Lawrenson, Holmes, Daly, Grealish, Brady, McGee (Stapleton), Givens (Grimes), Ryan.
England: Clemence; Neal, Watson (Thompson), Hughes, Mills, Wilkins, Keegan, Brooking, Coppell, Latchford, Barnes (Woodcock).

October 25 1978, Belfast
N Ireland (0) 2 (*Spence, Anderson*)
Denmark (0) 1 (*Jensen H*) 25,000
N Ireland: Jennings; Rice, Nicholl (C), Hunter, Nelson, McCreery, Armstrong, O'Neill, McIlroy, Morgan (Spence) (Anderson), Cochrane.
Denmark: Kjaer; Nielsen F, Rontved, Larsen, Andersen, Rasmussen, Nielsen B, Flindt-Bjerg, Agerbeck (Sorensen), Jensen H, Kristensen.

November 29 1978, Sofia
Bulgaria (0) 0
N Ireland (1) 2 (*Armstrong, Nicholl J*) 30,000
Bulgaria: Goranov; Grantcharov, Stankov P, Karakolev, Dimitrov, Sredkov, Gotchev, Slavkov, Mladenov (Djevizov), Panov, Stankov A (Zvetkov).
N Ireland: Jennings; Hamilton, Nicholl J, Nicholl C, Nelson, O'Neill, McCreery, McIlroy (Moreland), Cochrane (McGrath), Armstrong, Caskey.

February 7 1979, Wembley
England (1) 4 (*Keegan, Latchford 2, Watson*)
N Ireland (0) 0 92,000
England: Clemence; Neal, Watson, Hughes, Mills, Currie, Brooking, Coppell, Latchford, Keegan, Barnes.
N Ireland: Jennings; Rice, Nicholl (C), Nicholl (J), Nelson, McIlroy, McCreery, O'Neill, Cochrane (McGrath), Armstrong, Caskey (Spence).

May 2 1979, Belfast
N Ireland (2) 2 (*Nicholl C., Armstrong*)
Bulgaria (0) 0 18,700
N Ireland: Jennings; Hamilton, Nicholl (J) (Moreland), Nicholl (C), Nelson, McCreery, O'Neill, McIlroy, Armstrong, Caskey (Spence), Cochrane.
Bulgaria: Stojanov; Vassilev, Ivkov, Rainov, Bonev (G), Kolev, Sredkov, Panov, Zdravkov (Iliev), Djevizov, Tsvetkov.

May 2 1979, Dublin
Eire (1) 2 (*Daly, Givens*)
Denmark (0) 0 26,000
Eire: Peyton; Gregg, Martin, Mulligan, Holmes, Daly, Giles, Brady, Hayes (Walsh), Stapleton, Givens (McGee).
Denmark: Kjaer; Nielsen F, Rontved, Larsen, Lerby, Lund, Arnesen, Olsen, Simonsen, Nielsen B (Agerbeck), Elkjaer.

May 19 1979, Sofia
Bulgaria (0) 0
Eire (0) 1 (*Tsvetkov*) 20,000
Bulgaria: Filipov; Grancharov, Ivkov, Iliev, Vassilev, Zdravkov, Borissov, Panov, Voinov, Jeliaskov, Tsvetkov.
Eire: Peyton; Gregg, O'Leary, Martin, Holmes (Mulligan), Daly, Giles, Brady, Walsh (McGee), Givens, Heighway.

June 6 1979, Copenhagen
Denmark (2) 4 (*Elkjaer 3, Simonsen*)
N Ireland (0) 0 16,800
Denmark: Kjaer; Hoygaard, Ziegler, Busk, Andersen, Olsen, Arnesen, Lerby, Norregard, Simonsen, Elkjaer.
N Ireland: Jennings; Rice, Nicholl (J), Hunter, Nelson, O'Neill (Sloan), McCreery, Hamilton, McIlroy, Spence, Armstrong (Caskey).

June 6 1979, Sofia
Bulgaria (0) 0
England (1) 3 (*Keegan, Watson, Barnes*) 47,500
Bulgaria: Filipov; Grancharov, Iliev, Ivkov, Bonev (G), Zdravkov (Gotchev), Borissov, Panov, Voinov (Barzov), Jeliaskov, Tsvetkov.

	P	W	D	L	F	A	Pts
England	4	3	1	0	12	4	7
Northern Ireland	6	3	1	2	6	9	7
Eire	5	1	3	1	6	5	5
Denmark	6	1	2	3	13	13	4
Bulgaria	5	1	1	3	3	9	3

GROUP 2

August 30 1978, Oslo
Norway (0) 0
Austria (2) 2 (*Pezzey, Krankl*) 15,000
Norway: Jacobsen; Karlsen (Berntsen), Birkelund, Grondalen, Pedersen, Aas, Johansen, Thunberg, Mathisen, Iversen (Larsen-Okland), Thoresen.
Austria: Fuchsbichler; Robert Sara, Obermayer, Pezzey, Strasser, Prohaska, Weber, Kreuz, Jara (Hintermaier), Schachner, Krankl.

September 20 1978, Lokeren
Belgium (0) 1 (*Cools*)
Norway (1) 1 (*Larsen-Okland*) 7400
Belgium: Pfaff; Gerets (Van der Elst), Meeuws, Leekens, Cools, Verheyen, Van der Eycken, Coeck, Van Gool, Courant (Geurts), Voordeckers.
Norway: Jacobsen T R; Pedersen, Kordahl, Aas, Grondalen, Albertsen, Berntsen, Johansen, Thoresen, Mathisen (Thunberg), Larsen-Okland (Jacobsen, P).

September 20 1978, Vienna
Austria (1) 3 (*Pezzey, Schachner, Kreuz*)
Scotland (0) 2 (*McQueen, Gray, A*) 71,500
Austria: Fuchsbichler; Robert Sara, Obermayer, Pezzey, Strasser, Prohaska (Oberacher), Weber, Jara, Kreuz, Schachner, Krankl.
Scotland: Rough; Kennedy, Donachie, Buchan, McQueen, Souness, Gemmill, Hartford, Dalglish, Jordan (Graham), Gray A.

October 11 1978, Lisbon
Portugal (1) 1 (*Gomes*)
Belgium (1) 1 (*Vercauteren*) 35,000
Portugal: Bento; Gabriel, Eurico, Humberto, Sheu (Artur), Alves, Oliveira, Costa, Manuel Fernandes (Nene), Gomes.
Belgium: Pfaff; Gerets, Meeuws, Broos, Renquin, Cools, Coeck, Van der Eycken, Vercauteren, Dardenne (Van der Elst), Voordeckers (Ceulemans).

October 25 1978, Glasgow
Scotland (1) 3 (*Dalglish 2, Gemmill pen.*)
Norway (1) 2 (*Aas, Larsen-Okland*) 40,000
Scotland: Stewart; Donachie, McQueen, Buchan, Gray F, Gemmill, Hartford, Souness, Dalglish, Gray A, Graham.
Norway: Jacobsen T R; Pedersen (Karlsen), Birkelund, Kordahl, Grondalen, Aas, Jacobsen T (Hansen J), Johansen, Thoresen, Larsen-Okland, Mathisen.

November 15 1978, Vienna
Austria (0) 1 (*Schachner*)
Portugal (1) 2 (*Nene, Alberto*) 72,000
Austria: Koncilia; Robert Sara, Pezzey, Obermayer, Strasser, Prohaska, Hattenberger, Jara (Baumeister), Schachner, Kreuz (Gasselich), Krankl.
Portugal: Bento; Artur, Humberto, Alhinho, Alberto, Pietra, Teixeira, Alves, Oliveira (Sheu), Costa, Nene (Gomes).

November 29 1978, Lisbon
Portugal (1) 1 (*Alberto*)
Scotland (0) 0 70,400
Portugal: Bento; Artur, Humberto, Alhinho, Alberto, Pietra, Alves, Oliveira (Eurico), Nene, Gomes, Costa (Sheu).
Scotland: Rough; Kennedy, Buchan, McQueen, Gray F (Donachie), Gemmill, Narey, Hartford, Robertson, Jordan (Wallace), Dalglish.

March 28 1979, Brussells
Belgium (1) 1 (*Vandereycken pen*).
Austria (0) 1 (*Krankl*) 9900
Belgium: Pfaff; Gerets, Meeuws, Broos, Renquin, Cools (Geurts), Vandereycken, Vercauteren, Cluytens, Van der Elst, Janssens.
Austria: Koncilia; Robert Sara, Obermayer, Pezzey, Mirnegg, Hattenberger, Baumeister, Weber, Kruez, Schachner, Krankl.

May 2 1979, Vienna
Austria (0) 0
Belgium (0) 0 40,000
Austria: Koncilia; Robert Sara, Obermayer, Pezzey, Mirnegg, Prohaska (Gasselich), Hattenberger, Baumeister, Schachner, Kreuz (Hintermaier), Krankl.
Belgium: Preud'homme; Gerets, Meeuws, Broos, Renquin, Cools, Van der Elst, Vandereycken, Vercauteren, Jacobs (Dardenne), Janssens.

May 9 1979, Oslo
Norway (0) 0
Portugal (1) 1 (*Alves*) 9800
Norway: Amundsen; Pedersen, Kordahl, Einer Aas Grondalen, Hansen, Albertsen, Johansen (T E) (Thunberg), Lund, Mathisen (Refvik), Okland.
Portugal: Bento; Artur, Humberto, Alhino, Alberto, Eurico, Pietra, Alves, Nene (Gomes), Costa (Bastos Lopes), Oliveira.

June 7 1979, Oslo
Norway (0) 0
Scotland (3) 4 (*Jordan, Dalglish, Robertson, McQueen*) 17,269
Norway: Jacobsen; Karlsen, Kordahl, Grondalen, Pedersen P (Hansen), Aas, Albertsen, Thunberg (Svendsen), Thoresen, Mathisen, Okland.
Scotland: Rough; Burley (Hegarty) (Wark), Munro, Burns, McQueen, Gemmill, Graham, Dalglish, Jordan, Hartford, Robertson.

	P	W	D	L	F	A	Pts
Portugal	4	3	1	0	5	2	7
Austria	5	2	2	1	7	5	6
Scotland	4	2	0	2	9	6	4
Belgium	4	0	4	0	3	4	4
Norway	5	0	1	4	3	11	1

GROUP 3

October 4 1978, Zagreb
Yugoslavia (1) 1 (*Halilhodzic*)
Spain (2) 2 (*Juanito, Santillana*) 60,000
Yugoslavia: Stincic; Dzoni, Muzinic, Zajec (Cukrov), Rozic, Stoijkovic, Zungul (Savic), Vukotic, Halilhodzic, Surjak, Susic.
Spain: Miguel Angel; Marcelino, Migueli, Cundi, Olmo, Del Bosque, Juanito (Sanchez), Villar, Santillana (Ruben Cano), Asensi, Uria.

October 25 1978, Bucharest
Rumania (0) 3 (*Sames 2, Jordanescu pen.*)
Yugoslavia (1) 2 (*Petrovic, Desnica*) 28,000
Rumania: Raducanu; Anghelini, Sames, Stefanescu, Vigu, Romila, Boloni, Jordanescu, Crisan, Dobrin, Doru Nicolae (Radulescu).
Yugoslavia: Borota; Muzinic, Trifunovic (Rozic), Hadziabdic, Stojkovic, Surjak, Petrovic, Zungul (Desnica), Halilhodzic, Susic, Cukrov.

November 15 1978, Valencia
Spain (1) 1 (*Asensi*)
Rumania (0) 0 60,000
Spain: Miguel Angel; Carrete, Migueli, Alesanco, Marcelino, Del Bosque, Villar, Asensi, Heredia (Saura), Santillana, Rojo (Ruben Cano).
Rumania: Coman; Zamfir, Sames, Stefanescu, Vigu, Boloni, Romila, Jordanescu, Crisan, Georgescu, Radulescu.

December 13, 1978, Salamanca
Spain (2) 5 (*Asensi, Del Bosque, Santillana 2, Ruben Cano*)
Cyprus (0) 0 20,000
Spain: Miguel Angel; Marcelino, Migueli, Alesanco, Cundi, Villar (Leal), Asensi, Del Bosque, Heredia (Ruben Cano), Santillana, Argote.
Cyprus: Panziaras G; Panziaras N, Kizas, Stefanos, Kalothe, Christon, Savva, Papadopoulos, Economou, Kanaris, Phoebus.

April 1 1979, Nicosia
Cyprus (0) 0
Yugoslavia (1) 3 (*Vujovic* 2, *Surjak pen.*) 4500
Cyprus: Phanos; Kalothe, Violaris, Stefanos, Pandjaris, Gregory, Miamiliotis, Kalimeras, Kissonerghis, Koudas, Kanaris.
Yugoslavia: Svilar; Hadzic, Starovlah, Stojkovic, Peruzovic, Muzinic, Vujovic, Surkov, Savic, Mirocevic, Surjak.

April 4 1979, Craiova
Rumania (0) 2 (*Georgescu* 2, 1 *pen.*)
Spain (0) 2 (*Dani* 2) 40,000
Rumania: Lungu; Zamfir, Sames, Dinu, Lucuta, Dumitru (Stefanescu), Romila, Boloni, Lucescu (Crisan), Georgescu, Marcu.
Spain: Arconada; San Jose, Alesanco, Felipe, Marcelino, Asensi, Del Bosque (Cundi), Villar, Quini (Carrasco), Ruben Cano, Dani.

May 13 1979, Limassol
Cyprus (1) 1 (*Kaiafas*)
Rumania (1) 1 (*Ankustia*) 8000
Cyprus: Panziaras (G); Patikis, Kolothe, Stefanos, Panziaras (N), Papadopoulos, Mavrodisgregori, Kaiafas, Antoniu, Kisson, Irghi (Fivos).
Rumania: Andrey; Zamfir, Kiseu, Stefanescu, Ivan, Ankustia, Doru, Iovanescu, Radu, Barbulescu, Stan.

	P	W	D	L	F	A	Pts
Spain	4	3	1	0	10	3	7
Rumania	4	1	2	1	6	6	4
Yugoslavia	3	1	0	2	6	5	2
Cyprus	3	0	1	2	1	9	1

GROUP 4

September 6 1978, Reykjavik
Iceland (0) 0
Poland (1) 2 (*Kusto, Lato*) 7000
Iceland: Stefansson; Torfasson, Sveinsson, Petursson J, Edvaldsson J, Thordarsson, Hilmarsson (Albertsson), Edvaldsson A, Gudlaugsson, Thorbjornsson, Petursson P.
Poland: Kukla; Szymanowski, Maculewicz, Majewski, Rudy, Blachno, Cmikiewicz, Masztaler, Lato, Boniek, Kusto.

September 20 1978, Nijmegen
Holland (1) 3 (*Krol, Brandts, Rensenbrink*)
Iceland (0) 0 17,000
Holland: Schrijvers; Poortvliet, Krol, Brandts, Wildschut, Jansen, Haan, Willy Van der Kerkhof, Kosters (Peters), Nanninga, Rensenbrink.
Iceland: Bjarnason; Gudlaugsson, Sveinsson, Edvaldsson J, Petursson J, Edvaldsson A, (Gudmundsson), Thordarsson, Sigurvinsson, Thorbjornsson, Petursson P, Albertsson.

October 4 1978, Halle
E. Germany (2) 3 (*Peter, Riediger, Hoffmann*)
Iceland (0) 1 (*Petursson P pen.*) . 12,000
E. Germany: Croy; Weise, Hause, Dorner, Weber, Hafner (Lindemann), Pommerenke, Eigendorf, Peter, Riediger, Hoffmann.
Iceland: Bjarnasson (Stefansson), Bjorgvinsson, Gudlaugsson, Petursson L, Sveinsson (Albertsson), Thordarsson K, Edvaldsson A, Thorbjornsson, Sigurdsson, Thordarsson T, Petursson P.

October 11 1978, Berne
Switzerland (1) 1 (*Tanner*)
Holland (1) 3 (*Wildschut, Brandts, Geels*) 23,000
Switzerland: Burgener; Brechbuhl, Chapuisat, Montandon, Bizzini, Barberis, Tanner (Wehrli), Schnyder (Ponte), Sulser, Elsener, Botteron.
Holland: Schrivers; Wildschut, Krol, Brandts, Poortvliet, Haan, Willy Van der Kerkhof (Peters), Hovenkamp (Dusbaba), Geels, Nanninga, Rensenbrink.

November 15 1978, Rotterdam
Holland (1) 3 (*Kische o.g., Geels* 2, 1 *a pen.*)
E. Germany (0) 0 60,000
Holland: Schrijvers; Van Kraay, Krol, Brandts, Hovenkamp, Wildschut, Neeskens (Metgod), Peters, Rene Van der Kerkhof (Koster), Geels, Rensenbrink.
E. Germany: Croy; Kische, Dorner, Schnuphase, Weber, Hafner, Lindemann, Eigendorf (Netz), Schade (Peter), Riediger, Hoffmann.

November 15 1978, Wroclaw
Poland (1) 2 (*Boniek, Ogaza*)
Switzerland (0) 0 45,000
Poland: Kukla; Szymanowski, Maculewicz, Zmuda, Cmikiewicz, Majewski (Rudy), Boniek, Nawalka, Lato, Ogaza, Terlecki.
Switzerland: Engel; Brechbuhl, Chapuisat, Montandon, Bizzini, Barberis, Botteron, Meyer, Schnyder, Sulser, Elsener (Ponte).

March 28 1979, Eindhoven
Holland (0) 3 (*Kist, Metgod, Peters*)
Switzerland (0) 0 27,000
Holland: Schrijvers; Wildschut (Stevens), Brandts, Jansen, Poortvliet, Neeskens, Willy Van der Kerkhof (Metgod), Peters, Rene Van der Kerkhof, Kist, Rensenbrink.
Switzerland: Burgener; Brechbuhl, (Ponte), Chapuisat, Montadon, Bizzini (Wehrli), Botteron, Barberis, Hermann, Schnyder, Sulser, Elsener.

April 18 1979, Leipzig
E. Germany (0) 2 (*Streich, Lindemann*)
Poland (1) 1 (*Boniek*) 55,000
E. Germany: Grapenthein; Kische, Dorner, Weise, Weber, Hafner, Schade (Pommerenke), Lindemann, Riediger, Streich, Hoffmann.
Poland: Kukla; Dziuba (Rudy), Zmuda, Janas, Szymanowski, Majewski (Wrobel), Cmikiewicz, Boniek, Nawalka, Lato, Ogaza.

May 2 1979, Chorzow
Poland (1) 2 (*Boniek, Mazur pen.*)
Holland (0) 0 100,000
Poland: Kukla; Dziuba, Zmuda, Szymanowski, Plaszewski, Nawalka, Boniek, Lilka, Lato, Ogaza, Terlecki (Mazur)
Holland: Schrijvers; Stevens, Brandts, Krol, Hovenkamp, Jansen, Peters, Willy Van der Kerkhof, Rene Van der Kerkhof (Geels), Kist, Rensenbrink (Metgod).

May 5 1979, St Gallen
Switzerland (0) 0
E. Germany (1) 2 (*Lindemann, Streich*) 9000
Switzerland: Berbig; Ludi, Wehrli, Bizzini, Heinz Hermann, Maissen, Barberis, Tanner, Zwahlen (Herbert Herrmann), Brigger, (Botteron) Ponte.
E. Germany: Grapenthein; Kische, Dorner, Weise, Weber, Hafner, Pommerenke, Linedmann, Riediger, Streich, Hoffman.

May 22 1979, Berne
Switzerland (1) 2 (*Herbert Hermann, Zappa*)
Iceland (0) 0 25,000
Switzerland: Eichenberger; Brechbuhl, Ludi, Zappa, Heinz Hermann, Maissen, Barberis, Wehrli, Ponte, Botteron, Herbert Hermann.
Iceland: Olafsson; Gudlaugsson, Edvaldsson J (Gudmundsson), Petursson J, Sveinsson, Edvaldsson A, Giersson, Thorbjonsson, Sigurvinsson, Gudjohnsen, Petursson P.

June 9 1979, Reykjavik
Iceland (0) 1 (*Gudlaugsson*)
Switzerland (0) 2 (*Ponte, Heinz Hermann*) 10,300
Iceland: Olafsson; Edvaldsson J, Gudlaugsson, Geirsson, Harladson, Torbjornsson (Sveinsson), Sigurvinsson, Edvaldsson A, Gudjohnen, Thordarsson T (Thordarsson K), Petursson P.
Switzerland: Berbig; Ludi, Brechbuhl, Zappa, Wehrli, Barberis, Heinz Hermann, Andrey, Ponte, Herbert Hermann (Egli), Botteron (Tanner).

	P	W	D	L	F	A	Pts
Holland	5	4	0	1	12	3	8
Poland	4	3	0	1	7	2	6
E Germany	4	3	0	1	7	5	6
Switzerland	6	2	0	4	5	11	4
Iceland	5	0	0	5	2	12	0

GROUP 5

September 1 1978, Paris
France (0) 2 (*Berdoll, Six*)
Sweden (0) 2 (*Nordgren, Gronhagen*) 46,200
France: Rey; Battiston, Rio, Lopez, Bossis, Bathenay, Michel, Jouve, Rouyer, Gemmrich (Berdoll), Six (Giresse).
Sweden: Hellstrom; Borg, Nordqvist, Aman, Arvidsson, Lennart Larsson, Linderoth, Nordgren, Gronhagen, Sjoberg (Berggren), Wendt.

October 4 1978, Stockholm
Sweden (1) 1 (*Borg pen.*) 6000
Czechoslovakia (1) 3 (*Kroupa, Masny, Nehoda*)
Sweden: Hellstrom; Borg, Aman, Nordqvist, Arvidsson, Lennart Larsson, Linderoth, Nordgren, Gronhagen, Berggren (Ohlsson B), Wendt.
Czechoslovakia: Michalik; Barmos, Ondrus, Vojecek, Gogh, Pollak, Stambacher, Gajdusek, Masny, Kroupa (Kozak), Nehoda.

October 7 1978, Luxembourg
Luxembourg (0) 1 (*Michaux*)
France (1) 3 (*Six, Tresor, Gemmrich*) 12,000
Luxembourg: Moes; Meunier (Catani), Rohmann, Raths (Fandel), Margue, Weis, Dresch, Philipp, Michaux, Dussier, Neumann.
France: Dropsy; Battiston, Tresor, Lopez, Bossis, Larios (Petit), Jouve, Piasecki, Rocheteau (Gemmrich), Lacombe, Six.

February 25 1979, Paris
France (1) 3 (*Petit, Emon, Larios*)
Luxembourg (0) 0 25,000
France: Dropsy; Battiston, Specht, Tresor, Bossis, Petit, Piasecki (Larios), Michel, Rocheteau, Berdoll (Pecout), Emon.
Luxembourg: Moes; Meunier, Margue, Raths, Rohmann, Wies (Neumann), Philipp, Dresch, Michaux Wagner, Swally (Bossi).

May 1 1979, Luxembourg
Luxembourg (0) 0 3500
Czechoslovakia (1) 3 (*Masny, Gajdusek, Stambacher*)
Luxembourg: Moes; Meunier, (Fondl) Rohmann, Mond, Margue, Weis, Wagner, Dresch, Michaux, Di Domenico, Zwally (Neumann).
Czechoslovakia: Netolicka; Barmos, Vojacek, Ondrus, Gogh, Kozak, Panenka, Stambacher (Dobias), Masny, Kroupa (Micek), Gajdusek.

April 4 1979, Bratislava
Czechoslovakia (0) 2 (*Panenka, Stambacher*)
France (0) 0 50,000
Czechoslovakia: Netolicka; Barmos, Ondrus, Vojacek, Gogh, Kozak, Panenka, Stambacher, Masny, Nehoda, Gajdusek.
France: Dropsy; Domenech, Lopez, Specht, Bossis, Petit, Larios, Platini, Emon, Berdoll, Amisse.

June 7 1979, Stockholm
Sweden (2) 3 (*Gronhagen, Cervin, Borg pen*)
Luxembourg (0) 0 8000
Sweden: Hellstrom; Borg, Arvidsson (Johansson), Aaman, Fredriksson, Nordin, Linderoth, Nordgren, Gronhagen, Cervin, Ohlsson.
Luxembourg: Moes; Meunier, Rohmann, Kramer, Weis, Dresch (Bianchini), Scheitler, Michaux, Di Domenici, Girres.

	P	W	D	L	F	A	Pts
Czechoslovakia	3	3	0	0	8	1	6
France	4	2	1	1	8	5	5
Sweden	3	1	1	1	6	5	3
Luxembourg	4	0	0	4	1	12	0

GROUP 6

May 24 1978, Helsinki
Finland (0) 3 (*Ismail 2, Nieminen*)
Greece (0) 0 7800
Finland: Alaja; Vihtila, Tosla, Makynen, Ranta, Jantunen, Houtsonen (Rissanen), Aki Heiskanen, Toivola, Ismail, Nieminen.
Greece: Christidis; Pallas (Karavitis), Nikolaou, Firos, Iosifidis, Damanakis, Ardizoglou (Semertzidis), Papaioannou, Terzanidis, Galakos, Mavros.

September 20 1978, Helsinki
Finland (1) 2 (*Ismail, Pyykko*)
Hungary (0) 1 (*Tieber*) 4800
Finland: Alaja; Vihtila, Salonen, Tolsa, Ranta, Jantunen, Pyykko (Vimonen), Suomalainen (Helin), Toivola, Nieminen, Ismail.
Hungary: Gujdar; Paroczai, Balint, Kereki, Lukacs, Kovacs (Szokolai), Tatar, Gyimesi, Pinter, Kardos, Tieber.

September 20 1978, Erevan
USSR (1) 2 (*Tchesnokov, Bessonov*)
Greece (0) 0 55,000
USSR: Degtiarev; Konkov, Zupikov, Bereznoi, Bubnov, Prigoda, Burjak, Tchesnokov, Bessonov, Hidijatulin An, Blokhin.
Greece: Christidis; Kyrastas, Pallas, Ravousis, Firos, Terzanidis, Damanakis, Nikoloudis, Mitropoulos, Delikaris, Mavros.

October 11 1978, Budapest
Hungary (0) 2 (*Varadi, Szokolai*)
USSR (0) 0 35,000
Hungary: Katzirz; Martos, Kocsis, Kereki, Lukacs, Pal, Tatar, Pinter, Szokolai (Gyimesi), Kovacs (Fekete), Varadi.
USSR: Degtarev (Gontar); Bereschnoi, Bubnov, Shipikov, Machovikov, Konkov, Bessonov, Burjak (Zartzev), Hidiatulin, Gutzaev, Blokhin.

October 11 1978, Athens
Greece (5) 8 (*Mavros 4, 1 pen, Nikoloudis, Delikaris 2, Galakos*)
Finland (0) 1 (*Heiskanen*) 6000
Greece: Constantinou; Kyrastas, Pallas, Ravousis, Firos, Ardizoglou, Nikoloudis, Delikaris, Mitropoulos (Semertzidis), Galakos (Ziakos), Mavros.
Finland: Alaja; Vihtila, Salonen, Ranta, Tolsa, Jantunen, Heiskanen, Suomalainen (Nieminen, K.), Ismial, Pyykko (Uimonen), Nieminen J.

October 25 1978, Salonika
Greece (0) 4 (*Galakos 2, Ardizoglou, Mavros*)
Hungary (0) 1 (*Varadi*) 15,000
Greece: Constantinou; Xanthopoulos, Ravousis, Firos, Iosifidis, Nikoloudis, Delikaris (Damanakis), Koudas, Ardizoglou (Mitropoulos), Galakos, Mavros.
Hungary: Katzirz; Martos, Kocsis, Lukacs, Kereki, Zombori, Pal, Pinter, Szokolai (Kovacs, I.), Tatar, Varadi.

May 2 1979, Budapest
Hungary (0) 0
Greece (0) 0   25,000
Hungary: Katzirz; Torok, Kocsis, Balint, Kutasi, Kovacs, Csapo, Zombori, Fazekas, Torocsik, Fekete.
Greece: Kalisidis; Josifidis, Firos, Gounaris, Kapsis, Damanakis, Nikoloudis, Livanthinos, Mavros, Kostikos, Ardizoglou.

May 19, 1979 Tbilisi
USSR (1) 2 (*Chesnokov, Shengelia*)
Hungary (1) 2 (*Tatar, Pusztai*)   80,000
USSR: Gontar; Berezhnoi, Azhdem, Bubnov, Makhovikov, Daraselia, Machaidze, Koridze (Kipiani), Chesnokov (Joulokov), Shengelia, Blokin.
Hungary: Gujdar; Torok (Martos), Kocsis, Balint, Toth (J) (Rab), Tatar, Nyilasi, Zombori, Magyar, Pusztai, Torocsik.

July 4 1979, Helsinki
Finland (0) 1 (*Ismail*)
USSR (1) 1 (*Khapsalis*)   13,119
Finland: Alaja; Lampi, Tolsa, Houtsonen, Ranta, Rautiainen, Pyykko (Salonen), Toivola (Kokko), Kupianinen, Ismail.
USSR: Remenski; Prigoda, Shintjegasvili, Mahovikov, Bubnov, Daraselja, Khetejatulin, Bessonov, Chessnokov, Kipiani (Shengelija), Khapsalis.

	P	W	L	D	F	A	Pts
Greece	5	2	1	2	12	7	5
Finland	4	2	1	1	7	10	5
USSR	4	1	2	1	5	5	4
Hungary	5	1	2	2	6	8	4

GROUP 7

October 25 1978, Wrexham
Wales (3) 7 (*Edwards* 4, *O'Sullivan, Thomas, Flynn*)
Malta (0) 0   11,500
Wales: Davies; Jones, Stevenson, Phillips, Page, Thomas (M), Harris, Flynn, Edwards, James, Cartwright (O'Sullivan).
Malta: Gatt; Ciantar, Farrugia (Consiglio), Tortell, Schembri, Holland, Magro, Aquilina, Xuereb G, Xuereb R, Seychell.

November 29 1978, Wrexham
Wales (0) 0 (*Deacy*)
Turkey (0) 0   11,800
Wales: Davies; Stevenson, Jones, Phillips, Yorath, Thomas M, Flynn, Dwyer, Harris, Deacy, James.
Turkey: Senol; Turgay, Erdogan, Cem, Necati, Fatih, Necdet, Mehmet, Eksi, Sedat, Onder (Ahmet).

February 25 1979, Valletta
Malta (0) 0
West Germany (0) 0   13,000
Malta: Sciberras; Buckingham, Buttigieg, Holland, Ed Farrugia, Em Farrugia, Xuereb R, Xuereb J, Magro, Spiteri-Gonzi (Seychell), Xuereb G.
West Germany: Maier; Kaltz, Zewe (Kelsch), Forster, Dietz, Muller (H), Cullmann, Bonhof, Rummenigge (Allofs), Fischer, Abramczik.

March 18 1979, Izmir
Turkey (1) 2 (*Sedat, Fatih*)
Malta (0) 1 (*Spiteri-Gonzi*)   30,000
Turkey: Senol; Turgay, Cem, Necati, Fatih, Erhan, Mehmet, Tuna, Bahtiar, Sedat, Mustapha.
Malta: Sciberras; Ciantar, Ed Farrugia, Xuereb G, Holland, Buttigieg, Spiteri-Gonzi, Magro, Xuereb J, Em Farrugia, Xuereb R.

April 1 1979, Izmir
Turkey (0) 0
West Germany (0) 0   50,000
Turkey: Senol; Turgay, Fatih, Necati, Cem, Engin, Sedat III, Onal, Necdet (Tuna), Cemil, Buyuk, Mustafa.
West Germany: Burdenski; Kaltz, Bonhof, Stielike, Dietz, Cullmann, Zimmermann (Forster), Muller H, Rummenigge (Kelsch), Toppmoller, Borchers.

May 2 1979, Wrexham
Wales (0) 0
West Germany (1) 2 (*Zimmermann, Fischer*) 30,000
Wales: Davies; Page, Phillips, Berry, Jones J, Mahoney, Thomas, Yorath (James), Harris, Edwards (Toshack), Curtis.
West Germany: Maier; Kaltz, Cullmann, Forster, Dietz, Bonhof, Stielike (Martin), Zimmermann, Rummenigge, Fischer, Allofs.

June 2 1979, Valletta
Malta (0) 0
Wales (1) 2 (*Nicholas, Flynn*)   9000
Malta: Sciberras; Buckingham, Ed Farrugia, Holland, Buttigieg, Em Farrugia, Magre, Xuereb J, Spiteri-Gonzi (Hahri), Xuereb R, Xuereb G.
Wales: Davies; Stevenson, Phillips, Jones J, Harris (Thomas), Nicholas, Flynn (Dwyer), Mahoney, Curtis, Toshack, James.

	P	W	D	L	F	A	Pts
Wales	4	3	0	1	10	2	6
W Germany	3	1	2	0	2	0	4
Turkey	3	1	1	1	2	2	3
Malta	4	0	1	3	1	11	1

UNDER-21 EUROPEAN CHAMPIONSHIP 1978-80

Group 1
Denmark v England 1–2
Denmark v Bulgaria 2–0
Bulgaria v England 1–3

	P	W	D	L	F	A	Pts
England	2	2	–	–	5	2	4
Denmark	2	1	–	1	3	2	2
Bulgaria	2	–	–	2	1	5	–

Group 2
Belgium v Norway 4–0
Portugal v Belgium 0–0
Scotland v Norway 5–1
Portugal v Scotland 0–3
Norway v Portugal 0–0
Norway v Scotland 2–2

	P	W	D	L	F	A	Pts
Scotland	3	2	1	–	10	3	5
Belgium	2	1	1	–	4	0	3
Portugal	3	–	2	1	0	3	2
Norway	4	–	2	2	3	11	2

Group 3
Spain v Yugoslavia 0–1
Cyprus v Spain 0–0
Yugoslavia v Cyprus 1–0

	P	W	D	L	F	A	Pts
Yugoslavia	2	2	–	–	2	0	4
Cyprus	2	–	1	1	0	1	1
Spain	2	–	1	1	0	1	1

Group 4
E Germany v Holland 2–0
Poland v E Germany 1–1
Holland v Poland 2–3

	P	W	D	L	F	A	Pts
E Germany	2	1	1	–	3	1	3
Poland	2	1	1	–	4	3	3
Holland	2	–	–	2	2	5	–

Group 5
France v Sweden 2–1
Sweden v Czechoslovakia 0–1
Czechoslovakia v France 1–0

	P	W	D	L	F	A	Pts
Czechoslovakia	2	2	–	–	2	0	4
France	2	1	–	1	2	2	2
Sweden	2	–	–	2	1	3	–

Group 6
Finland v Greece 0–1
Greece v USSR 0–3
Greece v Finland 3–1
Finland v USSR 0–2

	P	W	D	L	F	A	Pts
USSR	2	2	–	–	5	0	4
Greece	3	2	–	1	4	4	4
Finland	3	–	–	3	1	6	–

Group 7
*Turkey v Hungary 0–3
Hungary v Rumania 1–0
*Rumania v Turkey 3–0
Turkey v Rumania 2–0
Hungary v Turkey 5–0

	P	W	D	L	F	A	Pts
Hungary	3	3	–	–	9	0	6
Rumania	3	1	–	2	3	3	2
Turkey	4	1	–	3	2	11	2

*Turkey fielded ineligible players—results were annulled by UEFA and the two points were awarded to opponents with a 3–0 scoreline.

Group 8
Luxembourg v Switzerland 0–3
Switzerland v Italy 0–0

	P	W	D	L	F	A	Pts
Switzerland	2	1	1	–	3	0	3
Italy	1	–	1	–	–	–	1
Luxembourg	1	–	–	1	0	3	–

European Club Tournaments 1978-79

EUROPEAN CUP

First Round, first leg
Juventus 1 (*Virdis*)
Rangers 0
Real Madrid 5 (*Jensen, Juanito* 2, *Del Bosque, Wolff*)
Progres Niedercorn 0
AEK Athens 6 (*Bajevic* 2, *Ardizoglou, Tassos, Nikolau, Mavros*)
Porto 1 (*Oliveira*)
Fenerbahce 2 (*Rasit, Cemil*)
PSV Eindhoven 1 (*Brandts*)
Nottingham F 2 (*Birtles, Barrett*)
Liverpool 0
Vllaznia 2 (*Zhega, Ballgjini*)
Austria/WAC 0
Malmo 0
Monaco 0
Linfield 0
Lillestrom 0
Cologne 4 (*Littbarski, Neumann* 2, *Konopka*)
Akranes 1 (*Hallgrimsson*)
Zbrojovka Brno 2 (*Kroupa, Janecka*)
Ujpest Dozsa 2 (*Fekete, Torocsik*)
Partizan Belgrade 2 (*Prekazi, Djurovic*)
Dynamo Dresden 0
Grasshoppers 8 (*Sulser* 5, *Ponte* 2, *Wehrli*)
Valletta 0
Bruges 2 (*Cuelemans, Cools*)
Wisla Krakow 1 (*Kapka*)
Odense 2 (*Jensen M* 2)
Lokomotive Sofia 2 (*Kolev, Veliotzkov*)
Valkeakosken 0
Dynamo Kiev 1 (*Boltatsha*)
Omonia 2 (*Kanaris, Gootkrtou*)
Bohemians 1 (*O'Connor*)

First Round, second leg
Rangers 2 (*MacDonald, Smith*)
Juventus 0
Progress Niedercorn 0
Real Madrid 7 (*Pirri, Jensen, Stielike, Santillana* 2, *Hernandez, Bossi og*)
Porto 4 (*Vital* 2, *Teixeira, Gomes*)
AEK Athens 1 (*Bajevic*)
PSV Eindhoven 6 (*Van der Kuylen* 4, *Deykers* 2)
Fenerbahce 1 (*Rasit*)
Liverpool 0
Nottingham F 0
Austria/WAC 4 (*Parits, Schachner* 2, *Robert Sara*)
Vllaznia 1 (*Hafizi*)
Monaco 0
Malmo 1 (*Kinnvall*)
Lillestrom 1 (*Lonstad*)
Linfield 0
Akranes 1 (*Hein og*)
Cologne 1 (*Van Gool*)
Ujpest Dozsa 0
Zbrojovka Brno 2 (*Dosek, Kroupa*)
Dynamo Dresden 2 (*Dorner, Weber*)
Partizan Belgrade 0
Valletta 3 (*Seychell, Agius, Farrugia*)
Grasshoppers 5 (*Sulser, Ponte, Heinz Hermann, Traber* 2)
Wisla Krakow 3 (*Kmiecik, Lipka, Krupinski*)
Bruges 1 (*Van der Eycken*)
Lokomotiv Sofia 2 (*Mihailov, Kostov*)
Odense 1 (*Erikson*)
Dynamo Kiev 3 (*Veremeev, Khapsalis, Buriak*)
Valkeakosken 1 (*Ronkainen*)
Bohemians 1 (*Joyce*)
Omonia 0

Second Round, first leg
Real Madrid 3 (*Juanito, Garcia, Santillana*)
Grasshoppers 1 (*Sulser*)
AEK Athens 1 (*Mavros*)
Nottingham F 2 (*McGovern, Birtles*)
Dynamo Kiev 0
Malmo 0
Lokomotive Sofia 0
Cologne 1 (*Zimmermann*)
Bohemians 0
Dynamo Dresden 0
Austria/WAC 4 (*Gasselich* 2, *Robert Sara, Schachner*)
Lillestrom 1 (*Dokker*)
Rangers 0
PSV Eindhoven 0
Zbrojovka Brno 2 (*Pesice, Kroupa*)
Wisla Krakow 2 (*Kmiecik, Maculewicz*)

Second Round, second leg
Grasshoppers 2 (*Sulser* 2)
Real Madrid 0
Nottingham F 5 (*Needham, Woodcock, Anderson, Birtles* 2)
AEK Athens 1 (*Bajevic*)
Malmo 2 (*Kinnvall, Cervin*)
Dynamo Kiev 0
Cologne 4 (*Dieter Muller* 2, *Van Gool, Glowacz*)
Lokomotiv Sofia 0
Dynamo Dresden 6 (*Trautmann* 2, *Dorner, Schmuch, Riedl, Kotte*)
Bohemians 0
Lillestrom 0
Austria/WAC 0
PSV Eindhoven 2 (*Lubse, Deykers*)
Rangers 3 (*MacDonald, Watson, Johnstone*)
Wisla Krakow 1 (*Kapka*)
Zbrojovka Brno 1 (*Dosek*)

Quarter-finals, first leg
Nottingham F 4 (*Birtles, Robertson pen, Gemmill, Lloyd*)
Grasshoppers 1 (*Sulser*)
Cologne 1 (*Dieter Muller*)
Rangers 0
Wisla Krakow 2 (*Nawalka, Kmiecik*)
Malmo 1 (*Hansson*)
Austria/WAC 3 (*Schachner* 2, *Zach*)
Dynamo Dresden 1 (*Weber*)

Quarter-finals, second leg

Grasshoppers 1 (*Sulser pen*)
Nottingham F 1 (*O'Neill*)
Rangers 1 (*McLean*)
Cologne 1 (*Dieter Muller*)
Malmo 4 (*Ljungberg 3, 2 pens, Cervin*)
Wisla Krakow 1 (*Kmiecik*)
Dynamo 1 (*Riedl pen*)
Austria/WAC 0

Semi-finals, first leg

Nottingham F 3 (*Birtles, Bowyer, Robertson*)
Cologne 3 (*Van Gool, Dieter Muller, Okudera*)
Austria/WAC 0
Malmo 0

Semi-finals, second leg

Cologne 0
Nottingham F 1 (*Bowyer*)
Malmo 1 (*Hansson*)
Austria/WAC 0

Final 1978–79: Nottingham F (1) 1 (*Francis*)
Malmo (0) 0
(in Munich, May 30 1979, 57,500)

Nottingham F: Shilton; Anderson, Lloyd, Burns, Clark, Francis, McGovern, Bowyer, Robertson, Woodcock, Birtles.
Malmo: Moller; Roland Andersson, Jonsson, Magnus Andersson, Erlandsson, Tapper (Malmberg), Ljungberg, Prytz, Kinnvall, Hansson (Tommy Andersson), Cervin.

EUROPEAN CUP-WINNERS' CUP

First Round, first leg

Floriana 1 (*Xuereb R*)
Inter-Milan 3 (*Altobelli 3*)
Valur 1 (*Albertsson*)
Magdeburg 1 (*Steinbach*)
Sporting Lisbon 0
Banik Ostrava 1 (*Antalik*)
Beveren 3 (*Albert, Stevens, Schonberger*)
Ballymena 0
Ferencvaros 2 (*Nyilasi, Major*)
Kalmar 0
Marek Stanke Dimitrov 3 (*Petrov V, Petrov I 2*)
Aberdeen 2 (*Jarvie, Harper*)
Barcelona 3 (*Krankl 2, Sanchez*)
Shakhtor 0
PAOK Salonika 2 (*Karmanides, Sarafis*)
Servette 0
Uni Craiova 3 (*Camataru 2, Crisau*)
Fortuna Dusseldorf 4 (*Fanz 2, Allofs, Zimmermann*)
Zaglebie Sosnowiec 2 (*Zarichta, Starinski*)
SW Innsbruck 3 (*Peter Koncilia, Oberacher, Brasoler*)
AZ 67 0
Ipswich T 0
Apoel 0
Shamrock Rovers 2 (*Giles, Lynex*)
Rijeka 3 (*Tomic, Durkalic, Curkov*)
Wrexham 0
Bodo Glimt 4 (*Solhang 2, Berg, Hanssen*)
Union Luxembourg 1 (*Teitgen*)
Frem 2 (*Jacobsen, Hansen*)
Nancy 0

First Round, second leg

Inter-Milan 5 (*Muraro 2, Fedele 2, Chierico*)
Floriana 0
Magdeburg 4 (*Seguin, Steinbach, Hoffmann, Streich*)
Valur 0
Banik Ostrava 1 (*Licka*)
Sporting Lisbon 0
Ballymena 0
Beveren 3 (*Jansen 2, Wissmann*)
Kalmar 2 (*Magnusson, Nyberg*)
Ferencvaros 2 (*Ebedli, Szokolai*)
Aberdeen 3 (*Strachan, Jarvie, Harper*)
Marek Stanke Dimitrov 0

Shakhtor 1 (*Resnik*)
Barcelona 1 (*Krankl*)
Servette 4 (*Pfister, Hamberg, Elia 2*)
PAOK Solonika 0
Fortuna Dusseldorf 1 (*Bommer*)
Uni Craiova 1 (*Marcu*)
SW Innsbruck 1 (*Koterva og*)
Zaglebie Sosnowiec 1 (*Dvorczik*)
Ipswich T 2 (*Mariner, Wark*)
AZ 67 0
Shamrock Rovers 1 (*Lynex*)
Apoel 0
Wrexham 2 (*McNeil, Cartwright*)
Rijeka 0
Union Luxembourg 1 (*Teitgen*)
Bodo Glimt 0
Nancy 4 (*Curbelo, Jeannol 2, Zenter*)
Frem 0

Second Round, first leg

Servette 2 (*Hamberg, Barberis*)
Nancy 1 (*Robio*)
Banik Ostrava 3 (*Knapp, Radimec, Rygel*)
Shamrock Rovers 0
Ipswich T 1 (*Wark*)
SW Innsbruck 0
Anderlecht 3 (*Van der Elst 2, Coeck*)
Barcelona 0
Inter-Milan 5 (*Beccalossi, Altobelli 3, Muraro*)
Bodo Glimt 0
Fortuna Dusseldorf 3 (*Gunther 2, Zimmermann*)
Aberdeen 0
Rijeka 0
Beveren 0
Magdeburg 1 (*Streich*)
Ferencvaros 0

Second Round, second leg

Nancy 2 (*Zenier, Umpierrez*)
Servette 2 (*Elia, Schnyder*)
Shamrock Rovers 2 (*Giles*)
Banik Ostrava 3 (*Licka 2, Albrecht*)
SW Innsbruck 1 (*Oberacher*)
Ipswich T 1 (*Burley*)
Barcelona 3 (*Krankl, Heredia, Zuviria*)
Anderlecht 0

Bodo Glimt 1 (*Hansen*)
Inter-Milan 2 (*Altobelli, Scanziani*)
Aberdeen 2 (*McLelland, Jarvie*)
Fortuna Dusseldorf 0
Beveren 2 (*Baecke* 2)
Rijeka 0
Ferencvaros 2 (*Pusztai, Szokolai*)
Magdeburg 1 (*Stachmann*)

Quarter-finals, first leg
Inter-Milan 0
Beveren 0
Fortuna Dusseldorf 0
Servette 0
Ipswich T 2 (*Gates* 2)
Barcelona 1 (*Esteban*)
Magdeburg 2 (*Streich* 2)
Banik Ostrava 1 (*Antalik*)

Quarter-finals, second leg
Beveren 1 (*Stevens*)
Inter-Milan 0
Servette 1 (*Andrey*)
Fortuna Dusseldorf 1 (*Bommer*)
Barcelona 1 (*Migueli*)
Ipswich T 0
Banik Ostrava 4 (*Rygel* 2, *Albrecht, Nemec*)
Magdeburg 2 (*Sparwasser, Pommerenke*)

Semi-finals, first leg
Fortuna Dusseldorf 3 (*Klaus Allofs* 2, *Thomas Allofs*)
Banik Ostrava 1 (*Nemec*)
Barcelona 1 (*Rexach pen*)
Beveren 0

Semi-finals, second leg
Banik Ostrava 2 (*Licka, Antalik*)
Fortuna Dusseldorf 1 (*Zewe*)
Beveren 0
Barcelona 1 (*Krankl pen*)

Final 1978–79: Barcelona (2) (2) 4 (*Sanchez, Asensi, Rexach, Krankl*)
Fortuna Dusseldorf (2) (2) 3 (*Klaus Allofs, Seel* 2) aet
(in Basle, May 16 1979)
Barcelona: Artola; Zuviria, Migueli, Costas (Martinez), Albaladejo (De la Cruz), Sanchez, Neeskens, Asensi, Rexach, Krankl, Carrasco.
Fortuna: Daniel; Baltes, Zewe, Zimmermann (Lund), Brei (Weikl), Kohnen, Bommer, Schmitz, Thomas Allofs, Klaus Allofs, Seel.

UEFA CUP

First round, first leg

Dukla Prague 1 (*Nehoda*)
Lanerossi Vicenza 0
AC Milan 1 (*Novellino*)
Lokomotive Kosice 0
CSKA Sofia 2 (*Djevizov, Christov*)
Valencia 1 (*Solsona*)
Borussia Moenchengladbach 5 (*Bruns 2, Gores, Nielsen, Simonsen*)
Sturm Graz 1 (*Jurtin*)
Arges Pitesti 3 (*Toma, Moiceanu 2*)
Panathinaikos 0
Athletic Bilbao 2 (*Van Dord og, Vidal*)
Ajax 0
Everton 5 (*King 2, Thomas Walsh, Latchford*)
Finn Harps 0
Jeunesse Esch 0
Lausanne 0
Nantes 0
Benfica 2 (*Chalana, Nene*)
Gijon 3 (*Ferrero, Moran 2*)
Torino 0
Sporting Braga 5 (*Chico Gordo 4, Lito*)
Hibernian 0
Galatasaray 1 (*Fatih*)
WBA 3 (*Robson, Regis, Cunningham*)
Dynamo Berlin 5 (*Riediger 3, Netz, Brillat*)
Red Star Belgrade 2 (*Sestic, Savic*)
Palloseura 2 (*Monkkanen, Eiskanen*)
1903 Copenhagen 1 (*Haarbye*)
Basle 2 (*Tanner, Stohler*)
Stuttgart 3 (*Ohlicher 2, Dieter Hoeness*)
Torpedo Moscow 4 (*Vassilev, Mironov, Grijsin, Sutsijlin*)
Molde 0
Elfsborg 2 (*Svensson, Magnusson*)
Strasbourg 0
Duisburg 5 (*Jara, Alhaus, Bussers, Worm 2*)
Lech Poznan 0
Standard Liege 1 (*Denier*)
Dundee United 0
Start Kristiansand 0
Esbjerg 0
Arsenal 3 (*Stapleton 2, Sunderland*)
Lokomotive Leipzig 0
Carl Zeiss Jena 1 (*Topfer*)
Lierse 0
Glentoran 0
IBV Vestmann 0
Twente 1 (*Thorsen*)
Manchester City 1 (*Watson*)
Hibernian 3 (*Higgins 2, Temperley*)
IFK Norrkoping 2 (*Ohlsson, Andersson*)
Timisoara 2 (*Cotec, Paltinisan*)
MTK Budapest 0
Pezoporikos 2 (*Teofonu 2*)
Slask Wroclaw 2 (*Pawlowski, Sybis*)
Olympiakos 2 (*Kritikopoulos, Kaltzas*)
Levski Spartak 1 (*Panov*)
Dynamo Tbilisi 2 (*Kipiani, Shengelja*)
Napoli 0
Hajduk Split 2 (*Kop, Luchetin*)
Rapid Vienna 0
Hertha Berlin 0
Trakia Plovdiv 0
Honved 6 (*Lukacs, Weimper 2, Gijmesi, Bodoyni, Nagy*)
Adanaspor 0

First Round, Second leg

Lanerossi Vicenza 1 (*Briaschi*)
Dukla Prague 1 (*Roselli og*)
Lokomotive Kosice 1 (*Kozak*)
AC Milan 0
Valencia 4 (*Saura 2, Kempes, Felman*)
CSKA Sofia 1 (*Christov*)
Sturm Graz 1 (*Schilcher*)
Borussia Moenchengladbach 2 (*Simonsen, Bruns*)
Panathinaikos 1 (*Gonios*)
Arges Pitesti 2 (*Duru, Radu*)
Ajax 3 (*Clarke 2, Lerby*)
Athletico Bilbao 0
Finn Harps 0
Everton 5 (*King, Latchford, Walsh, Ross, Dobson*)
Lausanne 2 (*Dizerens, Sanpedro*)
Jeunesse Esch 0
Benfica 0
Nantes 0
Torino 1 (*Graziani*)
Gijon 0
Hibernian 3 (*Spiteri Gonzi, Mizzi 2*)
Sporting Braga 2 (*Chico Gordo, Reinaldo*)
WBA 3 (*Robson, Cunningham, Trewick*)
Galatasaray 1 (*Turgay*)
Red Star Belgrade 4 (*Borovnicka 2, Savic, Sestic*)
Dynamo Berlin 1 (*Riediger*)
1903 Copenhagen 4 (*Christensen, Smidt, Larsen, Dam*)
Palloseura 4 (*Eiskanen 2, Heinalainen, Rautio*)
Stuttgart 4 (*Kelsch 3, Hansi Muller*)
Basle 1 (*Schonberger*)
Molde 3 (*Brakstad, Bjoraa, Fuglseth*)
Torpedo Moscow 3 (*Vassilev 2, Zotijlin*)
Strasbourg 4 (*Piasecki, Tanter, Marx, Wagner*)
Elfsborg 1 (*Ahlstrom*)
Lech Poznan 2 (*Kasalik, Okonski*)
Duisburg 5 (*Bussers, Worm 2, Wenten, Buttgereit*)
Dundee United 0
Standard Liege 0
Esbjerg 1 (*Iversen*)
Start Kristiansand 0
Lokomotive Leipzig 1 (*Stapleton og*)
Arsenal 4 (*Price, Sunderland, Stapleton 2*)
Lierse 2 (*Bosche, Van den Bergh*)
Carl Zeiss Jena 2 (*Schupase, Topfer*)
IBV Westmann 1 (*Oskarsson*)
Glentoran 1 (*McFall*)
Manchester C 3 (*Kidd, Bell, Overweg og*)
Twente 2 (*Wildschut, Gritter*)
IFK Norrkoping 0
Hibernian 0
MTK Budapest 2 (*Koritar, Nadu og*)
Timisoara 1 (*Petrescu*)
Slask Wroclaw 5 (*Garlowski, Faber, Olesiak, Kwiatkowski, Sybis*)
Pezoporikos 1 (*Lambrou*)
Levski Spartak 3 (*Milkov, Panov, Voinov*)
Olympiakos 1 (*Kaltzas*)
Napoli 1 (*Savoldi*)
Dynamo Tbilisi 1 (*Daraselia*)
Rapid Vienna 2 (*Krejcirik, Francker*)
Hajduk Split 1 (*Zungul*)
Trakia Plovdiv 1 (*Argirov*)
Hertha Berlin 2 (*Granitza 2*)
Adanaspor 2 (*Irfan, Necip*)
Honved 2 (*Sener og, Pinter*)

Second Round, first leg
Ajax 1 (*Lerby*)
Lausanne 0
Benfica 0
Borussia Moenchengladbach 0
Everton 2 (*Latchford, King*)
Dukla Prague 1 (*Macela*)
Arges Pitesti 2 (*Dobrin, Moiceanu*)
Valencia 1 (*Felman*)
Sporting Braga 0
WBA 2 (*Regis 2*)
Torpedo Moscow 2 (*Vassilev, Sakharov*)
Stuttgart 1 (*Dieter Hoeness*)
Strasbourg 2 (*Gemmrich, Piasecki*)
Hibernian 0
Gijon 0
Red Star Belgrade 1 (*Misa og*)
Carl Zeiss Jena 0
Duisburg 0
Palloseura 0
Esbjerg 2 (*Bach, Nielsen*)
IBV Westmann 0
Slask Wrocław 2 (*Kwiatkowski, Halgrimsson og*)
Manchester C 4 (*Hartford, Palmer, Kidd 2*)
Standard Liege 0
Honved 4 (*Weimper 2, Gijmesi, Pinter*)
Timisoara 0
Hertha Berlin 2 (*Nussing, Granitza*)
Dynamo Tbilisi 0
Hajduk Split 2 (*Kop, Djordjevic*)
Arsenal 1 (*Brady*)
Levski Spartak 1 (*Milkov*)
AC Milan 1 (*Chiodi*)

Second Round, second leg
WBA 1 (*Brown A*)
Sporting Braga 0
Stuttgart 2 (*Hansi Muller, Volkert*)
Torpedo Moscow 0
Hibernian 1 (*MacLeod*)
Strasbourg 0
Red Star Belgrade 1 (*Petrovic*)
Gijon 1 (*Borovnika og*)
Duisburg 3 (*Dietz, Jara, Fruck*)
Carl Zeiss Jena 0
Esbjerg 4 (*Berthelsen, Thoresen, Stergaard, Bach*)
Palloseura 1 (*Loikkanen*)
Slask Wrocław 2 (*Nocko, Kwiatkowski*)
IBV Westmann 1 (*Halgrimsson*)
Standard Liege 2 (*Sigurvinsson 2*)
Manchester C 0
Timisoara 2 (*Rosca, Paltinislan*)
Honved 0
Dynamo Tbilisi 1 (*Shengelja*)
Hertha Berlin 0
Arsenal 1 (*Young*)
Hajduk Split 0
AC Milan 3 (*Maldera, Bigon, Chiodi*)
Levski Spartak 0
Dukla Prague 1 (*Gajdusek*)
Everton 0
Lausanne 0
Ajax 4 (*Erkens, Clarke 2, Arnesen*)
Valencia 5 (*Kempes 2, Bonhof, Saura, Solrona*)
Arges Pitesti 2 (*Moiceanu, Doru Nicolae*)
Borussia Moenchengladbach 2 (*Bruns pen, Klinkhammer*)
Benfica 0

Third Round, first leg
Stuttgart 4 (*Volkert 2, 1 a pen, Kelsch, Ohlicher*)
Dukla Prague 1 (*Gajdusek*)
Honved 4 (*Nagy 2, Lukacs, Weimper pen*)
Ajax 1 (*Clarke pen*)
Red Star Belgrade 1 (*Blagojevic*)
Arsenal 0
Esbjerg 2 (*Hansen pen, Jaspersen*)
Hertha Berlin 1 (*Milewski*)
Borussia Moenchengladbach 1 (*Kulik pen*)
Slask Wrocław 1 (*Olesiak*)
Valencia 1 (*Felman*)
WBA 1 (*Cunningham*)
Strasbourg 0
Duisburg 0
AC Milan 2 (*Bigon 2*)
Manchester C 2 (*Kidd, Power*)

Third Round, second leg
Dukla Prague 4 (*Dieter Hoeness og, Vizek, Pelc pen, Gajdusek*)
Stuttgart 0
Ajax 2 (*Clarke pen, Tahamata*)
Honved 0
Arsenal 1 (*Sunderland*)
Red Star Belgrade 1 (*Savic*)
Hertha Berlin 4 (*Milewski 4*)
Esbjerg 0
Slask Wrocław 2 (*Pawlowski 2, 1 a pen*)
Borussia Moenchengladbach 4 (*Simonsen 3, Nielsen*)
WBA 2 (*Brown T 2*)
Valencia 0
Duisburg 4 (*Worm, Weber 2, Fruck*)
Strasbourg 0
Manchester C 3 (*Booth, Hartford, Kidd*)
AC Milan 0

Quarter-finals, first leg
Honved 2 (*Varga II, Weimper pen*)
Duisburg 3 (*Worm 2, Seliger*)
Red Star Belgrade 1 (*Savic*)
WBA 0
Manchester C 1 (*Channon*)
Borussia Moenchengladbach 1 (*Lienen*)
Hertha Berlin 1 (*Nussing*)
Dukla Prague 1 (*Pelc*)

Quarter-finals, second leg
Duisburg 1 (*Bussers*)
Honved 2 (*Karalyos, Pal*)
WBA 1 (*Regis*)
Red Star Belgrade 1 (*Sestic*)
Borussia Moenchengladbach 3 (*Kulik, Bruns, Del Haye*)
Manchester C 1 (*Deyna*)
Dukla Prague 1 (*Nehoda*)
Hertha Berlin 2 (*Agerbeck, Milewski*)

Semi-finals, first leg
Red Star Belgrade 1 (*Savic*)
Hertha Berlin 0
Duisburg 2 (*Worm, Fruck*)
Borussia Moenchengladbach 2 (*Simonsen, Lausen*)

Semi-finals, second leg
Hertha Berlin 2 (*Beer, Sidka*)
Red Star Belgrade 1 (*Miloslavjevic*)
Borussia Moenchengladbach 4 (*Simonsen 2, Kulik, Lienen*)
Duisburg 1 (*Bussers*)

Final 1978–79: Red Star Belgrade (1) 1 (*Sestic*)
Borussia Moenchengladbach (0) 1 (*Jurisic og*)
(First leg in Belgrade, May 9 1979, 87,500)
Red Star: Stojanovic; Jovanovic, Miletovic, Jurisic, Jovin, Muslin (Krmpotic), Petrovic, Blagojevic, Milosavljevic (Milovanovic), Savic, Sestic.
Borussia: Kneib; Vogts, Hannes, Schaffer, Ringles, Schafer, Kulik, Nielsen (Danner), Wohlers (Gores), Simonsen, Lienen.
Borussia Moenchengladbach (1) 1 (*Simonsen pen*)
Red Star Belgrade (0) 0
Second leg in Dusseldorf, May 23 1979, 45,000)
Borussia: Kneib; Vogts, Hannes, Schaffer, Ringles, Schafer, Kulik (Koppel), Gores, Wohlers, Simonsen, Lienen.
Red Star: Stojanovic; Jovanovic, Miletovic, Jurisic, Jovin, Muslin, Petrovic, Blagojevic, Milovanovic (Sestic), Savic, Milosavljevic.

THE LORD'S TAVERNERS' STICKY WICKET BOOK

Edited by Tim Rice, aided and abetted by Willie Rushton

A marvellous compendium of wit, humour, reminiscence and lunacy from the pens and cameras of some of the best-known stars of stage and screen, all of whom have one thing in common – an insatiable appetite for cricket.

Contributors include Henry Cooper, Eric Morecambe, James Hunt, Brian Johnston, Patrick Mower, John Cleese, Brian Clough, Ernie Wise, Sir Donald Bradman, Patrick Moore and many others.

Foreword by H.R.H. The Duke of Edinburgh

All royalties will go to the Lord's Taverners' charities.

£5.50   144 pp
cartoons by Willie Rushton
publishing October 18th

Available from booksellers, or in case of difficulty write to QAP Direct Sales, 9 Partridge Drive, Orpington, Kent, England, enclosing cheque/PO payable to Macdonald & Jane's + 45p per copy p&p (UK only). Allow 28 days for delivery, subject to availability.

M&J Queen Anne Press

EUROPEAN CHAMPIONS CUP FINALS 1956–79

Year	Winners		Runners-up		Venue
1956	Real Madrid	4	Stade de Rheims	3	Paris
1957	Real Madrid	2	AC Fiorentina	0	Madrid
1958	Real Madrid	3	AC Milan	2	Brussels
1959	Real Madrid	2	Stade de Rheims	0	Stuttgart
1960	Real Madrid	7	Eintracht Frankfurt	3	Glasgow
1961	Benfica	3	Barcelona	2	Berne
1962	Benfica	5	Real Madrid	3	Amsterdam
1963	AC Milan	2	Benfica	1	London
1964	Inter-Milan	3	Real Madrid	1	Vienna
1965	Inter-Milan	1	Benfica	0	Milan
1966	Real Madrid	2	Partizan Belgrade	1	Brussels
1967	Celtic	2	Inter-Milan	1	Lisbon
1968	Manchester U.	4	Benfica	1	London
1969	AC Milan	4	Ajax Amsterdam	1	Madrid
1970	Feyenoord	2	Celtic	1	Milan
1971	Ajax Amsterdam	2	Panathinaikos	0	London
1972	Ajax Amsterdam	2	Inter-Milan	0	Rotterdam
1973	Ajax Amsterdam	1	Juventus	0	Belgrade
1974	Bayern Munich	4	Atletico Madrid	0	Brussels
	(after 1-1 draw in Brussels)				
1975	Bayern Munich	2	Leeds U.	0	Paris
1976	Bayern Munich	1	St. Etienne	0	Glasgow
1977	Liverpool	3	Bor. Moenchengladbach	1	Rome
1978	Liverpool	1	FC Bruges	0	London
1979	Nottingham F	1	Malmo	0	Munich

EUROPEAN CUP-WINNERS' CUP FINALS 1961–79

Year	Winners		Runners-up		Venue
1961	AC Fiorentina	4	Rangers	1	on aggregate
1962	Atletico Madrid	3	AC Fiorentina	0	Stuttgart
	(after 1-1 draw in Glasgow)				
1963	Tottenham H	5	Atletico Madrid	1	Rotterdam
1964	Sporting Club Lisbon	1	MTK Budapest	0	Antwerp
	(after 3-3 draw in Brussels)				
1965	West Ham U	2	TSV Munich 1860	0	London
1966	Borussia Dortmund	2	Liverpool	1	Glasgow
1967	Bayern Munich	1	Rangers	0	Nuremberg
1968	AC Milan	2	SV Hamburg	0	Rotterdam
1969	Slovan Bratislava	3	Barcelona	2	Basel
1970	Manchester C	2	Gornik Zabrze	1	Vienna
1971	Chelsea	2	Real Madrid	1	Athens
	(after 1-1 draw in Athens)				
1972	Rangers	3	Dynamo Moscow	2	Barcelona
1973	AC Milan	1	Leeds U	0	Salonika
1974	FC Magdeburg	2	AC Milan	0	Rotterdam
1975	Dynamo Kiev	3	Ferencvaros	0	Basel
1976	Anderlecht	4	West Ham U	2	Brussels
1977	SV Hamburg	2	Anderlecht	0	Amsterdam
1978	Anderlecht	4	Austria/WAC	0	Paris
1979	Barcelona	4	Fortuna Dusseldorf	3	Basel

EUROPEAN FAIRS CUP FINALS 1958–71

1958	Barcelona 8, London 2*	1966	Barcelona 4, Real Zaragoza 3*
1960	Barcelona 4, Birmingham C. 1*	1967	Dynamo Zagreb 2, Leeds U 0*
1961	A. S. Roma 4, Birmingham C. 2*	1968	Leeds U. 1, Ferencvaros 0*
1962	Valencia 7, Barcelona 3*	1969	Newcastle U 6, Ujpest Dozsa 2*
1963	Valencia 4, Dynamo Zagreb 1*	1970	Arsenal 4, Anderlecht 3*
1964	Real Zaragoza 2, Valencia 1	1971	Leeds U 3, Juventus 3*
1965	Ferencvaros 1, Juventus 0		(Leeds won on away goals)

UEFA CUP 1972–79

1972 Tottenham H 3, Wolverhampton W 2*
1973 Liverpool 3, Bor Moenchengladbach 2*
1974 Feyenoord 4, Tottenham H 2*
1975 Bor. Moenchengladbach 5, Twente Enschede 1*
1976 Liverpool 4, FC Bruges 3*
1977 Juventus 2, Athletic Bilbao 2*
  (Juventus won on away goals)
1978 PSV Eindhoven 3, Bastia 0*
1979 Bor. Moenchengladbach 2, Red Star Belgrade 1*

*aggregate scores

EUROPEAN CUP HISTORY

Note: The first team given played at home in the first leg. Aggregate score in brackets.

EUROPEAN CUP 1955–56

First Round
Sporting Lisbon v Partizan Belgrade (5-8) 3-3, 2-5
Voros Lobogo v Anderlecht (10-4) 6-3, 4-1
Servette Geneva v Real Madrid (0-7) 0-2, 0-5
Rot Weiss Essen v Hibernian (1-5) 0-4, 1-1
Aarhus v Stade de Reims (2-4) 0-2, 2-2
Rapid Vienna v PSV Eindhoven (6-2) 6-1, 0-1
Djurgaarden v Gwardia Warsaw (4-1) 0-0, 4-1
AC Milan v Saarbrücken (7-5) 3-4, 4-1

Quarter-Final
Hibernian v Djurgaarden (4-1) 3-1, 1-0
Stade de Reims v Voros Lobogo (8-6) 4-2, 4-4
Real Madrid v Partizan Belgrade (4-3) 4-0, 0-3
Rapid Vienna v AC Milan (3-8) 1-1, 2-7

Semi-Final
Stade de Reims v Hibernian (3-0) 2-0, 1-0
Real Madrid v AC Milan (5-4) 4-2, 1-2

Final 1955–56: Real Madrid 4 Stade de Rheims 3
(In Paris, June 13, 1956, 38,000)
Read Madrid: Alonso; Atienza, Lesmes, Munoz, Marquitos, Zarraga; Joseito, Marchal, Di Stefano, Rial, Gento.
Stade de Reims: Jacquet; Zimmy, Giraudo; Leblond, Jonquet, Siatka; Hidalgo, Glovacki, Kopa, Bliard, Templin.
Scorers—Real Madrid: Di Stefano, Rial 2, Marquitos. Stade de Rheims: Leblond, Templin, Hidalgo.

EUROPEAN CUP 1956–57

Byes: Real Madrid; Rapid Heerlen; Rangers; Honved; Red Star; CDNA; Grasshoppers; Fiorentina; Norrköping.

Preliminary Round
Borussia Dortmund v Spora Lux (12-5) 4-3, 1-2, 7-0
Dynamo Bucharest v Galatasaray (4-3) 3-1, 1-2
Slovan Bratislava v CWKS Warsaw (4-2) 4-0, 0-2
Anderlecht v Manchester U (0-12) 0-2, 0-10
Aarhus v Nice (2-6) 1-1, 1-5
Porto v Atletico Bilbao (3-5) 1-2, 2-3

First Round
Manchester U v Borussia Dortmund (3-2) 3-2, 0-0
CDNA Sofia v Dynamo Bucharest (10-4) 8-1, 2-3
Slovan Bratislava v Grasshoppers (1-2) 1-0, 0-2
Rangers v Nice (4-6) 2-1, 1-2, 1-3

Real Madrid v Rapid Vienna (7-5) 4-2, 1-3, 2-0
Rapid Heerlen v Red Star Belgrade (3-6) 3-4, 0-2
Fiorentina v Norrköping (2-1) 1-1, 1-0
Atletico Bilbao v Honved (6-5) 3-2, 3-3

Quarter-Final
Atletico Bilbao v Manchester U (5-6) 5-3, 0-3
Fiorentina v Grasshoppers (5-3) 3-1, 2-2
Red Star Belgrade v CDNA Sofia (4-3) 3-1, 1-2
Real Madrid v Nice (6-2) 3-0, 3-2

Semi-Final
Red Star Belgrade v Fiorentina (0-1) 0-1, 0-0
Real Madrid v Manchester U (5-3) 3-1, 2-2

Final 1956–57: Real Madrid 2 Fiorentina 0
(In Madrid, May 30, 1957, 124,000)
Real Madrid: Alonso; Torres, Lesmes, Munoz, Marquitos, Zarraga; Kopa, Mateos, Di Stefano, Rial, Gento.
Fiorentina: Sarti; Magnini, Cervato; Scaramucci, Orzan, Segato; Julinho, Gratton, Virgili, Montuori, Bizzarri.
Scorers: Di Stefano (penalty), Gento.

EUROPEAN CUP 1957–58

Byes: Ajax; Young Boys; Dukla; Norrköping; Dortmund; Real Madrid; Antwerp; CCA Bucharest.

Preliminary Round
Rangers v St. Etienne (4-3) 3-1, 1-2
CDNA Sofia v Vasas Budapest (3-7) 2-1, 1-6
Stade Dudelange v Red Star Belgrade (1-14) 0-5, 1-9
Aarhus v Glenavon (3-0) 0-0, 3-0
Gwardia Warsaw v Wismut Karl-Marx-Stadt
(5-5) 3-1, 1-3, 1-1 (Wismut won the toss)
Seville v Benfica (3-1) 3-1, 0-0
Shamrock R v Manchester U (2-9) 0-6, 2-3
AC Milan v Rapid Vienna (10-8) 4-1, 2-5, 4-2

First Round
Antwerp v Real Madrid (1-8) 1-2, 0-6
Norrköping v Red Star Belgrade (3-4) 2-2, 1-2
Wismut Karl-Marx-Stadt v Ajax Amsterdam
(1-4) 1-3, 0-1

Manchester U v Dukla Prague (3-1) 3-0, 0-1
Young Boys Berne v Vasas Budapest (2-3) 1-1, 1-2
Rangers v AC Milan (1-6) 1-4, 0-2
Seville v Aarhus (4-2) 4-0, 0-2
Borussia Dortmund v CCA Bucharest (8-6) 4-2, 1-3, 3-1

Quarter-Final
Manchester U v Red Star Belgrade (5-4) 2-1, 3-3
Real Madrid v Seville (10-2) 8-0, 2-2
Ajax Amsterdam v Vasas Budapest (2-6) 2-2, 0-4
Borussia Dortmund v AC Milan (2-5) 1-1, 1-4

Semi-Final
Real Madrid v Vasas Budapest (4-2) 4-0, 0-2
Manchester U v AC Milan (2-5) 2-1, 0-4

Final 1957–58: Real Madrid 3 Milan 2 (after extra time)
(In Brussels, May 28, 1958, 67,000)
Real Madrid: Alonso; Atienza, Lesmes, Santisteban; Santamaria, Zarraga; Kopa, Joseito, Di Stefano, Rial, Gento.
Milan: Soldan; Fontana, Beraldo, Bergamaschi; Maldini, Radice; Danova, Liedholm, Schiaffino, Grillo, Cucchiaroni.
Scorers—Real Madrid: Di Stefano, Rial, Gento. Milan: Schiaffino, Grillo.

EUROPEAN CUP 1958–59

Holders: Real Madrid, exempt until First Round.
Byes: CDNA Sofia; Palloseura Helsinki; Wolverhampton W.

Qualifying Round
Juventus v Wiener SK (3-8)	3-1, 0-7
Dynamo Zagreb v Dukla Prague (3-4)	2-2, 1-2
KB Copenhagen v Schalke' 04 (6-8)	3-0, 2-5, 1-3
Atletico Madrid v Drumcondra (13-1)	8-0, 5-1
Polonia Bytom v MTK Budapest (0-6)	0-3, 0-3
Wismut Karl-Marx-Stadt v Petrolul Ploesti (9-4)	4-2, 0-2, 5-0
Gothenburg v Jeunesse Esch (7-3)	2-1, 0-1, 5-1
DOS Utrecht v Sporting Lisbon (4-6)	3-4, 1-2
Standard Liege v Hearts (6-3)	5-1, 1-2
Ards v Stade de Reims (3-10)	1-4, 2-6
Besiktas (walked over) v Olympiakos Piraeus (withdrew)	
Young Boys Berne (walked over) v Manchester United (withdrew)	

First Round
Real Madrid v Besiktas (3-1)	2-0, 1-1
Wiener SK v Dukla Prague (3-2)	3-1, 0-1
Atletico Madrid v CDNA Sofia (5-3)	2-1, 0-1, 3-1
Wolverhampton W v Schalke '04 (3-4)	2-2, 1-2
Gothenburg v Wismut Karl-Marx-Stadt (2-5)	0-3, 2-2
MTK Budapest v Young Boys Berne (2-6)	1-2, 1-4
Sporting Lisbon v Standard Liege (2-6)	2-3, 0-3
Stade de Reims v Palloseura (7-0)	4-0, 3-0

Quarter-Finals
Wiener SK v Real Madrid (1-7)	0-0, 1-7
Atletico Madrid v Schalke '04 (4-1)	3-0, 1-1
Young Boys Berne v Wismut Karl-Marx-Stadt (4-3)	0-0, 2-2, 2-1
Standard Liege v Stade de Reims (2-3)	2-0, 0-3

Semi-Final
Real Madrid v Atletico Madrid (4-3)	2-1, 0-1, 2-1
Young Boys Berne v Stade de Reims (1-3)	1-0, 0-3

Final 1958–59: Real Madrid 2 Stade de Reims 0
(In Stuttgart, June 2, 1959, 80,000)

Real Madrid: Dominguez; Marquitos, Zarraga; Santisteban, Santamaria, Ruiz; Kopa, Mateos, Di Stefano, Rial, Gento.

Stade de Reims: Colonna; Rodzik, Giraudo; Penverne, Jonquet, Leblond; Lamartine, Bliard, Fontaine, Piantoni, Vincent.

Scorers: Mateos, Di Stefano.

EUROPEAN CUP 1959–60

Holders: Real Madrid, exempt until First Round.
Byes: Odense BK 09; Young Boys Berne; Sparta Rotterdam; Red Star Belgrade.

Qualifying Round
Jeunesse Esch v LKS Lodz (7-2)	6-0, 1-2
Nice v Shamrock Rovers (4-3)	3-2, 1-1
Fenerbahce v Csepel (4-3)	1-1, 3-2
CDNA Sofia v Barcelona (4-8)	2-2, 2-6
AC Milan v Olympiakos Piraeus (5-3)	2-2, 3-1
Vorwaerts v Wolverhampton W (2-3)	2-1, 0-2
Linfield v Gothenburg (3-7)	2-1, 1-6
Red Star Bratislava v Porto (4-1)	2-1, 2-0
Rangers v Anderlecht (7-2)	5-2, 2-0
Petrolul Ploesti v Wiener SK (1-2)	0-0, 1-2
Eintracht Frankfurt (walked over) v Kuopion Palloseura (withdrew)	

First Round
AC Milan v Barcelona (1-7)	0-2, 1-5
Red Star Belgrade v Wolverhampton W (1-4)	1-1, 0-3
Fenerbahce v Nice (4-8)	2-1, 1-2, 1-5
Real Madrid v Jeunesse Esch (12-2)	7-0, 5-2
Young Boys Berne v Eintracht Frankfurt (2-5)	1-4, 1-1
Odense BK 09 v Wiener SK (2-5)	0-3, 2-2
Sparta Rotterdam v Gothenburg (7-5)	3-1, 1-3, 3-1
Rangers v Red Star Bratislava (5-4)	4-3, 1-1

Second Round
Barcelona v Wolverhampton W (9-2)	4-0, 5-2
Nice v Real Madrid (3-6)	3-2, 0-4
Eintracht Frankfurt v Wiener SK (3-2)	2-1, 1-1
Sparta Rotterdam v Rangers (5-6)	2-3, 1-0, 2-3

Semi-Final
Real Madrid v Barcelona (6-2)	3-1, 3-1
Eintracht Frankfurt v Rangers (12-4)	6-1, 6-3

Final 1959–60: Real Madrid 7 Eintracht Frankfurt 3
(In Glasgow, May 18, 1960, 135,000)

Real Madrid: Dominguez; Marquitos, Pachin; Vidal, Santamaria, Zarraga; Canario, Del Sol, Di Stefano, Puskas, Gento.

Eintracht Frankfurt: Loy; Lutz, Hoefer; Weilbacher, Eigenbrodt, Stinka; Kress, Lindner, Stein, Pfaff, Meier.

Scorers—Real Madrid; Di Stefano, 3, Puskas 4. Eintracht-Frankfurt: Kress, Stein 2.

EUROPEAN CUP 1960-61

Byes: Real Madrid; Panathinaikos; Hamburg S.V.; Burnley;

Preliminary Round
Barcelona v Lierse SK (5-0)	2-0, 3-0
CCA Bucharest v Spartak Kralove (0-3)	0-3†
Limerick v Young Boys Berne (2-9)	0-5, 2-4
Stade de Reims v Jeunesse Esch (11-1)	6-1, 5-0
Rapid Vienna v Besiktas (4-1)	4-0, 0-1
HIFK Helsinki v IFK Malmo (2-5)	1-3, 1-2
Juventus v CDNA Sofia (3-4)	2-0, 1-4
Aarhus v Legia Warsaw (3-1)	3-0, 0-1
Fredrikstad v Ajax (4-3)	4-3, 0-0
Red Star Belgrade v Ujpest Dozsa (1-5)	1-2, 0-3
Hearts v Benefica (1-5)	1-2, 0-3
Wismut Karl-Marx-Stadt v Glenavon (withdrew)	
Young Boys Berne v SV Hamburg (3-8)	0-5, 3-3
Burnley v Stade de Reims (4-3)	2-0, 2-3
Rapid Vienna v Wismut Karl-Marx-Stadt (4-3)	3-1, 0-2, 1-0
IFK Malmo v CDNA Sofia (2-1)	1-0, 1-1
Aarhus v Fredrikstad (4-0)	3-0, 1-0
Benfica v Ujpest Dozsa (7-4)	6-2, 1-2

Quarter-Final
Barcelona v Spartak Kralov (5-1)	4-0, 1-1
Burnley v SV Hamburg (4-5)	3-1, 1-4
Rapid Vienna v IFK Malmo (4-0)	2-0, 2-0
Benfica v Aarhus (7-2)	3-1, 4-1

First Round
Real Madrid v Barcelona (3-4)	2-2, 1-2
Spartak Kralov v Panathinaikos (1-0)	1-0, 0-0

Semi-Final
Barcelona v SV Hamburg (3-2)	1-0, 1-2, 1-0
Benfica v Rapid Vienna (4-1)	3-0, 1-1

†Withdrew after first leg.

Final 1960-61: Benfica 3 Barcelona 2
(In Berne, March 31, 1961, 28,000)

Benfica: Costa Pereira; Joao, Angelo; Neto, Germano, Cruz; Augusto, Santana, Aguas, Coluna, Cavem.
Barcelona: Ramallets; Foncho, Gracia; Verges, Gensana, Garay; Kubala, Kocsis, Evaristo, Suarez, Czibor.
Scorers—Benfica: Aguas, Ramallets (own goal), Coluna. Barcelona: Kocsis, Czibor.

EUROPEAN CUP 1961-62

Holders: Benfica, exempt until First Round.
Byes: Valkeakosken; Fenerbahce.

Preliminary Round
Vasas Budapest v Real Madrid (1-5)	0-2, 1-3
Spora Lux v Odense BK 1913 (2-15)	0-6, 2-9
Panathinaikos v Juventus (2-3)	1-1, 1-2
Sporting Lisbon v Partizan Belgrade (1-3)	1-1, 0-2
Standard Liege v Fredrikstad (4-1)	2-1, 2-0
Monaco v Rangers (4-6)	2-3, 2-3
Vorwaerts Berlin v Linfield (3-0)	3-0†
Gornik Zabrze v Tottenham H (5-10)	4-2, 1-8
Gothenburg v Feyenoord (2-11)	0-3, 2-8
CDNA Sofia v Dukla Prague (5-6)	4-4, 1-2
Servette Geneva v Hibernians Valletta (7-1)	5-0, 2-1
Nuremberg v Drumcondra (9-1)	5-0, 4-1
CCA Bucharest v FK Austria (0-2)	0-0, 0-2
Partizan Belgrade v Juventus (1-7)	1-2, 0-5
Standard Liege v Valkeakosken (7-1)	5-1, 2-0
Vorwaerts Berlin v Rangers (2-6)	1-2, 1-4
Feyenoord v Tottenham H (2-4)	1-3, 1-1
Servette Geneva v Dukla Prague (4-5)	4-3, 0-2
Fenerbahce v Nuremberg (1-3)	1-2, 0-1
FK Austria v Benfica (2-6)	1-1, 1-5

Quarter-Final
Juventus v Real Madrid (2-4)	0-1, 1-0, 1-3
Standard Liege v Rangers (4-3)	4-1, 0-2
Dukla Prague v Tottenham H (2-4)	1-0, 1-4
Nuremberg v Benfica (3-7)	3-1, 0-6

First Round
Odense BK 1913 v Real Madrid (0-12)	0-3, 0-9

Semi-Final
Real Madrid v Standard Liege (6-0)	4-0, 2-0
Benfica v Tottenham H (4-3)	3-1, 1-2

†Linfield withdrew.

Final 1961-62: Benfica 5 Real Madrid 3
(In Amsterdam, May 2, 1962, 65,000)

Benfica: Costa Pereira; Joao, Angelo; Cavem, Germano, Cruz; Augusto, Eusebio, Aguas, Coluna, Simoes.
Real Madrid: Araquistain; Cassado, Miera; Felo, Santamaria, Pachin; Tejada, Del Sol, Di Stefano, Puskas, Gento.
Scorers—Benfica: Aguas, Cavem, Coluna, Eusebio 2. Real Madrid: Puskas 3.

EUROPEAN CUP 1962-63

Holders: Benfica, exempt until First Round.
Bye: Stade de Reims.

Preliminary Round
AC Milan v Luxembourg (14-0)	8-0, 6-0
Floriana Valletta v Ipswich T (1-14)	1-4, 0-10
Dynamo Bucharest v Galatasaray (1-4)	1-1, 0-3
Polonia Bytom v Panathinaikos (6-2)	2-1, 4-1
Dundee v Cologne (8-5)	8-1, 0-4
Shelbourne v Sporting Lisbon (1-7)	0-2, 1-5
Real Madrid v Anderlecht (3-4)	3-3, 0-1
CDNA Sofia v Partizan Belgrade (6-2)	2-1, 4-1
Servette Geneva v Feyenoord (5-7)	1-3, 3-1, 1-3
Fredrikstadt v Vasas Budapest (1-11)	1-4, 0-7
FK Austria v HIFK Helsinki (7-3)	5-3, 2-0
Linfield v Esbjerg (1-2)	1-2, 0-0
Vorwaerts Berlin v Dukla Prague (0-4)	0-3, 0-1
Norrköping v Partizan Tirana (3-1)	2-0, 1-1

First Round
AC Milan v Ipswich T (4-2)	3-0, 1-2
Galatasaray v Polonia Bytom (4-2)	4-1, 0-1
Sporting Lisbon v Dundee (2-4)	1-0, 1-4
CDNA Sofia v Anderlecht (2-4)	2-2, 0-2
Feyenoord v Vasas Budapest (4-3)	1-1, 2-2, 1-0
FK Austria v Stade de Reims (3-7)	3-2, 0-5
Esbjerg v Dukla Prague (0-5)	0-0, 0-5
Norrköping v Benfica (2-6)	1-1, 1-5

Quarter-Final
Galatasaray v AC Milan (1-8)	1-3, 0-5
Anderlecht v Dundee (2-6)	1-4, 1-2
Stade de Reims v Feyenoord (1-2)	0-1, 1-1
Benfica v Dukla Prague (2-1)	2-1, 0-0

Semi-Final
AC Milan v Dundee (5-2)	5-1, 0-1
Feyenoord v Benfica (1-3)	0-0, 1-3

Final 1962-63: AC Milan 2 Benfica 1
(At Wembley Stadium, May 22, 1963, 45,000)

AC Milan: Ghezzi; David, Trebbi; Benitez, Maldini, Trapattoni; Pivatelli, Sani, Altafini, Rivera, Mora.
Benfica: Costa Pereira; Cavem, Cruz; Humberto, Raul, Coluna; Augusto, Santana, Torres, Eusebio, Simoes.
Scorers—Milan: Altafini 2. Benfica: Eusebio.

EUROPEAN CUP 1963-64

Holders: AC Milan, exempt until First Round.

Preliminary Round
Everton v Inter-Milan (0-1)	0-0, 0-1
Monaco v AEK Athens (8-3)	7-2, 1-1
Valkeakosken v Jeunesse Esch (4-5)	4-1, 0-4
Partizan Belgrade v Anorthosis (6-1)	3-0, 3-1
Distillery v Benfica (3-8)	3-3, 0-5
Lyn Oslo v Borussia Dortmund (3-7)	2-4, 1-3
Gornik Zabrze v FK Austria (3-2)	1-0, 2-1
Dukla Prague v FC Valletta (8-0)	6-0, 2-0
Dundalk v Zurich (2-4)	0-3, 2-1
Galatasaray v Ferencvaros (4-2)	4-0, 0-2
Partizan Tirana v Spartak Plovdiv (2-3)	1-0, 1-3
Esbjerg v PSV Eindhoven (4-11)	3-4, 1-7
Standard Liege v Norrkoping (1-2)	1-0, 0-2
Dynamo Bucharest v Motor Jena (3-0)	2-0, 1-0
Rangers v Real Madrid (0-7)	0-1, 0-6

First Round
Inter-Milan v Monaco (4-1)	1-0, 3-1
Jeunesse Esch v Partizan Belgrade (4-7)	2-1, 2-6
Benefica v Borussia Dortmund (2-6)	2-1, 0-5
Gornik Zabrze v Dukla Prague (3-4)	2-0, 1-4
Zurich v Galatasaray (4-4)	2-0, 0-2, 2-2†
Spartak Plovdiv v PSV Eindhoven (0-1)	0-1, 0-0
Norrköping v AC Milan (3-6)	1-1, 2-5
Dynamo Bucharest v Real Madrid (4-8)	1-3, 3-5

Quarter-Final
Partizan Belgrade v Inter-Milan (1-4)	0-2, 1-2
Dukla Prague v Borussia Dortmund (3-5)	0-4, 3-1
PSV Eindhoven v Zurich (2-3)	1-0, 1-3
Real Madrid v AC Milan (4-3)	4-1, 0-2

Semi-Final
Borussia Dortmund v Inter Milan (2-4)	2-2, 0-2
Zurich v Real Madrid (1-8)	1-2, 0-6

†Winner decided by toss of coin.

Final 1963-64: Inter-Milan 3 Real Madrid 1
(In Vienna, May 27, 1964, 74,000)

Inter-Milan: Sarti; Burgnich, Facchetti; Tagnin, Guarneri, Picchi; Jair, Mazzola, Milani, Suarez, Corso.
Real Madrid: Vicente; Isidro, Pachin, Muller; Santamaria, Zoco; Amancio, Felo, Di Stefano, Puskas, Gento.
Scorers—Inter-Milan: Mazzola 2, Milani. Real Madrid: Felo.

EUROPEAN CUP 1964-65

Holders: Inter-Milan, exempt First Round.

Preliminary Round

Sliema Wanderers v Dynamo Bucharest (0-7)	0-2, 0-5
Rangers v Red Star Belgrade (8-6)	3-1, 2-4, 3-1
Rapid Vienna v Shamrock R (5-0)	3-0, 2-0
Glentoran v Panathinaikos (4-5)	2-2, 2-3
Partizan Tirana v Cologne (0-2)	0-0, 0-2
KR Reykjavik v Liverpool (1-11)	0-5, 1-6
Anderlecht v Bologna (2-2)	1-0, 1-2, 0-0†
Chemie Leipzig v Vasas Gyor (2-6)	0-2, 2-4
Locomotiv Sofia v Malmo FF (8-5)	8-3, 0-2
DWS Amsterdam v Fenerbahce (4-1)	3-1, 1-0
Lahden Reipas v Lyn Oslo (2-4)	2-1, 0-3
Odense BK 09 v Real Madrid (2-9)	2-5, 0-4
Dukla Prague v Gornik Zabrze (4-4)	4-1, 0-3, 0-0†
St Etienne v La Chaux de Fonds (3-4)	2-2, 1-2
Aris Bonnevoie v Benfica (2-10)	1-5, 1-5

First Round

Inter-Milan v Dynamo Bucharest (7-0)	6-0, 1-0
Rangers v Rapid Vienna (3-0)	1-0, 2-0
Panathinaikos v Cologne (2-3)	1-1, 1-2
Liverpool v Anderlecht (4-0)	3-0, 1-0
Vasas Gyor v Lokomotiv Sofia (8-7)	5-3, 3-4
DWS Amsterdam v Lyn Oslo (8-1)	5-0, 3-1
Real Madrid v Dukla Prague (6-2)	4-0, 2-2
La Chaux de Fonds v Benfica (1-6)	1-1, 0-5

Quarter-Final

Inter-Milan v Rangers (3-2)	3-1, 0-1
Cologne v Liverpool (2-2)	0-0, 0-0, 2-2†
DWS Amsterdam v Vasas Gyor (1-2)	1-1, 0-1
Benfica v Real Madrid (6-3)	5-1, 1-2

Semi-Final

Liverpool v Inter-Milan (3-4)	3-1, 0-3
Vasas Gyor v Benfica (0-5)	0-1, 0-4

†Winner decided by toss of coin.

Final 1964-65: Inter-Milan 1 Benfica 0

(In Milan, May 28, 1965, 80,000)

Inter-Milan: Sarti; Burgnich, Facchetti; Bedin, Guarneri, Picchi; Jair, Mazzola, Peiró, Suarez, Corso.
Benfica: Costa Pereira; Cavem, Cruz; Neto, Germano, Raul; Augusto, Eusebio, Torres, Coluna, Simoes.
Scorer: Jair.

EUROPEAN CUP 1965-66

Holders: Inter-Milan, exempt until First Round.

Preliminary Round

Feyenoord v Real Madrid (2-6)	2-1, 0-5
Nendori, Tirana v Kilmarnock (0-1)	0-0, 0-1
Fenerbahce v Anderlecht (1-5)	0-0, 1-5
Lyn Oslo v Derry (6-8)	5-3, 1-5
Dynamo Bucharest v Odense BK 09 (7-2)	3-2, 4-0
Keflavik v Ferencvaros (2-13)	1-4, 1-9
Panathinaikos v Sliema Wanderers (4-2)	4-1, 0-1
HJK Helsinki v Manchester U (2-9)	2-3, 0-6
Drumcondra v Vorwaerts Berlin (1-3)	1-0, 0-3
Stade Dudelange v Benfica (0-18)	0-8, 0-10
Djurgaarden v Levski (2-7)	2-1, 0-6
Lausanne v Sparta Prague (0-4)	0-0, 0-4
ASK Linz v Gornik Zabrze (2-5)	1-3, 1-2
Apoel Nicosia v Werder Bremen (0-10)	0-5, 0-5
Partizan Belgrade v Nantes (4-2)	2-0, 2-2

First Round

Kilmarnock v Real Madrid (3-7)	2-2, 1-5
Anderlecht v Derry C (9-0)	9-0†
Dynamo Bucharest v Inter-Milan (2-3)	2-1, 0-2
Ferencvaros v Panathinaikos (3-1)	0-0, 3-1
Vorwaerts Berlin v Manchester U (1-5)	0-2, 1-3
Levski v Benfica (4-5)	2-2, 2-3
Sparta Prague v Gornik Zabrze (5-1)	3-0, 2-1
Partizan Belgrade v Werder Bremen (3-1)	3-0, 0-1

Quarter-Final

Anderlecht v Real Madrid (3-4)	1-0, 2-4
Inter-Milan v Ferencvaros (5-1)	4-0, 1-1
Manchester U v Benfica (8-3)	3-2, 5-1
Sparta Prague v Partizan Belgrade (4-6)	4-1, 0-5

Semi-Final

Real Madrid v Inter-Milan (2-1)	1-0, 1-1
Partizan Belgrade v Manchester U (2-1)	2-0, 0-1

†Withdrew after first leg

Final 1966-66: Real Madrid 2 Partizan Belgrade 1

(In Brussels, May 11, 1966, 55,000)

Real Madrid: Araquistain; Pachin, Sanchis; Pirri, De Felipe, Zoco; Serena, Amancio, Grosso, Velazquez, Gento.
Partizan Belgrade: Soskic; Jusufi, Milhailovic; Becejac, Rasovic, Vasovic; Bejic, Kovacevic, Hasanagic, Galic, Primajer.
Scorers—Real Madrid; Amancio, Serena. Partisan: Vasovic.

EUROPEAN CUP 1966-67

Preliminary Round
Sliema Wanderers v CSKA Sofia (1-6)   1-2, 0-4
Waterford v Vorwaerts Berlin (1-12)   1-6, 0-6

First Round
Inter-Milan v Torpedo Moscow (1-0)   1-0, 0-0
Vasas Budapest v Sporting Lisbon (7-0)   5-0, 2-0
Munich 1860 v Omonia Nicosia (10-1)   8-0, 2-1
CSKA Sofia v Olympiakos Piraeus (3-2)   3-1, 0-1
Gornik Zabrze v Vorwaerts Berlin (6-4)   2-1, 1-2, 3-1
Valerengen v Nendori Tirana (withdrew)
Aris Bonnevoie v Linfield (4-9)   3-3, 1-6
Esbjerg v Dukla Prague (0-6)   0-2, 0-4
Valkeakosken v Anderlecht (1-12)   1-10, 0-2
Ajax v Besiktas (4-1)   2-0, 2-1
Liverpool v Petrolul Ploesti (5-3)   2-0, 1-3, 2-0
Malmo FF v Atletico Madrid (1-5)   0-2, 1-3
Admira v Vojvodina (0-1)   0-1, 0-0
Reykjavik FC v Nantes (4-8)   2-3, 2-5
Celtic v Zurich (5-0)   2-0, 3-0

Second Round
Inter-Milan v Vasas Budapest (4-1)   2-1, 2-0
Munich 1860 v Real Madrid (2-3)   1-0, 1-3
CSKA Sofia v Gornik Zabrze (4-3)   4-0, 0-3
Valerengen v Linfield (2-5)   1-4, 1-1
Dukla Prague v Anderlecht (6-2)   4-1, 2-1
Ajax v Liverpool (7-3)   5-1, 2-2
Vojvodina v Atletico Madrid (6-5)   3-1, 0-2, 3-2
Nantes v Celtic (2-6)   1-3, 1-3

Quarter-Final
Inter-Milan v Real Madrid (3-0)   1-0, 2-0
Linfield v CSKA Sofia (2-3)   2-2, 0-1
Ajax v Dukla Prague (2-3)   1-1, 1-2
Vojvodina v Celtic (1-2)   1-0, 0-2

Semi-Final
Inter-Milan v CSKA Sofia (3-2)   1-1, 1-1, 1-0
Celtic v Dukla Prague (3-1)   3-1 0-0

Final 1966-67: Celtic 2 Inter-Milan 1
(In Lisbon, May 25, 1967, 56,000)

Celtic: Simpson; Craig, Gemmell; Murdoch, McNeill, Clark; Johnstone, Wallace, Chalmers, Auld, Lennox.

Inter-Milan: Sarti; Burgnich, Facchetti; Bedin, Guarneri; Picchi; Bicicli, Mazzola, Cappellini, Corso, Domenghini.

Scorers—Celtic; Gemmell, Chalmers.   Inter-Milan: Mazzola (penalty).

EUROPEAN CUP 1967-68

First Round
Manchester U v Hibernians Valletta (4-0)   4-0, 0-0
Olympiakos Nicosia v Sarajevo (3-5)   2-2, 1-3
Gornik Zabrze v Djurgaarden (4-0)   1-0, 3-0
Celtic v Dynamo Kiev (2-3)   1-2, 1-1
Ajax v Real Madrid (2-3)   1-1, 1-2
Basle v Hvidovre (4-5)   1-2, 3-3
Skeid Oslo v Sparta Prague (1-2)   0-1, 1-1
Wismut Karl-Marx-Stadt v Anderlecht (2-5)   1-3, 1-2
Olympiakos Piraeus v Juventus (0-2)   0-0, 0-2
Botev Plovdiv v Rapid Bucharest (2-3)   2-0, 0-3
Eintracht Brunswick v Dyn. Tirana (withdrew)
Besiktas v Rapid Vienna (0-4)   0-1, 0-3
Dundalk v Vasas Budapest (1-9)   0-1, 1-8
*Valur Reykjavik v Jeunesse Esch (4-4)   1-1, 3-3
St Etienne v Kuopion Palloseura (5-0)   2-0, 3-0
*Glentoran v Benfica (1-1)   1-1, 0-0

Second Round
Sarajevo v Manchester U (1-2)   0-0, 1-2

Dynamo Kiev v Gornik Zabrze (2-3)   1-2, 1-1
Hvidovre v Real Madrid (3-7)   2-2, 1-4
Sparta Prague v Anderlecht (6-5)   3-2, 3-3
Juventus v Rapid Bucharest (1-0)   1-0, 0-0
Rapid Vienna v Eintracht Brunswick (1-2)   1-0, 0-2
Vasas Budapest v Valur Reykjavik (11-1)   6-0, 5-1
Benfica v St Etienne (2-1)   2-0, 0-1

Quarter-Final
Manchester U v Gornik Zabrze (2-1)   2-0, 0-1
Real Madrid v Sparta Prague (4-2)   3-0, 1-2
Eintracht Brunswick v Juventus (3-4)   3-2, 0-1, 0-1
Vasas Budapest v Benfica (0-3)   0-0, 0-3

Semi-Final
Manchester U v Real Madrid (4-3)   1-0, 3-3
Benfica v Juventus (3-0)   2-0, 1-0

*Won on away goals counting double.

Final 1967-68: Manchester U 4 Benfica 1 (*aet*)
(At Wembley Stadium, May 29, 1968, 100,000)

Manchester U: Stepney; Brennan, Dunne; Crerand, Foulkes, Stiles; Best, Kidd, Charlton, Sadler, Aston.
Benfica: Henrique; Adolfo, Humberto, Jacinto, Cruz; Graça, Coluna; Augusto, Eusebio, Torres, Simoes.
Scorers—Manchester U: Charlton 2, Best, Kidd.   Benfica: Graça.

EUROPEAN CUP 1968–69

First Round
Malmo FF v AC Milan (3-5)	2-1, 1-4
St Etienne v Celtic (2-4)	2-0, 0-4
Waterford v Manchester U (2-10)	1-3, 1-7
Anderlecht v Glentoran (5-2)	3-0, 2-2
Rosenborg v Rapid Vienna (4-6)	1-3, 3-3
Real Madrid v Union Limassol (12-0)	6-0, 6-0
Steaua Bucharest v Spartak Trnava (3-5)	3-1, 0-4
Floriana v Lahden Reipas (1-3)	1-1, 0-2
AEK Athens v Jeunesse Esch (5-3)	3-0, 2-3
Zurich v AB Copenhagen (3-4)	1-3, 2-1
Valur Reykjavik v Benfica (1-8)	0-0, 1-8
Manchester C v Fenerbahce (1-2)	0-0, 1-2
Nuremburg v Ajax (1-5)	1-1, 0-4
Celtic v Red Star Belgrade (6-2)	5-1, 1-1
Manchester U v Anderlecht (4-3)	3-0, 1-3
†Rapid Vienna v Real Madrid (2-2)	1-0, 1-2
Lahden Reipas v Spartak Trnava (2-16)	1-9, 1-7
AEK Athens v AB Copenhagen (2-0)	0-0, 2-0
Ajax v Fenerbahce (4-0)	2-0, 2-0

Second Round
Bye: AC Milan
Bye: Benfica

Quarter-Final
AC Milan v Celtic (1-0)	0-0, 1-0
Manchester U v Rapid Vienna (3-0)	3-0, 0-0
Spartak Trnava v AEK Athens (3-2)	2-1, 1-1
Ajax v Benfica (7-4)	1-3, 3-1, 3-0

Semi-Final
AC Milan v Manchester U (2-1)	2-0, 0-1
Ajax v Spartak Trnava (3-2)	3-0, 0-2

†Won on away goals counting double.

Final 1968-69: AC Milan 4 Ajax 1
(In Madrid, May 28, 1969, 50,000)

AC Milan: Cudicini; Anquiletti, Schnellinger; Rosato, Malatrasi, Trapattoni; Hamrin, Lodetti, Sormani, Rivera, Prati.

Ajax: Bals; Suurbier, Hulshoff; Vasovic, Van Duivenbode, Pronk; Groot, Swart, Cruyff, Danielsson, Keizer.

Scorers—Milan: Prati 3, Sormani. Ajax: Vasovic (penalty).

EUROPEAN CUP 1969–70

Preliminary Round
Turun Palloseura v KB Copenhagen (0-5)	0-1, 0-4

First Round
Leeds U v Lyn Oslo (16-0)	10-0, 6-0
CSKA Sofia v Ferencvaros (3-5)	2-1, 1-4
Standard Liege v Nendori Tirana (4-1)	1-1, 3-0
Real Madrid v Olympiakos Nicosia (14-1)	8-0, 6-1
Basle v Celtic (0-2)	0-0, 0-2
Benfica v KB Copenhagen (5-2)	2-0, 3-2
FK Austria v Dynamo Kiev (2-5)	1-2, 1-3
Fiorentina v Oester (3-1)	2-1, 1-0
Galatasaray v Waterford (5-2)	2-0, 3-2
Hibernians Valletta v Spartak Trnava(2-6)	2-2, 0-4
UT Arad v Legia Warsaw (1-10)	1-2, 0-8
Bayern Munich v St Etienne (2-3)	2-0, 0-3
Vorwaerts Berlin v Panathinaikos (3-1)	1-1, 2-0
Red Star Belgrade v Linfield (12-2)	8-0, 4-2
AC Milan v Avenir Beggen (8-0)	5-0, 3-0
Feyenoord v KR Reykjavik (16-0)	12-0, 4-0

Second Round
Leeds U v Ferencvaros (6-0)	3-0, 3-0
Standard Liege v Real Madrid (4-2)	1-0, 3-2
*Celtic v Benfica (3-3)	3-0, 0-3
Dynamo Kiev v Fiorentina (1-2)	1-2, 0-0
*Galatasaray v Spartak Trnava (1-1)	1-0, 0-1
Legia Warsaw v St Etienne (3-1)	2-1, 1-0
†Vorwaerts Berlin v Red Star Belgrade (4-4)	2-1, 2-3
AC Milan v Feyenoord (1-2)	1-0, 0-2

Quarter-Final
Standard Liege v Leeds U (0-2)	0-1, 0-1
Celtic v Fiorentina (3-1)	3-0, 0-1
Galatasaray v Legia Warsaw (1-3)	1-1, 0-2
Vorwaerts Berlin v Feyenoord (1-2)	1-0, 0-2

Semi-Final
Leeds U v Celtic (1-3)	0-1, 1-2
Legia Warsaw v Feyenoord (0-2)	0-0, 0-2

*Won on toss of coin.
†Won on away goals counting double.

Final 1969-70: Feyenoord 2 Celtic 1 (*aet*)
(In Milan, May 6, 1970, 50,000)

Feyenoord: Graafland; Romeyn (Sub. Haak), Laseroms; Israel, Van Duivenbode, Hasil; Jansen, Van Hanegem, Wery, Kindvall, Moulijn.

Celtic: Williams; Hay, Gemmell; Murdoch, McNeill, Brogan; Johnstone, Lennox, Wallace, Auld (Sub. Connelly), Hughes.

Scorers—Feyenoord: Israel, Kindvall. Celtic: Gemmell.

EUROPEAN CUP 1970-71

First Round
Jeunesse Esch v Panathinaikos (1-7)	1-2, 0-5
Slovan Bratislava v BK 1903 Copenhagen (4-3)	2-1, 2-2
Everton v Keflavik (9-2)	6-2, 3-0
Bor. Moenchengladbach v EPA Larnaca (16-0)	6-0, 10-0
Fenerbahce v Carl Zeiss Jena (0-5)	0-4, 0-1
Sporting Lisbon v Floriana (9-0)	5-0, 4-0
Ujpest Dozsa v Red Star Belgrade (2-4)	2-0, 0-4
†Feyenoord v UT Arad (1-1)	1-1, 0-0
Atletico Madrid v ‡FK Austria (4-1)	2-0, 2-1
Cagliari v St. Etienne (3-1)	3-0, 0-1
Gothenburg v Legia Warsaw (1-6)	0-4, 1-2
Rosenborg v Standard Liege (0-7)	0-2, 0-5
Celtic v KPV Kokkola (14-0)	9-0, 5-0
Glentoran v Waterford (1-4)	1-3, 0-1
Moscow Spartak v Basle (4-4)†	3-2, 1-2
Nendori Tirana v Ajax Amsterdam (2-4)	2-2, 0-2

Second Round
Panathinaikos v Slovan Bratislava (4-2)	3-0, 1-2
Bor. Moenchengladbach v Everton* (2-2)	1-1, 1-1
Carl Zeiss Jena v Sporting Lisbon (4-2)	2-1, 2-1
Red Star Belgrade v UT Arad (6-1)	3-0, 3-1
Cagliari v Atletico Madrid (2-4)	2-1, 0-3
Standard Liege v Legia Warsaw (1-2)	1-0, 0-2
Waterford v Celtic (2-10)	0-7, 2-3
Ajax Amsterdam v Basle (5-1)	3-0, 2-1

Quarter-Finals
Everton v Panathinaikos†(1-1)	1-1, 0-0
Carl Zeiss Jena v Red Star Belgrade (3-6)	3-2, 0-4
Atletico Madrid† v Legia Warsaw (2-2)	1-0, 1-2
Ajax Amsterdam v Celtic (3-1)	3-0, 0-1

Semi-Finals
Red Star Belgrade v Panathinaikos† (4-4)	4-1, 0-3
Atletico Madrid v Ajax Amsterdam (1-3)	1-0, 0-3

*Won on penalties
†Won on away goals counting double
‡Levski Spartak lost to FK Austria 3-1, 0-3 in preliminary round.

Final 1970-71: Ajax 2 Panathinaikos 0
(At Wembley, June 2, 1971—90,000, £183,000)

Ajax: Stuy; Vasovic, Suurbier; Hulshoff, Rijnders (Sub Haan), Neeskens; Swart (Sub Blankenburg), Muhren, Keizer, Van Dijk, Cruyff.

Panathinaikos: Economopoulos; Tomaros, Vlahos; Elefterakis, Kamaras, Sourpis; Grammos, Filokouris, Antoniadis, Domazos, Kapsis.

Scorers: Van Dijk, Kapsis og.

EUROPEAN CUP 1971-72

Preliminary Round
Valencia v US Luxembourg (4-1)	3-1, 1-0

First Round
Galatasaray v CSKA Moscow (1-4)	1-1, 0-3
Standard Liege v Linfield (5-2)	2-0, 3-2
BK 1903 Copenhagen v Celtic (2-4)	2-1, 0-3
Feyenoord v Olympiakos Nicosia (17-0)	8-0, 9-0
Inter-Milan v AEK Athens (6-4)	4-1, 2-3
Ujpest Dozsa v Malmo FF (4-1)	4-0, 0-1
*Valencia v Hajduk Split (1-1)	0-0, 1-1
Cork Hibs v Bor. Moenchengladbach (1-7)	0-5, 1-2
Wacker Innsbruck v Benfica (1-7)	0-4, 1-3
Ajax Amsterdam v Dynamo Dresden (2-0)	2-0, 0-0
Stromsgodset v Arsenal (1-7)	1-3, 0-4
*Dynamo Bucharest v Spartak Trnava (2-2)	0-0, 2-2
Marseille v Gornik Zabrze (3-2)	2-1, 1-1
CSKA Sofia v Partizan Tirana (4-0)	3-0, 1-0
Lahden Reipas v Grasshoppers (1-9)	1-1, 0-8
Akranes v Sliema Wanderers (0-4)	0-4, 0-0

Second Round
CSKA Moscow v Standard Liege (1-2)	1-0, 0-2
Dynamo Bucharest v Feyenoord (0-5)	0-3, 0-2
Valencia v Ujpest Dozsa (1-3)	0-1, 1-2
Inter-Milan v Bor. Moenchengladbach (4-2)	4-2, 0-0
Benfica v CSKA Sofia (2-1)	2-1, 0-0
Grasshoppers v Arsenal (0-5)	0-2, 0-3
Marseille v Ajax (2-6)	1-2, 1-4
Celtic v Sliema Wanderers (7-1)	5-0, 2-1

Quarter-Finals
Ajax v Arsenal (3-1)	2-1, 1-0
Feyenoord v Benfica (2-5)	1-0, 1-5
Ujpest Dozsa v Celtic (2-3)	1-2, 1-1
*Inter-Milan v Standard Liege (2-2)	1-0, 1-2

Semi-Finals
Ajax v Benfica (1-0)	1-0, 0-0
‡Inter-Milan v Celtic (0-0)	0-0, 0-0

*Won on away goals rule †Won on penalty kicks.
‡Won on penalty kicks after extra time

Final 1971-72: Ajax 2 Inter-Milan 0
(in Rotterdam, May 31, 1972, 67,000)

Ajax: Stuy; Suurbier, Blankenburg, Hulshoff, Krol, Neeskens, Haan, Muhren (G), Swart, Cruyff, Keizer.

Inter-Milan: Bordon; Burgnich, Bellugi, Oriali, Facchetti, Bedin, Mazzola, Giubertoni (Bertini), Jair (Pellizzaro), Boninsegna, Frustalupi.

Scorers: Cruyff 2.

R.F. 79/80—38

EUROPEAN CUP 1972-73

First Round
Real Madrid v Keflavik (4-0)	3-0, 1-0
Anderlecht v Vejle (7-2)	4-2, 3-0
Ujpest Dozsa v Basle (4-3)	2-0, 2-3
Celtic v Rosenborg (5-2)	2-1, 3-1
Galatasaray v Bayern Munich (1-7)	1-1, 0-6
Marseille v Juventus (1-3)	1-0, 0-3
Malmö FF v Benfica (2-4)	1-0, 1-4
TS Innsbruck v Dynamo Kiev (0-3)	0-1, 0-2
CSKA Sofia v Panathinaikos (4-1)	2-1, 2-0
Sliema Wand v Gornik Zabrze (0-10)	0-5, 0-5
FC Magdeburg v Turun Palloreura (9-1)	6-0, 3-1
Aris Bonnevoie v Arges Pitesti (0-6)	0-2, 0-4
Derby Co v Zeljeznicar (4-1)	2-0, 2-1
Waterford v Omonia Nicosia (2-3)	2-1, 0-2
Ajax	bye
Spartak Trnava	bye

Second Round
Omonia Nicosia v Bayern Munich (0-13)	0-9, 0-4
Spartak Trnava v Anderlecht (2-0)	1-0, 1-0
Derby Co v Benfica (3-0)	3-0, 0-0
Celtic v Ujpest Dozsa (2-4)	2-1, 0-3
Dynamo Kiev v Gornik Zabrze (3-2)	2-0, 1-2
Juventus v FC Magdeburg (2-0)	1-0, 1-0
Arges Pitesti v Real Madrid (3-4)	2-1, 1-3
CSKA Sofia v Ajax (1-7)	1-3, 0-3

Quarter-Finals
*Juventus v Ujpest Dozsa (2-2)	0-0, 2-2
Spartak Trnava v Derby Co (1-2)	1-0, 0-2
Dynamo Kiev v Real Madrid (0-3)	0-0, 0-3
Ajax v Bayern Munich (5-2)	4-0, 1-2

Semi-Finals
Juventus v Derby Co (3-1)	3-1, 0-0
Ajax v Real Madrid (3-1)	2-1, 1-0

*Won on away goals rule.

Final 1972–73: Ajax Amsterdam 1 Juventus 0
(in Belgrade, May 30, 1973, 93,500)

Ajax: Stuy; Suurbier, Krol, Neeskens, Hulshoff, Blankenburg, Rep, Haan, Cruyff, Gerrie Muhren, Keizer.
Juventus: Zoff; Longobucco, Marchetti, Furino, Morini, Salvadore, Altafini, Causio (Cuccureddu), Anastasi, Capello, Bettega (Haller).
Scorer: Rep

EUROPEAN CUP 1973-74

First Round
Waterford v Ujpest Dozsa (2-6)	2-3, 0-3
†Bayern Munich v Atvidaberg (4-4)	3-1, 1-3
Benfica v Olympiakos Pireaus (2-0)	1-0, 1-0
Turku v Celtic (1-9)	1-6, 0-3
Dynamo Dresden v Juventus (4-3)	2-0, 2-3
Sarja Voroshilovgrad v Apoel Nicosia (3-0)	2-0, 1-0
Red Star Belgrade v Stal Mielec (3-1)	2-1, 1-0
Bruges v Floriana (10-0)	8-0, 2-0
Jeunesse D'Esch v Liverpool (1-3)	1-1, 0-2
Atlètico Madrid v Galatasaray (1-0)	0-0, 1-0
Viking Stavanger v Spartak Trnava (1-3)	1-2, 0-1
Vejle v Nantes (3-2)	2-2, 1-0
CSKA Sofia v SW Innsbruck (4-0)	3-0, 1-0
Frem Reykjavik v Basle (2-11)	0-5, 2-6
Crusaders v Dinamo Bucharest (0-12)	0-1, 0-11
Ajax	bye

Second Round
Benfica v Ujpest Dozsa (1-3)	1-1, 0-2
Celtic v Vejle (1-0)	0-0, 1-0
Spartak Trnava v Sarja Voroshilovgrad (1-0)	0-0, 1-0
Red Star Belgrade v Liverpool (4-2)	2-1, 2-1
Bruges v Basle (6-7)	2-1, 4-6
Dinamo Bucharest v Atlètico Madrid (2-4)	0-2, 2-2
Ajax v CSKA Sofia (1-2)	1-0, 0-2
Bayern Munich v Dynamo Dresden (7-6)	4-3, 3-3

Quarter-Finals
†Spartak Trnava v Ujpest Dozsa (2-2)	1-1, 1-1
Bayern Munich v CSKA Sofia (5-3)	4-1, 1-2
Red Star Belgrade v Atlètico Madrid (0-2)	0-2, 0-0
Basle v Celtic (5-6)	3-2, 2-4

Semi-Finals
Ujpest Dozsa v Bayern Munich (1-4)	1-1, 0-3
Celtic v Atlètico Madrid (0-2)	0-0, 0-2

†Won on penalty kicks

Final 1973–74: Bayern Munich 1, Atlètico Madrid 1
(at Brussels, May 15, 1974, 65,000)

Bayern Munich: Maier; Hansen, Breitner, Schwarzenbeck, Beckenbauer, Roth, Torstensson (Durnberger), Zobel, Muller, Hoeness, Kappelmann.
Atlètico Madrid: Reina; Melo, Capon, Adelardo, Heredia, Eusebio, Ufarte (Becerra), Luis, Garate, Irueta, Salcedo (Alberto).
Scorers: Bayern Munich, Schwarzenbeck; Atlètico Madrid, Luis.

Replay: Bayern Munich 4, Atlètico Madrid 0
(at Brussels, May 17, 1974, 65,000)

Bayern Munich: Maier, Hansen; Breitner, Schwarzenbeck, Beckenbauer, Roth, Torstensson, Zobel, Muller, Hoeness, Kappelmann.
Atlètico Madrid: Reina; Melo, Capon, Adelardo (Benegas), Heredia, Eusebio, Luis, Garate, Salcedo Alberto, Ufarte (Becerra).
Scorers: Muller (2), Hoeness (2).

EUROPEAN CUP 1974-75

First Round, First Leg
Leeds U 4 (*Lorimer pen, Clarke 2, Jordan*)
Zurich 1 (*Katic*)
Celtic 1 (*Wilson*)
Olympiakos Pireaus 1 (*Viera*)
Uni. Craiova 2 (*Oblemenco 2*)
Atvidaberg 1 (*Bo Augustsson*)
Valetta 1 (*Magro*)
HJK Helsinki 0
Levski Spartak 0
Ujpest Dozsa 3 (*Horvath, Bene, Antal Dunai*)
Jeunesse D'Esch 2 (*Mond, Guiliani*)
Fenerbahce 3 (*Osman, Cemel, Ender*)
Viking Stavanger 0
Ararat Erevan 2 (*Markarov 2*)
Hvidovre 0
Ruch Chorzow 0
Slovan Bratislava 4 (*Novotny, Masny 2, Svehlik*)
Anderlecht 2 (*Coeck, Van Himst*)
Feyenoord 7 (*Schoenmaker, Kreuz 3, Van Hanegem 2, Ressel*)
Coleraine 0
St Etienne 2 (*Herve Revelli, Bereta*)
Sporting Lisbon 0
VOEST Linz 0
Barcelona 0
Hajduk Split 7 (*Zungul 2, Surjak 2, Jerkovic, Buljan, Boljat*)
Keflavik 1

First Round, Second Leg
Zurich 2 (*Katic, Rutschmann pen*)
Leeds U 1 (*Clarke*)
Olympiakos Pireaus 2 (*Kritikopoulos, Stravropoulos*)
Celtic 0
Atvidaberg 3 (*Andersson, Almqvist 2*)
Uni. Craiova 1 (*Badin*)
HJK Helsinki 4 (*Rahja, Peltonen, Hamalainen, Forsell*)
Valetta 1 (*Gigilo*)
Ujpest Dozsa 4 (*Bene 2, Antal Dunai 2*)
Levski Spartak 1 (*Voinov*)
Fenerbahce 2 (*Cemil, Yilmaz*)
Jeunesse D'Esch 0
Ararat Erevan 4 (*Markarov 3, Bondarenko*)
Viking Stavanger 2
Ruch Chorzow 2 (*Bula 2*)
Hvidovre 1 (*Pedersen, B*)
Anderlecht 3 (*Van Himst, Coeck, Thissen*)
Slovan Bratislava 1 (*Masny*)
Coleraine 1 (*Simpson*)
Feyenoord 4 (*Schoenmaker 3, Kreuz*)
Sporting Lisbon 1 (*Yazalde*)
St Etienne 1 (*Herve Revelli*)
Barcelona 5 (*Clares 2, Asensi, Juan Carlos, Cruyff*)
VOEST Linz 0
Keflavik 0
Hajduk Split 2 (*Dzoni, Mijac*)
Bayern Munich and Madgeburg received byes; Cork Celtic had a walkover when Omonia Nicosia withdrew.

Second Round, First Leg
Ujpest Dozsa 1 (*Fazekas pen*)
Leeds U 2 (*Lorimer, McQueen*)
Bayern Munich 3 (*Muller,2 Wunder*)
Magdeburg 2 (*Hoffmann, Sparwasser*)
Hajduk Split 4 (*Jerkovic 2, Zungul, Mijac*)
St Etienne 1 (*Herve Revelli*)
Feyenoord 0
Barcelona 0
Cork Celtic 1 (*Tambling*)
Ararat Erevan 2 (*Zanazanyan, Kazaryan*)
Ruch Chorzow 2 (*Kopicera, Beniger*)
Fenerbahce 1 (*Niazi*)
HJK Helsinki 0
Atvidaberg 3 (*Almqvist 2, Hasselberg*)
Anderlecht 5 (*Rensenbrink 3, 2 pens, Ladinszky Van der Elst*)
Olympiakos Piraeus 1 (*Persides pen*)

Second Round, Second Leg
Leeds U 3 (*McQueen, Yorath, Bremner*)
Ujpest Dozsa 0
Magdeburg 1 (*Sparwasser*)
Bayern Munich 2 (*Muller 2*)
St Etienne 5 (*Triantafilos 2, Barthenay, Synaeghel, Larque*)
Hajduk Split 1 (*Jovanic*)
Barcelona 3 (*Rexach 3*)
Feyenoord 0
Ararat Erevan 5 (*Markarov 2, Andriassian, Kazaryan 2*)
Cork Celtic 0
Fenerbahce 0
Ruch Chorzow 2 (*Kopicera, Chojnacki*)
Atvidaberg 1 (*Almqvist*)
HJK Helsinki 0
Olympiakos Piraeus 3 (*Galakos 3*)
Anderlecht 0

Quarter-Final, First Leg
Bayern Munich (0) 2 (*Hoeness, Torstensson*)
Ararat Erevan (0) 0
Leeds U (2) 3 (*Jordan, McQueen, Lorimer*)
Anderlecht (0) 0
Ruch Chorzow (2) 3 (*Maszczyk, Beniger, Bula pen*)
St Etienne (0) 2 (*Larque, Triantafilos*)
Barcelona (1) 2 (*Mario Marinho, Clares*)
Atvidaberg (0) 0

Quarter-Final, Second Leg
Atvidaberg (0) 0
Barcelona (1) 3 (*Gallego, Asensi, Neeskens*)
St Etienne (1) 2 (*Janvion, Herve Revelli pen*)
Ruch Chorzow (0) 0
Ararat Erevan (1) 1 (*Andriassian*)
Bayern Munich (0) 0
Anderlecht (0) 0
Leeds U (0) 1 (*Bremner*)

Semi-Final, First Leg
St Etienne (0) 0
BayernMunich (0) 0
Leeds U (1) 2 (*Bremner, Clarke*)
Barcelona (0) 1 (*Asensi*)

Semi-Final, Second Leg
Bayern Munich (1) 2 (*Beckenbauer, Durnberger*)
St Etienne (0) 0
Barcelona (0) 1 (*Clares*)
Leeds U (1) 1 (*Lorimer*)

Final 1974-75: Bayern Munich 2 Leeds 0
(at Paris, May 28, 1975, 50,000)

Bayern Munich: Maier; Durnberger, Andersson (Weiss), Schwarzenbeck, Beckenbauer, Roth, Torstensson, Zobel, Muller, Hoeness (Wunder), Kapellmann.
Leeds U: Stewart; Reaney, F Gray, Bremner, Madeley, Hunter, Lorimer, Clarke, Jordan, Giles, Yorath (E Gray).
Scorers: Bayern Munich: Roth, Muller

EUROPEAN CUP 1975-76

First Round, First Leg
Benfica 7 (*Sheu, Nene* 3, *Jordao* 3)
Fenerbahce 0
Borussia Moenchengladbach 1 (*Simonsen pen.*)
Swarowski Innsbruck 1 (*Welzl*)
KB Copenhagen 0
St Etienne 2 (*P. Revelli, Larque*)
CSKA Sofia 2 (*Denev, Marashliev*)
Juventus 1 (*Anastasi*)
Floriana 0
Hajduk Split 5 (*Zungul* 3, *Buljan, Surjak*)
Jeunesse D'Esch 0
Bayern Munich 5 (*Wunder, Schuster* 2, *Rummenigge* 2)
Linfield 1 (*P Malone*)
PSV Eindhoven 2 (*Rene Van der Kerkhof, Edstrom*)
Malmo 2 (*Cervin, Bo Larsson*)
Magdeburg 1 (*Hoffmann*)
Olympiakos 2 (*Kritikopoulos, Aidiniou*)
Dynamo Kiev 2 (*Kolotov, Burjak*)
Rangers 4 (*Fyfe, Burge o.g., O'Hara, Johnstone*)
Bohemians 1 (*Flanagan*)
Real Madrid 4 (*Santillana* 2, *Roberto Martinez, Netzer*)
Dinamo Bucharest 1 (*Lucescu*)
Ruch Chorzow 5 (*Marx* 2, *Bula, Beniger, Kopicera*)
Kuopion Palloseura 0
Slovan Bratislava 1 (*Masny*)
Derby Co 0
Ujpest Dozsa 4 (*Fazekas, Dunai, Toth, pen., Keleman*)
Zurich 0
RWD Molenbeek 3 (*Boskamp, Teugals, Wellens*)
Viking Stavanger 2 (*Johansson, Kvia*)
Omonia Nicosia 2 (*Philippou* 2)
Akranes 1 (*Alfredsson*)

First Round, Second Leg
Akranes 4 (*M Hallgrimsson* 2, *T Thordarson, K Thordarson*)
Omonia Nicosia 0
Viking Stavanger 0
RWD Molenbeek 1 (*Neilsen*)
Bayern Munich 3 (*Schuster* 3)
Jeunesse D'Esch 1 (*Zwally*)
Bohemians 1 (*T O'Connor*)
Rangers 1 (*Johnstone*)
Derby Co 3 (*Bourne, Lee* 2)
Slovan Bratislava 0
Dinamo Bucharest 1 (*Satmareanu*)
Real Madrid 0
Dynamo Kiev 1 (*Onischenko*)
Olympiakos 0
Fenerbahce 1 (*Engin*)
Benfica 0
Hajduk Split 3 (*Buljan, Djordjevic, Salvov*)
Floriana 0
Juventus 2 (*Furino, Anastasi*)
CSKA Sofia 0
Kuopion Palloseura 2 (*Toernroos, Heiskanen*)
Ruch Chorzow 2 (*Chojnacki, Faber*)
Magdeburg 2 (*Hoffmann, Streich*)
Malmo 1 (*Andersson*)
PSV Eindhoven 8 (*Lubse* 2, *Dahlqvist, Willy Van der Kerkhof, Van der Kuylen, Edstrom, Deacy* 2)
Linfield 0
St Etienne 3 (*Rocheteau, Patrick Revelli, Larque*)
KB Copenhagen 1 (*Petersen*)
Swarowski Innsbruck 1 (*Flindt*)
Borussia Moenchengladbach 6 (*Stielike, Simonsen, Heynckes* 4)
Zurich 5 (*Katic, Risi* 3, *Kuhn*)
Ujpest Dozsa 1 (*Nagy*)

Second Round, First Leg
Benfica 5 (*Moinhos, Sheu, Vitor Baptista* 2, *Toni*)
Ujpest Dozsa 2 (*Dunai A., Fazekas*)
Borussia Moenchengladbach 2 (*Heynckes, Simonsen*)
Juventus 0
Derby Co 4 (*George* 3, 2 pens., *Nish*)
Real Madrid 1 (*Pirri*)
Dynamo Kiev 3 (*Burjak* 2, *Blokhin*)
Akranes 0
Hajduk Split 4 (*Zungul, Rozic, Surjak, Mijak*)
RWD Molenbeek 0
Malmo 1 (*Andersson T*)
Bayern Munich 0
Ruch Chorzow 1 (*Bula*)
PSV Eindhoven 3 (*Lubse, Edstrom, Rene Van der Kerkhof*)
St Etienne 2 (*Patrick Revelli, Bathenay*)
Rangers 0

Second Round, Second Leg
Akranes 0
Dynamo Kiev 2 (*Onischenko, Gunnlaugsson og*)
Bayern Munich 2 (*Durnberger pen, Torstensson*)
Malmo 0
Juventus 2 (*Gori, Bettega*)
Borussia Moenchengladbach 2 (*Danner, Simonsen*)
PSV Eindhoven 4 (*Rene Van der Kerkhof, Van der Kuylen* 2, *Lubse*)
Ruch Chorzow 0
Rangers 1 (*MacDonald*)
St Etienne 2 (*Rocheteau, Herve Revelli*)
Real Madrid 5 (*Roberto Martinez* 2, *Santillana* 2, *Pirri pen*)
Derby Co 1 (*George*)
RWD Molenbeek 2 (*Teugels, Nielsen pen*)
Hajduk Split 3 (*Surjak, Zungul, Jovanic*)
Ujpest Dozsa 3 (*Bene* 2, *Nagy L*)
Benfica 1 (*Nene*)

Quarter-finals, First Leg
Benfica 0
Bayern Munich 0
Borussia Moenchengladbach 2 (*Jensen, Wittkamp*)
Real Madrid 2 (*Roberto Martinez, Pirri*)
Dynamo Kiev 2 (*Konkov, Blokhin*)
St Etienne 0
Hajduk Split 2 (*Mijac, Surjak*)
PSV Eindhoven 0

Quarter-finals, Second Leg
Bayern Munich 5 (*Durnberger* 2, *Rummenigge, Muller* 2)
Benfica 1 (*Barros*)
PSV Eindhoven 3 (*Dahlqvist, Lubse, Van der Kuylen*)
Hajduk Split 0
Real Madrid 1 (*Santillana*)
Borussia Moenchengladbach 1 (*Heynckes*)
St Etienne 3 (*Herve Revelli, Larque, Rocheteau*)
Dynamo Kiev 0 (after extra time)

Semi-finals, First Leg
Real Madrid 1 (*Roberto Martinez*)
Bayern Munich 1 (*Muller*)
St Etienne 1 (*Larque*)
PSV Eindhoven 0

Semi-finals, Second Leg
Bayern Munich 2 (*Muller* 2)
Real Madrid 0
PSV Eindhoven 0
St Etienne 0

Final 1975–76: Bayern Munich 1 St Etienne 0
(at Hampden Park, May 12, 1976, 54,864)

Bayern: Maier; Hansen, Schwarzenbeck, Beckenbauer, Horsmann, Roth, Durnberger, Kapellmann, Rummenigge, Muller, Hoeness.

St Etienne: Curkovic; Repellini, Piazza, Lopez, Janvion, Bathenay, Santini, Larque, Patrick Revelli, Herve Revelli, Sarramagna (Rocheteau).

Scorer: Bayern: Roth

EUROPEAN CUP 1976-77

First Round, First Leg
Akranes 1 (*Sveinsson*)
Trabzonspor 3 (*Perikli, Ali Kemal 2*)
Austria/WAC 1 (*Daxbacher*)
Borussia Moenchengladbach 0
FC Bruges 2 (*Davies pen., Verbeeke*)
Steaua Bucharest 1 (*Troi*)
CSKA Sofia 0
St Etienne 0
Dynamo Dresden 2 (*Kotte pen., Riedel*)
Benfica 0
Dundalk 1 (*McDowell*)
PSV Eindhoven 1 (*Van der Kuylen*)
Ferencvaros 5 (*Nyilasi 2, Magyar, Onhaus, Ebedli*)
Jeunesse Esch 1 (*Giuliani*)
Dynamo Kiev 3 (*Onishenko, Troshkin, Blokhin pen.*)
Partizan Belgrade 0
Omonia Nicosia 0
PAOK Salonika 2 (*Koudas, Sarafis*)
Rangers 1 (*Parlane*)
Zurich 1 (*Cucinotta*)
Stal Mielec 1 (*Sekulski*)
Real Madrid 2 (*Santillani, Del Bosque*)
Viking Stavanger 2 (*Valen, Johanessen*)
Banik Ostrava 1 (*Slany*)
Torino 2 (*Mozzini, Graziani*)
Malmo 1 (*Jonsson*)
Liverpool 2 (*Neal pen., Toshack*)
Crusaders 0
Koge 0
Bayern Munich 5 (*Torstensson 2, Muller 2, Durnberger*)
Sliema Wanderers 2 (*E. Aquilina 2*)
Turun Palloseura 1 (*Mannien*)

First Round, Second Leg
Turun Palloseura 1 (*Suhonen*)
Sliema Wanderers 0
Crusaders 0
Liverpool 5 (*Keegan, Johnson 2, McDermott, Heighway*)
Banik Ostrava 2 (*Vojacek 2*)
Viking Stavanger 0
Bayern Munich 2 (*Beckenbauer, Torstensson*)
Koge 1 (*Poulsen*)
Borussia Moenchengladbach 3 (*Stielike, Bonhof pen., Heynckes*)
Austria/WAC 0
Jeunesse Esch 2 (*Zwallay 2*)
Ferencvaros 6 (*Nyilasi 2, 1 pen., Pusztai 2, Szabo 2, 1 pen*)
Malmo 1 (*Ljungberg pen*)
Torino 1 (*Claudio Sala*)
PAOK Salonika 1 (*Sarafis*)
Omonia Nicosia 1 (*Philippos pen*)
Partizan Belgrade 0
Dynamo Kiev 2 (*Muntian pen., Slobodan*)
PSV Eindhoven 6 (*Van der Kuylen, Postuma, Rene Van der Kerkhof 4*)
Dundalk 0
St Etienne 1 (*Piazza*)
CSKA Sofia 0
Steaua Bucharest 1 (*Vigu*)
FC Bruges 1 (*Lambert*)
Trabzonspor 3 (*Huseyin 2, Engin*)
Akranes 2 (*Pogarson 2, 1 pen*)
Zurich 1 (*Martinelli*)
Rangers 0
Real Madrid 1 (*Pirri*)
Stal Mielec 0
Benfica 0
Dynamo Dresden 0

Second Round, First Leg
Dynamo Kiev 4 (*Burjak 2, Kolotov, Slobodan*)
PAOK Salonika 0
Ferencvaros 1 (*Onhaus*)
Dynamo Dresden 0
Real Madrid 0
FC Bruges 0
St Etienne 1 (*Piazza*)
PSV Eindhoven 0
Torino 1 (*Wittkamp o.g.*)
Borussia Moenchengladbach 2 (*Vogts, Klinkhammer*)
Trabzonspor 1 (*Cemil pen*)
Liverpool 0
Zurich 2 (*Cucinotta, Scheiwiler*)
Turun Palloseura 0
Banik Ostrava 2 (*Lorenc, Licka*)
Bayern Munich 1 (*Muller*)

Second Round, Second Leg
Bayern Munich 5 (*Muller 2, Rummenigge, Kapellmann, Torstensson*)
Banik Ostrava 0
Borussia Moenchengladbach 0
Torino 0
FC Bruges 2 (*Le Fevre, Camacho o.g.*)
Real Madrid 0
Dynamo Dresden 4 (*Heidler, Schmuck, Riedel, Kotte*)
Ferencvaros 0
Liverpool 3 (*Highway, Johnson, Keegan*)
Trabzonspor 0
Turun Palloseura 0
Zurich 1 (*Cucinotta*)
PAOK Salonika 0
Dynamo Kiev 2 (*Kolotov, Blokhin*)
PSV Eindhoven 0
St Etienne 0

Quarter-finals, First Leg
Bayern Munich 1 (*Kunkel*)
Dynamo Kiev 0
Borussia Moenchengladbach 2 (*Kulik, Simonsen*)
FC Bruges 2 (*Cools, Courant*)
St Etienne 1 (*Bathenay*)
Liverpool 0
Zurich 2 (*Cucinotta, Risi*)
Dynamo Dresden 1 (*Kreische*)

Quarter-finals, Second Leg
FC Bruges 0
Borussia Moenchengladbach 1 (*Hannes*)
Dynamo Dresden 3 (*Schade pen., Kreische 2*)
Zurich 2 (*Cucinotta, Risi*)
Dynamo Kiev 2 (*Burjak pen., Slobodan*)
Bayern Munich 0
Liverpool 3 (*Keegan, Kennedy, Fairclough*)
St Etienne 1 (*Bathenay*)

Semi-finals, First Leg
Dynamo Kiev 1 (*Onishenko*)
Borussia Moenchengladbach 0
Zurich 1 (*Risi pen*)
Liverpool 3 (*Neal 2, 1 pen., Heighway*)

Semi-finals, Second Leg
Borussia Moenchengladbach 2 (*Bonhof pen., Wittkamp*)
Dynamo Kiev 0
Liverpool 3 (*Case 2, Keegan*)
Zurich 0

Final 1976-77: Liverpool (1) 3 Borussia Moenchengladbach (0) 1
(in Rome, May 25 1977, 57,000)

Liverpool: Clemence; Neal, Jones, Smith, Kennedy, Hughes, Keegan, Case, Heighway, Callaghan, McDermott.
Borussia: Kneib; Vogts, Klinkhammer, Wittkamp, Bonhof, Wohlers (Hannes), Simonsen, Wimmer (Kulik), Stielike, Schaffer, Heynckes.
Scorers: Liverpool: McDermott, Smith, Neal pen.
Borussia: Simonsen.

EUROPEAN CUP 1977-78

First Round, first leg
Basel 1 (*Von Wartburg*)
SW Innsbruck 3 (*Welzl 2, 1 pen, Constantini*)
Celtic 5 (*McDonald, Wilson, Craig 2, McLaughlin*)
Jeunesse Esch 0
Benfica 0
Moscow Torpedo 0
Dynamo Dresden 2 (*Heidler, Schade*)
Halmstad 0
Dukla Prague 1 (*Vizek*)
Nantes 1 (*Amisse*)
Floriana 1 (*George Xuereb*)
Panathinaikos 1 (*Aslanidis*)
Kuopion Palloseura 0
FC Bruges 4 (*Vandereycken, Cools, Lambert, Davies*)
Levsky Spartak 3 (*Panov, Milanov 2*)
Slask Wroclaw 0
Lillestrom 2 (*Lonsdal, Johansen*)
Ajax 0
Omonia 0
Juventus 3 (*Bettega, Fanna, Virdis*)
Red Star Belgrade 3 (*Dzajic 2, Filipovic*)
Sligo Rovers 0
Trabzonspor 1 (*Necdet*)
BK 03 Copenhagen 0
Vasas 0
Borussia Moenchengladbach 3 (*Schaefer, Simonsen, Wohlers*)
Valur 1 (*Magnus Bergs*)
Glentoran 0
Dinamo Bucharest 2 (*Vrinceanu, Georgescu*)
Atletico Madrid 1 (*Luis Pereira*)

First round, second leg
Ajax 4 (*Birkelund og, Geels, La Ling 2*)
Lillestrom 0
Atletico Madrid 2 (*Benegas, Ruben Cano*)
Dinamo Bucharest 0
BK 03 Copenhagen 2 (*Francker 2*)
Trabzonspor 0
Borussia Moenchengladbach 1 (*Simonsen*)
Vasas 1 (*Izso*)
FC Bruges 5 (*Davies 2, Vandereycken, Simoen, Maes*)
Kuopion Palloseura 2 (*Rissanen, Laikonen*)
Halmstad 2 (*Johansson, Larsson*)
Dynamo Dresden 1 (*Heidler*)
Jeunesse Esch 1 (*Giuliano*)
Celtic 6 (*Lennox 2, Glavin, McLaughlin, Edvaldsson 2*)
Juventus 2 (*Boninsegna, Virdis*)
Omonia 0
Nantes 0
Dukla Prague 0
Panathinaikos 4 (*Alvarez, Antoniadis 2, 1 pen, Gonios*)
Floriana 0
Slask Wroclaw 2 (*Pawlowsky, Kopycky*)
Levski Spartak 2 (*Panov 2*)
Sligo Rovers 0
Red Star Belgrade 3 (*Filipovic 2, Jovanovic*)
SW Innsbruck 0
Basel 1 (*Miessen*)
Moscow Torpedo 0
Benfica 0 (*Benfica won 4-1 on penalties*)
Glentoran 2 (*Robson, Jamison*)
Valur 0

Second Round, first leg
Benfica 1 (*Pietra pen*)
BK 03 Copenhagen 0
FC Bruges 2 (*Davies pen, Cools*)
Panathinaikos 0
Celtic 2 (*Craig, Burns*)
SW Innsbruck 1 (*Kriess*)
Glentoran 0
Juventus 1 (*Causio*)
Levski Spartak 1 (*Voinov pen*)
Ajax 2 (*Geels, Erkens*)
Liverpool 5 (*Hansen, Case 2, Neal pen, Kennedy*)
Dynamo Dresden 1 (*Hafner*)
Nantes 1 (*Lacombe*)
Atletico Madrid 1 (*Marcial*)
Red Star Belgrade 0
Borussia Moenchengladbach 3 (*Schaffer, Heynckes, Simonsen*)

Second round, second leg
Ajax 2 (*Lerby, Geels*)
Levski Spartak 1 (*Milanov*)
Atletico Madrid 2 (*Ruben Cano, Luis Pereira*)
Nantes 1 (*Lacombe*)
Borussia Moenchengladbach 5 (*Simonsen 2, Heynckes, Nikolic og, Wittkamp*)
Red Star Belgrade 1 (*Susic*)
BK 03 Copenhagen 0
Benfica 1 (*Pietra*)
Dynamo Dresden 2 (*Kotte, Sachse*)
Liverpool 1 (*Highway*)
SW Innsbruck 3 (*Welzl, Stering, Oberacher*)
Celtic 0
Juventus 5 (*Virdis 2, Boninsegna, Fanna, Benetti*)
Glentoran 0
Panathinaikos 1 (*Gonios*)
FC Bruges 0

Quarter-finals, first leg
Benfica 1 (*Nene*)
Liverpool 2 (*Case, Hughes*)
Ajax 1 (*Van Dord*)
Juventus 1 (*Causio*)
FC Bruges 2 (*Courant, De Cubber*)
Atletico Madrid 0
SW Innsbruck 3 (*Peter Koncilia, Kriess, Werner Schwarz*)
Borussia Moenchengladbach 1 (*Heynckes*)

Quarter-finals, second leg
Juventus 1 (*Tardelli*)
Ajax 1 (*La Ling*) *Juventus won 3-0 on penalties*
Atletico Madrid 3 (*Benegas, Marcial 2*)
FC Bruges 2 (*Cools, Lambert*)
Liverpool 4 (*Callaghan, Dalglish, McDermott, Neal*)
Benfica 1 (*Nene*)
Borussia Moenchengladbach 2 (*Bonhof pen, Heynckes*)
SW Innsbruck 0

Semi-finals, first leg
Borussia Moenchengladbach 2 (*Hannes, Bonhof*)
Liverpool 1 (*Johnson*)
Juventus 1 (*Bettega*)
FC Bruges 0

Semi-finals, second leg
Liverpool 3 (*Kennedy, Dalglish, Case*)
Borussia Moenchengladbach 0
FC Bruges 2 (*Bastijns, Vandereycken*)
Juventus 0

Final 1977-78: Liverpool (0) 1 FC Bruges (0) 0
(at Wembley, May 10 1978, 92,000)

Liverpool: Clemence; Neal, Thompson, Hansen, Hughes, McDermott, Kennedy, Souness, Case (Heighway), Fairclough, Dalglish.
FC Bruges: Jensen; Bastijns, Krieger, Leekens, Maes (Volders), Cools, De Cubber, Vandereycken, Ku (Sanders), Simoen, Sorensen.
Scorers: Liverpool: Dalglish.

CUP-WINNERS' CUP HISTORY

EUROPEAN CUP-WINNERS' CUP 1960-61

Qualifying Round
Vorwaerts Berlin v Red Brno (2-3)   2-1, 0-2
Rangers v Ferencvaros (5-4)   4-2, 1-2

Quarter-Final
Red Star Brno v Dynamo Zagreb (0-2)   0-0, 0-2
FK Austria v Wolverhampton W (2-5)   2-0, 0-5

Borussia Moenchengladbach v Rangers (0-11)   0-3, 0-8
Lucerne v Fiorentina (2-9)   0-3, 2-6

Semi-Final
Fiorentina v Dynamo Zagreb (4-2)   3-0, 1-2
Rangers v Wolverhampton W (3-1)   2-0, 1-1

Final 1960-61: Rangers 0 Fiorentina 2
(First leg, Glasgow, May 17 1961)
Rangers: Ritchie; Shearer, Caldow; Davis, Paterson, Baxter, Wilson, McMillan, Scott, Brand, Hume.
Fiorentina: Albertosi; Robotti, Castelletti; Gonfiantini, Orzan, Rimbaldo; Hamrin, Micheli, Da Costa, Milani, Petris.
Scorer: Milan 2.

Fiorentina 2 Rangers 1
(Second leg, Florence, 27 May, 1961)
Fiorentina: Albertosi; Robotti, Castelletti; Gonfiantini, Orzan, Rimbaldo; Hamrin, Micheli, Da Costa, Milani, Petris.
Rangers: Ritchie; Shearer, Caldow; Davis, Paterson, Baxter; Scott, McMillan, Millar, Brand, Wilson
Scorers—Fiorentina: Milan, Hamrin. Rangers: Scott. Fiorentina won Cup on aggregate 4-1

EUROPEAN CUP-WINNERS' CUP 1961-62

Holders: Fiorentina, exempt until Second Round.
Byes: Ajax; Werder; Aarhus; Dudelange; Progresul; Vardar; Zilina; Olympiakos.

First Round
Glenavon v Leicester C (2-7)   1-4, 1-3
Dunfermline Ath v St Patrick's (8-1)   4-1, 4-0
Swansea T v Motor Jena (3-7)   2-2, 1-5
La Chaux de Fonds v Leixoes (6-7)   6-2, 0-5
Sedan v Atletico Madrid (3-7)   2-3, 1-4
Rapid Vienna v Spartak Varna (5-2)   0-0, 5-2
Floriana v Ujpest (4-15)   2-5, 2-10

Second Round
Fiorentina v Rapid Vienna (9-3)   3-1, 6-2
Leicester C v Atletico Madrid (1-3)   1-1, 0-2
Dunfermline Ath v Vardar Skoplje (5-2)   5-0, 0-2
Werder Bremen v Aarhus (5-2)   2-0, 3-2

Ajax v Ujpest (3-4)   2-1, 1-3
Olympiakos Piraeus v Dynamo Zilina (2-4)   2-3, 0-1
Leixoes v Progresul (2-1)   1-1, 1-0
Motor Jena v Alliance Dudelange (9-2)   7-0, 2-2

Quarter-Final
Werder Bremen v Atletico Madrid (2-4)   1-3, 1-1
Ujpest v Dunfermline Ath. (5-3)   4-3, 1-0
Dynamo Zilina v Fiorentina (3-4)   3-2, 0-2
Motor Jena v Leixoes (4-2)   1-1, 3-1

Semi-Final
Fiorentina v Ujpest (3-0)   2-0, 1-0
Motor Jena v Atletico Madrid (0-5)   0-1, 0-4

Final 1961-62: Fiorentina 1 Atletico Madrid 1 (In Glasgow, May 10, 1962)
Fiorentina: Albertosi; Robotti, Castelletti; Malatrasi, Orzan, Marchesi; Hamrin, Ferretti, Milani, Dell'Angelo, Petris.
Atletico Madrid: Madinabeytia; Rivilla, Calleja, Ramirez, Griffa, Glaria; Jones, Adelardo, Mendonça, Peiró, Collar.
Scorers—Fiorentina: Hamrin. Atletico Madrid: Peiró.

Replay: Atletico Madrid 3 Fiorentina 0   No change in teams.
(In Stuttgart, September 5, 1962)   Scorers: Jones, Mendonça, Peiró.

EUROPEAN CUP-WINNERS' CUP 1962-63

Holders: Atletico Madrid, exempt until Second Round.
Byes: Graz; Nuremberg; Portadown; Shamrock; Slovan; Spurs.

First Round
Lausanne v Sparta Rotterdam (5-4)   3-0, 2-4
St. Etienne v Vitoria Setubal (4-1)   1-1, 3-0
Alliance Dudelange v Odense BK 09 (2-9)   1-1, 1-8
Rangers v Seville (4-2)   4-0, 0-2
OFK Belgrade v Chemie Halle (5-3)   2-0, 3-3
Steaua Bucharest v Botev Plovdiv (4-7)   3-2, 1-5
Ujpest v Zaglebie Sosnowiec (5-0)   5-0, 0-0
Bangor C v Napoli (4-5)   2-0, 1-3, 1-2

Second Round
St Etienne v Nuremberg (0-3)   0-0, 0-3
Atletico Madrid v Hibernians Valletta (5-0)   4-0, 1-0
Shamrock R v Botev Plovdiv (0-5)   0-4, 0-1
Sturm Graz v Odense Bk 09 (4-6)   1-1, 3-5

Tottenham H v Rangers (8-4)   5-2, 3-2
OFK Belgrade v Portadown (7-4)   5-1, 2-3
Lausanne v Slovan Bratislava (1-2)   1-1, 0-1
Ujpest v Napoli (3-5)   1-1, 1-1, 1-3

Quarter-Final
Slovan Bratislava v Tottenham H (2-6)   2-0, 0-6
Odense BK 09 v Nuremberg (0-7)   0-1, 0-6
Botev Plovdiv v Atletico Madrid (1-5)   1-1, 0-4
OFK Belgrade v Napoli (6-4)   2-0, 1-3, 3-1

Semi-Final
OFK Belgrade v Tottenham H (2-5)   1-2, 1-3
Nuremberg v Atletico Madrid (2-3)   2-1, 0-2

Final 1962-63: Tottenham H. 5 Atletico Madrid 1 (In Rotterdam, May 15, 1963)
Tottenham H: Brown; Baker, Henry, Blanchflower, Norman, Marchi; Jones, White, Smith, Greaves, Dyson.
Atletico Madrid: Madinabeytia; Rivilla, Rodrigues, Ramiro, Griffa, Glaria; Jones, Adelardo, Chuzo, Mendonça, Collar.
Scorers—Tottenham H: Greaves 2, White, Dyson 2. Atletico Madrid: Collar (penalty)

EUROPEAN CUP-WINNERS' CUP 1963-64

Holders: Tottenham H, exempt until Second Round.
Byes: Linfield, Zwickau.

First Round

Fenerbahce v Petrolul Ploesti (4-2)	4-1, 0-1
Basle v Celtic (1-10)	1-5, 0-5
Tilburg Willem II v Manchester U (2-7)	1-1, 1-6
SV Hamburg v US Luxembourg (7-2)	4-0, 3-2
Olympiakos Piraeus v Zaglebie Sosnowiec (4-2)	2-1, 0-1, 2-0
Shelbourne v Barcelona (1-5)	0-2, 1-3
Lyon v Odense BK 09 (6-2)	3-1, 3-1
MTK Budapest v Slavia Sofia (2-1)	1-0, 1-1
ASK Linz v Dynamo Zagreb (2-2)	1-0, 0-1, 1-1
(Linz lost the toss)	
Sliema Wanderers v Borough U (0-2)	0-0, 0-2
Atlanta v Sporting Lisbon (4-6)	2-0, 1-3, 1-3
Apoel Nicosia v Gjoevik Lyn (6-1)	6-0, 0-1
Helsinki Palloseura v Slovan Bratislava (2-12)	1-4, 1-8

Second Round

Tottenham H v Manchester U (3-4)	2-0, 1-4
Fenerbahce v Linfield (4-3)	4-1, 0-2
Barcelona v SV Hamburg (6-7)	4-4, 0-0, 2-3
Sporting Lisbon v Apoel Nicosia (18-1)	16-1, 2-0
Lyon v Olympiakos Piraeus (5-3)	4-1, 1-2
Motor Zwickau v MTK Budapest (1-2)	1-0, 0-2
Celtic v Dynamo Zagreb (4-2)	3-0, 1-2
Borough U v Slovan Bratislava (0-4)	0-1, 0-3

Quarter-Final

Manchester U v Sporting Lisbon (4-6)	4-1, 0-5
SV Hamburg v Lyon (1-3)	1-1, 0-2
Celtic v Slovan Bratislava (2-0)	1-0, 1-0
MTK Budapest v Fenerbahce (4-3)	2-0, 1-3, 1-0

Semi-Final

Celtic v MTK Budapest (3-4)	3-0, 0-4
Lyon v Sporting Lisbon (1-2)	0-0, 1-1, 0-1

Final 1963-64: MTK Budapest 3 Sporting Lisbon 3 (after extra time)
(In Brussels, May 13, 1964)

MTK Budapest: Kovalik; Keszei, Dansky, Jenei, Nagy, Kovacs; Sandor, Vasas, Kuti, Bodor, Halapi.
Sporting Lisbon: Carvalho; Gomez, Perdis; Battista, Carlos, Geo; Mendes, Oswaldo, Mascarenhas, Figueiredo, Morais.
Scorers—MTK Budapest: Sandor 2, Kuti. Sporting Lisbon: Figueiredo 2, Dansky (own goal).

Replay 1963-64: Sporting Lisbon 1 MTK Budapest 0
(at Antwerp, May 15, 1964)

Teams unchanged.
Scorer—Lisbon: Mendes.

EUROPEAN CUP-WINNERS' CUP 1964-65

Holders: Sporting Lisbon, exempt until Second Round.
Bye: Dundee.

First Round

Admira Vienna v Legia Warsaw (1-4)	1-3, 0-1
Lausanne v Honved (2-1)	2-0, 0-1
US Luxembourg v Munich 1860 (0-10)	0-4, 0-6
Valletta v Real Zaragoza (1-8)	0-3, 1-5
AEK Athens v Dynamo Zagreb (2-3)	2-0, 0-3
Steaua Bucharest v Derry C (5-0)	3-0, 2-0
Magdeburg v Galatasaray (3-3)	1-1, 1-1, 1-1
(Galatasaray won toss)	
Esbjerg v Cardiff C (0-1)	0-0, 0-1
Skeid Oslo v Valkeakosken (1-2)	1-0, 0-2
Porto v Lyon (4-0)	3-0, 1-0
Sparta Prague v Anorthosis (16-0)	10-0, 6-0
La Gantoise v West Ham U (1-2)	0-1, 1-1
Torino v Fortuna Geelen (5-3)	3-1, 2-2
Slavia Sofia v Cork Celtic (3-1)	1-1, 2-0

Second Round

Dundee v Real Zaragoza (3-4)	2-2, 1-2
Slavia Sofia v Lausanne (4-5)	1-0, 1-2, 2-3
Legia Warsaw v Galatasaray (3-2)	2-1, 0-1, 1-0
West Ham U v Sparta Prague (3-2)	2-0, 1-2
Porto v Munich 1860 (1-2)	0-1, 1-1
Steaua Bucharest v Dynamo Zagreb (1-5)	1-3, 0-2
Sporting Lisbon v Cardiff C (1-2)	1-2, 0-0
Torino v Valkeakosken (6-0)	5-0, 1-0

Quarter-Final

Real Zaragoza v Cardiff C (3-2)	2-2, 1-0
Legia Warsaw v Munich 1860 (0-4)	0-4, 0-0
Torino v Dynamo Zagreb (3-2)	1-1, 2-1
Lausanne v West Ham U (4-6)	1-2, 3-4

Semi-Final

West Ham U v Real Zaragoza (3-2)	2-1, 1-1
Torino v Munich 1860 (3-5)	2-0, 1-3, 0-2

Final 1964-65: West Ham U 2 Munich 1860 0
At Wembley Stadium, May 19, 1965)

West Ham U: Standen; Kirkup, Burkett; Peters, Brown, Moore; Sealey, Boyce, Hurst, Dear, Sissons.
Munich 1860: Radenkovic; Wagner, Kohlars; Bena, Reich, Luttrop; Heiss, Kuppers, Brunnenmeier, Grosser, Rebele.
Scorer: Sealey 2.

EUROPEAN CUP-WINNERS' CUP 1965-66

Holders: West Ham U, exempt until Second Round.

First Round

Juventus v Liverpool (1-2)	1-0, 0-2
Cardiff C v Standard Liege (1-3)	1-2, 0-1
Lahden Reipas v Honved (2-16)	2-10, 0-6
Dukla Prague v Stade Rennes (2-0)	2-0, 0-0
Go Ahead Deventer v Celtic (0-7)	0-6, 0-1
Aarhus v Vitoria Setubal (4-2)	2-1, 2-1
Coleraine v Dynamo Kiev (1-10)	1-6, 0-4
KR Rekyjavik v Rosenborg (2-6)	1-3, 1-3
Omonia Nicosia v Olympiakos Piraeus (1-2)	0-1, 1-1
Magdeburg v Spora Luxembourg (3-0)	1-0, 2-0
Sion v Galatasaray (6-3)	5-1, 1-2
Atletico Madrid v Dynamo Zagreb (5-0)	1-0, 4-0
Wiener Neustadt v Stjnta Cluj (0-3)	0-1, 0-2
Limerick v CSKA Sofia (1-4)	1-2, 0-2
Fioriana v Borussia Dortmund (1-13)	1-5, 0-8

Second Round

Liverpool v Standard Liege (5-2)	3-1, 2-1
Dukla Prague v Honved* (4-4)	3-2, 1-2
Aarhus v Celtic (0-3)	0-1, 0-2
Rosenborg v Dynamo Kiev (1-6)	1-4, 0-2
West Ham U v Olympiakos Piraeus (6-2)	4-0, 2-2
Magdeburg v Sion (10-3)	8-1, 2-2
Stijnta Cluj v Atlètico Madrid (0-6)	0-2, 0-4
Borussia Dortmund v CSKA Sofia (5-4)	3-0, 2-4

Quarter-Final

Honved v Liverpool (0-2)	0-0, 0-2
Celtic v Dynamo Kiev (4-1)	3-0, 1-1
West Ham U v Magdeburg (2-1)	1-0, 1-1
Atlètico Madrid v Borussia Dortmund (1-2)	1-1, 0-1

Semi-Final

Celtic v Liverpool (1-2)	1-0, 0-2
West Ham U v Borussia Dortmund (2-5)	1-2, 1-3

*Honved won on away goals rule.

Final 1965–66: Borussia Dortmund 2 Liverpool 1 (after extra time)
(In Glasgow, May 5, 1966)

Borussia Dortmund: Tilkowski; Cyliax, Redder; Kurrat, Paul, Assauer; Libuda, Schmidt, Held, Sturm, Emmerich.
Liverpool: Lawrence; Lawler, Byrne; Milne, Yeats, Stevenson; Callaghan, Hunt, St John, Smith, Thompson.
Scorers: Borussia Dortmund: Held, Yeats (og). Liverpool: Hunt.

EUROPEAN CUP-WINNERS' CUP 1966–67

Holders: Borussia Dortmund, exempt until Second Round.

Preliminary Round

Valur Reykjavik v Standard Liege (2-9)	1-1, 1-8

First Round

Tatran Presov v Bayern Munich (3-4)	1-1, 2-3
Shamrock R v Spora Luxembourg (8-2)	4-1, 4-1
OFK Belgrade v Spartak Moscow (1-6)	1-3, 0-3
Rapid Vienna v Galatasaray (9-3)	4-0, 5-3
Fiorentina v Vasas Gyor (3-4)	1-0, 2-4
AEK Athens v Sporting Braga (2-4)	0-1, 2-3
Chemie Leipzig v Legia Warsaw (5-2)	3-0, 2-2
Standard Liege v Apollon Limassol (6-1)	5-1, 1-0
Servette Geneva v Kamraterna (3-2)	1-1, 2-1
Fioriana v Sparta Rotterdam (1-7)	1-1, 0-6
Swansea T v Slavia Sofia (1-5)	1-1, 0-4
Strasbourg v Steaua Bucharest (2-1)	1-0, 1-1
Skeid Oslo v Real Zaragoza (4-5)	3-2, 1-3
Aalborg v Everton (1-2)	0-0, 1-2
Glentoran v Rangers (1-5)	1-1, 0-4

Second Round

Shamrock R v Bayern Munich (3-4)	1-1, 2-3
Spartak Moscow v Rapid Vienna (1-2)	1-1, 0-1
Vasas Gyor v Sporting Braga (3-2)	3-0, 0-2
†Chemie Leipzig v Standard Liege (2-2)	2-1, 0-1
Servette Geneva v Sparta Rotterdam (2-1)	2-0, 0-1
Strasbourg v Slavia Sofia (1-2)	1-0, 0-2
Real Zaragoza v Everton (2-1)	2-0, 0-1
Rangers v Borussia Dortmund (2-1)	2-1, 0-0

Quarter-Final

Rapid Vienna v Bayern Munich (1-2)	1-0, 0-2
Vasas Gyor v Standard Liege (2-3)	2-1, 0-2
Servette Geneva v Slavia Sofia (1-3)	1-0, 0-3
*Rangers v Real Zaragoza (2-2)	2-0, 0-2

Semi-Final

Bayern Munich v Standard Liege (5-1)	2-0, 3-1
Slavia Sofia v Rangers (0-2)	0-1, 0-1

*Won on toss of a disc.   †Won on away goals counting double.

Final 1966–67: Bayern Munich 1 Rangers 0 (after extra time)
(At Nuremberg, May 31, 1967)

Bayern Munich: Maier; Nowak, Kupferschmidt; Roth, Beckenbauer, Olk; Nafziger, Ohlhauser, Muller, Koulmann, Brenninger.
Rangers: Martin; Johansen, Provan; Jardine, McKinnon, Greig; Henderson Smith A, Hynd, Smith D, Johnston.
Scorer: Roth.

EUROPEAN CUP-WINNERS' CUP 1967–68

First Round

AC Milan v Levski Sofia (6-2)	5-1, 1-1
Vasas Gyor v Apollon Limassol (9-0)	5-0, 4-0
Altay Izmir v Standard Liege (2-3)	2-3, 0-0
Aberdeen v KR Reykjavik (14-1)	10-0, 4-1
Bayern Munich v Panathinaikos (7-1)	5-0, 2-1
Frederikstad v Vitoria Setubal (2-7)	1-5, 1-2
Valencia v Crusaders (4-0)	4-0, 4-2
FK Austria v Steaua Bucharest (1-4)	0-2, 1-2
Shamrock R v Cardiff C (1-3)	1-1, 0-2
Fioriana v NAC Breda (1-3)	1-2, 0-1
Moscow Torpedo v Motor Zwickau (1-0)	0-0, 1-0
Lausanne v Spartak Trnava (3-4)	3-2, 0-2
Aris Bonneweg v Lyon (1-5)	0-3, 1-2
Hajduk Split v Tottenham H (3-6)	0-2, 3-4
HJK Helsinki v Wisla Krakow (1-8)	1-4, 0-4
SV Hamburg v Randers Freja (7-3)	5-3, 2-0

Second Round

*Vasas Gyor v AC Milan (3-3)	2-2, 1-1
Standard Liege v Aberdeen (3-2)	3-0, 0-2
Bayern Munich v Vitoria Setubal (7-3)	6-2, 1-1
Valencia v Steaua Bucharest (3-1)	3-0, 0-1
NAC Breda v Cardiff C (2-5)	1-1, 1-4
Moscow Torpedo v Spartak Trnava (6-1)	3-0, 3-1
*Lyon v Tottenham H (4-4)	1-0, 3-4
Wisla Krakow v SV Hamburg (0-5)	0-1, 0-4

Quarter-Final

Standard Liege v AC Milan (2-4)	1-1, 1-1, 0-2
Valencia v Bayern Munich (1-2)	1-1, 0-1
Cardiff C v Moscow Torpedo (2-1)	1-0, 0-1, 1-0
SV Hamburg v Lyon (4-2)	2-0, 0-2, 2-0

Semi-Final

AC Milan v Bayern Munich (2-0)	2-0, 0-0
SV Hamburg v Cardiff C (4-3)	1-1, 3-2

Final 1967–8: AC Milan 2 SV Hamburg 0
(In Rotterdam, May 23, 1968)

Milan: Cudicini; Anquilletti, Schnellinger; Trappatoni, Rosato Scala; Hamrin Lodetti, Sormani, Rivera, Prati.
SV Hamburg: Ozcan; Sondemann, Kurbjohn; Dieckemann, Horst, Schulz H, Dorfel II, Kramer, Seeler, Hornig, Dorfel I.
Scorer: Hamrin 2.

EUROPEAN CUP-WINNERS' CUP 1968–69

First Round
Slovan Bratislava v Bor (3-2)	3-0, 2-0
Cardiff C v Porto (3-4)	2-2, 1-2
Partizan Tirana v Torino (2-3)	1-3, 1-0
Dunfermline Ath v Apoel Nicosia (12-1)	10-1, 2-0
Olympiakos Piraeus v Fram Reykjavik (4-0)	2-0, 2-0
Bruges v WBA* (3-3)	3-1, 0-2
Bordeaux v Cologne (2-4)	2-1, 0-3
AK Graz v ADO The Hague (1-6)	1-4, 0-2
Randers Freja v Shamrock R (3-1)	1-0, 2-1
Rumelange v Sliema Wanderers* (2-2)	2-1, 0-1
Altay Izmir v Lyn Oslo (4-5)	3-1, 1-4
Crusaders v Norrköping (3-6)	2-2, 1-4
Lugano v Barcelona (0-4)	0-1, 0-3

Second Round
Porto v Slovan Bratislava (1-4)	1-0, 0-4
Dunfermline Ath v Olympiakos Piraeus (4-3)	4-0, 0-3
Dynamo Bucharest v WBA (1-5)	1-1, 0-4
ADO The Hague v Cologne (0-4)	0-1, 0-3
Randers Freja v Sliema Wanderers (8-0)	6-0, 2-0
Lyn Oslo v Norrköping (4-3)	2-0, 2-3
Torino	bye
Barcelona	bye

QuarterFinal
Torino v Slovan Bratislava (1-3)	0-1, 1-2
Dunfermline Ath v WBA (1-0)	0-0, 1-0
Cologne v Randers Freja (5-1)	2-1, 3-0
Barcelona v Lyn Oslo (5-4)	3-2, 2-2

Semi-Final
Dunfermline Ath v Slovan Bratislava (1-2)	1-1, 0-1
Cologne v Barcelona (3-6)	2-2, 1-4

*Won on away goals counting double.

Final 1968–69: Slovan Bratislava 3 Barcelona 2
(In Basle, 40,000, May 21, 1969)

Slovan Bratislava: Vencel; Filo, Hrivnak; Jan Zlocha, Horvath, Hrdlicka, Cvetler; Moder, Josef Capkovic, Jokl, Jan Capkovic.

Barcelona: Sadurni; Franch (Pereda), Eladio; Rife, Olivella, Zabalza; Pellicer, Castro (Mendoca), Zaluda, Fuste, Rexach.

Scorers: Slovan Bratislava: Cvetler, Hrivnak, Jan Capkovic. Barcelona: Zaluda, Rexach.

EUROPEAN CUP-WINNERS' CUP 1969–70

Preliminary Round
*Rapid Vienna v Moscow Torpedo (1-1)	0-0, 1-1

First Round
Olympiakos Piraeus v Gornik Zabrze (2-7)	2-2, 0-5
Rangers v Steaua Bucharest (2-0)	2-0, 0-0
IBV Reykjavik v Levski Sofia (0-8)	0-4, 0-4
Frem Copenhagen v St. Gallen*(2-2)	2-1, 0-1
Ards v AS Roma (1-3)	0-0, 1-3
Rapid Vienna v PSV Eindhoven (3-6)	2-4, 1-2
Goztepe Izmir v US Luxembourg (6-2)	3-0, 3-2
Mjoendalen v Cardiff C (2-12)	1-7, 1-5
Shamrock R v Schalke 04 (2-4)	2-1, 0-3
Norrköping v Sliema Wanderers (5-2)	5-1, 0-1
Dukla Prague v Marseille (1-2)	1-0, 0-2
Dynamo Zagreb v Slovan Bratislava (3-0)	3-0, 0-0
Magdeburg v MTK Budapest (2-1)	1-1, 1-0
Academica Coimbra v Kuopion Pallo. (1-0)	0-0, 1-0
Lierse v Apoel Nicosia (11-1)	10-1, 1-0
Atlètico Bilbao v Manchester C (3-6)	3-3, 0-3

Second Round
Gornik Zabrze v Rangers (6-2)	3-1, 3-1
Levski Sofia v St Gallen (4-0)	4-0, 0-0
†AS Roma v PSV Eindhoven (1-1)	1-0, 0-1
Goztepe Izmir v Cardiff C (3-1)	3-0, 0-1
Norrköping v Schalke 04 (0-1)	0-0, 0-1
Marseille v Dynamo Zagreb (1-3)	1-1, 0-2
Magdeburg v Academica Coimbra (1-2)	1-0, 0-2
Lierse v Manchester C (0-8)	0-3, 0-5

Quarter-Finals
Levski Sofia v *Gornik Zabrze (4-4)	3-2, 1-2
AS Roma v Goztepe Izmir (2-0)	2-0, 0-0
Dynamo Zagreb v Schalke 04 (1-4)	1-3, 0-1
Academica Coimbra v Manchester C (0-1)	0-0, 0-1

Semi-Final
AS Roma v †Gornik Zabrze (4-4)	1-1, 2-2, 1-1
Schalke 04 v Manchester C (2-5)	1-0, 1-5

*Won on away goals counting double. †Won on toss of coin after extra time.

Final 1969–70: Manchester C 2, Gornik Zabrze 1
(In Vienna, 10,000, April 29, 1970)

Manchester C: Corrigan; Book, Pardoe; Doyle (Sub Bowyer), Booth, Oakes, Heslop, Bell, Lee, Young, Towers.

Gornik Zabrze: Kostka; Gorgan, Ozlizlo; Latogha, Forenski, Szoltysik; Wilczek, Olek, Banas, Lubanski, Szaryniski.

Scorers: Manchester C: Young, Lee (pen). Gornik Zabrze: Ozlizlo.

EUROPEAN CUP-WINNERS' CUP 1970-71

Preliminary Round
Atvidaberg v Partizan Tirana (1-3)	0-2, 1-1
Bohemians v Gottwaldov (3-4)	1-2, 2-2

First Round
*Manchester C v Linfield (2-2)	1-0, 1-2
Olympija Ljubljana v Benfica (2-9)	1-1, 1-8
Akureyri v Zurich (1-14)	1-7, 0-7
Cardiff C v Pezoporikos (8-0)	8-0, 0-0
Offenbach Kickers v Bruges (2-3)	2-1, 0-2
Hibernians Valletta v Real Madrid (0-5)	0-0, 0-5
*Vorwaerts Berlin v Bologna (1-1)	0-0, 1-1
Steaua Bucharest v Karpaty Lvov (4-3)	3-3, 1-0
CSKA Sofia v Valkeakosken (11-1)	9-0, 2-1
Aberdeen v Honved† (4-4)	1-3, 3-1
Stromsgodset v Nantes (3-7)	0-5, 3-2
Aalborg v Gornik Zabrze (1-9)	0-1, 1-8
Goztepe Izmir v US Luxembourg (5-1)	5-0, 0-1
Wacker Innsbruck v Partizan Tirana (5-3)	3-2, 2-1
Gottwaldov v PSV Eindhoven* (2-2)	2-1, 0-1
Aris Salonika v Chelsea (2-6)	1-1, 1-5

Second Round
CSKA Sofia v Chelsea (0-2)	0-1, 0-1
Honved v Manchester C (0-3)	0-1, 0-2
Cardiff C v Nantes (7-2)	5-1, 2-1
Bruges v Zurich (4-3)	2-0, 2-3
PSV Eindhoven v Steaua Bucharest (7-0)	4-0, 3-0
Goztepe Izmir v Gornik Zabrze (0-4)	0-1, 0-3
Real Madrid v Wacker Innsbruck (2-1)	0-1, 2-0
Benfica v Vorwaerts Berlin† (2-2)	2-0, 0-2

Quarter-Finals
Manchester C v Gornik Zabrze (5-3)	2-0, 0-2, 3-1
PSV Eindhoven v Vorwaerts Berlin (2-1)	2-0, 0-1
Cardiff C v Real Madrid (1-2)	1-0, 0-2
Bruges v Chelsea (2-4)	2-0, 0-4

Semi-Finals
Chelsea v Manchester C (2-0)	1-0, 1-0
PSV Eindhoven v Real Madrid (1-2)	0-0, 1-2

*Won on away goals counting double.
†Won on penalty contest when teams level on two games, second after extra time.

Final 1970-71: Chelsea 2 Real Madrid 1
(after 1-1 draw, both games in Athens)
(First game, May 19, 1971, 42,000, after extra time)

Chelsea: Bonetti; Boyle, Harris; Hollins, Dempsey, Webb; Weller, Hudson, Osgood, Cooke, Houseman.
Real Madrid: Borja; Luis, Zunzunegui; Pirri, Benito, Zoco; Perez, Amancio, Grosso, Valasquez, Gento.
Scorers: Chelsea, Osgood, Real Madrid, Zoco.

(Second game, May 21, 1971, 24,000)

Chelsea: Bonetti; Boyle, Harris; Cooke, Dempsey, Webb; Weller, Baldwin, Osgood (Smethurst), Hudson, Houseman.
Real Madrid: Borja; Luis, Zunzunegui; Pirri, Benito, Zoco; Fleitas, Amancio, Grosso, Velasquez (Gento), Bueno (Grande).
Scorers: Chelsea, Dempsey, Osgood, Real Madrid, Fleitas.

EUROPEAN CUP-WINNERS' CUP 1971-72

Preliminary Round
Odense BK 09 v FK Austria* (4-4)	4-2, 0-2
Hibernians Valletta v Fram Reykjavik (3-2)	3-0, 0-2

First Round
Servette Geneva v Liverpool (2-3)	2-1, 0-2
Distillery v Barcelona (1-7)	1-3, 0-4
†Dynamo Berlin v Cardiff C (2-2)	1-1, 1-1
Jeunesse Hautcharage v Chelsea (0-21)	0-8, 0-13
Limerick v Torino (0-5)	0-1, 0-4
Dynamo Tirana v FK Austria (1-2)	1-1, 0-1
Rennes v Rangers (1-2)	1-1, 0-1
Hibernians Valletta v Steaua Bucharest (0-1)	0-0, 0-1
Sporting Lisbon v Lyn Oslo (7-0)	3-0, 4-0
Skoda Pilzen v Bayern Munich (1-7)	0-1, 1-6
Komlo Banyasi v Red Star Belgrade (4-8)	2-7, 2-1
Olympiakos Piraeus v Dynamo Moscow (2-3)	0-2, 2-1
Levski Sofia v Sparta Rotterdam (1-3)	1-1, 0-2
Zaglebie Sosnowiec v Atvidaberg (4-5)	3-4, 1-1
Mikkeli v Eskisehirspor (0-4)	0-0, 0-4
Beerschot v Famagusta (8-0)	7-0, 1-0

Second Round
Liverpool v Bayern Munich (1-3)	0-0, 1-3
*Atvidaberg v Chelsea (1-1)	0-0, 1-1
Torino v FK Austria (1-0)	1-0, 0-0
†Rangers v Sporting Lisbon (6-6)	3-2, 3-4
Beerschot v Dynamo Berlin (2-6)	1-3, 1-3
Sparta Rotterdam v Red Star Belgrade (2-3)	1-1, 1-2
Barcelona v Steaua Bucharest (1-3)	0-1, 1-2
Eskisehirspor v Dynamo Moscow (0-2)	0-1, 0-1

Quarter-Finals
Torino v Rangers (1-2)	1-1, 0-1
Steaua Bucharest v Bayern Munich* (1-1)	1-1, 0-0
Atvidaberg v Dynamo Berlin (2-4)	0-2, 2-2
Red Star Belgrade v Dynamo Moscow (2-3)	1-2, 1-1

Semi-Finals
Bayern Munich v Rangers (1-3)	1-1, 0-2
Dynamo Berlin v Dynamo Moscow † (2-2)	1-1, 1-1

* Won on away goals rule. † Won on penalty kicks.

Final 1971-72: Rangers 3 Dynamo Moscow 2
(in Barcelona, May 24, 1972, 35,000)

Rangers: McCloy; Jardine, Mathieson, Greig, Johnstone, Smith, McLean, Conn, Stein, MacDonald, Johnston.
Dynamo: Pilgui; Basalev, Dolmatov, Zykov, Dobbonosov, (Gerschkovitch), Zhukov, Baidatchini, Jakubik (Estrekov), Sabo, Makovikov, Evryuzhikhin.
Scorers: Rangers, Stein, Johnstone 2. Dynamo, Estrekov, Makovikov.
Referee: Ortiz de Mendibil (Spain).

EUROPEAN CUP-WINNERS' CUP 1972-73

First Round
Bastia v Atlético Madrid (1-2)	0-0, 1-2
Floriana Valetta v Ferencvaros (1-6)	1-0, 0-6
Schalke 04 v Slavia Sofia (5-2)	2-1, 3-1
Standard Liège v Sparta Prague (3-4)	1-0, 2-4
Spartak Moscow v FC Den Haag (1-0)	1-0, 0-0
Vikingur Reykjavik v Legia Warsaw (0-11)	0-2, 0-9
Ankaragucu v Leeds U (1-2)	1-1, 0-1
Hajduk Split v Fredrikstad (2-0)	1-0, 1-0
*Rapid Vienna v PAOK Saloniki (2-2)	0-0, 2-2
Zurich v Wrexham (2-3)	1-1, 1-2
Sporting Lisbon v Hibernian (3-7)	2-1, 1-6
Rapid Bucharest v Landskrona (3-1)	3-0, 0-1
Pezoporikos v Cork Hibs (2-6)	1-2, 1-4
Fremad Amager v Besa*(1-1)	1-1, 0-0
Carl Zeiss Jena v Mikkeli (8-4)	6-1, 2-3
Red Boys Differdingen v AC Milan (1-7)	1-4, 0-3

Second Round
Rapid Vienna v Rapid Bucharest (2-4)	1-1, 1-3
Carl Zeiss Jena v Leeds U (0-2)	0-0, 0-2
Wrexham v Hajduk Split*(3-3)	3-1, 0-2
Cork Hibs v Schalke 04 (0-3)	0-0, 0-3
Atlético Madrid v Spartak Moscow*(5-5)	3-4, 2-1
Hibernian v Besa (8-2)	7-1, 1-1
Ferencvaros v Sparta Prague (3-4)	2-0, 1-4
Legia Warsaw v AC Milan (2-3)	1-1, 1-2

Quarter-Final
Leeds U v Rapid Bucharest (8-1)	5-0, 3-1
Hibernian v Hajduk Split (4-5)	4-2, 0-3
Schalke 04 v Sparta Prague (2-4)	2-1, 0-3
Spartak Moscow v AC Milan (1-2)	0-1, 1-1

Semi-Finals
Leeds U v Hajduk Split (1-0)	1-0, 0-0
AC Milan v Sparta Prague (2-0)	1-0, 1-0

*won on away-goals rule.

Final 1972-73: AC Milan 1, Leeds U 0
(in Salonika, May 16, 1973, 45,000)

AC Milan: Vecchi; Sabadini, Zigno Anquilletti, Turone, Rosato (Dolci), Sogliano, Benetti, Bigon, Rivera, Chiarugi.

Leeds U: Harvey; Reaney, Cherry, Bates, Madeley, Hunter, Lorimer, Jordan, Jones, Gray E, Yorath (McQueen).

Scorer: Chiarugi.

EUROPEAN CUP-WINNERS' CUP 1973-74

First Round
Legia Warsaw v PAOK Salonika (1-2)	1-1, 0-1
Anderlecht v Zurich*(3-3)	3-2, 0-1
Vestmannajar v Bor Moenchengladbach (1-16)	0-7, 1-9
Vasas Budapest v Sunderland (0-3)	0-2, 0-1
Ankaragucu v Rangers (0-6)	0-2, 0-4
AC Milan v Dinamo Zagreb (4-1)	3-1, 1-0
Torpedo Moscow v Atlètico Bilbao (0-2)	0-0, 0-2
Gzira v Brann Bergen (0-9)	0-2, 0-7
NAC v Magdeburg (0-2)	0-0, 0-2
Randers Freja v Rapid Vienna (1-2)	0-0, 1-2
Chimia Ramnicu v Glentoran (2-4)	2-2, 0-2
Larnaca v Malmo (0-11)	0-0, 0-11
Fola Esch v Beroe Stara (1-11)	0-7, 1-4
Banik Ostrava v Cork Hibs (3-1)	1-0, 2-1
Reipas Lahti v Lyon (0-2)	0-0, 0-2
Cardiff C v Sporting Lisbon (1-2)	0-0, 1-2

Second leg
Lyon v PAOK Salonika (3-7)	3-3, 0-4

Bor Moenchengladbach v Rangers (5-3)	3-0, 2-3
Brann Bergen v Glentoran (2-4)	1-1, 1-3
Banik Ostrava v Magdeburg (2-3)	2-0, 0-3
*Zurich v Malmo (1-1)	0-0, 1-1
Beroe Stara v Atlètico Bilbao (3-1)	3-0, 0-1
Sunderland v Sporting Lisbon (2-3)	2-1, 0-2
AC Milan v Rapid Vienna (2-0)	0-0, 2-0

Quarter-finals
Magdeburg v Beroe Stara (3-1)	2-0, 1-1
Glentoran v Bor Moenchengladbach (0-7)	0-2, 0-5
Sporting Lisbon v Zurich (4-1)	3-0, 1-1
AC Milan v PAOK Salonika (5-2)	3-0, 2-2

Semi-finals
AC Milan v Bor Moenchengladbach (2-1)	2-0, 0-1
Sporting Lisbon v Magdeburg (2-3)	1-1, 1-2

*won on away goals rule

Final 1973-74: FC Magdeburg 2, AC Milan 0
(at Rotterdam, May 8, 1974, 5000)

FC Magdeburg: Schultz; Enge, Zapf, Gaube, Abraham, Tyll, Pommerenke, Seguin, Raugust, Sparwasser, Hoffman.

AC Milan: Pizzaballa; Anquilletti, Sabadini, Lanzi, Schnellinger, Maldera, Tresoldi, Benetti, Bigon, Rivera, Bergamaschi.

Scorers: Lanzi og, Seguin.

EUROPEAN CUP-WINNERS' CUP 1974-75

First Round, First Leg
Liverpool 11 (*Lindsay pen, Boersma 2, Thompson 2, Heighway, Cormack, Hughes, Callaghan, Smith, Kennedy*)
Stromsgodset 0
Dundee United 3 (*Narey, Copland, Gardener*)
Jiul Petrosani 0
Ferencvaros 2 (*Nyilasi, Szabo*)
Cardiff City 0
Bursaspor 4 (*Turan 2, Ali, Sinan pen*)
Finn Harps 2 (*Ferry, Bradley*)
Sliema Wanderers 2 (*Camilleri 2*)
Reipas Lahti 0
Dynamo Kiev 1 (*Blokhin*)
CSKA Sofia 0
Malmo 1 (*Cervin*)
Sion 0
Gwardia Warsaw 2 (*Sroka, Kraska*)
Bologna 1 (*Savoldi*)
Slavia Prague 1 (*Herda*)
Carl Zeiss Jena 0
Waregem 2 (*Delesie 2*)
Austria/WAC 1 (*Pirkner*)
PAOK Salonika 1 (*Terzanides*)
Red Star Belgrade 0
PSV Eindhoven 10 (*Van der Kuylen 3, Lubse 3, Kemper, Deykers, Edstrom, Van Kraay*)
Ards 0
Fram Reykjavik 0
Real Madrid 2 (*Roberto Martinez 2*)
Benfica 4 (*Jordao 2, Humberto, Nene*)
Vanlose 0
Eintracht Frankfurt 3 (*Holzenbein 2, Rohrbach*)
Monaco 0

First Round, Second Leg
Stromsgodset 0
Liverpool 1 (*Kennedy*)
Jiul Petrosani 2 (*Rosnai, Tonca*)
Dundee United 0
Cardiff City 1 (*Dwyer*)
Ferencvaros 4 (*Takacs, Szabo, Pusztai, Mate*)
Finn Harps 0
Bursaspor 0
Reipas Lahti 4 (*Salonen, Lehtanen, Sandberg 2*)
Sliema Wanderers 1 (*Aquilina*)
CSKA Sofia 0
Dynamo Kiev 1 (*Blokhin*)
Sion 1 (*Suiza*)
Malmo 0
Bologna 2 (*Savoldi 2*)
Gwardia Warsaw 1 (*Terlecki*)
Carl Zeiss Jena 1 (*Stein*)
Slavia Prague 0
Austria/WAC 4 (*Pirkner 2, Weigel, Fiala*)
Waregem 1 (*Koudijzer*)
Red Star Belgrade 2 (*V. Petrovic, Savic*)
PAOK Salonika 0
Ards 1 (*Guy*)
PSV Eindhoven 4 (*Van der Kuylen, Edstrom, Dahlqvist 2*)
Real Madrid 6 (*Pirri 2, Santillana, Netzer, Macanas, Aguilar*)
Fram Reykjavik 0
Vanlose 1 (*Petersen*)
Benfica 4 (*Nene, Jordao 2, Barros*)
Monaco 2 (*Onnis, Petit*)
Eintracht Frankfurt 2 (*Beverungen, Nickel*)
Avenir Beggen had a walkover when Paralimni withdrew.

Second Round, First Leg
Liverpool 1 (*Keegan*)
Ferencvaros 1 (*Mate*)
Dundee United 0
Bursaspor 0
Real Madrid 3 (*Krieger og, Santillana, Roberto Martinez*)
Austria/WAC 0
Gwardia Warsaw 1 (*Malkiewicz*)
PSV Eindhoven 5 (*Willy Van der Kerkhof, Kialak og, Deykers, Lubse, Van der Kuylen*)
Carl Zeiss Jena 1 (*Vogel*)
Benfica 1 (*Nene*)
Red Star Belgrade 6 (*Sestic 3, Filipovic 2, Rajkovic*)
Avenir Beggen 1 (*Sinner*)
Malmo 3 (*Larsson 2, Sjoberg*)
Reipas Lahti 1 (*Kautonen*)
Eintracht Frankfurt 2 (*Nickel, Koerbel*)
Dynamo Kiev 3 (*Kolotov, Blokhin, Muntian*)

Second Round, Second Leg
Ferencvaros 0
Liverpool 0
Bursapor 1 (*Vahit*)
Dundee United 0
Austria/WAC 2 (*Pirkner, Fiala*)
Real Madrid 2 (*Roberto Martinez, Netzer*)
PSV Eindhoven 3 (*Van der Kuylen 2, pen, Lubse*)
Gwardia Warsaw 0
Benfica 0
Carl Zeis sJena 0
Avenir Beggen 1 (*Dresch*)
Red Star Belgrade 5 (*Rajkovic 2, Filipovic, Sestic, Savic*)
Reipas Lahti 0
Malmo 0
Dynamo Kiev 2 (*Onischenko 2*)
Eintracht Frankfurt 1 (*Rohrbach*)

Quarter Finals, First Leg
Real Madrid (1) 2 (*Santillana, Netzer pen*)
Red Star Belgrade (0) 0
PSV Eindhoven (0) 0
Benfica (0) 0
Malmo (0) 1 (*Sjoberg*)
Ferencvaros (1) 3 (*Nyilasi, Magyar, Mate*)
Bursaspor (0) 0
Dynamo Kiev (1) 1 (*Onischenko*)

Quarter-Finals, Second Leg
Benfica (1) 1 (*Humberto*)
PSV Eindhoven (1) 2 (*Willy Van der Kerkhof, Quaars*)
Ferencvaros (0) 1 (*Mate*)
Malmo (1) 1 (*Sjoberg*)
Dynamo Kiev (0) 2 (*Kolotov pen, Muntian*)
Bursaspor (0) 0
Red Star Belgrade (1) 2 (*Dzajic, O. Petrovic pen*)
Real Madrid (0) 0 (*Red Star won on penalties*)

Semi-Finals, First Leg
Ferencvaros (1) 2 (*Branikovits, Magyar*)
Red Star Belgrade (0) 1 (*Savic*)
Dynamo Kiev (2) 3 (*Kolotov, Onischenko, Blokhin*)
PSV Eindhoven (0) 0

Semi-Finals, Second Leg
Red Star Belgrade (0) 2 (*Keri, Filipovic*)
Ferencvaros (1) 2 (*Pusztai, Megyesi pen*)
PSV Eindhoven (1) 2 (*Edstrom 2*)
Dynamo Kiev (0) 1 (*Burjak*)

Final 1974-75: Dynamo Kiev 3, Ferencvaros 0
(at Basel, May 14 1975, 13,000)

Dynamo Kiev: Rudakov; Fomenko, Troshkin, Reshko, Matvienko, Muntian, Konkov, Burjak, Kolotov, Onischenko, Blokhin.
Ferencvaros: Geczi; Pataki, Martos, Rab, Megyesi, Nyilasi (Onhaus), Juhas z, Mucha, Szabo, Mate, Magyar.
Scorers: Dynamo Kiev, Onischenko (2), Blokhin.

EUROPEAN CUP-WINNERS' CUP 1975-76

First Round, First Leg
Ararat Erevan 9 (*Markarov 5, 1 pen, Oganiesian 2, Petrosian S, Bondarenko*)
Anorthosis 0
Basel 1 (*Schoenberger*)
Atletico Madrid 2 (*Garate, Ayala*)
Besiktas 0
Fiorentina 3 (*Caso 2, Casarsa*)
Borac Banja Luka 9 (*Cetina 3, Ibrahimbegovic 5, Jurkovic*)
US Rumelange 0
Eintracht Frankfurt 5 (*Korbel, Beverungen, Holzenbein, Nickel 2*)
Coleraine 1 (*Cochrane*)
Haladas Szombathely 7 (*Fedor 2, Horath 2, Frakas, og Halmosi*)
Valetta 0
Home Farm 1 (*Brophy*)
Lens 1 (*Hopquin*)
Lahden Reipas 2 (*Lindholm, Tupasela*)
West Ham U 2 (*Brooking, Bonds*)
Panathinaikos 0
Sachsenring Zwickau 0
Rapid Bucharest 1 (*Thissen og*)
Anderlecht 0
Spartak Trnava 0
Boavista 0
Skeid Oslo 1 (*B Skjoensberg*)
Stal Rzeszow 4 (*Kozierski 2, Curylo, Krawczyk*)
Sturm Graz 3 (*Stendal 2 pens, Kulmer*)
Slavia Sofia 1 (*Kostov*)
Valur Reykjavik 0
Celtic 2 (*Dalglish, McDonald*)
Vejle 0
Den Haag 2 (*Jol, Van Leeuwen*)
Wrexham 2 (*Griffiths, Davis*)
Djurgaardens 1 (*Krantz*)

First Round, Second Leg
Anderlecht 2 (*Van Binst, Rensenbrink*)
Rapid Bucharest 0
Anorthosis 1 (*Fivos pen*)
Ararat Erevan 1 (*Bondarenko*)
Atletico Madrid 1 (*Becerra*)
Basel 1 (*Demarmels*)
Boavista 3 (*Mane, Celse, Salvador*)
Spartak Trnava 0
Celtic 7 (*Edvaldsson, Dalglish, McCluskey pen, Hood 2, Deans, Callaghan*)
Valur 0
Den Haag 2 (*Perazic, Mansveld*)
Vejle 0
Djurgaarden 1 (*Lovfors*)
Wrexham 1 (*Whittle*)
Lens 6 (*Northeaux, Mujica pen, Kaiser 3, Llorens*)
Home Farm 0
Sachsenring Zwickau 2 (*Schykowski, Dietzsch pen*)
Panathinaikos 0
Slavia Sofia 1 (*Kostov*)
Sturm Graz 0
West Ham 3 (*Robson 2, Jennings*)
Reipas Lahden 0
US Rumelange 1 (*Rohmann*)
Borac Banja Luka 5 (*Smilevski, Reso, Kovahevic, Vidacek, Marjonaovic*)
Coleraine 2 (*McCurdy, Cochrane*)
Eintracht Frankfurt 6 (*Grabowski 3, Nickel, Lorenz, Holzenbein*)
Valetta 1 (*Giglio*)
Haladas Szombathely 1 (*Karaci*)
Fiorentina 3 (*Caso 2, Casarsa*)
Besiktas 0
Stal Rzeszow 4 (*Kozierski, Miler, Krawczyk Napieracz*)
Skeid Oslo 0

Second Round, First Leg
Anderlecht 3 (*Rensenbrink 2, Coeck*)
Borac Banja Luka 0
Ararat Erevan 1 (*Petrosian S*)
West Ham U 1 (*Taylor A*)
Atletico Madrid 1 (*Bacerra*)
Eintracht Frankfurt 2 (*Holzenbein 2*)
Boavista 0
Celtic 0
Den Haag 3 (*Schoenmaker, Van Vliet, Van Leeawen*)
Lens 2 (*Zuraszek, Janovic*)
Fiorentina 1 (*Speggiorin*)
Sachsenring Zwickau 0
Sturm Graz 2 (*Stendal, Stenier pen*)
Haladas Szombathely 0
Wrexham 2 (*Ashcroft 2*)
Stal Rzeszow 0

Second Round, Second Leg
Borac Banja Luka 1 (*Ibrahimbegovic*)
Anderlecht 0
Celtic 3 (*Dalglish, Edvaldsson, Deans*)
Boavista 0 (*Mane*)
Eintracht Frankfurt 1 (*Reichel*)
Atletico Madrid 0
Haladas Szombathely 1 (*Horvath*)
Sturm Grax 1 (*Jurtin*)
Lens 1 (*Mujica pen*)
Den Haag 3 (*Shoenmaker 2, Van Leeuwen*)
Sachsenring Zwickau 1 (*Schykowski, J*)
Fiorentina 0
Stal Rzeszow 1 (*Kozierski*)
Wrexham 1 (*Sutton*)
West Ham U 3 (*Paddon, Robson, Taylor A*)
Ararat Erevan 1 (*Petrosian, N*)

Quarter-Finals, First Leg
Anderlecht 1 (*Van Binst*)
Wrexham 0
Celtic 1 (*Dalglish*)
Sachsenring Zwickau 1 (*Blank*)
Den Haag 4 (*Mansveld 3, 2 pens, Schoenmaker*)
West Ham U 2 (*Jennings 2*)
Sturm Graz 0
Eintracht Frankfurt 2 (*Holzenbein, Wenzel*)

Quarter-finals, Second Leg
Eintracht Frankfurt 1 (*Holzenbein*)
Sturm Graz 0
Sachsenring Zwickau 1 (*Blank*)
Celtic 0
West Ham U 3 (*Taylor A, Lampard, Bonds pen*)
Den Haag 1 (*Schoenmaker*)
Wrexham 1 (*Lee*)
Anderlecht 1 (*Rensenbrink*)

Semi-finals, First Leg
Eintracht Frankfurt 2 (*Neuberger, Kraus*)
West Ham U 1 (*Paddon*)
Sachsenring Zwickau 0
Anderlecht 3 (*Van der Elst 2, Rensenbrink*)

Semi-fiinals, Second Leg
Anderlecht 2 (*Rensenbrink, Van der Elst*)
Sachsenring Zwickau 0
West Ham U 3 (*Brooking 2, Robson*)
Eintracht Frankfurt 1 (*Beverungen*)

Final 1975-76: **Anderlecht 4 West Ham U 2**
(at Heysel Stadium, Brussels, May 5 1976, 58,000)

Anderlecht: Ruiter; Lomme, Broos, Van Binst, Thissen, Dockx, Coeck (Vercauteren), Van der Elst, Ressel, Haan, Rensenbrink.
West Ham U: Day; Coleman, Bonds, Taylor (T), Lampard (Taylor A), McDowell, Brooking, Paddon, Holland, Jennings, Robson.
Scorers: Anderlecht: Rensenbrink 2, 1 pen, Van der Elst 2. West Ham U: Holland, Robson.

EUROPEAN CUP-WINNERS' CUP 1976-77

Preliminary Round, First Leg
Cardiff City 1 (*Evans*)
Servette 0
Preliminary Round, Second Leg
Servette 2 (*Bizzini, Pfister*)
Cardiff City 1 (*Showers*)
First Round, First Leg
Lierse 1 (*Ceulemans*)
Hajduk Split 0
MTK Budapest 3 (*Kunszt, Kovacs, Borso*)
Sparta Prague 1 (*Cermak*)
AIK Stockholm 1 (*Wallgren*)
Galatasaray 2 (*Gokmen, Nehmet*)
Anderlecht 2 (*Van der Elst, Rensenbrink*)
Roda JC 1 (*Toonstra*)
Bodo Glimt 0
Napoli 2 (*Speggiorin 2*)
Bohemians 2 (*Ryan, B Hansen og*)
Esbjerg 1 (*H. Nielsen*)
Cardiff City 1 (*Alston*)
Dynamo Tbilisi 0
Carrick Rangers 3 (*Prenter 2, Connor*)
Aris Bonnevoie 1 (*Pissinger*)
Hamburg 3 (*Zaczyk, Reimann, Hidien*)
Keflavik 0
Iraklis 0
Apoel Nicosia 0
Lokomotive Leipzig 2 (*Sekora, Fritsche*)
Hearts 0
Southampton 4 (*Waldron, Channon 2, 1 pen, Osgood*)
Marseille 0
Levski Spartak 12 (*Yordanov 2, Milanov 6, Panov 2, Spassov 2*)
Reipas Lahden 2 (*Sandberg, Tupasela*)
Floriana 1 (*Vassallo*)
Slask Wroclaw 4 (*Gavslovski 2, Kwiatkowski, Farrugia o.g.*)
Rapid Vienna 1 (*Krankl*)
Atletico Madrid 2 (*Cano, Ayala*)
CSU Galati 2 (*Simionescu, Holzer*)
Boavista 3 (*Mane 2, Salvador*)
First Round, Second Leg
Apoel Nicosia 2 (*Marcou 2*)
Iraklis 0
Atletico Madrid 1 (*Leivinha*)
Rapid Vienna 1 (*Krejcirik*)
Boavista 2 (*Mane 2*)
CSU Galati 0
Esbjerg 0
Bohemians 1 (*Mitten*)
Galatasaray 1 (*Gokmen*)
AIK Stockholm 1 (*Wallgren*)
Hajduk Split 3 (*Zungul 2, Jerkovic*)
Lierse 0
Hearts 5 (*Kay, Gibson 2, Brown, Busby*)
Lokomotive Leipzig 1 (*Fritsche*)
Keflavik 1 (*S. Johansson*)
Hamburg 1 (*Hidien*)
Reipas Lahden 1 (*Sandberg*)
Levski Spartak 7 (*Panov, Milanov 4, 2 pens, Spassov, Krastanov*)
Marseille 2 (*Nogues, Emon*)
Southampton 1 (*Peach*)
Napoli 1 (*Massa*)
Bodo Glimt 0
Roda JC 2 (*Vermeulen, Van der Lem pen.*)
Anderlecht 3 (*Rensenbrink, Van der Elst 2*)
Slask Wroclaw 2 (*Pawlowski, Ehrlich*)
Floriana 0
Sparta Prague 1 (*Urban*)
MTK Budapest 1 (*Kunszt*)
Tbilisi Dynamo 3 (*Gutsaev, Kipiani, Kandeladze pen.*)
Cardiff City 0
Aris Bonnevoie 2 (*Werner, Langers*)
Carrick Rangers 1 (*Irwin*)
Second Round, First Leg
Anderlecht 5 (*Coeck, Vercauteren, Rensenbrink 2, 1 pen.*)
Galatasaray 1 (*Ozdewak*)
Apoel Nicosia 1 (*Leonidas*)
Napoli 1 (*Savoldi pen.*)
Atletico Madrid 1 (*Cano*)
Hajduk Split 0
Boavista 3 (*Celso 2, Mane*)
Levski Spartak 1 (*Milanov*)
Carrick Rangers 1 (*Irwin, Prenter*)
Southampton 5 (*Channon 2, Stokes, McCalliog, Osgood*)
Hamburg 4 (*Bjornmose, Eigl, Reimann, Gallacher o.g.*)
Hearts 2 (*Busby, Park*)
Dynamo Tbilisi 1 (*Macheidze*)
MTK Bupadest 4 (*Shyloshi, Takach 2, Kish*)
Slask Wroclaw 3 (*Kwiatkowski, Sybis 2*)
Bohemians 0
Second Round, Second Leg
Bohemians 0
Slask Wroclaw 1 (*Pawlowski*)
Galatasaray 1 (*Gokmen*)
Anderlecht 5 (*Rensenbrink 2, Haan, Ressel, Coeck*)
Hearts 1 (*Gibson*)
Hamburg 4 (*Eigl 2, Magath 2*)
Levski Spartak 2 (*Panov, Milanov*)
Boavista 0
MTK Budapest 1 (*Koritar*)
Dynamo Tbilisi 0
Southampton 4 (*Williams, Hayes 2, Stokes*)
Carrick Rangers 1 (*Reid*)
Napoli 2 (*Speggiorin, Massa*)
Apoel Nicosia 0
Hajduk Split 1 (*Zungul*)
Atletico Madrid 2 (*Ayala, Leal*)
Quarter-finals, First Leg
Anderlecht 2 (*Resse l, Rensenbrink*)
Southampton 0
Levski Spartak 2 (*Tsvetkov, Milanov*)
Atletico Madrid 1 (*Ayala*)
MTK Budapest 1 (*Borso*)
Hamburg 1 (*Volkert*)
Slask Wroclaw 0
Napoli 0
Quarter-finals, Second Leg
Atletico Madrid 2 (*Ayala 2 pens*)
Levski Spartak 0
Hamburg 4 (*Reimann 2, Kaltz pen, Zaczyk*)
MTK Budapest 1 (*Siklosi*)
Napoli 2 (*Massa, Chiarugi*)
Slask Wroclaw 0
Southampton 2 (*Peach pen, MacDougall*)
Anderlecht 1 (*Van der Elst*)
Semi-finals, First Leg
Napoli 1 (*Bruscolotti*)
Anderlecht 0
Atletico Madrid 3 (*Cano 2, Leal*)
Hamburg 1 (*Magath*)
Semi-finals, Second Leg
Hamburg 3 (*Capon og, Reimann, Keller*)
Atletico Madrid 0
Anderlecht 2 (*Thissen, Van der Elst*)
Napoli 0

Final 1976-77: Hamburg (0) 2 Anderlecht (0) 0
(in Amsterdam, May 11 1977, 65,000)

Hamburg: Kargus; Kaltz, Ripp, Nogly, Hidien, Steffenhagen, Keller, Reimann, Memering, Magath, Volkert.
Anderlecht: Ruiter; Van Binst, Vanden Daele, Broos, Thissen, Van der Elst, Coeck, Haan, Dockx (Van Poucke), Ressel, Rensenbrink.
Scorers: Hamburg: Volkert pen, Magath.

EUROPEAN CUP-WINNERS' CUP 1977-78

Preliminary Round, First Leg
Glasgow Rangers 1 (*Greig*)
Young Boys 0
Preliminary Round, Second Leg
Young Boys 2 (*Jackson og, Leuzinger*)
Glasgow Rangers 2 (*Johnstone, Smith*)
First Round, First Leg
Lokomotiv Sofia 1 (*Kolev*)
Anderlecht 6 (*Van der Elst 4, 1 pen, Nielsen, Van Poucke*)
Besiktas 2 (*Zeferiya Burth, Paunovic*)
Diosgyor 0
Betis 2 (*Garcia Soriano, Eulate*)
AC Milan 0
Brann Bergen 1 (*Aase*)
IA Akranes 0
Cardiff 0
Austria/WAC 0
Coleraine 1 (*Tweed*)
Lokomotiv Leipzig 4 (*Eichhorn 1, Kuhn, Lowe 2*)
Dundalk 1 (*Flanagan*)
Hajduk Split 0
Hamburg 8 (*Keller, 4 Volkert pen, Buljan, Steffenhagen, Reimann*)
Lahden Reipas 1 (*Riotto*)
FC Cologne 2 (*Lohr, Muller*)
Porto 2 (*Gabriel, Octavio*)
Lokomotiv Kosice 0
Oster Vaxjo 0
PAOK Salonika 2 (*Pelios, Anastasiadis*)
Zaglebie Sosnowiec 0
Progres Niedercorn 0
Vejle 1 (*Steen Tychosen*)
Glasgow Rangers 0
Twente 0
St Etienne 1 (*Synaeghel*)
Manchester United 1 (*Hill*)
Olympiakos Nicosia 1 (*Aristidou*)
Uni. Craiova 6 (*Balaci 2, Girtsu, Marcu, Crisan, Irinescu*)
Valletta 0
Moscow Dynamo 2 (*Kazachenok, Maximenkov*)
First Round, Second Leg
IA Akranes 0
Brann Bergen 4 (*Aase 2, Dahlhaug, Tronstad*)
Anderlecht 2 (*Van der Elst, Bouvy*)
Lokomotiv Sofia 0
Austria/WAC 1 (*Baumeister*)
Cardiff 0
Diosgyor 5 (*Fuko, Olah 2, 1 pen, Fekete 2*)
Besiktas 0
Hajduk Split 4 (*Vujovic, McManus og, Rukljac, McConville og*)
Dundalk 0
Lahden Reipas 2 (*Riotto 2*)
Hamburg 5 (*Volkert pen, Keegan, Magath, Keller, Steffenhagen*)
Lokomotiv Leipzig 2 (*Altmann, Fritsche pen*)
Coleraine 2 (*Guy 2*)
AC Milan 2 (*Tosetto, Capello*)
Betis 1 (*Lopez*)
Oster Vaxjo 2 (*Bild, Evesson*)
Lokomotiv Kosice 2 (*Jozsa, Dobrovic*)
Porto 1 (*Murca*)
FC Cologne 0
Twente 3 (*Gritter, Arnold Muhren, Van der Vall*)
Glasgow Rangers 0
Uni. Craiova 2 (*Marcu, Cirtu*)
Olympiakos Nicosia 0
Vejle 9 (*Sorensen, Ostergaard 2, Eg, Norgaard 3, Schacke, Tychosen*)
Progres Niedercorn 0
Zaglebie Sosnowiec 0
PAOK Salonika 2 (*Kermanidis, Damanikis*)
Moscow Dynamo 5 (*Kolyesov 3, Jakubik, Kazachenkov*)
Valletta 0
Manchester United 2 (*Pearson, Coppell*)
St Etienne 0
Second Round, First Leg
Austria/WAC 0
Lokomotiv Kosice 0
Diosgyor 2 (*Tatar, Varadi*)
Hajduk Split 1 (*Muzinic*)
Hamburg 1 (*Keller*)
Anderlecht 2 (*Coeck, Rensenbrink*)
Lokomotiv Leipzig 1 (*Grobner*)
Betis 1 (*Lopez*)
Moscow Dynamo 2 (*Kazachenov, Minaev*)
Uni. Craiova 0
Twente 2 (*Gritter 2*)
Brann Bergen 0
Vejle 3 (*Eg, Jaquet, Ostergaard*)
PAOK Salonika 0
Porto 4 (*Duda 3, Oliveira*)
Manchester United 0
Second Round, Second Leg
Anderlecht 1 (*Van der Elst*)
Hamburg 1 (*Keegan*)
Betis 2 (*Garcia Soriano 2*)
Lokomotiv Leipzig 1 (*Liebers*)
Brann Bergen 1 (*Tronstad*)
Twente 2 (*Gritter, Thoresen*)
Uni. Craiova 2 (*Cirtu, Beideanu*)
Moscow Dynamo 0 *Dynamo won 3-0 on penalties*
Hajduk Split 2 (*Vujovic, Rukljac pen*)
Diosgyor 1 (*Tatar*) *Hajduk Split won 4-3 on penalties*
Lokomotiv Kosice 1 (*Farkas pen*)
Austria/WAC 1 (*Morales*)
Manchester United 5 (*Coppell 2, Murca 2 ogs, Nicholl*)
Porto 2 (*Seninho 2*)
PAOK Salonika 2 (*Orfanos, Kermanides*)
Vejle 1 (*Jaquet*)
Quarter-Finals, First Leg
Vejle 0
Twente 3 (*Arnold Muhren, Gritter, Thijssen*)
Austria/WAC 1 (*Parits*)
Hajduk Split 1 (*Surjak*)
Betis 0
Moscow Dynamo 0
Porto 1 (*Gomes*)
Anderlecht 0
Quarter-Finals, Second Leg
Hajduk Split 1 (*Cop*)
Austria/WAC 1 (*Daxbacher*) (*Austria/WAC won 3-0 on penalties*)
Moscow Dynamo 3 (*Gershkovich, Kazachenov, Maximenkov*)
Betis 0
Anderlecht 3 (*Rensenbrink pen, Nielsen, Vercauteren*)
Porto 0
Twente 4 (*Thijssen, Overweg, Gritter, Van der Vall*)
Vejle 0
Semi-finals, first leg
Moscow Dynamo 2 (*Tseretli, Gershkovich*)
Austria/WAC 1 (*Baumeister*)
Twente 0
Anderlecht 1 (*Nielsen*)
Semi-finals, second leg
Anderlecht 2 (*Haan, Rensenbrink pen*)
Twente 0
Austria/WAC 2 (*Pirkner pen, Morales*)
Moscow Dynamo 1 (*Yakubik*)

Final 1977-78: Anderlecht (3) 4 Austria/WAC (0) 0
(in Paris, May 3 1978, 48,679)
Anderlecht: De Bree; Van Binst, Broos, Dusbaba, Thissen, Van der Elst, Hann, Nielsen, Coeck, Vercauteren (Dockx), Rensenbrink.
Austria/WAC: Baumgartner; Robert Sara, Josef Sara, Obermayer, Baumeister, Prohaska, Daxbacher (Martinez), Gasselich, Morales (Drazen), Pirkner, Parits.
Scorers: Anderlecht: Rensenbrink 2, Van Binst 2.

FAIRS & UEFA CUP HISTORY

FAIRS CUP 1955–58

GROUP A
Barcelona 6, Copenhagen 2
Copenhagen 1, Barcelona 1
Vienna withdrew

	P	W	D	L	F	A	Pts
Barcelona	2	1	1	0	7	3	3
Copenhagen	2	0	1	1	3	7	1

GROUP B
Inter-Milan 0, Birmingham C 0
Zagreb 0, Birmingham C 1
Zagreb 0, Inter-Milan 1
Birmingham C 3, Zagreb 0
Inter-Milan 4, Zagreb 0
Birmingham C 2, Inter-Milan 1

	P	W	D	L	F	A	Pts
Birmingham C	4	3	1	0	6	1	7
Inter-Milan	4	2	1	1	6	2	5
Zagreb	4	0	0	4	0	9	0

GROUP C
Leipzig 6, Lausanne 3
Lausanne 7, Leipzig 3
Cologne withdrew

	P	W	D	L	F	A	Pts
Lausanne	2	1	0	1	10	9	2
Leipzig	2	1	0	1	9	10	2

GROUP D
Basle 0, London 5
London 3, Frankfurt 2
London 1, Basle 0
Frankfurt 5, Basle 1
Frankfurt 1, London 0
Basle 6, Frankfurt 2

	P	W	D	L	F	A	Pts
London	4	3	0	1	9	3	6
Frankfurt	4	2	0	2	10	10	4
Basle	4	1	0	3	7	13	2

Semi-Final
Birmingham C v Barcelona (5-6)   4-3, 0-1, 1-2
Lausanne v London (2-3)   2-1, 0-2

Final
London v Barcelona (2-8)   2-2, 0-6

FAIRS CUP 1958–60

First Round
Basle v Barcelona (3-7)   1-2, 2-5
Inter-Milan v Lyon (8-1)   7-0, 1-1
Belgrade v Lausanne (11-4)   6-1, 5-3
Frem Copenhagen v Chelsea (2-7)   1-3, 1-4
Union St Gilloise v Leipzig (6-1)   6-0, 0-1
Hanover 96 v AS Roma (2-4)   1-3, 1-1
Zagreb v Ujpest Dozsa (4-3)   4-2, 0-1
Cologne v Birmingham C (2-4)   2-2, 0-2

Quarter-Finals
Barcelona v Inter-Milan (8-2)   4-0, 4-2
Chelsea v Belgrade (2-4)   1-0, 1-4
Union St Gilloise v AS Roma (3-1)   2-0, 1-1
Birmingham C v Zagreb (4-3)   1-0, 3-3

Semi-Finals
Belgrade v Barcelona (2-4)   1-1, 1-3
Union St Gilloise v Birmingham C (4-8)   2-4, 2-4

Final:
Birmingham C v Barcelona (1-4)   0-0, 1-4

FAIRS CUP 1960–61

First Round
Union St Gilloise v AS Roma (1-4)   0-0, 1-4
Lyon v Cologne (3-4)   1-3, 2-1
*Lausanne v Hibernian (0-2)   0-2
Zagreb v Barcelona (4-5)   1-1, 3-4
Leipzig v Belgrade (6-8)   5-2, 1-4, 0-2
Inter-Milan v Hanover 96 (14-3)   8-2, 6-1
Copenhagen v Basle (11-4)   8-1, 3-3
Birmingham C v Ujpest Dozsa (5-3)   3-2, 2-1

Quarter-Finals
Cologne v AS Roma (3-6)   0-2, 2-0, 1-4
Barcelona v Hibernian (6-7)   4-4, 2-3
Inter-Milan v Belgrade (5-1)   5-0, 0-1
Copenhagen v Birmingham C (4-9)   4-4, 0-5

Semi-Finals
Hibernian v AS Roma (5-11)   2-2, 3-3, 0-6
Inter-Milan v Birmingham C (2-4)   1-2, 1-2

Final
Birmingham C v AS Roma (2-4)   2-2, 0-2

*Lausanne withdrew.

FAIRS CUP 1961-62

First Round

Valencia v Nottingham F (7-1)	2-0, 5-1
Lausanne	bye
Cologne v Inter-Milan (7-9)	4-2, 0-2, 3-5
Union St Gilloise v Hearts (1-5)	1-3, 0-2
Spartak Brno v Leipzig (3-6)	2-2, 1-4
Strasbourg v MTK Budapest (3-13)	1-3, 2-10
AC Milan v Novisad (0-2)	0-0, 0-2
Iraklis Salonika	bye
Basle v Red Star Belgrade (2-5)	1-1, 1-4
Hibernian v Belenenses (6-4)	3-3, 3-1
Hanover 96 v Espanol (0-3)	0-1, 0-2
Birmingham C	bye
Lyon v Sheffield W (6-7)	4-2, 2-5
AS Roma	bye
Copenhagen v Dynamo Zagreb (4-9)	2-7, 2-2
West Berlin v Barcelona (1-3)	1-0, 0-3
Hearts v Inter-Milan (0-5)	0-1, 0-4
MTK Budapest v Leipzig (5-3)	3-0, 0-3, 2-0
Iraklis Salonika v Novisad (3-10)	2-1, 1-9
Red Star Belgrade v Hibernian (5-0)	4-0, 1-0
Espanol v Birmingham C (5-3)	5-2, 0-1
Sheffield W v AS Roma (4-1)	4-0, 0-1
Barcelona v Dynamo Zagreb (7-3)	5-1, 2-2

Second Round

Lausanne v Valencia (3-4)	3-4*

*Second leg not played.

Quarter-Finals

Valencia v Inter-Milan (5-3)	2-0, 3-3
Novisad v MTK Budapest (2-6)	1-4, 1-2
Espanol v Red Star Belgrade (2-6)	2-1, 0-5
Sheffield W v Barcelona (3-4)	3-2, 0-2

Semi-Finals

Valencia v MTK Budapest (10-3)	3-0, 7-3
Red Star Belgrade v Barcelona (1-6)	0-2, 1-4

Final

Valencia v Barcelona (7-3)	6-2, 1-1

FAIRS CUP 1962-63

First Round

Valencia v Celtic (6-4)	4-2, 2-2
Everton v Dunfermline Ath (1-2)	1-0, 0-2
Hibernian v Copenhagen (7-2)	4-0, 3-2
DOS Utrecht v Tasmania Berlin (5-3)	3-2, 2-1
Altay Izmir v AS Roma (3-13)	2-3, 0-0
Glentoran v Real Zaragoza (2-8)	0-2, 1-6
Rapid Vienna v Red Star Belgrade (1-2)	1-1, 0-1
Barcelona v Belenenses (5-4)	1-1, 1-1, 3-2
Viktoria Cologne v Ferencvaros (5-7)	4-3, 1-4
Sampdoria v Aris Luxembourg (3-0)	1-0, 2-0
Petrolul Ploesti v Spartak Brno (4-3)	4-2, 0-1
Vojvodina v Leipzig (1-2)	1-0, 0-2
Basle v Bayern Munich (0-3)	0-3[1]
Drumcondra v Odense BK 09 (6-5)	4-1, 2-4
Marseille v Union St Gilloise (3-4)	1-0, 2-4
Porto v Dynamo Zagreb (1-2)	1-2, 0-0
Real Zaragoza v AS Roma (3-6)	2-4, 1-2
Red Star Belgrade v Barcelona (4-3)	3-2, 0-1, 1-0
Sampdoria v Ferencvaros (1-6)	1-0, 0-6
Petrolul Ploesti v Leipzig (2-1)	1-0, 0-1, 1-0
Bayern Munich v Drumcondra (6-1)	6-0, 0-1
Dynamo Zagreb v Union St Gilloise (5-4)	2-1, 0-1, 3-2

Second Round

Valencia v Dunfermline Ath (7-6)	4-0, 2-6, 1-0
DOS Utrecht v Hibernian (1-3)	0-1, 1-2

Quarter-Finals

Valencia v Hibernian (6-2)	5-0, 1-2
AS Roma v Red Star Belgrade (3-2)	3-0, 0-2
Ferencvaros v Petrolul Ploesti (2-1)	2-0, 0-1
Bayern Munich v Dynamo Zagreb (1-4)	1-4, 0-0

Semi-Finals

Valencia v AS Roma (3-1)	3-0, 0-1
Ferencvaros v Dynamo Zagreb (1-3)	0-1, 1-2

Final

Dynamo Zagreb v Valencia (1-4)	1-2, 0-2

[1]Second leg not played.

FAIRS CUP 1963-64

First Round

Real Zaragoza v Iraklis Salonika (9-1)	3-0, 6-1
Lausanne v Hearts (9-8)	2-2, 4-4, 3-2
Atletico Madrid v Porto (2-1)	2-1, 0-0
Juventus v OFK Belgrade (4-3)	2-1, 1-2, 1-0
Aris Luxembourg v Liège (0-2)	0-2, 0-0
Staevnet Copenhagen v Arsenal (4-9)	1-7, 3-2
Glentoran v Partick T (1-7)	1-4, 0-3
Spartak Brno v Servette Geneva (7-1)	5-0, 2-1
Cologne v La Gantoise (4-2)	3-1, 1-1
DOS Utrecht v Sheffield W (2-8)	1-4, 1-4
Hertha Berlin v AS Roma (1-5)	1-3, 0-2
Tresnjevka Zagreb v Belenenses (1-4)	0-2, 1-2
Ujpest Dozsa v Locomotiv Leipzig (3-2)	0-0, 3-2
Red Flag Brasov v Locomotiv Plovdiv (2-5)	1-3, 1-2
Rapid Vienna v Racing Club de Paris (4-2)	1-0, 3-2
Shamrock Rovers v Valencia (2-3)	0-1, 2-2
Juventus v Atletico Madrid (3-1)	1-0, 2-1
Arsenal v Liège (2-4)	1-1, 1-3
Partick T v Spartak Brno (3-6)	3-2, 0-4
Cologne v Sheffield W (5-3)	3-2, 2-1
AS Roma v Belenenses (3-1)	2-1, 1-0
Ujpest Dozsa v Locomotiv Plovdiv (3-1)	0-0, 3-1
Rapid Vienna v Valencia (2-3)	0-0, 2-3

Second Round

Lausanne v Real Zaragoza (1-5)	1-2, 0-3

Quarter-Finals

Real Zaragoza v Juventus (3-2)	3-2, 0-0
Liège v Spartak Brno (3-2)	2-0, 0-2, 1-0
AS Roma v Cologne (3-5)	3-1, 0-4
Valencia v Ujpest Dozsa (6-5)	5-2, 1-3

Semi-Finals

Liège v Real Zaragoza (2-4)	1-0, 1-2, 0-2
Valencia v Cologne (4-3)	4-1, 0-2

Final: at Barcelona

Real Zaragoza v Valencia	2-1

FAIRS CUP 1964-65

First Round
Union St Gilloise v Juventus (0-2)	0-1, 0-1
Betis v Stade Francais (1-3)	1-1, 0-2
Goztepe Izmir v Petrolul Ploesti (1-3)	1-2, 0-1
Vojvodina v Lokomotiv Plovdiv (2-4) 1-1,	1-1, 0-2
KB Copenhagen v DOS Utrecht (4-6)	3-4, 1-2
Valencia v Liège (2-4)	1-1, 1-3
Belenenses v Shelbourne (2-3) 1-1,	0-0, 1-2
Servette Geneva v Atletico Madrid (3-8)	2-2, 1-6
Basle v Spora Luxembourg (2-1)	2-0, 0-1
Strasbourg v AC Milan (2-1)	2-0, 0-1
Barcelona v Fiorentina (2-1)	0-1, 2-0
Leixoes v Celtic (1-4)	1-1, 0-3
Borussia Dortmund v Bordeaux (4-3)	4-1, 0-2
Manchester U v Djurgaarden (7-2)	1-1, 6-1
Eintracht Frankfurt v Kilmarnock (4-5)	3-0, 1-5
Valerengen v Everton (4-9)	2-5, 2-4
Atletico Bilbao v OFK Belgrade (4-2)	2-2, 2-0
Hertha Berlin v Antwerp (2-3)	2-1, 0-2
Odense BK13 v Stuttgart (1-4)	1-3, 0-1
Dunfermline Ath v Oergryte (4-2)	4-2, 0-0
Dynamo Zagreb v Graz (9-2)	3-2, 6-0
Aris Salonika v AS Roma (0-3)	0-0, 0-3
Wiener SK v Lokomotive Leipzig (3-1)	2-1, 1-0
Ferencvaros v Spartak Brno (2-1)	2-0, 0-1

Second Round
Stade Francais v Juventus (0-1)	0-0, 0-1
Petrolul Ploesti v Lokomotiv Plovdiv (1-2)	1-0, 0-2
DOS Utrecht v Liège (0-4)	0-2, 0-2

*Won on toss of coin.

Shelbourne v Atletico Madrid (0-2)	0-1, 0-1
Basle v Strasbourg (2-6)	0-1, 2-5
Barcelona v Celtic (3-1)	3-1, 0-0
Borussia Dortmund v Manchester U (1-10)	1-6, 0-4
Kilmarnock v Everton (1-6)	0-2, 1-4
Atlético Bilbao v Antwerp (3-0)	2-0, 1-0
Dunfermline Ath v Stuttgart (1-0)	1-0 0-0
Dynamo Zagreb v AS Roma (1-2)	1-1, 0-1
Ferencvaros v Wiener SK (4-2)	0-1, 2-1, 2-0

Third Round
Juventus v Lokomotive Plovdiv (4-3)	1-1, 1-1, 2-1
Liège v Atletico Madrid (1-2)	1-0, 0-2
*Strasbourg v Barcelona (2-2)	0-0, 2-2, 0-0
Manchester U v Everton (3-2)	1-1, 2-1
Atletico Bilbao v Dunfermline Ath (3-2)	1-0, 0-1, 2-1
AS Roma v Ferencvaros (1-3)	1-2, 0-1

Quarter-Finals
Juventus	bye
Atletico Madrid	bye
Strasbourg v Manchester U (0-5)	0-5, 0-0
Ferencvaros v Atletico Bilbao (5-2)	1-0, 1-2, 3-0

Semi-Finals
Atletico Madrid v Juventus (5-7)	3-1, 1-3, 1-3
Manchester U v Ferencvaros (4-5)	3-2, 0-1, 1-2

Final: at Turin
Juventus v Ferencvaros	0-1

FAIRS CUP 1965-66

First Round
DOS Utrecht v Barcelona (1-7)	0-0, 1-7
Antwerp v Glentoran (4-3)	1-0, 3-3
Hanover 96	bye
Stade Francais v Porto (0-1)	0-0, 0-1
Bordeaux v Sporting Lisbon (1-10)	0-4, 1-6
Espanol	bye
Liège v Dynamo Zagreb (1-2)	1-0, 0-2
Red Flag Brasov	bye
Goztepe Izmir	bye
Munich 1860 v Malmö FF (7-0)	4-1, 3-0
AIK Stockholm v Daring (3-1)	3-1, 0-0
Servette Geneva	bye
*AC Milan v Strasbourg (3-3)	1-0, 1-2, 1-1
CUF	bye
Wiener SK v PAOK Salonika (7-2)	6-0, 1-2
Chelsea v AS Roma (4-1)	4-1, 0-0
Lokomotiv Leipzig	bye
Leeds U v Torino (2-1)	2-1, 0-0
Basle	bye
Hibernian v Valencia (2-5)	2-0, 0-2, 0-3
Aris Salonika	bye
US Luxembourg v Cologne (0-17)	0-4, 0-13
Ujpest Dozsa	bye
Nuremberg v Everton (1-2)	1-1, 0-1
Dunfermline Ath	bye
KB Copenhagen	bye
Red Star Belgrade v Fiorentina (1-7)	0-4, 1-3
Spartak Brno v Lokomotiv Plovdiv (2-1)	2-0, 0-1
Hearts	bye
Valerengen	bye
Shamrock Rovers	bye
Real Zaragoza	bye

Second Round
Antwerp v Barcelona (2-3)	2-1, 0-2
Hanover 96 v Porto (6-2)	5-0, 1-2

*Won on toss after extra time.

Sporting Lisbon v Espanol (6-7)	2-1, 3-4, 1-2
Dynamo Zagreb v Red Flag Brasov (2-3)	2-2, 0-1
Goztepe Izmir v Munich 1860 (3-10)	2-1, 1-9
AIK Stockholm v Servette Geneva (3-5)	2-1, 1-4
CUF v Milan (2-3)	2-0, 0-2, 0-1
Weiner SK v Chelsea (1-2)	1-0, 0-2
Lokomotive Leipzig v Leeds U (1-2)	1-2, 0-0
Basle v Valencia (2-8)	1-3, 1-5
Aris Salonika v Cologne (2-3)	2-1, 0-2
Ujpest Dozsa v Everton (4-2)	3-0, 1-2
Dunfermline Ath v KB Copenhagen (9-2)	5-0, 4-2
Fiorentina v Spartak Brno (2-4)	2-0, 0-4
Hearts v Valerengen (4-1)	1-0, 3-1
Shamrock Rovers v Real Zaragoza (2-3)	1-1, 1-2

Third Round
Hanover 96 v Barcelona* (3-3)	2-1, 0-1, 1-1
Espanol v Red Flag Brasov (6-5)	3-1, 2-4, 1-0
Servette Geneva v Munich 1860 (2-5)	1-1, 1-4
AC Milan v Chelsea* (4-4)	2-1, 1-2, 1-1
Leeds U v Valencia (2-1)	1-1, 1-0
Cologne v Ujpest Dozsa (3-6)	3-2, 0-4
Dunfermline Ath v Spartak Brno (2-0)	2-0, 0-0
Hearts v Real Zaragoza (5-6)	3-3, 2-2, 0-1

Quarter-Finals
Barcelona v Espanol (2-0)	1-0, 1-0
Munich 1860 v Chelsea (2-3)	2-2, 0-1
Leeds U v Ujpest Dozsa (5-2)	4-1, 1-1
Dunfermline Ath v Real Zaragoza (3-4)	1-0, 2-4

Semi-Finals
Barcelona v Chelsea (7-2)	2-0, 0-2, 5-0
Real Zaragoza v Leeds U (5-3)	1-0, 1-2, 3-1

Final
Barcelona v Zaragoza (4-3)	0-1, 4-2

EUROPEAN FAIRS CUP 1966–67

First Round
Leeds U	bye
DWS Amsterdam	bye
Nuremburg v Valencia (1-4)	1-2, 0-2
Red Star Belgrade v Atletico Bilbao (5-2)	5-0, 0-2
WBA	bye
DOS Utrecht v Basle (4-3)	2-1, 2-2
Bologna v Goztepe Izmir (5-2)	2-1, 3-1
Sparta Prague	bye
Liège	bye
Djurgaarden v Lokomotiv Leipzig (2-5)	1-3, 1-2
Benfica	bye
Spartak Plovdiv	bye
Kilmarnock	bye
US Luxembourg v Antwerp (0-2)	0-1, 0-1
La Gantoise	bye
Porto v Bordeaux* (3-3)	2-1, 1-2
Drumcondra v Eintracht Frankfurt (1-8)	0-2, 1-6
Hvidovre	bye
Nice v Oergryte (3-4)	2-2, 1-2
Olympija Ljubljana v Ferencvaros (3-6)	3-3, 0-3
Stuttgart v Burnley (1-3)	1-1, 0-2
Lausanne	bye
Wiener SK v Napoli (2-5)	1-2, 1-3
Odense BK 09	bye
Juventus v Aris Salonika (7-0)	5-0, 2-0
Vitoria Setubal	bye
Dundee U	bye
Barcelona	bye
Toulouse	bye
Dynamo Pitesti v Seville (4-2)	2-0, 2-2
Frigg Oslo v Dunfermline Ath (2-6)	1-3, 1-3
Spartak Brno v Dynamo Zagreb* (2-2)	0-2, 2-0

Second Round
DWS Amsterdam v Leeds U (2-8)	1-3, 1-5
Valencia v Red Star Belgrade (3-1)	1-0, 2-1
WBA v DOS Utrecht (6-3)	5-2, 1-1
Sparta Prague v Bologna (3-4)	2-2, 1-2
Liège v Lokomotiv Leipzig (1-2)	0-0, 1-2
Spartak Plovdiv v Benfica (1-4)	1-1, 0-3
Antwerp v Kilmarnock (2-8)	0-1, 2-7
La Gantoise v Bordeaux (1-0)	1-0, 0-0
Eintracht Frankfurt v Hvidovre (7-3)	5-1, 2-2
Oergryte v Ferencvaros (1-7)	0-0, 1-7
Lausanne v Burnley (1-8)	1-3, 0-5
Odense BK09 v Napoli (2-6)	1-4, 1-2
Juventus v Vitoria Setubal (5-1)	3-1, 2-0
Barcelona v Dundee U (1-4)	1-2, 0-2
Toulouse v Dynamo Pitesti (4-5)	3-0, 1-5
Dunfermline Ath v Dynamo Zagreb† (4-4)	4-2, 0-2

Third Round
Leeds U v Valencia (3-1)	1-1, 2-0
Bologna v WBA (6-1)	3-0, 3-1
Lokomotiv Leipzig v Benfica (4-3)	3-1, 1-2
Kilmarnock v La Gantoise (3-1)	1-0, 2-1
Eintracht Frankfurt v Ferencvaros (5-3)	4-1, 1-2
Burnley v Naples (3-0)	3-0, 0-0
Juventus v Dundee U (3-1)	3-0, 0-1
Dynamo Pitesti v Dynamo Zagreb (0-1)	0-1, 0-0

Quarter-Finals
Bologna v Leeds U* (1-1)	1-0, 0-1
Lokomotiv Leipzig v Kilmarnock (1-2)	1-0, 0-2
Eintracht Frankfurt v Burnley (3-2)	1-1, 2-1
Juventus v Dynamo Zagreb (2-5)	2-2, 0-3

Semi-Finals
Leeds U v Kilmarnock (4-2)	4-2, 0-0
Eintracht Frankfurt v Dynamo Zagreb (3-4)	3-0, 0-4

Final
Dynamo Zagreb v Leeds U (2-0)	2-0, 0-0

*Won on toss. †Won on away goals rule.

EUROPEAN FAIRS CUP 1967–68

First Round
Spora Luxemburg v Leeds U (0-16)	0-9, 0-7
PAOK Salonika v Liège (2-5)	0-2, 2-3
Wiener SK v Atletico Madrid (3-7)	2-5, 1-2
St Patrick's Athletic v Bordeaux (4-9)	1-3, 3-6
DOS Utrecht v Real Zaragoza (4-5)	3-2, 1-3
Napoli v Hanover 96 (5-1)	4-0, 1-1
Bologna v Lyn Oslo (2-0)	2-0, 0-0
Nice v Fiorentina (0-5)	0-1, 0-4
Dynamo Dresden v Rangers (2-3)	1-1, 1-2
Servette Geneva v Munich 1860 (2-6)	2-2, 0-4
Argesul Pitesti v Farencvaros (3-5)	3-1, 0-4
Malmo FF v Liverpool (1-4)	0-2, 1-2
Hibernian v Porto (4-3)	3-0, 1-3
Eintracht Frankfurt v Nottingham F (0-5)	0-1, 0-4
Dynamo Zagreb v Petrolul Ploesti (5-2)	5-0, 0-2
Bruges v Sporting Lisbon (1-2)	0-0, 1-2
Frem Copenhagen v Atletico Bilbao (2-4)	0-1, 2-3
Zurich v Barcelona (3-2)	3-1, 0-1
Lokomotiv Leipzig v Linfield (5-2)	5-1, 0-1
DWS Amsterdam v Dundee (2-4)	2-1, 0-3
Partizan Belgrade v Lokomotiv Plovdiv (6-2)	5-1, 1-1
Vojvodina v CUF (4-1)	1-0, 3-1
Cologne v Slavia Prague (4-2)	2-0, 2-2
Antwerp v Goztepe Izmir (1-2)	1-2, 0-0

Second Round
Nottingham F v Zurich* (2-2)	2-1, 0-1

*Won on away goals rule.

Bordeaux v Atletico Bilbao (1-4)	1-3, 0-1
Dundee v Liège (7-2)	3-1, 4-1
Vojvodina v Lokomotiv Leipzig (2-0)	0-0, 2-0
Real Zaragoza v Ferencvaros (2-4)	2-1, 0-3
Liverpool v Munich 1860 (9-2)	8-0, 1-2
Rangers v Cologne (4-3)	3-0, 1-3
Bologna v Dynamo Zagreb (2-1)	0-0, 2-1
Napoli v Hibernian (4-6)	4-1, 0-5
Partizan Belgrade v Leeds U (2-3)	1-2, 1-1
Fiorentina v Sporting Lisbon (2-3)	1-1, 1-2
Atletico Madrid v Goztepe Izmir (2-3)	2-0, 0-3

Third Round
Ferencvaros v Liverpool (2-0)	1-0, 1-0
Leeds U v Hibernian (2-1)	1-0, 1-1
Vojvodina v Goztepe Izmir (2-0)	1-0, 1-0
Zurich v Sporting Lisbon (3-1)	3-0, 0-1
Byes: Atletico Bilbao, Bologna, Dundee and Rangers	

Quarter-Finals
Ferencvaros v Atletico Bilbao (4-2)	2-1, 2-1
Rangers v Leeds U (0-2)	0-0, 0-2
Dundee v Zurich (2-0)	1-0, 1-0
Bologna v Vojvodina (2-0)	0-0, 2-0

Semi-Finals
Dundee v Leeds U (1-2)	1-1, 1-2
Ferencvaros v Bologna (5-4)	3-2, 2-2

Final
Leeds U v Ferencvaros (1-0)	1-0, 0-0

EUROPEAN FAIRS CUP 1968-69

Byes: Argesul, Leipzig, Ujpest.

First Round

Chelsea v Morton (9-3)	5-0, 4-3
Newcastle U v Feyenoord (4-2)	4-0, 0-2
*Atletico Bilbao v Liverpool (3-3)	2-1, 0-2
Rangers v Vojvodina (2-1)	2-0, 0-1
Ljubljana v Hibernian (1-5)	0-3, 1-2
Rapid Bucharest v OFK Belgrade (4-7)	3-1, 1-6
Wiener SK v Slavia Prague (1-5)	1-0, 0-5
Skeid Oslo v AIK Stockholm (2-3)	1-1, 1-2
Trakia Plovdiv v Real Zaragoza† (3-3)	3-1, 0-2
Dynamo Zagreb v Fiorentina (2-3)	1-1, 1-2
Legia Warsaw v Munich 1860 (9-2)	6-0, 3-2
Daring v Panathinaikos (2-3)	2-1, 0-2
Wacker Innsbruck v Eintracht Frankfurt (2-5)	2-2, 0-3
Sporting Lisbon v Valencia (5-4)	4-0, 1-4
Bologna v Basle (6-2)	4-1, 2-1
Aris Salonika v Hibernians Valletta (7-0)	1-0, 6-0
DOS Utrecht v Dundalk (2-3)	1-1, 1-2
Atletico Madrid v Waregem* (2-2)	2-1, 0-1
Hansa Rostock v Nice (4-3)	3-0, 1-2
*Goztepe Izmir v Marseille (2-2)	2-0, 0-2
Metz v SV Hamburg (3-7)	1-4, 2-3
*Lyon v Academica Coimbra (1-1)	1-0, 0-1
Lausanne v Juventus (0-4)	0-2, 0-2
Beerschot v DWS Amsterdam (2-3)	1-1, 1-2
Hanover 96 v Odense BK 09 (4-2)	3-2, 1-0
Vitoria Setubal v Linfield (6-1)	3-0, 3-1
Standard Liège v Leeds U (2-3)	0-0, 2-3
Napoli v Grasshoppers (3-2)	3-1, 0-1
Slavia Sofia v Aberdeen (0-2)	0-0, 0-2
Rangers v Dundalk (9-1)	6-1, 3-0
Aberdeen v Real Zaragoza (2-4)	2-1, 0-3
Chelsea v DWS Amsterdam * (0-0)	0-0, 0-0
Sporting Lisbon v Newcastle U (1-2)	1-1, 0-1
Vitoria Setubal v Lyon (7-1)	5-0, 2-1
Goztepe Izmir v Argesu Pitesti (5-3)	3-0, 2-3
Hansa Rostock v Fiorentina †(4-4)	3-2, 1-2
SV Hamburg v Slavia Prague (5-4)	4-1, 1-3
Panathinaikos v Atletico Bilbao (0-0)	0-0, 0-1
OFK Belgrade v Bologna (2-1)	1-0, 1-1
Aris Salonika v Ujpest Dozsa (2-11)	1-2, 1-9
AIK Stockholm v Hanover 96 (6-7)	4-2, 2-5
Waregem v Legia Warsaw (1-2)	1-0, 0-2
Juventus v Eintracht Frankfurt (0-1)	0-0, 0-1

Third Round

Leeds U v Hanover 96 (7-2)	5-1, 2-1
†SV Hamburg v Hibernian (2-2)	1-0, 1-2
Legia Warsaw v Ujpest Dozsa (2-3)	0-1, 2-2
Real Zaragoza v Newcastle U† (4-4)	3-2, 1-2
OFK Belgrade v Goztepe Izmir† (3-3)	3-1, 0-2
Eintracht Frankfurt v Atletico Bilbao (1-2)	1-1, 0-1
DWS Amsterdam v Rangers (1-4)	0-2, 1-2
Vitoria Setubal v Fiorentina (4-2)	3-0, 1-2

Quarter-Finals

Newcastle U v Vitoria Setubal (6-4)	5-1, 1-3
Rangers v Atletico Bilbao (4-3)	4-1, 0-2
Leeds U v Ujpest Dozsa (0-3)	0-1, 0-2
Goztepe Izmir v SV Hamburg	(Hamburg scr)

Second Round

Hibernian v Lokomotiv Leipzig (4-1)	3-1, 1-0
*Leeds U v Napoli (2-2)	2-0, 0-2

Semi-Finals

Goztepe Izmir v Ujpest Dozsa (1-8)	1-4, 0-4
Rangers v Newcastle U (0-2)	0-0, 0-2

Final 1968–69: Newcastle U 3 Ujpest Dozsa 0
(At Newcastle, May 29, 1969)

Newcastle U: McFaul; Craig, Clark; Gibb, Burton, Moncur; Scott, Robson, Davies, Arentoft, Sinclair (Foggon).
Ujpest Dozsa: Szentimihalyi; Kaposza, Solymosi; Bankuti, Nosko, Dunai E; Fazekas, Gorocs, Bene Dunai A, Zambo.
Scorers: Newcastle U Moncur, 2 Scott.
*Won on toss. †Won on away goals rule.

Ujpest Dozsa 2 Newcastle U 3
(At Budapest, June 11, 1969)

Ujpest Dozsa: Unchanged from first leg.
Newcastle U: Unchanged from first leg – Foggon substituted for Scott.
Scorers: Ujpest, Bene, Gorocs. Newcastle U Moncur, Arentoft, Foggon.
Newcastle U won 6-2 on aggregate.

EUROPEAN FAIRS CUP 1969-70

First Round

Arsenal v Glentoran (3-1)	3-0, 0-1
Dundee U v Newcastle U (1-3)	1-2, 0-1
Liverpool v Dundalk (14-0)	10-0, 4-0
Partizan Belgrade v Ujpest Dozsa (2-3)	2-1, 0-2
Sabadell v Bruges (3-5)	2-0, 1-5
Las Palmas v Hertha Berlin (0-1)	0-0, 0-1
Wiener SK v Ruch Chorzow (5-6)	4-2, 1-4
Rouen v Twente (2-1)	2-0, 0-1
Vitoria Guimaraes v Banik Ostrava (2-1)	1-0, 1-1
Sporting Lisbon v ASK Linz (6-2)	4-0, 2-2
Carl Zeiss Jena v Altay Izmir (1-0)	1-0, 0-0
Lausanne v Vasas Gyor (2-4)	1-2, 1-2
Rosenborg v Southampton (1-2)	1-0, 0-2
Hansa Rostock v Panionios (3-2)	3-0, 0-2
Dynamo Bacau v Floriana (7-0)	6-0, 1-0
Slavia Sofia v Valencia (3-1)	2-0, 1-1
Inter-Milan v Sparta Prague (4-0)	3-0, 1-0
Juventus v Lokomotiv Plovdiv (5-2)	3-1, 2-1
Stuttgart v Malmo FF (4-1)	3-0, 1-1
Hanover 96 v Ajax (2-4)	2-1, 0-3
Aris Salonika v Cagliari (1-4)	1-1, 0-3
Metz v Napoli (2-3)	1-1, 1-2
Barcelona v Odense BK 09 (6-0)	4-0, 2-0
Gwardia Warsaw v Vojvodina (2-1)	1-0, 1-1
Dunfermline Ath v Bordeaux (4-2)	4-0, 0-2
Zurich v Kilmarnock (4-5)	3-2, 1-3
Munich 1860 v Skied Oslo (3-4)	2-2, 1-2
Valur Reykjavik v Anderlecht (0-8)	0-6, 0-2
SC Charleroi v ZNK Zagreb (5-2)	2-1, 3-1
Hvidovre v Porto (1-4)	1-2, 0-2
Jeunesse Esch v Coleraine (3-6)	3-2, 0-4
Vitoria Setubal v Rapid Bucharest (7-2)	3-1, 4-1
SC Charleroi v Rouen† (3-3)	3-1, 0-2
Skeid Oslo v Dynamo Bacau (0-2)	0-0, 0-2
Kilmarnock v Slavia Sofia (4-3)	4-1, 0-2
Ajax v Ruch Chorzow (9-1)	7-0, 2-1
Stuttgart v Napoli (0-1)	0-0, 0-1
Carl Zeiss Jena v Cagliari (3-0)	2-0, 1-0
Bruges v Ujpest Dozsa† (5-5)	5-2, 0-3
Hansa Rostock v Inter-Milan (2-4)	2-1, 0-3
Vasas Gyor v Barcelona (2-5)	2-3, 0-2
Hertha Berlin v Juventus (3-1)	3-1, 0-0
Vitoria Setubal v Liverpool (3-3)	1-0, 2-3
Porto v Newcastle U (0-1)	0-0, 0-1
Vitoria Guimaraes v Southampton (4-8)	3-3, 1-5
Dunfermline Ath v Gwardia Warsaw (3-1)	2-1, 1-0
Anderlecht v Coleraine (13-4)	6-1, 7-3

Third Round

Rouen v Arsenal (0-1)	0-0, 0-1
Kilmarnock v Dynamo Bacau (1-3)	1-1, 0-2
Napoli v Ajax (1-4)	1-0, 0-4
Carl Zeiss Jena v Ujpest Dozsa (4-0)	1-0, 3-0
Barcelona v Inter-Milan (3-2)	1-2, 1-1
Vitoria Setubal v Hertha Berlin (1-2)	1-1, 0-1
Newcastle U† v Southampton (1-1)	0-0, 1-1
Anderlecht† v Dunfermline Ath (3-3)	1-0, 2-3

Quarter-Finals

Dynamo Bacau v Arsenal (1-9)	0-2, 1-7
Carl Zeiss Jena v Ajax (4-6)	3-1, 1-5
Hertha Berlin v Inter-Milan (1-2)	1-0, 0-2
Anderlecht† v Newcastle U (3-3)	2-0, 1-3

Second Round

Sporting Lisbon v Arsenal (0-3)	0-0, 0-3

Semi-Finals

Arsenal v Ajax (3-1)	3-0, 0-1
Anderlecht v Inter-Milan (2-1)	0-1, 2-0

Final 1969–70: Anderlecht 3 Arsenal 1
(First leg at Brussels, April 22, 1970, 37,000)

Anderlecht: Trappeniers; Heylens, Velkeneers; Nordahl, Kialunda, Cornelis (Peeters); Desanghere Devrindt, Mulder, Van Himst, Puis.
Arsenal: Wilson; Storey, McNab; Kelly, McLintock, Simpson; Armstrong, Sammels, Radford, George, (Kennedy), Graham.
Scorers: Anderlecht, Devrindt, Mulder 2. Arsenal, Kennedy.

Arsenal 3 Anderlecht 0
(Second leg at Highbury, April 28, 1970, 51,612)

Arsenal: Wilson; Storey, McNab; Kelly, McLintock, Simpson;' Armstrong, Sammels, Radford, George' Graham.
Anderlecht: Trappeniers; Heylens, Maartens; Nordahl, Velkeneers, Kialunda; Desanghere, Devrindt Mulder, Van Himst, Puis.

†Won on away goals counting double.

EUROPEAN FAIRS CUP 1970–71

First Round

AEK Athens v Twente (0-4)	0-1, 0-3
Zeljeznicar v Anderlecht (7-9)	4-5, 3-4
La Gantoise v SV Hamburg (1-8)	0-1, 1-7
Seville v Eskisehirspor (2-3)	1-0, 1-3
Coleraine v Kilmarnock (4-3)	1-1, 3-2
Dundee U v Grasshoppers (3-2)	3-2, 0-0
Sarpsborg v Leeds U (0-6)	0-1, 0-5
*Spartak Trnava v Marseille (2-2)	2-0, 0-2
Cologne v Sedan (5-2)	5-1, 0-1
Lausanne v Vitoria Setubal (1-4)	0-2, 1-2
Hibernian v Malmo FF (9-2)	6-0, 3-2
Liverpool v Ferencvaros (2-1)	1-0, 1-1
Trakia Plovdiv v Coventry C (1-6)	1-4, 0-2
Lazio v Arsenal (2-4)	2-2, 0-2
Bayern Munich v Rangers (2-1)	1-0, 1-1
Dynamo Bucharest v PAOK Salonika (5-1)	5-0, 0-1
Uni Craiova v Pecs Dozsa (2-4)	2-1, 0-3
Katowice v Barcelona (2-4)	0-1, 2-3
Wiener SK v Beveren (0-5)	0-2, 0-3
Ilves Kissat v Sturm Graz (4-5)	4-2, 0-3
Barreirense v Dynamo Zagreb (3-6)	2-0, 1-6
Hajduk Split v Slavia Sofia (3-1)	3-0, 0-1
Cork Hibs v Valencia (1-6)	0-3, 1-3
Sparta Prague v Atletico Bilbao (3-1)	2-0 1-1
Partizan Belgrade v Dynamo Dresden (0-6)	0-0, 0-6
AB Copenhagen v Sliema Wanderers (10-2)	7-0, 3-2
Juventus v Rumelange (11-0)	7-0, 4-0
Nykoping v Hertha Berlin (3-8)	2-4, 1-4
Ruch Chorzow v Fiorentina (1-3)	1-1, 0-2
Inter-Milan v Newcastle U (1-3)	1-1, 0-2
Sparta Rotterdam v Akranes (15-0)	6-0, 9-0
Vitoria Guimaraes v Angouleme (4-3)	3-0, 1-3

Second Round

Hibernian v Vitoria Guimaraes (3-2)	2-0, 1-2
Sparta Rotterdam v Coleraine (4-1)	2-0, 2-1
Bayern Munich v Coventry C (7-3)	6-1, 1-2
Barcelona v Juventus (2-4)	1-2, 1-2
Fiorentina v Cologne (1-3)	1-2, 0-1
Sturm Graz v Arsenal (1-2)	1-0, 0-2
†Leeds U v Dynamo Dresden (2-2)	1-0, 1-2
Liverpool v Dynamo Bucharest (4-1)	3-0, 1-1
AB Copenhagen v Anderlecht (1-7)	1-3, 0-4
Newcastle U v Pecs Dozsa (2-2)	2-0, 0-2
Sparta Prague v Dundee U (3-2)	3-1, 0-1
Hertha Berlin v Spartak Trnava (2-3)	1-0, 1-3
Dynamo Zagreb v Hamburg (4-1)	4-0, 0-1
Vitoria Setubal v Hajduk Split (3-2)	2-0, 1-2
Valencia v Beveren (1-2)	0-1, 1-1
Eskisehir v Twente (4-8)	3-2, 1-6

Third Round

Spartak Trnava v Cologne (0-4)	0-1, 0-3
Bayern Munich v Sparta Rotterdam (5-2)	2-1, 3-1
Leeds U v Sparta Prague (9-2)	6-0, 3-2
Arsenal v Beveren (4-0)	4-0, 0-0
Pecs Dozsa v Juventus (0-3)	0-1, 0-2
Dynamo Zagreb v Twente (2-3)	2-2, 0-1
Anderlecht v Vitoria Setubal (3-4)	2-1, 1-3
Hibernian v Liverpool (0-3)	0-1, 0-2

Quarter-Finals

Juventus v Twente (4-2)	2-0, 2-2
Arsenal v Cologne†(2-2)	2-1, 0-1
Leeds U v Setubal (3-2)	2-1, 1-1
Liverpool v Bayern Munich (4-1)	3-0, 1-1

Semi-Finals

Liverpool v Leeds U (0-1)	0-1, 0-0
Cologne v Juventus (1-3)	1-1, 0-2

Final 1970–71: Juventus 2, Leeds U 2
at Turin, May 29, 1971, 45,000)

Juventus: Piloni; Spinosi, Marchetti, Furino, Morini, Salvadore, Haller, Causio, Anastasi, (Novellini), Capello, Bettega.
Leeds U: Sprake; Reaney, Cooper, Bremner, Charlton, Hunter, Lorimer, Clarke, Jones, (Bates), Giles, Madeley.
Scorers: Juventus, Bettega, Capello, Leeds U, Madeley, Bates.

Leeds U 1, Juventus 1
(at Leeds, June 2, 1971, 42,483)

Leeds U: Sprake; Reaney, Cooper, Bremner, Charlton, Hunter, Lorimer, Clarke, Jones, Giles, Madeley, (Bates).
Juventus: Tancredi; Spinosi, Marchetti, Furino, Morini, Salvadore, Haller, Causio, Anastasi, Capello, Bettega
Scorers: Leeds U, Clarke, Juventus, Anastasi.
Leeds U won on away goals rule.

*Won on penalty kicks. †Won on away goals rule.

UEFA CUP 1971–72

First Round
Hertha Berlin v Elfsborg (7-2)	4-1, 3-1
Dundee v Akademisk Copenhagen (5-2)	4-2, 1-0
Rosenborg v IFK Helsinki (4-0)	3-0, 1-0
Vasas Budapest v Shelbourne (2-1)	1-0, 1-1
Glentoran v Eintracht Brunswick (1-7)	0-1, 1-6
Keflavik v Tottenham H (1-15)	1-6, 0-9
Celta Vigo v Aberdeen (0-3)	0-2, 0-1
FC Den Haag v Aris Luxembourg (6-1)	5-0, 1-1
Wolverhampton W v Academica Coimbra (7-1)	4-1, 3-0
St Etienne v Cologne (2-3)	1-1, 1-2
Lugano v Legia Warsaw (1-3)	1-3, 0-0
Porto v Nantes (1-3)	0-2, 1-1
SV Hamburg v St Johnstone (2-4)	2-1, 0-3
Southampton v Atletico Bilbao (2-3)	2-1, 0-2
Bologna v Anderlecht (3-1)	2-0, 1-1
Napoli v Rapid Bucharest (1-2)	1-0, 0-2
Vitoria Setubal* v Nimes (2-2)	1-0, 1-2
Atletico Madrid v Panionios* (2-2)	2-1, 0-1
Carl Zeiss Jena v Lokomotiv Plovdiv (4-3)	3-0, 1-3
Basle v Real Madrid (2-4)	1-2, 1-2
Marsa v Juventus (0-11)	0-6, 0-5
Dynamo Zagreb v Botev Vratza (8-2)	6-1, 2-1
UT Arad v Austria Salzburg (5-4)	4-1, 1-3
Fenerbahce v Ferencvaros (4-2)	1-1, 1-3
AC Milan v Dighenis (7-0)	4-0, 3-0
Spartak Moscow v VSS Kosice (3-2)	1-2, 2-0
OFK Belgrade v Djurgaarden (6-3)	2-2, 4-1
Rapid Vienna	Bye
Zeljeznicar v Bruges (4-3)	3-0, 1-3
Chemie Halle v PSV Eindhoven (0-0) (withdrawn)	0-0, –
Zaglebie Walbrzych v Union Teplice (4-2)	1-0, 3-2
Lierse v Leeds U (4-2)	0-2, 4-0

Second Round
Rosenborg v Lierse* (4-4)	4-1, 0-3
Rapid Bucharest v Legia Warsaw (4-2)	4-0, 0-2
Cologne v Dundee (4-5)	2-1, 2-4
FC Den Haag v Wolverhampton W (1-7)	1-3, 0-4
Zeljeznicar* v Bologna (3-3)	1-1, 2-2
Nantes v Tottenham H (0-1)	0-0, 0-1
Eintracht Brunswick v Atletico Bilbao (4-3)	2-1, 2-2
St Johnstone v Vasas Budapest (2-1)	2-0, 0-1
Spartak Moscow v Vitoria Setubal (0-4)	0-0, 0-4
Hertha Berlin v AC Milan (4-5)	2-1, 2-4
OFK Belgrade v Carl Zeiss Jena (1-5)	1-1, 0-4
Zaglebie Walbrzych v UT Arad (2-3)	1-1, 1-2
Dynamo Zagreb v Rapid Vienna* (2-2)	2-2, 0-0
Real Madrid v PSV Eindhoven* (3-3)	3-1, 0-2
Juventus v Aberdeen (3-1)	2-0, 1-1
Ferencvaros v Panionios (6-0) (disqualified)	6-0 –

Third Round
AC Milan v Dundee (3-2)	3-0, 0-2
Carl Zeiss Jena v Wolverhampton W (0-4)	0-1, 0-3
Eintracht Brunswick v Ferencvaros (3-6)	1-1, 2-5
PSV Eindhoven v Lierse (1-4)	1-0, 0-4
Rapid Vienna v Juventus (1-5)	0-1, 1-4
St Johnstone v Zeljeznicar (2-5)	1-0, 1-5
Tottenham H v Rapid Bucharest (5-0)	3-0, 2-0
UT Arad v Vitoria Setubal (3-1)	3-0, 0-1

Quarter-Finals
AC Milan v Lierse (3-1)	2-0, 1-1
UT Arad v Tottenham H (1-3)	0-2, 1-1
Ferencvaros† v Zeljeznicar (3-3)	1-2, 2-1
Juventus v Wolverhampton W (2-3)	1-1, 1-2

Semi-Finals
Tottenham H v AC Milan (3-2)	2-1, 1-1
Ferencvaros v Wolverhampton W (3-4)	2-2, 1-2

Final 1971–72: Wolverhampton W 1 Tottenham H 2
(First leg at Wolverhampton, May 3, 1972, 45,000)
Wolverhampton W: Parkes; Shaw, Taylor, Hegan, Munro, McAlle, McCalliog, Hibbitt, Richards, Dougan Wagstaffe.
Tottenham H: Jennings; Kinnear, Knowles, Mullery, England, Beal, Coates (Pratt), Perryman, Chivers, Peters, Gilzean.
Scorers: Wolverhampton W McCalliog, Tottenham H Chivers 2.

Tottenham H 1 Wolverhampton W 1
(second leg at White Hart Lane, May 17, 1972)
Tottenham H: Jennings; Kinnear, Knowles, Mullery, England, Beal, Coates, Perryman, Chivers, Peters, Gilzean.
Wolverhampton W: Parkes; Shaw, Taylor, Hegan, Munro, McAlle, MaCalliog, Hibbitt (Bailey), Richards Dougan (Curran), Wagstaffe.
Scorers: Tottenham H Mullery, Wolverhampton W Wagstaffe.
*Won on away goals rule. †Won on penalty kicks.

UEFA CUP 1972–73

First Round
Aberdeen v Bor Moenchengladbach (5-9)	2-3, 3-6
Atvidaberg v Bruges (5-6)	3-5, 2-1
Manchester C v Valencia (3-4)	2-2, 1-2
Lyn Oslo v Tottenham H (3-12)	3-6, 0-6
Cologne v Bohemians (5-1)	2-1, 3-0
Honved v Partick T (4-0)	1-0, 3-0
Viking Stavanger v IBV Vastmannejar (1-0)	1-0, 0-0
Feyenoord v US Rumelange (21-0)	9-0, 12-0
Liverpool v Eintracht Frankfurt (2-0)	2-0, 0-0
Grasshoppers v Nimes (4-2)	2-1, 2-1
Vitoria Setubal v Zaglebie Sosnowiec (6-2)	6-1, 0-1
Stoke C v Kaiserslautern (4-5)	3-1, 0-4
Racing White v CUF Barrierense (0-3)	0-1, 0-2
Torino v Las Palmas (2-4)	2-0, 0-4
Sochaux v Frem Copenhagen (2-5)	1-3, 1-2
Olympiakos Piraeus v Cagliari (3-1)	2-1, 1-0
Angers v Dynamo Berlin (2-3)	3-1, 1-0
Porto v Barcelona (4-1)	3-1, 1-0
Univ Cluj v Levski Sofia (5-6)	4-1, 1-5
Red Star Belgrade v Lausanne (7-4)	5-1, 2-3
Inter-Milan v FC Valetta (7-1)	6-1, 1-0
Beroe Stara v FK Austria (10-1)	7-0, 3-1
UT Arad v Norrköping (4-4)	1-2, 0-2
EPA Larna v Ararat Erevan (0-2)	0-1, 0-1
AEK Athens v Salgotarjan (4-2)	3-1, 1-1
Eskisehirspor v Fiorentina (1-1)	1-2, 0-3
Dukla Prague v OFK Belgrade (3-5)	2-2, 1-3
Slovan Bratislava v Voivodina (8-1)	6-0, 2-1
Dynamo Tbilisi v FC Twente (3-4)	3-2, 0-2
Ruch Chorzow v Fenerbahce (3-1)	3-0, 0-1
Dynamo Dresden v Voest Linz (4-2)	2-0, 2-2
Hvidovre Copenhagen	bye

Second Round
Dynamo Berlin v Levski Sofia (3-2)	3-0, 0-2
Bor Moenchengladbach v Hvidovre Copenhagen (6-1)	3-0, 3-1
Porto v Bruges (5-3)	3-0, 2-3
Tottenham H v Olympiakos Piraeus (4-1)	4-0, 0-1
Red Star Belgrade v Valencia (4-1)	3-1, 1-0
Inter-Milan v Norrköping (4-3)	2-2, 2-0
Viking Stavanger v Cologne (2-9)	1-0, 1-9
Beroe Stara v Honved (3-1)	3-0, 0-1
Feyenoord v OFK Belgrade* (5-5)	4-3, 1-2
Liverpool v AEK Athens (6-1)	3-0, 3-1
*Vitoria Setubal v Fiorentina (2-2)	1-0, 1-2
Grasshoppers v Ararat Erevan (3-7)	1-3, 2-4
CUF Barreirense v Kaiserslautern (2-3)	1-3, 1-0
Las Palmas v Slovan Bratislava (3-2)	2-2, 1-0
Ruch Chorzow v Dynamo Dresden (0-4)	0-1, 0-3
Frem Copenhagen v FC Twente (0-9)	0-5, 0-4

Third Round
Ararat Erevan v Kaiserslautern† (2-2)	2-0, 0-2
Cologne v Bor Moenchengladbach (0-5)	0-0, 0-5
Tottenham H v Red Star Belgrade (2-1)	2-0, 0-1
FC Twente v Las Palmas (4-2)	3-0, 1-2
OFK Belgrade v Beroe Stara (3-1)	0-0, 3-1
Vitoria Setubal v Inter-Milan (2-1)	2-0, 0-1
Dynamo Berlin v Liverpool (0-3)	0-0, 1-3
Porto v Dynamo Dresden (1-3)	1-2, 0-1

Quarter-Finals
Kaiserslautern v Bor Moenchengladbach (2-9)	1-2, 1-7
OFK Belgrade v FC Twente (3-4)	3-2, 0-2
Tottenham H *v Vitoria Setubal (2-2)	1-0, 1-2
Liverpool v Dynamo Dresden (3-0)	2-0, 1-0

Semi-Finals
Liverpool* v Tottenham H (2-2)	1-0, 1-2
Bor Moenchengladbach v FC Twente (5-1)	3-0, 2-1

*won on away goals rule
†won on penalty kicks

Final 1972-73: Liverpool 3, Borussia Moenchengladbach 0
(First leg at Liverpool, May 10 1973, 41,169)

Liverpool: Clemence; Lawler, Lindsay, Smith, Lloyd, Hughes, Keegan, Cormack, Toshack, Heighway (Hall), Callaghan.
Borussia Moenchengladbach: Kleff; Danner, Michallik, Vogts, Bonhof, Kulik, Jensen, Wimmer, Rupp (Simonsen), Netzer, Heynckes.
Scorers: Keegan 2, Lloyd.

Borussia Moenchengladbach 2, Liverpool 0
(Second leg at Moenchengladbach, May 23, 1973, 35,000)

Borussia Moenchengladbach: Kleff; Vogts, Surau, Netzer, Bonhof, Danner, Wimmer, Kulik, Jensen, Rupp, Heynckes.
Liverpool: Clemence; Lawler, Lindsay, Smith, Lloyd, Hughes, Keegan, Cormack, Heighway, (Boersma), Toshack, Callaghan.
Scorer: Heynckes 2.

UEFA CUP 1973-74

First Round
Fredrikstad v Dynamo Kiev (0-5)	0-1, 0-4
Ruch Chorzow v Wuppertal (8-6)	4-1, 4-5
BK 1903 Copenhagen v AIK (3-2)	2-1, 1-1
Carl Zeiss Jena v Mikkelin (6-0)	3-0, 3-0
Stroemsgodset v Leeds U (2-7)	1-1, 1-6
Oesters v Feyenoord (2-5)	1-3, 1-2
Hibernian v Keflavik (3-1)	2-0, 1-1
Nice v Barcelona (3-2)	3-0, 0-2
Fortuna Dusseldorf v Naestved (3-2)	1-0, 2-2
Grasshoppers v Tottenham H (2-9)	1-5, 1-4
Aberdeen v Finn Harps (7-2)	4-1, 3-1
Dundee v FC Twente (3-7)	1-3, 2-4
Espanol v RWD Molenbeek (2-4)	0-3, 2-1
Belenenses v Wolverhampton W (1-4)	0-2, 1-2
US Luxembourg v Marseille (1-12)	0-5, 1-7
Setubal v Beerschot (4-0)	2-0, 2-0
Ipswich T v Real Madrid (1-0)	1-0, 0-0
Lazio v Sion (4-3)	3-0, 1-3
Sliema Wanderers v Lok Plovdiv (0-3)	0-2, 0-1
Fiorentina v Univ Craiova (0-1)	0-0, 0-1
Ferencvaros v Gwardia Warsaw (1-3)	0-1, 1-2
Stuttgart v Olympiakos Nicosia (13-0)	9-0, 4-0
Tatran Presov v Velez (5-3)	4-2, 1-1
Dynamo Tbilisi v Slavia Sofia (4-3)	4-1, 0-2
Panathinaikos v OFK Belgrade* (2-2)	1-2, 1-0
*Admira-Wacker v Inter-Milan (2-2)	1-0, 1-2
Fenerbahce v Agres Pitesti (6-2)	5-1, 1-1
VSS Kosice v Honved (3-5)	1-0, 2-5
Torino v Lok Leipzig (2-4)	1-2, 1-2
Eskisehirspor v Cologne (0-2)	0-0, 0-2
Panachaiki v AK Graz (3-1)	2-1, 1-0
Ards v Standard Liège (4-8)	3-2, 1-6

Second Round
Admira-Wacker v Fortuna Dusseldorf (2-4)	2-1, 0-3
Aberdeen v Tottenham H (2-5)	1-1, 1-4
Dynamo Tbilisi v OFK Belgrade (8-1)	3-0, 5-1
Nice v Fenerbahce (4-2)	4-0, 0-2
*Lok Leipzig v Wolverhampton W (4-4)	3-0, 1-4
Panachaiki v FC Twente (1-8)	1-1, 0-7
*Setubal v RWD Molenbeek (2-2)	1-0, 1-2
Marseille v Cologne (2-6)	2-0, 0-6
Ipswich T v Lazio (6-4)	4-0, 2-4
Dynamo Kiev v BK 1903 Copenhagen (3-1)	1-0, 2-1
Lok Plovdiv v Honved (5-7)	3-4, 2-3
Ruch Chorzow v Carl Zeiss Jena (3-1)	3-0, 0-1
Stuttgart v Tatran Presov (8-4)	3-1, 5-3
†Leeds U v Hibernian (0-0)	0-0, 0-0
Feyenoord v Gwardia Warsaw (3-2)	3-1, 0-1
Standard Liege v Univ Craiova (3-1)	2-0, 1-1

Third Round
Dynamo Kiev v Stuttgart (2-3)	2-0, 0-3
Dynamo Tbilisi v Tottenham H (2-6)	1-1, 1-5
Ipswich T v FC Twente (3-1)	1-0, 2-1
Honved v Ruch Chorzow (2-5)	2-0, 0-5
Fortuna Dusseldorf v Lok Leipzig (2-4)	2-1, 0-3
Nice v Cologne (1-4)	1-0, 0-4
Standard Liege v Feyenoord* (3-3)	3-1, 0-2

Quarter-Finals
Ipswich T v Lok Leipzig† (1-1)	1-0, 0-1
Cologne v Tottenham H (1-5)	1-2, 0-3
Stuttgart v Setubal (3-2)	1-0, 2-2
Ruch Chorzow v Feyenoord (2-4)	1-1, 1-3

Semi-Finals
Lok Leipzig v Tottenham H (1-4)	1-2, 0-2
Feyenoord v Stuttgart (4-3)	2-1, 2-2

*won on away goals. †won on penalties

Final 1973-74: Tottenham Hotspur 2, Feyenoord 2
(First leg at White Hart Lane May 21, 1974, 46,281)

Tottenham: Jennings; Evans, Naylor, Pratt, England, Beal, McGrath, Perryman, Chivers, Peters, Coates.
Feyenoord: Treytel; Rijsbergen, Van Daele, Israel, Vos, De Jong, Jansen, Van Hanegem, Ressel, Schoenmaker, Kristensen.
Scorers: Tottenham, England, Van Daele og; Feyenoord, Van Hanegem, De Jong.

Feyenoord 2, Tottenham Hotspur 0
(Second leg at Rotterdam, May 29, 1974, 68,000)

Feyenoord: Treytel; Rijsbergen, Van Daele, Israel, Vos, Ramljak, Jansen, De Jong, Ressel, Schoenmaker, Kristensen (Boskamp) (Wery).
Tottenham: Jennings; Evans, Naylor, Pratt, (Holder), England, Beal, McGrath, Perryman, Chivers Peters, Coates.
Scorers: Rijsbergen, Ressel.

UEFA CUP 1974-75

First Round, First Leg
Lyon 7 (*Lacombe 3, Maillard 3, Maniero*)
Red Boys 0
Valur 0
Portadown 0
Derby Co 4 (*Hector 2, Daniel, Lee*)
Servette 1 (*Petrovic*)
Ipswich T 2 (*Talbot, Hamilton*)
Twente 2 (*Zuidema, Pahlplatz*)
Stoke C 1 (*Smith*)
Ajax 1 (*Krol*)
RWD Molenbeek 1 (*Wellens*)
Dundee 0
Rosenborg 2 (*Iversen 2*)
Hibernian 3 (*Stanton, Gordon, Cropley*)
Porto 4 (*McAlle og, Cubillas, Flavio, Gomes*)
Wolves 1 (*Bailey*)
Etar 0
Inter-Milan 0
Gornik Zabrze 2 (*Kurzeja, Kwasny*)
Partizan Belgrade 2 (*Zavitic, Vukotic*)
Start 1 (*Mathiesen M*)
Djurgaarden 2 (*Svensson M., Skotte*)
Boluspor 0
Dynamo Bucharest 1 (*Deleanu*)
Spartak Moscow 3 (*Piscarov, Gladulin, Lovchev*)
Velez Mostar 1 (*Bajevic*)
Besiktas 2 (*Sinan, Tezcan*)
Steagul Brasov 0
SW Innsbruck 2 (*Flindt 2*)
Borussia Moenchengladbach 1 (*Heynckes*)
Sturm Graz 2 (*Stendal, Kulmer*)
Antwerp 1 (*Heyligen*)
Randers Freja 1 (*Nielsen*)
Dynamo Dresden 1 (*Dorner*)
Hamburg 3 (*Volkert 2, Kaltz*)
Bohemians 0
Rapid Vienna 3 (*Pajenk, Ritter, Krankl*)
Aris Salonika 1 (*Alexiadis*)
Real Sociedad 0
Banik Ostrava 1 (*Micka*)
Lokomotiv Plovdiv 3 (*Kourbanov, Bonev, Stamboliev*)
Raba ETO 1 (*Glazer*)
Oesters 3 (*Mattsson 2, Nordenberg pen*)
Dynamo Moscow 2 (*Koslov, Pavlenkov*)
Nantes 2 (*Rampillon, Michel*)
Legia Warsaw 2 (*Bialad 2*)
Napoli 2 (*Massa, Pogliana*)
Videoton 0
Vorwaerts 2 (*Schutz, Krautzk*)
Juventus 1 (*Capello*)
Grasshoppers 2 (*Elsener, Grahn*)
Panathinaikos 0
Torino 1 (*Pulici*)
Fortuna Dusseldorf 1 (*Zewe*)
Cologne 5 (*Muller 2, Flohe 2, Lohr*)
Kokkolan 1 (*Makela*)
FC Amsterdam 5 (*Jansen 2, Otto, Koopman, Husers*)
Hibernian Malta 0
KB Copenhagen 1 (*Sorensen, Holstrom, Bernborg*)
Atletico Madrid 2 (*Ayala, Salcedo*)
Vitoria Setubal 1 (*Vicente*)
Real Zaragoza 1 (*Arrua*)

First round, Second Leg
Red Boys 1 (*Cristophe*)
Lyon 4 (*Domenech 2, Mariot, Bernard*)
Portadown 2 (*McFaul, Morrison pen*)
Valur 1 (*Albertson*)
Servette 1 (*Martin*)
Derby Co 2 (*Lee, Hector*)
Twente 1 (*Bos*)
Ipswich T 1 (*Hamilton*)
Ajax 0
Stoke C 0

Dundee 2 (*Duncan, Jocky Scott*)
RWD Molenbeek 4 (*Teugels, Boskamp, Wellens 2*)
Hibernian 9 (*Harper 2, Munro 2, Stanton 2, Cropley, Gordon*)
Rosenborg 1 (*Iversen*)
Wolves 3 (*Richards, Dougan, Daley*)
Porto 1 (*Cubillas*)
Inter-Milan 3 (*Oriali, Boninsegna 2*)
Etar 0
Partizan Belgrade 3 (*Dordevic, Vukotic, Todozevic*)
Gornik Zabrze 0
Djurgaarden 5 (*Skotte, Stenbach, Karlsson 2, Samuelsson*)
Start 1 (*Mathiesen*)
Dynamo Bucharest 3 (*Dinu, Dumitrache, Lucescu*)
Boluspor 0
Velez Mostar 2 (*Colic, Popic*)
Spartak Moscow 0
Steagul Brasov 3 (*Serbaniou 3*)
Besiktas 0
Borussia Moenchengladbach 3 (*Heynckes, Jensen, Vogts*)
SW Innsbruck 0
Antwerp 1 (*Kodat*)
Sturm Graz 0
Dynamo Dresden 0
Randers Freja 0
Bohemians 0
Hamburg 1 (*Bertl*)
Aris Salonika 1 (*Alexiadis*)
Rapid Vienna 0
Banik Ostrava 4 (*Vojacek, Slany, Albrecht, Kolecko*)
Real Sociedad 0
Raba ETO 3 (*Sebo, Penzes, Proczik*)
Lokomotiv Plovdiv 1 (*Kichekov*)
Dynamo Moscow 2 (*Evryuzhikhin, Petrushin*)
Oesters 1 (*Svensson*)
Legia Warsaw 0
Nantes 1 (*Merigot*)
Videoton 1 (*Wollek*)
Napoli 1 (*Braglia*)
Juventus 3 (*Anastasi, Altafini, Hause og*)
Vorwaerts 0
Panathinaikos 2 (*Antoniadis 2*)
Grasshoppers 1 (*Santrac*)
Fortuna Dusseldorf 3 (*Zimmerman, Seel, Geye pen*)
Torino 1 (*Agroppi*)
Kokkolan 1 (*Lamberg*)
Cologne 4 (*Neumann, Lohr, Simmet 2*)
Hibernian Malta 0
FC Amsterdam 7 (*Karte, 2 Jansen 2, Franz, Husers, Dekkers*)
Atletico Madrid 4 (*Leal, Garate, Irureta 2*)
KB Copenhagen 0
Real Zaragoza 4 (*Arrua, Diarte, Castany, Leiros*)
Vitoria Setubal 0
Dukla Prague had a walkover when Pezoporikos withdrew

Second Round, First Leg
Derby County 2 (*Nish, Rioch pen*)
Atletico Madrid 2 (*Luis pen, Ayala*)
Hibernian 2 (*Stanton, Cropley*)
Juventus 4 (*Gentile, Altafini 2, Cuccurredu*)
Partizan Belgrade 5 (*Kosic 2, Zavajic, Nikolic, Vukotic*)
Portadown 0
Nantes 1 (*Bossis*)
Banik Ostrava 0
Dynamo Bucharest 1 (*Dinu*)
Cologne 1 (*Luscher*)
Raba ETO 2 (*Varsanyi, Stolz*)
Fortuna Dusseldorf 0
Rapid Vienna 1 (*Ritter*)
Velez Mostar 1 (*Halaldiz*)

Dynamo Dresden 1 (*Sasche*)
Dynamo Moscow 0
Grasshoppers 2 (*Grahn, Santrac*)
Real Zaragoza 1 (*Arrua*)
Borussia Moenchengladbach 1 (*Simonsen*)
Lyon 0
Hamburg 8 (*Volkert 2, Bertl, Zaczyk, Memering, Nogly, Ripp, Krobach*)
Steagul Brasov 0
Twente 2 (*Thijssen, Van der Vall*)
RWD Molenbeek 1 (*Koens*)
Djurgaarden 0
Dukla Prague 2 (*Nehoda, Gajdusek*)
Inter-Milan 1 (*Boninsegna*)
FC Amsterdam 2 (*Jansen 2*)
Napoli 1 (*Orlandini*)
Porto 0
Ajax 1 (*Gerrie Muhren*)
Antwerp 0

Second Round, Second Leg

Atletico Madrid 2 (*Luis 2*)
Derby County 2 (*Rioch, Hector*) Derby won 7-6 on penalties
Juventus 4 (*Bettega, Anastasi, 2 Altafini*)
Hibernian 0
Portadown 1 (*Malcolmson*)
Partizan Belgrade 1 (*Tordevic*)
Banik Ostrava (*Klement 2*)
Nantes 0
Cologne 3 (*Overath, Muller, Neumann*)
Dynamo Bucharest 2 (*Custov, Georgescu*)
Fortuna Dusseldorf 3 (*Herzog, Szernotzky, Brucken*)
Raba ETO 0
Velez Mostar 1 (*Halaldiz*)
Rapid Vienna 0
Dynamo Moscow 1 (*Korneev*)
Dynamo Dresden 0
Real Zaragoza 5 (*Rubial 2, Soto, Olhauser og, Niggl og*)
Grasshoppers 0
Lyon 2 (*Valette, R Domenech*)
Borussia Moencheggladbach 5 (*Bonhof 2, Simonsen 2, Kulik*)
Steagul Brasov 1 (*Curbaniou*)
Hamburg 2 (*Kaltz, Bjornmose*)
RWD Molenbeek 0
Twente 1 (*Zuidema*)
Dukla Prague 3 (*Nehoda 2, Macela*)
Djurgaarden 1 (*Svensson*)
FC Amsterdam 0
Inter-Milan 0
Porto 0
Napoli 1 (*Juliano*)
Antwerp 2 (*Kodat, Riedl pen*)
Ajax 1 (*Geels*)

Third Round, First Leg

Napoli 0
Banik Ostrava 2 (*Albrecht, Kolecko*)
Hamburg 4 (*Bjornmose 2, Volkert, Nogly*)
Dynamo Dresden 1 (*Schmuck*)
Dukla Prague 3 (*Dvorak, Krumich, Nehoda*)
Twente 1 (*Jeuring*)

Partizan Belgrade 1 (*Vukotic*)
Cologne 0
Borussia Moenchengladbach 5 (*Heynckes 2, Simonsen 2, Bonhof*)
Real Zaragoza 0
FC Amsterdam 3 (*Husers 2, Kriegler og*)
Fortuna Dusseldorf 0
Juventus 1 (*Damiani*)
Ajax 0
Derby County 3 (*Bourne 2, Hinton*)
Velez Mostar 1 (*Vladic*)

Third Round, Second Leg

Banik Ostrava 1 (*Slany*)
Napoli 1 (*Ferrandini*)
Dynamo Dresden 2 (*Dorner, Hafner*)
Hamburg 2 (*Bertl 2*)
Twente 5 (*Zuidema 3, Notten 2*)
Dukla Prague 0
Cologne 5 (*Overath, Lohr, Muller, Glowacz, Flohe*)
Partizan Belgrade 1 (*Povlovic*)
Real Zaragoza 2 (*Vileta, Galdos*)
Borussia Moenchengladbach 4 (*Simonsen, Heynckes 2, Stielike*)
Fortuna Dusseldorf 1 (*Seel*)
FC Amsterdam 2 (*Husers, Jansen*)
Ajax 2 (*Blankenburg, Gerrie Muhren*)
Juventus 1 (*Damiani pen*)
Velez Mostar 4 (*Bajevic pen, Pecelj, Vladic, Primorac pen*)
Derby County 1 (*Hector*)

Quarter-finals, First Leg

Juventus (2) 2 (*Capello, Viola*)
Hamburg (0) 0
Cologne (1) 5 (*Flohe 2, 1 a pen, Muller 3*)
Amsterdam (1) 1 (*Visser*)
Velez Mostar (0) 1 (*Kvesic*)
Twente (0) 0
Banik Ostrava (0) 0
Borussia Moenchengladbach (0) 1 (*Heynckes*)

Quarter-finals, Second Leg

Hamburg (0) 0
Juventus (0) 0
Borussia Moenchengladbach (1) 3 (*Micka og, Heynckes, Vogts*)
Banik Ostrava (0) 1 (*Hudecek*)
Amsterdam (0) 2 (*Jansen 2*)
Cologne (2) 3 (*Strack, Muller, Lohr*)
Twente (1) 2 (*Zuidema, Overweg*)
Velez Mostar (0) 0

Semi-finals, First Leg

Twente (1) 3 (*Jeuring, Zuidema 2*)
Juventus (0) 1 (*Altafini*)
FC Cologne (0) 1 (*Lohr*)
Borussia Moenchengladbach (2) 3 (*Simonsen 2, Danner*)

Semi-finals, Second Leg

Juventus (0) 0
Twente (0) 1 (*Zuidema*)
Borussia Moenchengladbach (0) 1 (*Danner*)
FC Cologne (0) 0

Final 1974-75: Borussia Moenchengladbach 0, Twente Enschede 0
(First leg at Dusseldorf, May 7, 1975, 45,000)

Bor Moenchengladbach: Kleff; Wittkamp, Stielike, Vogts, Surau, Bonhof, Wimmer, Danner (Del Haye), Kulik (Schaffer), Simonsen, Jensen.

Twente Enschede: Gross; Drost, Van Ierssel, Overweg, Oranen, Thijssen, Pahlplatz, Van der Vall, Bos, Jeuring (Achterberg), Zuidema.

Twente Enschede 1, Borussia Moenchengladbach 5
(Second leg at Enschede, May 21, 1975, 24,500)

Twente Enschede: Gross, Drost, Van Ierssel, Overweg, Oranen, Bos (Muhren), Thijssen, Pahlplatz (Achterberg), Van der Vall, Jeuring, Zuidema.

Bor Moenchengladbach: Kleff; Wittkamp, Vogts, Surau (Schafer), Klinkhammer, Bonhof, Wimmer (Koppel), Danner, Simonsen, Jensen, Heynckes.

Scorers: Bor Moenchengladbach; Heynckes (3), Simonsen (2, 1 a pen), Twente Enschede; Drost.

UEFA CUP 1975-76

First Round, First Leg
Duisburg 7 (*Mertakas og, Lehmann 3, Worm 2, Thies*)
Paralimni 1 (*Chatzyannis*)
Glentoran 1 (*Jamieson*)
Ajax 6 (*Geels, 4 Meyer, Notten*)
Grasshoppers 3 (*Elsener, Santrac, Bosco*)
Real Sociedad 3 (*Satrustegui 2, Murillo*)
PAOK Salonika 1 (*Koudas*)
Barcelona 0
AIK Stockholm 1 (*Leback pen*)
Spartak Moscow 1 (*Lovchev*)
Antwerp 4 (*Heylingen, Kodat 3*)
Aston Villa 1 (*Graydon*)
Bohemians Prague 1 (*Masnik*)
Honved 2 (*Pinter, Toth*)
Carl Zeiss Jena 3 (*Sengewald 2, Kurbjuweit*)
Marseille 0
Uni Craiova 1 (*Oblemenco*)
Red Star Belgrade 3 (*Filipovic 2, Savic*)
Everton 0
AC Milan 0
Feyenoord 1 (*De Jong*)
Ipswich 2 (*Whymark, Johnson*)
GAIS Gothenburg 2 (*Palsson 2, 1 a pen*)
Slask Wroclaw 1 (*Kwaitkowski*)
Hertha Berlin 4 (*Kostedde 2, Hoor 2*)
HJK Helsinki 1 (*Kangaslorpi*)
Hibernian 1 (*Harper*)
Liverpool 0
Holbaek 0
Stal Mielec 1 (*Domarski*)
Cologne 2 (*Glowacz, Lohr*)
B 1903 Copenhagen 0
Lyon 4 (*Jodar, Millard 2, Mihajlovic*)
Bruges 3 (*Van der Eycken, 3, 1 pen*)
Molde 1 (*Wetterdahl*)
Oesters Vaxjo 0
Tirgu Mures 2 (*Muresan, Faxekas*)
Dynamo Dresden 2 (*Schade, Heidler*)
Chernomonretz Odessa 1 (*Doroschenko*)
Lazio 0
Porto 7 (*Julio, Cubillas 3, 1 a pen, Oliveira, Octavio, Gomes*)
Avenir Beggen 0
Rapid Vienna 1 (*Widmann*)
Galatasaray 0
Roma 2 (*Pellegrini, Petrini*)
Dounav Russe 0
Moscow Torpedo 4 (*Grishken 2, Sakharov pen, Belenkov*)
Napoli 1 (*Savoldi*)
VOEST Linz 2 (*Scharmann, Stering*)
Vasas Budapest 0
Vojvodina 0
AEK Athens 0
Young Boys 0
Hamburg 0
Athlone T 2 (*Martin, Davis 2*)
Valerengen 1 (*Olsen*)
Inter Bratislava 5 (*Levicky, Luprich, Petras, Jurkemik, Sajanek*)
Zaragoza 0
Keflavik 0
Dundee U 2 (*Narey 2*)
Levski Spartak 3 (*Spassov 2, Panov*)
Eskisehirspor 0
Sliema Wanderers 1 (*Azzopardi*)
Sporting Lisbon 2 (*Marinho, Fernandez*)

First Round, Second Leg
Paralimni 2 (*Konstantinou A, Mertakas*)
Duisburg 3 (*Dietz, Krause, Seliger*)
Dundee U 4 (*Hall 2, Hegarty pen, Sturrock*)
Keflavik 0
Liverpool 3 (*Toshack 3*)
Hibernian 1 (*Edwards*)
AEK Athens 3 (*Papaioannou, Papadopoulos, Wagner*)
Vojvodina 1 (*Buikov*)

Ajax 8 (*Notten, Van Dord, Geels 3, G Muhren, Brokamp 2*)
Glentoran 0
Aston Villa 0
Antwerp 1 (*Kodat*)
Barcelona 6 (*Neeskens 2 pens, Rexach 3, Cruyff*)
PAOK Salonika 1 (*Anastasiadis*)
Bruges 3 (*Van der Eycken, Valette og, Chnier og*)
Lyon 0
Avenir Beggen 0
Porto 3 (*Julio, Grilli og, Seninho*)
Marseille 0
Carl Zeiss Jena 1 (*Irmscher*)
B 1903 Copenhagen 2 (*Christiansen 2*)
Cologne 3 (*Brucken 3*)
Dounav Russe 1 (*Ivanov*)
Roma 0
Dynamo Dresden 4 (*Heidler 3, Kreische*)
Tirgu Mures 1 (*Muresan*)
Eskisehirspor 1 (*Mehmet*)
Levski Spartak 4 (*Spassov 2, Panov, Milanov*)
Galatasaray 3 (*Sevki, Gokmen 2*)
Rapid Vienna 1 (*Krankl*)
Hamburg 4 (*Reimann, Bertl 2, Bjornmose*)
Young Boys 2 (*Siegenthaler 2*)
HJK Helsinki 1 (*Salo*)
Hertha Berlin 2 (*Sidka, Grau*)
Honved 1 (*Kocsis pen*)
Bohemians Prague 1 (*Panenka*)
Ipswich 2 (*Woods, Whymark*)
Feyenoord 0
Lazio 3 (*Chinaglia 3, 1 a pen*)
Chernomoretz Odessa 0
AC Milan 1 (*Calloni pen*)
Everton 0
Napoli 1 (*Braglia*)
Moscow Torpedo 1 (*Filatov*)
Oesters Vaxjo 6 (*Svensson, Matsson 2, Evesson, Ejderstedt, Isaxsson*)
Molde 0
Red Star Belgrade 1 (*Filipovic pen*)
Uni Craiova 1 (*Krizan*)
Real Sociedad 1 (*Urreisti*)
Grasshoppers 1 (*Santrac*)
Slask Wroclaw 4 (*Sybis 3, Pawlowski*)
GAIS Gothenburg 2 (*Hans Johanson 2*)
Moscow Spartak 1 (*Andreyev*)
AIK Stockholm 0
Sporting Lisbon 3 (*Baltazar, Da Costa, Manue Fernades pen*)
Sliema Wanderers 1 (*Loporto*)
Stal Mielec 2 (*Karas, Krawczyk*)
Holbaek 1 (*Torben Hansen*)
Valerengen 1 (*Dag Olvavason*)
Athlone T 1 (*Martin*)
Vasas Budapest 4 (*Varadi 2, Kovacs, Izso*)
VOEST Linz 0
Zaragoza 2 (*Pepe Gonzalez pen, Arrua*)
Inter Bratislava 3 (*Jurkemik, Petras, Mraz*)

Second Round, First Leg
Duisburg 3 (*Schneider W, Worm, Krause*)
Levski Spartak 2 (*Panov 2*)
Athlone T 0
AC Milan 0
Carl Zeiss Jena 1 (*Kurbjuweit*)
Stal Mielec 0
Dundee U 1 (*Rennie*)
Porto 2 (*Oliveira, Seninho*)
Galatasaray 2 (*Sevki, Gokmen*)
Moscow Torpedo 4 (*Enver og, Hrobroskin, Sakharov pen, Maksimenkov*)
Hertha Berlin 1 (*Kostedde*)
Ajax 0
Honved 2 (*Weimper 2*)
Dynamo Dresden 2 (*Heidler 2*)
Inter Bratislava 2 (*Luprich pen, Mraz*)
AEK Athens 0
Ipswich 3 (*Gates, Peddelty, Austin*)
Bruges 0

Spartak Moscow 2 (*Lovchev 2*)
Cologne 0
Oesters Vaxjo 1 (*Evansson*)
Roma 0
Real Sociedad 1 (*Amas*)
Liverpool 3 (*Heighway, Callaghan, Thompson*)
Red Star Belgrade 1 (*Susic*)
Hamburg 1 (*Bjornmose*)
Slask Wroclaw 1 (*Pawlowski*)
Antwerp 1 (*Houwaart*)
Vasas Budapest 3 (*Kovacs 2, Varad pen*)
Sporting Lisbon 1 (*Chico*)
Lazio 0
Barcelona 3 (*Lazio refused to play because of possible political demonstrations against the Spaniards. FIFA thus awarded the game to Barcelona 3-0*).

Second Round, Second Leg
Levski Spartak 2 (*Ivkov, Panov pen*)
Duisburg 1 (*Worm*)
Liverpool 6 (*Toshack, Kennedy 2, Fairclough, Heighway, Neal*)
Real Sociedad 0
Ajax 4 (*Brokamp, Geels 2, 1 a pen, Meyer*)
Hertha Berlin 1 (*Kostedde*)
Antwerp 1 (*De Schrijver*)
Slask Wroclaw 2 (*Sybis, Pawlowski*)
AEK Athens 3 (*Tassos 2, 1 a pen, Wagner*)
Inter Bratislava 1 (*Novotny*)
Barcelona 4 (*Sotil, Cruyff, Neeskens, Fortes*)
Lazio 0
Bruges 4 (*Lambert 1 pen, De Cubber, Le Fevre, Van der Eycken*)
Ipswich 0
Dynamo Dresden 1 (*Dorner pen*)
Honved 0
Hamburg 4 (*Reimann 2, Ettmayer, Memering*)
Red Star Belgrade 0
Cologne 0
Moscow Spartak 1 (*Andreyev*)
AC Milan 3 (*Vincenzi, Benetti 2, 1 a pen*)
Athlone T
Moscow Torpedo 3 (*Degtyarev, Sahkarov pen, Budulakin*)
Galatasaray 0
Porto 1 (*Seninho*)
Dundee U 1 (*Hegarty*)
Roma 2 (*Pellegrini, Boni*)
Oesters Vaxjo 0
Sporting Lisbon 2 (*Manuel Fernandes 2*)
Vasas Budapest 1 (*Grass*)
Stal Mielec 1 (*Karas*)
Car Zeiss Jena 0

Third Round, First Leg
Ajax 2 (*Geels, Steffenhagen*)
Levski Spartak 1 (*Voinov*)
Barcelona 3 (*Migueli, Rexach, Neeskens*)
Vasas Budapest 1 (*Muller*)
Bruges 1 (*Cools*)
Roma 0
Dynamo Dresden 3 (*Riedel 2, Kreische*)
Moscow Torpedo 0
Hamburg 2 (*Zaczyk, Volkert pen*)
Porto 0
Inter Bratislava 1 (*Saljanek*)
Stal Mielec 0
Slask Wroclaw 1 (*Pawlowski*)
Liverpool 2 (*Faber og, Toshack*)
AC Milan 4 (*Calloni 2, Bigon, Maldera*)
Moscow Spartak 0

Third Round, Second Leg
Levski Spartak 2 (*Panov 2*)
Ajax 1 (*Geels*)
Liverpool 3 (*Case 3*)
Slask Wroclaw 0
Moscow Spartak 2 (*Papayev, Ovchev*)
AC Milan 0
Moscow Torpedo 3 (*Dedtyaryov 2, Petrenko*)
Dynamo Dresden 1 (*Heidler*)
Porto 2 (*Julio, Cubillas*)
Hamburg 1 (*Reimann*)
Roma 0
Bruges 1 (*Lambert*)
Stal Mielec 2 (*Sekulski, Karas*)
Inter Bratislava 0
Vasas Budapest 0
Barcelona 1 (*Fortes*)

Quarter-finals, First Leg
Barcelona 4 (*Neeskens pen, Marcial, Asensi, Heredia*)
Levski Spartak 0
Bruges 2 (*Le Fevre, Krieger*)
AC Milan 0
Dynamo Dresden 0
Liverpool 0
Hamburg 1 (*Bertl*)
Stal Mielec 1 (*Oratowski*)

Quarter-finals, Second Leg
Levski Spartak 5 (*Panov 2, 1 a pen, Yordanov 2, Spassov*)
Barcelona 4 (*Marcial, Asensi, Heredia, Neeskens pen*)
Liverpool 2 (*Case, Keegan*)
Dynamo Dresden 1 (*Heidler*)
AC Milan 2 (*Chiarugi 2*)
Bruges 1 (*Sanders*)
Stal Mielec 0
Hamburg 1 (*Nogly*)

Semi-finals, First Leg
Barcelona 0
Liverpool 1 (*Toshack*)
Hamburg 1 (*Reimann*)
Bruges 1 (*Lambert*)

Semi-finals, Second Leg
Bruges 1 (*Kaltz og*)
Hamburg 0
Liverpool 1 (*Thompson*)
Barcelona 1 (*Rexach*)

Final 1975–76: Liverpool 3, Bruges 2
(First leg at Anfield, April 28 1976, 56,000)

Liverpool: Clemence; Smith, Neal, Thompson, Kennedy, Hughes, Keegan, Fairclough, Heighway, Toshack (Case), Callaghan.
Bruges: Jensen; Bastyns, Krieger, Leekens, Volders, Cools, Van der Eycken, De Cubber, Van Gool, Lambert, Le Fevre.
Scorers: Liverpool: Kennedy, Case, Keegan pen. Bruges: Lambert, Cools.

Bruges 1, Liverpool 1
(Second leg at Olympia Stadium, Bruges, May 19 1976, 32,000)

Bruges: Jensen; Bastyns, Krieger, Leekens, Volders, Cools, Van der Eycken, Van Gool, Lambert (Sanders), De Cubber (Hinderyckx), Le Fevre.
Liverpool: Clemence; Smith, Neal, Thompson, Kennedy, Hughes, Keegan, Case, Heighway, Toshack (Fairclough), Callaghan.
Scorers: Bruges: Lambert, pen. Liverpool: Keegan.

UEFA CUP 1976-77

First Round, First Leg
Porto 2 (*Rodolfo, Cubillas*)
Schalke 04 2 (*Erwin Kremers, Fischer*)
Fram Reykjavik 0
Slovan Bratislava 3 (*Haraslin 2, Mrva*)
Glentoran 3 (*Feeney 2, Dickinson*)
Basle 2 (*Maissen, Ramseier*)
Paralimni 1 (*Mertakas*)
Kaiserslautern 3 (*Rinderl, Meier, Spiergerl*)
AEK Athens 2 (*Nikoloudis, Papaioannou*)
Moscow Dynamo 0
Ajax 1 (*Krol*)
Manchester U 0
Austria Salzburg 5 (*Schwarz 3, 1 pen, Haider 2*)
Adanaspor 0
Belenenses 2 (*Quaresma, Horta*)
Barcelona 2 (*Heredia 2*)
Celtic 2 (*McDonald, Dalglish*)
Wisla Krakow 2 (*Kmiecik, Wrobel*)
Derby C 12 (*Hector 5, Rioch, James 3, George 3*)
Finn Harps 0
Dynamo Bucharest 0
AC Milan 0
Eintracht Brunswick 7 (*Hollmann, Stoltenburg 2, Frank 3, Gersdorff*)
Holbaek 0
Espanol 3 (*Cuesta, Maranon, Caszely*)
Nice 1 (*Toko*)
Feyenoord 3 (*Schneider pen, Kreuz, Vreysen*)
Djurgaarden 0
Fenerbahce 2 (*Cemil 2*)
Videoton 1 (*Nagy*)
Grasshoppers 7 (*Bosco, Ponte, Seiler 2, Bauer, Corniοley 2, 1 pen*)
Hibernian Malta 0
Hibernian 1 (*Brownlie*)
Sochaux 0
Internazionale 0
Honved 1 (*Kozma*)
Cologne 2 (*Flohe pen, Van Gool*)
GKS Tychy 0
Kuopion Palloseura 3 (*Toernroos, Rissanen 2*)
Oester Vaxjo 2 (*Stromberg, Ejderstedt*)
Magdeburg 3 (*Steinbach, Streich 2, 1 pen*)
Cesena 0
Manchester C 1 (*Kidd*)
Juventus 0
Naestved 0
RWD Molenbeek 3 (*Boskamp, Wellens 2*)
QPR 4 (*Bowles 3, Masson*)
Brann Bergen 0
Red Boys Differdange 0
Lokeren 3 (*Verheyen 2, Dalving*)
Slavia Prague 2 (*Herda, Radolsky*)
Akademik Sofia 0
Schachtjor Donetzk 3 (*Rogovsky, Sokolvsky, Starukhin*)
Dynamo Berlin 0
Sportul Studentes 3 (*Grosu, Ionescu 2*)
Olympiakos 0
Wacker Innsbruck 2 (*Sterig, Pezzey*)
Start Kristiansand 1 (*Mathiesen pen*)
ASA Tirgu Mures 0
Dynamo Zagreb 1 (*Jurisic*)
Ujpest Dozsa 1 (*Dunai II*)
Athletic Bilbao 0
Lokomotiv Plovdiv 2 (*Fidanov, Bonev*)
Red Star Belgrade 1 (*Filipovic*)

First Round, Second Leg
Adanaspor 2 (*Isa, Sener*)
Austria Salzburg 0
Akademik Sofia 3 (*Dimitrov 2, Yankov*)
Slavia Prague 0
Barcelona 3 (*Rexach, Asensi, Clares*)
Belenenses 2 (*Vasques, Rocha*)
Basle 3 (*Nielsen, Mundschin, Demarmels*)
Glentoran 0
Dynamo Berlin 1 (*Noak*)
Schachtjor Donetzk 1 (*Rogowski*)

Athletic Bilbao 5 (*Rojo 2, Dani 3*)
Ujpest Dozsa 0
Brann Bergen 0
QPR 7 (*Webb, Givens 2, Bowles 3, Thomas*)
Cesena 2 (*Mariani, Pepe, Macchi*)
Magdeburg 1 (*Sparwasser*)
Djurgaarden 2 (*K Karlsson, Stenbaek*)
Feyenoord 1 (*Nico Jansen*)
Dynamo Zagreb 3 (*Sensen 2, Bogdan*)
ASA Tirgu Mures 0
Finn Harps 1 (*McFarland og*)
Derby C 4 (*Hector 2, George 2*)
Hibernian Malta 0
Grasshoppers 2 (*Sieler, Cornioley pen*)
Holbaek 1 (*Tofte*)
Eintracht Brunswick 0
Honved 1 (*Poczik*)
Internazionale 1 (*Mariani*)
Juventus 2 (*Scirea, Boninsegna*)
Manchester C 0
Lokeren 3 (*Mommens, Hansen, Lubanski*)
Red Boys Differdange 1 (*Flenghi pen*)
Manchester U 2 (*Macari, McIlroy*)
Ajax 0
Moscow Dynamo 2 (*Bubnov, Yukubik pen*)
AEK Athens 1 (*Tassos pen*)
Nice 2 (*Toko, Bjekovic*)
Esponal 1 (*Aquino pen*)
Oester Vaxjo 2 (*Stromberg, Svensson*)
Kuopion Palloseura 0
Olympiakos 2 (*Galakos, Karavitis pen*)
Sportul Studentes 1 (*Radacanu*)
RWD Molenbeek 4 (*Koons, Boskamp 2, 1 pen, Cordier*)
Naestved 0
Schalke 04 3 (*Fichtel, Abramczik, Fischer*)
Porto 2 (*Oliveira 2*)
Slovan Bratislava 5 (*Pekarik, Ondrus, Barto, Capkovic, Atlasson eg*)
Fram Reykjavik 0
Sochaux 0
Hibernian 0
Start Kristiansand 0
Wacker Innsbruck 5 (*Koncilia 2, Sterling 2, 1 pen, Wltzl*)
GKS Tychy 1 (*Ogaza*)
Cologne 1 (*Muller*)
Videoton 4 (*Wollek, J Kovacs, Szalmasy 2*)
Fenerbahce 0
Wisla Krakow 2 (*Kmiecik 2*)
Celtic 0
Kaiserslautern 8 (*Toppmuller 4, Pirrung 2, Meier, Riedl*)
Paralimni 0
AC Milan 2 (*Calloni, Silva*)
Dinamo Bucharest 1 (*Satmareanu*)
Red Star Belgrade 4 (*Bolicevic, Filipovic 2, Stamenkovic*)
Lokomotiv Plovdiv 1 (*Bonev*)

Second Round, First Leg
AEK Athens 2 (*Wagner 2*)
Derby County 0
Akademik Sofia 4 (*Paunov 2, Manolov, Dimitrov*)
AC Milan 3 (*Capello 2, Colovatti*)
Austria Salzburg 2 (*P. Schwarz, W. Schwarz pen.*)
Red Star Belgrade 1 (*Filipovic*)
Barcelona 2 (*Cruyff, Clares*)
Lokeren 0
Basle 1 (*Marti*)
Athletic Bilbao 1 (*Madariaga*)
Eintracht Brunswick 2 (*Frank, Stolzenburg*)
Espanol 1 (*Maranon*)
Hibernian 2 (*Blackley, Brownlie*)
Oester Vaxjo 0
Swarowski Innsbruck 1 (*Sterling*)
Videoton 1 (*Czeczeli pen*)
Kaiserslautern 2 (*Briegel 2*)
Feyenoord 2 (*De Jong, Nico Jansen*)

Cologne 2 (*Konopka, Muller*)
Grasshoppers 0
Magdeburg 2 (*Steinbach, Zapf*)
Dynamo Zagreb 0
Manchester United 1 (*Hill*)
Juventus 0
Schachtjor Donetzk 3 (*Shevluch, Starukhin, Vasin*)
Honved 0
Slovan Bratislava 3 (*Novotny, Haraslin, Ondrus*)
QPR 3 (*Bowles 2, Givens*)
Sportul Studentesc 0
Schalke 04 1 (*Fischer*)
Wisla Krakow 1 (*Kapka*)
RWD Molenbeck 1 (*Olsen*)

Second Round, Second Leg
Athletic Bilbao 3 (*Villar, Carlos, Rojo* 1)
Basle 1 (*Marti*)
Derby County 2 (*George, Rioch*)
AEK Athens 3 (*Nikoloudis, Tassos, Wagner*)
Dynamo Zagreb 2 (*Kranjcar* 2)
Magdeburg 2 (*Streich, Pommerenke*)
Espanol 2 (*Jeremias, Ortiz Aquino pen*)
Eintracht Brunswick 0
Feyenoord 5 (*Wim Jansen, Nico Jansen, De Jong, Van Deinsen, Schneider pen*)
Kaiserslautern 0
Grasshoppers 2 (*Bauer pen., Bosco*)
FC Cologne 3 (*Muller, Larsen* 2)
Honved 2 (*Kozma* 2, 1 a pen)
Schachtjor Donetzk 3 (*Shevluik, Reznik* 2)
Juventus 3 (*Boninsegna* 2, *Benetti*)
Manchester United 0
AC Milan 2 (*Calloni, Morini*)
Akademik Sofia 0
Oester Vaxjo 4 (*Linderoth* 2, *Ejderstedt* 2)
Hibernian 1 (*Smith*)
QPR 5 (*Givens* 3, 1 a pen, *Bowles, Clement*)
Slovan Bratislava 2 (*Ondrus, Jan Capkovic*)
Red Star Belgrade 1 (*Filipovic*)
Austria Salzburg 0
RWD Molenbeek 1 (*Nielsen*)
Wisla Krakow 1 (*Maculewicz*)
Schalke 4 (*Bongartz* 2, *Fischer* 2)
Sportul Bucharest 0
Videoton 1 (*Nagy*)
SW Innsbruck 0
Lokeren 2 (*Verheyen, Dalving*)
Barcelona 1 (*Cruyff*)

Third Round, First Leg
AEK Athens 2 (*Papaioannou, Marvos*)
Red Star Belgrade 0
Athletic Bilbao 4 (*Dani* 2, 1 a pen, *Carlos* 2)
AC Milan 1 (*Capello*)
Espanol 0
Feyenoord 1 (*De Felipe og*)
Juventus 3 (*Bettega, Tardelli, Boninsegna*)
Schachtjor Donetzk 0

Magdeburg 5 (*Streich, Tyll* 2, *Mewes, Pommerenke*)
Videoton 0
Oester Vaxjo 0
Barcelona 3 (*Clares* 2, *Neeskens*)
QPR 3 (*Givens, Webb, Bowles*)
Cologne 0
RWD Molenbeek 1 (*Lafont*)
Schalke 04 0

Third Round, Second Leg
Cologne 4 (*Muller* 2, *Lohr, Weber*)
QPR 1 (*Masson*)
Barcelona 5 (*Clares, Cruyff, Asensi* 2, *Heredia*)
Oester Vaxjo 1 (*Everson*)
Feyenoord 2 (*Krauz, Nico Jansen*)
Espanol 0
AC Milan 3 (*Calloni* 2, 1 a pen, *Biasiolo*)
Athletic Bilbao 1 (*Madariaga pen*)
Red Star Belgrade 3 (*Baralic, Filipovic, Savic*)
AEK Athens 1 (*Wagner*)
Schalke 04 1 (*Abramczik*)
RWD Molenbeek 1 (*Teugels*)
Schachtjor Donetsk 1 (*Shevluk*)
Juventus 0
Videoton 1 (*J. Nagy*)
Magdeburg 0

Quarter-finals, First Leg
Athletic Bilbao 2 (*Churruca, Dani pen*)
Barcelona 1 (*Asensi*)
Feyenoord 0
RWD Molenbeek 0
Magdeburg 1 (*Streich*)
Juventus 3 (*Cuccureddu, Benetti, Boninsegna*)
QPR 3 (*Francis*, 2 pens, *Bowles*)
AEK Athens 0

Quarter-finals, Second Leg
AEK Athens 3 (*Mavros* 2, *Papaioannou*)
QPR 0
Barcelona 2 (*Cruyff* 2)
Athletic Bilbao 2 (*Irureta* 2)
Juventus 1 (*Cuccureddu*)
Magdeburg 0
RWD Molenbeek 2 (*Wellens, Teugels pen*)
Feyenoord 1 (*De Jong*)

Semi-finals, First Leg
RWD Molenbeek 1 (*Teugels*)
Athletic Bilbao 1 (*Churruca*)
Juventus 4 (*Cucureddu, Bettega* 2, *Causio*)
AEK Athens 1 (*Papadopoulos*)

Semi-finals, Second Leg
AEK Athens 0
Juventus 1 (*Bettega*)
Athletic Bilbao 0
RWD Molenbeek 0

Final 1976–77: Juventus (1) 1 Athletic Bilbao (0) 0
(First leg in Turin, May 4 1977, 75,000)

Juventus: Zoff; Cuccureddu, Gentile, Scirea, Morini, Tardelli, Furino, Benetti, Causio, Boninsegna (Gori), Bettega.
Bilbao: Iribar; Villar, Escalza, Guoicoechea, Guisasola, Quaderra, Irureta, Rojo II, Dani, Churruca, Rojo I.
Scorer: Juventus: Tardelli.

Athletic Bilbao (1) 2 Juventus (1) 1
(Second leg in Bilbao, May 18 1977, 43,000)

Bilbao: Iribar; Lasa (Carlos), Guisasola, Alesanco, Escalza, Villar, Churruca, Irureta, Amarrortu, Dani, Rojo I.
Juventus: Zoff; Cuccureddu, Morini, Scirea, Gentile, Causio, Tardelli, Furino, Benetti, Boninsegna (Spinosi), Bettega.
Scorers: Bilbao: Irureta, Carlos. Juventus: Bettega.

UEFA CUP 1977-78

First round, first leg

Eintracht Frankfurt 5 (*Nickel 2, Wenzel, Kraus, Grabowski*)
Sliema Wanderers 0
AZ 67 11 (*Van Hanegem, Arntz, Nygaard 3, Peters 4, Kist 2*)
Red Boys 1 (*Christoph pen*)
Aston Villa 4 (*Gray, Deehan 2, Little*)
Fenerbahce 0
Barcelona 5 (*Heredia 2, Cruyff pen, Clares, Zuviria*)
Steaua 1 (*Nastase*)
Bastia 3 (*Felix 3*)
Sporting Lisbon 2 (*Jordao pen, Fraguito*)
Bayern Munich 8 (*Oblak, Rummenigge 3, Hoeness, Muller 3*)
Mjondalen 0
Boavista 1 (*Jorge Gomes*)
Lazio 0
Bohemians 0
Newcastle United 0
Carl Zeiss Jena 5 (*Trocha 2, Vogel 2, 1 pen, Topfer*)
Altay Izmir 1 (*Mustafa pen*)
Dundee United 1 (*Sturrock*)
KB Copenhagen 0
Fiorentina 0
Schalke 04 0
Frem Copenhagen 0
Grasshoppers 2 (*Elsener, Becker*)
Glenavon 2 (*Malone pen, McDonald*)
PSV Eindhoven 6 (*Van der Kuylen 2, Van Kraay, Deijkers, Deacy, Lubse*)
Gornik Zabrze 5 (*Gizil 3, Radecki, Wasilewski*)
Haka Valkeakosken 3 (*Jarzyna og, Vimomen, Pivinen*)
Internazionale 0
Dynamo Tbilisi 1 (*Kipiani*)
Dynamo Kiev 1 (*Vermeeyev*)
Eintracht Brunswick 1 (*Frank*)
Landskrona 0
Ipswich 1 (*Whymark*)
Las Palmas 5 (*Maciel 2, 1 pen, Juani, Morete 2*)
Sloboda Tuzla 0
Lens 4 (*Bosudira, Francoise, Djeballi, Elie*)
Malmo 1 (*Sjoberg*)
Linz ASK 3 (*Koegelberger 2, Vokovic*)
Ujpest Dozsa 2 (*Torocsik 2*)
Odra Opole 1 (*Decker*)
Magdeburg 2 (*Sparwasser*)
Olympiakos Piraeus 2 (*Karavisis, Losanda, Galakos*)
Dynamo Zagreb 1 (*Zedec*)
Manchester City 2 (*Barnes, Channon*)
Widzew Lodz 2 (*Boniek 2, 1 pen*)
Marek Stanke Dimitrov 3 (*Pargov, Petrov 2*)
Ferencvaros 0
Rapid Vienna 1 (*Walzer*)
Inter Bratislava 0
RWD Molenbeek 0
Aberdeen 0
Servette 1 (*Barberis*)
Athletic Bilbao 0
Standard Liege 1 (*Nickel*)
Slavia Prague 0
Start Kristiansand 6 (*Myhre, Skuse, Haugen 2, Mathisen 2, 1 a pen*)
Fram Reykjavik 0
ASA Tirgu Mures 1 (*Fanici*)
AEK Athens 0
Torino 3 (*Pulici 2, Claudio Sala*)
Apoel 0
Zurich 1 (*Risi*)
CSKA Sofia 0

First round, Second leg

Aberdeen 1 (*Jarvie*)
RWD Molenbeek 2 (*Gorez, Wellens*)
AEK Athens 3 (*Papaioannou, Viera, Moussouris*)
ASA Tirgu Mures 0
Altay Izmir 4 (*Mustafa 2, Murat 2*)
Carl Zeiss Jena 1 (*Lindemann*)
Apoel 1 (*Marcou*)
Torino 1 (*Garritano*)
Athletic Bilbao 2 (*Dani, Amorrortu*)
Servette 0
CSKA Sofia 1 (*Markov*)
Zurich 1 (*Cuccinotta*)
Eintracht Brunswick 0
Dynamo Kiev 0
Fenerbahce 0
Aston Villa 2 (*Deehan, Little*)
Ferencvaros 2 (*Pusztai, Ebedli pen*)
Marek Stanke 0
Grasshoppers 6 (*Meyer 2, Becker, Elsener, Ponte 2*)
Frem Copenhagen 1 (*Mikkelsen*)
Inter Bratislava 3 (*Novotny 2, Levicky 2*)
Rapid Vienna 0
Ipswich 5 (*Whymark 4, 1 a pen, Mariner*)
Landskrona 0
Lazio 5 (*Garlaschelli 2, Giordano 3*)
Boavista 0
Magdeburg 1 (*Streich*)
Odra Opole 1 (*Kiose*)
Malmo FF 2 (*Cervin, Ljungberg*)
Lens 0
Mjondalen 0
Bayern Munich 4 (*Rausch, Gruber, Kunkel, Niedermaier*)
Newcastle 4 (*Gowling 2, Craig T 2*)
Bohemians 0
PSV Eindhoven 5 (*Rene Van der Kerkhof, Lubse 2, Deijkers 2*)
Glenavon 0
Schalke 04 2 (*Abramczik, Helmut Kremers*)
Fiorentina 1 (*Desolati*)
Slavia Prague 3 (*Vesely, Notovy, Nachtman*)
Standard Liege 2 (*Nickel, Sigurvinsson*)
Sliema Wanderers 0
Eintracht Frankfurt 0
Sloboda Tuzla 4 (*Gec, Kovacevic 2, Mulahasonovic*)
Las Palmas 3 (*Morete 2, Maciel*)
Sporting Lisbon 1 (*Manuel Fernandes*)
Bastia 2 (*Rep, Desvignes*)
Steaua 1 (*Dumitru pen*)
Barcelona 3 (*Cruyff, Asensi, Sanchez*)
Dynamo Tbilisi 0
Internazionale 0
Ujpest Dozsa 7 (*Fazekas 2, Toth 2, Torocsik 2, Sarlos, Fekete*)
Linz ASK 0
Valkeakosken 0
Gornik Zabrze 0
Widzew Lodz 0
Manchester City 0
Dynamo Zagreb 5 (*Cerin 2, Senzen, Zajec pen, Bonic*)
Olympiakos Piraeus 1 (*Caravitis pen*)
Start Kristiansand 2 (*Skuseth, Ole Olsen*)
Fram Reykjavik 0
Red Boys 0
AZ 67 5 (*Kist 3, Van Hanegem, Van Rijnsoer*)
KB Copenhagen 3 (*Andersen 3*)
Dundee United 0

Second Round, First Leg
AEK Athens 2 (*Mavros, Nikoloudis*)
Standard Liege 2 (*Sigurvinsson, Poul*)
AZ 67 1 (*Nygaard*)
Barcelona 1 (*Neeskens*)
Aston Villa 2 (*McNaught 2*)
Gornik Zabrze 0
Bastia 2 (*Papi 2*)
Newcastle United 1 (*Cannell*)
Bayern Munich 3 (*Muller, Rummenigge 2*)
Marek Stanke 0
Inter Bratislava 1 (*Sajanek*)
Grasshoppers 0
Ipswich 1 (*Gates*)
Las Palmas 0
KB Copenhagen 1 (*Laudrup*)
Dynamo Tbilisi 4 (*Chiwadze, Kipiani, Chelebadze, Shengekiya*)
Lazio 2 (*Wilson, Giordano*)
Lens 0
Magdeburg 4 (*Sparwasser 3, Steinbach*)
Schalke 04 2 (*Demange, Abramczik*)
RWD Molenbeek 1 (*Wellens*)
Carl Zeiss Jena 1 (*Lindemann*)
Start Kristiansand 1 (*Helge Haugen*)
Eintracht Brunswick 0
Torino 3 (*Pulici, Patrizio Sala, Pecci*)
Dynamo Zagreb 1 (*Cerin*)
Ujpest Dozsa 2 (*Torocsik, Viczko*)
Athletic Bilbao 0
Widzew Lodz 3 (*Rozborsky, Kowenicki, Boniek*)
PSV Eindhoven 5 (*Deijkers 2, Deacy, Van der Kuylen, Francois*)
Zurich 0
Eintracht Frankfurt 3 (*Holzenbien, Wenzel 2*)

Second Round, Second Leg
Barcelona 1 (*Rexach pen*)
AZ 67 1 (*Kist*) (*Barcelona won on penalties 5-4*)
Athletic Bilbao 3 (*Dani 2, Tirapu*)
Ujpest Dozsa 0
Eintracht Brunswick 4 (*Breitner, Handschuh, Hollman 2*)
Start Kristiansand 0
Carl Zeiss Jena 1 (*Lindemann pen*)
RWD Molenbeek 1 (*Alhino*) (*Carl Zeiss won 6-5 on penalties*)
Dynamo Zagreb 1 (*Senzen*)
Torino 0
Eintracht Frankfurt 4 (*Kraus, Grabowski, Stepanovic, Krobach*)
Zurich 3 (*Risi 2, 1 pen, Torstensson*)
Gornik Zabrze 1 (*Marcinkowski*)
Aston Villa 1 (*Gray*)
Grasshoppers 5 (*Elsener, Ponte, Sulser, Hey*)
Inter Bratislava 1 (*Jurkemik*)
Marek Stanke 2 (*Petrov, Pargov*)
Bayern Munich 0
Las Palmas 3 (*Morete 2, Felix*)
Ipswich 3 (*Mariner 2, Tibbott*)
Lens 6 (*Six 3, Bousdira, Djebali 2*)
Lazio 0
Newcastle United 1 (*Gowling*)
Bastia 3 (*De Zerbi, Rep 2*)
PSV Eindhoven 1 (*Deijkers*)
Widzew Lodz 0
Schalke 04 1 (*Kremers*)
Magdeburg 3 (*Pommerenke 2, Steinbach*)
Standard Liege 4 (*Labarbe, Riedl, Nickel, Gorez*)
AEK Athens 1 (*Ardizoglou*)
Dynamo Tbilisi 2 (*Kipiani, Chelebadze*)
KB Copenhagen 1 (*Andersen*)

Third Round, First Leg
Aston Villa 2 (*Iribar og, Deehan*)
Athletic Bilbao 0
Bastia 2 (*Papi, Rep*)
Torino 1 (*Pulici*)
Carl Zeiss Jena 2 (*Schnuphase, Lindemann*)
Standard Liege 0
Eintracht Frankfurt 4 (*Grabowski, Holzenbein, Kraus, Skala*)
Bayern Munich 0
Ipswich Town 3 (*Gates, Whymark, Talbot*)
Barcelona 0
Magdeburg 4 (*Zapf, Pommerenke pen, Mewis, Steinbach*)
Lens 0
PSV Eindhoven 2 (*Lubse, Van der Kuylen*)
Eintrach Brunswick 0
Dynamo Tbilisi 1 (*Shengeliva*)
Grasshoppers 0

Third Round, Second Leg
Athletic Bilbao 1 (*Dani*)
Aston Villa 0 (*Mortimer*)
Barcelona 3 (*Cruyff 2, Rexach pen*)
Ipswich 0 (*Barcelona won 3-1 on penalties*)
Bayern Munich 1 (*Rummenigge*)
Eintracht Frankfurt 2 (*Wenzel, Holzenbein*)
Eintracht Brunswick 1 (*Bruns*)
PSV Eindhoven 2 (*Van Kraay ,Deijkers*)
Grasshoppers 4 (*Sulser, Ponte, 2 1 pen, Elsener*)
Dynamo Tbilisi 0
Lens 2 (*Bousdira 2*)
Magdeburg 0
Standard Liege 1 (*Nickel*)
Carl Zeiss Jena 2 (*Szengewald Weise pen*)
Torino 2 (*Graziani 2*)
Bastia 3 (*Larios, Krimau 2*)

Quarter Finals, First Leg
Aston Villa 2 (*McNaught, Deehan*)
Barcelona 2 (*Cruyff, Zuviria*)
Bastia 7 (*Larios, Papi, Mariot, Felix 2, Cazes, Franceschetti*)
Carl Zeiss Jena 2 (*Raab 2*)
Magdeburg 1 (*Streich*)
PSV Eindhoven 0
Eintracht Frankfurt 3 (*Kraus, Holzenbein 2, 1 pen*)
Grasshoppers 2 (*Bosco, Ponte pen*)

Quarter Finals, Second Leg
Grasshoppers 1 (*Ponte pen*)
Eintracht Frankfurt 0
Carl Zeiss Jena 4 (*Raab, Lindemann, Vogel, Topfer pen*)
Bastia 2 (*Papi, Krimau*)
PSV Eindhoven 4 (*Brandst 2, Seguin og, Lubse*)
Magdeburg 2 (*Hoffman, Pommerenke*)
Barcelona 2 (*Migueli, Asensi*)
Aston Villa 1 (*Little*)

Semi-Finals, First Leg
Grasshoppers 3 (*Hermann, Ponte pen, Montandon*)
Bastia 2 (*Krimau, Rep pen*)
PSV Eindhoven 3 (*Olmo og, Lubse, Postuma*)
Barcelona 0

Semi-Finals, Second Leg
Barcelona 3 (*Rexach 2 pens, Fortes*)
PSV Eindhoven 1 (*Deacy*)
Bastia 1 (*Papi*)
Grasshoppers 0

Final 1978-78: Bastia (0) 0 PSV Eindhoven (0) 0
(First Leg in Corsica, April 26 1978, 15,000)

Bastia: Hiard; Burkhard, Guesdon, Orlanducci Cazes, Papi, Lacuseta (Felix), Larios, Rep, Krimau, Mariot.
PSV: Van Beveren; Van Kraay, Krijgh, Stevens, Brandts, Poortvliet, Van der Kuylen, Willy Van der Kerkhof, Deijkers, Rene Van der Kerkhof, Lubse.

PSV Eindhoven (1) 3 (*Willy Van der Kerkhof, Deijkers, Van der Kuylen*) **Bastia (0) 0**
(Second leg in Eindhoven, May 9 1978, 27,000)

PSV: Van Beveren; Krijgh, Stevens, Van Kraay (Deacy), Brandts, Willy Van der Kerkhof, Poortvliet, Van der Kuylen, Lubse, Deijkers, Rene Van der Kerkhof.
Bastia: Hiard (Weller); Marchioni, Orlanducci, Guesdon, Cazes, Lacuesta, Larios, Papi, Rep, Krimau, Mariot (De Zerbi).

England's full international teams 1872-1978

Substitute in brackets † World Cup final stages

1872 Scotland	1873 Scotland	1874 Scotland	1875 Scotland	1876 Scotland
1 Maynard	1 Morton	1 Welch	1 Carr	1 Savage
2 Greenhalgh	2 Greenhalgh	2 Ogilvie	2 Haygarth	2 Green
3 Welch	3 Howell	3 Stratford	3 Rawson	3 Field
4 Maddison	4 Goodwyn	4 Ottaway	4 Birley	4 Bambridge
5 Barker	5 Vidal	5 Birley	5 von Donop	5 Jarrett
6 Brockbank	6 von Donop	6 Wollaston	6 Wollaston	6 Heron H
7 Clegg J C	7 Chenery	7 Kingsford	7 Alcock	7 Cursham A W
8 Smith A K	8 Clegg J C	8 Edwards	8 Rawson	8 Heron F
9 Ottaway	9 Bonsor	9 Chenery	9 Bonsor	9 Smith C E
10 Chenery	10 Capt. Kenyon-Slaney	10 Heron	10 Heron	10 Buchanan
11 Morice	11 Heron	11 Owen	11 Greaves	11 Maynard
Glasgow Nov 30: 0-0	Kennington Oval Mar 8: 4-2 *Kenyon-Slaney 2, Bonsor, Chenery*	Glasgow Mar 7: 1-2 *Kingsford*	Kennington Oval Mar 6: 2-2 *Wollaston, Alcock*	Glasgow Mar 4: 0-3

1877 Scotland	1878 Scotland	1879 Wales	1879 Scotland	1880 Scotland
1 Betts	1 Walker	1 Anderson	1 Birkett	1 Swepstone
2 Lindsay	2 Hon E Lyttelton	2 Bury	2 Morse	2 Brindle
3 Bury	3 Hunter	3 Wilson	3 Christian	3 Luntley
4 Rawson	4 Bailey	4 Bailey	4 Bailey	4 Bailey
5 Jarrett	5 Jarrett	5 Clegg W E	5 Prinsep	5 Hunter
6 Wollaston	6 Cursham A W	6 Parry	6 Hills	6 Wollaston
7 Cursham A W	7 Fairclough	7 Sorby	7 Goodyer	7 Bastard
8 Hon A Lyttelton	8 Wace	8 Cursham A W	8 Wace	8 Sparks
9 Wingfield-Stratford	9 Wylie	9 Wace	9 Sparks	9 Widdowson
10 Bain	10 Heron H	10 Mosforth	10 Bambridge E C	10 Mosforth
11 Mosforth	11 Mosforth	11 Mosforth	11 Mosforth	11 Bambridge E C
Kennington Oval Mar 3: 1-3 *Lyttelton*	Glasgow Mar 2: 2-7 *Wylie, Cursham*	Kennington Oval Jan 18: 2-1 *Sorby, Whitfield*	Kennington Oval April 5: 5-4 *Mosforth, Bambridge 2, Goodyer, Bailey*	Glasgow Mar 13: 4-5 *Mosforth, Bambridge 2, Sparks*

1880 Wales	1881 Wales	1881 Scotland	1882 Ireland	1882 Scotland
1 Sands	1 Hawtrey	1 Hawtrey	1 Rawlinson	1 Swepstone
2 Luntley	2 Harvey	2 Field	2 Dobson	2 Greenwood
3 Brindle	3 Bambridge A L	3 Wilson	3 Greenwood	3 Jones A
4 Hunter	4 Hunter	4 Bailey	4 Hargreaves	4 Bailey
5 Hargreaves	5 Hargreaves	5 Hunter	5 King	5 Hunter
6 Marshall	6 Marshall	6 Holden	6 Bambridge	6 Cursham H A
7 Cursham H A	7 Rostron	7 Rostron	7 Barnet	7 Parry
8 Sparks	8 Brown J	8 Macauley	8 Brown A	8 Brown A
9 Mitchell	9 Tait	9 Mitchell	9 Brown J	9 Vaughton
10 Johnson	10 Hargreaves	10 Bambridge E C	10 Vaughton	10 Mosforth
11 Mosforth	11 Mosforth	11 Hargreaves	11 Cursham H A	11 Bambridge E C
Wrexham Mar 15: 3-2 *Sparks 2, Brindle*	Blackburn Feb 26: 0-1	Kennington Oval Mar 12: 1-6 *Bambridge*	Belfast Feb 18: 13-0 *Vaughton 5, Brown A 4, Brown J 2, Cursham, Bambridge*	Glasgow Mar 11: 1-5 *Vaughton*

1882 Wales	1883 Wales	1883 Ireland	1883 Scotland	1884 Ireland
1 Swepstone	1 Swepstone	1 Swepstone	1 Swepstone	1 Rose
2 Hunter	2 Paravacini	2 Paravacini	2 Paravacini	2 Dobson
3 Jones A	3 Jones A	3 Moore	3 Jones A	3 Beverley
4 Bailey	4 Bailey	4 Hudson	4 Bailey	4 Bailey
5 Bambridge E C	5 Macrae	5 Macrae	5 Macrae	5 Macrae
6 Parry	6 Cursham A W	6 Whateley	6 Cursham H A	6 Johnson
7 Cursham H A	7 Whateley	7 Pawson	7 Cobbold	7 Holden
8 Parr	8 Mitchell	8 Goodhart	8 Mitchell	8 Bambridge A L
9 Brown A	9 Goodhart	9 Dunn	9 Goodhart	9 Dunn
10 Vaughton	10 Cursham H A	10 Cobbold	10 Cursham A W	10 Bambridge E C
11 Mosforth	11 Cobbold	11 Cursham H A	11 Whateley	11 Cursham H A
Wrexham Mar 13: 3-5 *Mosforth, Parry, Cursham*	Kennington Oval Feb 3: 5-0 *Mitchell 3, Cursham A W, Bambridge*	Liverpool Feb 24: 7-0 *Cobbold 2, Dunn 2, Whateley 2, Pawson*	Sheffield Mar 10: 2-3 *Mitchell, Cobbold*	Belfast Feb 25: 8-1 *Johnson 2, Bambridge E 2, Cursham 3, Bambridge A*

1884 Scotland	1884 Wales	1885 Ireland	1885 Wales	1885 Scotland
1 Rose	1 Rose	1 Arthur	1 Arthur	1 Arthur
2 Dobson	2 Dobson	2 Walters P M	2 Moore	2 Walters P M
3 Beverley	3 Beverley	3 Walters A M	3 Ward	3 Walters A M
4 Bailey	4 Bailey	4 Bailey	4 Bailey	4 Bailey
5 Macrae	5 Forrest	5 Forrest	5 Forrest	5 Forrest
6 Wilson C P	6 Wilson C P	6 Lofthouse	6 Lofthouse	6 Amos
7 Bromley-Davenport	7 Holden	7 Spilsbury	7 Davenport	7 Brown J
8 Gunn	8 Vaughton	8 Brown E	8 Brown E	8 Lofthouse
9 Bambridge E C	9 Bromley-Davenport	9 Pawson	9 Mitchell	9 Danks
10 Vaughton	10 Gunn	10 Cobbold	10 Dixon	10 Bambridge E C
11 Holden	11 Bambridge E C	11 Bambridge E C	11 Bambridge E C	11 Cobbold
Glasgow Mar 15: 0-1	Wrexham Mar 17: 4-0 *Bromley-Davenport 2, Gunn, Bailey*	Manchester Feb 28: 4-0 *Bambridge E C, Spilsbury, Brown, Lofthouse*	Blackburn Mar 14: 1-1 *Mitchell*	Kennington Oval Mar 21: 1-1 *Bambridge E C*

1886 Ireland	1886 Scotland	1886 Wales	1887 Ireland	1887 Wales
1 Rose	1 Arthur	1 Arthur	1 Arthur	1 Arthur
2 Walters P M	2 Walters A M	2 Squire	2 Howarth R	2 Walters P M
3 Baugh	3 Walters P M	3 Walters P M	3 Mason	3 Walters A M
4 Shutt	4 Bailey	4 Bailey	4 Howarth G	4 Howarth G
5 Squire	5 Squire	5 Amos	5 Brayshaw	5 Bailey
6 Dobson	6 Forrest	6 Forrest	6 Forrest	6 Forrest
7 Leighton	7 Cobbold	7 Dewhurst	7 Sayer	7 Lofthouse
8 Dewhurst	8 Bambridge E C	8 Brann	8 Dewhurst	8 Dewhurst
9 Lindley	9 Lindley	9 Lindley	9 Lindley	9 Lindley
10 Spilsbury	10 Spilsbury	10 Cobbold	10 Cobbold	10 Cobbold
11 Pike	11 Brann	11 Bambridge E C	11 Bambridge E C	11 Bambridge E C
Belfast Mar 13: 6-1 *Spilsbury 4, Dewhurst, Lindley*	Glasgow Mar 31: 1-1 *Lindley*	Wrexham Mar 29: 3-1 *Dewhurst, Bambridge E C, Lindley*	Sheffield Feb 5: 7-0 *Cobbold 2, Lindley 3, Dewhurst 2*	Kennington Oval Feb 26: 4-0 *Cobbold 2, Lindley 2*

1887 Scotland	1888 Wales	1888 Scotland	1888 Ireland	1889 Wales
1 Roberts	1 Moon	1 Moon	1 Roberts	1 Moon
2 Walters A M	2 Howarth R	2 Howarth R	2 Aldridge	2 Walters A M
3 Walters P M	3 Mason	3 Walters P M	3 Walters P M	3 Walters P M
4 Bailey	4 Saunders	4 Allen H	4 Holmes	4 Fletcher
5 Howarth G	5 Allen H	5 Howarth G	5 Allen H	5 Shelton
6 Forrest	6 Holden-White	6 Holden-White	6 Shelton	6 Betts
7 Bambridge E C	7 Woodall	7 Woodhall	7 Bassett	7 Bassett
8 Cobbold	8 Goodall	8 Goodall	8 Dewhurst	8 Goodall
9 Lofthouse	9 Lindley	9 Lindley	9 Lindley	9 Southworth
10 Dewhurst	10 Dewhurst	10 Hodgetts	10 Allen G	10 Dewhurst
11 Lindley	11 Hodgetts	11 Dewhurst	11 Hodgetts	11 Townley
Blackburn Mar 19: 2-3 *Dewhurst, Lindley*	Crewe Feb 4: 5-1 *Dewhurst 2, Woodhall, Goodall, Lindley*	Glasgow Mar 17: 5-0 *Lindley, Hodgetts, Dewhurst 2, Goodall*	Belfast Mar 31: 5-1 *Dewhurst, Allen 3, Lindley*	Stoke Feb 23: 4-1 *Bassett, Goodall, Southworth, Dewhurst*

1889 Ireland	1889 Scotland	1890 Wales	1890 Ireland	1890 Scotland
1 Rowley	1 Moon	1 Moon	1 Roberts	1 Moon
2 Clare	2 Walters A M	2 Walters A M	2 Baugh	2 Walters A M
3 Aldridge	3 Walters P M	3 Walters P M	3 Mason	3 Walters P M
4 Wreford-Brown	4 Hammond	4 Fletcher	4 Barton	4 Howarth G
5 Weir	5 Allen	5 Holt	5 Perry	5 Allen
6 Shelton	6 Forrest	6 Shelton	6 Forrest	6 Shelton
7 Lofthouse	7 Brodie	7 Bassett	7 Lofthouse	7 Bassett
8 Burton	8 Goodall	8 Currey	8 Davenport	8 Currey
9 Brodie	9 Bassett	9 Lindley	9 Geary	9 Lindley
10 Daft	10 Weir	10 Daft	10 Walton	10 Wood
11 Yates	11 Lindley	11 Wood	11 Townley	11 Daft
Everton Mar 2: 6-1 *Weir, Yates 3, Lofthouse, Brodie*	Kennington Oval April 13: 2-3 *Bassett, Weir*	Wrexham Mar 15: 3-1 *Currey 2, Lindley*	Belfast Mar 15: 9-1 *Townley 2, Davenport 2, Geary 3, Lofthouse, Barton*	Glasgow April 5: 1-1 *Wood*

1891 Wales	1891 Ireland	1891 Scotland	1892 Wales	1892 Ireland
1 Wilkinson	1 Rose	1 Moon	1 Toone	1 Rowley
2 Porteous	2 Marsden	2 Howarth	2 Dunn	2 Underwood
3 Jackson	3 Underwood	3 Holmes	3 Lilley	3 Clare
4 Smith A	4 Bayliss	4 Smith A	4 Hossack	4 Cox
5 Holt	5 Perry	5 Holt	5 Winckworth	5 Holt
6 Shelton	6 Brodie	6 Shelton	6 Kinsey	6 Whittam
7 Brann	7 Bassett	7 Bassett	7 Gosling	7 Athersmith
8 Goodall	8 Cotterill	8 Goodall	8 Cotterill	8 Pearson
9 Southworth	9 Lindley	9 Geary	9 Henfrey	9 Devey
10 Milward	10 Henfrey	10 Chadwick	10 Schofield	10 Daft
11 Chadwick	11 Daft	11 Milward	11 Sandilands	11 Hodgetts
Sunderland Mar 7: 4-1 *Goodall, Southworth, Chadwick, Milward*	Wolverhampton Mar 7: 6-1 *Cotterill, Daft, Henfrey, Lindley 2, Bassett*	Blackburn April 6: 2-1 *Goodall, Chadwick*	Wrexham Mar 5: 2-0 *Henfrey, Sandilands*	Belfast Mar 5: 2-0 *Daft 2*

1892 Scotland	1893 Ireland	1893 Wales	1893 Scotland	1894 Ireland
1 Toone	1 Charsley	1 Sutcliffe	1 Gay	1 Reader
2 Dunn	2 Clare	2 Clare	2 Harrison	2 Howarth
3 Holmes	3 Pelly	3 Holmes	3 Holmes	3 Holmes
4 Holt	4 Smith A	4 Reynolds	4 Reynolds	4 Reynolds
5 Reynolds	5 Winckworth	5 Perry	5 Holt	5 Holt
6 Shelton	6 Cooper	6 Turner	6 Kingsley	6 Crabtree
7 Bassett	7 Topham	7 Bassett	7 Bassett	7 Chippendale
8 Goodall	8 Smith G O	8 Whitehead	8 Gosling	8 Whitehead
9 Chadwick	9 Cotterill	9 Goodall	9 Cotterill	9 Devey
10 Hodgetts	10 Gilliatt	10 Schofield	10 Chadwick	10 Hodgetts
11 Southworth	11 Sandilands	11 Spiksley	11 Spiksley	11 Spiksley
Glasgow April 2: 4-1 Southworth, Goodall 2, Chadwick	Birmingham Feb 25: 6-1 Sandilands, Gilliatt 3, Winckworth, Smith G O	Stoke Mar 13: 6-0 Spiksley 2, Goodall, Bassett, Schofield, Reynolds	Richmond April 1: 5-2 Spiksley 2, Gosling, Cotterill, Reynolds	Belfast Mar 1: 2-2 Devey, Spiksley

1894 Wales	1894 Scotland	1895 Ireland	1895 Wales	1895 Scotland
1 Gay	1 Gay	1 Sutcliffe	1 Raikes	1 Sutcliffe
2 Lodge	2 Clare	2 Crabtree	2 Lodge	2 Crabtree
3 Pelly	3 Pelly	3 Holmes	3 Oakley	3 Lodge
4 Hossack	4 Reynolds	4 Howell	4 Henfrey	4 Needham
5 Wreford Brown	5 Holt	5 Crawshaw	5 Wreford Brown	5 Holt
6 Topham A G	6 Needham	6 Turner	6 Barker	6 Reynolds
7 Topham R	7 Bassett	7 Bassett	7 Stanbrough	7 Gosling
8 Gosling	8 Smith G O	8 Bloomer	8 Dewhurst	8 Smith S
9 Smith G O	9 Goodall	9 Goodall	9 Smith G O	9 Goodall
10 Veitch	10 Chadwick	10 Becton	10 Gosling	10 Bassett
11 Sandilands	11 Spiksley	11 Schofield	11 Sandilands	11 Bloomer
Wrexham Mar 12: 5-1 Veitch 3, Gosling, 1 og	Glasgow April 7: 2-2 Goodall, Reynolds	Derby Mar 9: 9-0 Bloomer 2, Goodall 2, Bassett, Howell, Becton 2, 1 og	Queens Club Mar 18: 1-1 Smith	Goodison Park April 6: 3-0 Bloomer, Smith, Gibson og

1896 Ireland	1896 Wales	1896 Scotland	1897 Ireland	1897 Wales
1 Raikes	1 Raikes	1 Raikes	1 Robinson	1 Foulke
2 Lodge	2 Oakley	2 Lodge	2 Oakley	2 Oakley
3 Oakley	3 Crabtree	3 Oakley	3 Williams	3 Spencer
4 Crabtree	4 Henfrey	4 Crabtree	4 Middleditch	4 Reynolds
5 Crawshaw	5 Crawshaw	5 Crawshaw	5 Crawshaw	5 Crawshaw
6 Kinsey	6 Kinsey	6 Henfrey	6 Needham	6 Needham
7 Bassett	7 Bassett	7 Goodall	7 Athersmith	7 Athersmith
8 Bloomer	8 Bloomer	8 Bassett	8 Bloomer	8 Bloomer
9 Smith G O	9 Smith G O	9 Smith G O	9 Smith G O	9 Smith G O
10 Chadwick	10 Goodall	10 Wood	10 Wheldon	10 Beeton
11 Spiksley	11 Sandilands	11 Burnup	11 Bradshaw	11 Milward
Belfast Mar 7: 2-0 Bloomer, Smith	Cardiff Mar 16: 9-1 Bloomer 5, Smith 2, Goodall, Bassett	Glasgow April 4: 1-2 Bassett	Nottingham Feb 20: 6-0 Bloomer 2, Wheldon 3, Athersmith	Sheffield Mar 29: 4-0 Bloomer, Needham, Milward 2

1897 Scotland	1898 Ireland	1898 Wales	1898 Scotland	1899 Ireland
1 Robinson	1 Robinson	1 Robinson	1 Robinson	1 Hillman
2 Oakley	2 Oakley	2 Oakley	2 Williams	2 Bach
3 Spencer	3 Williams	3 Williams	3 Oakley	3 Williams
4 Reynolds	4 Forman (Frank)	4 Perry	4 Needham	4 Forman (Frank)
5 Crawshaw	5 Morren	5 Booth	5 Wreford Brown	5 Crabtree
6 Needham	6 Turner	6 Needham	6 Forman (Frank)	6 Needham
7 Athersmith	7 Athersmith	7 Athersmith	7 Spiksley	7 Athersmith
8 Bloomer	8 Richards	8 Goodall	8 Wheldon	8 Bloomer
9 Smith G O	9 Smith G O	9 Smith G O	9 Smith G O	9 Smith G O
10 Chadwick	10 Garfield	10 Wheldon	10 Bloomer	10 Settle
11 Milward	11 Wheldon	11 Spiksley	11 Athersmith	11 Forman (Fred)

Crystal Palace
April 3: 1-2
Bloomer

Belfast
Mar 5: 3-2
Morren, Athersmith, Smith

Wrexham
Mar 28: 3-0
Smith, Wheldon 2

Glasgow
April 2: 3-1
Bloomer 2, Wheldon

Sunderland
Feb 18: 13-2
Frank Forman Bloomer 2, Athersmith, Settle 3, Smith 4, Fred Forman 2

1899 Wales	1899 Scotland	1900 Ireland	1900 Wales	1900 Scotland
1 Robinson	1 Robinson	1 Robinson	1 Robinson	1 Robinson
2 Thickett	2 Thickett	2 Oakley	2 Spencer	2 Oakley
3 Williams	3 Crabtree	3 Crabtree	3 Oakley	3 Crabtree
4 Needham	4 Forman (Frank)	4 Johnson	4 Johnson	4 Johnson
5 Crabtree	5 Howell	5 Holt	5 Chadwick A	5 Chadwick A
6 Forman (Frank)	6 Needham	6 Needham	6 Crabtree	6 Needham
7 Athersmith	7 Athersmith	7 Turner	7 Athersmith	7 Athersmith
8 Bloomer	8 Bloomer	8 Cunliffe	8 Foster	8 Bloomer
9 Smith G O	9 Smith G O	9 Smith G O	9 Smith G O	9 Smith G O
10 Settle	10 Settle	10 Sagar	10 Wilson	10 Wilson
11 Forman (Fred)	11 Forman (Fred)	11 Priest	11 Spouncer	11 Plant

Bristol
Mar 20: 4-0
Bloomer 2, Fred Forman, Needham

Birmingham
April 8: 2-1
Smith, Settle

Dublin
Mar 17: 2-0
Johnson, Sagar

Cardiff
Mar 26: 1-1
Wilson

Glasgow
April 7: 1-4
Bloomer

1901 Ireland	1901 Wales	1901 Scotland	1902 Wales	1902 Ireland
1 Robinson	1 Kingsley	1 Sutcliffe	1 George	1 George
2 Fry	2 Crabtree	2 Iremonger	2 Crompton	2 Crompton
3 Oakley	3 Oakley	3 Oakley	3 Crabtree	3 Iremonger
4 Jones W	4 Wilkes	4 Wilkes	4 Wilkes	4 Wilkes
5 Crawshaw	5 Bannister	5 Forman (Frank)	5 Abbott	5 Bannister
6 Needham	6 Needham	6 Needham	6 Needham	6 Forman (Frank)
7 Turner	7 Bennett	7 Bennett	7 Hogg	7 Hogg
8 Foster	8 Bloomer	8 Bloomer	8 Bloomer	8 Bloomer
9 Hedley	9 Beats	9 Smith G O	9 Sagar	9 Calvey
10 Banks	10 Foster	10 Foster	10 Foster	10 Settle
11 Cox	11 Corbett	11 Blackburn	11 Lipsham	11 Blackburn

Southampton
Mar 9: 3-0
Foster 2, Crawshaw

Newcastle
Mar 18: 6-0
Bloomer 4, Foster, Needham

Crystal Palace
Mar 30: 2-2
Blackburn, Bloomer

Wrexham
Mar 3: 0-0

Belfast
Mar 22: 1-0
Settle

1902 Scotland	1903 Ireland	1903 Wales	1903 Scotland	1904 Wales
1 George	1 Baddeley	1 Sutcliffe	1 Baddeley	1 Baddeley
2 Crompton	2 Spencer	2 Crompton	2 Crompton	2 Crompton
3 Molyneux	3 Molyneux	3 Molyneux	3 Molyneux	3 Burgess
4 Wilkes	4 Johnson	4 Johnson	4 Johnson	4 Lee
5 Forman (Frank)	5 Holford	5 Forman (Frank)	5 Booth	5 Crawshaw
6 Houlker	6 Hadley	6 Houlker	6 Houlker	6 Ruddlesdin
7 Hogg	7 Davis	7 Davis	7 Davis	7 Brawn
8 Bloomer	8 Sharp	8 Garraty	8 Humphreys	8 Common
9 Beats	9 Woodward	9 Woodward	9 Woodward	9 Brown A
10 Settle	10 Settle	10 Bache	10 Capes	10 Bache
11 Cox	11 Lockett	11 Corbett	11 Cox	11 Davis
Birmingham May 3: 2-2 *Wilkes, Settle*	Wolverhampton Feb 14: 4-0 *Sharp, Davis, Woodward 2*	Portsmouth Mar 2: 2-1 *Bache, Woodward*	Sheffield April 4: 1-2 *Woodward*	Wrexham Feb 29: 2-2 *Common, Bache*

1904 Ireland	1904 Scotland	1905 Ireland	1905 Wales	1905 Scotland
1 Baddeley	1 Baddeley	1 Williamson	1 Linacre	1 Linacre
2 Crompton	2 Balmer	2 Carr	2 Spencer	2 Spencer
3 Burgess	3 Burgess	3 Carr	3 Smith H	3 Smith H
4 Ruddlesdin	4 Wolstenholme	4 Wolstenholme	4 Wolstenholme	4 Ruddlesdin
5 Crawshaw	5 Wilkinson	5 Roberts	5 Roberts	5 Roberts
6 Leake	6 Leake	6 Leake	6 Leake	6 Leake
7 Brawn	7 Rutherford	7 Bond	7 Bond	7 Sharp
8 Common	8 Bloomer	8 Bloomer	8 Bloomer	8 Bloomer
9 Woodward	9 Woodward	9 Woodward	9 Woodward	9 Woodward
10 Bache	10 Harris	10 Harris	10 Harris	10 Bache
11 Davis	11 Blackburn	11 Booth	11 Hardman	11 Bridgett
Belfast Mar 12: 3-1 *Common, Bache, Davis*	Glasgow April 9: 1-0 *Bloomer*	Middlesbrough Feb 25: 1-1 *Bloomer*	Liverpool Mar 27: 3-1 *Woodward 2, Harris*	Crystal Palace April 1: 1-0 *Bache*

1906 Ireland	1906 Wales	1906 Scotland	1907 Ireland	1907 Wales
1 Ashcroft	1 Ashcroft	1 Ashcroft	1 Hardy	1 Hardy
2 Crompton	2 Crompton	2 Crompton	2 Crompton	2 Crompton
3 Smith H	3 Smith H	3 Burgess	3 Carr	3 Pennington
4 Warren	4 Warren	4 Warren	4 Warren	4 Warren
5 Veitch	5 Veitch	5 Veitch	5 Wedlock	5 Wedlock
6 Houlker	6 Houlker	6 Makepeace	6 Hawkes	6 Veitch
7 Bond	7 Bond	7 Bond	7 Rutherford	7 Rutherford
8 Day	8 Day	8 Day	8 Coleman	8 Bloomer
9 Brown A	9 Common	9 Shepherd	9 Hilsdon	9 Thornley
10 Harris	10 Harris	10 Bache	10 Bache	10 Stewart
11 Gosnell	11 Wright	11 Conlin	11 Hardman	11 Wall
Belfast Feb 17: 5-0 *Bond 2, Day, Harris, Brown*	Cardiff Mar 19: 1-0 *Day*	Glasgow April 7: 1-2 *Shepherd*	Everton Feb 16: 1-0 *Hardman*	Fulham Mar 18: 1-1 *Stewart*

1907 Scotland	1908 Ireland	1908 Wales	1908 Scotland	1908 Austria
1 Hardy	1 Maskrey	1 Bailey	1 Hardy	1 Bailey
2 Crompton	2 Crompton	2 Crompton	2 Crompton	2 Crompton
3 Pennington	3 Pennington	3 Pennington	3 Pennington	3 Corbett
4 Warren	4 Warren	4 Warren	4 Warren	4 Warren
5 Wedlock	5 Wedlock	5 Wedlock	5 Wedlock	5 Wedlock
6 Veitch	6 Lintott	6 Lintott	6 Lintott	6 Hawkes
7 Rutherford	7 Rutherford	7 Rutherford	7 Rutherford	7 Rutherford
8 Bloomer	8 Woodward	8 Woodward	8 Woodward	8 Woodward
9 Woodward	9 Hilsdon	9 Hilsdon	9 Hilsdon	9 Bradshaw
10 Stewart	10 Windridge	10 Windridge	10 Windridge	10 Windridge
11 Hardman	11 Wall	11 Hardman	11 Bridgett	11 Bridgett

Newcastle
April 6: 1-1
Bloomer

Belfast
Feb 15: 3-1
Woodward,
Hilsdon 2

Wrexham
Mar 16: 7-1
Wedlock,
Windridge,
Hilsdon 2,
Woodward 3

Glasgow
April 4: 1-1
Windridge

Vienna
June 6: 6-1
Hilsdon 2,
Windridge 2,
Bridgett,
Woodward

1908 Austria	1908 Hungary	1908 Bohemia	1909 Ireland	1909 Wales
1 Bailey	1 Bailey	1 Bailey	1 Hardy	1 Hardy
2 Crompton	2 Crompton	2 Crompton	2 Crompton	2 Crompton
3 Pennington	3 Corbett	3 Corbett	3 Cottle	3 Pennington
4 Warren	4 Warren	4 Warren	4 Warren	4 Warren
5 Wedlock	5 Wedlock	5 Wedlock	5 Wedlock	5 Wedlock
6 Hawkes	6 Hawkes	6 Hawkes	6 Lintott	6 Veitch
7 Rutherford	7 Rutherford	7 Rutherford	7 Berry	7 Pentland
8 Woodward	8 Woodward	8 Woodward	8 Woodward	8 Woodward
9 Bradshaw	9 Hilsdon	9 Hilsdon	9 Hilsdon	9 Freeman
10 Windridge	10 Windridge	10 Windridge	10 Windridge	10 Holley
11 Bridgett	11 Bridgett	11 Bridgett	11 Bridgett	11 Bridgett

Vienna
June 8: 11-1
Woodward 4, Bridgett
Bradshaw 3, Warren,
Rutherford,
Windridge

Budapest
June 10: 7-0
Hilsdon 4,
Windridge,
Woodward,
Rutherford

Prague
June 13: 4-0
Hilsdon 2,
Windridge,
Rutherford

Bradford
Feb 13: 4-0
Hilsdon 2,
Woodward 2

Nottingham
Mar 15: 2-0
Holley,
Freeman

1909 Scotland	1909 Hungary	1909 Hungary	1909 Austria	1910 Ireland
1 Hardy	1 Hardy	1 Hardy	1 Hardy	1 Hardy
2 Crompton	2 Crompton	2 Crompton	2 Crompton	2 Morley
3 Pennington	3 Pennington	3 Pennington	3 Pennington	3 Cowell
4 Warren	4 Warren	4 Warren	4 Warren	4 Ducat
5 Wedlock	5 Wedlock	5 Wedlock	5 Wedlock	5 Wedlock
6 Lintott	6 Lintott	6 Lintott	6 Richards	6 Bradshaw
7 Pentland	7 Pentland	7 Pentland	7 Pentland	7 Bond
8 Fleming	8 Fleming	8 Fleming	8 Halse	8 Fleming
9 Freeman	9 Woodward	9 Woodward	9 Woodward	9 Woodward
10 Holley	10 Holley	10 Holley	10 Holley	10 Bache
11 Wall	11 Bridgett	11 Bridgett	11 Bridgett	11 Hall

Crystal Palace
April 3: 2-0
Wall 2

Budapest
May 29: 4-2
Woodward 2,
Fleming, Bridgett

Budapest
May 31: 8-2
Woodward 4,
Fleming,
Holley 2

Vienna
June 1: 8-1
Woodward 3,
Warren, Halse 2,
Holley 2

Belfast
Feb 12: 1-1
Fleming

1910 Wales	1910 Scotland	1911 Ireland	1911 Wales	1911 Scotland
1 Hardy	1 Hardy	1 Williamson	1 Williamson	1 Williamson
2 Crompton	2 Crompton	2 Crompton	2 Crompton	2 Crompton
3 Pennington	3 Pennington	3 Pennington	3 Pennington	3 Pennington
4 Ducat	4 Ducat	4 Warren	4 Warren	4 Warren
5 Wedlock	5 Wedlock	5 Wedlock	5 Wedlock	5 Wedlock
6 Bradshaw	6 Makepeace	6 Sturgess	6 Rev Hunt	6 Rev Hunt
7 Bond	7 Bond	7 Simpson	7 Simpson	7 Simpson
8 Fleming	8 Hibbett	8 Fleming	8 Fleming	8 Stewart
9 Parkinson	9 Parkinson	9 Shepherd	9 Webb	9 Webb
10 Holley	10 Hardinge	10 Woodger	10 Woodward	10 Bache
11 Wall	11 Wall	11 Evans	11 Evans	11 Evans
Cardiff Mar 14: 1-0 *Ducat*	Glasgow April 2: 0-2	Derby Feb 11: 2-1 *Shepherd, Evans*	Millwall Mar 13: 3-0 *Woodward 2, Webb*	Everton April 1: 1-1 *Stewart*

1912 Ireland	1912 Wales	1912 Scotland	1913 Ireland	1913 Wales
1 Hardy	1 Williamson	1 Williamson	1 Williamson	1 Scattergood
2 Crompton	2 Crompton	2 Crompton	2 Crompton	2 Crompton
3 Pennington	3 Pennington	3 Pennington	3 Benson	3 Pennington
4 Brittleton	4 Brittleton	4 Brittleton	4 Cuggy	4 Moffatt
5 Wedlock	5 Wedlock	5 Wedlock	5 Boyle	5 McCall
6 Bradshaw	6 Makepeace	6 Makepeace	6 Utley	6 Bradshaw
7 Simpson	7 Simpson	7 Simpson	7 Mordue	7 Wallace
8 Fleming	8 Jefferis	8 Jefferis	8 Buchan	8 Fleming
9 Freeman	9 Freeman	9 Freeman	9 Elliott	9 Hampton
10 Holley	10 Holley	10 Holley	10 Smith, Joe	10 Latheron
11 Mordue	11 Evans	11 Wall	11 Wall	11 Hodkinson
Dublin Feb 10: 6-1 *Fleming 3, Freeman, Holley, Simpson*	Wrexham Mar 11: 2-0 *Holley, Freeman*	Glasgow Mar 23: 1-1 *Holley*	Belfast Feb 15: 1-2 *Buchan*	Bristol Mar 17: 4-3 *Fleming, McCall, Latheron, Hampton*

1913 Scotland	1914 Ireland	1914 Wales	1914 Scotland	1919 Ireland
1 Hardy	1 Hardy	1 Hardy	1 Hardy	1 Hardy
2 Crompton	2 Crompton	2 Crompton	2 Crompton	2 Smith, Joe (WBA)
3 Pennington	3 Pennington	3 Colclough	3 Pennington	3 Knight
4 Brittleton	4 Cuggy	4 Brittleton	4 Sturgess	4 Bagshaw
5 McCall	5 Buckley	5 Wedlock	5 McCall	5 Bowser
6 Watson	6 Watson	6 McNeal	6 McNeal	6 Watson
7 Simpson	7 Wallace	7 Simpson	7 Walden	7 Turnbull
8 Fleming	8 Shea	8 Shea	8 Fleming	8 Carr
9 Hampton	9 Elliott	9 Hampton	9 Hampton	9 Cock
10 Holley	10 Latheron	10 Smith, Joe	10 Smith, Joe	10 Smith, Joe (Bolton W)
11 Hodkinson	11 Martin	11 Mosscrop	11 Mosscrop	11 Hodkinson
Chelsea April 5: 1-0 *Hampton*	Middlesbrough Feb 14: 0-3	Cardiff Mar 16: 2-0 *Smith, Wedlock*	Glasgow April 4: 1-3 *Fleming*	Belfast Oct 25: 1-1 *Cock*

1920 Wales	1920 Scotland	1920 Ireland	1921 Wales	1921 Scotland
1 Hardy	1 Hardy	1 Mew	1 Coleman	1 Gough
2 Clay	2 Longworth	2 Downs	2 Cresswell	2 Smart
3 Pennington	3 Pennington	3 Bullock	3 Silcock	3 Silcock
4 Ducat	4 Ducat	4 Ducat	4 Bamber	4 Smith B
5 Barson	5 McCall	5 McCall	5 Wilson	5 Wilson
6 Grimsdell	6 Grimsdell	6 Grimsdell	6 Bromilow	6 Grimsdell
7 Chedgzoy	7 Wallace	7 Chedgzoy	7 Chedgzoy	7 Chedgzoy
8 Buchan	8 Kelly	8 Kelly	8 Kelly	8 Kelly
9 Elliott	9 Cock	9 Walker	9 Buchan	9 Chambers
10 Smith, Joe	10 Morris	10 Morris	10 Chambers	10 Bliss
11 Quantrill	11 Quantrill	11 Quantrill	11 Quantrill	11 Dimmock
Arsenal Mar 15: 1-2 *Buchan*	Sheffield April 10: 5-4 *Kelly 2, Cock, Morris, Quantrill*	Sunderland Oct 23: 2-0 *Kelly, Walker*	Cardiff Mar 14: 0-0	Glasgow April 9: 0-3

1921 Belgium	1921 Ireland	1922 Wales	1922 Scotland	1922 Ireland
1 Baker H	1 Dawson	1 Davison	1 Davison	1 Taylor
2 Fort	2 Clay	2 Clay	2 Clay	2 Smith, Joe (WBA)
3 Longworth	3 Lucas	3 Titmuss	3 Wadsworth	3 Harrow
4 Read	4 Moss	4 Smith B	4 Moss	4 Moss
5 Wilson	5 Wilson	5 Woosnam	5 Wilson	5 Wilson
6 Barton	6 Barton	6 Bromilow	6 Bromilow	6 Grimsdell
7 Rawlings	7 Chedgzoy	7 Walden	7 York	7 Mercer
8 Seed	8 Kirton	8 Kelly	8 Kelly	8 Seed
9 Buchan	9 Simms	9 Rawlings	9 Rawlings	9 Osborne
10 Chambers	10 Walker	10 Walker	10 Walker	10 Chambers
11 Harrison	11 Harrison	11 Smith W H	11 Smith W H	11 Williams
Brussels May 21: 2-0 *Buchan, Chambers*	Belfast Oct 22: 1-1 *Kirton*	Liverpool Mar 13: 1-0 *Kelly*	Birmingham April 8: 0-1	West Bromwich Oct 21: 2-0 *Chambers 2*

1923 Wales	1923 Belgium	1923 Scotland	1923 France	1923 Sweden
1 Taylor	1 Taylor	1 Taylor	1 Alderson	1 Williamson
2 Longworth	2 Longworth	2 Longworth	2 Cresswell	2 Ashurst
3 Titmuss	3 Wadsworth	3 Wadsworth	3 Jones H	3 Harrow
4 Magee	4 Kean	4 Kean	4 Plum	4 Patchitt
5 Wilson	5 Wilson	5 Wilson	5 Seddon	5 Seddon
6 Grimsdell	6 Bromilow	6 Tresadern	6 Barton	6 Tresadern
7 Carr	7 Mercer	7 Chedgzoy	7 Osborne	7 Thornewell
8 Seed	8 Seed	8 Kelly	8 Buchan	8 Moore
9 Watson	9 Bullock	9 Watson	9 Creek	9 Bedford
10 Chambers	10 Chambers	10 Chambers	10 Hartley	10 Walker
11 Williams	11 Hegan	11 Tunstall	11 Hegan	11 Urwin
Cardiff Mar 5: 2-2 *Chambers, Watson*	Arsenal Mar 19: 6-1 *Hegan 2, Chambers, Mercer, Seed, Bullock*	Glasgow April 14: 2-2 *Kelly, Watson*	Paris May 10: 4-1 *Hegan 2, Buchan, Creek*	Stockholm May 21: 4-2 *Walker 2, Moore, Thornewell*

R.F. 79/80—40

1923 Sweden	1923 Ireland	1923 Belgium	1924 Wales	1924 Scotland
1 Williamson	1 Taylor	1 Hufton	1 Sewell	1 Taylor
2 Ashurst	2 Bower	2 Cresswell	2 Smart	2 Smart
3 Silcock	3 Wadsworth	3 Bower	3 Mort	3 Wadsworth
4 Magee	4 Pantling	4 Moss	4 Kean	4 Moss
5 Seddon	5 Wilson	5 Seddon	5 Wilson	5 Spencer
6 Patchitt	6 Meehan	6 Barton	6 Barton	6 Barton
7 Thornewell	7 Hegan	7 Hegan	7 Chedgzoy	7 Butler
8 Moore	8 Kelly	8 Brown W	8 Jack	8 Jack
9 Walker	9 Bradford	9 Roberts	9 Roberts	9 Buchan
10 Miller	10 Chambers	10 Doggart	10 Stephenson	10 Walker
11 Urwin	11 Tunstall	11 Urwin	11 Tunstall	11 Tunstall
Stockholm May 24: 3-1 Moore 2, Miller	Belfast Oct 20: 1-2 Bradford	Antwerp Nov 1: 2-2 Brown, Roberts	Blackburn Mar 3: 1-2 Roberts	Wembley April 12: 1-1 Walker

1924 France	1924 Ireland	1924 Belgium	1925 Wales	1925 Scotland
1 Taylor	1 Mitchell	1 Hardy	1 Pym	1 Pym
2 Lucas	2 Cresswell	2 Ashurst	2 Ashurst	2 Ashurst
3 Mort	2 Wadsworth	3 Bower	3 Bower	3 Wadsworth
4 Ewer	4 Keen	4 Magee	4 Hill	4 Magee
5 Wilson	5 Healless	5 Butler	5 Spencer	5 Townrow
6 Blackburn	6 Barton	6 Ewer	6 Graham	6 Graham
7 Thornewell	7 Chedgzoy	7 Osborne	7 Kelly	7 Kelly
8 Earle	8 Kelly	8 Roberts	8 Roberts	8 Seed
9 Gibbins	9 Bedford	9 Bradford	9 Cook	9 Roberts
10 Storer	10 Walker	10 Walker	10 Walker	10 Walker
11 Tunstall	11 Tunstall	11 Dorrell	11 Dorrell	11 Tunstall
Paris May 17: 3-1 Gibbins 2, Storer	Liverpool Oct 22: 3-1 Kelly, Bedford Walker	West Bromwich Dec 8: 4-0 Bradford 2, Walker 2	Swansea Feb 28: 2-1 Roberts 2	Glasgow April 4: 0-2

1925 France	1925 Ireland	1926 Wales	1926 Scotland	1926 Belgium
1 Fox	1 Baker H	1 Pym	1 Taylor	1 Ashmore
2 Parker	2 Smart	2 Cresswell	2 Goodall	2 Lucas
3 Felton	3 Hudspeth	3 Wadsworth	3 Mort	3 Hill
4 Magee	4 Kean	4 Edwards	4 Edwards	4 Kean
5 Bryant	5 Armitage	5 Townrow	5 Hill	5 Cowan
6 Green	6 Bromilow	6 Green	6 Green	6 Green
7 Thornewell	7 Austin	7 Urwin	7 York	7 Spence
8 Roberts	8 Puddefoot	8 Kelly	8 Puddlefoot	8 Carter J S
9 Gibbins	9 Ashton	9 Bullock	9 Harper	9 Osborne
10 Walker	10 Walker	10 Walker	10 Walker	10 Johnson
11 Dorrell	11 Dorrell	11 Dimmock	11 Ruffell	11 Dimmock
Paris May 21: 3-2 Gibbins, Dorrell, 1 og	Belfast Oct 24: 0-0	Selhurst Mar 1: 1-3 Walker	Manchester April 17: 0-1	Antwerp May 24: 5-3 Osborne 3, Carter Johnson

1926 Ireland	1927 Wales	1927 Scotland	1927 Belgium	1927 Luxembourg
1 McInroy	1 Brown J	1 Brown J	1 Brown J	1 Brown J
2 Cresswell	2 Bower	2 Goodall	2 Goodall	2 Goodall
3 Wadsworth	3 Waterfield	3 Jones H	3 Jones H	3 Jones H
4 Edwards	4 Edwards	4 Edwards	4 Edwards	4 Edwards
5 Hill	5 Seddon	5 Hill	5 Hill	5 Kean
6 Green	6 Green	6 Bishop	6 Bishop	6 Bishop
7 Spence	7 Pease	7 Hulme	7 Hulme	7 Kelly
8 Brown G	8 Brown G	8 Brown G	8 Brown G	8 Brown G
9 Bullock	9 Dean	9 Dean	9 Dean	9 Dean
10 Walker	10 Walker	10 Rigby	10 Rigby	10 Rigby
11 Ruffell	11 Page	11 Page	11 Page	11 Page
Liverpool Oct 20: 3-3 *Brown, Spence, Bullock*	Wrexham Feb 12: 3-3 *Dean 2, Walker*	Glasgow April 2: 2-1 *Dean 2*	Brussels May 11: 9-1 *Dean 3, Brown 2, Rigby 2, Page, Hulme*	Luxembourg May 21: 5-2 *Dean 3, Kelly, Bishop*

1927 France	1927 Ireland	1927 Wales	1928 Scotland	1928 France
1 Brown J	1 Hufton	1 Tremelling	1 Hufton	1 Olney
2 Goodall	2 Cooper	2 Goodall	2 Goodall	2 Goodall
3 Jones H	3 Jones H	3 Osborne	3 Jones H	3 Blenkinsop
4 Edwards	4 Nuttall	4 Baker	4 Edwards	4 Edwards
5 Hill	5 Hill	5 Hill	5 Wilson	5 Matthews
6 Bishop	6 Storer	6 Nuttall	6 Healless	6 Green
7 Hulme	7 Hulme	7 Hulme	7 Hulme	7 Bruton
8 Brown G	8 Earle	8 Brown G	8 Kelly	8 Jack
9 Dean	9 Dean	9 Dean	9 Dean	9 Dean
10 Rigby	10 Ball	10 Rigby	10 Bradford	10 Stephenson
11 Page	11 Page	11 Page	11 Smith W H	11 Barry
Paris May 26: 6-0 *Dean 2, Brown 2, Rigby, Rollet og*	Belfast Oct 22: 0-2	Burnley Nov 28: 1-2 *Keenor og*	Wembley Mar 31: 1-5 *Kelly*	Paris May 17: 5-1 *Stephenson 2, Dean 2, Jack*

1928 Belgium	1928 Ireland	1928 Wales	1929 Scotland	1929 France
1 Olney	1 Hacking	1 Hacking	1 Hacking	1 Hufton
2 Goodall	2 Cooper	2 Cooper	2 Cooper	2 Blenkinsop
3 Blenkinsop	3 Blenkinsop	3 Blenkinsop	3 Blenkinsop	3 Cooper
4 Edwards	4 Edwards	4 Edwards	4 Edwards	4 Kean
5 Matthews	5 Barrett	5 Hart	5 Seddon	5 Hill
6 Green	6 Campbell	6 Campbell	6 Nuttall	6 Peacock
7 Bruton	7 Hulme	7 Hulme	7 Bruton	7 Adcock
8 Jack	8 Hine	8 Hine	8 Brown G	8 Kail
9 Dean	9 Dean	9 Dean	9 Dean	9 Camsell
10 Stephenson	10 Bradford	10 Bradford	10 Wainscoat	10 Bradford
11 Barry	11 Ruffell	11 Ruffell	11 Ruffell	11 Barry
Antwerp May 19: 3-1 *Dean 2, Matthews*	Liverpool Oct 22: 2-1 *Hulme, Dean*	Swansea Nov 17: 3-2 *Hulme 2, Hine*	Glasgow April 13: 0-1	Paris May 9: 4-1 *Kail 2, Camsell 2*

1929 Belgium	1929 Spain	1929 Ireland	1929 Wales	1930 Scotland
1 Hufton	1 Hufton	1 Brown J	1 Hibbs	1 Hibbs
2 Cooper	2 Cooper	2 Cresswell	2 Smart	2 Goodall
3 Blenkinsop	3 Blenkinsop	3 Blenkinsop	3 Blenkinsop	3 Blenkinsop
4 Oliver	4 Kean	4 Edwards	4 Edwards	4 Strange
5 Hill	5 Hill	5 Hart	5 Hart	5 Webster
6 Peacock	6 Peacock	6 Barrett	6 Marsden	6 Marsden
7 Adcock	7 Adcock	7 Adcock	7 Adcock	7 Crooks
8 Kail	8 Kail	8 Hine	8 Hine	8 Jack
9 Camsell	9 Bradford	9 Camsell	9 Camsell	9 Watson
10 Carter J S	10 Carter J S	10 Bradford	10 Johnson	10 Bradford
11 Barry	11 Barry	11 Brook	11 Ruffell	11 Rimmer
Brussels May 11: 5-1 *Camsell 4, Carter*	Madrid May 15: 3-4 *Carter 2, Bradford*	Belfast Oct 19: 3-0 *Camsell 2, Hine*	Chelsea Nov 20: 6-0 *Adcock, Camsell 3, Johnson 2*	Wembley April 5: 5-2 *Jack, Watson 2, Rimmer 2*

1930 Germany	1930 Austria	1930 Ireland	1930 Wales	1931 Scotland
1 Hibbs	1 Hibbs	1 Hibbs	1 Hibbs	1 Hibbs
2 Goodall	2 Goodall	2 Goodall	2 Goodall	2 Goodall
3 Blenkinsop	3 Blenkinsop	3 Blenkinsop	3 Blenkinsop	3 Blenkinsop
4 Strange	4 Strange	4 Strange	4 Strange	4 Strange
5 Webster	5 Webster	5 Leach	5 Leach	5 Roberts
6 Marsden	6 Cowan	6 Campbell	6 Campbell	6 Campbell
7 Crooks	7 Crooks	7 Crooks	7 Crooks	7 Crooks
8 Jack	8 Jack	8 Hodgson	8 Hodgson	8 Hodgson
9 Watson	9 Watson	9 Hampson	9 Hampson	9 Dean
10 Bradford	10 Bradford	10 Burgess	10 Bradford	10 Burgess
11 Rimmer	11 Rimmer	11 Houghton	11 Houghton	11 Crawford
Berlin May 10: 3-3 *Bradford 2, Jack*	Vienna May 14: 0-0	Sheffield Oct 20: 5-1 *Burgess 2, Crooks, Hampson, Houghton*	Wrexham Nov 22: 4-0 *Hodgson, Bradford, Hampson 2*	Glasgow Mar 28: 0-2

1931 France	1931 Belgium	1931 Ireland	1931 Wales	1931 Spain
1 Turner	1 Turner	1 Hibbs	1 Hibbs	1 Hibbs
2 Cooper	2 Goodall	2 Goodall	2 Cooper	2 Cooper
3 Blenkinsop	3 Blenkinsop	3 Blenkinsop	3 Blenkinsop	3 Blenkinsop
4 Strange	4 Strange	4 Strange	4 Strange	4 Strange
5 Graham	5 Cowan	5 Graham	5 Gee	5 Gee
6 Tate	6 Tate	6 Campbell	6 Campbell	6 Campbell
7 Crooks	7 Crooks	7 Crooks	7 Crooks	7 Crooks
8 Stephenson	8 Roberts	8 Smith J	8 Smith J	8 Smith J
9 Waring	9 Waring	9 Waring	9 Waring	9 Dean
10 Burgess	10 Burgess	10 Hine	10 Hine	10 Johnson
11 Houghton	11 Houghton	11 Houghton	11 Bastin	11 Rimmer
Paris May 14: 2-5 *Crooks, Waring*	Brussels May 16: 4-1 *Burgess 2, Houghton, Roberts*	Belfast Oct 17: 6-2 *Waring 2, Smith, Hine, Houghton 2*	Liverpool Nov 18: 3-1 *Smith, Crooks, Hine*	Arsenal Dec 9: 7-1 *Smith 2, Johnson 2, Crooks 2, Dean*

1932 Scotland	1932 Ireland	1932 Wales	1932 Austria	1933 Scotland
1 Pearson	1 Hibbs	1 Hibbs	1 Hibbs	1 Hibbs
2 Shaw	2 Goodall	2 Goodall	2 Goodall	2 Cooper
3 Blenkinsop	3 Blenkinsop	3 Blenkinsop	3 Blenkinsop	3 Blenkinsop
4 Strange	4 Strange	4 Stoker	4 Strange	4 Strange
5 O'Dowd	5 O'Dowd	5 Young	5 Hart	5 Hart
6 Weaver	6 Weaver	6 Tate	6 Keen	6 Weaver
7 Crooks	7 Crooks	7 Crooks	7 Crooks	7 Hulme
8 Barclay	8 Barclay	8 Jack	8 Jack	8 Starling
9 Waring	9 Dean	9 Brown G	9 Hampson	9 Hunt
10 Johnson	10 Johnson	10 Sandford	10 Walker	10 Pickering
11 Houghton	11 Cunliffe	11 Cunliffe	11 Houghton	11 Arnold
Wembley April 9: 3-0 Waring, Crooks, Barclay	Blackpool Oct 17: 1-0 Barclay	Wrexham Nov 16: 0-0	Chelsea Dec 7: 4-3 Hampson 2, Houghton, Crooks	Glasgow April 1: 1-2 Hunt

1933 Italy	1933 Switzerland	1933 Ireland	1933 Wales	1933 France
1 Hibbs	1 Hibbs	1 Hibbs	1 Hibbs	1 Hibbs
2 Goodall	2 Goodall	2 Goodall	2 Goodall	2 Goodall
3 Hapgood	3 Hapgood	3 Hapgood	3 Hapgood	3 Fairhurst
4 Strange	4 Strange	4 Strange	4 Strange	4 Strange
5 White	5 O'Dowd	5 Allen	5 Allen	5 Rowe
6 Copping	6 Copping	6 Copping	6 Copping	6 Copping
7 Geldard	7 Geldard	7 Crooks	7 Crooks	7 Crooks
8 Richardson J R	8 Richardson J R	8 Grosvenor	8 Grosvenor	8 Grosvenor
9 Hunt	9 Hunt	9 Bowers	9 Bowers	9 Camsell
10 Furness	10 Bastin	10 Bastin	10 Bastin	10 Hall
11 Bastin	11 Brook	11 Brook	11 Brook	11 Brook
Rome May 13: 1-1 Bastin	Berne May 20: 4-0 Bastin 2, Richardson 2	Belfast Oct 14: 3-0 Brook, Grosvenor, Bowers	Newcastle Nov 15: 1-2 Brook	Tottenham Dec 6: 4-1 Camsell 2, Brook, Grosvenor

1934 Scotland	1934 Hungary	1934 Czechoslovakia	1934 Wales	1934 Italy
1 Moss	1 Moss	1 Moss	1 Hibbs	1 Moss
2 Cooper	2 Cooper	2 Cooper	2 Cooper	2 Male
3 Hapgood	3 Hapgood	3 Hapgood	3 Hapgood	3 Hapgood
4 Stoker	4 Stoker	4 Gardner	4 Britton	4 Britton
5 Hart	5 Hart	5 Hart	5 Barker	5 Barker
6 Copping	6 Burrows	6 Burrows	6 Bray	6 Copping
7 Crooks	7 Crooks	7 Crooks	7 Matthews	7 Matthews
8 Carter H S	8 Carter H S	8 Beresford	8 Bowden	8 Bowden
9 Bowers	9 Tilson	9 Tilson	9 Tilson	9 Drake
10 Bastin	10 Bastin	10 Bastin	10 Westwood	10 Bastin
11 Brook	11 Brook	11 Brook	11 Brook	11 Brook
Wembley April 14: 3-0 Brook, Bastin, Bowers	Budapest May 10: 1-2 Tilson	Prague May 16: 1-2 Tilson	Cardiff Sept 29: 4-0 Tilson 2, Brook, Matthews	Arsenal Nov 14: 3-2 Brook 2, Drake

1935 Ireland	1935 Scotland	1935 Holland	1935 Ireland	1935 Germany
1 Hibbs	1 Hibbs	1 Hibbs	1 Sagar	1 Hibbs
2 Male	2 Male	2 Male	2 Male	2 Male
3 Hapgood	3 Hapgood	3 Hapgood	3 Hapgood	3 Hapgood
4 Britton	4 Britton	4 Gardner	4 Smith S	4 Crayston
5 Barker	5 Barker	5 Barker	5 Barker	5 Barker
6 Copping	6 Alsford	6 Burrows	6 Bray	6 Bray
7 Crooks	7 Geldard	7 Worrall	7 Birkett	7 Matthews
8 Bestall	8 Bastin	8 Eastham	8 Bowden	8 Carter H S
9 Drake	9 Gurney	9 Richardson W G	9 Tilson	9 Camsell
10 Bastin	10 Westwood	10 Westwood	10 Westwood	10 Westwood
11 Brook	11 Brook	11 Boyes	11 Brook	11 Bastin
Everton Feb 6: 2-1 *Bastin 2*	Glasgow April 6: 0-2	Amsterdam May 18: 1-0 *Worrall*	Belfast Oct 19: 3-1 *Tilson 2, Brook*	Tottenham Dec 4: 3-0 *Camsell 2, Bastin*

1936 Wales	1936 Scotland	1936 Austria	1936 Belgium	1936 Wales
1 Hibbs	1 Sagar	1 Sagar	1 Sagar	1 Holdcroft
2 Male	2 Male	2 Male	2 Male	2 Sproston
3 Hapgood	3 Hapgood	3 Hapgood	3 Hapgood	3 Catlin
4 Crayston	4 Crayston	4 Crayston	4 Crayston	4 Smalley
5 Barker	5 Barker	5 Barker	5 Joy	5 Barker
6 Bray	6 Bray	6 Copping	6 Copping	6 Keen
7 Crooks	7 Crooks	7 Spence	7 Spence	7 Crooks
8 Bowden	8 Barclay	8 Bowden	8 Barkas	8 Scott
9 Drake	9 Camsell	9 Camsell	9 Camsell	9 Steele
10 Bastin	10 Bastin	10 Bastin	10 Cunliffe	10 Westwood
11 Brook	11 Brook	11 Hobbis	11 Hobbis	11 Bastin
Wolverhampton Feb 5: 1-2 *Bowden*	Wembley April 4: 1-1 *Camsell*	Vienna May 6: 1-2 *Camsell*	Brussels May 9: 2-3 *Camsell, Hobbis*	Cardiff Oct 17: 1-2 *Bastin*

1936 Ireland	1936 Hungary	1937 Scotland	1937 Norway	1937 Sweden
1 Holdcroft	1 Tweedy	1 Woodley	1 Woodley	1 Woodley
2 Male	2 Male	2 Male	2 Male	2 Male
3 Catlin	3 Catlin	3 Barkas	3 Catlin	3 Catlin
4 Britton	4 Britton	4 Britton	4 Britton	4 Britton
5 Gee	5 Young	5 Young	5 Young	5 Young
6 Keen	6 Keen	6 Bray	6 Copping	6 Copping
7 Worrall	7 Crooks	7 Matthews	7 Kirchen	7 Kirchen
8 Carter H S	8 Bowden	8 Carter H S	8 Galley	8 Galley
9 Steele	9 Drake	9 Steele	9 Steele	9 Steele
10 Bastin	10 Carter H S	10 Starling	10 Goulden	10 Goulden
11 Johnson	11 Brook	11 Johnson	11 Johnson	11 Johnson
Stoke Nov 18: 3-1 *Carter, Bastin, Worrall*	Arsenal Dec 2: 6-2 *Drake 3, Brook, Britton, Carter*	Glasgow April 17: 1-3 *Steele*	Oslo May 14: 6-0 *Steele 2, Kirchen, Galley, Goulden, Holmsen og*	Stockholm May 17: 4-0 *Steele 3, Johnson*

1937 Finland	1937 Ireland	1937 Wales	1937 Czechoslovakia	1938 Scotland
1 Woodley	1 Woodley	1 Woodley	1 Woodley	1 Woodley
2 Male	2 Sproston	2 Sproston	2 Sproston	2 Sproston
3 Hapgood	3 Barkas	3 Barkas	3 Barkas	3 Hapgood
4 Willingham	4 Crayston	4 Crayston	4 Crayston	4 Willingham
5 Betmead	5 Cullis	5 Cullis	5 Cullis	5 Cullis
6 Copping	6 Copping	6 Copping	6 Copping	6 Copping
7 Kirchen	7 Geldard	7 Matthews	7 Matthews	7 Matthews
8 Robinson	8 Hall	8 Hall	8 Hall	8 Hall
9 Payne	9 Mills	9 Mills	9 Mills	9 Fenton
10 Steele	10 Goulden	10 Goulden	10 Goulden	10 Stephenson
11 Johnson	11 Brook	11 Brook	11 Morton	11 Bastin
Helsinki May 20: 8-0 *Payne 2, Steele 2, Kirchen, Willingham, Johnson, Robinson*	Belfast Oct 23: 5-1 *Mills 3, Hall, Brook*	Middlesbrough Nov 17: 2-1 *Matthews, Hall*	Tottenham Dec 1: 5-4 *Crayston, Morton, Matthews 3*	Wembley April 9: 0-1

1938 Germany	1938 Switzerland	1938 France	1938 Wales	1938 FIFA
1 Woodley	1 Woodley	1 Woodley	1 Woodley	1 Woodley
2 Sproston	2 Sproston	2 Sproston	2 Sproston	2 Sproston
3 Hapgood	3 Hapgood	3 Hapgood	3 Hapgood	3 Hapgood
4 Willingham	4 Willingham	4 Willingham	4 Willingham	4 Willingham
5 Young	5 Young	5 Young	5 Young	5 Cullis
6 Welsh	6 Welsh	6 Cullis	6 Copping	6 Copping
7 Matthews	7 Matthews	7 Broome	7 Matthews	7 Matthews
8 Robinson	8 Robinson	8 Matthews	8 Robinson	8 Hall
9 Broome	9 Broome	9 Drake	9 Lawton	9 Lawton
10 Goulden	10 Goulden	10 Goulden	10 Goulden	10 Goulden
11 Bastin	11 Bastin	11 Bastin	11 Boyes	11 Boyes
Berlin May 14: 6-3 *Robinson 2, Bastin, Broome, Matthews, Goulden*	Zurich May 21: 1-2 *Bastin*	Paris May 26: 4-2 *Drake 2, Broome, Bastin*	Cardiff Oct 22: 2-4 *Lawton, Matthews*	Arsenal Oct 26: 3-0 *Hall, Lawton, Goulden*

1938 Norway	1938 Ireland	1939 Scotland	1939 Italy	1939 Yugoslavia
1 Woodley	1 Woodley	1 Woodley	1 Woodley	1 Woodley
2 Sproston	2 Morris	2 Morris	2 Male	2 Male
3 Hapgood	3 Hapgood	3 Hapgood	3 Hapgood	3 Hapgood
4 Willingham	4 Willingham	4 Willingham	4 Willingham	4 Willingham
5 Cullis	5 Cullis	5 Cullis	5 Cullis	5 Cullis
6 Wright D	6 Mercer	6 Mercer	6 Mercer	6 Mercer
7 Matthews	7 Matthews	7 Matthews	7 Matthews	7 Matthews
8 Broome	8 Hall	8 Hall	8 Hall	8 Hall
9 Lawton	9 Lawton	9 Lawton	9 Lawton	9 Lawton
10 Dix	10 Stephenson	10 Goulden	10 Goulden	10 Goulden
11 Smith J R	11 Smith J R	11 Beasley	11 Beasley	11 Broome
Newcastle Nov 9: 4-0 *Smith 2, Dix, Lawton*	Manchester Nov 16: 7-0 *Hall 5, Lawton, Matthews*	Glasgow April 15: 2-1 *Beasley, Lawton*	Milan May 13: 2-2 *Lawton, Hall*	Belgrade May 18: 1-2 *Broome*

1939 Rumania	1946 N Ireland	1946 Rep of Ireland	1946 Wales	1946 Netherlands
1 Woodley	1 Swift	1 Swift	1 Swift	1 Swift
2 Male	2 Scott	2 Scott	2 Scott	2 Scott
3 Morris	3 Hardwick	3 Hardwick	3 Hardwick	3 Hardwick
4 Mercer	4 Wright W	4 Wright W	4 Wright W	4 Wright W
5 Cullis	5 Franklin	5 Franklin	5 Franklin	5 Franklin
6 Copping	6 Cockburn	6 Cockburn	6 Cockburn	6 Johnston
7 Broome	7 Finney	7 Finney	7 Finney	7 Finney
8 Goulden	8 Carter	8 Carter	8 Carter	8 Carter
9 Lawton	9 Lawton	9 Lawton	9 Lawton	9 Lawton
10 Welsh	10 Mannion	10 Mannion	10 Mannion	10 Mannion
11 Smith L C	11 Langton	11 Langton	11 Langton	11 Langton
Bucharest May 24: 2-0 Goulden, Welsh	Belfast Sept 28: 7-2 Carter, Mannion 3, Finney, Lawton, Langton	Dublin Sept 30: 1-0 Finney	Maine Rd Manchester Oct 19: 3-0 Mannion 2, Lawton	Huddersfield Nov 27: 8-2 Lawton 4, Carter 2, Mannion, Finney

1947 Scotland	1947 France	1947 Switzerland	1947 Portugal	1947 Belgium
1 Swift	1 Swift	1 Swift	1 Swift	1 Swift
2 Scott	2 Scott	2 Scott	2 Scott	2 Scott
3 Hardwick	3 Hardwick	3 Hardwick	3 Harwick	3 Hardwick
4 Wright W	4 Wright W	4 Wright W	4 Wright W	4 Ward
5 Franklin	5 Franklin	5 Franklin	5 Franklin	5 Franklin
6 Johnston	6 Lowe	6 Lowe	6 Lowe	6 Wright W
7 Matthews S	7 Finney	7 Matthews S	7 Matthews S	7 Matthews S
8 Carter	8 Carter	8 Carter	8 Mortensen	8 Mortensen
9 Lawton	9 Lawton	9 Lawton	9 Lawton	9 Lawton
10 Mannion	10 Mannion	10 Mannion	10 Mannion	10 Mannion
11 Mullen	11 Langton	11 Langton	11 Finney	11 Finney
Wembley April 12: 1-1 Carter	Highbury May 3: 3-0 Finney, Mannion, Carter	Zurich May 18: 0-1	Lisbon May 27: 10-0 Lawton 4 Mortensen 4, Finney, Matthews S	Brussels Sept 21: 5-2 Lawton 2, Mortensen, Finney 2

1947 Wales	1947 N Ireland	1947 Sweden	1948 Scotland	1948 Italy
1 Swift	1 Swift	1 Swift	1 Swift	1 Swift
2 Scott	2 Scott	2 Scott	2 Scott	2 Scott
3 Hardwick	3 Hardwick	3 Hardwick	3 Hardwick	3 Howe J
4 Taylor P	4 Taylor P	4 Taylor P	4 Wright W	4 Wright W
5 Franklin	5 Franklin	5 Franklin	5 Franklin	5 Franklin
6 Wright W	6 Wright W	6 Wright W	6 Cockburn	6 Cockburn
7 Matthews S	7 Matthews S	7 Finney	7 Matthews S	7 Matthews S
8 Mortensen	8 Mortensen	8 Mortensen	8 Mortensen	8 Mortensen
9 Lawton	9 Lawton	9 Lawton	9 Lawton	9 Lawton
10 Mannion	10 Mannion	10 Mannion	10 Pearson	10 Mannion
11 Finney	11 Finney	11 Langton	11 Finney	11 Finney
Cardiff Oct 18: 3-0 Finney, Mortensen, Lawton	Everton Nov 5: 2-2 Mannion, Lawton	Highbury Nov 19: 4-2 Mortensen 3, Lawton (pen)	Glasgow April 10: 2-0 Finney, Mortensen	Turin May 16: 4-0 Mortensen, Lawton, Finney 2

1948 Denmark	1948 N Ireland	1948 Wales	1948 Switzerland	1948 Scotland
1 Swift	1 Swift	1 Swift	1 Ditchburn	1 Swift
2 Scott	2 Scott	2 Scott	2 Ramsey	2 Aston
3 Aston	3 Howe J	3 Aston	3 Aston	3 Howe J
4 Wright W	4 Wright W	4 Ward	4 Wright W	4 Wright W
5 Franklin	5 Franklin	5 Franklin	5 Franklin	5 Franklin
6 Cockburn	6 Cockburn	6 Wright W	6 Cockburn	6 Cockburn
7 Matthews S	7 Matthews S	7 Matthews S	7 Matthews S	7 Matthews S
8 Hagan	8 Mortensen	8 Mortensen	8 Rowley J	8 Mortensen
9 Lawton	9 Milburn	9 Milburn	9 Milburn	9 Milburn
10 Shackleton	10 Pearson	10 Shackleton	10 Haines	10 Pearson
11 Langton	11 Finney	11 Finney	11 Hancocks	11 Finney
Copenhagen Sept 26: 0-0	Belfast Oct 9: 6-2 *Matthews S, Mortensen 3, Milburn, Pearson*	Villa Park Nov 10: 1-0 *Finney*	Highbury Dec 1: 6-0 *Haines 2, Hancocks 2, Rowley, Milburn*	Wembley April 9: 1-3 *Milburn*

1949 Sweden	1949 Norway	1949 France	1949 Rep of Ireland	1949 Wales
1 Ditchburn	1 Swift	1 Williams	1 Williams	1 Williams
2 Shinwell	2 Ellerington	2 Ellerington	2 Mozley	2 Mozley
3 Aston	3 Aston	3 Aston	3 Aston	3 Aston
4 Wright W	4 Wright W	4 Wright W	4 Wright W	4 Wright W
5 Franklin	5 Franklin	5 Franklin	5 Franklin	5 Franklin
6 Cockburn	6 Dickinson	6 Dickinson	6 Dickinson	6 Dickinson
7 Finney	7 Finney	7 Finney	7 Harris P	7 Finney
8 Mortensen	8 Morris	8 Morris	8 Morris	8 Mortensen
9 Bentley	9 Mortensen	9 Rowley J	9 Pye	9 Milburn
10 Rowley J	10 Mannion	10 Mannion	10 Mannion	10 Shackleton
11 Langton	11 Mullen	11 Mullen	11 Finney	11 Hancocks
Stockholm May 13: 1-3 *Finney*	Oslo May 18: 4-1 *Mullen, Finney Spydevolde, og Morris*	Paris May 22: 3-1 *Morris 2, Wright W*	Goodison Park Everton Sept 21: 0-2	Cardiff Oct 15: 4-1 *Mortensen, Milburn 3*

1949 N Ireland	1949 Italy	1950 Scotland	1950 Portugal	1950 Belgium
1 Streten	1 Williams	1 Williams	1 Williams	1 Williams
2 Mozley	2 Ramsey	2 Ramsey	2 Ramsey	2 Ramsey
3 Aston	3 Aston	3 Aston	3 Aston	3 Aston
4 Watson	4 Watson	4 Wright W	4 Wright W	4 Wright W
5 Franklin	5 Franklin	5 Franklin	5 Jones W H	5 Jones W H
6 Wright W	6 Wright W	6 Dickinson	6 Dickinson	6 Dickinson
7 Finney	7 Finney	7 Finney	7 Milburn	7 Milburn (Mullen)
8 Mortensen	8 Mortensen	8 Mannion	8 Mortensen	8 Mortensen
9 Rowley J	9 Rowley J	9 Mortensen	9 Bentley	9 Bentley
10 Pearson	10 Pearson	10 Bentley	10 Mannion	10 Mannion
11 Froggatt J	11 Froggatt J	11 Langton	11 Finney	11 Finney
Maine Rd Manchester Nov 16: 9-2 *Rowley 4, Froggatt J, Pearson 2, Mortensen 2*	Tottenham Nov 30: 2-0 *Rowley, Wright W*	Glasgow April 15: 1-0 *Bentley*	Luton May 14: 5-3 *Finney 4 (2 pens), Mortensen*	Brussels May 18: 4-1 *Mullen, Mortensen, Mannion, Bentley*

1950 Chile†	1950 USA†	1950 Spain†	1950 N Ireland	1950 Wales
1 Williams	1 Williams	1 Williams	1 Williams	1 Williams
2 Ramsey	2 Ramsey	2 Ramsey	2 Ramsey	2 Ramsey
3 Aston	3 Aston	3 Eckersley	3 Aston	3 Smith L
4 Wright W	4 Wright W	4 Wright W	4 Wright W	4 Watson
5 Hughes L	5 Hughes L	5 Hughes L	5 Chilton	5 Compton L
6 Dickinson	6 Dickinson	6 Dickinson	6 Dickinson	6 Dickinson
7 Finney	7 Finney	7 Matthews S	7 Matthews S	7 Finney
8 Mannion	8 Mannion	8 Mannion	8 Mannion	8 Mannion
9 Bentley	9 Bentley	9 Milburn	9 Lee J	9 Milburn
10 Mortensen	10 Mortensen	10 Baily E	10 Baily E	10 Baily E
11 Mullen	11 Mullen	11 Finney	11 Langton	11 Medley
Rio de Janeiro June 15: 2-0 *Mortensen, Mannion*	Belo Horizonte June 29: 0-1	Rio de Janeiro July 2: 0-1	Belfast Oct 7: 4-1 *Baily 2, Lee J, Wright W*	Sunderland Nov 15: 4-2 *Baily 2, Mannion, Milburn*

1950 Yugoslavia	1951 Scotland	1951 Argentina	1951 Portugal	1951 France
1 Williams	1 Williams	1 Williams	1 Williams	1 Williams
2 Ramsey	2 Ramsey	2 Ramsey	2 Ramsey	2 Ramsey
3 Eckersley	3 Eckersley	3 Eckersley	3 Eckersley	3 Willis
4 Watson	4 Johnston	4 Wright W	4 Nicholson	4 Wright W
5 Compton L	5 Froggatt J	5 Taylor J	5 Taylor J	5 Chilton
6 Dickinson	6 Wright W	6 Cockburn	6 Cockburn	6 Cockburn
7 Hancocks	7 Matthews S	7 Finney	7 Finney	7 Finney
8 Mannion	8 Mannion	8 Mortensen	8 Pearson	8 Mannion
9 Lofthouse	9 Mortensen	9 Milburn	9 Milburn	9 Milburn
10 Baily E	10 Hassall	10 Hassall	10 Hassall	10 Hassall
11 Medley	11 Finney	11 Metcalfe	11 Metcalfe	11 Medley
Highbury Nov 22: 2-2 *Lofthouse 2*	Wembley April 14: 2-3 *Hassall, Finney*	Wembley May 9: 2-1 *Mortensen 2*	Goodison Park Everton May 19: 5-2 *Nicholson, Milburn 2, Finney, Hassall*	Highbury Oct 3: 2-2 *Firoud, og Medley*

1951 Wales	1951 N Ireland	1951 Austria	1952 Scotland	1952 Italy
1 Williams	1 Merrick	1 Merrick	1 Merrick	1 Merrick
2 Ramsey	2 Ramsey	2 Ramsey	2 Ramsey	2 Ramsey
3 Smith L	3 Smith L	3 Eckersley	3 Garrett	3 Garrett
4 Wright W	4 Wright W	4 Wright W	4 Wright W	4 Wright W
5 Barrass	5 Barrass	5 Froggatt J	5 Froggatt J	5 Froggatt J
6 Dickinson	6 Dickinson	6 Dickinson	6 Dickinson	6 Dickinson
7 Finney	7 Finney	7 Milton	7 Finney	7 Finney
8 Thompson T	8 Sewell	8 Broadis	8 Broadis	8 Broadis
9 Lofthouse	9 Lofthouse	9 Lofthouse	9 Lofthouse	9 Lofthouse
10 Baily E	10 Phillips	10 Baily E	10 Pearson	10 Pearson
11 Medley	11 Medley	11 Medley	11 Rowley J	11 Elliott
Cardiff Oct 20: 1-1 *Baily*	Villa Park Nov 14: 2-0 *Lofthouse 2*	Wembley Nov 28: 2-2 *Ramsey (pen), Lofthouse*	Glasgow April 5: 2-1 *Pearson 2*	Florence May 18: 1-1 *Broadis*

1952 Austria	1952 Switzerland	1952 N Ireland	1952 Wales	1952 Belgium
1 Merrick	1 Merrick	1 Merrick	1 Merrick	1 Merrick
2 Ramsey	2 Ramsey	2 Ramsey	2 Ramsey	2 Ramsey
3 Eckersley	3 Eckersley	3 Eckersley	3 Smith L	3 Smith L
4 Wright W	4 Wright W	4 Wright W	4 Wright W	4 Wright W
5 Froggatt J	5 Froggatt J	5 Froggatt J	5 Froggatt J	5 Froggatt J
6 Dickinson	6 Dickinson	6 Dickinson	6 Dickinson	6 Dickinson
7 Finney	7 Allen R	7 Finney	7 Finney	7 Finney
8 Sewell	8 Sewell	8 Sewell	8 Froggatt R	9 Bentley
9 Lofthouse	9 Lofthouse	9 Lofthouse	9 Lofthouse	9 Lofthouse
10 Baily E	10 Baily E	10 Baily E	10 Bentley	10 Froggatt R
11 Elliott	11 Finney	11 Elliott	11 Elliott	11 Elliott
Vienna May 25: 3-2 *Lofthouse 2, Sewell*	Zurich May 28: 3-0 *Sewell, Lofthouse 2*	Belfast Oct 4: 2-2 *Lofthouse, Elliott*	Wembley Nov 12: 5-2 *Finney, Lofthouse 2, Froggatt J, Bentley*	Wembley Nov 26: 5-0 *Elliott 2, Lofthouse 2, Froggatt R*

1953 Scotland	1953 Argentina	1953 Chile	1953 Uruguay	1953 USA
1 Merrick	1 Merrick	1 Merrick	1 Merrick	1 Ditchburn
2 Ramsey	2 Ramsey	2 Ramsey	2 Ramsey	2 Ramsey
3 Smith L	3 Eckersley	3 Eckersley	3 Eckersley	3 Eckersley
4 Wright W	4 Wright W	4 Wright W	4 Wright W	4 Wright W
5 Barrass	5 Johnston	5 Johnston	5 Johnston	5 Johnston
6 Dickinson	6 Dickinson	6 Dickinson	6 Dickinson	6 Dickinson
7 Finney	7 Finney	7 Finney	7 Finney	7 Finney
8 Broadis	8 Broadis	8 Broadis	8 Broadis	8 Broadis
9 Lofthouse	9 Lofthouse	9 Lofthouse	9 Lofthouse	9 Lofthouse
10 Froggatt R	10 Taylor T	10 Taylor T	10 Taylor T	10 Froggatt R
11 Froggatt J	11 Berry	11 Berry	11 Berry	11 Froggatt J
Wembley April 18: 2-2 *Broadis 2*	Buenos Aires May 17: 0-0 (abandoned after 23 mins)	Santiago May 24: 2-1 *Taylor T Lofthouse*	Montevideo May 31: 1-2 *Taylor T*	New York June 8: 6-3 *Broadis, Finney 2, Lofthouse 2, Froggatt R*

1953 Wales	1953 Rest of Europe	1953 N Ireland	1953 Hungary	1954 Scotland
1 Merrick	1 Merrick	1 Merrick	1 Merrick	1 Merrick
2 Garrett	2 Ramsey	2 Rickaby	2 Ramsey	2 Staniforth
3 Eckersley	3 Eckersley	3 Eckersley	3 Eckersley	3 Byrne R
4 Wright W	4 Wright W	4 Wright W	4 Wright W	4 Wright W
5 Johnston	5 Ufton	5 Johnston	5 Johnston	5 Clarke H
6 Dickinson	6 Dickinson	6 Dickinson	6 Dickinson	6 Dickinson
7 Finney	7 Matthews S	7 Matthews S	7 Matthews S	7 Finney
8 Quixall	8 Mortensen	8 Quixall	8 Taylor E	8 Broadis
9 Lofthouse	9 Lofthouse	9 Lofthouse	9 Mortensen	9 Allen R
10 Wilshaw	10 Quixall	10 Hassall	10 Sewell	10 Nicholls
11 Mullen	11 Mullen	11 Mullen	11 Robb	11 Mullen
Cardiff Oct 10: 4-1 *Wilshaw 2, Lofthouse 2*	Wembley Oct 21: 4-4 *Mullen 2, Mortensen, Ramsey (pen)*	Goodison Park Everton Nov 11: 3-1 *Hassall 2, Lofthouse*	Wembley Nov 25: 3-6 *Sewell, Mortensen, Ramsey (pen)*	Glasgow April 3: 4-2 *Broadis, Nicholls, Allen, Mullen*

1954 Yugoslavia	1954 Hungary	1954 Belgium†	1954 Switzerland†	1954 Uruguay†
1 Merrick	1 Merrick	1 Merrick	1 Merrick	1 Merrick
2 Staniforth	2 Staniforth	2 Staniforth	2 Staniforth	2 Staniforth
3 Byrne R	3 Byrne R	3 Byrne R	3 Byrne R	3 Byrne R
4 Wright W	4 Wright W	4 Wright W	4 McGarry	4 McGarry
5 Owen	5 Owen	5 Owen	5 Wright W	5 Wright W
6 Dickinson	6 Dickinson	6 Dickinson	6 Dickinson	6 Dickinson
7 Finney	7 Harris P	7 Matthews S	7 Finney	7 Matthews S
8 Broadis	8 Sewell	8 Broadis	8 Broadis	8 Broadis
9 Allen R	9 Jezzard	9 Lofthouse	9 Taylor T	9 Lofthouse
10 Nicholls	10 Broadis	10 Taylor T	10 Wilshaw	10 Wilshaw
11 Mullen	11 Finney	11 Finney	11 Mullen	11 Finney
Belgrade May 16: 0-1	Budapest May 23: 1-7 *Broadis*	Basle June 17: 4-4 (aet), *Broadis* 2, *Lofthouse* 2	Berne June 29: 2-0 *Wilshaw, Mullen*	Basle Oct 2: 2-4 *Lofthouse, Finney*

1954 N Ireland	1954 Wales	1954 W Germany	1955 Scotland	1955 France
1 Wood	1 Wood	1 Williams	1 Williams	1 Williams
2 Foulkes	2 Staniforth	2 Staniforth	2 Meadows	2 Sillett P
3 Byrne R	3 Byrne R	3 Byrne R	3 Byrne R	3 Byrne R
4 Wheeler	4 Phillips	4 Phillips	4 Armstrong	4 Flowers
5 Wright W	5 Wright W	5 Wright W	5 Wright W	5 Wright W
6 Barlow	6 Slater	6 Slater	6 Edwards	6 Edwards
7 Matthews S	7 Matthews S	7 Matthews S	7 Matthews S	7 Matthews S
8 Revie	8 Bentley	8 Bentley	8 Revie	8 Revie
9 Lofthouse	9 Allen R	9 Allen R	9 Lofthouse	9 Lofthouse
10 Haynes	10 Shackleton	10 Shackleton	10 Wilshaw	10 Wilshaw
11 Pilkington	11 Blunstone	11 Finney	11 Blunstone	11 Blunstone
Belfast Oct 2: 2-0 *Haynes, Revie*	Wembley Nov 10: 3-2 *Bentley* 3	Wembley Dec 1: 3-1 *Bentley, Allen, Shackleton*	Wembley April 2: 7-2 *Wilshaw* 4, *Lofthouse* 2, *Revie*	Paris May 18: 0-1

1955 Spain	1955 Portugal	1955 Denmark	1955 Wales	1955 N Ireland
1 Williams	1 Williams	1 Baynham	1 Williams	1 Baynham
2 Sillett P	2 Sillett P	2 Hall	2 Hall	2 Hall
3 Byrne R	3 Byrne R	3 Byrne R	3 Byrne R	3 Byrne R
4 Dickinson	4 Dickinson	4 McGarry	4 McGarry	4 Clayton
5 Wright W	5 Wright W	5 Wright W	5 Wright W	5 Wright W
6 Edwards	6 Edwards	6 Dickinson	6 Dickinson	6 Dickinson
7 Matthews S	7 Matthews S	7 Milburn	7 Matthews S	7 Finney
8 Bentley	8 Bentley	8 Revie	8 Revie	8 Haynes
9 Lofthouse	9 Lofthouse (Quixall)	9 Lofthouse	9 Lofthouse	9 Jezzard
10 Quixall	10 Wilshaw	10 Bradford	10 Wilshaw	10 Wilshaw
11 Wilshaw	11 Blunstone	11 Finney	11 Finney	11 Perry
Madrid May 18: 1-1 *Bentley*	Oporto May 22: 1-3 *Bentley*	Copenhagen Oct 2: 5-1 *Revie* 2 (1 a pen), *Lofthouse, Bradford*	Cardiff Oct 22: 1-1 *Charles J, og*	Wembley Nov 2: 3-0 *Wilshaw* 2, *Finney*

1955 Spain	1956 Scotland	1956 Brazil	1956 Sweden	1956 Finland
1 Baynham	1 Matthews R	1 Matthews R	1 Matthews R	1 Wood
2 Hall	2 Hall	2 Hall	2 Hall	2 Hall
3 Byrne R	3 Byrne R	3 Byrne R	3 Byrne R	3 Byrne R
4 Clayton	4 Dickinson	4 Clayton	4 Clayton	4 Clayton
5 Wright W	5 Wright W	5 Wright W	5 Wright W	5 Wright W
6 Dickinson	6 Edwards	6 Edwards	6 Edwards	6 Edwards
7 Finney	7 Finney	7 Matthews S	7 Berry	7 Astall
8 Atyeo	8 Taylor T	8 Atyeo	8 Atyeo	8 Haynes
9 Lofthouse	9 Lofthouse	9 Taylor T	9 Taylor T	9 Taylor T (Lofthouse 40 min)
10 Haynes	10 Haynes	10 Haynes	10 Haynes	10 Wilshaw
11 Perry	11 Perry	11 Grainger	11 Grainger	11 Grainger
Wembley Nov 30: 4-1 *Atyeo, Perry 2, Finney*	Glasgow April 14: 1-1 *Haynes*	Wembley May 9: 4-2 *Taylor T 2, Grainger 2*	Stockholm May 16: 0-0	Helsinki May 20: 5-1 *Wilshaw, Haynes, Astall, Lofthouse 2*

1956 W Germany	1956 N Ireland	1956 Wales	1956 Yugoslavia	1956 Denmark
1 Matthews R	1 Matthews R	1 Ditchburn	1 Ditchburn	1 Ditchburn
2 Hall	2 Hall	2 Hall	2 Hall	2 Hall
3 Byrne R	3 Byrne R	3 Byrne R	3 Byrne R	3 Byrne R
4 Clayton	4 Clayton	4 Clayton	4 Clayton	4 Clayton
5 Wright W	5 Wright W	5 Wright W	5 Wright W	5 Wright W
6 Edwards	6 Edwards	6 Dickinson	6 Dickinson	6 Dickinson
7 Astall	7 Matthews S	7 Matthews S	7 Matthews S	7 Matthews S
8 Haynes	8 Revie	8 Brooks	8 Brooks	8 Brooks
9 Taylor T	9 Taylor T	9 Finney	9 Finney	9 Taylor T
10 Wilshaw	10 Wilshaw	10 Haynes	10 Haynes (Taylor T)	10 Edwards
11 Grainger	11 Grainger	11 Grainger	11 Blunstone	11 Finney
Berlin May 26: 3-1 *Edwards, Grainger, Haynes*	Belfast Oct 6: 1-1 *Matthews S*	Wembley Nov 14: 3-1 *Haynes, Brooks, Finney*	Wembley Nov 28: 3-0 *Brooks, Taylor T 2*	Wolverhampton Dec 5: 5-2 *Taylor T 3, Edwards 2*

1957 Scotland	1957 Rep of Ireland	1957 Denmark	1957 Rep of Ireland	1957 Wales
1 Hodgkinson	1 Hodgkinson	1 Hodgkinson	1 Hodgkinson	1 Hopkinson
2 Hall	2 Hall	2 Hall	2 Hall	2 Howe D
3 Byrne R	3 Byrne R	3 Byrne R	3 Byrne R	3 Byrne R
4 Clayton	4 Clayton	4 Clayton	4 Clayton	4 Clayton
5 Wright W	5 Wright W	5 Wright W	5 Wright W	5 Wright W
6 Edwards	6 Edwards	6 Edwards	6 Edwards	6 Edwards
7 Matthews S	7 Matthews S	7 Matthews S	7 Finney	7 Douglas
8 Thompson T	8 Atyeo	8 Atyeo	8 Atyeo	8 Kevan
9 Finney	9 Taylor T	9 Taylor T	9 Taylor T	9 Taylor T
10 Kevan	10 Haynes	10 Haynes	10 Haynes	10 Haynes
11 Grainger	11 Finney	11 Finney	11 Pegg	11 Finney
Wembley April 6: 2-1 *Kevan, Edwards*	Wembley May 8: 5-1 *Taylor T 3, Atyeo 2*	Copenhagen May 15: 4-1 *Haynes, Taylor T 2, Atyeo*	Dublin May 19: 1-1 *Atyeo*	Cardiff Oct 19: 4-0 *Hopkins, og, Haynes 2, Finney*

1957 N Ireland	1957 France	1958 Scotland	1958 Portugal	1958 Yugoslavia
1 Hopkinson	1 Hopkinson	1 Hopkinson	1 Hopkinson	1 Hopkinson
2 Howe D	2 Howe D	2 Howe D	2 Howe D	2 Howe D
3 Byrne R	3 Byrne R	3 Langley	3 Langley	3 Langley
4 Clayton	4 Clayton	4 Clayton	4 Clayton	4 Clayton
5 Wright W	5 Wright W	5 Wright W	5 Wright W	5 Wright W
6 Edwards	6 Edwards	6 Slater	6 Slater	6 Slater
7 Douglas	7 Douglas	7 Douglas	7 Douglas	7 Douglas
8 Kenyon	8 Robson R	8 Charlton R	8 Charlton R	8 Charlton R
9 Taylor T	9 Taylor T	9 Kevan	9 Kevan	9 Kevan
10 Haynes	10 Haynes	10 Haynes	10 Haynes	10 Haynes
11 A'Court	11 Finney	11 Finney	11 Finney	11 Finney
Wembley Nov 6: 2-3 *A'Court, Edwards*	Wembley Nov 27: 4-0 *Taylor T 2, Robson 2*	Glasgow April 19: 4-0 *Douglas, Kevan 2, Charlton R*	Wembley May 7: 2-1 *Charlton R 2*	Belgrade May 11: 0-5

1958 USSR	1958 USSR†	1958 Brazil†	1958 Austria†	1958 USSR†
1 McDonald	1 McDonald	1 McDonald	1 McDonald	1 McDonald
2 Howe D	2 Howe D	2 Howe D	2 Howe D	2 Howe D
3 Banks T	3 Banks T	3 Banks T	3 Banks T	3 Banks T
4 Clamp	4 Clamp	4 Clamp	4 Clamp	4 Clayton
5 Wright W	5 Wright W	5 Wright W	5 Wright W	5 Wright W
6 Slater	6 Slater	6 Slater	6 Slater	6 Slater
7 Douglas	7 Douglas	7 Douglas	7 Douglas	7 Brabrook
8 Robson R	8 Robson R	8 Robson R	8 Robson R	8 Broadbent
9 Kevan	9 Kevan	9 Kevan	9 Kevan	9 Kevan
10 Haynes	10 Haynes	10 Haynes	10 Haynes	10 Haynes
11 Finney	11 Finney	11 A'Court	11 A'Court	11 A'Court
Moscow May 18: 1-1 *Kevan*	Gothenburg June 8: 2-2 *Kevan, Finney* (pen)	Gothenburg June 11: 0-0	Boras June 15: 2-2 *Haynes, Kevan*	Gothenburg June 17: 0-1

1958 N Ireland	1958 USSR	1958 Wales	1959 Scotland	1959 Italy
1 McDonald	1 McDonald	1 McDonald	1 Hopkinson	1 Hopkinson
2 Howe D	2 Howe D	2 Howe D	2 Howe D	2 Howe D
3 Banks T	3 Shaw G	3 Shaw G	3 Shaw G	3 Shaw G
4 Clayton	4 Clayton	4 Clayton	4 Clayton	4 Clayton
5 Wright W	5 Wright W	5 Wright W	5 Wright W	5 Wright W
6 McGuinness	6 Slater	6 Flowers	6 Flowers	6 Flowers
7 Brabrook	7 Douglas	7 Clapton	7 Douglas	7 Bradley
8 Broadbent	8 Charlton R	8 Broadbent	8 Broadbent	8 Broadbent
9 Charlton R	9 Lofthouse	9 Lofthouse	9 Charlton R	9 Charlton R
10 Haynes	10 Haynes	10 Haynes	10 Haynes	10 Haynes
11 Finney	11 Finney	11 A'Court	11 Holden	11 Holden
Belfast Oct 4: 3-3 *Charlton R 2, Finney*	Wembley Oct 22: 5-0 *Haynes 3, Charlton R* (pen), *Lofthouse*	Villa Park Nov 26: 2-2 *Broadbent 2*	Wembley April 11: 1-0 *Charlton R*	Wembley May 6: 2-2 *Charlton R, Bradley*

1959 Brazil	1959 Peru	1959 Mexico	1959 USA	1959 Wales
1 Hopkinson	1 Hopkinson	1 Hopkinson	1 Hopkinson	1 Hopkinson
2 Howe D	2 Howe D	2 Howe D	2 Howe D	2 Howe D
3 Armfield	3 Armfield	3 Armfield	3 Armfield	3 Allen A
4 Clayton	4 Clayton	4 Clayton	4 Clayton	4 Clayton
5 Wright W	5 Wright W	5 Wright W	5 Wright W	5 Smith T
6 Flowers	6 Flowers	6 McGuiness (Flowers)	6 Flowers	6 Flowers
7 Deeley	7 Deeley	7 Holden (Bradley)	7 Bradley	7 Connelly
8 Broadbent	8 Greaves	8 Greaves	8 Greaves	8 Greaves
9 Charlton R	9 Charlton R	9 Kevan	9 Kevan	9 Clough
10 Haynes	10 Haynes	10 Haynes	10 Haynes	10 Charlton R
11 Holden	11 Holden	11 Charlton R	11 Charlton R	11 Holliday
Rio de Janeiro May 13: 0-2	Lima May 17: 1-4 *Greaves*	Mexico City May 24: 1-2 *Kevan*	Los Angeles May 28: 8-1 *Charlton R 3, Flowers 2, Bradley, Kevan, Haynes*	Cardiff Oct 17: 1-1 *Greaves*

1959 Sweden	1959 N Ireland	1960 Scotland	1960 Yugoslavia	1960 Spain
1 Hopkinson	1 Springett R	1 Springett R	1 Springett R	1 Springett R
2 Howe D	2 Howe D	2 Armfield	2 Armfield	2 Armfield
3 Allen A	3 Allen A	3 Wilson	3 Wilson	3 Wilson
4 Clayton	4 Clayton	4 Clayton	4 Clayton	4 Robson R
5 Smith T	5 Brown	5 Slater	5 Swan	5 Swan
6 Flowers	6 Flowers	6 Flowers	6 Flowers	6 Flowers
7 Connelly	7 Connelly	7 Connelly	7 Douglas	7 Brabrook
8 Greaves	8 Haynes	8 Broadbent	8 Haynes	8 Haynes
9 Clough	9 Baker	9 Baker	9 Baker	9 Baker
10 Charlton R	10 Parry	10 Parry	10 Greaves	10 Greaves
11 Holliday	11 Holliday	11 Charlton R	11 Charlton R	11 Charlton R
Wembley Oct 28: 2-3 *Connelly, Charlton R*	Wembley Nov 18: 2-1 *Baker, Parry*	Glasgow April 19: 1-1 *Charlton R (pen)*	Wembley May 11: 3-3 *Douglas, Greaves, Baker*	Madrid May 15: 0-3

1960 Hungary	1960 N Ireland	1960 Luxembourg	1960 Spain	1960 Wales
1 Springett R	1 Springett R	1 Springett R	1 Springett R	1 Hodgkinson
2 Armfield	2 Armfield	2 Armfield	2 Armfield	2 Armfield
3 Wilson	3 McNeil	3 McNeil	3 McNeil	3 McNeil
4 Robson R	4 Robson R	4 Robson R	4 Robson R	4 Robson R
5 Swan	5 Swan	5 Swan	5 Swan	5 Swan
6 Flowers	6 Flowers	6 Flowers	6 Flowers	6 Flowers
7 Douglas	7 Douglas	7 Douglas	7 Douglas	7 Douglas
8 Haynes	8 Greaves	8 Greaves	8 Greaves	8 Greaves
9 Baker	9 Smith R	9 Smith R	9 Smith R	9 Smith R
10 Viollet	10 Haynes	10 Haynes	10 Haynes	10 Haynes
11 Charlton R	11 Charlton R	11 Charlton R	11 Charlton R	11 Charlton R
Budapest May 22: 0-2	Belfast Oct. 8: 5-2 *Smith, Greaves 2, Charlton R, Douglas*	Luxembourg Oct. 19: 9-0 *Greaves 3, Charlton R 3, Smith 2, Haynes*	Wembley Oct 26: 4-2 *Greaves, Douglas, Smith 2*	Wembley Nov 23: 5-1 *Greaves 2, Charlton R, Smith, Haynes*

1961 Scotland	1961 Mexico	1961 Portugal	1961 Italy	1961 Austria
1 Springett R	1 Springett R	1 Springett R	1 Springett R	1 Springett R
2 Armfield	2 Armfield	2 Armfield	2 Armfield	2 Armfield
3 McNeil	3 McNeil	3 McNeil	3 McNeil	3 Angus
4 Robson R	4 Robson R	4 Robson R	4 Robson R	4 Miller
5 Swan	5 Swan	5 Swan	5 Swan	5 Swan
6 Flowers	6 Flowers	6 Flowers	6 Flowers	6 Flowers
7 Douglas	7 Douglas	7 Douglas	7 Douglas	7 Douglas
8 Greaves	8 Kevan	8 Greaves	8 Greaves	8 Greaves
9 Smith R	9 Hitchens	9 Smith R	9 Hitchens	9 Hitchens
10 Haynes	10 Haynes	10 Haynes	10 Haynes	10 Haynes
11 Charlton R	11 Charlton R	11 Charlton R	11 Charlton R	11 Charlton R
Wembley April 15: 9-3 Robson, Greaves 3, Douglas, Smith 2, Haynes 2	Wembley May 10: 8-0 Hitchens, Charlton R 3, Robson, Douglas 2, Flowers (pen)	Lisbon May 21: 1-1 Flowers	Rome May 24: 3-2 Hitchens 2, Greaves	Vienna May 27: 1-3 Greaves

1961 Luxembourg	1961 Wales	1961 Portugal	1961 N Ireland	1962 Austria
1 Springett R	1 Springett R	1 Springett R	1 Springett R	1 Springett R
2 Armfield	2 Armfield	2 Armfield	2 Armfield	2 Armfield
3 McNeil	3 Wilson	3 Wilson	3 Wilson	3 Wilson
4 Robson R	4 Robson R	4 Robson R	4 Robson R	4 Anderson
5 Swan	5 Swan	5 Swan	5 Swan	5 Swan
6 Flowers	6 Flowers	6 Flowers	6 Flowers	6 Flowers
7 Douglas	7 Connelly	7 Connelly	7 Douglas	7 Connelly
8 Fantham	8 Douglas	8 Douglas	8 Byrne J	8 Hunt
9 Pointer	9 Pointer	9 Pointer	9 Crawford	9 Crawford
10 Viollet	10 Haynes	10 Haynes	10 Haynes	10 Haynes
11 Charlton R	11 Charlton R	11 Charlton R	11 Charlton R	11 Charlton R
Highbury Sept 28: 4-1 Pointer, Viollet, Charlton R 2	Cardiff Oct 14: 1-1 Douglas	Wembley Oct 25: 2-0 Connelly, Pointer	Wembley Nov 22: 1-1 Charlton R	Wembley April 4: 3-1 Crawford, Flowers (pen), Hunt

1962 Scotland	1962 Switzerland	1962 Peru	1962 Hungary†	1962 Argentina†
1 Springett R	1 Springett R	1 Springett R	1 Springett R	1 Springett R
2 Armfield	2 Armfield	2 Armfield	2 Armfield	2 Armfield
3 Wilson	3 Wilson	3 Wilson	3 Wilson	3 Wilson
4 Anderson	4 Robson R	4 Moore	4 Moore	4 Moore
5 Swan	5 Swan	5 Norman	5 Norman	5 Norman
6 Flowers	6 Flowers	6 Flowers	6 Flowers	6 Flowers
7 Douglas	7 Connelly	7 Douglas	7 Douglas	7 Douglas
8 Greaves	8 Greaves	8 Greaves	8 Greaves	8 Greaves
9 Smith R	9 Hitchens	9 Hitchens	9 Hitchens	9 Peacock
10 Haynes	10 Haynes	10 Haynes	10 Haynes	10 Haynes
11 Charlton R	11 Charlton R	11 Charlton R	11 Charlton R	11 Charlton R
Glasgow April 14: 0-2	Wembley May 9: 3-1 Flowers, Hitchens, Connelly	Lima May 20: 4-0 Flowers (pen), Greaves 3	Rancagua May 31: 1-2 Flowers, (pen)	Rancagua June 2: 3-1 Flowers (pen), Charlton R, Greaves

1962 Bulgaria†	1962 Brazil†	1962 France	1962 N Ireland	1962 Wales
1 Springett R	1 Springett R	1 Springett R	1 Springett R	1 Springett R
2 Armfield	2 Armfield	2 Armfield	2 Armfield	2 Armfield
3 Wilson	3 Wilson	3 Wilson	3 Wilson	3 Shaw G
4 Moore	4 Moore	4 Moore	4 Moore	4 Moore
5 Norman	5 Norman	5 Norman	5 Labone	5 Labone
6 Flowers	6 Flowers	6 Flowers	6 Flowers	6 Flowers
7 Douglas	7 Douglas	7 Hellawell	7 Hellawell	7 Connelly
8 Greaves	8 Greaves	8 Crowe	8 Hill F	8 Hill F
9 Peacock	9 Hitchens	9 Charnley	9 Peacock	9 Peacock
10 Haynes	10 Haynes	10 Greaves	10 Greaves	10 Greaves
11 Charlton R	11 Charlton R	11 Hinton A	11 O'Grady	11 Tambling
Rancagua June 7: 0-0	Vina del Mar June 10: 1-3 *Hitchens*	Hillsborough Sheffield Oct 20 Oct 3: 1-1 *Flowers* (pen)	Belfast Oct 20: 3-1 *Greaves, O'Grady 2*	Wembley Nov 21: 4-0 *Connelly, Peacock 2, Greaves*

1963 France	1963 Scotland	1963 Brazil	1963 Czechoslovakia	1963 E Germany
1 Springett R	1 Banks G	1 Banks G	1 Banks G	1 Banks G
2 Armfield	2 Armfield	2 Armfield	2 Shellito	2 Armfield
3 Henry	3 Byrne G	3 Wilson	3 Wilson	3 Wilson
4 Moore	4 Moore	4 Milne	4 Milne	4 Milne
5 Labone	5 Norman	5 Norman	5 Norman	5 Norman
6 Flowers	6 Flowers	6 Moore	6 Moore	6 Moore
7 Connelly	7 Douglas	7 Douglas	7 Paine	7 Paine
8 Tambling	8 Greaves	8 Greaves	8 Greaves	8 Hunt
9 Smith R	9 Smith R	9 Smith R	9 Smith R	9 Smith R
10 Greaves	10 Melia	10 Eastham	10 Eastham	10 Eastham
11 Charlton R	11 Charlton R	11 Charlton R	11 Charlton R	11 Charlton R
Paris Feb 27: 2-5 *Smith, Tambling*	Wembley April 6: 1-2 *Douglas*	Wembley May 8: 1-1 *Douglas*	Bratislava May 20: 4-2 *Greaves 2, Smith, Charlton R*	Leipzig June 2: 2-1 *Hunt, Charlton R*

1963 Switzerland	1963 Wales	1963 R of World	1963 N Ireland	1964 Scotland
1 Springett R	1 Banks G	1 Banks G	1 Banks G	1 Banks G
2 Armfield	2 Armfield	2 Armfield	2 Armfield	2 Armfield
3 Wilson	3 Wilson	3 Wilson	3 Thomson R	3 Wilson
4 Kay	4 Milne	4 Milne	4 Milne	4 Milne
5 Norman	5 Norman	5 Norman	5 Norman	5 Norman
6 Flowers	6 Moore	6 Moore	6 Moore	6 Moore
7 Douglas	7 Paine	7 Paine	7 Paine	7 Paine
8 Greaves	8 Greaves	8 Greaves	8 Greaves	8 Hunt
9 Byrne J	9 Smith R	9 Smith R	9 Smith R	9 Byrne J
10 Melia	10 Eastham	10 Eastham	10 Eastham	10 Eastham
11 Charlton R	11 Charlton R	11 Charlton R	11 Charlton R	11 Charlton R
Basle June 5: 8-1 *Charlton, R 3, Byrne, J 2, Douglas, Kay, Melia*	Cardiff Oct 12: 4-0 *Smith 2, Greaves, Charlton R*	Wembley Oct 23: 2-1 *Paine, Greaves*	Wembley (first by floodlight) Nov 20: 8-3 *Greaves 4, Paine 3, Smith*	Glasgow April 11: 0-1

1964 Uruguay	1964 Portugal	1964 Rep of Ireland	1964 USA	1964 Brazil
1 Banks G	1 Banks G	1 Waiters	1 Banks G	1 Waiters
2 Cohen	2 Cohen	2 Cohen	2 Cohen	2 Cohen
3 Wilson	3 Wilson	3 Wilson	3 Thomson R	3 Wilson
4 Milne	4 Milne	4 Milne	4 Bailey M	4 Milne
5 Norman	5 Norman	5 Flowers	5 Norman	5 Norman
6 Moore	6 Moore	6 Moore	6 Flowers	6 Moore
7 Paine	7 Thompson P	7 Thompson P	7 Paine	7 Thompson P
8 Greaves	8 Greaves	8 Greaves	8 Hunt	8 Greaves
9 Byrne J	9 Byrne J	9 Byrne J	9 Pickering	9 Byrne J
10 Eastham	10 Eastham	10 Eastham	10 Eastham (Charlton R)	10 Eastham
11 Charlton R	11 Charlton R	11 Charlton R	11 Thompson P	11 Charlton R
Wembley May 6: 2-1 *Byrne J 2*	Lisbon May 17: 4-3 *Byrne J 3, Charlton R*	Dublin May 24: 3-1 *Eastham, Byrne J, Greaves*	New York May 27: 10-0 *Hunt 4, Pickering 3, Paine 2, Charlton R*	Rio de Janeiro May 30: 1-5 *Greaves*

1964 Portugal	1964 Argentina	1964 N Ireland	1964 Belgium	1964 Wales
1 Banks G	1 Banks G	1 Banks G	1 Waiters	1 Waiters
2 Thomson R	2 Thomson R	2 Cohen	2 Cohen	2 Cohen
3 Wilson	3 Wilson	3 Thomson R	3 Thomson R	3 Thomson R
4 Flowers	4 Milne	4 Milne	4 Milne	4 Bailey M
5 Norman	5 Norman	5 Norman	5 Norman	5 Flowers
6 Moore	6 Moore	6 Moore	6 Moore	6 Young
7 Paine	7 Thompson P	7 Paine	7 Thompson P	7 Thompson P
8 Greaves	8 Greaves	8 Greaves	8 Greaves	8 Hunt
9 Byrne J	9 Byrne J	9 Pickering	9 Pickering	9 Wignall
11 Hunt	10 Eastham	10 Charlton R	10 Venables	10 Byrne J
11 Thompson P	11 Charlton R	11 Thompson P	11 Hinton A	11 Hinton A
Sao Paulo June 4: 1-1 *Hunt*	Rio de Janeiro June 6: 0-1	Belfast Oct 3: 4-3 *Pickering, Greaves 3*	Wembley Oct 21: 2-2 *Pickering, Hinton*	Wembley Nov 18: 2-1 *Wignall 2*

1964 Netherlands	1965 Scotland	1965 Hungary	1965 Yugoslavia	1965 W Germany
1 Waiters	1 Banks G	1 Banks G	1 Banks G	1 Banks G
2 Cohen	2 Cohen	2 Cohen	2 Cohen	2 Cohen
3 Thomson R	3 Wilson	3 Wilson	3 Wilson	3 Wilson
4 Mullery	4 Stiles	4 Stiles	4 Stiles	4 Flowers
5 Norman	5 Charlton J	5 Charlton J	5 Charlton J	5 Charlton J
6 Flowers	6 Moore	6 Moore	6 Moore	6 Moore
7 Thompson P	7 Thompson P	7 Paine	7 Paine	7 Paine
8 Greaves	8 Greaves	8 Greaves	8 Greaves	8 Ball
9 Wignall	9 Bridges	9 Bridges	9 Bridges	9 Jones M
10 Venables	10 Byrne J	10 Eastham	10 Ball	10 Eastham
11 Charlton R	11 Charlton R	11 Connolly	11 Connolly	11 Temple
Amsterdam Dec 9: 1-1 *Greaves*	Wembley April 10: 2-2 *Charlton R, Greaves*	Wembley May 5: 1-0 *Greaves*	Belgrade May 9: 1-1 *Bridges*	Nuremberg May 12: 1-0 *Paine*

1965 Sweden	1965 Wales	1965 Austria	1965 N Ireland	1965 Spain
1 Banks G	1 Springett R	1 Springett R	1 Banks G	1 Banks G
2 Cohen	2 Cohen	2 Cohen	2 Cohen	2 Cohen
3 Wilson	3 Wilson	3 Wilson	3 Wilson	3 Wilson
4 Stiles	4 Stiles	4 Stiles	4 Stiles	4 Stiles
5 Charlton J	5 Charlton J	5 Charlton J	5 Charlton J	5 Charlton J
6 Moore	6 Moore	6 Moore	6 Moore	6 Moore
7 Paine	7 Paine	7 Paine	7 Thompson P	7 Ball
8 Ball	8 Greaves	8 Greaves	8 Baker	8 Hunt
9 Jones M	9 Peacock	9 Bridges	9 Peacock	9 Baker (Hunter)
10 Eastham	10 Charlton R	10 Charlton R	10 Charlton R	10 Eastham
11 Connolly	11 Connolly	11 Connolly	11 Connolly	11 Charlton R
Gothenburg May 16: 2-1 Ball, Connolly	Cardiff Oct 2: 0-0	Wembley Oct 20: 2-3 Charlton R, Connolly	Wembley Nov 10: 2-1 Baker, Peacock	Madrid Dec 8: 2-0 Baker, Hunt

1966 Poland	1966 W Germany	1966 Scotland	1966 Yugoslavia	1966 Finland
1 Banks G	1 Banks G	1 Banks G	1 Banks G	1 Banks G
2 Cohen	2 Cohen	2 Cohen	2 Armfield	2 Armfield
3 Wilson	3 Newton K (Wilson)	3 Newton K	3 Wilson	3 Wilson
4 Stiles	4 Moore	4 Stiles	4 Peters	4 Peters
5 Charlton J	5 Charlton J	5 Charlton J	5 Charlton J	5 Charlton J
6 Moore	6 Hunter	6 Moore	6 Hunter	6 Hunter
7 Ball	7 Ball	7 Ball	7 Paine	7 Callaghan
8 Hunt	8 Hunt	8 Hunt	8 Greaves	8 Hunt
9 Baker	9 Stiles	9 Charlton R	9 Charlton R	9 Charlton R
10 Eastham	10 Hurst G	10 Hurst G	10 Hurst G	10 Hurst G
11 Harris G	11 Charlton R	11 Connolly	11 Tambling	11 Ball
Liverpool Jan 5: 1-1 Moore	Wembley Feb 23: 1-0 Stiles	Glasgow April 2: 4-3 Hurst, Hunt 2, Charlton R	Wembley May 4: 2-0 Greaves, Charlton R	Helsinki June 26: 3-0 Peters, Hunt, Charlton J

1966 Norway	1966 Denmark	1966 Poland	1966 Uruguay†	1966 Mexico†
1 Springett R	1 Bonetti	1 Banks G	1 Banks G	1 Banks G
2 Cohen	2 Cohen	2 Cohen	2 Cohen	2 Cohen
3 Byrne G	3 Wilson	3 Wilson	3 Wilson	3 Wilson
4 Stiles	4 Stiles	4 Stiles	4 Stiles	4 Stiles
5 Flowers	5 Charlton J	5 Charlton J	5 Charlton J	5 Charlton J
6 Moore	6 Moore	6 Moore	6 Moore	6 Moore
7 Paine	7 Ball	7 Ball	7 Ball	7 Paine
8 Greaves	8 Greaves	8 Greaves	8 Greaves	8 Greaves
9 Charlton R	9 Hurst G	9 Charlton R	9 Charlton R	9 Charlton R
10 Hunt	10 Eastham	10 Hunt	10 Hunt	10 Hunt
11 Connolly	11 Connolly	11 Peters	11 Connolly	11 Peters
Oslo June 29: 6-1 Greaves 4, Connolly, Moore	Copenhagen July 3: 2-0 Charlton J, Eastham	Chorzhow July 5: 1-0 Hunt	Wembley July 11: 0-0	Wembley July 16: 2-0 Charlton R, Hunt

1966 France†	1966 Argentina†	1966 Portugal†	1966 W Germany†	1966 N Ireland
1 Banks G	1 Banks G	1 Banks G	1 Banks G	1 Banks G
2 Cohen	2 Cohen	2 Cohen	2 Cohen	2 Cohen
3 Wilson	3 Wilson	3 Wilson	3 Wilson	3 Wilson
4 Stiles	4 Stiles	4 Stiles	4 Stiles	4 Stiles
5 Charlton J	5 Charlton J	5 Charlton J	5 Charlton J	5 Charlton J
6 Moore	6 Moore	6 Moore	6 Moore	6 Moore
7 Callaghan	7 Ball	7 Ball	7 Ball	7 Ball
8 Greaves	8 Hurst G	8 Hurst G	8 Hurst G	8 Hurst G
9 Charlton R	9 Charlton R	9 Charlton R	9 Charlton R	9 Charlton R
10 Hunt	10 Hunt	10 Hunt	10 Hunt	10 Hunt
11 Peters	11 Peters	11 Peters	11 Peters	11 Peters
Wembley July 20: 2-0 *Hunt 2*	Wembley July 23: 1-0 *Hurst*	Wembley July 26: 2-1 *Charlton R 2*	Wembley (*World Cup Final: aet*) July 30: 4-2 *Hurst 3, Peters*	Belfast Oct 22: 2-0 *Hunt, Peters*

1966 Czechoslovakia	1966 Wales	1967 Scotland	1967 Spain	1967 Austria
1 Banks G	1 Banks G	1 Banks G	1 Bonetti	1 Bonetti
2 Cohen	2 Cohen	2 Cohen	2 Cohen	2 Newton K
3 Wilson	3 Wilson	3 Wilson	3 Newton K	3 Wilson
4 Stiles	4 Stiles	4 Stiles	4 Mullery	4 Mullery
5 Charlton J	5 Charlton J	5 Charlton J	5 Labone	5 Labone
6 Moore	6 Moore	6 Moore	6 Moore	6 Moore
7 Ball	7 Ball	7 Ball	7 Ball	7 Ball
8 Hurst G	8 Hurst G	8 Greaves	8 Greaves	8 Greaves
9 Charlton R	9 Charlton R	9 Charlton R	9 Hurst G	9 Hurst G
10 Hunt	10 Hunt	10 Hurst G	10 Hunt	10 Hunt
11 Peters	11 Peters	11 Peters	11 Hollins	11 Hunter
Wembley Nov 2: 0-0	Wembley Nov 16: 5-1 *Hurst 2, Charlton R, Charlton J, Hennessy og*	Wembley April 15: 2-3 *Charlton J, Hurst G*	Wembley May 24 2-0 *Greaves, Hunt*	Vienna May 27: 1-0 *Ball*

1967 Wales	1967 N Ireland	1967 USSR	1968 Scotland	1968 Spain
1 Banks G	1 Banks G	1 Banks G	1 Banks G	1 Banks G
2 Cohen	2 Cohen	2 Knowles C	2 Newton K	2 Knowles C
3 Newton K	3 Wilson	3 Wilson	3 Wilson	3 Wilson
4 Mullery	4 Mullery	4 Mullery	4 Mullery	4 Mullery
5 Charlton J	5 Sadler	5 Sadler	5 Labone	5 Charlton J
6 Moore	6 Moore	6 Moore	6 Moore	6 Moore
7 Ball	7 Thompson P	7 Ball	7 Ball	7 Ball
8 Hunt	8 Hunt	8 Hunt	8 Hurst G	8 Hunt
9 Charlton R	9 Charlton R	9 Charlton R	9 Summerbee	9 Summerbee
10 Hurst G	10 Hurst G	10 Hurst G	10 Charlton R	10 Charlton R
11 Peters	11 Peters	11 Peters	11 Peters	11 Peters
Cardiff Oct 21: 3-0 *Peters, Charlton R, Ball*	Wembley Nov 22: 2-0 *Hurst G, Charlton R*	Wembley Dec 6: 2-2 *Bull, Peters*	Glasgow Feb 24: 1-1 *Peters*	Wembley April 3: 1-0 *Charlton R*

1968 Spain	1968 Sweden	1968 W Germany	1968 Yugoslavia	1968 USSR
1 Bonetti	1 Stepney	1 Banks G	1 Banks G	1 Banks G
2 Newton K	2 Newton K	2 Newton K	2 Newton K	2 Wright T
3 Wilson	3 Knowles C	3 Knowles C	3 Wilson	3 Wilson
4 Mullery	4 Mullery	4 Hunter	4 Mullery	4 Stiles
5 Labone	5 Labone	5 Labone	5 Labone	5 Labone
6 Moore	6 Moore	6 Moore	6 Moore	6 Moore
7 Ball	7 Bell	7 Ball	7 Ball	7 Hunter
8 Peters	8 Peters	8 Bell	8 Peters	8 Hunt
9 Charlton R	9 Charlton R (Hurst G)	9 Summerbee	9 Charlton R	9 Charlton R
10 Hunt	10 Hunt	10 Hurst G	10 Hunt	10 Hurst G
11 Hunter	11 Hunter	11 Thompson P	11 Hunter	11 Peters
Madrid May 8: 2-1 *Peters, Hunter*	Wembley May 22: 3-1 *Peters, Charlton R, Hunt*	Hanover June 1: 0-1	Florence June 5: 0-1	Rome June 8: 2-0 *Charlton R, Hurst*

1968 Rumania	1968 Bulgaria	1969 Rumania	1969 France	1969 N Ireland
1 Banks G	1 West	1 Banks G	1 Banks G	1 Banks G
2 Wright T (McNab)	2 Newton K (Reaney)	2 Wright T	2 Newton K	2 Newton K
3 Newton K	3 McNab	3 McNab	3 Cooper	3 McNab
4 Mullery	4 Mullery	4 Stiles	4 Mullery	4 Mullery
5 Labone	5 Labone	5 Charlton J	5 Charlton J	5 Labone
6 Moore	6 Moore	6 Hunter	6 Moore	6 Moore
7 Ball	7 Lee F	7 Radford	7 Lee F	7 Ball
8 Hunt	8 Bell	8 Hunt	8 Bell	8 Lee F
9 Charlton R	9 Charlton R	9 Charlton R	9 Hurst G	9 Charlton R
10 Hurst G	10 Hurst G	10 Hurst G	10 Peters	10 Hurst G
11 Peters	11 Peters	11 Ball	11 O'Grady	11 Peters
Bucharest Nov 6: 0-0	Wembley Dec 11: 1-1 *Hurst G*	Wembley Jan 15: 1-1 *Charlton J*	Wembley Mar 12: 5-0 *Hurst G 3, O'Grady, Lee*	Belfast May 3: 3-1 *Peters, Lee F, Hurst G (pen)*

1969 Wales	1969 Scotland	1969 Mexico	1969 Uruguay	1969 Brazil
1 West	1 Banks G	1 West	1 Banks G	1 Banks G
2 Newton K	2 Newton K	2 Newton K (Wright T)	2 Wright T	2 Wright T
3 Cooper	3 Cooper	3 Cooper	3 Newton K	3 Newton K
4 Moore	4 Mullery	4 Mullery	4 Mullery	4 Mullery
5 Charlton J	5 Labone	5 Labone	5 Labone	5 Labone
6 Hunter	6 Moore	6 Moore	6 Moore	6 Moore
7 Lee F	7 Lee F	7 Lee F	7 Lee F	7 Ball
8 Bell	8 Ball	8 Ball	8 Bell	8 Bell
9 Astle	9 Charlton R	9 Charlton R	9 Hurst G	9 Charlton R
10 Charlton R	10 Hurst G	10 Hurst G	10 Ball	10 Hurst G
11 Ball	11 Peters	11 Peters	11 Peters	11 Peters
Wembley May 7: 2-1 *Charlton R, Lee F*	Wembley May 10: 4-1 *Peters 2, Hurst G 2 (1 a pen)*	Mexico City June 1: 0-0	Montevideo June 8: 2-1 *Lee F, Hurst G*	Rio de Janeiro June 12: 1-2 *Bell*

1969 Netherlands	1969 Portugal	1970 Netherlands	1970 Belgium	1970 Wales
1 Bonetti	1 Bonetti	1 Banks G	1 Banks G	1 Banks G
2 Wright T	2 Reaney	2 Newton K	2 Wright T	2 Wright T
3 Hughes E	3 Hughes E	3 Cooper	3 Cooper	3 Hughes E
4 Mullery	4 Mullery	4 Peters	4 Moore	4 Mullery
5 Charlton J	5 Charlton J	5 Charlton J	5 Labone	5 Labone
6 Moore	6 Moore	6 Hunter	6 Hughes E	6 Moore
7 Lee F (Thompson P)	7 Lee F	7 Lee F (Mullery)	7 Lee F	7 Lee F
8 Bell	8 Bell (Peters)	8 Bell	8 Ball	8 Ball
9 Charlton R	9 Astle	9 Jones M (Hurst G)	9 Osgood	9 Charlton R
10 Hurst G	10 Charlton R	10 Charlton R	10 Hurst G	10 Hurst G
11 Peters	11 Ball	11 Moore I	11 Peters	11 Peters
Amsterdam Nov 5: 1-0 *Bell*	Wembley Dec 10: 1-0 *Charlton J*	Wembley Jan 14: 0-0	Brussels Feb 25: 3-1 *Ball 2, Hurst G*	Cardiff April 18: 1-1 *Lee F*

1970 N Ireland	1970 Scotland	1970 Colombia	1970 Ecuador	1970 Rumania†
1 Banks G	1 Banks G	1 Banks G	1 Banks G	1 Banks G
2 Newton K (Bell)	2 Newton K	2 Newton K	2 Newton K	2 Newton K (Wright T)
3 Hughes E	3 Hughes E	3 Cooper	3 Cooper	3 Cooper
4 Mullery	4 Stiles	4 Mullery	4 Mullery	4 Mullery
5 Moore	5 Labone	5 Labone	5 Labone	5 Labone
6 Stiles	6 Moore	6 Moore	6 Moore	6 Moore
7 Coates	7 Thompson P (Mullery)	7 Lee F	7 Lee F (Kidd)	7 Lee F (Osgood)
8 Kidd	8 Ball	8 Ball	8 Ball	8 Ball
9 Charlton R	9 Astle	9 Charlton R	9 Charlton R (Sadler)	9 Charlton R
10 Hurst G	10 Hurst G	10 Hurst G	10 Hurst G	10 Hurst G
11 Peters	11 Peters	11 Peters	11 Peters	11 Peters
Wembley April 21: 3-1 *Peters, Hurst G, Charlton R*	Glasgow April 25: 0-0	Bogata May 20: 4-0 *Peters 2, Charlton R, Ball*	Quito May 24: 2-0 *Lee F, Kidd*	Guadalajara June 2: 1-0 *Hurst G*

1970 Brazil†	1970 Czechoslovakia†	1970 W Germany†	1970 E Germany	1971 Malta
1 Banks G	1 Banks G	1 Bonetti	1 Shilton	1 Banks G
2 Wright T	2 Newton K	2 Newton K	2 Hughes	2 Reaney
3 Cooper	3 Cooper	3 Cooper	3 Cooper	3 Cooper
4 Mullery	4 Mullery	4 Mullery	4 Mullery	4 Mullery
5 Labone	5 Charlton J	5 Labone	5 Sadler	5 McFarland
6 Moore	6 Moore	6 Moore	6 Moore	6 Hunter
7 Lee F (Astle)	7 Bell	7 Lee F	7 Lee F	7 Ball
8 Ball	8 Charlton R (Ball)	8 Ball	8 Ball	8 Chivers
9 Charlton R (Bell)	9 Astle (Osgood)	9 Charlton R (Bell)	9 Hurst G	9 Royle
10 Hurst G	10 Clarke A	10 Hurst G	10 Clarke A	10 Harvey
11 Peters	11 Peters	11 Peters (Hunter)	11 Peters	11 Peters
Guadalajara June 7: 0-1	Guadalajara June 11: 1-0 *Clarke* (pen)	Leon June 14: 2-3 (aet) *Mullery, Peters*	Wembley Nov 25: 3-1 *Lee, Peters, Clarke*	Valletta Feb 3: 1-0 *Peters*

1971 Greece	1971 Malta	1971 N Ireland	1971 Wales	1971 Scotland
1 Banks G	1 Banks G	1 Banks G	1 Shilton	1 Banks G
2 Storey	2 Lawler	2 Madeley	2 Lawler	2 Lawler
3 Hughes	3 Cooper	3 Cooper	3 Cooper	3 Cooper
4 Mullery	4 Moore	4 Storey	4 Smith	4 Storey
5 McFarland	5 McFarland	5 McFarland	5 Lloyd	5 McFarland
6 Moore	6 Hughes	6 Moore	6 Hughes	6 Moore
7 Lee F	7 Lee F	7 Lee F	7 Lee F	7 Lee F (Clarke)
8 Ball (Coates)	8 Coates	8 Ball	8 Coates (Clark)	8 Ball
9 Chivers	9 Chivers	9 Chivers	9 Hurst G	9 Chivers
10 Hurst G	10 Clarke	10 Clarke	10 Brown A	10 Hurst G
11 Peters	11 Peters (Ball)	11 Peters	11 Peters	11 Peters
Wembley April 21: 3-0 *Chivers, Hurst G, Lee F*	Wembley May 12: 5-0 *Chivers 2, Lee, Clarke (pen), Lawler*	Belfast May 15: 1-0 *Clarke*	Wembley May 19: 0-0	Wembley May 22: 3-1 *Peters, Chivers 2*

1971 Switzerland	1971 Switzerland	1971 Greece	1971 W Germany	1972 W Germany
1 Banks G	1 Shilton	1 Banks G	1 Banks G	1 Banks G
2 Lawler	2 Madeley	2 Madeley	2 Madeley	2 Madeley
3 Cooper	3 Cooper	3 Hughes	3 Hughes	3 Hughes
4 Mullery	4 Storey	4 Bell	4 Bell	4 Storey
5 McFarland	5 Lloyd	5 McFarland	5 Moore	5 McFarland
6 Moore	6 Moore	6 Moore	6 Hunter	6 Moore
7 Lee F	7 Summerbee (Chivers)	7 Lee F	7 Lee F	7 Ball
8 Madeley	8 Ball	8 Ball	8 Ball	8 Bell
9 Chivers	9 Hurst G	9 Chivers	9 Chivers	9 Chivers
10 Hurst G (Radford)	10 Lee F (Marsh)	10 Hurst G	10 Hurst G (Marsh)	10 Marsh (Summerbee)
11 Peters	11 Hughes	11 Peters	11 Peters	11 Hunter (Peters)
Basle Oct 13: 3-2 *Hurst, Chivers, Weibel, og*	Wembley Nov 10: 1-1 *Summerbee*	Athens Dec 1: 2-0 *Hurst, Chivers*	Wembley April 29: 1-3 *Lee F*	Berlin May 13: 0-0

1972 Wales	1972 N Ireland	1972 Scotland	1972 Yugoslavia	1972 Wales
1 Banks G	1 Shilton	1 Banks G	1 Shilton	1 Clemence
2 Madeley	2 Todd	2 Madeley	2 Mills	2 Storey
3 Hughes	3 Hughes	3 Hughes	3 Lampard	3 Hughes
4 Storey	4 Storey	4 Storey	4 Storey	4 Hunter
5 McFarland	5 Lloyd	5 McFarland	5 Blockley	5 McFarland
6 Moore	6 Hunter	6 Moore	6 Moore	6 Moore
7 Summerbee	7 Summerbee	7 Ball	7 Ball	7 Keegan
8 Bell	8 Bell	8 Bell	8 Channon	8 Chivers
9 Macdonald	9 Macdonald (Chivers)	9 Chivers	9 Royle	9 Marsh
10 Marsh	10 Marsh	10 Marsh (Macdonald)	10 Bell	10 Bell
11 Hunter	11 Currie (Peters)	11 Hunter	11 Marsh	11 Ball
Cardiff May 20: 3-0 *Hughes, Bell, Marsh*	Wembley May 23: 0-1	Hampden May 27: 1-0 *Ball*	Wembley Oct 11: 1-1 *Royle*	Cardiff Nov 15: 1-0 *Bell*

1973 Wales	1973 Scotland	1973 N Ireland	1973 Wales	1973 Scotland
1 Clemence	1 Shilton	1 Shilton	1 Shilton	1 Shilton
2 Storey	2 Storey	2 Storey	2 Storey	2 Storey
3 Hughes	3 Hughes	3 Nish	3 Hughes	3 Hughes
4 Hunter	4 Bell	4 Bell	4 Bell	4 Bell
5 McFarland	5 Madeley	5 McFarland	5 McFarland	5 McFarland
6 Moore	6 Moore	6 Moore	6 Moore	6 Moore
7 Keegan	7 Ball	7 Ball	7 Ball	7 Ball
8 Bell	8 Channon	8 Channon	8 Channon	8 Channon
9 Chivers	9 Chivers	9 Chivers	9 Chivers	9 Chivers
10 Marsh	10 Clarke	10 Richards	10 Clarke	10 Clarke
11 Ball	11 Peters	11 Peters	11 Peters	11 Peters
Wembley Jan 24: 1-1 *Hunter*	Glasgow Feb 14: 5-0 *Lorimer, og, Clarke 2, Channon, Chivers*	Liverpool May 12: 2-1 *Chivers 2*	Wembley May 15: 3-0 *Chivers, Channon, Peters*	Wembley May 19: 1-0 *Peters*

1973 Czechoslovakia	1973 Poland	1973 USSR	1973 Italy	1973 Austria
1 Shilton	1 Shilton	1 Shilton	1 Shilton	1 Shilton
2 Madeley	2 Madeley	2 Madeley	2 Madeley	2 Madeley
3 Storey	3 Hughes	3 Hughes	3 Hughes	3 Hughes
4 Bell	4 Storey	4 Storey	4 Storey	4 Bell
5 McFarland	5 McFarland	5 McFarland	5 McFarland	5 McFarland
6 Moore	6 Moore	6 Moore	6 Moore	6 Hunter
7 Ball	7 Ball	7 Currie	7 Currie	7 Currie
8 Channon	8 Bell	8 Channon (Summerbee)	8 Channon	8 Channon
9 Chivers	9 Chivers	9 Chivers	9 Chivers	9 Chivers
10 Clarke A	10 Clarke A	10 Clarke A (Macdonald)	10 Clarke A	10 Clarke
11 Peters	11 Peters	11 Peters (Hunter)	11 Peters	11 Peters
Prague May 27: 1-1 *Clarke*	Chorzow June 6: 0-2	Moscow June 10: 2-1 *Chivers, Khurtislava, og*	Turin June 14: 0-2	Wembley Sept 26: 7-0 *Channon 2, Clark 2, Chivers, Currie, Bell*

1973 Poland	1973 Italy	1974 Portugal	1974 Wales	1974 N Ireland
1 Shilton	1 Shilton	1 Parkes	1 Shilton	1 Shilton
2 Madeley	2 Madeley	2 Nish	2 Nish	2 Nish
3 Hughes	3 Hughes	3 Pejic	3 Pejic	3 Pejic
4 Bell	4 Bell	4 Dobson	4 Hughes	4 Hughes
5 McFarland	5 McFarland	5 Watson	5 McFarland	5 McFarland (Hunter)
6 Hunter	6 Moore	6 Todd	6 Todd	6 Todd
7 Currie	7 Currie	7 Bowles	7 Keegan	7 Keegan
8 Channon	8 Channon	8 Channon	8 Bell	8 Weller
9 Chivers (Hector)	9 Osgood	9 Macdonald (Ball)	9 Channon	9 Channon
10 Clarke	10 Clarke (Hector)	10 Brooking	10 Weller	10 Bell
11 Peters	11 Peters	11 Peters	11 Bowles	11 Bowles (Worthington)
Wembley Oct 17: 1-1 *Clarke* (pen)	Wembley Nov 14: 0-1	Lisbon April 3: 0-0	Cardiff May 11: 2-0 *Bowles, Keegan*	Wembley May 15: 1-0 *Weller*

1974 Scotland	1974 Argentina	1974 East Germany	1974 Bulgaria	1974 Yugoslavia
1 Shilton	1 Shilton	1 Clemence	1 Clemence	1 Clemence
2 Nish	2 Hughes	2 Hughes	2 Hughes	2 Hughes
3 Pejic	3 Lindsay	3 Lindsay	3 Todd	3 Lindsay
4 Hughes	4 Todd	4 Todd	4 Watson	4 Todd
5 Hunter (Watson)	5 Watson	5 Watson	5 Lindsay	5 Watson
6 Todd	6 Bell	6 Dobson	6 Dobson	6 Dobson
7 Channon	7 Keegan	7 Keegan	7 Brooking	7 Keegan
8 Bell	8 Channon	8 Channon	8 Bell	8 Channon
9 Worthington (Macdonald)	9 Worthington	9 Worthington	9 Keegan	9 Worthington (Macdonald)
10 Weller	10 Weller	10 Bell	10 Channon	10 Bell
11 Peters	11 Brooking	11 Brooking	11 Worthington	11 Brooking
Hampden Park May 18: 0-2	Wembley May 22: 2-2 *Channon, Worthington*	Leipzig May 29: 1-1 *Channon*	Sofia June 1: 1-0 *Worthington*	Belgrade June 5: 2-2 *Channon, Keegan*

1974 Czechoslovakia	1974 Portugal	1975 West Germany	1975 Cyprus	1975 Cyprus
1 Clemence	1 Clemence	1 Clemence	1 Shilton	1 Clemence
2 Madeley	2 Madeley	2 Whitworth	2 Madeley	2 Whitworth
3 Hughes	3 Watson	3 Gillard	3 Watson	3 Beattie (Hughes)
4 Dobson (Brooking)	4 Hughes	4 Bell	4 Todd	4 Hudson
5 Watson	5 Cooper (Todd)	5 Watson	5 Beattie	5 Todd
6 Hunter	6 Brooking	6 Todd	6 Bell	6 Bell
7 Bell	7 Francis	7 Ball	7 Ball	7 Thomas
8 Francis	8 Bell	8 Macdonald	8 Hudson	8 Ball
9 Worthington (Thomas)	9 Thomas	9 Channon	9 Channon (Thomas)	9 Channon
10 Channon	10 Channon	10 Hudson	10 Macdonald	10 Macdonald
11 Keegan	11 Clarke (Worthington)	11 Keegan	11 Keegan	11 Keegan (Tueart)
Wembley Oct 30: 3-0 *Channon, Bell 2*	Wembley Nov 20: 0-0	Wembley Mar 12: 2-0 *Bell, Macdonald*	Wembley April 16: 5-0 *Macdonald 5*	Limassol May 11: 1-0 *Keegan*

1975 N Ireland	1975 Wales	1975 Scotland	1975 Switzerland	1975 Czechoslovakia
1 Clemence	1 Clemence	1 Clemence	1 Clemence	1 Clemence
2 Whitworth	2 Whitworth	2 Whitworth	2 Whitworth	2 Madeley
3 Hughes	3 Gillard	3 Beattie	3 Todd	3 Gillard
4 Bell	4 Francis	4 Bell	4 Watson	4 Francis G
5 Watson	5 Watson	5 Watson	5 Beattie	5 McFarland (Watson)
6 Todd	6 Todd	6 Todd	6 Bell	6 Todd
7 Ball	7 Ball	7 Ball	7 Currie	7 Keegan
8 Viljoen	8 Channon (Little)	8 Channon	8 Francis G	8 Channon (Thomas)
9 Macdonald (Channon)	9 Johnson	9 Johnson	9 Channon	9 Macdonald
10 Keegan	10 Viljoen	10 Francis	10 Johnson (Macdonald)	10 Clarke
11 Tueart	11 Thomas	11 Keegan (Thomas)	11 Keegan	11 Bell
Belfast May 17: 0-0	Wembley May 21: 2-2 *Johnson 2*	Wembley May 24: 5-1 *Francis 2, Beattie, Bell, Johnson*	Basle Sept 3: 2-1 *Keegan, Channon*	Bratislava Oct 30: 1-2 *Channon*

1975 Portugal	1976 Wales	1976 Wales	1976 N. Ireland	1976 Scotland
1 Clemence	1 Clemence	1 Clement	1 Clemence	1 Clemence
2 Whitworth	2 Cherry (Clement)	2 Clement	2 Todd	2 Todd
3 Beattie	3 Mills	3 Mills	3 Mills	3 Mills
4 Francis G	4 Neal	4 Towers	4 Thompson	4 Thompson
5 Watson	5 Thompson	5 Greenhoff B	5 Greenhoff B	5 McFarland (Doyle)
6 Todd	6 Doyle	6 Thompson	6 Kennedy	6 Kennedy
7 Keegan	7 Keegan	7 Keegan	7 Keegan (Royle)	7 Keegan
8 Channon	8 Channon (Taylor)	8 Francis G	8 Francis G	8 Francis G
9 Macdonald (Thomas)	9 Boyer	9 Pearson	9 Pearson	9 Pearson (Cherry)
10 Brooking	10 Brooking	10 Kennedy	10 Channon	10 Channon
11 Madeley (Clarke)	11 Kennedy	11 Taylor	11 Taylor (Towers)	11 Taylor
Lisbon Nov 19: 1-1 *Channon*	Wrexham Mar 24: 2-1 *Kennedy, Taylor*	Cardiff May 8: 1-0 *Taylor*	Wembley May 11: 4-0 *Francis, Channon 2 (1 pen), Pearson*	Glasgow May 15: 1-2 *Channon*

1976 Brazil	1976 Italy	1976 Finland	1976 Eire	1976 Finland
1 Clemence	1 Rimmer (Corrigan)	1 Clemence	1 Clemence	1 Clemence
2 Todd	2 Clement	2 Todd	2 Todd	2 Todd
3 Doyle	3 Neal (Mills)	3 Mills	3 Madeley	3 Beattie
4 Thompson	4 Thompson	4 Thompson	4 Cherry	4 Thompson
5 Mills	5 Doyle	5 Madeley	5 McFarland	5 Greenhoff
6 Francis G	6 Towers	6 Cherry	6 Greenhoff	6 Wilkins
7 Cherry	7 Wilkins	7 Keegan	7 Keegan	7 Keegan
8 Brooking	8 Brooking	8 Channon	8 Wilkins	8 Channon
9 Keegan	9 Royle	9 Pearson	9 Pearson	9 Royle
10 Pearson	10 Channon	10 Brooking	10 Brooking	10 Brooking (Mills)
11 Channon	11 Hill	11 Francis G	11 George (Hill)	11 Tueart (Hill)
Los Angeles May 23: 0-1	New York May 28: 3-2 *Channon 2, Thompson*	Helsinki June 13: 4-1 *Keegan 2, Channon, Pearson*	Wembley Sept 8: 1-1 *Pearson*	Wembley Oct 13: 2-1 *Tueart, Royle*

1976 Italy	1977 Holland	1977 Luxembourg	1977 N Ireland	1977 Wales
1 Clemence	1 Clemence	1 Clemence	1 Shilton	1 Shilton
2 Clement (Beattie)	2 Clement	2 Gidman	2 Cherry	2 Neal
3 Mills	3 Beattie	3 Cherry	3 Mills	3 Mills
4 Greenhoff	4 Doyle	4 Kennedy	4 Greenhoff	4 Greenhoff
5 McFarland	5 Watson	5 Watson	5 Watson	5 Watson
6 Hughes	6 Madeley (Pearson)	6 Hughes	6 Todd	6 Hughes
7 Keegan	7 Keegan	7 Keegan	7 Wilkins (Talbot)	7 Keegan
8 Channon	8 Greenhoff (Todd)	8 Channon	8 Channon	8 Channon
9 Bowles	9 Francis T	9 Royle (Mariner)	9 Mariner	9 Pearson
10 Cherry	10 Bowles	10 Francis T	10 Brooking	10 Brooking (Tueart)
11 Brooking	11 Brooking	11 Hill	11 Tueart	11 Kennedy
Rome Nov 17: 0-2	Wembley Feb 9: 0-2	Wembley Mar 30: 5-0 *Keegan, Francis T, Kennedy, Channon 2 (1 pen)*	Belfast May 28: 2-1 *Channon, Tueart*	Wembley May 31: 0-1

1977 Scotland	1977 Brazil	1977 Argentina	1977 Uruguay	1977 Switzerland
1 Clemence	1 Clemence	1 Clemence	1 Clemence	1 Clemence
2 Neal	2 Neal	2 Neal	2 Neal	2 Neal
3 Mills	3 Cherry	3 Cherry	3 Cherry	3 Cherry
4 Greenhoff (Cherry)	4 Greenhoff	4 Greenhoff (Kennedy)	4 Greenhoff	4 McDermott
5 Watson	5 Watson	5 Watson	5 Watson	5 Watson
6 Hughes	6 Hughes	6 Hughes	6 Hughes	6 Hughes
7 Francis T	7 Keegan	7 Keegan	7 Keegan	7 Keegan
8 Channon	8 Francis T	8 Channon	8 Channon	8 Channon (Hill)
9 Pearson	9 Pearson (Channon)	9 Pearson	9 Pearson	9 Francis T
10 Talbot	10 Wilkins (Kennedy)	10 Wilkins	10 Wilkins	10 Kennedy
11 Kennedy (Tueart)	11 Talbot	11 Talbot	11 Talbot	11 Callaghan (Wilkins)
Wembley June 4: 1-2 *Channon* (pen)	Rio June 8: 0-0	Buenos Aires June 12: 1-1 *Pearson*	Montevideo June 15: 0-0	Wembley Sept 7: 0-0

1977 Luxembourg	1977 Italy	1978 W Germany	1978 Brazil	1978 Wales
1 Clemence	1 Clemence	1 Clemence	1 Corrigan	1 Shilton
2 Cherry	2 Neal	2 Neal	2 Mills	2 Mills
3 Watson (Beattie)	3 Cherry	3 Mills	3 Cherry	3 Cherry (Currie)
4 Hughes	4 Wilkins	4 Wilkins	4 Greenhoff	4 Greenhoff
5 Kennedy	5 Watson	5 Watson	5 Watson	5 Watson
6 Callaghan	6 Hughes	6 Hughes	6 Currie	6 Wilkins
7 McDermott (Whymark)	7 Keegan (Francis T)	7 Keegan (Francis T)	7 Keegan	7 Coppell
8 Wilkins	8 Coppell	8 Coppell	8 Coppell	8 Francis T
9 Francis T	9 Latchford (Pearson)	9 Pearson	9 Latchford	9 Latchford (Mariner)
10 Mariner	10 Brooking	10 Brooking	10 Francis T	10 Brooking
11 Hill	11 Barnes	11 Barnes	11 Barnes	11 Barnes
Luxembourg Oct 12: 2-0 *Kennedy, Mariner*	Wembley Nov 16: 2-0 *Keegan, Brooking*	Munich Feb 22: 1-2 *Pearson*	Wembley April 19: 1-1 *Keegan*	Cardiff May 13. 3-1 *Latchford, Currie, Barnes*

1978 N Ireland	1978 Scotland	1978 Hungary
1 Clemence	1 Clemence	1 Shilton
2 Neal	2 Neal	2 Neal
3 Mills	3 Mills	3 Mills
4 Wilkins	4 Currie	4 Wilkins
5 Watson	5 Watson	5 Watson (Greenhoff)
6 Hughes	6 Hughes (Greenhoff)	6 Hughes
7 Currie	7 Wilkins	7 Keegan
8 Coppell	8 Coppell	8 Coppell
9 Pearson	9 Mariner (Brooking)	9 Francis T
10 Woodcock	10 Francis T	10 Brooking (Currie)
11 Greenhoff	11 Barnes	11 Barnes
Wembley May 16: 1-0 *Neal*	Glasgow May 20: 1-0 *Coppell*	Wembley May 24: 4-1 *Barnes, Neal* (pen), *Francis T, Currie*

Ireland's full international teams 1882-1978

Substitutes in brackets   †World Cup final stages

1882 England	1882 Wales	1883 England	1883 Wales	1884 Scotland
1 Hamilton	1 Hamilton	1 Rankine	1 Rankine	1 Hunter
2 McAleny	2 Crone W	2 Watson	2 Watson	2 Wilson
3 Rattray	3 McAleny	3 Rattray	3 Rattray	3 Crone W
4 Martin	4 Martin	4 Molyneux	4 Molyneux	4 Hastings
5 Hastings	5 Hastings	5 Martin	5 Hastings	5 Molyneux
6 Buckle	6 Crone W	6 Morrow	6 Morrow	6 Dill
7 McWha	7 McWha	7 Potts	7 Potts	7 Spiller
8 Davison	8 Condy	8 McWha	8 McWha	8 Gibb
9 Sinclair	9 Sinclair	9 Davison	9 Davison	9 Morrow
10 Dill	10 Dill	10 Buckle	10 Spiller	10 Davison
11 McCaw	11 Johnston	11 Dill	11 Dill	11 Gaussen
Belfast Feb 18: 0-13	Wrexham Feb 25: 1-7 *Johnston*	Liverpool Feb 24: 0-7	Belfast Mar 17: 1-1 *Morrow*	Belfast Jan 26: 0-5

1884 Wales	1884 England	1885 England	1855 Scotland	1885 Wales
1 Hunter	1 Hunter	1 Henderson	1 Henderson	1 Henderson
2 Wilson	2 Wilson	2 Hewison	2 Hewison	2 Johnston
3 Crone W	3 Crone W	3 Moorehead	3 Johnson	3 Eames
4 Molyneux	4 Hastings	4 Molyneux	4 Muir	4 Molyneux
5 Lockhart	5 Molyneux	5 Houston	5 Houston	5 Muir
6 Redmond	6 Dill	6 Eames	6 Eames	6 McWha
7 Davison	7 Spiller	7 McWha	7 McLean	7 Hamilton W J
8 Gibb	8 McWha	8 Davison	8 Sherrard	8 Hamilton W D
9 Reid	9 Johnson	9 Gibb	9 Gibb	9 Gibb
10 Spiller	10 Davison	10 McGee	10 McGee	10 McGee
11 Dill	11 Gaussen	11 Dill	11 Dill	11 Dill
Wrexham Feb 9: 0-6	Belfast Feb 23: 1-8 *McWha*	Manchester Feb 28: 0-4	Glasgow Mar 14: 2-8 *Gibb 2*	Belfast April 11: 2-8 *Molyneux, Dill*

1886 Wales	1886 England	1886 Scotland	1887 England	1887 Scotland
1 Gillespie	1 Gillespie	1 Gillespie	1 Gillespie	1 Gillespie
2 Watson	2 Watson	2 Watson	2 Browne	2 Fox
3 Devine	3 Devine	3 Crone W	3 Fox	3 Watson
4 Molyneux	4 Molyneux	4 Molyneux	4 Rosbotham	4 Moore
5 Crone W	5 Crone W	5 Williams	5 Leslie	5 Rosbotham
6 McArthur	6 Hastings	6 Hastings	6 Crone W	6 Baxter
7 McClatchey	7 Turner	7 McClatchey	7 Allen	7 Reid
8 Smyth	8 Condy	8 Johnson	8 Gibb	8 Stanfield
9 Whitfield	9 Johnson	9 Gibb	9 Stanfield	9 Browne
10 Lemon	10 McClatchey	10 Condy	10 Small	10 Peden
11 Raper	11 Williams	11 Turner	11 Whitfield	11 Gibb
Wrexham Feb 27: 0-5	Belfast Mar 13: 1-6 *Williams*	Belfast Mar 20: 2-7 *Condy, Johnson*	Sheffield Feb 5: 0-7	Glasgow Feb 19: 1-4 *Browne*

1887 Wales	1888 Wales	1888 Scotland	1888 England	1889 England
1 Gillespie	1 Clugston	1 Lowther	1 Lowther	1 Clugston
2 Browne	2 Forbes	2 Wilson	2 McVickers	2 Goodbody
3 Watson	3 Crone W	3 Browne	3 Browne	3 Watson
4 Sherrard	4 Sherrard	4 Forsyth	4 Forsyth	4 Crawford
5 Rosbotham	5 Rosbotham	5 Rosbotham	5 Rosbotham	5 Rosbotham
6 Devine	6 Devine	6 Molyneux	6 Crone W	6 Cooke
7 Moore	7 Gaussen	7 Dalton	7 Gaussen	7 Gaussen
8 Baxter	8 Stanfield	8 Stanfield	8 Stanfield	8 Stanfield
9 Gibb	9 Berry	9 Berry	9 Silo	9 Berry
10 Stanfield	10 Wilton	10 Lemon	10 Wilton	10 Wilton
11 Peden	11 Peden	11 Turner	11 Peden	11 Peden
Belfast Mar 12: 4-1 *Stanfield, Browne, Peden, Sherrard*	Wrexham Mar 3: 0-11	Belfast Mar 24: 2-10 *Lemon and another*	Belfast April 7: 1-5 *Crone*	Liverpool Mar 2: 1-6 *Wilton*

1889 Scotland	1889 Wales	1890 Wales	1890 England	1890 Scotland
1 Clugston	1 Clugston	1 Galbraith	1 Clugston	1 Clugston
2 McVickers	2 Elleman	2 Crone R	2 Stewart	2 Stewart
3 Crone R	3 Watson	3 Stewart	3 Crone R	3 Crone R
4 Thomson	4 Crawford	4 Crone W	4 Williamson	4 Reid
5 Christian	5 Bennett	5 Reynolds	5 Spencer	5 Spencer
6 Crone W	6 Reid	6 Reid	6 Cooke	6 Cooke
7 Torrans S	7 Gaussen	7 Dalton	7 Elleman	7 Dalton
8 Stanfield	8 Stanfield	8 Gaffikin	8 Stanfield	8 Gaffikin
9 Gibb	9 Percy	9 Johnston	9 Wilton	9 Stanfield
10 Wilton	10 Lemon	10 Torrans S	10 McIlvenny	10 Torrans S
11 Peden	11 Gillespie	11 Peden	11 Reynolds	11 Peden
Glasgow Mar 9: 0-7	Belfast April 27: 1-3 *Lemon*	Shrewsbury Feb 8: 2-5 *Dalton 2*	Belfast Mar 15: 1-9 *Reynolds*	Belfast Mar 29: 1-4 *Peden*

1891 Wales	1891 England	1891 Scotland	1892 Wales	1892 England
1 Clugston	1 Clugston	1 Loyal	1 Clugston	1 Clugston
2 Goodbody	2 Forbes	2 Gordon	2 Gordon	2 Gordon
3 Morris	3 Morrison	3 Forbes	3 Stewart	3 Stewart
4 Crawford	4 Crawford	4 Crawford	4 McKeown	4 McKeown
5 Reynolds	5 Reynolds	5 Reynolds	5 Spencer	5 Spencer
6 Moore	6 Moore	6 Moore	6 Cunningham	6 Cunningham
7 Dalton	7 Whitehead	7 Dalton	7 Dalton	7 Dalton
8 Gaffikin	8 Stanfield	8 Gaffikin	8 Gaffikin	8 Gaffikin
9 Stanfield	9 McCabe	9 Stanfield	9 Stanfield	9 Stanfield
10 Torrans S	10 McIlvenny	10 Brisby	10 Torrans S	10 Torrans S
11 Peden	11 Peden	11 Torrans S	11 Peden	11 Peden
Belfast Feb 7: 7-2 *Dalton 3, Stanfield 2, Gaffikin 2*	Wolverhampton Mar 7: 1-6 *Whitehead*	Glasgow Mar 28: 1-2 *Stanfield*	Bangor Feb 27: 1-1 *Stanfield*	Belfast Mar 5: 0-2

1892 Scotland	1893 England	1893 Scotland	1893 Wales	1894 Wales
1 Clugston	1 Clugston	1 Clugston	1 Clugston	1 Gordon
2 Gordon	2 Gordon	2 Gordon	2 Gordon	2 Stewart
3 Stewart	3 Stewart	3 Torrans R	3 Stewart	3 Torrans S
4 McKeown	4 Crawford	4 McKeown	4 Crawford	4 McKeown
5 Spencer	5 Spencer	5 Johnston	5 McKeown	5 Burnett
6 Cunningham	6 Cunningham	6 Torrans S	6 Johnston	6 Milne
7 Dalton	7 Small	7 Small	7 Small	7 Dalton
8 Gaffikin	8 Gaffikin	8 Gaffikin	8 Gaffikin	8 Gaffikin
9 Williamson	9 Stanfield	9 Williamson	9 Stanfield	9 Stanfield
10 Stanfield	10 Torrans S	10 Wilton	10 Wilton	10 Gibson
11 Torrans S	11 Peden	11 Peden	11 Peden	11 Barron
Belfast Mar 19: 2-3 *Williamson, Gaffikin*	Birmingham Feb 25: 1-6 *Gaffikin*	Glasgow Mar 25: 1-6 *Gaffikin*	Belfast April 5: 4-3 *Peden 3, Wilton*	Swansea Feb 24: 1-4 *Stanfield*

1894 England	1894 Scotland	1895 England	1895 Wales	1895 Scotland
1 Scott T	1 Scott T	1 Gordon T	1 Scott T	1 Scott T
2 Stewart	2 Stewart	2 Gordon H	2 Gordon H	2 Ponsonby
3 Torrans S	3 Torrans S	3 Torrans S	3 Scott L J	3 Scott L J
4 Johnston	4 McKeown	4 McKie	4 McKie	4 McKie
5 Burnett	5 Burnett	5 Milne	5 Milne	5 Alexander
6 Milne	6 Milne	6 Burnett	6 Burnett	6 McClatchey
7 Dalton	7 Dalton	7 Morrison	7 Morrison	7 Morrison
8 Gaffikin	8 Gaffikin	8 Gaffikin	8 Sherrard	8 Sherrard
9 Stanfield	9 Stanfield	9 Stanfield	9 Jordan	9 Stanfield
10 Gibson	10 Gibson	10 Sherrard	10 Gawkrodger	10 Gibson
11 Barron	11 Barron	11 Jordan	11 Gaffikin	11 Barron
Belfast Mar 3: 2-2 *Stanfield, Gibson*	Belfast Mar 31: 1-2 *Stanfield*	Derby Mar 9: 0-9	Belfast Mar 16: 2-2 *Gawkrodger, Sherrard*	Glasgow Mar 30: 1-3 *Sherrard*

1896 Wales	1896 England	1896 Scotland	1897 England	1897 Wales
1 Scott T	1 Scott T	1 Scott T	1 Scott T	1 Scott T
2 Ponsonby	2 Ponsonby	2 Ponsonby	2 Ponsonby	2 Gibson
3 Torrans S	3 Torrans S	3 Torrans S	3 Torrans S	3 Torrans S
4 McCoy	4 Fitzpatrick	4 Gordon	4 Pyper, John	4 Pyper, John
5 Milne	5 Milne	5 Milne	5 Milne	5 Ponsonby
6 Campbell	6 Gordon H	6 Fitzpatrick	6 McMaster	6 McMaster
7 Turner	7 Baird	7 Baird	7 Campbell	7 Campbell
8 Baird	8 Kelly	8 Morrogh	8 Hall	8 Stanfield
9 Stanfield	9 Stanfield	9 Stanfield	9 Stanfield	9 Pyper, James
10 McCashin	10 Turner	10 Barron	10 Darling	10 Peden
11 Peden	11 Peden	11 Peden	11 Barron	11 Barron
Wrexham Feb 29: 1-6 *Turner*	Belfast Mar 7: 0-2	Belfast Mar 28: 3-3 *Barron 2, Milne (pen)*	Nottingham Feb 20: 0-6	Belfast Mar 6: 4-3 *Barron, Stanfield, John Pyper, Peden*

1897 Scotland	1898 Wales	1898 England	1898 Scotland	1899 England
1 Thompson	1 Scott T	1 Scott T	1 Scott T	1 Lewis
2 Ponsonby	2 Gibson	2 Gibson	2 Gibson	2 Pyper, John
3 Torrans S	3 Cochrane	3 Torrans S	3 Torrans S	3 Torrans S
4 Pyper, John	4 Anderson	4 Anderson	4 Anderson	4 Ponsonby
5 Milne	5 Milne	5 Milne	5 Milne	5 Milne
6 McMaster	6 Little	6 Cochrane	6 Cochrane	6 Cochrane
7 Campbell	7 Campbell	7 Campbell	7 Campbell	7 Campbell
8 Stanfield	8 Mercer	8 Mercer	8 Mercer	8 Mercer
9 Pyper, James	9 Pyper, James	9 Pyper, James	9 Pyper, James	9 Waring
10 Darling	10 McCartney	10 Peden	10 McCashin	10 McWhattie
11 Peden	11 Peden	11 McAllen	11 Peden	11 McAllen
Glasgow Mar 27: 1-5 *James Pyper*	Llandudno Feb 19: 1-0 *Peden*	Belfast Mar 5: 2-3 *Pyper, Mercer*	Belfast Mar 26: 0-3	Sunderland Feb 18: 2-13 *McAllen, Campbell*

1899 Wales	1899 Scotland	1900 Wales	1900 Scotland	1900 England
1 Lewis	1 Lewis	1 Scott T	1 Lewis	1 Reilly
2 Pyper, John	2 Swan	2 Pyper, John	2 Pyper, John	2 Pyper, John
3 Torrans S	3 Forman	3 Cochrane	3 Cochrane	3 Cochrane
4 Goodall	4 Anderson	4 McShane	4 McShane	4 McShane
5 Milne	5 Goodall	5 Goodall	5 Berry	5 Goodall
6 Taggart	6 McShane	6 Maginnis	6 Maginnis	6 Maginnis
7 Morrison	7 Sheehan	7 Sheehan	7 Campbell	7 Sheehan
8 Meldon	8 Meldon	8 Morrison	8 Darling	8 Campbell
9 Hannah	9 Pyper, James	9 Kirwan	9 McAuley	9 Pyper, James
10 McAllen	10 McCashin	10 Kearns	10 McAllen	10 McAllen
11 Peden	11 McAllen	11 McAllen	11 Kearns	11 Kearns
Belfast Mar 4: 1-0 *Meldon*	Glasgow Mar 25: 1-9 *Goodall*	Llandudno Feb 24: 0-2	Belfast Mar 3: 0-3	Dublin Mar 17: 0-2

1901 Scotland	1901 England	1901 Wales	1902 Wales	1902 Scotland
1 McAlpine	1 Nolan-Whelan	1 Nolan-Whelan	1 Nolan-Whelan	1 Nolan-Whelan
2 Gibson	2 Gibson	2 Gibson	2 Gibson	2 Gibson
3 Boyle	3 Boyle	3 Torrans S	3 McCracken W	3 Pyper, John
4 Farrell	4 Connor	4 Farrell	4 Darling	4 Darling
5 Connor	5 Goodall	5 Milne	5 Milne	5 Goodall
6 Cochrane	6 Burnison	6 Burnison	6 Nicholl	6 Milne
7 Scott J	7 Black	7 Campbell	7 Mercer	7 Campbell
8 Smith J	8 Rea	8 Smith J	8 Maxwell	8 Morrison
9 Campbell	9 Mansfield	9 McKelvie	9 Gara	9 Gara
10 O'Reilly	10 Doherty	10 O'Reilly	10 Kearns	10 Kearns
11 Clarke	11 Clarke	11 McAllen	11 Kirwan	11 McAllen
Glasgow Feb 23: 0-11	Southampton Mar 9: 0-3	Belfast Mar 23: 0-1	Cardiff Feb 22: 3-0 *Gara 3*	Belfast Mar 1: 1-3 *Milne*

1902 England	1903 England	1903 Scotland	1903 Wales	1904 England
1 Reilly	1 Scott W	1 Scott W	1 Scott W	1 Scott W
2 McCracken W	2 McCracken W	2 McCartney	2 McCartney	2 McCracken W
3 Boyle	3 McMillan	3 Boyle	3 Boyle	3 Boyle
4 Darling	4 Darling	4 Darling	4 Darling	4 Milne
5 Milne	5 Milne	5 Milne	5 Goodall	5 Goodall
6 Nicholl	6 Goodall	6 Maginnis	6 Maginnis	6 Maginnis
7 Mercer	7 Campbell	7 Mercer	7 Mercer	7 Mercer
8 Morrison	8 Maxwell	8 Sheridan	8 Maxwell	8 Sheridan
9 Gara	9 Sheridan	9 Connor	9 Connor	9 Connor
10 Kearns	10 Sloan	10 Shanks	10 Sheridan	10 Kirwan
11 Kirwan	11 Kirwan	11 Kirwan	11 Kirwan	11 Buckle
Belfast Mar 22: 0-1	Wolverhampton Feb 14: 0-4	Glasgow Mar 21: 2-0 *Connor, Kirwan*	Belfast Mar 28: 2-0 *Goodall, Sheridan*	Belfast Mar 12: 1-3 *Kirwan*

1904 Wales	1904 Scotland	1905 England	1905 Scotland	1905 Wales
1 Scott W	1 Scott W	1 Scott W	1 Scott W	1 Reynolds
2 McCracken W	2 McCracken W	2 McCracken W	2 McCartney	2 McCracken
3 McCartney	3 McCartney	3 McCartney	3 McCracken W	3 McMillan
4 McConnell	4 McConnell	4 Darling	4 Darling	4 Darling
5 Milne	5 Milne	5 Connor	5 Connor	5 Connor
6 Maginnis	6 Maginnis	6 Nicholl	6 McConnell	6 Johnstone
7 Mercer	7 Campbell	7 Sloan	7 Mercer	7 Hunter
8 Shanks	8 Sheridan	8 Sheridan	8 Maxwell	8 Maxwell
9 Goodall	9 O'Reilly	9 Murphy	9 Murphy	9 Murphy
10 Kirkwood	10 Sloan	10 Shanks	10 O'Hagan	10 O'Hagan
11 Kirwan	11 Kirwan	11 Kirwan	11 Kirwan	11 Kirwan
Bangor Mar 21: 1-0 *McCracken* (pen)	Dublin Mar 26: 1-1 *Sheridan*	Middlesbrough Feb 25: 1-1 *Williamson og*	Glasgow Mar 18: 0-4	Belfast April 8: 2-2 *Murphy, O'Hagan*

1906 England	1906 Scotland	1906 Wales	1907 England	1907 Wales
1 Sherry	1 McKee	1 McKee	1 Scott W	1 Sherry
2 Darling	2 Willis	2 Willis	2 McCracken W	2 Seymour
3 McIlroy	3 Darling	3 Darling	3 McCartney	3 McCartney
4 Wright	4 Wright	4 Wright	4 Wright	4 Wright
5 Milne	5 Milne	5 Milne	5 Connor	5 Crothers
6 McConnell	6 Ledwidge	6 Ledwidge	6 McConnell	6 McClure
7 Hunter	7 Hunter	7 Hunter	7 Blair	7 Blair
8 Mulholland	8 Mulholland	8 Maxwell	8 Harris	8 Harris
9 Harris	9 Waddell	9 O'Hagan	9 Sloan	9 Sloan
10 O'Hagan	10 O'Hagan	10 Sloan	10 O'Hagan	10 O'Hagan
11 Kirwan	11 Kirwan	11 Kirwan	11 Young	11 Kirwan
Belfast Feb 17: 0-5	Dublin Mar 17: 0-1	Wrexham April 2: 4-4 *Maxwell 2, Sloan 2*	Liverpool Feb 16: 0-1	Belfast Feb 23: 2-3 *O'Hagan, Sloan*

1907 Scotland	1908 England	1908 Scotland	1908 Wales	1909 England
1 Scott W	1 Scott W	1 Scott W	1 Scott W	1 Scott W
2 Willis	2 Craig	2 Craig	2 Craig	2 Balfe
3 McCartney	3 McCartney	3 McCartney	3 McCartney	3 McCartney
4 Wright	4 Harris	4 Harris	4 Darling	4 Harris
5 Connor	5 Connor	5 Connor	5 McConnell	5 Darling
6 McClure	6 McClure	6 McConnell	6 Harris	6 McClure
7 Blair	7 Blair	7 Blair	7 Hunter	7 Hunter
8 Maxwell	8 Hannon	8 Hannon	8 Hamilton	8 Lacey
9 McGuire	9 Mercer	9 Andrews	9 Sloan	9 Greer
10 O'Hagan	10 Burnison	10 O'Hagan	10 O'Hagan	10 O'Hagan
11 Young	11 Young	11 Young	11 Buckle	11 Young
Glasgow Mar 16: 0-3	Belfast Feb 15: 1-3 *Hannon*	Dublin Mar 14: 0-5	Aberdare April 11: 1-0 *Sloan*	Bradford Feb 13: 0-4

1909 Scotland	1909 Wales	1910 England	1910 Scotland	1910 Wales
1 Scott W	1 Scott W	1 Scott W	1 Scott W	1 O'Hehir
2 Craig	2 Seymour	2 Burnison	2 Burnison	2 Balfe
3 McCartney	3 McCartney	3 McCann	3 McCann	3 McCann
4 Harris	4 Harris	4 Harris	4 Harris	4 Harris
5 McConnell	5 Connor	5 McConnell	5 McConnell	5 McConnell
6 Sloan	6 McConnell	6 Darling	6 Darling	6 Darling
7 Hunter	7 Hunter	7 Renneville	7 Renneville	7 Renneville
8 Lacey	8 Lacey	8 Lacey	8 Lacey	8 Lacey
9 Greer	9 Greer	9 Murray	9 Murray	9 Murray
10 Webb	10 Webb	10 Murphy	10 Murphy	10 Murphy
11 Kirwan	11 Slemin	11 Thompson	11 Thompson	11 Thompson
Glasgow Mar 15: 0-5	Belfast Mar 20: 2-3 *Lacey, Hunter*	Belfast Feb 12: 1-1 *Thompson*	Belfast Mar 19: 1-0 *Thompson*	Wrexham April 11: 1-4 *Darling* (pen)

1911 Wales	1911 England	1911 Scotland	1912 England	1912 Scotland
1 Scott W	1 Scott W	1 Scott W	1 Scott W	1 Hanna
2 Burnison	2 Burnison	2 Burnison	2 Burnison	2 Willis
3 Thunder	3 McCann	3 McCann	3 McCann	3 Craig
4 Harris	4 Harris	4 Harris	4 Harris	4 Darling
5 Connor	5 Connor	5 Connor	5 O'Connell	5 O'Connell
6 Hampton	6 Hampton	6 Hampton	6 Hampton	6 Moran
7 Renneville	7 Lacey	7 Lacey	7 Lacey	7 Houston
8 Lacey	8 Hannon	8 Hannon	8 Hamill	8 McKnight
9 Halligan	9 McDonnell	9 McDonnell	9 Halligan	9 Macauley
10 Macauley	10 Macauley	10 Webb	10 Macauley	10 Enright
11 Thompson	11 Thompson	11 Walker	11 Thompson	11 Young
Belfast Jan 28: 1-2 *Halligan*	Derby Feb 11: 1-2 *Macauley*	Glasgow Mar 18: 0-2	Dublin Feb 10: 1-6 *Hamill*	Belfast Mar 16: 1-4 *McKnight* (pen)

1912 Wales	1913 Wales	1913 England	1913 Scotland	1914 Wales
1 Hanna	1 Scott W	1 Scott W	1 Scott W	1 McKee
2 Craig	2 Burnison	2 McConnell	2 McConnell	2 McConnell
3 McConnell	3 McCann	3 Warren	3 Warrren	3 Craig
4 Hampton	4 Rollo	4 Hampton	4 Andrews	4 Harris
5 Brennan	5 Donnelly	5 Harris	5 Harris	5 O'Connell
6 Rollo	6 Hampton	6 Andrews	6 Hampton	6 Rollo
7 Houston	7 Houston	7 Houston	7 Houston	7 Seymour
8 Hannon	8 Lacey	8 Hannon	8 McKnight	8 Young
9 McDonnell	9 McDonnell	9 Gillespie	9 Gillespie	9 Gillespie
10 McCandless J	10 McCandless J	10 Macauley	10 Macauley	10 Lacey
11 Thompson	11 Thompson	11 Thompson	11 Thompson	11 Bookman
Cardiff April 13: 3-2 *McCandless 2, Brennan*	Belfast Jan 18: 0-1	Belfast Feb 15: 2-1 *Gillespie 2*	Dublin Mar 15: 1-2 *McKnight*	Wrexham Jan 19: 2-1 *Young, Gillespie*

1914 England	1914 Scotland	1919 England	1920 Wales	1920 Scotland
1 McKee	1 McKee	1 O'Hagan	1 O'Hagan	1 Scott E
2 McConnell	2 McConnell	2 McCandless	2 Manderson	2 Manderson
3 Craig	3 Craig	3 McCracken W	3 Rollo	3 Rollo
4 Hampton	4 Harris	4 Emerson	4 McCandless W	4 Hamill
5 O'Connell	5 O'Connell	5 Hamill	5 Hamill	5 Lacey
6 Hamill	6 Hamill	6 Lacey	6 Emerson	6 Emerson
7 Rollo	7 Houston	7 Ferris	7 Lyner	7 Robinson
8 Young	8 Nixon	8 Snape	8 Lacey	8 Gallagher
9 Gillespie	9 Young	9 Gowdy	9 Gillespie	9 Brookes
10 Lacey	10 Lacey	10 Gallagher	10 Ferris	10 Gillespie
11 Thompson	11 Thompson	11 Lyner	11 McCandless J	11 McCandless J
Middlesbrough Feb 14: 3-0 *Lacey 2, Gillespie*	Belfast Mar 14: 1-1 *Young*	Belfast Oct 25: 1-1 *Ferris*	Belfast Feb 14: 2-2 *McCandless J, Emerson*	Glasgow Mar 13: 0-3

1920 England	1921 Scotland	1921 Wales	1921 England	1922 Scotland
1 Scott E	1 Scott E	1 Scott E	1 Scott E	1 Collins
2 Rollo	2 Mulligan	2 Rollo	2 McCracken W	2 McCracken W
3 McCandless W	3 Rollo	3 McCandless W	3 Rollo	3 McCandless W
4 McCracken R	4 Lacey	4 Lacey	4 McCracken R	4 McCracken R
5 Lacey	5 Smith E E	5 Scragg	5 Scragg	5 O'Brien
6 Emerson	6 O'Brien	6 Harris J	6 Emerson	6 Emerson
7 Kelly	7 McGregor	7 Robinson	7 Lacey	7 Lacey
8 Ferris	8 Ferris	8 Brown J	8 Gillespie	8 Gallagher
9 Doran	9 McKinney	9 Chambers	9 Doran	9 Irvine
10 Gillespie	10 Hamill	10 Mathieson	10 Mathieson	10 Gillespie
11 McCandless J	11 Bookman	11 Bookman	11 Bookman	11 Lyner
Sunderland Oct 23: 0-2	Belfast Feb 26: 0-2	Swansea April 9: 1-2 *Chambers*	Belfast Oct 22: 1-1 *Gillespie*	Glasgow Mar 4: 1-2 *Gillespie*

1922 Wales	1922 England	1923 Scotland	1923 Wales	1923 England
1 Mehaffy	1 Harland	1 Farquharson	1 Farquharson	1 Farquharson
2 McCracken W	2 Rollo	2 McCracken W	2 Mackie	2 McCluggage
3 Curran	3 Curran	3 Curran	3 Kennedy	3 Curran
4 McCracken R	4 Emerson	4 Irving	4 Irving	4 Irving
5 O'Brien	5 Smith E E	5 Moorhead	5 Smith E E	5 Smith E E
6 Emerson	6 Morgan	6 Emerson	6 Emerson	6 Emerson
7 Lyner	7 Lyner	7 McKenzie	7 Lyner	7 Brown J
8 Crooks	8 Irvine	8 Gallagher	8 Gallagher	8 Croft
9 Doran	9 Nelis	9 Reid	9 Irvine	9 Irvine
10 Gillespie	10 Gillespie	10 Gillespie	10 Gillespie	10 Gillespie
11 Toner	11 Burns	11 Moore	11 Toner	11 Toner
Belfast April 1: 1-1 *Gillespie*	West Bromwich Oct 21: 0-2	Belfast Mar 3: 0-1	Wrexham April 14: 3-0 *Irvine 2, Gillespie*	Belfast Oct 20: 2-1 *Gillespie, Croft*

1924 Scotland	1924 Wales	1924 England	1925 Scotland	1925 Wales
1 Farquharson	1 Farquharson	1 Farquharson	1 Farquharson	1 Scott E
2 Rollo	2 Rollo	2 Manderson	2 Manderson	2 Rollo
3 McCandless W	3 McCandless W	3 Kennedy	3 McCandless W	3 McConnell
4 Irving	4 Gowdy	4 Chatton	4 Chatton	4 Garrett
5 O'Brien	5 O'Brien	5 O'Brien	5 O'Brien	5 O'Brien
6 Morgan	6 Irving	6 Irving	6 Irving	6 Irving
7 McKinney	7 Brown J	7 Lacey	7 Martin	7 Cowan
8 Gallagher	8 Gallagher	8 Gallagher	8 Gallagher	8 Gallagher
9 Irvine	9 McIlvenny	9 Irvine	9 Carroll	9 Sloan
10 Gillespie	10 Gillespie	10 Gillespie	10 Gillespie	10 Meek
11 McGrillen	11 Toner	11 Toner	11 Toner	11 Wilson
Glasgow Mar 1: 0-2	Belfast Mar 15: 0-1	Liverpool Oct 22: 1-3 *Gillespie*	Belfast Feb 28: 0-3	Wrexham April 18: 0-0

1925 England	1926 Wales	1926 Scotland	1926 England	1927 Scotland
1 Scott E	1 Scott E	1 Scott E	1 Scott E	1 Scott E
2 Rollo	2 Brown J	2 Manderson	2 Rollo	2 McCluggage
3 McConnell	3 McConnell	3 Watson	3 McConnell	3 McConnell
4 Gowdy	4 Irving	4 Irving	4 Gowdy	4 Gowdy
5 Chatton	5 O'Brien	5 Gowdy	5 Morgan	5 Sloan
6 Sloan	6 Sloan	6 Sloan	6 Irving	6 McMullan
7 Bothwell	7 Bothwell	7 Bothwell	7 Bothwell	7 McGrillen
8 Irvine	8 Steele	8 Steele	8 Irvine	8 Gallagher
9 Davey	9 Curran	9 Curran	9 Davey	9 Davey
10 Hopkins	10 Gillespie	10 Gallagher	10 Gillespie	10 Irving
11 McMullan	11 McMullan	11 McLean	11 Toner	11 Toner
Belfast Oct 24: 0-0	Belfast Feb 13: 3-0 *Gillespie, Curran 2*	Glasgow Feb 27: 0-4	Liverpool Oct 20: 3-3 *Gillespie, Davey, Irvine*	Belfast Feb 26: 0-2

1927 Wales	1927 England	1928 Wales	1928 Scotland	1928 England
1 Scott E	1 Scott E	1 Scott E	1 Scott E	1 Scott E
2 McCluggage	2 McCluggage	2 McCluggage	2 McCluggage	2 McCluggage
3 McConnell	3 McConnell	3 McConnell W	3 Hamilton	3 Hamilton
4 Irving	4 Irving	4 Irving	4 Irving	4 Irving
5 Sloan	5 Morgan	5 Morgan	5 Moorhead	5 Sloan
6 O'Brien	6 Sloan	6 Sloan	6 Morgan	6 Morgan
7 Bothwell	7 Chambers	7 Chambers	7 Chambers	7 Chambers
8 Irvine	8 Irvine	8 Dunne	8 Irvine	8 Irvine
9 Johnston	9 Davey	9 Davey	9 Curran	9 Bambrick
10 Gillespie	10 Gillespie	10 McConnell P	10 Ferris	10 Gillespie
11 McCaw	11 Mahood	11 Mahood	11 Mahood	11 Mahood
Cardiff April 9: 2-2 *Johnston 2*	Belfast Oct 22: 2-0 *Jones, og, Mahood*	Belfast Feb 4: 1-2 *Chambers*	Glasgow Feb 25: 1-0 *Chambers*	Liverpool Oct 22: 1-2 *Bambrick*

1929 Wales	1929 Scotland	1929 England	1930 Wales	1930 Scotland
1 Scott E	1 Scott E	1 Scott	1 Gardiner	1 Gardiner
2 McCluggage	2 McCluggage	2 Russell	2 McCluggage	2 Russell
3 McCandless	3 Flack	3 Hamilton	3 Fulton	3 Hamilton
4 Miller	4 Miller	4 Miller	4 McCleery	4 McDonald
5 Elwood	5 Moorhead	5 Elwood	5 Cpl J Jones	5 Cpl J Jones
6 Steele	6 Steele	6 McCleery	6 Sloan	6 Sloan
7 Chambers	7 Chambers	7 Duggan	7 Chambers	7 Chambers
8 Rowley	8 Rowley	8 Rowley	8 Rowley	8 Irvine
9 Bambrick	9 Bambrick	9 Bambrick	9 Bambrick	9 Bambrick
10 Cumming	10 Cumming	10 Cumming	10 McCambridge	10 McCambridge
11 Mahood	11 Mahood	11 Kavanagh	11 Mahood	11 McCaw
Wrexham Feb 2: 2-2 *Mahood, McCluggage (pen)*	Belfast Feb 23: 3-7 *Bambrick 2, Rowley*	Belfast Oct 19: 0-3	Belfast Feb 1: 0-7	Glasgow Feb 22: 1-3 *McCaw*

1930 England	1931 Scotland	1931 Wales	1931 Scotland	1931 England
1 Scott E	1 Gardiner	1 Diffin	1 Gardiner	1 Gardiner
2 McCluggage	2 McNinch	2 McCluggage	2 McNinch	2 Russell
3 Fulton	3 Fulton	3 Fulton	3 Hamilton R	3 Fulton
4 Jones J	4 McCleery	4 Irving	4 McCleery	4 McDonald
5 Reid	5 Jones J	5 Jones J	5 Jones J	5 Jones J
6 McCleery	6 Sloan	6 McCleery	6 Gowdy	6 Mitchell
7 Duggan	7 Blair	7 Duggan	7 Blair	7 Chambers
8 Irvine	8 Falloon	8 Rowley	8 Rowley	8 McConnell
9 Dunne	9 Roberts	9 Dunne	9 Dunne	9 Dunne
10 Gillespie	10 Geary	10 McCambridge	10 Geary	10 McCambridge
11 McCaw	11 McCaw	11 McCaw	11 Chambers	11 Kelly
Sheffield Oct 20: 1-5 *Dunne*	Belfast Feb 21: 0-0	Wrexham April 22: 2-3 *Dunne, Rowley*	Glasgow Sept 19: 1-3 *Dunne*	Belfast Oct 17: 2-6 *Dunne, Kelly*

1931 Wales	1932 Scotland	1932 England	1932 Wales	1933 Scotland
1 Scott E	1 Scott E	1 Scott E	1 Scott E	1 Scott E
2 McNinch	2 Cook	2 Cook	2 Cook	2 Willingham
3 Fulton	3 Fulton	3 Fulton	3 Willingham	3 Fulton
4 McCleery	4 Falloon	4 Mitchell W	4 Mitchell W	4 McMahon
5 Pyper	5 Jones J	5 Jones J	5 Jones J	5 Jones J
6 Mitchell W	6 Gowdy	6 McCleery	6 McCleery	6 Mitchell W
7 Chambers	7 Mitchell E	7 Duggan	7 Houston	7 Blair
8 Irvine	8 Priestley	8 Moore	8 English	8 Stevenson
9 Bambrick	9 Millar	9 Dunne	9 Dunne	9 Martin
10 Millar	10 English	10 Doherty J	10 Doherty J	10 Coulter
11 Kelly	11 Kelly	11 Kelly	11 Kelly	11 Mahood
Belfast Dec 5: 4-0 *Kelly 2, Millar, Bambrick*	Belfast Sept 12: 0-4	Blackpool Oct 17: 0-1	Wrexham Dec 7: 1-4 *English*	Glasgow Sept 16: 2-1 *Martin 2*

1933 England	1933 Wales	1934 Scotland	1935 England	1935 Wales
1 Scott E	1 Scott E	1 Scott E	1 Breen	1 Breen
2 Reid	2 Reid	2 Mackie	2 Cook	2 Mackie
3 Fulton	3 Fulton	3 Fulton	3 Fulton	3 Fulton
4 McMillen	4 Mitchell W	4 McMillen	4 Gowdy	4 McCullough
5 Jones J	5 Jones J	5 Jones J	5 Jones J	5 Jones J
6 Jones S	6 Jones S	6 Mitchell W	6 Mitchell W	6 Gowdy
7 Duggan	7 Mitchell C	7 Duggan	7 Brown J	7 Duggan
8 Stevenson	8 Stevenson	8 Gowdy	8 Doherty P	8 Brown J
9 Martin	9 Martin	9 Martin	9 Martin	9 Bambrick
10 Coulter	10 Coulter	10 Stevenson	10 Stevenson	10 Doherty P
11 Priestley	11 Kelly	11 Coulter	11 Coulter	11 Coulter
Belfast Oct 14: 0-3	Belfast Nov 4: 1-1 *Jones S*	Belfast Oct 20: 2-1 *Martin, Coulter*	Liverpool Feb 6: 1-2 *Stevenson*	Wrexham Mar 27: 1-3 *Bambrick*

1935 England	1935 Scotland	1936 Wales	1936 Scotland	1936 England
1 Scott E	1 Scott E	1 Scott E	1 Breen	1 Breen
2 Reid	2 Cook	2 Cook	2 Cook	2 Cook
3 Allen	3 Fulton	3 Fulton	3 Fulton	3 Fulton
4 Mitchell W	4 McCullough	4 Gowdy	4 McMillen	4 McCullough
5 Jones J	5 Jones J	5 Jones J	5 Jones J	5 Jones J
6 Browne R	6 Mitchell W	6 Browne R	6 Mitchell W	6 Mitchell W
7 Brown J	7 Duggan	7 Kernoghan	7 Kernoghan	7 Brown J
8 McCullough	8 Stevenson	8 Gibb	8 McCullough	8 Stevenson
9 Bambrick	9 Bambrick	9 Martin	9 Martin	9 Davis
10 Doherty P	10 Doherty P	10 Stevenson	10 Coulter	10 Doherty P
11 Kelly	11 Kelly	11 Kelly	11 Kelly	11 Kelly
Belfast Oct 19: 1-3 *Brown*	Edinburgh Nov 13: 1-2 *Kelly*	Belfast Mar 11: 3-2 *Gibb, Stevenson, Kernoghan*	Belfast Oct 31: 1-3 *Kernoghan*	Stoke-on-Trent Nov 18: 1-3 *Davis*

1937 Wales	1937 England	1937 Scotland	1938 Wales	1938 Scotland
1 Breen	1 Breen	1 Breen	1 Twoomey	1 Breen
2 Cook	2 Hayes	2 Hayes	2 Cook	2 Hayes
3 Fulton	3 Cook	3 Cook	3 Fulton	3 Cook
4 Brolly	4 Mitchell W	4 Doherty J	4 Brolly	4 McMillen
5 Jones J	5 Jones J	5 McMillen	5 McMillen	5 O'Mahoney
6 Mitchell W	6 Browne R	6 Mitchell W	6 Browne R	6 Browne R
7 Brown J	7 Kernoghan	7 Brown J	7 Brown J	7 Brown J
8 Doherty P	8 Stevenson	8 McAlinden	8 Farrell	8 McAlinden
9 Banks	9 Martin	9 Martin	9 Bambrick	9 Martin
10 Stevenson	10 Doherty P	10 Doherty P	10 Stevenson	10 Stevenson
11 Coulter	11 Madden	11 Coulter	11 Coulter	11 Coulter
Wrexham Mar 17: 1-4 *Stevenson*	Belfast Oct 23: 1-5 *Stevenson*	Aberdeen Nov 10: 1-1 *Doherty P*	Belfast Mar 16: 1-0 *Bambrick*	Belfast Oct 8: 0-2

1938 England	1939 Wales	1946 England	1946 Scotland	1947 Wales
1 Twoomey	1 Breen	1 Russell	1 Hinton	1 Hinton
2 Hayes	2 Cook	2 Gorman	2 Gorman	2 Gorman
3 Cook	3 Butler	3 Ahearne	3 Feeney	3 Carey
4 Brolly	4 Brolly	4 Carey	4 Martin	4 Sloan
5 McMillen	5 Leatham	5 Vernon	5 Vernon	5 Vernon
6 Browne R	6 Weir	6 Douglas	6 Farrell	6 Farrell
7 Cochrane	7 Cochrane	7 Cochrane	7 Cochrane	7 Cochrane
8 Stevenson	8 Stevenson	8 McAlinden	8 Carey	8 Stevenson
9 Baird	9 Milligan	9 McMorran	9 Walsh D	9 Walsh D
10 Doherty P	10 Doherty P	10 Doherty	10 Stevenson	10 Doherty
11 Brown J	11 Brown J	11 Lockhart	11 Eglington	11 Eglington
Manchester Nov 16: 0-7	Wrexham Mar 15: 1-3 *Milligan*	Belfast Sept 28: 2-7 *Lockhart 2*	Hampden Nov 27: 0-0	Belfast April 16: 2-1 *Stevenson, Doherty*

1947 Scotland	1947 England	1948 Wales	1948 England	1948 Scotland
1 Hinton	1 Hinton	1 Hinton	1 Smyth	1 Smyth
2 Martin	2 Martin	2 Martin	2 Carey	2 Carey
3 Ahearne	3 Carey	3 Gorman	3 Martin	3 Keane
4 Walsh W	4 Walsh W	4 Walsh W	4 Walsh W	4 McCabe
5 Vernon	5 Vernon	5 Vernon	5 Vernon	5 Vernon
6 Farrell	6 Farrell	6 Farrell	6 Farrell	6 Walsh W
7 Cochrane	7 Cochrane	7 Cochrane	7 O'Driscoll	7 Cochrane
8 Smyth	8 Smyth	8 Smyth	8 McAlinden	8 Smyth
9 Walsh D	9 Walsh D	9 Walsh D	9 Walsh D	9 Walsh D
10 Stevenson	10 Doherty	10 Doherty	10 Tully	10 Doherty
11 Eglington	11 Eglington	11 Eglington	11 Eglington	11 O'Driscoll
Belfast Oct 4: 2-0 *Smyth 2*	Everton Nov 5: 2-2 *Doherty, Walsh D*	Wrexham Mar 10: 0-2	Belfast Oct 9: 2-6 *Walsh D 2*	Hampden Nov 17: 2-3 *Walsh D 2*

1949 Wales	1949 Scotland	1949 England	1950 Wales	1950 England
1 Moore	1 Kelly P	1 Kelly	1 Kelly	1 Kelly
2 Carey	2 Bowler	2 Feeney	2 Bowler	2 Gallogly
3 Ahearne	3 McMichael	3 McMichael	3 Ahearne	3 McMichael
4 McCabe	4 Blanchflower	4 Bowler	4 Blanchflower	4 Blanchflower
5 Vernon	5 Vernon	5 Vernon	5 Martin	5 Vernon
6 Farrell	6 Ferris	6 McCabe	6 Ryan	6 Cush
7 Cochrane	7 Cochrane	7 Cochrane	7 McKenna	7 Campbell
8 Smyth	8 Smyth	8 Smyth	8 Smyth	8 Crossan
9 Walsh D	9 Brennan	9 Brennan	9 Walsh D	9 McMorran
10 Brennan	10 Crossan	10 Tully	10 Brennan	10 Brennan
11 O'Driscoll	11 McKenna	11 McKenna	11 Lockhart	11 McKenna
Belfast Mar 9: 0-2	Belfast Oct 1: 2-8 *Smyth 2*	Maine Road, Manchester Nov 6: 2-9 *Smyth, Brennan*	Wrexham Mar 8: 0-0	Belfast Oct 7: 1-4 *McMorran*

1950 Scotland	1951 Wales	1951 France	1951 Scotland	1951 England
1 Kelly	1 Hinton	1 Hinton	1 Uprichard	1 Uprichard
2 Gallogly	2 Graham	2 Graham	2 Graham	2 Graham
3 McMichael	3 Cunningham	3 McMichael	3 McMichael	3 McMichael
4 Blanchflower	4 McCabe	4 Blanchflower	4 Dickson	4 Dickson
5 Vernon	5 Vernon	5 Vernon	5 Vernon	5 Vernon
6 Cush	6 Dickson	6 Ferris	6 Ferris	6 McCourt
7 Campbell	7 Hughes	7 Bingham	7 Bingham	7 Bingham
8 McGarry	8 McMorran	8 McGarry	8 McIlroy	8 Smyth
9 McMorran	9 Simpson	9 Simpson	9 McMorran	9 McMorran
10 Doherty	10 McGarry	10 Dickson	10 Peacock	10 McIlroy
11 McKenna	11 Lockhart	11 McKenna	11 Tully	11 McKenna
Hampden Nov 1: 1-6 *McGarry*	Belfast Mar 7: 1-2 *Simpson*	Belfast May 12: 2-2 *Ferris, Simpson*	Belfast Oct 6: 0-3	Villa Park Nov 20: 0-2

1952 Wales	1952 England	1952 Scotland	1952 France	1953 Wales
1 Uprichard	1 Uprichard	1 Uprichard	1 Uprichard	1 Uprichard
2 Graham	2 Cunningham	2 Graham	2 Graham	2 McCabe
3 McMichael	3 McMichael	3 McMichael	3 McMichael	3 McMichael
4 Blanchflower	4 Blanchflower	4 Blanchflower	4 Blanchflower	4 Blanchflower
5 Dickson	5 Dickson	5 Dickson	5 Dickson	5 Dickson
6 McCourt	6 McCourt	6 McCourt	6 McCourt	6 McCourt
7 Bingham	7 Bingham	7 Bingham	7 Bingham	7 Bingham
8 D'Arcy	8 D'Arcy	8 D'Arcy	8 D'Arcy	8 McIlroy
9 McMorran	9 McMorran	9 McMorran	9 McMorran	9 McMorran
10 McIlroy	10 McIlroy	10 McIlroy	10 Peacock	10 D'Arcy
11 Lockhart	11 Tully	11 Tully	11 Tully	11 Tully
Swansea Mar 19: 0-3	Belfast Oct 4: 2-2 *Tully 2*	Hampden Nov 5: 1-1 *D'Arcy*	Paris Nov 11: 1-3 *Tully*	Belfast April 15: 2-3 *McMorran 2*

1953 Scotland	1953 England	1954 Wales	1954 England	1954 Scotland
1 Smyth	1 Smyth	1 Gregg	1 Uprichard	1 Uprichard
2 Cunningham	2 Graham	2 Graham	2 Montgomery	2 Graham
3 McMichael	3 McMichael	3 McMichael	3 McMichael	3 Cunningham
4 Blanchflower	4 Blanchflower	4 Blanchflower	4 Blanchflower	4 Blanchflower
5 McCabe	5 Dickson	5 Dickson	5 Dickson	5 McCavana
6 Cush	6 Cush	6 Peacock	6 Peacock	6 Peacock
7 Bingham	7 Bingham	7 Bingham	7 Bingham	7 Bingham
8 McIlroy	8 McIlroy	8 Blanchflower J	8 Blanchflower J	8 Blanchflower J
9 Simpson	9 Simpson	9 McAdams	9 Simpson	9 McAdams
10 Tully	10 McMorran	10 McIlroy	10 McIlroy	10 McIlroy
11 Lockhart	11 Lockhart	11 McParland	11 McParland	11 McParland
Belfast Oct 3: 1-3 *Lockhart*	Everton Nov 11: 1-3 *McMorran*	Wrexham Mar 31: 2-1 *McParland 2*	Belfast Oct 2: 0-2	Hampden Nov 3: 2-2 *Bingham, McAdams*

1955 Wales	1955 Scotland	1955 England	1956 Wales	1956 England
1 Uprichard	1 Uprichard	1 Uprichard	1 Uprichard	1 Gregg
2 Graham	2 Graham	2 Cunningham	2 Cunningham	2 Cunningham
3 McMichael	3 Cunningham	3 Graham	3 McMichael	3 McMichael
4 Blanchflower	4 Blanchflower	4 Blanchflower	4 Blanchflower	4 Blanchflower
5 McCleary	5 McCavana	5 McCavana	5 Blanchflower J	5 Blanchflower J
6 Casey	6 Peacock	6 Peacock	6 Casey	6 Casey
7 Bingham	7 Bingham	7 Bingham	7 Bingham	7 Bingham
8 Crossan	8 Blanchflower J	8 McIlroy	8 McIlroy	8 McIlroy
9 Walker	9 Coyle	9 Coyle	9 Jones J	9 Jones J
10 McIlroy	10 McIlroy	10 Tully	10 McMorran	10 McAdams
11 Lockhart	11 McParland	11 McParland	11 Lockhart	11 McParland
Belfast April 20: 2-3 *Crossan, Walker*	Belfast Oct 8: 2-1 *Blanchflower J, Bingham*	Wembley Nov 2: 0-3	Cardiff April 11: 1-1 *Jones*	Belfast Oct 6: 1-1 *McIlroy*

1956 Scotland	1957 Portugal	1957 Wales	1957 Italy	1957 Portugal
1 Gregg	1 Gregg	1 Gregg	1 Gregg	1 Gregg
2 Cuningham	2 Cunningham	2 Cunningham	2 Cunningham	2 Cunningham
3 McMichael	3 McMichael	3 McMichael	3 McMichael	3 McMichael
4 Blanchflower	4 Blanchflower	4 Blanchflower	4 Blanchflower	4 Blanchflower
5 Blanchflower J	5 Blanchflower J	5 Cush	5 Cush	5 Cush
6 Casey	6 Casey	6 Peacock	6 Casey	6 Casey
7 Bingham	7 Bingham	7 Bingham	7 Bingham	7 Bingham
8 McIlroy	8 McIlroy	8 McIlroy	8 Simpson	8 Simpson
9 Shields	9 Coyle	9 Jones	9 McMorran	9 McMorran
10 Dickson	10 Cush	10 Casey	10 McIlroy	10 McIlroy
11 McParland	11 McParland	11 McParland	11 Peacock	11 Peacock
Hampden Nov 7: 0-1	Lisbon Jan 16: 1-1 *Bingham*	Belfast April 10: 0-0	Rome April 25: 0-1	Belfast May 1: 3-0 *Simpson, McIlroy, Casey*

1957 Scotland	1957 England	1957 Italy	1958 Italy	1958 Wales
1 Uprichard	1 Gregg	1 Gregg	1 Uprichard	1 Gregg
2 Cunningham	2 Keith	2 Keith	2 Cunningham	2 Cunningham
3 McMichael	3 McMichael	3 McMichael	3 McMichael	3 McMichael
4 Blanchflower	4 Blanchflower	4 Blanchflower	4 Blanchflower	4 Blanchflower
5 Blanchflower J	5 Blanchflower J	5 Blanchflower J	5 Blanchflower J	5 Keith
6 Peacock	6 Peacock	6 Peacock	6 Peacock	6 Peacock
7 Bingham	7 Bingham	7 Bingham	7 Bingham	7 Bingham
8 Simpson	8 McCrory	8 McIlroy	8 Cush	8 Cush
9 McAdams	9 Simpson	9 McAdams	9 Simpson	9 Simpson
10 McIlroy	10 McIlroy	10 Cush	10 McIlroy	10 McIlroy
11 McParland	11 McParland	11 McParland	11 McParland	11 McParland
Belfast Oct 5: 1-1 *Bingham*	Wembley Nov 6: 3-2 *McIlroy, McCrory, Simpson*	Belfast Dec 4: 2-2 *Cush 2*	Belfast Jan 15: 2-1 *McIlroy, Cush*	Cardiff April 16: 1-1 *Simpson*

1958 Czechoslovakia†	1958 Argentina†	1958 W Germany†	1958 Czechoslovakia†	1958 France†
1 Gregg	1 Gregg	1 Gregg	1 Uprichard	1 Gregg
2 Keith	2 Keith	2 Keith	2 Keith	2 Keith
3 McMichael	3 McMichael	3 McMichael	3 McMichael	3 McMichael
4 Blanchflower	4 Blanchflower	4 Blanchflower	4 Blanchflower	4 Blanchflower
5 Cunningham	5 Cunningham	5 Cunningham	5 Cunningham	5 Cunningham
6 Peacock	6 Peacock	6 Peacock	6 Peacock	6 Cush
7 Bingham	7 Bingham	7 Bingham	7 Bingham	7 Bingham
8 Cush	8 Cush	8 Cush	8 Cush	8 Casey
9 Dougan	9 Coyle	9 Casey	9 Scott	9 Scott
10 McIlroy	10 McIlroy	10 McIlroy	10 McIlroy	10 McIlroy
11 McParland	11 McParland	11 McParland	11 McParland	11 McParland
Halmstad June 8: 1-0 *Cush*	Halmstad June 11: 1-3 *McParland*	Malmo June 15: 2-2 *McParland 2*	Malmo June 17: 2-1 *McParland 2*	Norrkoping June 19: 0-4

1958 England	1958 Spain	1958 Scotland	1959 Wales	1959 Scotland
1 Gregg	1 Uprichard	1 Uprichard	1 Gregg	1 Gregg
2 Keith	2 Keith	2 Keith	2 Keith	2 Keith
3 Graham	3 McMichael	3 McMichael	3 McMichael	3 McMichael
4 Blanchflower	4 Blanchflower	4 Blanchflower	4 Blanchflower	4 Blanchflower
5 Cunningham	5 Forde	5 Cunningham	5 Cunningham	5 Cunningham
6 Peacock	6 Casey	6 Peacock	6 Peacock	6 Peacock
7 Bingham	7 Bingham	7 Bingham	7 Bingham	7 Bingham
8 Cush	8 Cush	8 Cush	8 McIlroy	8 Cush
9 Casey	9 McParland	9 Simpson	9 Cush	9 Dougan
10 McIlroy	10 McIlroy	10 McIlroy	10 Hill	10 McIlroy
11 McParland	11 Tully	11 McParland	11 McParland	11 McParland
Belfast Oct 4: 3-3 *Cush, Peacock, Casey*	Madrid Oct 15: 2-6 *Bingham, McIlroy*	Hampden Nov 5: 2-2 *(opponent og) McIlroy*	Belfast April 22: 4-1 *McParland 2, Peacock, McIlroy*	Belfast Oct 3: 0-4

1959 England	1960 Wales	1960 England	1960 W Germany	1960 Scotland
1 Gregg	1 Gregg	1 Gregg	1 McClelland	1 Gregg
2 Keith	2 Elder	2 Keith	2 Keith	2 Keith
3 McMichael	3 McMichael	3 Elder	3 Elder	3 Elder
4 Blanchflower	4 Blanchflower	4 Blanchflower	4 Blanchflower	4 Blanchflower
5 Cunningham	5 Cunningham	5 Forde	5 Forde	5 Forde
6 Peacock	6 Cush	6 Peacock	6 Peacock	6 Peacock
7 Bingham	7 Bingham	7 Bingham	7 Bingham	7 Bingham
8 Crossan	8 McIlroy	8 McIlroy	8 McIlroy	8 Bruce
9 Cush	9 Lawther	9 McAdams	9 McAdams	9 McAdams
10 McIlroy	10 Hill	10 Dougan	10 Hill	10 Nicholson
11 McParland	11 McParland	11 McParland	11 McParland	11 McParland
Wembley Nov 18: 1-2 *Bingham*	Wrexham April 6: 2-3 *Bingham, Blanchflower*	Belfast Oct 8: 2-5 *McAdams* 2	Belfast Oct 26: 3-4 *McAdams* 3	Hampden Nov 9: 2-5 *Blanchflower, McParland*

1961 Wales	1961 Italy	1961 Greece	1961 W Germany	1961 Scotland
1 McClelland	1 McClelland	1 McClelland	1 McClelland	1 Gregg
2 Keith	2 Keith	2 Keith	2 Keith	2 Magill
3 Elder	3 McCullough	3 Elder	3 Elder	3 Elder
4 Blanchflower	4 Harvey	4 Cush	4 Blanchflower	4 Blanchflower
5 Cunningham	5 Neill	5 Neill	5 Neill	5 Neill
6 Nicholson	6 Peacock	6 Peacock	6 Peacock	6 Peacock
7 Stewart	7 Bingham	7 Bingham	7 Bingham	7 Wilson
8 Dougan	8 Dougan	8 McIlroy	8 Cush	8 McIlroy
9 McAdams	9 Lawther	9 McAdams	9 McAdams	9 Lawther
10 McIlroy	10 McAdams	10 Dougan	10 McIlroy	10 Hill
11 McParland	11 McParland	11 McParland	11 McParland	11 McLaughlin
Belfast April 12: 1-5 *Dougan*	Bologna April 25: 2-3 *Dougan, McAdams*	Athens May 3: 1-2 *McIlroy*	Berlin May 10: 1-2 *McIlroy*	Belfast Oct 7: 1-6 *McLaughlin*

1961 Greece	1961 England	1962 Wales	1962 Netherlands	1962 Poland
1 Gregg	1 Hunter	1 Briggs	1 Irvine R	1 Irvine R
2 Magill	2 Magill	2 Keith	2 Keith	2 Magill
3 Elder	3 Elder	3 Cunningham	3 Cunningham	3 Elder
4 Blanchflower	4 Blanchflower	4 Blanchflower	4 Harvey	4 Blanchflower
5 Neill	5 Neill	5 Neill	5 Blanchflower	5 Hatton
6 Nicholson	6 Nicholson	6 Nicholson	6 Nicholson	6 Nicholson
7 Bingham	7 Bingham	7 Humphries	7 Humphries	7 Humphries
8 McIlroy	8 Barr H	8 Johnston W	8 Lawther	8 Barr
9 McAdams	9 McAdams	9 O'Neill	9 McAdams	9 Dougan
10 Cush	10 McIlroy	10 McLaughlin	10 McIlroy	10 McIlroy
11 McLaughlin	11 McLaughlin	11 Braithwaite	11 McParland	11 Bingham
Belfast Oct 17: 2-0 *McLaughlin* 2	Wembley Nov 22: 1-1 *McIlroy*	Cardiff April 11: 0-4	Rotterdam May 9: 0-4	Katowice Oct 10: 2-0 *Dougan, Humphries*

1962 England	1962 Scotland	1962 Poland	1963 Wales	1963 Spain
1 Irvine R	1 Irvine R	1 Irvine R	1 Irvine R	1 Irvine R
2 Magill	2 Magill	2 Magill	2 Magill	2 Magill
3 Elder	3 Elder	3 Elder	3 Elder	3 Elder
4 Blanchflower	4 Blanchflower	4 Blanchflower	4 Harvey	4 Harvey
5 Neill	5 Hatton	5 Neill	5 Campbell	5 Neill
6 Nicholson	6 Nicholson	6 Nicholson	6 Neill	6 McCullough
7 Humphries	7 Humphries	7 Bingham	7 Humphries	7 Bingham
8 Barr	8 McMillan	8 Crossan	8 Crossan	8 Humphries
9 McMillan	9 Dougan	9 Dougan	9 Irvine W	9 Irvine W
10 McIlroy	10 McIlroy	10 McIlroy	10 McIlroy	10 Crossan
11 Bingham	11 Bingham	11 Braithwaite	11 McLaughlin	11 Braithwaite
Belfast Oct 20: 1-3 *Barr*	Hampden Nov 7: 1-5 *Bingham*	Belfast Nov 28: 2-0 *Crossan, Bingham*	Belfast April 3: 1-4 *Harvey*	Bilbao May 30: 1-1 *Irvine W*

1963 Scotland	1963 Spain	1963 England	1964 Wales	1964 Uruguay
1 Gregg	1 Hunter	1 Gregg	1 Jennings	1 Jennings
2 Magill	2 Magill	2 Magill	2 Magill	2 Magill
3 Parke	3 Parke	3 Parke	3 Elder	3 Elder
4 Harvey	4 Harvey	4 Harvey	4 Harvey	4 Harvey
5 Neill	5 Neill	5 Neill	5 Neill	5 Neill
6 McCullough	6 McCullough	6 McCullough	6 McCullough	6 McCullough
7 Bingham	7 Bingham	7 Bingham	7 Best	7 Best
8 Humphries	8 Humphries	8 Humphries	8 Crossan	8 Crossan
9 Wilson	9 Wilson	9 Wilson	9 Wilson	9 Wilson
10 Crossan	10 Crossan	10 Crossan	10 McLaughlin	10 McLaughlin
11 Hill	11 Hill	11 Hill	11 Braithwaite	11 Braithwaite
Belfast Oct 12: 2-1 *Bingham, Wilson*	Belfast Oct 30: 0-1	Wembley Nov 20: 3-8 *Crossan, Wilson 2*	Swansea April 15: 3-2 *McLaughlin, Wilson, Harvey*	Belfast April 29: 3-0 *Crossan 2, Wilson*

1964 England	1964 Switzerland	1964 Switzerland	1964 Scotland	1965 Netherlands
1 Jennings	1 Jennings	1 Jennings	1 Jennings	1 Briggs
2 Magill	2 Magill	2 Magill	2 Magill	2 Parke
3 Elder	3 Elder	3 Elder	3 Elder	3 Elder
4 Harvey	4 Harvey	4 Harvey	4 Harvey	4 Harvey
5 Neill	5 Neill	5 Campbell	5 Neill	5 Neill
6 McCullough	6 McCullough	6 Parke	6 Parke	6 Nicholson
7 Best	7 Best	7 Best	7 Best	7 Humphries
8 Crossan	8 Crossan	8 Crossan	8 Humphries	8 Crossan
9 Wilson	9 Wilson	9 Irvine W	9 Irvine W	9 Irvine W
10 McLaughlin	10 McLaughlin	10 McLaughlin	10 Crossan	10 Clements
11 Braithwaite	11 Braithwaite	11 Braithwaite	11 Braithwaite	11 Best
Belfast Oct 3: 3-4 *Wilson McLaughlin 2*	Belfast Oct 14: 1-0 *Crossan*	Lausanne Nov 14: 1-2 *Best*	Hampden Nov 25: 2-3 *Best, Irvine W*	Belfast Mar 17: 2-1 *Crossan, Neill*

1965 Wales	1965 Netherlands	1965 Albania	1965 Scotland	1965 England
1 Irvine R	1 Jennings	1 Jennings	1 Jennings	1 Jennings
2 Parke	2 Magill	2 Magill	2 Magill	2 Magill
3 Elder	3 Elder	3 Elder	3 Elder	3 Elder
4 Harvey	4 Harvey	4 Harvey	4 Harvey	4 Harvey
5 Neill	5 Neill	5 Neill	5 Neill	5 Neill
6 Nicholson	6 Parke	6 Parke	6 Nicholson	6 Nicholson
7 Humphries	7 Best	7 Humphries	7 McIlroy	7 McIlroy
8 Crossan	8 Crossan	8 Crossan	8 Crossan	8 Crossan
9 Irvine W	9 Irvine W	9 Irvine W	9 Irvine W	9 Irvine W
10 McLaughlin	10 Nicholson	10 Nicholson	10 Dougan	10 Dougan
11 Clements	11 Braithwaite	11 Best	11 Best	11 Best
Belfast March 31: 0-5	Rotterdam April 7: 0-0	Belfast May 7: 4-1 *Crossan 3, Best*	Belfast Oct 2: 3-2 *Dougan, Crossan, Irvine W*	Wembley Nov 10: 1-2 *Irvine W*

1965 Albania	1966 Wales	1966 W Germany	1966 Mexico	1966 England
1 Jennings	1 Jennings	1 Jennings	1 McClelland	1 Jennings (McFaul)
2 Magill	2 Magill	2 Magill	2 Magill	2 Parke
3 Elder	3 Elder	3 Parke	3 Elder	3 Elder
4 Harvey	4 Harvey	4 Harvey	4 Harvey	4 Todd
5 Neill	5 Neill	5 Napier	5 Neill	5 Harvey
6 Nicholson	6 Nicholson	6 Neill	6 Nicholson	6 McCullough
7 McIlroy	7 Welsh	7 Welsh	7 Welsh	7 Ferguson
8 Crossan	8 Wilson	8 Crossan	8 Ferguson	8 Crossan
9 Irvine W	9 Irvine W	9 Wilson	9 Irvine (Johnston)	9 Irvine W
10 Dougan	10 Dougan	10 Dougan	10 Dougan	10 Dougan
11 Best	11 McLaughlin	11 McKinney	11 Clements	11 Best
Tirana Nov 24: 1-1 *Irvine W*	Cardiff Mar 30: 4-1 *Irvine W, Wilson, Welsh, Harvey*	Belfast May 7: 0-2	Belfast June 22: 4-1 *Johnston, Elder, Nicholson, Ferguson*	Belfast Oct 22: 0-2

1966 Scotland	1967 Wales	1967 Scotland	1967 England	1968 Wales
1 Jennings	1 McKenzie	1 Jennings	1 Jennings	1 Jennings
2 Parke	2 Craig	2 McKeag	2 Parke	2 Craig
3 Elder	3 Elder	3 Parke	3 Elder	3 Elder
4 Harvey	4 Stewart	4 Stewart	4 Stewart	4 Harvey
5 Neill	5 Neill	5 Neill	5 Neill	5 Todd
6 Nicholson	6 Nicholson	6 Clements	6 Harvey	6 McKeag
7 Wilson	7 Welsh	7 Campbell	7 Campbell	7 Irvine
8 Crossan	8 Trainor	8 Crossan	8 Irvine	8 Stewart
9 Irvine W	9 Dougan	9 Dougan	9 Wilson	9 Dougan
10 Dougan	10 Bruce	10 Nicholson	10 Nicholson	10 Nicholson
11 Clements	11 Clements	11 Best	11 Clements	11 Harkin
Hampden Nov 16: 1-2 *Nicholson*	Belfast April 12: 0-0	Belfast Oct 21: 1-0 *Clements*	Wembley Nov 22: 0-2	Wrexham Feb 28: 0-2

1968 Israel	1968 Turkey	1968 Turkey	1969 England	1969 Scotland
1 Jennings	1 Jennings	1 Jennings	1 Jennings	1 Jennings
2 Rice	2 Craig (Stewart)	2 Craig	2 Craig	2 Craig
3 Jackson	3 Harvey	3 Harvey	3 Harvey (Elder)	3 Elder
4 Stewart	4 Nicholson	4 Nicholson	4 Todd	4 Todd
5 Neill	5 Neill	5 Neill	5 Neill	5 Neill
6 Harvey	6 Clements	6 Stewart	6 Nicholson	6 Nicholson
7 Sloan	7 Campbell	7 Hamilton	7 McMordie	7 Best
8 McMordie	8 McMordie	8 McMordie	8 Jackson	8 McMordie
9 Dougan (Gaston)	9 Dougan	9 Dougan	9 Dougan	9 Dougan
10 Irvine W	10 Irvine W	10 Harkin	10 Irvine W	10 Jackson
11 Ross	11 Best	11 Clements	11 Best	11 Clements
Jaffa Sept 10: 3-2 *Irvine 2, Dougan*	Belfast Oct 23: 4-1 *Best, McMordie, Dougan, Campbell*	Istanbul Dec 11: 3-0 *Harkin 2, Nicholson*	Belfast May 3: 1-3 *McMordie*	Hampden May 6: 1-1 *McMordie*

1969 Wales	1969 USSR	1969 USSR	1970 Scotland	1970 England
1 Jennings	1 Jennings	1 Jennings	1 Jennings	1 Jennings
2 Craig	2 Rice	2 Craig	2 Craig	2 Craig
3 Elder	3 Elder	3 Harvey	3 Clements	3 Clements
4 Todd	4 Todd	4 Hunter	4 Todd (O'Kane)	4 O'Kane
5 Neill	5 Neill	5 Neill	5 Neill	5 Neill
6 Nicholson	6 Nicholson	6 Nicholson	6 Nicholson	6 Nicholson
7 Best	7 Campbell	7 Hegan	7 Campbell (Dickson)	7 McMordie
8 McMordie	8 McMordie	8 Jackson	8 Lutton	8 Best
9 Dougan	9 Dougan	9 Dougan	9 Dougan	9 Dougan
10 Jackson	10 Clements (Jackson)	10 Harkin	10 McMordie	10 O'Doherty (Nelson)
11 Clements (Harkin)	11 Best	11 Clements	11 Best	11 Lutton (Cowan)
Belfast May 10: 0-0	Belfast Sept 10: 0-0	Moscow Oct 22: 0-2	Belfast April 18: 0-1	Wembley April 21: 1-3 *Best*

1970 Wales	1970 Spain	1971 Cyprus	1971 Cyprus	1971 England
1 McFaul	1 McFaul	1 Jennings	1 Jennings	1 Jennings
2 Craig	2 Craig	2 Craig	2 Craig	2 Rice
3 Nelson	3 Nelson	3 Nelson	3 Clements	3 Nelson
4 O'Kane	4 Jackson	4 Hunter	4 Harvey	4 O'Kane
5 Neill	5 Neill	5 Neill	5 Hunter	5 Hunter
6 Nicholson	6 O'Kane	6 Todd	6 Todd (Watson)	6 Nicholson
7 Campbell (O'Doherty)	7 Sloan	7 Hamilton	7 Hamilton	7 Hamilton
8 Best	8 Best	8 McMordie	8 McMordie	8 McMordie (Cassidy)
9 Dickson	9 Dougan (Todd)	9 Dougan	9 Dougan	9 Dougan
10 McMordie	10 Harkin	10 Nicholson	10 Nicholson	10 Clements
11 Clements	11 Clements	11 Best	11 Best	11 Best
Swansea April 25: 0-1	Seville Nov 11: 0-3	Nicosia Feb 3: 3-0 *Nicholson, Dougan, Best*	Belfast April 21: 5-0 *Dougan, Best 3, Nicholson*	Belfast May 15: 0-1

1971 Scotland	1971 Wales	1971 USSR	1971 USSR	1972 Spain
1 Jennings	1 Jennings	1 McFaul	1 Jennings	1 Jennings
2 Rice	2 Rice	2 Craig (Hamilton)	2 Rice	2 Rice
3 Nelson	3 Nelson	3 Neill	3 Nelson	3 Nelson
4 O'Kane	4 O'Kane	4 Hunter	4 Nicholson	4 Neill
5 Hunter	5 Hunter	5 Nelson	5 Hunter	5 Hunter
6 Nicholson	6 Nicholson (Harvey)	6 Hegan	6 O'Kane	6 Clements
7 Hamilton	7 Hamilton	7 Clements	7 McMordie	7 Hamilton (O'Neill)
8 McMordie (Craig)	8 McMordie	8 Nicholson	8 Hamilton (O'Neill)	8 McMordie
9 Dougan	9 Dougan	9 O'Kane	9 Neill	9 Morgan
10 Clements	10 Clements	10 Dougan	10 Dougan (Cassidy)	10 McIlroy
11 Best	11 Best	11 Best	11 Clements	11 Best
Hampden May 18: 1-0 *opponent og*	Belfast May 22: 1-0 *Hamilton*	Moscow Sept 22: 0-1	Belfast Oct 13: 1-1 *Nicholson*	Hull Feb 16: 1-1 *Morgan*

1972 Scotland	1972 England	1972 Wales	1972 Bulgaria	1973 Cyprus
1 Jennings	1 Jennings	1 Jennings	1 Jennings	1 Jennings
2 Rice	2 Rice	2 Rice	2 Rice	2 Rice
3 Nelson	3 Nelson	3 Nelson	3 Nelson	3 Neill
4 Neill	4 Neill	4 Neill	4 Hunter	4 Hunter
5 Hunter	5 Hunter	5 Hunter	5 Neill	5 Craig
6 Clements (Craig)	6 Clements	6 Clements	6 Clements	6 Hegan
7 Hegan	7 Hegan	7 Hegan	7 Hamilton (Morgan)	7 Clements
8 McMordie (McIlroy)	8 McMordie	8 McMordie	8 Hegan	8 Hamilton
9 Dougan	9 Dougan	9 Dougan (O'Neill)	9 McMordie	9 Dickson
10 Irvine	10 Irvine	10 Irvine	10 Dougan	10 Dougan
11 Jackson	11 Jackson	11 Jackson	11 Best	11 Nelson
Hampden May 20: 0-2	Wembley May 23: 1-0 *Neill*	Wrexham May 27: 0-0	Sofia Oct 18: 0-3	Nicosia Feb 14: 0-1

1973 Portugal	1973 Cyprus	1973 England	1973 Scotland	1973 Wales
1 Jennings	1 McFaul	1 Jennings	1 Jennings	1 Jennings
2 O'Kane	2 O'Kane	2 Rice	2 Rice	2 Rice
3 Nelson	3 Hunter (Coyle)	3 Craig	3 Craig	3 Craig
4 Neill	4 Neill	4 Neill	4 Neill	4 Neill
5 Hunter	5 Craig	5 Hunter	5 Hunter	5 Hunter
6 Clements	6 Hamilton (Lutton)	6 Clements	6 Clements	6 Clements
7 Hamilton	7 Jackson	7 Hamilton	7 Hamilton	7 Hamilton (Lutton)
8 Coyle	8 Clements	8 Jackson	8 Jackson	8 Jackson
9 Morgan	9 Morgan	9 Morgan	9 Morgan	9 Morgan
10 Dickson	10 O'Neill	10 O'Neill	10 O'Neill	10 O'Neill
11 O'Neill	11 Anderson	11 Anderson	11 Anderson (Lutton)	11 Anderson (Coyle)
Coventry Mar 28: 1-1 *O'Neill*	London May 8: 3-0 *Morgan, Anderson 2*	Liverpool May 12: 1-2 *Clements (pen)*	Glasgow May 16: 2-1 *O'Neill, Anderson*	Liverpool May 19: 1-0 *Hamilton*

1973 Bulgaria	1973 Portugal	1974 Scotland	1974 England	1974 Wales
1 McFaul	1 Jennings	1 Jennings	1 Jennings	1 Jennings
2 Rice	2 Rice	2 Rice	2 Rice	2 Rice
3 Craig	3 Craig	3 Nelson	3 Nelson (Jackson)	3 Dowd
4 O'Kane	4 Lutton	4 O'Kane	4 O'Kane	4 O'Kane
5 Hunter	5 O'Kane	5 Hunter	5 Hunter	5 Hunter
6 Clements	6 Clements	6 Clements	6 Clements	6 Clements
7 Hamilton	7 Jackson	7 Hamilton (Jackson)	7 Hamilton (O'Neill)	7 Hamilton (Jackson)
8 Jackson (Coyle)	8 O'Neill	8 Cassidy	8 Cassidy	8 Cassidy
9 Morgan	9 Morgan	9 Morgan	9 Morgan	9 McIlroy
10 Anderson	10 Anderson	10 McIlroy	10 McIlroy	10 McGrath
11 O'Neill (Cassidy)	11 Best	11 McGrath	11 McGrath	11 O'Neill
Hillsborough Sept 26: 0-0	Lisbon Nov 14: 1-1 *O'Kane*	Hampden May 11: 1-0 *Cassidy*	Wembley May 15: 0-1	Wrexham May 18: 0-1

1974 Norway	1974 Sweden	1975 Yugoslavia	1975 England	1975 Scotland
1 Jennings	1 Jennings	1 Jennings	1 Jennings	1 Jennings
2 Rice	2 O'Kane	2 Rice	2 Rice	2 Rice
3 Craig (Dowd)	3 Nelson (Blair)	3 Nelson	3 O'Kane	3 O'Kane
4 O'Kane	4 Dowd	4 Nicholl	4 Nicholl	4 Nicholl
5 Hunter	5 Hunter	5 Hunter	5 Hunter	5 Hunter (Blair)
6 Clements	6 Nicholl	6 Clements	6 Clements	6 Clements
7 Hamilton	7 Jackson	7 Hamilton	7 Hamilton (Finney)	7 Finney
8 Cassidy	8 O'Neill	8 O'Neill	8 O'Neill	8 O'Neill (Anderson)
9 Finney	9 Morgan	9 Spence	9 Spence	9 Spence
10 McIlroy	10 McIlroy	10 McIlroy	10 McIlroy	10 McIlroy
11 McGrath (Jackson)	11 Hamilton	11 Jackson	11 Jackson	11 Jackson
Oslo Sept 4: 1-2 *Finney*	Solna Oct 30: 2-0 *O'Neill, Nicholl*	Belfast March 16: 1-0 *Hamilton*	Belfast May 17: 0-0	Hampden May 20: 0-3

1975 Wales	1975 Sweden	1975 Norway	1975 Yugoslavia	1976 Israel
1 Jennings	1 Jennings	1 Jennings	1 Jennings	1 Jennings (Platt)
2 Scott	2 Rice	2 Rice	2 Rice	2 Scott
3 Rice	3 Nelson	3 Nelson	3 Scott	3 Nicholl J
4 Nicholl	4 Clements	4 Nicholl	4 Nicholl	4 Hunter
5 Hunter	5 Hunter	5 Hunter	5 Hunter	5 Rice
6 Clements	6 Nicholl	6 Jackson	6 Clements	6 Blair
7 Blair	7 Blair	7 Hamilton	7 Hamilton	7 Nelson
8 Jackson	8 Hamilton (Morgan)	8 McIlroy	8 McIlroy	8 Hamilton
9 Spence	9 Spence	9 Morgan (Cochrane)	9 Morgan	9 Anderson (McGrath)
10 McIlroy	10 McIlroy	10 Jamison	10 Jackson (O'Neill)	10 Spence
11 Finney	11 Jackson	11 Finney	11 Finney	11 Finney
Belfast May 23: 1-0 *Finney*	Belfast Sept 3: 1-2 *Hunter*	Belfast Oct 29: 3-0 *Morgan, McIlroy, Hamilton*	Belgrade Nov 19: 0-1	Tel Aviv Mar 24: 1-1 *Lev, og*

1976 Scotland	1976 England	1976 Wales	1976 Netherlands	1976 Belgium
1 Jennings	1 Jennings	1 Jennings	1 Jennings	1 Jennings
2 Scott	2 Rice	2 Scott	2 Nicholl J	2 Nicholl J
3 Nicholl C	3 Nelson (Scott)	3 Rice	3 Jackson	3 Rice (Nelson)
4 Hunter	4 Clements	4 Nicholl C	4 Rice	4 Jackson
5 Rice	5 Hunter	5 Hunter	5 Hunter	5 Hunter
6 Hamilton	6 Nicholl C	6 Clements	6 Hamilton B	6 Hamilton B
7 Cassidy	7 Hamilton	7 Hamilton	7 Best	7 Best
8 Sharkey (McCreery)	8 Cassidy	8 McIlroy	8 McIlroy	8 McIlroy
9 McIlroy	9 McCreery	9 Spence (Morgan)	9 McGrath (Spence)	9 McGrath
10 Morgan (Spence)	10 Spence	10 Cassidy (Nicholl J)	10 McCreery	10 McCreery
11 Finney	11 McIlroy	11 McCreery	11 Anderson	11 Anderson
Glasgow May 8: 0-3	Wembley May 11: 0-4	Swansea May 14: 0-1	Rotterdam Oct 13: 2-2 McGrath, Spence	Liège Nov 10: 0-2

1977 W Germany	1977 England	1977 Scotland	1977 Wales	1977 Iceland
1 Jennings	1 Jennings	1 Jennings	1 Jennings	1 Jennings
2 Rice	2 Nicholl J	2 Nicholl J	2 Nicholl J	2 Rice
3 Nelson	3 Rice	3 Rice	3 Nelson	3 Nelson
4 Jackson	4 Jackson	4 Jackson	4 Nicholl C	4 Nicholl J
5 Hunter	5 Hunter	5 Hunter	5 Hunter	5 Hunter
6 McCreery (Cassidy)	6 Hamilton B	6 Hamilton B	6 Hamilton B	6 Hamilton B
7 Hamilton B	7 McGrath	7 McGrath	7 McGrath	7 McGrath
8 Best	8 McIlroy	8 McIlroy	8 McIlroy	8 McIlroy
9 Armstrong (Spence)	9 Armstrong (O'Neill)	9 O'Neill (Spence)	9 Jackson	9 Jackson
10 McGrath	10 McCreery	10 McCreery	10 McCreery (Armstrong)	10 McCreery
11 Anderson	11 Anderson (Spence)	11 Anderson	11 Anderson (Spence)	11 Anderson
Cologne April 27: 0-5	Belfast May 28: 1-2 McGrath	Glasgow June 1: 0-2	Belfast June 3: 1-1 Nelson	Reykjavik June 11: 0-1

1977 Iceland	1977 Netherlands	1977 Belgium	1978 Scotland	1978 England	1978 Wales
1 Jennings	1 Jennings	1 Jennings	1 Platt	1 Platt	1 Platt
2 Rice	2 Rice	2 Rice	2 Hamilton B	2 Hamilton B	2 Hamilton B
3 Nicholl J	3 Nelson	3 Nelson	3 Scott	3 Scott	3 Scott (Nelson)
4 Nelson	4 Nicholl J	4 Nicholl J	4 Nicholl C	4 Nicholl C	4 Nicholl C
5 Hunter	5 Hunter	5 Hunter (Nicholl C)	5 Nicholl J	5 Nicholl J	5 Nicholl J
6 McCreery	6 O'Neill	6 McIlroy	6 McIlroy	6 McIlroy	6 O'Neill
7 McGrath	7 McIlroy	7 McGrath	7 McCreery	7 McCreery	7 McCreery
8 Best	8 Best	8 McCreery	8 O'Neill	8 O'Neill	8 McIlroy
9 McIlroy	9 McCreery	9 Armstrong	9 Anderson (Hamilton W)	9 Anderson	9 Anderson (Cochrane)
10 O'Neill	10 McGrath	10 Stewart	10 Armstrong	10 Armstrong	10 Armstrong
11 Anderson	11 Anderson	11 Anderson	11 McGrath (Cochrane)	11 McGrath (Cochrane)	11 McGrath
Belfast Sept 21: 2-0 McGrath, McIlroy	Belfast Oct 12: 0-1	Belfast Nov 16: 3-0 Armstrong 2, McGrath	Glasgow May 13: 1-1 O'Neill	Wembley May 16: 0-1	Wrexham May 19: 0-1

DENIS LAW

An Autobiography

Denis Law, one of the all-time great footballers, tells his life story in his own inimitable and engaging way.

illustrated   176pp   £4.95

Available from bookshops or in case of difficulty send cheque/PO payable to Macdonald & Jane's to: QAP Direct Sales, 9 Partridge Drive, Orpington, Kent, England, including 10% postage and packing (UK only). Please allow up to 28 days for delivery, subject to availability.

Scotland's full international teams 1872-1978

Substitutes in brackets

1872 England	1873 England	1874 England	1875 England	1876 England
1 Gardner	1 Gardner	1 Gardner	1 Gardner	1 McGeoch
2 Ker	2 Ker	2 Hunter	2 Hunter	2 Hunter
3 Taylor	3 Taylor	3 Taylor	3 Taylor	3 Taylor
4 Thomson	4 Gibb	4 Thomson	4 McLintock	4 McLintock
5 Smith, James	5 Smith, Robert	5 Campbell C	5 Kennedy	5 Kennedy
6 Smith, Robert	6 Wotherspoon	6 Weir	6 Weir	6 McNeil H
7 Leckie	7 Renny-Tailyour	7 Mackinnon W	7 Mackinnon W	7 Highet
8 Rhind	8 Kinnaird	8 Ferguson	8 Highet	8 Mackinnon W
9 McKinnon	9 Blackburn	9 Mackinnon A	9 McNeil H	9 Miller
10 Weir	10 Thomson	10 McNeil H	10 Andrew	10 Ferguson
11 Wotherspoon	11 McKinnon	11 Anderson	11 McPherson	11 Baird
Glasgow Nov 30: 0-0	London Mar 8: 2-4 *Renny-Tailyour, Gibb*	Glasgow Mar 7: 2-1 *Mackinnon A, Anderson*	London Mar 6: 2-2 *McNeil, Andrews*	Glasgow Mar 4: 3-0 *Mackinnon, McNeil, Highet*

1876 Wales	1877 England	1877 Wales	1878 England	1878 Wales
1 McGeoch	1 McGeoch	1 McGeoch	1 Gardner	1 Parlane
2 Taylor	2 Neill	2 Neill	2 McIntyre	2 Neill
3 Neill	3 Vallance	3 Vallance	3 Vallance	3 Duncan
4 Kennedy	4 Campbell C	4 Phillips	4 Campbell C	4 Phillips
5 Campbell C	5 Phillips	5 Campbell C	5 Kennedy	5 Davidson
6 Highet	6 Richmond	6 Smith J	6 Richmond	6 Lang
7 Ferguson	7 Mackinnon W	7 McGregor	7 Mackinnon W	7 Weir
8 Lang	8 McGregor	8 Ferguson	8 McGregor	8 Watson
9 McKinnon	9 McDougall	9 McDougall	9 McDougall	9 Campbell P
10 McNeil M	10 Smith J	10 McNeil H	10 Highet	10 Ferguson
11 McNeil H	11 Ferguson	11 Hunter	11 McNeil H	11 Baird
Glasgow Mar 25: 4-0 *Ferguson, Lang, McKinnon, McNeil H*	London Mar 3: 3-1 *Ferguson 2, Richmond*	Wrexham Mar 5: 2-0 *Campbell, Powell, og*	Glasgow Mar 2: 7-2 *McDougall 3, McGregor, McNeil 2, Mackinnon*	Glasgow Mar 23: 9-0 *Campbell, Weir 2, Ferguson 3, Baird, Watson and one other*

1879 Wales	1879 England	1880 England	1880 Wales	1881 England
1 Parlane	1 Parlane	1 Rowan	1 Gillespie	1 Gillespie
2 Vallance	2 Somers	2 Neill	2 Somers	2 Watson
3 Somers	3 Vallance	3 McLintock	3 Lang	3 Vallance
4 McPherson	4 Campbell C	4 Campbell C	4 Davidson	4 Campbell C
5 Davidson	5 McPherson	5 McPherson	5 McIntyre	5 Davidson
6 McNeil H	6 Beveridge	6 Smith J	6 Douglas	6 McGuire
7 McDougall	7 Smith J	7 McNeil M	7 McAdam	7 Hill
8 Campbell P	8 McDougall	8 Ker	8 Frazer	8 Ker
9 Paton	9 Paton	9 McGregor	9 Lindsay	9 Lindsay
10 Beveridge	10 Mackinnon W	10 Baird	10 Campbell J	10 McNeil H
11 Smith J	11 McNeil H	11 Kay	11 Beveridge	11 Smith J
Wrexham April 7: 3-0 *Campbell, Smith 2*	London April 5: 4-5 *Mackinnon 2, McDougall, Smith*	Glasgow Mar 13: 5-4 *Ker 3, Baird, Kay*	Glasgow Mar 27: 5-1 *Davidson, Beveridge, Lindsay, McAdam, Campbell*	London Mar 12: 6-1 *Smith J 3, Ker 2, McGuire*

1881 Wales	1882 England	1882 Wales	1883 England	1883 Wales
1 Gillespie	1 Gillespie	1 Rowan	1 McAulay (Dumbarton)	1 McAulay (Dumbarton)
2 Vallance	2 Watson	2 Holm	2 Holm	2 Arnott
3 Watson	3 McIntyre	3 Duncan	3 Paton	3 Holm
4 McPherson	4 Campbell C	4 Kennedy	4 Miller	4 Miller
5 Davidson	5 Miller	5 Campbell C	5 McPherson	5 McPherson
6 Smith J	6 Fraser	6 Fraser	6 Fraser	6 Smith Dr J
7 McNeil H	7 Anderson	7 Hill	7 Anderson	7 Inglis
8 Lindsay	8 Ker	8 Ker	8 Smith Dr J	8 Mackinnon W
9 McGuire	9 Harrower	9 McAulay (Arthurlie)	9 Inglis	9 Rowan
10 Ker	10 Kay	10 Kay	10 Kay	10 Kay
11 Hill	11 McPherson	11 Richmond	11 Mackinnon W	11 Fraser
Wrexham Mar 14: 5-1 *Smith 2, Ker 2, Lindsay*	Glasgow Mar 11: 5-1 *Horrower, Ker 2, Kay, McPherson*	Glasgow Mar 25: 5-0 *Kay, Ker, Fraser 2, McAulay*	Sheffield Mar 10: 3-2 *Smith Dr 2, Fraser*	Wrexham Mar 12: 3-0 *Smith Dr, Fraser, Anderson*

1884 Ireland	1884 England	1884 Wales	1885 Ireland	1885 England
1 Inglish	1 McAulay (Dumbarton)	1 Turner	1 Chalmers	1 McAulay (Dumbarton)
2 Forbes	2 Arnott	2 Forbes	2 Niven	2 Arnott
3 Kennedy	3 Forbes	3 Paton	3 McHardy	3 Paton
4 Graham	4 Campbell C	4 Kennedy	4 McPherson	4 Campbell C
5 Fulton	5 McPherson	5 McIntyre	5 Kelso	5 Gow
6 Brown R	6 Shaw	6 Kay	6 Turner	6 Anderson
7 Thomson	7 Anderson	7 Lindsay	7 Lamont	7 Hamilton
8 Gossland	8 Lindsay	8 Shaw	8 Barbour	8 Sellar
9 Goudie	9 Smith Dr J	9 Mackinnon	9 Calderwood	9 Lindsay
10 Mackinnon W	10 Christie	10 Thomson	10 Marshall	10 Allan
11 McAulay (Arthurlie)	11 Mackinnon W	11 Brown R	11 Higgins	11 Calderwood
Belfast Jan 26: 5-0 *Goudie, Harrower 2, Gossland 2*	Glasgow Mar 15: 1-0 *Smith Dr*	Glasgow Mar 29: 4-1 *Kay 2, Lindsay, Shaw*	Glasgow Mar 14: 8-2 *Higgins 4, Kelso, Barbour, McPherson, Calderwood*	London Mar 21: 1-1 *Lindsay*

1885 Wales	1886 Ireland	1886 England	1886 Wales	1887 Ireland
1 McAulay (Dumbarton)	1 Connor	1 McAulay (Dumbarton)	1 Gillespie	1 Doig
2 Arnott	2 McLeod	2 Arnott	2 Lundie	2 Whitelaw
3 Paton	3 Thomson	3 Paton	3 Semple	3 Smellie
4 Kelso	4 Keir	4 Campbell C	4 Kelso	4 Weir
5 McCall	5 Cameron	5 McDonald	5 McCall	5 McMillan
6 Hamilton	6 Turner	6 Sellar	6 Jackson	6 Hutton
7 Anderson	7 Heggie	7 Hamilton	7 McCormack	7 Jenkinson
8 Lindsay	8 Dunbar	8 Somerville	8 Marshall	8 Lambie
9 Calderwood	9 Fleming	9 Lindsay	9 Harrower	9 Watt
10 Brown R jun	10 Kelly	10 Gray	10 McGhee	10 Lowe
11 Allan	11 Gourlay	11 Aitken	11 Allan	11 Johnstone
Wrexham Mar 23: 8-1 *Anderson 3, Lindsay 2, Allan 2, Calderwood*	Belfast Mar 20: 7-2 *Heggie 5, Dunbar, Gourlay*	Glasgow Mar 31: 1-1 *Somerville*	Glasgow April 10: 4-1 *Harrower 2, Allan 2*	Glasgow Feb 19: 4-1 *Watt, Jenkinson, Johnstone, Lowe*

1887 England	1887 Wales	1888 Wales	1888 England	1888 Ireland
1 McAulay (Dumbarton)	1 McAulay (Dumbarton)	1 Wilson	1 Lindsay	1 McLeod
2 Arnott	2 Arnott	2 Hannah	2 Arnott	2 Jackson
3 Forbes	3 Forbes	3 Smellie	3 Gow	3 Stewart D
4 Kelso	4 Keir	4 Gourlay	4 Kelso	4 Stewart A
5 Auld	5 Auld	5 Johnston J	5 Kelly	5 Dewar
6 Keir	6 Kelso	6 McLaren	6 Keir	6 Kelso
7 Marshall	7 Robertson	7 Latta	7 Hamilton	7 Gow
8 Robertson	8 McCall	8 McPherson	8 Berry	8 Brackenridge
9 Sellar	9 Allan	9 Groves	9 Sellar	9 Dickson
10 Allan	10 Marshall	10 Paul	10 McCall	10 Aitken
11 McCall	11 Sellar	11 Munro	11 Lambie	11 McCallum
Blackburn Mar 19: 3-2 *McCall, Allan 2*	Wrexham Mar 21: 2-0 *Robertson, Marshall*	Edinburgh Mar 10: 5-1 *Paul 2, McPherson 2, Groves*	Glasgow Mar 17: 0-5	Belfast Mar 24: 10-2 *Dewar, Dickson, Aitken, McCallum, Brackenridge, Wilson, og, and 3 others*

1889 Ireland	1889 England	1889 Wales	1890 Wales	1890 Ireland
1 Doig	1 Wilson	1 McLeod	1 Gillespie	1 McLeod
2 Adams	2 Arnott	2 Thomson	2 Whitelaw	2 Hunter
3 McKeown	3 Smellie	3 Rae	3 Murray	3 Rae
4 Robertson	4 Kelly	4 Stewart	4 McQueen	4 Russell
5 Calderhead	5 Dewar	5 Auld	5 Brown A	5 Begbie
6 Buchanan	6 McLaren	6 Lochead	6 Wilson	6 Mitchell
7 Watt	7 Latta	7 Watt	7 Watt	7 Wyllie
8 McInnes	8 Berry	8 Campbell H	8 Brown J	8 Rankin
9 Groves	9 Oswald	9 Paul	9 Paul	9 McPherson
10 Boyd	10 McPherson	10 Johnstone	10 Dunlop	10 Bell
11 Black	11 Munro	11 Hannah	11 Bruce	11 Baird
Glasgow Mar 9: 7-0 *Watt, McInnes 2, Black, Groves 3*	London April 13: 3-2 *McLaren, Oswald, Munro*	Wrexham April 15: 0-0	Glasgow Mar 22: 5-0 *Paul 4, Wilson*	Belfast Mar 29: 4-1 *Wyllie, Rankin 2, McPherson*

1890 England	1891 Wales	1891 Ireland	1891 England	1892 Ireland
1 Wilson	1 McCorkindale	1 Gillespie	1 Wilson	1 Baird
2 Arnott	2 Ritchie	2 Sillars	2 Arnott	2 Bowman
3 McKeown	3 Hepburn	3 Paul	3 Smellie	3 Drummond
4 Robertson	4 McQueen	4 Hamilton	4 Begbie	4 Marshall
5 Kelly	5 Brown A	5 Cleland	5 McPherson	5 Robertson
6 McLaren	6 Robertson	6 Campbell (Kilm'k)	6 Hill	6 Dowds
7 Groves	7 Gulliland	7 Lowe	7 Rankin	7 Gulliland
8 Berry	8 Buchanan	8 Bowie	8 Watt	8 McPherson
9 Johnstone W	9 Boyd	9 Fraser	9 Sellar	9 Ellis
10 McPherson	10 Logan	10 Clements	10 Berry	10 Keillor
11 McCall	11 Keillor	11 Waddell	11 Baird	11 Lambie
Glasgow April 5: 1-1 *McPherson*	Wrexham Mar 21: 4-3 *Logan, Buchanan, Boyd 2*	Glasgow Mar 28: 2-1 *Waddell, Lowe*	Blackburn April 6: 1-2 *Watt*	Belfast Mar 19: 3-2 *Keillor, Lambie, Ellis*

1892 Wales	1892 England	1893 Wales	1893 Ireland	1893 England
1 Downie	1 McLeod	1 McLeod	1 Lindsay	1 Lindsay
2 Adams	2 Doyle	2 Doyle	2 Adams	2 Arnott
3 Orr	3 Arnott	3 Foyers	3 Smellie	3 Smellie
4 Begbie	4 Kelly	4 Sillars	4 Maley	4 Maley
5 Campbell (Kilm'k)	5 Sillars	5 McCreadie	5 Kelly	5 Kelly -
6 Hill	6 Mitchell	6 Stewart	6 Mitchell	6 Mitchell
7 Taylor	7 McPherson	7 Taylor	7 Waddell	7 Sellar
8 Thomson	8 Taylor	8 Thomson	8 Campbell (Celtic)	8 Waddell
9 Hamilton	9 Waddell	9 Madden	9 Hamilton	9 Hamilton
10 McPherson	10 McMahon	10 Lambie	10 Sellar	10 McMahon
11 Baird	11 Bell	11 Barker	11 McMahon	11 Campbell (Celtic)
Edinburgh Mar 26: 6-1 *Thomson, Hamilton 2, McPherson, Baird 2*	Glasgow April 2: 1-4 *Bell*	Wrexham Mar 18: 8-0 *Madden 4, Barker 3, Lambie*	Glasgow Mar 25: 6-1 *Sellar 2, Kelly, McMahon, Hamilton, 1 og*	Richmond April 1: 2-5 *Sellar 2*

1894 Wales	1894 Ireland	1894 England	1895 Wales	1895 Ireland
1 Baird	1 Barrett	1 Haddow	1 Barrett	1 McArthur
2 Crawford	2 Crawford	2 Sillars	2 Sillars	2 Doyle
3 Foyers	3 Drummond	3 Doyle	3 Glen	3 Drummond
4 Johnstone	4 Marshall	4 Begbie	4 Simpson	4 Simpson
5 Kelly	5 Stewart	5 McCreadie	5 McColl	5 Russell
6 McBain	6 Longair	6 Mitchell	6 Keillor	6 Gibson
7 Chalmers	7 Taylor	7 Gulliland	7 Fyfe	7 Taylor
8 Stewart	8 Blessington	8 Blessington	8 Murray	8 Waddell
9 Alexander	9 Alexander	9 McMahon	9 Madden	9 McPherson
10 Berry	10 Scott	10 McPherson	10 Sawers	10 Walker
11 Barker	11 Keillor	11 Lambie	11 Divers	11 Lambie
Kilmarnock Mar 24: 5-2 *Berry, Barker, Chalmers Alexander, Johnstone*	Belfast Mar 31: 2-1 *Taylor, Torrans, og*	Glasgow April 7: 2-2 *Lambie, McMahon*	Wrexham Mar 23: 2-2 *Madden, Divers*	Glasgow Mar 30: 3-1 *Lambie, Walker 2*

1895 England	1896 Wales	1896 Ireland	1896 England	1897 Wales
1 McArthur	1 McFarlane	1 Anderson	1 Doig	1 Patrick
2 Drummond	2 McLean	2 Meechan	2 Brandon	2 Ritchie
3 Doyle	3 Glen	3 Drummond	3 Drummond	3 Gardner
4 Russell	4 Gillespie	4 Gibson	4 Gibson	4 Breslin
5 Simpson	5 Neil	5 Kelly	5 Cowan	5 Russell
6 Gibson	6 Blair	6 Hogg	6 Hogg	6 Keillor
7 Lambie	7 Thomson	7 Murray	7 Bell	7 Kennedy
8 McPherson	8 Paton	8 Blessington	8 Blessington	8 Murray
9 Oswald	9 McColl	9 McColl	9 Hyslop	9 Oswald
10 Waddell	10 King	10 Cameron	10 King	10 McMillan
11 Gulliland	11 Keillor	11 Lambie	11 Lambie	11 Walker
Liverpool April 6: 0-3	Dundee Mar 21: 4-0 *Neil 2, Keillor 2*	Belfast Mar 28: 3-3 *McColl 2, Drummond*	Glasgow April 4: 2-1 *Lambie, Bell*	Wrexham Mar 20: 2-2 *Ritchie (pen), Jones og*

1897 Ireland	1897 England	1898 Wales	1898 Ireland	1898 England
1 Dickie	1 Patrick	1 Watson	1 Anderson	1 Anderson
2 McLean	2 Smith N	2 Smith N	2 Kelso	2 Drummond
3 Drummond	3 Doyle	3 Scott	3 Doyle	3 Doyle
4 Gibson	4 Gibson	4 Thomson	4 Thomson	4 Gibson
5 Stewart	5 Cowan	5 Christie	5 Russell	5 Cowan
6 Baird	6 Wilson	6 Campbell P	6 King	6 Robertson
7 Low	7 Bell	7 Gillespie	7 Stewart	7 Bell
8 King	8 Miller	8 Miller	8 Campbell (Celtic)	8 Campbell (Celtic)
9 McColl	9 Allan	9 McKie	9 McColl	9 Maxwell
10 McPherson	10 Hyslop	10 Morgan	10 Walker	10 Miller
11 Lambie	11 Lambie	11 Findlay	11 Robertson	11 Smith A

Glasgow Mar 27: 5-1 *McPherson 2, Gibson, McColl, King*

London April 3: 2-1 *Hyslop, Miller*

Motherwell Mar 19: 5-2 *Gillespie 3, McKie 2*

Belfast Mar 26: 3-0 *Robertson, McColl, Stewart*

Glasgow April 2: **1**-3 *Miller*

1899 Wales	1899 Ireland	1899 England	1900 Wales	1900 Ireland
1 McArthur	1 Dickie	1 Doig	1 Dickie	1 Rennie
2 Smith N	2 Smith N	2 Smith N	2 Smith N	2 Smith N
3 Storrier	3 Storrier	3 Storrier	3 Crawford	3 Glen
4 Gibson	4 Gibson	4 Gibson	4 Irons	4 Marshall
5 Marshall	5 Christie	5 Christie	5 Neil	5 Orr
6 King	6 King	6 Robertson	6 Robertson	6 Gibson
7 Campbell (Rangers)	7 Campbell (Rangers)	7 Campbell (Rangers)	7 Bell	7 Stewart
8 Hamilton	8 Hamilton	8 Hamilton	8 Wilson	8 Walker
9 McColl	9 McColl	9 McColl	9 McColl	9 Campbell (Celtic)
10 Bell	10 Bell	10 Morgan	10 Hamilton	10 Callaghan
11 Berry	11 Berry	11 Bell	11 Smith A	11 Smith A

Wrexham Mar 18: 6-0 *Campbell 2, McColl 3, Marshall*

Glasgow Mar 25: 9-1 *McColl 3, Hamilton 2, Campbell 2, Bell, Christie*

Birmingham April 8: 1-2 *Hamilton*

Aberdeen Feb 3: 5-2 *Bell, Wilson 2, Hamilton, Smith A*

Belfast Mar 3: 3-0 *Campbell 2, Smith A*

1900 England	1901 Ireland	1901 Wales	1901 England	1902 Ireland
1 Rennie	1 McWhattie	1 McWhattie	1 Rennie	1 Rennie
2 Smith N	2 Smith N	2 Smith N	2 Battles	2 Smith N
3 Drummond	3 Battles	3 Battles	3 Drummond	3 Drummond
4 Gibson	4 Russell	3 Gibson	4 Aitken	4 Key
5 Raisbeck	5 Anderson	5 Russell	5 Raisbeck	5 Buick
6 Robertson	6 Robertson	6 Robertson	6 Robertson	6 Robertson
7 Walker	7 Campbell (Rangers)	7 Bell	7 Walker	7 McCartney
8 Campbell (Celtic)	8 Campbell (Celtic)	8 Walker	8 Campbell (Celtic)	8 Walker
9 McColl	9 Hamilton	9 McColl	9 McColl	9 Hamilton
10 Bell	10 McMahon	10 Campbell (Celtic)	10 Hamilton	10 Campbell (Celtic)
11 Smith A	11 Smith A	11 Smith A	11 Smith A	11 Smith A

Glasgow April 7: 4-1 *McColl 3, Bell*

Glasgow Feb 23: 11-0 *Campbell (Celtic) 2, McMahon 4, Hamilton 4, Russell*

Wrexham Mar 2: 1-1 *Robertson*

London Mar 30: 2-2 *Campbell, Hamilton*

Belfast Mar 1: 5-1 *Hamilton 3, Buick, Walker*

1902 Wales	1902 England	1903 Wales	1903 Wales	1903 England
1 Rennie	1 Rennie	1 Rennie	1 Rennie	1 Doig
2 Allan	2 Smith N	2 McCombie	2 Gray	2 McCombie
3 Drummond	3 Drummond	3 Watson	3 Drummond	3 Watson
4 Wilson	4 Aitken	4 Aitken	4 Cross	4 Aitken
5 Buick	5 Raisbeck	5 Raisbeck	5 Robertson	5 Raisbeck
6 Robertson	6 Robertson	6 Robertson	6 Orr	6 Robertson
7 Campbell (Celtic)	7 Templeton	7 Templeton	7 Lindsay	7 Templeton
8 Walker	8 Walker	8 Walker	8 Walker	8 Walker
9 Hamilton	9 McColl	9 Campbell (Celtic)	9 Porteous	9 Hamilton
10 McMahon	10 Orr	10 Speedie	10 Speedie	10 Speedie
11 Smith A	11 Smith A	11 Smith A	11 Smith A	11 Smith A
Greenock Mar 15: 5-1 *Smith 3, Buick, Drummond*	Birmingham May 3: 2-2 *Templeton, Orr*	Cardiff Mar 9: 1-0 *Speedie*	Glasgow Mar 21: 0-2	Sheffield April 4: 2-1 *Speedie, Walker*

1904 Wales	1904 Ireland	1904 England	1905 Wales	1905 Ireland
1 Skene	1 Rennie	1 McBride	1 Rennie	1 Howden
2 Jackson	2 Jackson	2 Jackson	2 McCombie	2 McLeod
3 Sharp	3 Cameron	3 Watson	3 Jackson	3 McIntosh
4 Orr	4 Henderson	4 Aitken	4 Aitken	4 Gibson
5 Sloan	5 Thomson	5 Raisbeck	5 Thomson	5 Thomson
6 Robertson	6 Robertson	6 Robertson	6 Robertson	6 Hay
7 Walker J	7 Walker J	7 Niblo	7 Templeton	7 McMenemy
8 Walker R	8 Walker R	8 Walker R	8 Walker R	8 Walker
9 Bennett	9 Hamilton	9 Brown A	9 Kennedy	9 Quinn
10 McFarlane	10 Wilson	10 Orr	10 Fitchie	10 Somers
11 Wilson	11 Smith A	11 Templeton	11 Smith A	11 Wilson
Dundee Mar 12: 1-1 *Walker R*	Dublin Mar 26: 1-1 *Hamilton*	Glasgow April 9: 0-1	Wrexham Mar 6: 1-3 *Robertson*	Glasgow Mar 18: 4-0 *Thomas 2 (2 pens), Walker, Quinn*

1905 England	1906 Wales	1906 Ireland	1906 England	1907 Wales
1 Lyall	1 Raeside	1 Rennie	1 McBride	1 McBride
2 McCombie	2 McLeod	2 McLeod	2 McLeod	2 Jackson
3 Watson	3 Richmond	3 Hill	3 Dunlop	3 Sharp
4 Aitken	4 McNair	4 Young	4 Aitken	4 Aitken
5 Thomson	5 Thomson	5 Thomson	5 Raisbeck	5 Thomson
6 McWilliam	6 Hay	6 May	6 McWilliam	6 McWilliam
7 Walker	7 Stewart	7 Hamilton	7 Stewart	7 Stewart
8 Howie	8 McFarlane	8 Walker R	8 Howie	8 Livingstone
9 Young	9 Quinn	9 Quinn	9 Menzies	9 Young
10 Somers	10 Fitchie	10 Fitchie	10 Livingstone	10 Fitchie
11 Wilson	11 Wilson	11 Smith A	11 Smith A	11 Smith A
London April 1: 0-1	Edinburgh Mar 3: 0-2	Dublin Mar 17: 1-0 *Fitchie*	Glasgow April 7: 2-1 *Howie 2*	Wrexham Mar 4: 0-1

1907 Ireland	1907 England	1908 Wales	1908 Ireland	1908 England
1 Muir	1 McBride	1 Rennie	1 Rennie	1 McBride
2 Jackson	2 Thomson	2 Agnew	2 Mitchell	2 McNair
3 Agnew	3 Sharp	3 Chaplin	3 Agnew	3 Sharp
4 Key	4 Aitken	4 McNair	4 May	4 Aitken
5 Thomson	5 Raisbeck	5 Thomson	5 Thomson	5 Thomson
6 McNair	6 McWilliam	6 Galt	6 Galt	6 May
7 Bennett	7 Bennett	7 Bennett	7 Templeton	7 Howie
8 Walker R	8 Walker R	8 Walker R	8 Walker R	8 Walker R
9 O'Rourke	9 Wilson A	9 Spiers	9 Quinn	9 Wilson A
10 Somers	10 White	10 McFarlane	10 McColl	10 White
11 Fraser	11 Wilson G	11 Lennie	11 Lennie	11 Quinn
Glasgow Mar 16: 3-0 O'Rourke, Walker, Thomson (pen)	Newcastle April 6: 1-1 Crompton, og	Dundee Mar 7: 2-1 Bennett, Lennie	Dublin Mar 14: 5-0 Quinn 4, Galt	Glasgow April 4: 1-1 Wilson

1909 Wales	1909 Ireland	1909 England	1910 Wales	1910 Ireland
1 McBride	1 Brownlie	1 Brownlie	1 Brownlie	1 Brownlie
2 Collins	2 Main	2 Cameron	2 Law	2 Law
3 Sharp	3 Watson	3 Watson	3 Mitchell	3 Mitchell
4 May	4 Walker W	4 McNair	4 McNair	4 Walker W
5 Thomson	5 Stark	5 Stark	5 Loney	5 Loney
6 McWilliam	6 Hay	6 McWilliam	6 Hay	6 Hay
7 Bennett	7 Bennett	7 Bennett	7 Bennett	7 Sinclair
8 Hunter	8 McMenemy	8 Walker R	8 McMenemy	8 McTavish
9 Walker R	9 Thomson	9 Quinn	9 Quinn	9 Quinn
10 Somers	10 McFarlane	10 Wilson G	10 Devine	10 Higgins
11 Paul	11 Paul	11 Paul	11 Robertson	11 Templeton
Wrexham Mar 1: 2-3 Walker, Paul	Glasgow Mar 15: 5-0 McMenemy 2, McFarlane, Thomson, Paul	London April 3: 0-2	Kilmarnock Mar 5: 1-0 Devine	Belfast Mar 19: 0-1

1910 England	1911 Wales	1911 Ireland	1911 England	1912 Wales
1 Brownlie	1 Brownlie	1 Brownlie	1 Lawrence	1 Brownlie
2 Law	2 Colman	2 Colman	2 Colman	2 McNair
3 Hay	3 Walker J	3 Walker J	3 Walker J	3 Walker J
4 Aitken	4 Tait	4 Aitken	4 Aitken	4 Mercer
5 Thomson	5 Low	5 Thomson	5 Low	5 Thomson
6 McWilliam	6 McWilliam	6 Hay	6 Hay	6 Hay
7 Bennett	7 Bennett	7 Douglas	7 Bennett	7 Sinclair
8 McMenemy	8 McMenemy	8 McMenemy	8 McMenemy	8 McMenemy
9 Quinn	9 Reid	9 Reid	9 Reid	9 Quinn
10 Higgins	10 McFarlane	10 Higgins	10 Higgins	10 Walker R
11 Templeton	11 Hamilton	11 Smith A	11 Smith A	11 Robertson
Glasgow April 2: 2-0 McMenemy, Quinn	Cardiff Mar 6: 2-2 Hamilton 2	Glasgow Mar 18: 2-0 Reid, McMemeny	Liverpool April 1: 1-1 Higgins	Edinburgh Mar 2: 1-0 Quinn

1912 Ireland	1912 England	1913 Wales	1913 Ireland	1913 England
1 Brownlie	1 Brownlie	1 Brownlie	1 Brownlie	1 Brownlie
2 McNair	2 McNair	2 Orrock	2 Colman	2 McNair
3 Walker J	3 Walker J	3 Walker J	3 Walker J	3 Walker J
4 Gordon	4 Gordon	4 Gordon	4 Mercer	4 Gordon
5 Low	5 Thomson	5 Thomson	5 Logan	5 Thomson
6 Bell	6 Hay	6 Campbell	6 Nellies	6 Wilson D
7 Sinclair	7 Templeton	7 McAtee	7 Bennett	7 Donnachie
8 Walker R	8 Walker R	8 Walker R	8 Gordon	8 Wilson R
9 Reid	9 McLean	9 Reid	9 Reid	9 Reid
10 Aitkenhead	10 Wilson A	10 Wilson A	10 Croal	10 Wilson A
11 Templeton	11 Quinn	11 Templeton	11 Robertson	11 Robertson
Belfast Mar 16: 4-1 *Aitkenhead 2, Reid, Walker R*	Glasgow Mar 23: 1-1 *Wilson*	Wrexham Mar 3: 0-0	Dublin Mar 15: 2-1 *Reid, Bennett*	Stamford Bridge April 5: 0-1

1914 Wales	1914 Ireland	1914 England	1920 Wales	1920 Ireland
1 Brownlie	1 Brownlie	1 Brownlie	1 Campbell	1 Campbell
2 Kelso	2 Dodds	2 McNair	2 McNair	2 McNair
3 Dodds	3 McNair	3 Dodds	3 Thomson	3 Blair
4 Nellies	4 Gordon	4 Gordon	4 Gordon	4 Bowie
5 Pursell	5 Thomson	5 Thomson	5 Cringen	5 Low
6 Anderson	6 Hay	6 Hay	6 McMullen	6 Gordon
7 Donaldson	7 Donaldson	7 Donaldson	7 Reid	7 Donaldson
8 McMenemy	8 McMenemy	8 McMenemy	8 Crosby	8 McMenemy
9 Reid	9 Reid	9 Reid	9 Wilson A N	9 Wilson A N
10 Croal	10 Wilson A	10 Croal	10 Cairns	10 Cunningham
11 Browning	11 Donnachie	11 Donnachie	11 Morton	11 Morton
Glasgow Feb 28: 0-0	Belfast Mar 14: 1-1 *Donnachie*	Glasgow April 4: 3-1 *Thomson, McMenemy, Reid*	Cardiff Feb 26: 1-1 *Cairns*	Glasgow Mar 13: 3-0 *Wilson, Morton, Cunningham*

1920 England	1921 Wales	1921 Ireland	1921 England	1922 Wales
1 Campbell	1 Campbell	1 Campbell	1 Ewart	1 Campbell
2 McNair	2 Marshall	2 Marshall	2 Marshall	2 Marshall
3 Blair	3 McStey	3 McStey	3 Blair	3 McKinlay
4 Bowie	4 Harris	4 Harris	4 Davidson	4 Meiklejohn
5 Low	5 Pringle	5 Graham	5 Brewster	5 Gilhooley
6 Gordon	6 McMullen	6 McMullen	6 McMullen	6 Collier
7 Donaldson	7 Archibald	7 McNab	7 McNab	7 Archibald
8 Miller	8 Cunningham	8 Miller	8 Miller	8 White
9 Wilson A N	9 Wilson A N	9 Wilson A N	9 Wilson A N	9 Wilson A N
10 Paterson	10 Cassidy	10 Cassidy	10 Cunningham	10 Walker F
11 Troup	11 Troup	11 Troup	11 Morton	11 Morton
Sheffield April 10: 4-5 *Miller 2 Wilson Donaldson*	Aberdeen Feb 12: 2-1 *Wilson 2*	Belfast Feb 26: 2-0 *Wilson* (pen) *Cassidy*	Glasgow April 9: 3-0 *Wilson, Morton, Cunningham*	Wrexham Feb 4: 1-2 *Archibald*

1922 Ireland	1922 England	1923 Ireland	1923 Wales	1923 England
1 Campbell	1 Campbell	1 Harper	1 Harper	1 Harper
2 Marshall	2 Marshall	2 Hutton	2 Hutton	2 Hutton
3 McKinlay	3 Blair	3 Blair	3 Blair	3 Blair
4 Hogg	4 Gilchrist	4 Steele	4 McNab	4 Steele
5 Cringan	5 Cringan	5 Morris	5 Cringan	5 Cringan
6 Muirhead	6 McBain	6 McBain	6 Steele	6 Muirhead
7 Donaldson	7 Archibald	7 Archibald	7 Ritchie	7 Lawson
8 Kinloch	8 Crosbie	8 White	8 Cunningham	8 Cunningham
9 Wilson A N	9 Wilson A N	9 Wilson A N	9 Wilson A N	9 Wilson A N
10 Cunningham	10 Cairns	10 Cassidy	10 Cairns	10 Cairns
11 Troup	11 Morton	11 Morton	11 Morton	11 Morton
Glasgow Mar 4: 2-1 *Wilson 2*	Birmingham April 8: 1-0 *Wilson*	Belfast Mar 3: 1-0 *Wilson*	Glasgow Mar 17: 2-0 *Wilson 2*	Glasgow April 14: 2-2 *Cunningham, Wilson*

1924 Wales	1924 Ireland	1924 England	1925 Wales	1925 Ireland
1 Harper	1 Harper	1 Harper	1 Harper	1 Harper
2 Marshall	2 Hutton	2 Smith J	2 Nelson	2 Nelson
3 Blair	3 Hamilton	3 McCloy	3 McStay	3 McStay
4 Meiklejohn	4 Kerr	4 Clunas	4 Meiklejohn	4 Meiklejohn
5 McBain	5 Morris	5 Morris	5 Morris	5 Morris
6 Muirhead	6 McMullan	6 McMullan	6 Bennie	6 Bennie
7 Archibald	7 Reid	7 Archibald	7 Jackson	7 Jackson
8 Russell	8 Cunningham	8 Cowan	8 Dunn	8 Dunn
9 Cassidy	9 Gallacher	9 Harris	9 Gallacher	9 Gallacher
10 McKay	10 Cairns	10 Cunningham	10 Cairns	10 Cairns
11 Morton	11 Morton	11 Morton	11 Morton	11 Morton
Cardiff Feb 16: 0-2	Glasgow Mar 1: 2-0 *Cunningham, Morris*	Wembley April 12: 1-1 *Taylor, og*	Edinburgh Feb 14: 3-1 *Meiklejohn, Gallacher 2*	Belfast Feb 28: 3-0 *Meiklejohn, Gallacher, Dunn*

1925 England	1925 Wales	1926 Ireland	1926 England	1926 Wales
1 Harper	1 Robb	1 Harper	1 Harper	1 McClory
2 McStay	2 Hutton	2 Hutton	2 Hutton	2 McStay
3 McCloy	3 McStay	3 McStay	3 McStay	3 Wiseman
4 Meiklejohn	4 Clunas	4 Wilson	4 Gibson	4 Gibson
5 Morris	5 Townsley	5 McDougall	5 Summers	5 Gillespie
6 McMullan	6 McMullan	6 Bennie	6 McMullan	6 McMullan
7 Jackson	7 Jackson	7 Jackson	7 Jackson	7 Jackson
8 Russell	8 Duncan	8 Cunningham	8 Thomson	8 Cunningham
9 Gallacher	9 Gallacher	9 Gallacher	9 Gallacher	9 Gallacher
10 Cairns	10 James	10 McInally	10 Cunningham	10 McInally
11 Morton	11 McLean	11 McLean	11 Troup	11 McLean
Glasgow April 4: 2-0 *Gallacher 2*	Cardiff Oct 31: 3-0 *Duncan, McLean, Clunas*	Glasgow Feb 27: 4-0 *Gallacher 3, Cunningham*	Manchester April 17: 1-0 *Jackson*	Glasgow Oct 30: 3-0 *Gallacher, Jackson 2*

1927 Ireland	1927 England	1927 Wales	1928 Ireland	1928 England
1 Harkness	1 Harkness	1 Robb	1 McClory	1 Harkness
2 Hutton	2 McStay	2 Hutton	2 Hutton	2 Nelson
3 McStay	3 Thomson	3 McStay	3 McStay	3 Law
4 Muirhead	4 Morrison	4 Meiklejohn	4 Muirhead	4 Gibson
5 Gibson	5 Gibson	5 Gibson	5 Meiklejohn	5 Bradshaw
6 Craig	6 McMullan	6 McMullan	6 Craig	6 McMullan
7 Jackson	7 McLean	7 Jackson	7 Ritchie	7 Jackson
8 Dunn	8 Cunningham	8 McKay	8 Dunn	8 Dunn
9 Gallacher	9 Gallacher	9 Gallacher	9 McGrory	9 Gallacher
10 Howieson	10 McPhail	10 Stevenson	10 Stevenson	10 James
11 Morton	11 Morton	11 Morton	11 Morton	11 Morton
Belfast Feb 26: 2-0 *Morton 2*	Glasgow April 2: 1-2 *Morton*	Wrexham Oct 29: 2-2 *Gallacher, Hutton*(pen)	Glasgow Feb 25: 0-1	Wembley Mar 31: 5-1 *Jackson 3, James, Gibson*

1928 Wales	1929 Ireland	1929 England	1929 Norway	1929 Germany
1 Harkness	1 Harkness	1 Harkness	1 McLaren	1 McLaren
2 Gray	2 Gray	2 Crapnell	2 Crapnell	2 Gray
3 Blair	3 Blair	3 Nibloe	3 Nibloe	3 Crapnell
4 Muirhead	4 Muirhead	4 Buchanan	4 Imrie	4 Morton
5 King	5 Meiklejohn	5 Meiklejohn	5 Craig A	5 Imrie
6 McMullan	6 McMullan	6 McMullan	6 Craig T	6 Craig T
7 Jackson	7 Jackson	7 Jackson	7 Nisbet	7 Nisbet
8 Dunn	8 Chalmers	8 Cheyne	8 Cheyne	8 Cheyne
9 Gallacher	9 Gallacher	9 Gallacher	9 McCrae	9 McCrae
10 McPhail	10 James	10 James	10 Rankin	10 Rankin
11 Morton	11 Morton	11 Morton	11 Howe	11 Fleming
Glasgow Oct 27: 4-2 *Gallacher 3, Dunn*	Belfast Feb 23: 7-3 *Gallacher 4, Jackson 2, James*	Glasgow April 13: 1-0 *Cheyne*	Bergen May 26: 7-3 *Cheyne 3, Nisbet 2, Craig T, Rankin*	Berlin June 1: 1-1 *Imrie*

1929 Holland	1929 Wales	1930 Ireland	1930 England	1930 France
1 McClaren	1 Harkness	1 Middleton	1 Harkness	1 Thomson
2 Gray	2 Gray	2 Gray	2 Gray	2 Nelson
3 Nibloe	3 Nibloe	3 Wiseman	3 Law	3 Crapnell
4 Morton	4 Gibson	4 Gibson	4 Buchanan	4 Wilson
5 Craig A	5 Johnstone	5 Meiklejohn	5 Meiklejohn	5 Walker
6 Craig T	6 Craig	6 Craig	6 Craig	6 Hill
7 Nisbet	7 Jackson	7 Jackson	7 Jackson	7 Jackson
8 Cheyne	8 Muirhead	8 Stevenson	8 James	8 Cheyne
9 Fleming	9 Gallacher	9 Gallacher	9 Fleming	9 Gallacher
10 Rankin	10 James	10 James	10 Stevenson	10 Stevenson
11 Howe	11 Morton	11 Morton	11 Morton	11 Connor
Amsterdam June 4: 2-0 *Fleming, Rankin*	Cardiff Oct 26: 4-2 *Gallacher 2, James, Gibson*	Glasgow Feb 22: 3-1 *Gallacher 2, Stevenson*	Wembley April 5: 2-5 *Fleming 2*	Paris May 18: 2-0 *Gallacher 2*

1930 Wales	1931 Ireland	1931 England	1931 Austria	1931 Italy
1 Thomson	1 Thomson	1 Thomson	1 Jackson	1 Jackson
2 Gray	2 Crapnell	2 Blair	2 Blair	2 Blair
3 Gilmour	3 Nibloe	3 Nibloe	3 Nibloe	3 Nibloe
4 McNab	4 Wilson P	4 McNab	4 McNab	4 McNab
5 Gillespie	5 Walker	5 Meiklejohn	5 McDougal	5 McDougal
6 Hill	6 Hill	6 Miller	6 Miller	6 Miller
7 McRorie	7 Murdoch	7 Archibald	7 Love	7 Love
8 Brown G	8 Scarff	8 Stevenson	8 Paterson	8 Paterson
9 Battles	9 Yorston	9 McGrory	9 Boyd	9 Boyd
10 Stevenson	10 McPhail	10 McPhail	10 Robertson	10 Robertson
11 Morton	11 Morton	11 Morton	11 Liddell D	11 Liddell D
Glasgow Oct 25: 1-1 *Battles*	Belfast Feb 21: 0-0	Glasgow Mar 28: 2-0 *Stevenson, McGrory*	Vienna May 16: 0-5	Rome May 20: 0-3

1931 Switzerland	1931 Ireland	1931 Wales	1932 England	1932 France
1 Jackson	1 Hepburn	1 Harkness	1 Hamilton T	1 Harkness
2 Crapnell	2 Blair	2 Blair	2 Crapnell	2 Crapnell
3 Nibloe	3 McAulay	3 McAulay	3 Nibloe	3 Nibloe
4 McNab	4 Massie	4 Massie	4 McNab	4 Massie
5 Walker G	5 Meiklejohn	5 Meiklejohn	5 Craig	5 Gillespie
6 Miller	6 Brown G	6 Brown G	6 Brown G	6 Miller
7 Love	7 Crawford	7 Thomson R	7 Archibald	7 Crawford
8 Paterson	8 Stevenson	8 Stevenson	8 Marshall	8 Thomson A
9 Boyd	9 McGrory	9 McGrory	9 Dewar	9 Dewar
10 Easson	10 McPhail	10 McPhail	10 Napier	10 McPhail
11 Liddell D	11 Connor	11 Morton	11 Morton	11 Morton
Geneva May 24: 3-2 *Easson, Boyd, Love*	Glasgow Sept 19: 3-1 *Stevenson, McGrory, McPhail*	Wrexham Oct 31: 3-2 *Stevenson, Thomson, McGrory*	Wembley April 9: 0-3	Paris May 8: 3-1 *Dewar 3*

1932 Ireland	1932 Wales	1933 England	1933 Ireland	1933 Wales
1 McLaren	1 McLaren	1 Jackson	1 Harkness	1 Kennaway
2 Gray	2 Gray	2 Anderson	2 Anderson	2 Anderson
3 Crapnell	3 Blair	3 McGonagle	3 McGonagle	3 Urquhart
4 Massie	4 Wales	4 Wilson P	4 Massie	4 Busby
5 Johnstone	5 Johnstone	5 Gillespie	5 Lowe	5 Blair
6 Telfer	6 Thomson J	6 Brown G	6 Telfer	6 McLuckie
7 Crawford	7 Crawford	7 Crawford	7 Boyd	7 McGurk
8 Stevenson	8 Thomson A	8 Marshall	8 Venters	8 McMenemy
9 McGrory	9 Dewar	9 McGrory	9 McGrory	9 McFadyen
10 McPhail	10 James	10 McPhail	10 McPhail	10 Easson
11 King	11 Duncan	11 Duncan	11 King	11 Duncan
Belfast Sept 19: 4-0 *McPhail 2, King, McGrory*	Edinburgh Oct 26: 2-5 *Dewar, Duncan*	Glasgow April 1: 2-1 *McGrory 2*	Glasgow Sept 16: 1-2 *McPhail*	Cardiff Oct 4: 2-3 *Duncan, McFadyen*

1933 Austria	1934 England	1934 Ireland	1934 Wales	1935 England
1 Kennaway	1 Jackson	1 Dawson	1 McClory	1 Jackson
2 Anderson	2 Anderson	2 Anderson	2 Anderson	2 Anderson
3 McGonagle	3 McGonagle	3 McGonagle	3 McGonagle	3 Cummings
4 Meiklejohn	4 Massie	4 Massie	4 Massie	4 Massie
5 Watson P	5 Smith T	5 Simpson	5 Simpson	5 Simpson
6 Brown G	6 Miller	6 Herd	6 Brown G	6 Brown G
7 Ogilvie	7 Cook	7 Cook	7 Cook	7 Napier
8 Bruce	8 Marshall	8 Stevenson	8 Walker T	8 Walker T
9 McFadyen	9 Gallacher	9 Smith J	9 McCulloch	9 Gallacher
10 McPhail	10 Stevenson	10 Gallacher	10 Napier	10 McPhail
11 Duncan	11 Connor	11 Connor	11 Duncan	11 Duncan
Glasgow Nov 29: 2-2 *Meiklejohn, McFadyen*	Wembley April 14: 0-3	Belfast Oct 20: 1-2 *Gallacher*	Aberdeen Nov 21: 3-2 *Duncan, Napier 2*	Glasgow April 6: 2-0 *Duncan 2*

1935 Wales	1935 Ireland	1936 England	1936 Germany	1936 Ireland
1 Jackson	1 Jackson	1 Dawson	1 Dawson	1 Dawson
2 Anderson	2 Anderson	2 Anderson	2 Anderson	2 Anderson
3 Cummings	3 Cummings	3 Cummings	3 Cummings	3 Ancell
4 Massie	4 Massie	4 Massie	4 Massie	4 Massie
5 Simpson	5 Simpson	5 Simpson	5 Simpson	5 Simpson
6 Brown G	6 Hastings	6 Brown G	6 Brown G	6 Brown G
7 Delaney	7 Delaney	7 Crum	7 Delaney	7 Munro
8 Walker T	8 Walker T	8 Walker T	8 Walker T	8 Walker T
9 Armstrong	9 Armstrong	9 McCulloch	9 Armstrong	9 McCulloch
10 Mills	10 Mills	10 Venters	10 McPhail	10 Napier
11 Duncan	11 Duncan	11 Duncan	11 Duncan	11 Duncan
Cardiff Oct 5: 1-1 *Duncan*	Edinburgh Nov 13: 2-1 *Walker, Duncan*	Wembley April 4: 1-1 *Walker*	Glasgow Oct 14: 2-0 *Delaney 2*	Belfast Oct 31: 3-1 *Napier, Munro, McCulloch*

1936 Wales	1937 England	1937 Austria	1937 Czechoslovakia	1937 Wales
1 Dawson	1 Dawson	1 Dawson	1 Dawson	1 Dawson
2 Anderson	2 Anderson	2 Anderson	2 Hogg	2 Anderson
3 Ancell	3 Beattie	3 Beattie	3 Beattie	3 Cummings
4 Massie	4 Massie	4 Massie	4 Thomson	4 Massie
5 Simpson	5 Simpson	5 Simpson	5 Simpson	5 Simpson
6 Brown G	6 Brown G	6 McNab	6 Brown G	6 Brown G
7 Munro	7 Delaney	7 Delaney	7 Delaney	7 Main
8 Walker T	8 Walker T	8 Walker T	8 Walker T	8 Walker T
9 McCulloch	9 O'Donnell F	9 O'Donnell F	9 O'Donnell F	9 O'Donnell F
10 Mills	10 McPhail	10 Napier	10 McPhail	10 McPhail
11 Duncan	11 Duncan	11 Gillick	11 Gillick	11 Duncan
Dundee Dec 2: 1-2 *Walker*	Glasgow April 17: 3-1 *O'Donnell, McPhail 2*	Vienna May 9: 1-1 *O'Donnell*	Prague May 22: 3-1 *Simpson, McPhail, Gillick*	Cardiff Oct 30: 1-2 *Massie*

1937 Ireland	1937 Czechoslovakia	1938 England	1938 Holland	1938 Ireland
1 Dawson	1 Waugh	1 Cumming	1 Dawson	1 Dawson
2 Anderson	2 Anderson	2 Anderson	2 Anderson	2 Carabine
3 Cummings	3 Cummings	3 Beattie	3 Carabine	3 Beattie A
4 McKenzie	4 Robertson	4 Shankly	4 McKillop	4 Shankly
5 Simpson	5 Johnston	5 Smith T	5 Dykes	5 Dykes
6 Hastings	6 Brown G	6 Brown G	6 Brown G	6 Paterson
7 Delaney	7 Buchanan	7 Milne	7 Munro	7 Delaney
8 Walker T	8 Walker T	8 Walker T	8 Walker T	8 Walker T
9 Smith J	9 McCulloch	9 O'Donnell F	9 O'Donnell F	9 Crum
10 McPhail	10 Black	10 Mutch	10 Black	10 Divers
11 Reid	11 Kinnear	11 Reid	11 Murphy	11 Gillick
Aberdeen Nov 10: 1-1 *Smith*	Glasgow Dec 8: 5-0 *McCulloch 2, Black, Buchanan, Kinnear*	Wembley April 9: 1-0 *Walker*	Amsterdam May 21: 3-1 *Black, Murphy, Walker*	Belfast Oct 8: 2-0 *Delaney, Walker*

1938 Wales	1938 Hungary	1939 England	1946 Wales	1946 N Ireland
1 Brown J	1 Dawson	1 Dawson	1 Miller	1 Brown
2 Anderson	2 Anderson	2 Carabine	2 Stephen	2 Young
3 Beattie A	3 Beattie A	3 Cummings	3 Shaw D	3 Shaw D
4 Shankly	4 Shankly	4 Shankly	4 Brown	4 Campbell
5 Baxter	5 Baxter	5 Baxter	5 Brennan	5 Brennan
6 Miller	6 Symon	6 McNab	6 Husband	6 Long
7 Delaney	7 McSpadyen	7 McSpadyen	7 Waddell	7 Smith
8 Walker	8 Walker T	8 Walker T	8 Dougall	8 Hamilton
9 McCulloch	9 McCulloch	9 Dougall	9 Thornton	9 Thornton
10 Beattie R	10 Black	10 Venters	10 Blair	10 Duncanson
11 Gillick	11 Gillick	11 Milne	11 Liddell	11 Liddell
Edinburgh Nov 9: 3-2 *Walker 2, Gillick*	Glasgow Dec 7: 3-1 *Black, Walker Gillick*	Glasgow April 15: 1-2 *Dougall*	Wrexham Oct 19: 1-3 *Waddell*	Hampden Nov 27: 0-0

1947 England	1947 Belgium	1947 Luxembourg	1947 N Ireland	1947 Wales
1 Miller	1 Miller	1 Miller	1 Miller	1 Miller
2 Young	2 Young	2 Young	2 Young	2 Govan
3 Shaw J	3 Shaw J	3 Shaw J	3 Shaw J	3 Stephen
4 Macaulay	4 Brown	4 Brown	4 Macaulay	4 Macaulay
5 Woodburn	5 Woodburn	5 Woodburn	5 Woodburn	5 Woodburn
6 Forbes	6 Forbes	6 Forbes	6 Forbes	6 Forbes
7 Smith	7 Campbell	7 McFarlane	7 Delaney	7 Smith
8 McLaren	8 McLaren	8 McLaren	8 Watson	8 McLaren
9 Delaney	9 Flavell	9 Flavell	9 Thornton	9 Delaney
10 Steel	10 Steel	10 Steel	10 Steel	10 Steel
11 Pearson	11 Pearson	11 Campbell	11 Liddell	11 Liddell
Wembley April 12: 1-1 *McLaren*	Brussels May 18: 1-2 *Steel*	Luxembourg May 24: 6-0 *McLaren 2, Steel 2, Flavell 2*	Belfast Oct 4: 0-2	Hampden Nov 12 :1-2 *McLaren*

1948 England	1948 Belgium	1948 Switzerland	1948 France	1948 Wales
1 Black	1 Cowan	1 Cowan	1 Cowan	1 Cowan
2 Govan	2 Govan	2 Govan	2 Govan	2 Howie
3 Shaw D	3 Shaw D	3 Shaw D	3 Shaw D	3 Shaw D
4 Campbell	4 Campbell	4 Campbell	4 Campbell	4 Evans
5 Young	5 Young	5 Young	5 Young	5 Young
6 Macaulay	6 Macaulay	6 Macaulay	6 Macaulay	6 Redpath
7 Delaney	7 Smith	7 Smith	7 Rutherford	7 Waddell
8 Combe	8 Combe	8 Combe	8 Steel	8 Mason
9 Thornton	9 Johnstone	9 Johnstone	9 Smith	9 Reilly
10 Steel	10 Turnbull	10 Turnbull	10 Cox	10 Steel
11 Liddell	11 Duncan	11 Duncan	11 Duncan	11 Kelly
Hampden April 10: 0-2	Hampden April 28: 2-0 *Combe, Duncan*	Berne May 17: 1-2 *Johnstone*	Paris May 23: 0-3	Cardiff Oct 23: 3-1 *Howie, Waddell 2*

1948 N Ireland	1949 England	1949 France	1949 N Ireland	1949 Wales
1 Brown	1 Cowan	1 Cowan	1 Cowan	1 Cowan
2 Govan	2 Young	2 Young	2 Young	2 Young
3 Shaw D	3 Cox	3 Cox	3 Cox	3 Cox
4 Evans	4 Evans	4 Evans	4 Evans	4 Evans
5 Young	5 Woodburn	5 Woodburn	5 Woodburn	5 Woodburn
6 Redpath	6 Aitken	6 Aitken	6 Aitken	6 Aitken
7 Waddell	7 Waddell	7 Waddell	7 Waddell	7 Liddell
8 Mason	8 Mason	8 Thornton	8 Mason	8 McPhail
9 Houliston	9 Houliston	9 Houliston	9 Morris	9 Linwood
10 Steel	10 Steel	10 Steel	10 Steel	10 Steel
11 Kelly	11 Reilly	11 Reilly	11 Reilly	11 Reilly
Hampden Nov 17: 3-2 *Houliston 2, Mason*	Wembley April 9: 3-1 *Mason, Steel, Reilly*	Hampden April 27: 2-0 *Steel 2*	Belfast Oct 1: 8-2 *Morris 3, Waddell 2, McPhail, Linwood Steel, Reilly, Mason*	Hampden Nov 9: 2-0

1950 England	1950 Switzerland	1950 Portugal	1950 France	1950 Wales
1 Cowan	1 Cowan	1 Cowan	1 Cowan	1 Cowan
2 Young	2 Young	2 Young	2 Young	2 Young
3 Cox	3 Cox	3 Cox	3 Cox	3 McNaught
4 McColl	4 Evans	4 Evans	4 McColl	4 McColl
5 Woodburn	5 Dougan	5 Woodburn	5 Woodburn	5 Woodburn
6 Forbes	6 Aitken	6 Forbes	6 Forbes	6 Forbes
7 Waddell	7 Campbell	7 Campbell	7 Campbell	7 Collins
8 Moir	8 Brown	8 Brown	8 Brown	8 McPhail
9 Bauld	9 Bauld	9 Bauld	9 Reilly	9 Reilly
10 Steel	10 Steel	10 Steel	10 Steel	10 Steel
11 Liddell	11 Reilly	11 Liddell	11 Liddell	11 Liddell
Hampden April 15: 0-1	Hampden April 26: 3-1 *Bauld, Campbell, Brown*	Lisbon May 25: 2-2 *Brown, Bauld*	Paris May 27: 1-0 *Brown*	Cardiff Oct 21: 3-1 *Reilly 2, Liddell*

843

1950 N Ireland	1950 Austria	1951 England	1951 Denmark	1951 France
1 Cowan	1 Cowan	1 Cowan	1 Cowan	1 Cowan
2 Young	2 Young	2 Young	2 Young	2 Young
3 McNaught	3 McNaught	3 Cox	3 Cox	3 Cox
4 McColl	4 Evans	4 Evans	4 Scoular	4 Scoular
5 Woodburn	5 Woodburn	5 Woodburn	5 Woodburn	5 Woodburn
6 Forbes	6 Forbes	6 Redpath	6 Redpath	6 Redpath
7 Collins	7 Collins	7 Waddell	7 Waddell	7 Waddell
8 Mason	8 Turnbull	8 Johnstone	8 Johnstone	8 Johnstone
9 McPhail	9 McPhail	9 Reilly	9 Reilly	9 Reilly
10 Steel	10 Steel	10 Steel	10 Steel	10 Steel
11 Liddell	11 Liddell	11 Liddell	11 Mitchell	11 Mitchell
Hampden Nov 1: 6-1 McPhail 2, Steel 4	Hampden Dec 13: 0-1	Wembley April 14: 3-2 Johnstone, Reilly, Liddell	Hampden May 12: 3-1 Steel, Reilly, Mitchell	Hampden May 16: 1-0 Reilly

1951 Belgium	1951 Austria	1951 N Ireland	1951 Wales	1952 England
1 Cowan	1 Cowan	1 Cowan	1 Cowan	1 Brown
2 Young	2 Young	2 Young	2 Young	2 Young
3 Cox	3 Cox	3 Cox	3 Cox	3 McNaught
4 McColl	4 Scoular	4 Evans	4 Docherty	4 Scoular
5 Woodburn	5 Woodburn	5 Woodburn	5 Woodburn	5 Woodburn
6 Redpath	6 Redpath	6 Redpath	6 Forbes	6 Redpath
7 Waddell	7 Waddell	7 Waddell	7 Waddell	7 Smith
8 Mason	8 Mason	8 Johnstone	8 Orr	8 Johnstone
9 Hamilton	9 Hamilton	9 Reilly	9 Reilly	9 Reilly
10 Steel	10 Steel	10 Orr	10 Steel	10 McMillan
11 Reilly	11 Reilly	11 Liddell	11 Liddell	11 Liddell
Brussels May 20: 5-0 Hamilton 3, Mason, Waddell	Vienna May 27: 0-4	Belfast Oct 6: 3-0 Johnstone 2, Orr	Hampden Nov 28: 0-1	Hampden April 5: 1-2 Reilly

1952 USA	1952 Denmark	1952 Sweden	1952 Wales	1952 N Ireland
1 Cowan	1 Cowan	1 Cowan	1 Farm	1 Farm
2 Young	2 Young	2 Young	2 Young	2 Young
3 Cox	3 Cox	3 Cox	3 Cox	3 Cox
4 Scoular	4 Scoular	4 Scoular	4 Scoular	4 Scoular
5 Woodburn	5 Paton	5 Paton	5 Brennan	5 Brennan
6 Kelly	6 Forbes	6 Forbes	6 Aitken	6 Aitken
7 Smith	7 Reilly	7 Reilly	7 Wright T	7 Wright T
8 McMillan	8 McMillan	8 Humphries	8 Brown	8 Logie
9 Reilly	9 Thornton	9 Thornton	9 Reilly	9 Reilly
10 Brown	10 Brown	10 Brown	10 Steel	10 Steel
11 Liddell	11 Liddell	11 Liddell	11 Liddell	11 Liddell
Hampden April 30: 6-0 Reilly 3, McMillan 2, opponent (og)	Copenhagen May 25: 2-1 Thornton, Reilly	Stockholm May 30: 1-3 Liddell	Cardiff Oct 15: 2-1 Brown, Liddell	Hampden Nov 5: 1-1 Reilly

1953 England	1953 Sweden	1953 N Ireland	1953 Wales	1954 England
1 Farm	1 Farm	1 Farm	1 Farm	1 Farm
2 Young	2 Young	2 Young	2 Young	2 Haughney
3 Cox	3 Little	3 Cox	3 Cox	3 Cox
4 Docherty	4 Evans	4 Evans	4 Evans	4 Evans
5 Brennan	5 Cowie	5 Brennan	5 Telfer	5 Brennan
6 Cowie	6 Docherty	6 Cowie	6 Cowie	6 Aitken
7 Wright T	7 Henderson	7 Waddell	7 McKenzie	7 McKenzie
8 Johnstone	8 Johnstone	8 Fleming	8 Johnstone	8 Johnstone
9 Reilly	9 Reilly	9 McPhail	9 Reilly	9 Henderson
10 Steel	10 Steel	10 Watson	10 Brown	10 Brown
11 Liddell	11 Ring	11 Henderson	11 Liddell	11 Ormond
Wembley April 18: 2-2 *Reilly 2*	Hampden May 6: 1-2 *Johnstone*	Belfast Oct 3: 3-1 *Fleming 2, Henderson*	Hampden Nov 4: 3-3 *Brown, Johnstone, Reilly*	Hampden April 3: 2-4 *Brown, opponent (og)*

1954 Norway	1954 Norway	1954 Finland	1954 Austria	1954 Uruguay
1 Martin	1 Martin	1 Anderson	1 Martin	1 Martin
2 Cunningham	2 Cunningham	2 Wilson	2 Cunningham	2 Cunningham
3 Aird	3 Aird	3 Cunningham	3 Aird	3 Aird
4 Docherty	4 Docherty	4 Evans	4 Docherty	4 Docherty
5 Davidson	5 Davidson	5 Cowie	5 Davidson	5 Davidson
6 Evans	6 Cowie	6 Mathers	6 Cowie	6 Cowie
7 Johnstone	7 McKenzie	7 McKenzie	7 McKenzie	7 McKenzie
8 Hamilton	8 Hamilton	8 Johnstone	8 Fernie	8 Fernie
9 Buckley	9 Henderson	9 Brown	9 Mochan	9 Mochan
10 Brown	10 Brown	10 Fernie	10 Brown	10 Brown
11 Ormond	11 Mochan	11 Ormond	11 Ormond	11 Ormond
Hampden May 5: 1-0 *Hamilton*	Oslo May 19: 1-1 *McKenzie*	Helsinki May 25: 2-1 *Ormond, Johnstone*	Zurich June 16: 0-1	Basle June 19: 0-7

1954 Wales	1954 N Ireland	1954 Hungary	1955 England	1955 Portugal
1 Fraser	1 Fraser	1 Martin	1 Martin	1 Younger
2 Young	2 Young	2 Cunningham	2 Cunningham	2 Parker
3 Cunningham	3 McNaught	3 Haddock	3 Haddock	3 Haddock
4 Docherty	4 Evans	4 Docherty	4 Docherty	4 Evans
5 Davidson	5 Davidson	5 Davidson	5 Davidson	5 Young
6 Cowie	6 Cowie	6 Cumming	6 Cumming	6 Cumming
7 Waddell	7 Waddell	7 McKenzie	7 McKenzie	7 Smith
8 Yorston	8 Johnstone	8 Johnstone	8 Johnstone	8 Robertson
9 Buckley	9 Buckley	9 Reilly	9 Reilly	9 Reilly
10 Fernie	10 Fernie	10 Wardhaugh	10 McMillan	10 Gemmell
11 Ring	11 Ring	11 Ring	11 Ring	11 Liddell
Cardiff Oct 16: 1-0 *Buckley*	Hampden Nov 3: 2-2 *Davidson, Johnstone*	Hampden Dec 8: 2-4 *Ring, Johnstone*	Wembley April 2: 2-7 *Reilly, Docherty*	Hampden May 16: 3-0 *Reilly, Gemmell, Liddell*

1955 Yugoslavia	1955 Austria	1955 Hungary	1955 N Ireland	1955 Wales
1 Younger	1 Younger	1 Younger	1 Younger	1 Younger
2 Parker	2 Parker	2 Kerr	2 Parker	2 Parker
3 Haddock	3 Kerr	3 Haddock	3 McDonald	3 McDonald
4 Evans	4 Docherty	4 Docherty	4 Evans	4 Evans
5 Young	5 Evans	5 Evans	5 Young	5 Young
6 Cumming	6 Cowie	6 Cowie	6 Glen	6 Cowie
7 Smith	7 Smith	7 Smith	7 Smith	7 Smith
8 Collins	8 Collins	8 Collins	8 Collins	8 Johnstone
9 Reilly	9 Reilly	9 Reilly	9 Reilly	9 Reilly
10 Gemmell	10 Robertson	10 Robertson	10 Johnstone	10 Collins
11 Liddell	11 Liddell	11 Liddell	11 Liddell	11 Henderson
Belgrade May 15: 2-2 *Reilly, Smith*	Vienna May 19: 4-1 *Robertson, Smith, Liddell, Reilly*	Budapest May 29: 1-3 *Smith*	Belfast Oct 8: 1-2 *Reilly*	Hampden Nov 9: 2-0 *Johnstone 2*

1956 England	1956 Austria	1956 Wales	1956 N Ireland	1956 Yugoslavia
1 Younger	1 Younger	1 Younger	1 Younger	1 Younger
2 Parker	2 Parker	2 Parker	2 Parker	2 Parker
3 Hewie	3 Hewie	3 Hewie	3 Hewie	3 Hewie
4 Evans	4 Evans	4 McColl	4 McColl	4 McColl
5 Young	5 Young	5 Young	5 Young	5 Young
6 Glen	6 Cowie	6 Cowie	6 Cowie	6 Docherty
7 Leggat	5 McKenzie	5 Leggat	7 Scott	7 Scott
8 Johnstone	8 Conn	8 Mudie	8 Mudie	8 Mudie
9 Reilly	9 Reilly	9 Reilly	9 Reilly	9 Reilly
10 McMillan	10 Baird	10 Collins	10 Wardhaugh	10 Baird
11 Smith	11 Cullen	11 Fernie	11 Fernie	11 Fernie
Hampden April 14: 1-1 *Leggat*	Hampden May 2: 1-1 *Conn*	Cardiff Oct 20: 2-2 *Fernie, Reilly*	Hampden Nov 7: 1-0 *Scott*	Hampden Nov 21: 2-0 *Mudie, Baird*

1957 England	1957 Spain	1957 Switzerland	1957 W Germany	1957 Spain
1 Younger	1 Younger	1 Younger	1 Younger	1 Younger
2 Caldow	2 Caldow	2 Caldow	2 Caldow	2 Caldow
3 Hewie	3 Hewie	3 Hewie	3 Hewie	3 Hewie
4 McColl	4 McColl	4 McColl	4 McColl	4 Mackay
5 Young	5 Young	5 Young	5 Evans	5 Evans
6 Docherty	6 Docherty	6 Docherty	6 Docherty	6 Docherty
7 Collins	7 Smith	7 Smith	7 Scott	7 Smith
8 Fernie	8 Collins	8 Collins	8 Collins	8 Collins
9 Reilly	9 Mudie	9 Mudie	9 Mudie	9 Mudie
10 Mudie	10 Baird	10 Baird	10 Baird	10 Baird
11 Ring	11 Ring	11 Ring	11 Ring	11 Ring
Wembley April 6: 1-2 *Ring*	Hampden May 8: 4-2 *Mudie 3, Hewie (pen)*	Basle May 19: 2-1 *Mudie, Collins*	Stuttgart May 22: 3-1 *Collins 2, Mudie*	Madrid May 26: 1-4 *Smith*

1957 N Ireland	1957 Switzerland	1957 Wales	1958 England	1958 Hungary
1 Younger	1 Younger	1 Younger	1 Younger	1 Younger
2 Parker	2 Parker	2 Parker	2 Parker	2 Caldow
3 Caldow	3 Caldow	3 Caldow	3 Haddock	3 Hewie
4 McColl	4 Fernie	4 Docherty	4 McColl	4 Turnbull
5 Evans	5 Evans	5 Evans	5 Evans	5 Evans
6 Docherty	6 Docherty	6 Fernie	6 Docherty	6 Cowie
7 Leggat	7 Scott	7 Scott	7 Herd	7 Leggat
8 Collins	8 Collins	8 Collins	8 Murray	8 Murray
9 Mudie	9 Mudie	9 Gardiner	9 Mudie	9 Mudie
10 Baird	10 Robertson	10 Mudie	10 Forrest	10 Collins
11 Ring	11 Ring	11 Ewing	11 Ewing	11 Imlach
Belfast Oct 5: 1-1 *Leggat*	Hampden Nov 6: 3-2 *Robertson, Mudie, Scott*	Hampden Nov 13: 1-1 *Collins*	Hampden April 19: 0-4	Hampden May 7: 1-1 *Mudie*

1958 Poland	1958 Yugoslavia	1958 Paraguay	1958 France	1958 Wales
1 Younger	1 Younger	1 Younger	1 Brown	1 Brown
2 Caldow	2 Caldow	2 Parker	2 Caldow	2 Grant
3 Hewie	3 Hewie	3 Caldow	3 Hewie	3 Caldow
4 Turnbull	4 Turnbull	4 Turnbull	4 Turnbull	4 Mackay
5 Evans	5 Evans	5 Evans	5 Evans	5 Toner
6 Cowie	6 Cowie	6 Cowie	6 Mackay	6 Docherty
7 Leggat	7 Leggat	7 Leggat	7 Collins	7 Leggat
8 Murray	8 Murray	8 Collins	8 Murray	8 Collins
9 Mudie	9 Mudie	9 Mudie	9 Mudie	9 Herd
10 Collins	10 Collins	10 Robertson	10 Baird	10 Law
11 Imlach	11 Imlach	11 Fernie	11 Imlach	11 Henderson
Warsaw June 1: 2-1 *Collins 2*	Vasteraas June 8: 1-1 *Murray*	Norrkoping June 11: 2-3 *Mudie, Collins*	Orebro June 15: 1-2 *Baird*	Cardiff Oct 18: 3-0 *Leggat, Law, Collins*

1958 N Ireland	1959 England	1959 W Germany	1959 Holland	1959 Portugal
1 Brown	1 Brown	1 Farm	1 Farm	1 Farm
2 Grant	2 McKay	2 McKay	2 McKay	2 McKay
3 Caldow	3 Caldow	3 Caldow	3 Caldow	3 Caldow
4 Mackay	4 Docherty	4 Mackay	4 Smith	4 Smith
5 Toner	5 Evans	5 Evans	5 Evans	5 Evans
6 Docherty	6 Mackay	6 McCann	6 Hewie	6 Hewie
7 Leggat	7 Leggat	7 Leggat	7 Leggat	7 Scott
8 Collins	8 Collins	8 White	8 Collins	8 Collins
9 Herd	9 Herd	9 St John	9 White	9 White
10 Law	10 Dick	10 Collins	10 Law	10 Law
11 Henderson	11 Ormond	11 Weir	11 Auld	11 Auld
Hampden Nov 5: 2-2 *Herd, Collins*	Wembley April 11: 0-1	Hampden May 6: 3-2 *White, Weir, Leggat*	Amsterdam May 27: 2-1 *Collins, Leggat*	Lisbon June 3: 0-1

1959 N Ireland	1959 Wales	1960 England	1960 Poland	1960 Austria
1 Brown	1 Brown	1 Haffey	1 Brown	1 Brown
2 Caldow	2 Caldow	2 McKay	2 McKay	2 McKay
3 Hewie	3 Mackay	3 Caldow	3 Hewie	3 Caldow
4 Mackay	4 Hewie	4 Cumming	4 Mackay	4 Mackay
5 Evans	5 Evans	5 Evans	5 Evans	5 Evans
6 McCann	6 McCann	6 McCann	6 Cumming	6 Cumming
7 Leggat	7 Leggat	7 Leggat	7 Leggat	7 Leggat
8 White	8 White	8 Young	8 White	8 White
9 St John	9 St John	9 St John	9 St John	9 St John
10 Law	10 Law	10 Law	10 Law	10 Law (Young)
11 Mulhall	11 Auld	11 Weir	11 Weir	11 Weir
Belfast Oct 3: 4-0 *Leggat, Hewie, White, Mulhall*	Hampden Nov 14: 1-1 *Leggat*	Hampden April 9: 1-1 *Leggat*	Hampden May 4: 2-3 *Law, St John*	Vienna May 29: 1-4 *Mackay*

1960 Hungary	1960 Turkey	1960 Wales	1960 N Ireland	1961 England
1 Brown	1 Brown	1 Leslie	1 Leslie	1 Haffey
2 McKay	2 McKay	2 McKay	2 McKay	2 Shearer
3 Caldow	3 Caldow	3 Caldow	3 Caldow	3 Caldow
4 Cumming	4 Mackay	4 Gabriel	4 Mackay	4 Mackay
5 Evans	5 Evans	5 Martins	5 Plenderleith	5 McNeill
6 Mackay	6 Cumming	6 Mackay	6 Baxter	6 McCann
7 Leggat	7 White	7 Herd	7 Herd	7 McLeod
8 Herd	8 Herd	8 White	8 Law	8 Law
9 Young	9 Young	9 Young	9 Young	9 St John
10 Hunter	10 Hunter	10 Hunter	10 Brand	10 Quinn
11 Weir	11 Weir	11 Wilson	11 Wilson	11 Wilson
Budapest June 5: 3-3 *Hunter, Herd, Young*	Ankara June 8: 2-4 *Caldow, Young*	Cardiff Oct 22: 0-2	Hampden Nov 9: 5-2 *Law, Caldow, Young, Brand 2*	Wembley April 15: 3-9 *Mackay, Wilson, Quinn*

1961 Rep of Ireland	1961 Rep of Ireland	1961 Czechoslovakia	1961 Czechoslovakia	1961 N Ireland
1 Leslie	1 Leslie	1 Leslie	1 Brown	1 Brown
2 Shearer	2 Shearer	2 Shearer	2 McKay	2 McKay
3 Caldow	3 Crerand	3 Caldow	3 Caldow	3 Caldow
4 Crerand	4 Caldow	4 Crerand	4 Crerand	4 Crerand
5 McNeill	5 McNeill	5 McNeill	5 McNeill	5 McNeill
6 Baxter	6 Baxter	6 Baxter	6 Baxter	6 Baxter
7 McLeod	7 McLeod	7 McLeod	7 Scott	7 Scott
8 Quinn	8 Quinn	8 McMillan	8 White	8 White
9 Herd	9 Young	9 Herd	9 St John	9 St John
10 Brand	10 Brand	10 Brand	10 Law	10 Brand
11 Wilson	11 Wilson	11 Wilson	11 Wilson	11 Wilson
Hampden May 3: 4-1 *Brand 2, Herd 2*	Dublin May 7: 3-0 *Young 2, Brand*	Bratislava May 14: 0-4	Hampden Sept 26: 3-2 *St John, Law 2*	Belfast Oct 7: 6-1 *Wilson, Scott 3 Brand 2*

1961 Wales	1961 Czechoslovakia	1962 England	1962 Uruguay	1962 Wales
1 Brown	1 Connachan	1 Brown	1 Connachan	1 Brown
2 Hamilton	2 Hamilton	2 Hamilton	2 Hamilton	2 Hamilton
3 Caldow	3 Caldow	3 Caldow	3 Caldow	3 Caldow
4 Crerand	4 Crerand	4 Crerand	4 Crerand	4 Crerand
5 Ure	5 Ure	5 McNeill	5 McNeill	5 Ure
6 Baxter	6 Baxter	6 Baxter	6 Baxter	6 Baxter
7 Scott	7 Brand	7 Scott	7 Scott	7 Henderson
8 White	8 White	8 White	8 Quinn	8 White
9 St John	9 St John	9 St John	9 St John	9 St John
10 Brand	10 Law	10 Law	10 Brand	10 Law
11 Wilson	11 Robertson	11 Wilson	11 Wilson	11 Wilson
Hampden Nov 8: 2-0 *St John 2*	Brussels Nov 29: 2-4 *St John 2*	Hampden April 14: 2-0 *Wilson, Caldow*	Hampden May 2: 2-3 *Baxter, Brand*	Cardiff Oct 20: 3-2 *Caldow, Law, Henderson*

1962 N Ireland	1963 England	1963 Austria	1963 Norway	1963 Rep of Ireland
1 Brown	1 Brown	1 Brown	1 Blacklaw	1 Lawrence
2 Hamilton	2 Hamilton	2 Hamilton	2 Hamilton	2 Hamilton
3 Caldow	3 Caldow	3 Holt	3 Holt	3 Holt
4 Crerand	4 Mackay	4 Mackay	4 Mackay (McLintock)	4 McLintock
5 Ure	5 Ure	5 Ure	5 Ure	5 McNeill
6 Baxter	6 Baxter	6 Baxter	6 Baxter	6 Baxter
7 Henderson	7 Henderson	7 Henderson	7 Henderson	7 Henderson
8 White	8 White	8 Gibson	8 Gibson	8 Gibson
9 St John	9 St John	9 Millar	9 St John	9 Millar (St John)
10 Law	10 Law	10 Law	10 Law	10 Law
11 Mulhall	11 Wilson	11 Wilson	11 Wilson	11 Wilson
Hampden Nov 7: 5-1 *Law 4, Henderson*	Wembley April 6: 2-1 *Baxter 2*	Hampden May 8: 4-1 *Wilson 2, Law 2 (abandoned after 79 mins)*	Bergen June 4: 3-4 *Law 3*	Dublin June 9: 0-1

1963 Spain	1963 N Ireland	1963 Norway	1963 Wales	1964 England
1 Blacklaw	1 Brown	1 Brown	1 Brown	1 Forsyth
2 McNeill	2 Hamilton	2 Hamilton	2 Hamilton	2 Hamilton
3 Holt	3 Provan	3 Provan	3 Kennedy	3 Kennedy
4 McLintock	4 Crerand	4 Mackay	4 Mackay	4 Greig
5 Ure	5 Ure	5 Ure	5 McNeill	5 McNeill
6 Baxter	6 Mackay	6 Baxter (Gabriel)	6 Baxter	6 Baxter
7 Henderson	7 Henderson	7 Scott	7 Henderson	7 Henderson
8 Gibson	8 White	8 White	8 White	8 White
9 St John	9 St John	9 Gilzean	9 Gilzean	9 Gilzean
10 Law	10 Gibson	10 Law	10 Law	10 Law
11 Wilson	11 Mulhall	11 Henderson	11 Scott	11 Wilson
Madrid June 13: 6-2 *St John, Wilson, Law, Henderson, Gibson, McLintock*	Belfast Oct 12: 1-2 *St John*	Hampden Nov 7: 6-1 *Law 4, Mackay 2*	Hampden Nov 20: 2-1 *White, Law*	Hampden April 11: 1-0 *Gilzean*

1964 W Germany	1964 Wales	1964 Finland	1964 N Ireland	1965 England
1 Cruickshank	1 Forsyth	1 Forsyth	1 Forsyth	1 Brown
2 Hamilton (Holt)	2 Hamilton	2 Hamilton	2 Hamilton	2 Hamilton
3 Kennedy	3 Kennedy	3 Kennedy	3 Kennedy	3 McCreadie
4 Greig	4 Greig	4 Greig	4 Greig	4 Crerand
5 McNeill	5 Yeats	5 McGrory	5 McGrory	5 McNeill
6 Baxter	6 Baxter	6 Baxter	6 McLintock	6 Greig
7 Henderson	7 Johnstone	7 Johnstone	7 Wallace	7 Henderson
8 White	8 Gibson	8 Gibson	8 Law	8 Collins
9 Gilzean	9 Chalmers	9 Chalmers	9 Gilzean	9 St John
10 Law	10 Law	10 Law	10 Baxter	10 Law
11 Wilson	11 Robertson	11 Scott	11 Wilson	11 Wilson
Hanover May 12: 2-2 Gilzean 2	Cardiff Oct 3: 2-3 Chalmers, Gibson	Hampden Oct 21: 3-1 Law, Chalmers, Gibson	Hampden Nov 25: 3-2 Wilson 2, Gilzean	Wembley April 10: 2-2 Law, St John

1965 Spain	1965 Poland	1965 Finland	1965 N Ireland	1965 Poland
1 Brown	1 Brown	1 Brown	1 Brown	1 Brown
2 Hamilton	2 Hamilton	2 Hamilton	2 Hamilton	2 Hamilton
3 McCreadie	3 McCreadie	3 McCreadie	3 McCreadie	3 McCreadie
4 Bremner	4 Greig	4 Crerand	4 Mackay	4 Crerand
5 McNeill	5 McNeill	5 McNeill	5 McNeill	5 McNeill
6 Greig	6 Crerand	6 Greig	6 Greig	6 Greig
7 Henderson	7 Henderson	7 Henderson	7 Henderson	7 Henderson
8 Collins	8 Collins	8 Law	8 Law	8 Bremner
9 Law	9 Martin	9 Martin	9 Gilzean	9 Gilzean
10 Gilzean	10 Law	10 Hamilton	10 Baxter	10 Law
11 Hughes	11 Hughes	11 Wilson	11 Hughes	11 Johnston
Hampden May 8: 0-0	Chorzow May 23: 1-1 Law	Helsinki May 27: 2-1 Wilson, Greig	Belfast Oct 2: 2-3 Gilzean 2	Hampden Oct 13: 1-2 McNeill

1965 Italy	1965 Wales	1965 Italy	1966 England	1966 Netherlands
1 Brown	1 Ferguson	1 Blacklaw	1 Ferguson	1 Ferguson
2 Greig	2 Greig	2 Provan	2 Greig	2 Greig
3 Provan	3 McCreadie	3 McCreadie	3 Gemmell	3 Provan
4 Murdoch	4 Murdoch	4 Murdoch	4 Murdoch	4 Stanton
5 McKinnon	5 McKinnon	5 McKinnon	5 McKinnon	5 McKinnon
6 Baxter	6 Baxter	6 Greig	6 Baxter	6 Smith
7 Henderson	7 Henderson	7 Forrest	7 Johnstone	7 Henderson
8 Bremner	8 Cooke	8 Bremner	8 Law	8 Penman
9 Gilzean	9 Forrest	9 Yeats	9 Wallace	9 Scott
10 Martin	10 Gilzean	10 Cooke	10 Bremner	10 Wallace
11 Hughes	11 Johnston	11 Hughes	11 Johnston	11 Johnston
Hampden Nov 9: 1-0 Greig	Hampden Nov 24: 4-1 Murdoch 2, Henderson, Greig	Naples Dec 7: 0-3	Hampden April 2: 3-4 Law, Johnston 2	Hampden May 11: 0-3

1966 Portugal	1966 Brazil	1966 Wales	1966 N Ireland	1967 England
1 Ferguson	1 Ferguson	1 Ferguson	1 Ferguson	1 Simpson
2 Bell	2 Greig	2 Greig	2 Greig	2 Gemmell
3 McCreadie	3 Bell	3 Gemmell	3 Gemmell	3 McCreadie
4 Greig	4 Bremner	4 Bremner	4 Bremner	4 Greig
5 McGrory	5 McKinnon	5 McKinnon	5 McKinnon	5 McKinnon
6 Bremner	6 Clark	6 Clark	6 Clark	6 Bremner
7 Scott	7 Scott	7 Johnstone	7 Henderson	7 McCalliog
8 Cooke	8 Cooke	8 Law	8 Murdoch	8 Law
9 Young (Chalmers)	9 Chalmers	9 McBride	9 McBride	9 Wallace
10 Baxter	10 Baxter	10 Baxter	10 Chalmers	10 Baxter
11 Sinclair	11 Cormack	11 Henderson	11 Lennox	11 Lennox
Hampden June 18: 0-1	Hampden June 25: 1-1 *Chalmers*	Cardiff Oct 22: 1-1 *Law*	Hampden Nov 16: 2-1 *Murdoch, Lennox*	Wembley April 15: 3-2 *Law, Lennox, McCalliog*

1967 USSR	1967 N Ireland	1967 Wales	1968 England	1968 Netherlands
1 Simpson	1 Simpson	1 Clark	1 Simpson	1 Clark
2 Gemmell	2 Gemmell	2 Craig	2 Gemmell	2 Fraser
3 McCreadie	3 McCreadie	3 McCreadie	3 McCreadie	3 McCreadie
4 Clark	4 Greig	4 Greig	4 McNeill	4 Moncur
5 McNeill	5 McKinnon	5 McKinnon	5 McKinnon	5 McKinnon
6 Baxter	6 Ure	6 Baxter	6 Greig	6 Smith D
7 Johnstone	7 Wallace	7 Johnstone	7 Cooke	7 Henderson
8 McLintock	8 Murdoch	8 Bremner	8 Bremner	8 Hope (Smith J)
9 McCalliog	9 McCalliog	9 Gilzean	9 Hughes	9 McLean
10 Law (Wallace)	10 Law	10 Johnston	10 Johnston	10 Greig
11 Lennox	11 Morgan	11 Lennox	11 Lennox	11 Cooke
Hampden May 10: 0-2	Belfast Oct 21: 0-1	Hampden Nov 22: 3-2 *Gilzean 2, McKinnon*	Hampden Feb 24: 1-1 *Hughes*	Amsterdam May 30: 0-0

1968 Denmark	1968 Austria	1968 Cyprus	1969 W Germany	1969 Wales
1 Herriot	1 Simpson	1 Herriot	1 Lawrence	1 Lawrence (Herriot)
2 Gemmell	2 Gemmell	2 Fraser	2 Gemmell	2 Gemmell
3 McCreadie	3 McCreadie	3 McCreadie	3 McCreadie	3 McCreadie
4 Bremner	4 Bremner	4 Bremner	4 Murdoch	4 Bremner
5 McKinnon	5 McKinnon	5 McKinnon (McNeill)	5 McKinnon	5 McNeill
6 Greig	6 Greig	6 Greig	6 Greig	6 Greig
7 McLean	7 Johnstone	7 McLean	7 Johnstone	7 McLean
8 McCalliog (Cormack)	8 Cooke	8 Murdoch	8 Bremner	8 Murdoch
9 Stein	9 Hughes	9 Stein	9 Law	9 Stein
10 Hope	10 Law (Gilzean)	10 Gilzean	10 Gilzean	10 Gilzean
11 Lennox	11 Lennox	11 Cooke (Lennox)	11 Lennox (Cooke)	11 Cooke
Copenhagen Oct 16: 1-0 *Lennox*	Hampden Nov 6: 2-1 *Law, Bremner*	Nicosia Dec 11: 5-0 *Gilzean 2, Stein 2, Murdoch*	Hampden April 16: 1-1 *Murdoch*	Wrexham May 3: 5-3 *McNeill, Stein, Gilzean, Bremner, McLean*

1969 N Ireland	1969 England	1969 Cyprus	1969 Rep of Ireland	1969 W Germany
1 Herriot	1 Herriot	1 Herriot	1 McGarr (Herriot)	1 Herriot
2 McCreadie	2 McCreadie	2 McCreadie	2 Greig	2 Greig
3 Gemmell	3 Gemmell	3 Gemmell	3 Gemmell (Callaghan)	3 Gemmell
4 Bremner	4 Murdoch	4 Bremner	4 Stanton	4 Bremner
5 Greig	5 McNeill	5 McNeill	5 McKinnon	5 McKinnon
6 Stanton	6 Greig	6 Greig	6 Moncur	6 McNeill
7 Henderson	7 Henderson	7 Henderson	7 Henderson	7 Johnstone
8 Murdoch	8 Bremner	8 Cooke	8 Bremner	8 Cormack
9 Stein	9 Stein	9 Stein	9 Stein	9 Gilzean
10 Law	10 Gilzean (Wallace)	10 Gilzean	10 Cormack	10 Gray
11 Cooke (Johnston)	11 Gray	11 Gray	11 Hughes	11 Stein
Hampden May 6: 1-1 Stein	Wembley May 10: 1-4 Stein	Hampden May 12: 8-0 Gray, McNeill, Stein 4, Henderson	Dublin Sept 21: 1-1 Stein	Hamburg Oct 22: 2-3 Johnstone, Gilzean

1969 Austria	1970 N Ireland	1970 Wales	1970 England	1970 Denmark
1 McGarr	1 Clark	1 Cruickshank	1 Cruickshank	1 Cruickshank
2 Greig	2 Hay	2 Callaghan	2 Gemmell	2 Hay (Jardine)
3 Burns	3 Dickson	3 Dickson	3 Dickson	3 Greig
4 Murdoch	4 McLintock	4 Greig	4 Greig	4 Stanton
5 McKinnon	5 McKinnon	5 McKinnon	5 McKinnon	5 McKinnon
6 Stanton	6 Moncur	6 Moncur	6 Moncur (Gilzean)	6 Moncur
7 Cooke (Stein)	7 McLean	7 McLean (Lennox)	7 Johnstone	7 Johnstone
8 Bremner	8 Carr	8 Hay	8 Hay	8 Carr
9 Gilzean	9 O'Hare	9 O'Hare	9 Stein	9 Stein
10 Curran (Lorimer)	10 Gilzean (Stein)	10 Stein	10 O'Hare	10 O'Hare (Cormack)
11 Gray	11 Johnston	11 Carr	11 Carr	11 Johnston
Vienna Nov 5: 0-2	Belfast April 18: 1-0 O'Hare	Hampden April 22: 0-0	Hampden April 25: 0-0	Hampden Nov 11: 1-0 O'Hare

1971 Belgium	1971 Portugal	1971 Wales	1971 N Ireland	1971 England
1 Cruickshank	1 Clark	1 Clark	1 Clark	1 Clark
2 Hay	2 Hay	2 Hay	2 Hay	2 Greig
3 Gemmell	3 Brogan	3 Brogan	3 Brogan	3 Brogan
4 Stanton (Green)	4 Stanton (Green)	4 Bremner (Greig)	4 Greig	4 Bremner
5 McKinnon	5 McKinnon	5 McLintock	5 McLintock (Munro)	5 McLintock
6 Moncur	6 Moncur	6 Moncur	6 Moncur	6 Moncur
7 Gemmill	7 Henderson	7 Lorimer	7 Lorimer	7 Johnstone
8 Greig	8 McCalliog (Jarvie)	8 Robb	8 Green	8 Robb
9 Stein (Forrest)	9 Robb	9 O'Hare	9 O'Hare (Jarvie)	9 Curran (Munro)
10 O'Hare	10 Cormack	10 Cormack	10 Curran	10 Green (Jarvie)
11 Cooke	11 Gilzean	11 Gray	11 Gray	11 Cormack
Liege Feb 3: 0-3	Lisbon April 21: 0-2	Cardiff May 15: 0-0	Hampden May 18: 0-1	Wembley May 22: 1-3 Curran

1971 Denmark	1971 USSR	1971 Portugal	1971 Belgium	1971 Netherlands
1 Clark	1 Clark	1 Wilson	1 Clark	1 Wilson
2 Munro	2 Brownlie	2 Jardine	2 Jardine	2 Jardine
3 Dickson	3 Dickson	3 Colquhoun (Buchan)	3 Hay	3 Hay
4 Stanton	4 Munroe	4 Stanton	4 Bremner	4 Bremner
5 McKinnon	5 McKinnon	5 Hay	5 Buchan	5 Colquhoun
6 Moncur	6 Stanton	6 Bremner	6 Stanton	6 Stanton
7 McLean	7 Forrest	7 Cropley	7 Johnstone (Hansen)	7 Johnstone (O'Hare)
8 Forsyth (Robb)	8 Watson	8 Graham	8 Murray	8 Gemmill
9 Stein	9 Stein (Curran)	9 Johnstone	9 O'Hare	9 Dalglish
10 Curran	10 Robb	10 O'Hare	10 Gray	10 Graham
11 Forrest (Scott)	11 Scott	11 Gemmill	11 Cropley (Dalglish)	11 Gray (Cormack)
Copenhagen June 9: 0-1	Moscow June 14: 0-1	Hampden Oct 13: 2-1 O'Hare, Gemmill	Aberdeen Nov 10: 1-0 O'Hare	Amsterdam Dec 1: 1-2 Graham

1972 Peru	1972 N Ireland	1972 Wales	1972 England	1972 Yugoslavia
1 Hunter	1 Clark	1 Clark	1 Clark	1 Hunter
2 Brownlie	2 Brownlie	2 Stanton	2 Brownlie	2 Forsyth
3 Donachie	3 Donachie	3 Buchan	3 Donachie (Green)	3 Buchan
4 Carr	4 Bremner	4 Bremner	4 Bremner	4 Hansen
5 Colquhoun	5 McNeill	5 McNeill	5 McNeill	5 Donachie
6 Moncur	6 Moncur	6 Moncur	6 Moncur	6 Bremner
7 Morgan	8 Johnstone (Lorimer)	7 Lorimer	7 Gemmill (Johnstone)	7 Hartford
8 Hartford	8 Gemmill	8 Green	8 Hartford	8 Graham
9 O'Hare	9 O'Hare	9 O'Hare (Macari)	9 Lorimer	9 Morgan
10 Law	10 Law	10 Law	10 Macari	10 Law (Bone)
11 Gemmill	11 Graham	11 Gemmill (Hartford)	11 Law	11 Macari
Hampden April 26: 2-0 O'Hare, Law	Hampden May 20: 2-0 Law, Lorimer	Hampden May 24: 1-0 Lorimer	Hampden May 27: 0-1	Belo Horizonte June 29: 2-2 Macari 2

1972 Czechoslovakia	1972 Brazil	1972 Denmark	1972 Denmark	1973 England
1 Clark	1 Clark	1 Clark	1 Harvey	1 Clark
2 Forsyth	2 Forsyth	2 Brownlie	2 Brownlie	2 Forsyth
3 Colquhoun	3 Colquhoun	3 Forsyth	3 Donachie	3 Donachie
4 Buchan	4 Buchan	4 Bremner	4 Bremner	4 Bremner
5 Donachie	5 Donachie	5 Colquhoun	5 Colquhoun	5 Colquhoun
6 Bremner	6 Bremner	6 Buchan	6 Buchan	6 Buchan
7 Graham	7 Graham	7 Lorimer	7 Lorimer	7 Lorimer
8 Law	8 Hartford	8 Macari (Dalglish)	8 Dalglish (Carr)	8 Dalglish
9 Hartford	9 Morgan	9 Bone	9 Harper	9 Macari
10 Morgan	10 Law	10 Graham	10 Graham	10 Graham
11 Macari	11 Macari	11 Morgan	11 Morgan	11 Morgan (Stein)
Porto Alegre July 2: 0-0	Rio July 5: 0-1	Copenhagen Oct 18: 4-1 Macari, Bone, Harper, Morgan	Glasgow Nov 15: 2-0 Dalglish, Lorimer	Glasgow Feb 14: 0-5

1973 Wales	1973 N Ireland	1973 England	1973 Switzerland	1973 Brazil
1 McCloy	1 McCloy	1 Hunter	1 McCloy	1 McCloy
2 McGrain	2 McGrain	2 Jardine	2 Jardine	2 Jardine
3 Donachie	3 Donachie	3 McGrain	3 McGrain	3 McGrain
4 Graham	4 Graham (Macari)	4 Bremner	4 Bremner	4 Bremner
5 Holton	5 Holton	5 Holton	5 Holton	5 Holton
6 Johnstone	6 Johnstone	6 Johnstone	6 Johnstone	6 Johnstone
7 Dalglish (Macari)	7 Dalglish	7 Morgan	7 Dalglish	7 Morgan
8 Stanton	8 Stanton (Bremner)	8 Macari (Jordan)	8 Hay	8 Hay
9 Parlane (Stein)	9 Stein	9 Dalglish	9 Parlane	9 Parlane
10 Hay	10 Hay	10 Hay	10 Connolly (Jordan)	10 Jordan
11 Morgan	11 Morgan	11 Lorimer (Stein)	11 Morgan	11 Dalglish (Graham)
Wrexham May 12: 2-0 Graham 2	Glasgow May 16: 1-2 Dalglish	Wembley May 19: 0-1	Berne June 22: 0-1	Glasgow June 30: 0-1

1973 Czechoslovakia	1973 Czechoslovakia	1973 W Germany	1974 W Germany	1974 N Ireland
1 Hunter	1 Harvey	1 Harvey	1 Allan	1 Harvey
2 Jardine	2 Jardine	2 Jardine	2 Jardine	2 Jardine
3 McGrain	3 McGrain	3 McGrain	3 Schaedler	3 Donachie (Smith)
4 Bremner	4 Forsyth	4 Bremner	4 Hay	4 Bremner
5 Holton	5 Blackley	5 Holton	5 Buchan	5 Holton
6 Connolly	6 Hay	6 Connolly	6 Stanton	6 Buchan
7 Hay	7 Morgan	7 Morgan	7 Morgan	7 Morgan
8 Law	8 Jordan	8 Smith (Lorimer)	8 Dalglish	8 Hay
9 Morgan	9 Law (Ford)	9 Law (Jordan)	9 Law (Ford)	9 Law (Jordan)
10 Dalglish (Jordan)	10 Dalglish	10 Dalglish	10 Hutchison	10 Dalglish
11 Hutchison	11 Hutchison	11 Hutchison	11 Burns (Robinson)	11 Hutchison
Hampden Sept 26: 2-1 Holton, Jordan	Bratislava Oct 17: 0-1	Hampden Nov 14: 1-1 Holton	Frankfurt March 27: 1-2 Dalglish	Hampden May 11: 0-1

1974 Wales	1974 England	1974 Belgium	1974 Norway	1974 Zaire
1 Harvey	1 Harvey	1 Harvey	1 Allan	1 Harvey
2 Jardine	2 Jardine	2 Jardine	2 Jardine	2 Jardine
3 Hay	3 McGrain	3 McGrain	3 McGrain	3 McGrain
4 Bremner	4 Bremner	4 Bremner	4 Bremner	4 Bremner
5 Holton	5 Holton	5 McQueen	5 Holton	5 Holton
6 Buchan (McGrain)	6 Blackley	6 Blackley	6 Buchan	6 Blackley
7 Johnstone	7 Lorimer	7 Johnstone (Morgan)	7 Johnstone (Dalglish)	7 Dalglish (Hutchison)
8 Dalglish	8 Johnstone	8 Dalglish (Hutchison)	8 Lorimer	8 Hay
9 Ford	9 Jordan	9 Jordan	9 Jordan	9 Lorimer
10 Jordan	10 Dalglish	10 Hay	10 Hay	10 Jordan
11 Hutchison (Smith)	11 Hay	11 Lorimer	11 Hutchison	11 Law
Hampden May 14: 2-0 Dalglish, Jardine	Hampden May 18: 2-0 Jordan, Todd (og)	Bruges June 1: 1-2 Johnstone	Oslo June 6: 1-2 Jordan, Dalglish	Dortmund June 14: 2-0 Lorimer, Jordan

1974 Brazil	1974 Yugoslavia	1974 E Germany	1974 Spain	1975 Spain
1 Harvey	1 Harvey	1 Harvey	1 Harvey	1 Harvey
2 Jardine	2 Jardine	2 Jardine	2 Jardine	2 Jardine
3 McGrain	3 McGrain	3 Forsyth A	3 Forsyth	3 McQueen
4 Holton	4 Holton	4 Souness	4 McQueen	4 Buchan
5 Buchan	5 Buchan	5 Holton (Burns)	5 Burns	5 McGrain
6 Bremner	6 Bremner	6 Buchan	6 Bremner	6 Bremner
7 Hay	7 Dalglish (Hutchison)	7 Johnstone J	7 Souness	7 Cooke
8 Dalglish	8 Hay	8 Dalglish (Johnstone D)	8 Hutchison (Dalglish)	8 Hutchison
9 Morgan	9 Morgan	9 Deans	9 Johnstone	9 Dalglish
10 Jordan	10 Jordan	10 Jordan	10 Deans (Lorimer)	10 Jordan (Parlane)
11 Lorimer	11 Lorimer	11 Hutchison	11 Jordan	11 Burns (Wilson)
Frankfurt June 18: 0-0	Frankfurt June 22: 1-1 *Jordan*	Hampden Oct 30: 3-0 *Hutchison (pen), Burns, Dalglish*	Hampden Nov 20: 1-2 *Bremner*	Valencia Feb 5: 1-1 *Jordan*

1975 Sweden	1975 Portugal	1975 Wales	1975 N Ireland	1975 England
1 Kennedy	1 Kennedy	1 Kennedy	1 Kennedy	1 Kennedy
2 Jardine	2 Jardine	2 Jardine	2 Jardine (Forsyth)	2 Jardine
3 McGrain	3 McGrain	3 McGrain	3 McGrain	3 McGrain
4 Munro	4 Buchan (Jackson)	4 Jackson (Munro)	4 Munro	4 Munro
5 Jackson	5 McQueen	5 McQueen	5 McQueen	5 McQueen
6 Robinson	6 Rioch	6 Rioch	6 Rioch	6 Rioch
7 Dalglish	7 Cooke (Macari)	7 Macari	7 Dalglish	7 Dalglish
8 Souness (Johnstone D)	8 Dalglish	8 Dalglish	8 Robinson (Conn)	8 Conn
9 Parlane	9 Parlane	9 Parlane	9 Parlane	9 Parlane
10 MacDougall	10 MacDougall	10 MacDougall	10 MacDougall	10 MacDougall (Macari)
11 Macari (Hughes)	11 Hutchison (Duncan)	11 Duncan	11 Duncan	11 Duncan (Hutchison)
Gothenburg April 16: 1-1 *MacDougall*	Hampden May 13: 1-0 *Artur (og)*	Cardiff May 17: 2-2 *Jackson, Rioch*	Hampden May 20: 3-0 *MacDougall, Dalglish, Parlane*	Wembley May 24: 1-5 *Rioch (pen)*

1975 Rumania	1975 Denmark	1975 Denmark	1975 Rumania	1976 Switzerland
1 Brown	1 Harvey	1 Harvey	1 Cruickshank	1 Rough
2 McGrain	2 McGrain	2 McGrain	2 Brownlie	2 McGrain
3 Forsyth	3 Forsyth	3 Houston	3 Donachie	3 Gray F
4 Munro	4 Bremner	4 Greig	4 Buchan	4 Forsyth
5 McQueen	5 McQueen	5 Jackson	5 Jackson	5 Blackley
6 Rioch (Hutchison)	6 Buchan	6 Rioch	6 Rioch	6 Craig
7 Dalglish	7 Lorimer	7 Lorimer	7 Doyle (Lorimer)	7 Dalglish (Bremner D)
8 Miller	8 Dalglish	8 Dalglish	8 Hartford	8 Pettigrew (McKean)
9 Parlane	9 Harper	9 MacDougall (Parlane)	9 Gray	9 Gray A
10 Macari (Robinson)	10 Rioch	10 Hartford	10 Dalglish (MacDougall)	10 MacDonald
11 Duncan	11 Hutchison (Duncan)	11 Gemmill	11 Gemmill	11 Johnstone
Bucharest June 1: 1-1 *McQueen*	Copenhagen Sept 3: 1-0 *Harper*	Glasgow Oct 29: 3-1 *Dalglish, Rioch, MacDougall*	Glasgow Dec 17: 1-1 *Rioch*	Glasgow April 7: 1-0 *Pettigrew*

1976 Wales	1976 N Ireland	1976 England	1976 Finland	1976 Czechoslovakia
1 Rough	1 Rough	1 Rough	1 Rough (Harvey)	1 Rough
2 McGrain	2 McGrain	2 McGrain	2 McGrain	2 McGrain
3 Donachie	3 Donachie	3 Donachie	3 Donachie	3 Donachie
4 Forsyth T	4 Forsyth T	4 Forsyth T	4 Rioch	4 Buchan
5 Jackson	5 Jackson	5 Jackson	5 Forsyth	5 McQueen
6 Rioch	6 Rioch (Hartford)	6 Rioch	6 Buchan	6 Rioch
7 Pettigrew	7 Masson	7 Masson	7 Dalglish	7 Dalglish (Burns)
8 Masson	8 Gemmill	8 Gemmill	8 Gemmill	8 Masson (Hartford)
9 Jordan	9 Pettigrew (Johnstone)	9 Dalglish	9 Gray A	9 Jordan
10 Gemmill	10 Jordan	10 Jordan	10 Masson	10 Gray A
11 Gray E	11 Dalglish	11 Gray E (Johnstone)	11 Gray E	11 Gemmill
Glasgow May 6: 3-1 Pettigrew, Rioch, Gray E	Glasgow May 8: 3-0 Gemmill, Masson, Dalglish	Glasgow May 15: 2-1 Masson, Dalglish	Glasgow Sept 8: 6-0 Rioch, Masson (pen), Dalglish, Gray A 2, Gray E	Prague Oct 13: 0-2

1976 Wales	1977 Sweden	1977 Wales	1977 N Ireland	1977 England
1 Rough	1 Rough	1 Rough	1 Rough	1 Rough
2 McGrain	2 McGrain	2 McGrain	2 McGrain	2 McGrain
3 Donachie	3 Forsyth	3 Donachie	3 Donachie	3 Donachie
4 Blackley	4 Blackley (Narey)	4 Rioch (Johnston)	4 Forsyth	4 Forsyth
5 McQueen	5 Donachie	5 McQueen	5 McQueen	5 McQueen
6 Rioch (Hartford)	6 Glavin (Jardine)	6 Forsyth	6 Rioch	6 Rioch
7 Burns	7 Dalglish	7 Masson	7 Masson	7 Masson (Gemmill)
8 Dalglish	8 Hartford	8 Gemmill	8 Hartford	8 Dalglish
9 Jordan	9 Burns (Craig J)	9 Jordan (Burns)	9 Jordan (Macari)	9 Jordan (Macari)
10 Gemmill	10 Pettigrew	10 Dalglish	10 Dalglish	10 Hartford
11 Gray E (Pettigrew)	11 Johnston	11 Hartford	11 Johnston (Gemmill)	11 Johnston
Glasgow Nov 17: 1-0 Evans (og)	Glasgow April 27: 3-1 Hartford, Dalglish, Craig J	Wrexham May 28: 0-0	Glasgow June 1: 3-0 Dalglish 2, McQueen	Wembley June 4: 2-0 McQueen, Dalglish

1977 Chile	1977 Argentina	1977 Brazil	1977 E Germany	1977 Czechoslovakia
1 Rough (Stewart)	1 Rough	1 Rough	1 Stewart	1 Rough
2 McGrain	2 McGrain	2 McGrain	2 McGrain	2 Jardine
3 Donachie	3 Donachie	3 Donachie	3 Donachie	3 McGrain
4 Buchan	4 Gemmill	4 Rioch	4 Masson	4 Forsyth
5 Forsyth	5 Forsyth	5 Forsyth	5 McQueen	5 McQueen
6 Rioch (Gemmill)	6 Buchan	6 Buchan	6 Buchan	6 Rioch
7 Masson	7 Masson	7 Masson	7 Dalglish	7 Dalglish
8 Dalglish	8 Dalglish	8 Gemmill	8 Hartford (Gemmill)	8 Masson
9 Macari	9 Macari	9 Dalglish	9 Jordan	9 Jordan
10 Hartford (Jardine)	10 Hartford	10 Hartford	10 Macari	10 Hartford
11 Johnston	11 Johnston	11 Johnston (Jardine)	11 Johnston (Graham)	11 Johnston
Santiago June 15: 4-2 Dalglish, Macari 2, Hartford	Buenos Aires June 18: 1-1 Masson (pen)	Rio June 23: 0-2	East Berlin Sept 7: 0-1	Glasgow Sept 21: 3-1 Jordan Hartford, Dalglish

1977 Wales	1978 Bulgaria	1978 N Ireland	1978 Wales	1978 England
1 Rough	1 Blyth	1 Rough	1 Blyth	1 Rough
2 Jardine (Buchan)	2 Kennedy	2 Jardine	2 Kennedy	2 Kennedy
3 Donachie	3 Donachie	3 Buchan (Burns)	3 Donachie	3 Burns
4 Masson	4 Souness	4 Forsyth	4 Burns	4 Forsyth
5 McQueen	5 McQueen	5 McQueen	5 McQueen (Forsyth)	5 Donachie
6 Forsyth	6 Miller	6 Rioch	6 Gemmill	6 Rioch (Souness)
7 Dalglish	7 Dalglish (Wallace)	7 Masson	7 Souness	7 Masson (Gemmill)
8 Hartford	8 Hartford	8 Gemmill	8 Hartford	8 Hartford
9 Jordan	9 Jordan (Johnstone)	9 Jordan (Dalglish)	9 Johnstone	9 Dalglish
10 Macari	10 Macari	10 Johnstone	10 Dalglish	10 Jordan
11 Johnston	11 Gemmill	11 Robertson	11 Johnston (Robertson)	11 Johnston
Liverpool Oct 12: 2-0 *Masson (pen), Dalglish*	Glasgow Feb 22: 2-1 *Gemmill (pen), Wallace*	Glasgow May 13: 1-1 *Johnstone*	Glasgow May 17: 1-1 *Johnstone*	Glasgow May 20: 0-1

1978 Peru	1978 Iran	1978 Netherlands
1 Rough	1 Rough	1 Rough
2 Burns	2 Buchan (Forsyth)	2 Donachie
3 Kennedy	3 Jardine	3 Buchan
4 Forsyth	4 Burns	4 Kennedy
5 Buchan	5 Donachie	5 Forsyth
6 Rioch (Macari)	6 Macari	6 Rioch
7 Masson (Gemmill)	7 Gemmill	7 Hartford
8 Hartford	8 Hartford	8 Gemmill
9 Dalglish	9 Jordan	9 Souness
10 Jordan	10 Dalglish (Harper)	10 Dalglish
11 Johnston	11 Robertson	11 Jordan
Cordoba June 3: 1-3 *Jordan*	Cordoba June 7: 1-1 *Eskandarian (og)*	Mendoza June 11: 3-2 *Dalglish, Gemmill 2, (1 a pen)*

Wales' full international teams 1876-1978

1876 Scotland	1877 Scotland	1878 Scotland	1879 England	1879 Scotland
1 Thompson	1 Burnett	1 Phennah	1 Glascodine	1 Davies, John
2 Evans W A W	2 Evans W A W	2 Higham	2 Kenrick	2 Kenrick
3 Kenrick	3 Kenrick	3 Powell	3 Higham	3 Morgan J R
4 Cross	4 Morgan	4 Edwards H	4 Williams W	4 Cross
5 Williams W	5 Cross	5 Williams W	5 Owen T	5 Williams W
6 Dr Gray	6 Davies W H	6 Savin	6 Davies W H	6 Lloyd J W
7 Davies W H	7 Davies A	7 Davies, James	7 Shone	7 Woosnam
8 Thomson	8 Price	8 Dr Gray	8 Heywood	8 Hughes A J
9 Edwards J H	9 Jones A F	9 Britten	9 Price	9 Roberts J
10 Jones J	10 Hughes J	10 Price	10 Owen D	10 Roberts W
11 Davies A	11 Thomson	11 Edwards C	11 Roberts W	11 Vaughan
Glasgow Mar 25: 0-4	Wrexham Mar 5: 0-2	Glasgow Mar 23: 0-9	London Jan 18: 1-2 *Davies*	Wrexham April 7: 0-3

1880 England	1880 Scotland	1881 England	1881 Scotland	1882 Ireland
1 Hibbott	1 Hibbott	1 McMillan	1 McMillan	1 Adams
2 Morgan J R	2 Morgan J R	2 Morgan J R	2 Morgan J R	2 Morgan J R
3 Powell	3 Powell	3 Kenrick	3 Roberts (Ruthin)	3 Powell
4 Edwards H	4 Bowen	4 Williams W	4 Williams W	4 Hughes F W
5 Williams W	5 Williams W	5 Bell	5 Bell	5 Williams W
6 Owen W P	6 Owen W P	6 Owen W P	6 Owen W P	6 Owen W P
7 Davies W H	7 Roberts J	7 Lewis T	7 Lewis T	7 Shaw
8 Boden	8 Roberts J	8 Cross	8 Price	8 Ketley
9 Price	9 Price	9 Price	9 Cross	9 Price
10 Roberts J	10 Britten	10 Goodwin	10 Roberts W	10 Roberts J
11 Roberts W	11 Vaughan	11 Vaughan	11 Vaughan	11 Vaughan
Wrexham Mar 15: 2-3 *Roberts J, Roberts W*	Glasgow Mar 27: 1-5 *Roberts W*	Blackburn Feb 26: 1-0 *Vaughan*	Wrexham Mar 14: 1-5 *Cross*	Wrexham Feb 25: 7-1 *Price 4, Morgan, Owen 2*

1882 England	1882 Scotland	1883 England	1883 Scotland	1883 Ireland
1 Adams	1 Phoenix	1 Adams	1 Gough	1 Gough
2 Morgan J R	2 Morgan J R	2 Powell	2 Powell	2 Powell
3 Powell	3 Powell	3 Morgan J R	3 Hughes F W	3 Hughes F W
4 Edwards H	4 Edwards H	4 Hughes F W	4 Bowen	4 Bowen
5 Hughes F W	5 Williams W	5 Burke	5 Jones J	5 Williams W
6 Williams W	6 Roberts J (Ruthin)	6 Roberts W H	6 Edwards H	6 Eyton-Jones
7 Owen W P	7 Owen W P	7 Owen W P	7 Price	7 Price
8 Roberts W H	8 Roberts W H	8 Davies J P	8 Owen W P	8 Vaughan
9 Price	9 Price	9 Roberts W	9 Roberts W H	9 Roberts W H
10 Roberts J	10 Roberts J (Corwen)	10 Roberts J	10 Vaughan	10 Owen W P
11 Vaughan	11 Vaughan	11 Vaughan	11 Roberts W	11 Davies R
Wrexham Mar 13: 5-3 *Owen 2, Morgan, Vaughan 1 (og)*	Glasgow Mar 25: 0-5	London Feb 3: 0-5	Wrexham Mar 12: 0-3	Belfast Mar 17: 1-1 *Roberts*

1884 Ireland	1884 England	1884 Scotland	1885 England	1885 Scotland
1 Owen	1 Owen	1 Owen	1 Mills-Roberts	1 Mills-Roberts
2 Conde	2 Powell	2 Roberts R	2 Jones F R	2 Powell
3 Davies W	3 Conde	3 Conde	3 Thomas G	3 Thomas G
4 Foulkes	4 Evans M	4 Hughes F W	4 Davies R	4 Burke
5 Griffiths	5 Williams J H	5 Burke	5 Jones H	5 Jones H
6 Edwards H	6 Griffiths	6 Jones J	6 Davies J E	6 Foulkes
7 Owen W P	7 Owen W P	7 Owen W P	7 Vaughan	7 Hibbott
8 Davies R	8 Owen W	8 Roberts W H	8 Farmer	8 Farmer
9 Shaw	9 Vaughan	9 Shaw	9 Lewis	9 Lloyd
10 Eyton-Jones	10 Eyton-Jones	10 Eyton-Jones	10 Burke	10 Jones R A
11 Jones R A	11 Jones R A	11 Jones R A	11 Wilding	11 Wilding
Wrexham Feb 9: 6-0 *Shaw 2, Owen W P 2, Jones, Eyton-Jones*	Wrexham Mar 17: 0-4	Glasgow Mar 29: 1-4 *Roberts R*	Blackburn Mar 14: 1-1 *Wilding*	Wrexham Mar 23: 1-8 *Jones R A*

1885 Ireland	1886 Ireland	1886 England	1886 Scotland	1887 England
1 Mills-Roberts	1 Hersee M	1 Mills-Roberts	1 Hersee M	1 Mills-Roberts
2 Jones T	2 Roberts R	2 Davies A O	2 Davies A O	2 Davies A O
3 Davies A O	3 Powell	3 Powell	3 Jones F R	3 Powell
4 Burke	4 Vaughan	4 Vaughan	4 Vaughan	4 Jones H
5 Vaughan	5 Bell	5 Bell	5 Bell	5 Burke
6 Jones H	6 Jones H	6 Jones H	6 Jones H	6 Evelyn
7 Davies R	7 Wilding	7 Wilding	7 Williams R P	7 Challen
8 Owen W	8 Roberts W	8 Roberts W	8 Roberts W	8 Owen
9 Wilding	9 Sisson	9 Davies T	9 Sisson	9 Wilding
10 Sisson	10 Bryan	10 Bryan	10 Lewis	10 Turner
11 Roach	11 Hersee R	11 Lewis	11 Doughty J	11 Lewis
Belfast April 11: 8-2 *Owen, Burke, Sisson 3, Roach 2, Jones H*	Wrexham Feb 27: 5-0 *Roberts W, Wilding, Hersee R, Sisson, Bryan*	Wrexham Mar 29: 1-3 *Lewis*	Glasgow April 10: 1-4 *Lundie (og)*	London Feb 26: 0-4

1887 Ireland	1887 Scotland	1888 England	1888 Ireland	1888 Scotland
1 Roberts E	1 Trainer	1 Mills-Roberts	1 Mills-Roberts	1 Trainer
2 Townsend	2 Davies A O	2 Davies A O	2 Davies A O	2 Jones D
3 Jones S	3 Powell	3 Roberts R	3 Powell	3 Powell
4 Hughes P W	4 Morris	4 Powell	4 Jones D	4 Burke
5 Hunter	5 Burke	5 Griffiths	5 Humphreys	5 Davies R
6 Edwards H	6 Roberts R	6 Davies Jos	6 Davies Jos	6 Roberts Jos
7 Sabine	7 Challen	7 Challen	7 Doughty J	7 Doughty J
8 Doughty J	8 Doughty J	8 Doughty J	8 Howell	8 Doughty R
9 Turner	9 Lewis	9 Lewis	9 Pryce-Jones	9 Pryce-Jones
10 Roberts W	10 Pryce-Jones	10 Pryce-Jones	10 Doughty R	10 Owen G
11 Griffiths	11 Jones R	11 Owen	11 Wilding	11 Wilding
Belfast Mar 12: 1-4 *Sabine*	Wrexham Mar 21: 0-2	Crewe Feb 4: 1-5 *Doughty J*	Wrexham Mar 3: 11-0 *Wilding 2, Doughty J 4, Howell 2, Doughty R 2, Pryce-Jones*	Edinburgh Mar 10: 1-5 *Doughty J*

1889 England	1889 Scotland	1889 Ireland	1890 Ireland	1890 England
1 Trainer	1 Gillam (Pugh)	1 Gillam	1 Gillam	1 Gillam
2 Jones W P	2 Davies A O	2 Jones W P	2 Jones D	2 Davies A O
3 Jones D	3 Jones D	3 Jones D	3 Jones W P	3 Jones D
4 Hughes	4 Roberts R	4 Hughes	4 Griffiths	4 Davies J (Heath N)
5 Jones H	5 Davies J (Heath N)	5 Carty	5 Hayes	5 Jones H
6 Roberts R	6 Jones H	6 Leary	6 Jones R	6 Evans W G
7 Hallam	7 Davies J (Everton)	7 Davies J (Everton)	7 Bowdler J C H	7 Challen
8 Jones R	8 Owen W	8 Owen W	8 Willcocks	8 Jones R
9 Lewis	9 Doughty J	9 Owen G	9 Pryce-Jones	9 Doughty R
10 Lea	10 Owen G	10 Jarrett	10 Owen W	10 Howell
11 Owen	11 Lewis	11 Lewis	11 Lewis	11 Lewis
Stoke-on-Trent Feb 23: 1-4 Owen	Wrexham April 15: 0-0	Belfast April 27: 3-1 Jarrett 3	Shrewsbury Feb 8: 5-2 Lewis 2, Pryce-Jones 2, Owen	Wrexham Mar 15: 1-3 Lewis

1890 Scotland	1891 Ireland	1891 England	1891 Scotland	1892 Ireland
1 Trainer	1 Turner	1 Turner	1 Trainer	1 Trainer
2 Jones W P	2 Roberts R (Wrexham)	2 Evans W G	2 Powell	2 Arridge
3 Jones S	3 Lloyd	3 Powell	3 Jones D	3 Jones D
4 Griffiths	4 Griffiths	4 Hughes W	4 Lea	4 Hughes
5 Jones H	5 Mates	5 Jones H	5 Jones H	5 Jenkyns
6 Roberts R	6 Lea	6 Parry	6 Parry	6 Roberts R
7 Lewis	7 Davies J	7 Davies J	7 Davies J	7 Davies R L
8 Davies O	8 Owen W	8 Owen W	8 Owen W	8 Bostock
9 Owen	9 Davies O	9 Turner	9 Turner	9 Lewis B
10 Jarrett	10 Roberts R (Rhos)	10 Howell	10 Bowdler J C H	10 Bowdler J C H
11 Turner	11 Lewis	11 Lewis	11 Lewis	11 Lewis W
Glasgow Mar 22: 0-5	Belfast Feb 7: 2-7 Lewis 2	Sunderland Mar 7: 1-4 Howell	Wrexham Mar 21: 3-4 Bowdler 2, Owen	Bangor Feb 27: 1-1 Lewis B

1892 England	1892 Scotland	1893 England	1893 Scotland	1893 Ireland
1 Mills-Roberts	1 Trainer	1 Trainer	1 Jones S	1 Jones S
2 Evans	2 Arridge	2 Jones D	2 Taylor	2 Townsend
3 Powell	3 Powell	3 Parry	3 Jones F W	3 Taylor
4 Davies J (Wolves)	4 Hughes	4 Williams E	4 Williams G	4 Lea
5 Jenkyns	5 Jenkyns	5 Davies J (Wolves)	5 Williams E	5 Evans J
6 Owen G	6 Roberts R	6 Morris E	6 Morris E	6 Morris E
7 Owen W	7 Wilding	7 Butler	7 Vaughan	7 Vaughan
8 Turner	8 Owen W	8 Vaughan	8 Butler	8 Owen W
9 Lewis B	9 Lewis B	9 James	9 Owen W	9 Butler
10 Davies R L	10 Egan	10 Lewis B	10 Lewis B	10 Owen G
11 Lewis W	11 Lewis W	11 Roberts R	11 Bowdler H E	11 James
Wrexham Mar 5: 0-2	Edinburgh Mar 26: 1-6 Lewis B	Stoke-on-Trent Mar 13: 0-6	Wrexham Mar 18: 0-8	Belfast April 5: 3-4 Owen G 2, Stewart (og)

1894 Ireland	1894 England	1894 Scotland	1895 Ireland	1895 England
1 Trainer	1 Trainer	1 Gillam	1 Trainer J	1 Trainer J
2 Arridge	2 Parry	2 Taylor	2 Arridge	2 Parry
3 Taylor	3 Jones D	3 Hughes	3 Edwards	3 Jones D
4 Jones R S	4 Evans J	4 Williams G	4 Williams G	4 Williams G
5 Chapman	5 Chapman	5 Chapman	6 Chapman	5 Jenkyns
6 Hayes	6 Hughes	6 Worthington	6 Jones J L	6 Jones J L
7 Evans J	7 James	7 Morris H	7 Meredith W	7 Meredith W
8 Lewis B	8 Lewis B	8 Lewis B	8 Davies Jos	8 Davies Jos
9 Lewis W	9 Lewis W	9 Lewis W	9 Trainer H	9 Trainer H
10 Rea	10 Rea	10 Rea	10 Parry	10 Pryce-Jones
11 James	11 Bowdler J C H	11 James	11 Lewis W	11 Lewis W
Swansea Feb 24: 4-1 Lewis W 2, James 2	Wrexham Mar 12: 1-5 Bowdler	Kilmarnock Mar 24: 2-5 Morris 2	Belfast Mar 16: 2-2 Trainer H 2	London Mar 18: 1-1 Lewis

1895 Scotland	1896 Ireland	1896 England	1896 Scotland	1897 Ireland
1 Jones S	1 Jones S	1 Jones S	1 Trainer	1 Trainer
2 Lloyd	2 Parry	2 Arridge	2 Parry	2 Edwards
3 Parry	3 Matthias	3 Parry	3 Matthias	3 Parry
4 Williams G	4 Rogers	4 Rogers	4 Rogers	4 Darvell
5 Chapman	5 White	5 Chapman	5 Jenkyns	5 Jenkyns
6 Jones J L	6 Jones J L	6 Jones J L	6 Jones J L	6 Jones J L
7 Davies Jos	7 Meredith W	7 Meredith W	7 Pugh	7 Meredith W
8 Lewis B	8 Pugh	8 Davies Jos	8 Garner	8 Pugh
9 Trainer H	9 Morris A G	9 Morris, A G	9 Morris A G	9 Morgan-Owen
10 Lewis W	10 Rea	10 Morris H	10 Lewis W	10 Rea
11 Rea	11 Lewis W	11 Lewis W	11 Rea	11 Nock
Wrexham Mar 23: 2-2 Lewis W, Chapman	Wrexham Feb 29: 6-1 Lewis 2, Meredith 2, Pugh, Morris	Cardiff Mar 16: 1-9 Chapman	Dundee Mar 21: 0-4	Belfast Mar 6: 3-4 Meredith 2, Jenkyns

1897 Scotland	1897 England	1898 Ireland	1898 Scotland	1898 England
1 Trainer	1 Trainer	1 Morris J	1 Trainer	1 Trainer
2 Jones W R	2 Matthias	2 Parry	2 Parry	2 Parry
3 Matthias	3 Edwards	3 Arridge	3 Jones D	3 Arridge
4 Darvell	4 Chapman	4 Williams G	4 Jones R S	4 Taylor
5 Mates	5 Mates	5 Edwards	5 Jenkyns	5 Jenkyns
6 Jones J L	6 Jones J L	6 Jones J L	6 Jones J L	6 Jones J L
7 Meredith W	7 Meredith W	7 Meredith W	7 Roberts J (Chirk)	7 Meredith W
8 Pugh	8 Davies Jos	8 Thomas	8 Thomas	8 Bartley
9 Morgan-Owen	9 Morris A G	9 Lewis W	9 Morgan-Owen	9 Morgan-Owen
10 Rea	10 Morris H	10 Lockley	10 Morris A G	10 Watkins
11 Lewis W	11 Lewis W	11 Rea	11 Watkins	11 James
Wrexham Mar 20: 2-2 Pugh, Morgan-Owen	Sheffield Mar 29: 0-4	Llandudno Feb 19: 0-1	Motherwell Mar 19: 2-5 Thomas, Morgan-Owen	Wrexham Mar 28: 0-3

R.F. 79/80—44

1899 Ireland	1899 Scotland	1899 England	1900 Scotland	1900 Ireland
1 Trainer	1 Trainer	1 Jones W	1 Griffiths	1 Roose
2 Blew	2 Matthias	2 Blew	2 Thomas	2 Jones D
3 Thomas	3 Blew	3 Arridge	3 Morris C	3 Morris C
4 Richards	4 Richards	4 Richards	4 Meredith S	4 Brookes
5 Jones J L	5 Jones J L	5 Buckland	5 Jones J L	5 Morris R
6 Hughes	6 Hughes	6 Harrison	6 Harrison	6 Harrison
7 Kelly	7 Kelly	7 Vaughan	7 Pugh	7 Meredith W
8 Atherton	8 Owen T	8 Meredith W	8 Butler	8 Butler
9 James	9 Morgan-Owen	9 Owen T	9 Jones R	9 Jones R
10 Davies C	10 Jones R	10 Morris A G	10 Parry	10 Parry
11 Jackson	11 Morris A G	11 Atherton	11 Watkins	11 Davies C
Belfast Mar 4: 0-1	Wrexham Mar 18: 0-6	Bristol Mar 20: 0-4	Aberdeen Feb 3: 2-5 *Butler, Parry*	Llandudno Feb 24: 2-0 *Parry, Meredith (pen*

1900 England	1901 Scotland	1901 England	1901 Ireland	1902 Ireland
1 Griffiths	1 Roose	1 Roose	1 Roose	1 Evans R O
2 Jones D	2 Meredith S	2 Meredith S	2 Meredith S	2 Blew
3 Morris C	3 Morris C	3 Morris C	3 Morris C	3 Jones H
4 Brookes	4 Parry M	4 Parry M	4 Parry M	4 Parry M
5 Morris R	5 Jones W J	5 Jones W J	5 Morris R	5 Hughes
6 Harrison	6 Hughes	6 Hughes	6 Harrison	6 Jones J L
7 Meredith W	7 Pugh	7 Meredith W	7 Meredith W	7 Kelly
8 Davies Jos	8 Jones J O	8 Pugh	8 Jones J O	8 Kenkins
9 Morgan-Owen	9 Morgan-Owen	9 Morgan-Owen	9 Green	9 Evans R
10 Watkins	10 Parry T D	10 Parry T D	10 Parry T D	10 Williams E
11 Parry	11 Williams E	11 Williams E	11 Williams	11 Morris R
Cardiff Mar 26: 1-1 *Meredith*	Wrexham Mar 2: 1-1 *Parry*	Newcastle Mar 18: 0-6	Belfast Mar 23: 1-0 *Jones*	Cardiff Feb 22: 0-3

1902 England	1902 Scotland	1903 England	1903 Scotland	1903 Ireland
1 Roose	1 Roose	1 Evans R O	1 Evans R O	1 Evans R O
2 Meredith S	2 Blew	2 Blew	2 Blew	2 Meredith S
3 Morris C	3 Morris C	3 Morris C	3 Morris C	3 Morris C
4 Parry M	4 Parry M	4 Parry M	4 Parry M	4 Richards
5 Jones J L	5 Jones J L	5 Morris R	5 Morgan-Owen	5 Morris R
6 Jones W J	6 Jones W J	6 Davies T	6 Davies T	6 Davies T
7 Meredith W	7 Meredith W	7 Meredith W	7 Meredith W	7 Meredith W
8 Watkins W M	8 Griffiths	8 Watkins W M	8 Watkins W M	8 Wynn
9 Parry T D	9 Morgan-Owen	9 Green	9 Morris A G	9 Davies W
10 Williams E	10 Morris R	10 Morris A G	10 Morris R	10 Morris R
11 Morris R	11 Owen J	11 Atherton	11 Atherton	11 Atherton
Wrexham Mar 3: 0-0	Greenock Mar 15: 1-5 *Meredith*	Portsmouth Mar 2: 1-2 *Watkins*	Cardiff Mar 9: 0-1	Belfast Mar 28: 0-2

1904 England	1904 Scotland	1904 Ireland	1905 Scotland	1905 England
1 Roose	1 Davies D	1 Davies D	1 Roose	1 Roose
2 Meredith S	2 Blew	2 Blew	2 Blew	2 Jones A T
3 Blew	3 Davies T	3 Morris C	3 Morris C	3 Morris C
4 Parry M	4 Richards	4 Parry M	4 Lathom	4 Lathom
5 Hughes	5 Hughes	5 Hughes	5 Hughes E	5 Hughes E
6 Jones J L	6 Jones J L	6 Jones J L	6 Hughes J	6 Hughes J
7 Meredith W	7 Davies A	7 Watkins A E	7 Meredith W	7 Meredith W
8 Atherton	8 Watkins W M	8 Watkins W M	8 Davies A	8 Jones W L
9 Watkins W M	9 Green	9 Green	9 Watkins M	9 Watkins M
10 Morris R	10 Morris R	10 Atherton	10 Morris A G	10 Morris A G
11 Davies Lloyd	11 Atherton	11 Morris R	11 Oliver	11 Oliver
Wrexham Feb 29: 2-2 *Watkins, Davies*	Dundee Mar 12: 1-1 *Atherton*	Bangor Mar 21: 0-1	Wrexham Mar 6: 3-1 *Morris A G, Meredith, Watkins*	Liverpool Mar 27: 1-5 *Morris A G*

1905 Ireland	1906 Scotland	1906 England	1906 Ireland	1907 Ireland
1 Morgan	1 Roose	1 Roose	1 Roose	1 Roose
2 Blew	2 Blew	2 Jones A T	2 Blew	2 Roberts
3 Morris C	3 Morris C	3 Blew	3 Roberts	3 Davies Lloyd
4 Richards	4 Hughes E	4 Parry M	4 Hughes E (N Forest)	4 Lathom
5 Hughes E	5 Morgan-Owen M M	5 Morgan-Owen M M	5 Morgan-Owen M M	5 Williams G O
6 Hughes J	6 Lathom	6 Hughes E	6 Hughes E (Spurs)	6 Davies Llew
7 Matthews	7 Jones W L	7 Jones W L	7 Jones W L	7 Meredith W
8 Watkins	8 Morris R	8 Morgan-Owen H	8 Morgan-Owen H	8 Jones W L
9 Davies W	9 Jones J L	9 Green	9 Green	9 Hughes A
10 Jones W L	10 Jones R	10 Lewis	10 Jones R	10 Morris R
11 Atherton	11 Evans R	11 Evans R	11 Evans R	11 Jones G P
Belfast April 8: 2-2 *Watkins, Atherton*	Edinburgh Mar 3: 2-0 *Jones W L, Jones J L*	Cardiff Mar 19: 0-1	Wrexham April 2: 4-4 *Green 3, Morgan-Owen H*	Belfast Feb 23: 3-2 *Morris, Meredith, Jones W L*

1907 Scotland	1907 England	1908 Scotland	1908 England	1908 Ireland
1 Roose	1 Roose	1 Roose	1 Roose (Davies D)	1 Evans R O
2 Blew	2 Davies Lloyd	2 Blew	2 Blew	2 Blew
3 Morris C	3 Meredith S	3 Morris C	3 Morris C	3 Jones J
4 Lathom	4 Hughes E (Spurs)	4 Hughes E (N Forest)	4 Hughes E (N Forest)	4 Peake
5 Davies Lloyd	5 Morgan-Owen M M	5 Parry M	5 Parry M	5 Parry M
6 Price	6 Lathom	6 Davies Lloyd	6 Lathom	6 Price
7 Meredith W	7 Meredith W	7 Davies W C	7 Meredith W	7 Meredith W
8 Jones W L	8 Jones W L	8 Jones W L	8 Matthews	8 Morris R
9 Morgan-Owen	9 Green	9 Davies W	9 Davies W	9 Watkins W M
10 Morris A G	10 Morris A G	10 Green	10 Morris A G	10 Hodgkinson
11 Jones G P	11 Evans R	11 Evans R	11 Evans R	11 Jones T D
Wrexham Mar 4: 1-0 *Morris A G*	Fulham Mar 18: 1-1 *Jones*	Dundee Mar 7: 1-2 *Jones*	Wrexham Mar 16: 1-7 *Davies W*	Aberdare April 11: 0-1

1909 Scotland	1909 England	1909 Ireland	1910 Scotland	1910 England
1 Roose	1 Roose	1 Roose	1 Roose	1 Roose
2 Blew	2 Blew	2 Morris C	2 Jones J	2 Blew
3 Morris C	3 Morris C	3 Jones J	3 Morris C	3 Morris C
4 Parry M	4 Parry M	4 Lathom	4 Hughes (N Forest)	4 Hughes (N Forest)
5 Peake	5 Peake	5 Peake	5 Peake	5 Lathom
6 Price	6 Price	6 Davies Lloyd	6 Davies Llew	6 Davies Llew
7 Meredith W	7 Meredith W	7 Meredith W	7 Meredith W	7 Meredith W
8 Wynn	8 Wynn	8 Wynn	8 Davies W C	8 Wynn
9 Davies W	9 Davies W	9 Davies W	9 Jones E	9 Jones W L
10 Jones W L	10 Jones W L	10 Jones W L	10 Morris A G	10 Morris A G
11 Evans R	11 Davies W C	11 Price	11 Evans R	11 Evans R
Wrexham Mar 1: 3-2 Davies 2, Jones	Nottingham Mar 15: 0-2	Belfast Mar 20: 3-2 Jones W L, Wynn, Meredith	Kilmarnock Mar 5: 0-1	Cardiff Mar 14: 0-1

1910 Ireland	1911 Ireland	1911 Scotland	1911 England	1912 Scotland
1 Roose	1 Evans R O	1 Roose	1 Evans R O	1 Evans R O
2 Davies Lloyd	2 Hewitt	2 Morris C	2 Morris C	2 Davies Llew
3 Morris C	3 Morris C	3 Hewitt	3 Hewitt	3 Davies Lloyd
4 Hughes (N Forest)	4 Hughes (N Forest)	4 Hughes (N Forest)	4 Hughes (N Forest)	4 Jones J T
5 Peake	5 Peake	5 Davies Lloyd	5 Davies Lloyd	5 Hughes (W'ham)
6 Davies Llew	6 Davies Llew	6 Davies Llew	6 Jones W L	6 Russell
7 Meredith W	7 Meredith W	7 Meredith W	7 Meredith W	7 Meredith W
8 Jones J L	8 Wynn	8 Jones E	8 Jones E	8 Wynn
9 Jones E	9 Davies W	9 Davies W	9 Davies W	9 Jones E
10 Morris A G	10 Morris A G	10 Morris A G	10 Morris A G	10 Williams J W
11 Evans R	11 Vizard	11 Vizard	11 Vizard	11 Vizard
Wrexham April 11: 4-1 Evans 2, Morris A G 2	Belfast Jan 28: 2-1 Davies, Morris A G	Cardiff Mar 6: 2-2 Morris A G 2	London Mar 13: 0-3	Edinburgh Mar 2: 0-1

1912 England	1912 Ireland	1913 Ireland	1913 Scotland	1913 England
1 Evans R O	1 Evans R O	1 Bailiff	1 Bailiff	1 Bailiff
2 Davies Llew	2 Davies Llew	2 Hewitt	2 Hewitt	2 Hewitt
3 Davies Lloyd	3 Russell	3 Davies Llew	3 Davies Llew	3 Davies Lloyd
4 Hughes (Wrexham)	4 Hughes (Wrexham)	4 Lathom	4 Hughes (Man City)	4 Hughes (Man City)
5 Peake	5 Newton	5 Peake	5 Davies Lloyd	5 Peake
6 Jones J T	6 Jones J T	6 Jones J T	6 Jones W L	6 Jones J T
7 Meredith W	7 Meredith W	7 Meredith W	7 Meredith W	7 Meredith W
8 Wynn	8 Williams J W	8 Davies D W	8 Wynn	8 Wynn
9 Jones E	9 Davies W	9 Davies W	9 Davis W	9 Davis W
10 Morris A G	10 Davies D W	10 Roberts	10 Roberts	10 Jones W L
11 Vizard	11 Evans J	11 Evans J	11 Vizard	11 Davies Llew
Wrexham Mar 11: 0-2	Cardiff April 13: 2-3 Davies W, Davies D W	Belfast Jan 18: 1-0 Roberts	Wrexham Mar 3: 0-0	Bristol Mar 17: 3-4 Davis, Meredith, Peake

1914 Ireland	1914 Scotland	1914 England	1920 Ireland	1920 Scotland
1 Peers	1 Peers	1 Peers	1 Bailiff	1 Peers
2 Davies Llew	2 Hewitt	2 Hewitt	2 Millership	2 Millership
3 Davies Lloyd	3 Jennings	3 Russell	3 Russell	3 Russell
4 Hughes (Man City)	4 Mathias	4 Mathias	4 Mathias	4 Mathias
5 Peake	5 Davies Lloyd	5 Davies Lloyd	5 Jones J T	5 Jones J T
6 Jones J T	6 Jones J T	6 Jennings	6 Keenor	6 Jennings
7 Meredith W	7 Meredith W	7 Meredith W	7 Meredith W	7 Meredith W
8 Jones E	8 Wynn	8 Wynn	8 Jones W L	8 Jones I
9 Davis W	9 Davis W	9 Rowlands	9 Davies S	9 Davies S
10 Jones W L	10 Jones W L	10 Davies W C	10 Jones I	10 Richards
11 Vizard	11 Evans J	11 Vizard	11 Evans J	11 Evans J
Wrexham Jan 19: 1-2 *Jones E* (pen)	Glasgow Feb 28: 0-0	Cardiff Mar 16: 0-2	Belfast Feb 14: 2-2 *Davies 2*	Cardiff Feb 26: 1-1 *Evans*

1920 England	1921 Scotland	1921 England	1921 Ireland	1922 Scotland
1 Peers	1 Peers	1 Peers	1 Peers	1 Peers
2 Millership	2 Millership	2 Millership	2 Russell	2 Parry E
3 Russell	3 Russell	3 Russell	3 Millership	3 Evans J H
4 Mathias	4 Keenor	4 Keenor	4 Keenor	4 Evans H P
5 Jones J T	5 Jones J T	5 Jones J T	5 Matthews	5 Jones J T
6 Keenor	6 Mathias	6 Mathias	6 Mathias	6 Mathias
7 Meredith W	7 Williams R	7 Williams R	7 Hole	7 Davies S
8 Jones W L	8 Collier	8 Jones I	8 Jones I	8 Jones I
9 Davies S	9 Hoddinott	9 Hoddinott	9 Davies S	9 Davies L
10 Richards	10 Davies S	10 Davies S	10 Richards	10 Richards
11 Vizard	11 Vizard	11 Vizard	11 Vizard	11 Vizard
London Mar 15: 2-1 *Davies* (pen), *Richards*	Aberdeen Feb 12: 1-2 *Collier*	Cardiff Mar 16: 0-0	Swansea April 9: 2-1 *Hole, Davies*	Wrexham Feb 4: 2-1 *Davies L, Davies S*

1922 England	1922 Ireland	1923 England	1923 Scotland	1923 Ireland
1 Peers	1 Peers	1 Peers	1 Godding	1 Godding
2 Russell	2 Russell	2 Parry	2 Russell	2 Russell
3 Evans J H	3 Evans J H	3 Russell	3 Evans J H	3 Parry
4 Evans H P	4 Evans H P	4 Keenor	4 Mathias	4 John
5 Jones J T	5 Jones J T	5 Matthews	5 Keenor	5 Keenor
6 Mathias	6 Mathias	6 Jennings	6 John	6 Jennings
7 Hole	7 Davies S	7 Hole	7 Williams R	7 Hole
8 Davies S	8 Keenor	8 Jones I	8 Davies I	8 Jones I
9 Davies L	9 Davies L	9 Davies L	9 Davies S	9 Davies L
10 Richards	10 Jones I	10 Vizard	10 Davies L	10 Vizard
11 Vizard	11 Evans J	11 Evans J	11 Nicholas	11 Evans J
Liverpool Mar 13: 0-1	Belfast April 1: 1-1 *Davies L*	Cardiff Mar 5: 2-2 *Keenor, Jones*	Glasgow Mar 17: 0-2	Wrexham April 14: 0-3

1924 Scotland	1924 England	1924 Ireland	1925 Scotland	1925 England
1 Gray	1 Gray	1 Gray	1 Gray	1 Gray
2 Russell	2 Russell	2 Russell	2 Jenkins	2 Morley
3 Jenkins	3 Jenkins	3 Jenkins	3 Russell	3 Russell
4 Evans H P	4 Evans H P	4 Evans H P	4 Davies S	4 Jenkins E
5 Keenor	5 Kennor	5 Keenor	5 Keenor	5 Keenor
6 Jennings	6 Jennings	6 Jennings	6 Williams W	6 Thomas E
7 Davies W	7 Davies W	7 Davies W	7 Davies W	7 Davies W
8 Jones I	8 Nicholls	8 Nicholls	8 Nicholls	8 Nicholls
9 Davies L	9 Davies L	9 Davies L	9 Davies L	9 Fowler
10 Richards	10 Richards	10 Richards	10 Beadles	10 Beadles
11 Vizard	11 Vizard	11 Vizard	11 Cook	11 Cook
Cardiff Feb 16: 2-0 *Davies W, Davies L*	Blackburn Mar 3: 2-1 *Davies W, Vizard*	Belfast Mar 15: 1-0 *Russell* (pen)	Edinburgh Feb 14: 1-3 *Williams*	Swansea Feb 28: 1-2 *Bower (og)*

1925 Ireland	1925 Scotland	1926 Ireland	1926 England	1926 Scotland
1 Gray	1 Gray	1 Brown	1 Gray	1 Gray
2 Parry	2 Russell	2 Parry	2 Russell	2 Evans T J
3 Jenkins	3 Jenkins	3 Jones T	3 Jenkins	3 Jenkins
4 Mousdale	4 Bennion	4 Newnes	4 Davies S	4 Bennion
5 Keenor	5 Kennor	5 Matthews	5 Pullen	5 Keenor
6 John	6 Lewis	6 Evans D	6 John	6 Jennings
7 Davies W	7 Williams R	7 Davies W	7 Davies W	7 Davies W
8 Davies S	8 Davies W	8 Davies L	8 Davies L	8 Davies S
9 Jones J	9 Davies S	9 Fowler	9 Fowler	9 Fowler
10 Davies L	10 Richards	10 Davies S	10 Jones C	10 Jones C
11 Williams J	11 Vizard	11 Jones I	11 Vizard	11 Vizard
Wrexham April 18: 0-0	Cardiff Oct 31: 0-3	Belfast Feb 13: 0-3	London Mar 1: 3-1 *Fowler 2, Davies W*	Glasgow Oct 30: 0-3

1927 England	1927 Ireland	1927 Scotland	1927 England	1928 Ireland
1 Lewis	1 Evans L	1 Gray	1 Gray	1 Lewis
2 Jones T	2 Jones T	2 Russell	2 Williams B	2 Williams B
3 John	3 Jennings	3 Evans T J	3 Evans T J	3 Evans T J
4 Keenor	4 Keenor	4 Bennion	4 Bennion	4 Bennion
5 Griffiths T	5 Griffiths T	5 Keenor	5 Keenor	5 Keenor
6 Evans D	6 Evans D	6 Davies S	6 John	6 John
7 Williams R	7 Williams R	7 Hole	7 Hole	7 Hole
8 Lewis	8 Lewis	8 Davies L	8 Davies L	8 Davies W
9 Davies L	9 Davies L	9 Fowler	9 Lewis	9 Lewis
10 Nicholas	10 Jones C	10 Curtis	10 Jones C	10 Davies L
11 Thomas	11 Nicholas	11 Cook	11 Cook	11 Rev H Davies
Wrexham Feb 14: 3-3 *Davies L 2, Lewis*	Cardiff April 9: 2-2 *Williams 2*	Wrexham Oct 29: 2-2 *Curtis, Gibson (og)*	Burnley Nov 28: 2-1 *Lewis, Hill (og)*	Belfast Feb 4: 2-1 *Davies W, Lewis*

1928 Scotland	1928 England	1929 Ireland	1929 Scotland	1929 England
1 Gray	1 Gray	1 Gray	1 Gray	1 Lewis D
2 Morley	2 Morley	2 Morley	2 Williams B	2 Williams B
3 Jennings	3 Russell	3 Lumberg	3 Lumberg	3 Lumberg
4 Bennion	4 Griffiths	4 Bennion	4 Bennion	4 Keenor
5 Keenor	5 Keenor	5 Keenor	5 Keenor	5 Griffiths T
6 Evans D	6 Bennion	6 Bowsher	6 John	6 John
7 Hole	7 Hole	7 Davies W	7 Davies W	7 Davies W
8 Davies W	8 Davies W	8 O'Callaghan	8 O'Callaghan	8 Davies L
9 Lewis	9 Fowler	9 Mays	9 Davies L	9 Lewis W
10 Davies L	10 Davies L	10 Davies L	10 Jones C	10 Jones C
11 Williams R	11 Williams R	11 Warren	11 Cook	11 Cook
Glasgow Oct 27: 2-4 *Davies W* 2	Swansea Nov 17: 2-3 *Fowler, Keenor*	Wrexham Feb 2: 2-2 *Mays, Warren*	Cardiff Oct 26: 2-4 *O'Callaghan Davies L*	London Nov 20: 0-6

1930 Ireland	1930 Scotland	1930 England	1931 Ireland	1931 Scotland
1 Finnigan	1 Evans L	1 Evans L	1 John	1 Gray
2 Pugh	2 Dewey	2 Dewey	2 Williams B	2 Richards
3 Jones T	3 Crompton	3 Crompton	3 Crompton	3 Lumberg
4 Lawrence	4 Rogers	4 Rogers	4 Keenor	4 Edwards
5 Keenor	5 Keenor	5 Keenor	5 Griffiths T	5 Griffiths T
6 Pugsley	6 Ellis	6 Ellis	6 Richards	6 Lawrence
7 Davies W	7 Collins	7 Williams L	7 Phillips	7 Griffiths P
8 Williams B	8 Neal	8 Neal	8 Astley	8 O'Callaghan
9 Martin	9 Bamford	9 Bamford	9 Bamford	9 Glover
10 Davies S	10 Robbins	10 Robbins	10 James	10 Robbins
11 Cook	11 Thomas	11 Thomas	11 Warren	11 Curtis
Belfast Feb 1: 0-7	Glasgow Oct 25: 1-1 *Bamford*	Wrexham Nov 22: 0-4	Wrexham April 22: 3-2 *Phillips, Griffiths, Warren*	Wrexham Oct 31: 2-3 *Curtis* 2

1931 England	1931 Ireland	1932 Scotland	1932 England	1932 Ireland
1 Gray	1 Gray	1 John W	1 John W	1 John W
2 Williams B	2 Lawrence	2 Williams B	2 Williams B	2 Williams B
3 Ellis	3 Foulkes	3 Ellis	3 Ellis	3 John R
4 Jones C	4 Bennion	4 Keenor	4 Murphy	4 Murphy
5 Griffiths T	5 Griffiths T	5 Griffiths T	5 Griffiths T	5 Griffiths T
6 John	6 Ellis	6 Richards	6 Richards	6 Richards D
7 Phillips	7 Jones T J	7 Phillips	7 Warren	7 Richards W
8 O'Callaghan	8 James	8 O'Callaghan	8 O'Callaghan	8 O'Callaghan
9 Astley	9 Bamford	9 Astley	9 Astley	9 Astley
10 Robbins	10 Robbins	10 Robbins	10 Robbins	10 Robbins
11 Cook	11 Parris	11 Lewis	11 Lewis	11 Evans W
Liverpool Nov 18: 1-3 *Robbins*	Belfast Dec 5: 0-4	Edinburgh Oct 26: 5-2 *O'Callaghan* 2, *Griffiths, Astley, Thomson J* (og)	Wrexham Nov 16: 0-0	Wrexham Dec 7: 4-1 *Astley* 2, *Robbins* 2

1933 France	1933 Scotland	1933 Ireland	1933 England	1934 England
1 John W	1 John W	1 Evans L	1 John W	1 John W
2 John R	2 Lawrence	2 Lawrence	2 Lawrence	2 Lawrence
3 Lawrence	3 Ellis	3 Jones D O	3 Jones D O	3 Jones D O
4 Murphy	4 Murphy	4 Day	4 Murphy	4 Murphy
5 Griffiths T	5 Griffiths T	5 Hanford	5 Griffiths T	5 Griffiths T
6 Jones C	6 Richards	6 Richards	6 Richards	6 Richards
7 Phillips	7 Phillips	7 Phillips	7 Phillips	7 Phillips
8 Jones T	8 O'Callaghan	8 O'Callaghan	8 O'Callaghan	8 O'Callaghan
9 Bamford	9 Astley	9 Glover	9 Astley	9 Williams R
10 Robbins	10 Robbins	10 Mills	10 Mills	10 Mills
11 Warren	11 Evans W	11 Curtis	11 Evans W	11 Evans W
Paris May 25: 1-1 *Griffiths*	Cardiff Oct 4: 3-2 *Evans, Robbins, Astley*	Belfast Nov 4: 1-1 *Glover*	Newcastle-upon-Tyne Nov 15: 2-1 *Mills, Astley*	Cardiff Sept 29: 0-4

1934 Scotland	1935 Ireland	1935 Scotland	1936 England	1936 Ireland
1 John W	1 Hughes	1 John W	1 John W	1 John W
2 Lawrence	2 Williams B	2 Lawrence	2 Jones D O	2 Griffiths
3 Jones D O	3 John R	3 John R	3 Ellis	3 Jones D O
4 Murphy	4 Murphy	4 Murphy	4 Murphy	4 Murphy
5 Hanford	5 Griffiths	5 Griffiths	5 Hanford	5 Hanford
6 Richards	6 Richards	6 Richards	6 Richards	6 Richards
7 Hopkins	7 Phillips	7 Phillips	7 Hopkins	7 Hopkins
8 Williams R	8 Jones L	8 Jones B	8 Phillips	8 Phillips
9 Astley	9 Jones C W	9 Glover	9 Astley	9 Astley
10 Mills	10 Jones B	10 Jones L	10 Jones B	10 Jones B
11 Phillips	11 Phillips	11 Robbins	11 Evans W	11 Evans W
Aberdeen Nov 21: 2-3 *Phillips, Astley*	Wrexham Mar 27: 3-1 *Jones C W, Phillips, Hopkins*	Cardiff Oct 5: 1-1 *Phillips*	Wolverhampton Feb 5: 2-1 *Astley, Jones B*	Belfast Mar 11: 2-3 *Astley, Phillips*

1936 England	1936 Scotland	1937 Ireland	1937 Scotland	1937 England
1 Gray	1 Gray	1 Gray	1 Gray	1 Gray
2 Turner	2 Turner	2 Turner	2 Turner	2 Turner
3 John	3 Ellis	3 Jones D	3 Hughes	3 Hughes
4 Warner	4 Murphy	4 Murphy	4 Murphy	4 Murphy
5 Griffiths T	5 Griffiths T	5 Griffiths T	5 Hanford	5 Hanford
6 Richards	6 Richards	6 Richards	6 Richards	6 Richards
7 Hopkins	7 Hopkins	7 Hopkins	7 Phillips	7 Hopkins
8 Jones B	8 Jones B	8 Jones B	8 Jones L	8 Jones L
9 Glover	9 Glover	9 Glover	9 Perry	9 Perry
10 Jones L	10 Jones L	10 Jones L	10 Jones B	10 Jones B
11 Morris	11 Morris	11 Warren	11 Morris	11 Morris
Cardiff Oct 17: 2-1 *Morris, Glover*	Dundee Dec 2: 2-1 *Glover 2*	Wrexham Mar 17: 4-1 *Glover 2, Jones B, Warren*	Cardiff Oct 30: 2-1 *Jones B, Morris*	Middlesbrough Nov 17: 1-2 *Perry*

1938 Ireland	1938 England	1938 Scotland	1939 Ireland	1939 France
1 Gray	1 John	1 John	1 Poland	1 Poland
2 Turner	2 Whatley	2 Whatley	2 Turner	2 Turner
3 Hughes	3 Hughes	3 Hughes	3 Hughes	3 Hughes
4 Green	4 Green	4 Dearson	4 Green	4 Green
5 Jones T G	5 Jones T	5 Jones T G	5 Jones T G	5 Hanford
6 Richards	6 Richards	6 Richards	6 Dearson	6 Warner
7 Hopkins	7 Hopkins	7 Hopkins	7 Hopkins	7 Williams J
8 Jones L	8 Jones L	8 Jones L	8 Boulter	8 Astley
9 Perry	9 Astley	9 Astley	9 Glover	9 Jones W
10 Jones B	10 Jones B	10 Jones B	10 Jones B	10 Dearson
11 Warren	11 Cumner	11 Cumner	11 Cumner	11 Morris
Belfast Mar 16: 0-1	Cardiff Oct 22: 4-2 *Astley 2, Hopkins, Jones B*	Edinburgh Nov 9: 2-3 *Astley, Jones L*	Wrexham Mar 15: 3-1 *Cumner, Glover, Boulter*	Paris May 20: 1-2 *Astley*

1946 Scotland	1946 England	1947 N Ireland	1947 England	1947 Scotland
1 Sidlow	1 Sidlow	1 Shortt	1 Sidlow	1 Sidlow
2 Lambert	2 Sherwood	2 Sherwood	2 Lambert	2 Sherwood
3 Hughes	3 Hughes	3 Hughes	3 Barnes	3 Barnes
4 Witcomb	4 Witcomb	4 Witcomb	4 Powell I	4 Powell I
5 Jones T G	5 Jones T G	5 Humphreys	5 Jones T G	5 Jones T G
6 Burgess	6 Burgess	6 Burgess	6 Burgess	6 Burgess
7 Jones E	7 Jones E	7 Griffiths	7 Thomas S	7 Thomas S
8 Powell A	8 Powell A	8 Morris	8 Powell A	8 Powell A
9 Ford	9 Richards	9 Ford	9 Lowrie	9 Ford
10 Jones B	10 Powell I	10 Jones B	10 Jones B	10 Lowrie
11 Edwards	11 Edwards	11 Edwards	11 Edwards	11 Edwards
Wrexham Oct 19: 3-1 *Jones B, Ford Stephen (og)*	Maine Road Manchester Nov 13: 0-3	Belfast April 16: 1-2 *Ford*	Cardiff Oct 18: 0-3	Hampden Nov 12: 2-1 *Ford, Lowrie*

1948 N Ireland	1948 Scotland	1948 England	1949 N Ireland	1949 Portugal
1 Sidlow	1 Sidlow	1 Hughes	1 Hughes	1 Hughes
2 Sherwood	2 Sherwood	2 Barnes	2 Barnes	2 Sherwood
3 Barnes	3 Barnes	3 Sherwood	3 Sherwood	3 Lambert
4 Powell I	4 Paul	4 Paul	4 Paul	4 Paul
5 Jones T G	5 Stansfield	5 Jones T G	5 Jones T G	5 Jones T G
6 Baker	6 Burgess	6 Burgess	6 Burgess	6 Burgess
7 Thomas S	7 Thomas S	7 Jones E	7 Williams	7 Griffiths
8 Powell A	8 Lucas	8 Powell A	8 Rees	8 Lucas
9 Ford	9 Ford	9 Ford	9 Ford	9 Ford
10 Lowrie	10 Jones B	10 Morris	10 Lucas	10 Lowrie
11 Edwards	11 Jones E	11 Clarke	11 Edwards	11 Edwards
Wrexham Mar 10: 2-0 *Lowrie, Edwards*	Cardiff Oct 23: 1-3 *Jones B*	Villa Park Nov 10: 0-1	Belfast Mar 9: 2-0 *Edwards, Ford*	Lisbon May 15: 2-3 *Ford 2*

1949 Belgium	1949 Switzerland	1949 England	1949 Scotland	1949 Belgium
1 Hughes	1 Hughes	1 Sidlow	1 Jones K B	1 Shortt
2 Roberts	2 Sherwood	2 Barnes	2 Barnes	2 Barnes
3 Lambert	3 Lambert	3 Sherwood	3 Sherwood	3 Sherwood
4 Powell I	4 Paul	4 Paul	4 Powell I	4 Powell I
5 Jones T G	5 Jones T G	5 Jones T G	5 Jones T G	5 Jones T G
6 Burgess	6 Burgess	6 Burgess	6 Burgess	6 Burgess
7 Griffiths	7 Williams	7 Griffiths	7 Griffiths	7 Griffiths
8 Rees	8 Rees	8 Lucas	8 Paul	8 Paul
9 Ford	9 Ford	9 Ford	9 Ford	9 Ford
10 Lucas	10 Lucas	10 Scrine	10 Clarke	10 Powell A
11 Edwards	11 Edwards	11 Edwards	11 Edwards	11 Clarke
Liege May 23: 1-3 *Ford*	Berne May 26: 0-4	Cardiff Oct 15: 1-4 *Griffiths*	Hampden Nov 9: 0-2	Cardiff Nov 23: 5-1 *Clarke, Paul, Ford 3*

1950 N Ireland	1950 Scotland	1950 England	1951 N Ireland	1951 Portugal
1 Shortt	1 Parry	1 Hughes	1 Hughes	1 Hughes
2 Barnes	2 Barnes	2 Barnes	2 Barnes	2 Barnes
3 Sherwood	3 Sherwood	3 Sherwood	3 Sherwood	3 Sherwood
4 Paul	4 Powell I	4 Paul	4 Paul	4 Paul
5 Charles J	5 Paul	5 Daniel	5 Daniel	5 Daniel
6 Burgess	6 Burgess	6 Lucas	6 Burgess	6 Burgess
7 Williams	7 Williams	7 Griffiths	7 Griffiths	7 Griffiths
8 Rees	8 Allen	8 Allen	8 Kinsey	8 Kinsey
9 Ford	9 Ford	9 Ford	9 Ford	9 Ford
10 Scrine	10 Powell A	10 Allchurch I	10 Allchurch I	10 Allchurch I
11 Clarke	11 Clarke	11 Clarke	11 Clarke	11 Clarke
Wrexham Mar 8: 0-0	Cardiff Oct 21: 1-3 *Powell A*	Sunderland Nov 15: 2-4 *Ford 2*	Belfast Mar 7: 2-1 *Clarke 2*	Cardiff May 12: 2-1 *Griffiths, Ford*

1951 Switzerland	1951 England	1951 Scotland	1951 Rest of UK	1952 N Ireland
1 Hughes	1 Shortt	1 Shortt	1 Shortt	1 Shortt
2 Williams	2 Barnes	2 Barnes	2 Barnes	2 Barnes
3 Sherwood	3 Sherwood	3 Sherwood	3 Sherwood	3 Sherwood
4 Paul	4 Paul	4 Paul	4 Paul	4 Paul
5 Charles J	5 Daniel	5 Daniel	5 Daniel	5 Daniel
6 Burgess	6 Burgess	6 Burgess	6 Burgess	6 Burgess
7 Griffiths	7 Foulkes	7 Foulkes	7 Foulkes	7 Foulkes
8 Kinsey	8 Kinsey	8 Morris	8 Morris	8 Morris
9 Ford	9 Ford	9 Ford	9 Ford	9 Ford
10 Allchurch I	10 Allchurch I	10 Allchurch I	10 Allchurch I	10 Allchurch I
11 Clarke	11 Clarke	11 Clarke	11 Clarke	11 Clarke
Wrexham May 16: 3-2 *Ford 2 Burgess*	Cardiff Oct 20: 1-1 *Foulkes*	Hampden Nov 20: 1-0 *Allchurch*	Cardiff Dec 5: 3-2 *Allchurch 2, Ford*	Swansea Mar 19: 3-0 *Barnes, Allchurch Clarke*

1952 Scotland	1952 England	1953 N Ireland	1953 France	1953 Yugoslavia
1 Shortt	1 Shortt	1 Shortt	1 Shortt	1 Shortt
2 Lever	2 Stitfall	2 Sullivan	2 Sullivan	2 Sullivan
3 Sherwood	3 Sherwood	3 Sherwood	3 Sherwood	3 Sherwood
4 Paul	4 Paul	4 Paul	4 Paul	4 Paul
5 Daniel	5 Daniel	5 Daniel	5 Daniel	5 Daniel
6 Burgess	6 Burgess	6 Burgess	6 Burgess	6 Burgess
7 Foulkes	7 Foulkes	7 Medwin	7 Medwin	7 Medwin
8 Davies R	8 Davies R	8 Charles J	8 Charles J	8 Charles J
9 Ford	9 Ford	9 Ford	9 Ford	9 Ford
10 Allchurch I	10 Allchurch I	10 Allchurch I	10 Allchurch I	10 Allchurch I
11 Clarke	11 Clarke	11 Griffiths	11 Foulkes	11 Foulkes
Cardiff Oct 18: 1-2 *Ford*	Wembley Nov 12: 2-5 *Ford 2*	Belfast April 15: 3-2 *Charles 2, Ford*	Paris May 14: 1-6 *Allchurch*	Belgrade May 21: 2-5 *Ford 2*

1953 England	1953 Scotland	1954 N Ireland	1954 Austria	1954 Yugoslavia
1 Howells	1 Howells	1 Kelsey	1 Kelsey	1 Kelsey
2 Barnes	2 Barnes	2 Sullivan	2 Williams S	2 Barnes
3 Sherwood	3 Sherwood	3 Sherwood	3 Sherwood	3 Sherwood
4 Paul	4 Paul	4 Paul	4 Harris	4 Paul
5 Daniel	5 Daniel	5 Daniel	5 Charles J	5 Charles J
6 Burgess	6 Burgess	6 Burgess	6 Burgess	6 Bowen
7 Foulkes	7 Foulkes	7 Foulkes	7 Griffiths	7 Reed
8 Davies R	8 Davies R	8 Kinsey	8 Tapscott	8 Tapscott
9 Charles J	9 Charles J	9 Charles J	9 Ford	9 Ford
10 Allchurch I	10 Allchurch I	10 Allchurch I	10 Allchurch I	10 Allchurch I
11 Clarke	11 Clarke	11 Clarke	11 Jones C	11 Clarke
Cardiff Oct 10: 1-4 *Allchurch*	Hampden Nov 4: 3-3 *Charles 2, Allchurch*	Wrexham Mar 31: 1-2 *Charles*	Vienna May 9: 0-2	Cardiff Sept 22: 1-3 *Allchurch*

1954 Scotland	1954 England	1955 N Ireland	1955 England	1955 Scotland
1 Kelsey	1 King	1 Kelsey	1 Kelsey	1 Kelsey
2 Barnes	2 Williams S	2 Williams S	2 Williams S	2 Williams S
3 Sherwood	3 Sherwood	3 Sherwood	3 Sherwood	3 Sherwood
4 Paul	4 Paul	4 Charles M	4 Charles M	4 Charles M
5 Charles J	5 Daniel	5 Daniel	5 Charles J	5 Charles J
6 Bowen	6 Sullivan	6 Sullivan	6 Paul	6 Paul
7 Reed	7 Tapscott	7 Tapscott	7 Tapscott	7 Tapscott
8 Tapscott	8 Ford	8 Ford	8 Kinsey	8 Kinsey
9 Ford	9 Charles J	9 Charles J	9 Ford	9 Ford
10 Allchurch I	10 Allchurch I	10 Allchurch I	10 Allchurch I	10 Allchurch I
11 Clarke	11 Clarke	11 Allchurch L	11 Jones C	11 Jones C
Cardiff Oct 16: 0-1	Wembley Nov 10: 2-3 *Charles 2*	Belfast April 20: 3-2 *Charles J 3*	Cardiff Oct 22: 2-1 *Tapscott, Jones*	Hampden Nov 9: 0-2

1955 Austria	1956 N Ireland	1956 Scotland	1956 England	1957 N Ireland
1 Kelsey	1 Kelsey	1 Kelsey	1 Kelsey	1 Kelsey
2 Williams S	2 Sherwood	2 Sherwood	2 Sherwood	2 Edwards
3 Hopkins	3 Hopkins	3 Hopkins	3 Hopkins	3 Hopkins
4 Charles M	4 Harrington	4 Harrington	4 Harrington	4 Charles M
5 Charles J	5 Charles J	5 Daniel	5 Daniel	5 Daniel
6 Paul	6 Paul	6 Sullivan	6 Sullivan	6 Bowen
7 Allchurch L	7 Jones C	7 Medwin	7 Medwin	7 Medwin
8 Tapscott	8 Tapscott	8 Charles J	8 Charles M	8 Tapscott
9 Ford	9 Ford	9 Ford	9 Charles J	9 Charles J
10 Allchurch I	10 Allchurch I	10 Allchurch I	10 Allchurch I	10 Vernon
11 Jones C	11 Clarke	11 Jones C	11 Jones C	11 Jones C
Wrexham Nov 23: 1-2 Tapscott	Cardiff April 11: 1-1 Clarke	Cardiff Oct 20: 2-2 Ford, Medwin	Wembley Nov 14: 1-3 Charles J	Belfast April 10: 0-0

1957 Czechoslovakia	1957 E Germany	1957 Czechoslovakia	1957 E Germany	1957 England
1 Kelsey	1 Kelsey	1 Kelsey	1 Vearncombe	1 Kelsey
2 Stitfall	2 Edwards	2 Thomas	2 Thomas	2 Williams S
3 Hopkins	3 Hopkins	3 Hopkins	3 Hopkins	3 Hopkins
4 Charles M	4 Harris	4 Charles M	4 Harris	4 Harris
5 Charles J	5 Charles J	5 Daniel	5 Charles M	5 Charles M
6 Bowen	6 Bowen	6 Harris	6 Bowen	6 Bowen
7 Medwin	7 Medwin	7 Medwin	7 Allchurch L	7 Medwin
8 Tapscott	8 Tapscott	8 Palmer	8 Davies R	8 Davies R
9 Webster	9 Charles M	9 Charles J	9 Palmer	9 Palmer
10 Vernon	10 Vernon	10 Vernon	10 Vernon	10 Vernon
11 Jones C	11 Jones C	11 Jones C	11 Jones C	11 Jones C
Cardiff May 1: 1-0 Vernon	Leipzig May 19: 1-2 Charles M	Prague May 26: 0-2	Cardiff Sept 25: 4-1 Palmer 3, Jones	Cardiff Oct 19: 0-4

1957 Scotland	1958 Israel	1958 Israel	1958 N Ireland	1958 Hungary†
1 Kelsey	1 Kelsey	1 Kelsey	1 Kelsey	1 Kelsey
2 Williams S	2 Williams S	2 Williams S	2 Williams S	2 Williams S
3 Hopkins	3 Hopkins	3 Hopkins	3 Hopkins	3 Hopkins
4 Harrington	4 Harrington	4 Harrington	4 Harrington	4 Sullivan
5 Charles M	5 Charles M	5 Charles M	5 Sullivan	5 Charles M
6 Bowen	6 Bowen	6 Bowen	6 Bowen	6 Bowen
7 Allchurch L	7 Allchurch	7 Medwin	7 Allchurch L	7 Webster
8 Harris	8 Charles J	8 Hewitt	8 Hewitt	8 Medwin
9 Medwin	9 Medwin	9 Charles J	9 Medwin	9 Charles J
10 Vernon	10 Allchurch I	10 Allchurch I	10 Allchurch I	10 Allchurch I
11 Jones C	11 Jones C	11 Jones C	11 Jones C	11 Jones C
Hampden Nov 13: 1-1 Medwin	Tel-Aviv Jan 15: 2-0 Allchurch I, Bowen	Cardiff Feb 5: 2-0 Allchurch I, Jones	Cardiff April 16: 1-1 Hewitt	Sandviken June 8: 1-1 Charles J

1958 Mexico†	1958 Sweden†	1958 Hungary†	1958 Brazil†	1958 Scotland
1 Kelsey	1 Kelsey	1 Kelsey	1 Kelsey	1 Kelsey
2 Williams S	2 Williams S	2 Williams S	2 Williams S	2 Williams S
3 Hopkins	3 Hopkins	3 Hopkins	3 Hopkins	3 Hopkins
4 Baker	4 Sullivan	4 Sullivan	4 Sullivan	4 Sullivan
5 Charles M	5 Charles M	5 Charles M	5 Charles M	5 Charles M
6 Bowen	6 Bowen	6 Bowen	6 Bowen	6 Bowen
7 Webster	7 Vernon	7 Medwin	7 Medwin	7 Allchurch L
8 Medwin	8 Hewitt	8 Hewitt	8 Hewitt	8 Vernon
9 Charles J	9 Charles J	9 Charles J	9 Webster	9 Medwin
10 Allchurch I	10 Allchurch I	10 Allchurch I	10 Allchurch I	10 Allchurch I
11 Jones C	11 Jones C	11 Jones C	11 Jones C	11 Woosnam
Stockholm June 11: 1-1 *Allchurch I*	Stockholm June 15: 0-0	Stockholm June 17: 2-1 *Allchurch I, Medwin*	Gothenburg June 19: 0-1	Cardiff Oct 18: 0-3

1958 England	1959 N. Ireland	1959 England	1959 Scotland	1960 N. Ireland
1 Kelsey	1 Rouse	1 Kelsey	1 Kelsey	1 Kelsey
2 Williams S	2 Williams S	2 Williams S	2 Williams S	2 Williams S
3 Hopkins	3 Hopkins	3 Hopkins	3 Hopkins	3 Williams G
4 Crowe	4 Crowe	4 Crowe	4 Sullivan	4 Crowe
5 Charles M	5 Sullivan	5 Nurse	5 Charles J	5 Nurse
6 Bowen	6 Bowen	6 Sullivan	6 Baker	6 Baker
7 Medwin	7 Medwin	7 Medwin	7 Medwin	7 Medwin
8 Ward	8 Tapscott	8 Woosnam	8 Woosnam	8 Woosnam
9 Tapscott	9 Rowley	9 Moore	9 Moore	9 Moore
10 Allchurch I	10 Allchurch I	10 Allchurch I	10 Allchurch I	10 Vernon
11 Woosnam	11 Jones C	11 Jones C	11 Jones C	11 Jones C
Villa Park Nov 26: 2-2 *Tapscott Allchurch I*	Belfast April 22: 1-4 *Tapscott*	Cardiff Oct 17: 1-1 *Moore*	Hampden Nov 4: 1-1 *Charles*	Wrexham April 6: 3-2 *Medwin 2, Woosnam*

1960 Rep. of Ireland	1960 Scotland	1960 England	1961 N. Ireland	1961 Spain
1 Vearncombe	1 Kelsey	1 Kelsey	1 Kelsey	1 Kelsey
2 Williams S	2 Harrington	2 Harrington	2 Williams S	2 Williams S
3 Williams G	3 Williams G	3 Williams G	3 Hopkins	3 Hopkins
4 Crowe	4 Crowe	4 Crowe	4 Charles M	4 Charles M
5 Nurse	5 Nurse	5 Nurse	5 Nurse	5 Nurse
6 Baker	6 Baker	6 Baker	6 Crowe	6 Crowe
7 Medwin	7 Medwin	7 Medwin	7 Jones C	7 Medwin
8 Woosnam	8 Woosnam	8 Woosnam	8 Woosnam	8 Woosnam
9 Moore	9 Leek	9 Leek	9 Leek	9 Leek
10 Vernon	10 Vernon	10 Vernon	10 Allchurch I	10 Allchurch I
11 Jones C	11 Jones C	11 Jones C	11 Williams G	11 Williams G
Dublin Sept 28: 3-2 *Jones 2, Woosnam*	Cardiff Oct 22: 2-0 *Vernon, Jones*	Wembley Nov 23: 1-5 *Leek*	Belfast April 12: 5-1 *Charles, Jones 2 Allchurch, Leek*	Cardiff April 19: 1-2 *Woosnam*

1961 Spain	1961 Hungary	1961 England	1961 Scotland	1962 N. Ireland
1 Kelsey	1 Kelsey	1 Kelsey	1 Kelsey	1 Kelsey
2 Williams S	2 Williams S	2 Harrington	2 Harrington	2 Williams S
3 Hopkins	3 Hopkins	3 Williams S	3 Williams S	3 Hopkins
4 Charles M	4 Charles M	4 Charles M	4 Crowe	4 Lucas
5 Nurse	5 Nurse	5 Charles J	5 Charles M	5 England
6 Crowe	6 Crowe	6 Crowe	6 Baker	6 Hennessey
7 Jones C	7 Jones C	7 Jones C	7 Allchurch L	7 Allchurch L
8 Moore	8 Woosnam	8 Woosnam	8 Woosnam	8 Woosnam
9 Leek	9 Leek	9 Ward	9 Leek	9 Charles M
10 Allchurch I	10 Allchurch I	10 Allchurch I	10 Allchurch I	10 Vernon
11 Williams G	11 Williams G	11 Williams G	11 Jones C	11 Jones C
Madrid May 18: 1-1 *Allchurch*	Budapest May 28: 2-3 *Allchurch, Jones*	Cardiff Oct 14: 1-1 *Williams G*	Hampden Nov 8: 0-2	Cardiff April 11: 4-0 *Charles M 4*

1962 Brazil	1962 Brazil	1962 Mexico	1962 Scotland	1962 Hungary
1 Kelsey	1 Kelsey (Hollins)	1 Hollins	1 Millington	1 Millington
2 Williams S	2 Williams S	2 Williams S	2 Williams S	2 Williams S
3 Hopkins	3 Hopkins	3 Hopkins	3 Hopkins	3 Hopkins
4 Hennessey	4 England	4 Lucas	4 Hennessey	4 Hennessey
5 Charles J	5 Charles J	5 England	5 Charles J	5 Nurse
6 Crowe	6 Hennessey	6 Crowe	6 Lucas	6 Crowe
7 Allchurch L	7 Woosnam	7 Vernon	7 Jones B	7 Medwin
8 Vernon	8 Vernon	8 Allchurch I	8 Allchurch I	8 Allchurch I
9 Charles M	9 Moore (Leek)	9 Charles J	9 Charles M	9 Charles M
10 Allchurch I	10 Allchurch I	10 Leek	10 Vernon	10 Vernon
11 Jones C	11 Jones C	11 Jones C	11 Jones C	11 Jones B
Rio May 12: 1-3 *Allchurch I*	Sao Paulo May 16: 1-3 *Leek*	Mexico City May 22: 1-2 *Charles J*	Cardiff Oct 20: 2-3 *Allchurch, Charles J*	Budapest Nov 7: 1-3 *Medwin*

1962 England	1963 Hungary	1963 N. Ireland	1963 England	1963 Scotland
1 Millington	1 Hollins	1 Hollins	1 Hollins	1 Sprake
2 Williams S	2 Williams S	2 Hopkins	2 Williams S	2 Williams S
3 Sear	3 Williams G	3 Williams G	3 Williams G	3 Williams G
4 Hennessey	4 Hennessey	4 Burton	4 Hennessey	4 Hennessey
5 Nurse	5 England	5 England	5 England	5 England
6 Lucas	6 Burton	6 Hole	6 Burton	6 Nurse
8 Jones B	7 Jones B	7 Jones B	7 Allchurch	7 Jones B
8 Allchurch I	8 Woosnam	8 Woosnam	8 Vernon	8 Moore
9 Leek	9 Moore	9 Moore	9 Davies W	9 Charles J
10 Vernon	10 Allchurch I	10 Allchurch I	10 Allchurch I	10 Vernon
11 Medwin	11 Jones C	11 Jones C	11 Jones C	11 Jones C
Wembley Nov 21: 0-4	Cardiff Mar 20: 1-1 *Jones C*	Belfast April 3: 4-1 *Woosnam, Jones, C 3*	Cardiff Oct 12: 0-4	Hampden Nov 20: 1-2 *Jones B*

1964 N Ireland	1964 Scotland	1964 Denmark	1964 England	1964 Greece
1 Sprake	1 Sprake	1 Sprake	1 Millington	1 Sprake
2 Evans R	2 Williams S	2 Williams S	2 Williams S	2 Rodrigues
3 Williams G	3 Williams G	3 Williams G	3 Williams G	3 Williams G
4 Johnson	4 Hole	4 Hennessey	4 Hennessey	4 Hennessey
5 England	5 Charles J	5 England	5 England	5 England
6 Hole	6 Hennessey	6 Hole	6 Hole	6 Hole
7 Jones B	7 Jones C	7 Jones B	7 Rees	7 Rees
8 Moore	8 Leek	8 Godfrey	8 Davies R	8 Leek
9 Davies R	9 Davies W	9 Davies W	9 Davies W	9 Davies W
10 Godfrey	10 Allchurch I	10 Jones C	10 Allchurch I	10 Williams H
11 Jones C	11 Rees	11 Rees	11 Jones C	11 Jones C
Swansea April 15: 2-3 *Godfrey, Davies R*	Cardiff Oct 3: 3-2 *Davies W, Leek 2*	Copenhagen Oct 21: 0-1	Wembley Nov 18: 1-2 *Jones C*	Athens Dec 9: 0-2

1965 Greece	1965 N Ireland	1965 Italy	1965 USSR	1965 England
1 Hollins	1 Hollins	1 Hollins	1 Millington	1 Sprake
2 Rodrigues	2 Rodrigues	2 Green	2 Green	2 Rodrigues
3 Williams G	3 Williams G	3 Williams G	3 Williams G	3 Green
4 Williams H	4 Lea	4 Lea	4 Hennessey	4 Hennessey
5 England	5 England	5 England	5 England	5 England
6 Hole	6 Hole	6 Hole	6 Hole	6 Hole
7 Jones C	7 Jones C	7 Jones C	7 Jones C	7 Rees
8 Allchurch I	8 Allchurch I	8 Allchurch I	8 Allchurch I	8 Vernon
9 Leek	9 Davies W	9 Godfrey	9 Davies W	9 Davies W
10 Vernon	10 Vernon	10 Vernon	10 Charles J	10 Allchurch I
11 Rees	11 Rees	11 Rees	11 Rees	11 Reece
Cardiff May 17: 4-1 *Allchurch 2 England, Vernon*	Belfast Mar 31: 5-0 *Vernon 2, Jones C Williams G Allchurch I*	Florence May 1: 1-4 *Godfrey*	Moscow May 30: 1-2 *Davies W*	Cardiff Oct 2: 0-0

1965 USSR	1965 Scotland	1965 Denmark	1966 N Ireland	1966 Brazil
1 Sprake	1 Hollins	1 Hollins	1 Sprake	1 Hollins
2 Rodrigues	2 Rodrigues	2 Rodrigues	2 Rodrigues	2 Green
3 Green	3 Green	3 Williams S	3 Williams G	3 Rodrigues
4 Hennessey	4 Hennessey	4 Hennessey	4 Hennessey	4 Hennessey
5 England	5 England	5 England	5 England	5 James
6 Hole	6 Hole	6 Hole	6 Hole	6 Hole
7 Rees	7 Rees	7 Rees	7 Rees	7 Rees
8 Vernon	8 Vernon	8 Vernon	8 Vernon	8 Davies R
9 Davies W	9 Davies W	9 Davies W	9 Davies W	9 Davies W
10 Allchurch I	10 Allchurch I	10 Allchurch I	10 Moore	10 Allchurch I
11 Reece	11 Reece	11 Pring	11 Reece	11 Williams G
Cardiff Oct 27: 2-1 *Vernon Allchurch I*	Hampden Nov 24: 1-4 *Allchurch I*	Wrexham Dec 1: 4-2 *Vernon 2, Davies W, Rees*	Cardiff Mar 30: 1-4 *Davies W*	Rio May 14: 1-3 *Davies R*

1966 Brazil	1966 Chile	1966 Scotland	1966 England	1967 N Ireland
1 Millington	1 Millington	1 Sprake	1 Millington	1 Millington
2 Green	2 Rodrigues	2 Rodrigues	2 Green	2 Thomas
3 Rodrigues	3 Williams G	3 Williams G	3 Williams G	3 Williams G
4 Hennessey	4 Hennessey	4 Hennessey	4 Hennessey	4 Jarvis
5 James	5 James (Rankmore)	5 England	5 England	5 James
6 Hole	6 Hole	6 Hole	6 Hole	6 Hole
7 Rees (Durban)	7 Rees	7 Reece	7 Rees	7 Rees
8 Davies R	8 Moore	8 Davies W	8 Davies W	8 Durban
9 Davies W	9 Davies R	9 Davies R	9 Davies R	9 Davies R
10 Allchurch I	10 Allchurch I	10 Jones C	10 Jones C	10 Vernon
11 Williams G	11 Pring (Davies W)	11 Jarvis	11 Jarvis	11 Pring
Belo Horizonte May 18: 0-1	Santiago May 22: 0-2	Cardiff Oct 22: 1-1 *Davies R*	Wembley Nov 16: 1-5 *Davies W*	Belfast April 12: 0-0

1967 England	1967 Scotland	1968 N Ireland	1968 W Germany	1968 Italy
1 Sprake	1 Sprake	1 Millington	1 Millington	1 Millington
2 Rodrigues	2 Rodrigues	2 Rodrigues	2 Thomas	2 Thomas
3 Green	3 Green	3 Green	3 Green	3 Williams G
4 Hennessey	4 Hennessey	4 Hennessey	4 Powell	4 Burton
5 England	5 James	5 England	5 England	5 Powell
6 Hole	6 Hole	6 Hole	6 Hole	6 Hole
7 Rees	7 Rees	7 Rees	7 Rees	7 Rees
8 Durban	8 Davies W	8 Davies W	8 Davies W	8 Davies W
9 Mahoney	9 Davies R	9 Davies R	9 Davies R	9 Davies R
10 Vernon	10 Durban	10 Durban	10 Durban	10 Green (Jones B)
11 Jones C	11 Jones C	11 Williams G	11 Jones C	11 Jones C
Cardiff Oct 21: 0-3	Hampden Nov 22: 2-3 *Davies R, Durban*	Wrexham Feb 28: 2-0 *Rees, Davies W*	Cardiff May 8: 1-1 *Davies W*	Cardiff Oct 23: 0-1

1969 W Germany	1969 E Germany	1969 Scotland	1969 England	1969 N Ireland
1 Sprake	1 Millington	1 Sprake	1 Sprake	1 Sprake
2 Thomas	2 Rodrigues	2 Derrett (Rees)	2 Rodrigues	2 Rodrigues (Green)
3 Derrett	3 Burton	3 Green	3 Thomas	3 Thomas
4 Powell	4 Hennessey	4 Durban	4 Durban	4 Durban
5 Hennessey	5 England	5 Burton	5 Powell	5 Powell
6 Hole	6 Hole	6 Powell	6 Burton	6 Burton
7 Jones B	7 Jones B	7 Moore	7 Jones B	7 Jones B
8 Durban	8 Durban	8 Toshack	8 Davies R	8 Davies R
9 Davies R	9 Toshack	9 Davies R	9 Toshack	9 Toshack
10 Toshack	10 Mahoney	10 Davies W	10 Davies W	10 Davies W
11 Rees	11 Rees	11 Jones B	11 Moore	11 Moore
Frankfurt Mar 26: 1-1 *Jones B*	Dresden April 16: 1-2 *Toshack*	Wrexham May 3: 3-5 *Davies R 2, Toshack*	Wembley May 7: 1-2 *Davies R*	Belfast May 10: 0-0

1969 Rest of UK	1969 E Germany	1969 Italy	1969 England	1970 Scotland
1 Sprake	1 Sprake	1 Sprake	1 Millington	1 Millington
2 Rodrigues	2 Rodrigues	2 Thomas	2 Rodrigues	2 Rodrigues
3 Thomas	3 Thomas	3 Derrett	3 Thomas	3 Thomas
4 Hennessey	4 Hennessey	4 Durban	4 Hennessey	4 Hennessey
5 England	5 England	5 England	5 England	5 England
6 Moore	6 Powell	6 Moore	6 Powell	6 Powell
7 Jones B	7 Durban	7 Yorath	7 Krzywicki	7 Krzywicki
8 Jones C	8 Krzywicki	8 Toshack	8 Durban	8 Durban
9 Davies R	9 Davies W	9 Hole	9 Davies R	9 Davies R
10 Toshack	10 Toshack	10 Krzywicki	10 Moore	10 Moore
11 Rees (Reece)	11 Rees	11 Rees (Reece)	11 Rees	11 Rees
Cardiff July 28: 0-1	Cardiff Oct 22: 1-3 *Powell*	Rome Nov 4: 1-4 *England*	Cardiff April 18: 1-1 *Krzywicki*	Hampden April 22: 0-0

1970 N. Ireland	1970 Rumania	1971 Czechoslovakia	1971 Scotland	1971 England
1 Millington	1 Sprake	1 Millington	1 Sprake	1 Sprake
2 Rodrigues	2 Rodrigues	2 Rodrigues	2 Rodrigues	2 Rodrigues
3 Thomas	3 Thomas	3 Thomas	3 Thomas	3 Thomas
4 Hennessey	4 Powell	4 Phillips	4 James	4 James
5 England	5 England	5 James	5 Roberts	5 Roberts
6 Powell	6 Hole	6 Walley	6 Yorath	6 Yorath
7 Krzywicki	7 Krzywicki	7 Rees	7 Phillips	7 Phillips
8 Durban	8 Durban	8 Durban	8 Durban	8 Durban
9 Davies R	9 Davies W	9 Davies R	9 Davies R	9 Davies R
10 Moore	10 Moore	10 Davies W	10 Toshack	10 Toshack
11 Rees	11 Rees	11 Mahoney	11 Reece	11 Reece (Rees)
Swansea April 25: 1-0 *Rees*	Cardiff Nov 11: 0-0	Swansea April 21: 1-3 *Davies R*	Cardiff May 15: 0-0	Wembley May 18: 0-0

1971 N Ireland	1971 Finland	1971 Finland	1971 Czechoslovakia	1971 Rumania
1 Sprake	1 Millington	1 Sprake (Millington)	1 Millington	1 Millington
2 Rodrigues	2 Page	2 Rodrigues	2 Rodrigues	2 Rodrigues
3 Thomas	3 Derrett	3 Thomas	3 Phillips	3 Thomas
4 James	4 Durban	4 Roberts	4 Burton	4 Phillips
5 Roberts	5 Roberts	5 England	5 Thomas	5 Williams
6 Yorath	6 Mielczarek	6 Hennessey	6 Yorath	6 Hockey
7 Phillips (Rees)	7 Krzywicki	7 Evans	7 Hennessey (Rees)	7 James
8 Durban	8 Jones W	8 Reece	8 Durban	8 Hill (Davies C)
9 Davies R	9 Rees	9 Toshack	9 Evans (Krzywicki)	9 Davies R
10 Toshack	10 Toshack	10 Durban	10 Hill	10 Reece
11 Reece	11 Reece	11 Hockey	11 James	11 Rees
Belfast May 22: 0-1	Helsinki May 26: 1-0 *Toshack*	Swansea Oct 13: 3-0 *Durban, Toshack Reece*	Prague Oct 27: 0-1	Bucharest Nov 24: 0-2

1972 England	1972 Scotland	1972 N Ireland	1972 England	1973 England
1 Sprake	1 Sprake	1 Sprake	1 Sprake	1 Sprake
2 Rodrigues	2 Page	2 Page	2 Rodrigues (Reece)	2 Rodrigues (Page)
3 Thomas	3 Thomas	3 Thomas	3 Thomas	3 Thomas
4 Hennessey	4 Hennessey (James)	4 Yorath (Rodrigues)	4 Hennessey	4 Hockey
5 England	5 England	5 England	5 England	5 England
6 Roberts (Reece)	6 Yorath	6 Roberts	6 Hockey	6 Roberts J
7 Yorath	7 Durban	7 Durban	7 Phillips	7 Evans
8 Davies R	8 Davies W	8 Davies W	8 Mahoney	8 Mahoney
9 Davies W	9 Reece	9 Reece	9 Davies W	9 Toshack
10 Toshack	10 Davies R	10 Davies R	10 Toshack	10 Yorath
11 Durban	11 Phillips	11 Phillips	11 James	11 James
Cardiff May 20: 0-3	Hampden May 24: 0-1	Wrexham May 27: 0-0	Cardiff Nov 15: 0-1	Wembley Jan 24: 1:1 *Toshack*

1973 Poland	1973 Scotland	1973 England	1973 N. Ireland	1973 Poland
1 Sprake	1 Sprake	1 Phillips	1 Sprake	1 Sprake
2 Rodrigues	2 Rodrigues	2 Rodrigues	2 Rodrigues	2 Rodrigues
3 Thomas	3 Thomas	3 Thomas	3 Thomas	3 Thomas
4 Roberts D	4 Hockey	4 Hockey	4 Hockey (Emanuel)	4 Mahoney (Phillips)
5 Roberts J	5 England	5 England (Roberts D)	5 Roberts D	5 England
6 Hockey	6 Roberts J	6 Roberts J	6 Roberts J	6 Roberts J
7 James	7 James	7 James	7 James	7 Evans (Reece)
8 Yorath	8 Mahoney	8 Mahoney	8 Mahoney	8 Yorath
9 Toshack	9 Toshack	9 Toshack	9 Reece	9 Davies W
10 Mahoney	10 Yorath (Davies W)	10 Page (Emanuel)	10 Page	10 Hockey
11 Evans	11 Evans (O'Sullivan)	11 Evans	11 Davies W	11 James
Cardiff Mar 28: 2-0 *James, Hockey*	Wrexham May 12: 0-2	Wembley May 15: 0-3	Liverpool May 19: 0-1	Chorzow Sept 26: 0-3

1974 England	1974 Scotland	1974 N Ireland	1974 Austria	1974 Hungary
1 Phillips	1 Sprake	1 Sprake	1 Sprake	1 Sprake (Phillips J)
2 Roberts P (Cartwright)	2 Thomas	2 Page	2 Roberts P	2 Thomas
3 Thomas	3 Page	3 Thomas	3 Phillips	3 Roberts P
4 Mahoney	4 Mahoney	4 Mahoney	4 Roberts D	4 Mahoney
5 Roberts J	5 Roberts J	5 Roberts J	5 Roberts J	5 England
6 Roberts D	6 Roberts D	6 Reece	6 Yorath	6 Phillips L
7 Reece	7 Reece (Smallman)	7 Yorath	7 Mahoney	7 Griffiths
8 Villars	8 Villars	8 James	8 Griffiths	8 Yorath
9 Davies R (Smallman)	9 Yorath	9 Smallman (Villars)	9 Reece	9 Reece
10 Yorath	10 Cartwright	10 Phillips	10 Toshack	10 Toshack
11 James	11 James	11 Cartwright	11 James	11 James
Cardiff May 11: 0-2	Hampden May 14: 0-2	Wrexham May 18: 1-0 *Smallman*	Vienna Sept 4: 1-2 *Griffiths*	Cardiff Oct 30: 2-0 *Griffiths, Toshack*

1974 Luxembourg	1975 Hungary	1975 Luxembourg	1975 Scotland	1975 England
1 Sprake	1 Davies	1 Davies	1 Davies	1 Davies
2 Thomas	2 Thomas	2 Page	2 Thomas	2 Thomas
3 England	3 Page	3 Yorath	3 Page	3 Page
4 Roberts P	4 Phillips L	4 Thomas	4 Yorath	4 Mahoney
5 Phillips L	5 Roberts J	5 Roberts D	5 Roberts J	5 Roberts J
6 Mahoney (Flynn)	6 Yorath	6 Mahoney	6 Phillips	6 Phillips
7 Yorath	7 Mahoney	7 Phillips	7 Mahoney	7 Griffiths
8 Griffiths	8 Griffiths	8 Griffiths (Flynn)	8 Flynn	8 Flynn
9 James	9 Reece (Smallman)	9 Reece	9 Reece	9 Smallman (Showers)
10 Reece	10 Toshack	10 Toshack	10 Toshack	10 Toshack
11 Toshack	11 James (Flynn)	11 James	11 James	11 James
Swansea Nov 20: 5-0 *Toshack, England Roberts P, Griffiths Yorath*	Budapest April 16: 2-1 *Toshack, Mahoney*	Luxembourg May 1: 3-1 *Reece, James 2 (1 pen)*	Cardiff May 17: 2-2 *Toshack, Flynn*	Wembley May 21: 2-2 *Toshack, Griffiths*

1975 N Ireland	1975 Austria	1976 England	1976 Yugoslavia	1976 Scotland
1 Davies	1 Lloyd	1 Lloyd	1 Davies	1 Lloyd
2 Thomas	2 Thomas	2 Page	2 Thomas	2 Jones D
3 Page	3 Jones	3 Jones	3 Page	3 Jones J
4 Mahoney	4 Mahoney	4 Yorath	4 Mahoney	4 Roberts D
5 Roberts D	5 Evans	5 Phillips	5 Phillips	5 Roberts J
6 Phillips	6 Phillips	6 Evans	6 Evans	6 Yorath
7 Griffiths	7 Griffiths	7 Harris	7 James (Curtis)	7 Griffiths
8 Flynn	8 Flynn	8 Flynn	8 Flynn	8 Harris (Cartwright)
9 Reece (Smallman)	9 Yorath	9 Curtis	9 Yorath	9 Curtis
10 Showers	10 Smallman	10 Roberts J	10 Toshack	10 O'Sullivan
11 James	11 James	11 Griffiths	11 Griffiths	11 James
Belfast May 23: 0-1	Wrexham Nov 19: 1-0 *Griffiths*	Wrexham Mar 24: 1-2 *Curtis*	Zagreb April 24: 0-2	Glasgow May 6: 1-3 *Griffiths* (pen)

1976 England	1976 N Ireland	1976 Yugoslavia	1976 W Germany	1976 Scotland
1 Davies	1 Davies	1 Davies	1 Davies	1 Davies
2 Thomas (Jones D)	2 Phillips	2 Phillips	2 Page (Cartwright)	2 Page
3 Page	3 Page	3 Roberts D	3 Jones	3 Jones
4 Mahoney	4 Mahoney	4 Evans	4 Mahoney	4 Phillips
5 Phillips	5 Roberts D	5 Page	5 Phillips	5 Evans
6 Evans	6 Evans	6 Griffiths (Curtis)	6 Evans	6 Griffiths
7 Yorath	7 Griffiths	7 Yorath	7 James	7 Thomas M
8 Flynn	8 Flynn	8 Mahoney	8 Yorath	8 Flynn
9 Curtis (Griffiths)	9 Yorath	9 Flynn	9 Curtis	9 Yorath
10 Toshack	10 Curtis	10 Toshack	10 Thomas M	10 Toshack
11 James	11 James	11 James	11 Griffiths (Flynn)	11 James (Curtis)
Cardiff May 8: 0-1	Swansea May 14: 1-0 *James*	Cardiff May 22: 1-1 *Evans*	Cardiff Oct 6: 0-2	Glasgow Nov 17: 0-1

1977 Czechoslovakia	1977 Scotland	1977 England	1977 N Ireland	1977 Kuwait
1 Davies	1 Davies	1 Davies	1 Davies	1 Davies
2 Thomas R	2 Thomas R	2 Thomas R	2 Thomas R	2 Thomas R (Page)
3 Jones	3 Jones	3 Jones	3 Jones	3 Jones
4 Mahoney	4 Mahoney	4 Mahoney	4 Mahoney	4 Mahoney
5 Phillips	5 Phillips	5 Phillips (Roberts D)	5 Roberts	5 Phillips
6 Evans	6 Evans	6 Evans	6 Evans	6 Roberts D
7 Sayer	7 Sayer	7 Sayer	7 Sayer (Curtis)	7 Sayer (Deacy)
8 Flynn	8 Flynn	8 Flynn	8 Flynn	8 Flynn
9 Yorath	9 Yorath	9 Yorath	9 Yorath	9 Yorath
10 Deacy	10 Deacy	10 Deacy	10 Deacy	10 Toshack
11 James	11 James (Thomas M)	11 James	11 James (Thomas M)	11 James
Wrexham Mar: 30: 3-0 *James 2, Deacy*	Wrexham May 28: 0-0	Wembley May 31: 1-0 *James* (pen)	Belfast June 3: 1-1 *Deacy*	Wrexham Sept 6: 0-0

1977 Kuwait	1977 Scotland	1977 Czechoslovakia	1977 W Germany	1978 Iran
1 Phillips J	1 Davies	1 Davies	1 Davies	1 Davies
2 Page	2 Thomas R	2 Thomas R	2 Page	2 Page
3 Jones	3 Jones J	3 Jones J	3 Jones J	3 Jones J
4 Mahoney	4 Mahoney	4 Mahoney	4 Jones D	4 Davis
5 Phillips L	5 Jones D	5 Jones D	5 Phillips	5 Jones D
6 Evans	6 Phillips	6 Phillips	6 Harris	6 Mahoney (Flynn)
7 Sayer	7 Flynn	7 Nardiello	7 Flynn	7 Harris (Cartwright)
8 Flynn	8 Sayer	8 Flynn	8 Yorath	8 Yorath
9 Yorath (Roberts D)	9 Yorath	9 Yorath	9 Deacy	9 Dwyer
10 Toshack (Edwards I)	10 Toshack	10 Toshack	10 James	10 Deacy
11 James (Thomas M)	11 Thomas M	11 Thomas M (Deacy)	11 Curtis (Nardiello)	11 Thomas M
Kuwait Sept 20: 0-0	Liverpool Oct 12: 0-2	Prague Nov 16: 0-1	Dortmund Dec 14: 1-1 *Jones D*	Teheran April 18: 1-0 *Dwyer*

1978 England	1978 Scotland	1978 N Ireland
1 Davies	1 Davies	1 Davies
2 Page	2 Page (Deacy)	2 Jones J
3 Jones	3 Jones J	3 Stevenson
4 Phillips	4 Roberts D	4 Roberts D
5 Jones D (Davis)	5 Phillips	5 Davis
6 Yorath (Mahoney)	6 Yorath	6 Mahoney
7 Harris	7 Mahoney	7 Yorath (Thomas M)
8 Flynn	8 Flynn	8 Flynn
9 Curtis	9 Harris	9 Harris
10 Dwyer	10 Dwyer	10 Dwyer
11 Thomas M	11 Curtis	11 Deacy
Cardiff May 13: 1-3 *Dwyer*	Glasgow May 17: 1-1 *Donachie* (og)	Wrexham May 19: 1-0 *Deacy* (pen)

EUROPEAN CUP 1978-79
BRITISH CLUBS FULL RECORD

FIRST ROUND, FIRST LEG

Juventus (1) 1 (*Virdis*)   60,000
Rangers (0) 0
Juventus: Zoff; Cuccureddu, Cabrini, Furino, Morini, Scirea, Causio, Tardelli, Virdis, Benetti (Fanna), Bettega.
Rangers: McCloy; Jardine, Forsyth A, Forsyth T, Jackson, MacDonald, Miller, Russell, Parlane, Smith, Watson.

Linfield (0) 0   6000
Lillestrom (0) 0
Linfield: Barclay; Fraser, Garrett, Coyle, Rafferty, Dornan, Nixon, Jameson, Martin, Kirk, Murray.
Lillestrom: Amundsen; Hammer, Birkeland, Kordahl, Berg, Gronlund, Hansen L, Lonstad, Hansen V, Lund, Tomteberget.

Nottingham F (1) 2 (*Birtles, Barrett*)   38,316
Liverpool (0) 0
Nottingham F: Shilton; Anderson, Barrett, McGovern, Lloyd, Burns, Gemmill, Bowyer, Birtles, Woodcock, Robertson.
Liverpool: Clemence; Neal, Kennedy A, Thompson, Kennedy R, Hughes, Dalglish, Case, Heighway, McDermott (Johnson), Souness.

FIRST ROUND, SECOND LEG

Lillestrom (1) 1 (*Lonstad*)   5600
Linfield (0) 0
Lillestrom: Amundsen; Hammer, Birkelund, Kordahl, Berg, Gronlund, Hansen L, (Dokken), Lonstad, Hansen V, Lund, Tomteberget.
Linfield: Barclay; Fraser, Garrett, Kirk, Rafferty, Dornan, Nixon, Jameson, Martin, Hewitt (Dunlop), Murray.

Liverpool (0) 0   51,679
Nottingham F (0) 0
Liverpool: Clemence; Neal, Kennedy A, Thompson, Kennedy R, Hughes, Dalglish, Case (Fairclough), Heighway, McDermott (Johnson), Souness.
Nottingham F: Shilton; Anderson, Clark, McGovern, Lloyd, Burns, Gemmill, Bowyer, Birtles, Woodcock, Robertson.

Rangers (1) 2 (*MacDonald, Smith*)   44,000
Juventus (0) 0
Rangers: McCloy; Jardine, Forsyth A, Forsyth T, Jackson, MacDonald, McLean, Russell, Parlane, Johnstone, Smith.
Juventus: Zoff; Cuccureddu, Cabrini, Furino (Benetti), Morini, Scirea, Causio, Tardelli (Fanna), Virdis, Gentile, Bettega.

SECOND ROUND, FIRST LEG

AEK Athens (0) 1 (*Tassos pen*)   35,000
Nottingham F (2) 2 (*McGovern, Birtles*)
AEK Athens: Stergioudas; Moussouris, Idzoglou (Damlanidas), Ravousis, Nikolaou, Viera, Tassos (Tsamis), Nikoloudis, Bajevic, Ardizoglou, Mavros.
Nottingham F: Shilton; Anderson, Clark, McGovern, Lloyd, Burns, Bowyer, Gemmill, Birtles, Woodcock, Robertson.

R.F. 79/80—45

Rangers (0) 0   44,000
PSV Eindhoven (0) 0
Rangers: McCloy; Jardine, Forsyth A, Forsyth T, Jackson (Miller), McDonald, McLean, Russell, Parlane (Cooper), Johnstone, Smith.
PSV Eindhoven: Van Engelen; Deijkers, Stevens, Brandts, Poortvliet, Lubse, Postuma, Willy Van der Kerkhof (Hooyer), Van Kraay, Krigh, Van der Kuylen (Jansen).

SECOND ROUND, SECOND LEG

Nottingham F (3) 5 (*Needham, Woodcock, Anderson, Birtles 2*)   38,069
AEK Athens (0) 1 (*Bajevic*)
Nottingham F: Shilton; Anderson, Clark (Mills), O'Hare, Lloyd, Needham, Gemmill, Bowyer, Birtles, Woodcock, Robertson.
AEK Athens: Christidis; Moussouris, Idzoglou, Ravousis, Nikolaou, Domazos, Tassos, Nikoloudis, Bajevic, Ardizoglou, Mavros.

PSV Eindhoven (1) 2 (*Lubse, Deijkers*)   28,000
Rangers (0) 3 (*MacDonald, Johnstone, Russell*)
PSV Eindhoven: Van Engelen; Krijgh (Smits), Stevens, Van Kraay, Brandts, Willy Van der Kerkhof, Jansen, Poortvliet, Rene Van der Kerkhof, Lubse, Deijkers.
Rangers: McCloy; Jardine, Forsyth A, Forsyth T, Johnstone, MacDonald, McLean, Russell, Parlane, Smith, Watson.

QUARTER-FINALS, FIRST LEG

Cologne (0) 1 (*Muller*)   40,000
Rangers (0) 0
Cologne: Schumacher; Konopka, Zimmermann, Schuster, Gerber, Cullmann, Glowacz (Prestin), Flohe, Muller, Neumann, Littbarski.
Rangers: McCloy; Jardine, Dawson, Forsyth, Jackson, MacDonald, McLean, Russell, Parlane (Urquhart), Smith, Denny (Miller).

Nottingham F (1) 4 (*Birtles, Robertson pen, Gemmill, Lloyd*)   31,949
Grasshoppers (1) 1 (*Sulser*)
Nottingham F: Shilton; Anderson, Clark, McGovern, Lloyd, Needham, O'Neill, Gemmill, Birtles, Woodcock, Robertson.
Grasshoppers: Berbig; Wehrli, Heinz Hermann, Montandon, Hey, Bauer, Meyer, Eigl, Sulser, Ponte, Herbert Hermann.

QUARTER-FINALS, SECOND LEG

Grasshoppers (1) 1 (*Sulser pen*)   17,800
Nottingham F (1) 1 (*O'Neill*)
Grasshoppers: Berbig; Wehrli, Heinz Hermann, Montandon, Hey, Bauer, Traber, Egli, Sulser, Ponte, Herbert Hermann.
Nottingham F: Shilton; Anderson, Barrett, McGovern, Lloyd, Needham, O'Neill, Gemmill, Birtles, Woodcock, Robertson.

Rangers (0) (*McLean*) 44,000
Cologne (0) 1 (*Muller*)
Rangers: McCloy; Jardine, Dawson (Johnstone), Forsyth, Jackson, MacDonald, McLean, Russell, Urquhart (Parlane), Smith, Cooper.
Cologne: Schumacher; Konopka, Zimmermann, Strack (Prestin), Gerber, Cullmann, Schuster, Flohe, Muller, Neumann, Van Gool (Glowacz).

SEMI-FINAL, FIRST LEG

Nottingham F (1) 3 (*Birtles, Bowyer, Robertson*) 40,804
Cologne (2) 3 (*Van Gool, Muller, Okudera*)
Nottingham F: Shilton; Barrett, Bowyer, McGovern, Lloyd, Needham, O'Neill, Gemmill (Clark), Birtles, Woodcock, Robertson.
Cologne: Schumacher; Konopka, Zimmermann, Schuster, Gerber, Cullmann, Van Gool, Glowacz (Okudera), Muller, Neumann, Prestin.

SEMI-FINAL, SECOND LEG

Cologne (0) 0 40,000
Nottingham F (0) 1 (*Bowyer*)
Cologne: Schumacher; Konopka, Zimmermann, Strack, Schuster, Cullmann, Van Gool, Glowacz (Okudera), Muller (Flohe), Neumann, Prestin.
Nottingham F: Shilton; Anderson, Clark, McGovern, Lloyd, Burns, O'Neill, Bowyer, Birtles, Woodcock, Robertson.

FINAL

Nottingham F (1) 1 (*Francis*) 60,000
Malmo (0) 0 (*at Munich*)
Nottingham F: Shilton; Anderson, Clark, McGovern, Lloyd, Burns, Francis, Bowyer, Birtles, Woodcock, Robertson.
Malmo: Moller; Roland Andersson, Erlandsson, Jonsson, Magnus Andersson, Tapper (Malmberg), Ljungberg, Prytz, Hansson (Tommy Andersson), Cervin, Kinnvall.

EUROPEAN CUP-WINNERS' CUP 1978-79
BRITISH CLUBS FULL RECORD

FIRST ROUND, FIRST LEG

AZ 67 (0) 0 18,000
Ipswich T (0) 0
AZ 67: Meskovic; Arntz, Spelbos, Metgod, Van Rijnsoever (Tol), Peters, Ressel, Van Hanegem, Kist, Nygaard (Hovenkamp), De Graaf.
Ipswich T: Cooper; Burley, Osman, Beattie, Tibbott, Talbot, Wark, Mills, Mariner, Whymark (Geddis), Woods.

Marek Stanke Dimitrov (0) 3 (*Petrov V*) 20,000
Petrov I 2)
Aberdeen (1) 2 (*Jarvie, Harper*)
Marek Stanke Dimitrov: Stoyanov; Sevdin, Kolev, Karakolev, Palev, Rainov, Pargov, Tomov, Petrov I, Ventislav, Petrov V.
Aberdeen: Leighton; Kennedy, McLelland, McMaster, Garner (Rougvie), Miller, Sullivan, Jarvie, Harper, Archibald, Scanlon.

Beveren (2) 3 (*Albert, Stevens, Schoenberger* 17,000 pen)
Ballymena (0) 0
Beveren: Pfaff; Jaspers, Buyl, Van Genechten, Baecke, Schoenberger, Hofkens, Cluytens, Stevens, Albert, Janssens.
Ballymena: Brown; Donald, McCulloch, Jackson, Butcher, Sloan, Simpson, McQuiston, Mullan, McLean, Shaw.

Rijeka (2) 3 (*Tomic, Durkalic, Cukrov*) 9000
Wrexham (0) 0
Rijeka: Auramovic (Ravnic); Makin, Hrstic, Cukrov, Radin, Juricic, Durkalic, Fegic (Bursdc), Tomic, Ruzik, Desnica.
Wrexham: Davies; Hill, Whittle, Davis, Roberts, Thomas, Shinton, Sutton, McNeil (Williams), Lyons, Cartwright.

FIRST ROUND, SECOND LEG

Aberdeen (0) 3 (*Strachan, Jarvie, Harper*) 25,000
Marek Stanke Dimitrov (0) 0
Aberdeen: Leighton; Kennedy, McLelland, McMaster, McLeish, Miller, Sullivan (Strachan), Archibald, Harper, Jarvie, Scanlon.
Marek Stanke Dimitrov: Stoinov; Sevdin, Kolev, Karakolev, Pavlev, Rainov, Pargov (Brankov), Tomov, Petrov I, Petrov V, Dimitrov.

Ballymena (0) 0 4000
Beveren (0) 3 (*Janssens 2, Wissmann*)
Ballymena: Brown; Donald, Butcher, McCullough, Jackson, Shaw (Spence), McQuiston, McAvoy, Mullan, Simpson, McClean.
Beveren: Pfaff; Jaspers, Van Genechten, Buyl, Baecke, Hofkens, Schoenberger, Albert (Truyens), Stevens (Wissmann), Cluytens, Janssens.

Ipswich T (1) 2 (*Mariner, Wark pen*) 23,814
AZ 67 (0) 0
Ipswich T: Cooper; Burley, Tibbott, Talbot, Osman, Beattie, Mills, Wark, Mariner, Whymark, Woods.
AZ 67: Vooys; Van Rijnsoever, Spelbos, Metgod, Hovenkamp, Peters, Ressel, Van Hanegem, Kist, Arntz, De Graaf (Nygaard).

Wrexham (0) 2 (*McNeil, Cartwright*) 10,469
Rijeka (0) 0
Wrexham: Davies; Hill, Whittle, Davis, Cegielski, Thomas, Shinton, Sutton, McNeil, Williams, Cartwright.
Rijeka: Avramovic; Makin, Hristic, Cukrov, Radin, Juricic, Durkalic, Desnica, Fegic, Tomic, Ruzic.

SECOND ROUND, FIRST LEG

Fortuna Dusseldorf (0) 3 (*Gunther 2, Zimmermann*) 10,500
Aberdeen (0) 0
Fortuna Dusseldorf: Woyke; Brei, Zewe, Zimmermann, Baltes, Kohnen, Gunther, Schmitz, Weikl, Allofs, Seel.
Aberdeen: Leighton; Kennedy, McLeish, Miller, McLelland, Rougvie, McMaster (Scanlon), Jarvie (Strachan), Sullivan, Archibald, Harper.

Ipswich T (0) 1 (*Wark pen*) 20,394
SW Innsbruck (0) 0
Ipswich T: Cooper; Burley, Tibbott, Talbot, Hunter, Osman, Mills, Wark, Mariner (Geddis), Whymark, Woods.
SW Innsbruck: Friedl Koncilia; Zanon, Auer, Silkio, Werner Schwarz (Gartner), Hanschitz, Scharman, Peter Koncilia, Oberacher Hickersberger, Braschler (Wolfgang Schwarz).

SECOND ROUND, SECOND LEG

Aberdeen (0) 2 (*McLelland, Jarvie*)   16,800
Fortuna Dusseldorf (0) 0
Aberdeen: Clark; Rougvie, McLelland, McMaster, McLeish, Miller, Sullivan, Archibald, Harper, Jarvie, Strachan.
Fortuna Dusseldorf: Woyke; Brei, Zewe, Zimmerman, Bates, Kohnen, Wael, Lund, Gunther, Allofs, Seel.

SW Innsbruck (0) 1 (*Oberacher*)   18,400
Ipswich T (0) 1 (*Burley*)
SW Innsbruck: Friedl Koncilia; Zanon, Forstinger, Auer, Sikic (Muller), Hanschitz, Scharmann, Peter Koncilia, Hickersberger, Oberacher (Wolfgang Schwarz), Braschler.
Ipswich T: Cooper; Burley, Tibbott, Talbot, Hunter, Osman, Mills, Wark, Mariner, Geddis (Whymark), Woods (Gates).

QUARTER-FINAL, FIRST LEG

Ipswich T (0) 2 (*Gates 2*)   28,000
Barcelona (0) 1 (*Esteban*)
Ipswich T: Cooper; Burley, Tibbott, Mills, Osman, Butcher, Wark, Muhren, Brazil, Gates, Geddis (Hunter).
Barcelona: Artola; Zuviria, Migueli, Olmo, De la Cruz, Neeskens (Costas), Esteban, Heredia, Krankl, Asensi, Martinez.

QUARTER-FINAL, SECOND LEG

Barcelona (1) 1 (*Migueli*)   100,000
Ipswich T (0) 0
Barcelona: Artola; Zuviria, Migueli, Olmo, Albaladejo, Asensi, Neeskens, Martinez, Rexach, Krankl, Heredia.
Ipswich T: Cooper; Burley, Osman, Butcher, Beattie, Wark (Parkin), Muhren, Mills, Gates (Geddis), Brazil, Woods.

UEFA CUP 1978-79
BRITISH CLUBS FULL RECORD

FIRST ROUND, FIRST LEG

IBV Westman (0) 0
Glentoran (0) 0   1000
IBV Westman: Sveinsson A, Oskarsson, Fropjofsson, Hallgrimsson, Finnbogasson, Sveinsson S, Sigporsson, Vairysson, Porleifsson, Palsson, Baldvinsson.
Glentoran: Matthews; Dougan, McFall R, Porter, Cranston, Moreland, Caskey J, Jamison, Caskey W, McFall G, O'Neill.

Finn Harps (0) 0   5000
Everton (2) 5 (*Thomas, King 2, Latchford, Walsh*)
Finn Harps: Mahon (Harper); McDowell, Hutton, O'Docherty, Sheridan, Healy, Logan, Minnock, McGuinness (Stephenson), Duffy, Ferry.
Everton: Wood, Darracott, Pejic, Lyons (Higgins), Wright, Nulty, King, Ross, Latchford, Walsh, Thomas.

Standard Liege (1) 1 (*Denier*)
Dundee U (0) 0 (*in Ghent*)   18,000
Standard Liege: Preud'homme; Gerets, Piessers, Garot, Poel, Labarbe, Denier, Graf, Wellens Sigurvinsson, Marechal (Onal).
Dundee U: McAlpine; Kirkwood, Kopel, Robinson, Hegarty, Narey, Smith, Addison, Sturrock (Dodds), Holt, Payne (Frye).

Arsenal (0) 3 (*Stapleton 2, Sunderland*)
Lokomotive Leipzig (0) 0   34,233
Arsenal: Jennings; Rice, Nelson, Price, Walford, Young, Brady (Gatting), Sunderland, Stapleton, Harvey (Heeley), Rix.
Lokomotive Leipzig: Stotzner; Sekora (Roth), Hammer, Grobner, Fritsche, Altmann, Moldt, Liebers, Kinne, Lowe (Eichhorn), Kuhn.

Galatasaray (0) 1 (*Fatih pen*)
WBA (1) 3 (*Robson, Regis, Cunningham*)   50,000
Galatasaray: Eser; Mufit, Erdogan, Gungor, Fatih, Mehmet, Oner, Ali, Cuneyt, Gokmen, Tuncay.
WBA: Godden; Batson, Statham, Cunningham, Wile, Robertson, Robson, [Brown A, Regis, Trewick, Cantello.

Hibernian (1) 3 (*Higgins 2, Temperley*)
Norrkoping (0) 2 (*Ohlsson, Andersson*)   10,000
Hibernian: McDonald; Duncan, Smith, Rae, Fleming, McNamara, Murray, McLeod, Higgins, Carroll (Hutchinson), Temperley.
Norrkoping: Jonsson; Eek, Andersson, Fredriksson, Ohlsson, Bernsten, Eriksson, Lundqvist, Lilijedahl, Svensson (Helberg), Larsson.

Twente (0) 1 (*Thoresen*)
Manchester C (1) 1 (*Watson*)   12,000
Twente: Pasveer; Van Ierssel, Drost, Overweg, Wildschut, Thijssen, Van der Vall, Otto, Bos (Smard), Gritter, Thoresen.
Manchester C: Corrigan; Clements, Power. Viljoen, Watson, Futcher P, Channon, Owen, Palmer, Hartford, Barnes.

FIRST ROUND, SECOND LEG

Glentoran (1) 1 (*Caskey W*)
IBV Westman (0) 1 (*Oskarsson*)   5000
Glentoran: Matthews; Dougan, McFall R, Porter, Cranston, Moreland, Caskey J, Jameson, Caskey W, McFall Q, O'Neill.
IBV Westman: Sveinsson A; Oskarsson, Fropjofsson, Hallgrimsson, Finnbogasson, Sviensson S, Sigporsson, Vairysson, Porleifsson, (Earlingsson), Palsson (Porsteinsson), Baldvinsson.

Everton (2) 5 (*King, Latchford, Walsh, Ross, Dobson*)
Finn Harps (0) 0   21,611
Everton: Wood; Darracott, Pejic, Lyons (Higgins), Wright, Ross, King, Dobson, Latchford, Walsh, Thomas (Robinson).
Finn Harps: Harper (Mahon); McDowell, Hutton, O'Doherty T, Sheridan, McGuinness P, Logan, Healy F, McGuinness T, Ferry, Minnock.

Dundee U (0) 0
Standard Liege (0) 0   9150
Dundee U: McAlpine; Stewart, Kopel, Holt, Hegarty, Narey, Smith, Addison (Fleming), Payne, Sturrock, Dodds.
Standard Liege: Preud'homme; Gerets, Renquin, Garot, Poel, Labarbe, Denier, Graf, Wellens, Sigurvinsson, De Matos.

Lokomotive Leipzig (0) 1 (*Stapleton og*) 22,000
Arsenal (1) 4 (*Brady, Stapleton 2, Sunderland*)
Lokomotive Leipzig: Stotzner; Hammer, Grobner, Fritsche, Moldt, Kinne, Kuhn Dennstedt, Baum (Altmann), Eichhorn, Liebers.
Arsenal: Jennings; Rice, Nelson, Price (Vaessen), O'Leary, Young (Walford), Brady, Sunderland, Stapleton, Devine, Rix.

Manchester C (1) 3 (*Wildschut og, Kidd, Bell*)
Twente (0) 2 (*Overweg, Gritter*) 29,330
Manchester C: Corrigan; Clements, Power, Viljoen (Bell), Watson, Futcher P, Channon, Owen, Kidd, Hartford, Barnes.
Twente: Pasveer; Van Ierssel, Overweg, Drost, Wildschut, Thijssen, Van der Vall, Pahlplatz, Gritter, Bos (Bruggnink), Thoresen.

Norrkoping (0) 0
Hibernian (0) 0 1300
Norrkoping: Johnson; Eek, Andersson, Fredriksson, Bernsten, Eriksson, Lundqvist, Lilijedahl, Ohlsson, Svensson, Larsson.
Hibernian: McDonald; Duncan, Smith, Rae, Fleming, McNamara, McLeod, Higgins, Stewart, Hutchinson, Bremner.

WBA (2) 3 (*Robson, Cunningham pen., Trewick*)
Galatasaray (1) 1 (*Turgay*) 22,380
WBA: Godden (Grew); Batson, Statham, Trewick (Brown T). Wile, Robertson, Robson, Brown A, Regis, Cantello, Cunningham.
Galatasaray: Bahatin; Mufit, Erdogan, Gungor, Tuncay, Fatih, Oner, Gurcan, Cuneyt, Tacettin, Turgay.

SECOND ROUND, FIRST LEG

Everton (1) 2 (*Latchford, King*)
Dukla (0) 1 (*Macela*) 32,857
Everton: Wood; Darracott (Robinson), Pejic, Lyons, Wright, Ross, King, Dobson, Latchford, Walsh, Thomas.
Dukla: Stromsik; Barmos, Macela, Samek, Fiala, Rott, Pelc (Bilsky), Novac, Stambacher, Nehoda, Gajdusek.

Hajduk Split (2) 2 (*Cop, Djordjevic*)
Arsenal (1) 1 (*Brady*) 30,000
Hajduk Split: Cosic; Primorac, Krsticevic (Maricic), Jovanic, Peruzovic, Rozic, Zungul, Musinic, Cop (Vujovic), Djordjevic, Surjak.
Arsenal: Jennings; Rice, Nelson, Price, O'Leary, Young, Brady, Kosmina, Stapleton, Heeley, Rix.

Manchester C (1) 4 (*Hartford, Kidd 2, 1 a pen, Palmer*)
Standard Liege (0) 0 27,498
Manchester C: Corrigan; Clements, Donachie, Booth, Watson, Viljoen (Keegan), Palmer, Bell, Kidd, Hartford, Barnes.
Standard Liege: Preud'homme; Gerets, Renquin, Garot, Poel, Onal, Denier, Graf, Wellens, Sigurvinsson, De Matos.

Sporting Braga (0) 0
WBA (0) 2 (*Regis 2*) 20,000
Sporting Braga: Conhe; Artur, Fernando, Serra, Cardoso, Paulo, Rocha, Jose Artur, Rodrigo, Chico Faria, Lito, Nelinho.
WBA: Godden; Batson, Statham, Cunningham, Wile, Robertson, Robson, Brown A, Regis, Cantello, Brown T.

Strasbourg (1) 2 (*Gemmrich, Piasecki pen*)
Hibernian (0) 0 25,000
Strasbourg: Dropsy; Marx (Deutschmann), Specht, Novi, Domenech, Jouve (Ehrlacher), Dugueperoux, Piasecki, Wagner, Tanter, Gemmrich.
Hibernian: McDonald; Duncan, Stewart, McNamara, Smith, Bremner, McLeod, Campbell, Rae, Hutchinson, Higgins.

SECOND ROUND, SECOND LEG

Arsenal (0) 1 (*Young*)
Hajduk Split (0) 0 41,787
Arsenal: Jennings; Rice, Nelson, Price, O'Leary, Young, Brady, Gatting, Stapleton, Heeley (Kosmina), Rix.
Hajduk Split: Budincevic; Primorac, Krsticevic, Luketin (Cop), Peruzovic, Rozic, Zungul, Muzinic, Jovanic, Djordjevic, Surjak.

Dukla Prague (0) 1 (*Gajdusek*)
Everton (0) 0 35,000
Dukla Prague: Stromsik; Macela, Samek, Novak, Barmos, Pelc (Berger), Vizek, Bilsky, Nehoda, Gajdusek, Stambacher.
Everton: Wood; Darracott, Pejic, Kenyon, Wright, Nulty (King), Ross, Dobson, Latchford, Walsh, Thomas.

Hibernian (0) 1 (*McLeod pen*)
Strasbourg (0) 0 14,662
Hibernian: McDonald; Duncan, Smith, Bremner, Stewart, McNamara, Rae, McLeod, Hutchinson, Higgins, Murray.
Strasbourg: Dropsy; Marx, Domenech, Specht, Novi, Dugueperoux, Tanter, Piasecki, Wagner, Gemmrich, Deutschmann.

Standard Liege (0) 2 (*Sigurvinsson 2, 1 a pen*)
Manchester C (0) 0 30,000
Standard Liege: Preud'homme; Gerets, Renquin, Garot, Poel, Labarbe, Onal, Graf, Wellens (Denier), Sigurvinsson, De Matos (Plessers).
Manchester C: Corrigan; Clements, Donachie, Booth, Watson, Owen, Channon, Bell, Kidd, Hartford, Palmer.

WBA (0) 1 (*Brown A*)
Sporting Braga (0) 0 26,019
WBA: Godden; Batson, Statham, Cunningham, Wile, Robertson, Robson (Trewick), Brown A, Regis, Cantello (Martin), Brown T.
Sporting Braga: Cohne; Correira, Serra, Cardoso, Bilala (Mendes), Paulo Rocha, Jose Artur, Garcia (Fontes), Chico Faria, Lito, Nelinho.

THIRD ROUND, FIRST LEG

Red Star Belgrade (1) 1 (*Blagojevic*)
Arsenal (0) 0 50,000
Red Star Belgrade: Stojanovic; Jovanovic, Jovin, Muslin, Keri, Jurisic, Petrovic, Blagojevic (Milosavljevic), Savic, Sestic, Lukic (Simic).
Arsenal: Jennings; Rice, Nelson, Price, O'Leary, Young, Heeley, Sunderland, Stapleton, Walford, Rix.

Valencia (1) 1 (*Felman*)
WBA (0) 1 (*Cunningham*) 50,000
Valencia: Pereira; Cervero, Castellano, Arias, Butubot, Cabral, Saura, Bonhof, Felman, Solsona, Kempes.
WBA: Godden; Batson, Statham, Trewick, Wile, Robertson, Robson, Brown A, Regis, Cantello, Cunningham.

AC Milan (0) 2 (*Bigon* 2)
Manchester C (1) 2 (*Kidd, Power*) 40,000
AC Milan: Albertosi; Collovati, Maldera, De Vecchi, Bet, Baresi, Buriani, Bigon, Novellino, Rivera, Chiodi.
Manchester C: Corrigan; Clements, Donachie, Booth, Watson, Power, Viljoen (Keegan), Bell, Kidd, Hartford, Palmer.

THIRD ROUND, SECOND LEG

Arsenal (0) 1 (*Sunderland*)
Red Star Belgrade (0) 1 (*Savic*) 41,566
Arsenal: Jennings; Rice, Nelson, Price, O'Leary, Young, Heeley (Kosmina), Gatting, Stapleton, Sunderland, Rix (Macdonald).
Red Star: Stojanovic; Jovanovic, Krmpotic, Muslin, Keri, Jurisic, Petrovic, Blagojevic, Savic, Milosavljevic, Borovnica.

Manchester C (3) 3 (*Booth, Hartford, Kidd*)
AC Milan (0) 0 38,026
Manchester C: Corrigan; Keegan, Donachie, Booth, Watson, Power, Channon, Viljoen, Kidd, Hartford, Barnes.
AC Milan: Albertosi; Collovati, Maldera, De Vecchi, Bet, Baresi, Buriani, Antonelli, Novellino, Rivera (Boldini), Sartori.

WBA (1) 2 (*Brown T* 2, 1 *a pen*)
Valencia (0) 0 38,000
WBA: Godden; Batson, Statham, Brown T, Wile, Robertson, Robson, Brown A, Regis, Cantello (Trewick), Cunningham.
Valencia: Manzadedo; Carrette, Cordero, Arias, Botubot, Bonhof, Saura, Cabral, Kempes, Solsona Felman (Diarte).

QUARTER-FINAL, FIRST LEG

Manchester C (1) 1 (*Channon*)
Bor Moenchengladbach (0) 1 (*Lienen*) 39,005
Manchester C: Corrigan; Donachie, Power, Reid, Watson, Booth, Channon, Viljoen, Kidd, Hartford, Barnes.
Bor Moenchengladbach: Kneib; Schaffer, Hannes, Schafer, Klinkhammer, Bruns, Simonsen, Kulik, Del Haye, Nielsen, Lienen.

Red Star Belgrade (0) 1 (*Savic*)
WBA (0) 0 95,000
Red Star Belgrade: Stojanovic; Jovanovic, Krmpotic, Muslin, Miletovic, Jurisic, Petrovic (Milosavljevic), Blagojevic, Savic, Milovanovic, Sestic (Simic).
WBA: Godden; Batson, Statham, Trewick, Wile, Robertson, Robson, Brown A, Regis, Brown T, Cunningham.

QUARTER-FINAL, SECOND LEG

Bor Moenchengladbach (1) 3 (*Kulik, Bruns, Del Haye*)
Manchester C (0) 1 (*Deyna*) 35,000
Bor Moenchengladbach: Kneib; Schaffer, Hannes, Schafer, Ringels, Bruns, Simonsen, Kulik, Del Haye (Amrath), Wohlers, Lienen.
Manchester C: Corrigan; Donachie, Power, Reid (Deyna), Watson, Booth, Channon, Viljoen, Henry, Hartford, Barnes.

WBA (1) 1 (*Regis*)
Red Star Belgrade (0) 1 (*Sestic*) 31,110
WBA: Godden; Batson, Statham, Brown T, Wile, Robertson, Robson, Brown A, Regis, Cantello, Cunningham.
Red Star Belgrade: Stojanovic; Jovanovic, Krmpotic, Muslin, Jurisic, Jelikic, Sestic, Blagojevic, Savic, Borovnica, Milosavljevic.

PROGRESS OF BRITISH AND IRISH CLUBS IN EUROPE

1955–56
EUROPEAN CUP Hibernian (Semi-Final)

1955–58
EUROPEAN INTER-CITIES FAIRS CUP London beat Basle, Frankfurt and Lausanne before losing to Barcelona 2-2, 2-6 in the Final.
Birmingham C. knocked out Inter and Zagreb before losing to Barcelona 4-3, 0-1 and 1-2 at Basle.

1956–57
EUROPEAN CUP Manchester U. (Semi-Final)   Rangers (First Round Proper)

1957–58
EUROPEAN CUP Manchester U. (Semi-Final)   Glenavon (Preliminary Round)
Rangers (First Round Proper)   Shamrock R. (Preliminary Round)

1958–60
FAIRS CUP Birmingham C. (Runners-Up)   Chelsea (Second Round)

1958–59
EUROPEAN CUP Wolverhampton W. (First Round)   Drumcondra (Preliminary Round)
Ards (Preliminary Round)   Hearts (Preliminary Round)
Manchester U. were invited to compete, but were withdrawn by the Football League.

1959–60
EUROPEAN CUP Rangers (Semi-Final)   Linfield (Preliminary Round)
Wolverhampton W. (Quarter-Final)   Shamrock R. (Preliminary Round)

1960–61
EUROPEAN CUP Burnley (Quarter-Final)   Limerick (Preliminary Round)
Hearts (Preliminary Round)   Glenavon—Withdrew

EUROPEAN CUP-WINNERS' CUP Rangers (Runners-Up)   Wolverhampton W. (Semi-Final)

FAIRS CUP Birmingham C. (Runners-Up)   Hibernian (Semi-Final)

1961–62
EUROPEAN CUP Tottenham H. (Semi-Final)   Drumcondra (Preliminary Round)
Rangers (Quarter-Final)   Linfield (Preliminary Round)

EUROPEAN CUP-WINNERS' CUP Dunfermline Ath. (Quarter-Final)   Swansea T. (First Round)
Leicester C. (Second Round)   Glenavon (First Round)
  St Patrick's Ath. (Preliminary Round)

FAIRS CUP Sheffield W. (Quarter-Final)   Nottingham F. (First Round)
Hearts (Second Round)   Birmingham C. (Second Round)
  Hibernian (Second Round)

1962–63
EUROPEAN CUP Dundee (Semi-Final)   Shelbourne (Preliminary Round)
Ipswich T. (First Round)   Linfield (Preliminary Round)

EUROPEAN CUP-WINNERS' CUP Tottenham H. (Winners)   Shamrock R. (Second Round)
Rangers (Second Round)   Bangor C. (First Round)
  Portadown (First Round)

FAIRS CUP Hibernian (Quarter-Final)   Everton (First Round)
Dunfermline Ath. (Second Round)   Celtic (First Round)
Glentoran (First Round)   Drumcondra (Second Round)

1963–64
EUROPEAN CUP Rangers (Preliminary Round)   Dundalk (Preliminary Round)
Everton (Preliminary Round)   Distillery (Preliminary Round)

EUROPEAN CUP-WINNERS' CUP Celtic (Semi-Final)   Borough U. (Second Round)
Manchester U. (Quarter-Final)   Tottenham H. (Second Round)
Linfield (Second Round)   Shelbourne (First Round)

FAIRS CUP Partick T. (Second Round)   Hearts (First Round)
Arsenal (Second Round)   Glentoran (First Round)
Sheffield W. (Second Round)   Shamrock R. (First Round)

1964–65

EUROPEAN CUP	Liverpool (Semi-Final)	Shamrock R. (Preliminary Round)
	Rangers (Quarter-Final)	Glentoran (Preliminary Round)
EUROPEAN CUP-WINNERS' CUP	West Ham U. (Winners)	Cork Celtic (First Round)
	Cardiff C. (Quarter-Final)	Derry C. (First Round)
	Dundee (Second Round)	
FAIRS CUP	Manchester U. (Semi-Final)	Celtic (Second Round)
	Dunfermline Ath. (Third Round)	Shelbourne (Second Round)
	Everton (Third Round)	Kilmarnock (Second Round)

1965–66

EUROPEAN CUP	Manchester U. (Semi-Final)	Kilmarnock (First Round)
	Derry C. (First Round)	Drumcondra (Preliminary Round)
EUROPEAN CUP-WINNERS' CUP	Liverpool (Runners-Up)	Limerick (First Round)
	Celtic (Semi-Final)	Cardiff C. (First Round)
	West Ham U. (Semi-Final)	Coleraine (First Round)
FAIRS CUP	Leeds U. (Semi-Final)	Everton (Second Round)
	Chelsea (Semi-Final)	Glentoran (First Round)
	Dunfermline Ath. (Quarter-Final)	Hibernian (First Round)
	Hearts (Third Round)	Shamrock R. (Second Round)

1966–67

EUROPEAN CUP	Celtic (Winners)	Liverpool (First Round)
	Linfield (Quarter-Final)	Waterford (Preliminary Round)
EUROPEAN CUP-WINNERS' CUP	Rangers (Runners-Up)	Glentoran (First Round)
	Everton (Second Round)	Swansea T. (First Round)
	Shamrock R. (Second Round)	
FAIRS CUP	Leeds U. (Runners-Up)	W.B.A. (Third Round)
	Kilmarnock (Semi-Final)	Dunfermline Ath. (Second Round)
	Burnley (Quarter-Final)	Drumcondra (First Round)
	Dundee U. (Third Round)	

1967–68

EUROPEAN CUP	Manchester U. (Winners)	Celtic (First Round)
	Dundalk (First Round)	Glentoran (First Round)
EUROPEAN CUP-WINNERS' CUP	Cardiff C. (Semi-Final)	Crusaders (First Round)
	Aberdeen (Second Round)	Shamrock R. (First Round)
	Tottenham H. (Second Round)	
FAIRS CUP	Leeds U. (Winners)	Rangers (Quarter-Final)
	Dundee (Semi-Final)	Nottingham F. (Second Round)
	Hibernian (Third Round)	Linfield (First Round)
	Liverpool (Third Round)	St. Patricks (First Round)

1968–69

EUROPEAN CUP	Manchester U. (Semi-Final)	Glentoran (First Round)
	Celtic (Quarter-Final)	Waterford (First Round)
	Manchester C. (First Round)	
EUROPEAN CUP-WINNERS' CUP	Dunfermline Ath. (Semi-Final)	Cardiff C. (First Round)
	W.B.A. (Quarter-Final)	Shamrock R. (First Round)
	Crusaders (First Round)	
FAIRS CUP	Newcastle U. (Winners)	Chelsea (Second Round)
	Rangers (Semi-Final)	Dundalk (Second Round)
	Leeds U. (Quarter-Final)	Liverpool (First Round)
	Hibernian (Third Round)	Linfield (First Round)
	Aberdeen (Second Round)	Morton (First Round)

1969–70

EUROPEAN CUP	Celtic (Runners-Up)	Waterford (First Round)
	Leeds U. (Semi-Final)	Linfield (First Round)
EUROPEAN CUP-WINNERS' CUP	Manchester C. (Winners)	Ards (First Round)
	Rangers (Second Round)	Shamrock R. (First Round)
	Cardiff C. (Second Round)	
EUROPEAN FAIRS CUP	Arsenal (Winners)	Kilmarnock (Third Round)
	Newcastle U. (Quarter-Finals)	Dundee U. (First Round)
	Dunfermline Ath. (Third Round)	Coleraine (Second Round)
	Southampton (Third Round)	Dundalk (First Round)
	Liverpool (Second Round)	Glentoran (First Round)

1970-71
EUROPEAN CUP
Celtic (Quarter Final)
Everton (Quarter Final)
Waterford (Second Round)
Glentoran (First Round)

EUROPEAN CUP-WINNERS' CUP
Manchester C. (Semi-Final)
Chelsea (Winners)
Cardiff C. (Quarter Final)
Linfield (First Round)
Aberdeen (First Round)
Bohemians (Preliminary Round)

EUROPEAN FAIRS CUP
Leeds U. (Winners)
Arsenal (Quarter Final)
Liverpool (Semi-Final)
Newcastle U. (Second Round)
Coleraine (Second Round)
Dundee U. (Second Round)
Coventry C. (Second Round)
Cork Hibernians (First Round)
Rangers (First Round)
Kilmarnock (First Round)
Hibernian (Third Round)

1971-72
EUROPEAN CUP
Arsenal (Quarter-Final)
Celtic (Semi-Final)
Linfield (First Round)
Cork Hibs. (First Round)

EUROPEAN CUP-WINNERS' CUP
Liverpool (Second Round)
Chelsea (Second Round)
Cardiff C. (First Round)
Rangers (Winners)
Distillery (First Round)
Limerick (First Round)

UEFA CUP
Tottenham H. (Winners)
Wolverhampton W. (Runners-up)
Leeds (First Round)
Southampton (First Round)
Shelbourne (First Round)
Glentoran (First Round)
Dundee (Third Round)
Aberdeen (Second Round)
St. Johnstone (Third Round)

1972-73
EUROPEAN CUP
Derby Co. (Semi-Final)
Celtic (Second Round)
Waterford (First Round)

EUROPEAN CUP-WINNERS' CUP
Leeds U. (Runners-up)
Hibernian (Quarter-Final)
Wrexham (Second Round)
Cork Hibs. (Second Round)

UEFA CUP
Liverpool (Winners)
Tottenham H. (Semi-Final)
Stoke C. (First Round)
Manchester C. (First Round)
Aberdeen (First Round)
Partick T. (First Round)
Bohemians (First Round)

1973-74
EUROPEAN CUP
Liverpool (Second Round)
Celtic (Semi-Final)
Waterford (First Round)
Crusaders (First Round)

EUROPEAN CUP-WINNERS' CUP
Sunderland (Second Round)
Rangers (Second Round)
Cardiff C. (First Round)
Glentoran (Quarter-Finals)
Cork Hibs. (First Round)

UEFA CUP
Tottenham H. (Runners-up)
Ipswich T. (Quarter-Finals)
Leeds U. (Third Round)
Wolverhampton W. (Second Round)
Aberdeen (Second Round)
Hibernian (Second Round)
Finn Harps (First Round)
Ards (First Round)

1974-75
EUROPEAN CUP
Leeds U. (Runners-up)
Celtic (First Round)
Coleraine (First Round)
Cork Celtic (Second Round)

EUROPEAN CUP-WINNERS' CUP
Liverpool (Second Round)
Ards (First Round)
Cardiff (First Round)
Finn Harps (First Round)
Dundee U. (Second Round)

UEFA CUP
Derby Co. (Third Round)
Ipswich T. (First Round)
Stoke C. (First Round)
Wolverhampton W. (First Round)
Bohemians (First Round)
Dundee (First Round)
Portadown (Second Round)
Hibernian (Second Round)

1975-76
EUROPEAN CUP
Derby Co. (Second Round)
Linfield (First Round)
Rangers (Second Round)
Bohemians (First Round)

EUROPEAN CUP-WINNERS' CUP
West Ham U. (Runners-up)
Celtic (Quarter-Final)
Home Farm (First Round)
Wrexham (Quarter-Final)
Coleraine (First Round)

UEFA CUP
Liverpool (Winners)
Aston Villa (First Round)
Glentoran (First Round)
Athlone T. (Second Round)
Ipswich T. (Second Round)
Everton (First Round)
Hibernian (First Round)
Dundee U. (Second Round)

1976-77
EUROPEAN CUP
- Liverpool (Winners)
- Crusaders (First Round)
- Dundalk (First Round)
- Rangers (First Round)

EUROPEAN CUP-WINNERS' CUP
- Southampton (Quarter-Finals)
- Cardiff C. (First Round)
- Hearts (Second Round)
- Bohemians (Second Round)
- Carrick Rangers (Second Round)

UEFA CUP
- Manchester C. (First Round)
- Derby Co. (Second Round)
- Manchester U. (Second Round)
- Q.P.R. (Quarter-Finals)
- Hibernian (Second Round)
- Glentoran (First Round)
- Celtic (First Round)
- Finn Harps (First Round)

1977-78
EUROPEAN CUP
- Liverpool (Winners)
- Sligo Rovers (First Round)
- Celtic (Second Round)
- Glentoran (Second Round)

EUROPEAN CUP-WINNERS' CUP
- Rangers (First Round)
- Dundalk (First Round)
- Coleraine (First Round)
- Cardiff C (First Round)
- Manchester U (Second Round)

UEFA CUP
- Aston Villa (Quarter-Finals)
- Manchester C (First Round)
- Bohemians (First Round)
- Glenavon (First Round)
- Ipswich T (Third Round)
- Newcastle U (Second Round)
- Dundee U (First Round)
- Aberdeen (First Round)

1978-79
EUROPEAN CUP
- Nottingham F (Winners)
- Liverpool (First Round)
- Linfield (First Round)
- Rangers (Quarter-Final)
- Bohemians (Second Round)

EUROPEAN CUP-WINNERS CUP
- Ipswich (Quarter-Final)
- Ballymena (First Round)
- Wrexham (First Round)
- Aberdeen (Second Round)
- Shamrock R (Second Round)

UEFA CUP
- Manchester C (Quarter-Final)
- Arsenal (Third Round)
- Dundee U (First Round)
- Finn Harps (First Round)
- WBA (Quarter-Final)
- Everton (Second Round)
- Hibernian (Second Round)
- Glentoran (First Round)

SUMMARY OF APPEARANCES BY BRITISH AND IRISH CLUBS IN EUROPE

THE EUROPEAN CUP (1955–79)

English clubs	Appearances
Liverpool	6
Manchester U	5
Derby Co	2
Wolverhampton W	2
Everton	2
Leeds U	2
Burnley	1
Tottenham H	1
Ipswich T	1
Manchester C	1
Arsenal	1
Nottingham F	1

Scottish clubs	
Celtic	10
Rangers	9
Hearts	2
Dundee	1
Kilmarnock	1
Hibernian	1

Clubs from Northern Ireland	Appearances
Linfield	8
Glentoran	5
Crusaders	2
Glenavon	1
Ards	1
Distillery	1
Derry C	1
Coleraine	1

Clubs from Eire	
Waterford	6
Drumcondra	3
Shamrock R	3
Dundalk	3
Bohemians	2
Limerick	1
Shelbourne	1
Cork Hibs	1
Cork Celtic	1
Sligo Rovers	1

Winners: Celtic 1966-67; Manchester U 1967-68; Liverpool 1976-77, 1977-78; Nottingham F 1978-79
Finalists: Celtic 1969-70; Leeds U 1974-5

THE EUROPEAN CUP-WINNERS' CUP (1960–79)

English clubs	Appearances
Tottenham H	3
Liverpool	3
West Ham U	3
Chelsea	2
Manchester C	2
Manchester U	2
Wolverhampton W	1
Leicester C	1
Everton	1
WBA	1
Leeds U	1
Sunderland	1
Southampton	1
Ipswich T	1

Scottish clubs	
Rangers	7
Celtic	3
Aberdeen	3
Dunfermline Ath	2
Dundee	1
Dundee U	1
Hibernian	1
Hearts	1

Welsh clubs	
Cardiff C	11
Wrexham	3
Swansea C (then Town)	2
Bangor C	1

Clubs from Northern Ireland	Appearances
Coleraine	3
Crusaders	2
Glentoran	2
Ards	2
Linfield	2
Glenavon	1
Derry C	1
Distillery	1
Portadown	1
Carrick Rangers	1
Ballymena	1

Clubs from Eire	
Shamrock R	6
Limerick	2
Cork Hibs	2
Bohemians	2
Shelbourne	1
Cork Celtic	1
St Patrick's Ath	1
Finn Harps	1
Home Farm	1
Dundalk	1

Winners: Tottenham H 1962-63; West Ham U 1964-65; Manchester C 1969-70; Chelsea 1970-71; Rangers 1971-72
Finalists: Liverpool 1965-66; Rangers 1960-61; 1966-67; Leeds U 1972-73; West Ham U 1975-76

THE EUROPEAN FAIRS CUP & UEFA CUP (1955–79)

English clubs
7 Leeds U
6 Liverpool
5 Everton
4 Arsenal, Manchester C, Birmingham C, Newcastle U, Ipswich T.
3 Chelsea, Tottenham H, Wolverhampton W.
2 WBA, Sheffield W, Nottingham F, Southampton, Stoke C, Manchester U, Derby Co, Aston Villa.
1 Burnley, Coventry C, London Rep XI, QPR.

Scottish clubs
12 Hibernian
5 Dundee U, Dunfermline Ath
4 Kilmarnock, Aberdeen
3 Hearts, Rangers, Dundee, Celtic
2 Partick T
1 Morton, St Johnstone

Clubs from Northern Ireland
8 Glentoran
2 Linfield, Coleraine
1 Ards, Portadown, Glenavon

Clubs from Eire
3 Bohemians, Finn Harps
2 Dundalk, Shelbourne, Shamrock R, Drumcondra
1 St Patrick's Ath, Cork Hibs, Athlone T

Winners: Leeds U 1967-68, 1970-71; Newcastle U 1968-69; Arsenal 1969-70; Tottenham H 1971-72; Liverpool 1972-73, 1975-76
Finalists: Birmingham C 1958-60, 1960-61; Leeds U 1966-67; Wolverhampton W 1971-72; Tottenham H 1973-74

Rothmans
Book of
Football League Records 1888-89 to 1978-79

Ian Laschke

How to settle who won which game and when!

A new addition to the famous Rothmans sports book series, listing the result of every Football League match since the inaugural season, and other fascinating facts and figures.

£10.00 hardback   352pp   November 5th

Available from bookshops or in case of difficulty send cheque/PO payable to Macdonald & Jane's to: QAP Direct Sales, 9 Partridge Drive, Orpington, Kent, England, including 10% postage and packing (UK only). Please allow up to 28 days for delivery, subject to availability.

EUROPEAN NATIONS SECTION

Details have been listed for all European footballing nations, but unfortunately due to other countries seasons finishing at different times from our own, some league champions and cup winners are unknown for the current season. Total number of championship and cup wins is given with winners' present names, with previous names in brackets. In the tables of league champions and cup winners, contemporary names are used.

ALBANIA

President: Mustafa Celkupa
Secretary: Ilia Shuke.
Address of Association: Federation Albanaise de Football, Rruga, Kongresi I Permetit, 41 Tirana.
Telephone: 7256, 2426
Cable: Albsport Tirana.
Area: 11,100 square miles.
Population: 2,405,000. *Number of Clubs:* 42.
Teams: 215
Number of Players: 4,730.
Year of Formation: 1932.
National Colours: Red shirts, black shorts, black stockings with red stripe.
Second Choice of Colours: White shirts, white shorts, white stockings.
Name, Address and Capacity of National Stadium: Qemal Stafa, Tirana, 30,000.
Names and Capacity of Other Principal Football Grounds: Dinamo, 15,000; Shkodra, 13,000; Durresi, 15,000; Korca, 13,000; Fier, 10,000; Vlora, 13,000.
Season: September-May

International matches 1978
No games

League Championship wins (1945–79)
Dinamo Tirana 14; Partizan Tirana 11; 17 Nendori 5; Vlaznia 4.

Cup wins (1948–79)
Dinamo Tirana 12; Partizan Tirana 8; 17 Nendori 4; Vlaznia 2; Besa 1; Labinoti 1.

League Champions	Cup Winners
1945 Vlaznia	
1946 Vlaznia	
1947 Partizan Tirana	
1948 Partizan Tirana	Partizan Tirana
1949 Partizan Tirana	Partizan Tirana
1950 Dinamo Tirana	Dinamo Tirana
1951 Dinamo Tirana	Dinamo Tirana
1952 Dinamo Tirana	Dinamo Tirana
1953 Dinamo Tirana	Dinamo Tirana
1954 Partizan Tirana	Dinamo Tirana
1955 Dinamo Tirana	No competition
1956 Dinamo Tirana	No competition
1957 Partizan Tirana	Partizan Tirana
1958 Partizan Tirana	Partizan Tirana
1959 Partizan Tirana	No competition
1960 Dinamo Tirana	Dinamo Tirana
1961 Partizan Tirana	Partizan Tirana
1963*Dinamo Tirana	17 Nendori
1964 Partizan Tirana	Partizan Tirana
1965 17 Nendori	Dinamo Tirana
1966 17 Nendori	Dinamo Tirana
1967 Dinamo Tirana	Vlaznia
1968 17 Nendori	Dinamo Tirana
1969 17 Nendori	17 Nendori
1970 17 Nendori	Partizan Tirana
1971 Partizan Tirana	Dinamo Tirana
1972 Vlaznia	Besa
1973 Dinamo Tirana	Partizan Tirana
1974 Vlaznia	Dinamo Tirana
1975 Dinamo Tirana	Labinoti
1976 Dinamo Tirana	17 Nendori
1977 Dinamo Tirana	17 Nendori
1978 Dinamo Tirana	Dinamo Tirana
1979 Partizan Tirana	Vlaznia

Final League Table 1978–79

	P	W	D	L	F	A	Pts.
Partizan	26	14	8	4	38	20	36
17 Nendori	26	13	9	4	41	27	35
Besa	26	11	9	6	36	25	31
Flamurtari	26	11	8	7	25	20	30
Dinamo	26	8	13	5	35	24	29
Labinoti	26	10	8	8	25	22	28
Lokomotiva	26	6	13	7	30	29	25
Tomori	26	7	11	8	21	21	25
Vlaznia	26	8	7	11	37	33	23
Naftetari	26	6	11	9	21	36	23
Shkendija	26	5	11	10	20	29	21
Luftetari	26	8	5	13	21	32	21
Beselidhja	26	10	0	16	19	38	20
Traktori	26	3	11	12	19	32	17

*Changed from calendar season to overlapping season from autumn to spring.

AUSTRIA

President: Karl Sekanina.
Secretary: Otto Demuth.
Address of Association: Oesterreichischer Fussball-Bund, Mariahilferstrasse 99, Postfach 161, Wien A-1061.
Telephone: 57-15-36.
Cable: Football Wien.
Telex: 11919oefb a
Area: 32,374 square miles.
Population: 7,457,000
Number of Clubs: 2,041. *Teams:* 6,466.
Number of Players: 255,125.
Year of Formation: 1904.
National Colours: White shirts, black shorts, black stockings.
Second Choice of Colours: Red shirts, white shorts, red stockings.
Name, Address and Capacity of National Stadium: Wiener Stadion, Prater, Vienna, 70,714.

Names, Addresses and Capacities of Other Principal Football Grounds: Linzer Stadion, Linz, 22,000; Stadion Salzburger, Bundesstadion Liebenau, Graz, 19,000; Salzburg, Tivoli Stadion, Innsbruck, 14,400; Stadion, Wiener Neustadt, 12,600; Bodenseestadion, Bregenz, 12,000; Stadion Klagenfurt, Klagenfurt, 11,000; Hohe Warte, Vienna Weststadion, Vienna, 20,000 Bundesstadion Sudstadt, Maria Enzersdort, 15,600;
Season: August-December; February-June

Principal Honours
Olympic Games: runners-up 1936
European Cup Winners Cup: runners-up Austria/WAC, 1978

Austria
International matches 1978
15 Feb, Athens: v Greece (a) drew 1-1 (*Krankl*)
22 Feb, Charleroi: v Belgium (a) lost 0-1
4 April, Basle: v Switzerland (a) won 1-0 (*Jara*)
20 May, Vienna: v Holland (h) lost 0-1
3 June, Buenos Aires: v Spain (a) won 2-1 (WC) (*Schachner, Krankl*)
7 June, Buenos Aires: v Sweden (a) won 1-0 (WC) (*Krankl*)
11 June, Mar del Plata: v Brazil (a) lost 0-1 (WC)
14 June, Cordoba: v Holland (a) lost 1-5 (WC) (*Obermayer*)
18 June, Buenos Aires: v Italy (a) lost 0-1 (WC)
21 June, Cordoba: v West Germany (a) won 3-2 (WC) (*Vogts og, Krankl* 2)
30 Aug, Oslo: v Norway (a) 2-0 (EC) *Pezzey, Krankl*).
20 Sept, Vienna: v Scotland (h) won 3-2 (EC) (*Pezzey, Schachner, Kreuz*).
15 Nov, Vienna: Portugal (h) lost 1-2 (EC) (*Schachner*).

League Championship wins (1912–79)
Rapid Vienna 25; Austria/WAC (previously FK Austria and WAC) 14; Admira-Energie-Wacker (prev. Sportklub Admira & Admira-Energie) 8; First Vienna 6, Tirol-Svarowski-Innsbruck (prev. Wacker Innsbruck) 5; Wiener Sportklub 3; FAC 1; Hakoah 1; Linz ASK 1; Wacker Vienna 1; WAF 1; Voest Linz 1.

Cup wins (1919–79)
FK Austria 19; Rapid Vienna 9; Admira-Energie-Wacker (prev. Sportklub Admira & Admira-Energie) 5; SW Innsbruck (prev. Wacker Innsbruck) 5; First Vienna 3; Linz ASK 1; Wacker Vienna 1; WAF 1; Wiener Sportklub 1.

	League Champions	Cup Winners
1946	Rapid Vienna	Rapid Vienna
1947	Wacker Vienna	Wacker Vienna
1948	Rapid Vienna	FK Austria
1949	FK Austria	FK Austria
1950	FK Austria	No competition
1951	Rapid Vienna	No competition
1952	Rapid Vienna	No competition
1953	FK Austria	No competition
1954	Rapid Vienna	No competition
1955	First Vienna	No competition
1956	Rapid Vienna	No competition
1957	Rapid Vienna	No competition
1958	Wiener Sportklub	No competition
1959	Wiener Sportklub	Wiener AC
1960	Rapid Vienna	FK Austria
1961	FK Austria	Rapid Vienna
1962	FK Austria	FK Austria
1963	FK Austria	FK Austria
1964	Rapid Vienna	Admira-Energie
1965	Linz ASK	Linz ASK
1966	Admira-Energie	Admira-Energie
1967	Rapid Vienna	FK Austria
1968	Rapid Vienna	Rapid Vienna
1969	FK Austria	Rapid Vienna
1970	FK Austria	Wacker Innsbruck
1971	Wacker Innsbruck	FK Austria
1972	T.-S. Innsbruck	Rapid Vienna
1973	T.-S. Innsbruck	T.-S. Innsbruck
1974	Voest Linz	Austria/WAC
1975	T.-S. Innsbruck	T.-S. Innsbruck
1976	Austria/WAC	Rapid Vienna
1977	Austria/WAC	Austria/WAC
1978	Austria/WAC	SW Innsbruck
1979	Austria/WAC	SW Innsbruck

Final League Table 1978–79

	P	W	D	L	F	A	Pts.
Austria/WAC	36	25	5	6	88	44	55
Wiener SK/Post	36	14	12	10	69	55	40
Rapid Vienna	36	13	14	9	53	40	40
Sturm Graz	36	14	9	13	43	50	37
Voest Linz	36	11	14	11	41	44	36
Austria Salzburg	36	13	10	13	38	53	36
Admira/Wacker	36	13	8	15	42	43	34
Vienna	36	9	11	16	48	62	29
Graz AK	36	7	15	14	36	53	29
SW Innsbruck	36	8	8	20	41	55	24

BELGIUM

President: M. Louis Wouters.
Secretary: Albert Roosens.
Address of Association: Union Royale Belge des Sociétés de Football Association, Rue de la Loi 43, B-1040 Bruxelles.
Telephone: 02/230.07.30
Telex: 23257 bvbfbt b
Cable: UBSFA Bruxelles.
Area: 11,779 square miles.

Population: 9,250,000.
Number of Clubs: 3,071. *Teams:* 8,694.
Number of Players: 279,420.
Year of Formation: 1895.

National Colours: White shirts with tricoloured (black-yellow-red) collar and cuffs, white shorts, white stockings with tricoloured (black-yellow-red) tops.

Second Choice of Colours: Red shirts, black shorts, yellow stockings.
Name, Address and Capacity of National Stadium: Centenary Stadium, Marathon Avenue, Brussels (Heysel), 70,000.
Names, Addresses and Capacities of Other Principal Football Grounds: R. Antwerp F.C.-Bosuilbaan, at Deurne (Antwerp), 62,000; R.F.C. Liégeois-Chaussée de Tongres, at Rocourt (Liège), 43,000; R. Standard C. Liégeois-2 rue de la Centrale at Sclessin (Liège), 43,000; R.S.C. Anderlechtois-2, avenue Théo Verbeeck, Anderlecht (Brussels), 38,000.
Season: September–May.

Principal Honours

Olympic Games: winners 1920
Fairs Cup: runners-up Anderlecht 1970
European Champions Cup: runners-up FC Bruges 1978
European Cup Winners Cup: winners Anderlecht 1976, 1978; runners-up Anderlecht 1977
UEFA Cup: runners-up F.C. Bruges 1976
Super Cup: Anderlecht 1978

Belgium

International matches 1978

22 March, Charleroi: v Austria (h) won 1-0 (*Geurts*).
19 April, Magdeburg: v East Germany (a) drew 0-0.
20 Sept, Lokeren: v Norway (h) drew 1-1 (EC) (*Cools*).
11 Oct, Lisbon: v Portugal (a) drew 1-1 (EC) (*Vercauteren*).
15 Nov, Tel Aviv: v Israel (a) lost 0-1.

League Championship wins (1896–1979)

Anderlecht 16; Union St. Gilloise 11; Beerschot 7; Standard Liege 6; RC Brussels 6; FC Liege 5; FC Bruges 5; Daring Brussels 5; Antwerp 4; Lierse SK 3; Malines 3; CS Bruges 3; R.W.D. Molenbeek 1; Beveren 1.

Cup wins (1954–79)

Anderlecht 5; Standard Liege 3; FC Bruges 3; Beerschot 2; Antwerp 1; La Gantoise 1; Lierse SK 1; Tournai 1; Waregem 1; Beveren 1.

League Champions	Cup Winners
1946 Malines	
1947 Anderlecht	
1948 Malines	
1949 Anderlecht	
1950 Anderlecht	
1951 Anderlecht	
1952 FC Liege	
1953 FC Liege	
1954 Anderlecht	Standard Liege
1955 Anderlecht	Antwerp
1956 Anderlecht	Tournai
1957 Antwerp	No competition
1958 Standard Liege	No competition
1959 Anderlecht	No competition
1960 Lierse S.K.	No competition
1961 Standard Liege	No competition
1962 Anderlecht	No competition
1963 Standard Liege	No competition
1964 Anderlecht	La Gantoise
1965 Anderlecht	Anderlecht
1966 Anderlecht	Standard Liege
1967 Anderlecht	Standard Liege
1968 Anderlecht	FC Bruges
1969 Standard Liege	Lierse SK
1970 Standard Liege	FC Bruges
1971 Standard Liege	Beerschot
1972 Anderlecht	Anderlecht
1973 FC Bruges	Anderlecht
1974 Anderlecht	Waregem
1975 R.W.D. Molenbeek	Anderlecht
1976 FC Bruges	Anderlecht
1977 FC Bruges	FC Bruges
1978 FC Bruges	Beveren
1979 Beveren	Beerschot

Final League Table 1978-79

	P	W	D	L	F	A	Pts.
Beveren-Wass	34	19	11	4	62	24	49
Anderlecht	34	21	3	10	76	41	45
Standard Liege	34	17	10	7	46	30	44
Lokeren	34	16	10	8	54	33	42
RWD Molenbeek	34	17	7	10	57	41	41
FC Bruges	34	14	10	10	51	49	38
SC Charleroi	34	13	8	13	43	47	34
Antwerp	34	10	14	10	42	40	34
Lierse SK	34	13	7	14	44	48	33
Winterslag	34	10	13	11	45	47	33
Waterschei	34	10	12	12	42	44	32
Beerschot	34	12	7	15	46	51	31
Beringen	34	9	11	14	38	47	29
Waregem	34	7	15	12	33	47	29
Berchem	34	8	12	14	30	46	28
FC Liege	34	10	6	18	49	55	26
La Louviere	34	8	8	18	45	79	24
Kortrijk	34	5	10	19	27	61	20

BULGARIA

President: Ivan Nikolov.
Secretary: Assen Mladenov.
Address of Association: Federation Bulgare de Football, Boul. Tolboukhin 18, Sofia
Telephone: 8651. *Cable:* Besefese Sofia.
Area: 42,830 square miles.
Population: 9,000,000.
Number of Clubs: 3,923. *Teams:* 5,737.
Number of Players: 117,280.
Year of Formation: 1923.

National Colours: White shirts, green shorts, red stockings.
Second Choice of Colours: Red Sshirts, green shorts, white stockings.
Name, Address and Capacity of National Stadium: "Vassil Levski", Sofia, 55,000.
Names, Addresses and Capacities of Other Principal Football Grounds: Stade Narodna Armia, Parc de la Liberté, Sofia, 43,000; Levski-Gerena, Sofia, 40,000; Stade Slavia,

Ovtcha Koupel, Sofia, 35,000; Stade Rakovski, quarter Ivan Vasoc, Sofia, 29,000; Stade Guerena, quartier Podouene, Sofia, 33,000; Stade 9 Septembre, Plovdiv, 40,000; Stade Christo Botev, Plovdiv, 30,000; Stade Yuri Gagarine, Varna, 40 000; Stade de la ville de Rousse, 20,000; Stade 9 Septembre, Bourgass, 15,000.
Season: August-December; March-June

Principal Honours
Olympic Games: runners-up 1968

Bulgaria
International matches 1978
22 Feb, Glasgow: v Scotland (a) lost 1-2 (*Mladenov*).
30 March, Buenos Aires: v Argentina (a) lost 1-3 (*Grantcharov*).
2 April, Lima: v Peru (a) drew 1-1 (*Manolov*).
5 April, Mexico City: v Mexico (a) lost 0-3.
23 April, Brno: v Czechoslovakia (a) drew 0-0.
26 April, Warsaw: v Poland (a) lost 0-1.
3 May, Bucharest: v Rumania (a) lost 0-2.
31 May, Sofia: v Rumania (h) drew 1-1 (*Mladenov*).
4 Aug, Varna: v Rumania (h) won 2-0 (*Markov, Ivanov*).
30 Aug, Erfurt: v East Germany (a) drew 2-2 (*Panov, Stankov*).
20 Sept, Turin: v Italy (a) lost 0-1.
11 Oct, Copenhagen: v Denmark (a) drew 2-2 (EC) (*Panov, Iliev*).
29 Nov, Sofia: v Northern Ireland (h) lost 0-2 (EC)

League Championship wins (1925–79)
CSKA Sofia (prev. CDNA) 19; Levski Spartak (prev. Levski Sofia) 13, Slavia Sofia 6; Vladislav Varna 3; Lokomotiv Sofia 3; AS 23 Sofia 1; Botev Plovdiv 1; SC Sofia 1; Sokol Varna 1; Spartak Plovdiv 1; Tichka Varan 1; Trakia Plovdiv 1; ZSK Sofia 1.

Cup wins (1946–79)
Levski Spartak (prev. Levski Sofia) 13; CSKA Sofia (prev. CDNA) 10; Slavia Sofia 5; Lokomotiv Sofia 2; Botev Plovdiv 1; Spartak Plovdiv 1; Spartak Sofia 1; Marek Stanke 1.

	League Champions	Cup Winners
1946	Levski Sofia	Levski Sofia
1947	Levski Sofia	Levski Sofia
1948	CDNA Sofia	Lokomotiv Sofia
1949	Levski Sofia	Levski Sofia
1950	Levski Sofia	Levski Sofia
1951	CDNA Sofia	CDNA Sofia
1952	CDNA Sofia	Slavia Sofia
1953	Levski Sofia	Lokomotiv Sofia
1954	CDNA Sofia	CDNA Sofia
1955	CDNA Sofia	CDNA Sofia
1956	CDNA Sofia	Levski Sofia
1957	CDNA Sofia	Levski Sofia
1958	CDNA Sofia	Spartak Plovdiv
1959	CDNA Sofia	Levski Sofia
1960	CDNA Sofia	CDNA Sofia
1961	CDNA Sofia	CDNA Sofia
1962	CDNA Sofia	Botev Plovdiv
1963	Spartak Plovdiv	Slavia Sofia
1964	Lokomotiv Sofia	Slavia Sofia
1965	Levski Sofia	CSKA Sofia
1966	CSKA Sofia	Slavia Sofia
1967	Trakia Plovdiv	Levski Sofia
1968	Levski Sofia	Spartak Sofia
1969	CSKA Sofia	CSKA Sofia
1970	Levski Spartak	Levski Spartak
1971	CSKA Sofia	Levski Spartak
1972	CSKA Sofia	CSKA Sofia
1973	CSKA Sofia	CSKA Sofia
1974	Levski Spartak	CSKA Sofia
1975	CSKA Sofia	Slavia Sofia
1976	CSKA Sofia	Levski Spartak
1977	Levski Spartak	Levski Spartak
1978	Lokomotiv Sofia	Marek Stanke
1979	Levski Spartak	Levski Spartak

Final League Table 1978–79

	P	W	D	L	F	A	Pts
Levski Spartak	30	18	7	5	54	29	43
CSKA Sofia	30	14	12	4	49	26	40
Lokomotiv Sofia	30	14	9	7	35	22	37
Slavia	30	16	4	10	52	33	36
Bourgass	30	13	8	9	45	43	34
Marek Stanke	30	13	7	10	42	39	33
Beroe	30	14	5	11	45	47	33
Pirin	30	9	11	10	37	39	29
Trakia Plovdiv	30	9	11	10	45	45	29
Chernomore	30	8	10	12	29	40	26
Plevene	30	9	7	14	25	27	25
Botev Vratza	30	9	7	14	36	42	25
Sliven	30	8	9	13	35	42	25
Lokomotiv Plovdiv	30	10	4	16	35	43	24
Akademik Svishtov	30	6	10	14	27	50	22
Haskovo	30	7	5	18	35	59	19

CYPRUS

President: Takis Hadjioaunou.
General Secretary: Andreas Matsoukaris.
Address of Association: Cyprus Football Association, Stasinos Street I, Engomi 114, P.O. Box 5071, Nicosia.
Telephone: 45341
Cable: Kop Nicosia.
Area: 3,572 square miles.
Population: 630,000.
Number of Clubs: 41.   *Teams:* 57.
Number of Players: 12,000.
Year of Formation: 1934.

National Colours: Sky blue shirts, white shorts, blue and white stockings.
Second Choice of Colours: White shirts, blue shorts, white stockings.
Name, Address and Capacity of National Stadium: G.S.P., Nicosia, 12,000.
Names, Addresses and Capacities of Other Principal Football Grounds: Tsition, Limassol, 20,000; G.S.E., Famagusta, 10,000; G.S.O. Limassol, 10,000; G.Sj., Larnaca, 8,000.
Season: October–June.
All Players are Amateurs.

Cyprus

International matches 1978
11 Jan, Limassol: v Greece (h) lost 0-2
13 Dec, Salamanca: v Spain (a) lost 0-5 (EC)

League Championship wins (1935–79)
Apoel 11; Omonia 9; Anorthosis 6; AEL 5; EPA 3; Olympiakos 3; Chetin Kayal 1; Pezoporikos 1; Trast 1.

Cup wins (1935–79)
Apoel 10; EPA 5; AEL 3; Trast 3; Chetin Kaya 2; Omonia 2; Apollon 2; Pezoporikos 2; Anorthosis 2; Paralimni 1; Olympiakos 1.

League Champions	Cup Winners
1946 EPA	EPA
1947 Apoel	Apoel
1948 Apoel	AEL
1949 Apoel	Anorthosis
1950 Anorthosis	EPA
1951 Chetin Kaya	Apoel
1952 Apoel	Chetin Kaya
1953 AEL	EPA
1954 Pezoporikos	Chetin Kaya
1955 AEL	EPA
1956 AEL	No competition
1957 Anorthosis	No competition
1958 Anorthosis	No competition
1959 No competition	No competition
1960 Anorthosis	No competition
1961 Omonia	No competition
1962 Anorthosis	Anorthosis
1963 Anorthosis	Apoel
1964 No competition	No competition
1965 Apoel	Omonia
1966 Omonia	Apollon
1967 Olympiakos	Apollon
1968 AEL	Apoel
1969 Olympiakos	Apoel
1970 EPA	Pezoporikos
1971 Olympiakos	Anorthosis
1972 Omonia	Omonia
1973 Apoel	Pezoporikos
1974 Omonia	Paralimni
1975 Omonia	Anorthosis
1976 Omonia	Apoel
1977 Omonia	Olympiakos
1978 Omonia (WC)	Apoel
1979 Omonia	Apoel

Final League Table 1978–79

	P	W	D	L	F	A	Pts.
Omonia	30	18	9	3	66	17	45
Apoel	30	20	4	6	54	18	44
Alki	30	12	9	9	41	39	33
Aris	30	12	8	10	36	34	32
Anorthosis	30	10	11	9	26	21	31
Pezoporikos	30	9	12	9	32	24	30
Apollon	30	10	10	10	25	28	30
Paralimni	30	9	10	11	37	30	28
AEL	30	6	16	8	24	28	28
EPA	30	9	9	12	32	35	27
Arradipu	30	6	15	9	26	37	27
Evagoras	30	8	11	11	26	35	27
Olympiakos	30	10	7	13	26	40	27
Apop	30	8	11	11	34	49	27
Salamis	30	10	6	14	42	48	26
Dighenis	30	4	10	16	21	65	18

CZECHOSLOVAKIA

President: Jaromir Tomanek.
Secretary: Rudolf Bata.
Address of Association: Czechoslovak Football, 12, Na Porící, Prague, 1.
Telephone: 24 98 41, 22 58 36.
Cable: Sportsvaz.
Area: 49,370 square miles.
Population: 15,000,000.
Number of Clubs: 6,776. *Teams:* 26,847.
Number of Players: 352,227.
Year of Formation: 1906.
National Colours: Red shirts, white shorts, blue stockings.
Second Choice of Colours: White shirts, white shorts, white stockings.
Name, Address and Capacity of National Stadium: Stadion ceskoslovenské armády, Praha-Strahov, 60,000.
Names, Addresses and Capacities of Other Principal Football Grounds: Slovan Bratislava, Bratislava-Tehelné pole, 63,000; Zbrojovka Brno, Brno, 70,000; Slavia Prague, Prague, 43,000; International, Bratislava, 40,000; Sparta Praha, Prague, 38,000.
Season: August-November; February-June.

Principal Honours
World Cup: runners-up 1934, 1962
European Championship: winners 1976.
Olympic Games: runners-up 1964.
Cup-Winners Cup: winners Slovan Bratislava (1969)

International matches 1978
22 March, Salonika: v Greece (a) won 1-0 (*Kroupa*).
15 April, Budapest: v Hungary (a) lost 1-2 (*Kroupa*).
23 April, Brno: v Bulgaria (h) drew 0-0.
20 May, Rio de Janeiro: v Brazil (a) lost 0-2.
20 May, Stockholm: v Sweden (a) drew 0-0.
6 Sept, Leipzig: v East Germany (a) lost 1-2 (*Ondrus*).
4 Oct, Stockholm: v Sweden (a) won 3-1 (EC) (*Kroupa, Masny pen, Nehoda*).
11 Oct, Prague: v West Germany (h) lost 3-4 (*Stambacher 2, Masny*).
8 Nov, Bratislava: v Italy (h) won 3-0 (*Jarusek, Panenka, Masny pen*).
29 Nov, Wembley: v England (a) lost 0-1.

League Championship wins (1926–79)
Sparta Prague 13; Slavia Prague 12; Dukla Prague (prev. UDA) 10; Slovan Bratislava 6; Spartak Trnava 5; Inter-Bratislava 1; Spartak Hradec Kralove 1; Viktoria Zizkov 1; Banik Ostrava 1; Zbrojovka Brno 1.

897

Cup wins (1961–79)
Dukla Prague 4; Slovan Bratislava 4; Spartak Trnava 3; Sparta Prague 3; Banik Ostrava 2, Lokomotiv Kosice 2.

League Champions	Cup Winners
1946 Sparta Prague	
1947 Slavia Prague	
1948 Sparta Prague	
1949 Slovan Bratislava	
1950 Slovan Bratislava	
1951 Slovan Bratislava	
1952 Sparta Prague	
1953 Dukla Prague	
1954 Sparta Prague	
1955 Slovan Bratislava	
1956 Dukla Prague	
1957 No competition	
1958 Dukla Prague	
1959 Inter-Bratislava	
1960 Hradec Kralove	
1961 Dukla Prague	Dukla Prague
1962 Dukla Prague	Slovan Bratislava
1963 Dukla Prague	Slovan Bratislava
1964 Dukla Prague	Sparta Prague
1965 Sparta Prague	Dukla Prague
1966 Dukla Prague	Dukla Prague
1967 Sparta Prague	Spartak Trnava
1968 Spartak Trnava	Slovan Bratislava
1969 Spartak Trnava	Dukla Prague
1970 Slovan Bratislava	TJ Gottwaldov
1971 Spartak Trnava	Spartak Trnava
1972 Spartak Trnava	Sparta Prague
1973 Spartak Trnava	Banik Ostrava
1974 Slovan Bratislava	Slovan Bratislava
1975 Slovan Bratislava	Spartak Trnava
1976 Banik Ostrava	Sparta Prague
1977 Dukla Prague	Lokomotiv Kosice
1978 Zbrojovka Brno	Banik Ostrava
1979 Dukla Prague	Locomotiv Kosice

Final League Table 1978–79

	P	W	D	L	F	A	Pts.
Dukla Prague	30	18	5	7	65	24	41
Banik Ostrava	30	16	9	5	44	22	41
Zbrojovka Brno	30	13	9	8	55	32	35
Bohemians	30	12	8	10	44	43	32
Sparta Prague	30	12	7	11	43	37	31
Inter	30	11	8	11	40	34	30
Slavia	30	12	5	13	40	45	29
Banska Bystrica	30	10	9	11	42	49	29
ZTS Kosice	30	12	5	13	42	56	29
Slovan	30	8	12	10	35	32	28
Lokomotive Kosice	30	11	6	13	47	48	28
Spartak Trnava	30	7	13	10	34	37	27
Trencin	30	10	6	14	38	45	26
Pilzen	30	9	8	13	27	47	26
Presov	30	7	11	12	24	51	25
Teplice	30	8	7	15	30	48	23

DENMARK

President: Carl Nielsen.
Secretary: Erik Hyldstorp.
Address of Association: Dansk Boldspil–Union, P. W. Ligns Alle 4, Copenhngen, 2100.
Telephone: 424540.
Cable: Danksboldspil.
Area: 17,159 square miles.
Population: 4,750,000.
Number of Clubs: 1,453. *Teams:* 7,400.
Number of Players: 208,000.
Year of Formation: 1889.
National Colours: Red shirts, white shorts, red stockings.
Second Choice of Colours: White shirts, white shorts, red stockings.
Name, Address and Capacity of National Stadium: Kobenhavns Idraetspark, P.H.-Lings-Alle 2, 50,000.
Names, Addresses and Capacities of Other Principal Football Grounds: Odense stadium, Odense, 20,000; Aarhus stadium, Aarhus, 24,000; Aalborg stadium, Aalborg, 22,000; Esbjerg stadium, Esbjerg, 18,000; Vejle stadium, Vejle, 18,000.
Season: April–November. Break: December to March.

Principal Honours
Olympic Games: runners-up 1908, 1912, 1960

International matches 1978
8 Feb, Tel Aviv: v Israel (a) lost 0–2.
24 May, Copenhagen: v Republic of Ireland (h) drew 3–3 (EC) (*Henning Jensen, Benny Nielsen, Lerby*).
31 May, Oslo: v Norway (a) won 2–1 (*Jan Sorensen, Larsen*).
28 June, Reykjavik: v Iceland (a) drew 0–0.
16 Aug, Copehagen: v Sweden (h) won 2–1 (*Benny Nielsen, Rontved*).
20 Sept, Copenhagen: v England (h) lost 3–4 (EC) (*Simonsen pen, Arnesen, Rontved*).
11 Oct, Copenhagen: v Bulgaria (h) drew 2–2 (EC) (*Benny Nielsen, Lerby*).
25 Oct, Belfast: v Northern Ireland (a) lost 1–2 (EC) (*Henning Jensen*).

League Championship wins (1913–78)
KB Copenhagen 14; B 93 Copenhagen 9; AB (Akademisk) 9; B 1903 Copenhagen 7; Frem 6; AGF Aarhus 4; Esbjergs FK 4; Vejle BK 4; B 1909 Odense 2; Hvidovre 2; Koge BK 2; Odense BK 1.

Cup wins (1955–78)
Aarhus GF 5; Vejle 5; BK 09 Odense 3; Randers Freja 3; Aalborg BK 2; Esbjerg BK 2; Frem 2; KB Copenhagan 1; Vanlose 1.

League Champions	Cup Winners
1946 BK 93	
1947 Akademisk	
1948 KB Copenhagen	
1949 KB Copenhagen	
1950 KB Copenhagen	
1951 Akademisk	
1952 Akademisk	
1953 KB Copenhagen	
1954 Koge BK	
1955 Aarhus GF	Aarhus GF
1956 Aarhus GF	Frem

1957	Aarhus GF	Aarhus GF	1975	Koge BK	Vejle
1958	Vejle	Vejle	1976	BK 03 Copenhagen	Esbjerg
1959	BK 09 Odense	Vejle	1977	Odense BK	Vejle
1960	Aarhus GF	Aarhus GF	1978	Vejle	Frem
1961	Esbjerg BK	Aarhus GF			
1962	Esbjerg BK	BK Odense 09			
1963	Esbjerg BK	BK Odense 09			
1964	BK 09 Odense	Esbjerg			
1965	Esbjerg BK	Aarhus GF			
1966	Hvidovre	Aalborg BK			
1967	Akademisk	Randers Freja			
1968	KB Copenhagen	Randers Freja			
1969	BK 03 Copenhagen	KB Copenhagen			
1970	BK 03 Copenhagen	Aalborg BK			
1971	Vejle	BK 09 Odense			
1972	Vejle	Vejle			
1973	Hvidovre	Randers Freja			
1974	KB Copenhagen	Vanlose			

Final League Table 1978

	P	W	D	L	F	A	Pts.
Vejle	30	19	6	5	64	33	44
Esbjerg	30	16	8	6	50	32	40
Aarhus GF	30	15	9	6	52	39	39
Odense BK	30	15	8	7	63	39	38
B 1903 Copenhagen	30	13	9	8	48	32	35
KB Copenhagen	30	15	4	11	54	39	34
B 93 Copenhagen	30	12	9	9	45	40	33
Slagelse IF	30	10	10	10	50	53	30
Skovb. Aarhus	30	10	8	12	47	49	28
Frem Copenhagen	30	10	8	12	30	34	28
Kastrup	30	9	7	14	38	40	25
B 1901 Nykobing	30	8	8	14	49	59	24
Nastved BK	30	9	6	15	36	47	24
IFK Fredrikshavn	30	7	7	16	27	43	21
Koge	30	7	7	16	28	53	21
Randers Freja	30	6	4	20	39	88	16

FINLAND

President: Jouko Loikkanen.

Secretary: Erkki Poroila.

Address of Association: Suomen Palloliitto—Finlands Bollförbund, Stadion, 00250 Helsinki 25.

Telephone: 44 12 81, 49 93 99

Cable: Suomifotboll.

Area: 130,119 square miles.

Population: 4,741,000.

Number of Clubs: 900.   *Teams:* 2,437.

Year of Formation: 1907.

National Colours: White shirts, blue shorts, white stockings.

Second Choice of Colours: Blue shirts, white shorts, blue stockings.

Name, Address and Capacity of National Stadium: Olympiastadion, Helsinki, 50,000.

Names, Addresses and Capacities of Other Principal Football Grounds: Ratina, Tampere, 25,000; Urhei Lukeskus kotka, 14,500; Kupittaa, Turku, 11,000; VainoLanniemi, Kuopio, 10,100.

All Amateur Players.

Season: April-October

International matches 1978

5 April, Erevan: v USSR (a) lost 2-10 (*Heiskanen, Nieminen*).

3 May, Helsinki: v Mexico (h) lost 0-1.

24 May, Helsinki: v Greece (h) won 3-0 (EC) (*Ismail 2, Nieminen*).

26 June, Boras: v Sweden (a) lost 1-2 (*Ismail*).

9 Aug, Helsinki: v Norway (h) drew 1-1 (*Ismail*).

30 Aug, Helsinki: v Poland (h) lost 0-1

20 Sept, Helsinki: v Hungary (h) won 2-1 (EC) (*Ismail, Pyykko*).

11 Oct, Athens: v Greece (a) lost 1-8 (EC) (*Heiskanen*).

Championship wins (1949-78)

Turun Palloseura 5; Kupion Palloseura 5; Valkeakosken Haka 4; Helsinki JK 3; Lahden Reipas 3; IF Kamraterna 2; Kotkan TP 2; Turun Pyrkivä 1; IF Kronohagens 1; Helsinki PS 1; Ilves-Kissat 1; Kokkolan PV 1; IF Kamraterna I Vasa 1.

Cup wins (1955-78)

Lahden Reipas 7; Valkeakosken Haka 6; Kotkan TP 3; Mikkelin 2; IFK Abo 1; Drott 1; Helsinki JK 1; Helsinki PS 1; Kuopion Palloseura 1; Pallo-Peikot 1.

	League Champions	Cup Winners
1949	Turun Palloseura	
1950	Ilves-Kissat	
1951	Kotkan TP	
1952	Kotkan TP	
1953	IF Kamraterna I Vasa	
1954	Turun Pyrkivä	
1955	IF Kronohagens	Valkeakosken Haka
1956	Kuopion Palloseura	Pallo-Peikot
1957	Helsinki PS	Drott
1958	Kuopion Palloseura	Kotkan TP
1959	IF Kamraterna	Valkeakosken Haka
1960	Valkeakosken Haka	Valkeakosken Haka
1961	IF Kamraterna	Kotkan TP
1962	Valkeakosken	Helsinki PS
1963	Lahden Reipas	Valkeakosken Haka
1964	Helsinki JK	Lahden Reipas
1965	Valkeakosken Haka	IFK Abo
1966	Kuopion Palloseura	Helsinki JK
1967	Lahden Reipas	Kotkan TP
1968	Turun Palloseura	Kuopion Palloseura
1969	Kokkolan PV	Valkeakosken Haka

Year	Champion	Cup Winner
1970	Lahden Reipas	Mikkelin
1971	Turun Palloseura	Mikkelin
1972	Turun Palloseura	Lahden Reipas
1973	Helsinki JK	Lahden Reipas
1974	Kuopion Palloseura	Lahden Reipas
1975	Turun Palloseura	Lahden Reipas
1976	Kuopion Palloseura	Lahden Reipas
1977	Valkeakosken Haka	Valkeakosken Haka
1978	Helsinki JK	Lahden Reipas

Final League Table 1978

	P	W	D	L	F	A	Pts
HJK Helsinki	22	13	7	2	52	29	33
KPT Kuopio	22	12	8	2	35	15	32
Valkeakosken Haka	22	12	7	3	42	19	31
Palloseura Turku	22	12	2	8	57	29	26
Palloseura Oulu	22	11	4	7	34	21	26
Mikkelin Pallokissat	22	11	3	8	29	22	25
Pallos. Kuopio	22	9	3	10	33	31	21
Kokkolan Palloveikot	22	9	3	10	26	31	21
Reipas Lahti	22	5	9	8	20	35	19
Prykiva Turku	22	4	9	9	14	28	17
Kiffen Helsinki	22	2	3	17	13	58	7
TP Oulo	22	1	4	17	15	52	6

FRANCE

President: Fernand Sastre.
Secretary: Michel Cagnion (Dir. Gen.)
Address of Association: Federation Francaise de Football, 60 bis, Avenue d'Iena, Paris 16e.
Telephone: 720 65-40.
Cable: Cefi Paris 034.
Telex: Fedfoot 620837 F
Area: 209,454 square miles.
Population: 52,000,000.
Number of Clubs: 18,285. *Teams:* 52,000.
Number of Players: 1,194,189
Year of Formation: 1919.
National Colours: Blue shirts, white shorts, red stockings.
Second Choice of Colours: Red shirts, white shorts, blue stockings.
Name, Address and Capacity of National Stadium: Stade du Parc de Princes, 24 rue du Commandant Guilbaud, 75, Paris 16ème, 50,000.
Names, Addresses and Capacities of Other Principal Football Grounds: Stade Vélodrome Jean Bouin, Marseille, 45,000; Stade Municipal de Bordeaux, Avenue de la Côte d'Argent, 33, Bordeaux, 30,000; Stade Municipal de Gerland, Lyon, 45,000; Stade Geoffroy Guichard Saint Etienne, 42,000; Stade Marcel Saupin, Nantes, 33,000; Stade de la Meinau, Strasbourg, 30,000; Stadium Municipal de Toulouse, Parc des Sports, 31 Toulouse, 30,000.
Season: August to June.

Principal Honours

European Champions Cup: runners-up Stade de Reims (1956, 1959), St. Etienne (1976). UEFA Cup: runners-up Bastia (1978).

International matches 1978

8 Feb, Naples: v Italy (a) drew 2-2 (*Bathenay, Platini*).
8 March, Paris: v Portugal (h) won 2-0 (*Baronchelli, Berdoll*).
1 April, Paris: v Brazil (h) won 1-0 (*Platini*).
11 May, Toulouse: v Iran (h) won 2-1 (*Gemmrich, Six*).
19 May, Lille: v Tunisia (h) won 2-0 (*Platini, Dalger*).
2 June; Mar del Plata: v Italy (a) lost 1-2 (WC) (*Lacombe*).
6 June, Buenos Aires: v Argentina (a) lost 1-2 (WC) (*Platini*).
10 June, Mar del Plata: v Hungary (a) won 3-1 (WC) (*Lopez, Berdoll, Rocheteau*).
1 Sept, Paris: v Sweden (h) drew 2-2 (EC) (*Berdoll, Six*).
7 Oct, Luxembourg: v Luxembourg (a) won 3-1 (EC) (*Six, Tresor, Gemmrich*).
8 Nov, Paris: v Spain (h) won 1-0 (*Specht*).

League Championship wins (1933–79)

Saint Etienne 9; Stade de Reims 6; OGC Nice 5; Olympique Marseilles 4; Nantes 4; Lille OSC 3; AS Monaco 3; FC Sete 2; Sochaux 2; Racing Club Paris 1; Roubaix-Tourcoing 1; Girondins Bordeaux 1; Strasbourg 1.

Cup wins (1918–79)

Olympique Marseilles 9; Saint Etienne 6; Lille OSC 5; Racing Club Paris 5; Red Star 5; Olympique Lyon 3; CAS Genereaux 2; AS Monaco 2; OGC Nice 2; Racing Club Strasbourg 2; Sedan 2; FC Sete 2; Stade de Reims 2; Stade Rennes 2; AS Cannes 1; Club Francais 1; Excelsior Roubaix 1; Girondins Bordeaux 1; Le Havre 1; SO Montpelier 1; Nancy-Lorraine 1; Olympique de Pantin 1; CA Paris 1; Sochaux 1; Toulouse 1; Nancy 1; Nantes 1.

Year	League Champions	Cup Winners
1946	Lille OSC	Lille OSC
1947	Roubaix-Tourcoing	Lille OSC
1948	Ol. Marseilles	Lille OSC
1949	Stade de Reims	Racing Paris
1950	Girondins Bordeaux	Stade de Reims
1951	OGC Nice	Racing Strasbourg
1952	OGC Nice	OGC Nice
1953	Stade de Reims	Lille OSC
1954	Lille OSC	OGC Nice
1955	Stade de Reims	Lille OSC
1956	OGC Nice	Sedan
1957	Saint Etienne	Toulouse
1958	Stade de Reims	Stade de Reims
1959	OGC Nice	Le Havre

Year	Winner	Runner-up
1960	Stade de Reims	AS Monaco
1961	AS Monaco	Sedan
1962	Stade de Reims	Saint Etienne
1963	AS Monaco	AS Monaco
1964	Saint Etienne	Ol. Lyon
1965	Nantes	Stade Rennes
1966	Nantes	Racing Strasbourg
1967	Saint Etienne	Ol. Lyon
1968	Saint Etienne	Saint Etienne
1969	Saint Etienne	Ol. Marseilles
1970	Saint Etienne	Saint Etienne
1971	Ol. Marseilles	Stade Rennes
1972	Ol. Marseilles	Ol. Marseilles
1973	Nantes	Ol. Lyon
1974	Saint Etienne	Saint Etienne
1975	Saint Etienne	Saint Etienne
1976	Saint Etienne	Ol. Marseilles
1977	Nantes	Saint Etienne
1978	Monaco	Nancy
1979	Strasbourg	Nantes

Final League Table 1978–79

	P	W	D	L	F	A	Pts.
Strasbourg	38	22	12	4	68	28	56
Nantes	38	23	8	7	85	33	54
St.-Etienne	38	24	6	8	77	34	54
Monaco	38	18	8	12	70	51	44
Metz	38	19	6	13	61	56	44
Lille	38	11	18	9	67	62	40
Lyon	38	15	10	13	53	56	40
Nimes	38	15	9	14	61	50	39
Sochaux	38	15	9	14	63	53	39
Bordeaux	38	12	15	11	45	42	39
Nancy	38	15	8	15	77	61	38
Marseille	38	12	13	13	50	55	37
St.-Germain	38	14	8	16	59	66	36
Bastia	38	13	9	16	53	65	35
Nice	38	11	10	17	58	75	32
Laval	38	8	14	16	53	73	30
Angers	38	8	14	16	37	68	30
Valenciennes	38	9	10	19	36	65	28
Paris	38	9	10	19	42	77	28
Reims	38	3	11	24	26	71	17

EAST GERMANY

President: Gunter Schneider.
Secretary: Werner Lempert.
Address of Association: Deutscher Fussball-Verband, Storkower Strasse 118, 1055 Berlin.
Telephone: 438 43 88/91/93
Cable: Fussball Verband Berlin.
Telex: 0112119. *Area:* 41,802 square miles.
Population: 17,000,000.
Number of Clubs: 4,981. *Teams:* 25,043.
Number of Players: 557,055.
Year of Formation: 1948.
National Colours: White shirts, blue shorts, white stockings.
Second choice of Colours: Blue shirts, white shorts, blue stockings
Name, Address and Capacity of National Stadium: Sportforum-Leipzig, 95,000.
Names, Addresses and Capacities of Other Principal Football Grounds: Festival Stadion, Berlin; Dynamo-Stadion, Dresden, 37,000; Ernst-Thälmann-Stadion, Karl-Marx-Stadt, 45,000; Georg-Dimitroff-Stadion, Erfurt, 50,000; Kurt-Wabbel-Stadion, Halle, 32,000; Ernest-Abbe-Stadion, Jena, 25,000; Ostsee-Stadion, Rostock, 30,000; Friedrich-Ludwig-Jahn-Sportpark, Berlin, 25,000; Ernest-Grube-Stadion, Magdeburg, 45,000.
Season: August-June (with winter break)

Principal Honours

Cup-Winners' Cup
Winners: FC Magdeburg 1974.
Olympic Games Winners 1976

International matches 1978

8 March, Karl-Marx-Stadt: v Switzerland (h) won 3-1 (*Riediger, Hoffmann* 2).
4 April, Leipzig: v Sweden (h) lost 0-1.
19 April, Magdeburg: v Belgium (h) drew 0-0.
30 Aug, Erfurt: v Bulgaria (h) drew 2-2 (*Eigendorf* 2).
6 Sept, Leipzig: v Czechoslovakia (h) won 2-1 (*Pommerenke, Eigendorf*).
4 Oct, Halle: v Iceland (h) won 3-1 (EC) (*Peter, Riediger, Hoffman*).
15 Nov, Rotterdam: v Holland (a) lost 0-3.

League Championship wins (1950–79)

ASK Vorwaerts 6; Dynamo Dresden 6; Wismut Karl-Marx-Stadt 4; Carl Zeiss Jena (prev. Motor Jena) 3; FC Magdeburg 3; Chemie Leipzig 2; Turbine Erfurt 2; Turbine Halle 1; Zwickau Horch 1; Empor Rostock 1, Dynamo Berlin 1.

Cup wins (1949–79)

Carl Zeiss Jena (prev. Motor Jena) 4; FC Magdeburg 4; Chemie Leipzig 2; Magdeburg Aufbau 2; Motor Zwickau 2; ASK Vorwaerts 2; Lokomotiv Leipzig 2; Dynamo Dresden 2; Dresden Einheit SC 1; Dresden VP 1; Dynamo Berlin 1; Halle Chemie SC 1; North Dessau Waggonworks 1; Thale EHW 1; Union East Berlin 1; Wismut Karl-Marx-Stadt 1; Sachsenring Zwickau 1.

Year	League Champions	Cup Winners
1949		North Dessau Waggonworks
1950	Zwickau Horch	Thale EHW
1951	Chemie Leipzig	No competition
1952	Halle Turbine	Dresden VP
1953	Dynamo Dresden	No competition
1954	Turbine Erfurt	ASK Vorwaerts
1955	Turbine Erfurt	Wismut Karl-Marx-Stadt
1956	Wismut Karl-Marx-Stadt	Chemie Leipzig
1957	Wismut Karl-Marx-Stadt	Lokomotiv Leipzig
1958	ASK Vorwaerts	Dresden Einheit SC
1959	Wismut Karl-Marx-Stadt	Dynamo Berlin
1960	ASK Vorwaerts	Motor Jena

1961	Empor Rostock	Motor Jena
1962	ASK Vorwaerts	Halle Chemie SC
1963	Motor Jena	Motor Zwickau
1964	Leipzig Chemie	Magdeburg Aufbau
1965	ASK Vorwaerts	Magdeburg Aufbau
1966	ASK Vorwaerts	Chemie Leipzig
1967	Wismut Karl-Marx-Stadt	Motor Zwickau
1968	Carl Zeiss Jena	Union East Berlin
1969	ASK Vorwaerts	FC Magdeburg
1970	Carl Zeiss Jena	ASK Vorwaerts
1971	Dynamo Dresden	Dynamo Dresden
1972	FC Magdeburg	Carl Zeiss Jena
1973	Dynamo Dresden	FC Magdeburg
1974	FC Magdeburg	Carl Zeiss Jena
1975	FC Magdeburg	Sachsenring Zwickau
1976	Dynamo Dresden	Lokomotiv Leipzig
1977	Dynamo Dresden	Dynamo Dresden
1978	FC Magdeburg	Dynamo Dresden
1979	Dynamo Berlin	FC Magdeburg

Final League Table 1978–79

	P	W	D	L	F	A	Pts
Dynamo Berlin	26	21	4	1	75	18	46
Dynamo Dresden	26	15	9	2	59	19	39
Carl Zeiss Jena	26	14	6	6	38	21	34
Magdeburg	26	14	5	7	63	32	33
Lokomotiv Leipzig	26	11	7	8	41	40	29
Chemie Halle	26	10	7	9	36	32	27
Rot-Weiss Erfurt	26	9	6	11	37	46	24
Karl-Marx-Stadt	26	9	4	13	32	38	22
Stahl Riesa	26	8	5	13	33	47	21
Union Berlin	26	7	7	12	22	39	21
Wismut Aue	26	8	3	15	34	49	19
Sachsenring Zwickau	26	7	4	15	23	63	18
Chemie Bohlen	26	5	6	15	33	66	16
Hansa Rostock	26	5	5	16	30	46	15

WEST GERMANY

President: Hermann Neuberger
Secretary: Hans Passlack.
Address of Association: Deutscher Fussball-Bund, Otto-Fleck-Schneise 6, Frankfurt (Main) 71.
Telephone: (0611) 63 10 63
Cable: Fussball, Frankfurt.
Telex: 041 6815 dfbd.
Area: 95,097 square miles.
Population: 61,510,000.
Number of Clubs: 17,549. *Teams:* 115,145.
Number of Players: 3,611,431.
Year of Formation: 1900.
National Colours: White shirts, black shorts, white stockings.
Second Choice of Colours: Green shirts, white shorts, white stockings.
Name, Address and Capacity of National Stadium: There is no stadium which could be considered as the National Stadium.
Names, Addresses and Capacities of Principal Football Grounds: Olympiastadion Berlin, 80,000 (61,800 seats); Olympiastadion München, 75,600 (44,200 seats); Neckarstadion Stuttgart, 72,200 (34,400 seats); Parkstadion Gelsenkirchen, 70,000 (36,000 seats); Rheinstadion Düsseldorf, 69,600 (31,800 seats); Waldstadion Frankfurt 61,000 (29,900 seats); Volksparkstadion Hamburg, 61,400 (27,800 seats); Niedersachsenstadion Hannover 60,500 (39,000 seats); Westfalen stadion Dortmund 53,600 (16,600 seats). Müngersdorfer Stadion, Cologne 60,000 (28,000 *seats).*
Season: August to June.

Principal Honours

World Cup: winners 1954, 1974; runners-up 1966
European Championship: winners 1972; runners-up 1976
World Club Champions: Bayern Munich (1976)
European Champions Cup: winners, Bayern Munich (1974), (1975), (1976), runners-up Eintracht Frankfurt (1960), Borussia Moenchengladbach (1977)
Cup-Winners' Cup: winners Borussia Dortmund (1966), Bayern Munich (1967), SV Hamburg (1977); runners-up Munich 1860 (1965), SV Hamburg (1968), Fortuna Dusseldorf (1979)
UEFA Cup:
Borussia Moenchengladbach winners (1975), runners-up (1973), winners (1979)

International matches 1978

22 Feb, Munich: v England (h) won 2-1 (*Worm, Bonhof*).
8 March, Frankfurt: v USSR (h) won 1-0 (*Russmann*).
5 April, Hamburg: v Brazil (h) lost 0-1.
19 April, Stockholm: v Sweden (a) lost 1-3 (*Bonhof*).
1 June, Buenos Aires: v Poland (a) drew 0-0 (WC).
6 June, Cordoba: v Mexico (a) won 6-0 (WC) (*Dieter Muller, Hansi Muller, Rummenigge 2, Flohe 2*).
10 June, Cordoba: v Tunisia (a) drew 0-0 (WC).
14 June, Buenos Aires: v Italy (a) drew 0-0 (WC).
18 June, Cordoba: v Holland (a) drew 2-2 (WC) (*Abramczik, Dieter Muller*).
21 June, Cordoba: v Austria (a) lost 2-3 (WC) (*Rummenigge, Holzenbein*).
11 Oct, Prague: v Czechoslovakia (a) won 4-3 (*Abramczik, Bonhof 2, 1 a pen, Hansi Muller*).
15 Nov, Frankfurt: v Hungary (h) drew 0-0 (*abandoned after 60 minutes fog*).
20 Dec, Dusseldorf: v Holland (h) won 3-1 (*Rummenigge, Fischer, Bonhof*).

League Championship wins (1903–79)

1FC Nuremberg 9; Schalke 7; Bayern Munich 5; Borussia Moenchengladbach 5; SV Hamburg 4; VfB Leipzig 3; SpVgg Fürth 3; Borussia Dortmund 3; 1FC Cologne 3; Viktoria Berlin 2; Hertha Berlin 2; Hanover 96 2; Dresden SC 2; VfB Stuttgart 2; 1FC Kaiserslautern 2; Munich 1860 1; SV

Werder Bremen 1; Union Berlin 1; FC Freibourg 1; Phoenix Karlsruhe 1; Karlsruher FV 1; Holstein Kiel 1; Fortuna Düsseldorf 1; Rapid Vienna 1; VfR Mannheim 1; Rot-Weiss Essen 1; Eintracht Frankfurt 1; Eintracht Brunswick 1.

Cup wins (1935-79)

Bayern Munich 5; 1FC Nuremberg 3; IFC Cologne 3; Dresden SC 2; Karlsruher SC 2; Munich 1860 2; Schalke 04 2; VfB Stuttgart 2; Borussia Moenchengladbach 2; Eintracht Frankfurt 2; SV Hamburg 2; Borussia Dortmund 1; First Vienna 1; VfB Leipzig 1; Kickers Offenbach 1; Rapid Vienna 1; Rot-Weiss Essen 1; SW Essen 1; Werder Bremen 1, Fortuna Dusseldorf 1.

	League Champions	Cup Winners
1948	1FC Nuremberg	No competition
1949	VfR Mannheim	No competition
1950	VfB Stuttgart	No competition
1951	1FC Kaiserslautern	No competition
1952	VfB Stuttgart	No competition
1953	1FC Kaiserslautern	Rot-Weiss Essen
1954	Hanover 96	VfB Stuttgart
1955	Rot-Weiss Essen	Karlsruhe SC
1956	Borussia Dortmund	Karlsruhe SC
1957	Borussia Dortmund	Bayern Munich
1958	Schalke 04	VfB Stuttgart
1959	Eintracht Frankfurt	SW Essen
1960	SV Hamburg	Borussia Moenchengladbach
1961	1FC Nuremberg	Werder Bremen
1962	1FC Cologne	IFC Nuremberg
1963	Borussia Dortmund	SV Hamburg
1964	1FC Cologne	Munich 1860
1965	Werder Bremen	Borussia Dortmund
1966	Munich 1860	Bayern Munich
1967	Eintracht Brunswick	Bayern Munich
1968	1FC Nuremberg	IFC Cologne
1969	Bayern Munich	Bayern Munich
1970	Borussia Moenchengladbach	Kickers Offenbach
1971	Borussia Moenchengladbach	Bayern Munich
1972	Bayern Munich	Schalke 04
1973	Bayern Munich	Borussia Moenchengladbach
1974	Bayern Munich	Eintracht Frankfurt
1975	Borussia Moenchengladbach	Eintracht Frankfurt
1976	Borussia Moenchengladbach	SV Hamburg
1977	Borussia Moenchengladbach	IFC Cologne
1978	Cologne	Cologne
1979	SV Hamburg	Fortuna Dussledorf

Final League Table 1978-79

	P	W	D	L	F	A	Pts.
Hamburger SV	34	21	7	6	78	32	49
VfB Stuttgart	34	20	8	6	73	34	48
Kaiserslautern	34	16	11	7	62	47	43
Bayern Munich	34	16	8	10	69	46	40
Eintracht Frankfurt	34	16	7	11	50	49	39
Cologne	34	13	12	9	55	47	38
Fortuna Dusseldorf	34	13	11	10	70	59	37
VfL Bochum	34	10	13	11	47	46	33
E. Braunschweig	34	10	13	11	50	55	33
B. Moenchengladbach	34	12	8	14	50	53	32
Werder Bremen	34	10	11	13	48	60	31
Borussia Dortmund	34	10	11	13	54	70	31
Duisburg	34	12	6	16	43	56	30
Hertha Berlin	34	9	11	14	40	50	29
Schalke 04	34	9	10	15	55	61	28
Arm. Bielefeld	34	9	8	17	43	56	26
Nurnberg	34	8	8	18	36	67	24
Darmstadt	34	7	7	20	40	75	21

GREECE

President: Dr. Basile Hadzijannis.
Secretary: Constantin Gourtsoulis.
Address of Association: Federation Hellenique de Football Association, 93 Rue de L'Académie, Athénes.
Telephone: 362 22 02/03 *Cable:* Football Athenes. *Telex:* 215328. *Area:* 50,547 square miles. *Population:* 9,500,000. *Number of Clubs:* 1,762. *Teams:* 1,762. *Number of Players:* 91,020. *Year of Formation:* 1926.
National Colours: White shirts, blue shorts, white stockings.
Second Choice of Colours: Blue shirts, white shorts, blue stockings.
Name, Address and Capacity of National Stadium: Karaïskaki, Neon Faliron, 42,000.
Names, Addresses and Capacities of Other Principal Football Grounds: Kaftatzoglion, Salonika, 47,000; A.E.K., Athens, 35,000; Panathinaïkos, Athénes, 25,000; PAOK, Salonika, 40,000; Aris, Salonika, 30,000.

Principal Honours
European Champions Cup: runners-up Panathinaïkos (1971)

International matches 1978
11 Jan, Limassol: v Cyprus (a) won 2-0 (*Delikaris, Livathinos*).
15 Feb, Athens: v Austria (h) drew 1-1 (*Galakos*).
22 Feb, Salonika: v Czechoslovakia (h) lost 0-1.
5 April, Poznan: v Poland (a) lost 2-5 (*Orfanos, Mavros*).
24 May, Helsinki: v Finland (a) (FC) lost 0-3
20 Sept, Erevan: v USSR (a) 0-2.
11 Oct, Athens: v Finland (h) won 8-1 (EC) (*Mavros 4, 1 a pen, Nikoloudis, Delikaris 2, Galakos*).
25 Oct, Salonika: Hungary (h) won 4-1 (EC) (*Galakos 2, Ardizoglou, Mavros*).
15 Nov, Skoplje: v Yugoslavia (a) lost 1-4 (*Mavros*).
13 Dec, Athens: v Rumania (h) won 2-1

League Championship wins (1928–79)
Olympiakos 20; Panathinaikos 12; AEK Athens 7; Aris Salonika 3; PAOK Salonika 1.

Cup wins (1932–79)
Olympiakos 17; AEK Athens 8; Panathinaikos 6, PAOK Salonika 2; Aris Salonika 1; Ethnikos 1; Iraklis 1; Panionios 1.

League Champions	Cup Winners
1946 Aris Salonika	No competition
1947 Olympiakos	Olympiakos
1948 Olympiakos	Panathinaikos
1949 No competition	AEK Athens
1950 Panathinaikos	AEK Athens
1951 Olympiakos	Olympiakos
1952 No competition	Olympiakos
1953 Panathinaikos	Olympiakos
1954 Olympiakos	Olympiakos
1955 Olympiakos	Panathinaikos
1956 Olympiakos	AEK Athens
1957 Olympiakos	Olympiakos
1958 Olympiakos	Olympiakos
1959 Olympiakos	Olympiakos
1960 Panathinaikos	Olympiakos
1961 Panathinaikos	Olympiakos
1962 Panathinaikos	Olympiakos
1963 AEK Athens	Olympiakos
1964 Panathinaikos	AEK Athens
1965 Panathinaikos	Olympiakos
1966 Olympiakos	AEK Athens
1967 Olympiakos	Panathinaikos
1968 AEK Athens	Olympiakos
1969 Panathinaikos	Panathinaikos
1970 Panathinaikos	Aris Salonika
1971 AEK Athens	Olympiakos
1972 Panathinaikos	PAOK Salonika
1973 Olympiakos	Olympiakos
1974 Olympiakos	PAOK Salonika
1975 Olympiakos	Olympiakos
1976 PAOK Salonika	Iraklis
1977 Panathinaikos	Panathinaikos
1978 AEK Athens	AEK Athens
1979 AEK Athens	Panionios

Final League Table 1978–79

	P	W	D	L	F	A	Pts
AEK Athens	34	25	6	3	90	30	56
Olympiakos	34	26	5	4	61	25	56
Aris Salonika	34	22	6	6	63	26	50
PAOK Salonika	34	18	9	7	73	23	45
Panathinaikos	34	14	10	10	46	37	38
Heraklis	34	12	10	12	48	46	34
OFI Crete	34	14	6	14	37	42	34
Ethnikos	34	14	4	16	36	50	32
Kastoria	34	10	11	13	31	42	31
Apollon	34	10	9	15	37	42	29
Rhodes	34	13	3	18	50	64	29
Larissa	34	12	5	17	34	53	29
Iannina	34	9	10	15	28	40	28
Panionios	34	9	10	15	37	50	28
Patras	34	9	9	16	26	37	27
Kavala	34	12	3	19	34	56	27
Aigaleo	34	10	6	18	34	56	26
Senes	34	4	5	25	17	63	13

HUNGARY

President: Gyorgy Szepesi.
Secretary: Jozsef Krizsan.
Address of Association: Fédération Hongroise de Football, Népköztársaság utja 47, Budapest VI.
Telephone: 22 58 17, 42 13 16
Cable: Mlsz–Budapest.
Area: 35,919 square miles.
Population: 10,500,000.
Year of Formation: 1901
Number of Clubs: 2,440.   *Teams:* 5,326
Number of Players: 138,461.
National Colours: Red shirts, white shorts, green stockings.
Second choice of Colours: All white.
Name, Address and Capacity of National Stadium: Népstadion Budapest XIV, István Mezei ut 3/5, 80,000.
Names, Addresses and Capacities of Other Principal Football Grounds: Ferencvaros, Budapest IX Ullöi-ut, 30,000; BP. Vasas SC. Budapest XIII. Fay-u. 58, 20,000; Ujpesti Dozsa SE. Budapest IV. Mergyeri ut 13, 25,000; MTK-VM Budapest VIII. Hungaria krt. 6, 20,000; Csepel SE. Budapest XXI. Béke tér, 22,000 Györi Raba ETO Györ, 20,000; Pécs MSC. Pécs, 25,000; Szegedi Egyetemi OL. Szeged, 25,000; Djösgyöri VTK Diösgyör, 25,000; Bp. Honved, Budapest, 30,000.
Season: September-December; March-June.

Principal Honours
World Cup: runners-up 1938, 1954
Olympic Games: winners 1952, 1964, 1968; runners-up 1972
Cup-Winners' Cup: runners-up MTK Budapest (1964); Ferencvaros (1975)
Fairs Cup: winners Ferencvaros (1965); runners-up Ferencvaros (1968), Ujpest Dozsa (1969)

International matches 1978
15 April, Budapest: v Czechoslovakia (h) won 2-1 (*Nyilasi* 2).
23 May, Wembley: v England (a) lost 1-4 (*Nagy*).
2 June, Buenos Aires: v Argentina (a) lost 1-2 (WC) (*Csapo*).
6 June, Mar del Plata: v Italy (a) lost 1-3 (WC) (*Andras Toth*).
10 June, Mar del Plata: v France (a) lost 1-3 (WC) (*Zombori*).
20 Sept, Helsinki: v Finland (a) lost 1-2 (EC) (*Tieber*).
11 Oct, Budapest: v USSR (h) won 2-0 (EC) (*Varadi, Szokolai*).
25 Oct, Salonika: v Greece (a) lost 1-4 (EC) (*Varadi*).
15 Nov, Frankfurt: v West Germany (a) drew 0-0 (*abandoned after 60 minutes fog*).

League Championship wins (1901–79)
Ferencvaros (prev FTC.) 22; MTK-VM Budapest (prev. Hungaria, Bastay, & Vörös Lobogo) 18; Ujpest Dozsa 18; Vasas Budapest 6; Honved 5; Csepel 4; BTC 2; Nagyvarad 1; Vasas Györ 1.

Cup wins (1910–79)*
Ferencvaros (prev. FTC) 14; MTK-VM Budapest (prev. Hungaria, Bastya, & Vörös Lobogo) 9; Ujpest Dozsa 4; Raba Györ (formerly Vasas Györ) 4; Vasas Budapest 1; Bocskai 1; Honved 1; III Ker 1; Kispesti AC 1; Soroksar 1; Szolnoki MAV 1; Diösgyör 1.
*Cup not held regularly until 1964

League Champions	Cup Winners
1946 Ujpest Dozsa	No competition
1947 Ujpest Dozsa	No competition
1948 Vasas Csepel	No competition
1949 Ferencvaros	No competition
1950 Honved	No competition
1950*Honved	No competition
1951 Bastya	No competition
1952 Honved	Bastya
1953 Vörös Lobogo	No competition
1954 Honved	No competition
1955 Honved	Vasas Budapest
1956 Champ. abandoned	No competition
1957 Vasas Budapest	No competition
1958 MTK Budapest	Ferencvaros
1959 Vasas Csepel	No competition
1960 Ujpest Dozsa	No competition
1961 Vasas Budapest	No competition
1962 Vasas Budapest	No competition
1963 Ferencvaros	No competition
1963*Vasas Györ	
1964 Ferencvaros	Honved
1965 Vasas Budapest	Vasas Györ
1966 Vasas Budapest	Vasas Györ
1967 Ferencvaros	Vasas Györ
1968 Ferencvaros	MTK Budapest
1969 Ujpest Dozsa	Ujpest Dozsa
1970 Ujpest Dozsa	Ujpest Dozsa
1971 Ujpest Dozsa	Ujpest Dozsa
1972 Ujpest Dozsa	Ferencvaros
1973 Ujpest Dozsa	Vasas Budapest
1974 Ujpest Dozsa	Ferencvaros
1975 Ujpest Dozsa	Ujpest Dozsa
1976 Ferencvaros	Ferencvaros
1977 Vasas Budapest	Diösgyör
1978 Ujpest Dozsa	Ferencvaros
1979 Ujpest Dozsa	Raba Györ

*(Short season)

Final League Table 1978–79

	P	W	D	L	F	A	Pts.
Ujpest Dozsa	34	21	10	3	84	38	52
FTC	34	18	11	5	75	44	47
DVTK	34	19	6	9	60	37	44
Vasas Budapest	34	16	10	8	62	49	42
Honved	34	16	9	9	57	39	41
Raba Eto Gyor	34	12	11	11	40	33	35
Tatabanya	34	12	11	11	50	47	35
PMSC	34	10	15	9	38	42	35
Videoton	34	12	10	12	46	49	34
ZTE	34	10	12	12	46	46	32
Dunaujvaros	34	10	12	12	50	54	32
Bekescsaba	34	11	9	14	49	52	31
STC	34	9	13	12	43	50	31
MTK/VM	34	11	8	15	42	50	30
MAV E.	34	10	9	15	31	54	29
Csepel	34	5	15	14	35	48	25
Haladas	34	9	5	20	40	74	23
V. Izzo	34	4	6	24	35	77	14

ICELAND

President: Ellert B. Schram.
Secretary: Karl Gudmundsson.
Address of Association: Football Association of Iceland, P.O. Box 1011, Reykjavik.
Telephone: 8–4444. *Cable:* KSI Reykjavik.
Telex: 2110 (att. E. Schram)
Area: 39,768 square miles.
Population: 222,055. *Number of Clubs:* 67.
Teams: 427. *Number of Players:* 13,856.
Year of Formation: 1929.
National Colours: Blue shirts, white shorts and blue stockings.
Second Choice of Colours: White shirts, blue shorts, white stockings.
Name, Address and Capacity of National Stadium: Laugardalsvöllur, Reykjavik, 14,800.
Names and Addresses of Other Principal Football Grounds: Melavöllur, Reykjavik. Ibrottavöllurinn, Akureyri. Ibróttavöllurinn, Akranesi. Ibrottavollurinn, Keflavik 10,000.
Season: April–October.

International matches 1978
28 June, Reykjavik: v Denmark (h) drew 0–0.
3 Sept, Reykjavik: v USA (h) drew 0–0.
6 Sept, Reykjavik: v Poland (h) lost 0–2 (EC).
20 Sept, Nijmegen: v Holland (a) lost 0–3 (EC).
4 Oct, Halle: v East Germany (a) lost 1–3 (EC) (*Petursson* pen).

League Championship wins (1912–78)
KR 20; Valur 16; Fram 15; IA Akranes 10; IBK Keflavik 3; Vikingur 2; IBV Vestmann 1.

Cup wins (1960–78)
KR 7; Valur 4; IBV Vestmann 2; Fram 2; IBA Akureyri 1; Vikingur 1; IBK Keflavik 1, IA Akranes 1.

League Champions	Cup Winners
1946 Fram	
1947 Fram	
1948 KR	
1949 KR	
1950 KR	
1951 IA Akranes	
1952 KR	
1953 IA Akranes	
1954 IA Akranes	
1955 KR	
1956 Valur	
1957 IA Akranes	
1958 IA Akranes	
1959 KR	
1960 IA Akranes	KR
1961 KR	KR
1962 Fram	KR
1963 KR	KR
1964 IBK Keflavik	KR
1965 KR	Valur
1966 Valur	KR

1967	Valur	KR
1968	KR	IBV Vestmann
1969	IBK Keflavik	IBV Akureyri
1970	IA Akranes	Fram
1971	IBV Vestmann	Vikingur
1972	Fram	IBV Vestmann
1973	IBK Keflavik	Fram
1974	IA Akranes	Valur
1975	IA Akranes	IBK Keflavik
1976	Valur	Valur
1977	IA Akranes	Valur
1978	Valur	IA Akranes

Final League Table 1978

	P	W	D	L	F	A	Pts.
Valur	18	17	1	0	45	8	35
IA Akranes	18	13	3	2	47	13	29
IB Keflavik	18	8	4	6	31	25	20
Vestmann	18	8	3	7	29	24	19
Vikingur	18	9	1	8	27	31	19
Fram	18	7	2	9	23	31	16
Throttur, Reykjavik	18	4	6	8	22	27	14
KA. Akureyri	18	3	5	10	14	38	11
FH Hafnafirdi	18	2	6	10	22	37	10
UB Breidablik Kopavogi	18	3	1	14	19	45	7

REPUBLIC OF IRELAND

President: F. Davis.
Secretary: P. J. O'Driscoll P.C.
Address of Association: The Football Association of Ireland, 80 Merrion Square, Dublin 2
Telephone: 76 68 64
Cable: Soccer Dublin
Population: 4,500,000
Year of formation: 1921
Number of Clubs: 2,914. *Teams:* 2,928.
Number of Players: 54,596.
National colours: Green shirts, white shorts, green stockings.
Second Choice of Colours: White
Name, Address and Capacity of National Stadium: Dalymount Park, Dublin, 45,000; and Lansdowne Road, Dublin, 48,000;
Names, Addresses and Capacities of Other Principal Football Grounds: Glenmalure Park, Milltown, Dublin, 25,000; Flower Lodge, Cork, 25,000; Lourdes Stadium, Drogheda, 25,000; Tolka Park, Dublin, 20,000; Oriel Park, Dundalk, 15,000; Richmond Park, Dublin, 10,000; Markeis Field, Limerick, 10,000; Kilcohan Park, Waterford, 15,000.
Season: August- May.

International matches 1978

5 April, Dublin: v Turkey (h) won 4-2 (*Giles, McGee, Treacy* 2).
12 April, Lodz: v Poland (a) lost 0-3.
21 May, Oslo: v Norway (a) drew 0-0.
24 May, Copenhagen: v Denmark (a) drew 3-3 (EC) (*Stapleton, Grealish, Daly*).
20 Sept, Dublin: v Northern Ireland (h) drew 0-0 (EC).
25 Oct, Dublin: v England (h) drew 1-1 (EC) (*Daly*).

League Championship wins (1922-79)

Shamrock Rovers 10; Shelbourne 7; Bohemians 7; Waterford 6; Cork United 5; Drumcondra 5; Dundalk 5; St. Patrick's Athletic 3; St. James's Gate 2; Cork Athletic 2; Sligo Rovers 2; Limerick 1; Dolphin 1; Cork Hibernians 1; Cork Celtic 1.

Cup wins (1922-79)

Shamrock Rovers 21, Dundalk 6; Drumcondra 5; Bohemians 4; Shelbourne 3; Cork Athletic 2; Cork United 2; St. James's Gate 2; St. Patrick's Athletic 2; Cork Hibernians 2; Alton United 1; Athlone Town 1; Cork 1; Fordsons 1; Limerick ;1 Transport 1; Waterford 1; Finn Harps 1; Home Farm 1.

	League Champions	Cup Winners
1946	Cork United	Drumcondra
1947	Shelbourne	Cork United
1948	Drumcondra	Shamrock Rovers
1948	Drumcondra	Shamrock Rovers
1949	Drumcondra	Dundalk
1950	Cork Athletic	Transport
1951	Cork Athletic	Cork Athletic
1952	St. Patrick's Ath.	Dundalk
1953	Shelbourne	Cork Athletic
1954	Shamrock Rovers	Drumcondra
1955	St. Patrick's Ath.	Shamrock Rovers
1956	St. Patrick's Ath.	Shamrock Rovers
1957	Shamrock Rovers	Drumcondra
1958	Drumcondra	Dundalk
1959	Shamrock Rovers	St. Patrick's Ath.
1960	Limerick	Shelbourne
1961	Drumcondra	St. Patrick's Ath.
1962	Shelbourne	Shamrock Rovers
1963	Dundalk	Shelbourne
1964	Shamrock Rovers	Shamrock Rovers
1965	Drumcondra	Shamrock Rovers
1966	Waterford	Shamrock Rovers
1967	Dundalk	Shamrock Rovers
1968	Waterford	Shamrock Rovers
1969	Waterford	Shamrock Rovers
1970	Waterford	Bohemians
1971	Cork Hibernians	Limerick
1972	Waterford	Cork Hibernians
1973	Waterford	Cork Hibernians
1974	Cork Celtic	Finn Harps
1975	Bohemians	Home Farm
1976	Dundalk	Bohemians
1977	Sligo Rovers	Dundalk
1978	Bohemians	Shamrock Rovers
1979	Dundalk	Dundalk

Final League Table 1978-79

	P	W	D	L	F	A	Pts
Dundalk	30	19	7	4	57	25	45
Bohemians	30	18	7	5	53	21	43
Drogheda Utd.	30	18	6	6	60	40	42
Waterford	30	17	8	5	48	32	42
Limerick	30	14	8	8	39	25	36
Shamrock Rov.	30	17	3	10	45	25	37
Athlone Town	30	14	7	9	56	41	35
Finn Harps	30	14	6	10	56	41	34
Home Farm	30	13	7	10	47	33	33
Sligo Rov.	30	9	7	14	35	40	25
Cork Alberts	30	7	9	14	35	49	23
Thurles Town	30	9	5	16	35	62	23
Shelbourne	30	6	9	15	41	58	21
St. Patrick's Ath.	30	7	6	17	36	62	20
Galway Rov.	30	4	5	21	41	79	13
Cork Celtic	30	2	4	24	16	67	8

ITALY

President: Dr. Franco Carraro.
Secretary: Dr. Dario Borgogno.
Address of Association: Federazione Italiana Giuoco Calcio, via Gregorio Allegri, 14, Rome.
Telephone: 84 91.
Cable: Federcalcio Roma
Area: 97,068 square miles.
Population: 54,134,846.
Number of Clubs: 21,845. *Teams:* 22,132.
Number of Players: 833,564.
Year of Formation: 1898.
National Colours: Blue shirts, white shorts, blue stockings with white tops.
Second Choice of Colours: White with light blue stripe.
Name, Address and Capacity of National Stadium: Stadio Olimpico, Roma, 90,000.
Names, Addresses and Capacities of Other Principal Football Grounds: Bologna, Stadio Comunale, Via A. Costa 176, 50,000; Firenze, Stadio Comunale, Viale M. Fanti 4/6, 67,000; Milano, Stadio Comunale San Siro, Via Fetonte, 85,000; Torino, Stadio Comunale, Corso Sebatopoli 123, 71,000; Napoli, Stadio S. Paolo, Fuorigrotta, 82,000; Genova, Stadio Luigi, Ferraris, Via del Piano, 64,000.
Season: September- June.

Principal Honours

World Cup: winners 1934, 1938; runners-up 1970
European Championship: winners 1968
Olympic Games: winners 1936
World club champions: Inter-Milan (1964, 1965), AC Milan (1969)
European Champions Cup: winners AC Milan (1963, 1969), Inter-Milan (1964, 1965); runners-up Fiorentina (1957), AC Milan (1958), Inter-Milan (1967, 1972), Juventus (1973)
Cup-Winners' Cup: winners Fiorentina (1961), AC Milan (1968, 1973); runners-up Fiorentina (1962), A. C. Milan (1974)
Fairs Cup: winners AS Roma (1961); runners-up Juventus (1965, 1971)
UEFA Cup: winners Juventus (1977)

International matches 1978

25 Jan, Madrid: v Spain (a) lost 1-2 (*Tardelli*).
8 Feb, Naples: v France (h) drew 2-2 (*Graziani* 2, 1 *a pen*).
18 May, Rome: v Yugoslavia (h) drew 0-0.
2 June, Mar del Plata: v France (a) won 2-1 (WC) (*Rossi, Zacarelli*).
6 June, Mar del Plata: v Hungary (a) won 3-1 (WC) (*Rossi, Bettega, Benetti*).
10 June, Buenos Aires: v Argentina (a) won 1-0 (WC) (*Bettega*).
14 June, Buenos Aires: v West Germany (a) drew 0-0 (WC).
18 June, Buenos Aires: v Austria (a) won 1-0 (WC) (*Rossi*).
21 June, Buenos Aires: v Holland (a) lost 1-2 (WC) (*Brandts og*).
24 June, Buenos Aires: v Brazil (a) lost 1-2 (WC) (*Causio*).
20 Sept, Turin: v Bulgaria (h) won 1-0 (*Cabrini*).
24 Sept, Florence: v Turkey (h) won 1-0 (*Graziani*).
8 Nov, Bratislava: v Czechoslovakia (a) lost 0-3.
20 Dec, Rome: v Spain (h) won 1-0 (*Rossi*).

League Championship wins (1898-1979)

Juventus 18; Inter-Milan 11; AC Milan 10; Genoa 9; Torino 8; Pro Vercelli 7; Bologna 7; Fiorentina 2; Casale 1; Novese 1; AS Roma 1; Cagliari 1; Lazio 1.

Cup wins (1922-79)

Juventus 6; Torino 4; Fiorentina 4; AC Milan 4; Napoli 2; AS Roma 2; Bologna 2; Inter-Milan 2; Atalanta 1; Genoa 1; Lazio 1; Vado 1; Venezia 1.

	League Champions	Cup Winners
1946	Torino	No competition
1947	Torino	No competition
1948	Torino	No competition
1949	Torino	No competition
1950	Juventus	No competition
1951	AC Milan	No competition
1952	Juventus	No competition
1953	Inter-Milan	No competition
1954	Inter-Milan	No competition
1955	AC Milan	No competition
1956	Fiorentina	No competition
1957	AC Milan	No competition
1958	Juventus	Lazio
1959	AC Milan	Juventus
1960	Juventus	Juventus
1961	Juventus	Fiorentina
1962	AC Milan	Napoli
1963	Inter-Milan	Atalanta
1964	Bologna	AS Roma
1965	Inter-Milan	Juventus

1966	Inter-Milan	Fiorentina
1967	Juventus	AC Milan
1968	AC Milan	Torino
1969	Fiorentina	AS Roma
1970	Cagliari	Bologna
1971	Inter-Milan	Torino
1972	Juventus	AC Milan
1973	Juventus	AC Milan
1974	Lazio	Bologna
1975	Juventus	Fiorentina
1976	Torino	Napoli
1977	Juventus	AC Milan
1978	Juventus	Inter-Milan
1979	AC Milan	Juventus

Final League Table 1978–79

	P	W	D	L	F	A	Pts.
AC Milan	30	17	10	3	46	19	44
Perugia	30	11	19	0	34	16	41
Juventus	30	12	13	5	40	23	37
Inter-Milan	30	10	16	4	38	24	36
Torino	30	11	14	5	35	23	36
Napoli	30	9	14	7	23	21	32
Fiorentina	30	10	12	8	26	26	32
Lazio	30	9	11	10	35	40	29
Catanzaro	30	6	16	8	23	30	28
Ascoli	30	7	12	11	26	31	26
Avellino	30	6	14	10	19	26	26
Roma	30	8	10	12	24	32	26
Bologna	30	4	16	10	23	28	24
Vicenza	30	5	14	11	29	42	24
Atalanta	30	6	12	12	20	35	24
Verona	30	2	11	17	14	39	15

LIECHTENSTEIN

President: Herbert Moser.
Secretary: Werner Ospelt.
Address of Association: Liechtensteiner, Fussball-Verband, 9490 Vaduz.
Telephone: 23 879
Year of Formation: 1933.
National colours: Blue/red shirts, red shorts, blue stockings.
Second Choice od colours: Yellow/red shirts, red shorts, yellow stockings.
Name Address and Capacity of National Stadium: Landessportplatz, Vaduz, 10,000.
Population: 25,000.
Number of Clubs: 7. *Teams:* 60.
Number of Players: 1,200.
Liechtenstein has no national league. Teams compete in Swiss regional leagues.
Season: August-July.

LUXEMBOURG

President: M. Rene van den Bulcke.
Secretary: Mlle Eliane Cremona.
Address of Association: Fédération Luxembourgeoise de Football, 50 Rue de Strasbourg, Luxembourg.
Telephone: 48-86-61.
Area: 999 square miles.
Population: 350,000.
Number of Clubs: 209. *Teams:* 532.
Number of Players: 15,730.
Year of Formation: 1908.
National Colours: Red shirts, white shorts, blue stockings.
Second Choice of Colours: Blue shirts, white shorts, blue stockings.
Name, Address and Capacity of National Stadium: City Stadium Luxembourg, 15,100.
Names, Addresses and Capacities of Other Principal Football Grounds: Stade Emile Mayrisch, Esch-sur-Alzette, 11,000; Stade Municipal, Differdange, 10,000.
Season: August – June.

International matches 1978

22 March, Luxembourg: v Poland (h) lost 1-3 (*Reiter*).
7 Oct, Luxembourg: v France (h) lost 1-3 (EC) (*Michaux*).

League Championship wins (1910–79)

Jeunesse Esch 16; Spora Luxembourg 10; Stade Dudelange 10; Red Boys Differdange 6; US Hollerich-Bonnevoie 5; Fola Esch 5; US Luxembourg 3; Sporting Luxembourg 2; Aris Bonnevoie 3; Progres Niedercorn 2; Racing Luxembourg 1; National Schiffige 1; Avenir Beggen 1.

Cup wins (1922–79)

Red Boys Differdange 14; Spora Luxembourg 7; Jeunesse Esch 7; US Luxembourg 6; Stade Dudelange 4; Progres Niedercorn 4; US Rumelange 2; Aris Bonnevoie 1; Us Dudelange 1; Jeunesse Hautcharage 1; National Schiffige 1; Racing Luxembourg 1; SC Tetange 1.

League Champions	Cup Winners
1946 Stade Dudelange	Jeunesse Esch
1947 Stade Dudelange	US Luxembourg
1948 Stade Dudelange	Stade Dudelange
1949 Spora Luxembourg	Stade Dudelange
1950 Stade Dudelange	Spora Luxembourg
1951 Jeunesse Esch	SC Tetange
1952 National Schiffige	Red Boys Differdange
1953 Progres Niedercorn	Red Boys Differdange
1954 Jeunesse Esch	Jeunesse Esch
1955 Stade Dudelange	Fola Esch
1956 Spora Luxembourg	Stade Dudelange
1957 Stade Dudelange	Spora Luxembourg
1958 Jeunesse Esch	Red Boys Differdange
1959 Jeunesse Esch	US Luxembourg
1960 Jeunesse Esch	National Schiffige
1961 Spora Luxembourg	Alliance Dudelange
1962 US Luxembourg	Alliance Dudelange
1963 Jeunesse Esch	US Luxembourg
1964 Aris Bonnevoie	US Luxembourg

1965	Stade Dudelange	Spora Luxembourg	
1966	Aris Bonnevoie	Spora Luxembourg	
1967	Jeunesse Esch	Aris Bonnevoie	
1968	Jeunesse Esch	US Rumelange	
1969	Avenir Beggen	US Luxembourg	
1970	Jeunesse Esch	US Luxembourg	
1971	US Luxembourg	Jeunesse Hautcharage	
1972	Aris Bonnevoie	Red Boys Differdange	
1973	Jeunesse Esch	Jeunesse Esch	
1974	Jeunesse Esch	Jeunesse Esch	
1975	Jeunesse Esch	US Rumelange	
1976	Jeunesse Esch	Jeunesse Esch	
1977	Jeunesse Esch	Progres Niedercorn	
1978	Progres Niedercorn	Progres Niedercorn	
1979	Red Boys	Red Boys	

Final League Table 1978–79

	P	W	D	L	F	A	Pts.
Red Boys	22	14	6	2	60	19	34
Progres Niedercorn	22	13	8	1	61	25	34
Union	22	11	3	8	55	31	25
Avenir Beggen	22	7	10	5	34	26	24
Jeunesse Esch	22	9	6	7	35	34	24
Etzella Ettelbruck	22	8	6	8	43	48	22
Aris Bonneweg	22	7	6	9	24	46	20
Grevenmacher	22	6	7	9	23	33	19
Chiers Rodange	22	9	1	12	30	48	19
Rumelingen	22	5	8	9	22	26	18
Alliance Dudelingen	22	5	7	10	20	32	17
YoungBoysDiekirch	22	3	2	17	28	67	8

MALTA

President: Dr. Gius Mifsud Bonnici LL.D.
Secretary: Frank Attard.
Address of Association: Malta Football Association, 84 Old Mint Street, Valetta, Malta.
Telephone: 22697, 67 43 72.
Cable: Football Malta Valletta
Area: 122 square miles.
Population: 300,000.
Number of Clubs: 231.
Number of Players: 7,460.   *Teams:* 362.
Year of Formation: 1900.
National Colours: Red.
Second Choice of Colours: White.
Name, Address and Capacity of National Stadium: The Stadium, Gzira, 30,000.
Name, Address and Capacity of Other Principal Football Grounds: Schreiber Sports Ground, Paola, 8,000. Manoel Island Upper Ground, 10,000.
Season: September-May.

International matches 1978

25 Oct, Wrexham: v Wales (a) lost 0-7 (EC).

League Championship wins (1910–1979)

Floriana 24; Sliema Wanderers 21; Valletta 10; Hibernians 4; Hamrum Spartans 3; St. George's 1; K.O.M.R. 1.

Cup wins (1935–1979)

Sliema Wanderers 16; Floriana 14; Valletta 5; Hibernians 3; Gzira United 1; Melita 1.

League Champions	Cup Winners
1946 Valletta	Sliema Wanderers
1947 Hamrun Spart.	Floriana
1948 Valletta	Sliema Wanderers
1949 Sliema Wand.	Floriana
1950 Floriana	Floriana
1951 Floriana	Sliema Wanderers
1952 Floriana	Sliema Wanderers
1953 Floriana	Floriana
1954 Sliema Wand.	Floriana
1955 Floriana	Floriana
1956 Sliema Wand.	Sliema Wanderers
1957 Sliema Wand.	Floriana
1958 Floriana	Floriana
1959 Valletta	Sliema Wanderers
1960 Valletta	Valletta
1961 Hibernians	Floriana
1962 Floriana	Hibernians
1963 Valletta	Sliema Wanderers
1964 Sliema Wand.	Valletta
1965 Sliema Wand.	Sliema Wanderers
1966 Sliema Wand.	Floriana
1967 Hibernians	Floriana
1968 Floriana	Sliema Wanderers
1969 Hibernians	Sliema Wanderers
1970 Floriana	Hibernians
1971 Sliema Wand.	Hibernians
1972 Sliema Wand.	Floriana
1973 Floriana	Gzira
1974 Valletta	Sliema Wanderers
1975 Floriana	Valletta
1976 Sliema Wand.	Floriana
1977 Floriana	Valletta
1978 Valletta	Valletta
1979 Hibernians	Sliema Wanderers

Final League Table 1978–79

	P	W	D	L	F	A	Pts.
Group A							
Hibernians	6	5	1	0	12	3	11
Valletta	6	2	2	2	7	6	6
Sliema Wanderers	6	2	0	4	7	9	4
Floriana	6	1	1	4	5	10	3
Group B (relegation)							
Hamrun	10	8	2	0	23	4	19
Marsa	10	5	3	2	22	8	15
St Georges	10	4	1	5	13	9	11
Qormi	10	3	4	3	17	13	10
Chaxaq	10	3	1	6	9	19	8
Msida	10	1	3	8	6	25	3

NETHERLANDS

President: W. A. G. M. Meuleman.
Secretary/Treasurer: Drs. E. J. Van Eijk.
Address of Association: Koninklijke Nederlandsche Voetbalbond, (KNVB) Woudenbergseweg 56-58, Zeist Netherlands.
Telephone: 03439 922
Cable: Voetbal Zeist
Telex: 40497
Area: 12,616 square miles.
Population: 13,000,000.

Number of Clubs: 7,635.   *Teams:* 54,048.
Number of Players: 964,215.
Year of Formation: 1889.
National Colours: Orange shirts, white shorts, orange stockings.
Second Choice of colours: All white.
Name, Address and Capacity of National Stadium: "Olympisch Stadion", Stadionplein. 20, Amsterdam, 67,000
Names, Addresses and Capacities of Other Principal Football Grounds: Stadion Feijenoord, Olympiaweg 50, Rotterdam, 67,000; Ground of Sparta, Spartastraat 5, Rotterdam, 30,000; Stadium De Goffert, Nijmegen, 30,000; Sportpark Diekman, J. J. van Deinselaan 30, Enschede, 27,564; PSV Eindhoven, Eindhoven, 27,500; Ajax Middemweg, Amsterdam, 29,000; A. Z. Alkmaar Dehout, 23,000.
Season: August–June.

Principal Honours
World Cup: Runners-up 1974, 1978.
World club champions: Feyenoord (1970), Ajax Amsterdam (1972).
European Champions Cup: winners Feyenoord (1970), Ajax Amsterdam (1971, 1972, 1973); runners-up Ajax (1969).
UEFA-Cup: winners Feyenoord (1974), PSV Eindhoven (1978); runners-up Twente Enschede (1975).
Super Cup: Ajax (1972), (1973).

International matches 1978
25 Jan, Alkmaar: v Dutch Foreigners (h) won 1-0 (*Rep*).
22 Feb, Tel Aviv: v Israel (a) won 2-1 (*Rensenbrink pen, La Ling*).
5 April, Tunis: v Tunisia (a) won 4-0 (*Nanninga 2, Van Leeuwen, Chebbi og*).
20 May, Vienna: v Austria (a) won 1-0 (*Haan*).
3 June, Mendoza: v Iran (a) won 3-0 (WC) (*Rensenbrink 3, 2 pens*).
7 June, Mendoza: v Peru (a) drew 0-0 (WC).
11 June, Mendoza: v Scotland (a) lost 2-3 (WC) (*Rensenbrink, Rep*).
14 June, Cordoba: v Austria (a) won 5-1 (WC) (*Brandts, Rensenbrink, Rep 2, Willy Van der Kerkhof*).
18 June, Cordoba: v West Germany (a) drew 2-2 (WC) (*Haan, Rene Van der Kerkhof*).
21 June, Buenos Aires: v Italy (a) won 2-1 (WC) (*Brandts, Haan*).
25 June, Buenos Aires: v Argentina (a) lost 1-3 (WC) (*Nanninga*).
20 Sept, Nijmegen: v Iceland (h) won 3-0 (EC) (*Krol, Brandts, Rensenbrink*).
11 Oct, Berne: v Switzerland (a) won 3-1 (EC) (*Wildschut, Brandts, Geels*).
15 Nov, Rotterdam: v East Germany (h) won 3-0 (*Kische og, Geels* 2).
20 Dec, Dusseldorf: v West Germany (h) lost 1-3 (*La Ling*).

League Championship wins (1898–1979)
Ajax Amsterdam 18; Feyenoord 12; HVV The Hague 8; PSV Eindhoven 7; Sparta Rotterdam 6; Go Ahead Deventer 4; HBS The Hague 3; Willem II Tilburg 3; RCH Haarlem 2; RAP 2; Heracles 2; ADO The Hague 2; Quick The Hague 1; BVV Scheidam 1; NAC Breda 1; Eindhoven 1; Enschede 1; Volewijckers Amsterdam 1; Limburgia 1; Rapid JC Haarlem 1; DOS Utrecht 1; DWS Amsterdam 1; Haarlem 1; Be Quick Groningen 1; SVV Scheidam 1.

Cup wins (1899–1979)
Ajax Amsterdam 8; Feyenoord 4; Quick The Hague 4; PSV Eindhoven 4; HEC 3; Sparta Rotterdam 3; DFC 2; Fortuna Geleen 2; Haarlem 2; HBS The Hague 2; RCH 2; VOC 2; Wageningen 2; Willem II Tilburg 2; F.C. Den Haag 2; Concordia Rotterdam 1; CVV 1; Eindhoven 1; HVV The Hague 1; Longa 1; Quick Njimegen 1; RAP 1; Roermond 1; Schoten 1; Velocitas Breda 1; Velocitas Groningen 1; VSV 1; VUC 1; VVV 1; ZFC 1; N.A.C. Breda 1, Twente Enschede 1; AZ 67 Alkmaar 1.

	League Champions	Cup Winners
1946	Haarlem	No competition
1947	Ajax Amsterdam	No competition
1948	BVV Scheidam	Wageningen
1949	SVV Scheidam	Quick Njimegen
1950	Limburgia	PSV Eindhoven
1951	PSV Eindhoven	No competition
1952	Willem II Tilburg	No competition
1953	RCH Haarlem	No competition
1954	Eindhoven	No competition
1955	Willem II Tilburg	No competition
1956	Rapid JC Haarlem	No competition
1957	Ajax Amsterdam	Fortuna Geleen
1958	DOS Utrecht	Sparta Rotterdam
1959	Sparta Rotterdam	VVV Groningen
1960	Ajax Amsterdam	No competition
1961	Feyenoord	Ajax Amsterdam
1962	Feyenoord	Sparta Rotterdam
1963	PSV Eindhoven	Willem II Tilburg
1964	DWS Amsterdam	Fortuna Geleen
1965	Feyenoord	Feyenoord
1966	Ajax Amsterdam	Sparta Rotterdam
1967	Ajax Amsterdam	Ajax Amsterdam
1968	Ajax Amsterdam	ADO The Hague
1969	Feyenoord	Feyenoord
1970	Ajax Amsterdam	Ajax Amsterdam
1971	Feyenoord	Ajax Amsterdam
1972	Ajax Amsterdam	Ajax Amsterdam
1973	Ajax Amsterdam	N.A.C. Breda
1974	Feyenoord	PSV Eindhoven
1975	PSV Eindhoven	F.C. Den Haag.
1976	PSV Eindhoven	PSV Eindhoven
1977	Ajax Amsterdam	Twente Enschede
1978	PSV Eindhoven	AZ 67 Alkmaar
1979	Ajax Amsterdam	Ajax Amsterdam

Final League Table 1978-79

	P	W	D	L	F	A	Pts.
Ajax Amsterdam	34	24	6	4	93	31	54
Feyenoord	34	19	13	2	62	19	51
PSV Eindhoven	34	20	9	5	65	23	49
AZ 67 Alkmaar	34	19	7	8	84	43	45
Roda JC Kerkrade	34	18	8	8	58	33	44
Sparta Rotterdam	34	14	5	15	47	48	33
Den Haag	34	11	11	12	43	55	33
PEC Zwolle	34	7	18	9	36	46	32
Go Ahead Deventer	34	11	9	14	48	48	31
NAC Breda	34	8	15	11	41	51	31
MVV Maastricht	34	9	13	12	26	45	31
Twente Enschede	34	9	12	13	54	58	30
Utrecht	34	10	10	14	43	55	30
Vitesse Arnheim	34	7	15	12	42	63	29
NEC Nijmegen	34	7	14	13	35	49	28
Haarlem	34	6	13	15	31	64	25
Volendam	34	7	8	19	42	63	22
VV Venlo	34	4	6	24	23	79	14

NORWAY

President: Einar Jorum.
Secretary: Nicolai Johansen.
Address of Association: Norges Fotballforbund, Boks 3823, Ullevål Hageby, Oslo 8.
Telephone: 46.98.30.
Cable: Fotballforbund Oslo.
Area: 125,064 square miles.
Population: 4,000,000.
Number of Clubs: 3,100. *Teams:* 6,790.
Number of Players: 124,000.
Year of Formation: 1902.
National Colours: Red shirts, white shorts, blue and white stockings.
Second Choice of Colours: Blue shirts, white shorts, blue stockings.
Name, Address and Capacity of National Stadium: Ulleval Stadium, Sognsveien 75, Oslo, 24,500
Names, Addresses and Capacities of Other Principal Football Grounds: Bislet Satdium, Oslo, 24,000; Brann Stadium, Bergen, 26,000; Lerkendal Stadium, Trondheim, 30,000; Stavanger Stadium, Stavanger, 19,800
Season: April-November.

International matches 1978

29 March, Gijon: v Spain (a) lost 0-3.
21 May, Oslo: v Republic of Ireland (h) drew 0-0.
31 May, Oslo: v Denmark (h) lost 1-2 (*Thoresen*).
9 Aug, Helsinki: v Finland (a) drew 1-1 (*Johansen*).
30 Aug, Oslo: v Austria (h) lost 0-2 (EC).
20 Sept, Lokeren: v Belgium (a) drew 1-1 (EC) (*Larsen-Oakland*).
25 Oct, Glasgow: v Scotland (a) lost 2-3 (EC) (*Aas, Larsen-Oakland*).

Strömgodset IF Drammen 3; Mercantile 2; Viking Stavanger 2; Lillestroem 2; Grane Nordstrand 1; Kvik Halden 1; Sparta 1; Gjovik 1; Bodo-Glimt 1. (*Until 1937 the cup-winners were regarded as champions.*)

	League Champions	Cup Winners
1946	No competition	Lyn Oslo
1947	No competition	Skeid Oslo
1948	Freidig	Sarpsborg FK
1949	Fredrikstad	Sarpsborg FK
1950	Fram	Fredrikstad
1951	Fredrikstad	Sarpsborg FK
1952	Fredrikstad	Sparta Sarpsborg
1953	Larvik Turn	Viking Stavanger
1954	Fredrikstad	Skeid Oslo
1955	Larvik Turn	Skeid Oslo
1956	Larvik Turn	Skeid Oslo
1957	Fredrikstad	Fredrikstad
1958	Viking Stav.	Skeid Oslo
1959	Lillestroem	Viking Stav.
1960	Fredrikstad	Rosenborg Tr.
1961	Fredrikstad	Fredrikstad
1962	Brann Bergen	Gjovik Lyn
1963	Brann Bergen	Skeid Oslo
1964	Lyn Oslo	Rosenborg Tr.
1965	Valerengen	Skeid Oslo
1966	Skeid Oslo	Fredrikstad
1967	Rosenborg Tr.	Lyn Oslo
1968	Lyn Oslo	Lyn Oslo
1969	Rosenborg Tr.	Strömgodset Dr.
1970	Strömgodset Dr.	Strömgodset Dr.
1971	Rosenborg Tr.	Rosenborg Tr.
1972	Viking Stav.	Brann Bergen
1973	Viking Stav.	Strömgodset Dr.
1974	Viking Stav.	Skeid Oslo
1975	Viking Stav.	Bodo-Glimt
1976	Lillestroem	Brann Bergen
1977	Lillestroem	Lillestroem
1978	IK Start	Lillestroem

League Championship wins (1938-78)

Fredrikstad 9; Viking Stavanger 5; Rosenborg Trondheim 3; Larvik Turn 3; Lillestroem 3; Brann Bergen 2; Lyn Oslo 2; Valerengen 1; Friedig 1; Fram 1; Skeid Oslo 1; Stromgodset Drammen 1; IK Start 1.

Cup wins (1902-78)

Odds Bk, Skien 11; Fredrikstads Fk 9; Lyn Oslo 8; Skeid Oslo 8; Sarpsborgs Fk 6; Ørn Fk Horten 4; Brann Bergen 4; Miondalens IF 3; Rosenborgs BK Trondheim 3;

Final League Table 1978

	P	W	D	L	F	A	Pts.
IK Start	22	13	7	2	30	13	33
Lillestroem	22	11	9	2	45	22	31
Viking Stavanger	22	12	7	3	42	44	31
Skeid	22	12	2	8	38	33	26
SK Brann	22	11	3	8	52	42	25
Valerengen	22	9	6	7	44	34	24
Bryne	22	7	8	7	27	30	22
Moss	22	8	4	10	39	28	20
SoFK Bodo/Glimt	22	6	6	10	37	37	18
Molde	22	5	2	15	36	58	12
Lyn	22	3	5	14	23	53	11
Strinkjer	22	1	9	12	20	51	11

POLAND

President: Edward Sznajder.
Secretary: Stanislaw Winczewski.
Address of Association: Polish Football Association, Al. Ujazdowskie 22, Warszawa.
Telephone: 28-93-44; 29-24-89.
Area: 120,359 square miles.
Population: 34,528,000.
Number of Clubs: 5,334. *Teams:* 11,223.
Number of Players: 234,052.
Year of Formation: 1923.
National Colours: White shirts, red shorts, white and red stockings.
Second Choice of Colours: Red shirts, white shorts, red stockings.
Name, Address and Capacity of National Stadium: Stadium of the "X Anniversary" Warszawa, 87,000.
Names, Addresses and Capacities of Other Principal Football Grounds: Stadium Slaski, Chorzow, 93,000; Stadium "Warta", Poznan, 45,000; Stadium "Olimpijski", Wroclaw, 72,000; Stadium "Wisla" Kraków 45,000; Stadium "Ruch", Chorzów, 40,000; Stadium "Legia", Warszawa, 35,000; Stadium "Piast", Gliwice, 55,000; Stadium "Pgoon", Szczecin, 36,000; Stadium "Polonia", Bytom, 35,000. Stade KS Zawisza, Bydgoszcz, 55,000.
Season: August–November; March–June

Principal Honours
Olympic Games: winners 1972; runners-up 1976. Cup-Winners' Cup: runners-up Gornik Zabrze (1970).

International matches 1978

22 March, Luxembourg: v Luxembourg (a) won 3-1 (*Lubanski, Szarmach* 2).
5 April, Poznan: v Greece (h) won 5-2 (*Lato, Deyna* 2, *Zmuda, Boniek*).
12 April, Lodz: v Republic of Ireland (h) won 3-0 (*Boniek, Deyna, Mazur*).
26 April, Warsaw: v Bulgaria (h) won 1-0 (*Lato*).
1 June, Buenos Aires: v West Germany (a) drew 0-0 (WC).
6 June, Rosario: v Tunisia (a) won 1-0 (WC) (*Lato*).
10 June, Rosario: v Mexico (a) won 3-1 (WC) (*Boniek* 2, *Deyna*).
14 June, Rosario: v Argentina (a) lost 0-2 (WC).
18 June, Mendoza: v Peru (a) won 1-0 (WC) (*Szarmach*).
21 June, Mendoza: v Brazil (a) lost 1-3 (WC) (*Lato*).
30 Aug, Helsinki: v Finland (a) won 1-0 (*Majewski*).
6 Sept, Reykjavik: v Iceland (a) won 2-0 (EC) (*Kusto, Lato*).
11 Oct, Bucharest: v Rumania (a) lost 0-1.
15 Nov, Wroclaw: v Switzerland (h) won 2-0 (EC) (*Boniek, Ogaza*).

League Championship wins (1921-79)
Ruch Chorzow 12; Gornik Zabrze 10; Wisla Krakow 6; Cracovia 5; Pogon Lwow 4; Legia Warsaw 4; Warta Poznan 2; Polonia Bytom 2; Stal Mielec 2; Garbarnia Krakow 1; Polonia Warsaw 1; LKS Lodz 1; Slask Wroclaw 1.

Cup wins (1951-79)
Gornik Zabrze 6; Legia Warsaw 5; Zaglebie Sosnowiec 4; Ruch Chorzow 2; Gwardia Warsaw 1; LKS Lodz 1; Polonia Warsaw 1; Wisla Krakow 1; Stal Rzeszow 1, Slask Wroclaw 1; Arka Gdynia 1.

	League Champions	Cup Winners
1946	Polonia Warsaw	
1947	Warta Poznan	
1948	Cracovia	
1949	Wisla Krakow	
1950	Wisla Krakow	
1951	Wisla Krakow	Ruch Chorzow
1952	Ruch Chorzow	Polonia Warsaw
1953	Ruch Chorzow	No competition
1954	Polonia Bytom	Gwardia Warsaw
1955	Legia Warsaw	Legia Warsaw
1956	Legia Warsaw	Legia Warsaw
1957	Gornik Zabrze	LKS Lodz
1958	LKS Lodz	No competition
1959	Gornik Zabrze	No competition
1960	Ruch Chorzow	No competition
1961	Gornik Zabrze	No competition
1962	Polonia Bytom	Zaglebie Sosnowiec
1963	Gornik Zabrze	Zaglebie Sosnowiec
1964	Gornik Zabrze	Legia Warsaw
1965	Gornik Zabrze	Gornik Zabrze
1966	Gornik Zabrze	Legia Warsaw
1967	Gornik Zabrze	Wisla Krakow
1968	Ruch Chorzow	Gornik Zabrze
1969	Legia Warsaw	Gornik Zabrze
1970	Legia Warsaw	Gornik Zabrze
1971	Gornik Zabrze	Gornik Zabrze
1972	Gornik Zabrze	Gornik Zabrze
1973	Stal Mielec	Legia Warsaw
1974	Ruch Chorzow	Ruch Chorzow
1975	Ruch Chorzow	Stal Rzeszow
1976	Stal Mielec	Slask Wroclaw
1977	Slask Wroclaw	Zaglebie Sosnowiec
1979	Ruch Chorzow	Arka Gdynia

Final League Table 1978–79

	P	W	D	L	F	A	Pts.
Ruch Chorzow	30	16	7	7	44	27	39
Widzew Lodz	30	14	11	5	37	26	39
Stal Mielec	30	14	8	8	43	27	36
Szombierki Bytom	30	11	13	6	42	27	35
Odra Opole	30	14	6	10	42	28	34
Legia Warsaw	30	13	7	10	32	28	33
Lech Poznan	30	11	8	11	34	38	30
GKS Katowice	30	10	10	10	28	36	30
Zaglebie Sosnowiec	30	7	15	8	22	25	29
Slask Wroclaw	30	11	7	12	23	27	29
Arka	30	11	7	12	29	35	29
Wisla Krakow	30	9	8	13	42	43	26
LKS Lodz	30	9	8	13	30	36	26
Polonia	30	9	6	15	23	39	24
Pogon Szczecin	30	7	8	15	31	41	22
Gwardia Warsaw	30	5	9	16	22	41	19

PORTUGAL

President: Dr. Antonio Marques.
Secretary: Cesar Gracio.
Address of Association: Federação Portuguesa de Futebol, Praça de Alegria, 25, Lisboa.
Telephone: 32 82 07/08/09, 32 82 00
Cable: Futebol Lisboa.
Telex: 13 489 FPFP
Area: 34,139 square miles.
Population: 8,668,267.
Number of Clubs: 880. *Teams:* 224.
Number of Players: 40,815.
Year of Formation: 1914.
National Colours: Red shirts, white shorts, green stockings.
Second Choice of Colours: White shirts, blue shorts, blue stockings.
Name, Address and Capacity of National Stadium: National Stadium, Lisbon, 51,000.
Names, Addresses and Capacities of Other Principal Football Grounds: Estadio de Luz, Lisbon, 69,000; Estadio Jose Alvalade, Lisbon, 47,000; Eastadio do Restelo, Lisbon, 35,000; Estadio das Antas, Porto, 40,000; Estadio 28 de Maio, Braga, 30,000; Estadio Bonfim, Setubal, 20,000; Estadio Alfredo da Silva, 23,000; Estadio Municipal, Coimbra, 25,000; Estadio Municipal, Guimaraes, 25,000.
Season: September-July.

Principal Honours

European Champions Cup: winners Benfica (1961, 1962); runners-up Benfica (1963, 1965, 1968)

Cup-Winners' Cup: winners Sporting Lisbon (1964)

International matches 1978

8 March, Paris: v France (a) lost 0-2.
20 Sept, Setubal: v USA (h) won 1-0 (*Costa*).
11 Oct, Lisbon: v Belgium (h) drew 1-1 (EC) (*Gomes*).
15 Nov, Vienna: v Austria (a) won 2-1 (EC) (*Nene, Alberto*).
29 Nov, Lisbon: v Scotland (h) won 1-0 (EC) (*Alberto*).

League Championship wins (1935-79)

Benfica 23; Sporting Lisbon 14; FC Porto 7; Belenenses 1.

Cup wins (1939-79)

Benfica 15; Sporting Lisbon 9; FC Porto 4; Boavista 3; Belenenses 2, Vitoria Setubal 2; Academica Coimbra 1; Leixoes Porto 1; Sporting Braga 1.

	League Champions	Cup Winners
1946	Belenenses	Sporting Lisbon
1947	Sporting Lisbon	No competition
1948	Sporting Lisbon	Sporting Lisbon
1949	Sporting Lisbon	Benfica
1950	Benfica	No competition
1951	Sporting Lisbon	Benfica
1952	Sporting Lisbon	Benfica
1953	Sporting Lisbon	Benfica
1954	Sporting Lisbon	Sporting Lisbon
1955	Benfica	Benfica
1956	FC Porto	FC Porto
1957	Benfica	Benfica
1958	Sporting Lisbon	FC Porto
1959	FC Porto	Benfica
1960	Benfica	Belenenses
1961	Benfica	Leixoes
1962	Sporting Lisbon	Benfica
1963	Benfica	Sporting Lisbon
1964	Benfica	Benfica
1965	Benfica	Vitoria Setubal
1966	Sporting Lisbon	Sporting Braga
1967	Benfica	Vitoria Setubal
1968	Benfica	FC Porto
1969	Benfica	Benfica
1970	Sporting Lisbon	Benfica
1971	Benfica	Sporting Lisbon
1972	Benfica	Benfica
1973	Benfica	Sporting Lisbon
1974	Sporting Lisbon	Sporting Lisbon
1975	Benfica	Boavista
1976	Benfica	Boavista
1977	Benfica	FC Porto
1978	FC Porto	Sporting Lisbon
1979	FC Porto	Boavista

Final League Table 1978-79

	P	W	D	L	F	A	Pts.
Porto	30	21	8	1	70	19	50
Benfica	30	23	3	4	75	21	49
Sporting Lisbon	30	17	8	5	46	22	42
Braga	30	16	5	9	49	35	37
Varzim	30	11	10	9	30	29	32
Guimaraes	30	12	7	11	44	38	31
Setubal	30	12	7	11	38	38	31
Belenenses	30	10	9	11	47	43	29
Maritimo Funchal	30	11	5	14	36	37	27
Boavista Porto	30	12	3	15	36	40	27
Estoril	30	8	10	12	24	42	26
Beira-Mar	30	11	2	17	44	56	24
Famalicao	30	9	6	15	30	45	24
Barreirense	30	8	6	16	24	45	22
Academico	30	5	8	17	20	41	18
Viseu	30	5	1	24	13	75	11

RUMANIA

President: Anghel Parashiv.
Secretary: Florea Tanasescu.
Address of Association: Federatia Romana de Fotbal, Vasile Conta 16, Bucarest 6.
Telephone: 12-10-60. 12-09-40. *Cable:* Sportrom Bucaresti. *Telex:* 11180 Bucaresti.
Area: 91,699 square miles. *Population:* 23,000,000. *Number of Clubs:* 5,453. *Teams:* 5,577. *Number of Players:* 179,987.
Year of Formation: 1908.
National Colours: Yellow shirts, blue shorts, red stockings.
Second Choice of Colours: Blue shirts, yellow shorts, red stockings.
Name, Address and Capacity of National Stadium: 23 August, Bucharest, 95,000.
Names, Addresses and Capacities of Other Principal Football Grounds: Republicii, Bucharest, 37,000; Giulesti, Bucharest, 20,000; Municipal, Cluj, 40,000; 1 Mai, Timisoara, 30,000; 23 August, Iasi, 20,000; 1 Mai, Constanta, 20,000; Petrolul, Ploiesti, 20,000; 1 Mai, Pitesti, 20,000. Stade Central Craiova, 40,000.
Season: August-July (with winter break).

International matches 1978

22 March, Istanbul: v Turkey (a) drew 1-1 (*Georgescu*).
5 April, Buenos Aires: v Argentina (a) lost 0-2.
3 May, Bucharest: v Bulgaria (h) won 2-0 (*Jordanescu, Balaci*).
14 May, Bucharest: v USSR (h) lost 0-1.
31 May, Sofia: v Bulgaria (a) drew 1-1 (*Jordanescu*).
4 Aug, Varna: v Bulgaria (a) lost 0-2.
11 Oct, Bucharest: v Poland (h) won 1-0 (*Jordanescu*).
25 Oct, Bucharest: v Yugoslavia (h) won 3-2 (EC) (*Sames 2, Jordanescu pen*).
15 Nov, Valencia: v Spain (a) lost 0-1 (EC).
13 Dec, Athens: v Greece (a) lost 1-2.

League Championship wins (1910-79)

Dynamo Bucharest 9; Steaua Bucharest (prev. CCA) 9; Venus Bucharest 7; CSC Temesvar 6; UT Arad 6; Rapid Bucharest Ripensia Temesvar 3; Petrolul Ploesti 3; Olimpia Bucharest 2; CAC Bucharest 2; Arges 2; Soc. RA Bucharest 1; Prahova Ploesti 1; CSC Brasov 1; Juventus Bucharest 1; SSUD Reita 1; Craiova Bucharest 1; Progresul 1; Ploesti United 1; Uni. Craiova 1.

Cup wins (1934-79)

Steaua Bucharest (prev. CCA) 13; Rapid Bucharest 7; Dynamo Bucharest 3; UT Arad 2; CFR Bucharest 2; Progresul 2; RIP Timisoara 2; Uni Craiova 2; ICO Oradeo 1, Metal Ochimia Resita 1; Petrolul Ploesti 1; Stinta Cluj 1; Stinta Timisoara 1; Turnu Severin 1; Chimia Ramnicu 1; Jiul Petroseni 1.

League Champions	Cup Winners
1947 UT Arad	No competition
1948 UT Arad	UT Arad
1949 Progresul	CCA Bucharest
1950 UT Arad	CCA Bucharest
1951 CCA Bucharest	CCA Bucharest
1952 CCA Bucharest	CCA Bucharest
1953 CCA Bucharest	UT Arad
1954 UT Arad	Metal Och. Resitta
1955 Dynamo Bucharest	CCA Bucharest
1956 CCA Bucharest	ICO Oradea
1957 No competition	No competition
1958 Petrolul Ploesti	Stinta Timisoara
1959 Petrolul Ploesti	Dynamo Bucharest
1960 CCA Bucharest	Progresul
1961 CCA Bucharest	Progresul
1962 Dynamo Bucharest	Steaua Bucharest
1963 Dynamo Bucharest	Petrolul Ploesti
1964 Dynamo Bucharest	Dynamo Bucharest
1965 Dynamo Bucharest	Stinta Cluj
1966 Petrolul Ploesti	Steaua Bucharest
1967 Rapid Bucharest	Steaua Bucharest
1968 Steaua Bucharest	Dynamo Bucharest
1969 UT Arad	Steaua Bucharest
1970 UT Arad	Steaua Bucharest
1971 Dynamo Bucharest	Steaua Bucharest
1972 Arges Pitesti	Rapid Bucharest
1973 Dynamo Bucharest	Chimia Ramnicu
1974 Uni Craiova	Jiul Petroseni
1975 Dynamo Bucharest	Rapid Bucharest
1976 Steaua Bucharest	Steaua Bucharest
1977 Dynamo Bucharest	Uni Craiova
1978 Steaua Bucharest	Uni Craiova
1979 Arges Pitesti	Steaua Bucharest

Final League Table 1978-79

	P	W	D	L	F	A	Pts.
Arges Pitesti	34	20	5	9	54	29	45
Dynamo Bucharest	34	16	9	9	51	28	41
Steaua Bucharest	34	18	4	14	57	32	40
Uni Craiova	34	15	8	11	40	25	38
Baia Mare	34	17	4	13	42	38	38
Sportul	34	14	7	13	42	41	35
Tirgoviste	34	15	5	14	38	38	35
Bacau	34	14	6	14	37	38	34
Tirgu Mures	34	13	6	15	49	59	32
Olimpia Bucharest	34	14	4	16	38	52	32
Timisoara	34	13	5	16	35	37	31
Iassy	34	11	9	14	37	44	31
Buzau	34	13	5	16	34	46	31
Petrosani	34	13	5	16	38	51	31
Valcea	34	13	5	16	38	54	31
Corvinul	34	13	4	17	45	50	30
UT Arad	34	11	7	16	45	46	29
Bihor	34	10	8	16	37	49	28

SPAIN

President: Pablo Porta Bussoms.
Secretary: Augustin Dominguez.
Address of Association: Real Federación Española de Futbol, Calle Alberto Bosch 13, Apartado 347, Madrid 14.
Telephone: 2391000, 2391008, 2391009.
Cable: Futbol.
Area: 190,115 square miles.
Population: 35,400,000.
Number of Clubs: 5,578.   *Teams:* 5,578.
Number of Players: 202,574.
Year of Formation: 1913.
National Colours: Red shirts, dark blue shorts, black with yellow border stockings.
Second Choice of Colours: Blue shirts, dark blue shorts.
No National Stadium.
Names, Addresses and Capacities of Principal Football Grounds: Santiago Bernabeu, Madrid, 101,663; Campo nuevo, Barcelona, 90,138; Manzanares, Madrid, 70,000; Mestalla, Valencia, 53,100; Sánchez Pizjuan, Sevilla, 46,000; San Mamés, Bilbao, 41,400; Sarriá, Barcelona, 38,295; Riazor, La Coruña, 35,860; La Romareda, Zaragoza, 32,416.
Season: September–June.

Principal Honours
European Nations Cup: winners 1964
Olympic Games: runners-up 1920
European Champions Cup: winners Real Madrid (1956, 1957, 1958, 1959, 1960, 1966); runners-up Real Madrid (1962, 1964), Barcelona (1961), Atletico Madrid (1974)
World club champions: Real Madrid (1960), Atletico Madrid (1975).
Cup-Winners Cup: winners Atletico Madrid (1962), Barcelona (1979); runners-up Atletico Madrid (1963), Barcelona (1969), Real Madrid (1971).
Fairs Cup: winners Barcelona (1958, 1960, 1966), Valencia (1962, 1963), Zaragoza (1964); runners-up Barcelona (1962), Valencia (1964), Zaragoza (1966)
UEFA Cup: runners-up Athletic Bilbao (1977)

International matches 1978
25 Jan, Madrid: v Italy (h) won 2-1 (*Pirri* pen, *Dani*).
29 March, Gijon: v Norway (h) won 3-0 (*Quini, Villar, Dani*).
26 April, Grenada: v Mexico (h) won 2-0 (*Quini, Dani*).
24 May, Montevideo: v Uruguay (a) drew 0-0.
3 June, Buenos Aires: v Austria (a) lost 1-2 (WC) (*Dani*).
7 June, Mar del Plata: v Brazil (a) drew 0-0 (WC).
11 June, Buenos Aires: v Sweden (a) won 1-0 (WC) (*Asensi*).
4 Oct, Zagreb: v Yugoslavia (a) won 2-1 (EC) (*Juanito, Santillana*).
8 Nov, Paris: v France (a) lost 0-1.
15 Nov, Valencia: v Rumania (h) won 1-0 (EC) (*Asensi*).
13 Dec, Salamanca: v Cyprus (h) won 5-0 (EC) (*Asensi, Del Bosque, Santillana* 2, *Ruben Cano*).
20 Dec, Rome: Italy (a) lost 0-1.

League Championship wins (1929–79)
Real Madrid 19; Barcelona 9; Atletico Madrid 8; Atletico Bilbao 6; Valencia 4; Betis 1; Seville 1.

Cup wins (1902–79)
Atletico Bilbao 22; Barcelona 18; Real Madrid 13; Atletico Madrid 5; Valencia 5; Real Union de Irun 3; Seville 3; Espanol 2; Real Zaragoza 2; Arenas 1; Ciclista Sebastian 1; Racing de Irun 1; Vizcaya Bilbao 1; Real Betis 1.

	League Champions	Cup Winners
1946	Seville	Real Madrid
1947	Valencia	Real Madrid
1948	Barcelona	Seville
1949	Barcelona	Valencia
1950	Atletico Madrid	Atletico Bilbao
1951	Atletico Madrid	Barcelona
1952	Barcelona	Barcelona
1953	Barcelona	Barcelona
1954	Real Madrid	Valencia
1955	Real Madrid	Atletico Bilbao
1956	Atletico Bilbao	Atletico Bilbao
1957	Real Madrid	Barcelona
1958	Real Madrid	Atletico Bilbao
1959	Barcelona	Barcelona
1960	Barcelona	Atletico Madrid
1961	Real Madrid	Atletico Madrid
1962	Real Madrid	Real Madrid
1963	Real Madrid	Barcelona
1964	Real Madrid	Real Zaragoza
1965	Real Madrid	Atletico Madrid
1966	Atletico Madrid	Real Zaragoza
1967	Real Madrid	Valencia
1968	Real Madrid	Barcelona
1969	Real Madrid	Atletico Bilbao
1970	Atletico Madrid	Real Madrid
1971	Valencia	Barcelona
1972	Real Madrid	Atletico Madrid
1973	Atletico Madrid	Atletico Bilbao
1974	Barcelona	Real Madrid
1975	Real Madrid	Real Madrid
1976	Real Madrid	Atletico Madrid
1977	Atletico Madrid	Real Betis
1978	Real Madrid	Barcelona
1979	Real Madrid	Valencia

Final League Table 1978-79

	P	W	D	L	F	A	Pts.
Real Madrid	34	16	15	3	61	36	47
Gijon	34	17	9	8	50	35	43
Atletico Madrid	34	14	13	7	55	37	41
Real Sociedad	34	18	5	11	53	36	41
Barcelona	34	16	6	12	69	37	38
Las Palmas	34	14	9	11	49	43	37
Valencia	34	14	7	13	44	38	35
Espanol Barcelona	34	15	5	14	37	46	35
Atletico Bilbao	34	12	10	12	56	46	34
Salamanca	34	13	8	13	36	40	34
Seville	34	12	9	13	47	48	33
Hercules Alicante	34	13	6	15	32	38	32
Burgos	34	10	12	12	37	47	32
Real Zaragoza	34	12	6	16	56	59	30
Rayo Vallecano	34	9	11	14	31	54	29
Celta Vigo	34	9	10	15	35	55	28
Santander	34	9	4	21	36	63	22
Huelva	34	8	5	21	39	65	21

SWEDEN

President: Tore Brodd
Secretary: Åke Barrling
Address of Association: Svenska Fotbollförbundet, Box 1216 S-171 23, Solna.
Telephone: 08/27 25 00. 27 2900.
Cable: Fotball. *Telex:* 17711 Fotball s.
Area: 173,665 square miles.
Population: 8,268,086.
Number of Clubs: 3,220. *Teams:* 6,011.
Number of Players: 152,548.
Year of Formation: 1904.
National Colours: Yellow shirts, blue shorts, yellow and blue stockings.
Second Choice of Colours: Blue shirts, white shorts, yellow stockings.
Name, Address and Capacity of National Stadium: Fotbollstadion, Solna, 52,000.
Names, Addresses and Capacities of Other Principal Football Grounds: Nya Ullevi, Göteborg, 52,000; Malmö stadion, Malmö, 35,000; Idrottsparken, Norrköping, 35,000; Olympia, Helsingborg, 25,000; Stadion, Stockolm 25,000.
Season: April–October.

Principal Honours
Olympic Games: winners 1948
World Cup: runners-up 1958
European Champions Cup: runners-up Malmö FF (1979)

International matches 1978
4 April, Leipzig: v East Germany (a) won 1-0 (*Aslund*).
19 April, Stockholm: v West Germany (h) won 3-1 (*Sjoberg, Lennart Larsson* 2).
20 May, Stockholm: v Czechoslovakia (h) drew 0-0.
3 June, Mar del Plata: v Brazil (a) drew 1-1 (WC) (*Sjoberg*).
7 June, Buenos Aires: v Austria (a) lost 0-1 (WC).
11 June, Buenos Aires: v Spain (a) lost 0-1 (WC).
28 June, Boras: Finland (h) won 2-1 (*Tommy Nilsson, Magnus Anderson*).
16 Aug, Copenhagen: v Denmark (a) lost 1-2 (*Berggren*).
1 Sept, Paris: v France (a) drew 2-2 (EC) (*Nordgren, Gronhagen*).
4 Oct, Stockholm: v Czechoslovakia (h) lost 1-3 (EC) (*Borg pen*).

League Championship wins (1896–1978)
Malmo FF 12; Oergryte IS Gothenburg 11; IFK Norrkoping 11; Djurgaarden 8; IFK Gothenburg 8; AIK Stockholm 8; GAIS Gothenburg 4; Boras IF Elfsborg 4; IF Halsingborg 3; Oester Vaexjoe 2; Atvidaberg 2; IFK Ekilstune 1; IF Gavle Brynas 1; IF Gothenburg Fassbergs 1; Norrköping IK Sleipner 1; Halmstad 1.

Cup wins (1941–78)
Malmo FF 11; IFK Norrköping 3; AIK Stockholm 3; Atvidaberg 2; GAIS Gothenburg 1; IFK Halsingborg 1; Raa 1; Landskrona 1.

	League Champions	Cup Winners
1946	IFK Norrköping	Malmö FF
1947	IFK Norrköping	Malmö FF
1948	IFK Norrköping	Raa
1949	Malmö FF	AIK Stockholm
1950	Malmö FF	AIK Stockholm
1951	Malmö FF	Malmö FF
1952	IFK Norrköping	No competition
1953	Malmö FF	Malmö FF
1954	GAIS Gothenburg	No competition
1955	Djurgaarden	No competition
1956	IFK Norrköping	No competition
1957	IFK Norrköping	No competition
1958	IFK Gothenburg	No competition
1959	Djurgaarden	No competition
1960	IFK Norrköping	No competition
1961	Boras Elfsborg	No competition
1962	IFK Norrköping	No competition
1963	IFK Norrköping	No competition
1964	Djurgaarden	No competition
1965	Malmö FF	No competition
1966	Djurgaarden	No competition
1967	Malmö FF	Malmö FF
1968	Oester Vaexjoe	No competition
1969	IFK Gothenburg	IFK Norrköping
1970	Malmö FF	Atvidaberg
1971	Malmö FF	Atvidaberg
1972	Atvidaberg	Landskrona
1973	Atvidaberg	Malmö FF
1974	Malmö FF	Malmö FF
1975	Malmö FF	Malmö FF
1976	Halmstad BK	AIK Stockholm
1977	Malmö FF	Malmö FF
1978	Oester Vaexjoe	Malmö FF

Final League Table 1978

	P	W	D	L	F	A	Pts.
Oester Vaexjoe	26	15	8	3	46	20	38
Malmö FF	26	12	8	6	29	15	32
IFK Gotsborg	26	13	5	8	39	29	31
Kalmar FF	26	11	9	6	35	30	31
Djurgaarden	26	10	10	6	50	32	30
Elfsborg Boras	26	10	9	7	44	37	29
AIK	26	10	7	9	31	35	27
Halmstad	26	7	11	8	24	29	25
Hammarby	26	9	5	12	32	38	23
Landskrona	26	6	10	10	28	38	22
IFK Norrköping	26	7	7	12	33	39	21
Atvidaberg FF	26	9	1	16	31	42	19
Orebro	26	5	8	13	31	45	18
Vasteras SK	26	6	6	14	20	44	18

SWITZERLAND

President: Walter Baumann.
Secretary: Edgar Obertufer.
Address of Association: Schweizerischer Fussballverband, Laubeggstrasse 70 B.P. 24, 3000 Berne 32.
Telephone: (031) 44–62–23.
Cable: Fussballverband Berne.
Telex: 33582 SFV CH.
Area: 15,941 square miles.
Population: 6,000,000.
Number of Clubs: 1,382. *Teams:* 7,314.
Number of Players: 146,188.
Year of Formation: 1895.
National Colours: Red jerseys, white shorts, white stockings.
Second Choice of Colours: White jersey, white shorts, red stockings.
Name, Address and Capacity of National Stadium: Wankdorf Stadium, Berne, 60,000
Names, Addresses and Capacities of Other Principal Football Grounds: St. Jakob Stadium, Basle, 60,000; Stade Olympique, Lausanne, 45,000; Parc des Sports des Charmilles, Genève, 38,800; Sportplatz Hardturm, Zurich, 37,200.
Season: September–May.

Principal Honours

Olympic Games: runners-up 1924

International matches 1978

8 March, Karl-Marx-Stadt: v East Germany (a) lost 1-3 (*Sulser*).
4 April, Basle: v Austria (h) lost 0-1.
6 Sept, Lucerne: v USA (h) won 2-0 (*Elsener, Schnyder*).
11 Oct, Berne: v Holland (h) lost 1-3 (EC) (*Tanner*).
15 Nov, Wroclaw: v Poland (a) lost 0-2 (EC).

League Championship wins (1898–1979)

Grasshoppers 17; Servette 14; Young Boys Berne 10; FC Zurich 8; Lausanne 7; FC Basle 7; La Chaux-de-Fonds 3; FC Lugano 3; Winterthur 3; FC Aarau 2; FC Anglo-Americans 1; St. Gallen 1; FC Brühl 1; Cantonal-Neuchatel 1; Biel 1; Bellinzona 1; FC Etoile la Chaux de Fonds 1.

Cup wins (1926–79)

Grasshoppers 13; La Chaux-de-Fonds 6; Lausanne 6; FC Basle 5; FC Zurich 5; Young Boys Berne 5; Servette 5; FC Lugano 2; FC Sion 2; FC Granges 1; Lucerne 1; St. Gallen 1; Urania Geneva 1; Young Fellows Zurich 1.

League Champions / Cup Winners

Year	League Champions	Cup Winners
1946	Servette	Grasshoppers
1947	Biel	FC Basle
1948	Bellinzona	La Chaux-de-Fonds
1949	FC Lugano	Servette
1950	Servette	Lausanne
1951	Lausanne	La Chaux-de-Fonds
1952	Grasshoppers	Grasshoppers
1953	FC Basle	Young Boys Berne
1954	La Chaux-de-Fonds	La Chaux-de-Fonds
1955	La Chaux-de-Fonds	La Chaux-de-Fonds
1956	Grasshoppers	Grasshoppers
1957	Young Boys, Berne	La Chaux-de-Fonds
1958	Young Boys, Berne	Young Boys, Berne
1959	Young Boys, Berne	FC Granges
1960	Young Boys, Berne	Lucerne
1961	Servette	La Chaux-de-Fonds
1962	Servette	Lausanne
1963	FC Zurich	FC Basle
1964	La Chaux-de-Fonds	Lausanne
1965	Lausanne	FC Sion
1966	FC Zurich	FC Zurich
1967	FC Basle	FC Basle
1968	FC Zurich	FC Lugano
1969	FC Basle	St. Gallen
1970	FC Basle	FC Zurich
1971	Grasshoppers	Servette
1972	FC Basle	FC Zurich
1973	FC Basle	FC Zurich
1974	FC Zurich	FC Sion
1975	FC Zurich	FC Basle
1976	FC Zurich	FC Zurich
1977	FC Basle	Young Boys, Berne
1978	Grasshoppers	Servette
1979	Servette	Servette

Final Qualifying League Table 1978–79

	P	W	D	L	F	A	Pts
Zurich	22	13	6	3	51	19	32
Servette	22	12	6	4	56	23	30
Grasshoppers	22	9	9	4	35	24	27
Basle	22	10	6	6	36	29	26
St Gallen	22	11	4	7	39	34	26
Young Boys	22	11	4	7	34	34	26
Neuchatel Xamax	22	8	8	6	42	33	24
Chenois	22	8	6	8	30	32	22
Lausanne	22	6	3	13	28	40	15
Chiasso	22	5	3	14	20	46	13
Nordstern	22	2	8	12	19	44	12
Sion	22	3	5	14	20	52	11

Championship play-off 1978–79

	P	W	D	L	F	A	Pts	Qual	T
Servette	10	10	0	0	23	5	20	+15	35
Zurich	10	6	1	3	19	14	13	+16	29
Grasshoppers	10	3	3	4	11	13	9	+14	23
St. Gallen	10	2	3	5	8	10	7	+13	20
Young Boys	10	1	4	5	5	17	6	+13	19
Basle	10	2	1	7	17	24	5	+13	18

Relegation play-off 1978–79

	P	W	D	L	F	A	Pts	Qual	T
Chenois	10	4	5	1	21	14	13	+11	24
Sion	10	5	4	1	15	8	14	+ 6	20
Chiasso	10	5	3	3	16	10	13	+ 7	20
Lausanne	10	5	2	3	20	16	12	+ 8	20
Xamax	10	2	1	7	11	19	5	+12	17
Nordst	10	1	1	8	8	24	3	+ 6	9

TURKEY

President: Sahir Gurkan.
Secretary: Haluk Ozbek.
Address of Association: Federation Turque de Football, Ulus is Hani, A Blok, Ket 4, Ankara.
Telephone: 24 39 34/5, 24 39 38.
Cable: Futbolsport.
Telex: 42251 tff tr.
Area: 296,185 square miles.
Population: 40,000,000.
Number of Clubs: 1,432. *Teams:* 1,540.
Number of Players: 43,229.
Year of Formation: 1923.
National Colours: White shirts with white crescent and star on red hoop, white shorts, red and white stockings.
Second Choice of Colours: Red shirts, white shorts, red and white stockings.
Name, Address and Capacity of National Stadium: Stade 19, Mayis, Ankara, 35,000.
Names, Addresses and Capacities of Other Principal Football Grounds: Stade Ali Sam, Yen Istanbul, 40,000; Stade Mithatpasat Istanbul, 45,000; Stade Alsancak, Izmiri 30,000; Stade d'Ataturk, Eskisehir, 35,000; Stade d'Ataturk, Adana, 30,000; Stade de Ville, Kayseri, 25,000; Stade d'Ataturk Izmir, 70,000.
Season: September–June.

International matches 1978

22 March, Istanbul: v Rumania (h) drew 1-1 (Sedat).
5 April, Dublin: v Republic of Ireland (a) lost 2-4 (Cemil, Onder).
24 Sept, Florence: v Italy (a) lost 0-1.
4 Oct, Ankara: v USSR (h) lost 0-2.
29 Nov, Wrexham: v Wales (a) lost 0-1 (EC).

League Championship wins (1960–1979)

Fenerbahce 8; Galatasaray 5; Besiktas 3; Trabzonspor 3.

Cup wins (1963–1979)

Galatasaray 6; Fenerbahce 3; Goztepe Izmir 2; Trabzonspor 3; Altay Izmir 1; Ankaragucu 1; Eskisehirspor 1; Besiktas 1.

League Champions	Cup Winners
1960 Besiktas	
1961	
1962 Fenerbahce	
1963 Galatasaray	Galatasaray
1964 Fenerbahce	Galatasaray
1965 Fenerbahce	Galatasaray
1966 Besiktas	Galatasaray
1967 Besiktas	Altay Izmir
1968 Fenerbahce	Fenerbahce
1969 Galatasaray	Goztepe Izmir
1970 Fenerbahce	Goztepe Izmir
1971 Galatasaray	Eskisehirspor
1972 Galatasaray	Ankaragücü
1973 Galatasaray	Galatasaray
1974 Fenerbahce	Fenerbahce
1975 Fenerbahce	Besiktas
1976 Trabzonspor	Galatasaray
1977 Trabzonspor	Trabzonspor
1978 Fenerbahce	Trabzonspor
1979 Trabzonspor	Fenerbahce

Fina League Table 1978–79

	P	W	D	L	F	A	Pts.
Trabzonspor	30	13	16	1	34	7	42
Galatasaray	30	17	7	6	47	17	41
Fenerbahce	30	15	8	7	40	22	38
Orduspor	30	13	8	9	31	27	34
Diyarbakir	30	13	6	11	26	31	32
Altay Izmir	30	10	11	9	37	29	31
Eskisehirspor	30	10	11	9	26	24	31
Zonguldakspor	30	11	7	12	28	24	29
Besiktas	30	10	9	11	33	32	29
Goztepe	30	9	10	11	30	40	28
Adanaspor	30	8	11	11	33	33	27
Bursaspor	30	7	13	10	25	33	27
Adanasdemispor	30	9	9	12	23	32	27
Boluspor	30	9	8	13	33	32	26
Samsun	30	6	8	16	18	37	20
Kirikhale	30	5	8	17	20	64	18

USSR

President: Boris Fedosov.
Secretary: Anatoly Chetirko.
Address of Association: Federation De Football De L'URSS, Skatertnyi, Pereulok 4, Moscow, 69.
Telephone: 291 5796. *Cable:* Sportkomitet USSR. *Area:* 8,598,678 square miles. *Population:* 255,524,000. *Number of Clubs:* 50,664. *Teams:* 164,000. *Number of Players:* 4,505,000. *Year of Formation:* 1912. *National Colours:* Red shirts, white shorts, red stockings.
Second Choice of Colours: White.
Name, Address and Capacity of National Stadium: Lenin Stadium, Moscow, 102,000.
Names, Addresses and Capacities of Other Principal Football Grounds: Kirov Stadium, Victory Park, Leningrad, 84,000; "Pakhtakov" Central Stadium, Tashkent, Socialism Street 23, 60,000; Ukraine Republic Stadium, Kiev, Krasnoarmeiskaya Street 51, 100,000; Dynamo Stadium, Moscow, Leningrad Prospect 36, 54,000; Dynamo Stadium, Tbilisi, Tseretely Street 2, 75,000.
Season: South: March–December.
Central: April–October.
North: May–September.

Principal Honours
Olympic Games: winners 1956
European Nations Cup: winners 1960; runners-up 1964
European Championship: runners-up 1972;
Cup-Winners' Cup: winners Dynamo Kiev (1975); runners-up Dynamo Moscow (1972)
Super Cup: Dynamo Kiev (1975)

International matches 1978

26 Feb, Marrakech: v Morocco (a) won 3-2 (*Blokhin, Konkov, Tchesnokov*).
8 March, Frankfurt: v West Germany (a) lost 0-1.
5 April, Erevan: v Finland (h) won 10-2 (*Konkov, Kipiani, Tchesnokov, Blokhin* 4, *Kolotov* 2, *Pietrakov*).
14 May, Bucharest: v Rumania (a) won 1-0 (*Blokhin*).
20 Sept, Erevan: v Greece (h) won 2-0 (EC) (*Tchesnokov, Bessonov*).
4 Oct, Ankara: v Turkey (a) won 2-0 (*Gutzaev, Blokhin*).
11 Oct, Budapest: v Hungary (a) lost 0-2 (EC).
19 Nov, Tokyo: v Japan (a) won 4-1 (*Darasella, Gazzaev* 2, *Gavrilov*).
28 Nov, Tokyo: v Japan (a) won 4-1 (*Kipiani, Khidiathullin, Kostava, Kipiani*).
26 Nov, Osaka: v Japan (a) won 3-0 (*Gazzaev, Gavrilov, Bessonov*).

League Championship wins (1936–78)

Dynamo Moscow 11; Spartak Moscow 9; Dynamo Kiev 8; CSKA Moscow 6; Torpedo Moscow 3; Dynamo Tbilisi 2; Saria Voroshilovgrad 1; Ararat Erevan 1.

Cup wins (1936–78)

Spartak Moscow 9; Torpedo Moscow 5; Dynamo Moscow 5; Dynamo Kiev 5; CSKA Moscow 4; Donets Shaktyor 2; Lokomotiv Moscow 2; Ararat Erevan 2; Karpaty Lvov 1; Zenit Leningrad 1; Dynamo Tbilisi 1.

	League Champions	Cup Winners
1946	CSKA Moscow	Spartak Moscow
1947	CSKA Moscow	Spartak Moscow
1948	CSKA Moscow	CSKA Moscow
1949	Dynamo Moscow	Torpedo Moscow
1950	CSKA Moscow	Spartak Moscow
1951	CSKA Moscow	CSKA Moscow
1952*	Spartak Moscow	Torpedo Moscow
1953	Spartak Moscow	Dynamo Moscow
1954	Dynamo Moscow	Dynamo Kiev
1955	Dynamo Moscow	CSKA Moscow
1956	Spartak Moscow	No competition
1957	Dynamo Moscow	Lokomotiv Mos.
1958	Spartak Moscow	Spartak Moscow
1959	Dynamo Moscow	No competition
1960	Torpedo Moscow	Torpedo Moscow
1961	Dynamo Kiev	Donets Shaktyor
1962	Spartak Moscow	Donets Shaktyor
1963	Dynamo Moscow	Spartak Moscow
1964	Dynamo Tbilisi	Dynamo Kiev
1965	Torpedo Moscow	Spartak Moscow
1966	Dynamo Kiev	Dynamo Kiev
1967	Dynamo Kiev	Dynamo Moscow
1968	Dynamo Kiev	Torpedo Moscow
1969	Spartak Moscow	Karpaty Lvov
1970	CSKA Moscow	Dynamo Moscow
1971	Dynamo Kiev	Spartak Moscow
1972	Saria Voroshilovgrad	Torpedo Moscow
1973	Ararat Erevan	Ararat Erevan
1974	Dynamo Kiev	Dynamo Kiev
1975	Dynamo Kiev	Ararat Erevan
1976	Dynamo Moscow / Torpedo Moscow	Dynamo Tbilisi
1977	Dynamo Kiev	Dynamo Moscow
1978	Dynamo Tbilisi	Dynamo Kiev

*Short league season

Final League Table 1978

	P	W	D*	L	F	A	Pts.
Dynamo Tbilisi	30	17	8	5	45	24	42
Dynamo Kiev	30	15	9	6	42	20	38
Schachtjor Donezk	30	16	5	9	42	31	37
Dynamo Moscow	30	14	10	6	37	23	36
Spartak Moscow	30	14	5	11	42	33	33
Tchernomorets Odessa	30	12	10	8	41	26	32
CSKA Moscow	30	14	4	12	36	40	32
Torpedo Moscow	30	11	11	8	36	29	30
Pachtakor Taschkent	30	9	8	13	42	43	26
Voroschilovgrad	30	9	8	13	38	44	26
Zenit Leningrad	30	9	8	13	31	46	26
Kairat Alma-Ata	30	9	7	14	29	41	25
Neftschi Baku	30	8	7	15	28	39	23
Lokomotiv Moscow	30	7	9	14	26	40	22
Ararat Erevan	30	8	6	16	20	42	22
Dnjepropetrowsk	30	9	3	18	25	39	21

(Only eight drawn games are allowed. No points are given for further draws.)

YUGOSLAVIA

President: Tore Florjancic.
General Secretary: Milan Lazarevic.
Address of Association: Yugoslav Football Association, Terazije No. 35, BP 263, Belgrade.
Telephone: 33 34 33, 33 34 47.
Cable: Jugofutbal.
Telex: 11666 yu fsj.
Area: 98,766 square miles.
Population: 20,500,000.
Number of Clubs: 4,289. *Teams:* 4,289.
Number of Players: 172,225.
Year of Formation: 1919.
National Colours: Blue shirts, white shorts, red stockings.
Second Choice of Colours: White shirts, white shorts, white stockings.
No National Stadium.

Names, Addresses and Capacities of Principal Football Grounds: Red Star Stadium, Belgrade, 95,000; Yugoslav National Army, Belgrade, 55,000; Yuth Stadium, Belgrade, 25,000; Dinamo, Zagreb, 55,000; Kosevo, Sarajevo, 40,000.

Principal Honours

Olympic Games: winners 1960; runners-up 1948, 1952, 1956
European Nations Cup: runners-up 1960
European Championship: runners-up 1968
European Champions Cup: runners-up Partizan Belgrade (1966)
Fairs Cup: winners Dynamo Zagreb (1967); runners-up Dynamo Zagreb (1963)
UEFA Cup runners up: Red Star Belgrade (1979)

International matches 1978

5 April, Tehran: v Iran (a) drew 0-0.
18 May, Rome: v Italy (a) drew 0-0.
4 Oct, Zagreb: v Spain (h) lost 1-2 (EC) (*Halilhodzic*).
25 Oct, Bucharest: v Rumania (a) lost 2-3 (EC) (*Petrovic, Desnica*).
15 Nov, Skoplje: v Greece (h) won 4-1 (*Savic, Halilhodzic* 3).

League Championship wins (1923–79)

Red Star Belgrade 12; Hajduk Split 9; Partizan Belgrade 8; Gradjanski Zagreb 5; BSK Belgrade 5; Dynamo Zagreb 3; Jugoslovija Belgrade 2; Concordia Zagreb 2; HASK Zagreb 1; Vojvodina Novi Sad 1; F.C. Sarajevo 1, Zeljeznicar 1.

Cup wins (1947–79)

Red Star Belgrade 9; Partizan Belgrade 4; Dynamo Zagreb 6; Hajduk Split 5; BSK Belgrade 2; FK Belgrade 2; Rijeka 2; Vardar Skoplje 1.

League Champions	Cup Winners
1947 Partizan Belgrade	Partizan Belgrade
1948 Dynamo Zagreb	Red Star Belgrade
1949 Partizan Belgrade	Red Star Belgrade
1950 Hajduk Split	Red Star Belgrade
1951 Red Star Belgrade	Dynamo Zagreb
1952 Hajduk Split	Partizan Belgrade
1953 Red Star Belgrade	BSK Belgrade
1954 Dynamo Zagreb	Partizan Belgrade
1955 Hajduk Split	BSK Belgrade
1956 Red Star Belgrade	No competition
1957 Red Star Belgrade	Partizan Belgrade
1958 Dynamo Zagreb	Red Star Belgrade
1959 Red Star Belgrade	Red Star Belgrade
1960 Red Star Belgrade	Dynamo Zagreb
1961 Partizan Belgrade	Vardar Skoplje
1962 Partizan Belgrade	OFK Belgrade
1963 Partizan Belgrade	Dynamo Zagreb
1964 Red Star Belgrade	Red Star Belgrade
1965 Partizan Belgrade	Dynamo Zagreb
1966 Vojvodina Novi Sad	OFK Belgrade
1967 FC Sarajevo	Hajduk Split
1968 Red Star Belgrade	Red Star Belgrade
1969 Red Star Belgrade	Dynamo Zagreb
1970 Red Star Belgrade	Red Star Belgrade
1971 Hajduk Split	Red Star Belgrade
1972 Zeljeznicar	Hajduk Split
1973 Red Star Belgrade	Dynamo Zagreb
1974 Hajduk Split	Hajduk Split
1975 Hajduk Split	Hajduk Split
1976 Partizan Belgrade	Hajduk Split
1977 Red Star Belgrade	Hajduk Split
1978 Partizan Belgrade	Rijeka
1979 Hajduk Split	Rijeka

Final League Table 1978–79

	P	W	D	L	F	A	Pts.
Hajduk Split	34	20	10	4	62	28	50
Dynamo Zagreb	34	21	8	5	67	38	50
Red Star Belgrade	34	16	9	9	51	33	41
Sarajevo	34	17	5	12	55	52	39
Velez Mostar	34	15	8	11	50	41	38
Buducnost Titograd	34	15	8	11	32	35	38
Radnicki	34	11	13	10	37	34	35
Sloboda Tuzla	34	11	10	13	33	34	32
Zeljeznicar	34	14	4	16	44	51	32
Rijeka	34	10	11	13	35	34	31
Borac Banja Luka	34	11	9	14	45	56	31
Vojvodina	34	11	7	16	35	38	29
Partizan Belgrade	34	9	11	14	38	45	29
Osijek	34	8	13	13	32	39	29
Napredak	34	9	11	14	43	51	29
Olimpija Ljubljana	34	11	7	16	35	53	29
Zagreb	34	7	12	15	32	39	26
OFK Belgrade	34	6	12	16	30	55	24

THE WORLD CUP, PREVIOUS FINALS

URUGUAY 1930

POOL 1
France 4, Mexico 1
Argentina 1, France 0
Chile 3, Mexico 0
Chile 1, France 0
Argentina 6, Mexico 3
Argentina 3, Chile 1

	P	W	D	L	F	A	Pts.
Argentina	3	3	0	0	10	4	6
Chile	3	2	0	1	5	3	4
France	3	1	0	2	4	3	2
Mexico	3	0	0	3	4	13	0

POOL 2
Yugoslavia 2, Brazil 1
Yugoslavia 4, Bolivia 0
Brazil 4, Bolivia 0

	P	W	D	L	F	A	Pts.
Yugoslavia	2	2	0	0	6	1	4
Brazil	2	1	0	1	5	2	2
Bolivia	2	0	0	2	0	8	0

POOL 3
Rumania 3, Peru 1
Uruguay 1, Peru 0
Uruguay 4, Rumania 0

	P	W	D	L	F	A	Pts.
Uruguay	2	2	0	0	5	0	4
Rumania	2	1	0	1	3	5	2
Peru	2	0	0	2	1	4	0

POOL 4
United States 3, Belgium 0
United States 3, Paraguay 0
Paraguay 1, Belgium 0

	P	W	D	L	F	A	Pts.
United States	2	2	0	0	6	0	4
Paraguay	2	1	0	1	1	3	2
Belgium	2	0	0	2	0	4	0

SEMI-FINALS
Argentina 6, United States 1
Uruguay 6, Yugoslavia 1

FINAL
Uruguay 4, Argentina 2 (1-2)

Uruguay: Ballesteros; Nasazzi (capt.), Mascheroni, Andrade, Fernandez, Gestido, Dorado, Scarone, Castro, Cea, Iriarte.

Argentina: Botasso; Della Torre, Paternoster, Evaristo J., Monti, Suarez, Peucelle, Varallo, Stabile, Ferreira (capt.), Evaristo M.

Scorers: Dorado, Cea, Iriarte, Castro for Uruguay; Peucelle, Stabile for Argentina.

Leading scorer: Stabile (Argentina) 8.

ITALY 1934

FIRST ROUND
Italy 7, United States 1
Czechoslovakia 2, Rumania 1
Germany 5, Belgium 2
Austria 3, France 2
Spain 3, Brazil 1
Switzerland 3, Holland 2
Sweden 3, Argentina 2
Hungary 4, Egypt 2

SECOND ROUND
Germany 2, Sweden 1
Austria 2, Hungary 1
Italy 1, Spain 1
Italy 1, Spain 0 *replay*
Czechoslovakia 3, Switzerland 2

SEMI-FINALS
Czechoslovakia 3, Germany 1
Italy 1, Austria 0

THIRD PLACE MATCH
Germany 3, Austria 2

FINAL
Italy 2, Czechoslovakia 1 (0-0) (1-1) after extra time. *Rome.*

Italy: Combi (capt.); Monzeglio, Allemandi; Ferraris IV, Monti, Bertolini, Guaita, Meazza, Schiavio, Ferrari, Orsi.

Czechoslovakia: Planicka (capt.); Zenisek, Ctyroky, Kostalek, Cambal, Krcil; Junek, Svoboda, Sobotka, Nejedly, Puc.

Scorers: Orsi, Schiavio for Italy; Puc for Czechoslovakia.

Leading Scorers: Schiavio (Italy), Nejedly (Czechoslovakia), Conen (Germany) each 4.

FRANCE 1938

FIRST ROUND
Switzerland 1, Germany 1
Switzerland 4, Germany 2 *replay*
Cuba 3, Rumania 3
Cuba 2, Rumania 1 *replay*
Hungary 6, Dutch East Indies 0
France 3, Belgium 1
Czechoslovakia 3, Holland 0
Brazil 6, Poland 5
Italy 2, Norway 1

SECOND ROUND
Sweden 8, Cuba 0
Hungary 2, Switzerland 0
Italy 3, France 1
Brazil 1, Czechoslovakia 1
Brazil 2, Czechoslovakia 1 *replay*

SEMI-FINALS
Italy 2, Brazil 1
Hungary 5, Sweden 1

THIRD PLACE MATCH
Brazil 4, Sweden 2

FINAL
Italy 4, Hungary 2 (3-1). *Paris*
Italy: Olivieri; Foni, Rava; Serantoni, Andreolo, Locatelli; Biavati, Meazza (capt.), Piola, Ferrari, Colaussi.
Hungary: Szabo; Polgar, Biro; Szalay, Szucs, Lazar; Sas, Vincze, Sarosi (capt.), Szengeller, Titkos.
Scorers: Colaussi (2), Piola (2) for Italy, Titkos, Sarosi for Hungary.
Leading Scorer: Leonidas (Brazil) 8.

BRAZIL 1950

POOL 1
Brazil 4, Mexico 0
Yugoslavia 3, Switzerland 0
Yugoslavia 4, Mexico 1
Brazil 2, Switzerland 2
Brazil 2, Yugoslavia 0
Switzerland 2, Mexico 1

	P	W	D	L	F	A	Pts.
Brazil	3	2	1	0	8	2	5
Yugoslavia	3	2	0	1	7	3	4
Switzerland	3	1	1	1	4	6	3
Mexico	3	0	0	3	2	10	0

POOL 2
Spain 3, United States 1
England 2, Chile 0
United States 1, England 0
Spain 2, Chile 0
Spain 1, England 0
Chile 5, United States 2

	P	W	D	L	F	A	Pts.
Spain	3	3	0	0	6	1	6
England	3	1	0	2	2	2	2
Chile	3	1	0	2	5	6	2
United States	3	1	0	2	4	8	2

POOL 3
Sweden 3, Italy 2
Sweden 2, Paraguay 2
Italy 2, Paraguay 0

	P	W	D	L	F	A	Pts.
Sweden	2	1	1	0	5	4	3
Italy	2	1	0	1	4	3	2
Paraguay	2	0	1	1	2	4	1

POOL 4
Uruguay 8, Bolivia 0

	P	W	D	L	F	A	Pts.
Uruguay	1	1	0	0	8	0	2
Bolivia	1	0	0	1	0	8	0

Final pool replaced knock-out system.

FINAL POOL
Uruguay 2, Spain 2
Brazil 7, Sweden 1
Uruguay 3, Sweden 2
Brazil 6, Spain 1
Sweden 3, Spain 1
Uruguay 2, Brazil 1

FINAL POSITIONS

	P	W	D	L	F	A	Pts.
Uruguay	3	2	1	0	7	5	5
Brazil	3	2	0	1	14	4	4
Sweden	3	1	0	2	6	11	2
Spain	3	0	1	2	4	11	1

Leading Scorers: Ademir (Brazil) 7, Schiaffino (Uruguay), Basora (Spain) 5.

GOALSCORING IN WORLD CUP FINAL ROUNDS, ATTENDANCES AND AVERAGE

Year	Goals	Per match	Attendance	Average
1930:	70 goals in 18 matches	(3.8 per match)	434,500	24,139
1934:	70 goals in 17 matches	(4.1 per match)	395,000	23,235
1938:	84 goals in 18 matches	(4.6 per match)	483,000	26,833
1950:	88 goals in 22 matches	(4.0 per match)	1,337,000	60,772
1954:	140 goals in 26 matches	(5.3 per match)	943,000	36,270
1958:	126 goals in 35 matches	(3.6 per match)	868,000	24,800
1962:	89 goals in 32 matches	(2.7 per match)	776,000	24,250
1966:	89 goals in 32 matches	(2.7 per match)	1,614,677	50,458
1970:	95 goals in 32 matches	(2.9 per match)	1,673,975	52,312
1974:	97 goals in 38 matches	(2.5 per match)	1,774,022	46,685
1978:	102 goals in 38 matches	(2.6 per match)	1,610,215	42,374

SWITZERLAND 1954

GROUP 1
Yugoslavia 1, France 0
Brazil 5, Mexico 0
France 3, Mexico 2
Brazil 1, Yugoslavia 1

	P	W	D	L	F	A	Pts.
Brazil	2	1	1	0	6	1	3
Yugoslavia	2	1	1	0	2	1	3
France	2	1	0	1	3	3	2
Mexico	2	0	0	2	8	0	

GROUP 2
Hungary 9, Korea 0
W. Germany 4, Turkey 1
Hungary 8, W. Germany 3
Turkey 7, Korea 0
PLAY-OFF W. Germany 7, Turkey 2

	P	W	D	L	F	A	Pts.
Hungary	2	2	0	0	17	3	4
W. Germany	2	1	0	1	7	9	2
Turkey	2	1	0	1	8	4	2
Korea	2	0	0	2	0	16	0

GROUP 3
Austria 1, Scotland 0
Uruguay 2, Czechoslovakia 0
Austria 5, Czechoslovakia 0
Uruguay 7, Scotland 0

	P	W	D	L	F	A	Pts.
Uruguay	2	2	0	0	9	0	4
Austria	2	2	0	0	6	0	4
Czechoslovakia	2	0	0	2	0	7	0
Scotland	2	0	0	2	0	8	0

GROUP 4
England 4, Belgium 4
England 2, Switzerland 0
Switzerland 2, Italy 1
Italy 4, Belgium 1
PLAY-OFF Switzerland 4, Italy 1

	P	W	D	L	F	A	Pts.
England	2	1	1	0	6	4	3
Italy	2	1	0	1	5	3	2
Switzerland	2	1	0	1	2	3	2
Belgium	2	0	1	1	5	8	1

QUARTER-FINALS
W. Germany 2, Yugoslavia 0
Hungary 4, Brazil 2
Austria 7, Switzerland 5
Uruguay 4, England 2

SEMI-FINALS
West Germany 6, Austria 1
Hungary 4, Uruguay 2

THIRD PLACE MATCH
Austria 3, Uruguay 1

FINAL
West Germany 3, Hungary 2

West Germany: Turek; Posipal, Kohlmeyer; Eckel, Liebrich, Mai; Rahn, Morlock, Walter, O., Walter, F. (capt.), Schaefer.
Hungary: Grosics; Buzansky, Lantos; Bozsik, Lorant, Zakarias; Czibor, Kocsis, Hidegkuti, Puskas (capt.), Toth, J.
Scorers: Morlock, Rahn (2) for Germany, Puskas, Czibor for Hungary.
Leading Scorer: Kocsis (Hungary) 11.

SWEDEN 1958

GROUP 1
W. Germany 3, Argentina 1
N. Ireland 1, Czechoslovakia 0
W. Germany 2, Czechoslovakia 2
Argentina 3, N. Ireland 1
W. Germany 2, N. Ireland 2
Czechoslovakia 6, Argentina 1

	P	W	D	L	F	A	Pts.
West Germany	3	1	2	0	7	5	4
Czechoslovakia	3	1	1	1	8	4	3
Ireland	3	1	1	1	4	5	3
Argentina	3	1	0	2	5	10	2

PLAY-OFF MATCH
N. Ireland 2, Czechoslovakia 1

GROUP 2
France 7, Paraguay 3
Yugoslavia 1, Scotland 1
Yugoslavia 3, France 2
Paraguay 3, Scotland 2
France 2, Scotland 1
Yugoslavia 3, Paraguay 3

	P	W	D	L	F	A	Pts.
France	3	2	0	1	11	7	4
Yugoslavia	3	1	2	0	7	6	4
Paraguay	3	1	1	1	9	12	3
Scotland	3	0	1	2	4	6	1

GROUP 3
Sweden 3, Mexico 0
Hungary 1, Wales 1
Wales 1, Mexico 1
Sweden 2, Hungary 1
Sweden 0, Wales 0
Hungary 4, Mexico 0

	P	W	D	L	F	A	Pts.
Sweden	3	2	1	0	5	1	5
Hungary	3	1	1	1	6	3	3
Wales	3	0	3	0	2	2	3
Mexico	3	0	1	2	1	8	1

PLAY-OFF MATCH
Wales 2, Hungary 1

GROUP 4
England 2, Russia 2
Brazil 3, Austria 0
England 0, Brazil 0
Russia 2, Austria 0
Brazil 2, Russia 0
England 2, Austria 2

	P	W	D	L	F	A	Pts.
Brazil	3	2	1	0	5	0	5
England	3	0	3	0	4	4	3
Russia	3	1	1	1	4	4	3
Austria	3	0	1	2	2	7	1

PLAY-OFF MATCH
Russia 1, England 0

QUARTER-FINALS
France 4, Ireland 0
W. Germany 1, Yugoslavia 0
Sweden 2, Russia 0
Brazil 1, Wales 0

SEMI-FINALS
Brazil 5, France 2
Sweden 3, West Germany 1

THIRD PLACE MATCH
France 6, West Germany 3

FINAL
Brazil 5, Sweden 2 (2-1) *Stockholm*

Brazil: Gilmar; Santos, D., Santos, N.; Zito, Bellini, Orlando, Garrincha, Didi, Vava, Pele, Zagalo.
Sweden: Svensson; Bergmark, Axbom; Boerjesson, Gustavsson, Parling, Hamrin, Gren, Simonsson, Liedholm, Skoglund.
Scorers: Vava (2), Pele (2), Zagalo for Brazil. Liedholm, Simonsson for Sweden.
Leading Scorer: Fontaine 13 (present record total).

CHILE 1962

GROUP 1
Uruguay 2, Colombia 1
Russia 2, Yugoslavia 0
Yugoslavia 3, Uruguay 1
Russia 4, Colombia 4
Russia 2, Uruguay 1
Yugoslavia 5, Colombia 0

	P	W	D	L	F	A	Pts.
Russia	3	2	1	0	8	5	5
Yugoslavia	3	2	0	1	8	3	4
Uruguay	3	1	0	2	4	6	2
Colombia	3	0	1	2	5	11	1

GROUP 2
Chile 3, Switzerland 1
W. Germany 0, Italy 0
Chile 2, Italy 0
W. Germany 2, Switzerland 1
W. Germany 2, Chile 0
Italy 3, Switzerland 0

	P	W	D	L	F	A	Pts.
W. Germany	3	2	1	0	4	1	5
Chile	3	2	0	1	5	2	4
Italy	3	1	1	1	3	2	3
Switzerland	3	0	0	3	2	8	0

GROUP 3
Brazil 2, Mexico 0
Czechoslovakia 1, Spain 0
Brazil 0, Czechoslovakia 0
Spain 1, Mexico 0
Brazil 2, Spain 1
Mexico 3, Czechoslovakia 1

	P	W	D	L	F	A	Pts.
Brazil	3	2	1	0	4	1	5
Czechoslovakia	3	1	1	1	2	3	3
Mexico	3	1	0	2	3	4	2
Spain	3	1	0	2	2	3	2

GROUP 4
Argentina 1, Bulgaria 0
Hungary 2, England 1
England 3, Argentina 1
Hungary 6, Bulgaria 1
Argentina 0, Hungary 0
England 0, Bulgaria 0

	P	W	D	L	F	A	Pts.
Hungary	3	2	1	0	8	2	5
England	3	1	1	1	4	3	3
Argentina	3	1	1	1	2	3	3
Bulgaria	3	0	1	2	1	7	1

QUARTER-FINALS
Yugoslavia 1, W. Germany 0
Brazil 3, England 1
Chile 2, Russia 1
Czechoslovakia 1, Hungary 0

SEMI-FINALS
Brazil 4, Chile 2
Czechoslovakia 3, Yugoslavia 1

THIRD PLACE MATCH
Chile 1, Yugoslavia 0

FINAL
Santiago
Brazil 3, Czechoslovakia 1 (1-1)

Brazil: Gilmar; Santos, D., Mauro, Zozimo, Santos, N.; Zito, Didi; Garrincha, Vavà, Amarildo, Zagalo.

Czechoslovakia: Schroiff; Tichy, Novak; Pluskal, Popluhar, Masopust, Pospichal, Scherer, Kvasniak, Kadraba, Jelinek.

Scorers: Amarildo, Zito, Vavà for Brazil, Masopust for Czechoslovakia.

Leading Scorers: Albert (Hungary), Ivanov (Russia), Sanchez, L. (Chile), Garrincha, Vavà (Brazil), Jerkovic (Yugoslavia) each 4.

ENGLAND 1966

GROUP 1
England 0, Uruguay 0
France 1, Mexico 1
Uruguay 2, France 1
England 2, Mexico 0
Uruguay 0, Mexico 0
England 2, France 0

	P	W	D	L	F	A	Pts.
England	3	2	1	0	4	0	5
Uruguay	3	1	2	0	2	1	4
Mexico	3	0	2	1	1	3	2
France	3	0	1	2	2	5	1

GROUP 2
W. Germany 5, Switzerland 0
Argentina 2, Spain 1
Spain 2, Switzerland 1
Argentina 0, W. Germany 0
Argentina 2, Switzerland 0
W. Germany 2, Spain 1

	P	W	D	L	F	A	Pts.
West Germany	3	2	1	0	7	1	5
Argentina	3	2	1	0	4	1	5
Spain	3	1	0	2	4	5	2
Switzerland	3	0	0	3	1	9	0

GROUP 3
Brazil 2, Bulgaria 0
Portugal 3, Hungary 1
Hungary 3, Brazil 1
Portugal 3, Bulgaria 0
Portugal 3, Brazil 1
Hungary 3, Bulgaria 1

	P	W	D	L	F	A	Pts.
Portugal	3	3	0	0	9	2	6
Hungary	3	2	0	1	7	5	4
Brazil	3	1	0	2	4	6	2
Bulgaria	3	0	0	3	1	8	0

GROUP 4
Russia 3, N. Korea 0
Italy 2, Chile 0
Chile 1, N. Korea 1
Russia 1, Italy 0
N. Korea 1, Italy 0
Russia 2, Chile 1

	P	W	D	L	F	A	Pts.
Russia	3	3	0	0	6	1	6
North Korea	3	1	1	1	2	4	3
Italy	3	1	0	2	2	2	2
Chile	3	0	1	2	2	5	1

QUARTER-FINALS
England 1, Argentina 0
West Germany 4, Uruguay 0
Portugal 5, North Korea 3
Russia 2, Hungary 1

SEMI-FINALS
West Germany 2, Russia 1
England 2, Portugal 1

THIRD PLACE MATCH
Portugal 2, Russia 1

FINAL *Wembley*
England 4, West Germany 2 (1-1) (2-2) after extra time

England: Banks; Cohen, Wilson; Stiles, Charlton, J., Moore; Ball, Hurst, Hunt, Charlton, R., Peters.

West Germany: Tilkowski; Hottges, Schulz, Weber, Schnellinger; Haller, Beckenbauer; Overath, Seeler, Held, Emmerich.

Scorers: Hurst 3, Peters for England, Haller, Weber for Germany.

Leading scorer: Eusebio (Portugal) 9.

MEXICO 1970

GROUP A
Mexico 0, Russia 0
Belgium 3, El Salvador 0
Russia 4, Belgium 1
Mexico 4, El Salvador 0
Russia 2, El Salvador 0
Belgium 0, Mexico 1

	P	W	D	L	F	A	Pts.
Russia	3	2	1	0	6	1	5
Mexico	3	2	1	0	5	0	5
Belgium	3	1	0	2	4	5	2
El Salvador	3	0	0	3	0	9	0

GROUP B
Uruguay 2, Israel 0
Italy 1, Sweden 0
Uruguay 0, Italy 0
Israel 1, Sweden 1
Sweden 1, Uruguay 0
Israel 0, Italy 0

	P	W	D	L	F	A	Pts.
Italy	3	1	2	0	1	0	4
Uruguay	3	1	1	1	2	1	3
Sweden	3	1	1	1	2	2	3
Israel	3	0	2	1	1	3	2

GROUP C
England 1, Rumania 0
Brazil 4, Czechoslovakia 1
Rumania 2, Czechoslovakia 1
Brazil 1, England 0
Brazil 3, Rumania 2
England 1, Czechoslovakia 0

	P	W	D	L	F	A	Pts.
Brazil	3	3	0	0	8	3	6
England	3	2	0	1	2	1	4
Rumania	3	1	0	2	4	5	2
Czechoslovakia	3	0	0	3	2	7	0

GROUP D
Peru 3, Bulgaria 2
W. Germany 2, Morocco 1
Peru 3, Morocco 0
W. Germany 5, Bulgaria 2
W. Germany 3, Peru 1
Bulgaria 1, Morocco 1

	P	W	D	L	F	A	Pts.
W. Germany	3	3	0	0	10	4	6
Peru	3	2	0	1	7	5	4
Bulgaria	3	0	1	2	5	9	1
Morocco	3	0	1	2	2	6	1

QUARTER FINALS
Uruguay 1, Russia 0
Italy 4, Mexico 1
Brazil 4, Peru 2
West Germany 3, England 2

SEMI-FINALS
Italy 4, West Germany 3
Brazil 3, Uruguay 1

THIRD PLACE MATCH
West Germany 1, Uruguay 0

FINAL *Mexico City*
Brazil 4, Italy 1.

Brazil: Felix; Carlos Alberto, Brito, Piazza, Everaldo; Gerson, Clodoaldo; Jairzinho, Pele, Tostao, Rivelino. No subs.

Italy: Albertosi; Burgnich, Cera, Rosato, Facchetti; Bertini, Riva; Domenghini, Mazzola, De Sisti, Boninsegna. Subs: Juliano for Bertini, Rivera for Boninsegna.

Scorers: Pele, Gerson, Jairzinho, Carlos Alberto for Brazil; Boninsegna for Italy.

Leading scorer: Muller (West Germany) 10.

WORLD CUP 1930-78 FINAL SERIES

	P	W	D	L	F	A		P	W	D	L	F	A
Brazil	52	33	10	9	119	56	United States	7	3	0	4	12	21
W Germany	47	28	9	10	110	68	Wales	5	1	3	1	4	4
Italy	36	20	6	10	62	40	N Ireland	5	2	1	2	6	10
Uruguay	29	14	5	10	57	39	Rumania	8	2	1	5	12	17
Argentina	29	14	5	10	55	43	Bulgaria	12	0	4	8	9	29
Hungary	26	13	2	11	73	42	Tunisia	3	1	1	1	3	2
Sweden	28	11	6	11	48	46	North Korea	4	1	1	2	5	9
England	24	10	6	8	34	28	Cuba	3	1	1	1	5	12
Yugoslavia	25	10	5	10	45	34	Belgium	9	1	1	7	12	25
Russia	19	10	3	6	30	21	Turkey	3	1	0	2	10	11
Holland	16	8	3	5	32	19	Israel	3	0	2	1	1	3
Poland	14	9	1	4	27	17	Morocco	3	0	1	2	2	6
Austria	18	9	1	8	33	36	Australia	3	0	1	2	0	5
Czechoslovakia	22	8	3	11	32	36	Colombia	3	0	1	2	5	11
France	20	8	1	11	43	38	Iran	3	0	1	2	2	8
Chile	18	7	3	8	23	24	Norway	1	0	0	1	1	2
Spain	18	7	3	8	22	25	Egypt	1	0	0	1	2	4
Switzerland	18	5	2	11	28	44	Dutch East Indies	1	0	0	1	0	6
Portugal	6	5	0	1	17	8	El Salvador	3	0	0	3	0	9
Mexico	24	3	4	17	21	62	South Korea	2	0	0	2	0	16
Peru	12	4	1	7	17	25	Haiti	3	0	0	3	2	14
Scotland	11	2	4	5	12	21	Zaire	3	0	0	3	0	14
E Germany	6	2	2	2	5	5	Bolivia	3	0	0	3	0	16
Paraguay	7	2	2	3	12	19							

Only six countries have won the World Cup: Brazil (1958, 1962 and 1970), Italy (1934 and 1938), Uruguay (1930 and 1950), West Germany (1954 and 1974), England (1966) and Argentina (1978).
1,050 goals have been scored in 308 matches in the 11 final tournaments for an overall average of 3.4 per match.

WEST GERMANY 1974

GROUP 1
West Germany 1, Chile 0
East Germany 2, Australia 0
West Germany 3, Australia 0
East Germany 1, Chile 1
East Germany 1, West Germany 0
Chile 0, Australia 0

	P	W	D	L	F	A	Pts.
East Germany	3	2	1	0	4	1	5
West Germany	3	2	0	1	4	1	4
Chile	3	0	2	1	1	2	2
Australia	3	0	1	2	0	5	1

GROUP 2
Brazil 0, Yugoslavia 0
Scotland 2, Zaire 0
Brazil 0, Scotland 0
Yugoslavia 9, Zaire 0
Scotland 1, Yugoslavia 1
Brazil 3, Zaire 0

	P	W	D	L	F	A	Pts.
Yugoslavia	3	1	2	0	10	1	4
Brazil	3	1	2	0	3	0	4
Scotland	3	1	2	0	3	1	4
Zaire	3	0	0	3	0	14	0

GROUP 3
Holland 2, Uruguay 0
Sweden 0, Bulgaria 0
Holland 0, Sweden 0
Bulgaria 1, Uruguay 1
Holland 4, Bulgaria 1
Sweden 3, Uruguay 0

	P	W	D	L	F	A	Pts.
Holland	3	2	1	0	6	1	5
Sweden	3	1	2	0	3	0	4
Bulgaria	3	0	2	1	2	5	2
Uruguay	3	0	1	2	1	6	1

GROUP 4
Italy 3, Haiti 1
Poland 3, Argentina 2
Argentina 1, Italy 1
Poland 7, Haiti 0
Argentina 4, Haiti 1
Poland 2, Italy 1

	P	W	D	L	F	A	Pts.
Poland	3	3	0	0	12	3	6
Argentina	3	1	1	1	7	5	3
Italy	3	1	1	1	5	4	3
Haiti	3	0	0	3	2	14	0

GROUP A
Brazil 1, East Germany 0
Holland 4, Argentina 0
Holland 2, East Germany 0
Brazil 2, Argentina 1
Holland 2, Brazil 0
Argentina 1, East Germany 1

	P	W	D	L	F	A	Pts.
Holland	3	3	0	0	8	0	6
Brazil	3	2	0	1	3	3	4
East Germany	3	0	1	2	1	4	1
Argentina	3	0	1	2	2	7	1

GROUP B
Poland 1, Sweden 0
West Germany 2, Yugoslavia 0
Poland 2, Yugoslavia 1
West Germany 4, Sweden 2
Sweden 2, Yugoslavia 1
West Germany 1, Poland 0

	P	W	D	L	F	A	Pts.
West Germany	3	3	0	0	7	2	6
Poland	3	2	0	1	3	2	4
Sweden	3	1	0	2	4	6	2
Yugoslavia	3	0	0	3	2	6	0

THIRD PLACE MATCH
Poland 1, Brazil 0

FINAL
Munich

West Germany 2, Holland 1 (2-1)

West Germany: Maier; Vogts, Schwarzenbeck, Beckenbauer, Breitner, Bonhof, Hoeness, Overath, Grabowski, Muller, Holzenbein.

Holland: Jongbled; Suurbier, Rijsbergen (De Jong), Haan, Krol, Jansen, Van Hanegem, Neeskens, Rep, Cruyff, Rensenbrink (Van der Kerkhof R).

Scorers: Breitner (*pen*), Muller for West Germany; Neeskens (*pen*) for Holland.

Leading scorer: Lato (Poland) 7.

ARGENTINA 1978

GROUP 1
Italy 2, France 1
Argentina 2, Hungary 1
Italy 3, Hungary 1
Argentina 2, France 1
France 3, Hungary 1
Italy 1, Argentina 0

	P	W	D	L	F	A	Pts.
Italy	3	3	0	0	6	2	6
Argentina	3	2	0	1	4	3	4
France	3	1	0	2	5	5	2
Hungary	3	0	0	3	3	8	0

GROUP 2
West Germany 0, Poland 0
Tunisia 3, Mexico 1
Poland 1, Tunisia 0
West Germany 6, Mexico 0
Poland 3, Mexico 1
West Germany 0, Tunisia 0

	P	W	D	L	F	A	Pts.
Poland	3	2	1	0	4	1	5
West Germany	3	1	2	0	6	0	4
Tunisia	3	1	1	1	3	2	3
Mexico	3	0	0	3	2	12	0

GROUP 3
Austria 2, Spain 1
Brazil 1, Sweden 1
Austria 1, Sweden 0
Brazil 0, Spain 0
Spain 1, Sweden 0
Brazil 1, Austria 0

	P	W	D	L	F	A	Pts.
Austria	3	2	0	1	3	2	4
Brazil	3	1	2	0	2	1	4
Spain	3	1	1	1	2	2	3
Sweden	3	0	1	2	1	3	1

GROUP 4
Peru 3, Scotland 1
Holland 3, Iran 0
Scotland 1, Iran 1
Holland 0, Peru 0
Peru 4, Iran 1
Scotland 3, Holland 2

	P	W	D	L	F	A	Pts.
Peru	3	2	1	0	7	2	5
Holland	3	1	1	1	5	3	3
Scotland	3	1	1	1	5	6	3
Iran	3	0	1	2	2	8	1

GROUP A
West Germany 0, Italy 0
Holland 5, Austria 1
Italy 1, Austria 0
Holland 2, West Germany 2
Holland 2, Italy 1
Austria 3, West Germany 2

	P	W	D	L	F	A	Pts.
Holland	3	2	1	0	9	4	5
Italy	3	1	1	1	2	2	3
West Germany	3	0	2	1	4	5	2
Austria	3	1	0	2	4	8	2

GROUP B
Brazil 3, Peru 0
Argentina 2, Poland 0
Poland 1, Peru 0
Argentina 0, Brazil 0
Brazil 3, Poland 1
Argentina 6, Peru 0

	P	W	D	L	F	A	Pts.
Argentina	3	2	1	0	8	0	5
Brazil	3	2	1	0	6	1	5
Poland	3	1	0	2	2	5	2
Peru	3	0	0	3	0	10	0

THIRD PLACE MATCH
Brazil 2, Italy 1

FINAL
Buenos Aires
Argentina 3, Holland 1 (1-0) after extra time

Argentina: Fillol; Passarella, Olquin, Galvan (L), Tarantini, Ardiles (Larrosa), Gallego, Ortiz (Houseman), Bertoni, Luque, Kempes.

Holland: Jongbloed; Krol, Poortvliet, Brandts, Jansen (Suurbier), Haan, Neeskens, Van der Kerkhof(W), Rep (Nanninga), Van der kerkhof(R), Rensenbrink.

Scorers: Kempes 2, Bertoni for Argentina; Nanninga for Holland.

Leading scorer: Kempes (Argentina) 6.

ALL-TIME RECORD OF WORLD CUP FINALISTS '78

Argentina (7 appearances)
1930 Runners-up; 1934 First round; 1938 Withdrew; 1950 Withdrew; 1954 Did not enter; 1958 Group stage; 1962 Group stage; 1966 Quarter-finalists; 1970 Did not qualify; 1974 Second stage; 1978 Winners.

Austria (4 appearances)
1930 Did not enter; 1934 Fourth place; 1938 Withdrew; 1950 Withdrew; 1954 Third place; 1958 Group stage; 1962 Did not enter; 1966 Did not qualify; 1970 Did not qualify; 1974 Did not qualify; 1978 Second stage.

Brazil (11 appearances)
1930 Group stage; 1934 First round; 1938 Third place; 1950 Runners-up; 1954 Quarter-finalists; 1958 Winners; 1962 Winners; 1966 Group stage; 1970 Winners; 1974 Fourth place; 1978 Third place.

France (7 appearances)
1930 Group stage; 1934 First round; 1938 Quarter-finalists; 1950 Did not qualify; 1954 Group stage; 1958 Third place; 1962 Did not qualify; 1966 Group stage; 1970 Did not qualify; 1974 Did not qualify 1978 Group stage.

Holland (4 appearances)
1930 Did not enter; 1934 First round; 1938 First round; 1950 Did not enter; 1954 Did not enter; 1958 Did not qualify; 1962 Did not qualify; 1966 Did not qualify; 1970 Did not qualify; 1974 Runners-up; 1978 Runners-up.

Hungary (7 appearances)
1930 Did not enter; 1934 Quarter-finalists; 1938 Runners-up; 1950 Did not enter; 1954 Runners-up; 1958 Group stage; 1962 Quarter-finalists; 1966 Quarter-finalists; 1970 Did not qualify; 1974 Did not qualify; 1978 Group stage.

Iran (1 appearance)
1930–74 Did not enter; 1978 Group stage.

Italy (9 appearances)
1930 Did not enter; 1934 Winners; 1934 Winners; 1950 Group stage; 1954 Group stage; 1958 Did not qualify; 1962 Group stage; 1966 Group stage; 1970 Runners-up; 1974 Group stage; 1978 Fourth place.

Mexico (8 appearances)
1930 Group stage; 1934 Did not qualify; 1938 Withdrew; 1950 Group stage; 1954 Group stage; 1958 Group stage; 1962 Group stage; 1966 Group stage; 1970 Quarter-finalists; 1974 Did not qualify; 1978 Group stage.

Peru (3 appearances)
1930 Group stage; 1934 Withdrew; 1938 Did not enter; 1950 Withdrew; 1954 Did not enter; 1958 Did not qualify; 1962 Did not qualify; 1966 Did not qualify; 1970 Quarter-finalists; 1974 Did not qualify; 1978 Second stage.

Poland (3 appearances)
1930 Did not enter; 1934 Did not qualify; 1938 First round; 1950 Did not enter; 1954 Withdrew; 1958 Did not qualify; 1962 Did not qualify; 1966 Did not qualify; 1970 Did not qualify; 1974 Third place; 1978 Second stage.

Scotland (4 appearances)
1930 Did not enter; 1934 Did not enter; 1938 Did not enter; 1950 Declined final place; 1954 Group stage; 1958 Group stage; 1962 Did not qualify; 1966 Did not qualify; 1970 Did not qualify; 1974 Group stage; 1978 Group stage.

Spain (5 appearances)
1930 Did not enter; 1934 Quarter-finalists; 1938 Did not enter; 1950 Fourth place; 1954 Did not qualify; 1958 Did not qualify; 1962 Group stage; 1966 Group stage; 1970 Did not qualify; 1974 Did not qualify; 1978 Group stage.

Sweden (7 appearances)
1930 Did not enter; 1934 Quarter-finalists; 1938 Fourth place; 1950 Third place; 1954 Did not qualify; 1958 Runners-up; 1962 Did not qualify; 1966 Did not qualify; 1970 Group stage; 1974 Second stage; 1978 Group stage.

Tunisia (1 appearance)
1930–1958 Did not enter; 1962 Did not qualify; 1966 Withdrew; 1970 Did not qualify; 1974 Did not qualify. 1978 Group stage.

West Germany (9 appearances)
1930 Did not qualify; 1934 Third place; 1938 First round; 1950 Did not enter; 1954 Winners; 1958 Fourth place; 1962 Quarter-finalists; 1966 Runners-up; 1970 Third place; 1974 Winners; 1978 Second stage.

WORLD CLUB CHAMPIONSHIP

Played annually up to 1974 between the winners of the European Cup and the winners of the South American Champions Cup—known as the Copa Libertadores.

1960 Real Madrid beat Penarol 0-0, 5-1
1961 Penarol beat Benfica 0-1, 5-0, 2-1
1962 Santos beat Benfica 3-2, 5-2
1963 Santos beat AC Milan 2-4, 4-2, 1-0
1964 Inter-Milan beat Independiente 0-1, 2-0, 1-0
1965 Inter-Milan beat Independiente 3-0, 0-0
1966 Penarol beat Real Madrid 2-0, 2-0
1967 Racing Club beat Celtic 0-1, 2-1, 1-0
1968 Estudiantes beat Manchester United 1-0, 1-1
1969 AC Milan beat Estudiantes 3-0, 1-2
1970 Feyenoord beat Estudiantes 2-2, 1-0
1971 Nacional beat Panathinaikos 1-1, 2-1
1972 Ajax beat Independiente 1-1, 3-0
1973 Independiente beat Juventus 1-0
1974 Atlético Madrid beat Independiente 0-1, 2-0
1975 Independiente and Bayern Munich could not agree dates; no matches.
1976 Bayern Munich beat Cruzeiro 2-0, 0-0
1977 Boca Juniors beat Borussia Moenchengladbach 2-2, 3-0

SOUTH AMERICAN CHAMPIONSHIPS

Year	Winner	Year	Winner	Year	Winner
1916	Uruguay	1927	Argentina	1949	Brazil
1917	Uruguay	1929	Argentina	1953	Paraguay
1919	Brazil	1935	Uruguay	1955	Argentina
1920	Uruguay	1937	Argentina	1956	Uruguay
1921	Argentina	1939	Peru	1957	Argentina
1922	Brazil	1941	Argentina	1959	Argentina
1923	Uruguay	1942	Uruguay	1959	Uruguay
1924	Uruguay	1945	Argentina	1963	Bolivia
1925	Argentina	1946	Argentina	1967	Uruguay
1926	Uruguay	1947	Argentina	1975	Peru

SOUTH AMERICAN CHAMPIONSHIP RECORD 1917-1975

	P	W	D	L	F	A
Argentina	87	61	11	15	243	84
Uruguay	92	56	7	29	230	122
Brazil	76	43	9	24	207	106
Paraguay	88	42	9	37	164	175
Peru	73	31	13	29	123	125
Chile	81	23	15	43	129	180
Bolivia	48	11	6	31	56	157
Colombia	35	8	5	22	37	91
Ecuador	51	2	9	40	48	163
Venezuela	9	1	0	8	8	42

Table includes only 23 championships considered as 'official' tournaments

COPA LIBERTADORES (South American Cup)

Year	Winners	Year	Winners	Year	Winners
1960	Penarol (Uruguay)	1966	Penarol	1972	Independiente
1961	Penarol	1967	Racing (Argentina)	1973	Independiente
1962	Santos (Brazil)	1968	Estudiantes (Argentina)	1974	Independiente
1963	Santos			1975	Independiente
1964	Independiente (Argentina)	1969	Estudiantes	1976	Cruzeiro (Brazil)
		1970	Estudiantes	1977	Boca Juniors
1965	Independiente	1971	Nacional	1978	Boca Juniors

UNDER-23 APPEARANCES 1954-76

ENGLAND

A'Court, A. (Liverpool): 1957 v F, Bul, Cz; 1958 v Bul, R, S, W. (7)
Allen, A. (Stoke C) : 1959, v P, Cz, F, It, WG; 1960 v Hun, S. (7)
Allen, L. (Tottenham H): 1961 v W. (1)
Anderson, S. (Sunderland): 1955 v S (sub); 1956 v D; 1957 v F, Bul. (4)
Angus, J. (Burnley): 1959 v WG; 1960 v EG, P, Is; 1961 v It, W; 1962 v S. (7)
Armfield, J. (Blackpool): 1957 v D, Bul, R, Cz; 1958 v R; 1959 v P, Cz, F, It. (9)
Armstrong, D. (Middlesbrough): 1975 v P, W; 1976 v Cz, P. (4)
Armstrong, G. (Arsenal): 1956 v Cz, WG, A; 1966 v Y, T. (5)
Ashurst, L. (Sunderland): 1961 v WG. (1)
Aston, J. (Manchester U) 1970 v W. (1)
Atyeo, J. (Bristol C): 1955 v It, S. (2)
Ayre, R. (Charlton Ath): 1955 v It, S. (2)

Badger, L. (Sheffield U): 1964 v S, Hun, Is, T; 1965 v W, R, S, Cz, A; 1966 v T; 1968 v W, Hun (sub), WG. (13)
Bailey, M. (Charlton Ath): 1964 v S, F, Hun, Is, T. (5)
Baker, J. (Hibernian): 1959 v P Cz; 1960 v F. Ho; 1961 v It; (Arsenal) 1963 v Y. (6)
Baldwin, T. (Chelsea): 1968 v It, WG. (2)
Ball, A. (Blackpool): 1965 v W, R, S, Cz, WG, Cz, A; 1966 v F. (8)
Banks, G. (Leicester C): 1961 v W, S. (2)
Barnwell, J. (Arsenal): 1961 v WG. (1)
Barrett, L. (Fulham): 1967 v G. (1)
Barrowclough, S. (Newcastle U): 1973 v W, S, Cz, D, Ho. (5)
Beattie, K. (Ipswich T): 1973 v W, Ho, S; 1974 v Pol, W, T, Y, F; 1975 v W. (9)
Bell, C. (Manchester C): 1968 v S, Hun. (2)
Bennett, A. (Rotherham): 1965 v W. (1)
Bernard, M. (Stoke C): 1971 v WG (sub), Se (sub), W. (3)
Birchenall, A. (Sheffield U): 1966 v T; 1968 v W. (Chelsea) It, WG. (4)
Blockley, J. (Coventry C): 1972 v Sw, W, S, EG, USSR, Pol; (Arsenal) 1973 v S, D, Ho, Cz. (10)
Bloomfield, J. (Arsenal): 1957 v D, Bul. (2)
Blunstone, F. (Chelsea): 1954 v It; 1955 v It, S; 1956 v D; 1957 v D. (5)
Bonds, W. (West Ham U): 1969 v W, Ho. (2)
Bonetti, P. (Chelsea): 1962 v S, T; 1963 v Bel, G, Y, Y, R; 1964 v F, Hun, Is, T; 1965 v A. (12)
Booth, C. (Wolverhampton W) :1957 v F. (sub) (1)
Booth, T. (Manchester C): 1969 v Pt; 1972 v Sw, W, S. (4)
Boyer, P. (Norwich C): 1975 v S; 1976 v Cz. (2)
Brabrook, P. (Chelsea): 1958 v Bul, R, S; 1959 v P, Cz, It, WG; 1960 v Hun; 1961 v S. (9)
Broadbent, P. (Wolverhampton W): 1954 v It. (1)
Brooking, T. (West Ham U): 1972 v Sw. (1)
Buckley, M. (Everton): 1975 v P; 1976 v Cz (2)
Burnside, D. (WBA): 1962 v T. (1)
Burrows, H. (Aston Villa): 1963 v G. (1)
Burne, G. (Liverpool): 1961 v W. (1)
Byrne, J. (Crystal Palace): 1961 v W S, WG; 1962 v Is, Ho, S; (West Ham U) T. (7)

Callaghan, I. (Liverpool): 1963 v G, Y, Y, R. (4)
Cantello, L. (WBA): 1972 v EG; 1973 v W, Ho (2) D, Cz; 1974 v Pol, D. (8)
Case, J. (Liverpool): 1976 v H. (1)
Cattlin, C. (Coventry C) :1969 v W, Ho. (2)
Channon, M. (Southampton): 1971 v Se, W, S; 1972 v Sw, W, S, EG. (2) USSR (sub). (9)
Charlton, R. (Manchester U): 1959 v P, Cz, F; 1960 v Hun, S; 1961 v It. (6)
Cheesebrough, A. (Burnley): 1957 v F. (1)
Chisnall, P. (Manchester U): 1964 v W, WG, S, F. (4)

Chivers, M. (Southampton): 1964 v F. (sub), Hun; 1965 v W, R (sub), S, Cz, WG, Cz, A (sub); 1966 v F, Y; 1968 v It, (Tottenham H) S, Hun, It, Hun, WG. (17)
Clark, C. (WBA): 1961 v W. (1)
Clarke, A. (Fulham): 1967 v W, A, G, Bul, T; (Leicester) 1969 v Pt. (6)
Clayton, R. (Blackburn R): 1956 v D, S; 1957 v D, S, R, Cz. (6)
Clemence, R. (Liverpool): 1968 v W; 1971 v Se, W, S. (4)
Clough, B. (Middlesbrough): 1957 v S, Bul; 1958 v W. (3)
Coates, R. (Burnley): 1967 v W, G, Bul, T; 1969 v Ho, Pt, N, Bel. (8)
Cohen, G. (Fulham): 1960 v Hun, F, S, Ho; 1961 v S, WG; 1963 v Y, R. (8)
Connelly, J. (Burnley): 1961 v It.(1)
Coppell, S. (Manchester U): 1976 v H. (1)
Corrigan, J. (Manchester C): 1970 v USSR (1)
Crawford, B. (Blackpool): 1962 v S. (1)
Cross, G. (Leicester C): 1963 v Y, Y, R; 1964 v W, WG, S, F, Hun, Is, T; 1966 v T. (11)
Crowe, C. (Leeds U): 1960 v F, S; (Blackburn) 1961 v W, S. (4)
Crowther, S. (Aston Villa): 1958 v Bul, R, S. (3)
Currie, A. (Sheffield U): 1970 v W, Bul; 1971 v WG, S; 1972 v W, S, EG, Pol, USSR; 1973 v W, Ho, S, Cz. (13)
Curry, W. (Newcastle): 1958 v R. (1)

Davies, R. (Derby Co): 1974 v S. (sub) (1)
Day, M. (West Ham U): 1974 v Y, F. (sub); 1975 v S, W; 1976 v P. (5)
Deakin, A. (Aston Villa): 1962 v Is, T; 1963 v Y (2) R; 1964 v T (sub) (6)
Dobing, P. (Blackburn): 1959 v WG; 1960 v F, EG, P, Is; 1961 v It, S. (7)
Dobson, C. (Sheffield W): 1963 v Y (sub), R. (2)
Dobson, M. (Burnley): 1970 v Bul. (1)
Dodd, A. (Stoke C): 1975 v Cz, P, S; 1976 v Cz, P, H. (6)
Dodgin, W. (Arsenal): 1954 v It. (1)
Douglas, B. (Blackburn): 1957 v D, F, Bul, R, Cz. (5)
Doyle, M. (Manchester C): 1968 v Hun, It, Hun, WG; 1969 v Pt, Ho, Bel, Pt. (8)
Dyson, J. (Manchester C): 1957 v S. (1)
Dyson, K. (Newcastle U): 1970 v Bul. (1)

Eastham, G. (Newcastle U): 1960 v F, S, Ho, EG, P, Is. (6)
Edwards, D. (Manchester U): 1954 v It; 1955 v It, S; 1956 v S; 1957 v R, Cz. (6)
Edwards, P. (Manchester U): 1970 v Bul (sub); 1971 v WG, Se. (3)
Ellis, S. (Sheffield W):1969 v W; 1970 v W, USSR. (3)
Ellis, S. (Charlton Ath): 1954 v It. (1)
Evans, A. (Liverpool): 1969 v Ho, Pt, Bel, Pt. (4)

Fantham, J. (Sheffield W): 1961 v It. (1)
Farmer, E. (Wolverhampton W): 1962 v Is, Ho. (2)
Farmer, J. (Stoke C): 1967 v W. (1)
Finney, A. (Sheffield W): 1954 v It; 1956 v S; 1957 v S. (3)
Fletcher, P. (Burnley): 1974 v D (sub), W, Y, F (sub). (4)
Flowers, R. (Wolverhampton W): 1955 v It, S. (2)
Ford, D. (Sheffield W): 1967 v W, S. (2)
Foulkes, W. (Manchester U): 1955 v It, S. (2)
Francis, G. (QPR): 1974 v D, S, T, Y (sub), F; 1976 v H. (6)
Francis, T. (Birmingham C): 1974 v Pol, D, W; 1976 v P, H. (5)

Garland, C. (Bristol C): 1970 v Bul (sub). (1)
George, C. (Arsenal): 1973 v W, Ho, Cz; 1974 v Pol, D. (5)

Gidman, J. (Aston Villa): 1975 v Cz; 1976 v Cz, P, H. (4)
Gillard, I. (QPR): 1974 v S, T, Y, F; 1975 v S. (5)
Glazier, W. (Coventry C): 1965 v R, S, Cz. (3)
Gowling, A. (Manchester U): 1972 v Sw. (1)
Greaves, J. (Chelsea): 1958 v Bul, R, S, W; 1959 v P, Cz, F, It; 1960 v Hun, S, Ho; (Tottenham H) 1962 v S. (12)
Greenhoff, B. (Manchester U): 1974 v Y, F (sub); 1975 v Cz; 1976 v H. (4)
Greenhoff, J. (Birmingham C): 1969 v W, Ho, Ho (sub), Bel; 1976 v H. (5)
Groves, V. (Arsenal): 1957 v F. (1)
Grummitt, P. (Nottingham F): 1962 v Ho; 1964 v W, WG. (3)
Gunter, P. (Portsmouth): 1954 v It. (1)

Hankin, R. (Burnley): 1975 v Cz (sub), S, W. (3)
Harris, Gordon (Burnley): 1962 v Is; 1963 v Y. (2)
Harris, Gerry (Wolverhampton W): 1958 v Bul, R, S, W. (4)
Harris, J. (Everton): 1956 v S. (1)
Harris, R. (Chelsea): 1967 v W; 1968 v It, Hun, WG. (4)
Harrison, M. (Chelsea): 1961 v WG; 1962 v S, T. (3)
Harvey, J. (Everton): 1967 v S, A, G, Bul, T. (5)
Hayes, J. (Manchester C): 1958 v S, W. (2)
Haynes, J. (Fulham): 1955 v It, S; 1956 v D, S; 1957 v S, R, Cz; 1958 v Bul. (8)
Hibbitt, K. (Wolverhampton W): 1971 v W. (sub) (1)
Hill, F. (Bolton W): 1961 v WG; 1962 v Is, Ho, S, T; 1963 v Bel, G, Y, Y, R. (10)
Hill, G. (Manchester U): 1976 v H. (1)
Hill, S. (Blackpool): 1962 v Is, Bel, S, T. (4)
Hindley, P. (Nottingham F): 1967 v G. (1)
Hinton, A. (Wolverhampton W): 1963 v Y, R; 1964 v W. (Nottingham F) Hun, Is, T; 1965 v R. (7)
Hinton, M. (Charlton Ath): 1962 v S, T; 1963 v Bel. (3)
Hitchens, G. (Cardiff C): 1957 v D. (1)
Hodgkinson, A. (Sheffield U): 1957 v D, F, S; 1958 v R, W; 1959 v P, Cz. (7)
Holiday, E. (Middlesbrough): 1960 v Hun, Ho, EG, P, Is. (5)
Hollins, J. (Chelsea): 1965 v W, Cz, A; 1966 v F, Y; 1967 v W, S, A; 1968 v W, It, S, Hun. (12)
Hooper, H. (West Ham U): 1955 v It, S. (2)
Hopkinson, E. (Bolton W): 1957 v Bul, R, Cz; 1958 v Bul, S; 1959 v F. (6)
Howe, D. (WBA): 1956 v S; 1957 v F, S; 1958 v Bul, S, W. (6)
Hudson, A. (Chelsea): 1970 v S; 1971 v W, S; 1972 v S, EG; (with Stoke C), 1974 v S, T, Y, F; 1976 v H. (10)
Hughes, E. (Liverpool): 1968 v W, It, S; 1969 v Ho, Bel, Pt (sub); 1970 v R, Bul. (8)
Hunt, R. P. (Swindon T): 1963 v R; (Wolverhampton W): 1966 v Y, T. (3)
Hunter, N. (Leeds U): 1965 v W, R, S. (3)
Hurst, G. (West Ham U): 1964 v W, F, Is, T. (4)
Hurst, J. (Everton): 1967 v G, Bul, T; 1969 v W, Ho, Ho, Bel, Pt; 1970 v USSR. (9)
Husband, J. (Everton): 1967 v A (sub), G, Bul; 1970 v USSR, S. (5)
Hutchinson, I. (Chelsea): 1971 v W, S. (2)

Iley, J. (Tottenham H): 1958 v W. (1)

Jeffrey, A. (Doncaster R): 1957 v D, F. (2)
Jeffries, D. (Manchester C): 1972 v EG. (1)
Johnson, D. (Ipswich T): 1973 v Cz (2), Ho; 1974 v Pol; 1975 v Cz, P, W; 1976 v P, H. (9)
Jones, G. (Middlesbrough): 1962 v Is, Ho, S, T; 1963 v Bel, G, Y; 1974 v W, WG. (9)
Jones, M. (Sheffield U): 1965 v R, S, Cz, WG, A; 1966 v F, Y, T; 1967 v A. (9)
Jones, R. (Bournemouth): 1968 v Hun. (1)

Kay, A. (Sheffield W): 1959 v It, WG; 1960 v S, Ho, EG, P, Is. (7)
Kaye, A. (Barnsley): 1956 v D. (1)

Keegan, K. (Liverpool): 1972 v S, EG. (2), Pol USSR. (5)
Kember, S. (Crystal Palace): 1971 v WG; (Chelsea) 1972 v Sw, EG. (3)
Kendall, H. (Everton): 1968 v W, It, It, Hun; 1969 v W, Ho. (6)
Kennedy, A. (Newcastle U): 1975 v Cz, P; 1976 v Cz, P, H (2). (6)
Kennedy, R. (Arsenal): 1972 v W; 1973 v Ho, (1+1 sub), D, Cz (sub); 1974 v Pol. (6)
Kevan, D. (WBA): 1957 v Bul, R, Cz; 1958 v Bul. (4)
Kidd, B. (Manchester U): 1968 v W, It, S; 1969 v Ho, Bel (sub); 1970 v W, USSR, S; 1971 v WG, Se. (10)
Kirkham, J. (Wolverhampton W): 1961 v W, S. (2)
Kirkup, J. (West Ham U): 1962 v Is, Ho, T. (3)
Knowles, C. (Tottenham H): 1965 v W; 1967 v W, S, G, Bul, T. (6)
Knowles, P. (Wolverhampton W): 1968 v W, It; 1969 v W, Ho. (4)

Labone, B. (Everton): 1961 v It, W, S; 1962 v Is, Ho; 1963 v Y, R. (7)
Lampard, F. (West Ham U): 1972 v Sw, EG, Pol, USSR. (4)
Latchford, P. (WBA): 1974 v Pol, W. (2)
Latchford, R. (Birmingham C): 1974 v D, W; (Everton), S, T, Y, F. (6)
Lawler, C. (Liverpool): 1966 v F, Y; 1967 v S, A. (4)
Leary, S. (Charlton Ath): 1954 v It. (1)
Le Flem, R. (Nottingham F): 1962 v Ho. (1)
Lloyd, L. (Liverpool): 1971 v WG, Se, W, S; 1972 v EG (2), Pol, USSR. (8)
Lock, K. (West Ham U): 1973 v D, Ho, Cz; 1976 v H. (4)
Lyons, M. (Everton): 1975 v Cz, P, S, W (sub); 1976 v Cz. (5)

Maddren, W. (Middlesbrough): 1973 v Cz; 1974 v D, S, Y (sub), F. (5)
Macedo, E. (Fulham): 1959 v It, WG; 1960 v Hun, F, Ho, EG, P, Is; 1961 v It, WG. (10)
Mannion, G. (Wolverhampton W): 1960 v P, Is. (2)
Marsh, R. (QPR): 1968 v S, Hun. (2)
Marshall, G. (Hearts): 1960 v S. (1)
Matthews, R. (Coventry C): 1955 v It, S; 1965 v D, S. (4)
McDermott, T. (Newcastle U): 1974 v W. (1)
Macdonald, M. (Newcastle U): 1972 v W, S, EG; 1973 v W. (4)
McDowell, J. (West Ham U): 1973 v W, Ho (2), S, Cz(2), D; 1974 v Pol, D, S, T, Y (sub), F. (13)
McFarland, R. (Derby Co): 1969 v Ho (2), Bel, Pt; 1970 v S. (5)
McGrath, J. (Newcastle U): 1961 v WG. (1)
McGuinness, W. (Manchester U): 1959 v P, Cz, F; 1960 v Hun. (4)
McNeil, M. (Middlesbrough): 1960 v F, Ho, EG, P, Is; 1961 v It, S; 1963 v Bel, G. (9)
Miller, B. (Burnley): 1960 v EG, P, Is. (3)
Mills, D. (Middlesbrough): 1974 v S, T, Y, F; 1975 v Cz; 1976 v Cz, P (sub), H (sub). (8)
Mills, M. (Ipswich T): 1971 v W; 1972 v S, EG, Pol, USSR. (5)
Mills, S. J. (Southampton), 1974 v W. (1)
Mobley, V. (Sheffield W): 1965 v W, R, S, Cz, WG, Cz, A; 1966 v F, Y; 1967 v A, G, Bul, T. (13)
Montgomery, J. (Sunderland): 1964 v S; 1967 v S, A, G, Bul, T. (6)
Moore, I. (Nottingham F): 1967 v S, A. (2)
Moore, R. (West Ham U): 1961 v It, W, S, WG, 1962 v Is, Ho, S, T. (8)
Moores, I. (Stoke C): 1975 v W; 1976 v Cz. (2)
Morgan, R. (Tottenham H): 1970 v Bul. (1)
Morley, M. (Preston NE): 1975 v W (sub) (1)
Mortimer, D. (Coventry C): 1973 v W, Ho. (2), S, Cz (2). (6)
Mullery, A. (Fulham): 1961 v It; 1962 Ho; 1963 v Bel. (3)
Murray, A. (Chelsea): 1965 v R, S, Cz, WG, Cz, A. (6)

Murray, J. (Wolverhampton W): 1958 v S; 1959 v F. (2)

Nattrass, I. (Newcastle U): 1976 v H. (1)
Neal, R. (Lincoln): 1957 v D, F, S; (Birmingham C) Bul. (4)
Newton, H. (Nottingham F): 1965 v R, Cz; 1967 v Bul, T. (4)
Newton, K. (Blackburn R): 1964 v S, Hun, Is, T. (4)
Nicholls, J. (WBA): 1954 v It. (1)
Nisbet, G. (WBA): 1972 v EG. (1)
Nish, D. (Leicester C): 1969 v Pt (sub), Bel, Pt; 1970 v W, USSR, S, Bul; 1971 v Se, W, S. (10)
Norman, M. (Tottenham H): 1956 v S; 1957 v R, Cz. (3)

O'Grady, M. (Huddersfield): 1961 v S; 1963 v Bel; (Leeds) 1966 v F. (3)
O'Neil, B. (Burnley): 1966 v T. (1)
O'Rourke, J. (Middlesbrough): 1967 v T. (1)
Osgood, P. (Chelsea): 1968 v W, S, Hun; 1970 v W, USSR, S. (6)

Pacey, D. (Luton T): 1959 v WG. (1)
Paine, T. (Southampton): 1960 v Ho, EG; 1961 v WG; 1962 v T (sub). (4)
Paddon, G. (West Ham U): 1976 v H (1)
Palmer, G. (Wolverhampton W): 1974 v W; 1975 v P. (2)
Pardoe, G. (Manchester C): 1968 v Hun; 1969 Pt, Bel, Pt. (4)
Parkes, P. (QPR): 1972 v W, S, EG; 1973 v D, Cz; 1976 v Cz. (6)
Parkin, D. (Wolverhampton W): 1970 v W, USSR, Bul, S; 1971 v S. (5)
Parry, R. (Bolton): 1958 v R; 1959 v F, It, WG. (4)
Payne, D. (Crystal Palace): 1968 v W (sub). (1)
Pearson, S. (Manchester U): 1976 v H. (1)
Pegg, D. (Manchester U): 1956 v S; 1957 v S, R. (3)
Pejic, M. (Stoke C): 1972 v Pol, USSR; 1973 v W, Ho (2), S, D, Cz. (8)
Perryman, S. (Tottenham H): 1972 v EG, Pol, USSR; 1973 v S, ID, Ho, Cz; 1974 v Pol, D, W, S, T, Y; 1975 v Cz, P, S, W. (17)
Peters, M. (West Ham U): 1963 v Bel, G; 1964 v WG; 1966 v T. (5)
Pickering, F. (Blackburn R): 1964 v W; WG, S. (3)
Piper, N. (Plymouth Arg): 1970 v Bul; (Portsmouth) 1971 v WG, Se, S. (4)
Pointer, R. (Burnley): 1959 v It; 1960 v Hun, EG, P, Is. (5)
Powell, B. (Wolverhampton W): 1974 v S; 1975 v Cz, P (sub), S. (4)
Powell, S. (Derby Co): 1975 v S. (1)
Pugh, J. (Sheffield W): 1970 v W. (1)

Quixall, A. (Sheffield W): 1956 v S. (1)

Radford, J. (Arsenal): 1969 v W, Ho (2), Pt. (4)
Rankin, A. (Everton): 1965 v W. (1)
Reaney, P. (Leeds U): 1964 v F; 1965 v S, WG, Cz; 1967 v S. (5)
Richards, J. (Wolverhampton W): 1972 v EG, Pol, USSR; 1973 v S; 1974 v Pol (sub), W. (6)
Riley, H. (Leicester C): 1959 v W; 1961 v W. (2)
Robson, B. (Newcastle U): 1967 v S; 1969 v Pt. (2)
Robson, Jimmy (Burnley): 1959 v WG. (1)
Robson, John (Derby): 1971 v WG, Se, S; 1972 v W, S, EG; (Aston Villa) 1973 v Cz. (7)
Robson, R. (Fulham): 1956 v D. (1)
Rofe, D. (Leicester C): 1973 v Cz (sub). (1)
Rogers, D. (Swindon T): 1966 v Y; 1968 v W. (2)
Royle, J. (Everton): 1968 v Hun (sub), Hun; 1969 Ho, Bel (sub), Pt; 1970 v USSR, S (sub); 1971 v WG, Se; 1972 v Sw. (10)

Sadler, D. (Manchester U): 1967 v S; 1968 v W; 1969 v Pt. (3)
Sammels, J. (Arsenal): 1967 v W, A, G, Bul, T; 1968 v It, It, Hun, WG. (9)
Scanlon, A. (Manchester U): 1959 v P, Cz, F, It, WG. (5)
Scott, M. (Chelsea): 1959 v P, Cz, F; 1960 v Hun. (4)

Setters, M. (WBA): 1958 v Bul, R, S, W; 1959 v P, Cz, F, It, WG; 1960 v Hun, F (with Manchester U) S, Ho, EG, P, Is. (16)
Shaw, B. (Sheffield U): 1968 v It, Hun. (2)
Shaw, G. (Sheffield U): 1956 v D; 1957 v D, F, S, Bul. (5)
Shawcross, D. (Manchester C): 1961 v WG. (1)
Shellito, K. (Chelsea): 1963 v Y. (1)
Shilton, P. (Leicester C): 1969 v W, Ho, Pt, Ho, Pt; 1970 v W, Bul, S; 1971 v WG; 1972 v Sw, EG, Pol, USSR. (13)
Sillett, P. (Chelsea): 1955 v It, S; 1956 v D. (3)
Sissons, J. (West Ham U): 1965 v W, S; 1967 v W; 1968 v Hun, WG; 1969 v W, Pt, Ho, Bel, Pt. (10)
Sleeuwenhoek, J. (Aston Villa): 1963 v G, Y. (2)
Smith, J. (West Ham U): 1960 v F. (1)
Smith, Tommy (Liverpool): 1965 v Cz, WG, Cz, A; 1966 v F, Y; 1967 v S, A; 1968 v It, S. (10)
Smith, Trevor (Birmingham C): 1955 v It, S; 1956 v D, S; 1957 v D, F, S, Bul, R, Cz; 1958 v Bul, R, S, W; 1959 v It. (15)
Smith, W. (Sheffield W): 1969 v Pt, Ho, Pt; 1970 v W, Bul, S. (6)
Springett, P. (Sheffield W): 1968 v It, S, Hun, It, WG; 1969 v Bel. (6)
Stephenson, A. (Crystal Palace): 1967 v W; 1968 v It, S; (West Ham U) Hun, It, Hun, WG. (7)
Stepney, A. (Millwall): 1966 v F, Y, T. (3)
Stevens, D. (Bolton W): 1957 v R, Cz. (2)
Stevenson, A. (Burnley): 1973 v W, Ho (2), S, Cz; 1974 v D, S, T, F; 1975 v Cz, P. (11)
Stiles, N. (Manchester U): 1965 v S, WG, Cz. (3)
Stokes, A. (Tottenham H): 1956 v D. (1)
Stokes, D. (Huddersfield): 1963 v Bel, G, Y, R (sub). (4)
Suddick, A. (Newcastle U): 1963 v Bel, Y. (2)
Sullivan, C. (Plymouth A): 1974 v Pol, D (2)
Summerbee, M. (Manchester C): 1966 v T. (1)
Sunderland, A. (Wolverhampton W): 1974 v S (sub). (1)
Swan, P. (Sheffield W): 1960 v F, S, Ho. (3)
Sydenham, J. (Southampton): 1960 v F, S. (2)

Talbut, J. (Burnley): 1964 v W, WG, S, F, Hun, Is, T. (7)
Tambling, R. (Chelsea): 1963 v Bel, G, Y; 1964 v WG, S, F, Hun, Is, T; 1965 v W (sub), R, Cz, A. (13)
Taylor, P. (Crystal Palace): 1975 v Cz, P; 1976 v Cz (sub), P. (4)
Taylor, T. (West Ham U): 1972 v EG (sub); 1973 v W, Ho, Cz; 1974 v Pol, D, W, S, T, Y; 1976 v P. (11)
Thomas, D. (Burnley): 1970 v Bul, S; 1971 v WG, Se, W; 1972 v Sw, S, EG; (QPR) 1974 v D (sub), T, F. (11)
Thompson, P. (Liverpool): 1964 v WG, S, F; 1966 v F. (4)
Thompson, P. B. (Liverpool): 1975 v W; 1976 v H. (2)
Thomson, R. (Wolverhampton W): 1963 v Y, R; 1964 v W, WG, F; 1965 v R, Cz, WG, Cz, A; 1966 v F, Y, T; 1967 v W, A. (15)
Todd, C. (Sunderland): 1968 v Hun, Hun (sub), WG; 1969 v W, Ho (sub); 1970 v W, USSR, S; 1971 v WG, Se, W (Derby) S; 1972 v W; 1975 v W. (14)
Towers, A. (Manchester C): 1972 v USSR, R (sub); 1973 v D, Cz (with Sunderland); 1975 v W; 1976 v Cz, P, H. (8)
Tueart, D. (Manchester C): 1975 v S. (1)

Usher, B. (Sunderland): 1964 v F. (1)

Venables, T. (Chelsea): 1963 v G; 1964 v Hun, Is, T. (4)

Wallington, M. (Leicester C): 1976 v H (2). (2)
West, A. (Burnley): 1972 v W. (1)
West, G. (Blackpool): 1962 v Is; (Everton) 1965 v WG, Cz. (3)
Whitefoot, G. (Manchester U): 1954 v It. (1)

Whitham, J.(Sheffield W): 1969 v W (sub).(1)
Whittle, A.(Everton): 1971 v W,(1)
Whitworth, S. (Leicester C): 1972 v Sw, W; 1974 v Y, F; 1975 v S, S, W. (6)
Whymark, T. (Ipswich T): 1973 v Ho (2), S, Cz, (2), D; 1975 v P. (7)
Wilkins, R.(Chelsea): v P, H. (2)
Wilson, D. (Preston NE): 1964 v W .WG, S., Hun, Is, T; 1965 v W. (7)
Wood, R. (Manchester U): 1954 v It. (1)
Worthington, F. (Huddersfield T): 1972 v Pol, USSR. (2)
Wright, T. (Everton): 1967 v Bul. T; 1968 v It. S, Hun, It, Hun. (7)

NORTHERN IRELAND
(all matches against Wales)

Briggs, R. (Manchester U): 1962; (with Swansea T.) 1965.(2)
Burke, R.(Portadown): 1963.(1)

Campbell, W. (Distillery): 1964; (with Sunderland) 1965 (with Dundee) 1967.(3)
Clarke, F. (Arsenal): 1962, 1963, 1964, 1965. (4)
Clarke, N. (Ballymena): 1962; (with Sunderland) 1963. (2)
Clements, D. (Coventry C): 1965, 1967, 1968. (3)
Craig, D. (Newcastle U): 1965, 1967.(2)
Craig, W.(Linfield): 1965.(1)

Dunlop, J.(Coleraine): 1965, 1968. (2)

Elder, A.(Burnley): 1964.(1)
Elwood, J.(Orient): 1962.(1)

Hamilton, B.(Linfield): 1968.(1)
Harkin, T.(Port Vale): 1963.(1)
Harvey, M. (Sunderland): 1962, 1963, 1964. (3)

Irvine, R.(Linfield): 1963.(1)
Irvine, W. (Burnley): 1963, 1964, 1965. (3)

Jackson, T.(Everton): 1968.(1)
Jennings, P.(Watford): 1964.(1)
Johnston, W. (Glenavon): 1962.(1)

Magill, J.(Arsenal): 1962.(1)
McAvoy, W. (Ards.): 1968.(1)
McCaffrey G. (Leicester C): 1963.(1)
McKeag, W. (Glentoran): 1967, 1968.(2)
McKenzie, R. (Airdrieonians): 1967, 1968.(2)
McKinney, V. (Falkirk): 1967.(1)
McLaughlin, J. (Shrewsbury T): 1963 (with Swansea T), 1964.(2)
McMillan, S. (Wrexham); 1964.(1)

McMordie, E. (Middlesbrough): 1967.(1)
McNeill, A. (Middlesbrough): 1968.(1)
Morrow, T. (Glentoran): 1968. (1)

Napier, J. (Bolton W): 1967; (with Brighton) 1968. (2)
Neill, T. (Arsenal): 1962, 1963, 1964, 1965. (4)
Nicholson, J. (Manchester U): 1962, 1963, 1964, (with Huddersfield T), 1965. (4)

O'Neill, J. (Sunderland): 1962.(1)

Rice, P. (Arsenal): 1968.(1)
Ross, E. (Glentoran): 1967.(1)

Sloan, D.(Scunthorpe U): 1964.(1)

Todd, S. (Burnley): 1965, 1967, 1968. (3)
Trainor, D. (Crusaders): 1967.(1)

Welsh, E.(Distillery): 1962.(1)

Ireland also played an under 23 international v Italy on 26 March, 1969 at Brescia losing 1-2.

Team:—
Gaston, R. (Oxford U)
Hamilton, B. (Linfield)
Hunter, A. (Oldham Ath)
Johnston, J. (Blackpool)
McKenzie, R. (Airdrieonians)
Morrow, T. (Glentoran)
Mullan, B. (Fulham)
Nelson, S. (Arsenal)
O'Doherty, A. (Coleraine)
Rice, P. (Arsenal)
Todd, S. (Burnley)

SCOTLAND

Aitken, C.(Aston Villa): 1962 v E, W; 1963 v W. (3)
Alderson, B. (Coventry C.): 1973 v E.(1)
Allan, W. (Aberdeen): 1963 v W.(1)
Anderson, G. (Morton): 1973 v W.(1)

Baillie, D. (Airdrieonians): 1955 v E; 1959 v W. (2)
Baird, D. (Partick T): 1959 v W.(1)
Baxter, James (Raith R): 1959 v W.(1)
Baxter, John (Hibernian): 1959 v W.(1)
Baxter, T. (Queen of the South): 1956 v E.(1)
Beattie, R. (Celtic): 1958 v Ho (2), E. (3)
Blacklaw, A. (Burnley): 1960 v E, W. (2)
Blackley, J. (Hibernian): 1970 v F, E, W; 1971 v E. (4)
Bone, J. (Norwich C): 1972 v E, W; 1973 v E. (3)
Brand, R. (Rangers): 1958 v E.(1)
Bremner, D. (Hibernian): 1975 v E, W, Se; 1976 v D. (2), R, W, Ho (2). (9)
Bremner, W. (Leeds U): 1964 v E, F; 1965 v W, E. (4)
Brown, H. (Kilmarnock): 1963 v W.(1)
Brown, J. (Chesterfield): 1974 v W (sub), E (sub) (with Sheffield U): 1975 v E (sub), Se (sub). (4)
Brownie, J. (Hibernian): 1972 v E, W; 1976 v W, Ho (2). (5)
Bruce, A. (Newcastle U): 1974 v E.(1)
Buchan, M. (Aberdeen): 1971 v W; 1972 v W, E. (3)
Burley, G. (Ipswich T): 1975 v E, Se. (2)
Burns, F. (Manchester U): 1968 v E.(1)

Burns, K. (Birmingham C): 1974 v W; 1976 v Ho. (2)

Calderwood, R. (Birmingham C): 1974 v E.(1)
Caldow, E. (Rangers): 1955 v E; 1957 v E. (2)
Campbell, A. (Charlton): 1970 v W. (1)
Carr, W. (Coventry C): 1970 v F, W; 1971 v W; 1972 v E. (4)
Clark, R. (Aberdeen): 1967 v W, E. (2)
Clunie, J. (Hearts): 1970 v E, W. (2)
Colquhoun, E. (WBA): 1968 v E. (1)
Colrain, J. (Celtic): 1958 v Ho. (1)
Conn, A. (Tottenham H): 1975 v R; 1976 v D, R. (3)
Connelly, G. (Celtic): 1970 v E; 1971 v E; 1972 v E. (3)
Connolly, J. (Everton): 1971 v W; 1973 v W. (2)
Cooke, C. (Aberdeen): 1963 v W; 1964 v W; 1965 v W; (with Dundee) 1965 v E.(4)
Cormack, P. (Hibernian): 1965 v W, E; 1967 v W, E; 1968; v E. (5)
Cousin, A. (Dundee): 1958 v Ho; 1960 v E, Bel. (3)
Craig, J. (Partick T): 1976 v D, R, W, Ho. (4)
Craig, T. (Sheffield W): 1974 v E (with Newcastle U): 1975 v W, Se, R; 1976 v D (2), R, W, Ho. (9)
Crawford, I. (Hearts): 1957 v E.(1)
Crerand, P. (Celtic): 1961 v E. (1)
Cropley, A. (Hibernian): 1972 v W; 1973 v E; 1974 v W. (3)
Cruickshank, J. (Queen's Park): 1960 v Bel; (with Hearts); 1964 v W, E. (3)
Currie, D. (Clyde): 1958 v Ho (2), E. 1959 v W. (4)

Dalglish, K. (Celtic): 1972 v W, E; 1973 v W; 1976 v H. (4)
Davie, A. (Dundee U): 1964 v F. (1)
Dickson, P. (Queen of the S.): 1976 v H (sub). (1)
Dickson, W. (Kilmarnock): 1970 v E. (1)
Donachie, W. (Manchester C): 1972 v W, E. (2)
Donaldson, A. (Dundee): 1965 v W, E. (2)
Doyle, J. (Ayr U): 1973 v E, W; 1974 v W (sub).(3)
Duff, W. (Hearts): 1955 v E. (1)
Duncan, A. (Hibernian): 1971 v E. (1)

Eston, J. (Hibernian): 1964 v W. (1)
Edwards, A. (Dunfermline Ath): 1976 v W. (1)
Ewen, R. (Aberdeen): 1959 v W. (1)

Ferguson, R. (West Ham U): 1968 v E. (1)
Forrest, J. (Rangers): 1964 v W; 1965 v E. (2)
Forsyth, A. (Manchester U): 1974 v W. (1)
Forsyth, C. (St Mirren): 1957 v E. (1)
Forsyth, T. (Motherwell): 1971 v E. (1)
Fraser, C. (Dunfermline Ath): 1962 v W; (with Aston Villa) 1963 v W. (2)

Gabriel, J. (Dundee): 1960 v W (with Everton), E, Bel; 1962 v W; 1963 v W, E. (6)
Gemmill, A. (Preston NE): 1970 v E. (1)
Gibb, T. (Partick T): 1968 v E. (sub). (1)
Gibson, I. (Middlesbrough): 1964 v W, F. (2)
Gillies, D. (Bristol C): 1974 v E. (1)
Gilzean, A. (Dundee): 1961 v E; 1962 v W, E. (3)
Glen, A. (Queen's Park): 1957 v E. (1)
Gow, G. (Bristol C): 1974 v E (sub). (1)
Graham, A. (Aberdeen): 1975 v W, E, Se, R (sub). (3)
Graham, G. (Chelsea): 1965 v W, E. (2)
Gray, A. (Dundee U): 1975 v E, W, R; (with Aston Villa), 1976 v D. (4)
Gray, E. (Leeds U): 1967 v W, E. (2)
Gray, F. (Leeds U): 1974 v E; 1976 v D (2), R, Ho. (5)
Greig, J. (Rangers): 1964 v W, E. (2)

Hamilton, J. (Hearts); 1956 v E; 1957 v E. (2)
Hamilton, R. (Kilmarnock): 1965 v W. (1)
Hansen, A. (Partick T): 1975 v Se; 1976 v R, W (sub). (3)
Harper, J. (Aberdeen): 1970 v W (sub); 1971 v W. (2)
Harrower, J. (Hibernian): 1958 v Ho. (1)
Hartford, A. (WBA): 1970 v W; 1971 v W; 1972 v E; 1973 v E, W. (5)
Hay, D. (Celtic): 1970 v F; 1971 v E, W. (3)
Henderson, W. (Rangers): 1962 v W, E. (2)
Herd, G. (Clyde): 1958 v Ho. (2)
Hermiston, J. (Aberdeen): 1971 v W. (1)
Hewie, J. (Charlton Ath): 1957 v E. (1)
Higgins, W. (Hearts): 1960 v E, W, Bel; 1962 v E.(4)
Hill, A. (Clyde): 1955 v E, (1)
Hilley, D. (Third Lanark): 1961 v E. (1)
Hogan, J. (Partick T): 1961 v E. (1)
Hollywood, D. (Southampton): 1965 v E. (1)
Holmes, R. (St Mirren): 1955 v E. (1)
Holt, D. (Queen's Park): 1958 v Ho; (with Hearts). (1)
Holton, J. (Manchester U): 1973 v W. (1)
Hood, H. (Clyde): 1968 v E. (1)
Hope, R. (WBA): 1967 v W. (1)
Houston, S. (Manchester U): 1975 v Se, R. (2)
Hughes, J. (Celtic): 1961 v E; 1962 v W, E; 1964 v E. (4)
Hughes, T. (Chelsea): 1970 v F, E. (2)
Hunter, A. (Kilmarnock): 1971 v E (sub); 1972 v W, E. (3)
Hunter, W. (Motherwell): 1960 v W, E, Bel; 1962 v E. (4)
Hutchison, T. (Blackpool): 1971 v W. (1)

Jackson, C. (Rangers): 1976 v Ho. (1)
Jardine, S. (Rangers): 1971 v E, W (sub); 1972 v W, E. (4)
Jarvie, A. (Airdrieonians): 1971 v E. (1)
Jeffrey, R. (Celtic): 1963 v W. (1)
Jordan, J. (Leeds U): 1976 v Ho. (1)
Johnston, W. (Rangers): 1970 v F, E. (2)
Johnstone, D. (Rangers): 1974 v W. E; 1975 v E; 1976 v W. Ho (2). (6).

Johnstone, J. (Celtic): 1964 v F, E. (2)

Kelly, E. (Arsenal): 1971 v E, W; 1974 v W. (3)
Kennedy, J. (Kilmarnock): 1958 v N. (1)
Kennedy, S. (Falkirk): 1973 v E, W; 1975 v W. (3)
Kennedy, S. (Rangers): 1975 v W. (1)
King, A. (Kilmarnock): 1964 v W, F; 1965 v W. (3)

Lamb, A. (Preston NE): 1974 v E (sub). (1)
Law, D. (Huddersfield T): 1960 v W, E; 1961 v E, (3)
Lawrence, T. (Liverpool): 1963 v W. (1)
Leggat, G. (Aberdeen): 1955 v E. (1)
Lochhead, A. (Burnley): 1963 v W. (1)
Lorimer, P. (Leeds U): 1970 v W, F. (2)

Macari, L. (Celtic): 1972 v W, E. (2)
Mackay, D. (Hearts): 1955 v E; 1957 v E; 1958 v Ho, E. (4)
Mackay, D. (Celtic): 1959 v W; 1960 v E, W, Bel.(4)
Malone, D. (Ayr U): 1970 v F. (1)
Martin, N. (Hibernian): 1964 v F. (1)
Martis, J. (Motherwell): 1960 v E. (1)
Marinello, P. (Hibernian): 1970 v F (sub), (with Arsenal) v E (sub), (2)
McCalliog, J. (Sheffield W): 1967 v W, E. (2)
McCluskey, P. (Celtic): 1973 v E, W (sub); 1975 v E, W, R; 1976 v D. (6)
McCulloch, W. (Cardiff C): 1973 v W (sub). (1)
McDonald, I. (St Johnstone): 1974 v E. (1)
McDonald, R. (Celtic)
McDougall, I. (Rangers): 1975 v W. (1)
McGillivray, A. (Third Lanark): 1962 v E. (1)
McGovern, J. (Derby Co): 1972 v W; 1973 v W. (2)
McGrain, D. (Celtic): 1973 v W, E. (2)
McGrory, J. (Kilmarnock): 1964 v F, E; 1935 v W (3)
McIntosh, J. (Falkirk): 1956 v E; 1958 v E, Ho. (3)
McLelland, C. (Aberdeen): 1976 v W, Ho. (2)
McLeod, J. M. (Hibernian): 1961 v E. (1)
McLintock, F. (Leicester C): 1962 v E. (1)
McMillan, T. (Aberdeen): 1967 v W, E. (2)
McNeill, W. (Celtic): 1960 v Bel; 1961 v E; 1962 v W, E; 1963 v W. (5)
McParland, D. (Partick T): 1955 v E. (1)
McQuade, D. (Partick T): 1972 v W (sub). (1)
MacRae, K. (Motherwell): 1971 v E, W. (2)
McVie, W. (Motherwell): 1976 v W, Ho. (2)
Milne, A. (Cardiff C): 1960 v W. (1)
Mitchell, I. (Dundee U): 1967 v W, E. (2)
Morgan, W. (Burnley): 1968 v E. (1)
Miller, W. (Aberdeen): 1974 v E; 1975 v E, W, Se; 1976 v D, R, W, Ho (2). (9)
Morrison, R. (Aberdeen): 1956 v E. (1)
Moncur, R. (Newcastle U): 1968 v E. (1)
Munro, F. (Wolverhampton W): 1970 v F, E, W (sub), 1971 v W. (4)
Murdoch, R. (Celtic): 1964 v E. (1)
Murray, D. (Cardiff C): 1965 v E. (1)
Murray, G. (Motherwell): 1964 v F; 1965 v W, E. (3)
Murray, M. (Rangers): 1956 v E; 1957 v E. (2)
Murray, S. (Dundee): 1968 v E. (1)

Narey, D. (Dundee U): 1975 v R; 1976 v D (2), (3)
Nicol, R. (Hibernian): 1956 v E, 1958 v Ho. (2)

Ogston, J. (Aberdeen): 1961 v E; 1962 v W, E. (3)
O'Hara, E. (Falkirk): 1958 v Ho (2), E. (3)
O'Hare, J. (Derby Co): 1970 v F, E. W. (3)
Oliver, J. (Hearts): 1971 v W (sub). (1)

Parker, A. (Falkirk): 1955 v E; 1956 v E; 1957 v E; 1958 v Ho (2), E. (6)
Parlane, D. (Rangers): 1973 v E (sub), W; 1974 v W; 1975 v E, W. (5)
Pearson, J. (St Johnstone): 1974 v W, E; 1975 (with Everton) v W (sub), Se, R; 1976 v D. (6)
Penman, A. (Dundee): 1960 v Bel; 1962 v W; 1964 v W; 1965 v E. (4)
Pettigrew, W. (Aberdeen): 1975 v Se, R; 1976 v D (2), R, W, Ho. (7)
Phillip, I. (Crystal Palace): 1973 v E (1)

Plenderleith, J. (Hibernian): 1957 v E; 1958 v Ho. (2), E; 1960 v W. (5)
Prentice, R. (Hearts): 1974 v W; 1976 v D (sub), R. (3)
Price, W. (Airdrieonians): 1956 v E; 1958 v Ho. (2)
Provan, D. (Rangers): 1964 v E. (1)
Purdie, I. (Aberdeen): 1975 v E (sub)

Rae, I. (Falkirk): 1956 v E. (1)
Reilly, F. (Dunfermline Ath): 1957 v E. (1)
Riddell, I. (St Mirren): 1960 v E; 1961 v E. (2)
Robb, D. (Aberdeen): 1970 v F, W; 1971 v E. (3)
Roberts, R. (Motherwell): 1962 v W. (1)
Robertson, H. (Dundee): 1962 v W. (1)
Robertson, J. (St Mirren): 1964 v W; (with Tottenham H): 1964 v F; 1965 v W; 1968 v E. (4)
Robinson, R. (Dundee): 1974 v W. (1)
Rough, A. (Partick T): 1973 v E; 1975 v Se, R; 1976 v D. (2), R, W, Ho. (2), (9)

St John, I. (Motherwell): 1960 v E, Bel. (2)
Scott, A. (Rangers): 1958 v E. (1)
Sharkey, D. (Sunderland): 1964 v F, E. (2)
Shevlane, C. (Hearts): 1964 v W, F, E; 1965 v W. (4)
Slater, R. (Falkirk): 1959 v W. (1)
Smith, D. (Aberdeen): 1963 v W; 1964 v W. (2)
Smith, G. (Kilmarnock): 1975 v W, Se, R (sub); 1976 v W (sub) (4)
Smith, G. (St Johnstone): 1975 v R; 1976 v D. (2), R. (4)

Smith, J. (Aberdeen): 1967 v E. (1)
Smith, J. (Aberdeen): 1976 v Ho. (1)
Sneddon, D. (Dundee): 1959 v W. (1)
Souness, G. (Middlesbrough): 1974 v E; 1976 v Ho. (2)
Stanton, P. (Hibernian): 1967 v W, E; 1968 v E. (3)
Stein, C. (Hibernian): 1968 v E. (1)
Stewart, D. (Ayr U): 1970 v W. (1)
Stewart, J. (Kilmarnock): 1973 v W; 1974 v W, E; 1975 v E; 1976 v W (sub) (5)
Sullivan, D. (Clyde): 1975 v E, W (sub) (2)

Thomson, A. (Hearts): 1970 v F, E, W. (3)
Thomson, J. (Hearts): 1958 v E; 1960 v Bel. (2)
Tinney, H. (Partick T): 1967 v W, E. (2)

Ure, J. F. (Dundee): 1961 v E. (1)

Wallace, J. (Dunfermline Ath): 1974 v W. (1)
Walsh, J. (Celtic): 1955 v E. (1)
Weir, A. (Motherwell): 1960 v E, Bel, W. (3)
White, J. (Tottenham H): 1960 v W. (1)
Whyte, J. (Aberdeen): 1967 v W, E. (2)
Wilson, D. (Rangers): 1959 v W. (1)
Wilson, R. (WBA): 1970 v W. (1)
Wishart, R. (Aberdeen): 1955 v E; 1956 v E. (2)

Young, A. (Hearts): 1956 v E; 1957 v E; 1958 v E, Ho; 1959 v W; 1960 v W. (6)
Young, I. (Celtic): 1965 v E. (1)
Young, Q. (Ayr U): 1971 v E. (1)
Young, W. (Aberdeen): 1972 v W; 1973 v E; 1975 v W, R; 1976 v D.

WALES

Aitken, P. (Bristol R): 1975 v E, S; 1976 v S (sub). (3)
Aizlewood, S. (Newport Co): 1972 v E, S; 1973 v S; 1974 v E; 1976 v S. (5)

Baker, C. (Cardiff C): 1958. (1)
Baker, T. (Plymouth Arg): 1958 v E; 1959 v S. (2)
Barry, M. (Carlisle U): 1975 v E (sub). (1)
Blore, R. (Southport): 1962 v S; (with Blackburn R) 1965 v E, S, Ni. (4)
Burton, O. (Newport Co): 1961 v E; (with Norwich C), 1963 v S, Ni; (with Newcastle U) 1965 v E, S. (5)

Cartwright, L. (Coventry C): 1974 v S; 1975 v E, S; 1976 v S. (4)
Charles, M. (Swansea T): 1958 v E. (1)
Coldrick, G. (Cardiff C): 1967 v S; 1968 v E. (2)
Collins, J. (Portsmouth): 1967 v E, Ni; (with Tottenham) 1968 v E, Ni; 1969 v E; (with Portsmouth) 1972 v E, S. (7)
Curtis, A. (Swansea C): 1976 v S (sub) (1)

Davies, C. (Charlton Ath): 1971 v E, S; 1972 v E, S (sub) (4)
Davies, D. (Swansea C): 1971 v E; (with Everton) S; 1975 v E. (3)
Davies, D. L. (Cardiff C): 1967 v E. (1)
Davies, R. (Norwich C): 1964 v S, Ni; 1965 v S. (3)
Davies, W. (Bolton W): 1963 v S; 1964 v E; 1965 v S, Ni. (4)
Davis, G. (Wrexham): 1970 v E, S; 1971 v E, S. (4)
Deacy, N. (PSV Eindhoven): 1976 v S. (1)
Derrett, S. (Cardiff C): 1970 v E; 1971 v E, S. (3)
Draper, D. (Swansea C): 1965 v E. (1)
Durban, A. (Cardiff C): 1963 v Ni; (with Derby Co) 1964 v E, S, Ni. (4)
Dwyer, P. (Cardiff C): 1974 v E, S; 1975 v E, S; 1976 v S. (5)

Edwards, M. (Bolton W): 1958 v E; 1959 v S. (2)
Edwards, N. (Chester): 1973 v E, S; 1974 v E. (3)
Edwards, T. (Charlton Ath): 1958 v E; 1959 v S, Ni. (2)
Emmanuel, G. (Birmingham C): 1975 v S. (1)
England, M. (Blackburn R): 1960 v S; 1961 v E; 1962 v S, Ni; 1963 v Ni; 1964 v E, S, Ni; 1965 v E, S, Ni. (11)

Evans, B. C. (Swansea T): 1965 v E, S. (2)
Evans, M. (QPR): 1973 v E; 1974 v S. (2)
Evans, M. (Wrexham): 1967 v Ni; 1970 v E. (2)
Evans, R. (Swansea T): 1963 v Ni; 1964 v E, Ni. (3)

Flynn, B. (Burnley): 1975 v E, S. (2)
Fox, A. (Wrexham): 1959 v S. (1)

Gammon, S. (Cardiff C): 1960 v S; 1962 v Ni. (2)
Green, C. (Everton): 1962 v S, Ni; 1963 v S (with Birmingham C) Ni; 1964 v E, S; 1965 v Ni. (7)
Griffiths, A. (Arsenal): 1961 v E (sub) 1962 v Ni; 1963 v S; (with Wrexham) 1964
Griffiths, C. (Manchester U): 1974 v E, S. (2)
Godfrey, B. (Scunthorpe U): 1962 v Ni. (1)
Gwyther, D. (Swansea C): 1972 v E, S. (2)

Harris, C. (Leeds U): 1976 v S. (1)
Hawkins, D. (Leeds U): 1976 v S, Ni; 1968 v E, Ni; 1969 v E; (with Shrewsbury T) 1970 v S. (6)
Hennessey, T. (Birmingham C): 1962 v Ni; 1963 v Ni; 1964 v S, Ni; 1965 v E, S. (6)
Hole, B. (Cardiff C): 1961 v S; 1962 v S; 1963 v S; 1965 v S, Ni. (5)
Hollins, D. (Brighton): 1960 v S; 1961 v E. (2)
Hopkins, M. (Tottenham H): 1958 v E. (1)
Hubbard, T. (Swindon T): 1973 v S. (sub); 1974 v E. (2)
Hughes, B. (Swansea T): 1960 v S; 1961 v E. (2)
Hughes, J. (Blackpool): 1971 v E (sub) S. (2)
Humphreys, G. (Everton): 1965 v Ni; 1967 v E, S, Ni; 1969 v E. (5)

James, G. (Blackpool): 1965 v E, Ni. (2)
James, L. (Burnley): 1972 v E, S; 1973 v E, S; 1974 v E; 1975 v E, S. (7)
John, D. (Cardiff C): 1965 v S. (1)
Johnson, J. (Crystal Palace): 1974 v S; 1976 v S. (2)
Johnson, M. (Swansea T): 1963 v S; 1964 v E. (2)
Jones, A. (Swansea T): 1967 v E. (1)
Jones, B. (Bristol R) 1971 v E. (1)
Jones, B. (Swansea T): 1961 v E; 1962 v S, Ni; 1963 v S, Ni; 1964 v E, Ni; (with Plymouth Arg) 1965 v S. (8)
Jones, C. (Tottenham H): 1958 v E. (1)
Jones, D. (Bournemouth): 1973 v S; 1974 v E, S. (4)

Jones, F. (Brighton): 1959 v S; (with Swindon) 1961 v E. (2)
Jones, J. (Wrexham): 1974 v S; 1975 v E, S (with Liverpool); 1976 v S. (4)
Jones, K. (Cardiff C): 1958 v E. (1)
Jones, W. (Bristol R): 1968 v E, Ni; 1969 v E; 1970 v S; 1971 v E, S. (6)
Jones, T. L. (Wrexham): 1963 v S. (1)

Kryzwicki, R. (WBA): 1967 v E, S; 1970 v S. (3)

Leek, K. (Northampton T): 1958 v E. (1)
Letheran, G. (Leeds U): 1976 v S. (1)
Lewis, B. (Cardiff C): 1965 v Ni; 1967 v E, S; 1968 v E; (with Watford) 1968 v Ni. (5)
Lewis, J. (Grimsby T): 1976 . (1)
Llewellyn, D. (West Ham U): 1972 v S. (1)
Lloyd, B. (Southend U): 1970 v E, S. (2)
Lucas, A. (Wrexham): 1967 v S. (1)
Lucas, M. (Orient): 1962 v S.

Mahoney, J. (Crewe Alex): 1967 v Ni; (with Stoke C) 1969 v E; 1970 v E. (3)
Mielczarek, R. (Huddersfield T): 1968 v E, Ni. (2)
Millington, T. (WBA): 1962 v S, Ni; 1963 v S, Ni. (4)
Moore, G. (Cardiff C): 1960 v S; 1961 v E; 1962 v S; (with Chelsea) 1962 v Ni; 1963 v S, Ni; (with Manchester U) 1964 v E,S, Ni. (9)
Morgan, R. (Cardiff): 1970 v S. (1)
Morgans, K. (Manchester U): 1959 v S; 1960 v S. (2)

Nurse, M. (Swansea T): 1960 v S; 1961 v E. (2)

Orritt, B. (Birmingham C): 1958 v E; 1959 v S; 1960 v S. (3)
O'Sullivan, P. (Brighton): 1971 v S (sub), 1972 v E, S; 1973 v E, S; 1976 v S. (6)

Page, M. (Blackburn C): 1976 v E, S; 1968 v Ni; 1969 v E; 1970 v E, S. (6)
Parton, J. (Burnley): 1972 v E, S; 1974 v E. (3)
Pearson, D.; 1970 v S. (1)
Phillips, J. (Chelsea): 1973 v E, S; 1974 v S; 1975 v S. (4)
Phillips, L. (Cardiff C): 1971 v S; 1972 v S; 1973 v E, S (with Aston Villa). (4)
Powell, D. (Wrexham): 1967 v E, Ni; 1968 v E, Ni. (4)
Price, P. (Peterborough U): 1970 v E, S; 1971 v E, S. (4)
Prince, F. (Bristol R): 1971 v S; 1972 v E, S; 1973 v E. (4)
Pugh, D. (Newport Co): 1967 v E, S. (2)

Randell, C. (Plymouth Arg): 1975 v E. (1)

Rankmore, F. (Cardiff C): 1962 v S, Ni. (2)
Rees, R. (Coventry C): 1963 v S, Ni; 1964 v E, S, Ni; 1965 v E, Ni. (7)
Rodrigues, P. (Cardiff C): 1964 v S, Ni; 1964 v E, S, Ni. (5)
Roberts, D. (Oxford U): 1973 v E, S; 1975 v E, (with Hull C) S. (4)
Roberts, J. (Swansea T): 1967 v Ni; 1968 v E; (with Northampton T) 1968 v Ni (sub); 1969 v E; 1970 v E. (5)
Roberts, P. (Bristol R): 1971 v E, S; 1972 v E, S; 1973 v E, S. (6)
Roberts, R. (Wrexham): 1962 v S, Ni. (2)
Rouse, V. (Crystal Palace): 1959 v S. (1)
Rowland, J. (Newport Co): 1959 v S. (1)
Ryan, J. (Charlton Ath): 1965 v E. (1)

Screen, A. L. (Swansea C): 1971 v S (sub). (1)
Screen, W. (Swansea T): 1968 v Ni; 1961 v E. (2)
Sear, C. (Manchester C): 1959 v S; 1960 v S. (2)
Showers, J. (Cardiff C): 1973 v E, S; 1974 v E, S; 1975 v E, S. (6)
Simpkins, K. (Hartlepools U): 1967 v S. (1)
Smallman, D. (Wrexham): 1973 v E; 1974 v E, S, 1975 v E, (with Everton) S. (5)
Sprake, G. (Leeds U): 1964 v E, S, Ni; 1965 v E, Ni. (5)
Stephens, J. (Hull C): 1958 v E. (1)
Summerhayes, D. (Cardiff C): 1967 v S. (1)

Thomas, G. (Swansea T): 1968 v E; 1971 v E, S. (3)
Thomas, M. (Wrexham): 1976 v S (sub). (1)
Thomas, J. (Newport Co): 1967 v Ni. (1)
Thomas, R. (Swindon T): 1967 v S, Ni; 1968 v Ni; 1969 v E; 1970 v E, S. (6)
Todd, K. H. (Swansea T): 1963 v Ni. (1)
Toshack, J. (Cardiff C): 1967 v E (with Liverpool) 1971 v E; 1972 v E. (3)

Vernon, R. (Blackburn R): 1959 v S. (2)
Villars, A. (Cardiff C): 1974 v E, S. (2)

Walker, M. (York C): 1967 v Ni; 1968 v E, Ni. (3) (Watford): 1969 v E. (4)
Walley, T. (Arsenal): 1967 v E, Ni; (with Watford) 1968 v E, Ni. (4)
Williams, D. (Bristol R): 1967 v S. (1)
Williams, G. (Swansea T): 1960 v S. (1)
Williams, G. E. (WBA): 1960 v S; 1961 v E. (2)
Williams, H. (Swansea T): 1961 v E; 1962 v S; 1964 v S, E, Ni. (5)

Yorath, T. (Leeds U): 1969 v E; 1970 v E, S; 1971 v E; 1972 v E, S; 1973 v E. (7)
Young, G. (Newport Co): 1970 v E. (1)

UNDER-21 APPEARANCES 1976-79

ENGLAND

Anderson, V. A. (Nottingham F), 1978 v I (1)
Bailey, G. R. (Manchester U), 1979 v W, Bul (2)
Barnes, P. S. (Manchester C), 1977 v W (sub), S, Fi, N; 1978 v N, Fi, I (2), Y (9)
Bertschin, K. E. (Birmingham C), 1977 v S; 1978 v Y (2) (3)
Blissett, L. L. (Watford), 1979 v W, Bul (sub), Se (3)
Bradshaw, P. W. (Wolverhampton W), 1977 v W, S; 1978 v Fi, Y (4)
Butcher, T. I. (Ipswich T) 1979 v Se (1)

Corrigan, J. T. (Manchester C) 1978 v I (2), Y (3)
Cowans, G. S. (Aston Villa), 1979 v W, Se (2)
Cunningham, L. (WBA), 1977 v S, Fi, N (sub); 1978 v N, Fi, I (6)

Daniel, P. W. (Hull C), 1977 v S, Fi, N; 1978 v Fi, I, Y (2) (7)
Deehan, J. M. (Aston Villa), 1977 v N; 1978 v N, Fi, I; 1979 v Bul, Se (sub) (6)

Futcher, P. (Luton T), 1977 v W, S, Fi, N; (Manchester C), 1978 v N, Fi, I (2), Y (2); 1979 v D (11)
Fairclough, D. (Liverpool), 1977 v W (1)

Gilbert, W. A. (C Palace), 1979 v W, Bul (2)

Haigh, P. (Hull C), 1977 v N (sub) (1)
Hazell, R. J. (Wolverhampton W), 1979 v D (1)
Hinshelwood, P. A. (C Palace), 1978 v N (1)
Hoddle, G. (Tottenham H), 1977 v W (sub); 1978 v Fi (sub), I (2), Y; 1979 v D, W, Bul (8)

Jones, D. R. (Everton), 1977 v W (1)
Jones, C. H. (Tottenham H), 1978 v Y (sub) (1)

Keegan, G. A. (Manchester C), 1977 v W (1)
King, A. E. (Everton), 1977 v W; 1978 v Y (2)

Langley, T. W. (Chelsea), 1978 v I (sub) (1)

Middleton, J. (Nottingham F), 1977 v Fi, N; (Derby Co.), 1978 v N (3)

Osman, R. C. (Ipswich T), 1979 v W (sub), Se (2)
Owen, G. A. (Manchester C), 1977 v S, Fi, N; 1978 v N, Fi, I (2), Y; 1979 v D, W, (WBA), Bul, Se (sub) (12)

Parkes, P. B. F. (QPR), 1979 v D (1)
Peach, D. S. (Southampton), 1977 v S, Fi, N; 1978 v N, I (2), Y (2) (8)

Reeves, K. P. (Norwich C), 1978 v I, Y (2); 1979 v N, W, Bul, Se (7)
Regis, C. (WBA), 1979 v D, Bul, Se (3)
Reid, P. (Bolton W), 1977 v S, Fi, N; 1978 v Fi, I, Y (6)
Richards, J. P. (Wolverhampton W), 1977 v Fi, N (2)
Rix, G. (Arsenal), 1978 v Fi (sub), Y; 1979 v D, Se (4)
Robson, B. (WBA), 1979 v W, Bul (sub), Se (3)
Rowell, G. (Sunderland), 1977 v Fi (1)

Sansom, K. G. (C Palace), 1979 v D, W, Bul, Se (4)
Sims, S. (Leicester C), 1977 v W, S, Fi, N; 1978 v N, Fi, I (2), Y (2) (10)
Statham, D. J. (WBA), 1978 v Fi; 1979 v W, Bul, Se (4)
Sunderland, A. (Wolverhampton W), 1977 v W (1)
Swindlehurst, D. (C Palace), 1977 v W (1)

Talbot, B. (Ipswich T), 1977 v W (1)

Ward, P. D. (Brighton), 1978 v N (1)
Wilkins, R. C. (Chelsea), 1977 v W (1)
Williams, S. C. (Southampton), 1977 v S, Fi, N; 1978 v N, I (sub), I, Y (2); 1979 v D, Bul, Se (sub) (11)
Woodcock, A. S. (Nottingham F), 1978 v Fi, I (2)
Woods, C. C. E. (Nottingham F), 1979 v W (sub), Se (2)
Wright, W. (Everton), 1979 v D, W, Bul (3)

SCOTLAND

Aitken, R. (Celtic), 1977 v Cz, W, Sw; 1978 v Cz, W; 1979 v P, N (2) (8)
Albiston, A. (Manchester U), 1977 v Cz, W, Sw; 1978 v Sw, Cz (5)

Bannon, E. J. P. (Hearts), 1979 v US, (Chelsea), P, N (2) (4)
Brazil, A. (Hibernian), 1978 v W (1)
Brazil, A. (Ipswich T), 1979 v N (2)
Burley, G. E. (Ipswich T), 1977 v Cz, W, Sw; 1978 v Sw, Cz (5)
Burns, T. (Celtic), 1977 v Cz, W, E; 1978 v Sw (4)

Casey, J. (Celtic), 1978 v W (1)
Clark, R. (Aberdeen), 1977 v Cz, W, Sw (3)
Cooper, D. (Clyde), 1977 v Cz, W, Sw, E; (Rangers), 1978 v Sw, Cz (6)
Craig, T. (Newcastle U), 1977 v E (1)

Dawson, A. (Rangers), 1979 v P, N (2) (3)
Dodds, D. (Dundee U), 1978 v W (1)

Ferguson, R. (Hamilton A), 1977 v E (1)
Fitzpatrick, A. (St Mirren), 1977 v W (sub), Sw (sub), E; 1978 v Sw, Cz (5)

Gillespie, G. (Coventry C), 1979 v US (1)

Hartford, R. A. (Manchester C), 1977 v Sw (1)

Jardine, I. (Kilmarnock), 1979 v US (1)

Lindsey, J. (Motherwell), 1979 v US (1)

MacLeod, A. (Hibernian), 1979 v P, N (2) (3)
MacLeod, M. (Dumbarton), 1979 v US, (Celtic), P (sub) N (2) (4)
McGarvey, F. (St Mirren), 1977 v E; 1978 v Cz (2)
McLeish, A. (Aberdeen), 1978 v W; 1979 v US (2)
McNab, N. (Tottenham H), 1978 v W (1)
McNichol, J. (Brentford), 1979 v P, N (2) (3)
McNiven, D. (Leeds U), 1977 v Cz, W (sub), Sw (sub) (3)
Melrose, J. (Partick T), 1977 v Sw; 1979 v US, P, N (2) (5)
Miller, W. (Aberdeen), 1978 v Sw, Cz (2)
Muir, L. (Hibernian), 1977 v Cz (sub) (1)
McCluskey, G. (Celtic), 1979 v US, P (2)

Narey, D. (Dundee U), 1977 v Cz, Sw; 1978 v Sw, Cz (4)

Orr, N. (Morton), 1978 v W (sub); 1979 v US, P, N (2) (5)

Parlane, D. (Rangers), 1977 v W (1)
Payne, G. (Dundee U), 1978 v Sw, Cz, W (3)
Provan, D. (Kilmarnock), 1977 v Cz (sub) (1)

Reid, R. (St Mirren), 1977 v W, Sw, E (3)
Robertson, C. (Rangers), 1977 v E (sub) (1)
Ross, T. W. (Arsenal), 1977 v W (1)
Russell, R. (Rangers), 1978 v W (1)

Sinclair, G. (Dumbarton), 1977 v E (1)
Smith, G. (Rangers), 1978 v W (1)
Sneddon, A. (Celtic), 1979 v US (1)
Stanton, P. (Hibernian), 1977 v Cz (1)
Stevens, G. (Motherwell), 1977 v E (1)
Stewart, J. (Kilmarnock), 1978 v Sw, Cz; (Middlesbrough), 1979 v P (3)

Stewart, R. (Dundee U), 1979 v P, N (2) (3)
Sturrock, P. (Dundee U), 1977 v Cz, W, Sw, E; 1978 v Sw, Cz (6)

Thomson, W. (Partick T), 1977 v E (sub); 1978 v W; (St Mirren), 1979 v US, N (2) (5)

Wallace, I. (Coventry C), 1978 v Sw (1)
Wark, J. (Ipswich T), 1977 v Cz, W, Sw; 1978 v W; 1979 v P (5)
Watson, K. (Rangers), 1977 v E; 1978 v Sw (sub) (2)

WALES

Aizlewood, M. (Luton T), 1979 v E (1)

Bater, P. T. (Bristol R), 1977 v E, S (2)

Cegielski, W. (Wrexham), 1977 v E (sub), S (2)
Charles, J. M. (Swansea C), 1979 v E (1)
Clark, J. (Manchester U), 1978 v S; (Derby Co), 1979 v E (2)
Curtis, A. T. (Swansea C), 1977 v E (1)

Davies, I. C. (Norwich C), 1978 v S (sub) (1)
Deacy, N. (PSV Eindhoven), 1977 v S (1)
Doyle, S. C. (Preston NE), 1979 v E (sub) (1)
Dwyer, P. J. (Cardiff C), 1979 v E (1)

Edwards, R. I. (Chester), 1977 v S; 1978 v W (2)
Evans, A. (Bristol R), 1977 v E (1)

Giles, D. C. (Cardiff C), 1977 v S; 1978 v S (2)

Hughes, W. (WBA), 1977 v E, S; 1978 v S (3)

James, R. M. (Swansea C), 1977 v E, S; 1978 v S (3)
Jones, V. (Bristol R), 1979 v E (1)

Kendall, M. (Tottenham H), 1978 v S (1)

Letheran, G. (Leeds U), 1977 v E, S (2)
Lowndes, S. R. (Newport Co), 1979 v E (1)

Nardiello, D. (Coventry C), 1978 v S (1)
Nicholas, P. (C Palace), 1978 v S; 1979 v E (2)

Phillips, L. (Swansea C), 1979 v E (1)
Pontin, K. (Cardiff C), 1978 v S (1)

Roberts, J. G. (Wrexham), 1977 v E (1)

Sayer, P. A. (Cardiff C), 1977 v E, S (2)
Stevenson, W. B. (Leeds U), 1977 v E, S; 1978 v S (3)

Martin, R. Thomas (Bristol R), 1979 v E (1)
Mickey, R. Thomas (Wrexham), 1977 v E; 1978 v S (2)
Tibbott, L. (Ipswich T), 1977 v E, S (2)
Thomas, D. G. (Leeds U), 1977 v E; 1979 v E (2)

Walsh, I. P. (C Palace), 1979 v E (1)

NORTHERN IRELAND

Team v Eire 1978; Johnston; Nicholl, Hayes, Moreland, O'Neill, Donaghy, Sloan (sub), Harley, Brotherston, Blackledge, Hamilton, McCreery.

'B' INTERNATIONAL MATCHES

v AUSTRIA
			England	Austria
*1979 June	12	Klagenfurt	1	0

v CZECHOSLOVAKIA
			England	Czechoslovakia
1978 Nov.	28	Prague	1	0

v FINLAND
			England	Finland
1949 May	15	Helsinki	4	0

v FRANCE
			England	France
1952 May	22	Le Havre	1	7

v WEST GERMANY
			England	West Germany
1954 Mar.	24	Gelsenkirchen	4	0
1955 Mar.	23	Sheffield	1	1
1978 Feb.	21	Augsburg	1	2

v ITALY
			England	Italy
1950 May	11	Milan	0	5

v LUXEMBOURG
			England	Luxembourg
1950 May	21	Luxembourg	2	1

v MALAYSIA B
			England	Malaysia
1978 May	30	Kuala Lumpur	1	1

*Abandoned after an hour's play.

v NETHERLANDS
			England	Netherlands
1949 May	18	Amsterdam	4	0
1950 Feb.	22	Newcastle	1	0
1950 Mar.	17	Amsterdam	0	3
1952 Mar.	26	Amsterdam	1	0

v NEW ZEALAND
			England	New Zealand
1978 June	7	Christchurch	4	0
1978 June	11	Wellington	3	1
1978 June	14	Auckland	4	0

v SCOTLAND
			England	Scotland
1953 Mar.	11	Edinburgh	2	2
1954 Mar.	3	Sunderland	1	1
1956 Feb.	29	Dundee	2	2
1957 Feb.	6	Birmingham	4	1

v SWITZERLAND
			England	Switzerland
1950 Jan.	18	Sheffield	5	0
1954 May	22	Basle	0	2
1956 Mar.	21	Southampton	4	1

v YUGOSLAVIA
			England	Yugoslavia
1954 May	16	Lubljana	1	2
1955 Oct.	19	Manchester	5	1

UNOFFICIAL INTERNATIONAL MATCHES

v SCOTLAND
Year Date	Venue	England	Scotland
D1902 April 5	Glasgow	1	1
†1919 April 26	Everton	2	2
†1919 May 3	Glasgow	4	3
J1935 Aug. 21	Glasgow	2	4
*1939 Dec. 2	Newcastle	2	1
*1940 May 11	Glasgow	1	1
*1941 Feb. 8	Newcastle	2	3
*1941 May 3	Glasgow	3	1
*1941 Oct. 4	Wembley	2	0
*1942 Jan. 17	Wembley	3	0
*1942 April 18	Glasgow	4	5
*1942 Oct. 10	Wembley	0	0
*1943 April 17	Glasgow	4	0
*1943 Oct. 16	Manchester	8	0
*1944 Feb. 19	Wembley	6	2
*1944 April 22	Glasgow	3	2
*1944 Oct. 14	Wembley	6	2
*1945 Feb. 3	Aston Villa	3	2
*1945 April 14	Glasgow	6	1
†1946 April 13	Glasgow	0	1

v SWITZERLAND
		England	Switzerland
†1946 May 11	Chelsea	4	1

v FRANCE
		England	France
*1945 May 26	Wembley	2	2

v WALES
Year Date	Venue	England	Wales
†1919 Oct. 11	Cardiff	1	2
†1919 Oct. 18	Stoke	2	0
*1939 Nov. 11	Cardiff	1	1
*1939 Nov. 18	Wrexham	3	2
*1940 April 13	Wembley	0	1
*1941 April 26	Nottingham	4	1
*1941 June 7	Cardiff	3	2
*1941 Oct. 25	Birmingham	2	1
*1942 May 9	Cardiff	0	1
*1942 Oct. 24	Wolverhampton	1	2
*1943 Feb. 27	Wembley	5	3
*1943 May 8	Cardiff	1	1
*1943 Sept. 25	Wembley	8	3
*1944 May 6	Cardiff	2	0
*1944 Sept. 16	Liverpool	2	2
*1945 May 5	Cardiff	3	2
†1945 Oct. 20	West Bromwich	0	1

v IRELAND
		England	Ireland
†1945 Sept. 15	Belfast	1	0

v BELGIUM
		England	Belgium
†1946 Jan. 19	Wembley	2	0

v TEAM AMERICA
		England	Team America
B1976 May 30	Philadelphia	3	1

DDeclared unofficial owing to disaster at ground. †Victory. JJubilee. *War-time. BAmerican Bicentennial Tournament.

UEFA YOUTH TOURNAMENT 1978-79

Group A

				P	W	D	L	F	A	Pts.
France v Belgium	5-1									
Holland v Switzerland	2-1									
France v Switzerland	1-1	France		3	2	1	—	8	3	5
Belgium v Holland	2-1	Belgium		3	2	—	1	7	7	4
France v Holland	2-1	Holland		3	1	—	2	4	5	2
Belgium v Switzerland	4-1	Switzerland		3	—	1	2	3	7	1

Group B

				P	W	D	L	F	A	Pts.
West Germany v Malta	5-0									
England v Czechoslovakia	3-0									
England v Malta	3-0	England		3	3	—	—	8	0	6
Czechoslovakia v West Germany	2-0	Czechoslovakia		3	2	—	1	8	3	4
England v West Germany	2-0	West Germany		3	1	—	2	5	4	2
Czechoslovakia v Malta	6-0	Malta		3	—	—	3	0	14	0

Group C

				P	W	D	L	F	A	Pts.
Austria v Norway	2-0									
Yugoslavia v Hungary	2-0									
Yugoslavia v Austria	2-1	Yugoslavia		3	3	—	—	7	2	6
Hungary v Norway	2-1	Hungary		3	2	—	1	5	3	4
Yugoslavia v Norway	3-1	Austria		3	1	—	2	3	5	2
Hungary v Austria	3-0	Norway		3	—	—	3	2	7	0

Group D

				P	W	D	L	F	A	Pts.
Scotland v Poland	3-2									
Bulgaria v Denmark	1-0									
Denmark v Poland	2-1	Bulgaria		3	3	—	—	7	1	6
Bulgaria v Scotland	2-0	Scotland		3	2	—	1	5	5	4
Bulgaria v Poland	4-1	Denmark		3	1	—	2	3	4	2
Scotland v Denmark	2-1	Poland		3	—	—	3	4	9	0

Semi-Final

Yugoslavia v France	3-0
Bulgaria v England	1-0

Final

Yugoslavia v Bulgaria	1-0

Third Place Play-Off

England v France (England won on penalties) 0-0

UEFA YOUTH TOURNAMENT FINALS 1948–79

Year	Winners		Runners-up		Venue
1948	England	3	Netherlands	2	London
1949	France	4	Netherlands	1	Rotterdam
1950	Austria	3	France	2	Vienna
1951	Yugoslavia	3	Austria	2	Cannes
1952	*Spain	0	Belgium	0	Barcelona
1953	Hungary	2	Yugoslavia	0	Brussels
1954	*Spain	2	West Germany	2	Cologne
1955-56	Played in groups only				
1957	Austria	3	Spain	2	Madrid
1958	Italy	1	England	0	Luxembourg
1959	Bulgaria	1	Italy	0	Sofia
1960	Hungary	2	Rumania	1	Vienna
1961	Portugal	4	Poland	0	Lisbon
1962	Rumania	4	Yugoslavia	1	Bucharest
1963	England	4	Northern Ireland	0	London
1964	England	4	Spain	0	Amsterdam
1965	East Germany	3	England	2	Essen
1966	†Italy	0	USSR	0	Belgrade
1967	U.S.S.R.	1	England	0	Istanbul
1968	Czechoslovakia	2	France	1	Cannes
1969	*Bulgaria	1	East Germany	1	Leipzig
1970	*East Germany	1	Holland	1	Glasgow
1971	England	3	Portugal	0	Prague
1972	England	2	West Germany	0	Barcelona
1973	England	3	East Germany	2	Florence
1974	Bulgaria	1	Yugoslavia	0	Malmoe
1975	England	1	Finland	0	Berne
1976	U.S.S.R.	1	Hungary	0	Budapest
1977	Belgium	2	Bulgaria	1	Brussels
1978	Russia	3	Yugoslavia	0	Krakow
1979	Yugoslavia	1	Bulgaria	0	Vienna

* Won on toss of a coin.   † Joint holders.

ENGLISH YOUTH INTERNATIONAL MATCHES 1978-79

Youth Tournament Las Palmas
8 October 1978
Las Palmas Select 2
England XI 4 (*Allen* 3, *Falco*) 2000
England: Lukic (Cherry); Falconer (Hamilton), Sisman, Harper (Canavan), Hindmarch, McCall, Mills (Quow), Proctor, Allen (C), Falco (Russell) Moss.

10 October 1978
USSR 0
England 1 (*Falco*) 3000
England: Cherry; Hamilton, Harper, Hindmarch, Sisman, Mills, Proctor, McCall, Allen (C), Falco, Moss.

12 October 1978
Las Palmas 0
England XI 3 (*Falco* 2, *Allen*) 5000
England: Cherry; Hamilton, Sisman, Harper, Hindmarch, Proctor, McCall, Mills, Allen (C), Falco, Russell (Moss)

Youth Tournament Monaco
13 November 1978
Portugal 0
England 2 (*Allen, Falco*) 3000
England: Lukic; Sisman, Ormsby, Hindmarch, Watson, Allen (C), Hamilton, Fillery, Jenkins, Shaw, Falco.

15 November 1978
Yugoslavia 1
England 1 (*Hindmarch*) 3000
England: Lukic; Hamilton, Ormsby, Hindmarch, Watson, Allen (C), (Clarke), Klug, McCall, Fillery, Shaw, Falco.

17 November 1978
Spain 1
England 1 (*Hamilton*) 2500
England: Lukic; Hamilton, Watson, Hindmarch, Ormsby, Allen (C) (Jenkins), Klug, McCall, Clarke, Shaw, Falco.

19 November 1978
Italy 2
England 1 (*Shaw*) 6000
England: Cherry; Ormsby, Hindmarch, Canavan, Sisman (Watson), Hamilton, Klug, Fillery (McCall), Jenkins, Shaw, Clarke.

Friendly
17 January 1979
Belgium 0 (in Brussels)
England 4 (*Clarke* 2, *Carter, McDermott*) 1000
England: Lukic (Knight); James, Dennis (Burke, D), Mackenzie, Bruce, Ormsby, Mills (Allen, P), Clarke, Allen C, (Fashanu), Carter, Burke (S), (McDermott)

International Youth Tournament Qualifying Competition
28 February 1979
Italy 0
England 1 (*Carter*) (in Rome) 2000
England: Knight; James, Dennis, Mackenzie, Bruce, Ormsby, Allen P, Carter, Allen C, Burke D, Burke S.

4 April 1979
England 2
Italy 0 (at Villa Park) 2777
England: Lukic; James, Dennis, Mackenzie, Bruce, Ormsby, Paul, McDermott (Fashanu), Carter, Allen P, Burke S (Gibson).

International Youth Tournament in Austria
24 May 1979
England 3 (*McDermott* 2, *Shaw*)
Czechoslovakia 0 (at Bischofshofen) 3000
England: Lukic; James, Dennis, Bruce, Ormsby, Paul (Proctor), Mackenzie, Allen P, Burke S, Shaw, McDermott.

26 May 1979
England 3 (*Allen C, Shaw, Bruce*)
Malta 0 (at Salzburg-Lehen) 2500
England: Knight; James, Dennis, Ormsby (Banfield), Bruce, Proctor, Mackenzie, Allen P, McDermott (Buchanan), Allen C, Shaw.

28 May 1979
England 2 (*Shaw, McDermott*)
West Germany 0 (at Salzburg-Itzling) 2500
England: Lukic; James, Dennis, Bruce, Ormsby, Proctor, Mackenzie, Allen P, Burke S (Buchanan), Shaw (Allen C), McDermott.

31 May 1979
England 0
Bulgaria 1 (at Sudstadt) 1500
England: Lukic; James, Dennis, Bruce, Ormsby, Proctor (Banfield), Mackenzie, Allen P, Allen C, Shaw, McDermott (Buchanan).

2 June 1979
England 0
France 0 (at Wiener Westadion) 3500
England: Lukic; James, Dennis, Bruce, Ormsby, Mackenzie (Proctor), Banfield, Allen P, Burke S, McDermott, Shaw (Allen C).
England won 4-3 on penalties to secure third place in the tournament.

YOUTH INTERNATIONAL MATCHES 1947-78

ENGLAND v SCOTLAND	Eng-land	Scot-land
1947 Oct 25 Doncaster	4	2
1948 Oct 30 Aberdeen	1	3
UYT 1949 April 21 Utrecht	0	1
1950 Feb 4 Carlisle	7	1
1951 Feb 3 Kilmarnock	6	1
1952 Feb 15 Sunderland	3	1
1953 Feb 7 Glasgow	4	3
1954 Feb 6 Middlesbrough	2	1
1955 Mar 5 Kilmarnock	3	4
1956 Mar 3 Preston	2	2
1957 Mar 9 Aberdeen	3	1
1958 Mar 1 Hull	2	0
1959 Feb 28 Aberdeen	1	1
1960 Feb 27 Newcastle	1	1
1961 Feb 25 Elgin	3	2
1962 Feb 24 Peterborough	4	2
*UYT 1963 April 19 White City	1	0
1963 May 18 Dumfries	3	1
1964 Feb 22 Middlesbrough	1	1
1965 Feb 27 Inverness	1	2
1966 Feb 5 Hereford	5	3
1967 Feb 4 Aberdeen	0	1
*UYT 1967 Mar 1 Southampton	1	0
*UYT 1967 Mar 15 Dundee	0	0
1968 Feb 3 Walsall	0	5
1969 Feb 1 Stranraer	1	1
1970 Jan 31 Derby	1	2
1971 Jan 30 Greenock	1	2
1972 Jan 30 Bournemouth	2	0
1973 Jan 20 Kilmarnock	3	2
1974 Jan 26 Brighton	2	2

ENGLAND v WALES

Year	Date	Venue	England Goals	Wales Goals
1948	Feb 28	High Wycombe	4	2
UYT1948	April 15	Shepherds Bush	4	0
1949	Feb 26	Swansea	0	0
1950	Feb 25	Worcester	1	0
1951	Feb 17	Wrexham	1	1
1952	Feb 23	Plymouth	6	0
1953	Feb 21	Swansea	4	2
1954	Feb 20	Derby	2	1
1955	Feb 19	Milford Haven	7	2
1956	Feb 18	Shrewsbury	5	1
1957	Feb 9	Cardiff	7	1
1958	Feb 8	Reading	8	2
1959	Feb 14	Portmadoc	3	0
1960	Mar 19	Canterbury	1	1
1961	Mar 18	Newtown	4	0
1962	Mar 17	Swindon	4	0
1963	Mar 16	Haverfordwest	1	0
1964	Mar 15	Leeds	2	1
1965	Mar 20	Newport	2	2
1966	Mar 19	Northampton	4	1
1967	Mar 18	Cwmbran	3	3
1968	Mar 16	Watford	2	3
1969	Mar 15	Haverfordwest	3	1
*UYT1970	Feb 25	Newport	0	0
*UYT1970	Mar 18	Leyton	1	2
1970	April 20	Reading	0	0
1971	Feb 20	Aberystwyth	1	2
1972	Feb 19	Swindon	4	0
1973	Feb 24	Portmadoc	4	1
*UYT1974	Jan 9	West Bromwich	1	0
1974	Mar 2	Shrewsbury	2	1
*UYT1974	Mar 13	Cardiff	0	1
*UYT1976	Feb 11	Cardiff	1	0
*UYT1976	Mar 3	Maine Rd	2	3
*UYT1977	Mar 9	West Bromwich	1	0
*UYT1977	Mar 23	Cardiff	1	1

ENGLAND v IRELAND

Year	Date	Venue	England	Ireland
1948	May 15	Belfast	2	2
1949	April 18	Haarlem	3	3
1949	May 14	Hull	4	2
1950	May 6	Belfast	0	1
1951	May 5	Liverpool	5	2
1952	April 19	Belfast	0	2
1953	April 11	Wolverhampton	0	0
UYT1954	April 10	Bruehl	5	0
1954	May 8	Newtownards	2	2
1955	May 14	Watford	3	0
1956	May 12	Belfast	0	1
1957	May 11	Leyton	6	2
1958	May 10	Bangor	2	4
1959	May 9	Liverpool	5	0
1960	May 14	Portadown	5	2
1961	May 13	Manchester	2	0
1962	May 12	Londonderry	1	2
*UYT1963	April 23	Wembley	4	0
1963	May 11	Oldham	1	1
1964	Jan 25	Belfast	3	1
1965	Jan 22	Birkenhead	2	3
1966	Feb 26	Belfast	4	0
1967	Feb 25	Stockport	3	0
1968	Feb 23	Belfast	0	2
1969	Feb 28	Birkenhead	0	2
1970	Feb 28	Lurgan	1	3
1971	Mar 6	Blackpool	1	1
1972	Mar 11	Chester	1	1
*UYT1972	May 17	Sabadell	4	0
1973	Mar 24	Telford	3	0
1974	April 19	Birkenhead	1	2
*UYT1975	May 13	Kriens	3	0

ENGLAND v AUSTRIA

Year	Date	Venue	England	Austria
UYT1949	April 19	Zeist	4	2
UYT1952	April 17	Barcelona	5	5
UYT1957	April 16	Barcelona	0	3
1958	Mar 4	Highbury	3	2
1958	June 1	Graz	4	3
UYT1960	April 20	Vienna	0	1
*UYT1964	April 1	Rotterdam	2	1

ENGLAND v BELGIUM

Year	Date	Venue	England	Belgium
UYT1948	April 16	West Ham	3	1
UYT1951	Mar 22	Cannes	1	1
UYT1953	Mar 31	Brussels	2	0
†1956	Nov 7	Brussels	3	2
1957	Nov 13	Sheffield	2	0
*UYT1965	April 15	Ludwigshafen	3	0
*UYT1969	Mar 11	West Ham	1	0
*UYT1969	Mar 26	Waregem	2	0
UYT1972	May 13	Palma	0	0
UYT1973	June 4	Viareggio	0	0
*UYT1977	May 19	Lokeren	1	0
1979	Jan 17	Brussels	4	0

ENGLAND v BULGARIA

Year	Date	Venue	England	Bulgaria
UYT1956	Mar 28	Salgotarjan	1	2
UYT1960	April 16	Graz	0	1
UYT1962	April 24	Ploesti	0	0
*UYT1968	April 7	Nimes	0	0
*UYT1979	May 31	Vienna	0	1

ENGLAND v CZECHOSLOVAKIA

Year	Date	Venue	England	Czechoslovakia
UYT1955	April 7	Lucca	0	1
*UYT1966	May 21	Rijeka	2	3
*UYT1969	May 20	Leipzig	3	1
*UYT1979	May 24	Bischofshofen	3	0

ENGLAND v DENMARK

Year	Date	Venue	England	Denmark
*1955	Oct 1	Plymouth	9	2
1956	May 20	Esbjerg	2	1

ENGLAND v FINLAND

Year	Date	Venue	England	Finland
*UYT1975	May 19	Berne	1	1

ENGLAND v FRANCE

Year	Date	Venue	England	France
1957	Mar 24	Fontainebleau	1	0
1958	Mar 22	Eastbourne	0	1
*UYT1966	May 23	Rijeka	1	2
*UYT1967	May 11	Istanbul	2	0
*1968	Jan 25	Paris	0	1
*UYT1978	Feb 8	Selhurst Park	3	1
*UYT1978	Mar 1	Paris	0	0
*UYT1979	June 2	Vienna	0	0

ENGLAND v EAST GERMANY

Year	Date	Venue	England	East Germany
UYT1958	April 7	Neunkirchen	1	0
1959	Mar 8	Zwickau	3	4
1960	April 2	Portsmouth	1	1
*UYT1965	April 25	Essen	2	3
*UYT1969	May 22	Magdeburg	0	4
*UYT1973	June 10	Florence	3	2

ENGLAND v WEST GERMANY

Year	Date	Venue	Goals	
			England	West Germany
UYT1953	April 4	Boom	3	1
UYT1954	April 15	Gelsenkirchen	2	2
UYT1956	April 1	Sztalinvaros	2	1
1957	Mar 31	Oberhausen	4	1
1958	Mar 12	Bolton	1	2
1961	Mar 12	Flensberg	0	2
*1962	Mar 31	Northampton	1	0
*1967	Feb 14	Moenchengladbach	1	0
UYT1972	May 22	Barcelona	2	0
1975	Jan 25	Las Palmas	4	2
1976	Nov 14	Monte Carlo	1	1
*UYT1979	May 28	Salzburg	2	0

ENGLAND v GREECE

Year	Date	Venue	England	Greece
UYT1957	April 18	Barcelona	2	3
UYT1959	April 2	Dimitrovo	4	0
UYT1977	May 23	Beveren	1	1

ENGLAND v HUNGARY

Year	Date	Venue	England	Hungary
UYT1954	April 11	Dusseldorf	1	3
UYT1956	Mar 31	Tatabanya	2	4
*1956	Oct 23	Tottenham	2	1
*1956	Oct 25	Sunderland	2	1
*UYT1965	April 21	Wuppertal	5	0
*UYT1975	May 16	Olten	3	1
*UYT1977	Oct 10	Las Palmas	3	0

ENGLAND v ICELAND

Year	Date	Venue	England	Iceland
*UYT1973	May 31	Viareggio	2	0
*UYT1977	May 21	Turnhout	0	0

ENGLAND v REPUBLIC OF IRELAND

Year	Date	Venue	England	Rep. of Ireland
UYT1953	April 5	Leuven	2	0
*UYT1964	Mar 30	Middleburg	6	0
*UYT1968	Feb 7	Dublin	0	0
*UYT1968	Feb 28	Portsmouth	4	1
*UYT1970	Jan 14	Dublin	4	1
*UYT1970	Feb 4	Luton	10	0
*UYT1975	May 9	Brunnen	1	0

ENGLAND v ISRAEL

Year	Date	Venue	England	Israel
*1962	May 20	Tel Aviv	3	1
*1962	May 22	Haifa	1	2

ENGLAND v ITALY

Year	Date	Venue	England	Italy
UYT1958	Apr 113	Luxembourg	0	1
UYT1959	Mar 25	Sofia	0	3
UYT1961	April 4	Braga	2	3
*UYT1965	April 23	Marl-Huels	3	1
*UYT1966	May 25	Rijeka	1	1
*UYT1967	May 5	Izmir	0	0
1973	Feb 14	Cava dei Tirreni	0	1
1973	Mar 14	Highbury	1	0
*UYT1973	June 6	Viareggio	1	0
1978	Nov 19	Monte Carlo	1	2
*UYT1979	Feb 28	Rome	1	0
*UYT1979	Apr 4	Villa Park	2	0

ENGLAND v LUXEMBOURG

Year	Date	Venue	England	Luxembourg
UYT1950	May 25	Vienna	1	2
UYT1954	April 17	Bad Neuenahr	0	2
1957	Feb 2	West Ham	7	1
1957	Nov 17	Luxembourg	3	0
UYT1958	April 9	Eschsalzette	5	0

ENGLAND v MALTA

Year	Date	Venue	England	Malta
*UYT1969	May 18	Wolfen	6	0
*UYT1979	May 26	Salzburg	3	0

ENGLAND v NETHERLANDS

Year	Date	Venue	England	Netherlands
UYT1948	April 17	Tottenham	3	2
UYT1951	Mar 26	Cannes	2	1
*1954	Nov 21	Arnhem	2	3
*1955	Nov 5	Norwich	3	1
1957	Mar 2	Brentford	5	5
UYT1957	April 14	Barcelona	1	2
1957	Oct 2	Amsterdam	3	2
1961	Mar 9	Utrecht	0	1
*1962	Jan 31	Brighton	4	0
UYT1962	April 22	Ploesti	0	3
*UYT1963	April 13	Wimbledon	5	0
*UYT1968	April 9	Nimes	1	0
*UYT1974	Feb 13	West Bromwich	1	1
*UYT1974	Feb 27	The Hague	1	0

ENGLAND v POLAND

Year	Date	Venue	England	Poland
UYT1960	April 18	Graz	4	2
*UYT1964	Mar 26	Breda	1	1
*UYT1971	May 26	Presov	0	0
UYT1972	May 20	Valencia	1	0
1975	Jan 21	Las Palmas	1	1
*UYT1978	May 9	Chorzow	0	2

ENGLAND v PORTUGAL

Year	Date	Venue	England	Portugal
UYT1954	April 18	Bonn	0	2
UYT1961	April 2	Lisbon	0	4
*UYT1964	April 3	The Hague	4	0
*UYT1971	May 30	Prague	3	0
1978	Nov 13	Monte Carlo	2	0

ENGLAND v RUMANIA

Year	Date	Venue	England	Rumania
1957	Oct 15	Tottenham	4	2
UYT1958	April 11	Luxembourg	1	0
UYT1959	Mar 31	Pazardjic	1	2
*UYT1963	April 15	Highbury	3	0

UYT UEFA Youth Tournament.

ENGLAND v SARR

Year	Date	Venue	England	Sarr
UYT1954	April 13	Dortmund	1	1
UYT1955	April 9	Prato	3	1

ENGLAND v SPAIN

Year	Date	Venue	England	Spain
UYT1952	April 15	Barcelona	1	4
1957	Sept 26	Birmingham	4	4
UYT1958	April 5	Saarbrucken	2	2
*1958	Oct 8	Madrid	4	2
UYT1961	Mar 30	Lisbon	0	0
1964	Feb 27	Murcia	2	1
*1964	April 5	Amsterdam	4	0
*UYT1965	April 17	Heilbronn	0	0
*1966	Mar 30	Swindon	3	0
*UYT1967	May 7	Manisa	2	1
*1971	Mar 31	Pamplona	2	3
*1971	April 20	Luton	1	1
1972	Feb 9	Alicante	0	0
1972	Mar 15	Sheffield	4	1
*UYT1975	Feb 25	Bristol	1	1
*UYT1975	Mar 18	Madrid	1	0
1976	Nov 12	Monte Carlo	3	0
*UYT1978	May 7	Bukowno	1	0
1978	Nov 17	Monte Carlo	1	1

ENGLAND v SWEDEN

Year	Date	Venue	England	Sweden
*UYT1971	May 24	Poprad	1	0

ENGLAND v SWITZERLAND

Year	Date	Venue	England	Switzerland
UYT1950	May 26	Stockerau	2	1
UYT1951	Mar 27	Nice	3	1
UYT1952	April 13	Barcelona	4	0
UYT1955	April 11	Florence	0	0
1956	Mar 11	Schaffhausen	2	0
1956	Oct 13	Brighton	2	2
1958	May 26	Zurich	3	0
*1960	Oct 8	Leyton	4	3
*†1962	Nov 22	Coventry	1	0

ENGLAND v TURKEY

Year	Date	Venue	England	Turkey
*1963	Mar 21	Bienne	7	1
*UYT1973	June 2	Forte dei Marim	2	0
*UYT1975	May 11	Buochs	4	0

Year	Date	Venue	England	Turkey
UYT1959	Mar 29	Dimitrovo	1	1
UYT1978	May 5	Wodzislaw	1	1

ENGLAND v URUGUAY

Year	Date	Venue	England	Uruguay
1977	Oct 9	Las Palmas	1	1

ENGLAND v USSR

Year	Date	Venue	England	USSR
*UYT1963	April 17	Tottenham	2	0
*UYT1967	May 13	Istanbul	0	1
*UYT1968	April 11	Nimes	1	1
*UYT1971	May 28	Prague	1	1
1978	Oct 10	Las Palmas	1	0

ENGLAND v YUGOSLAVIA

Year	Date	Venue	England	Yugoslavia
UYT1953	April 2	Liege	1	1
1958	Feb 4	Chelsea	2	2
UYT1962	April 20	Ploesti	0	5
*UYT1967	May 9	Izmir	1	1
*UYT1971	May 22	Bardejor	1	0
1972	May 18	Barcelona	1	0
1976	Nov 16	Monte Carlo	0	3
1978	Nov 15	Monte Carlo	1	1

†Abandoned. *Professionals.

FA YOUTH CHALLENGE CUP 1978-79

Preliminary Round
Wrexham v Chorley	1-0
Tamworth v Enderby T	1-3
Sutton Coldfield T v Alvechurch	4-0
Hitchin T v Bedford T	0-2
Ware v Barking	2-2
Hertford T v Aylesbury U	1-2
Wycombe W v Leytonstone	5-2
Welwyn Garden v Harefield U	2-2
Margate v Dover	0-4
Ringmer v Bognor Regis T	6-1
Wealdstone v Ruislip Manor	1-4
Wycombe W v Stevenage Bor	3-1
†Viking Sports v Maidenhead U	1-7
Hendon v St Albans C	0-0
Southall & Ealing Borough v Harrow Boro	4-2
Harefield U v Ilford	2-3
*Wokingham T v Kingstonian	
Hounslow v Molesey	3-0
Wimbledon v Eastbourne U	13-1
Aldershot v Hampton	6-0
Maidstone U v Folkestone & Shepway	2-1
Dover v Gillingham	0-9
Gosport Bor v Chichester C	1-2
Ringmer v Fareham T	0-0
Trowbridge T v Mangotsfield PF	0-0
Exeter C v Poole T	1-2

†at *Maidenhead U FC*
*WO for Wokingham T FC over Kingstonian FC

Replays
Barking v Ware	2-0
Harefield U v Welwyn Garden	8-0
Long Eaton U v Normanby Park Works	1-2
Syston Juniors v Bedworth U	1-0
Fareham T v Ringmer (aet)	4-1
Mangotsfield PF v Trowbridge T	3-0
Notts Co v Enderby T (aet)	2-0
St Albans C v Hendon	2-1

First Round Qualifying
Yorkshire Amateur v Gateshead	2-0
Farsley Celtic v Grainger Park BC	2-0
Southport v Preston North End	0-1
Wrexham v Rhyl	3-0
Rochdale v Doncaster R	3-2
Crewe Alexandra v Halifax T	2-0
Normanby Park Works v Long Eaton U	3-3
Clifton All Whites v Louth U	1-0
Oldswinford v Hednesford T	2-0
Enderby T v Notts Co	1-1
Walsall v Coalville T	7-0
Bedworth U v Syston Juniors	2-2
Northampton T v Atherstone T	3-2
Sutton Coldfield T v Coventry C	2-7
Histon v Cambridge C	7-6
Bedford T v Corby T	5-2
Southend U v Colchester U	2-2
Barking v Ford U	2-1
Letchworth GC v Banbury U	3-1
Aylesbury U v Harpenden T	17-0

Second Round Qualifying
Yorkshire Amateur v Farsley Celtic	4-1
Preston North End v Wrexham	2-1
Rochdale v Crewe Alexandra	1-1
Normanby PW v Clifton All Whites	1-2
Oldswinford v Notts Co	2-2
Walsall v Syston Juniors	3-0
Northampton T v Coventry C	1-5
*Histon v Bedford T	1-6
Southend U v Barking	4-1

Letchworth GC v Aylesbury U	1-4	Cardiff C v Newport Co	4-1
Ruislip Manor v Wycombe W (aet)	2-1	Hereford U v Birmingham C	2-1
Maidenhead U v St Albans C	2-2	Peterborough U v Arsenal	0-0
Southall & Ealing Bor v Ilford	1-1	West Ham U v Tottenham H	1-2
Wokingham T v Hounslow	1-5	Norwich C v Orient	3-0
Wimbledon v Aldershot	1-1	Bedford T v Luton T	1-1
Maidstone U v Gillingham	0-1	Ipswich T v Watford	3-0
Chichester C v Fareham T	2-2	Fulham v Crystal Palace	0-2
Mangotsfield U v Poole T	0-4	Staines T v Portsmouth	1-1
*at Bedford T FC		Oxford U v Chelsea	0-3
		Brighton & Hove Albion v Gillingham	3-0
Replays		Charlton Ath v Queen's Park Rangers	3-2
Crewe Alexandra v Rochdale	0-1	Millwall v Slough T	3-0
St Albans C v Maidenhead U	1-0	Bristol R v Bristol C	5-1
Ilford v Southall & Ealing Bor	1-3	Southampton v Plymouth Argyle	2-1
Aldershot v Wimbledon	2-2	*at Leicester C FC	
Fareham T v Chichester C	1-0		
Notts Co v Oldswinford	3-1	**Replays**	
		Bolton W v Sheffield W	2-1
Second Replay		Wolverhampton W v Coventry C	0-1
Wimbledon v Aldershot	1-0	Aston Villa v West Bromwich Albion	1-0
at Wimbledon FC		Arsenal v Peterborough U	4-2
		Luton T v Bedford T	2-1
First Round Proper		Portsmouth v Staines T	2-1
Hartelpool U v Nunthorpe Ath	0-2		
New Hartley Juniors v Newcastle U	2-6	**Third Round Proper**	
Hull C v York C	2-0	Middlesbrough v Blackpool	3-1
Bradford C v Huddersfield T	0-1	Bolton W v Leeds U	1-1
Scunthorpe U v Yorkshire Amateur	1-1	Newcastle U v Manchester C	0-0
Preston North End v Blackpool	1-1	Sunderland v Rotherham U	3-1
Port Vale v Rochdale	0-1	Manchester U v Derby Co	0-3
Tranmere R v Stoke C	3-1	Chester v Bristol R	0-1
Barnsley v Chester	2-2	Hereford U v Everton	0-3
Sheffield W v Sheffield U	2-1	Leicester C v Aston Villa	1-1
Clifton All Whites v Notts Co	0-5	Lincoln C v Nottingham F	1-2
Chesterfield v Lincoln C	2-4	Coventry C v Cardiff C	3-0
Nuneaton Bor v Mansfield T	4-1	Millwall v Norwich C	3-0
Swansea C v Cardiff C	0-3	Tottenham H v Crystal Palace	0-2
Birmingham C v Shrewsbury T	9-2	Portsmouth v Brighton & Hove Albion	2-0
Northfield T v Walsall	1-4	Luton T v Arsenal	1-0
Swindon T v Oxford U	0-2	Charlton Ath v Ipswich T	3-2
Coventry C v Cheltenham T	2-2	Chelsea v Southampton	0-1
Luton T v Coventry Sporting	5-0		
Bedford T v Aylesbury U	1-1	**Replays**	
Cambridge U v Norwich C	1-3	Leeds U v Bolton W	3-1
West Ham U v Southend U	4-3	Manchester C v Newcastle U	3-0
Watford v Ruislip Manor	2-0	Aston Villa v Leicester C	1-0
Orient v St Albans C	3-0		
Hounslow v Queen's Park Rangers	0-4	**Fourth Round Proper**	
Welling U v Gillingham	0-1	Crystal Palace v Manchester C	1-2
Staines T v Southall & Ealing Bor	4-1	Leeds U v Charlton Ath	1-3
Wimbledon v Fulham	2-2	Millwall v Sunderland	2-1
Slough T v Croydon	4-1	Middlesbrough v Southampton	0-1
Portsmouth v Fareham T	6-0	Bristol R v Everton	2-2
Reading v Brighton & Hove Albion	1-3	Luton T v Aston Villa	2-1
Southampton v Redhill	7-1	Coventry C v Derby Co	1-1
Torquay U v Plymouth Argyle	0-3	Nottingham F v Portsmouth	6-0
Bristol R v Poole T	1-1		
		Replays	
Replays		Everton v Bristol R	2-2
Yorkshire Amateur v Scunthorpe U	1-0	Derby Co v Coventry C	1-2
Blackpool v Preston North End	2-1		
Chester v Barnsley	4-0	**Second Replay**	
Cheltenham T v Coventry C	0-3	Bristol R v Everton	1-4
Aylesbury U v Bedford T	1-2		
Fulham v Wimbledon	4-0	**Fifth Round Proper**	
Poole T v Bristol R	1-2	Southampton v Charlton Ath	4-0
		Coventry C v Everton	1-6
Second Round Proper		Manchester C v Luton T	1-1
Hull C v Newcastle U	0-3	Millwall v Nottingham F	3-3
Sunderland v Nunthorpe Ath	2-1		
Yorkshire Amateur v Leeds U	0-2	**Replays**	
Burnley v Middlesbrough	0-1	Luton T v Manchester C	1-3
Derby C v Tranmere R	1-0	Nottingham F v Millwall	0-1
Oldham Ath v Manchester C	0-1		
Sheffield W v Bolton W	2-2	**Semi-Final Ties**	
Huddersfield T v Chester	0-5	**First Leg**	
Rochdale v Blackpool	0-1	Everton v Millwall	0-0
Everton v Liverpool	2-0	Manchester C v Southampton	1-0
Manchester U v Blackburn R	6-2	**Second Leg**	
Rotherham U v Grimsby T	6-2	Millwall v Everton	2-0
Lincoln C v Notts Co	4-1	Southampton v Manchester C	0-3
*Nuneaton Bor v Leicester C	2-6	**Final Tie**	
Walsall v Nottingham F	1-2	**First Leg**	
Coventry C v Wolverhampton W	3-3	Manchester C v Millwall	0-0
West Bromwich Albion v Aston Villa	1-1	**Second Leg**	
		Millwall v Manchester C	2-0

ENGLAND YOUTH INTERNATIONAL PLAYERS 1947-79

Abrahams, R (Essex) 1952
Adlard, S (Lincoln C) 1968, 1969
Adlem, R (Dorset FA) 1965
Aitken, G (Chelsea) 1971
Albert T (Middlesex) 1949
Allder, D (Millwall) 1970
Albeson, B (Bury) 1965
Allen, A (Stoke) 1958
Allen, C D (QPR) 1978, 1979
Allen, G (Newcastle U) 1965
Allen, P K (West Ham U) 1979
Allner, G (Walsall) 1968
Amphlett, A (Worcestershire) 1950
Anderson T (Arsenal) 1961
Angus, J (Burnley) 1957, 1958
Armour, D (Northumberland) 1953
Armstrong, G (Arsenal) 1962
Armstrong, G (Fulham) 1973
Arnold, G (Aston Villa) 1963
Ash, M (Sheffield U) 1961
Ashe, N (Aston Villa) 1960
Ashurst, L (Liverpool Co) 1957
Aslett, G W (Ipswich T) 1967
Atkins, G (Berks & Bucks) 1951, 1952
Atyeo, P J (Wiltshire) 1950
Ayris, J D (West Ham U) 1971

Bacuzzi, D (Arsenal) 1959
Badger, L (Sheffield U) 1963
Bailey, J (Hampshire) 1956
Baker, A (Aston Villa) 1960, 1961, 1962
Baker, G (Worcestershire Co FA) 1970
Baker, J (Kingstonian) 1968
Banfield, N A (Crystal Palace) 1979
Bannister, K (Sheffield & Hallam) 1948
Barber, D (Barnsley) 1958
Barnham, R (West Ham U) 1968
Barley, D (Berks & Bucks) 1950
Barnes, P (London) 1953
Barnes, P S (Manchester C) 1975
Barnett, G (Everton) 1965
Barrett, J (Birmingham Co) 1949
Barnwell, J (Northumberland) 1956 (Middlesex) 1957
Barratt, S T (Winsford U) 1972
Bartley, D R (Bristol C) 1966
Barton, A (Middlesex) 1954 (Fulham) 1955
Barton, F (Scunthorpe U) 1966
Batchelor, C (West Ham U) 1973
Bates, P (Berks & Bucks) 1953
Beal, P (Tottenham H) 1963
Beard, M (Birmingham C) 1959
Beattie, T K (Ipswich T) 1972
Beaumont, F (Barnsley) 1958
Beavon, C (Wolves) 1957
Beeby, O (Leicestershire) 1953
Belger, W (Barnet) 1961
Bell, G (Oldham Ath) 1973
Bellett, W (Essex) 1952
Bennett, A (Staffs) 1949
Bennett, A (Rotherham U) 1962
Bennett, D (Middlesex) 1951, 1952
Bennett, D (London) 1956
Bennett, R (Northampton T) 1963
Bentley, W (Stoke C) 1966
Berick, R (Manchester Co) 1949
Bernard, M (Stoke C) 1966
Bertschin K E (Ipswich T) 1975
Betts, A T (Aston Villa) 1972
Bickles, D (West Ham U) 1961
Bidois, D (Oxfordshire) 1951, 1952
Bielby, P A (Manchester U) 1975
Billington S (Liverpool Co) 1955
Birch, B (Manchester Co) 1949
Birch, B (Lancashire) 1955
Bird, R (Birmingham C) 1958

Birtles, B (Sheffield U) 1966
Bishop, P (Sheffield) 1963
Black, S (Fulham) 1973
Block, M (Chelsea) 1958
Bloomfield R (Arsenal) 1961, 1963
Bloor, A (Stoke C) 1960
Blunstone, F (Cheshire) 1951
Bond, D J (Watford) 1965
Boorn, A (Folkestone) 1971
Boseley, G (Gloucestershire) 1951, 1952
Bowtell, S J (Orient) 1969
Boyce, R (West Ham U) 1960, 1061
Brabrook, P (Middlesex) 1955 (Chelsea) 1957
Bradley, R (WBA) 1956
Bradshaw, P (Burnley) 1971, 1972
Bradshaw, P W (Blackburn R) 1974
Bragger, P (West Ham U) 1967
Bramhall, J (Hillsborough BC) 1958
Brennan, D (Cheshire) 1950
Brickley, D (West Riding) 1948
Bridges, B (Chelsea) 1957, 1958
Brindley, J C (Nottingham F) 1964, 1965
Britt, M (West Ham U) 1963
Broad, W (Crystal Palace) 1968
Bromilow, G J (Liverpool Co) 1949
Bromley, B (Bolton W) 1964
Brookes, E (Barnsley) 1961, 1962
Brooking, T D (West Ham U) 1967
Brown, G (Staffs) 1951, 1952
Brown, R (Derbyshire) 1950
Brown, T (Liverpool Co) 1948
Bruce, S R (Gillingham) 1979
Bruntlett, G (Newcastle U) 1963
Bryant, J (Fulham) 1973
Buchanan, D (Leicester C) 1979
Buckley, D W (Stoke C) 1971
Buckley, I (Oldham Ath) 1972
Buckley, M J (Everton) 1972
Bullock, P (Stoke C) 1958, 1959
Bulmer, J (Leyton O) 1964
Bunce, F (Watford) 1956, 1957
Bunch, P (WBA) 1957
Bunkell, R K (Tottenham H) 1968
Burbeck, R (Leicestershire) 1952
Burckitt, J (Coventry C) 1965
Burgess, G (Gloucestershire) 1954
Burke, D I (Bolton W) 1979
Burke, S J (Nottingham F) 1978, 1979
Burkhill, K (Liverpool Co) 1948
Burnside, D (Staffs) 1957 (WBA) 1958
Burton, K O (Sheffield W) 1968
Busby, M G (QPR) 1971
Butler, I (Rotherham U) 1962
Butterfield, G (Southend U) 1966
Byford, G J (Southend U) 1974
Byrne, J (Surrey) 1956
Byrom, J (Blackburn R) 1962

Cahill, P G (Coventry C) 1974
Cakebread, G (Middlesex) 1954
Caldwell, T (Huddersfield T) 1957, 1958
Calvert, C A (York C) 1972
Campbell, D (Liverpool Co) 1950
Campbell, J (Bedford T) 1973
Campbell, R (Liverpool) 1954
Cammack, S R (Sheffield U) 1972
Canavan, P (Ipswich T) 1979
Cantello, L (WBA) 1970
Capewell, M C (Leicester C) 1974
Carlin, W (Liverpool) 1958, 1959
Carr, G (Northampton T) 1962
Carter, L A (Crystal Palace) 1979
Cartwright, J (West Ham U) 1957
Catley, S W (Bristol R) 1970
Cavell, C (Kent) 1951, 1952
Chadburn, A (Quorn) 1957

Challis, R (Gillingham) 1961
Chamberlain, T (Middlesex) 1950
Charles, C (West Ham U) 1970
Charles, J (West Ham U) 1962, 1963
Charles, R (Southampton) 1959
Charlton, M (Hampshire) 1952
Charlton, R (Manchester County) 1954
Chatterley, L C (Aston Villa) 1963
Cheesewright, A (Leyton O) 1964
Cherry, S R (Derby Co) 1978
Child, P C (Aston Villa) 1971
Church, D (Gloucestershire) 1950
Clapton, D (Arsenal) 1958
Clark, F A (Crook T) 1962
Clark, P D (Southend U) 1977
Clarke, J L (Northampton T) 1965
Clarke, N (Birmingham County) 1952, 1953
Clarke, R C (Tottenham H) 1971
Clarke, W (Wolverhampton W) 1979
Clayton, G (Manchester U) 1955
Clement, D T (QPR) 1966
Cliss, D (Chelsea) 1957
Close, D B (West Riding) 1949
Cocker, L (Wolves) 1958
Cockroft, V (Wolves) 1959
Collier, A (Bedfordshire) 1955 (Luton T) 1956, 1957
Collinson, R (Doncaster R) 1958
Colton, E (Sheffield W) 1957
Connaughton, J P (Manchester U) 1968
Connelly, T (Barnsley) 1960
Connolly, M (Sheffield & Hallam) 1957
Conroy, M (Middlesex) 1952
Cooke, B (Staffs) 1955 (WBA) 1956, 1957
Cooper, L (Staffs) 1953
Cooper, S (Worcestershire FA) 1974
Corbett, A (Wolves) 1959
Cotton, R W L (Brentford) 1974
Cowans, G S (Aston Villa) 1977
Cowen, J (Chelsea) 1963
Cox, C V (Oxford U) 1968
Craddock, T (Herts) 1954
Craggs, J E (Newcastle U) 1966, 1967
Craven, T (Barnsley) 1963
Crickson, C (Kent) 1951
Crosby, J (WBA) 1959
Cross, G F (Leicester C) 1962
Crossman, D (Tottenham H) 1964
Crowe, C (West Riding) 1956
Cruickshank, R (Vauxhall Motors) 1968
Curbishley, L C (West Ham U) 1975, 1976
Currie, A W (Watford/Sheffield U) 1968
Curtis, G (Birmingham County) 1956 (Coventry C) 1957, 1958

Dagless, M N (Peterborough U) 1966
Daines, B (Tottenham H) 1970
Dale, M A (Hull C) 1969
Daley, S (Wolves) 1971
Dalrymple, M (Luton T) 1970
Dangerfield, C G (Wolves) 1974
Dare, K J (Crystal Palace) 1978
Darwin, N (Durham) 1948
Davey, S (Plymouth Arg) 1967
Davids, N G (Leeds U) 1974
Dawkins, T (West Ham U) 1964
Dawson, O (Portsmouth) 1960
Day, M R (West Ham U) 1971
Dean, D (Aston Villa) 1962
Dean, J (Manchester County) 1956 (Bolton W) 1957, 1958
Deehan, J M (Aston Villa) 1976
Deeman, S (Thorneywood Ath) 1965
Dellar, B (London) 1957
Dennis, A (Tottenham H) 1961
Dennis, M E (Birmingham C) 1979
De Placido, N S (York C) 1972
Detchon, J (Derbyshire) 1956
Dickson, J (Liverpool County) 1952
Dillon, K P (Birmingham C) 1978
Dillon, M L (Tottenham H) 1971
Dillon, T (Orient) 1972
Dilworth, J R (Middlesex) 1966
Docherty, M (Burnley) 1969

Dodkins, H (Essex) 1948
Dodson, D (Middlesex) 1956, 1957
Donaghy, B (WBA) 1973, 1974
Donaghy, R (Liverpool County) 1950
Donaldson, D J (Arsenal) 1972
Doyle, J (Manchester County) 1955
Draper, J (Northamptonshire) 1953
Drury, C (Staffs) 1955
Duffy, A (Newcastle U) 1968
Dugdale, A (Coventry C) 1971
Durrant, A (Orient) 1970
Dyer, J (Alvechurch) 1967

Eastoe, P R (Wolves) 1971, 1972
Eccleshare, K (Bury) 1969
Edmonds, D J (Leeds U) 1968
Edmondson, S J (Lincolnshire FA) 1968
Edwards, D (Manchester U) 1955
Ellery, L (Cornwall County FA) 1970
Ellis, R W (Bolton W) 1970
Elms, J (Manchester U) 1958
Entwistle, W P (Bury) 1977
Etheridge, B (Northampton T) 1962
Evans, A (Manchester County) 1950
Evans, A W (Wolves) 1967, 1968
Evans, D (Middlesex) 1953
Evans, M (Middlesex) 1954
Evans, R (Chelsea) 1965
Evans, R L (Tottenham H) 1968

Fairclough, P (Liverpool County) 1952
Falco, M P (Tottenham H) 1979
Farrimond, S (Bolton W) 1958
Fashanu, J S (Norwich C) 1979
Favager, J (Cheshire) 1953
Feely, P (Ipswich T) 1968
Feist, R (Middlesex) 1957
Felton, G M (Northampton T) 1967
Fenton, S J (Middlesbrough) 1969
Fenwick, T W (Crystal Palace) 1978
Fergey, R (Middlesex) 1954
Fidler, M (Barnsley) 1964
Field, J (Tottenham H) 1972
Fillery, M C (Chelsea) 1979
Finney, R J (Rotherham U) 1973, 1974
Fisher, A R (Hull C) 1969
Fisher, S (Portsmouth) 1973
Flanagan, M A (Tottenham H) 1971
Fletcher, M (Derby Co) 1970
Foggon, A (Newcastle U) 1968
Ford, A (Bristol C) 1962
Foster, B (Mansfield T) 1970
Fox, J (West Riding) 1952
France, K (Bolton W) 1959
Francis, T J (Birmingham C) 1971, 1972
French, G E (Shrewsbury T) 1963
French, M J (Eastbourne U) 1971

Gaddes, R (Portsmouth) 1960
Gale, A P (Fulham) 1978
Galvin, C (Leeds U) 1970
Gardner, T K (Liverpool County) 1948
Garner, P (Huddersfield T) 1974
Garrett, L (London) 1954
Garwood, C (Peterborough U) 1967
Gaskell, D (Manchester U) 1957, 1958, 1959
Gates, W (Spennymoor G/T School) 1961
Geddis, D (Ipswich T) 1976
Gibson, M (Derbyshire) 1957
Gibson, T B (Tottenham H) 1979
Gidman, J (Aston Villa) 1972
Gilbert, W A (Crystal Palace) 1978
Giles, P (Staffs) 1948
Gillingwater, D (Gillingham) 1961
Gillott, P (Sheffield & Hallam) 1953
Glover, G (Everton) 1965
Gonzalez, R (Crystal Palace) 1969
Goodwin, R (East Riding) 1953
Gould, T R (Coventry C) 1968
Gould, W T (Gloucestershire) 1949
Gover, P J (Bristol C) 1972
Gray, T I (Leeds Ashley Road) 1972
Graydon, R (Bristol R) 1965
Greaves, J (Chelsea) 1957

Greaves, T (Birmingham County) 1956
Green, A P (Coventry C) 1972
Greendale, M (Hull C) 1970
Gregory, H (Leyton Orient) 1961
Gregory, A (Bedfordshire) 1954
Groves, V (Essex) 1951, 1952
Grummett, J (Lincoln C) 1963
Gradkowski, M (Bristol R) 1967
Guest, B J (Lincoln C) 1977

Hagger, D R (Luton T) 1969
Hague, N (Rotherham U) 1968
Haines, K (Leicestershire & Rutland) 1956
Hall, A. (Manchester County) 1955
Hall, C (Nottingham F) 1966
Hall, I (Wolves) 1958
Hall, J (Northampton T) 1963
Hames, B (Crystal Palace) 1962
Hamilton, D (Sunderland) 1979
Hamilton, I (Crystal Palace) 1967
Hamilton, I (Chelsea) 1968 (Southend U) 1969
Hammond, K L (Harwich & P) 1967
Hampton, P J (Leeds U) 1973
Hankin, R (Burnley) 1973
Harding, D (Sussex County FA) 1973
Hardwick, S (Chesterfield) 1974
Harfield, L (Southampton) 1971
Harper, A (Liverpool) 1979
Harper, D (Millwall) 1957
Harper, R (Woodside/Wealdstone) 1967
Harris, A (Chelsea) 1961
Harris, B (Cheshire) 1953
Harris, R E (Chelsea) 1961, 1962, 1963
Harrison, F (East Riding) 1949
Hart, B (Cambridge U) 1959
Haslam, I (Lancs County FA) 1970
Havenhand, K. (Chesterfield) 1957
Hawksby, J (Leeds U) 1959
Hawksworth, A (Manchester County) 1955
Haynes, J (Middlesex) 1952
Hayzelden, G (Tottenham H) 1973
Hazell, A P (QPR) 1965, 1966
Hazel, R (Wiltshire) 1949
Hazell, R J (Wolves) 1977
Hazelden, W (Aston Villa) 1958
Healey, G (Hull C) 1963
Heaney, A (Southampton) 1958
Heard, J (Arsenal) 1959
Heard, T P (Everton) 1978
Hennin, D (Liverpool County) 1949
Hesford, I (Blackpool) 1978
Hewitt, C (Dorset) 1952
Hewitt, R (Manchester U) 1961
Heyes, K (Liverpool County) 1953
Heys, G (Macclesfield) 1974
Hicks, K (Oldham Ath) 1973
Higgins, M N (Everton) 1977
Higgs, K (Staffs) 1954
High, D (Reading) 1958
Hilaire, V M (Crystal Palace) 1977, 1978
Hill, G A (Southend U) 1972
Hill, R A (Luton T) 1977
Hillsdon, I (Liverpool) 1954 (Everton) 1955
Hincks, K (Leicestershire) 1949
Hindmarch, R (Sunderland) 1979
Hines, D (Leicestershire) 1948
Hinton, A (Wolves) 1959
Hoddle, G (Tottenham H) 1975, 1976
Hoadley, P (Crystal Palace) 1970
Hodgson, G H (Newcastle U) 1971
Holden, D (Lancashire) 1949
Holder, P (Tottenham H) 1970
Holland, R (Manchester U) 1957, 1958
Hollins, J (Chelsea) 1964
Holmes, C (Southampton) 1957
Holsgrove, J (Crystal Palace) 1964
Hornsby, B G (Arsenal) 1973
Horsfield, A (Middlesbrough) 1964
Houghton, W (Barnsley) 1957, 1958
Howlett, M G (West Ham U) 1971
Hoy, R (Huddersfield T) 1968
Hughes, L J (WBA) 1969
Hulse, R (Nantwich T) 1967

Hunt, H (Cheshire) 1949
Hunt, P (Southend U) 1970
Hunt, R L (Hull C) 1971
Hurrell, R (Middlesex) 1953
Hurst, G (West Ham U) 1959
Husband, J (Everton) 1966
Hutchins, R (Redhill) 1964
Huxford, C (Chelsea) 1962
Huxley, G (Brentford) 1973

Impey, J E (Cardiff C) 1973
Ingham, G P A (Luton T) 1978
Irving, D (Workington) 1970
Irwin, C (Sunderland) 1959

Jackson, D (Liverpool County) 1955
Jackson, J (St Clement Danes School) 1961
Jacobs, D (Alleyns School) 1957
Jago, G (London) 1951, 1952
James, K A (Portsmouth) 1974
James, R S (Manchester U) 1968
James, T P W (Cambridge U) 1967
Jarrold, B (Kent) 1954
Jeffrey, A (Sheffield & Hallam) 1955
Jenkins, L (Aston Villa) 1979
Jennings, R L (Wiltshire) 1950
Jennings, W (Watford) 1970
Jewkes, T (Wolves) 1965
Johnson, D (Durham Co FA) 1974
Johnson, G (Arsenal) 1970
Johnson, R (Leeds U) 1962
Jolley, G (Cheshire) 1953
Jones, A (WBA) 1961
Jones, D (Birmingham C) 1958
Jones, D K (Bolton W) 1973
Jones, D R (Everton) 1975
Jones, G (Bury) 1962, 1963
Jones, G (Middlesbrough) 1961
Jones, G A (Birmingham County) 1948
Jones, Glyn (Sheffield & Hallam) 1953, 1954
Jones, M C (Hereford U) 1974
Jones, P (Manchester U) 1956
Jones, P (Burnley) 1968
Joy, D (Durham Johnston HS) 1962
Jones, T E (Liverpool County) 1948

Keeley, A J (Tottenham H) 1975
Keeley, G M (Ipswich T) 1973
Keeley, J (Liverpool County) 1954
Kellard, R (Southend U) 1960
Kelly, B J (Liverpool County) 1951
Kelly, J J (Doncaster R) 1964
Kember, S D (Crystal Palace) 1967
Kendall, H (Preston N E) 1964
Kenworthy, A D (Sheffield U) 1977
Kerry, D (Derbyshire) 1955
Kerslake, M N (Fulham) 1976
Kettle, B (Liverpool) 1974
Kidd, B (Manchester U) 1967
Kilmore, K (Scunthorpe U) 1978
Kindon, S M (Burnley) 1968, 1969
Kingston, A K (Oxford U) 1977
Kirkham, J (Wolves) 1959
Kirkup, J (West Ham U) 1957
Klug, B P (Ipswich T) 1978, 1979
Knapman, J (Torquay U) 1968, 1969
Knight, A E (Portsmouth) 1979
Knight, J (Gloucestershire) 1953
Knott, W (West Riding) 1951, 1952
Knowles, P (Wolves) 1964

Lackenby, A (North Shields Cors) 1959
Lakin, J (Grimsby T) 1964
Lampard, F (West Ham U) 1966, 1967
Lampe, D (Middlesex) 1954 (Fulham) 1957
Langley, T W (Chelsea) 1975
Laraman, P (Charlton Ath) 1958
Latchford, R D (Birmingham C) 1969
Laurel, J (Middlesex) 1952
Laverick, R. (Chelsea) 1955
Lawler, C (Liverpool) 1961
Lawson, I (Burnley) 1958
Leach M (QPR), 1963, 1965

Leadbeater, P (Sheffield FA) 1962
Leake, A G (Staffs) 1948
Leather, D (Southampton) 1960
Leather, M P (Hampshire) 1948
Lee, F (Bolton W) 1961
Lee, G (Sheffield U) 1962
Lee, S (Liverpool) 1977
Leeke, A (Worcestershire) 1954
Leslie, S R (Colchester U) 1971
Lewington, G (Middlesex) 1949
Lewis, A T (Derby Co) 1972, 1973
Lewis, J (Orient) 1972
Lewis, K (Sheffield U) 1958
Lill, M (Essex) 1954
Lindsay, A (Bury) 1966
Llewellyn, H (Liverpool County) 1956 (Everton) 1957
Lloyd, B (Chelsea) 1967
Lloyd, L (Bristol R) 1967
Lock, K J (West Ham U) 1971, 1972
Locke, G R (Chelsea) 1972
Lockwood, R (Leicestershire) 1951, 1952
Love, J (Oxfordshire) 1955
Lukic, J (Leeds U) 1979
Lyall, J (West Ham U) 1957

Mabbutt, K A (Bristol C) 1977
McCabe, K (Liverpool) 1959
McCaffery, A (Newcastle U) 1976
McCaffrey, J (Nottingham F) 1970
McCall S H (Ipswich T) 1979
McCarthy, K (Coventry C) 1958
McDermott, B J (Arsenal) 1979
Mackenzie, S (Crystal Palace) 1979
McDonagh, J M (Rotherham U) 1971
MacDonald, J (Wiltshire) 1948
McDonald, S (Chelsea) 1974
McDonald, T (Essex) 1956
McDowell, J (West Ham U) 1970
McGonagle, I (Charlton Ath) 1971
McGowan, A (Northamptonshire FA) 1974
McGowan, G (Liverpool) 1970
McGuinness, W (Manchester County) 1954 (Manchester U) 1956, 1957, 1958
McGuire, M (Coventry C) 1971
McHale, K (West Riding) 1957 (Huddersfield T)
McLaughlin, J (Colchester U) 1973
McPartland, D (Middlesbrough) 1966
Madeley, P (Leeds U) 1962
Malcolm A (Essex) 1950
Manley, K (Plymouth Arg) 1967
Mann, M (Fulham) 1974
Mannion, G (Wolves) 1958
Mansfield, P (Derby Co) 1963
Marchi A (London) 1950
Marriott, T (Bedford T) 1966
Martin, A E (West Ham U) 1976
Martin, D (Northampton T) 1962
Martin, E (Port Vale) 1965
Mason, S J (Wrexham) 1966
Massey, R (St Paul's Coll, Cheltenham) 1963
Maxwell, D (Carlisle U) 1965
Mayhew, B (Ipswich T) 1974
Melia, J (Liverpool) 1956, 1958
Mellor, P (Manchester C) 1966
Mellows, M (Sutton U) 1966
Melville, L (Liverpool County) 1949
Merrick, A R (WBA) 1968
Metcalfe, S M (Blackburn R) 1969
Metchick, D (Fulham) 1961
Middleton, H (Wolves) 1955
Middleton, J (Nottingham F) 1975
Milkins, J (Portsmouth) 1961
Mills, G R (Nottingham F) 1979
Mills, M (Ipswich T) 1967
Mills, R (Northamptonshire) 1951, 1952
Minton, A (Staffs) 1954
Mitchell, R D (Cornwall) 1949
Mitten, J (Mansfield T) 1958 (Newcastle U) 1959
Moffit, D (Swindon T) 1970
Mole, L (Middlesbrough) 1964
Molyneux, J A (Cheshire) 1949
Monaghan, D J (WBA) 1977
Montgomery, J (Sunderland) 1962

Moorcroft, M (Sheffield & Hallam) 1948
Moore, R (West Ham U) 1958, 1959
Morgan, R (QPR) 1965
Morley, W A (Preston NE) 1973
Morris, D J (Westbury U) 1963
Morris, E (Cheshire) 1948
Mortimer, D (Coventry C) 1970
Mortimore, J (Hampshire) 1952
Morton, R S (Manchester U) 1972
Moseley, G (Derby Co) 1972
Moss, C (Wolves) 1979
Munday, B (Gloucestershire) 1955
Munks, D (Sheffield U) 1965
Munro, M G (Leicester C) 1971
Murray, A (Chelsea) 1961
Mustill, P R (Huddersfield T) 1964

Nicholas, A (Chelsea) 1956, 1957
Nicholas, K (Middlesex) 1955 (Arsenal) 1956
Nightingale, M B D (Bournemouth) 1975
Nish, D J (Leicester C) 1965, 1966
Noble, R (Manchester U) 1964
Norman, D (Alvechurch) 1964
Norman, G D (Essex) 1949
Norris, R (Nottingham F) 1965
North, R G (West Ham U) 1972
Northcott, T (Devon) 1949
Novacki, Y (Bolton W) 1977

Oakes, M (Leicester C) 1962
Oakley, H (Chesterfield) 1962
Oakley, T (St Neots T) 1970
Oates, R A (Leeds Ashley Road) 1974
Oliver, J (Tottenham H) 1970
Ormsby, B T (Aston Villa) 1979
O'Rourke, J (Arsenal) 1961, 1962
Osgood, K (Tottenham H) 1973
Osgood, P (Chelsea) 1965
Osman, R (Derbyshire) 1949
Osman, R C (Ipswich T) 1977
Osmond, C (Hampshire) 1954
Owen, D (Helsby GS) 1957
Owen, G A (Manchester C) 1976
Owens, M (Newcastle U) 1976
Oxford, K (Manchester County) 1948

Packham, M (Sheffield & Hallam) 1955
Pamment, M I (Bradford C) 1963
Parker, R (Coventry C) 1971
Parkinson, N D (Ipswich T) 1978
Parnell, D (Aldershot) 1958
Parry, R (Lancashire) 1952
Passey, P (Birmingham C) 1970
Patching, M (Wolves) 1976, 1977
Paul, A G (Crystal Palace) 1979
Pawley, J (Leicester C) 1970
Peacock, A (Middlesbrough) 1956
Peaper, G L (Oxford U) 1968
Pearson, M (Manchester U) 1957
Peddelty, J (Ipswich T) 1973
Pegram, S F (Enfield) 1965
Perry, R (Wolves) 1958
Perryman, S (Tottenham H) 1970
Peters, M (West Ham U) 1960, 1961, 1962
Peters, R (Bristol C) 1962
Petts, J (Middlesex) 1955, 1956 (Arsenal) 1957
Philipson, F (Durham FA) 1965
Phillips, S E (Birmingham C) 1973
Phillips, T (Rotherham U) 1970, 1971
Phythian, E (Bolton W) 1959
Piekalnietis, J (Nottingham F) 1969
Pimlott, C (Lancs County FA) 1970
Piper, N J (Plymouth Arg) 1966
Platts, G (Leicestershire & Rutland) 1954
Pleat, D (Nottingham F) 1961, 1962, 1963
Pollard, B (York C) 1971, 1972
Pollard, C J (Birmingham County) 1948
Pople, S (Fulham) 1973
Powell, S (Derby County) 1973, 1974
Pountain, M J (Pershore U) 1965
Powling, R (Arsenal) 1974
Price, A J (Leicester C) 1974
Price, D J (Arsenal) 1973
Prince, G (Louth U) 1972

Probert, E (Burnley) 1970
Proctor, M G (Middlesbrough) 1979
Purchase, P (Somerset) 1952
Punter, B (Staffs) 1953

Rankin, G (Liverpool County) 1948
Rands, L (West Ham U) 1971
Ranson, R (Manchester C) 1978
Rathbone, M J (Birmingham C) 1977
Reader, P (West Ham U) 1958, 1959
Redknapp, H (West Ham U) 1964
Redmond, P (Liverpool County) 1957
Redrobe, E (Bolton W) 1961
Reeves, K P (AFC Bournemouth) 1976
Reeves, P J (Charlton Ath) 1967
Reeves, R (Berks & Bucks) 1949
Reynolds, R (Plymouth Arg) 1966
Richardson, G C (Hartlepool) 1976
Richardson, P (Nottingham F) 1968
Riches, K (North Shields) 1968
Ricketts, G (Gloucestershire) 1956
Ridler, E (Somerset) 1949
Riley, E B (Manchester U) 1971
Riley, H (Leicestershire & Rutland) 1955
Rioch, N G (Luton T) 1969
Riordan, J (Huddersfield T) 1970
Ritchie, A T (Manchester U) 1978
Roach, J (Birmingham C) 1955
Roberts, J D (Ipswich T) 1975
Roberts, R (Bristol C) 1967
Roberts, T (Scunthorpe U) 1964
Robinson, B (Bolton W) 1961
Robinson, W (Surrey) 1952
Robson, B (WBA) 1975
Robson, T H (Northampton T) 1962
Rogers, D (Swindon T) 1964
Rogers, M (Bristol C) 1973
Rogers, M (Manchester U) 1978
Roost, G (Gloucestershire Co FA) 1969
Roper, D (Bradford C) 1963
Rose, F (Huddersfield T) 1972
Rossiter, D (London) 1952
Rowland, A (Derby Co) 1973
Rowlands, J (Nottingham F) 1959
Royle, J (Everton) 1967
Rucker, N (Manchester County) 1954
Rumjahn, J R (WBA) 1974

Sadler, D (Manchester U) 1963, 1964
Saile, M A (Bury) 1969
Salkeld, E W (Sheffield U) 1969
Salman, D M M (Brentford) 1978
Sammels, J (Arsenal) 1963
Sanchez, J (Arsenal) 1957
Sansom, K G (Crystal Palace) 1977
Saul, F (Tottenham H) 1960
Saunders, R (Liverpool County) 1951
Saunders, R (East Riding) 1948
Saxby, B (Arsenal) 1956, 1957
Scott, A (West Ham U) 1958, 1959
Scott, M (Middlesex) 1957 (Chelsea) 1958
Scott, P (Prescot T) 1967
Seaborne, K (Essex) 1950
Seacole, J P (Oxford U) 1978
Sellens, C J (Charlton Ath) 1966
Setters, M (WBA) 1957
Shanks, D (Luton T) 1971
Sharp, C (Northampton T) 1961
Sharples, S (Everton) 1961
Shaw, B (Sheffield U) 1963
Shaw, C (Chelsea) 1961
Shaw, G (Aston Villa) 1979
Shaw, N (Middlesex) 1951, 1952
Shawcross, D (Manchester C) 1959
Shilton, P (Leicester C) 1967, 1968
Shreeve, D (Middlesex) 1950
Shrewsbury, P (Notts Co) 1965
Sibley, F (QPR) 1966
Siddall, B (Bolton W) 1973
Sidney, W (Durham Co) 1949
Sillett, P (Hampshire) 1950
Simons, G (Brentford) 1964
Sisman, G (Luton T) 1979
Sissons, J (West Ham U) 1963, 1964

Skull, J (Wiltshire) 1949
Sleeuwenhoek, J (Aston Villa) 1960, 1962
Smailes, J (Essex) 1950
Smart, B (Chelsea) 1958
Smillie, A (West Ham U) 1958, 1959
Smith, B (Manchester U) 1958, 1959
Smith, B (Bolton W) 1973, 1974
Smith, D (Gloucestershire) 1953
Smith, I R (Tottenham H) 1975
Smith, J (Essex) 1953
Smith, J (West Ham U) 1957
Smith, P (Sheffield & Hallam) 1956
Smith, R (Manchester U) 1961
Smith, S J (Birmingham C) 1975
Smith, T (Liverpool) 1963
Smith, W (Sheffield W) 1965
Smithson, R (Arsenal) 1962
Sparrow, J P (Chelsea) 1975
Spence, A (Sunderland) 1958
Spector, M (Middlesex) 1952
Spencer, J R (Sheffield & Hallam) 1952, 1953
Spencer, M (Staffs) 1951, 1952
Spencer-Smith, D (Penzance) 1974
Spilsbury, J (Worcestershire) 1952
Spiring, P J (Bristol C) 1968
Spratt, T (Manchester U) 1959
Springett, P (QPR) 1964
Stainrod, S A (Sheffield U) 1977
Starks, B (Southampton) 1962
Statham, D J (WBA) 1977
Staton, B (Sheffield & Hallam) 1956 (Doncaster R) 1957
Stenson, J A (Charlton Ath) 1968
Stiles, N (Manchester U) 1959
Stirk, J (Ipswich T) 1974
Stokes, R W (Southampton) 1969
Stonehouse, D (North Riding) 1951, 1952
Storton, B (Huddersfield T) 1957
Stratton, R (Woking) 1957
Stringer, J (Norwich C) 1963
Styles, A (Everton) 1968
Suddick, A (Newcastle U) 1962
Suggett, C (Durham FA) 1965
Sullivan, B (Fulham) 1959
Sullivan, C (Plymouth Arg) 1969
Summerfield K (WBA) 1977
Summerill, P E (Birmingham C) 1966
Sutcliffe, P D (Manchester U) 1975
Sutton, R (Winsford U) 1969
Swain, D (Liverpool) 1970
Swan, P (Sheffield W) 1955
Swindells, J (Manchester County) 1955
Swindlehurst, D (Crystal Palace) 1974
Sydenham, J (Southampton) 1957, 1958
Sykes, F (West Riding) 1956
Sykes, N (Gloucestershire) 1953
Syrett, D K (Swindon T) 1974

Tait, A (Northumberland) 1952
Tate, G (Leicestershire & Rutland) 1955
Taylor, R H (Huddersfield T) 1974, 1975
Taylor, T (Orient) 1969, 1970
Temple, D (Everton) 1958
Templeton, S J (Scunthorpe U) 1972
Tether, C (Staffs) 1955
Thomas, B (Leicester C) 1955
Thomas, D (Burnley) 1968, 1969
Thomas, E (Wiltshire) 1951, 1952
Thompson, C D (Bolton W) 1978
Thompson, P B (Liverpool) 1972
Thursby, R (Durham) 1956
Thwaites, D (Birmingham C) 1961, 1962
Tilsed, R (Bournemouth) 1970, 1971
Tindall, M (Aston Villa) 1958
Tinnion, B (Workington T) 1966
Toase, D (Durham) 1948
Todd, C (Sunderland) 1967
Tomkins, L (Crystal Palace) 1967
Tomkys, M (Middlesex) 1951
Tomlinson, J (Liverpool) 1952
Towers, M A (Manchester C) 1969, 1970
Townsend, N R (Northampton T) 1968
Trenchard, C (Widemarsh U) 1962
Trewick, J (WBA) 1975

Trigg, G Chesterfield) 1959
Trunkfield, M (Manchester C) 1970
Turbitt, P (Bradford C) 1969
Turner, C R (Sheffield W) 1977
Turner, M (Bridport) 1957
Turner, R D (Ipswich T) 1974
Twist, F (Liverpool) 1958, 1959
Twitchin, I (Torquay U) 1969
Tynan, R (Tranmere R) 1973, 1974

Valentine, J (Lancashire) 1955
Venables, T (Chelsea) 1960
Vickets, P (West Riding) 1951
Vincent, J (Birmingham C) 1965
Vine, P (Southampton) 1958

Wagstaffe, D (Manchester C) 1960
Wainman, W H (Grimsby T) 1964
Waite, J (Grimsby T) 1960
Wales, A (Doncaster R) 1960
Walford, S J (Tottenham H) 1976
Walker, R (West Ham U) 1957
Wallington, F M (Lincolnshire Co FA) 1971
Wanklin, J (Portsmouth) 1962
Want, A G (Tottenham H) 1967
Ward, G (London & Essex) 1953
Ward, M B (Shrewsbury T) 1971
Ware, N G (Tranmere R) 1970, 1971
Warman, P (Charlton Ath) 1968
Warner, R (Leicestershire) 1949
Warnes, R (Tooting & Mitcham) 1962
Watkins, J (Gloucestershire) 1951, 1952
Watson, G (Oxford U) 1979
Watts, G (Chesterfield) 1962
Watts, R (Essex) 1952
Webb, D (St Albans C) 1973
Webster, M W (Arsenal) 1969
Weir, A (Sunderland) 1978
Welch, R G (Sheffield U) 1969
Went, P F (Leyton Orient) 1967 (Charlton Ath) 1968
West, G (Blackpool) 1960, 1961

Westburgh, M (West Ham U) 1968
White, J (Portsmouth) 1959
Whitear J (Surrey) 1953
Whitehead, C (Bristol C) 1973
Whitington, E (Chelsea) 1964
Whittaker, R (Arsenal) 1962, 1963
Whittle, A (Everton) 1968
Whitworth, S (Leicester C) 1970
Wicks, P (Sheffield W) 1966
Wicks, S J (Chelsea) 1975
Wilcox, R J (Leicestershire) 1975
Wileman, A (Measham Imperial) 1958
Wilkins, R C (Chelsea) 1975
Wilkinson, G (Durham) 1953
Wilkinson, H (Sheffield W) 1962
Willder, F (Blackpool) 1962
Williams, A (Bristol C) 1960
Williams, E (Canterbury C) 1974
Williams, J (Manchester County) 1950
Williams, W (Portsmouth) 1960
Willis, R G (Chelsea) 1965
Wilson, H (Burnley) 1971
Winstanley, E (Barnsley) 1962
Wojciechowicz, A (Blackpool) 1970
Wood, A E (Manchester C) 1964
Woodley, D (West Ham U) 1959
Woods, A (Tottenham H) 1955
Woods, B (Manchester C) 1968
Woods, C (Nottingham F) 1977, 1978
Woods, J (Gillingham) 1966
Woodward, A (Sheffield U) 1965
Woolley, P D (Chesterfield) 1968
Wootton, R (Essex) 1954
Worley, L (Berks & Bucks)
Wright, B (Leicester C) 1955
Wright, B (Leeds U) 1964
Wright, D (Barnsley GS) 1957, 1958
Wright, J M (Aston Villa) 1964, 1965
Wright, V (Lancashire) 1949

Young, E (Manchester U) 1971
Young, N (Manchester C) 1962

F.A. COUNTY YOUTH CHALLENGE CUP 1978-79

First Round
Durham v Westmorland 3-0
Lancashire v North Riding 6-1
East Riding v Sheffield & Hallamshire 0-3
Shropshire v Staffordshire 1-3
Nottinghamshire v Derbyshire 1-0
Birmingham v Northamptonshire 2-1
Huntingdonshire v Norfolk 5-2
Cambridgeshire v Hertfordshire 0-1
Surrey v Hampshire 0-1
London v Bedfordshire 1-2
RAF v Oxfordshire 0-3
Herefordshire v Worcestershire 1-4
Royal Navy v Somerset 2-2
Devon v Cornwall 0-2

Replay
Somerset v Royal Navy 4-1

Second Round
Northumberland v Durham 1-2
Cumberland v Lancashire 0-3
Liverpool v Manchester 2-1
West Riding v Sheffield & Hallamshire 6-1
Cheshire v Staffordshire 5-3
Lincolnshire v Nottinghamshire 4-4
Leicestershire & Rutland v Birmingham 1-3
Essex v Huntingdonshire 2-0
Suffolk v Hertfordshire 0-2
Middlesex v Hampshire 0-4
Army v Bedfordshire 4-3
Kent v Sussex 2-3
Berks & Bucks v Oxfordshire 5-0
Gloucestershire v Worcestershire (aet) 3-5
Wiltshire v Somerset 5-1
Dorset v Cornwall 1-0

Replay
Nottinghamshire v Lincolnshire 4-2

Third Round
Durham v Lancashire 1-3
Liverpool v West Riding 2-2
Cheshire v Nottinghamshire 0-1
Birmingham v Worcestershire 1-1
Essex v Hertfordshire 1-3
Army v Berks & Bucks 1-0
Hampshire v Dorset 3-0
Wiltshire v Dorset 1-2

Replays
West Riding v Liverpool 0-3
Worcestershire v Birmingham 2-2

Fourth Round
Birmingham v Lancashire 0-1
Nottinghamshire v Liverpool 0-2
Dorset v Hertfordshire 1-4
Hampshire v Army 7-1

Semi-Final Ties
Liverpool v Lancashire 2-0
Hertfordshire v Hampshire 4-1

Final Tie
Liverpool v Hertfordshire 1-4
at Burscough FC

THE SOUTHERN FOOTBALL LEAGUE 1978-79

PREMIER DIVISION

	P	W	D	L	F	A	Pts
Worcester C	42	27	11	4	92	33	65
Kettering T	42	27	7	8	109	43	61
Telford U	42	22	10	10	60	39	54
Maidstone U	42	18	18	6	55	35	54
Bath C	42	17	19	6	59	41	53
Weymouth	42	18	15	9	71	51	51
AP Leamington	42	19	11	12	65	53	49
Redditch U	42	19	10	13	70	57	48
Yeovil T	42	15	16	11	59	49	46
Witney T	42	17	10	15	53	52	44
Nuneaton Bor	42	13	17	12	59	50	43
Gravesend & Northfleet	42	15	12	15	56	55	42
Barnet	42	16	10	16	52	64	42
Hillingdon Bor	42	12	16	14	50	41	40
Wealdstone	42	12	12	18	51	59	36
Atherstone T	42	9	17	16	46	65	35
Dartford	42	10	14	18	40	56	34
Cheltenham T	42	11	10	21	38	72	32
Margate	42	10	9	23	44	75	29
Dorchester T	42	7	11	24	46	86	25
Hastings U	42	5	13	24	37	85	23
Bridgend T	42	6	6	30	39	90	18

FIRST DIVISION NORTH

	P	W	D	L	F	A	Pts
Grantham	38	21	10	7	70	45	52
Merthyr Tydfil	38	22	7	9	90	53	51
Alvechurch	38	20	10	8	70	42	50
Bedford T	38	19	9	10	74	49	47
King's Lynn	38	17	11	10	57	46	45
Oswestry T	38	18	8	12	63	43	44
Gloucester C	38	18	8	12	76	59	44
Burton Albion	38	16	10	12	51	40	42
Kidderminster H	38	13	14	11	70	60	40
Bedworth U	38	13	14	11	41	34	40
Tamworth	38	15	8	15	47	45	38
Stourbridge	38	15	7	16	64	61	37
Barry T	38	14	9	15	51	53	37
Enderby T	38	14	8	16	46	55	36
Banbury U	38	10	13	15	42	58	33
Wellingborough T	38	13	6	19	50	71	32
Cambridge C	38	9	9	20	37	62	27
Bromsgrove R	38	6	14	18	33	61	26
Milton Keynes C	38	7	9	22	37	87	23
Corby T	38	5	6	27	40	85	16

Leading Goalscorers (League and League Cup)

PREMIER DIVISION
34 Kellock (Kettering T)
26 Clayton (Kettering T)
25 Phipps (Kettering T)
22 Henderson (Weymouth)
20 Roberts (Dorchester T)
20 Tuohy (Redditch U)
19 Cleary (Barnet)
19 Bastable (Redditch U)
19 Phelps (Worcester C)
19 Vincent (AP Leamington)
18 Gardener (AP Leamington)
18 Leitch (Weymouth)

FIRST DIVISION NORTH
39 Cooke (Grantham)
34 Pratt (Merthyr Tydfil)
26 Mullen (Kidderminster H)
25 Cunningham (Stourbridge)
19 Mortimore (Bedford T)
18 Kaviel (Bedford T)
18 Roberts (Bedford T)
17 Harper (Alvechurch)

FIRST DIVISION SOUTH

	P	W	D	L	F	A	Pts
Dover	40	28	9	3	88	20	65
Folkestone & Shepway	40	22	6	12	84	50	50
Gosport Bor	40	19	11	10	62	47	49
Chelmsford C	40	20	7	13	65	61	47
Minehead	40	16	13	11	58	39	45
Poole T	40	15	15	10	48	44	45
Hounslow	40	16	12	12	56	45	44
Waterlooville	40	17	10	13	52	43	44
Trowbridge T	40	15	12	13	65	61	42
Aylesbury U	40	16	9	15	54	52	41
Taunton T	40	16	9	15	53	51	41
Bognor Regis T	40	17	7	16	58	58	41
Dunstable	40	18	4	18	57	55	40
Tonbridge AFC	40	15	10	15	43	47	40
Salisbury	40	13	10	17	47	51	36
Basingstoke T	40	12	11	17	49	62	35
Addlestone	40	12	9	19	56	64	33
Andover	40	12	6	22	47	69	30
Ashford T	40	10	10	20	28	53	30
Crawley T	40	9	9	22	44	75	27
Canterbury C	40	6	3	31	31	98	15

FIRST DIVISION SOUTH
31 Ovard (Folkestone & Shepway)
23 Coulbert (Gosport Bor)
21 Green (Andover)
20 Morris (Addlestone)
19 Peterson (Chelmsford C)
19 Unit (Bognor Regis T)
17 Francis (Hounslow)
17 Melisi (Aylesbury U)
16 Hawes (Gosport Bor)
15 Brown (Minehead)
15 Legg (Trowbridge T)

THE NORTHERN PREMIER LEAGUE 1978-79

	P	W	D	L	F	A	Pts
Mossley	44	32	5	7	117	48	69
Altrincham	44	25	11	8	93	39	61
Matlock T	44	24	8	12	100	59	56
Scarborough	44	19	14	11	61	44	52
Southport	44	19	14	11	62	49	52
Boston U	44	17	18	9	40	33	52
Runcorn	44	21	9	14	79	54	51
Stafford R	44	18	14	12	67	41	50
Goole T	44	17	15	12	56	61	49
Northwich Vic	44	18	11	15	64	52	47
Lancaster C	44	17	12	15	62	54	46
Bangor C	44	15	14	15	65	66	44
Worksop T	44	13	14	17	55	67	40
Workington	44	16	7	21	62	74	39
Netherfield	44	13	11	20	39	69	37
Barrow	44	14	9	21	47	78	37
Gainsborough Tr	44	12	12	20	52	67	36
Morecambe	44	11	13	20	55	65	35
Frickley Ath	44	13	9	22	58	70	35
South Liverpool	44	12	10	22	48	85	34
Gateshead	44	11	11	22	42	63	33
Buxton	44	11	9	24	50	84	31
Macclesfield T	44	8	10	26	40	92	26

Leading Goalscorers—League and League Cup
38, Moore (Mossley); 33, Smith (Mossley); 30, O'Keefe (Mossley); 29, Rogers (Altrincham); 24, Cullerton (Stafford R), (2 with Northwich Victoria); 24, Skeete (Mossley); 22, Johnson (Altrincham); 21, Whitbread (Runcorn); 19, Heathcote (Altrincham); 19, Thompson (Goole T); 18, Cowperthwaite C, (Barrow); 18, Owen (Bangor C); 18, Scott (Matlock T).

SOUTHERN LEAGUE PREMIER DIVISION 1978-79

	Atherstone T	AP Leamington (formerly Lockheed Leamington)	Barnet	Bath C	Bridgend T	Cheltenham T	Dartford	Dorchester T	Gravesend and Northfleet	Hastings U	Hillingdon Bor	Kettering T	Maidstone U	Margate	Nuneaton Bor	Redditch U	Telford U	Wealdstone	Weymouth	Witney T	Worcester C	Yeovil T
Atherstone T	—	1-3	2-1	1-1	2-0	2-2	1-1	0-1	0-1	2-2	1-0	0-2	2-2	1-1	2-2	1-3	0-2	2-2	1-0	0-1	1-3	1-1
AP Leamington (formerly Lockheed Leamington)	0-1	—	1-3	1-1	5-1	1-0	2-0	3-2	1-0	3-1	2-2	2-1	1-0	2-0	0-0	1-1	1-0	0-0	2-2	2-0	1-1	3-0
Barnet	1-1	2-1	—	1-1	0-0	2-0	1-0	3-3	0-0	4-0	0-2	0-4	0-2	2-0	0-2	2-1	1-4	3-2	0-4	1-0	2-3	1-1
Bath C	1-1	1-1	4-0	—	5-0	2-1	1-0	2-0	1-0	1-0	0-2	0-0	0-1	1-1	3-2	1-1	1-2	1-0	1-1	1-0	0-0	3-0
Bridgend T	1-0	3-2	0-2	1-2	—	0-1	0-2	1-2	1-2	2-3	0-1	1-2	1-2	1-2	1-2	1-1	1-0	3-1	1-1	3-5	3-3	1-1
Cheltenham T	4-2	0-0	1-0	0-2	2-0	—	1-0	2-1	0-2	1-0	0-0	0-4	1-1	3-2	1-2	3-1	2-1	2-4	2-4	1-0	0-2	1-1
Dartford	1-2	0-2	2-1	1-1	0-1	—	—	2-1	3-1	0-0	0-1	0-1	0-2	2-1	1-0	2-3	0-0	1-0	1-3	1-1	1-1	0-0
Dorchester T	0-1	0-0	0-1	1-1	3-3	1-0	3-2	—	—	2-1	1-4	0-6	0-0	1-2	1-0	0-2	1-1	5-1	0-0	2-1	1-5	3-1
Gravesend and Northfleet	3-3	2-1	1-4	2-2	5-1	3-0	5-1	3-1	—	0-0	1-1	1-1	2-2	2-1	3-1	2-1	1-0	5-2	0-0	2-0	0-1	0-1
Hastings U	1-4	2-3	0-0	2-2	0-0	3-1	1-1	4-0	1-1	—	0-0	0-3	1-0	0-2	2-2	1-2	1-0	2-4	1-2	0-1	0-4	0-2
Hillingdon Bor	2-0	1-1	0-0	4-0	3-0	2-0	1-1	2-4	1-1	3-0	—	1-3	0-1	1-1	1-1	2-0	1-1	1-0	0-0	3-0	0-1	0-0
Kettering T	5-0	4-2	4-0	6-1	5-0	2-1	0-0	3-1	3-0	5-0	2-2	—	1-2	3-0	2-1	2-3	1-3	1-0	4-3	2-1	3-5	5-1
Maidstone U	1-1	1-1	1-1	0-0	1-0	3-1	2-2	3-1	1-0	3-1	3-2	1-0	—	—	2-1	1-1	0-1	0-0	1-1	1-1	1-2	2-2
Margate	0-3	4-2	0-2	1-4	1-0	2-3	1-1	3-1	1-3	2-2	4-1	3-2	0-2	—	1-1	1-1	0-1	1-0	2-3	0-2	0-2	0-0
Nuneaton Bor	2-0	1-0	0-2	2-1	3-1	5-1	1-1	3-0	0-0	3-0	0-0	0-3	3-3	4-1	—	1-1	0-1	4-0	2-2	1-2	1-1	0-0
Redditch U	2-1	3-5	5-0	1-1	2-1	3-0	3-0	1-0	0-0	1-1	3-2	1-1	3-0	4-1	0-2	—	0-2	1-0	1-0	1-2	0-1	3-1
Telford U	0-0	4-0	1-2	1-1	1-0	3-0	0-0	4-1	3-1	2-0	2-0	0-5	0-2	2-1	0-2	1-0	—	2-2	1-1	3-1	0-0	2-0
Wealdstone	1-0	0-1	1-1	0-0	3-0	0-0	3-4	2-2	2-1	1-2	1-0	0-5	2-1	1-0	0-0	3-0	3-0	—	0-0	0-1	0-0	4-0
Weymouth	1-1	2-1	4-1	1-3	4-1	3-0	3-0	2-1	2-1	3-0	1-0	2-2	0-1	0-0	4-0	2-2	0-1	2-1	—	1-0	1-0	3-3
Witney T	1-1	2-3	4-3	1-2	2-2	0-0	3-3	1-0	1-0	5-0	1-1	1-1	1-0	0-0	1-1	2-1	0-2	3-1	—	—	1-2	3-2
Worcester C	7-1	1-2	2-1	0-1	2-1	5-0	3-3	3-0	1-1	4-1	1-0	1-1	0-0	3-0	1-1	3-0	5-2	3-1	3-0	3-0	—	1-0
Yeovil T	0-0	3-1	0-1	1-1	1-0	0-0	2-1	3-0	4-0	3-1	2-1	0-1	0-0	2-0	3-1	4-0	3-3	4-1	4-0	2-0	1-1	—

SOUTHERN LEAGUE—FIRST DIVISION (NORTH)—1978-79

	Alvechurch	Banbury U	Barry T	Bedford T	Bedworth U	Bromsgrove R	Burton A	Cambridge C	Corby T	Enderby T	Gloucester C	Grantham	Kidderminster H	King's Lynn	Merthyr Tydfil	Milton Keynes C (formerly Bletchley T)	Oswestry T	Stourbridge	Tamworth	Wellingborough T
*Alvechurch	—	1-1	2-1	3-2	1-1	3-1	2-0	5-1	1-0	4-0	1-1	1-1	4-2	2-2	1-0	6-0	1-2	2-1	1-2	3-1
Banbury U	1-1	—	1-0	1-3	0-2	1-1	1-1	1-3	3-2	2-1	2-2	1-3	3-3	2-1	2-1	3-0	1-4	1-2	0-0	0-1
Barry T	2-0	1-2	—	1-3	1-0	1-2	5-2	2-0	4-1	1-2	3-1	3-1	1-4	4-1	1-0	3-1	2-0	0-2	0-2	2-2
Bedford T	1-2	3-0	1-1	—	0-0	3-2	3-1	2-0	3-1	2-3	3-1	5-0	5-2	2-3	1-1	0-3	0-2	2-1	2-0	3-1
Bedworth U	0-0	1-0	0-0	1-3	—	1-0	3-1	1-2	4-0	4-1	0-2	1-2	1-1	0-0	1-1	1-1	0-2	1-1	2-0	1-0
Bromsgrove R	1-2	1-2	1-4	2-2	1-1	—	1-1	1-0	2-1	0-0	2-3	0-1	2-2	1-4	1-3	2-2	0-3	1-1	0-1	0-0
Burton Albion	3-1	2-0	2-0	2-2	2-1	1-3	—	1-0	4-2	0-1	1-1	0-1	2-2	1-0	0-1	4-0	3-1	1-0	3-0	2-0
Cambridge C	1-0	0-0	1-1	1-3	0-2	2-2	—	—	4-0	1-3	0-0	0-0	0-2	0-3	3-1	0-1	1-0	1-0	3-0	2-3
Corby T	0-1	4-1	1-1	0-2	2-3	1-1	0-0	0-0	—	0-1	3-1	0-0	0-0	0-3	1-2	2-3	2-1	0-1	3-0	0-2
Enderby T	1-1	1-1	1-1	3-1	1-0	2-0	0-2	0-0	1-5	—	3-1	1-2	2-0	3-0	0-2	2-1	4-1	3-4	1-0	3-0
Gloucester C	0-3	2-1	1-1	3-1	1-2	1-1	1-1	0-2	4-1	4-1	—	1-2	2-2	3-0	5-0	2-1	4-3	2-2	1-0	3-0
Grantham	3-3	3-0	0-0	1-1	3-2	1-2	2-0	1-1	3-2	3-1	3-0	—	2-2	3-0	3-0	3-0	1-1	2-1	1-0	6-0
Kidderminster H	1-0	1-1	4-0	1-3	2-2	3-0	1-1	1-2	6-1	1-1	3-0	—	—	0-3	2-5	5-1	1-2	4-2	0-2	2-1
King's Lynn	3-1	0-0	0-0	3-2	1-1	1-0	0-2	3-4	4-2	1-0	4-1	2-4	0-0	—	0-3	1-1	0-0	1-0	0-0	2-1
Merthyr Tydfil	4-2	3-1	2-1	2-1	1-1	3-0	0-1	6-2	9-0	3-2	3-2	2-2	0-0	2-1	—	4-2	4-0	1-3	5-0	5-2
Milton Keynes C (formerly Bletchley T)	0-2	1-2	0-0	1-4	0-0	1-0	2-0	2-0	1-4	1-0	0-7	0-3	1-2	1-2	3-6	—	1-5	2-5	5-0	0-0
Oswestry T	0-0	3-0	4-0	0-0	0-1	1-0	1-0	2-0	1-1	3-0	1-0	2-0	0-2	0-2	1-1	3-1	—	3-1	3-2	5-0
Stourbridge	0-3	1-1	3-0	1-3	4-2	0-1	1-0	4-1	2-0	1-1	3-4	1-2	2-2	1-3	5-3	1-2	1-1	—	2-1	2-0
Tamworth	1-2	2-0	0-1	1-1	1-0	0-0	2-1	2-1	2-0	2-0	4-3	4-2	1-2	1-1	0-1	3-2	1-1	—	—	5-0
Wellingborough T	1-2	1-3	4-1	1-1	0-1	5-0	3-1	5-1	3-2	0-2	1-2	1-0	0-2	1-1	1-2	0-0	3-2	3-2	3-2	—

*First season in the Southern League

SOUTHERN LEAGUE—FIRST DIVISION (SOUTH)—1978-79

	Addlestone	Andover	Ashford T	Aylesbury U	Basingstoke T	Bognor Regis T	Canterbury C	Chelmsford C	Crawley T	Dover	Dunstable (formerly Dunstable T)	Folkestone and Shepway (formerly Folkestone)	Gosport Bor	Hounslow	Minehead	Poole T	Salisbury	Taunton T	Tonbridge AFC (formerly Tonbridge)	Trowbridge T	Waterlooville
Addlestone	—	4-1	1-3	2-0	5-1	2-0	3-0	2-3	1-2	0-1	0-0	1-3	1-0	2-1	2-3	0-0	0-0	1-2	1-1	1-3	1-2
Andover	3-0	—	1-1	2-3	2-5	0-2	2-1	1-2	0-1	1-1	2-1	5-2	0-1	0-2	3-1	0-0	2-1	0-0	2-1	3-1	1-2
Ashford T	0-2	2-1	—	2-0	1-0	0-2	1-0	1-1	1-0	0-1	1-0	1-0	0-0	0-2	0-3	0-1	1-1	0-2	1-1	0-0	2-0
Aylesbury U	3-3	1-1	3-1	—	1-0	1-1	3-2	2-0	4-0	1-2	2-0	3-2	4-0	1-3	0-6	2-1	1-1	2-2	0-2	2-0	0-2
Basingstoke T	2-0	0-0	0-1	1-1	—	1-0	3-1	0-1	0-0	0-1	1-2	2-1	3-0	1-3	0-6	1-3	1-1	0-1	2-2	2-1	4-1
Bognor Regis T	2-1	2-0	1-0	1-3	5-2	—	0-2	1-2	3-1	2-1	2-0	3-3	2-2	2-0	1-0	2-1	1-2	1-3	3-3	2-0	2-1
Canterbury C	0-2	0-1	2-0	1-0	0-1	0-2	—	1-3	1-3	0-2	1-3	2-5	1-1	2-1	2-0	1-4	0-3	1-3	3-3	1-3	0-2
Chelmsford C	3-1	1-1	4-0	2-3	1-0	4-1	2-0	—	2-1	2-1	2-1	3-2	1-1	0-1	2-0	3-3	0-3	1-3	3-2	1-1	0-2
Crawley T	0-3	1-2	1-1	0-0	2-4	3-1	3-1	1-1	—	2-1	2-3	0-3	0-2	0-1	0-2	1-2	4-3	4-0	2-2	1-2	1-1
Dover	7-1	4-2	2-1	2-0	2-0	4-0	7-0	5-0	7-1	—	2-0	1-0	4-1	0-0	1-1	0-0	4-0	4-0	1-1	1-1	3-1
*Dunstable (formerly Dunstable T)	2-1	3-1	1-0	0-0	2-0	4-2	4-0	3-0	3-0	1-3	—	1-0	2-0	3-1	0-1	2-1	1-3	1-2	1-1	0-1	1-0
Folkestone and Shepway (formerly Folkestone)	2-4	4-0	4-1	2-2	3-1	4-2	1-2	4-4	3-0	0-1	2-1	—	6-2	2-1	0-0	1-0	2-1	4-0	1-0	3-2	2-0
†Gosport Bor	4-0	2-0	3-0	0-3	0-0	2-2	4-0	3-1	1-1	0-2	2-1	5-2	—	2-1	1-0	2-1	1-0	3-0	5-0	1-1	1-1
Hounslow	1-1	1-3	2-0	1-2	2-2	5-0	2-1	0-0	0-0	0-1	2-3	0-3	0-1	—	2-0	0-0	2-0	1-1	2-0	2-1	4-2
Minehead	2-2	0-0	2-1	4-0	1-1	4-0	4-0	0-0	2-2	0-2	7-3	0-0	1-0	1-3	—	2-0	2-0	1-1	0-0	5-2	1-1
Poole T	0-0	1-4	1-1	1-0	2-1	3-2	2-2	3-1	2-1	1-1	2-1	0-2	0-0	2-2	1-1	—	2-1	1-0	0-0	2-2	0-1
Salisbury	1-0	1-2	3-0	4-1	0-0	1-0	1-0	3-0	2-0	0-2	3-1	0-4	0-3	1-1	1-0	0-1	—	2-4	0-1	3-0	0-0
Taunton T	0-1	0-1	1-0	1-0	1-1	1-1	3-0	4-0	2-0	0-2	2-1	2-3	2-2	0-1	0-0	1-2	0-0	—	0-2	3-0	1-1
Tonbridge AFC (formerly Tonbridge)	0-3	2-0	1-0	1-0	1-2	0-3	2-0	2-1	1-3	0-2	2-0	1-1	0-0	0-0	2-0	0-1	4-2	2-1	—	2-0	1-0
Trowbridge T	4-2	3-2	1-1	2-2	3-3	3-0	3-1	1-2	4-2	0-0	2-0	1-1	1-2	2-2	0-1	2-1	2-1	3-1	2-0	—	1-3
Waterlooville	2-0	3-0	1-1	3-0	0-0	1-2	4-1	1-4	0-1	0-0	0-0	2-0	2-0	3-1	0-0	3-0	1-0	2-1	2-1	1-3	—

*—Last season they were in the (North) section of the Southern League
†—First season in the Southern League

NORTHERN PREMIER LEAGUE—1978-79

	Altrincham	Bangor C	Barrow	Boston U	Buxton	Frickley Ath	Gainsborough Tr	Gateshead	Goole T	Lancaster C	Macclesfield T	Matlock T	Morecambe	Mossley	Netherfield	Northwich Vic	Runcorn	Scarborough	South Liverpool	Southport	Stafford Rangers	Workington	Worksop T
Altrincham	—	3-2	4-0	3-0	0-1	1-2	3-0	2-0	2-1	0-0	0-1	3-1	1-1	0-1	1-0	1-1	2-1	2-0	5-1	1-3	0-0	3-2	4-1
Bangor C	1-1	—	1-3	1-1	1-1	4-2	1-1	1-2	0-0	2-1	2-1	3-3	4-0	3-1	1-1	1-0	1-2	0-0	3-0	0-2	0-2	2-0	2-4
Barrow	1-6	0-1	—	*0-0	1-0	1-0	2-1	4-2	2-0	2-1	1-2	3-2	0-0	2-5	3-3	2-4	1-2	0-1	0-0	0-2	*1-1	1-2	1-1
Boston U	1-4	1-1	*2-0	—	1-0	2-0	1-0	1-1	0-0	0-0	2-0	2-1	*3-0	1-0	0-0	1-0	0-0	0-3	1-0	1-0	0-1	2-1	2-2
Buxton	0-4	5-1	*2-1	0-0	—	2-0	1-1	1-1	1-2	3-1	*2-1	1-3	1-6	1-3	1-1	0-2	0-2	1-0	4-1	1-1	0-1	0-4	1-2
Frickley Ath	0-4	1-3	1-2	1-1	1-0	—	4-0	1-1	1-2	3-2	3-1	1-3	1-6	0-2	5-0	1-3	0-2	1-0	6-0	1-3	0-3	3-1	1-1
Gainsborough Tr	2-4	1-1	1-2	2-0	1-1	—	—	0-1	1-2	1-0	2-1	3-3	2-1	1-0	0-1	0-1	2-3	1-2	1-2	3-0	*1-0	3-0	1-2
Gateshead	0-3	2-4	1-2	0-1	1-0	1-0	1-0	—	0-1	0-1	0-1	1-2	2-0	1-3	*1-3	2-2	1-1	1-0	1-1	*2-1	1-1	0-1	*0-2
Goole T	1-1	3-1	3-1	0-2	3-3	2-0	0-0	0-0	—	0-0	2-0	1-1	3-2	0-4	1-0	1-0	3-0	2-2	2-1	0-2	2-1	2-1	1-2
Lancaster C	0-4	3-1	0-1	0-2	4-1	1-3	3-0	1-0	—	—	5-3	0-0	4-2	2-3	0-0	1-0	3-0	1-0	4-0	2-2	1-0	4-1	1-1
Macclesfield T	1-5	0-0	1-1	0-2	2-2	0-2	2-2	0-1	1-2	0-1	—	0-4	0-0	1-1	1-1	1-0	2-3	1-1	3-2	1-2	1-0	3-0	1-0
Matlock T	2-0	1-2	0-1	1-0	4-1	1-0	2-3	4-1	2-2	2-0	5-0	—	*1-1	2-4	3-1	3-2	2-3	6-0	3-1	1-3	3-2	5-1	1-1
Morecambe	2-4	3-1	0-1	0-0	3-1	1-1	*2-2	3-3	3-2	2-0	4-0	0-1	—	1-2	2-0	0-0	1-0	1-3	2-1	0-1	0-1	2-0	1-4
Mossley	1-1	3-0	6-1	1-1	3-1	4-3	2-0	1-2	5-1	3-1	5-0	1-6	3-2	—	2-0	2-3	4-2	2-2	6-0	3-1	2-1	4-1	4-0
Netherfield	0-0	1-0	0-1	0-2	3-1	1-0	0-2	0-0	*3-0	0-0	2-0	0-1	3-2	1-3	—	3-1	4-2	*1-0	3-1	2-1	1-1	1-0	*2-0
Northwich Vic	1-0	1-2	3-0	3-0	0-0	4-0	1-2	3-1	0-0	2-2	3-0	2-1	0-0	2-0	3-1	—	2-3	2-0	0-0	2-2	2-0	*2-1	1-1
Runcorn	0-0	0-0	2-1	4-2	6-0	0-1	3-0	2-0	4-0	1-3	6-0	2-3	2-0	0-2	3-0	1-2	—	0-0	4-1	0-0	3-2	0-0	2-0
Scarborough	1-2	1-1	1-0	0-0	0-0	2-0	3-0	2-0	3-1	1-3	2-2	0-1	0-0	2-1	5-0	4-0	1-2	—	2-0	0-1	3-2	0-1	2-0
South Liverpool	1-1	1-1	2-0	*3-1	3-0	2-2	2-2	0-1	2-0	0-2	1-1	0-3	3-1	0-1	2-1	2-1	4-1	3-0	—	0-1	0-1	1-1	1-0
Southport	3-1	0-0	1-2	1-0	2-1	0-0	3-3	0-2	1-1	2-2	3-2	2-1	1-0	0-1	3-1	2-2	0-3	1-2	2-2	—	1-2	3-1	2-0
Stafford Rangers	1-1	3-2	4-2	0-0	4-3	1-0	*0-1	1-1	3-0	1-1	2-0	1-2	0-0	0-2	7-0	3-0	4-0	*0-0	5-1	1-1	—	0-2	0-0
Workington	0-4	3-1	1-0	1-2	2-1	2-2	0-0	3-2	3-3	0-0	2-0	1-0	3-1	0-6	0-1	4-1	1-1	3-2	6-1	0-2	1-0	—	3-0
Worksop T	1-2	1-3	3-1	1-1	0-1	3-3	1-1	2-1	0-1	0-1	3-1	2-5	3-2	1-2	1-0	2-0	1-1	2-2	1-1	*0-2	2-2	1-0	—

†—First season in the Northern Premier League
*—Match played on a Sunday

SOUTHERN LEAGUE CUP 1978-79

First Round
Cambridge City received a bye into the Second Round.
Addlestone v Hounslow	0-1, 1-0
Alvechurch v Bromsgrove R	3-2, 1-1
Ashford T v Gravesend & Northfleet	0-2, 1-3
A P Leamington v Banbury U	1-4, 1-3
Aylesbury U v Dunstable	2-0, 1-1
Basingstoke T v Andover	2-3, 2-2
Bedford T v Wellingborough T	4-1, 0-0
Bedworth T v Milton Keynes C	2-2, 1-2
Bognor Regis T v Tonbridge AFC	2-1, 1-1
Bridgend T v Barry T	0-2, 1-0
Burton Albion v Nuneaton Bor	1-1, 1-5
Canterbury C v Folkestone & Shepway	0-4, 2-2
Chelmsford C v Barnet	0-3, 2-6
Corby T v Grantham	0-1, 0-0
Crawley T v Hastings U	1-1, 0-0
Dartford v Margate	0-0, 3-3
Dorchester T v Salisbury	5-0, 2-1
Dover v Maidstone U	0-1, 0-3
Enderby T v Atherstone T	2-1, 1-4
Gloucester C v Cheltenham T	2-1, 4-2
Hillingdon Bor v Wealdstone	2-1, 0-3
Kettering T v King's Lynn	4-0, 3-0
Kidderminster H v Telford U	1-2, 1-3
Merthyr Tydfil v Bath C	2-3, 1-2
Poole T v Weymouth	1-1, 0-3
Redditch U v Stourbridge	2-3, 1-2
Tamworth v Oswestry T	0-0, 0-0
Taunton T v Minehead	0-0, 1-0
Waterlooville v Gosport Bor	1-0, 2-3
Witney T v Worcester C	0-1, 1-5
Yeovil T v Trowbridge T	2-0, 0-2

First Round Replays
Crawley T v Hastings U	2-0
Dartford v Margate	*aet 0-0
Gosport Bor v Waterlooville	aet 2-3
Hounslow v Addlestone	2-3
Tamworth v Oswestry T	1-0
Trowbridge T v Yeovil T	1-2

*Decided by penalties – Dartford won 4-3

Second Round
Addlestone v Dartford	0-3
Andover v Taunton T	2-2
Atherstone v Alvechurch	2-0
Barnet v Wealdstone	1-0
Barry T v Bognor Regis T	2-1
Bath C v Gloucester C	1-0
Bedford T v Crawley T	1-1
Cambridge C v Maidstone U	1-0
Dorchester T v Yeovil T	0-0
Grantham v Aylesbury U	2-2
Gravesend & Northfleet v Folkestone & Shepway	5-2
Kettering T v Telford U	3-3
Stourbridge v Milton Keynes C	1-2
Tamworth v Banbury U	0-2
Waterlooville v Weymouth	1-2
Worcester C v Nuneaton Bor	4-0

Second Round Replays
Aylesbury U v Grantham	0-2
Crawley T v Bedford T	aet 0-2
Taunton T v Andover	0-1
Telford U v Kettering T	4-2
Yeovil T v Dorchester T	3-0

Third Round
Andover v Weymouth	1-1
Atherstone T v Banbury U	0-0
Bath City v Barnet	4-1
Bedford T v Gravesend & Northfleet	3-0
Dartford v Cambridge C	2-1
Milton Keynes C v Worcester C	0-2
Telford U v Grantham	1-2
Yeovil T v Barry T	3-0

Third Round Replays
Banbury U v Atherstone T	3-0
Weymouth v Andover	2-0

Fourth Round
Banbury U v Bath C	0-3
Dartford v Bedford T	0-2
Weymouth v Grantham	2-1
Worcester C v Yeovil T	3-3

Fourth Round Replay
Yeovil T v Worcester C	4-1

Semi-Finals
Bath C v Bedford T	2-1
Bedford T v Bath C	1-2
Weymouth v Yeovil T	1-1
Yeovil T v Weymouth	1-0

Final
Bath C v Yeovil T	1-0
Yeovil T v Bath C	0-0

Final – First Leg: Bath City 1 Yeovil Town 0
(1,569, 7 April 1979)

Bath City: Book; Ryan, Rogers; Brown, Bourn, Cover; Wheeler, Broom, Jenkins (Bryant), Crompton, Tavener.
Scorer: Brown
Yeovil Town: Parker; Thompson, Cottle; Gold, Cotton, Harrison; Morrall, Platt, Green, Finnigan, Clancy.

Second Leg: Yeovil Town 0 Bath City 0
(3,111, 14 April 1979)

Yeovil Town: Parker; Thompson, Cottle; Leigh (Flay), Cotton, Harrison; Morrall, Platt, Green, Finnigan, Clancy.
Bath City: Book; Ryan, Rogers; Brown, Bourne, Cover; Wheeler, Broom (Higgens), Jenkins, Crompton, Tavener.

CHAMPIONSHIP MATCH

Bath City 1 Gravesend & Northfleet 3
(Played at Bath on 28 August 1978, attendance 930)

This is a match played between the League winners Bath City, and the Cup Winners Gravesend & Northfleet.

JOHN SMITH'S NORTHERN PREMIER LEAGUE CHALLENGE CUP 1978-79

The following clubs received byes into the Second Round:—Altrincham, Bangor City, Boston United, Lancaster City, Matlock Town, Northwich Victoria, Runcorn, Scarborough and Stafford Rangers.

First Round
Buxton v Worksop T	1-2
Frickley Ath v Gainsborough T	1-0
Goole T v Gateshead	1-0
Morecambe v Barrow	0-0
Mossley v Macclesfield T	7-1
Southport v South Liverpool	1-1
Workington v Netherfield	1-1

First Round Replays
Barrow v Morecambe	3-0
Netherfield v Workington	0-1
South Liverpool v Southport	*2-2

Second Replay
Southport v South Liverpool	†2-4

*after extra-time, score after 90 minutes 0-0
†after extra-time, score after 90 minutes 1-1

Second Round
Barrow v Boston U	2-2
Frickley Ath v Bangor C	2-1
Goole T v Matlock T	0-1
Lancaster C v Worksop T	1-3
Northwich Vic v Workington	2-1
Runcorn v Altrincham	2-2
Scarborough v Mossley	0-4
South Liverpool v Stafford R	0-0

Second Round Replays
Altrincham v Runcorn	3-0
Boston U v Barrow	2-0
Stafford R v South Liverpool	3-1

Third Round
Boston U v Northwich Vic	1-4
Frickley Ath v Altrincham	0-2
Mossley v Worksop T	5-1
Stafford R v Matlock T	2-0

Semi-Finals
Altrincham v Mossley	5-4
Mossley v Altrincham	5-1
Stafford R v Northwich Vic	2-2
Northwich Vic v Stafford R	2-0

Final
Mossley v Northwich Victoria 4-1
score after 90 minutes 1-1
(Played at Maine Road on 8 May 1979, attendance 5,025)

Mossley: Fitton; Brown, Vaughan; O'Keefe, Pollitt, Roberts; Smith, Grundy (Moore), Skeete, O'Connor, Gorman.
Scorers: Smith, Moore 2, Gorman.

Northwich Victoria: Ryan; Jones P., Collier; Wain, Nieman, Jones K.; Garrity, Hall, O'Connor, Bailey (Becket), Williams.
Scorer: O'Connor.

NORTHERN PREMIER LEAGUE CHALLENGE SHIELD 1978

Boston United 0 Matlock Town 1
(Played at Boston on 23 August 1978, attendance 1,387)

This is a match played between last season's League Champions, Boston United and the Cup Winners, Matlock Town.

NORTHERN PREMIER LEAGUE CHAMPIONS
v
SOUTHERN FOOTBALL LEAGUE CHAMPIONS

Boston United v Bath City   2-0 on 6 December 1978
Bath City v Boston United   4-1 on 11 December 1978

BERGER ISTHMIAN FOOTBALL LEAGUE

FINAL TABLES 1978-79
PREMIER DIVISION

	P	W	D	L	F	A	Pts.	Penalty Points C	D
Barking	42	28	9	5	92	50	93	11	—
Dagenham	42	25	6	11	83	63	81	12	—
Enfield	42	22	11	9	69	37	77	12	—
Dulwich Hamlet	42	21	13	8	69	39	76	8	—
Slough Town	42	20	12	10	61	44	72	14	—
Wycombe Wanderers	42	20	9	13	59	44	69	8	—
Woking	42	18	14	10	79	59	68	13	3
Croydon	42	19	9	14	61	51	66	6	—
Hendon	42	16	14	12	55	48	62	7	8
Leatherhead	42	17	9	16	57	45	60	5	—
Sutton United	42	17	9	16	62	51	60	4	—
Tooting & Mitcham	42	15	14	13	52	52	59	15	5
Walthamstow Avenue	42	15	6	21	61	69	51	3	—
Tilbury	42	13	11	18	60	76	50	30	5
Boreham Wood	42	13	10	19	50	67	49	13	5
Hitchin Town	42	12	11	19	59	71	47	11	—
Carshalton Ath.	42	10	16	16	49	69	46	16	10
Hayes	42	9	18	15	45	58	45	15	5
Oxford City	42	12	7	23	50	80	43	17	—
Staines Town	42	6	16	20	40	64	34	13	10
Leytonstone	42	8	7	27	36	75	31	13	15
Kingstonian	42	3	15	24	35	72	24	9	—

FIRST DIVISION

	P	W	D	L	F	A	Pts.	C	D
Harlow Town	42	31	7	4	93	32	100	9	—
Harrow Borough	42	26	8	8	85	49	86	19	—
Maidenhead Utd	42	25	6	11	72	50	81	9	3
Bishop's Stortford	42	22	11	9	68	40	77	20	5
Hertford Town	42	21	11	10	62	41	74	24	—
Horsham	42	22	8	12	62	47	74	14	—
Harwich & Parkstone	42	22	5	15	90	57	71	15	5
Bromley	42	18	12	12	76	50	66	19	5
Hampton	42	17	11	14	59	47	62	10	—
Epsom & Ewell	42	18	7	17	69	57	61	6	—
Wembley	42	15	14	13	57	50	59	23	14
Aveley	42	17	7	18	57	66	58	15	—
Wokingham Town	42	17	8	17	64	68	56*	11	10
Clapton	42	15	8	19	67	80	53	26	8
Metropolitan Police	42	12	13	17	58	55	49	19	—
Walton & Hersham	42	12	9	21	47	71	45	15	—
Ilford	42	13	5	24	48	80	44	16	—
Ware	42	11	10	21	46	69	43	21	—
Chesham United	42	11	9	22	46	66	42	15	5
Finchley	42	7	15	20	43	74	36	9	11
St Albans City	42	7	7	28	43	90	28	16	5
Southall & E.B.	42	5	5	32	41	114	20	11	5

*3 points deducted

SECOND DIVISION

	P	W	D	L	F	A	Pts.	C	D
Farnborough Town	34	26	3	5	77	34	81	13	5
Camberley Town	34	21	8	5	71	32	71	16	10
Molesey	34	19	11	4	55	33	68	20	—
Lewes	34	19	6	9	66	50	63	3	5
Feltham	34	16	7	11	47	36	55	9	5
Letchworth G.C.	34	14	10	10	56	48	52	18	8
Eastbourne Utd	34	16	4	14	47	46	52	3	—
Hemel Hempstead	34	13	11	10	46	37	50	7	—
Epping Town	34	14	7	13	49	44	49	14	—
Rainham Town	34	13	10	11	42	41	49	14	14
Cheshunt	34	11	8	15	43	49	41	14	10
Hungerford Town	34	11	8	15	48	58	41	8	—
Worthing	34	9	8	17	40	50	35	5	5
Hornchurch	34	9	8	17	38	61	35	16	—
Egham Town	34	7	12	15	49	54	33	7	10
Tring Town	34	6	8	20	33	56	26	3	—
Willesden	34	6	8	20	41	77	26	11	—
Corinthian Casuals	34	4	7	23	23	65	19	9	—

BERGER ISTHMIAN LEAGUE — PREMIER DIVISION — 1978-79

	Barking	Boreham Wood	Carshalton Ath	Croydon	Dagenham	Dulwich H	Enfield	Hayes	Hendon	Hitchin Town	Kingstonian	Leatherhead	Leytonstone	Oxford C	Slough Town	Staines Town	Sutton Utd	Tilbury	Tooting & M	Walthamstow	Woking	Wycombe W
Barking	—	3-1	2-0	1-0	2-3	1-1	2-3	5-3	1-0	5-2	1-0	2-0	1-0	3-1	4-1	1-1	2-1	1-1	4-2	1-2	1-0	2-2
Boreham Wood	1-2	—	1-1	0-2	0-1	0-2	0-2	1-0	3-1	2-0	2-1	2-3	1-3	2-4	1-0	1-1	0-1	5-0	1-1	3-1	2-4	1-1
Carshalton A	1-1	2-2	—	1-0	0-3	1-1	0-3	0-5	1-0	0-0	1-0	1-1	5-1	3-1	1-1	2-2	3-2	2-0	0-0	1-0	0-4	2-3
Croydon	0-4	1-2	0-0	—	3-2	2-3	1-1	1-0	1-3	1-1	1-0	2-1	5-1	3-1	4-2	2-1	4-0	4-1	1-1	2-0	1-3	3-0
Dagenham	0-3	0-0	4-3	3-0	—	0-2	2-6	4-1	1-1	3-1	3-2	2-1	0-1	3-1	4-2	2-1	0-2	1-1	1-0	5-4	5-3	1-0
Dulwich H	0-0	9-2	1-1	1-0	0-1	—	0-2	2-1	2-1	2-2	4-0	1-0	1-0	5-0	2-0	2-1	2-0	1-1	1-2	1-0	4-1	3-1
Enfield	1-1	0-0	2-0	2-1	2-0	2-0	—	1-1	1-2	4-0	4-1	2-0	2-0	5-2	0-1	3-0	1-0	2-1	0-2	4-4	1-1	1-4
Hayes	2-2	2-1	1-1	1-3	2-0	0-0	—	—	1-0	1-1	2-0	1-1	2-2	3-1	0-1	0-0	1-1	1-3	2-5	1-1	1-1	0-1
Hendon	0-1	1-1	2-1	5-2	3-0	0-1	1-1	2-0	—	3-2	2-2	1-1	3-0	3-1	3-2	1-1	1-0	4-1	3-2	1-1	1-1	1-0
Hitchin Town	6-2	1-1	0-1	0-0	1-3	1-1	2-1	5-1	0-1	—	1-1	1-0	5-1	0-0	1-2	1-1	0-1	1-2	0-1	2-0	1-0	2-1
Kingstonian	1-1	1-2	2-2	1-3	1-1	0-0	0-1	—	1-1	1-1	—	1-1	0-1	2-0	0-1	0-1	0-2	4-1	1-0	2-4	1-3	0-2
Leatherhead	2-0	0-1	1-2	0-2	1-1	1-2	0-1	0-1	0-0	3-1	4-1	—	2-0	3-0	1-3	3-0	5-2	3-0	3-0	1-0	2-0	1-2
Leytonstone	1-3	1-2	3-0	0-1	1-1	0-1	0-3	1-1	1-1	2-3	1-1	1-0	—	1-3	1-1	2-1	0-4	0-2	0-0	1-0	2-0	1-2
Oxford C	1-2	0-1	3-0	0-3	2-3	3-2	0-1	1-0	1-0	1-3	3-2	3-2	0-0	—	1-1	3-2	2-2	0-2	4-3	1-0	0-2	0-3
Slough Town	2-4	2-0	2-0	0-0	2-0	3-2	2-1	0-0	2-1	4-1	3-1	1-2	2-1	1-0	—	1-1	1-0	0-0	5-0	3-2	1-2	0-0
Staines Town	0-2	4-0	1-1	0-0	0-2	1-1	1-0	0-0	0-0	4-1	3-3	0-1	0-1	2-0	1-2	—	0-2	1-2	1-1	1-1	1-3	2-1
Sutton United	1-2	2-2	2-0	3-0	0-2	0-3	1-1	2-0	2-0	1-0	4-0	1-2	0-1	0-0	1-2	5-1	—	1-0	0-1	1-1	3-0	1-1
Tilbury	2-3	2-1	4-3	3-3	2-2	2-0	0-2	0-1	1-1	3-2	0-0	1-2	4-2	3-2	0-1	1-0	4-0	—	1-2	2-5	2-1	0-1
Tooting & Mitcham U	0-2	2-0	1-1	0-0	3-1	1-1	1-2	0-0	1-3	3-0	1-1	3-0	2-1	0-3	1-1	0-0	1-0	2-2	—	1-0	0-1	2-0
Walthamstow A	1-4	1-2	4-1	1-0	4-1	1-2	2-1	1-1	1-2	0-1	0-1	1-3	1-0	2-1	1-0	4-1	1-5	4-1	0-1	—	0-6	2-0
Woking	2-3	1-0	3-2	3-1	3-4	1-1	1-1	1-1	2-2	3-1	2-0	0-0	2-2	4-1	2-0	2-0	3-3	2-2	2-2	1-1	—	1-1
Wycombe W	1-4	1-0	0-2	0-0	1-1	1-0	0-0	3-2	5-0	2-1	2-1	2-0	2-0	2-0	0-1	1-1	1-2	2-0	3-1	1-2	3-1	—

BERGER ISTHMIAN LEAGUE DIVISION 1 1978-79

	Aveley	Bishop's Stortford	Bromley	Chesham Utd	Clapton	Epsom & Ewell	Finchley	Hampton	Harlow Town	Harrow Borough	Harwich & Parkeston	Hertford Town	Horsham	Ilford	Maidenhead Utd	Met. Police	Southall & E.B.	St Albans City	Walton & Hersham	Ware	Wembley	Wokingham Town
Aveley	—	1-1	1-0	1-1	0-1	3-1	3-0	2-2	1-2	3-1	4-2	3-0	1-0	2-1	1-1	0-1	2-0	3-1	2-0	3-2	1-2	2-1
Bishop's Stortford	1-0	—	1-1	3-0	2-1	0-1	2-3	0-2	2-0	1-0	2-1	1-1	5-1	3-0	2-0	1-5	3-1	5-1	0-2	1-0	2-0	3-2
Bromley	1-1	2-1	—	4-0	4-3	3-0	1-1	4-2	0-0	0-0	1-4	1-1	1-2	1-2	1-2	3-1	5-1	1-1	4-0	3-0	4-0	0-1
Chesham United	0-1	1-2	1-1	—	3-0	2-0	1-0	4-2	1-3	0-0	0-2	0-2	0-2	1-2	0-0	0-1	2-0	1-1	0-2	0-0	2-2	3-1
Clapton	3-1	0-1	1-4	3-1	—	1-3	3-1	1-2	2-4	4-1	0-2	1-4	0-3	2-1	2-5	1-1	1-1	1-0	3-2	1-1	2-3	1-2
Epsom & Ewell	3-0	0-2	0-4	3-0	1-1	—	4-0	1-1	1-2	4-1	2-3	3-1	0-3	1-2	1-0	1-1	1-1	4-0	2-0	4-1	0-0	1-0
Finchley	2-2	0-0	0-0	2-1	3-5	3-2	—	1-1	1-2	1-4	1-1	1-2	1-3	3-1	1-4	1-1	3-2	1-1	0-1	0-0	0-1	0-2
Hampton	1-2	0-0	1-2	1-1	1-0	4-0	2-2	—	0-1	1-3	4-0	1-3	0-2	3-0	0-1	2-1	2-1	1-0	3-0	2-2	0-0	0-1
Harlow Town	3-1	4-1	2-0	2-1	1-0	0-0	2-1	0-0	—	4-0	2-2	2-1	2-0	5-1	3-0	2-1	8-0	3-0	3-0	3-1	3-1	0-3
Harrow Borough	4-2	1-1	2-1	1-1	3-0	3-1	3-1	1-2	—	—	4-3	1-1	3-1	2-2	2-1	0-2	1-2	1-2	2-0	2-0	3-1	0-3
Harwich & Parkeston	3-0	2-1	4-1	1-2	0-1	5-1	4-0	2-1	1-2	—	—	0-1	1-0	2-2	2-3	4-1	6-1	3-0	4-0	3-2	1-0	1-2
Hertford Town	1-0	2-0	1-1	0-2	1-2	1-0	3-0	2-1	1-2	0-4	3-1	—	1-1	1-1	1-3	0-0	2-0	2-0	4-0	0-0	1-2	2-1
Horsham	2-1	2-1	2-1	2-0	2-2	1-0	2-1	0-2	2-4	1-1	1-2	1-1	—	2-0	0-1	1-0	0-0	1-2	3-3	3-1	1-0	2-0
Ilford	1-1	1-0	0-2	1-2	1-6	2-1	0-1	1-1	2-3	3-4	1-2	2-0	2-1	—	—	0-5	5-1	2-1	1-1	1-2	1-0	0-3
Maidenhead United	0-1	1-1	1-4	2-0	3-1	1-0	1-1	1-2	1-4	1-1	3-1	1-2	3-2	1-0	—	1-0	3-2	1-0	1-1	3-0	2-1	3-1
Met. Police	2-0	2-3	0-1	2-2	1-1	1-3	0-0	2-3	1-2	0-1	2-0	1-1	1-0	1-2	1-0	—	3-0	1-2	0-0	2-1	1-1	6-0
Southall & E.B.	3-1	1-1	0-2	3-1	0-3	3-2	1-2	0-1	0-6	2-3	0-4	1-2	1-2	1-2	1-2	1-5	—	5-2	1-2	1-6	0-2	2-3
St Albans City	2-2	0-3	1-3	3-1	1-3	2-2	5-4	1-1	1-1	0-3	1-5	1-2	1-0	1-0	1-3	2-2	5-0	—	0-1	0-1	0-1	3-2
Walton & Hersham	4-1	1-1	1-1	2-3	0-2	2-4	2-0	1-1	0-2	1-3	1-2	1-1	1-3	0-1	0-1	2-2	1-0	5-0	—	2-0	0-3	1-1
Ware	2-1	1-1	2-1	1-3	0-1	1-1	0-0	0-1	0-2	0-4	2-1	1-0	1-2	1-1	0-1	0-0	1-0	4-0	3-2	—	4-3	2-3
Wembley	0-1	1-1	1-1	2-1	0-0	1-1	1-1	0-0	0-3	4-4	0-3	3-1	1-0	3-1	2-2	5-1	1-1	1-0	0-1	6-0	—	1-1
Wokingham Town	2-2	0-0	4-0	3-1	5-2	0-2	1-1	2-1	2-1	1-3	0-2	1-4	1-1	0-3	3-2	1-2	3-1	2-0	1-2	1-0	2-2	—

BERGER ISTHMIAN LEAGUE DIVISION 2 1978-79

	Camberley Town	Cheshunt	Corinthian C.	Eastbourne Utd	Egham Town	Epping Town	Farnborough Town	Feltham	Hemel Hempstead	Hornchurch	Hungerford Town	Letchworth GC	Lewes	Molesey	Rainham Town	Tring Town	Worthing	Willesden
Camberley Town	—	2-0	3-0	4-0	2-0	2-2	1-0	1-0	0-0	4-0	2-1	0-0	1-2	2-2	1-0	2-0	2-0	7-0
Cheshunt	2-0	—	2-0	1-0	2-2	1-0	0-2	0-1	1-1	1-1	1-1	2-2	4-2	2-3	1-0	2-2	0-1	1-0
Corinthian C.	1-5	1-1	—	1-0	0-0	1-1	2-0	0-3	0-3	1-3	1-3	0-3	2-4	0-1	0-3	0-0	1-1	2-1
Eastbourne United	2-3	3-1	4-1	—	0-0	1-0	1-0	0-3	1-0	0-1	3-0	3-0	1-3	0-1	1-0	3-0	2-1	2-3
Egham Town	1-1	1-3	4-0	6-0	—	0-1	1-2	0-1	3-2	2-1	2-2	1-3	1-3	2-2	0-0	0-1	2-3	1-1
Epping Town	1-2	1-0	3-1	1-2	0-0	—	1-2	2-0	2-0	2-0	4-0	2-4	2-0	2-1	1-2	4-3	3-0	2-0
Farnborough Town	3-4	4-1	2-0	3-2	3-1	1-1	—	2-1	3-2	4-1	3-0	1-0	2-1	4-0	2-1	6-1	4-3	2-0
Feltham	2-1	4-5	0-2	3-1	2-1	2-0	1-3	—	2-2	1-1	1-2	1-1	1-0	1-0	1-2	2-0	1-0	0-0
Hemel Hempstead	0-2	2-2	3-2	0-1	2-1	2-0	1-2	0-1	—	3-1	3-3	3-1	1-0	1-1	1-0	1-2	1-0	1-1
Hornchurch	2-1	1-1	2-1	3-1	1-0	2-1	0-3	0-2	1-3	—	1-0	3-1	2-3	1-1	0-3	2-1	2-3	5-3
Hungerford Town	0-1	2-1	3-0	1-1	2-2	1-2	0-3	1-3	3-1	3-1	—	3-1	4-0	0-2	1-4	3-0	1-0	4-0
Letchworth G.C.	2-1	2-1	3-0	1-3	4-1	2-2	1-1	2-1	0-0	2-2	1-0	—	3-1	3-4	1-1	2-0	2-1	4-2
Lewes	1-2	4-1	0-0	2-1	1-1	2-0	2-5	3-2	2-2	3-1	3-1	1-2	—	2-2	3-2	2-0	1-0	2-1
Molesey	1-1	2-1	1-0	0-0	4-1	1-2	0-0	1-1	1-0	3-2	0-0	0-0	1-1	—	3-2	2-0	3-1	0-5
Rainham Town	1-1	1-0	0-0	3-3	3-0	0-3	0-1	0-3	2-1	1-1	2-1	0-0	0-3	1-1	—	2-1	2-2	1-2
Tring Town	2-3	1-0	0-0	2-1	2-1	0-1	0-1	0-1	1-1	3-0	2-3	3-2	1-1	1-3	0-1	—	2-2	1-2
Worthing	2-2	2-2	2-1	2-3	1-1	1-0	0-2	1-1	0-0	4-0	0-0	3-1	0-1	0-1	2-0	2-2	—	0-4
Willesden	2-5	0-1	1-0	1-4	2-5	2-2	1-2	1-1	2-4	2-1	0-0	2-2	1-3	0-2	0-2	0-0	0-4	—

R.F. 79/80—49

F.A. TODAY

The voice of the Football Association will be published as a new quarterly magazine giving full coverage of all football in the jurisdiction of the Football Association.

Features covered in FA Today will include:

Internationals at all levels

FA competitions — FA Cup, FA Trophy, FA Vase

FA Coaching (incorporating Insight, the official FA coaching magazine)

Refereeing — Administration

Plus official FA views on national and international football topics.

FA Today can be ordered by subscription only. Cheques for £2·65 should be sent to: The Football Association Quarterly Department, 16 Lancaster Gate, London W2 3LW.

F.A. CHALLENGE TROPHY 1978-79

Preliminary Round

Bootle v Connahs Quay Nomads	4-1
Kirkby T v Skelmersdale U	1-0
Colwyn Bay v Oswestry T	1-0
Alfreton T v Bridlington Tr	1-3
Boston v Spalding U	2-0
Heanor T v Alvechurch	1-3
Arnold v Stourbridge	1-1
Eastwood (Hanley) v Bedworth U	1-1
Bilston v Moor Green	2-1
Eastwood T v Belper T	6-1
Darlaston v Tamworth	1-0
Clacton T v Gorleston	3-0
Harwich & Parkeston v Sudbury T	4-0
Hertford v Chesham U	6-1
Corby T v St Albans C	1-0
Maidenhead U v Aylesbury U	3-2
Dunstable v Wokingham T	3-1
Epsom & Ewell v Hounslow	1-1
Clapton v Aveley	4-0
Walton & Hersham v Corinthian-Casuals	1-1
Hornchurch v Hampton	2-0
Wembley v Metropolitan Police	2-1
Ilford v Addlestone	2-1
Finchley v Crawley T	0-1
Ashford T v Bromley	3-1
Medway v Ramsgate	0-0
Folkestone & Shepway v Sheppey U	3-1
Tonbridge AFC v Sittingbourne	2-0
Fareham T v Andover	3-0
Basingstoke T v Welton R	2-1
Glastonbury v Clevedon T	1-3
Paulton R v Salisbury	1-2
Mangotsfield PF v Shepton Mallet T	2-1
Cinderford T v Barry T	0-1
Trowbridge T v Gloucester C	2-2
Dawlish v Bridgwater T	1-1
Bridport v Tiverton T	2-3
Darlaston v AP Leamington	0-1
Corby T v Lye T	0-2
Dudley T v Bedworth U	2-2
Arnold v Wellingborough T	4-2
Highgate U v Bilston	1-1
Harrow Bor v Ware	5-3
Cambridge C v Wealdstone	2-2
Leytonstone v Boreham Wood	1-1
Wisbech T v Chelmsford C	1-1
Wembley v Barnet	1-1
Clapton v Kings Lynn	2-2
Harlow T v Harwich & Parkeston	1-1
Dunstable v Hayes	1-2
*Barking v Clacton T	7-0
Milton Keynes C v Lowestoft T	1-0
Hertford v Tilbury	0-1
Croydon v Epsom & Ewell	5-0
Woking v Waterlooville	2-2
Maidenhead U v Kingstonian	1-1
Dulwich Hamlet v Carshalton Ath	1-0
Bognor Regis T v Ashford T	3-1
Folkestone & Shepway v Crawley T	3-1
Tonbridge AFC v Fareham T	2-1
Corinthian-Casuals v Basingstoke T	3-3
Medway v Horsham	2-0
Mangotsfield PF v Redditch U	0-2
*Ilford v Hornchurch	1-0
at Leytonstone FC	
Trowbridge T v Barry T	1-1
Alvechurch v Witney T	2-2
Clevedon T v Weston-super-Mare	0-3
Bridgend T v Llanelli	0-2
Ton Pentre v Oxford C	0-3
Salisbury v Tiverton T	1-1
Bridgwater T v Poole T	3-1
Frome T v Taunton T	1-2
Bideford v Dorchester T	1-1

Replays

Stourbridge v Arnold	0-1
Bedworth U v Eastwood (Hanley)	aet 1-0
Hounslow v Epsom & Ewell	0-1
Corinthian-Casuals v Walton & Hersham	0-0
Ramsgate v Medway	0-1
Gloucester C v Trowbridge T	1-2
Bridgwater T v Dawlish	2-1
Penrith v Emley	aet 1-4
Bridlington T v Shildon	2-1
Netherfield v North Shields	1-3
South Liverpool v New Brighton	3-2
Eastwood T v Louth U	4-3
Bedworth U v Dudley T	aet 1-2
Bilston v Highgate U	aet 3-2
Wealdstone v Cambridge C	0-0
Boreham Wood v Leytonstone	2-2
Chelmsford C v Wisbech T	2-2
Barnet v Wembley	2-3
Kings Lynn v Clapton	3-1
Harwich & Parkeston v Harlow T	0-1
Waterlooville v Woking	3-3
Kingstonian v Maidenhead U	0-1
Basingstoke T v Corinthian-Casuals	aet 4-1
Barry T v Trowbridge T	2-1
Witney T v Alvechurch	0-4
Tiverton T v Salisbury	2-1
Dorchester T v Bideford	

Second Replay

Walton & Hersham v Corinthian-Casuals	1-2
at Walton & Hersham FC	

First Round Qualifying

Horden CW v Durham C	2-0
Prestwich Heys v Gateshead	2-5
Emley v Penrith	1-1
Tow Law T v West Auckland T	1-0
Whitley Bay v Horwich RMI	1-4
Mexborough T v Droylsden	1-2
South Bank v Darwen	0-4
Barrow v Billingham Synthonia	2-1
Evenwood T v Accrington Stanley	0-2
Shildon v Bridlington Tr	0-0
Radcliffe Bor v Ferryhill Ath	2-1
North Shields v Netherfield	0-0
Bootle v Pwllheli & District	3-1
Kirkby T v St Helens T	0-0
New Brighton v South Liverpool	0-0
Burscough v Rhyl	1-0
Colwyn Bay v Formby	0-2
Boston v Ashton U	2-0
Nantwich T v Stalybridge Celtic	0-2
Witton Albion v Middlewich Ath	2-1
Long Eaton U v Worksop T	2-0
Leek T v Mossley	1-2
Sutton U v Hyde U	2-0
Louth U v Eastwood T	2-2
New Mills v Buxton	1-2
Enderby T v Sutton Coldfield T	2-1

Second Replays

Cambridge C v Wealdstone	1-2
at Wealdstone FC	
Leytonstone v Boreham Wood	0-4
at Leytonstone FC	
Wisbech T v Chelmsford C	2-3
at Wisbech T FC	
Woking v Waterlooville	0-0
at Waterlooville FC	

Third Replay

Waterlooville v Woking	0-1
at Woking FC	

Second Round Qualifying

Emley v Gateshead	1-1
Bridlington T v North Shields	1-1
Darwen v Tow Law T	1-1

Horden CW v Radcliffe Bor	0-0
Burscough v Barrow	2-3
Droylsden v Accrington Stanley	0-1
Horwich RMI v Ashington	3-0
Mossley v Formby	2-2
Buxton v South Liverpool	1-1
Bootle v Witton Albion	0-3
Stalybridge Celtic v Kirkby T	4-0
Arnold v Eastwood T	0-3
Bilston v Sutton T	1-5
Boston v Bedworth U	3-0
Enderby T v Long Eaton U	1-1
Kings Lynn v Ilford	2-1
Wealdstone v Harlow T	1-2
Barking v Chelmsford C	10-2
Corinthian-Casuals v Wembley	0-4
Harrow Bor v AP Leamington	2-1
Southall & Ealing Bor v Oxford C	0-1
Hayes v Milton Keynes C	2-1
Boreham Wood v Tilbury	3-3
Tonbridge AFC v Dulwich Hamlet	2-3
Medway v Maidenhead U	0-1
Croydon v Folkestone & Shepway	3-1
Bognor Regis T v Woking	1-1
Barry T v Weston-super-Mare	2-1
Lye T v Witney T	1-1
Llanelli v Redditch U	1-4
Bridgwater T v Salisbury	1-1
Taunton T v Dorchester T	3-2

Replays

Gateshead v Emley	2-1
North Shields v Bridlington Tri	0-2
Tow Law T v Darwen	aet 7-2
Radcliffe Bor v Horden CW	1-2
*Formby v Mossley	2-3
South Liverpool v Buxton	0-2
†Long Eaton U v Enderby T	2-4
Tilbury v Boreham Wood	2-1
Woking v Bognor Regis T	2-0
Witney T v Lye T	1-0
Salisbury v Bridgwater T	2-1
*at Southport FC	
†at Enderby Town FC	

Third Round Qualifying

Tow Law T v Horwich RMI	1-1
Frickley Ath v Barrow	1-2
Bishop Auckland v Willington	4-0
Bridlington Tri v Chorley	1-3
Stalybridge Celtic v Mossley	1-1
Workington v Goole T	2-2
Accrington Stanley v Gateshead	6-1
Horden CW v Consett	0-1
Eastwood T v Telford U	1-0
Burton Albion v Grantham	1-1
Enderby T v Boston	1-1
Macclesfield T v Witton Albion	0-0
Buxton v Gainsborough Tri	1-1
Hednesford T v Northwich Vic	0-2
Kings Lynn v Sutton T	2-1
Hayes v Hitchin T	1-0
Hillingdon Bor v Bishops Stortford	2-0
Wembley v Dover	0-3
Woking v Tilbury	0-0
Harrow Bor v Gravesend & Northfleet	2-0
Sutton U v Walthamstow Ave	4-0
Harlow T v Croydon	1-1
Staines T v Hastings U	1-2
Dulwich Hamlet v Barking	1-2
Margate v Dartford	4-1
Cheltenham T v Banbury U	4-2
Maidenhead U v Minehead	1-2
Salisbury v Taunton T	0-2
Bromsgrove R v Witney T	0-2
Redditch U v Barry T	3-0
Oxford C v Kidderminster H	1-4
Yeovil T v Merthyr Tydfil	8-1

Replays

Horwich RMI v Tow Law T	6-0
Mossley v Stalybridge Celtic	2-3
Goole T v Workington	3-0
Grantham v Burton Albion	1-0

Boston v Enderby T	1-1
Witton Albion v Macclesfield T	3-1
Gainsborough Tri v Buxton	3-2
Tilbury v Woking	0-1
Croydon v Harlow T	0-1

Second Replay

Enderby T v Boston	3-0
at Worksop T FC	

First Round Proper

Barrow v Southport	2-1
Spennymoor U v Horwich RMI	2-1
Consett v Accrington Stanley	3-2
Goole T v Blyth Spartans	0-0
Whitby T v Lancaster C	1-3
Bishop Auckland v Crook T	0-0
Stalybridge Celtic v Chorley	2-2
Morecambe v Scarborough	0-1
Grantham v Runcorn	2-3
Kettering T v Nuneaton Bor	1-1
Eastwood T v Worcester C	0-5
Kings Lynn v Redditch U	1-0
Kidderminster H v Witton Albion	2-2
Atherstone T v Boston U	1-2
Marine v Bangor C	3-1
Altrincham v Cheltenham T	1-2
Stafford Rangers v Matlock T	1-1
Enderby T v Winsford U	3-0
Gainsborough Tri v Northwich Vic	1-2
Hendon v Witney T	1-2
Sutton U v Enfield	0-1
Slough T v Woking	3-0
Leatherhead v Hillingdon Bor	2-1
Wycombe W v Barking	1-0
Hayes v Harrow Bor	2-0
Maidstone U v Harlow T	3-0
Dover v Bedford T	0-0
Dagenham v Tooting & Mitcham U	1-1
Margate v Hastings U	2-1
Weymouth v Taunton T	5-1
Minehead v Bath C	2-1
Yeovil T v Falmouth T	3-0

Replays

Blyth Spartans v Goole T	2-1
Chorley v Stalybridge Celtic	2-1
Nuneaton Bor v Kettering T	0-1
Witton Albion v Kidderminster H	4-2
Matlock T v Stafford Rangers	1-2
Bedford T v Dover	3-2
Tooting & Mitcham U v Dagenham	0-0
Crook v Bishop Auckland	1-1

Second Replay

Dagenham v Tooting & Mitcham U	3-1
at Hayes FC	
Bishop Auckland v Crook T	2-0
at Bishop Auckland FC	

Second Replay

Bishop Auckland v Kings Lynn	4-2
Witney T v Dagenham	0-2
Yeovil T v Barrow	5-0
Margate v Marine	3-0
Kettering v Scarborough	3-0
Northwich Vic v Enfield	1-3
Weymouth v Stafford Rangers	0-1
Enderby T v Minehead	1-0
Chorley v Cheltenham T	2-2
Blyth Spartans v Wycombe W	1-1
Witton Albion v Spennymoor U	1-0
Bedford T v Runcorn	1-3
Hayes v Consett	0-0
Lancaster C v Leatherhead	0-0
Boston U v Worcester C	4-0
Maidstone U v Slough T	3-1

Replays

Cheltenham T v Chorley	2-1
Wycombe W v Blyth Spartans	3-0
Leatherhead v Lancaster C	aet 4-1

Third Round Proper
Runcorn v Margate	0-0
Enderby T v Bishop Auckland	2-2
Cheltenham T v Enfield	0-4
Hayes v Wycombe W	2-2
Leatherhead v Yeovil T	0-1
Stafford Rangers v Boston U	2-1
Witton Albion v Dagenham	1-1
Kettering T v Maidstone U	2-0

Replays
Margate v Runcorn	aet 0-2
Bishop Auckland v Enderby T	aet 4-2
Wycombe W v Hayes	2-3
Dagenham v Witton Albion	1-1

Second Replay
Witton Albion v Dagenham at Kidderminster Harriers FC	1-3

Fourth Round Proper
Runcorn v Hayes	2-1
Kettering T v Enfield	1-1
Bishop Auckland v Stafford Rangers	1-1
Dagenham v Yeovil T	2-0

Replays
Enfield v Kettering T	0-3
Stafford Rangers v Bishop Auckland	3-1

Semi-Final Ties
First Leg
Dagenham v Kettering T	0-0
Runcorn v Stafford Rangers	1-2

Second Leg
Kettering T v Dagenham	1-0
Stafford Rangers v Runcorn	1-1

Final at Wembley
Stafford Rangers 2 (*Wood A* 2)
Kettering Town 0   32,000

Stafford Rangers: Arnold; Wood F, Willis; Sargeant, Seddon, Ritchie; Secker, Chapman, Wood A, Cullerton, Chadwick.
Kettering Town: Lane; Ashby, Lee; Easthall, Dixey, Suddards, Flannagan, Kellock, Phipps, Clayton, Evans.

Previous Finals
1970	Macclesfield T 2; Telford U 0; (28,000)
1971	Telford U 3; Hillingdon 2; (29,500)
1972	Stafford R 3; Barnet 0; (24,000)
1973	Scarborough 2; Wigan Ath 1; (23,000)
1974	Morecambe 2; Dartford 1; (19,000)
1975	Matlock T 4; Scarborough 0; (21,000)
1976	Scarborough 3; Stafford R 2 (aet); (21,000)
1977	Scarborough 2; Dagenham 1; (20,000)
1978	Altrincham 3; Leatherhead 1; (19,999)

HITACHI CUP 1978-79

First Round
Metropolitan Police v Corinthian Casuals	4-0
Epsom & E v Lewes	6-1
Worthing v Bromley	1-3
Horsham v Walton & H	1-0
Tring T v Egham T	4-5
Hampton v Chesham U	1-2
Southall & EB v Clapton	2-1
Ilford v Willesden	3-0
St Albans v Hemel Hempstead	0-1
Aveley v Finchley	0-3
Ware v Bishops Stortford	1-4
Harwich & P v Cheshunt	2-1
Harrow B v Hungerford T	1-4
Camberley T v Farnboro' T	0-1
Rainham T v Wembley	0-1
Epping T v Harlow T	0-0, 1-2
Molesey v Eastbourne U	2-0
Wokingham T v Maidenhead U	2-1
Hornchurch v Feltham	1-1, 1-3
Hertford T v Letchworth GC	4-1
Egham T v Enfield	0-4
Dulwich Hamlet v Working	3-1
Wycombe Wanderers v Leatherhead	1-2
Sutton U v Walthamstow Av	2-0
Ilford v Hendon	2-1
Dagenham v Oxford C	6-2
Croydon v Hemel Hempstead	4-0
Bishops Stortford v Harrow Borough	0-2
Slough T v Staines T	3-0
Tilbury v Carshalton Ath	3-1
Boreham Wood v Hitchin T	2-0
Harlow T v Wokingham T	1-2
Hayes v Hertford T	4-1

Second Round
Metropolitan Police v Epsom & E	3-0
Bromley v Horsham	2-0
Egham T v Chesham U	2-1
Southall & EB v Ilford	2-2, 1-2
Hemel H v Finchley	2-1
Bishops Stortford v Harwich & P	3-0
Harrow B v Farnboro' T	3-0
Wembley v Harlow T	1-2
Molesey v Wokingham T	0-1
Feltham v Hertford T	0-3

Third Round
Metropolitan Police v Bromley	1-2
Barking v Leytonstone	3-1
Kingstonian v Tooting & M U	0-4

Fourth Round
Bromley v Barking	4-4, 1-1, 4-3
Tooting & M U v Enfield	1-3
Dulwich Hamlet v Leatherhead	3-0
Sutton U v Ilford	1-0
Dagenham v Croydon	1-5
Harrow Borough v Slough T	2-0
Tilbury v Boreham Wood	2-1
Wokingham T v Hayes	1-2

Fifth Round
Bromley v Enfield	0-4
Dulwich Hamlet v Sutton U	4-3
Croydon v Harrow Borough	0-3
Tilbury v Hayes	1-3

Semi-Finals
Enfield v Dulwich Hamlet	0-0, 0-0, 3-2
Harrow Borough v Hayes	1-2

Final
Enfield v Hayes	2-1

FA SUNDAY CUP 1978-79

First Round

Bedlington Station SC v The Sportsman	0-2
Durham Boilers v Coundon WMC	2-1
Cumberland Star v Willington Belle Vue	3-4
Hartlepool Lion Htl v Peterlee M'cock "A"	2-1
Newton Ayciffe WMC v Morton Cmty Ctre	1-5
Newbiggin Dolphin v Ye Olde England	3-1
Black Bull Taverners v Raysel	4-3
North Chadderton v Dingle Rail	2-6
Lobster v Woodhouse R	3-2
Magnet Southerns v Hull Fish Trades	4-0
Piper Club v Tindale Crescent WMC	2-1
Monson U v Hull Fruit Trades BC	3-3
Priory v White Swan	3-0
Hoyland T Jaguars v Adelaide Park	1-0
Sutton Sports v Swanfield	1-2
Harrowby Villa v Corby Kingfisher	1-1
Ruston Dorman v Taverners	2-0
Byron Ath v Bordesley R	7-1
Club Lafayette v Halesowen H	1-5
Counts XI v Cobblers	2-2
Newtown Unity v Old Horns	4-2
Lodge Cottrell & Ladywood Scl v Codsall 440	3-0
Pinvin U v Slade Celtic	0-1
Hawkins Sports v Eastfield OB	3-2
Lea Hall RBL v Rydell Mount	2-1
Enderby Rangers v Brereton T	0-4
Marstons v Uplands	4-2
Ogley Hay v Jumbos XI	0-1
Sandwell v Springfield Social	1-4
Isham U v Cold Arbour	2-0
Stewartby v Waren R	1-5
Loke U v Eye U	7-4
Needingworth U v Phoenix	2-1
Girton Eagles v Fox & Duck Sports	4-2
Oak Hill U v Twin Foxes	0-3
Greenleys v Chesthunt	1-3
Pools U v Potton Casuals	5-1
*Carlton U v Avica Sports	
Odhams OB v Queensmead	3-0
Brentwood East v Berwick Rangers	4-1
Nicholas Breakspear OB v Sheffield Hse R	0-1
Clifda v Buxton Ath	2-1
Tesco v Westwood	2-1
Nova v Apsley Sports	1-1
†Old Walpolians v Roman U	
Evergreen v Coopers	2-2
Tate & Lyle (London) Sports v Thameside W	3-2
Rainham WMC v Oxford Road Social	1-3
The Tavern v Two-Seven-Nine	0-6
Southern Argyle v Northcliffe & Dormobile	3-1
Sun v Walmer	4-4
Moorgreen v Headington Ath	4-3
Robin Hoods Retreat v Tabular-Beaufort	1-0
Hallen Sunday v George Inn Colts	2-2
Hunt & Broadhurst v Road Sea	2-6
Cowley Workers v Colden Common	0-2
North Stoneham v Ollis Transport Comb	1-2
Clyst Honiton Sports v Bonnet Electrics	0-4
Plymstock Club v Redifusion Bedminster Down Sunday	1-0

*WO for Carlton United FC
†WO for Old Walpolians FC

Replays

Hull Fruit Trades BC v Monson U	3-2
Corby Kingfisher v Harrowby Villa	1-0
Cobblers v Counts XI	3-4
Apsley Sports v Nova	1-1
Coopers v Evergreen	0-2
Walmer v Sun	1-0
George Inn Colts v Hallen Sunday	1-2

Second Replay

Nova v Apsley Sports	0-2

Second Round

Durham Boilers v Newbiggin Dolphin	2-2
Hartlepool Lion Hotel v The Sportsman	5-0
Willington BV v Langley Park SW	0-1
Magnet Southerns v Morton Community Ctre	2-0
Priory v Hull Fruit Trades BC	1-4
Piper Club v Black Bull Taverners	2-1
Swanfield v Hoyland T	5-2
Dingle Rail v Brereton T	2-0
Marstons v Lobster	1-2
Corby Kingfisher v Isham U	2-0
Springfield Social v Ruston Dorman	4-0
Halesowen Harriers v Counts XI	0-1
Hawkins Sports v Byron Ath	1-2
Needingworth U v Newton U	3-3
Lodge Cottrell & Ladywood Scl v Twin Foxes	2-2
Lion Rangers v Warren R	1-0
Jumbos XI v Evergreen	0-1
Robin Hoods Retreat v Olympic Star	1-1
Slade Celtic v Lea Hall RBL	1-3
Girton Eagles v Cheshunt	2-1
Arras v Loke U	4-1
Clifda v Tesco	5-0
Carlton U v Pools U	2-1
Odhams OB v Sheffield House Rangers	0-2
Two-Seven-Nine v Apsley Sports	5-0
Tate & Lyle (London) Sports v Troy Ath	4-4
Walmer v Oxford Road Social	2-1
Old Walpolians v Colden Common	0-3
Southern Argyle v Road Sea	0-3
Brentford East v Moorgreen	1-2
Hallen Sunday v Plymstock Club	2-0
Ollis Transport Combined v Bonnet Eltcs	2-0

Replays

Newbiggin Dolphin v Durham Boilers	1-2
Newtown Unity v Needingworth U	3-0
Twin Foxes v Lodge Cottrell & Ladywood Social	2-1
Olympic Star v Robin Hoods Retreat	1-2
Troy Ath v Tate & Lyle (London) Sports	3-2

Third Round

Hull Fruit Trades BC v Langley Park SW	0-2
Durham Boilers v Hartlepool Lion Hotel	1-0
Dingle Rail v Swanfield	4-2
Piper Club v Magnet Southerns	1-2
Lea Hall RBL v Springfield Social	0-2
Lobster v Byron Ath	3-1
Lion Rangers v Hallen Sunday	5-3
Robin Hoods Retreat v Counts XI	0-1
Sheffield House Rangers v Twin Foxes	4-2
Newtown Unity v Corby Kingfisher	0-1
Troy Ath v Carlton U	1-2
Girton Eagles v Clifda	0-6
Road Sea v Two-Seven-Nine	1-4
Evergreen v Walmer	3-0
Ollis Transport Combined v Colden Common	2-1
Arras v Moorgreen	0-0

Replay

Moorgreen v Arras	2-0

Fourth Round

Magnet Southerns v Langley Park Scl Wlfe	0-2
Dingle Rail v Durham Boilers	0-4
Corby Kingfisher v Ollis Transport Comb'd	1-3
Springfield Social v Lobster	0-3
Lion Rangers v Counts XI	1-2
Moorgreen v Evergreen	1-3
Carlton U v Sheffield House Rangers	3-2
Clifda v Two-Seven-Nine	1-0

Fifth Round

Langley Park Scl Welfre v Durham Boilers	2-1
Lobster v Counts XI (aet)	2-1
Carlton U v Evergreen	3-1
Clifda v Ollis Transport Combined	1-0

Semi-Final Ties

Lobster v Langley Park Social Welfare	1-0
Clifda v Carlton U	0-1

Final Tie

Lobster v Carlton U	3-2

at Southport FC

OTHER LEAGUE TABLES 1978-79

Cheshire County Football League
FIRST DIVISION

	P	W	D	L	F	A	Pts
Horwich RMI	42	35	2	5	89	45	72
Witton Albion	42	30	4	8	114	38	64
Marine	42	29	5	8	104	38	63
Stalybridge Celtic	42	25	5	12	93	47	55
Burscough	42	19	15	8	59	31	53
Winsford United	42	21	11	10	74	49	53
Chorley	42	21	8	13	66	43	50
Formby	42	20	9	13	73	57	49
Leek Town	42	19	10	13	62	43	48
Droylsden	42	18	9	15	62	61	45
Nantwich Town	42	18	8	16	76	72	44
Fleetwood Town	42	17	10	15	70	68	44
Hyde United	42	15	12	15	59	57	42
St Helens Town	42	16	9	17	59	57	41
Darwen	42	15	9	18	52	53	39
Rhyl	42	15	8	19	53	60	38
Ashton United	42	13	5	24	63	94	31
New Mills	42	9	11	22	58	82	29
Rossendale United	42	11	6	25	51	108	28
Radcliffe Borough	42	4	7	31	37	115	15
New Brighton	42	3	5	34	36	115	11
Middlewich Athletic	42	3	4	35	43	120	10

SECOND DIVISION

	P	W	D	L	F	A	Pts
Bootle	34	19	9	6	61	35	47
Curzon Ashton	34	18	9	7	57	32	45
Prescot Town	34	20	5	9	68	37	*43
Kirkby Town	34	18	6	10	66	42	42
Accrington Stanley	34	18	6	10	65	43	42
Irlam Town	34	16	10	8	47	33	42
Congleton Town	34	14	13	7	52	31	41
Prescot BI	34	15	11	8	55	42	41
Eastwood (Hanley)	34	15	9	10	60	47	39
Prestwich Heys	34	17	5	12	53	41	*37
Maghull	34	11	7	16	41	50	29
Ford Motors	34	9	10	15	38	52	28
Anson Villa	34	10	7	17	39	60	27
Warrington Town	34	11	5	18	45	69	27
Atherton Collieries	34	8	9	17	43	56	25
Skelmersdale United	34	9	6	19	36	53	24
Glossop	34	6	6	22	42	83	18
Ashton Town	34	3	5	26	22	84	11

*Two points deducted

Hellenic Football League
PREMIER DIVISION

	P	W	D	L	F	A	Pts
Newbury Town	26	14	8	4	52	31	36
Fairford Town	26	14	7	5	53	39	35
Forest Green Rvrs	26	15	4	7	52	35	34
Thame United	26	15	3	8	37	26	33
Bicester Town	26	12	9	5	47	38	33
Chipping Norton T	26	14	4	8	51	27	32
Moreton Town	26	12	7	7	42	31	31
Flackwell Heath	26	10	8	8	37	33	28
Clanfield	26	9	4	13	36	47	22
Wallingford Town	26	8	4	14	41	48	20
Abingdon Town	26	6	7	13	34	51	19
Didcot Town	26	4	9	13	33	52	17
Garrard Athletic	26	4	8	14	35	51	16
Abingdon United	26	2	4	20	24	65	8

Kent Football League

	P	W	D	L	F	A	Pts
Sheppey United	34	22	11	1	73	28	55
Hythe Town	34	21	7	6	71	34	49
Faversham	34	22	5	7	71	37	49
Medway	34	18	10	6	64	27	46
Whitstable	34	18	7	9	52	35	43
Sittingbourne	34	16	7	11	57	42	39
Tunbridge Wells	34	15	6	13	51	52	36
Darenth Heathside	34	10	12	12	42	38	32
Deal Town	34	13	6	15	40	50	32
Ramsgate	34	14	4	16	42	59	32
Slade Green	34	8	13	13	46	47	29
Dartford Glentw'th	34	9	10	15	40	52	28
Herne Bay	34	10	10	14	47	59	*28
Cray Wanderers	34	9	9	16	50	65	27
Erith & Belvedere	34	8	9	17	49	48	25
Kent Police	34	10	4	20	46	67	24
Crockenhill	34	7	7	20	43	73	21
Snowdon	34	4	7	23	29	102	15

*Two goals and two points deducted for playing an ineligible player

Hampshire League
DIVISION ONE

	P	W	D	L	F	A	Pts
Newport	30	23	5	2	64	11	51
Fareham Town	30	18	7	5	75	34	43
Brockenhurst	30	14	9	7	46	35	37
Waterloo Reserves	30	14	8	8	41	34	36
Swaythling	30	13	9	8	42	35	35
Pirelli General	30	10	12	8	44	30	32
Sholing Sports	30	14	3	13	47	37	31
Southampton 'A'	30	10	10	10	43	37	30
East Cowes Vics	30	12	4	14	38	52	*27
BAT	30	11	6	13	34	38	*27
Netley Cent. Spts.	30	11	3	16	39	44	25
Gosport Bor. Res	30	9	6	15	39	60	24
Moneyfield Sports	30	7	9	14	27	48	23
Brading Town	30	8	7	15	22	47	23
Portsmouth RN	30	7	5	18	25	53	*18
Havant Town	30	5	7	18	41	69	17

*One point deducted

Leicestershire Senior Football League
DIVISION ONE

	P	W	D	L	F	A	Pts
Shepshed Charter'se	30	21	5	4	64	15	47
Anstey Nomads	30	17	9	4	63	18	43
Friar Lane OB	30	17	6	7	57	27	40
Oadby Town	30	14	11	5	58	37	39
Hinckley Town	30	17	4	9	59	37	38
Stapenhill	30	15	7	8	59	40	37
Wigston Fields	30	12	10	8	30	31	34
Hillcroft	30	14	3	13	44	58	31
Newfoundpool WMC	30	11	8	11	42	42	30
Enderby Res	30	10	9	11	33	36	29
Melton Town	30	11	5	14	31	40	27
Birstall United Soc	30	7	8	15	34	41	22
Thringstone MW	30	8	6	16	31	53	22
Lutterworth Town	30	6	7	17	35	63	19
Earl Shilton Albion	30	3	7	20	26	65	13
Corby Res	30	2	5	23	28	91	9

London Spartan Football League
PREMIER DIVISION

	P	W	D	L	F	A	Pts
Swanley Town	34	25	5	4	78	33	55
Fisher Athletic	34	20	7	7	54	27	47
Merstham	34	19	6	9	62	28	44
Bracknell Town	34	19	6	9	71	42	44
Malden Vale	34	16	8	10	49	40	40
Beckenham Town	34	14	9	11	56	46	37
Banstead Athletic	34	9	19	6	46	46	37
Berkhamsted Town	34	12	10	12	52	46	34
Farnham Town	34	13	8	13	48	46	34
Horley Town	34	12	8	14	43	40	32
Amersham Town	34	12	8	14	54	57	32
Alma Swanley	34	10	10	14	44	52	30
Chingford	34	10	8	16	36	53	28
East Thurrock U	34	8	10	16	33	47	26
Whyteleafe	34	11	4	19	32	53	26
Frimley Green	34	7	10	17	33	60	24
Hatfield Town	34	8	6	20	38	81	22
Ulysses	34	6	8	20	41	73	20

South Midlands Football League
PREMIER DIVISION

	P	W	D	L	F	A	Pts
Barton Rovers	30	25	4	1	81	12	54
Pirton	30	23	4	3	63	23	50
Arlesey Town	30	17	9	4	49	32	43
Royston Town	30	16	6	8	50	37	38
Stotfold	30	12	10	8	32	18	34
Selby	30	12	7	11	48	43	31
Electrolux	30	11	9	10	35	32	31
Sandy Albions	30	11	7	12	41	50	29
Baldock Town	30	10	8	12	32	33	28
Shillington	30	10	7	13	43	35	27
Winslow United	30	9	7	14	40	44	25
New Bradwell St Peter	30	5	13	12	35	49	23
Waterlows	30	7	5	18	31	51	19
Langford	30	6	7	17	33	69	19
Harpenden Town	30	7	4	19	30	68	18
Eaton Bray United	30	4	3	23	26	73	11

Midland Football Combination
DIVISION ONE

	P	W	D	L	F	A	Pts
Sutton Coldfield T	38	26	9	3	104	30	61
Oldbury United	38	20	11	7	49	29	51
Bridgnorth Town	38	19	11	8	54	31	49
Boldmere St Michaels	38	20	9	9	44	35	49
Walsall Sportsco	38	18	11	9	58	41	47
Blakenall	38	17	10	11	57	38	44
Solihull Borough	38	18	8	12	59	46	44
Paget Rangers	38	16	10	12	50	41	42
Knowle	38	17	7	14	51	44	41
Mile Oak Rovers	38	15	10	13	42	37	40
Moor Green	38	16	7	15	70	55	39
Highgate United	38	13	7	18	46	54	33
Malvern Town	38	9	15	14	39	51	33
West Midlands Police	38	11	11	16	32	46	33
Racing Club Warwick	38	11	10	17	41	46	32
Walsall Wood	38	10	11	17	43	65	31
Cinderford Town	38	10	10	18	36	64	30
Northfield Town	38	12	5	21	41	62	29
Evesham United	38	7	5	26	29	80	19
Coleshill Town	38	1	11	26	22	72	13

Sussex County Football League
DIVISION ONE

	P	W	D	L	F	A	Pts
Peacehaven and Telscombe	30	18	9	3	61	28	45
Southwick	30	16	9	5	60	33	41
Horsham YMCA	30	18	5	7	58	33	41
Steyning	30	15	7	8	56	45	37
Littlehampton Town	30	14	7	9	54	34	35
Ringmer	30	13	8	9	41	44	34
Arundel	30	13	7	10	44	37	33
Shoreham	30	10	10	10	43	40	30
Haywards Heath	30	9	12	9	44	47	30
Bexhill Town	30	11	5	14	56	56	27
Eastbourne Town	30	10	6	14	47	51	26
Chichester City	30	10	5	15	51	64	25
Burgess Hill Town	30	8	6	16	34	56	22
Rye United	30	8	5	17	31	42	21
East Grinstead	30	5	8	17	40	65	18
Sidley United	30	5	5	20	22	67	15

Midland Counties Football League
PREMIER DIVISION

	P	W	D	L	F	A	Pts
Boston	36	24	6	6	71	27	54
Skegness Town	36	23	8	4	65	31	54
Mexborough T Ath	36	21	8	7	57	35	50
Eastwood Town	36	19	10	7	56	35	48
Bridlington Trinity	36	15	11	9	76	43	43
Arnold	36	14	14	8	56	50	42
Sutton Town	36	16	7	13	53	50	39
Long Eaton United	36	16	6	14	51	40	38
Brigg Town	36	12	9	15	52	54	33
Ashby	36	13	7	16	36	48	33
Retford Town	36	12	8	16	49	49	32
Appleby Frodingham Athletic	36	13	6	17	55	63	32
Ilkeston Town	36	11	9	16	52	61	31
Kimberley Town	36	7	16	13	46	54	30
Louth United	36	10	7	19	43	72	27
Spalding United	36	7	12	17	44	68	26
Alfreton Town	36	6	13	17	39	61	25
Heanor Town	36	7	10	19	37	64	24
Belper Town	36	6	11	19	43	76	23

Town and Country Football League

	P	W	D	L	F	A	Pts
Haverhill Rovers	42	29	9	4	90	36	67
Gt Yarmouth Town	42	28	10	4	112	44	66
Lowestoft Town	42	24	15	3	89	40	63
Bury Town	42	27	7	8	99	56	61
Sudbury Town	42	19	11	12	78	50	49
Ely City	42	16	11	13	50	57	47
Gorleston	42	21	4	17	74	67	46
Braintree & Crittall Athletic	42	18	9	15	78	72	45
Wisbech Town	42	17	11	14	68	69	45
Brantham Athletic	42	16	11	15	62	61	43
March Town United	42	16	9	17	65	69	41
Cambridge U Res	42	16	9	17	58	67	41
Soham T Rangers	42	18	4	20	70	74	40
Thetford Town	42	14	9	19	73	78	37
Histon	42	15	6	21	61	73	36
Saffron Walden	42	13	9	20	64	68	35
Felixstowe Town	42	11	10	21	43	64	32
Colchester U Res	42	11	8	23	54	78	30
Stowmarket	42	10	9	23	62	84	29
Clacton Town	42	8	13	21	38	62	29
Chatteris Town	42	10	7	25	80	120	27
Newmarket Town	42	5	4	33	34	107	14

Wearside Football League

	P	W	D	L	F	A	Pts
Wallsend Town	32	21	5	6	88	42	47
Wingate	32	21	4	7	81	46	46
Whickham	32	17	10	5	66	36	44
Boldon CA	32	18	7	7	77	43	43
South Shields	32	16	11	5	80	50	43
Hartlepool Reserves	32	15	5	11	61	52	37
Chester le Street Tn	32	13	10	9	55	48	36
Blue Star	32	20	5	8	90	42	*35
Annfield Plain	32	13	6	13	67	69	32
Easington CW	32	11	8	13	50	73	30
Ryhope CW	32	8	11	13	49	50	27
Eppleton CW	32	8	6	18	52	71	22
Washington	32	7	8	17	32	59	†20
Reyrolles	32	8	4	20	52	90	20
Roker	32	5	8	19	38	79	18
Heaton Stannington	32	6	5	21	43	86	17
Murton CW	32	4	9	19	27	75	17

*Ten points deducted †Two points deducted

Kingsmead Athenian Football League

	P	W	D	L	F	A	Pts
Billericay Town	36	26	5	5	86	29	57
Burnham	36	22	10	4	86	37	54
Edgware	36	19	11	6	83	34	49
Windsor & Eton	36	21	6	9	62	30	48
Haringey Borough	36	16	15	5	60	42	47
Uxbridge	36	17	12	7	45	22	46
Welling United	36	17	9	10	60	46	43
Leyton-Wingate	36	16	10	10	67	48	42
Grays Athletic	36	17	8	11	55	46	42
Alton Town	36	15	9	12	51	45	39
Hoddesdon Town	36	13	7	16	63	60	33
Chalfont St Peter	36	12	8	16	41	58	32
Harefield United	36	11	7	18	53	70	29
Dorking Town	36	10	7	19	39	64	27
Harlow	36	9	4	23	48	92	22
Ruislip Manor	36	8	4	24	35	71	20
Fleet Town	36	6	7	23	37	73	19
Redhill	36	6	7	23	29	79	19
Chertsey Town	36	4	8	24	36	90	16

Yorkshire Football League
DIVISION ONE

	P	W	D	L	F	A	Pts
Winterton Rangers	30	19	5	6	54	21	43
Emley	30	18	5	7	58	31	41
North Ferriby	30	16	9	5	55	31	41
Guiseley	30	11	9	10	35	32	31
Thackley	30	13	5	12	41	39	31
Ossett Town	30	12	2	14	42	37	30
Scarborough	30	10	10	10	34	36	30
Sheffield	30	9	11	10	26	28	29
Leeds Ashley Road	30	10	8	12	34	37	28
Hallam	30	12	4	14	33	42	28
Bridlington Town	30	11	6	13	36	48	28
Frecheville CA	30	7	13	10	33	42	27
Tadcaster Albion	30	9	8	13	33	39	26
Bentley VW	30	9	7	14	34	38	25
Kiveton Park	30	8	7	15	44	54	23
Lincoln United	30	5	9	16	28	65	19

DIVISION TWO

	P	W	D	L	F	A	Pts
Ossett Albion	30	17	9	4	77	18	43
Fryston CW	30	15	6	9	56	36	36
Thorne Colliery	30	12	12	6	45	34	36
Liversedge	30	13	9	8	39	33	35
Brook Sports	30	12	8	10	45	48	32
Farsley Celtic	30	11	9	9	49	38	31
Hatfield Main	30	11	9	10	39	36	31
Maltby MW	30	8	12	10	37	38	28
Denaby United	30	10	7	13	47	51	27
Norton Woodseats	30	10	7	13	38	47	27
Yorkshire Amateur	30	9	9	12	34	46	27
Barton Town	30	10	6	14	43	47	26
Rawmarsh Welfare	30	8	10	12	45	51	26
Worsbrough Bridge MW	30	11	4	15	39	48	26
Leeds Carnegie Polytechnic	30	11	3	16	55	58	25
Wombwell SA	30	9	6	15	33	52	24

Western Football League
PREMIER DIVISION

	P	W	D	L	F	A	Pts
Frome Town	38	36	12	5	60	29	75
Bideford	38	22	8	8	76	39	74
Saltash United	38	19	10	9	65	39	67
Barnstaple Town	38	18	10	10	65	35	64
Tiverton Town	38	17	9	12	71	60	60
Clandown	38	16	11	11	58	49	59
Weston-super-Mare	38	14	15	9	65	48	57
Falmouth Town	38	15	9	14	51	47	54
Paulton Rovers	38	15	9	14	40	48	54
Bridport	38	13	13	12	54	50	52
Bridgwater Town	38	14	9	15	57	53	51
Keynsham Town	38	13	12	13	47	57	51
Mangotsfield PF	38	15	2	21	53	64	47
Ilminster Town	38	11	12	15	45	55	45
Welton Rovers	38	11	8	19	44	59	41
Exeter City	38	12	5	21	48	75	41
Clevedon Town	38	11	7	20	50	64	40
Dawlish	38	10	10	18	43	61	40
Shepton Mallet Tn	38	10	10	18	48	74	40
Glastonbury	38	8	9	21	42	76	33

FIRST DIVISION

	P	W	D	L	F	A	Pts
AFC Bournemouth	36	25	6	5	101	41	81
Portway-Bristol	36	23	5	8	81	43	74
Bristol Manor Farm	36	20	5	11	59	47	65
Chippenham Town	36	19	7	10	56	43	64
Torquay United	36	20	4	12	82	47	†62
Melksham Town	36	18	4	14	58	57	58
Devizes Town	36	16	9	11	71	54	57
Wellington	36	18	3	15	48	46	57
Chard Town	36	15	6	15	57	58	51
Brixham United	36	15	5	16	55	61	50
Elmore	36	15	3	18	48	65	48
Ottery St Mary	36	13	5	18	51	60	*43
Larkhall Athletic	36	12	6	18	52	56	42
Westland-Yeovil	36	11	9	16	43	53	42
Heavitree United	36	12	5	19	39	61	41
Swanage Town & Herston	36	11	6	19	51	60	39
Odd Down	36	10	5	21	38	71	35
Exmouth Town	36	8	9	19	41	72	33
Yeovil Town	36	5	10	21	30	65	*24

*One point deducted for playing an ineligible player.
†Two points deducted for playing ineligible players.

Northern Football League

	P	W	D	L	F	A	Pts
Spennymoor United	38	25	6	7	96	43	81
Bishop Auckland	38	25	5	8	96	38	80
Ashington	38	23	7	8	79	47	76
Crook Town	38	21	10	7	63	38	73
Blyth Spartans	38	19	12	7	81	39	69
Consett	38	21	9	8	84	52	*69
North Shields	38	21	4	13	76	55	67
South Bank	38	16	11	11	58	47	59
Horden Colliery Welfare	38	17	8	13	64	56	59
Durham City	38	15	9	14	63	62	54
Billingham Synthonia	38	12	12	14	60	55	48
Tow Law Town	38	12	8	18	54	63	44
Shildon	38	11	10	17	52	69	43
Whitby Town	38	11	12	15	55	68	*42
Whitley Bay	38	9	9	20	54	77	36
West Auckland Tn	38	9	9	20	54	87	36
Ferryhill Athletic	38	10	5	23	43	74	35
Willington	38	7	10	21	41	75	31
Penrith	38	8	7	23	35	82	31
Evenwood Town	38	4	5	29	31	112	*14

*Three points deducted

Lancashire Football Combination

	P	W	D	L	F	A	Pts
Wren Rovers	28	21	5	2	51	10	47
Leyland Motors	28	18	6	4	63	26	42
Whitworth Valley	28	15	8	5	49	35	38
Colne Dynamos	28	13	8	7	50	32	34
Bacup Borough	28	14	6	8	48	36	34
Padiham	28	14	5	9	40	35	33
Lytham	28	11	8	9	41	34	30
Nelson	28	7	10	11	31	33	24
Blackpool Mech	28	7	10	11	21	33	24
Chorley Res	28	6	11	11	34	37	23
Wigan Rovers	28	6	9	13	25	40	21
Barrow Res	28	6	8	14	25	39	20
Daisey Hill	28	5	10	13	26	45	20
Clitheroe	28	7	5	16	31	46	19
Ashton Athletic	28	3	5	20	17	67	11

West Midlands (Regional) League
PREMIER DIVISION

	P	W	D	L	F	A	Pts
Willenhall Town	34	23	7	4	82	32	53
Lye Town	34	21	11	2	62	33	53
Dudley Town	34	21	8	5	53	23	50
Hednesford Town	34	19	10	5	59	26	48
Tividale	34	19	6	9	63	40	44
Bilston	34	15	10	9	50	34	40
Brierley Hill Alliance	34	17	5	12	67	47	39
Brereton Social	34	17	5	12	48	40	39
Darlaston	34	15	5	14	52	51	35
Coventry Sporting	34	12	6	16	39	48	30
Hinckley Athletic	34	12	5	17	42	52	29
Ledbury Town	34	10	7	17	57	63	27
VS Rugby	34	9	9	16	29	41	27
Wednesfield Social	34	7	12	15	27	45	26
Halesowen Town	34	8	8	18	35	55	24
Armitage	34	7	6	21	44	69	20
Gresley Rovers	34	4	7	23	27	67	15
Gornal Athletic	34	4	5	25	21	91	13

The Central League

	P	W	D	L	F	A	Pts
Liverpool	42	30	7	5	89	34	67
Nottingham Forest	42	26	6	10	82	38	58
Stoke City	42	23	11	8	65	45	57
Manchester City	42	23	9	10	70	45	55
Wolverhampton Wanderers	42	21	11	10	79	42	53
West Bromwich A	42	18	12	12	80	51	48
Coventry City	42	19	8	15	87	71	46
Sheffield Wednesday	42	19	6	17	74	68	44
Leeds United	42	14	16	12	50	49	44
Aston Villa	42	16	11	15	67	54	43
Manchester United	42	17	9	16	66	58	43
Derby County	42	17	9	16	67	64	43
Everton	42	18	7	17	50	49	43
Burnley	42	15	9	18	42	56	39
Huddersfield Town	42	13	11	18	52	58	37
Blackburn Rovers	42	11	13	18	53	69	35
Bolton Wanderers	42	11	13	18	61	83	35
Sheffield United	42	12	9	21	55	88	33
Newcastle United	42	12	8	22	44	72	32
Blackpool	42	11	6	25	41	68	28
Bury	42	9	4	29	54	104	22
Preston North End	42	6	7	29	46	107	19

The United Counties Football League
PREMIER DIVISION

	P	W	D	L	F	A	Pts
Irthlingborough Diamonds	36	25	5	6	88	31	55
Rushden Town	36	22	7	7	72	29	51
Kempston Rovers	36	20	7	9	55	23	47
Desborough Town	36	20	3	13	82	59	43
Potton United	36	18	7	11	59	49	43
Wolverton Town	36	17	9	10	61	52	43
Rothwell Town	36	14	12	10	56	50	40
Stamford AFC	36	15	9	12	61	47	39
St Neots Town	36	16	7	13	59	51	39
Wootton Blue Cross	36	15	8	13	77	63	38
Stewart & Lloyds (Corby)	36	16	5	15	48	46	37
Olney Town	36	14	9	13	36	43	37
Buckingham Town	36	10	11	15	46	52	31
Long Buckby AFC	36	12	6	18	41	58	30
Ampthill Town	36	10	5	21	44	74	25
Bourne Town	36	9	6	21	51	86	24
Northampton Spencer OB	36	7	9	20	47	76	23
Holbeach United	36	9	4	23	51	94	22
Eynesbury Rovers	36	6	5	25	28	79	17

South East Counties League
DIVISION ONE

	P	W	D	L	F	A	Pts
Tottenham H	30	19	6	5	80	45	44
Ipswich T	30	17	6	7	66	38	40
Millwall	30	15	7	8	51	38	37
Arsenal	30	15	6	9	49	32	*35
Portsmouth	30	15	5	10	52	51	35
Gillingham	30	15	4	11	54	41	34
Crystal P	30	14	5	11	58	54	33
West Ham U	30	11	7	12	52	51	29
Chelsea	30	14	4	12	65	59	*28
Orient	30	12	3	15	42	49	27
Charlton A	30	11	3	16	54	62	25
Watford	30	8	6	16	30	48	22
Norwich C	30	9	6	15	40	62	*22
Southend U	30	9	3	18	48	68	21
Queens P R	30	9	3	18	44	68	21
Fulham	30	7	6	17	35	54	20

* Points Deducted

The Football Combination

	P	W	D	L	F	A	Pts
Tottenham Hotspur	42	30	6	6	105	42	66
Ipswich Town	42	29	7	6	94	38	65
Queens Park Rangers	42	27	8	7	103	57	62
West Ham United	42	25	11	6	86	43	61
Norwich City	42	21	13	8	81	45	55
Fulham	42	21	10	11	78	50	52
Chelsea	42	18	14	10	74	54	50
Bristol City	42	20	8	14	73	68	48
Bristol Rovers	42	18	10	14	72	72	46
Arsenal	42	13	18	11	55	44	44
Southampton	42	17	9	16	68	63	43
Crystal Palace	42	11	16	15	60	59	38
Plymouth Argyle	42	14	9	19	58	72	37
Cardiff City	42	13	8	21	54	75	34
Hereford United	42	10	12	20	54	83	32
Oxford United	42	11	9	22	68	78	31
Birmingham City	42	9	12	21	38	61	30
Swindon Town	42	9	12	21	38	76	30
Leicester City	42	8	11	23	47	72	27
Reading	42	10	6	26	55	117	26
Luton Town	42	9	7	26	37	74	25
Orient	42	9	4	29	45	100	22

Northern Football Alliance

	P	W	D	L	F	A	Pts
Brandon United	34	27	4	3	105	35	58
Guisborough Town	34	25	7	2	107	24	57
Seaham CW Red Star	34	23	7	4	111	33	53
Ryhope CA	34	16	10	8	67	46	42
Peterlee Newtown	34	19	2	13	63	50	40
Wallington	34	18	3	13	73	49	39
Carlisle City	34	15	8	11	60	45	38
Newcastle Utd 'A'	34	15	7	12	82	53	37
Marine Park	34	13	9	12	59	50	35
Morpeth Town	34	13	7	14	69	68	33
Stobswood	34	14	5	15	46	74	33
Percy Main	34	11	7	16	47	74	29
Belford	34	11	4	19	46	82	26
Aliywick Town	34	10	6	18	49	88	26
Cramlington Newtown	34	10	5	19	54	83	25
Sunderland Pyrex	34	8	5	21	31	63	21
Bedlington Town	34	6	5	23	51	97	17
Durham University	34	1	1	32	24	130	3

Gloucestershire County League

	P	W	D	L	F	A	Pts
Almondsbury Greenway	32	23	3	6	112	36	49
Hambrook	32	22	4	6	73	44	48
Worrall Hill	32	18	7	7	64	45	43
Port of Bristol	32	16	10	6	72	45	42
Matson Athletic	32	16	9	7	67	44	41
Sharpness	32	16	3	13	64	48	35
Yate Town	32	13	9	10	58	44	35
Hanham Athletic	32	15	5	12	55	44	35
Old Georgians	32	13	9	10	53	48	35
Stonehouse	32	12	10	10	47	55	34
Bristol St George	32	10	5	17	45	54	25
Lydbrook Athletic	32	8	9	15	42	69	25
Patchway	32	7	9	16	39	75	23
Wilton Rovers	32	9	4	19	33	68	22
Oldland	32	6	9	17	33	61	21
Shortwood United	32	3	10	19	43	88	16
Gloucester City Res	32	3	9	20	33	65	15

South Western League

	P	W	D	L	F	A	Pts
Liskeard	36	26	5	5	98	42	57
Wadebridge	36	23	7	6	91	36	53
Newquay	36	22	9	5	74	33	53
Plymouth Civil Service	36	20	7	9	71	45	47
St Blazey	36	17	7	12	60	49	41
Torpoint Athletic	36	16	9	11	73	69	41
Louis International	36	15	10	11	57	52	40
Truro City	36	15	9	12	69	57	39
Holsworth	36	15	8	13	66	59	38
St Austell	36	15	7	14	57	59	37
Tavistock	36	11	11	14	61	64	33
Penzance	36	11	10	15	63	65	32
Bugle	36	11	7	18	43	71	29
Appledore	36	10	8	18	47	58	28
Bodmin	36	9	7	20	43	81	25
Illogan RBL	36	6	12	18	58	88	24
Torrington	36	8	9	19	50	80	*23
Newton Abbot Dynamos	36	8	6	22	33	59	22
Plymouth Command	36	6	8	22	34	82	20

*Points deducted.

Essex Senior Football League

	P	W	D	L	F	A	Pts
Basildon	32	26	5	1	86	14	57
Canvey Island	32	22	8	2	73	21	52
Eton Manor	32	19	6	7	68	37	44
Heybridge	32	17	9	6	50	32	43
Brentwood	32	15	9	8	64	49	39
East Ham	32	16	6	10	57	42	38
Witham	32	14	7	11	47	43	35
Tiptree	32	11	11	10	42	32	33
Brightlingsea	32	12	9	11	53	51	33
Bowers	32	12	8	12	41	47	32
Chelmsford Res	32	11	6	15	41	47	28
Maldon	32	7	14	11	43	60	28
Woodford	33	10	7	15	46	62	27
Ford	32	4	9	19	28	47	17
Stansted	32	7	2	23	34	72	16
Coggeshall	32	2	10	20	40	82	14
Sawbridgeworth	32	3	2	27	29	104	8

AFA FOOTBALL 1978-79

AMATEUR FOOTBALL ALLIANCE SENIOR CUP FINAL 1978-79

Lloyds Bank 2   Carshalton 0
(At National Westminster Bank Ground, Norbury)

Lloyds Bank: Kaplanski; Norbury, Roberts, Williams, Rouse, Lockwood, Foster, Cavalli, Fraser, Allan, Dyer.

Carshalton: Walker; Butcher, Wigham, Dunkley, Stewart, Cocker, Dobbs, McBey (Kotas), Irwin, Strong, Benham.

OTHER COMPETITION WINNERS 1978-79

AFA Middlesex Senior Cup: East Barnet Old Grammarians (*Beat Old Ignatians* 2-1)
AFA Surrey Senior Cup: Clapham Old Xaverians (*beat Old Josephians* 4-1)
AFA Essex Senior Cup: Old Fairlopians (*beat Old Buckwellians* 1-0)
Southern Amateur League: Catford Wanderers
Old Boys' League: Old Salesians
Southern Olympian League: Old Finchleians

FA VASE 1978-79

Preliminary Round
Darlington RA v Wallington	3-1
Ryhope v Whickham	2-3
Carlisle C v Billingham Social	1-3
Brandon U v Norton CCT	0-1
Peterlee Newtown v Carlisle Spartans	1-2
Heaton Stannington v Boys Welfare	2-1
Boldon CA v Smith's Dock	2-1
Wallsend T v Guisborough T	2-1
Seaham CW Red Star v Appleby	4-2
Pickering v Washington	0-3
Wingate v Sunderland Pyrex	1-0
Teesside Polytechnic v Eppleton CW	0-1
Wren R v Little Lever	1-2
Nelson v Old Blackburnians	6-2
Leyland Motors v Stork	6-2
Waterloo Dock v Newton	5-0
Salford Amateurs v Blackpool Mechanics	3-1
Lytham v Whalley Range Amateur	6-2
Wythenshawe Amateurs v North Withington	0-1
Prescot BI v Hoylake Ath	1-3
East Chorlton Amateur v Kidsgrove Ath	0-4
*Linotype v Heswall	3-2
Glossop v Chadderton	2-3
BSC Parkgate v Ossett T	0-6
Thackley v Clitheroe	1-0
Harrogate T v Bradley Rangers	1-0
Fryston Colliery v Normanby PW	1-3
Guiseley v North Ferriby U	1-0
Birkenshaw R v Bentley Vic	2-3
Brook Sports v Hatfield Main	3-0
Yorkshire Amateur v Gainsborough U	1-2
Hall Road Rangers v Ashby Institute	2-1
Immingham T v Retford T	1-4
Ruston Sports v Pilkington Recreation	0-0
Rawmarsh Welfare v Barton T	4-2
Skegness T v Kiveton Park	2-0
Oakham U v Ruston Bucyrus	0-0
Thringstone v Newfoundpool WMC	2-3
*Norton Woodseats v Staveley Works	3-2
Shepshed Charterhouse v Carrvale U	5-0
Clay Cross Works v Paget Rangers	2-3
*Long Eaton Grange v Tividale	2-1
Walsall Sportsco v Oadby T	1-0
*Solihull Bor v Hinckley T	0-2
Wednesfield Social v GKN Sankey	5-2
Boldmere St Michaels v Brierley Hill	0-2
†Coventry Sporting v Long Buckby	
Willenhall T v Desborough T	3-2
Knowle v Coleshill T	3-1
Walsall Wood v Northfield T	0-4
*Rothwell T v Valley Sports Rugby	1-0
Ely C v Leverington	3-0
Stowmarket v Holbeach U	2-2
Holt U v Beccles	3-1
Soham T Rangers v Bungay T	5-1
March Town U v Norwich Union	4-2
Chatteris T v Watton U	0-3
Melton T v Mirrlees Blackstone	2-2
Royston T v Diss T	4-0
*Felixstowe T v Maldon T	2-0
Stratford T v Bicester T	0-2
*Eaton Bray U v Northampton Spencer	0-1
Knebworth v Olney T	2-3
Stansted v Langford	2-0
Letchworth GC v Huntingdon U	8-1
*Wolveron & BR v Hemel Hempstead	2-1
Sandy Albions v Sun Sports	0-2
Cheshunt v Potton U	4-2
Tiptree U v Haverhill R	0-1
Leggatts OB v Baldock T	1-2
Hatfield T v Thame U	1-6
*Wootton Blue Cross v Rolls Royce Engines	3-2
Sawbridgeworth v Arlesey T	1-4
Witham T v Eynesbury R	3-1
Pirton v Saffron Walden T	3-1
Chingford v Selby	0-3
Vauxhall Motors v Edgware	2-0
Heybridge Swifts v Braintree & Crittall	4-1
Wallingford T v Harefield U	2-1
Tansley v Stotfold	2-1
Willesden v Didcot T	3-1
Harpenden T v Shillington	1-2
Woodford T v Kingsbury T	2-1
*Norsemen v Swanley T	3-4
Windsor & Eton v Eton Manor	2-0
Ford U v Whyteleafe	0-0
‡West Wickham v Darenth Heathside	2-0
Erith v Belvedere v LB of Greenwich	0-1
Bracknell T v Malden Vale	0-2
Thatcham T v BAC (Weybridge)	0-2
Chalfont St Peter v Banstead Ath	0-1
Civil Service v Frimley Green	3-1
Malden T v Feltham	1-2
Flackwell Heath v Chertsey T	1-4
*Ulysses v Egham T	1-3
Kew Association v Marlow	2-2
Cobham v Shoreham	1-1
Steyning v Horsham YMCA	1-0
Old Salesians v Camberley T	2-3
*Dartford Glentworth v Canvey Island	5-4
Crockenhill v Crown & Manor	6-2
East Grinstead v Whitstable T	2-2
Faversham T v Sidley U	5-1
Bexley v Welling U	1-4
Herne Bay v Hythe T	3-0
Wigmore Ath v Merstham	2-3
Ringmer v Three Bridges	2-1
Dorking T v Southwick	2-1
Tunbridge Wells v Horley T	1-0
Littlehampton T Bexhill T	2-1
Worthing v Farnham T	1-0
Newport IOW v Selsey	5-0
Brading T v Swanage & Herston	4-2
Chichester C v Cowes	1-0
Alton T v Swaythling	3-2
First Tower T v Havant T	2-1
Brockenhurst v Sholing Sports	1-3
Fleet T v St Martins	0-1
Amesbury v Wantage T	6-0
Clandown v Larkhall Ath	0-0
Ledbury T v Wilton R	6-2
Pegasus Juniors v West Midlands Police	2-5
Worrall Hill v Fairford T	3-1
Malmesbury Vic v Shortwood U	1-3
Calne T v Radstock T	0-1
Sharpness v Chippenham T	3-1
Cirencester T v Bristol St George	0-0
Ilminster T v Port of Bristol	6-3
Westbury U v Odd Down	4-2
*Peasedown Ath v Glenside St Gabriels	1-0
Bristol Manor Farm v Keynsham T	1-1
Stonehouse v Clanfield	1-2
Forest Green R v Avon Bradfort	12-1
Brixham U v Ottery St Mary	3-1
Exmouth T v Holsworthy	2-1

*After extra time
†WO for Coventry Sporting as Long Buckby have withdrawn
‡At Darenth Heathside FC

Replays
Pilkington Recreation v Ruston Sports	0-1
Ruston Bucyrus v Oakham U	0-2
Holbeach U v Stowmarket (aet)	2-3
Mirrlees Blackstone v Melton T	3-2
Whyteleafe v Ford U	2-0
Marlow v Kew Association	1-3
Shoreham v Cobham	1-2
Whitstable T v East Grinstead	3-2
Larkhall Ath v Clandown	0-0
Bristol St George v Cirencester T	2-1
Keynsham T v Bristol Manor Farm	3-0

Second Replay
Clandown v Larkhall Ath	0-2

at Bath C FC

First Round

Wingate v Wallsend T	1-0
*Carlisle Spartans v Washington	2-4
Billingham Social v Boldon CA	1-3
Heaton Stannington v Seaham CW Red Star	1-2
Norton CCT v Annfield Plain	1-3
Whickham v Eppleton CW	4-0
Guiseley v Tadcaster Albion	0-1
Leeds Polytechnic v Darlington RA	0-2
Harrogate T v Thackley	0-5
Irlam T v Leyland Motors	1-1
Fleetwood T v Little Lever	3-0
Linotype v Hoylake Ath	2-1
Lytham v Warrington T	2-1
Salford Amateurs v Nelson	2-1
Waterloo Dock v Curzon Ashton	3-0
Brook Sports v Chadderton	4-1
Norton Woodseats v Anson Villa	1-0
North Withington v Ossett Albion	3-2
*Appleby FA v Denaby U	2-1
Ossett T v Ruston Sports	2-0
Bentley Vic v Normanby PW	2-1
Hall Road Rangers v Brigg T	5-1
Clipstone Welfare v Gainsborough U	0-1
Rawmarsh Welfare v Retford T	2-3
Bourne T v Oakham U	2-0
Skegness T v Mirrlees Blackstone	5-0
Hinckley T v Paget Rangers	0-1
Rothwell T v Long Eaton Grange	0-0
Gresley R v Newfoundpool WMC	0-1
Walsall Sportsco v Knowle	1-0
Oldbury U v Shepshed Charterhouse	1-3
Coventry Sporting v Gornal Ath	2-0
Northfield T v Armitage	2-4
Kidsgrove Ath v Bridgnorth T	2-0
Willenhall T v West Midlands Police	3-2
Evesham U v Anstey Nomads	0-2
*Racing Club (Warwick) v Brierley Hill A	1-0
Malvern T v Astwood Bank	3-1
Moreton T v Wednesfield Social	2-6
Halesowen T v Ledbury T	4-4
Felixstowe T v Watton U	3-1
Soham T Rangers v Beccles	2-0
CNSOBU v Stowmarket	2-1
Haverhill R v Royston T	0-2
Vauxhall Motors v March U	0-1
St Neots T v Shillington	6-1
Pirton v Bicester T	0-2
Northampton Spencer v Berkhamsted T	1-2
Stansted v Baldock T	1-4
Rushden T v Ely C	2-0
Histon v Ampthill T	2-2
Wootton Blue Cross v Olney T	3-1
Thame U v Letchworth GC	0-1
Arlesey T v Wolverton T & BR	1-0
Kidlington v Amersham T	1-2
Witham T v Basildon U	0-4
Brightlingsea U v Rainham T	1-1
Leyton-Wingate v Heybridge Swifts	2-2
Coggeshall T v Bowers U	2-1
Faversham T v Ringmer	1-1
Swanley U v Herne Bay	3-0
Whitstable T v Tunbridge Wells	1-2
West Wickham v Tansley	2-0
Crockenhill v Cheshunt	0-6
Selby v Woodford T	3-1
Banstead Ath v Whyteleafe	2-0
Dartford Glentworth v Grays Ath	0-3
Hoddesdon T v Welling U	3-2
Sun Sports v Kew Association	4-4
Willesden v Ruislip Manor	1-3
*Feltham v Cray W	4-1
Civil Service v Redhill	1-2
Merstham v LB of Greenwich	2-1
Uxbridge v Chessington U	3-0
Arundel v Alton T	1-4
First Tower U v Littlehampton T	4-4
*Amesbury v St Martins	1-2
Sholing Sports v Newbury T	0-1
Worthing v Brading T	2-0
Newport IOW v Chichester C	7-0
Malden Vale v Dorking T	2-0
Ash United v Shoreham	4-0
Steyning v Egham T	1-3
Camberley T v Wallingford T	4-3
Windsor & Eton v Chertsey T	2-1
BAC (Weybridge) v Chobham	2-1
Abingdon T v Hazells	1-0
Larkhall Ath v Peasedown Ath	1-2
Worrall Hill v Bristol St George	1-1
Clanfield v Cadbury Heath	2-0
*Westbury U v Shortwood U	3-2
Forest Green R v Yate T	1-1
Sharpness v Westland-Yeovil	1-2
Radstock T v Keynsham T	1-2
Illogan RBL v Exmouth T	0-1
Ilminster T v Brixham U	3-2

after extra time

Replays

Leyland Motors v Irlam T	0-1
Ossett Albion v North Withington	2-1
Long Eaton Grange v Rothwell T	2-1
Ledbury T v Halesowen T	1-3
Ampthill T v Histon	0-2
Rainham T v Brightlingsea U	1-0
Heybridge Swifts v Leyton-Wingate	1-3
Ringmer v Faversham T	0-4
Kew Association v Sun Sports	1-0
Littlehampton T v First Tower U	0-2
Bristol St George v Worrall Hill	0-2
Yate T v Forest Green R	aet 1-3

Second Round

Blue Star v Wingate	2-1
Seaham CW Red Star v Annfield Plain	4-1
Washington v Boldon CA	1-3
Whickham v Darlington RA	3-0
Thackley v Fleetwood T	1-1
Prescot T v Hallam	4-3
Lytham v Salford Amateurs	4-0
Ossett Albion v Waterloo Dock	2-1
Leeds Ashley Road v Linotype	4-2
Norton Woodseats v Irlam T	2-0
Ossett T v Tadcaster Albion	0-2
Gainsborough U v Winterton Rangers	0-2
Appleby FA v Hall Road Rangers	3-1
Lincoln U v Brook Sports	6-3
Retford T v Kidsgrove Ath	2-1
Frecheville Community v Bentley Vic	0-1
Sheffield v Congleton T	4-1
Shepshed Charterhouse v Armitage	4-0
Wigston Fields v Skegness T	0-1
Rushden T v Newfoundpool WMC	5-1
Bourne T v Stamford	0-1
Coventry Sporting v Friar Lane OB	0-1
Wednesfield Social v Long Eaton Grange	2-1
Paget Rangers v Hinckley Ath	1-2
Anstey Nomads v Blakenhall	1-0
Racing Club (Warwick) v Irthlingborough	0-0
Willenhall T v Walsall Sportsco	3-1
Halesowen T v Malvern T	5-1
Buckingham T v Bicester T	1-3
CNSOBU v Soham T Rangers	0-7
Felixstowe T v Coggeshall T	2-1
Egham T v Leyton-Wingate	1-4
Barton R v Wootton Blue Cross	aet 3-1
Feltham v Epping T	aet 2-3
Hoddesdon T v Royston T	aet 0-1
St Neots T v Letchworth GC	aet 4-3
Histon v March T U	aet 3-1
Arlesey T v Kempston R	2-1
Selby v Camberley T	0-2
Tring T v Ruislip Manor	2-0
Berkhamsted T v Burnham	2-3
Billericay T v Rainham T	aet 2-1
Baldock T v Cheshunt	0-5
East Ham U v Basildon U	2-0
Grays Ath v Swanley T	1-0
Windsor & Eton v Banstead Ath	4-1
Kew Association v Haringey Bor	3-5
Molesey v Malden Vale	3-2
Amersham T v Farnborough T	0-1
BAC (Weybridge) v Uxbridge	1-2
Abingdon T v Newbury T	1-3
Eastbourne U v Faversham T	3-1
Merstham v Alma Swanley	1-2

Eastbourne T v Tunbridge Wells	1-2
Redhill v West Wickham	0-2
Newport IOW v Gosport Bor	0-1
Worthing v Ash U	4-2
St Martins v First Tower U	1-0
Hungerford T v Alton T	3-4
Clanfield v Worrall Hill	2-1
Westbury U v Peasedown Ath	0-1
Almondsbury Greenway v Forest Green R	5-0
Exmouth T v Ilminster T	aet 1-4
Westland-Yeovil v Keynsham T	1-0

Replays

Fleetwood T v Thackley	0-3
*Irthlingborough D v Racing Club (Warwick)	2-1

*after extra time

Third Round

Seaham CW Red Star v Ossett T	4-0
Leeds Ashley Road v Winterton Rangers	1-1
Bentley Vic v Bolden CA	3-2
Blue Star v Whickham	2-4
Ossett Albion v Prescot T	0-2
Thackley v Lytham	1-1
Friar Lane OB v Sheffield	aet 4-2
Skegness T v Bourne T	7-2
Lincoln U v Appleby Frodingham Ath	1-1
Willenhall T v Retford T	3-1
Norton Woodseats v Shepshed Charterhouse	1-2
St Neots T v Irthlingborough D	2-4
Anstey Nomads v Halesowen T	7-0
Hinckley Ath v Wednesfield Social	2-1
Rushden T v Bicester T	0-3
Billericay T v Epping T	5-0
Royston T v Histon	2-1
Felixstowe T v Soham T Rangers	4-4
Haringey Bor v Tring T	3-1
Cheshunt v East Ham U	5-2
Arlesley T v Leyton-Wingate	0-2
Tunbridge Wells v Uxbridge	0-0
Eastbourne U v Alma Swanley	3-0
Molesey v Grays Ath	1-0
West Wickham v Farnborough T	2-2
Windsor & Eton v Newbury T	4-2
Clanfield v Camberley T	0-2
Barton R v Burnham	2-1
Alton T v Worthing	1-2
Gosport Bor v St Martins	3-1
Westland-Yeovil v Almondsbury Greenway	0-2
Peasedown Ath v Ilminster T	2-1

Replays

Winterton Rangers v Leeds Ashley Road	3-2
Lytham v Thackley	aet 1-2
Appleby Frodingham Ath v Lincoln U	3-3
Soham T Rangers v Felixstowe T	3-1
Uxbridge v Tunbridge Wells	aet 1-2
Farnborough T v West Wickham	3-2

Second Replay

Lincoln U v Appleby Frodingham Ath	3-0

Fourth Round

Seaham CW Red Star v Prescot T	1-1
Thackley v Wickham	2-2
Bentley Vic v Winterton Rangers	0-2
Irthlingborough D v Anstey Nomads	2-1
Lincoln U v Willenhall T	2-3

Shepshed Charterhouse v Skegness T	1-0
Friar Lane OB v Hickley Ath	1-0
Billericay T v Royston T	2-0
Haringey Bor v Barton R	1-2
Bicester T v Cheshunt	0-2
Soham Town Rangers v Leyton-Wingate	1-2
Windsor & Eton v Almondsbury Greenway	0-2
Camberley T v Eastbourne U	1-2
Molesey v Farnborough T	2-4
Gosport Bor v Tunbridge Wells	4-2
Worthing v Peasedown Ath	5-2

Replays

Prescot T v Seaham CW Red Star	1-3
Whickham v Thackley	2-0

Fifth Round

Shepshed Charterhouse v Winterton R	4-2
Whickham v Seaham CW Red Star	5-2
Friar Lane OB v Barton R	2-4
Willenhall T v Irthlingborough D	2-1
Leyton-Wingate v Eastbourne U	0-0
Cheshunt v Farnborough T	0-4
Worthing v Billericay T	1-2
Gosport Bor v Almondsbury Greenway	1-1

Replays

Leyton-Wingate v Eastbourne U	0-2
Almondsbury Green v Gosport Bor	4-3

Sixth Round

Whickham v Willenhall T	3-2
Barton R v Shepshed Charterhouse	*2-3
Eastbourne U v Billericay T	0-1
Almondsbury Greenway v Farnborough T	3-1

*after extra time

Semi-Final Ties

First Leg

Billericay T v Shepshed Charterhouse	2-0
Almondsbury Greenway v Whickham	1-0

Second Leg

Shepshed Charterhouse v Billericay	2-0
Whickham v Almondsbury Greenway	1-1

Replay

Billericay T v Shepshed Charterhouse	2-0
at Cambridge C FC	

Final at Wembley

Billericay T 4 (*Young* 3, *Clayden*)		16,792
Almondsbury Greenway 1 (*Price*)		

Billericay T: Norris; Blackaller, Bingham, Whettell, Bone, Reeves, Pullen, Scott, Clayden, Young, Groom (Carrigan)

Almondsbury Greenway: Hamilton; Bowers Phil, Scarrett, Sullivan, Tudor (Kilbaine), Wookey, Bowers Peter, Shehean, Kerr, Butt, Price

Previous Finals

1975	Hoddesdon 2; Epsom 1 (10,000)
1976	Billericay T 1; Stamford 0 (12,000)
1977	Billericay T 1, 2; Sheffield 1, 1 (15,150)
1978	Blue Star 2; Barton R 1 (16,000)

FA REPRESENTATIVE MATCHES 1934-78

FA XI v ROYAL NAVY

Year	Date	Venue	FA	RN
1934	Dec	Portsmouth	0	0
1935	Dec	Plymouth	3	4
1936	Dec	Chatham	7	0
1937	Dec	Devonport	5	0
1938	Dec	Portsmouth	6	2
1947	Feb	Portsmouth	3	0
1947	Dec	Portsmouth	4	0
1948	Dec	Plymouth	1	1
1949	Dec	Plymouth	4	1
1950	Dec	Portsmouth	1	2
1951	Dec	Portsmouth	4	1
1952	Dec	Plymouth	4	0
1953	Dec	Portsmouth	1	0
1954	Dec	Portsmouth	2	1
1955	Dec	Portsmouth	5	5
1957	Jan	Portsmouth	5	1
1957	Dec	Portsmouth	5	2
1958	Dec	Portsmouth	4	1
1959	Dec	Portsmouth	5	3
1960	Dec	Portsmouth	6	2
1961	Dec	Portsmouth	7	3
1962	Dec	Portsmouth	4	0
1963	Dec	Portsmouth	2	0
1964	Dec	Portsmouth	4	1
1965	Dec	Portsmouth	9	0
1966	Nov	Portsmouth	1	0
1967	Nov	Portsmouth	3	0
1968	Nov	Portsmouth	2	0
1969	Nov	Portsmouth	1	0
1970	Dec	Portsmouth	2	2
1971	Dec	Portsmouth	3	2
1972	Nov	Portsmouth	2	1
1973	Nov	Portsmouth	2	0

FA XI v OXFORD UNIVERSITY

Year	Date	Venue	FA	OU
1934	Nov	Oxford	6	1
1935	Nov	Oxford	3	2
1936	Nov	Oxford	5	1
1937	Nov	Oxford	6	2
1938	Nov	Oxford	2	0
1945	Nov	Oxford	7	0
1946	Nov	Oxford	4	3
1947	Nov	Oxford	2	0
1948	Nov	Oxford	1	1
1949	Nov	Oxford	2	1
1950	Nov	Reading	3	3
1951	Nov	Oxford	2	1
1952	Nov	Oxford	4	2
1953	Nov	Oxford	4	2
1954	Nov	Oxford	5	0
1955	Nov	Oxford	2	1
1956	Nov	Oxford	3	0
1957	Nov	Oxford	1	1
1958	Nov	Oxford	5	0
1959	Nov	Malvern	4	1
1960	Nov	Eastbourne	3	0
1961	Nov	Oxford	6	0
1962	Nov	Eastbourne	3	3
1963	Nov	Oxford	4	0
1964	Oct	Eastbourne	4	1
1965	Nov	Oxford	6	0
1966	Nov	Eastbourne	3	0
1967	Nov	Oxford	6	0
1968	Nov	Eastbourne	5	0
1969	Nov	Oxford	0	1
1970	Nov	Eastbourne	1	0
1971	Nov	Oxford	1	0
1972	Nov	Eastbourne	5	0
1973	Nov	Oxford	5	0
1976	Nov	Oxford	1	0
1977	Nov	Oxford	4	0
1978	Nov	Oxford	3	1

FA XI v THE ARMY

Year	Date	Venue	FA	Army
1934	Nov	Tidworth	1	1
1935	Nov	Colchester	4	4
1936	Nov	Aldershot	6	3
1937	Nov	Aldershot	4	2
1938	Nov	Colchester	1	1
1946	Nov	Stoke	3	8
1947	Nov	Brighton	4	0
1948	Nov	Ipswich	0	2
1949	Nov	Charlton	4	1
1950	Nov	Highbury	3	2
1951	Nov	Highbury	4	2
1952	Nov	Leeds	4	4
1953	Nov	Newcastle	3	1
1954	Nov	Sheffield	1	1
1955	Nov	Newcastle	2	2
1956	Nov	Manchester	7	3
1957	Oct	Manchester	6	3
1958	Oct	Newcastle	4	1
1959	Oct	Newcastle	3	1
1960	Oct	Sheffield	2	1
1961	Oct	Sunderland	1	2
1962	Oct	Aldershot	6	2
1963	Oct	Aldershot	4	2
1964	Feb	Catterick	2	2
1964	Oct	Aldershot	1	4
1965	Feb	Catterick	1	2
1965	Oct	Aldershot	1	1
1966	Oct	Aldershot	1	1
1967	Oct	Aldershot	3	1
1968	Oct	Aldershot	1	1
1969	Oct	Aldershot	3	0
1970	Oct	Aldershot	2	0
1972	Oct	Aldershot	3	2
1973	Oct	Bordon	0	4

FA XI v UNIVERSITIES ATHLETIC UNION

Year	Date	Venue	FA	UAU
1934	Feb	Newcastle	5	2
1935	Feb	Manchester	0	5
1936	Feb	Manchester	2	2
1937	Feb	Exeter	1	4
1938	Feb	Leeds	4	1
1939	Feb	Southampton	0	2
1946	Feb	Darlington	10	1
1947	Feb	Southampton	4	1
1948	Feb	Bristol	2	1
1949	Feb	Sheffield	2	0
1950	Feb	Exeter	4	0
1951	Feb	Hull	2	1
1952	Mar	Doncaster	1	4
1953	Feb	Nottingham	4	1
1954	Feb	Bristol	3	1
1955	Feb	Sheffield	5	0
1956	Feb	Reading	0	3
1957	Mar	Stoke	4	1
1958	Mar	Leicester	1	1
1959	Mar	Peterborough	1	2
1960	Mar	Norwich	3	0
1961	Feb	Reading	1	2
1963	Apr	Sheffield	3	0
1964	Feb	Birmingham	8	0
1965	Mar	Coventry	1	3
1966	Mar	Rugby	5	0
1967	Mar	Sheffield	2	1
1968	Feb	Nottingham	1	1
1969	Apr	Sheffield	6	0
1970	Feb	Morecambe	3	1
1971	Apr	Durham	1	1
1971	Oct	Aldershot	0	2
1973	Feb	Newcastle	2	3
1974	Feb	Nuneaton	2	2
1976	Feb	York	2	2
1977	Mar	York	2	2
1978	Mar	Altrincham FC	2	1
1979	Mar	Altrincham FC	1	1

FA XI v ROYAL AIR FORCE

Year	Date	Venue	FA	RAF
1934	Jan	Cranwell	2	0
1935	Jan	Watford	4	0
1936	Jan	Uxbridge	3	3
1937	Jan	Uxbridge	9	1
1937	Nov	Uxbridge	4	4
1938	Dec	Cranwell	3	2
1946	Oct	Reading	4	1
1947	Oct	Highbury	3	0
1948	Oct	Highbury	9	2
1949	Oct	Fulham	2	1
1950	Oct	Fulham	6	1
1951	Oct	Stamford Bridge	4	0
1952	Oct	Stamford Bridge	8	1
1953	Oct	Tottenham	4	0
1954	Oct	Highbury	3	1
1955	Oct	Bristol	9	0
1956	Oct	Sheffield	2	1
1957	Oct	Nottingham	5	2
1958	Oct	Bristol	1	4
1959	Oct	Norwich	9	2
1960	Oct	Manchester	2	2
1961	Oct	Peterborough	13	0
1962	Oct	Uxbridge	4	2
1963	Oct	Uxbridge	4	2
1964	Sept	Uxbridge	5	1
1969	Oct	Halton	2	2
1970	Oct	Halton	5	0
1971	Oct	Halton	1	0
1972	Oct	Uxbridge	2	1
1973	Oct	Uxbridge	4	0
1976	Jan	Wealdstone	2	1

FA XI v CAMBRIDGE UNIVERSITY

Year	Date	Venue	FA	CU
1934	Nov	Cambridge	5	0
1935	Nov	Cambridge	6	1
1936	Nov	Cambridge	5	0
1937	Nov	Cambridge	3	1
1938	Nov	Cambridge	6	2
1946	Feb	Cambridge	5	1
1946	Nov	Cambridge	3	2
1947	Nov	Cambridge	6	1
1948	Nov	Cambridge	7	1
1949	Nov	Cambridge	3	1
1950	Nov	Cambridge	4	2
1951	Nov	Cambridge	4	1
1952	Nov	Cambridge	8	0
1953	Nov	Cambridge	2	3
1954	Nov	Cambridge	4	2
1955	Nov	Cambridge	5	1
1956	Nov	Cambridge	6	1
1957	Nov	Cambridge	5	0
1958	Nov	Cambridge	1	1
1959	Nov	Eastbourne	1	2
1960	Nov	Cambridge	3	4
1961	Nov	Eastbourne	3	2
1962	Nov	Cambridge	abandoned	
1963	Oct	Eastbourne	2	0
1964	Nov	Cambridge	3	1
1965	Nov	Eastbourne	4	0
1966	Nov	Cambridge	5	1
1967	Nov	Eastbourne	1	1
1968	Nov	Cambridge	2	1
1969	Nov	Eastbourne	3	0
1970	Nov	Cambridge	7	0
1971	Nov	Eastbourne	4	0
1972	Nov	Cambridge	1	0
1973	Nov	Eastbourne	3	0
1976	Nov	Cambridge	1	0
1977	Nov	Cambridge	4	0
1978	Nov	Cambridge	6	1

FA XI v LONDON UNIVERSITY

Year	Date	Venue	FA	LU
1958	Mar	Motspur Park	7	1
1959	Mar	Motspur Park	0	1
1960	Mar	Motspur Park	5	1
1961	Mar	Kingston	2	2
1962	Mar	Motspur Park	7	0
1964	Mar	Kingston	5	1
1965	Mar	Motspur Park	6	2
1966	Mar	Motspur Park	2	1
1967	Mar	Hayes	3	1
1968	Mar	Motspur Park	3	0
1969	Mar	Motspur Park	3	0
1970	Mar	Woking	9	0
1971	Mar	Motspur Park	4	0
1973	Mar	Motspur Park	4	1
1974	Mar	Motspur Park	8	1
1976	Mar	Kingston	4	1
1976	Dec	Wealdstone	3	0
1977	Dec	Metropolitan Police FC	2	0
1978	Dec	Harrow Borough FC	5	1

FA XI v AMATEUR FOOTBALL ALLIANCE

Year	Date	Venue	FA	AFA
1958	Jan	Maidstone	4	2
1959	Jan	Barking	3	1
1960	Feb	Maidstone	5	0
1961	Feb	Bromley	2	2
1962	Feb	Wimbledon	3	1
1963	Feb	Kingston	7	1
1964	Feb	Tooting	3	0
1965	Feb	Wealdstone	2	2
1966	Feb	Kingston	3	0
1967	Feb	Bromley	1	2
1968	Feb	Enfield	1	0
1969	Feb	Dulwich	Ground unfit	
1970	Feb	Clapton	2	2
1971	Feb	Tooting	4	0
1973	Feb	B Stortford	3	1
1974	Feb	Leytonstone	2	1
1976	Apr	Dulwich	4	0
1977	Mar	Leytonstone	2	2
1978	Feb	Wealdstone FC	4	1
1979	Feb	Metropolitan Police FC	5	2

FA XI v BRITISH COLLEGES SPORTS ASSOCIATION

Year	Date	Venue	FA	BC
1972	Dec	Chorley	2	1
1973	Dec	Spennymoor	0	1
1976	Mar	Cheltenham	0	1
1977	Feb	Cheltenham	4	0
1978	Feb	Cheltenham	0	1

FA XI v SUNDERLAND

Year	Date	Venue	FA	Sund
1973	Dec	Sunderland	0	4

FA XI v COMBINED SERVICES

Year	Date	Venue	FA	CS
1977	Apr	Aldershot	2	2
1978	Apr	Aldershot	1	1
1979	Apr	Aldershot	1	1

FA XI v NORTHERN LEAGUE

Year	Date	Venue	FA	NL
1977	Mar	Blyth Spartans FC	2	3
1978	Apr	Consett FC	2	3
1979	Apr	North Shields FC	0	2

FA XI v SOUTH WEST COUNTIES

Year	Date	Venue	FA	SWC
1977	Oct	Exeter City FC	0	1
1978	Oct	Southampton FC	1	1

LAWS OF THE GAME

The Laws of the Game and Decisions of the International Board that follow are reproduced with the special permission of FIFA, and the text is the official text as published by FIFA.

LAW 1
THE FIELD OF PLAY

The Field of Play and appurtenances shall be as shown in the following plan:

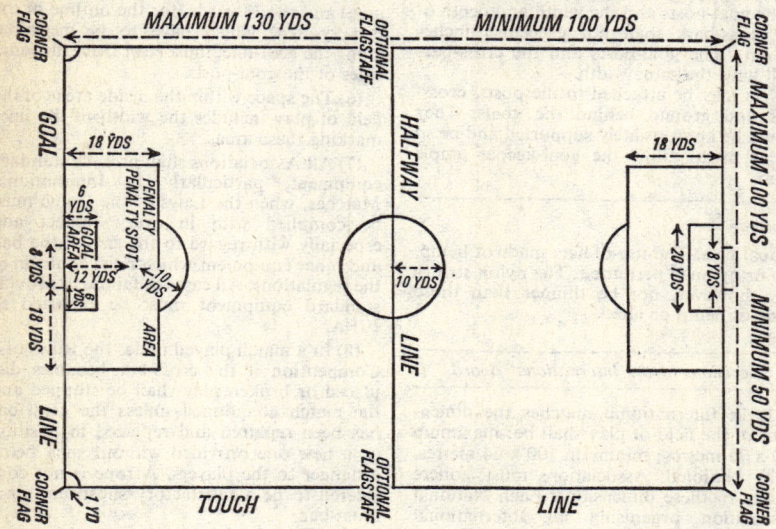

(1) **Dimensions.** The field of play shall be rectangular, its length being not more than 130 yards nor less than 100 yards and its breadth not more than 100 yards nor less than 50 yards. (In International Matches the length shall be not more than 120 yards nor less than 110 yards and the breadth not more than 80 yards nor less than 70 yards.) The length shall in all cases exceed the breadth.

(2) **Marking.** The field of play shall be marked with distinctive lines, not more than 5 inches in width, not by a V-shaped rut, in accordance with the plan, the longer boundary lines being called the touch-lines and the shorter the goal-lines. A flag on a post not less than 5 ft. high and having a non-pointed top, shall be placed at each corner; a similar flag-post may be placed opposite the halfway line on each side of the field of play, not less than 1 yard outside the touch-line. A halfway-line shall be marked out across the field of play. The centre of the field of play shall be indicated by a suitable mark and a circle with a 10 yards radius shall be marked round it.

(3) **The Goal-Area.** At each end of the field of play two lines shall be drawn at right-angles to the goal-line, 6 yards from each goal-post. These shall extend into the field of play for a distance of 6 yards and shall be joined by a line drawn parallel with the goal-line. Each of the spaces enclosed by these goal lines and the goal-line shall be called a goal-area.

(4) **The Penalty-Area.** At each end of the field of play two lines shall be drawn at right-angles to the goal-line, 18 yards from each goal-post. These shall extend into the field of play for a distance of 18 yards and shall be joined by a line drawn parallel with the goal-line. Each of the spaces enclosed by these lines and the goal-line shall be called a penalty-area. A suitable mark shall be made within each penalty-area, 12 yards from the mid-point of the goal-line, measured along an undrawn line at right-angles thereto. These shall be the penalty-kick marks. From each penalty-kick mark an arc of a circle, having a radius of 10 yards, shall be drawn outside the penalty-area.

(5) **The Corner-Area.** From each corner-

flag post a quarter circle, having a radius of 1 yard, shall be drawn inside the field of play.

(6) **The Goals.** The goals shall be placed on the centre of each goal-line and shall consist of two upright posts, equidistant from the corner-flags and 8 yards apart (inside measurement), joined by a horizontal cross-bar the lower edge of which shall be 8 ft from the ground. The width and depth of the goal-posts and the width and depth of the cross-bars shall not exceed 5 inches (12 cm). The goal-posts and the cross-bars shall have the same width.

Nets may be attached to the posts, cross-bars and ground behind the goals. They should be appropriately supported and be so placed as to allow the goal-keeper ample room.

Footnote

Goal nets. The use of nets made of hemp, jute or nylon is permitted. The nylon strings may, however, not be thinner than those made of hemp or jute.

Decisions of the International Board

(1) In International matches the dimensions of the field of play shall be: maximum 110 x 75 metres; minimum 100 x 64 metres.

(2) National Associations must adhere strictly to these dimensions. Each National Association organising an International Match must advise the visiting Association, before the match, of the place and the dimensions of the field of play.

(3) The Board has approved this table of measurements for the Laws of the Game:

130 yards	120 Metres
120 yards	110
110 yards	100
100 yards	90
80 yards	75
70 yards	64
50 yards	45
18 yards	16.50
12 yards	11
10 yards	9.15
8 yards	7.32
6 yards	5.50
1 yard	1
8 feet	2.44
5 feet	1.50
28 inches	0.71
27 inches	0.68
9 inches	0.22
5 inches	0.12
3/4 inch	0.019
1/2 inch	0.0127
3/8 inch	0.010
14 ounces	396 grams
16 ounces	453 grams
15 lb./sq.in.	1 kg/cm^2

(4) The goal-line shall be marked the same width as the depth of the goal-posts and the cross-bar, so that the goal-line and goal-post will conform to the same interior and exterior edges.

(5) The 6 yards (for the outline of the goal-area) and the 18 yards (for the outline of the penalty-area) which have to be measured along the goal-line, must start from the inner sides of the goal-posts.

(6) The space within the inside areas of the field of play includes the width of the lines marking these areas.

(7) All Associations shall provide standard equipment, particularly in International Matches, when the Laws of the Game must be complied with in every respect and especially with regard to the size of the ball and other equipment which must conform to the regulations. All cases of failure to provide standard equipment must be reported to FIFA.

(8) In a match played under the Rules of a Competition if the cross-bar becomes displaced or broken play shall be stopped and the match abandoned unless the cross-bar has been repaired and replaced in position or a new one provided without such being a danger to the players. A rope is not considered to be a satisfactory substitute for a cross-bar.

In a Friendly Match, by mutual consent, play may be resumed without the cross-bar provided it has been removed and no longer constitutes a danger to the players. In these circumstances, a rope may be used as a substitute for a cross-bar. If a rope is not used and the ball crosses the goal-line at a point which in the opinion of the Referee is below where the cross-bar should have been he shall award a goal.

The game shall be restarted by the Referee dropping the ball at the place where it was when play was stopped.

(9) National Associations may specify such maximum and minimum dimensions for the cross-bars and goal-posts, within the limits laid down in Law I, as they consider appropriate.

(10) Goal-posts and cross-bars must be made of wood, metal or other approved material as decided from time to time by the International F.A. Board. They may be square, rectangular, round, half-round or elliptical in shape. Goal-posts and cross-bars made of other materials and in other shapes are not permitted.

(11) 'Curtain-raisers' to International

matches should only be played following agreement on the day of the match, and taking into account the condition of the field of play, between representatives of the two Associations and the Referee (of the International Match).

(12) National Associations, particularly in International Matches, should
— restrict the number of photographers around the field of play,
— have a line ("photographers' line") marked behind the goal-lines at least two metres from the corner flag going through a point situated at least 3.5 metres behind the intersection of the goal-line with the line marking the goal area to a point situated at least six metres behind the goal-posts,
— prohibit photographers from passing over these lines,
— forbid the use of artificial lighting in the form of "flashlights".

LAW II.—THE BALL

The ball shall be spherical; the outer casing shall be of leather or other approved materials. No material shall be used in its construction which might prove dangerous to the players.

The circumference of the ball shall not be more than 28 in and not less than 27 in. The weight of the ball at the start of the game shall not be more than 16 oz nor less than 14 oz. The pressure shall be equal to 0.6-0.7 atmosphere, which equals 9.0-10.5 lb/sq in (= 600-700 gr/cm^2) at sea level. The ball shall not be changed during the game unless authorised by the Referee.

Decisions of the International Board

(1) The ball used in any match shall be considered the property of the Association or Club on whose ground the match is played, and at the close of play it must be returned to the Referee.

(2) The International Board, from time to time, shall decide what constitutes approved materials. Any approved material shall be certified as such by the International Board.

(3) The Board has approved these equivalents of the weights specified in the Law: 14 to 16 ounces = 396 to 453 grammes.

(4) If the ball bursts or becomes deflated during the course of a match, the game shall be stopped and restarted by dropping the new ball at the place where the first ball became defective.

(5) If this happens during a stoppage of the game (place-kick, goal-kick, corner-kick, free-kick, penalty-kick or throw-in) the game shall be restarted accordingly.

LAW III.—NUMBER OF PLAYERS

(1) A match shall be played by two teams, each consisting of not more than eleven players, one of whom shall be the goalkeeper.

(2) Substitutes may be used in any match played under the rules of a competition, subject to the following conditions:

(a) that the authority of the international association(s) or national association(s) concerned, has been obtained,

(b) that, subject to the restriction contained in the following paragraph (c) the rules of a competition shall state how many, if any, substitutes may be used, and

(c) that a team shall not be permitted to use more that two substitutes in any match.

(3) Substitutes may be used in any other match, provided that the two teams concerned reach agreement on a maximum number, not exceeding five, and that the terms of such agreement are intimated to the Referee, before the match. If the Referee is not informed, or if the teams fail to reach agreement, no more than two substitutes shall be permitted.

(4) Any of the other players may change places with the goalkeeper, provided that the Referee is informed before the change is made, and provided also, that the change is made during a stoppage in the game.

(5) When a goalkeeper or any other player is to be replaced by a substitute, the following conditions shall be observed:

(a) the Referee shall be informed of the proposed substitution, before it is made,

(b) the substitute shall not enter the field of play until the player he is replacing has left, and then only after having received a signal from the Referee,

(c) he shall enter the field during a stoppage in the game, and at the half-way line.

Punishment:

(a) Play shall not be stopped for an infringement of paragraph 4. The players concerned shall be cautioned immediately the ball goes out of play.

(b) For any other infringement of this law, the player concerned shall be cautioned, and if the game is stopped by the Referee, to administer the caution, it shall be restarted by an indirect free-kick, to be taken by a player of the opposing team, from the place where the ball was, when play was stopped. If the free-kick is awarded to a side within its own goal area, it may be taken from any point within that half of the goal area in which the ball was when play was stopped.

Decisions of the International Board

(1) The minimum number of players in a team is left to the discretion of National Associations.

(2) The Board is of the opinion that a match should not be considered valid if there are fewer than seven players in either of the teams.

(3) A competition may require that the referee shall be informed, before the start of the match, of the names of not more than five players, from whom the substitutes (if any) must be chosen.

(4) A player who has been ordered off before play begins may only be replaced by one of the named substitutes. The kick-off must not be delayed to allow the substitute to join his team.

A player who has been ordered off after play has started may not be replaced.

A named substitute who has been ordered off, either before or after play has started, may not be replaced (this decision only relates to players who are ordered off under Law XII. It does not apply to players who have infringed Law IV.)

(5) A player who has been replaced shall not take any further part in the game.

(6) A substitute shall be deemed to be a player and shall be subject to the authority and jurisdiction of the Referee whether called upon to play or not. For any offence committed on the field of play a substitute shall be subject to the same punishment as any other player whether called upon or not.

LAW IV.—PLAYERS' EQUIPMENT

(1) A player shall not wear anything which is dangerous to another player.

(2) Footwear (boots or shoes) must conform to the following standard:

(a) Bars shall be made of leather or rubber and shall be transverse and flat, not less than half an inch in width and shall extend the total width of the sole and be rounded at the corners.

(b) Studs which are independently mounted on the sole and are replaceable shall be made of leather, rubber, aluminium, plastic or similar material and shall be solid. With the exception of that part of the stud forming the base, which shall not protrude from the sole more than one quarter of an inch, studs shall be round in plan and not less than half an inch in diameter. Where studs are tapered, the minimum diameter of any section of the stud must not be less than half an inch. Where metal seating for the screw type is used, this seating must be embedded in the sole of the footwear and any attachment screw shall be part of the stud. Other than the metal seating for the screw type of stud, no metal plates even though covered with leather or rubber shall be worn, neither studs which are threaded to allow them to be screwed on to a base screw that is fixed by nails or otherwise to the soles of footwear, nor studs which, apart from the base, have any form of protruding edge rim or relief marking or ornament should be allowed.

(c) Studs which are moulded as an integral part of the sole and are not replaceable shall be made of rubber, plastic, polyurethane or similar soft materials. Provided that there are no fewer than ten studs on the sole, they shall have a minimum diameter of three eighths of an inch (10 mm). Additional supporting material to stabilise studs of soft materials, and ridges which shall not protrude more than 5 mm from the sole and moulded to strengthen it, shall be permitted provided that they are in no way dangerous to other players. In all other respects they shall conform to the general requirements of this Law.

(d) Combined bars and studs may be worn, provided the whole conforms to the general requirements of this Law. Neither bars nor studs on the soles shall project more than three-quarters of an inch. If nails are used they shall be driven in flush with the surface.

(3) The goalkeeper shall wear colours which distinguish him from the other players and from the Referee.

Punishment: For any infringement of this Law, the player at fault shall be sent off the field of play to adjust his equipment and he shall not return without first reporting to the Referee, who shall satisfy himself that the player's equipment is in order; the player shall only re-enter the game at a moment when the ball has ceased to be in play.

Decisions of the International Board

(1) The usual equipment of a player is a jersey or shirt, shorts, stockings and footwear. In a match played under the rules of a competition, players need not wear boots or shoes, but shall wear jersey or shirt, shorts, or track suit or similar trousers, and stockings.

(2) The Law does not insist that boots or shoes must be worn. However, in competition matches Referees should not allow one or a few players to play without footwear when all the other players are so equipped.

(3) In International Matches, International Competitions, International Club Competitions and friendly matches between clubs of different National Associations, the Referee, prior to the start of the game, shall inspect the players' footwear, and prevent any player whose footwear does not conform to the requirements of this Law from playing until such time as it does comply,

The rules of any competition may include a similar provision.

(4) If the Referee finds that a player is wearing articles not permitted by the Laws and which may constitute a danger to other

players, he shall order him to take them off. If he fails to carry out the Referee's instruction, the player shall not take part in the match.

(5) A player who has been prevented from taking part in the game or a player who has been sent off the field for infringing Law IV must report to the Referee during a stoppage of the game and may not enter or re-enter the field of play unless and until the Referee has satisfied himself that the player is no longer infringing Law IV.

(6) A player who has been prevented from taking part in a game or who has been sent off because of an infringement of Law IV, and who enters or re-enters the field of play to join or re-join his team, in breach of the conditions of Law XII, shall be cautioned. If the Referee stops the game to administer the caution, the game shall be restarted by an indirect free-kick, taken by a player of the opposing side, from the place where the ball was when the Referee stopped the game. If the free-kick is awarded to a side within its own goal area, it may be taken from any point within that half of the goal area in which the ball was when play was stopped.

LAW V.—REFEREES

A Referee shall be appointed to officiate in each game. His authority and the exercise of the powers granted to him by the Laws of the Game commence as soon as he enters the field of play.

His power of penalising shall extend to offences committed when play has been temporarily suspended, or when the ball is out of play. His decision on points of fact connected with the play shall be final, so far as the result of the game is concerned. He shall:

(a) Enforce the Laws.

(b) Refrain from penalising in cases where he is satisfied that, by doing so, he would be giving an advantage to the offending team.

(c) Keep a record of the game, act as timekeeper and allow the full or agreed time, adding thereto all time lost through accident or other cause.

(d) Have discretionary power to stop the game for any infringement of the Laws and to suspend or terminate the game whenever, by reason of the elements, interference by spectators, or other cause, he deems such stoppage necessary. In such a case he shall submit a detailed report to the competent authority, within the stipulated time, and in accordance with the provisions set up by the National Association under whose jurisdiction the match was played. Reports will be deemed to be made when received in the ordinary course of post.

(e) From the time he enters the field of play, caution any player guilty of misconduct or ungentlemanly behaviour and, if he persists, suspend him from further participation in the game. In such cases the Referee shall send the name of the offender to the competent authority, within the stipulated time, and in accordance with the provisions set up by the National Association under whose jurisdiction the match was played. Reports will be deemed to be made when received in the ordinary course of post.

(f) Allow no person other than the players and linesmen to enter the field of play without his permission.

(g) Stop the game if, in his opinion, a player has been seriously injured; have the player removed as soon as possible from the field of play, and immediately resume the game. If a player is slightly injured, the game shall not be stopped until the ball has ceased to be in play. A player who is able to go to the touch or goal-line for attention of any kind, shall not be treated on the field of play.

(h) Send off the field of play, any player who, in his opinion, is guilty of violent conduct, serious foul play, or the use of foul or abusive language.

(i) Signal for recommencement of the game after all stoppages.

(j) Decide that the ball provided for a match meets with the requirements of Law II.

Decisions of the International Board
---

(1) Referees in International Matches shall wear a blazer or blouse the colour of which is distinct from the colours worn by the contesting teams.

(2) Referees for International Matches will be selected from a neutral country unless the countries concerned agree to appoint their own officials.

(3) The Referee must be chosen from the official list of International Referees. This need not apply to Amateur and Youth International Matches.

(4) The Referee shall report to the appropriate authority misconduct or any misdemeanour on the part of spectators, officials, players, named substitutes or other persons which take place either on the field of play or in its vicinity at any time prior to, during, or after the match in question so that appropriate action can be taken by the Authority concerned.

(5) Linesmen are assistants of the Referee. In no case shall the Referee consider the intervention of a Linesman if he himself has seen the incident and from his position on

the field, is better able to judge. With this reserve, and the Linesman neutral, the Referee can consider the intervention and if the information of the Linesman applies to that phase of the game immediately before the scoring of a goal, the Referee may act thereon and cancel the goal.

(6) The Referee, however, can only reverse his first decision so long as the game has not been restarted.

(7) If the Referee has decided to apply the advantage clause and to let the game proceed, he cannot revoke his decision if the presumed advantage has not been realised, even though he has not, by any gesture, indicated his decision. This does not exempt the offending player from being dealt with by the Referee.

(8) The Laws of the Game are intended to provide that games should be played with as little interference as possible, and in this view it is the duty of Referees to penalise only deliberate breaches of the Law. Constant whistling for trifling and doubtful breaches produces bad feeling and loss of temper on the part of the players and spoils the pleasure of spectators.

(9) By para. (d) of Law V the Referee is empowered to terminate a match in the event of grave disorder, but he has no power or right to decide, in such event, that either team is disqualified and thereby the loser of the match. He must send a detailed report to the proper authority who alone has power to deal further with this matter.

(10) If a player commits two infringements of a different nature at the same time, the Referee shall punish the more serious offence.

(11) It is the duty of the Referee to act upon the information of neutral Linesmen with regard to incidents that do not come under the personal notice of the Referee.

(12) The Referee shall not allow any person to enter the field until play has stopped, and only then, if he has given him a signal to do so, nor shall he allow coaching from the boundary lines.

LAW VI.—LINESMEN

Two Linesmen shall be appointed, whose duty (subject to the decision of the Referee) shall be to indicate when the ball is out of play and which side is entitled to the corner-kick, goal-kick or throw-in. They shall also assist the Referee to control the game in accordance with the Laws. In the event of undue interference or improper conduct by a Linesman, the Referee shall dispense with his services and arrange for a substitute to be appointed. (The matter shall be reported by the Referee to the competent authority.) The Linesmen should be equipped with flags by the Club on whose ground the match is played.

Decisions of the International Board

(1) Linesmen, where neutral, shall draw the Referee's attention to any breach of the Laws of the Game of which they become aware if they consider that the Referee may not have seen it, but the Referee shall always be the judge of the decision to be taken.

(2) National Associations are advised to appoint official Referees of neutral nationality to act as Linesmen in International Matches.

(3) In International Matches Linesmen's flags shall be of a vivid colour, bright reds and yellows. Such flags are recommended for use in all other matches.

(4) A Linesman may be subject to disciplinary action only upon a report of the Referee for unjustified interference or insufficient assistance.

LAW VII.—DURATION OF THE GAME

The duration of the game shall be two equal periods of 45 minutes, unless otherwise mutually agreed upon, subject to the following: (a) Allowance shall be made in either period for all time lost through accident or other cause, the amount of which shall be a matter for the discretion of the Referee; (b) Time shall be extended to permit a penalty-kick being taken at or after the expiration of the normal period in either half.

At half-time the interval shall not exceed five minutes except by consent of the Referee.

Decisions of the International Board

(1) If a match has been stopped by the Referee, before the completion of the time specified in the rules, for any reason stated in Law V it must be replayed in full unless the rules of the competition concerned provide for the result of the match at the time of such stoppage to stand.

(2) Players have a right to an interval at half-time.

LAW VIII.—THE START OF PLAY

(a) At the beginning of the game, choice of ends and the kick-off shall be decided by the toss of a coin. The team winning the toss shall have the option of choice of ends or the kick-off. The Referee having given a signal, the game shall be started by a player taking a place-kick (i.e., a kick at the ball while it is stationary on the ground in the centre of the field of play) into his opponents' half of the field of play. Every player shall be in his own half of the field and every player of the team opposing that of the kicker shall remain not less than 10 yards from the ball until it is kicked-off; it shall not be deemed in play until it has travelled the distance of its own circumference. The kicker shall not play the ball a second time until it has been touched or played by another player.

(b) **After a goal is scored**, the game shall be restarted in like manner by a player of the team losing the goal.

(c) **After half-time:** when restarting after half-time, ends shall be changed and the kick-off shall be taken by a player of the opposite team to that of the player who started the game.

Punishment. For any infringement of this Law, the kick-off shall be retaken, except in the case of the kicker playing the ball again before it has been touched or played by another player; for this offence, an indirect free-kick shall be taken by a player of the opposing team from the place where the infringement occurred, unless the offence is committed by a player in his opponent's goal area, in which case the free-kick shall be taken from a point anywhere within that half of the goal area in which the offence occurred. A goal shall not be scored direct from a kick-off.

(d) **After any other temporary suspension:** when restarting the game after a temporary suspension of play from any cause not mentioned elsewhere in these Laws, provided that immediately prior to the suspension the ball has not passed over the touch or goal-lines, the Referee shall drop the ball at the place where it was when play was suspended and it shall be deemed in play when it has touched the ground; if, however, it goes over the touch or goal-lines after it has been dropped by the Referee, but before it is touched by a player, the Referee shall again drop it. A player shall not play the ball until it has touched the ground. If this section of the Law is not complied with the Referee shall again drop the ball.

Decisions of the International Board

(1) If, when the Referee drops the ball, a player infringes any of the Laws before the ball has touched the ground, the player concerned shall be cautioned or sent off the field according to the seriousness of the offence, but a free-kick cannot be awarded to the opposing team because the ball was not in play at the time of the offence. The ball shall therefore be again dropped by the Referee.

(2) Kicking-off by persons other than the players competing in a match is prohibited.

LAW IX.—BALL IN AND OUT OF PLAY

The ball is out of play:
(a) When it has wholly crossed the goal-line or touch-line, whether on the ground or in the air.
(b) When the game has been stopped by the Referee.

The ball is in play at all other times from the start of the match to the finish including:
(a) If it rebounds from a goal-post, cross-bar or corner-flag post into the field of play.
(b) If it rebounds off either the Referee or Linesmen when they are in the field of play.
(c) In the event of a supposed infringement of the Laws, until a decision is given.

Decisions of the International Board

(1) The lines belong to the areas of which they are the boundaries. In consequence, the touch-lines and the goal-lines belong to the field of play.

LAW X.—METHOD OF SCORING

Except as otherwise provided by these Laws, a goal is scored when the whole of the ball has passed over the goal-line, between the goal-posts and under the cross-bar, provided it has not been thrown, carried or intentionally propelled by hand or arm, by a player of the attacking side, except in the case of a goalkeeper, who is within his own penalty-area.

The team scoring the greater number of goals during a game shall be the winner; if no goals, or an equal number of goals are scored, the game shall be termed a "draw".

Decisions of the International Board

(1) Law X defines the only method according to which a match is won or drawn; no variation whatsoever can be authorised.

(2) A goal cannot in any case be allowed if the ball has been prevented by some outside agent from passing over the goal-line. If this happens in the normal course of play, other than at the taking of a penalty-kick: the game must be stopped and restarted by the Referee dropping the ball at the place where the ball came into contact with the interference.

(3) If, when the ball is going into goal, a spectator enters the field before it passes wholly over the goal-line, and tries to prevent a score, a goal shall be allowed if the ball goes into goal unless the spectator has made contact with the ball or has interfered with play, in which case the Referee shall stop the game and restart it by dropping the ball at the place where the contact or interference occurred.

LAW XI.—OFF-SIDE

1. A player is in an off-side position if he is nearer to his opponents' goal-line than the ball, **unless**:

(a) He is in his own half of the field of play, or

(b) There are at least two of his opponents nearer their own goal-line than he is.

2. A player shall only be declared off-side and penalised for being in an off-side position, if, at the moment the ball touches, or is played by, one of his team, he is, in the opinion of the referee

(a) interfering with play or with an opponent, or

(b) seeking to gain an advantage by being in that position.

3. A player shall not be declared off-side by the referee

(a) merely because of his being in an off-side position, or

(b) if he receives the ball, direct, from a goal-kick, a corner-kick, a throw-in, or when it has been dropped by the referee.

4. If a player is declared off-side, the referee shall award an indirect free-kick, which shall be taken by a player of the opposing team from the place where the infringement occurred, unless the offence is committed by a player in his opponents' goal area, in which case, the free-kick shall be taken from a point anywhere within that half of the goal area in which the offence occurred.

Decisions of the International Board

(1) Off-side shall not be judged at the moment the player in question receives the ball, but at the moment when the ball is passed to him by one of his own side. A player who is not in an off-side position when one of his colleagues passes the ball to him or takes a free-kick, does not therefore become off-side if he goes forward during the flight of the ball.

LAW XII.—FOULS AND MISCONDUCT

A player who intentionally commits any of the following nine offences:

(a) Kicks or attempts to kick an opponent;

(b) Trips an opponent, i.e., throwing or attempting to throw him by the use of the legs or by stooping in front of or behind him;

(c) Jumps at an opponent;

(d) Charges an opponent in a violent or dangerous manner;

(e) Charges an opponent from behind unless the latter be obstructing;

(f) Strikes or attempts to strike an opponent;

(g) Holds an opponent;

(h) Pushes an opponent;

(i) Handles the ball, i.e., carries, strikes or propels the ball with his hand or arm. (This does not apply to the goalkeeper within his own penalty-area);

shall be penalised by the award of a direct free-kick to be taken by the opposing side from the place where the offence occurred, unless the offence is committed by a player in his opponents' goal area in which case, the free-kick shall be taken from a point anywhere within that half of the goal area in which the offence occurred.

Should a player of the defending side intentionally commit one of the above nine offences within the penalty-area he shall be penalised by a **penalty-kick**.

A penalty-kick can be awarded irrespective of the position of the ball, if in play, at the time an offence within the penalty-area is committed.

A player committing any of the five following offences:

(1) Playing in a manner considered by the Referee to be dangerous, e.g., attempting to kick the ball while held by the goalkeeper;

(2) Charging fairly, i.e., with the shoulder, when the ball is not within playing distance of the players concerned and they are definitely not trying to play it;

(3) When not playing the ball, intentionally obstructing an opponent, i.e., running between the opponent and the ball, or interposing the body so as to form an obstacle to an opponent;

(4) Charging the goalkeeper except when he

(a) is holding the ball;

(b) is obstructing an opponent;

(c) has passed outside his goal-area;

(5) When playing as goalkeeper,

(a) takes more than 4 steps whilst holding, bouncing or throwing the ball in the air and catching it again without releasing it so that it is played by another player, or

(b) indulges in tactics which, in the opinion of the Referee, are designed merely to hold up the game and thus waste time and so give an unfair advantage to his own team — shall be penalised by the award of an **indirect free-kick** to be taken by the opposing side from the place where the infringement occurred, unless the offence is committed by a player in his opponents' goal area, in which case the free-kick shall be taken from a point anywhere within that half of the goal area in which the offence occurred.

A player shall be **cautioned** if:

(j) he enters or re-enters the field of play to join or rejoin his team after the game has commenced, or leaves the field of play during the progress of the game (except through accident) without, in either case, first having received a signal from the Referee showing him that he may do so. If the Referee stops the game to administer the caution the game shall be restarted by an indirect free-kick taken by a player of the opposing team from the place where the ball was when the Referee stopped the game. If the free-kick is awarded to a side within its own goal area it may be taken from any point within the half of the goal area in which the ball was when play was stopped. If, however, the offending player has committed a more serious offence he shall be penalised according to that section of the law he infringed;

(k) he persistently infringes the Laws of the Game;

(l) he shows by word or action, dissent from any decision given by the Referee;

(m) he is guilty of ungentlemanly conduct.

For any of these last three offences, in addition to the caution, an **indirect free-kick** shall also be awarded to the opposing side from the place where the offence occurred unless a more serious infringement of the Laws of the Game was committed. If the offence is committed by a player in his opponents' goal area, a free-kick shall be taken from a point anywhere within that half of the goal area in which the offence occurred.

A player shall be **sent off** the field of play, if:

(n) in the opinion of the Referee he is guilty of violent conduct or serious foul play;

(o) he uses foul or abusive language;

(p) he persists in misconduct after having received a caution.

If play is stopped by reason of a player being ordered from the field for an offence without a separate breach of the Law having been committed, the game shall be resumed by an **indirect free-kick** awarded to the opposing side from the place where the infringement occurred, unless the offence is committed by a player in his opponents' goal area, in which case, the free-kick shall be taken from a point anywhere within that half of the goal area in which the offence occurred.

Decisions of the International Board

(1) If the goalkeeper either intentionally strikes an opponent by throwing the ball vigorously at him or pushes him with the ball while holding it, the Referee shall award a penalty-kick, if the offence took place within the penalty-area.

(2) If a player deliberately turns his back to an opponent when he is about to be tackled, he may be charged but not in a dangerous manner.

(3) In case of body-contact in the goal-area between an attacking player and the opposing goalkeeper not in possession of the ball, the Referee, as sole judge of intention, shall stop the game if, in his opinion, the action of the attacking player was intentional, and award an indirect free-kick.

(4) If a player leans on the shoulders of another player of his own team in order to head the ball, the Referee shall stop the game, caution the player for ungentlemanly conduct and award an indirect free-kick to the opposing side.

(5) A player's obligation when joining or rejoining his team after the start of the match to 'report to the Referee' must be interpreted as meaning 'to draw the attention of the Referee from the touch-line'. The signal from the Referee shall be made by a definite gesture which makes the player understand that he may come into the field of play; it is not necessary for the Referee to wait until the game is stopped (this does not apply in respect of an infringement of Law IV), but the Referee is the sole judge of the moment in which he gives his signal of acknowledgement.

(6) The letter and spirit of Law XII do not oblige the Referee to stop a game to administer a caution. He may, if he chooses, apply the advantage. If he does apply the advantage, he shall caution the player when play stops.

(7) If a player covers up the ball without touching it in an endeavour not to have it played by an opponent, he obstructs but does not infringe Law XII para. 3 because he is already in possession of the ball and covers it for tactical reasons whilst the ball remains within playing distance. In fact, he is actually playing the ball and does not commit an infringement; in this case, the player may be charged because he is in fact playing the ball.

(8) If a player intentionally stretches his arms to obstruct an opponent and steps from one side to the other, moving his arms up and down to delay his opponent, forcing him to change course, but does not make "bodily contact" the Referee shall caution the player for ungentlemanly conduct and award an indirect free-kick.

(9) If a player intentionally obstructs the opposing goalkeeper, in an attempt to prevent him from putting the ball into play in accordance with Law XII, 5(a), the Referee shall award an indirect free-kick.

(10) If after a Referee has awarded a free-kick a player protests violently by using abusive or foul language and is sent off the field, the free-kick should not be taken until the player has left the field.

(11) Any player, whether he is within or outside the field of play, whose conduct is ungentlemanly or violent, whether or not it is directed towards an opponent, a colleague,

the Referee, a linesman or other person, or who uses foul or abusive language, is guilty of an offence, and shall be dealt with according to the nature of the offence committed.

(12) If, in the opinion of the Referee a goalkeeper intentionally lies on the ball longer than is necessary, he shall be penalised for ungentlemanly conduct and

(a) be cautioned and an indirect free-kick awarded to the opposing team;

(b) in case of repetition of the offence, be sent off the field.

(13) The offence of spitting at opponents, officials or othe persons, or similar unseemly behaviour shall be considered as violent conduct within the meaning of section (n) of Law XII.

(14) If, when a Referee is about to caution a player, and before he has done so, the player commits another offence which merits a caution, the player shall be sent off the field of play.

LAW XIII. – FREE-KICK

Free-kicks shall be classified under two headings: "Direct" (from which a goal can be scored direct against the offending side), and "Indirect" (from which a goal cannot be scored unless the ball has been played or touched by a player other than the kicker before passing through the goal).

When a player is taking a direct or an indirect free-kick inside his own penalty-area, all of the opposing players shall remain outside the area, and shall be at least ten yards from the ball whilst the kick is being taken. The ball shall be in play immediately it has travelled the distance of its own circumference and is beyond the penalty-area. The goalkeeper shall not receive the ball into his hands, in order that he thereafter kick it into play. If the ball is not kicked direct into play, beyond the penalty-area, the kick shall be retaken.

When a player is taking a direct or an indirect free-kick outside his own penalty-area, all of the opposing players shall be at least ten yards from the ball, until it is in play, unless they are standing on their own goal-line, between the goal-posts. The ball shall be in play when it has travelled the distance of its own circumference.

If a player of the opposing side encroaches into the penalty-area, or within ten yards of the ball, as the case may be, before a free-kick is taken, the Referee shall delay the taking of the kick, until the Law is complied with.

The ball must be stationary when a free-kick is taken, and the kicker shall not play the ball a second time, until it has been touched or played by another player.

Notwithstanding any other reference in these Laws to the point from which a free-kick is to be taken, any free-kick awarded to the defending side, within its own goal area, shall be taken from any point within that half of the goal area in which the free-kick has been awarded.

Punishment. If the kicker, after taking the free-kick, plays the ball a second time before it has been touched or played by another player an indirect free-kick shall be taken by a player of the opposing team from the spot where the infringement occurred.

Decisions of the International Board

(1) In order to distinguish between a direct and an indirect free-kick, the Referee, when he awards an indirect free-kick, shall indicate accordingly by raising an arm above his head. He shall keep his arm in that position until the kick has been taken and retain the signal until the ball has been played or touched by another player or goes out of play.

(2) Players who do not retire to the proper distance when a free-kick is taken must be cautioned and on any repetition be ordered off. It is particularly requested of Referees that attempts to delay the taking of a free-kick by encroaching should be treated as serious misconduct.

(3) If, when a free-kick is being taken, any of the players dance about or gesticulate in a way calculated to distract their opponents, it shall be deemed ungentlemanly conduct for which the offender(s) shall be cautioned.

LAW XIV – PENALTY-KICK

A penalty-kick shall be taken from the penalty-mark and, when it is being taken, all players with the exception of the player taking the kick, and the opposing goalkeeper, shall be within the field of play but outside the penalty-area, and at least 10 yards from the penalty-mark. The opposing goalkeeper must stand (without moving his feet) on his own goal-line, between the goal-posts, until the ball is kicked. The player taking the kick must kick the ball forward; he shall not play the ball a second time until it has been touched or played by another player. The ball shall be deemed in play directly it is kicked, i.e., when it has travelled the distance of its circumference, and a goal may be scored direct from such a penalty-kick. If the ball touches the goalkeeper before passing between the posts, when a penalty-kick is being taken at or after the expiration of half-time or full-time, it does not nullify a goal. If necessary, time of play shall be extended at half-time or full-time to allow a penalty-kick to be taken.

Punishment

For any infringement of this Law:

(a) by the defending team, the kick shall be retaken if a goal has not resulted.

(b) by the attacking team other than by the player taking the kick, if a goal is scored it shall be disallowed and the kick retaken.

(c) by the player taking the penalty-kick, committed after the ball is in play, a player of the opposing team shall take an indirect free-kick from the spot where the infringement occurred. If, in the case of paragraph (c), the offence is committed by the player in his opponents' goal area, the free-kick shall be taken from a point anywhere within that half of the goal area in which the offence occurred.

Decisions of the International Board

(1) When the Referee has awarded a penalty-kick, he shall not signal for it to be taken, until the players have taken up position in accordance with the Law.

(2) (a) If, after the kick has been taken, the ball is stopped in its course towards goal, by an outside agent, the kick shall be retaken.

(b) If, after the kick has been taken, the ball rebounds into play, from the goalkeeper, the cross-bar or a goal-post, and is then stopped in its course by an outside agent, the Referee shall stop play and restart it by dropping the ball at the place where it came into contact with the outside agent.

(3) (a) If, after having given the signal for a penalty-kick to be taken, the Referee sees that the goalkeeper is not in his right place on the goal-line, he shall, nevertheless, allow the kick to proceed. It shall be retaken, if a goal is not scored.

(b) If, after the Referee has given the signal for a penalty-kick to be taken, and before the ball has been kicked, the goalkeeper moves his feet, the Referee shall, nevertheless, allow the kick to proceed. It shall be retaken, if a goal is not scored.

(c) If, after the Referee has given the signal for a penalty-kick to be taken, and before the ball is in play, a player of the defending team encroaches into the penalty-area, or within ten yards of the penalty-mark, the Referee shall, nevertheless, allow the kick to proceed. It shall be retaken, if a goal is not scored.

The player concerned shall be cautioned.

(4) (a) If, when a penalty-kick is being taken, the player taking the kick is guilty of ungentlemanly conduct, the kick, if already taken, shall be retaken, if a goal is scored.

The player concerned shall be cautioned.

(b) If, after the Referee has given the signal for a penalty-kick to be taken, and before the ball is in play, a colleague of the player taking the kick encroaches into the penalty-area or within ten yards of the penalty-mark, the Referee shall, nevertheless, allow the kick to proceed. If a goal is scored, it shall be disallowed, and the kick retaken.

The player concerned shall be cautioned.

(c) If, in the circumstances described in the foregoing paragraph, the ball rebounds into play from the goalkeeper, the crossbar or a goal-post, the Referee shall stop the game, caution the player and award an indirect free-kick to the opposing team from the place where the infringement occurred.

(5) (a) If, after the referee has given the signal for a penalty-kick to be taken, and before the ball is in play, the goalkeeper moves from his position on the goal-line, or moves his feet, and a colleague of the kicker encroaches into the penalty-area or within 10 yards of the penalty-mark, the kick, if taken, shall be retaken.

The colleague of the kicker shall be cautioned.

(b) If, after the Referee has given the signal for a penalty-kick to be taken, and before the ball is in play, a player of each team encroaches into the penalty-area, or within 10 yards of the penalty-mark, the kick, if taken, shall be retaken.

The players concerned shall be cautioned.

(6) When a match is extended, at half-time or full-time, to allow a penalty-kick to be taken or retaken, the extension shall last until the moment that the penalty-kick has been completed, i.e. until the Referee has decided whether or not a goal is scored.

A goal is scored when the ball passes wholly over the goal-line.

(a) direct from the penalty-kick,

(b) having rebounded from either goalpost or the cross-bar, or

(c) having touched or been played by the goalkeeper.

The game shall terminate immediately the Referee has made his decision.

(7) When a penalty-kick is being taken in extended time:

(a) the provisions of all of the foregoing paragraphs, except paragraphs (2) (b) and (4) (c) shall apply in the usual way, and

(b) in the circumstances described in paragraphs (2) (b) and (4) (c) the game shall terminate immediately the ball rebounds from the goalkeeper, the cross-bar or the goalpost.

LAW XV – THROW-IN

When the whole of the ball passes over a touch-line, either on the ground or in the air, it shall be thrown in from the point where it crossed the line, in any direction, by a player of the team opposite to that of the player who last touched it. The thrower at the moment of delivering the ball must face the field of play and part of each foot shall be either on the touch-line or on the ground outside the touch-line. The thrower shall use both hands and shall deliver the ball from behind and over his head. The ball shall be in play immediately it enters the field of play, but the thrower shall not again play the ball until it has been touched or played by another player. A goal shall not be scored direct from a throw-in.

Punishment:

(a) If the ball is improperly thrown in the throw-in shall be taken by a player of the opposing team.

(b) If the thrower plays the ball a second time before it has been touched or played by another player, an indirect free-kick shall be taken by a player of the opposing team from the place where the infringement occurred, unless the offence is committed by a player in his opponents' goal area, in which case, the free-kick shall be taken from a point anywhere within that half of the goal area in which the offence occurred.

Decisions of the International Board

(1) If a player taking a throw-in, plays the ball a second time by handling it within the field of play before it has been touched or played by another player, the Referee shall award a direct free-kick.

(2) A player taking a throw-in must face the field of play with some part of his body.

(3) If, when a throw-in is being taken, any of the opposing players dance about or gesticulate in a way calculated to distract or impede the thrower, it shall be deemed ungentlemanly conduct, for which the offender(s) shall be cautioned.

LAW XVI – GOAL-KICK

When the whole of the ball passes over the goal-line excluding that portion between the goal-posts, either in the air or on the ground, having last been played by one of the attacking team, it shall be kicked direct into play beyond the penalty-area from a point within that half of the goal-area nearest to where it crossed the line, by a player of the defending team. A goalkeeper shall not receive the ball into his hands from a goal-kick in order that he may thereafter kick it into play. If the ball is not kicked beyond the penalty-area, i.e., direct into play, the kick shall be retaken. The kicker shall not play the ball a second time until it has touched – or been played by – another player. A goal shall not be scored direct from such a kick. Players of the team opposing that of the player taking the goal-kick shall remain outside the penalty-area whilst the kick is being taken.

Punishment:

If a player taking a goal-kick plays the ball a second time after it has passed beyond the penalty-area, but before it has touched or been played by another player, an indirect free-kick shall be awarded to the opposing team, to be taken from the place where the infringement occurred, unless the offence is committed by a player in his opponents' goal area, in which case, the free-kick shall be taken from a point anywhere within that half of the goal area in which the offence occurred.

Decisions of the International Board

(1) When a goal-kick has been taken and the player who has kicked the ball touches it again before it has left the penalty-area, the kick has not been taken in accordance with the Law and must be retaken.

LAW XVII – CORNER-KICK

When the whole of the ball passes over the goal-line, excluding that portion between the goal-posts, either in the air or on the ground, having last been played by one of the defending team, a member of the attacking team shall take a corner-kick, i.e., the whole of the ball shall be placed within the quarter circle at the nearest corner-flag-post, which must not be moved, and it shall be kicked from that position. A goal may be scored direct from such a kick. Players of the team opposing that of the player taking the corner-kick shall not approach within 10 yards of the ball until it is in play, i.e., it has travelled the distance of its own circumference, nor shall the kicker play the ball a second time until it has been touched or played by another player.

Punishment:

(a) If the player who takes the kick plays the ball a second time before it has been touched or played by another player, the Referee shall award an indirect free-kick to the opposing team, to be taken from the place where the infringement occurred, unless the offence is committed by a player in his opponents' goal area, in which case the free-kick shall be taken from a point anywhere within that half of the goal area in which the offence occurred.

(b) For any other infringement the kick shall be retaken.

LIST OF REFEREES FOR SEASON 1979-80

Ashley, N. J. (Nantwich)
Baker, K.W. (Rugby)
Baker, M. R. (Wolverhampton)
Banks, R. A. (Manchester)
Bates, S. G. (Bristol)
Bidmead, M. J. (Chessington)
Bombroff, W. H. (Bristol)
Bray, J. E. (Hinckley, Leics.)
Bridges, R. (Deeside)
Bune, T. G. (Billingshurst)
Burden, L. F. (Corfe Mullen, Dorset)
Butcher, J. K. (Kendal)
Callow, V. G. (Solihull)
Chadwick, R. (Darwen)
Challinor, A. (Rotherham)
Challis, R. C. (Tonbridge)
Civil, D. W. (Birmingham)
Clarke, D. E. (Accrington)
Courtney, G. (Spennymoor)
Cox, A. D. (South Croydon)
Daniels, B. H. (Brentwood)
Dobson, A. (Blackburn)
Downey, C. (Hounslow)
Farley, T. (Newton Aycliffe)
Flint, G. E. (Kirkby-in-Ashfield)
Glasson, A. R. (Salisbury)
Glover, N. H. (Chorley)
Grey, A. W. (Great Yarmouth)
Gunn, A. (Burgess Hill, Sussex)
Hackett K. S. (Sheffield)
Hamil, A. J. (Wolverhampton)
Heath, M. J. (Stoke)
Hedges, D. A. (Oxford)
Hill, B. (Wellingborough)
Hough, J. D. (Macclesfield)
Hunting, J. (Leicester)
Hutchinson, D. (Bourn, Cambs.)
Letts, D. (Basingstoke)
Lewis, R. S. (Great Bookham, Surrey)
Lloyd, D. W. (Fernhill Heath)
Lovatt, J. (Crewe)
Lowe, M. (Sheffield)
McNally, K. (South Wirral)
Martin, B. (Keyworth, Notts.)
Martin, J. E. (Alton, Hants.)
Maskell, C. A. (Cambridge)
Midgley, N. (Salford)
Mills, T. (Barnsley)
Morris, T. L. (Leeds)
Napthine, G. J. (Loughborough)
Newsome, C. L. (Broseley, Salop)
Nolan, G. (Stockport)
Owen, D. (Wirral)
Owen, G. P. (Anglesey)
Partridge, P. (Cockfield, Co. Durham)
Peck, M. G. (Doncaster)
Phipps, F. (Wrexham)
Porter, A. (Bolton)
Read, E. A. (Bristol)
Redfern, K. A. (Whitley Bay)
Reeves, D. V. (Uxbridge)
Reeves, P. G. (Leicester)
Richardson, D. (Great Harwood)
Richardson, D. T. (Lincoln)
Richardson, P. J. (Lincoln)
Robinson, A. (Portsmouth)
Robinson, H. R. (Norwich)
Robinson, L. M. (Sutton Coldfield)
Salmon, K. G. (Barnet)
Saunders, A. (Newcastle)
Scott, M. P. (Nottingham)
Seel, C. N. (Carlisle)
Seville, A. (Birmingham)
Sewell, J. (Birstall, Leicester)
Shapter, L. C. (Newton Abbot)
Shaw, D. (Sandbach)
Spencer, T. D. (Salisbury, Wilts.)
Stevens, B. T. (Stonehouse, Glos.)
Taylor, M. J. (Deal, Kent)
Thomas, C. (Porthcawl)
Toseland, R. W. (Market Harborough, Leics.)
Tyldesley, P. A. (Stockport)
Tyson G. M. (Sunderland)
Vickers, D. S. (Ilford)
Walmsley, K. (Thornton, Blackpool)
Warner, J. M. (Wednesbury, W. Mid.)
Webb, D. A. (Radcliffe)
White, C. B. (Harrow)
Willis, P. N. (Meadowfield, Co. Durham)
Worrall, J. B. (Warrington)

FOOTBALL LEAGUE FIXTURES 1979-80

(Subject to confirmation; copyright of the Football League Ltd and may not be reproduced in whole or in part without their consent)

DIVISION ONE

	Arsenal	Aston Villa	Bolton W	Brighton & HA	Bristol C	Coventry C	Crystal Palace	Derby Co	Everton	Ipswich T	Leeds U	Liverpool	Manchester C	Manchester U	Middlesbrough	Norwich C	Nottingham F	Southampton	Stoke C	Tottenham H	WBA	Wolverhampton W
Arsenal		9-2	23-2	3-11	8-3	8-12	22-3	19-1	17-11	21-8	12-1	24-11	6-10	25-8	15-9	21-12	12-4	5-4	20-10	26-12	26-4	29-9
Aston Villa	22-9		3-11	22-8	25-8	21-12	2-2	1-3	12-1	22-3	24-11	8-12	1-1	8-9	16-2	12-4	5-4	6-10	17-11	26-4	13-10	8-3
Bolton W	13-10	18-8		12-1	1-12	2-2	27-10	14-3	26-12	15-12	22-9	9-10	17-11	7-4	8-4	16-2	1-3	25-8	19-4	22-3	8-9	3-5
Brighton & HA	18-8	9-10	1-9		7-4	1-3	26-12	1-12	3-5	15-9	13-10	10-11	29-12	14-3	19-4	27-10	29-3	22-9	15-12	19-1	16-2	8-4
Bristol C	27-10	29-12	12-4	1-1		9-10	1-3	10-11	16-2	19-1	18-8	14-3	24-11	13-10	29-3	26-4	22-9	21-12	15-9	8-12	5-4	1-9
Coventry C	3-5	8-4	15-9	20-10	21-8		19-4	7-4	6-10	1-12	10-11	19-1	9-2	15-12	1-1	1-9	29-12	23-2	3-11	29-9	8-3	29-3
Crystal Palace	10-11	15-9	8-3	5-4	20-10	24-11		1-9	23-2	29-9	12-4	26-4	3-11	29-3	29-12	1-1	8-12	21-8	9-2	6-10	21-12	19-1
Derby Co	8-9	20-10	6-10	12-4	22-3	26-12	12-1		25-8	17-11	5-4	21-12	26-4	2-2	22-9	8-12	24-11	16-2	8-3	23-2	3-11	22-8
Everton	29-3	1-9	5-4	8-12	29-9	14-3	13-10	29-12		9-2	9-10	1-3	21-12	27-10	10-11	18-8	1-1	26-4	19-1	24-11	12-4	15-9
Ipswich T	9-10	19-4	26-4	2-2	8-9	12-4	16-2	29-3			14-3	13-10	8-12	1-3	27-10	5-4	18-8	24-11	1-9	21-12	1-1	29-12
Leeds U	1-9	19-4	9-2	23-2	3-11	22-3	1-12	1-1	22-8	6-10		15-9	29-9	3-5	7-4	29-12	19-1	8-3	8-4	20-10	17-11	15-12
Liverpool	19-4	3-5	21-8	22-3	6-10	8-9	15-12	8-4	20-10	23-2	2-2		29-9	3-5	26-12	16-2	12-1	4-4	17-11	25-8	8-3	3-11
Manchester C	14-3	7-4	29-3	25-8	19-4	22-9	18-8	15-12	8-4	3-5	16-2	27-10		10-11	10-10	1-3	13-10	8-9	26-12	12-1	2-2	1-12
Manchester U	29-12	19-1	1-1	6-10	23-2	26-4	17-11	15-9	8-3	20-10	8-12	5-4	22-3		1-9	24-11	21-12	3-11	29-9	12-4	22-8	9-2
Middlesbrough	2-2	29-9	21-12	24-11	17-11	5-4	25-8	9-2	22-3	8-3	26-12	12-4	21-8	12-1		8-9	26-4	8-12	23-2	3-11	6-10	20-10
Norwich C	8-4	1-12	29-9	8-3	15-12	12-1	7-4	3-5	3-11	26-12	25-8	9-2	20-10	19-4	19-1		15-9	17-11	6-10	22-8	22-3	23-2
Nottingham F	1-12	26-12	20-10	17-11	9-2	25-8	3-5	19-4	7-4	3-11	8-9	29-9	23-2	8-4	15-12	2-2		22-3	22-8	8-3	12-1	6-10
Southampton	1-1	14-3	29-12	9-2	8-4	13-10	9-10	29-9	15-12	19-4	27-10	1-9	19-1	18-8	3-5	29-3	10-11		1-12	15-9	1-3	7-4
Stoke C	1-3	29-3	24-11	26-4	2-2	18-8	22-9	27-10	8-9	12-1	21-12	1-1	5-4	16-2	13-10	14-3	10-10	12-4		25-8	8-12	10-11
Tottenham H	7-4	15-12	10-11	8-9	3-5	16-2	14-3	13-10	19-4	4-4	1-3	29-3	1-12	18-10	10-10	27-10	2-2	29-12			1-1	1-1
WBA	15-12	23-2	19-1	29-9	26-12	27-10	4-4	18-8	1-12	7-4	29-3	29-12	15-9	10-10	14-3	10-11	1-9	20-10	3-5	9-2		19-4
Wolverhampton W	16-2	27-10	8-12	21-12	12-1	17-11	8-9	9-10	2-2	25-8	26-4	18-8	12-4	22-9	1-3	13-10	14-3	26-12	22-3	5-4	24-11	

DIVISION TWO

	Birmingham C	Bristol R	Burnley	Cambridge U	Cardiff C	Charlton Ath	Chelsea	Fulham	Leicester C	Luton T	Newcastle U	Notts Co	Oldham Ath	Orient	Preston NE	QPR	Shrewsbury T	Sunderland	Swansea C	Watford	West Ham U	Wrexham
Birmingham C	—	1-9	15-12	10-11	29-12	15-9	19-1	18-8	1-12	19-4	29-9	3-5	8-4	9-2	14-3	1-1	27-10	9-10	20-10	29-3	7-4	23-2
Bristol R	12-1	—	1-12	2-2	29-9	20-10	23-2	4-4	7-4	21-8	17-11	6-10	15-12	8-3	9-2	3-11	25-8	19-4	26-12	8-9	3-5	22-3
Burnley	26-4	12-4	—	24-11	13-10	21-8	6-10	2-2	22-3	17-11	26-12	25-8	8-9	3-11	1-3	8-3	5-4	22-9	12-1	8-12	16-2	21-12
Cambridge U	22-3	15-9	19-4	—	9-2	23-2	29-9	15-12	21-8	3-11	8-3	8-4	26-12	20-10	3-5	1-12	12-1	19-1	6-10	25-8	4-4	17-11
Cardiff C	25-8	16-2	23-2	22-9	—	8-3	20-10	26-12	8-4	6-10	22-3	3-11	1-12	17-11	15-12	22-8	8-9	3-5	7-4	2-2	19-4	12-1
Charlton Ath	2-2	1-3	9-10	13-10	27-10	—	29-3	8-4	15-12	4-4	25-8	26-12	10-11	12-1	18-8	19-4	22-9	18-8	15-12	16-2	1-12	8-9
Chelsea	8-9	13-10	14-3	16-2	1-3	17-11	—	27-10	26-12	7-4	12-1	19-4	3-5	2-3	1-12	4-4	2-2	18-8	22-9	10-11	22-9	25-8
Fulham	3-11	21-12	15-9	26-4	5-4	1-1	8-3	—	27-10	26-12	20-10	29-3	3-5	22-8	1-9	19-1	8-12	29-12	23-2	24-11	10-11	6-10
Leicester C	12-4	1-1	10-11	10-10	21-12	26-4	5-4	22-9	—	1-9	2-2	8-9	1-3	29-3	29-3	29-12	14-3	27-10	16-2	18-8	13-10	24-11
Luton T	24-11	9-10	29-3	18-8	14-3	21-12	1-1	16-2	12-1	—	8-12	2-2	22-9	25-8	27-10	10-11	12-4	13-10	8-9	5-4	1-3	26-4
Newcastle U	16-2	29-3	7-4	27-10	10-11	29-12	1-1	1-12	15-9	3-5	—	4-4	18-8	19-1	10-10	15-12	13-10	1-1	19-4	1-3	14-3	22-9
Notts Co	8-12	14-3	29-12	1-1	18-8	5-4	24-11	1-3	19-1	15-9	21-12	—	13-10	26-4	10-11	15-12	13-10	9-10	22-9	12-4	27-10	16-2
Oldham Ath	21-12	26-4	19-1	5-4	12-4	22-3	8-12	17-11	20-10	9-2	3-11	23-2	—	6-10	15-9	29-9	24-11	29-3	8-3	1-1	29-12	21-8
Orient	22-9	27-10	18-8	1-3	29-3	1-9	10-11	9-10	3-5	29-12	8-9	15-12	14-3	—	19-4	7-4	16-2	1-12	4-4	13-10	1-1	2-2
Preston NE	6-10	22-9	20-10	8-12	26-4	3-11	12-4	17-11	25-8	8-3	21-8	12-1	16-2	26-12	—	23-2	26-12	16-2	25-8	21-12	8-9	5-4
QPR	5-4	18-8	27-10	12-4	9-10	24-11	21-12	8-9	25-8	22-3	26-4	21-8	12-1	26-12	13-10	—	17-11	1-3	2-2	14-3	22-9	8-12
Shrewsbury T	8-3	29-12	1-1	1-9	19-1	9-2	15-9	3-5	6-10	1-12	23-2	21-8	19-4	29-9	7-4	29-3	—	8-4	3-11	10-11	15-12	20-10
Sunderland	22-8	24-11	9-2	8-9	8-12	6-10	3-5	25-8	8-3	23-2	5-4	17-11	12-1	12-4	29-9	20-10	21-12	—	22-3	26-4	2-2	26-12
Swansea C	29-2	5-4	1-9	14-3	1-1	8-12	26-4	13-10	29-9	18-1	24-11	9-2	27-10	21-12	29-12	15-9	18-8	10-11	—	9-10	29-3	12-4
Watford	17-11	19-1	3-5	29-12	15-9	29-9	9-2	19-4	3-11	26-12	20-10	1-12	7-4	23-2	8-4	6-10	22-3	15-12	21-8	—	1-9	8-3
West Ham U	26-12	8-12	29-9	21-12	24-11	12-4	20-8	22-3	23-2	20-10	6-10	8-3	25-8	5-4	19-1	9-2	26-4	15-9	17-11	12-1	—	3-11
Wrexham	13-10	10-11	4-4	29-3	1-9	19-1	29-12	14-3	19-4	15-12	9-2	29-9	8-10	15-9	1-1	3-5	1-3	7-4	1-12	27-10	18-8	—

DIVISION THREE

	Barnsley	Blackburn R	Blackpool	Brentford	Bury	Carlisle U	Chester	Chesterfield	Colchester U	Exeter C	Gillingham	Grimsby T	Hull C	Mansfield T	Millwall	Oxford U	Plymouth Arg	Reading	Rotherham U	Sheffield U	Sheffield W	Southend U	Swindon T	Wimbledon
Barnsley	—	2-10	21-12	14-3	6-11	1-3	27-10	9-10	16-2	10-11	13-10	5-4	29-3	8-9	22-9	26-1	26-4	25-8	1-1	2-2	18-8	1-12	12-1	12-4
Blackburn R	19-9	—	9-2	1-3	3-5	10-10	7-11	10-11	27-10	5-1	14-3	1-9	4-4	26-12	18-8	8-12	13-10	19-4	29-9	7-4	26-1	15-9	12-1	19-1
Blackpool	4-4	22-9	—	13-10	10-10	7-4	3-5	7-11	1-3	14-3	18-8	26-1	26-12	19-4	29-3	5-1	16-2	8-12	15-9	3-10	10-11	19-1	29-3	1-9
Brentford	6-10	20-10	23-2	—	8-4	19-4	26-12	1-9	10-11	17-9	5-1	15-9	8-12	7-4	3-5	20-8	8-3	3-11	29-3	22-10	19-1	29-9	27-10	9-2
Bury	23-10	29-12	21-8	21-12	—	26-1	1-9	1-12	1-1	19-1	29-3	18-9	15-9	23-2	10-11	9-2	22-3	8-3	22-10	12-4	19-1	29-12	29-12	29-9
Carlisle U	20-10	21-8	1-1	1-12	25-8	—	29-9	5-4	26-4	9-2	8-9	21-12	23-2	23-10	12-1	8-3	6-10	2-2	5-4	20-10	12-4	6-10	26-4	6-10
Chester	8-3	24-10	29-12	5-4	12-1	16-2	—	1-1	12-4	23-2	2-2	22-8	20-10	17-11	8-9	22-3	6-10	18-9	21-12	25-8	1-12	3-11	12-4	6-10
Chesterfield	21-8	22-3	23-10	12-1	19-4	26-12	7-4	—	8-9	3-5	8-4	23-2	18-9	3-11	8-12	2-3	6-10	25-8	17-11	9-2	1-12	26-4	3-10	3-11
Colchester U	29-9	8-3	20-10	22-3	7-4	7-12	5-1	19-1	—	8-4	26-12	9-2	3-11	18-9	19-4	3-5	17-11	6-10	29-12	21-8	15-9	23-2	31-8	20-10
Exeter C	22-3	12-4	6-10	3-10	8-9	22-9	13-10	26-1	21-12	—	16-2	3-11	8-3	25-8	2-2	17-11	1-1	1-3	1-12	12-1	26-4	24-10	5-4	23-10
Gillingham	23-2	6-10	3-11	12-4	17-11	19-1	15-9	21-12	5-4	29-9	—	20-10	9-2	8-3	25-8	23-10	3-5	12-1	26-4	22-3	1-1	21-8	1-12	22-8
Grimsby T	26-12	12-1	25-8	2-2	2-10	4-4	9-10	13-10	22-9	18-8	1-3	—	7-4	8-12	14-3	19-4	8-9	5-1	27-10	3-5	6-11	22-3	16-2	18-9
Hull C	17-11	21-12	5-4	26-4	2-2	13-10	1-3	2-10	18-8	27-10	22-9	1-1	—	12-1	16-2	25-8	12-4	22-3	6-11	8-9	9-10	3-5	14-3	17-11
Mansfield T	19-1	5-4	1-12	1-1	13-10	5-11	29-3	18-8	1-10	29-12	27-10	26-4	1-9	—	1-3	15-9	21-12	16-2	8-10	22-9	14-3	12-4	10-11	1-12
Millwall	9-2	3-11	17-11	26-1	22-3	1-9	19-1	26-4	1-12	15-9	29-12	6-10	29-9	20-10	—	23-2	21-8	23-10	12-4	8-3	18-9	1-1	21-12	26-1
Oxford U	1-9	26-4	12-4	10-10	22-9	27-10	19-1	14-3	12-1	29-3	7-11	6-12	29-12	2-2	13-10	—	3-10	8-9	18-8	16-2	1-3	5-4	1-1	5-4
Plymouth Arg	8-12	23-2	29-9	27-10	18-8	10-11	14-3	29-12	29-3	7-4	26-1	19-1	5-1	8-4	9-10	18-9	—	16-2	20-10	19-4	1-9	9-2	6-11	21-12
Reading	29-12	1-12	26-4	18-8	27-10	15-9	9-2	29-3	14-3	20-10	1-9	12-4	10-11	29-9	7-11	19-1	5-4	—	26-1	23-2	21-12	19-9	10-10	15-9
Rotherham U	7-4	16-2	2-2	17-11	26-12	2-10	8-4	22-9	25-8	19-4	8-12	8-3	23-10	21-8	5-1	3-11	1-3	3-5	—	6-10	13-10	12-1	8-9	1-1
Sheffield U	15-9	1-1	18-9	6-11	1-3	29-3	26-1	1-9	10-11	1-9	10-11	29-12	19-1	9-2	27-10	29-9	1-12	13-10	14-3	—	5-4	21-12	18-8	22-3
Sheffield W	3-11	25-8	22-3	8-9	5-1	3-5	19-4	16-2	2-2	8-12	7-4	23-10	21-8	6-10	2-10	20-10	12-1	8-4	23-2	26-12	—	17-11	22-9	26-4
Southend U	19-4	2-2	8-9	16-2	14-3	18-8	8-12	27-10	13-10	5-11	8-10	10-11	26-1	5-1	7-4	26-12	22-9	1-10	1-9	4-4	29-3	—	1-3	8-3
Swindon T	3-5	17-11	8-3	25-8	8-12	5-1	18-9	15-9	26-1	26-12	19-4	29-9	6-10	22-3	8-4	7-4	23-10	21-8	19-1	17-11	9-2	20-10	—	29-12
Wimbledon	5-1	8-9	12-1	22-9	16-2	14-3	18-8	1-3	6-11	9-10	2-10	28-3	19-4	3-5	26-12	8-4	2-2	7-4	9-11	8-12	27-10	25-8	13-10	—

DIVISION FOUR

	Aldershot	AFC Bournemouth	Bradford C	Crewe Alex	Darlington	Doncaster R	Halifax T	Hartlepool U	Hereford U	Huddersfield T	Lincoln C	Newport Co	Northampton T	Peterborough U	Portsmouth	Port Vale	Rochdale	Scunthorpe U	Stockport Co	Torquay U	Tranmere R	Walsall	Wigan Ath	York C
Aldershot	—	26-12	6-10	22-9	2-2	19-4	17-11	12-1	8-3	3-11	23-10	2-10	21-8	2-10	7-4	25-8	22-3	8-9	5-1	1-3	8-4	16-2	3-5	8-12
AFC Bournemouth	5-4	—	8-3	26-4	29-12	17-11	22-9	12-9		20-10	22-3	1-12	25-8	1-12	2-10	12-4		12-1	2-2	1-1	16-2	21-8	8-9	23-2
Bradford C	14-3	27-10	—	18-8	5-4	26-1	7-11	21-12	26-4	10-11	8-9	12-1	2-2	12-1	1-3	3-10	1-1	22-9	13-10	12-4	25-8	1-12	16-2	29-3
Crewe Alex	9-2	8-12	3-11	—	17-11	6-10	12-1	8-3	23-2	19-9	22-8	2-2	10-11		5-1	8-9	20-10	7-4	19-4	25-8	26-12	24-10	4-4	3-5
Darlington	15-9	3-5	26-12	29-3	—	4-4	13-10	19-1	26-1	8-4	5-1	29-9	27-10	2-2	14-3	1-3	1-9	6-11	2-10	16-2	8-12	22-9	18-8	9-10
Doncaster R	1-12	29-3		14-3	21-12	—	9-10	1-1	12-4	29-12	2-2	18-8	9-11	27-10	14-3	12-1	26-4	16-2	1-3	7-9	2-10	5-4	13-10	6-11
Halifax T	29-3	9-2	23-10	1-9	23-2	21-8	—	29-9	15-9	26-12	2-2	12-4	29-12	18-8	26-12	10-11	18-9	4-4	26-1	8-3	3-11	20-10	5-1	7-4
Hartlepool U	1-9	14-3	4-4	27-10	8-9	8-4	16-2	—	10-11	26-1	19-4	8-4	19-1	29-12	1-3	18-8	13-10	29-12	9-10	6-11	22-9	2-2	2-10	26-12
Hereford U	27-10	7-11	8-12	13-10	25-8	5-1	2-2	22-3	—	19-4	8-4	7-4	6-11	14-3	16-2	26-12	10-10	17-11	3-5	8-9	12-1	12-4	9-10	27-10
Huddersfield T	18-8	1-3	22-3	1-1	25-8	5-4	3-5	22-3	1-12	—	12-1	8-9	6-11	14-3	13-10	22-9	21-12	3-5	16-2	3-10	12-4	12-1	22-9	18-8
Lincoln C	7-11	10-11	19-1	10-10	12-4	25-8	5-4	30-10	21-12	1-9	—	16-2	1-1	18-8	29-3	14-3	5-4	13-10	27-10	26-1	12-4	29-12	29-12	29-12
Newport Co	9-10	26-1	15-9	10-11	1-12	9-2	14-3	26-4	17-11	18-1	29-9	—	18-9	21-12	6-11	18-8	12-4	29-2	29-3	5-4	13-10	25-8	19-4	1-9
Northampton T	23-2	8-4	21-8	16-2	22-3	3-11	8-9	17-11	20-10	23-10	7-4	22-9	—	2-2	3-5	2-2	8-3	8-12	26-12	12-1	6-10	25-8	19-4	5-1
Peterborough U	19-9	19-4	3-5	5-1	8-3	22-3	25-8	20-10	29-9	6-10	3-11	9-2	8-4	—		26-1	23-2	5-1	7-4	24-10	22-8	17-11	26-12	19-1
Portsmouth	1-1	18-9	20-10	12-4	6-10	8-3	1-12	3-11	5-4	23-2	17-11	23-10	29-12	26-4	—	21-12	9-2	25-8	8-9	21-8	2-2	22-3	12-1	29-9
Port Vale	29-12	5-1	17-9	19-1	20-10	3-5	22-3	23-2	20-8	9-2	6-10	3-11	15-9	1-9	8-4	—	29-9	26-12	7-12	17-11	22-10	8-3	7-4	19-4
Rochdale	10-11	18-8	7-4	1-3	12-1	8-12	2-10	21-8	29-3	4-4	26-12	5-1	25-4	13-10	22-9	16-2	—	19-4	9-10	2-2	3-5	8-9	6-11	14-3
Scunthorpe U	19-1	1-9	9-2	1-1	23-10	28-9	21-12	21-8	29-12	15-9	23-2	20-10	5-4	12-4	26-1	5-4	30-11	—	10-11	3-11	8-3	6-10	29-3	18-9
Stockport Co	12-4	15-9	23-2	1-12	17-9	20-10	3-5	22-10	6-10	29-9	8-3	17-11	5-4	1-1	19-1	26-4	20-8	22-3	—	21-12	12-1	3-11	25-8	9-2
Torquay U	20-10	7-4	5-1	29-12	29-9	19-1	27-10	9-2	19-9	8-12	3-5	7-11	1-9	7-11	10-10	29-3	15-9	18-8	2-4	—	19-4	23-2	14-3	10-11
Tranmere R	21-12	29-9	29-12	5-4	26-4	17-9	18-8	12-4	19-1	29-3	9-2	23-2	14-3	8-10	15-9	5-11	26-1	27-10	1-9	1-12	—	1-1	10-11	19-10
Walsall	29-9	9-10	19-4	6-11	9-2	26-1	1-3	15-9	1-9	5-1	18-9	14-3	26-1	29-3	10-11	27-10	19-1	14-3	18-8	13-10	7-4	—	8-12	8-4
Wigan Ath	26-1	19-1	29-9	21-12	3-11	23-2	12-4	19-9	9-2	22-8	20-10	8-3	1-12	5-4	1-9	1-1	24-10	17-11	29-12	6-10	22-3	26-4	—	15-9
York C	26-4	12-10	17-11	26-1	21-8	23-10	1-1	5-4	3-11	8-3	25-8	12-1	12-4	8-9	16-2	1-12	6-10	2-10	22-9	22-3	1-3	21-12	2-2	—

993

Coaching and Coaches

The Football Association Coaching Scheme has considerably extended its range in the last 18 months, and therefore the numbers and variety of its courses has expanded. Apart from the long established Preliminary and Full Coaching Awards, which were supplemented by a Teachers' Certificate, there are three further courses now in existence.

These are the Local Team Managers' Award; the Youth Team Managers' Certificate; and the School Team Managers' Certificate. Thus there is an overall opportunity for all interested groups to participate in the teaching of soccer in this country and full details of the courses are available from the F.A.'s Headquarters at 16 Lancaster Gate, London W2 3LW.

Situated also at Lancaster Gate are the Director of Coaching, Mr Allen Wade and his Assistant Director, Mr Charles Hughes. To cover the Regions there are the Regional Coaches and the Regional Coaching Organisers as follows:—

Regional Coaches:

Midland West Region: Kevin Verity, 25 Gresham Chambers, 14 Litchfield Street, Wolverhampton WV1 1DG, Staffs.
Midland East Region: Keith Wright, 29B High Street, Oakham, Rutland.
North East Region: Howard Wilkinson, 3rd floor, 22 High Street, Sheffield S1 2GD, Yorks.
London Region North: Colin Murphy
London Region South: Robin Russell
both c/o The FA Regional Offices, Lancaster Gate, London W2 3LW.

Coaching Organisers:

South West Region: Peter Amos, 20 Tuckers Meadow, Crediton, Devon.
East Anglia Region: Graham Morgan, 52 Christchurch Road, Norwich.
Midlands West Region: J. A. Jones, 19 The Rank, North Bradley, Trowbridge, Wilts.

The above are supplemented by the various Staff Coaches both in and out of the professional game, who are as follows: Adams, J. W.; Adamson, J.; Ainsley, G. E.; Armfield, J.; Beaglehole, E. W.; Blenkinsop, E. B.; Blunt, K. R. W.; Bond, C. E.; Brown, A.; Brown, A. W.; Burnside, D.; Burton, K.; Calvert, J. S.; Cann, S. T.; Cartwright, J.; Casey, T.; Charlton, J.; Churchill, T.; Curtis, G.; Detchon, J.; Dobson, C.; Ford, F.; Gradi, D.; Hassall, H. W.; Henderson, J. R. E.; Hill, J. W. T.; Howe, D.; Hughes, C. F. C.; Jago, G.; Jarman, J. E.; Jones, C.; Kelly, M. J.; Lawrence, T. E.; Lee, B. R.; Lewin, R.; McAnearney, J.; Mansell, J.; Megson, D. H.; Mercer, J.; Minshull, R.; Nicholson, W. E.; Powell, E. W.; Robson, R. W.; Saunders, T. W.; Sayer, C.; Sexton, D. J.; Shannon, L.; Sirrell, J.; Slater, W. J.; Smith, G. C.; Smith, M. J.; Summers, G.; Taylor, G.; Tranter, T. G.; Truman, J. B.; Wade, A.; Waiters, A. K.; Walker, M.; Wardle, G.; Watson, T.; Welton, P.; Wigmore, S. T.; Wilkinson, H.; Williams, B.; Woosnam, P. A.; Worthington, E. S.; Wright, W. A.

SCHOOLS INTER-ASSOCIATION TROPHY

Fifth Round

Barking v Swindon	0-2
Slough v Hillingdon	5-2
Southampton v Redbridge	1-0
Bristol v West Herts	1-0
Hull v Leeds	0-4
Walsall v Salford	2-1
East Durham v Bradford	0-1
Barnsley v Langbaurgh	3-1
Worksop v Manchester	1-2
South Birmingham v Leicester	2-2, 3-0
Watford v Norwich	0-1
Croydon v East Cornwall	4-1
Brent v East Berks	2-1
North Kent v Reading	0-2
Stoke v Coventry	2-1
Bolton v Flint	3-1
Southampton v Bristol	0-2
Leeds v Walsall	3-0
Bradford v Barnsley	3-2
Manchester v South Birmingham	2-1
Norwich v Croydon	1-2
Brent v Reading	0-1
Stoke v Bolton	3-1

Quarter-finals

Slough v Bristol	0-1
Leeds v Bradford	0-2
Manchester v Croydon	1-2
Reading v Stoke	0-0, 1-2

Sixth Round

Swindon v Slough	0-3

Semi-finals

Bristol v Bradford	3-0
Croydon v Stoke	4-4, 4-1

Final

Bristol v Croydon	2-0, 2-0

ENGLISH SCHOOLS' TROPHY WINNERS 1905-78

	Winners	Runners up		Winners	Runners up
1905	London	Sheffield	1946	Leicester	Stockton-on-Tees
1906	Sheffield	Manchester	1947	Salford	Leicester
1907	West Ham	Sunderland	1948	*Stockport	*Liverpool
1908	Derby	Oxford	1949	Barnsley	Derby County
1909	Sheffield	Birmingham N	1950	Swansea	Manchester
1910	Sunderland	Walsall	1951	Liverpool	Brieley Hill & Sedgeley
1911	Chester-le-Street	Tottenham			
1912	West Ham	Birkenhead	1952	Ilford	Swansea
1913	Watford	Sunderland	1953	Swansea	Chesterfield
1914	Sheffield	West Ham	1954	Liverpool	Southampton
1915	Cardiff	Manchester	1955	Swansea	Manchester
1916	Bradford	West Ham	1956	Liverpool	Brighton
1917	West Ham	Grimsby	1957	*Southampton	*Barnsley
1918	Liverpool	West Ham	1958	Bristol	Swansea
1919	Grimsby	Sunderland	1959	*Brierley Hill, Sedgeley & Tipton	*Doncaster
1920	Reading	Grimsby			
1921	Liverpool	West Ham	1960	Manchester	East London
1922	S London	Grimsby	1961	Barnsley	Liverpool
1923	Sheffield	Birmingham	1962	Stoke	Liverpool
1924	N Staffs	Reading	1963	Stoke	Bristol
1925	Sheffield	Brighton	1964	Erdington and Saltley	Chester-le-Street
1926	Grimsby	Liverpool			
1927	E Northumberland	Rotherham	1965	*Swansea	*Leicester
1928	N Staffordshire	Brighton	1966	East London	Oxford
1929	S Northumberland	Southampton	1967	Liverpool	East London
1930	Newcastle	Chesterfield	1968	*Manchester	*Waltham Forest
1931	Islington	Wolverhampton	1969	Liverpool	Swindon
1932	*Manchester	*Southampton	1970	Liverpool	East London
1933	Sunderland	Edmonton	1971	Huyton	Stoke
1934	Manchester	Swansea	1972	Chelmsford	Oxford
1935	Manchester	Swansea	1973	Liverpool	Chelmsford
1936	*Preston	*West Ham	1974	Manchester	Oxford
1937	Liverpool	Blyth (N'th'bld)	1975	Barking	Havering
1938	Manchester	Bootle	1976	Liverpool	Slough
1939	Swansea	Chesterfield	1977	South London	Islington
1940	Abandoned		1978	Newham	Ealing
1941-5	No Competition		1979	Bristol	Croydon

*Joint Winners

ESFA ASSOCIATED BISCUITS TROPHY 1978-79

Second Round
Suffolk v Essex A	3-0
Essex B v Norfolk A	4-1
Surrey v Inner London A	0-1
Sussex A v Middlesex B	6-1
Humberside A v Northants	1-1, 2-1
Nottinghamshire v Lincolnshire	1-0
Durham A v Northumberland	0-1
Cleveland A v North Yorkshire	3-2
Berkshire v Oxfordshire	1-1, 2-2, 0-1
West Glamorgan v Avon	3-1
Devon B v Wiltshire	2-1
Devon A v Hampshire A	1-0
West Midlands A v Derbyshire	9-0
Cheshire B v Shropshire	1-1, 3-2
Cumbria v Gt. Manchester B	3-1
Merseyside A v Gt. Manchester A	2-1
Humberside A v Nottinghamshire	2-1
Northumberland v Cleveland A	2-1
Oxfordshire v West Glamorgan	1-0
Devon B v Devon A	2-1
West Midlands A v Cheshire B	2-5
Cumbria v Merseyside A	4-1

Third Round
Suffolk v Essex B	1-4
Inner London A v Sussex A	8-1

Fourth Round
Essex B v Inner London A	3-4
Humberside A v Northumberland	3-1
Oxfordshire v Devon B	1-1, 0-1
Cheshire B v Cumbria	3-0

Semi-finals
Inner London A v Humberside A	0-5
Devon B v Cheshire B	2-2, 1-0

Final
Humberside A v Devon B	0-1

(Riddings School, Scunthorpe v Public Secondary, Plymouth)

VICTORY SHIELD AND FRIENDLY INTERNATIONALS

VICTORY SHIELD (UNDER-15)

N Ireland	4	Wales	0	Ballymena	3 March
England	0	N Ireland	0	Carlisle	10 March
Scotland	1	N Ireland	0	Aberdeen	11 April
Wales	1	England	2	Wrexham	27 April
Scotland	0	Wales	1	Airdrie	4 May
England	1	Scotland	1	Newcastle	7 May

	P	W	D	L	F	A	Pts
England	3	1	2	0	3	2	4
N Ireland	3	1	1	1	4	1	3
Scotland	3	1	1	1	2	2	3
Wales	3	1	0	2	2	6	2

CENTENARY SHIELD (UNDER 18)

Scotland	1	England	1	Falkirk	31 March
England	0	Wales	2	Ipswich	7 April
Wales	1	Scotland	3	Cwmbran	18 May

	P	W	D	L	F	A	Pts
Scotland	2	1	1	0	4	2	3
Wales	2	1	0	1	3	3	2
England	2	0	1	1	1	3	1

OTHER INTERNATIONALS (UNDER 18)

England	2	Scotland	2	Scarborough	28 April

(UNDER 15)

England	1	Wales	1	Wembley	24 March
England	2	W Germany	2	Wembley	9 June

THE NATIONAL PRESS

These are the names of some of the men who spend most of their working lives in the newspaper, TV, and Radio world reporting football matches and generally covering the game:

Daily Express
- David Miller
- Steve Curry
- Jim Lawton
- Alan Thompson
- Alan Williams
- Malcolm Folley

Daily Mail
- Jeff Powell
- Ronald Crowther
- Brian Scovell
- Bill Mallinson
- Brian James
- Ian Wooldridge
- John Parsons

Daily Mirror
- Frank McGhee
- Harry Miller
- Derek Wallis
- Kevin Moseley
- Frank Taylor
- Nigel Clarke
- Jack Steggles

Daily Telegraph
- Donald Saunders
- Bob Oxby
- Denis Lowe
- Roger Malone
- Radford Barrett

The Times
- Norman Fox
- Tom Freeman

The Guardian
- David Lacey
- Richard Yallop
- Patrick Barclay
- Robert Armstrong
- John Roberts
- Paul Fitzpatrick

Sporting Life
- Derrick Shaw

Financial Times
- Trevor Bailey

Belfast Telegraph
- Malcolm Brodie
- Bill Ireland

BBC Radio
- Bryon Butler
- Peter Jones
- Alan Parry

Radio London
- Norman De Mesquita

Manchester Evening News
- David Meek
- Peter Gardner

Associated Press
- Geoff Miller
- Windsor Dobbin

The Sun
- Frank Clough
- Mike Ellis
- Alex Montgomery
- John Sadler
- Brian Woolnough
- Alasdair Ross
- Ian Jarrett
- Hugh Jamieson

Sunday Mirror
- Ken Jones
- Ken Montgomery
- Vince Wilson
- Rodger Baillie

Sunday Express
- Alan Hoby
- James Mossop
- Ray Bradley

Sunday Telegraph
- Colin Malam
- John Moynihan
- Jack Rollin

The Observer
- Hugh McIlvanney
- Julie Welch
- Tony Pawson

News of the World
- Frank Butler
- Reg Drury
- Terry McNeill
- Don Evans
- Martin Frizell

The Sunday People
- Mike Langley
- Brian Madley
- Sam Bartram
- David Barnes

The Sunday Times
- Brian Glanville
- James Wilson
- Rob Hughes
- Chris Lightbown

Daily Star
- Peter Batt
- Bob Driscoll
- Steve Stammers
- John Pyke
- John Ragg
- Mike Beale
- Matt D'Arcy

BBC TV
- Jimmy Hill
- David Coleman
- Barry Davies
- John Motson
- Bob Wilson
- Frank Bough
- Tony Gubba

Radio Times
- Brian Gearing

Evening News
- John Oakley
- Harry Harris
- Martin Marks
- Patrick Collins

Evening Standard
- Michael Hart
- Peter Blackman
- Neil Allen

Exchange Telegraph Co. Ltd.
- Ken Mays
- Eric Brown
- John Bowles

Reuters Limited
- Howard Whittem
- Steven Bierley

Press Association
- Tony Smith
- Peter West
- Graham Otway
- Rob King

Reg Hayter Ltd., Sports Services
- Alan Hughes

UPI
- Morley Myers
- Alex Frere
- David Cowell

Thomson Regional Newspapers, London
- Basil Easterbrook
- Bob Harris
- Michael Green

D. C. Thomson
- Charles Holloway
- Bob Hammond

ITV
- Brian Moore
- Hugh Johns
- Gerry Harrison
- Gerald Sinstadt
- Paul Doherty
- Martin Tyler
- Kenneth Wolstenholme
- Dickie Davies
- Ian St. John

Visnews
- Neil Mallard

Freelance
- Don Aldridge
- Eric Batty
- Eric Nicholls
- Pat Collins
- Lionel Francis
- Pat Garrow
- Dennis Signy
- Norman Giller
- Tony Pullein
- Arthur Rotmil
- Leslie Vernon
- Leslie Yates
- Max Marquis
- Harold Mayes
- Tony Rand

FOOTBALL PUBLICATIONS

Weekly
Football Weekly News. Editor: Paul Parish 30p, Websters Publications.
Shoot. Editor: Peter Stewart 20p, IPC Magazines Ltd.

Monthly
Football Magazine. Editorial Director: Philip Osborn, 45p. Plenhurst Publications.
Soccer Monthly. Editor: David Gregory, 40p, IPC Magazines Ltd.
World Soccer. Editor: Philip Rising, 45p, Websters Publications.

OLYMPIC FOOTBALL 1908-1976

LONDON 1908

Semi-Finals
Gt. Britain v Holland — 4-0
Denmark v France 'A' — 17-1

Third Place Final
Holland v Sweden* — 2-1

Final
Gt. Britain v Denmark — 2-0

*Sweden were nominated for the third-place final in preference to France 'A', who had been awarded a bye into the semis.

STOCKHOLM 1912

Semi-Finals
Gt. Britain v Finland — 4-0
Denmark v Holland — 4-1

Third Place Final
Holland v Finland — 9-0

Final
Gt. Britain v Denmark — 4-2

ANTWERP 1920

Semi-Finals
Belgium v Holland — 3-0
Czechoslovakia v France — 4-1

Play-off for Second and Third Places
Spain v Holland — 3-1

Final
Belgium v Czechoslovakia — 2-0
(Czechoslovakia were disqualified for walking off during the Final. Placings Belgium – Olympic Champions, Spain – Second, Holland – Third, France – Fourth.)

PARIS 1924

Semi-Finals
Uruguay v Holland — 2-1
Switzerland v Sweden — 2-1

Third Place Final
Sweden v Holland — 1-1, 3-1

Final
Uruguay v Switzerland — 3-0

AMSTERDAM 1928

Semi-Finals
Uruguay v Italy — 3-2
Argentina v Egypt — 6-0

Third Place Final
Italy v Egypt — 11-3

Final
Uruguay v Argentina — 1-1, 2-1

BERLIN 1936

Semi-Finals
Italy v Norway (after extra time) — 2-1
Austria v Poland — 3-1

Third Place Final
Norway v Poland — 3-2

Final
Italy v Austria (after extra time) — 2-1

LONDON 1948

Semi-Finals
Sweden v Denmark — 4-2
Yugoslavia v Gt. Britain — 3-1

Third Place Final
Denmark v Gt. Britain — 5-3

Final
Sweden v Yugoslavia — 3-1

HELSINKI 1952

Semi-Finals
Hungary v Sweden — 6-0
Yugoslavia v West Germany — 3-1

Third Place Final
Sweden v West Germany — 2-0

Final
Hungary v Yugoslavia — 2-0

MELBOURNE 1956

Semi-Finals
USSR v Bulgaria (after extra time) — 2-1
Yugoslavia v India — 4-1

Third Place Final
Bulgaria v India — 3-0

Final
USSR v Yugoslavia — 1-0

ROME 1960

Semi-Finals
Yugoslavia v Italy — 1-1
(Yugoslavia won on toss-up)
Denmark v Hungary — 2-0

Third Place Final
Italy v Hungary — 2-1

Final
Yugoslavia v Denmark — 3-1

TOKYO 1964

Semi-Finals
Czechoslovakia v East Germany — 2-1
Hungary v United Arab Republic — 6-0

Third Place Final
East Germany v U.A.R. — 3-1

Final
Hungary v Czechoslovakia — 2-1

MEXICO CITY 1968

Semi-Finals
Hungary v Japan — 5-0
Bulgaria v Mexico — 3-2

Third Place Final
Japan v Mexico — 2-0

Final
Hungary v Bulgaria — 4-1

MUNICH 1972

Second round qualifiers
Hungary, East Germany, Poland, USSR

Third Place Final
USSR v East Germany — 2-2

Final
Poland v Hungary — 2-1

MONTREAL 1976

Semi-Finals
Poland v Brazil — 2-0
East Germany v USSR — 2-1

Third Place Final
USSR v Brazil — 2-0

Final
East Germany v Poland — 3-1

PREVIOUS EDITIONS OF ROTHMANS FOOTBALL YEARBOOK

This is the tenth edition of Rothmans Football Yearbook. Because of the limitation on space and the need to revise and broaden the scope of the work, some items that appeared in previous years have been omitted. In previous years we have invited readers to apply direct to the publisher for back issues of the yearbook and the response has been so great that we are now able only to offer the following editions in this way. You can obtain copies of the editions mentioned below by writing to:

Department QAP, 9 Partridge Drive, Orpington, Kent

enclosing a cheque or PO together with your name and address.

ROTHMANS FOOTBALL YEARBOOK 1973-74
Limp edition £1.30 + 50p p&p

ROTHMANS FOOTBALL YEARBOOK 1975-76
Limp edition £2.25 + 50p p&p

ROTHMANS FOOTBALL YEARBOOK 1976-77
Limp edition £2.50 + 50p p&p

ROTHMANS FOOTBALL YEARBOOK 1977-78
Limp edition £2.95 + 50p p&p

ROTHMANS FOOTBALL YEARBOOK 1978-79
Limp edition £3.25 + 50p p&p

INTERNATIONAL, REPRESENTATIVE AND CUP DATES 1979-80

1979

August
11 FA Charity Shield Match
11 Football League Cup First Round First Leg
15 Football League Cup First Round Second Leg
29 Football League Cup Second Round First Leg

September
1 FA Challenge Cup Preliminary Round
5 Football League Cup Second Round Second Leg
8 FA Challenge Trophy Preliminary Round
8 FA Vase Extra Preliminary Round
11 England v Denmark (UEFA Under-21) at Watford
12 England v Denmark (EC)
15 FA Challenge Cup First Round Qualifying
19 European Cups First Round First Leg
26 Football League Cup Third Round
29 FA Vase Preliminary Round

October
3 European Cups, First Round Second Leg
6 FA Challenge Cup Second Round Qualifying
13 FA Challenge Trophy First Round Qualifying
17 Northern Ireland v England (EC) in Belfast; Scotland v Austria (EC); West Germany v Wales (EC)
20 FA Challenge Cup Third Round Qualifying
24 European Cups Second Round First Leg
27 FA Vase First Round
31 Football League Cup Fourth Round

November
3 FA Challenge Cup Fourth Round Qualifying
7 European Cups Second Round Second Leg
10 FA Challenge Trophy Second Round Qualifying
20 England v Bulgaria (UEFA Under-21) at Leicester
21 England v Bulgaria (EC) at Wembley; Scotland v Belgium (EC); Northern Ireland v Eire (EC); Turkey v Wales (EC)
24 FA Challenge Cup First Round Proper
    FA Vase Second Round
28 UEFA Cup Third Round First Leg

December
1 FA Challenge Trophy Third Round Qualifying
5 Football League Cup Fifth Round
12 UEFA Cup Third Round Second Leg
15 FA Challenge Cup Second Round Proper
    FA Vase Third Round

1980

January
5 FA Challenge Cup Third Round Proper
12 FA Challenge Trophy First Round Proper
16 Football League Cup Semi-finals First Leg
19 FA Vase Fourth Round
26 FA Challenge Cup Fourth Round Proper

February
2 FA Challenge Trophy Second Round Proper
6 England v Republic of Ireland (EC) at Wembley; Scotland v Portugal (EC)
9 FA Vase Fifth Round
16 FA Challenge Cup Fifth Round Proper
23 FA Challenge Trophy Third Round Proper

March
1 FA Vase Sixth Round
5 European Cups Quarter-Finals First Leg
8 FA Challenge Cup Sixth Round Proper
15 Football League Cup Final at Wembley
19 European Cups Quarter-Finals Second Leg
22 FA Vase Semi-Final First Leg
26 Spain v England (friendly); England "B" v Spain "B"; Scotland v Belgium (EC)
29 FA Vase Semi-Final Second Leg

April
9 European Cups Semi-finals First Leg
12 FA Challenge Cup Semi-Finals
    FA Challenge Trophy Semi-Finals First Leg
19 FA Challenge Trophy Semi-Finals Second Leg
23 European Cups Semi-Finals Second Leg
26 FA Vase Final

May
7 UEFA Cup Final First Leg
10 FA Challenge Cup Final at Wembley
13 England v Argentina (friendly) at Wembley
14 European Cup Winners Cup Final
17 Wales v England (BC); Northern Ireland v Scotland (BC)
    FA Challenge Trophy Final
20 England v Northern Ireland (BC)
21 Scotland v Wales (BC)
    UEFA Cup Final Second Leg
23 Northern Ireland v Wales (BC)
24 Scotland v England (BC)
28 European Cup Final